Vienna in 1815, when the major European powers re-drew the map of Europe after the defeat of Napoleon and the dismantlement of the massive empire France had acquired under his leadership. The settlement agreed upon at Vienna was intended to maintain a balance of power in the West. Map 4 shows Europe after World War I, when the map of Europe changed dramatically with the collapse of the old authoritarian empires and the creation of independent nation-states in eastern Europe. What neither Map 3 nor Map 4 can show, however, is the expansion of "the West" beyond European borders to embrace cultures on other continents, including Australia, Africa, and North America.

MAP 3
Europe After the Congress of Vienna, 1815

MAP 4
Europe After World War I

THE WEST

ENCOUNTERS & TRANSFORMATIONS

BRIAN LEVACK
University of Texas at Austin

EDWARD MUIR
Northwestern University

MICHAEL MAAS
Rice University

MEREDITH VELDMAN
Louisiana State University

PEARSON
Longman

New York   San Francisco   Boston
London   Toronto   Sydney   Tokyo   Singapore   Madrid
Mexico City   Munich   Paris   Cape Town   Hong Kong   Montreal

Vice President and Publisher: Priscilla McGeehon
Acquisitions Editor: Erika Gutierrez
Development Manager: Lisa Pinto
Senior Development Editor: Dawn Groundwater
Executive Marketing Manager: Sue Westmoreland
Supplements Editor: Kristi Olson
Media Editor: Patrick McCarthy
Production Manager: Donna DeBenedictis
Project Coordination and Electronic Page Makeup: Elm Street Publishing Services, Inc.
Interior Design: Pearson Education Development
Cover Art: A Moor and a Christian playing the lute. Miniature in a book of music from the "Cantigas" of Alfonso X "the
    Wise" (1221–84). 13th century (manuscript). Monasterio de El Escorial. Spain. Index/The Bridgeman Art Library.
Cover Designer/Manager: John Callahan
Cartography: Maps.com
Photo Researcher: Photosearch, Inc.
Manufacturing Buyer: Roy L. Pickering, Jr.
Printer and Binder: Quebecor World Versailles
Cover Printer: Coral Graphic Services, Inc.

Library of Congress Cataloging-in-Publication Data

Levack, Brian P.
    The West : encounters & transformations / Brian Levack . . . [et al.].
        p. cm.
    Includes bibliographical references and index.
    ISBN 0-321-19833-6
    1. Civilization, Western—History.   I. Title.

CB245.L485 2004
909'.09821—dc22

2003062213

Please visit our website at http://www.ablongman.com/levack

ISBN 0-321-19833-6 (single volume edition)
ISBN 0-673-98250-5 (volume I)
ISBN 0-673-98251-3 (volume II)
ISBN 0-321-18315-0 (volume A)
ISBN 0-321-18317-7 (volume B)
ISBN 0-321-18314-2 (volume C)

3 4 5 6 7 8 9 10—QWV—06 05 04

Brief Contents

Detailed Contents

CHAPTER 3

Building the Classical World: Hebrews, Persians, and Greeks, 1100–336 B.C.E. *77*

JUSTICE IN HISTORY

CHAPTER 8

Empires and Borderlands:
The Early Middle Ages,
750–1050   *259*

JUSTICE IN HISTORY

CHAPTER 9

The West Asserts Itself:
The High Middle Ages,
1050–1300   *291*

CHAPTER 23

The West and the World: Cultural Crisis and the New Imperialism, 1870–1914 *753*

CHAPTER 24

The First World War *789*

JUSTICE IN HISTORY

THE HUMAN BODY IN HISTORY

CHAPTER 25

Reconstruction, Reaction, and Continuing Revolution: The 1920s and 1930s   *827*

JUSTICE IN HISTORY
The Sentencing of Salman Rushdie 988

THE HUMAN BODY IN HISTORY
The Pill: Controlling the Female Body 972

Documents

Maps

Features

Chronologies

Preface

We wrote this textbook to answer questions about the identity of the civilization in which we live. Journalists, politicians, and scholars often refer to our civilization, its political ideologies, its economic systems, and its cultures as "Western" without fully considering what that label means and why it might be appropriate. The classification of our civilization as Western has become particularly problematic in the age of globalization. The creation of international markets, the rapid dissemination of ideas on a global scale, and the transmission of popular culture from one country to another often make it difficult to distinguish what is Western from what is not. *The West: Encounters & Transformations* offers students a history of Western civilization in which these issues of Western identity are given prominence. Our goal is neither to idealize nor to indict that civilization but to describe its main characteristics in different historical periods.

The West: Encounters & Transformations gives careful consideration to two basic questions. The first is how did the definition of the West change over time? In what ways did its boundaries shift and how did the distinguishing characteristics of its cultures change? The second question is by what means did the West—and the idea of the West—develop? We argue that the West is the product of a series of cultural encounters that occurred both outside and within its geographical boundaries. We explore these encounters and the transformations they produced by detailing the political, social, religious, and cultural history of the regions that have been, at one time or another, a part of the West.

Defining the West

What is the West? How did it come into being? How has it developed throughout history? Many textbooks take for granted which regions or peoples of the globe constitute the West. They treat the history of the West as a somewhat expanded version of European history. While not disputing the centrality of Europe to any definition of the West, we contend that the West is not only a geographical realm with ever-shifting boundaries but also a cultural realm, an area of cultural influence extending beyond the geographical and political boundaries of Europe. We so strongly believe in this notion that we have written the essay "What Is the West?" to encourage students to think about their understanding of Western civilization and to guide their understanding of each chapter. Many of the features of what we call Western civilization originated in regions that are not geographically part of Europe (such as northern Africa and the Middle East), while ever since the fifteenth century various social, ethnic, and political groups from non-European regions (such as North and South America, eastern Russia, Australia, New Zealand, and South Africa) have identified themselves, in one way or another, with the West. Throughout the text, we devote considerable attention to the boundaries of the West and show how borderlines between cultures have been created, especially in eastern and southeastern Europe.

Considered as a geographical and cultural realm, "the West" is a term of recent origin, and the civilization to which it refers did not become clearly defined until the eleventh century, especially during the Crusades, when western European Christians developed a distinct cultural identity. Before that time we can only talk about the powerful forces that created the West, especially the dynamic interaction of the civilizations of western Europe, the Byzantine Empire, and the Muslim world.

Over the centuries Western civilization has acquired many salient characteristics. These include two of the world's great legal systems (civil law and common law), three of the world's monotheistic religions (Judaism, Christianity, and Islam), certain political and social philosophies, forms of political organization (such as the modern bureaucratic state and democracy), methods of scientific inquiry, systems of economic organization (such as industrial capitalism), and distinctive styles of art, architecture, and music. At times one or more of these characteristics has served as a primary source of Western identity: Christianity in the Middle Ages, science and rationalism during the Enlightenment, industrialization in the nineteenth and twentieth centuries, and a defense of individual liberty and democracy in the late twentieth century. These sources of Western identity, however, have always been challenged and contested, both when they were coming into prominence and when they appeared to be most triumphant. Western culture has never been monolithic, and even today references to the West imply a wide range of meanings.

Cultural Encounters

The definition of the West is closely related to the central theme of our book, which is the process of cultural encounters. Throughout *The West: Encounters & Transformations,* we examine the West as a product of a series of cultural encounters both outside the West and within it. We show that the West originated and developed through a continuous process of inclusion and exclusion resulting from a series of encounters among and within different groups. These encounters can be described in a general sense as external, internal, or ideological.

EXTERNAL ENCOUNTERS

External encounters took place between peoples of different civilizations. Before the emergence of the West as a clearly defined entity, external encounters occurred between such diverse peoples as Greeks and Phoenicians, Macedonians and Egyptians, and Romans and Celts. After the eleventh century, external encounters between Western and non-Western peoples occurred mainly during periods of European exploration, expansion, and imperialism. In the sixteenth and seventeenth centuries, for example, a series of external encounters took place between Europeans on the one hand and Africans, Asians, and the indigenous people of the Americas on the other. Two chapters of *The West: Encounters & Transformations* (Chapters 12 and 19) and a large section of a third (Chapter 23) explore these external encounters in depth and discuss how they affected Western and non-Western civilizations alike.

INTERNAL ENCOUNTERS

Our discussion of encounters also includes similar interactions between different social groups *within* Western countries. These internal encounters often took place between dominant and subordinate groups, such as between lords and peasants, rulers and subjects, men and women, factory owners and workers, masters and slaves. Encounters between those who were educated and those who were illiterate, which recur frequently throughout Western history, also fall into this category. Encounters just as often took place between different religious and political groups, such as between Christians and Jews, Catholics and Protestants, royal absolutists and republicans.

IDEOLOGICAL ENCOUNTERS

Ideological encounters involve the interaction between comprehensive systems of thought, most notably religious doctrines, political philosophies, and scientific theories about the nature of the world. These ideological conflicts usually arose out of internal encounters, when various groups within Western societies subscribed to different theories of government or rival religious faiths. The encounters between Christianity and polytheism in the early Middle Ages, between liberalism and conservatism in the nineteenth century, and between fascism and communism in the twentieth century were ideological encounters. Some ideological encounters had an external dimension, such as when the forces of Islam and Christianity came into conflict during the Crusades and when the Cold War developed between Soviet communism and Western democracy in the second half of the twentieth century.

* * *

The West: Encounters & Transformations illuminates the variety of these encounters and clarifies their effects. By their very nature encounters are interactive, but they have taken different forms: they have been violent or peaceful, coercive or cooperative. Some have resulted in the imposition of Western ideas on areas lying outside the geographical boundaries of the West or the perpetuation of the dominant culture within Western societies. More often than not, however, encounters have resulted in a more reciprocal process of exchange in which both Western and non-Western cultures or the values of both dominant and subordinate groups have undergone significant transformation. Our book not only identifies these encounters but also discusses their significance by returning periodically to the issue of Western identity.

Coverage

The West: Encounters & Transformations offers both balanced coverage of political, social, and culture history and a broader coverage of the West and the world.

BALANCED COVERAGE

Our goal throughout the text has been to provide balanced coverage of political, social, and cultural history and to include significant coverage of religious and military history as well. Political history defines the basic structure of the book, and some chapters, such as those on building the classical world, the age of confessional divisions, absolutism and state building, the French Revolution, and the coming of mass politics, include sustained political narratives. Because we understand the West to be a cultural as well as a geographical realm, we give a prominent position to cultural history. Thus we include rich sections on Hellenistic philosophy and literature, the cultural environment of the Italian Renaissance, the creation of a new political culture at the time of the French Revolution, and the atmosphere of cultural despair and desire that prevailed in Europe after World War I. We also devote special attention to religious history, including the history of Islam as well as that of Christianity and Judaism. Unlike many other textbooks, our coverage of religion continues into the modern period.

The West: Encounters & Transformations also provides extensive coverage of the history of women and gender. Wherever possible the history of women is integrated into the broader social, cultural, and political history of the period. But there are also separate sections on women in our chapters on classical Greece, the Renaissance, the Reformation, the Enlightenment, the Industrial Revolution, World War I, World War II, and the postwar era.

THE WEST AND THE WORLD

Our book provides broad geographical coverage. Because the West is the product of a series of encounters, the external areas with which the West interacted are of major importance. Three chapters deal specifically with the West and the World.

- Chapter 12, "The West and the World: The Significance of Global Encounters, 1450–1650"
- Chapter 19, "The West and the World: Empire, Trade, and War, 1650–1850"
- Chapter 23, "The West and the World: Cultural Crisis and the New Imperialism, 1870–1914"

These chapters present substantial material on sub-Saharan Africa, Latin America, the Middle East, India, and East Asia. Our text is also distinctive in its coverage of eastern Europe and the Muslim world, areas which have often been considered outside the boundaries of the West. These regions were arenas within which significant cultural encounters took place. Finally we include material on the United States and Australia, both of which have become part of the West. We recognize that most American college and university students have the opportunity to study American history as a separate subject, but treatment of the United States as a Western nation provides a different perspective from that usually given in courses on American history. For example, this book treats the American Revolution as one of four Atlantic Revolutions, its national unification in the nineteenth century as part of a broader western European development, its pattern of industrialization as related to that of Britain, and its central role in the Cold War as part of an ideological encounter that was global in scope.

Organization

·····················■·····················

The chronological and thematic organization of our book conforms in its broad outline to the way in which Western civilization courses are generally taught. We have limited the number of chapters to twenty-nine, an effort to make the book more compatible with the traditional American semester calendar and to solve the frequent complaint that there is not enough time to cover all the material in the course. We have also made some significant changes in organization:

- Chapter 2, which covers the period from ca. 1600 to 550 B.C.E., is the first in a Western civilization textbook to examine the International Bronze Age and its aftermath as a period important in its own right because it saw the creation of expansionist, multiethnic empires, linked by trade and diplomacy.
- In Chapter 4 the Roman Republic, in keeping with contemporary scholarship, has been incorporated into a discussion of the Hellenistic world, dethroned slightly to emphasize how it was one of many competing Mediterranean civilizations.
- Chapter 12 covers the first period of European expansion, from 1450 to 1650. It examines the new European encounters with the civilizations of sub-Saharan Africa, the Americas, and East Asia. By paying careful attention to the characteristics of

these civilizations before the arrival of the Europeans, we show how this encounter affected indigenous peoples as well as Europeans.

■ Chapter 16 is devoted entirely to the scientific revolution of the seventeenth century in order to emphasize the central importance of this development in the creation of Western identity.

■ Chapter 19, which covers the second period of European expansion, from 1650 to 1850, studies the growth of European empires, the beginning of global warfare, and encounters between Europeans and the peoples of Asia and Africa.

■ Chapter 27, "The Holocaust, the Bomb, and the Legacy of Mass Killing," explores the moral fissure in the history of the West created by World War II. This unique chapter looks in detail at the age of mass destruction inaugurated, in very different ways, by the Holocaust and by the aerial bombings of civilian centers that culminated in the use of the atomic bomb in August 1945.

Features and Pedagogical Aids

In writing this textbook we have endeavored to keep both the student reader and the classroom instructor in mind at all times. The text includes the following features and pedagogical aids, all of which are intended to support the themes of the book.

WHAT IS THE WEST?

The West: Encounters & Transformations begins with an essay to engage students in the task of defining the West and to introduce them to the notion of cultural encounters. "What Is the West?" guides students through the text by providing a framework for understanding how the West was shaped. Structured around the six questions of What? When? Where? Who? How? and Why?, this framework encourages students to think about their understanding of Western civilization. The essay serves as a blueprint for using this textbook.

JUSTICE IN HISTORY

Found in every chapter, the goal of this feature is to present a historically significant trial or episode in which different notions of justice (or injustice) were debated and resolved. The *Justice in History* features illustrate cultural encounters within communities as they try to determine the fate of individuals from all walks of life. Many famous trials dealt with conflicts over basic religious, philosophical, or political values, such as those of Socrates, Jesus, Joan of Arc, Charles I, Galileo, and Adolf Eichmann. Other *Justice in History* features show how judicial institutions, such as the ordeal, the inquisition, and revolutionary tribunals, handled adversarial situations in different societies. These essays, therefore, illustrate the way in which the basic values of the West have evolved through attempts to resolve disputes, contention, and conflict.

Each *Justice in History* feature includes two pedagogical aids. "Questions of Justice" helps students explore the historical significance of the episode just examined. These questions can also be used in classroom discussion or as student essay topics. "Taking It Further" provides the student with a few references that can be consulted in connection with a research project.

What Is the West?

MANY OF THE PEOPLE WHO INFLUENCE PUBLIC OPINION—POLITICIANS, teachers, clergy, journalists, and television commentators—frequently refer to "Western values," "the West," and "Western civilization." But what *do* these terms mean? The West has always been an arena within which different cultures, religions, values, and philosophies have interacted, and any definition of the West will inevitably arouse controversy.

The most basic definition of the West is of a place. Western civilization is now typically thought to comprise the regions of Europe, the Americas, Australia, and New Zealand. As we shall see, however, over time these boundaries have shifted considerably. In addition to being a place, Western civilization also encompasses a history—a tradition stretching back thousands of years to the ancient world. Over this long period the civilization we now identify as Western gradually took shape. The many characteristics that identify any civilization emerged over this time: forms of governments, economic systems, and methods of scientific inquiry, as well as religions, languages, literature, and art.

Throughout the development of Western civilization, the ways in which people identified themselves changed as well. People in the ancient world had no such idea of the common identity of the West, only of being subjects of an em-

JUSTICE IN HISTORY

The Trial of Joan of Arc

After only fifteen months as the inspiration of the French army, Joan of Arc fell into the hands of the English, who brought her to trial for witchcraft. The English needed to stage a kind of show trial to demonstrate to their own demoralized forces that Joan's remarkable victories had been the result not of military superiority but rather of witchcraft. In the English trial, conducted at Rouen in 1431, Joan testified that her mission to save France was in response to voices she heard that commanded her to wear men's clothing. On the basis of this evidence of a confused or double gender identity, the ecclesiastical tribunal de-

voices had the authority of divine commands. The problem the English judges faced was to demonstrate that the voices came not from God but from the Devil. If they could prove that, then they had evidence of witchcraft and sorcery. Following standard inquisitorial guidelines, the judges knew that authentic messages from God would always conform to church dogma. Any deviation from official doctrines would constitute evidence of demonic influence. Thus, during Joan's trial the judges demanded that she make theological distinctions that were alien to her. When they wanted to know if the voices were those of

naive ar
tic visio
were on
during
had bee
mystics
Catheri
Sweden
cepted
English
they we
had to
showin
logicall
not do.

If th
theolog
for supe
tempt t
charges
sisted o
magic,
a magic
demons
behavio
man ha
count o
serted t
rious w
sorcery.
howeve

THE HUMAN BODY IN HISTORY

Found in most chapters, these features show that the human body, which many people tend to understand solely as a product of biology, also has a history. These essays reveal that the ways in which various religious and political groups have represented the body in art and literature, clothed it, treated it medically, and abused it tell a great deal about the history of Western culture. These features include essays on the classical nude male body, the signs of disease during the Black Death, bathing the body in the East and the West, and the contraceptive pill. Concluding each essay is a single question for discussion that directs students back to the broader issues with which the chapter deals.

THE HUMAN BODY IN HISTORY

Shell Shock: From Woman's Malady to Soldier's Affliction

Broken in mind as well as body, the casualties of World War I forced medical practitioners to think anew about the connections among emotional anguish, physical disabilities, and gender roles. Doctors discovered to their horror and surprise that in the trenches of total war, men's bodies began to act like women's. Pouring into hospital units came thousands of men with the symptoms of a malady that before the war was considered a woman's disease—hysteria.

The word *hysteria* comes from the Greek word *hystera*, for "womb" or "uterus," and for much of Western history doctors believed that women were doomed to suffer from hysteria because of their physical makeup—because they were afflicted with wombs. Physicians long considered the uterus to be an inherently weak and unstable organ, prone even to detach itself from its proper place and wander about the body causing havoc. By the end of the nineteenth century, however, the diagnosis had changed. Doctors continued

to regard hysteria as primaril[...] were more inclined to view it [...] emotional disorder. The sym[...] included bouts of shrieking, [...] pression or breakdown, and [...] clear physical cause—rangin[...] somnia to the inability to wal[...]

With war came thousands of hysteria—men who could[...] healthy limbs who could not [...] were nibbling at their bodies. symptoms as signs of coward[...] ness to avoid doing their dut[...] accounting for 40 percent of [...] zones alone, doctors realized demic of male hysteria.

The war illustrated that h[...] uterus or the weak female ne[...] environment of immobility [...] length of time a soldier had [...] horror of his combat experie[...] ducing breakdowns. Instead, his level of immobility. Men [...] found themselves in positio[...] ment. Deprived of the ability[...] mine their future, to act, ma[...]

Yet the reincarnation of wl[...] woman's malady as a soldier's [...]

PLACES OF ENCOUNTER

Found in four chapters of the book, these features show that cultural exchanges between groups of people often occurred in specific places. The four features discuss the Roman Colosseum, Protestant and Catholic churches at the time of the Reformation, the French salon during the Enlightenment, and the twentieth-century soccer stadium. Accompanied by innovative visuals and graphics, these features reinforce the theme of encounters and also show that culture, which students often think of in abstract terms, has a material dimension. Each essay concludes with a question for discussion.

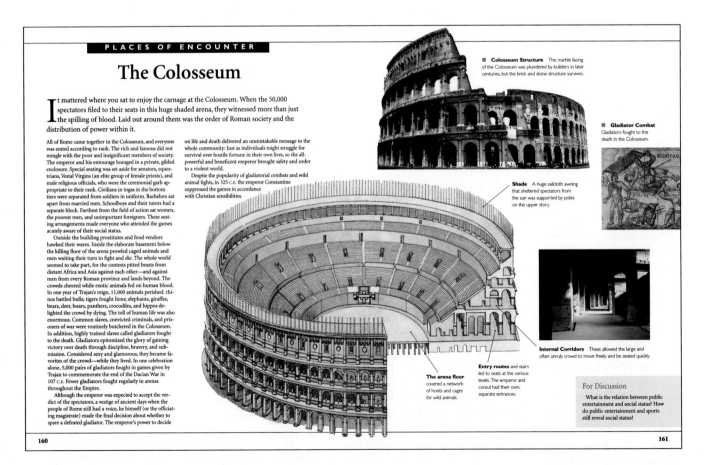

PLACES OF ENCOUNTER

The Colosseum

It mattered where you sat to enjoy the carnage at the Colosseum. When the 50,000 spectators filed to their seats in this huge shaded arena, they witnessed more than just the spilling of blood. Laid out around them was the order of Roman society and the distribution of power within it.

All of Rome came together in the Colosseum, and everyone was seated according to rank. The rich and famous did not mingle with the poor and insignificant members of society. The emperor and his entourage lounged in a private, gilded enclosure. Special seating was set aside for senators, equestrians, Vestal Virgins (an elite group of female priests), and male religious officials, who wore the ceremonial garb appropriate to their rank. Civilians in togas in the bottom tiers were separated from soldiers in uniform. Bachelors sat apart from married men. Schoolboys and their tutors had a separate block. Farthest from the field of action sat women, the poorest men, and unimportant foreigners. These seating arrangements made everyone who attended the games acutely aware of their social status.

Outside the building prostitutes and food vendors hawked their wares. Inside the elaborate basement below the killing floor of the arena prowled caged animals and men waiting their turn to fight and die. The whole world seemed to take part, for the contests pitted beasts from distant Africa and Asia against each other—and against men from every Roman province and lands beyond. The crowds cheered while exotic animals fed on human blood. In one year of Trajan's reign, 11,000 animals perished: rhinos battled bulls; tigers fought lions; elephants, giraffes, bears, deer, boars, panthers, crocodiles, and hippos delighted the crowd by dying. The toll of human life was also enormous. Common slaves, convicted criminals, and prisoners of war were routinely butchered in the Colosseum. In addition, highly trained slaves called gladiators fought to the death. Gladiators epitomized the glory of gaining victory over death through discipline, bravery, and submission. Considered sexy and glamorous, they became favorites of the crowd—while they lived. In one celebration alone, 5,000 pairs of gladiators fought in games given by Trajan to commemorate the end of the Dacian War in 107 C.E. Fewer gladiators fought regularly in arenas throughout the Empire.

Although the emperor was expected to accept the verdict of the spectators, a vestige of ancient days when the people of Rome still had a voice, he himself (or the officiating magistrate) made the final decision about whether to spare a defeated gladiator. The emperor's power to decide

on life and death delivered an unmistakable message to the whole community: Just as individuals might struggle for survival over hostile fortune in their own lives, so the all-powerful and beneficent emperor brought safety and order to a violent world.

Despite the popularity of gladiatorial combats and wild animal fights, in 325 C.E. the emperor Constantine suppressed the games in accordance with Christian sensibilities.

■ **Colosseum Structure** The marble facing of the Colosseum was plundered by builders in later centuries, but the brick and stone structure survives.

■ **Gladiator Combat** Gladiators fought to the death in the Colosseum.

Shade A huge sailcloth awning that sheltered spectators from the sun was supported by poles on the upper story.

Internal Corridors These allowed the large and often unruly crowd to move freely and be seated quickly.

The arena floor covered a network of hoists and cages for wild animals.

Entry routes and stairs led to seats at the various levels. The emperor and consul had their own, separate entrances.

For Discussion

What is the relation between public entertainment and social status? How do public entertainment and sports still reveal social status?

PRIMARY SOURCE DOCUMENTS

In each chapter we have presented a number of excerpts from primary source documents—from "Tales of the Flood" to "A Ghetto Diary"—in order to reinforce or expand upon the points made in the text and to introduce students to the basic materials of historical research.

MAPS AND ILLUSTRATIONS

Artwork is a key component of our book. We recognize that many students often lack a strong familiarity with geography, and so we have taken great care to develop maps that help sharpen their geographic skills. Complementing the book's standard map program, we include maps focusing on areas outside the borders of Western civilization. These maps include a small thumbnail globe that highlights the geographic area under discussion in the context of the larger world. Fine art and photos also tell the story of Western civilization and we have included over 350 images to help students visualize the past: the way people lived, the events that shaped their lives, and how they viewed the world around them.

CHRONOLOGIES AND SUGGESTED READINGS

Each chapter includes chronological charts and suggested readings. Chronologies outline significant events, such as "The Road to the Atom Bomb," and serve as convenient references for students. Each chapter concludes with an annotated list of suggested readings. These are not scholarly bibliographies aimed at the professor, but suggestions for students who wish to explore a topic in greater depth or to write a research paper. A comprehensive list of suggested readings is available on our book-specific website, www.ablongman.com/levack.

GLOSSARY

We have sought to create a work that is accessible to students with little prior knowledge of the basic facts of Western history or geography. Throughout the book we have explained difficult concepts at length. For example, we present in-depth explanations of the concepts of Zoroastrianism, Neoplatonism, Renaissance humanism, the various Protestant denominations of the sixteenth century, capitalism, seventeenth-century absolutism, nineteenth-century liberalism and nationalism, fascism, and modernism. Key concepts such as these are identified in the chapters with a degree symbol (°) and defined as well in the end-of-text Glossary.

A NOTE ABOUT DATES AND TRANSLITERATIONS

In keeping with current academic practice, *The West: Encounters & Transformations* uses B.C.E. (before the common era) and C.E. (common era) to designate dates. We also follow the most current and widely accepted English transliterations of Arabic. Qur'an, for example, is used for Koran; Muslim is used for Moslem. Chinese words appearing in the text for the first time are written in *pinyin,* followed by the older Wade-Giles system in parentheses.

Supplements

FOR QUALIFIED COLLEGE ADOPTERS

Instructor's Resource Manual
0-673-97563-0
Written by Sharon Arnoult, Midwestern State University, each chapter contains a chapter outline, significant themes, learning objectives, lesson enrichment ideas, discussion suggestions, and questions for discussing the primary source documents in the text.

Test Bank
0-673-97564-9
Written by Susan Carrafiello, Wright State University, this supplement contains more than 1,200 multiple-choice, true/false, and essay questions. Multiple-choice and true/false questions are referenced by topic and text page number.

TestGen-EQ Computerized Testing System
0-673-97565-3
This flexible, easy-to-master computerized test bank on a dual-platform CD includes all of the items in the printed test bank and allows instructors to select specific questions, edit existing questions, and add their own items to create exams. Tests can be printed in several different fonts and formats and can include figures, such as graphs and tables.

Companion Website
www.ablongman.com/levack
Instructors can take advantage of the Companion Website that supports this text. The instructor section includes teaching links, downloadable maps, tables, and graphs from the text for use in PowerPoint™, PowerPoint™ lecture outlines, and a link to Supplements Central.

Supplements Central™
http://suppscentral.ablongman.com
A helpful website where instructors can download supplements including: Instructor's Manuals, Test Banks, TestGens, and PowerPoint™ presentations, as well as CourseCompass®, WebCT, and Blackboard materials. Instructors will need to request a password from their sales representative to gain access.

PowerPoint™ Presentations
These presentations contain an average of 15 PowerPoint™ slides for each chapter and may include key points and terms for a lecture on the chapter, as well as full-color slides of important maps, graphs, and charts. The presentations are available for download from www.ablongman.com/levack.

Text-Specific Transparency Set
0-673-97568-1
A set of full-color transparency map acetates taken from the text.

History Video Program

A list of over 100 videos from which qualified adopters can choose. Restrictions apply.

History Digital Media Archive CD-ROM

0-321-14976-9

This CD-ROM contains electronic images and interactive and static maps, along with media elements such as video. It is fully customizable and ready for classroom presentation. All images and maps are available in PowerPoint™ as well.

CourseCompass

http://www.ablongman.com/techsolutions

Focus on teaching the course, not the technology! CourseCompass combines the strength of Longman content with state-of-the-art technology that simplifies online course management for you.This easy-to-use and customizable program enables you to tailor the content and functionality to meet your individual needs. You can create an on-line presence—for ANY course you teach—in under an hour. This course contains several dozen primary sources, Western civilization maps from Longman textbooks, and the map exercises from both *Mapping Western Civilization* and *Western Civilization Map Workbook,* all of which you can customize for your own class and text.

BlackBoard

http://www.ablongman.com/techsolutions

Longman's rich Western civilization content is available in BlackBoard's course management system. The BlackBoard format enables you to quickly and easily customize any course to meet your specific needs. This course contains several dozen primary sources, Western civilization maps from Longman textbooks, and the map *Workbook,* all of which you can customize for your own class and text.

WebCT

http://www.ablongman.com/techsolutions

WebCT offers a host of online course management tools. Qualified college adopters can customize their own WebCT course with Longman content in a number of ways. Available content includes several dozen primary sources, Western civilization maps from Longman textbooks, and the map exercises from both *Mapping Western Civilization* and *Western Civilization Map Workbook,* all of which you can customize for your own class and text. Contact your sales representative for more information.

Discovering Western Civilization Through Maps and Views

0-673-97499-5

Created by Gerald Danzer, University of Illinois at Chicago, and David Buisseret, this unique set of 140 full-color acetates contains an introduction to teaching history through maps and a detailed commentary on each transparency. The collection includes cartographic and pictorial maps, views and photos, urban plans, building diagrams, and works of art. Available to qualified college adopters.

FOR STUDENTS

Study Guide

Volume I 0-673-98252-1
Volume II 0-673-98253-X

Containing activities and study aids for every chapter in the text, each chapter of the *Study Guide* written by Paul Brasil, Western Oregon University, includes a thorough chapter outline; timeline; map exercise; identification, multiple-choice, and thought questions; and critical-thinking questions based on primary source documents from the text.

Companion Website

www.ablongman.com/levack

Providing a wealth of resources for students using *The West: Encounters & Transformations,* this Companion Website contains chapter summaries, interactive practice test questions, and Web links for every chapter in the text.

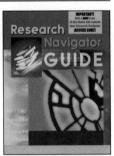

Research Navigator and Research Navigator Guide

0-205-40838-9

Research Navigator is a comprehensive website comprising three exclusive databases of credible and reliable source material for research and for student assignments: EBSCO's ContentSelect Academic Journal Database, the New York Times Search by Subject Archive, and "Best of the Web" Link Library. The site also includes an extensive help section. The Research Navigator Guide provides your students with access to the Research Navigator website and includes reference material and hints about conducting online research. **Free to qualified college adopters when packaged with the text.**

Multimedia Edition CD-ROM for
The West: Encounters & Transformations

0-321-18788-1

This unique CD-ROM takes students beyond the printed page, offering them a complete multimedia learning experience. It contains the full annotatable textbook on CD-ROM, with contextually placed media—audio, video, interactive maps, photos, and figures— that link students to additional content directly related to key concepts in the text. The CD also contains the *Study Guide,* Map Workbooks, a primary source reader, and more than a dozen supplementary books, most often assigned in Western civilization courses, including Plato, *The Republic,* and Machiavelli, *The Prince.* **Free to qualified college adopters when packaged with the text.**

Mapping Western Civilization:
Student Activities

0-673-53774-9

Created by Gerald Danzer, University of Illinois at Chicago, this FREE map workbook for students is designed as an accompaniment to *Discovering Western Civilization Through Maps and Views.* It features exercises designed to teach students to interpret and analyze cartographic materials such as historical documents. **Free to qualified college adopters when packaged with the text.**

Western Civilization Map Workbook

Volume I 0-321-01878-8

Volume II 0-321-01877-X

The map exercises in these volumes by Glee Wilson test and reinforce basic geography literacy while building critical-thinking skills. **Free to qualified college adopters when packaged with the text.**

Full-Color Longman Western Civilization Timeline

0-321-13004-9

Noting key events and trends in political and diplomatic, social and economic, and cultural and technological history, this fold-out illustrated timeline provides a thorough and accessible chronological reference guide for Western civilization. **Free to qualified college adopters when packaged with the text.**

Longman Atlas of Western Civilization

0-321-21626-1

This 52-page atlas features carefully selected historical maps that provide comprehensive coverage for the major historical periods. Each map has been designed to be colorful, easy-to-read, and informative, without sacrificing detailed accuracy. This atlas makes history—and geography—more comprehensible.

A Short Guide to Writing About History, Fourth Edition

0-321-09300-3

Written by Richard Marius, late of Harvard University, and Melvin E. Page, Eastern Tennessee State University, this engaging and practical text helps students get beyond merely compiling dates and facts; it teaches them how to incorporate their own ideas into their papers and to tell a story about history that interests them and their peers. Covering both brief essays and the documented resource paper, the text explores the writing and researching processes, identifies different modes of historical writing, including argument, and concludes with guidelines for improving style.

Longman World History—Primary Sources and Case Studies

Longmanworldhistory.com

The core of this website is its large database of thought-provoking primary sources, case studies, maps, and images—all carefully chosen and edited by scholars and teachers of world history. The content and organization of the site encourage students to analyze the themes, issues, and complexities of world history in a meaningful, exciting, and informative way. Offered at a significant discount to *The West: Encounters & Transformations* users, professors can visit the site for a free three-day trial.

PENGUIN-LONGMAN PARTNERSHIP

The partnership between Penguin Books and Longman Publishers offers your students a discount on the titles below when instructors bundle them with any Longman survey. Visit www.ablongman.com/penguin for more information.

Available Titles

Peter Abelard, *The Letters of Abelard and Heloise*

Dante Alighieri, *Divine Comedy: Inferno*

Dante Alighieri, *The Portable Dante*

Anonymous, *The Song of Roland*

Anonymous, *The Epic of Gilgamesh*

Anonymous, *Vinland Sagas*

Aristophanes, *The Knights, Peace, The Birds, Assemblywomen, Wealth*

Louis Auchincloss, *Woodrow Wilson* (Penguin Lives Series)

Jane Austen, *Emma*

Jane Austen, *Pride and Prejudice*

Jane Austen, *Persuasion*

Jane Austen, *Sense and Sensibility*

Edward Bellamy, *Looking Backward*

Richard Bowring, *Diary of Lady Murasaki*

Charlotte Brontë, *Jane Eyre*

Charlotte Brontë, *Villette*

Emily Brontë, *Wuthering Heights*

Benvenuto Cellini, *The Autobiography of Benvenuto Cellini*

Geoffrey Chaucer, *The Canterbury Tales*

Marcus Tullius Cicero, *Cicero: Selected Political Speeches*

Miguel de Cervantes, *The Adventures of Don Quixote*

Bartolome de las Casas, *A Short Account of the Destruction of the West Indies*

René Descartes, *Discourse on Method and The Meditations*

Charles Dickens, *Hard Times*

Charles Dickens, *Great Expectations*

John Dos Passos, *Three Soldiers*

Einhard, *Two Lives of Charlemagne*

Olaudah Equiano, *The Interesting Narrative and Other Writings*

Jeffrey Gantz (tr.), *Early Irish Myths and Sagas*

Peter Gay, *Mozart* (Penguin Lives Series)

William Golding, *Lord of the Flies*

Kenneth Grahame, *The Wind in the Willows*

Grimm & Grimm, *Grimms' Fairy Tales*

Thomas Hardy, *Jude the Obscure*

Herodotus, *The Histories*

Thomas Hobbes, *Leviathan*

Homer, *The Iliad*

Homer, *Odyssey: Revised Prose Translation*

Homer, *Odyssey Deluxe*

The Koran

Lemisch, *B. Franklin*

Primo Levi, *If Not Now, When?*

Machiavelli, *The Prince*

Karl Marx, *The Communist Manifesto*

John Stuart Mill, *On Liberty*

Jean-Baptiste Molière, *Tartuffe and Other Plays*

Charles-Louis Montesquieu, *Persian Letters*

Sir Thomas More, *Utopia and Other Essential Writings*

Sherwin Nuland, *Leonardo DaVinci*

George Orwell, *1984*

George Orwell, *Animal Farm*

Plato, *Great Dialogues of Plato*

Plato, *The Republic*

Plato, *The Last Days of Socrates*

Marco Polo, *The Travels*

Procopius, *The Secret History*

Jean-Jacques Rousseau, *The Social Contract*

Sallust, *The Jugurthine Wars, The Conspiracy of Cataline*

William Shakespeare, *Hamlet*

William Shakespeare, *Macbeth*

William Shakespeare, *The Merchant of Venice* (Pelican Series)

William Shakespeare, *The Merchant of Venice* (Signet Classics)

William Shakespeare, *Othello*

William Shakespeare, *The Taming of the Shrew*

William Shakespeare, *Twelfth Night*

William Shakespeare, *King Lear*

William Shakespeare, *Four Great Comedies: The Taming of the Shrew, A Midsummer's Night Dream, Twelfth Night, The Tempest*

William Shakespeare, *Four Great Tragedies: Hamlet, Macbeth, King Lear, Othello*

William Shakespeare, *Four Histories: Richard II, Henry IV: Part I, Henry IV: Part II, Henry V*

William Shakespeare, *The Tempest*

Mary Shelley, *Frankenstein*

Aleksandr Solzhenitsyn, *One Day in the Life of Ivan Denisovich*

Sophocles, *The Three Theban Plays*

St. Augustine, *The Confessions of St. Augustine*

Robert Louis Stevenson, *The Strange Case of Dr. Jekyll and Mr. Hyde*

Suetonius, *The Twelve Caesars*

Jonathan Swift, *Gulliver's Travels*

Tacitus, *The Histories*

Voltaire, *Candide, Zadig and Selected Stories*

Goethe, *Faust, Part 1*

Goethe, *Faust, Part 2*

Edith Wharton, *Ethan Frome*

M. Willet, *The Signet World Atlas*

Gary Wills, *Saint Augustine* (Penguin Lives Series)

Virginia Woolf, *Jacob's Room*

Acknowledgments

In writing this book we have benefited from the guidance of many members of the superb editorial staff at Longman. Our first acquisitions editor, Bruce Borland, encouraged us to write a book emphasizing the theme of cultural encounters, while Jay O'Callaghan and Erika Gutierrez helped us refine that theme as the book progressed. Dawn Groundwater, our senior development editor, gave us valuable line-by-line criticisms of all our chapters and helped us keep our audience in mind as we revised them. Lisa Pinto, the director of development, read our chapters at different stages of composition and made sure that our arguments were logical and consistent. Priscilla McGeehon, publisher for the social sciences, facilitated the progress of the project at a number of crucial junctures. Susan Gallier superintended the copyediting and proofreading with skill and efficiency, while Jullie Chung helped us locate the most appropriate illustrations. Sue Westmoreland, the executive marketing manager for history, offered many creative ideas for promoting the book.

The authors wish to thank the following friends and colleagues for their assistance: Joseph Alehermes, Kenneth Alder, Karl Appuhn, Sharon Arnoult, Nicholas Baker, Paul-Alain Beaulieu, Paula Baskovits, Kamilia Bergen, Timothy Breen, Peter Brown, Peter Carroll, Patricia Crone, Tracey Cullen, Arthur Eckstein, Susanna Elm, Benjamin Frommer, Cynthia Gladstone, Dena Goodman, Matthias Henze, Stanley Hilton, Kenneth Holum, Mark Jurdjevic, Werner Kelber, Cathleen Keller, Anne Kilmer, Jacob Lassner, Robert Lerner, Nancy Levack, Richard Lim, David Lindenfeld, Sarah Maza, Laura McGough, Roderick McIntosh, Susan K. McIntosh, Glenn Markoe, William Monter, Randy Nichols, Scott Noegel, Monique O'Connell, Carl Petry, Michael Rogers, Karl Roider, Sarah Ross, Michele Salzman, Paula Sanders, Regina Schwartz, Ethan Shagan, Julia M. H. Smith, and James Sidbury.

We would also like to thank the many historians who gave generously of their time to review our manuscript at various stages of development. Their comments and suggestions have helped to improve the book. Thank you:

Henry Abramson, *Florida Atlantic University*

Patricia Ali, *Morris College*

Joseph Appiah, *J. Sergeant Reynolds Community College*

Sharon L. Arnoult, *Midwestern State University*

Arthur H. Auten, *University of Hartford*

Clifford Backman, *Boston University*

Suzanne Balch-Lindsay, *Eastern New Mexico University*

Wayne C. Bartee, *Southwest Miami State University*

Brandon Beck, *Shenandoah University*

James R. Belpedio, *Becker College*

Richard Berthold, *University of New Mexico*

Cynthia S. Bisson, *Belmont University*

Richard Bodek, *College of Charleston*

Melissa Bokovoy, *University of New Mexico*

William H. Brennan, *University of the Pacific*

Morgan R. Broadhead, *Jefferson Community College*

Theodore Bromund, *Yale University*

April A. Brooks, *South Dakota State University*

Nathan M. Brooks, *New Mexico State University*

Michael Burger, *Mississippi University for Women*

Susan Carrafiello, *Wright State University*

Kathleen S. Carter, *High Point University*

William L. Combs, *Western Illinois University*

Joseph Coohill, *Pennsylvania State University—New Kensington*

Richard A. Cosgrove, *University of Arizona*

Leonard Curtis, *Mississippi College*

Miriam Davis, *Delta State University*

Alexander DeGrand, *North Carolina State University*

Marion Deshmukh, *George Mason University*

Janusz Duzinkiewicz, *Purdue University, North Central*

Mary Beth Emmerichs, *University of Wisconsin, Sheboygan*

Steven Fanning, *University of Illinois at Chicago*

Bryan Ganaway, *University of Illinois at Urbana-Champaign*

Frank Garosi, *California State University—Sacramento*

Christina Gold, *Loyola Marymount University*

Ignacio Götz, *Hofstra University*

Louis Haas, *Duquesne University*

Linda Jones Hall, *Saint Mary's College of Maryland*

Paul Halsall, *University of North Florida*

Donald J. Harreld, *Brigham Young University*

Carmen V. Harris, *University of South Carolina at Spartanburg*

James C. Harrison, *Siena College*

Mark C. Herman, *Edison Community College*

Curry A. Herring, *University of Southern Alabama*

Patrick Holt, *Fordham University*

W. Robert Houston, *University of South Alabama*

Lester Hutton, *Westfield State College*

Jeffrey Hyson, *Saint Joseph's University*

Paul Jankowski, *Brandeis University*

Padraic Kennedy, *McNeese State University*

Joanne Klein, *Boise State University*

Theodore Kluz, *Troy State University*

Skip Knox, *Boise State University*

Cynthia Kosso, *Northern Arizona University*

Ann Kuzdale, *Chicago State University*

Lawrence Langer, *University of Connecticut*

Oscar E. Lansen, *University of North Carolina at Charlotte*

Michael V. Leggiere, *Louisiana State University at Shreveport*

Rhett Leverett, *Marymount University*

Alison Williams Lewin, *Saint Joseph's University*

Wendy Liu, *Miami University, Middletown*

Elizabeth Makowski, *Southwest Texas State University*

Daniel Meissner, *Marquette University*

Isabel Moreira, *University of Utah*

Kenneth Moure, *University of California—Santa Barbara*

Melva E. Newsom, *Clark State Community College*

John A. Nichols, *Slippery Rock University*

Susannah R. Ottaway, *Carleton College*

James H. Overfield, *University of Vermont*

Brian L. Peterson, *Florida International University*

Hugh Phillips, *Western Kentucky University*

Jeff Plaks, *University of Central Oklahoma*

Thomas L. Powers, *University of South Carolina, Sumter*

Carole Putko, *San Diego State University*

Barbara Ranieri, *University of Alabama at Birmingham*

Elsa M. E. Rapp, *Montgomery County Community College*

Marlette Rebhorn, *Austin Community College*

Roger Reese, *Texas A&M University*

Travis Ricketts, *Bryan College*

Thomas Robisheaux, *Duke University*

Bill Robison, *Southeastern Louisiana University*

Mark Ruff, *Concordia University*

Frank Russell, *Transylvania University*

Marylou Ruud, *The University of West Florida*

Michael Saler, *University of California—Davis*

Timothy D. Saxon, *Charleston Southern University*

Daniel A. Scalberg, *Multnomah Bible College*

Ronald Schechter, *College of William and Mary*

Philip Skaggs, *Grand Valley State University*

Helmut Walser Smith, *Vanderbilt University*

Eileen Solwedel, *Edmonds Community College*

Sister Maria Consuelo Sparks, *Immaculata University*

Ilicia J. Sprey, *Saint Joseph's College*

Charles R. Sullivan, *University of Dallas*

Frederick Suppe, *Ball State University*

Frank W. Thackery, *Indiana University Southeast*

Frances B. Titchener, *Utah State University*

Katherine Tosa, *Muskegon Community College*

Lawrence A. Tritle, *Loyola Marymount University*

Clifford F. Wargelin, *Georgetown College*

Theodore R. Weeks, *Southern Illinois University*

Elizabeth A. Williams, *Oklahoma State University*

Mary E. Zamon, *Marymount University*

BRIAN LEVACK
EDWARD MUIR
MICHAEL MAAS
MEREDITH VELDMAN

Meet the Authors

Brian Levack grew up in a family of teachers in the New York metropolitan area. From his father, a professor of French history, he acquired a love for studying the past, and he knew from an early age that he too would become a historian. He received his B.A. from Fordham University in 1965 and his Ph.D. from Yale in 1970. In graduate school he became fascinated by the history of the law and the interaction between law and politics, interests that he has maintained throughout his career. In 1969 he joined the History Department of the University of Texas at Austin, where he is now the John Green Regents Professor in History. The winner of several teaching awards, Levack teaches a wide variety of courses on British and European history, legal history, and the history of witchcraft. For eight years he served as the chair of his department, a rewarding but challenging assignment that made it difficult for him to devote as much time as he wished to his teaching and scholarship. His books include *The Civil Lawyers in England, 1603–1641: A Political Study* (1973), *The Formation of the British State: England, Scotland and the Union, 1603–1707* (1987), and *The Witch-Hunt in Early Modern Europe* (1987 and 1995), which has been translated into eight languages.

His study of the development of beliefs about witchcraft in Europe over the course of many centuries gave him the idea of writing a textbook on Western civilization that would illustrate a broader set of encounters between different cultures, societies, and ideologies. While writing the book, Levack and his two sons built a house on property that he and his wife, Nancy, own in the Texas hill country. He found that the two projects presented similar challenges: It was easy to draw up the design, but far more difficult to execute it. When not teaching, writing, or doing carpentry work, Levack runs along the jogging trails of Austin, and he has recently discovered the pleasures of scuba diving.

Edward Muir grew up in the foothills of the Wasatch Mountains in Utah, close to the Emigration Trail along which wagon trains of Mormon pioneers and California-bound settlers made their way westward. As a child he loved to explore the broken-down wagons and abandoned household goods left at the side of the trail and from that acquired a fascination with the past. Besides the material remains of the past, he grew up with stories of his Mormon pioneer ancestors and an appreciation for how the past continued to influence the present. During the turbulent 1960s, he became interested in Renaissance Italy as a period and a place that had been formative for Western civilization. His biggest challenge is finding the time to explore yet another new corner of Italy and its restaurants.

Muir received his Ph.D. from Rutgers University, where he specialized in the Italian Renaissance and did archival research in Venice and Florence, Italy. He is now the Clarence L. Ver Steeg Professor in the Arts and Sciences at Northwestern University and former chair of the History Department. At Northwestern he has won several teaching awards. His books include *Civic Ritual in Renaissance Venice* (Princeton, 1981); *Mad Blood Stirring: Vendetta in Renaissance Italy* (Johns Hopkins, 1993 and 1998); and *Ritual in Early Modern Europe* (Cambridge, 1997).

Some years ago Muir began to experiment with the use of historical trials in teaching and discovered that students loved them. From that experience he decided to write this textbook, which employs trials as a central feature. He lives beside Lake Michigan in Evanston, Illinois. His twin passions are skiing in the Rocky Mountains and rooting for the Chicago Cubs, who manage every summer to demonstrate that winning isn't everything.

Michael Maas was born in the Ohio River Valley, in a community that had been a frontier outpost during the late eighteenth century. He grew up reading the stories of the early settlers and their struggles with the native peoples, and seeing in the urban fabric how the city had subsequently developed into a prosperous coal and steel town with immigrants from all over the world. As a boy he developed a lifetime interest in the archaeology and history of the ancient Mediterranean world and began to study Latin. At Cornell University he combined his interests in cultural history and the Classical world by majoring in Classics and Anthropology. A semester in Rome clinched his commitment to these fields—and to Italian cooking. Maas went on to get his Ph.D. in the Graduate Program in Ancient History and Mediterranean Archaeology at University of California at Berkeley.

He has traveled widely in the Mediterranean and the Middle East and participated in several archaeological excavations, including an underwater dig in Greece. Since 1985 he has taught ancient history at Rice University in Houston, Texas, where he founded and directs the interdisciplinary B.A. Program in Ancient Mediterranean Civilizations. He has won several teaching awards.

Maas's special area of research is Late Antiquity, the period of transition from the Classical to the Medieval worlds, which saw the collapse of the Roman Empire in western Europe and the development of the Byzantine state in the east. During his last sabbatical, he was a member of the Institute for Advanced Study in Princeton, New Jersey, where he worked on his current book, *The Conqueror's Gift: Ethnography, Identity, and Imperial Power at the End of Antiquity* (forthcoming). His other books include *John Lydus and the Roman Past: Antiquarianism and Politics in the Age of Justinian* (1992); *Readings in Late Antiquity: A Sourcebook* (2000); and *Exegesis and Empire in the Early Byzantine Mediterranean* (2003).

Maas has always been interested in interdisciplinary teaching and the encounters among different cultures. He sees *The West: Encounters & Transformations* as an opportunity to explain how the modern civilization that we call "the West" had its origins in the diverse interactions among many peoples of antiquity.

Meredith Veldman grew up in the western suburbs of Chicago in a close-knit, closed-in Dutch Calvinist community. In this immigrant society, history mattered: the "Reformed tradition" structured not only religious beliefs but also social identity and political practice. This influence certainly played some role in shaping Veldman's early fascination with history. But probably just as important were the countless World War II reenactment games she played with her five older brothers. Whatever the cause, Veldman majored in history at Calvin College in Grand Rapids, Michigan, and then earned a Ph.D. in modern European history, with a concentration in nineteenth- and twentieth-century Britain, from Northwestern University in 1988.

As Associate Professor of History at Louisiana State University, Veldman teaches courses in nineteenth- and twentieth-century British history and twentieth-century Europe, as well as the second half of "Western Civ." In her many semesters in the Western Civ. classroom, Veldman tried a number of different textbooks but found herself increasingly dissatisfied. She wanted a text that would convey to beginning students at least some of the complexities and ambiguities of historical interpretation, introduce them to the exciting work being done now in cultural history, and, most important, tell a good story. The search for this textbook led her to accept the offer made by Levack, Maas, and Muir to join them in writing *The West: Encounters & Transformations*.

The author of *Fantasy, the Bomb, and the Greening of Britain: Romantic Protest, 1945–1980* (1994), Veldman is also the wife of a Methodist minister and the mother of two young sons. They reside in Baton Rouge, Louisiana, where Veldman finds coping with the steamy climate a constant challenge. She and her family recently returned from Manchester, England, where they lived for three years and astonished the natives by their enthusiastic appreciation of English weather.

THE WEST

What Is the West?

MANY OF THE PEOPLE WHO INFLUENCE PUBLIC OPINION—POLITICIANS, teachers, clergy, journalists, and television commentators—frequently refer to "Western values," "the West," and "Western civilization." They often use these terms as if they do not require explanation. But what *do* these terms mean? The West has always been an arena within which different cultures, religions, values, and philosophies have interacted, and any definition of the West will inevitably arouse controversy.

The most basic definition of the West is of a place. Western civilization is now typically thought to comprise the regions of Europe, the Americas, Australia, and New Zealand. As we shall see, however, over time these boundaries have shifted considerably. In addition to being a place, Western civilization also encompasses a history—a tradition stretching back thousands of years to the ancient world. Over this long period the civilization we now identify as Western gradually took shape. The many characteristics that identify any civilization emerged over this time: forms of governments, economic systems, and methods of scientific inquiry, as well as religions, languages, literature, and art.

Throughout the development of Western civilization, the ways in which people identified themselves changed as well. People in the ancient world had no such idea of the common identity of the West, only of being subjects of an empire. But with the rise of Christianity and Islam between the third and seventh centuries C.E., the notion of a distinct civilization in these "Western" lands subtly changed. People came to identify themselves less as subjects of a particular empire and more as members of a community of faith—whether that community comprised followers of Christianity, Judaism, or Islam (see Chapter 7). These communities of faith drew lines of inclusion and exclusion that still exist today. Starting about 1,600 years ago, Christian monarchs obliterated polytheism (the worship of many gods) and marginalized Jews. Several centuries later they strove to expel Muslims from Christian kingdoms (see Chapter 9). Europeans developed definitions of the West that did not include Islamic communities. The Islamic countries themselves erected their own barriers, isolating themselves from the West. During the Renaissance in the fifteenth century an identity based on a continuous historical experience dating back to the ancient world was added to these religious definitions of the identity of the West.

The Temple of Hera at Paestum, Italy: Greek colonists in Italy built this temple in the sixth century B.C.E. Greek ideas and artistic styles spread throughout the ancient world both from Greek colonists, such as those at Paestum, and from other peoples who imitated the Greeks.

The definition of the West has also changed as a result of European colonialism, which began about 500 years ago. When European powers assembled large overseas empires, they introduced Western languages, religions, technology, and culture to many distant places in the world, making Western identity a transportable concept (see Chapters 12, 19, and 23). In some of these colonized areas—such as North America, Argentina, Australia, and New Zealand—the European newcomers so outnumbered the indigenous people that these regions became as much a part of the West as Britain, France, and Spain. In other European colonies, especially in European trading outposts on the Asian continent, Western culture failed to exercise a widespread influence.

As a result of colonialism Western culture sometimes merged with other cultures. Brazil, a South American country inhabited by large numbers of indigenous peoples, the descendants of African slaves, and European settlers, epitomizes the complexity of what defines the West. In Brazil, almost everyone speaks a Western language (Portuguese), practices a Western religion (Christianity), and enjoys the benefits of Western political and economic institutions (democracy and capitalism). Yet in Brazil all of these features of Western civilization have become part of a distinctive culture, in which indigenous, African, and European elements have been blended. During Carnival, for example, Brazilians dressed in indigenous costumes dance in African rhythms to the accompaniment of music played on European instruments.

For many people today, the most important definition of the West involves adherence to a certain set of values, the "Western" values. Values are the moral and philosophical principles that are held in esteem by a particular culture. The values typically identified as Western include universal human rights, toleration of religious diversity, equality before the law, democracy, and freedom of inquiry and expression. These values have a long history. Yet these values have not always been embraced by Western societies. For example, the rulers of ancient Rome extended the privileges of citizenship, the right to own property, and the ability to participate in trade to a select few inhabitants of their empire (see Chapter 5)—thus only the privileged enjoyed the benefits of equality before the law. The majority of medieval Europeans, who were Christian, expressed an intense intolerance for religious diversity expressed in the Crusades against Muslims and heretics and pogroms against Jews (see Chapter 9). As late as the nineteenth century, white men living in the United States enslaved blacks and into the twentieth excluded women from voting and equal access to jobs. And in Nazi Germany and the Soviet Union, totalitarian regimes terrorized their own population and millions of others beyond their borders (see Chapter 25). The history

■ **A Satellite View of Europe**

What is the West? Western civilization has undergone numerous transformations throughout history, but it has always included Europe.

of the West is riddled with examples of leaders who stifled free inquiry and who censored their followers. What are we to make of this contradiction in values? This text highlights and examines these contradictions, demonstrating how hard values were to formulate in the first place and how difficult they have been to preserve.

The Shifting Borders of the West

The geographical setting of the West has also shifted over time. This textbook begins about 10,000 years ago in southwestern Asia and Egypt. At that time the domestication of animals and crops began, and vast trading networks were being established. Cities, kingdoms, and empires gave birth to the first civilizations. By about 500 B.C.E., the civilizations that are the cultural ancestors of the modern West had spread from the Middle East to include the Mediterranean basin—areas influenced by Egyptian, Hebrew, Greek, and Roman thought, art, law, and religion. By the first century C.E. the Roman Empire drew the map of what historians consider the heartland of the West: most of western and southern Europe, the coastlands of the Mediterranean Sea, and the Middle East.

The West is now usually thought to include Europe and the Americas. However, the borders of the West have in recent decades come to be less about geography than identity. When Japan, an Asian country, accepted some Western values such as human rights and democracy after World War II, did it become part of the West? Or consider the Republic of South Africa, which until 1994 was ruled by the white minority, people descended from European immigrants. The oppressive regime violated human rights, rejected full legal equality for all citizens, and jailed or murdered those who questioned the government. Only when that government was replaced through democratic elections and a black man became president did South Africa grant full rights to non-Europeans. To what degree was South Africa part of the West before and after these developments?

Russia long saw itself as a Christian country with a tradition of culture, economic, and political ties with the rest of Europe. The Russians have intermittently identified with their western neighbors, but their neighbors were not always sure about the Russians. After the Mongol invasions of the thirteenth and fourteenth centuries much of Russia was isolated from the rest of the West (see Chapter 10) and during the Cold War from 1949 to 1989 (see Chapters 27–29) Russian communism and the Western democracies were polarized. When was Russia "Western" and when not?

Thus, when we talk about where the West is, we are almost always talking about the Mediterranean basin and much of Europe (and later, the Americas). But we will also show that countries that border "the West," and even countries far from it, might be considered Western in many aspects as well.

Asking the Right Questions

So how can we make sense of the West as a place and an identity, the shifting borders of the West, and Western civilization in general? In short, what has Western civilization been over the course of its long history—and what is it today?

Answering these questions is the friendly challenge this book poses. You may be alarmed to learn that there are no simple answers to any of these questions. On the other hand, you may be relieved to discover that there is a method for finding answers that have meaning for the different periods of history covered in this book. The method

■ **The Astrolabe**
The mariner's astrolabe was a navigational device intended for use primarily at sea. The astrolabe originated in the Islamic world and was adopted by Europeans in the twelfth century—a cultural encounter that enabled Europeans to embark on long ocean voyages around the world.

is straightforward. Always ask the *what*, the *when*, the *where*, the *who*, the *how*, and the *why* questions of the text. If you do so, you will surmount the challenge the book poses. To aid you, every chapter addresses the question of "What is the West," or "How was the West made" at its beginning following the story or event that opens the chapter. We revisit the question in the Conclusion at the end of every chapter. For example, in Chapter 11 we look at how the Italian Renaissance helped refashion the very concept of Western civilization. In the Conclusion, we see that the Renaissance interest in the history of the ancient world transformed the idea of the West from one defined primarily by religious identification with Christianity to one created by a common historical experience.

THE "WHAT" QUESTION

What is Western civilization? The answer to this question will vary according to time and place. In fact, for much of the early history covered in this book, Western civilization as we know it today did not exist as a single cultural entity. Rather, a number of distinctive civilizations were taking shape in the Middle East, northern Africa, and Europe, each of which contributed to what later became Western civilization (see Chapters 1–3). But throughout time the idea of Western civilization slowly began to form. Thus our understanding of Western civilization will change from chapter to chapter. For example, in Chapters 12, 19, and 23, we examine how the place of the West changed through the colonial expansion of the European nations. In Chapter 16 we learn how the West came to prize the values of scientific inquiry for solving human and philosophical problems, an approach that did not exist before the seventeenth century but became central to Western civilization.

THE "WHEN" QUESTION

When did the defining characteristics of Western civilization first emerge, and for how long did they prevail? To explore these questions you will want to refer to the dates that frame and organize each chapter, as well as the numerous short chronologies offered in each chapter. These resources will help you keep track of what happened when. Dates have no meaning by themselves, but the connections *between* them can be very revealing. For example, dates show that the agricultural revolution that permitted the birth of the first civilizations (see Chapter 1) unfolded over a long span of about 10,000 years—which is more time than was taken by all the other events and developments covered in this textbook. Wars of religion (see Chapter 14) plagued Europe for nearly 200 years before Enlightenment thinkers articulated the ideals of religious toleration (see Chapter 17). The American Civil War—the war to preserve the union as President Abraham Lincoln termed it—took place at exactly the same time as other wars were being fought to achieve national unity in Germany and Italy (see Chapter 21).

By learning when things happened, you can identify the major causes and consequences of events, and thus you can see the transformations of Western civilization. For instance, the ability to produce a surplus of food through agriculture and the domestication of animals was a prerequisite for the emergence of civilizations. The violent collapse of religious unity after the Protestant Reformation in the sixteenth century led some Europeans to propose the separation of church and state two centuries later. And during the nineteenth century many Western states—in response to the enormous diversity among their own peoples—became preoccupied with maintaining or establishing national unity.

THE "WHERE" QUESTION

Where has Western civilization been located? Geography, of course, does not change very rapidly, but the idea of where the West is does. The location of the West is not so much a matter of changing borders but of how people identify themselves. The key to understanding the shifting borders of the West is to study how the peoples within the West

■ **Map 1　Core Lands of the West**
The geographical borders of the West have changed substantially throughout history.

■ Cortés Meets Montezuma

As the Spanish fought, traded, and intermarried with the native peoples of the Americas during the fifteenth and sixteenth centuries, each culture changed.

Tenochtitlan.

thought of themselves. These groups include Muslims and the peoples of eastern Europe (such as the Soviet Union during the Cold War), which some people have wanted to exclude from the West. In addition, the chapters help you trace the relationships between the West (as it was constituted in different periods) and other, more distant civilizations with which it interacted. Those civilizations include not only those of East Asia and South Asia but also the indigenous peoples of sub-Saharan Africa, the Americas, and the Pacific islands (see Chapters 12, 19, and 23).

THE "WHO" QUESTION

Who were the people responsible for making Western civilization? Sometimes they were anonymous, such as the unknown geniuses who invented the mathematical systems of ancient Mesopotamia. At other times the makers of the West were famous—conquerors such as Julius Caesar, creative thinkers such as Galileo Galilei, or generals such as Napoleon. But history is not only made by great and famous people. Humble people, such as the many millions who migrated from Europe to North America or the unfortunate millions who suffered and died in the trenches of World War I, can also influence the course of events.

Perhaps most often in this book you will encounter people who were less the shapers of their own destinies than the subjects of forces that conditioned the kinds of choices they could make, often with unanticipated results. When during the eleventh century farmers throughout Europe began to employ a new kind of plow to till their fields, they were merely trying to do their work more efficiently. They certainly did not recognize that the increase in food they produced would stimulate the enormous population growth that made possible the medieval civilization of thriving cities and magnificent cathedrals. In answering the who question, you will always want to evaluate how much individuals and groups of people were in control of events and how much events controlled them.

THE "HOW" QUESTION

How did Western civilization develop? This is a question about processes—about how things change or stay the same over time. This book will help you identify these processes in several ways. First, we have woven the theme of encounters throughout the story. What do we mean by encounters? Here is an example from Chapter 12: When the Spanish *conquistadores* arrived in the Americas some 500 years ago, they came into contact with the cultures of the Caribs, the Aztecs, the Incas, and other peoples who had lived in the Americas for thousands of years. As the Spanish fought, traded with, and intermarried with the natives, each culture changed. The Spanish, for their part, borrowed from the Americas new plants for cultivation and responded to what they considered serious threats to their worldview. Many native Americans, in turn, adopted European religious practices and learned to speak European languages. At the same time, they were decimated by

European diseases to which they had never been exposed. They also witnessed the destruction of their own civilizations and governments at the hands of the colonial powers. Through many centuries of interaction and mutual influence, both sides became something other than what they had been.

The European encounter with the Americas is an obvious example of what was, in fact, a continuous process of encounters with other cultures. These encounters often occurred between peoples from different civilizations, such as the struggles between Greeks and Persians in the ancient world (see Chapter 3) or between Europeans and Chinese in the nineteenth century (see Chapter 23). Other encounters took place among people living in the same civilization. These include interactions between lords and peasants, men and women, Christians and Jews, Catholics and Protestants, factory owners and workers, and capitalists and communists. Western civilization developed and changed through a series of external and internal encounters.

Second, features in the chapters can also help you formulate answers to the question of how Western civilization developed. For example, each chapter contains an essay titled "Justice in History". These essays discuss a trial or some other episode involving questions of justice. Some "Justice in History" essays illustrate how Western civilization was forged in struggles over conflicting values, such as the discussion of the trial of Galileo in Chapter 16, which examines the conflict between religious and scientific concepts of truth. Others show how efforts to resolve internal cultural, political, and religious tensions helped shape Western ideas about justice, such as the essay on the *auto da fé* in Chapter 14, which illustrates how authorities attempted to enforce religious conformity. At the end of each "Justice in History" feature, you will find several questions tying that essay to the theme of the chapter. These questions will also ask you to explore the value-based conflicts or disputes embodied in the incident described in the essay.

Some chapters include two other features as well. Essays titled "The Human Body in History" demonstrate that even the body, which we typically understand as a product of genetics and biology, has a history. These essays show that the ways in which Western people understand their bodies, how they cure them, how they cover and uncover them, and how they adorn them tell us a great deal about the history of Western culture. We explore, for example, how the bodies of World War I soldiers afflicted with shell shock were treated differently from women experiencing similar symptoms of hysteria (see Chapter 24). Shell-shocked soldiers gave people a sense of the horrors of war and stimulated powerful movements in Europe to outlaw war as an instrument of government policy.

The "Places of Encounter" features show how encounters between different groups of people were not abstract historical processes but events that occurred in actual places, such as in the nineteenth-century soccer stadium (see Chapter 23). In the nineteenth century soccer was a sport reserved for gentlemen, but in the great industrial cities it became the favorite sport of the industrial workers. In the soccer stadiums they began to experience their common identity as a class.

THE "WHY" QUESTION

Why should you study Western civilization? Because everything around you depends on it—the education you receive, the books you read, the language you speak and those you study, the legal system that protects you, and the political one that guarantees you certain rights. The buildings you inhabit, the music and art you enjoy, and the science and technology that provides you with health, comfort, and prosperity are all artifacts of Western civilization. To appreciate all that, to contribute to it more fully yourself, and when necessary to question and critique it, requires that you understand the West was sometimes very different from the present—it was like a foreign country—and how it was sometimes very much like the present, the foundation upon which your world was made.

The Beginnings of Civilization, 10,000–2000 B.C.E.

IN 1991 HIKERS TOILING THEIR WAY ACROSS A GLACIER IN THE ALPS BETWEEN Austria and Italy made a startling discovery: a man's body stuck in the ice. They alerted the police, who soon turned the corpse over to archaeologists. The scientists determined that the middle-aged man had frozen to death about 5,300 years ago. Otzi the Ice Man (his name comes from the Ötztal Valley where he perished) quickly became an international celebrity as the world's oldest freeze-dried human.

The scientists who examined Otzi believe that he was a shepherd herding flocks of sheep and goats to mountain pastures when he died. A few grains of wheat on his clothing suggested that he lived in a farming community. Copper dust in his hair hinted that Otzi may also have been a metalworker, perhaps looking for ores during his journey. An arrowhead lodged in his back indicated a violent cause of death, but the exact circumstances remain mysterious.

Otzi's gear was state-of-the-art for his era. His possessions showed deep knowledge of the natural world. During thousands of years of careful observation and interaction with the environment, Otzi's ancestors had learned what materials were best suited to specific tasks. Otzi benefited from their experience—but made use of new technology as well. He wore leather boots insulated with dense grasses chosen for protection against the cold. The pouch around his waist contained stone tools and fire-lighting equipment. He wore carefully stitched leather leggings, a loincloth, and a knee-length tunic and may have used a grass mat for protection against the elements. The wood selected for his bow offered special strength and flexibility. In his light wooden backpack Otzi carried containers to hold burning embers, as well as dried meat and nutritious seeds to eat on the trail. The arrows in his quiver featured a natural adhesive that tightly bound bone and wooden points to the shafts. The most noteworthy find among

Chapter Outline

- Culture, Agriculture, and Civilization
- The Birth of Civilization in Southwest Asia
- The Emergence of Egyptian Civilization
- The Transformation of Europe

Wall Plaque: This Sumerian wall plaque shows King Ur-Nanshe of the city of Lagash in Mesopotamia. He carries a basket of bricks that will be used to build a temple. Cuneiform writing identifies the king and his project. In the lower right corner he drinks a beer to celebrate the completion of the temple.

■ **Otzi the Ice Man**
This most recent artist's recreation of Otzi shows him with his
state-of-the-art tools.

Otzi's possessions was his axe. Its handle was made of
wood but its head was copper—a remarkable innovation
at a time when most tools were made of stone. Otzi was
ready for almost anything—except the person who shot
him in the back.

Otzi lived near the end of what archaeologists call the
Neolithic Age, or "New Stone Age," when people made refinements in tool-making techniques over those of previous
ages. For example, Neolithic artisans carved remarkably
delicate arrowheads and blades that could be used for a variety of tasks, from hunting to sewing. The Neolithic Age
was a long period of revolutionary change lasting from
about 10,000 to 3000 B.C.E. that altered human existence on
Earth forever. Even the most advanced technological developments of the twentieth century did not reshape human
life as profoundly as did the technological and social shifts
of the Neolithic era.

This chapter traces humanity's first steps toward the civilizations that developed in Southwest Asia, Egypt, and
Europe—regions that made fundamental contributions to
the development of Western civilization. First we will
consider the most fundamental encounter of all—the rela-

tionship between humans and the natural world. Many
thousands of years of human interaction with nature led to
food production through agriculture and the domestication of animals. This revolutionary achievement let humans develop new, settled forms of communities: villages,
cities, and eventually kingdoms and empires. Civilizations
with quite different religious and political systems grew
from the foundations of agriculture and the domestication
of animals. The growth of civilization also depended on
constant interaction among communities who lived far
apart. Once people were settled in a region, they began
trading for commodities that were not available in their
homelands. As trade routes extended over long distances
and interactions among diverse peoples proliferated, ideas
and technology spread.

In this chapter we will address several major questions
about humanity's first civilizations: (1) What is the link between the food-producing revolution of the Neolithic era
and the emergence of civilizations? (2) What transformed
the earliest settled communities in Southwest Asia into the
first cities, kingdoms, and empires in history? (3) How did
civilization take shape along the Nile River in Egypt?
(4) How and why did food production and the use of metals transform the lives of the men and women who populated Europe in the Neolithic Age?

Culture, Agriculture, and Civilization

Anthropologists use the term *culture* to describe the
knowledge and adaptive behavior created by a
group of people that helps them to mediate between themselves and the natural world through time.
Indeed, culture° encompasses all the different ways that humans collectively adjust to their environment and organize
and transmit their experiences and knowledge to future
generations.

In the animal world, any successful adaptation takes a
very long time. The paleontological record is full of vanished species—such as the woolly mammoth and the giant
tree sloth—that failed to adapt quickly enough to changing environments and new predators. Humanity has survived by assessing constant changes in the natural world
and making the necessary adjustments to these new circumstances. Our evolution as a species over the last several
million years has depended on this adaptability. We are not
as strong as rhinoceroses or as fast as cheetahs, but through
culture we have an advantage over all the other creatures
with whom we share the planet—the ability to adapt to new
environments extremely quickly.

More specifically, humans possess three crucial adaptive
mechanisms. The primary adaptive behavior of humans is

language. Language allows us to exchange information and share experiences from one generation to the next, a skill that animals lack. We do not simply respond biologically. We can imagine powerful forces at work in our lives that we cannot see, and we can discuss our ideas. This ability to think abstractly and to share our thoughts through spoken language lets us employ our innate curiosity productively. We accumulate knowledge and use it to modify the world in which we live.

Our ability to speak and to put ideas into action drives us to create new technologies, the second adaptive mechanism that gives humans a competitive advantage over other species. Humans are careful observers of nature, acquiring knowledge from our experience that helps us respond creatively to the challenges that we encounter. As a result, we constantly refine our tools so that they become more efficient. With these tools we build shelters that allow us to live in a wide range of environments, from the icy Arctic to tropical rain forests. We create calendars that help us track time, and we write textbooks that interpret the past and give it meaning. We devise technologies—everything from Otzi's humble gear to space stations orbiting Earth—that alter natural processes, exploit natural resources, and help us understand our world.

Perhaps the most important adaptive mechanism of all is our capacity to experience and to express emotions such as love, pity, guilt, and shame. This ability shapes our collective behavior. We organize ourselves into families and other groups in which these feelings play an integral role. Thanks to our emotions we have the capacity to create long-lasting social relationships, such as families and friendships that have profound meaning for us. These bonds are the foundation of all human communities. Patterns of social relationships are transmitted through the generations, forming the backbones of our cultures and our civilizations. Emotional bonds enable communities to survive even while responding to challenges and change.

Culture is the medium through which these transmissions and adaptations take place over time. We can understand a people's culture as a web of interconnected meanings that enable them to understand themselves and their place in the world and transmit their experience and knowledge to future generations. Each culture is distinctive; thus we use labels—"Greek culture" or "American culture." Yet all cultures constantly borrow from their neighbors and change over time.

We often use *culture* and *civilization* interchangeably, yet in the history of human development, civilization has a specific definition. Archaeologists define civilization° as a society differentiated by levels of wealth and occupation in which people lived in cities. With cities, human populations achieved the critical mass necessary to develop specialized occupations, as well as a level of economic production high enough to sustain complex religious and cultural practices. In earlier village communities, social classes— groups considered to have different degrees of importance

and status—developed when the people to whom food and other vital resources were distributed became dependent upon the elites who distributed them. With the appearance of stark differences in wealth, the lines between social classes became more rigid. Rulers emerged who dictated the distribution of economic resources. As villages evolved into cities, their social organization grew more complicated. The labor of most people supported a small group of political administrators and religious leaders, as these city elites used taxation and control of trade to gain access to the economic resources of the countryside. Thus, as we will see shortly, in early civilizations three kinds of power— economic, political, and religious—converged. A city's rulers controlled the mechanisms of not only government and warfare but also the distribution of food and wealth. They augmented their authority by building temples to the gods and participating in religious rituals that linked divinity with kingship.

THE EMERGENCE OF HUNTER-GATHERER SOCIETIES

Between 200,000 and 100,000 years ago—after several million years of biological evolution—physically and intellectually modern humans, known as Homo sapiens sapiens° ("most intelligent people"), first appeared in Africa and began to spread to other continents. Scientists refer to this stage of human history as the Paleolithic Age, or Old Stone Age, because people made tools by cracking rocks and using their sharp edges to cut and chop. These people were our direct ancestors, but they were not alone on the planet. Other less advanced species of humans had been evolving for about four million years, and they too had migrated from Africa to many regions across the globe. *Homo sapiens sapiens* coexisted with these less advanced peoples, such as Neanderthals, for thousands of years during the Paleolithic Age.

Homo sapiens sapiens' use of tools shows the difference between their mental capacities and those of other less advanced groups. The tools of the non–*Homo sapiens sapiens* groups remained virtually unchanged over the hundreds of thousands of years of their evolution. By contrast, those of *Homo sapiens sapiens* demonstrated rigid adaptation to new environments and practical needs. They learned quickly through experience and observation and shared their knowledge through language. Their ability to develop new tools enabled *Homo sapiens sapiens* to live almost everywhere on the planet. For example, hunters learned to make razor-sharp blades with which to skin hides, which in turn could be used to make warm clothes suitable for cold climates. *Homo sapiens sapiens* successfully adapted to a broad range of environments, including tropical jungles, dry savannas, and mountain woodlands.

These humans developed other skills as well. They mastered the art of making fire, which they used to cook food and keep warm. They scavenged for wild food and became shrewd observers of the natural environment. They followed migrating herds of animals, hunting with increasing efficiency as their weapons improved. Archaeologists have unearthed skillfully crafted arrowheads, spear tips, and other blades, as well as fishhooks and harpoons carved from bone. These tools show that Paleolithic peoples learned to exploit the natural resources of a wide variety of ecological zones. They also created beautiful works of art by carving bone and painting on cave walls. Sadly, their music, poems, languages, and beliefs have all vanished from the human record.

By 45,000 years ago, these humans had reached most of Earth's habitable regions, except for Australia, the islands of the South Pacific, and North and South America. They continued to live as nomadic hunter-gatherers, foraging for wild foods, fishing, and tracking herds of game. But about 15,000 years ago, when the last Ice Age ended, the Earth's climate became warmer, causing changes in vegetation. Humans began to interact with the natural environment in new ways. The warmer climate allowed cereal grasses to spread quickly over large areas; hunter-gatherers learned to collect these wild grains and grind them up for food. Sometimes, groups of hunter-gatherers settled in semi-permanent camps, returning to them regularly to take advantage of the wild foods that flourished during different seasons. They established some camps near rivers and wetlands, where wild grains grew and provided a reliable source of food to supplement their hunting and fishing. When people learned that the seeds of wild grasses could be transplanted and grown in new areas, the domestication of plants was under way.

THE FOOD-PRODUCING REVOLUTION

Until about 8000 B.C.E., human beings acquired their food in the same ways they had since our species began evolving. They hunted, fished, and gathered foods that grew in the wild. But over the course of the next 8,000 years, a revolutionary change took place. Farming crops and herding domesticated animals gradually replaced hunting and gathering as the source of virtually all human nourishment. The long transition to food production° brought about the most profound change in human society since the appearance of *Homo sapiens sapiens:* Food production made civilization possible (see Map 1.1).

There was no single reason for the shift to food production, but archaeologists agree that population growth, ecological changes brought about by the warming environment, and the dwindling of game due to overkill by hunters all increased the demand for food. Driven by need, humans began to recognize that cultivation of the earth and domestication of animals could provide a dependable food supply. By trial and error they learned to plant crops in accordance with the seasons and natural growing cycles. They also dis-

CHRONOLOGY	
Prehistory to Civilization	
4.5 MILLION YEARS AGO	Humans originate in Africa
1 MILLION YEARS AGO	Humans learn to control fire
200,000 YEARS AGO	Origins of anatomically modern humans
150,000 YEARS AGO	Modern humans (*Homo sapiens sapiens*) appear in Africa
45,000 YEARS AGO	Modern humans spread through Europe, Africa, and Asia
13,000 YEARS AGO	Ice Age ends
10,000 YEARS AGO	Food production begins
3000 B.C.E.	Sumerian civilization develops in Mesopotamia
2500 B.C.E.	Egyptian civilization begins

covered that if they fertilized, weeded, harvested, and stored their crops at the right times and under favorable climatic circumstances, they would get bigger yields. In hunter-gatherer societies men hunt and fish while women generally collect wild foods. Thus it was probably women who first observed how plants spread in nature and first discovered that they could achieve the same effect by sowing seeds.

At the same time that people discovered the benefits of planting seeds, they also began domesticating pigs, sheep, goats, and cattle, which eventually replaced wild game as the main source of meat. Domestication° involves more than just taming wild animals. It requires entering into a complex process of control and intervention that lasts through several of the animals' generations. Domestication occurs when humans manipulate the breeding of animals in order to serve their own purposes—for example, making wool (lacking on wild sheep), laying extra eggs (not done by undomesticated chickens), and producing extra milk (wild cows produce only enough milk for their offspring).

Hunters had practiced some techniques of domestication when they began to spare the females and young males of a wild herd in order to maintain a steady food supply. Perhaps some young animals were captured alive and taken back to the camp, where they were partially tamed as pets. As flocks of animals were penned, the effects of breeding eventually were noticed and systematically developed. The first signs of goat domestication occurred about 8900 B.C.E. in the Zagros Mountains in Southwest Asia. Pigs, which adapt very well to human settlements because they eat

■ **Map 1.1   The Beginnings of Food Production**

This map shows early farming sites discovered by archaeologists where the first known production of food occurred in ancient Southwest Asia (the Middle East).

garbage, were first domesticated around 7000 B.C.E. By around 6500 B.C.E domesticated cattle, goats, and sheep had become widespread.

Farming and herding required hard work, but the payoff was enormous. Even simple agricultural methods could produce about fifty times more food than hunting and gathering. Thanks to the increased food supply, more newborns survived past infancy. Populations expanded, and so did human settlements. When the food-producing revolution began, humans numbered only about eight million people. Today, about 6.5 billion people live on the planet. Food production made this growth in world population possible.

In Southwest Asia, food production fostered the development of two new kinds of human communities that now exist around the globe: agricultural societies° and pastoralist societies°. In agricultural societies, people live in fixed communities. They plant crops and perhaps maintain herds of domesticated animals, often grazing them in meadows some distance away. In pastoralist societies, people lead a nomadic way of life, constantly moving their flocks from place to place in search of pasture where the animals can graze. Pastoralism developed in ancient Southwest Asia as a response to the arid conditions of most of the region. It spread widely around the globe from its

Southwest Asian origins, but few traces of it exist in the archaeological record.

With the mastery of food production, human societies developed the mechanisms not only to feed themselves, but also to produce a surplus, which could then be traded for other resources. Such economic activity allowed for economic specialization and fostered the growth of social, political, and religious hierarchies. As villages developed and then grew into cities, the first human civilization emerged.

The Birth of Civilization in Southwest Asia

By 6000 B.C.E., settled communities that depended on farming and herding had become the norm throughout Southwest Asia. With better and more plentiful food, such communities expanded steadily. Prosperity further stimulated commerce, and merchants from different regions began traveling regularly to one another's villages to trade. Mesopotamia, the dry floodplain bounded by the

Tigris and Euphrates Rivers, became the meeting place of ideas and peoples from across an enormous geographical area. The cultures of these trading communities remained quite distinct—they had different ways of building houses, decorating pottery, and selecting locations for their settlements. Historians assume that their beliefs and languages differed as well. Over time, however, these Mesopotamian village communities began to resemble one another and a more uniform culture developed. The development of this more uniform culture set the stage for the emergence of civilization in Southwest Asia.

THE FIRST FOOD-PRODUCING COMMUNITIES

In Southwest Asia, where sufficient annual rainfall enabled crops to grow without irrigation, people began cultivating food in three separate areas. Archaeologists have named the first area the Levantine Corridor° (also known as the Fertile Crescent°)—a twenty-five-mile-wide strip of land that runs from Jericho in the Jordan River valley of modern Israel to the Euphrates River valley in Iraq. The second region was the hilly land north of Mesopotamia at the base of the Zagros Mountains in the western part of modern Iran. The third was Anatolia, or what is now the central region of Turkey. Although humans mastered agriculture and domestication of animals independently in these three areas, contact among traders may have accelerated the spread of crops and knowledge about food production. Examination of human settlement in each of these three regions illuminates the diverse processes by which human beings learned to control their natural environment and to organize their societies.

The small settlement of Abu Hureyra in Syria on the Euphrates River, which was inhabited from about 9500 to 5000 B.C.E., illustrates how agriculture developed over a long period at a single site. The first settlers here fed themselves primarily by hunting gazelles and gathering wild cereals. But sometime between 8000 and 7700 B.C.E., they began to plant and harvest a small number of grains. By 7000 B.C.E. Abu Hureyra had grown into a farming settlement, covering nearly thirty acres that sustained a population of about 400. A few generations later, the inhabitants of Abu Hureyra began herding sheep and goats to supplement their meat supply. These domesticated animals became the community's primary source of meat when the gazelle herds were depleted about 6500 B.C.E.

Families in Abu Hureyra lived in small dwellings built of mud brick containing several rooms. The inhabitants discovered that crop rotation—planting different crops in a field each year—would result in a much higher yield. Archeological evidence shows that many women in the community developed arthritis in their knees, probably from crouching for hours on end as they ground grains. Thus we assume that while men hunted and harvested crops, women performed the labor of grinding the grains. This division of labor along gender lines indicates a growing complexity of social relations within communities.

At the other end of the Levantine Corridor, the farming village of Jericho began to develop rapidly after 8500 B.C.E. Located at an old hunting-gathering site along a stream in the Jordan River valley near modern Jerusalem, Jericho expanded to encompass nearly ten acres after its inhabitants started cultivating crops, including wheat, barley, lentils, and peas. In addition, they learned a valuable lesson: If they let a field lie fallow for a season, the soil would be richer and more productive the following year.

Archaeological evidence shows how Jericho's growing wealth enabled the community to develop. The inhabitants developed more complex political, religious, and economic structures. Fairly sophisticated engineering projects, such as the digging of a nine-foot-deep ditch around the village as a flood control device and the erection of a massive stone wall to protect against attackers, indicate the emergence of some form of political organization. Other findings hint at religious beliefs. Jericho's people buried their dead within the settlement, sometimes under the floors of their houses. They placed plastered skulls of their deceased on the walls, a practice that may suggest worship of the family's ancestors. Archaeological evidence also reveals that long-distance commerce played a part in the lives of these villagers. They exchanged agricultural goods for turquoise from the Sinai Peninsula, shells from the Mediterranean and Red Seas, and most important of all, obsidian from Anatolia. This volcanic stone was the most important commodity in the Neolithic Age because it could be used for making sharp-edged tools such as arrowheads, spear points, and sickles for harvesting crops.

The second region of village settlement, the lands at the foot of the Zagros Mountains north of Mesopotamia, reveals a different sort of development pattern from that exhibited in either Jericho or Abu Hureyra. Archaeologists have unearthed a hunter-gatherer camp at Sawi Chemi Shanidar, dating to about 9000 B.C.E. In this settlement, the domestication of animals long predated the development of agriculture. The settlers herded animals, but they did not cultivate crops for more than a thousand years. At the site of Ganj Dareh, a similar pattern occurred. First occupied as a seasonal camp in 8500 B.C.E., Ganj Dareh became a permanent mud-brick village with a few two-story houses by 7000 B.C.E. Its villagers herded cattle and goats. Evidently they slaughtered most male livestock but kept the females for breeding.

The third region of early settled communities, Anatolia, followed patterns more like those of the Levantine Corridor. Around 8500 B.C.E. a few simple settlements appeared. The villagers raised pigs and traded obsidian for materials from far away, such as the highly prized blue lapis lazuli stones from northeastern Afghanistan. A thousand years later, about 7400 B.C.E., Anatolians began cultivating a variety of crops, including wheat and lentils. They started herding sheep at roughly the same time as the Abu Hureyra villagers, and domesticated dogs for hunting, herding, and protection. Many new villages sprang up in this region during the next millennium. The farmers lived in rectangular houses. More than mere huts, these houses featured plastered walls, hearths, courtyards, and ovens for baking breads.

Some time after 6000 B.C.E. Anatolian communities grew more complex, with the emergence of religious beliefs and social hierarchies. For example, the Anatolian town of Çatal Hüyük consisted of thirty-two acres of tightly packed houses that the townspeople rebuilt more than a dozen times as their population expanded. Çatal Hüyük controlled the obsidian trade from Anatolia to the Levantine Corridor. The wealth from this trade fostered the emergence of social differences. For example, we know that the townspeople buried some of their dead with jewelry and other riches, a practice that indicates distinctions between wealthy and poor members of the society. In addition, the community was wealthy enough to sustain what appears to be some type of communal religious practice. The walls of several buildings display paintings of bulls and women giving birth to bulls, while the homes contain altars decorated with horns and figurines of rams and bulls.

The long-distance obsidian trade sped up the development of communities in the Levantine Corridor, the Zagros Mountains, and Anatolia. Enterprising merchants began carrying the valuable stone from the rich deposits of Anatolia to the Levantine Corridor, the Zagros Mountains, and the Sinai Peninsula. In village markets, they traded obsidian for turquoise, for decorative shells from the Mediterranean and Red Seas, and for timber from the hills of Lebanon. These trade networks of the Neolithic Age laid the foundation for commercial and cultural encounters that would shape the development of civilizations for the next 5,000 years.

SUMER: A CONSTELLATION OF CITIES IN SOUTHERN MESOPOTAMIA

About 5300 B.C.E. the villages in Sumer, an ancient name for southern Mesopotamia, began a dynamic civilization that would flourish for 3,000 years. At the height of this civilization, Sumerians (who called themselves "the black-headed people" because of their characteristic dark hair) lived in thriving cities governed by leaders who controlled

CHRONOLOGY	
Mesopotamia and Anatolia	
CA. 9500–5000 B.C.E.	Settled community at Abu Hureyra develops on the Euphrates River
CA. 8500–7000 B.C.E.	Humans domesticate animals at Ganj Dareh
CA. 8500–6000 B.C.E.	Humans domesticate animals, engage in agriculture, and create settled communities in Anatolia
CA. 6000 B.C.E.	Çatal Hüyük in Anatolia prospers from trade and agriculture
CA. 5300–3000 B.C.E.	Villages develop into cities in Mesopotamia; Sumerian culture emerges
CA. 4600–2500 B.C.E.	Uruk in Mesopotamia becomes powerful, with temples, kings, and economic regulation
CA. 3200 B.C.E.	First known written documents in cuneiform appear
CA. 2350 B.C.E.	Akkadian king Sargon conquers Sumer and other lands
CA. 2100 B.C.E.	Akkad falls; Ur becomes powerful in Mesopotamia
CA. 2000 B.C.E.	Amorites begin to enter Mesopotamia
CA. 1900 B.C.E.	Assyria grows powerful through trade and conquest
CA. 1800 B.C.E.	Babylonian civilization emerges; Hammurabi prepares his Law Code

agricultural production, regulated long-distance trade, and presided over the worship of the gods.

The Origins of Sumerian Cities

Sumerian civilization was linked to water. Over centuries, the Sumerians learned to control the unpredictable waters of the Tigris and Euphrates Rivers. In the process, they developed the structures of civilization. Initially, Sumerian villagers dug their own small channels to divert floodwaters from the two great rivers to irrigate their dry lands. Then they discovered that by combining the labor force of several villages, they could build and maintain irrigation channels on a large scale. These channels directed the rushing floodwaters of the rivers every spring in time for planting. The lands irrigated by river water provided rich yields of crops that fed Sumer's growing population. Villages blossomed into cities that became the foundation of Sumerian civilization.

By 2500 B.C.E., about twelve major cities in Sumer had emerged that controlled the Mesopotamian floodplain in an organized fashion. They used the floodwaters of the Tigris and Euphrates Rivers in order to irrigate agricultural lands, create new fields, and increase the food supply. Some cities achieved impressive dimensions. Uruk, for example, covered about two square miles by 2500 B.C.E. and had a population estimated at between 10,000 and 50,000 people, including the peasants living in the countryside. Many villagers living in the countryside surrounding the main cities labored to provide food for the urban populations as well as for themselves.

Sumerian Economic and Political Life

Sumerian cities served as the economic centers of southern Mesopotamia. Craft specialists such as potters, toolmakers, weavers, and artists gathered in these urban settings to purchase food, swap information, and sell their goods. By providing markets for outlying towns, the cities spun a web of economic interdependence. Long-distance trade, made easier by the introduction of wheeled carts drawn by oxen, enabled merchants to bring timber, ores, and luxury items unavailable in Mesopotamia from Anatolia, the Levantine Corridor, Afghanistan, and Iran. With the introduction of the potter's wheel, Sumerian artisans could mass-produce containers for trade and storage of grain and other commodities. Fishermen thrived as well. They fished on the rivers of Mesopotamia and in the Persian Gulf and traded their catch in the markets of villages and cities.

Within the cities, centralized authorities directed the necessary labor for irrigation and water control. The rulers of Uruk, for example, organized large-scale irrigation projects with canals leading to the rivers. They also maintained warehouses for storing surplus grains, and they distributed food to workers who labored on building projects for the king. Ultimate power to direct labor lay in the hands of the king. The people dedicated all the resources of the kingdom to supporting him and maintaining the city's ziggurat, the temple where everyone gathered to worship the city's main gods. Monumental temples and palaces demonstrated the king's power over the economic and human resources of the city—as well as the vast inequality of wealth between governing elites and the peasant workers. Archaeological excavations reveal that Uruk's elite—its priests, aristocrats, important civil administrators, and wealthy merchants—lived in luxurious houses near the temples, while everyone else crowded into small mud-brick houses with few comforts. Similar divisions characterized Sumer's other cities as well.

The economic resources of their cities enabled kings to supply armies and lead them into battle. Sumerian kings frequently waged war against one another in an effort to increase their territory and power. Long walls punctuated by tall gates and towers protected the inhabitants of Sumerian cities from the attacks of rival cities and the persistent raids of nomadic pastoralists who hovered on the outskirts of settled lands.

Rivalry among the kings prevented Sumerian cities from uniting politically, but the kings maintained diplomatic relations with one another as well as with rulers throughout Southwest Asia and Egypt, primarily to protect their trading networks. Safe trade links helped tie each Sumerian city to the common culture of Sumerian lands.

Through trade and warfare and from the many diplomats, soldiers, travelers, and slaves who passed through Mesopotamia's cities, the Sumerians knew much about the natural resources, economic organization, and customs that characterized the foreign peoples around them. The world known to them extended from India in the east to the Caucasus Mountains in the north; to Egypt and Ethiopia in the south; and to the Mediterranean Sea in the west. Sumerians strongly believed that the gods favored them over all other peoples, and they developed intense prejudices against their neighbors, accusing them of cowardice, stupidity, and treachery.

Sumerian Religious Life

Religion—powerfully influenced by Mesopotamia's volatile climate—played a central role in daily life. Sumerians knew firsthand the famine and destruction that could come from sudden floods, storms, and winds. They envisioned each of these natural forces as a god who, like a human king or queen, had to be pleased and appeased. Sumerians believed that in order to survive they must continually demonstrate their subservience to the gods, and their practice of constantly feeding these deities with sacrifices was one way of doing so.

Some scholars maintain that an important reason for the growth of Sumerian cities was the desire to "nourish" the gods, primarily through sacrifices of meat. The need to fulfill such expensive religious obligations may have led Sumerians to develop the complex economic and political arrangements that are the hallmarks of Sumerian civilization. It is clear that the bulk of each city's resources went to maintaining the temples, priests, and herds of sacrificial animals. Every day priests carried several sumptuous meals to the statues of the gods. The deities would consume the "immaterial essence" of the food, and then the priests and temple attendants would eat the leftovers. Ordinary people offered smaller gifts of nourishment to the gods at family shrines. By performing the right rituals and giving the appropriate offerings, Sumerians hoped that the gods would answer their humble prayers. For instance, one queen made a private offering to a goddess on behalf of her son, pleading, "May the statue, to which let my mistress the goddess turn her ear, speak my prayers."[1] There were, however, no guarantees of divine assistance.

Each Sumerian city was protected by one god or goddess. The deity's temples served as the center of the city and the focus of religious life. In Uruk, for example, two enormous temples dominated the community: the Ziggurat of Anu (the supreme sky god) and the Temple of Heaven Precinct. This latter complex of buildings contained a colonnaded courtyard and a large limestone temple dedicated to Inanna

THE CLASH BETWEEN CIVILIZATION AND NATURE: THE TAMING OF ENKIDU

········

The Sumerians saw their civilization as tightly linked to nature, as this passage from the tale of Gilgamesh suggests. This excerpt tells how Enkidu, Gilgamesh's companion, first became civilized. Originally living like a wild animal, Enkidu prevents hunters from trapping game. But city officials send him a prostitute who tames him by having sex with him for a week. The prostitute represents natural forces controlled by the city. As a result of this epic sexual encounter, Enkidu loses his ability to talk to the animals. Then, by consuming cooked food and beer and wearing cloth garments for the first time, he becomes a civilized man. The episode teaches that civilization imposes control on natural forces, transforming them in the process—a metaphor for the Sumerians' civilization.

In the wilderness the goddess Aruru created valiant
   Enkidu . . .
He knew neither people nor settled living . . .
He ate grasses like gazelles,
And jostled at the watering hole with the animals . . .
Then Shamhat [the prostitute] saw him—a primitive,
A savage fellow from the depths of the wilderness! . . .
Shamhat unclutched her bosom, exposed her sex,
And Enkidu took in her voluptuousness.
She was not restrained, but took his energy . . .

For six days and seven nights Enkidu stayed aroused,
And had intercourse with the prostitute,
Until he was sated with her charms.
But when he turned his attention to the animals,
The gazelles saw Enkidu and darted off,
The wild animals distanced themselves from his body . . .
Enkidu knew nothing about eating bread for food,
[nor] of drinking beer he had not been taught to.
The prostitute spoke to Enkidu, saying:
"Eat the food, Enkidu, it is the way one lives.
Drink the beer, as it is the custom of our land."
Enkidu ate the food until he was sated,
He drank the beer—seven jugs!—and became expansive
   and sang with joy!
He was elated and his face glowed.
He splashed his shaggy body with water,
And rubbed himself with oil and turned into a human.
He put on some clothing and became like a warrior.
He took up weapons and chased lions so shepherds could
   rest at night.
With Enkidu as their guard, the herders could lie down.

(also known as Ishtar), the goddess of love and war and the city's special guardian. All Sumerian cities had similar temples that towered over the city, reminding all the inhabitants of the omnipresent gods who controlled their destiny.

Sumerians believed that everything in the universe, from the mightiest god to the most insignificant pebble, contained a divine presence. They assumed, however, that the mightiest gods took human form. The all-powerful king Anu, the father of the gods, ruled the sky. Enlil was master of the wind and guided humans in the proper use of force. Enki ruled the Earth and rivers and guided human creativity and inventions. Inanna was the goddess of love, sex, fertility, and warfare. Ninhursaga, another female divinity, was considered a source of royal power. Sumerians also worshiped hundreds of lesser gods at home and in shrines throughout their cities and in the countryside.

Sumerians told exciting stories about their gods and heroes. One of the most popular figures in Sumerian ballads was the legendary king Gilgamesh of Uruk. Part god and part man, Gilgamesh—accompanied by his stalwart companion, Enkidu—embarked on many adventures that delighted Mesopotamian audiences for thousands of years. Originally told in the Sumerian language, the tales of Gilgamesh and Enkidu excited the imaginations of other Mesopotamian peoples as well, who later recorded them in their own languages.

The vastly entertaining story of Gilgamesh reveals Sumerian concerns about the proper behavior of a king and the limits of human ambition. The tale describes how the gods created Enkidu to be Gilgamesh's companion and balance the king's rash disposition. Together the two men battled monsters and set out on long journeys in search of adventure. When Enkidu died, Gilgamesh tried to find the secret of immortality, but learned that humans cannot live forever. As a result of his travels, Gilgamesh became a wiser king and his subjects benefited from his new wisdom.

Sumerian Cultural Achievements

Sumerian culture exerted an enormous impact on the peoples of ancient Southwest Asia, and remnants of it continue to influence today's world. Some archaeologists believe that the Sumerians invented the wheel. They also devised the potter's wheel, the wagon, and the chariot, which proved essential for daily transportation and warfare.

Perhaps the Sumerians' most important cultural innovation was their development of writing. The Sumerians

■ Cuneiform Texts

The first of these clay tablets, left, written in cuneiform, or "wedge-shaped" letters, is early in the development of the script. Dating from about 3000 B.C.E., it lists what are probably temple offerings under the categories day one, day two, and day three. The second text, below, was produced in Babylonia about 1750 B.C.E. It contains problems in geometry. Unlike the first tablet, which is written in the Sumerian language, the geometry tablet is in the Semitic language spoken by the Babylonians.

devised a unique script used to record their language. Historians call the symbols that were pressed onto clay tablets with sharp objects cuneiform°, or wedge-shaped, writing. The earliest known documents written in this language come from Uruk about 3200 B.C.E. In the following excerpt, a Sumerian storyteller marvels at the invention and usefulness of writing:

> This speech was too difficult; its contents were too long;
> The Messenger's mouth was too slow; he could not repeat it.
> Since the Messenger's mouth was too slow, and he could not repeat it,
> The Lord of Kulab patted some clay and set down the words as on a tablet.
> Before that day, there was no putting of words on clay;
> But now, when the Sun rose, it verily was so:
> The Lord of Kulab had verily put words on clay![2]

Researchers believe that the roots of cuneiform writing date back 10,000 years, when people began to cultivate crops and domesticate animals in Southwest Asia. To keep track of quantities of produce and numbers of livestock, villagers began using small clay tokens of different shapes to represent and record these quantities. Each marker had a separate meaning. For example, cones and spheres indicated certain quantities of grain, and an oval meant a container of oil. New shapes could be added to represent new commodities. The tokens took the uncertainty out of transactions, reducing conflict because parties to a transaction no longer had to rely simply on memory or spoken agreements.

About 3400 B.C.E. people began to store these tokens in small clay envelopes and to impress their markings on the outsides of the envelopes to convey what was inside. After several centuries, people stopped using the envelopes entirely and simply impressed the shapes on a flat piece of clay or tablet to record transactions. Eventually, traders started impressing information about quantities or objects directly onto clay with a pointed stick, thus eliminating the need for tokens entirely. As commodities and trading became more complex, the number of symbols multiplied. By 3000 B.C.E. the number of symbols had been streamlined from about a thousand to approximately 500, but learning even 500 signs required intensive study. The scribes, the people who mastered these signs, became valued members of the community. Sumerian cuneiform writing spread, and other peoples of Mesopotamia and Southwest Asia began adapting it to record information in their own languages.

The Sumerians also made impressive innovations in mathematics. The first numerals (symbols for numbers) emerged around the same time as writing. Derived from the impressions of tokens, numerals proved to be valuable in the royal bureaucracy and in trade. Over time, the Sumerians became highly skilled in mathematics. Archaeologists have found many Sumerian tablets used as school texts that contain problems in advanced algebra and plane and solid geometry. They also show multiplication tables, square and cube roots, and exponents, as well as other practical information such as how to calculate compound interest on loans. Sumerian numeracy has left a lasting imprint on Western culture. It was the Sumerians who developed a counting system based on sixty in multiples of ten—a system still in use in the way we tell time—and it was the Sumerians who divided the circle into 360 degrees.

In addition to mathematics, the Sumerians excelled in many other fields. They were skilled architects, as their ziggurats and city walls reveal. Their irrigation systems show their mastery of hydraulic engineering. They also developed detailed knowledge about the movement of the stars, planets, and the moon—especially as these movements pertained to agricultural cycles. But despite their invention of writing, they recorded none of their architectural, technological, and astrological knowledge. Instead, they passed it orally from generation to generation. The Babylonians, members of a civilization that arose later in Mesopotamia, inherited this knowledge, expanded it, and ultimately shared it with the Greeks, the Persians, the Phoenicians, and other peoples of later ages. In this way scientific traditions that began in ancient Sumer contributed to the scientific thought of Western civilization.

FROM AKKAD TO THE AMORITE INVASIONS

Around 2340 B.C.E., the political independence of Sumer's cities ended. Conquered by a warrior who took the name Sargon ("true king"), Sumer's cities found themselves swallowed up by Mesopotamia's first great empire. Sargon came from Akkad, a region in Mesopotamia north of Sumer. Sargon's people, the Akkadians, had lived in Mesopotamia for more than a thousand years.

The Akkadians began to migrate into Mesopotamia from their original homes somewhere in the Levantine Corridor during the late fourth millennium B.C.E. Their settlements grew in size, and although they intermingled with the native Sumerian population they preserved their own language and customs. During the third millennium B.C.E., a number of Akkadian cities grew strong. The inhabitants of these cities spoke Akkadian, a Semitic language that became the common language of trade throughout ancient Mesopotamia and Southwest Asia until about 500 B.C.E. The Akkadians' most significant contribution to Western civilization, however, came with their creation of a new kind of political entity: the multiethnic empire.

By bringing cities with very different languages, culture, and traditions under his rule, Sargon (r. ca. 2340–ca. 2305 B.C.E.) created a dynamic empire that endured for more than a century (see Map 1.2). The realm that Sargon had established reached its greatest extent about 2220 B.C.E. The empire's diverse subjects, including peoples in Mesopotamia, Syria, Anatolia, and western Iran, struggled to win back their independence, but Akkadian kings crushed their revolts.

Controlling such a large empire posed new challenges for Akkadian rulers. To surmount them, Sargon and his successors imitated and expanded upon the governing methods they observed in individual Sumerian cities. For example, to secure the loyalty of their many subjects, Akkadian kings presented themselves as symbols of unity in the form of semidivine figures. After a king's

death, his subjects worshiped him as a god. Some monarchs claimed to be gods while they were alive.

Raising the revenues to meet the costs of running their enormous empire presented another problem for Akkadian kings. The king paid for all the public buildings, irrigation projects, and temples throughout his realm, as well as for the immense army required to defend, control, and expand the empire. Monarchs generated revenues in several ways. A key source of revenue was the leasing out of the vast farmlands that belonged to the king. Kings also required conquered peoples to pay regular tribute in the form of trade goods, produce, and gold and silver. In addition, Akkadian kings depended on the revenue generated by commerce. They placed heavy taxes on raw materials imported from foreign lands. In fact, most Akkadian kings made long-distance trade the central objective of their foreign policy. They signed treaties with foreign kings and sent military expeditions as far as Anatolia and Iran to obtain timber, metals, luxury goods, and construction materials. Akkadian troops protected these international trade routes and managed the maritime trade in the Persian Gulf, where merchants brought goods by ship from India and southern Arabia.

The cities of Mesopotamia prospered under Akkadian rule. A wealthy upper class developed that owned a great deal of private property obtained from trade and agriculture. Even so, Akkadian rulers could not hold their empire together for reasons that historians do not completely understand. One cause was marauding tribes from the Zagros Mountains, who repeatedly infiltrated the kingdom and caused tremendous damage. Suddenly Akkadian kings lost control of their lands and a period of anarchy began about 2103 B.C.E. "Who was king? Who was not king?" lamented a

■ **Map 1.2 Sargon's Empire, 2220 B.C.E.**
Sargon of Akkad created an empire that included many distinct ethnic groups. For the first time in history, rulers had to struggle with the resistance of diverse subject peoples.

writer during this time of troubles. The kingdom finally collapsed about 2100 B.C.E.

With the fall of Akkad, the cities of Sumer regained their independence, but they were quickly reunited under Ur-Nammu (r. ca. 2112–ca. 2095 B.C.E.), king of the Sumerian city of Ur. Ur-Nammu established a powerful dynasty that lasted for more than a century. The kings of Ur strengthened the central government by turning formerly independent cities and their territories into provinces and appointing administrators to govern them. To prevent these provincial governors from becoming too powerful and possibly developing royal ambitions, the kings routinely rotated them to new administrative posts.

Ur's kings also centralized economic production in their empire. The royal administration controlled most long-distance trade and developed a vigorous industry in woolen garments and leather goods. Ur's rulers supported many thousands of artisans and laborers who were paid in beer and various agricultural products. The materials the artisans produced were traded throughout Southwest Asia. Wealth also flowed to the kings of Ur from farming and herding. The kings owned huge herds of livestock that grazed on royal estates, but ordinary individuals were not permitted to possess agricultural lands. Most of Ur's citizens worked either as tenant farmers on estates owned by the king and the political leaders, or as slaves. Each year government officials collected tens of thousands of cattle and hundreds of thousands of sheep and redistributed them to temples throughout the kingdom for use in sacrifices.

The most important innovation in Ur occurred in the realm of the law. Ur-Nammu compiled the first known collection of laws in ancient Mesopotamia. His laws reveal his determination to provide social justice for his subjects. He established courts in which a panel of judges made decisions about family controversies and business disputes such as debt, inheritance, contracts, and the sale of property and slaves. The custom of writing down laws so that citizens and later generations could refer to them became a strong tradition in Western civilization.

The kings of Ur used political innovations, economic centralization, and legal codification to strengthen their hold over Sumer's cities; they did not, however, challenge or change the key facets of Sumerian culture. Ur's monarchs continued the long Mesopotamian tradition of building elaborate temple complexes featuring ziggurats, palaces, and tombs to demonstrate their piety. Like earlier Mesopotamian rulers, Ur's kings considered themselves gods. They placed their tombs in the temple complex of the moon god Nanna, Ur's special protector.

Despite their sophisticated governmental structures, the kings of Ur could not stave off political fragmentation. About 2000 B.C.E., seminomadic peoples known as Amorites began invading Mesopotamia from the steppes to the west and north. They seized fortified towns, taking food and supplies and causing widespread destruction. By 2004 B.C.E.

THE LEGEND OF KING SARGON

The Akkadian king Sargon inspired many legends. The following story tells how his mother, a priestess, bore him in secret and put him in a basket in the river, from which a water bearer rescued him. The document explains how Sargon eventually became king of the Mesopotamians through the favor of the goddess Ishtar. The tale of a baby found in the bulrushes who achieves greatness was a Sumerian story already old in Sargon's day. A similar tale about the prophet Moses would be recorded in the Hebrew Bible more than a thousand years later. The recurrence of such literary motifs over a period of more than 3,000 years indicates the pervasive influence of Sumerian culture on subsequent civilizations of Southwest Asia.

Sargon, the mighty king, king of Agade, am I.
My mother was a high priestess, my father I knew not . . .
My mother, the high priestess, conceived me, in secret she bore me.
She set me in a basket of rushes, with bitumen she sealed my lid.
She cast me into the river which rose not over me.
The river bore me up and carried me to Akki, the drawer of water. . . .
Akki, the drawer of water, took me as his son and reared me.
Akki, the drawer of water, appointed me as his gardener.
While I was a gardener, Ishtar granted me her love.
And for four and [. . .] years I exercised kingship.
The black-headed people I ruled, I governed. . . .

Source: From *Chronicles Concerning Early Babylonian Kings*, by L. W. King. London: British Museum, 1907.

they had destabilized the economy of Mesopotamia as well as of other regions of Southwest Asia. Peasants fled from the fields, and with no food or revenues, inflation and famine overcame the empire. Ur collapsed, and Mesopotamia shattered once again into a scattering of squabbling cities. Taking advantage of the political turmoil, tribes of Amorites settled in Mesopotamian lands, because food was more abundant there than on the steppe. They abandoned their nomadic way of life in favor of agriculture.

NEW MESOPOTAMIAN KINGDOMS: ASSYRIA AND BABYLONIA

Within a few generations, the Amorites absorbed the culture of the Mesopotamian urban communities they had conquered. Two new kingdoms, Babylonia and Assyria, emerged in the lands once controlled by Sumer and Akkad

■ **Ziggurat of Ur**

Built of mud bricks, the Ziggurat of Ur was the focal point of religious life. This vast temple was built by King Ur-Nammu of the Third Dynasty (2113–2096 B.C.E.) and restored by the British archeologist Sir Leonard Woolley in the 1930s. Similar structures have been found in all the major cities of ancient Sumer and were typically surrounded by public buildings and palaces of the elite.

■ **Aerial View of the Ziggurat of Ur**

This photograph reveals how the great temple dominated the flat cityscape that surrounded it.

and coexisted for more than two centuries. The phenomenon of invaders absorbing the culture of sophisticated communities they conquered and then creating something new would often be repeated as Western civilization evolved.

Assyria: A Kingdom of Commerce

Ashur, the major city in Assyria, had its start on the upper Tigris River some time before 2000 B.C.E. Ashur's inhabitants, called Assyrians, spoke a Semitic language related to Akkadian. International commerce formed the basis of the Assyrian economy, and Ashur held a privileged place as a hub of trading routes.

Assyria's power began to expand around 2000 B.C.E., perhaps due in part to the discovery of bronze making. Bronze is an easily worked but very hard metal, made by combining molten copper with small quantities of tin. It quickly became very highly valued both for military and ornamental uses. Because the sources of copper and tin were in southern Arabia, Anatolia, and Afghanistan, trade in metals became increasingly important throughout Southwest

■ Map 1.3 Empire of Assyria, ca. 1800 B.C.E.
The Assyrians combined warfare and commerce to create their empire in Mesopotamia and Anatolia.

Asia. The Assyrians controlled much of the metals trade among these various regions.

By 1900 B.C.E. the Assyrians had established an extensive trading network that reached as far as Anatolia and Syria (see Map 1.3). They also controlled and operated about a dozen trading colonies throughout these regions. Assyrian merchants sent donkey caravans to these colonies loaded with tin (obtained in Afghanistan) and textiles (acquired in southern Mesopotamia) to exchange for copper, gold, and silver. In order to encourage long-distance commerce, Assyrian kings did not tax silver, gold, copper, tin, barley, and wool. The whole process of trading was recorded by Assyrian scribes who kept commercial records dealing with accounting, credit, prices, and transportation costs.

An assembly of leading merchants called "the City" amassed great power in Assyria. The City controlled diplomatic relations with foreign kingdoms, established economic policy, and determined taxes on commerce. It also passed binding legal decisions that affected the entire region. By contrast, the authority of Assyrian kings was limited to performing religious duties, maintaining the system of justice, and building irrigation works, walls, and other public projects.

By 1762 B.C.E., however, independent Assyria had ceased to exist. It, and all of Mesopotamia, fell under the rule of King Hammurabi of Babylon, one of humanity's first great empire builders.

Babylon: A Kingdom of Law and Order

The kingdom of Babylonia, a mixture of Sumerian and Amorite cultures, emerged about 1800 B.C.E. as the dominant power in southern Mesopotamia. To secure their rule and enrich their coffers, Babylonian kings embarked on the conquest of neighboring lands. Their capital city, Babylon,

grew wealthy. Under the leadership of King Hammurabi (r. 1792–1750 B.C.E.), Babylonia gained control of all of Mesopotamia, including the Assyrian realm. Impressed by his own victories, Hammurabi called himself "King of the Four Quarters of the World."

Hammurabi also called himself the "King of Justice," a title he deserves, because his historical legacy is a rigorous system of justice codified in law. The Law Code of Hammurabi, the most complete surviving legal text of ancient Mesopotamia, demonstrates the careful thought this monarch devoted to matters of justice.

The 282 civil, commercial, and criminal laws contained in the Code unveil the social assumptions and specific concerns of Babylonia's rulers. For example, the irrigation system on which Babylonian agriculture depended is a frequent focus of the Code. Many laws related specifically to damages and personal responsibility with regard to irrigation. Similarly, the Code buttressed Babylon's social hierarchy by drawing legal distinctions between classes of people. The crimes of aristocratic elites were treated far more leniently than were the offenses of nonaristocrats, while slaves were given no rights at all.

At the same time, however, Hammurabi's Code introduced one of the fundamentals of Western jurisprudence: the idea that the punishment must suit the crime. For example, one law reads: "If a man has opened his channel for irrigation and has been negligent and allowed the water to wash away a neighbor's field, he shall pay grain equivalent to the crops of his neighbors."[3] Through its introduction of such abstract principles as "an eye for an eye," Hammurabi's Code helped shape legal thought in Southwest Asia for a millennium. It later influenced the laws of the Hebrews, and through the Hebrew Bible continues to mold ideas about justice to this day.

The great temples of Mesopotamian cities influenced the lives of Babylonians by providing the opportunity to worship the gods upon whom success depended. In addition, the priests at the temples controlled large tracts of land in the name of the gods they served. The farmers who labored on these lands gave their produce to the priests, and the temples enjoyed great prosperity. Other groups in Babylonian society also grew wealthy.

Babylonian society contained a private sector of merchants, craftspeople, farmers, and sailors. These free people, who were not tied to the temples or the king, grew prosperous. For example, merchants traveling by land and sea brought textiles and metals as well as luxury items such as gold and silver jewelry and gems from Anatolia, Egypt, Iran,

Afghanistan, and lands along the Persian Gulf and Red Sea. This private sector enjoyed a degree of personal freedom unique in ancient Mesopotamia.

The most important person in Babylonian society, however, was the king. Babylonian monarchs had the responsibility of building and repairing city walls, temples to the gods, irrigation systems to improve agriculture, and warehouses for storing grain. Hammurabi and his successors imposed increasingly heavy taxes on their subjects. These financial demands provoked great resentment, and when Hammurabi died, many Babylonian provinces successfully revolted. As a result, Babylonian rulers were weakened by loss of revenues. They tried to maintain their control by increasing the number of bureaucrats. This only made the government top-heavy, and by 1500 B.C.E. it collapsed.

The Emergence of Egyptian Civilization

A s the civilizations of Mesopotamia rose and fell, another emerged far to the south, in Egypt—a long and narrow strip of land in the northeast corner of the African continent. Egypt's lifeline is the Nile, the world's longest river, which flows north into the Mediterranean Sea from its origin in east Africa 4,000 miles away. The northernmost part of Egypt, where the Nile enters the Mediterranean, is a broad and fertile delta. In ancient times, Egypt controlled an 850-mile strip of land along the Nile. Until the completion of the Aswan Dam in 1970 C.E., the

■ **Women's Work**
This sculpture from the Old Kingdom, made about 2400 B.C.E., shows a woman grinding grain by hand and then sieving it to remove the chaff. Small particles of stone from the grinding block entered the wheat and ground down everyone's teeth.

CHRONOLOGY

Egyptian Civilization

CA. 5000 B.C.E.	First agricultural communities on Nile
CA. 3500 B.C.E.	Hierakonpolis and other kingdoms established
CA. 3100 B.C.E.	Narmer unifies Upper and Lower Egypt
CA. 3000–2200 B.C.E.	Old Kingdom
2200–2040 B.C.E.	First Intermediate Period
CA. 2040–1785 B.C.E.	Middle Kingdom
1785–1560 B.C.E.	Second Intermediate Period; Hyksos rule in delta

river flooded annually from mid-July to mid-October, leaving behind rich deposits of silt ideal for planting crops. In its ancient days, the Nile abounded with fish, water birds, and game on the shore. The rich banks of the Nile provided an ideal setting for agriculture and settled communities.

Historians organize the long span of ancient Egyptian history into four main periods: Predynastic (10,000–3000 B.C.E.), the Old Kingdom (3000–2200 B.C.E.), the Middle Kingdom (2040–1785 B.C.E.), and the New Kingdom (1600–1100 B.C.E., discussed in Chapter 2). Times of political disruption between the kingdoms are called intermediate periods. Despite these periods of disruption, the Egyptians maintained a remarkably stable civilization throughout millennia.

THE BEGINNINGS OF SETTLED LIFE

Human beings had lived as hunter-gatherers in Egypt for tens of thousands of years before they began to settle in agricultural communities. Like the people of other civilizations we have discussed, the Egyptians were originally hunter-gatherers who slowly turned to growing crops and domesticating animals. Small villages, in which people could coordinate their labor most easily, appeared along the banks of the Nile between 5000 and 4000 B.C.E.

By 3500 B.C.E., Egyptians could survive comfortably through agriculture and herding. With hunting and foraging for food no longer a major focus of everyday life, the transition to settled life was complete, and Egyptian society began to develop in many new ways. Small

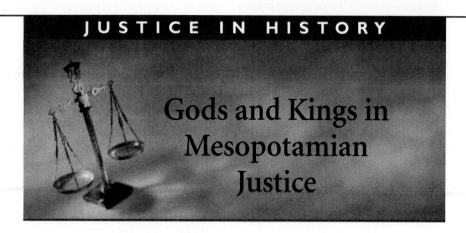

Gods and Kings in Mesopotamian Justice

Mesopotamian kings placed a high priority on ruling their subjects justly. Shamash, the sun god and protector of justice, named two of his children Truth and Fairness. In the preface to his law code, Hammurabi explained the relationship between his rule and divine justice:

> At that time, Anu and Enlil [two of the greatest gods], for the well-being of the people, called me by name, Hammurabi, the pious, god-fearing prince, and appointed me to make justice appear in the land [and] to destroy the evil and wicked, so that the strong might not oppress the weak, [and] to rise like Shamash over the black-headed people [the people of Mesopotamia].[4]

Courts in Mesopotamian cities handled cases involving property, inheritance, boundaries, sale, and theft. A special panel of royal judges and officials handled cases involving the death penalty, such as treason, murder, sorcery, theft of temple goods, or adultery. Mesopotamians kept records of trials and legal decisions on clay tablets so that others might learn from them and avoid additional lawsuits.

A lawsuit began when an individual brought a dispute before a court for trial and judgment. The court consisted of three to six judges chosen from among the town's leading men, who typically included merchants, scribes, and officials in the town assembly. The judges could speak with authority about the community's principles of justice.

Individuals involved in the dispute spoke on their own behalf and presented testimony through witnesses, written documents, or statements made by leading officials. Witnesses took strict oaths to tell the truth in a temple before the statue of a god. Once the parties presented all the evidence, the judges made their decision and pronounced the verdict and punishment.

Sometimes the judges asked the defendants to clear themselves by letting the god in whose name the oath was taken make the judgment. The accused person would then undergo an ordeal or test in which he or she had to jump into a river and swim a certain distance underwater. Individuals who survived were considered innocent. Drowning constituted proof of guilt and a just punishment rendered by the gods.

The following account of one such ordeal comes from the city of Mari, about 1770 B.C.E. In this case a queen was accused of casting spells on her husband. The maid whom she forced to undergo the ordeal on her behalf drowned, and we do not know whether the queen received further punishment:

> Concerning Amat-Sakkanim . . . whom the river god overwhelmed . . . : "We made her undertake her plunge, saying to her, 'Swear that your mistress did not perform any act of sorcery against Yarkab-Addad her lord; that she did not reveal any palace secret nor did another person open the missive of her mistress; that your mis-

> tress did not commit a transgression against her lord.' In connection with these oaths they had her take her plunge; the river god overwhelmed her, and she did not come up alive."[5]

This account illustrates the Mesopotamian belief that sometimes only the gods could make decisions about right and wrong. Kings willingly allowed the gods to administer justice in their kingdoms. In this way, divine justice and royal justice became part of the same system.

By contrast, the following trial excerpts come from a homicide case in which humans, not gods, made the final judgment. About 1850 B.C.E., three men murdered a temple official named Lu-Inanna. For unknown reasons they told the victim's wife, Nin-dada, what they had done. King Ur-Ninurta of the city of Isin sent the case to be tried in the city of Nippur, the site of an important court. When the case came to trial, nine accusers asked that the three murderers be executed. They also requested that Nin-dada should be put to death because she had not reported the murder to the authorities. The accusers said:

> They who have killed a man are not worthy of life. Those three males and that woman should be killed in front of the chair of Lu-Inanna, the son of Lugal-apindu, the religious official.

In her defense, two of Nin-dada's supporters pointed out that she had not been involved in the murder and therefore should be released:

■ The Law Code of Hammurabi

This stone copy of Hammurabi's code stands taller than seven feet. Written in Babylonian cuneiform script, it shows Hammurabi receiving the law directly from the sun god, Shamash, seated on a throne. The god wears a crown of horns, a scepter, and a ring, and has flames coming from his shoulders. Hammurabi stands because his status is lower than Shamash's. He raises his hand in a gesture of respect and speaks directly to the god.

Granted that the husband of Nin-dada, the daughter of Lu-Ninurta, has been killed, but what had the woman done that she should be killed?

The court agreed with this latter argument on the grounds that Nin-dada was justified in keeping silent because her husband had not provided for her properly. Then the members of the Assembly of Nippur faced the three murderers and said:

A woman whose husband did not support her . . . why should she not remain silent about him? Is it she who killed her husband? The punishment of those who actually killed him should suffice.

In accordance with the decision of the court, the defendants were executed.

This approach to justice—using witnesses, evaluating evidence, and rendering a verdict in a court protected by the king—demonstrates the Mesopotamians' desire for fairness. This court decision became an important precedent that later judges frequently cited. ■

Questions of Justice

1. How would a city benefit by letting a panel of royal officials make judgments about life-and-death issues? How would the king benefit?

2. These trials demonstrate that the enforcement of justice in Mesopotamia depended on the interaction of religious, social, and political beliefs. How does this interaction help us understand Mesopotamian civilization?

Taking It Further

Greengus, Samuel. "Legal and Social Institutions of Ancient Near Mesopotamia," in *Civilizations of the Ancient Middle East*, ed. Jack M. Sasson, vol. 1, 469–484. 1995. Describes basic principles of law and administration of justice, with a bibliography of ancient legal texts.

Kuhrt, Amelie. *The Ancient Middle East: ca. 3000–330 B.C.*, vol. 1. 1995. An authoritative survey combining archaeological and textual evidence.

towns grew quickly in number along the Nile, and market centers connected by roads emerged as hubs where artisans and merchants exchanged their wares. After the potter's wheel was introduced from Mesopotamia, the production of pottery became more sophisticated. Some towns specialized in producing certain kinds of pots for trade, such as the elegant clay vessels found in the tombs of the wealthy along the Nile. As the quality of tools improved, artisans made ever more intricate copper, gold, and silver vessels.

These technological advances had drastic ecological consequences, however. As potters cut down more and more trees to burn in their kilns and as flocks of sheep and goats devoured the grasses and plants on the forests' edge, the ecological balance of grassland and desert collapsed. Farmers were pushed to cultivate land closer to the banks of the Nile River.

With this ecological shift, the social balance of Egyptian communities changed as well. The men who controlled the fertile river banks grew wealthy from the increase in grain production. As wealth grew in the fourth millennium B.C.E., social divisions widened between rich and poor Egyptians. Rich people built large houses and tombs and filled them with expensive items such as jewelry and fine pottery. Archaeologists have discovered clusters of such graves, a clue that generations of prosperous families were buried together and that the community viewed lineage as vital. At the same time, the wealthy members of the community began to experiment with mummification to preserve their bodies after death. Thus, not even death erased the distinctions between rich and poor.

To meet these wealthy landowners' demand for luxuries, professional merchants traded busily up and down the Nile. Assembling donkey caravans (camels would not come into use for another 3,000 years), they traveled to the Red Sea, Sinai, Mesopotamia, Palestine, Syria, and Nubia for gold, silver, ivory, copper beads, and other prized goods. These voyages established the foundations of long-lasting international trade routes.

Between 3500 and 3000 B.C.E., during the Predynastic period, energetic trade along the Nile River resulted in a shared culture and unified way of life. Towns along the Nile grew into small kingdoms. Despite shared social structures, religious beliefs, and ideas, rulers of these small kingdoms constantly warred with one another, attempting to grab more land and extend their power. The big gobbled up the small, and by 3000 B.C.E., all the

towns had been absorbed into just two kingdoms: Upper Egypt in the south and Lower Egypt in the north. These two then united, forming what historians term the Old Kingdom. There is no written record or other evidence to show how the process of political unification unfolded, but Egyptian legends give some clues. According to tradition, King Narmer of Hierakonpolis (the "City of the Falcon") in Upper Egypt united the two kingdoms about 3100 B.C.E. Narmer established control from Aswan, a city in the southernmost part of Egypt, all the way north to the Mediterranean Sea.

UNITED EGYPT:
THE OLD KINGDOM, CA. 3000–2200 B.C.E.

With the unification of Egypt under one king, a new era dawned for this civilization. Soon after Narmer brought all of Egypt under his command, cultural and political power moved north from Hierakonpolis to the newly built capital city of Memphis. There the Egyptian kings established themselves as the focal points of religious, social, and political life. Under the kings' careful supervision, the Old Kingdom stabilized and took on many of the characteristics of early civilizations we have seen in Mesopotamia, such as semidivine kingship, literate bureaucracies, a centralized

■ **Narmer the Unifier of Egypt**

This piece of slate, twenty-nine inches long, is carved on both sides. Carved pieces of stone, called palettes, were originally crafted in the Predynastic period as holders for cosmetics, but they evolved into objects with important religious and symbolic functions. This sample shows King Narmer of Hierakonpolis, who lived about 3100 B.C.E. With his right hand he holds a mace and is about to smash the skull of an enemy. He stands on two dead enemies, as a servant behind him carries his sandals. A falcon god, Horus (Hierakonpolis means "City of the Falcon"), sits in a papyrus plant holding an enemy's severed head. Narmer wears the White Crown of Upper Egypt and a bull's tail, symbolizing his virility. On the other side, he wears the Red Crown of Lower Egypt, which he has conquered.

Mediterranean Sea

DELTA

Gaza
Sakkara
Fayyum (Oasis)
Herakleopolis
LOWER EGYPT
Sinai
Desert

Desert
UPPER EGYPT
Abydos
Hierakonpolis

Alternative caravan route to Nubia

Caravan route to Yam

Red Sea

NUBIA

Yam

KINGDOM OF YAM

PUNT

Nile R.

Old Kingdom Egypt, ca. 3000–2200 B.C.E.
→ Trade routes
▬ Area under Egyptian dominance

■ **Map 1.4 Old Kingdom Egypt, ca. 3000–2200 B.C.E.**

During the Old Kingdom, Egyptians traded with the kingdom of Yam, Nubia, and the land of Punt. Egyptian rulers built pyramids in lower (northern) Egypt.

that the kingdom was protected against forces of disorder and destruction. The rulers steadily amassed more power, and by 2600 B.C.E. they owned the largest and richest agricultural lands.

The power of the kings was highly centralized. Authority began with the king and passed to his court officials and then to provincial governors who delegated power to the mayors of cities and villages. Administrators collected Egypt's surplus produce—coinage would not be invented for another 2,500 years—and then the kings' officials redistributed it wherever it was needed: to feed the armies that protected Egyptian territories and long-distance trade and the peasants who labored on public works such as temples, roads, and irrigation projects.

A complex bureaucracy organized the enormous resources controlled by the pharaohs. The job of keeping records of the kings' possessions and supervising food production fell to the scribes, who were trained in hieroglyph writing. This form of writing involved a set of several thousand signs called hieroglyphs, literally "sacred words." Hieroglyphs represent both sounds (as in our alphabet) and objects (as in a pictorial system). The hieroglyph system was very complex; all the more so because it diverged from the spoken Egyptian language. Consequently, learning hieroglyphs for literary or administrative purposes meant acquiring a second language and took years of schooling to master. It was worth the effort, however, for knowledge of hieroglyphs gave scribes and administrators great power. For 3,000 years, the royal bureaucrats kept the machinery of Egyptian government running despite the rise and fall of dynasties.

Scribes kept their records on papyrus, a durable and lightweight paper made from the pulp of the stalk of the papyrus plant, which grows in abundance along the banks of the Nile. Egyptians began to manufacture papyrus paper about 3000 B.C.E., and it quickly became an essential tool for the kings' bureaucracy. The government kept a monopoly on papyrus, and merchants exported it to Southwest Asia, where scribes in other kingdoms used papyrus as well as clay tablets to record information.

Like bureaucrats, priests in the king's service grew powerful. Priests came from elite families, often the king's, and their positions passed from father to son. They owned vast estates, including the temples to the god they served, and they became enormously wealthy. In addition, they often played a major role in political life. Kings sought their

economy, and strong support of long-distance trade (see Map 1.4).

Egyptian monarchs considered themselves to be gods as well as kings, believing that Ra, the sun god and creator of the universe, had chosen them to rule as his representatives. A text called *King as Priest of the Sun* explains the king's role: "Ra has placed the king on the earth of the living for ever and eternity to judge humanity and to pacify the gods, to realize Right and annihilate Wrong; he gives divine offerings to the gods, funerary offerings to the transfigured dead, the name of the king is in the sky like that of Ra. . . ."[6]

In their role as religious leaders, kings claimed to control even the Nile and its life-giving floods. To the Egyptians, the presence of the kings meant that cosmic order reigned, and

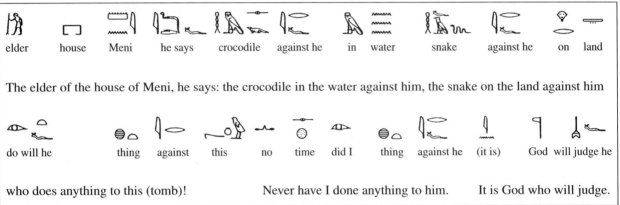

| elder | house | Meni | he says | crocodile | against he | in | water | snake | against he | on | land |

The elder of the house of Meni, he says: the crocodile in the water against him, the snake on the land against him

| do will he | | thing | against | this | no | time | did I | thing | against he | (it is) | God | will judge he |

who does anything to this (tomb)!   Never have I done anything to him.   It is God who will judge.

Source: From Regine Schulz and Matthias Seidel, *Egypt, the World of Pharaohs*, Koenemann, 1998, p. 347.

■ Hieroglyph Writing

One consequence of long-distance trade with Mesopotamia was the importation of the idea of writing, which became firmly established in Egypt about 3100 B.C.E. Egyptian script combines pictures and signs for sounds. Egyptians wrote on paper made from papyrus reeds, plentiful on the banks of the Nile. They also wrote on wood and pottery, and they carved on walls. *Hieroglyph,* the word used for Egyptian writing signs, means "sacred words" in Greek. Writing came into use for keeping business records. As a tool for organization it helped unify Egypt.

advice to ensure that in their leadership they were implementing the will of the gods.

Religious Beliefs in the Old Kingdom

Egypt's religion was polytheistic°. Ra, the sun god, was at the center of the belief system. Embodying the power of Heaven over Earth, Ra had created the universe and everything in it. He journeyed across the sky every day in a boat, rested at night, and returned in the morning to resume his eternal journey. By endlessly repeating the cycle of rising and setting, the sun symbolized the harmonious order of the universe that Ra established. The sun's reappearance at dawn every day gave Egyptians the hope of life after death.

Evil, however, constantly threatened the order of the universe in the form of Apopis, a serpent god whose coils could trap Ra's boat like a reef in the Nile. Ra's cosmic journey could continue only if proper worship and justice existed among humans. To make this possible, Ra created Egypt's kings, who shared in his divine nature and who ruled as his representatives on Earth.

Egyptians worshiped many gods in addition to Ra. Ptah, the patron of craftsmen, embodied the impulse to create and to speak. Min, depicted with a huge, erect phallus, represented male sexual potency and protected expeditions of trade and exploration. Bes, symbolized as a dwarf lion, protected women during childbirth. Hapy, the god of the annual Nile floods that enabled agriculture, was depicted as a man with pendulous breasts carrying armloads of crops.

Egyptians also worshiped Osiris, the son of the sky and the Earth, as god of the dead. According to Egyptian belief, Osiris was murdered by his brother Seth, god of chaos, after Osiris married their sister Isis, goddess of fertility. Seth cut Osiris into pieces and scattered them over the Earth, but Isis gathered the pieces and restored Osiris to life. The death and resurrection of Osiris symbolized the natural cycles of regeneration and rebirth that the Egyptians witnessed each spring as their fields bore new crops. After his regeneration, Osiris became king of the underworld, where he judged the dead. Egyptians associated this powerful deity with mummification, by which they tried to preserve bodies after death. Representations of Osiris appeared in pyramids, where the mummies of pharaohs rested for eternity.

The Mummy

The burial practices of the ancient Egyptians provide a window into their society. They reveal Egyptian attitudes about life, death, and the afterlife. Egyptians believed that a person could have an afterlife only if the person's body remained in recognizable form after death.

The Egyptians also thought that every human possessed three spirits active after death: the Ka, Ba, and Akh. The Ka was a person's life force, created at birth but set free at death to live in his or her tomb, where the spirit inhabited the deceased's statue and cared for the body. The Ba could take many shapes and travel outside the tomb, and it accompanied the corpse to final judgment. The Ba comprised all the qualities that made a person unique; without a body to return to, the Ba and the deceased's personality would vanish forever. The Akh represented a person's immortality and lived among the stars. These three spirits could survive only if the body did not decay, and so preserving the corpse became a central issue in burial practice.

Egyptians began experimenting with embalming or mummification between 3000 and 2600 B.C.E. and continued to develop the art for the next 3,000 years. The rise of Christianity in Egypt in the second and third centuries C.E. ended the practice of preserving corpses. Ancient records and modern scientific investigation have uncovered the secrets of mummification. Embalming took place within seventy days after death. By means of a metal hook, highly trained experts extracted the brains through the nostrils and discarded them. Sometimes they filled the skull with linen cloth and resin. Through an incision below the ribs the embalmers removed all the organs except for the heart. (That organ represented a person's life and would be examined by the gods on Judgment Day.) The embalmers wrapped the liver, lungs, stomach, and intestines individually and placed them in separate containers within a chest carved from alabaster. Next the embalmers thoroughly dried the corpse by packing it with natrun, a natural compound of sodium carbonate and bicarbonate. After drying for forty days, the skin shriveled and the embalmers padded the body with aromatic packing materials to re-create as lifelike an appearance as possible. The priests then added hairpieces and artificial eyes. They applied a layer of resin over the face and body followed by a coat of paint—red for men and yellow for women.

Customarily, embalmers placed magical amulets on the corpse to protect the deceased in the next world. They also decorated the body with expensive jewelry and insignia of rank. Then they tightly wrapped the corpse in long strips of linen. Before placing the corpse in a shroud, they fitted the face with a painted linen mask. The masks of royalty were made of gold.

Finally the corpse was placed in its coffin, which was painted with a stylized portrait of the deceased. The dead person's family and friends carried the coffin to the tomb. After the proper prayers, the priest conducting the burial ceremony touched the eyes, ears, nose, and mouth painted on the coffin to enable the dead person to see, hear, smell, and breathe for eternity. Then the priest and family sealed the tomb. When prepared in such a fashion, a body could last forever. ■

■ Mummy of Ramesses II

Both a science and an art, mummification preserved the body of King Ramesses II (r. 1279–1213 B.C.E.) for more than 3,000 years. This near-perfect example of a mummy is the product of an Egyptian tradition of preserving the body after death that began at the beginning of Egyptian history.

For Discussion

What does the practice of mummification reveal about Egyptian attitudes toward death and the boundaries between life and death?

■ **Shabtis**

Shabtis were small carved figures placed in tombs to serve the deceased in the afterlife. This elaborate group of shabtis in a Theban tomb, around 1900 B.C.E., shows officials assessing a herd of cattle for taxation purposes and scribes seated in a small pavilion taking careful notes. The deceased sits with them, watching a farmer being beaten by an official.

The Pyramids

With their emphasis on the afterlife, Egyptians took great pains to provide proper housing for the dead. Many tombs were built as monuments to the dead person's wealth and social status. These structures provided not only a resting place for the corpse but a symbolic entryway to the next life. Members of the elite were buried in expensive tombs filled with ivory furniture and other luxurious goods, but kings had the grandest tombs of all.

Burial customs in the Old Kingdom grew ever more elaborate. For the first several centuries of the Old Kingdom, kings built their tombs in the city of Abydos, in the homeland of the first kings. The tombs consisted of an underground room with a special compartment for the royal corpse. The king's treasures filled nearby underground rooms. Above the ground sat a small palace featuring courtyards and halls suitable for a royal afterlife. The earliest of these tombs, dating to about 2800 B.C.E., contains the bones of animals and people sacrificed to accompany the ruler into the next world. These included servants, entertainers, women, dogs, and pet lions. The practice of killing attendants ended a few centuries later.

About 2680 B.C.E., architects began building a new kind of royal tomb. The defining feature was a great four-sided monument of stone in the shape of a pyramid. Elaborate temples in which priests worshiped statues of the king surrounded the monument. The structure also included compartments where the king could dwell in the afterlife in the same luxury he enjoyed during his life on Earth. King Djoser, the founder of the Old Kingdom, built the first pyramid complex at Saqqara near Memphis. Known today as the Step Pyramid, this structure rests above Djoser's burial place and rises high into the air in six steps, which represent a ladder to heaven.

For the next 2,000 years, kings continued building pyramids for themselves and smaller ones for their queens, with each tomb becoming more architecturally sophisticated. The walls grew taller and steeper and contained hidden burial chambers and treasure rooms. The Great Pyramid at Giza, built around 2600 B.C.E. by king Khufu (or Cheops), stood as the largest humanmade structure in the ancient

■ **The Pyramids**

The cemetery of King Djoser, built at Saqqara about 2680 B.C.E., is the oldest monumental structure in the world built entirely of cut stone. The pyramid has steps and is surrounded by courts and chapels.

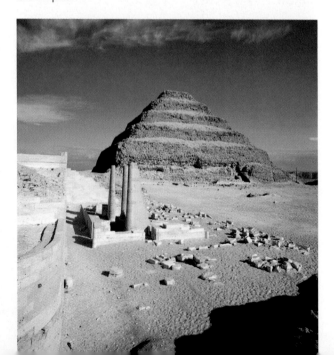

world. It consists of more than two million stones that weigh an average of two and a half tons each. Covering thirteen acres, it reaches more than 481 feet into the sky.

Building the pyramid complexes was an unending and enormously costly task. In addition to the architects, painters, sculptors, carpenters, and other specialists employed on the site throughout the year, stone masons supervised the quarrying and transportation of the colossal building blocks. Peasants, who were organized into work gangs and paid and fed by the king, provided the heavy labor when the Nile flooded their fields every year. As many as 70,000 workers out of a total population estimated at one and a half million sweated on the pyramids every day. Entire cities sprang up around pyramid building sites to house the workmen, artisans, and farmers. The construction of enormous pyramids stopped after 2400 B.C.E., probably because of the expense, but smaller burial structures continued to be built for many centuries.

THE MIDDLE KINGDOM, CA. 2040–1785 B.C.E.

Around 2200 B.C.E. the Old Kingdom collapsed, dragged down by economic decline, the deterioration of royal authority, and a cycle of terrible droughts that triggered a breakdown of law and order. As the kingdom endured years of famine, rulers lost their power to control Egypt, and provincial governors seized political and religious power in their provinces.

For 200 years, anarchy and civil war raged in Egypt during what historians call the First Intermediate Period. Finally, the governors of Thebes, a city in Upper Egypt, set out to reunify the kingdom. In 2040 B.C.E., Mentuhotep II consolidated his rule and established a vigorous new monarchy, initiating the Middle Kingdom (see Map 1.5).

Rulers in the Middle Kingdom defined a new role for themselves. They still viewed themselves as gods, but their rule became less despotic. The highly centralized bureaucracy that regulated most aspects of everyday life was open to men of any social standing, as long as they could read and write hieroglyphs. Wealth spread more widely, and private tombs were no longer the monopoly of the royal elite. Although they continued building large temple complexes to house themselves in the afterlife, these structures were not as grandiose as the Old Kingdom pyramids. Even more important, many Middle Kingdom kings directed more of Egypt's resources toward their subjects' welfare.

The kings also launched many public-works projects for the benefit of their subjects. For example, Amenemhet I (r. 1991–1962 B.C.E.) and his successors transformed the marshy Fayyum Oasis, fifty miles southwest of Memphis, into a well-irrigated agricultural community that yielded abundant crops even in dry years. In the planned city of Kahun, near the Fayyum Oasis, the houses were laid out on a grid pattern, with larger homes for the officials. Each of

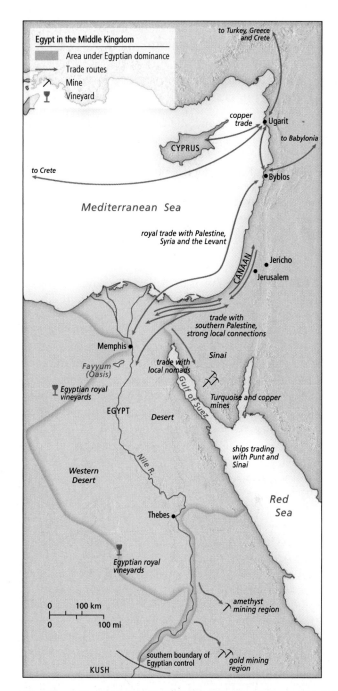

■ **Map 1.5 Egypt in the Middle Kingdom**
During the Middle Kingdom, Egyptian merchants traded extensively with Southwest Asia and the cities of the eastern Mediterranean. Turquoise and copper mines in the Sinai were heavily exploited.

these had its own granary, from which workers in the community received regular allotments of grain.

Even the religious life of the Middle Kingdom was characterized by greater concern for the lives and needs of ordinary people. Because it stressed moral conduct more than the performance of rituals open only to the wealthy, the religion of the Middle Kingdom comforted more people with the hope of a satisfying afterlife.

EGYPTIAN ENCOUNTERS WITH OTHER CIVILIZATIONS

During both the Old and Middle Kingdoms, the major foreign policy goal of Egypt's kings was to protect the trade routes along which raw materials and luxury goods were imported. Rulers did not hesitate to use force when necessary to protect their commercial interests. Some of them sent their armies to make punitive attacks in the western desert and in Sinai to stop raiders from robbing trade caravans. More positively, kings tried to maintain good relations with the chief trading cities of Syria and Palestine in order to stimulate trade.

From the earliest years of the Old Kingdom, Egypt cultivated friendly ties with the Mediterranean port city of Byblos, north of Beirut in modern Lebanon, an area known as the Levant. Exchanges between Byblos and Egypt benefited both sides. Egypt had no forests, and so the Egyptians imported timber from Byblos for the construction of tombs and learned many shipbuilding techniques from Byblos's experienced seamen. For their part, the people of Byblos gained technical skills, especially in masonry and engineering, from the Egyptians. They were also influenced by Egypt's religious beliefs. The Egyptian god of writing, Thoth, became Taut in Byblos, while Byblos's god of craftsmen, Kothar, was believed to have his home in the Egyptian city of Memphis.

During the Old and Middle Kingdoms, Egyptian interactions with Nubia, the territory to the south, also proved economically important. Egyptian merchants systematically exploited its natural resources of gold, timber, and animal skins. They also enslaved many Nubians and transported them for labor in Egypt. Agents of Egyptian rulers, called Keepers of the Gateway of the South, tried to protect the merchants by keeping the peace with the warlike Nubian tribes. When diplomacy failed, Egyptian armies would invade for short periods of time to create peaceful conditions. Slowly, Egyptian monarchs made their presence more permanent. About 1900 B.C.E., king Amenemhet built ten forts at strategic locations where trade routes from the interior of Africa reached the Nile River. Egyptian merchants placed the gold, ivory, and other natural resources that reached these forts into boats, which they sailed northward along the Nile to Egypt. Egyptians came to depend on the vast resources of Nubia.

Commercial connections between Egypt and other African lands were less important. Egyptian merchants traded with the land of Punt (modern Somalia) for spices and rare woods, and they opened turquoise mines in the

---

HYMNS OF PRAISE TO A VICTORIOUS KING

....

These passages come from a collection of hymns of praise to King Sesostris III of the Middle Kingdom. Written on a papyrus scroll, the hymns were probably read aloud in an elaborate ritual when Sesostris, who lived in the northern city of Memphis, visited a town in southern (Upper) Egypt. References to "Two Lands" and his "double crown" refer to the symbolic unity of all of Egypt that this king represents. The Bowmen are raiders from Nubia, evidently a considerable problem during Sesostris's reign. The praise includes more general allusions to other enemies as well. Needless to say, the king triumphs over all of them and wins the universal devotion of his subjects.

I.

Hail to you, Son of Re [the sun god], our Horus,
   Divine of Form!
Land's protector who widens its borders,
Who smites foreign countries with his crown;
Who holds the Two Lands in his arms' embrace;
Who subdues foreign lands by a motion of his hands;
Who slays Bowmen without a blow of the club;
Who shoots the arrow without drawing the string;

Whose terror strikes the Bowmen in their land,
Fear of whom smites the Nine Bows.
Whose slaughter brought death to thousands of Bowmen,
Who had come to invade his borders. . . .
His majesty's tongue restrains Nubia.
His utterances make Asiatics flee. . . .

II.

How the gods rejoice:
You have strengthened their offerings!
How the people rejoice:
You have made safe their frontiers!
How your forbears rejoice:
You have enriched their portions!
How Egypt rejoices in your strength:
You have protected its customs!
How the people rejoice in your guidance:
Your might has won increase for them! . . .

Source: From Miriam Lichtheim, *Ancient Egyptian Literature: The Old and Middle Kingdoms*, Volume 1. Copyright © 1973 by The Regents of the University of California. Reprinted by permission.

Sinai. During the Old Kingdom, some merchants traded for skins, ivory, incense, and slaves among the peoples living in the Kingdom of Yam, located at the tributaries of the Nile River in the interior of eastern Africa. Because the peoples of the interior of Africa attacked Egyptian merchants and took their goods, this trading activity proved too dangerous, and the Egyptians abandoned trade with Africa south of Nubia during the Middle Kingdom.

With the desert on both sides of the Nile Valley protecting Egypt from invasion by foreign enemies, the Egyptians developed a distinctive culture characterized not only by economic prosperity but also by a powerful sense of self-confidence and optimism. Attracted by Egypt's stability and prosperity during both the Old and Middle Kingdom eras, peoples from different lands sought to settle in the Nile Valley. They came from Syria, Nubia, and the deserts that border the Nile River. They took Egyptian names and assimilated into Egyptian culture. The government settled these immigrants, as well as war captives, throughout the kingdom where they could mix quickly with the local inhabitants. This willingness to accept newcomers into their kingdom lent Egyptian civilization even more vibrancy. During the last years of the Middle Kingdom, many merchants and large numbers of settlers moved into Egypt from Syria and Palestine. Around 1750 B.C.E., one such group from Syria, called the Hyksos, took control of Egypt and changed the direction of Egyptian history. As we shall see in Chapter 2, the Second Intermediate Period was marked by both foreign invasion and internal division.

The Transformation of Europe

Europe, which has become the core territory of Western civilization, occupies the westernmost part of the Eurasian land mass stretching from western Russia to the Atlantic Ocean. Because the climate was colder and forests had to be cleared, food production was more difficult in Europe than in the floodplains of Mesopotamia and the Levantine Corridor. Consequently people made the transition from hunting and gathering to food production very gradually. The food-producing revolution that had begun in Southwest Asia around 8000 B.C.E. spread to Europe a thousand years later when farmers, probably from Anatolia, ventured to northern Greece and the Balkans. It took another 4,000 years for the inhabitants of Europe to clear forests and establish farms and grazing lands. By 2500 B.C.E., most of Europe's hunting and gathering cultures had given way to farming societies. This transition to food production laid the economic foundations of subsequent European cultures (see Map 1.6).

Food production in Europe spread slowly but steadily in two interrelated ways: through the migration of groups

Neolithic Europe

CA. 45,000 B.C.E.	*Homo sapiens sapiens* begin to spread throughout Europe
CA. 7000–2500 B.C.E.	Agriculture spreads throughout Europe
CA. 5000 B.C.E.	Linear Pottery culture emerges in northern Europe; cultures grow diverse
CA. 4500 B.C.E.	Copper is first mined in Europe
CA. 3500–2000 B.C.E.	Battle Axe cultures and megalith-building cultures flourish
CA. 3300 B.C.E.	Otzi the Ice Man dies

that knew how to farm and breed livestock and by the adoption of agriculture and animal domestication by hunter-gatherers. Archaeologists have discovered thousands of small outposts of food producers in Europe who were greatly outnumbered by the hunter-gatherers around them. In these frontier settlements, farmers and hunter-gatherers traded food, hides, and tools. Perhaps necessity eventually compelled hunter-gatherers to abandon their old ways of life. Clearing the lands for farming meant the forests disappeared in many areas, and so hunter-gatherers who depended on forest animals and plants had to adapt

■ **Map 1.6 Neolithic Cultures in Europe**

During the Neolithic period, most of the peoples of Europe changed their way of life from hunting and gathering to food production. In the process, many new cultures developed.

■ **Neolithic Farm, ca. 5000 B.C.E.**
This artist's reconstruction of a Linear Pottery farm is based on the excavation of many sites in northern Europe around 5000 B.C.E.

to farming and animal domestication for their survival. Hunting continued to supplement food production in Europe during the Neolithic Age, but it would never again stand as the primary way to obtain food.

As farmers and herders spread across Europe, people adapted to different climates and terrain. A variety of cultures evolved from these differences. We will never know the names these people called themselves, the languages they spoke, or their religious beliefs because no writings or oral traditions have survived from their time. So, archaeologists have named the different cultures of Neolithic Europe after some distinguishing feature of their pottery, tools, methods of constructing houses, or burial customs.

THE LINEAR POTTERY CULTURE

By 5000 B.C.E. one of the most important of these cultures, the Linear Pottery culture, had spread across Europe from Holland to Russia. Archaeologists call it the Linear Pottery culture because its people decorated their pottery with parallel lines. Their customs varied slightly in different regions, but they shared many similarities as well. For example, the Linear Pottery farmers lived in small villages of about sixty people. They built clusters of permanent family farmsteads made of timber and thatch, and rebuilt them over many generations. These farm families cultivated barley and other grains and kept sheep, goats, dogs, and, most important, cattle, which provided wealth and prestige. From gifts of jewelry and other luxury goods left in graves, archaeologists

theorize that women were held in high esteem, perhaps because the people in these communities traced ancestry through them.

After about 4500 B.C.E., villages consisting of several hundred people began to appear in northern Europe, and the trend toward cultural diversity accelerated. In different regions, people used different kinds of pottery and probably spoke distinct languages.

As Linear Pottery settlements slowly spread, competition for farmlands and grazing lands stiffened. Archaeologists believe that men who controlled the livestock—the source of wealth and prestige—developed political authority. These early European elites tried to increase their influence by seizing the lands and herds of others. Conflicts broke out among groups, and people fortified their villages with defensive works. These struggles marked the beginnings of warfare in Europe.

At the same time that the power of elites in Linear Pottery communities was growing, they began building communal tombs with huge stones called *megaliths* in the regions from Scandinavia to Spain and on islands in the western Mediterranean. Archaeologists disagree about the meaning of the megaliths. Some believe that these tombs were the burying places of the elites who controlled the livestock and lands in Linear Pottery communities. They argue that the tombs symbolized the power of these influential, wealthy families—and perhaps new religious beliefs involving these family groups in the afterlife. Other archaeologists, however, reject the religious interpretation of the megaliths. Instead, they argue that farming communities built the structures to announce their claim to frontier lands, for which they competed with hunting-gathering communities. The megalith builders may also have wished to display their power and wealth to families with whom they were competing for prestige.

The best-known example of a megalithic structure is Stonehenge, a monument in England. People began to build Stonehenge about 3000 B.C.E. as a ring of pits. Later generations reconstructed it several times, adding large stones. Stonehenge took its final form about 1600 B.C.E., when builders positioned immense stones, each weighing several tons, in standing positions. Stonehenge possibly measured the movement of stars, the sun, and the planets, and perhaps served as a place for religious ceremonies of some kind.

Around the same time Europeans began experimenting with metallurgy, the art of using fire to shape metals such as copper into items such as tools or jewelry. The idea of shaping metals probably originated when potters noticed that bits of metal ore that accidentally mixed with pottery clay melted in the hot kilns and then hardened again after cooling. Knowledge of metallurgy spread slowly across Europe from the Balkans, where people started to mine copper about 4500 B.C.E. Metallurgy would eventually prove as revolutionary as food production, but its beginnings were very modest. At first, people worked with copper only part of the year. Otzi the Ice Man, for example, may have been both a shepherd and a coppersmith. Gradually, as copper tools and ornaments became more widely used, metalworkers became specialists. As villages became larger, wealthier inhabitants demonstrated their social status by wearing precious copper jewelry. Trade in metals flourished, changing Europe's economy by creating long-distance trading networks. In turn, these networks provided the basis for cultural encounters—for the meeting and blending of different cultural assumptions and ideas.

THE BATTLE AXE CULTURES

Between 3500 B.C.E. and 2000 B.C.E. the Battle Axe cultures flourished in Europe. Fanning across Europe, they gradually replaced the Linear Pottery cultures. Battle Axe peoples cultivated many different types of crops, lived in rectangular single-family thatched dwellings, and used stone and copper battle axes. They may also have been the first peoples to domesticate the horse.

One of the better understood Battle Axe cultures is that of the Kurgan peoples, who made their homes on the edges of the Russian steppes beginning about 3000 B.C.E. Their name comes from a burial custom in which each male corpse was buried under a mound of earth (*kurgan* in Russian) with a copper or stone axe. Kurgans were a warrior culture in which weapons not only were used for fighting but had an important symbolic meaning as well, although the symbolism is not clearly understood by archaeologists. Because Kurgan people had to cross long distances to trade for the copper they needed for their weapons, their culture spread far to the west and south. They traveled by means of wheeled carts and domesticated horses that they obtained from seminomadic pastoralists whom they encountered on the steppe. One of the most important things the Kurgan peoples may have carried with them was a language that was the ancestor of the tongues spoken by half the world's population today.

Historians of languages believe that the majority of the languages spoken today in Europe, the Americas, and other lands colonized by Europeans, as well as several languages spoken in Southwest Asia, such as Persian and Armenian, descend from an ancient family of languages that Europeans spoke about 5,000 years ago. Historians call this family of languages Indo-European. All Indo-European languages share similarities in vocabulary and grammar inherited from their ancient parent language.

■ **Stonehenge**

This megalithic monument consists of two circles of standing stones with large blocks capping the circles. It was built without the aid of wheeled vehicles or metal tools, and the stones were dragged from many miles away.

Many historians believe that Indo-European languages began to develop among the ancestors of the Kurgan peoples, who first lived in southern Russia more than 5,000 years ago. When the Kurgan peoples began to migrate from southern Russia about 3500 B.C.E. they spoke the Indo-European parent language, which then spread throughout Europe in the course of their migrations. The spread and development of Indo-European languages represents a foundation of Western civilization: the languages we speak.

TECHNOLOGY AND SOCIAL CHANGE

As the peoples of Europe developed their diverse cultures, their societies became socially stratified. Historians link the emergence of social hierarchies to technological and economic change. One important tool that helped alter human relationships in early Europe was the plow. European farmers had used wooden plows to cultivate their fields as early as 3600 B.C.E., but the use of plows did not become widespread until about 2600 B.C.E. Once plow technology took hold, however, agricultural life in Europe underwent substantial changes over the course of a mere 200 years. European soils are heavy and difficult to cultivate; hence, the use of plows meant that fewer people were needed to cultivate land. With more people available to clear forest lands, new settlements sprang up and farming communities spread into new regions.

The expansion of land under cultivation led to the development of new ways of organizing society. Because farmers could move out from old family-controlled lands and start new homes, opportunities for individual initiative and the accumulation of wealth increased. Some farmers could afford trade goods of high prestige, and they passed their lands and possessions to their descendants, who used their inherited resources to acquire even more wealth. By exchanging these expensive and prestigious objects, men cultivated friendships and loyalty, established political and military ties, and formalized mutual obligations. Growing divisions resulted between rich and poor, the powerful and the subordinate.

Such changes were evident in western Europe between about 2600 and 2400 B.C.E. For the first time, individual graves played a prominent role in burial customs, which may indicate the emergence of new forms of authority based on the preeminence of individual men in the community, particularly those who controlled land and inheritances. The tombs contain weapons and luxury goods such as jewelry and drinking cups, suggesting not only that these individuals were wealthy and powerful men who could afford expensive symbols of their prestige and power, but also that they were warriors as well as or instead of farmers. As influential warriors gained power, wealth, and influence in their communities, they emerged as political leaders, and they passed their wealth, political power, and social status down to their sons. These families came to dominate their societies. Today we call these elite groups nobles or aristocrats. The presence of male-dominated groups, designated by birth, that controlled the greatest wealth and enjoyed the greatest privileges in society remained unchallenged in Europe until the eighteenth century.

CONCLUSION
Civilization and the West

Civilization is a recent phenomenon in human history. Humans with intellectual capacities equal to our own have existed on the planet for about 200,000 years, but the elements that produced civilization in ancient Southwest Asia and Egypt began to appear only about 10,000 years ago. Western history claims the cultures that developed in these regions as remote ancestors.

This chapter has described the change in human patterns of life from nomadic hunting and gathering to living in settled communities in which food was produced through agriculture and domestication of animals. This transformation took more than 8,000 years. The changes in food production led to the development of village settlements. Powerful elites emerged, and an individual's social status and gender defined what kind of work he or she performed.

Soon human communities took on new characteristics. In Southwest Asia and Egypt, civilizations arose by about 3000 B.C.E. that were based on cities that devoted their resources to irrigation, warfare, and worship. The invention of writing enabled communities to record their laws and traditions. It also reinforced the long-distance trade that linked communities together throughout Southwest Asia and beyond. Long-distance trade among these cities led to the encounters of different peoples. They exchanged new food production technologies, advances in crafts, new approaches to government and administration, and stories and religious ideas.

These changes unfolded over many centuries and did not happen everywhere at the same time. In Europe new patterns of wealth, prestige, and inheritance had begun reshaping some communities by the end of the Neolithic Age, but Europeans did not yet live in cities. Without the critical mass of people and possessions that accompanied city life, Europeans could not yet develop the specialized religious, economic, and political classes that characterize a "civilization." The West did not yet exist, but from the civilizations of Egypt and Southwest Asia, Western civilization would inherit such crucial components as systems of writing and numeracy, the idea of a law code based on abstract principles, and perhaps gender-based divisions of labor and power.

By 3000 B.C.E., the rulers of Egypt and Mesopotamia had spun a web of interrelated economies and shared political interests. For the next millennium, civilizations waxed and waned. Cities such as Ur and Ashur grew powerful under the watchful eyes of ambitious kings who constantly fought with one another. But these kings did not yet possess the skills needed to rule vast empires for an extended period of time. As we will see in the next chapter, they would soon learn.

Suggestions for Further Reading

For a comprehensive list of suggested readings, please go to www.ablongman.com/levack/chapter1

Andrews, Anthony P. *First Cities*. 1995. An excellent introduction to the development of urbanism in Southwest Asia, Egypt, India, China, and the Americas.

Bogucki, Peter. *Forest Farmers and Stockherders: Early Agriculture and Its Consequences*. 1988. A clear synthesis of archaeological evidence from northern Europe.

Cunliffe, Barry, ed. *The Oxford Illustrated Prehistory of Europe*. 1994. An important synthesis of recent research by leading archaeologists.

Fagan, Brian. *People of the Earth: An Introduction to World Prehistory*. 1998. A comprehensive textbook that introduces basic issues with a wealth of illustrations and explanatory materials.

Harris, David R., ed. *The Origins and Spread of Agriculture and Pastoralism in Eurasia*. 1996. A collection of detailed essays by noted experts that draw on the latest research.

Kemp, Barry J. "Unification and Urbanization of Ancient Egypt," in *Civilizations of the Ancient Middle East*, ed. Jack M. Sasson, vol. 2, 679–690. 1995. Describes the emergence of towns and political unification of the early phases of Egyptian history.

Kuhrt, Amelie. *The Ancient Middle East: ca. 3000–330 B.C.*, vol. 1. 1995. An authoritative and up-to-date survey that combines archaeological and textual evidence in a lucid narrative with rich documentation.

Murnane, William J. "The History of Ancient Egypt: An Overview," in *Civilizations of the Ancient Middle East*, ed. Jack M. Sasson, vol. 2, 691–718. 1995. A good place to start for a "big picture" of ancient Egyptian history.

Quirke, Stephen. *Ancient Egyptian Religion*. 1992. A brilliant synthesis and explanation of basic Egyptian beliefs and practices.

Redford, Donald B. *Egypt, Canaan, and Israel in Ancient Times*. 1993. A distinguished Egyptologist discusses 3,000 years of uninterrupted contact between Egypt and southwestern Asia.

Schmandt-Besserat, Denise. *How Writing Came About*. 1996. A highly readable and groundbreaking argument that cuneiform writing developed from a method of counting with tokens.

Shaw, I., ed. *The Oxford History of Ancient Egypt*. 2001. Provides excellent discussions of all aspects of Egyptian life.

Spindler, Konrad. *The Man in the Ice: The Discovery of a 5,000-Year-Old Body Reveals the Secrets of the Stone Age*. 1994. A leader of the international team of experts interprets the corpse of a Neolithic hunter found in the Austrian Alps.

Trigger, Bruce G. *Early Civilizations: Ancient Egypt in Context*. 1995. A leading cultural anthropologist examines Old and Middle Kingdom Egypt through comparison with the early civilizations of China, Peru, Mexico, Mesopotamia, and Africa.

Notes

1. J. N. Postgate, *Early Mesopotamia: Society and Economy at the Dawn of History* (1992), p. 132.
2. H. Vanstiphout, "Memory and Literacy in Ancient Western Asia," in David R. Harris, ed., *The Origins and Spread of Agriculture and Pastoralism in Eurasia* (1996) p. 2185.
3. *Code of Hammurabi* (trans. J. N. Postgate), 55–56. Cited in Postgate, *Early Mesopotamia*, p. 160.
4. Samuel Greengus, "Legal and Social Institutions of Ancient Near Mesopotamia," in *Civilizations of the Ancient Middle East*, ed. Jack M. Sasson, vol. 1 (1995), p. 471.
5. Ibid., p. 474.
6. Translated in Stephen Quirke, *Ancient Egyptian Religion* (1992), p. 38.

The International Bronze Age and Its Aftermath: Trade, Empire, and Diplomacy, 1600–550 B.C.E.

I N 1984, SCUBA-DIVING ARCHAEOLOGISTS BEGAN TO EXCAVATE THE WRECK OF A RICH merchant ship that sank about 1300 B.C.E. at Uluburun, off the southern coast of Turkey. Its cargo of raw materials and exotic luxury objects reveals a prosperous world of international trade and cultural exchange. A partial inventory includes ebony logs, ostrich eggshells, elephant tusks, and a trumpet carved from a hippopotamus tooth from Egypt. From the Middle East came exquisitely worked gold jewelry as well as nearly a ton of scented resin, perhaps intended for use as incense in religious worship. The ship's stone anchors had been made in Syria. Finely painted storage jars from the island of Cyprus held pomegranates and probably olive oil. The archaeologists also recovered swords, daggers, and arrowheads; scrap gold and silver that might be sold in any port; and hinged wooden writing boards with a thick wax surface on which business accounts could be recorded.

The most valuable portion of the cargo that the divers lifted from the ocean floor, however, consisted of 354 flat copper bars, each weighing about fifty pounds, and several bars of tin. When melted and mixed together, these metals produce bronze°. This alloy, which is much tougher than copper or tin, lends itself to the making of dishes, jewelry, tools, and especially weapons. The use of bronze ushered in a new era in the ancient world.

About 3200 B.C.E. people living in northern Syria and Iraq began making bronze. The technology spread slowly throughout the Middle East and into Egypt and Europe. Because deposits of tin and copper are not always present in the same areas, merchants traded over long distances to obtain the ores with which to forge the prized alloy. As they traded, they spread knowledge about

House of the Admiral: This lively wall painting, which may depict a religious celebration, comes from the so-called House of the Admiral on the island of Thera, midway between Crete and Greece. The painting is about twenty-two feet long and a foot and a half high. Created about 1500 B.C.E., before a volcanic explosion destroyed the settlement on Thera, this painting shows scenes of busy maritime activity outside a harbor town.

■ **Map 2.1 The International Bronze Age, ca. 1600–1100 B.C.E.**
For five hundred years, networks of commerce and diplomacy tied together the distinct cultures of Egypt, Greece, Anatolia, and the Middle East.

bronze technology among diverse peoples. By 1600 B.C.E., when peoples throughout the Middle East, Egypt, and Europe had mastered bronze making, the International Bronze Age began (see Map 2.1).

The new international trade in bronze provides the key to understanding how five separate regions in the Middle East, Africa, and Europe became linked in a large area of political and cultural influence and thus began to lay the foundations of Western civilization. The regions were the lands controlled by Egypt in northeast Africa and the Middle East, the territories ruled by the Hittite kingdom in Anatolia (modern Turkey), the Assyrian and Babylonian kingdoms in Mesopotamia, the maritime kingdoms of Minoan Crete and Mycenaean Greece in the eastern Mediterranean, and the small mercantile kingdoms of Troy and Ugarit, also situated in the eastern Mediterranean. The people in these different regions spoke different languages, worshiped different gods, and had different systems of government, but they were linked by trade and diplomacy, and they engaged in a series of commercial, technological, and

cultural exchanges. Those exchanges formed the basis of what we now call the West.

These five regions depended on an international trade network to obtain the metals and other goods they needed for everyday life. Their rulers encouraged this trade because they needed bronze, mainly to develop new weapons, especially horse-drawn chariots, a new military technology. Chariot fighting was expensive, however, and therefore rulers constantly sought the acquisition of wealth and vital resources through trade and conquest.

The use of horse-drawn chariots and the continued quest for new sources of wealth to support them led to two major developments in international affairs. The first was the growth of empire—the expansion of the territories under the control of individual kingdoms. During the International Bronze Age rulers in Egypt, the Hittite kingdom, Assyria, and Babylonia used their superior military strength to build large, multiethnic empires. The growth of these empires became one of the main features of this historical period. The second development was the recognition that warfare, which these kingdoms had used to conquer foreign peoples, could interrupt trade and interfere with the successful management of a ruler's territories. Discovering the advantages of international cooperation for the first time, rulers during this period developed a system of diplomacy that produced long periods of peace—an unprecedented achievement. Trade was so important that royal families intermarried and exchanged precious gifts to maintain good international relations. That the Uluburun cargo ship could stop at so many ports and take on board merchandise from so many different kingdoms illustrates the benefit of these peaceful times.

The elaborate economic, diplomatic, and cultural networks of the International Bronze Age disintegrated about 1100 B.C.E. International trade in copper and tin broke down. Destructive raiders who had learned how to overcome chariot warriors destroyed the Hittite Empire as well as many smaller kingdoms. At the same time, Mycenaean power collapsed and the empires of Egypt and Mesopotamia went into a steep decline as well. After a period of slow recovery, however, powerful new empires emerged in Mesopotamia, while Phoenician civilization emerged in the Mediterranean. The Phoenicians, who were master mariners, took their culture to North Africa and Spain, creating a new civilization based on trade.

This chapter examines how the peoples of the International Bronze Age and the period immediately following its demise engaged in a series of commercial, technological, and cultural exchanges. To understand these changes we shall consider the following questions: (1) How did Egypt during the New Kingdom use warfare and diplomacy to develop an empire that reached from Nubia to Mesopotamia? (2) What were the political, religious, and cultural traditions of the Hittite Empire in Anatolia and the Assyrian and Babylonian Empires in Mesopotamia? (3) What were the characteristics of the Mediterranean civilizations of Minoan Crete, Mycenaean Greece, Ugarit, and Troy, and what roles did they play in international trade and politics? (4) What forces brought the International Bronze Age to a close and how did the Phoenicians, Assyrians, and Babylonians build new kingdoms and empires in its wake, generating new international economic, cultural, and political traditions?

The Egyptian Empire

A prosperous new phase of Egyptian history began when the Middle Kingdom ended about 1650 B.C.E. During the next 500-year period, Egyptians made use of a new military technology to create a vast multi-ethnic empire stretching from Africa to the Middle East. The term empire° identifies a kingdom or any other type of state that controls several foreign territories, either on the same continent or overseas. During this period Egyptian forces conquered Nubia in the south, and in Mesopotamia they marched as far east as the Euphrates River. Pharaohs combined military expansion with diplomacy and encouraged foreign trade, making Egypt a major force in international affairs.

THE HYKSOS AND THE REVOLUTION IN MILITARY TECHNOLOGY

Egyptian history changed course abruptly at the end of the Middle Kingdom when the Hyksos, a people from northern Palestine whose name meant "peoples of foreign lands," invaded Egypt and established a new regime in the northern Delta region. The Hyksos' rule had a lasting impact on Egyptian society in two ways.

First, through their ties with the Middle East, the Hyksos linked Egypt to the international network of commerce, technology, and diplomacy that was emerging in the International Bronze Age. The Hyksos maintained diplomatic and economic ties with kingdoms of Mesopotamia, Syria, and the Mediterranean. These connections encouraged cultural exchanges, such as when the Hyksos employed artists from Crete to paint vivid scenes on the walls of the royal palace at Avaris, their capital city.

Second, the Hyksos introduced an advanced military technology that was revolutionizing warfare throughout the Middle East, Anatolia, and Greece. The new military technology consisted of a chariot with lightweight wheels with bronze spokes drawn by a team of trained horses. Two young men wearing bronze chain-mail armor would ride into battle on each chariot, one driving the horses, the other shooting bronze-tipped arrows at the enemy. The archers used costly composite bows made of laminated layers of wood, horn, and sinew. It took between five and ten years for a composite bow to age properly, but they permitted archers to fire arrows as far as 200 yards—double or triple the range of simple wooden bows. This military technology enabled the Hyksos to conquer Egypt and later helped the Egyptians acquire a vast overseas empire.

Troops of trained charioteers and bowmen could easily outmaneuver the traditional massed infantry forces and inflict terrible casualties from a distance. Chariot squadrons would advance in a broad line with infantry marching behind them. When two armies with similar armament began a battle, the opposing lines of chariots would race toward each other, hoping to disable the enemy with dense arrow fire. Then they would wheel away in formation, and the infantrymen, also wearing bronze-plated armor and brandishing bronze swords and lances, would charge.

Chariot warfare reshaped the economic policies and foreign relations of Egypt and all the other kingdoms and empires of the International Bronze Age. To meet the enormous expenses of training and supplying armies of charioteers, rulers carefully organized domestic resources and tried to acquire more wealth through trade and conquest.

ADMINISTRATION AND GOVERNMENT DURING THE NEW KINGDOM

About 1550 B.C.E. Pharaoh Ahmose I (r. ca. 1569–ca. 1545 B.C.E.) expelled the Hyksos from Egypt. Ahmose came from Thebes in southern Egypt, which had remained independent of Hyksos control, and he enjoyed the support of the majority of the Egyptian population. His mastery of the new military tactics enabled him to defeat the Hyksos and reunify Egypt under his command. Historians call the period of renewed Egyptian self-rule that began with Ahmose the New Kingdom (ca. 1550–1150 B.C.E.) During this period Egypt extended its territorial boundaries, acquiring lands in Asia and reaching the Euphrates River. Ahmose's new dynasty continued the highly centralized system of government that had been developed in the Middle Kingdom, adding a powerful new force: a permanent, or standing, army. For the first time in Egyptian history, a ruler could count on the readiness of highly trained regiments of charioteers and infantrymen to go to war whenever he wished. Troops would also remain as garrisons in conquered lands. The standing army extended the ruler's reach and influence abroad.

During the New Kingdom, Egypt's kings first took the title pharaoh, which means "great house"—or master of all Egyptians. Pharaohs exercised wide-ranging and unrivaled political power. Egyptians believed that the gods entrusted their safekeeping to the pharaoh's care and that he had the final authority in matters of government, law, and religion. As supreme commander of the military forces, he made all decisions about war and peace, and he supervised diplomatic ties with foreign nations. In return for the authority granted him by the gods, the pharaoh had the duty of maintaining peace and order in Egypt and bringing this order to the entire world. He did this by caring for the temples and cults of the gods, conquering Egypt's enemies, and ruling wisely.

In his role as supreme ruler, the pharaoh therefore served as a vital link between humanity and Heaven. All of his activities as pharaoh, whether protecting his people from foreigners, conquering enemies abroad, building huge temples in honor of the gods, governing his territories, or feeding his subjects, symbolized his fight against the forces of chaos on behalf of the gods. The total

power of the pharaoh represented the divine will of Heaven at work on Earth.

As a consequence of its strong centralized system of government, Egypt during the New Kingdom developed a highly organized bureaucracy that helped the pharaoh maintain order. The chief minister of state and the highest official in the land was the vizier. As the pharaoh's chief executive officer the vizier superintended the administration of the entire kingdom, and he was responsible for guaranteeing that justice prevailed. Every year the vizier decided when to open the canal locks on the Nile, so that farmers' fields could be irrigated. He supervised the Egyptian treasury and the warehouses into which produce was paid as taxes. In addition to the vizier, four administrators chosen by the pharaoh directed the army, religious affairs, the pharaoh's properties, and internal administration.

During the New Kingdom, Egypt was divided into two major administrative regions. The southern region, called Upper Egypt, was governed from the city of Thebes, while Lower Egypt, in the north, was ruled from the city of Memphis. Regional administrators raised taxes and organized men to work on the pharaoh's building projects. Smaller cities were ruled by mayors who collected taxes and otherwise served as middlemen between the central gov-

■ **Scribe Nebmertuf**

Scribe Nebmertuf, who lived in Egypt about 1360 B.C.E., was a minor official who helped keep the tightly organized bureaucracy functioning. He writes on a scroll made of papyrus that he has unrolled in his lap. The baboon who watches him is the sacred animal of Thoth, the god of wisdom.

■ **Enemies of Egypt**

These tiles found at the mortuary temple of Pharaoh Ramesses III were made around 1170 B.C.E. They depict Egypt's enemies with such great attention to details of clothing, hairstyle, and stereotyped physical features that we can know the ethnicity of the men. From left to right: a Libyan with tattooed arms, a Nubian with black skin, and a bearded Syrian. All wear handcuffs, a sign of their defeat and Egypt's triumph. Other figures in the series not shown here include a bedouin nomad and a Hittite.

ernment and the local population. Thousands of state officials labored in this complex administrative system. Called scribes, these literate officials maintained the careful records on which the bureaucracy depended.

Temples played an essential part in the government of Egypt. Many of the temples to the great gods, and the priests who managed them, acquired enormous wealth and influence because they possessed huge tracts of land. The temple of Amun at Karnak, for example, owned nearly one-quarter of all Egypt's grain fields and controlled a workforce of nearly 100,000 people. The high priests, whom the pharaoh appointed from among his most trusted advisers, had responsibility for building the tombs of the pharaoh and his family, the imperial granaries, and other public works. Priests also participated in the administration of imperial affairs. They managed the many thousands of peasants who labored in the vast estates attached to the temples, collecting taxes, organizing building projects, and administering justice.

MILITARY EXPANSION: BUILDING AN EMPIRE IN CANAAN AND NUBIA

During the New Kingdom, pharaohs conquered territories far beyond the borders of Egypt. The military power that came from chariot warfare technology, and the ability of the pharaoh to use the great wealth of the country to support a large army, made these conquests possible. A well-developed logistical system also contributed to Egypt's military strength. With food and supplies carefully prepared in advance by government administrators, the Egyptian army regularly waged war far from home. The army was efficient, highly mobile, and extremely well trained.

Egyptian attitudes toward non-Egyptians also encouraged the imperial expansion of the New Kingdom. Egyptians believed that the pharaoh should extend Egyptian power throughout the world. They divided the world into two groups: themselves (whom they referred to as "The People") and everyone else. Egyptians were people who lived in the Nile Valley and spoke Egyptian. The other peoples known to the Egyptians were the inhabitants of the Middle East (called Asians), Nubians, and Libyans. At the beginning of the New Kingdom, Egyptians considered the foreign people they encountered through trade and diplomacy inferior and naturally subordinate to themselves. They believed that forces of chaos resided in foreign lands where the pharaoh had not yet imposed his will. Thus it was the pharaoh's responsibility to crush all foreign peoples and bring order to the world. By the end of the New Kingdom, however, constant interaction with foreign peoples broadened the Egyptian worldview. By that time, for example, pharaohs treated foreign kings as equals and called them "brothers"—something not possible during earlier periods of Egypt's history.

In their drive to establish order in the world, Egyptian rulers in the New Kingdom clashed with kingdoms in Anatolia, Syria, and Mesopotamia, as we will see later in this chapter. Under the dynamic leadership of Thutmose I (r. 1504–1492 B.C.E.), the armies of Egypt conquered southern Palestine. A coalition of Syrian cities slowed further

Egyptian Tomb Robbers on Trial

In New Kingdom Egypt a council called a *kenbet,* composed of the local governor and temple priests, combined the functions of prosecutor, judge, and jury. There was no counsel for the defendants. At the village level people might bring lawsuits against one another at the *kenbet,* and women and men alike represented themselves at trial. Another court, the Great Kenbet, handled all cases of property and taxation affecting state revenues as well as all offenses against the pharaoh and the government. This court consisted of high officials of the government and was headed by the pharaoh's chief administrator, the vizier.

One of the most serious crimes in Egypt was robbing tombs. People accused of this crime were interrogated by the authorities, who routinely used beatings and torture to extract confessions. The Great Kenbet then delivered a verdict. Conviction of tomb robbing carried the death penalty. Lesser crimes not related to tomb robbing could result in confiscation of property, beatings, forced labor, and body mutilation.

The following document comes from the trial record of tomb robbers in the Great Tombs of the pharaohs in the Valley of the Kings.[1] These tombs were situated a few miles from the Nile River at Thebes, where most of the New Kingdom pharaohs and their families were buried. The trials were conducted over a period of several summer days during the reign of Ramesses IX (r. 1125–1107 B.C.E.). The vizier, assisted by the overseer of the granary and treasury and two royal stewards, conducted the proceedings, which were written on a papyrus scroll unearthed in 1872 C.E. The account shows how justice was carried out in the New Kingdom.

Examination. The herdsman Bukhaaf of the temple of Amun was brought. The Vizier said to him, "When you were about that business in which you engaged and the god caught you and brought and placed you in the hand of pharaoh, tell me all the men who were with you in the Great Tombs." Bukhaaf replied, "As for me, I am a field worker of the temple of Amun. The woman came to the place where I was and she said to me, 'some men have found something that can be sold for bread; let's go so you may eat it with them.'" [Bukhaaf gives some misleading testimony that does not deceive the Kenbet.] Bukhaaf was examined with the stick [i.e., beaten]. "Stop, I will tell," he said. The Vizier said to him, "Tell the story of your going to attack the Great and Noble Tombs." Bukhaaf said, "It was Pewer, a workman of the City of the Dead [the Tombs] who showed us the tomb of Queen Hebrezet." The Vizier and the others said to him, "In what condition was the tomb that you went to?" Bukhaaf said, "I found it already open." He was examined with the stick again. "Stop," he said, "I will tell." The Vizier said to him, "Tell what you did." He said, "I brought away the inner coffin of silver and a shroud of gold and silver together with the men who were with me. And we broke them up and divided them among ourselves."

[Bukhaaf's punishment is not recorded, but it was in all likelihood death.]

On the third day of the trial of thieves, a carpenter Thewenani was examined for a different robbery. He proclaimed his innocence and swore a great oath, "If I speak untruth may I be mutilated and sent to Ethiopia."

Despite several beatings and torture, Thewenani would not confess, and the vizier let him off with the warning that if he were accused again, he would be sentenced to death. Later that day, Ese, the wife of the gardener Ker who had been implicated in stealing silver from the Great Tombs in still another case, was brought before the Kenbet. She swore an oath to be truthful or be mutilated and placed on a stake. She denied any connection with the robbery, but one of the officials at the trial asked her how she had suddenly gotten rich enough to buy several slaves. Her answer that she had saved the money from selling the produce of her garden did not convince the Kenbet, which brought in her slave to give testimony against her. Her fate is not recorded.

Why did Egyptian officials prosecute tomb robbers with such energy? They considered tomb robbing a serious crime for both religious and economic reasons. Egyptians were deeply concerned about the afterlife and stressed the proper treatment of the dead. They believed that when people died they were judged by the god Osiris. If they had lived good lives, their bodies would live again. The families of the deceased had the obligation to provide food and water at the graveside for the dead to eat. They also were required to remember the name of the dead. "Provide water for your father and mother who rest in the desert valley . . . Let the people know that you are doing it and then your son will do the same for you," advised one religious text.[2] In Egyptian eyes, robbing a tomb violated basic principles of religious behavior. It was a monstrous sacrilege.

The many gifts placed in a grave with the dead person were intended to make the deceased person's afterlife as comfortable as possible. Pharaohs and the wealthy elite of Egypt filled their tombs with luxury items of incalculable value—an irresistible lure for thieves. In addition to their profound desire to prevent sacrilege, Egyptian officials worried that plundering this treasure and putting it back into circulation would cause prices to fall and thereby derail the economy. From the point of view of Egyptian officials, tomb robbers deserved nothing less than death. Only this way would justice be served. ▪

Questions of Justice

1. What values made tomb robbing "criminal" in Egypt during the New Kingdom? What does the crime reveal about the organization of Egyptian society?

2. What was the notion of justice that determined these trials and their outcome? What principles of justice are the judges trying to uphold?

3. To what extent do both the living and the dead play a part in this trial?

Taking It Further

Goelet, Ogden. "Tomb Robbery Papyri," in *The Oxford Encyclopedia of Ancient Egypt*, ed. Donald B. Redford, vol. 3, pp. 417–418. 2001. Provides the latest analysis of the documents relating to the trials of tomb robbers as well as further bibliography.

Kruchten, Jean-Marie. "Law," in *The Oxford Encyclopedia of Ancient Egypt*, ed. Donald B. Redford, vol. 2, pp. 277–282. 2001. An excellent overview of Egyptian law with helpful suggestions for further reading.

■ **Judgment Day**

Painted about 1285 B.C.E., this papyrus scroll shows the trial of a man called Hunefer on the day of judgment. The jackal-headed god Anubis leads Hunefer into the courtroom, where his heart is weighed against a feather on giant scales. Because the feather and the heart weigh the same, it means that the court decides that Hunefer has led a just life. The god of wisdom, Thoth, stands by the scale, records the result of the weighing, and leads Hunefer to the great god Osiris who judges and rules the dead. Hunefer can look forward to a peaceful eternity.

advance, but by the end of the reign of the great conqueror Thutmose III (r. 1458–1425 B.C.E.), Egypt had extended its control over all the lands between the Orontes River in Syria and the Euphrates in Mesopotamia. The western portion of this region, which today includes modern Lebanon, Israel, and parts of Jordan and Syria, was called Canaan.

The Egyptians conquered Canaan because of its great wealth. After Canaan had fallen under Egyptian control, a steady stream of caravans transported its natural resources and manufactured goods to Egypt. Fine Canaanite garments and tapestries, as well as grain, wine, opium, incense, honey, and olive oils were highly valued in Egypt. Canaan also provided many resources lacking in Egypt, such as timber and copper, which was used to create bronze for chariots and weapons. Silver came in large quantities from Jerusalem and nearby towns. Egyptian officials also demanded that the Canaanites supply horses, chariots, and highly trained charioteers as tribute.

Because Canaan was a trading center with ties to Mesopotamia and beyond, Egyptian merchants gained access to goods from distant lands not controlled by Egypt. Precious gems came from Afghanistan; incense for burning in temples came from Arabia; Cyprus, an island in the eastern Mediterranean Sea, was a main source of copper; and wines, luxury metalwork, textiles, oil, and expensive pottery came from Crete, another Mediterranean island. Syria provided cedar wood used for construction as well as other rare woods used to make luxury furniture and temple implements.

To maintain their grip on the rich resources of Canaan, the pharaohs chose a loyal and reliable leader in each Canaanite city to be the mayor. Like the mayors of Egyptian towns, these local officials swore an oath of allegiance to the pharaoh. Their sons were sent to Egypt to be hostages in exchange for their fathers' good behavior and to learn the ways of Egyptian culture. The mayors collected the heavy taxes that the central government required, and they administered the forced labor of the civilian population that was regularly demanded to build temples and maintain public buildings.

The New Kingdom also expanded its territorial grip southward, seizing the populous and prosperous African land known in antiquity as Nubia or Kush (modern Sudan). Nubia was extremely rich in gold and other natural resources, while trade routes from central and eastern Africa that converged in Nubia further augmented its wealth. In order to gain control of these riches, Egyptian forces conquered Nubia about 1500 B.C.E. and established an administration there that had a degree of self-rule (see Map 2.2).

An Egyptian governor, called the King's Son of Kush, ruled a vast region in the pharaoh's name and saw to its systematic economic exploitation. Egyptian control depended on the cooperation of Nubian princes, who organized local labor and guaranteed the regular delivery of tribute demanded by the pharaoh's agents. In return for this collaboration, the princes were permitted to govern their communities. As in Canaan, the pharaohs required local rulers to send their sons to Egypt to be educated. This practice ensured the loyalty of the boys' fathers. It also strengthened Egyptian control of Nubia, for when the

■ **Map 2.2   Egypt in the New Kingdom**

During the New Kingdom, Egyptians conquered Nubia, Canaan, and parts of the Middle East as far as the Euphrates River. They created a prosperous, multiethnic empire.

"Egyptianized" young men returned to Nubia to govern their communities after the death of their fathers, they brought with them a respect for Egyptian power and an appreciation for Egyptian culture.

Another strategy for maintaining the Nubians' allegiance was through worship of the pharaoh. In order to bring the presence of the pharaoh to the people of Nubia, the Egyptians built temples to their ruler and his ancestral gods in all the major commercial and garrison cities of the country. With the presence of the pharaoh all around them—and the threat of overwhelming force that it subtly implied—the people of Nubia would think twice before rebelling. They also were encouraged to participate in the worship of the pharaoh and the Egyptian gods.

To strengthen their grip over Nubia, pharaohs encouraged Egyptians to migrate to Nubia and establish communities along the Nile River. These Egyptian colonies increased the population of Nubia and exploited the fertile river lands for the benefit of the pharaoh.

Egypt gained enormous wealth from its empire in Nubia and Canaan. Conquest and centralized administration enabled the Egyptians to collect tribute and taxes from their subjects, and the resulting economic growth led to vigorous private commerce and many cultural encounters between Egyptians and other peoples. Even though Egyptians viewed the foreign peoples they ruled with contempt, they slowly absorbed many things from their subjects during the 400-year interaction. Egyptian speech, for example, adopted hundreds of Canaanite words, especially those pertaining to military affairs and the natural resources coveted by Egyptians. In addition, many fairy tales about exotic lands modeled on the Middle East made their way into Egyptian literature. Numerous gods of conquered peoples entered Egyptian life as well. For example, Baal and Astarte, who were worshiped widely in the Middle East, became popular Egyptian divinities. The cultural encounter between Egyptians and the people they conquered, therefore, resulted in an exchange of ideas and traditions, not just the imposition of the Egyptian culture on the people brought into their empire.

PHARAOHS: THE SOURCE OF EGYPT'S SUCCESS

Egypt's success during the New Kingdom hinged in large part on the talents of its pharaohs. These rulers defined all aspects of Egyptian life, from empire building and trade to agriculture and worship. Several pharaohs left a particularly impressive mark during this era of Egyptian history.

Hatshepsut the Female Pharaoh and Thutmose III the Conqueror

One of the most remarkable rulers of the New Kingdom was Hatshepsut, the daughter of Thutmose I. Hatshepsut became co-ruler with her infant stepson Thutmose III

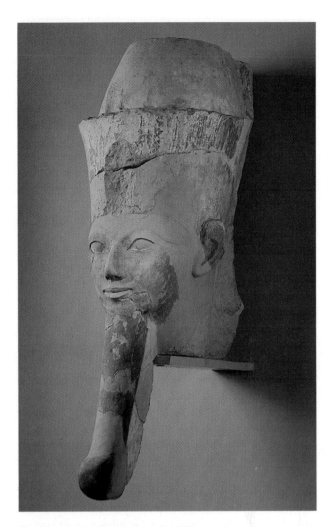

■ **Hatshepsut as a Bearded Pharaoh**
Although she was a woman, tradition required that Hatshepsut be depicted as a man.

when her husband, the pharaoh Thutmose II, died in 1479 B.C.E. Six years later, she seized power for herself, becoming the first female pharaoh.

Hatshepsut held power from 1479 to 1458 B.C.E., a period in which Egypt enjoyed great prosperity. With the aid of trusted advisers, Hatshepsut pursued policies of peace, though her armies waged war when necessary to secure Egypt's possessions in the Middle East. With Hatshepsut's encouragement, trade with the land of Punt (modern Somalia) flourished. Egyptians exchanged weapons, jewelry, and manufactured goods for ivory, gold, ebony, incense, myrrh, live animals, and exotic animal skins with merchants from Punt.

Because pharaohs had always been men, all of the images of kingly power were male, and all of the elaborate rituals of ruling presumed a male ruler. Hatshepsut very carefully adapted her image to these expectations. For example, in the inscriptions and paintings of the great funerary temple that she built in the holy valley of Deir el-Bahari near Thebes, Hatshepsut is represented as a man, the son of the god Amun-Re. In more private contexts, she referred to herself as a woman. Several decades after Hatshepsut's death, her name was systematically removed from monuments throughout Egypt, probably to inform the gods that Egypt had returned to "proper" male kingship.

Thutmose III (r. 1458–1425 B.C.E.) succeeded Hatshepsut and began a reign marked by military glory. When he ascended the throne, Egypt was in danger of losing its grip on Nubia, as well as Canaan and parts of Syria. Interfering in Egyptian affairs, the kingdom of Mittani in northern Syria stirred up revolts and rivalries among Egypt's subjects in the Middle East. In order to reassert Egyptian control, Thutmose led his armies into Canaan seventeen times during his reign. In one of his greatest victories at Megiddo (in modern Israel) Thutmose captured more than 900 war chariots from his enemies.

Thutmose restored Egyptian power as far as the Euphrates River in Mesopotamia. He also harshly suppressed revolts in Nubia. To maintain Egyptian authority throughout his empire, Thutmose established permanent garrisons in conquered territories, just as Ahmose had done when the territory had first been conquered. Thutmose closely supervised local government in the areas under Egyptian control. He also cultivated a triumphant military atmosphere at court that was quite different from that of Hatshepsut.

A man of high culture as well as a brilliant general, Thutmose wrote literary works and pursued an interest in science. From Syria he brought back samples of the region's flowers and plants and had them painted on temple walls. Under his influence, Egyptian artists perfected their ability to capture detail, movement, and emotion in painting and sculpture.

The Amarna Period: Religious Ferment and the Beginnings of Diplomacy

For more than a thousand years, Egyptians had worshiped the sun, Amun-Re, mightiest of all their deities. Pharaoh Amenhotep III (r. 1388–1351 B.C.E.) turned away from traditional Egyptian religion, however, believing that Amun-Re was not just the god of Egyptians but a universal deity who ruled all peoples. Amenhotep called the sun Aten and worshipped his physical form, the sun seen in the sky. He no longer recognized the other gods.

The pharaoh's son, Amenhotep IV (r. 1351–1334 B.C.E.), changed his own name to Akhenaten ("One useful to Aten") and took the revolutionary step of declaring that Aten was the only god. A contemporary hymn proclaimed, "O sole god unlike any other, you created the world according to your desire, while you were alone." Akhenaten attacked the worship of other gods, closed down many temples, and appropriated their wealth and lands for himself.

> ## A HYMN TO ATEN SUNG BY THE PHARAOH
> ···················
>
> *The following Egyptian hymn was sung to Aten, the sun god, by the pharaoh. It describes a single god who created the universe:*
>
> Splendid you rise, O living Aten, eternal lord!
> You are radiant, beauteous, mighty,
> Your love is great, immense.
> Your rays light up all faces,
> Your bright hue gives life to hearts,
> When you fill the Two Lands with your love.
> August God who fashioned himself,
> Who made every land, created what is in it,
> All peoples, herds, and flocks,
> All trees that grow from soil; they live when you dawn
>   for them,
> You are mother and father of all that you made.
> I am your son who serves you, who exalts your name,
> Your power, your strength, are firm in my heart;
> You are the living Aten whose image endures,
> You have made the far sky to shine in it,
> To observe all that you made. . . .
>
> Source: From Miriam Lichtheim, *Ancient Egyptian Literature: The Old and Middle Kingdoms, Volume II.* Copyright © 1976 by the Regents of the University of California. Reprinted by permission.

He forbade the celebration of ancient public festivals to the other gods and even the mention of their names. His agents chiseled their names from monuments and buildings across the land.

Full of religious enthusiasm, Akhenaten and his queen, Nefertiti, abandoned the capital of Thebes and built a new city called Horizon of Aten in a valley in middle Egypt where no temples to other gods had ever stood. Because the modern name for this site is Tell el-Amarna, historians refer to this period of religious ferment as the Amarna Period. Left open to the sun, the city received the first rays of light as each day dawned. These rays touched the main temple of Aten through a natural break in the surrounding cliffs. Paintings and sculptures no longer depicted Aten in the traditional way, as a falcon-headed god, but instead represented the deity as a simple disc with radiating beams of light.

Akhenaten went too far in his enforcement of these regulations, losing the support of the general population as well as that of the priests who administered the temples of other gods. The people of Egypt were unwilling to abandon the many traditional gods who played such an important role their daily lives. Aten stood for light, love, and universal life, but Akhenaten's tight control of the government and suppression of all opposition to his rule made everyday existence dark during his reign.

In another deliberate break with tradition Akhenaten changed the standard representation of a pharaoh. Rather than a masculine figure with a taut body and highly symmetrical limbs, his statutes show him with an exaggerated stomach and hips and elongated face. Declaring that he was the mother as well as the father of his people, Akhenaten emphasized female traits in his statues.

These radical and abstract ideas did not survive Akhenaten. After his death, the royal court abandoned Horizon of Aten and returned to Memphis and then to Thebes. Akhenaten's religious beliefs do indicate, however, the cosmopolitan nature of New Kingdom Egypt. Taking into account the diverse people whom Egypt ruled, the religious thinkers around Akhenaten developed the idea of a single, transcendent god for all humanity.

The pharaohs of the Amarna Period immersed themselves as deeply in foreign policy as they did in religious innovation. Evidence of their diplomacy comes from an archive of documents discovered at Tell el-Amarna in Egypt in 1887 C.E. Written in Akkadian, the Mesopotamian language used for international communication, these letters show that Egyptian pharaohs were in regular contact with the rulers of neighboring peoples, such as the Hittites, Assyrians, Babylonians, and the leaders of much smaller city-states in the Middle East, as well as with their own officials in Canaan and Syria.

In their correspondence, the monarchs referred to themselves as "Great Kings" and addressed one another as "brother," despite their constant rivalry. By using these titles, the rulers recognized each other's authority and created a sense of international community. Though prepared for war, they preferred to cement their ties by arranging marriages among the royal families and exchanging lavish gifts. By these means they could guard their frontiers and protect the merchants who crisscrossed their territories.

Diplomacy did not always succeed. Ancient records describe murder, a failed marriage alliance, and the calamity that followed when ties between the Hittites and Egyptians broke down. When Pharaoh Tutankhamun died in 1333 B.C.E., his widow wrote to the Hittite king: ". . . My husband is dead. I have no son! I shall never take a servant of mine [that is, any Egyptian] and make him my husband. I have written to no other country. I have written only to you; so give me one son of yours . . . He will be my husband. In Egypt he will be king!"[3] No doubt delighted to extend Hittite influence, the Hittite monarch sent his fourth son, Prince Zannanza, to Egypt. On the journey, however, Zannanza was murdered, and the mystery of his death has never been solved. Furious at his son's death and seeking vengeance, the Hittite king invaded the Egyptian Empire in Syria, sacked several cities, and seized many thousands of

■ **Amarna Altar Panel**
Carved about 1340 B.C.E., this stone panel was found in an Egyptian home where it served as the focus of daily prayers. On the left, Akhenaten kisses his infant child. Facing him, his wife Nefertiti holds an older girl on her knee while resting another baby on her shoulder. The sun god Aten sends his rays down as a blessing to the entire royal family and so to all Egyptians. The oddly elongated heads and body shapes, especially of the pharaoh, typify a new way of depicting the royal family in the Amarna period.

prisoners. Although he soon withdrew his forces, tensions between the two empires continued to mount.

The mysterious murder of Prince Zannanza and the war that followed illustrate that open conflict among the empires remained a constant threat in the fourteenth century B.C.E. Nevertheless, for the first time in the ancient world, international relations among sovereign powers brought periods of peace and prosperity to different cultures over a huge area.

The Age of Ramesses

After Akhenaten's death, rule of Egypt passed through the hands of several men before Ramesses I took the throne in 1292 B.C.E. and established a new dynasty, the nineteenth in Egyptian history. The rulers in this dynasty used military force to control the provinces of Canaan, Syria, and Nubia, where revolts continually broke out. During their reign they confronted a further threat to Egyptian security on the northwestern frontier, where peoples from Libya called the Labu and the Meshwesh attempted unsuccessfully to enter the northern delta of the Nile.

The greatest king of the nineteenth dynasty was Ramesses II (r. 1279–1213 B.C.E.), who ruled for sixty-six years. A tireless builder of temples and monuments, he constructed a new imperial city, called City of Ramesses, in the eastern delta. Ramesses's greatest accomplishments, however, were in military action abroad.

Ramesses's efforts to restore Egyptian authority in Syria brought him into conflict with the king of the Hittites, Muwatallis, who wanted to conquer some of Egypt's possessions for himself. In 1274 B.C.E. the armies of Ramesses and Muwatallis clashed in a battle at the city of Kadesh on the Orontes River in northern Syria. At stake was the limit of expansion of both empires. Ramesses's goal was to smash Hittite power in Syria and regain the influence that Egypt had enjoyed during the great days of Thutmose III and his successors in the fifteenth and fourteenth centuries B.C.E. Muwatallis hoped to enlarge the Hittite sphere of influence by pushing south and taking more lands away from the Egyptian Empire.

The pharaoh struck first, leading his regiments north in two columns that converged on the Syrian city of Kadesh. A huge Hittite army, with perhaps 3,500 chariots and 37,000 infantry under the command of Muwatallis himself, caught the Egyptians by surprise. An attack of the Hittite chariots nearly destroyed Ramesses's forces, but in a last-minute counterattack led by the pharaoh himself, Egyptian troops rallied and pushed their enemy back across the Orontes. The battle ended in a stalemate, with heavy losses on both sides.

The Battle of Kadesh°, despite its indecisive outcome, produced a treaty between the two empires. Writing in Akkadian, the Egyptian and Hittite monarchs signed a treaty of friendship and cooperation in 1269 B.C.E. According to its terms, Ramesses recognized the new Hittite

CHRONOLOGY

Egypt in the Bronze Age

1650–1550 B.C.E.	The Hyksos rule Egypt
1550 B.C.E.	Ahmose I expels Hyksos; New Kingdom begins
1479–1458 B.C.E.	The first female pharaoh, Hatshepsut, reigns
1458–1425 B.C.E.	Thutmose III reigns
1388–1351 B.C.E.	Amenhotep III reigns
1351–1334 B.C.E.	Amenhotep IV (Akhenaten) rules; Amarna period
1292 B.C.E.	Nineteenth Dynasty begins; Ramesses I reigns
1279–1213 B.C.E.	Ramesses II reigns
1274 B.C.E.	Egyptians and Hittites fight the Battle of Kadesh

king Hattusili and formally abandoned Egyptian claims to the city of Kadesh and northern Syria. In return, the Hittite monarch acknowledged Egypt's right to control Canaan, establishing a boundary between the two states. The two powers also agreed to give one another aid and military assistance in case of invasion by a third party or in the event of internal rebellions. Plans for the Hittite king to visit Egypt did not materialize, but after further negotiations a dynastic marriage was arranged between a daughter of the Hittite king and Ramesses in 1256 B.C.E. A second Hittite woman entered the pharaoh's harem a few years later.

The Battle of Kadesh yielded nearly a century of peace between the Hittites and the Egyptians. During this period commerce flourished in the Near East, benefiting both realms. With peace established with the Hittites, Nubia pacified, and the Libyan border fortified, Egypt enjoyed many decades of prosperity under Ramesses II's rule. The Hittite king turned his attention to problems presented by the growing power of Assyria to his east. He also signed a treaty of alliance with the Kassite monarch of Babylonia in Mesopotamia. Rulers had discovered that thoughtful diplomacy offered far more benefits than warfare.

WOMEN IN THE NEW KINGDOM

Under Egyptian law, women and men had complete equality in matters of property, business, and inheritance. In case of a divorce the wife's dowry (the wealth a woman brings to her husband in marriage) was returned to her and the couple's property divided. Women and men generally married within their own social class, and often within the same family occupations. For example, the daughter or sister of a shoemaker would likely marry a shoemaker. As a result, women frequently helped their husbands in the family business. They could earn on their own by weaving or selling garden produce.

Except for dynastic marriages in the royal family, Egyptian marriages were a private matter between two individuals and their families. The newlyweds celebrated their marriage with a party and the exchange of gifts. The union lasted as long as the husband and wife provided fidelity, love, and care for one another. Many elaborate marriage contracts, wills, and other financial documents that survive from the New Kingdom reveal careful planning for the welfare of family members and preserving family property through inheritance.

In the New Kingdom, women played an important role in religious worship. The wives of priests and officials formed musical groups called "Singers of Amun" that sang, clapped, and danced to the accompaniment of stringed instruments during religious rituals. These prestigious groups performed in communities throughout Egypt. Some women held priesthoods on their own. The most powerful was the "God's Wife of Amun." This priestess, often a member of the royal family, had administrative responsibilities as well as the obligation to perform religious rituals such as burning images of the god's enemies and summoning the god to meals.

The many female divinities prominent in Egyptian religion reflected Egyptian reverence for women. For example, Isis had fearsome powers as the protector of women and men against evil. She could cure the sick and revive the dead. Egyptians loved and feared her at the same time. Another goddess, Nut, was depicted as enveloping the entire Earth. At sunset Nut swallowed the sun and protected it in her body throughout the night until giving birth to it again in the morning, dramatizing the solar cycle with images of childbirth.

Egyptian families cherished their daughters as much as their sons, and women had a valued place in the household. In addition to preparing foods, weaving cloth, and caring for livestock and children, women arranged burials and worshiped at tombs to ensure an afterlife for departed parents and family members. In return they inherited a fair share of property from their parents.

The highly centralized government of the pharaohs created peaceful conditions that let Egypt prosper during the New Kingdom. Additional wealth came to Egypt through international commerce and from its empire in Canaan, Syria, and Nubia. Under the direction of talented and aggressive rulers, Egyptian imperial civilization reached its greatest height.

The Hittite, Assyrian, and Babylonian Empires

Egypt was only one of several large, highly centralized empires that developed during the International Bronze Age. Its main counterparts and rivals were the Hittite empire in Anatolia and the Assyrian and Babylonian empires in Mesopotamia.

THE GROWTH OF HITTITE POWER: CONQUEST AND DIVERSITY

By about 1650 B.C.E., the Hittites, who spoke an Indo-European language, had established control over the rich plateau of Anatolia (modern Turkey). Like the Egyptians, the warlike Hittites were among the first people to make use of the new chariot warfare technology. From their capital city at Hattushas, they not only maintained tight control over their subjects in Anatolia but also actively participated in long-distance commerce, established diplomatic ties with foreign states, and extended their power through military conquest.

Hittite imperial expansion was rooted in a long tradition of exploiting the resources of their neighbors. One early Hittite ruler, Hattusili I (ca. 1650–1620 B.C.E.), recorded his "manly deeds" in the following terms: ". . . three times I brought battle into the city gates of Hahha (a city to the southeast of Hattushas). I destroyed Hahha, but its goods I took away and brought them to Hattushas, my city. Two complete four-wheeled carts were loaded with silver . . . I, the Great King . . . destroyed [Hassuwa and] Hahha and gave them over to fire totally, but their smoke I showed to the God of Storms . . . and the king of Hahha I yoked to the four-wheeled cart . . ."[4]

CHRONOLOGY

The Hittites

CA. 1650 B.C.E.	The Hittite kingdom emerges
1380–1346 B.C.E.	Suppiluliuma I gains control of Syria
CA. 1300 B.C.E.	A Hittite king negotiates with a Mycenaean King about Millawanda
1274 B.C.E.	Egyptians and Hittites fight the Battle of Kadesh
CA. 1150 B.C.E.	The Hittite kingdom collapses

For two centuries Hittite power gradually expanded into northern Syria, Mesopotamia, and western Anatolia. About 1400 B.C.E. as they pushed southward, the Hittites became entangled in the quarrels of Syrian kingdoms over control of the trade routes to the Euphrates River. The kingdom of Mittani presented the chief obstacle to Hittite expansion into Syria. But under the rule of King Suppiluliuma I (ca. 1380–1346 B.C.E.) the Hittites crushed the kingdom of Mittani. This victory led to greater risks, for it brought the Hittites face to face with the Egyptian Empire, which stretched as far north as Palestine and the Euphrates. Within a century Hittite conflict with Egypt led to the Battle of Kadesh, as we saw earlier.

Expansion into western Anatolia brought Hittites into contact with the peoples of Greece and the Aegean Sea known as Mycenaeans. Some Mycenaeans established bases for piracy and trade on the western coast of Anatolia. Because the Hittites had no ships of their own, they were powerless to control these interlopers, who could always escape on their fast ships. Sometimes, however, Hittite kings were able to establish diplomatic ties with Mycenaean kings and thus create conditions of peace in which trade could flourish.

Cities played an important role in the Hittite imperial system because they functioned as administrative centers that gathered the resources of the countryside. Many of the cities had stone fortifications to guard royal residences and storehouses where the textiles, grains, and metals produced by the rural population were stored. From the carefully kept inventory tablets that have survived, historians know that the Hittites made great profits by trading these products to markets as far away as Cyprus and the Aegean, Syria, and Mesopotamia in return for metals and luxury goods.

As the Hittite Empire expanded, it grew increasingly multiethnic, absorbing many smaller kingdoms with their own languages and cultural traditions. The Hittites solved the thorny problem of administering this linguistically and culturally mixed empire by using Hittite, which was only one of many Indo-European languages spoken in Anatolia, as the official language of law and government. Nevertheless, the empire's cultural diversity and ties abroad forced the Hittites to keep records in other languages as well. An archive of more than 150,000 clay tablets unearthed by archaeologists at Hattushas in 1910 C.E. contains documents in seven languages in addition to Hittite, such as Akkadian and Luwian, the language possibly spoken at Troy. These tablets are written in cuneiform script, which the Hittites borrowed from nearby Mesopotamia, evidence of extensive cultural interaction with that region.

The Great King

Archaeologists have learned much about how the Hittite Empire functioned from the Hattushas archives. At the top of the Hittite Empire was the Great King, who ruled in the name of the supreme God of Storms. Like Egyptian rulers, the Great King owned the land of all his subjects, and he

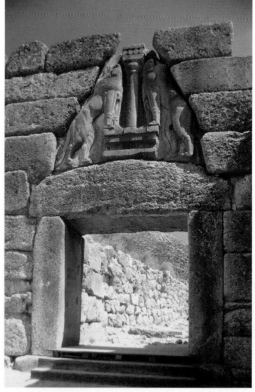

■ **Lion Gates at Imperial Palaces: Hattushas and Mycenae**
On this monumental entrance gate to Hattushas, above, the fortified capital of the Hittite Empire, massive stone lions flank the gate. On the right, stone lions guard the main entrance to the citadel of Mycenae in Greece. Lions symbolized royal strength in many kingdoms of the International Bronze Age. Their presence at fortress gates also suggests an international style of military architecture.

gave agricultural estates to the noblemen who served as his officials. In return they obeyed him and supplied the soldiers and charioteers he demanded for the army. The Great King also strengthened ties of allegiance throughout his empire by requiring his officials and subordinate monarchs to swear oaths of loyalty to the main Hittite gods. The Great King gave further unity to the empire by playing the role of chief priest of all the gods who were worshiped by the many different communities under his control.

Hittite kings worked hard to provide uniform justice throughout their realm for rich and poor, male and female alike. This proved a complex undertaking because the many different peoples who made up the Hittite Empire were permitted to follow their own customs and laws. Administering justice required close cooperation between subject peoples' local authorities and the Great King's legal officials.

Hittite Religion: "A Thousand Gods"

The Hittites spoke of their "thousand gods" because their religion drew from the empire's many subjects as well as from the neighboring people of Mesopotamia. The imperial government deliberately brought the statues of the gods of its subjects to Hattushas and built many temples for them in an effort to promote the unity of all the people under the Great King's rule.

The archive at Hattushas contained thousands of mythological and religious texts that reveal basic Hittite attitudes. Hittites believed that their gods were present in the form of their statues and that the gods wished to communicate with their human worshipers. Priests appointed by the Great King managed this "conversation" by making appropriate offerings to the deities at fixed intervals maintained in an elaborate calendar of festivals and holy days. The most important deity, Teshub, the God of Storms, presided over numerous gods, who controlled the heavens and involved themselves intimately in human affairs. According to Hittite belief, properly worshiped gods would protect the empire as well as any individuals who might pray to them privately. If a person sinned by violating standards of morality and piety set by the gods, such as committing murder or theft, breaking oaths, having sexual relations with certain animals, or neglecting the gods, the gods would punish that person as well as his or her entire family.

In addition to worshiping numerous gods, the Hittites relied heavily on magic to ward off evils, to stir up trouble for their enemies, and to gain the favor of certain gods. Hittites hired specialists to perform these magical rites, which often required the sacrifice of animals or humans, generally prisoners of war.

The Hittites believed in an afterlife in which the souls of the deceased continued their earthly occupations or lived in a huge palace ruled by the Goddess of Death in the Underworld, located far below the Earth's surface. Hittite rulers maintained a cult of dead kings in Hattushas, and it

HITTITE MILITARY RITUALS

Religious rituals and magic played an important role in every aspect of Hittite life, including warfare. Hittite warriors believed that the gods were usually on their side in battle. They thought that if the gods saw them as impure, they would suffer defeat in combat. After a purification ritual, defeated Hittite soldiers could return to soldiering with renewed morale and vigor. The following document explains the ritual of purification that soldiers performed after a military defeat:

If our troops are defeated by the enemy, they perform the Far-Side-Of-The-River-Ritual. On the far side of the river, they cut in half a person, a billy goat, a puppy, and a piglet. Half of each they place on this side and half on that side (of the river). In front they build a gate of hawthorn. . . . Over the top they draw a rope. In front, on either side, they light a fire. The troops go through the middle. When they reach the river, they sprinkle them with water. Afterward they perform the Ritual-of-The-Battlefield for them in the usual way [and can return to battle].

Source: From Richard H. Beal, "Hittite Military Organization" in *Civilizations of the Ancient Near East 4V*, edited by Jack Sasson, Charles Scribner's Sons, © 1995 by Charles Scribner's Sons. Reprinted by permission of The Gale Group.

is likely that families worshiped their ancestors and made sacrifices to them as well.

The militaristic and deeply religious Hittite Empire grew strong from conquering and ruthlessly exploiting the resources of its subjects. As it expanded, it played a prominent role in the network of trade and communication of the International Bronze Age. Hittite kings maintained diplomatic ties with rulers in Syria, Egypt, Mycenaean lands, and Mesopotamia, and Hittite merchants traded with their counterparts in these same areas. These commercial interconnections fostered an era of unprecedented cultural and political exchange among great empires.

THE MESOPOTAMIAN EMPIRES

The kingdoms of Mesopotamia, which rivaled the Hittite Empire in wealth and power, had an equally vital place in the political, commercial, and cultural networks of the International Bronze Age. As we discussed in Chapter 1, highly organized agriculture and urbanism produced distinctive cultures in northern and southern Mesopotamia. The political scene in these regions changed as small cities were transformed into large kingdoms that included many peoples. Because of their size and diversity, these kingdoms, like those of the Egyptians and Hittites, are properly referred to as empires.

During this period, two powerful empires emerged in Mesopotamia: Babylonia in the south and Assyria in the north. Their rulers controlled the economic production of their subjects, and they maintained diplomatic ties with the Egyptians and Hittites. Groups of people called Hapiru also lived in Mesopotamia beyond the control of the Assyrian and Babylonian states. Their seminomadic way of life on the outskirts of settled communities offered an alternative to the tightly controlled, sedentary agricultural societies of Babylonia and Assyria.

The Kingdom of Babylonia: Prosperity Under Kassite Rule

By about 1600 B.C.E. people known as Kassites infiltrated Mesopotamia as raiders, soldiers, and laborers. Their language and precise place of origin are unknown, but by 1400 B.C.E. they had gradually gained control of most of southern Mesopotamia. For the next 250 years, until about 1150 B.C.E., Kassite monarchs maintained order and prosperity in Babylonia, establishing the longest-ruling dynasty in ancient Middle Eastern history.

During these centuries, Babylonia enjoyed a golden age. Kassite kings politically unified Babylonia's many cities through a highly centralized administration that closely controlled both urban centers and countryside. These skilled monarchs won the loyalty of individuals of all ranks and temple priesthoods by giving them tracts of land. The Kassite kings gained a reputation for fair rule and for that reason were popular with their subjects. The government spent lavishly on temples, public buildings, and projects such as canals throughout the kingdom. Bureaucrats kept careful track of revenues. From these resources the government supported a large number of soldiers, artisans, officials, and temple officials.

A minority within the population, the Kassites quickly assimilated into Babylonian culture. They adopted Akkadian, the language of Babylonia, and abandoned their original tongue in an effort to fit in. Under Kassite rule, Babylonia became renowned as a center of trade, culture, and learning.

Babylonia's reputation for learning was linked primarily to science, medicine, and literature, which flourished during this period. With encouragement from the Kassite kings, who wished to demonstrate their full integration into Babylonian society, scribes systematically copied the works of earlier Mesopotamian cultures to preserve their intellectual legacy. Treatises on omens, astrology, and medicine gathered an enormous body of knowledge. This learning passed to future generations, adding to the foundations of the Western tradition.

Owing to their learning and skill, especially with herbal remedies and magic, Babylonian doctors earned fame throughout the Middle East. Gula, the goddess of healing known as the Great Physician, was the divine patron of a religious center where doctors received their training. A hymn of praise to Gula gives a glimpse of medical practices of the age. "I am a physician, I can heal. I carry around all healing herbs. I drive away disease. I gird myself with the leather bag containing health-giving incantations. I carry around texts which bring recovery. I give cures to mankind."[5]

In literature, the Babylonian creation epic *Enuma Elish* tells the story of the origin of the world by Marduk, the god of Babylon and sole lord of the universe. The order that Marduk creates reflects the organized rule that the Kassite kings provided for Babylonia. Babylonian authors also wrote versions of the *Epic of Gilgamesh*, the Sumerian story about the establishment of civilization that we discussed in Chapter 1. These two great works were translated into many languages and entertained people throughout the Middle East for more than a thousand years.

The Kingdom of Assyria: Expansion and Trade

As we saw in Chapter 1, around 1350 B.C.E. the Assyrian kingdom in northern Mesopotamia recovered from more than a century of submission to the neighboring kingdom of Mittani in Syria. When Hittite armies crushed the Mittanians, the Assyrians took advantage of the confusion and reestablished their independence. They began to build a new empire by conquering neighboring peoples. Under the skillful rule of Ashur-Uballit (ca. 1365–1330 B.C.E.) the Assyrian kingdom began a new phase of expansion by grabbing some former Mittanian territories that were rich in grain.

Ashur-Uballit wanted Assyria to stand on equal footing with the Egyptian and Hittite Empires and to take part in the long-distance network of trade and diplomacy that characterized the International Bronze Age. As a letter found in Egypt reveals, he tried to win the favor of the pharaoh in Egypt:

Thus speaks Ashur-Uballit, king of Assyria. May everything be well with you, your house, your land, your chariots and your troops. I am sending a messenger to you to visit you and to visit your country. Until now, my predecessors did not write; but today I am writing. I am sending you a beautiful chariot, two horses, and a bead of authentic lapis-lazuli [a valuable gemstone] as your greeting gift . . . My messenger will see how you are and how your country is, and then may he come back to me.[6]

Ashur-Uballit and his successors understood the value of close diplomatic ties with Egypt and other great powers. They also knew that their own power depended on control of natural resources and trade routes, and so they were quite willing to go to war to safeguard their economic interests. To that end, Assyrian kings pushed westward, clashing with the Hittites over trade, metal ores, and timber. The Assyrians built a string of garrisons on their border with the Hittite kingdom and seized territories in northern Syria that had come under Hittite control.

Assyrian kings also competed with Babylonia for control of copper, tin, horses, and other prized natural resources in the hilly lands to Mesopotamia's north and east. The mighty ruler Tukulti-Ninurta I (r. 1244–1208 B.C.E.) led his armies to victory over the Babylonian state, and by the time of his death Assyria controlled all the lands extending from northern Syria to southern Iraq—the greatest reach Assyria would ever attain. Even though Babylonia would reassert its independence within the next twenty years, Assyria dominated Mesopotamian affairs for the next two centuries.

Assyrian power expanded again during the reign of Tiglath-Pileser I (r. 1114–1076 B.C.E.). This capable ruler waged wars against the seminomadic pastoral tribes living on his frontiers, threatening essential Assyrian trade routes. Assyria had become a major consumer of materials imported from abroad, such as timber, copper, cedar, ivory, and tin. In order to protect his sources of supply, Tiglath-Pileser led an expedition to the Mediterranean coast, where he established cordial relations with many trading cities such as Byblos that supplied many of these valued items.

Military victories allowed Assyrian monarchs to sponsor grand public works. Tukulti-Ninurta, for example, celebrated his successes by building a new royal city, called the Harbor of Tukulti-Ninurta, on the banks of the Tigris River. The new capital included a grand canal to facilitate trade, and boasted many palaces and temples decorated with colorful tiles. The chief temple, built in the form of a huge mud-brick ziggurat, honored the Assyrian god Ashur. Assyrian rulers also established many administrative centers throughout their lands from which they could control the wealth produced by their subjects.

The Hapiru: On the Edges of Settled Life

Although they had fierce armies and abundant wealth, the kingdoms of Babylonia and Assyria could not control the diverse peoples called Hapiru, or "landless peoples," who lived on the margins of their lands. Unlike the Kassites, who had settled in Babylonia and achieved political power, different groups of Hapiru maintained a seminomadic existence that was an alternative to life in the highly centralized, agriculture-based empires. They never achieved any political unity.

The Hapiru comprised peoples of diverse origins. Historians believe some were fugitives from economic exploitation by the centralized governments of the Mesopotamian kingdoms or refugees from the constant wars among them. Others were pastoral peoples who had never lived in cities or practiced agriculture. Regardless of their origin, the Hapiru demonstrate that there was room for unsettled peoples on the boundaries between the great empires. Some Hapiru raided urban communities and lived as bandits and occasionally as mercenaries. Others were en-

slaved and forced to labor on government building projects in Mesopotamia and as far away as Egypt.

At the end of the International Bronze Age, when the great Mesopotamian empires collapsed, the Hapiru nearly disappeared from the historical record. As we will see in the next chapter, however, one group of landless Hapiru entered the land of Canaan about 1100 B.C.E. Some historians believe that these wandering landless people were the ancestors of the people known in the Bible as Hebrews.

The Civilizations of the Mediterranean

During the International Bronze Age, two vigorous and distinctive civilizations developed in the eastern Mediterranean: the Minoan civilization of Crete (a large island south of Greece) and the Mycenaean civilization on mainland Greece. These were the first civilizations in Europe. Both developed from native peoples who had been in Crete and Greece since the Neolithic period. They prospered from agriculture and long-distance trade, rivaling the empires of Assyria and Babylonia in wealth and influence. The political history of these two civilizations has been forgotten, but the myths and legends of Greek civilization in later centuries preserve some memories of their achievements. Archaeologists have unearthed their palaces, tombs, and objects of everyday life, which provide glimpses into their civilizations.

Also situated on the eastern Mediterranean, and serving as buffer states between Egypt, Mycenaean Greece, and the

CHRONOLOGY

The Peoples of Mesopotamia

CA. 1400 B.C.E.	The Kassites gain control of Babylonia
1365–1330 B.C.E.	Ashur-Uballit renews Assyrian power
1244–1208 B.C.E.	Tukulti-Ninurta I conquers Babylonia; literature, science, and medicine flourish
1114–1076 B.C.E.	Assyrian king Tiglath-Pileser reigns
CA. 1200–1000 B.C.E.	Hapiru live on fringes of settled life
CA. 1000	Arameans invade Assyria

Hittite Empire, were several small coastal cities and kingdoms. These states participated in the brisk trade that developed in this region during the International Bronze Age. The two most prosperous of these states, the mercantile kingdoms of Ugarit and Troy, played a "middle-man" role in the trading and diplomatic networks that developed during these centuries.

MINOAN CRETE

About 2000 B.C.E. small urban communities on the island of Crete, which lies midway between Greece and Egypt in the Mediterranean Sea, began to import copper and tin from the eastern Mediterranean. Sir Arthur Evans, the British archaeologist who discovered the remains of the palaces and shrines of Bronze Age Crete in 1899 C.E., called their society Minoan, from the legendary Cretan king Minos in Greek mythology. Minoans raised livestock and cultivated grapes, olives, and cereals that were introduced to the island from the Middle East during the food-producing revolution. Protected from enemies by the surrounding sea, the population of Crete slowly grew in size and prosperity.

In the course of the second millennium B.C.E., the Minoans became highly skilled navigators. They developed a busy merchant navy that traded with Greece, Egypt, and the coastal communities of the eastern Mediterranean. Crete became a thriving center of long-distance trade. The Minoans imported metals, especially copper and tin to make bronze, and they exported textiles, jewelry, wine, and olive oil in beautifully painted ceramic pots. Their civilization was the most brilliant in the Mediterranean until the sixteenth century B.C.E., when it was surpassed by that of the Mycenaeans.

Palace Administration: Collecting and Redistributing Wealth

The Minoan economy revolved around four major urban administrative centers, called palaces, at Knossos, Phaistos, Mallia, and Zakros. A network of roads linked the palaces, suggesting highly centralized political authority. Minoan rulers collected agricultural produce from farmers in the countryside and stored it in the palaces. Palace administrators told farmers how much to grow and collected the produce from them, then gave back sufficient food for their

■ **The Palace of Minos at Knossos, Crete**
This detailed reconstruction of the palace of a Minoan king at Knossos, Crete, is based on archaeological excavations. In one of the rooms adjacent to the central court, the royal family and palace officials worshiped the Snake Goddess (see illustration on page 60).

subsistence. Palace officials also controlled the specialized artists who produced crafts, such as delicately painted pottery, jewelry, and fabrics, that were traded abroad.

Archaeologists believe that the three-acre palace complex at Knossos was the most important in Crete. At its center stood a courtyard surrounded by hundreds of rooms intended as living quarters for the governing and religious elite, administrative headquarters, shrines for religious worship, and warehouses for storing crops and wine in huge clay jars. Archaeologists estimate that the warehouses at Knossos could hold more than a quarter of a million gallons of wine or olive oil. Some rooms functioned as workshops for weaving, pottery manufacture, and metalwork. These warehouses show the Minoan rulers' tight control over the production of wealth on Crete.

The Minoan elites lived in great luxury in palaces connected to warehouses. Built with carefully fitted blocks of smooth limestone cut to a standard unit of measure, with beams of wood and columns wider with flared tops, the palaces had several stories—Knossos sported five. Vivid frescoes (plaster painted while it is still wet) of sea creatures, flowers, court officials and acrobats in bright garments, and scenes of daily life adorned their walls. The residents enjoyed indoor plumbing and running water, comforts that most people in the West would not enjoy until the nineteenth century C.E. The palaces had no fortifications, suggesting that the Minoans felt quite safe on their island.

Like other monarchs, Minoan rulers carefully kept precise records of their wealth and possessions on clay tablets. Accountants recorded long lists of the livestock, produce, raw materials, and merchandise brought to the palace warehouses, as well as the amounts given back to the community. They also kept track of land holdings, debts, and payments made to the palace. These administrators used a form of writing known as Linear A, a simplified hieroglyphic script that developed on Crete around 1700 B.C.E., probably influenced by Egyptian writing. Linguists have not entirely deciphered the script. Minoan mercantile documents found in ports along the eastern coast of the Mediterranean (the Levant) as well as on Crete reveal the international reach of Minoan travel and commerce.

Minoan merchants and artists cultivated extensive commercial links abroad, especially throughout the eastern Mediterranean. For example, archaeologists have excavated Minoan trading posts on the islands of the central Aegean Sea, on the island of Rhodes, and in other locations along the eastern Mediterranean coast. The artists produced beautiful jewelry of precious metals and stones, painted sophisticated designs of sea creatures on vases, and carved delicate figures in ivory, gold, and a deep blue gemstone called lapis lazuli° obtained from the Middle East. Minoan merchants sold their wares on the Greek mainland, and Minoan delegations brought rich gifts to the courts of Egyptian pharaohs. Exporting these luxury goods to eager foreign buyers made the Minoans extremely rich.

CHRONOLOGY

Minoan Crete and Mycenaean Greece

CA. 6000 B.C.E.	First settlements on Crete
CA. 3000 B.C.E.	Minoans begin trading with the Levant
CA. 2300 B.C.E.	Bronze technology enters Aegean region
CA. 2000 B.C.E.	First palaces are built on Crete
CA. 1700 B.C.E.	Linear A script develops (still undeciphered)
CA. 1600 B.C.E.	Mycenaean civilization emerges on Greek mainland; shaft graves constructed at Mycenae
CA. 1450 B.C.E.	First palaces built at Mycenae; Linear B script develops
CA. 1400 B.C.E.	Mycenaean cities fortified
CA. 1375 B.C.E.	Mycenaeans control Crete and eastern sea routes
CA. 1200 B.C.E.	Raiders of Land and Sea appear
CA. 1150 B.C.E.	Mycenaean palaces and towns destroyed on mainland, Cyprus, and coast of Asia Minor

Some Minoan artists traveled abroad to work for wealthy patrons. Frescoes painted by artists from Crete have been found in the Hyksos capital of Avaris in the Egyptian delta and at sites in Canaan and Syria. Historians believe that these painters might have accompanied Minoan princesses who married foreign leaders to cement diplomatic relations. These clues suggest the elaborate commercial ties that developed in the eastern Mediterranean during the International Bronze Age.

The Mystery of Minoan Religion

The many frescoes and ritual artifacts unearthed from Bronze Age Crete provide archaeologists with a tantalizing but incomplete glimpse of Minoan religious observance. Minoans set aside rooms in their houses as shrines where they worshiped the gods and offered sacrifices. Religious rituals took place in the countryside as well. Worshipers brought offerings of swords, miniature axes, and figurines to more than twenty-five sacred caves in the mountains of Crete. On mountaintop sanctuaries people built bonfires into which they threw clay figurines of humans and animals. Archaeologists have found traces of human sacrifice at some sites, but their meaning remains unclear.

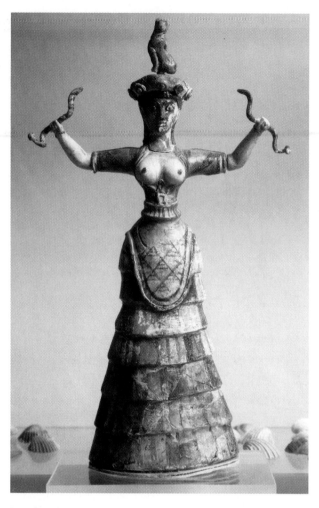

■ **Snake Goddess**

One of the most important divinities of Minoan civilization was the Snake Goddess. Here she (or her priestess) is captured in typical pose and dress: She grasps a snake in each outstretched hand and wears a tight-fitting, layered dress that exposes her breasts. A sacred bird perches on her head.

Historians believe that female divinities dominated Minoan religion. Minoans worshiped the powerful Mistress of Animals at some mountaintop shrines, and in their homes they prayed to a goddess whom they always depicted as holding a snake. Statues show this Snake Goddess (or her priestess) wearing a many-tiered skirt, with breasts exposed and snakes coiled around her outstretched arms. Minoans also worshiped the Goddess of Childbirth and a Dove Goddess, who was perhaps the goddess of love, as well as an assortment of demons and male gods.

Despite the rich array of artifacts and sites unearthed by archaeologists, we know very little about the basic beliefs of Minoan religion because no written texts that discuss them have been found. The beliefs of the Minoans remain a mystery.

The Collapse of Minoan Prosperity

Minoan prosperity and power came to a sudden and unexplained end around 1450 B.C.E., when all of the Cretan towns and palaces were destroyed except for Knossos, which fell about 1375 B.C.E. Excavations reveal that immediately after the destruction of the Minoan palaces, artifacts from mainland Greece appeared on Crete and throughout the Aegean. Goods from the Greek mainland, such as pottery painted with distinctive patterns and nautical images, weapons, and wine replaced Minoan products in Syria and the western Mediterranean. Graves on Crete began to contain Greek-style weapons and armor. Archaeologists do not know whether Mycenaean Greeks from the mainland caused the collapse of Minoan power or merely took advantage of it, but it is certain that invaders from Greece took control of Crete and its trade networks around this time. The international economy and the balance of maritime power in the eastern Mediterranean shifted from the island of Minoan Crete to the mainland of Mycenaean Greece.

MYCENAEAN GREECE

A German archaeologist, Heinrich Schliemann, first brought the Bronze Age civilization of mainland Greece to light in 1876 C.E. Determined to prove that the epic poems of the Greek poet Homer about the Trojan war were based in fact, Schliemann first dug at Troy (see next section) and then at the fortress of Mycenae, the home of the Greek king Agamemnon in Homer's *Iliad.* He made spectacular finds of golden treasures and sophisticated architecture at Mycenae, which archaeologists today believe was only one of perhaps six kingdoms on the Greek mainland.

The name *Mycenaean* refers to the kingdom of Mycenae, but since we do not know its ancient name or that of any of the other kingdoms of Greece, the term is also applied generally to the culture of Greece during the International Bronze Age. Historians believe that Mycenaean civilization lasted from around 1600 to 1100 B.C.E.

Mycenaean Civilization

Mycenaean civilization emerged among the native populations of the Peloponnese, the southern portion of Greece. The larger Mycenaean communities consisted of heavily fortified palaces with outlying agricultural lands. Historians do not know anything about the political organization of Mycenaean Greece, but the palace fortifications suggest that the rulers of different palaces frequently warred with one another and that there was no political unity in Greece. Extensive excavation also shows that the strongest fortresses stood at Mycenae, Tiryns, Pylos, Gla, and Thebes. Archaeologists assume that these fortified palaces represented different kingdoms, perhaps linked by alliances.

As on Crete, the Mycenaean palaces functioned as administrative centers of food collection, storage, and distribution. They also served as manufacturing centers that produced pottery, jewelry, tapestries, and other trade goods. Literate bureaucrats living in the palaces were essential in governing the Mycenaean kingdoms. These administrators kept a sharp eye on all aspects of economic production. Like their counterparts in Crete and the Middle East, they recorded long lists of livestock, slaves, farm produce, land holdings, taxes, and tribute taken from peasants and slaves. They also kept detailed records of imported and exported luxury goods and raw materials. The lists include foreign terms for many of the exotic objects found in the Uluburun shipwreck, further evidence of a flourishing international market (see Map 2.3).

By 1400 B.C.E. a uniform Mycenaean civilization had reached its apex throughout southern Greece and in Mycenaean settlements abroad. The similarity of pottery and other manufactured goods from Mycenaean sites in Greece and abroad prevents us from knowing which of the fortress kingdoms traded with a foreign land or campaigned on foreign shores.

Administrative records of the Mycenaean kings demonstrate that the Mycenaeans were Greeks. We know this because palace administrators recorded their lists on clay tablets in a script known as Linear B, which developed around 1450 B.C.E. A British scholar who deciphered Linear B in the early 1950s C.E. proved that it was an early form of the Greek language still spoken today. Moreover, even though the Linear B tablets contain only palace bookkeeping records and do not record literature or history, some of them included the names of gods, such as Poseidon, Zeus, Hera, and Hermes. Greeks worshiped these gods until Christianity took hold during the Roman Empire in the sixth century C.E.

Mycenaean kings controlled their realms in ways similar to those of their counterparts in Egypt and Anatolia. Kings stood at the top of the administrative hierarchy. They led their people in wartime, formed diplomatic alliances with other monarchs, and tried to become richer and more powerful through trade and conquest.

The Warrior Kingdom of Mycenae

The most influential kingdom in southern Greece during this period was located at Mycenae, where kings governed from a citadel looking down on a broad agricultural plain. This center of power, which lasted until around 1100 B.C.E., reveals much about in life in Bronze Age Greece. Thirty royal burials consisting of deep shafts arranged in two circles on the citadel and dating from 1600 to 1450 B.C.E. suggest a highly warlike people. The graves contain bronze swords, daggers, spearheads, and stone arrowheads and blades. The skeletons of the rulers buried in these graves stood nearly six feet tall, which made them tower over the general population. Apparently they enjoyed better nutrition than their subjects, whose graves reveal more diminutive skeletons. The many gold and silver drinking vessels and pieces of jewelry found in the graves further demonstrate that the Mycenaean leaders enjoyed tremendous luxury.

The rulers of Mycenae possessed enough wealth to construct beehive-shaped vaulted tombs, bigger than any other buildings previously built in the Mediterranean. More than fifty such tombs survive. One king's tomb had a diameter of nearly fifty feet, stood forty-three feet high, and was topped by a capstone weighing more than a hundred tons.

The Mycenaean kings also relied on aristocratic warriors, who enforced the monarchs' decisions and served as

■ **Map 2.3 Mycenaean Trade and Contacts, ca. 1200 B.C.E.**
The Mycenaean Greeks traded extensively with communities throughout the eastern Mediterranean world, including Egypt, the coastal towns of Asia Minor, and Canaan. Sometimes their commerce was little more than raiding and piracy.

■ **Mycenaean Decorated Pot**

This Warrior Vase, dating to about 1200 B.C.E., shows a marching troop of infantrymen, an indication of the Mycenaeans' military activities throughout the eastern Mediterranean.

military officers during wartime. As in Egypt, Anatolia, and the Middle East, elite warriors used light, fast-moving chariots pulled by horses. They also took their favorite weapons of war with them to the grave, suggesting that they valued military prowess very highly.

Infantrymen ranked below the aristocrats in the military organization of the Mycenaean states. These soldiers followed the chariots into battle and engaged in hand-to-hand combat using spears and swords. The infantry was drawn from farmers who leased lands from aristocrats and kings. Aristocratic women with religious titles controlled some estates independently, and they may have supplied soldiers to the king's armies as well.

Overseas Trade and Settlement

The Mycenaeans took advantage of the peaceful conditions in the eastern Mediterranean that diplomatic ties between Egypt and the Hittite Empire had helped to create. With the collapse of Minoan Crete, they assumed control of the commerce across the Aegean Sea and the eastern Mediterranean. During the fourteenth and thirteenth centuries B.C.E., Mycenaean merchants extended Minoan commercial routes, establishing strong links with Egyptians, Hittites, and the inhabitants of Ugarit and other Middle Eastern coastal towns. During this time of expansion and commercial success, the treasuries of the Mycenaean rulers were filled.

Like other rulers of their time, the Mycenaeans cultivated extensive commercial and diplomatic contacts with foreign peoples. As participants in the international trading networks, they imported many goods. From Minoan Crete came artistic influences in stone- and goldworking. From the Middle East came knowledge of the war chariot. Merchants brought amber from the Baltic seacoast of northern Europe and metal ores from Italy and western Mediterranean lands. In return for these goods, the Mycenaeans traded tapestries, wine, and perfumed olive oil. Vessels painted with distinctive Mycenaean designs carried the liquid commodities to Egypt and the Middle East, and as far west as Spain and northern Italy.

Mycenaean rulers also forged diplomatic ties with Hittite and Egyptian monarchs. Ambassadors of Pharaoh Amenhotep III visited Crete and the Greek mainland, including Mycenae, where they presented ceremonial plaques bearing the pharaoh's name. Expensive gifts from Mycenaean rulers to pharaohs also have been discovered in Egypt.

In the interest of maintaining good relations and brisk commerce, Egyptian and Mycenaean rulers avoided war with each other during this period. Mycenaean relations with the Hittites were not quite so cordial. To extend and protect their trade routes, some Mycenaean Greeks settled on the coast of Asia Minor, a sphere of Hittite influence. There they engaged in trade, piracy, and warfare with surrounding communities. Hittite documents dating to the fourteenth century B.C.E. tell of meddling Mycenaean kings who slipped away to sea in their ships, out of the reach of landbound Hittite forces. The pottery of the Mycenaeans in these settlements shows that they shared the culture of the Greek mainland. Nevertheless, historians do not know how they were connected to the great palace-fortresses of the Greek mainland.

The Mycenaeans also coveted the copper mines on Cyprus, an island south of modern Turkey in the eastern Mediterranean Sea (*Cyprus* means "copper" in Greek). To gain control of the deposits of this prized ore, Mycenaean traders established numerous trading colonies on Cyprus beginning in the fourteenth century B.C.E. They traded extensively with the local inhabitants and with the peoples of Syria and Palestine. Archaeologists have found rich deposits of pottery painted in the styles of the Greek mainland, but also showing the influence of Cypriot, Syrian, and Palestinian styles, evidence of the varied cultural encounters that international trade facilitated.

TWO COASTAL KINGDOMS: UGARIT AND TROY

Many independent cities existed along the border regions between Egypt, Mycenaean Greece, and the Hittite Empire. Overshadowed by their more powerful neighbors, each city survived by acknowledging the superiority of one of the great empires and following its lead in trade, diplomacy, and warfare. A string of these small communities stretched along the seacoast from the Aegean Sea to the Gaza Strip and served as a buffer between the three major powers. The two most notable cities were Ugarit and Troy.

THE MILLAWANDA LETTER

....

About 1300 B.C.E., a Hittite king wrote the following letter to an unknown Mycenaean king, complaining of the behavior of a lesser ruler on the Aegean coast of Asia Minor who had defied the Hittite king's commands. It reveals the limitations placed on the Hittites by their lack of a navy. Millawanda was the Hittite name for the coastal town in Asia Minor where the Mycenaeans had established a stronghold.

The author's insistence on the formalities of diplomatic communication is striking. The letter indicates the significant role of international diplomatic relations among the great powers, but it leaves some questions unanswered: Was the Mycenaean kingdom of Ahhijawa on Rhodes, on Cyprus, or in Greece? What was the previous trouble over the city of Wilusa (another name for Troy)?

I have to complain of the insolent and treacherous conduct of . . . Tawagalawas. We came into contact in the land of Luqqa [in southwest Asia Minor]; and he offered to become a vassal of the Hittite Emperor . . . I order him, if he desires to become a vassal of mine, to make sure that no troops of his are to be found in Ijalanda [an unknown location] when I arrive there. And what do I find when I arrive at Ijalanda? The troops of Tawagalawas fighting on the side of my enemies. I defeat them, take many prisoners, devastate the district, scrupulously keeping the fortress of Atrija intact out of respect for my treaty with you. Now comes a Hittite subject, Pijamaradus, . . . who steals my 7000 prisoners, and makes off to your city Millawanda (Miletus). I command him to return to me:

he disobeys. I write to you: you send a surly message, unaccompanied by gift or greeting. . . . So I go to fetch him. I enter your city Millawanda, for I have something to say to Pijamaradus, and it would be well that your subjects there should hear me say it. But my visit is not a success. I ask for Tawagalawas: he is not at home. I should like to see Pijamaradus: he has gone to sea. . . . Are you aware, and is it with your blessing, that Pijamaradus is going around saying that he intends to leave his wife and family, and incidentally my 7000 prisoners, under your protection, while he makes continual inroads into my territory? Kindly tell him either to settle down peacefully in your country, or to return to my country. Do not let him use Ahhijawa as a base for operations against me. You and I are friends. There has been no quarrel between us since we came to terms in the matter of Wilusa [Troy]: the trouble there was all my fault, and I promise you that it shall not happen again. As for my military occupation of your city Millawanda, please consider it a friendly visit. I am sorry that in the past you have had occasion to accuse me of being aggressive and of sending impolite messages: I was young then and carried away in the heat of action. I may add that I also have had harsh words from you, and I suggest that the fault may not lie with ourselves but with our messengers. Let us bring them to trial, cut off their heads, mutilate their bodies, and live henceforward in perfect friendship.

Source: From Denys L. Page, *History and the Homeric Iliad,* Copyright © 1959 by The Regents of the University of California. Reprinted by permission.

Ugarit: A Mercantile Kingdom

Directly east of Cyprus on the Syrian coast lay the port city of Ugarit, which controlled a small but influential kingdom of about 2,000 square miles. Ugarit was one of several small kingdoms dotting the coast that grew wealthy from maritime trade and agriculture. Lying in the area known as Canaan, Ugarit shared Canaanite gods, customs, and social organization with other communities in the region.

Ugarit became a highly cultured city with international connections because of its rich natural resources. The fertile plain offered arable land for grape vines, olive trees, and grains, while the heavily forested surrounding hills provided timber for shipbuilding and construction. Perhaps Ugarit's greatest asset was a fine natural harbor that made the city a hub of international trade. Merchant ships like the one that sank at Uluburun sailed to Ugarit from Cyprus and the Aegean, the coast of western Anatolia, and Egypt. Caravans laden with goods arrived from Mesopotamia, the Hittite lands, and Canaan. People from all these places set-

tled in Ugarit, whose population is estimated at 10,000 inhabitants. Another 25,000 people lived as farmers in the Ugarit countryside.

The city of Ugarit consisted of two major sections. An enormous, fortified palace occupying about 10,000 square yards dominated the city. It contained residential quarters with running water and sewage disposal facilities, administrative buildings, and imposing temples to the gods Baal and Dagan, who protected the city. In a second section of the city, wealthy inhabitants lived in spacious homes with elaborate family tombs under the floor of one room. In these spacious houses archaeologists have excavated numerous baked clay tablets containing legal, financial, literary, diplomatic, and religious texts written in Ugaritic, the local Semitic language. The tablets demonstrate the literacy of the Ugaritic elite. Young people studied their own language in school while also mastering foreign languages useful in trade and diplomacy. The tablets show an innovative alphabet. In it, each spoken sound was represented by just one letter or sign. This Ugaritic alphabet was the ancestor of all modern alphabets that follow the same principle of one sign per spoken sound.

The kings of Ugarit controlled a substantial military force in the form of an elite corps of 2,000 aristocratic charioteers. These warriors supplied their own horses, a sign of the city's enormous wealth. The rulers could also afford to hire battalions of mercenary troops from neighboring lands. Even with these forces, however, Ugarit was always overshadowed by mighty Egypt to the south and the combative Hittite Empire to the north. To maintain Ugarit's independence, the port city's rulers had to be clever diplomats. Archaeologists have unearthed records of treaties made between the kings of Ugarit and Hittite, Mitannian, Assyrian, and other rulers in the Middle East. These treaties show that Ugarit played a crucial role in international diplomacy.

Troy: A City of Legend

Troy, the best known and yet most mysterious of all Bronze Age cities, has captured the popular imagination for 3,000 years, but archaeology cannot explain the origins of the people who lived there, or even their language. Situated in northwest Asia Minor on a promontory overlooking a bay about six miles from the Aegean Sea, this city has become immortal as the site of the Trojan War in Homer's epic poems the *Iliad* and the *Odyssey*.

Composed about 750 B.C.E., these stories were legends, not history. Still, they formed part of an enduring oral tradition that began in the International Bronze Age. In some ways they reflect social conditions and perhaps even events that actually occurred. Archaeologists began excavating Troy, Mycenae, and other sites specifically to investigate the reliability of Homer's accounts. Today, however, historians appreciate Troy primarily as a city embedded in the intricate web of trade, diplomacy, and warfare that linked the societies of the International Bronze Age.

Archaeologists have unearthed numerous distinct layers of occupation and construction in Troy, as generations of inhabitants rebuilt their city from about 3000 to 1200 B.C.E. Around 1700 B.C.E. the inhabitants of Troy VI (meaning the sixth major layer of occupation) constructed huge gateways and a royal palace consisting of many roomy mansions. A fortified citadel, Troy VI was built with monumental blocks of masonry similar to that used by the Hittites and the Mycenaeans, suggesting that techniques of military engineering had spread among these kingdoms. Sandwiched between the Hittite Empire and the kingdoms of Mycenaean Greece, Troy retained its independence, though it probably remained under the shadow of the Hittite Empire.

The Trojans prospered in the fifteenth and fourteenth centuries B.C.E. by trading with Mycenaean Greeks, Hittites, Cypriots (from Cyprus), and merchants from Ugarit. They produced woolen fabrics and fine tapestries for export. They also won notice as breeders of fine horses, which warrior aristocrats used in chariot combat. The skipper of the

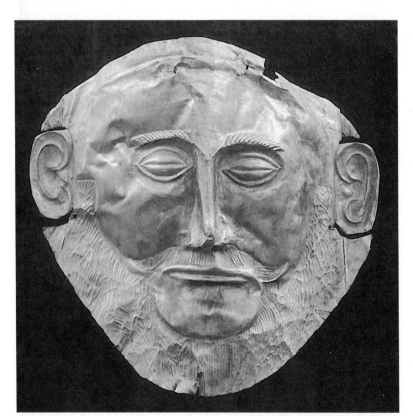

■ **The "Death Mask of Agamemnon"**
This thin gold mask, about 11 inches long, was found at the citadel of Mycenae in the tomb of a ruler who died about 1550 B.C.E. Heinrich Schliemann, who excavated the tomb, mistakenly jumped to the conclusion that it was the death mask of King Agamemnon, who led the Greek forces during the Trojan War, as told in Homer's *Iliad*. Later archaeologists have discovered that this king died several centuries before the period that Homer described.

ship wrecked at Uluburun likely stopped at Troy during one of his many voyages.

Around 1270 B.C.E., an earthquake tumbled the mighty walls of Troy VI and the city went up in flames. The Trojans' prosperity and influence ended. Heinrich Schliemann, the first archaeologist to excavate Troy, erroneously concluded that Troy VI was the city destroyed by Mycenaean Greeks in Homer's *Iliad*. Later archaeologists proved that Greeks had nothing to do with the city's collapse.

The survivors of the earthquake rebuilt the city, which archaeologists have named Troy VIIa, on a very modest scale. Situated within the rubble of Troy VI's fortress walls, this new version of the city also fell to ruin about 1190 B.C.E. The presence of human bones in the debris suggest that warfare destroyed it. Most archaeologists believe that if there is even a kernel of truth in Homer's stories about the Greek destruction of Troy, it must lie in the violent end of Troy VIIa, not Troy VI.

We have no hope of reconstructing an accurate account of these events. Nevertheless, Hittite royal documents indicate that Mycenaeans raided the coastlands of Asia Minor in search of slaves and booty, and Linear B tablets from the Greek mainland list slaves captured on the Asia Minor coast. These records suggest that Troy VIIa may well have fallen prey to a Mycenaean attack. Some historians believe that in the centuries following Troy VIIa's destruction, the story of a Mycenaean raid slowly took on epic proportions as generations of Greek bards told and retold it. Older tales recounting the glory of Troy VI may have augmented the legend of the Trojan War.

The End of the International Bronze Age and Its Aftermath

The intricate diplomatic, cultural, and economic interconnections between Egypt, the Middle East, Anatolia, and Greece broke between 1200 and 1100 B.C.E. These formerly vibrant civilizations plummeted into a dark age, marked by invasions, migrations, and the collapse of stable governments. The era of prosperity and international cooperation came to an abrupt end.

THE RAIDERS OF THE LAND AND SEA

For Mycenaean Greece, warfare among the mainland's many competitive kingdoms probably began a chain of disasters. Some archaeologists argue that overpopulation and competition for resources may have sparked these struggles. These conflicts resulted in the breakdown of the palace-centered economic system about 1150 B.C.E. When

CHRONOLOGY	
Ugarit and Troy	
CA. 1700–1270 B.C.E.	Troy VI flourishes; trades with Mycenaeans and Hittites
CA. 1700 B.C.E.	Ugarit emerges as important trading center
CA. 1270 B.C.E.	Troy VI falls
CA. 1270–1150 B.C.E.	Troy VIIa inhabited
CA. 1150 B.C.E.	Troy VIIa falls; Raiders of the Land and Sea burn Ugarit

the Mycenaean kingdoms collapsed, the economy disintegrated as well. Literacy disappeared because there was no need for scribes to learn Linear B and keep palace inventories. Trade and population declined rapidly, and many Greeks migrated to the coast of Asia Minor in search of new homes. Village life dragged on, though at an impoverished level. The Greek language and some religious beliefs survived, but the crafts, artistic styles, and architectural traditions of Mycenaean life were forgotten. Some memories of Mycenaean fighting on the coast of Asia Minor were preserved in distorted form in Greek legends of later centuries. These stories claimed that a wave of invaders from the north entered the Greek mainland at this time, but there is no archaeological evidence to support this assertion. In contrast to the brilliance of Mycenaean civilization, the poverty and hardship of the era that followed merit the name "dark age."

For the Hittite Empire, a deadly combination of economic decline and invasions early in the twelfth century B.C.E. triggered the government's collapse. The subject kingdoms in the western regions of the Hittite Empire began to rebel, and peasants fled their lands, perhaps due to droughts. The Hittites became ever more dependent on foreign sources of grain, forcing their rulers to import larger supplies from Egypt and Syria. Sometimes rebellions blocked these shipments, worsening the Hittites' plight.

When seaborne raiders invaded from the west, the Hittites, who had no navy of their own, made a desperate, defensive alliance with the kings of the maritime city of Ugarit. The combined effort of the allied war fleets and Hittite troops temporarily protected the empire's western flank, but by the first decade of the twelfth century B.C.E. an enemy force of uncertain origin stormed through the Hittite Empire and burned the capital city of Hattushas. With no effective leadership, Hittite power soon crumbled. Within just a few generations, the empire's glory was forgotten.

■ **Map 2.4 Routes of the Raiders of the Land and Sea, ca. 1200–1150 B.C.E.**
Migrating peoples, known as the Raiders of the Land and Sea, destroyed the network of commerce and diplomacy that had flourished during the International Bronze Age. Traveling along the eastern Mediterranean coast, these displaced peoples destroyed many kingdoms and cities before being stopped and dispersed by Egyptian forces.

The collapse of Hittite and Mycenaean power contributed to migrations throughout the eastern Mediterranean. People fled their homes in search of new lands to settle. Overcoming all resistance, these displaced groups plundered cities and brought destruction to the entire eastern Mediterranean as they moved south toward Egypt.

In Egyptian documents these people are referred to as Raiders of the Land and Sea°. They came from many places and there is no single explanation of what set them in motion (see Map 2.4). Earthquakes, plague, climate change, political instability, and economic decline likely spurred them to migrate. Some of the raiders came from the Aegean region and included Mycenaean Greeks. Others originated in Cyprus and the territories seeking to break free from Hittite control. Perhaps some came from the region of Troy. Still more originated in the Middle East. Although they included pirates and mercenaries, the raiders were not simply a coalition of violent bandits. They included migrating groups that traveled with their families and livestock in search of new lands.

Moving south through Syria and Palestine, the raiders destroyed Ugarit and other coastal cities that formerly had ties with the Hittites and Egyptians. "Now the ships of the enemy have come, and they have burned my cities in fire and have committed atrocities in my land!" lamented the last king of Ugarit in a letter to the ruler of Cyprus. Bound together in a loose confederation, the raiders moved further south toward Egypt in search of land and food.

Taking advantage of Egypt's preoccupation with the raiders, the Labu and Meshwesh people, who originated in Libya, invaded the Nile's western delta. Pharaoh Merenptah (r. 1213–1203 B.C.E.) stopped them after a long and bloody battle. Within twenty-five years the Labu and the Meshwesh entered the delta again, this time settling there. They allied themselves with the Raiders of the Land and Sea from the north, making common cause with groups who had participated in the destruction of the Hittite capital, as well as Ugarit and other cities on Cyprus and the Mediterranean coast. Ramesses III (r. 1185–1153 B.C.E.) overcame this coalition in battle, but the worst was yet to come. In 1177 B.C.E., another huge coalition of raiders from the north invaded Egypt territory. Ramesses defeated their land forces in a fierce battle in Palestine and then crushed their sea forces off the Nile delta. The pharaoh recorded his victory in a huge stone carving at Medinet Habu. The inscriptions on his mortuary temple gloat over his triumph:

The foreign lands made a convocation in their islands, bursting forth and scattering in the strife of the lands at one time; no land could stand before their arms, beginning with the Kingdom of the Hittites . . . They laid their hands on countries as far as the circuit of the earth trusting and confident: "Our plans will succeed! . . . Those who came upon the sea, the consuming flame faced them at the Nile mouths . . . they were dragged up, surrounded and cast down upon the shore, slaughtered in heaps from head to tail."[7]

Egypt avoided destruction at the hands of the Raiders of the Land and Sea, but nevertheless slipped into a long economic and military decline. Within fifteen years of Ramesses III's death in 1153 B.C.E., the empire had lost control of Syria and Canaan. Groups of raiders settled on the Mediterranean coast and extended their power inland, where they destroyed the last of the Bronze Age cities by about 1100 B.C.E. In Egypt, drought, poor harvests, and inflation ruined the economy, while weak rulers struggled unsuccessfully to hold Egypt together. The bonds between Upper and Lower Egypt were severed, and the land of Egypt split once again into separate kingdoms.

Some raiders who escaped Egyptian troops spread across the Mediterranean. Some probably settled in Sicily, Sardinia, and Etruria. Others, the Peleset People, eventually settled on the coast of Canaan. These people are known to us as the Philistines, a name that survives in the modern word *Palestine.*

In Mesopotamia, the kingdoms of Babylonia and Assyria experienced an economic and political breakdown, though not as great as that of the Mycenaeans and Hittites. Historians are uncertain of the precise causes of the decline of these two great Mesopotamian powers. They attribute it primarily to invasions by Arameans, who were seminomadic peoples originating in Syria and areas to the west of Mesopotamia. The Arameans invaded Assyrian territories, destroying harvests and causing famines. They seized control of portions of the Assyrian kingdom and established their own rule. Assyrian monarchs retained authority over a much reduced kingdom. Babylonia, for its part, endured frequent invasions by different peoples from the Iranian plateau, called Elamites. Babylonia's leaders, too, lost power and political influence. The Assyrians and Babylonians nevertheless maintained their identity as distinct peoples throughout these troubled centuries.

After the International Bronze Age ended about 1100 B.C.E., the people of the Middle East from the Mediterranean coast to Mesopotamia gradually evolved into new and powerful kingdoms with distinctive cultures. Long-distance trade in tin and copper broke down but did not disappear. People began to rely on iron rather than bronze for making weapons and other tools because it existed in many sites throughout the Mediterranean and Middle East and so was cheaper to use. It took several centuries for iron to displace bronze as the preferred metal for weapons, and bronze continued to be used for many other purposes.

During this time, two regions acquired special importance: the eastern coast of the Mediterranean, where the Phoenicians developed a maritime culture built on the traditions of cities like Ugarit, and Mesopotamia, the land between the Tigris and Euphrates rivers, where the kingdoms of Assyria and Babylonia revived. (We will examine the Middle Eastern civilization of the Hebrews, which emerged in the aftermath of the International Bronze Age, in Chapter 3.)

THE PHOENICIANS: MERCHANTS OF THE MEDITERRANEAN

Two hundred years after the International Bronze Age drew to a close, a dynamic maritime civilization took shape in the cities that stretched along the eastern Mediterranean seaboard. These seafaring people, whom historians call Phoenicians, continued the commercial traditions of Ugarit and other small Bronze Age kingdoms. Historians do not know what Phoenicians called themselves, but they probably used the term Canaanites, as they spoke a Semitic Canaanite language. The name *Phoenician* apparently derives from a Greek word meaning "red," in reference to the valuable dark red dye extracted from murex shells that was essential to the Phoenician textile industry, a basic part of their commerce.

Phoenicians are known mainly as accomplished sailors and merchants. By 950 B.C.E. they established extensive trade and political connections with peoples of the Levant and spread their civilization into the Mediterranean world as far as North Africa, Italy, and Spain. The independent port cities of Byblos, Tyre, and Sidon were the main centers

---

CHRONOLOGY

The Aftermath of the International Bronze Age

1100–900 B.C.E.	Emergence of Phoenicians in eastern Mediterranean
950 B.C.E.	Phoenician trading voyages extend as far west as Spain; trading posts established in Spain, North Africa, and Sicily
800 B.C.E.	Tyrian traders found Carthage and voyage to Britain and West Africa; children sacrificed to gods in Phoenician communities
CA. 750 B.C.E.	Phoenician alphabet reaches Greece; Neo-Assyrian Empire emerges
730s B.C.E.	Phoenicians begin competing with Greek colonists in Sicily and Italy
721 B.C.E.	Assyria conquers Israel (Northern Kingdom)
603 B.C.E.	Assyrian Empire falls
612–539 B.C.E.	Neo-Babylonian Empire emerges; astronomers are active

of Phoenician life and served as the original departure points for movement to the western Mediterranean. Phoenicians did not, however, form a large, centralized state. Their cities, therefore, became vulnerable to attack and lost their independence in the fifth century B.C.E., but their strong mercantile and seafaring culture lasted into Roman times.

Economic Expansion

The search for metal ores, such as tin, copper, iron, silver, and gold, motivated Phoenician commerce. Merchants from Tyre led the rapid expansion of Phoenician trade westward into Mediterranean markets, where they created a large commercial empire by following old Minoan and Mycenaean trade routes of the International Bronze Age that had not been forgotten (see Map 2.5). Phoenician sailors were legendary for their skills in navigation and shipbuilding. Hundreds of their ships crisscrossed the Mediterranean and ventured into the Atlantic Ocean in

search of trade. Phoenician metal prospectors located deposits of precious ores in North Africa, Spain, Italy, Britain, and France. They did business with the local inhabitants in these regions who had been working the mines for centuries. In this way Phoenician traders established economic connections with lands that would later become the center of Western civilization.

The enterprising Phoenicians also learned techniques of smelting metals (including iron) for weapons, tools, and jewelry that had been developing in European lands since the International Bronze Age, and they transmitted this knowledge to Middle Eastern peoples. In return, they brought back Middle Eastern and Egyptian artistic styles to western Mediterranean lands. These transactions in metal ores, manufactured goods, and timber occurred at the trading posts that Phoenician merchants established.

By 800 B.C.E., Carthage ("New City"), a colony from Tyre located on the northern coast of modern Tunisia, had become the chief Phoenician city in the west. For this reason, Phoenician culture in the western Mediterranean is

■ **Map 2.5 Phoenician Expansion, ca. 600 B.C.E.**
Several centuries after the collapse of the International Bronze Age, adventurous merchants from the eastern Mediterranean coast developed a commercial empire across the Mediterranean Sea. By 600 B.C.E. Carthage had become the chief Phoenician city in the western Mediterranean. It controlled the resources of North Africa and parts of Spain.

Phoenician Bowl

People from many different cultures admired the beautiful metal bowls with elaborate patterns made by skilled Phoenician craftworkers. The artists drew their inspiration from the traditions they encountered throughout the Mediterranean world, which they then used to create their own style. The silver bowl shown here was found in Cyprus. In the center is a common Egyptian motif, a king clubbing an enemy on the head. Compare with the illustration on page 28.

often called Carthaginian. With its magnificent harbor and strategic location midway between the Levant and the straits of Gibraltar, Carthage controlled trade between the eastern and western Mediterranean. Its inhabitants developed a land-based empire on the North African coast and in Spain. Merchants from the city explored the Spanish deposits of tin, which was used as an alloy with other metals, and silver, which was prized for jewelry. Some merchants ventured as far north as Britain to exploit that country's rich tin deposits.

As we will see in Chapter 3, Phoenician and Greek merchants competed for trade in the western Mediterranean, but they controlled different spheres of influence. Phoenician colonies clung to the southern shore of the Mediterranean, while Greek colonies held the northern shore. Unlike the Greeks, who established their colonies on land taken by force from the local inhabitants, Phoenicians were more interested in trading than settling. Their approach to business facilitated good relations with the southern Mediterranean's native inhabitants, especially in Sicily and Italy.

Religion and Culture

Phoenician religion showed remarkable continuity through time and across the Mediterranean. Many of their gods and goddesses had also been worshiped by Middle Eastern peoples during the International Bronze Age. Even though the deities' names differed among many Phoenician cities, their roles as protectors and warriors remained the same. The chief gods were Baalat ("Lady of the Heavens") and her husband Baal ("Lord of the Heavens"), who represented the order of the natural world and protected the Phoenicians from danger. In one religious festival, celebrated throughout the Phoenician world every spring, worshipers burned a statue of the Lord of the Heavens on a ritual pyre to mark his annual death. After a sacred ritual marriage with the Lady of the Heavens he was reborn. This festival celebrated the rebirth of nature and the restoration of heavenly order. The idea of a god's death and resurrection during springtime was widely shared throughout the Mediterranean world, and eventually influenced later religions of the Greek and Roman world, including Christianity.

In the Carthaginian cities of the western Mediterranean, the Lady of the Heavens became associated with the practice of sacred prostitution. Within her temples, women fulfilled vows taken in the goddess's name and made themselves sexually available to male visitors. Every sexual union symbolized the fertility and regenerative power of the Lady of the Heavens. In addition, many parents killed their firstborn son as an offering to the Lord and Lady of the Heavens at moments of crisis or as an offering for the fulfillment of a personal vow. Child sacrifice continued at Carthage and other Carthaginian settlements, often secretly, as late as 200 C.E.

Because Phoenicians traveled so widely, they encountered many foreign gods and goddesses and often adopted some as their own. Some Egyptian divinities, such as Bes, the goddess of childbirth and protector of women and children, and Isis, who offered a special sense of security and comfort, became extremely popular among the Phoenicians, an indication of the close contact between Phoenician and Egyptian cultures. The religious interactions between the Phoenicians and other peoples throughout the Mediterranean world powerfully illustrate how cultural encounters can transmit influential ideas and beliefs.

The Phoenicians' most lasting cultural contribution to the peoples of the Mediterranean world was the alphabet, a system of writing based on that of Ugarit in which each letter represented a single sound. Thus the alphabet could be used to record the sounds of any language. The Phoenician alphabet spread throughout the Mediterranean world, where the Greeks and then the Romans adopted it. In this way it became the source of all alphabets and writing in the West.

MESOPOTAMIAN KINGDOMS: ASSYRIA AND BABYLON, 1050–550 B.C.E.

The decline of both Assyria and Babylonia at the end of the International Bronze Age did not result in their disappearance as kingdoms. Torn apart by invasions, they nevertheless managed to survive, and beginning in about 1050 B.C.E., Assyria and then Babylonia began to regain effective control over their territories, re-establish their commercial power, and reconquer neighboring lands.

Neo-Assyrian Imperialism

After 1000 B.C.E., the Assyrian kings slowly reasserted their dominance in northern Mesopotamia and overseas by regaining control of the trade routes that had made them rich in earlier centuries and by gradually reconquering old and new lands. In 745 B.C.E., Tiglath-Pileser III (r. 745–727 B.C.E.) ascended the Assyrian throne and ushered in a century of astonishing expansion. Historians call the realm he acquired the Neo-Assyrian Empire.

Because Tiglath-Pileser and his successors believed that Ashur, their chief god, had commanded them to expand their empire's borders, they went to war frequently. As a result, the Assyrians overran the peoples of Canaan (including the Israelites), Phoenicians, Babylonians, many Iranian peoples, and much of Egypt. They created the first empire to control the Tigris, Euphrates, and Nile River valleys, where civilization had first emerged two millennia before (see Map 2.6). By 500 B.C.E., Nineveh, the empire's capital city, boasted at least 500,000 inhabitants drawn from all of these regions.

Neo-Assyrian rulers, who called themselves "Kings of the Universe," developed a highly militarized empire. To terrify their victims and aid their conquests, they cultivated a reputation for extreme cruelty. Assyrian armies tortured, butchered, and enslaved the inhabitants of defeated cities. Then, after carting off everything of value, they burned the cities to the ground. They immediately spread the news of their atrocities to neighboring areas, which quickly and understandably surrendered.

As the Assyrians conquered more and more peoples, they faced problems that have troubled empires ever since:

How can subject peoples be controlled and what degree of cultural independence should they be permitted to retain? Assyrian solutions were thoughtful yet violent. Assyrian rulers permitted their subjects to continue their traditions and religious practices without interference. If they rebelled against Assyrian authority, however, the army would crush them and deport entire populations to distant corners of the empire. Some Assyrian rulers depopulated entire regions, forcing perhaps as many as a million and a half people from their homes. Many deportees perished and others lost their cultural identity after years of assimilation.

Like their predecessors during the International Bronze Age, the Neo-Assyrian rulers grew wealthy from agriculture and trade. They also exploited their subjects more harshly than previously. Provincial administrators imposed crippling taxes and systematically drained away their subjects' resources. With these revenues, the kings could maintain armies of more than 100,000 men and supply them with iron weapons. At the same time, the government strengthened the economy by rebuilding cities, increasing the amount of land under cultivation, and building roads to improve trade and communications throughout the empire.

Ashurbanipal (r. 669–626 B.C.E.), the last strong ruler of the Neo-Assyrian empire, attempted to create a uniform culture throughout his vast realm. At his command, scholars collected subject people's written knowledge, translated it into Akkadian, and distributed copies on clay tablets throughout Assyrian lands. Ashurbanipal did not succeed in imposing a standardized culture on the empire, but he was the first monarch to try to organize the diverse cultural inheritance of his multiethnic empire. Many subsequent empires, such as those of the Hellenistic world (discussed in Chapter 4) and Rome (discussed in Chapter 5) gained stability by cultivating a dominant culture shared by the empires' elites.

Despite its prosperity and efficient administration, the Neo-Assyrian model of imperial rule failed to bring lasting unity to its peoples. Serious internal dynastic struggles and ineffective leadership after Ashurbanipal's death weakened the empire. Most destructive of all, subject peoples who had endured brutal treatment at the hands of Assyrian administrators nursed a bitter resentment and revolted as soon as possible. The most significant of these rebels was the Babylonian king Nabopolassar in southern Mesopotamia (r. 625–605 B.C.E.). He allied himself with Iranian kings and began a successful revolt against Assyrian rule. By 603 B.C.E., the Assyrian Empire collapsed again.

The Neo-Babylonian Empire

After Nabopolassar acquired Assyrian territory, he built the Neo-Babylonian (or Chaldean) Empire into the most powerful in the Middle East, which lasted until 539 B.C.E.

■ **Map 2.6　The Neo-Assyrian Empire at Its Greatest Extent, ca. 630 B.C.E.**
By 630 B.C.E., the Assyrians had recovered their strength and established the Neo-Assyrian Empire. This huge realm included Mesopotamia, the Israelite kingdoms, Phoenicia, and parts of Egypt.

His son, the brilliant general Nebuchadnezzar II (r. 604–562 B.C.E.), conquered lands that had broken free when Assyrian rule collapsed (see Map 2.7). Babylonian armies seized Egypt, Syria, Phoenicia, and the kingdom of Judah, where they destroyed the city of Jerusalem and exiled many Jews to Babylon. (We will learn more about this exile in Chapter 3.)

With the wealth acquired from these conquests, Nebuchadnezzar made his capital city, Babylon, one of the most luxurious in the ancient world. A moat flooded with waters from the Euphrates River surrounded Babylon's eight miles of walls. The emperor also built the Ishtar Gate, which his artisans decorated with glazed, brightly colored tiles. The gate opened onto a grand avenue leading to the temple of Marduk, Babylon's greatest god. According to tradition, Nebuchadnezzar also built the "Hanging Gardens of Babylon" for a favorite wife who missed her mountainous homeland. Splendid flowers and plants cascaded down

the slopes of a terraced hillside that from a distance seemed to float in the air. In ancient times, people considered the Hanging Gardens to be one of the great wonders of the world.

The Neo-Babylonian Empire comprised a constellation of wealthy cities in which life revolved around the uninterrupted worship of Marduk. At the center of each community stood a magnificent temple to the all-powerful god. Each city also had complex religious, political, and economic arrangements with the king. For example, the Babylonians considered proper worship essential for the prosperity of their communities. They looked to the king to provide the peaceful conditions in which they could worship their gods without interruption. The king, for his part, expected his subjects to obey his commands, and he counted on the priests to bolster his authority. In return he granted the most cooperative cities privileges and benefits, such as exemption from taxes. If city dwellers detected even

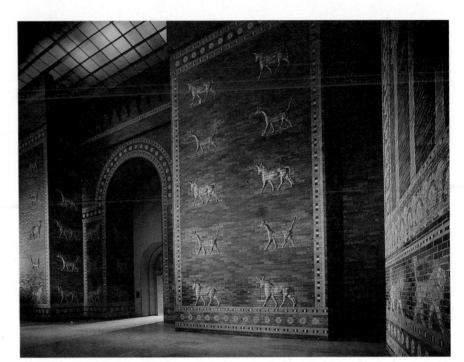

■ **Ishtar Gate**

The magnificently tiled Ishtar Gate, right, provided a dramatic entrance to Babylon, the capital city of the Neo-Babylonian Empire. Babylonian artists used brightly colored tiles to create complicated three-dimensional depictions of animals, including lions which represented royal power. The gate now rests in a museum in Berlin. An artist's reconstruction is shown below.

a hint of weakness on the part of their ruler, they might revolt in search of a more effective king.

Religion not only gave the Babylonians a profound sense of spiritual security, it also expanded their scientific knowledge. Babylonians believed that the Earth and the sky were interrelated. In their view, proper interpretation of the celestial bodies through astronomy could help them understand the meaning of daily events as well as the will of the gods. Building on the Sumerians' mathematical and astronomical legacy, Babylonian astronomers patiently observed and recorded the movements of the stars, the planets, and the moon. They kept a continuous log of observations between 747 b.c.e. and 61 c.e., an astonishing achievement. Starting around 500 b.c.e., they had accumulated so much information about the movements of the planets and stars that they could perform complicated mathematical computations to predict eclipses of the moon and sun. They also calculated the first appearance of the new moon every month, which enabled them to devise a calendar. These astronomers' brilliant calculations, which Persians and Greeks would later adopt, have helped lay the foundation of Western science. From these able scientists, the West has inherited the names of many constellations, the zodiac, and many complex mathematical models of astronomical phenomena.

By ca. 580 B.C.E., the Neo-Babylonian Empire had replaced the Neo-Assyrian Empire as the dominant power in the Middle East.

CONCLUSION

The International Bronze Age and the Emergence of the West

The International Bronze Age marked an early but crucial phase in the formation of Western civilization. Within a large geographical area centered on the eastern Mediterranean but stretching far beyond its shores, an intricate network of political, commercial, and cultural ties was established among cities and kingdoms that had previously lived in relative isolation from each other. During the International Bronze Age this geographical area extended to Mesopotamia in the east, Nubia in the south, and Greece and Anatolia in the north. The forces that exposed the cultures of these areas to each other were the expansion of international trade, the development of a new military technology, the growth of large, multiethnic empires, and the establishment of diplomatic relations among rulers.

The encounters that took place among the peoples of these lands contributed to the emergence of Western civilization. Long before it was possible to identify what we now call the West, the exchange of commodities, the spread of religious ideas, the growth of common political traditions, the dissemination of scientific and technological techniques, and the borrowing of one language from another created a complex pattern of cultural diffusion over a vast geographical area.

During subsequent centuries the content of such cultural exchange would change, and the geographical area within which the exchanges took place would shift, first to the lands controlled by Persia, then to the Hellenistic world conquered by Alexander the Great, and later still to the sprawling Roman Empire. All these shifts took place as the result of imperial expansion and consolidation, a process that began with the formation of multiethnic empires discussed in this chapter. Each period of expansion, moreover, involved new cultural encounters between different peoples. The first of these periods, in which a series of encounters took place between Hebrews, Persians, and Greeks, will be the subject of the next chapter.

Suggestions for Further Reading

For a comprehensive list of suggested readings, please go to www.ablongman.com/levack/chapter2

Bryce, Trevor. *The Kingdom of the Hittites* 1998. The latest synthesis of Hittite history and culture.

Cline, Eric H., and Diane Harris-Cline, eds. *The Aegean and the Orient in the Second Millennium: Proceedings of the 50th Anniversary Symposium, Cincinnati, 18–20 April 1997, Aegaeum* 18. 1998. A collection of papers by experts providing state-of-the-art discussions of all aspects of the connections among Bronze Age civilizations of the eastern Mediterranean and Middle East.

Dickinson, Oliver. *The Aegean Bronze Age.* 1994. Now the standard treatment of the complex archaeological data.

Dothan, Trude, and Moshe Dothan. *People of the Sea: The Search for the Philistines.* 1992. A recent, highly popularized survey of the archaeological material.

Drews, Robert. *The End of the Bronze Age: Changes in Warfare and the Catastrophe ca. 1200 B.C.* 1993. A controversial but well-argued analysis that offers new solutions to the question of why the Bronze Age ended.

Fitton, J. Lesley. *The Discovery of the Greek Bronze Age.* 1996. A lucid and well-illustrated study of the archaeologists who brought the Greek Bronze Age to light in the nineteenth and early twentieth centuries.

Harding, A. F. *The Mycenaeans in Europe.* 1984. Exploration of the trade and cultural connections between Mycenaeans and the rest of Europe.

Hornung, Erik. *History of Ancient Egypt: An Introduction,* trans. David Lorton. 1999. A concise and lucid overview of Egyptian history and life.

Knapp, A. Bernard. *The History and Culture of Ancient Western Asia and Egypt.* 1988. A reliable archaeological and historical overview without excessive detail.

Kuhrt, Amelie. *The Ancient Middle East, ca. 3000–330 B.C.,* 2 vols. 1995. A magisterial, up-to-date overview, with excellent bibliography. The place to start for a continuous historical narrative of the region.

Macqueen, James G. *The Hittites and Their Contemporaries in Asia Minor.* 1986. This account stresses the interconnections of Hittites and other peoples.

Markoe, Glenn. *Phoenicians.* 2000. The best and most up-to-date treatment of Phoenician society by a noted expert.

Page, Denys. *History and the Homeric Iliad.* 1959. An entertaining and provocative examination of the historical context of the events described in Homer's *Iliad.*

Redford, Donald B. *Egypt, Canaan and Israel in Ancient Times.* 1992. An excellent, detailed synthesis of textual and archaeological evidence that emphasizes interconnections among cultures.

Schulz, Regine, and Matthias Seidel, eds. *Egypt: The World of the Pharaohs.* 1999. A sumptuously illustrated collection of essays on all aspects of Egyptian society and life by leading experts.

Traill, David. *Schliemann of Troy: Treasure and Deceit.* 1995. A fascinating discussion of the motivations and methods of the archaeologist who discovered the Bronze Age.

Walker, Christopher, ed. *Astronomy Before the Telescope.* 1996. A fascinating collection of essays about astronomy in the premodern period, which makes clear Western civilization's enormous debt to the Babylonians.

Wood, Michael. *In Search of the Trojan War.* 1985. A valuable introductory discussion of the archaeological and historical problems of placing Homer's Trojan War in its Bronze Age context.

Notes

1. T. Eric Peet, *The Great Tomb Robberies of the Twentieth Egyptian Dynasty,* I–II, (Oxford, 1930) reprinted in one volume (Hildesheim, 1977). (Contains texts and translations of this and other trials.)
2. Regina Schulz and Matthias Seidel, eds., *Egypt: The World of the Pharaohs* (1998), p. 485.
3. Trevor Bryce, *The Kingdom of the Hittites* (1998), pp. 195–199.
4. A. Khurt, *The Ancient Middle East,* vol. I (1995), p. 242.
5. W. G. Lambert, "The Gula Hymn of Bullutsa-rabi," *Orientalia* n.s.36 (1967), p. 121.
6. Translated in Kuhrt, pp. 350–351.
7. Donald Redford, *Egypt, Canaan, and Israel in Ancient Times* (1992), 251, 256, with some changes.

Building the Classical World: Hebrews, Persians, and Greeks, 1100–336 B.C.E.

N THE SECOND HALF OF THE SIXTH CENTURY B.C.E., CYRUS THE GREAT, A PERSIAN king from southern Iran, created the largest empire the world had ever seen, with territories in Asia, the Middle East, Africa, and Europe. According to one of the many legends surrounding this celebrated ruler, Cyrus grew restless as a young man under the rule of another king. He summoned the Persian tribal leaders who owed him allegiance and instructed them to spend a day clearing land with sickles. When they finally stopped their backbreaking labor, he invited them to a magnificent banquet. After the men had devoured the last delicacy, Cyrus asked them which they enjoyed more, tasting the wonderful food or sweating in the fields. The chieftains shouted in unison that they preferred the wine and fine foods. Cyrus then proclaimed:

> *Men of Persia, follow me and I promise that you will enjoy this sort of luxury for the rest of your lives, but if you do not, your lives will be full of painful toil with no such rewards from your present masters.*[1]

Without hesitation the men joined Cyrus in his successful revolt. Under his able leadership the Persians conquered more than twenty-three different peoples in territories ranging from the eastern Mediterranean coast to central Asia. Cyrus's successors added Egypt and parts of Greece and India to the Persian Empire. With its huge expanse and the stable government it provided to an enormous mix of cultures, the Persian Empire marked a turning point in the history of the ancient world.

This chapter examines the civilizations that developed during the six centuries following the collapse of the International Bronze Age around 1100 B.C.E. When long-distance trade in copper and tin broke down at that time, iron

Persian Art: Persian artists drew freely from the artistic traditions of their subject peoples. This illustration shows how they put their own stamp on the Babylonian art of ceramic tile. The tiles show two members of the elite imperial guard, known as the Immortals. The details of their uniforms appear in vivid color. Soldiers like these in Xerxes's army attacked the Greeks in the fifth century B.C.E.

became the preferred metal for making tools and weapons throughout the ancient world. As a result of the widespread use of iron, archaeologists refer to the new period as the Iron Age. Most historians, however, refer to the period that began after 1100 B.C.E. as the Classical Age because of the distinctive religious, political, and cultural innovations and transformations that resulted from Persian encounters with other peoples, particularly the Hebrews and Greeks.

For two centuries after Cyrus's death, the Persian Empire prospered as its leaders methodically expanded their territory abroad and shrewdly managed their many subject peoples. The interaction of local cultures with Persian culture made an indelible impression on the history of the West. From their Assyrian and Babylonian subjects, the Persians inherited—and improved upon—a political legacy of ruling a multiethnic empire. They also benefited from a scientific legacy that stretched back to the Sumerians. The Persians' capacity to borrow and adapt the most useful features of other cultures strengthened their own highly organized and justly administered empire.

In addition to developing their own dynamic culture, the Persians made possible the spread of two highly influential ideas in the Western tradition, although they did not originally conceive of them. The first of these ideas was monotheism°, the belief in only one god. This concept originated with the Hebrews about 1000 B.C.E. During the Classical Age, the Hebrews came under Persian rule. As a consequence, Hebrew religion was transformed into Judaism under the blanket of Persian imperial administration. The idea of monotheism became the core principle of Judaism and Christianity. Followers of Islam also link their faith to the tradition of biblical monotheism.

The second idea was democracy°, the conviction that people should share equally in the government of their community, devise their own governing institutions, and select their own leaders. Originating in the Greek city-state of Athens in the sixth century B.C.E., democratic institutions helped the Athenians repel several Persian invasions in the fifth century B.C.E. When the Persian threat ended, democratic institutions in Athens grew stronger. Athenian victory over the Persians gave Athens the economic stability and security needed for their governmental institutions to become more democratic. Artists and thinkers flourished in Athens's creative atmosphere during the Classical Age. They established philosophical schools where students learned to examine the validity of every assumption and to explain natural phenomena without referring to the gods. Drama became a powerful moral voice in Greek society, providing a mirror in which the audience could judge themselves and their community. In sculpture, architecture, and other arts, they created the distinctive Greek classical style, which influenced the Romans, and has continued to be a source of inspiration in Western civilization up to the present day.

In many respects, the Classical Age created the most lasting cultural foundations of the West, foundations built on Hebrew monotheism and ethics and Greek government, philosophy, and arts—all against the backdrop of Persian imperial power.

To understand how the Classical Age came together from so many cultural elements, we will explore these questions: (1) What political and religious beliefs and institutions gave Hebrew civilization its unique character, and what consequences came of its interactions with the Assyrians, Babylonians, and Persians? (2) How did the Persian Empire bring these peoples of the Middle East together in a stable realm, and what elements of Persian religion and government have influenced Western thought? (3) How did Greek city-states develop in the framework of a larger world dominated by Persia? (4) What were the intellectual, social, and political innovations of Greece in the Classical Age?

Hebrew Civilization and Religion

One of the most influential civilizations in the West has been that of the Jews, a people who originated in the Middle East when the International Bronze Age came to an end. As we saw in Chapter 2, the Raiders of the Land and Sea destroyed many Canaanite cities around 1100 B.C.E. and caused great upheaval among the local populations. At about the same time, different groups of semi-nomadic pastoralists, called *Hapiru* ("landless people"), began to migrate into the hill country of Canaan, where they settled, herded their flocks, and began farming. Some historians think that this settlement was the origin of the biblical Hebrews, who gradually cohered into tribes and then kingdoms.

THE SETTLEMENT IN CANAAN

If these historians are correct, sometime around 1100 B.C.E. one small group of wandering Hapiru arrived in Canaan from Egypt, bringing with them the seeds of a powerful new religious belief. They gave allegiance to only one god. Belief in this deity gave them a strong sense of identity and distinguished them from the Canaanite peoples, who worshiped many gods. These followers of one god became known as Hebrews, then Israelites, and later Jews. Many centuries later, their traditions explained that a leader called Moses had led them from slavery in Egypt to freedom in Canaan, and that he had communicated God's law to them. Known today as the Ten Commandments, these laws forbid such acts as murder, theft, lying, and worshiping other gods. Later Biblical laws were built on these principles.

By absorbing new members and conquering other groups, a loose confederation of tribes gained control of most of .Canaan during the eleventh century B.C.E. Impressed by the Hebrew victories, many Canaanites began to worship the Hebrew God and joined the Hebrew tribes. Gradually these various tribes came to believe that they all shared a common history and a common ancestor, Abraham, who had traveled to Canaan from his home in Mesopotamia long before Moses. According to biblical tradition, Abraham was the first person to worship only one god. For this reason, he is considered the first Hebrew monotheist and the ancestor of the Jews.

The Hebrew tribes built shrines to their God throughout Canaan. The most important religious site was the shrine in the town of Shiloh, where they celebrated their allegiance to their God and settled disputes about property, inheritance, and crime. They kept their most sacred object, the Ark of the Covenant, in this shrine. The Ark of the Covenant was a gold-covered box that reputedly contained a divine and mysterious power. Concealed from the sight of everyone but the priests who organized God's worship, the Ark symbolized the connection between God and his followers as well as the unity of all the Hebrew tribes.

The confederation of Hebrew tribes faced many enemies in Canaan. The most serious threat came from the Philistines, who were descendants of a group of Raiders of the Land and Sea called the Peleset. They controlled the Mediterranean coastal plain in Canaan and pushed relentlessly at the Hebrews living in the inland hills. Around 1050 B.C.E., a Philistine army defeated the Hebrew tribes in battle, captured the Ark of the Covenant, and destroyed Shiloh. According to traditions recorded in the Bible, the desperate Hebrews chose a king to give them stronger leadership, even though tribal tradition was hostile to the notion of kings. The tribes chose Saul to be the first king about 1020 B.C.E, and he retrieved the Ark from the Philistines. Some twenty years later, a popular warrior in Saul's court named David succeeded Saul as king and reigned from approximately 1000 to 962 B.C.E.

■ Map 3.1 The Israelite Monarchy
The kingdom established by David (ca. 1000–962 B.C.E.) and expanded by his son Solomon (ca. 962–922 B.C.E.) unified the Hebrew tribes of Canaan. At Solomon's death, the realm split into two smaller kingdoms. Assyrian armies destroyed the northern kingdom of Israel in 722 B.C.E., and Babylonian forces destroyed the southern kingdom of Judah in 586 B.C.E.

THE ISRAELITE KINGDOMS

David was a talented monarch. By establishing a strong alliance among the Hebrew tribes of northern and southern Canaan, he defeated the Philistines permanently and built a prosperous kingdom. Called the Israelite monarchy by historians, this kingdom lay sandwiched between the empires of Egypt and Mesopotamia (see Map 3.1). By imitating the government institutions of these neighboring states, David transformed the nature of Israelite society. He set up a centralized bureaucracy run by professional soldiers, administrators, and scribes. David established a census as the basis for tax collection and military conscription, and he created a royal court complete with a harem. Jerusalem, an old

Canaanite city, served as the capital of his new kingdom. He moved the Ark of the Covenant from Shiloh to Jerusalem, bringing the worship of the Hebrew God under the control of the monarchy.

During the reign of David's son Solomon (ca. 962–922 B.C.E.), the kingdom of Israel enjoyed peace and prosperity. One of Solomon's greatest achievements was the construction of a grand temple in Jerusalem to serve as the house of God and a resting place for the Ark of the Covenant. Constructed with the technical assistance of architects and craftsmen from the neighboring Phoenician kingdom of Tyre and the forced labor of Solomon's subjects, the

Jerusalem temple became the focal point of religious worship in his kingdom.

Solomon pursued an ambitious foreign policy devoted to developing long-distance commerce. He controlled the major trade routes running from Egypt and Arabia to Syria, and under his supervision Israelite merchants prospered as middlemen in an expanding system of international commerce. Under his leadership, the kingdom enjoyed substantial control over the trade of horses sent south from Asia Minor and chariots sent north from Egypt. Solomon developed his own corps of charioteers to protect these trade routes from bandits.

With the assistance of Phoenician shipbuilders, Solomon constructed a merchant fleet for trade in the Red Sea. His merchants sailed as far south as Somalia, the portion of the African coast that touches the Arabian Sea, from where they brought jewels, gold, ivory, and other items of luxury. In addition, Solomon also developed overland trade with Arabia and established economic ties with the kingdom of Sabaea (Sheba) in Yemen. According to tradition, the Queen of Sheba visited Solomon, bringing delightful gifts including spices from east Asia. What Solomon's merchants traded in return is uncertain. Solomon developed diplomatic relations with Egypt, as well as the seafaring Phoenicians, and other kingdoms in Africa and Middle East. He married foreign princesses in order to cement diplomatic ties, and he permitted his wives to build shrines in Jerusalem to gods of their homelands.

When Solomon died in 922 B.C.E., his heirs' inability to placate the northern Israelite tribes, which felt that Solomon had favored his own tribe of Judah at their expense, caused the Israelite kingdom to break into two parts. The kingdom of Israel, in the northern region of the former kingdom, established its capital at Shechem and remained reasonably stable in comparison to its southern rival. In the southern kingdom of Judah, Solomon's successors retained Jerusalem as its capital, but political stability remained elusive for them due to dynastic instability and quarrels among the leaders. Only for two brief periods did the kingdom of Judah enjoy stable government. During the two centuries after 922 B.C.E., however, both of the two successor kingdoms struggled to survive under the shadow of the far more powerful neighboring empires of Assyria and Babylonia. The gap between the rich and the poor in both kingdoms widened in the course of these tumultuous centuries. The upper classes grew extremely wealthy from trade and the accumulation of land, which they acquired from the indebted poor. In their anguish the poor called out for social justice, a cry heard by the prophets.

The Hebrew Prophets

Rapacious kings, greedy aristocrats, and high taxes meant that more and more debt-ridden peasants lost their farms to rich landholders. The poor found champions in the Hebrew prophets. These men spoke out on behalf of the downtrodden with words they believed to be inspired by God. These social critics strongly censured what they saw as religious and moral decay among the landowners and kings, such as the worship of Canaanite gods, a practice that remained widespread. They urged the entire population toward moral reform and spiritual consciousness. The prophet Elijah, who lived in the ninth century B.C.E., proclaimed that kings should not break the laws with impunity but should conform to the same laws as everyone else. The principle that kings and rulers are not above the law remained as a basic political idea in what eventually became the West. In the next century, another champion of social justice named Amos mocked the irony and hypocrisy of the royal court's celebrating lavish religious ceremonies in God's name while the poor starved. Isaiah, a prophet who lived in Jerusalem, demanded that people attempt to establish a just society in order to avert divine punishment. He had no patience for religious observance empty of personal commitment. According to Isaiah, God said:

> What need have I of all your sacrifices? . . . I am sated with burnt offerings of sacrificial rams . . . Incense is offensive to me. . . . Though you pray at length, I will not listen. Your hands are stained with crime. Wash yourselves clean; Put your evil doings away from my sight. Cease to do evil; learn to do good; devote yourself to justice; aid the wronged. Uphold the rights of the orphan. Defend the cause of the widow. [Isaiah 1: 11–17]

Preoccupied with internal problems, the Israelites failed to note the growing power of the neighboring Assyrian Empire. As we saw in Chapter 2, Assyrian armies under the command of king Tiglath-Pileser conquered the Israelite kingdom in 733 B.C.E. Eleven years later, when the Israelite ruler refused to pay tribute, the Assyrians destroyed the kingdom and deported nearly 30,000 Israelites to Mesopotamia, a standard Assyrian practice with defeated enemies. The deported Israelites, who became known as the Lost Ten Tribes, eventually forgot their cultural identity in their new homes and disappeared from the historical record. The kingdom of Israel had come to an undignified end.

The kingdom of Judah, however, survived. By accepting the overlordship of the Assyrians and later the Babylonians, who had replaced the Assyrians as the dominant power in the Middle East by the late seventh century B.C.E., Judah escaped Israel's fate. After the destruction of the northern kingdom, a mood of religious reform spread throughout Judah. People began to believe that God had destroyed the kingdom of Israel in anger, though they disagreed about the causes of his rage and how to appease him.

To regain God's favor, some of Judah's leaders insisted on the absolute primacy of the temple in Jerusalem as the place for religious worship on the assumption that God disapproved of his followers worshiping him at many shrines instead of only one. By insisting on Jerusalem as the sole place of worship, the priests of Jerusalem increased their power. With the help of the king's soldiers, the temple priests in Jerusalem violently suppressed all other shrines to God scattered across the land. The consequences were greater uniformity of worship among the Hebrews and a centralized religious authority. These developments enhanced a sense of Hebrew identity.

Some Hebrew prophets, however, sought to appease God by countering this trend. They challenged the supremacy of the Jerusalem priests and emphasized the need for personal reform and the creation of a just society. One of these prophets was Jeremiah, who began preaching in 627 B.C.E. In the tradition of Isaiah, he placed little value on the strength of the temple priesthood's prayers on Judah's behalf. He predicted that God would cause the Babylonians to destroy Judah because its people were corrupt. Jeremiah's predictions proved correct. When Judah revolted against the Babylonians in 598 B.C.E., the Babylonian king Nebuchadnezzar sent a large army to crush the rebellion. The next year he captured Jerusalem and deported Judah's king and high priests to Babylonia. Ten years later, when another revolt broke out, Babylonian forces burned Jerusalem to the ground and demolished Solomon's temple, the spiritual and political center of the kingdom of Judah. Perhaps as many as 20,000 people were deported to Babylonia, an event historians call the Babylonian Exile°.

The Babylonian Exile

After the destruction of the Jerusalem temple in 587 B.C.E., the Hebrew exiles living in Babylonia struggled to maintain their cultural and religious identity. But Babylonian culture influenced their religious practice. Babylonian astronomy contributed to the institution of a seven-day week (and perhaps sabbath worship on the seventh day). The Hebrews developed a calendar that adopted Babylonian names of months. For example, the Babylonian month Nissanu is the same as the Hebrew month Nisan. Like the Babylonians, the Hebrew exiles structured their calendar around seasonal festivals. The exiles added their own new religious celebrations to the structure provided by the Babylonian calendar. The Hebrews observed a New Year's Day and a Day of Atonement in the autumn. In the spring they celebrated Passover, the commemoration of the departure of the Hebrews from Egypt under the leadership of Moses.

Sometime after the year 538 B.C.E., an anonymous author, referred to as Second Isaiah, comforted the dispirited Hebrews in Babylonia. Trying to find meaning in the destruction of the kingdoms of Israel and Judah, he explained that God's primary interest lay in the human spirit, not in earthly kingdoms. The God described by Second Isaiah was a truly universal God who alone governs all creation and shapes the lives of all the peoples of the world. This vision of a single, universal God not bound by time or place was perhaps the greatest legacy of Hebrew civilization to the West.

Second Isaiah promised that God would return his people to Jerusalem and that Cyrus the Great King of Persia would serve as God's agent in this task. The reference to the Persian king suggests that Second Isaiah wrote sometime around 538 B.C.E., when Cyrus instituted a policy permitting all peoples exiled by the Babylonians to return to their homelands (we will learn more about this policy shortly). Many of the Hebrew exiles in Babylonia returned to their old homes, now governed by Persia, and attempted to revive traditional religious life in Jerusalem.

The Second Temple and Jewish Religious Practice

Nearly two generations passed before the Hebrews, with Persian assistance, finished building a new temple in Jerusalem, called the Second Temple. In 458 B.C.E., with the authority of the Persian king, a leader called Ezra the Scribe began to organize and regulate religious practices. He instituted regular sabbath worship and began a program of teaching religious law to the population. For the next 500 years this restored temple worship would be the center of religious life. Historians call the Hebrews who lived after the completion of the Second Temple Jews. Henceforth, the people are known as Jews and their religion is called Judaism.

Ezra and other religious thinkers believed that God had destroyed the kingdoms of Israel and Judah before the Babylonian Exile because the people had failed to observe religious law properly. For this reason, knowledge of the law

CHRONOLOGY

The Israelite Kingdom

CA. 1100 B.C.E.	The International Bronze Age ends; Hapiru arrive in Canaan
CA. 1000–922 B.C.E.	David and Solomon rule the Israelite kingdom
922 B.C.E.	The Israelite kingdom splits into Judah (southern kingdom) and Israel (northern kingdom)
CA. 800 B.C.E.	Prophets begin to preach moral reform
721 B.C.E.	Assyrians destroy northern kingdom (Israel)
587 B.C.E.	Babylonians defeat southern kingdom (Judah) and destroy Jerusalem and Solomon's temple
538 B.C.E.	Cyrus of Persia permits Israelites to return to Palestine and rebuild the temple

■ Isaiah Scroll

Discovered in a cave near the Dead Sea in 1947 and now housed in the Shrine of the Book in Jerusalem, this text of the biblical book of Isaiah was written between about 300 and 100 B.C.E., making it nearly a thousand years older than the next surviving manuscript of Isaiah. The two copies of the book of Isaiah differ in only a few minor details, demonstrating the care with which biblical texts were copied and passed on by generations of scribes.

(or Torah) through study and observance now became all-important for the preservation of the Jewish community and Jewish identity. In particular, the priesthood in Jerusalem, who controlled secular and religious affairs, insisted on very strict observance of laws concerning temple sacrifice and ritual. The priests also made decisions that determined the status of women in Jewish society. By deciding that descent through the mother determined Jewish identity, they gave women a crucial role within Judaism. Membership in the Jewish community depended on descent through the mother, a situation that enhanced the status of Jewish wives.

Despite these reforms, the public role of women in organized worship grew quite restricted. Prior to the Babylonian exile, women participated in worship as priestesses, singers, and dancers. Canaanite religion gave a high status to female goddesses of fertility, and Israelite women sometimes participated in their cults. In the Second Temple period, however, the Jews worshiped only one male god and denied all other deities. Women could not enter the most sacred portions of the temple where the main sacrifices were performed because according to religious law the blood of menstruation and childbirth made them ritually unclean.

Many of these ancient attitudes regarding the place of women in religious and family life have survived to the present day, especially in the exclusion of women from the most sacred rituals and responsibilities in some forms of Judaism and Christianity.

The Hebrew Bible

After the Second Temple was built in 515 B.C.E., the Hebrew Bible (called the Old Testament by Christians) slowly took the shape it has today. Like many other peoples in the ancient Middle East, the Jews believed that their God had chosen them to serve him. They believed that historical events described in the Bible illustrate and interpret that relationship. As a historical document, the Bible provides a chronology of the world from the moment of its creation and gives an account of the early development of the Hebrew people. Drawn from a variety of oral and written sources, and composed many centuries after the events they describe, the biblical accounts condense and simplify a very complex process of migration, settlement, and religious development.

Many details in the Bible have been confirmed by non-Hebrew sources, but the Bible must be understood primar-

TALES OF THE FLOOD

In one of the most popular tales of the Classical Age, a god destroys the earth in a great flood but permits some humans to survive on a boat and repopulate the earth once the waters subside. Here we see excerpts from three versions of the flood story composed by Babylonians, Hebrews, and Greeks. The similarities indicate encounters among these cultures through the oldest of pleasures: telling stories.

THE EPIC OF GILGAMESH: HOW THE GODS SPARED UT-NAPISHTI

[Everything I owned] I loaded aboard:
all the silver I owned I loaded aboard,
all the gold I owned I loaded aboard,
all the living creatures I had I loaded aboard.
I sent on board all my kith and kin,
the beasts of the field, the creatures of the wild, and
members of every skill and craft . . .
. . . . . For six days and [seven] nights,
there blew the wind, the downpour,
the gale, the Deluge, it flattened land.
But the seventh day when it came,
the gale relented, the Deluge ended.
The ocean grew calm, that had thrashed like a woman in
    labour,
the tempest grew still, the Deluge ended . . .
Enlil [a powerful god] came up inside the boat,
[and blessed Uta-napishti and his wife, saying:]
In the past Uta-napishti was a mortal man,
but now he and his wife shall become like us gods!

THE HEBREW BIBLE: THE STORY OF NOAH AND THE ARK

Then the Lord said to Noah, "Go into the ark with all your household, for you alone have I found righteous before Me in this generation. Of every clean animal you shall take seven pairs, males and their mates, and of every animal that is not clean, two, a male and its mate. Of the birds of the sky, also . . . . . For in seven days I will make it rain upon the earth, forty days and forty nights, and I will blot out from the earth all existence that I created. And Noah did just as the Lord commanded him. . . . And on the seventh day the waters of the Flood came upon the earth. . . . [When the Flood had ended] God spoke to Noah, saying, come out of the ark, together with your wife, your sons, and your sons' wives. Bring out with you every living thing of all flesh that is there with you: birds, animals, and everything that creeps on earth; and let them swarm on the earth and be fertile and increase on earth.

GREEK MYTHOLOGY: DEUCALION'S STORY

In this Greek tale, King Deucalion survives because his father, the god Prometheus, warns him.

When Zeus, the king of the gods, decided to destroy humankind . . . Deucalion by the advice of Prometheus constructed a chest, and having stored it with provisions he embarked in it with Pyrrha, his wife. But Zeus, by pouring heavy rain from heaven flooded the greater part of Greece, so that all men were destroyed, except for a few who fled to high mountains in the neighborhood. . . . But Deucalion, floating in the chest over the sea for nine days and as many nights, drifted to Mount Parnassus, and there, when the rain ceased, he landed and sacrificed to Zeus . . . And Zeus . . . allowed Deucalion to choose whatever he wished, and he chose to create men. At the bidding of Zeus, he picked up stones and threw them over his head, and the stones became men, and the stones that Pyrrha threw became women. . . .

Sources: From *The Epic of Gilgamesh: The Babylonian Epic Poem and Other Texts in Akkadian and Sumerian*, translated by Andrew George (Allen Lane The Penguin Press, 1999). Translation copyright © 1999 by Andrew George. Reproduced by permission of Penguin Books Ltd.; from *Tanakh, A New Translation of The Holy Scriptures According to the Traditional Hebrew Text*, 1985, Exodus 7-8. Published by the Jewish Publication Society; and Reprinted by permission of the publishers and the Trustees of the Loeb Classical Library from *Apollodorus: Volume I,* Loeb Classical Library Volume L 121, translated by J. G. Frazer, Cambridge, Mass.: Harvard University Press, 1921. The Loeb Classical Library® is a registered trademark of the President and Fellows of Harvard College.

ily as an expression of religious meaning through historical traditions of different sorts. It combines highly detailed narratives with folklore, prophecies, parables, stories, and poems. The Bible provides far more than the narration of events. It explains God's presence in human lives and establishes a moral vision of human existence. As a result no book has had more influence on the religious thought of the West.

For historians, the significance of the Hebrew Bible lies in the religious principles that its stories illustrate. The book describes a single God who protects the Earth and his chosen people, the Hebrews. Historical events demonstrate his concern for them, for he punishes and rewards his people in accordance with their actions. In the Hebrew Bible, events such as the restoration of the temple in Jerusalem by Cyrus have significance in terms of a divine plan and the fulfillment of prophecy. As part of this divine plan, God expects his followers to follow a strict code of compassionate, ethical behavior toward their fellow human beings. As a religious work the Hebrew Bible provides the basis of

Judaism. In conjunction with the New Testament, written in the first century C.E., it is the core text of Christianity. Muslims also recognize both the Hebrew and Christian texts as holy writings, superceded only by the Qur'an.

The Second Temple was built and the Hebrew Bible took shape under Persian rule. We turn now to see how the Persian Empire developed and gained control over the peoples of the Middle East.

Classical Persia:
An Empire on Three Continents

Persian history began about 1400 B.C.E., when small groups of people started migrating with their herds and flocks into western Iran from areas north of the Caspian Sea. Over five centuries these settlers slowly coalesced into two closely related groups, the Medes and the Persians.

The Medes organized a loose confederation of tribes in western Iran and began to expand their territory. By about 900 B.C.E., they established mastery over all the peoples of the Iranian plateau, including the Persians. In 612 B.C.E., with the assistance of the Babylonians, the Medes conquered the Assyrians. Then they pushed into central Asia Minor (modern Turkey), Afghanistan, and possibly farther into central Asia. In the sixth century, under the leadership of Cyrus the Great (r. 550 B.C.E.–530 B.C.E.), Persia broke away from Medean rule and soon conquered the kingdom of the Medes. Under the guidance of this brilliant monarch and his successors, the Persians acquired a vast empire. They followed a monotheistic religion, Zoroastrianism, and governed their subjects with a combination of tolerance and firmness.

CYRUS THE GREAT AND PERSIAN EXPANSION

After ascending the Persian throne about 550 B.C.E., Cyrus embarked on a dazzling twenty-year career of conquering neighboring peoples. His military genius and organizational skills transformed the small kingdom near the Persian Gulf into a giant, multiethnic empire that stretched from India to the Mediterranean Sea. Cyrus's swift victory over the Medes put Persia at the cen-

ter of the Middle East and thrust it into face-to-face encounters with a diverse array of peoples.

Cyrus expanded his empire beyond Persia in several stages. In 547 B.C.E. he conquered Asia Minor, where he first came into contact with Greeks living on the westernmost coast and islands, a region called Ionia. Cyrus conquered these Ionian Greek cities and installed loyal Greek administrators. Next he defeated the kingdom of Babylonia in 539 B.C.E., thus gaining control of the entire Mesopotamian region. After that he brought Afghanistan under his control and fortified it against the raids of the Scythian nomads who lived on the steppe lands to the north of his realm. These fierce warriors posed a perpetual threat to the settled territories of Persia.

With his borders expanded and secured, Cyrus turned his attention to the welfare of his Persian homeland. Dissatisfied with his capital city of Susa, he founded a spacious new capital city called Pasargadae. Builders, craftsmen, artists, and merchants flocked to it from Asia Minor, Egypt, Mesopotamia, and Greece. Inspired by Cyrus's leadership, these artisans turned the new capital into a cosmopolitan city of tremendous ethnic diversity.

After Cyrus died in 530 B.C.E. while fighting against steppe nomads north of Persia, his son Cambyses II (r. 529–522 B.C.E.) continued his father's policy of expansion by subduing Egypt and the wealthy Phoenician port cities. The capture of Phoenicia gave the Persians a new strategic advantage. With control of Phoenician naval resources, the Persian Empire could reach overseas in a way that the landlocked Hittites could not during the International Bronze Age. Phoenician fleets became an integral part in Persia's invasion of Greece, as we will see later in this chapter. By the time of Cambyses' death in 522 B.C.E., Persia had become the mightiest empire in the world, with territorial possessions spanning Europe, Asia, the Middle East, and Africa (see Map 3.2).

To ensure that they could easily communicate with their subjects, the Great Kings of Persia established an elaborate system of roads to link their provinces.

■ **Scythian Nomads**
A Scythian nomad strings his bow. The Greek artist who made this vase pays scrupulous attention to the details of the Scythian's clothing, including his leggings, peaked cap, and tunic.

Special officials maintained supply stations at regular intervals along these roads. The chief branch of this system, called the Royal Road, stretched between Asia Minor and the Persian homeland. Persian road building was an indication of the sophistication of the Great Kings in managing an empire. Along these roads flowed not just soldiers but merchants and goods, and with this trade subjects of the Persian Empire exchanged ideas as well.

A Government of Tolerance

The key to maintaining power in such a diverse empire lay in the Persian government's treatment of its many ethnic groups. The highly centralized Persian government wielded absolute power, but it rejected the brutal model of the Assyrian and Babylonian imperial system in favor of a more tolerant approach.

As we saw in the case of the Hebrews, Cyrus began a popular policy of allowing peoples exiled by the Babylonians to return to their homelands. Though Cyrus was Zoroastrian, he made a proclamation to the Babylonians presenting himself as an agent of their chief god, Marduk:

> *I am Cyrus, the king of the world. Marduk, the great god, rejoices at my pious acts . . . I gathered all their peoples and led them back to their abodes . . . and at the order of Marduk . . . I had all the gods [of exiled peoples] installed in their sanctuaries . . . May all the gods whom I have led back to their cities pray daily for the length of my days.*[2]

Subject peoples were permitted to worship freely if they acknowledged the political supremacy of the Great King. In this way the Persians won the loyalty and gratitude of their ethnically diverse subjects throughout the empire.

■ **Map 3.2   The Persian Empire at Its Greatest Extent**

The Persian Empire begun by Cyrus about 550 B.C.E. grew to include all of the Middle East as far as India, Egypt, and northern Greece. This multiethnic, multireligious empire governed its many peoples firmly but tolerantly.

The firm but tolerant methods of governing developed by the Persian government provided a legacy for Western civilization. As we will see in Chapter 4, Greek rulers continued to permit subjects to worship as they wished in the Hellenistic period following Alexander the Great's conquest of Persia.

Zoroastrianism: An Imperial Religion

The Great Kings of Persia and the Persian people followed Zoroastrianism°, a monotheistic religion that still exists today. Its founder, the prophet Zoroaster, lived and preached between 1500 and 1200 B.C.E. His message spread widely throughout Iran for a thousand years before it became Persia's chief faith.

Persians transmitted Zoroaster's teachings, known collectively as the *Avesta*, through oral tradition until scribes recorded them in the sixth century C.E. According to Zoroaster, Ahura Mazda (Lord Wisdom), the one and only God of all creation, is the cause of all good things in the universe. He represents wisdom, justice, and proper order among all created things. Another eternal being, Angra Mainyu (or Ahriman), opposes him. This spirit of destruction and disorder threatens Ahura Mazda's benevolent arrangement of creation.

In Zoroastrian belief, Ahura Mazda will eventually triumph in this struggle with the forces of evil, leaving all creation to enjoy a blissful eternity. Until then, the cosmic fight between Ahura Mazda's forces of light and Angra Mainyu's forces of darkness gives meaning to human existence and lays the foundation for a profoundly ethical way of life. Ahura Mazda requires humans to contribute to the well-being of the world. Everyone has the responsibility of choosing between right and wrong actions.

At the last Day of Judgment, sinners who have not listened to Ahura Mazda's instructions, such as those succumbing to the "filth of intoxication," will suffer eternal torment in a deep pit of terrible darkness. Those who have lived ethical lives will live eternally in a world purged of evil. In a period of transformation called "the Making Wonderful," the dead will be resurrected, and all will live together in the worship of Ahura Mazda.

The Great Kings of Persia believed themselves to be Ahura Mazda's earthly representatives. They committed their energies to fighting the forces of disorder active in their world. In this way, Zoroastrianism provided an ideological support for the Persian Empire's wars of conquest and consolidation at home. The Great Kings lavishly supported the Zoroastrian church, and its priests, called magi, established the faith as the empire's official religion. They built grand temples with sacred fires throughout Persian lands. Because Zoroastrian worship at fire altars occurred wherever Persian power expressed itself, the religion became a reminder to subject peoples of an enduring imperial presence around them. Although the Persian Empire toler-

ated other religions, Zoroastrianism became the official religion that supported the emperor.

Zoroastrian beliefs have played an important role in shaping Western religious thought. The idea of a final judgment followed by an afterlife in heaven or hell became a central concept in Christianity and Islam. Likewise, the idea of a final combat between the Devil and God, followed by the judgment of humanity and the establishment of the kingdom of God on Earth, is still important in many Christian communities.

THE ACHAEMENID DYNASTY

In 522 B.C.E., a Persian nobleman, Darius, seized the imperial throne by murdering one of the sons of Cyrus the Great, and initiated the Achaemenid dynasty. Named for a legendary ancestor, Achaemenes, the new dynasty inaugurated an epoch of territorial expansion and cultural activity that lasted until the Macedonian conqueror Alexander the Great overwhelmed Persia in 330 B.C.E. Darius built a new capital city at Persepolis. Like Cyrus before him, Darius drew workmen, artists, and material resources from among the many peoples of his vast empire. Greeks, Egyptians, Babylonians, and Scythians, among others, made the imperial capital a glittering city crowded with luxurious palaces where people of many cultures came together in the service of the Great King.

From this power center, Darius controlled an efficient administration. He expanded and improved Persia's roads, set up a postal system, and standardized measures and

CHRONOLOGY	
Persia	
550 B.C.E.	Cyrus starts the Persian Empire; Zoroastrianism becomes the empire's religion
546 B.C.E.	The Persians conquer Asia Minor
539 B.C.E.	The Persians capture Babylon
530 B.C.E.	Cyrus dies fighting Scythian steppe nomads
525 B.C.E.	Persian troops conquer Egypt
522 B.C.E.	Darius becomes king; the Achaemenid dynasty begins
490 B.C.E.	Greeks stop Persian invasion of Greece at Marathon
480–479 B.C.E.	Xerxes' invasion of Greece fails

coinage. He also reorganized Cyrus's system of provincial government, dividing the empire into twenty provinces called *satrapies*. Each province paid an annual sum to the central government based on its productivity. The provincial governors, Persian noblemen called *satraps*, collected these taxes and gathered military recruits. In addition, the provincial capitals imitated Persepolis, maintaining administrative archives and serving as local centers of tax collection and bureaucracy. As we will see in the next chapter, this system of administration served as a model for later empires, particularly that of Alexander the Great.

By 513 B.C.E. Darius had greatly expanded his empire. On his northeastern frontier he annexed portions of India as far as the Indus River. He built a canal in Egypt that linked the Mediterranean and Red Seas. But his conquests on the northwestern frontier of the Persian Empire had the greatest impact on Western civilization because they brought Persia into direct contact with the Greeks. Eager to conquer Greece, Darius sent troops across the Hellespont, the channel of water that separates Europe from Asia, in order to establish military bases in the north of Greece. Such incursions along the Greek frontier were only a small part of Darius's grand imperial strategy, but to the Greeks the growing Persian presence caused tremendous anxiety. The stage was now set for the confrontation between the Persians and the Greeks, a confrontation that demonstrated the limits of Persian imperialism.

Greece Rebuilds, 1100–479 B.C.E.

As we saw in Chapter 2, at the end of the International Bronze Age Greek civilization entered a period of bitter poverty and political instability. This period, known as the Dark Age, lasted until about 750 B.C.E., when the Archaic Age began. The Archaic Age was marked by economic growth at home and many Greek encounters with Phoenicians and Persians abroad (see Map 3.3). This period of revival set the stage for Greece's Classical Age, a time of great cultural achievement.

THE DARK AGE, CA. 1100–750 B.C.E.

Compared with the wealth and splendor of the Bronze Age Mycenaean communities, Greek life in the Dark Age was quite gloomy. Few new settlements were established on the mainland and urban life disappeared. Linear B writing dropped out of use entirely, and extensive maritime trade ended. A serious decline in agriculture led to a steep decrease in food production and population.

A slow economic recovery began in the Greek world about 850 B.C.E., for reasons that remain obscure. Because of the harsh living conditions on the mainland during the Dark Age, many Greeks had abandoned their homes and moved to a region called Ionia that encompassed the coasts and islands of western Asia Minor. Relatively isolated from other Greek communities, these pioneers developed their own distinctive Ionian variation of the Greek language. By 800 B.C.E. the Ionian Greeks were regularly interacting with the Phoenicians in the eastern Mediterranean. These seafarers forged a connection between Greeks and the cultures of the Middle East that exerted a lasting impact on Greek society because it marked the end of Greek isolation (see map on page 68).

THE ARCHAIC AGE, CA. 750–479 B.C.E.

Between about 750 and 650 B.C.E., many fresh ideas poured into Greece from the Middle East through contact with the Phoenicians and other peoples. Historians call this exciting period the Archaic Age. Encounters with Middle Eastern poets, merchants, artisans, refugees, doctors, slaves, and spouses brought innovations to Greece: new words such as tyrant and gold; new economic practices such as the use of coinage and charging interest on loans; new myths and literary themes (such as the story of the flood; see document on page 83); new ritual procedures for sacrificing animals; new gods and goddesses (such as Dionysus, the god of wine); and new inventions of convenience (such as parasols to provide shade).

By far the most valuable import from the Phoenicians was the alphabet. As we saw in Chapter 2, the Phoenicians, who had been using an alphabet of twenty-two letters for at least three centuries, introduced the system to Greece sometime just before 750 B.C.E. The adoption of the alphabet was one of the developments that marked the beginning of the Archaic Age. Because an alphabet records sounds, not words, it can be adjusted easily for any language. Greeks quickly recognized the potential of the new system, and quickly adopted it throughout their communities. Greeks learned to write and read, first for business purposes and then for pleasure. They began to record their oral traditions, legends, and songs. At the same time, they began to compose an entirely new literature and write down their laws.

Homer's Epic Poems

Two of the greatest works of epic literature ever composed, the *Iliad* and the *Odyssey*, were soon written down in the new alphabet. A Greek poet named Homer, who probably lived around 750 B.C.E., is credited with composing these poems, but they were certainly not his personal invention. The stories of the *Iliad* and the *Odyssey* drew from a large and widely recited cycle of tales about the legendary Trojan

MACEDONIA

M. Olympus

Troy

Aegean Sea

Greece in the Archaic and Classical Ages
- Sparta and Allies
- Attica
- Other Greek communities

M. Parnassos
Ithaca
Delphi
Thebes
Plataea
Eleusis Marathon
Salamis Piraeus
Corinth Athens
ATTICA

IONIA

Ephesus

Olympia

Miletus

Delos

MESSENIA
Sparta

Halicarnassus

LACONIA

0   50 km
0   50 mi

Rhodes

■ **Map 3.3   Greece in the Archaic and Classical Ages**
During the Archaic and Classical Ages, Greek cities spread from Greece to the shores of the Black Sea and as far west as Italy and southern France. This map shows the Greek heartland: the mainland, the islands of the Aegean Sea, and Ionia. Although never unified politically in the Archaic and Classical Ages, the people in these cities spoke Greek, worshiped the same gods, and shared a similar culture.

War that wandering poets had recited for centuries. The poets had elaborated upon the stories so much over time that all historical accuracy was lost. Nevertheless, many details in the poems, especially about weapons and armor no longer used in Homer's day, suggest that the earliest versions of the poems were first recited in the International Bronze Age and may be very loosely based on events of that time.

The body of poems of which the *Iliad* and the *Odyssey* were a part tells how an army of Greek warriors sailed to Troy, a wealthy city on the northwest coast of Asia Minor, to recover a beautiful Greek princess, Helen, who had been stolen by a Trojan prince. After ten years of savage fighting, the Greeks finally stormed Troy and won the war, though their greatest fighters had died in battle. When the surviving heroes returned home to Greece, they were met with treachery and bloodshed.

The genius of Homer lay in his retelling of these old stories. He did not relate the entire saga of the Trojan War because he knew that his audiences were familiar with it. Instead, he selected certain episodes in which he emphasized aspects of human character and emotion in the midst of violent conflict in fresh ways. In the *Iliad*, for example, he describes how the hero Achilles, the mightiest of all the Greeks fighting at Troy, grows angry when his commander-in-chief Agamemnon steals his favorite concubine. In a rage, Achilles withdraws from the battle and returns to fight only to avenge his best friend who had been killed by Hector, the mainstay of the Trojan defense. Achilles eventually slays Hector, but does not relinquish his fury until Hector's father, Priam, the king of Troy, begs him to return his son's corpse for proper burial. "Honor the Gods, Achilles, and take pity upon me, remembering your own father," implores King Priam, "Yet I am still more pitiful than he. I have endured more than any other mortal: I kiss the hand of the man who has killed my sons." Achilles relents and weeps, his humanity finally restored after so much killing. In Homer's hands, the story of Achilles' anger becomes a profound investigation into human alienation and redemption.

The *Odyssey* tells a different kind of story. The hero of this poem, the Greek king Odysseus, wants nothing more than to return to his wife after the fall of Troy. His trek takes ten years, full of suspenseful adventures as he sails about in the Mediterranean Sea. Odysseus's endless patience, relentless cunning, intellectual curiosity, and deep love for his family finally brings him home. Due to their very human strengths and weaknesses, Achilles and Odysseus are two of the most finely drawn characters in Western literature.

One of the best known episodes of the Trojan saga (though Homer does not relate it) tells how the Greeks won their final victory by means of a ruse—the most famous deception in literature. The Greeks pretended to abandon their siege of Troy but left behind a hollow wooden horse filled with Greek soldiers. The Trojans dragged the horse into their city, only to permit the Greeks to climb out after dark and open the city gates for their companions. By the next morning, Troy was a smoking ruin.

The Polis

In addition to telling epic tales that glorified heroes of the past, Greeks in the Archaic Age experimented with new forms of social and political life. They developed a new style of community called the polis° (plural *poleis*), or city-state. A polis was a self-governing community consisting of an urban center with a defensible hilltop called an acropolis° and all the surrounding land farmed by citizens of the polis. Greek cities varied in size from a few square miles to several hundred. All contained similar institutions: an assembly in which the men of the community gathered to discuss and make decisions about public business; a council of male elders who offered advice on public matters; temples to gods who protected the polis and whose goodwill was necessary for the community's prosperity; and an open area in the center of town called an *agora,* which served as a market and a place for informal discussions.

Living in a polis provided an extremely strong sense of community. A person could be a citizen of only one polis, and every citizen was expected to place the community's interests above all other concerns. Even the women, who were citizens but not permitted to play a role in public life, felt powerful ties to their polis. While only citizens had full membership in a polis, enjoying the greatest rights and bearing the greatest responsibilities, every city had noncitizens from other communities. Some of these noncitizens had limited rights and obligations. Others were slaves, who had no rights at all.

Colonization and the Settlement of New Lands

A population boom during the Archaic Age forced Greeks to emigrate because the rocky soil of the mainland could not provide enough food. From about 750 to 550 B.C.E., cities such as Corinth and Megara on the mainland and Miletos in Ionia established more than 200 colonies overseas.

Greek emigrants traveled by boat to foreign shores. Many colonists settled on the Aegean coast north into the Black Sea region, which offered plentiful farmlands. The important settlement at Byzantium controlled access to the agricultural wealth of these Black Sea colonies. Greeks established many new cities in Sicily and southern Italy, as well as on the southern coast of France and the eastern coast of Spain. By 600 B.C.E. Greeks had founded colonies in North Africa in the region of modern Libya and on the islands of Cyprus and Crete. Greek merchants also set up a trading community on the Syrian coast and another in the Egyptian delta, with the pharaoh's permission.

New Greek cities like Syracuse and Tarentum in Italy, Massilia (Marseilles) in France, and Neapolis (Naples) in Italy gave land-hungry settlers the opportunity to prosper through farming, manufacturing, and trade. The colonists obtained metal ores, timber, and slaves from the regions they settled and began growing wheat, olives, and wine for export. Merchants carried the goods to markets all over the Mediterranean. The overseas world of the Greeks prospered, and a vibrant Greek culture with common language, gods, and social institutions spread throughout the Mediterranean and into the Black Sea.

Although all of the Greek colonies maintained some formal religious ties with their mother city-states, or *metropoleis,* they were self-governing and independent. Some colonies failed, but others grew rich and populous enough to send out their own colonies. Because the Greek colonists seized territory by force and sometimes slaughtered the local inhabitants, relations with the people already living in these lands were often quite tense.

The Greek adoption of coinage spurred commercial activity among many Greek communities. Coinage first replaced barter as a medium of exchange in western Asia Minor about 630 B.C.E. as a form of portable wealth that could be used to buy goods and services. Minted from precious metals and uniform in weight, coins helped people standardize the value of goods, a development that revolutionized commerce. By 600 B.C.E. Greeks living in Ionia and on the Greek mainland began to mint their own coins. Each city-state used a distinctive emblem to mark its currency. When Athens became the dominant economic power in the Aegean during the second half of the fifth century B.C.E., Athenian coinage became the standard throughout the Greek world and far beyond.

Greek colonization played a critical role in shaping Western civilization by creating wealthy centers of Greek culture in Italy and the western Mediterranean. Sometimes

Athenian

(front)   (back)

Jewish Second Temple Period

(front)   (back)

■ **Athenian Coinage**
The coins made in Athens displayed the head of Athena on one side, and her sacred bird, the owl, on the other side. The coin shown at the top dates to the height of the Athenian Empire, about 450 B.C.E. On the bottom, another coin of similar weight and appearance is called a Jehud (from the Persian name of the province of Judah). Minted near Jerusalem, its front shows a face based on Athena. Its back shows an owl and Hebrew writing. The similarities of these coins reveal the international influence of Athenian coinage and the importance of standard weights in long-distance trade.

overshadowed in the historical record by city-states of the Greek mainland, such as Athens, Sparta, and Corinth, the impressive new poleis spread Greek civilization, language, literature, religion, and art far beyond Greece itself. The colony of Syracuse in Sicily, for example, grew to be larger than any city in Greece. Greek communities deeply influenced local cultures and would make a tremendous impact on Etruscan and Roman civilization in Italy, as we will see in Chapter 4. Overseas colonies also prepared the way for the rapid explosion of Greek culture that followed the conquests of Alexander the Great.

Elite Athletic Competition in Greek Poleis

Athletic contests called panhellenic° games, because they drew participants from the entire Greek world, were a mainstay of aristocratic Greek culture in the Archaic Age. As many as 150 cities regularly offered aristocratic men the chance to win glory through competition in chariot racing, discus throwing, wrestling, foot racing and other field events. Through sports the Greeks found a common culture

that allowed them to express their Greek identity and honor the gods at the same time.

The Olympic games, which originated in 776 B.C.E., carried the most prestige. Every four years Greek athletes from southern Italy to the Black Sea gathered in the sacred grove of Olympia in central Greece to take part in games dedicated to Zeus, the chief Greek god. The rules required the poleis to call truces to any wars, even if they were in the middle of battle, and allow safe passage to all athletes traveling to Olympia. Records show the naming of champions at Olympia from 776 B.C.E to 217 C.E. The Roman emperor Theodosius I, who was a Christian, abolished the games in 393 C.E. because they involved the worship of Greek gods.

The Hoplite Revolution

The new wealth flowing through the panhellenic world transformed Greek life. For the first time, men who were not aristocrats could afford to purchase weapons of war. Called hoplites°, these men had the means to acquire helmets, shields, swords, shin guards, and thrusting spears. Hoplites developed a completely different method of fighting. Rather than galloping into battle on horseback, the method preferred by aristocrats with their expensive mounts, or engaging in individual hand-to-hand combat to win personal glory, hoplites entered the battlefield as a phalanx°, fighting as a group that moved in unison. Standing shoulder to shoulder in rows eight men deep, each fighter relied on the man to his right to shield him while he struck forward with his sword or spear. If the line broke, the enemy could easily rout the soldiers. Thus the hoplites' success depended on intense training and, above all, cooperation.

Greeks glorified battling in this close-knit manner. Hoplite fighting generated a sense of pride and common purpose that had political consequences, as hoplites demanded a political voice in the communities for which they fought. Their growing confidence directly challenged aristocratic families who traditionally held tight control over community decision making.

In many poleis, new political leaders arose to champion the cause of the hoplite citizenry. These political leaders were known as tyrants°, a word borrowed from the Middle East that originally did not have the negative connotation it carries today. Tyrants typically came from the ruling classes, but they found their political support among the hoplites and the poor who felt otherwise left out of the political life of the community. When tyrants seized power in a polis, they served the interests of the community as a whole, not just the aristocrats. They promoted overseas trade, built harbors, protected farmers, and began public-works projects to employ citizen workers and to beautify their cities. They also cultivated alliances with other tyrants in other poleis to establish peace and prosperity. Most important, the tyrants' authority enabled a broad range of Greek citizens to participate in government for the first time.

But tyrannies contained a fatal flaw. The power of the tyrant was handed down from father to son, successors rarely inherited their fathers' qualities of leadership. As a result, the tyrannies often became oppressive and unpopular, especially among the hoplites and poor who had supported the tyrants in the first place. Few of them lasted more than two generations.

Two of the most important poleis on the Greek mainland, Sparta and Athens, dealt with tyranny in radically opposing ways. As a result, they created very different political and social systems for their citizens: Sparta became the model for an authoritarian, military society, while Athens was the model for democracy.

Sparta: A Militarized Society

Cut off from the rest of Greece by high mountain ranges to the west and north, Sparta dominated the Peloponnese, the southernmost part of Greece. Until about 700 B.C.E. Spartans lived very much like other Greeks except that their

hoplite forces achieved political power without the aid of tyrants, whom they despised. Rapid expansion in the Peloponnese prompted Spartans to develop a highly militarized way of life among the Greeks. All political power rested with a corps of warrior hoplites that comprised the entire population of male citizens. The Spartan hoplites, who called themselves "the Equals," controlled all the polis's land and spent their time in military training.

The Spartan military system grew more elaborate after 700 B.C.E. when the Spartans conquered Messenia, a fertile region in the western Peloponnese. To maintain control over the Messenians, who vastly outnumbered them, the Spartans brutally reduced the Messenians to the status of helots°, a level barely higher than beasts of burden. Technically free, helots were nevertheless bound to the land and forced to farm. If a Spartan master sold the land to another Spartan, the helots stayed with the land. Helots paid

TYRTAEUS: THE GLORY OF HOPLITE WARFARE

....

During the mid-seventh century B.C.E., the Spartan poet Tyrtaeus wrote many poems glorifying warfare on behalf of the polis. Spartan troops sang his poems as they marched into combat. This poem explains why young men should seek glory and avoid shame by fighting in the front ranks.

It is a noble thing for a good man to die fighting in the
    front lines for his country;
but to abandon his city and fertile fields, to be reduced to
    poverty,
this is most grievous of all things, for then a man wanders
    from place to place
with his beloved mother and elderly father, his small
    children and lawful wife....
And so, since a wanderer receives no recognition, neither
    honor nor respect nor mercy,
let us fight with all our might for this land, and die for our
    children,
never caring to spare our lives.
Stand together and fight, then, O young men; take no step
    in shameful flight.
Be not overcome by fear, but let the heart be great and
    strong in your breast,
never flinching when you face the enemy....
So let every man bite his lip, and, with both feet firmly on
    the ground,
take his place for battle.

Source: From *Ancient Greece: Documentary Perspectives, Second Edition* by Stylianos V. Spyridakis and Bradley P. Nystrom. Copyright © 1997 by Kendall/Hunt Publishing Co. Used with permission.

half of their produce to their Spartan masters and could be murdered with impunity. Controlling the helots through terror became the Spartans' preoccupation.

In Sparta's social hierarchy free subjects stood one level above the helots. These individuals included merchants, manufacturers, and other businessmen who lived in communities throughout Spartan territories. Free subjects paid taxes and served in the army when necessary, but they were not Spartan citizens.

The male and female citizens of Sparta stood at the top of the social pyramid. They devoted themselves completely to a military way of life. The greatest responsibility of all Spartan citizens was to fulfill the needs of the polis. From early childhood, boys trained to become soldiers and girls trained to become the mothers of soldiers. Boys left home at seven years of age to live in barracks, where they mastered the skills of battle. They learned that their comrades-in-arms played a more important role in their lives than their own families. Young married Spartans were not permitted to live with their wives, but had to sneak away from their barracks at night to visit them.

Contempt for pain and hardship, blind obedience to orders, simplicity in word and deed, and unabashed courage were the chief Spartan virtues. Cowardice had no place in this society. Before sending their men to war, wives and mothers warned, "Come home with your shield—or on it!" Sparta's splendidly trained armies won a reputation as the most ferocious force in all of Greece.

After its conquest of Messenia, Sparta strengthened its presence further by organizing the Peloponnesian League, an informal alliance of most of the poleis in the Peloponnese. Spartans avoided wars far from home, but they and their allies joined with the Athenians and other Greeks in resisting Persia's aggression against Greece, as we will see shortly.

Athens: Toward Democracy

Athens, the best known polis of ancient Greece, made an incalculably rich contribution to the political, philosophical, artistic, and literary traditions of Western civilization. The first democracy in the ancient world, Athens developed principles of government that remain alive today. Athens's innovative form of government and the flowering of its intellectual life stemmed directly from its response to tyranny and Persian aggression.

In the eighth and seventh centuries B.C.E., the Athenians settled Attica, the territory surrounding their city, rather than sending colonists abroad. In this way, Athens gained more land and a larger population than any other polis. By the beginning of the sixth century, aristocrats controlled

CHRONOLOGY	
Greece Rebuilds	
CA. 1100 B.C.E.	Mycenaean palaces collapse; the Dark Age begins
850 B.C.E.	Greek population begins to grow; trade and settlements increase
776 B.C.E.	Traditional date of first Olympic games
750–720 B.C.E.	Homer composes the *Iliad* and the *Odyssey*
750 B.C.E.	City-states emerge, overseas colonization begins; Greeks adopt the alphabet from the Phoenicians
700–650 B.C.E.	Hoplite armor and tactics develop; Spartans conquer Messenia
670–500 B.C.E.	Tyrants rule many city-states
600 B.C.E.	Coins are first minted in Lydia in Asia Minor; science and philosophy start in Ionia
594 B.C.E.	Solon reforms Athenian Constitution
CA. 560–514 B.C.E.	Peisistratus and sons become tyrants in Athens; Sparta is dominant in Peloponnese
507 B.C.E.	Cleisthenes' democratic reforms unify Attica

most of the wealth of Attica, and many of the Athenian peasants became heavily indebted to them, pledging their bodies as collateral on loans. They risked being sold into slavery abroad if they could not repay the debt.

With civil war between the debt-ridden peasantry and the aristocracy on the horizon, both segments of the population of Attica agreed to let Solon, an Athenian statesman known for his practical wisdom, reform the political system. In 594 B.C.E. Solon (ca. 650–570 B.C.E.) enacted several reforms that limited the authority of the aristocracy and enabled all male citizens to participate more fully in Athenian public life. These reforms created the institutions of public political life from which democracy eventually developed. Solon cancelled debts, eliminated debt-slavery, and raised enough funds to buy back enslaved Athenians. Then he took additional steps to give all Athenian men a greater voice in governing their city. Taking advantage of a rise in literacy, Solon directed scribes to record his new laws on wooden panels for the whole community to see. This diminished aristocratic control of the interpretation of Athenian law and ensured that the laws would be enforced fairly for all Athenian citizens, regardless of their status.

Solon next organized the population into four classes based on wealth. Only men in the two richest classes could hold the highest administrative office of *archon* and be elected to the highest court, traditionally a base of aristocratic authority. From the third class, Solon created the *boule,* a council of 400 men who prepared the agenda for the general citizen assembly. Men from the fourth and poorest class, who could not afford hoplite weapons, could vote in the citizen assembly, though they could not be elected to any office. Finally, men of any class could serve on a new court that Solon established. Women and slaves had no voice in government at all. These changes provided a temporary solution to Athens's problems.

After a generation of internal peace, Athenian aristocrats began to chafe at their loss of power and rebelled against Solon's system. In ca. 560 B.C.E. a nobleman named Peisistratus (ca. 590–528 B.C.E.) seized power and ruled Athens as a tyrant. Like other tyrannies in Greece, Peisistratus's regime initially enjoyed widespread support. He sponsored building projects, supported religious festivals, encouraged trade and economic development, and supported the arts. He initiated a vigorous tradition of Athenian intellectual life by inviting artists and poets to come to Athens from all over Greece. His sons, however, abused their power, and jealous aristocrats assisted by Sparta toppled the family's rule in 510. Peisistratus's surviving son fled to Persia.

Two years later, the assembly selected a nobleman named Cleisthenes to reorganize Athens. By cleverly rearranging the basic political units of Attica, Cleisthenes unified Attica and made Athens the center of all important political activity. Building upon Solon's reforms, he set the basic institutions of democracy in place with a new council of 500 male citizens drawn from throughout Attica, which made decisions for the community. He ensured every male citizen a permanent voice in government, broke the power of aristocratic families, and set up the lasting, fundamental structures of Athenian democracy. The strength of Cleisthenes' new system would be tested in the face of invasions by Persia in the fifth century B.C.E.

THE PERSIAN WARS, 490–479 B.C.E.

Around 510 B.C.E. the Persian king Darius conquered the Ionian Greek poleis. The Persians ruled their new subjects fairly, but the Ionian Greeks nevertheless revolted in 499 B.C.E. Ionian Greek rebels traveled to Sparta and Athens to ask for assistance against the Persians. The Spartans refused to send any troops when they learned how far away Ionia was. The Athenians, however, sent an expeditionary force that helped the rebels burn Sardis, a Persian provincial capital. The Persians crushed the rebellion in 494 B.C.E., but they did not forget Athens's role in it.

The Marathon Campaign

In 490 B.C.E., after four years of meticulous planning, a Persian army crossed the Aegean Sea in the ships of their Phoenician subjects. They landed at the beach of Marathon, some twenty-six miles from Athens. The vicinity around Marathon was the traditional stronghold of Peisistratus, the former Athenian tyrant. The Persians brought Peisistratus's

son Hippias with them, planning to install him as the new tyrant of Athens.

To save their city, the Athenians marched to Marathon, and with the aid of troops from a neighboring polis (Spartan reinforcements arrived too late), the outnumbered Greek army overcame the Persian forces. Their surprising victory at Marathon demonstrated that a well-trained hoplite force could defeat a far more numerous foe. It also showed that Cleisthenes' democratic reforms had unified Attica so firmly that its citizens had no interest in helping the Persians restore tyranny. Democracy worked.

Athenian Naval Power and the Salamis Campaign

After Marathon, Athens embraced even more dramatic reforms. A new political leader named Themistocles persuaded his fellow citizens to spend the proceeds from a rich silver mine in Attica on a new navy and port. By 480 B.C.E. Athens possessed nearly 200 battleships, called triremes°. With three banks of oars manned by the poorest citizens of the polis, the triremes transformed Athens into a naval powerhouse. The entire male citizen body of Athens, not just the aristocrats and hoplites, could now be called to arms. The Athenian navy embodied Athenian democracy in action in which every male citizen had an obligation to defend his homeland.

The battle of Marathon dealt a shameful blow to the Persians' pride that they resolved to avenge, but a major revolt in Egypt and Darius's death in 486 B.C.E. prevented them from invading Greece again for nearly a decade. In 480 B.C.E., Xerxes I, the new Persian Great King, launched a massive invasion of Greece. He brought an overwhelming force of some 150,000 soldiers, a navy of nearly 700 mostly Phoenician vessels, and ample supplies. His troops crossed from Asia into Europe by means of a bridge of boats over the Hellespont, while the navy followed a parallel path by sea in order to supply the troops. They intended to smash Athens.

Terrified by the magnitude of the Persian army, fewer than 40 of the more than 700 Greek poleis joined the defensive coalition that had formed in anticipation of the invasion. Under the leadership of Sparta, the Greek allies planned to hold back the Persian land force in the north, while the Athenian navy sailed north to attack the invaders at sea. The Spartan king Leonidas led the coalition. Under his command, a Greek force stopped the Persians at the pass of Thermopylae until a traitor revealed an alternate path through the mountains. On the last day of the battle, Leonidas, his entire force of 300 valiant Spartans, and several thousand allies, died fighting.

Their sacrifice was not in vain. The disaster at Thermopylae gave the Athenians precious time to evacuate their city and to station their highly maneuverable fleet in the narrow straits of Salamis, just off the Athenian coast. In a stunning display of naval skill, the Athenian triremes defeated the Persian navy in a single day of heavy fighting.

■ **Warfare at Sea**
In the classical world navies relied on the trireme, a long rowed vessel propelled by 170 oarsmen with a bronze battering ram at the water line. Invented in either Egypt or Phoenicia about 650 B.C.E., the trireme became the backbone of the Athenian fleet. Highly trained rowers could reach a speed of more than nine knots over short distances.

Xerxes withdrew most of his forces to Asia Minor, but left a large army in northern Greece.

Early in 479 B.C.E., a combined Greek army once again stopped the Persians at the battle of Plataea, north of Attica. In this battle a large contingent of Spartans led a decisive final charge. That same year, the combined naval forces of Greece defeated the Persian navy off the Ionian coast. Without a single substantial military success, Xerxes gave up the attempt to conquer Greece and returned to Persia.

The Classical Age of Greece, 479–336 B.C.E.

The defeat of mighty Persia by a handful of Greek cities shocked the Mediterranean world. Xerxes' failure did not seriously weaken Persian society, but it greatly strengthened the Greeks, not only by boosting their economy and by enhancing their own position in the Mediterranean but also for what we would now call their self-image. After the defeat of the Persians, the Greeks exhibited immense confidence in their ability to shape their political institutions and to describe and analyze their society and the world around them. In the political realm, the emboldened Athenians created a powerful empire that made them the dominant power in the Greek world. During this time democratic institutions flourished in Athens. Yet the very success of Athens sowed the seeds of its demise. After alienating many of the other Greek poleis, Athens lost the long and bitter Peloponnesian War with Sparta.

The distinguishing feature of the Classical Age was its remarkable level of creativity, especially in drama, science, history writing, philosophy, and the visual arts. Despite the turmoil of the Persian and Peloponnesian Wars, Greek society remained rigidly hierarchic with strictly defined gender roles and a large class of slaves who performed much of the heavy labor. The structures of Greek society provided many male citizens with the leisure time for debating public affairs in a democratic fashion, for attending plays, and for speculating about philosophical issues. The many deities of the Greek pantheon were the subject of much Greek art. Greeks worshiped these gods in temples that established the Classical style, which was imitated by Romans and other peoples throughout subsequent centuries. None of the Greek cities produced as many creative men as Athens, which makes its experience as an empire and a democracy particularly revealing.

THE RISE AND FALL OF THE ATHENIAN EMPIRE

With the Persian threat to Greece nearly eliminated, Athens began a period of rapid imperial expansion. This aggressive foreign policy backfired. It set off waves of discord among the other Greek city-states that led to war and the eventual collapse of the Athenian Empire.

From Defensive Alliance to Athenian Empire

After the battle of Plataea, the Greek defensive alliance set out to clear the Persians once and for all from the Ionian coast. The Spartans soon grew disillusioned with the effort and withdrew their troops, leaving Athenians in charge. In the winter of 478 B.C.E., Athens reorganized the alliance, creating the Delian League° named for the small island of Delos where the members met. Athens contributed approximately 200 warships to continue attacks against the Persians, while the other members supplied ships or funds to pay for them. The league ultimately gathered a naval force of 300 ships. By 469 B.C.E. it drove the last Persians from the Aegean.

With the Persians ousted, several poleis tried to leave the league, but the Athenians forced them to remain. The Athenians were rapidly turning the Delian League into an Athenian Empire organized for their own benefit. In subsequent decades the Athenians established military garrisons and interfered in the political life of many cities of the league by imposing heavy taxes and establishing many rules and financial regulations. Several open revolts broke out, but no polis in the empire could overcome Athens's might. In 460 B.C.E. Athens sent approximately 4,000 men and 200 warships to assist in an Egyptian revolt against Persia, but Persian troops destroyed the entire expeditionary force. Sobered by this fiasco, the Athenians moved the treasury of the Delian League from Delos to Athens, claiming that they were protecting it from Persian retaliation. In fact, the Athenians spent the league treasury on public buildings in Athens, including the Parthenon. Athenian policy had become indifferent to the original purpose of the league, but the revenues generated by the league's exploitation simultaneously enabled democracy to flourish at home.

Democracy in the Age of Pericles

The chief designer of the Athenian Empire was Pericles, an aristocrat who dominated Athenian politics from 461 B.C.E. until his death in 429 B.C.E. During the so-called "Age of Pericles," Athenian democracy at home and empire abroad reached their peak.

CHRONOLOGY	
Classical Greece	
490 B.C.E.	Battle of Marathon; first Persian invasion stopped
480–478 B.C.E.	Xerxes invades Greece and is defeated
478 B.C.E.	Delian League formed; expansion of Athenian democracy and imperialism
450s B.C.E.	Pericles ascendant in Athens; Herodotus writes his *Investigations* (*Histories*)
477–432 B.C.E.	Parthenon built in Athens; Sophists active
431–404 B.C.E.	Peloponnesian War; Thucydides writes his *History*
429 B.C.E.	Death of Pericles; Euripides and Sophocles active
415–413 B.C.E.	Athens's campaign in Sicily fails
404–403 B.C.E.	Sparta defeats Athens
399 B.C.E.	Trial and death of Socrates
399–347 B.C.E.	Plato writes *Dialogues* and founds Academy

During the Age of Pericles, about 40,000 citizen men lived in Athens. Only men over age 18 could participate in the city's political life. Women, foreigners, slaves, and other imperial subjects had no voice in public life.

The representative council of 500 men established by Cleisthenes continued to administer public business. The citizen assembly met every ten days and probably never had more than 5,000 citizens in attendance, except for the most important occasions. The assembly made final decisions on issues of war, peace, and public policy by majority vote. Because men gained political power through debate in the assembly, a politician's rhetorical skills played an all-important role in convincing voters.

Ten officials called *generals* were elected every year by popular vote to handle high affairs of state and to direct Athens's military forces. Generals typically were aristocrats who had proven their expertise. Pericles, for example, was reelected almost continually for more than twenty years.

The vast increase in public business multiplied the number of public administrators running the empire. By the middle of the fifth century, Athens had about 1,500 officials in its bureaucracy. Now responsible for administrating the Delian League, boards of assessors determined the amount of money its members would pay. Many legal disputes arose among cities in the league, forcing Athens to increase the number of its courts. Because of the constant need for jurors and other office holders, Pericles began

■ Map 3.4 The Peloponnesian War

During this long conflict that lasted from 431 to 404 B.C.E., the forces of Athens and its allies struggled with Sparta and its allies for control of mainland Greece. Though Sparta defeated the Athenian Empire, Athens survived as an influential force in Greek social, political, and economic life.

paying wages for public service, the first such policy in history. Jurors were chosen by lot, and trials lasted no more than a day to expedite cases, save money, and prevent jury tampering.

Athenians took steps to ensure honesty in public affairs. Every official who spent public revenues had his account books examined at the beginning and at the end of his term in office. Citizens meeting in the assembly had regular opportunities to write down the name of any other citizen they disliked or distrusted on a broken piece of pottery called an *ostrakon*. If a sufficient number of citizens singled out the same person, he would be expelled from Athenian lands for ten years, though his property would remain intact for his return. This procedure, called ostracism°, provided a way to get rid of corrupt or overly ambitious politicians. A strong sense of shared identity and common purpose resulted from these democratic institutions and attracted men of all social classes to public service.

Additional reforms by Pericles gave women a more important role in Athenian society. Before 451 B.C.E., children born to Athenian men and their foreign wives attained full citizenship. Pericles' new law allowed citizenship only if both parents were Athenian citizens. As a result, Athenian citizen women took pride in giving birth to the polis's only legitimate citizens. Nevertheless, citizen women continued to be denied full freedom of action in public life.

Conflict with Sparta: The Peloponnesian War

Sparta and its allies felt threatened by growing Athenian power. Between 460 and 431 B.C.E., Athens and a few allies fought intermittently with Sparta and the Peloponnesian League. War broke out between the two sides in 431 B.C.E., dragging on until 404 B.C.E.(see Map 3.4). In the beginning of the conflict, called the Peloponnesian War, the Spartans repeatedly raided Attica in the hope of defeating Athenian forces in open battle.

Thanks to Athens's fortifications and the two parallel five-mile-long walls connecting the city to its main port of Piraeus, the Athenians endured the devastating Spartan invasions. Safe behind their fortifications, they relied on their navy to deliver food and supplies from cities of the Athenian Empire that Spartan armies could not reach. The

Athenians also launched attacks from the sea against Spartan territory almost at will. With the hope that their greater resources would sustain them until victory, the Athenians fought on. Although plague struck the overcrowded city in 430 B.C.E., killing almost one-third of the population including Pericles, Athens and Sparta continued to fight.

In 421 B.C.E., Spartan and Athenian generals agreed to a fifty-year truce, but a mere six years later war broke out again. The reckless policies of Alcibiades, an Athenian general, started a new round of warfare. A nephew of Pericles, Alcibiades lacked his uncle's wisdom. In 415 B.C.E. he persuaded the Athenians to send an expeditionary force of 5,000 hoplites to invade Sicily and take its resources for the war effort. Just as the fleet was about to sail, Alcibiades's enemies accused him of profaning a religious festival, and he fled to Sparta. After two years of heavy fighting, the Athenian expedition ended in utter disaster. Syracusan soldiers captured every Athenian ship and either slaughtered the Athenian soldiers or sold them into slavery.

The Collapse of Athenian Power

The Peloponnesian War dragged on for another ten years, but Athens never fully recovered from the catastrophic loss of men and ships in Sicily. At the suggestion of Alcibiades, the Spartans established a permanent military base within sight of Athens, which enabled them to control Attica. When 20,000 slaves in the Athenian silver mines escaped to freedom under the Spartans, Athens lost its main source of revenue. The final blow came when Lysander, the Spartan commander-in-chief, obtained money from Persia to build a navy strong enough to challenge Athenian sea power. At the battle of Aegospotami on the Hellespont, Lysander's navy sank every Athenian ship. Athens surrendered in 404 B.C.E.

The victorious Spartan forces pulled down Athens's long walls stretching to Piraeus, but they refused to burn the city to the ground as some enemies of Athens demanded, because Athens had been Sparta's valiant ally in the Persian Wars. Instead, the Spartans set up an oligarchy°, or government by a few. Led by the "Thirty Tyrants," a violent and conservative political faction, the oligarchy soon earned the hatred of Athenian citizens. Within a year they overthrew the tyrants and restored democracy.

Sparta's victory did not bring peace to the Greek world. Following the defeat of the Athenian Empire, the Spartans began a shortsighted attack on Persian provinces in Asia Minor. Angered by Sparta's aggression, the Persians retaliated by financing Athens and other poleis to fight Sparta. Bitter war raged among the Greek poleis, but finally agents of the Persian Great King negotiated the King's Peace in 386 B.C.E. With this treaty the Persians promised not to interfere again in Greek affairs. In return the Greek cities of Asia Minor would remain under Persian control. The war-weary Greek states eagerly agreed. For the next two decades, the Greek city of Thebes dominated Greek affairs after defeating Sparta in 371 B.C.E., but wars among different poleis continued on a small scale. When not fighting other Greeks, many Greek hoplites fought as mercenaries for Persian kings in the period after the Peloponnesian War. These Greek soldiers learned that well-trained, highly disciplined hoplite troops were more than a match for the Persian army. In the next chapter we will see how the kingdom of Macedonia to the north of Greece benefited from this important lesson.

THE SOCIAL AND RELIGIOUS FOUNDATIONS OF CLASSICAL GREECE

Amid the violence of the Classical Age, the Greek poleis developed a vibrant way of life, in which men and women had distinct roles to play, one that freed men for involvement in public affairs. Greek men and women lived very different lives, guided by strict rules of behavior. A hierarchy of gender roles determined individuals' access to public space, legal rights, and opportunities to work. In this emphatically patriarchal society, only men held positions of public authority, controlled wealth and inheritance, and enjoyed the right to participate in political life. Women were expected to engage in domestic activities, out of sight of non–family members. At the bottom of society were slaves of both genders, who had no rights at all.

Gender Roles

Greek women were expected to marry early in puberty, typically to men at least ten years older. Through marriage legal control of women passed from father to husband. In the case of divorce, which only men could instigate, the husband had to return his wife's dowry to her father. Greek houses were small and usually divided into two parts. In the brighter front rooms husbands entertained their male friends at dinner and enjoyed active conversation and social interaction with other males. Wives spent the majority of their time in the more secluded portions of the home, supervising the household slaves, raising children, dealing with their mothers-in-law, and weaving cloth.

Greek men feared that their wives would commit adultery, which carried the risk of illegitimate offspring and implied that husbands could not control their possessions or access to their homes. Consequently, Greek men strictly monitored and closely controlled women's sexual activity. Because men considered females powerless to resist seduction, respectable women rarely ventured out in public without a chaperone. Slaves went to market and ran errands. To the typical Greek husband, the ideal wife stayed out of public sight, dutifully obeyed him, and was satisfied by sexual relations with him three times a month. She was

■ Male Views of Women: Subservient or Out of Control?

In male-dominated Greek communities, men idealized passive women and had great anxiety about losing control over them. (a) This Athenian vase of the fifth century B.C.E. reflects Greek men's view of a properly subordinate woman. In the image, the wife bids goodbye to her young husband, who is going off to war. Her place is at home, tending to chores until his return. (b) This vase depicts male fears about females freed from social constraints. It depicts women as wild, drunken, and potentially murderous followers of Dionysus, god of wine. (c) Greek men's worst nightmare was women fighting back. This vase portrays an Amazon, a mythological female warrior, fighting on horseback. According to myth, Amazons fought in battle like men and ruled themselves.

not supposed to mind if he had relations with prostitutes or adolescent boys. Above all, she was expected to produce legitimate children, preferably sons, who would continue the family line and honorably serve the polis.

Women who worked outside the home did so primarily in three capacities: as vendors of farm produce or cloth in the marketplace, as priestesses, and as prostitutes. Female vendors in the marketplace came from the lower classes. Their skills in weaving cloth and making garments, as well as in growing vegetables in their gardens, gave them the opportunity to supplement the family income.

Priestesses served the temples of goddesses such as Hera in Argos and Athena in Athens. In classical Athens, more than forty publicly sponsored religious cults had female priests. These women gained high prestige in their communities. Greeks believed that some women possessed a special spirituality that made them excellent mediums through whom divinities often spoke. Such women served as oracles, as in the temple of Apollo at Delphi. They attracted visitors from all over the Mediterranean world who wanted to discern the gods' wishes or learn what the future might bring.

Prostitutes lived in all Greek cities, but unlike priestesses, their profession was considered shameful. In Athens, most prostitutes were slaves from abroad. Some women worked as elite courtesans called *hetairai*°. Because Greek men did not think it possible to have intellectual exchanges with their spouses, they hired hetairai to accompany them to social gatherings and to participate in stimulating conversations about politics, philosophy, and the arts. Like ordinary prostitutes, hetairai also were expected to be sexually available for pay.

The most famous of all hetairai was Aspasia, who came to Athens from the Ionian city of Miletus. She became Pericles' companion, and their son gained Athenian citizenship by special vote of the assembly. Aspasia participated fully in the circle of scientists, artists, and intellectuals who surrounded Pericles and made Athens "the school of Greece." According to legend, she taught rhetoric and regularly conversed with the philosopher Socrates.

The Athenian orator Demosthenes famously summed up Greek attitudes toward women with these words: "We have hetairai for the sake of pleasure, regular prostitutes to care for our physical needs, and wives to bear legitimate children and be loyal custodians of our households."[3]

In classical Greece, where men considered women to be intellectually and emotionally inferior, many men believed that the best sort of friendship was found in male homosexual unions. Greek men frequently courted adolescent youths. The older man became a mentor and a good example for his younger lover. Some poleis institutionalized such relationships. In the city of Thebes, for example, the elite "Sacred Band" of 150 male couples led the city's hoplites into battle during the fourth century B.C.E. These men were considered the best warriors because they would not endure the shame of showing cowardice to their lovers. The Sacred Band could defeat even Spartan warriors.

Slavery: The Source of Greek Prosperity

Unlike free citizens of a polis, slaves were totally under the control of other people and had no political or legal rights. Masters could kill them without serious penalty and could demand sexual favors at any time. Slavery existed in every polis at every social level. The slave population expanded in the period after 600 B.C.E. as poleis prospered and demands for labor increased.

Most information about Greek slavery comes from Athens, which was the first major slave society that is well-documented. Between about 450 and 320 B.C.E., the thriving polis had a total population of perhaps a quarter of a million people, one-third of whom were enslaved. The proportion of slaves to free persons was similar in other poleis. In the Archaic Age the Athenian aris-

tocracy began to rely on slave labor to work their large landed estates. Most of these slaves had fallen into bondage for debt, but after Solon made the enslavement of Athenian citizens illegal in 594 B.C.E., the wealthy turned to sources outside Attica. Many slaves were captured during the Persian Wars, but most slaves were either the children of slaves or purchased from the thriving slave trade in non-Greek peoples from around the Aegean.

Athenians and other Greeks relied on slaves to perform an enormous variety of tasks. The city of Athens owned slaves who served as a police force, as public executioners, as clerks in court, and in other public capacities. Most slaves, however, were privately owned. Some labored as highly skilled artisans and businessmen who lived apart from their owners but were required to pay them a high percentage of their profits. Every Greek household had male and female slaves who performed menial tasks. Some rich landowners owned gangs of slaves who worked in the fields. Others rented slaves to the polis to labor in the silver mines, where they were worked to death under hideous conditions.

Slavery did not necessarily last until a person's death. A few slaves won their freedom through the generosity of their owners. Others saved enough money from their trades to buy their freedom. Freed slaves could not become citizens. Instead, they lived as resident foreigners in the polis of their former masters and often maintained close ties of loyalty and obligation to them.

Slavery was so widespread in Athens because it was extremely profitable. The Athenian political system evolved to permit and support the exploitation of noncitizen slaves to benefit the citizen class. The slaves were primarily responsible for the prosperity of Athens and gave the aristocrats the leisure to engage in intellectual pursuits and to create the rich culture that became part of the core of Western civilization.

■ **Male Homosexuality**

This painted vase displays a common homoerotic scene, the courting of an unbearded youth by an older man. The youth holds a garland that suggests athletic victory.

Religion and the Gods

Religion permeated Greek life. It provided a structured way for Greeks to interact with the deities who exercised considerable influence over their lives. Greeks worshiped many gods, whom they asked for favors and advice. Every city kept a calendar of religious observances established for certain days. Festivals marked phases in the agricultural year, such as the harvest or sowing seasons, and initiation ceremonies marked an individual's transition from childhood to adulthood.

Above all, Greeks gave their devotion to the gods who protected the city. For instance, during the annual Panathenaea festival in Athens, the entire population, citizens and noncitizens alike, honored the city's patron goddess Athena with a grand procession and numerous sacrifices. Every fourth year, the celebration was expanded to include major athletic and musical competitions. In a joyous parade, the citizens would convey a robe embroidered with mythological scenes to the statue of Athena in her temple, called the Parthenon, or House of the Virgin Goddess, that stood on the Acropolis hill in the center of the city.

Although every polis had its own set of religious practices, people throughout the Greek world shared many ideas about the gods. Like the Greek language, these common religious attitudes gave a common identity to Greeks. They also distinguished them from so-called barbarians who worshipped strange gods in ways the Greeks considered uncivilized.

Most Greeks believed that immortal and enormously powerful gods and goddesses were all around them. These deities often embodied natural phenomena like the sun or moon, but Greeks attributed very human personalities and desires to them. Because these divine forces touched every aspect of daily life, human interactions with them were unavoidable and risky, for the gods could be as harmful as they were helpful to humans.

The Greeks believed that the twelve greatest gods lived on Mount Olympus in northern Greece as a large and quite dysfunctional family. Zeus was the father and king; Hera was his sister and wife; and Aphrodite was the goddess of sex and love. The jealous clan also included Apollo, god of the sun, prophecy, and medicine; Ares, the god of war; and Athena, the goddess of wisdom. Greek mythology developed a set of stories about the Olympian gods that have passed into Western literature and art.

In addition to their home on Mount Olympus, the gods also maintained residences in cities. Temples served as the gods' living quarters. They displayed the wealth and piety of every polis, for Greek cities spared no expense to employ the finest architects and best materials. Rows of carved marble columns surrounded the central room and supported the temple's roof. Sculptural decorations on the temple walls that told stories about the gods were brilliantly painted, but today they have been bleached white by centuries of sunlight and weathering. The gods' likeness, typically a large statue, stood at the center of these rectangular marble structures, facing an altar in front of the building.

Worship at Greek temples consisted of offerings and sacrifices. Outside in the open air, the worshipers made offerings, perhaps a small bouquet of flowers, a pinch of incense, or a small grain cake. On especially important festivals the Greeks sacrificed live animals to their gods. Priests and priestesses supervised these rituals. The god inside the temple watched the priests prepare the sacrifice, heard the sacrificial animals bleat as their throats were slit, and listened

■ **The Acropolis and the Parthenon**
The Acropolis of Athens, crowned by the Parthenon, stood as a symbol of Athenian imperial culture.

■ Dragons and Serpents

Current archaeological research suggests that the dragons and serpents appearing in Greek mythology represent ancient attempts to explain dinosaur fossils. Greek vase painters illustrated these stories with such accuracy that paleontologists today can identify the dinosaur. This vase, painted about 550 B.C.E., shows the hero Hercules and the princess Hesione fighting the sea monster that had been holding her captive. Scientists believe that the monster's head might have been modeled on the skull of *Samotherium,* a giant giraffe that lived about eight million years ago. Many fossils of this creature have been found in Greece and Turkey.

to women howl as blood poured from the beasts. Finally, the god smelled the aroma of burning meat as the victim was cooked over the flames. Satisfied, the god awaited the next sacrifice.

In addition, Greeks took pains to discern the future. They hired religious experts to analyze their dreams and to predict the future based on the examination of the internal organs of specially sacrificed birds. Greeks and non-Greeks alike traveled to consult the priestess of Apollo, the so-called Oracle of Delphi, at a shrine in central Greece. If the god chose to reply to a particular query, he spoke through the mouth of his oracle, a priestess who would lapse into a trance. Priests stood nearby to record and explain the oracle's utterances, which often could have more than one interpretation. When King Croesus of Lydia asked the oracle what would happen if he went to war with the Persians, Apollo told him that "a great kingdom will fall." Croesus never dreamed it would be his own.

INTELLECTUAL LIFE

In the Classical Age, Greeks investigated the natural world and explored the human condition with astonishing freshness and vigor. Their legacy in drama, science, philosophy, and the arts continued to inspire people in many subsequent periods of history. The term *Renaissance,* which is applied to several cultural movements in later periods, refers to attempts to recapture the intellectual vitality of the Greek Classical Age as well as that of the Romans, which drew heavily from it.

Greek Drama

Greek men examined their society's values through public dramatic performances. Peisistratus, the tyrant of Athens, introduced plays around 550 B.C.E. Initially, plays were performed in annual festivals dedicated to Dionysus, the god of wine, and authors entered their plays in competition. Dramatic productions soon became a mainstay of Greek life. In their plays set in the mythical past, the playwrights explored issues relevant to contemporary society. Above all, Greeks who attended the plays (only men were allowed) could expect to be educated and entertained. Fewer than fifty plays from the Greek classical period have survived, but they count among the most powerful examples of literature in the Western tradition.

In tragedies Athenian men watched stories about the terrible suffering underlying human society. In many of these plays an important aristocrat or ruler is destroyed by a fatal personal flaw beyond his or her ability to control. With an unflinching gaze, playwrights examined conflicts between violent passion and reason and between the laws of the gods and those of human communities. Their dramas depicted the terrible consequences of vengeance, the brutality of war, and the relationship of the individual to the polis. In the plays of the three great Athenian tragedians—Aeschylus, Sophocles, and Euripides—characters learn vital lessons through their suffering, and the audience learns them, too.

Aeschylus (525–456 B.C.E.) believed that the gods were just and that human suffering stemmed directly from human error. His most powerful works include a trilogy called the *Oresteia.* This collection of three plays expresses the notion that a polis can survive only when courts made up of citizens settle matters of murder, rather than leaving justice to family vendettas. The cycle of retaliation that tormented the family of King Agamemnon of Mycenae for generations finally ends when Athena and her citizens provide the hideous deities of violent revenge an honorable resting place in Athens.

Another of his plays, called *The Persians,* put Athenians in a triumphal mood after the defeat of the Persians at Salamis and the subsequent Persian withdrawal from Greece. This play shows the tragic consequences of Xerxes' limitless arrogance and ambition. Aeschylus also makes a sharp distinction, for the first time in Greek literature, between Greek civilization and foreign barbarism. This distinction developed into a major theme in Greek thought, and it still is used to categorize cultures today.

In the plays of Sophocles (ca. 496–406 B.C.E.), humans are free to act, but they are trapped by their own weaknesses, their history, and the will of the gods. In *Antigone,* a young woman buries her outlaw brother in accordance with divine principles but in defiance of her city's laws, knowing that she will be executed for her brave act. The misguided king who wrote the law and ordered her death realizes too late that a polis will prosper only if human and divine laws come into proper balance. In *Oedipus the King,* Oedipus unknowingly kills his father and marries his mother. When he learns what he has done, Oedipus blinds himself. Although he knows that a god caused his tragedy, he understands that he was the one who committed the immoral acts.

Like Sophocles' works, the plays of Euripides (ca. 484–406 B.C.E.) portray humans struggling against their fates. In these works, the gods have no human feeling and are capable of bestial action against humans. Unlike other writers of his day, Euripides showed remarkable sympathy for women, who often fall victim to war and male deceit in his plays. At the end of *The Trojan Women,* the despairing Trojan queen Hecuba stands amid the smoldering ruins of her vanquished city, lamenting the cruel life as a slave that awaits her: "Lead me, who walked soft-footed once in Troy, lead me a slave where earth falls sheer away by rocky edges, let me drop and die withered away with tears."[4]

In addition to the tragedies, Greeks delighted in irreverent comedies. Performances of comedy probably began in the seventh century B.C.E. as lewd sketches associated with Dionysus, the god of wine and fertility. The playwright Aristophanes of Athens (ca. 450–388 B.C.E.) proved a master at presenting comedy as social commentary. No person, god, or institution escaped his mockery. Although fully committed to Athenian democracy, Aristophanes had no patience for hypocritical politicians or self-important intellectuals. His comic plays are full of raunchy sex and allusions to the day's issues, containing withering sarcasm, silly puns, and outrageous insults. Audiences howled at the fun,

---

GREEK VERSUS BARBARIAN
....

In the following excerpt Hippocrates of Kos (d. ca. 400 B.C.E.), known as the Father of Medicine, explains the forms of government of the Near East and the character of the people, whom he calls Asiatics. Like other Greeks of his time, Hippocrates believed in the superiority of Greek civilization. In this passage, he explains that the climatic zones in which people live determine the characteristics of their culture.

The small variations of climate to which the Asiatics are subject, extremes of both heat and of cold being avoided, account for their mental flabbiness and cowardice . . . They are less warlike than Europeans and tamer of spirit, for they are not subject to those physical changes and the mental stimulation that sharpen tempers and induce recklessness and hot-headedness . . . Such things appear to me to be the cause of the feebleness of the Asiatic race, but a contributory cause also lies in their customs; for the greater part is under monarchical rule . . . Even if a man be born brave and of stout heart, his character is ruined by this form of government.

Source: From Paul Cartledge, *The Greeks: A Portrait of Self and Others,* 1993. Reprinted by permission of Oxford University Press.

---

but these plays always carried a thought-provoking message as well. *The Birds* is an apt example. In this satire, Aristophanes tells the story of two down-on-their-luck Athenians who flee the city looking for peace and quiet. On their trek they have to deal with an endless stream of Athenian bureaucrats and frauds whom Aristophanes mercilessly skewers. Finally the travelers seize power over the Kingdom of the Birds—and then transform it into a replica of Athens. This satire of Athenian imperialism shows Athenians helpless to avoid their own worst instincts.

Scientific Thought in Ionia

Greek science began about 600 B.C.E. in the cities of Ionia, when a handful of men began to ask new questions about the natural world. Living on the border between Greek and Persian civilizations, these Greek thinkers encountered the vigorous Babylonian scientific and mathematical traditions that still flourished in the Persian Empire. Inspired by these methods of carefully observing the natural world and systematically recording data, Greek thinkers started pulling away from traditional Greek explanations for natural phenomena.

They rejected old notions of gods who arbitrarily inflicted floods, earthquakes, and other disasters on humanity. Instead, they looked for general principles that could explain each natural phenomenon. To these investigators, the natural world was orderly, knowable by means of careful inquiry, and therefore ultimately predictable. These scientists inquired about the physical composition of the natural world, tried to formulate the principles of why change occurs, and began to think about proving their theories logically.

Thales of Miletus (ca. 625–547 B.C.E.), the first of these investigators, theorized that the Earth was a disk floating on water. When the Earth rocked in the water, he proposed, the motion caused earthquakes. Thales traveled to Egypt to study geometry and established the pyramids' height by calculating the length of their shadows. Perhaps influenced by Egyptian and Babylonian teachings, he believed that water gave rise to everything else. His greatest success as an astronomer came when he predicted a solar eclipse in 585 B.C.E.

One of Thales's students, Anaximander (ca. 610–547 B.C.E.), wrote a pioneering essay about natural science called *On the Nature of Things*. Anaximander became the first Greek to create a map of the inhabited world. He also argued that the universe was rational and symmetrical. In his view, it consisted of Earth as a flat disk at its center, held in place by the perfect balance of the limitless space around it. Anaximander also believed that change occurred on Earth through the tension between opposites, such as hot versus cold and dry versus wet.

A third great thinker from Miletus, Anaximenes (ca. 545–525 B.C.E.), suggested that air is the fundamental substance of the universe. Through different processes, air could become fire, wind, water, earth, or even stone. His conclusions, along with those of Thales and Anaximander, may seem odd and unsatisfactory today, but these men were pioneers of science exploration of the natural world. Their brave willingness to remove the gods from explanations of natural phenomena, and their effort to provide arguments in defense of their theories, established the foundations of modern scientific inquiry and observation.

These Milesian thinkers sparked inquiry in other parts of the classical Greek world as well. Soon other investigators developed their own theories. Heraclitus of Ephesus (ca. 500 B.C.E.) argued that fire, not gods, provided the true origin of the world. Leucippus of Miletus (fifth century B.C.E.) and Democritus of Abdera (ca. 460–370 B.C.E.) proposed that the universe consisted entirely of an endless number of material atoms. Too small to be seen, these particles floated everywhere. When the atoms collided or stuck together, they produced the elements of the world we live in, including life itself. These atomists had no need for gods in their explanations of the natural world.

The Origins of Writing History

The Western tradition of writing history has its roots in the work of Herodotus (ca. 484–420 B.C.E.), who grew to adulthood in the Ionian city of Halicarnassus. This Greek author concerned himself with finding the general causes of human events, not natural phenomena. He called his work *Investigations* (the original Greek meaning of the word *history*), and he attempted to explain the Persian War. He believed this conflict deserved to be analyzed and remembered because it had been the greatest war ever fought. For Herodotus, "the war between the Greeks and the non-Greeks" was just one episode in an unending cycle of violence between East and West, between barbarian and civilized, between oppressed and free.

Gods appear in Herodotus's narrative, but do not play a causal role in events. Instead, he attempted to show that humans always act in accordance with the general principle of reciprocity; that is, people predictably respond in equal measure to what befalls them. He sketched the reciprocal violence between East and West in legends, such as that of the Trojan War, and then described the conquest of Lydia by the Persian King Cyrus in the sixth century. He tells how the Greeks became involved in Persian affairs and finally triumphed over Persian aggression.

Herodotus traveled widely. He frequently visited Athens, where he read portions of his analysis of the Persian War to appreciative audiences. He also made voyages to Egypt, Babylonia, and other foreign lands, gathering information about local religions and customs. Herodotus relished the differences among cultures, and his narrative brims with vivid descriptions of exotic habits in far-off lands.

Although he considered Greeks superior to other peoples, Herodotus raised basic questions about cultural encounters that still engage us today. How can we judge whether one culture's customs are better than another's? Is it possible to evaluate a foreign culture on its own terms or are we doomed to view things through our own eyes and experiences only? Herodotus made description and analysis of foreign cultures an integral part of his "investigations." Today historians justly refer to him as the "Father of History."

Western civilization also owes an incalculable debt to Thucydides of Athens (d. ca. 400 B.C.E.), who further advanced the science of writing history. His brilliant *History of the Peloponnesian War* stands as perhaps the single most influential work of history in the Western tradition because it provides a model for analyzing the causes of human events and the outcomes of individual decisions. In it he combines meticulous attention to accuracy and detail with a broad moral vision. To Thucydides, the Peloponnesian War represented a profound tragedy. At one time under the wise leadership of Pericles, Athens epitomized all that was good about a human community. In this "school of Greece," culture flourished and creativity and political accomplishment had no limits. Unfortunately, Athenians, like all humans, possessed a fatal flaw, the unrelenting desire to possess more. Never satisfied, they followed unprincipled leaders

The Classical Nude Male Figure

The Ideal Youth, ca. 530 B.C.E.

Classical Greek culture celebrated the human male body in literature and art. Men dominated polis life, and considered the male body the standard of human beauty. In the eyes of Greek men, males embodied the most admirable virtues; in the physical world the male body came closest to perfection. Greeks considered beauty an active force that "attracted the eyes like a magnet."[5] Throughout the Greek world, from the Black Sea to Spain, freestanding marble and bronze statues of men filled the public spaces of cities. By attracting viewers to their beauty, statues became a vibrant presence in public life, conveying these masculine values to the people who admired them.

As Greek society changed so did the statues. By considering how the statues of men changed over time, we can learn about the development of the Greek attitudes that lay behind them.

Egyptian statues originally inspired Greek sculptors. For more than a thousand years, Egyptians had made statues according to the same conventions. The rigidly symmetrical figure with one leg forward was best viewed from the front. In their sculptures, the forward leg was just simply made longer. Egyptian artists had no interest in exploring how the body moves or how its weight shifts.

Greeks sculptors first encountered Egyptian art about 650 B.C.E. Intrigued, they began to make statues of young men. Like their Egyptian models, these works tended to be stiff. As techniques for carving marble developed, Greek artists became fascinated with representing human anatomy more realistically.

For a Greek artist, how the body moves, how it relates to surrounding space, and how it evokes emotions became matters of intense interest. For these artists, a *kouros,* an adolescent male at the height of his physical perfection, served as the ideal subject. Carved from white marble, the *kouros* shown here (top) was made in Athens about 530 B.C.E. It depicts a young man stepping forward and putting his weight on his left foot, which causes his right heel to rise. His arms are held tightly at his side, and he stares straight ahead. Although the statue captures the shifting of weight in the man's stride, his muscles are too symmetrical to be lifelike, and his posture is quite rigid. This statue presents an idealized image of a perfect adolescent.

In the burst of creative excitement that followed victory over the Persians, Greek sculptors turned away from the rigid style that the *kouros* represents and energetically began exploring all the possibilities of rendering the human body in a more lifelike fashion. The ideal was an autonomous man, in control of his emotions and with a disciplined body, well-trained for combat and victory over others.

Polyclitus of Argos, a sculptor who worked between about 460 and 410 B.C.E., created a bronze statue of a warrior, probably Achilles, that became the standard for masculine perfection and for precise representation of anatomy. Called the Spear-Carrier, or *Doryphoros,* this statue (bottom) was widely copied in antiquity, but the original has not survived. This Roman replica is proportioned according to Polyclitus's meticulous measuring of the ideal male figure. The Spear-Carrier's anatomy is accurately and purposefully depicted. The beautiful muscles indicate the self-discipline necessary for much physical training, and their power implies the force of male strength in warfare in defense of the polis. The Doryphoros is the perfect male citizen, balanced and controlled, yet poised to fight. ■

Polyclitus's Spear-Carrier: The Ideal Man, ca. 430 B.C.E.

For Discussion

How does depicting the human body in Greek art reveal basic assumptions held by Greek culture?

after Pericles' death, embarking on foolhardy adventures that eventually destroyed them.

In Thucydides' analysis, humans, not the gods, are entirely responsible for their own triumphs and defeats. As an analyst of the destructive impact of uncontrolled power on a society, Thucydides has no match. Even more than Herodotus, he set the standard for historical analysis in the West.

Nature Versus Customs and the Origins of Philosophical Thought

The Greeks believed that their communities could prosper only when governed by just political institutions and fair laws. They questioned whether the political and moral standards of the day were rooted in nature or whether humans had invented them and preserved them as customs. They wondered whether absolute standards should guide polis life or whether humans are the measure of all things. No one has answered these questions satisfactorily to this day, but one of the legacies of classical Greece is that they were asked at all.

During the fifth century B.C.E., a group of teachers known as sophists°, or wise men, traveled throughout the Greek-speaking world. They shared no common doctrines, and they taught everything from mathematics to political theory with the hope of instructing individuals in the best ways to lead better lives. The best-known among them was Protagoras (ca. 485–440 B.C.E.), who denied the existence of gods and absolute standards of truth. All human institutions, Protagoras argued, were created through human custom or law and not through nature. Thus, because truth is relative, an individual should be able to argue either side of an argument persuasively.

Socrates (469 B.C.E.–399 B.C.E.), an Athenian citizen, challenged the sophists' notion that there were no absolutes to guide human life. He spent his days trying to help his fellow Athenians understand the basic moral concepts that governed their lives by relentlessly asking them questions. Because Socrates wrote nothing himself, we know of his ideas chiefly through the accounts of his student Plato of Athens (ca. 428–347 B.C.E.), who made his teacher the central figure in his own philosophical essays.

Plato established a center called the Academy in Athens for the purpose of teaching and discussion, and earned a towering reputation among Greek philosophers. Like Socrates, he rejected the notion that truth and morality are relative concepts. Plato taught that absolute virtues such as goodness, justice, and beauty do exist, but on a higher level of reality than human existence. He called these eternal, unchanging absolutes Forms°. In fact, in Platonic thought, the Forms represent true reality. Like shadows that provide only an outline of an object, what we experience in daily life is merely an approximation of this true reality. Plato's theories about the existence of absolute truths and how humans can discover them continue to shape Western thought. In par-

ticular, Platonic theory emphasizes how the senses deceive us and how the truth is often hidden. Truth can be discovered only through careful, critical questioning rather than through observation of the physical world. As a result, Platonic thought emphasizes the superiority of theory over scientific investigation.

According to Plato, humans can gain knowledge of the Forms. This is possible because we have souls that are small bits of a larger eternal Soul that enters our bodies at birth, bringing knowledge of the Forms with it. Our individual bits of Soul always seek to return to their source, but they must fight the constraints of the body and physical existence that stand in the way of their return. Mortals can aid the Soul in its struggle to overcome the material world by using reason to seek knowledge of the Forms. This rational quest for absolutes, Plato argued, is the particular responsibility of the philosophers, but all of us should do our best to embark on this search.

In his treatise *The Republic,* Plato described how people might construct an ideal community based on the principles he had established. In this ideal state, educated men and women called the Guardians would lead the polis because they were capable of comprehending the Forms. They would supervise the brave Auxiliaries who defended the city. At the bottom of society were the Workers who produced the basic requirements of life. Workers were the least capable of abstract thought.

Plato and his student Aristotle (384–322 B.C.E.) stand as the two greatest thinkers of classical Greece. Aristotle founded his own school in Athens, called the Lyceum. Unlike his teacher, Aristotle did not envision the Forms as separate from matter. In his view, form and matter are completely bound together. For this reason, we can acquire knowledge of the Forms by carefully observing the world around us and classifying what we find. Following this theory, Aristotle rigorously investigated a huge range of subjects, including animal and plant biology, mechanics, and physics. His many books made him the most influential natural scientist in the Western tradition before the modern period.

In his treatise *Politics,* Aristotle discussed the difference between Greeks and non-Greeks, whom he refers to collectively as "barbarians." He argued that barbarians were slaves by nature, while Greeks were free. Furthermore, Greeks were truly noble in every way, while barbarians were noble only in accordance with their own customs. Aristotle used this argument to justify Greek imperialism abroad; his notions of cultural superiority survive to this day as justifications for racism and imperialism.

The Arts: Sculpture, Painting, and Architecture

Like philosophers and dramatists during the Classical Age, Greek sculptors, painters, and architects pursued ideal beauty and truth. Classical artists believed the human body was beautiful and an appropriate subject of their

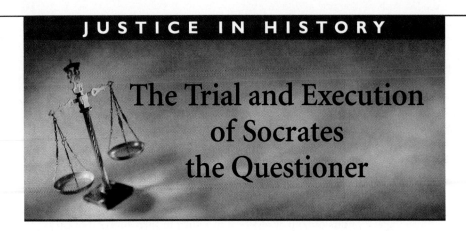

The Trial and Execution of Socrates the Questioner

In 399 B.C.E. the people of Athens tried and executed Socrates, their fellow citizen, for three crimes: for not believing in Athenian gods, for introducing new gods, and for corrupting the city's young men. The charges were paradoxical, for Socrates had devoted his life to investigating how to live ethically and morally. Although Socrates could have escaped, he chose to die rather than betray his most fundamental beliefs. Socrates wrote nothing down, yet his ideas and the example that he set by his life and death make him one of the most influential figures in the history of Western thought.

Born in Athens in 469 B.C.E., Socrates fought bravely during the Peloponnesian War. Afterward he openly defied the antidemocratic Thirty Tyrants whom the Spartans had installed in Athens. Socrates did not seek a career in politics or business. Instead he spent his time thinking and talking, which earned him a reputation as an eccentric. His friends, however, loved and deeply respected Socrates.

Socrates did not give lectures. Instead, he questioned people who believed they knew the truth. By asking them such questions as What is justice? Beauty? Courage? What is the best way to lead a good life? Socrates revealed that they—and most people—do not truly understand their most basic assumptions. Socrates did not claim to know the answers, but he did believe in the relentless application of rational argument in the pursuit of answers.

This style of questioning, known as the Socratic method, infuriated complacent men because it made them seem foolish. But Socrates' method delighted people interested in taking a hard look at their most cherished beliefs.

Socrates attracted many followers. His brightest student was the philosopher Plato, to whom Socrates was not only a mentor, but a hero. Plato wrote a number of dialogues, or dramatized conversations, in which Socrates appears as a questioner, pursuing the truth about an important topic. Four of his dialogues—*Euthyphro, Apology, Crito,* and *Phaedo,* involve Socrates' trial and death.

The trial began when three citizens named Lycon, Meletus, and Anytus accused Socrates before a jury of 501 men. The accusers charged Socrates with corrupting the youth of Athens, failing to believe in the gods, and introducing new gods to the city. Socrates spoke in his own defense, but instead

of showing any remorse, he boldly defended his method of questioning. Annoyed by Socrates' stubbornness, the jury convicted him.

Athenian law permitted accusers as well as defendants to suggest alternative penalties. When the accusers asked for death, Socrates responded with astonishing arrogance. He suggested instead that Athens pay him a reward for making the city a better place. Outraged by Socrates' behavior, the jury chose death by an even wider margin. Socrates accepted their verdict calmly.

While Socrates sat in prison waiting for his execution, a friend named Crito offered to help him escape. Socrates refused to flee. He told Crito that only a man who did not respect the law would break it, and that such a man would indeed be a corrupting influence on the young. Socrates pointed out that he had lived his life as an obedient Athenian citizen and would certainly not break the law now. Human laws may be imperfect, he admitted, but they permit a society to function. Private individuals should never disregard them. To the end he remained a loyal citizen.

On his final day, with his closest friends around him, Socrates drank a cup of poison and died bravely. Plato

■ **Athenian Coin**
This Athenian silver coin dating from the fifth century B.C.E. shows an owl, the sacred bird of the goddess Athena. Both the owl and the goddess symbolized wisdom.

Many sculptors made portraits of Socrates in the centuries after his death. Though Socrates was viewed as a hero who died for his beliefs, this sculptor did nothing to glamorize him in this portrait. Socrates was famous for the beauty of his thoughts—and the ugliness of his face.

wrote, "This is the way our dear friend perished. It is fair to say that he was the bravest, the wisest, and the most honorable man of all those we have ever known."[6]

Historians and philosophers have discussed Socrates' case since Plato's time. Were the accusations fair? What precisely was his crime? In the matter of corrupting Athens's youth, there is no doubt that at least two of his most fervent young followers, Alcibiades and Critias, had earned terrible reputations. Alcibiades had betrayed his city in the Peloponnesian War. Critias was one of the most violent of the Thirty Tyrants. Many Athenians suspected Socrates of influencing them, even though these men represented everything he opposed.

Charges of impiety were harder to substantiate, but Athenians took them seriously. His fellow citizens knew that Socrates always participated in Athenian religious life. But during his defense Socrates admitted that his views were not exactly the same as those of his prosecutors. His claim to have a divine *daimon* or "sign" who sat on his shoulder and gave him advice was eccentric though not actually sacrilegious. Many Athenians thought this daimon was a foreign god, and not Socrates' metaphor for his own mental processes.

The reasons for Socrates' prosecution lie much deeper than the official charges. His trial and execution emerged from an anti-intellectual backlash bred in the frustrations of Athens's defeat in the Peloponnesian War and in the Thirty Tyrants' rule. Even though Athenians had restored democracy, deep-seated resentments sealed Socrates' fate. In many societies throughout history, especially democratic ones like that of Athens that grant freedom to explore new ideas, people who fear change and creativity often strike out at artists, intellectuals, and innovators in times of stress.

Athenians resented Socrates because he challenged them to think. He wanted them to live better lives, and they killed him. ■

Questions of Justice

1. What threat did Socrates' prosecutors imagine he presented to the community? Do you think they were right?
2. Under what circumstances can an individual benefit society by breaking its laws? Under what circumstances can an individual harm society by obeying its laws?

Taking It Further

Brickhouse, Thomas C., and Nicholas D. Smith. *Socrates on Trial*. 1989. A thorough analysis of Socrates' trial.

Stokes, Michael. *Plato: Apology, with Introduction, Translation, and Commentary*. 1997. The best translation, with important commentary.

attention. They also valued the human capacity to represent in art the ideals of beauty, harmony, and proportion found in nature. Classical Greek men celebrated their ability to make rational judgments about what was beautiful and pleasing to the eye—and to create art that embodied those judgments.

To create a statue that was an image of physical perfection, sculptors copied the best features of several human models while ignoring their flaws. They strove to depict the muscles, movement, and balance of the human figure in a way that was both lifelike in its imitation of nature and yet idealized in the harmony and symmetry of the torso and limbs. The balance between realism and idealism has continually inspired artists in the Western tradition.

Greek painters explored movement of the human body as well as colors and the optical illusion of depth. The figures that they depicted on vases and on walls became increasingly lively and realistic as the Classical Age unfolded. Artists portrayed every sort of activity from religious worship to erotic fun, but regardless of the subject, they shared a similar goal: to create a lifelike depiction of the human figure.

In a similar effort to capture ideals of perfection, Greek architects designed their buildings, especially temples, to be symmetrical and proportional. They used mathematical ratios that they observed in nature to shape their designs. The buildings they created show a grace, balance, and harmony that have inspired architects for more than two millennia.

The temple of Athena in Athens called the Parthenon or "House of the Virgin Goddess," stood as the greatest triumph of classical Greek architecture (see illustration on page 100). Built on the Acropolis of Athens, the temple symbolized Athens's imperial glory. Using funds appropriated from the Delian League, Athenians dedicated the huge temple to their divine protector between 447 and 432 B.C.E. The architects Ictinus and Callicrates achieved a superb example of structural harmony, perfectly balancing all the building's elements according to mathematical proportions copied from nature. For the Parthenon's sacred inner room, Phidias, a friend of Pericles, sculpted a statue of Athena made of gold and ivory over a wooden core and decorated it with gems and other precious metals. The temple also displayed an elaborate series of carved and brightly painted marble panels depicting the mythology of Athena. The Parthenon remained nearly intact until 1687 C.E., when powder kegs stored inside exploded, causing irreparable damage.

CONCLUSION
Classical Foundations of the West

During the Classical Age, which ended about 336 B.C.E, several of the elements of what would later be considered the cultural inheritance of the West came into being. These ancient peoples did not have a conception of "the West" as a cultural realm. What they did is to create things that have had a lasting influence. The legacy of the Hebrews has been their religious and ethical teachings, encapsulated in the Hebrew Bible. The Persians supplied a model for an efficient empire that was inherited by later conquerors, most notably Alexander the Great and his followers. They also established a model for other imperial systems of the future, including the Roman Empire. By permitting forms of worship other than the official Zoroastrianism, the Persians limited dissent, and by allowing exiled peoples, such as the Hebrews, to return to their homes, they knitted together an efficient multiethnic, multireligious empire. Throughout that empire the older Middle Eastern traditions of science, mathematics, astronomy, and navigation (discussed in Chapter 2) passed on to the Greeks and then into the western Mediterranean, North African, and eventually Europe. Zoroastrian religious ideas of heaven and hell and the struggle between God and the Devil also found their way into other western religions, most notably Christianity.

The stumbling blocks for Persian imperial expansion to the West were the hoplite armies and fleets of the Greeks. When the Persians arrived on the shores of Greece, the institutions of the poleis were well established. However, the Greek victory strengthened those institutions and facilitated the further development of Athenian democracy. Under the political and cultural leadership of Athens, Greek civilization thrived, producing the most lasting artistic and philosophical contributions from the ancient world to the history of the West.

The Classical Age demonstrated that well-trained, highly disciplined Greek hoplite troops were more than a match for the Persian army. In the next chapter, we will see how the kingdom of Macedonia to the north of Greece also learned this important lesson. After conquering Greece, the Macedonians, led by Alexander the Great, overwhelmed the entire Persian Empire. Alexander's conquests inaugurated a new era in history, the Hellenistic Age, in which classical Greek civilization spread over an enormous region.

Suggestions for Further Reading

For a comprehensive list of suggested readings, please go to www.ablongman.com/levack/chapter3

Boardman, John. *Persia and the West: An Archaeological Investigation of the Genesis of Achaemenid Art.* 2000. A brilliantly illustrated study that stresses intercultural influences in every aspect of Persian art.

Boyce, Mary. *A History of Zoroastrianism.* Vol. 2, 1975. This authoritative examination provides a masterful overview of the religion of the Persian Empire.

Burkert, Walter. *The Orientalizing Revolution: Near Eastern Influence on Greek Culture in the Early Archaic Age,* trans. Margaret Pinder and Walter Burkert. 1993. Explains how the Semitic East influenced the development of Greek society in the Archaic Age.

Cohn, Norman. *Cosmos, Chaos, and the World to Come: The Ancient Roots of Apocalyptic Faith.* 1993. Expert critical analysis of apocalyptic religions in the West, including Zoroastrianism, ancient Judaism, Christianity, and other faiths.

Finkelstein, Israel, and Neil Asher Silberman. *The Bible Unearthed: Archaeology's New Vision of Ancient Israel and the Origin of the Sacred Texts.* 2001. An important archaeological interpretation that challenges the narrative of the Hebrew Bible and offers a reconsideration of biblical history.

Gottwald, Norman K. *The Hebrew Bible: A Socio-Literary Introduction.* 1985. Combines a close reading of the Hebrew Bible with the latest archaeological and historical evidence.

Just, Roger. *Women in Athenian Law and Life.* 1989. Provides an overview of the social context of women in Athens.

Kuhrt, Amélie. *The Ancient Near East, ca. 3000–330 B.C.* Vol. 2. 1995. This rich and comprehensive bibliography is a remarkably concise and readable account of Persian history with excellent discussion of ancient textual evidence. Many important passages appear in fluent translation.

Lindberg, David C. *The Beginnings of Western Science: The European Scientific Tradition in Philosophical, Religious, and Institutional Context, 600 B.C. to A.D. 1450.* 1992. This highly readable study provides an exciting survey of the main developments in western science.

Markoe, Glenn. *Phoenicians.* 2000. The best and most up-to-date treatment of Phoenician society by a noted expert.

Murray, Oswyn. *Early Greece.* 1983. A brilliant study of all aspects of the emergence of Greek society between the Dark Age and the end of the Persian Wars.

Osborne, Robin. *Greece in the Making, 1200–479 B.C.* 1996. An excellent narrative of the development of Greek society with special regard to the archaeological evidence.

Stewart, Andrew. *Art, Desire, and the Body in Ancient Greece.* 1997. A provocative study that examines Greek attitudes toward sexuality and art.

Walker, Christopher, ed. *Astronomy Before the Telescope.* 1996. A fascinating collection of essays about astronomy in the premodern period, which makes clear our enormous debt to the Babylonians.

Wieshöfer, Josef. *Ancient Persia from 550 B.C. to A.D. 650,* trans. Azizeh Azodi. 1996. A fresh and comprehensive overview of Persian cultural, social, and political history that relies on Persian evidence more heavily than biased Greek and Roman sources.

Notes

1. Based on Herodotus, *History,* vol. 1, trans. Rex Warner (2000), pp. 125–126.
2. James B. Pritchard, *Ancient Near Eastern Texts Relating to the Old Testament.* 3rd edition with supplement (1969) pp. 315–316.
3. Demosthenes, *Orations,* 59.122.
4. From Euripides, *The Trojan Women.* Translated by Peter Levi in *The Oxford History of the Classical World,* eds. John Boardman, Jasper Griffith, and Oswyn Murray (1986), p. 169.
5. Andrew Stewart, *Art, Desire, and the Body in Ancient Greece* (Cambridge: Cambridge University Press, 1997), p. 19.
6. Plato, *Phaedo,* l. 118.

The Hellenistic Age, 336–31 B.C.E.

ONE EVENING AFTER DINNER IN 193 B.C.E., AT THE PALACE OF A GREEK KING in Asia Minor, two battle-hardened generals from different lands debated the identity of the greatest military commander of all time. Both generals came from aristocratic backgrounds. One had grown up in Rome, Italy; the other in Carthage, an imperial city on the coast of North Africa. They conversed in Greek, the language of diplomacy and culture that was used throughout the Mediterranean and the Middle East. The Carthaginian was Hannibal, a military genius who had led the armies of Carthage in a savage war against Rome between 218 and 201 B.C.E., and who now lived in exile. The Roman, who was visiting Asia Minor as part of a diplomatic mission, was Publius Cornelius Scipio Africanus. This equally brilliant general had defeated Hannibal and ended the bloodiest war in Rome's history. When Scipio asked Hannibal who he thought was the world's greatest general, Hannibal named the legendary Macedonian conqueror Alexander the Great. With a smile Scipio then asked his former foe, "What if *you* had defeated *me?*" "In that case," replied the Carthaginian in a flattering tone, "I would be the greatest general of them all."

This anecdote illuminates some fundamental elements of a period that historians call the Hellenistic Age. First, it reveals a cosmopolitan, Greek-based culture in which a Carthaginian general, whose native tongue was a Semitic language, and a Latin-speaking Roman aristocrat could easily communicate. Second, these two warriors shared knowledge of the history of Mediterranean lands, politics, and diplomatic etiquette. Most of all, both admired Alexander the Great, who had made their cosmopolitan world possible. Scipio, Hannibal, and doubtless their host sought to imitate the Macedonian king. Alexander and the

Celt and Wife: This dramatic statue epitomizes the mixing of cultures in the Hellenistic Age. The statue is a Roman copy in marble of a bronze original made at Pergamum in Asia Minor by a Greek sculptor. The artist tells the tragic story of a defeated Celt. Rather than be captured alive, he has just killed his wife and is at the precise moment of taking his own life. In typically Hellenistic style, the artist combines anatomical accuracy with psychological agony.

civilization he had inaugurated had set the standard for success in the minds of men from very different cultural backgrounds.

The Hellenistic period began when Alexander (r. 336–323 B.C.E.) conquered the Persian Empire, extending Greek culture as far east as Afghanistan and India. Greeks called themselves *Hellenes,* and thus historians use the terms *Hellenism* and *Hellenistic* to describe the complex cosmopolitan civilization that developed in the wake of Alexander's conquests. This civilization offered a rich variety of goods, technologies, and ideas to anyone who knew or was willing to learn Greek. Just as people throughout the world today study English because it is the primary language used in high technology, global business, and international politics, Greek became the common tongue used in trade, politics, and intellectual life.

Political borders did not limit Hellenistic civilization. After Alexander died, the empire he had built fragmented into smaller kingdoms that often fought one another. Despite the instability and warfare, however, Hellenistic culture thrived within Alexander's successor kingdoms. It also spread far beyond the lands conquered by Alexander, mainly in the western Mediterranean, where it had a profound effect on the civilizations of North Africa, Europe, and especially Rome. Romans, Jews, Persians, Celts, Carthaginians, and other peoples all absorbed elements of Greek culture—its philosophy, religion, literature, and art. Hellenism gave a common language of science and learning to diverse peoples speaking different languages and worshiping different gods. Hellenism thus gave a cultural unity to a vast area stretching from Europe in the west to Afghanistan in the east. Large portions of this cultural realm ultimately became what historians call the West.

The spread of Hellenistic culture over this vast area involved a series of cultural exchanges. Greek culture offered great prestige and possessed a powerful intellectual appeal to non-Greek peoples, but it also posed a threat to their local, traditional identities. Instead of simply accepting Greek culture, these non-Greek peoples engaged in a process of cultural adaptation and synthesis. In this way Hellenism, which throughout this period remained open to outside influences, absorbed foreign scientific knowledge, religious ideas, and many other elements of culture. These elements then entered the mainstream of Hellenistic culture and were transmitted to the greater Hellenistic world. Some of the basic components of Western civilization originated in these cultural encounters between Greek and non-Greek peoples. These include the seven-day week, beliefs in Hell and Judgment Day, the study of astrology and astronomy, and technologies of metallurgy, agriculture, and navigation.

The Hellenistic era and the age of independent Hellenistic kingdoms came to a close in 31 B.C.E., when the Roman politician and military commander Octavian (later known as Augustus) won control of the Mediterranean world, the Middle East, Egypt, and parts of Europe. This political development did not, however, put an end to the influence of Hellenistic culture. By forging a new, more resilient civilization in which Greeks, Romans, and many other peoples intermingled in peace, the Romans created their own version of Hellenism and introduced it to western Europe.

To understand the Hellenistic Age, this chapter will explore four questions: (1) How did Alexander the Great create an empire in which Greek civilization flourished in the midst of many diverse cultures? (2) What were the distinguishing features of Hellenistic society and culture, and what was the result of encounters between Greeks and non-Greeks? (3) How did the Roman Republic come to dominate the Mediterranean world during the Hellenistic Age, and how did Roman rule over the Hellenistic East affect Rome's development? (4) What political and social changes brought the Roman Republic to an end?

The Warlike Kingdom of Macedon

The Hellenistic Age had its roots in Macedon, a kingdom to the north of Greece that was rich in timber, grain, horses, and fighting men. Most Macedonians lived in scattered villages and made a living by engaging in small-scale farming, raiding their neighbors, and trading over short distances. Relentless warfare against wild Thracian and Illyrian tribesmen to the north and west kept Macedonians constantly ready for battle.

Macedonians spoke a dialect of Greek, but their customs and political organization differed from those of the urbanized Greek communities that lay to their south. Unlike democratic Athens, Macedon had a hereditary monarchy. Cutthroat struggles for ascendancy in the royal family trained Macedonian kings to select the best moment to deliver a lethal blow to any enemy. Maintaining centralized political control over their territory proved a constant problem for Macedon's kings because independent-minded nobles resented their rule. Only the army of free citizens could legitimize a king's reign. In return for their support, the soldiers demanded the spoils of war. As a result, Macedonian kings had to wage war continuously to obtain that wealth and keep their precarious position on the throne.

UNITY AND EXPANSION UNDER KING PHILIP

Throughout most of the classical period (ca. 700–335 B.C.E.), these fierce Macedonian highlanders knew little of city life and seemed like savages to sophisticated Greeks. When cities started to appear in Macedon in the fifth cen-

■ **Map 4.1   Before Alexander: Major Cultural Areas, ca. 350 B.C.E.**

During the Hellenistic Age, Greek culture influenced many cultures. This map shows the realms of the Persians, Celts, Romans, Carthaginians, and Phoenicians, whose societies would participate in the Hellenistic Age.

tury B.C.E., Macedonian aristocrats began to emulate the culture of classical Greece. The members of the royal family, for example, claimed the Greek hero Hercules as their ancestor. This move won them the right to compete in the Olympic Games, which were open only to Greeks. Macedonian aristocrats also offered rich stipends to Greek playwrights and scholars to lure them to their capital city of Pella.

In the political realm, however, Macedon shrewdly avoided Greek affairs. During the Persian Wars (490 B.C.E. and 480–479 B.C.E.), Macedonian kings pursued a cautious and profitable policy of friendship with the Persian invaders. During the convulsions of the Peloponnesian War (431–404 B.C.E.) and its turbulent aftermath, Macedon refrained from exploiting Athens, Sparta, and the other Greek

cities as they bled to exhaustion. The lack of Greek entanglements, however, could not ease the tensions between kings and nobles. In 399 B.C.E., Macedon slipped into a forty-year period of anarchy. Just as Macedon was on the verge of disintegration, King Philip II (382–336 B.C.E.) stepped forward and transformed the Macedonian kingdom.

A ruthless opportunist with a gift for military organization, Philip consolidated his power by eliminating his rivals, killing many of them in battle. He unified the unruly nobles who controlled different regions of Macedon by demonstrating the advantages of cooperation under his leadership. As Philip led the nobles to victory after victory over hostile frontier tribes and shared his plunder with them and with the common soldiers, the Macedonians embraced his leadership (see Map 4.1).

Philip created a new army in which the nobles had a special role as cavalry armed with heavy lances. Called the Companions, they formed elite regiments bound to their king by oaths of loyalty. Philip reorganized the infantry, or foot soldiers, into military units called phalanxes. Armed with lances nearly fourteen feet long, the infantry held off the enemy while the cavalry galloped in to strike a fatal blow. This new strategy gave Philip's armies an enormous tactical advantage over traditional hoplite formations. After seizing the gold and silver mines of the north Aegean coast of Greece, Philip had ample funds to hire additional armies of mercenaries to augment his Macedonian troops.

With Macedon firmly under his control, its borders secure and his army eager for loot, Philip stood poised to strike at Greece. In 349 B.C.E. he seized several cities in northern and central Greece, inaugurating a decade of diplomacy, bribery, and threats as he maneuvered for power over the rest of the Greek *poleis.*

Recognizing that Philip represented a threat to Greek liberty, the brilliant Athenian orator Demosthenes organized resistance among the city-states. In 340 B.C.E., when Philip attempted to seize the Bosporus, the link to Athens's vital Black Sea trade routes, the *poleis* took action. Demosthenes delivered a series of blistering speeches against Philip known as "the Philippics" and assembled an alliance of cities. In 338 B.C.E., however, Philip crushed the allied armies at the battle of Chaeronea in central Greece. In this confrontation Philip's 18-year-old son Alexander led the Companions in a charge that won the day for the Macedonians.

Philip imposed Macedonian rule over Greece by establishing a coalition of Greek cities called the League of Corinth, of which he was the leader. He also established Macedonian garrisons at strategic sites and forbade Greek cities to change their form of government without his approval. For the Greek *poleis,* the age of autonomy had passed forever.

Philip next cast his eyes on the Persian Empire. In 337 B.C.E. he cloaked himself in the mantle of Greek culture and announced that he would lead his armies and the forces of Greece against the empire to the east. His reason? To avenge Persia's invasion of Greece in the previous century. Philip's shrewd linking of classical Greek civilization with Macedonian force now became a rallying cry for imperialist expansion under Philip's direction. But as Philip laid plans for his assault on Persia 336 B.C.E. an assassin murdered him. Philip's son Alexander replaced him and continued his plans to invade the east.

THE CONQUESTS OF ALEXANDER

A man of immense personal charisma and political craftiness, Alexander won the support of his soldiers by demonstrating fearlessness in combat and displaying military ge-

■ **The Macedonian Phalanx**

This reconstruction drawing shows the Macedonian phalanx advancing into battle. The soldiers hold long spears called sarissas. Men in the first rank level their sarissas at the enemy. The soldiers behind them will lower their spears in turn as they advance. Cavalry regiments of Companions wait for an opportunity to attack.

nius on the battlefield. He combined a predatory instinct for conquest and glory with utter ruthlessness in the pursuit of power. These traits proved to be the key to his success. By the time of his death, at the age of just 33, Alexander had won military victories as far east as India, creating a vast empire. Alexander's successes made him a legend during his lifetime, and millions of his subjects worshiped him as a god. Historians consider him a pivotal figure in the history of Western civilization because his conquests led to the dissemination of Hellenistic culture in lands that were to become important components of the West.

After brutally consolidating power in Macedonia and Greece following his father's death, Alexander launched an invasion of Persia. With only about 40,000 infantry and 5,000 cavalry, Alexander crossed the Hellespont—the narrow strait dividing Europe from Asia where the Black Sea meets the Aegean Sea—and marched into Persian territory in 334 B.C.E.. Darius III, the Great King of Persia who had ascended the throne two years earlier, proved no match for Alexander's tactical brilliance. The young Macedonian king won his first great victory in battle over Persian forces at the Granicus River, giving him control over Asia Minor with its rich Greek coastal cities and fleets. A few weeks later he marched into Syria, where he broke the main Persian army near the town of Issus. Just as he had done at the battle of the Granicus River, Alexander led the Macedonian cavalry's victorious charge into the teeth of the enemy. From this victory Alexander gained control of the entire eastern coast of the Mediterranean Sea and the Persian naval bases located there.

When the maritime city of Tyre succumbed to Alexander's siege in 332 B.C.E., Darius panicked and offered the young Macedonian his daughter and all of his empire west of the Euphrates River in return for peace. Alexander rejected the offer and marched into Egypt, where the inhabitants welcomed him as a liberator from their Persian masters. From Egypt he advanced into Mesopotamia, where he crushed Darius once again on the battlefield at Gaugamela near the Tigris River.

When Alexander entered Babylon in triumph he once again received an enthusiastic welcome as a liberator. From Babylon his forces ventured southeast to Persepolis, the Persian capital, which Alexander captured in January 330 B.C.E. He plundered the city and burned it to the ground. The enormous wealth he acquired from Persepolis paid for all of his military activities for the next dozen years and invigorated the entire Macedonian economy. Darius escaped the destruction of his capital but was soon murdered by his own nobles. The once-powerful Persian Empire lay in ruins.

Alexander had fulfilled his father's pledge to gain vengeance against Persia, but he had no intention of slowing down his march of conquest (see Map 4.2). He pushed past the tribesmen of the harsh Afghan mountain ranges to

CHRONOLOGY

Alexander the Great and the Greek East

359–336 B.C.E.	Philip II rules Macedon
338 B.C.E.	Philip II conquers Greece (Battle of Chaeronea)
336–323 B.C.E.	Alexander the Great reigns
334 B.C.E.	Battle of Granicus River fought
333 B.C.E.	Battle of Issus fought
331 B.C.E.	Battle of Gaugamela fought; Alexander founds Alexandria in Egypt
330 B.C.E.	Alexander destroys Persepolis, capital of Persia
327 B.C.E.	Alexander reaches India
323 B.C.E.	Alexander dies at Babylon
323–CA. 300 B.C.E.	Successors to Alexander establish kingdoms

penetrate Central Asia. Then in 327 B.C.E. he entered the territory that is modern Pakistan through the Khyber Pass. There he defeated the Indian king, but then the tide of fortune slowly turned against him. He planned to cross the Indus River and advance into India, but his exhausted armies refused to follow. He had little choice but to begin a long and arduous return westward. Most of his soldiers died on the way, and Alexander himself suffered nearly fatal wounds. While recuperating at Babylon in 323 B.C.E., where he had begun to plan further conquests, Alexander succumbed to fever after a drinking bout. He had never lost a battle.

In strategic locations through the lands he had conquered, Alexander established cities as garrisons for his troops. More than a dozen of these cities received the name Alexandria in his honor. Thousands of Greeks migrated east to settle in the new cities to take advantage of the expanded economic opportunities for trade and farming. These Greek settlers became the cultural and political elite of the new cities.

Governing an empire of this size proved to be a difficult challenge. It was much easier for Alexander to conquer an enormous empire than to rule it. The Macedonian kingdom that he led was geared to seizing land and plundering cities. It was another task entirely to create the infrastructure and discipline necessary for ruling an immense territory that had little linguistic or cultural unity. Alexander understood that he was no longer king of just Macedon. He recognized that the only model of rule suitable to such a diverse empire was that devised by his Persian predecessors: a Great King presiding over a hierarchy of nobles who governed Persian territory, and subject kings who ruled non-Persian regions.

Necessity thus forced Alexander to bring his Macedonian troops and his new Persian subjects together in an uneasy balance. To that end, Alexander persuaded his army to proclaim him "King of Asia"—that is, the new Great King. With his Companions he simply took over the government of the former Persian Empire from the top. He included a handful of loyal Persians in his administration by making them regional governors or satraps, while offering other Persians minor roles in his regime.

These practical steps promised to bring order to the empire. By adopting the elaborate Persian role of the Great King, Alexander demonstrated to his foreign subjects that his regime stood for security and continuity of orderly rule. His proud Macedonian soldiers, however, ultimately stymied his efforts. They refused to grovel before him as Persian royal ceremony dictated. And though Alexander may well have thought of himself as a god, they refused to worship him while he lived. Instead, they saw Alexander's recruitment of 30,000 Persian troops into their army as a threat to the traditional relationship between Macedonian soldiers and their king. They also resented the marriages with the daughters of Persian noblemen that Alexander forced upon them in order to unite Macedonians and Persians—although no Persian nobles received Greek wives. The Macedonian troops expected to keep all the spoils of victory for themselves. They wanted to be conquerors, not partners in a new government. They failed to understand that men of other cultures within the new empire might be equally loyal to Alexander and thus deserve a share of power and public honor. Alexander's charismatic personality held his conquests together, but his death destroyed any dreams of cooperation between Persians and Greeks.

■ **Map 4.2   Macedon and the Conquests of Alexander the Great**

Alexander led troops from his Macedonian homeland as far east as the Indus Valley. He defeated the Persian Empire and incorporated it into his kingdom. This map shows the route of Alexander's march of conquest and the sites of his most important victories.

SUCCESSOR KINGDOMS: DISTRIBUTING THE SPOILS

Alexander left no adult heir, and the Macedonian nobles who served as his generals fought viciously among themselves for control of his conquered territory. Eventually these generals created a number of kingdoms out of lands Alexander had acquired (see Map 4.3). One general, Ptolemy, established the Ptolemaic dynasty in Egypt, which would last until 30 B.C.E. Antigonus "the One-Eyed" gained control of the Macedonian homeland and established the Antigonid dynasty, which survived until Rome defeated it in 167 B.C.E. The largest portion of Alexander's conquests, comprising the bulk of the old Persian Empire, fell to his general Seleucus. But in the mid-third century B.C.E., the Parthians, a people from northeastern Persia, shook off Seleucid rule and created a vigorous state. By 150 B.C.E. the Seleucids ruled only Syria.

Smaller kingdoms were also carved out of the areas Alexander had conquered. Bactria (in northern Afghanistan) came under the rule of a Greek-speaking government that would control it well into the second century B.C.E. In 303 B.C.E. the Indian king Chandragupta Maurya conquered the easternmost Indian territories and incorporated them into his own non-Greek kingdom in India. Another lesser successor kingdom emerged in Asia Minor. Centered on the city of Pergamum, a buffer between the Seleucid and Antigonid kingdoms, was ruled by the Attalid dynasty.

Following the example of Macedon itself, the Hellenistic successor states all acquired a monarchical form of government, in which a king ruled the with the support of the army and highly regimented bureaucracies. The members of the administrative hierarchy were all Greeks and Macedonians; indigenous people were not recruited into the ruling elite. Greek was the language of rule in the successor kingdoms. The talented queen Cleopatra (69–30 B.C.E.), who was the last descendant of Ptolemy to rule in Egypt, was the first of her line ever to speak Egyptian. Greek-speaking monarchs were nonetheless aware that they needed to cultivate the goodwill of their non-Greek-speaking subjects. As one monarch asked in a Hellenistic political dialogue, "How can I accommodate myself to all the different races in my kingdom?" A subject answered: "By adopting the appropriate attitude to each, making justice one's guide."

The king towered over Hellenistic society, holding authority over all his subjects and bearing ultimate responsibility for their welfare. Following the example of Alexander, Hellenistic monarchs earned legitimacy by leading their troops into wars of conquest. A king embodied the entire community that he ruled. He was at once the ruler, father, protector, savior, source of law, and god of all his subjects. His garb reinforced his elevated position—kings arrayed themselves in battle gear with a helmet or Macedonian sombrero, crowns, purple robes, scepters, and special seal

■ **Ptolemaic King of Egypt**

This golden ring depicts Ptolemy VI, who ruled Egypt from 176 to 145 B.C.E. Although he and his court spoke only Greek, he is depicted as a pharaoh wearing a double crown, the age-old symbol of Egyptian monarchy. The image on the ring demonstrated the integration of old and new political symbols in Egypt during the Hellenistic Age.

rings. Monarchs earned the loyalty of their subjects and glorified their own rule by establishing cities, constructing public buildings, and rewarding their inner circle.

Ptolemy II, who ruled in Egypt from 283 to 246 B.C.E., exemplifies these notions of Hellenistic kingship. Ptolemy expanded his dominions by conquering parts of Asia Minor and Syria from rival monarchs. He also expanded the bureaucracy, refined the taxation system, and funded many new military settlements. With his support, merchants established new trading posts on the Red Sea, where they engaged in commerce with merchants from India and other eastern lands. Ptolemy patronized the arts and sciences by building impressive research institutes and libraries. He transformed Egypt's capital city of Alexandria, founded by Alexander in Egypt in 331 B.C.E., into the leading center of Greek culture and learning in the Hellenistic world. To reinforce his authority and majesty, he encouraged his subjects to worship him as a god.

■ **Map 4.3 After Alexander: Major Successor Kingdoms, ca. 300 B.C.E.**
After Alexander's death, his generals quarreled and broke the empire into several smaller kingdoms.

This worship of Hellenistic monarchs drew from indigenous traditions throughout the Middle East, but in its Hellenistic form it had a political rather than a spiritual significance. People worshipped their kings as a spontaneous expression of gratitude for the protection and the peace that good government made possible. For example, when the Antigonid king Demetrius "the Besieger" captured Athens in 308 B.C.E., the pragmatic Athenians sang a song in honor of their new master: "The other gods either do not exist or are far off, either they do not hear, or they do not care; but you are here and we can see you, not in wood and stone but in living truth".[1] Deification legitimized a king's right to rule. In turn the ruler cult, in which monarchs were worshiped as gods, channeled all-important loyalty directly to the king.

In addition to the loyalty of their subjects, Hellenistic kings also depended on permanent professional armies to wage the military campaigns so essential to maintaining their authority and to defending their territories. Hellenistic kings fought wars over much larger territories than those that had led to squabbles among Greek city-states in previous centuries. The conquest of such territories required an increase in the size of field armies. The Athenian hoplites had numbered about 10,000 in the fifth century B.C.E., but in the Hellenistic Age kings routinely mustered armies of between 60,000 and 80,000 men. Many soldiers came from military colonies established by the kings. In return for land, the men of these Greek-speaking colonies were obliged to serve generation after generation in the king's army and to police the native, non-Greek populations.

Hellenistic Society and Culture

Chronic warfare among Hellenistic monarchs made political unity among the Hellenistic kingdoms impossible. Nevertheless, the social institutions and cultural orientation of Greek-speaking people in all these kingdoms gave them a unity that their monarchs could achieve.

CITIES: THE HEART OF HELLENISTIC LIFE

Alexander and his successors seized dozens of Greek city-states scattered across the eastern Mediterranean and founded dozens of new glittering urban communities in all the territories they conquered. Hellenistic cities were much more than garrisons put in place to enforce the conquerors' power. They continued traditions of learning, art, and architecture, as well as traditions of citizen participation in public life that had flourished in the classical *poleis*. Most important, people in cities throughout the Hellenistic world spoke a standard version of Greek called koine° that gave them a sense of common identity. Greek city life defined Hellenistic civilization.

On the surface, many of the institutions of the classical *poleis* remained the same: magistrates, councils, and popular assemblies ran the cities' affairs, and some form of democracy remained the ideal in local government. Yet beneath the surface, the *poleis* had undergone radical changes. Because kings wielded absolute power, once-independent cities such as Athens and Corinth lost their freedom to make peace or wage war. They now served as the bureaucratic centers that administered their rulers' huge kingdoms.

Hellenistic kings preferred to maintain the illusion of the cities' independence and rarely intervened in urban affairs, permitting considerable freedom in local government. Nonetheless, Hellenistic methods and those of classical Greece differed in one important way. Democracies had developed in Greece during the Archaic and Classical Ages to protect the interests of the poor as well as the rich. Now, in the Hellenistic Age, the wealthy dominated society and government while the condition of the poor deteriorated. Rich men appointed by the king controlled all the courts, held all the magistracies, and represented all the cities at the court of the kings, who in return showered these civic leaders with honors. Through land grants, tax immunities, and other favors, the monarchs developed networks of personal ties that bound civic leaders to them. In return, these urban elites did more than serve their king. They spent their vast fortunes on behalf of their cities, building magnificent temples, gymnasiums, and other structures for their fellow citizens.

Hellenistic kings and aristocrats spent fortunes turning their cities into showcases of art and design. Distinctive styles of building and ornamentation quickly spread from the east to Italy, Carthage, and Rome. Laying out streets on a grid plan became standard in the Mediterranean world, lending a sense of order to urban space. Stone theaters for plays and spectacles, council halls, and roofed colonnades called *stoas* sprang up everywhere, as did baths with heated pools and gymnasium complexes with sports facilities and classrooms.

In all the major Greek cities of the Hellenistic world, architects built on a monumental scale, integrating sculpture with surrounding buildings and the natural landscape. Temple precincts reveal designers' delight in sweeping

■ Greek Athletics and Culture

Athletic competition, such as wrestling, was a significant part of Greek culture. Every self-respecting Greek city had a gymnasium. Great cities like Pergamum might have half a dozen. More than just sports centers, gymnasiums served as centers of education and social life for Greek-speaking communities. In these clusters of colonnaded porticoes, wealthy young men of the city learned the basics of Greek literature, rhetoric, science, and music from teachers paid with public funds. For centuries gymnasiums produced leaders and carriers of Hellenistic culture. Here lies the paradox of Hellenism: At the same time that gymnasiums created a shared culture and sense of unity over an enormous geographical extent, they also established a sense of exclusivity and distance from people who did not speak Greek.

vistas across carefully planned terraces and grand stairways. Redefined by these features, the natural setting served as a backdrop for the temple and its processions and rituals.

The freestanding sculpture that decorated public spaces in Hellenistic cities took classical Greek forms in new directions. Turning away from representations of ideal perfection, Hellenistic artists delighted in exploring the movement of the human body and varieties of facial expression. Their subjects ranged from alluring love goddesses to drunks and haggard old boxers. Artists enjoyed portraying the play of fabrics across the human body to accentuate the contours of male and female flesh. Sometimes painted in bright colors, these statues explored human frailty and homeliness as often as they celebrated beauty and lofty emotions.

As we saw in Chapter 3, citizenship in the city-states of classical Greece was a carefully limited commodity that gave people a sense of identity, guaranteed desirable rights and privileges, and demanded certain responsibilities. The territories controlled by any city-state were relatively small, yet even Athens at the height of its empire never considered giving Athenian citizenship to all of the people it ruled outside Attica. In contrast, during the Hellenistic Age, large kingdoms containing many cities were the basic political unit. People were subjects of a king and citizens of their particular cities. To be sure, some philosophers played with the idea of a universal citizenship of all humankind, but there was no notion of a citizenship shared by all the people in one kingdom. Citizenship lost its political force because individual cities had lost their political autonomy. In a sharp break with earlier practice, important individuals sometimes gained the honor of citizenship in more than one city, something that Greeks in the Classical Age would have found inconceivable.

Hellenistic cities contained more diverse populations than had classical *poleis*. Alexandria, in Egypt, the largest and most cosmopolitan of Greek cities, boasted large communities of Macedonians, Greeks, Jews, Syrians, and Egyptians. Although these groups lived in different areas of town and often fought violently with one another, they all participated to varying degrees in the Hellenistic culture of the city. For example, Alexandrian Jews who spoke Greek translated the Hebrew Bible into Greek, a version called the Septuagint°, so that they could more easily read and understand it.

In some older cities such as Babylon and Jerusalem, deep-seated cultural and religious traditions prevented the complete penetration of Greek civilization. Many traditional customs and forms of religious worship, such as the Babylonian worship of the great god Marduk, continued untouched by the Greek way of life. Even the Greek language found limited use in local government. In Mesopotamian cities, for example, local administrators continued to use Aramaic, the local language. The leading families of these cities learned Greek, however, so they could communicate with the members of the king's government and gain political influence.

NEW OPPORTUNITIES FOR WOMEN

One measure of the status of women in a society is the amount of female infanticide permitted. Greek parents in the Classical Age routinely abandoned unwanted female babies, leaving them to die. In Hellenistic families, however, particularly those of the Ptolemaic nobility, baby girls were raised in greater numbers than before. Greek women in Egypt, as well as many other Hellenized lands, enjoyed full citizenship and held religious offices. Many owned land and property, paying taxes as men did, but they could enter into business contracts only of minimal value.

Women in the upper levels of Hellenistic society had the opportunity to wield considerably more power than was conceivable for aristocratic women in the classical Greek period. The wives of Hellenistic kings emerged as models of the new, more powerful Hellenistic woman. Inscriptions engraved in stone praise Hellenistic queens for demonstrating such traditional female virtues as piety and for producing sons. As public benefactors, these women built sanctuaries and public works, sponsored charioteers at the Olympic games, and provided dowries for poor brides. Queens sometimes exerted real authority, supporting and commanding armies. For example, in Egypt the Ptolemaic queen Arsinoë II (r. 276–270 B.C.E.), sister and wife of Ptolemy II of Egypt, directed the armies and navies of the Ptolemaic kingdom in their conquest of Phoenicia and much of the coast of Asia Minor. Egyptian sources refer to her as Pharaoh, a royal title usually reserved for men. The reverence paid to her was also related to the worship of the goddess Isis, with whom she was often identified.

To a lesser extent, opportunities for nonaristocratic Greek women also increased during the Hellenistic Age. In Alexandria young women received education in dancing, music, rudimentary reading and writing, and scholarship and philosophy. Often the daughters of scholars became scholars in their own right. Although their work is lost, we know that women wrote about astronomy, musical theory, and literature, and many female poets competed for honors. A few Hellenistic women distinguished themselves as portrait painters, architects, and harpists. Despite these accomplishments, women still had fewer rights and opportunities than men, and they remained under the supervision of their male relatives. In Egypt, a woman still could not travel overnight without her husband's permission.

HELLENISTIC LITERATURE, PHILOSOPHY, AND SCIENCE

The Hellenistic Age witnessed the continuation of some trends in classical Greek scholarship while promoting some striking innovations in literature, philosophy, and science.

Literature: Poetry and History Writing

Much Hellenistic literature has vanished, but some surviving works give a glimpse of creativity and originality, which often combined urbanity and thoughtful scholarship. Hellenistic poets turned to frivolous themes because the repressive political climate discouraged questioning of authority. Light comedy became immensely popular, especially in the hands of the playwright Menander of Athens (ca. 300 B.C.E.). This clever author delighted audiences with escapist, frothy tales of temporarily frustrated love and happy endings. These plays, known now as New Comedy, developed from the risqué satires of classical Athens. They featured vivid street language and a cast of stock characters: crotchety parents, naive young men and silly young women, tricky slaves, and wicked pimps.

Theocritus (ca. 300–ca. 260 B.C.E.), who came from Syracuse but wrote in Alexandria in the 270s B.C.E., invented a new genre called pastoral poetry. His verses described idyllic life in the countryside, but his coarse herdsmen reflect the sadness and tensions of city life. Of all the Hellenistic poets, Theocritus has had the most wide-ranging and enduring influence, providing a model for pastoral verse in Rome, Shakespeare's England, and even in nineteenth-century Russia. The other great poet from Alexandria, Callimachus (ca. 305–240 B.C.E.), combined playfulness with extraordinary learning in works ranging from *Collections of Wonders of the World* to his moving love poems, the *Elegies*. His poetry provides the best example of the erudite style known as Alexandrianism, which demonstrated a command of meter and language and which appealed more to the intellect than to the emotions.

Powerful Hellenistic monarchs influenced the writing of history. Kings wanted flattering accounts of their deeds, not the probing, critical independence of mind that Thucydides had offered in the classical period. Some writers resisted these pressures, however. Hieronymous of Cardia, a professional administrator who lived to age 104, described nearly three generations of political intrigue that followed Alexander's death. His conclusion? Fortune, not the efforts of mighty kings, determines the affairs of men.

Philosophy: The Quest for Peace of Mind

The study of philosophy continued to flourish in the Hellenistic world. Plato's Academy and Aristotle's Lyceaum remained in operation in Athens, drawing intellectually curious men from around the Mediterranean. In this environment several new schools of philosophy arose. Three of them in particular—the Epicureans, the Stoics, and the Cynics—shared the common goal of overcoming what they called disturbance, thereby acquiring an inner tranquility or peace of mind. According to Xenocrates (d. 314 B.C.E.), the head of the Platonic Academy, the purpose of studying philosophy "is to allay what causes disturbance in life."

HONORING A FAMOUS WOMAN POET

In the third century B.C.E., a distinguished female poet named Aristodama visited the city of Lamia in Thessaly, where she recited from her work. The Lamians enjoyed her performances so much that they made her a citizen of their town and gave her several honorific titles to show their appreciation. The remarkable inscription on a marble plaque from Lamia recording the town's decision to honor Aristodama reveals that in the Hellenistic Age a person's citizenship was not confined to one city. It also shows the greater freedom and status available to women in the Hellenistic Age. It would have been almost unthinkable in Classical Greece for a woman to become a famous poet.

. . . Resolved by the city of the Lamians. Since Aristodama, daughter of Amyntas, a citizen of Smyrna in Ionia, epic poetess, while she was in our city gave several public recitations of her poems in which [our] ancestors were worthily commemorated and since the performance was done with great enthusiasm, she shall be a Special Friend of the city and a Benefactress, and she shall be given citizenship and the right to possess land and a house and the right of pasture and inviolability and security on land and sea in war and peace for herself and her descendants and their property for all time together with all other privileges that are given to other foreign guests and benefactors.

Source: From *The Hellenistic Age: From the Battle of Ipsos to the Death of Kleopatra VII*, edited and translated by Stanley M. Burstein. Copyright © 1985 by Cambridge University Press. Reprinted by permission.

The first of these philosophical schools, the Epicureans°, was founded by Epicurus of Samos (341–271 B.C.E.). Known by its meeting place, the Garden, this school was open to women and slaves as well as free men. Because Epicurus believed that "the entire world lives in pain," he urged people to gain tranquility in their troubled souls through the rational choice of pleasure. The word *epicurean* today denotes a person of discriminating taste who takes pleasure in eating and drinking, but the pleasure Epicurus sought was intellectual, a perfect harmony of body and mind. To achieve this harmony Epicurus recommended a virtuous and simple life, characterized by plain living and withdrawal from the stressful world of politics and social competition. Epicurus also reassured his students that they should fear neither death nor the gods. There was no reason to fear death because the soul was material; hence there was no afterlife. Nor was there any reason to fear the gods, who lived in a happy condition far from Earth, unconcerned

Aphrodite of Melos: The Hellenistic Portrayal of the Perfect Female

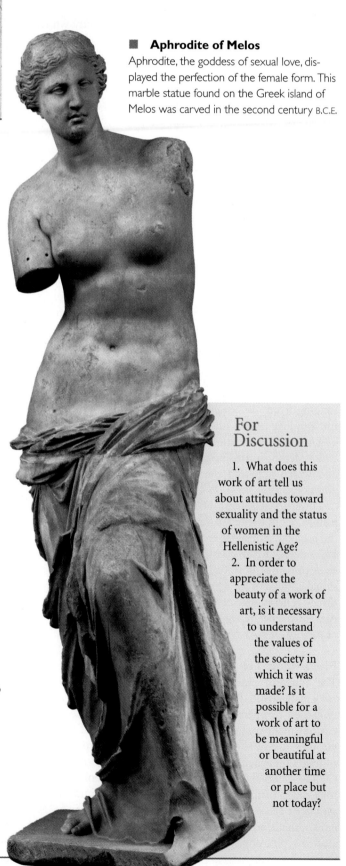

■ **Aphrodite of Melos**
Aphrodite, the goddess of sexual love, displayed the perfection of the female form. This marble statue found on the Greek island of Melos was carved in the second century B.C.E.

Perhaps the best-known female statue surviving from antiquity is that of Aphrodite of Melos, popularly known as the Venus di Milo (her Italian name). Sculpted from marble in the second century B.C.E., the goddess is half-nude. She rests on her right foot and seems to step forward toward the viewer. Though her arms are missing today, originally one arm was probably raised to cover her breasts in a gesture of modesty. Her facial expression is serene. The garment draped loosely around her hips gave an artist the opportunity to explore the play of thin cloth over her thighs, expressing his delight in movement and physicality. Somewhat more sedate than other voluptuous representations of Aphrodite, the goddess of love, this statue portrays a male vision of a perfect woman, highly sexual but also charmingly modest.

Nude statues of Aphrodite meant to be erotic and provoke sexual feelings in men became popular in the Hellenistic Age as the result of changing male attitudes about women. Greek women in the Classical Age led secluded lives at home, with no role to play in warfare, politics, debate, or intellectual pursuits. Men appreciated women primarily as mothers and maintainers of the household, not as objects of sexual desire. Statues of women in the Classical Age generally presented them as heavily draped to protect their bodies from the stares of men. In this misogynistic environment, homoeroticism flourished, and men idealized young men as suitable objects of their love and sexual desire.

In the Hellenistic Age, Greek women achieved more social freedom. Although still excluded from politics, women won greater legal rights and participated more fully in activities outside the home. One consequence of women's changed status in the polis was that men began to appreciate them more fully as objects of sexual desire. Male intellectuals debated whether sex with young men or with young women was better for men, and male artists began portraying women as an erotic ideal. Men created nudes like Aphrodite of Melos for other men to enjoy. It is not known what Hellenistic women thought of these statues. ■

For Discussion

1. What does this work of art tell us about attitudes toward sexuality and the status of women in the Hellenistic Age?

2. In order to appreciate the beauty of a work of art, is it necessary to understand the values of the society in which it was made? Is it possible for a work of art to be meaningful or beautiful at another time or place but not today?

■ **Comedy Mosaic from Pompeii**
Brilliant decorative mosaics have survived in great numbers from the Hellenistic world. Often derived from Greek paintings, which have entirely disappeared, these scenes give a vivid glimpse into everyday life. This mosaic is based on a scene from a comedy performed in a theater. We can almost hear the music as street entertainers play and dance in front of a rich man's house.

with human activity. With these fears assuaged, humans could find inner peace.

The main rival to Epicureanism was Stoicism°, the school established by Zeno of Citium (ca. 335–ca. 263 B.C.E.) at Athens in 300 B.C.E. Taking its name from the Stoa Poikile (the Painted Portico) where Zeno and his successors taught, Stoicism remained influential well into the time of the Roman Empire. Stoics believed that all human beings have an element of divinity in them and therefore participate in one single indissoluble cosmic process. They could find peace of mind by submitting to that cosmic order, which Stoics identified with nature or fate. Thus the word *stoic* today carries the meaning of a person who responds to pain or misfortune without showing passion or feeling. Stoics believed that wise men did not allow the vicissitudes of life to distract them. Rather than calling for withdrawal from the world, like the Epicureans, Stoicism encouraged people to participate actively in public life. Because Stoicism accepted the status quo, many kings and aristocrats embraced it. They wanted to believe that their success formed part of a cosmic, divine plan.

The members of the Cynic° school took a different approach to gaining peace of mind. Founded by Antisthenes (ca. 445–360 B.C.E.), a devoted follower of Socrates, the Cynic school taught that the key to happiness was the rejec-

tion of all needs and desires. To achieve this goal, Cynics rejected all pleasures and possessions, leading a life of asceticism. Diogenes (ca. 412–324 B.C.E.), the chief representative of the school, made his home in an empty barrel. Cynics manifested contempt for the customs and conventions of society, including wealth, social position, and prevailing standards of morality. One prominent Cynic, Crates of Thebes (ca. 328 B.C.E.), caused a public scandal when he did the unthinkable: He took his wife, the philosopher Hipparchia, out for a meal in public instead of leaving her at home where respectable women belonged. The word *cynic* today usually refers to a person who sneeringly denies the sincerity of human motives and actions. Some Cynics took the doctrine of Diogenes to extremes by satisfying, rather than denying, their simplest natural needs. Their behavior, which included public masturbation and defecation, repelled so many people that their philosophy failed to have a lasting impact.

Explaining the Natural World: Scientific Investigation

While Athens remained the hub of philosophy in the Hellenistic Age, the Ptolemaic kings made Alexandria the preeminent center of scientific learning. These monarchs sponsored scientific research and lectures on the natural world by professional scholars at an institution called the Museum. Nearby, the Library housed hundreds of thousands of texts that attempted to organize the knowledge of the world. In addition to summarizing the work of previous scholars, Hellenistic scientists sought to depict the world as it actually was. This emphasis on realism involved the rejection of some of the more speculative notions that had characterized classical Greek science.

In mathematics, Euclid (ca. 300 B.C.E.) produced a masterful synthesis of the knowledge of geometry in his great work, the *Elements*, which remained the standard geometry textbook until the twentieth century. Euclid demonstrated how one could attain knowledge by rational methods alone—by mathematical reasoning through the use of deductive proofs and theorems. Equally famous as a theorist and engineer was Archimedes of Syracuse (ca. 287–212 B.C.E.), who calculated the value of *pi* (the ratio of a circle's circumference to its diameter) and measured the diameter of the sun. A sophisticated mechanical engineer, Archimedes reputedly said: "Give me a fulcrum and I will move the world." Archimedes put his scientific knowledge to work in wartime. During the Roman siege of Syracuse in 212 B.C.E., he built a huge reflecting mirror that focused the bright Sicilian sun on Roman warships, burning holes in their decks.

Astronomy advanced as well during the Hellenistic Age. In their research, Hellenistic investigators borrowed from the long tradition of precisely recorded observation of the heavens that Babylonian and Egyptian scholars had established. This intersection of Middle Eastern and Greek astronomical work produced one of the richest new areas of knowledge in the Hellenistic world. For example, Heraclides of Pontus (ca. 390–310 B.C.E.) anticipated a heliocentric (sun-centered) theory of the universe when he observed that Venus and Mercury orbit the sun, not the Earth. Aristarchus of Samos (ca. 310–230 B.C.E.) established the idea that the planets revolve around the sun while spinning on their own axes. Eratosthenes of Cyrene (ca. 276–194 B.C.E.) made a calculation of the Earth's circumference that came within 200 miles of being accurate.

The sun-centered view never caught on because of fierce opposition from the followers of Aristotle, whose geocentric (Earth-centered) theories had become canonical. Instead, Hipparchus of Nicaea (ca. 146–127 B.C.E.), who produced the first catalogue of stars, insisted that the Earth was the center of the universe. The geocentric view of the universe prevailed until the sixteenth century C.E., when the Polish astronomer Nicholas Copernicus, who had read the work of Heraclides and Aristarchus, provided mathematical data to support the heliocentric theory (see Chapter 16).

Medical theory and research also flourished in the great Hellenistic cities. Diocles, a Greek doctor of the fourth century B.C.E. who combined theory and practice, wrote the first handbook on human anatomy and invented a spoon-

like tool for removing arrowheads from the human body that physicians used on King Philip of Macedon. Doctors during this period believed that human behavior as well as disease were products of the interactions of fluids in the body, called humors. They argued about whether to categorize the humors as hot, cold, wet, and dry; as earth, water, fire, and air; or as blood, phlegm, yellow bile, and black bile. Praxagoras of Cos (late fourth century B.C.E.) argued that the body contained more than a dozen kinds of humors. He also studied the relation of the brain to the spinal cord. Other doctors, like Herophilus and Erasistratus, who lived in Alexandria in the fourth century B.C.E., systematically dissected human cadavers. They also may have practiced vivisection, operating on living subjects to study living organs. There is some evidence that with the king's permission they conducted experiments on condemned criminals who had not yet been executed, a practice that is outlawed today. Through dissection these physicians learned a great deal about the human nervous system, the structure of the eye, and reproductive physiology.

The Hellenistic medical tradition outlasted the Hellenistic Age and flourished in the Roman Empire. Galen (129–199 C.E.), the greatest doctor of antiquity, organized Hellenistic medical knowledge, producing accurate, realistic descriptions of human anatomy, and formulated a theory regarding the motion of the blood from the liver to the veins that was not replaced until William Harvey discovered the circulation of the blood in the seventeenth century (see Chapter 16). Galen's theories, like many other aspects of Hellenistic culture, had a profound impact on Western scholarship during the Middle Ages.

ENCOUNTERS WITH FOREIGN PEOPLES

During the Hellenistic Age, Greeks encountered large numbers of foreign peoples, and the effects of these interactions laid some of the foundations of the West. The encounters took place when Greeks explored the unknown regions in Africa and Europe; when Hellenistic culture met with resistance from Babylonians, Egyptians, and Hebrews; and when Celtic peoples migrated to the boundaries of the Hellenistic world.

Exploring the Hellenistic World

A spirit of inquiry—combined with hunger for trade and profit—drove men to explore and map the unknown world during the Hellenistic Age (see Map 4.4). Explorers backed by monarchs ventured into the Caspian, Aral, and Red Seas. By the second century B.C.E., Greeks had established trading posts along the coasts of modern Eritrea and Somalia, where merchants bought goods, particularly ivory, transported from the interior of Africa. Hellenistic people also craved pepper, cinnamon, and other spices and luxury goods from India, but Arab middlemen made direct trade nearly impossible. One intrepid navigator named Eudoxus made an unsuccessful attempt to find a sea route to India by sailing down both the east and west coasts of Africa, but he never got farther than Morocco.

The most ambitious and successful of all Hellenistic explorers was Pytheas of Marseilles (ca. 310–306 B.C.E.). Setting out from the Greek city of Gades (the modern Spanish port of Cadiz), he sailed around Britain and reported the existence of either Iceland or Norway. He may even have reached the Vistula River in Poland. Throughout his journeys Pytheas contributed much to navigational knowledge by recording astronomical bearings and natural wonders such as the Northern Lights.

As these explorers expanded geographical horizons, Greeks developed a lively though condescending interest in the different peoples of the world. Greeks considered themselves culturally superior to non-Greek-speaking peoples, including Jews, Babylonians, Celts, steppe nomads, and sub-Saharan Africans who lived beyond the borders of Hellenistic kingdoms. Greeks considered all of these peoples inferior barbarians. Despite this prejudice, educated men and women throughout the Hellenistic world enjoyed reading accounts in Greek of foreign peoples' customs, myths, natural history, and forms of government.

Knowledge about different peoples often came from non-Greek intellectuals who translated their accounts into Greek. For example, Berosus, a Babylonian priest, wrote a history of his people that provided Greek readers with extensive astronomical knowledge as well. Manetho, an Egyptian priest, composed a history of his land. Hecataeus of Abdera, a Greek, wrote a popular history arguing that

■ **Map 4.4   Hellenistic Trade and Exploration**

During the Hellenistic Age, merchants traveled widely across the breadth of the Mediterranean and throughout the Near East. They sailed into the Persian Gulf and Indian Ocean on commercial ventures. Some explorers sailed along the east and west coasts of Africa as well as Europe's Atlantic coast, reaching Britain and the North Sea.

Egypt was the site of the origin of civilization. Most of what was known in the West about India until the Middle Ages derived from the reports of Megasthenes, a Seleucid diplomat. Information about the histories and belief systems of their neighbors entertained intellectuals and helped Hellenistic rulers govern their conquered peoples.

Resistance to Hellenistic Culture

Despite this curiosity among educated Greeks about foreign customs, a great barrier of mutual incomprehension and suspicious resentment separated Greeks and their subjects. Language was one such barrier. In most kingdoms, administrators conducted official business only in Greek. Few Greek settlers in the cities or even in far-flung, isolated military colonies ever bothered to learn the local languages, and only a small percentage of the local populations learned Greek. Many communities preferred to ignore their Greek rulers completely. In Babylonia, for example, age-old patterns of urban life centering on temple worship continued outside the influence of Greek culture. Some non-Greeks, however, hoped to rise in the service of their Greek masters. They made an effort to learn Greek and to assimilate into Hellenistic culture. Their collaboration with Greek rulers alienated them from their own people and provoked divisions within native societies.

Many people conquered by the Greeks continued to practice their traditional religions. Still stunned by the loss of their empire, some aristocratic Persians found solace in practicing Zoroastrianism, the traditional Persian religion. Zoroastrianism teaches that the world is in the grip of an eternal struggle between the good forces of light, represented by the divine creator, Ahura Mazda, and the evil forces of darkness, represented by Angra Mainyu, the demonic destroyer. These Persians interpreted Alexander as Angra Mainyu's agent. In the aftermath of the Persian defeat an important religious text (composed in Greek, ironically) predicted that a military messiah would soon restore Persia's true religion and rulers. In Babylon a book known as the *Dynastic Prophecy* (ca. 300 B.C.E.) expressed similar hopes for Babylonians.

Resentful voices also rang out in Egypt. The *Demotic Chronicle* (ca. 250 B.C.E.) and *The Oracle of the Potter* (ca. 250 B.C.E.) maintained that the Ptolemies had brought the punishment of the gods to Egypt by displacing the pharaohs and interfering with religious customs. One day, the book assured readers, a mighty king would expel the conquerors. Not coincidentally, a series of open rebellions

CHRONOLOGY

Hellenistic Science and Philosophy

CA. 445–360 B.C.E.	Antisthenes founds the Cynic School at Athens
390–320 B.C.E.	Heraclides of Pontus notes that some planets orbit the sun
CA. 350 B.C.E.	First books on human anatomy are written
310–230 B.C.E.	Aristarchus of Samos establishes heliocentric theory
CA. 310–306 B.C.E.	Pytheas of Marseilles explores coasts of the North Sea
CA. 295 B.C.E.	Ptolemy I founds Museum and Library in Alexandria in Egypt; Menander of Athens writes New Comedy; Zeno of Cition teaches Stoicism at Athens; Euclid writes *Elements of Geometry*
287–212 B.C.E.	Archimedes of Syracuse calculates the value of *pi*
276–194 B.C.E.	Eratosthenes of Cyrene calculates the Earth's circumference
CA. 147–127 B.C.E.	Hipparchus of Nicaea argues that the Earth is the center of the universe
140S B.C.E.	Polybius writes history of Rome's rise to world power
60S–40S B.C.E.	Cicero writes on rhetoric and philosophy at Rome
129–199 C.E.	Galen codifies Hellenistic medical knowledge

erupted in Egypt about the same time that these works gained popularity.

The Jewish response to Hellenism produced the best-known account of resistance, preserved in the Hebrew Bible as the First and Second Book of Maccabees. After Alexander's conquest of the Persian Empire in 333 B.C.E., Jerusalem and Jewish Palestine passed to the control of the Ptolemies and then the Seleucids. The Ptolemaic monarchs at first tolerated Jewish religion and welcomed the rapid assimilation of Jerusalem's priestly aristocracy into Greek culture. Under the rule of these Hellenized priests, a gymnasium and other elements of Greek culture first appeared in Jerusalem. At the same time, however, traditional Jewish worship at the temple in Jerusalem continued.

The situation changed in 167 B.C.E., when the Seleucid king Antiochus IV Epiphanes tried to demonstrate his authority by further Hellenizing the city; when the Jews resisted, his soldiers desecrated the temple by introducing foreign worship there, an abomination in Jewish eyes. Initially, Antiochus intended to advertise his own strength, not to suppress Jewish practice, but his plan backfired. A family of Jewish priests, the Maccabees, began a religious war of liberation. They drove Antiochus's armies out of Palestine, purified the Temple in Jerusalem, and established an independent Jewish kingdom under their rulership. Later, when Jewish writers sought to explain their actions to the Greek-speaking Jews of Alexandria, they described their struggle in terms of resistance to Hellenism. However, the Maccabean dynasty that had led the victorious struggle against Hellenism soon adopted many Greek customs, causing deep rifts within Jewish society.

Celts on the Fringes of the Hellenistic World

In addition to the Greek culture that spread throughout the Mediterranean and Near East, Celtic civilization flourished in Europe during the Hellenistic Age. Celtic peoples emerged in continental Europe north of the Alps about 750 B.C.E. The Celts, who lived in tribes that were never politically unified on a large scale, shared common dialects, metal- and pottery-making techniques, and agricultural and home-building methods. They are the ancestors of many peoples of northern and central Europe today.

Through trade and war, Celts played an influential role on the northern margins of the Hellenistic world from Asia Minor to Spain. Trading routes were established as early as the eighth century B.C.E., but commerce was often interrupted by war. The military activities of Celtic tribes restricted the expansion of Hellenistic kingdoms, thereby pressuring them to strengthen their military capacities.

Archaeologists call the first Celtic civilization in central Europe Hallstatt culture, because of excavations in Hallstatt, Austria. Around 750 B.C.E., Hallstatt° Celts started to spread from their homeland into Italy, the Balkans, Ireland, Spain, and Asia Minor, conquering local peoples on the way. These people left no written records, so we know little of their political practices. The luxury goods and weapons left in their graves, however, indicate a stratified society led by a warrior elite. Hallstatt sites were heavily fortified, suggesting frequent warfare among communities. Men gained status through competitive exchange of gifts, raiding, and valor in battle. In southern France, Celts encountered Hellenistic civilization at the Greek city of Massilia (modern Marseilles). There they participated in lively trade along the Rhône River for Greek luxury goods, including wine and drinking goblets.

In the middle of the fifth century B.C.E. a new phase in Celtic civilization began, called La Tène° culture, which takes its name from a site in modern Switzerland. More weapons appeared in tombs than in the Halstatt period, indicating intensified warfare. La Tène Celts developed new centers of wealth and power, especially in the valleys of the Rhine and Danube Rivers. They also founded large,

A JEWISH MARTYR FOR A HELLENISTIC AUDIENCE

·················

This excerpt from the narrative of II Maccabees in the Greek version of the Hebrew Bible tells the tragic tale of an old Jew who endured martyrdom for his refusal to compromise with Hellenistic life. Written for a Greek-speaking Jewish audience in Alexandria, the story is told with many allusions to Plato's account of the death of Socrates, demonstrating how Greek ideas had influenced even the enemies of Hellenism.

Eleazar, one of the foremost teachers of the Law, a man already advanced in years and of most noble appearance, had his mouth forced open, to make him eat a piece of pork. But he, resolving to die with honour rather than to live disgraced, walked of his own accord to the torture of the wheel. . . . The people supervising the ritual meal, forbidden by the law, because of the time for which they had known him, took him aside and privately urged him to have meat brought of a kind he could properly use, prepared by himself, and only pretend to eat the portions of sacrificial meat as prescribed by the king; this action would enable him to escape death, by availing himself of an act of kindness prompted by their long friendship. But having taken a noble decision worthy of his years and the dignity of his great age and the well-earned distinction of his grey hairs, worthy too of his impeccable conduct from boyhood and about all of the holy legislation established by God himself, he answered accordingly, telling them to send him at once to Hades. "Pretence, he said, does not befit our time of life. Many young people would suppose that Eleazar at the age of ninety had conformed to the foreigners' way of life and because I had played this part for the sake of a paltry brief spell of my life, might themselves be led astray on my account; I should only bring defilement and disgrace on my old age. Even though for the moment I avoid execution by man, I can never elude the grasp of the Almighty. Therefore if I am man enough to quit this life here and now, I shall have left the young a noble example of how to make a good death, eagerly and generously, for the venerable and holy laws." So saying he walked straight to the wheel . . .

Source: Excerpt from *The New Jerusalem Bible*, copyright © 1985 by Darton, Longman & Todd, Ltd. and Doubleday, a division of Random House, Inc. Reprinted by permission.

fortified settlements in these regions as well as in present-day France and England.

La Tène craftsmen benefited from new trade routes across the Alps to northern Italy, the home of Etruscan merchants and artisans. Etruscans traded bronze statuettes to the Celtic north, and they may have also introduced the two-wheeled fighting chariots found in aristocratic Celtic tombs. Greek styles in art reached the Celts through these Etruscan intermediaries, but Celtic artists developed their own distinctive style of metalwork and sculpture. Many Celtic communities began to use coinage, which they adopted from the Greeks.

For about a century relations between the Celtic and Mediterranean peoples centered on trade, but around 400 B.C.E. overpopulation in central Europe instigated massive migrations of Celtic tribes. Around 390 B.C.E.

one migrating group of Celts sacked the city of Rome. Their invasion had an unexpected effect on Roman military technology: The Romans began to use the highly effective Celtic short sword, which became the standard weapon of the Roman legions.

This period of hostile migrations lasted until 200 B.C.E. Some Celts traveled to lands that are Slavic today (Slovakia and southern Poland), while others established new homes in the Po Valley in northern Italy, as well as Spain, Britain, and Ireland. Other groups of Celts invaded the Balkans, plundered Greece, and finally settled in Asia Minor, where they established a kingdom, called Galatia, known for the bravery and cruelty of its soldiers. These fighters played an important role as mercenaries in the constant wars among the Hellenistic successor kingdoms. Ultimately the Celts would be absorbed, together with the peoples in the Hellenistic kingdoms in the eastern Mediterranean, into the Roman Empire (see Map 4.5).

Rome's Rise to Power

From Rome's Capitoline Hill a tourist today can look down upon the Roman Forum and see a large field of broken monuments. These remains lie at the heart of what was once an enormous empire extending from northern England to Iraq, and from Morocco to the Black Sea. A few yards away on the western slope of the neighboring Palatine Hill, archaeologists have uncovered hut foundations from the city's earliest occupants in the tenth century B.C.E. How the Roman Empire emerged from this crude village above a swamp remains one of the most remarkable stories in the history of the West.

During the Hellenistic Age, Rome expanded from being a relatively small city-state with a republican form of government into a vast and powerful empire. As it conquered the peoples who ringed the Mediterranean—the Carthaginians, the Celts, and the Hellenistic kingdoms of Alexander's successors—Rome incorporated these newcomers into the political structure of the republic. Trying to govern these sprawling territories with institutions and social traditions suited for a city-state overwhelmed the Roman republic° and led to the establishment of

■ **Celtic Warriors**

These two Celtic statuettes of fighting men reveal the impact of Hellenistic art on native traditions. The first warrior, who stands stiffly and without a well-articulated anatomy, is the product of Celtic artistic traditions untouched by Greek art. The second figure shows the influence of Greek styles. He is well-balanced to throw a spear. His muscles are clearly understood and he turns convincingly in space.

a new form of government, the Roman Empire, by the end of the first century B.C.E.

ROMAN ORIGINS AND ETRUSCAN INFLUENCES

Interaction with outsiders shaped the story of Rome from its very beginning. Resting on low but easily defensible hills covering a few hundred acres above the Tiber River, Rome lies at the intersection of north-south and east-west trade routes that had been used in Italy since the Neolithic Age. Romans used these same routes to develop a thriving commerce with other peoples, many of whom they eventually conquered and absorbed into their Roman polity.

Settlements began in Rome about 1000 B.C.E., but we know little about the lives of these first inhabitants. So small was the scale of village life that clusters of huts on the different hills may have constituted entirely different communities. What would one day be the Forum°—the place of assembly for judicial and other public business—was an undrained marsh, which villagers used as protection and burial grounds.

Control of the Tiber river crossing and trade allowed Rome to grow quickly. Excavated graves from the eighth century B.C.E. reveal that a wealthy elite or aristocracy had already emerged. Women evidently shared the benefits of increased prosperity. One grave contained a woman buried with her chariot, a symbol of authority and status. In the course of the seventh century the Roman population increased rapidly. Extended families or clans emerged as a force in Roman life. Throughout this early period of Roman history, according to Roman legend, kings exercised political authority.

Historians think that Latin, the Roman language, was only one of at least 140 distinct languages and dialects spoken by Italy's frequently warring communities during the

■ **Map 4.5 Celtic Expansion, Fifth to Third Century B.C.E.**
During the Hellenistic Age, Celtic peoples migrated into many parts of Europe and Asia Minor. This map shows their routes.

■ **View of the Forum from Capitoline Hill**
This view down into the Forum valley was taken from the site of the Temple to Jupiter, Rome's mightiest god. All victory processions after a successful war would have ended at this temple, where sacrifices were made. Now tourists visit the remains of buildings from which Rome ruled an international empire.

first four centuries of Rome's existence. During this period, Romans developed their military skills in order to defend themselves against their neighbors. Nevertheless, the Romans had amicable relations with some neighbors—particularly the Etruscans, who lived northwest of Rome.

In the sixth and seventh centuries B.C.E., Etruscan culture strongly influenced that of Rome. Like the Romans, the Etruscans° descended from indigenous prehistoric Italian peoples. By 800 B.C.E., they were firmly established in Etruria (modern Tuscany), a region in central Italy between the Arno and the Tiber rivers. By the sixth century B.C.E. they controlled territory as far south as the Bay of Naples and east to the Adriatic Sea. The Etruscans maintained a loose confederation of independent cities that often waged war against other Italian peoples.

Etruscans carried on a lively trade with Greek merchants, exchanging native iron ore and other resources for Greek vases and other luxury goods. Commerce became the conduit through which Etruscans and later Romans absorbed many aspects of Greek culture. The Etruscans, for example, adopted the Greek alphabet and subscribed to

many Greek myths, which they later transmitted to the Romans.

During the sixth century B.C.E., the Etruscans ruled Rome, influencing its religion and temple architecture. Although the Etruscans and Romans spoke different languages, a common culture deriving from native Italian, Etruscan, and Greek communities gradually evolved, especially in religious practice. The three main gods of Rome—Jupiter, Minerva, and Juno—were first worshiped in Etruria. (The Greek equivalents were Zeus, Athena, and Hera.) In addition, Romans learned from Etruscans seers how to interpret omens, especially how to learn the will of the gods by examining the entrails of sacrificed animals. Etruscans also gave the Romans a distinctive temple architecture that differed from that of the Greeks. While people could walk around a Greek temple and see it from all sides, Etruscan and eventually Roman temples featured deep porches and were placed on a high platform at the back of a long sacred enclosure. This positioning directed the worshippers' attention to the god's temple and the altar in front of it rather than the building's placement in the landscape.

THE BEGINNINGS OF THE ROMAN STATE

By about 600 B.C.E. Romans had prospered sufficiently to drain the marsh that lay at the center of their city, which would be called the Forum. At the same time they began to construct temples and public buildings, including the first senate house, where the elders met to discuss community affairs. Under the rule of its kings, some of whom were of Etruscan origin, Rome became an important military power in Italy. Only free male inhabitants of the city who could afford their own weapons voted in the citizen assembly, which made public decisions with the advice of the senate. Poor men could fight but not vote. Thus began the struggle between rich and poor that would plague Roman life for centuries.

About 500 B.C.E., when Rome had become a powerful city, with perhaps as many as 35,000 inhabitants, the Romans put an end to kingship and began a new system of government that historians call the Roman Republic. According to legend, in 509 B.C.E. a courageous aristocrat named Brutus overthrew the tyrannical Etruscan king, Tarquin the Arrogant. After the coup, Roman aristocrats established several new institutions in place of the kingship that structured political life for 500 years. An assembly comprising Rome's male citizens, called the Centuriate Assembly because of the units of 100 into which the population was divided, managed the city's legislative, judicial, and administrative affairs. As in the Greek *poleis,* only men participated in battle and public life. Each year, the assembly elected two chief executives called consuls, who could apply the law but whose decisions could be appealed. As time went on, the assembly also selected additional officers to deal with legal and financial responsibilities. A body of elders, called the Senate, comprising about 300 Romans who had held administrative offices, advised the consuls, though they had no formal authority. Priests performed religious ceremonies on behalf of the city.

Hatred of kings, which became a staple of Roman political thought, prevented any one man from becoming too prominent. A relatively small group of influential families held real power within the political community, by both holding offices and working behind the scenes. This kind of government is known as an oligarchy, or "the rule of the few."

To celebrate the end of the monarchy, the people of Rome built a grand new temple to Jupiter on the Capitoline Hill, looking down on the Forum. Probably at the same time the Romans also established the community of Vestal Virgins as caretakers of the sacred fire and hearth in the Temple of Vesta, one of Rome's most ancient religious sites. In such ways the welfare of Rome became a shared public concern.

Tensions between the rich and the poor shaped political and social life at Rome in the first two centuries of the Republic. At the top of the social hierarchy stood the patricians°, aristocratic clans whose high status extended to the days of the kings. These men, including the legendary Brutus, had been responsible for toppling the monarchy. Because they monopolized the magistracies and the priesthoods, they occupied most of the seats in the Senate. Other rich landowners and senators with lesser pedigrees, as well as the prosperous farmers who made up the army's phalanxes, joined the patricians in resisting the plebeians°, the poorest segments of society. The plebeians demanded more political rights, such as a fair share of distributed public land and freedom from debt bondage. These efforts of poor Romans to acquire a political voice, called the Struggle of the Orders°, accelerated during the fifth century B.C.E., when Rome experienced a severe economic recession.

A victory in the plebeians' struggle came in 494 B.C.E., when they won the right to elect two tribunes each year as their spokesmen. Tribunes could veto magistrates' decisions and so block arbitrary judicial actions by the patricians. Then, in 471 B.C.E., a new Plebeian Assembly gave plebeians the opportunity to express their political views in a formal setting, although without the formal authority to enact actual legislation. About 450 B.C.E., the plebeians took another major step forward with the publication of the Law of the Twelve Tables. Until that time, Romans did not write down their laws, and aristocrats often arbitrarily interpreted and applied laws to the disadvantage of the poor. The plebeians pressed for codification and public display of the law to ensure that the rights of all free Romans would be recognized and respected. The Twelve Tables covered all aspects of life from the proper protection of women ("Women shall remain under the guardianship [of a man] even when they have reached legal adulthood") and debt bondage ("Unless he pays his debt or someone stands surety for him in court, bind him in a harness, or in chains . . .") to religious matters. Even when cruel, the law could now be applied uniformly.

The plebeians continued to make their presence felt in Roman life. In 445 B.C.E., a new law permitted marriage between plebeians and patricians. This enabled wealthy plebeians to marry into aristocratic families. A high point came in 367 B.C.E., when politicians agreed that one of each year's two consuls should come from the plebeian class. The plebeians now were fully integrated within the Roman government. Moreover, around the same time Romans limited the amount of public land that could be distributed to any citizen. The new arrangement prevented aristocrats from seizing the lion's share of conquered territories and permitted poor citizen soldiers to receive a share of captured land. The last concession to the plebeians came in 287 B.C.E., when the decisions of the Plebeian Assembly became binding on the whole state. The plebeians acquired their political strength and full acceptance in the political arena by simple extortion: They threatened to leave the army if the aristocratic elite filed to meet their demands. Without the

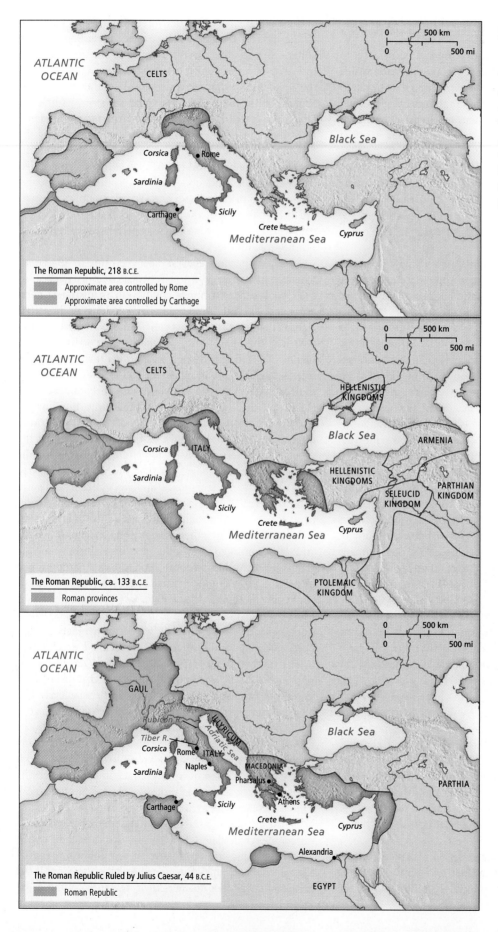

The Roman Republic, 218 B.C.E.
- Approximate area controlled by Rome
- Approximate area controlled by Carthage

The Roman Republic, ca. 133 B.C.E.
- Roman provinces

The Roman Republic Ruled by Julius Caesar, 44 B.C.E.
- Roman Republic

■ **Map 4.6 The Roman Conquest of the Mediterranean During the Republic**

Armies of the Roman Republic conquered the Mediterranean world during the Hellenistic Age, overcoming the Carthaginian Empire, the Hellenistic successor kingdoms, and many Celtic peoples in Spain and Gaul.

plebeians, who constituted the bulk of the Roman army, the Republic could not protect itself from invaders or conquer new lands.

At the same time a new underclass of slaves emerged as the result of military expansion in Italy. Poor Roman farmers eagerly settled in newly conquered territories. These farmers in turn served as soldiers in further wars of expansion in which Romans enslaved other conquered peoples. Thus a self-perpetuating cycle of conquest, settlement, and enslavement began to take shape, reaching full development after 200 B.C.E.

ROMAN TERRITORIAL EXPANSION

During the period of the Republic, Rome conquered and incorporated all of Italy, the vast Carthaginian Empire in northern Africa, and Spain, and many of the lands inhabited by Celtic people to the north and west of Italy (see Map 4.6). As a result of these conquests, the Roman state found it necessary to change the methods of government established in the fifth century B.C.E.

Winning Control of Italy

The new political and military institutions that developed in Rome enabled the Romans to conquer the entire Italian peninsula by 263 B.C.E. In the process the Romans learned the fundamental lessons necessary for ruling much larger territories abroad. Romans began to expand their realm by allying with neighboring cities in Italy. For centuries, Rome and the other Latin-speaking peoples of Latium (the region of central Italy where Rome was situated) had belonged to a loose coalition of cities called the Latin League. Citizens of these cities shared close commercial and legal ties and could intermarry without losing citizenship rights in their native cities. More important, they forged close military alliances with one another.

In 493 B.C.E. Rome successfully led the Latin cities in battle against fierce hill tribes who coveted Latium's rich farmlands. From the success of this venture, Rome learned the value of political alliances with neighbors. Rome and its allies next confronted the Etruscans. In 396 B.C.E. they overcame the Etruscan city of Veii through a combination of military might and shrewd political maneuvering. From this experience, the Romans discovered the uses of careful diplomacy.

A temporary setback to Rome's expansion occurred in 386 B.C.E., when a raiding band of Celts from the Po Valley in the north of Italy defeated a Roman army and plundered the city of Rome before returning home. Only after a generation did Romans recover from this disaster and reassert their preeminence among their allies. Still, they had learned that tenacity and discipline enabled them to endure even a serious military reversal.

The next major step in Rome's expansion came in 338 B.C.E., when Roman troops smashed a three-year revolt of its Latin allies, who had come to resent Rome's overlordship. The peace settlement set the precedent for Rome's future expansion: Rome permitted defeated peoples to become citizens, giving them either partial or full citizenship depending on the treaty it struck with each community. The conquered allies were permitted to continue their own customs, and were not forced to pay tribute. Rome asked for only two things in return: loyalty and troops. All allied communities had to contribute soldiers to the Roman army in wartime. With the huge new pool of troops, Rome became the strongest power in Italy.

In return for their military service and support of Rome, the newly incorporated citizens, especially aristocrats from the allied communities, received a share of the profits of war. They also received the guarantee of Roman protection from internal dissension or outside threats. Those communities not granted full Roman citizenship rights could hope to earn it if they served Roman interests faithfully. Some communities joined the Roman state willingly. Others, particularly the Samnites of south central Italy, resisted bitterly, but to no avail.

Romans continued their march through Italy, becoming embroiled in the affairs of Greek cities of the "toe"

CHRONOLOGY

Rome's Rise to Power

CA. 509 B.C.E.	Roman Republic is created
508 B.C.E.	Romans sign treaty with Carthage
494 B.C.E.	Tribunes of the Plebeians created
474 B.C.E.	Plebeian Assembly is created
451 B.C.E.	Twelve Tables of Law is published
387 B.C.E.	Celts sack Rome
287 B.C.E.	Laws of Plebeian Assembly become binding on all Romans
280 B.C.E.	Pyrrhus of Epirus is defeated
264–241 B.C.E.	First Punic War
218–201 B.C.E.	Second Punic War
215–167 B.C.E.	Wars with Macedon
148–146 B.C.E.	Macedon and Greece become a Roman province
67–62 B.C.E.	Pompey establishes Roman control over Asia Minor, Syria, and Palestine

and "heel" of the boot-shaped Italian peninsula. Some of these Greek cities invited King Pyrrhus of Epirus, a Hellenistic adventurer, to wage war against Rome on their behalf. Pyrrhus invaded southern Italy with 25,000 men and twenty elephants. Though he defeated Roman armies in two great battles in 280 B.C.E., he lost nearly two-thirds of his own troops and withdrew from Italy. "Another victory like this and I'm finished for good!" he said to a comrade, giving rise to the expression "a Pyrrhic victory," which is a win so costly that it is ruinous. Without Pyrrhus's protection, the Greeks in southern Italy could not withstand Rome's legions, and by 263 B.C.E. Rome ruled all of Italy.

The Struggle with Carthage

By the third century B.C.E., imperial Carthage dominated the western Mediterranean region. From the capital city of Carthage located on the north African coast near modern Tunis, Carthaginians held rich lands along the African coast from modern Algeria to Morocco, controlled the natural resources of southern Spain, and dominated the sea lanes of the entire region. Phoenician traders had founded Carthage in the eighth century B.C.E., and the city's energetic merchants carried on business with Greeks, Etruscans, Celts, and eventually Romans.

Hellenistic culture deeply affected Carthage as it did other Mediterranean and Middle Eastern cities. During the Classical Age, Carthaginian trade with the Greek cities in Sicily, and likely with Greek artisans in north Africa, introduced many elements of Greek culture to Carthage. For example, Carthaginians worshiped the Greek goddess of agriculture, Demeter, and her daughter, Kore (also called Persephone), in an elegant temple served by Carthaginian priests and priestesses. By the fourth century B.C.E. the Carthaginian Empire was playing an integral role in the economy of the Hellenistic world by exporting agricultural products, raw materials, metal goods, and pottery.

Rome and Carthage were old acquaintances. Eager for widespread recognition at the beginning of the Republic, Roman leaders signed a commercial treaty with Carthage. Several centuries of wary respect and increasing trade followed. In 264 B.C.E., just as Rome established power throughout the Italian peninsula, a complicated war between Greek cities in Sicily drew Rome and Carthage into conflict. When a Carthaginian fleet went to help a Greek city in Sicily, another city asked Rome for assistance in dislodging them. The aristocratic Senate refused, but the Plebeian Assembly, eager for the spoils of war, voted to intercede. Rome invaded Sicily, setting off the First Punic War, so called because the word Punic comes from the Latin word for Phoenician.

The First Punic War between Rome and Carthage for control of Sicily lasted from 264 to 241 B.C.E. During this time the Romans learned how to fight at sea, cutting off the Carthaginian supply lines to Sicily. In 241 B.C.E. Carthage

CHRONOLOGY	
Imperial Carthage	
CA. 850 B.C.E.	Phoenicians found Carthage
600S B.C.E.	Carthage expands in North Africa, Sardinia, southern Spain, and Sicily
508 B.C.E.	Carthage makes treaty with Rome
500–200 B.C.E.	Conflicts with Greeks in Sicily
264–241 B.C.E.	Carthage fights First Punic War against Rome
218–203 B.C.E.	Hannibal fights in Italy
218–201 B.C.E.	Carthage fights Second Punic War against Rome
202 B.C.E.	Battle of Zama; Hannibal is defeated near Carthage
149–146 B.C.E.	Carthage fights Third Punic War against Rome; end of Carthaginian Empire
146 B.C.E.	Destruction of the city of Carthage

signed a treaty in which it agreed to surrender Sicily and the surrounding islands and to pay a war indemnity over the course of a decade. Roman treachery, however, wrecked the agreement. While the Carthaginians struggled to suppress a revolt of mercenary soldiers, Rome seized Corsica and Sardinia, over which Carthage had lost effective control, and demanded larger reparations. Roman bad faith stoked Carthaginian hatred and desire for revenge.

War did not resume for another two decades. Under the able leadership of Hamilcar Barca (r. 238–229 B.C.E.), Carthage put its energy into developing resources in Spain, while Rome campaigned against Celts living in the Po Valley and fierce tribes on the Adriatic coast. During these years trade between Rome and Carthage continued, reaching new heights. Soon, however, the rapid growth of Carthaginian power in Spain led to renewed conflict with Rome. The Second Punic War (218–201 B.C.E.) erupted when Hamilcar's son, Hannibal, 25 years old and eager for vengeance, ignored a Roman warning and captured Saguntum, a Spanish town with which Rome had formal ties of friendship. In an imaginative and daring move, Hannibal then launched a surprise attack on Italy by crossing the Alps and invading from the north. With an army of nearly 25,000 men and eighteen elephants, he crushed the Roman armies sent against him. In the first major battle, at the Trebia River in the Po Valley, 20,000 Romans died. At Lake Trasimene in Etruria in 216 B.C.E., another 25,000

Romans fell. In the same year at Cannae, 50,000 men perished in Rome's worst defeat ever.

Despite these staggering losses, the Romans persevered and eventually defeated the Carthaginian general. They succeeded, first of all, because Hannibal lacked sufficient logistical support from Carthage to capitalize on his early victories and take the city of Rome. Second, most of Rome's allies in Italy proved loyal. They had often seen Romans prevail in the past and knew that the Romans took fierce revenge on disloyal friends. Thus the Roman policy of including and protecting allies paid off. A third reason for Hannibal's defeat was the indomitable Roman spirit. The Romans simply refused to stop fighting, even after suffering devastating causalities.

The turning point in the war came when Roman commanders devised a new strategy. After incurring so many defeats, the army dared not face Hannibal in open battle. Instead, Fabius, the Roman commander in Italy, avoided open battle and used guerilla tactics to pin down Hannibal in Italy, thus earning the nickname "the Delayer," while Publius Cornelius Scipio Africanus, the Roman general introduced at the beginning of this chapter, took command of Roman forces in Spain. Within a few years he defeated Carthaginian forces there, cutting completely the thin lines of logistical support to Hannibal. In 204 B.C.E., Scipio led Roman legions into Africa, forcing Carthage to recall Hannibal from Italy in order to protect the city.

In one last effort Hannibal confronted Scipio on Carthaginian soil. At the battle of Zama near Carthage in 202 B.C.E., fortune finally deserted Hannibal. Scipio put an end to his string of victories, forcing him into exile. Hannibal had won every battle but his last. Though Scipio spared Hannibal's life and did not destroy Carthage, the peace treaty transferred all of Carthage's overseas territories to Roman control.

Because the war against Hannibal had claimed so many Roman lives, many vengeful Romans agitated for the total destruction of Carthage. In particular, the statesman Marcus Porcius Cato (234–149 B.C.E.), who ended every public utterance with the demand "Carthage must be destroyed!" goaded Romans to violate the peace treaty and resume war with its old adversary. The Third Punic War (149–146 B.C.E.) resulted in the destruction of Carthage. Survivors were enslaved, and the city was burned to the ground and plowed under with salt. Its territories were reorganized as the Roman provinces of Africa.

Conflict with the Celts

Celtic peoples in western Europe fiercely resisted Roman military expansion. After Carthaginian power ended in the Iberian peninsula (modern Spain and Portugal) following the Punic Wars, Romans struggled for more than a century to establish their control over the region's natural resources, particularly its metals and rich farmlands. Not until the reign of Augustus (31 B.C.E.–14 C.E.) did the Romans bring the Iberian peninsula under complete control. The constant fighting drained Rome's manpower and contributed to severe economic and political turmoil in the Republic during the second century B.C.E.

Relations with the Celts had not always been acrimonious. The Roman colonies along the Mediterranean coast that formed an administrative unit called "the Province" (modern Provence) traded peacefully and actively with their Gallic Celtic neighbors. By the late second century B.C.E., Rome had made military alliances with the Aedui, a Celtic tribe that lived further inland. Peace with the Celts, however, ended in 58 B.C.E., when the Roman general Julius Caesar invaded the part of Gaul that lies across the Alps. There he found numerous Celtic tribes with sophisticated political systems dominated by warrior aristocrats. After eight years of bloody conquest and massacre, Caesar conquered Gaul, turning the region into several Roman provinces that within a century became an integral part of the Roman Empire.

From the sack of Rome by Celts in the fourth century B.C.E. to the incorporation of some Celtic lands into the Roman state at the end of the Republic, the Celts were a significant factor in Roman life. In his *History*, Polybius suggested that the constant threat of Celtic invasion contributed to the growth of Roman military force. The Roman Republic was geared for constant warfare, and the Celts frequently were the enemy. Thus the Celts shaped Roman foreign policy as well as the Roman allocation of military resources.

ROME AND THE HELLENISTIC WORLD

By the end of the Punic Wars, Rome had become involved in the affairs of the vigorous Hellenistic kingdoms of the East. Initially reluctant to take direct control of these regions, Roman leaders gradually changed their policies.

CHRONOLOGY

The World of the Celts

CA. 400 B.C.E.	Celts expand from central Europe
CA. 390–386 B.C.E.	Celts invade Italy and plunder Rome
281 B.C.E.	Celts kill Macedonian king in battle
279 B.C.E.	Celts invade Greece
270s B.C.E.	Celts establish kingdom in Asia Minor
100s B.C.E.	Romans campaign against Celts in Spain
58–49 B.C.E.	Julius Caesar fights Celts in Gaul

They assumed responsibility for maintaining order and gradually established absolute control over the entire eastern Mediterranean region.

The Macedonian Wars

Rome waged three wars against Macedon between 215 and 168 B.C.E. that resulted in mastery of Macedon and Greece. The First Macedonian War (215–205 B.C.E.) began when the Macedonian king, Philip V (221–179 B.C.E.), had made an alliance with Hannibal after the Roman defeat at the battle of Cannae. The results of the conflict were inconclusive.

Rome entered a second war with Macedon (205–197 B.C.E.) because Philip and the Seleucid king Antiochus III of Syria had agreed to split the eastern Mediterranean between them. The *poleis* of Greece begged Rome for help, and Rome responded by ordering Philip to cease meddling in Greek affairs. Philip refused, and Roman forces easily defeated him with the support of Greek cities. In 196 B.C.E. the Roman general Titus Quinctius Flamininus declared the cities of Greece free and withdrew his forces.

These cities were not truly free, however. Rome installed oligarchic governments on whose support the Romans could rely. These unpopular regimes perpetuated the class distinctions of Rome. When Antiochus III sent an army to Greece to free it of Roman control, Rome struck back again, defeating him in 189 B.C.E. Rome imposed heavy reparations but claimed no territory, preferring to protect the newly freed Greek cities of Asia Minor and Greece from a distance.

Rome's policy of control from a distance changed after a third war with Macedon (172–168 B.C.E.). A harsher attitude took hold in Rome when a new Macedonian king tried to supplant Rome as protector of Greece. After a smashing victory, Rome imposed crippling terms of surrender on Macedon. Rome chopped Macedon into four separate republics, and strictly forbade marriage and trade across the new borders. Roman troops ruthlessly stamped out all opposition, destroying seventy cities that objected to Rome's presence and selling 150,000 people into slavery.

When some Greek cities tried to pull away from Roman control and assert their independence, the heel of Rome came down hard. To set an example of the danger of resistance, the Roman commander Mummius burned the opulent city of Corinth to the ground and enslaved its inhabitants. For weeks afterward, ships carrying plunder and slaves from the fallen city docked in Italy.

The Encounter Between Greek and Roman Culture

Romans had interacted with Greek culture to some degree for centuries, first indirectly through Etruscan intermediaries, and then through direct contact with Greek communities in southern Italy and Sicily. During the second century B.C.E., when Rome acquired the eastern Mediterranean through its wars with Macedon, the pace of Hellenism's intellectual influence on Rome accelerated. In addition to fine statues and paintings, Greek ideas about literature, art, philosophy, rhetoric, and education poured into Rome after the Macedonian wars.

This Hellenistic legacy challenged many Roman assumptions about the world. But there was a paradox in the reaction of Roman aristocrats to Hellenism. Many noblemen in Rome felt threatened by the novelty of Hellenistic ideas. They preferred to maintain their conservative traditions of public life and thought. They also wanted to present to the world the image of a strong and independent Roman culture, untainted by traditions from other cultures. Thus during the second century B.C.E., Romans occasionally tried to expel Greek philosophers from their city because they worried that Greek culture might corrupt traditional Roman values. At the same time, many truly admired the sophistication of Greek political thought, art, and literature, and they wished to participate in the Hellenistic community.

Consequently many aristocrats learned Greek but refused to speak it while on official business in the East. While Latin remained the language spoken in the Senate house, senators hired Greek tutors to instruct their sons at home in philosophy, literature, science and the arts, and Greek intellectuals found a warm welcome with Rome's upper class. Cato the Censor, the senator who had insisted that Rome destroy Carthage, embodied the paradox of maintaining public distance from Greek culture while privately cherishing it. He cultivated an appearance of forthrightness and honesty, traditional Roman values that he claimed were threatened by Greek culture. He publicly denounced Greek oratory as unmanly, while drawing upon his deep knowledge of Greek rhetoric and literature to write his speeches praising Roman culture.

Before their exposure to the Hellenistic world in the second century B.C.E., Romans had little interest in literature. Their written efforts consisted mainly of inscriptions of laws and treaties on bronze plaques hung from the outer walls of public buildings. Families kept records of the funeral eulogies of their ancestors, while priests maintained simple lists of events and religious festivals. By ca. 240 B.C.E., Livius Andronicus, a former Greek slave, began to translate Greek dramas into Latin. In 220 B.C.E., a Roman senator, Quintus Fabius Pictor, wrote a history of Rome in the Greek language—the first major Roman prose work. In the next century, Polybius, a Greek historian who stood watching with Scipio Aemilianus while Carthage burned, made a major contribution to the writing of Roman history. Taken to Rome from Greece as a hostage in the 160s B.C.E., Polybius came to realize the futility of opposing Roman force. His *History,* written in the analytical tradition of the Greek historian Thucydides, traces Rome's astounding rise to world dominance in a mere fifty-three years and includes moralizing attacks on the abuse of power.

Hellenistic culture also had a major impact on Roman drama. Two Roman playwrights, Plautus (ca. 250–184 B.C.E.) and Terence (ca. 190–159 B.C.E.), took their inspiration from Hellenistic New Comedy and injected some fun into Roman literature. Their surviving works offer entertaining glimpses into the pitfalls of everyday life while also reinforcing the aristocratic values of the rulers of Rome's vast new domains.

Many educated Romans found Greek philosophy extremely attractive. The theory of matter advanced by the Hellenistic philosopher Epicurus, whose ethical philosophy we have already discussed, gained wide acceptance among Romans. Epicurus believed that everything has a natural cause; that "nothing comes from nothing." Romans learned about Epicurus's theories of matter and the infinity of the universe from the poem *On the Nature of the Universe* by the Roman poet Lucretius (d. ca. 51 B.C.E.), who wrote in Latin. The Hellenistic ethical philosophy that held the greatest appeal to Romans was Stoicism, because it encouraged an active public life. Stoic emphasis on the mastery of human difficulties appealed to aristocratic Romans' sense of duty and dignity. The great Roman orator and politician

Marcus Tullius Cicero (106–43 B.C.E.), in particular combined Stoic ideas in a highly personal yet fully Roman way. He stressed moral behavior in political life while urging the attainment of a broad education. Cicero's high-minded devotion to the Republic won him the enmity of unscrupulous politicians, and he was murdered in 43 B.C.E. for his defense of Roman republican liberty.

Despite their openness to Greek philosophy, many members of the Roman ruling elite objected to foreign religious practices. In 186 B.C.E., for example, the Senate suppressed the popular orgiastic cult of the wine god Bacchus, not simply to protect public morals, as they claimed, but to demonstrate and extend their authority over religious worship. Nevertheless, at crucial moments Rome welcomed foreign gods. In 204 B.C.E., two years before the end of the war with Hannibal, the Senate imported the image of the nature goddess Cybele, called the Great Mother, to Rome in order to inspire and unify the city. The cult of Cybele flourished in the Hellenistic kingdom of Pergamum, where devotees worshiped her in the form of an ancient and holy rock. A committee of leading citizens brought this sacred

■ **Magna Mater**

Romans worshiped Magna Mater (The Great Mother) after her cult was introduced in Rome during the Second Punic War against Hannibal. People had worshiped this goddess throughout the eastern Mediterranean since remote antiquity. This statue expresses her majestic power.

boulder to a new temple on the Palatine Hill amid rejoicing. When the ship carrying the rock got stuck in the Tiber River, legend has it that a noble lady, Claudia Quinta, towed the ship with her sash. Not only did Rome defeat Hannibal soon after the arrival of Cybele's sacred stone, but the move cemented Roman relations with Pergamum.

The massive infusion of Hellenistic art following the Macedonian wars inevitably affected public taste. The most prestigious works of art decorated public shrines and spaces throughout the city. Many treasures went to private collectors. Greek artists soon moved to Rome to enjoy the patronage of wealthy Romans. Although copyists made replicas of Greek masterpieces, distinctively Roman artistic styles also emerged, just as they did in rhetoric, literature, philosophy, and history writing. In portrait sculpture, especially, a style developed that unflinchingly depicted all the wrinkles of experience on a person's face. In this way the venerable Roman tradition of carving ancestral busts merged with Greek art.

In architecture, the magnificent temple of Fortune at Praeneste (first century B.C.E.), a town near Rome, combined Italian and Hellenistic concepts to produce the first great monument demonstrating a genuinely Greco-Roman style. By the end of the Republic, Romans had gained enough confidence to adopt the intellectual heritage of Greece and put it to their own ends without fear of seeming "too Greek."

LIFE IN THE ROMAN REPUBLIC

During the Hellenistic Age, Rome prospered from the acquisition of new territories. A small number of influential families dominated political life, sometimes making decisions about war from which they could win wealth and prestige. The Roman Republic remained strong because these ruling families took pains to limit the amount of power any one man or extended political family might attain.

Patrons and Clients

The ruling families of Rome established political networks that extended their influence through all levels of Roman society. These relationships depended on the traditional Roman institution of patrons and clients°. By exercising influence on behalf of a social subordinate, a powerful man (the patron) would bind that man (the client) to him in anticipation of future support. In this way complex webs of personal interdependency influenced the entire Roman social system. The patron-client system operated at every level of society, and it was customary for a man of influence to receive his clients on matters of business at his home the first thing in the morning. In a modest household the discussion might involve everyday business such as shipping fish, arranging a marriage, or making a loan. But in the mansion of a Roman aristocrat a patron might be more in-

terested in forging a political alliance. When several patron-client groups joined forces, they became significant political factions under the leadership of one patron.

Pyramids of Wealth and Power

Like its political organization, Rome's social organization demonstrated a well-defined hierarchy. By the first century B.C.E., a new, elite class of political leaders had emerged in Rome, composed of both the old noble families and those families of plebeian origin who had been able to attain membership in the Senate through their service in the various public offices. The men of this leadership class dominated the Senate and formed the inner circle of government. From their ranks came most of the consuls. They set foreign and domestic policy, led armies to war, held the main magistracies, and siphoned off the lion's share of the Republic's resources.

Beneath this elite group came the equestrian class. Equestrians normally abstained from public office, but were often tied to political leaders by personal obligation. They were primarily businessmen who prospered from the financial opportunities that Rome's expansion provided. For example, during the Republic, equestrian businessmen could bid on contracts to collect taxes in different areas. The man awarded the contract was permitted to collect taxes—with few restraints on his methods. After paying the Senate the amount agreed upon in the contract, he could keep any other tax funds that he had gathered. Many equestrians accumulated fortunes in this way.

Next in rank came the plebeians, the mass of citizens who lived in Rome and throughout Italy. As we have seen, though protected by law with certain hard-won rights and offices, the Plebeian Assembly had gradually come under the control of plebeian politicians who were the clients of aristocratic patrons. These plebeian politicians and their patrons had little interest in the condition of the poor. This left the plebeians with no direct way to express their political will. The demands of army service kept many peasants away from their small farms for long periods of time. Rich investors took the opportunity to create huge estates by grabbing the bankrupt farms and replacing the free farmers with slaves captured in war. Sometimes impoverished plebeians became dependent tenant farmers on land they had once owned themselves. As a result, the citizen peasantry turned more and more to leaders who would protect them and give them land.

Rome's Italian allies had even fewer rights than the plebeians, despite their service in the Roman armies. Although millions of allies inhabited lands controlled by Rome, only a privileged few of the local elites received Roman citizenship. The rest could only hope for the goodwill of Roman officials.

At the bottom of the Roman hierarchy were slaves. By the first century B.C.E., about two million slaves captured in war or born in captivity lived in Italy and Sicily, amounting to about one-third of the population. Romans considered the slaves to be pieces of property, "talking tools," whom their owners could exploit at will. Freed slaves owed legal obligations to their former masters and were their clients. The brutal inequities of this system led to violence. The slave gangs who farmed vast estates in Sicily revolted first. In 135 B.C.E. they began an ill-fated struggle for freedom that lasted three years and involved more than 200,000 slaves.

Thirty years later another unsuccessful outburst began in southern Italy and Sicily because slave owners refused to comply with a senatorial decree to release any slaves who once had been free allies of Rome. Thirty thousand slaves took up arms between 104 and 101 B.C.E. The most destructive revolt occurred in Italy during the years from 74 to 71 B.C.E. An army of more than 100,000 slaves led by the Thracian gladiator Spartacus (gladiators were slaves who fought for public entertainment) battled eight Roman legions totaling about 50,000 men before being crushed by the superior Roman military organization.

The Roman Family

A Roman *familia* typically included not just the husband, wife, and unmarried children, but also their slaves and often freedmen and others who were dependent on the household. Legitimate marriages required the agreement of both husband and wife. Women usually married at puberty, and men did so in their twenties. Because few babies survived infancy, most families had only two or three children. Although Roman men could have only one wife at a time, men frequently cohabited with women to whom they were not married (concubines). Having a concubine was perfectly acceptable, but doing so was legal only if both parties involved had no living spouse.

The Roman family mirrored the patterns of authority and dependency found in the political arena. Just as a patron commanded the support of his clients regardless of their status in public life, so the male head of the household directed the destiny of all his subordinates within the *familia*. A man ruled his *familia* with full authority over the purse strings and all of his descendants until he died. The head of the family, or *paterfamilias,* held power of life and death over his wife, children, and slaves, though few men exercised this power. In reality, women and grown children often had a great deal of independence, and aristocratic women often exerted a strong influence in political life, though always from behind the scenes.

Upper-class Romans placed great value on the continuity of the family name, family traditions, and control of family property through the generations. For these reasons they often adopted males, even of adult age, to be heirs, especially if they had no legitimate sons of their own. Legitimate offspring always took the name of their father,

and in case of divorce, which could be easily obtained, continued to live with him. Illegitimate offspring stayed with the mother.

With very few exceptions Roman women remained legally dependent on a male relative. In the most common form of marriage, a wife remained under the formal control of the *paterfamilias* to whom she belonged before her marriage—in most cases, her father. In practice this meant that the wife retained control of her own property and the inheritance she had received from her father. A husband in this sort of marriage would have to be careful to avoid the anger of his wife's father or brothers, and so he might be inclined to treat his wife more justly. Another form of marriage brought the wife under the full control of her husband after the wedding. She had to worship the family gods of her husband's household and accept his ancestors as her own. If her husband died, one of his male relatives became the woman's legal protector.

The stability of family life through the generations desired by free Romans was impossible for slaves to attain. Former female slaves (freedwomen) remained tied to their former masters with bonds of dependency and obligation. Roman law did not recognize marriage between slaves. Some Roman handbooks explaining how to use slaves to maximum advantage advocated letting slaves establish conjugal arrangements. Owners could shatter such alliances by selling the enslaved partners or their offspring.

Beginnings of the Roman Revolution

························■························

The inequalities of wealth and power in Roman society led to the disintegration of the Republic. The rapid acquisition of territories and enormous wealth overseas heightened those differences. Roman reformers' attempts to face the new economic realities met with fierce resistance from those who profited the most from imperial rule: politicians, governors, high military personnel, and businessmen. These men sought personal glory and political advantage even if it came at the Republic's expense. Their quest for political prominence through military adventure, coupled with deep-seated flaws of political institutions, eventually overwhelmed the Republic's political structure and brought about a revolution—a decisive, fundamental change in the political system.

THE GRACCHI

During the second century B.C.E., more and more citizen farmers in Italy lost their fields to powerful landholders, who replaced them with slaves on their estates. As a result, the slave population of Italy increased dramatically. Some members of the political elite feared the danger inherent in these developments. If citizen farmers failed to meet the property requirements for military service and pay for their own weapons, as they traditionally had done, Rome would lose its supply of recruits for its legions.

Two young brothers, Tiberius and Gaius Gracchus, attempted some reforms. Although their mother was an aristocrat (the daughter of Scipio Africanus), she had married a wealthy plebeian. Thus, the brothers were legally plebeian, and they sought influence through the tribunate, an office limited to plebeians. As a tribune, Tiberius Gracchus (162–133 B.C.E.) convinced the Plebeian Assembly to pass a bill limiting the amount of public land that one man could possess. The new law required that the excess land from wealthy landholders be redistributed in small lots to poor citizens. While the land redistribution was in progress, conservative senators ignited a firestorm of opposition to Tiberius Gracchus. He responded by running for a second term as tribune, which was a break with precedent. Fearing revolution, a clique of senators in 133 B.C.E. arranged for assassins to club Tiberius to death. Land redistribution did not cease, but a terrible precedent of public violence had been set.

A decade later, when Tiberius's brother Gaius Gracchus became tribune in 123 B.C.E., he turned his attention to the problem of extortion in the provinces. With no checks on their authority, many corrupt governors forced provincials to give them money, valuable goods, and crops. Gaius Gracchus attempted to stop these abuses. In an attempt to dilute the power of corrupt provincial administrators chosen from the Senate and to win the political support of equestrians in Rome, he permitted equestrian tax collectors to operate in the provinces and to serve on juries that tried extortion cases. Gaius also tried to speed up land redistribution. But when he attempted to give citizenship to Rome's Italian allies in order to protect them from having their land confiscated by Romans, he lost the support of the Roman people, who did not wish to share the benefits of citizenship with non-Romans. In 121 B.C.E. Gaius committed suicide rather than allow himself to be murdered by a mob sent by his senatorial foes.

The ruthless suppression of the Gracchi (the Latin plural form of Gracchus) and their supporters lit the fuse of political and social revolution at Rome. By attempting to effect change through the Plebeian Assembly, the Gracchi unwittingly paved the way for less scrupulous aristocrats to seek power by falsely claiming to represent the interests of the poor. The introduction of assassinations into the public debate signaled the end of political consensus among the oligarchy. Rivalry among the elite combined with the desperation of the poor in an explosive blend, with the army as the wild card. If an unscrupulous politi-

THE RUINOUS EFFECTS OF CONQUEST

Roman conquests in Italy damaged the economy of newly captured rural areas. The following description by the Roman historian Appian describes the process of Roman settlement in newly taken territories in Italy, and the consequences of that settlement. The reforms of the Gracchi were intended to correct some of these problems.

The Romans, as they subdued the Italian peoples successively in war, seized a part of their lands and built towns there, or established their own colonies in already existing towns, using them as garrisons. Of the land thus acquired by war they assigned the cultivated part forthwith to settlers, or leased or sold it. Since they had no leisure as yet to allot the part which then lay desolated by war (this was generally the greater part), they proclaimed that in the meantime those who were willing to work it might do so for a share of the yearly crops—a tenth of the grain and a fifth of the fruit. From those who kept flocks, a tax was fixed for the animals, both oxen and small cattle. This they did in order to multiply the Italian race, which they considered to be the most laborious of peoples, so that that they might have plenty of allies at home. But the very opposite happened; for the rich, getting possession of the greater part of the undistributed lands, and being emboldened by the lapse of time to believe that they would never be dispossessed, and adding to their holding the small farms of their poor neighbors, partly by purchase and partly by force, came to cultivate vast tracts instead of single estates, using for this purpose slaves as laborers and herdsmen, lest free laborers be drawn from agriculture into the army. . . . Thus the governing class became enormously rich and number of slaves multiplied throughout the country, while the Italian peoples dwindled in numbers and strength . . .

Source: From *A History of Rome through the Fifth Century, Volume 1, The Republic,* edited by A. H. M. Jones (New York: Walker and Company, 1968), p. 104.

cian were to join forces with poverty-stricken soldiers, the Republic would be in peril.

Gaius Marius (157–86 B.C.E.) became the first Roman general to play this wild card. He rose to power when the angry Roman poor made him their champion. Despite his equestrian origins, this experienced general won the consulship in 107 B.C.E. A special law of the Plebeian Assembly put him in command of the legions fighting King Jugurtha in Numidia in North Africa, and he brought the war to a quick and successful conclusion. Then in response to a new threat from Germanic tribes seeking to invade Italy, Marius trained a new army and trounced the invaders.

In organizing his army Marius made some radical changes. He eliminated the property requirement for enlistment, thereby opening the ranks to the very poorest citizens in the countryside and in Rome. These soldiers swore an oath of loyalty to their commander-in-chief, who in return promised them farms after a victorious campaign. Marius's reforms put generals in the crossfire of the long-running political struggle between the Senate and the Plebeian Assembly, the two groups authorized to allocate lands won in war.

Marius achieved great personal power, but he did not use it against the institutions of the Republic. When he left public life in old age, the Roman Republic lurched ahead to its next major crisis: a revolt of the Italian allies.

THE SOCIAL WAR

In 90 B.C.E. Rome's loyal allies in Italy could no longer endure being treated as inferiors when it came to distribution of land and booty. They launched a revolt against Rome known as the Social War (from the Latin word *socii*, which means "allies"). The confederation of allies demanded not independence but participation in the Roman Republic. They wanted full citizenship rights because they had been partners in all of Rome's wars and thus felt entitled to share in the fruits of victory. The allies lost this war, but once they were defeated, Rome granted all their demands. All of Rome's Italian allies, consisting of the entire population of the peninsula, obtained Roman citizenship and quickly became a potent force in Roman political life. Their presence in the political arena tilted the political scales away from the wealthy in Rome toward the population of Italy in general.

The Social War in Italy was followed by wars abroad. The aristocrat Lucius Cornelius Sulla (138–78 B.C.E.), consul in 88 B.C.E., was setting out with an army to put down a serious provincial revolt in Asia Minor when the Plebeian Assembly turned command of his troops over to Marius, whose military reforms had aided the poor. In response, Sulla marched from southern Italy to Rome and reestablished his control by placing his own supporters into positions of authority in the Senate, the Plebeian Assembly, and various administrative offices.

However, only a year later, when Sulla returned to Asia Minor to resume command of the war against King Mithradates of Pontus, Marius and the other consul, Cinna, won back political control of Rome. They declared Sulla an outlaw and slaughtered his supporters. When Sulla returned to Italy in 82 B.C.E., at the head of a triumphant and loyal army, he seized Rome after a battle in which about

CHRONOLOGY

Social Conflict in Rome and Italy

133 B.C.E.	Tiberius Gracchus initiates reforms
123–122 B.C.E.	Gaius Gracchus initiates reforms
107 B.C.E.	Marius serves his first consulship
104–100 B.C.E.	Marius holds consecutive consulships
90–88 B.C.E.	Rome fights "Social War" with Italian allies
88 B.C.E.	Sulla takes Rome
82–79 B.C.E.	Sulla serves as dictator
77–71 B.C.E.	Pompey fights Celts in Spain
73–71 B.C.E.	Spartacus's slave revolt
70 B.C.E.	Cicero prosecutes Verres in court

60,000 Roman soldiers died, and then murdered 3,000 of his political opponents. The Senate named him dictator, which gave him complete power. With the support of the aristocratic Senate, whose power he hoped to restore, Sulla crippled the political power of the plebeians. In particular, he restricted the powers of tribunes to propose legislation because they had stirred up so much political instability for fifty years. After restoring the peace and the institutions of the state, Sulla surprised many people by resigning as dictator in 80 B.C.E. Like Marius, Sulla was unwilling to destroy the Republic's institutions for the sake of his own ambition. It was enough for him to have restored peace and the preeminence of the Senate. Nevertheless, he had set a precedent for using armies in political rivalries. In the next fifty years the Senate conspicuously failed to restrain private generals backed by public armies, thereby contributing to the collapse of the Republic.

THE FIRST TRIUMVIRATE

The Roman Republic's final downward spiral of social turmoil was provoked by three men: Pompey (Gnaeus Pompeius, 106–48 B.C.E.), Marcus Licinius Crassus (ca. 115–53 B.C.E.), and Gaius Julius Caesar (100–44 B.C.E.). Pompey, the general who suppressed a revolt in Spain, and Crassus, the wealthiest man in Rome who had been one of Sulla's lieutenants, joined forces to crush the slave revolt of Spartacus in 71 B.C.E. Backed by their armies, they then coerced the Senate into naming them consuls for 70 B.C.E.,

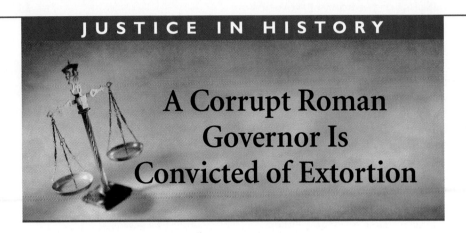

A Corrupt Roman Governor Is Convicted of Extortion

Governors sent by the Roman Senate to rule the provinces wielded absolute power, which often corrupted them. One such man was Gaius Verres, who was convicted in 70 B.C.E. in a court in Rome for his flagrant abuse of power while governor of Sicily. The courtroom drama in which Verres was found guilty reveals one of the deepest flaws of the Roman Republic: the unprincipled exploitation of lands under Roman control. It also reveals one of Rome's greatest strengths: the presence of men of high ethical standards who believed in honest government and fair treatment of Roman subjects. The trial and its result reveals Republican Rome at its best and worst.

While governor from 73 to 71 B.C.E., Verres had looted Sicily with shocking thoroughness. In his pursuit of gold and Greek art, Verres tortured and sometimes killed Roman citizens. His outraged victims employed the young and ambitious lawyer Marcus Tullius Cicero (106–43 B.C.E.) to prosecute Verres. They could not have chosen a better advocate.

The prosecution of Verres marks the beginning of Cicero's illustrious career as one of the most active politicians and certainly the greatest orator of the Republic. Cicero also stands as one of the most influential political philosophers of Western civilization, one who hated the corruption of political life and opposed tyranny in any form. His many works have influenced political thinkers from antiquity to the present.

In the Roman Republic, only senators and equestrians between ages 30 and 60 could serve on juries for civil crimes like those committed by Verres. All adult male citizens had the right to bring a case to court, but women had less freedom to do so. After swearing oaths of good faith, accusers read the charges in the presence of the accused, who in turn agreed to accept the decision of the court.

When trials began, the prosecutor was expected to be present, but the accused could decline to attend. The prosecution and the defense both produced evidence, then cross-examined witnesses. Since a Roman lawyer could discuss any aspect of the defendant's personal or public life, character assassination became an important—and amusing—rhetorical tool.

After deliberating, the jury delivered its verdict and the judge gave the penalty required by law, generally fines or periods of exile. No provisions for appeal existed, but pardon could be obtained by a legislative act.

Cicero worked this system to his advantage in his prosecution of Verres. He nimbly quashed an attempt to delay the trial until 69 B.C.E., when the president of the court would be a crony of Verres. Then, with a combination of ringing oratory and irrefutable evidence of Verres's crimes, Cicero made his case. The following excerpt from his speech shows Cicero's mastery of persuasive rhetoric:

Judges: at this grave crisis in the history of our country, you have been offered a peculiarly desirable gift . . . For you have been given a unique chance to make your Senatorial Order less unpopular, and to set right the damaged reputation of these courts. A belief has taken root which is having a fatal effect on our nation—and which to us who are senators, in particular, threatens grave peril. This belief is on everyone's tongue, at Rome and even in foreign countries. It is this: that in these courts, with their present membership, even the worst criminal will never be convicted provided that he has money. . . . And at this very juncture Gaius Verres has been brought to trial. Here is a man whose life and actions the world has already condemned—yet whose enormous fortune, according to his own loudly expressed hopes, has already brought him acquittal! Pronounce a just and scrupulous verdict against Verres and you will keep the good name which ought always to be yours. . . . I spent fifty days on a careful investigation of the entire island of Sicily; I got to know every document, every wrong suffered either by a community or an individual. . . .

For three long years he so thoroughly despoiled and pillaged the province that its restoration to its previous state is out of the question. . . .

This portrait of Cicero captures his uncompromising personality. The style of depicting every wrinkle conforms both to Hellenistic interest in psychological portraiture and traditional Roman directness. In the Republican period this type of portraiture was enormously popular.

All the property that anyone in Sicily still has for his own today is merely what happened to escape the attention of this avaricious lecher, or survived his glutted appetites. . . . It was an appalling disgrace for our country.

. . . In the first stage of the trial, then, my charge is this. I accuse Gaius Verres of committing acts of lechery and brutality against the citizens and allies of Rome, and many crimes against God and man. I claim that he has illegally taken from Sicily sums amounting to forty million sesterces. By the witnesses and documents, public and private, which I am going to cite, I shall convince you that these charges are true.[2]

Cicero's speech was persuasive and the jury found Verres guilty. Verres went into exile in Marseilles to avoid his sentence, but he did not avoid punishment altogether. Justice—relentless and ironic—caught up with him some years later during the civil wars that followed Julius Caesar's death. Mark Antony, who was also a connoisseur of other people's wealth, wanted Verres's art collection for himself and so put Verres's name on a death list to obtain it. The former governor of Sicily was murdered in 43 B.C.E.

In his prosecution of Verres, Cicero delivered more than an indictment of one corrupt man; for a brief moment he revealed some of the deepest, fatal flaws of the Roman Republic. The trial inspired some short-term reforms, but not until the reforms of the emperor Augustus did the relationship between Roman administrators and provincial populations become more fair. ■

Questions of Justice

1. What does Verres's trial reveal about weaknesses in the Roman Republic?
2. Cicero's speech illustrates his disdain for corruption and tyranny. What are the tensions between personal morality and the requirements of governing a large empire?

Taking It Further

Rawson, Elizabeth. *Cicero, A Portrait.* 1975. This book gives a balanced account of Cicero's life.

Gruen, Erich S. *The Last Generation of the Roman Republic.* 1974. A magisterial analysis of the Republic's decline, with emphasis on legal affairs.

even though Pompey was legally too young and had not yet held the prerequisite junior offices.

During their consulship, Pompey and Crassus made modest changes to Sulla's reforms. They permitted the tribunes to propose laws again and let equestrians serve on juries. After their year in office they retired without making further demands. Pompey continued his military career. He received a special command in 67 B.C.E. to clear pirates from the Mediterranean in order to protect Roman trade. The following year Pompey crushed another rebellion in Asia Minor. He reorganized Asia Minor and territories in the Middle East, creating new provinces and more client kingdoms subservient to Rome.

When Pompey returned to Rome he asked the Senate to grant land to his victorious troops. The Senate, jealous of his success and afraid of the power he would gain as the patron of so many troops, would not comply. To gain land for his soldiers and have his political arrangements in Asia Minor and the Middle East ratified, Pompey made an alliance with two men even more ambitious and less scrupulous than he: his old ally Crassus and Gaius Julius Caesar, the ambitious descendant of an ancient patrician family. The three formed an informal alliance historians call the First Triumvirate°. With their influence now combined, no man or institution could oppose them. Caesar obtained the consulship in 59 B.C.E., despite the objections of many senators. By using illegal means that would return to haunt him, he directed the Senate to ratify Pompey's arrangements in the Middle East and Asia Minor and to grant land to his troops. He arranged for Crassus's clients, the equestrian tax collectors, to have their financial problems resolved at public expense.

As a reward for his efforts on behalf of the triumvirate, the perpetually debt-ridden Caesar arranged to receive the governorship of the Po Valley and the Illyrian coast for five years after his consulship ended. Later he extended that term for ten years. During this time, he planned to enrich himself at the expense of the provincials. As he set out for his governorship, he assumed command of Transalpine Gaul (northwest of the Alps) when its governor died. This put Caesar in a position to operate militarily in all of Gaul—and ultimately to conquer it.

JULIUS CAESAR AND THE END OF THE REPUBLIC

Caesar's determination to conquer Gaul lay in pursuing personal advantage. He knew that he would win glory, wealth, and prestige in Rome by conquering new lands, and so he promptly began a war (58–50 B.C.E.) against the Celtic tribes of Transalpine Gaul. A military genius, Caesar chronicled his ruthless tactics and military successes in his *Commentaries on the Gallic War,* as famous today for its elegant Latin as for its unflinching glimpse of Roman methods and justifications of conquest. In eight years Caesar conquered the area of modern France and Belgium, turning these territories into Roman provinces. He even briefly invaded Britain. His intrusion into Celtic lands led to their eventual Romanization. The French language developed from the Latin spoken by Roman soldiers. Similarly Spanish, Italian, Portuguese, and Romanian also derived from the tongue of Roman conquerors and are called "Romance" languages.

Meanwhile, the other members of the triumvirate, Crassus and Pompey, also sought military glory. The wealthy Crassus raised an army out of his own pocket, reputedly asserting, "If you can't afford to pay for an army, you shouldn't command it!" His attempt to conquer the Parthians, the successors to the Persian Empire, ended in disaster in 53 B.C.E. in Syria. The Parthians killed Crassus, destroyed his army, and captured the military insignia (metal eagles on staffs, called standards) that each legion proudly carried into battle. Pompey again assumed the governorship of Spain, but stayed in Rome while subordinates waged war there against Spain's Celtic inhabitants.

In Rome, a group of senators grew fearful of Caesar's power, ambitions, and arrogance. They appealed to Pompey for assistance, and he brought the armies loyal to him to the aid of the Senate against Caesar. The Senate then asked Caesar to lay down his command in Gaul and return to Rome. Caesar knew that if he complied with this request he would be indicted on charges of improper conduct or corruption as soon as he returned to Rome. Facing certain conviction, Caesar refused to return for a trial. In 49 B.C.E. he left Gaul and marched south with his loyal troops against the forces of the Senate in Rome. Recognizing the enormity of his gamble ("I've thrown the dice!" he said when he crossed the Rubicon River, the boundary of land under direct control of the Senate), he deliberately plunged Rome into civil war. Because of his victories in Gaul and his generosity to the people of Rome, Caesar could pose as the people's champion while seeking absolute power for himself. Intimidated by Caesar's forces and public support, Pompey hastily withdrew to Greece, but Caesar overtook and defeated him at Pharsalus, a town in Thessaly, in 48 B.C.E. When Pompey fled to Egypt high officials of the Ptolemaic pharaoh's court immediately murdered him to win Caesar's favor.

It took Caesar more than two years to crush remnants of senatorial resistance to his authority before he could return to Italy in 45 B.C.E. In 44 B.C.E., back in Rome, he had himself proclaimed dictator for life and assumed complete control over all aspects of government, flagrantly disregarding the precedents of the Republic. Because his plans did not reach fulfillment, Caesar's long-term goals for the Roman state remain unclear, but some version of Hellenistic monarchy seems to have been his goal.

Once in power, Caesar permanently ended the autonomy of the Senate. He enlarged the Senate from 600 (its size at the time of Sulla) to 900 men, and then filled it with his supporters. He also established military colonies in Spain, North Africa, and Gaul to provide land for his veterans and to secure those territories. He adjusted the chaotic Republican calendar by adding one day every leap year, creating a year of 365.25 days. The resulting "Julian" calendar lasted until the sixteenth century C.E. He regularized gold coinage and urban administration and planned a vast public library. At his death, plans for a major campaign against Parthia were underway, suggesting that conquest would have remained a basic feature of his rule.

Caesar seriously miscalculated by assuming he could win the support of his enemies by showing clemency to them and by making administrative changes that disregarded Republican precedent. These changes earned Caesar the resentment of traditionalist senators who failed to recognize that the Republic could never be restored. On March 15, 44 B.C.E., a group of idealistic senators, led by Cassius and Brutus, stabbed Caesar to death at a Senate meeting. The assassins claimed that they wanted to restore the Republic, but in reality they had only unleashed another brutal civil war.

Marcus Antonius (Mark Antony), who had been Caesar's right-hand man, stepped forward to oppose the conspirators. He was soon joined by Octavian, Caesar's grandnephew and legal heir. Though Octavian was only 19, he gained control of some of Caesar's legions and compelled the Senate to name him consul. Marcus Lepidus, commander of Caesar's cavalry, joined Mark Antony and Octavian to form the Second Triumvirate°. The new trio coerced the Senate into granting them power to rule Rome legally.

At the battle of Philippi, a town in Macedonia, in 42 B.C.E., forces of the Second Triumvirate crushed the army of the senators who had assassinated Caesar. But soon Antony, Octavian, and Lepidus began to struggle among themselves for absolute authority. Lepidus soon dropped out of the contest, while Antony and Octavian maneuvered for control of Rome. Reluctant to begin open warfare, they agreed to separate spheres of influence. Octavian took Italy and Rome's western provinces, while Antony took the eastern provinces.

In Egypt, Antony joined forces with Cleopatra VII, the last descendent of the Hellenistic monarch Ptolemy. Both stood to gain from this alliance: Antony would gain the resources of Egypt in his quest to gain complete power over the eastern provinces, while Cleopatra would strengthen her rule in Egypt. In response to this alliance, Octavian launched a vicious propaganda campaign. Posing as the conservative protector of Roman tradition, he accused Antony of surrendering Roman values and territory to an evil foreign seductress. The inevitable war broke out in 31

CHRONOLOGY

The Collapse of the Roman Republic

60 B.C.E.	The First Triumvirate is established
59–49 B.C.E.	Julius Caesar conquers northern and central Gaul
53 B.C.E.	Crassus is killed in the Parthian War
49 B.C.E.	Caesar crosses Rubicon River and begins civil war
48 B.C.E.	Battle of Pharsalus; Pompey is killed in Egypt
45 B.C.E.	Caesar wins civil war
47–44 B.C.E.	Caesar serves as dictator
44 B.C.E.	Caesar is murdered; civil war breaks out
43 B.C.E.	The Second Triumvirate is formed; Cicero is murdered
42 B.C.E.	Battle of Philippi; Caesar's assassins are defeated
31 B.C.E.	Octavian defeats Antony and Cleopatra and gains absolute power

B.C.E. At the battle of Actium, in Greece, Octavian's troops defeated Antony and Cleopatra's land and naval forces. The couple fled to Alexandria, in Egypt, where they committed suicide a year later.

The 31-year-old Octavian now stood as absolute master of the Roman world. He had a clear vision of the problems that had destroyed the Republic, and from its ashes he planned to rebuild the Roman state. Under the leadership of Octavian, who came to be known as the emperor Augustus, Rome created a new political system, the Roman Empire, in which Octavian had unprecedented power over a vast geographical area.

The new world order that Octavian created brought an end to the Hellenistic Age. Rome now ruled all the lands that Alexander the Great had conquered, except for Persia and the territories farther to the east, and Hellenistic culture would now have to accommodate the realities of Roman rule. As we will see in the next chapter, Octavian succeeded where Alexander had failed: He created a world empire that had the infrastructure it needed to endure, and the peaceful conditions that enabled its culture to flourish and spread.

CONCLUSION

Defining the West in the Hellenistic Age

During the Hellenistic Age the cultural and geographical boundaries of what would later be called the West began to take shape. These boundaries encompassed the regions where Hellenistic culture penetrated and had a lasting influence. The lands within the empire of Alexander the Great, all of which lay to the east of Greece and Egypt, formed the core of this cultural realm, but the Hellenistic world also extended westward across the Mediterranean, embracing the lands ruled by Carthage from North Africa to Spain. Hellenism also reached the edges of the lands inhabited by Celtic peoples. Most of all, Hellenistic culture left a distinctive mark on Roman civilization in Italy. In all these locations Greek culture interacted with those of the areas it penetrated, and the synthesis that resulted became one of the main foundations of Western civilization.

During the period of the Roman Empire, which will be the subject of the next chapter, a new blend of Hellenistic and Latin cultures, in which Hellenism was an important but not the dominant component, took shape. The geographical arena within which this culture flourished was that of the vast Roman Empire, covering a large part of Europe, North Africa, and the Middle East. The culture that characterized this empire gave a new definition to what we now call the West.

Suggestions for Further Reading

For a comprehensive list of suggested readings, please go to www.ablongman.com/levack/chapter4

Boardman, John, Jasper Griffin, and Oswyn Murray, eds. *Greece and the Hellenistic World, The Oxford History of the Classical World.* 1988. A synthesis of all aspects of Hellenistic life, with excellent illustrations and bibliography.

Cohn, Norman. *Cosmos, Chaos, and the World to Come: The Ancient Roots of Apocalyptic Faith.* 1993. This brilliant study explains the development of ideas about the end of the world in the cultures of the ancient world.

Cornell, T. J. *The Beginnings of Rome: Italy and Rome from the Bronze Age to the Punic Wars (ca. 1000–264 B.C.).* 1996. A synthesis of the latest evidence with many important new interpretations.

Crawford, Michael. *The Roman Republic,* 2nd ed. 1992. This overview by a leading scholar lays a strong foundation for further study.

Cunliffe, Barry. *The Ancient Celts.* 1997. This source analyzes the archaeological evidence for the Celtic Iron Age, with many illustrations and maps.

Cunliffe, Barry, ed. *The Oxford Illustrated Prehistory of Europe.* 1996. A collection of well-illustrated essays on the development of European cultures from the end of the Ice Age to the Classical period.

Gardner, Jane F. *Women in Roman Law and Society.* 1986. Explains the legal position of women in the Roman world.

Green, Peter. *Alexander to Actium: The Historical Evolution of the Hellenistic Age.* 1990. A vivid interpretation of the world created by Alexander until the victory of Augustus.

Gruen, Erich S. *The Hellenistic World and the Coming of Rome.* 1984. An extremely important study of how Rome entered the eastern Mediterranean world.

Kuhrt, Amélie, and Susan Sherwin-White, eds. *Hellenism in the East: The Interaction of Greek and Non-Greek Civilizations from Syria to Central Asia After Alexander.* 1987. These studies help us understand the complexities of the interaction of Greeks and non-Greeks in the Hellenistic world.

Pollitt, J. J. *Art in the Hellenistic Age.* 1986. A brilliant interpretation of the development of Hellenistic art.

Notes

1. Athenaios, 253 D; cited and translated in J. J. Pollitt, *Art in the Hellenistic Age* (1986), p. 271.
2. From *Selected Works* by Cicero, translated by Michael Grant (Penguin Classics 1960, second revised edition 1971).

Enclosing the West: The Early Roman Empire and Its Neighbors, 31 B.C.E.–235 C.E.

N THE MIDDLE OF THE SECOND CENTURY C.E., AELIUS ARISTIDES, AN ARISTOCRATIC Greek writer who held Roman citizenship, visited Rome, where he gave a long public oration in honor of the imperial capital. His words reveal what the Roman Empire meant to a wealthy, highly educated man from Rome's eastern provinces: "Rome is to the whole world what an ordinary city is to its suburbs and surrounding countryside . . . you have given up the division of nation from nation . . . you have separated the human race into Roman and non-Romans."

Aristides' description of the empire as one grand city with a unified culture set off from the "barbarian" peoples in the world is an exaggeration. Nevertheless it points to the key element of the Romans' success—a willingness to share their culture with their subjects and to assimilate them into the political and social life of the empire. Aristides understood that Roman culture flourished primarily in cities, and he saw that Roman urban life was the mark of civilization. He dismissed with a contemptuous sniff those not fortunate enough to live as Romans. In Aristides's opinion, Rome's destiny was to bring civilization to the rest of the world. His satisfied view of the Roman Empire demonstrates how successfully Rome had created a sense of common purpose among its elite citizens.

During its first two and a half centuries of existence, the Roman Empire brought cultural unity and political stability to an astonishingly diverse area stretching from the Atlantic Ocean to the Persian Gulf. Imperial rule disseminated Roman culture throughout not only the Mediterranean region and the Middle East, but also northwestern Europe. Within imperial Rome's parameters—intellectual, religious, political, and geographic—the basic outlines of what we call the West today were drawn.

This chapter examines the Roman Empire at the height of its power (ca. 31 B.C.E.–235 C.E.). We will see how its encounters with far-flung subject populations helped shape its development. Autocratic and exploitative, the

Marcus Aurelius: This magnificent bronze statue shows the emperor Marcus Aurelius (r. 161–180) raising his right hand in a gesture of command, compelling the viewer to obey. A triumph of the art of bronze casting, this statue conveys the majesty of the Roman Empire.

Roman imperial system nonetheless provided the climate for rich developments in social, religious, and political life. Military force maintained the imperial system, but the peace and prosperity that accompanied Roman rule persuaded many subject peoples of its benefits. The new regime established a stable governing system that brought a nearly unbroken peace to the Mediterranean world for more than two centuries. Historians call this era the *Pax Romana°*, the Roman peace. In these centuries Roman culture slowly took root across western Europe, North Africa, and the Middle East, transforming the lives of local populations. In the eyes of millions of people during these years, Rome ceased to be an unfamiliar and predatory occupying power. They came to regard Rome as a "civilizing agent" that provided unity and common culture. But others, particularly the slaves whose labor fueled the Roman economy and the small farmers whose taxes supported the Roman state, experienced Rome as an oppressive ruler.

This chapter analyzes imperial Rome's constantly evolving political and cultural community as three concentric circles of power—the imperial center, the provinces, and the frontiers and beyond. The imperial center served as the site of the main agents of control—the emperor, the Roman senate, the chief legal and administrative institutions, and the army. In the second circle, provincial populations struggled with the challenges raised by the imposition of Roman culture and politics and in the process contributed to the construction of a new imperial culture. The outermost circle of the empire, its frontier zones and the lands beyond, included Romans living within the empire's borders as well as those peoples who lived on the other side, but who nonetheless interacted with Rome through trading and warfare. Throughout the chapter we will explore what it meant to be a Roman in each of these concentric circles. Four questions guide this exploration: (1) How did the Roman imperial system develop and what roles did the emperor, senate, army, and Rome itself play in this process? (2) How did provincial peoples assimilate to or resist Roman rule? (3) How did Romans interact with peoples living beyond the imperial borders? (4) What was the social and cultural response to the emergence and consolidation of empire?

The Imperial Center

After civil wars left the Roman Republic in ruins, a new political system emerged from its ashes. Rome continued to acquire and rule huge territories far from Italy. Its form of government, however, changed from a republic, in which members of an oligarchy competed for power that they shared by serving in elected offices, to an empire, in which one man, the emperor, held absolute power for life. Roman culture, with its strict social divisions

and political structures, its distinctive forms of architecture and art, its shared intellectual and religious life, and its legal system defining the rights of citizens and subjects, was now securely anchored by an imperial system based on force. The city of Rome, the center of imperial operations, became the model for social life, political processes, and architectural styles throughout the empire. At the same time, Roman law united Roman citizens throughout the empire and distinguished them from conquered peoples, who kept their own laws and customs. After 212 C.E. all free people in the empire gained Roman citizenship, a sign of growing cultural unity and the Romanization of the diverse peoples under imperial rule (see Map 5.1).

IMPERIAL AUTHORITY: AUGUSTUS AND AFTER

As we saw in Chapter 4, Julius Caesar's heir, Octavian, destroyed the Republic while pretending to preserve it. Octavian wrenched the state from the spiral of civil war and claimed that he had restored normal life to the Republic. In his own eyes, as well as those of a people weary of bitter civil war, Octavian was the savior of Republican Rome. In public affairs, however, nothing could have been further from the truth. Behind a carefully crafted façade of restored Republican tradition, Octavian created a Roman version of a Hellenistic monarchy, like those of Alexander the Great's successors in the eastern Mediterranean. By neutralizing all of his political enemies in the Roman Senate; vanquishing his military rivals, such as Antony and Cleopatra; and establishing an iron grip on every visible mechanism of power, Octavian succeeded where Julius Caesar and the other less able Republican politicians had failed: He achieved total mastery of the political arena at Rome. No one successfully challenged his authority.

To mask his tyranny, Octavian never wore a crown and modestly referred to himself as *Princeps,* or First Citizen. He took several steps to create a political position in Rome that was all-powerful and at the same time unobtrusive. In 27 B.C.E., as he boasted in the official account of his reign, Octavian "transferred the Republic from his power into that of the Senate and the Roman people." This abdication was a carefully organized sham. In reality, he maintained absolute political control over Rome. Following his instructions, the powerless Senate showered honors upon him, including the title "Augustus." This invented title best illustrates the political cleverness of Rome's absolute master. "Augustus" implied a uniquely exalted, godlike authority in the community, but the word had no previous associations with kingship. Augustus "accepted" the Senate's plea to remain consul and agreed to exercise control over the frontier provinces where the most troops were stationed, including Spain, Gaul, and Syria. The senators rejoiced, calling Augustus "sole savior of the entire empire."

In 23 B.C.E. Augustus took further steps to establish his paramount position. He had held the consulship every year since the end of the civil war in 31 B.C.E., but he recognized that holding the power of a consul year after year was inconsistent with his claim to have restored the Republic. So, in 23 C.E. he renounced the consulship and shrewdly arranged for the Senate to grant him unprecedented power, but disguised by Republican trappings. He assumed the powers of a tribune, which included the right to conduct business in the Senate, the right to veto, and immunity from arrest and punishment. He could now legally intercede in all government activities and military affairs by virtue of "greater authority" granted to him by the Senate. Other generals continued to lead the legions into battle, but always in his name. Other magistrates continued to administer the state in accordance with the traditional responsibilities of their office, but no one was chosen without his approval.

Augustus selected or approved all his provincial governors. He assumed direct control over particularly rich provinces, such as Egypt, and those, like Germany, that required a strong military presence to ward off invaders and control the recently conquered population. The Roman Senate maintained authority over peaceful provinces like Greece and Sicily. Yet even in these provinces, Augustus intervened whenever he wished.

Later rulers, accepting the trappings of monarchy more openly than Augustus, abandoned the fiction of the "Princeps" and used the title *imperator,* or emperor. Despite this change, the imperial system established by Augustus long survived his death, even when the throne was occupied by brutal men such as Caligula (r. 37–41 C.E.), who tried to have his favorite horse elected to the Senate, or Nero (r. 54–68 C.E.), who murdered both his wife and his mother.

■ **Map 5.1 The Roman Empire at Its Greatest Extent**

The Roman Empire reached its greatest extent during the reign of Trajan (98–117 C.E.). Stretching from the north of Britain to the Euphrates River, the empire brought together hundreds of distinct ethnic groups.

The Problem of Succession

Augustus, following the example of the Hellenistic world, hoped to establish a hereditary monarchy, in which power passed down through his family. When he died in 14 C.E., his stepson Tiberius (r. 14–37 C.E.) took control of the empire without opposition. A hereditary monarchy was now firmly in place. Some senators muttered occasionally about restoring the Republic, but this remained an idle—and very dangerous—dream. Neither the army nor the people would have supported a Senate-led anti-imperial rebellion.

The hereditary principle remained unchallenged for centuries, in part because it staved off the instability that would have come with open competition for the throne. In the dynasty inaugurated by Augustus, which is known as the Julio-Claudian dynasty and which lasted almost 100 years, every ruler came from Augustus's extended family. But when Nero, the last of Augustus's family line, committed suicide in 68 C.E. he left no heirs and so there were no obvious successors to the throne. Civil war broke out among four contenders.

During this "Year of the Four Emperors," Rome learned what the historian Tacitus later called the "secret of empire"—that troops far from the imperial city could choose emperors. Four different emperors took the throne in quick succession, as different Roman armies competed to put their commanders on the throne. The winner of this contest, the general Titus Flavius Vespasianus, or Vespasian (r. 69–79 C.E.), after breaking the back of a great Jewish rebellion that raged from 66–70 C.E., moved to seize power when he learned of Nero's death. Vespasian carefully consulted with other Roman commanders to obtain their support for his imperial ambitions before embarking for Italy. By the end of 69 C.E. he had defeated his rivals and became the first emperor who did not come from the Roman nobility. Born into the equestrian class, he built his reputation on his military prowess.

The Flavian dynasty that Vespasian established lasted twenty-five years until the death of his last son, Domitian (r. 81–96 C.E.). A conscientious and able monarch, Domitian nevertheless ruled with an openly autocratic style. He executed many aristocratic senators, creating a reign of terror among Rome's elite. Fittingly, a group of senators murdered him.

To avoid the chaos of another succession crisis, the Senate cooperated with the army in choosing a new emperor, the elderly Nerva (r. 96–98 C.E.). They hoped that this

CHRONOLOGY

Emperors of Rome

27 B.C.E.–14 C.E.	Augustus	
14–37 C.E.	Tiberius	
37–41 C.E.	Caligula	JULIO-CLAUDIAN DYNASTY
41–54 C.E.	Claudius	
54–68 C.E.	Nero	
68–69 C.E.	Galba	
69 C.E.	Otho	
69 C.E.	Vitellius	
69–79 C.E.	Vespasian	
79–81 C.E.	Titus	FLAVIAN DYNASTY
81–96 C.E.	Domitian	
96–98 C.E.	Nerva	
98–117 C.E.	Trajan	
117–138 C.E.	Hadrian	
138–161 C.E.	Antoninus Pius	
161–180 C.E.	Marcus Aurelius	ANTONINE DYNASTY
161–169 C.E.	Lucius Verus	
180–192 C.E.	Commodus	
193 C.E.	Pertinax	
193 C.E.	Didius Julianus	
193–211 C.E.	Septimius Severus	
211–217 C.E.	Caracalla	
211–212 C.E.	Geta	SEVERAN DYNASTY
217–218 C.E.	Macrinus	
218–222 C.E.	Elagabalus	
222–235 C.E.	Severus Alexander	

elderly, highly respected man who had no sons would ensure a smooth transition to the next regime, and so he did. Under pressure from the restless military establishment, Nerva adopted the vigorous and experienced general Trajan (r. 98–117 C.E.) as his son and heir. He thus inaugurated the era historians call the Antonine Age. For almost a century, Rome enjoyed competent rule, to a large degree because

Nerva's practice of adopting highly qualified successors continued. After Trajan adopted Hadrian (r. 117–138 C.E.), Hadrian in turn adopted Antoninus Pius (r. 138–161 C.E.). Antoninus adopted Marcus Aurelius (r. 161–180 C.E.) to succeed him. Historians consider the Antonine age a high point of Roman peace and prosperity. The Roman historian Tacitus, who survived Domitian's tyranny to live during Nerva's and Trajan's reigns, praised these latter emperors for establishing "the rare happiness of times, when we may think what we please, and express what we think."

Yet again the murder of an emperor brought an end to peace. Marcus Aurelius unfortunately abandoned the custom of picking a highly qualified successor, and instead was followed to the throne by his incompetent, cruel, and eventually insane son Commodus (r. 180–192 C.E.). In 192 C.E., several senators arranged to have Commodus strangled, triggering another civil war.

A senator from North Africa, Septimius Severus, emerged victorious from this conflict and assumed the imperial throne in 193 C.E. Fluent in Latin, Greek, and Punic, the Phoenician language still widely spoken in North Africa, Septimius Severus exemplified the ascent of provincial aristocrats to the highest levels of the empire. The Severan dynasty he established lasted until 235 C.E. Septimius Severus could afford to ignore the Senate because he was popular with the army—he raised its pay for the first time in more than 100 years. But when the last emperor of his dynasty, Severus Alexander (r. 222–235 C.E.), attempted to negotiate with the German tribes in 235 C.E. by offering them bribes, his own troops killed him because they wanted the cash for themselves. Once again, the murder of an emperor provoked civil war. Fifty years of political and economic crises followed the end of the Severan dynasty. As we will see in the next chapter, the imperial structure that emerged after this time of crisis differed significantly from the Augustan model.

The Emperor's Role:
The Nature of Imperial Power

Under the Augustan imperial system, four main responsibilities defined the emperor's role. First, the emperor both protected and expanded imperial territory. Only the emperor determined foreign policy and made treaties with other nations. Only the emperor waged war—both defensive wars to protect the empire from its enemies and aggressive campaigns of conquest. Generals fighting under Augustus's orders conquered huge tracts of Spain, Germany, and the Balkans. The emperor Trajan won great glory by conquering the rich Dacian kingdom north of the Danube River between 101 and 106 C.E. Other emperors smashed internal revolts or fought long border wars. From Augustus's reign onward, the northern frontier with Germany was particularly troublesome. Marcus Aurelius had to pawn palace treasures to finance campaigns against confederations of Germanic tribes.

The emperor's second responsibility was to administer justice and to provide good government throughout his dominions. In theory all citizens could appeal to the emperor directly for justice. In addition, the emperor and his staff responded to questions on points of law and administration from provincial governors and other officials who ruled in the emperor's name. Emperors provided emergency relief after natural disasters, looked after the roads and infrastructure of the empire, and financed public buildings in cities in all the provinces.

The emperor's third responsibility stemmed from his religious role. As *Pontifex Maximus,* or High Priest, the emperor supervised the public worship of the great gods of Rome, particularly Jupiter, as well as the goddess Roma as his deified imperial ancestors. Emperors and subjects alike believed that in order to fulfill Rome's destiny to rule the world, they must make regular sacrifices to the gods.

Finally, the emperor gradually became a symbol of unity for all the peoples of the empire. He embodied the empire and served as the focal point around which all life in the empire revolved. Inevitably, the emperor seemed more than human, even worthy of worship, for he was the guarantor of peace, prosperity, and victory for Rome, and he had infinitely more power than anyone else alive.

CHRONOLOGY

Political and Military Events

31 B.C.E.	Octavian defeats Mark Antony and controls Mediterranean world
27 B.C.E.	Octavian adopts the name Augustus
9 C.E.	Varus and three legions are defeated; Romans abandon Germany
63 C.E.	Revolt of Boudica crushed in Britain
66-70 C.E.	Jewish Revolt; Jerusalem destroyed
69 C.E.	"Year of the Four Emperors"
113–117 C.E.	Trajan conquers Mesopotamia and Dacia; Rome at greatest extent
120s C.E.	Hadrian's Wall built in Britain
168–175 C.E.	Marcus Aurelius fights Marcomanni and other tribes
212 C.E.	Antonine Constitution grants Roman citizenship to all free inhabitants of the empire
235 C.E.	Fifty years of political turmoil begin

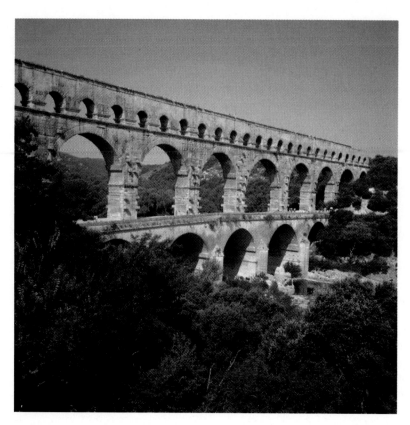

■ **Aqueducts: The Pont du Gard**
This graceful aqueduct, now known as the Pont du Gard, was built about 14 C.E. to carry water to the city of Nîmes, in the south of France, from its surrounding hills. Romans were highly sophisticated hydraulic engineers, and waterworks like this aqueduct were a common feature of all the large cities of the empire.

Worship of the emperor began with Augustus. He was reluctant to call himself a god because Roman tradition opposed such an idea, but he permitted his spirit to be worshiped in a paternal way, as a sort of *paterfamilias* or head of a universal family of peoples of the empire. He also referred to himself as the "son of a god"—in this case Julius Caesar, whom the Senate had declared divine. After Augustus, imperial worship became more pronounced, although only a few emperors, such as Domitian, emphasized their divinity during their lifetimes. Most were content to be worshiped after death, assuming that the Senate would declare them gods after their funerals. On his deathbed, Vespasian managed to joke, "I guess I'm becoming a god now."

In Rome's eastern provinces such as Egypt and Syria, where people for thousands of years had considered their kings divine, the worship of the emperor spread quickly. Each city's official calendar marked the emperor's day of accession to the throne. Soon, cities across the empire worshiped the emperor on special occasions through games, speeches, sacrifices, and free public feasts in which people ate the flesh of the animals sacrificed in the emperor's honor. Within magnificent temples, priests conducted elaborate public rituals to venerate the emperor.

This cult of the emperor provided a focus of allegiance for the diverse peoples of the empire and so served as a unifying force. Although most people would never see their ruler, he was in their prayers and their public spaces every day. In addition to encouraging worship or veneration in public ceremonies throughout the empire, emperors made their presence felt by building and restoring roads, temples, harbors, aqueducts, and fortifications. These public works demonstrated the emperor's unparalleled patronage and concern for the public welfare. In turn, local leaders emulated his generosity in their own cities.

Other elements of material culture also made the imperial presence real for the emperor's subjects. Coins, for example, provided a glimpse of the emperor's face and a phrase that characterized some aspect of his reign. Slogans such as "Restorer of the World," "Concord with the Gods," and "The Best Ruler—Sustenance for Italy" brought the ruler's message into every person's pocket. Statues of the emperor served a similar purpose. (One statue of an emperor found in Carthage had a removable head, so that when a new ruler ascended the throne, the town leaders could save money by replacing only the head.) In his own portraits, Augustus tended toward the conventions of classical Greek portraiture that presented him as remote and ageless. On the other hand, most emperors were willing to place fairly realistic portraits of their faces on their coins and statues.

Emperors also used military and sporting victories to make their presence felt throughout the empire. In the Republic, conquest had brought wealth and glory to its many generals. In contrast, in the new imperial system, only

■ Augustus: A Commanding Presence

This imposing statue of Augustus dating to 19 B.C.E. depicts him as a warrior making a gesture of command. His face is ageless, the carving on his armor celebrates peace and prosperity, and his posture is balanced and forceful.

the emperor could take credit for victory in war. Imperial propaganda described the emperor as eternally triumphant. Sporting events, too, glorified the emperor. At the Circus Maximus in Rome, a chariot racetrack where a quarter of a million people could gather to cheer their favorite charioteer, as well as in racetracks throughout the empire, victory in every race belonged symbolically to the emperor.

THE AGENTS OF CONTROL

The emperor stood at the heart of the imperial system devised by Augustus. But the imperial center also included other agents of control. The Roman Senate continued to play a significant administrative role in the new system. As it grew to represent not just the aristocracy of the city of Rome, but a new ruling elite drawn from the provinces, the Senate solidified new networks of power and communications that tied the imperial center to its outlying regions. The army, too, constituted an important element of the imperial center. It not only conquered new territories and ensured the emperor's rule throughout the empire, it also served as a Romanizing force, bringing Roman cultural and political practices to distant regions.

The Roman Senate: A Loss of Autonomy

In the imperial system fashioned by Augustus, the Senate continued to function, but with a more restricted role. To maintain the illusion that he had saved rather than destroyed the Republic, Augustus took pains to show respect for the Senate. He allowed its members to compete among themselves for promotion and honor in his service. He permitted the old Republican offices such as tribune and consul to remain in place, and encouraged ambitious men in Rome to compete for them. Augustus also emphasized integrity in the service of the state and sent able senators to govern provinces, thereby reducing corruption. In these ways the basic machinery of government inherited from

the Republic continued to operate—but in conformity with the emperor's wishes. In the new imperial system, the emperor, not the Senate, controlled military, financial, and diplomatic policy. Free political debate was silenced. Because he wanted to avoid the ruthless competition for power that had destroyed the Republic, Augustus eliminated his opponents and filled the Senate with loyal supporters.

At the same time, Augustus both restructured the Senate and revised its political role. He trimmed the number of senators to a manageable 600 men, a number that remained standard for several centuries. He recruited able men from the ranks of the equestrians and so ensured that nonaristocrats entered the Senate in greater numbers. He also gave the Senate legislative powers that had once belonged to the popular assemblies—but he retained the right to veto any legislation for himself. Deprived of its autonomy, the Senate became an administrative arm of imperial rule.

Augustus and the emperors who followed him allowed the Senate to exist because they needed a pool of skilled administrators to manage the empire's day-to-day affairs. Senators served as provincial governors, army commanders, judges, and financial officers. They managed the water and grain supplies of the city of Rome, and some of them served on the emperor's advisory council. In return for their cooperation, emperors let senators bear responsibility and earn honor in public service. As a result, aristocratic senators learned to serve the empire faithfully even if they disliked the emperor.

Emperors often brought new men into the Senate from the provinces as a reward for their support, with the belief that Rome grew strong through admitting the best of its provincials to the highest levels of government. Broadening Senate membership in this way enabled more and more of the Romanized elites of the empire to feel they had a stake in the imperial enterprise. Participation in the Senate at Rome was the ultimate reward for a provincial citizen. Some Roman-born senators, however, balked at such inclusiveness. The emperor Claudius (r. 41–54 C.E.) caused considerable dismay among the snobbish Roman senators when he admitted a few new members from Gaul. Nevertheless, the numbers of provincials in the Roman

Senate increased in the first two centuries. By the end of the third century C.E. more than half of Rome's senators came from outside of Italy.

The Roman Army: Conquest and Coercion

Like the Senate, the Roman army was a crucial component of the imperial center. Soldiers enforced peace in the provinces, defended the borders, and conquered new lands to win glory for the emperor. The emperor, in turn, relied on the army's support to remain in power. The army could make or break an emperor—something that every ruler understood. Without the army's support, Augustus would never have succeeded in transforming the Republic into his imperial system. In 41 C.E., after the death of Caligula, soldiers of the palace guard dragged the lame, stammering Claudius from behind a curtain and forced him to take the throne, as a means of ensuring imperial continuity—and their own livelihoods. When Vespasian took the throne in 69 C.E. with the support of his troops, no one in Rome, least of all the emperors, could doubt the power of the army to influence political affairs. After 235 C.E., many emperors, including Aurelian (r. 270–275 C.E.) and Diocletian (r. 284–305 C.E.), rose through the ranks and became emperor due to the support of their fellow soldiers.

Augustus created a highly efficient professional army that would be the bulwark of the empire for nearly two and a half centuries. His first step was to reduce the army from 60 to 28 legions, so that the troops now totaled 150,000 citizens. (Trajan later added two more legions.) This force included the elite Praetorian Guard, which consisted of one and a half legions stationed in Rome to serve as a ceremonial escort for the emperor, maintain order in the city, and enforce the emperor's will throughout Italy. The strength of the army was augmented by subject peoples who had not been granted citizenship, the prerequisite for service in the legions. These subjects served as auxiliary troops. The combined legions and auxiliaries brought the military strength of the Roman army to 300,000 men.

Legionnaires enlisted for twenty-five years but only about half survived this term of service. Short life expectancy rather than death in battle kept the figure low, although regular rations and medical care may have helped soldiers live longer than civilians. A soldier with special skills, such as literacy, could rise through the ranks to have significant responsibilities and perhaps become an officer. For those who survived their period of enlistment, Augustus established military colonies in Italy and the provinces of Africa, Spain, and Asia. He rewarded more than 100,000 veterans with grants of land in return for

■ **Oplontis**

Painted on the wall of a private villa at the foot of Mount Vesuvius, near Naples, Italy, this vividly colored fresco imitated the interior architecture of a palace. When Mount Vesuvius exploded in 79 C.E., hot ash enveloped the building and preserved the painting.

their military service. Later emperors continued the same practice.

THE CITY OF ROME

At the center of the imperial system stood the city of Rome. This urban hub was a monument to the power of the ruling elite and celebrated the paramount authority of the emperor. Augustus boasted that he had found Rome built of brick and left it built of marble. Though an exaggeration, this claim nevertheless reveals the effect of monarchy on Rome's urban fabric. Every emperor wanted to leave his mark on the city of Rome as a testimony to his generosity and power. As Rome grew, it became the model for cities throughout the empire. Its public spaces and buildings provided a stage for the acting out of basic principles of imperial rule (see Map 5.2).

The center of political and public life in the city of Rome was the Forum, an area filled with many imposing buildings—administrative headquarters such as the treasury and

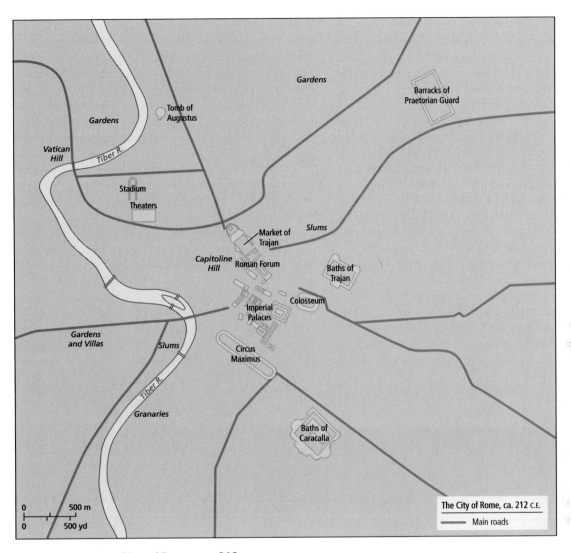

■ **Map 5.2 The City of Rome, ca. 212 C.E.**
This diagram shows the main public buildings of the imperial capital. Most cities elsewhere in the empire imitated this urban plan.

records office, law courts, and the Senate House. An altar to the goddess Victory stood in the Senate, where generals took oaths of allegiance to the emperor before marching to war. Roman laws were inscribed on gleaming bronze tablets and placed on the outer walls of these buildings, testimony to the principles of justice and order that formed the framework of the Roman state. Basilicas, a kind of colonnaded hall in which Romans conducted public business ranging from finance to law courts, crowded against the sides of the Forum. Because public and religious life were intertwined, the Forum also contained many grand temples of the gods who controlled Rome's destiny. For example, the goddess Concordia, who represented political agreement among Romans, had a gleaming shrine. Jupiter, Rome's chief god, had a huge marble temple on the Capitoline Hill looking down on the Forum. The Forum lay at the physical center

of Rome—just as the political power it represented lay at the center of the imperial system and just as the laws so visibly displayed marked the center of Roman citizenship.

The Forum particularly highlighted the emperor's power within the imperial system. Emperors built huge arches in the Roman forum to celebrate their triumphs. After a victorious military campaign, emperors would parade through the Forum on the Sacred Way, pass under the arches, and finish at the temple of Jupiter. Delighted crowds would see defeated kings pass by in chains and marvel at huge floats piled high with loot. In the victory parade, slaves carried huge paintings that depicted important battles and other scenes of the war. Each emperor from Augustus through Trajan built a new marble forum adjacent to the original Forum in the center of Rome. These new forums met the need for additional space to conduct administrative and legal business as the empire grew. Trajan's Forum, by far the biggest, included huge libraries of Greek and Latin texts, a multistoried marketplace not unlike a modern mall, shops, and a huge marble column on which was carved the story of Trajan's victorious Dacian Wars.

The might of the emperor was on display throughout the city of Rome. Emperors spent gigantic sums on public waterworks and entertainment. They built colossal bathhouses and aqueducts that carried water into Rome from outlying hills. The emperor Caracalla was renowned for constructing the biggest and most expensive bathing complex. The Colosseum, built by Vespasian and Titus, replaced Nero's private pleasure pond and provided a spot in the very heart of the city where as many as 50,000 happy spectators could watch the slaughter of men and animals at the emperor's expense. Romans could also go to the Circus Maximus to see horse-drawn chariots compete for victory under the emperor's auspices. Emperors built and maintained theaters, libraries, parks, and markets for the public's enjoyment. The camp of the Praetorian Guard lay at a discreet distance from the Forum, a reminder that the emperor could summon crippling force to suppress dissent.

Other impressive monuments dotted the city's landscape. The tombs of Augustus and his family and of Hadrian were exceptions to the rule that burials must take place beyond the city's walls. A great map of the empire built by Augustus delighted viewers while at the same time asserting imperial claims to control of the world. Emperors built their palaces on the Palatine Hill, which looked down on the Forum from the east, and great men's mansions covered nearby hills.

To erect these monumental buildings, the Romans pioneered certain architectural techniques and styles. They were the first to build extensively in concrete, which allowed them to develop new methods of construction. The concrete vault, for example, made possible the enormous baths and public buildings that graced the streets of Rome. The Pantheon, built by Hadrian, is the largest ancient roofed building still standing today. With a diameter of 142 feet, its dome has no interior supports.

In stark contrast to the gleaming homes and public buildings were the filthy slums of the poor. Unlike wealthy Romans, the impoverished majority of Rome's inhabitants lived in the valleys between Rome's seven hills or by the

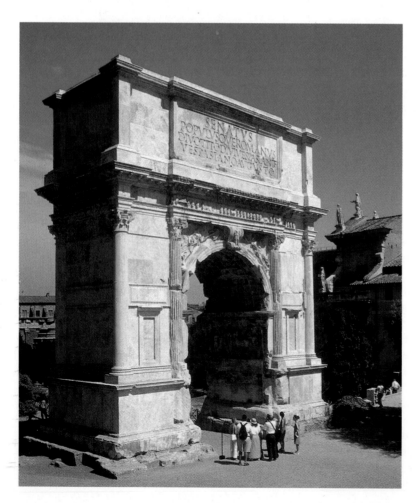

■ **Arch of Titus**

This triumphal arch built at the end of the first century C.E. honors the recently deceased Titus for crushing the Jewish revolt of 66–70 C.E. Marble reliefs inside the arch represent the loot from the Temple of Jerusalem in the triumphal parade.

More than a thousand cities dotted the imperial map, connected by more than 40,000 miles of roads (see Map 5.3). In regions where Roman urban traditions were little-known, the Romans created new urban centers. Cities such as Lugdunum (Lyons) in France or Eburacum (York) in Britain were created in the first years of conquest as centers of Roman culture and authority. In contrast, in regions throughout the Mediterranean where urban culture had deep roots, provincial cities such as Athens or Jerusalem had long been centers of learning or religion. Some urban hubs, such as Carthage and Alexandria, teemed with several hundred thousand people. In these immense provincial cities, governors and their staffs represented the Roman order in grand fashion.

In their physical layout and architecture, these provincial cities modeled themselves on the imperial capital. Each had gladiator arenas; bathhouses; a forum; a council house; and temples to its gods, to Rome, and to the emperor. Worship of the emperor linked these new communities to the larger imperial system.

All cities governed themselves. A city council modeled on the Roman Senate presided over each city's affairs. Only a handful of the community's wealthiest men served in the city council and held the various magistracies and priesthoods. Council membership passed from father to son. Wealthy women held no administrative office and had no role in public decision making, though they presided as priestesses in civic religious observances. The male citizens of each city voted on local issues and elected town officials.

City councilors had many responsibilities, which they viewed as great honors. The imperial government could rely on city councils to control the agricultural resources of the surrounding farmlands, thus reducing the need for a top-heavy imperial bureaucracy. City councils managed the grain supply, arranged for army recruitment, supervised the marketplaces, administered justice in local law courts, and most important of all, collected taxes for the central government. Councilors paid out of their own pockets for the upkeep of public works, aqueducts, and baths. They also funded religious festivals and celebrations of the imperial cult. In addition, they sponsored gladiatorial games, wild-beast slaughters, chariot races, and other forms of public amusement. This system of making private donations for the public good permitted aristocrats to compete for recognition and public offices in ways that benefited the city and its people. As provincial officials performed their public responsibilities on behalf of their hometowns, they imitated the efforts of that greatest patron of all, the emperor himself. The city councilors were the "mouthpiece of Rome."

When Romans took over the lands of others and organized provinces during the era of the Republic they did not try to impose a uniform legal and administrative sys-

AGRICOLA THE GENERAL

The historian Tacitus wrote a biography of his father-in-law, the general and administrator Gnaeus Julius Agricola (49–93 C.E.). Agricola had a glittering military career under the Flavian emperors. As commander-in-chief of Roman forces in Britain from 78 to 83 C.E., he subdued most of the island and advanced deep into Scotland. Agricola encouraged urbanization and Mediterranean customs such as public bathing and chariot racing. In the following selection, Tacitus considers the implications of deliberate "Romanization."

The following winter passed without disturbance, and was employed in salutary measures. For, to accustom to rest and repose through the charms of luxury a population scattered and barbarous and therefore inclined to war, Agricola gave private encouragement and public aid to the building of temples, courts of justice and dwelling houses, praising the energetic and reproving the indolent. Thus an honourable rivalry took the place of compulsion. He likewise provided a liberal education for the sons of the chiefs, and showed such a preference for the natural powers of the Britons over the industry of the Gauls that they who lately disdained the tongue of Rome now coveted its eloquence. Hence, too, a liking sprang up for our style of dress and the toga became fashionable. Step by step they were led to things which dispose to vice, the lounge, the bath, the elegant banquet. All this in their ignorance they called civilization, when it was but a part of their servitude.

Source: From Tacitus, "Agricola 21" in *Complete Works of Tacitus*, edited by Moses Hadas, translated by Alfred John Church and William Jackson Brodribb, (New York: The Modern Library, 1942).

tem. Once a victorious general ended a war of conquest, he established the terms of peace with Rome's new subjects in legal charters, city by city, tribe by tribe. These separate arrangements collectively were called the Law of the Province. This system continued during the imperial era. When a governor assumed command of his province, he issued an edict stating the legal terms of his rule and describing the structure of his administration. Although they were under no obligation, subsequent governors generally accepted the arrangements of their predecessors. This provided a certain smoothness of transition, but it also meant that different provinces might experience Roman government in quite different ways.

THE COUNTRYSIDE

The wealth that enabled aristocratic men throughout the empire to gain an education, enter public service, and pay for public buildings, festivals, and games came from agriculture. Control of the countryside was the key to the prosperity of the imperial system. The wealthiest men owned the most land. Landholdings, however, varied greatly in size and distribution. The emperor was the greatest property owner, controlling millions of acres of land throughout the empire. Augustus, for example, personally owned the entire province of Egypt. Like Augustus, wealthy Roman investors owned properties in many different areas, some bridging entire continents. Some of these landed magnates chose to enter a life of public service either in Rome or in their home cities. Others preferred to enjoy the benefits of their enormous wealth away from the risks of political life.

At the bottom of the pyramid toiled the peasants, who lived in the countryside and performed the agricultural labor that made local landowners rich. The circumstances of peasant life varied greatly throughout the empire. Some peasants owned small farms sufficient to maintain their families, perhaps with the assistance of seasonal wage laborers or a few slaves. Others rented their lands from landlords to whom they owed payment in the form of produce, money, or labor. Degrees of dependency on landlords var-

■ **Map 5.3   Major Cities and Roads of the Roman Empire**

Thousands of miles of roads linked the cities of the Roman Empire. Used primarily as military highways, the roads also helped merchants travel with their wares. When they crossed imperial frontiers, merchants traded with many peoples eager for Roman goods, especially wine and luxury objects.

ied as well. Extremely fierce penalties for inability to pay rents ranged from enslavement to other forms of bondage.

All landowning peasants faced one constant threat—the possibility that a more powerful landowner might seize their fields by force. When this happened, peasants had little hope of getting their land back. The imperial system favored the property rights of the wealthy and worked to the disadvantage of the rural poor. Cities gobbled up the peasants' crops; government officials extorted taxes from them; and landlords and soldiers bullied them. Rabbi Hanina ben Hama, who lived in Palestine about 240 C.E., stated bluntly that the empire established cities "in order to impose upon the people forced labor, extortion and oppression." In addition to this relentless exploitation, the specters of famine, natural disasters, and debt constantly threatened the peasants' very survival.

Despite these hardships, the peasantry during the empire's first three centuries managed to produce enough surplus crops to maintain the imperial system, especially the army with its ravenous demands for supplies and foods. Indeed, agricultural productivity during this era was remarkable, considering the low yields of farms, the difficulty and expense of transportation (it was less expensive to ship a load of grain all the way across the Mediterranean Sea than to send it 100 miles overland), and the rudimentary farming technology of the time. Some historians estimate that Europe did not see a comparable level of agricultural productivity again until the seventeenth century.

Food staples in the Mediterranean region included olives, grains, and wines, while in more northern regions butter replaced oil and beer substituted for wine. Large flocks of sheep and herds of cattle provided necessary wool and leather. Farmers did not export their produce over long distances; the vast Roman road network was developed to move troops, not crops. But if famine struck, relief supplies could be obtained quickly from fields a few days' transport away—provided the political organization existed to make the arrangements.

Terrain and climate as much as investment and local farming custom determined the methods of agricultural exploitation. In Sicily and parts of southern Italy, chain gangs of slaves predominated, working on vast estates. Migrant workers labored in the olive groves of North Africa, while seasonal movement of grazing animals predominated in hilly regions of Italy and the Balkans. In Egypt, the annual flooding of the Nile determined the rhythms of agricultural life and made the Nile Valley one of the empire's chief producers of grain.

REVOLTS AGAINST ROME

Conquest by Roman armies could be a long and brutal ordeal. After the shock of military defeat and surrender to Roman generals came the imposition of the administrative structures of Roman rule and the mechanisms of economic exploitation. Not surprisingly, resentment simmered among conquered peoples. Revolts against Roman authority often followed soon after a subject people's initial defeat, while freedom was still a living memory. The stories of several revolts illustrate that subject peoples rarely adjusted smoothly to Roman rule, and that with only one exception, Roman force proved overwhelming.

Arminius and the Revolt in Germany

In 9 C.E. Arminius, chieftain of a Germanic tribe called the Cherusci, led the only successful revolt against Roman rule. As a young man serving in an auxiliary regiment in the Roman army, Arminius earned Roman citizenship, learned to speak Latin, and gained the rank of equestrian. Arminius seemed to be a real friend of Rome, but the Cherusci had a history of belligerence and resistance. Arminius's tribal ties proved stronger than his loyalty to the empire. The Romans underestimated the pugnacity of their new Germanic subjects and sent the wrong man, Lucius Varus, to be their governor. Varus was a peacetime administrator, not a general. His previous experience in Syria and North Africa had not prepared him for the challenges he encountered east of the Rhine River. He imposed economic exploitation and taxation—the hallmarks of the Roman peace—upon the Cherusci too quickly. Not used to a monetary economy, debt, and foreign control, the Germanic tribe rose in revolt led by Arminius.

Arminius lured the unsuspecting Varus into a trap in the Teutoburg Forest, slaughtering Varus and three entire Roman legions. A relief army under the command of the future emperor Tiberius contained the disaster, but nevertheless, when Augustus died in 14 C.E., all of Rome's legions were on the west side of the Rhine. No emperor ever again attempted to conquer Germany. One lasting result of Arminius's successful revolt is the linguistic distinction that still cuts across Europe. Whereas French and Italian derive from Latin, German does not because the tribes living between the Rhine and Elbe Rivers managed to throw off the Roman yoke in 9 C.E.

Boudica's Revolt in Britain

Fifty years after Arminius's victory, another major uprising broke out in Britain, led by Boudica, the queen of the people known as the Iceni. The revolt had a long, complex history. In the decades following the initial conquest of the island by the emperor Claudius in 43 C.E., the Romans consolidated their power by playing favorites among the local tribes. They also encouraged those tribes not under Roman control to ally themselves with Rome as client states. Under King Prasutagus, the Iceni were one of these client states that supplied troops to the Roman army in return for Roman protection. Before King Prasutagus died in

60 C.E., he named the Roman emperor his co-heir with his wife, Boudica, and his daughters. Within a few years the emperor Nero pushed Boudica aside and incorporated the kingdom of the Iceni directly into the Roman state. Emboldened by their new dominance over the Iceni, the agents of the tyrannical Roman governor abused Boudica and raped her daughters.

The queen then led her forces into open rebellion. With the aid of several neighboring tribes who also resented the Roman presence in Britain, Boudica destroyed a legion and leveled several cities, including Camulodunum, a major imperial cult center with a temple dedicated to Rome and the emperor. Resistance ended quickly after Roman force routed Boudica's troops and the queen took her own life.

The Britons learned that resistance to Rome was futile. The Romans learned a lesson as well: Subject peoples should be treated more justly. The next Roman governor of Britain adopted more lenient administrative policies.

The Revolt of Julius Civilis in Gaul

Like Arminius, Julius Civilis was a Germanic tribal leader who had served in the Roman army. Julius Civilis was both a Roman citizen and a prince of his tribe, the Batavi. Like the Iceni in Britain, the Batavi had supplied troops but not tribute to Rome for several decades. Civilis was serving as a commander of Roman auxiliary troops in Gaul when civil war broke out in Rome in 69 C.E. following Nero's death. Quick to seize an opportunity, Julius Civilis led an army—consisting not only of Batavians but also men from several unconquered German tribes and some restless Gallic tribes—against Roman legionary bases depleted by the civil war.

Despite his career in Roman military service and his involvement in provincial politics, Civilis presented himself to his Batavian followers in religious terms, with native-style oaths of allegiance sworn in a sacred grove. He also maintained close ties with a Batavian prophet, who may have predicted that Civilis would lead his people to freedom. But unlike the revolt of Arminius, the revolt of Civilis came to an end when the new emperor Vespasian brought stability back to the frontier through a combination of diplomacy and swift military action.

Jewish Revolts

Augustus had created the province of Judaea and annexed it to the Empire in 6 C.E. With Roman rule came mediocre governors and heavy taxation that caused Judaea's economy to decline. Famines and banditry became common, and political discontent mounted among the Jews. Open rebellion almost broke out when the emperor Caligula (r. 37–41 C.E.) ordered that his statue be placed in the Temple in Jerusalem, an unthinkable sacrilege for the Jews. Only his

GALEN THE PHYSICIAN

Galen, the greatest physician of the imperial age, described in vivid terms how peasants in the countryside often were very close to starvation.

As soon as summer was over, those who live in the cities, in accordance with their universal practice of collecting a sufficient supply of grain to last a whole year, took from the fields all the wheat, with the barley, beans and lentils, and left to the rustics only those annual products which are called pulses and leguminous fruits; they even took away a good part of these to the city. So the people in the countryside, after consuming during the winter what had been left, were compelled to use unhealthy forms of nourishment. Through the spring they ate twigs and shoots of trees, bulbs and roots of unwholesome plants, and they made unsparing use of what are called wild vegetables, whatever they could get hold of, until they were surfeited; they ate them after boiling them whole like green grasses, of which they had not tasted before even as an experiment. I myself in person saw some of them at the end of spring and almost all at the beginning summer afflicted with numerous ulcers covering their skin and inflamed tumours, others from spreading boils, others had an eruption resembling . . . leprosy.

Source: From Galen, translated by G. E. M. de Ste. Croix in *The Class Struggle in the Ancient Greek World.* Copyright © 1981 by G. E. M. de Ste. Croix. Reprinted by permission of Gerald Duckworth & Co. Ltd.

death in 41 C.E. prevented the beginning of war between Rome and the Jews of Judaea.

Under Roman rule, a significant divide opened up within the Jewish community. The Jewish priestly caste grew to appreciate many aspects of Hellenistic culture, and the landed elite benefited directly from Roman rule. Ordinary Jews, however, suffered from high taxation and viewed their leaders as collaborators with an occupying and godless power. These Jews gave their loyalty and respect to the scribes, men of learning who devoted their lives to copying religious texts and interpreting the Bible. These learned and religious men had little stake in preserving Roman rule.

Sixty years of Roman mismanagement combined with a desire for independence sparked a massive revolt in Judaea in 66 C.E. Jews stopped offering sacrifices for the emperor's health and formed their own government. They appointed regional military commanders, chose a leader by lot, abolished debt, and issued their own coinage imprinted with messages of freedom. Internal political conflicts within the Jewish community, however, weakened the rebellion and proved as fatal to their cause as the might of Roman legions. In 70 C.E. imperial forces captured Jerusalem, destroyed the Temple, and enslaved an estimated two million people. The victorious generals were Vespasian and his son Titus, both of whom later became emperors.

Despite their overwhelming defeat in 70 C.E., Jewish communities continued to resist Rome. During Trajan's reign, minor revolts broke out in the eastern Mediterranean (115–118 C.E.). Revolts erupted again in 132–135 C.E., prompted by Hadrian's attempt to forbid the Jewish ritual circumcision of male infants. This latter revolt was led by Simon Bar Kochba, or "Son of the Star," who claimed to be the messiah, a leader who would end foreign oppression and inaugurate a new era for the Jewish nation. Other rebellions occurred under the emperors Antoninus Pius (r. 138–161 C.E.) and Septimius Severus (r. 193–211 C.E.). The last major Jewish uprising occurred in Palestine in the fourth century C.E. All of these revolts failed.

Several conclusions may be drawn from these instances of resistance. In each of the western revolts, the Romans overestimated their ability to pacify subject peoples soon after conquering them. Even a tribal leader's service in the Roman auxiliary forces did not blunt tribal identity and allegiance. The rebel leaders appealed to their fellow tribesmen in traditional rather than in Roman terms. It required more than one generation after conquest for tribal elites to embrace the imperial system.

In the case of the Jewish revolt of 66–70 C.E., the Romans misunderstood the nature of leadership and loyalty in Judaea's Jewish society. The Romans allied themselves with members of the Jewish elite whom the majority of Jews distrusted and refused to follow. The continuation of Jewish opposition to Roman rule demonstrates that a population with a strong sense of religious identity rooted in a set of sacred texts could resist—and survive—the overwhelming power of Rome. Rebels in western Europe lacked this focus. Within a few generations these unsuccessful rebels assimilated fully into Roman society. The Jews never did so.

FORCES OF ROMANIZATION

Two very different institutions worked as Romanizing forces in the provinces of the empire. The first, the army, proved vital in not only establishing the geographic limits of the empire but also in transmitting Roman culture within those limits. The second, Roman law, helped erode the local loyalties and traditions of the diverse provincial peoples and so furthered this process of creating a Roman imperial culture.

The Roman Army

More than any other institution, the army mirrored the growth of the Roman Empire from a diverse collection of conquests to a well-organized state with a common culture. The army was a significant force of Romanization° throughout the imperial era. During the Republic, soldiers tended to be drawn from the city of Rome and surrounding regions—a natural consequence of the fact that Roman soldiers were required to be Roman citizens. In the course of the first two and a half centuries of imperial rule, however, the number of troops from Italy steadily diminished as territories under Roman rule increased. After 212 C.E., when all free men and women within imperial borders gained citizenship, the army drew recruits from all the provinces.

Army bases in far-flung regions provided the first taste of Roman culture and language to provincial peoples. The army introduced provincial recruits to the Latin language, Roman religion, social organization, and values. Oaths of loyalty bound soldiers to the emperor and Rome, neither of which most legionnaires would ever see. Latin, the language of command and army administration, provided another common bond to men whose mother tongues reflected the empire's ethnic diversity. Many inscriptions on soldiers' tombstones reveal that a simplified version of Latin developed in the army. (This language became the ancestor of French, Spanish, and other Romance languages.)

Roman soldiers who settled in the provinces also served as a Romanizing force. Soldiers could not legally marry during their military service because Romans believed that family obligations reduced troops' willingness to be stationed far from home. Many men reared families anyway with local women. Septimius Severus pragmatically abandoned the restriction against marriage in the army at the end of the second century C.E. At retirement, most soldiers stayed near the bases in which they had been stationed. Many towns arose full of former military personnel and their friends, families, and small businesses. These towns helped transmit Roman culture and values to provincial peoples.

The imperial army maintained a very high degree of organization, discipline, and training—characteristics on which Romans prided themselves. Each of the legions with a contingent of auxiliary troops was stationed as a permanent garrison in a province with an elaborate logistical infrastructure to provide weapons, food, and housing. Legions had a standard chain of command to organize officers and men. The architecture of camps and fortification, as well as weapons, armor, and tactics, followed the same conventions across the empire, thus reinforcing the army's role as a Romanizing force. Generals and staff officers often had postings in different provinces during their careers, so there developed a strong sense of shared enterprise in the command structure as well as a common body of knowledge about how the army worked from the inside.

Romans knew that strict military discipline distinguished their soldiery from disorganized "barbarians." Military punishments were notoriously ferocious. For example, if a soldier fell asleep during sentry duty, his barrackmates were required to beat him to death. But tight discipline and vigorous training did produce highly professional fighters. To keep in fighting trim, troops constantly drilled in weaponry, camp building, and battle formations.

The army also confronted Romans with new cultural ideas. Some provincial troops seemed exotic to Roman eyes. For example, sun-worshipping legionnaires from Syria stationed in Rome raised eyebrows by saluting their god at dawn. Soldiers from the Rhine who felt uncomfortable in the noonday heat of Rome once baffled onlookers by drinking water from the Tiber, which everyone in Rome knew was contaminated.

Roman Citizenship and Law

Roman law, like the Roman army, constituted a strong force for Romanization. In the early days of the empire, Roman law set Romans apart from the bulk of the empire's peoples, who followed their own laws. For example, Jews could live according to Jewish law or Athenians by Athenian law, as long as they paid their taxes to the emperor and did not cause trouble. If a Jew or an Athenian held Roman citizenship, however, he or she could also enjoy the rights and benefits of Roman law. A Roman citizen possessed crucial legally defined rights, including the guarantee of freedom from enslavement. Male citizens had the right to compete for public magistracies, vote in public assemblies, serve in the legions, and make an appeal in a criminal trial. As the Roman Empire expanded during the first and second centuries C.E., conditions of peace and prosperity encouraged the spread of both Roman-style cities and Roman citizenship, and thus the dominance of Roman law. In this way, Roman law tied the vast empire together. No matter where they lived in the empire, Roman citizens took pride in their centuries-old legal tradition, and in their rights of citizenship.

Then, in 212 C.E., Emperor Aurelius Antoninus (r. 211–217 C.E.), nicknamed Caracalla, issued what became known as the Antonine Decree°. This ruling was a milestone because it granted citizenship to all free men and women within the empire, presumably to increase the tax base. By formally eliminating the distinction between Roman conquerors and subject peoples, the Antonine Decree enabled Roman law to embrace the entire population. This legal uniformity further strengthened provincial loyalty to Rome. Provincial allegiances to their own traditions and laws that had coexisted with Roman imperial law for centuries began to diminish.

Roman law distinguished between civil law and criminal law. Civil law dealt with all aspects of family life, property and inheritance, slavery, and citizenship. It also dealt with legal procedure, trial, appeal, and the settling of disputes.

Civil law, therefore, defined relations among different classes of Roman society and enabled courts to judge disputes among citizens. Criminal law addressed theft, homicide, sexual crimes, treason, and offenses against the government. These distinctions between civil and criminal law created by the Romans have become standard in the legal systems of nations that are part of Western civilization.

The significance of Roman law extended beyond the imperial age. One of the most important aspects of Roman law was the development of the concept of the "law of nature." This concept stemmed from Stoicism, with its ideal of an underlying rational order to all things. From this Stoic assumption of rational order the idea developed that certain principles of justice are part of nature itself. Ideally, at least, laws of human societies should conform to the law of nature. Hence the Romans developed the idea that codes of law, although the product of particular societies and circumstances, were based on universally applicable principles. This idea would become a foundation of Western civilization. Building on this Roman idea, later thinkers would insist that all human beings had inalienable rights and that all individuals should be treated as equals under the law.

Equality under the law did not, however, exist in the Roman imperial age. Roman citizens had more rights than noncitizens. In the first century C.E. the vast differences in wealth that divided citizens took on legal significance. The wealthy upper class, generally called *honestiores,* and the poor, called *humiliores,* acquired different legal rights, especially in criminal law. For example, *honestiores* convicted of crimes were spared the most gruesome punishments, such as being crucified or being thrown to wild animals in the arena.

Responsibility for making laws shifted as the Republic gave way to the empire. During the Republic the Senate gave advice on legal matters to magistrates or citizen assemblies that had official authority to issue laws. During the empire these lawmaking procedures changed, as the control of law shifted into the emperor's hands. Whether the emperor was issuing a decree on his own initiative, making a general policy in response to an inquiry from a provincial administrator, or making a technical ruling on a point of law in consultation with legal experts on his staff, his decisions had the same status as any law issued by a citizen assembly during the Republic. The idea that the emperor was above the law and that his wishes had the force of law was widely accepted by the early third century C.E.

Legal experts also played a critical part in the evolution of Roman law. In the Republic these legal experts had been aristocratic, independent scholars, entrusted with the task of understanding and interpreting the law. They served as an invaluable resource to the practice of law. Their methods of interpretation made it possible to apply the law to new circumstances as the precedents they established became the basis for future law.

During the empire, legal experts lost their independence but continued their work in imperial service. Combining legal scholarship, teaching, and administrative careers, the legal experts of the Roman Empire collected and analyzed earlier laws and the opinions of their predecessors. Papinian, Paul, and Ulpian, who lived in the early third century C.E., were the greatest of these specialists. They wrote hundreds of books of commentary that shaped the interpretation of Roman law for centuries. Their opinions, collected and organized during the reign of Justinian in the sixth century C.E., were passed on to the lawyers of medieval and Renaissance Europe. Roman law remains the foundation of Italian, French, and Spanish legal traditions today, as well as the legal system of the state of Louisiana.

The Frontier and Beyond

The third concentric circle of the Roman world consisted of the frontier—the outermost regions of the empire, and beyond. In this section we will see how boundaries and border zones took shape on the edges of the empire and how cultural distinctions emerged between "civilized" Romans and "barbarians" living across the borders. Some contacts between the two groups, such as trade with sub-Saharan Africa, India, and China, only temporarily affected the empire. Other encounters with foreign peoples, such as the Parthians in the Middle East and the Germanic peoples living north of the Danube and Rhine Rivers, profoundly influenced Rome and the shaping of the West.

FRONTIER ZONES: CIVILIZATION AND BARBARIANS

By the early second century C.E., the empire's northern border was marked by regularly spaced military bases and fortresses. Armed naval forces patrolled the Rhine and Danube, and the great wall of Hadrian stretched across the north of Britain. In the East, another line of military defenses extended from the Black Sea to the Nile. In North Africa as well, a perimeter of fortifications marked the limits of cultivable land along the empire's southernmost edge. This demarcation of the empire's edges and the gradual emergence of the idea of perimeter defense reveals much about the evolution of the imperial government, as well as the spread of Roman culture and ideas about empire.

As in so many other areas, the Augustan regime provided the catalyst. After 9 C.E., when three of his best legions perished in the revolt of Arminius in Germany, Augustus realized that the empire lacked the resources to expand indefinitely. Augustus put a stop to unlimited imperial expansion, but Jupiter's promise that Romans would have empire without limits, as described by Virgil (70–19 B.C.E.) in the *Aeneid* (ca. 26–19 B.C.E.), nevertheless remained an official conceit.

Only as the pace of conquest slowed and as the empire absorbed the client kingdoms on the fringes of the empire did imperial policies change. By the end of the first century C.E., emperors turned their attention to consolidating conquests systematically and developing fortified lines of defense across areas that lacked rivers or other natural obstacles. As we have seen, the contrasting policies of Trajan and Hadrian illustrate this shift. Trajan saw himself as an old-fashioned conqueror, seizing lands as far as his legions could push. His troops conquered Dacia (modern Romania) and Mesopotamia. Trajan's successor Hadrian looked at the empire differently. Hadrian abandoned the conquests that he thought Rome could not maintain, and then he secured the frontier with a strong line of border defenses.

The borders established by Roman forces in the initial phase of conquest were intended to control newly conquered peoples and to protect against enemies beyond Rome's borders. After conquest Roman armies remained in place as occupying forces. The Romans spoke a different language than that of their subjects, worshiped different gods, and enforced strange and unwelcome rules. The tension between Roman armies and provincial populations never entirely went away, but gradually the conquered peoples became Romanized. As the occupying Roman forces settled in and raised families with local women, defeated peoples started to assimilate into Roman culture. They adopted Roman customs and language, and provincial elites began to enter Roman politics. Romanization transformed the provinces from occupied zones where shattered communities obeyed foreign masters to well-integrated territories in which Roman culture flourished.

Natural boundaries such as the Rhine and Danube Rivers, and humanmade ones, such as Hadrian's Wall in the north of Britain, separated the Roman Empire from its unconquered neighbors. For the Romans, these boundaries symbolized a cultural division between civilization and barbarism. In the Romans' view, all peoples who did not live under Roman rule were barbarians and therefore hostile. As a result, the most important borders separated Romanized provinces from lands beyond the limits of Roman control. Emperors systematically and heavily fortified these lines of political and cultural demarcation. Romans used this distinction to help define their place in the world and to justify their conquest and absorption of other peoples. Despite the resources spent on maintaining these borders, they remained highly permeable. These borders represented the limits of Roman authority, but they could not prevent non-Romans from entering the empire altogether.

ROME AND THE PARTHIAN EMPIRE

Although the Roman Empire dominated a huge expanse of territory, it did have one formidable rival: the Parthian Empire (Parthia) to the east. This realm stretched from the Euphrates River to the Indus River (covering modern Iraq, Iran, and Pakistan). Unlike the poorly organized and politically unstable Celtic and Germanic tribes the Romans confronted in western Europe, the Parthian Empire was highly structured and enormously powerful. It replaced the successor states of Alexander the Great in Iran in the mid-third century B.C.E. The Parthian Empire ended in 224 C.E., when another Iranian dynasty, the Sasanian, rose to power.

The structure of the highly stratified Parthian society included a king and warrior aristocracy; a middle range of doctors, artisans, and traders; and a large class of peasants. In addition Parthia contained many subject peoples with their own cultures, such as Babylonians, Jews, and Armenians. Unlike Rome, Parthia did not permit subject peoples and internal minorities to enter the ruling elite. The Parthian Empire did tolerate practice of various religions, although Zoroastrianism was the main religion of the Parthian state.

The Romans knew the Parthians as fierce warriors. Parthia's specially bred battle horses, which were famous as far away as China, made heavily armed Parthian cavalrymen and their archers worthy opponents of Rome's legions. Glory-seeking Roman generals of the late Republic found Parthia an attractive but dangerous target. Marcus Licinius Crassus (the associate of Julius Caesar and Pompey in the First Triumvirate) invaded the Parthian Empire, but died there in battle in 53 B.C.E. Most of his troops perished as well, but a few survivors may have ended their days in central Asia fighting as mercenaries for the emperor of China, who maintained ties with the Parthian emperor. After defeating his rivals in 45 B.C.E., Julius Caesar was preparing another invasion of Parthia, but he was assassinated before the attack could begin.

Augustus inaugurated a new Roman policy toward Parthia, just as he initiated changes in so many other aspects of Roman rule. He avenged Crassus's death and regained Roman honor through diplomatic means. Like Augustus, most Roman emperors preferred diplomacy to open conflict with Parthia because they knew they could not conquer and assimilate such a vast territory. Trajan, however, proved an exception. He conquered the Parthian provinces of Armenia and Mesopotamia in ambitious campaigns in 115–116 C.E., when Parthia was weakened by civil war. But Trajan's triumph proved short-lived. His successor, Hadrian, abandoned these conquests because he knew that they overextended Rome's resources.

The most important result of the rivalry between Parthia and Rome was the exchange of ideas and technology between their peoples. Romans highly prized Parthian steel and leather, as well as the exotic spices traded through

Parthia from even farther east. The Romans also adopted some military technology and tactics from Parthia, particularly the use of heavily armed cavalry. By the fourth century C.E. these units constituted the core of Roman military might.

There was also an erratic exchange of nonmilitary technological expertise between the two empires. From the Parthians, the Romans learned new techniques of irrigating fields. In turn, Roman hydraulic engineers and masons went to Persia to help construct a great dam for the Parthian king. *Via,* the Latin word for "paved road," entered the Persian language, an indication that other Roman specialists worked in Parthia as well.

Religious ideas also flowed in both directions. Many people in the Roman Empire studied Parthian astrology and magic, while Jewish scholars in the Roman Empire maintained close ties with the Jewish academies in the Parthian province of Babylonia. It was Christianity, however, that was the most directly influenced by this religious interchange between the Parthians and the Romans. The Persian Mani (216–276 C.E.), founder of a religion called Manichaeism, preached that an eternal conflict between forces of light and darkness caused good and evil to intermingle. God's soul had become trapped in matter, and Jesus, the son of God, had come to Earth to retrieve God's soul. Mani taught that all those who followed him and turned their back on earthly possessions would be redeemed. These ideas deeply influenced some Christians in the Roman Empire. Small Christian communities also appeared in Parthia during the imperial period.

ROMAN ENCOUNTERS WITH GERMANIC PEOPLES

The peoples living north of the Rhine and Danube Rivers, not the Parthians, posed the greatest threat to Rome during the first two and a half centuries C.E. Called "Germans" by the Romans, these peoples never used that term among themselves or thought of themselves as one group. Numbering in the tens of millions, most of them spoke their own dialects and did not understand the language of other tribes. Lacking political unity, different Germanic peoples constantly grouped and regrouped, taking new names and following new leaders. Led by aristocratic warriors, they often fought bitterly among themselves. Occasionally for short periods of time they formed loose confederations under the leadership of charismatic warlords in order to defend themselves from Roman aggression or to invade the empire themselves. For example, the Marcomanni, meaning "men of the borderlands," constituted one of these hostile confederations during the reign of Marcus Aurelius. Seeking land and booty, this confederation of many armed groups attacked the Roman Empire with more than a hundred thousand men. Only after fourteen years of brutal war did Marcus Aurelius crush them.

In the early years of Augustus's reign, Roman legions conquered large portions of what is now called Germany between the Rhine and the Elbe Rivers. Arminius's successful revolt in 9 C.E. drove out the Romans, however, and Roman civilization never took root in Germany. The Rhine and Danube Rivers became the symbolic boundary between Romans and their northern enemies. Most of Rome's legions were stationed along this boundary to defend against attacks from their northern neighbors. Tribes along the northern border sometimes fragmented into pro- and anti-Roman factions. Romans supported kings who would favor their cause by fighting Rome's enemies beyond the borders and supplying troops to the auxiliary regiments of the Roman army.

During long periods of peace, the people on either side of the border had the opportunity to interact with one another through military service and trade. Through extensive trade with Roman merchants, mostly Italians and Syrians, many Germanic aristocrats developed a taste for Mediterranean luxuries, including wine and jewelry. By the second century C.E. some chose to live in Roman-style villas in imitation of Roman aristocrats. Many Germanic men gained exposure to Roman civilization when they served in the Roman army as auxiliary troops. As members of the Roman army, they fought wherever they were sent in the empire, even if that meant warfare with other Germanic tribes to the north. Discharged after the standard twenty-five years of service, many of these men returned to their homes with Roman money in their purses, a smattering of Latin, and knowledge of the riches and power of the Roman Empire.

By the end of the second century C.E. the weight of different peoples pressing on Rome's northern borders began to crack the imperial defenses. With the end of the Severan dynasty in 235 C.E., the empire entered a period of unrelieved disasters that lasted nearly fifty years. Invading groups from north of the Rhine and Danube Rivers pushed into the empire as far south as central Italy in search of plunder and land on which to settle. The Romans ultimately marshaled the military resources to repel the invaders and restore the empire's security late in the third century C.E. As we will see in the next chapter, however, the restored Roman Empire differed radically from the system Augustus inaugurated.

ROMAN ENCOUNTERS WITH ASIANS AND AFRICANS

More than 3,000 forbidding miles separated the empires of Rome and China, but commerce brought them together. China produced silk, the luxurious tex-tile coveted in the West. Merchants risked great dangers to bring silk and other luxury goods westward from China in their caravans. Chinese documents from the first century C.E. mention Chinese ambassadors sent to Rome who reached as far as the Persian Gulf. Emperor Marcus Aurelius sent ambassadors to China in 166 C.E., but the two empires never established formal ties.

India came to the attention of the Hellenistic world and later to Rome through the campaigns of Alexander the Great. For centuries the Indian subcontinent inspired Greek fantasy writers, who were intrigued by rumors of enormous wealth, exotic animals, and very different social customs in the Indian subcontinent brought back to the Hellenistic world by traders and travelers. In the first and second centuries C.E. India also played a crucial role in the silk trade as the main depot for silk coming from China on its way to Rome.

Indian trade with merchants coming from the Roman Empire, particularly from Alexandria, was brisk and highly profitable in the first several centuries C.E. Trade routes linked the Mediterranean basin, the East African coast, the Persian Gulf, and the Red Sea with India's western Malabar coast, as well as with lands across the Bay of Bengal in Southeast Asia and China. One Roman account from the first century C.E., *Voyage Around the Red Sea,* written by an unknown author, describes a vast international commercial network.

Roman demand for spices (especially pepper) and luxury items from the Far East meant that Roman trading networks extended as far as Java in East Asia. In the first century C.E., Pliny the Elder griped, "And by the lowest

■ **Wineship**

Found in Germany, this energetic but unsophisticated sculpture of the second century C.E. depicts wine merchants hurrying their cargo to thirsty customers somewhere on the Rhine River. Because grapes could not be cultivated in this northern region, wine was a luxury there. Common people drank beer.

reckoning India, China, and the Arabian Peninsula take from our Empire many thousands of pounds of gold every year—that is the sum which our luxuries and our women cost us." Pliny's concern was not unfounded: Archaeologists have discovered thousands of Roman coins in India and even in Thailand, evidence of commerce's extensive reach. Only the rise of Islam in the seventh century C.E. would disconnect Rome and Mediterranean lands from this far-reaching Asian trade network.

In addition to trading with China and India, Romans did some exploring in sub-Saharan Africa. Roman coins found deep in the interior of Africa suggest that they may have had commercial dealings with peoples there as well. To the Romans, however, "Africa" was one of their provinces bordering the Mediterranean Sea—the region we know as North Africa today—not the vast continent that lay to the south, beyond the Sahara Desert. Only in the European Middle Ages would the name Africa come to stand for the entire land mass of the continent.

The Romans knew little about sub-Saharan Africa. In 146 B.C.E., the Roman general Scipio sent the historian Polybius on an expedition down the west coast of Africa. Polybius's expedition got as far as Senegal and a place Scipio called Crocodile River. In the first century C.E., a Roman military expedition that marched south from a base in North Africa in pursuit of some raiders may have reached Chad. One hundred years later, an intrepid Roman officer named Julius Maternus traveled south for four months, reaching a place "where the rhinoceroses gather." He emerged in the Sudan, where he found the Nile and returned home.

The Romans used the word *Aethiopians* ("the People with Burned Faces") to refer to the peoples who lived south of the Sahara desert. Most of their knowledge of these peoples came from the Egyptians, who regularly traded with peoples living in the extreme south of the Nile River valley. From the Egyptians they learned of a place of fabulous wealth and exotic creatures. It would take many centuries, however, before European peoples viewed Africa as anything other than a fantasyland.

Society and Culture in the Imperial Age

The same central theme that characterized Roman politics after Augustus also characterized Roman society in the imperial age—the illusion of continuity with the Republic, masking fundamental change. The social pyramid described in Chapter 4 remained intact— aristocrats at the top, followed by equestrians, plebeians and peasants, freedmen, and slaves. Important changes, however, occurred within the pyramid, as imperial rule altered social and economic relationships. The shift from republic to empire also had a profound influence on Roman culture and religious belief. In their works, writers, poets, and historians explored the ambivalence of life under stable but autocratic rule. At the same time, the spread of religious cults promising salvation hinted that many people under Roman rule found life less than stable, and looked outside the political sphere for safety. Christianity, which emerged during the Augustan era, possessed a special appeal to those classes of society that benefitted the least from imperial governance.

THE UPPER AND LOWER CLASSES

In the Roman Empire, aristocrats continued to stand at the top of the social pyramid, enjoying the greatest wealth, power, and prestige. Roman emperors recognized three social groups, or orders, as having aristocratic status. The first order, the senators of Rome, occupied a place of honor at the very top of the social pyramid. Augustus attempted to rebuild the Roman Senate and boost its morale after the civil war by recruiting new members and dismissing men whom he considered of low moral character. The Roman Senate was not a hereditary aristocracy, but Augustus encouraged the sons of senators to follow in their fathers' footsteps, and he offered financial incentives to senators to have children and perpetuate their family line. Despite these efforts, most of the oldest Roman senatorial families died out by the end of the first century C.E., due to death in war, failure to protect heirs, and falling victim to political intrigues. With the approval of the emperor, new aristocratic families emerged to take their place and serve in the Senate. These senators came from Roman families that had grown in wealth and prestige through service to the emperor. Many new senators also stemmed from the provinces and came to Rome to be in the Senate and serve as imperial officials. All senators, and their descendants for three generations, had the right to wear a broad purple stripe on their togas (formal clothing) as a badge of honor.

Below the senators stood the equestrian order, which was much larger than the senatorial order. Like senators, equestrians had to possess high birth and wealth—but to a lesser degree. The equestrian order flourished in the imperial age. Many equestrians continued to follow business careers as they had during the Republic, but the expansion of the Republic provided them with new opportunities for public service. Equestrians staffed the diplomatic, fiscal, and military services. Many served in the Roman Senate. They constituted an increasing percentage of Rome's senators in the first centuries of the empire.

The third aristocratic order consisted of the city councilors who served in the councils of every Roman city throughout the provinces. Like senators and equestrians, they were expected to be wealthy, of respectable birth, and of good moral character. In many cities, the sons of freedmen (men who had once been slaves) were permitted to be city councilors.

These three aristocratic orders represented only a tiny fraction of the empire's population. Below them came the plebeians—Rome's poor but free underclass of citizens. Though not included in political life, plebeians living throughout the empire benefited in some ways from imperial rule. In the city of Rome, for example, they received a daily allotment of free grain. (Approximately half of Rome's population of one million depended on the daily gifts of grain.) With little incentive to work and deprived of the rights and responsibilities of political participation, the plebeians enjoyed much leisure time. By the first century C.E., Romans had approximately 100 days designated as holidays. The plebeians demanded a steady diet of bloody entertainment, such as the gladiatorial combats in the Colosseum and the chariot races in the Circus Maximus. Thus plebeian life in the city of Rome was degraded into "bread and circuses": free grain and free entertainment.

In the city of Rome, the plebeians needed bread and circuses to compensate not only for their loss of political power but also for their poor living conditions. Crowded into vile tenement slums with little light and no plumbing, the poor lived in misery. The streets flowed with human and animal excrement and other sewage. Vultures picked at the refuse dumped outside butcher shops. Fire was a constant threat, and the Tiber flooded frequently. The urban poor had no access to education or political power. Disease kept the birth rate and life expectancy very low. Probably more than a quarter of all infants died within their first five years, and a third of those who survived were dead by age 10. The average Roman man died at age 45, and the average woman at age 34.

Poor people lived in similarly wretched conditions in every Roman city, but without the free distributions of grain. They relied on local aristocrats to provide food in times of emergency and to provide public entertainments. Plebeians in the countryside made their living primarily by farming, and they provided the bulk of troops in the Roman army.

SLAVES AND FREEDMEN

Slavery was one of the harshest facts of life in the Roman Empire. Slaves made up a huge percentage of Roman society, at the very bottom of the social order. Of the city of Rome's approximately one million inhabitants, an estimated 400,000 were slaves during the early empire. When Augustus took control of Rome, slaves constituted 35 to 40 percent of the total population of Italy.

Everyone accepted that humans could be reduced to property. Millions of slaves inhabited the empire, holding the lowest possible status in a society in which social and le-

gal status meant everything. No Roman citizen ever objected to slavery as an institution. Some high-minded Stoic philosophers, who noted the common humanity of slaves and owners, did criticize slavery, but only because they feared its corrupting effect on the masters. They had no concern for the condition of the slaves themselves. Later Christian writers living within the empire stressed that slaves should obey their masters "with fear and trembling."

The victims of a brisk international trade in humans, most slaves entered the empire through conquest. Others were enslaved from birth, having been born of a slave mother. There was never a shortage of slaves, and sometimes after a successful military campaign, such as Trajan's defeat of the Dacians in 106 C.E., the market was glutted.

Ownership of slaves reflected a person's status. The emperor himself owned tens of thousands of slaves who labored on his estates throughout the empire. Rich men, too, possessed them in huge numbers. Even poor artisans and teachers might hold one or two. Former slaves who had gained their freedom (freedmen) also owned slaves. Slaves were permitted to earn money, with the result that even some slaves owned slaves.

Slaves used for domestic service or in commerce and crafts were the lucky ones. Many slaves worked on the great plantations, or latifundia°, as part of large slave gangs. The absentee owners cared little for the welfare of these slaves. Latifundia slaves often labored in chains and slept in underground prisons. The slaves sent to work in the mines experienced even worse conditions. For them, only a wretched death lay ahead. Female slaves were spared the horrors of working in the fields and mines, but they were valued far less than were male slaves.

Dehumanized by their enslavement and stripped of their identity when taken from family and home, slaves lived in fear of their masters, who could abuse them physically or sexually with impunity. Violence lay at the heart of this institution, for ultimate control of slaves rested on force. In 61 C.E. when Pedanius Secundus, the chief administrator of the city of Rome, was killed by one of his slaves, all the other 400 slaves in his household were executed in accordance with Roman custom, on the assumption that some of them surely must have known the killer's intention. The Senate affirmed this decision as the right thing to do. Romans, in common with the Greeks and other ancient peoples, believed that the only way to compel a slave to tell the truth was through torture. Thus, any testimony provided by a slave in court was valid only if it was extracted by torture. Galen, the great physician, did recommend that owners not beat their slaves, but only because of its medical benefits to the owners: "If a man adheres to the practice of never striking any of his slaves with his hand, he will be less likely to succumb to a fit of anger later on. . . . I have criticized many of my friends when I saw how they had bruised their hands by hitting their slaves on the mouth." In the face of such brutality, slaves had few options. Slaves could try to escape, but if caught were branded on the forehead. Slave revolts never succeeded.

Despite their utter lack of freedom, many slaves formed emotional and sexual relationships with one another. Epitaphs on graves demonstrate that they used conventional terms of affection and marriage bonds such as husband and wife, although Roman law did not recognize these informal slave marriages. Some slave owners permitted slave marriages because they understood that slaves with families would be less likely to rebel. Complete submissiveness and the goodwill of their masters were necessary to hold a slave family together.

Slavery was not, however, necessarily a permanent condition. Slaves might obtain their freedom through manumission. Through this carefully regulated legal procedure, a master granted freedom to a slave as a reward for faithful service or docile behavior, or even out of genuine affection. Of course manumission worked to the best interests of the owner: The merest hope of manumission kept most slaves docile. Moreover, Roman law established limits to manumission. No more than 100 slaves could be freed at the death of an owner, and the slave had to be at least 30 years old and the owner at least 25.

Despite these restrictions, the freedmen constituted an important class in Roman society. Freedmen made up only about 5 percent of Rome's population, but their enterprise and ambition marked them as some of the more successful members of Roman society. Many former slaves worked in business or as skilled laborers, teachers, and doctors. Unlike in other ancient societies, freedmen rid themselves of the taint of slavery in only one generation. A freed slave had only partial citizen rights, but his or her children became full Roman citizens, who could freely marry other citizens. The historian Tacitus records a remark made in a senatorial debate about this phenomenon: "Not without good reason had our ancestors, in distinguishing the position of the different orders, thrown freedom open to all." Tacitus noted that some senators and many equestrians could point to ex-slaves among their ancestors.

Slavery remained a part of Mediterranean economic and social life until the early Middle Ages, but in the second century C.E. the role of slaves in the economy began to diminish. As Roman emperors concentrated on consolidating rather than expanding the borders of the empire, the supply of slaves dwindled, and the cost of slaves rose. Thus, slave owning may have become less economically viable.

WOMEN IN THE ROMAN EMPIRE

Women in the senatorial and equestrian ranks possessed far more freedom than was usual in the ancient world. By 250 C.E., the form of marriage by which a woman passed from the control of her father to that of her husband had al-

most entirely died out. Women remained, at least theoretically, under the control of their father or legal guardian. In practice, this form of marriage gave a woman more freedom, in large part because her husband no longer controlled her dowry. Some women used this freedom to move more into the public view, taking part in banquets, attending the gladiatorial battles at the Colosseum and the races at the Circus Maximus, and even presiding over literary salons. Many women were educated in the liberal arts and lived a cultivated lifestyle. Their surviving portraits (carved in stone) reveal a restrained physical elegance. The portraits of several wives and daughters of emperors even appeared on coins.

As these coins suggest, at the highest level of society some women possessed real political power, though expressed behind the scenes. Livia, married to Augustus for fifty-two years, possessed a great deal of influence during his reign and worked actively to ensure the succession of her son Tiberius. The emperor Hadrian may have received his throne in part because of the influence of his cousin Trajan's wife, Plotina. At Plotina's funeral, Hadrian admitted, "She often made requests of me, and I never once refused her." The empress Julia Domna survived her husband Septimius Severus to become an important political power during the reign of her son Caracalla.

Although literary evidence demonstrates that many aristocratic Roman men cherished their daughters, the practice of female infanticide remained common throughout Roman society. In addition, some children born outside marriage, and those born deformed or ill, were regularly exposed—left on a pile of garbage or by the roadside. Not all the exposed children died. Sometimes they were rescued and raised as slaves by ordinary people. In other cases, slave dealers picked up the abandoned babies and sold them.

LITERATURE AND EMPIRE

As in the Republic, in the empire Roman writers continued to look to Greek Hellenistic culture for their models. But the presence of the empire itself influenced Roman writers. No author could avoid the political facts of life, whether he cynically ignored them, enthusiastically embraced them, or cautiously probed their limits. The presence of imperial autocracy, as well as Rome's expanding might, affected literary production in different ways.

Writers during the reign of Augustus embodied the tensions and uncertainties of living in a society that had exchanged freedom for stability. Livy (59 B.C.E.–12 C.E.) wrote a massive history of Rome, called *From the Foundation of the City*, that traced Rome from its origins until his own time. Though less than a fifth of this work survives, we see that Livy presented Rome's rise to world mastery as a series of instructive moral and patriotic lessons. He showed how

Rome grew to world power through vanquishing many enemies. Although proud of Rome's greatness, Livy also believed that with power came decadence. He expressed the hope that Augustus would restore Rome's glory and put an end to what he perceived as its moral and political decline.

The tragic career of Ovid (43 B.C.E.–17 C.E.) demonstrates the risks of offending an emperor. Ovid's brilliant love elegies had made him the darling of Rome. But in 8 C.E., his erotic poem "The Art of Love," along with an obscure scandal involving Augustus's family, earned him the hostility of the prudish emperor. Augustus exiled Ovid to a squalid village on the Black Sea, where he died in sorrow.

The poet Horace (65–8 B.C.E.), son of a wealthy freedman, walked a more careful path. He avoided political entanglements and maintained close ties to Augustus. His poetry on public themes praised Augustus for bringing peace and the hope of a moral life to the world. Throughout his work, Horace urged serene appreciation of life's transient joys. In his most famous verse (*Odes* I.11.6ff) he sings, "Be wise, taste the wine, and since our time is brief, be moderate in your aspirations. Even as we speak, greedy life slips away from us. Grasp each day (*carpe diem*) and do not pin your hopes on tomorrow."

Virgil stands as the greatest of the Roman poets. Drawing on Hellenistic poetic forms, Virgil wrote of the wisdom, safety, and serenity found in an idealized country life—with the terrible uncertainties of civil war providing a silent backdrop. At Augustus' request Virgil composed the *Aeneid*°, an epic poem that legitimized and celebrated the emperor's reign. Ostensibly the poem was about the mythic foundation of the Roman state by the hero Aeneas, a Trojan prince fleeing the destruction of his native city by the Greeks. But through a series of cinematic "flash-forwards," Virgil presented the entire history of the Roman people as culminating in the reign of Augustus. In the *Aeneid*, the emperor brings to completion the nearly unendurable efforts of his Trojan ancestor.

Although the *Aeneid* praises Augustus, Virgil was not just a propagandist for the imperial regime. Virgil remained his own man throughout his lifetime, praising those aspects of peace and fulfillment of duty that he genuinely valued, but nevertheless questioning the costs of warfare and the demands of empire on human beings. Virgil subtly investigated the effects of warfare and public duty on individual character. In the *Aeneid* Virgil's hero Aeneas was deeply tempted by his love for the Carthaginian queen Dido to abandon his mission of founding Rome. But Aeneas overcame his private desire in favor of the destiny of Rome. He willingly abandoned Dido to continue his divinely inspired mission. At the end of the poem, Aeneas stands victorious—but a psychological ruin. He had given everything to his duty. Virgil makes his readers wonder about the costs of such utter public service. If any writer understood the promise and the threat of the imperial system, it was Virgil.

Seneca (ca. 4 B.C.E.–41 C.E.), who combined philosophical interests with literary skill, accepted the imperial system. His integrity and rhetorical brilliance earned him the unenviable task of being Nero's tutor when the emperor was still an impressionable 12-year-old boy. For eight years Seneca guided Nero, and the empire enjoyed good government. As Nero matured, however, he found other, less decent advisers. Appalled by his student's descent into corruption, Seneca plotted to kill Nero. When he was caught, he killed himself.

In the Middle Ages Seneca's works were so highly regarded that many people believed he had exchanged letters with the Christian Paul of Tarsus. Stoic beliefs deeply influenced Seneca's writing. He intended his writings to give sound advice to rulers. Seneca courageously acknowledged how hard it was to control one's human weaknesses and live a truly moral life.

Other writers analyzed the imperial system differently. Practitioners of the art of public speaking (rhetoric) had to grapple with new realities during the imperial age. The new autocratic government made free political debate impossible. Nevertheless, opportunities for public speech still abounded: Law cases still had to be tried in court, and emperors had to be bathed in praise at regular intervals. Thus, rhetoric blossomed in the new imperial world. Quintilian (ca. 35–ca. 90 C.E.) exemplifies the new kind of imperial rhetorician. He rose to prominence in Rome as a teacher and speaker, becoming the tutor in the royal household of the emperor Domitian. His masterpiece, *Training in Oratory*, calls for clarity and balance in speaking. It also rather wistfully suggests that an orator might guide the Senate and the state, as Quintilian's model Cicero had done during the days of the Republic.

The historian and rhetorician Tacitus (ca. 56–ca. 118 C.E.) took a more realistic approach than Quintilian. In his *Dialogue on Orators* he argued—correctly—that political autocracy had killed true oratory, reducing it to mere public entertainment and ceremonial flourishes. Sardonic and terse, Tacitus's historical accounts covering the first century of the Augustan age displayed a deep understanding of human psychological reaction to the harsh political realities of early imperial tyranny. Although Tacitus's career flourished under the tyrannical Domitian, he hated political oppression and he never abandoned his love for the best of Roman ideals. In the *Agricola*, his biography of his father-in-law, Tacitus affirmed that good men could serve their country honorably, even under bad rulers. The *Agricola* thus inadvertently revealed an important accomplishment of Augustus's imperial system: It had tamed the competitive energies of Rome's aristocrats, transforming them into an efficient governing class.

Eager to contemplate the cultural superiority of the Roman Empire over other peoples, Rome's ruling elite took a strong interest in the habits of non-Romans. In his

Geography, Strabo (64 B.C.E.–ca. 25 C.E.), a native Greek and a Roman citizen, wrote a detailed account of the many peoples ruled by Rome, stressing how Roman civilization could change foreign cultures for the better. He suggested that Rome's rulers and administrators should "bring together cities and peoples into a single Empire and political management." Drawing on Hellenistic and Greek traditions of writing about foreign cultures, Strabo placed the Roman Empire at the center of the inhabited world.

In addition to geography, other forms of scientific writing made great strides in the early centuries of the Roman Empire. Claudius Ptolemy of Alexandria maintained the high standards of the Hellenistic science tradition that continued to flourish under Roman rule. Writing in the second half of the second century C.E. (historians cannot be precise about the dates of his birth or death), Ptolemy composed definitive works in many fields. Using the division of spheres into units of 60 first developed by the Sumerians and perfected by the Babylonians, Ptolemy's *Almagest* proved the theories and tables necessary to compute the positions of the sun, the moon, and five known planets. He accepted the Greek theory that the sun revolves around the Earth. Western astronomers used his maps of the heavens for nearly 1,500 years. His *Geography* gave readings in longitude and latitude and provided information for drawing a world map, which remained the basis of cartography until the sixteenth century. Translated from Greek into Arabic, Ptolemy's books became standard in the medieval Islamic world. Eventually they were translated into Latin and so passed back into use in western Europe during the Middle Ages.

RELIGIOUS LIFE

Religious expression in the Roman Empire took many forms. The imperial government made no effort to impose uniform belief, so subject peoples freely worshiped many gods and maintained their traditional religious rituals. Within many religious cultures, trends that first appeared in the Hellenistic Age continued, but important new changes emerged during the imperial era. Judaism was transformed during this period. At the same time, an entirely new religion, Christianity, emerged from Jewish roots. This new faith grew to become the dominant religion in the empire by 400 C.E. and eventually suppressed polytheistic religions.

Polytheism in the Empire

Syncretism°, the practice of equating two gods and fusing their cults, was a common feature of imperial religious life. Like many other Mediterranean peoples, the Romans often identified a foreign god with their own deities. For example, Julius Caesar described the Gallic god of commerce as

Mercury, because Mercury served the same function in Roman religion. Romans did not care that other people throughout the empire might worship Jupiter or Juno or any other Roman god in different ways, or might give the gods different attributes. Syncretism, then, helped unify the diverse peoples and regions under Roman rule. Through syncretism, shared religious experiences spread across the empire.

Roman religious practice was a public, not private, phenomenon. Imperial subjects worshiped the emperor and Rome, the protectors of the entire empire. In addition, each city in the empire had its own gods, whom people imagined as dwelling within the temples dedicated to them. Worshipers gathered in front of the temples to offer sacrifices at altars located in front of the shrines. On religious holidays, thousands of city dwellers participated in parades and feasted at the great banquets that followed the sacrifice of many specially selected animals at temple altars. Particularly elaborate celebrations even attracted pilgrims and visitors from afar.

The gods worshiped in specific cities and at specific holy sites generally were of great antiquity. Gods such as Athena in Athens or Jupiter in Rome were as old as the town itself. People believed that these gods would protect and benefit their communities if the residents made the proper sacrifices. Although a deity might be associated with a similar god in another town, its worship in each city had a unique quality, deeply intertwined with the history and architecture of the town itself. For example, Hercules protected many places, but his temple in each town was connected to a different local myth about him.

Some religious cults transcended their places of origin and spread widely, particularly among slaves, freedmen, and the urban poor who felt lost in the sprawl of the empire's big cities. As we have seen, large numbers of the urban poor had no stake in the success of the Roman system. The anonymity of life in big cities for the poor contributed to the spread of religions that offered a measure of identity and community and a kind of salvation as well. Religions that promised victory over death or liberation from the abuses and pain of daily existence possessed a wide appeal and spread quickly across the empire. The goddess Isis, for example, who originated in Egypt, offered freedom from the arbitrary abuses of fate to her many followers throughout the empire. Her cult particularly attracted women. Because she was often depicted holding her baby son Horus, she represented the universal mother. In his work *The Golden Ass,* the Roman writer Apuleius (ca. 125–ca. 170 C.E.) describes the goddess's protective power. Full of eroticism and magic, the work tells the story of Lucius, a carefree young Romeo, who is turned into a miserable donkey when caught spying on a gorgeous witch. After many comic misadventures in which Lucius learns how uncertain fate can be, Isis restores him

■ **Mummy Wrapping from Egypt**

This painted linen cloth was wrapped around a mummy in an Egyptian burial during the second century C.E. It shows the Egyptian god Osiris (on the left) and the jackal-headed god Anubis (on the right). Between them is the deceased man, dressed in Roman clothing. His portrait has been carefully painted and added separately. This wrapping and portrait show the continuity of ancient Egyptian religion during Roman imperial rule.

to human form. In gratitude, Lucius joins her religion and becomes her priest.

Another popular religion that promised salvation to its initiates was that of Mithras, a sun god. Artists depicted Mithras slaying a bull, an archetypal sacrifice that his followers reenacted in secret ceremonies. Limited to men, worship of Mithras took place in underground chambers in which small groups held banquets, recited sacred lessons about the celestial journey of the soul after death, and made sacrifices to the god in imitation of his killing of the bull. Because this religion stressed both physical courage and performance of duty, it particularly attracted soldiers and administrators.

The most important religion of an eastern god whose worship spread throughout the Roman Empire was that of the Unconquered Sun. Originating in Syria, this deity came to be associated with Apollo and Helios, two Greco-Roman sun gods. When Elagabalus, the high priest of the Syrian sun god (El-Gabal), became Roman emperor (r. 218–222 C.E.), he built a huge temple dedicated to his god in Rome, and designated December 25 as a special day of worship to the deity. Within fifty years, the Unconquered Sun became the chief god of imperial and official worship. Only the rise of Christianity would displace the worship of the Unconquered Sun.

Gnosticism, which originated in the Hellenistic Age, continued its influence in the Roman Empire, affecting Judaism, Christianity, and many polytheistic religions. Gnostics believed that the material world of daily life is incompatible with the supreme god. They thought that sparks of divinity (sometimes considered the human soul) are imprisoned within the body. Only a redeemer sent from the supreme god could release these divine sparks.

The Origins of Rabbinic Judaism

Following the Roman devastation of Judaea and the destruction of the Temple in Jerusalem in 70 C.E., Judaism began to take the shape it has today. Since priests could no longer make sacrifices at the Temple and provide a focus for Jewish worship, a new kind of community-based religious life began to develop among Jews in Judaea and other lands. Rabbis replaced priests in the roles of religious instructors and community guides. Unlike the priests who had served as intermediaries between the community and God by offering prayers and animal sacrifices on the people's behalf, the rabbis had no sacred function. *Rabbi*, a Hebrew term of respect meaning "my master," was the term that Jews applied to teachers. Men with legal training, rabbis interpreted and taught the Jewish law contained in the Torah, the first five books of the Hebrew Bible. Rabbis placed tremendous importance upon studying the Torah. "It is the unlearned who bring trouble into the world," said Rabbi Judah the Prince, a Jewish scholar of the late second century C.E.

Rabbis became more important after the failed Jewish revolt against Rome (66–70 C.E.). According to Jewish tradition, a rabbi named Johannon ben Zakkai, who had opposed the revolt, was smuggled out of Jerusalem around 68 C.E. Johannon ben Zakkai gained permission from the Romans to establish an academy at Jamnia in Judaea, where men might study and interpret Jewish law. Judaea remained a center of rabbinic teaching until the Bar Kochba revolt of 132–135 C.E. In the aftermath of this bloodily suppressed rebellion in which more than half a million Jews were killed, the emperor Hadrian built a new city on the site of ruined Jerusalem and barred Jews from admission all but one day a year. Galilee (a region to the north of Jerusalem)

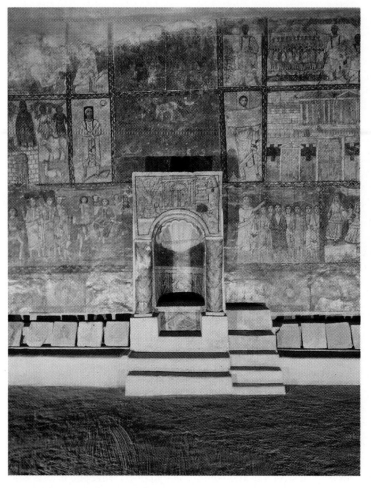

■ **Dura Europus**

Located on the Euphrates River, the town of Dura Europus was on the eastern frontier of the Roman Empire, and had a large and prosperous Jewish community in the third century C.E. The walls of the community's synagogue were painted with many scenes illustrating stories from the Hebrew Bible.

material for reference and teaching, rabbis undertook a task not unlike that of the Roman jurists. But unlike Roman compilations, which drew from written texts, the Mishnah drew largely from oral law that had been memorized and transmitted through many generations.

Compiled by Rabbi Judah the Prince and his school, the Mishnah consists of sixty-three books, each dealing with a particular aspect of law, ranging from matters of ritual purity to calendrical issues to civil and criminal law. Because legal opinions are attributed to the rabbi who gave the original judgment, we can trace the development of Jewish law in the first and second centuries C.E. Among the many moral principles stressed by the Mishnah, saving life was paramount. According to the Mishnah, no person could save his or her own life by causing another's death, and no person could be sacrificed for the welfare of the community. Moreover, to save a life, any person could break any Jewish religious law, except those forbidding idolatry, adultery, incest, or murder. In Jewish thought, saving one life symbolized saving humanity. A radical idea slowly emerged from this principle: Since all humans are made in God's image, they should all have equal rights. This idea contributed to the gradual decline of slave holding among Jews.

In addition to the rabbis who led individual Jewish communities, an official called the Patriarch represented the Jews as a whole to the emperor. The Romans appointed the Patriarch and gave him the highest political authority in Jewish affairs in the empire. The Patriarch's responsibilities included collecting taxes for Rome and choosing judges for Jewish courts. The Romans gave the Patriarch the rank of senator, as the representative of all the Jews in the empire. This arrangement, a clear example of how Roman authorities let local populations manage their own laws, continued until Christianity became the official religion of the empire in the fifth century C.E. Christian emperors then began persecuting Jews and limiting their participation in public life.

The Emergence of Christianity

So far in this chapter we have considered the interaction of the Roman government with communities that had existed for many centuries. The emergence of Christianity, however, forced the Romans to deal with an entirely new community within the empire. Christians had a new sense of shared identity, a new sense of history, and a new perception of the Roman system. Christianity gradually became the most widespread religion in the Roman Empire, and within 400 years of the death of its founder became the official religion of the empire.

and the coastal city of Caesarea then became important rabbinic centers. Historians have found little evidence that rabbis taught elsewhere in the Roman Empire for many centuries afterward.

By 200 C.E., synagogues emerged as communal centers that served many functions for Jews. In these buildings rabbis studied Jewish law and passed judgment on disputes. Members of the community gathered there to celebrate sacred meals on the Sabbath and to hear the Jewish law read aloud and explained. Gradually synagogues developed into centers where the Jewish community would pray together.

The greatest product of the rabbinic academies was the Mishnah, a collection of legal opinions, legal decisions, and homilies to explain the law to unlearned people. Jewish teachers had begun accumulating this material in Hellenistic times, but it was completed around the year 220 C.E. In their desire to prepare a manageable body of

The founder of Christianity was a Jew named Yeshua ben Yosef, known today as Jesus of Nazareth (ca. 4 B.C.E.–ca. 30 C.E.). Born to a poor couple in Galilee during the reign of Augustus, Jesus grew to manhood in the Jewish community. Around age 30 he began to travel through Palestine with a band of followers, urging men and women to repent their sins because God would soon come to rule the Kingdom of Heaven on Earth. Jesus probably believed himself to be the messiah whose death would inaugurate a new age and a new covenant with God. By means of this covenant, God's earthly kingdom would begin and all humanity would be freed from sin, death, and the power of the Devil.

Jesus was a holy man and a healer. Like other contemporary Jewish teachers, he insisted that having the right intent in carrying out God's law mattered more than conforming to the outward performance of the law. When asked what the greatest commandment is, Jesus replied, "You must love the Lord your God with all your heart, with all your soul, and with all your mind. This is the greatest and the first commandment. The second resembles it: You must love your neighbor as yourself. On these two commandments hang the whole Law." (Matthew 22:37–39)

In 30 C.E. Jesus entered Jerusalem to preach his message. The Roman authorities arrested and tried him as a revolutionary. They executed Jesus by crucifixion, the usual Roman death penalty for noncitizens. Jesus' followers, however, insisted that he still lived. They believed that he rose from the dead three days after being executed, and that forty days later he entered heaven to be united with God. His followers came to believe that Jesus was the Son of God, and that he had died on the cross as part of a divine plan. In Christian theology, Jesus' brutal death at the hands of the Romans became a loving sacrifice: Jesus took the punishment for sin due to all human beings. Christians, then, regarded Jesus as their savior, as the God whose intervention in human history guaranteed them eternal life.

Jesus recorded none of his ideas in writing, but his followers transmitted his teachings orally for several decades after his death before beginning to write them down. By about 120 C.E. they had compiled an authoritative body of texts that recorded Jesus' life and words, which Christians call the New Testament. Much early writing about Jesus was not included in the New Testament, but enough of this material survives to show that many different interpretations of Jesus, his death, and his message existed even during his lifetime.

For many decades after Jesus' death, his followers still thought of themselves as Jews. The word *Christian* (which comes from the Greek word *Christos,* meaning "the anointed one" or "messiah") was first used in the Syrian city of Antioch in the second half of the first century C.E. Christianity drew much from Judaism. For example, both faiths believe that that there is only one God, with whom contact is direct and immediate, that this God has a plan for his people on Earth, and that he wishes them to live by a moral and ethical code elaborated in his law.

Christianity diverges from Judaism in several ways. Unlike Jews, Christians have a strong sense of mission. Proselytizing (preaching to nonbelievers in order to convert them) became a central activity for followers of the new faith. As we have seen, the destruction of the Jerusalem Temple in 70 C.E. forced Jews to abandon ritual sacrifice. By contrast, Christians created a priesthood to maintain the sacrament of the Eucharist (Holy Communion), a ritual that recalls Jesus' death on the cross in order to fulfill Jesus' instructions: "Jesus . . . broke some bread, and he said, 'this is my body, which is for you; do this as a memorial of me.' And in the same way, with the cup after supper, saying, 'Whenever you eat this bread, then, and drink this cup, you are proclaiming the Lord's death until he comes.'" (1 Corinthians 11:23–26) In this ritual, the Christian tastes bread and wine, representing the flesh and blood of Jesus. The Christian is thus united to God through Jesus. At the same time, this tasting of the Eucharist reminds the Christian of Jesus' sacrifice to ensure his or her salvation.

Christians and Jews further disagree about how to interpret texts that both communities consider fundamental. For example, Christians hold that Jesus' teachings (contained in the New Testament) build on the teachings of the Hebrew Bible, which they called the Old Testament. Consequently, they interpret the Hebrew Bible solely in light of Christianity. For example, Christians believe that the prophetic writings of the Hebrew Bible predict Jesus' birth, death, and resurrection. They also believe that baptism, the ritual that signals an individual's membership in the Christian community, replaces circumcision as a sign of God's promise to his people. Thus, unlike Judaism, Christianity does not require male circumcision for its adherents.

For all their fundamental differences of belief, Christianity and Judaism share some characteristics that distinguish them from other religions of antiquity. First, both Christianity and Judaism combine a statement of belief with a social ethic. Their ethical systems, which they believe stems from divine revelation, are embodied in values that strengthen the religious community. In antiquity Christians and Jews married within their own communities and both protected the underprivileged in their communities—widows, orphans, and the poor. Second, both religious communities had an internal organization that did not depend on Rome. Their leaders (bishops for Christians and rabbis for Jews) gave judgments based on law that was separate from the Roman justice system. Finally, both Judaism and Christianity were monotheistic. To the Romans, who believed in many gods, this monotheism was the strangest aspect of the two faiths. Worshiping only one god made no sense to Romans, with their tradition of making sacrifices to many gods.

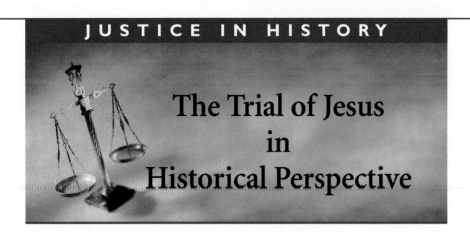

The Trial of Jesus in Historical Perspective

In 30 C.E. Roman authorities in Jerusalem tried and executed a Jewish teacher known today as Jesus of Nazareth or Jesus Christ, whose teachings lie at the foundation of Christianity, the faith of hundreds of millions of people in the world today. Although an insignificant event at the time, the trial of Jesus and its interpretation made a profound impact on Western civilization. We can learn much about the West by understanding the ways in which the trial has been interpreted through the ages.

Information about Jesus' trial comes from the New Testament books of Matthew, Mark, Luke, and John. These narratives, called the Gospels, were written thirty to sixty years after Jesus' death. They relate that during three years of teaching and miraculous healing, Jesus earned the resentment of some Jewish religious leaders by disregarding aspects of Jewish religious law. According to the Gospels, when Jesus entered the Temple precinct in Jerusalem, he started a riot by overturning the tables of money changers who served pilgrims and by denouncing the hypocrisy of the priestly elite, who then conspired to kill him. The priests paid one of Jesus' followers to reveal his whereabouts, arrested him on either the night before or the night of the Passover feast, and tried him immediately before the Sanhedrin, the highest Jewish court, which met that same night in the house of the Jewish high priest.

The Gospels say that the Sanhedrin found Jesus guilty of blasphemy for claiming to be the Messiah and the Son of God. Lacking the authority to put Jesus to death, the Jewish leaders brought Jesus before Pontius Pilate, the Roman governor, and demanded that he execute Jesus. Pilate was reluctant to do so, but the priests persuaded him by insisting that Jesus threatened the emperor's authority with his claim to be King of the Jews. Pilate's soldiers crucified Jesus—a terrible punishment in which the condemned person was tied or nailed to a wooden cross and left to die. According to the Gospel accounts, however, the real blame for Jesus' death rests with the Jews, who had demanded his execution. In all four Gospel accounts, Jewish crowds in Jerusalem reject Jesus and cry out, "Crucify him!" to a reluctant Pontius Pilate.

The Gospel narratives, however, do not correspond to what historians know about the conduct of trials by Jewish authorities or Roman administrators. For example, the Sanhedrin could not hold trials at night; it never met in the house of the High Priest, only in the Hall of Justice in the Temple precinct; and it never met on a Jewish feast day or the night before a feast. The most important difference, however, is that according to Jewish law it was not a crime to claim to be the messiah. Originating in ceremonies of anointing kings, the word *messiah* had many interpretations as a kingly figure of power—but not as a god.

If Jesus had not committed a crime under Jewish law by claiming to be the messiah, what then was his offense? Jesus had committed a very dangerous act by denouncing the priests in Jerusalem. These men, especially the High Priest himself, owed their positions of power to the Roman overlords and were responsible for maintaining order. These Jewish elites saw Jesus as an agitator who posed a threat to their authority.

■ The Scales of Justice
This coin shows the goddess Aequitas, who represents the idea of fairness in Roman justice.

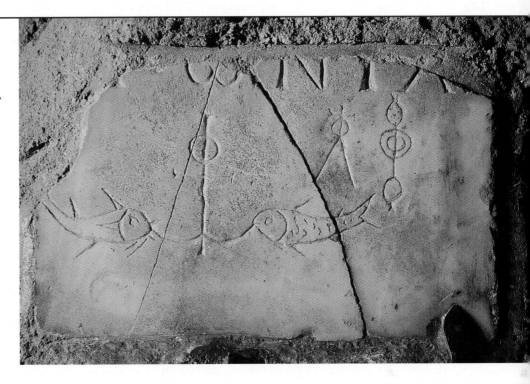

■ Early Christian Symbols
This Roman tombstone is decorated with some of the earliest Christian symbols. The anchor represents hope, while the fish stand for Jesus. The Greek word for fish, *icthus*, is an anagram of the Greek words for "Jesus Christ Son of God and Savior."

For this reason Jesus was first brought before the Sanhedrin, the Jewish court permitted by the Romans to deal with affairs within the Jewish community. The Romans had appointed all seventy-one members of the court, including Caiaphas, the high priest who led it. These court members knew that if they could not control Jesus, the Romans would certainly replace them. The Sanhedrin could not punish Jesus under Jewish law, but it could send him before Roman magistrates on a charge that the Romans would not hesitate to prosecute—stirring up rebellion.

Jesus' popularity with the common people and the riot in the Temple precinct would have been enough to arouse Roman suspicion. It is also likely that the Roman authorities did not understand the concept of messiah or how Jesus understood the term. Any uncertainty in Pontius Pilate's mind about Jesus' claims would quickly have led to a death sentence. Roman officials usually responded to real or imagined threats to the political order by crucifixion. In the eyes of Pontius Pilate, a cautious magistrate, Jesus constituted a threat to public order, and so deserved execution.

Why, then, do the Gospels shift the blame for Jesus' death from Pontius Pilate and place it on the Jewish community as whole? The Gospel narratives began to be written down in an atmosphere of growing hostility and suspicion between Jews and Christians. After Roman armies destroyed the Jerusalem Temple in the Jewish rebellion of 66–70 C.E., Christians wanted to disassociate themselves from Jews in Roman eyes, hoping to persuade Roman authorities to think of them not as rebels but rather as followers of a lawful religion. The Gospels link the death of Jesus in 30 C.E. and the destruction of the Temple in 70 C.E., by saying that Jesus predicted the Temple's destruction. These accounts interpret both events from a post–70 C.E. perspective. They present Jesus' death as willed by Jewish leaders, and they suggest that the Roman officials in fact did not want to kill him. According to the Gospels, the destruction of the Temple was punishment for the Jews who had caused Jesus' death.

This interpretation of Jesus' trial and execution helped poison Christian–Jewish relations for two millennia. From the first century C.E. through the twentieth, the Christian community blamed Jews for Jesus' crucifixion. ■

Questions of Justice

1. What does the trial of Jesus show about Roman provincial administration?
2. From the point of view of a member of the Sanhedrin, why was the execution of Jesus justifiable?

Taking It Further

Crossan, John Dominic. *Who Killed Jesus: Exposing the Roots of Anti-Semitism in the Gospel Story of the Death of Jesus.* 1997. A highly engaging investigation.

Johnson, Luke Timothy, John Dominic Crossan, and Werner H. Kelber. *The Jesus Controversy.* 1999. Three experts discuss the problems of finding who Jesus "really was."

Sherwin-White, A. N. *Roman Society and Roman Law in the New Testament.* 1963. A leading Roman historian puts the New Testament in its Roman context.

The Spread of Christianity

Christianity drew many of its first converts from socially marginalized groups, such as women, noncitizens, and slaves. Indeed, Jesus' message was revolutionary in the way it overturned conventional boundaries of class, gender, and ethnicity. The writings of Paul of Tarsus° (d. ca. 65 C.E.) in the New Testament illustrate this perspective. Paul became the most effective early Christian missionary. He preached to non-Jewish audiences that Jesus had inaugurated a new age in human history, and that the end of the current age was imminent. Paul encouraged a communal life in which all followers of Jesus were equal in the eyes of God. As he wrote to a small Christian community in Galatia in Asia Minor, "For in Christ Jesus . . . there is no longer Jew or Greek, there is no longer slave or free, there is no longer male or female; for all of you are one in Christ Jesus." Paul therefore urged the entry of gentiles (non-Jews) into the Christian community, believing that Jesus' teachings would one day unify the entire human race.

Christianity continued to attract the poor and outcast, but by the middle of the second century C.E., an important change occurred within the ranks of Christian adherents. Many new converts to the faith were men and women who had already been educated in Greek philosophy. They began to analyze and understand Christianity in the terms with which they were familiar: the abstract ideas of the Hellenistic philosophical tradition. Rather than dismiss the philosopher Plato, for example, they argued that his ideas about the supremacy of the soul and what it meant to lead a good life anticipated the teachings of Jesus. Because it eventually led to Christianity's assimilation of much of classical culture, this encounter between Christians and the intelligentsia of the Mediterranean world transformed the Christian faith. As Christians explained their faith to educated gentiles in the language of traditional philosophical education, they won even more converts. They developed methods of analyzing biblical texts drawn from philosophy and rhetoric. The language of Christianity and Greek and Latin intellectual life fused.

Much of this development centered on the works of a group of Christian writers, whom historians call Apologists°. The Apologists publicly defended their faith to learned non-Christian audiences (just as Socrates had defended his beliefs in Plato's *Apology*—hence the name *Apologists*.) In the process, they helped shape the Christian response to the challenges of Hellenist philosophy and cosmology. One of the most important of the Apologists, Justin Martyr (ca. 100–165 C.E.), sought to make Christianity comprehensible to other intellectuals like himself who had not grown up as Christians. Justin insisted that Christian beliefs accorded with rational thought. He interpreted Christianity as the culmination of intellectual developments that had begun in the classical past. For example, he believed that Plato had anticipated some Christian truths, such as the existence of a single, transcendent God.

CHRONOLOGY	
Cultural and Religious Events	
59–12 B.C.E.	Livy writes *History of Rome*
70–19 B.C.E.	Virgil writes poetry, completes *Aeneid*
65–8 B.C.E.	Horace writes poetry
43 B.C.E.–17 C.E.	Ovid writes poetry
4 B.C.E.–30 C.E.	Life of Jesus of Nazareth
4 B.C.E.–41 C.E.	Seneca writes works of Stoic philosophy
CA. 35–90 C.E.	Quintilian writes about rhetoric
CA. 56–CA. 118 C.E.	Tacitus writes about recent Roman history
CA. 100 C.E.	New Testament completed
CA. 100–165 C.E.	Justin Martyr explains Christianity
125–170 C.E.	Apuleius writes *The Golden Ass*
CA. 160–240 C.E.	Tertullian defends Christianity and criticizes Rome
184–255 C.E.	Origen writes about the theory and practice of Christianity

Justin Martyr's embrace of Greek philosophy was typical of Apologist thought. Another Apologist, Clement of Alexandria (ca. 150–216 C.E.), wrote that the study of Greek philosophy could prepare a Christian to understand Jesus' teachings. Origen (ca. 184–255 C.E.), the most profound thinker among the Apologists, was as much a classical scholar as a churchman. A talented editor and commentator on biblical texts, he also made significant contributions to Christian theology. He and Clement laid the groundwork for the integration of classical Greek philosophy and culture with Christianity. This complex step was of unparalleled importance in the development of Western civilization because it not only enhanced the appeal of Christianity among educated believers but also ensured the transmission of many Greek philosophical ideas to what would become Western culture.

The Apologists faced stiff opposition from within the Christian community because many churchmen viewed classical learning with deep suspicion. Tertullian (ca. 160–240 C.E.), Origen's influential contemporary, argued forcefully for the separation of Christianity from the learning and culture of the non-Christian world. He worried that the mingling of religious cults so common in his day might corrupt Christianity. Tertullian summed up his opposition to classical culture: "What has Athens to do with Jerusalem? What is there in common between the philosopher and the Christian? . . . After the Gospel we have no need for further research." Christians like Tertullian mistrusted the power of the human intellect and stressed the need to remain focused on the divine revelation of the Christian Scriptures. Yet Tertullian could not stop the integration of Christianity with classical learning. By the third century C.E. Christians could no longer ignore the Mediterranean world in which they lived.

And that world could no longer ignore them. Many of Christianity's core concepts, such as its ideas about personal salvation, the equality of individual men and women before God, and the redemption of humanity from sin, distinguished it from the empire's polytheistic faiths. Perhaps the greatest difference between polytheists and Christians, however, was Christianity's intolerance of other people's forms of worship. Christians referred to all polytheist forms of worship collectively as "paganism" and tried to convert pagans to Christianity.

Through their proselytizing and their hostility to other forms of religious expression, Christians gained enemies. Their close community life meant they kept to themselves; this failure to engage in the public life of Roman culture won them suspicion. As a result, Christians sometimes endured persecution, though the danger in these early years was never as severe as later Christian writers claimed.

Claudius expelled Christians from Rome, and in 64 C.E., the Roman emperor Nero blamed Christians for a destructive fire that consumed central Rome. (Popular legend blamed him, equally wrongly.) Hundreds of Christians died in the arena before cheering crowds.

By the second half of the first century C.E., many Roman officials perceived Christians as potential enemies of the state because they refused to join in the worship of the emperor. Christians who refused to renounce their religious beliefs were sometimes executed. During an inspection tour in Asia Minor for the emperor Trajan in 112 C.E., the lawyer Pliny interrogated people suspected of being Christians. Pliny tried to follow proper legal procedure and to avoid unwarranted harrassment of the suspects, but he did execute anyone found guilty of being a Christian. Christians believed that these victims of religious persecution had died gloriously and called them martyrs, or witnesses for their faith. Tertullian chided his Roman persecutors, "We multiply whenever we are mown down by you; the blood of Christians is [like] seed."

In their vision of all humanity united under a single God and their desire to suppress other forms of religious expression, Christians were truly revolutionary. Christians eventually succeeded in displacing all polytheist religions within the Roman Empire. Although polytheism still exists in many parts of the world today, it is virtually absent from the West. As a consequence, the Western world has lost touch with a fundamental part of how many peoples understood—or still understand—the world.

CONCLUSION
Rome Shapes the West

The map of the Roman Empire outlined the heart of the regions included in the West today. Rome was the means by which cultural and political ideas developed in Mediterranean societies and spread into Europe. This quilt of lands and peoples was acquired mostly by conquest. An autocratic government held the pieces together. Although Roman authorities permitted no dissent in the provinces, they allowed provincial peoples to become Roman. Being Roman meant that one had specific legal rights of citizenship, not that one belonged to a particular race or ethnic group. Thus, in addition to expanding the boundaries of the empire and patrolling its borders, the Roman army brought a version of Roman society to subject peoples. Provincial cities became "little Romes." By imitating Roman styles of architecture and urban life, the cities, too, helped spread Roman civilization. Moreover, the elites of these cities helped funnel the resources of the countryside into the emperor's coffers, and so sustain the imperial system.

For two and a half centuries the *Pax Romana* inaugurated by Augustus fostered a remarkable degree of cultural uniformity within the empire's boundaries. Rome's civilization, including its legal system, its development of cities, and its literary and artistic legacy, made it the foundation of Western civilization as we know it today. The legal precedents established by Roman jurists remain valid in much of Europe. Latin and Greek literature of the early Roman Empire has entertained, instructed, and inspired readers in the West for nearly 2,000 years. Until very recently all educated people in the West could read Latin and looked to the works of the Romans for their model in prose style. Many of our public buildings and memorial sculptures continue to adhere to the artistic and architectural models first outlined in Rome. Of equal importance, the monotheism and ethical teachings of Judaism and Christianity have been prominent forces in shaping Western ideals and attitudes.

A debilitating combination of economic weakness, civil war, and invasions by northern peoples would almost destroy the Roman Empire in the third century C.E. How the Roman Empire recovered and was transformed in the process is the story of the next chapter.

Suggestions for Further Reading

······················· ▬ ·······················

For a comprehensive list of suggested readings, please go to www.ablongman.com/levack/chapter5

Beard, Mary, John North, and Simon Price. *Religions of Rome.* 1995. The first volume contains essays on polytheist religions, and the second contains translated ancient sources.

Gardner, Jane F. *Women in Roman Law and Society.* 1987. Discusses issues pertaining to women in Rome.

Garnsey, Peter, and Richard Saller. *The Roman Empire: Economy, Society, and Culture.* 1987. Stresses the economic and social foundations of the Roman Empire.

Hornblower, Simon, and Antony Spawforth, eds. *The Oxford Classical Dictionary,* 3rd ed. 1996. This encyclopedia treats all aspects of Roman culture and history.

Markus, Robert. *Christianity in the Roman World.* 1974. An excellent study of the growth of Christianity.

Romm, James. *The Edges of the Earth in Ancient Thought: Geography, Exploration, and Fiction.* 1992. An exciting introduction to the Roman understanding of real and imaginary peoples.

Talbert, Richard, ed. *The Barrington Atlas of the Classical World.* 2000. This atlas contains the best maps available.

Webster, Graham. *The Roman Imperial Army,* 3rd ed. 1985. Discusses military organization and life in the empire.

Wiedemann, Thomas. *Emperors and Gladiators.* 1992. An important study of the ideology and practice of gladiatorial combat.

Wolfram, Herwig. *The Roman Empire and Its Germanic Peoples.* 1997. Examines the interrelation of Romans and Germans over several centuries.

Woolf, Greg. *Becoming Roman: The Origins of Provincial Civilization in Gaul.* 1998. The best recent study of Romanization.

ΚΑΙΜΕΝΟΜΡΘΕΚΗΜΕΝΗΠΕΡΕΥΠΟΠΑΤΟΧΕΙΜΩΝΔΗ
ΛΟΟΘΗΓΑΗΓΟΥΓΟΜΡΘΑΠΑΡΑΜΟΗΤΙΝΑΔΑΤΟΥ ΓΟΗΧΥΟΘΕΗ
ΠΟΓΗΧΗΛΟΥΤΙΗΛΓΓΗΚΙΗ ΤΟΤΟΟΟΤΙΑΝΑ ΤΟΥ ΑΤΟ
ΟΔΩΝΕΟΤΙΠΑ ΠΟΡΟΟΤΟΜΟΗΤΙΝΑ ΠΙΤΥΟΥ ΗΟΓΘΟΥ
ΔΗΓΟΗΗΟΥΑΕΟΟΘΗΗΤΙΗΥΤΟΝΕΝΗΑΟΜΕΝΑ ΤΟΗ
ΤΟΟΟΤΟΗ ΕΠΙΑΙΟΥΟΟΩΗ ΟΟΟΟΟΥ ΝΝΗΤΟΑΗ
ΚΑΙΧΥΠΙΟ ΠΑΙΗΟΟΟΟΟΙΗΙΟΟΝΜ ΧΩΗ ΥΟΗΙΤ
ΓΛΥΓΗΕΩΧ ΠΙΛΗΗΑΧΙΙΑ ΚΗΗΜΟΝ ΝΟΟΟΜΕΩ
ΗΤΜΟΜΕΝΑΔΑΠΟΝΙΝ ΚΑΗΡΕΠΛΗΛΗΝΛΟΛΗ
ΠΟΜΜΑΠΑΧΧΧΙΛΑΟΤΗΓΠΕΟΤΜΟΑΗ ΤΟΝΟΟΜΗΟΙ
ΤΟΥ ΠΛΟΗΝΙΛΙΟ ΠΟΝΛΟΠΟΤΗΛΧΟΙΟ ΗΗ
ΤΟΟΘΟΛΟΙΠΟΗΠΑΗΤΟΑΠΙΟΙΑΗ ΝΕΟ ΗΟΟΠΟ
ΟΟΙΑΤΟΙ ΑΗΠΑΟΠΟΛΙΟΤΗΟΕΗΙΟ
ΕΛΙΑ ΟΛΤΟΗΤΟ ΤΟΒ̄ΤΕΕ ΘΟΤΑΡ Ο
ΤΛΟΟΤΤΗΟΥΗ ΗΙΚΤΟΡΟΠΛΧΙ

Late Antiquity: The Age of New Boundaries, 250–600

DURING THE LAST WEEK OF AUGUST IN 410, AN EVENT OCCURRED THAT stunned the Roman world. A small army of landless warriors—no more than a few thousand men—led by their king Alaric forced their way into the city of Rome and plundered it for three days. For more than a year Alaric had been threatening the city in an attempt to extort gold and land for his people. When his attempts at extortion failed, he resorted to attacking the great city of Rome. Because Alaric's followers, the Visigoths, were Christian, they spared Rome's churches and took care not to violate nuns. But that left plenty of loot—gold, silver, and silks—for them to cart away.

For these migrating warriors and their families, who had first invaded the Roman Empire from their homelands in southern Russia thirty years earlier, pillaging the most opulent city in the Mediterranean world was a pleasant interlude in a long struggle to secure a permanent home. For the Romans, however, the looting of Rome was an unfathomable disaster. They could scarcely believe that their capital city, the gleaming symbol of world rule, had fallen to an army made up of people they regarded as barbarian. "If Rome is sacked, what can be safe?" lamented the churchman Jerome when he heard the news in far-off Jerusalem. His remark captures the outrage and astonishment felt by Roman citizens everywhere, Christian and non-Christian alike, who believed that their empire was divinely protected and would last forever.

To understand how the Visigoths managed to sack Rome, we must examine late antiquity, the period between about 250 and 600, which bridged the classical world and the Middle Ages. During this critical era in the development of

Chapter Outline

- Crisis and Recovery in the Third Century
- Christianizing the Empire
- New Christian Communities and Identities
- The Breakup of the Roman Empire

The Vienna Genesis: Written in silver ink on purple-dyed parchment, this sumptuous manuscript of the first book of the Bible, now in a museum in Vienna, Austria, was created in the sixth century, probably for a member of the imperial court in Constantinople. The Greek text at the top portion of the page tells the story of Susanna at the Well, which is illustrated at the bottom of the page. Though the illustration tells a biblical story, certain details reflect conditions in late antiquity, such as fortified cities and the growing importance of camels in travel and commerce. The seated, semi-nude female in the lower left is derived from polytheist religion. She personifies the stream from which the more modestly dressed Susanna gathers water.

Western civilization, the Roman Empire underwent radical transformation. After its recovery from a half century of near-fatal civil war, foreign invasion, and economic crisis, Rome experienced a hundred years of political reform and economic revival. Yet by the middle of the fifth century, the political unity of the Mediterranean world had come to an end. The Roman Empire collapsed in western Europe. In its place, new Germanic kingdoms developed in Italy, Gaul, Britain, Spain, and North Africa. These kingdoms would serve as the foundation of western medieval Europe.

In contrast, the Roman Empire in the east managed to hold together and prosper. Rome's eastern provinces formed the nucleus of what historians call the Byzantine Empire, based in the city of Constantinople (modern Istanbul in Turkey). Until their empire fell to the Turks in 1453, the inhabitants of this eastern realm considered themselves Romans. The Byzantine Empire served as the most important cultural center in Europe throughout the Middle Ages. In both Byzantium (where Roman political administration was maintained) and the new kingdoms of the West (where it was not) Rome's cultural legacy continued, although in very different ways.

The late antique era witnessed not only the collapse of the Roman Empire in the West but also the emergence of Christianity as the dominant religion throughout the imperial realm. From there it spread beyond the imperial borders, bringing new notions of civilization to the people of Europe, North Africa, and the Middle East. In this era one did not have to be Roman to be Christian, but it was necessary to be Christian to be civilized. New cultural boundary lines divided Christian communities from Jews and polytheists, and as we will see in Chapter 7, the followers of another emerging faith, Islam.

To explore this complex age of consolidation, transformation, and cultural transmission, we will consider the following questions: (1) How did the Roman Empire successfully reorganize following the instability of the third century? (2) How did Christianity become the dominant religion in the Roman Empire, and what impact did it exert on Roman society? (3) How did Christianity enable the transformation of communities, religious experience, and intellectual traditions inside and outside the empire? (4) How and why did the Roman Empire in the West disintegrate?

Crisis and Recovery in the Third Century

In the years between 235 and 284, the Roman Empire staggered under waves of political and economic turmoil. Rival generals competed for the throne, chronic civil war shook the empire's very foundation, and invaders hungry for land and plunder broke through the weakened imperial

borders. The economy collapsed and the imperial administration broke down. But in 284, a new emperor seized power and halted the process of decline, shoring up the empire with drastic administrative and social reforms and religious persecution.

THE BREAKDOWN OF THE IMPERIAL GOVERNMENT

In 235, the assassination of Emperor Severus Alexander, the last member of the Severan dynasty, sent the imperial administration into a tailspin. Military coup followed military coup as ruthless generals with nicknames like "Sword-in-Hand" competed for the throne. In the latter half of this century, not one of more than four dozen emperors and would-be emperors died a natural death. Gallienus clung to the throne longest: his reign lasted fifteen years (253–268). Most emperors held power for only a few months. Preoccupied with merely staying on the throne, they neglected the empire's borders, leaving them vulnerable to attack.

This situation had dire consequences for the empire. Foreign invaders attacked both eastern and western provinces throughout late antiquity. To the Romans' deep

■ **The Walls of Rome**
The emperor Aurelian built a twelve-mile circuit of walls around Rome in the 270s to protect the city from Germanic invaders. Twenty feet high and twelve feet thick, the walls had eighteen major gates. The Gate of Saint Sebastian, seen here, had additional towers added in later years. That Rome should need protective walls would have been unthinkable during the early empire.

■ Subjugation of Valerian

Persian kings built their tombs in a cliff six miles north of Persepolis, the old Persian capital. Here at Naqsh-i Rustam, a carving depicts the Great King Shapur I (239–272) on horseback holding the arm of his prisoner, the Roman emperor Valerian. The previous Roman emperor, Philip (known as "the Arab"), kneels in supplication. Shapur bragged about his accomplishments: "When I first came to rule, the Roman emperor Gordian gathered an army from the whole empire of the Romans, Goths, and Germans and came to Mesopotamia against my empire. . . . and we annihilated the Roman army. Then the Romans proclaimed Philip the new emperor . . . and he came to plead with me, and he paid 500,000 gold pieces as ransom and became our tributary . . . And when I marched against Carrhae and Edessa [Roman cities in Syria], the Emperor Valerian advanced against us . . . We fought a great battle . . . and I captured the Emperor Valerian myself with my own hands."

shame, Emperor Valerian was captured in battle by the Great King of Persia in 260. Warbands from across the Rhine River reached as far south as Italy, forcing the emperor Aurelian to build a great wall around the city of Rome in 270. Many other cities across the empire constructed similar defenses. The Roman military system and the Roman economy buckled under the pressure of invasions and civil war. Inflation spun out of control and coins lost their value. The government paid soldiers in produce and supplies rather than cash. Not surprisingly, resentment boiled among the troops.

The seat of power now shifted from Rome to provincial cities. Unlike their predecessors, the soldier-emperors of this era, who came mostly from frontier provinces, had little time to cultivate the support of the Roman Senate. Instead, they held court in cities close to the embattled frontiers. Towns far from Rome, such as York in Britain or Trier in Gaul, had long functioned as military bases and supply distribution centers. Now they served as imperial capitals whenever the emperor resided there.

With the emperor on the move and with armies slipping from imperial control, political power fragmented. Political decentralization injured the empire further. Some cities and provinces took advantage of the weakened government to try to break away from Roman control. In the early 260s and 270s a large portion of Gaul known as the Gallic

Empire briefly established independence. A few years later, Zenobia, the queen of Palmyra (r. 267–272), a city in Syria that had grown wealthy from the caravan trade, rebelled against Rome, and a bitter war ensued. The emperor Aurelian's troops finally crushed Palmyra in 272 and led Zenobia in chains through the streets of Rome in a triumphal procession. Such triumphs, however, were few and far between in these years.

THE RESTORATION OF IMPERIAL GOVERNMENT

Fortunately for the Romans, Diocletian (r. 284–305) stepped in to rescue the empire from total ruin near the end of the third century. Diocletian launched a succession of military, administrative, and economic reforms that had far reaching consequences. Not since the reign of Augustus had the Roman Empire been so fundamentally transformed.

Diocletian's Reforms

After ruling alone for nine years, Diocletian recognized that the enormous responsibilities of imperial rule overburdened a single ruler, and so he took the dramatic step of dividing the empire into two parts. In 286 he chose a co-ruler, Maximian, to govern the western half of the empire, while he continued to rule in the east. Maximian maintained a separate administrative system and his own army. Then, in 293, Diocletian and Maximian subdivided their territories by appointing two junior-level emperors. These junior rulers administered their territories in the eastern and western parts of the empire with their own bureaucracies and armies.

Through this system of government called the tetrarchy°, Diocletian hoped not only to make the imperial government more efficient, but also to put an end to the bloody cycle of imperial assassinations. Although he had gained the throne by murdering his predecessor, he knew that the empire's survival depended on a reliable succession strategy. To that end, Diocletian dictated that the junior emperors were to step into the senior emperors' place when they retired. Then they themselves were to select two new talented and reliable men to be junior emperors and their eventual replacements. Thus supreme power was to be handed down from capable ruler to capable ruler, and the constant cycle of assassinations and civil wars was to be broken.

Diocletian sought to enhance imperial authority by heightening the grandeur of the emperor's office. He used the title *dominus,* or lord, more freely than any emperor before him. Everything that had to do with the emperor was referred to as sacred or divine. During public ceremonies he arrayed himself in gorgeous robes of purple silk. He required his officials to prostrate themselves before him and kiss the hem of his gown before they spoke to him. Diocletian as well as his fellow tetrarchs claimed that spe-

■ **The Tetrarchs**

Stolen by crusaders during the Middle Ages from its original site near Constantinople, this statue of the tetrarchs now is built into a wall of the cathedral of San Marco in Venice. To depict their solidarity and readiness for war, the tetrarchs are presented as fierce soldiers in military uniform, holding their swords with one hand and clasping their colleague's shoulder with the other. Each pair of figures shows one junior emperor and one senior emperor, who has more worry lines in his forehead as a sign of his greater responsibilities.

cific gods had singled them out for glory and victory. Jupiter was Diocletian's special protector, while Mars (the god of war) and Hercules guarded other tetrarchs. By insisting on his own divinity and emphasizing his special ties to the mightiest god of Rome, Diocletian set himself apart from the rest of the imperial court. Increasingly, the imperial palaces resembled the court of the Great Kings of Persia. Even the geographical location of the center of power shifted eastward, with Diocletian residing for much of his early rule in the city of Nicomedia (in modern Turkey), strategically located at the point where Asia meets Europe.

To restore Roman military power that had been weakened during the crises of earlier decades, Diocletian reorganized the Roman army. He nearly doubled its size to about 400,000 men. In order to protect the empire from invaders, he stationed these troops along the borders of the empire and built military roads from Britain in the west to the Euphrates River in the east. At the same time, Diocletian sought to reduce the army's involvement in political affairs. Although he was a soldier himself, he recognized that the army had played a disruptive role in earlier decades by constantly engaging in civil wars. He reduced the size of each legion in order to limit its commander's power as well as to increase its maneuverability. He placed the legions under new, loyal commanders. With these military reforms effected, Diocletian was able to secure the empire's borders once again and suppress internal revolts (see Map 6.1).

Reorganizing the army was only one part of Diocletian's vision of reform. To restore efficient government, he also embarked upon a thorough reorganization of the empire's administrative system. He redrew the map of the realm, drastically reducing the size of provinces and setting up separate civilian and military bureaucracies within each. These changes further reduced the risk of rebellion by limiting the power of any single civilian official. This administrative overhaul resulted in a significant expansion of the numbers of bureaucrats and military commanders.

Maintaining the bloated civilian and military apparatus created by the tetrarchy demanded full utilization of the empire's financial resources as well as far-reaching economic reforms—particularly in an era of rampant inflation. To halt the declining value of money, Diocletian attempted—none too successfully—to freeze wages and prices by imperial decree. He also increased taxes and endeavored to make tax collection more effective through the establishment of a regular—and deeply resented—census to register all taxpayers. The new tax system generated enough revenues to fund the now enormous machinery of government.

This tax system was, however, riddled with loopholes and inequities. Senators, army officers, and other influential citizens were undertaxed or not taxed at all, and rich landowners often used bribery and force to fend off imperial tax collectors. Consequently the greatest burden fell on those least able to bear it: the peasants. In hopes of increasing economic productivity, Diocletian's administrators used the census to enforce laws that required peasants and craftsmen to remain at their work by insisting that they not move from the place at which they were registered. During the late antique era, then, the gap between rich and poor continued to grow. Fewer rich men controlled more of the empire's land and the wealth it generated than ever before. The emperor himself was the wealthiest of all, adding to his possessions through confiscation of lands owned by cities and private individuals.

Diocletian did nothing to address the widening social and economic division in his empire; instead, he attempted to reinforce the cultural unity of the empire through religious persecution. In 303, he and his junior emperor Galerius initiated an attack on Christians that is now known as the Great Persecution°. The two emperors believed that failure to worship the traditional Roman gods had angered the deities and brought hardship to the empire. In the interest of unity, these rulers tried to destroy Christianity in the eastern part of the empire, which was under their rule. Diocletian and Galerius forbade Christians to assemble for worship and ordered the destruction of all churches and sacred books. Several thousand women and men refused to cooperate and were executed.

Unintended Consequences

Diocletian's reforms stabilized and preserved the Roman Empire. They also had three unintended consequences that altered the character of the empire. First, urban life slowly changed under the impact of his reorganization of imperial government. As we saw in Chapter 5, cities played an essential role in imperial Rome's economic, religious, and cultural life: Romans saw themselves as civilized because they lived in cities. The number of Roman cities remained stable in late antiquity, but the weight of new government economic demands transformed many traditions of urban daily life. Although cities continued to serve as local centers of tax collection, helping to link the provinces to the imperial government, the increasingly centralized and costly bureaucracy put new pressures upon them. Emperors confiscated most city-owned lands and revenues, resulting in a reduction of funds to spend on civic life: games, chariot races, public buildings, and maintenance of urban infrastructure.

Furthermore, the city councilors, who had the responsibility of raising the tax revenues required by the central government, were frustrated. They knew that failure to provide the imperial government with the sums it demanded could lead to public flogging with lead-tipped whips—a punishment as humiliating as it was painful. Understandably, the idea of holding civic office, which most men had considered a great honor, began to lose its appeal. Because a position in the imperial bureaucracy granted immunity from service in city government, with its crushing fiscal obligations (not to mention its risk of public flogging), many ambitious men turned to the imperial bureaucracy to win the honors, status, and power that used to come with positions in the city government. Meanwhile, both the wealth and numbers of city aristocrats, the traditional leaders and patrons of their communities, dwindled.

One result of this shift in power away from the traditional urban aristocracy was a deterioration in the fabric of urban life. The inscriptions in marble attached to public buildings reveal a gradual decline in public spending by all but the very wealthiest citizens. As civic monuments and public buildings decayed, restoration and repair rather than new building became the order of the day in cities throughout the empire.

The second unintended consequence of Diocletian's reforms was an acceleration in the long-term decentralization and fragmentation of economic and political power within the western provinces of the empire. As some men grew richer and more powerful, poor people turned to them for protection against other landowners and ruthless imperial tax collectors. In return for this protection, peasants gave their wealthy patrons the ownership of the farms on which they continued to work. These peasants, called *coloni*, lost the right to leave their farms and move elsewhere. Coloni had to perform labor for their landlords and had only limited control of their own possessions, although they could not be evicted and were still considered free Roman citizens.

The imperial government supported this form of near-slavery because it benefited the biggest landholders—including the emperor—who needed a stable workforce tied to the land to make agriculture as profitable as possible. The coloni system also promised the emperor a reliable source of tax revenues. But over time, landowners began to develop private armies to protect their vast country estates and the peasants who labored on them. This usurpation of the role of the central government weakened the authority of the emperor and his administration in the western provinces. In contrast, the eastern provinces of the empire remained prosperous into the sixth century. Private estates grew in size, but the imperial administrators in Constantinople maintained tight control of the economy.

The final unintended consequence of Diocletian's reforms, then, is that under Diocletian the center of gravity within the empire shifted decisively to the east, where the empire's wealth and political might were increasingly concentrated. Diocletian's own style of rule contributed to this process. He not only delegated the government of the western (and by implication less important) provinces to his co-emperor, Maximian, he also lived for much of his reign in the east.

■ **Map 6.1 The Roman Empire in Late Antiquity**

Following the reforms of Diocletian, the Roman Empire enjoyed a century of stable government, with the same borders as in earlier centuries.

■ Free Grain for the City of Rome

This carving from the Arch of Constantine in Rome, built in 312, shows citizens lining up to receive grain allotments from imperial officials. Bureaucrats, shown in little offices above the heads of the citizens, check the eligibility lists. In the panel's center, the emperor sits on a throne surrounded by his staff.

Christianizing the Empire

When Diocletian died, he left the empire stronger militarily, administratively, and economically than it had been for nearly a century. The steps he had taken to confine the growing power of Christianity, however, turned out to be a failure. The new faith gathered momentum despite all the efforts of polytheist emperors. Eventually, it captured the imagination of an ambitious young Roman who would become the empire's first Christian emperor.

CONSTANTINE: THE FIRST CHRISTIAN EMPEROR

In 305, Diocletian stepped down from the imperial throne and insisted that his co-emperor in the west, Maximian, retire as well. Diocletian expected a peaceful succession to occur. It did, but just barely. The two junior emperors, Galerius and Constantius, took Diocletian's and Maximian's places. But just one year later, Constantius died in Britain. Abandoning the principles of the tetrarchy, the troops stationed in Britain proclaimed Constantius's son, Constantine (r. 306–337), to be his replacement. The ambitious young general set out to claim sole rule of the Roman Empire. In 312 he smashed the army of Maxentius, his last rival in the west, at the battle of the Milvian Bridge over the Tiber River at Rome. Twelve years later he defeated Licinius, the tetrarch ruling in the east. Constantine then joined the empire together with himself as absolute ruler. Thus both the four-part rule of the empire and the system of succession that Diocletian implemented came to an end.

In other ways, however, Constantine continued along Diocletian's reformist path. Under Constantine the empire's eastern and western sectors retained separate administrations. To overcome the dangers of decentralization Constantine installed new officials called praetorian prefects in each sector. These rulers were directly accountable to the emperor. He also retained Diocletian's emphasis on a large field army, but ensured that heavily armored cavalry troops were trained for rapid deployment to trouble spots.

Moreover, Constantine, like Diocletian, did little to ease the economic burden weighing down the peasants and poor townsfolk. The imperial bureaucracy remained immense, the army remained huge, and so taxes remained high. To reinforce the economic structures of the empire, Constantine tried to reform the coinage system. He recognized that the existing coins had become so debased they were effectively worthless, so he created a unique gold coin—the solidus. (Seventy-two solidi equaled one pound of gold.) The creation of the solidus stabilized the economy by restoring the value of currency. The new coin ended the devastating inflationary spiral that had contributed so much to the political and social turmoil of the third century. The solidus remained the standard coin in the Mediterranean world for 800 years.

Constantine followed the path of military emperors in the third century C.E. by founding a new capital city as the seat of his power. To glorify his name and monarchy, Constantine founded Constantinople, the "City of Constantine," on the site of the Greek city Byzantium in 324. (Today Constantinople is the city of Istanbul in Turkey.) Constantine's choice of location reveals a shrewd eye for strategy. The city lay at the juncture of two military roads that linked Europe and Asia and controlled access to the Black Sea. From this convenient spot the emperor could monitor the vast resources of the empire's eastern provinces. Like Diocletian, Constantine recognized that the wealth and power of the empire lay in the east.

Unlike Diocletian, Constantine embraced the new religion of Christianity. Most emperors had associated themselves with a divine protector. Constantine chose the sun god Apollo as his first divine companion. During the night before the pivotal battle at the Milvian Bridge in 312, however, Constantine experienced a new revelation, which he interpreted as a sign from the Christian God. After triumphing in battle, Constantine attributed his success to Christ's favor. Later in his reign, writers described Constantine's victory as a miracle. Though it was not unusual for an emperor to embrace a new god, Constantine's particular choice made a difference. Because monotheistic Christianity repudiated rival gods and alternative forms of worship, Constantine's conversion led to the eventual Christianization of the entire empire. Constantine did not order his subjects to accept Christianity or forbid polytheist worship. He did, however, encourage widespread practice of his new faith and he lavished funds on church buildings. He obtained the gold for his new solidus coinage by looting the treasures that had been stored for centuries in polytheist temples. Now yoked to the imperial office, Christianity very quickly gained strength across the empire and became a potent challenge to traditional modes of religious expression.

The growth of Constantine's new city of Constantinople paralleled the growth of Christianity. Constantine did not intend to establish an exclusively Christian city as an alternative to Rome. He built no more than three churches and left the city's many temples to older gods intact. Within a generation, however, Constantinople became a Christian center, and the traces of polytheism in the city disappeared. Constantinople continued to grow in size and splendor, as palaces, monuments, churches, bathhouses, public buildings, and colonnaded streets appeared on a scale befitting the New Rome, as Constantinople came to be known. Constantine's capital also became a fortified city. In response to the threat of attack by Vandal pirates, the emperor Theodosius II erected massive defensive walls around the city in 413. In future centuries these fortifications would protect the city—and indeed, the empire—from ruin on several occasions. With a new Senate formed on the model of the Senate of the city of Rome, a steady supply of grain from Egypt to feed the capital's inhabitants, and plenty of opportunities for trade, Constantinople attracted people from all over the empire. The city rapidly grew in size, reaching perhaps several hundred thousand inhabitants by the early sixth century.

In addition to serving as an administrative center and an imperial capital, Constantinople came to symbolize the kingdom of Heaven in the minds of Christians. As God ruled from his throne in the court of Heaven, so the emperor ruled in Constantinople. The emperor, whom God had chosen to rule, thus provided the essential link between the celestial and earthly kingdoms. With one Roman law wedded to one orthodox faith for all its subjects and led by an emperor who was God's representative on Earth, Constantinople became the center of a monotheistic empire.

THE SPREAD OF CHRISTIANITY

Backed by Rome's emperors, Christianity spread rapidly throughout the empire during the fourth century. With imperial support, church leaders transformed the face of cities by building churches and leading attacks on the institutions and temples of polytheist worship.

The Rise of the Bishops

As Christianity spread, it grew more complex in its internal organization. Shortly after Paul of Tarsus (ca. 5–67) had established much of the theological grounding of the new religion, a distinction developed between the laity—the ordinary worshipers—and the priests, who led the worship and administered the central rituals, or sacraments. Much of the early growth of the Christian community occurred in cities and so it is perhaps not surprising that as this community developed its own administrative structures and leadership hierarchy, it patterned itself along the lines of the imperial urban administration. Just as an imperial official directed each city's political affairs with a staff of assistants, so each city's Christian community came to be led by a bishop who in turn had a staff of priests and administrators. Moreover, just as a provincial governor controlled the political affairs of all of the cities and rural regions in his province, so the bishop of the main city of a province held authority over the other bishops and priests in the province. This main or head bishop came to be called a *metropolitan* in the east, an *archbishop* in the west. Through this hierarchy of archbishops/metropolitans, bishops, and priests, the scattered Christian communities were linked into what emerged as the Christian Church.

With its sophisticated administrative structure, the Church grew quickly and bishops emerged as important powers in their cities. A bishop's main task was to supervise the religious life of his *see,* which comprised not only the city itself but also its surrounding agricultural regions. Thus a central task of each bishop was to explain Christian principles and teach the Bible to these communities. Bishops soon became far more than simply religious teachers. As the Church grew wealthy from the massive donations of emperors like Constantine and the humbler offerings of pious women and men throughout the empire, bishops often used these resources to help the poor. They cared for the general welfare of orphans, widows, sick people, prisoners, and travelers. When famine struck southern Gaul in the fifth century, for example, the bishop of Lyons sent so much food from his church estates that the Rhône and Saône Rivers as well as all the roads to the south were jammed with grain transports.

The Church's bishops soon became entangled in secular politics as Constantine incorporated them into the imperial government by permitting them to act as judges in civil actions. Litigants could choose to be tried before a bishop rather than a civil judge. The decisions of a bishop had the same legal authority as those made by civil judges and could not be appealed. Using the rhetorical skills they had learned in Roman schools, bishops were also the advocates of their cities before provincial governors or the imperial court. In many ways they usurped the role of the traditional urban aristocracy. For example, when the people of Antioch in Syria rioted and smashed a statue of the emperor, it was the local bishop, not a local aristocrat, who intervened with the emperor to prevent imperial troops from massacring the city's people.

Bishops also administered the financial affairs of their communities. Some sees remained poor, but the churches in the largest cities accumulated phenomenal wealth through donations of land and money received from the faithful. Sometimes bishops used this money for political purposes. In an attempt to win influence and political support, Cyril, bishop of Alexandria from 412 to 444, spent 2,500 pounds of gold on general expenses and bribes to court officials and other clergymen during just one visit to Constantinople. In contrast, British bishops going to a Church conference in 359 could do so only with financial assistance from the government.

By 400 Rome had become the most important see in western Europe, and the bishop of Rome was called the "pope"—the papa or father of the other western bishops. By the middle of the fifth century the emperor formally recognized the pope's claim to have preeminence and the right of appeal over other bishops. A number of factors explain why the office of the bishop of Rome evolved into the papacy°. Together with Jerusalem, Rome was a site of powerful symbolic importance to Christians. Both the Apostle Peter, the first among Jesus' disciples, and Paul of Tarsus, the traveling teacher who took a leading role in spreading Christianity beyond its Jewish origins, died as martyrs in Rome, and popular Christian tradition held that Peter himself was the first bishop in the city. Thus all Roman bishops were believed to have inherited the authority of Peter.

This tradition received support from a conversation between Jesus and Peter recorded in the Gospel of Matthew. Punning on Peter's name, Jesus told him, "You are Peter [*petrus*] and upon this rock [*petram*] I will build my church, and the gates of Hell shall not avail against it. And I will give to you the keys of the kingdom of heaven." Early Christians interpreted these words to mean that Jesus had given Peter special authority, including the power to absolve a sinner's guilt, and that the Church was to be led by those who inherited Peter's position. What came to be called the doctrine of the Petrine Succession declared that just as Peter was specially anointed by Jesus, so subsequent bishops in Rome (the popes) were anointed with special, God-given powers.

In this way popes claimed to be the chief bishops of the Christian world. They insisted that their spiritual authority took precedence over rival bishops in four other imperial cities: Constantinople, Jerusalem, Alexandria in Egypt, and Antioch in Syria. The bishops of these leading religious centers, however, also claimed spiritual descent from Jesus' apostles. They did not accept papal authority and often quarreled bitterly over matters of faith and politics with the pope. The tensions among the leaders of the empire's most important Christian communities led to deep divisions between the eastern and western parts of the empire that have lasted until the present day.

Through these changes, the Church began functioning almost as an administrative arm of the government, although it still had its own internal organization. Indeed, when Roman rule collapsed in western Europe in the fifth century, the Church survived the crisis and stepped in to fill the vacuum of public leadership.

Christianity and the City of Rome

As Christianity spread, new church buildings transformed the appearance of Roman cities. Constantine set an example of public and private spending on churches, hospitals, and monastic communities that conformed to Christian values, and so construction of traditional buildings such as temples, bathhouses, and buildings for public entertainments such as circuses gradually declined. In addition, Christian festivals, processions, and holidays gradually replaced traditional celebrations. These developments can be seen in all the cities of the empire, but the Christianization of Rome during the fourth century offers especially vivid examples.

The first churches in Rome were built to honor Christian martyrs of earlier centuries. Because Roman custom forbade burials within city walls, martyrs had been buried outside the walls of Rome. One of the great churches that Constantine built in Rome was called "Saint Paul Outside the Walls." This imposing structure marked the burial spot of Paul of Tarsus. Constantine also financed the construction of another grand church on the presumed site of Peter's martyrdom and burial, in an obscure cemetery on what was called the Vatican hill, just outside Rome's northwest wall and across the Tiber River. St. Peter's Church was an enormous structure, with five aisles punctuated with marble columns. Its altar rested over Peter's grave. (Today the papal cathedral of St. Peter stands on that same spot, in the heart of the Vatican, the city of the pope.) The construction of these churches signaled that Jesus' disciples Peter and Paul had replaced Rome's mythical founders Romulus and Remus as the city's sacred patrons. In other places, too, Christian saints took the place of traditional gods and heroes as protectors of city life.

Although Rome became a vital center of Christianity, the city's inhabitants did not adopt the Christian faith overnight. Throughout the fourth century, the huge temples and shrines of the old gods clustered in Rome's center continued to attract many worshipers, including influential senators. Church authorities hesitated to close these time-honored precincts because they did not have legal authority to do so. Even after imperial laws in 391 and 392 forbade polytheist worship, sacrifices, and other religious rites, temples stood empty for a long time, for Christians believed that demons inhabited them. At the prompting of Rome's bishops, other public buildings that originally had had no religious connotations were turned into churches.

With the proliferation of new Christian houses of worship in Rome and other cities came new religious festivals and rituals. Christians marked the anniversaries of the martyrdom of saints on the calendar. Sometimes a Christian holiday (a holy day) competed with a non-Christian holiday. For example, Rome's churchmen designated December 25 as the birthday of Christ to challenge the popular festival of the Unconquered Sun, which fell on the same day. Other Christian holidays also aimed to draw worshipers away from the rites of older gods. By the early sixth century the Church had filled the calendar with many days devoted to Christian ceremonies. Christmas and Easter (which commemorates Jesus' death and resurrection) as well as days for worshiping specific martyrs supplanted traditional Roman holidays. These festivals thus changed the patterns of urban community life throughout the empire. Not all of the traditional Roman holidays disappeared, however. Those that Christians considered harmless continued to be observed as civic holidays. These included New Year's Day, the accession days of the emperors, and the days that celebrated the founding of Rome and Constantinople.

One additional development in the Christian shaping of time was the use of the letters A.D. as a dating convention. A.D. stands for *anno domini,* or "in the year of our Lord," referring to the year of Jesus' birth. Today it is the standard dating convention used around the world. It began in 531, when Dionysius Exiguus, a monk in Rome, established a simple system for determining the date of Easter every year.

He began his calendar with the birth of Jesus in the year 1 (zero was unknown in Europe at this time), and started counting from there. Although he was probably a few years off in his determination of the year of Jesus' birth, his system slowly came into general use by the tenth century. In modern secular societies, many people prefer not to use A.D. because of its association with Christianity. Instead, they use C.E.—meaning "in the Common Era"—to designate years (as is done in this textbook). In both systems, however, the year 1 still refers to Jesus' birth, and thus the calendar remains linked to Christianity regardless of what dating convention is used.

Old Gods Under Attack

Many people today identify themselves as members of a religious community—as Christians, Buddhists, Jews, or Muslims. For the most part these faiths are mutually exclusive—there are no Muslim Christians, for example. In late antiquity, however, before Christianity became the dominant religion in the Roman Empire, people prayed to gods of all sorts. Different deities met different needs, and the worship of one did not preclude worship of another. Some divinities—such as Isis, who promised life after death—had elaborate cults throughout the empire. The empire's great gods—Jupiter, Juno, and Minerva—had temples in cities everywhere, and were formally worshiped on state occasions. In the countryside as well a variety of deities protected laborers and ensured fertility of plants, animals, and the farmers themselves.

To Christians, this diverse range of religious expression was intolerable. They labeled all polytheistic worship with the derogatory term paganism° and made a determined effort to eradicate it. Christians attacked polytheism on two fronts: public practice and private belief.

After converting to Christianity in 312, Constantine ordered the end of the persecution of Christians. Although Christianity did not become the "official" religion of the empire for nearly a century, tolerance for non-Christian beliefs and practices began to fade. In the fourth century, imperial laws forbade sacrificing animals on the altars outside of the old gods' temples. Constantine's son, Constantius II (r. 337–361), ordered the Altar of Victory removed from the Senate House in Rome. Since Augustus's reign, generals had sworn oaths of allegiance to the emperor at this altar before marching to battle. State funding for polytheistic worship gradually stopped. Instead of temples, emperors built churches with money collected from the taxpayers.

During the fourth century bishops and monks, often in collusion with local administrators, led attacks on polytheist shrines and holy places. For example, in 392 the bishop and parishioners of Alexandria destroyed the city's Temple of Serapis, known for its huge size, its magnificent architecture, and the devotion of the local community to it. Similar clashes erupted in many cities across the empire. Libanius, an aristocrat from Antioch, complained to Emperor Theodosius in 390 about the destruction caused by gangs of zealous monks: "This black-robed tribe . . . hasten to attack the temples with sticks and stones and bars of iron, and in some cases, disdaining these, with hands and feet. Then utter desolation follows, with the stripping of roofs, demolition of walls, the tearing down of statues and the overthrow of altars, and the priests must either keep quiet or die."[1]

One emperor tried to restore traditional religion. Julian the Apostate (r. 360–363), who had been raised as a Christian in Constantine's court, rejected Christianity and tried to reinstate the old religions when he came to the throne. But his death during a campaign against Persia eliminated any hope for a restoration of pre-Christian ways. Emboldened by this turn of events, an increasingly zealous Church establishment attacked polytheism with renewed vigor. Theodosius I (r. 379–395) and his grandson Theodosius II (r. 402–450) forbade all forms of polytheistic worship, and non-Christian practice lost the protection of the law.

The attack on polytheism intensified during the reign of Theodosius. Because polytheism was not a single, organized religion, it offered no systematic opposition to government-supported Christian attacks. The most vocal opponents to this Christianization of the empire lived in Rome. In sharp contrast to the pious court at Constantinople, the conservative aristocracy of the city of Rome clung hard to the old gods. In 384, their spokesman unsuccessfully begged the emperor for tolerance. Quintus Aurelius Symmachus, a highly respectable nobleman who had pleaded unsuccessfully for the return of the Altar of Victory, argued that Rome's greatness had resulted from the observance of ancient rites. His pleas fell on deaf ears. By the middle of the fifth century the aristocracy of the city of Rome had accepted Christianity.

Humble people also struggled to maintain ancient forms of worship. Sometimes they brawled with monks to preserve the shrines of the gods their families had worshiped for generations. But with the empire's resources pitted against them, they could not resist for long. People began to join Christian communities, though often without fully understanding what the religion required of them. Surviving records of sermons reveal that church leaders preached for centuries afterward against the surprising persistence of "pagan" habits among their congregants. Priests repeatedly explained the risks to salvation that lurked in age-old festivals, bawdy public entertainments, and even regular bathing, which was considered a sinful pleasure.

Eventually, this priestly diligence paid off. The pace of conversion accelerated in the fifth and sixth centuries. Emperor Justinian (r. 527–565) helped things along by sponsoring programs of forced conversion in the countryside of Asia Minor, where tens of thousands of his subjects still followed ancient ways. Eradicating polytheism in the Roman Empire meant far more than the substitution of one religion for another. Polytheism lay at the heart of every community, influencing every activity, every habit of social life, in the pre-Christian world. To replace the worship of the old gods required a true revolution in social and intellectual life.

New Christian Communities and Identities

The spread of Christianity produced new kinds of identities based on faith and language. Christianity solidified community loyalties and allegiances by providing a shared belief system and new opportunities for participation in religious culture. Yet at the same time, Christianity opened up new divisions and gave rise to new hostilities. Certain new groups were respected and revered; others found themselves marginalized or persecuted. As Christians debated how to interpret the doctrines of their faith, sharp divisions emerged among them. Because Christians spoke Greek, Latin, Coptic, Syriac, Armenian, and other languages, different religious interpretations and rituals sometimes took hold, creating distinct communities. As a result, new religious zones identified with different spoken languages and different interpretations of Christian texts appeared within the empire.

THE CREATION OF NEW COMMUNITIES

Christianity fostered the growth of large-scale communities of faith by providing a well-defined set of beliefs and values. These basic principles had to be integrated with daily life and older ways of thinking. Thus Christianity required followers to study and interpret the Bible—the religion's sacred text. The religion also demanded allegiance to one God and a complex set of doctrines, and it dictated a distinctive lifestyle. Weaving these elements into daily life resulted in a strong sense of Christian identity and common purpose. This new Christian identity competed with and at times replaced older identities linked to Roman citizenship or shaped by regional or urban loyalties.

Christian Doctrine and Heresy

The Old and New Testaments gave a focal point to Christian worship, and their interpretation shaped Christian communities. Every week the priest read to parishioners from these sacred texts. As Christian communities developed, interpretation of that faith by its followers became all-important. The Church decided what interpretations of the Bible were correct, and expected all members of the community to accept these doctrines. In this way, Christian teaching contrasted sharply with secular (nonreligious) education in the Roman Empire, which was intended only for the urban elite. Christian teaching was meant for all. It required all people to live their lives based on a shared interpretation of the Bible and the meaning of Jesus' life, death, and resurrection.

The Church soon ran into difficulties over interpretation of the texts, as Church leaders disagreed about the meanings of many biblical passages. Councils of bishops met frequently to try to resolve doctrinal differences and produce statements of the faith that all parties could accept. Two theological questions generated particularly tense discussion and drove wedges between several groups—the nature of the Trinity and the nature of Jesus Christ.

Christians are monotheists: They believe that one God created and governs Heaven and Earth. This monotheistic foundation, however, undergirded a complex theological system in which the one God was understood to have three aspects or "persons," each fully and absolutely God—God the Father, God the Son, and God the Holy Spirit—or the Holy Trinity. Such a complex theology generated endless debates. Church leaders argued about the precise relation of the three persons to one another and within the Trinity. Were the Son and the Holy Spirit of the same essence as the Father? Were they equally divine? Did the Father exist before the Son?

These debates over the Trinity were intimately connected to the second issue of contention with the early Church—the question of the nature of Jesus. At one extreme, some Christian scholars believed that Jesus was entirely divine and had no human nature. This emphasis on Jesus' divinity made his death on the cross and his resurrection irrelevant, for God could not suffer and die. It also severed the links between Jesus and his human followers by emphasizing that Jesus was entirely "transcendent" or "other," entirely beyond human comprehension or human limitations. At the other extreme, some Christians taught that Jesus was entirely human and not at all divine, thus challenging both the Christian belief in the Trinity and the Christian understanding of Jesus' mission on earth.

The questions of the nature of the Trinity and the nature of Jesus erupted in the first great Christian controversy of late antiquity: the dispute between the Arians and the Athanasians. The Arians followed Arius of Alexandria, a priest who used Greek philosophy to argue that the idea that Jesus, God the Son, was both fully divine and fully human was illogical. Arians argued that God the Father created Jesus and so Jesus could not be equal to or of the same essence as God the Father. The Athanasians, followers of the Bishop Athanasius of Alexandria (293–373), were horrified by what they saw as the Arians' attempt to degrade Jesus' divinity. They argued that Christian truths were beyond human logic, and that Jesus was fully God, equal to and of the same substance as God the Father, yet fully human.

The Arian-Athanasian dispute resulted in perhaps the most influential of the many church meetings held in late antiquity: the Council of Nicaea. In 325, Emperor Constantine summoned the bishops to Nicaea, a town near Constantinople, to reach a decision about the relationship among the divine members of the Holy Trinity. The bishops produced the Nicene Creed, which is still recited in Christian worship today. The creed states that God the Son (Jesus Christ) is identical in nature and essence to God the Father. In other words, the Athanasians won. More than a century later, the Council of Chalcedon of 451 drove the point home: The assembled bishops agreed that Jesus was both fully human and fully divine, and that these two natures were entirely distinct though united.

The Nicene Creed and the decisions of the Council of Chalcedon became the correct, or orthodox°, interpretation of Christian teaching because they had the support of most bishops and the imperial court. Still, some bishops and other religious leaders continued to debate conflicting interpretations of the Bible, and many ordinary Christians continued to hold beliefs that clashed with those defined as orthodox. People who held the orthodox point of view considered such alternative doctrines to be false beliefs, or heresies°, and they labeled their supporters *heretics*.

Communities of Faith and Language

The doctrinal differences between orthodox and unorthodox Christian groups created and helped cement different communal and ethnic identities in late antiquity. Several geographic zones of Christians emerged that held different interpretations of Christian doctrine. They produced Bibles, sermons, and religious ceremonies in their native languages. A central zone based in Constantinople and including North Africa, Gaul, Italy, and the Balkans contained Christians called Chalcedonians°, or orthodox. (In the Latin-speaking western provinces they were also called Catholics.) These believers followed the decision of the Council of Chalcedon in 451 that defined Christ's divine and human natures as equal but entirely distinct. In late antiquity, the emperors in Constantinople and the popes in Rome—as well as the bulk of the population of the Roman empire—were Chalcedonian Christians.

In the eastern regions of the empire most of the Christians were Monophysites° who did not accept the teaching of the Council of Chalcedon. They believed that Jesus Christ had only one nature rather than two. Three separate Monophysite communities had developed by the end of late antiquity. The first was in Armenia, a region in the Caucasus mountains of eastern Asia Minor. Around 300, Armenia became the first kingdom in the world to accept Christianity. The religion gave the Armenians a new sense of ethnic solidarity. A century later a translation of the Bible into Armenian fostered the development of a rich Christian literature among Armenia's clans. After the Council of Chalcedon, the Armenian church accepted the doctrines of Monophysite Christianity, which it still follows today.

Another Monophysite community arose in Egypt, among the native Egyptian speakers called Copts. Like the Armenians, the Copts accepted Monophysite Christianity after the Council of Chalcedon and developed a vibrant Christian culture expressed in the Egyptian language. They wrote their native tongue in Greek letters adopted during the Hellenistic Age, when their land was ruled by Greek speakers. Christianity took root in Egypt during the first century, and a Coptic Bible, completed in late antiquity, solidified a Coptic community that has survived to the present day.

In the Middle East, Christianity helped forge another new collective identity among the inhabitants of Syria. These Christians spoke Syriac, a Semitic language spoken by many cultures within the region. The Syriac Bible probably appeared in the second century. As was the case with Armenian and Coptic peoples, a vast literature of biblical interpretation, sermons, commentaries, and church documents slowly arose, forming the basis of a new Syriac-speaking Christian culture. Monophysite Christianity flourished among the Christians of Syria. In the sixth century the Syriac church developed its own hierarchy of priests and bishops independent of the Chalcedonian church in Constantinople. Monophysite beliefs kept the Syriac Church at odds with the emperor and his Chalcedonian followers.

In addition to the Chalcedonian and Monophysite regions, a third zone of Christians existed in late antiquity comprised of Arian Christians. As described earlier, Arians° believed that Jesus was not equal to or of the same essence as God the Father. Most of the people who followed Arian Christianity were the Goths and other Germanic settlers who seized political control of Rome's western provinces in the fifth century. The Goths had converted to Christianity in the fourth century, when they still lived north of the Danube River and in southern Russia. A Gothic priest named Ulfila created a Gothic alphabet and used it to translate the Bible and spread the faith. When the settlers who followed Arian Christianity entered the Roman Empire, their faith kept them from marrying Roman Christians who followed Chalcedonian Christianity. In this way, the Arians' faith helped define their community in the face of the much larger Roman populations whom they ruled.

In all of these three zones, variations of the Christian faith expressed in different languages formed the seedbed of ethnic traditions, some of which survive to the present day, such as the Armenians, Copts, and Greek-speaking Orthodox Christians. Yet at the same time, the spread of Christianity weakened other local groupings. As language-based Christian communities spread inside and outside the empire, many local dialects and languages disappeared. Throughout most of western Europe the Celtic languages began to fade away during late antiquity. In the east the old languages of Asia Minor were gone by the end of the sixth century. Only those languages in which Christian thinking found textual expression survived.

In western Europe, Latin was the language of Christian literature and church ritual. About 410, the churchman Jerome finished a new Latin translation of the Bible, which replaced earlier Latin versions. This translation, called the Vulgate Bible, became the standard Bible in European churches for many centuries.

The western Church's use of Latin kept the door open for the transmission of all Latin texts into a world defined by Christianity. This ensured the survival of Roman legal, scientific, and literary traditions, even after Roman rule had evaporated in western Europe. Latin also forged a common bond among different political communities of the empire's western sector. Latin served as an international language among the ruling elites in western Europe, even though they spoke different languages in their daily lives. Thus, church-based Latin served as a powerful unifying and stabilizing influence. The Latin language combined with Christianity to spur the development of Christendom°—the many peoples and kingdoms in western Europe united by their common religion and shared language of worship and intellectual life.

In the eastern Mediterranean, Christianity had a different voice. There a Greek-based Church developed. Greek was the language of imperial rule and common culture in that region, and Greek became the language of the eastern Christian Church. In addition to the New Testament, which had been originally written in Greek, eastern Christians used a Greek version of the Hebrew Bible (the Old Testament) called the Septuagint, which Greek-speaking

The Ascetic Alternative

T he idea that the human body, with all its physical needs, stands in the way of spiritual progress had long existed in the ancient Mediterranean world. Over the centuries, it has become deeply rooted in Western culture. As we saw in Chapter 3, in the fifth century B.C.E. Plato had argued that human souls are only bits of the great Soul that dwells in an unchanging celestial realm far above our earthly world. These bits of soul reside only temporarily in the human body during a person's life. By pursuing the philosophical life people might overcome the constraints of the human body and the material world and free these bits of soul to return to their source. Living a philosophical life meant combining a rigorous intellectual pursuit of knowledge with a disregard for physical needs. Greek and Roman philosophers following Plato dreamed of freeing their souls to ascend to a higher realm.

Christian ascetics took a different direction. They sought to suppress their physical needs to the extent that God might enter their bodies and work through them. Making contact with God required constant preparation, as one might prepare for an athletic competition. For this reason Christian ascetics struggled to deny the physical self in all its manifestations. Many relied on deprivation, going without food and sleep. They would also punish their bodies through self-flagellation. Still others rejected human contact, living in uncomfortable places such as atop a pillar or at the bottom of a dry well. All ascetics struggled to abstain from sex and to reject social standards of cleanliness, which they viewed as mere vanity.

Christian ascetic practice could also take subtler forms than physical abuse. Some followers rejected their families and communities, spurned all knowl-

edge except for the content of the Bible, and even denied the significance of the passage of time by insisting that each day was a new beginning. In all of these ways ascetics freed themselves from the practices that ordered and gave meaning to everyday life. In monasteries and nunneries men and women submitted to the absolute rule of abbots and abbesses in their quest to suppress individual aspirations.

Winning the endless battles against the desires of the self and the lures of the Devil made ascetics holy in the eyes of their fellow Christians. Once an ascetic achieved communion with God, that divine presence within the ascetic radiated a curative power. Uniquely situated on the border between the divine and the human, holy ascetics sometimes channeled their power to the benefit of the human community by performing healing miracles and mediating disputes.

The ascetic movement revealed a profound shift in ideas about the body, the accessibility of divinity, and the nature of sexuality. From the ascetic perspective, the human body ceased to be a beautiful gift to be glorified in statuary and song. Instead it became an obstacle to spiritual communion with God. An ascetic life was not just a suppression of sexual desires but a victory over them. For Christians, following an ascetic life was not a cowardly flight from the problems of the world. Rather, it represented a courageous encounter with personal demons and the evils of society. Through ascetic discipline, men and women challenged their own physical existence as well as the basic values of the everyday Mediterranean world. ■

■ Symeon the Pillar Saint

The fifth-century ascetic saint Symeon lived atop a pillar in Syria. Crowds gathered to watch him perform holy acts of bodily mortification and to ask his advice and blessing. In this silver plaque Symeon is threatened by the Devil, who has taken the form of a serpent. Symeon, who wears the robes of a monk, resists with the help of a holy text that he holds on his lap. The shell above his head symbolizes his sainthood.

For Discussion

How did religious beliefs affect the ways that Christians understood their bodies in late antiquity? What do these beliefs about the human body and sexuality tell us about late antique society?

Jews had prepared in Alexandria in the second century B.C.E. for their own community. The Septuagint combined with the Greek New Testament to become the authoritative Christian Bible throughout Rome's eastern provinces.

The Monastic Movement

Near the end of the third century, then, a new Christian spiritual movement took root in the Roman Empire. Known today as asceticism°, it both challenged the emerging connection between the political and religious hierarchies and rejected the growing wealth of the Church. Asceticism called for Christians to subordinate their physical needs and temporal desires to a quest for spiritual union with God.

The founder of the ascetic movement was Antony, an Egyptian Christian. Around 280 Antony sold all his property and walked away from his crowded village near the Nile into the desert in search of spiritual union with God. A few decades later, Bishop Athanasius composed a biography, the *Life of Antony,* telling how Antony overcame all the temptations the Devil could conjure up, from voluptuous naked women to opportunities for power and fame. Vividly describing the struggle between asceticism ("the discipline") and the demonic lures of everyday life ("the household"), Athanasius's work became one of the most influential books in Western literature. It captured the spiritual yearnings of many thousands of men and women, inspiring them to imitate Antony by following "the discipline" to seek spiritual communion with God.

Ascetic discipline required harsh and often violent treatment of the body. The first ascetics, called anchorites or hermits, lived alone in the most inaccessible and uncomfortable places they could find, such as a cave in a cliffside, a hole in the ground, or on top of a pillar. In addition to praying constantly in their struggle to overcome the Devil and make contact with God, these men and women starved and whipped themselves, rejecting every comfort, including human companionship.

Over time, however, many Egyptian ascetics began to construct communities for themselves. The result was the monastic movement°. Because these communities, called monasteries, often grew to hold a thousand or more members, they required organization and guidance. Leaders like the Egyptian Pachomius (ca. 292–346), known as the "Searcher of Hearts," emerged to provide clear instructions for regulating monastic life and to offer spiritual guidance to the members of the monasteries. (The male inhabitants of monasteries are called monks, or solitary men; women are called nuns.)

Monastic communities soon multiplied in the eastern provinces of the Roman Empire, especially near Jerusalem in Palestine, where Jesus had lived centuries earlier. Basil of Caesarea (ca. 330–379) wrote a set of guidelines that was widely followed in eastern lands. Highly educated in Greek and Roman literature and philosophy as well as Christian theology, Basil repudiated extreme ascetic practices. He viewed the monastery as a community of individuals living and working together while pursuing their individual spiritual growth. Through his writings, Basil encouraged monks to discipline their souls through productive labor and voluntary poverty rather than through long bouts of self-inflicted physical tortures. He also insisted that monks should devote the greater part of their day to religious contemplation and prayer. In the monasteries, the monks typically shared meals and worship but engaged in ascetic discipline and prayer alone.

After spreading throughout the eastern provinces, monasticism made its way into western Europe. The desert, so accessible to monks in Egypt, became a metaphor for any desolate place where a person could live as an ascetic in the quest for God. John Cassian (ca. 365–ca. 433), for example, carried monastic ideas from Egypt to Gaul, where he found his "desert" in the rugged islands of the coast near modern Marseilles. He established two monasteries there. Cassian and other monks wrote rule books explaining how to organize and govern monastic life for the many communities that sprang up in Italy and Gaul. Drawing from the ideas of these earlier monks, Benedict of Nursia (ca. 480–547) wrote a *Rule* that became the most influential set of instructions in western Europe. Benedict founded a monastery on Monte Cassino near Naples in 529. Like Basil of Caesarea, Benedict emphasized voluntary poverty and a life devoted to prayer. Benedict, however, placed a greater stress on labor. Fearing that the Devil could easily tempt an idle monk, Benedict wanted his monks to keep busy. He therefore ordered that all monks perform physical labor for parts of every day when they were not sleeping or praying. In Roman society, which held manual labor in contempt, Benedict's orders were quite radical.

Monasticism, Women, and Sexuality

The monastic movement had a powerful impact on women. Ascetic life in a monastic community certainly opened new avenues for female spirituality. In monastic communities, men and women lived separately to reduce sexual temptation, but within the confines of these communities, gender was irrelevant. It was just one more difficult physical boundary to cross over on the path to finding God. By joining monastic communities and leaving the routines of daily life behind, women could gain independence from the obligations of male-dominated society. In all the lands where Christianity was followed, ascetic women created communities of their own. They lived as celibate sisterhoods of nuns, dedicated to spiritual quest and service to God. Perhaps not surprisingly, church leaders approved of this lifestyle for women.

Some wives or daughters of wealthy and powerful families rejected traditional expectations to be wives and mothers by founding monastic communities. Such women wielded an authority and influence that would not have

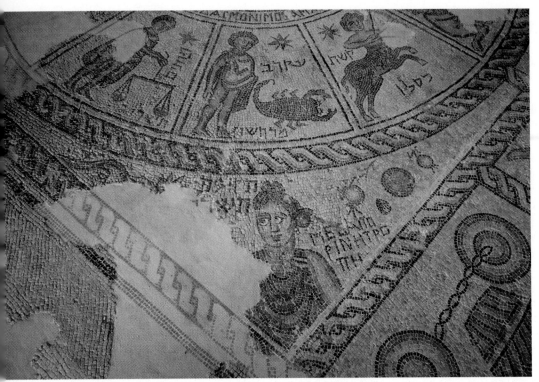

In late antiquity, Jews living in Palestine sometimes decorated their synagogues with mosaic floors depicting the zodiac. Although these mosaics appeared in synagogues and often contained Hebrew writing, the scenes and style of the mosaics were typical of Greek and Roman art. This blending demonstrates that members of the Jewish congregation also participated in the general non-Jewish culture of the province.

been available to them otherwise. For example, Melania the Younger (383–439), the daughter of a wealthy Roman senatorial family, decided to sell her vast estates and spend the proceeds in religious pursuits. When the Roman Senate objected to the breaking up of Melania's family estates, Melania successfully appealed to the empress, who interceded with the legal authorities to enable her to dispose of her property. (Melania's slaves also objected because they did not want to be sold separately to raise cash for her religious projects, but Melania ignored them.) Melania spent her fortune on building monasteries in the Holy Land of Palestine. Most women lacked the financial resources to make such dramatic gestures, but they could imitate Melania's accomplishment on a modest scale, developing a new kind of religious life over which they exercised control.

Monasticism also reinforced negative ideas about women and sexuality in the Church. Male ascetics preached and practiced sexual abstinence as an important self-denying discipline. In ascetic thought, women were linked to the corrupt world of the flesh against which the Christian must exercise unceasing vigilance. The ascetic retreat into the desert or monastery was a flight from temptation, and that meant a flight from women. As ascetic ideas gained in prominence, celibacy became a Christian ideal, with sexual relations within the confines of marriage viewed as distinctly second-best.

The increasingly negative view of women within Christian thought is apparent in the writings of churchmen of the late antique era. Christian writers branded women as disobedient, sexually promiscuous, innately sinful, and nat-

urally inferior to men. They interpreted Genesis, the first book of the Bible, to mean that women bore a special curse. In their reading of the Genesis account, Eve, the first woman, seduced Adam, the first man. For this reason late antique Christians blamed Eve—and women collectively—for humanity's expulsion from the Garden of Eden and for all the woes human beings had suffered ever since. Ambrose, the influential bishop of Milan from 373 to 397, wrote, "Since a woman is not the image of God, a woman ought to veil her head, to show herself subject. And since falsehood began through her, she ought to have this sign, that her head be not free, but covered with a veil."[2] Yet, at the same time, Christians also believed that God would save the souls of women as well as men, and they honored Mary for her role in bringing Jesus, and therefore salvation, into the world. In many ways women occupied a position in the Christian religious imagination comparable to that held by Jews: They were considered guilty as a group of a terrible deed, yet they were accepted as a necessary part of God's plan for humanity. For these reasons Christian women never achieved full equality with men in daily life during late antiquity.

Jews in a Christian World

Until Christianity became the official religion of the Roman Empire, Jews had been simply one group of people among hundreds who lived under Roman rule. Although polytheist Romans considered Jews eccentric because they worshiped only one god and refused to make statues of him, they still respected the antiquity of the Jewish people's faith. Throughout the empire, Jews had enjoyed full citizenship rights and appeared in all professions and at all levels of society.

Christianity erased all this. According to Christian belief, Jews had been the chosen people of God until the appearance of Jesus, who displaced them from their place in God's plan. Christians criticized Jews for failing to accept that Jesus' teachings had supplanted those of the Hebrew Bible, and blamed them collectively for Jesus' crucifixion. As Christians saw it, the Diaspora (the dispersion of Jews around the world after the destruction of Jerusalem by the Roman army in 70) was God's way of punishing the Jews.

With the advance of Christianity within the empire, the Jewish position worsened. Beginning in the fourth century, Roman laws began to discriminate against Jews, forbidding them to marry Christians, own Christian slaves, or accept converts into their faith. Church leaders sometimes forced entire communities of Jews to convert to Christianity on pain of death. A notable exception to this downward spiral was that Jews still retained the right to remain members of city councils. Although organized resistance among scattered Jewish communities was impossible, many Jews refused to accept the deepening oppression. Their resistance ranged from acts of violence against Jews who had converted to Christianity to armed revolt against Roman authorities.

Despite their marginal position in the empire, Jews did retain some security because most emperors honored traditional obligations to protect all their subjects. Roman emperors repeatedly issued laws forbidding the destruction of synagogues. They permitted Jews to worship on the sabbath, and excused them from performing public or private business on that day, as Jewish law required. Zealous bishops often objected to such fair treatment of Jews, and some bishops goaded Christians into attacking synagogues. For example, in 388 the bishop of Callinicum, a town on the Euphrates River, destroyed the local synagogue with the assistance of his Christian congregation. When the emperor Theodosius I tried to punish the guilty citizens, Bishop Ambrose of Milan wrote a long letter stiffly rebuking the emperor: "Will you give the Jews this triumph over the Church of God, this victory over the people of Christ?" asked Ambrose. The emperor backed down, and the Christians of Callinicum went unpunished.

In 429, Roman officials abolished the office of Jewish Patriarch. The Roman emperors had long recognized the Patriarch as leader of the Jews throughout the empire, and had given the Patriarch certain legal and administrative duties. With the office abolished, the Roman treasury now collected for itself the special taxes that had been paid by Jews for the Patriarch's administration. The end of the Patriarchate shows that Jews had lost their status as an ethnic community in the eyes of the empire.

Individual Jewish communities continued to administer their own affairs under the leadership of rabbis—men who served as teachers and interpreters of Jewish law. With the completion of the Mishnah°, the final organization and transcription of Jewish oral law, by the end of the third century and the production of the Jerusalem and Babylonian Talmuds°, or commentaries on the law, by the end of the fourth and fifth centuries, rabbis and their courts now dominated Jewish community life. These learned men established academies of legal study in Roman Palestine and Persian Babylonia, where they produced authoritative interpretations of law that guided everyday Jewish life.

Although some Jewish women served as leaders of synagogues in late antiquity, in general rabbinic Judaism legitimized the subordination of women in Jewish society. Jewish women did not benefit from the education at the Jewish academies. Excluded from the formal process of interpreting the Bible, Jewish women did not acquire highly prized religious knowledge. Instead, men expected them to conform to traditional roles as daughters, wives, and mothers, much as women in other religious communities were expected to do.

ACCESS TO HOLINESS: CHRISTIAN PILGRIMS

Christianity not only created new communities and condemned others, it also offered new avenues of participation in religious culture. In late antiquity, Christians of all social ranks began to make religious journeys, which they called going on a pilgrimage°. Their goal was to visit sacred places, especially places where holy objects, known as relics°, were housed. They believed these relics were inherently holy because they were physical objects associated with saints and martyrs, or with Jesus himself. The most highly valued relics were the bones from the skeleton of the venerated person. Christians believed that contact with such relics could cure them of an illness, heighten their spiritual awareness, or improve their lives.

The mortal remains of Christian martyrs provided the first relics and the first objects of veneration for pilgrims, but after persecution of Christians ceased in 312, believers resorted to the bodies of great bishops and ascetic monks and nuns. From the fourth century onward, Christians regularly dug up saintly skeletons, chopped them up, and distributed the pieces to churches. The more important the holy person, the fiercer the competition for the bones and other objects associated with him or her. Churches in the largest cities of the empire, such as Rome, Constantinople, Alexandria, and Jerusalem, acquired fine collections. For example, the robe of the Virgin Mary, the mother of Jesus, was kept in a church in Constantinople. Residents of the city believed that the Virgin's robe drove away enemies when it was carried in procession along the city's battlements.

Emperors and important bishops acquired the greatest and most powerful relics of all—those that had reportedly touched Jesus himself. These included the crown of thorns he wore when crucified, the cross on which he died, and the nails that fastened him to the wood. Relics reminded Christians that Jesus' own death was symbolically repeated in the martyrdom of his followers. For this reason church altars where followers celebrated the Eucharist, the rite in which bread and wine are offered as Jesus' body and blood in memory of his death, were built over the graves or relics of martyrs.

Traveling to touch a relic was the primary motive for going on a pilgrimage, but there were other reasons as well. Palestine became a frequent destination of Christian pilgrims because it contained the greatest number of sacred sites and relics associated with events described in the Bible and particularly with Jesus' life and death. Between the fourth and seventh centuries, thousands of earnest Christian pilgrims from the Mediterranean and Middle Eastern worlds flocked to Palestine to visit holy sites and pray for divine assistance and forgiveness for their sins. Helena, the mother of Emperor Constantine, made pilgrimage fashionable. In the early fourth century she visited Jerusalem, where she reportedly found remnants of the cross on which Jesus was crucified, as well as many of the sites pertaining to Jesus' life.

Inspired by his mother's journey, Constantine funded the construction of lavish shrines and monasteries at these sites, as well as guest houses for pilgrims. Practically overnight Palestine was transformed from a provincial backwater to the spiritual focus of the Christian world. Religious men and women—rich and poor, old and young, sick and healthy—streamed to Palestine and Jerusalem. There they joined processions that made their way from holy place to holy place. At each site clergymen permitted them to view and sometimes kiss or touch holy relics. On the most important holidays, such as Easter, priests held special ceremonies at the different sites of Jesus' last day on earth—at the Mount of Olives where he was arrested by Roman soldiers, at the place of his trial, at the hill of his crucifixion, and at his tomb, called the Holy Sepulchre.

Palestine did not have a monopoly on holy places, however. Pilgrims traveled to places throughout the Roman world wherever saints had lived and died and where their relics rested. Their pilgrimages contributed to the growth of a Christian view of the world in several ways. Because pilgrimage was a holy enterprise, Christian communities gave hospitality and lodging to religious travelers. This fostered a shared sense of Christian community among people from many lands. Christians envisioned a Christian "map" dominated by spiritually significant places. Travel guides that explained this "spiritual geography" became popular among pilgrims. Most of all, pilgrims who returned home enriched in their faith and perhaps cured in mind or spirit inspired their home communities with news of a growing Christian world directly linked to the biblical lands they heard about in church.

CHRISTIAN INTELLECTUAL LIFE

In late antiquity, many Christians actively participated in the empire's intellectual life. Highly educated in Christian learning as well as the traditional studies of the Roman elite, writers examined the meaning of Christian life in the context of classical literature, philosophy, and the study of history.

Early Christian Hostility to Classical Learning

In Roman schools, the sons of wealthy families, as well as some poor boys with ambition and talent, studied the poets, dramatists, philosophers, and rhetoricians of the classical Greek, Hellenistic, and Roman periods. By late antiquity this curriculum, known today as classical learning, had become formalized into seven liberal arts: grammar, logical argument, and rhetoric (collectively called the Trivium); and geometry, arithmetic, astronomy, and music (the Quadrivium). Law and medicine were taught separately, for those who aspired to those professions. This education prepared students for careers in the imperial bureaucracy and various other fields. Equally important, it provided aristocratic men with a common cultural bond—a shared version of history, a value system that legitimized their exercise of power, an appreciation of the benefits of city life, and a common understanding of how the universe functioned. No other institution before the rise of Christianity, not even the army, exerted such a powerful influence on the minds of the men who controlled Rome's destiny.

Classical learning and the educational system that kept it alive posed a challenge to Christian educators. Specifically, how should Christians reconcile classical teachings with the doctrines of their faith, particularly when the two conflicted? Did the classics of Greek and Roman literature constitute a threat to Christianity? Could Christians learn anything of value from non-Christian cultures? Should educated men turn their backs on classical learning in order to avoid being corrupted by it?

During the first three centuries after Jesus' death, when Christians were marginalized and at times persecuted in Roman society, many church leaders strongly criticized classical learning. Churchmen argued that the learning of pagan intellectuals was false wisdom, that it distracted the Christian from what was truly important—contemplation of Jesus Christ and the eternal salvation he offered—and therefore that it corrupted young Christians.

The Reconciliation of Christianity and the Classics

After Constantine's conversion in 312, however, the Church became an increasingly influential voice in the empire and classical learning no longer seemed so dangerous to Christians. Many church leaders now came from the empire's urban elite, where they had benefited from classical learning. Christian officials grudgingly approved secular education as churchmen recognized that the traditional curriculum still had practical value. Training in classical rhetoric, grammar, and literature became an integral part of upper-class Christian life. By the fifth century most Christians accepted traditional schooling as a useful if vaguely risky enterprise. As Basil the Great (ca. 330–379), bishop of Caesarea in Cappadocia (in modern Turkey), explained to young men about to embark on their studies, classical learning had both benefits and dangers: "It is sufficiently proved that this pagan learning is not without use to the soul . . . It is necessary . . . to watch incessantly in guarding our souls, lest that, charmed by the attraction of the words, we receive in our ignorance some bad impressions and with the honey introduce into our bosoms poisonous fluids."[3]

Influential churchmen, writing in Greek and Latin, now drew freely from classical texts and methods of discussion, even though they considered the Christian scriptures the sole source of truth. The career of Augustine (354–430) shows how a classical education could serve Christian purposes. Born to parents of modest means, Augustine attended traditional Roman schools as a youth. His talent and schooling had prepared him for a high position in public life. After his conversion to Christianity, Augustine became the influential bishop of the city of Hippo Regius in North Africa. Using his episcopal office as a platform from which to launch his attacks on polytheism and heresy and to define all aspects of the Christian faith, Augustine displayed a sincere respect for certain aspects of Roman cultural and intellectual accomplishments—especially rhetoric and history—but he always believed Christianity was superior. For Augustine, the last enemy of all true Christians was "antiquity, mothers of all evils"—the source of false beliefs.

Like Augustine, Cassiodorus (ca. 490–ca. 585), an Italian statesman in the court of Ostrogothic rulers of Italy, regarded classical learning as an intellectual inheritance of high value. Cassiodorus was appalled by the waning of the traditional classical educational system in the chaotic final days of the Roman Empire in the west. In response, he founded a monastery at Vivarium in the south of Italy, to which he retired at the end of his political career. Eager to preserve the liberal arts, Cassiodorus instructed his monks to copy classical literature in the monastery's library. "Let the task of the ancients be our task,"[4] he told them.

As the example of Cassiodorus shows, in the western Roman Empire monasticism played a central role in preserving classical learning and thus allowing its integration into Christian culture in later centuries. Much of the responsibility for the preservation of the classical intellectual tradition lay with the monasteries founded by Benedict of Nursia. This group of monks, called the Benedictine order, established many monasteries throughout western Europe, modeled on the monastery of Monte Cassino that Benedict established. They followed Benedict's *Rule* that spelled out the duties of the monks and nuns. Benedict himself was wary of classical teaching, but he wanted the monks and nuns under his supervision to be able to read religious books. At least basic education had to become part of monastic life. Benedictine monasteries provided an educa-

tion not only to their inhabitants but also to any eager scholar from the surrounding communities. The Benedictine definition of "manual labor" expanded to include the copying of ancient manuscripts and Benedictine monasteries developed significant libraries. As monasteries that followed Benedict's *Rule* spread throughout Europe, they served as centers of education and also succeeded in preserving much Latin literature.

Traditional schooling flourished throughout the empire as long as cities could afford to pay for teachers. In most of the towns in western Europe, schools gradually disappeared in the course of the fifth century as a result of the Germanic invasions. With the exception of a few major urban centers, such as Carthage in North Africa, where traditional Roman schooling continued after the establishment of the Vandal kingdom, cities no longer had the funds to pay for teachers. Classical education all but disappeared from urban life by the end of the fifth century. In the eastern half of the empire, classical learning lasted well into the sixth century as a basic part of elite education. Traditional education declined in Byzantium not because of a decline in wealth but because of the growing influence of Christianity on daily life. After the emperor Justinian (r. 527–565) forbade non-Christians to teach, the number of schools declined. By the end of the seventh century, traditional schools of grammar and rhetoric had disappeared. The Psalter (the collection of Psalms in the Bible) became the primer for reading, and religious literature supplanted classical works. As we will see in Chapter 7, however, classical learning revived in Byzantium after the seventh century.

Neoplatonism and Christianity

Greek and Roman philosophy continued to be enormously influential in late antiquity. One branch of this tradition, called Neoplatonism°, originated with Plotinus (205–270), a non-Christian. His teachings greatly influenced Christianity, an example of how classical and Christian thought intertwined in late antiquity. Plotinus, who taught in the city of Rome, traced his intellectual roots primarily to the works of Plato (ca. 429–327 B.C.E.). He also drew ideas from Aristotle (384–322 B.C.E.) and various Stoic philosophers (third century B.C.E.), as well as the writings of their followers. In a series of essays called the *Enneads,* Plotinus applied Plato's views to the issues addressed in ancient philosophy, including ethical behavior, the physical structure of the cosmos, and the nature of perception, consciousness, and memory. He also turned Neoplatonism in religious directions, arguing that all things that exist, whether intangible ideas or matter, originate in a single force called the One. Iamblichus (ca. 245–ca. 325) and other Neoplatonist teachers established a school curriculum based on Plotinus' teachings.

According to Neoplatonists, the One has no physical existence; it is eternal and unchanging. The One is separated from the world of matter and physical change in which humans live by three descending grades of reality: the World Mind, the World Soul, and finally Nature. The World Mind contains the Forms that Plato described (see Chapter 3) and holds them all together as pure knowledge. The World Soul produces time and space. Nature is the lowest of these creative principles, consisting of things that come into being, change, and go out of existence. In Neoplatonic thinking, the human soul is a microcosm of these three levels of reality. The human soul "fell" from the One into the world of Nature and into the human body, thereby losing its connection with the One. Yet the human soul can be redeemed. Humans have the potential to reunite their souls with the One by overcoming their passions and physical desires. Many Neoplatonists believed that by gaining the help of the gods through magical rites (called theurgy) and by studying divine revelations, the human soul can reconnect with the One and fulfill its fullest potential.

With its emphasis on the fall and return of the soul to the One, Neoplatonism appealed to many Christians. For them, the One was God, and the Bible provided the divine revelations that could lead to the salvation of the human soul and reunification with God. The churchmen Gregory of Nyssa in the Greek East and Augustine in the Latin West were only two of the many churchmen who incorporated Neoplatonism into their own works in the later fourth century. Yet Christian and non-Christian Neoplatonists soon argued over such issues as whether the identity of "the One" could be equated with the Christian God and whether the use of theurgy constituted a pagan practice. In 529 the emperor Justinian closed Plato's Academy in Athens and forbade non-Christians to teach philosophy.

The impact of Neoplatonism on Christian theology remained profound. Neoplatonic thought helped to shape the Christian doctrine of the immortality of the human soul. It also reinforced the ascetic ideal. Thus, contempt for the material, temporal world and the physical body took deep root in Christian culture.

Christianity's View of the Empire in History

Christianity not only influenced the way people saw themselves in relation to philosophy and faith, it also shaped their view of the Roman Empire's role in human history. Eusebius, the bishop of Caesarea in Palestine from 313 to 339 and an advisor to Constantine, developed a theory of history that linked the development of the Roman Empire to a divine plan for humanity's salvation. Like other Christians before him, Eusebius believed that the Bible described the main events of human history, such as the creation of the first man and woman, God's revelation of his law to the Hebrews, and the appearance of Jesus. Events still to come, according to Eusebius, included the appearance of the Antichrist, who would inaugurate a brutal reign of evil on Earth, the return of Jesus, the overthrow of the Antichrist, and the End of Days, when God would judge all human beings, reward the pious, and punish the wicked.

CHRONOLOGY

Christianity, Polytheism, and Judaism

CA. 280	Antony goes into the Egyptian desert
CA. 300	Armenia becomes the first Christian kingdom
303	Great Persecution of Christians
306–337	Reign of Constantine the Great
312	Constantine converts to Christianity
325	Council of Nicaea writes the Nicene Creed
360–363	Julian the Apostate reigns
391	Polytheist worship forbidden by Roman law
396–430	Augustine is Bishop of Hippo
CA. 400	Jerusalem Talmud completed
410	Jerome completes Latin translation of Hebrew Bible (Vulgate)
429	End of Jewish Patriarchate
451	Council of Chalcedon
CA. 500	Babylonian Talmud finished
529	Academy in Athens closed; non-Christians forbidden to teach; Benedict founds monastery at Monte Cassino in Italy
534	Benedict writes *Rule* for monastic life

Eusebius added the Roman Empire to this historical plan. He argued that God had sent Jesus to Earth at a divinely appointed place and time—during the reign of the emperor Augustus and thus at a time when much of the known world had been united under imperial rule. The *Pax Romana,* according to Eusebius, provided the perfect, indeed the divinely ordained, conditions for the rapid spread of Christian teaching and the rapid growth of the Christian Church. In Eusebius's view, Constantine's conversion to Christianity marked the next step in God's plan. With one world empire now united under the one true religion, it would be the emperor's job to bring this religion to all of humankind. This triumphal vision of history struck a powerful chord among the empire's Christian elite. It gave Rome a crucial role to play in human destiny. It also enabled aristocrats to justify their traditional roles as political leaders.

By the fifth century, Romans found Eusebius's triumphalism less satisfying as troubling questions surfaced. As we saw in the chapter introduction, in 410 the

Visigoths plundered the city of Rome itself. This epic event challenged Christians' confidence in Eusebius's vision. Did Rome really have a special role in God's divine plan for humanity? If God favored Rome, as Eusebius explained, why had he allowed Visigoths to humiliate the great city? Was God punishing Romans because they had not eradicated paganism?

Such questions prompted Augustine to reexamine conventional notions about Rome's place in the world. In his book *The City of God*, completed in 423, Augustine developed a new interpretation of history. Though Augustine admired the Romans for their many virtues, he concluded that Rome played no significant role in salvation history and that the sack of Rome had no special meaning for Christians. Augustine's theory disconnected Christian ideas of human destiny from the fate of the Roman Empire. In his view, the Roman Empire was just one among many that had existed and that would exist before Jesus' return. According to Augustine, the only dates humanity should view as spiritually significant were Jesus' time on Earth and the End of Days sometime in the future. The significance of all events in between remained known only to God.

Augustine's theory proved quite timely. Within a few years of his death the Vandals seized North Africa and the Roman Empire lost control of all of its provinces in western Europe. Augustine thus gave Roman Christians a new perspective with which to view this loss: Rome had contributed to world civilization and to the growth of the Christian Church, but now Christianity would grow on its own without the support of Roman emperors.

Other churchmen explained the collapse of Roman power in western Europe differently. Salvian, a clergyman from the south of France who found himself living in a new Germanic kingdom in the first half of the fifth century, believed that the Romans deserved to lose their empire in the west because of their sinful lives and oppressive social order. The Visigoths, while less sophisticated than Romans, were nevertheless purer at heart—better Christians despite their heretical Arian views. Salvian's views demonstrate that for many devout Christians, Roman civilization had come to the end of the road. In their eyes, it was time to build a new, Christian world.

The Breakup of the Roman Empire

During the fifth century, the Roman Empire split into two parts: the Latin-speaking provinces in western Europe, and the largely Greek- and Syriac-speaking provinces in the east. As the Roman government lost control of its western domains, independent Germanic kingdoms emerged there. The eastern provinces remained under the control of the Roman emperor, whose capital city was not Rome, but Constantinople. In this section we will discuss the breakup of the empire and explore its consequences.

THE FALL OF ROME'S WESTERN PROVINCES

Why did Roman rule remain strong in the eastern Mediterranean while collapsing in western Europe? This is one of the most hotly debated subjects in European history. Most Christians of the time attributed the collapse of Roman rule to God's anger at the stubborn persistence of polytheist worship. Polytheists, for their part, blamed Christians for destroying the temples of the gods who had protected Rome so well in the past. In later centuries, the explanations varied. Edward Gibbon, an eighteenth-century writer whose *Decline and Fall of the Roman Empire* has influenced all historians of Rome and remains one of the most widely read history books of all time, criticized the Catholic Church for diverting able men away from public service and into religious life. Other historians attributed Rome's collapse in the west to enormous waves of savage barbarian invasions. The reason the Romans lost their western provinces is, unfortunately, more complicated and less dramatic than any of these one-dimensional explanations.

Invasions from the North

During the first century, the Romans established the northern limits of their empire on the European continent along the Rhine and Danube Rivers. From that time forward, Roman generals and emperors withstood invasions of many different northern tribes looking for plunder and new lands. The Roman legions parried their attacks, maintaining a relatively stable northern frontier through not only military might and but also diplomacy. Since the time of Augustus, Roman emperors had made treaties with newcomers, permitting them to settle on Roman lands. The empire had always been able to absorb the settlers. Why did this state of affairs break down in late antiquity—to the degree that the Romans lost their western provinces? The rather undramatic answer is that the end of Roman rule in western Europe came in a haphazard and gradual fashion as the cumulative result of unwise decisions, weak leadership, and military failure.

In the fourth century, the sudden appearance in southern Russia of the Huns, a fierce nomadic people from central Asia, set in motion a series of events that helped bring about the eventual collapse of Roman rule in western Europe. Unlike the settled farmers who lived in Europe, the Huns were highly mobile nomads who herded their flocks over the plains (or *steppes*) that stretched from southern Russia to central Asia. Able to travel vast distances very quickly on their rugged horses, the Huns had earned a reputation for ferocity in battle. Always living under the specter of starvation, they lusted after the great riches and easy lifestyles they observed in the urbanized empires of Rome and Persia.

In 376, in what is now south Russia, an army of Huns drove a group of Visigoths from their farmlands. The refugees gained permission from the Roman emperor Valens to cross the Danube and settle in the Balkans in return for supplying troops to the Roman army. In the past, Roman rulers had frequently made this sort of arrangement with newcomers eager to settle in the empire. The Roman officials in charge of this resettlement, however, flagrantly exploited the refugees by charging them exorbitant fees for food and supplies. The situation grew so unendurable that in 378 the Visigoths revolted. At the battle of Adrianople in Thrace they killed Valens and an entire Roman army.

The Visigoths' successful rebellion wounded the empire, but not fatally. Rome's response to the disaster, however, sowed the seeds for a serious loss of imperial power in the west. Necessity forced the new emperor, Theodosius the Great (r. 379–395), to permit Visigothic soldiers to serve in the Roman army under their own Visigothic commanders. As Theodosius and the rest of Rome would unhappily discover, this precedent of letting independent military forces of dubious loyalty operate freely within the empire was a

terrible mistake. The consequences of Theodosius's decision became all too clear in the mid-390s when Alaric, the Visigoths' king, attacked and plundered Roman cities in the Balkans and Greece. In 401 Alaric invaded Italy, but was driven out. Seven years later the Visigoths appeared again at the walls of Rome and extorted a huge payment of gold and the precious spice pepper from the angry but powerless Senate.

Alaric's success only expanded his ambitions. In 409 he returned to the city of Rome and ordered that parts of northern Italy and the western coast of the Balkans be turned over to him. When the Senate refused, Alaric and his men sacked the city. Disbelieving senators and citizens alike could only watch as the Visigoths rampaged through their streets. Ironically, Alaric died soon after his triumph. To keep his burial place secret, his followers diverted the Busento River in Italy, buried their fallen leader and all his loot, and then executed the grave diggers. Finally, they returned the river to its original course. The exact location of Alaric's grave remains a mystery to this day, awaiting an archaeologist's spade.

The Visigoths' sack of Rome not only dealt a psychological blow to the empire's inhabitants, it also led indirectly to the loss of many of Rome's western provinces. To fight Alaric, the Roman general Stilicho had withdrawn legions

THE HUNS, MONSTROUS INVADERS

Shortly after the Huns rode in from the steppelands of central Asia and drove the Visigoths into the Roman Empire in the 370s, a Roman historian wrote this description of the event. His picture of the Huns, though filled with misconceptions and errors, reveals the fear that the nomadic tribesmen inspired in the settled communities of the Mediterranean world. By describing the ways in which he views the Huns as uncivilized, the writer provides a good picture of Roman ideas of civilization.

The people of the Huns . . . exceed every degree of savagery. Since the cheeks of the children are deeply furrowed with steel knives from their very birth, in order that the growth of hair, when it appears at the proper time, may be checked by the wrinkled scars, they grow old without beards and without any beauty, like eunuchs. They all have compact, strong limbs and thick necks, and are so monstrously ugly and misshapen, that one might take them for two-legged beasts . . . They are so hardy that they have no need of fire or of savory food, but eat the roots of wild plants and the half-raw flesh of any kind of animal whatever, which they put between their thighs and the backs of their horses, and thus warm it a

little. They are never protected by any buildings, but they avoid these like tombs . . . They are almost glued to their horses . . . They are subject to no royal restraint, but they are content with the disorderly government of their important men, and led by them they force their way through every obstacle. . . . You would not hesitate to call them the most terrible of warriors, because they fight from a distance with missiles having sharp bone . . . joined to the shafts . . . then they gallop over the intervening spaces and fight hand to hand with swords, regardless of their own lives . . . No one in their country ever plows a field. . . . They are all without fixed abode, without hearth, or law, or settled mode of life . . . Like unreasoning beasts they are utterly ignorant of the difference between right and wrong, they are deceitful and ambiguous in speech, never bound by any reverence for religion . . . They burn with an infinite thirst for gold . . .

Source: Reprinted by permission of the publishers and the Trustees of the Loeb Classical Library from *Ammianus Marcellinus, Volume III*, Loeb Classical Library Volume LCL 331, translated by John C. Rolfe, Cambridge, Mass.: Harvard University Press, 1939. The Loeb Classical Library ® is a registered trademark of the President and Fellows of Harvard College.

■ Stilicho and His Family

Between 395 and 408 the general Stilicho ruled the western half of the empire as the regent for Honorius, the son of Theodosius I. Though his father was a Vandal, Stilicho was completely loyal to Rome. Carved in traditional Roman style, these ivory panels show Stilicho dressed in Vandal clothing, accompanied by his wife and son.

from the empire's northwestern defenses, leaving the Rhine frontier vulnerable. In December 406, the Rhine River froze, enabling an array of migrating Germanic tribes to enter the empire with little opposition from Roman forces. In the aftermath of the invasions of the winter of 406–407, the military situation in the western provinces became chaotic.

In Britain, Rome abandoned its control entirely after an ambitious general, styling himself Constantine III, led Britain's last legions across the English Channel in an unsuccessful attempt to seize the imperial throne. This action left Britain defenseless, vulnerable to groups of Saxons already settled on British soil. Originally from the shores of the North Sea near modern Denmark, the Saxons had been fighting in Britain as allies of Roman forces. Now they turned on their former partners and attacked Roman-held Britain. The desperate inhabitants begged for help from the emperor Honorius. According to one contemporary, in 410 the beleaguered ruler merely told the Britons to fend for themselves.

Elsewhere the chaos continued. Small bands of marauding tribes such as Alans, Burgundians, and Sueves roamed through Gaul, while the Vandals and their allies raided their way through Spain. For over a decade, the various invaders tried to secure territory for themselves within the imperial borders by force. Vastly outnumbered by the provincial populations, they survived by plundering the countryside.

Although the invading bands were small, the imperial government in the west no longer possessed the administrative capacity to marshal its military resources and push the invaders out. Instead, it turned to diplomacy, offering the invaders a place within the Roman Empire. In Gaul, for example, the treaty of 418 granted the Visigoths a home in Aquitania (a region of southwestern Gaul). According to the treaty, the Visigoths received lands on which to settle permanently, something they had sought for nearly two generations. In return they would pay taxes and fight under Rome's banner to combat peasant rebels and other invading tribes. Within a generation, however, the Visigoths shook off their subordinate status to Rome. Refusing to pay taxes to Roman officials or send troops to fight in Roman armies, they established a kingdom of their own in Gaul by 450. A similar process of encroachment and settlement took place elsewhere in the western provinces. In 429 the Vandals

■ **Map 6.2 Germanic Kingdoms, ca. 525**

In little more than a century after their entry into the Roman Empire, different Germanic peoples had established several powerful kingdoms in western Europe.

moved from Spain to North Africa where they soon established an independent kingdom. In 439 they seized Carthage and made it their capital.

Thus, encroaching bands of Germanic peoples established independent kingdoms in the regions of Britain, Gaul, Spain, and North Africa through a gradual process (see Map 6.2). The empire was not invaded by overwhelming numbers of savage invaders. In fact, their numbers were puny compared to the millions of Roman provincials they pitted themselves against. And although the Germans plundered and pillaged, they could not hold on to imperial lands and settle there without the active cooperation of Roman administrators. Once they put down roots, however, they steadily consolidated their strength and established rule on their own. By then, Roman authorities lacked both the organization and the strength to defeat them.

Even though most of the western provinces had fallen to invaders by 450, the Romans managed to hold on to Italy for a short while longer. The city of Rome remained the home of the Senate, while the emperor of the western provinces resided in Ravenna, a town on Italy's northeast coast. Military strongmen, however, held the real power in

Italy, although they were formally subordinate to the emperor. These soldiers were usually not Romans by birth, but they adopted Roman culture and fought for Rome's advantage. In 476 one of these strongmen, a Germanic general named Odovacar, ended the charade of obedience to the emperor. He deposed the last emperor in the west, a boy named Romulus Augustulus. Odovacar then assumed full power over the Italian peninsula, naming himself king of Italy. For many historians the year 476 symbolizes the end of the Roman Empire in the west. In actuality, however, 476 is a date of little significance. The Romans' control of their western provinces had all but slipped away decades earlier.

The Empire of Attila

The Huns, who had driven the Visigoths into the Balkans and sparked the series of events that led to Rome's loss of its western provinces, continued to advance on Europe. By 400 they had carved out a powerful kingdom on the great plain of Hungary, where they could graze their horses and flocks. Throughout the first half of the fifth century the Huns remained a violent and disruptive presence on the European continent, relentlessly raiding the Balkans and western Europe. They forced conquered peoples to fight under Hunnic banners.

By 445, a charismatic and ruthless conqueror emerged as the sole leader of the Hunnic tribes and their allies. Named Attila, this ambitious warrior began to expand the Huns' empire from southern Russia to France. His aggression brought him face to face with the Roman Empire in the east. To their surprise, Roman diplomats from Constantinople who visited Attila's court found the Hunnic king to be a sophisticated bargainer as well as an able administrator. Attila, they discovered, included chieftains of subject peoples among his trusted assistants. The diplomats also found Roman merchants and craftsmen who had been attracted to Attila's camp, where they enjoyed freedom from oppressive Roman taxation and corrupt Roman officials.

Yet the Hunnic ruler had a shockingly brutal side as well. From his base of operations on the Hungarian plain, Attila hammered the Balkan provinces and forced the Roman emperor in Constantinople to pay him tribute in gold every year. In 450, when a new emperor refused to submit any longer to Attila's extortion, the Hun turned westward and invaded Gaul with an immense army. The savagery of his attack and the fear he inspired earned him the title "the Scourge of God."

The next year, the tide began to turn against Attila. A force of Visigoths (who still hated the Huns for having driven them from their homelands in south Russia nearly a century earlier) joined with Romans and other allies from the Germanic kingdoms in western Europe. This allied force stopped Attila's advance in a battle at the Catalaunian Fields in central Gaul in 451. The following year the tenacious warrior launched a new attack on Italy but failed to take the city of Rome, perhaps because his army was weakened by disease.

Soon after the ill-fated invasion of Italy, Attila died while in bed with a young bride. His sons divided the Hunnic Empire among themselves, but the realm could not endure without its great leader. Soon the Huns' subject peoples rebelled against their oppressors and reclaimed their independence. The mighty empire of the Huns fragmented and disappeared. Within a century another nomadic people, the Avars, would replace the Huns as the biggest menace to the Roman Empire and its successor kingdoms (see Map 6.3). The Huns seem to have made no material or intellectual contribution to Western civilization. But they did leave a chilling cultural legacy. As a common enemy of the peoples of the settled Mediterranean world, they embedded in Western culture a frightening memory of bloodthirsty steppe peoples who attacked from the east.

A ROMAN ARISTOCRAT LEARNS GOTHIC

·················

Sidonius Apollinaris was a Roman aristocrat who lived in Gaul in the fifth century when Germanic kingdoms replaced Roman imperial rule. In this letter, he gently teases a Roman friend, Syagrius, who has been trying to find a place in the new power structure in the kingdom established in southern Gaul by the Burgundians, a Germanic tribe. Syagrius served as a legal advisor at the Burgundian court, where separate legal systems were enforced for Burgundians and Romans. Syagrius was one of a long succession of Romans who kept Roman culture and law working for several generations after the empire fell in the west—but he had to learn a new language:

Sidonius sends greetings to his friend, Syagrius:

You are the great-grandson of a consul . . . and you are descended from a poet . . . and the culture of his descendants has not declined one bit from his standard . . . I am therefore inexpressibly amazed that you have quickly acquired a knowledge of the German tongue with such ease. And yet I remember that your boyhood had a good schooling in liberal studies and I know for certain that you

often declaimed with spirit and eloquence before your professor of oratory. This being so, please tell me how you have managed to absorb so swiftly into your inner being the exact sounds of an alien race, so that now after reading Vergil under the schoolmaster's cane and toiling and working through the rich fluency of . . . Cicero, you burst forth like a young falcon from an old nest. You have no idea what amusement it gives me, and others too, when I hear that in your presence the barbarian is afraid to perpetrate a barbarism in his own language. The bent elders of the Germans are astounded at you when you translate letters, and they adopt you as umpire and arbitrator in their mutual dealings . . . Only one thing remains, most clever of men: continue with undiminished zeal, even in your hours of ease, to devote some attention to reading; and like the man of refinement that you are, observe a just balance between the two languages: retain your grasp of Latin, lest you be laughed at, and practice the other, in order to have the laugh on them. Farewell.

Source: Reprinted by permission of the publishers and Trustees of the Loeb Classical Library from *Sidonius Poems and Letters, Volume II,* Loeb Classical Library Volume LCL 420, translated by W. B. Anderson, Cambridge, Mass.: Harvard University Press, 1935. The Loeb Classical Library ® is a registered trademark of the President and Fellows of Harvard College.

■ **Map 6.3   Nomad Empires**

During late antiquity, the Huns and later the Avars established powerful empires based on the Hungarian plain. These fierce horsemen terrified the settled peoples of the Roman world.

Cultural Encounters
After the End of Roman Rule

By the mid-fifth century, when the fighting between Germanic invaders and the Romans stopped, the two sides had to learn to live with one another. The Germanic rulers possessed military power but were vastly outnumbered by the Romans. For example, only 40,000 Vandals controlled North Africa, which had a population of several million Romans. And although the Romans had no military power, they dominated urban life and agricultural production. Both sides faced unique challenges. The newcomers had the special problem of staying separate from the population they ruled. The Romans in turn had to adapt traditions of urban life and education to the new realities of life under Germanic masters.

Of course, Roman culture did not abruptly come to an end with the last vestiges of Roman rule. It remained a vital presence in most regions, but it took different forms in the various lands now ruled by Germanic leaders. In Britain, Roman culture perhaps fared the worst. Little of it survived into later ages. Yet legends hint at a fierce resistance against the invaders. The stories about King Arthur that have captivated English-speaking audiences since the Middle Ages are based on memories of valiant resistance to the Saxon invaders in the mid-fifth century.

In Gaul, North Africa, Italy, and Spain, the new settlers were Christian, which softened the shock of their presence. They followed Arian Christianity, however, a creed that viewed Jesus Christ as subordinate to God the Father. The Romans, on the other hand, followed orthodox Christianity and thus saw the invaders as heretics. Although this religious difference caused considerable friction between the two peoples, it also worked to their mutual advantage. Roman law forbade intermarriage between orthodox and Arian Christians, so the settlers remained a distinct minority in their new domains. This enabled them to maintain a separate Arian clergy and separate churches and hence a distinct identity in the midst of the vastly superior numbers of Roman provincials they ruled.

Confident in their position of power, the newcomers easily slipped into the role of military protectors of the Roman provincials they now ruled. For example, Vandal forces fought against Berber nomads from the foothills of the Atlas Mountains who tried to raid North Africa's fertile farmlands. To many Roman peasants, the new masters provided a welcome alternative to the callous imperial officials who had exploited them for so long. Salvian of Marseilles, a churchman who wrote in southern Gaul in the mid-fifth century, described the situation:

> The Roman poor are despoiled, the widows groan, the orphans are tread underfoot, so much so that many of them . . . flee to the enemy . . . Although these Romans differ in religion and language from the barbarians to whom they flee, and differ from them in respect to filthiness of body and clothing, nevertheless . . . they prefer to bear among the barbarians a worship unlike their own rather than rampant injustice among the Romans. They prefer to live as freemen under an outward form of captivity than as captives under an appearance of liberty.[5]

Of all the former empire's western provinces, Italy prospered the most under Germanic rule, particularly under the long reign of Theodoric the Ostrogoth (r. 493–526). In 493 Theodoric left the Balkans for Italy at the suggestion of the Roman emperor in Constantinople. The emperor told Theodoric that he could rule Italy if he was able to capture it from Odovacar, who was currently ruling there. The crafty emperor calculated that if Odovacar defeated Theodoric, the situation in Italy would remain unchanged, but a menace would be gone from the Balkans. If Theodoric won, the Balkans would be safe and there would be another barbarian ruling Italy. Either way he had little to lose and much to gain. Theodoric accepted the challenge and murdered Odovacar in Italy. Once on the throne of Italy, Theodoric took care to affirm his support for the Roman Empire and to acknowledge the emperor's superior status. In politics, Theodoric sought to create an atmosphere of mutual respect between Ostrogoths and Romans by maintaining two separate administrations—one for his Ostrogoths, the other for the Romans—so that both communities could manage their own affairs under his supervision. He also included aristocratic Romans among his closest advisers

CHRONOLOGY

Roman Empire, East and West

235–284	Crisis in Roman government
284	Diocletian begins imperial reforms
293	Tetrarchy established
312	Constantine wins control of western empire
324	Constantinople founded
378	Battle of Adrianople; Visigoths invade empire
406	Vandals and other tribes cross the Rhine
410	Romans withdraw from Britain; Visigoths plunder Rome
418	Visigoths settle in Gaul
429–439	Vandals take North Africa
445–453	Attila rules the Hunnic Empire
476	Romulus Augustulus, last western emperor, deposed
493–526	Theodoric the Ostrogoth rules Italy

and most trusted administrators. Even in his religious policies Theodoric pursued mutual tolerance. As an Arian Christian, Theodoric supported a separate clergy, but he also maintained excellent ties with the pope, leader of the orthodox Roman Christians. Theodoric united Visigothic kingdoms in Spain and Gaul with his own in Italy, ultimately wielding great influence throughout western Europe. Italy prospered under his rule, and the communities of Ostrogoths and Romans lived together amicably.

Throughout the western provinces, however, links to the Roman Empire in the east began to weaken. Most of the invaders had brought with them their traditional practice of pledging fidelity and obedience to a local chieftain, and this tradition began to eat away at loyalty to the far-off Roman emperor in Constantinople. By pledging themselves to a Germanic king, men gained a place in the "tribe" of their new chieftain. Many of these soldiers had served in units of the Roman army under their own officers, but now they looked to their king—not to the emperor—to provide gifts and the opportunities to win prestige, honor, and land. Thus service to the empire gradually gave way to oaths of loyalty to local chieftains. Over time, new warrior-based aristocracies took shape in which landowning noblemen forged ties of personal loyalty to their local king.

Some deeply rooted Roman ways remained, however. Except for Britain, where the language spoken by the Saxon invaders and their Angle allies took hold and began developing into the English spoken today, the settlers quickly learned the tongues of the provincials they ruled. Within several centuries these Latin-based "Romance" (based on the Roman speech) languages grew into the early versions of Italian, Spanish, and French. Latin continued as the language of literacy, and the settlers borrowed heavily from Roman literary forms. Writing in Latin, they produced histories of their tribal kingdoms in imitation of Roman historians. They also developed law codes composed in Latin influenced by Roman models.

THE BIRTH OF BYZANTIUM

The Roman Empire endured in the eastern Mediterranean without interruption in late antiquity, despite the profound alterations wrought by Christianity and Rome's loss of the western provinces. Constantinople, the imperial city founded by Constantine in 324, became the center of a remodeled empire that over several centuries acquired both Christian and Roman characteristics. Historians have named this realm the Byzantine Empire, or Byzantium, although the inhabitants of the realm continued to think of themselves as Romans for a thousand years.

■ **The Cathedral of Holy Wisdom (Haghia Sophia)**
When Justinian entered his newly completed cathedral of Holy Wisdom (Haghia Sophia) in Constantinople, he boasted, "Solomon, I have outdone you!" He meant that his church was bigger than the Jerusalem Temple built by the biblical King Solomon. For centuries Haghia Sophia was the largest building in Europe. In 1453 the church became a mosque. Today it is a public museum.

Christianity and Law Under Justinian

The most important amalgamation of Christian and Roman traditions took place during the reign of the emperor Justinian (r. 527–565). Born in the Balkans, Justinian was the last native Latin-speaking emperor. When his uncle became emperor in 518, Justinian was the real power behind the throne. He combined a powerful intellect, an unshakable Christian faith, and a driving ambition to reform the empire. He defied convention by marrying Theodora, a strong-willed former actress, and included her in imperial decision making once he became emperor in 527.

Justinian inaugurated a number of changes that highlighted his role as a Christian emperor. First of all, he emphasized the position of the emperor at the center of society in explicitly Christian terms. He was the first emperor to use the title "Beloved of Christ" and he amplified the emperor's role in Church affairs. Justinian considered it his duty as emperor to enforce uniform religious belief throughout his domain. By bullying clergymen and writing his own works on doctrinal matters he tried to usurp the bishops' control of the definition of orthodox Christianity. He ruthlessly purged non-Christians and heretical Christians from public life so that only men who were orthodox Christians could now hold government offices. In addition, Justinian directed Christian priests to force the conversion of surviving pockets of polytheists to orthodox Christianity.

Justinian attempted to create a Christian society by using Roman law coupled with military force. Unlike rulers of Rome's early empire, who permitted subject peoples to maintain their own customary laws, Justinian suppressed local laws throughout his realm. He envisioned all of his subjects obeying only Roman law—law that he defined and that God approved. (Justinian was sure that if God did not approve of his legislative changes, God would not allow him to continue as emperor.) Justinian believed that by spreading orthodox Christianity throughout the empire he was spreading civilization.

Thus, in his God-given mission as emperor-legislator, Justinian reformed Roman law. In an effort to simplify the vast body of civil law, he ordered his lawyers to sort through all the laws that had accumulated over the centuries and determine which of them should still be enforced. This monumental effort, which was completed in 534, is known as the *Code of Justinian*. His lawyers also prepared a handbook of basic Roman law for law students, called the *Institutes,* as well as the *Digest,* a collection and summary of several centuries' worth of commentary on Roman law by legal experts. Justinian then banned any additional commentary on the law, naming himself as the only interpreter of existing laws and the sole source of new laws. While the *Code, Digest,* and *Institutes* were composed in Latin, the traditional legal language of Rome, Justinian's new legislation, called the *Novels,* was issued in Greek, the common language of the eastern empire. Collectively, this legal work is called the *Corpus of Civil Law*°. Roman law passed down to later generations primarily through this compilation. At the end of the eleventh century, scholars in Italy discovered manuscripts of Justinian's legal works in church libraries, and interest in Roman law began to revive. The *Digest* became the most influential legal text in medieval Europe. Thus the Corpus of Civil Law became a pillar of Latin-speaking European civilization.

Reconquering the Provinces in the West
Once he had reorganized Byzantium's legal system, Justinian turned his attention to Rome's fallen western provinces. He wanted to reestablish imperial control over

AN EMPRESS REFUSES TO PANIC

As Justinian's wife, Theodora exerted a strong influence at court and throughout the empire. Early in his reign, Justinian was almost driven from the throne in an urban riot called the Nika Revolt. When the emperor and his advisers were frantically discussing whether they should flee from Constantinople, Theodora's proud remarks persuaded her husband not to give up. His soldiers bolted the gates to the Hippodrome, where the protesters had gathered, and slaughtered at least 30,000 of them. The revolt ended.

As to the belief that a woman ought not to be daring among men or to assert herself boldly among those who are holding back from fear, I consider that the present crisis most certainly does not permit us to discuss whether the matter should be regarded in this or in some other way. For in the case of those whose interests have come into the greatest danger nothing else seems best except to settle the issue immediately before them in the best possible way. My opinion then is that at the present time, above all others, is inopportune for flight, even though it bring safety. For while it is impossible for a man who has seen the light also not to die, for one who has been emperor it is unendurable to be a fugitive. May I never be separated from this purple [the color of the imperial robes], and may I not live that day on which those who meet me shall not address me as mistress. If now it is your wish to save yourself, O Emperor, there is no difficulty. For we have much money, and there is the sea, here are the boats. However consider whether it will not come about that after you have been saved that you would gladly exchange that safety for death. For as for myself, I approve a certain ancient saying that royal robes are a good burial shroud.

Source: Reprinted by permission of the publishers and the Trustees of the Loeb Classical Library from *Procopius, Volume I,* Loeb Classical Library Volume LCL 48, translated by H. B. Dewing, Cambridge, Mass.: Harvard University Press, 1914. The Loeb Classical Library ® is a registered trademark of the President and Fellows of Harvard College.

these territories, now ruled by Germanic kings. Between 533 and 554 Justinian's armies snatched back North Africa from the Vandals, seized Sicily and Italy from the Ostrogoths, and won parts of Spain from the Visigoths. With the empire nearly restored to its former glory, Justinian's plan was to impose his version of Christian orthodoxy upon the Arian Christian Vandals and Ostrogoths still living in his western domains. He would also force them to live under his version of Roman law and government.

Two Martyrdoms: Culture and Religion on Trial

Between the reigns of Diocletian (r. 284–305) and Justinian (r. 527–565), the status of Christians changed dramatically. Christians went from being a religious minority persecuted by the imperial government to a majority that persecuted non-Christians with the Roman government's backing. One thing did not change during this period, however. Whether polytheist or Christian, emperors used force to compel their subjects to believe and worship in prescribed ways, hoping to keep the empire in the gods' good graces. To ensure religious conformity, emperors used the Roman judicial system. A comparison of the trials of a Christian soldier named Julius in 303, and Phocas, an aristocrat in Constantinople accused of paganism in 529 and 545, illustrates the objectives and methods of the Roman government's religious prosecution.

In 303 officials arrested a veteran soldier named Julius and brought him before the prefect Maximus. The following excerpt comes from a description of the trial[6]:

> "Who is this?" asked Maximus. One of the staff replied: "This is a Christian who will not obey the laws." "What is your name?" asked the prefect. "Julius," was the reply. "Well, what say you, Julius?" asked the prefect. "Are these allegations true?" "Yes, they are," said Julius. "I am indeed a Christian. I do not deny that I am precisely what I am." "You are surely aware," said the prefect, "of the emperors' edicts which order you to sacrifice to the gods?" "I

am aware of them," answered Julius. "I am indeed a Christian and cannot do what you want; for I must not lose sight of my living and true God.". . . "If you think it a sin," answered the prefect Maximus, "let me take the blame. I am the one who is forcing you, so that you may not give impression of having consented voluntarily. Afterwards you can go home in peace, you will pick up your ten-year bonus, and no one will ever trouble you again. . . . If you do not respect the imperial decrees and offer sacrifice, I am going to cut your head off." "That is a good plan," answered Julius, "Only I beg . . . that you execute your plan and pass sentence on me so that my prayers may be answered. . . . I have chosen death for now so that I might live with the saints forever." The prefect Maximus then delivered the sentence as follows: "Whereas Julius has refused to obey the imperial edicts, he is sentenced to death."

After Constantine's conversion to Christianity in 312, persecution of Christians stopped, and Christian officials began to attack polytheism with the government's support. The emperor Justinian severely enforced laws against polytheists, executing anyone who sacrificed animals to non-Christian gods. During Justinian's reign, the imperial government launched three major persecutions of polytheists. In the first episode of persecution in 528–529, one year after Justinian ascended to the throne, a handful of government officials were charged with the crime of worshiping pagan gods.

One of these men was Phocas the Patrician, an aristocratic lawyer with an illustrious career in the emperor's service. After serving as the chief of protocol at court, he was sent to Antioch with funds to rebuild the city after a ruinous earthquake in 526. Cleared of charges of practicing paganism in 529, he continued to enjoy Justinian's trust and earn further promotions. In 532 he served for a year as Praetorian Prefect, the most powerful position in the realm after the emperor. During this time, Phocas was responsible for raising revenues and administering the empire. He assisted in the construction of the new Cathedral of Holy Wisdom (Haghia Sophia; see illustration on page 214) in Constantinople by raising revenues. He also spent his personal funds in supporting smaller churches and ransoming hostages captured by Byzantium's enemies. Justinian next made him a judge and sent him on a mission to investigate the murder of a bishop. Then, in 545–546, during the second wave of persecution, despite his publicly recognized activities in support of the church and his faithful service to Justinian, Phocas was arrested again. He was among the doctors, teachers, and government officials suddenly charged with being pagans. A contemporary historian described a time of terror in Constantinople, when officials accused of worshiping the old gods in secret were driven from public office, had their property confiscated by the emperor, and were executed. In a

■ Justinian

This mid-sixth-century ivory panel depicts the emperor Justinian in a standard pose of Roman emperors. He rides a horse, while beneath his feet subject barbarians in native clothing bring offerings of gold and ivory. An angel of victory hovers next to the emperor; another supports his foot. An attendant carries a statue adorned with a wreath of victory. At the top is a representation of Jesus holding a cross and making a gesture of blessing. The panel sends the message that Justinian rules the world with the approval and support of God.

panic, some of the accused men took their own lives. Phocas was one of them. Rather than undergo the humiliation of public execution, Phocas committed suicide. The furious emperor ordered that Phocas' body be buried in a ditch like an animal, without prayer or ceremony of any sort.

Phocas thus missed the third purge of 562, when polytheists were arrested throughout the empire, paraded in public, imprisoned, tried, and sentenced. Zealous crowds threw thousands of non-Christian books into bonfires in the empire's cities.

Why did the government use such a heavy hand in persecuting polytheists during Justinian's reign? Men like Phocas who were attacked as pagans were highly educated in the traditional learning of the Greco-Roman world. Indeed, it was this learning that was really on trial. Phocas and other victims had a deep commitment to traditional Roman culture; their "paganism" was not the furtive worship of old gods like Zeus or Apollo. Rather, Phocas was considered a pagan because he was loyal to classical philosophy, literature, and rhetoric, without any Christian overlay or interpretation. In Justinian's eyes, this sort of classical learning had no place in a Christian empire. ■

Questions of Justice

1. How did the change from polytheism to Christianity alter the ways in which the Roman government understood religious persecution in late antiquity?

2. What did justice mean to the author of the trial of Julius the veteran soldier?

Taking It Further

Helgeland, John. *Christians in the Military: The Early Experience.* 1985. An introduction to the persecutions of Christians in the Roman army and their depiction in Christian literature.

Maas, Michael. *John Lydus and the Roman Past: Antiquarianism and Politics in the Age of Justinian.* 1992. This book explains how Justinian's policies about religion also involved an encounter with the empire's classical heritage.

In 533, Justinian sent a fleet of 10,000 men and 5,000 cavalry under the command of his general Belisarius to attack the Vandal kingdom in North Africa. The Vandal kingdom fell quickly, and within a year Belisarius celebrated a triumph in Constantinople. Encouraged by this easy victory, Justinian set his sights on Italy, where the Ostrogothic ruling family was embroiled in political infighting. This time Justinian had underestimated his opponents. The Ostrogoths, who had won the support of the Roman population in Italy, mounted a fierce resistance to Belisarius's invasion in 536. Justinian, for his part, did not trust his own general and failed to support him with adequate funds and soldiers. Bitter fighting between Justinian's troops and the Ostrogothic armies dragged on for two decades. Justinian's armies eventually wrestled Italy back under imperial control, but the long-term effects of the protracted reconquest had disastrous consequences for Justinian's empire. The many years of fighting devastated Italy's cities and countryside. Between pouring precious financial resources into the Italy campaign and maintaining his grip on North Africa, Justinian was draining his empire's resources dry.

One of the reasons Justinian's reconquest of Italy took decades was the impact of the bubonic plague. The plague struck the empire in 542 and spread throughout Justinian's realm, migrating swiftly to Italy, North Africa, and Gaul. The first onslaught took the lives of perhaps half the population of Constantinople—about a quarter of a million people. An estimated one-third of the entire population of the empire's inhabi-

tants succumbed to the dreaded disease. With the population devastated by the plague, Justinian's army could not recruit the large number of soldiers it needed to fight on several fronts; the protracted battle for Italy was the result. The plague's impact also extended far beyond slowing Justinian's military adventures. Farms lay deserted and city populations shriveled. More than any other single factor, the bubonic plague weakened the Roman Empire and contributed to the eventual collapse of Mediterranean unity in the mid-seventh century.

After Justinian's death, Byzantine emperors would never again attempt to reestablish control over the entire Mediterranean world (see Map 6.4). Instead, they focused their attention on matters of more pressing interest closer to home. Justinian's ill-fated reconquests did, however, leave a mark on religious affairs in Mediterranean lands. The

■ **Map 6.4   The Byzantine Empire at the Death of Justinian**

When Justinian died in 565, the territories of Italy, North Africa, and part of Spain that had been lost in the fifth century were restored, temporarily, to imperial rule.

The Byzantine Empire at the Death of Justinian

- Roman Empire in 527 at Justinian's accession
- Conquests under Justinian (ruled by Arians prior to reconquest)
- Kingdom of the Franks, Chalcedonian (Catholic) after ca. 508
- Kingdom of the Visigoths (ruled by Arians)
- Chalcedonians
- Monophysites

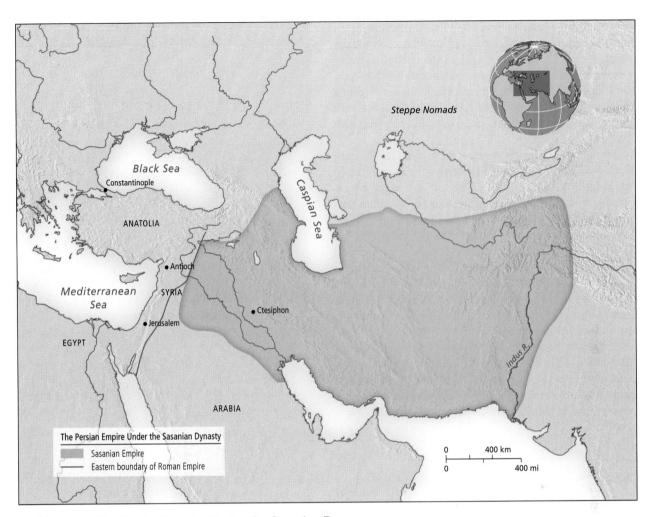

■ **Map 6.5   The Persian Empire Under the Sasanian Dynasty**
Under the dynamic Sasanian dynasty, the Persian Empire fought many wars with the Roman Empire.
Neither empire had an advantage because they were roughly the same size and possessed equivalent
resources of wealth and manpower.

bishops of North Africa and Italy deeply resented Justinian's attempts to meddle in doctrinal matters. As a result a bitter division arose between Christian churches in the eastern and western Mediterranean—a chasm that would endure for centuries.

The Struggle with Persia

Although Justinian's greatest military successes were in the western Mediterranean, his most dangerous enemy was the Persian Empire on his eastern flank. This huge, multi-ethnic empire, under the rule of the Sasanian dynasty (ca. 220–633), had been Rome's main rival throughout late antiquity (see Map 6.5). The tension stemmed chiefly from competition over Armenia, which was a source of skilled troops, and Syria, which possessed enormous wealth. From the time that Emperor Julian died in combat against Persia in 363, emperors at Constantinople kept up their guard against this eastern threat. Though wars were

frequent, neither side could win permanent superiority over the other.

Justinian fought several brutal wars with Persia. The emperor gave top priority to the struggle on his eastern frontier by supplying more than half of the Byzantine troops, led by his best generals. He also provided more financial resources to the struggle in the east than to the wars of reconquest in the west. Chosroes I, the aggressive and ambitious Great King of Persia, proved to be a worthy adversary for Justinian. Chosroes often invaded the Byzantine Empire, causing great damage. In 540, for example, he sacked Antioch, the wealthiest city in Syria. Because war with Persia was extraordinarily expensive, Justinian made peace by paying thousands of pounds of gold to the Persian monarch in order to bring the fighting to a close. Even this great cost was less than continuing to fight every year.

By the time of Justinian's death, the two superpowers had established an uneasy coexistence, but the basic animosity between them remained unresolved. For the next half century, Justinian's successors engaged in intermittent bitter warfare with the Persian rulers. This protracted struggle between Byzantium and Persia demonstrates how the Byzantines' most important enemies lay to the east. Fighting to regain provinces in the west brought glory, but war with Persia was a matter of life and death for the Byzantine Empire.

By fighting expensive wars on the eastern and western flanks of his empire, Justinian hastened the disintegration of Byzantine imperial rule. The overextension of resources ensured that Byzantium could not maintain lasting control of the western Mediterranean region. When new invaders descended on Italy and the Balkans in the late sixth century, the empire would not have the strength to resist them. The drain of resources on the Persian front helped weaken Byzantium as well. If Justinian had been less ambitious, it is likely that the Byzantine Empire could have withstood the attack of Muslim armies in the seventh centuries and retained control of provinces in North Africa, Egypt, and Syria. Nevertheless, Justinian succeeded in creating a Christian-Roman society, united under one God, one emperor, and one law. On the basis of the unified culture created by Justinian, the Byzantine Empire would survive for nearly a millennium—though on a smaller scale.

CHRONOLOGY	
The Reign of Justinian	
429	Plato's Academy in Athens closed
527–565	Reign of Justinian
529–532	War with Persia
532	Nika Revolt in Constantinople
527–533	Law Code of Justinian
534	Reconquest of North Africa
534–561	Reconquest of Italy
540–562	War with Persia
542	Plague strikes empire
565	Death of Justinian

CONCLUSION
A Transformed World

The transformation of the Roman world in late antiquity helped create the West as we understand it today. Christianity became the dominant religion throughout the Roman Empire. It assimilated much of classical culture and became the official religion by 400. During late antiquity Europe split into two parts. After Roman rule in the West collapsed, Germanic rulers established new kingdoms in the old Roman provinces. These kingdoms spoke Romance languages derived from Latin, and used Latin in church and law. In the eastern Mediterranean, the Roman Empire developed in new ways. Christianity and Roman civilization merged to create the vibrant Byzantine civilization. Greek remained the dominant tongue of daily life and Christian worship.

When Islam emerged as a powerful religious and political entity at the end of the late antique period, as we will see in the next chapter, its adherents were by definition excluded from the European communities of Christian believers. As a result, the North African, Middle Eastern, and Balkan lands that Islamic conquerors seized from the Byzantine Empire lost their place in the roster of "Western" communities, while those lands not conquered by Islam became the bastion of a medieval civilization that defined itself primarily as European and Christian.

Suggestions for Further Reading

For a comprehensive list of suggested readings, please go to www.ablongman.com/levack/chapter6

Bowersock, G. W. *Hellenism in Late Antiquity.* 1990. Explains the important role of traditional Greek culture in shaping late antiquity.

Bowersock, G. W., Peter Brown, and Oleg Grabar, eds. *Late Antiquity: A Guide to the Postclassical World.* 1999. An indispensable handbook containing synthetic essays and shorter encyclopedia entries.

Brown, Peter. *The Cult of the Saints: Its Rise and Function in Late Antiquity.* 1981. A brilliant and highly influential study.

Brown, Peter. *The Rise of Western Christendom: Triumph and Diversity.* 1996. An influential and highly accessible survey.

Brown, Peter. *The World of Late Antiquity.* 1971. A classic treatment of the period.

Cameron, Averil. *The Later Roman Empire.* 1993. *The Mediterranean World in Late Antiquity.* 1997. Excellent textbooks with bibliography and maps.

Clark, Gillian. *Women in Late Antiquity: Pagan and Christian Life-Styles.* 1993. The starting point of modern discussion; lucid and reliable.

Harries, Jill. *Law and Empire in Late Antiquity.* 1999. Explores the presence and practice of law in Roman society.

Lee, A. D. *Information and Frontiers: Roman Foreign Relations in Late Antiquity.* 1993. An exciting and original investigation.

Maas, Michael. *Readings in Late Antiquity: A Sourcebook.* 2000. Hundreds of ancient sources in translation illustrating all aspects of late antiquity.

Markus, Robert. *The End of Ancient Christianity.* 1995. Excellent introduction to the transformation of Christianity in late antiquity.

Rich, John, ed. *The City in Late Antiquity.* 1992. Important studies of changes in late antique urbanism.

Thompson, E. A. *The Huns,* rev. Peter Heather. 1996. The best introduction to major issues.

Notes

1. Libanius, *On the Temples,* in A. F. Norman, *Libanius: Selected Works* (1977), 107–109.

2. Ambrose, *Commentary on Paul's First Letter to the Corinthians,* trans. Karl Frederick Morrison, *Rome and the City of God* (1964), 46–47.

3. Nigel G. Wilson, ed, *Saint Basil on the Value of Greek Literature* (1975).

4. Marcia L. Colish, *Medieval Foundations of the Western Intellectual Tradition* (1997), p. 49.

5. Salvian, *On the Government of God,* trans. Jeremiah O'Sullivan, *Fathers of the Church: The Writings of Salvian the Presbyter* (1947), 132–137, with some slight changes.

6. John Helgeland, *Christians in the Military: The Early Experience* (1985), p. 64–65.

Byzantium, Islam, and the Latin West: The Foundations of Medieval Europe, 550–750

One gray day in central Germany in 740, an English monk named Boniface swung his axe at an enormous oak tree. This was the sacred Oak of Thor, where German men and women had prayed for centuries to one of their mightiest gods. Some local Christians cheered and applauded the monk. But an angry crowd of men and women gathered as well, cursing Boniface for attacking their sacred tree. Then something extraordinary occurred. Though Boniface had only taken one small chop, the entire tree came crashing down, split neatly into four parts. Boniface's biographer, a monk named Willibald, explained the strange event as God's judgment against "pagan" worshipers. In Willibald's account of the incident, the hostile crowd was so impressed by the miracle that they immediately embraced Christianity. As the news spread, more and more Germans accepted the faith, and Boniface's fame grew. According to Willibald, "The sound of Boniface's name was heard through the greater part of Europe. From the land of Britain, a great host of monks came to him—readers, and writers, and men trained in other skills."[1]

Whether or not the miracle at the Oak of Thor actually occurred, Boniface, a skilled diplomat who cooperated closely with the pope in Rome, played a leading role in spreading Christianity among the peoples of northern Europe. The Christian missionaries who traveled to lands far beyond the Mediterranean world brought Latin books and established monasteries, where a few men and women learned to read and write. Through Christianity and the literacy that spread from these monastic centers, the monks established unbreakable ties to Roman learning and the late antique world.

But Boniface was not Roman. He was English, a descendant of the Anglo-Saxon invaders who took control of much of Britain after the Roman legions

Chapter Outline

- Byzantium: The Survival of the Roman Empire
- The New World of Islam
- The Birth of Latin Christendom

Theodolinda's Gospel Book: Pope Gregory the Great gave a valuable copy of the Gospels to the Lombard queen Theodolinda when her son was christened in 603. Jewels, enamels, and Roman cameos decorated the book's covers. By giving lavish gifts to the polytheist rulers of Germanic states, Gregory hoped to encourage their conversion to Christianity.

abandoned it in the early fourth century. Boniface's England (as southern Britain is called after the Anglo-Saxon settlements) was just one of the former Roman provinces in western Europe in which Germanic and Roman cultures had mixed. In Spain, Italy, France, and North Africa as well, the new settlers grafted their societies onto a still-living Roman stalk. The intermingling of these cultures produced Christian kingdoms on a Roman foundation. Historians refer to these kingdoms collectively as Latin Christendom.

The Latin Christendom that came to dominate western Europe was only one of three major civilizations that emerged on the ruins of the late antique Roman world and that constituted the West during this period. A second major cultural force was taking shape as Boniface chopped down the Oak of Thor. This was the Byzantine Empire, which consisted of the eastern provinces of the Roman Empire. Roman rule continued uninterrupted in the Byzantine Empire, and its citizens continued to call themselves Roman. Because their capital was Constantinople, a city previously known as Byzantium, historians today refer to the inhabitants of the empire as Byzantines. By the time of Boniface the Byzantine Empire, also known as Byzantium, had dramatically shrunk in size and endured many hardships, especially in its wars with the Islamic Empire. Yet in the process Byzantium developed a vibrant Christian culture that spread through the Balkans and influenced eastern Europe and eventually Russia. As the dominant Christian power in the eastern Mediterranean, Byzantium played a significant role in Western political and cultural life for a thousand years as a vigorous, militaristic empire; as a center of learning; and as the most important intermediary between the peoples of western Europe and the Middle East.

During this same period, another religion—Islam—shook the foundations of the late antique world, creating a third major civilization. In the century after the death of its founder, the prophet Muhammad, in 632, Islam's followers burst from their home in Arabia to conquer an empire stretching from Spain to central Asia. Muslims (believers in Islam) rejected Christianity and did not adopt Roman law. Nevertheless they absorbed some Roman institutions of imperial government, which played a fundamental role in shaping their empire.

These three civilizations—Latin Christendom, Byzantium, and Islam—transformed the world of late antiquity. Historians call the new era they inaugurated the Middle Ages (550–1450), or the West's medieval period. We consider all three of these medieval civilizations parts of Western civilization because they emerged in the Middle East and Europe, the core lands where civilization began. Moreover, all three drew from Rome's cultural, administrative, and religious legacy, although in different ways. Finally, these civilizations all centered on monotheistic religions that shared basic beliefs about God and the origin of their faiths. However, because each of these medieval civilizations defined itself as an exclusive community of faith, cultural and political boundaries developed between them that are still visible today. Byzantium and Latin Christendom grew apart, and Islam gained an adversarial status in Christian eyes that continues in the minds of some people to this day.

To understand the impact of this era, we will explore three questions in this chapter: (1) How did the Roman Empire's eastern provinces evolve into the Byzantine Empire? (2) How did Islam develop in Arabia, and how did its followers create a vast empire so quickly? (3) How did Latin Christendom—the new kingdoms of western Europe—build on Rome's legal and governmental legacies and how did Christianity spread in these new kingdoms?

Byzantium: The Survival of the Roman Empire

The emperor Justinian (r. 527–565) tried to restore the glory of the Roman Empire by reconquering Roman provinces in North Africa, Italy, and parts of Spain from Germanic rulers who had established kingdoms in these territories in the fifth century. When Justinian died, his realm extended from southern Spain to the Persian frontier. As we saw in Chapter 6, it was an empire in which many of the institutions and traditions of the late antique Roman state, such as the imperial bureaucracy and provincial organization, still functioned. Despite these continuities with the Roman Empire of earlier centuries, Justinian brought profound changes to his empire. By insisting that his subjects follow Orthodox Christianity and by eradicating the last traces of polytheist worship, he gave religious unity and strength to his empire. By emphasizing the role of Christianity in every aspect of government, education, and other aspects of daily life, he made classical culture a part of Christian life. Because of these profound changes in imperial life that Justinian's reign inaugurated, historians refer to the Roman Empire during his reign and afterwards as the Byzantine Empire. After Justinian's death in 565, the Byzantine Empire began losing territory to enemies who surrounded the empire on all sides. The economy changed due to the loss of rich territories to Islamic conquerors. In response, emperors reorganized Byzantium for military purposes. Several important Roman institutions remained from late antiquity, however: the emperor with his imperial bureaucracy, the army, and the Orthodox Church. These institutions gave strength to the Byzantine Empire and helped it endure many challenges.

AN EMBATTLED EMPIRE

By 750, the Byzantine Empire was reduced to a much smaller regional power struggling for survival against many enemies. Avars and Slavs seized the Balkans. Italy fell to Lombard invaders. Persia continued its attacks against Byzantium. The worst threat came from the Muslim armies that conquered Egypt, North Africa, and Syria, the empire's richest territories. As the Byzantines struggled to recover from these catastrophic losses, their fragile empire began to change.

The Balkan Front: Avars, Slavs, and Bulgars

The Avars were a nomadic people with a bone-chilling reputation for cruelty and ferocity in warfare who first appeared on the steppes north of the Black Sea in the sixth century. Based in the plains of present-day Hungary, the Avars' territory extended into central Europe. These tenacious warriors posed a constant menace to the new kingdoms taking shape in Italy and France as well as Byzantium (see Map 7.1).

Like the Huns in the fifth century, the Avars created an empire by forcing conquered peoples to serve in their armies. Some of the peoples were Slavs. Between about 400 and 600, Slavic societies had formed from a blending of many cultures and ethnic groups, including Dacians, Goths, and Sarmatians. The Slavic communities that developed in eastern Europe between the Baltic Sea and the Balkans lay outside Byzantium's borders. Thus, they knew little of Roman models of politics, administration, agriculture, and social organization. Their Avar conquerors ruled by brute force, and most Slavs could not win back their independence. A few Slavic communities managed to overthrow Avar rule, however. In the middle of the seventh

■ **Map 7.1 The Byzantine Empire, ca. 600**

By 600 the Byzantine Empire consisted of Anatolia, Greece, part of the Balkans, Syria, Egypt, and some territories in North Africa and Spain. Until the rise of Islam, the Persian Empire remained its greatest enemy.

(a)

■ Avar Stirrups and Saber

Originally a nomadic people from central Asia, the Avars settled in Hungary and created an empire in central Europe. They depended on their heavily armed cavalry in battle. Byzantine military writers carefully studied Avar cavalry tactics and maneuvers. This pair of iron stirrups (a) supported the weight of heavily armed cavalry and gave an Avar rider extra striking power with a slashing saber (b).

(b)

century, for example, in the territory of the modern Czech Republic, the Slavic king Samo led a successful revolt against the Avars and ruled a small, independent kingdom for nearly forty years.

In the second half of the sixth century, bands of Slavs began to migrate south across the Danube River into the Balkans, searching for new homes. Collaborating with groups of marauding Avars, the Slavs settled in sparsely populated frontier lands in the northern Balkans. As the Slavs pushed south, many Byzantines fled their cities, abandoning them to the invaders.

By 600, Slavic groups had seized most Byzantine lands from the Danube to Greece. In 626, Slav and Avar forces attacked Constantinople from the northwest, while their Persian allies approached from the east. The capital city survived their combined assault, but the Byzantines never reasserted control over their old territories.

Farther north, in the territory between the Danube River, the Black Sea, and the Balkans, nomadic peoples called Bulgars established rule over the largely Slavic inhab-

itants. The Bulgars destroyed old Roman cities there and expelled Christians. Between the late seventh and ninth centuries, the Slavs and Bulgars merged into an independent Slavic-speaking kingdom called Bulgaria. As we will see in the next chapter, this new kingdom frequently waged war with Byzantium.

The Italian and North African Fronts

At the end of the sixth century, Byzantine emperors reorganized their possessions in Italy and North Africa into two new administrative units called *exarchates*. Because of their distance from Constantinople and the weight of the local problems they confronted, the two exarchates remained somewhat independent of the rest of the Byzantine Empire. Governors called exarchs ruled the exarchates, holding authority over civilian as well as military affairs—a break from Roman tradition. This joint command augmented the exarch's authority and independence. The Exarchate of Carthage, which consisted of North Africa and southern Spain, lasted until 698 when it fell to Muslim armies.

In Italy, the exarchate was based in the capital city of Ravenna, located in an easily defensible marshy area on the northeastern coast. The Exarchate of Ravenna consisted of Byzantine possessions in Italy and Sicily, including the city of Rome, where the support of the pope was important for implementing Byzantine policies. After the Lombard invasion in the late sixth century, the Exarchs of Ravenna struggled to maintain control of Italy. The Lombards eventually captured Ravenna and put an end to the exarchate in 751.

The Persian Front

Ruled by the Sasanian dynasty, Persia continued to threaten Byzantium after Justinian's death. The two powers fought intermittently for the rest of the sixth century. In 602 the struggle entered a new and final phase when the Persian ruler Chosroes II launched a series of devastating attacks against Byzantium. In 614 Chosroes seized Antioch, the richest Roman city in Syria. Then he captured Jerusalem, the holiest Christian city in the Byzantine Empire, and stole the holiest relic in the Christian world: a fragment of the cross on which Jesus reportedly had been crucified, known as the True Cross.

Motivated by a desire to avenge these losses and regain the holy relics, the Byzantine emperor Heraclius (r. 610–641) devoted his life to crushing the Persians once and for all. This resourceful and tenacious emperor spent most of his reign locked in a life-and-death struggle against Persia. In 622 Heraclius took a huge gamble. Leaving Constantinople in the hands of its capable patriarch Sergius, he led the Byzantine army deep into Persian territory, where he campaigned for years at a time. Believing that Constantinople now lay vulnerable due to the emperor's absence, the Persians made an alliance with the Avars in 626 and attacked the Byzantine capital. The city's massive walls, however, thwarted their assault. After two more years of desperate fighting, Heraclius finally defeated Chosroes on Persian territory.

When Heraclius defeated the Persian emperor, he recovered the fragment of Jesus' cross that had been stolen from Jerusalem. When the Byzantine emperor returned the cherished relic to Jerusalem, he won a spiritual as well as a military and political triumph. Writers of the day described his struggle with Persia as a victory of Christianity. Heraclius announced his victory to the inhabitants of Constantinople with these words: "Let all the earth raise a cry to God . . . and let all we Christians, praising and glorifying, give thanks to the one God, rejoicing with great joy in his holy name, for fallen is the arrogant Chosroes, opponent of God." Despite the rejoicing, Heraclius's victory over Persia had exacted a huge toll. It left the Byzantines (and the Persians) too exhausted to resist the sudden onslaught of a new enemy, the Muslim Arab armies.

■ **King David Plate**

Nine silver plates made in Constantinople about 630 illustrate scenes from the career of the biblical King David. The largest plate (about 20 inches in diameter) shows David battling the giant Goliath. Though the subject matter is biblical, the style of representing clothing, human bodies, and spatial relationships comes directly from the classical tradition. The artist may have intended to show a connection between the warrior king of the Bible and the emperor Heraclius, who defeated the mighty Persian emperor Chosroes II.

The Islamic Front

A ferocious new enemy challenged Byzantium from the east after the defeat of the Persian emperor: the armies of Islam. After the establishment of the Islamic caliphate in the 630s, Islamic armies in search of booty attacked the Byzantine Empire continually from the east, raiding deep into Anatolia (modern Turkey) and sometimes threatening Constantinople itself. In 636, the formidable enemy crushed a Byzantine army at the battle of the Yarmuk River, forcing the Byzantines to abandon the wealthy province of Syria. A few years later Arab troops seized Egypt from Byzantine hands. Encouraged by their victories, an enormous Arab force of more than 100,000 men and 1,800 ships besieged Constantinople itself between 716 and 718. The

FAILURE OF COMMUNICATION BETWEEN EMPEROR AND CALIPH

....

The Byzantine emperor Leo III (r. 717–741) corresponded with the Caliph Umar II (r. 717–720). This letter from Leo demonstrates the importance of religious beliefs in defining relations between the two empires. Leo's letter sarcastically criticizes Muslim beliefs and refuses to address Umar by his Muslim religious title "Commander of the Believers." There would be little progress in the mutual understanding of Muslims and Christians for the next thousand years.

Emperor Flavianus Leo, the Servant of Jesus Christ . . . to Umar, the Chief of the Saracens:

What exact reply can I make to all the arguments you advance against me? . . . As a matter of fact, nothing would induce us to discuss with you our doctrines, since our Lord and Master Himself (Jesus Christ) has bidden us refrain from exposing our unique and divine doctrine before heretics, for fear it be turned into ridicule, and least of all before those to whom the predictions of the Prophets of the Bible and the testimony of the Apostles are as something strange. This is the rule we preserve towards others. It is true that we have several times written to you, and shall write to you again as necessity demands, but it has always been about mundane affairs, never about affairs divine. Still, Holy Writ bids us reply to those who question us and maintain silence before those who do not. You call

"the Way of God" these devastating raids which bring death and captivity to all peoples. Behold your religion and its recompence. Behold your glory, you who pretend to live an angelic life. As for us, instructed in and convinced of the marvelous mystery of our redemption, we hope, after our resurrection, to enjoy the celestial kingdom, so we are submissive to the doctrines of the Gospel, and wait humbly for a happiness such that "eyes have never seen it, nor ears ever heard it, but which God has prepared for those who love Him" (I Cor. II,9). We do not hope to find there springs of wine, honey or milk. We do not expect to enjoy there commerce with women who remain forever virgin, and to have children by them, for we put no faith in such silly tales engendered by extreme ignorance and by paganism. May such dreams, such fables remain distant from us. "The kingdom of God consisteth not in eating and drinking" (Rom. XIV,17), as saith the Holy Spirit, "but in justice," and "at the resurrection men will not marry women, nor women men, but they shall be as the angels" (Matt. XXII,30). For you who are given up to carnal vices, and who have never been known to limit the same, you who prefer your pleasures to any good, it is precisely for that reason that you consider the celestial realm of no account if it is not peopled with women.

Source: From Arthur Jeffery, "Ghevond's Text of the Correspondence between 'Umar II and Leo III," *Harvard Theological Review* 37 (1944): pp. 269–332. Reprinted with permission from Harvard Theological Review.

---

attack failed because of the strength of Constantinople's walls, the courage of the defenders, and logistical problems among the Arabs. Some Byzantines claimed that the Virgin Mary had helped defend their capital.

Undismayed by their failure to capture Constantinople, Arab troops soon resumed their annual raids into Byzantine territory, defeating every Byzantine army that opposed them. Finally, in 740, Emperor Leo III (r. 717–741) won the Byzantine Empire's first important victory over the Muslim armies at the battle of Akroinon in western Asia Minor. Exhausted Byzantine troops could not go on the offensive, but they had slowed Arab momentum against their empire.

EMPEROR, ARMY, AND CHURCH

Despite assaults from so many directions, three institutions enabled the Byzantine Empire to survive the turmoil of this period: the emperor, who set policies and safeguarded his subjects' welfare; the army that defended the realm's frontiers; and the Christian Church, which provided spiritual guidance.

Imperial Administration and Economy

Based in the capital city of Constantinople, the emperor stood at the very center of Byzantine society. His authority, which his people believed had been granted by God, reached to every corner of the empire. This supreme ruler governed with the assistance of a large bureaucracy that he tightly controlled. In this hierarchical bureaucracy different clothing indicated different levels of importance. Only the emperor or members of his household, for example, could wear the color purple, a symbol of royalty. High dignitaries wore silk garments of different colors encrusted with jewels; the higher the official, the more gems he was permitted to display. Courtiers lined up in elaborate processions in order of their importance, as indicated by the color of their clothing and shoes.

Men fortunate enough to obtain a position in the imperial government acquired considerable wealth and influence. For this reason leading provincial families sent their sons to Constantinople in search of positions in the imperial hierarchy. Through this method of recruitment Constantinople remained in close touch with the outlying regions of the empire. However, many men obtained their positions by bribing court officials who worked for the emperor. This practice produced corruption throughout the system as officials gave jobs to men on the basis of bribes rather than talent.

From his position at the head of this elaborate hierarchy, the emperor controlled Byzantium's economy. When Justinian died, the imperial taxation system that Constantine had established in the early fourth century still generated the funds that kept the imperial system working. Imperial officials also minted coins, enriching many cities and spurring a flourishing cash-based economy.

By the end of the seventh century, however, when the rich provinces of Egypt and Syria and the wealthy cities of Alexandria, Antioch, Jerusalem, and many others had fallen to the Arabs, the Byzantine economy stumbled. Thousands of refugees from lands conquered by Muslims streamed into the empire and strained its dwindling resources. In conquered provinces, Muslim rulers monopolized Middle Eastern trade revenues and prevented Byzantine merchants from participating in long-distance commerce. Cut off from foreign markets, Byzantines stopped manufacturing goods for export. As the economy shriveled, Byzantines stopped building new homes and churches. By 750, the standard of living in most Byzantine cities steeply declined.

The Military System

Byzantine society was organized in constant preparation for war. Emperors relied on their armies to protect Constantinople, the nerve center of the shrinking Byzantine state, and defend against invaders. By about 650, emperors abandoned the late antique system of provinces and reorganized their forces in Asia Minor into four military districts called themes, each with its own army and administration commanded by a general chosen by the emperor. The theme's armies developed strong traditions of local identity and prided themselves on their expert military skills, a legacy the Byzantine Empire inherited from Rome. These military forces remained strong enough to keep the empire from collapsing in spite of devastating losses to Islamic armies throughout the seventh century.

By 750 the themes developed considerable independence from Constantinople and were the basis of further reorganization of the agricultural economy and procedures for recruitment. Soldiers and sailors who were once paid in cash from the emperor's tax revenues now were granted land on which to support themselves. Fighting men had to provide their own weapons from their income as farmers.

Even with reorganized defenses, Constantinople could not be protected without naval power. During the seventh and eighth centuries, the Byzantine fleet successfully kept Arab forces at bay through the use of "Greek Fire," a kind of napalm hurled against enemy ships to ignite them. Muslims soon learned how to use "Greek Fire," but the Byzantines used it more effectively in battle.

The Church and Religious Life

Most Byzantines identified themselves as Orthodox Christians, meaning that they followed the kind of Christianity practiced by the emperor and the court in Constantinople. They accepted the doctrines established by the Council of Chalcedon in 451 that defined Christ's human and divine natures as being united in one divine "person" without any separation, division, or change. This distinguished Byzantine Christians from other Christian communities that interpreted the nature of Christ differently, as we saw in Chapter 6. Constantinople boasted so many churches and sacred relics that by 600 Byzantines had begun to think of it as a holy city, protected by God and under the special care of the Virgin Mary, Jesus' human mother. Churchmen taught that Constantinople was a "New Jerusalem" that would be at the center of events at the end of days when God would bring history to an end and judge humanity.

Like the empire itself, the Byzantine clergy had a hierarchical organization. The Patriarch, or chief bishop, of Constantinople led the Orthodox Church, administering several thousand clergymen in the capital and directing church affairs throughout the empire. Emperors generally controlled the Patriarchs, and often they worked closely together, serving Byzantium's spiritual needs. The Patriarch helped impose religious unity throughout Byzantium by controlling the network of bishops based in cities. As leaders of urban religious life, bishops supervised the veneration of the saints' relics stored in each city's churches.

Byzantines believed that the relics protected each community, as the pagan gods had done in the pre-Christian past. Bishops often came from the city's elite. They continued the

■ Christ on Byzantine Coins: An Emperor's Piety

Coins often indicate beliefs important to the society that minted them. The emperor Justinian II (r. 685–695) introduced a new kind of coin that for the first time depicted the head of Christ. The emperor moved his own image holding a cross to the back of the coin, a statement of his subordination to Christ.

Continuity in Portraits of God from Polytheism to Christianity

This fine icon of Christ Pantokrator (Lord of All), left, is located in the monastery of Saint Catherine at Mount Sinai in Egypt. Painted in the last decades of the seventh century, it portrays Christ's face in the same style that we can see on coins of the period (see the illustration on the previous page). The icon demonstrates the highest level of Roman painting techniques. With its long hair and beard, Christ's portrait echoes ancient representations of Zeus, chief of the old Greek gods. We can see similarities between the portrait and this marble head of Zeus, below, from the fourth century B.C.E.

centuries-old Mediterranean tradition of leadership and decision making on the local level.

Many cities also had monasteries, which played a significant role in the empire's daily life. Men and women went to separate monasteries to live a spiritual life, praying for their salvation and that of other people. People in need of assistance, such as orphans, the elderly, battered wives, and the physically and mentally ill, found refuge and assistance in many monasteries. Monks and nuns regularly distributed food and clothing to the needy outside the monastery walls. Generous donors gave lavishly to monasteries to fund these activities, and many monasteries grew extremely wealthy through these gifts. Some monks championed the use of images of Jesus, the Virgin Mary, and the saints as means of reaching God.

As the Islamic Empire absorbed groups whom the Orthodox Christian Byzantines considered heretical, such as Monophysite Christians living in Syria and Egypt, Byzantium's population became almost entirely Orthodox. The resulting unity of faith and culture helped hold the

empire together during its darkest hours in the seventh century.

During the seventh and eighth centuries, the traditional Roman educational system gave way to Christian instruction. As we saw in Chapter 6, by about 600, city leaders had stopped paying schoolmasters to offer traditional instruction because they lacked funds. Pious Christians also developed a deep suspicion of classical learning, with its references to ancient gods and customs frowned on by the Church. People now learned how to read by studying the Bible, not the classics of Greek antiquity. Knowledge of classical literature and science disappeared everywhere except in Constantinople, and even there the academic community was tiny. Byzantines nearly forgot the history and knowledge of classical antiquity. Many Byzantines, for example, thought that the marble statues from earlier centuries adorning their cities were sinister demons.

During the seventh century, most Byzantines could neither read nor write. Only a few people obtained an education in law, literature, mathematics, or philosophy. Use of

Latin disappeared except among those scribes who communicated with the kingdoms of western Europe. No more than a handful of Byzantines could write the elegant Greek that had been the language of learning for nearly 2,000 years.

Icons and the Iconoclastic Controversy

As the Muslims and other enemies tore at the empire, Byzantines wondered why God was punishing them so severely. Their answer was that somehow they were failing God. Convinced that only appeasing God could save them, Emperor Leo III (r. 717–741) took action. He forcibly converted communities of Jews to Christianity in order to make a uniformly Christian empire. More significantly, he challenged the use of icons°, the images of God and saints found everywhere in Byzantine worship.

Byzantine theologians understood icons as vehicles through which the divine presence could make itself accessible to believers. Churchmen cautioned that God or saints do not actually reside within the icons, and so believers should not worship the images themselves. Rather, they should consider icons as doorways to a spiritual world, enabling believers to encounter a holy presence. Thus Byzantines treated icons with great love and respect.

The first Christians refused to make images of Christ and other holy individuals. They had two reasons for banning such representations. First, the Hebrew Bible forbids creating any representations of God. Second, they thought that Christians might start to worship their images in the same way that polytheists worshiped statues in their temples. "When images are put up, the customs of the pagans do the rest," wrote one church leader in the fourth century.

Despite such warnings, Christians responded to the beautiful polytheist statues and images that filled the cities in which they lived. Christian sculptors and painters started to create a uniquely Christian art that combined religious beliefs with the styles and techniques of classical art. After Constantine converted to Christianity in 312 and put an end to the persecution of Christians, this new art flourished. Artists routinely portrayed Christ and the saints in churches. During the sixth and seventh centuries Byzantines used religious images with greater zeal than ever before. By 600, for example, the emperor placed a large image of Christ above the Bronze Gate, the main entrance to the imperial palace in Constantinople. Smaller paintings became intensely popular in churches and in people's homes.

Some Byzantine religious thinkers in the eighth century advised Emperor Leo that icon veneration should be halted because too many people believed icons were divine themselves. Following their advice, Leo decided to forbid use of icons, but public resistance forced him to move very carefully. For example, when he ordered workers to remove the image of Christ from the Bronze Gate at the imperial palace in 726, the people of Constantinople rioted. Four years later, Leo forbade the presence and veneration of holy images (except for crucifixes) throughout the empire on his own authority as the ruler chosen by God. The prohibition and destruction of icons, known as iconoclasm° (image breaking), sparked a bitter controversy that divided Byzantine society until 842.

Leo's iconoclasm backfired because the veneration of icons was such a vital part of popular religious life. He found it difficult to enforce iconoclasm outside Constantinople. Revolts broke out in Greece and southern Italy when imperial messengers arrived with orders to destroy images. The iconoclastic controversy affected international politics as well. Outraged by the emperor's prohibition of icons, the pope excommunicated Leo. In retaliation the emperor deprived the pope of political authority over southern Italy, Sicily, and Illyricum (the Balkan coast of the Adriatic Sea). The Roman popes never forgave the emperor for this slight. This conflict contributed to a growing rift between Greek Orthodox and Latin Christianity.

CHRONOLOGY

The Byzantine World

527–565	Reign of Justinian I
542	Bubonic plague spreads through Mediterranean
568	Lombards invade Italy
610	Heraclius arrives from Carthage and begins reign
614–616	Persians take Jerusalem and Egypt
624	Heraclius campaigns against Persia
626	Avars and Persians besiege Constantinople
630	Heraclius defeats Persian king and restores True Cross to Jerusalem
636	Byzantines lose Battle of Yarmuk: Arabs take Syria and Jerusalem
642	Muslims take Egypt
698	Muslims take Carthage
716–718	Muslims besiege Constantinople
740	Byzantines defeat Arabs at Akroinon
751	Lombards conquer Ravenna and end the Exarchate of Italy

After years of turmoil, two Byzantine empresses who sympathized with their subjects' religious convictions restored icons to churches. In 797, the empress Irene called a general church council that reversed Leo's ruling. After a brief renewal of iconoclasm, in 843 the empress Theodora introduced a religious ceremony for commemorating images, which Orthodox Christians still celebrate annually. Icons remain an integral part of Orthodox worship today.

■ **An Icon that Survived Iconoclasm:**
St. Peter in the Monastery at Mount Sinai
This image of St. Peter, painted sometime during the sixth century, is in the Monastery of St. Catherine on Mount Sinai in Egypt. Because Egypt was in Muslim hands when the iconoclastic controversy broke out, this image survived.

The New World of Islam

T he Muslim armies that battered Byzantium created a thriving civilization that transformed the Mediterranean world. Today more than one billion Muslims around the globe adhere to Islam, playing a significant role in world affairs. This rapidly growing faith has left an indelible stamp not only on the West but also on the rest of the world.

Islam originated in the early seventh century among the inhabitants of the Arabian peninsula. Like Christianity 600 years earlier, the new religion's emergence surprised the settled communities of the Middle Eastern and Mediterranean worlds. Through conquest and expansion, Muslims created a single Islamic Empire stretching from Spain to central Asia by 750 (see Map 7.2). In this section, we will examine the origins of Islam, its impact on neighboring empires, and how the Arab peoples created an imperial realm.

ARABS BEFORE ISLAM

Before the emergence of Islam, Arabs were tribal people from the Arabian peninsula and the Middle East who spoke Arabic, a semitic language related to Hebrew, Aramaic, and Akkadian. Despite their shared language, Arab communities took different forms. Those living in the interior of the Arabian peninsula led a nomadic life herding camels. On the edges of the desert they raised goats and sheep. In south Arabia, they farmed and lived in towns. These communities, however, were not unified into a single state.

Arabs have a long history in the Middle East. They were first mentioned in the Hebrew Bible about 1000 B.C.E., and Middle Eastern, Greek, and Roman historical records continued to describe them for 1,500 years as raiders of settled communities, but never as serious military threats. The Arabs became more threatening to their enemies after 300 B.C.E. because of a military innovation. They developed a new kind of saddle that let them ride the one-humped Arabian camel with greater comfort and efficiency in battle. Up to this time it took two men to use a camel in warfare, one to hold the reins and the other to hold the weapons. The new saddle let one rider grasp the camel's reins with one hand while slashing downward at enemy troops with a sword in his other hand. Warriors on camels could attack with speed and crushing force. As a result of this innovation, Arab military power developed rapidly.

Military strength combined with trade in luxury goods made some Arab communities wealthy and powerful. By the first century B.C.E. Arabs had seized control of Petra, a merchant city in modern Jordan that controlled the incense trade. Merchants brought this precious, fragrant spice used in religious rituals across the Arabian peninsula

■ **Map 7.2   The Expansion of Islam: The Umayyad Caliphate, ca. 750**

By about 750 the Umayyad caliphate had reached its greatest extent. It provided political unity to territories stretching from central Asia to Spain. Islam became the dominant religion in this vast empire.

from ports on the Red Sea and the Persian Gulf to Petra, where it was sold to other merchants from throughout the Middle East and the Mediterranean region. Petra also received merchandise such as ivory and gold from Egyptian traders. Other Arab cities such as Mecca and Medina, located on the western coast of the Arabian peninsula, also flourished due to long-distance caravan trade. Their merchants traded throughout the Middle East, sailed to India, and had extensive contacts with eastern Africa. At the same time, Arabs in north Arabia bred sturdier camels that could endure the harsh, arid terrain of central Asia. This enabled Arab merchants to travel to China along the silk route.

Most Arab communities organized themselves into tribes, each of which claimed descent from a common male ancestor. There was no formal government holding each tribe together. The chiefs who led their tribes did so by personal prestige and by the common consent of the tribesmen. Arab tribes protected the lives and property of all their members. Arabs constantly feuded with one another, killing the men and stealing the herds and women of other tribes. Honor required retribution for every grievance, and so cycles of violence often lasted for generations. An injury to any member of a tribe obliged fellow tribesmen to seek either vengeance or compensation. Some feuding men chose to settle their grievances through mediation. If both parties agreed, mediators would set fair terms of compensation.

Before the rise of Islam in the seventh century, most Arabs worshiped many gods, including natural objects such as the sun and certain rocks or trees. Some Arabs worshiped only a single deity. Unlike their Egyptian and Greco-Roman neighbors, however, they did not erect huge temples to these deities. Through their encounters with Jews, Christians, and Zoroastrians in Syria, Palestine, Mesopotamia, and Arabia, Arabs also learned about different sorts of monotheism, especially as revealed in sacred texts such as the Bible and the Avesta, the sacred text of Zoroastrians. Large Jewish communities existed in the cities of western Arabia as well as in Yemen, the southwest corner of the Arabian peninsula. Christianity had spread on Arabia's southern coast, and small groups of Zoroastrians lived in eastern Arabia. Arabs developed ideas about heaven and hell, about the individual judgment of the human soul after death, and about divinely inspired prophecy.

THE RISE OF ISLAM

Islam is based on the Qur'an and the teachings of the prophet Muhammad (ca. 570–632). Muhammad was born in 570 to the powerful Quraysh tribe in the cosmopolitan and wealthy west Arabian trading city of Mecca. This city was the site of the Kaaba, a sacred stone where polytheist Arabs worshiped various deities. As a young man Muhammad married a widowed businesswoman, Khadija, and worked as a caravan merchant. In this profession he earned a reputation as a skilled arbitrator of disputes. When he was meditating in solitude at about age 40, an angel appeared before him, saying, "Muhammad, I am Gabriel and you are the Messenger of God. Recite!" The angel gave him a message to convey to the people of Mecca. Muhammad's message was a call to the Arabs to worship the one true God (the god of Abraham) and to warn of the fires of hell if they failed to answer that call. Muhammad continued to receive these revelations for the rest of his life. They were written down as the Qur'an (meaning "recitation"), the holy book of Islam. Though Muhammad won some followers among friends and family, the people of Mecca initially did not accept his monotheist message.

In 622, Muhammad and his followers moved from Mecca to Medina, a city 200 miles to the north. Aware of Muhammad's skill as a mediator, several feuding tribes in Medina had invited him to settle their long-lasting disputes. Muhammad's emigration to Medina, known as the *Hijra,* is the starting date of the Muslim calendar. The event marks a historical turning point in the development of Islam. For the first time Muhammad and his followers lived as an independent community. As the prophet of God, Muhammad strictly regulated the internal affairs of his new community and its relations with outsiders, creating a society that was political as well as religious. At the center of this Islamic community lay the mosque°, the place where his followers gathered to pray and hear Muhammad recite the Qur'an.

Initially, Muhammad and his followers enjoyed good relations with the Jews in Medina. He and his followers even abided by some Jewish rituals, like turning toward Jerusalem while praying. But because the Jewish tribes refused to accept Muhammad's political authority, even though he did not demand that they convert, violence broke out. Muhammad changed the direction of prayer to Mecca and expelled a tribe of Jews from Medina in 625. Two years later Muhammad's followers massacred the men of another Jewish tribe, enslaving its women and children. With Jewish opposition eliminated and control of Medina secured, Muhammad and an army of his followers attacked Mecca, which surrendered in 630.

Using a combination of force and negotiating skills, Muhammad drew many Arab tribes into his new religious community. By the time of his death in 632 he had unified most of Arabia under Islam. Muhammad harnessed the enormous energy of the Arabian population, creating a tightly controlled community that was inspired by his teachings.

Islam as Revealed to Muhammad

Islam teaches that Allah (which means "God" in Arabic) revealed his message to Muhammad, the last prophet in a line that included Abraham, Moses, and David, all pivotal biblical figures in the Jewish tradition who transmitted divine instruction to humanity, and Jesus Christ, whom Muslims accept as a prophet but not the son of God. Muslims claimed Abraham as their ancestor because he was the father of Ishmael, whom they consider to be the father of the Arab peoples.

Muhammad taught his followers five basic principles called the Pillars of Islam°. *Islam* means "submission," and by performing these acts of faith Muslims demonstrate submission to the will of God. First, all Muslims must acknowledge that there is only one God and that Muhammad is his prophet. Second, they must state this belief in prayer five times a day. On Fridays, the noon prayers must be recited in the company of other believers. Muslims may say their prayers anywhere. Third, Muslims must fast between sunrise and sunset during Ramadan, the ninth month of the Muslim calendar. Fourth, Muslims must give generous donations of money and food to the needy in their community. Islam expects its followers to be kind to one another, especially to orphans and widows, and to work for the good of the entire Islamic community. Fifth, Muslims must make a pilgrimage to Mecca at least once in their lives if it is possible.

As the focus of prayer and pilgrimage, Mecca quickly became the center of the Muslim world. The Qur'an affirmed Mecca's special role in Islam with these words:

Announce the Pilgrimage to the people. They will come to you on foot and riding along distant roads on lean and slender beasts, in order to reach the place of advantage (the Kaaba) for them, and to pronounce the name of God on appointed days over cattle he has given them as food; then eat the food and feed the needy and the poor. (Qur'an 22:26)

The Kaaba in Mecca
In pre-Islamic times, Arabs worshiped a large, black stone at the Kaaba shrine in the center of Mecca. When Muhammad established Islam in Mecca in 629, he rejected the polytheist past and transformed the Kaaba into the holiest place in the Islamic world, revered as the House of God. Muslim teachers interpreted polytheist rituals that continued under Islam, such as walking around the Kaaba seven times, as symbols of the Muslim believer's entry into God's presence. Muslims from all over the world make pilgrimages to the Kaaba. These journeys foster a sense of shared religious identity among them, no matter where their homelands lie.

With the spread of Islam to Persia, Asia, and parts of Europe in the seventh century, Muslims from many different lands encountered one another in Mecca, developing a shared Islamic identity.

The Qur'an contains many examples of proper behavior for the community to follow, and Muslims look also to the prophet Muhammad's example as a guide. Muhammad taught his followers to struggle for the good of the community morally, spiritually, intellectually, and when necessary by force of arms. This combined effort is called *jihad*. Often translated as "holy war," *jihad* is a commitment to confront a community's problems through the teachings of a moral faith.

The Islamic Community After Muhammad

Muhammad had demonstrated a remarkable talent for leadership during his lifetime, but he did not choose anyone to succeed him. His death in 632 caused a profound crisis among his followers. Would the Islamic community stay united under a single new leader or break up into smaller groups? After many deliberations, the leaders of the community chose the prophet's father-in-law, Abu Bakr, to lead them. Abu Bakr (r. 632–634) became the first caliph, or successor to Muhammad. The form of Islamic government that evolved under his leadership is called the caliphate°.

Most Muslims supported Abu Bakr wholeheartedly, but some opposed him. One group claimed that Muhammad's son-in-law and cousin, Ali, should have become the first

caliph instead. Called the Shi'a (party) of Ali, this group developed into one of Islam's major sects, the Shiites. Other Arab tribes rejected not only Abu Bakr's succession, but Islam itself. They rebelled, claiming that their membership in the Islamic community had been valid only when Muhammad was alive. Abu Bakr crushed these forces in a struggle called the Wars of Apostasy (a word meaning renunciation of a previous faith). By the time of his death in 634, Abu Bakr had brought most of Arabia back under his control. In the course of these wars, he created a highly trained Muslim army eager to spread the faith and gain additional wealth and power. The rich Persian and Byzantine Empires became an irresistible target.

Attacks on the Byzantine and Persian Empires

Under the leadership of the second caliph, Umar (r. 634–644), Muslim forces moved north from the Arabian peninsula and invaded Byzantine and Persian territory. As we saw earlier, they seized Syria in 636. The next year they crushed the main Persian army and captured the Persian capital city, Ctesiphon. Within just a decade Islamic troops had conquered Egypt, Syria, and all of Persia as far east as India. Meanwhile, Muslim navies, manned by subject Egyptian and Syrian sailors and Arab troops, seized Cyprus, raided in the eastern Mediterranean, and defeated a large Byzantine fleet. Muslim armies were racing across North Africa without serious opposition when civil war broke out in 655 and temporarily halted their advance.

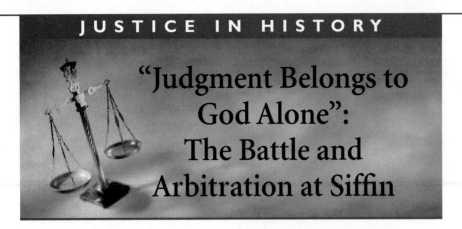

"Judgment Belongs to God Alone": The Battle and Arbitration at Siffin

On a spring day in 657, two Muslim armies confronted each other at Siffin, a village on the Euphrates River in Mesopotamia. The armies were commanded by men who had been longtime rivals, the Caliph Ali (r. 656–661) and Muawiya, the governor of Syria. Their rivalry stemmed from Muawiya's refusal to accept Ali's authority as caliph. The Battle of Siffin became a defining moment in the development of the Islamic state. Basic Islamic ideas about divine judgment were put to the test, leading to passionate debate about how God makes his judgment known to Muslims.

Ali had taken power after the assassination of his predecessor, Caliph Uthman, in 656. The murder went unpunished, but many people considered Ali responsible because when he became caliph he appointed officials known to have taken part in the murder and because he had never disavowed the crime. Uthman belonged to the influential Umayyad clan, and his supporters and family felt an obligation to avenge their kinsman's death. Chief among Ali's opponents was Muawiya, a leading member of the Umayyad clan. Muawiya maintained a strong army and powerful support in Syria.

The immediate provocation of the confrontation between Muawiya and Ali was Uthman's murder, but the men's quarrel also stemmed from tensions about status and membership in the Muslim community. The earliest converts to Islam and their descendants believed that their association with Muhammad entitled them to greater status than the many new non-Arab converts to the religion, most of whom supported Ali. Resenting Ali's popularity among the newer members of the Islamic community, the early converts supported Muawiya. Further support for Muawiya came from many tribal leaders who opposed the caliph's growing authority.

The new converts to Islam also had complaints. In their view, the earliest Muslims, including the Umayyad clan, unfairly enjoyed a privileged position in the Islamic community even though all Muslims were supposed to be treated equally.

When Ali and Muawiya confronted each other at Siffin, they hesitated to fight because many of their soldiers felt strongly that Muslims should not shed the blood of other Muslims. As one of Ali's followers said,

It is one of the worst wrongs and most terrible trials that we should be sent against our own people and they against us. . . . Yet, if we do not assist our community and act faithfully toward our leader, we deny our faith, and if we do that, we abandon our honor and extinguish our fire.[2]

So for three months, the armies engaged in only occasional skirmishes.

Finally, in July 657, real fighting broke out. Ali encouraged his men with these words: "Be steadfast! May God's spirit descend on you, and may God make you firm with conviction so that he who is put to flight knows that he displeases his God . . . "

The furious battle came to a sudden halt in July when Muawiya's soldiers held up pages of the Qur'an on the ends of their spears and appealed for arbitration. When Ali's men saw this symbolic gesture, they stopped fighting and demanded that their leader settle his differences with Muawiya peacefully through arbitration.

Mediation of conflicts by third-party arbitrators frequently occurred among Arab tribes. Muhammad himself had earned renown as a skilled mediator before Islam was revealed to him. However, the arbitration between Ali and Muawiya failed to resolve the conflict. The two men and their armies separated without having reached an agreement. Ali continued to rule as caliph for six more years, but his authority declined rapidly because many Arabs interpreted his willingness to go to arbitration as a sign of weakness. In 661 Ali was assassinated.

In contrast, Muawiya's power grew after the Battle of Siffin. He openly claimed the caliphate for himself and began making deals with the tribal leaders for their support in order to form his own coalition. After Ali's assassination, Muawiya became caliph.

The fact that the arbitration at Siffin occurred at all had long-lasting consequences. Most important, a small but influential Muslim faction emerged when the two leaders first confronted one another. They objected to Ali's initial agreement to arbitration, arguing that God was the only true arbitrator. They believed that Ali should pull out of the arbitration and submit to God's judgment, which they believed could be known only through battle. These Muslims wanted to fight Muawiya in order to find out what God wanted. This splinter group became known as the Kharijites or "seceders." The Kharijites expressed their view in the phrase "Judgment belongs to God alone."

The Kharijites went one step further in their beliefs. They declared not only that Ali was wrong to accept human arbitration, but that he and his supporters should no longer be considered Muslims. In their view, Ali and his supporters had committed an unpardonable grave sin by accepting arbitration. The Kharijites claimed that they were the only true Muslims. Small in numbers, they established several independent communities in the Islamic Empire and turned their back on Islamic society. They lived as bandits until the tenth century, when they disappeared from the historical record.

Other Muslims who disagreed with the Kharijites proclaimed that neither the Kharijites nor any other human being could know whether sinners were still Muslims in the eyes of God. In their opinion, believers would discover God's judgment on these matters only at the End of Days, when God will judge all humanity. ■

■ The Qur'an

Muslim artists devised elaborate Arabic scripts to enhance the beauty of the Qur'an, the holiest text of their faith. This page of the Qur'an, dating to the Umayyad caliphate, is written in the elegant and highly decorative Kufic script.

Questions of Justice

1. During this formative period of the Islamic Empire, how did different Arab groups explain how God makes his justice known to humans?

2. How did these ideas influence their beliefs about arbitration and authority?

Taking It Further

W. M. Watt. *The Formative Period of Islamic Thought.* 1973. This account discusses the formation of sects and political groups in early Islamic history.

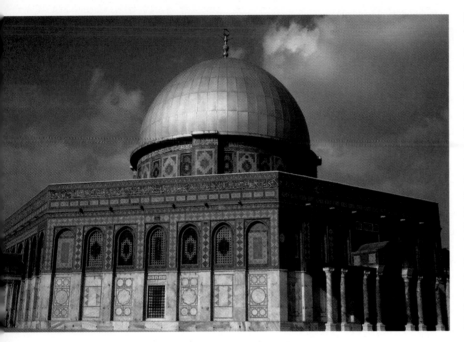

■ **The Dome of the Rock in Jerusalem**
The Dome of the Rock, an eight-sided building with a gilded dome, dominates Jerusalem's skyline. Completed in 692 on the Temple Mount (the site of the Jewish Temple destroyed by the Romans in 69 C.E.), the building encloses a rock projecting from the floor. Scholars disagree about the structure's original purpose. A Muslim of the tenth century thought it had been built as a statement of Islam's triumph at the heart of the holiest Christian city. During the sixteenth century the story began to circulate that when Muhammad ascended to heaven at night, his winged horse took one leap from Mecca to the rock and then sprang skyward. The artists who completed the dome's interior mosaics probably came from Constantinople, the only place where art of such high quality was being produced. The mosaic patterns also draw from contemporary styles in the Mediterranean world and Persia.

Two groups struggled for control of the caliphate in this civil war, which lasted for six years. On one side were Muhammad's son-in-law Ali, who had become caliph in 656, and his supporters. On the other side was the wealthy Umayyad family who opposed him. In 661 they arranged Ali's assassination and took control of the caliphate, creating a new dynasty that would last until 750. The Umayyads established Damascus in Syria as their new capital city, which shifted Islam's power center away from Mecca.

THE UMAYYAD CALIPHATE

The Umayyad dynasty produced brilliant administrators and generals. At the end of the civil war in 661, these talented leaders consolidated their control of conquered territories and established peaceful conditions in the empire. Then they resumed wars of conquest to spread the Islamic state's political sovereignty and to gain wealth.

Conquests

As we saw in Chapter 5, the Romans distinguished themselves from uncivilized "barbarians" who had not yet come under Roman rule. In a similar fashion, the Umayyads viewed the world as consisting of two parts: the "House of Islam," which contained the territories under their political control, and the "House of War," which included all non-Muslim lands, which they hoped to conquer. By 700, Muslim armies had rolled west across North Africa as far as the Atlantic Ocean in order to conquer non-Muslim lands.

Eleven years later, they invaded Spain and overthrew the Visigothic kingdom in just one battle. From Spain they attacked France, but in 732, Charles Martel "the Hammer," king of the warlike Franks, stopped their advance into Europe at the Battle of Poitiers. After their defeat, the Umayyad armies retreated to their territories in Spain.

Umayyad caliphs attempted to conquer the Christian kingdom of Nubia south of Egypt to obtain its gold and spread Islam. The Nubians successfully repelled the Muslim invaders, however, and in 661 a lasting peace treaty was signed between the Umayyad caliphate and Nubian kingdoms. This treaty was unique, because the Nubians belonged to the "House of War," which meant that they were enemies still to be conquered.

While struggling with the Nubians, Umayyad armies continued to strike at the Byzantine Empire. After seizing Egypt and Syria, they made regular attacks on the Byzantine territories, sometimes reaching as far as Constantinople, which remained protected by its formidable walls. After the last massive land and sea attacks failed in 717, Umayyad armies made no further attempt to conquer the Byzantine Empire. They did, however, continue to invade Byzantine Anatolia (in modern Turkey) every year to gain plunder.

Umayyad armies moved eastward with equal speed and success. They reached the territories of modern Pakistan and India and even penetrated central Asia, where they captured the caravan city of Samarkand in 710. During the Umayyad caliphate, this city served as a commercial hub on the trade route to China. In 751, just after the death of the last Umayyad caliph, Muslim armies defeated Chinese troops of the expansionist Chinese Tang dynasty at the Battle of Talas, beyond the Jaxartes River in central Asia. Despite their victory, the Muslims decided to halt their expansion and did not advance further into Chinese-controlled areas in central Asia. One unexpected consequence of this encounter was the introduction of paper from China into the Islamic world, from where it spread into Europe 500 years later.

Like the battle of Poitiers, which marked the limit of the Umayyads' expansion into western Europe, the battle of Talas marked the limit of Muslim military expansion into central Asia. For the next four centuries, these borders would define the Islamic world. Within a century the Umayyads built an empire that reached from southern France to central Asia and India. Never again would the entire world of Islam be united under one government.

Governing the Islamic Empire

Drawing heavily on the administrative systems of the Byzantine and Persian provinces they had conquered, the Umayyads developed a highly centralized and autocratic regime that changed the political character of the Muslim community. The first Umayyad caliph, Muawiya (r. 661–680), established a hereditary monarchy to ensure orderly succession of power. This was a major change in the caliphate. Unlike the first four caliphs who ruled by virtue of their prestige (as did Arab tribal chiefs), the Umayyads made the caliphate an authoritarian institution. Because of this, the soldiers protested that the Umayyads had turned "God's servants into slaves," corrupted the faith, and seized the property of God. A second civil war broke out (683–692), and the Umayyads emerged victorious.

In order to control their vast empire, Umayyad rulers developed a new administrative system. They designed new provinces that replaced old Roman and Persian administrative units. In addition, the Umayyads developed a professional bureaucracy based in the capital of Damascus to meet their expanding financial needs and to ensure that the taxes collected in the provinces came to the central treasury. Most of the administrators were local officials who had served the Roman or Persian empires. Many of them were non-Muslims, but a large number also converted to Islam. They provided significant administrative continuity between the caliphate and the empires that it conquered.

The Umayyads used the Arabic language to unify their empire. Arabic gradually replaced the languages of the conquered peoples. Only in Iran did Persian survive as a widely spoken language, and even there Arabic served as the language of government. In the Umayyad caliphate, the Arabic language functioned as Latin had done in the Roman Empire: It provided a common language for diverse subject peoples. By 800 Arabic had become the essential language of administration and international commerce in lands from Morocco to central Asia.

Settlements and Cities

The rapid expansion of Islam created problems for Umayyad rulers eager to consolidate their power. Arab armies had conquered enormous territories, but were only a small minority among the huge non-Muslim populations whose great wealth and manpower resources they controlled. Umayyad policy was to establish garrison cities in conquered lands to hold down the more numerous local populations. Just as Greek colonists followed in the footsteps of Alexander the Great in the fourth century B.C.E., Arab settlers from the Arabian peninsula migrated to newly conquered lands in great numbers. They established themselves first in the garrison towns where government officials were based, and then they became a significant presence in major cities, such as Alexandria, Jerusalem, and Antioch. Some immigrants were nomadic tribes that adopted a settled way of life for the first time. Others were farmers from the highlands of Yemen, who brought sophisticated irrigation systems and agricultural traditions to their new homes. Arab migrations to cities ended many old Arab traditions of nomadic life.

In addition to settling in existing cities, Arabs founded many new ones. In Egypt they built Fustat, which would later become Cairo. In North Africa, they established Kairouan in Tunisia. In Mesopotamia they created Basra, an important port city, as well as Kufa on the Euphrates River. Though built on a smaller scale than the major urban centers of the Roman and Persian Empires, most new Arab cities drew from Hellenistic town planning. They had a square shape, walls with gates on all four sides, towers, and a central plaza. In the heart of all of these cities, Umayyad caliphs built a mosque to emphasize the central role of Islam in community life and to celebrate their own authority. The magnificent mosques in Damascus, Jerusalem, and other cities were intended to surpass the grand Christian churches in prestige.

Urban life continued in the Byzantine cities such as Jerusalem, Antioch, and Alexandria that Muslim armies conquered, but with significant changes, especially in urban street patterns. Winding, narrow streets in which camels could easily maneuver replaced the long, straight, wide streets appropriate for wagons that typified Hellenistic and Roman cities. Wheeled vehicles gradually disappeared from use. Especially in markets, the old, wide streets and sidewalks filled up with small shops, and pedestrians walked through narrow alleys behind the shops.

Patterns of daily activity also changed under Muslim rule. With Islam now dominating public life, cities ceased to carry Greco-Roman culture. Theaters fell out of use because there was no Arabic tradition of publicly performed drama and comedy. The exercise fields, sports buildings, libraries, and schools associated with public baths and gymnasiums in the Classical Age also fell out of use, though people continued to enjoy bathhouses with heated pools.

Revenues once earmarked for gymnasiums and other public buildings now went to local mosques. These centers of Islamic urban culture replaced the forums and agoras of the Roman and Greek world as the chief public space for men. Mosque schools provided education for the community. Muslims gathered at mosques for public festivals and, of course, for religious worship. In their capacity as administrative centers, mosques provided courtrooms, assembly halls, and treasuries for the community. Judges, tax collectors, bureaucrats, and emissaries from the caliph conducted their affairs in the mosque precinct.

During the Umayyad caliphate, many Muslim farmers and craftsworkers lived in prosperous villages. Many of these small communities stood on the vast estates of rich landowners who controlled the workers' labor. The caliphate also sponsored huge land reclamation projects on the edges of the desert in Syria and Mesopotamia. Officials of the imperial government drew revenues directly from the villages that sprang up in these new farmlands.

Becoming Muslims

Islam sharply defined the differences between Muslims and their ethnically diverse subjects. The conquerors understood themselves as a community of faith. Only individuals who converted to Islam could gain full participation in the Islamic community. Their ethnicity did not matter. Therefore Muslims defined their new subjects by their religions, something Egyptians, Assyrians, Persians, Greeks, or Romans had never done. The Qur'an states that "there is no compulsion in religion," meaning that monotheists (Jews, Christian, and Zoroastrians) cannot be forced to convert to Islam. Muslims viewed polytheists differently. Polytheists had the choice of conversion to the Muslim faith or dying.

Throughout the Umayyad period, the number of Muslims grew slowly, reaching perhaps only 10 percent of the total population. Many Christians, Jews, and Zoroastrians willingly converted to the new religion. Other converts were slaves in the households of their Muslim owners. Still others were villagers who migrated to garrison cities and converted in the hope of sharing in the spoils of conquest—and avoiding the taxes demanded of non-Muslims. Their eagerness to convert threatened the tax base, and many Muslim officials refused to acknowledge their conversion and sent them back to their villages.

Conversion to Islam increased as Muslim armies fought their way across North Africa. In the huge area that stretches from Egypt to the Atlantic Ocean, the Muslims conquered many distinct polytheist ethnic groups whom the Arab conquerors collectively called Berbers. Faced with the choice of conversion or death, huge numbers of Berbers joined the victorious Muslim armies. Islam unified the Berber populations and brought them into a wider Islamic world. With the aid of these troops, Islamic power spread even more quickly across North Africa and into Spain.

Peoples of the Book

How do empires govern subject peoples? Do they have the same privileges and obligations as their rulers? Can they freely enter into the society of their masters? In previous chapters we have seen how the Assyrians, Persians, Hellenistic Greeks, and Romans answered these questions. Though their solutions differed, none of these great empires considered the religions of their subjects when deciding their place in society.

By distinguishing their subjects on religious, not ethnic grounds, the Umayyad caliphate took a different approach to governing their subject peoples. Jews, Christians, and Zoroastrians constituted the main religions among conquered peoples. Islamic law called them "Peoples of the Book" because each of these religious communities had a sacred book. They had lower status than Muslims, and they had to pay extra taxes, but they were free to practice their religion. Islamic law forbade their persecution or forcible conversion. For this reason, large communities of Christians, Jews, and Zoroastrians lived peacefully under Muslim rule.

Several Christian communities, separated by old controversies about doctrinal issues, coexisted within the Islamic Empire since the caliphate was indifferent to which Christian doctrine they followed. Followers of the Chalcedonian Orthodox church changed the language of prayer from Greek to Syriac and then to Arabic. Though these Christians had no direct ties with Constantinople, they followed the Byzantine emperors' Chalcedonian Orthodoxy. Thus their church was called the Melkite, or Royal, church. The Melkite church continues to be the largest Christian community in Muslim lands in the Middle East today. Another Christian church, called the Jacobite church, was formed by Monophysite Christians in the late sixth century, as we saw in Chapter 6. Its Bible and prayers are in Syriac. The Nestorian church, comprised of Christians who emphasized Jesus' humanity rather than the combination of his humanity and divinity, also flourished under Muslim rule in Persia, Syria, and northern Arabia. Nestorians also established communities in India, central Asia, and China. The variety of Christian communities in the caliphate was greater than in Byzantium and Latin Christendom.

Jewish communities also flourished throughout Umayyad lands, notably in Spain and Mesopotamia. Jews found their subordinate but protected status under Islam preferable to the open persecution they suffered in many Christian kingdoms. In Persia, Zoroastrian communities fared less well. As they were slowly forced into remote regions of central Iran, their numbers gradually dwindled. In the tenth century, many Zoroastrians migrated to India, where they are known today as Farsis, a word that means "Persians."

Commercial Encounters

The economic system of the Muslim world changed under Umayyad rule. From the time of the first conquests, revenues derived primarily from the huge amounts of gold and

THE PACT OF UMAR: ISLAM ENCOUNTERS THE GREAT FAITHS OF THE ANCIENT MIDDLE EAST

··················

Islam recognized Christians, Jews, and Zoroastrians as "Peoples of the Book" because they were monotheists and because their religions were based on holy texts. The Pact of Umar, *issued by the Caliph Umar I (r. 634–644), introduced the idea that Muslim authorities would protect them, though with restrictions. This letter was sent by the Christians of Syria to Umar I, spelling out the restrictions they accepted.*

When Umar . . . may God be pleased with him, accorded a peace to the Christians in Syria, we wrote to him as follows:

In the name of God, the Merciful and Compassionate.

This is a letter to the servant of God Umar, Commander of the Faithful, from the Christians of such-and-such a city. When you came against us, we asked you for safe-conduct for ourselves, our descendants, our property, and the people of our community, and we undertook the following obligations toward you:

We shall not build, in our cities or in their neighborhood, new monasteries, churches, convents, or monks' cells, nor shall we repair, by day or night, such of them as fall in ruins or are situated in the quarters of the Muslims.

We shall not give shelter in our churches or in our dwellings to any spy, nor hide him from the Muslims.

We shall not teach the Qur'an to our children.

We shall not manifest our religion publicly nor convert anyone to it.

We shall not prevent any of our kin from entering Islam if they wish it.

We shall show respect toward the Muslims, and we shall rise from our seats when they wish to sit.

We shall not seek to resemble the Muslims by imitating any of their garments, the headgear, the turban, footwear, or the parting of the hair.

We shall not mount our saddles, nor shall we gird swords nor bear any kind of arms nor carry them on our persons.

We shall not engrave Arabic inscriptions on our seals.

We shall not sell fermented drinks.

We shall not display our crosses or our books in the roads or markets of the Muslims. We shall only use clappers in our churches very softly. We shall not raise our voices in our church services or in the presence of Muslims, nor shall we raise our voices when following our dead (in funeral processions). We shall not show lights on any of the roads of the Muslims or in their markets. We shall not bury our dead near the Muslims.

We shall not take slaves who have been allotted to the Muslims.

We shall not build houses overtopping the houses of the Muslims.

We accept these conditions for ourselves and for the people of our community, and in return we receive safe-conduct.

If we in any way violate these undertakings for which we ourselves stand surety, we forfeit our covenant, and we become liable to the penalties for contumacy [resistance to authority] and sedition.

Source: From *Islam: From the Prophet Muhammad to the Capture of Constantinople, Volume 2: Religion and Society,* edited by Bernard Lewis, translated by Bernard Lewis, copyright © 1987 by Bernard Lewis. Used by permission of Oxford University Press, Inc.

---

silver taken in war, taxes, and contributions made by Muslims to support widows and orphans. To increase their revenues further, Umayyad rulers introduced a land tax for Muslim landowners, in imitation of Byzantine and Persian systems of taxation. Even the proud Arab tribesmen, for whom paying taxes was a humiliation because it implied subordination to a greater authority, had to pay taxes, though not as much as non-Muslims. With land tax revenues Umayyad caliphs could afford to establish a standing professional army. This further reduced the fighting role of individual Arab tribes. It also enabled caliphs to cement their authority more firmly.

Long-distance overland trade rapidly expanded due to the peaceful conditions in Umayyad lands. Although merchants could travel safely from Morocco to central Asia and earn great sums, such long-distance expeditions were ex-

pensive. Merchants had to invest considerable sums of money to cover the costs of a trading expedition in the hopes of making a profit at the end of the journey. The Qur'an approves of mercantile trading, and Islamic law permitted letters of credit, loans, and other financial instruments that made commerce over huge distances possible long before they were known in Europe.

Umayyad rulers further stimulated international commerce by creating a new currency that imitated Persian and Roman coinage. The Persian silver *drahm* (a word derived from the Greek *drachma*) inspired the Umayyad *dirham*, which became the standard coin throughout the caliphate by the 780s. Muslim merchants, as well as businessmen as far away as western Europe, Scandinavia, and Russia, used silver *dirhams* to pay for goods. For gold coinage the Umayyads minted the *dinar* (a word derived from a Roman

Islamic coin

(front)   (back)

Byzantine prototypes

(back)   (back)

■ Designing Muslim Coins:
The Encounter with Byzantine Prototypes

In the early years of the Umayyad state, caliphs experimented with the design of Islamic coins. Because Arabs had no tradition of minting coins, they borrowed freely from the images they saw on Persian and Byzantine coins. Then they made the necessary adjustments to change Christian or Persian symbols to Islamic ones. On a *dinar* of Abd al-Malik (r. 685–705) (top), the artist changed the Byzantine emperor Heraclius and his heirs, who carry globes with small crosses (shown on the back of a Byzantine coin at bottom left), to the caliph and his heirs, holding globes without crosses. On the Islamic coin's reverse side, Muhammad's scepter replaced the Christian cross (shown bottom right, on the back of another Byzantine coin). By the end of his reign, Abd al-Malik did away with images altogether and decorated his coins entirely with written quotations from the Qur'an.

coin, the *denarius*). Like the *dirham,* the *dinar* also became a standard coin in the caliphate as well as in distant lands. Merchants could depend on the value of this currency wherever they did business.

Camels played a significant role in the expanding Islamic economy because they made long-distance trade extremely profitable. Merchants had used domesticated camels throughout the Arabian peninsula for many centuries, but the caliphate's huge size and peaceful conditions brought new opportunities for long-distance camel-borne trade. Camels can carry heavy cargoes through harsh terrain for long periods, and they require little water. Because these "ships of the desert" do not need paved roads, caravan routes did not have to stick to Roman road systems. New trade routes suited for camels developed from Morocco to central Asia. Camel-based commerce proved so successful that between 700 and 1500, paved roads, as well as the carts and wagons that traveled on them, nearly disappeared. Furthermore, because of long-distance camel caravans, the Mediterranean Sea, the great superhighway of the Roman Empire, lost its primary place in international trade. The revenues earned from the camel caravans helped make the Umayyad caliphate extremely rich.

In addition to supporting long-distance overland trade by camel caravans, Umayyad caliphs also developed maritime trade. The Egyptian city of Alexandria became the chief Mediterranean naval base for Arab commercial shipping. The Syrian port cities of Acre and Tyre also contributed to maritime shipping in the eastern Mediterranean region. The Umayyads maintained peaceful conditions in the Persian Gulf and the Indian Ocean. Arab merchants sailed past Zanzibar and India to Canton in southern China, following sea routes established by Persian navigators. Arab traders also sailed down the coast of East Africa to obtain slaves and natural resources brought from the interior. In later centuries Muslim navigators reached Malaysia, Indochina, and eventually Indonesia and the Philippines.

By 850, Muslims in cities throughout the caliphate could buy many exotic luxuries. These goods included panther skins, rubies, and coconuts from India; paper, silk, fine ceramics, eunuchs (castrated men), slaves, and marble workers from China; hawks from North Africa; Egyptian papyrus; and furs and sugar cane from central Asia. People could also buy less-expensive fabrics and manufactured items crafted locally.

Arab traders also brought back valuable ideas and scientific knowledge from the peoples encountered through trade in the East. Many Arabic nautical terms derive from Persian, and late in the eighth century scholars translated Persian and Indian astronomical works into Arabic, the beginning of an explosion of scientific knowledge in the Islamic world.

Throughout the formative period of Islam and the Umayyad caliphate, Muslims took firm hold of territories stretching from North Africa to central Asia, creating a single political realm there for the first time in history. The inhabitants of the entire Arabian peninsula, with their trade connections to Africa and Asia, for the first time joined the peoples of the Middle East and the Mediterranean in an intricate system of commerce and government. These new commercial networks affected the economy of the Mediterranean world and Europe, making a deep impact on Europe's development. By replacing Roman civilization in North Africa and the Middle East, Muslims introduced a new monotheistic religion to the Mediterranean world.

CHRONOLOGY

The New World of Islam

CA. 570	Muhammad born in Mecca
622	Muhammad flees to Medina (the Hijra)
632	Muhammad dies in Medina
633–640	Muslims conquer Syria, Palestine, and Mesopotamia
640–642	Byzantines abandon Alexandria; Muslims conquer Egypt
651	Muslims conquer Persia
661	Caliph Ali is assassinated
661–750	Umayyad dynasty rules from Damascus
CA. 691–692	Dome of the Rock built in Jerusalem
706–715	Great Mosque of Damascus built
710	Muslim army reaches the Indus River in India
711	Muslims conquer Spain
732	Charles Martel defeats Muslims at Poitiers
751	Abbasid dynasty begins; Muslim armies defeat Chinese forces at Talas in central Asia

The Birth of Latin Christendom

By 750, several new kingdoms had emerged in the lands that once constituted the western part of the Roman Empire. The Lombards ruled in Italy; the Visigoths in Spain; and the Franks in modern-day France, Germany, and the Netherlands. Various Anglo-Saxon kings controlled most of England. These territories were not politically united as they had been under the Roman Empire (see Map 7.3). Though their populations were quite diverse ethnically and linguistically, they shared certain social and religious characteristics. They had enough in common that historians refer to these kingdoms collectively as Latin Christendom.

GERMANIC KINGDOMS ON ROMAN FOUNDATIONS

Historians describe these new kingdoms of Christendom as Germanic because the peoples who established them spoke languages related to modern German. Although most of these kingdoms borrowed from Roman law while establishing government institutions, they maintained their own cultural identity and relied on German methods of rule. For example, in the new kingdoms kinship obligations to a particular clan of blood relatives rather than citizenship, as in the Roman Empire, defined a person's place in society and his or her relationship to rulers. In the Germanic kingdoms personal loyalty rather than legal rights unified society.

Christianity became the dominant religion in the kingdoms, providing another powerful unifying force. Indeed, the faith united the disparate regions, as these realms' rulers followed the same form of Christianity as their subjects. The Germanic settlers and remaining Romans merged quickly through intermarriage. The particular kind of Christianity that spread into these kingdoms was Latin Christianity or Catholicism. Latin served as the language of worship, learning, and diplomacy in these kingdoms.

■ **Map 7.3   Europe, ca. 750**

By about 750 the kingdom of the Franks had become the dominant power in western Europe. The Umayyad caliphate controlled Spain, and the Lombard kingdom governed most of Italy. The Byzantine Empire held power in Greece, as well as its core lands in Asia Minor.

Anglo-Saxon England

Roman civilization collapsed more completely in Britain during the fifth century than it did on the European continent, largely because of Britain's long distance from Rome and the small number of Romans who had settled there. About 400, the Roman economic and administrative infrastructure of Britain fell apart, and the last Roman legions left the island to fight on the continent. Raiders from the coast of the North Sea called Angles and Saxons (historians refer to them as Anglo-Saxons) took advantage of Britain's weakened defenses and launched invasions. In their light, fast ships, they began to probe the island's southeast coast, pillaging the small villages they found there and establishing permanent settlements of their own. Many Roman Britons fled to Brittany on the northern coast of modern France, while others retreated to Cornwall, southern Scotland, and Wales.

The economic situation in Britain continued to deteriorate. By 420 coinage had fallen out of use on the island, and barter became the sole means of exchange. By 450, cities either shrank to very small villages or lay abandoned. A century later, fortified villas in the countryside—the last vestige of Roman life—had disappeared.

Christian worship evaporated temporarily in southeast England around this time due to the settlement of the polytheist Anglo-Saxons. Christianity hung on, however, in Wales, Cornwall, and southern Scotland. Due to the efforts of missionaries from Italy, Gaul, and Ireland, by 750 Christianity had re-emerged and become deeply embedded in Anglo-Saxon culture.

Because the small bands of Anglo-Saxon settlers fought as often among themselves as they did with the Roman Britons, the island remained fragmented politically during the first few centuries of the invaders' rule. But by 750, three warring kingdoms managed to seize enough land to coalesce and dominate Britain: Mercia, Wessex, and Northumbria.

Because Roman culture had virtually disappeared in these areas, Roman legal traditions did not influence Anglo-Saxon law. Moreover, Roman and Anglo-Saxon societies did not merge as they did in Spain, Italy, and Gaul. We can see evidence of this in the English language, which derives primarily from the Germanic languages spoken by the Anglo-Saxon settlers of Britain. In contrast, the Romance (or Roman-based) languages of Spanish, Italian, and French developed from Latin spoken in Rome's former provinces on the continent where Roman civilization was more deeply rooted. In Wales, which the Anglo-Saxons did not conquer, the Welsh language shows a combination of Latin and the region's older Celtic tongues.

The Franks: A Dual Heritage

The encounter between Roman and Frankish cultures from the third to the seventh century produced the largest and most powerful state in western Europe, the kingdom of the Franks. Yet the Franks had modest origins. In the third cen-

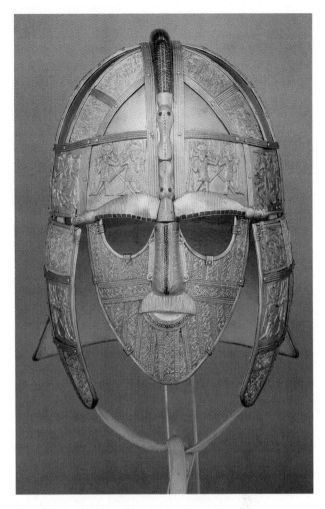

■ **Sutton Hoo: A King Proclaims His Power**

Around 625, the Anglo-Saxon ruler of a kingdom in eastern England was buried in his raiding ship under a massive mound at Sutton Hoo. This method of burial is entirely Germanic. An extremely rich array of military equipment, jewelry, and coins accompanied this monarch into the next world. These treasures illustrate the wealth and long-distance connections of his dynasty. The king's magnificent iron helmet with face mask and decorations in gold, silver, and precious stones is based on Roman ceremonial helmets of the late empire, but is in keeping with the armor of Anglo-Saxon warrior kings.

tury a number of small tribes living in what is now the Netherlands and the northwestern part of Germany organized themselves into a loose confederation. According to Roman records, Frankish warbands launched destructive attacks on northern Gaul (now northern France) and raided Spain and North Africa during the second half of the third century. The armies of the Roman emperor Constantine finally brought the Franks under control in the early fourth century. After that those Franks who lived beyond Roman borders did not dare to attack Rome, and those Franks living within the empire served faithfully as soldiers in the Roman army. These men retained dual identities, remaining both Frankish and Roman. As a third century soldier's gravestone proudly states: "I am a Frank, a Roman citizen, and an armed soldier."[3] Several Franks even became important Roman generals.

But in the course of the fifth century, as Roman imperial control of western Europe disintegrated, Frankish power grew. One group among the Franks, called Salians, gradually gained preeminence among the Frankish people. The Salians' leading family called themselves Merovingians because they claimed descent from a legendary warrior named Merovech. A crafty Merovingian war chief named Childeric ruled the Franks from about 460 until his death in 482.

During his long reign, Childeric set the stage for the rapid consolidation and expansion of Frankish power. Childeric gave Frankish warriors the opportunity to participate in campaigns to seize control of Gaul, rewarding them handsomely with loot. But the complex political situation in Gaul posed a problem for the Merovingian leader. After Roman imperial government collapsed throughout most of Gaul by the 420s, some independent groups of Romans continued to fight for control of territory against Huns, Visigoths, and other peoples who had settled there. In a few places Roman churchmen and aristocrats managed to hold on to some authority. Although Childeric was not Christian, he cooperated with these Romans in an effort to win their support and consolidate his power in northern Gaul, and the result was a stronger kingdom than any other in western Europe during this troubled period.

With the support of loyal Frankish soldiers, Childeric laid the foundation for the Merovingian kingdom. His energetic and ruthless son Clovis (r. 481–511) made the Franks the leading power in western Europe. Clovis aggressively expanded his father's power base through conquest of Gaul and neighboring territories. He also murdered many of his relatives and other Frankish chieftains whom he considered rivals. In 486 he overcame the last Roman stronghold in northern Gaul and stood as the most powerful ruler in western Europe.

Clovis's wife, Clotild, followed Latin or Catholic Christianity, the religion followed by most of the inhabitants of the former Roman Empire in western Europe. Historians refer to this version of Christianity as Latin Christianity because its followers used a Latin Bible, performed church services in Latin, and were native Latin speakers. Catholic Christianity, like the Greek-based Orthodox Christianity in the Byzantine Empire, teaches the full equality of the Father, the Son, and the Holy Spirit in the Trinity. In contrast to Catholic Christianity in the western provinces was the Arian Christianity practiced by the Germanic kings and their subjects, who had established new kingdoms in western Europe during the fifth century.

Arians believed that Christ was divine, but inferior to God the Father in rank, authority, and glory.

The theological distinction between Catholic and Arian Christians in western Europe was a crucial political issue that divided the Roman and Germanic populations. Around 500, perhaps influenced by his wife's beliefs, the polytheist Clovis converted to Catholic Christianity. About 3,000 warriors, the core of his army, joined their king in this change to the new faith. Clovis had practical reasons to convert as well. He intended to attack the Visigothic kingdom in southern Gaul. The Visigoths followed Arian Christianity, but their subjects, the Roman inhabitants of the region, followed Catholic Christianity. By converting to Catholicism, Clovis won the support of the Visigoths' subjects. With their help Clovis and his Frankish army crushed the Visigothic king Alaric II at the battle of Vouillé in the summer of 507, forcing him to retreat to Visigothic territories in Spain. Clovis now controlled almost all of Gaul as far as Spain.

Clovis also conquered other Germanic peoples as well. His armies overran the kingdom of the Thuringians to the east of his homeland. They also defeated the Alemanni, who lived in what are now Switzerland and southwest Germany. In order to consolidate his authority in these varied lands, Clovis needed recognition from both the emperor in Constantinople and the Roman Church in Gaul. He shrewdly achieved both. After defeating Alaric II, the Merovingian ruler won the Gallic clergy's support by donating much of the booty from his victory to the church of the most important saint in Gaul, Martin of Tours. Clovis then earned the recognition of the Byzantine emperor by formally acknowledging his authority. At the pageant when Clovis brought the treasure to Martin's church, ambassadors of the Byzantine emperor made him an honorary consul. Wearing a Roman military uniform, Clovis celebrated a Roman-style victory parade in which he scattered gold coins to the crowd. For the next three centuries, Merovingian kings followed Catholic Christianity and received similar honors from Byzantine emperors.

The Frankish kingdom thrived under several able monarchs in the sixth and seventh centuries. Continuing their father's expansionist policies, Clovis's sons conquered the Burgundian kingdom in 534 and acquired Provence (the southern coast of Gaul) two years later. They also carved out a foothold in northern Italy.

Despite these successes, the Merovingian dynasty gradually grew weak as a result of conflicts among kings, their quarrelsome sons, and independent-minded aristocrats. As a result of these squabbles, Clovis's kingdom split into three separate realms: Neustria in the west; Austrasia, which included lands east of the Rhine River as well as in Gaul; and Burgundy in the south. Rulers of these independent kingdoms issued their own law codes, collected taxes from their subjects—and quarreled bitterly with one another. As they went their separate ways politically, striking linguistic differences emerged. For example, in Neustria, the people

ENCOUNTERING CHRISTIANITY: THE COURTESY AND CONVERSION OF KING ETHELBERT OF KENT

················

When Pope Gregory the Great sent missionaries to England in 597, King Ethelbert of Kent treated them with kindness. In this passage, the English historian Bede (ca. 673–735) presents the point of view of the unconverted English as well as the missionaries' piety.

Reassured by the encouragement of the blessed father Gregory, Augustine and his fellow-servants of Christ resumed their work in the word of God, and arrived in Britain. The King of Kent at this time was the powerful King Ethelbert. To the east of Kent lies the large island of Thanet. It was here that God's servant Augustine landed with companions, who are said to have been forty in number. At the direction of blessed Pope Gregory, they had brought interpreters from among the Franks, and they sent these to Ethelbert, saying that they came from Rome bearing very glad news, which infallibly assured all who would receive it of eternal joy in heaven, and an everlasting kingdom with the living and true God. On receiving this message, the king ordered them to remain in the island where they had landed, and gave directions that they were to be provided with all necessaries until he should decide what action to take. For he had already heard of the Christian religion, having a Christian wife of the Frankish royal house . . . After some days, the king came to the island, and sitting down in the open air, summoned Augustine and his companions. But he took precautions that they should not approach him in a house, for he held an ancient superstition that if they were practisers of magical arts, they might have opportunity to deceive and master him. But the monks were endowed with power from God, not the Devil, and approached the king carrying a silver cross as their standard, and the likeness of our Lord and Saviour painted on a board. . . . And when, at the king's command, Augustine had sat down and preached the word of life to the king and his court, the king said: "Your words and promises are fair indeed, but they are new and strange to us, and I cannot accept them and abandon the age-old beliefs of the whole English nation. But since you have travelled far, and I can see that you are sincere in your desire to instruct us in what you believe to be true and excellent, we will not harm you. We will receive you hospitably, and take care to supply you with all that you need; nor will we forbid you to preach and win any people you can to your religion."

Source: From *A History of the English Church and People* by Bede, translated by Leo Sherley-Price, revised by R. E. Latham (Penguin Classics 1955, Revised edition 1968.) Copyright © 1955, 1968 by Leo Sherley-Price. Reproduced by permission of Penguin Books Ltd.

---

spoke an early form of French, while in Austrasia they spoke a German language. These communities stood as the foundations of medieval France and Germany.

Though Merovingian kings still ruled in Neustria, Austrasia, and Burgundy, they had become so ineffectual that real power passed to the official in charge of the royal household called the "Mayor of the Palace." One of these mayors, Charles Martel "the Hammer" (r. 714–741), established his personal power by regaining control over regions that had slipped away from Merovingian rule, and by defeating an invading Muslim army at Poitiers in 732. Martel's son, Pepin the Short (r. 751–768), dethroned the last of the Merovingian monarchs and in 751 made himself king of the Franks. As we will see in Chapter 8, the new royal house established by Charles Martel, called the Carolingian dynasty, initiated the most glorious period in Frankish history.

Visigoths in Spain

In contrast to the Frankish kings who after Clovis accepted Catholic Christianity, during the sixth century the Visigothic kings, who controlled southern Gaul and most of Spain, adhered to Arian Christianity. These kings attempted to force Arian conversion on the indigenous population. In southern Gaul, where much of the population accepted the Roman Church, forced conversion to Arianism caused hostility toward the Visigoths. When the Frankish king Clovis invaded southern Gaul in 507, many Catholics welcomed him and provided the Franks with military assistance. As a consequence of defeat, the Visigoth kings retreated to Spain, where they concentrated on unifying the people through the spread of Arianism and the acceptance of Roman law, which influenced the Visigoth law codes.

By 600, Visigoth kings ruled over most of the Spanish peninsula and had even managed to drive the last Byzantine forces from its southern coast. Under the Visigoths Spain thrived. From its vast, rich estates, surpluses of grain, olive oil, and leather were exported by international merchants, including a substantial community of Jews as well as Greeks and even Syrians. By taxing this trade the Visigoth kings filled their treasuries with gold and became the envy of their neighbors.

Despite their best efforts the Visigoth kings failed to enforce Arianism on the population, and when King Reccared

(r. 586–601) converted to Catholicism most of the population followed. The kings began to imitate the Byzantine emperors with the elaborate court ceremonies of Constantinople and used frequent Church councils as assemblies that enforced their will. Thus, the key to their success was the ability to employ the spiritual authority of the Church to enhance the secular authority of the king. However, King Reccared's conversion was accompanied by growing intolerance for minority religions and even more ardent attempts to create religious unity through forced conversions. The principal victims of these conversion campaigns were the Jews, who were ordered to be baptized or leave the kingdom in 613. The forced conversion of the Jews was never carried out, but it created distrust and opposition among them that weakened the kingdom. The autocratic instincts of the Visigoth kings also alienated many of the substantial landowners who were easily lured by the promise of alternative kings.

In 711 invading armies of Muslims from North Africa vanquished the last Visigothic king. As a result, Spain became part of the Umayyad caliphate. The Jews, in particular, welcomed the Muslim conquerors because Islam granted them a measure of religious toleration they had not experienced under the Visigoths. Many Christians from the upper classes converted to Islam to preserve the property and offices of authority. Some survivors of the Visigoth kingdoms held on in the northwest of Spain, where they managed to keep Christianity alive.

Lombards in Italy

Between 568 and 774, a people known as the Lombards controlled most of northern and central Italy. These Germanic men and women lived in the area of modern Germany during the first five centuries C.E. They called themselves *Langobardi*, or "Long Beards," from which the name *Lombard* derives. In the first part of the sixth century under their ruler Waccho, Lombards established a kingdom in the area of modern Hungary. As we have seen, Justinian's wars and a devastating plague drained the Byzantine Empire's strength. Without imperial troops to defend Italy, the peninsula became vulnerable to invasion. The Lombard king Alboin (ca. 565–572) took advantage of the situation and invaded Italy in 568. Alboin's army contained soldiers of different ethnic backgrounds. In addition to Lombards, his forces included smaller bands of Goths, Avars, Saxons, and other non-Romans. Some were Arian Christians; others were Catholic Christians. Still others practiced polytheism. Alboin's highly diverse army indicated his ability to attract followers but also implied a lack of common purpose among them other than taking the opportunity to pillage. That lack of common purpose meant that Alboin lacked the ability to build a strong, lasting kingdom.

The Romans living in Italy put up a feeble resistance. Within three years Alboin controlled all of northern Italy, Tuscany, and parts of southern Italy in the region of Spoleto, near Naples. Yet until 700, the Lombard kings proved weak. Throughout their lands real power lay in the hands of semi-independent dukes based in heavily populated urban centers such as Benevento and Spoleto. These dukes gradually expanded their possessions within Italy, jockeying among themselves for land and power. After 700, the Lombard kings reasserted their authority by developing a royal bureaucracy of judges and legal officials, compensating somewhat for the weaknesses of the Lombard system evident in the initial conquest. The new infrastructure enabled them to overshadow the dukes' local authority.

Despite the Lombard kings' newfound strength, they still faced two formidable external enemies. The most dangerous of these were the Byzantine forces who remained in the Exarchate of Ravenna. These soldiers hoped to crush the Lombards and regain control of Italy in the name of the Byzantine emperors. Again and again they battled with Lombards in an attempt to crush their kingdom, but their efforts proved futile. In 751 the Lombard ruler Aistulf defeated the Exarchate of Ravenna. The Franks posed the second threat to the Lombards. These hardy warriors marched into Italy several times during the seventh century, trying to crush the Lombards and seize their lands. Sometimes they joined with Byzantine forces from the Exarchate of Ravenna. During other attacks, the Franks had the backing of the popes in Rome, who resented the Lombards' power. Despite their diplomatic and military efforts, however, the Franks failed to achieve their goals of conquest. The Lombards always drove them out of Italy.

The tide of battle soon turned against the Lombards. In the middle of the eighth century, internal political disputes once again tore at the kingdom. The Lombards' diplomatic relations with the papacy and their uneasy standoff with the Franks deteriorated. As we will see in Chapter 8, the Frankish king Charlemagne, responding to a call for assistance from Pope Leo III, invaded Italy and crushed the Lombards in 774.

The Growth of the Papacy

In theory, the Byzantine emperors still controlled the city of Rome and its surrounding lands during this violent time. However, strapped for cash and troops, these distant rulers proved unequal to the task of defending the city from internal or external threats. In the resulting power vacuum, the popes stepped in to manage local affairs and became, in effect, princes who ruled over a significant part of Italy.

Gregory the Great (r. 590–604) stands out as the most powerful of these popes. The pragmatic Gregory realized that Rome could no longer count on Byzantium for protection. The Roman Church's future, he concluded, instead lay with the Frankish kingdoms in western Europe. Through clever diplomacy, Gregory successfully cultivated the goodwill of the Christian communities of western Europe by offering religious sanction to the authority of friendly kings. He negotiated skillfully with his Lombard, Frankish, and Byzantine neighbors to gain their support and establish the authority of the Roman church. He also encouraged Christian missionaries to spread the faith in England and Germany. In addition, he took steps to train educated clergymen for future generations, in this way securing Christianity's future in western Europe.

Gregory had set the stage for a dramatic increase in papal power. As his successors' authority expanded over the next few centuries, relations between Rome and the Byzantine emperors slowly soured. By the early eighth century the popes abandoned the fiction that they were still subject to the Byzantines and sought protection from the Frankish kings. The popes established political independence during the period but remained dependent on the Franks for military assistance when necessary.

DIFFERENT KINGDOMS, SHARED TRADITIONS

With the exception of England, where Anglo-Saxon invaders drove out the Roman population, the leaders of the new Germanic kingdoms faced a common problem: how should the Germanic minority govern subject peoples who vastly outnumbered them? These rulers found a solution to this problem by blending Roman and Germanic traditions. For example, the kings served as administrators of the civil order in the style of the Roman emperor, issuing laws and managing a bureaucracy. They also served as war leaders in the Germanic tradition, leading their men into battle in search of glory and loot. As the Germanic kings defined new roles for themselves, they discovered that Christianity could bind all their subjects together into one community of believers. The merging of Roman and Germanic traditions could also be traced in the law, which eventually erased the distinctions between Romans and Germans, and in the ability of women to own property, a right far more common among the Romans than the Germans.

Civil Authority: The Roman Legacy

In imitation of Roman practice, the monarchs of Latin Christendom designated themselves the source of all law and believed that they ruled with God's approval. Kings controlled all appointments to civil, military, and religious office. Accompanied by troops and administrative assistants, they also traveled throughout their lands to dispense justice, collect taxes, and enforce royal authority.

Frankish Gaul provides an apt example of how these monarchs adopted preexisting Roman institutions. When Clovis conquered the Visigoths in Gaul, he inherited the nearly intact Roman infrastructure and administrative system that had survived the collapse of Roman imperial authority. Merovingian kings (as well as Visigoth and Lombard rulers in Spain and Italy) gladly maintained parts of the preexisting system and kept the officials who ran them. For instance, Frankish kings relied on the bishops

and counts in each region to deal with local problems. Because Roman aristocrats were literate and had experience in Roman administration on the local level, they often served as counts. Based in cities, these officials presided in local law courts, collected revenues, and raised troops for the king's army. Most bishops also stemmed from the Roman aristocracy. In addition to performing their religious responsibilities, bishops aided their king by providing for the poor, ransoming hostages who had been captured by enemy warriors from other kingdoms, and bringing social and legal injustices to the monarch's attention. Finally, the kings used dukes, most of whom were Franks, to serve as local military commanders and community patrons.

War Leaders and *Wergild:* The Germanic Legacy

The kingdoms of Latin Christendom developed from war bands led by chieftains. By rewarding brave warriors with land and loot taken in war, as well as with revenues skimmed from subject peoples, chieftains created political communities of loyal men and their families, called clans or kin groups°. Though these followers sometimes came from diverse backgrounds, they all owed military service to the clan chiefs. Because leadership in Germanic society was hereditary, networks of loyalty and kinship expanded through the generations.

Though the principle of loyalty to a superior defined life in these Germanic communities, many men ignored this principle in the pursuit of their own interests. Rivalries among warriors unwilling to follow their chieftain and among power-hungry men who competed for the kingship within the royal families often led to bloody struggles that weakened the political fabric of the kingdoms. Frankish leaders proved particularly vicious in their quest for power, thinking nothing of betrayal and assassination of their rivals. Despite the bloodshed and brutal competition for power, the various political communities gradually evolved into distinct ethnic groups led by a king, such as the Lombards and the Franks. These ethnic groups developed a sense of shared history, kinship, and culture. The coalescence of these kingdoms resulted from the Germanic settlers' pride in their new homelands as well as from their allegiance to their monarchs who governed them fairly at home and who protected them from foreign enemies.

The new Germanic kingdoms had highly hierarchical societies geared for warfare. Kinship-based clans stood as the most basic unit of Germanic society. The clan consisted of all the households and blood relations loyal to the clan chief, and a warrior who protected them and spoke on their behalf before the king on matters of justice. Clan chieftains in turn swore oaths of loyalty to their kings and agreed to fight for him in wars against other kingdoms. The clan leaders formed an aristocracy among the Germanic peoples. Like the Roman elites before them, the royal house and the clan-based aristocracy consisted of rich men and women who controlled huge estates. The new Germanic aristocrats intermarried with the pre-existing Roman elites of wealthy landholders, thus maintaining control of most of the land. These people stood at the very top of the social order, winning the loyalty of their followers by giving them gifts and parcels of land. Under the weight of this new upper class, the majority of the population, the ordinary farmers and artisans, slipped into a deepening dependence on these nobles. Eventually, ordinary farmers merged with the Roman peasantry. Most peasants could not enter into legal transactions in their own name, and they had few protections and privileges under the law. Even so, they were better off than the slaves who toiled at society's very lowest depths. Valued simply as property, these men, women, and children had virtually no rights in the eyes of the law.

Though this social hierarchy showed some similarities to societies in earlier Roman times, the new kingdoms' various social groups were defined by law in a fundamentally different way. Unlike Roman law, which defined people by citizenship rights and obligations, the laws of the new kingdoms defined people by their wergild°. A Germanic concept, *wergild* referred to what an individual was worth in case he or she suffered some grievance at the hands of another. If someone injured or murdered someone else, *wergild* was the amount of compensation in gold that the wrongdoer's family had to pay to the victim's family.

In the wergild system, every person had a price that depended on social status. For example, among the Lombards service to the king increased a free man's worth—his *wergild* was higher than that of a peasant. In the Frankish kingdom, if a freeborn woman of childbearing age was murdered, the killer's family had to pay 600 pieces of gold. Two-thirds of that sum went to the victim's family. The king received the rest. Noble women and men had higher *wergild* than peasants, while slaves and women past childbearing age were worth very little.

If proper *wergild* was not paid, the injured party's kin group felt obligated to gain vengeance for their loss. The desire for revenge and compensation frequently led to vicious feuding. In order to minimize the bloodletting that could sometimes drag on for generations after a crime had been committed, representatives of the king or a local aristocrat urged families to accept *wergild*.

Unity Through Law and Christianity

Within the kingdoms of Latin Christendom, rulers achieved unity by merging Germanic and Roman legal principles and by accepting Roman Christianity (Catholicism). Religious diversity among the peoples in their kingdoms made this unity difficult to establish. As we saw in Chapter 6, many of the tribes that invaded the Roman Empire during the fifth century practiced Arian Christianity. They kept themselves apart from the Latin or Catholic Christians by force of law. For example, they declared marriage between Arian and Catholic Christians illegal.

These barriers began to collapse when some Germanic kings converted to the Catholic Christianity of their Roman subjects. Some converted for reasons of personal belief, or because their wives were Catholic. Others decided to become Catholic to gain wider political support. For instance, when Clovis converted to Catholic Christianity about 500 and drove the Arian Visigoths into Spain, laws against intermarriage in Gaul disappeared. More and more Franks and Romans began to marry one another, blending the two formerly separate communities into one and reinforcing the strength of Catholicism. Similarly in 587, when the Visigothic King Reccared converted from Arianism to Catholicism, he made Catholic Christianity the official religion of Spain. Soon Visigoths and Romans began to intermarry legally. In Italy, the Lombards had become Catholic by about 650 and they, too, began to marry Romans. By 750, all of the western European kingdoms had become Catholic.

Germanic kings adopted Roman Catholic Christianity, but they had no intention of abandoning their own Germanic law, which differed from Roman law on many issues, especially relating to the family and property. Instead, they offered their Roman subjects the opportunity to turn their back on Roman law, which still governed their lives, in favor of living under the Germanic law that governed the king. Clovis's *Law Code* or *Salic Law*, published sometime between 508 and 511, illustrates this development. The *Law Code* applied to Franks and to any other non-Roman peoples in his realm who chose to live according to Frankish law. Because the Romans dwelling in the Frankish kingdom technically still followed the laws of Byzantium, Clovis did not presume to legislate for them. Romans could follow their own law if they wished, or they could follow his laws and become Franks.

Permitting his subjects to switch to Frankish law helped Clovis strengthen his kingdom. It fostered a shared sense of Frankish identity throughout his kingdom. Eventually the Frankish king's policies eroded distinctions among Romans, Franks, and other ethnic groups within his realm. By 750, most Romans had chosen to abandon their legal identity as Romans and live according to Frankish law, and the distinction between Roman and Frank lost all meaning.

A similar process occurred in other Germanic kingdoms. The Lombards slowly mixed with the Romans living in Italy. By 750 their law, which originally protected only Lombards, now applied to all the Catholic inhabitants of Italy. In Spain, the Roman and Visigothic populations merged once the religious barriers came down. In 654 the Visigothic King Recceswinth abolished the separate Roman law entirely and brought his entire population under Visigothic law. As in the Frankish and Lombard kingdoms, this unification of two peoples under one law happened without protest, a sign that various groups had blended politically, religiously, and culturally.

Women and Property

Roman law influenced more than just local administration in Latin Christendom. It also prompted Germanic rulers to reconsider the question of a woman's right to inherit land. In the Roman Empire, women had inherited land without difficulty. Indeed, perhaps as much as 25 percent of the land in the entire realm had been owned by women. In many Germanic societies, however, men could inherit land and property far more easily than women. Attitudes about female inheritance began to shift when the Germanic settlers established their homes in previously Roman provinces—and began to marry Roman women who owned property.

By comparing the law codes of the new kingdoms over time, historians have detected the impact of Roman customs on Germanic inheritance laws. By the late eighth century women in Frankish Gaul, Lombard Italy, and Visigothic Spain could inherit land, though often under the restriction that they must eventually pass it on to their sons. Germanic rulers adopted the custom of female inheritance

because it enabled the new settlers to keep within their own families the property that their Roman wives had inherited and brought to the marriage. Despite these limitations, the new laws transformed women's lives. A woman who received an inheritance of land could live more independently, support herself if her husband died, and have a say in the community's decisions.

THE SPREAD OF CATHOLIC CHRISTIANITY IN THE NEW KINGDOMS OF WESTERN EUROPE

As Catholic Christianity slowly spread through the new kingdoms, churchmen decided that they had a moral responsibility to convert all the people of the world to their faith. They sent out missionaries to explain the religion to nonbelievers and challenge the worship of polytheist gods. Their hard work paid off. By 750 everyone living in the new kingdoms except Jews had become Catholic Christians (see Map 7.4).

■ **Map 7.4 Spread of Latin Christianity in Western Europe**

By about 750 Catholicism had spread throughout western Europe. Travelling monks converted many polytheists to Christianity. They established monasteries that served as centers of education and places where Latin literature was copied and preserved. Because Latin was the language of worship and education throughout these lands, historians refer to Christianity in western Europe as Latin Christianity. This term distinguishes western Europe from Byzantine lands in the eastern Mediterranean, where Greek served as the main language of worship and education.

Meanwhile, bishops based in cities directed people's spiritual lives, instilling the moral and social conventions of Christianity through sermons delivered in church. Monks such as Boniface traveled from their home monasteries in Ireland, England, and Gaul to spread the faith into Germany and other areas. Monasteries became centers of intellectual life, and monks replaced urban aristocrats as the keepers of books and learning.

Converting the Irish

Though the Romans had conquered most of Britain during the imperial period, they never attempted to bring Ireland into their empire. Thus the island off England's west coast had had only minimal contact with Christianity. This changed after 432. According to a pious legend, at some point in the early 400s, Irish slavers stole a young boy named Patrick (ca. 410–ca. 492) from his Christian family in England and transported him to Ireland, where they sold him into bondage. Patrick learned Irish during his years in captivity. He managed to escape to Britain, where he eventually became a bishop. In 432 Patrick returned to Ireland as a missionary. There, he converted thousands of polytheist worshipers by preaching Catholic Christianity.

But Ireland was still a rural place. Patrick and his fellow missionaries wondered how to Christianize the Irish without a Roman urban foundation to build on. Elsewhere in the West Christianity spread out into the countryside from cities, with bishops administering the local church from their city cathedrals. However, the island lacked cities in which to build churches and housing for bishops. No one living in Ireland knew Latin, Greek, or any of the other languages into which the Bible had been translated. And no schools existed where churchmen might teach the Gospel to new converts.

Irish churchmen found solutions to these problems in monasteries, places where priests could receive training and men and women from the surrounding communities could learn to read Latin and absorb the basics of Christian education. By 750, the Irish scholars produced by these monasteries gained a reputation in their own lands as well as across western Europe. Irish monasteries sent out dozens of missionaries, who in turn founded new monasteries in England, France, and Germany. Irish scholars produced magnificently illustrated manuscripts in their libraries. These books brought Irish art to all the lands where the missionaries traveled.

Irish monasteries sometimes grew rich from the gifts of money and property provided by kings and other pious folk. Such centers, especially those that became bishops' headquarters, acquired substantial economic and political influence in their local communities by settling disputes, caring for the sick, and employing local laborers. Having proved its value in Ireland, the monastery system spread from the island to England and then to the European continent.

Converting the Anglo-Saxons

By 600, numerous Irish missionaries had begun to travel to England and the European continent to establish new monasteries. Columbanus (543–615), for example, founded several monasteries on the Irish model in the kingdom of Burgundy. The most notable among these were the monastery of Luxeuil in the Rhône River valley, and Bobbio in northern Italy. These centers inspired the founding of many additional nunneries and monasteries in northern Gaul. From there Catholicism spread east of the Rhine River, into lands where the religion had not yet penetrated.

Irish missionaries also expanded their monastic network in their own land. Columba (521–597), for instance, founded several new monasteries in Ireland as well as one on the island of Iona, Scotland's western coast. From this thriving community missionaries began to bring Catholicism to the men and women of Scotland. The offshoot monastery of Lindisfarne in northern England also became a dynamic center of learning and missionary activity. During the seventh century, missionaries based there carried Christianity to many other parts of England. They also began converting the people of Frisia on the North Sea, in the area of the modern Netherlands.

Irish monks who went to Anglo-Saxon England sometimes found themselves working side by side with monks sent from Rome by Pope Gregory the Great (r. 590–604) and his successors. Gregory believed that the Catholic Church should fill the void left by the collapse of Roman government. By filling this void, Catholics could forge a Christian society throughout Europe. Gregory understood that the first step in creating that new community was to convert as many people as possible to the faith. Deep learning about the religion could come later. To that end he instructed missionaries to permit local variations in worship and to accommodate harmless vestiges of pre-Christian worship practices. "Don't tear down their temples," Gregory advised; "put a cross on the roofs!"

Following Gregory's pragmatic suggestion, missionaries in England accepted certain Anglo-Saxon calendar conventions that stemmed from polytheist worship. For example, in the Anglo-Saxon calendar, the weekdays took their names from old gods: Tuesday derived from Tiw, a war god; Wednesday from Woden, king of the gods; Thursday from Thor, god of thunder; and Friday from Freya, goddess of agriculture. Anglo-Saxon deities eventually found their way into the Christian calendar as well. Eostre, for example, a goddess whose festival came in April, gave her name to the Christian holiday Easter.

The Irish and Roman monks working throughout England disagreed strongly about proper Catholic practice. For instance, they argued over how to perform baptism, the ritual of anointing someone with water to admit him or her into the Christian community. They bickered about how monks should shave the tops of their heads to show their religious dedication, and they squabbled about the correct

(a)

(b)

■ **A Mixture of Cultural Traditions in Anglo-Saxon England**

This box, which is about 10 inches long, 6 inches high, and 8 inches wide, was carved from whalebone early in the first half of the eighth century in England. The style continues the Roman art of ivory carving, but the writing on the box is Anglo-Saxon. The box depicts scenes from Roman, Jewish, Christian, and Germanic traditions. The top panel (a) shows the Roman capture of Jerusalem in 70 C.E. The lower panel (b) shows the Germanic hero Aegili defending his home from armed invaders. Other scenes not shown here include Romulus and Remus (the legendary twin founders of Rome), the Adoration of the Magi (wise men who worshiped the infant Jesus in his manger crib), and Weland, a magical artisan from Germanic mythology. Used to hold precious objects at a monastery, this box illustrates the broad range of cultural interests and the rich intellectual life that thrived at these religious centers in England. The box captures encounters among Christianity, Anglo-Saxon culture, and the legacy of classical antiquity.

means of calculating the date of Easter. These disputes threatened to create deep divisions among England's Christians. The overall conflict finally found resolution in 664 in the Anglo-Saxon kingdom of Northumbria, where monastic life flourished. At a council of monks and royal advisers called the Synod of Whitby, the Northumbrian monarch commanded that the Roman version of Catholicism would prevail in his kingdom. His decision eventually was accepted throughout England.

Monastic Intellectual Life

The missionaries from Rome were members of the vigorous monastic movement initiated by Benedict of Nursia (ca. 480–547) from his monastery at Monte Cassino in Italy (see Chapter 6). These monks followed Benedict's *Rule,* a

guidebook for the management of monastic life and spirituality. In the *Rule* Benedict had written that individual monks should live temperate lives devoted to spiritual contemplation, communal prayer, and manual labor. So that their contemplations might not depart from the path of truth, monks must also seek guidance in the Bible, in the writings of the renowned theologians, and in works of spiritual edification. For Benedict, contemplative reading constituted a fundamental part of monastic life. Thus, monks had to be literate in Latin. They needed training in the Latin classics, which required books.

Medieval monasteries set aside at least two rooms—the scriptorium° and the library—to meet the growing demand for books. In the scriptorium, scribes laboriously copied Latin and Greek manuscripts letter by letter and word by word, often without understanding what they were copying. Because copying manuscripts was an act of religious devotion, the monks persevered. Monastery libraries were small in comparison to the public libraries of fourth-century Rome, but the volumes were cherished and carefully controlled. Because books were precious possessions, these libraries set forth strict rules for their use. Some librarians chained books to tables to prevent theft. Others pronounced a curse against anyone who failed to return a borrowed book. Nevertheless, librarians also generously lent books to other monasteries to copy.

Monks preferred to read Christian texts with a spiritual message, so these books were the most frequently copied.

■ The Lindisfarne Gospels

Eadfrith, a monk and later bishop of the Lindisfarne monastery in England, completed the writing and illustration of this Gospel book by 698 to honor a saint whose relics had come to the altar that year. A monk wrote an Anglo-Saxon translation of the book between the lines of Latin sometime during the tenth century. The artist painted soft, bright colors into elaborate interconnected designs that characterize Celtic art, showing continuity of Celtic artistic traditions through the Roman and early medieval periods. The page shown here is the first page of the Gospel of John and was the most complicated of Eadfrith's designs.

In many monasteries, however, monks preserved non-Christian texts. By doing so, they kept knowledge of Latin and classical learning alive. Indeed, every surviving work by an author of the Classical Age was copied and passed on by monks in the sixth and seventh centuries. In addition to Christian works, monks also studied the writings of Latin poets such as Virgil and Juvenal, scientists such as Pliny the Elder, and philosophers such as Boethius and Cicero, as well as the works of grammarians, mathematicians, scientists, and physicians from the ancient world. Without the monasteries and scriptoria, we would know almost nothing about the literature of the classical world today.

Sometimes classical works survived merely by accident. Because parchment, the specially prepared sheepskin on which writers copied their manuscripts, was expensive, many monks scrubbed old manuscripts clean and reused them to copy religious texts. By studying these reused parchment sheets, called palimpsests°, modern scholars have succeeded in reclaiming vital classical texts that otherwise would have been lost forever. Cicero's treatise *On the Republic,* which has influenced many political thinkers including the writers of the U.S. Constitution, is one example. This work survived only because in the seventh century, at the monastery of Bobbio in northern Italy, a monk erased Cicero's text and copied an interpretation of the Psalms by Augustine onto the parchment. Modern scholars can read Cicero's words below Augustine's.

Monks did far more than merely copy ancient texts, however. Some wrote original books of their own. At the English monastery at Jarrow, for example, Bede (d. 735) became the most distinguished scholar in eighth-century Europe. He wrote many books, including the *History of the English Church and People.* This work provides an invaluable source of information about the early Anglo-Saxon kingdoms.

Monks carried books with them when they embarked on missionary journeys. They also acquired new books during their travels. For instance, Benedict Biscop, the founder of the monasteries of Wearmouth (674) and Jarrow (682) in England, made six trips to Italy. Each time he brought back crates of books on all subjects, including works written by classical authors whom a handful of monks studied with interest. Other Anglo-Saxon missionaries transported this literary heritage to the monasteries they founded in Germany during the eighth century. As monks avidly read, copied, wrote, and transported books of all sorts, knowledge and intellectual discourse flourished in the monasteries.

Monks shared their expanding knowledge with Christians outside the monastery walls. They established schools at monasteries where boys (and in some places girls) could learn to read and write. Most of the very few literate people who lived between 550 and 750 gained their education at monastery schools. The men trained in these schools played an important role in society as officials and bureaucrats. Their skills in reading and writing were necessary for keeping records and writing business and diplomatic letters.

Jews in a Christian World

For Jews during this era, quality of life varied in the different western European kingdoms. Jews continued to work in every profession, own land, serve in the army, and engage in trade. Most of the time monarchs protected the Jewish minorities living in their kingdoms. Thus many Jews prospered in the Frankish, Visigothic, and Lombard realms (no Jews lived in England during this period). At times, theological curiosity led to intellectual encounters between Jews and Christians. In Lombard Italy, for example, Jews and Christians sometimes engaged in public debates about their religious beliefs.

Yet churchmen still blamed Jews collectively for Jesus' death. Consequently, Jews sometimes suffered severe discrimination at the hands of Christian rulers. For example, in Visigothic Spain, kings passed new laws attempting to force Jews to convert to Christianity or endure terrible penalties, including torture, exile, and enslavement.

Leading churchmen in the western kingdoms also developed theological reasons for wanting Jews to convert to Christianity. Pope Gregory urged conversion because he believed that Christ would return to Earth only when Jews embraced Christianity. Nevertheless, Gregory advocated the use of persuasion and kindness to encourage conversion, rather than force or terror. On numerous occasions he intervened to stop Christians from committing violence against Jews. Other Christian writers, such as the Isidore of Seville (in Spain), further developed

CHRONOLOGY	
The Birth of Latin Christendom	
482–511	Clovis reigns; Frankish kingdom divided at his death
CA. 525	Benedict founds monastery at Monte Cassino
520s–560s	Slavs penetrate Balkans
542	Bubonic plague strikes Mediterranean
554	Justinian's armies defeat Ostrogoths in Italy
568	Lombards invade Italy
582	Avars enter Balkans
587	Visigothic king of Spain converts to Catholicism; Columbanus travels to Gaul from Ireland
597	Augustine of Canterbury begins conversions in England
672	Lombards accept Catholicism
727–743	Lombards attack Byzantine holdings in Italy
732	Charles Martel defeats Muslims at Poitiers
751	Pepin overthrows last Merovingian king; Exarchate of Ravenna falls to Lombards

the idea that Jews had a place in Christian society because of their role in bringing about Christ's return and then the Day of Judgment. Highly ambivalent, Christians both persecuted and protected Jews. They permitted Jews to live in their midst, but granted them fewer rights than Christians had. Violence against Jews might flare up suddenly, yet its perpetrators neither applied it systematically nor sustained it for very long.

CONCLUSION

Three Cultural Realms

The death of the Byzantine emperor Justinian I in 565 marked the last time the territory spanning from Spain to Carthage to Constantinople would be united under one imperial ruler. The Persian Empire still menaced Byzantium's eastern frontier, and except for Italy and some coastal areas of Spain, western Europe was now ruled by Germanic kings. During the next two centuries western Europe, the Mediterranean world, and the Middle East as far as India and central Asia were utterly reconfigured politically and culturally. By ca. 750, three new realms had come into sharp focus: the Christian Byzantine Empire based at Constantinople; the vast Umayyad caliphate created by Muhammad's Islamic followers; and

Latin Christendom in western Europe, which was fragmented politically but united by Catholic Christianity. Each of these regions was a community of uncompromising religious faith. The cultural foundations they established as well as the bitter divisions that emerged among them are still shaping the West today.

These three cultural realms of the West each borrowed from the heritage of ancient Rome, especially its network of cities, which survived most completely in the Mediterranean and the Middle East. They were each influenced by the religious traditions of antiquity, especially the emphasis on monotheism in Judaism. They each adapted parts of Roman law but reshaped it to suit changing needs and new cultural influences. The heritage of Rome remained strongest in Byzantium. Indeed, the Byzantines continued to call themselves Romans. But between the sixth and eighth centuries these three cultural realms came to be distinguished by the language that dominated intellectual life and by the forms of monotheism practiced. In Byzantium the Greek language and Orthodox Christianity with its distinctively elaborate ceremonies defined the culture. In the Umayyad caliphate a similar function was performed by the Arabic language and the five Pillars of Islam. In western Europe, many languages were spoken but Latin became the universal language of Catholicism and government. None of these cultural realms, however, had yet achieved the level of uniformity and monolithic authority they would achieve during the subsequent centuries of the Middle Ages.

The year 750 saw the end of the Umayyad caliphate and the limit of Muslim expansion in western Europe and central Asia. After that the Byzantine Empire struggled for survival. In the Latin West, the Merovingian dynasty lost control of the Frankish kingdom. In the next chapter we will see how the Carolingian dynasty that succeeded the Merovingians led the Franks to predominance in western Europe. We will also discover how the Abbasid caliphate inaugurated a new, rich period in Islamic life, and how Byzantium began to reassert itself politically and culturally.

Suggestions for Further Reading

For a comprehensive list of suggested readings, please go to www.ablongman.com/levack/chapter7

Bowersock, Glen, Peter Brown, and Oleg Grabar, eds. *Late Antiquity: A Guide to the Post-Classical World.* 1999. Interpretive essays combined with encyclopedia entries make this a starting point for discussion.

Brown, Peter. *The Rise of Western Christendom: Triumph and Diversity A.D. 200–1000.* 2001. A brilliant interpretation of the development of Christianity in its social context.

Brown, Thomas S. *Gentlemen and Officers: Imperial Administration and Aristocratic Power in Byzantine Italy, A.D. 554–800.* 1984. The basic study of Byzantine rule in Italy between Justinian and Charlemagne.

Bulliet, Richard W. *The Camel and the Wheel.* 1990. A fascinating investigation of the importance of the camel in history.

Cohen, Jeremy. *Living Letters of the Law: Ideas of the Jew in Medieval Christianity.* 1999. A masterful investigation of early medieval Judaism.

Cook, Michael. *Muhammad.* 1996. A short, incisive account of Muhammad's life that questions the traditional picture.

Cormack, Robin. *Writing in Gold: Byzantine Society and Its Icons.* 1985. An expert discussion of icons in the Byzantine world.

Crone, Patricia, and Michael Cook. *Hagarism: The Making of the Islamic World.* 1977. A challenging view of the origins of Islam.

Donner, Fred M. *The Early Islamic Conquests.* 1981. Discusses the first phases of Islamic expansion.

Geary, Patrick J. *The Peoples of Europe in the Early Middle Ages.* 2002. Discusses the emergence of the new kingdoms of Europe, stressing the incorporation of Roman elements.

Hourani, George. *Arab Seafaring in the Indian Ocean in Ancient and Early Medieval Times.* 1995. The standard discussion of Arab maritime activity.

Robinson, Francis, ed. *The Cambridge Illustrated History of the Islamic World.* 1977. Many excellent and well-illustrated articles that will be useful for beginners.

Strayer, Joseph B., ed. *Dictionary of the Middle Ages.* 1986. An indispensable reference work.

Treadgold, Warren. *A History of the Byzantine State and Society.* 1997. A reliable narrative of Byzantine history.

Webster, Leslie and Michelle Brown, eds. *The Transformation of the Roman World, A.D. 400–900.* 1997. A well-illustrated synthesis with maps and bibliography.

Wickham, Chris. *Early Medieval Italy: Central Government and Local Society, 400–1000.* 1981. Examines the economic and social transformation of Italy.

Notes

1. Willibald, *The Life of Boniface*, in *Anglo-Saxon Saints and Heroes*, trans. Clinton Albertson (1967), 308–310.

2. Al-Tabari, *The History of Al-Tabari. vol. XVII. The First Civil War*, trans. and annotated by G. R. Hawting (1985), 50.

3. Kent Rigsby, *Zeitschrift für Papyrologie and Epigraphik*, 126 (1999), 175–176.

Empires and Borderlands: The Early Middle Ages, 750–1050

N 860 FIERCE RUS TRIBESMEN ABOARD A FLEET OF SLEEK DRAGON SHIPS RAIDED THE villages along the shores of the Black Sea and then stomped up to the gates of Constantinople, ready for pillage and rape. Completely taken by surprise, the Byzantines were gripped with panic. The Byzantine patriarch Photius called upon the people to repent of their sins to avoid God's wrath, and when the Rus unexpectedly broke camp and departed, it was interpreted as an act of divine intervention.

Throughout the tenth century, the barbarian Rus tribes mounted sporadic raids on and eventually trading visits to civilized Byzantine cities, particularly Constantinople, the largest city in the Western world. The Byzantines clearly considered even the Rus merchants as little more than savages, prone to the worst kinds of violence, and tried to keep them under control while in Constantinople by signing treaties. The treaties stipulated that no more than fifty Rus could enter the city at one time, all must be unarmed, and they all had to leave by autumn. In exchange for civilized behavior, however, the Rus received during their stay free baths, food, provisions for a month, and equipment for their return. The Rus inhabited the river valleys of present-day Ukraine and Russia in eastern Europe. After spending the winters collecting tribute from the Slavic tribes, the Rus set off in their boats, risking dangerous rapids and water-falls on the Dnieper River and ambush from hostile tribes, to reach the Black Sea and the splendid emporium of the world, Constantinople, which they called simply the "Great City."

Accustomed to the rough life of long winter treks, grubby little villages, and constant danger, the Rus were dazzled by the sight of the Great City, with its half

Reliquary Bust of Charlemagne, ca. 1350: This bust was made more than 500 years after the death of Charlemagne, which means it is unlikely to be an accurate portrait of him. Medieval portraits, however, were not intended to represent the individuals as they actually looked but to represent their status or spiritual qualities. The majesty of this work, which housed some of the bones of Charlemagne, encouraged veneration of the great ruler considered a saint by many during the Middle Ages.

a million inhabitants, the gilded cupolas of its churches, the marble palaces of the aristocrats and emperor, the cavernous wharves and warehouses of its merchants, and the twelve miles of fortifications and walls that protected the city. The people of Constantinople were equally astonished by the sight of the Rus merchants—sun-worn, fur-clad, and armed to the teeth—whom they met with fascination and no little fear. The usual purpose of these repeated visitations was trade. The merchants of Constantinople traded Byzantine and Chinese silks, Persian glass, Arabian silver (highly prized by the Rus), and Indian spices for honey, wax, slaves, and musty bales of furs from Scandinavia and what is now northern Russia.

In the merchant stalls of Constantinople, traders from many cultures met, haggled, and came to know something of one another. None perhaps were more unlike each other than the rough Rus and the refined Byzantines, but their mutual desires for profit kept them in a persistent, if tentative, embrace. These repeated interactions among very different peoples who traded, competed, and fought with one another offer clues for understanding the medieval world, also known as the Middle Ages.

The term *Middle Ages* refers to the period between the ancient and modern civilizations, that is from ca. 550 to 1500. The culture of that period rested on the foundations of three great civilizations: the Latin-Christian kingdoms of western Europe; the Greek Christianity of Byzantium; and the Arabic-speaking Islamic caliphates of the Middle East, North Africa, and Spain. The dynamic interactions among these three civilizations, distinguished by religion and language, lay at the heart of medieval culture. But the great civilizations also encountered barbarian peoples outside Christian and Islamic civilization—traders, raiders, and nomads from the North and East.

During the Early Middle Ages, the period from ca. 750 to 1050, the Latin, Greek, and Islamic kingdoms and empires began to form a distinctively Western civilization, but there were vast borderlands between them and at the frontiers with barbarian peoples that escaped Western domination and cultural influence. In this crucial phase in forming Western civilization, expansive empires made possible greater political cohesion that brought together ethnically and linguistically diverse peoples under obedience to an emperor, or caliph in the case of the Islamic empires. The empires enforced or encouraged uniformity of religion, spread a common language among the ruling elite, and instituted systematic principles for governing. The most important innovation from this period was that a distinctive Latin Christian or Roman Catholic culture began to emerge in western Europe. The Carolingian empire, which lasted from 800 to 843 and controlled much of western Europe, re-established the Roman Empire in the West for the first time in more than 300 years and sponsored a revival of interest in antiquity called the Carolingian Renaissance. The Carolingian empire's collapse was followed by a period of anarchy as Europe faced wave after

wave of hostile invaders. Only during the late tenth and eleventh centuries did the kingdoms of western Europe become strong enough to resist the invaders and to convert many of them to Roman Catholicism. At the same time the strength of the Byzantine empire was sapped by invaders and internal strife, but it too revived and experienced a remarkable Renaissance under the Macedonian dynasty (867–1056). The most energetic of the three civilizations during this period was certainly Islam, which threatened militarily both the Latin Christian kingdoms and Byzantium, supported important philosophical and scientific work, and produced a thriving economy.

It was during the period from 750 to 1050 that the first signs appeared of a shift in the balance of military and cultural power away from Byzantium and the Islamic states toward the kingdoms of western Europe. The principal task of this and the following chapter is to trace how that happened. This chapter will address four questions: (1) How did the Carolingian empire contribute to establishing a distinctive western European culture? (2) After the collapse of the Carolingian empire, how did the Western kingdoms consolidate in the core of the European continent and how did Roman Catholicism spread to its periphery? (3) Why did Byzantium revive after a series of invasions and then decline? (4) What were the sources of dynamism and weakness within the Islamic states?

The Carolingians

Among the successor kingdoms to the Roman Empire in the West, as we saw in Chapter 7, none was more powerful militarily than the kingdom of the Franks, which encompassed much of the ancient Roman province of Gaul. The Merovingian dynasty ruled the kingdom of the Franks during the sixth and seventh centuries. But the Merovingian dynasty was plagued by factions, royal assassinations, and do-nothing kings. The Merovingians were so weak that real power passed to the "mayor of the palace," the official in charge of the royal household. In 751 one of these mayors, Pepin the Short (ca. 714–768), deposed the last of the Merovingian kings and made himself king of the Franks. Pepin inaugurated the Carolingian dynasty, which vastly expanded the political and cultural reach of the Franks to encompass much of western Europe.

Both the weak Merovingians and the strong Carolingians illustrated how the problem of succession from one king to another destabilized early medieval monarchies. The kingdom was considered the private property of the royal family, and according to Frankish custom, a father was obliged to divide his estates among his legitimate sons. As a result, whenever a king of the Franks died, the kingdom was divided up. When Pepin died in 768, the kingdom was divided between his sons, Charlemagne and Carloman. When Carloman died suddenly in 771, Charlemagne ignored the inheritance rights of Carloman's sons and may even have had them killed, making himself the sole ruler of the Franks.

THE LEADERSHIP OF CHARLEMAGNE

Charlemagne's (r. 768–814) ruthlessness with his own nephews epitomized the crafty leadership that made him the mightiest ruler in western Europe and gave him the nickname of Charles the Great. One of his court poets labeled him "The King Father of Europe"; no monarch in European history has enjoyed such posthumous fame.

An unusually tall and imposing figure, Charlemagne was a superb athlete and swimmer, a lover of jokes and high living, but also a deeply pious Christian. As Pepin's eldest son,

he had frequently accompanied the army during his father's campaigns, and these youthful experiences gave him an unbending will and a fighting spirit.

During his reign, Charlemagne engaged in almost constant warfare, especially against polytheistic tribes that when defeated were usually compelled to accept Christianity. He went to war some eighteen times against the Germanic tribe the Saxons, whose forced conversion only encouraged future rebellions. The causes for Charlemagne's persistent warfare were complex. He believed he had an obligation to spread Christianity. He also needed to control his borders from incursions by hostile tribes. Perhaps most important, however, was his need to satisfy his followers, especially the members of the aristocracy, by providing them with opportunities for plunder and new lands. As a result of these wars, he established a network of subservient kingdoms that owed tribute to the Frankish empire (see Map 8.1).

■ **Map 8.1 Carolingian Empire**

Charlemagne's conquests were the greatest military achievement of the Early Middle Ages. The Carolingian armies successfully reunified all western European territories of the ancient Roman Empire except for southern Italy, Spain, and Britain. However, the empire was fragile due to Frankish inheritance laws that required all legitimate sons to inherit lands from their father. By the time of Charlemagne's grandsons the empire began to fragment.

The extraordinary expansion of the Frankish empire represented a significant departure from the small, loosely governed kingdoms that had prevailed in the wake of the collapse of the Roman Empire. Charlemagne's empire covered all of western Europe except for southern Italy, Spain, and the British Isles. His military ambitions had brought the Franks into direct confrontation with other cultures—the polytheistic German tribes, Scandinavians, and Slavs; the Orthodox Christians of Byzantium; and the Muslims in Spain. These confrontations were usually hostile and violent, characterized as they were by the imposition of Frankish rule and faith.

Coronation of Charlemagne as Emperor

Charlemagne's coronation as Roman emperor at the hands of Pope Leo III (r. 795–816) conferred extraordinary authority on the Frankish kingdom. In 799 Pope Leo found himself embroiled in a vicious dispute with a faction of Roman nobles who accused him of adultery and lying. Kidnapped on the streets of Rome, he barely escaped having his tongue and eyes cut out before he was rescued by some of his attendants. Charlemagne put together a commission of prominent churchmen and nobles to conduct a judicial inquiry into the charges against the pope, and then in the autumn of 800 the king himself set out for Rome to restore order to the church. After Leo was cleared of the accusations against him, on Christmas Day 800 in front of a large crowd at St. Peter's Basilica, Pope Leo presided over a ceremony in which Charlemagne was crowned emperor. Historians have debated exactly what happened, but according to one report, the assembled throng acclaimed Charlemagne as Augustus and emperor, and the pope prostrated himself before the new emperor in a public demonstration of submission. Charlemagne's biographer later stated that the coronation came as a surprise to the king, but that seems unlikely. Charlemagne may have wished to make it appear that he was reluctant to accept the crown because he knew the coronation was certain to antagonize Constantinople, where there already was a Roman emperor. Nevertheless, Charlemagne became the first Roman emperor in the West since the fifth century.

The coronation exemplified two of the most prominent characteristics of the Carolingians. The first was the conscious imitation of the ancient Roman Empire, especially the late Roman Christian empire of Constantine. Charlemagne's conquests approximated the former territory of the western Roman Empire, and the churches built during his reign were modeled after the fourth- and fifth-century basilicas of Rome. The second characteristic of Carolingian rule was the obligation of the Frankish kings to protect the Roman popes, an obligation that began under Charlemagne's father Pepin. In exchange for this protection, the popes offered the Carolingian monarchs the legitimacy of divine sanction.

The imperial title bestowed on Charlemagne tremendous prestige and tremendous risk. With the imperial crown came the rulership of northern Italy and theoretical superiority over all other rulers in the West. But it made dangerous enemies of the Byzantine emperors. They had been calling themselves Roman emperors since the fourth century and justly claimed to be the true heirs of the legal authority of the ancient Roman Empire. To them Charlemagne was nothing more than a usurper of the imperial crown. In their minds the pope had no right to crown anyone emperor. Instead of reuniting the eastern and western halves of the ancient Roman Empire, the coronation of Charlemagne drove them further apart.

Carolingian Rulership

Even under the discerning and strong rulership of Charlemagne, the Carolingian empire never enjoyed the assets that had united the ancient Roman Empire for so many centuries. The Carolingians lacked a standing army and navy, professional civil servants, properly maintained roads, regular communications, and a money economy. There was not even a capital city in which Charlemagne could show off his power and establish a governmental bureaucracy, a stark contrast with the splendid Byzantine capital of Constantinople. From Christmas to Easter and sometimes longer, Charlemagne wintered in one of the imperial palaces, usually in the Frankish heartland. In the summer he and his court traveled about, camping out or living as guests in the castles of friendly lords, where he dispensed justice, decided disputes, and enforced obedience to his rule. During these summer travels he frequently conducted campaigns against the Saxon tribes.

Such a system of government depended more on personal than institutional forms of rule. Personal loyalty to the Carolingian monarch, expressed in an oath of allegiance, provided the strongest bonds unifying the realm, but betrayals were frequent. The Carolingian system required a monarch with outstanding personal abilities and unflagging energy, such as Charlemagne possessed, but a weak monarch threatened the collapse of the entire empire. Until the reign of Charlemagne, royal commands had been delivered orally, and there were few written records of what decisions had been made. Charlemagne's decrees (capitularies) gradually came to be written out. Although first presented in a hodgepodge fashion that combined different issues, the written capitularies began to strengthen and institutionalize governmental procedures through written aids to memory. In addition, Charlemagne's leading adviser, Alcuin, insisted that all official communications be stated in the appropriate Latin form, which would help prevent falsification because only the educated members of Charlemagne's court were well enough educated to know the proper forms.

One of the weaknesses of the Merovingian dynasty had been the decentralization of power, as local dukes appropriated royal resources and public functions for themselves. To combat this weakness, Charlemagne followed his father's lead in reorganizing government around territorial units called counties°, each administered by a count. The counts were rewarded with lands from the king and sent to areas where they had no family ties to serve as a combined provincial governor, judge, military commander, and representative of the king. To check on the counts, traveling circuit inspectors reviewed the counts' activities on a regular basis and remedied abuses of office. On the frontiers of their sprawling kingdom, the Franks established special territories called marches°, which were ruled by margraves with extended powers necessary to defend vulnerable borders.

In many respects, however, the Church provided the most vital foundations for the Carolingian system of rulership. During the last years of the ancient Roman Empire, the administration of the Church was organized around the office of the bishop. By the late seventh century this system had almost completely collapsed, as many bishoprics were left vacant or were occupied by royal favorites and relatives who lacked qualifications for church office. Because Carolingian monarchs took responsibility for the welfare of Christianity, they took charge of the appointment of bishops and reorganized church administration into a strict hierarchy of archbishops who supervised bishops who, in turn, supervised parish priests. Pepin and Charlemagne also revitalized the monasteries and endowed new ones, which provided the royal court with trained personnel—scribes, advisers, and spiritual assistants. Most laymen of the time were illiterate, so monks and priests wrote the emperor's letters for him, kept government records, composed histories, and promoted education—all essential for Carolingian rule.

The Carolingian Renaissance

In addition to organizing efficient political administration, Charlemagne sought to make the royal court an intellectual center. He gathered around him prominent scholars from throughout the realm and other countries. Under Charlemagne's patronage, these scholars were responsible for the flowering of culture that is called the Carolingian Renaissance.

The Carolingian Renaissance° ("rebirth") was one of a series of revivals of interest in ancient Greek and Latin literature. Charlemagne understood that both governmental efficiency and the propagation of the Christian faith required the intensive study of Latin, which was the language of the law, learning, and the Church. The Latin of everyday speech had evolved considerably since antiquity. During Charlemagne's time, spoken Latin had already been transformed into early versions of the Romance languages of Spanish, Italian, and French. Distressed that the poor Latin of many clergymen meant they misunderstood the Bible, Charlemagne ordered that all prospective priests undergo a rigorous education and recommended the lib-

■ **Copying Manuscripts**
This manuscript illumination of the Ascension from the Sacramentary of Archbishop Drogo of Metz, ca. 842, reveals the pious care that went into the copying of manuscripts during the Carolingian period. The faded letters around the illumination are examples of the Carolingian minuscule writing style.

eral application of physical punishment if a pupil was slow in his lessons.

Charlemagne's patronage was crucial for the Carolingian Renaissance, which took place in the monasteries and the imperial court. Many of the heads of the monastic writing rooms wrote literary works of their own, including poetry and theology. The Carolingian scholars developed a beautiful new style of handwriting called the Carolingian minuscule, in which each letter was carefully and clearly formed. Texts collected by Carolingian librarians provided the foundation for the laws of the Church (called canon law) and codified the liturgy, which consisted of the prayers offered, texts read, and chants sung on each day of the year.

As we saw in Chapter 7, monastic scribes helped preserve ancient Latin literature. During the Carolingian period, the copying and studying of ancient Latin texts intensified. Much of what has survived of classical Latin learning, including the works of some seventy ancient authors, was preserved by Carolingian scribes. Some 8,000 Carolingian manuscripts still exist, a small portion of the total number known to have been produced.

The brighter young clerics and some promising lay-men required instruction more advanced than the typical monastery could provide; to meet this need, Charlemagne established a school in his palace in Aachen. To staff his school and to serve as advisers, Charlemagne sought the best talent from within and outside the empire. Grammarians, historians, geographers, and astronomers from Ireland, England, Italy, Germany, and Spain flocked to Charlemagne's call.

The man most fully responsible for the Carolingian Renaissance was the English poet and cleric Alcuin of York (ca. 732–804), whom Charlemagne invited to head the palace school. Charlemagne himself joined his sons, his friends, and his friends' sons as a student, and under Alcuin's guidance the court became a lively center of dis-cussion and exchange of knowledge. They debated issues such as the existence or nonexistence of Hell, the meaning of solar eclipses, and the nature of the Holy Trinity. After fifteen years at court, Alcuin became the abbot of the monastery of St. Martin at Tours, where he expanded the library and produced a number of works on education, theology, and philosophy.

A brilliant young monk named Einhard (ca. 770–840) who studied in the palace school quickly became a trusted friend and adviser to Charlemagne. Based on twenty-three years of service to Charlemagne and research in royal docu-ments, Einhard wrote the *Life of Charlemagne* (830–833), which describes Charlemagne's family, foreign policy, con-quests, administration, and personal attributes. In Einhard's vivid Latin prose, Charlemagne comes alive as a great leader, a lover of hunting and fighting, who unlike his rough companions possessed a towering sense of responsi-bility for the welfare of his subjects and the salvation of their souls. In Einhard's biography, Charlemagne appears as an idealist, the first Christian prince in medieval Europe to imagine that his role was not just to acquire more posses-sions but to better humankind.

Charlemagne's rule and reputation has had lasting sig-nificance for western Europe. Around 776 an Anglo-Saxon monk referred to the vast new kingdom of the Franks as the Kingdom of Europe, reviving the Roman geographical term *Europa*. Thanks to the Carolingians, Europe became more than a geographical expression. It became the geographical center of a new civilization that supplanted the Roman civi-lization of the Mediterranean and transformed the culture of the West.

THE DIVISION OF WESTERN EUROPE

None of Charlemagne's successors possessed his personal skills, and without a permanent institutional basis for ad-ministration, the empire was vulnerable to fragmentation and disorder. When Charlemagne died in 814, the imper-ial crown passed to his only surviving son, Louis the Pious (r. 814–840). Louis's most serious problem was dividing

---

CHRONOLOGY

The Carolingian Dynasty

751	Pepin the Short deposes last Merovingian king
800	Charlemagne crowned emperor in Rome
843	Treaty of Verdun divides Frankish kingdom
987	Death of the last Carolingian king

---

the empire among his own three sons, as required by Frankish inheritance laws. Disputes among Louis's sons led to civil war, even before the death of their father, and while they were fighting the administration of the empire was neglected.

After years of fighting, the three sons—Charles the Bald (d. 877), Lothair (d. 855), and Louis the German (d. 876)—negotiated the Treaty of Verdun, which divided the Frankish kingdom. Charles the Bald received the western part of the territories, the kingdom of West Francia. Louis the German received the eastern portion, the kingdom of East Francia. Lothair obtained the imperial title as well as the central portion of the kingdom, the "Middle Kingdom," which ex-tended from Rome to the North Sea (see Map 8.1). In suc-ceeding generations, the laws of inheritance created further fragmentation of these kingdoms, and during the ninth and tenth centuries the descendants of Charlemagne died out or lost control of their lands. By 987 none were left.

The Carolingian empire lasted only a few generations. Carolingian military power, however, had been formidable, providing within the Frankish lands an unusual period of security from hostile enemies, measured by the fact that few settlements were fortified. After the empire's collapse virtu-ally every surviving community in western Europe required fortifications, represented by castles and town walls. Post-Carolingian Europe became fragmented as local aristocrats stepped into the vacuum created by the demise of the Carolingians—and it became vulnerable, as raiders plun-dered and invaders carved out land for themselves.

Invasions and Recovery in the Latin West

Despite Charlemagne's campaigns of conquest and conversion, the spread of Christianity throughout western Europe remained uneven and incomplete. By 900, Roman Catholicism was limited to a few regions that constituted the heartland of western Europe—the

■ **Map 8.2   Invasions of Europe, Seventh through Eleventh Centuries**

Especially after the division of the Carolingian empire, Europe came under severe pressure from invading Viking bands from Scandinavia. The effects of the Viking invasions were felt most gravely in the British Isles and northern France. From the east came the Magyars, who eventually settled in the vast Hungarian plain. From the south there were persistent raids and conquests from various Islamic states, some of which established a rich Muslim civilization in Europe.

Frankish lands, Italy, parts of Germany that had been under Carolingian rule, the British Isles, and a fringe in Spain. During the ninth and tenth centuries, hostile polytheistic tribes raided deep into the tightly packed Christian core of western Europe (see Map 8.2). Despite these attacks Christianity survived, and many of the polytheist tribes eventually accepted the Christian faith. These conversions were not always the consequence of Christian victories in battle, as had been the case during late antiquity and the Carolingian period. More frequently they resulted from organized missionary efforts by monks and bishops.

THE POLYTHEIST INVADERS OF THE LATIN WEST

Some of the raiders during the eighth to eleventh centuries plundered what they could from the Christian settlements

of the West and returned home. Others seized lands, settled down, and established new principalities. The two groups who took advantage of the weakness of the Latin West most often during this period were the Magyars and Vikings. The original homeland of the Magyars, later known as the Hungarians, was in the central Asian steppes. Gradually driven by other nomads to the western edge of the steppes, the Magyars began to penetrate Europe in the late ninth century. By 896 they had crossed en masse into the middle of the Danube river basin, occupying sparsely settled lands that were easily conquered. The grassy plains of this basin had long attracted nomads, including the Huns and Avars before them, and like other nomads, the Magyars were accomplished horsemen. Once established, the Magyar tribes divided the vast plain among themselves and pushed at the borders of the neighboring Slavic and German principalities.

Mounted raiding parties of Magyars ranged far into western Europe. Between 898 and 920 they sacked settlements in the prosperous Po River valley of Italy and then descended on the remnant kingdoms of the Carolingian empire. Wherever they went they plundered for booty and took slaves for domestic service or sale. The kings of western and central Europe were powerless against these fierce raiders, who were unstoppable until 955 when the Saxon king Otto I (who later became emperor) destroyed a band of marauders on their way home with booty. After 955, Magyar raiding subsided.

The definitive end of Magyar forays, however, may have had less to do with Otto's victory than with the consolidation of the Hungarian plain into its own kingdom under the Árpád dynasty, named after Árpád (d. 907), who had led seven Magyar tribes in their migration to Hungary. Both Orthodox and Catholic missionaries vied to convert the Magyars, but because of an alliance with German monarchs, the Árpáds accepted Roman Catholicism. On Christmas Day 1000, the Árpád king Stephen I (r. 997–1038) received the insignia of royalty directly from the pope and was crowned king. To help convert his people, King Stephen laid out a network of bishoprics and lavishly endowed monasteries.

The most devastating of the eighth- to eleventh-century invaders of western European settlements were the Vikings, also called Norsemen or Northmen. (These Viking warriors were ethnically related to the Rus who harassed Constantinople at the same time.) During this period, Danish, Norwegian, and Swedish Viking warriors sailed on long-distance raiding expeditions from their homes in

Scandinavia. Every spring the long Viking dragon ships sailed forth, each carrying 50 to 100 warriors avid for loot. Propelled by a single square sail or by oarsmen when the winds failed or were blowing in the wrong direction, Viking ships were unmatched for seaworthiness and regularly sailed into the wild seas of the North Atlantic. The shallow-draft vessels could also be rowed up the lazy rivers of Europe to plunder monasteries and villages far into the interior.

The causes for the enormous Viking onslaught were complex. Higher annual temperatures in the North may have stimulated a spurt in population that encouraged raiding and eventually emigration. But the primary motive seems to have been an insatiable thirst for silver, which was deemed the essential standard of social distinction in Scandinavian society. As a result, monasteries and cathedrals with their silver liturgical vessels were especially prized sources of plunder for Viking raiding parties. In 793, for example, the great English monastery at Lindisfarne was pillaged for silver and largely destroyed in the process.

By the middle of the ninth century, the Vikings began to maintain winter quarters in the British Isles and on the shores of the weak Carolingian kingdoms—locations that enabled them to house and feed ever-larger raiding parties. These raiders soon became invading armies that took land and settled their families on it. As a result, the Vikings moved from disruptive pillaging to permanent occupation, which created a lasting influence in Europe. In western Europe amid the ruins of the Carolingian empire, Viking settlements on the Seine River formed the beginnings of the duchy of Normandy ("Northman land"), whose soldiers

■ **A Norman Ship, Possibly Based on a Viking Design, Used in the Invasion of England in 1066**

Note the single sail, the horses and warriors in the hold of the ship, and the tiller, which was mounted on the starboard side toward the stern. Stern-mounted rudders, which gave the helmsman much greater control of the direction of the ship, were gradually introduced during the twelfth century.

would conquer during the eleventh century England, Sicily, and much of southern Italy.

The most long-lasting influence of the Vikings outside of Scandinavia was in the British Isles and North Atlantic. In 865 a great Viking army conquered large parts of northeastern England, creating a loosely organized network of territories known as the Danelaw. The Danish and Norse conquests in the British Isles left deep cultural residues in local dialects, geographical names, personal names, social structure, and literature. The most enduring example in Old English, the earliest form of spoken and written English, remains the epic of *Beowulf,* which recounts the exploits of a great Scandinavian adventurer in combat with the monster Grendel, Grendel's mother, and a fiery dragon.

In the North Atlantic, Vikings undertook long voyages into the unknown across cold rough seas. Beginning about 870, settlers poured into unsettled Iceland. Using Iceland as a base, they ventured farther asea and established new colonies in Greenland. In Iceland the adventures of these Viking warriors, explorers, and settlers were celebrated in poetry and sagas. The sagas of Erik the Red and the Greenlanders recount hazardous voyages to the coasts of Canada. In 930 the fiercely independent Icelanders founded a national parliament, the *althing,* an institution at which disputes were adjudicated through legal procedures rather than combat.

After the mid-ninth century, the kings of Scandinavia (Norway, Denmark, and Sweden) began to assert control over the bands of raiders who had constituted the vanguard of the Viking invasions. By the end of the tenth century, the great age of Viking raiding by small parties ended. The Scandinavian kings established a firm hold over the settled population and converted to Christianity, bringing their subjects with them into the new faith. Henceforth, the descendants of the Viking raiders settled down to become peaceable farmers and shepherds.

THE RULERS IN THE LATIN WEST

As a consequence of the disintegration of the Carolingian order and the subsequent invasions, people during the ninth and tenth centuries began to seek protection from local warlords who assumed responsibilities once invested in royal authorities.

Lords and Vassals

The society of warlords derived from Germanic military traditions in which a great chief attracted followers who fought alongside him. The relationship was voluntary and egalitarian. By the eighth century, however, the chief had become a lord° who dominated others, and his dependents were known as vassals°.

The bond of loyalty between lord and vassal was formalized by an oath. In the Carolingian period the vassal proved

---

AN OATH OF VOLUNTARY SUBMISSION TO A LORD

....

Many men who found themselves in desperate circumstances became vassals in order to feed themselves and to find protection from someone richer and stronger. This voluntary oath of obedience reflects the origins of the relationship of dominance and submission between lords and vassals. In the eighth century a destitute man addressed a certain "magnificent lord" as follows:

Inasmuch as it is known to all and sundry that I lack the wherewithal to feed and clothe myself, I have asked of your pity, and your goodwill has granted to me permission to deliver and commend myself into your authority and protection . . . in return you have undertaken to aid and sustain me in food and clothing, while I have undertaken to serve you and deserve well of you as far as lies in my power. And for as long as I shall live, I am bound to serve you and respect you as a free man ought, and during my lifetime I have not the right to withdraw from your authority and protection, but must, on the contrary for the remainder of my days remain under it.

And in virtue of this action, if one of us wishes to alter the terms of the agreement, he can do so after paying a fine of ten solidi to the other. But the agreement itself shall remain in force. Whence it has seemed good to us that we should both draw up and confirm two documents of the same tenor, and this they have done.

Source: This example of a voluntary oath of obedience comes from Tours, in the eighth century.

---

his loyalty to the lord by performing an act of homage, which made the vassal the "man" of the lord. The act of homage was a ritual in which the kneeling vassal placed his clasped hands between the hands of the lord and made a verbal declaration of intent, usually something such as, "Sir, I become your man." In return for the vassal's homage or fealty, as it came to be called, the lord swore to protect the vassal. The oath established a personal relationship in which the lord reciprocated the vassal's loyalty and willingness to obey the lord with protection and in some cases with a land grant called a fief°. Lords frequently called upon their vassals for military assistance to resist invaders or to fight with other lords. The fief supplied the vassal with an income to cover the expenses of armor and weapons and of raising and feeding horses, all of which were necessary to be an effective mounted soldier, known by the twelfth century as a knight°. This connection between lord-vassal relations and the holding of a fief is called feudalism°.

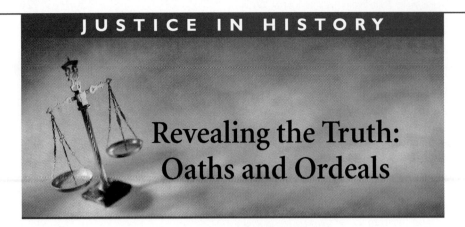

Revealing the Truth: Oaths and Ordeals

No participant in a lawsuit or criminal trial today would dream of entering the courtroom without an accompanying pile of documents to prove the case. In modern society we trust written over oral evidence because we are aware of how easily memories can be distorted. In an early medieval court, however, the participants usually arrived with nothing more than their own sworn testimony and personal reputations to support their cause. Papers alleging to prove one thing or another meant little in a largely illiterate society. Unable to read and perhaps aware that the few who could read might deceive them, most people trusted what they had personally seen and heard. Count Berthold of Hamm expressed the opinion of many when, after being presented with documents opposing his claim to a piece of land, he "laughed at the documents, saying that since anyone's pen could write what they liked, he ought not to lose his rights over it."

To settle disputes, medieval courts put much more faith in confession or in eyewitness testimony than in documents. In 1124 Pope Calixtus II pronounced that "we put greater faith in the oral testimony of living witnesses than in the written word."

Under normal trial procedures, a man would give his oath that what he was saying was true. If he was an established and respected member of the community, he would also have a number of "oath-witnesses" testify for his reliability, although not to the truth or

falsehood of his evidence. The court would also hear from witnesses in the case. This system worked well enough when two local men, known in the community, were at odds. But what happened when there was a trial involving a person who had a bad reputation, was a known liar, or was a stranger? What would happen in a case with no witnesses?

In these instances, medieval courts sometimes turned to trial by ordeal to settle the matter. The judicial ordeal was used only as a last resort, as a German law code of 1220 declared: "It is not right to use the ordeal in any case, except that the truth may be known in no other way." The wide range of situations and people handed over to the ordeal makes clear that in the eyes of the medieval courts, the ordeal was a fallback method when all else failed to reveal the truth.

What was a trial by ordeal? There were several types. The most common was trial by fire. The accused would plunge his or her arm into a cauldron of boiling water to retrieve a coin or a jewel, or alternately would pick up a red-hot iron and walk nine paces. A variation of this method was to walk over hot coals or red-hot ploughshares. After the accused suffered this ordeal, his or her hand or foot would be bound for three days and then examined. If the wound was healing "cleanly," meaning without infection, the accused was declared innocent. If not, he or she was adjudged guilty. Another common form of the ordeal

was immersion in cold water, or "swimming," made famous in later centuries by its use in witch trials. The accused would be thrown into a river or lake. If the water "rejected" her and she floated, then she was guilty. If the water "embraced" her and she sank, then she was innocent. The obvious complication that a sinking person, even though innocent, may have also been a drowning person did not seem to deter use of trial by water.

The ordeal was especially widespread in judging crimes such as heresy and adultery and in assigning paternity. In 1218, Inga of Varteig carried the hot iron to prove that her son, born out of wedlock, was the son of deceased King Hakon III, which if true would change the line of succession in Norway. The ordeal was also used to decide much more pedestrian matters. In 1090, Gautier of Meigné claimed a plot of land from the monks of Saint Auban at Angers, arguing that he had traded a horse in return for the property. He too carried the iron to prove his claim.

The belief that an ordeal could effectively reveal guilt or innocence in a judicial matter was based on the widespread conviction that God constantly and actively intervened in earthly affairs and that his judgment could be seen immediately. To focus God's attention on a specific issue, the participants performed the ordeal in a ritual manner. A priest was usually present to invoke God's power and to bless the implements employed in the ordeal. In one typical formula, the priest asked God "to bless and sanctify this fiery iron, which is used in the just examination of doubtful issues." Priests would also inform the accused, "If you are innocent of this charge . . . you may confidently receive this iron in your hand and the Lord, the just judge, will free you." The ritual element of the judicial ordeal emphasized the judgment of God over the judgment of men.

During the eleventh and twelfth centuries, the use of the ordeal waned. The recovery of Roman law, the rise of literacy and written documents in society at large, and a greater belief in the power of human justice to settle disputes all contributed to the gradual replacement of the ordeal with the jury trial or the use of torture to elicit a confession from the accused. In

England the common law began to entrust the determination of the truth to a jury of peers who listened to and evaluated all the testimony. The jury system valued the opinions of members of the community over the reliability of the ordeal to reveal God's judgment. These changes mark a shift in medieval society toward a growing belief in the power of secular society to organize and police itself, leaving divine justice to the afterlife. But the most crucial shift came from within the Church itself, which felt its spiritual mission compromised by the involvement of priests in supervising ordeals. In 1215 the Fourth Lateran Council forbade priests from participating, and their absence made it impossible for the ordeal to continue as a formal legal procedure. ■

Questions of Justice

1. Why would it have been so crucial during this troubled period to have a decisive verdict even in cases when the evidence of guilt was unknown or inconclusive?

2. Why was someone's reputation in the community so significant for determining the truth in a medieval trial? How do reputations play a role in trials today?

3. What do oaths and the trial by ordeal reveal about the relationship between human and divine justice during the Middle Ages?

Taking It Further

Bartlett, Robert. *Trial by Fire and Water: The Medieval Judicial Ordeal.* 1986. Associates the spread of the trial by ordeal with the expansion of Christianity. The best study of the ordeal.

van Caenegen, R. C. *An Historical Introduction to Private Law.* 1992. A basic narrative from late antiquity to the nineteenth century that traces the evolution of early medieval trial procedures.

During the ninth and tenth centuries, the lords often became the only effective rulers in a particular locality. After the collapse of public authority during the invasions and the dissolution of the Carolingian empire, lordship implied political and legal jurisdiction over the inhabitants of the land. These lords came to exercise many of the powers of the state, such as adjudicating disputes over property or inheritance and punishing thieves and murderers. The rendering of justice represented the most elementary attribute of government, and in the absence of a formal legal system and systematic record keeping, local lords rendered a rough and ready justice. The personal loyalties of those involved in a dispute were crucial for determining the outcome. Those well-connected to the lord, especially those who were his vassals, were always better off than those who were outsiders or had fallen into his disfavor. In a society in which personal ties meant everything, the truth of conflicting testimonies was often determined by the public reputations and personal connections of those who testified. When the reputations of disputants or an alleged criminal could not determine whom to believe, lords acting as judges relied on oaths and ordeals to determine the truth.

The mixture of personal lord-vassal obligations, property rights conveyed by the fief, and legal jurisdiction over communities caused endless complications. The king's vassals were also lords of their own vassals, who in turn were lords over lesser vassals down to the level of simple knight. In theory such a system created a hierarchy of authority that descended down from the king, but reality was never that simple. In France, for example, many of the great lords enjoyed as much land as the king, which made it very difficult for the king to force them to enact his will. Many vassals held different fiefs from different lords, which created a confusion of loyalties, especially when two lords of the same vassal went to war against one another.

Women could inherit fiefs and own property of their own, although they could not perform military services. They often managed royal and aristocratic property when men were absent or dead, made decisions about how property would be divided up among heirs, and functioned as lords when receiving the homage of male vassals. The lineage and accomplishments of prominent ladies enhanced their husbands' social prestige. A number of aristocratic families traced their descent from the female line, if it was more prestigious than the male line, and named their children after the wife's illustrious ancestors.

Lord-vassal relationships infiltrated many medieval social institutions and practices. Since most vassals owed military service to their lords, medieval armies were at least partially composed of vassal-knights who were obliged to fight for their lord for a certain number of days (often forty) per year. Vassals were required to provide their lord with other kinds of support as well. When summoned, they had to appear at the lord's court to offer advice or sit in judgment of other vassals who were their peers. When the

lord traveled, his vassal was obliged to provide food and shelter in the vassal's castle, sometimes for a large entourage of family and retainers who accompanied the lord. Vassals were obliged to pay their lord certain fees on special occasions, such as the marriage of the lord's daughter. If the lord was captured in battle, his vassals had to pay the ransom.

The Western European Kingdoms After the Carolingians

At a time when the bonds between lords and vassals were the only form of protection from invaders and marauders, lordship was a stronger social institution than the vague obligations all subjects owed to their kings. To rule effectively, a king was obliged to be a strong lord, in effect to be-

■ **Otto III**

The Emperor Otto III is represented here in a form usually reserved for Christ. The emperor sits on a throne, is surrounded by a mandorla (lines surrounding his body in the shape of an almond), and reaches out to the four evangelists—Matthew, Mark, Luke, and John—who are signified by the winged figures of an eagle, lion, bull, and man. The hand of God reaches down from the heavens to crown Otto. The idea of divine sanction of kingship could not be more graphic.

come the lord of all the other lords, who in turn would discipline their own vassals. Achieving this difficult goal took several steps. First, the king had to establish a firm hand over his own lands, the royal domain. With the domain supplying food, materiel, and fighting men, the king could attempt the second step—establishing control over lords who lived outside the royal domain. To hold sway over these independent-minded lords, kings sometimes employed force but frequently offered lucrative rewards by giving out royal prerogatives to loyal lords. These prerogatives included the rights to receive fines in courts of law, to collect taxes, and to perform other governmental functions. As a result, some medieval kingdoms, such as France and England, began to combine in the hands of the same people the personal authority of lordship with the legal authority of the king, creating feudal kingship.

The final step in the process of establishing royal authority was to emphasize the sacred character of kingship. With the assistance of the clergy, kings emulated the great Christian emperors of Rome, Constantine and Justinian. Medieval kings became quasi priests who demanded obedience from their subjects because kings represented the majesty of God on earth. The institution of sacred kingship gave kings an additional weapon for persuading the nobles to recognize the king's superiority over them.

Under the influence of ancient Roman ideas of rulership, some kings began to envision their kingdoms as something grander than private property. As the Germanic king and later emperor Conrad II (r. 1024–1039) put it, "If the king is dead the kingdom remains, just as the ship remains even if the helmsman falls overboard."[1] The idea slowly began to take hold that the kingdom had an eternal existence separate from the mortal person of the king and that it was superior to its component parts—its provinces, tribes, lords, families, bishoprics, and cities. This profound idea reached its fullest theoretical expression many centuries later. Promoting the sacred and eternal character of kingship required monarchs to patronize priests, monks, writers, and artists who could formulate and express these ideas.

The kingdoms of East and West Francia, which arose out of the remnants of the Carolingian empire, produced kings who attempted to expand the power of the monarchy and enhance the idea of kingship. East Francia largely consisted of Germanic tribes, each governed by a Frankish official called a duke. During the tenth century, several of these dukes became powerful lords, but they had to rule from the saddle, constantly on the road—being seen, making judgments, suppressing revolts, punishing disloyal vassals, and rewarding loyal ones.

After 919 the dukes of Saxony were elected the kings of East Francia, establishing the foundations for the Saxon dynasty. With few lands of their own, the Saxon kings maintained their power by acquiring other duchies and controlling appointments to high church offices, which went to family members or loyal followers. The greatest of

CHRONOLOGY

The Western European Kingdoms Emerge

787	First recorded raid by the Danes in Anglo-Saxon England
843–911	Carolingian dynasty in East Francia
843–987	Carolingian dynasty in West Francia
919–1024	Saxon or Ottonian dynasty
955	Otto I defeats Magyars
962	Otto crowned emperor in Rome
987–1328	Capetian dynasty in France
1066	William the Conqueror defeats last Anglo-Saxon king

the Saxon kings, Otto I the Great (936–973), combined deep Christian piety with formidable military ability. More than any other tenth-century king, he supported the foundation of missionary bishoprics in polytheist Slavic and Scandinavian lands, thereby pushing the boundaries of Christianity beyond what they had been under Charlemagne. Otto launched a major expedition to Italy, where he reestablished order in anarchic Rome, deposed one pope, and nominated another. As a consequence of his intervention in Italy, the new pope crowned him emperor in 962, reviving the Roman Empire in the West, as Charlemagne had done earlier. Otto and his successors in the Saxon dynasty attempted to rule a more restricted version of the western empire than had Charlemagne. By the 1030s the German Empire consisted of most of the Germanic duchies, north-central Italy, and Burgundy. In later centuries these regions collectively came to be called the Holy Roman Empire.

As had been the case under Charlemagne, effective rulership in the new German Empire included the patronage of learned men and women who enhanced the reputation of the monarch. Otto and his able brother Bruno, the archbishop of Cologne, initiated a cultural revival, the Ottonian Renaissance°, which centered around the imperial court. Learned Irish and English monks, Greek philosophers from Byzantium, and Italian scholars found positions there. Among the many intellectuals patronized by Otto, the most notable was Liutprand of Cremona (ca. 920–ca. 972), a vivid writer whose unabashed histories reflected the passions of the troubled times. For example, his history of contemporary Europe vilified his enemies and was aptly titled *Revenge.*

Like East Francia, West Francia included many groups with separate ethnic and linguistic identities, but the kingdom had been Christianized much longer because it had been part of the Roman Empire. Thus West Francia, although highly fragmented, possessed the potential for greater unity by using Christianity to champion the authority of the king.

Strengthening the monarchy became the crucial goal of the Capetian dynasty, which succeeded the last of the Carolingian kings. Hugh Capet (r. 987–996) was elevated king of West Francia in an elaborate coronation ceremony in which the prayers of the archbishop of Reims offered divine sanction to the new dynasty. The involvement of the archbishop established an important precedent for the French monarchy: From this point on, the monarchy and the church hierarchy were closely entwined. From this mutually beneficial relationship, the king received ecclesiastical and spiritual support while the upper clergy gained royal protection and patronage. The term *France* at first applied only to Capet's feudal domain, a small but rich region around Paris, but through the persistence of the Capetians West Francia became so unified that the name France came to refer to the entire kingdom.

The Capetians were especially successful in soliciting homage and services from the great lords of the land—despite some initial resistance. Hugh and his successors distinguished themselves by emphasizing that unlike other lords, kings were appointed by God. Shortly after his own coronation, Hugh had his son crowned—a strategy that ensured the succession of the Capetian family. Hugh's son, Robert II, the Pious (r. 996–1031), was apparently the first to perform the king's touch, the reputed power of the king to cure certain skin diseases. The royal coronation cult and the king's touch established the reputation of French kings as miracle workers.

Anglo-Saxon England had never been part of the Carolingian empire, but because it was Christian, England shared in the culture of the Latin West. England suffered extensive damage at the hands of the Vikings. After England was almost overwhelmed by a Danish invasion during the winter of 878–879, Alfred the Great (r. 871–899) finally defeated the Danes as spring approached. As king of only Wessex (not of all England), Alfred consolidated his authority and issued a new law code. Alfred's able successors cooperated with the nobility more effectively than the monarchs in either East or West Francia and built a broad base of support in the local units of government, the hundreds and shires. The Anglo-Saxon monarchy also enjoyed the support of the Church, which provided it with skilled servants and spiritual authorization.

During the late ninth and tenth centuries, Anglo-Saxon England experienced a cultural revival under royal patronage. King Alfred proclaimed that the Viking invasions had been God's punishment for the neglect of learning, without which God's will could not be known. Alfred accordingly promoted the study of Latin. He also desired that all men of wealth learn to read the language of the English people. Under Alfred a highly sophisticated literature appeared in Old English. This literature included poems, sermons, commentaries on the Bible, and translations of important Latin works. The masterpiece of this era was a history called the *Anglo-Saxon Chronicle*. It was begun during Alfred's reign but maintained over several generations.

During the late tenth and early eleventh centuries, England was weakened by a series of Viking raids and a succession of feeble kings. In 1066 William, the duke of Normandy and a descendant of Vikings who had settled in the north of France, defeated King Harold, the last Anglo-Saxon king. William seized the English throne. William the Conqueror opened a new era in which English affairs

■ **A Medieval Windmill**
The peasant on the left is carrying a sack of grain for milling. The entire mill was built on a pivot so that it could be rotated to catch the wind.

■ **A Heavy *Carruca* Plow**
At the center of the two-wheeled plow is a sturdy timber from which the coulter projects just in front of the plowshare, which is hidden by the earth.

became deeply intertwined with those of the duchy of Normandy and the kingdom of France.

THE COMMON PEOPLE

After the end of the invasions of the ninth and tenth centuries, the population of western Europe recovered dramatically. Technological innovations created the agricultural revolution° that increased the supply of food. With more food available, people were better nourished than they had been in more than 500 years. As a result of more and better food, the population began to grow. In the seventh century all of Europe was home to only about 14 million inhabitants. Much of the land cultivated in the ancient world had reverted to wild forests, simply because there were not enough people left to farm it due to the deaths from plague and the barbarian invasions. By 1300 the population had exploded to 74 million. From the seventh to the fourteenth centuries, then, the population grew many times over, perhaps as much as 500 percent. The most dramatic signs of population growth began after the year 1000.

The Medieval Agricultural Revolution

At the beginning of the eleventh century, the vast majority of people lived in small villages or isolated farmsteads. Peasants literally scratched out a living from a small area of cleared land around the village by employing a light scratch plow that barely turned over the soil. The farms produced mostly grain, which was consumed as bread, porridge, and ale or beer. Vegetables were rare, meat and fish uncommon. Over the course of the century, the productivity of the land was greatly enhanced by a number of innovations that came into widespread use.

The invention of new labor-saving devices ushered in the power revolution. This development, which occurred in the tenth to twelfth centuries, harnessed the first new sources of power since the domestication of oxen and the

invention of the ship in the ancient world. There would not be a technological discovery of similar magnitude until the development of steam power in the eighteenth century. Perhaps the most notable innovation was the exploitation of nonanimal sources of power from water and wind. The water mill was invented in late Roman times, but it came into widespread use only in the tenth and eleventh centuries. Water mills were first used to grind grain but were gradually adapted to a wide variety of tasks, including turning saws to mill timber. By the end of the twelfth century windmills also began to appear, which were used for similar purposes.

As important as the harnessing of water and wind power was the enhanced ability to use animal power. Knights began to breed large, powerful war-horses. They equipped their horses with metal armor and stirrups, which kept knights on their horses, and metal horseshoes (until then, horses' hooves had been bound in cloth), which gave horses better footing and traction. Improvements in this period also included a new type of horse collar, which increased the animal's pulling power. Earlier collars fit tightly around a horse's neck, which choked the animal if it pulled too great a weight. The new collar transferred the pressure points from the throat to the shoulders. Originally devised to make horses more effective at fighting, the collar was adapted to make both horses and oxen more efficient farm draft animals. With enhanced animal pulling power, farmers could plow the damp, heavy clay soils of northern Europe much more efficiently.

The centerpiece of the agricultural revolution was the heavy plow, which replaced the widely used Mediterranean scratch plow. Developed for light, sandy soils that were easily broken up, the scratch plow was barely able to dig into the poorly drained soils of the northern European plain.

The heavy plow had several distinctive advantages. It cut through and lifted the soil, aerating it and bringing to the surface minerals vital for plant growth. It created a furrow that channeled drainage, preventing the fields from

■ Twelfth-Century Village

Aerial photograph of the village of West Whelpington North (England), which was settled in the twelfth century but whose inhabitants died out during the Black Death of the fourteenth century (see Chapter 10). Outlines of the individual families' farm gardens can be seen in the left center. On the lower right are the ridges and furrows of the elongated fields required by the use of the heavy plow.

fallow field, what was called the open field, leaving their manure to recondition its soil. This practice, the two-field system, was gradually supplanted by the three-field system. In the three-field system one field was planted in the fall with grain; one was planted in the spring with beans, peas, or lentils; and one lay fallow. Both fall and spring plantings were harvested in the summer, after which all the fields shifted. The open three-field system produced extraordinary advantages: the amount of land under cultivation was increased from one-half to two-thirds; beans planted in the spring rotation returned nitrogen to the soil; and the crop rotation combined with animal manure reduced soil exhaustion from excessive grain planting.

The agricultural revolution had a significant effect on society. First, villagers learned to cooperate—by pooling draft animals for plow teams, by redesigning and elongating their fields, by coordinating the three-field rotation of crops, and by timing the harvest schedule. To accomplish these cooperative ventures, they created village councils and developed habits of collective decision making that were essential for stable community life. Second, the system produced not only more food, but better food. Beans and other vegetables grown in the spring planting were rich in proteins. Slaughtering cattle for meat was still out of the question for peasants, but a plate of beans had a nutritional value similar to that of beef.

Manors and Serfs

The medieval agricultural economy bound landlords and peasants together in a unit of management called the manor. A manor referred to the holding of a single lord and the community of farmers who worked it. A single village might be divided up to serve several small manors, or a large manor might draw from several villages. Some lords possessed several manors and traveled from one to another throughout the year. The lord of the manor usually had his own large house or stone castle and served as the presiding judge of the community. The lord's manor court was the only form of law that rural people knew. The lord typically appointed the priest of the parish church and was responsible for enforcing church attendance and maintaining the church buildings. The parish priest worked land loaned to him by the lord in exchange for his religious services to the village and manor.

Unlike in the ancient world, in which slaves performed most of the heavy farm work, slaves seldom worked on farms during the Middle Ages. A much more common status was that of serf. Unlike slaves, serfs° were not owned,

being flooded by the frequent rains of northern Europe. The heavy plow was very cumbersome, however. It required six or eight horses or oxen to pull it, and no single peasant family in the tenth or eleventh century was able to afford that many draft animals. Farmers had to pool their animals to create plow teams, a practice that required mutual planning and cooperation. A two-wheeled heavy plow pulled by a team of eight oxen was difficult to turn, which meant it was best to continue plowing in a straight line for as long as possible. Thus, the heavy plow required peasants to cooperate further in redesigning their fields—from compact square fields, which had been cross-plowed with the older scratch plow, to long narrow fields that minimized the number of turns and provided a headland at the end to permit the draft team to make a wide turn. The new plow created the elongated fields that were distinctive to northern Europe.

The necessity to replenish the soil meant that half the arable land lay fallow while the other half was planted with crops. The fields would be reversed in the following year. In northern Europe farm animals were allowed to graze in the but they were tied to a specific manor, which they could not leave. They had certain legal rights denied slaves, such as the right to a certain portion of what they produced, but they were obliged to subject themselves to the lord's will. In theory, at least, the relationship between the lord and his serfs was reciprocal. The lord supplied the land, sometimes tools and seed, and protection from invaders and bandits. In return serfs supplied the labor necessary to work the land. Serfs were most common in England and northern France.

There were also free peasants who worked as independent farmers and owned their land outright. Free peasants appeared in Scandinavia, northern Germany, southern France, Switzerland, and northern Italy. In many villages of Europe free peasants could be found scattered among larger communities of serfs.

At the bottom of rural society were the numerous impoverished cottagers who farmed smaller plots of land than serfs or free peasants but who did not have the right to pass the land down to succeeding generations as serfs and free peasants did. Even serfdom, which was onerous, was preferable to being a cottager or completely landless; at least serfdom provided peasants with the means to feed themselves and their families.

The most important social units on a medieval manor were families who worked the land together, each member performing tasks suitable to their abilities, strength, and age. The rigors of medieval farm labor did not permit a fastidious division of labor between women and men. Women did not usually drive the heavy plow, but they toiled at other physically demanding tasks. The life of one young girl—documented because she later achieved sainthood as Saint Alpaix—was probably typical. From age 12, Alpaix worked with her father in the fields, carrying heavy baskets of manure and sheep dung to fertilize the garden. When her arms became exhausted, she was harnessed to a sledge by a rope so that she could drag manure to the fields. During the critical harvest times, women and children worked alongside men from dawn to dusk. Young girls typically worked as gleaners, picking up the stalks and kernels that the male harvesters dropped or left behind, and girls were responsible for weeding and cleaning the fields. Before the use of water mills and windmills, women ground the grain by hand.

The fundamental fact of life on a medieval farm was the necessity of unremitting toil for women, men, girls, and boys. Even during the dormant winter months, no one stayed idle for long because of the need to make and repair farm tools, and to spin, weave, sew, brew, and bake.

The Growth of Cities

Before the eleventh century the vast majority of people in Europe lived in rural villages or perhaps small market towns of a few thousand people. The cities that survived from the ancient world remained small, except in the Mediterranean. Constantinople was by far the largest city, with a population in the hundreds of thousands. The vibrant Islamic cities of Spain were the largest in western Europe, and it was said that more people could fit into the mosque of Córdoba than lived in Rome. When the population began to grow as a consequence of the agricultural revolution, immigrants swelled the market towns into cities and repopulated the few cities that had survived from antiquity.

The newly thriving cities proved to be troublesome for the lords, bishops, and kings who usually had legal authority over them. As the population grew and the merchant classes became rich, city dwellers attempted to throw off their rulers to establish self-rule or, at least, substantial autonomy for their city. In the cities of north-central Italy, for example, the prominent townsmen began to chafe at the violent authority the rural lords held over them. The lords taxed or even stole the wealth that the townsmen earned through manufacturing and trade. The lords made life unsafe and unbearable, fighting among themselves and robbing from the humble inhabitants of the cities. To counter the power of the lords, townsmen formed sworn defensive associations called communes°, which quickly became the effective government of the towns. The communes evolved into city-states, which were self-governing cities that became small states by seizing control of the surrounding countryside. Perhaps as many as a hundred or more cities in north-central Italy formed communes after 1070.

Outside Italy the movement for urban liberty was strongest in southern France, the Christian parts of Spain, and the Netherlands. Kings fiercely resisted attempts to establish urban autonomy. Especially in northern Europe, urban liberty was often extracted at a high price. Townsmen bought their freedom by agreeing to pay higher taxes to kings, who were always desperate for cash. London, which had been an old Roman city and began to thrive again by the end of the eleventh century, gained urban rights in a piecemeal fashion from several kings.

As a result of the population explosion after the year 1000, growing cities became one of the defining features of medieval life. Most of these cities were modest in size—numbering in the tens of thousands rather than hundreds of thousands—but they became important as centers of trade and manufacturing and the source for new ideas.

THE SPREAD AND REFORM OF CHRISTIANITY IN THE LATIN WEST

As the core of the Latin West became politically stronger and economically more prosperous during the tenth and eleventh centuries, Christianity spread among the previously polytheistic tribes in northern and eastern Europe. Through conversion, Roman Catholicism became the dominant religion in Europe and came to distinguish itself more firmly from the Orthodox Christianity of Byzantium. Catholicism and Orthodoxy gradually grew apart during the Middle Ages, primarily over theological differences and

■ **A Silver Crucifix from Birka, Sweden, ca. 900**
The Viking fascination with silver was exploited by early missionaries, who had local silversmiths adapt the symbolism of Christianity to traditional Scandinavian art forms. Such objects assisted in the conversion of the Swedes.

disputes about the ultimate authority in the Church. For most Christians, however, the crucial differences were over liturgy and language. The liturgy° consists of the forms of worship—prayers, chants, and rituals. In the Middle Ages there was a great deal of variety in the Christian liturgy, and a number of languages were used, but followers of the Roman church gradually came to identify themselves with the Latin liturgy and the Latin language. As a result, the diverse peoples of medieval western Europe began to be called the "Latin people," although they spoke many different languages. The term *Latin* came to represent more than a liturgy or language; during the Middle Ages it became a religious and even cultural identity.

Conversions

Among the polytheistic tribes on the northern and eastern frontiers of the Latin West in Scandinavia, the Baltic Sea region, and parts of eastern Europe, the first Christian conversions usually took place when a king or chieftain accepted Christianity, and his subjects were expected to follow. Teaching Christian principles and forms of worship required much more time and effort, of course. Missionary monks usually arrived after a king's conversion, but these monks tended to take a tolerant attitude about variations in the liturgy. Because most Christians were isolated from one another, new converts tended to practice their own local forms of worship and belief. Missionaries and Christian princes discovered that the most effective way to combat this localizing tendency was to found bishoprics. The bishopric was a territorial unit (called the *diocese*), presided over by an official (called the *bishop*), who was responsible for enforcing correct worship, combating the vestiges of polytheism and false Christian beliefs (known as *heresy*), and disciplining immorality. Especially among the illiterate, formerly polytheist tribes in northern and eastern Europe, the foundation of bishoprics created cultural centers of considerable prestige that attracted members of the upper classes. Those educated under the supervision of these new bishops became influential servants to the ruling families, further enhancing the stature of Christian culture.

In eastern Europe both Byzantine Greek and Catholic Latin forms of Christianity spread. From the middle of the tenth century along the eastern frontiers of Germany, a line of newly established Catholic bishoprics became the base for the conversion of the polytheist Slavic tribes. Over a period of about sixty years, these German bishoprics pushed the Latin form of Christianity deep into east-central Europe. This effort ensured that the Poles, Bohemians (Czechs), and Magyars (Hungarians) looked to the West and the pope for their cultural models and religious leadership. These peoples remain overwhelmingly Catholic to this day.

The first bishoprics in Scandinavia were also established in the last half of the tenth century. Whereas Germans were primarily responsible for the spread of Catholicism among the Slavs, it was English missionaries who evangelized Scandinavia. Denmark had the first completely organized church in Scandinavia, represented by the establishment of nine bishoprics by 1060. The diffusion into Sweden, Norway, and Iceland came later after the strong kingdoms developed in those countries and a pro-Christian dynasty could assist the spread of the new religion. Christian conversion especially benefited women through the abandonment of polygamous marriages, common among the polytheist peoples. As a result, aristocratic women played an important role in helping convert their peoples to Christianity. That role gave them a lasting influence in the churches of the newly converted lands, both as founders and patrons of convents and as writers on religious subjects. By the end of the fourteenth century organized polytheistic worship had disappeared.

The Power of the Saints

Saints are holy persons whose moral perfection gives them a special relationship with the sacred. Ordinary Christians venerated saints to gain access to supernatural powers, protection, and intercession with God. A saintly intercessor was someone who could be trusted to obtain God's favor. In many places the newly converted simply transformed polytheistic deities into saints, a process that greatly facilitated the adoption of Christianity.

The relationship between Christian believers and the saints was profoundly intimate and intertwined with many aspects of life: Christian children were named after saints who became their special protectors; every church was dedicated to a saint; every town and city adopted a patron saint. And even entire peoples cherished a patron saint; for example, the Irish adopted Saint Patrick, who supposedly brought Christianity to the island.

A city gained protection from a patron saint by obtaining the saint's corpse or skeleton or part of the skeleton or some object associated with the saint. These body parts and material objects, called relics°, served as contacts between Earth and Heaven and were verified by miracles. The belief in the miraculous powers of relics created an enormous demand for them in the thriving medieval cities. But because the remains of the martyrs and early saints of the church were spread across the Middle East and Mediterranean from Jerusalem to Rome, relics first had to be discovered and transferred from where they were buried to new homes in the churches of the growing western European cities. The demand created a thriving market in saints' bones and body parts. They were bought or stolen, and there was ample room for fraud in passing off unauthentic bones to gullible buyers.

Possessing relics was also important for establishing the legitimacy of political authority. For example, the ruler of the city of Venice, the doge, claimed to possess the relics of Saint Mark, one of the four evangelists who wrote the gospels of the New Testament. Based on their possession of these prestigious relics, the Venetians argued that God had authorized the city's liberty from outside interference. They used this argument against their one-time imperial masters in Constantinople, against the Carolingians who attempted to conquer the thriving city, against bishops from the mainland who claimed authority over Venice's churches, and eventually even against the pope when he attempted to control the Venetian church. The great basilica of Saint Mark in Venice became a pilgrimage shrine visited by Catholics from all over Europe on their way to the Holy Land. Each pilgrim learned of Venice's intimate association with Saint Mark from the magnificent mosaics that adorned the basilica's ceilings and walls.

The Task of Church Reform

As Christianity expanded, its spiritual mission suffered from its success in the violent and materialistic world of secular affairs. The immense wealth of the Church made it prone to corruption. Many Roman popes who had benefited from the wealth of the Church were reluctant to promote reforms. Even those who wanted to eliminate corruption were slow to assemble the administrative machinery necessary to enforce their will across the unruly lands of Latin Christianity.

As we saw in Chapter 7, Pope Gregory the Great (r. 590–604) served as the moral guidepost of the western Church during his tenure. But after Gregory the papacy gradually fell into a degraded moral state. Popes were caught in a web of scandal spun by the ambitious aristocratic families of Rome that involved the theft of church property, sexual intrigue, and even murder. During the tenth century the Crescentii family became the virtual dictators of papal administration, were rumored to have murdered popes who got in their way, and set members of their own clan on the papal throne. The slow but determined

■ Mosaics in the Basilica of Saint Mark in Venice

Pilgrims learned of Venice's intimate association with Saint Mark from the magnificent mosaics that adorned the basilica's ceilings and walls. This scene shows a miracle that occurred after Saint Mark's body was lost during a fire in the basilica. After the leaders of Venice spent days in prayer, shown on the left, Saint Mark opened a door in a column shown at the far right to reveal the place where his body was hidden. In between these two scenes, those who witnessed the miracle turn to one another in amazement.

progress of the popes from this low point to regain their prominence as moral reformers is one of the most remarkable achievements of the eleventh century.

The movement for reform, however, did not begin with the popes. The idea and energy for the reform of the Church came out of the monasteries. Monks thought the best way to clean up corruption in the Church would be to improve the morals of individuals. If men conducted themselves with a sense of moral responsibility, the whole institution of the Church could be purified. The model for self-improvement was that provided by monks themselves, who set an example for the rest of the Church and for society at large. The most influential of the reform-minded monasteries was that of Cluny° in Burgundy, which was established in 910. Cluny itself became the center of a far-reaching reform movement that was sustained in more than 1,500 Cluniac monasteries.

From the very beginning Cluny was exceptional, for several reasons. First, its aristocratic founder offered the monastery as a gift to the pope. As a result, it was directly connected to Rome and completely independent from local political pressures, which were so often the source of corruption. The Rome connection positioned Cluniacs to assist in reforming the papacy itself. Second, the various abbots who headed Cluny over the years closely coordinated reform activities of the various monasteries in the Cluniac system. Some of these abbots were men of exceptional ability and learning who had a European-wide reputation for their moral stature. Third, Cluny regulated the life of monks much more closely than did other monasteries, so the monks there were models of devotion. To the Cluniacs moral purity required as complete a renunciation of the benefits of the material world as possible and a commitment to stimulating spiritual experiences. Cluniac purity was symbolized by the elegantly simple liturgy in which the text of the mass and other prayers were sung by the monks themselves. The beauty of the music enhanced the spiritual experience, and its simplicity clarified rather than obscured the meaning of the words. The Cluniac liturgy spread to the far corners of Europe.

The success of Cluny and other reformed monasteries provided the base from which reform spread beyond the isolated world of monks to the rest of the Church. The first candidates for reform were parish priests and bishops. Called the *secular clergy* (in Latin *saeculum,* meaning "secular") because they lived in the secular world, they differed from the regular clergy (in Latin *regula,* those who followed a "rule") who lived in monasteries apart from the world. The lives of many secular clergy differed little from their lay neighbors. (*Laypeople* or *the laity* referred to all Christians who had not taken religious vows to become a priest, monk, or nun.) In contrast to celibate monks, who were sexually chaste, many priests kept concubines or were married and tried to bequeath church property to their children. The Catholic Church had repeatedly forbidden priests to marry, but the prohibitions had been ineffective until Cluniac re-

form stressed the ideal of the sexually pure priest. During the eleventh century Catholic bishops, church councils, and reformist popes began to insist on a celibate clergy, a movement that differentiated the Catholic from the Orthodox Church, in which priests could marry.

The other objective of the clerical reform movement was the elimination of the corrupt practices of simony and lay investiture. Simony° was the practice of buying and selling church offices. Lay investiture° took place when nobles, kings, or emperors actually installed churchmen and gave them their symbols of office ("invested" them). Through this practice, the powerful laity dominated the clergy. Many nobles conceived of church offices as a form of vassalage and expected to be able to name their own candidates as priests and bishops in exchange for protecting the Church. The reformers saw as sinful any form of lay authority over the Church—whether that of the local lord or the emperor himself. The movement to eradicate simony and lay investiture contradicted the Carolingian ideal that obligated the emperor to oversee the Church. Now the reformers wanted the emperor and all other lords to keep their hands off. As a result of this controversy, the most troublesome issue of the eleventh century became establishing the boundaries between temporal and spiritual authorities.

Byzantium and Eastern Europe

In late antiquity Constantinople and Rome had been the capitals of the two halves of the Roman Empire. Once joined in a common Christian culture, eastern and western Christians had grown so far apart that by the late ninth century they began to constitute separate civilizations. There were still cultural exchanges among them as merchants, pilgrims, and scholars crossed back and forth, but the two civilizations had ceased to understand one another. They held different opinions about religious matters, such as the dating of Easter, the rituals of the liturgy, the role of images in worship, and the authority of the bishop in Rome, whom Orthodox Christians refused to recognize as pope. To Orthodox Christians, the pope was just one bishop among many Christian bishops. As the popes found protection from the Frankish kings and Carolingian emperors during the eighth and ninth centuries, their ties with the Byzantine emperor loosened. After the imperial coronation of Charlemagne, the eastern (Byzantine) and the western (Carolingian and later German) emperors became rival claimants to the authority of ancient Rome.

The East and West also spoke different languages. In the East, Greek was the language of most of the population, and Latin had been largely forgotten by the end of the sixth century. In the West, Latin or local dialects of Latin prevailed; except in southern Italy and Sicily, only a tiny few knew some Greek.

Eastern Europe, especially the Balkan peninsula, constituted a borderland between the rival Greek and Latin forms of Christianity. The two civilizations competed for converts and allies to their respective sides, and the struggle between the two has left permanent scars in the cultural divisions of the region.

BYZANTIUM

Like western Europe, the Byzantine empire suffered from a long period of instability provoked by wave after wave of invaders. During the eighth and early ninth centuries Byzantium was prey to a series of invasions by Muslim armies and by the Bulgars, who were a confederation of several groups of nomads from the steppes of central Asia. Resisting these invaders sapped the strength of the empire and its emperors. As we saw in Chapter 7, the iconoclastic controversy magnified internal dissension within Byzantium. When Emperor Leo III (r. 717–741) forbade religious images, except for crucifixes, he provoked rebellions and riots throughout the empire, especially among the laity, for whom the veneration of images was a vital part of spiritual life. During this troubled period, the pope in Rome excommunicated Emperor Leo and turned away from the Byzantine emperors to accept the protection of the Frankish kings, Pepin the Short and Charlemagne, a move that shifted the attention of the papacy toward the West.

The Macedonian Dynasty

Byzantium's weakness in the face of external enemies and its persistent internal dissension ceased during the Macedonian dynasty (867–1056), a line of emperors that lasted six generations. Byzantine emperors were elected, but after Basil I (r. 867–886) murdered his way to the throne he kept his family in power by naming his sons co-emperors and making imperial elections a mere formality. Under the Macedonian emperors, Byzantine armies took the field against the Arabs, and a missionary effort converted the Bulgars, the Russians, and many of the Slavic tribes.

Byzantium and Islam had been engaged in a life-and-death struggle since the seventh century. From the middle of the ninth century to the late tenth century, Byzantine armies and fleets fought Muslim armies on several fronts. In the East the Byzantines pushed into Syria and Palestine almost to Jerusalem. A large portion of the Mesopotamian river valley fell into their hands. They annexed the kingdom of Georgia and part of Armenia. In the Mediterranean the Byzantines retook the island of Cyprus and kept the Muslims from southern Italy, although they were unable to prevent Muslim conquests of Crete and Sicily, which became thriving centers of Muslim culture.

Whereas on the eastern borders the only option against the Muslims was a military one, in the polytheistic Balkans missionary efforts helped create new alliances. By conversion the Byzantines brought the southern Slavs and the

■ **Byzantine Manuscript**

In this ninth-century Byzantine manuscript the figure with a pole is shown whiting out an image of Christ.

Bulgars into their sphere of influence. The Bulgars, however, proved to be inconstant allies, and on several occasions threatened Constantinople itself.

As we saw at the beginning of this chapter, the Rus also threatened Constantinople by sailing down the Dneiper River from Kiev to the Black Sea. After resisting a series of assaults from the Rus, the Byzantines sought to break down their hostility through diplomatic contacts and trade. Through conversions among members of the ruling families, Byzantine missionaries spread Christianity and Greek culture, making the Rus less isolated and more open to Byzantine influence. By the end of the tenth century the Rus had converted en masse and accepted the subordination of their church to the patriarch of Constantinople. As a result the Rus remained culturally connected to Byzantium, a connection that helped determine the forms of worship within Russian Orthodoxy.

During the seventh century, the settlement of the Slavic tribes between Byzantium and the western European kingdoms had widened the separation between the Greek and Latin worlds. The Byzantine success at converting the Slavs magnified a growing bitterness with Catholic Christians. For their part, the Byzantines under the Macedonian dynasty took heart from their military successes and assumed it was only a matter of time before the West returned to obedience to the one true emperor in Constantinople. Needless to say, Latin Christians did not accept the Byzantine vision of an empire in which they played a subordinate role, and relations between East and West soured during the tenth and eleventh centuries. Especially after the Saxon king Otto I was crowned emperor in 962, the Macedonian dynasty was hostile to the Latins. Visiting western ambassadors were treated with scorn and a superior attitude that precluded cooperation between Orthodox and Catholic Christians, especially against their common Muslim foes.

Under the Macedonian dynasty, the economy of Constantinople thrived. Home to more than half a million people by the tenth century, the city became a great marketplace where goods from as far away as China and the British Isles were exchanged. It was also the center for the production of luxury goods, especially silk cloth and brocades, which were traded throughout Europe, Asia, and northern Africa. During this period aristocratic families, the Church, and monasteries became immensely rich, and devoted themselves to embellishing the city with magnificent buildings, mosaics, and icons, creating the Macedonian Renaissance°.

The settlement of the iconoclastic controversy in 842 by Empress Theodora released great creative energies by defining the religious dogmas of Orthodoxy and creating unity within the Byzantine Church. Some of those energies went into missionary work, but the educated classes of courtiers, churchmen, monks, and scholars also produced a remarkable body of work. The most original work was spiritual in nature, embodied in sermons, theological scholarship, and especially hymns, but thanks to generous imperial patronage Constantinople also became a center for philosophical study, even if much of the work was derivative and unoriginal.

The patriarch Photius (ca. 810–ca. 893) became the most eminent scholar in the history of Byzantium. He maintained a huge library, which became a major center for the study of ancient Greek literature based on the rare manuscripts Photius had collected. Photius was the author of several important works, including the *Library,* an encyclopedic compendium of classical, late antique, and early Byzantine writers in both theology and secular literatures. By summarizing and analyzing these writers, Photius pioneered the book review, and his summaries remain especially vital because many of these books have been lost since his time. In addition to writing, Photius was deeply involved in church politics. Elected patriarch while still a layman, he was twice deposed from office due to the shifts of political winds in Constantinople. A bitter critic of the Catholics, Photius is often blamed for widening the gap between the two churches.

The quasi-sacred office of the emperor came to be magnified in elaborate court ceremonies under the Macedonian dynasty. The historian Emperor Constantine VII Porphyrogenetus (r. 912–959) wrote *On the Administration of the Empire,* an important source for Byzantine history. He also wrote the *Book of Ceremonies,* which became a model for royal ceremony throughout the Christian world and was adapted in kingdoms across Europe from Spain to Russia. The accumulation of ancient manuscripts and the compilations of ancient philosophy created an important cultural link between the medieval and the ancient worlds.

CHRONOLOGY

Byzantium

CA. 810–CA. 893	Life of Photius, patriarch of Constinople
867–1056	Macedonian dynasty
1025	Death of Basil II, emperor
1071	Loss of Bari and southern Italy; Seljuk Turks defeat Byzantine army at the Battle of Manzikert

In these accomplishments the Macedonian Renaissance surpassed the Carolingian Renaissance in the West.

Instability and Decline

Despite the achievements of the Macedonians, new threats loomed on the horizon. Under the Macedonian emperors, Byzantium had never been completely free from the external threat of invasions. The extent to which the empire succeeded in meeting these threats had depended on two factors—the political stability guaranteed by the Macedonian dynasty, and the organization and recruitment of the army through the military districts of the themes.

Emperor Basil II died in 1025 and left no direct heirs, but members of his family continued to rule until 1056, largely because of the general assumption that the peace and prosperity of the empire depended on the dynasty. Basil's successors, however, were not the strong leaders that had distinguished the earlier Macedonian dynasty. Administration of the empire was highly centralized, with a tangled bureaucracy that supervised everything from diplomatic ceremony to the training of lowly craftsmen. Without energetic leadership, the Byzantine bureaucracy quickly degenerated into routine and failed to respond to new challenges.

The success in checking invasions of the early Macedonian emperors had been largely the result of Byzantium's superior military capacities, guaranteed by the systematic organization of the army and navy and the strength of the economy. As we saw in Chapter 7, the military districts of the themes had originally been created as buffer territories against Muslims in Anatolia. Over time the four original themes were subdivided and new ones added until by the end of the eleventh century there were thirty-eight themes. The military strength of the empire depended on the theme system in which free, tax-paying soldier-farmers lived in villages under the supervision of a military commander who was also civil administrator. These soldier-farmers usually fought in their own districts, which meant they were defending their homes and families, and they provided a formidable bulwark against invaders.

By the eleventh century the independence of these soldier-farmers was threatened by deteriorating economic conditions. The emperor controlled virtually all industry and trade, which meant that the only profitable form of investment for aristocrats was to buy land. Every time a crop failed or a drought or famine struck, starving soldier-farmers in the themes were forced to surrender their land and their independence to one of the prosperous aristocrats who offered them food. As the great landowners acquired more land, the small farmers who were the backbone of the army began to disappear or lose their freedom. Because only free landholders could perform military service, the concentration of land in the hands of a few was disastrous for the army. After the death of Basil II, none of his successors was able to control these land-grabbing aristocrats, and the army began to decay.

After 1025 Byzantium faced formidable new enemies. In the west the Normans, who were distant descendants of Viking settlers, advanced on southern Italy and Sicily, crushing Byzantine power in Italy forever. The Normans, however, preserved a great deal of Byzantine culture in these regions, even as the Byzantine empire became a distant memory. Official documents were issued in Latin, Greek, and Arabic, and the Norman princes acted as patrons of the Greek monasteries. Greek continued to be spoken in southern Italy for many centuries as remnants of Byzantine civilization survived alongside other languages and cultures.

In the East Byzantium faced an even more dangerous enemy. In 1071, the Seljuk Turks captured the Byzantine emperor himself at the battle of Manzikert in Turkish-held Armenia. The Seljuks advanced across Asia Minor and threatened the very survival of Byzantium. The situation looked bleak indeed, and over the succeeding centuries, western European armies and the Turks ate away at Byzantium until its final collapse in 1453.

BORDERLANDS IN EASTERN EUROPE

In much of the Balkan peninsula during the seventh through ninth centuries, the dissolution of Byzantine power created a power vacuum among peoples who were Christians and still considered themselves subjects of the Roman Empire. The peninsula was also home to substantial numbers of the more recently arrived polytheist Slavic and Bulgar peoples who had never been subject to Rome. During the ninth through eleventh centuries, most of these tribes converted to one or another form of Christianity, and the patterns of those conversions have had lasting consequences to this day. The religious dividing line between those who adhered to Roman Catholicism and those who followed Orthodox rites cut directly through Slavic Europe.

The various Slavic tribes in eastern Europe were extremely fragmented politically. The intricate distribution of ethnic and linguistic groups made this region more diverse than western Europe and complicated state building there.

■ **Map 8.3 The Expanding States of Eastern and Northern Europe**

Eastern Europe during the Early Middle Ages was home to a very diverse population of tribes and fledgling states. Within this diversity the states of Bulgaria, Kievan Rus, and Poland emerged by the beginning of the eleventh century.

The Expanding States of Eastern and Northern Europe

Throughout this region, tribal loyalties had long dominated society and prevented sophisticated political development. But by about 1000 the new kingdoms of Bulgaria, Kievan Rus, and Poland began to solidify as certain dominant families made dynastic claims to rule over clusters of tribes (see Map 8.3). Bulgaria and Kievan Rus became bastions of Orthodox Christianity, Poland of Roman Catholicism.

Even before it accepted Christianity, Bulgaria began to expand at the expense of the Byzantine empire. In 811, after annihilating the Byzantine army, the Bulgarian Khan (the head of a confederation of clans) Krum (r. 808–814) had the Byzantine emperor murdered and lined his skull with silver in order to turn the rival's head into a drinking cup. With this symbolic act of debasement, the Bulgarians gained a fierce reputation as enemies of Christianity. In 865, however, Khan Boris I (r. 852–889) accepted Orthodox Christianity from Byzantium. His conversion illustrates the politics of the period. During the ninth century Christianity had acquired a powerful allure among the polytheistic tribes, not the least because so-called pagans were considered by Christian rulers as legitimate objects of aggression, and their acceptance of Christianity opened the possibility for diplomatic ties and alliances. For Boris, therefore, conversion was a way to ward off Byzantine aggression. For some four years, Boris brilliantly negotiated with Rome, Constantinople, and German missionaries, all of whom sought to convert the Bulgars. In the end Boris got what he wanted—a Bulgarian Church that recognized the ultimate authority of the patriarch of Constantinople but was essentially autonomous.

The autonomy of the Bulgarian Church was further guaranteed later in the ninth century by the adoption of a Slavic rather than Latin or Greek liturgy. This was made possible by the missionary work in neighboring Moravia of Saint Cyril (ca. 826–869) and his brother Saint Methodius (815–885), who had invented an alphabet to write the Slavic language. They translated a church liturgy into a version of the Slavic language, now known as Old Church Slavonic. The acceptance of the Slavonic liturgy gradually led the ethnically and linguistically mixed peoples of Bulgaria to identify with Slavic culture and language. From a string of monasteries established by the Bulgarians, the Old Church Slavonic liturgy spread among the Serbs, Romanians, and Russians, creating cultural ties among these widespread peoples that have survived to the present.

Despite their conversion to Orthodox Christianity, the Bulgarians remained military rivals of Byzantium. A foolhardy Bulgarian attempt to capture impregnable

AN ARAB TRAVELER DESCRIBES THE RUS

·················

During the years 921–922 the Arab Ibn Fadlan was a member of a diplomatic mission sent from Baghdad to the Bulgars on the Volga River. Along the way, Ibn Fadlan encountered the Rus at a camp and trading post. In his description of them, which remains the most celebrated account of the Viking Rus, he betrayed a fascination with their exotic appearance and customs. He identified Rus culture in terms of dress and rituals.

I have seen the Rus as they came on their merchant journeys and encamped by the Atil (Volga river). I have never seen more perfect physical specimens, tall as date palms, blond and ruddy; they wear neither tunics nor caftans, but the men wear a garment which covers one side of the body and leaves a hand free. Each man has an axe, a sword, and a knife, and keeps each by him at all times. . . . Each woman wears on either breast a box of iron, silver, copper, or gold; the value of the box indicates the wealth of the husband. Each box has a ring from which depends a knife. The women wear neck-rings of gold and silver . . . Their most prized ornaments are green glass beads . . . They string them as necklaces for their women.

. . .

When they have come from their land and anchored on, or tied up at the shore of, the Volga, which is a great river, they build big houses of wood on the shore, each holding ten to twenty persons more or less. Each man has a couch on which he sits. With them are pretty slave girls destined for sale to merchants.

. . .

When the ships come to this mooring place, everybody goes ashore with bread, meat, onions, milk and *nabid* [an intoxicating drink, perhaps beer] and betakes himself to a long upright piece of wood that has a face like a man's and is surrounded by little figures [idols], behind which are long stakes in the ground. The Rus prostrates himself before the big carving and says, "O my Lord, I have come from a far land and have with me such and such a number of girls and such and such a number of sables," and he proceeds to enumerate all his other wares. Then he says, "I have brought you these gifts," and lays down what he has brought with him, and continues, "I wish that you would send me a merchant with many dinars and *dirhems* [coins], who will buy from me whatever I wish and will not dispute anything I say."

Source: Excerpts from H. M. Smyser, "Ibn Fadlan's Account of the Rus with Some Commentary and Some Allusions to Beowulf" in *Frunciplegius: Medieval and Linguistic Studies in Honor of Francis Peabody Magoun, Jr.*, eds. Jess B. Bessinger, Jr. and Robert P. Creed, 1965. Reprinted by permission of New York University Press.

Constantinople, safe behind its massive circuit of walls, provoked a formidable military reaction. By 1018 Bulgaria had lost its independence and was reincorporated into the Byzantine empire.

Like the Bulgars, the Rus eventually adopted a Slavic language and Slavic customs. The Rus commanded the river routes from the Baltic to the Black and Caspian Seas. They established a headquarters at Kiev on the Dnieper River and extended their domination over the local Slav tribes by collecting tribute. From among the merchant-warriors of the Rus arose the forebears of the princes of Kiev, who by the end of the tenth century ruled a vast forest domain through a loose collective of principalities. The term *Rus* (later *Russian*) came to be applied to all the lands ruled by the princes of Kiev.

The zenith of Kievan Rus was under Vladimir the Great (r. 980–1015) and his son Iaroslav the Wise (r. 1019–1054). A ruthless fighter, Vladimir consolidated into a single state the provinces of Kiev and Novgorod, a city in the far north that had grown rich from the fur trade. A polytheist by birth, Vladimir had seven wives and took part in human sacrifices. However, when offered a military alliance with Byzantium in 987, he abandoned his other wives, married the Byzantine emperor's sister, and accepted conversion to Orthodox Christianity. He then forced the inhabitants of Kiev and Novgorod to be baptized and had their idols cast into the rivers. The Byzantine Church established administrative control over the Rus Church by appointing an Orthodox archbishop for Kiev. The liturgy was in Old Church Slavonic, which provided a written language and the stimulus for the literature, art, and music at the foundations of Russian culture.

The religious and political connection between the Rus and Byzantium influenced the course of Russian history; it also limited the eastward spread of Roman Catholicism. Iaroslav helped establish a bulwark of Orthodox culture throughout the Kievan state by collecting books, employing scribes to translate Greek religious books into Old Slavonic, and founding new churches and monasteries.

Unlike Bulgaria and Kievan Rus, Poland favored Roman Catholicism, an association that helped create strong cultural ties to western Europe. The Slavic Poles inhabited a flat plain of forested land with small clearings for farming. First exposed to missionaries tied to Saint Methodius, Poland resisted Christianity until Prince Mieszko (ca. 960–992) created the most powerful of the Slav states and accepted Christianity in 966. To solve the problem of German religious and political interference in his lands, Mieszko subordinated his country to the Roman pope with the Donation of Poland (ca. 991). Thus began Poland's long and special relationship with the papacy.

Mieszko's successor, Boleslaw the Brave (992–1025), expanded his territories through conquest, making Poland one of the largest European kingdoms. He guaranteed the independence of the Polish church from German ecclesiastical control by obtaining the pope's approval for a Polish archdiocese, and within a few years a string of bishoprics were set up across Poland. In 1000 the German emperor recognized the independence of Poland. In 1025 the pope gave Boleslaw a royal crown, making him the equal of any monarch in Europe. Boleslaw's immediate successors, however, allowed the central authority of the government to slip away into the hands of the local nobility and even lost the title of king.

By the eleventh century the three great Christian kingdoms of eastern Europe had been established, but Bulgaria, Kievan Rus, and Poland rested on shaky foundations. All three were subject to dissolution whenever a succession crisis or a weak king opened the door for the nobility to seize power. Bulgaria and Kiev became bastions of Old Slavonic Orthodoxy. Poland had become the principal Catholic state among the Slavs.

The Dynamism of Islam

The principal reason for the rapid spread of the religion of the prophet Muhammad was the capacity of his message to unify many diverse communities in Arabia. Especially during its early centuries, Islam disseminated Muhammad's message by both force and persuasion. Islamic rule quickly spread from Arabia into Persia, Egypt, Palestine, Syria, and beyond. In the early years of the Islamic empire, the majority of conquered peoples—who were Jews, Christians, and Zoroastrians—did not become Muslims. Instead, they agreed to accept Islamic political control and to pay a poll tax in exchange for the right to continue to practice their religion. Only later did many of these people convert to Islam, often to avoid paying higher taxes.

One of the Islamic Empire's continuing problems was how to sustain political unity over time. The fundamental problem arose from disagreements about succession. After Muhammad's death in 632, the ruler of the Islamic state was called the caliph°. The first cracks in the unity of Islam broke open over the proper succession to the caliphate. To this day the principal sectarian divisions within Islam between the Shi'ites and the Sunnis derive from conflicts over succession that emerged after the death of Muhammad.

As we saw in Chapter 7, after the assassination of Muhammad's son-in-law Ali, the caliphate fell under the control of the Umayyad clan, who governed a vast Islamic Empire between 661 and 750. The Umayyads, however, were never firmly in control of the entire Islamic world and faced a series of rebellions, especially from the Shi'ites, the followers of Ali, and the Abbasid clan, who were descendants of Muhammad's uncle. These two groups—the Shi'ites and the Abbasids—were briefly allied in mutual hostility to the Umayyads. However, after the last Umayyad caliph died in a battle in 750, the Abbasids seized the caliphate and Shi'ite support for the Abbasids collapsed. Abbasid victory made permanent the split within Islam between the minority Shi'ites and the majority Sunni. While the Shi'ites and Sunni both considered the caliphate a hereditary office restricted to members of Muhammad's clan, the Quraysh, the Shi'ites believed that only direct descendants of Muhammad through his daughter Fatima and son-in-law Ali should rule the Islamic community. The Sunni, in contrast, devised a more flexible theory of succession that allowed them to accept the Abbasid caliphs and in later generations even foreign caliphs. The caliphate developed into an office that combined some governmental and some religious responsibilities.

Once they had secured the caliphate, the Abbasids engaged in a campaign to exterminate the entire Umayyad family. The only Umayyad to escape their extermination order, Abd al-Rahman I (r. 756–788), fled to Spain where he founded what would later become the Umayyad caliphate of Córdoba. In the tenth century the Fatimids established the Shi'ite caliphate in North Africa, which claimed direct succession from Muhammad's daughter, Fatima, and opposed both the Abbasids and the Umayyads of Spain. From this time on, the Muslim world split apart into rival caliphates.

THE ABBASID CALIPHATE

The Abbasid caliphate (750–945) quickly altered the character of the Muslim world. In 762–763 a new capital was established in Baghdad. In this new location, the Abbasids were exposed to the ceremonial and administrative traditions of Persia, which helped expand the intellectual horizons of the caliphs, their courtiers, and bureaucrats. The Abbasid caliphate continued to be dominated by Arabs, and Arabic remained the language of the court. Nevertheless, the Abbasids considered all Muslims equals, whether Arabs or not. This belief fostered a distinctive Islamic civilization that fused ideas and practices derived from Arabic, Persian, Byzantine, and Syrian cultures. Despite opposition from purists, the Abbasids married non-Arabs and recruited Turks, Slavs, and other non-Muslims to serve as palace guards.

The Abbasid caliphs expanded their control over society, but they were far from despots. The caliph was first and foremost an emir—that is, the commander of a professional army. He was also responsible for internal security, which meant suppressing rebellions, supervising officials, and making sure taxes were honestly collected. But the caliph did not become involved in other public institutions, such as the mosques, hospitals, and schools. The principal exception was the office of market inspector, through which the caliph guaranteed fair business practices. In this commitment to the integrity of markets and trade, the Islamic

caliphate was considerably more advanced than either Byzantium or the Latin states.

The period of Abbasid greatness lasted about a century (754–861), and its eclectic nature is reflected in its literature. The famous *Arabian Nights,* stories written down for the Caliph Harun al-Rashid (r. 786–809), were based on Hellenistic, Jewish, Indian, and Arab legends. The *Arabian Nights* and the rich tradition of Arabic poetry, which often recounted tales of thwarted love, in turn influenced Western Christian poetry of courtly love. Caliph Harun al-Rashid began the grand project of translating into Arabic the literature of ancient Greece, as well as texts from Syria, India, and Persia.

Philosophical and scientific inquiry thrived under Caliph al-Mamun (r. 813–833), who had an astronomical observatory built in Baghdad and who appreciated the work of al-Kindi (who died sometime after 870), the first outstanding Islamic philosopher. Al-Kindi grappled with questions specific to Islam but also with the works of Aristotle and problems in astrology, medicine, optics, arithmetic, cooking, and metallurgy—topics that made him well known outside the Islamic world. The work of the Arabic translators in the ninth and tenth centuries created a crucial cultural link between the ancient and medieval worlds. The Muslims supplied Arabic translations of ancient Greek texts to a later generation of Jews and Christians in Spain, who translated them into Latin. These secondhand and third-hand Latin translations of ancient philosophy and science became the core of the university curriculum in western Europe during the twelfth century.

Abbasid political power ceased in 945 when a clan of rough tribesmen from northwestern Iran seized Baghdad. The Abbasid caliphs remained figureheads, and there were occasional attempts to reinvigorate the caliphate, but its greatness as a ruling institution had ceased. However, the caliphate remained a vital symbol of Islamic unity and survived as formal institution, at least, for another 300 years.

ISLAMIC CIVILIZATION IN EUROPE

During the eighth and ninth centuries the Muslim armies chipped away at Christian territories in Europe. Unlike their fellow Muslims in the Middle East and North Africa, most of the Muslims in Europe conducted themselves more as raiders than conquerors. They plundered and pillaged but did not stay long and did not attempt a mass conversion of Christians to Islam. The effects of these raids cannot be underestimated, however. The populations of many Mediterranean cities were vulnerable and began to disappear as urban life became impossible. The only hope for survival was to disperse into the countryside, where families could live off the land and find protection with one of the many local lords who built castles for defense. Thus the Muslim raids contributed to the decline of cities along

A HUMBLE CHRISTIAN MONK MEETS THE CALIPH OF CÓRDOBA

·················

In 953 the German emperor Otto I sent the abbot John of Gorze on a diplomatic mission to the court of Abd al-Rahman III, the caliph of Córdoba, in order to enlist his help in stamping out piracy in the western Mediterranean. Unfortunately for John, because the letters he carried from the emperor were overtly hostile to Islam, he was put under house arrest for three years. The caliph also could not understand the commitment to poverty and filth required of a Christian monk and interpreted John's refusal to dress elegantly as a calculated slight. However, John's pious sincerity eventually changed the caliph's mind. In recognition of the power of John's convictions, the caliph extended him a sign of exceptional respect by allowing him to kiss the royal hand.

John, released from almost three years of cloistered seclusion, was ordered to appear in the royal presence. When he was told by the messengers to make himself presentable to royalty by cutting his hair, washing his body, and putting on clean clothes, he refused, lest they should tell the caliph that he had changed in his essential being beneath a mere change of clothes. The caliph then sent John ten pounds in coin, so that he might purchase clothing to put on and be decent in the royal eyes, for it was not right for people to be presented in slovenly dress.

John could not at first decide whether to accept the money, but eventually he reasoned that it would be better spent for the relief of the poor, and sent thanks for the caliph's generosity and for the solicitude he had deigned to show him. The monk added in his reply: "I do not despise royal gifts, but it is not permitted for a monk to wear anything other than his usual habit, nor indeed could I put on any garment of a color other than black." When this was reported to the caliph, he remarked: "In this reply I perceive his unyielding firmness of mind. Even if he comes dressed in a sack, I will most gladly receive him." . . .

When John arrived at the dais where the caliph was seated alone—almost like a godhead accessible to none or to very few—he saw everything draped with rare coverings, and floor-tiles stretching evenly to the walls. The caliph himself reclined upon a most richly ornate couch. As John came into his presence, the caliph stretched out a hand to be kissed. The hand-kissing not being customarily granted to any of his own people or to foreigners, and never to persons of low and middling mark, the caliph none the less gave John his hand to kiss.

Source: From Colin Smith, *Christians and Moors in Spain, Volume 1,* (Aris and Phillips, 1988).

the coastlines of the Christian Mediterranean. These cities revived only when Muslim raids tapered off in the eleventh century, allowing for the growth of cities discussed earlier.

The significant exceptions to the pattern of raiding were in Sicily and Spain. Muslim farmers and merchants began to settle in Sicily. Between 703 and 1060, large numbers of Arabs migrated there from North Africa, and Islam spread among the general population even though pockets of Christianity remained. In Spain, Muslim conquests in the early eighth century brought all of the peninsula into the orbit of Islam except for the mountains and coastal regions of the extreme north.

Sicily and Spain became the principal borderlands through which Arabic learning and science filtered into Catholic Europe. These borderlands became zones of particularly intense cultural interaction, where several languages were spoken and different faiths were practiced. Although small, Muslim Sicily and Spain were among the most dynamic places in Europe during the eighth to early eleventh centuries. Certainly no Christian city in western Europe could rival Córdoba, and even within the Muslim world, which enjoyed many splendid cities, only Córdoba was comparable to Baghdad. A German nun visiting Córdoba in Muslim Spain during the tenth century thought

the city embodied "the majesty and adornment of the world, the wondrous capital . . . radiating in affluence of all earthly blessings."[2] During the tenth century the caliphate of Córdoba became the most important intellectual capital in western Europe, renowned for the learning of both its Muslim and Jewish scholars. Córdoba's fame derived from the extensive authority and magnificent building projects encouraged by the caliph Abd al-Rahman III (r. 912–961) and his three successors.

With an ethnically mixed population of more than 100,000, Córdoba boasted 700 mosques, 3,000 public baths, 5,000 silk looms, and 70 libraries. The caliph alone possessed a library housing more than 400,000 volumes. The streets of the city were paved and illuminated at night, the best houses enjoyed indoor plumbing, and the rich enjoyed country villas as vacation retreats. (In contrast, the city of Rome did not erect street lamps for another thousand years.) Besides the great mosque, which was one of the most famous religious monuments in Islam, the architectural centerpiece of the city was Madinat az-Zahra, a colossal 400-room palace that Abd al-Rahman III built for his favorite concubine, Zahra. Adorned with marble and semiprecious stones from Constantinople, the palace took twenty years to build and housed 13,000 household

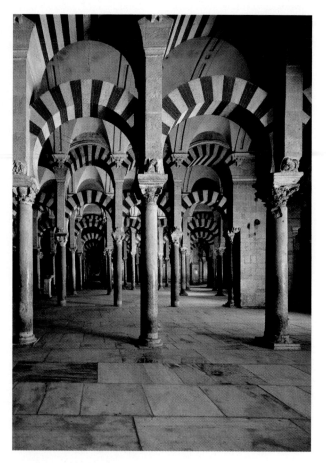

■ **Mosque of Córdoba**

The great mosque was one of the wonders of the world during the tenth century. Since Islam prohibited the depiction of the human body, mosques were embellished with geometrical forms and quotations from the Qur'an. The repetition of multiple arches creates an intricate pattern that changes as the viewer moves about in the space.

servants in addition to the diplomats and courtiers who attended the caliph.

The lasting influence of the golden age of Córdoba can be found in the legacy of the poets, scientists, physicians, astronomers, and architects who thrived under the caliphs' patronage. Despite some tensions among Muslims and Jews, many of the prominent intellectuals in the caliphs' court were Jews. Hasdai ibn Shaprut (915–970) was a courtier who became famous for his medical skills, in particular his antidotes for poisons. In the caliphs' court the demand for his cures was strong, because several princes had fallen victim to conspiracies hatched in the palace harem or had been poisoned by a lover. The trust that Hasdai gained from his medical skills led to political appointments to deal with sensitive customs and diplomatic disputes. Both Muslim and Christian rulers considered Jews

like Hasdai politically neutral, making them prized as diplomatic envoys. The Jew Samuel ibn Nagrela (993–1055) astonishingly rose to the position of vizier (prime minister) of the neighboring Muslim kingdom of Granada. An able Hebrew poet, biblical commentator, and philosopher, Samuel was also an effective commander of Muslim armies. His brilliant career reflected the value Muslims placed on learning and skill.

During the early eleventh century, the caliphate of Córdoba splintered into numerous small states. The disunity of Muslim Spain provided opportunities for the stubborn little Christian states to push against the frontiers of their opulent Muslim neighbors. The kingdom of Navarre under Sancho I (r. 1000–1035) was the first to achieve dramatic success against Muslims. After Sancho's death the division of his conquests created the three kingdoms of Navarre, Aragon, and Castile. During the reign of Alfonso VI (r. 1072–1109), Castile became the dominant military power on the peninsula. Forcing Muslims to pay tribute to him to finance further wars and gathering assistance from French knights eager for plunder and French monks ardent for converts, Alfonso launched a massive campaign known as the Spanish Reconquest that led to the capture of Toledo in 1085. Once the center of Spanish Christianity before the Muslim conquests, Toledo provided Alfonso with a glorious prize that made him famous throughout Christian Europe (see Map 8.4).

The loss of Toledo so shocked the Muslim states that they invited into Spain a sect of warriors called the Almoravids from northern Africa. The Almoravids defeated Alfonso VI and temporarily halted the Spanish Reconquest in 1086. The halt of active warfare against the Muslims provided the young Christian kingdoms time to mature by establishing the basic institutions of government. After the time of Alfonso VI, the Reconquest was seldom more than an occasional rallying cry to justify particular acts of aggression, and a few surviving remnants of Muslim power managed to hang on in Spain for another 400 years.

CHRONOLOGY

Islamic Civilization

661–750	Umayyad caliphate
703–1060	Arab occupation of Sicily
750–945	Abbasid caliphate
756–1031	Umayyad dynasty of Córdoba
AFTER 870	Death of al-Kindi
1085	Capture of Toledo from Muslims

■ **Map 8.4 Christian Reconquest of Muslim Spain**
The Spanish Reconquest refers to the numerous military campaigns by the Christian kingdoms of northern Spain to capture the Muslim-controlled cities and kingdoms of southern Spain. This long, intermittent struggle began with the capture of Toledo in 1085 and lasted until Granada fell to Christian armies in 1492.

LEGENDS OF THE BORDERLANDS

From the late eighth to the eleventh centuries, Muslim and Christian armies grappled in innumerable violent engagements. The border regions between their respective lands became militarized through building of fortresses and castles, assignment of territory to lords and generals willing to defend the borders, and settlement by soldier-farmers who served as infantrymen when required. The borderlands, however, were more than just places of conflict. During times of peace, Christians and Muslims traded with and even married one another, and in the confused loyalties typical of the times, soldiers and generals from both faiths frequently switched sides. One of the lasting fruits of these borderland societies were legends of great heroes. These legends began as stories recited in verse to entertain the aristocrats whose ancestors had fought in the borderlands, and several of these oral legends were eventually refashioned into epic poems that became extremely popular and much imitated. There were French, Byzantine, and Spanish versions of borderland epics, each strongly influencing language and culture.

The Song of Roland, an Old French epic poem that dates from around 1100, tells a story about the Battle of Roncesvalles, which took place in 778. The actual historical battle had been a minor skirmish between the soldiers of Charlemagne returning from a campaign in Spain against Basques who massacred the rear guard of the Frankish army in revenge for Charlemagne's brutal destruction of their homes. *The Song of Roland,* however, transforms this sordid episode into a great epic battle. It replaces the Basques with Muslims—the recurring enemies of the Christian Franks—and explores the psychology of family betrayal, a personality clash among friends, and the folly of heedless courage. In the climax of the poem, the hero Roland, seeking renown for his valor, rejects his companion Oliver's advice to blow a horn to alert Charlemagne of a Muslim attack. The battle is hopeless, and when the horn is finally sounded it is too late to save Roland or Oliver. For those who heard and cherished the poem, the disagreement between the prudent Oliver and the reckless Roland expressed the complicated values of bravery and loyalty, the most important values in medieval French society. In this poem the borderland conflicts be-

tween Christians and Muslims became a primal source for medieval aristocratic culture.

The epic tenth-century Greek poem *Digenes Akritas* describes the heroic feats of soldiers during the late eighth century on the eastern frontier of the empire, where Byzantine and Arab populations both fought and cooperated in a complex symbiosis. The father of the hero of the poem was an Arab soldier who abducted the daughter of a Byzantine general, married her, and converted to Christianity. The son of this mixed marriage was Digenes ("two-blooded"), a man of two peoples and two religions, who became a border fighter. This greatest Byzantine hero, who lived between two cultures, was the poetic embodiment of the engagement between Byzantium and Islam at a time when the former seemed clearly in the ascendant. Like *The Song of Roland* for the French, the legends surrounding *Digenes Akritas* had a profound influence on Greek literature. Later writers referred to it and retold its stories again and again.

In the border wars of eleventh-century Spain, the most effective soldier was Rodrigo Díaz de Vivar (ca. 1043–1099), known to history as El Cid (from the Arabic word for "lord"). Fighting for Alfonso VI, the king of Castile, El Cid was the most famous figure of the Spanish Reconquest. He is remembered in legend as a heroic Christian knight

287

fighting for God; however, El Cid did not in fact live out this role during his life. After a quarrel with Alfonso, El Cid went over to the Muslim side. For nearly ten years, this most prestigious of the Christian warriors defended the Muslim king of Saragossa. During this period of fighting his fellow Christians, El Cid added to his reputation as a general who had never suffered defeat. Even when the Almoravids invaded from North Africa and threatened the very existence of Christian Spain, El Cid did not come to the rescue of the Christian kingdoms. Instead he undertook a private adventure to carve out a kingdom for himself in Muslim Valencia. Under El Cid the city was partially Christianized and Christian immigrants began to move there, but Christian rule did not survive his death.

Soon after El Cid's death and despite his inconstant loyalty to Castile and Christianity, he was elevated to the status of the great hero of Christian Spain. Legend soon supplanted historical truth. The popularity of the twelfth-century epic poem *The Poem of My Cid* transformed this cruel, vindictive, and utterly self-interested man into a model of Christian virtue and self-sacrificing loyalty.

Similar to the western American frontier, the medieval borderlands created legends of heroism and epic struggles. The borderlands were a wild frontier into which desperate men fled to hide or to make opportunities for themselves. Like Digenes Akritas, many were the products of mixed ancestry because of Christian and Muslim abductions and marriages. The borderlands produced a class of professional warriors, such as El Cid, who took advantage of the perpetual conflicts of the Christian and Muslim kingdoms to enrich themselves and their followers. The meeting of Christians and Muslims that took place there stimulated medieval poetry and the values of knightly valor that characterized the Middles Ages.

CONCLUSION
An Emerging Unity in the Latin West

The most lasting legacy of the Early Middle Ages was the distinction between western and eastern Europe, established by the patterns of conversion to Christianity. Slavs in eastern Europe, such as the Poles, who were converted to Catholicism looked to Rome as a source for inspiration and eventually considered themselves part of the West. Those who converted to Orthodox Christianity, such as the Bulgarians and Russians, remained Europeans certainly but came to see themselves as culturally distinct from their Western counterparts. The southern border of Christian Europe was defined by the presence of the Islamic caliphates, which remained in a state of semipermanent enmity with the Christian kingdoms. The only groups to move freely between these hostile camps were soldiers of fortune in the borderlands and Jewish merchants whose trading interests pulled them across frontiers.

During this same period, however, a tentative unity began to emerge among western European Christians, just as Byzantium fell into decline and Islam divided among competing caliphates. That ephemeral unity was born in the hero worship of Charlemagne and the resurrection of the Roman Empire in the West, symbolized by his coronation in Rome. The collapse of the Carolingian empire created the basis for the European kingdoms that dominated the political order of Europe for most of the subsequent millennium. These new kingdoms were each quite distinctive, and yet they shared a heritage from ancient Rome and the Carolingians that emphasized the power of the law on the one hand and the intimate relationship between royal and ecclesiastical authority on the other. The most distinguishing mark of western Europe became the practice of Roman Catholicism, identifiable by the use of the Latin language and the celebration of the church liturgy in Latin.

By about 1050, three social institutions had emerged that became characteristic of Latin medieval society for the next 400 years or more. The first was the system of personal loyalties associated with lordship and vassalage. All medieval kings were obliged to build their monarchies upon the social foundations of lordship, which provided the only cohesive force available. The second institution was the agricultural economy built on manors, which took advantage of the productive capacities of the agricultural revolution and guaranteed a steady supply of agricultural labor through the institution of serfdom. The third institution distinctive to Latin medieval society was the demographic revival of cities, a development that energized western Europe, in particular, with economic vigor and with the idea of a community's freedom from external tyranny.

By the end of the eleventh century, emerging western Europe had recovered sufficiently from the many destructive invaders and had built new political and ecclesiastical institutions that enabled it to assert itself on a broader stage. The first move was sensational: The leaders of the Roman Church declared their intention to achieve what the Byzantines had failed to do—recapture Jerusalem from Islam. As we shall see in the next chapter, with the beginning of the Crusades, western Europeans began an aggressive engagement outside of their own continent.

Suggestions for Further Reading

For a comprehensive list of suggested readings, please go to www.ablongman.com/levack/chapter8

Bartlett, Robert. *The Making of Europe: Conquest, Colonization and Cultural Change: 950–1350.* 1993. The best, and often greatly stimulating, analysis of how Latin Christianity spread in post-Carolingian Europe.

Fletcher, Richard. *Moorish Spain.* 1992. Highly readable.

Franklin, Simon, and Jonathan Shepard. *The Emergence of Rus: 750–1200.* 1996. The standard text for this period.

Gimpel, Jean. *The Medieval Machine: The Industrial Revolution of the Middle Ages.* 1976. A short, lucid account of the power and agricultural revolutions.

Hollister, C. Warren. *Medieval Europe: A Short History.* 1997. This concise, crisply written text presents the development of Europe during the Middle Ages by charting its progression from a primitive rural society, sparsely settled and impoverished, to a powerful and distinctive civilization.

Jones, Gwyn. *A History of the Vikings.* 2001. A comprehensive, highly readable analysis.

McKitterick, Rosamond. *The Early Middle Ages.* 2001. The best up-to-date survey for the period 400–1000. It is composed of separate essays by leading specialists.

Reuter, Timothy. *Germany in the Early Middle Ages, c. 800–1056.* 1991. A lucid explanation of the complexities of German history in this period.

Reynolds, Susan. *Fiefs and Vassals: The Medieval Evidence Reinterpreted.* 1994. The most important reexamination of the feudalism problem.

Riché, Pierre. *The Carolingians: A Family Who Forged Europe.* 1993. Translated from the 1983 French edition, this book traces the rise, fall, and revival of the Carolingian dynasty, and shows how it molded the shape of a post-Roman Europe that still prevails today. This is basically a family history, but the family dominated Europe for more than two centuries.

Stenton, Frank M. *Anglo-Saxon England.* 2001. This classic history covers the period ca. 550–1087 and traces the development of English society from the oldest Anglo-Saxon laws and kings to the extension of private lordship.

Treadgold, Warren T. *A Concise History of Byzantium.* 2001. The best short survey.

Notes

1. Quoted in Edward Peters, *Europe and the Middle Ages* (1989), 158.

2. Quoted in Jane S. Gerber, *The Jews of Spain: A History of the Sephardic Experience* (1992), 28.

The West Asserts Itself: The High Middle Ages, 1050–1300

OUSAMA, A TWELFTH-CENTURY ARAB NOBLEMAN, MADE A BUSINESS TRIP TO Jerusalem, which at the time was occupied by Christian crusaders. To fulfill the obligation of his Muslim faith to pray daily, Ousama went to the Al-Aksa mosque, the oldest Muslim shrine in Jerusalem. He was struck by the contrast between those crusaders who had resided in Jerusalem for some time and had an understanding of Islam and those who had just arrived and "show themselves more inhuman." Some of the old-timers had even befriended him and made certain he had a place to pray. But the newcomers were far from friendly. He reported, "One day I went into [the mosque] and glorified Allah. I was engrossed in my praying when one of the Franks [as Muslims called all western Europeans] rushed at me, seized me and turned my face to the East, saying, 'That is how to pray!'" At that time Christians were supposed to pray facing the rising sun in the East. Muslims pray facing Mecca to the south of Jerusalem. On two occasions the Templars, members of a Christian military order who guarded the mosque, had to expel the zealous Frank from the mosque so Ousama could return to his prayers. The Templars apologized to Ousama, saying, "He is a stranger who has only recently arrived from Frankish lands. He has never seen anyone praying without turning to the East."

An uneasy familiarity developed among the Christians and Muslims in Jerusalem during this period. It was possible for an Arab such as Ousama to describe the Templars as his "friends," and they in turn protected him from the intolerance of the newly arrived Europeans. This peculiar mixture of friendliness and intolerance cut both ways. Muslims were shocked by what they perceived as the impiety of Christians. Ousama recounted another scene he witnessed when a descendant of Muhammad visited the Dome of the Rock, the place from which it was believed that Muhammad had ascended to heaven but which crusaders had transformed into a Christian church. A Templar came up to him and asked if he would like to see God as a child. When the Muslim answered "yes," the

Gothic Architecture: Interior view of stained-glass windows in Sainte-Chapelle, upper chapel, interior toward east, Paris.

Frankish knight displayed a painting of the Virgin Mary with the Christ child on her lap. The Muslims were shocked at the Christian's idolatry of referring to an image as God. "May Allah raise himself high above those who speak such impious things!"[1] Ousama exclaimed.

Throughout the Middle Ages, Muslims and Christians mixed mutual curiosity with militant hostility. Their tentative appreciation of each other was undermined by grotesque misunderstandings. The complexity of the relationship became especially clear in spiritual centers such as the mosques and churches of Jerusalem.

The cultural exchanges and clashes among the Catholic West, the Orthodox East, and the Muslim South were punctuated by the battles of the Crusades. Based on the efforts of the knights who fought in the Crusades and European merchants, the Catholic West began to assert itself both militarily and economically in Byzantium and in the Muslim world. As a result, western Europeans more sharply distinguished themselves from the Orthodox and Muslim worlds. The West became more exclusively Latin and Catholic. Westerners began to see themselves as culturally and religiously superior in comparison to their eastern and southern neighbors.

The consolidation of a distinctive Western identity and the projection of Western power outside Europe for the first time was made possible by internal developments within Europe. A number of vigorous kings created political stability in the West by consolidating their authority through financial and judicial bureaucracies. The most effective of these kings used a variety of strategies to force the most dangerous element in society, the landed aristocrats, to serve the royal interest. At the same time, the West experienced a period of creative ferment unequaled since antiquity. The Roman Catholic Church played a central role in encouraging intellectual and artistic activity, but there was also a flourishing literature in the languages of the common people—the vernaculars, such as French, German, and Italian.

During the twelfth and thirteenth centuries western Europe, in particular, was profoundly transformed. To understand this transformation, this chapter will address several fundamental questions: (1) What were the causes and consequences of the Crusades? (2) How did the Catholic Church consolidate its hold over the Latin West? (3) How did the western European monarchies strengthen themselves? (4) What made western European culture distinctive?

The West in the East: The Crusades

On a chilly November day in 1095 in a bare field outside of Clermont, France, Pope Urban II (r. 1088–1099) delivered a landmark sermon to the assembled French clergy and laypeople eager to hear the pope. In stirring words Urban recalled that Muslims in the East were persecuting Christians and that the holy places in Palestine had been ransacked. He called upon the knights "to take up the cross" to defend their fellow Christians in distress.

Urban's appeal for a Crusade was stunningly successful. When he finished speaking, the crowd chanted back, "God wills it." The news of Urban's call for a holy war in the East spread like wildfire, and all across France and the western part of the German Empire knights prepared for the journey to Jerusalem. Unexpectedly and probably contrary to the pope's intentions, the poor and dispossessed also became enthused about an armed pilgrimage to the Holy Land. The zealous Peter the Hermit (ca. 1050–1115) preached the Crusade among the poor and homeless and gathered a huge unequipped, undisciplined army, which left for Jerusalem well in advance of the knights. The army was annihilated along the way.

Urban's call for a Crusade gave powerful religious sanction to the western Christian military expeditions against Islam. Between 1095 and 1291, there were eight major Crusades and many smaller-scale expeditions (see Map 9.1).

THE ORIGINS OF HOLY WAR

The original impulse for the Crusades° was the perceived threat that Muslim armies posed to Christian peoples, pilgrims, and holy places in the eastern Mediterranean. By the middle of the eleventh century the Seljuk Turks, who had converted to Islam, were putting pressure on the Byzantine empire. In 1071 the Seljuks defeated the Byzantine army at Manzikert; their victory opened all of Asia Minor to Muslim occupation. Pope Urban's appeal for a Crusade in 1095 came in response to a request for military assistance from the Byzantine emperor Alexius Comnenus, who probably thought he would get yet another band of Western mercenaries to help him reconquer Byzantine territory lost to the Seljuks. Instead, he got something utterly unprecedented, a massive volunteer army of perhaps 100,000 soldiers devoted less to assisting their Byzantine Christian brethren than to wresting Jerusalem from Muslim hands.

To people in the eleventh century, the very idea of Jerusalem had a mystical allure. Enhancing this allure was a widespread confusion between the actual earthly city of Jerusalem in Palestine, where Jesus had been crucified more than a millennium before, and the fantastic heavenly city of Jerusalem with walls of dazzling precious stones as promised in the Bible (Revelation, 21:10ff). Many of the crusaders probably could not distinguish between the earthly and the heavenly cities and thought that when they abandoned their homes for Jerusalem, they were marching directly to Paradise. The promise of an eternal reward was reinforced by a special offer Pope Urban made in his famous sermon at Clermont to remit all penance for sin for those who went on the Crusade. Moreover, a penitential pilgrimage to a holy site such as Jerusalem provided a sinner with a pardon for capital crimes such as murder.

There was a significant difference between a pilgrim and a crusader, however. A pilgrim was always unarmed. A crusader carried weapons and was willing not just to defend other pilgrims from attack but to launch an assault on those he considered heathens. The innovation of the Crusades was to create the idea of armed pilgrims who received special rewards from the Church. The merger of a spiritual calling and military action was strongest in the knightly orders. The Templars, Hospitallers, and Teutonic Knights were soldiers who took monastic vows of poverty, chastity, and obedience. But rather than isolating themselves to pray in a monastery, they went forth, sword in hand, to conquer for Christ. These knightly orders exercised considerable political influence in Europe and amassed great wealth.

In the minds of crusader-knights, greed probably jostled with fervent piety. Growing population pressures and the spread of primogeniture (passing landed estates onto the eldest male heir) left younger sons with little to anticipate at home and much to hope for by seeking their fortunes in the Crusades.

Nevertheless, crusaders testified to the sense of community they enjoyed by participating in "the common enterprise of all Christians." The crusader Fulcher of Chartres was especially captivated by the unity displayed by crusaders from so many different countries: "Who has ever heard of speakers of so many languages in one army . . . If Breton or a German wished to ask me something, I was utterly without words to reply. But although we were divided by language, we seemed to be like brothers in the love of God and like near neighbors of one mind."[2] For many crusaders the exhilarating experience of brotherhood in the love of God seemed to be a sufficient motive.

CRUSADING WARFARE

The crusaders' enthusiasm for getting to Jerusalem diverted the knights from providing any direct help to the Byzantine emperor as originally planned. Instead the crusaders landed

■ **Map 9.1   The Major Crusades**
During the first three Crusades, Christian armies and fleets from western Europe attacked Muslim strongholds and fortresses in the Middle East in an attempt to capture and hold Jerusalem. The Fourth Crusade never arrived in the Middle East, as it was diverted to besiege Constantinople.

in the Middle East and struck out to capture Jerusalem itself from the Muslims. In achieving this goal, the First Crusade (1095–1099) was strikingly successful.

Several factors had weakened Muslim solidarity in the Middle East and the ability to resist the Crusaders. First, the onslaught of the Seljuk Turks threatened the Arab states that controlled access to Jerusalem as much as Byzantium. When the crusaders arrived, these states had already been weakened from fighting the Turks. Second, Muslims were divided internally. There were theological divisions between Sunnite and Shi'ite Muslims that prevented the Muslim caliphs from uniting against the Christians.

In 1099, after a little more than a month's siege, the crusaders scaled the walls of Jerusalem and slaughtered thousands of Muslims and Jews. The Christian triumph led to the establishment of the Latin principalities, which were devoted to maintaining a Western foothold in the Holy Land. The Latin principalities included all of the territory in contemporary Lebanon, Israel, and Palestine.

The subsequent crusades never achieved the success of the first. In 1144 Muslims captured the northernmost Latin principality, the county of Edessa—a warning to Westerners of the fragility of a defensive system that relied on a few scattered fortresses strung along a thin strip of coastline. In response to the loss of Edessa, Christians

CHRONOLOGY

The Crusades

1071	Battle of Manzikert; Seljuk Turks defeat the Byzantine emperor
1095	Council of Clermont; Urban II calls First Crusade
1095–1099	First Crusade
1099	Christians capture Jerusalem
1147–1149	Second Crusade
1189–1192	Third Crusade, led by Emperor Frederick Barbarossa (who drowned), King Richard the Lion-Heart of England, and King Philip II of France
1202–1204	Fourth Crusade, culminates in capture of Constantinople by Western crusaders
1208–1213	Albigensian Crusade

launched the Second Crusade. The ambitious offensive on several fronts failed so disastrously that the crusader movement lost credibility in the eyes of many. In 1187, the sultan of Egypt and Syria, Saladin (1137–1193), recaptured Jerusalem for Islam. In response to this dispiriting loss, the Third Crusade (1189–1192) assembled the most spectacular army of European chivalry ever seen, led by Europe's three most powerful kings: German Emperor Frederick Barbarossa, Philip Augustus of France, and Richard the Lion-Heart of England. After Frederick drowned wading in

■ **Krak des Chevaliers**
This crusader castle survives in northern Syria in what was once the County of Edessa, a Latin Christian principality constructed to defend the Holy Land. The word *krak* derives from an Arabic word meaning "strong fort."

a river en route and Philip went home, Richard the Lion-Heart negotiated a truce with Saladin.

The Fourth Crusade proved the most disastrous. In 1199, Pope Innocent III called for yet another Crusade to recapture Jerusalem, but the Frankish knights and Venetian sailors who provided transportation allowed themselves to be diverted from that mission. In 1204 in an attempt to assist an exiled candidate for the throne of the Byzantine empire, the crusaders and the Venetians besieged and captured the Byzantine capital Constantinople. The Westerners divided up the empire among themselves, set up a Latin regime that lasted until 1261, and forgot about their sacred obligation to reconquer Jerusalem. The Fourth Crusade dangerously weakened the Byzantine empire by making it a prize for Western adventurers and opened the path to its eventual destruction. None of the four subsequent Crusades achieved lasting success, even though they continued to preoccupy Westerners until 1291.

THE SIGNIFICANCE OF THE CRUSADES

Despite the capture of Jerusalem during the First Crusade, the crusaders could not maintain control of the city and for more than a century wasted enormous efforts on what proved to be a futile enterprise. Neither did any of the Latin principalities in the Middle East survive for very long. The crusaders who resided in these principalities were obliged to learn how to live and trade with their Muslim neighbors, but few of them learned Arabic or took seriously Muslim learning. The strongest Islamic cultural and intellectual influences on Christian Europe came through Sicily and Spain rather than via returning crusaders. Perhaps the deepest irony of the Crusades was the extent to which they destabilized the Byzantine empire, thus weakening the West's only Christian ally so that it became an easy target for Muslim conquest.

The most important immediate consequence of the Crusades was not the tenuous Western possession of the Holy Land but the expansion of trade and economic contacts the expeditions facilitated. No one profited more from the Crusades than the Italian cities that provided transportation and supplies to the crusading armies. During the Crusades, Genoa, Pisa, and Venice were transformed from small ports of regional significance into hubs of international trade. Genoa and Venice established their own colonial outposts in the eastern Mediterranean, and both vied to monopolize the rich commerce of Byzantium. The new trade controlled by these cities included luxury goods, such as silk, Persian carpets, medicine, and spices, all expensive, exotic consumer goods found in the bazaars of the Middle East. Profits from this trade helped galvanize the economy of western Europe, leading to an era of exuberant economic growth during the twelfth and thirteenth centuries.

The Consolidation of Roman Catholicism

································■································

The late eleventh through thirteenth centuries witnessed one of the greatest periods of religious vitality in the history of Roman Catholicism. Manifest by the rise of new religious orders, remarkable intellectual creativity, and the final triumphant battle with the surviving polytheistic tribes of northern and eastern Europe, the religious vitality of the era was due in no small part to the effective leadership of a series of able popes. They gave the Church the benefits of the most advanced, centralized government in Europe. However, the papacy's successful intervention in worldly affairs helped undermine its spiritual authority, opening the way to the degradation of the papacy in the fourteenth century.

THE POPE BECOMES A MONARCH

Religious vitality required unity within the Church. The most important step in building unity was to define what it meant to be a Catholic. Catholics began to define themselves in two ways. First, the Church insisted on conformity in rites. Rites consisted of the forms of public worship called the liturgy, which included certain prescribed prayers and chants, usually in Latin. Uniform rites meant that Catholics could hear the Mass celebrated in essentially the same way everywhere from Poland to Portugal, Iceland to Croatia. Conformity of worship created a cultural unity that transcended differences in language and ethnicity. When Catholics from far-flung locales encountered one another, they shared something meaningful to them all because of the uniformity of the rites. The second thing that defined a Catholic was obedience to the pope. Ritual uniformity and obedience to the pope were closely interrelated because both the ritual and the pope were Roman. There were many bishops in Christianity, but as one monk put it, "Rome is . . . the head of the world."

The task of the medieval popes was to make this theoretical claim to authority real—in short, to make the papacy a religious monarchy. In the last half of the eleventh century under a series of dynamic reformers, the papacy firmly reasserted itself as the head of the Roman Catholic world. Among the reformers who gathered in Rome was Hildebrand (ca. 1020–1085), one of the most remarkable figures in the history of the Church, a man considered saintly by his admirers, and considered an ambitious, self-serving megalomaniac by many others. From 1055 to 1073 during the pontificates of some four popes, Hildebrand became the power behind the throne, helping enact wide-ranging reforms that enforced uniformity of worship and establishing the rules for electing new popes by the college of cardinals. In 1073 Hildebrand was himself elected pope and took the name Gregory VII (r. 1073–1085).

Gregory's greatness lay in his leadership over the internal reform of the Church. Every year he held a church council in Rome where he decreed against simony (the buying and selling of church offices) and priests who married and attempted to bequeath church property to their children. Gregory centralized authority over the Church itself by sending out papal legates, representatives who delivered orders to local bishops, and attempted to free it from external influence by asserting the superiority of the pope over all other authorities. Gregory's theory of papal supremacy led him into direct conflict with the German Emperor Henry IV (r. 1056–1106). The issue was lay investiture, the power of kings and emperors to pick their own candidates for ecclesiastical offices, especially bishoprics. As we saw in Chapter 8, during the eighth and ninth centuries weak popes relied on the Carolingian kings and emperors to name suitable candidates for these offices in order to keep them out of the hands of local aristocrats. At stake was not only power and authority, but also the in-

come from the enormous amount of property controlled by the Church, which the emperor was in the best position to protect. During the eleventh century, Gregory VII and other reform-minded popes sought to regain control of this property. Without the ability to name his own candidates as bishops, Gregory recognized that his whole campaign for church reform would falter. When Pope Gregory tried to negotiate with the emperor over the appointment of the bishop of Milan, Henry was defiant, ordering Gregory to resign the papacy in a letter with the notorious salutation, "Henry, King not by usurpation, but by the pious ordination of God to Hildebrand now not Pope but false monk."

Gregory struck back in an escalating confrontation now known as the Investiture Controversy°. He deposed Henry from the imperial throne and excommunicated him. Excommunication° prohibited the sinner from participating in the sacraments and forbade any social contact whatsoever with the surrounding community. People caught talking to an excommunicated person or writing a letter or even offering a drink of water could themselves be excommunicated. Excommunication was a form of social death, a dire punishment indeed, especially if the excommunicated person was a king. Both sides marshaled arguments from scripture and history, but the excommunication was effective. Henry's friends started to abandon him, rebellion broke out in Germany, and the most powerful German lords called for a meeting to elect a new emperor. Backed into a corner, Henry plotted a clever counterstroke.

Early in the winter of 1077 Pope Gregory set out to cross the Alps to meet with the German lords. When Gregory reached the Alpine passes, however, he learned that Emperor Henry was on his way to Italy. In fear of what the emperor would do, Gregory retreated to the castle of Canossa, where he expected to be attacked. Henry surprised Gregory, however, by arriving not with an army but as a supplicant asking the pope to hear his confession. As a priest Gregory could hardly refuse to hear the confession of a penitent sinner, but he nevertheless attempted to humiliate Henry by making him wait for three days, kneeling in the snow outside the castle. Henry's presentation of himself as a penitent sinner posed a dilemma for Gregory. The German lords were waiting for Gregory to appear in his capacity as the chief justice of Christendom to judge Henry, but Henry himself was asking the pope to act in his capacity as priest to grant absolution for sin. The priest in Gregory won out over the judge, and he absolved Henry.

Even after the deaths of Gregory and Henry, the Investiture Controversy continued to poison relations between the popes and emperors until the Concordat of Worms in 1122 resolved the issue in a formal treaty. The emperor retained the right to nominate high churchmen, but in a concession to the papacy, the emperor lost the ceremonial privileges of investiture that conveyed spiritual authority. Without the ceremony of investiture, no bishop could exercise his office. By refusing to invest unsuitable

■ **Map 9.2   Universal Monarchy of Pope Innocent III**
Besides his direct control of the Papal States in central Italy, Pope Innocent III made vassals of many of the kings of Catholic Europe. These feudal ties provided a legal foundation for his claim to be the highest authority in Christian Europe.

nominees, the popes had the last word. Gregory VII's vision of papal supremacy over all kings and emperors persevered.

How the Popes Ruled

The most lasting accomplishment of the popes during the twelfth and thirteenth centuries derived less from dramatic confrontations with emperors than from the humdrum routine of the law. Beginning with Gregory VII, the papacy became the supreme court of the Catholic world by claiming authority over a vast range of issues. To justify these claims, Gregory and his assistants conducted a massive research campaign among old laws and treatises. These were organized into a body of legal texts called canon law°.

Canon law came to encompass many kinds of cases, including all those involving the clergy, disputes about church property, and donations to the Church. The law of the Church also touched on many of the most vital concerns of the laity—all those who were not priests, monks, or nuns—including annulling marriages, legitimating bastards, prosecuting bigamy, protecting widows and orphans, and resolving inheritance disputes. Most of the cases originated in the courts of the bishops, but the bishops' decisions could be appealed to the pope and cardinals sitting together in the papal consistory. The consistory could make exceptions from the letter of the law, called dispensations, giving it considerable power over kings and aristocrats who wanted to marry a cousin, divorce a wife, legitimate a bastard, or annul a will. By the middle of the twelfth century, Rome was awash with legal business. The functions of the canon law courts became so important that those who were elected popes were no longer monks but trained canon lawyers, men very capable in the ways of the world.

The pope also presided over the curia°, the administrative bureaucracy of the Church. The cardinals served as ministers in the papal administration and were sent off to foreign princes and cities as ambassadors, or legates. Because large amounts of revenue were flowing into the coffers of the Church, Rome became the financial capital of the West.

In addition to its legal, administrative, and financial authority, the papacy also made use of two powerful spiritual weapons against the disobedient. Any Christian who refused to repent of a sin could be excommunicated, as the Emperor Henry IV had been. The second spiritual weapon was the interdict°, which usually applied to a whole city or kingdom whose ruler had displeased the pope. During an interdict, the sacraments were not celebrated, and the churches closed their doors, creating panic among the faithful who could not baptize their children or bury their dead. The interdict, which encouraged a public outcry, could be a very effective weapon for undermining the political support of any monarch who ran afoul of the pope.

The Pinnacle of the Medieval Papacy: Pope Innocent III

The most capable of the medieval popes was Innocent III (r. 1198–1216). Only 37 when elected, Innocent was tough-minded and the ideal candidate to bolster the papal monarchy, because of both his extensive family connections in Italy and Germany and his training in theology and canon law (see Map 9.2). Innocent possessed a clear-sighted concept of the papal monarchy. To him the pope was the overlord and moral guide of the Christian community, with authority over the entire world. He recognized the right of kings to rule over the secular sphere, but he considered it his duty to prevent and punish sin, a duty that gave him wide latitude to meddle in the affairs of kings and princes. The indefatigable pope pummeled the world with commands and advice, which were not to be taken lightly. Under Innocent, the sheer volume of correspondence to Spain, for example, increased by some twenty-five times over what it had been under the hyperactive Pope Gregory VII.

Innocent's first task was to provide the papacy with a strong territorial base of support so that the popes could act with the same freedom as kings and princes. Innocent is generally considered to be the founder of the Papal State in central Italy, an independent state that lasted until 1870 and survives today in a tiny fragment as Vatican City.

Innocent's second task was keeping alive the crusading ideal. He called the Fourth Crusade, which went awry when the crusaders attacked Constantinople. He also expanded the very idea of crusading by attempting to use a Crusade to eradicate heretics within Europe. Innocent was deeply concerned about the spread of new heresies, which attracted enormous numbers of converts, especially in the growing cities of southern Europe. By crusading against Christian heretics, Innocent employed military methods to enforce uniformity of belief. He waged a fierce crusade against the heretical Cathars and Waldensians, which is described later in this chapter.

The third objective of this ambitious and energetic pope was to assert the power of the papacy over political affairs. Innocent managed the election of Emperor Frederick II; he also assumed the right to veto imperial elections. He excommunicated King Philip II of France to force him to take back an unwanted wife. And he placed England under the interdict to compel King John to cede his kingdom to the papacy and receive it back as a fief, a transaction that made the king of England the vassal of the pope. Using whatever means necessary, he made papal vassals of the rulers of Aragon, Bulgaria, Denmark, Hungary, Poland, Portugal, and Serbia. Through these manipulations of the feudal law of vassalage, Innocent brought the papacy to its closest approximation of a universal Christian monarchy.

Innocent's fourth and greatest accomplishment was to codify the rites of the liturgy and to define the dogmas of the faith. This monumental task was the achievement of the Fourth Lateran Council, held in Rome in 1215. This council, attended by more than 400 bishops, 800 abbots, and the ambassadors of the monarchs of Catholic Europe, issued decrees that reinforced the celebration of the sacraments as the centerpiece of Christian life. They included rules to educate the clergy, define their qualifications, and govern elections of bishops. The council condemned heretical beliefs, and it called yet another Crusade. It be-

came the guidepost that has governed many aspects of Catholic practice, especially with regard to the sacraments. It did more than any other council to fulfill the goal of uniformity of rites in Catholicism, and its influence survives to this day.

The Troubled Legacy of the Papal Monarchy

Innocent was a crafty, intelligent man who in single-minded fashion pursued the greater good of the Church as he saw it. His policies, however, had ruinous results in the hands of his less able successors. Their blunders undermined the pope's spiritual mission, especially when they attempted to influence the fate of the kingdom of Sicily, which lay on the southern border of the Papal State. Innocent's successors went beyond defending the Papal State and embroiled all Italy in a series of bloody civil wars between the Guelfs, who supported the popes, and the Ghibellines, who opposed them. The pope's position as a monarch superior to all others collapsed under the weight of immense folly and hypocrisy during the pontificate of Boniface VIII (r. 1294–1303). His personal faults, which included breathtaking vanity and rudeness, did little to help the papacy's blemished reputation. Widely believed to be a religious skeptic addicted to amulets and magic, Boniface enjoyed the company of riotous companions and loved to dress up in the regalia of an emperor.

In 1302 Boniface promulgated the most extreme theoretical assertion of papal superiority over lay rulers. Behind the statement was a specific dispute with King Philip IV of France (r. 1285–1314), who was attempting to try a French bishop for treason. The larger issue behind the dispute was similar to the Investiture Controversy of the eleventh century, but this time no one paid much attention to the pope. The loss of papal moral authority had taken its toll. In the heat of the confrontation, King Philip accused Pope Boniface of heresy, one of the few sins of which he was not guilty, and sent his agents to arrest the pope. They forced their way into his rooms at the papal palace of Anagni in

CHRONOLOGY	
The Papal Monarchy	
1073–1085	Reign of Pope Gregory VII
1075–1122	The Investiture Controversy
1095	Council of Clermont; Urban calls First Crusade
1198–1216	Reign of Pope Innocent III
1215	Fourth Lateran Council
1294–1303	Reign of Pope Boniface VIII

1303 where they found the 70-year-old Boniface in bed. Traumatized by the arrest and the threats of violence against him, the old man died shortly after he was released. With Boniface the papal monarchy died as well. It took more than a century for the popes to recover their independence from French influence and longer still to recapture their dignity.

DISCOVERING GOD IN THE WORLD

Even before the First Crusade, Catholic Europe began to experience an unprecedented spiritual awakening. The eleventh-century papal campaign to reform the morals of the clergy helped make priests more respectable. As a consequence, many laypeople who had previously been Christians in name only began to attend church services and to show genuine enthusiasm for the Church. Others were drawn to dedicating their lives to religion. In England, for example, the number of monks increased tenfold from the late eleventh century to 1200. The most vital indication of spiritual renewal was the success of new religious orders, which satisfied a widespread yearning to discover the hand of God in the world.

■ **Fontenay Abbey, a Cistercian House Founded in Burgundy in 1118**
The austere simplicity of the architecture is typical of the Cistercian style.

The New Religious Orders

By the eleventh century many men attracted to the religious life found the Benedictines too lax in their discipline and the Cluniacs too worldly with their elaborate liturgy and decorated churches. In 1098 a small group of Benedictine monks removed themselves to an isolated wasteland to establish the Cistercian Order. The Cistercians practiced a very strict discipline. They ate only enough to stay alive. Each monk possessed only one robe. Unlike other orders that required monks to attend frequent and lengthy services, the Cistercians spent more time in private prayer and manual labor. Their churches were bare of all decoration. Under the brilliant leadership of Bernard of Clairvaux (1090–1153), the Cistercians grew rapidly, as many men disillusioned with the sinful and materialistic society around them joined the new order. Bernard's asceticism led him to seek refuge from the affairs of the world, but he was also a religious reformer and activist, engaged with the important issues of his time. He even helped settle a disputed papal election and preached a crusade.

The Cistercians established their new monasteries in isolated, uninhabited places where they cleared forests and worked the land so that they could live in complete isolation from the troubled affairs of the world. Their hard work had an ironic result. By bringing new lands under the plow and by employing the latest technological innovations, such as water mills, many of the Cistercian monasteries produced more than was needed for the monks, and the sale of excess produce made the Cistercians very rich. The economic success of the Cistercians helped them expand even more rapidly. In their first century, the Cistercians built more than 500 new monasteries, many in places previously untouched by Western monasticism. Numerous colonies of Cistercian monks moved into northeastern Europe in areas recently converted to Catholicism. English Cistercians moved into Norway, Germans into Poland. There were also foundations in Greece and Syria, both bastions of Eastern Orthodoxy. The rapid Cistercian push beyond the frontiers of Catholic Europe helped disseminate the culture of Catholic Christianity through educating the local elites and attracting members of the aristocracy to join the Cistercians.

More than a century after the foundation of the Cistercians in France, two religious figures from Spain and Italy formulated a new kind of religious order composed of mendicant friars°. Instead of working in a monastery to feed themselves as did the Cistercians, friars ("brothers") wandered from city to city and throughout the countryside begging for alms (*mendicare* means "to beg", hence *mendicant*). Unlike monks who remained in a cloister, friars tried to help ordinary laypeople with their problems by preaching and administering to the sick and poor.

The Spaniard Dominic (1170–1221) founded the Dominican Order to convert Muslims and Jews and to combat heresy among Christians, especially the Albigensians, against whom he began his preaching mission while traveling through southern France. The ever-perceptive Pope Innocent III recognized Dominic's talents while he was visiting Rome and gave his new order provisional approval. Dominic believed the task of conversion could be achieved through persuasion and argument. To hone the Dominicans' persuasive skills, they created the first multigrade, comprehensive educational system. It connected schools located in individual friaries with more advanced regional schools that offered specialized training in languages, philosophy, and especially theology. Most Dominican friars never studied at a university but enjoyed, nevertheless, a highly sophisticated education that made them exceptionally influential in European intellectual life. Famed for their preaching skills, Dominicans were equally successful moving the illiterate masses and debating sophisticated opponents.

From the beginning, the Dominican order synthesized the contemplative life of the monastery and the active ministry of preaching to laypeople. Perhaps Dominic's greatest skill was as an innovative organizer. In contrast to traditional monastic orders, the Dominican order was organized like an army. Each province was under the supervision of a master general, and each Dominican was ready to travel wherever needed to preach and convert.

The Franciscan Order enjoyed a similar success. The Italian Francis of Assisi (1182–1226) was less an organizer than an intensely spiritual man and a visionary. The son of a prosperous merchant, Francis as a young man rebelled against the selfishness of his father's materialistic world. In a famous episode, he stripped naked in the town square as a symbol of his rejection of all possessions. Dressed in rags, he begged for food, preached repentance in the streets, and ministered to outcasts and lepers. Without training as a priest or license as a preacher, Francis at first seemed like a devout eccentric or even a dangerous heretic, but his rigorous imitation of Jesus began to attract like-minded followers. In 1210 Francis and his ragged brothers showed up in the opulent papal court of Innocent III seeking approval of a new religious order. A lesser man than Innocent would have sent the strange band packing or thrown them in prison as a danger to established society, but Innocent was impressed by Francis's sincerity and his willingness to profess obedience to the pope. Innocent's provisional approval of the Franciscans was a brilliant stroke, in that it gave the papacy a way to manage the widespread enthusiasm for a life of spirituality and purity.

Deeply influenced by Francis, Clare of Assisi (1194–1253) founded a parallel order for women, the Poor Clares. Like the Franciscans, she and her followers enjoyed the "privilege of perfect poverty," which forbade the ownership of any property even by the community itself. Clare devoted herself to penitential prayer, which was said to have twice saved the town of Assisi from besieging armies.

Both the Dominican and Franciscan Orders spread rapidly. Whereas the successful Cistercians had founded

THE SONG OF BROTHER SUN

Francis of Assisi is known as a nature mystic, which means he celebrated God's creation through a love of nature. In one of the most renowned celebrations of nature ever written, "The Song of Brother Sun," Francis transforms the inanimate forces of nature into his spiritual brothers and sisters.

Be praised, my Lord, with all Your creatures,
Especially Sir Brother Sun,
By whom You give us the light of day!
And he is beautiful and radiant with great splendor.
Of You, Most High, he is a symbol!
Be praised, my Lord, for Sister Moon and the Stars!
In the sky You formed them bright and lovely and fair.
Be praised, my Lord, for Brother Wind
And for the Air and cloudy and clear and all Weather,
By which You give sustenance to Your creatures!
Be praised, my Lord, for Sister Water,
Who is very useful and humble and lovely and chaste!
Be praised, my Lord, for Brother Fire,
By whom You give us light at night,
And he is beautiful and merry and mighty and strong!
Be praised, my Lord, for our Sister Mother Earth,
Who sustains and governs us,
And produces fruits with colorful flowers and leaves!

Source: From *The Little Flowers of St. Francis* by St. Francis of Assisi, translated by Raphael Brown, copyright ©1958 by Beverly Brown. Used by permission of Doubleday, a division of Random House, Inc.

500 new houses in their first century, the Franciscans established more than 1,400 in their first hundred years. Liberated from the obligation to live in a monastery, the mendicant friars traveled wherever the pope ordered them, making them effective agents of the papal monarchy. They preached Crusades. They pacified the poor. They converted heretics and non-Christians through their inspiring preaching revivals. Even more effectively than the Cistercians before them, they established Catholic colonies along the frontiers of the West and beyond. They became missionary scouts looking for opportunities to disseminate Christian culture. In 1254 the Great Khan in Mongolia sponsored a debate on the principal religions of the world. There, many thousands of miles from Catholic Europe, was a Franciscan friar ready to debate the learned men representing Islam, Buddhism, and Confucianism.

The Flowering of Religious Sensibilities

During the twelfth and thirteenth centuries the widespread enthusiasm for religion exalted spiritual creativity.

Experimentation pushed Christian piety in new directions, not just for aristocratic men, who dominated the Church hierarchy and the monasteries, but for women and laypeople of all classes.

Catholic worship concentrated on the celebration of the Eucharist° (Holy Communion or the Lord's Supper). The Eucharist, which was the crucial ritual moment during the Mass, celebrated Jesus' last meal with his apostles. The Eucharistic rite consecrated wafers of bread and a chalice of wine as the body and blood of Christ. After the consecration, the celebrating priest distributed to the congregation the bread, called the host. Drinking from the chalice, however, was a special privilege of the priesthood. More than anything else, belief in the miraculous change from bread to flesh and wine to blood, along with the sacrament of baptism, distinguished Christian believers from others. The Fourth Lateran Council in 1215 obligated all Christians to partake of the Eucharist:

> All the faithful of both sexes shall after they have reached the age of discretion faithfully confess all their sins at least once a year to their own priest, and perform to the best of their ability the penance imposed, receiving reverently, at least at Easter, the sacrament of the Eucharist, unless perchance at the advice of their own priest they may for a good reason abstain for a time from its reception; otherwise they shall be cut off from the Church during life, and deprived of Christian burial in death.[3]

This statement in its stark simplicity defined the core obligation of all medieval Catholics. As simple as it was as a ritual observance, belief in the Eucharistic miracle presented a vexing and complex theological problem—why the host still looked, tasted, and smelled like bread rather than flesh, and why the blood in the chalice still seemed to be wine rather than blood. After the Fourth Lateran Council, Catholics solved this problem with the doctrine of transubstantiation°. The doctrine rested on a distinction between the outward appearances of the object, which the five senses can perceive, and the substance of an object, which they cannot perceive. When the priest spoke the words of consecration during the Mass, the bread and wine were changed into the flesh and blood of Christ in substance ("transubstantiated") but not in outward appearances. Thus, the substance of the Eucharist literally became God's body, but the senses of taste, smell, and sight perceived it as bread.

Veneration of the Eucharist enabled the faithful to identify with Christ because believers considered the consecrated Eucharistic wafer to be Christ himself. By eating the host, they had literally ingested Christ, making his body part of their bodies. Eucharistic veneration became enormously popular in the thirteenth century and the climax of dazzling ritual performance. Priests enhanced the effect of the miracle by dramatically elevating the host at the moment of consecration, holding it in upraised hands. Altar screens had special peepholes so that many people could gawk at the elevation, and the faithful would rush from altar to altar or church to church to witness a succession of host elevations.

■ **St. Francis of Assisi Asks Pope Innocent III for a License to Preach**
The drama of the meeting between the simple brothers shown kneeling, presenting their rule to the pope, and the sumptuous prelates of the curia is captured by the greatest of all medieval painters, Giotto. This fresco was painted in the Franciscan church in Assisi shortly before 1300.

■ **Mary, the Model of Charity**

Etienne Chevalier, the minister of finance to the king of France, is shown here adoring the Virgin Mary, who is suckling the Christ child.

During the twelfth and thirteenth centuries public veneration of saints also began to undergo a subtle shift of emphasis, away from the cults of the local patron saints toward more universal figures such as Jesus and the Virgin Mary. The patron saints had functioned almost like the family deities of antiquity who served the particular interests of individuals and communities, but the papal monarchy encouraged uniform rites that were universal throughout Catholicism.

Christians had always honored the Virgin Mary, but beginning in the twelfth century her immense popularity provided Catholics with a positive female image that contradicted the traditional misogyny and mistrust associated with Eve. Clerics and monks had long depicted women as deceitful and lustful in luring men to their moral ruin. In contrast, the veneration of the Virgin Mary promoted the image of a loving mother who would intervene with her son on behalf of sinners at the Last Judgment. Theologians still taught that the woman Eve had brought sin into the world, but the woman Mary offered help in escaping the consequences of sin.

The popularity of Mary was evident everywhere. Most of the new cathedrals in the burgeoning cities of Europe were dedicated to her. She became the favorite example of preachers as a model for women, and numerous miracles were attributed to her. Part of her appeal derived from her image as the ideal mother with the bouncing Christ child on her knee. Countless paintings and sculptures of the Madonna and child adorned the churches of Europe, and Mary's tender humanity stimulated artists to find new ways to evoke human emotions. Mary became the center of a renewed interest in the family and the Christian value of love within the family.

Mary became a model with whom women could identify, presenting a positive image of femininity. In images of her suckling the Christ child, she became the perfect embodiment of the virtue of charity, the willingness to give without any expectation of reward. Through the image of the nursing Virgin Mary, the ability to nurture became associated not just with Mary but with Christ himself. In contrast to the early Christian saints who were predominantly martyrs and missionaries, during the twelfth and thirteenth centuries saints exhibited sanctity more through nurturing others, especially by feeding the poor and healing the sick. Nurturing was associated with women, and many more women became saints during this period than during the entire first millennium of Christianity. In 1100 fewer than 10 percent of all the saints were female. By 1300 the percentage had increased to 24 percent. During the fifteenth century about 30 percent were women. Far from a feminist

THE HUMAN BODY IN HISTORY

A Tale of Two Marys

Medieval thinking about women began with the fundamental dichotomy between Eve, the symbol of women as they are, and Mary, the ideal to which all women strived. These two female archetypes classified women by what they did or did not do with their bodies. Eve brought sin and sex into the world through her disobedience to God. Mary, the Virgin Mother, kept her body inviolate.

Into the gap between the two natures of women emerged Mary Magdalen, a repentant prostitute whose veneration reached a pinnacle in the twelfth century. The medieval image of Magdalen was a composite figure, based on confusion among several different women in the New Testament. In contrast to the perpetually virginal ideal of Mary, the mother of Christ, Magdalen offered the possibility of redemption to all women. The clerical discussion of the natures of these two Marys—the Virgin Mary and Mary Magdalen—reveals a complex and changing medieval discussion about the nature of women. This discussion was pursued through a theoretical examination of women's bodies and their sexuality.

The precise significance of Mary's virginity long preoccupied Christian thinkers. Two of the Gospels simply assert that Mary had not known a man before she became pregnant with the Christ child. Later Christian thinkers extended this idea to assert that she remained a virgin after the birth of Jesus and even that she miraculously managed to preserve her virginity "before, during, and after delivery" of the infant. By discussing her as a virgin who gave birth and still remained a virgin, these Christian thinkers relegated Mary to a heavenly realm where the physical facts of real women's lives did not apply.

Geoffroy of Vendôme (d. 1132), a cleric educated in a cathedral school, drew an astonishing conclusion from these speculations about Mary's reproductive anatomy:

> *Virtuous Mary gave birth to Christ, and in Christ she gave birth to Christians. Hence the mother of Christ is the mother of all Christians. If the mother of Christ is the mother of all Christians, then clearly Christ and Christians are brothers. Not only is Christ the brother of all Christians, he is also the father of all men and primarily of Christians. From which it follows that Christ is the Virgin's father and husband as well as her son.*[4]

Geoffroy collapsed all male family relationships into one: the lineage of father, husband, and son merges with the equality of brotherhood among all Christians. What is most remarkable about Geoffroy's way of thinking is that this great Christian drama takes place within the confines of a mother's womb, invisible to sight yet so mysteriously open to speculative examination. The problem with this way of thinking was that its implications were not merely theoretical. Geoffroy and other priests were pastors who offered practical advice to real women. The model of the Virgin Mary left them with only one avenue for giving advice: They recommended that women remain lifelong virgins, which was rather impractical advice for the vast majority of women who were married.

Mary Magdalen's life provided an alternative, more practical model to follow. Known in the early Church, her veneration spread after the abbey at Vézelay, Burgundy, changed its dedication from the Virgin Mary to Mary Magdalen in 1095 and began to flourish as a pilgrimage site. Throughout France, "Madeleine" became a popular name for girls. In 1105 Geoffroy of Vendôme assembled most of the known and presumed information about her in a sermon, "In Honor of the Blessed Mary Magdalen." All writers agreed she had been a prostitute. Some insisted she had been afflicted by insatiable lust. But she had redeemed herself. By confessing her sins, she saved herself, and Christ forgave her. Thus, a woman whose body had once been corrupted saved not only herself but through her example brought others to repentance. If Magdalen could achieve redemption from her degraded state, did she not offer hope to all women? This medieval understanding of human redemption was worked out through a discussion of woman's reproduction and sexuality. ∎

■ **Mary Magdalen**
The repentant prostitute, Mary Magdalen, represented the possibility of redemption for all sinners.

For Discussion

What did the medieval depiction of the two Marys reveal about the way people thought about women, sexuality, and moral worth?

religion, Catholicism nevertheless developed a sacred female principle and offered an ideal woman for veneration much more prominently than did Judaism or Islam.

Many Christians became attracted to mysticism, the attempt to achieve union of the self with God. To the mystic, complete understanding of the divine was spiritual, not intellectual, an understanding best achieved through asceticism, the repudiation of material and bodily comforts. Both men and women were mystics, but women concentrated on the more extreme forms of asceticism. For example, some women allowed themselves to be walled up in dark chambers to achieve perfect seclusion from the world and avoid distractions from their mystical pursuits. Others had themselves whipped, wore painful scratching clothing, starved themselves in a form of holy anorexia, or claimed to survive with the Eucharist as their only food. Female mystics, such as Juliana of Norwich (1342–ca. 1416), envisioned a holy family in which God the Father was almighty but the Mother was all wisdom. Some female mystics believed that Christ had a female body because he was the perfect nurturer, and they ecstatically contemplated spiritual union with him.

Saints and mystics were exceptional people, however. Most Christians contented themselves with the sacraments, especially baptism, penance, and the Eucharist; perhaps a pilgrimage to a saint's shrine; and a final attempt for salvation by making a pious gift to the Church on their deathbed. The benevolent process of discovering God also stimulated a related malevolent process of attempting to detect the influence of the Devil in the world. To eradicate the Devil's influence, Christians made some people the outcasts of Western society.

CREATING THE OUTCASTS OF EUROPE

As churchmen and kings sought to enforce religious unity and moral reform during the twelfth and thirteenth centuries, they were disturbed by peoples who did not seem to fit into official notions of Christian society. Some of these people, such as lepers and male homosexuals, were physically or socially different; others, such as heretics and Jews, actively rejected church authority. The Church began a dramatic wave of persecutions, including campaigns to convert, control, or suppress these minorities, who were made social outcasts.

The Heretics: Cathars and Waldensians

In its efforts to defend the faith, the Church during the first half of the thirteenth century began to authorize bishops and other clerics to conduct inquisitions (formal inquiries) into specific instances of heresy or perceived heresy. The so-called heretics tended to be faithful people who sought a form of religion purer than the Church provided. During the thirteenth and early fourteenth centuries, inquisitions

and systematic persecutions targeted the Cathars and Waldensians.

The Cathars were especially strong in northern Italy and southern France. Heavily concentrated around the French town of Albi, the Cathars were also known as Albigensians. They departed from Catholic doctrine, which held that God created the Earth, because they believed that an evil force had created all matter. To purify themselves, an elite few—known as "perfects"—rejected their own bodies as corrupt matter, refused to marry and procreate, and in extreme cases gradually starved themselves. These purified perfects provided a dramatic contrast to the worldly Catholic clergy. For many, Catharism became a form of protest against the wealth and power of the Church. By the 1150s the Cathars had organized their own churches, performed their own rituals, and even elected their own bishops. Where they became deeply rooted, as in the south of France, they practiced their faith openly and publicly mocked Catholics.

The Waldensians were the followers of Peter Waldo (died ca. 1184), a merchant of Lyons, France, who had abandoned all his possessions and taken a vow of poverty. Desiring to imitate the life of Jesus and live in simple purity, the Waldensians preached and translated the Gospels from the Latin into their own language so that common people could read and understand them. The Waldensians created an alternative church that became immensely popular in southern France, Rhineland Germany, and northern Italy.

Catholic authorities were unremittingly hostile to the Cathars and Waldensians. They declared heretics liable to the same legal penalties as those guilty of treason, which authorized the political authorities to proceed against them. In 1208 Pope Innocent III called the Albigensian Crusade, the first of several holy wars launched against heretics in the south of France. To eradicate the remaining Cathars and Waldensians, several kings and popes initiated inquisitions. By the middle of the thirteenth century the Cathars had been exterminated except for a few isolated pockets in the mountains, which were systematically mopped up by later inquisitors. The Waldensians were nearly wiped out by inquisitorial campaigns, but a few scattered groups have managed to survive to this day, mostly by retreating to the relative safety of the high Alps.

Systematic Persecution of the Jews

Before the Crusades, Christians and Jews had lived in relative harmony in Europe. In fact, during the Carolingian period the Frankish kings and emperors had protected Jewish communities from the occasional hostility of bishops who sought to expel them. The Crusades fomented increased violence against Jews, however. Discrimination and assaults against Jews soon became far more common than ever before. In 1182 Jews were expelled from France and allowed to return only under dire financial penalties. In England the monarchy discriminated against the Jews, opening the way for the massacre and mass suicide of the entire Jewish community of York in 1190. The 1215 decrees of the Fourth Lateran Council, which were the centerpiece of Innocent III's pontificate, attempted to regulate the activities of the Jews of Europe. These decrees prohibited Jews from holding public offices and required them to wear distinctive dress.

Christians justified their persecution of Jews during the twelfth and thirteenth centuries in two ways. First, they depicted Jews as the enemies of Christ. This bias was based on the belief that Jews were members of a conspiratorial organization devoted to the destruction of Christianity. Second, jurists began to consider Jews as royal serfs because they lived in a Christian kingdom at the king's sufferance. By classifying Jews as serfs, the law deprived them of the rights of private property. As the jurist Bracton put it, "The Jew can have nothing of his own, for whatever he acquires he acquires not for himself but for the king; for the Jews live not for themselves but for others and so they acquire not for themselves but for others."[5] This precept, which was promulgated in Spain, England, and the German Empire, justified the repeated royal confiscations of Jewish property. Especially when faced with a fiscal shortfall, kings were inclined to solve their financial problems by expropriating the property of the Jewish community.

"The Living Dead": Lepers

The widespread presence of lepers produced dramatically conflicting emotions in medieval Europe. Leprosy (Hansen's disease), which destroys the blood vessels, skin tissues, and ligaments of its victims, creating grotesque disfigurements and bone deformations, was greatly feared. Leviticus 13:45–46 says of the leper, "he is unclean: he shall dwell alone." Following these biblical precepts, many communities during the twelfth century established leper houses to segregate victims of leprosy and other disfiguring or repellent diseases. Lepers' separation from the world made them objects of admiration for some pious Christians. To wash the sores and kiss the lesions of lepers constituted a charitable act of special merit, especially for pious women.

Some medieval thinkers equated lepers with heretics and Jews. A monk was reported to have shouted to a heretical preacher, "you too are a leper, scarred by heresy, excluded from communion by the judgment of the priest, according

■ Burning of Heretics During the Early Thirteenth Century

These were followers of Amalric of Bène, whose body was dug up and burned in 1210. King Philip II of France supervises the burning.

JUSTICE IN HISTORY

Inquiring into Heresy: The Inquisition in Montaillou

In 1208 Pope Innocent III issued a call for a Crusade against the Cathars or Albigensians. Fighting on behalf of French King Philip II, Simon de Montfort decisively defeated the pro-Cathar barons of southern France at Muret in 1213. Catharism retreated to the mountains, where it was kept alive by a clandestine network of adherents. The obliteration of these stubborn remnants required methods more subtle than the blunt instrument of a Crusade. It required the techniques of inquisitors adept at interrogation and investigation.

Against the Cathar underground, the inquisition conducted its business through a combination of denunciations, exhaustive interrogations of witnesses and suspects, and confessions. Because its avowed purpose was to root out doctrinal error and to reconcile heretics to the Church, eliciting confessions was the preferred technique. But confessed heretics could not receive absolution until they informed on their friends and associates.

One of the last and most extensively documented inquisition cases against Catharism took place in Montaillou, a village in the Pyrenees Mountains, near the border of modern-day France and Spain. The Montaillou inquisition began in 1308, a century after the launch of the Albigensian Crusade and long after the heyday of Catharism.

However, the detailed records of the inquisitors provide a revealing glimpse into Catharism and its suppression as

well as the procedures of the inquisition. The first to investigate Montaillou was Geoffrey d'Ablis, the inquisitor of Carcassone. In 1308 he had every resident over age 12 seized and imprisoned. After the investigation, the villagers suffered the full range of inquisitorial penalties for their Cathar faith. Some were burned at the stake or sentenced to life in prison. Many who were allowed to return to Montaillou were forced to wear a yellow cross, the symbol of a heretic, sewn to the outside of their garments.

Unfortunately for these survivors, Montaillou was investigated again from 1318 to 1325 by the most fearsome inquisitor of the age, Jacques Fournier, who was later elected Pope Benedict XII. Known as an efficient, rigorous opponent of heresy, Fournier forced virtually all the surviving adults in Montaillou to appear before his tribunal. When the scrupulous Fournier took up a case, his inquiries were notoriously lengthy and rigorous. Both witnesses and defendants spoke of his tenacity, skill, and close attention to detail in conducting interrogations. If Fournier and his assistants could not uncover evidence through interrogation and confession, they did not hesitate to employ informers and spies to obtain the necessary information. When Pierre Maury, a shepherd who had been sought by the inquisitors for many years, returned to the village for a visit, an old friend received him with caution: "When we saw you again we

felt both joy and fear. Joy, because it was a long time since we had seen you. Fear, because I was afraid lest the Inquisition had captured you up there: if they had they would have made you confess everything and come back among us as a spy in order to bring about my capture."[6]

Fournier's success in Montaillou depended on his ability to play local factions against each other by encouraging members of one clan to denounce the members of another. Fournier's persistence even turned family members against one another. The clearest example of this convoluted play of local alliances and animosities, family ties, religious belief, and self-interest is the case of Montaillou's wealthiest family, the Clergues.

Bernard Clergue was the count's local representative, which made him a kind of sheriff, and his brother Pierre was the parish priest. Together they represented both the secular and religious arms of the inquisition in Montaillou. In his youth, Pierre had Cathar sympathies, and he reportedly had kept a heretical book or calendar in his home. Nevertheless, at some time before 1308, he and Bernard betrayed the local Cathars to the inquisition. In the proceedings that followed, they had the power to either protect or expose their neighbors and family members. When one of his relatives was summoned to appear before the inquisition, Bernard warned

Heretics Besiege the Church

In this fifteenth-century painting the Church is symbolized by a castle, which is defended by the pope and bishops. Many of the heretics attacking the Church wear blindfolds, which symbolized their inability to see the truth.

her to "say you fell off the ladder in your house; pretend you have broken bones everywhere. Otherwise it's prison for you."[7] Pierre relentlessly used his influence for his own and his family's benefit. A notorious womanizer, Pierre frightened women into sleeping with him by threatening to denounce them to the inquisition. Those he personally testified against were primarily from other prominent Montaillou families who represented a challenge to the Clergues' power. As one resident bitterly testified, "the priest himself cause[s] many inhabitants of Montaillou to be summoned by the Lord Inquisitor of Carcassone. It is high time the people of the priest's house were thrust as deep in prison as the other inhabitants of Montaillou."[8]

Despite the Clergues' attempted misuse of the inquisitorial investigation for their own purposes, the inquisitor Fournier persevered according to his own standards of evidence. In 1320 he finally had Pierre Clergue arrested as a heretic. The sly priest died in prison.

Questions of Justice

1. How did the methods of the inquisition help create outcasts from Catholic society? How did these methods help consolidate Catholic identity?

2. The trial of the people of Montaillou focused on differences of belief. How did the inquisition trial make these differences more apparent both to Cathars and Catholics?

3. The primary function of the inquisition was to investigate what people believed. In this sense the inquisition differed from secular criminal courts that investigated alleged criminal actions. What kinds of evidence would reveal what people believed as opposed to what people had done?

Taking It Further

Lambert, Malcolm. *The Cathars*. 1998. The best place to investigate the Cathar movement in the full sweep of its troubled history.

Le Roy Ladurie, Emmanuel. *Montaillou: The Promised Land of Error*, trans. Barbara Bray. 1978. The best-selling and fascinating account of life in a Cathar village based on the records of Fournier's inquisition.

Moore, R. I. *The Formation of a Persecuting Society: Power and Deviance in Western Europe, 950–1250*. 1987. Places the harassment of heretics in the broader context of medieval persecutions.

CRUSADERS MASSACRE THE JEWS OF RHINELAND GERMANY

··················

On May 25, 1096, a restless crusading army attacked the Jews living in the city of Mainz, one of the great Rhineland cities on the route to the Holy Land. The Jews had taken refuge in the courtyard of the archbishop's palace, where, surrounded by heavily armed soldiers, they were given a stark choice—convert to Christianity or die. Most chose to hold fast to their faith and accept death. A Hebrew narrative recounts how a mother realizing that her children were about to be captured by the crusaders killed them herself.

There was a notable lady, Rachel the daughter of Rabbi Isaac [son of Rabbi] Asher. She said to her companions: "I have four children. On them as well have no mercy, lest these uncircumcised come and seize them and they remain in their pseudo-faith. With them as well you must sanctify the Holy Name." One of her companions came and took the knife. When she [Rachel] saw the knife, she cried loudly and bitterly. She beat her face, crying and saying: "Where is your steadfast love, O Lord?" She took Isaac, her small son—indeed he was very lovely—and slaughtered him. She had said to her companions: "Wait! Do not slaughter Isaac before Aaron." But the lad Aaron, when he saw that his brother had been slaughtered, cried out: "Mother, Mother, do not slaughter me!" He then went and hid himself under a bureau. She took her two daughters, Bella and Matrona, and sacrificed them to the Lord God of Hosts, who commanded us not to abandon pure awe of him and to remain loyal to him. When the saintly one finished sacrificing her three children before our Creator, she then lifted her voice and called out to her son: "Aaron, Aaron, where are you? I shall not have pity on you either." She pulled him by the leg from under the bureau, where he had hidden, and sacrificed him before the sublime and exalted God. She then put them under her two sleeves, two on one side and two on the other, near her heart. [The soldiers] convulsed near her, until the crusaders seized the chamber. They found her sitting and mourning them. They said to her: "Show us the money which you have under your sleeves." When they saw the slaughtered children, they smote her and killed her.

Source: From *The Jews and the Crusaders,* translated from the Hebrew by Shlomo Eidelberg. Published by The University of Wisconsin Press, 1977. Reprinted by permission.

---

to the law, bare-headed, with ragged clothing, your body covered by an infected and filthy garment." In 1321 rumors alleged that a conspiracy between lepers and Jews had poisoned the wells in France. Heretics, lepers, and Jews became interchangeable co-conspirators in league with the Devil to destroy Christianity. As the assumed common enemy, they all became subject to persecution.

The Invention of Sexual Crimes

The Christian disapproval of men who engaged in sexual relations with other men derived from a medieval interpretation of the biblical condemnation of the Sodomites, the people of the city of Sodom and its sister cities. Ezekiel 16:49 states, "This was the guilt of your sister Sodom: she and her daughters had pride, excess of food, and prosperous ease, but did not aid the poor and needy." According to this passage, the sin of the people of Sodom was the failure to be charitable; sexual behavior was not mentioned. In fact, during the first millennium of Christianity, there was no particular concern about homosexuality. Christian theologians advocated chastity for everyone and did not consider homosexual relations between men to be any more sinful than any other form of sexual behavior.

During the eleventh century, however, the sin of Sodom came to be associated with homosexual relations, prompted perhaps by reports of forced child prostitution in Muslim lands. The first church legislation against the practice came in 1179. The reasons for this dramatic shift of opinion—from tolerating such behavior to treating it as criminal—are obscure, but the language of the time paired sodomy with leprosy. Male sodomites began to be persecuted, and by 1300 most governments had made male sodomy punishable by death, in many statutes death by burning. In the process of creating new outcasts, however, female homosexuals were never mentioned. It appears that the male authors of penal legislation could not imagine that erotic relationships between women were even possible.

By the thirteenth century, heretics, Jews, lepers, and male sodomites were identified as outcasts and subjected to legal discrimination, persecution, violence, and—in the case of heretics—even extermination. The so-called cleansing of Christian Europe of its outcasts was a particularly violent example of the use of power by the dominant society over certain minority groups within it. One of the ways medieval Catholic society became unified was by ostracizing certain groups of people from within its midst. The cleansing of Christian Europe was a tragedy for its victims, but it gave both church and government officials a greater sense of unity and control.

Strengthening the Center of the West

During the twelfth and thirteenth centuries, Catholic western Europe became the supreme political and economic power in the Christian world, eclipsing Byzantium—an achievement that made it a potent rival to the Islamic states. One reason was heightened political unity. The kings of France and England, in particular, achieved unprecedented power over their own dominions. A second reason was economic. From the city-states in Italy to the cities of the Hanseatic League on the shores of the Baltic Sea, Europe was bound together by an extensive trading network controlled by sophisticated merchants. As a result, by the thirteenth century Europeans enjoyed a high level of prosperity.

THE MONARCHIES OF WESTERN EUROPE

The three forms of government during the Middle Ages were empires, city-states, and monarchies. The best example of an empire was Byzantium, a potentially formidable military power, but too diverse and far flung to maintain the loyalty of its subjects. During the twelfth century the threads that held the Byzantine empire together began to fray. The other empire at the time was the German Empire, which boasted some impressive monarchs but lacked unity and thus never achieved its potential as the dominant power in Europe. Italian city-states, such as Venice, Milan, Florence, Pisa, and Genoa, thrived as the engines of economic innovation and vitality, but they were vulnerable to foreign conquest and frequently enfeebled by internal rivalries and feuds. In contrast to overextended empires and underdefended city-states, the western European monarchies gathered the military resources and created the bureaucratic structures necessary to surpass all other forms of government. These kingdoms created the foundations of the modern nation states, which remain to this day the dominant forms of government around the globe. What happened in France and England during the twelfth and thirteenth centuries, therefore, represents one of the most important and lasting contributions of the West to world history.

During the High Middle Ages, France and England began to exhibit the fundamental characteristics of modern states. Several developments explain how these states strengthened themselves. First, they formed political units that persisted. That is, these units had borders that survived despite changes in rulers and dynasties. Second, they developed lasting, impersonal institutions that managed finances and administration. That is, they created bureaucracies.

Third, they established a system for resolving disputes and rendering justice in which the final authority was the king. That is, they established the principle of sovereignty. Fourth, the medieval monarchies resolved that the fundamental loyalty of subjects should be to the laws of the state, a loyalty greater than the obligations of a vassal to a lord or even a son to a father. Stable borders, permanent bureaucracies, sovereignty, and the rule of law—these were the foundations on which France and England established strong states in the twelfth and thirteenth centuries (see Map 9.3).

Expansion of Power: France

For the French kings, the pressing task was to unify their hodge-podge kingdom. Through most of the twelfth century the only part of France the kings ruled directly was the royal domain, the Ile-de-France, an area roughly the size of Vermont but with the fertile soil of Illinois. Over the rest of the kingdom, the king of France was merely the overlord with vague obligations from his vassals, one of whom, the king of England, directly controlled more French territory than he did. Upon these unpromising foundations, the twelfth- and thirteenth-century French monarchs built the most powerful kingdom in Europe and one of the most unified. The kings of France achieved unity through military conquests and shrewd administrative reforms.

France was blessed with a continuous succession of kings who ruled for long periods of time, produced male heirs, and avoided succession disputes. In the turbulent Middle Ages, dynastic continuity was a key ingredient in building loyalty and avoiding chaos. The vigorous Philip I (r. 1060–1108) initiated a succession of extremely effective kings. Unpopular with the clergy because of his alleged adultery, he took charge of his own domain, where he countermanded the arbitrary justice of local lords by extending royal justice. By focusing his attention on establishing himself as the undisputed lord of his own domain, Philip provided his descendants with a powerful lordship upon which they built the French monarchy.

Louis VI, the Fat (r. 1108–1137), secured complete control of the Ile-de-France, thus providing the dynasty with a dependable income from the region's abundant farms and the thriving trade of Paris. He shoved aside the great barons who had dominated the royal administration and replaced them with career bureaucrats who were loyal only to the king. The most prominent of these was the highly talented Suger, a lower-class priest who had been Louis's tutor and served the king as a statesman of vision.

Louis's grandson, Philip II Augustus (r. 1180–1223), lacked education but proved himself a shrewd realist who outmaneuvered his vassal, the English King John, to recover much of western France for himself. To administer his domain and newly acquired lands, Philip introduced new royal officials, the *baillis*, who were paid professionals and often trained in Roman law. Directly responsible to the king, they had full administrative, judicial, and military powers in their districts. Philip tolerated considerable regional diversity, but the *baillis* laid the foundation for a bureaucracy that centralized French government. Many historians consider Philip Augustus the most important figure in establishing the unity of the French state.

The medieval French king who came closest to exemplifying the moral ideals of kingship was Louis IX (r. 1226–1270), who was canonized Saint Louis in 1297 for his exemplary piety and reputation for justice. A tall imposing figure, Louis was blessed with impeccable manners and a chivalrous nature. Prompted by an ardent desire to lead a Crusade to the Holy Land, he sought to strengthen the kingdom so that it could operate and survive in his absence. He introduced a system of judicial appeals that expanded royal justice and investigated the honesty of the *baillis*.

The reputation of the monarchy so carefully burnished by Louis IX suffered during the reign of his grandson, Philip IV, the Fair (r. 1285–1314)—known for his ruthless use of power. Philip greatly expanded the king's authority and also managed to bring the Church under his personal control, making the French clergy largely exempt from papal supervision. To pay for his frequent wars, Philip expelled the Jews after stripping them of their lands and goods, and then turned against the rich Order of the Knights Templar, a crusader order that had amassed a fortune as the papal banker and creditor of Philip. He confiscated the Templars' lands and tortured the knights to extort confessions to various crimes in a perverse campaign to discredit them. Philip was perhaps most effective in finding new ways to increase taxation. Under Philip, royal revenues grew tenfold from what they had been in the saintly reign of Louis IX.

■ **Map 9.3 Western European Kingdoms in the Late Twelfth Century**

The kings of England occupied Ireland as well as much of western France. France itself was consolidated around the Ile-de-France, the area around Paris. The kingdoms of Germany, Bohemia, Burgundy, and Italy were ruled by the German emperors.

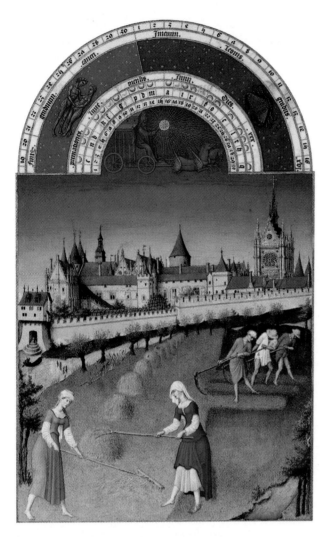

■ The Fertile Medieval Countryside
During the month of June everyone in the village participated in the wheat harvest. The men cut the grain while the women raked it. In the background is one of the great palaces of the dukes of Burgundy.

Lord of All Lords: The King of England

When the Norman William I, the Conqueror (r. 1066–1087), seized England in 1066, he claimed that as the conqueror he possessed all the land. The new king kept about one-fifth of the land under his personal rule and parceled out the rest to the loyal nobles, monasteries, and the churches. This policy ensured that every bit of England was held as a fief, directly or indirectly, from the king, a principle of lordship enforced by an oath of loyalty to the crown required of all vassals. About 180 great lords from among the Norman aristocracy held land directly from the king, and hundreds of lesser nobles were vassals of these great lords. William accomplished what other kings only dreamed about: He had truly made himself the lord of all lords. William's hierarchy of nobles

transformed the nature of the English monarchy, giving the Norman kings far greater authority over England than any of the earlier Anglo-Saxon kings had enjoyed and creating a more unified realm than any kingdom on the continent.

The legacy of the conquest provided William's successors with a decided advantage in centralizing the monarchy. Nevertheless, the system required the close personal attention of the king. King Henry II (r. 1154–1189) proved himself an indefatigable administrator and calculating realist who made England the best-governed kingdom in Europe at the time. Reacting to the anarchy that prevailed when he ascended to the throne, he strengthened the government of England and extended English authority—with varying degrees of success—over Ireland, Wales, and Scotland.

The greatest innovations of Henry's rule were judicial. His use of sheriffs to enforce the royal will produced the legends of Robin Hood, the bandit who resisted the nasty sheriff of Nottingham on behalf of the poor. But in reality the sheriffs probably did more good than evil in protecting the weak against the powerful. In attempting to reduce the jurisdiction of the nobles, Henry made it possible for almost anyone to obtain a writ that moved a case to a royal court. To make justice more available to those who could not travel to Westminster, just outside of London where the royal court usually sat, Henry introduced a system of itinerant circuit court° judges who visited every shire in the land four times a year. When this judge arrived, the sheriff was required to assemble a group of men familiar with local affairs to report the major crimes that had been committed since the judge's last visit. These assemblies were the origins of the grand jury° system, which persists to this day as the means for indicting someone for a crime.

For disputes over the possession of land, sheriffs assembled a group of twelve local men who testified under oath about the claims of the plaintiffs, and the judge made his decision on the basis of their testimony. These assemblies were the beginning of trial by jury°. The system was later extended to criminal cases and remains the basis for rendering legal verdicts in common-law countries, including Britain, the United States, and Canada.

With his usual directness, Henry tackled the special legal privileges of the clergy, the thorn in the side of medieval kings everywhere. According to canon law, priests could be tried only in church courts, which were notoriously easygoing in punishing even murderers with a simple penance. Moreover, these verdicts—however trivial—could be appealed to Rome, a process that could delay justice for years. Henry wanted to subject priests who had committed crimes to the jurisdiction of the royal courts in order to establish a universal justice that applied to everyone in the realm, a principle fiercely opposed by Thomas Becket, the archbishop of Canterbury. When four knights—believing they were acting on the king's wishes—murdered Becket before the altar of Canterbury cathedral, the public was outraged and Henry's attempts to subject the Church to royal justice were ruined. Becket was soon canonized and revered as England's most famous saint.

The royal powers assembled by Henry met strong reaction under King John (r. 1199–1216). In 1204 John lost to King Philip II of France the Duchy of Normandy, which had been one of the foundations of English royal power since William the Conqueror. After the French defeated King John at the Battle of Bouvines in 1214, the barons of England grew tired of being asked to pay for wars the king lost. In 1215 some English barons forced John to sign Magna Carta° ("great charter," in reference to its size), in which the king pledged to respect the traditional feudal privileges of the nobility, towns, and clergy. Contrary to widespread belief, Magna Carta had nothing to do with asserting the liberty of the common people or guaranteeing universal rights. It addressed only the privileges of a select few rather than the rights of the many. Subsequent kings, however, swore to uphold it, thereby accepting the fundamental principle that even the king was obliged to respect the law. After Magna Carta the lord of all lords became less so.

English government boasted two important innovations under King Edward I (r. 1272–1307). The first was the foundation of the English Parliament (from the French "talking together"). Edward called together the clergy, barons, knights, and townsmen in Parliament in order to raise large sums of money for his foreign wars. The members of Parliament had little choice but to comply with the king's demands, and all they received in return was Edward's explanation of what he was going to do with their money. The English Parliament differed from similar assemblies on the continent in that it more often included representatives of the "commons." The commons consisted of townsmen and prosperous farmers who lacked titles of nobility but whom the king summoned because he needed their money. The second governmental innovation during Edward's reign consisted of an extensive body of legal reforms. Edward curtailed the power of the local courts, which were dominated by rural landlords and aristocrats. And he began to issue statutes that applied to the entire kingdom. Under Edward, lawyers began to practice at the Inns of Court in London, where they transformed customary legal practices into the common law that still survives as the foundation of Anglo-American law.

A Divided Regime: The German Empire

The German Empire, heir to the old Carolingian kingdom of East Francia, suffered from the division between its principal component parts in Germany and northern Italy. Germany itself was an ill-defined region, subdivided by deep ethnic diversity and powerful dukes who ruled their lands with a spirit of fierce independence. As a result, emperors could not rule Germany directly but only by demanding homage from the dukes who became imperial vassals. These feudal bonds were fragile substitutes for the kinds of monarchic institutions that evolved in France and England. An effective emperor could call upon the dukes to help him crush rivals, but he could neither dictate to his vassals nor claim vacant fiefs for the crown, as in France and England. The emperor's best asset was the force of his personality and his willingness to engage in a perpetual show of force to prevent rebellion. In northern Italy, the other part of the emperor's dominion, he did not even enjoy these extensive ties of vassalage and could rely only on vague legal rights granted by the imperial title and his ability to keep an army on the scene.

The century between the election of Frederick I (r. 1152–1190), known as Barbarossa or "red-beard," and the death of his grandson Frederick II (r. 1212–1250) represented the great age of the medieval German Empire, a period of relative stability preceded and followed by disastrous phases of anarchy and civil war. Both of these Hohenstaufen emperors, however, faced hostility from the popes whose own monarchic pretensions clashed with imperial rule in Italy.

Barbarossa projected enormous personal charisma that helped him awe recalcitrant vassals. He became a careful student of the imperial dignities encoded in Roman law, surrounded himself with experts in that law, and considered himself the heir of the great emperors Constantine, Justinian, and Charlemagne. He even managed to have Charlemagne canonized a saint.

Barbarossa's lofty ambitions contrasted with the flimsy base of his support. His own ancestral lands were in Swabia, an impoverished region barely capable of subsistence let alone supporting Frederick's imperial adventures. To set himself on a firmer financial footing, Frederick launched a series of expeditions across the Alps to subdue the enormously wealthy Italian cities that were technically part of his realm, even though they acted as if they were independent. The campaign proved a disaster. It galvanized papal

CHRONOLOGY

Strengthening the Center of the West

1170	Murder of Thomas Becket
1176	Battle of Legnano; Lombard League defeats Emperor Frederick I Barbarossa
1214	Battle of Bouvines; Philip II of France allied to Emperor Frederick II defeats John of England and his allies
1215	Magna Carta
1231	Constitutions of Melfi

opposition to him and forced the Italian city-states to put aside their rivalries to form an anti-imperial coalition, the Lombard League. At the Battle of Legnano in 1176 the League decisively defeated the German imperial army, forcing Barbarossa to recognize the autonomy of the city-states.

Barbarossa's young grandson, Frederick II, turned the traditional policy of the German emperors upside down. Instead of residing in Germany and attempting to influence Italian affairs from afar, Frederick, who loved the warm climate and engaging society of the South, lived in Sicily and left Germany alone.

Frederick has long enjoyed a remarkable historical reputation as the "wonder of the world," the most cosmopolitan monarch of the Middle Ages, who laid out grand plans for a united Italy embodied in the Constitutions of Melfi, which he put forth in 1231 (see Map 9.4). Through them, he proposed to rule through a professional imperial bureaucracy, to employ itinerant inspectors to check corruption, and to introduce uniform statutes based on Roman law. In effect, he sought a level of uniformity similar to what France and England had achieved during this period, and he was probably subject to similar influences derived from ancient Roman political theory and law. However, the popes' enduring antagonism to these plans and Frederick's own despotic tendencies undermined these ambitious and potentially fruitful reforms. He cut himself off from honest advice by declaring it an act of sacrilege even to discuss, let alone question, any of his decisions. He so overtaxed southern Italy and Sicily that these lands, which were once the richest in Italy, became an economic backwater. And his abandonment of Germany to its feuding princes prevented the centralization and implementation of legal reforms that took place in France and England.

After Frederick II's death, his successors lost their hold on both Italy and Germany. During the nearly constant warfare and turmoil of the late thirteenth century, the exceedingly inappropriate name of "Holy Roman Empire" came into general use for the German Empire. The term suggested a universal empire ordained by God and descended from ancient Rome, but the lofty claims embedded in the name found no basis in the crude reality of the rebellious, disunited lands of Germany and Italy.

■ **Map 9.4   The Empire and the Papacy in Italy**
During the reign of Emperor Frederick II, the kingdom of Sicily became the most potent power in Italy and presented a challenge to the papacy. After Frederick's death, the peninsula suffered from a long series of wars as rival claimants attempted to replace him in Sicily and the popes attempted to control events.

THE ECONOMIC BOOM YEARS

The kingdoms of the medieval West thrived on an economic base of unprecedented prosperity. What made possible the twelfth- and thirteenth-century economic boom? As we saw in Chapter 8, the agricultural and power revolutions of the eleventh century certainly provided the necessary foundations, but three other factors also proved crucial.

First, there were advances in transportation networks. Trade in grain, woolen cloth, and other bulk goods depended on the use of relatively cheap water transportation for hauling goods. Where there were neither seaports nor navigable rivers, goods had to be hauled cross-country by pack train, a very expensive enterprise. To address the problem and to facilitate transportation and trade, new roads and bridges were built, and old Roman roads that had been neglected for a thousand years were repaired. These improvements, however, were unevenly distributed, leaving large parts of Europe without any effective form of transportation. Many roads were little more than deeply rutted tracks, blocked in places by bogs of mud or fallen trees. Without a cheap way to move grain to places of scarcity, one village could be suffering from famine while another nearby enjoyed a surplus.

The most lucrative trade was the international commerce in luxury goods. Because these goods were lightweight and high-priced, they could sustain the cost of long-distance transportation across land. Italian merchants virtually monopolized the European luxury trade. The Genoese distributed rare alum—the fixing agent for dyeing cloth—from the west coast of Asia Minor to the entire European cloth industry. Venetians and Genoese imported cotton from the Middle East. Raw silk, transported aboard camel caravans from China and Turkestan, was sold at trading posts on the shores of the Black Sea and in Constantinople to Italian merchants who earned enormous profits selling shimmering silk fabric to the ladies and gentlemen of the western European aristocracy. The silk trade was quite small in quantity, but it was of great value to international commerce because silk was so highly prized. One ounce of fine Chinese black silk sold on the London market for as much as a highly skilled mason would earn in a week's labor.

Rubies, pearls, coral, and diamonds were also easily transported for fantastic profits. Marco Polo of Venice, for example, specialized in trading jewels, which he sewed into the linings of his clothing for safety when he trekked across Asia from Venice to China and back. During the thirteenth century, he was only one of many, as countless European merchants crisscrossed the caravan routes of Asia and north Africa. Italian merchant fleets sailed the Mediterranean, but transportation from the European ports in the Mediterranean to northern Europe still employed costly pack trains traversing the Alpine passes north. By the end of the thirteenth century, however, first Genoese and then other Italian fleets ventured beyond the Straits of Gibraltar into the stormy Atlantic, dramatically improving transportation between northern and southern Europe.

Even the bulk commodities the Italians brought from the East were valuable enough to sustain the high transportation costs. Known by the generic term "spices," these included hundreds of exotic items: True spices such as pepper, sugar, cloves, nutmeg, ginger, saffron, mace, and cinnamon were used to enhance the otherwise boring, bland medieval cuisine; indigo and madder were used for dyes; and medicinal herbs including opiates were used as pain relievers. The profits from spices generated most of the capital in European financial markets.

The second factor responsible for the economic boom of the twelfth and thirteenth centuries was the creation of new business techniques that long-distance trade necessitated—for example, money. Coins had virtually disappeared in the West for nearly 400 years during the Early Middle Ages,

when most people lived self-sufficiently on manors and bartered for what they could not produce for themselves. The expansion of trade and new markets, however, required a moneyed economy. By the thirteenth century Venice and Florence were minting their own gold coins, which became the medium for exchange across much of Europe.

Merchants engaged in long-distance trade began to develop the essential business tools of capitalism during this period. They created business partnerships, uniform accounting practices, merchants' courts to enforce contracts and resolve disputes, letters of credit (used like modern traveler's checks), bank deposits and loans, and even insurance policies. The Italian cities established primary schools to train merchants' sons to write business letters and keep accounts—a sign of the growing professional character of business. Two centuries earlier an international merchant had been an itinerant peddler who led pack trains over dusty and muddy tracks to customers in small villages and castles. But by the end of the thirteenth century an interna-

■ **Map 9.5 European Fairs and Trade Routes**

Trade routes crisscrossed the Mediterranean Sea and hugged the Atlantic Ocean, North Sea, and Baltic Sea coastlines. Land routes converged in central France at the Champagne fairs. Other trade routes led to the large market cities in Germany and Flanders.

tional merchant could stay at home behind a desk, writing letters to business partners and ship captains and enjoying the profits from his labors in the bustling atmosphere of a thriving city.

At the center of the European market were the Champagne fairs in France, where merchants from northern and southern Europe met every summer to bargain and haggle (see Map 9.5). The Italians exchanged their spices for English raw wool, Dutch woolen cloth, German furs and linens, and Spanish leather. From the Champagne fairs, prosperity spread into previously wild parts of Europe. Cities along the German rivers and the Baltic coast thrived through the trade of raw materials such as timber and iron, livestock, salt fish, and hides. The most prominent of the North German towns was Lübeck, which became the center of a loose trade association of cities in Germany and the Baltic coast known as the Hanseatic League. Never achieving the level of a unified government, the league nonetheless provided its members mutual security and trading monopolies—necessary because of the weakness of the German imperial government.

The third factor in the economic prosperity of the period was cities. Cities both facilitated the commercial boom and were the primary beneficiaries of it. All across Europe, especially in Flanders, the Netherlands, and north-central Italy, cities exploded in size. Exact population figures are hard to come by, but there is ample evidence of stunning growth. Between 1160 and 1300 Ghent had to expand its city walls five times to accommodate all its inhabitants. During the thirteenth century the population of Florence grew by an estimated 640 percent.

Urban civilization, one of the major achievements of the Middle Ages, was an outgrowth of commerce. And from urban civilization came other achievements. All the cities built a large new cathedral to flaunt their accumulated wealth and to honor God. New educational institutions, especially universities, trained the sons of the urban, commercial elite in the professions. However, these merchants who commanded the booming urban economy were not necessarily society's heroes. The populace at large viewed them with deep ambivalence, despite the immeasurable ways in which they enriched society. The landed aristocrats treated merchants with withering disdain even when forced to borrow money from them and to tax them to finance grandiose expenditures. Many merchants themselves were ambivalent about trade and aspired to retire as soon as they could afford to buy land and take up life as a country gentleman.

Churchmen worried about the morality of making profits. Church councils condemned usury—the lending of money for interest—even though papal finances depended on it. Theologians promulgated the idea of a "just price," the idea that there should be a fixed price for any particular commodity. The just price was anathema to hardheaded merchants who were committed to the laws of supply and demand. Part of the ambivalence toward trade and mer-

chants came from an inequity in all market-based economies, even the primitive one of the Middle Ages—the rewards of the market were unevenly distributed, both socially and geographically. The prosperous merchants were the most visible signs of puzzling social changes, but they were also the dynamic force that made possible the intellectual and artistic flowering of the High Middle Ages.

Medieval Culture: The Search for Understanding

Cultural encounters during the High Middle Ages took many forms. Some were direct exchanges, as when Christians and Muslims in crusader Jerusalem discovered their different ways of praying. Other encounters were more indirect, as when medieval thinkers read the books of ancient philosophers and so were confronted with the thinkers of a more sophisticated culture. During the twelfth and thirteenth centuries, this second kind of encounter, based on the renewed availability of works of classical Greek philosophy, opened creative possibilities, especially in theology. The Greek philosophers had been dead for nearly 1,500 years, but the medieval thinkers who discovered ancient philosophy experienced a profound cultural shock. First Muslim and then Jewish and Christian writers struggled to reconcile the rational approach of Aristotle and other Greek philosophers with the faith demanded by Islam, Judaism, and Christianity. Some suffered from a crisis of faith. Others confronted the challenge presented by ancient philosophy and attempted to reconcile reason and faith by creating new philosophical systems.

The medieval intellectual engagement with new ideas spread in many directions. Lawyers began to look back to ancient Roman law for guidance about how to settle disputes, adjudicate crimes, and create governmental institutions. Muslim influences reinvigorated the Christian understanding of the sciences. Themes found in Persian love poetry, which were echoed in Arabic poems, found their way into the Christian notion of courtly love. Catholic western Europe experienced a cultural flowering through the spread of education, the growing sophistication of Latin learning, and the invention of the university. Distinctively Western forms developed in literature, music, drama, and above all the Romanesque and Gothic architecture of Europe's great cathedrals.

The city of Paris was the breeding ground for much of the creative activity. The dynamism of Paris attracted thinkers and artists from all over Europe. Thirteenth-century Paris represented the cultural pinnacle of the High Middle Ages, comparable to Athens in the fifth century B.C.E. or Florence in the fifteenth century.

REVIVAL OF LEARNING

The magnitude of the educational revolution in medieval western Europe is clear from simple statistics. In 1050 less than 1 percent of the population of western Europe could read, and most of these literate people were priests who knew just enough Latin to read the offices of the liturgy. Four hundred years later, as much as 40 percent of men and a smaller percentage of women were literate in the cities of western Europe. Europeans had embraced learning on a massive scale even before inexpensive printed books became available in the late fifteenth century. In fact, the printing revolution of the fifteenth century was not so much the stimulus for new learning as a response to the escalating demand for more books. How did this demand come about?

In 1050 education was available only in monasteries and cathedral schools, and the curriculum was very basic, usually only reading and writing. These two kinds of schools had different educational missions. Monastic education trained monks to read the books available in their libraries as an aid to contemplating the mysteries of the next world. In contrast, the cathedral schools, which trained members of the ecclesiastical hierarchy, emphasized the practical skills of rational analysis that would help future priests, bishops, and royal advisers solve the problems of this world.

By 1100 the number of cathedral schools had grown significantly and the curriculum expanded to include the study of the ancient Roman masters, Cicero and Virgil, who became models for clear Latin composition. These schools met the demand for trained officials from various sources—the thriving cities, the growing church bureaucracy, and the infant bureaucracies of the Western kingdoms. As the number of schools expanded, they became less exclusively devoted to religious training and began to provide a practical education for laymen. But the Church was still the dominant force.

Scholasticism: A Christian Philosophy

The cathedral schools, in addition to teaching Latin grammar, recognized a growing need for training in logic as well. Refuting heresies required precise logical arguments. Anselm of Canterbury (ca. 1033–1109), for example, employed strict logic in an attempt to prove the existence of God. He began with the question of how the mind conceived ideas. He could not imagine ideas coming from nothing, arguing that they must have some basis in reality. Did not the very presence of the idea of God in the mind, Anselm concluded, demonstrate that God must exist? Intrigued by such arguments, students began to seek more advanced instruction than that provided by the standard curriculum. They tended to gather around popular lecturers in the cathedral schools where they were trained in

scholasticism, which emphasized the critical methods of reasoning, pioneered by Anselm.

Scholasticism° literally means "of the schools," but the term also refers to a broad philosophical and theological movement that dominated medieval thought. In this broader sense, scholasticism refers to the use of logic learned from Aristotle to interpret the meaning of the Bible and the writings of the Church Fathers, who created Christian theology in its first centuries. Books were scarce in the cathedral schools because the only means of duplication before the invention of the printing press was hand copying onto expensive sheepskin parchment. So the principal method of teaching and learning was the lecture. Teachers read out loud texts in Latin verbatim, and students were obliged to memorize what they heard. In the classroom the lecturer would recite a short passage, present the comments of other authorities on it, and draw his own conclusions. He would then move onto another brief passage and repeat the process. Students heard the same lectures over and over again until they had thoroughly memorized the text under discussion. In addition to lectures, scholastics engaged in disputations. Participants in a disputation presented oral arguments for or against a particular thesis, a process called dialectical reasoning. Disputants were evaluated on their ability to investigate through logic the truth of a thesis. Disputations required several skills—verbal facility, a prodigious memory so that apt citations could be made, and the ability to think quickly. The process we know today as debate originated with these medieval disputations. Lectures and disputations became the core activities of the scholastics, who considered all subjects, however sacred, as appropriate for dialectical reasoning.

None of the scholastic teachers was more popular than the acerbic, witty, and daring Peter Abelard (1079–1142). Students from all over Europe flocked to hear Abelard's lectures at the cathedral school of Paris. Peter Abelard's clever criticisms of the ideas of other thinkers brought him hoards of delighted students. In *Sic et Non* ("Yes and No"), Abelard boldly examined some of the foundations of Christian truth. Employing the dialectical reasoning of a disputation, he presented both sides of 150 theological problems discussed by the Church Fathers. He left the conclusions open in order to challenge his students and readers to think further, but his intention seems to have been less to undermine accepted biblical truths than to point out how apparent disagreements among the experts masked a deeper level of agreement about Christian truth.

Universities: Organizing Learning

From the cathedral schools arose the first universities. The University of Paris evolved from the cathedral school where Abelard once taught. The universities were, at first, little more than guilds (trade associations), organized by either students or teachers to protect their interests. As members

■ **A Lecture in a Medieval University**
Some of the students are sleeping and others are chatting with their neighbors. The most earnest students are sitting in the front row. Some things never change.

of a guild, students bargained with their professors and townspeople as would other tradesmen over costs and established minimum standards of instruction. The guild of the law students at Bologna received a charter in 1158, which probably made it the first university. Some of the early universities were professional schools, such as the medical faculty at Salerno, but true to their origins as cathedral schools, most emphasized theology over other subjects.

The medieval universities formulated the basic educational practices that are still in place today. They established a curriculum, examined students, conferred degrees, and conducted graduation ceremonies. Students and teachers wore distinctive robes, which are still worn at graduation ceremonies. Teachers were clergymen—that is, they "professed" religion—hence the title of professor for a university instructor. In their first years students pursued the liberal arts curriculum, which consisted of the *trivium* (grammar, rhetoric, and logic) and the *quadrivium* (arithmetic, geometry, astronomy, and music). This curriculum is forerunner of the arts and sciences faculties and distribution requirements in modern universities. Medieval university students devoted many years to rigorous study and rote memorization. Completion of a professional doctorate in law, medicine, or theology typically required more than ten years.

Medieval universities did not admit women, in part because women were barred from the priesthood and most university students were training to become priests. (Women did not attend universities until the nineteenth century.) There was also a widespread fear of learned women who might think on their own. The few women who did receive advanced educations had to rely on a private tutor.

The Ancients: Renaissance of the Twelfth Century

The scholastics' integration of Greek philosophy with Christian theology represents a key facet of the Twelfth-Century Renaissance°, a revival of interest in the ancients comparable in importance to the Carolingian Renaissance of the ninth century and the Italian Renaissance of the fifteenth. During Peter Abelard's lifetime, very few western Europeans knew Greek, the language of ancient philosophy, and only a few works of the Greeks were available in Latin translations. Between about 1140 and 1260 this cultural isolation dramatically changed.

A flood of new Latin translations of the Greek classics came from Sicily and Spain, where Christians had close contacts with Muslims and Jews. Muslim philosophers had translated into Arabic the Greek philosophical and scientific classics, which were readily available in the Middle East and North Africa. These Arabic translations were then translated into Latin, often by Jewish scholars who knew both languages. Later a few Catholic scholars traveled to Byzantium, where they learned enough Greek to make even better translations from the originals.

As they encountered the philosophy of the ancients, Muslim, Jewish, and Christian thinkers faced profoundly disturbing problems. The principles of faith revealed in the Qur'an of Islam and the Hebrew and Christian Bibles were not easily reconciled with the philosophical method of reasoning found in Greek works, especially those by Aristotle. These religious thinkers recognized the obvious superiority of Greek thought over their own. They worried that the power of philosophical reasoning undermined religious truth. As men of faith they challenged themselves to demonstrate that philosophy did not contradict religious teaching, and some of them went even further to employ philosophical reasoning to demonstrate the truth of religion. However, they always faced opposition within their own religious faiths, especially from people who thought philosophical reason was an impediment to religious faith.

The first Muslim thinker to confront the questions raised by Greek philosophy, such as how to prove the existence of God or account for the creation of the world, was Avicenna (980–1037), an Iranian physician. His commentaries on Aristotle deeply influenced the Catholic scholastics, who quoted him extensively. Avicenna attempted a rational proof of the existence of God based on the "necessary existent." Without God nothing exists; therefore, if we exist, so must God. Following Avicenna's lead, Al-Ghazali (1058–1111) taught the ancient Greek philosophers to Muslim students. But from the daunting task of reconciling philosophy and religion he suffered a nervous breakdown, which forced him to abandon lecturing temporarily and turn to religious mysticism. After this experience, he wrote *The Incoherence of the Philosophers,* in which he argued that religious truth was more accessible through mystical experience than through rational and systematic analysis.

The most powerful answer to Al-Ghazali's critique of philosophy came from Averroës (1126–1198), who rose to become the chief judge of Córdoba, Spain, and an adviser to the caliph. In *The Incoherence of the Incoherence* (1179–1180), Averroës argued that the aim of philosophy is to explain the true, inner meaning of religious revelations. This inner meaning, however, should not be disclosed to the unlettered masses, who must be told only the simple, literal stories and metaphors of Scripture. Although lively and persuasive, Averroës's defense of philosophy failed to revive philosophical speculation within Islam. Philosophy and science within Islam, once far superior to that of the Catholic world, went into a steep decline as mysticism and rote learning were favored over rational debate. Averroës received a more sympathetic hearing among Jews and Catholics than among Muslims.

Within Judaism, many had attempted unsuccessfully a reconciliation of Greek philosophy with Hebrew law and scripture. Success was achieved by a contemporary of Averroës, also from Córdoba—the Jewish philosopher, jurist, and physician Moses Maimonides (1135–1204). His most important work in religious philosophy was *The Guide for the Perplexed* (ca. 1191), which synthesized Greek philosophy, science, and Judaism. Widely read in Arabic, Hebrew, and Latin versions, the book stimulated both Jewish and Christian philosophy. Maimonides's efforts, like those of Averroës, distressed many of his fellow Jews. Maimonides's tomb was desecrated, but as controversy abated he came to be recognized as a pillar of Jewish thought.

For medieval Catholic philosophers, one of the most difficult tasks was reconciling the biblical account of the divine creation with Aristotle's teaching that the universe was eternal. Even in this early clash between science and religion, creationism was the sticking point. Following the lead established by Avicenna, Averroës, and Maimonides, the great project of the scholastics became to demonstrate the fundamental harmony between Christian faith and the philosophical knowledge of the ancients.

The most effective resolution of this problem was found in the work of Thomas Aquinas (1225–1274), whose philosophy is called Thomism°. A Dominican friar, Thomas spent most of his career developing a school system for the Dominicans in Italy, but he also spent two short periods teaching at the University of Paris. The temperamental opposite of the fiery Abelard, Thomas avoided distracting controversies and academic disputes to concentrate on his two great summaries of human knowledge—the *Summary of the Catholic Faith against the Gentiles* (1261) and the *Summary of Theology* (1265–1274). In both of these massive scholastic works, reason fully confirmed Christian faith. Encyclopedias of knowledge, they rigorously examined whole fields through dialectical reasoning. Thomas's method was to pose a question derived from the Bible—such as "Whether woman was made from man?"—and then draw on the accumulated thought of the past to suggest answers, raise critical objections to the answers, refute the objections, and reach a conclusion. Then he proceeded to the next question, "Whether [woman was made] of man's rib?"

Building upon the works of Averroës, Thomas solved the problem of reconciling philosophy and religion by drawing a distinction between *natural truth* and *revealed truth.* For Thomas, natural truth meant the kinds of things anyone can know through the operation of human reason; revealed truth referred to the things that can be known only through revelation, such as the Trinity and the incarnation of Christ. Thomas argued that these two kinds of truths could not possibly contradict one another because both came from God. Apparent contradictions could be accommodated by an understanding of a higher truth. On the issue of creation, for example, Thomas argued that Aristotle's understanding of the eternal universe was inferior to the higher revealed truth of the Bible that God created the universe in seven days.

The most influential of the scholastic thinkers, Thomas asserted that to achieve religious truth one should start with faith and then use reason to reach conclusions. He was the first to understand theology systematically in this way, and in doing so he raised a storm of opposition among Christians who were threatened by philosophical reason. Like the work of Avicenna and Maimonides before him, Aquinas's writings were at first prohibited by the theological faculties in universities. Nevertheless, his method remains crucial for Catholic theology to this day.

Just as scholastic theologians looked to ancient Greek philosophy as a guide to reason, jurists revived ancient Roman law, especially at the universities of Bologna and

Pavia in Italy. In the law faculties, students were required to learn the legal work of the Emperor Justinian—the text of the *Body of the Civil Law,* together with the commentaries on it. The systematic approach of Roman law provided a way to make the legal system less arbitrary for judges, lawyers, bureaucrats, and advisers to kings and popes. Laws had long consisted of a contradictory mess of municipal regulations, Germanic customs, and feudal precepts. Under Roman law, judges were obliged to justify their verdicts according to prescribed standards of evidence and procedure. The revival of Roman law in the twelfth century made possible the legal system that still guides most of continental Europe.

EPIC VIOLENCE AND COURTLY LOVE

In addition to the developments in philosophy, theology, and the law, the Twelfth-Century Renaissance included a remarkable literary output in the vernacular languages, the tongues spoken in everyday life. The great heroic epics, most of which were adapted from oral tradition or composed between 1050 and 1150, were in English, German, Celtic, Slavonic, Nordic, Icelandic, French, and Spanish. These epics, often repeated from memory as popular entertainment, recounted adventure stories about medieval warriors. They were manly stories that celebrated the beauty and terror of battle and glorified cracked skulls and brutal death: "Now Roland feels that he is at death's door; Out of his ears the brain is running forth." Women hardly appear

at all in these epics, except as backdrops to the battles among men or as battered wives. As we saw in Chapter 8, *The Digenes Akritas* in Greek, *The Poem of El Cid* in Spanish, and *The Song of Roland* in French became national epics that formed the literary roots of the modern vernacular literatures.

By the end of the twelfth century, however, a new vernacular literature appeared, created by poets called troubadours°. Unlike the creators of national epics, the troubadour poets included women as well as men, and their literature reflected an entirely new sensibility about the relationships between men and women. The troubadours wrote poems of love, meant to be sung to music; their literary movement is called courtly love°. They composed in Provençal, one of the languages of southern France, and the first audience for their poems was in the courts of southern France. These graciously elegant poems clearly show influences from Arabic love poetry and especially from Muslim mystical literature in which the soul, depicted as feminine, seeks her masculine God/lover. The troubadours secularized this theme of religious union by portraying the ennobling possibilities of the love between a woman and a man. In so doing, they introduced the idea of romantic love, one of the most powerful concepts in all of Western history, an ideal that still dominates popular culture to this day. It is especially remarkable that romantic love between the sexes, which we now assume to be so natural, is a cultural invention, one that can be dated from the twelfth century.

THE LOVE OF TRISTAN AND ISEULT
··················

In Gottfried von Strassburg's thirteenth-century romance of Tristan and Iseult, love is a powerful, irresistible, ennobling force. At first the two lovers struggle to resist temptation and to doubt the other's love, but they find themselves unable to keep away from one another. His resistance is motivated by a sense of "faith and honor," hers by "maiden shame," but love triumphs and the two consummate their relationship.

Now, when the man and the maid, Tristan and Iseult, had drunk of the potion, Love, who never resteth but besetteth all hearts, crept softly into the hearts of the twain [the two], and ere [before] they were aware of it had she planted her banner on conquest therein, and brought them under her rule. They were one and undivided who but now were twain and at enmity. . . . But one heart had they—her grief was his sadness, his sadness her grief. Both were one in love and sorrow, and yet both would hide it in shame and doubt. She felt same of her love, and the like did he. She doubted of his love, and

he of hers. For though both their hearts were blindly bent to one will, yet was the chance and the beginning heavy to them, and both alike would hide their desire.

When Tristan felt the pangs of love, then he bethought him straightway of his faith and honor, and would fain have set himself free. . . . So would he turn his heart, fighting against his own will, and desiring against his own desire. . . . Yet ever the more he looked into his heart the more he found that therein was nought but Love—and Iseult.

Even so was it with the maiden: she was as a bird that is snared with lime. . . . Love drew her heart towards him, and shame drove her eyes away. Thus Love and maiden shame strove together till Iseult wearied of the fruitless strife, and did as many have done before her—vanquished, she yielded herself body and soul to the man, and to Love.

Source: From *The Love of Tristan and Iseult* by Gottfried von Strassburg, thirteenth century.

An innovative aspect of the courtly love poems of the troubadours was their idealization of women. The male troubadours, such as Chrétien de Troyes (1135–1183), placed women on a pedestal and treated men as the "love vassals" of beloved women to whom they owed loyalty and service. Female troubadours, such as Marie de France (dates unknown), did not place women on a pedestal but idealized emotionally honest and open relationships between lovers. Unlike the epics in which women were brutalized, the troubadours typically saw women as holding power over men or acting as their equals. From southern France, courtly love spread to Germany and elsewhere throughout Europe. Many of the German poems were romances, reinterpreting the stories of the epics to conform to the values of courtly love. The courtly love ideal, though often satirized as hopelessly unrealistic, has persisted across the centuries in innumerable popular revivals.

THE CENTER OF MEDIEVAL CULTURE: THE GREAT CATHEDRALS

When tourists visit a European city today, they usually want to see the town's cathedral. Most of these imposing structures were built between 1050 and 1300 and symbolize the soaring ambitions and imaginations of their largely unknown builders. During the great medieval building boom, old churches, which were often perfectly adequate but out of style, were ripped down. In their place hundreds of new cathedrals and thousands of other churches were erected, sparing no expense and reflecting the latest experimental techniques in architectural engineering and artistic fashion. These buildings became multimedia centers for the arts—incorporating architecture, sculpture, stained glass, and painting in their structure and providing a setting for the performance of music and drama.

Architecture: The Romanesque and Gothic Styles

The Romanesque° style spread throughout western Europe during the eleventh century and the first half of the twelfth century because the master masons who understood sophisticated stone construction techniques traveled from one building site to another, bringing with them a uniform style. The principal innovation of the Romanesque was the arched stone roofs, which were more aesthetically pleasing and less vulnerable to fire than the flat roofs they replaced. The rounded arches of these stone roofs were called barrel vaults because they looked like the inside of a barrel. Romanesque churches employed transepts, which fashioned the church into the shape of a cross if viewed from above, the vantage point of God. The intersection of the transept with the nave of the church required a cross vault, a construction that demanded considerable expertise. The high stone vaults of Romanesque churches and cathedrals required the support of massive stone pillars and thick

■ **Romanesque Cathedral Architecture**
The rounded arches, the massive columns, the barrel vaults in the ceilings, and the small windows were characteristic of the Romanesque style. The pointed arch over the apse is a later Gothic addition.

walls. As a result, windows were small slits that imitated the slit windows of castles. Romanesque churches had a dark, yet cozy appearance, which was sometimes enlivened by painted walls or sculpture.

The religious experience of worshiping in a Romanesque cathedral had an intimate, almost familiar quality to it. The worshiper was enveloped by a comforting space, surrounded by family and neighbors, and close to deceased relatives buried beneath the pavement or in tombs that lined the walls. Romanesque churches and cathedrals were the first architectural expression of the new and growing medieval cities, proud and wealthy places. In such a building, God became a fellow townsman, an associate in the grand new project of making cities habitable and comfortable.

More than a century after the urban revival began, during the late twelfth and thirteenth centuries, the Gothic° style replaced the Romanesque. The innovation of this style was the ribbed vault and pointed arches, which superseded the barrel vault of the Romanesque. These narrow pointed arches drew the viewer's eye upward toward God and gave the building the appearance of weightlessness that symbolized the Christian's uplifting reach for heaven. The neighborly solidity of the Romanesque style was abandoned for an effect that stimulated a mystical appreciation of God's utter otherness, the supreme divinity far above mortal men and women. The Gothic style also introduced the innovation of the flying buttress, an arched construction on the outside of the walls that redistributed the weight of the roof. This innovation allowed for thin walls, which were pierced by windows much bigger than was possible with Romanesque construction techniques.

The result was stunning. The stone work of a Gothic cathedral became a skeleton to support massive expanses of stained glass, transforming the interior spaces into a mystical haven from the outside world. At different times of the day, the multicolored windows converted sunlight into an ever-changing light show that offered sparkling hints of the secret truths of God's creation. See, for example, the image on page 290. The light that passed through these windows symbolized the light of God. The windows themselves contained scenes that were an encyclopedia of medieval knowledge and lore. In addition to Bible stories and the lives of

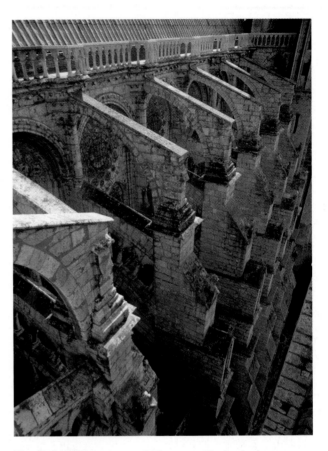

■ **Flying Buttresses of Chartres Cathedral**
The flying buttress did more than hold up the thin walls of Gothic cathedrals. The buttress created an almost lace-like appearance on the outside of the building, magnifying the sense of mystery evoked by the style.

■ **Interior of a Gothic Cathedral**
Narrow columns and the pointed arches characterized the Gothic style.

saints, these windows depicted common people at their trades, animals, plants, and natural wonders. These windows celebrated not only the promise of salvation but all the wonders of God's creation. They drew worshipers out of the busy city in which they lived and worked toward the perfect realm of the divine.

The first Gothic church was built at the abbey of St. Denis, outside Paris, under the direction of the abbot Suger. From northern France the style spread all across Europe. In France, Germany, Italy, Spain, and England, cities made enormous financial sacrifices to construct new Gothic cathedrals during the economic boom years of the thirteenth century. Gothic cathedrals expressed civic pride as well as Christian piety, and cities vied to build taller and taller cathedrals with ever more daringly thin walls. The French city of Beauvais pushed beyond reasonable limits by building its cathedral so high that it collapsed. Because costs were so high, many cathedrals remained unfinished, but even the incomplete ones became vital symbols of local identity.

Music and Drama: Reaching God's Ear and the Christian's Soul

The churches and cathedrals were devoted to the celebration of the Latin liturgy, which at the time was a chanted form of prayer. Because the function of chant was worship, music was one of the most exquisite expressions of medieval religious life. The liturgical chant that survives from the Middle Ages can still be sung today because the Benedictine monk Guido of Arezzo (ca. 990–1050) devised a system of musical notation, which forms the basis for modern Western musical notation. In Guido's time, chant was primarily plainchant°, a straightforward melody sung with simple harmony by a choir to accompany the recitation of the text of the liturgy. The simple clarity of plainchant matched the solid familiarity of the Romanesque style in church architecture.

In the Paris cathedral around 1170, however, musical experiments led to an important new breakthrough. Instead of using a simple plainchant melody to sing the liturgy, the simultaneous singing of two melodies was employed. This new form was called polyphony°, the singing of two or more independent melodies at the same time. Polyphony represented a major innovation in music by creating an enchanting sound to echo throughout the vast stone chambers of Gothic cathedrals, a musical form of praise that enhanced the mystical experience of worship.

In addition to its advances in architecture and music, Paris became the center for innovation in liturgical drama. Some time during the twelfth century, portions of the liturgy began to be acted out in short Latin plays, usually inside the church. These rudimentary plays were soon translated into the vernacular language so that everyone in the congregation could understand them. As they became more popular, the performances moved outside in front of the church. The function of these liturgical dramas was to educate as well as to worship. The priests who put on the plays wanted to teach Christian stories and provide moral examples to the young and to the uneducated laity. From these early liturgical plays arose the Western dramatic tradition that evolved into the secular theater of Shakespeare and the ubiquitous dramas of modern television and film.

CONCLUSION

Asserting Western Culture

During the twelfth and thirteenth centuries, western Europe matured into its own self-confident identity. The common culture of Catholic Christianity spread into the most distant corners of Europe by converting the remaining adherents of polytheistic religion. Through penal laws, discrimination, and extermination, heretical groups within Europe were systematically transformed into outcasts or eradicated altogether. The processes of creating outcasts within Europe and defining what it meant to be a Catholic accompanied the external assertion of Latin power. The West looked both inward and outward as it measured itself, defined itself, and promoted itself. The most dramatic outward assertion of Western identity was the series of Crusades, when European power was extended outside the continent for the first time since the fall of the Roman Empire in the West.

Less a semibarbarian backwater than it had been even in the time of Charlemagne, western Europe cultivated modes of thought that revealed an almost limitless capacity for creative renewal and critical self-examination. That capacity, first evident during the Twelfth-Century Renaissance, is what has most distinguished the West ever since. Part of the reason for this creative capacity rested in the cultivation of critical methods of thinking, codified in scholasticism. No medieval thinker followed these critical methods consistently, and they repeatedly caused alarm among the more intellectually timid. However, this tendency to question basic assumptions is among the greatest achievements of Western civilization. The process evident in the ancient philosophers emerged again in the medieval scholastics. The university system, which was based on teaching methods of critical inquiry, differed from the educational institutions in other cultures, such as Byzantium or Islam, that were devoted to passing on received knowledge. This distinctive critical spirit connects the cultures of the ancient, medieval, and modern West.

Suggestions for Further Reading

···

For a comprehensive list of suggested readings, please go to www.ablongman.com/levack/chapter9

Bony, Jean. *French Gothic Architecture of the Twelfth and Thirteenth Centuries.* 1983. With many beautiful illustrations, this is a good way to begin an investigation of these magnificent buildings.

Colish, Marcia L. *Medieval Foundations of the Western Intellectual Tradition, 400–1400.* 1997. The best general study.

Keen, Maurice. *Chivalry.* 1984. Readable and balanced in its coverage of this sometimes misunderstood phenomenon.

Keen, Maurice, ed. *Medieval Warfare: A History.* 1999. Lucid specialist studies of aspects of medieval warfare.

Lambert, Malcolm. *Medieval Heresy: Popular Movements from the Gregorian Reform to the Reformation.* 2nd ed. 1992. The best general study of heresy.

Lawrence, C. H. *The Friars: The Impact of the Early Mendicant Movement on Western Society.* 1994. The best general study of the influence of Dominicans and Franciscans.

Moore, R. I. *The Formation of a Persecuting Society: Power and Deviance in Western Europe, 950–1250.* 1987. A brilliant analysis of how Europe became a persecuting society.

Morris, Colin. *The Papal Monarchy: The Western Church from 1050 to 1250.* 1989. A thorough study that should be the beginning point for further investigation of the many fascinating figures in the medieval Church.

Mundy, John H. *Europe in the High Middle Ages, 1150–1309.* 3rd ed. 1999. A comprehensive introduction to the period.

Peters, Edward. *Europe and the Middle Ages.* 1989. An excellent general survey.

Riley-Smith, Jonathan Simon Christopher. *The Crusades: A Short History.* 1987. Exactly what the title says.

Strayer, Joseph R. *On the Medieval Origins of the Modern State.* 1970. Still the best short analysis.

Notes

···

1. *The Autobiography of Ousama (1995–1188),* trans. G. R. Potter, in Brian Tierney, ed., *The Middle Ages,* Vol. 1: *Sources of Medieval History,* 3rd. ed. (1978), 162.

2. Fulcher of Chartres, *Historia Hierosolymitana,* ed. Heinrich Hagenmeyer (1913), 202–203.

3. Edward Peters, *Heresy and Authority in the Middle Ages* (1980), 177.

4. Cited in Jacques Dalarun, "The Clerical Gaze," in Christiane Klapisch-Zuber, ed., *A History of Women in the West,* Vol. 2: *Silences of the Middle Ages* (1992), 27.

5. A. F. Pollock and F. W. Maitland, *The History of English Law,* Vol. 1 (1895), 468.

6. Cited in Emmanuel Le Roy Ladurie, *Montaillou: Promised Land of Error,* trans. Barbara Bray (1978), 130.

7. Ibid., 56.

8. Ibid., 63.

non essent regelvantes que non
et suturis ministrantes que per

The West in Crisis: The Later Middle Ages, 1300–1450

THE STORY WE ARE ABOUT TO TELL IS NOT A PLEASANT ONE, BUT IT SPEAKS TO the extraordinary scope of human experiences that occurred in Europe in the fourteenth and early fifteenth centuries. The fourteenth century dawned with a chill. In 1303 and then again during 1306–1307, the Baltic Sea froze over. No one had ever heard of that happening before, and the freezings foretold worse disasters. The cold spread beyond its normal winter season, arriving earlier in the autumn and staying later into the summer. Then it started to rain and did not let up. The Caspian Sea began to rise, flooding villages along its shores. In the summer of 1314 all across Europe, crops rotted in sodden fields. The meager harvest came late, precipitating a surge in prices for farm produce and forcing King Edward II of England to impose price controls. But capping prices did not grow more food.

In 1315 the situation got worse. In England during that year, the price of wheat rose 800 percent. Preachers compared the ceaseless rains to the great flood in the Bible, and floods did come, overwhelming dikes in the Netherlands and England, washing away entire towns in Germany, turning fields into lakes in France. Everywhere crops failed.

And then things got much worse. Torrential rains fell again in 1316, and for the third straight year the crops failed, creating the most severe famine in recorded European history. The effects were most dramatic in the far North. In Scandinavia agriculture almost disappeared, in Iceland peasants abandoned farming and turned to fishing and herding sheep, and in Greenland the European settlers began to die out. Already malnourished, the people of Europe became susceptible to disease and starvation. Desperate people resorted to desperate options. They ate cats, rats, insects, reptiles, animal dung, and tree leaves. Stories spread that some ate their own children. In Poland the starving were said to cut down criminals from the gallows for food.

A Time of Death: Burying the plague victims of Tournai, 1349. The fourteenth and early fifteenth centuries were a time of famine, war, and plague.

By the 1340s, nearly all of Europe was in an endless cycle of disease and famine. Then came the deadliest epidemic in European history, the Black Death, which killed at least one-third of the total population. The economy collapsed. Trade disappeared. Industry shriveled. Hopeless peasants and urban workers revolted against their masters, demanding relief for their families. Neither church nor state could provide it. The popes left the dangerous streets of Rome for Avignon, France, where they became the puppets of the kings of France and were obliged to extort money to survive. The two great medieval kingdoms of France and England became locked in an interminable struggle that depleted royal treasuries and wasted the aristocracy in a series of clashes that historians call the Hundred Years' War. European culture became obsessed with death.

Of all the frightening elements of these disasters, perhaps most frightening was that their causes were hidden or completely unknowable given the technology and medical understanding of the time. In many respects, the West was held captive by the climate, economic forces that no one completely understood, and microbes that would not be identified for another 550 years. During the twelfth and thirteenth centuries the West had asserted itself against Islam through the Crusades and spread Catholic Christianity to the far corners of Europe. During the fourteenth and early fifteenth centuries, however, the West drew into itself due to war, plague, and conflicts with the Mongol and Ottoman Empires. Western European contact with Russia became more intermittent, and the Byzantine Empire, once the bastion of Orthodox Christianity, fell to the Muslim armies of the Ottomans.

This chapter explores the multiple, interlocking crises of the fourteenth and fifteenth centuries. It addresses six questions: (1) What caused the deaths of so many Europeans? (2) How did forces outside Europe, in particular the Mongol and Ottoman Empires, influence conditions in the West? (3) How did disturbances in the rudimentary global economy of the Middle Ages precipitate almost complete financial collapse and widespread social discontent in Europe? (4) Why did the church fail to provide leadership and spiritual guidance during these difficult times? (5) How did incessant warfare transform the most powerful medieval states? (6) How did European culture offer explanations and solace for the otherwise inexplicable calamities of the times?

A Time of Death

Because of demographic research, we know a great deal about life and death during the fourteenth century. The magnitude of Europe's demographic crisis is evident from the raw numbers. In 1300 the population of Europe was about 74 million—roughly 15 percent of its current population. Population size can be an elementary measure of the success of a subsistence economy to keep people alive, and by this measure Europe had been very successful up to about 1300. It had approximately doubled its population over the previous three hundred years. After the 1340s, however, Europe's ability to sustain its population evaporated. Population fell to just 52 million.

The raw numbers hardly touch the magnitude of human suffering, however, which fell disproportionately on the poor, the very young, and the old. Death by starvation and disease became the fate of uncomprehending millions. The demographic crisis of the fourteenth century was the greatest natural disaster in Western civilization since the epidemics of antiquity. How did it happen?

MASS STARVATION

Widespread famine began during the decade of 1310–1320. During the famines in 1315 and 1316 alone, more than 10 percent of Europe's population probably died. One eyewitness described bands of people as thin as skeletons in 1315:

We saw a large number of both sexes, not only from nearby places but from places as much as five leagues away, barefooted, and many even, except the women, in a completely nude condition, with their priests coming together in procession at the church of the holy martyrs, and they devoutly carried bodies of the saints and other relics to be adored.[1]

A crisis in agriculture produced the famines.

As we saw in Chapter 8, the agricultural revolution of the eleventh century had made available more food and more nutritious food, triggering the growth of the population during the Middle Ages. During the twelfth and thirteenth centuries, vast tracks of virgin forests were cleared for farming, especially in eastern Europe. By the thirteenth century this region resembled the American frontier during the nineteenth century, as settlers flocked in, staked out farms, and established new towns. The additional land under the plow created an escape valve for population growth by preventing large numbers of people from going hungry. But by the fourteenth century no more virgin land was available for clearing, which meant that an ever-growing population tried to survive on a fixed amount of farming land. Because of the limitations of medieval agriculture, the ability of farmers to produce food could not keep up with unchecked population growth.

The imbalance between food production and population set off a dreadful cycle of famine and disease. Insufficient food resulted in either malnutrition or starvation. Those who suffered from prolonged malnutrition were particularly susceptible to epidemic diseases, such as typhus, cholera, and dysentery. By 1300, children of the poor faced the probability of extreme hunger once or twice during the course of their expected lifespan of thirty to thirty-five years. In Pistoia, Italy, priests kept the *Book of the*

Dead, which recorded the pattern: famine in 1313, famine in 1328–1329, famine and epidemic in 1339–1340 that killed one-quarter of the population, famine in 1346, famine and epidemic in 1347, and then the killing hammer blow—the Black Death in 1348 (see Map 10.1).

THE BLACK DEATH

In the spring of 1348 the Black Death arrived in Europe with brutal force. In the lovely hilltop city of Siena, Italy, all industry stopped, carters refused to bring produce and cooking oil in from the countryside, and on June 2 the daily records of the city council and civil courts abruptly ended, as if the city fathers and judges had all died or rushed home in panic. A local chronicler, Agnolo di Tura, wrote down his memories of those terrible days:

> *Father abandoned child, wife husband, one brother another; for this illness seemed to strike through the breath and sight. And so they died. And none could be found to bury the dead for money or friendship. Members of a household brought their dead to a ditch as best they could, without priest, without divine offices. Nor did the [death] bell sound. And in many places in Siena great pits*

were dug and piled deep with the multitude of dead. . . . And I, Agnolo di Tura, called the Fat, buried my five children with my own hands. And there were also those who were so sparsely covered with earth that the dogs dragged them forth and devoured many bodies throughout the city.[2]

During the summer of 1348 more than half of the Sienese died. The construction of Siena's great cathedral, planned to be the largest in the world, stopped and was never resumed due to a lack of workers. In fact, Siena, once among the most prosperous cities in Europe, never fully recovered and lost its economic preeminence to other cities.

Experts still dispute the cause of the Black Death, but most consider the bubonic plague° the most likely culprit. The bubonic plague can appear in two forms. In the classic form it is usually transmitted to humans by a flea that has bitten a rodent infected with the *Pasteurella pestis* bacillus, usually a rat. The infected flea then bites a human victim. The infection enters the bloodstream, causing inflamed swellings called buboes (hence, "bubonic" plague) in the glands of the groin or armpit, internal bleeding, and discoloration of the skin, which suggested the name "Black Death." The symptoms of bubonic plague were

■ **Map 10.1 Spread of the Black Death**

After the Black Death first appeared in the ports of Italy in 1348, it spread relentlessly throughout most of Europe, killing at least 20 million people in Europe alone.

Spread of the Black Death

- 1347
- 1348
- 1349
- 1350
- After 1350
- Area partially or totally spared

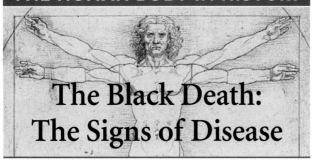

The Black Death: The Signs of Disease

Infectious diseases are invisible. They are carried by viruses or bacteria that infect the body, but until the invention of the microscope and the development of epidemiology in the nineteenth century the disease itself could not be directly observed. Diseases manifest themselves indirectly through symptoms: fevers, cold sweats, pain, coughing, vomiting, diarrhea, paleness, glandular swellings, skin lesions, and rashes. Through these symptoms, the disease leaves a distinctive sign on the body.

No disease left more distinctive and disturbing signs on the body than the bubonic plague. In the introduction to *The Decameron*, Giovanni Boccaccio described what he had witnessed of the symptoms:

> In the year 1348 after the fruitful incarnation of the Son of God, that most beautiful of Italian cities, noble Florence, was attacked by deadly plague. . . . The symptoms. . . began both in men and women with certain swellings in the groin or under the armpit. They grew to the size of a small apple or an egg, more or less, and were vulgarly called tumors. In a short space of time these tumors spread from the two parts named [to] all over the body. Soon after this the symptoms changed and black or purple spots appeared on the arms or thighs or any other part of the body, sometimes a few large ones, sometimes many little ones. These spots were a certain sign of death, just as the original tumor had been and still remained.[3]

The fear of the Black Death and the inability to discern its causes focused the attention of contemporaries on the bodies of the sick, and when someone fell ill there was intense concern to determine whether the signs of plague were present. As a result, almost any discoloration of the skin or glandular swellings could be interpreted as a sign of the presence of plague, and other diseases, such as smallpox, could be readily confused with plague. Physicians and surgeons, of course, were the experts in reading the signs of the body for disease. As victims and their distraught families soon discovered, however, physicians did not really know what the glandular swellings and discolorations of the skin meant. Boccaccio reported that "No doctor's advice, no medicine could overcome or alleviate this disease. . . . Either the disease was such that no treatment was possible or the doctors were so ignorant that they did not know what caused it, and consequently could not administer the proper remedy."[4] As it quickly became evident that very few recovered, respect for the medical profession declined.

Upon the advice of physicians, governmental authorities tried to stop the contagion by placing the houses of the sick and sometimes entire neighborhoods under quarantine when plague was suspected. Within the councils of city governments, greater attention began to be paid to the poor, largely because their bodies were more likely to manifest deformities and skin problems because of malnutrition and poor living conditions. The bodies of the poor became subject to systematic regulation. In general, the poor were much more likely to be quarantined than the rich. The deformed might even be driven out of town. Cities established hospitals to segregate the most wretched of the poor, and health officials set up border guards to prevent poor vagabonds from entering towns. To maintain quarantines and bury the dead, a public health bureaucracy was created, complete with its own staff physicians, grave diggers, and police force. The extraordinary powers granted to the public health authorities helped expand the authority of the state over its citizens in the name of pursuing the common good. The expansion of governmental bureaucracy that distinguished modern from medieval states was partly the result of the need to keep human bodies under surveillance and control—a need that began with the Black Death. ■

For Discussion

How did the government's need to control the Black Death contribute to the expansion of the state? How did it reveal the limits of the power of the state?

■ **Allegory of the Dance of Death**
During the plague years paintings such as these two panels depicted the fact that death did not discriminate. Death could arrive at any time and take anyone.

■ **The Triumph of Death**
A detail from Francesco Traini's fresco *The Triumph of Death,* in the Camposanto, Pisa, ca.1350. Frescoes such as this reflect the horror of the Black Death.

exceptionally disgusting, according to one quite typical contemporary description: "all the matter which exuded from their bodies let off an unbearable stench; sweat, excrement, spittle, breath, so fetid as to be overpowering; urine turbid, thick, black or red. . . ."[5]

The second form of plague was the pneumonic type, which infected the lungs and spread by coughing and sneezing. Either form could be lethal, but the complex epidemiology of bubonic plague meant that the first form could not be transmitted directly from one person to another. After being infected, however, many victims probably developed pneumonia as a secondary symptom, which then spread quickly to others. As one contemporary physician put it, one person could seemingly infect the entire world. In some cases, the doctor caught the illness and died before the patient did. The visitations of the bubonic plague in the twentieth century, which have been observed by physicians trained in modern medicine, provide some idea of mortality rates: Between 30 and 90 percent of those who received the bacillus through a flea bite died, but 100 percent of those who contracted pneumonic plague died, on average a mere 1.8 days after contracting it. Most historians think something similar to this must have happened in 1348, but the disease was so mysterious that some historians think the real culprit has not yet been found.

Two summers before the plague's appearance in Europe, sailors returning from the East had told stories about a terrible pestilence in China and India. Entire regions of India, they said, were littered with corpses with no survivors to bury them. But the vague information that arrived in European seaports in 1346 caused no particular alarm. Asia was far away and the source of stories so baffling that

most people could hardly credit them. No one knew that the plague bacillus was already on its way to Europe.

With the galley slaves dying at their oars, Genoese ships first brought the disease to ports in Italy, and by the spring of 1348 the Black Death began to spread throughout the Italian peninsula. Ironically, the very network of shipping that had connected the Mediterranean with northern European waters and propelled the great economic boom of the Middle Ages spread the deadly disease. By summer the pestilence had traveled as far north as Paris; by the end of the year it had crossed the English Channel, following William the Conqueror's old route from Normandy to England. From Italy the Black Death passed through the rugged Alpine passes into Switzerland and Hungary. In 1349 the relentless surge continued, passing from France into the Netherlands and from England to Scotland, Ireland, and Norway, where a ghost ship of dead men and live rats swarming among bales of wool ran aground near Bergen. From Norway the deadly disease migrated to Sweden, Denmark, Prussia, Iceland, and Greenland. By 1351 it had arrived in Russia.

Modern estimates indicate that during the late 1340s and early 1350s from India to Iceland, about one-third of the population perished. In Europe this would have meant that about twenty million people died, with the deaths usually clustered in a matter of a few weeks or months after the disease first appeared in a particular locale. The death toll, however, varied erratically from place to place, ranging from about 20 to 90 percent. So great was the toll that entire villages were depopulated or abandoned. In Avignon 400 died daily, in Pisa 500, in Paris 800. Paris lost half its population, Florence as much as four-fifths, and Venice two-thirds. Living in enclosed spaces, monks and nuns were especially hard hit. All the Franciscans of Carcassonne and Marseille in France died. In Montpellier, France, only 7 of the 140 Dominicans survived. In isolated Kilkenny, Ireland, Brother John Clyn found himself left alone among his dead brothers, and he began to write a diary of what he had witnessed because he was afraid he might be the last person left alive in the world.

Civic and religious leaders had neither the knowledge nor the power to prevent or contain the disease. Following the biblical passages that prescribed ostracizing lepers, governments began to treat plague victims as temporary lepers and quarantined them for forty days. Because such measures were ineffective, the plague kept coming back. In the Mediterranean basin where the many port cities formed a network of contagion, the plague reappeared between 1348 and 1721 in one port or another about every fifteen to twenty years. Some of the later outbreaks were just as lethal as the initial 1348 catastrophe. Florence lost half its population in 1400; Venice lost a third in 1575–1577 and a third again in 1630–1631. Half a million people died in northern Spain from an epidemic in 1596–1602. Less exposed than the Mediterranean, northern Europe suffered less and saw the last of the dread disease in the Great Plague of London of 1665.

Modern research has suggested that the homeland of the *Pasteurella pestis* bacillus is an extremely isolated area in Central Asia, from which the plague spread during the fourteenth century. It is evident that the fate of the West was largely in the hands of unknown forces that ensnared Eurasia from China to Iceland in a unified biological web. The strongest strands in that web were those of merchant traders and armies who were responsible for accidentally disseminating microbes. During the Later Middle Ages, no army was as important for the fate of Europe as the mounted warriors of the distant Mongol tribes, whose relentless conquests drove them from Outer Mongolia across central Asia toward Europe.

A Cold Wind from the East

The Mongols and Turks were nomadic peoples from central Asia. Closely related culturally but speaking different languages, these peoples exerted an extraordinary influence on world history despite a rather small population. Map 10.2 shows the place of origin of the Mongols and Turks and where they spread across a wide belt of open, relatively flat land stretching from the Yellow Sea between China and the Korean peninsula to the Baltic Sea and the Danube River basin in Europe. Virtually unwooded and interrupted only by a few easily traversed mountain ranges, the broad Eurasian plain has been the great migra-

tion highway of world history from prehistoric times to the medieval caravans and the modern trans-Siberian railway.

As the Mongols and Turks charged westward out of central Asia on their fast ponies, they put pressure on the kingdoms of the West. Mongol armies hobbled Russia, and Turks conquered Constantinople. As a consequence the potential Orthodox allies in the East of the Catholic Christian West were weakened or eliminated. Under the Ottomans, adherents to Islam were reinserted into the West, this time in the Balkans. In contrast to the era of the Crusades in the twelfth century, Catholic Europe found itself on the defensive against a powerful Muslim foe.

THE MONGOL INVASIONS

Whereas the Europeans became successful sailors because of their extensive coastlines and close proximity to the sea, the Mongols became roving horsemen because they needed to migrate several times a year in search of grass and water for their ponies and livestock. They also became highly skilled warriors because they competed persistently with other tribes for access to the grasslands.

In roughly fifty years (1206–1258), the Mongols transformed themselves from a collection of disunited tribes with a vague ethnic affinity to create the most extensive empire in the history of the world. The epic rise of the previously obscure Mongols was the work of a Mongol chief who succeeded in uniting the various quarreling tribes and transforming them into a world power. In 1206 he was proclaimed Genghis Khan (ca. 1162–1227) ("Very Mighty King"), the supreme ruler over all the Mongols. Genghis broke through the Great Wall of China, destroyed the Jin

CHRONOLOGY	
The Mongols	
1206–1227	Reign of Genghis Khan
1206–1258	Mongol armies advance undefeated across Eurasia
1241	Mongols defeat Poles, Germans, and Hungarians
1257–1294	Reign of Kubilai Khan in China
1260	Defeat in Syria of Mongols by Mamluks of Egypt
1369–1405	Reign of Tamerlane, Khan of Chagatay
1380–1489	Russians drive out Mongols
1462–1505	Tsar Ivan III unifies Russia and defeats Mongols

(Chin) empire in northern China, and occupied Beijing. His cavalry swept across Asia as far as Azerbaijan, Georgia, northern Persia, and Russia. Eventually, Mongol armies conquered territories that stretched from Korea to Hungary and from the Arctic Ocean to the Arabian Sea. They even attempted seaborne expeditions to overpower Japan, which ended in disaster, and Java, which they were only able to hold temporarily. These failures indicated that Mongol strength was in their army rather than their navy.

The Mongol success was accomplished through a highly disciplined military organization, tactics that relied on extremely mobile cavalry forces, and a sophisticated intelligence network. During the Russian campaign in the winter of 1223, the Mongol cavalry moved with lightning speed across frozen rivers to accomplish the only successful winter invasion of Russia in history. Although the Russian forces outnumbered the Mongol armies and had superior armor, they were crushed in every encounter with the Mongols.

The Mongol armies employed clever tactics. First they unnerved enemy soldiers with a hail of arrows. Then the Mongols would appear to retreat, only to draw the enemy into false confidence before the Mongol horsemen delivered a deadly final blow. European chroniclers at the time tried to explain their many defeats at the hands of the Mongols by reporting that the Mongol "hordes" had overwhelming numbers, but evidence clearly shows that their victories were the result not of superior numbers but of superior discipline and the sophistication of the Mongol intelligence network.

■ **Map 10.2   The Mongol Empire, 1206–1405**

The Mongols and Turks were nomadic peoples who spread out across Asia and Europe from their homeland in the region of Mongolia. The Mongol armies eventually conquered vast territories from Korea to the borders of Hungary and from the Arctic Ocean to the Arabian Sea.

The Mongol invasions completely altered the composition of Asia and much of eastern Europe—economically, politically, and ethnically. Once they had conquered new territories, they established the Mongol Peace by reopening the caravan routes across Asia, which had been closed for a thousand years, making trans-Eurasian trade possible and merchants safe from robbers. The most famous of the many who traversed this route were the Venetian merchants from the Polo family, including Marco Polo, who arrived at the court of the Great Khan in China in 1275. Marco Polo's book about his travels offers a vivid and often remarkably perceptive account of the Mongol Empire during the Mongol Peace. It also illustrates better than any other source the cultural engagement of the Christian West with the Mongol East during the late thirteenth century, an encounter in which both sides demonstrated an abiding fascination with the other's religion and social mores.

Mongol power climaxed in 1260. In that year the Mongols suffered a crushing defeat in Syria at the hands of the Mamluk rulers of Egypt, an event that ended the Mongol reputation for invincibility. Conflicts and succession disputes among the various Mongol tribes made them vulnerable to rivals and to rebellion from their unhappy subjects. The Mongol Empire did not disappear overnight, but its various successor kingdoms never recaptured the dynamic unity forged by Genghis Khan. During the fourteenth century the Mongol Peace came to an end.

In the wake of these upheavals, a warrior of Mongol descent known as Tamerlane (r. 1369–1405) created an army composed of Mongols, Turks, and Persians, which challenged the established Mongol khanates. Tamerlane's conquests rivaled those of Genghis Khan, but with very different results. His armies pillaged the rich cities that supplied the caravan routes. Thus, in his attempt to monopolize the lucrative trans-Eurasian trade, Tamerlane largely destroyed it. The collapse of the Mongol Peace broke the thread of commerce across Eurasia and stimulated the European search for alternative routes to China that ultimately resulted in the voyages of Christopher Columbus in 1492.

THE RISE OF THE OTTOMAN TURKS

The Mongol armies were never very large, so the Mongols had always augmented their numbers with Turkish tribes. The result was that outside of Mongolia, Turks gradually absorbed the Mongols. Turkish replaced Mongolian as the dominant language, and the Turks took over the govern-

---

MARCO POLO AND TIBETAN RELIGION

·················

In his travels to China, Marco Polo recorded numerous observations of the Mongol Empire. Polo was a merchant who spent more than two decades in Asia, but after he returned to his hometown of Venice, he was captured in battle by the Genoese, the enemies of the Venetians. While languishing in prison he dictated an account of his travels. His report of what he saw in Mongol China seemed so improbable to his contemporaries that his book was dubbed the "Million," from the seemingly million lies it contained. Modern historians, however, have established that Polo's observations were mostly accurate. He was particularly impressed by the influence of a class of astrologers and enchanters on the Mongol ruler Kublai Khan. Called the Bakhshi, *they were members of the Great Khan's court who came from Tibet and Kashmir.*

Let me tell you of a strange thing which I had forgotten. You must know that, when the Great Khan was staying in his palace and the weather was rainy or cloudy, he had wise astrologers and enchanters who by their skill and their enchantments would dispel all the clouds and the bad weather from above the palace so that, while bad weather continued all around, the weather above the palace was fine. The wise men who do this are called Tibetans and Kashmiris; these are two races of men who practise idolatry.

They know more of diabolic arts and enchantments than any other men. They do what they do by the arts of the Devil; but they make others believe that they do it by great holiness and by the work of God. For this reason they go about filthy and begrimed, with no regard for their own decency or for the persons who behold them; they keep the dirt on their faces, never wash or comb, but always remain in a state of squalor. . . .

Here is another remarkable fact about these enchanters, or *Bakhshi* as they are called. I assure you that, when the Great Khan is seated in his high hall at his table, which is raised more than eight cubits above the floor, and the cups are on the floor of the hall, a good ten paces distant from the table, and are full of wine and milk and other pleasant drinks, these *Bakhshi* contrive by their enchantment and their art that the full cups rise up of their own accord from the floor on which they have been standing and come to the Great Khan without anyone touching them. And this they do in the sight of 10,000 men. What I have told you is the plain truth without a word of falsehood. And those who are skilled in necromancy [magic] will confirm that it is perfectly feasible.

■ **Map 10.3 The Ottoman Empire**

The Ottoman state expanded from a small principality in Anatolia, which is south of the Black Sea. From there the Ottomans spread eastward into Kurdistan and Armenia. In the west they captured all of Greece and much of the Balkan peninsula.

ment of the central Asian empires that had been scraped together by the Mongol conquests. In contrast to the Mongols, many of whom remained Buddhists, the Turks became Muslims and created an exceptionally dynamic, expansionist society of their own (see Map 10.3).

Among the Turkish peoples, the most successful state builders were the Ottomans. Named for Osman I (d. 1326), who brought it to prominence, the Ottoman dynasty endured for more than six hundred years, until 1924. The nucleus of the Ottoman state was a small principality in Anatolia (a portion of present-day Turkey), which in the early fourteenth century began to expand at the expense of its weaker neighbors, including the Byzantine Empire. The Ottoman state was built not on national, linguistic, or ethnic unity, but on a purely dynastic network of personal and military loyalties to the Ottoman prince, called the sultan. Thus the vitality of the empire depended on the energy of the individual sultans. The Ottomans thought of themselves as

ghazis, warriors for Islam devoted to destroying polytheists, including Christians. (To Muslims the Christian belief in the Trinity and veneration of numerous saints demonstrated that Christians were not true monotheists.) During the fourteenth century, incessant Ottoman guerrilla actions gradually chipped away at the Byzantine frontier.

The Byzantine Empire in the middle of the thirteenth century was emerging from a period of domination by Frankish knights and Venetian merchants who had conquered Constantinople during the Fourth Crusade in 1204. In 1261, the Byzantine Emperor Michael VIII Palaeologus (r. 1260–1282) recaptured the great city. The revived Byzantine Empire, however, was a pale vestige of what it once had been, and the Palaeologi emperors desperately sought military assistance from western Europe to defend themselves from the Ottomans. Dependent on mercenary armies and divided by civil wars, the Byzantines offered only pathetic resistance to the all-conquering Ottomans.

From their base in Anatolia, the Ottomans raided far and wide, launching pirate fleets into the Aegean and gradually encircling Constantinople after they crossed over into Europe in 1308. By 1402 Ottoman territory had grown forty times greater than it had been a century earlier. During that century of conquests, the frontier between Christianity and Islam shifted. The former subjects of the Byzantines in the Balkans fell to the Ottoman Turks. Fragile Serbia, a bastion of Orthodox Christianity in the Balkans, broke under Ottoman pressure. First unified in the late twelfth century, Serbia established political independence from Byzantium and autonomy for the Serbian church. Although the Serbs had taken control over a number of former Byzantine provinces, they fell to the invincible Ottomans at the Battle of Kosovo in 1389. Lamenting the Battle of Kosovo has remained the bedrock of Serbian national identity to this day.

Serbia's western neighbors, the kingdoms of Bosnia and Herzegovina, deflated under Ottoman pressure during the late fifteenth century. Unlike Serbia, where most of the population remained loyal to the Serbian Orthodox Church, Bosnia and Herzegovina had long been divided by religious schisms. The dominant, educated classes were Serbian-speaking Muslims; the subjugated peasants, also Serbian-speaking, were Orthodox Christians who turned over one-third of everything they raised to their Muslim lords. The parallel divisions along religious and class lines long enfeebled Bosnian unity.

When Mehmed II, "The Conqueror" (r. 1451–1481), became the Ottoman sultan, he began to obliterate the last remnants of the Byzantine Empire. During the winter of 1451–1452, the sultan ordered the encirclement of Constantinople, a city that had once been the largest in the world but now was reduced from perhaps a million people to fewer than 50,000. The Ottoman siege strategy was to bombard Constantinople into submission with daily rounds from enormous cannons. The largest was a monster cannon, twenty-nine feet long, that could shoot 1,200-pound stones. It required a crew of 200 soldiers and sixty oxen to handle it, and each firing generated so much heat that it took hours to cool off before it could be fired again. The siege was a gargantuan task because the walls of Constantinople, which had been built, repaired, and improved over a period of a thousand years, were formidable. However, the new weapon of gunpowder artillery had rendered city walls a military anachronism. Brought from China by the Mongols, gunpowder had gradually revolutionized warfare, and breaching city walls in sieges was merely a matter of time as long as the heavy metal cannons could be dragged into position. Quarrels among the Christians also hampered the defense of the walls. Toward the end, the Byzantine emperor was forced to melt down church treasures so "that from them coins should be struck and given to the soldiers, the sappers and the builders, who selfishly cared so little for the public welfare that they were refusing to go to their work unless they were first paid."[6]

The final assault came in May 1453 and lasted less than a day. When the city fell, the Ottoman army spent the day plundering, raping, and enslaving the populace. The last Byzantine emperor, Constantine XI, was never found amid the multitude of the dead. The fall of Constantinople ended the Christian Byzantine Empire, the continuous remnant of the ancient Roman Empire. But the idea of Rome was not so easily snuffed out. The first Ottoman sultans resident in Constantinople continued to be called "Roman emperors."

Although the western European princes had done little to save Byzantium, its demise was a profound shock, rendering them vulnerable to the Ottoman onslaught. For the next 200 years the Ottomans used Constantinople as a base to threaten Christian Europe. Hungary and the eastern Mediterranean empire of Venice remained the last lines of defense for the West, and at various times in succeeding centuries the Ottomans launched expeditions against the great capitals of Europe, including Vienna and Rome.

Hundreds of years of attacks by the Mongol and Ottoman Empires redrew the map of the West. Events in western Europe did not and could not take place in isolation from the eastern pressures and influences. For more than 200 years Christian Russia was isolated from cultural influences in the rest of the Christian world. The experience made the Russians much more aware of their eastern neighbors, and when they did recover from the Mongol conquests in the fifteenth century, much of their energy and

CHRONOLOGY	
The Conquests of the Ottoman Turks	
1281–1326	Reign of Osman I
1308	Ottoman Empire advances into Europe
1366	Bulgaria conquered
1389	Battle of Kosovo; Prince Lazar of Serbia slain; Serbia becomes vassal state of the Ottomans
1451–1481	Reign of Mehmed II, "The Conqueror"
1453	Fall of Constantinople and death of last Byzantine emperor
1459	Serbia definitively incorporated into the Ottoman Empire
1463	Bosnia conquered
1483	Herzegovina conquered
1499	Montenegro conquered

military might was directed toward expanding eastward into the void left by the collapse of the Mongol Empire. The Ottoman conquests also created a lasting Muslim presence within the borders of Europe, especially in Bosnia and Albania. In succeeding centuries Christian Europe and the Muslim Ottoman Empire would be locked in a deadly competitive embrace, but they also benefited from innumerable cultural exchanges and regular trade. Hostility between the two sides was recurrent but never inevitable and was broken by long periods of peaceful engagement. In fact, the Christian kingdoms of western Europe went to war far more often with one another than with the Turks.

Economic Depression and Social Turmoil

Adding insult to injury in this time of famine, plague, and conquest, the West began to suffer a major economic depression during the fourteenth century. The economic boom fueled by the agricultural revolution and the revitalization of European cities during the eleventh century and the commercial prosperity of the twelfth and thirteenth centuries petered out in the fourteenth. The causes of this economic catastrophe were complex, but the consequences were obvious. Businesses went bust, banks collapsed, guilds were in turmoil, and workers rebelled.

THE COLLAPSE OF INTERNATIONAL TRADE AND BANKING

The Mongol Peace during the thirteenth century had stimulated vast, lucrative trade in exotic luxury items between Europe and Asia. When the Mongol Empire began to break up in the fourteenth century, the trade routes were cut off or displaced. Later in the century, Tamerlane's forcible channeling of the caravan trade through his own territory created a narrow trade corridor with outlets on the coast of the Middle East. Rulers along this path, such as the Mamluks in Egypt, took advantage of the situation to levy heavy tolls on trade, raising the price of goods beyond what the market could bear. As a result, trade dwindled. Alternative routes would have taken merchants through Constantinople, but Ottoman pressure on Byzantium endangered these routes.

The financial infrastructure of medieval Europe was tied to international trade in luxury goods. The successful, entrepreneurial Italian merchants who dominated the luxury trade deposited their enormous profits in Italian banks. The Italian bankers lent money to the aristocracy and royalty of northern Europe to finance the purchases of exotic luxuries and to fight wars. The whole system was mutually reinforcing, but it was very fragile. With the disruption of supply sources for luxury goods, the financial networks of Europe collapsed, precipitating a major and lasting depression.

For most of the thirteenth century the Italian city of Siena had been one of the principal banking centers of the world, the equivalent of New York or Tokyo today. In 1298, however, panic caused a run on its largest bank, which failed. Soon the lesser Sienese banks were forced to close, and the entire city fell into a deep economic depression. Siena never recovered its economic stature and is a major tourist attraction today simply because it is largely unchanged from the time when the banks went broke.

In nearby Florence, several local banks took advantage of Siena's collapse and became even bigger than the Sienese banks had been. Through these banks, the coinage of Florence, the florin, became the common currency of Europe. By 1346, however, all of these banks crashed due to a series of bad loans to several kings of Europe. With the bank crash, virtually all sources of credit dried up all across Europe. At the same time, wars between France and England deprived their aristocracies of the money to buy luxuries from the Italian merchants whose deposits had been the principal source of capital for the banks. With disruptions in the supply of Asian luxury goods, a catastrophic loss of capital by Italian bankers, and a decline in demand for luxuries in France and England, Europe entered a major depression.

REBELLIONS FROM BELOW

The luxury trade that brought exotic items from Asia to Europe represented only half of the economic equation. The other half was the raw materials and manufactured goods that Europeans sold in exchange, principally woolen cloth. The production of woolen cloth depended on a highly sophisticated economic system that connected shepherds in England, the Netherlands, and Spain with woolen cloth manufacturers in cities. The manufacture of cloth and other commodities was organized by guilds. The collapse of the luxury trade reduced the demand for the goods produced by the guilds, depriving guildsmen and urban workers of employment. The situation must have seemed ironic. Workers knew that the population decline from famine and pestilence had created a labor shortage, which according to the elementary laws of supply and demand should have produced higher wages for the workers who survived. However, wages stagnated because of the decline in business. Royal and local governments made matters worse by trying to control wages and raise taxes in a period of declining revenues. Frustrated and enraged, workers rebelled.

An Economy of Monopolies: Guilds

Central to the political and economic control of medieval cities were the guilds°. Because of their importance, guilds were at the center of the economic collapse of the fourteenth century and the turmoil that accompanied it. Guilds were professional associations devoted to protecting the special interests of a particular trade or craft and to monopolizing production and trade in the goods the guild produced. There were two dominant types of guilds. The first type, merchant guilds, attempted to monopolize the local market for a particular commodity. There were spice guilds, fruit and vegetable guilds, and apothecary guilds. The second type, craft guilds, regulated the manufacturing processes of artisans, such as carpenters, bricklayers, woolen-cloth manufacturers, glass blowers, and painters. These guilds were dominated by master craftsmen, who were the bosses of their own shops. Working for wages in these shops were the journeymen, who knew the craft but could not yet afford to open their own shops. Under the masters and journeymen were apprentices, who worked usually without pay for a specific number of years to learn the trade.

Guild regulations governed virtually all aspects of guildsmens' lives. In fact, until a youth passed from apprenticeship to become a journeyman, he could not marry or own property of his own. Craft guilds functioned like a modern professional association by guaranteeing that producers met certain standards of training and competence before they could practice a trade. Like merchant guilds, they also regulated competition and prices in an attempt to protect the masters' local monopoly in the craft.

In many cities the guilds expanded far beyond the economic regulation of trade and manufacturing to become the backbone of urban society and politics. The masters of the guilds constituted part of the urban elite, and guild membership was often a prerequisite for holding public office. The guilds unified the economic and political control of medieval cities; one of the obligations of city government was to protect the interests of the guildsmen, who in turn helped stabilize the economy through their influence in city hall. The guilds were often at the center of a city's social life as well, countering the anonymity of city life by offering fellowship and a sense of belonging. Medieval festivals were often organized by the guilds, whose members engaged in sports competitions with other guilds. In Nuremberg, for example, the butchers' guild organized and financed the elaborate carnival festivities that absorbed the energies of the entire city for days on end. In many places guilds supplied the actors for the Corpus Christi plays that acted out stories from the Bible or the lives of the saints for the entertainment and edification of their fellow citizens. In

WORKER REBELLIONS IN FLANDERS AND FRANCE

·····················

A Florentine businessman, Buonaccorso Pitti, who had witnessed the Ciompi revolt in Florence in 1378, found himself in Paris when the Maillotins *revolt broke out. Like his contemporaries, he concluded that the violence in Bruges and Ghent was somehow connected to the outbreak of violence in Rouen and Paris. This was a reasonable assumption, because the count of Flanders and the French royal court had many intimate ties. Thus, rebellion in one place had political implications elsewhere. Here is what Pitti reported.*

In 1381 the people of Ghent rebelled against their overlord, the count of Flanders, who was the father of the duchess of Burgundy. They marched in great numbers to Bruges, took the city, deposed the Count, robbed and killed all his officers, and dealt in the same way with all the other Flemish towns which fell into their hands. Their leader was Philip van Artevelde. As the number of Flemings rebelling against their overlords increased, they sent secret embassies to the populace of Paris and Rouen, urging them to do the like with their own lords, and promising them aid and succor in this undertaking. Accordingly, these two cities rebelled against the King of France. The first insurrection was that of the Paris mob, and was sparked off by a costermonger [someone who sells produce from a cart] who, when an official tried to levy a tax on the fruit and vegetables he was selling, began to roar "Down with the *gabelle* [a food tax]." At this cry the whole populace rose, ran to the tax-collectors' houses and robbed and murdered them. Then, since the mob was unarmed, one of their number led them to the Chatelet where Bertrand du Guesclin, a former High Constable, had stored 3000 lead-tipped cudgels in preparation for a battle which was to have been fought against the English. The rabble used axes to break their way into the tower where these cudgels or mallets (in French, *maillets*) were kept and, arming themselves, set forth in all directions to rob the houses of the King's representatives and in many cases to murder them. The. . . men of substance who in French are called *bourgeois*, fearing lest the mob (who were later called *Maillotins* and were of much the same kidney [nature] as the *Ciompi* in Florence) might rob them too, took arms and managed to subdue them. They then proceeded to take government into their own hands, and together with the *Maillotins*, continued the war against their royal lords.

Source: Reprinted by permission of Waveland Press, Inc. from Gene Brucker, ed., *Two Memoirs of Renaissance Florence: The Diaries of Buonaccorso Pitti and Gregorio Dati*, translated by Julia Martines. (Prospect Heights, IL; Waveland Press, Inc., 1967, reissued 1991) All rights reserved.

Florence the church of the guildsmen became a display case for works of sculpture by the city's most prominent artists, each work sponsored by a specific guild. The guilds endowed magnificent chapels and provided funeral insurance for their members and welfare for the injured and widows of masters.

When the economy declined during the fourteenth century, the urban guilds became lightning rods for mounting social tension. Guild monopolies produced considerable conflict, provoking anger among those who were blocked from joining guilds and thus excluded from the economic and political benefits available to guild members, and among young journeymen who earned low wages. These tensions exploded into dangerous revolts.

"Long Live the People, Long Live Liberty"

Economic pressures erupted into rebellion most dramatically among woolen-cloth workers in the urban centers in Italy, the Netherlands, and France. The most famous revolt involved the Ciompi, the laborers in the woolen-cloth industry of Florence, Italy, where guilds were a powerful force in city government. The Ciompi, who performed the heaviest jobs such as carting and the most noxious tasks such as dyeing, had not been allowed to have their own guild and were therefore deprived of the political and economic rights of guild membership. Fueling the Ciompi's frustration was the fact that by the middle of the fourteenth century woolen-cloth production in Florence dropped by two-thirds, leaving many workers unemployed. In 1378 the desperate Ciompi rebelled. A crowd chanting, "Long live the people, long live liberty," broke into the houses of prominent citizens, released political prisoners from the city jails, and sacked the rich convents that housed the pampered daughters of the wealthy. Over the course of a few months, the rebels managed to force their way onto the city council, where they demanded tax and economic reforms and the right to form their own guild. The Ciompi revolt is one of the earliest cases of workers demanding political rights. The disenfranchised workers did not want to eliminate the guilds' monopoly on political power; they merely wanted a guild of their own so that they could join the regime. That was not to be, however. After a few weeks of success, the Ciompi were divided and defeated.

Shortly after the Ciompi revolt faded, troubles broke out in the woolen-cloth centers of Ghent and Bruges in Flanders and in Paris and Rouen in France. In these cases, however, the revolt spread beyond woolen-cloth workers

■ **Slaughter of Peasants**
The slaughter of the peasant rebels during the Jacquerie on the bridge at Meaux.

to voice the more generalized grievances of urban workers. In Ghent and Bruges the weavers attempted to wrest control of their cities from the local leaders who dominated politics and the economy. In Paris and Rouen in 1380, social unrest erupted in resistance to high taxes and attacks by the poor on the rich. The pinnacle of the violence involved the *Maillotins* ("people who fight with mallets") in Paris during March 1382, when the houses of tax collectors were sacked and the inhabitants murdered. Although the violence in Flanders and France was precipitated by local issues, such as control of the town council and taxes, both cases were symptomatic of the widespread social conflicts that followed in the wake of the great depression of the fourteenth century that profoundly affected the crucial woolen-cloth industry.

Like urban workers, many rural peasants also rebelled during the troubled fourteenth century. In France in 1358 a peasant revolt broke out that came to be called the *Jacquerie*, a term derived from "Jacques Bonhomme" ("James Goodfellow"), the traditional name for the typical peasant. Jacquerie became synonymous with extreme, seemingly mindless violence. Filled with hatred for the aristocracy, the peasants indulged in pillaging, murder, and rape, but they offered no plan for an alternative social system or even for their own participation in the political order, so their movement had no lasting effects. They were quickly defeated by a force of nobles.

Unlike the French Jacquerie, the peasants who revolted in England in 1381 had a clear political vision for an alternative society, a fact that makes their revolt far more significant. In England the rebels' motives stemmed from the frustration of rising expectations that were never realized. The peasants believed that the labor shortage caused by the Black Death should have improved their condition, but the exact opposite was happening. Landlords clung to the old system that defined peasants as serfs who were tied to the land and unable to bargain for the price of their labor. Although the English peasants were probably better off than their fathers and grandfathers had been, their expectations of an even better life were blocked by the land-holding aristocracy. The clashing interests of the peasants and the aristocrats needed only a spark to ignite a conflagration. That spark came from the Poll Tax controversy.

The traditional means of raising revenue in England had been a levy on the more well-to-do landowners, who were taxed according to the size and value of their holdings. In 1381, however, the crown attempted to levy a Poll Tax, which taxed with little concern for the ability of each person to pay. The Poll Tax, in effect, shifted the burden of taxation to a lower social level, and the peasants bitterly resented it. As agents came to collect the Poll Tax in June 1381, riots broke out throughout eastern England, and rioters burned local tax records. The rebels briefly occupied London, where they lynched the lord chancellor and treasurer of the kingdom. The rebels demanded lower rents, higher wages, and the abolition of serfdom—all typical peasant demands—but to these they added a class-based argument against the aristocracy. They had been influenced by popular preachers who told them that in the Garden of Eden there had been no aristocracy. Following these preachers, the English rebels imagined a classless society, a utopian vision of an alternative to medieval society that was entirely structured around distinctive classes.

The 15-year-old English king, Richard II (r. 1377–1399), promised the rebels that their demands would be met. Satisfied that they had gotten what they wanted, including the abolition of serfdom, the peasants disbanded. The king then rescinded his promises and ordered that the peasant leaders be hunted down and executed. Thus, the greatest peasant rebellion in English history ended with broken promises and no tangible achievements.

None of the worker or peasant revolts of the fourteenth century met with lasting success. The universal failure of lower-class rebellion was due, in part, to the lack of any clear alternative to the existing economic and political system. The Ciompi wanted to join the existing guild system. The weavers of Ghent and Bruges were as much competing with one another as rebelling against the Flanders establishment. The extreme violence of the Jacquerie frightened away potential allies. Only the English rebels had precise revolutionary demands, but they were betrayed by King Richard.

CHRONOLOGY

Economic Depression and Social Turmoil

1298	Collapse of Sienese banks
1310–1320	Famines begin
1342–1346	Collapse of Florentine banks
1348	Arrival of Black Death in Europe
1358	Jacquerie revolt in France
1378	Ciompi revolt in Florence
1379–1385	Urban revolts in Flanders and France
1381	Peasants revolt in England

A Troubled Church and the Demand for Religious Comfort

In reaction to the suffering and widespread death during the fourteenth century, many people naturally turned to religion for spiritual consolation and for explanations of what had gone wrong. But the spiritual authority of the Church was so dangerously weakened during this period that it failed to satisfy the popular craving for solace. The moral leadership that had made the papacy such a powerful force for reform during the eleventh through thirteenth centuries was completely lacking in the fourteenth. Many laypeople gave up looking to the pope for guidance and found their own means of religious expression, making the Later Middle Ages one of the most religiously creative epochs in Christian history. Some of the new religious movements, especially in England and Bohemia, veered onto the dangerous shoals of heresy, breaking the fragile unity of the Church.

THE BABYLONIAN CAPTIVITY OF THE CHURCH AND THE GREAT SCHISM

Faced with anarchy in the streets of Rome as local aristocrats engaged in incessant feuding, a succession of seven consecutive popes chose to reside in the relative calm of Avignon, France. This period of voluntary papal exile is known as the Babylonian Captivity of the Church° (1305–1378), a biblical reference recalling the captivity of the Jews in Babylonia (587–539 B.C.E.). The popes' subservience to the kings of France during this period dangerously politicized the papacy, destroying its ability to rise above the petty squabbles of the European princes.

The loss of revenues from papal lands in Italy lured several popes into questionable financial schemes, which included accepting kickbacks from appointees to church offices, taking bribes for judicial decisions, and selling indulgences°. Indulgences were certificates that allowed penitents to atone for their sins and reduce their time in purgatory by paying money.

When Pope Urban VI (r. 1378–1389) was elevated to the papacy in 1378 and announced his intention to reside in Rome, a group of disgruntled French cardinals returned to Avignon and elected a rival French pope. The Church was then divided over allegiance to Italian and French claimants to the papal throne, a period called the Great Schism° (1378–1417). Toward the end of the schism there were actually four rival popes. Some of these antipopes completely lacked spiritual qualities. The most infamous was Baldassare Cossa, whom a faction of cardinals elected Pope John XXIII (r. 1410–1415) because he had been an effective commander of the papal troops. The cardinals who supported rival popes charged Pope John with the crimes of piracy, murder, rape, sodomy, and incest—charges without much substance—but the publication of the allegations further undermined the moral reputation of the papacy.

Urban VI's decision to return the papacy to Rome and end the Babylonian Captivity of the Church resulted from an intense demand for his presence in Italy. The reason was the growing influence of a young woman mystic. Catherine Benincasa (1347–1380), better known as St. Catherine of Siena, demonstrated her mystic tendencies at an early age by locking herself in a room of her parents' house for a year to devote herself to prayer and fasting. She soon became famous for her holiness and severe asceticism, which during the troubled times of the Babylonian Captivity gave her a powerful moral authority. She went to Avignon, and although the pope ignored her, she attracted the attention of others in the papal court. Catherine became the most important advocate for encouraging the return of the pope from Avignon to Rome and launching a new crusade against the Muslims. She helped Pope Urban VI reorganize the Church after he returned to Rome, and she sent out letters and pleas to the kings and queens of Europe to gain support for him during the schism. Although illiterate, Catherine produced an influential body of letters, prayers, and treatises by dictating to others. At a time when all of the great powers of Europe were failing to provide leadership, the void was filled by a young woman with a strong sense of moral mission.

The Great Schism created the need for a mechanism to sort out the competing claims of rival popes. That need led

The Government of the Church

Concern for the compromised authority of the Church during the Babylonian Captivity preoccupied churchmen everywhere. This elaborate allegory, *The Government of the Church*, was commissioned for the most important Dominican church in Florence, Santa Maria Novella, and painted by Andrea da Firenze in the Spanish Chapel, 1366–1368. The allegory demonstrates how the pope is assisted by the Dominicans, who fought heresy through preaching.

to the Conciliar Movement°. The conciliarists argued that a general meeting or council of the bishops of the Church had authority over the pope, it could be called to order by a king, and it could pass judgment on a standing pope or order a conclave to elect a new one. Several general councils were held during the early fifteenth century to resolve the schism and initiate reforms. The Council of Constance (1414–1417) finally succeeded in restoring unity to the Church and also in formally asserting the principle that a general council is superior to the pope and should be called frequently. The Council of Basel (1431–1449) approved a series of necessary reforms, although these were never implemented due to the hostility to conciliarism by Pope Eugene IV (r. 1431–1447). The failure of even the timid reforms of the Council of Basel opened the way for the more radical rejection of papal authority during the Protestant Reformation of the sixteenth century. The Conciliar Movement, however, was not a complete failure because it provided a model for how reform could take place. This model would later become central to the Catholic Reformation and the foundation of modern Catholicism (see Chapter 13).

THE SEARCH FOR RELIGIOUS ALTERNATIVES

The popes' loss of moral authority during the Babylonian Captivity and the Great Schism opened the way for a remarkable variety of reformers, mystics, and preachers, who appealed to lay believers crying out for a direct experience of God and a return to the message of the original apostles of Christ. Some of these movements were heretical, but the weakened papacy was unable to control them, as it had successfully done during the thirteenth century crusade against the Albigensians.

Protests Against the Papacy: New Heresies

For most Christians during the fourteenth century, religious life consisted of witnessing or participating in the seven sacraments, which were formal rituals celebrated by duly consecrated priests usually within the confines of churches. After baptism, which was universally performed on infants, the most common sacraments for lay adults were penance and communion. Both of these sacraments emphasized the power of the clergy over the laity and therefore were potential sources for resentment. The sacrament of penance required the layperson to confess his or her sins to a priest, who then prescribed certain penalties to satisfy the sin. At communion, it was believed, the priest changed the substance of an unleavened wafer of bread, called the Eucharist, into the body of Christ and a chalice of wine into his blood, a miraculous process called transubstantiation. Priest and lay recipients of communion both ate the wafer, but the chalice was reserved for the priest alone. More than anything else, the reservation of the chalice for priests profoundly symbolized the privileges of the clergy. Since medieval

CHRONOLOGY	
Troubles in the Church	
1305–1378	Babylonian Captivity of the Church; popes reside in Avignon
1320–1384	John Wycliffe
1347–1380	Catherine of Siena
1369–1415	Jan Hus
1378–1417	Great Schism; more than one pope
1414–1417	Council of Constance
1431–1449	Council of Basel
CA. 1441	*Imitation of Christ*

Catholicism was primarily a sacramental religion, reformers and heretics tended to concentrate their criticism on sacramental rituals, especially of their spiritual value compared to other kinds of worship such as prayer.

The most serious discontent about the authority of the popes, the privileges of the clergy, and the efficacy of the sacraments appeared in England and Bohemia (a region in the modern Czech Republic). An Oxford professor, John Wycliffe (1320–1384), criticized the power and wealth of the clergy, played down the moral value of the sacraments, and exalted the benefits of preaching, which promoted a sense of personal responsibility. During the Great Schism, Wycliffe rejected the authority of the rival popes and asserted instead the absolute authority of the Bible, which he wanted to make available to the laity in English rather than in Latin, which only priests understood.

Wycliffe's ideas found their most sympathetic audience outside England among a group of reformist professors at the University of Prague in Bohemia where Professor Jan Hus (1369–1415) regularly preached to a large popular following. Hus's most revolutionary act was to offer the chalice of consecrated communion wine to the laity, thus symbolically diminishing the special status of the clergy. When Hus also preached against indulgences, which he said converted the sacrament of penance into a cash transaction, Pope John XXIII excommunicated him. Hus attended the Council of Constance to defend his ideas. Despite a safe-conduct from the Holy Roman emperor (whose jurisdiction included Bohemia and Constance) that made him immune from arrest, he was imprisoned, his writings were condemned, and he was burned alive as a heretic.

Imitating Christ: The Modern Devotion

In the climate of religious turmoil of the fourteenth and fifteenth centuries, many sincere Christians sought deeper spiritual solace than the institutionalized Church could provide. By stressing individual piety, ethical behavior, and intense religious education, a movement called the Modern Devotion° became highly influential. Promoted by the Brothers of the Common Life, a religious order established in the Netherlands, the Modern Devotion was especially popular throughout northern Europe. In the houses for the Brothers, clerics and laity lived together without monastic vows, shared household tasks, joined in regular prayers, and engaged in religious studies. (A similar structure was devised for women.) The lay brothers continued their occupations in the outside world, thus influencing their neighbors through their pious example. The houses established schools that prepared boys for church careers through constant prayer and rigorous training in Latin. Many of the leading figures behind the Protestant Reformation in the sixteenth century had attended schools run by the Brothers of the Common Life.

The Modern Devotion was also spread by the best-seller of the late fifteenth century, the *Imitation of Christ*, written in 1441 by a Common Life brother, probably Thomas à Kempis. By emphasizing frequent private prayer and moral introspection, the *Imitation* provided a spiritual manual to guide laypeople in the path toward spiritual renewal that had traditionally been reserved for monks and nuns. There was nothing especially reformist or antisacramental about the *Imitation of Christ*, which emphasized the need for regular confession and communion. However, its popularity helped prepare the way for a broad-based reform of the Church by turning the walls of the monastery inside out, spilling out a large number of lay believers who were dedicated to becoming living examples of moral purity for their neighbors.

The moral and financial degradation of the papacy during the fourteenth and early fifteenth centuries was countered by a remarkable spiritual awakening among the laity, manifest in the Modern Devotion. As a result, throughout Europe laypeople began to take more responsibility, not only for their own salvation, but for the spiritual and material welfare of their entire community and of the Church itself. These pious people founded hospitals for the sick and dying, orphanages for abandoned children, and confraternities that engaged in a wide range of charitable good works—from providing dowries for poor women to accompanying condemned criminals to the gallows.

An Age of Continuous Warfare

·······················■·······················

Western Europe was further weakened during the fourteenth century by prolonged war between its two largest and previously most stable kingdoms, England and France. The Hundred Years' War° (1337–1453) was a struggle over England's attempts to assert its claims to territories in France. The prolonged conflict

drained resources from the aristocracies of both kingdoms, deepening the economic depression and making it last longer. The Hundred Years' War sowed the seeds of a military revolution that by the sixteenth century transformed the kingdoms of western Europe. Monarchies, ruled by relatively weak kings and strong aristocracies, evolved into modern states, ruled by strong monarchs who usurped many of the traditional privileges of the aristocracy in order to centralize authority and strengthen military prowess.

THE FRAGILITY OF MONARCHIES

The most dangerous threat to the kings of France and England during the fourteenth and fifteenth centuries came less from worker and peasant rebellions than from members of the aristocracy, who were fiercely protective of their

■ **Royal Justice**
English kings were preoccupied with extending their prerogatives over the judiciary as a way to express royal power. Despite the corruption of the many lower courts, the Court of the King's Bench attempted to assert a level of uniform procedures and royal control of justice.

jurisdictional privileges over their lands. The privilege of jurisdiction allowed aristocrats to act as judges for crimes committed in their territories, a privilege that was a crucial source of their power. In both kingdoms, royal officials asserted the legal principle that aristocratic jurisdictions originated with the crown and were subordinate to it. The problem behind this controversy was inherent in the system of rule in France and England—overlapping, conflicting, and sometimes contradictory jurisdictions and loyalties produced by many generations of inheritance. The system bred strife and limited the power of the monarch. Thus the Hundred Years' War was both a conflict between two kingdoms and a series of civil wars between aristocratic factions and imperiled monarchs.

Medieval monarchies depended on the king to maintain stability. Despite the remarkable legal reforms and bureaucratic centralization of monarchies in England and France during the twelfth and thirteenth centuries (see Chapter 9), weak or incompetent kings were all too common during the fourteenth. Weak kings created a perilous situation made worse by disputed successions. The career of Edward II (r. 1307–1327) of England illustrates the peril. Edward was unable to control the vital judicial and financial sinews of royal power. He continued the policy of his father, Edward I, by introducing resident justices of the peace who had replaced the inadequate system of itinerant judges who traveled from village to village to hear cases. In theory, these justices of the peace should have prevented the abuses of justice typical of aristocratic jurisdictions, but even though they were royal officials who answered to the king, most of those appointed were also local landowners who were deeply implicated in many of the disputes that came before them. As a result, justice in England became notoriously corrupt and the cause of discontent. Edward II was so incompetent to deal with the consequences of corrupted justice that he provoked a civil war in which his own queen joined his aristocratic enemies to depose him.

The French monarchy was no better. In fact, the French king was in an even weaker constitutional position than the English monarch. In France the king had effective jurisdiction over only a small part of his realm. Many of the duchies and counties of France were quasi-independent principalities, paying only nominal allegiance to the king, whose will was ignored with impunity. In these regions the administration of justice, the collection of taxes, and the recruitment of soldiers all remained in the hands of local lords. To explain why he needed to raise taxes, Philip IV, "The Fair" (r. 1285–1314), created a representative assembly, the Estates General, which met for the first time in 1302, but he still had to negotiate with each region and town individually to collect the taxes. Given the difficulty of raising taxes, the French kings resorted to makeshift solutions that hurt the economy, such as confiscating the property of vulnerable Jewish and Italian merchants and debasing the coinage to increase the value of scarce silver. Such a system made France especially vulnerable.

THE HUNDRED YEARS' WAR

The Hundred Years' War revealed the fragility of the medieval monarchies. The initial cause of the war involved disputes over the duchy of Aquitaine. The king of England also held the title of duke of Aquitaine, who was a vassal of the French crown, which meant that the English kings technically owed military assistance to the French kings whenever they asked for it. A long succession of English kings had reluctantly paid homage as dukes of Aquitaine to the king of France, but the unusual status of the duchy was a continuing source of contention.

The second cause of the war derived from a succession crisis over the French crown. When King Charles IV died in 1328, his closest surviving relative was none other than the archenemy of France, Edward III (r. 1327–1377), king of England. To the barons of France, the possibility of Edward's succession to the throne was unthinkable, and they excluded him because his relation to the French royal family was through his mother. Instead the barons elected to the throne a member of the Valois family, King Philip VI (r. 1328–1350), and at first Edward reluctantly accepted the decision. However, when Philip started to hear judicial appeals from the duchy of Aquitaine, Edward changed his mind. He claimed the title of king of

■ **Siege Warfare**
English soldiers pillaging and burning a French town.

■ **Map 10.4 The Hundred Years' War**

This map illustrates four phases of the Hundred Years' War. In the first phase (1337), England maintained a small foothold in the southwest of France. In the second phase (1360), England considerably expanded the territory around Aquitaine and gained a vital base in the north of France. In the third phase (ca. 1429), England occupied much of the north of France, and England's ally Burgundy established effective independence from French authority. In the fourth phase at the end of the war (1453), England had been driven from French soil except at Calais, and Burgundy maintained control over its scattered territories.

France for himself, sparking the beginning of more than a century of warfare (see Map 10.4).

The Hundred Years' War was not a continuous formal war but a series of occasional pitched battles, punctuated by long truces and periods of general exhaustion. The term *Hundred Years' War* was invented by nineteenth-century historians to describe a prolonged time of troubles between the two countries that lasted from 1337 to 1453. In terms of its potential for warfare, France, far richer and with three times the population, held the advantage over sparsely populated

England. In nearly every battle the French outnumbered the English, but the English were usually victorious because of superior discipline and the ability of their longbows to break up cavalry charges. As a rule, the English avoided open battle, preferring raids, sieges of isolated castles, and capturing French knights for ransom. For many Englishmen the objective in fighting in France was to get rich by looting. And because all the fighting took place on French soil, France suffered extensive destruction and significant civilian casualties from repeated English raids.

From English Victories to French Salvation

In the early phases of the war, the English enjoyed a stunning series of victories. At the Battle of Sluys in 1340, a small English fleet of 150 ships carrying the English invasion forces ran into a French blockade of more than 200 ships. In the heavy hand-to-hand combat, the English captured 166 French ships and killed some 20,000 men, so many that it was later said, "If fish could talk, they would speak French." At Crécy in 1346, the English longbowmen shot thousands of arrows "like thunderbolts" into the flanks of the charging French knights, killing men and horses in shocking numbers. The French knights mounted one disorderly, hopeless charge after another, until the piles of dead blocked further charges. Though wounded, King Philip escaped, leaving 3,000 of his men dead on the field, including 1,500 knights. The aristocracy of France was decimated. At Poitiers in 1356, King John of France (r. 1350–1364) encircled 6,000 English with a vastly superior royal army of 15,000, but—as at Crécy—the English archers broke up the overly hasty French cavalry charge, and the English counterassault crushed the French. Two thousand French knights died and another 2,000 were captured, including King John himself. With its king imprisoned in England, France was forced to pay a huge ransom and grant formal sovereignty over a third of France to the king of England.

At Agincourt in 1415, King Henry V (r. 1413–1422) and England's disease-racked army of 6,000 were cut off by a French force of about 20,000. In the ensuing battle the English archers repelled a hasty French cavalry charge and the fleeing, terrified horses trampled the French men-at-arms as they advanced. The English lost only a few hundred, but the French suffered nearly 10,000 casualties. After Agincourt, the French never again dared challenge King Henry in open battle, and were forced to recognize him as the heir to the French throne. By 1420 the English victory appeared complete. Now with the responsibility of ruling rather than conquering France, the English could no longer rely on their old strategy of mounted raiding and had to hold the French cities, which proved exceedingly difficult. By 1422, however, Henry V was dead, leaving two claimants to the French throne. The English asserted the rights of the infant King Henry VI of England, son of King Henry V, the victor at Agincourt. Most of the French defended the claim of the Dauphin Charles, the only surviving son of the late King Charles VI of France. The Hundred Years' War entered a new phase with factions of the French aristocracy supporting the two rivals in a bloody series of engagements.

By 1429 the English were on the verge of final victory. They occupied Paris and Rheims, and their army was besieging Orleans. The Dauphin Charles was penniless and indecisive. Even his own mother denied his legitimacy as king. At this point a 17-year-old illiterate peasant from Burgundy, Joan of Arc [Jeanne d'Arc, 1412?–1431], following "divine voices," went to Orleans to lead the French armies. Under her inspiration Orleans was relieved, French forces began to defeat the English, much of the occupied territory was regained, and the Dauphin was crowned King Charles VII (r. 1429–1461) in the cathedral of Rheims. After Joan failed to recapture Paris, however, her successes ceased.

Charles VII reorganized the French army and gradually chipped away at the English holdings in France, eventually taking away Aquitaine in 1453. The English lost all their possessions in France except Calais, which was finally surrendered in 1558. There was no peace treaty, just a fading away of war in France, especially after England stumbled into civil war—the War of the Roses (1455–1485).

The Hundred Years' War in Perspective

The Hundred Years' War had broad consequences. First, nearly continuous warfare between the two most powerful kingdoms in the West exacerbated other conflicts as

■ **The Battle of Sluys**

At the Battle of Sluys, ships lined up side by side to enable fierce hand-to-hand combat. Even in these close quarters, longbows were brought into play, giving the English a lethal advantage.

well. Scotland, the German princes, Aragon, Castile, and most importantly Burgundy were drawn into the conflict at various stages, making the English-French brawl a European-wide war at certain stages. The squabble between France and England made it much more difficult to settle the Great Schism that split the Church during the same period. Second, the war devastated France, which eventually regained control of most of its territory but still suffered the most from the fighting. During the century of the war, the population dropped by half, due to the ravages of combat, pillage, and plague. Agriculture languished after the repeated English mounted raids that destroyed crops and sacked peasant villages. Third, the deaths of so many nobles and destruction of their fortunes diminished the international luxury trade; merchants and banks as far away as Italy went broke; and the Flemish woolen industry was disrupted, causing further economic damage. Finally, the war helped make England more English. Before the war the Plantagenet dynasty in England was more French than English. The monarchs possessed extensive territories in France and were embroiled in French affairs. English aristocrats also had business in France, spoke French, and married their French cousins. After 1450 the English abandoned the many French connections that had stretched across the English Channel since William the Conqueror sailed from Normandy to England in 1066. Henceforth, the English upper classes cultivated English rather than French language and culture.

■ **English Archers**

English archers practicing the longbow. Note that the unpulled bows are the height of a man.

THE MILITARY REVOLUTION

The "military revolution," whose effects first became evident during the Hundred Years' War, refers to changes in warfare that marked the transition from the late medieval to the early modern state. The heavily armored mounted knights, who had dominated European warfare and society since the Carolingian period, were gradually supplanted by foot soldiers as the most effective fighting unit in battle. Infantry units were composed of men who fought on foot in disciplined ranks, which allowed them to break up cavalry charges by concentrating firepower in deadly volleys. Infantry soldiers could fight on a greater variety of terrains than mounted knights, who needed even ground and plenty of space for their horses to maneuver. The effectiveness of infantry units made battles more ferocious but also more decisive, which was why governments favored them. Infantry, however, put new requirements on the governments that recruited them. Armies now demanded large numbers of well-drilled foot soldiers who could move in disciplined ranks around a battlefield. Recruiting, training, and drilling soldiers made armies much more complex organizations than they had been, and officers needed to pos-

sess a wide range of management skills. Governments faced added expenses as they needed to arrange and pay for the logistical support necessary to feed and transport those large numbers. The creation of the highly centralized modern state resulted in part from the necessity to maintain a large army in which infantry played the crucial role.

CHRONOLOGY

An Age of Continuous Warfare

1285–1314	Reign of Philip IV, "The Fair," of France
1307–1327	Reign of Edward II of England
1327–1377	Reign of Edward III of England
1328–1350	Reign of Philip VI of France
1337–1453	Hundred Years' War
1340	Battle of Sluys
1346	Battle of Crécy
1356	Battle of Poitiers
1377–1399	Reign of Richard II of England
1399–1413	Reign of Henry IV of England
1412?–1431	Life of Joan of Arc
1413–1422	Reign of Henry V of England
1415	Battle of Agincourt
1429–1461	Reign of Charles VII of France
1455–1485	War of the Roses in England

The Trial of Joan of Arc

After only fifteen months as the inspiration of the French army, Joan of Arc fell into the hands of the English, who brought her to trial for witchcraft. The English needed to stage a kind of show trial to demonstrate to their own demoralized forces that Joan's remarkable victories had been the result not of military superiority but rather of witchcraft. In the English trial, conducted at Rouen in 1431, Joan testified that her mission to save France was in response to voices she heard that commanded her to wear men's clothing. On the basis of this evidence of a confused or double gender identity, the ecclesiastical tribunal declared her a witch and a relapsed heretic. The court sentenced her to be burned at the stake.

Political motivations governed the 1431 English trial for witchcraft, but Joan's testimony provides some clues to her own identity conflicts. One of the most compelling questions arising from the trial is why the English tried Joan as a heretic in a church court rather than in a military one as a prisoner of war. The answer can be found in the two pieces of evidence against Joan that ultimately resulted in her condemnation: the spiritual "voices" she claimed to hear and her cross-dressing in men's clothing.

From the beginning of her emergence onto the political scene, Joan's voices intrigued all who came into contact with her. Joan claimed that she was guided by the voices of St. Catherine, St. Margaret, and the Archangel Michael. To Joan, these voices had the authority of divine commands. The problem the English judges faced was to demonstrate that the voices came not from God but from the Devil. If they could prove that, then they had evidence of witchcraft and sorcery. Following standard inquisitorial guidelines, the judges knew that authentic messages from God would always conform to church dogma. Any deviation from official doctrines would constitute evidence of demonic influence. Thus, during Joan's trial the judges demanded that she make theological distinctions that were alien to her. When they wanted to know if the voices were those of angels or saints, Joan seemed perplexed and responded, "This voice comes from God. . . I am more afraid of failing the voices by saying what is displeasing to them than answering you."[7] The judges kept pushing, asking if the saints or angels had heads, eyes, and hair. Exasperated, Joan simply replied, "I have told you often enough, believe me if you will."

The judges reformulated Joan's words to reflect their own rigid scholastic categories and concluded that her "veneration of the saints seems to partake of idolatry and to proceed from a pact made with devils. These are less divine revelations than lies invented by Joan, suggested or shown to her by the demon in illusive apparitions, in order to mock at her imagination while she meddled with things that are beyond her and superior to the faculty of her condition."[8] In other words, Joan was just too naive and uneducated to have authentic visions. But the English judges were on dangerous ground because during the previous fifty years there had been a number of notable female mystics, including the illiterate St. Catherine of Siena and St. Bridget of Sweden, whose visions had been accepted as authentic by the pope. The English could not take the chance that they were executing a real saint. They had to prove Joan was a witch by showing that her visions were theologically unsound. But that they could not do.

If they could not convict her for bad theology, the English needed evidence for superstitious practices. In an attempt to do that, they drew up seventy charges against her. Many of these consisted of allegations of performing magic, such as chanting spells, visiting a magical tree at night, and invoking demons. They attempted to prove bad behavior by insinuating that a young man had refused to marry her on account of her immoral life. They asserted that her godmother was a notorious witch who had taught her sorcery. None of these ploys worked, however, because Joan consistently denied these charges. She did, however, admit to one allegation: she cross-dressed as a man.

Some of the charges against her and many of the questions she was asked concerned how she dressed:

The said Joan put off and entirely abandoned women's clothes, with her hair cropped short and round in the fashion of young men, she wore shirt, breeches, doublet, with hose joined together, long and fastened to the said doublet by twenty points, long leggings laced on the outside, a short mantle reaching to the knee, or thereabouts, a close-cut cap, tight-fitting boots or buskins, long spurs, sword, dagger, breastplate, lance and other arms in the style of a man-at-arms.[9]

The judges explained to her that "according to canon law and the Holy Scriptures" a woman dressing as a man or a man as a woman is "an abomination before God."[10] She replied simply

■ Joan of Arc

Joan of Arc appears before King Charles VII and his council. In this miniature taken from a chronicle of the period, Joan appears dressed in full armor and sword in the lower right corner. The label next to her knee reads, "La Pucelle," which means "The Young Girl." There are no contemporary portraits of Joan, and this image is clearly a generalized one of a young woman in armor rather than a portrait taken from the real Joan.

and consistently that "everything that I have done, I did by command of the voices" and that wearing male dress "would be for the great good of France."[11] When they asked her to put on a woman's dress in order to take the Eucharist on Easter Sunday, she refused, saying the miracle of the Eucharist did not depend on whether she wore a man's or a woman's clothing. On many occasions she had been asked to put on a woman's dress and refused. "And as for womanly duties, she said there were enough other women to do them."[12]

After a long imprisonment and psychological pressure from her inquisitors, Joan confessed to charges of witchcraft, signed a recantation of her heresy, and agreed to put on a dress. She was sentenced to life imprisonment on bread and water. Why did she confess? Some historians have argued that she was tricked into confessing because the inquisitors really wanted to execute her but could not do so unless she was a *relapsed* heretic. To be relapsed she had to confess and then somehow return to her heretical ways. If that was the inquisitors' intention, Joan soon obliged them. After a few days in prison, Joan threw off the women's clothes she had been given and resumed dressing as a man. As a witness put it, "The said Catherine and Margaret [instructed] this woman in the name of God to take and wear a man's clothes, and she had worn them and still wears them, stubbornly obeying the said command, to such an extent that this woman had declared she would rather die than relinquish these clothes."[13]

Joan was willing to be burned at the stake rather than dress as a woman. Why? Historians will never know for sure, but dressing as a man may have been necessary for her to fulfill her role as a military leader. The men who followed her into battle and trusted her voices accepted the necessity of this mutation of gender. In her military career, Joan had adopted the masculine qualities of chivalry: bravery, steadfastness, loyalty, and a willingness to accept pain and death. She made herself believable by dressing as a knight. A number of soldiers who had served with her testified that although they knew Joan was a woman, they had never felt any sexual desire for her, which suggests that she seemed androgynous to them. It was precisely Joan's gender ambiguity that the inquisitors found a dangerous sign of Satan's hand. And it was Joan's refusal to abandon her ambiguous gender identity that provided the inquisitors with the evidence they needed.

Joan's condemnation was much more than another example of men's attempt to control women. The inquisitors needed evidence of demonic influence, which to their minds Joan's transgressive gender behavior supplied. Joan's confused gender identity threatened the whole system of neat hierarchical distinctions upon which scholastic theology rested. To the theologians, everything in God's creation had its own proper place and anyone who changed his or her divinely ordained position in society presented a direct affront to God.

The English verdict and Joan's tragic fate greatly wounded French pride. In 1456 the French clergy reopened her case in a posthumous trial that sought to rehabilitate her in the eyes of the church. To these churchmen, she was an authentic visionary and a saint who listened to a direct command from God. To the French people ever since, she has become a national symbol of pride and of French unity against a foreign invader. In our own time, Joan has been characterized as many things—a saint, a madwoman, a female warrior, a woman exercising power in a male world, and a woman openly transgressing gender categories by dressing in men's clothes. ■

Questions of Justice

1. How did Joan's claim that she heard voices help her find her own voice and mission in life? Did she have any other way of finding her own voice and mission?

2. What motivated Joan? From our distant perspective, can we know her motivations?

3. In these ecclesiastical trials, what kinds of evidence were presented? What were the prosecutors trying to achieve by employing these kinds of evidence?

Taking It Further

Joan of Arc. *In Her Own Words*, trans. Willard Trask. 1996. The record of what Joan reputedly said at her trials.

Warner, Marina. *Joan of Arc: The Image of Female Heroism.* 1981. A highly readable feminist reading of the Joan of Arc story.

Infantry used a variety of weapons. The English demonstrated the effectiveness of longbowmen during the Hundred Years' War. Capable of shooting at a much more rapid rate than the French crossbowmen, the English longbowmen at Agincourt protected themselves behind a hurriedly erected stockade of stakes and rained a shower of deadly arrows on the French cavalry to break up charges. In the narrow battlefield, which was wedged between two forests, the French cavalry had insufficient room to maneuver, and when some of them dismounted to create more room, their heavy armor made them easy to topple over and spear through the underarm seam in their armor. Some infantry units deployed ranks of pikemen who created an impenetrable wall of sharp spikes.

The military revolution of the fourteenth and fifteenth centuries also introduced gunpowder to European warfare. Arriving from China with the Mongol invasions, gunpowder was first used in the West in artillery. Beginning in the 1320s huge wrought-iron cannons were used to shoot stone or iron against fortifications during sieges. By the early sixteenth century bronze muzzle-loading cannons were used in field battles. With the introduction during the late fifteenth century of the first handgun and the harquebus (a matchlock shoulder gun), properly drilled and disciplined infantrymen could deliver very destructive firepower. Gun shot pierced plate armor, whereas arrows bounced off. The slow rate of fire of these guns, however, necessitated carefully planned battle tactics. Around 1500 the Spanish introduced mixed infantry formations that pursued "shock" and "shot" tactics. Spanish pikemen provided the shock, which was quickly followed up by gun shot or missile fire. Spanish infantry formations were capable of defeating cavalry even in the open field without defensive fortifications, an unprecedented feat. By the end of the fifteenth century, trained infantry were necessary in every army.

The chivalric aristocrats, who made up the heavily armored cavalry forces and whose fighting ability justified their social privileges, tried to adapt to the changes by improving plate armor, employing longer lances, and drilling their horses for greater maneuverability. They were successful enough and retained enough political influence that heavy cavalry remained necessary in the professional armies that began to appear in the fifteenth century. However, the military revolution precipitated a major shift in European society as well as in battlefield tactics. The successful states were those that created the financial base and bureaucratic structures necessary to put into the field a well-trained professional army composed of infantry units and artillery. Armies now required officers who were capable of drilling infantry or understanding the science of warfare in order to serve as an artillery officer. The traditional landed aristocrats, accustomed to commanding armored knights, found that noble lineage was not as important as technical skills and talents.

The Culture of Loss

T o the influential Dutch historian Johan Huizinga the culture of fourteenth- and fifteenth-century northern Europe conveyed a passionate intensity of life:

When the world was half a thousand years younger all events had much sharper outlines than now. The distance between sadness

■ Calamities Stimulate Creative Literature

During the fourteenth and fifteenth centuries death was ever present, but some creative people responded by advocating social change. Here Christine de Pisan presents a copy of her poems to Isabeau of Bavaria, the wife of King Charles VI of France. Pisan championed the cause of women in literary work.

and joy, between good and bad fortune, seemed to be much greater than for us; every experience had that degree of directness and absoluteness that joy and sadness still have in the mind of a child.[14]

This childlike, passionate intensity of life, according to Huizinga, derived from the omnipresence of violence and death. Suffering and death became a common theme in the arts, and strangely the subject matter for jokes, fancy-dress masquerades, and wild dances. The preoccupation with death revealed an anxious attachment to fleeting life.

This widespread anxiety had many manifestations. Some people sought escape from the terror. Aristocrats indulged in a beautiful fantasy life of gallant knights and beautiful ladies. Others went on long penitential pilgrimages to the shrines of saints or to the Holy Land. During the fourteenth century the tribulations of the pilgrim's travels became a metaphor for the journey of life itself, stimulating creative literature. Still others tried to find someone to blame for calamities. When no other explanation could be found, alleged witches became handy scapegoats. The search for scapegoats also focused on minority groups, especially Jews and Muslims.

REMINDERS OF DEATH

In no other period of Western civilization has the idea of death constituted such a pervasive cultural theme as during the fourteenth and fifteenth centuries. The religious justification for this preoccupation was the Reminder of Death, a theme in a contemporary book of moral guidance advising the reader that "when he goes to bed, he should imagine not that he is putting himself to bed, but that others are laying him in his grave."[15] Reminders of Death became the everyday theme of preachers, and popular woodcuts represented death in simple but disturbing images. These representations emphasized the transitory nature of life, admonishing that every created thing perishes. The Reminder of Death tried to encourage ethical behavior in this life by showing that in everyone's future was neither riches, nor fame, nor love, nor pleasure, but only the decay of death.

The most macabre Reminder of Death was the Dance of Death. First appearing in a poem of 1376, the Dance of Death evolved into a street play, performed to illustrate sermons that called for repentance. It also appeared in church murals, depicting a procession led by a skeleton that included representatives of the social orders, from children and peasants to pope and emperor. All were being led to their inevitable deaths. At the Church of the Innocents in Paris, the mural depicting the Dance of Death is accompanied by an inscription that reads:

Advance, see yourselves in us, dead, naked, rotten and stinking. So will you be. . . . To live without thinking of this risks damnation. . . . Power, honor, riches are nothing; at the hour of death only good works count. . . . Everyone should think at least once a

■ Tomb Effigy of a Knight

This effigy above the tomb of Jean d'Alluy shows the deceased as if he were serenely sleeping, still dressed in the armor of his worldly profession.

day of his loathsome end [in order to escape] the dreadful pain of hell without end which is unspeakable.[16]

In earlier centuries, tombs had depicted death as serene: On top of the tomb was an effigy of the deceased, dressed in the finest clothes with hands piously folded and eyes open to the promise of eternal life. In contrast, during the fourteenth century tomb effigies began to depict putrefying bodies or naked skeletons, symbols of the futility of human status and achievements. These tombs were disturbingly graphic Reminders of Death. Likewise, poems spoke of the putrid smell of rotting flesh, the livid color of plague victims, the cold touch of the dead. Preachers loved to personalize death. They would point to the most beautiful young woman in the congregation and describe how she would look while rotting in the grave, how worms would crawl through the empty sockets that once held her alluring eyes.

In reminding people of the need to repent their sins in the face of their inevitable deaths, no sin was more condemned than pride, the high opinion of one's own qualities and conduct. In contrast to modern times, when pride

■ **Decomposing Cadaver**
The tomb effigy of Jean de Lagrange.

God and to separate the departed from their kin. According to the Art of Dying, which was prescribed in numerous advice books and illustrations, the sick or injured person should die in bed, surrounded by a room full of people, including children. It was believed that a dying person watched a supernatural spectacle visible to him or her alone as the heavenly host fought with Satan and his demon minions for the soul. The Art of Dying compared the deathbed contest to a horrific game of chess in which the Devil did all he could to trap the dying person into a checkmate just at the moment of death. In the best of circumstances, a priest arrived in time to hear a confession, offer words of consolation, encourage the dying individual to forgive his or her enemies and redress any wrongs, and perform the last rites.

is often understood as a virtue, late medieval moralists saw pride as an affront to God, a rejection of God's will that humanity should concentrate on spiritual rather than worldly things. Pride, in fact, was often discussed as the ultimate source of all the other deadly sins: lust, gluttony, avarice, sloth, wrath, and covetousness. The theme was encapsulated by the inscription on the tomb of a cardinal who died in 1402: "So, miserable one, what cause for pride?"[17]

Late medieval society was completely frank about the unpleasant process of dying, unlike modern societies that hide the dying in hospitals and segregate mourning to funeral homes. Dying was a public event, almost a theatrical performance. The last rites of the Catholic Church and the Art of Dying served to assist souls in their final test before

ILLUSIONS OF A NOBLE LIFE

Eventually death arrived for everyone, peasant and noble alike, a fact that the Reminders of Death were designed to keep foremost in the minds of all Christians. Some people, especially among the nobility, sought to ignore this funda-

■ **Nobles Hunting**
Nobles hunting deer with their ladies riding pillion. Hunts such as this one would have been a typical recreation of the dukes of Burgundy and their courtiers.

mental truth through escapist fantasies. These fantasies shielded nobles not only from the inevitability of death but also from all the other perils of the age—the worker and peasant rebellions, the economic depression that depleted their wealth, and the military revolution that challenged their monopoly on soldierly valor. As a result, the fantasy world of chivalry intensified. As discussed in Chapter 9, chivalric values among aristocratic knights and ladies emphasized honorable behavior and refined manners. During the Later Middle Ages, nobles indulged in chivalric escapism and idealized their class as the remedy for evil times. They thought God had placed them on earth to purify the world. Chivalry was an aesthetic ideal, a fantasy world of grace and beauty, that aspired to become an ethical ideal, a model for achieving virtue.

Much of the attraction of chivalry derived from its fanciful vision of the virtues of the ascetic life, the life that practices severe self-discipline and abstains from physical pleasures. The ideal medieval knight was as much a self-denying ascetic as the ideal medieval monk. The highest expression of the chivalric ideal was the knight-errant, a warrior who roamed in search of adventure. He was poor and free of ties to home and family, a man who lived a life of perfect freedom but whose virtue led him to do the right thing. In reality most knights were hardly ascetics but rich, propertied men who were completely involved in the world and who indulged in all of its pleasures.

The ideal of the ascetic knight-errant was pursued in an elaborately developed dream culture that occupied much of the time and cultural energy of the aristocracy. The French nobleman Philippe de Mézières (ca. 1327–1405), whose chivalric imagination knew no bounds, dreamed of establishing a new order of knights, the Order of the Passion, whose members would be spiritually removed from worldly affairs and devoted to reconquering the Holy Land. He drew up a plan for the order, but it never became a reality. He imagined that the knights in the Order of the Passion would peacefully end all wars among Christians and bind themselves together in a great crusade against the Mongols, Jews, Turks, and other Muslims. In reality, no serious crusade had been mounted since the failure of the Eighth Crusade in 1270. But several kings did found new crusading orders, which aristocrats joined with unbridled enthusiasm—the Order of the Garter in England, the Order of the Stars and Order of St. Michael in France, and the most fantastic of all, the Order of the Golden Fleece in Burgundy. Members of these orders indulged in extravagant acts of self-deprivation—for example, wearing fur coats in summer but refusing to wear a coat, hat, or gloves in freezing temperatures. They loved to take vows: One knight swore he would not sleep in a bed on Sundays until he had fought the Muslims; another took an oath that he would keep his right arm bare of any armor during battle with the Turks. None of these would-be crusaders came close to fighting Turks.

■ **A Sumptuous Aristocratic Banquet**
An aristocratic banquet with scenes of fighting in the background. Dining was the principal occasion at which nobles displayed refined manners showing their commitment to the beautiful life.

Many vows were taken in the name of ladies, revealing that the chivalric ideal also included a heavy dose of erotic desire. Besides ascetic self-denial, the most persistent chivalric fantasy was the motif of the young hero who liberates a virgin, either from a dragon or from a rioting mob of peasants. The myth of the noble knight suffering to save his beloved was the product of the male imagination, revealing how men wished to be admired in the eyes of women, but the myth has had a profound and lasting influence on Western culture.

The dream world of the noble life especially animated the duchy of Burgundy, a quasi-independent principality that paid nominal allegiance to the French king. Burgundy set the chivalric standards for all of Europe during the fifteenth century. Famous for his lavish life style, Duke Philip the Good (r. 1419–1467) was a notorious rake who seduced numerous noble ladies and produced many illegitimate children, but he also epitomized the ideals of chivalry in his love of horses, hunting, and court ceremonies. He was also an extravagant patron of the arts, which made him famous throughout Europe. Musicians, manuscript illuminators, painters, tapestry makers, and historians thrived with his support and made Burgundy the center of European aristocratic fashion.

The dukes of Burgundy sustained their power through their personal ties to the nobility and elites of the cities of their dominions. They were constantly on the move, visiting palaces, castles, and towns. They created a kind of theater state, staging elaborate entry ceremonies to the towns they visited; celebrating with fantastic splendor every event in the ducal family, such as marriages and births; entertaining the nobles with tournaments and the people with elaborate processions; and guaranteeing the loyalty of the nobles by inviting them to join the Order of the Golden Fleece, which occupied its members by training for a crusade.

PILGRIMS OF THE IMAGINATION

During the Middle Ages, a pilgrimage offered a religiously sanctioned form of escape from the omnipresent suffering and peril. Pious Christians could go on a pilgrimage to the Holy Land, Rome, or the shrine of a saint, such as Santiago de Compostela in Spain or Canterbury in England. The usual motive for a pilgrimage was to fulfill a vow or promise made to God, or to obtain an indulgence, which exempted the pilgrim from some of the time spent in punishment in Purgatory after death. The pilgrimage became the instrument for spiritual liberation and escape from difficulties. As a result, going on a pilgrimage became a compelling model for creative literature, especially during the fourteenth century. Not all of these great works of literature were fictional pilgrimages, but many evoked the pilgrim's impulse to find a refuge from the difficulties of daily life or to find solace in the promise of a better life to come.

Dante Alighieri and *The Divine Comedy*

In *The Divine Comedy* the Italian poet from Florence, Dante Alighieri (1265–1321), imagined the most fantastic pilgrimage ever attempted, a journey through Hell, Purgatory, and Paradise. A work of astounding originality, *The Divine Comedy* remains the greatest masterpiece of medieval literature. Little is known about Dante's early life except that somehow he acquired an encyclopedic education that gave him expertise in Greek philosophy, scholastic theology (the application of logic to the understanding of Christianity; see Chapter 9), Latin literature, and the newly fashionable poetic forms in Provençal, the language of southern France. Dante was involved in the dangerous politics of Florence, which led to his exile under pain of death if he ever returned. During his exile Dante wandered for years, suffering grievously the loss of his home: "bitter is the taste of another man's bread and . . . heavy the way up and down another man's stair" (*Paradiso*, canto 17). While in exile, Dante sustained himself by writing his great poetic vision of human destiny and God's plan for redemption.

In the poem Dante himself travels into the Christian version of the afterlife, but the poetic journey displays numerous non-Christian influences. The passage through Hell, for example, derived from a long Muslim poem reconstructing Mohammed's *miraj*, a night journey to Jerusalem and ascent to heaven. Dante's poem can be read on many levels—personal, historical, spiritual, moral, theological— as it recounts an allegorical pilgrimage to visit the souls of the departed. Dante connects his personal suffering with

■ **Peasants and a Ducal Castle in Burgundy**
Peasants sowing wheat and shearing sheep in the rich agricultural region that made possible the expensive court life of the duchy of Burgundy. One of the many great castles of the dukes appears in the background.

DANTE DESCRIBES HELL

....

In The Divine Comedy, *Dante imagined a series of circles in Hell into which were cast those guilty of a certain class of sin. In the eighth circle Dante and his guide Virgil came upon those guilty of fraud. They suffered for all eternity in the depths of stinking, filthy caverns in the ground. Dante and Virgil followed a path through Hell, and at this point the path led to a series of arches that spanned over the caverns.*

Here we heard people whine in the next chasm,
and knock and thump themselves with open palms,
and blubber through their snouts as if in a spasm.

Steaming from that pit, a vapor rose
over the banks, crusting them with a slime
that sickened my eyes and hammered at my nose.

That chasm sinks so deep we could not sight
its bottom anywhere until we climbed
along the rock arch to its greatest height.

Once there, I peered down; and I saw long lines
of people in a river of excrement
that seemed the overflow of the world's latrines.

I saw among the felons of that pit
one wraith who might or might not have been tonsured—
one could not tell, he was so smeared with shit.

He bellowed: "You there, why do you stare at me
more than at all the others in this stew?"
And I to him: "Because if memory

serves me, I knew you when your hair was dry.
You are Alessio Interminelli da Lucca.
That's why I pick you from this filthy fry."

And he then, beating himself on his clown's head:
"Down to this have the flatteries I sold
the living sunk me here among the dead."

And my Guide prompted then: "Lean forward a bit
and look beyond them, there—do you see that one
scratching herself with dungy nails, the strumpet

who fidgets to her feet, then to a crouch?
It is the whore Thais . . ."

Source: From *The Divine Comedy* by Dante Alighieri, translated by John Ciardi. Copyright 1954, 1957, 1960, 1961, 1965, 1967, 1970 by the Ciardi Family Publishing Trust. Used by permission of W. W. Norton & Company, Inc.

the historical problems of Italy, the warnings of the dead who had sinned in life, and the promise of rewards to those who had been virtuous. Dante's trip, initially guided by the Latin poet Virgil, the epitome of ancient wisdom, starts in Hell. While traveling deeper into its harsh depths, Dante is warned of the harmful values of this world by meeting a cast of sinful characters who inhabit the world of the damned. In Purgatory his guide becomes Beatrice, Dante's deceased beloved, who stands for the Christian virtues. In this section of the poem, he begins the painful process of spiritual rehabilitation where he comes to accept the Christian image of life as a pilgrimage. In Paradise he achieves spiritual fulfillment by speaking with figures from the past who have defied death.

The lasting appeal of this long, complex, and difficult poem is a wonder. Underlying the appeal of *The Divine Comedy* is perhaps its optimism, which expresses Dante's own cure to his depressing condition as an exile. The power of Dante's poetry established the form of the modern Italian language. Even in translation the images and stories can intrigue and fascinate.

Giovanni Boccaccio and *The Decameron*

Like Dante, Giovanni Boccaccio (1313–1375) was a Florentine. He grew up in a prosperous merchant banking family that was bankrupted during the Florentine financial crisis of the 1340s. Losing the shelter of economic and so-cial privilege, Boccaccio's life became one of poverty and endless adversity. In the freedom from business responsibilities created by enforced poverty, Boccaccio turned to writing tales of chivalry and love, which were immediately very popular and had lasting influence on other writers.

After witnessing the ravages of the Black Death in Florence in 1348 and 1349, Boccaccio turned to polishing his masterpiece, *The Decameron*, a collection of 100 humorous, satirical, majestic, and sometimes pornographic stories. The book begins with a somber description of the social chaos created by the plague and tells how ten young people (seven women and three men) escaped the plague in Florence for a refuge in the country. *The Decameron* is less a story of a pilgrimage than the depiction of a refuge, but it is no less an escape from the cruel realities of the world. In their luxurious fantasy world of the country, each of the ten tells a story every night for ten nights. Displaying an open-minded attitude toward human weaknesses, *The Decameron* represents Boccaccio's initial response to the Black Death. Believing there was no future other than death, Boccaccio responded with a celebration of life in stories full of heroism, romance, unhappy love, wit, trickery, sexual license, and laughter. Although *The Decameron* was often read as escapist fantasy literature designed to lift the gloom of events, it was also a literary masterpiece that created a vivid, swift moving narrative.

Geoffrey Chaucer and *The Canterbury Tales*

Boccaccio profoundly influenced Geoffrey Chaucer (ca. 1342–1400), the most outstanding English poet prior to Shakespeare. As a courtier and diplomat, Chaucer was a trusted adviser to three successive English kings. But he is best known for his literary output, including *The Canterbury Tales*, which exhibit some of the same earthy humor and tolerance for human folly as *The Decameron*.

In *The Canterbury Tales* a group of some thirty pilgrims tell stories as they travel on horseback to the shrine at Canterbury. By employing the pilgrimage as a framing device for telling the stories, Chaucer was able to bring together a collection of people from across the social spectrum, including a wife, indulgence hawker, miller, town magistrate, clerk, landowner, lawyer, merchant, knight, abbess, and monk. The variety of characters who told the tales allowed Chaucer to experiment with many kinds of literary forms, from a chivalric romance to a sermon. The pilgrimage combined the considerations of religious morality with the fun of a spring vacation more concerned with the pleasures of this world than preparing for the next, which was the avowed purpose of going on a pilgrimage. In this intertwining of the worldly and the spiritual, Chaucer brought the abstract principles of Christian morality down to a level of common understanding.

Margery Kempe and the Autobiographical Pilgrimage

As the daughter of a town mayor, Margery Kempe (1373–1440) was destined for a comfortable life as a middle-class wife in provincial England. After her first child was born, however, she experienced a bout of depression during which she had a vision of Christ. Her failure in the brewery business (women dominated brewing in the Middle Ages) led to more visions and the calling to a spiritual life. As a married woman she could not become a nun, which would have been the normal course for a woman with her spiritual inclinations. Instead, she accepted her marital duties and bore fourteen children.

At the age of about 40 she persuaded her husband to join her in a mutual vow of chastity and embarked on her own religious vocation. Always a bit of an eccentric, Kempe became a fervent vegetarian at a time when meat was scarce but highly desired. She also developed an insatiable wanderlust, undertaking a series of pilgrimages to Jerusalem, Rome, Germany, Norway, Spain, and numerous places in England. On these pilgrimages she sought out mystics and recluses for their spiritual advice. Her own devotions took the form of loud weeping and crying, which alienated many people who feared she might be a heretic or a madwoman. Toward the end of her life she dictated an account of her difficult dealings with her husband, her spells of madness, her ecstatic visions, and her widespread travels as a pilgrim. For Kempe the actual experience of undertaking pilgrimages made it possible for her to examine the course of her own life, which she understood as a spiritual pilgrimage. Her *Book* (1436) was the earliest autobiography in English.

Christine de Pisan and Early Feminism

The work of the poet Christine de Pisan (1364–1430) was neither escapist like Giovanni Boccaccio's nor a spiritual pilgrimage like Margery Kempe's but a thoughtful and passionate commentary on the tumultuous issues of her day. At age 15 Pisan married a notary of King Charles V of France, but by age 25 she was a widow with three young children. In order to support her family, she turned to writing and relied on the patronage of the royalty and wealthy aristocrats of France, Burgundy, Germany, and England, even though she continued to live in Paris.

Christine de Pisan was an early feminist who championed the cause of women in a male-dominated society that was often overtly hostile to them. Following the fashion of the times, she invented a new chivalric order, the Order of the Rose, whose members took a vow to defend the honor of women. She wrote a defense of women for a male readership and an allegorical autobiography. But she is most famous for the two books she wrote for women readers, *The Book of the City of Ladies* and *The Book of Three Virtues* (both about 1407). In these she recounted tales of the heroism and virtue of women and offered moral instruction for women in different social roles. In 1415 she retired to a convent where in the last year of her life she wrote a masterpiece of ecstatic lyricism that celebrated the early victories of Joan of Arc. Pisan's book turned the martyred Joan into a feminist heroine.

DEFINING CULTURAL BOUNDARIES

During the Later Middle Ages, systematic discrimination against certain ethnic and religious groups increased markedly in Europe. As European society enforced ever-higher levels of religious uniformity, intolerance spread in the ethnically mixed societies of the European periphery. Intolerance was marked in three especially troubled areas: Spain with its mixture of Muslim, Jewish, and Christian cultures; the German borderlands in east-central Europe, where Germans mingled with Slavs; and Ireland and Wales, where Celts came under the domination of the English. Within the heartland of Europe were other areas of clashing cultures—for example, Switzerland where the folk culture of peasants and shepherds living in the isolated mountains collided with the intense Christian religiosity of the cities.

During the eleventh and twelfth centuries, ethnic diversity had been more widely accepted. A Hungarian cleric wrote in an undated work from this period, "As immigrants come from various lands, so they bring with them various languages and customs, various skills and forms of armament, which adorn and glorify the royal household and quell the pride of external powers. A kingdom of one race and custom is weak and fragile."[18] By the fourteenth and fifteenth centuries, however, this optimistic celebration of diversity had faded. Ethnic discrimination and residential segregation created the first ghettos for ethnic and religious minorities.

Spain: Religious Communities in Tension

The Iberian peninsula was home to thriving communities of Muslims, Jews, and Christians. Since the eleventh century the aggressive northern Christian kingdoms of Castile and Aragon had engaged in a protracted program of Reconquest (*Reconquista*) against the Muslim states of the peninsula. By 1248 the Reconquest was largely completed, with only a small Muslim enclave in Granada holding out until 1492. The Spanish Reconquest placed former enemies in close proximity to one another. Hostilities between Christians and Muslims ranged from active warfare to tense stalemate, with Jews working as cultural intermediaries between the two larger communities.

During the twelfth and thirteenth centuries Muslims, called the Mudejars, who capitulated to the conquering Christians, received guarantees that they could continue to practice their own religion and laws. During the fourteenth century, however, Christian kings gradually reneged on these promises. In 1301 the king of Castile decreed that the testimony of any two Christian witnesses could convict a Jew or Muslim, notwithstanding any previously granted privileges that allowed them to be tried in their own courts. The Arabic language began to disappear in Spain as the Mudejars suffered discrimination on many levels. By the sixteenth century, the practice of Islam became illegal, and the Spanish state adopted a systematic policy to destroy Mudejar culture by prohibiting Muslim dress, customs, and marriage practices.

The Jews also began to feel the pain of organized, official discrimination. Christian preachers accused Jews of poisonings, stealing Christian babies, and cannibalism. When the Black Death arrived in 1348, the Jews of Aragon were accused of having poisoned the wells, even though Jews were dying just like Christians. Beginning in 1378, a Catholic prelate in Seville, Ferrant Martínez, commenced an anti-Jewish preaching campaign by calling for the destruction of all twenty-three of the city's synagogues, the confinement of Jews to a ghetto, the dislodging of all Jews from public positions, and the prohibition of any social contact between Christians and Jews. His campaign led to an attack on the Jews of Seville in 1391. Violence spread to other cities throughout the peninsula and the nearby Balearic Islands. Jews were given a stark choice: conversion or death. After a year of mob violence, about 100,000 Jews had been murdered and an equal number had gone into hiding or fled to more tolerant Muslim countries. The 1391 pogroms led to the first significant forced conversions of Jews in Spain. A century later in 1492, on the

heels of the final Christian victory of the Reconquest, all remaining Jews in Spain were compelled to either leave or convert.

German and Celtic Borderlands: Ethnic Communities in Tension

Other regions with diverse populations also witnessed discrimination and its brutal consequences. During the population boom of the twelfth and thirteenth centuries, German-speaking immigrants had established colonial towns in the Baltic and penetrated eastward, creating isolated pockets of German culture in Bohemia, Poland, and Hungary. During the fourteenth and fifteenth centuries, the bias of native populations against the colonizing Germans was manifest in various ways. One Czech prince offered 100 silver marks to anyone who brought him 100 German noses. The German settlers exhibited a similar intolerance of the natives. The Teutonic Knights, who had been the vanguard of the German migrations in the Baltic, began to require German ancestry for membership. In German-speaking towns along the colonized borderlands of east-central Europe, city councils and guilds began to restrict by ethnicity the qualification for holding certain offices or joining a guild. The most famous example was the "German Paragraph" in guild statutes, which required candidates for admission to a guild to prove German descent. As the statutes of a bakers' guild put it, "Whoever wishes to be a member must bring proof to the councillors and the guildsmen that he is born of legitimate, upright German folk." Others required members to be "of German blood and tongue," as if language were a matter of biological inheritance.[19] German guildsmen were also forbidden to marry non-Germans.

A similar process of exclusion occurred in the Celtic fringe of the British Isles. In Ireland the ruling English promulgated laws that attempted to protect the cultural identity of the English colonists. The English prohibited native Irish from citizenship in town or guild membership. The Statutes of Kilkenny of 1366 attempted to legislate ethnic purity: They prohibited intermarriage between English and Irish; they required English colonists to speak English, use English names, wear English clothes, and ride horses in the English way; and they forbade the English to play Irish games or listen to Irish music. The aggressive legislation of the English in Ireland was essentially defensive. The tiny English community was attempting to prevent its absorption into the majority culture. A similar pattern appeared in Wales, where the lines dividing the Welsh and English communities hardened during the fourteenth century.

Enemies Within

The Black Death and its aftermath transformed many segments of Europe into a persecuting society. The year 1348 represented a watershed; in the period that followed, vague biases and dislikes sharpened into systematic violence against minorities. The plague sparked assaults against lepers, people with handicaps and physical deformities, beggars, vagabonds, foreigners, priests, pilgrims, Muslims, and Jews. Anyone who looked strange, dressed differently, spoke with an accent, practiced a minority religion, or did not fit in was vulnerable to becoming a scapegoat for the miseries of others. Minorities took the blame for calamities that could not be otherwise explained.

Violence against minorities occurred in many places, but it was most systematic in German-speaking lands. Between November 1348 and August 1350, violence against Jews occurred in more than eighty German towns. Like the allegations in Aragon, the fear that Jews poisoned the wells led to massacres in German lands even *before* plague had arrived in these communities. The frequent occurrence of violence on Sundays or feast days suggests that preachers consciously or unconsciously encouraged the rioting mobs.

The troubles caused by the Great Schism (1378–1417, when there was more than one pope) also contributed to a heightened sensitivity to cultural differences. During the Council of Basel (1431–1449), German bishops and theologians in attendance began to exchange information about cases of alleged witchcraft they had heard about in the nearby Swiss Alps. What these learned priests and friars thought of as witchcraft was probably nothing more than harmless folk magic, but to them the strange details of peasant behavior seemed evidence of a vast Satanic conspiracy to destroy Christianity. For most of its history, the Catholic Church had denied that witchcraft existed, but the terrible events of the fourteenth century cried out for explanation. In 1484 Pope Innocent VIII changed official Catholic policy by calling upon two Dominican professors of theology to examine the alleged spread of witchcraft in Germany. As a guide to witch hunters, they wrote a detailed handbook on witchcraft, *The Hammer of Witches*, which went through twenty-eight editions between 1486 and 1600, evidence of its enormous success and influence.

The Hammer of Witches codified the folklore of the Alpine peasants as the basis for witchcraft practices. The book condemned as heretics those who disbelieved in the power of witches and established legal procedures for the prosecution of witches. It sanctioned torture as the most effective means for obtaining confessions, and it established much lower standards of evidence than in other kinds of cases. As an anthology of mythical stories about the activities of supposed witches, *The Hammer* summed up the worst of prevailing attitudes about women: "all witchcraft comes from carnal lust, which in women is insatiable." As we shall see in Chapter 14, most witchcraft persecutions came later in the sixteenth and seventeenth centuries, but

ANTI-GERMAN BIAS

The language of intolerance tends to borrow from a very limited repertoire of negative stereotypes. As a result, biased ideas have little if any relationship to reality. In this tract from fourteenth-century Bohemia, the Czech author applied to the hated German minority the very same stereotypes that Germans used against Jews. The author asserts that God had singled out the Germans to be a slave race, but they had usurped land and wealth of others. This tract called on Czechs to launch an anti-German pogrom.

The wise man should observe and the prudent man consider how this crafty and deceitful race has intruded itself into the most fertile prebends [church lands], the best fiefs [noble lands], the richest possessions, even into the prince's council. . . the sons of this race enter into the lands of others. . . . thus they plunder and devastate all lands; thus enriched they begin to oppress their neighbors and rebel against the princes and their other proper lords. Thus did Judas and Pilate behave. No one with any experience doubts that the Germans are wolves in the flock, flies in the food, serpents in the lap, whores in the house. . . .

It would be profitable, just and customary if the bear stayed in the wood, the fox in his den, the fish in water and the German in Germany. The world was healthy when the Germans were placed as a target for the arrow—in one place eyes were torn out, in another they were hung up by the foot, in one place they were thrown outside the walls, in another they gave their nose as a toll payment, in one place they were killed peremptorily in the sight of the princes, in another they were forced to eat their own ears, in one place they were punished one way and in another in a different way.

Source: From "De Theutonicis bonum dictamen" as quoted in Robert Bartlett, *The Making of Europe: Conquest, Colonization and Cultural Change, 950–1350.* Copyright 1993 by Robert Bartlett. Reprinted by permission of Princeton University Press.

the publication of *The Hammer of Witches* represented the culmination of the frenzied search to find enemies within European society, which was quickened by the events of the fourteenth and fifteenth centuries. With the dissemination of the idea of the reality of witchcraft, virtually anyone could be hauled before a court on charges of maintaining a secret liaison with Satan.

CONCLUSION
Looking Inward

U nlike the more dynamic, outward-looking thirteenth century, Europeans during the fourteenth and early fifteenth centuries turned their attention inward to their own communities and their own problems. Europe faced one calamity after another, each crisis compounding the misery. In the process the identity of the West became more defensive and the fragility of Christianity itself was laid bare. The process of changing Western identities can be seen in two ways. First, as a result of the Western encounters with the Mongol and Ottoman Empires, the political and religious frontiers of the West shifted. These two empires redrew the map of the West by ending the Christian Byzantine Empire and by leaving Christian Russia on the margins of the West. With the Mongol invasions, the eastward spread of Christianity into Asia ended. The Ottoman conquests left a lasting Muslim influence inside eastern Europe, particularly in Bosnia and Albania. Peoples who were predominantly Christian and whose political institutions were a heritage of the ancient Roman Empire now survived under the domination of Asiatic empires and in a tenuous relationship with the rest of the Christian West. Most of the new subjects of these empires remained Christian, but their Mongol and Ottoman masters destroyed their political autonomy. The Ottoman Empire remained hostile to and frequently at war with the Christian West for more than 200 years.

Second, in western Europe people reinforced their identity as Christians and became more self-conscious of the country in which they lived. At the same time Christian civilization was becoming eclipsed in parts of eastern Europe, however, it revived in the Iberian peninsula where the Muslim population, once the most extensive in the West, suffered discrimination and defeat. The northern Spanish kingdoms, for example, began to unify their subjects around a militant form of Christianity that was overtly hostile to Muslims and Jews. In many places in the West, religious and ethnic discrimination against minorities increased. A stronger sense of self-identification by country can be most dramatically seen in France and England as a consequence of the Hundred Years' War. The French rallied around a saintly national heroine, Joan of Arc. After dropping claims to France after the Hundred Years' War, the English aristocracy stopped speaking French and adopting the customs of the French court. They became less international and more English. The Western countries became more self-consciously characterized by an attitude of "us" versus "them."

Except for the very visible military conquests of the Mongols and the Ottomans, the causes of most of the calamities of the fourteenth century were invisible or unknown. No one recognized a climate change or understood the dynamics of the population crisis. No one could see the plague bacillus. No one grasped the role of the Mongol Empire in the world economy or the causes for the collapse of banking and trade. Unable to distinguish how these forces were changing their lives, western Europeans only witnessed their consequences. In the face of these calamities, European culture became obsessed with death and with finding scapegoats to blame for events that could not be otherwise explained. However, calamity also bred creativity, manifest in the passionate intensity of life. The search for answers to the question, "Why did this happen to us?" produced a new spiritual sensibility and a rich literature. Following the travails of the fourteenth century, moreover, there arose in the fifteenth a new, more optimistic cultural movement—the Renaissance. Gloom and doom was not the only response to troubles. During the Renaissance some people began to search for new answers to human problems in a fashion that would transform the West anew.

Suggestions for Further Reading

For a comprehensive list of suggested readings, please go to www.ablongman.com/levack/chapter10

Duby, Georges. *France in the Middle Ages, 987–1460: From Hugh Capet to Joan of Arc.* 1991. Traces the emergence of the French state.

Gordon, Bruce, and Peter Marshall, eds. *The Place of the Dead: Death and Remembrance in Late Medieval and Early Modern Europe.* 2000. A collection of essays that shows how the placing of the dead in society was an important activity that engendered considerable conflict and negotiation.

Herlihy, David. *The Black Death and the Transformation of the West.* 1997. A pithy, readable analysis of the epidemiological and historical issues surrounding the Black Death.

Holmes, George. *Europe: Hierarchy and Revolt, 1320–1450.* 1975. Excellent examination of rebellions.

Huizinga, Johan. *The Autumn of the Middle Ages,* trans. Rodney J. Payton and Urlich Mammitzsch. 1996. A new translation of the classic study of France and the Low Countries during the fourteenth and fifteenth century. Dated and perhaps too pessimistic, Huizinga's lucid prose and broad vision still make this an engaging reading experience.

Imber, Colin. *The Ottoman Empire, 1300–1481.* 1990. The basic work that establishes a chronology for the early Ottomans.

Lambert, Malcolm. *Medieval Heresy: Popular Movements from the Gregorian Reform to the Reformation.* 1992. Excellent general study of the Hussite and Lollard movements.

Le Roy Ladurie, Emmanuel. *Times of Feast, Times of Famine: A History of Climate since the Year 1000,* trans. Barbara Bray. 1971. The book that introduced the idea of the Little Ice Age and promoted the study of the influence of climate on history.

Lynch, Joseph H. *The Medieval Church: A Brief History.* 1992. A pithy, elegant survey of ecclesiastical institutions and developments.

Morgan, David O. *The Mongols.* 1986. Best introduction to Mongol history.

Nirenberg, David. *Communities of Violence: Persecution of Minorities in the Middle Ages.* 1996. An important analysis of the persecution of minorities that is deeply rooted in Spanish evidence.

Sumption, Jonathan. *The Hundred Years' War: Trial by Battle.* 1991. First volume goes only to 1347. When it is completed it will be the best comprehensive study.

Swanson, R. N. *Religion and Devotion in Europe, c. 1215–c. 1515.* 1995. The best up-to-date textbook account of late medieval religious practice.

Notes

1. Quoted in Emmanuel Le Roy Ladurie, *Times of Feast, Times of Famine: A History of Climate since the Year 1000,* trans. Barbara Bray (1971), 47.
2. Quoted in William Bowsky, "The Impact of the Black Death," in Anthony Molho, ed., *Social and Economic Foundations of the Italian Renaissance* (1969), 92.
3. Giovanni Boccaccio, *The Decameron,* trans. Richard Aldington (1962), 30.
4. Ibid.
5. Cited in Philip Ziegler, *The Black Death* (1969), 20.
6. Quoted in Mark C. Bartusis, *The Late Byzantine Army: Arms and Society, 1204–1453* (1992), 133.
7. Trial record as quoted in Marina Warner, *Joan of Arc* (1981), 122.
8. Ibid., 127.
9. Ibid., 143.
10. *The Trial of Joan of Arc,* trans. W. S. Scott (1956), 134.
11. Ibid., 106.
12. Ibid., 135.
13. Warner, *Joan of Arc,* 145.
14. Johan Huizinga, *The Autumn of the Middle Ages,* trans. Rodney J. Payton and Ulrich Mammitzsch (1996), 1.
15. Ibid., 156.
16. Quoted in Barbara W. Tuchman, *A Distant Mirror: The Calamitous 14th Century* (1978), 505–506. Translation has been slightly modified by the authors.
17. Ibid., 506
18. *Libellus de institutione morum,* ed. J. Balogh, *Scriptores rerum Hungaricarum 2* (1938), 625. Quoted in Robert Bartlett, *The Making of Europe: Conquest, Colonization and Cultural Change 950–1350* (1993), 239.
19. *Codex diplomaticus Brandenburgensis,* ed. Adolph Friedrich Riedel (41 vols., 1838–1869), 365–367. Cited in Bartlett, *The Making of Europe,* 238.

The Italian Renaissance and Beyond: The Politics of Culture, 1350–1550

FOR FIFTEEN YEARS NICCOLÒ MACHIAVELLI WORKED AS A DIPLOMAT AND POLITical adviser, a man always at the center of the action in his hometown of Florence. But in 1512 there was a change of regimes in the city-state of Florence. Distrusted by the new rulers and suspected of involvement in an assassination plot, he was abruptly fired from his job, imprisoned, tortured, and finally ordered to stay out of town. Exiled to his suburban farm, impoverished, and utterly miserable, Machiavelli survived by selling lumber from his wood lot to his former colleagues, who regularly cheated him. To help feed his family he snared birds; to entertain himself he played cards in a local inn with the innkeeper, a butcher, a miller, and two bakers. As he put it, "caught this way among these lice I wipe the mold from my brain [by playing cards] and release my feeling of being ill-treated by Fate."

In the evenings, however, Machiavelli transformed himself into an entirely different person. He entered his study, removed his mud-splattered clothes, and put on the elegant robes he had once worn as a government official. And then, "dressed in a more appropriate manner I enter into the ancient courts of ancient men and am welcomed by them kindly." Machiavelli was actually reading the works of the ancient Greek and Latin historians, but he described his evening reading as a conversation: He asked the ancients about the reasons for their actions, and in reading their books he found answers. For four hours, "I feel no boredom, I dismiss every affliction, I no longer fear poverty nor do I tremble at the thought of death: I become completely part of them."[1]

Machiavelli's evening conversations with the long-dead ancients perfectly expressed the sensibility of the Italian Renaissance. This wretched man, disillusioned with his own times and bored by his empty-headed neighbors, found in the ancients the stimulating companions he could not find in life. For him the

The Birth of Venus (1480): Sandro Botticelli's depiction of the birth of the ancient goddess of love exemplifies the Renaissance fascination with the culture of antiquity.

ancient past was more alive than the present. And in this sense Machiavelli was very much a Renaissance man, because feeling part of antiquity is what the Renaissance is all about. For those who were captivated by it, the ancient past and the examples of leadership and beauty it offered seemed to be a cure for the ills of a decidedly troubled time.

As we saw in Chapter 10, during the fourteenth and fifteenth centuries Europeans experienced a prevailing sense of loss, a morbid preoccupation with death, and a widespread pessimism about the human capacity for good. Yet in Florence during this same period a cultural movement began to express a more optimistic view of life. We now call that movement the Renaissance. The new optimism emerged from the desire to improve the human condition during times of trouble, and that desire was first manifest in the intellectually free environment of the independent city-states of Italy. Machiavelli—despite the bleak circumstances of his later life—was one of the Renaissance thinkers who thought the world could be improved. He strongly believed that human virtue derived from a blend of learning and political action, and in this respect he differed from the medieval writers who thought the contemplative life of the monk was the highest calling to which a man could aspire. The Renaissance was born and developed because the political structures of the Italian city-states encouraged cultural experimentation and fostered the idea that society could be reengineered according to the principles that made ancient Greece and Rome great.

The word Renaissance°, which means "rebirth," is a term historians invented to describe a movement that sought to imitate and understand the culture of antiquity. The fundamental Renaissance principle was the need to keep everything in balance and proportion, an aesthetic ideal derived from ancient literature. In political theory, this meant building a stable society upon the foundations of well-balanced individuals who conformed to a rigorous code of conduct. In the arts it meant searching for the underlying harmonies in nature, which typically meant employing geometry and the mathematics of proportion in drawing, painting, sculpting, and designing buildings. Renaissance artists thought geometry unlocked the secrets of nature and revealed the hidden hand of God in creation.

As we have seen in Chapters 8 and 9, the Italian Renaissance was not the first time the West experienced a revival of ancient learning and thought. In the Carolingian Renaissance of the ninth century, members of the Emperor Charlemagne's court reinvigorated education in Latin. And the European-wide Renaissance of the twelfth century led to the foundation of the universities, the reintroduction of Roman law, and the spread of scholastic philosophy and theology. The Renaissance considered in this chapter refers to a diffuse cultural movement that occurred at different times in different regions, and as a result its dates are very approximate. Most historians date the movement from about 1350 to 1550.

The Renaissance helped refashion the concept of Western civilization. From the fifth to the fourteenth centuries, the West identified itself primarily through conformity to Roman Catholicism, which meant the celebration of uniform religious rituals in Latin and obedience to the pope. The Renaissance added a new element to this identity. Although by no means anti-Christian, Renaissance thinkers began to think of themselves as the heirs of pre-Christian cultures—Hebrew, Greek, and Roman. In this sense, they began to imagine a Western civilization that was more than just Christian.

Through reading the texts and viewing the works of art of the long-dead ancients, people during the Renaissance gained historical and visual perspective on their own world and cultivated a critical attitude. To understand what was distinctive about their insights, this chapter will address four questions. (1) In what ways did the political and social climate peculiar to the Italian city-states help create Renaissance culture? (2) How did Renaissance thinkers create historical perspective and devise methods of criticism for interpreting texts? (3) How did various attempts to imitate antiquity in the arts alter perceptions of nature? (4) How did the monarchies of western Europe gather the strength to become more assertive and more effective?

The Cradle of the Renaissance: The Italian City-States

In comparison with the rest of Europe and other world civilizations, Renaissance Italy was distinguished by the large number and political autonomy of its thriving city-states. The Netherlands and parts of the Rhine Valley were as thoroughly urbanized, but only in Italy did cities have so much political power. The evolution of the Italian city-states can be encapsulated into two distinct phases.

The first phase in the evolution of the Italian city-states occurred during the eleventh and twelfth centuries. As we saw in Chapter 8, during this period about one hundred Italian towns became independent republics, also known as communes, and developed the laws and institutions of self-government. The male citizens of these tiny republics gathered on a regular basis in the town square to debate important issues such as assessing new taxes, improving the city walls, or going to war. To conduct the day-to-day business of government, they elected city officials from among themselves.

The governmental practices of these city-states produced the political theory of republicanism°, which described a state in which government officials were elected by the people or a portion of the people. The Renaissance theory of republicanism was first articulated by Marsilius of Padua (1270–1342) in *The Defender of the Peace,* a book that relied on the precedents established by the ancient Roman republic as a source of theory for the Italian Renaissance republics. Marsilius recognized two kinds of government—principalities and republics. Principalities relied upon the descending principle that political authority came directly from God and trickled down through kings and princes to the rest of humanity. According to this principle, the responsibility of government was to enforce God's laws. Marsilius, however, rejected the idea that the task of the political world was to express the will of God. His ascending principle of republicanism suggested that laws derive not from God but from the will of the people, who freely choose their own form of government and who are equally free to change it. In Marsilius's theory, citizens regularly expressed their will through voting. The first phase in the evolution of the Italian city-states established the institutions of self-government, the procedures for electing officials, and the theory of republicanism.

In the second phase of evolution, which occurred during the fourteenth century, most city-states abandoned or lost their republican institutions and came to be ruled by princes. The reasons for the transformation of these republics into principalities were related to the economic and demographic turmoil created by the international economic collapse and the Black Death. Two of the largest republics, however, did not go through this second phase and survived without losing their liberty to a prince. The Renaissance began in these two city-states, Florence and Venice (see Map 11.1). Their survival as republics, which made them exceptions to the rule by the fifteenth century, helps explain the origins of the Renaissance.

THE RENAISSANCE REPUBLICS: FLORENCE AND VENICE

In an age of despotic princes, Florence and Venice were keenly aware of how different they were from other cities, and they feared they might suffer the same fate as their neighbors if they did not defend their republican institutions and liberty. In keeping alive the traditions of republican self-government, these two cities created an environment of competition and freedom that stimulated creative ingenuity. Although neither of these cities were democracies, nor were they particularly egalitarian, they were certainly more open to new ideas than cities ruled by princes. In both Florence and Venice, citizens prized discussion and debate, the skills necessary for success in business and politics. By contrast, in the principalities all cultural activity tended to revolve around and express the tastes of the prince, who monopolized much of the wealth. In Florence and Venice a few great families called the *patriciate* controlled most of the property, but these patricians competed among themselves to gain recognition and fame by patronizing great artists and scholars. This patronage by wealthy men and women made the Renaissance possible. And because the tastes of these patricians dictated what writers and artists could do, understanding who they were helps explain Renaissance culture.

Florence Under the Medici

The greatest patron during the early Renaissance was the fabulously rich Florentine banker Cosimo de' Medici (1389–1464). Based on his financial power, Cosimo effectively took control of the Florentine republic in 1434, ushering in a period of unprecedented domestic peace and

■ **Map 11.1   Northern Italy in the Mid-Fifteenth Century**

During the Renaissance the largest city-states, such as Milan, Venice, and Florence, gained control of the surrounding countryside and smaller cities in the vicinity, establishing regional territorial states. Only Venice and Florence remained republics. Milan and Savoy were ruled by dukes. The Gonzaga family ruled Mantua and the Este Modena and Ferrara. The states of the Church were ruled by the pope in Rome.

Northern Italy in the Mid-Fifteenth Century

artistic splendor called the Medicean Age (1434–1494). Cosimo's style of rule was exceedingly clever. Instead of making himself a prince, which the citizens of Florence would have opposed, he managed the policies of the republic from behind the scenes. He seldom held public office, but he made himself the center of Florentine affairs through shrewd negotiating, the quiet fixing of elections, and the generous distribution of bribes, gifts, and jobs. Cosimo's behind-the-scenes rule illustrated a fundamental value of Renaissance culture—the desire to maintain appearances. In this case, the appearance of the Florentine republic was saved, even as the reality of Florentine liberty was subverted.

Cosimo's brilliant patronage of intellectuals and artists mirrored a similar ambition to maintain appearances. It helped make Cosimo appear a pious, generous man who modeled himself after the great statesmen of the ancient Roman republic. Cosimo appreciated intelligence and merit wherever he found it. He frequented the discussions of prominent scholars, some of whom became his lasting friends. Intrigued by what he learned from them, he personally financed the search for and acquisition of manuscripts of ancient Latin and Greek literature and philosophy for new libraries he helped establish. In return for his financial support, many Florentine scholars dedicated their works to Cosimo. He took particular interest in the revival of the ancient Greek philosopher Plato, and he set up the neo-Platonic philosopher Marsilio Ficino (1433–1499) with a house and steady income.

Cosimo's most significant patronage of the arts clustered in the neighborhood where he lived. He rebuilt the nearby monastery of San Marco. He personally selected Fra Angelico, a monk, to paint the austere yet deeply emotive frescoes throughout the monastery. As the centerpiece of his neighborhood beautification plans, Cosimo built for his own family a magnificent new palace, which he filled with innumerable objects of beauty and exquisite paintings.

Cosimo's artistic patronage helped create the image of a man who was an open-handed and benevolent godfather for his community. Since Cosimo had not been elected to rule Florence, his political influence was illegitimate and he needed to find a way to create a proper image that would justify his power. To do that he decorated the private chapel in his palace with frescoes that depicted him accompanying the magi, the wise men or kings who brought gifts to the baby Jesus. Thus, Cosimo made himself appear similar to those ancient kings who first recognized the divinity of Christ. By having himself depicted with the magi, Cosimo created an image that helped justify the fact that he controlled elections and dictated policies.

Cosimo's grandson Lorenzo the Magnificent (r. 1469–1492) expanded the family's dominance in Florentine politics through what has been called "veiled lordship." Lorenzo never took the title of prince but behaved very much like

---

COSIMO DE' MEDICI'S REPUTATION

....

Among the common genres of writing during the Renaissance were short biographies of illustrious men and women. Vespasiano da Bisticci's Lives of Illustrious Men, *written in the late fifteenth century, imitated the model of ancient biographies and was based on Vespasiano's personal recollections of many of his subjects. The owner of a bookshop that for many years served as a meeting place for learned men in Florence, Vespasiano knew and admired Cosimo de' Medici. In this example, Vespasiano recalls Cosimo's own views about his role as a patron.*

I once heard Cosimo say that the great mistake of his life was that he did not begin to spend his wealth ten years earlier; because, knowing well the disposition of his fellow-citizens, he was sure that, in the lapse of fifty years, no memory would remain of his personality or of his house save the few buildings he might have built. He went on, "I know that after my death my children will be in worse situation than those of any other Florentine who has died for many years past; moreover, I know I shall not wear the crown of laurel [a reference to an ancient sign of honor] more than any other citizen." He spoke like this because he knew the difficulty of ruling a state as he had ruled Florence, through the opposition of influential citizens who had rated themselves his equals in former times. He acted privately with the greatest discretion in order to safeguard himself, and whenever he sought to achieve something he tried to let it appear that the matter had been set in motion by someone else and thus he escaped envy and unpopularity. His manner was admirable; he never spoke ill of anyone, and it angered him greatly to hear slander spoken by others. He was kind and patient to all who sought a word with him: he was more a man of deeds than of words: he always did what he promised, and when this had been done he sent a message to let the petitioner know that his wishes had been granted. His replies were brief and sometimes obscure, so that they might be made to bear a double meaning.

Source: From Vespasiano, *Renaissance Princes, Popes, and Prelates,* translated by William George and Emily Waters, Harper Torchbooks, 1963. First English translation published by George Routledge & Sons, Ltd., London, 1926. Reprinted by permission of Thomson Publishing Services.

one by intervening publicly in the affairs of the state. In contrast to his grandfather's commitment to public patronage, Lorenzo's interest in the arts concentrated on building private villas, collecting precious gems, and commissioning small bronze statues, the kinds of things that gave him private pleasure rather than a public reputation. A fine poet and an intellectual companion of the most renowned scholars of his age, Lorenzo created a lasting reputation as a well-rounded, accomplished Renaissance man, but his princely style of rule, which ignored the republican sensibilities of the Florentines, created discontent and undermined public support for the Medicis. There were several conspiracies against him; during an attempted assassination of Lorenzo, his brother Giuliano was killed.

During the fifteenth century Florence became the first society that dedicated itself to the production and appreciation of what we now call Renaissance culture. As a republic on the perilous edge of financial survival, Florence had surrendered to the behind-the-scenes rule of the Medici family, who supported a movement in philosophy and the arts that, as we shall see, imitated and celebrated the heritage of pre-Christian antiquity, especially the culture of Greece and Rome.

Venice, the Cosmopolitan Republic

Venice resembled Florence in that it survived into the Renaissance period with its republican institutions intact, but it was far more politically stable. Situated in the midst of a vast lagoon, Venice's streets consisted of broad channels in which great seagoing merchant ships were moored and small canals choked with private gondolas for local transportation. To protect their fragile city from flooding, the Venetians recognized that they had to cooperate among themselves, and thus the imperative for survival helped create a republic that became a model of stability and ecological awareness. The Venetians, for example, created the world's first environmental regulatory agencies, which were responsible for hydrological projects, such as dikes and dredging canals, and for forestry management to prevent soil erosion and the consequent silting up of the lagoon.

Venice was among the first European powers to have colonies abroad. To guarantee its merchant ships access to the eastern Mediterranean and Constantinople, Venice conquered a series of ports, including a significant number in Greece (see Map 11.2). Its involvement in international trade and governing distant colonies made Venice unusually cosmopolitan. Many Venetian merchants spent years living abroad and some settled in the colonies. Moreover, people from all over Europe flocked to the city of Venice—Germans, Turks, Armenians, Albanians, Greeks, Slovenes, Croats, and Jews—each creating their own neighborhood communities and institutions. Venetian households owned Russian, Asian, Turkish, and African slaves, all of whom contributed to the remarkable diversity of the city.

■ **Map 11.2 Venetian Colonial Empire**
The Venetian colonies included the Greek-speaking islands in the Adriatic and a number of important islands in the Aegean. These colonies were threatened by the Ottoman Empire with its capital in Constantinople.

Of the many foreign groups in Venice, the most influential were the Greeks. Venice had long maintained close commercial and cultural ties with the Greek world. Its churches were modeled after the huge basilicas of Constantinople, and many Venetian merchants spoke Greek. After the fall of the Byzantine empire to the Ottoman Turks in 1453, many Greek Christian refugees found a new home in Venice and other Italian cities, including influential scholars who helped reintroduce Greek philosophy and literature to an eager Italian readership. One of these scholars was John Bessarion (1403–1472), a Byzantine archbishop who compiled a magnificent library of Greek manuscripts that he bequeathed to the republic of Venice. Venice also became the leading center in western Europe for the publication of Greek books, printing the important texts in Greek philosophy and science, and making them widely available for the first time in western Europe.

The defining characteristic of Venetian government was its social stability, a trait that made it the envy of other more troubled cities and the source of imitation by republican-minded reformers throughout Europe. Whereas the Florentine republic was notoriously unstable and subject to quiet subversion by the Medicis, Venice boasted a largely unchanging republican constitution that lasted from 1297 to 1797. Thus Venice is the longest-surviving republic in history. It was, however, a very exclusive republic. Out of a total population of nearly 150,000, only a small political elite consisting of some 2,500 nobles enjoyed voting privileges. From this elite and from Venice's many wealthy religious institutions came the resources to patronize Renaissance artists.

At the top of Venetian society was the *doge,* a member of the nobility who was elected to the job for life. The most notable Renaissance doge was Andrea Gritti (r. 1523–1538), whose reputation derived from his brilliant early career as a military administrator and diplomat. Gritti sometimes bent the laws in his favor, but he never manipulated elections or managed Venice's affairs as completely as Cosimo de' Medici did in Florence a century before. Like the Medicis, however, he used his own financial resources and his personal influence to transform his city into a major center of Renaissance culture.

Gritti hired some of the most prominent European artists, musicians, and poets to come to Venice. These included Pietro Aretino (1492–1556), the greatest master of satire of the sixteenth century, and the architect and sculptor Jacopo Sansovino (1486–1570). As official architect of the city, Sansovino transformed its appearance with his sculptures, palaces, and churches that imitated the styles of classical Greece and Rome. One of his most notable buildings is the Marciana Library, which was begun in 1537 to house Bessarion's collection of Greek manuscripts.

Artistic and scholarly creativity in Florence and Venice thrived on the competition among many different patrons. Neither the Medicis in Florence nor Gritti in Venice entirely dominated the cultural scene. Artistic patronage in these republics mirrored the dynamic political life that engaged many people. The diversity of patronage gave extensive employment to painters, sculptors, and architects, thereby attracting the best artists to these two cities. Later sections of the chapter will examine the works they produced.

PRINCES AND COURTIERS

Although the Renaissance began in the relative freedom of republics, such as Florence, it soon spread to principalities, those states ruled by one man, the prince. In contrast to the multiple sources of support for the arts and learning in the republics, patronage in the principalities was more constricted, confined to the prince and members of his court. The terms *lord* and *prince* refer to rulers who possessed formal aristocratic titles, such as the Marquis of Mantua, the Duke of Milan, or the King of Naples. Most Renaissance princes came from local aristocratic families who seized control of the government by force. Some, however, had been soldiers of fortune who had held on to a city as a spoil of war or had even overthrown a government that had once employed them to defend the city. Regardless of how a prince originally obtained power, his goal was to establish a dynasty, that is, to guarantee the rights of his descendants to

■ **Federico da Montefeltro as the Ideal Prince**
The papal tiara in the upper left alludes to the pope's authorization of his title as duke. Federico is shown studying a book while dressed in armor, reflecting his two sides as scholar and soldier. His dynastic ambitions are represented by the presence of his son and potential successor standing at his feet.

continue to rule the city. Some dynasties—such as that of the D'Este family, which ruled Ferrara from 1240 to 1597—were well established and quite popular.

The Ideal Prince, the Ideal Princess
Federico II da Montefeltro (1422–1482), Duke of Urbino, succeeded in achieving the lasting fame and glorious reputation that so many princes craved. Although he was illegit-

imate, his father gave him the best possible education by sending him to study at the most fashionable school in Italy and to apprentice as a soldier under the most renowned mercenary captain. In Renaissance Italy, an illegitimate boy could not inherit his father's property. Thus he usually had two career options: He could become a priest to obtain a living from the church, or he could become a mercenary and take his chances at war. Federico became a mercenary. From among the peasants of the duchy he recruited an army, which he hired out to the highest bidder. He soon earned a European-wide reputation for his many victories and enriched the duchy with the income from mercenary contracts and plunder. When his half-brother was assassinated in 1444, Federico became the ruler of Urbino, and by 1474 he obtained from the pope the title of duke. Federico epitomized the ideal Renaissance prince—a father figure to his subjects, astute diplomat, brilliant soldier, generous patron, avid collector, and man of learning. This was a prince who combined the insights of contemplative study with active involvement in the affairs of the world.

Federico's rule was paternalistic. He was concerned for the welfare of his subjects and personally listened to their complaints and adjudicated their disputes. His military adventures tripled the size of his duchy. Conquests brought the prosperity that financed his expensive building projects and his collection of Latin manuscripts. Federico's personal library surpassed that of any contemporary university library in Europe, and his wide-ranging reading interests showed his openness to the latest developments in learning. Federico's greatest achievement, however, was the building of a vast palace. At one stage the project was supervised by the architect Luciano Laurana (ca. 1420–1479), but it was Federico who clearly deserves most of the credit for what remains the single best example of Renaissance architectural ideals in a palace. Because of Federico, the small mountainous duchy of Urbino acquired a cultural importance far greater than its size warranted.

The best candidate for the ideal princess was Isabella d'Este (1474–1539), the Marchioness of Mantua. Such was her fame as a patron that she was known during her lifetime as "the first lady of the world." Enjoying an education that was exceptional for a girl in the fifteenth century, she grew up in the court at Ferrara, where she was surrounded by famous painters and poets and where she cultivated foreign ambassadors and leading intellectuals of the time. Such was her fame that her own clothing designs established the fashion for all of Europe. But her influence went far beyond that. When her husband was absent and after his death, she ruled Mantua by herself, earning a reputation for her just decisions and witty charm. She gained renown for her ability as a tenacious negotiator and behind-the-scenes diplomat. An avid reader and collector, she personally knew virtually all the great artists and writers of her age. Her influence spread far beyond Mantua, in part through her voluminous correspondence, which is estimated to include some 12,000 letters.

The Ideal Courtier

Just as the Renaissance republics developed a code of conduct for citizens, so the principalities created a model for the ideal courtier. A courtier was a man or woman who lived in or regularly visited the palace of a prince. Courtiers helped the prince's household function by performing all kinds of services, such as taking care of the family's wardrobe, managing servants, educating children, providing entertainment, keeping accounts, administering estates,

■ Courtiers Waiting on a Princely Family

The man at the far right is posing in a nonchalant manner. Members of the prince's family on the left congregate around him as he conducts business from the throne, which is just a chair with a dog resting underneath. In this scene the prince confers with a messenger who has brought him a letter.

going on diplomatic missions, and fighting battles. To best serve the princely family in whatever was needed, a courtier needed to cultivate a wide range of skills. Men trained in horsemanship, sword play, and all kinds of sports, which were useful for keeping in shape for war. Women learned to draw, dance, play musical instruments, and engage in witty conversation. Both men and women needed to be adept at foreign languages so that they could converse with visitors and diplomats. Men and some women in the courts knew Latin and Greek, which was the foundation of a formal education. The stability and efficiency of the princely states depended on the abilities of the courtiers, who performed many of the functions that elected officials did in the republics. It was also extremely important to prevent conflicts among the courtiers; otherwise the peace of the state would be compromised. The most influential guide to how a courtier should behave was *The Book of the Courtier* (composed between 1508 and 1528) by the cultivated diplomat, Baldassare Castiglione (1478–1529). Underlying the behavior and conversation of the ideal courtier described in this book were two general principles that governed all civilized manners—nonchalance and ease:

> *I have found quite a universal rule which . . . seems to me valid above all others, and in all human affairs whether in word or deed: and that is to avoid affectation in every way possible as though it were some very rough and dangerous reef; and (to pronounce a new word perhaps) to practice in all things a certain nonchalance, so as to conceal all art and make whatever is done or said appear to be without effort and almost without any thought about it. . . .*
>
> *Therefore we may call that art true art which does not seem to be art; nor must one be more careful of anything than of concealing it, because if it is discovered, this robs a man of all credit and causes him to be held in slight esteem.*[2]

In other words, nonchalance is the ability to do something that requires considerable training and effort while making it appear to be natural and without effort. The need to maintain appearances, which we first saw in the disguised rulership of Cosimo de' Medici in Florence, became one of the distinguishing traits of Italian Renaissance culture. According to Castiglione, all human action and communication should be moderate and balanced, creating the effect of ease. In effect, *The Book of the Courtier* translated the ideals of harmony and proportion so admired in Renaissance culture into a plan for human comportment. By using courtly manners, human beings governed the movements of the body according to an almost mathematical ideal of proportion.

Through *The Book of the Courtier* and its many imitators, the Renaissance ideal of courtly manners began to be widely disseminated during the sixteenth century. Written

CHRONOLOGY

The Cradle of the Renaissance: The Italian City-States

AFTER 1070	Founding of first city republics or communes
1270–1342	Marsilius of Padua, author of *The Defender of the Peace*
1434–1464	Rule of Cosimo de' Medici in Florence
1444–1482	Rule of Federico II da Montefeltro, Duke of Urbino
1469–1492	Rule of Lorenzo, the Magnificent, de' Medici in Florence
1474–1539	Life of Isabella d'Este, Marchioness of Mantua
1492–1503	Pontificate of Alexander VI
1508	Baldassare Castiglione begins writing *The Book of the Courtier*
1503–1513	Pontificate of Julius II
1513–1521	Pontificate of Leo X
1523–1538	Rule of Andrea Gritti, Doge of Venice

in a lucid Italian that made for lively reading, the book was translated into Latin, English, French, and Spanish and widely plagiarized, imitated, and absorbed into the literature of Europe. By studying these books, any young man or woman of talent and ambition could aspire to act and speak like a great aristocrat. The courtly ideal was completely accessible to anyone who could read, and many of its precepts were incorporated into the educational curriculum.

The Papal Prince

The Renaissance popes were the heads of the Church; they also had jurisdiction over the Papal State in central Italy. Thus they combined the roles of priest and prince. The Papal State was supposed to supply the pope with the income to run the affairs of the Church, but as we saw in Chapter 10, during the period when the popes left Rome and resided in Avignon (France) and during the Great Schism of 1305–1417, the popes lost control of the Papal State. After 1418 the popes saw that they had two main tasks—first, to regain the revenues of the Papal State; second, to restore the city of Rome, which had become a neglected ruin. To collect the taxes and revenues due them, many popes were obliged to use military force to bring the rebellious lords and cities into obedience. The popes also engaged in squabbles with the neighboring states that had taken advantage of the weakness of the papacy during the schism.

These military and diplomatic adventures thrust the popes into some very nasty quarrels—a situation that undermined the popes' ability to provide moral leadership. Pope Alexander VI (r. 1492–1503) financed his son Cesare Borgia's attempts to carve out a principality for himself along the northern fringe of the Papal State. He also married off his daughter, Lucrezia Borgia, in succession to several different Italian princes who were useful allies in the pope's military ambitions. The members of the Borgia family made many enemies who accused them of all kinds of evil deeds, including the poisoning of one of Lucrezia's husbands, brother-sister and father-daughter incest, and conducting orgies in the Vatican. Even though many of these allegations were false or exaggerated, the reputation of the papacy suffered. Alexander's successor, Pope Julius II (r. 1503–1513), continued to pursue military advantage in the Papal State. He took his princely role so seriously that he donned armor, personally led troops during the siege of Bologna, and rather presumptuously rewarded himself with a triumphal procession, an honor that had been granted in ancient Rome to victorious generals such as Julius Caesar.

Many of the Renaissance popes were embarrassed by the squalor of the city of Rome, an unfit place to serve as the capital of the Church. By the late fifteenth century a number of popes were ambitious to create a capital they felt worthy for Christendom. The most clear-sighted of the builders of Rome was Pope Leo X (r. 1513–1521), the second son of Lorenzo the Magnificent. Educated by the circle of scholars who surrounded the Medicis, Leo was destined for a clerical career at a young age. He received a doctorate in canon law and was made a cardinal at age seventeen. During Leo's pontificate, Rome was transformed into one of the centers of Renaissance culture. Leo transformed the University of Rome into a distinguished institution through the appointment of famous professors. For his own private secretaries he chose famous intellectuals. Leo's ambition can best be measured in his project to rebuild Saint Peter's Basilica as the largest church in the world. He tore down the old Basilica, which had been a major pilgrimage destination for more than a thousand years, and planned the great church that still dominates Rome today.

THE CONTRADICTIONS OF THE PATRIARCHAL FAMILY

The contradiction between the theory of the patriarchal family and realities of family life produced much of the creative energy of the Italian Renaissance. When theory dramatically departed from actual experience, many people began to distrust the theory and seek alternative ways of looking at society and the world. That is what happened in Renaissance Italy.

Advice books on family management, such as Leon Battista Alberti's *Four Books on the Family* (written in the 1430s), were popular and influential. Such books propounded the theory that husbands and fathers ruled. They

were the sources of social order and discipline, and not just within the family but of all of society. Groups of male relatives were responsible for rectifying injuries and especially for avenging any assault on a family member. Nearly all marriages were arranged by fathers or male guardians who sought beneficial financial and political alliances with other families, a situation that gave older men an advantage in the marriage market, as they were usually better off financially than younger ones. As a result, husbands tended to be much older than wives. In Florence in 1427, for example, the typical first marriage was between a 30-year-old man and an 18-year-old woman. Husbands were encouraged to treat their spouses with a kindly but distant paternalism. All women were supposed to be kept under strict male supervision, and the only honorable role for an unmarried woman was as a nun.

However, the reality of family life often departed from theory. A number of factors explain the disparity. First, a variety of circumstances made family life insecure and the very survival of families tenuous—death from epidemic diseases, especially plague, and separations due to marital strife, which were common enough even though divorce was not possible. Second, the wide age gap between husbands and wives meant that husbands were likely to die long before their wives, and thus many women became widows at a relatively young age with children still to raise. Third, many men, especially international merchants and migrant workers, were away from their families for long periods of time. Regardless of the patriarchal assertion that fathers should be in control, in reality they were often absent or dead.

The contradiction between the theory of patriarchy and the fragile reality of family life had far-reaching consequences. Unlike the strong hand fathers were supposed to wield over their families, most were remote figures who had little direct influence. Mothers who were supposed to be modest, obedient to their husbands, and invisible to the outside world not only had to raise children alone but often had to manage their dead or absent husband's business and political affairs. By necessity, many resilient, strong, and active women were deeply involved in the management of worldly affairs, and mothers had much more direct influence on children than fathers. Despite the theory of patriarchy, the families of Renaissance Italy were in fact matriarchies in which mothers ruled.

The contractions of family life became one of the most discussed problems in the Renaissance. Making fun of impotent old husbands married to beautiful but unfulfilled young wives became a major theme in comic drama. Given the demographic ravages of the plague, concern for the care of babies preoccupied preachers, while the many Renaissance paintings in which little cherubs seem to fall from the sky manifested a deep and widespread craving for healthy children. A widespread anxiety produced by the contradictions of family life and by the tenuous hold many

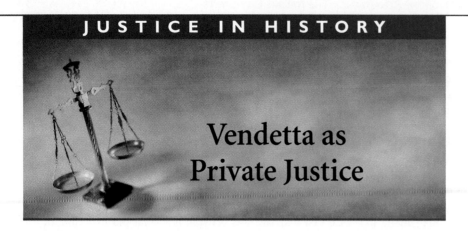

Vendetta as Private Justice

During the fourteenth and fifteenth centuries, the official justice provided by the law courts competed with the private justice of revenge. Private justice was based on the principle of retaliation. When someone was murdered or assaulted, it became the obligation of the victim's closest male relatives to avenge the injury by harming the perpetrator or one of his relatives to a similar degree. A son was obliged to avenge the death of his father, a brother the injury of his brother. Given the weakness of most governments, the only effective justice was often private justice or, as the Italians called it, *vendetta*. As the most significant source of disorder during the Renaissance, vendetta was a practice that all governments struggled to eradicate.

One of the attributes that distinguished an act of private justice from a simple violent crime was that avengers committed their acts openly and even bragged about what they had done. A criminal covered his tracks. An avenger did not. Therefore, the violence of an act of revenge was carried out in public so there would be witnesses, and often it was performed in a highly symbolic way in order to humiliate the victim as much as possible.

In Renaissance Italy private justice took many forms, but always such acts sought to do more than create another victim. They sought to deliver a message. After a period of disorder in 1342, the Florentines granted extraordinary judicial powers to a soldier of fortune, Walter of Brienne, known as the Duke of Athens. But Walter offended many Florentines by arresting and executing members of prominent families. In September of that year a crowd led by these families besieged the government palace and captured the duke's most hated henchmen, the "conservator" and his son. Even though the conservator had been the highest judge of Florence, the Florentines repudiated his authority by obtaining revenge. An eyewitness reported what happened next:

> The son was pushed out in front, and they cut him up and dismembered him. This done, they shoved out the conservator himself and did the same to him. Some carried a piece of him on a lance or sword throughout the city, and there were those so cruel, so bestial in their anger, and full of such hatred that they ate the raw flesh.[3]

This story of revenge in the most sophisticated city in Europe on the eve of the Renaissance illustrates the brutality of private justice, especially the need to make a public example of the victim.

Another account from nearly 200 years later tells of the murder of Antonio Savorgnan, a nobleman from Friuli who had killed a number of his enemies the previous year. Rather than attempting to have Antonio arrested as they could have, the murderers avenged their dead relatives through private justice. One eyewitness recounted that Antonio was attacked while leaving church, and then, "It was by divine miracle that Antonio Savorgnan was wounded: his head opened, he fell down, and he never spoke another word. But before he died, a giant dog came there and ate all his brains, and one cannot possibly deny that his brains were eaten."[4] This time a dog did the avengers' work for them. Perhaps the strangest detail in both of these accounts is that the writers wanted readers to believe that the victim had been eaten, either by humans or by a dog. Why was this an important message to get across?

The eating of a victim was one way avengers signaled that they were killing as an act of private justice. In both of the killings just described, the killers were retaliating for the murder of one of their close relatives and symbolically announcing to others that the attack was not an unjustifiable crime but a legitimate act of revenge. To convey that message, avengers could not ambush their opponent in the dark of night but were obliged to confront him openly in broad daylight before witnesses. There had to be the appearance, at least, of a fair fight. Murderers symbolized their revenge in several ways: They butchered the corpse as if it were the prey of a hunt or fed the remains to hunting dogs or even ate it themselves in what appeared to be a frenzy of revenge.

One of the major objectives of any government, whether a tiny city-state or a great monarchy, was to substitute public justice for private justice; but the persistence of tradition was strong. During the sixteenth century as governments sought to control violence and as the Renaissance values of moderation spread, a different kind of private justice appeared—the duel.

Private Justice

In Titian's painting, *The Bravo* (ca. 1515/1520), a man wearing a breast-plate and hiding a drawn sword behind his back grabs the collar of his enemy before assaulting him. To enact honorable revenge the attacker could not stab his enemy in the back but had to give him a chance in a fair fight.

Questions of Justice

1. How did the persistence of private justice present a challenge to an emerging state?
2. How would a person in the Renaissance likely defend himself against the charge that a crime had been committed through an act of private justice?

Taking It Further

Muir, Edward. *Mad Blood Stirring: Vendetta in Renaissance Italy.* 1998. A study of the most extensive and long-lasting vendetta in Renaissance Italy. It traces the evolution of vendetta violence into dueling.

Weinstein, Donald. *The Captain's Concubine: Love, Honor, and Violence in Renaissance Tuscany.* 2000. A delightfully engaging account of an ambush and fight among two nobles over a woman who was the concubine of the father of one of the fighters and the lover of the other. It reveals the disturbing relationship between love and violence in Renaissance society.

Traditionally, the duel had been a means of solving disputes among medieval knights, but during the sixteenth century duels became much more common, even among men who had never been soldiers. Dueling required potential combatants to conform to an elaborate set of rules: The legitimate causes for a challenge to a duel were few, the combatants had to recognize each other as honorable men, the actual fight took place only after extensive preparations, judges who were experts on honor had to serve as witnesses, and the combatants had to swear to accept the outcome and abstain from fighting one another in the future.

The very complexity of the rules of dueling limited the violence of private justice, and that meant that fewer fights actually took place. Dueling, in effect, civilized private justice. Although dueling was always against the law, princes tended to wink at duels because they kept conflicts among their own courtiers under control. At the same time, governments became far less tolerant of other forms of private justice, especially among the lower classes. They attempted to abolish feuds and vendettas and insisted that all disputes be submitted to the courts.

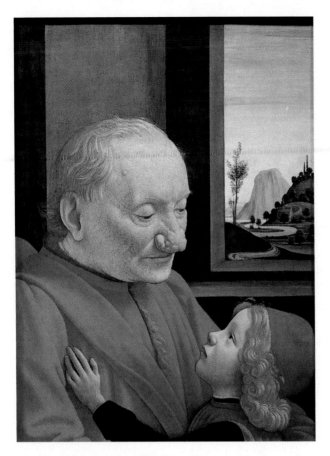

■ An Old Man and His Grandson

In Renaissance Italy, children barely knew their fathers and seldom their grandfathers, who were distant figures. This double portrait by Domenico Ghirlandio (ca. 1490) of an old man with his grandson visually expresses the ideal of patriarchy, which was the emotional bond between different generations. In fact, it is known that this little boy never knew his grandfather, who died years before he was born. Just as the painting idealizes the loving relationship between a grandfather and grandson who never knew each other, it is also realistic by depicting the grandfather's deformed nose. This combination of idealizing an emotional state while depicting the human body realistically is typical of the Renaissance style.

families had on survival stimulated the distinctive family theme in the culture of Renaissance Italy.

The Influence of Ancient Culture

The need in Renaissance Italy to provide effective models for how citizens, courtiers, and families should behave stimulated a reexamination of ancient culture. The civilizations of ancient Greece and Rome had long fascinated the educated classes in the West. In Italy

where most cities were built around or on top of the ruins of the ancient past, the seduction of antiquity was particularly pronounced. During the fourteenth and fifteenth centuries many Italian thinkers and artists attempted to foster a rebirth of ancient cultures. At first they merely attempted to imitate the Latin style of the best Roman writers. Then scholars tried to do the same thing with Greek, stimulated in part by direct contact with Greek-speaking refugees from Byzantium. Artists trekked to Rome to fill their notebooks with sketches of ancient ruins, sculptures, and medallions. Wealthy collectors hoarded manuscripts of ancient philosophy, built libraries to house them, bought up every piece of ancient sculpture they could find, and dug up ruins to find more antiquities to adorn their palaces. Patrons demanded that artists produce new works that imitated the styles of the ancients and that displayed a similar concern for rendering natural forms. Especially prized were lifelike representations of the human body.

Patrons, artists, and scholars during the Renaissance not only appreciated the achievements of the past but began to understand the enormous cultural distance between themselves and the ancients. That insight made their perspective historical. They also developed techniques of literary analysis to determine when a particular text had been written and to differentiate authentic texts from ones that had been corrupted by the mistakes of copyists. That ability made their perspective critical.

PETRARCH AND THE ILLUSTRIOUS ANCIENTS

The founder of the historical critical perspective that characterized the Renaissance was Francesco Petrarca (1304–1374), known in English as Petrarch. In contrast to the medieval thinkers who admired the ancients and treated their words as repositories of eternal wisdom, Petrarch discovered that the ancients were mere men much like himself. More than anything else, that insight might distinguish what was new about the Italian Renaissance, and Petrarch was the first to explore its implications.

Petrarch's early fame came from his poetry, in both his native Italian and in Latin. In an attempt to improve his Latin style, Petrarch engaged in a detailed study of the best ancient Roman writers and searched to find old manuscripts that were the least corrupted by copyists. In that search he was always watching for anything by the Roman orator Cicero (106–43 B.C.E.), who was the Latinist most revered for literary style. In 1345 Petrarch briefly visited Verona to see what he could find in the library of a local monastery. While thumbing through the dusty volumes, he excitedly happened upon a previously unknown collection of letters Cicero had written to his friend Atticus.

As Petrarch began to read the letters, however, he suffered a profound shock. Cicero had a reputation as the greatest sage of the Romans, a model of good Latin style, of philosophical sophistication, and most of all of high ethical standards. But in the letters Petrarch found not sage moral advice but gossip, rumors, and crude political calculations. Cicero looked like a scheming politician, a man of crass ambition rather than grand philosophical wisdom. Although Petrarch could never forgive Cicero for being less than what he had avowed in his philosophical writings, he had discovered the human Cicero rather than just the idealized Cicero, a man so human you could imagine having a conversation with him.

And having a conversation was precisely what Petrarch set out to do. Cicero, however, had been dead for 1,388 years. So Petrarch wrote a letter to Cicero's ghost. Adopting Cicero's own elegant Latin style, Petrarch lambasted the Roman for going against the moral advice he had given others. Petrarch quoted Cicero back to Cicero, asking him how he could be such a hypocrite.

> *Your letters I sought for long and diligently; and finally, where I least expected it, I found them. At once I read them, over and over, with the utmost eagerness. And as I read I seemed to hear your bodily voice, O Marcus Tullius [Cicero's given names], saying many things, uttering many lamentations, ranging through many phases of thought and feeling. I long had known how excellent a guide you have proved for others; at last I was to learn what sort of guidance you gave yourself. . . . Now it is your turn to be the listener.[5]*

Petrarch went on to lecture Cicero for his false dealings, his corruption, and his moral failures. The point of the exercise of writing a letter to a dead man was to compare the ideals Cicero had avowed in his philosophical work and the reality he seemed to have lived. Making comparisons is one of the elementary techniques of a critical method, and it became the hallmark of Petrarch's mode of analysis. Petrarch's letter reduced the stature of the ancients a bit, making them less like gods and more like other men who made mistakes and told lies. Petrarch ended this remarkable, unprecedented letter with a specific date, given in both the Roman and Christian ways, and a description of Verona's location in a way an ancient Roman would understand—as if he were making it possible for Cicero to find and answer him. This concern for historical precision typified the aspect that was most revolutionary about Petrarch's approach. No longer a repository of timeless truths, the ancient world became a specific time and place, which Petrarch perceived to be at a great distance from himself. The ancients had ceased to be godlike; they had become historical figures. After his letter to Cicero, Petrarch wrote a series of letters to other illustrious ancients in which he revealed the human qualities and shortcomings of each.

Petrarch developed his critical methods by editing classical texts, including parts of Livy's history of Rome, which was written about the time of Jesus. Petrarch compared different manuscript versions of Livy's work in an attempt to establish exactly the original words, a method very different from the medieval scribe's temptation to alter or improve a text as he saw fit. Petrarch strived to get the words right because he wanted to understand exactly what Livy had meant, a method now called the philological approach. Philology° is the comparative study of language, devoted to understanding the meaning of a word in a particular historical context. Petrarch's philology demonstrated that words do not have fixed meanings but take on different meanings depending on who is using them and when they were written. It was obvious to Petrarch, for example, that the word *virtue* had meant something quite different to the polytheist Livy than it did to Petrarch's contemporaries, who understood virtue in Christian terms. A concern for philology gave Petrarch access to the individuality of a writer. In the particularity of words, Petrarch discovered the particularity of actual individuals who lived and wrote many centuries before.

An interest in the meaning of words led Petrarch to study the rhetoric° of language. Rhetoric refers to the art of persuasive or emotive speaking and writing. From his studies of rhetoric, Petrarch became less confident about the ability of language to represent truth than he was about its capacity to motivate readers and listeners to action. He came to think that rhetoric was superior to philosophy because he preferred a good man over a wise one, and rhetoric offered examples worthy of emulation rather than abstract principles subject to debate. Petrarch wanted people to behave morally, not just talk or write about morality. And he believed that the most efficient way to inspire his readers to do the right thing was to write moving rhetoric.

THE HUMANISTS: THE LATIN POINT OF VIEW

Those who followed Petrarch's approach to the classical authors were the Renaissance humanists°. The Renaissance humanists studied Latin and sometimes Greek texts on grammar, rhetoric, poetry, history, and ethics. (The term *humanist* in the Renaissance meant something very different from what it means today—someone concerned with human welfare and dignity.) The humanists sought to resurrect a form of Latin that had been dead for more than a thousand years and was distinct from the living Latin used by the Church, law courts, and universities—which they thought was mediocre compared to ancient Latin. In this effort, humanists acquired a difficult but functional skill that opened a wide variety of employment opportunities to them and gave them great public influence. They worked as schoolmasters, secretaries, bureaucrats, official court or civic historians, and ambassadors. Many other humanists were wealthy men who did not need a job but were fascinated with the rhetorical capabilities of the new learning to persuade other people to do what they wanted them to do.

Because humanists could be found on different sides of almost all important questions of the day, the significance of their work lies less in what they said than in how they said it. They wrote about practically everything: painting

A HUMANIST LAMENTS THE RUINS OF ROME

························

In 1430 the distinguished humanist Poggio Bracciolini (1380–1459) was working in Rome as a papal secretary. In this account he describes his and a friend's response to seeing the ruins of the once-great city of Rome. Poggio's lament and those of other humanists stimulated popes to commit themselves to the rebuilding of the city, but the enthusiasm to return Rome to its ancient splendor had some unfortunate side effects. Many of the building materials for the new Rome were pillaged from the ruins of the old Rome. As a result, much of the destruction of the ancient city of Rome occurred during the Renaissance.

Not long ago, after Pope Martin left Rome shortly before his death for a farewell visit to the Tuscan countryside, and when Antonio Lusco, a very distinguished man, and I were free of business and public duties, we used to contemplate the desert places of the city with wonder in our hearts as we reflected on the former greatness of the broken buildings and the vast ruins of the ancient city, and again on the truly prodigious and astounding fall of its great empire and the deplorable inconstancy of fortune. And once when we had climbed the Capitoline hill, and Antonio, who was a little weary from riding, wanted to rest, we dismounted from our horses and sat down together within the very enclosures of the Tarpeian ruins, behind the great marble threshold of its very doors, as I believe, and the numerous broken columns lying here and there, whence a view of a large part of the city opens out.

Here, after he had looked about for some time, sighing and as if struck dumb, Antonio declared, "Oh, Poggio, how remote are these ruins from the Capitol that our Vergil celebrated: 'Golden now, once bristling with thorn bushes.' How justly one can transpose this verse and say: 'Golden once, now rough with thorns and overgrown with briars.'"

Source: "The Ruins of Rome" by Poggio Bracciolini, translated by Mary Martin McLaughlin, from *The Portable Renaissance Reader* by James B. Ross and Mary Martin McLaughlin, editors, copyright 1953, renewed © 1981 by Viking Penguin Inc. Used by permission of Viking Peguin, a division of Penguin Group (USA) Inc.

---

pictures, designing buildings, planting crops, draining swamps, raising children, managing a household, and educating women. They debated the nature of human liberty, the virtues of famous men, the vices of infamous ones, the meaning of Egyptian hieroglyphics, and the cosmology of the universe.

How did the humanists' use of Latin words and grammar influence the understanding of this vast range of subjects? Their approach was entirely literary. When they wanted to design a building, they read ancient books on architecture instead of consulting masons and builders. By studying the ancients, humanists organized experience into new categories that changed people's perceptions of themselves, the society they lived in, and the universe they inhabited. Humanist writing revealed what might be called the *Latin point of view*. Each language organizes experience according to the needs of the people who speak it, and all languages make arbitrary distinctions, dividing up the world into different categories. People who have studied a foreign language have run across these arbitrary distinctions when they learned that some expressions can never be translated exactly.

The humanists' recovery of the Latin point of view contributed new words, new sentence patterns, and new rhetorical models that often altered their own perceptions in very subtle ways. For example, when a fifteenth-century humanist examined what the ancient Romans had written about painting, he found the phrase *ars et ingenium*. *Ars* referred to skills that can be learned by following established rules and adhering to models provided by the best painters. Thus, the ability of a painter to draw a straight line, to mix colors properly, and to identify a saint with the correct symbol are examples of *ars* or what we would call craftsmanship. The meaning of *ingenium* was more difficult to pin down, however. It referred to the inventive capacity of the painter, to his ingenuity. The humanists discovered that the ancients had made a distinction between the craftsmanship and the ingenuity of a painter. As a result, when humanists and their pupils looked at paintings, they began to make the same distinction and began to admire the genius of artists whose work showed ingenuity as well as craftsmanship. Ingenuity came to refer to the ability of the painter to arrange his figures in a novel way, to employ unusual colors, or to create emotionally exciting effects that conveyed piety, sorrow, or joy as the subject demanded. So widespread was the influence of the humanists that the most ingenious artists demanded higher prices and became the most sought after. In this way, creative innovation was encouraged in the arts, but it all started very simply with the introduction of new words into the Latin vocabulary of the people who paid for paintings. A similar process of establishing new categories altered every subject the humanists touched.

The humanist movement spread rapidly during the fifteenth century. Leonardo Bruni (ca. 1370–1444), who became the chancellor of Florence (the head of the government's bureaucracy), employed humanist techniques to defend the republican institutions and values of the city. Bruni's defense of republican government is called civic humanism°. He argued that the truly ethical man should devote himself to active service to his city rather than to passive contemplation in scholarly retreat or monastic seclusion. Thus Bruni formulated the ethic of responsible citizenship that remains today as necessary to sustain a free society. Given the supreme value Christianity had long placed on the passive contemplation of divine truth, Bruni's assertion that active public service constituted an even higher vocation was radical indeed.

Lorenzo Valla (1407–1457) employed philological criticism to undermine papal claims to authority over secular rulers, such as the princes and republics of Italy. He did so by proving that a famous document, the Donation of Constantine, was a forgery. The Donation recorded that during the fourth century the Emperor Constantine had transferred his imperial authority in Italy to the pope, and although Renaissance popes could not get what they wanted just by citing this document, it was part of the legal arsenal popes used against secular rulers. Valla demonstrated that the Donation had actually been forged in the ninth century, a work of detection that showed how the historical analysis of documents could be immensely useful for resolving contemporary political disputes. The controversy between defenders and enemies of the papacy that followed Valla's discovery stimulated the demand for humanist learning because it became clear that humanist methods were necessary for political debate and propaganda.

The intellectual curiosity of the humanists led them to master many fields of endeavor. This breadth of accomplishment contributed to the ideal of the "Renaissance Man," a person who sought excellence in everything he did. No one came closer to this ideal than Leon Battista Alberti (1404–1472). As a young man, Alberti wrote Latin comedies and satirical works that drew on Greek and Roman models, but as he matured he tackled more serious subjects. Although he was a bachelor and thus knew nothing firsthand about marriage, he drew upon the ancient writers to create the most influential Renaissance book on the family, which included sections on relations between husbands and wives, raising children, and estate management. He composed the first grammar of the Italian language. He dabbled in mathematics and wrote on painting, law, the duties of bishops, love, horsemanship, dogs, agriculture, and flies. He mapped the city of Rome and wrote the most important fifteenth-century work on the theory and practice of architecture. His interest in architecture, moreover, was not just theoretical. In the last decades of his life, he dedicated much of his spare time to architectural projects that included restoring an ancient church in Rome, designing Renaissance façades for medieval churches, and building a palace for his most important patron. One of his last projects was the first significant work for making and deciphering secret codes in the West.

The humanists guaranteed their lasting influence through their innovations in the educational curriculum. The objective of humanist education was to create well-rounded male pupils (girls were not usually accepted in humanist schools) who were not specialists or professionals, such as the theologians, lawyers, and physicians trained in universities, but critical thinkers who could tackle any problems that life presented. It was a curriculum well suited for the active life of civic leaders, courtiers, princes, and churchmen. The influence of the humanist curriculum persists in the general-education requirements of modern universities, which require students, now of both sexes, to obtain intellectual breadth before they specialize in narrow professional training.

Historians have identified a few female humanists from the Renaissance. Because they were so unusual, learned humanist women were often ridiculed. Jealous men accused the humanist Isotta Nogarola (1418–1466) of promiscuity and incest, and other women insulted her in public. A famous male schoolmaster said that Isotta was too feminine in her writings and should learn how to find "a man within the woman."[6] Laura Cereta (1475–1506), who knew Greek as well as Latin and was adept at mathematics, answered the scorn of a male critic with rhetorical insult worthy of Petrarch himself:

I would have been silent, believe me, if that savage old enmity of yours had attacked me alone. . . . But I cannot tolerate your having attacked my entire sex. For this reason my thirsty soul seeks revenge, my sleeping pen is aroused to literary struggle, raging anger stirs mental passions long chained by silence. With just cause I am moved to demonstrate how great a reputation for learning and virtue women have won by their inborn excellence, manifested in every age as knowledge, the [purveyor] of honor. Certain, indeed, and legitimate is our possession of this inheritance, come to us from a long eternity of ages past.[7]

These few humanist women can be seen as among the first feminists. They advocated female equality and female education but also urged women to take control of their own lives. Nogarola answered her critics in a typical humanist fashion by reinterpreting the past. Thinking at this time suggested that all women were the daughters of Eve, who in her weakness had submitted to the temptation of the serpent, which led to the exile of humanity from the Garden of Eden. Nogarola pointed out that Eve had been no weaker than Adam, who also ate of the forbidden fruit, and therefore women should not be blamed for the Fall from God's grace. Cereta was the most optimistic of the women humanists. She maintained that if women paid as much attention to learning as they did to their appearances, they would achieve equality. Despite the efforts of Cereta and other female humanists, progress in women's education was extremely slow. The universities remained closed to talented women. The first woman to earn a degree from a university did so in 1678, and it took another two hundred years before very many others could follow her example.

Through the influence of the humanists, the Latin point of view permeated Renaissance culture. They educated generations of wealthy young gentlemen whose appreciation of antiquity led them to pay to collect manuscripts of ancient literature, philosophy, and science. These patrons were also responsible for encouraging artists to imitate the ancients. What began as a narrow literary movement became the stimulus to see human society and nature through entirely new eyes. As we shall see in Chapter 13, some humanists, especially in northern Europe, applied these techniques with revolutionary results to the study of the Bible and the sources of Christianity.

UNDERSTANDING NATURE: MOVING BEYOND THE SCIENCE OF THE ANCIENTS

The humanists' initial concern was to emulate the language of the ancients. Most of them preferred to spend time reading a book rather than observing the world around them. In fact, their methods were ill-suited to understanding nature, and when they wanted to explain some natural phenomenon such as the movement of blood through the body or the apparent movements of the planets and stars, they looked to ancient authorities for answers rather than to nature itself. The Renaissance humanists' most prominent contributions to science consisted of recovering classical texts and translating the work of ancient Greek scientists into the more widely understood Latin. This is in contrast to the scientific method with which we are familiar today, in which we form a hypothesis and then determine whether it is correct by observing the natural world as directly as possible. In contrast, Renaissance scientists searched for ancient texts about nature, and then debated about which ancient author had been correct.

These translated texts broadened the discussion of two subjects crucial to the scientific revolution of the late sixteenth and seventeenth centuries—astronomy and anatomy. In 1543 the Polish humanist Nicolaus Copernicus (1473–1543) resolved the complications in the cosmological system of the second-century astronomer Ptolemy. Whereas Ptolemy's writings had placed the earth at the center of the universe, Copernicus cited other ancient writers who put the sun in the center. Thus the first breakthrough in theoretical astronomy was achieved not by making new observations but by comparing ancient texts. Nothing was proven, however, until Galileo Galilei (1564–1642) turned his telescope to the heavens in 1610 to observe the stars through his own eyes rather than through an ancient text.

Andreas Vesalius (1514–1564) built upon recently published studies in anatomy from ancient Greece to write a survey of human anatomy, *On the Fabric of the Human Body* (1543), a book that encouraged dissection and anatomical observations. With Vesalius, anatomy moved away from relying exclusively on the authority of ancient books to encouraging medical students and physicians to examine the human body with their own eyes. Building upon Vesalius's work, Gabriele Falloppio (ca. 1523–1562)

made many original observations of muscles, nerves, kidneys, bones, and most famously the "Fallopian tubes," which he described for the first time. By the late sixteenth century, astronomy and anatomy had surpassed what the ancients had known.

Besides recovering ancient scientific texts, the most important Renaissance contributions to science came secondhand from developments in the visual arts and technology. A number of Florentine artists experimented during the early fifteenth century with the application of mathematics to the preliminary design of paintings. The goal was to make paintings more accurately represent reality by creating the visual illusion of the third dimension of depth on a two-dimensional rectangular surface, a technique known as linear perspective (see next section). These artists contributed to a more refined understanding of how the eye perceives objects, and their understanding of how the eye worked led to experiments with glass lenses. A more thorough knowledge of optics made possible the invention of the telescope and microscope.

Of all the developments in the fifteenth century, however, none matched the long-term significance of a pair of rather simple inventions—cheap manufactured paper and the printing press. Paper made from rags created an inex-

---

CHRONOLOGY

The Influence of Ancient Culture

106–43 B.C.E.	Marcus Tullius Cicero, Latin rhetorician
1304–1374	Francesco Petrarca (Petrarch), first humanist
CA. 1370–1444	Leonardo Bruni, chancellor of Florence
1404–1472	Leon Battista Alberti, humanist and architect
1407–1457	Lorenzo Valla, humanist
1418–1466	Isotta Nogarola, first female humanist
CA. 1454	Johann Gutenberg begins printing books
1473–1543	Nicolaus Copernicus, humanist and cosmological theorist
1475–1506	Laura Cereta, humanist
1514–1564	Andreas Vesalius, writer on anatomy
CA. 1523–1562	Gabriele Falloppio, conducted anatomical dissections
1564–1642	Galileo Galilei, astronomer

pensive alternative to sheepskins, which had been the preferred medium for medieval scribes. And just as paper replaced sheepskin, the printing press replaced the scribe. Several Dutch and German craftsmen had experimented with printing during the 1440s, but credit for the essential innovation of movable metal type has traditionally been accredited to Johannes Gutenberg (ca. 1398–1468) of Mainz in the 1450s. German immigrants brought printing to Italy, which rapidly became the publishing center of Europe, largely because it boasted a large, literate urban population who bought books.

Scientific books accounted for only about 10 percent of the titles of the first printed books, but the significance of printing for science was greater than the sales figures would indicate. In addition to making ancient scientific texts more readily available, print meant that new discoveries and new ideas reached a wider audience, duplication of scientific investigation could be avoided, illustrations were standardized, and scientists built upon each other's work. With the invention of the printing press, scientific work became closely intertwined with publishing, so that published scientific work advanced science, and scientific work that was not published went largely unnoticed. It is revealing that Leonardo da Vinci (1452–1519), the greatest Renaissance observer of nature, contributed nothing to science because he failed to publish his findings. The fundamental principle of modern science and, in fact, of all modern scholarship is that research must be made available to everyone through publication.

Antiquity and Nature in the Arts

More than any other age in Western history, the Italian Renaissance is identified with the visual arts. The unprecedented clusters of brilliant artists active in a handful of Italian cities during the fifteenth and sixteenth centuries overshadow any other contribution of Renaissance culture. Under the influence of the humanists, Renaissance artists began to imitate the sculpture, architecture, and painting of the ancients. At first they concerned themselves with merely copying ancient styles and poses. But soon they attempted a more sophisticated form of imitation. They wanted to understand the principles that made it possible for the artists from classical Greece and Rome to make their figures so lifelike. That led them to observe more directly nature itself, especially the anatomy of the human body. Renaissance art was driven by the passionate desire of artists and their patrons both to imitate ancient models and to imitate nature. These twin desires produced a certain creative tension in their work because the ancients, whose works of art often depicted gods and goddesses, had ideal-

ized and improved upon what they observed in nature. Renaissance artists sought to depict simultaneously the ideal and the real—an impossible goal, but one that sparked remarkable creativity.

All of the Renaissance arts displayed the mark of patrons, those discriminating and wealthy people who controlled the city-states and who had been educated in humanist schools. Until the end of the sixteenth century, all painters, sculptors, and even poets worked for a patron. An individual patron would commission a particular work of art, such as an altar painting, portrait bust, or palace. The patron and artist would agree to the terms of the work through a contract, which might spell out in considerable detail exactly what the artist was to do, what kinds of materials he was to use, how much they could cost, how much he was allowed to rely on assistants, how much he had to do himself, and even how he was to arrange figures. The same sort of contract was used when work was commissioned by a group—for example, a guild, lay religious society (called a confraternity), convent, or government. Michelangelo Buonarroti (1475–1564) sculpted *David*, which has become the most famous work of Renaissance art, to fulfill a contract that had been debated in a committee meeting. Regardless of their talent or ingenuity, artists were never free agents who could do whatever they wanted.

Another kind of patron supported the career of an artist for an extended period of time. Princes, in particular, liked to take on an artist, give him a regular salary and perhaps even some official title, in exchange for having him perform whatever duties the prince deemed necessary. In this kind of an arrangement, Duke Lodovico Sforza (1451–1508) brought Leonardo da Vinci to Milan, where Leonardo painted a portrait of the duke's mistress, devised plans for a giant equestrian statue of the duke's father, designed stage sets and carnival pageants, painted the interior decorations of the castle, and did engineering work. The artist Cosmè Tura (active ca. 1450–1495) probably spent more time painting furniture than canvases for the Duke of Ferrara.

Most patrons supported the arts in order to enhance their own prestige and power. Some, such as Pope Julius II, had exceptional influence on the work of artists. He persuaded the very reluctant Michelangelo, who saw himself as a sculptor, to become a painter in order to decorate the ceiling of the Sistine Chapel.

SCULPTURE, ARCHITECTURE, AND PAINTING: THE NATURAL AND THE IDEAL

Just as humanists recaptured antiquity by collecting, translating, and analyzing the writings of classical authors, so Renaissance artists made drawings of surviving classical medals, sculpture, and architecture. Collected in sketch books, these drawings often served as pattern books from which the apprentices in artists' workshops learned how to draw. Because artists believed that the classical world enjoyed an artistic tradition vastly superior to their own, these sketches became valuable models from which other artists could learn. Two of the most influential Florentine artists, the architect Filippo Brunelleschi (1377–1446) and the sculptor Donatello (1386–1466), may have gone to Rome together as young men to sketch the ancient monuments. No Roman paintings survived into the fifteenth century (Pompeii, which proved to have a treasure trove of Roman art buried under layers of volcanic ash, had not yet been excavated), and no Renaissance artist ever saw a Greek building, so the only examples of ancient art to copy were the ruins of Roman buildings and a few surviving Roman statues. As a result, architecture and sculpture led the way in the imitation of ancient art, but Renaissance artists imposed their own sensibilities on the ancients as much as they imitated them.

The Renaissance style evolved in Florence during the first few decades of the fifteenth century. In 1401 the 24-year-old Brunelleschi entered a competition to design

bronze relief panels for the north doors of the Baptistery. He narrowly lost to the even younger Lorenzo Ghiberti (1378–1455). Look at the illustrations on this page. The rules of the competition required both artists to fit their relief panels within a fancy decorative frame in the Gothic style, which had been in fashion for nearly 300 years. However, both competition relief panels seem constrained by the curves and angles of the frame. For example, some of the figures in the Brunelleschi panel project outside it as if trying to escape the restraints of the style. Ghiberti's relief shows the two characteristic elements of the early Renaissance style: The head of Isaac is modeled after a classical Roman sculpture, and the figures and horse on the left are depicted as realistically as possible. In these elements, Ghiberti was imitating both antiquity and nature.

Ghiberti worked on the north doors for twenty-one years and won such renown as a result that when he finished he was immediately offered a new commission to complete panels for the east portal. These doors, begun in 1425, took twenty-seven years to finish. In the east doors,

■ The Competition Panels of the Sacrifice of Isaac

These two panels were the finalists in a competition to design the cast bronze doors on the north side of the Baptistery in Florence. Each demonstrates a bold new design that attempted to capture the emotional trauma of the exact moment when an angel arrests Abraham's arm from sacrificing his son Isaac (Genesis 22:1–12). Both artists went on to be closely associated with the new style of the Renaissance. The panel on the left, by Filippo Brunelleschi, lost to the one on the right, by Lorenzo Ghiberti. Notice how the Ghiberti relief better conveys the drama of the scene by projecting the elbow of Abraham's upraised arm outward toward the viewer. As a result the viewer's line of sight follows the line of the arm and knife directly toward Isaac's throat.

■ **Linear Perspective**

In these panels Ghiberti broke out of the Gothic frame that had inhibited him in the panels on the north doors. Now he was free to explore the full potential of the newly discovered principles of linear perspective.

Ghiberti substituted a simple square frame for the Gothic frame of the north doors, thereby liberating his composition. In the illustration above, which also depicts the biblical story of Isaac, the squares in the pavement set up an underlying geometry to the scene. The background architecture of rounded arches and crisp-angled columns in the classical style creates the illusion of depth in the relief. This illusion is achieved through linear perspective°, that is, the use of geometrical principles to depict a three-dimensional space on a flat, two-dimensional surface. The rigorous geometry of the composition provided the additional benefit of allowing Ghiberti to divide up the space to depict several different scenes within one panel. In the panels of the east doors, he created the definitive Renaissance interpretation of the ancient principles of the harmony produced by geometry. Michelangelo later remarked that the doors were fit to serve as the "gates of paradise."

After failing to win the competition for the Baptistery doors, Brunelleschi turned to architecture. In his own time, Brunelleschi was considered to have revived ancient Roman principles, but it is evident now that he was less a student of antiquity than an astutely original thinker. In his buildings he employed a proportional system of design that is best seen in his masterpiece, the Pazzi Chapel, shown on the next page. He began with a basic geometric unit represented by each of the small rectangles clustered in groups of four on the upper third of the façade of the chapel. The height of each of these was approximately the height of an average man. All the other dimensions of the building were multiples of these basic rectangles. Thus, the building was formed from the proportions of a human being. Brunelleschi employed what he saw as the natural dimensions of humanity and transformed them into principles of architectural geometry. The result was a stunning impression of harmony in all the spaces of the building.

Later sculptors and architects built upon the innovations of Ghiberti and Brunelleschi. Florence became renowned for its tradition of sculpture, producing the two greatest Renaissance masters of the art, Donatello and Michelangelo. In their representations of the human form, both of these sculptors demonstrated the Renaissance preoccupation with the relationship between the ideal and the natural.

Conceptions of both the ideal and the natural are evident in the work of the most important painter of the early Florentine Renaissance, Masaccio (1401–ca. 1428), who worked in fresco. Fresco, a common form of decoration in

■ **The Geometry of Renaissance Architecture**
Filippo Brunelleschi designed the Pazzi Chapel in Florence to match the geometrical proportions of the human body.

churches, was the technique of applying paint to wet plaster on a wall. In his great fresco cycle for the Brancacci chapel painted in the 1420s, Masaccio depicted street scenes from Florence complete with portraits of actual people, including himself. These were examples of naturalism. On some other figures—Jesus, St. Peter, and St. John—he placed heads copied from ancient sculptures of gods. These were examples of idealized beauty, which were especially suitable for saints. In Masaccio's frescoes, both realistic and idealized figures appeared in the same work. The realistic figures helped viewers identify with the subject of the picture by allowing them to recognize people they actually knew. The idealized figures represented the saintly, whose superior moral qualities made them appear different from average people.

Masaccio developed the technical means for employing linear perspective in painting. To achieve the effect of perspective, he organized the entire composition around the position he assumed a viewer would take while looking at the picture. Once he established the point of view, he composed the picture to direct the viewer's gaze through the pictorial space. In *The Tribute Money*, he drew the spectator's eye to the head of Jesus, who is the figure in the middle pointing with his right hand. In addition, Masaccio recognized that the human eye perceives an object when light shines on it to create lighted surfaces and shadows. He used this understanding in creating a

■ *The Tribute Money:* **Combining Natural and Idealized Representations**
In this detail of a fresco of Christ and his Apostles, Masaccio mixed naturalism and idealized beauty. The figure on the right with his back turned to the viewer is a tax collector, who is depicted as a normal human being. The head of the fourth figure to the left of him, who represents one of the apostles, was copied from an ancient statue that represents ancient ideals of beauty.

The Natural and the Ideal Body in Renaissance Art

The Naturalistic Body

In the *contraposto* pose of Donatello's David, the weight of the figure is carried on one leg of the human form, which appears straight and taut while the other seems relaxed and slightly bent.

During the Italian Renaissance artists depicted the human body, especially the nude body, with a greater sensitivity to anatomy than at any time since antiquity. In attempting to portray the human body, Renaissance sculptors and painters explored two possible approaches. Should they attempt to imitate nature by depicting human bodies as they really appear, or should they improve upon nature by representing human bodies in an idealized way?

The Florentine sculptor Donatello (1386–1466) was the master of the first approach, the naturalistic representation of the human body. His major achievement was solving the difficult technical problem of creating a freestanding life-size statue of a human being that looked as if the person depicted were standing in a natural way. In his solution, called *contraposto,* one leg of the human form is kept straight and the other is slightly bent, with the hips slanting in the opposite direction from the slant of the shoulders. One contemporary described Donatello's statues as so lively that they appeared to move. Following Donatello's lead, Florentine sculptors dedicated themselves to "the return to nature," the attempt to make inanimate works of art imitate not just ancient sculpture, but nature itself.

During the later Renaissance, Michelangelo Buonarroti (1475–1564) perfected the second approach by idealizing the human body. He did not want just to imitate nature, he wanted to surpass nature. His figures, such as his famous *David,* often seemed super-human. In creating figures such as this, he brought the Renaissance preoccupation with antiquity full circle because many classical sculptors had intended to achieve the same effect. After all, most of their work was for polytheist temples, and by improving on nature they wanted to create images of the perfect bodies of the gods.

With Michelangelo, Western art entered an entirely new phase. He advanced art from the simple goal of imitating classical motifs and observing nature to a more grandiose goal of improving on the ancients and on nature. According to Michelangelo, since nature alone never achieved perfection, great art can be even more powerful than nature itself. ■

The Idealized Body

This larger-than-life figure of the biblical warrior King David transformed the young boy who slew the giant Goliath into a kind of superman whose physical bearing was greater than any normal man. Michelangelo altered the proportions of a natural man, making the head and hands significantly larger than normal. In its original placement on a staircase in a large open square, the statue towered above viewers.

For Discussion

How might the Renaissance humanist concerns for imitation produce both the artistic conceptions of naturalism and idealized beauty?

painting technique called *chiaroscuro* ("light and shade"). There is a single source of light in the painting coming from the same direction as the light in the room. That light defines figures and objects in the painting through the play of light and shadow. The strokes of Masaccio's paintbrush tried to duplicate the way natural light plays upon surfaces.

The techniques developed by Masaccio came to complete fulfillment in the career of Leonardo da Vinci (1452–1519). So compelling was Leonardo's curiosity and desire to tackle new problems that many of his paintings remained unfinished. He was a restless experimenter, never settling on simple solutions. Because of experiments Leonardo made with paint, his *Last Supper* fresco in Milan has seriously deteriorated. His mature works, such as *Mona Lisa*, completely reconciled the technical problems of representing human figures with realistic accuracy and the spiri-

tual goal of evoking deep emotions. Unlike some of his predecessors, who grouped figures in a painting as if they were statues, Leonardo managed to make his figures appear to interact and communicate with one another.

The technique of painting with oils achieved new levels among painters in the Netherlands and in Flanders (in present-day Belgium, but at the time a province in the Duchy of Burgundy). By carefully layering numerous coats of tinted oil glazes over the surface of the painting, these painters created a luminous surface that gave the illusion of depth. The use of glazes enabled painters to blend brush strokes in a way that made them virtually imperceptible. As a result Flemish and Dutch painters excelled in painting meticulous details, such as the textures of textiles, the reflections of gems, and the features of distant landscapes. Jan van Eyck (ca. 1395–1441) was the most famous Flemish painter. He worked as a court painter for the Duke of Burgundy, for whom he undertook many kinds of projects including decorating his palaces and designing stage sets and ornaments for festivals. His oil paintings were so famous that he was much praised by the Italian humanists, and numerous Italian patrons, including the Medicis, bought his works.

Most humanist theorists of painting linked artistic creativity with masculinity. By the sixteenth century, however, these theorists were proved wrong, as a number of female painters rose to prominence. The most notable was Sofonisba Anguissola (ca. 1532–1625). Born into an aristocratic family in Cremona, Italy, she received a humanist education along with her five sisters and brother. Because she was a woman, she was prohibited from studying anatomy or drawing male models. As a result she specialized in portraits, often of members of her family, and self-portraits. She developed a distinctive style of depicting animated faces. Her example inspired other aristocratic women to take up painting.

MUSIC OF THE EMOTIONS

Renaissance humanists' fascination with the visual arts of the ancients led them to assume that composers should imitate ancient music. But in attempting to turn humanist theories about music into real music, fifteenth-century composers faced a formidable problem—no one had the slightest clue what ancient Greek music actually sounded like. As a result, musical innovations lagged behind the other arts until the late sixteenth century, when a musical Renaissance finally took hold.

During the fourteenth and fifteenth centuries the principal composers came from France and the Netherlands. The greatest of them, Josquin de Prez (ca. 1440–1521), was born and trained in the Netherlands and later found patrons in Milan, Rome, and Ferrara. His finest talent as a composer consisted of his ability to enhance musically the meaning of lyrics. In contrast to Josquin's sensitivity to matching music

■ Depicting Human Emotions in Art

In this painting the maternal feelings of two mothers, Mary the mother of Jesus and St. Anne the mother of Mary, become the dominant message of the work. Leonardo da Vinci successfully united naturalism and idealism: The Virgin Mary is both a human mother who loves her fidgeting little boy and the perfectly beautiful eternal Mother who represents the love of God.

■ Northern Renaissance Art

In this mid-fifteenth century Flemish painting by Petrus Christus, the use of oil paint and glazes made it possible to convey the shimmering surfaces of the metal and gold in this goldsmith's shop. Shown in the mirror, which is leaning on the counter to the right, are a couple looking through a window into the shop. They are in the exact position of the viewers of the picture, and placing them in the mirror was a way to draw viewers into the scene.

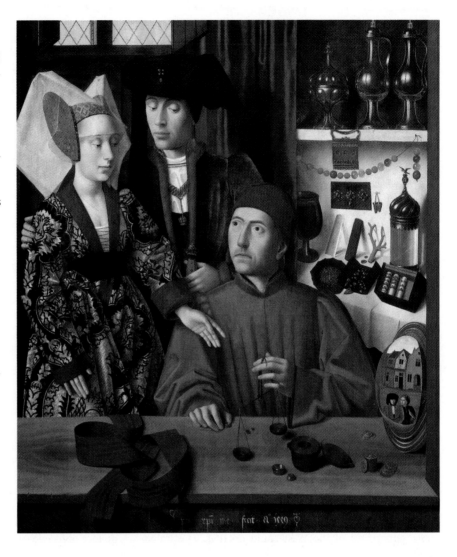

and lyric, most other composers relied on stereotypical rhythmic patterns and a simple melodic line that had no connection to the text. In fact, almost any lyric could be sung to the same music.

Recognizing that the music of their time did not measure up to what ancient writers had reported about the emotional intensity of their music, several prominent musician-humanists conducted extensive discussions about how to combine music and words in a way that would create a fuller aesthetic and emotional experience. The initial consequence of these discussions was the Renaissance madrigal, a type of song in which the music closely followed a poetic lyric to accentuate the shades of textual meaning. For example, when the text described a happy mood, the music would rise up the scale. A somber text would be lower-pitched. When the lyric described agitation or fear, the rhythm would quicken in imitation of the heart beating faster.

The most important consequence of the discussions about the need for a richer musical experience was the in-

vention of opera° during the final decades of the sixteenth century. A group of humanist thinkers called the *Camerata* thought the power of ancient Greek music could be recovered by writing continuous music to accompany a full drama. The drama was performed as a kind of speech-song with the range of pitch and rhythms closely following those of natural speech. Singers were accompanied by a small ensemble of musicians. The first operas composed in this vein were by Jacopo Peri (1561–1633) and Giulio Caccini (ca. 1550–1618), and were performed in Florence at the Grand Duke's court around 1600. These lengthy, bloated works attracted little attention among audiences, and opera likely would have sunk under its own weight had it not been for Claudio Monteverdi (1567–1643), who discovered its dramatic and lyrical potential. His sumptuous productions employed large ensembles of singers and instrumentalists, punctuated speech-song with arias (long sung solos) and dances, and included magnificent stage machines that simulated earthquakes, fires, and battles. Under Monteverdi's masterful hand, opera became the first complete multimedia art form. Arias from his productions became popular hits sung on every street corner, and opera moved from being a private amusement for princely courtiers to mass entertainment. The first public opera house opened in Venice in 1637. By the end of the seventeenth century, Venice boasted seventeen opera houses for a population of only 140,000. With the rise of opera houses and theaters for plays, the close bond between patrons and artists began to break down. Until then, artists were bound by the wishes of patrons. Now they began to serve the much larger marketplace for popular entertainment.

The Early Modern European State System

The civic independence that had made the Italian Renaissance possible was profoundly challenged during the Italian Wars (1494–1530). During these wars France, Spain, and the Holy Roman Empire attempted to carve up the peninsula for themselves, and the Italian city-states were thrown into turmoil. By 1530 the Italian city-states, with the exception of Venice, had lost their independence to the triumphant king of Spain. The surrender of the rich city-states of Italy was the first and most prominent sign of a major transformation in the European system of states. The age of city-states was over because they could never muster the level of materiel and manpower necessary to put and keep a large army in the field. Only the large monarchies of the West could do that. The Italian Wars revealed the outlines of the early modern European state system, which was built on the power of large countries that had been brought under control by their own kings. These kings amassed an unprecedented level of resources that not only crushed Italy but made possible, as we shall see in Chapter 12, the European domination of much of the globe through establishment of colonies in the Americas, Asia, and eventually Africa.

MONARCHIES: THE FOUNDATION OF THE STATE SYSTEM

During the last half of the fifteenth century, the monarchies of western Europe began to show signs of recovery from the turmoil of the fourteenth century, which had been marked by famine, plague, revolts, and continuous warfare. France and England ended the Hundred Years' War, which had bled both kingdoms of men and resources during the century before 1453. England escaped from its civil war, the War of the Roses, in 1485. The kingdoms of Castile and Aragon joined in 1479 to create the new kingdom of Spain, which in 1492 completed the reconquest of territories from

CHRONOLOGY

Antiquity and Nature in the Arts

1377–1446	Filippo Brunelleschi, Florentine sculptor and architect
1378–1455	Lorenzo Ghiberti, Florentine sculptor who created the "Gates of Paradise"
1386–1466	Donatello, Florentine sculptor
CA. 1395–1441	Jan van Eyck, Flemish painter
1401–CA. 1428	Masaccio, Florentine fresco painter
CA. 1440–1521	Josquin de Prez, composer
1452–1519	Leonardo da Vinci, Florentine painter and inventor
1475–1564	Michelangelo Buonarroti, Florentine sculptor, painter, architect, poet
CA. 1532–1625	Sofonisba Anguissola, painter
1567–1643	Claudio Monteverdi, opera composer

the Muslims that had been underway since the eleventh century. The Holy Roman Empire, which became allied to Spain through marriage, pursued a grand new vision for unifying the diverse principalities of Germany.

The early modern European state system was the consequence of five developments. First, governments established standing armies. As a result of the military revolution that brought large numbers of infantrymen to the field of battle and gunpowder cannons to besiege cities and castles, governments were obliged to modernize their armies or face defeat. Since the ninth century, kings had relied on feudal levies, in which soldiers were recruited to fulfill their personal obligation to a lord, but by the late fifteenth century governments began to organize standing armies. These armies enjoyed high levels of professionalism and skill, but they were very expensive to maintain because the soldiers had to be regularly paid. Moreover, the new artillery was costly, and improvements in the effectiveness of artillery bombardments necessitated extensive improvements in the walls of castles, fortresses, and cities. As a result, kings were desperate for new revenues.

The need for revenues led to the second development, the systematic expansion of taxation. Every European state struggled with the problem of taxation. The need to tax efficiently produced the beginnings of a bureaucracy of tax assessors and collectors in many states.

People naturally resisted the burden of new taxes, and monarchs naturally responded to the resistance. This tension led to the third development. Monarchs attempted to weaken the institutional seats of resistance by abolishing the tax-exempt privileges of local communities and ignoring regional assemblies and parliaments that were supposed to approve new taxes. During the twelfth and thirteenth centuries, effective government was local government, and kings seldom had the power to interfere in the affairs of towns and regions. During the fifteenth century, however, kings everywhere attempted to eliminate or erode the independence of towns and regional parliaments in order to raise taxes more effectively and to express the royal will throughout the realm.

The fourth development, closely linked to the third, can be seen in monarchs' attempts to constrain the independence of the aristocracy and the Church. In virtually every kingdom, the most significant threats to the power of the king were the powerful aristocrats. In England a civil war among aristocrats almost tore the kingdom apart. Kings everywhere struggled to co-opt or force submission from these aristocrats. Likewise, the autonomy of the Church threatened monarchial authority, and most monarchs took measures to oblige churchmen to act as agents of government policy.

The fifth development in the evolution of the European state system was the institution of resident ambassadors. During the Italian Wars, the kings of Europe began to exchange permanent, resident ambassadors who were responsible for informing their sovereign about conditions in the host country and representing the interests of their country abroad. Resident ambassadors became the linchpins in a sophisticated information network that provided intelligence about the intentions and capabilities of other kings, princes, and cities. These ambassadors typically enjoyed a humanist education, which helped them adapt to many strange and unpredictable situations, understand foreign languages, negotiate effectively, and speak persuasively. Ambassadors cultivated courtly manners, which smoothed over personal conflicts. For the development of the new state system, gathering reliable information became just as important as maintaining armies and collecting taxes.

France: Consolidating Power and Cultivating Renaissance Values

With the largest territory in western Europe and a population of more than 16 million, France had the potential to become the most powerful state in Europe if the king could figure out how to take advantage of the kingdom's size and resources. By 1453 the Hundred Years' War between France and England had come to an end. With the inspiration of Joan of Arc and with the reform of royal finances by the merchant-banker Jacques Coeur, King Charles VII (r. 1422–1461) expelled the English and regained control of his kingdom. Under Charles, France created its first professional army. Equally important, during the Hundred Years' War the Pragmatic Sanction of Bourges° (1438) guaranteed

the virtual autonomy of the French Church from papal control, giving the French king unparalleled opportunities to interfere in religious affairs and to exploit Church revenues for government purposes.

Louis XI (r. 1461–1483), called the "Spider King" because of his fondness for secret intrigue, took up the challenge of consolidating power over the great nobles of his kingdom, who thwarted his state building and threatened his throne. When Louis came to power, the Duchy of Brittany was virtually independent; one great aristocrat, René of Anjou, controlled more territory and was richer than the king himself; and, most dangerous of all, the dukes of Burgundy had carved out their own splendid principality, which celebrated extravagant forms of courtly ritual and threatened to eclipse the prestige of France itself.

Against these powerful rivals, Louis turned to an equally powerful new weapon—the *taille*. During the final years of the Hundred Years War, in order to support the army, the Estates General (France's parliament) granted the king the *taille*, the right to collect an annual direct tax. After the war, the tax continued and Louis turned it into a permanent source of revenue for himself and his successors. Armed with the financial resources of the *taille*, Louis took on his most rebellious vassal, Charles the Bold, the Duke of Burgundy, and in 1477 professional Swiss infantrymen in the pay of Louis defeated the plumed knights of Burgundy. Charles was killed in battle, and only his daughter Mary's hurried marriage to the Habsburg Archduke Maximilian bought the protection Burgundy needed from the Holy Roman Empire and prevented France from seizing all of the duchy.

The monarch most responsible for the spread of Renaissance culture in France was Francis I (r. 1515–1547), a sportsman and warrior who thrilled to the frenzy of battle. Much of his early career was devoted to pursuing French interests in the Italian Wars, until he was captured in battle in 1525 in Italy. Thereafter he focused more on patronizing Italian artists and humanists at his court and importing Italian Renaissance styles. He had the first Renaissance-style chateau built in the Loire Valley and hired artists, including Leonardo da Vinci. As a result of Francis's patronage, Italy was no longer the exclusive center of Renaissance culture.

Spain: Unification by Marriage

In the early fifteenth century the Iberian peninsula was a diverse place, lacking political unity. It was home to several different kingdoms—Portugal, Castile, Navarre, and Aragon, which were all Christian, and Granada, which was Muslim. Each kingdom had its own laws, political institutions, customs, and languages. Unlike France, the Christian kingdoms of medieval Iberia were poor, underpopulated, and preoccupied with the reconquest, the attempt to drive the Muslims from the peninsula. There was little reason to assume that this region would become one of the greatest powers in Europe, the rival of France.

Map 11.3 The Dynastic Marriages That Encircled France

Through skillfully arranging the marriages of their sons and daughters, Ferdinand of Aragon and Isabella of Castile managed to completely surround the rival kingdom of France with a network of alliances.

That rise to power began with a wedding. In 1469 Isabella, who later would become Queen of Castile (r. 1474–1504), married Ferdinand, who later would be King of Aragon (r. 1479–1516). The objective of this arranged marriage was to solidify an alliance between the two kingdoms, not to unify them, but in 1479 Castile and Aragon were combined into the kingdom of Spain. Of the two, Castile was the larger, with a population of perhaps six million, and the richer because of the government-supported sheep-raising industry called the *Mesta*. Aragon had less than a million people and was a hybrid of three very distinct regions that had nothing in common except that they shared the same king. Together Isabella and Ferdinand, each still ruling their own kingdoms, at least partially subdued the rebellious aristocracy and built up a bureaucracy of well-educated middle-class lawyers and priests to manage the administration of the government.

The Christian kings of Iberia had long aspired to making the entire peninsula Christian. In 1492 the armies of Isabella and Ferdinand defeated the last remaining Iberian

Muslim kingdom of Granada. While celebrating the victory over Islam, the monarchs made two momentous decisions. The first was to rid Spain of Jews as well as Muslims. Isabella and Ferdinand decreed that within six months all Jews must either convert to Christianity or leave. To enforce conformity to Christianity among the converted Jews who did not leave, the king and queen authorized an ecclesiastical tribunal, the Spanish Inquisition, to investigate the sincerity of conversions. The second decision was Isabella's alone. She financed a voyage by a Genoese sea captain, Christopher Columbus, to sail west into the Atlantic in an attempt to reach India and China. Isabella's intention seems to have been to outflank the Muslim kingdoms of the Middle East and find allies in Asia. As we shall see in the next chapter, Columbus's voyage had consequences more far-reaching than Isabella's intentions, adding to the crown of Castile immense lands in the Americas.

Despite the diversity of their kingdoms, Isabella and Ferdinand made Spain a great power. The clever dynastic marriages they arranged for their children allowed Spain to encircle rival France and established the framework for the diplomatic relations among European states for the next century and a half (see Map 11.3). Their eldest daughter and, after her death, her sister were married to the king of Portugal. Their son and another daughter, Joanna, married offspring of Mary of Burgundy and the Emperor Maximilian I of the Holy Roman Empire. Joanna's marriage produced a son, Charles V, who amassed extraordinary power. He succeeded to the Habsburg lands of Burgundy, inherited the crowns of Castile and Aragon (r. 1516–1556), was elected Holy Roman Emperor (r. 1519–1558), ruled over the Spanish conquests in Italy, and was the Emperor of the Indies, which included all of Spanish Central and South America. This was the greatest accumulation of territories by a European ruler since Charlemagne. The encirclement of France was completed with the wedding of Isabella and Ferdinand's daughter Catherine of Aragon to the Prince of Wales and after his death to his brother, King Henry VIII (r. 1509–1547) of England.

The Holy Roman Empire: The Costs of Decentralization

Like Spain, the Holy Roman Empire saw powerful France as its most dangerous enemy. And when the French king's invasion of Italy initiated the Italian Wars, it launched a struggle that pitted the empire and Spain against France for the next 200 years. Members of the Habsburg family had been elected to the throne of the Holy Roman Empire since 1438. As we have seen, Emperor Maximilian I (r. 1493–1519) wed Mary, the daughter of Charles the Bold of Burgundy, and although they were not able to preserve all of Burgundy from the French, they did keep substantial parts, including the extremely rich Netherlands.

In an era of coolly calculating monarchs, Maximilian cut an odd figure. Like his father-in-law, Charles the Bold, he loved chivalry and enjoyed nothing more than to play the role of a knight leading his men into battle. The problem was that he was not very good in that role. His military adventures led to a series of disasters, often at the hands of the rough Swiss mercenaries who were experts in using the pike (a long pole with a metal spearhead) to cut up aristocratic cavalrymen and who passionately hated everything about the autocratic Habsburgs who had once ruled their lands. Maximilian also came under the influence of Italian Renaissance culture and imagined himself another Caesar with a special mission to reconquer Italy for the Holy Roman Empire. The French invasion of Italy in 1494 drew him into the quagmire of Italian affairs as he attempted to counter French influence there. His erratic military policies, however, could not quite keep pace with these imperial ambitions.

Maximilian's inability to execute a consistent military policy in Italy was a consequence of the highly decentralized nature of the empire. Unlike the other European monarchs who inherited their thrones at the death of their predecessors, the emperor was selected by seven electors, who even after an election exercised considerable independent power. The German part of the Holy Roman Empire, home to 15 to 20 million people, was composed of some 300 sovereign and quasi-sovereign principalities and free cities (legally exempt from direct imperial rule). Besides the emperor, only a few institutions served to unify the empire. Most important was the imperial diet, an assembly that included the seven electors, other princes, and representatives of the imperial free cities. The imperial diet was established during the fifteenth century to control the relentless feuding among the German princes, but it often became instead a forum for resisting the emperor.

Maximilian's reign produced some limited reforms. These included a moratorium on feuds, a Supreme Court to impose ancient Roman law throughout Germany, a graduated property and income tax, and eventually an imperial council to exercise executive functions in the absence of the emperor. In practice, however, these institutions worked only to the degree that the emperor and German princes cooperated. The empire remained a fractured, dissent-ridden jumble with no real unity. Compared to the centralizing monarchies in France, Spain, and England, or even to the better managed among the Italian city-states such as tiny Venice, which recurrently defeated Maximilian in battle, the empire under Maximilian was little more than a glorious-sounding name.

England: From Civil War to Stability Under the Tudors

At the end of the Hundred Years' War in 1453, the English crown was defeated. Thousands of disbanded mercenaries were let loose in England and enlisted with one quarreling side or the other in feuds among aristocratic families. The mercenaries brought to England the evil habits of pillage, murder, and violence they had previously practiced in the wars with France. King Henry VI (r. 1422–1461) suffered from bouts of madness that made him unfit to rule and unable to control the disorder. Under the tensions caused by defeat and revolt, the royal family fractured into the two houses of Lancaster and York, which fought a vicious civil war, now known as the Wars of the Roses (1455–1485) from the red and white roses used to identify members of the two opposing sides.

After decades of bloody conflict, the cynical but able Richard III (r. 1483–1485) usurped the throne from his twelve-year-old nephew Edward V and had Edward and his brother imprisoned in the Tower of London, where they were murdered, perhaps on Richard's orders. Richard's apparent cruelty and his scandalous intent to marry Edward's young sister, now heir to the throne, precipitated open defections against him. When Henry Tudor challenged Richard, many nobles flocked to Henry's banner. At the

Battle of Bosworth Field (1485), Richard was slain and his crown discovered on the field of battle. His naked corpse was dragged off and buried in an unmarked grave.

When Henry Tudor became King Henry VII (r. 1485–1509), there was little reason to believe that exhausted England could again become a major force in European events. It took years of patient effort for Henry to become safe on his own throne. He revived the Court of Star Chamber as an instrument of royal will to punish unruly nobles who had long bribed and intimidated their way out of trouble with the courts. Because the king's own hand-picked councilors served as judges, Henry could guarantee that the court system became more equitable and obedient to his wishes. Henry confiscated the lands of the rebellious lords, thereby increasing his own income, and he prohibited all private armies except those that served his interests. By managing his administration efficiently, eliminating unnecessary expenses, and staying out of war, Henry governed without the need to call on Parliament for increased revenues.

England was still a backward country and, with fewer than three million people, a fraction of the size of France. By nourishing an alliance with newly unified Spain, Henry was able to bring England back into European affairs. When his son Henry VIII succeeded to the throne, the Tudor dynasty was more secure than any of its predecessors and England more stable than it had ever been before. As we shall see in Chapter 14, by the reign of Henry VII's granddaughter, Elizabeth I (r. 1558–1603), England could boast of a splendid Renaissance court and a fleet that would make it a world power.

THE ORIGINS OF MODERN HISTORICAL AND POLITICAL THOUGHT

The revival of the monarchies of western Europe and the loss of the independence of the Italian city-states forced a rethinking of politics. As in so many other fields, the Florentines led the way. In an attempt to understand their own troubled city-state, they analyzed politics by making historical comparisons between one kind of government and another and by carefully observing current events. Two crucial figures in these developments, Francesco Guicciardini and Niccolò Machiavelli, had both served Florence as diplomats, an experience that was crucial in forming their views.

History: The Search for Causes

During the fifteenth century there were two kinds of historians. The first kind were chroniclers who kept records of the important events in their city or principality. The chroniclers recorded a great deal of factual information in the simple form of one-occurrence-after-another. In so doing they established chronologies, which meant they

CHRONOLOGY	
The Early Modern European State System	
1422–1461	Reign of Charles VII of France
1455–1485	Wars of the Roses in England
1461–1483	Reign of Louis XI of France
1474–1504	Reign of Isabella of Castile
1479–1516	Reign of Ferdinand of Aragon
1479	Unification of Spain
1483–1485	Reign of Richard III of England
1485–1509	Reign of Henry VII of England
1492	Conquest of Granada; expulsion of the Jews from Spain; voyage of Christopher Columbus
1493–1519	Reign of Maximilian I, Holy Roman Emperor
1494–1530	The Italian Wars
1515–1547	Reign of Francis I of France
1515–1556	Reign of Charles I, King of Spain, who also became Charles V, Holy Roman Emperor (1519–1558)

arranged history according to a sequence of dates. But they lacked any sense of how one event caused another, and they failed to interpret the meaning and consequences of the decisions leaders and other people had made.

The second kind of historians were humanists. Petrarch established that the fundamental principle for writing humanist history was to maintain historical distance—the sense that the past was past and had to be reconstructed in its own terms. The most dangerous historical error in writing history became anachronism, that is, imposing present sensibilities and understandings on the past. Before the Renaissance the most common version of anachronism was for historians to interpret pre-Christian history in the light of Christian understandings of God's plan for humanity. In contrast to that approach, humanist historians attempted to offer explanations for why things had happened in human terms. When they interpreted past events, they tried to respect the limitations people had faced. For example, they understood that the moral code of the Roman orator and senator Cicero, who died two generations before Jesus was born, derived from Greek philosophy and Roman ethics rather than a premonition of Christianity. The humanists' interest in rhetoric, however, led them to make moral judgments about the past in an attempt to encourage morality among their readers. Thus, they were prone to pull especially compelling examples of good or bad conduct out of the historical context in which it had taken place and to compare it with other examples. For example, they might compare the behavior of the citizens in fifth-century B.C.E. Athens with the actions of citizens in fifteenth-century Florence.

The shock of the Italian Wars that began in 1494 stimulated a quest for understanding the causes of Italy's fall and prompted a new kind of history writing. The first person to write a successful history in the new vein was Francesco Guicciardini (1483–1540). Born to a well-placed Florentine family, educated in a humanist school, and experienced as a diplomat, governor, and adviser to the Medicis, Guicciardini combined literary skill and practical political experience. Besides collecting information about contemporary events, Guicciardini kept a record of how his own thoughts and values evolved in response to what he observed. One of the hallmarks of his work was that as he analyzed the motives of others, he engaged in self-scrutiny and self-criticism.

From this habit of criticizing himself and others, Guicciardini developed a strong interpretive framework for his histories. His masterpiece, *The History of Italy* (1536–1540), was the first account of events that occurred across the entire Italian peninsula. In many respects, this book originated the idea that Italy is more than just a geographical term and has had a common historical experience. Like the humanist historians, Guicciardini saw human causes for historical events rather than the hidden hand of God, but he refined the understanding of causation through his psychological insights. He suggested, for example, that emotions mattered more than rational calculation and noted that nothing ever turns out quite as anticipated.

Political Thought: Considering the End Result

Guicciardini's contemporary and Florentine compatriot Niccolò Machiavelli (1469–1527) also wrote histories, but he is best known as a political theorist. Trained as a humanist, he lacked the personal wealth and family connections that allowed Guicciardini to move as a matter of birthright in high social and political circles. As we saw in the story that opened this chapter, Machiavelli had worked as a diplomat and military official but had been exiled for complicity in a plot against the Medici family, who had retaken Florence in 1512. While in exile he wrote a book of advice for the Medicis in the vain hope that they would give him back his job. They probably never read his little book, *The Prince* (1513), but it became a classic in political thought. In it he encouraged rulers to understand the underlying principles of political power, which differed from the personal morality expected of those who were not rulers. He thought it was important for a prince to appear to be a moral per-

FRANCESCO GUICCIARDINI ON THE CHARACTER OF LODOVICO SFORZA

Guicciardini filled The History of Italy *with many insightful accounts of the leaders of the various European states during the Italian Wars. Here he analyzes the character and psychology of Lodovico Sforza, who rose to be duke of Milan after the death of his nephew in suspicious circumstances. Taken prisoner in 1500 after a defeat in battle, Lodovico spent the last ten years of his life in a French prison.*

Thus within a narrow prison were enclosed the thoughts and ambitions of one whose ideas earlier could scarcely be contained within the limits of all Italy—a prince certainly most excellent in eloquence, in skill and many other qualities of mind and nature, and worthy of obtaining a name for mildness and clemency if the infamy come upon him as a result of his nephew's death had not blemished that reputation. But on the other hand he was vain, and his mind full of ambitious, restless thoughts, and he violated his promises and his pledges; always presuming so much on the basis of his own knowledge that being highly offended whenever the prudence and counsels of others were praised, he convinced himself that he could turn everyone's ideas in whatever direction he pleased by means of his own industry and manipulations.

son, but Machiavelli pointed out that the successful prince might sometimes be obliged to be immoral in order to protect the interests of the state. How would the prince know when this might be the case?

Machiavelli's answer was that "necessity" forced political decisions to go against normal morality. The prince "must consider the end result," which meant that his highest obligation was preserving the very existence of the state, which had been entrusted to him and which provided security for all citizens of the state. This obligation was higher even than his obligation to religion.

Machiavelli's *The Prince* has sometimes been considered a blueprint for tyrants. However, as his more learned and serious work, *The Discourses of the First Decade of Livy* (1516–1519), makes clear, Machiavelli himself preferred a free republic over a despotic princely government. In some ways, *The Discourses* is an even more radical work than *The Prince* because it suggests that class conflict is the source of political liberty: "In every republic there are two different inclinations: that of the people and that of the upper class, and . . . all the laws which are made in favor of liberty are born of the conflict between the two."[8] In this passage, Machiavelli suggested that political turmoil was not necessarily a bad thing, because it was by provoking conflict that the lower classes prevented the upper classes from acting like tyrants.

In all his works, Machiavelli sought to understand the dynamics behind political events. To do this, he theorized that human events were the product of the interaction between two forces. One force was fortune, a term derived from the name of the ancient Roman goddess Fortuna. Fortune stood for all things beyond human control and could be equated with luck or chance. Machiavelli depicted fortune as extremely powerful, like an irresistible flood that swept all before it or the headstrong goddess who determined the fate of men. Fortune controlled perhaps half of all human events. The problem with fortune was its changeability and unpredictability: "since Fortune changes and men remain set in their ways, men will succeed when the two are in harmony and fail when they are not in accord." How could a ruler or even a simple citizen put

himself in harmony with fortune and predict its shifts? The answer could be found in the characteristics of the second force, virtue, which he understood as deriving from the Roman concept of *virtus,* literally "manliness." The best description of virtue could be found in the code expected of an ancient Roman warrior: strength, loyalty, and courage. If a man possessed these traits he was most likely to be able to confront the unpredictable. As Machiavelli put it, "I am certainly convinced of this: that it is better to be impetuous than cautious."[9] The man possessing virtue, therefore, looked for opportunities to take control of events before they took control of him. In that way he put himself in harmony with Fortune.

Through Guicciardini's analysis of human motivations and Machiavelli's attempt to discover the hidden forces behind events, history and political thought moved in a new direction. The key to understanding history and politics was in the details of human events. To Guicciardini these details provided clues to the psychology of leaders. To Machiavelli they revealed the hidden mechanisms of chance and planning that governed not just political decisions but all human events.

CONCLUSION

The Politics of Culture

The Renaissance began simply enough as an attempt to imitate the Latin style of the best ancient Latin authors and orators. Within a generation, however, humanists and artists pushed this narrowly technical literary project into a full-scale attempt to refashion human society on the model of ancient cultures. Reading about the ancients and looking at their works of art provoked comparisons with contemporary Renaissance society. The result was the development of a critical approach to the past and present. The critical approach was accompanied by an enhanced historical sensibility, which transformed the idea of the West from one defined primarily by religious identification with Christianity to one forged by a common historical experience.

During the sixteenth century, western Europeans absorbed the critical-historical methods of the Renaissance and turned them in new directions. As we shall see in the next chapter, Spanish and Portuguese sailors encountered previously unknown cultures in the Americas and only vaguely known ones in Africa and Asia. Because of the Renaissance, those who thought and wrote about these strange new cultures did so with the perspective of antiquity in mind. As we shall see in Chapter 13, in northern Europe the critical historical methods of the humanists were used to better understand the historical sources of Christianity, especially the Bible. With that development, Christianity began to take on new shades of meaning, and many thoughtful Christians attempted to make the practices of the church conform more closely to the Bible. The humanist approach to religion led down a path that permanently divided Christians into contending camps over the interpretation of Scripture, breaking apart the hard-won unity of the Roman Catholic West.

Suggestions for Further Reading

····························· ▬ ·····························

For a comprehensive list of suggested readings, please go to www.ablongman.com/levack/chapter11

Baxandall, Michael. *Painting and Experience in Fifteenth Century Italy: A Primer in the Social History of Pictorial Style.* 1988. A fascinating study of how the daily social experiences of Florentine bankers and churchgoers influenced how these individuals saw Renaissance paintings and how painters responded to the viewers' experience. One of the best books on Italian painting.

Brown, Howard M. *Music in the Renaissance.* 1976. Dated but still the best general study of Renaissance music.

Brown, Patricia Fortini. *Art and Life in Renaissance Venice.* 1997. A delightful study about how art fit into the daily lives and homes of the Venetian upper classes.

Brucker, Gene. *Florence: The Golden Age, 1138–1737.* 1998. A brilliant, beautifully illustrated history by the most prominent American historian of Florence.

Burke, Peter. *The Italian Renaissance.* 1999. A concise and readable synthesis of the most recent research.

Hale, J. R. *Renaissance Europe, 1480–1520.* 2000. A witty, engaging, and enlightening study of Europe during the formation of the early modern state system. Strong on establishing the material and social limitations of Renaissance society.

King, Margaret L. *Women of the Renaissance.* 1991. The best general study of women in Renaissance Europe. It is especially strong on female intellectuals and women's education.

Kohl, Benjamin G., and Alison Andrews Smith, eds. *Major Problems in the History of the Italian Renaissance.* 1995. A useful collection of articles and short studies of major historical problems in the study of the Renaissance.

Martines, Lauro. *Power and Imagination: City-States in Renaissance Italy.* 1988. An excellent general survey that is strong on class conflicts and patronage.

Nauert, Jr., Charles G. *Humanism and the Culture of Renaissance Europe.* 1995. The best survey of humanism for students new to the subject. It is clear and comprehensive.

Skinner, Quentin. *Machiavelli: A Very Short Introduction.* 2000. This is the place to begin in the study of Machiavelli. Always clear and precise, this is a beautiful little book.

Stephens, John. *The Italian Renaissance: The Origins of Intellectual and Artistic Change before the Reformation.* 1990. A stimulating analysis of how cultural change took place.

Vasari, Giorgio. *The Lives of the Artists.* 1998. Written by a sixteenth-century Florentine who was himself a prominent artist, this series of artistic biographies captures the spirit of Renaissance society.

Notes

····························· ▬ ·····························

1. *The Portable Machiavelli,* trans. and ed. Peter Bondanella and Mark Musa (1979), 67–69.
2. Baldesar Castiglione, *The Book of the Courtier,* trans. Charles S. Singleton (1959), 43.
3. Giovanni Villani, *Cronica,* vol. 7 (1823), p. 52. Translation by the authors.
4. Agostino di Colloredo, "Chroniche friulane, 1508–18," *Pagine friulane* 2 (1889), 6. Translation by the authors.
5. Francesco Petrarca, "Letter to the Shade of Cicero," in Kenneth R. Bartlett, ed., *The Civilization of the Italian Renaissance: A Sourcebook* (1992), 31.
6. Quoted in Margaret L. King, *Women of the Renaissance* (1991), 197.
7. "Laura Cereta to Bibulus Sempronius: Defense of the Liberal Instruction of Women," in Margaret King and Alfred Rabil, eds., *Her Immaculate Hand: Selected Words by and about the Women Humanists of Quattrocento Italy* (1983), 82.
8. *The Portable Machiavelli,* trans. and ed. Peter Bondanella and Mark Musa (1979), 183.
9. Ibid., 161–162.

The West and the World: The Significance of Global Encounters, 1450–1650

ON A HOT OCTOBER DAY IN 1492, CHRISTOPHER COLUMBUS AND HIS MEN, dressed in heavy armor, clanked onto the beach of an island in the Bahamas. The captain and his crew had been at sea sailing west from the Canary Islands for some five weeks, propelled by winds they thought would take them straight to Asia. As the ships under Columbus's command vainly searched among the islands of the Caribbean for the rich ports of Asia, Columbus thought he must be in India and thus called the natives he met "Indians." At another point he thought he might be among the Mongols of central Asia, which he described in his journal as the "people of the Great Khan." Both of Columbus's guesses about his location were incorrect, but they have left a revealing linguistic legacy in terms still in use: "Indians" for the native Americans, and both "cannibals" and "Caribbean" from Columbus's inconsistent spellings of Khan. Columbus believed that the people he called the Cannibals or Caribs ate human flesh. But he got that information—also incorrect—from their enemies. Thus began one of the most lasting misunderstandings from Columbus's first voyage.

Historians know very little about the natives' first thoughts of the arrival of their foreign visitors, but we know that the effects of the arrival were catastrophic. Within a few generations the Caribs nearly disappeared, replaced by African slaves who worked the plantations of European masters.

Western civilization by the end of the fifteenth century hardly seemed on the verge of encircling the globe with outposts and colonies. Its kingdoms had barely been able to reorganize themselves sufficiently for self-defense, let alone world exploration and foreign conquest. The Venetian and Genoese colonies in the Mediterranean were retreating from the advancing Ottoman Turks, who would

Chapter Outline

- Europeans in Africa
- Europeans in the Americas
- Europeans in Asia
- The Beginnings of the Global System

The Encounter of Three Cultures: On this wooden bottle painted in the Incan style about 1650, an African drummer leads a procession, followed by a Spanish trumpeter, and an Incan official. The mixing of cultures that occurred after the arrival of the Spanish and Portuguese is what distinguished the Americas from other civilizations.

continue to occupy the Balkans for at least four more centuries. The Ottoman threat was so great that all of southern Europe was on the defensive. And the hostilities had blocked the traditional trade routes to Asia, which had stimulated the great medieval economic expansion of Europe. Scandinavian voyages to North America had ceased in the fourteenth century, and the isolated Western outpost of Christianity in Greenland vanished under the onslaught of advancing ice by the middle of the fifteenth. In comparison with the Ottoman Empire or Ming China, Europe's puny, impoverished states seemed more prone to quarreling among themselves than to seeking expanded horizons.

Nevertheless, by 1500 Europeans could be found fighting and trading in Africa, the Americas, and Asia. A mere fifty years later, Europeans had destroyed the two greatest civilizations in the Americas, had begun the forced migration of Africans to the Americas through the slave trade, and had opened trading posts throughout South and East Asia.

Before 1500 the West, identified by its languages, religion, agricultural technology, literature, folklore, music, art, and common intellectual tradition that stretched back to pre-Christian antiquity, was largely confined to Europe and the Middle East. After 1500 the wandering Europeans began to export Western culture to the rest of the world.

Especially after large numbers of European settlers moved to the Americas, the culture and technology of western Europe began to spread around the globe. After the sixteenth century, European culture could be found in many distant lands, and western European languages and forms of Christianity were adopted by or forced upon other peoples. The West was now more of an idea than a place, a certain kind of culture that thrived in many different environments. The process was not all one-way, however: Western Europeans came under the influence of the far-flung cultures they visited, transforming Europe into the most cosmopolitan corner of the Earth. The European voyages integrated the globe biologically and economically. Microbes, animals, and plants that had once been isolated were now transported throughout the world. Because the Europeans possessed the ships for transport and the guns for coercion, they became the dominant players in international trade, even in places thousands of miles from the European homeland.

To understand the European encounters with the world during the fifteenth and sixteenth centuries, this chapter will address four central questions: (1) Why did the European incursions into sub-Saharan Africa lead to the vast migration of Africans to the Americas as slaves? (2) How did the arrival of Europeans in the Americas transform native cultures and life? (3) Why was the European encounter with Asian civilizations far less disruptive than those in Africa and the Americas? (4) How was the world tied together in a global biological and economic system?

Europeans in Africa

Geographers of the ancient world, writing in Greek and Latin, had accumulated a substantial knowledge about all of North Africa, but they were almost completely ignorant of the region south of the Sahara desert. Medieval writers remained equally ill-informed, reporting that sub-Saharan Africa was populated by man-eaters, "great giants of twenty-eight foot long . . . and they eat more gladly man's flesh than any other flesh" and Amazons, warrior women who cut off one breast to facilitate archery.

In reality, the interior of sub-Saharan Africa had been governed for centuries by highly developed kingdoms and boasted numerous wealthy cities. By the fifteenth century, Muslim contacts with sub-Saharan Africa made it clear that the region was a rich source of gold and slaves. In search of these, Europeans, especially the Portuguese, began to swarm down the west coast of Africa. Enabled by new developments in ship technology, the Europeans were capable of making long sea voyages. European settlers founded colonies in the Atlantic islands off the west coast of Africa, establishing precedents for colonies that would later be installed in the Americas.

SUB-SAHARAN AFRICA BEFORE THE EUROPEANS ARRIVED

During the Middle Ages a number of kingdoms that emulated ancient Egyptian forms of rulership arose south of the Sahara desert. Some kingdoms boasted large cities and consisted of as many as a million inhabitants who were subjects of strongly centralized regimes. The kingdoms were administered by public officials who could be transferred, demoted, or promoted according to the king's will in a bureaucratic system that paralleled what the European states had achieved.

For Europeans, the principal attraction to Africa were reports of its rich deposits of gold. These reports came from the Muslim kingdom of Mali, a landlocked empire between the Upper Senegal and Niger Rivers, to the north of the Guinea coast. The source of Mali's wealth was its monopoly of the gold caravans that carried the coveted metal from the fabled city of Timbuktu across the Sahara to the gold-greedy Mediterranean. The king of Mali, known as the Mansa, never owned the gold mines, the location of which was a closely kept secret, but he controlled the gold market. The gold from the mines went to the Mansa, whose agents traded it in distant lands for luxury goods. The Mansa's power rested on his cavalry, which by the middle of the fourteenth century had spread the rule of Mali from the Gambia and lower Senegal Rivers in the West through the Niger valley to South.

■ **Timbuktu, Mali**

This drawing was made by a nineteenth-century French explorer, René-Auguste Caillié, but it illustrates the city that had been built during the fourteenth century by the Mansa Musa. Built from the proceeds of the gold trade, Timbuktu became a major center of Islamic learning and was only one of several great Malian cities that arose during the fourteenth century.

The wealth of the Mansa became legendary after Mansa Musa (r. 1312–1337) conducted a spectacular pilgrimage to the Muslim holy city of Mecca in 1324. Mansa Musa made a magnificently opulent impression. A gold bird sat above the parasol that shaded him from the sun, and he carried a gilded staff, wore a gold skull cap, strung a gold quiver over his shoulder, and affixed a gold scabbard to his waist. The pilgrimage took more than a year, and Mansa Musa was so generous that his trip was remembered for centuries in Egypt, where he stayed for three months. He gave out so much gold that Egypt suffered a disastrous inflation of prices. Traveling with as many as a hundred camels, each loaded with 300 pounds of gold, the Mansa gave whole ingots of gold to officials along the way and to religious shrines he visited.

By 1400, however, the kingdom of Mali was in decline. Internal power struggles had split apart the once-vast empire. In 1482, when the Portuguese founded a gold-trading post at Elmina, some sixty miles west of the mouth of the Volta, they had to negotiate with a ruler called the Karamansa, whose title echoed the past glories of the Mansa

of Mali but whose power was a mere shadow of what the rulers of Mali exercised during the fourteenth century (see Map 12.1).

Influenced by Mali, the forest kingdoms of Guinea were built on a prosperous urban society and extensive trading networks. Benin was a particularly great city, which European travelers compared favorably with the principal European cities of the time. The towns of Guinea held regular markets, similar to the periodic fairs of Europe, and carefully scheduled them so they would not compete with each other. The staples of the long-distance trade routes in this region were high-value luxury goods, especially imported cloth, kola nuts (a mild stimulant popular in Muslim countries), metalwork such as cutlasses, ivory, and of course gold. For money, African traders used cowrie shells, brought all the way from the Indian Ocean.

Unlike the kingdoms of the western sub-Sahara, which tended to be Muslim, mountainous Ethiopia was predominantly Christian. In fact, Europeans saw Ethiopians as potential allies against Islam. The Roman Catholic pope sent a delegation to Ethiopia in 1316, and Ethiopian embassies

■ **Map 12.1 The Maghrib and West Africa, Fourteenth Century**

Long before the arrival of the Portuguese via sea routes, caravans of camels crisscrossed the Sahara desert during the fourteenth century, linking the sources of gold in Mali with the Maghrib (the coast of northwest Africa) and the seaports of the Mediterranean. The greatest medieval Arabic traveller, Ibn Battuta (1304–1368/69), crossed the Sahara and spent more than a year in Mali. He left the most extensive account of medieval West Africa.

occasionally appeared in Italy and Portugal during the fifteenth century. Diplomatic contacts between Rome and Ethiopia intensified at the time of the Council of Florence in 1439, which attempted to unify Christianity in defense against the onslaught of the Muslim Ottoman Turks. Learned Ethiopian churchmen became known in western Europe and created the impression that Ethiopia was an abundant land peopled by pious Christians.

Conditions during the later Middle Ages tended to confirm this image of Ethiopia. Threatened by Muslim invaders in 1270, the Ethiopian kingdom created a powerful army, rumors of which tantalized European Christians who sought allies against Islam. As the armies expanded Ethiopian power to the south and east, missionaries proselytized among the conquered peoples and helped unify the kingdom. Ethiopian expansion greatly enriched the kingdom through the control of trade in ivory, gold, slaves, and civet, a highly prized musky perfume. Portuguese visitors were duly impressed by the splendor of the emperor of Ethiopia, the Negus, who traveled with 2,000 attendants and 50,000 mules to carry provisions and tents.

By the early sixteenth century, the Ethiopian kingdom had become overextended. In the 1520s and 1530s Muslims attacked deep into the Ethiopian heartland, raiding and burning the wealthy Ethiopian monasteries. The raids severely weakened the power of the Negus. By destroying relics and religious images, the Muslims eradicated much of the great artistic heritage of Ethiopia. Ethiopia survived with the help of a Portuguese expeditionary force, but it was hobbled by competing Christian warlords and a weak central power, and it never regained its previous strength.

During the fifteenth and sixteenth centuries when European contacts with the sub-Sahara dramatically expanded, the once-strong kingdoms were either in decline or engaged in protracted struggles with regional rivals. The Europeans arrived at precisely the moment when they could take advantage of the weaknesses produced by internal African conflicts.

EUROPEAN VOYAGES ALONG THE AFRICAN COAST

Although sub-Saharan Africa represented something of a mystery to Europeans, merchants from Italy, Catalonia, Castile, and Portugal had long shown interest in the ports of the Maghreb, the collective name for the present-day regions of Morocco, Algeria, and Tunisia on the Mediterranean coast of North Africa. There they brought wool and woolen textiles, wine, dye stuffs, and clandestine items such as weapons, which they traded for various commodities, most significantly gold. Since at least the mid-thirteenth century, the Maghreb had been famous as the northern terminus of the gold caravans from Mali. In the thirteenth and fourteenth centuries, European traders obtained gold in the Maghreb in exchange for silver mined in Europe. They then resold the gold in the ports along the northern shore of the Mediterranean for more silver than they had originally paid to buy the gold. With the handsome silver profits made in the gold trade, merchants provided a steady supply that encouraged the general adoption of gold coinage throughout much of southern Europe. Gold was highly prized in Europe largely because it was rare in comparison to silver, and by the laws of supply and demand the commodity that is scarce is more valuable.

To gain more direct access to the sources of gold, European traders occasionally crossed the Sahara with the camel caravans—the "ships of the desert." For example, the

Florentine merchant Benedetto Dei told of traveling in 1470 as far as Timbuktu, where he saw many examples of European textiles on the local market. The efficient camel caravans created a vast trading network that stretched from Mali and Morocco in the west of Africa into central Asia, completely bypassing the Mediterranean. But Europeans had little hope of regularly using the "sea of sand" routes across North Africa because of the hostility of Muslim inhabitants who were wary about foreign interlopers, especially Christian ones.

The alternative for Europeans was to outflank the Muslims by crossing the sea of water. As early as the thirteenth century, European voyagers ventured down the west coast of Africa into uncharted waters. In 1291 the Vivaldi brothers left Genoa with the goal of circumnavigating Africa to reach the Indies. But their galleys were adapted to the relatively calm waters of the Mediterranean and were ill-suited for the voyage. Such ships, which required large crews of oarsmen, were easily swamped in the heavy seas of the Atlantic, and the long coastline of West Africa lacked protective harbors for refuge from storms. The Vivaldi expedition disappeared without a trace.

New Maritime Technology

The disadvantages of Mediterranean galleys were surmounted during the fifteenth century through changes in the technology of ocean sailing. The Iberian peninsula (the land of present-day Portugal and Spain), situated between the Mediterranean and the Atlantic, was uniquely located to develop a hybrid ship that combined features of Mediterranean and Atlantic types. The initial impulse for developing the shipping technology was to facilitate trade between the Mediterranean and northern Europe via the Atlantic. The resulting changes, however, also made possible much more ambitious voyages into the unknown southern regions.

The Iberians modified the cog design, the dominant ship in the Atlantic, by adding extra masts and creating a new kind of rigging that combined the square sails of Atlantic ships, suitable for sailing in the same direction as the wind was blowing, with the triangular "lateen" sails of Mediterranean galleys, which permitted sailing into the wind. The result was a ship that could sail in a variety of winds, carry large cargoes, be managed by a small crew, and be defended by guns mounted in the castle superstructure. These hybrid three-mast ships, called caravels°, appeared about 1450, and for the next 200 years Europeans sailed ships of this same basic design on long ocean voyages to the very ends of the Earth.

Also assisting European navigators were other technological innovations, the fruit of late medieval Mediterranean seafaring. The compass provided an approximate indicator of direction, and the astrolabe and naked-eye celestial navigation made it possible to estimate latitudes.

■ An Early Caravel

The caravel was typical of the hybrid ship developed during the fifteenth century on the Iberian peninsula. The ship on the lower right is rigged with a lateen sail on its main mast.

Books of sailing directions, called portolanos°, included charts and descriptions of ports and recorded the location of dangerous shoals and safe harbors for future voyages. The advances in maritime technology made it possible for Europeans motivated by economic need and religious fervor to sail wherever they wanted.

New Colonialism

During the fifteenth century, European colonialism departed somewhat from the patterns of the past. Mediterranean colonies established during the Crusades of the twelfth and thirteenth centuries had relied on native inhabitants to produce commodities that could be expropriated by the colonizers. These were either aristocratic colonies in which a few warriors occupied castles to dominate the native population or mercantile colonies built around a trading post for foreign merchants.

As Europeans ventured into the Atlantic more frequently and expanded their contacts with sub-Saharan Africa, they established new patterns of colonization. In search of fertile lands for agriculture, Castile and Portugal founded colonies in the Canary Islands, the Madeira archipelago, the Azores,

■ **Oceangoing Ship**
This is a Flemish version of the three-mast ship, square-rigged on the foremast and mainmast, lateen-rigged on the mizzenmast. Versions of this ship carried Europeans throughout the world.

and the Cape Verde Islands. The climate of these islands was similar to the Mediterranean and invited the cultivation of typical Mediterranean crops, such as grains and sugar cane, but the islands lacked a native labor force. When Europeans arrived, the Canaries were seriously underpopulated and the other islands were uninhabited. In response to the labor shortage, two new types of colonies emerged, both of which were later introduced into the Americas.

The first new type of colony during this period was the settler colony°. The settler colony derived from the medieval, feudal model of government, in which a private person obtained a license from a king to seize an island or some part of an island. The king supplied financial support and legal authority for the expedition. In return the settler promised to recognize the king as his lord and occasionally to pay a fee after the settlement was successful. The kings of Castile and Portugal issued such licenses for the exploitation of Atlantic islands. The actual expeditions to colonize

these islands were private enterprises, and adventurers from various parts of Europe vied for a license from any king who would grant them one. For example, the first European settlement in the Canary Islands was led by a Norman knight, Jean de Béthencourt, who could not obtain sufficient support from the king of France and thus switched loyalties to the king of Castile.

After the arrival of the Europeans, all the natives of the Canaries, called the Guanches, died off, creating the need for settler families from Europe to till the land and maintain the Castilian claim on the islands. These peasants and artisans, rather than living like islanders and adapting to the native culture, imposed their own culture. They brought with them their traditional family structures, customs, language, religion, seeds, livestock, and patterns of cultivation. Wherever settler colonies were found, whether in the Atlantic islands or the Americas, which the Europeans called the New World, they Europeanized the landscape and remade the lands they cultivated in the image of the Old World.

The second new type of colony was the plantation colony°. Until the occupation of the Cape Verde Islands in the 1460s, the Atlantic island colonies had relied on European settlers for labor. However, the Cape Verdes attracted few immigrants because of the rigors of the tropical climate, and yet the islands seemed especially well-suited for growing the lucrative sugar cane crop. The few permanent European colonists there tended to be exiled criminals, who had no choice but to stay, and the Cape Verdes became a haven for lawless ruffians who were disinclined to work. Because there was no indigenous population to exploit on the Cape Verdes, the few European colonizers began to look elsewhere for laborers and voyaged to the African coast where they bought slaves who had been captured from inland villages. These slaves worked as agricultural laborers in the Cape Verdes sugar cane fields. Thus, in the Cape Verdes began the tragic conjunction between African slavery and the European demand for sugar. When sugar began to replace honey as the sweetener of choice for Europeans, the almost insatiable demand was supplied by sugar cultivated by slaves in plantation colonies, first in the Atlantic islands and later in the West Indies and American mainland. Over the next 300 years, this pattern for plantation colonies was repeated for other valuable agricultural commodities, such as indigo for dyes, coffee, and cotton, which were grown to sell in European markets. The first loop of what would eventually become a global trading circuit was now completed.

The Portuguese in Africa

The first European voyages along the African coast during the fifteenth century were launched by the Portuguese. The sponsor of these voyages was Prince Henry the Navigator (1394–1460). As governor of Algarve, the southernmost province of Portugal, Henry established a headquarters at

Sagres and financed numerous exploratory voyages. Driven by the quest for fame and a profound faith in astrology, Henry had two objectives above all else: In order to enhance his reputation, he wanted to steal the Canary Islands from his archrival, the king of Castile; and to reward the men who sailed his ships, he desperately needed to get his hands on more gold.

The first Portuguese expeditions along the African coast were prompted by Henry's desire to capture the Canaries. He tried armed force, negotiations with the inhabitants, and entreaties to the pope, all with no success. He even purchased phony titles to the Canaries in a transparent attempt to fool the Castilians that he was really the lord of the islands. In the mid-1450s, however, Henry's disappointment over the Canaries subsided as it became evident that gold from Mali could be obtained further south from bases near the Senegal and Gambia rivers. Although the many voyages of Henry's sailors did not fulfill his dreams of conquest and enormous riches, he and other members of his family did help colonize Madeira and the Azores, and as a source of sugar, Madeira became a valuable colony (see Map 12.2).

CHRONOLOGY

Europeans in Africa

1270	Beginnings of the Ethiopian kingdom
1316	Papal delegation sent to Ethiopia
1324	Pilgrimage to Mecca by Mansa Musa of Mali
1394–1460	Life of Prince Henry the Navigator of Portugal
1450s	Appearance of new European ship designs, the caravel
CA. 1450	European slave trade in Africa begins
1460s	Occupation of Cape Verde Islands
1482	Portuguese gold-trading post founded at Elmina
1520s–1530s	Muslim attacks against Ethiopian kingdom

■ **Map 12.2 Europeans in the World, Fifteenth and Sixteenth Centuries**
During the fifteenth and sixteenth centuries European sailors opened sea lanes for commerce across the Atlantic, Pacific, and Indian Oceans. Dates indicate first arrival of Europeans.

After Henry's death, Portuguese exploration of the African coast accelerated. In only six years, a private merchant of Lisbon commissioned voyages that added 2,000 miles of coastline that was known to the Portuguese. In 1482 the exploration policy that had been a loose and haphazard enterprise under private contractors was transformed. That year the Portuguese royal house took control of trade with Africa; they required that all sailings be authorized and all cargoes inventoried, and they built a permanent fortress at Elmina near the mouth of the Volta River. At Elmina, Portuguese traders found local sources of gold and opportunities to obtain more upriver. Rather than establishing new settler or plantation colonies, the Portuguese on the African coast relied on trading posts that supplied gold, ivory, pepper, and slaves.

Europeans in the Americas

Like the Europeans who sailed along the African coast, the first European voyagers to the Americas coveted gold and an alternative route to India and China. The European impulse to reach Asia by sailing west came from the fact that the Ottoman Empire, which was pushing into the Mediterranean after the conquest of Constantinople in 1453, blocked the traditional trade routes through the Middle East and across the Black and Red Seas. Europeans relied on Asian sources for medicines, spices, and all kinds of luxury goods, which were unavailable elsewhere. Those who gained access to the source of these lucrative goods could make enormous profits. The desire to profit from this trade impelled men to take great risks to find an alternative route to East Asia. In the short run, the Americas proved to be an impediment to achieving these goals because the two continents stood in the way of getting to Asia. But in the long run, the European voyages to the Americas brought unimaginable consequences.

THE AMERICAS BEFORE THE CONQUISTADORES

Prior to their contact with Europeans, the peoples of the Americas displayed remarkable cultural variety. Nomadic hunters spread across the sub-Arctic regions, western North America, and the Amazon jungles, while farming settlements prevailed in much of South America and eastern North America. Some of these North American cultures, such as the Anasazi and Iroquois, developed highly sophisticated forms of political organization, but none matched the advanced civilizations of Mesoamerica and the central Andes to the south. On the eve of the arrival of Europeans, two great civilizations, the Aztecs of central Mexico and the Incas of highland Peru, had built extensive empires that dominated their neighbors.

The Aztec Empire of Mexico

Mesoamerica (the region we know today as Mexico and Central America) had been the home of a series of highly urbanized, politically centralized cultures: the Mayans (300–900), the Toltecs (900–1325), and finally the Aztecs (1325 to the Spanish conquest in 1522). The Aztecs found safety from incessant warfare with neighboring tribes on an island in Lake Texcoco, where they established the city of Tenochtitlán, now Mexico City. From their base at Tenochtitlán the Aztecs followed a brilliantly successful policy of divide and conquer, first allying with powerful neighbors to attack weaker groups, then turning against former allies.

The Aztec king, Montezuma I (r. 1440–1469), consolidated an empire that stretched across most of central Mexico. In order to provide food for his people during a severe famine between 1450 and 1454, Montezuma first conquered the breadbasket of Mexico, the rich coastal region of the Totonacs. In repeated attacks, swarms of Aztec troops took city after city, captured the local chief whenever possible, burned the temple, and extorted tribute payments from the population. With the riches gained from conquest, Montezuma transformed Tenochtitlán from a dusty town of mud houses to a great imperial capital built of stone with a grand botanical garden that displayed plants taken from various climates.

The Aztecs excelled in the perpetual state of war that had long been the dominant fact of life in Mexico, and as a result they attributed great religious value to war. From their predecessors they inherited the concept of the "flowery war," a staged occurrence when states agreed to a predetermined time and place for a battle, the only objective of which was to take prisoners for temple sacrifice. Sustaining the gods' hunger for human sacrifices became the most notorious feature of Aztec religion. The Aztecs attributed their military successes to their tribal god, Huitzilpochti, the giver of light and all things necessary for life, but Huitzilpochti could be nourished only with human blood, creating the need among the Aztec faithful to acquire human captives.

The rituals of sacrifice permeated Aztec society. It has been estimated that some 10,000 victims were sacrificed each year, with the number rising to 50,000 on the eve of the Spanish conquest. From the very first encounters, Europeans have been baffled by the paradox of Aztec culture. Despite their apparent practice of human sacrifice, the Aztecs displayed refined manners, a sensitivity to beauty, and a highly developed religion.

The Incan Empire of the Andes

At about the same time the Aztecs were thriving in Mexico, the Incas expanded their empire in Peru and developed a

■ **The Aztec Rite of Human Sacrifice**
Human victims had their hearts cut out by a priest at the top of the stairs to a temple.

comprehensive imperial ideal. Whereas the Aztecs created a loosely linked empire based on tribute payments, the Incas employed a more direct form of rulership. As they pushed out from their base in the south Andes during the fifteenth century, they imposed on conquered peoples their own form of economic organization, their culture, and their religion.

The first Incan emperor, Pachacuti Inca Yupanqui (r. 1438–1471), founded the empire around 1438 when he spread Incan rule beyond the valley of Cuzco. By the end of the fifteenth century, the Incas had begun to integrate by force the distinctive cultures of the various conquered regions. In this way, they created a mountain empire 200 miles wide and 2,000 miles long, stretching from modern-day Chile to Ecuador and comprising a population of about ten million. From his capital at Cuzco, the Incan emperor lived in luxury and established an elaborately hierarchic political structure. His authority was carried through layers of aristocrats down to officials who were responsible for every ten families in every village. These families supplied food and tribute for the empire, worked on roads and bridges, and served in the army. State-owned warehouses of food guaranteed the peasants freedom from starvation and provided for the sick and elderly.

Emperor Huayna Capac (r. 1493–1525) founded a second capital further south at Quito, established to decentralize the overextended empire, but at his death a bitter civil war broke out between the northern and southern halves of the empire, led respectively by his rival sons. This war weakened Incan unity on the eve of the Spanish conquest.

The Incas were impressive in creating a strong imperial administration, and as rulers they were as severe as the Aztecs. Huayna Capac slaughtered some 20,000 recalcitrant Caranqui and poisoned Lake Yahuar-Cocha with their corpses. After conquering a region, the Incas would kill the native population or remove them to a secure area and replace the inhabitants with loyal colonists. During the early sixteenth century, for example, Huayna Capac brought in 14,000 colonists from all over the empire to settle the Cochabamba valley. A superb network of roads and bridges covered more than 18,000 miles and made it possible to communicate with relays of runners who could cover as much as 140 miles a day. Troops could also be quickly dispatched to trouble spots via these roads. Despite this well-organized imperial system, the Incan Empire became overly centralized and decisions could only be made by the emperor himself, a fatal flaw that, as we shall see, allowed the Spanish invaders to crush it very quickly.

THE MISSION OF THE EUROPEAN VOYAGERS

The European arrival in the Americas was the result of a mistake promoted by Christopher Columbus's (1451–1506) stubborn sense of mission. Born in Genoa to an artisan family, Columbus followed the destiny of so many of his compatriots by becoming a sailor. "From my earliest

■ **Christopher Columbus**
A portrait of the navigator.

youth," he reported late in life, "I went to sea and I have remained at sea until this day. It has occupied me for more than forty years. Wherever men have sailed, I too have sailed." Of his skills as a navigator and seaman there can be no doubt, but his personality remains an enigma that has allowed a wide variety of interpretations. Historians once depicted Columbus as a practical-minded experimenter, who was opposed by ignorant fools, but now he is understood as a more complex figure whose defining characteristic was his religious devotion. Columbus believed that he had been predestined to fulfill biblical prophecies. If he could reach China, he could outflank the Ottoman Turks and recapture Jerusalem from the Muslims who had held it since 1187, an achievement that would usher in the Second Coming of Christ. In trying to convince Queen Isabella of Castile to finance his mission to voyage to China by sailing west, he later admitted that to make his case he ignored navigational data and, instead, relied "entirely on holy, sacred Scripture and certain prophetic texts by certain saintly persons, who by divine revelation have had something to say on this matter."[1]

It had long been recognized that it was theoretically possible to reach China, Columbus's goal, by sailing west. Most educated people, and certainly all those influenced by the Renaissance humanists, agreed the world was round. The problem was not a theoretical one about the shape of the Earth but a practical one about getting around it. During Columbus's life the most widely accepted authority on the circumference of the Earth was the ancient Greek geographer Ptolemy, who had estimated that the distance across the Atlantic Ocean from Europe to Asia was more than 10,000 miles. The practical problem was that no ship in Columbus's day could hope to sail that far without landfalls along the way for finding provisions and making repairs. In fact, Ptolemy had underestimated the size of the Earth by 25 percent, but Columbus decided that Ptolemy had overestimated the distance. Columbus also imagined that the wealthy island of Japan lay farther east of the Asian continent than it actually does, thus further minimizing the distance of the voyage. When he first presented his project for sailing west to Asia, King John II of Portugal consulted a committee of experts who quite correctly pointed out how seriously Columbus had miscalculated the distance. Skilled navigator that he was, Columbus was no geographer. His extremely inaccurate estimate of how close China was seems to have been more the result of wishful thinking and religious fervor than geographical expertise. King John's rejection led Columbus to seek patronage elsewhere. Columbus applied to Queen Isabella of newly unified Spain, whose own advisers at first recommended against the voyage for the same reasons the Portuguese experts had rejected his plan. When the Spanish defeated the Muslim kingdom of Granada in 1492, which completed the Christian reconquest of the Iberian peninsula, Isabella succumbed to the religious enthusiasm of the moment and relented. She offered Columbus a commission for the voyage in the hope that it would ensure a final Christian victory over Islam.

On August 3, 1492, Columbus set sail with three small ships—the Niña, Pinta, and Santa Maria—and a crew of some ninety men and boys. After refitting in the Canary Islands, the modest convoy entered unknown waters guided only by Columbus's faith in finding China, which was, in fact, many thousands of miles farther west than he thought it would be. At two in the morning on the moonlit night of October 12, a lookout spied land, probably Watling Island in the Bahamas.

In all, Columbus made four voyages across the Atlantic (1492, 1493, 1498, 1502), exploring the Caribbean Islands, the coast of Central America, and part of the coast of South America. He never abandoned the belief that he had arrived in Asia. His four voyages were filled with adventures. On the third voyage, he was arrested by the newly appointed Spanish governor of Hispaniola on false charges and sent home in chains for trial; on the fourth he was marooned for nearly a year on Jamaica after worms weakened the timbers of his ships. He garnered considerable wealth in gold found on his voyages, but he never received the titles and offices that Queen Isabella had promised him before his first voyage.

Soon after Columbus returned to Spain from his first voyage, the Spanish monarchs who had sponsored him tried to obtain a monopoly to explore the western Atlantic. They applied to Pope Alexander VI, who was himself a Spaniard and sympathetic to their request. In an effort to give the Spanish a firm legal monopoly to the lands across the Atlantic, the pope confirmed in 1493 the right of Spanish sailors to explore all lands to the west as long as they did not infringe upon the rights of another Christian ruler. Since all involved still thought Columbus had arrived in China, the obvious other Christian ruler was the king of Portugal, whose sailors had already pushed far enough south down the African coast to realize that they could eventually reach China by sailing east. The pope ordered a line of demarcation drawn along a north-south line 100 leagues (about 300 miles) west of the Azores and Cape Verde Islands. Spain received all lands to the west of the line; Portugal obtained the lands to the east. This line of demarcation seemed to limit the Portuguese to Africa, which alarmed them and led to direct negotiations between the Portuguese and the Spaniards. The result of the negotiations was the Treaty of Tordesillas in 1494, which moved the line of demarcation to 370 leagues (about 1,110 miles) west of the Cape Verde Islands, a decision that granted to Portugal all of Africa, India, and Brazil.

Despite Columbus's persistent faith that he had found a route to the East Indies, other voyagers began to suspect, even before Columbus's death, that he had not found Asia at all and that other routes had to be explored. Another Italian, the Florentine Amerigo Vespucci (1454–1512), met Columbus, helped him prepare for the third voyage, and later made at least two voyages of his own across the Atlantic. From his voyages, Vespucci recognized something of the immensity of the South American continent and was the first to use the term "New World." Because he used the term and because the account of his voyages got into print before Columbus's, Vespucci's given name, Amerigo, came to be attached to the New World rather than Columbus's. By the 1520s, Europeans had explored the Americas extensively enough to recognize that the New World was nowhere near India or China.

After the Treaty of Tordesillas, explorers followed two distinct strategies for finding a sea route to East Asia. The Portuguese continued to pursue routes to the south and east around Africa. Between 1487 and 1488, Bartholomew Dias (ca. 1450–1500) reached the Cape of Good Hope at the southern tip of the African continent. This discovery made it evident that passage to India could be achieved by sailing south, rounding the tip of Africa, and crossing the Indian Ocean. Political and financial problems in Portugal prevented a followup to Dias's voyage for ten years, however. Between 1497 and 1499, Vasco da Gama (ca. 1460–1524) finally succeeded in sailing from Lisbon to India around the Cape of Good Hope. This celebrated voyage included a great looping westward course far out into the Atlantic to escape the doldrums, an area in the ocean where the

COLUMBUS'S CHRISTIAN MISSION

One of the most common features of Christopher Columbus's writings is the prevalence of Christian images and themes. Expectations of Christian salvation and the second coming of Christ motivated Columbus in his attempts to reach Asia by sailing west. The Introduction to the journal of his first voyage offers a glimpse of Columbus's militant Christianity. It depicts the stirring moment of Christian triumph when the Muslim king of Granada surrendered to Ferdinand and Isabella in 1492.

I saw your Highnesses' banners victoriously raised on the towers of the Alhambra, the citadel of that city [of Granada], and the Moorish king come out of the city gates and kiss the hands of your Highnesses [Ferdinand and Isabella] . . . And later in that same month, on the grounds of information I had given your royal Highnesses concerning the lands of India and a prince who is called the Great Khan—which means in Spanish 'King of Kings'—and of his and his ancestors' frequent and vain applications to Rome for men learned in the holy faith who should instruct them in it, your Highnesses decided to send me, Christopher Columbus, to see these parts of India and the princes and peoples of those lands and consider the best means for their conversion. For, by the neglect of the Popes to send instructors, many nations had fallen to idolatory and adopted doctrines of perdition, and your Highnesses as Catholic princes and devoted propagators of the holy Christian faith have always been enemies of the sect of Mahomet and of all idolatries and heresies.

Your Highnesses ordained that I should not go eastward by land in the usual manner but by the western way which no one about whom we have positive information has ever followed. Therefore having expelled all the Jews from your dominions in that same month of January, your Highnesses commanded me to go with an adequate fleet to those parts of India.

Source: From *The Four Voyages of Christopher Columbus*, translated by J. M. Cohen (London: Penguin Classics, 1969). Copyright © 1969 by J. M. Cohen. Reproduced by permission of Penguin Books Ltd.

winds died. As a consequence of the route opened by da Gama, the Portuguese were the first Europeans to establish trading posts in Asia. They reached the Malabar coast of India in 1498 and soon found their way to the Spice Islands and China. By the middle of the sixteenth century, the Portuguese had assembled a string of more than fifty trading posts° and forts from Sofala on the east coast of Africa to Nagasaki in Japan.

The second strategy for reaching Asia consisted of Spanish attempts to pursue Columbus's proposed route west. The problem faced by those sailing under the Spanish flag was to find a way around the barrier presented by the American continents. A Portuguese sailor named Ferdinand Magellan (ca. 1480–1521), who had previously sailed to Asia aboard Portuguese ships, persuaded the king of Spain to sponsor a voyage to Asia sailing west around South America. That venture (1519–1522), which began under Magellan's command, passed through the strait named after him at the tip of South America and crossed the Pacific in a voyage of extreme hardship as his men suffered from thirst and hunger and died of scurvy. Magellan himself was killed by natives in the Philippines. After three years at sea, 18 survivors from the original 240 in Magellan's fleet reached Seville, having sailed around the world for the first time. Contemporaries immediately recognized the epic significance of the voyage, but the route opened by Magellan was too long and arduous for the Spanish to employ as a reliable alternative to the Portuguese route around Africa.

In the course of three centuries (about 1480–1780), European navigators linked the previously isolated routes of seaborne commerce, opened all the seas of the world to trade, and encountered many of the cultures and peoples of the world. For the first hundred years or so, the Portuguese and Spanish effectively maintained a monopoly over these trade routes, but gradually English, Dutch, and French sailors made their way all around the globe. In the Americas, inadvertently made known to Europeans by Christopher Columbus, the Spanish immediately began settlements and attempted to subdue the indigenous populations.

THE FALL OF THE AZTEC AND INCAN EMPIRES

Soon after the seafaring captains, such as Columbus and Magellan, came the conquistadores°, Spanish adventurers, usually from impoverished minor noble families. The conquistadores sought fortune and royal recognition through explorations and conquests of indigenous peoples. Spain was a poor land with few opportunities for advancement, a bleak situation that made the lands of the New World a powerful lure to many men seeking a fortune. Embroiled in almost continuous warfare in Europe, the Spanish crown was also perennially strapped for cash, which meant the king of Spain was highly motivated to encourage profitable

THE DIFFICULT LIFE OF SAILORS

During the expedition begun by Magellan, which completed the first circumnavigation of the globe, Antonio Pigafetta (ca. 1491–ca. 1536) kept a journal. The passage across the Pacific Ocean was especially difficult as food and water ran out. Sailors became so desperate that they ate sawdust from planks. The following entry is typical.

They sailed out from this strait [Strait of Magellan] into the Pacific Sea on the 28th of November in the year 1520, and they were three months and twenty days without eating anything [i.e., fresh food], and they ate biscuit, and when there was no more of that they ate the crumbs which were full of maggots and smelled strongly of mouse urine. They drank yellow water, already several days putrid. And they ate some of the hides that were on the largest shroud to keep it from breaking and that were very much toughened by the sun, rain and winds. And they softened them in the sea for four or five days, and then they put them in a pot over the fire and ate them and also much sawdust. A mouse would bring half a ducat or a ducat. The gums of some of the men swelled over their upper and lower teeth, so that they could not eat and so died. And nineteen men died from that sickness.

Source: From Antonio Pigafetta, *The Voyage of Magellan,* translated by Paula Spurlin Paige. Copyright © 1969 by The William L. Clements Library, University of Michigan. Reprinted by permission.

foreign conquests. Many of the conquistadores launched their own expeditions with little or no legal authority, hoping to acquire sufficient riches to impress the king to give them official sanction for additional conquests. Those who did acquire legal authority from the crown received the privilege to conquer new lands in the name of the king of Spain and to keep a portion of those territories for themselves. In return they were obliged to turn over to the king one fifth—the "royal fifth"—of everything of value they acquired, an obligation enforced by a notary sent along with the conquistadores to keep a record of everything valuable that was found. The conquistadores also extended Spanish sovereignty over new lands and opened the way for missionaries to bring millions, at least nominally, into the Christian fold.

All conquistadores were required to read a document, called the *requerimiento*°, to the natives before making war on them. The document briefly explained the principles of Christianity and commanded the natives to accept them immediately along with the authority of the pope and the sovereignty of the king of Spain. If the natives refused, they were warned that they would be forced through war to sub-

■ **Spanish Conquistadores Land on an Island in the New World**
The armored Spaniards are met by the naked inhabitants who offer them jewels and gold. As one of
their first acts, the Spaniards erect a cross, symbolizing the Christian conquest of the New World.

ject themselves "to the yoke and obedience of the Church
and of Their Highnesses. We shall take you and your wives
and your children, and shall make slaves of them, and as
such shall sell and dispose of them as Their Highnesses
may command. And we shall take your goods, and shall
do you all the mischief and damage that we can."[2] The
requerimiento revealed the conflicting motives behind the
Spanish conquest. On the one hand, the Spanish were sincerely interested in converting the natives to Christianity.
On the other, the conquistadores were trying to let themselves off the hook over the immorality of their actions by
suggesting that the natives had brought the attack on themselves by refusing to obey the Spanish king.

Hernán Cortés and the Conquest of Mexico

Among the first and most successful of the conquistadores
was Hernán Cortés (1485–1547). Cortés arrived on the
Yucatán peninsula of present-day Mexico in February
1519, beginning a conquest that culminated in the collapse
of the Aztec Empire and the Spanish colonization of
Mexico. He followed a policy of divide and conquer with
the natives, making alliances with peoples who hated the
Aztecs and then using their warriors on the front lines of
his battles where they absorbed most of the losses. If after a

reading of the *requerimiento* the native chieftains did not
immediately surrender, Cortés's men attacked them,
breaking through their lines on horses, which the natives
had never seen before.

After a number of bloody battles, Cortés set off with
some 450 Spanish troops, 15 horses, and 4,000 native
allies to conquer the great capital of the Aztec Empire,
Tenochtitlán, a city of at least 300,000 and defended by
thousands of warriors. As Cortés approached, Montezuma II
was slow to set up a strong defense, because he suspected
Cortés might be the white god, Quetzalcoatl, who according to prophecies would arrive one day from the east. The
result was disastrous for the Aztecs. Montezuma knew his
reign was doomed unless he could gain the assistance of
other gods to drive Quetzalcoatl away. Thus, rather than an
ardent military campaign, the king's defense primarily
took the form of ritual sacrifices, which failed. Cortés
captured Montezuma, who continued to rule for several
months as a puppet of the conquistadores. The city revolted, however, killing Montezuma and driving out the
Spanish. Cortés then gathered new troops and additional
allies, built ships for use on the lake that surrounded
Tenochtitlán, and besieged the city. By the time
Tenochtitlán finally surrendered, the shiny jewel that had

■ **Cortés Meets Montezuma in Tenochtitlán**
The figure on the right is the native woman who served as Cortés's translator, a position often occupied by native women who served as mediators between the indigenous and Spanish cultures.

■ **Spaniards Attacking Tenochtitlán, 1519**
Notice how the Spaniards had placed cannons on the bows of these small ships, which were built to sail on the lake.

WHAT MONTEZUMA BELIEVED ABOUT THE SPANISH

···················

After Cortés arrived in Tenochtitlán, he had an interview with Montezuma, the Aztec emperor. The following letter to the Emperor Charles V includes a speech Montezuma supposedly gave to Cortés in which the Aztec emperor surrendered authority to the Spanish because he assumed that Charles was an ancient god or ruler the Aztecs believed would return from the east. Just as Columbus was inspired by Christian prophecies to sail into the unknown, Montezuma was encouraged by Aztec prophecies to accept Cortés's invasion as a fulfillment of a religious obligation.

Long time have we been informed by the writings of our ancestors that neither myself nor any of those who inhabit this land are natives of it, but rather strangers who have come to it from foreign parts. We likewise know that from those parts our nation was led by a certain lord (to whom all were subject), and who then went back to his native land, where he remained so long delaying his return that at his coming those whom he had left had married the women of the land and had many children by them and had built themselves cities in which they lived, so that they would in no wise return to their own land nor acknowledge him as lord; upon which he left them. And we have always believed that among his descendants one would surely come to subject this land and us as rightful vassals. Now seeing the regions from which you [i.e., Cortés] say you come, which is from where the sun rises, and the news you tell of this great king and ruler [Emperor Charles V] who sent you hither, we believe and hold it certain that he is our natural lord: especially in that you say he has long had knowledge of us. Wherefore be certain that we will obey you and hold you as lord in place of that great lord of whom you speak, in which service there shall be neither slackness nor deceit: and throughout all the land, that is to say all that I rule, you may command anything you desire, and it shall be obeyed and done, and all that we have is at your will and pleasure. And since you are at your own land and house, rejoice and take your leisure from the fatigues of your journey and the battles you have fought; for I am well informed of all those that you have been forced to engage in on your way here. . . .

Source: From Hernán Cortés, "The Second Letter to Emperor Charles V" from Anthony Pagden, ed., *Letters from Mexico*. Copyright © 1986 by Yale University. Reprinted with the permission of Yale University Press.

so impressed the Spanish when they first glimpsed it from the surrounding mountains lay in smoldering ruins.

By 1522 Cortés controlled a territory in New Spain—as Mexico was renamed—larger than Old Spain itself. Aztec culture and its religion of human sacrifice disappeared as Franciscan friars arrived to evangelize the surviving population.

Francisco Pizarro and the Conquest of Peru

Like other conquistadores, Francisco Pizarro (ca. 1478–1541) was poor, but he bore the additional social liabilities of illegitimacy and illiteracy. With no prospects at home, Pizarro found his way to Panama where he accompanied Vasco Núñez de Balboa (1475–1519) on an expedition in 1513 across the Isthmus of Panama during which Europeans got their first look at the Pacific Ocean.

In 1531 Pizarro left Panama with a small expedition of some 180 men and 30 horses. His goal was to conquer Peru, known to be a land rich with gold. He gathered additional recruits along the way. He sailed to northern Peru and sent out spies who discovered that the Incan emperor, Atahuallpa, could be found in the highland city of Cajamarca. When Pizarro and his forces arrived there, the central square was empty, but Atahuallpa was encamped nearby with a large army. Pizarro treacherously invited Atahuallpa to come for a parlay, but instead took him captive. The news of the capture plunged the overly centralized Incan Empire into a crisis because no one dared take action without the emperor's orders. In an attempt to satisfy the Spaniards' hunger for gold and to win his freedom, Atahuallpa had a room filled with gold and silver for the conquistadores, but the treasure merely stimulated their appetite for more. In July 1533 Pizarro executed the emperor, and by the following November he had captured the demoralized Incan capital of Cuzco.

The conquest of Peru vastly increased the size of the Spanish Empire and began to satisfy the craving for gold that had impelled Columbus and the conquistadores in the first place. Through the collection of the royal fifth, gold and silver flowed into the royal coffers in Spain. The discovery in 1545 of the fabulous Peruvian silver mine of Potosí (in what is now in southern Bolivia) coincided with the introduction of the mercury amalgamation process that separated silver from ore. Mercury amalgamation enabled the Spaniards to replace surface gathering of silver ore with tunneling for ore, a procedure that led to greatly elevated yields of precious metals. For a century the silver of Peru helped provide otherwise impoverished Spain with the resources to become the most powerful kingdom in Europe.

■ **The Ransom of a King**

The Incas fill a room with gold objects to ransom Atahualpa.

SPANISH AMERICA: THE TRANSPLANTING OF A EUROPEAN CULTURE

With the defeat of the Aztec and Incan empires, the process of transplanting Spanish society to the Americas began in earnest. The arrival of Europeans was a catastrophe for most native peoples, some of whom—in the Caribbean, northern Argentina, and central Chile—completely disappeared through the ravages of conquest and disease. Whereas Spanish became the language of government and education, some native traditions survived and a mixed-blood immigrant and native population called *mestizos* gradually appeared. Through this process, Spanish America became the first lasting outpost of Western civilization outside of Europe.

The basic form of economic and social organization in Spanish America was the encomienda° system, which was created as an instrument to exploit native labor. An encomienda was a royal grant awarded for military or other services that gave the conquistadores and their successors the right to gather tribute from the Indians in a defined area. In return, the encomendero (the receiver of the royal grant and native tribute) was theoretically obliged to protect the natives and teach them the rudiments of the Christian faith. Because the encomiendas were very large, only a small number of Spanish settlers were actually encomenderos. In greater Peru, which included modern Peru, Ecuador, and Bolivia, there were never more than 500 encomenderos. By the seventeenth century these encomiendas had evolved to become great landed estates called haciendas°.

There were only a few prosperous encomenderos, but the stories about those who rose from rags to riches in the New World were so compelling that during the sixteenth century alone more than 200,000 Spaniards migrated there. They came from every part of the Iberian peninsula, from every class except the peasantry, and they practiced a wide variety of trades. There were nobles, notaries, lawyers, priests, physicians, merchants, artisans, and sailors; there were also vagabonds prone to crime and rebellion. In effect, these immigrants duplicated Spanish Catholic society in the New World, complete with its class divisions and tensions, except that the native population or African slaves substituted for the peasants as agricultural workers. Included among the immigrants were an unknown number of Jews who hid their faith and who escaped the rigors of the Spanish Inquisition by removing themselves to the Americas where they were less likely to suffer persecution.

For a long time the colonies suffered from a shortage of Spanish women. Only one in ten of Spanish immigrants were women. Although native Americans were usually excluded from Spanish society, many native women who were the mistresses and even wives of Spaniards partially assimilated to European culture and helped pass it on to their offspring. These native women learned Spanish and were converted to Christianity, but because of their origins they could mediate between the dominant Spanish and the subordinate native population. These women knew both languages, which made them valuable interpreters, and were familiar with both cultures, which enabled them to explain native customs to the Spanish. The progeny of European men and Indian women constituted the mestizo population.

Wherever they went in the Americas, the Spaniards brought African slaves with them. Most of the slaves remembered little about their original African cultures, however, because many had been born in Spain, the Caribbean, or the Cape Verde Islands, and Spanish had become their native language. At every stage from initial explorations to the building of new cities, Africans participated in helping make the Americas Spanish. In 1533, while Pizarro held the Incan emperor captive at Cajamarca, he sent to Cuzco an advance party of five men, including a black man who was entrusted to bring back a huge fortune in gold and silver. Unlike in the West Indies and the coastal regions where they became plantation workers, blacks in the interior of South America often fought and worked as partners with the Spanish, not as full equals but as necessary auxiliaries for and beneficiaries of the conquest.

The king of Spain was represented in the Americas by the two viceroys, who were the highest colonial officials. One in Mexico City governed the West Indies, the mainland north of Panama, Venezuela, and the Philippines; the other in Lima, Peru, had authority over all of Spanish South America, excluding Venezuela. However, the vast territory of Spanish America and the enormous cultural diversity within it precluded any rigorous centralized control either from Spain or from the viceregal capitals.

In Spanish America the church was a more effective presence than the state. Driven by the same religious fervor as Columbus, Catholic missionaries trekked into the farthest reaches of Spanish America, converting the native populations to Christianity with much more success than in Africa or Asia. Greed had enticed the conquistadores, but an ardent desire to spread the gospel of Christianity spurred the missionaries. As heirs to the long Christian struggle against Islam and, in particular, the reconquest of the Iberian peninsula from the Muslims, the missionaries found in the Americas an exceptional opportunity to expand Christianity. The most zealous missionaries were members of religious orders—Franciscans, Dominicans, and Jesuits—who were distinguished from the parish priests by their autonomy and special training for missionary work. Instead of answering to a bishop who had authority over a defined region, members of religious orders were organized like an army, followed the commands of the head of their order in Rome, and were willing to travel anywhere in the world. In fact, the head of the Society of Jesus, the official name of the Jesuits, was called a general.

The Spanish colonization of South America meant that missionaries did not have to contend with the opposition of local governments, as they did in Africa and Asia. Church officials generally assumed that it took ten years for the transition to a settled Christian society, a policy that meant that Christianity arrived in two stages. First, members of a religious order evangelized the population by learning the native language, then preaching and teaching in it. They also introduced the celebration of the Catholic sacraments. Once churches were built and Christianity was accepted by the local elite, the missionaries moved on to be replaced, in the second stage, by parish priests who expected to stay in one place for their entire lives. In the border regions, evangelizing never ceased and members of the missionary orders stayed on until the end of colonial times. In California, New Mexico, and Texas, missions formed outposts of Spanish society in regions that were otherwise often lawless borderlands. In Paraguay, the members of the Jesuit Order gathered the Guaraní peoples into *reductions*, highly disciplined and closed communities where the natives were subjected to a rigorous regime of labor and prayer, and even the most minute details of their daily lives were regulated.

PORTUGUESE BRAZIL: THE TENUOUS COLONY

In 1500 Pedro Cabral sighted the Brazilian coast, claiming it for Portugal under the Treaty of Tordesillas. While the Spaniards busied themselves with the conquest of Mexico and Peru, the Portuguese largely ignored Brazil, which lacked any obvious source of gold or temptingly rich civilizations to conquer. Instead, the Portuguese concentrated on developing their lucrative empire in Asia.

Brazil became a haven for pirates and castaways, especially French. In 1532 the Portuguese crown finally answered the French threat by devising a plan for Portuguese settlement and government of Brazil. Brazil was divided into fifteen captaincies, which were passed out to court favorites as compensation for services rendered or just to get them out of the way. The captains turned out to be tyrannical, incompetent, or absent, and they so completely failed to govern effectively that in 1549 the crown was forced to appoint a governor general and to establish a capital city at Salvador in eastern Brazil.

The impetus for the further colonization of Brazil was the growing European demand for sugar. The Brazilian climate was perfectly suited for cultivating sugar cane. Between 1575 and 1600, Brazil became the Western world's leading producer of sugar, luring thousands of poor young men from Portugal and the Azores who took native women as wives, thereby producing a distinctive mestizo population. In the coastal regions, the land was cleared for vast sugar cane plantations. Sugar cane production required back-breaking, dangerous labor to weed and especially to cut the cane. To work the plantations the Portuguese attempted to enslave the Tupí-Guaraní natives, but European diseases soon killed off this population.

The Portuguese increasingly looked to Africans to perform the hard labor they were unwilling to do themselves.

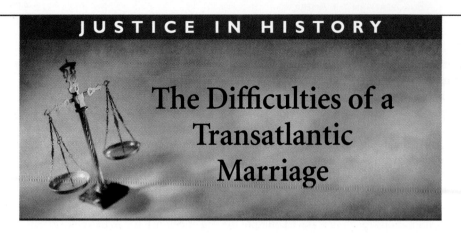

The Difficulties of a Transatlantic Marriage

In 1557 Francisco Noguerol de Ulloa, a Spanish conquistador who had fought in Peru, returned home to Spain. During his nearly two decades in the New World, he had amassed a sizable fortune and earned a great reputation for himself. He expected to enjoy his wealth and fame in a peaceful retirement, but instead almost immediately upon his return he was arrested on the charge of bigamy. During his long stay in Peru, he had neither seen nor heard from the Spanish woman he had married before he left, and when his sisters wrote to him that she had died he thought he was free to marry again. So he did. But when he returned to Spain, his first wife, Dona Beatriz, who was alive and well, heard about his second marriage and filed suit against him for bigamy.

The chance to escape Beatriz had impelled Francisco across the Atlantic in the first place. Many Spanish conquistadores were trying to flee troubles at home, such as a bad marriage. Francisco had married Beatriz under pressure from his widowed mother for the usual reasons parents forced their children into arranged marriages. Beatriz came with a large dowry and provided useful alliances for Francisco's mother and sisters, who felt vulnerable because of Francisco's father's untimely death.

But the marriage was a failure from the beginning. According to Francisco, they had never slept together, and in the eyes of the Church, at least, an unconsummated marriage was not a real marriage. Certainly Francisco and Beatriz never lived together, and she bore him no children. However, his lack of affection for his wife did not prevent him from accepting large payments for her dowry or from writing to his in-laws to ask for money when in his early years abroad he ran into difficulties in Peru. Even a letter of consolation on the death of his wife's sister included a request for more money. Francisco may never have had an affectionate or sexual relationship with Beatriz, but he certainly had a financial one.

Peru eventually rewarded Francisco with a great fortune. For his military prowess and devotion to the Spanish crown, he was granted one of the largest and most productive encomiendas in Peru, a vast tract of land that included the labor of thousands of Incas and a retinue of personal slaves, including a harem of female domestics. Once the false news of Beatriz's death spread throughout Peru, Francisco came to be regarded as the most eligible bachelor in the entire colony. Although many women were eager to become his wife, Francisco did not remarry for years after the news of his first wife's death.

Francisco's second wife, Dona Catalina, shared at least two attributes with his first wife: wealth and social prominence. Born into a respectable Castilian family, she was herself the widow of one of the most powerful Spaniards in Peru. She controlled her own vast fortune in property and other assets, which meant that she could bring a substantial dowry to her new husband. Her reputation as a woman of modesty and virtue was impeccable; she also possessed one vital asset that Beatriz apparently lacked—great beauty. Catalina was known as the "crown jewel of all the women of those parts." It is no wonder that Francisco chose her as his new wife. This time he consummated the marriage.

This case reveals much about the nature of marriage in imperial Spain, and the relative power of men and women in Spanish and colonial society. Marriage was the union of two families, not just two people. Social standing counted for more than affection in the choice of a spouse. Francisco, in fact, had to defend himself against the charge that he had fallen in love with Catalina and had, therefore, abandoned Beatriz so that he could marry Catalina. Love was not an acceptable reason for marriage, let alone an acceptable reason for leaving one marriage for another. In his trial and subsequent litigation, he never claimed to love his new wife and in fact denied that he knew her well at all before the wedding. As an honorable and respectable widow, she had lived a secluded life that would have made it impossible for Francisco to have had much contact with her at all, or so he said.

To escape Beatriz, Francisco had to prove that the marriage had never been a real marriage. To this end, he and his lawyers highlighted the fact that he had never consummated his first marriage, a fact that would have automatically invalidated it as a legal marriage according to the canon law of the Church. To keep Francisco as her husband, Beatriz had to prove that they had had sex together at least once. Francisco's belief that Beatriz was dead had no legal bearing on the case because she was not.

Despite Francisco's arguments that the marriage had never been valid, the judges initially decided in favor of Beatriz. Francisco was sentenced to pay a heavy fine to Beatriz, to serve time in jail, and to separate from his second wife, whom he was forbidden to ever see again. Perhaps most galling of all, he was obliged to resume marital relations with Beatriz, with whom he had certainly never lived before. Beatriz won the case largely because of the legal protection women enjoyed in sixteenth-century Spain. Husbands had obligations toward their wives that the courts consistently enforced.

One of the most important protections women had was the dowry itself. A man could enjoy the income from his wife's dowry, but legally she still had certain claims to it. If he died before she did—which was quite likely given the difference in age between men and women at first marriage—she had a claim on his estate to have the entire sum of her dowry restored to her, not to his family or his heirs but only to her. Beatriz supplied the court with extensive evidence of receipts for dowry payments, signed by Francisco himself. The judges respected the legal protections for women and would not allow Francisco to squander the dowry or relegate it entirely for himself. Francisco's repeated requests to his in-laws for more money made him look like an opportunistic fortune hunter rather than a valuable family ally. The court's judgment in favor of Beatriz had less to do with the emotions of love than the defense of the dowry system and its role in maintaining social stability.

Catalina did not accept lightly the loss of the man she considered her husband. She needed to protect her own dowry from Beatriz's claims. Catalina filed a countersuit to assert that much of Francisco's assets were profits earned from her own dowry, which could not, therefore, be transferred to Beatriz. Catalina was fighting not just for her dowry but for her good name and her marriage, and the courts eventually found a way to recognize the rights of both women—Beatriz to her dowry portion and Catalina to her honorable marriage to Francisco.

In the end, it was the women who resolved the legal struggle that surrounded Francisco. For both women, the courts and the dowry system served as a powerful form of protection for their financial well-being and their honor. Despite the overwhelming authority of men in Spanish society, women were not passive pawns. They found ways to assert control over their own lives. It is revealing that the distance between the Old and New Worlds had little bearing on the status of or legal protections for these women. Far from becoming a lawless frontier, early colonial Peru was for Spaniards at least, an extension of Spanish society. ■

■ A Spanish Couple

Francisco Noguerol de Ulloa and Catalina would have dressed much like this aristocratic couple out for a stroll.

Questions of Justice

1. How would you have resolved the conflicting claims of Beatriz and Catalina?
2. What does this case tell us about the nature of marriage in early modern Spain?

Taking It Further

Cook, Alexandra Parma, and Noble David Cook. *Good Faith and Truthful Ignorance: A Case of Transatlantic Bigamy.* 1991. A detailed study of the Noguerol de Ulloa case.

As a result, the Brazilian demand for slaves intensified the Portuguese presence in West Africa and the African presence in Brazil. In the search for ever more slaves, Portuguese slave buyers enlarged their area of operations in Africa south to Angola, where in 1575 they founded a trading post. This post became the embarkation point for slave traders who sailed directly to Brazil and sold slaves in exchange for low-grade Brazilian tobacco, which they exchanged for more slaves when they returned to Angola.

As in Spanish America, Portuguese authorities felt responsible for converting the natives to Christianity. In Brazil, the Jesuits took the lead during the last half of the sixteenth century by establishing a school for the training of missionaries on the site of the present city of São Paulo. São Paulo became the headquarters for the "Apostle of Brazil," José de Anchieta, who worked among the indigenous peoples. In the seventeenth century, Father Antonio Vieira established a string of missions in the Amazon valley. Once converted, natives were resettled into villages called aldeias°, which were similar to Spanish missions. The Jesuits attempted to protect the natives against the white colonists who wanted to enslave them, creating a lasting conflict between the Jesuit fathers and local landowners. Both Jesuits and colonists appealed to the king to settle their dispute; finally the king gave the Jesuits complete responsibility for all Indians in aldeias but allowed colonists to enslave Indians who had not been converted or who were captured in war. The Portuguese connected Christian conversion with settlement in aldeias, which meant that any unsettled native was, by definition, a heathen. Nevertheless, these restrictions on enslaving Indians created a perceived labor shortage and further stimulated the demand for African slaves.

More rural, more African, and less centrally governed than Spanish America, Brazil during its colonial history remained a plantation economy in which the few dominant white European landowners were vastly outnumbered by their African slaves. In certain areas a racially mixed population created its own vibrantly hybrid culture that combined native, African, and European elements, especially in the eclectic religious life that combined Catholic with polytheistic forms of worship. Although Brazil occupied nearly half of the South American continent, until the twentieth century most of the vast interior was unexplored by Europeans and unsettled except by the small native population.

NORTH AMERICA: THE LAND OF LESSER INTEREST

Compared with Central and South America, North America outside of Mexico held little attraction for Europeans during the sixteenth century. European experience in North America consisted of a number of exploratory missions and several failed attempts at colonization. By 1600, when hundreds of thousands of Europeans and Africans had settled in the Caribbean, Central and South America, the only European settlements in North America (except for New Spain) consisted of a tiny Spanish garrison at St. Augustine, Florida, a doomed Spanish colony on the upper Rio Grande in New Mexico, and a few marooned Frenchmen on Sable Island far off the coast of Nova Scotia. Even by 1700, when English, French, and Spanish colonies were finally thriving in North America, they still played a very minor role in the global picture of European economic interests.

At first the principal attraction of North America was the cod fisheries in the waters off Newfoundland, which every spring lured ships from England, France, Spain, and Portugal and which may have been frequented by Europeans even before Columbus. An Italian captain in the employ of England, John Cabot (ca. 1450–ca. 1498), landed in North America in 1497 and established the basis for an English claim in the New World, but after he disappeared on a return trip the following year no one else bothered to follow up on the claim. Occasionally, fishermen dropped anchor at the harbors at St. John's, Newfoundland, and came to know the coasts of Maine and the Gulf of St. Lawrence. In 1521 some Portuguese families founded a settlement on Nova Scotia, but they soon disappeared.

The second attraction of North America lay in the vain hope of a Northwest Passage to China and India through or around the continent to the North. After Magellan's voyage (1519–1522), the Spanish knew how to sail around South America, but they preferred overland transportation from Vera Cruz, Mexico, to reach the Pacific coast at Acapulco, which became an embarkation port for Spanish trade with Asia. In 1524 the French king sent the Italian Giovanni da Verrazano (ca. 1485–1528) to find a passage around North America, which resulted in the first geographical description of the coast from North Carolina to Newfoundland. Following up on Verrazano's voyage, Jacques Cartier (1491–1557) discovered the St. Lawrence River in 1534. Hard winters defeated two French attempts to found a colony in the St. Lawrence Valley between 1541 and 1543. The English explored further north in a series of voyages that led to the discovery of Hudson Bay, which was thought for some time to be part of the Pacific Ocean. Only in 1616 did William Baffin (ca. 1584–1622) determine that there was no ice-free passage around North America.

In the competition over North America, the English arrived late, devoting themselves at first to preying on Spanish shipping rather than building their own colonies. During most of the sixteenth century England was considerably less well prepared than Spain or Portugal to sustain a campaign of conquest and colonization in the Americas. At this time the English monarchy had a fragile hold on power, its naval fleet was tiny, and it lacked the financial backing for risky expeditions. In contrast to the great convoys of Spanish and Portuguese ships that plied the Atlantic, the English were represented by a few "privateers," which was a polite word for pirates. These men sought quick, easy profits rather than the rigors of settling and pacifying the country. John Hawkins, the most famous of the early English privateers, and his nephew, Francis Drake (ca. 1543–1596) specialized in harassing the Spanish fleet, both to steal the gold and silver that was being transported back to Spain and to sustain an intermittent war against England's most powerful enemy.

During the reign of Queen Elizabeth I (r. 1558–1603), English efforts finally turned to establishing colonies in the Americas. Two prominent courtiers, Humphrey Gilbert and his stepbrother, Walter Raleigh, sponsored a series of voyages intended to establish an English colony called Virginia in honor of Elizabeth, "The Virgin Queen." The shift of English interest from piracy to colonization was made possible by Elizabeth's success in strengthening the monarchy, building up the fleet, and encouraging investments in New World colonies. In 1585 the first English colonists in the Americas landed on Roanoke Island off the coast of North Carolina, but they were so poorly prepared that their attempt and a second one in 1587 failed. The inexperienced and naive English settlers did not even make provisions for planting crops.

The successful English colonies came a generation later. Learning from past mistakes, the colonists of Jamestown in Virginia, who landed in 1607, brought seeds for planting, built fortifications for protection, and established a successful form of self-government. From these modest beginnings, the English gradually established vast plantations along the rivers of Virginia. There they raised tobacco to supply the new European habit of smoking, which had been picked up from native Americans. In 1620 religious refugees from England settled in Massachusetts Bay, but in contrast to Central and South America, most of North America by 1650 remained only marginally touched by Europeans.

Europeans in Asia

··■··

India, the Malay peninsula, Indonesia, the Spice Islands, and China were the ultimate goal of the European explorers during the fifteenth and sixteenth centuries. They were eventually reached by many routes—by the Portuguese sailing around Africa, by the Spanish sailing around South America, and by the Russians trekking across the vastness of Siberia. Trade between Europe and Asia was very lucrative. Europeans were especially dependent on Asian sources for luxury goods such as silk, spices for cooking and preserving food, and medicines for pain relief and healing.

CHRONOLOGY

Europeans in the Americas

CA. 1438	Founding of Incan empire in Peru by Pachacuti Inca Yupanqui
1440–1469	Reign of Montezuma I of the Aztec empire
1492–1493	First two voyages of Christopher Columbus
1497	John Cabot lands in North America
1498	Third voyage of Columbus
1500	Cabral sights Brazil
1502	Fourth voyage of Columbus
1519–1522	Spanish conquer Mexico
1524	Giovanni da Verrazano explores North American coast for France
1534	Jacques Cartier discovers St. Lawrence River
1549	Portuguese establish a governor-general at Salvador, Brazil
1585	English establish colony on Roanoke Island, North Carolina
1607	English establish colony at Jamestown, Virginia
1616	William Baffin fails to discover Northwest Passage around North America
1620	English establish colony at Massachusetts Bay

ASIA BEFORE THE EUROPEAN EMPIRES

As we saw in Chapter 10, after the collapse of the Mongol Empire in the fourteenth century, direct access for European merchants to China and the Indian Ocean was blocked. Plague, political unrest, and Muslim hostility to Christians reduced trade to a mere trickle of what it had been. The elaborate trade networks that had helped drive the expansion of the economy of the West during the thirteenth century were in disarray.

The greatest potential rival to the Europeans who sought access to Asian trade was Ming China (1368–1644), a highly advanced civilization with maritime technology and organizational capability to launch exploratory voyages far superior to Europe's. Even before the Portuguese began their slow progress down the west coast of Africa, the Chinese organized a series of huge maritime expeditions into the

Indian Ocean that reached far down the east coast of Africa. Between 1405 and 1433 the Chinese established diplomatic contacts and demanded tribute in dozens of kingdoms in India and Africa. The size and ambition of these fleets far surpassed anything that sailed from Europe at this time, and the massive crews of as many as 27,500 men (compared to Columbus's crew of 90) included a complement of scholars to communicate with foreign kings and highly skilled technicians to make repairs to the fleet. The Chinese fleets took trade goods, such as silk, tea, and porcelains, and brought back to China strange animals, hostage kings, and possible trade items. After nearly thirty years of searching the Indian Ocean ports, the Ming emperors concluded that China already possessed all the goods that were available abroad, that China was indeed the center of civilization, and that further investments in oceangoing expeditions were unwarranted.

The European and Chinese voyages of the fifteenth century differed in their objectives and in the motives of the governments that sponsored them. The Europeans were mostly privateers seeking personal profit or captains who enjoyed official government backing in return for a portion of the profits. The economic motive behind the European voyages made them self-sustaining because the Europeans sailed only to places where they could make money. In contrast, the imperial Chinese expeditions were only partially motivated by the desire for economic gain. The official purpose of the Chinese voyages was to learn about the world, and once the Chinese found out what they wanted, they ceased the official voyages. Chinese merchant traders continued to ply the seas on their own, however, and when the Europeans arrived in East Asia, they simply inserted themselves into this already developed Chinese-dominated trade network.

In contrast to the trade in Africa and America, Europeans failed to monopolize trade in Asia. The Europeans were just one among many trading groups, some working under government sponsorship, such as the Portuguese, and others working alone, such as the Chinese.

THE TRADING POST EMPIRES

In 1497–1499 Vasco da Gama opened the most promising route for the Portuguese around Africa to South and East Asia. But the sailing distances were long, limiting the number of people who could be transported to Asia, and the Asian empires were well equipped to defend themselves against European conquest. As a result, European engagement with Asia was slight for some 300 years. Because Europeans lacked the support system provided by colonial conquest, few Europeans settled in Asia, and even missionary work proved much more difficult than in the Americas.

Unlike Brazil, where the Portuguese established colonial plantations, in Asia they established trading posts or factories along the coasts of India, China, and the Spice Islands.

When the Portuguese first arrived at a good location for a trading post—one that had a safe harbor and easy access to the hinterland—they built a fort and forced, bribed, or tricked the local political authority, usually a chieftain, to cede the land around the post to Portugal. The agents sent to trade in Asia were called factors and their trading posts were called factories. But they were not factories in the modern sense of sites for manufacturing; they were safe places where merchants could trade and store their merchandise. The factors lived in the factories with a few other Portuguese traders, a small detachment of troops, and servants recruited from the local population. Nowhere did Portuguese authority extend very far into the hinterland. The traditional political structures of local chieftains remained, and the local elites usually went along with the arrangement because they profited by reselling European wares, such as cloth, guns, knives, and many kinds of cheap gadgets. The factors acquired silks, gold, silver, raw cotton, pepper, spices, and medicines. Some of these outposts of the Portuguese Empire survived until late in the twentieth century, but their roots remained exceedingly shallow. Even in places such as East Timor, an island off Southeast Asia, and Macao on the south China coast, which were Portuguese outposts for more than four centuries, only a small native elite ever learned the Portuguese language or adapted to European culture.

The Portuguese and later other Europeans were motivated to establish colonies in Asia primarily by commercial considerations. Consider the search for the spice nutmeg, which illustrates something of the enticement of the Asia trade. In an account published in 1510, an Italian traveler, Ludovico di Varthema, described for the first time in a European language nutmeg trees, which he found growing in the Banda Islands, a small archipelago some thousand miles east of Java. These were the only places in the world where nutmeg grew. Besides adding flavor to foods, nutmeg was believed to possess powers to cure all kinds of diseases and to induce a hallucinatory euphoria. The demand for nutmeg was so great and the supply so limited that exporting it yielded enormous profits. At one time, nutmeg was the most valuable commodity in the world after gold and silver. In the early seventeenth century the markup on a pound of nutmeg transported from the Banda Islands to Europe was 60,000 percent. It is no wonder European traders were willing to risk their lives on long, dangerous sea voyages to obtain nutmeg and other spices.

In return for raw materials such as nutmeg, European merchants typically traded manufactured goods, and they made every effort to ensure that other European powers were excluded from competing in this trade. Given the high profit potential, there was a great temptation to break a European rival's trading monopoly on a rare commodity such as nutmeg. Crucial to enforcing the system was a network of factories and a strong navy, which was primarily used against other European and occasionally Muslim interlopers. Through the trading post empires, commercial rivalries among European states extended abroad to Asia. Competition over these trading posts foreshadowed the beginnings of a global economy dominated by Europeans. It also demonstrated the Europeans' propensity to transform European wars into world wars.

In addition to trade, the Portuguese and other European powers sought to spread Christianity among the local populations. Franciscan, Dominican, and later Jesuit missionaries preached to the indigenous peoples. To accomplish conversions, they tried persuasion, because without the backing of a full-scale conquest as in the Americas, resorting to force was usually not an option. The missionaries frequently drew the ire of local rulers, who viewed the converts as traitors—a situation that led to the persecution of some of the new Christians. To accomplish their task of conversion, Christian missionaries had to learn the native languages and something of the native culture and religion. In this effort, the Jesuits were particularly dedicated; they sent members of their order to the Chinese imperial court, where they lived incognito for decades, although they made few converts. Jesuits also traveled to Japan, where they established an outpost of Christianity at Nagasaki. With the exception of the Spanish Philippines, which was nominally converted to Catholicism by 1600, Christian missionaries were far less successful than in the Americas. Perhaps one million Asians outside the Philippines had been converted during this period, but many of these conversions did not last. Christians were most successful in converting Buddhists and least effective among Muslims, who almost never abandoned their faith.

By the end of the sixteenth century, Portuguese and Spanish shipping in Asian waters faced recurrent harassment from the English, French, and Dutch. The Dutch drove the Portuguese from their possessions in Ceylon, India, and the Spice Islands, except for East Timor. But none of these sixteenth-century European empires was particularly effective at imposing European culture on Asia in a way comparable with the Americas. In the Spanish Philippines, for example, few natives spoke Spanish, and there were fewer than 5,000 Spanish inhabitants as late as 1850. European states competed among themselves for trade and tried to enforce monopolies, but the Europeans remained peripheral to Asian culture until the late eighteenth and early nineteenth centuries, when the British expanded their power in India and colonized Australia and New Zealand.

The expansion of the Russian Empire into Asia depended not on naval power but on cross-country expeditions. The heartland of the Russian Empire was Muscovy, the area around Moscow, but the empire would eventually spread from the Baltic Sea to the Pacific Ocean. After 1552 Russians began to push across the Ural mountains into

CHRONOLOGY

Europeans in Asia

1487–1488	Bartholomew Dias reaches Cape of Good Hope
1497–1499	Vasco da Gama reaches India via Cape of Good Hope
1498	Portuguese reach Malabar coast of India
1514	Portuguese reach China
1519–1522	Ferdinard Magellan's crew circumnavigate the globe

Siberia, lured by the trade in exotic furs, which were in great demand among the upper classes of northern Europe, both to keep warm and as fashion statements. The Russians' search for furs was equivalent to the Spanish search for gold; like gold, fur attracted adventurous and desperate men. Following the navigable rivers and building strategic forts along the way, expeditions collected furs locally and then advanced deeper into the frozen wilds of Siberia. Several of the great aristocratic families of Russia acquired enormous wealth from the Siberian fur trade, which was so lucrative that Russian trappers kept pushing farther and farther east. In this quest for furs, expeditions reached the Pacific coast in 1649, by which time Russia had established a network of trading posts over all of northern Asia.

The significance of the European trading post empires lies less in the influence of Europe on Asia than in the influence of Asia on Europe. Asian products from spices and opium to silk cloth and oriental rugs became commonplace items in middle- and upper-class European households. European collectors became fascinated with Chinese porcelains, lacquered boxes, and screen paintings. At the same time, Asians began to visit Europe, a tradition begun when four Japanese converts to Christianity arrived in Lisbon in 1586 and made a celebrated tour of Europe.

The Beginnings of the Global System

As a result of the European voyages of the fifteenth and sixteenth centuries, a network of cultural, biological, and economic connections formed along intercontinental trading routes. These connections created a global system that has been sustained ever since. Today's global economy, based on the Internet, air transportation, and free trade, operates much more efficiently and quickly than its predecessors, but it is merely an extension and elaboration of a system that first appeared on a global scale during the sixteenth century. For many thousands of years, Europe, northern Africa, and Asia had been in contact with each other, but the system that took form during the sixteenth century began to encompass most of the globe, including sub-Saharan Africa and the Americas. Unlike earlier international trading systems that linked Europe and Asia, the new global system was dominated by Europeans. They turned large parts of the Americas into plantations that used African slave labor to grow crops for European consumers. This system transformed human society by bringing into contact elements that had previously been separate and isolated—regional cultures, biological systems, and local economies.

THE COLUMBIAN EXCHANGE

The most dramatic changes were at first produced by the trade of peoples, plants, animals, microbes, and ideas between the Old and New Worlds—a process known as the Columbian Exchange°. For the native Americans, the importation of Europeans, Africans, and microbes had devastating consequences—threatening indigenous religions, making native technology irrelevant, disrupting social life, and destroying millions of lives. For Europeans, the discovery of previously unknown civilizations profoundly shook their own understanding of human geography and history. Neither the ancient philosophers nor the Bible, which was understood to be a history of humankind since the creation of the world, had provided a hint about the peoples of the Americas.

The Slave Trade

All of the ancient civilizations had been slave societies with as many as one-third of the population in bondage. During the Middle Ages a small number of slaves were employed as domestic servants and concubines in the Christian cities of the Mediterranean, and in Muslim countries large numbers of slaves were found in harems, used as laborers, and even trained as soldiers. Many of the slaves in Christian cities were Muslims, and many slaves in Muslim countries were Christians, because both religions considered it legitimate to enslave members of the opposing faith. In the wars between Christians and Muslims, captives were habitually enslaved or held for ransom. Large-scale transportation of black Africans began during the ninth and tenth centuries, when Muslim traders took tens of thousands from the island of Zanzibar off the east coast of Africa to lower Iraq, where they performed the heavy labor of draining swamps and cutting sugar cane. Slavery was also widespread in Islamic West Africa. Mali depended heavily on slave labor, and in Muslim Ghana slaves constituted about one-third of the population. Thus the institution of slavery was well established in Africa long before the beginning of the transatlantic slave trade dominated by Europeans.

The slave trade flourished only when and where it was profitable. The necessary conditions for profitability were a strong demand for labor-intensive agricultural commodities, a perceived shortage of local labor, a supply of people who could be captured elsewhere, and a moral and legal climate that permitted slavery. These conditions, which came together for Europeans during the colonization of the Cape Verde Islands, were all present in the late fifteenth and sixteenth centuries. The growing population of Europe developed a taste for exotic products such as sugar, tobacco, coffee, and indigo dye. The European colonizers who sought to supply the demand for these goods needed agricultural workers, first for the colonies in the Atlantic islands and then for plantations in the Americas. In the Americas, European diseases decimated the indigenous population, creating a labor shortage. Europeans also found it difficult to enslave the native peoples, who knew the territory and could easily escape.

The flourishing demand for labor was supplied by the population of Africa. Once Europeans started to buy up slaves in the coastal trading posts, enterprising African chieftains sent slave-hunting expeditions into the interior. As a consequence, the slave-trading states of the Guinea coast gained power at the expense of their neighbors and spread the unwelcome web of the slave trade deep into African interior. The slave hunters sold captives to the Europeans for transportation across the Atlantic. Following the Portuguese in the trade came the Dutch, English, French, and Danes, who eventually established their own trading posts to obtain slaves.

In addition to the economic incentive for slavery, both Christianity and Islam provided a moral justification and legal protection for it. Enslaving others was considered legitimate punishment for unbelievers. Of all the Western religions, only Judaism demonstrated a consistent moral resistance to the slave trade because Jewish identity depended heavily on remembering the biblical account of the enslavement of the ancient Hebrews in Egypt. Notable exceptions were the few Jewish plantation owners in Surinam, who did use slave labor. The problem for Christian and Muslim slavers was that when a slave converted to Christianity or Islam, the pretext for enslavement disappeared. To solve this problem, Christians created a new rationalization by connecting slavery to race. As the African slave trade expanded during the seventeenth and eighteenth centuries, Europeans began to associate slavery with "blackness," which was considered inferior to "whiteness." Among Muslims, the justification for enslavement remained a religious one, and when a slave converted to Islam he or she was, at least theoretically, supposed to be freed.

During the nearly 400 years of the European slave trade (ca. 1500–1870), more than ten million Africans were transported to the Americas, the result of which was that large slices of the Americas were transformed into outposts of sub-Saharan African cultures. Blacks came to outnumber

PLAN OF A SLAVE VESSEL.

THE SLAVE TRADE.

THE motion in the House of Lords made by Lord Denman, on Tuesday night, has naturally revived the interest of the measures for the extinction of this vile traffic of " man-selling and man-stealing." The close of the session is marked by these humane exertions, as was its commencement, in the comprehensive speech of Lord George Bentinck, in the House of Commons, on February 3. His Lordship then held in his hand a communication from Captain Pilkington, of the Royal Navy, on the subject of the slave-trade, accompanied with a plan of one of the slave vessels (which we now Engrave). They were sit-

entertainment enlivened by some most exquisite performances on the national instrument, the harp, much to the delight of all assembled. From the dinner-table the company retired at an early hour to the School-rooms, where the *conversazioni* were held.

WEDNESDAY.

On Wednesday, as the Geological and Natural History Sections were unable to finish the business before them, they each held meetings; but as a great number of members had left Swansea that morning by the *Lord Beresford* steamer, and others were examining the works in the neighbourhood, the Sections were very slightly attended, and the papers communicated were of small general interest.

A dinner, given by Lewis W. Dillwyn, Esq., who is himself one of the oldest members of the Royal Society, may be regarded as the close of the proceedings.

The last General Meeting was held in the afternoon, when it appeared, that, notwithstanding the inferiority of Swansea as respects population, this meeting has added considerably to the funds of the Association.

In concluding our notice of an Association which numbers among its members all the most eminent men in every department of physical and natural science, we cannot but express our satisfaction at the business-like character of this meeting. It is true that it has not startled the word by the announcement of any great discovery ; but it will be found, upon examination, to present a fair average rate of progress. The vulnerable points have been less apparent than hitherto ; and by the exclusion from the sections of all subjects which were not purely scientific, and by particularly avoiding those communications which have frequently been introduced as mere trading advertisements, of which we witnessed but one, that on gutta percha, which in our opinion should not have been required, the Association has placed itself upon exalted ground, and en-

■ The Middle Passage
As human cargo slaves were packed together for the long voyage from a slave-trading post in Africa to the plantation colonies of the Americas.

the native Americans and constituted the majority of the colonial population in most of the Caribbean, and broad parts of coastal Central America, Venezuela, Guyana, and Brazil. Much of the male population of Angola was transported directly to Brazil, a forced migration that resulted in a dramatic excess of females over males in the most heavily depopulated areas of Angola. In the process, Portuguese Brazil became the single largest recipient of African slaves. It was the destination of some 3.6 million Africans—nearly ten times the number brought to all of English-speaking North America.

The slave ships that sailed the infamous Middle Passage across the Atlantic were so unhealthy, with humans "stacked like books on a shelf," that a significant portion of the human cargo died en route. The physical and psychological burdens that slavery placed on its victims can scarcely be imagined, in large part because few slaves were ever allowed to learn to read and write, and thus direct records of their experiences are rare. It is certain, however, that slaves were subjected to unhealthy living conditions, back-breaking work, and demoralization. The plantations of the New World mixed together Africans from different cultures and language groups, making it difficult for slaves to build the solidarity necessary to rebel successfully. In a few places, runaways established their own self-governing communities, such as the Saramakas of Surinam or the Cimarrón republic in Peru, but most found escape impossible because they had no place to go and certainly no way to return to their homeland. Despite these crushing hardships, and even within the harsh confines of white-owned plantations, black slaves created their own institutions, family structures, and cultures.

Biological Exchanges
Europeans certainly perpetuated atrocities in the New World, but the intentional genocide of whole peoples was exceedingly rare. Except for the first colonizers of the Canary Islands, even the most vicious colonizers wanted to enslave or exploit the natives, not destroy them. Nevertheless, the introduction of new diseases to the Americas and the disruption of traditional economies led to a form of unintentional genocide that resulted in the deaths of millions. The European, Asian, and African continents, on the one hand, and the Americas, on the other, had been isolated from each other for so long that they had become two biologically distinct worlds. After the voyages of

Christopher Columbus they were rejoined in ways that—for good or for ill—made them more alike culturally and, especially, biologically. As one historian has put it, the "trend toward biological homogeneity is one of the most important aspects of the history of life on this planet since the retreat of the continental glaciers."[3]

How did a few thousand Europeans so easily conquer the civilizations of the Americas, which were populated by millions of people? After all, the Aztecs, Incas, Tupinambas, and others put up a stubborn resistance to the conquistadores, and yet the Europeans triumphed time after time. The answer: epidemics. Along with their sense of superiority, the conquistadores' most effective allies were the invisible microbes of Old World diseases, such as smallpox. A native of the Yucatán peninsula recalled the better days before the conquest:

> There was then no sickness; they had no aching bones; they had then no high fever; they had then no smallpox; they had then no burning chest; they had then no abdominal pain; they had then no consumption; they had then no headache. At that time the course of humanity was orderly. The foreigners made it otherwise when they arrived here.[4]

Nearly every chronicler of the New World conquests was stunned by the toll that epidemic disease had on the natives soon after their initial contact with Europeans. Between 1520 and 1600, Mexico suffered fourteen major epidemics, and Peru suffered seventeen. By the 1580s the populations of the Caribbean islands, the Antilles, and the lowlands of Mexico and Peru had almost completely died off. Historians estimate the deaths in the tens of millions. The preconquest population of Mexico, which has been estimated at about 19 million, dropped in eighty years to 2.5 million. Even the infrequent contacts between European

fishermen and fur traders with natives on the coast of what is now Canada led to rapid depopulation.

The most deadly culprit was smallpox, but measles, typhus, scarlet fever, and chicken pox also contributed to the devastation. All of these were dangerous and even life-threatening to Europeans and Africans, but from exposure, people of the Old World had either died young or survived the illness with a resistance to infection from the disease. However, native Americans had never been exposed to these diseases, and as a population completely lacked immunities to them. As a result, all it took was for one infected person to arrive from the Old World to kill off many millions in the New World. After Cortés's men were first driven from Tenochtitlán, a Dominican friar reported that a new ally appeared: "When the Christians were exhausted from war, God saw fit to send the Indians smallpox, and there was a great pestilence in the city. . . ."[5] The epidemic undoubtedly impaired the fighting ability of the Aztecs. The Spaniards' immunity to the very diseases that killed off so many Indians reinforced the impression that the Europeans were favored agents of the gods or gods themselves. As a Mayan put it, "we were born to die."[6]

In exchange, the New World gave the Old World syphilis, or at least contemporary Europeans thought so. Historians and epidemiologists have long debated what they call the Columbian question° about the origins of syphilis. Some argue that syphilis or a venereal disease that might be classified as its ancestor came back from the New World with Columbus's sailors; others assert that syphilis was widespread in the Old World long before 1492. We still do not know the answer to the Columbian question, but it is true that after about 1492 there were epidemic outbreaks of sexually transmitted diseases, leading many to assume an American origin.

■ **The Columbian Exchange**
Aztecs fell victim to smallpox epidemics during the sixteenth century.

The exchange of other forms of life was less obviously disastrous. Following the Europeans came a flood of European animals and plants. With the conquistadores came pigs, cattle, goats, sheep, donkeys, and horses—all previously unknown in the New World. Pigs that escaped from the first Spanish ships to land in Florida were the ancestors of the ubiquitous wild razorback pigs of the southern United States. Vast areas of Mexico and Peru depopulated of humans were repopulated with enormous herds of sheep. The cattle herded by the present-day gauchos of Argentina derive from Iberian stock. The characteristic Latin American burro came from Europe as did the horse, which came to be so prized by the plains Indians of North America. Sheep, cattle, and horses, in particular, completely changed the way of life of the native American peoples.

From Europe came the lucrative plantation crops of sugar, cotton, rice, and indigo, crops that required a large supply of field hands. European varieties of wheat, grapes, and olives soon appeared as major crops in Mexico and elsewhere. In exchange, the Americas offered new crops to the Old World such as tobacco, cocoa, paprika, American cotton, pumpkins, beans, maize (corn), and potatoes. European peasant farmers discovered that maize and the potato provided an attractive substitute for wheat. In many places, the potato replaced wheat as the staple in the diet of the poor. By yielding more calories per acre than wheat or virtually any other traditional grain, the potato made it possible to support more people on a given amount of land. With the spread of the potato as a food source, European populations began to increase rapidly, a trend that created population pressures, which in turn stimulated additional European migrations to the Americas.

The Problem of Cultural Diversity

Before Columbus sailed west, Europeans possessed two systems of thought that seemed to explain everything to them—the Aristotelian and the Christian. The ancient Greek philosopher Aristotle and his followers provided a systematic explanation of geography and cosmology based on what they knew of the world. They had named the continents, described their peoples, and estimated the size of the globe. Particularly in the European universities, Aristotle was still considered practically infallible, the primary source of all human knowledge. But Aristotle had not even imagined the Americas, and that fact raised the possibility that he was wrong on other matters as well. He knew nothing of the llama, the potato, or syphilis—common knowledge to even the most ignorant conquistador. Aristotle had assumed that the heat of the equatorial zone was so great that no one could live there, but the Spanish had found great civilizations thriving astride the equator. In 1570, when Joseph de Acosta felt a chill in the tropics on his way to America, he observed, "what could I else do then but laugh at Aristotle's Meteors and his Philosophy."[7] Travelers

to the New World began to realize that the ancients had not known half the truth about the world.

For Christians and Jews, the Bible remained the unchallenged authority on the origins of the whole world, but the New World created numerous problems for biblical interpretation. The book of Genesis told of the creation and the great flood, which had destroyed all people and all animals except those saved in Noah's ark. The New World brought into question that vision of a single creation and cleansing flood simply because it could not explain why the plants and animals of the Americas were so different. If the only animals on Earth were those Noah preserved, then why were they different on the two sides of the Earth? About the New World a French writer asked, "How falls it out that the nations of the world, coming all of one father, Noah, do vary so much from one another, both in body and mind?"[8] Thinkers argued either that there must have been more than one creation or that the great flood must have covered only Palestine rather than the entire Earth. However, these solutions tacitly recognized that a literal reading of the words of Scripture could not produce a satisfactory account of the history of the world.

The greatest conceptual challenge to Christian Europe were the New World peoples themselves. If these people were not the children of God's Creation, then how did they get there? If they were God's children, then why were they so different from Europeans? In the terms available to sixteenth-century thinkers, there were three possible ways to answer these questions. One was to assume that the native Americans were subhumans, demons, or some strange form of animal life. This answer was the most convenient one to those who sought to exploit the natives. Often with little or no foundation, these Europeans believed that the natives practiced devil worship, incest, sexual promiscuity, polygamy, sodomy, and cannibalism—all signs of their demonic nature. If not demons, the natives must be unnatural beasts: wild men, dog men, or satyrs. In this extreme form of European belief, the natives did not even possess a human soul and were neither capable of converting to Christianity nor worthy of human rights. Most European thinkers insisted that the natives must be descendants of Adam and Eve, and thus they possessed souls, could be redeemed, and were subject to divine law. But even among otherwise intelligent thinkers, some of the subhuman prejudice survived. The English philosopher Francis Bacon (1561–1626), who did not wallow in the common intolerance of his day, shared the view that as naked cannibals, Indians had defaced humanity.

A second answer to why the peoples of the New World were so different sprung from a belief that the natives were complete innocents. The native peoples lived in a kind of earthly paradise, unspoiled by the corruption of European society. Some of the early English explorers of Virginia found the natives "most gentle, loving and faithful, void of any guile or treason," and one missionary found them "all the more children of God owing to their very lack of capacity and skill."[9] A tiny number of unconventional theological thinkers hypothesized that the native Americans had been created before the Hebrews as reported in the Bible, and, therefore, had not been subject to the Fall of Man and still lived in the earthly paradise. The English humanist Thomas More (1478–1535) located his Utopia, an imagined ideal community, in the New World to demonstrate how corrupt the social institutions of the Old World had become.

The most influential spokesman during the sixteenth century for this idea of native innocence was the powerful advocate of human rights Bartholomew de Las Casas (1474–1566), the bishop of arid, impoverished Chiapas in Mexico. Throughout his career, Las Casas forcefully argued against the enslavement and ill treatment of the native Americans, which was chronicled in his most important published work, *The Brief Relation of the Destruction of the West Indies* (1542). Through Las Casas's influence, Spanish royal policy toward the Indians became more peaceful and sympathetic. As beneficent as he was toward the natives, however, Las Casas did not accept native culture as in any way equal or superior to European. He merely saw the natives as innocents who needed to be guided rather than forced to accept Christianity and who did not deserve to be slaves. He did not, however, bother to make the same argument on behalf of black Africans.

The third response to the question of how to explain the "differentness" of New World peoples neither dehumanized them nor assumed them innocent but simply recognized their differences as the natural consequence of human diversity. Advocates of this position proposed some form of cultural toleration. The inconvenient facts of the New World brought to the forefront the inadequacy of traditional moral standards for judging the behavior of other people. Deciding whether a particular people were bad or good raised questions about the criteria for making such judgments, and these questions introduced the principle of cultural relativism. Cultural relativism° recognized that many (but not necessarily all) standards of judgment are specific to particular cultures rather than the fixed truths established by natural or divine law. In our own society, cultural relativists attempt to understand why other people think and act the way they do before they judge them. Such an approach can be traced to a small group of sixteenth-century European thinkers who tried to make sense of the new discoveries. Perplexed by the cultural diversity he had observed in the New World, Peter Martyr D'Anghiera (1457–1526), a pious priest and astute historian of Spanish explorations, noted that different peoples made judgments on the basis of different criteria: "the Ethiopian thinks the black color to be fairer than the white, and the white man thinks otherwise.... The bearded man supposes he is more comely than he that wants a beard. As appetite therefore moves, not as reason persuades, men run into these vanities, and every province is ruled by its own sense...."[10] What others thought fundamental moral truths, Martyr considered manifestations of superficial cultural differences.

The most eloquent voice for cultural toleration during the sixteenth century was Michel de Montaigne (1533–1592), the brilliant French essayist. After a career as a hardworking public official, he retired at age 38 to his estate to a life of study and contemplation. Among his many interests, he especially loved to read about travels to the New World. His essay "On Cannibals" pointed to the hypocrisy of Christians who condemned the alleged cannibalism of the native Americans but justified the torture and murder of other Christians over some minor theological dispute. Montaigne argued that a truly ethical, truly Christian person was not a rigid follower of biblical laws but was capable of understanding and tolerating cultural differences. The discovery in the New World that non-Christians could lead moral lives, love their families, practice humility and charity, and benefit from highly developed religious institutions shook the complacent sense of European superiority.

THE CAPITALIST GLOBAL ECONOMY

During the sixteenth century a truly global economy began to take shape as a consequence of the European encounters with the rest of the world. As the Europeans sailed the oceans of the world in search of profits, they pioneered a new form of economic organization—agrarian capitalism°. In agrarian capitalism Europeans organized the production of certain kinds of commercial crops, such as sugar, tobacco, and indigo, which were raised for sale to an expanding population in Europe. With land expropriated from native peoples in the Atlantic islands, the Americas, and parts of Asia, European capitalists began to raise commercial crops on an unprecedented scale. Unlike other forms of capitalism, which relied on workers who were paid a wage, agrarian capitalism relied on slave labor, mostly provided by transplanted Africans.

Agrarian capitalism depended on the creation of European empires—the settler colonies, plantation colonies, and trading post empires of the Portuguese, Spanish, Dutch, French, English, and Russians. These empires, however, were very different from those of the ancient world, medieval Europe, preconquest Americas, and Asia. In ancient Rome, medieval Byzantium, and early modern China, for example, imperial governments promoted monopolies and inhibited free access to the market and thus stymied the development of capitalism. These empires produced economic stagnation instead of growth. But in the European global empires of the sixteenth century, the organization of trade and the division of labor took place outside the authority of any one state, a fact that made it impossible for a single imperial government to monopolize completely economic resources. It was the competition among imperialist states, rather than control by a single powerful empire, that was new.

The creation of the European empires during the sixteenth century made it possible for capitalists to maximize their profits through regional specialization. Western Europe became the *core* of the global economy, the center of a complex variety of economic activities and institutions—banking, insurance, trade companies, gun manufacture, shipbuilding, and the production of cloth. In Europe agriculture was more and more devoted exclusively to producing food, and the labor supply was free—neither serfs, as had been the case in the Middle Ages, nor slaves, as was the case in parts of the Americas. The distant colonies, especially in Spanish and Portuguese America, became the *periphery* devoted to raising single cash crops, such as sugar, tobacco, cotton, coffee, or indigo for dyes. Agriculture in the periphery was produced on large estates by slaves.

The capitalist global economy has steadily and relentlessly expanded throughout the world since the sixteenth century. Much of the subsequent history of Western civilization can be understood only in terms of the triumph of capitalism and the economic integration of a world dominated by Westerners. The capitalist global economy has yielded many benefits in enhancing the material well-being of the middle classes of the West, increasing the available food supply of the world, and stimulating technological innovation. But there have been costs. Since the sixteenth century, the gap between rich and poor individuals and rich and poor countries has widened, and societies on the agrarian periphery have found it enormously difficult to break out of their disadvantaged position in the world economy.

CONCLUSION
The Significance of the Global Encounters

The world was forever changed by the European voyages from about 1450 to 1650. The significance of these encounters lay not so much in the Europeans' geographical discoveries as in the scale of permanent contact these voyages made possible among previously isolated peoples of the world. Europeans had been to the Americas before Columbus, and the Chinese had earlier engaged in long-distance voyages of reconnaissance as far as the east coast of Africa. But none of these early voyages had created a lasting economic system or lasting cultural contacts. The European voyages of the fifteenth and sixteenth centuries did.

As a result of the Portuguese slaving enterprises on the coast of West and Central Africa, millions of Africans were uprooted, transported in chains to a strange land, and forced to toil in subhuman conditions on plantations. There they grew crops for the increasingly affluent European consumers and generated profits often used to buy more slaves in Africa, parts of which became depopulated in the process. In Europe until the nineteenth century, every cup of coffee, every puff of tobacco, every sugar candy, and every cotton dress of indigo blue came from the sweat of a black slave.

Many of the native Americans lost their lives, their land, and their way of life as a result of European encounters. The most isolated of them retained their languages and religion, but other groups were assimilated to the point of nearly complete cultural loss. Everywhere in the Americas, native peoples suffered from the invasion of Old World microbes even more than from the invasion of Old World conquerors. The destruction of the Aztec and Incan empires were certainly the most dramatic, but everywhere native peoples struggled to adapt to an invasion of foreign beings from a foreign world.

Asia was far less altered by contact with Europeans. The most thorough Asian conquest—the Russians in Siberia—was of the least populated region of the entire Asian continent. European civilization remained on the cultural periphery of Asia. But European access to Asian luxury goods remained a crucial component in the expanding global economy that became one of the first fruits of European capitalism.

Coming to terms with the variety of world cultures became a persistent and absorbing problem in Western civilization. Most Europeans retained confidence in the inherent superiority of their civilization, but the realities of the world began to chip away at that confidence, and economic globalization profoundly altered Western civilization itself. Westerners began to confront the problem of understanding "other" cultures and in so doing changed themselves. The West came to mean less a place in Europe than a certain kind of culture that was exported throughout the world through conversion to Christianity, the acquisition of Western languages, and the spread of Western technology.

Suggestions for Further Reading

For a comprehensive list of suggested readings, please go to www.ablongman.com/levack/chapter12

Chaudhuri, K. N. *Trade and Civilization in the Indian Ocean: An Economic History from the Rise of Islam to 1750.* 1985. Arguing for the long-term unity of trade routes, the book lays out the importance of Asian merchants to maritime trade networks from the South China Sea to the Mediterranean.

Clendinnen, Inga. *Aztecs: An Interpretation.* 1991. A provocative, sometimes disturbing book that directly confronts the implications of human sacrifice and cannibalism among the Aztecs and offers an explanation for it by analyzing Aztec religion.

Crosby, Jr., Alfred W. *The Columbian Exchange: Biological and Cultural Consequences of 1492.* 1973. The most significant study on the implications of the biological exchanges for the cultural history of both the Old and New Worlds. It has the benefit of being an exciting book to read.

Curtin, Philip D. *African History: From Earliest Times to Independence.* 1995. An excellent survey by one of the most distinguished comparative historians.

Elvin, Mark. *The Pattern of the Chinese Past: A Social and Economic Interpretation.* 1973. An excellent overview of Chinese history that covers Chinese responses to Western encounters.

Fernández-Armesto, Felipe. *Before Columbus: Exploration and Colonization from the Mediterranean to the Atlantic, 1229–1492.* 1987. Engagingly written and original in scope, this is the best single account of early European colonization efforts.

Fernández-Armesto, Felipe. *Columbus.* 1991. The 500th anniversary of Columbus's voyage in 1492 provoked a wide-ranging reappraisal of his motives and career. This pithy, engaging book is by far the most convincing in revising Columbus's image, but it deflated much of the Columbus myth and caused considerable controversy.

Oliver, Roland. *The African Experience from Olduvai Gorge to the 21st Century.* 2000. A highly readable general survey.

Pagden, Anthony. *European Encounters with the New World: From Renaissance to Romanticism.* 1993. A fascinating examination of how Europeans interpreted their encounters with America.

Parry, J. H. *The Age of Reconnaissance.* 1982. An analysis of European shipping technology and the causes behind European explorations. It covers all the major voyages.

Parry, J. H. *The Spanish Seaborne Empire.* 1990. The standard study on the subject. It brings together an enormous range of material and presents it clearly and cogently.

Phillips, Jr., William D., and Carla Rahn Phillips. *The Worlds of Christopher Columbus.* 1992. A balanced analysis of Columbus's attempts to find financing for his voyage that pays equal attention to his personal ambition, Christian zeal, and navigational skills.

Notes

1. Christopher Columbus, quoted in Felipe Fernández-Armesto, *Columbus* (1991), 154.
2. Sir Arthur Helps, *The Spanish Conquest in America,* vol. 1 (1900), 1, 264–267.
3. Alfred W. Crosby, Jr., *The Columbian Exchange: Biological and Cultural Consequences of 1492* (1972), 3.
4. *The Book of Chilam Balam of Chumayel,* ed. and trans. Ralph L. Roy (1933), 83.
5. *The Conquistadores: First-Person Accounts of the Conquest of Mexico,* ed. and trans. Patricia de Fuentes (1963), 159.
6. *The Annals of the Cakchiquels and Title of the Lords of Totnicapán,* trans. Adrian Recinos, Dioniscio José Chonay, and Delia Goetz (1953), 116.
7. Quoted in Margaret T. Hodgen, *Early Anthropology in the Sixteenth and Seventeenth Centuries* (1964), 9.
8. Quoted in ibid., 207. Spelling has been modernized.
9. Quoted in ibid., 369.
10. Quoted in ibid., 373–374. Spelling and syntax have been modernized.

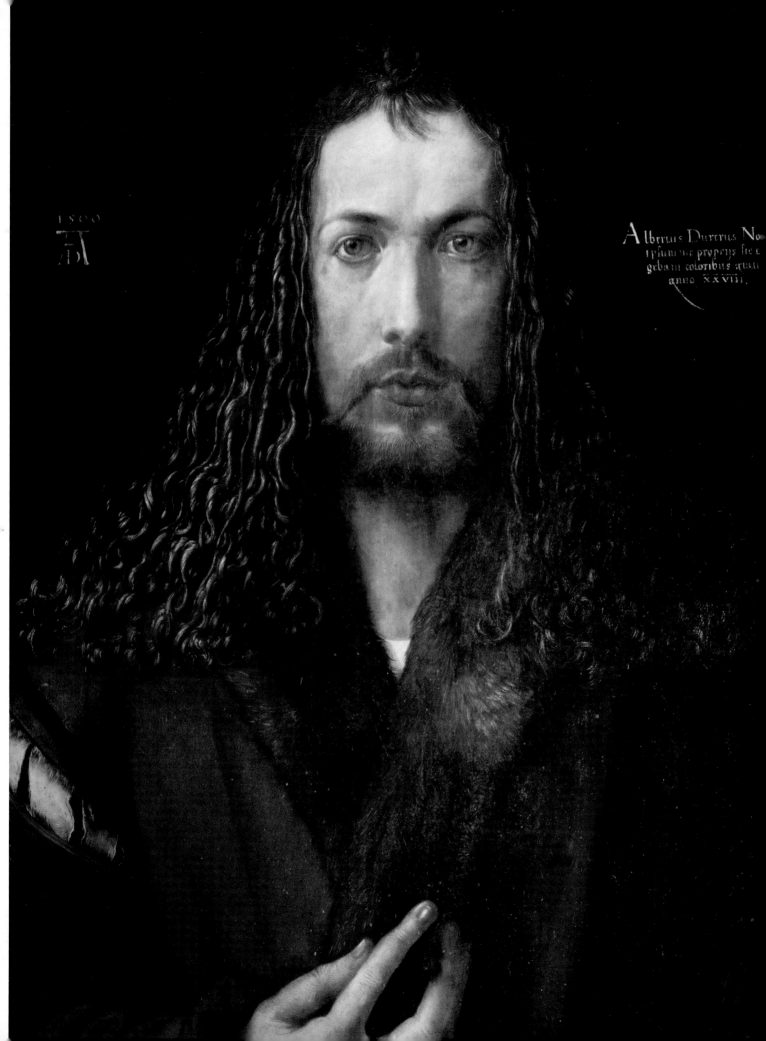

The Reformation of Religion, 1500–1560

O N OCTOBER 31, 1517, AN OBSCURE MONK-TURNED-UNIVERSITY-PROFESSOR nailed on the door of the cathedral in Wittenberg, Germany, an announcement containing ninety-five theses or debating propositions. Professor Martin Luther had no hint of the ramifications of this simple act—as common then as posting an announcement for a lecture or concert on a university bulletin board now. But Luther's seemingly harmless deed would spark a revolution. Within weeks all Germany was ablaze over what was widely seen as Luther's daring attack on the pope. Within a few short years Wittenberg became the European center for a movement to reform the Church. As the pope and high churchmen resisted the call for reform, much of Germany and eventually most of northern Europe and Britain broke away from the Catholic Church in a movement called the Protestant Reformation, which dominated European affairs from 1517 until 1555.

Martin Luther was successful because he expressed in print what many felt in their hearts—that the Church was failing in its most fundamental obligation to help Christians achieve salvation. In contrast, many Catholics considered the Protestants dangerous heretics who offended God with their errors. The division between Protestants and Catholics split the West into two distinctive religious cultures. The result was that the hard-won unity of the West, which had been achieved during the Middle Ages through the expansion of Christianity to the most distant corners of the European continent, was lost. Catholics and Protestants continued to share a great deal of the Christian tradition, but two fateful issues divided them: the Latin liturgy and obedience to the pope. After the Reformation of the sixteenth century, the common Christian culture was permanently severed by the Protestants' abandonment of Latin in the liturgy and their refusal to accept the authority of the pope.

Chapter Outline

- Causes of the Reformation
- The Lutheran Reformation
- The Diversity of Protestantism
- The Catholic and Counter Reformations
- The Reformation in the Arts

The Imitation of Christ: In Albrecht Dürer's self-portrait at age 28, he literally shows himself imitating Christ's appearance. The initials AD are prominently displayed in the upper left-hand corner. They stand for Albrecht Dürer but also for *anno domini*, "the year of our Lord."

Throughout western Europe, countries officially became either Catholic or Protestant—a situation that enforced obedience to the official faith through the police powers of the state and caused considerable suffering among adherents to unofficial religions. The fundamental conflict during the Reformation was about religion, but religion can never be entirely separated from politics or society. The competition among the kingdoms and the social tensions within the cities of central and northern Europe magnified the religious controversies, making the Reformation a broad cultural movement that seeped into all aspects of life.

This chapter will explore the Reformation controversies by addressing five central questions: (1) What caused the religious rebellion that began in German-speaking lands and spread to much of northern Europe? (2) How did the Lutheran Reformation create a new kind of religious culture? (3) How and why did Protestant denominations multiply to such an extent in northern Europe and Britain? (4) How did the Catholic Church respond to the unprecedented threat to its dominance of religious authority in the West? (5) How did the religious turmoil of the sixteenth century transform the role of the visual arts and music in public life?

Causes of the Reformation

························ ▬ ························

The Protestant Reformation was the culmination of nearly 200 years of turmoil within the Church. As we saw in Chapter 10, during the fourteenth and fifteenth centuries the Church was especially hampered by the contradiction between its divine mission and its obligations in this world. On the one hand, the Church taught that its mission was otherworldly, as the source of spiritual solace and the guide to eternal salvation. On the other hand, the Church was thoroughly of this world. It owned vast amounts of property, maintained a far-reaching judicial bureaucracy to enforce canon (Church) law, and was headed by the pope, who was also the territorial prince of the Papal State in central Italy. Whereas from the eleventh to the thirteenth centuries the popes had been the source of moral reform and spiritual renewal in the Church, by the fifteenth century they had become part of the problem. The problem was not so much that they had become corrupt but that they were unable to respond effectively to the demands of ordinary people who were increasingly concerned with their own salvation and the effective government of their communities.

Three developments, in particular, contributed to the demand for religious reform: the search for the freedom of private religious expression; the print revolution; and the Northern Renaissance interest in the Bible and sources of Christianity.

THE SEARCH FOR SPIRITUAL AND FISCAL FREEDOM

A series of events during the fourteenth century had weakened the authority of the popes and driven the Church to the point of splitting apart, more for political than theological reasons (see Chapter 10). Between 1305 and 1378 seven popes in a row abandoned Rome, which was plagued by dangerous feuds among its aristocratic families, and chose to reside in the relative calm of Avignon, France. The period came to be called the Babylonian Captivity of the Church, a pejorative term that reflected the opinion that the popes had become subservient to the kings of France. The loss of revenues from the Papal State in Italy forced the financial advisers of the popes into various shady financial schemes, which undermined the moral reputation of the papacy. The Babylonian Captivity was followed by an equally contentious period between 1378 and 1417, the Great Schism, when the Church was divided over allegiance to rival Italian and French popes, and eventually to three and four competing popes.

The degradation of the papacy during the Babylonian Captivity and the Great Schism led to the Conciliar Movement, an attempt by a group of bishops to solve the schism and to liberate the Church from the abuses of papal authority. The conciliarists argued that at a general meeting or council (hence, "conciliar"), the Church bishops would have authority over the pope and could depose him and arrange for the election of a new pope. Accordingly, the Council of Constance (1414–1417) ended the Great Schism, and the Council of Basel (1431–1449) voted for reforms. But the reforms were never implemented because of the uncompromising attitude of Pope Eugeneus IV (1431–1447). The failure of the moderate reforms of the Council of Basel opened the way for the more radical rejection of papal authority during the Protestant Reformation of the sixteenth century.

While the papacy's moral authority precipitously declined, lay Christians were drawn to new forms of worship. Particularly influential were the Modern Devotion, which was promoted by the Brothers of the Common Life, and the *Imitation of Christ*, written by a Common Life brother about 1441. By emphasizing frequent private prayer and moral introspection, the *Imitation* provided a kind of spiritual manual that helped laypeople follow the same path toward spiritual renewal that traditionally had been reserved for monks and nuns. The goal was to imitate Christ so thoroughly that Christ entered the believer's soul. For example, the 1500 self-portrait of Albrecht Dürer (1471–1528), a work influenced by the Modern Devotion, portrayed the artist as if he were Christ himself.

The religious fervor that drew many Christians to such profound forms of religious expression led them to question the moral authority of the papacy. They began to see the pope as a thieving foreigner who extorted money that could be better spent locally. German communities, in particular, protested against the financial demands and the questionable practices of the pope and higher clergy. Some bishops neglected their duties regarding the spiritual guidance of their flock. Some never resided in their dioceses (the district under the bishop's care), knew nothing of the problems of their people, and were concerned only with retaining their incomes and lavish living standards. Living amid the pleasures of Rome, these high clergymen were in no position to discipline parish priests, some of whom also ignored their moral responsibilities by living openly with concubines and even selling the sacraments. Although immorality of this sort was probably not widespread, a few notorious examples bred enormous resentment among the laity.

In an effort to assert control over the church in their own communities, city officials known as magistrates attempted to stem the financial drain and end clerical abuses. They restricted the amount of property ecclesiastical institutions could own, tried to tax the clergy, made priests subject to the town's courts of law, and eliminated the churchmen's exemption from burdensome duties, such as serving in the town militia or providing labor for public works. On the eve of the Reformation—especially in the cities of Germany and the Netherlands—magistrates had already begun to assert local control over the church, a tendency that prepared the way for the Protestants' efforts. For many laypeople, the overriding desire was to obtain greater spiritual and fiscal freedom from the Church.

THE PRINT REVOLUTION

Until the mid-fifteenth century, the only way in the West to reproduce any kind of text—a short business record or a long philosophical book—was to copy it laboriously by hand. As medieval scribes made copies on parchment, however, they often introduced errors or "improved" the original text as they saw fit. Thus, two different copies of the same text could read differently. Parchment books were also very expensive; a book as long as the Bible might require the skins of 300 sheep to make the parchment sheets and hundreds of hours of labor to copy the text. The high cost meant that books were limited to churchmen and to the very rich. Few Christians ever actually read the Bible simply because Bibles—like all books—were so rare.

Two fifteenth-century inventions revolutionized the availability of books. First, movable metal type was introduced around 1450, and after that time printed books first began to appear. Perhaps the very first was a Bible printed by Johannes Gutenberg in Mainz, Germany. Equally important, cheap manufactured paper replaced expensive sheepskins. These two developments reduced the cost of books to a level that made them available even to artisans of modest incomes.

■ The Printer
This woodcut depicts the new printing press. The verse that accompanied the woodcut celebrated the skills of the printer and the new art of printing.

The demand for inexpensive printed books was astounding. During the first forty years of print, more books were produced than had been copied by scribes during the previous thousand years. By 1500, presses in more than 200 cities and towns had printed six million books. Half of the titles were on religious subjects, and because the publishing industry (then as now) produced only what people wanted to buy, the predominance of religion is a telling indication of what was on the minds of the reading public.

The buyers of printed books included, of course, the traditionally literate classes of university students, churchmen, professionals, and aristocratic intellectuals. Remarkably, however, there was also an enormous demand among people for whom books had previously been an unimaginable luxury. During the fourteenth and fifteenth centuries literacy rates had steadily risen and the power of literate culture was strongly felt even by those who could not write. For example, an illiterate farmer near Siena, Italy, had someone else keep a farming diary for him because he recognized that a written record would give him greater power over his own affairs. Literacy rates varied enormously across Europe. They were highest in the cities, especially in northern Italy, Germany, and the Netherlands. In the rural areas, literacy was still rare, probably limited to the village priest, the notary, and perhaps the local nobility. Everywhere men were more often literate than women. However, the knowledge of what was in books spread widely beyond the literate few. The reason was that reading for most people in the fifteenth and sixteenth centuries was an oral, public activity rather than a silent, private one. In parish churches, taverns, and private houses the literate read books out loud to others for their entertainment and edification.

The expansion of the university system during this period also created more demand for books. Between 1300 and 1500 the number of European universities grew from twenty to seventy. The universities also developed a new way of reading. During the fifteenth century the Sorbonne in Paris and Oxford University decreed that libraries were to be quiet places, an indication of the spread of silent reading among the most highly educated classes. Compared to the tradition of reading aloud, silent reading was faster and more private. The silent reader learned more quickly and also decided independently the meaning of what had been read. Once many cheap books were available to the silent readers among the best educated, the interpretation of texts, especially the notoriously difficult text of the Bible, could no longer be easily regulated.

Would the Reformation have succeeded without the print revolution? It is impossible to imagine that it could have. Print culture radically changed how information was disseminated and gave people new ways to interpret their experiences. Between 1517 and 1520, Martin Luther wrote some thirty tracts, mostly in a riveting colloquial German; 300,000 copies were printed and distributed throughout Europe. No other author's ideas had ever spread so fast to so many.

THE NORTHERN RENAISSANCE AND THE CHRISTIAN HUMANISTS

As we saw in Chapter 11, the humanists were writers devoted to rediscovering the lost works of antiquity and imitating the style of the best Greek and Latin authors of the ancient world. As the humanists examined these ancient texts, they developed the study of philology, of how the meanings of words change over time. These endeavors stimulated a new kind of approach to the sources of Christianity. The humanist Lorenzo Valla (ca. 1407–1457), for example, evaluated the historical sources of papal authority, including the Donation of Constantine—a document that provided the legal justification for the Papal State and papal assertions of supreme authority in Italy. Because the Donation of Constantine used words that were not cur-

rent during the time when it was supposedly written, Valla argued that it was a forgery. He went on to question the accuracy of the Vulgate, the Latin translation of the Bible accepted by the Church.

The humanists who specialized in subjecting the Bible to philological study are called the Christian humanists°. In examining the sources of Christianity, their goal was not to criticize Christianity or the Church but to understand the precise meaning of its founding texts, especially the Bible and the writings of the Church fathers, who wrote in Greek and Latin and commented on the Bible during the early centuries of Christianity. The Christian humanists sought to correct what they saw as mistakes in interpreting Christian doctrine. They believed that the path to personal morality and to Church reform lay in imitating "the primitive church," which meant the practices of Christianity at the time of Jesus and the apostles. Most of the Christian humanists came from northern Europe. They constituted the most influential wing of the Northern Renaissance, a movement that built on the foundations of the Italian Renaissance. Through their efforts, the foundations of Christianity came under intense scrutiny during the early sixteenth century.

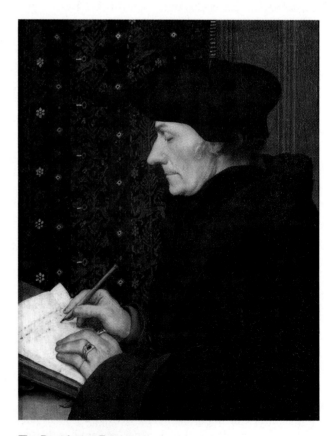

■ **Desiderius Erasmus**
This portrait showing the great humanist writing was painted by Hans Holbein the Younger in 1523.

By far the most influential of the Christian humanists was a Dutchman, Desiderius Erasmus (ca. 1469–1536). To remedy the evils of the world, Erasmus became an ardent advocate of education, especially for future priests, whom he wanted to learn "the philosophy of Christ." As a guide to that philosophy, he published an annotated text of the Greek New Testament, which he opened with the optimistic preface: "If the Gospel were truly preached, the Christian people would be spared many wars." He later translated the Greek New Testament into a new Latin version. His critical studies were the basis of many translations of the Hebrew and Greek Bible into vernacular languages, including the popular English translation, the King James Bible.

Exploiting the potential of the relatively new printing industry, Erasmus became the most inspiring moral critic of his times. During times of war he eloquently called for peace; he published a practical manual for helping children develop a sense of morality; and he laid out easy-to-follow guidelines for spiritual renewal in the *Handbook for the Militant Christian*. He was most popular for his biting criticisms of the Church that revealed a genuine spiritual sorrow shared by many of his readers:

> *I could see that the common body of Christians was corrupt not only in its affections but in its ideas. I pondered on the fact that those who profess themselves pastors and doctors for the most part misuse these titles, which belong to Christ, for their own advantage. . . . Is there any religious man who does not see with sorrow that this generation is far the most corrupt there has ever been?*[1]

Erasmus's penchant for moral criticism reached the level of high satire in his masterpiece, *The Praise of Folly* (1514). In it he attacked theologians preoccupied by silly questions, such as how many angels could dance on the head of a pin; he lampooned corrupt priests who took money from dying men to read the last rites; he ridiculed gullible pilgrims who bought phony relics as tourist souvenirs; and he parodied the vanity of monks who thought the color of their robes more important than helping the poor. He saved some of his most biting sarcasm for the monks by pointing out "their filthiness, their ignorance, their bawdiness, and their insolence."[2]

Despite these criticisms Erasmus refused to abandon Catholicism and engaged in a very public conflict with Luther and the Protestants. He thought the militants on both sides were driven more by egotism than by Christian humility. In the combative age of the Reformation, Erasmus

■ **Albrecht Dürer, *The Knight, Death, and the Devil***

This engraving of 1513 illustrates Erasmus's *Handbook for the Militant Christian* by depicting a knight steadfastly advancing through a frightening landscape. A figure of death holds an hourglass, indicating that the knight's time on Earth is limited. A devil follows behind him threateningly. His valiant horse and loyal dog represent the virtues that a pious Christian must acquire.

stood virtually alone as a voice of peace and moderation, and like many nonviolent men since that time, he was deeply hated. His lasting fame, however, rests on his perceptive philological analysis of the Bible and other early Christian texts. But he was also an eloquent popularizer, someone who demonstrated to a large public how individuals could apply to their daily lives previously obscure trends in humanist learning and how a better understanding of the Bible could purify faith and combat corruption within the Church.

Erasmus's friend, the Englishman Thomas More (1478–1535), is best known for his book, *Utopia* (1516). More's little book established the genre of utopian fiction, which describes imaginary, idealized worlds. It depicted a fantasy island in the New World, "Utopia," which in Greek

THOMAS MORE'S ARGUMENT AGAINST CAPITAL PUNISHMENT

....

In sixteenth-century England, there were literally hundreds of offenses, including simple theft, that could lead to capital punishment. Among the many aspects of contemporary society that Thomas More criticized in Utopia *(1516), capital punishment especially offended him because it was so clearly prohibited in the Bible. More combined moral precepts derived from Scripture and reasoned argument, a combination that is especially characteristic of the Christian humanists. Thomas More was himself a victim of capital punishment, executed by the courts of King Henry VIII.*

God said, "Thou shalt not kill"—does the theft of a little money make it quite all right for us to do so? If it's said that this commandment applies only to illegal killing, what's to prevent human beings from similarly agreeing among themselves to legalize certain types of rape, adultery, or perjury? Considering that God has forbidden us even to kill ourselves, can we really believe that purely human arrangements for the regulation of mutual slaughter are enough, without any divine author-

ity, to exempt executioners from the sixth commandment? Isn't that rather like saying that this particular commandment has no more validity than human laws allow it?—in which case the principle can be extended indefinitely, until in all spheres of life human beings decide just how far God's commandments may conveniently be observed.

. . .

Well, those are my objections on moral grounds. From a practical point of view, surely it's obvious that to punish thieves and murderers in precisely the same way is not only absurd but also highly dangerous for the public. If a thief knows that a conviction for murder will get him into no more trouble than a conviction for theft, he's naturally impelled to kill the person that he'd otherwise merely have robbed. It's no worse to him if he's caught, and it gives him a better chance of not being caught, and of concealing the crime altogether by eliminating the only witness. So in our efforts to terrorize thieves we're actually encouraging them to murder innocent people.

Source: From *Utopia*, by Thomas More, translated by Paul Turner (Penguin Classics, 1961). Copyright © 1961 by Paul Turner. Reproduced by permission of Penguin Books Ltd.

---

means "nowhere." Utopia was inhabited by monotheists who, although not Christians, intuitively understood pure religion, lived a highly regulated life, and shared their property in common. Utopia represented More's understanding of what a society based on the primitive church might look like. In particular he took the idea of abolishing all private property from Scripture, which states that the believers in Christ "were of one heart and soul, and no one claimed private ownership of any possessions, but everything they owned was held in common" (Acts 4:32). More shared some of Erasmus's ideas about the critical study of Scripture and a purer Church, but unlike Erasmus he was no pacifist. In his capacity as chancellor of England, he ruthlessly persecuted Protestants.

Erasmus and More remained loyal Catholics, and, as we shall see in the discussion of the English Reformation, More even sacrificed his own life to the faith. Nevertheless, their work helped popularize some of the principles that came to be associated with the Protestant reformers. To them, the test for the legitimacy of any religious practice was twofold: First, could it be found in the Bible; second, did it promote moral behavior? The Christian humanists' preoccupation with textual criticism focused attention on the sources of Christianity, and some were profoundly shaken by the deep disparity they perceived between the Christianity of the New Testament and the state of the Church in their own time.

The Lutheran Reformation

.... ▬ ....

The Protestant Reformation began with the protests of Martin Luther against the pope and certain Church practices. Like Erasmus and More, Luther used the Bible as the litmus test of what the Church should do. If a practice could not be found in the Bible, Luther thought, then it should not be considered Christian. But unlike Erasmus and More, he also introduced theological innovations that made compromise with the papacy impossible.

Luther and his followers would not have succeeded without the support of the local political authorities, who had their own grievances against the pope and the Holy Roman Emperor. The Lutheran Reformation first spread in Germany with the assistance and encouragement of those local authorities: the town magistrates and the territorial princes. Luther's ideas had a magnetic appeal to a wide spectrum of the population, especially women and peasants. When the peasants thought that Luther's ideas about the freedom of the Christian also meant economic freedom, they revolted against their feudal lords. The violence of that revolt forced Luther to retreat and to back the forces of order, the lords and princes. In so doing he made it clear that the Reformation was not to be a social revolution but a religious reform. Lutheranism would not threaten the established political order. Under the sponsorship of princes and kings, Lutheranism spread from Germany into Scandinavia.

MARTIN LUTHER AND THE BREAK WITH ROME

Martin Luther (1483–1546) suffered a grim childhood and uneasy relationship with his father, a miner who wanted his son to become a lawyer. During a break from the University of Erfurt where he was studying law, Luther was thrown from his horse in a storm and nearly died. That frightening experience impelled him to become a monk, a decision that infuriated his father because it meant young Luther abandoned a promising professional career. By becoming a monk, Luther replaced the control of his father with obedience to his superiors in the Augustinian Order. They sent him back to the University of Erfurt for advanced study in theology and then transferred him from the lovely garden city of Erfurt to Wittenberg in Saxony, a scruffy town "on the edge of beyond," as Luther described it. At Wittenberg Luther began to teach at an undistinguished university, far from the intellectual action. Instead of lamenting his isolation, Luther brought the world to his university by making it the center of the religious reform movement.

As a monk, Luther had been haunted by a deep lack of self-worth: "In the monastery, I did not think about women, or gold, or goods, but my heart trembled, and doubted how God could be gracious to me. Then I fell away from faith, and let myself think nothing less than that I had come under the Wrath of God, whom I must reconcile with my good works."[3] Obsessed by the fear that no amount of charitable good works, prayers, or religious ceremonies would compensate for God's contempt of him, Luther suffered from anxiety attacks and prolonged periods of depression. He understood his psychic turmoil and shaky faith as any monk would—the temptations of the Devil, who was a very powerful figure in Luther's life.

Over a number of years, while preparing and revising his university lectures on St. Paul, Luther gradually worked out a solution to his own spiritual crisis by reexamining the theology of penance. The sacrament of penance provided a way to confess sins and receive absolution for them. If a penitent had lied, for example, he could seek forgiveness for the sin by feeling sorry about it, confessing it to a priest, and receiving a penalty, usually a specified number of prayers. Penance took care of only those penalties the Church could inflict on sinners; God's punishment for sins would take place in Purgatory (a place of temporary suffering for dead souls) and at the Last Judgment. But Catholic theology held that penance in this world would reduce punishment in the next. In wrestling with the concept of penance, Luther long meditated on the meaning of a difficult passage in St. Paul's Epistle to the Romans (1:17): "The just shall live by faith." Luther came to understand this passage to mean that eternal salvation came not from performing the religious good works of penance but as a gift from God. That gift was called "grace" and was completely unmerited. In other words, corrupt humans were incapable of earning eternal salvation, but God in his love for humanity promised to give it to a select few, the "Elect." Luther called this process of receiving God's grace "justification by faith alone°," because the ability to have faith in Christ was a sign that one was among the Elect.

Luther's emphasis on justification by faith alone left no room for human free will in obtaining salvation, because Luther believed that faith could come only from God's grace. This did not mean that God controlled every human action, but it did mean that humans could not will to do good. They needed God's help. Those blessed with God's grace would naturally perform good works. This way of thinking about God's grace had a long tradition going back to St. Augustine, the Church father whose work profoundly influenced Luther's own thought. In the turmoil of the Reformation, however, Luther's interpretation of St. Augustine separated Lutheran from Catholic theology. The issue of free will became one of the most crucial differences between Protestants and Catholics.

For Luther this seemingly bleak doctrine of denying the human will to do good was tremendously liberating. He no longer had to worry whether he was doing enough to please God or could muster enough energy to fight the Devil. All he had to do was trust in God's grace. After this breakthrough, Luther reported that "I felt myself to be born anew, and to enter through open gates into paradise itself. From here, the whole face of the Scriptures was altered."[4]

The Ninety-Five Theses

In 1517 Luther became embroiled in a controversy that led to the separation of him and his followers from the Roman Catholic Church. In order to finance the building of a new St. Peter's Basilica in Rome, Pope Leo X had issued a special new indulgence. An indulgence was a particular form of penance whereby a sinner could remove years of punishment in Purgatory after death by performing a good work here on Earth. For example, pilgrims to Rome or Jerusalem were often in search of indulgences, which were concrete measures of the value of their penances. Indulgences formed one of the most intimate bonds between the Church and the laity because they offered a means for the forgiveness of specific sins.

During the fourteenth century popes in need of ready cash had begun to sell indulgences. But Pope Leo's new indulgence went far beyond the promise of earlier indulgences by offering a one-time-only opportunity to escape penalties for all sins. Moreover, the special indulgence could apply not only to the purchaser but to the dead already in Purgatory. The new indulgence immediately made all other indulgences worthless because it removed all penalties for sin whereas others removed only some of them.

Frederick the Wise, the Elector of Saxony (a princely title indicating that he was one of those who elected the emperors of the Holy Roman Empire) and the patron of Martin Luther's university, prohibited the sale of Pope Leo's special indulgence in Electoral Saxony, but it was sold just a few miles away from Wittenberg, across the border in the domain of Archbishop Albrecht of Mainz. Albrecht needed the revenues that the sale of indulgences would bring because he was in debt. He had borrowed enormous sums to bribe Pope Leo to allow him to hold simultaneously three ecclesiastical offices—a practice that was against Church law. To help Albrecht repay his debts, the pope allowed Albrecht to keep half of the revenue from the indulgence sale in his territories. Wittenbergers began to trek over the border to Albrecht's lands to listen to the sales pitch from the shameless indulgence hawker, the Dominican John Tetzel (1470–1519). Tetzel staged an ecclesiastical version of a carnival barker's act in which he harangued the crowd about their dead parents who could be immediately released from the flames of Purgatory for the sacrifice of a few coins. He allegedly ended his sermons with the notorious jingle,

> *As soon as gold in the basin rings,*
> *Right then the soul to heaven springs.*[5]

Some of the Wittenbergers who heard Tetzel asked Martin Luther for his advice about buying the indulgence. Luther responded less as a pastor offering comforting advice to his flock than as a university professor keen for debate. He prepared in Latin ninety-five theses—arguments or talking points—about indulgences that he announced he was willing to defend in an academic disputation. Luther had a few copies printed and posted one on the door of Wittenberg Cathedral. The Ninety-Five Theses were hardly revolutionary in themselves. They argued a simple point that salvation could not be bought and sold, a proposition that was sound, conservative theology; and they explicitly accepted the authority of the pope even as they set limits on that authority. On that point, Luther was merely following what the Church councils of the fifteenth century had decreed. Luther's tone was moderate. He simply suggested that Pope Leo may have been misled in issuing the new indulgence. No one showed up to debate Luther, but someone translated the Ninety-Five Theses into German and printed them, and within a few weeks, a previously unknown professor from an obscure university was the talk of the German lands.

The Dominicans counterattacked. Tetzel himself drew up opposing theses, which provoked a public clamor that Luther had tried to avoid. In 1519 at Leipzig before a raucous crowd of university students, Luther finally debated the theses and more with Johann Eck, a professor from the University of Ingolstadt. When Eck cleverly backed him into a logical corner, Luther refused to retreat; he insisted that the Bible was the sole guide to human conscience, and he questioned the authority of both popes and councils.

This was the very teaching for which earlier heretics had been burned at the stake. At this point Luther had no choice but to abandon his allegiance to the Church to which he had dedicated his life. By this time, Luther also had a large following in Wittenberg and beyond. The core of this group, who called themselves "evangelicals," were university students, younger humanists, and the well-educated, reform-minded priests and monks.

The Path to the Diet of Worms

In the wake of the Leipzig debate, Luther launched an inflammatory pamphlet campaign. Some pamphlets were first written in Latin, for learned readers, but all soon became available in Luther's acerbic German prose, which delighted readers. *Freedom of a Christian* (1520) argued that the Church's emphasis on good works had distracted Christians from the only source of salvation—faith. It proclaimed the revolutionary doctrine of the "priesthood of all believers°," which reasoned that all those of pure faith were themselves priests, a doctrine that undermined the authority of the Catholic clergy over the laity. The most inspirational pamphlet, *To the Christian Nobility of the German Nation* (1520), called upon the German princes to reform the Church and to defend Germany from exploitation by the corrupt Italians who ran the Church in Rome. When Pope Leo ordered Luther to retract his writings, he responded with a defiant demonstration in which he and his students burned the pope's decree and all of the university library's books of Church law. The die was cast.

The pope demanded that Luther be arrested, but the Elector Frederick answered by defending Luther. Frederick refused to make the arrest without first giving Luther a hearing at the Imperial Diet (parliament), which was set to meet at the town of Worms in 1521. Assembled at the Diet of Worms were haughty princes, grave bishops, and the resplendent young Emperor Charles V (r. 1519–1558), who was presiding over his first Imperial Diet. The emperor ordered Luther to disavow his writings, but Luther refused to do so. For several days the diet was in an uproar, divided by friends and foes of Luther's doctrines. Just before he was to be condemned by the emperor, Luther disappeared, and rumors flew that he had been assassinated. For days no one knew the truth. Frederick the Wise had kidnapped Luther for his own safety and hidden him in the castle at Wartburg, where for nearly a year he labored in quiet seclusion translating the New Testament into German.

THE LUTHERAN REFORMATION IN THE CITIES AND PRINCIPALITIES

Luther had escaped arrest and execution at the hands of the emperor, but he could not manage to control his own followers and allies. The Reformation quickly became a vast, sprawling movement far beyond the control of any individual, even in Luther's own Wittenberg. One of the characteristics of the Protestant Reformation was that once reform-

MARTIN LUTHER'S POWERS OF PERSUASION

....

Part of Martin Luther's appeal derived from his polemical style. The Freedom of a Christian (1520) was probably Luther's last serious attempt to reconcile himself with Pope Leo X. In the open letter to Pope Leo that introduces the tract, Luther asserts that he is criticizing corrupt advisers in the papal curia rather than the pope himself, but Luther's language seems more designed to embolden his own followers than to persuade the pope.

Living among the monsters of this age with whom I am now for the third year waging war, I am compelled occasionally to look up to you, Leo, most blessed father, and to think of you. Indeed, since you are occasionally regarded as the sole cause of my warfare, I cannot help thinking of you. To be sure, the undeserved raging of your godless flatterers against me has compelled me to appeal from your see [officials] to a future council [of all the bishops of the Church], despite the decrees of your predecessors Pius and Julius, who with a foolish tyranny forbade such an appeal.

. . .

I have truly despised your see, the Roman Curia, which, however, neither you nor anyone else can deny is more corrupt than any Babylon or Sodom [places condemned for sinfulness in the Bible] ever was, and which, as far as I can see, is characterized by a completely depraved, hopeless, and notorious godlessness. I have been thoroughly incensed over the fact that good Christians are mocked in your name and under the cloak of the Roman church. I have resisted and will continue to resist your see as long as the spirit of faith lives in me.

. . .

I never intended to attack the Roman Curia or to raise any controversy concerning it. But when I saw all efforts to save it were hopeless, I despised it, gave it a bill of divorce, and said, "let the evildoer still do evil, and the filthy still be filthy" [Revelations 22:11]. Then I turned to the quiet and peaceful study of the Holy Scriptures so that I might be helpful to my brothers around me. When I had made some progress in these studies, Satan opened his eyes and then filled his servant Johann Eck, a notable enemy of Christ, with an insatiable lust for glory and thus aroused him to drag me unawares to a debate, seizing me by means of one little word which I had let slip concerning the primacy of the Roman church. Then that boastful braggart, frothing and gnashing his teeth, declared that he would risk everything for the glory of God and the honor of the Apostolic See. Puffed up with the prospect of abusing your authority, he looked forward with great confidence to a victory over me. . . . When the debate ended badly for the sophist, an unbelievable madness overcame the man, for he believed that it was his fault alone which was responsible for my disclosing all the infamy of Rome.

Source: Excerpt from *Luther's Works, vol. 31, Career of the Reformer: I*, edited by Harold J. Grimm (Philadelphia: Muhlenberg Press, 1957). Translated by W. A. Lambert and revised by Harold J. Grimm.

ers rejected the supreme authority of the papacy, even minor differences about forms of worship or biblical interpretation led to division within the movement and eventually to the formation of separate churches.

In its early phases the Reformation spread most rapidly among the educated urban classes. During the sixteenth century, fifty of the sixty-five German imperial cities, at one time or another, officially accepted the Protestant Reformation. Besides these large imperial cities, most of the 200 smaller German towns with a population of more than 1,000 experienced some form of the Protestant movement. During the 1520s and 1530s, the magistrates of these towns took command of the Reformation movement by seizing control of the local churches. The magistrates implemented Luther's reform of worship, disciplined the clergy, and stopped the drain of revenues to irresponsible bishops and the distant pope.

The German princes of the Holy Roman Empire had their own reasons to resent the Church. They wanted to appoint their own nominees to ecclesiastical offices and to diminish the legal privileges of the clergy. During the 1520s Luther's enormous popularity gave many German princes the opportunity they had been waiting for. Despite his steadfast Catholicism, Emperor Charles V was in no position to resist their demands. During most of his reign, Charles faced a two-front war—against France and against the Ottoman Turks. Charles could ill afford additional trouble with the German princes because he desperately needed their military assistance. At the Imperial Diet of Speyer in 1526, Charles granted the princes territorial sovereignty in religion by allowing them to decide whether they would enforce the imperial edict of the Diet of Worms against Luther and his followers. To preserve the empire from external enemies, Charles was forced to allow its internal division along religious lines.

The Appeal of the Reformation to Women

Reformist theology had particular appeal to women. In the early days of the movement, women felt that Luther's description of "the priesthood of all believers" meant that women as well as men could participate fully in the religious life of the Church. Women understood Luther's phrase "the freedom of a Christian" as freeing them from the restrictive roles that had traditionally kept them silent and at home. Moreover, Luther and the other major reformers saw positive religious value in the role of wife and mother. Abandoning the Catholic Church's view that celibate monks and nuns were morally superior to married people, Luther declared marriage holy and set an example by taking a wife, the ex-nun Katherine von Bora. The wives of the reformers often became partners in the Reformation, taking particular responsibility for organizing charities and administering to the poor.

In the early phases of the Reformation, women preached and published on religious matters. These women demanded to be heard in churches and delivered inspiring sermons. They asked that their writings be accepted as authentic products of the Holy Spirit. In some cases, female rulers brought their entire land over to the Reformation. Elisabeth of Brunswick-Calenburg reformed the local church and invited Protestant preachers into her lands. In Germany the noblewoman Argula von Grumbach argued that even though St. Paul had warned that women should be silent in church, she felt driven by the word of God to profess her faith publicly. Marie Dentière, a former abbess of a French convent who joined the Reformation cause, asked, "Do we have two Gospels, one for men and the other for women? . . . For we [women] ought not, any more than men, hide and bury within the earth that which God has . . . revealed to us women?"[6]

Most women were soon disappointed. Women's preaching and writing threatened the male religious and political authorities. The authorities ordered Argula von Grumbach's husband to make her stop writing. Other women who defended the Reformation were silenced by the reformers

themselves, and women who spoke up in church were widely condemned. In some places laws were passed that prohibited groups of women from discussing religious questions. In England, noblewomen were even prevented from reading the Bible aloud to others. One kind of writing could not be controlled, however—the private diary. The Protestant imperative to discover the workings of faith within oneself helped promote writing private diaries. The practice spread rapidly with Protestantism, and many women used diaries as an outlet for personal expression and a way to develop a sense of their own personal identities.

The few women who were able to speak and act openly in public were either from the upper classes or the wives of prominent reformers. No man could silence Marguerite of Navarre and her daughter Jeanne d'Albret, who used their authority as queens to promote the Reformation. A body of religious literature developed that held up as models more humble women such as Katherine Zell, the wife of one of Strasbourg's reformers.

For most women participation in the Reformation was confined to the domestic sphere, where they instructed children, quietly read the Bible, and led prayer circles. Protestant authorities also allowed divorce, which was prohibited by Catholic Church law. However, the reform leaders were quite reluctant to grant women the same rights as their husbands in obtaining a divorce. During the early years of the Reformation, there were many marriages in which one spouse followed the old faith and the other the new. But if the woman converted and her husband did not, the Protestant reformers counseled that she obey her husband even if he forced her to act contrary to God's will. She could pray for his conversion but could not leave or divorce him. Most women were forced to remain married regard-

■ **The Destruction of a Monastery During the Peasants' Revolt**
Engravings such as this one depicted the violence of the peasants' revolt and helped galvanize Catholic support against the peasants.

less of their feelings. A few exceptional women left their husbands anyway and continued to proclaim their religious convictions to the world. One such woman, Anne Askew from England, was tortured and executed for her beliefs.

The German Peasants' Revolt

The Reformation also appealed to many peasants interested in purified religion and local control of the church. The peasants of Wendelstein, a typical South German village, had been complaining about the conduct of its priests for some time. In 1523, they hired a "Christian teacher" and told him in no uncertain terms: "We will not recognize you as a lord, but only as a servant of the community. We will command you, not you us, and we order you to preach the gospel and the word of God purely, clearly, and truthfully—without any human teachings—faithfully and conscientiously."[7] These villagers understood the Reformation to mean that they could take control of their local church and demand responsible conduct from the minister they hired. However, other peasants understood the Reformation as licensing radical social reforms as well.

In June 1524 a seemingly minor event sparked a revolt of peasants in many parts of Germany. When an aristocratic lady demanded that the peasants in her village abandon their grain harvest to gather snails for her, they rebelled and set her castle on fire. Over the next two years, the rebellion spread as peasants rose up against their feudal lords to demand the adoption of Lutheran reforms in the Church, a reduction of feudal privileges, the abolition of serfdom, and the self-government of their communities. Their rebellion was the largest and best organized peasant movement to that point in European history, a measure of the powerful effect of the Protestant reform message. Like the Reformation, the revolt was the culmination of a long period of discontent, but unlike the Reformation, it was a tragic failure.

These peasants were doing exactly what they thought Luther had advocated when he wrote about the "freedom of the Christian." They interpreted his words to mean complete social as well as religious freedom. However, Luther had not meant anything of the sort. To him the freedom of the Christian referred to inner, spiritual freedom, not liberation from economic or political bondage. Instead of supporting the rebellion begun in his name, Luther and nearly all the other reformers backed the feudal lords and condemned in uncompromising terms the violence of the peasant armies. In *Against the Thieving, Murderous Hordes of Peasants* (1525), Luther expressed his own fear of the lower classes and revealed that despite his acid-tongued attacks on the pope, he was fundamentally a conservative thinker who was committed to law and order. He urged that the peasants be hunted down and killed like rabid dogs. And so they were. Between 70,000 and 100,000 peasants died, a slaughter far greater than the Roman persecutions of the early Christians. To the peasants, Luther's

CHRONOLOGY	
\multicolumn{2}{c}{**The Lutheran Reformation**}	
1517	Luther posts the Ninety-Five Theses
1519	Luther debates Johann Eck at Leipzig; election of Charles V as Holy Roman Emperor
1521	Diet of Worms
1524–1525	German peasants revolt
1531	Formation of the Schmalkaldic League
1555	The Religious Peace of Augsburg

conservative position on social and economic issues felt like betrayal, but it enabled the Lutheran Reformation to retain the support of the princes, which was essential for its survival.

Lutheran Success

Soon after the crushing of the Peasants' Revolt, the Lutheran Reformation faced a renewed threat from its Catholic opponents. In 1530 Emperor Charles V bluntly commanded all Lutherans to return to the Catholic fold or face arrest. Enraged, the Lutherans refused to comply. The following year the Protestant princes formed a military alliance, the Schmalkaldic League, against the emperor. Renewed trouble with France and the Turks prevented a military confrontation between the League and the emperor for fifteen years, giving the Lutherans enough breathing space to put the Reformation on a firmer basis by creating new institutions to govern the churches in Germany. In place of the Catholic bishops, Lutherans established regional consistories (boards of clerics) to supervise the new Protestant churches. Educational reforms introduced a humanist curriculum, established schools for girls, and organized religious instruction for the laity. In the meantime Lutheranism spread beyond Germany into Scandinavia.

After freeing himself yet again from foreign wars and failing to effect a compromise solution in Germany, Charles V turned his armies against the Protestants. However, in 1552 the Protestant armies defeated in battle the Catholic forces of the emperor, and Charles was forced to relent. In 1555 the Religious Peace of Augsburg° established the principle of *cuius regio, eius religio,* which means "he who rules determines the religion of the land." Protestant princes were permitted to retain all church lands seized before 1552 and to enforce Protestant worship, but Catholic princes were also allowed to enforce Catholic worship in their territories. Those who disagreed with the religion of their ruler would not be tolerated; their only option was to emigrate elsewhere. With the Peace of Augsburg the religious division of

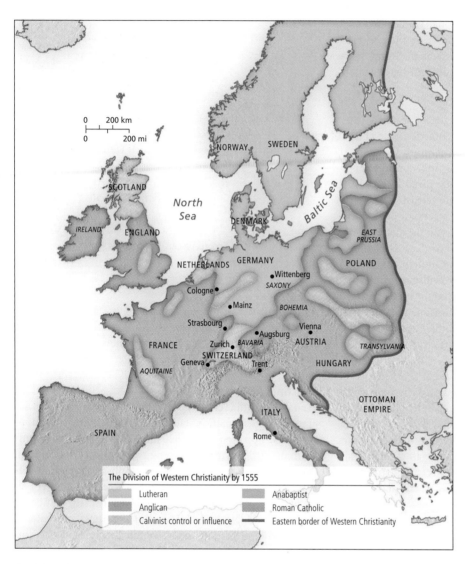

■ **Map 13.1 The Division of Western Christianity by 1555**

The West, which had been culturally unified by Christianity for more than a thousand years, split apart during the sixteenth century. These religious divisions persist to this day.

The Division of Western Christianity by 1555

Lutheran	Anabaptist
Anglican	Roman Catholic
Calvinist control or influence	Eastern border of Western Christianity

the Holy Roman Empire became permanent, and the legal foundations were in place for the development of the two distinctive religious cultures—Protestant and Catholic.

The following year, Emperor Charles, worn out from ceaseless warfare, the anxieties of holding his vast territories together, and nearly forty years of trying to stamp out Protestantism, abdicated and retired to a monastery where he died in 1558.

The Diversity of Protestantism

··■··

The term *Protestant* originally applied only to those followers of Luther who *protested* the decisions of the Imperial Diet of Speyer in 1529, but the term came to describe much more than that small group. It designated all western European Christians who refused to accept the authority of the pope. Protestantism encompassed innumerable churches and sects. Many of these have survived since the Reformation; some disappeared in the violence of the sixteenth century; others have sprung up since, especially in North America, where Protestantism has thrived.

The varieties of Protestantism can be divided into two types. The first type was the product of the Magisterial Reformation°, which refers to the churches that received official government sanction. These included the Lutheran churches in Germany and Scandinavia; the Reformed and Calvinist churches in Switzerland, Scotland, the Netherlands, and a few places in Germany; and the Anglican church in England. The second type was the product of the Radical Reformation° and includes the movements that failed to gain official recognition and were at best tolerated, at worst persecuted. This strict division into Magisterial and Radical Protestantism broke down in eastern Europe, where the states were too weak to enforce religious conformity. In eastern Europe religious variety prevailed over rigid conformity, at least for the sixteenth century (see Map 13.1).

THE REFORMATION IN SWITZERLAND

The governmental independence of Switzerland meant that local authorities could cooperate with the reformers without opposition from the emperor, as was the case in Germany. The Swiss Confederation bound together thirteen fiercely proud regions, called cantons, which had established their independence from the Habsburg dynasty of the Holy Roman Empire (see Map 13.2). Except for the leading cities of Bern, Basel, and Zürich, Switzerland remained an impoverished land of peasants who could not fully support themselves from the barren mountainous land. To supplement their meager incomes, young Swiss men fought as mercenaries in foreign armies, often those of the pope. Each spring, mercenary captains recruited able-bodied Swiss men from the mountain villages. The Swiss men left the women behind to tend the animals and farms. By summer, the villages were emptied of all men except the old and invalid. Each fall at the end of the fighting season, the survivors of that season's campaign trudged home, always bringing bad news to a fresh group of widows. The strain created by the mercenary's life stimulated the desire for sweeping reforms in Switzerland.

Zwingli's Zürich

Ulrich Zwingli (1484–1531) had served as a chaplain with the Swiss mercenaries serving the pope in Italy. In 1520, after being named the People's Priest of Zürich, Zwingli criticized his superior bishop for recruiting local young men to die in the papal armies. That same year he began to call for reform of the Church, advocating the abolition of the Roman Catholic mass, the marriage of priests, and the closing of monasteries. One of the novel features of Zwingli's reform was the strict emphasis on preaching the Word of Scripture during Church services, in contrast to the emphasis on ritual in the traditional Catholic liturgy. He ordered the removal of all paintings and statues from churches because they were too powerful a distraction from concentrating on the preaching. Zwingli was certainly influenced by the writings of Erasmus, but he denied that Luther had any effect on him at all. The Zwinglian Reformation began independently of the Lutheran Reformation and created a separate reform center from which initiatives spread throughout Switzerland, southern Germany, and England.

Two features distinguished the Zwinglian from the Lutheran Reformation. One was Zwingli's desire to involve reformed ministers in governmental decisions. In Lutheran Germany, church and state supported each other, but they remained legally separate, and the prince alone had the authority to determine the religion of the land. In Zürich, the moral Christian and the good citizen were one and the same, and Zwingli worked with the magistrates of the city council, who step-by-step legalized the Reformation and enforced conformity through its police powers. For Luther, the crucial task of the Christian was private, an introspec-

tive examination of the soul. For Zwingli the task of the Christian was public, an outward demonstration of conformity to the community's standards of morality.

Luther and Zwingli also differed in their understanding of the nature of the Eucharist, the sacrament that reenacted Christ's Last Supper with his apostles. Luther believed that Christ's body was spiritually present in the communion bread. "You will receive," as he put it, "as much as you believe you receive."[8] This emphasis on the inner, spiritual state of the believer was very characteristic of Luther's introspective piety. In contrast to Luther, Zwingli could not accept the idea of Almighty God making himself present in a humble piece of bread. To Zwingli the Eucharistic bread was just a symbol that stood for the body of Christ. The problem with the symbolic interpretation of the Eucharist was that the various reformers could not agree with Zwingli on exactly what the Eucharist symbolized. As early as 1524, it became evident that each reformer was committed to a different interpretation, and these different interpretations became the basis for different Protestant churches.

In 1529 Count Philip of Hesse (1504–1567) tried to forge a military alliance between the Protestants of Germany and Switzerland against the Catholics. The theological disputes over the Eucharist blocked full cooperation, however. Philip brought together Luther, Zwingli, and the other principal reformers for a formal discussion at the new Protestant university of Marburg. But Luther adamantly refused to compromise and shrugged off Zwingli's tearful pleas for cooperation. The failure of the Marburg Colloquy marked the permanent rupture of the Reformation movement.

Calvin's Geneva

In the next generation the momentum of the Reformation shifted to Geneva, Switzerland, under the leadership of John Calvin (1509–1564). Calvinism was closely associated with French-speaking Geneva's long struggle for independence from the Duke of Savoy and with the Genevan magistrates' attempts to build a holy community that was independent of the dictates of the Catholic bishop of the city. But Calvinism spread far beyond its Swiss home, becoming the dominant form of Protestantism in France, the Netherlands, Scotland, and New England. Zealous adherents to Calvinism insisted that society itself must be reformed so that people could say and do in public what they truly believed in private. Calvinists despised all forms of hypocrisy and valued personal sincerity, even at the cost of martyrdom.

Trained as a lawyer and exiled from his home in France in 1533 for his reformist views, Calvin spent several years wandering, searching for a quiet retreat and collaborating with other reformers. He eventually settled in Geneva, where he spent the rest of his life transforming the town into the City of God. The linchpin of the Genevan reform was the close cooperation between the magistrates of the city council and the clergy in enforcing the moral discipline of the citizens. To achieve this goal, Calvin convinced the magistrates in 1555 to grant the clergy the right to excommunicate sinners as well as those who disagreed in the slightest way with Calvinist theology. And in the Calvinist construction, excommunication meant more than banishment from church. Excommunicated people were completely shunned; no one could talk to them, including members of their own family; they effectively lost their property and ability to conduct business. Excommunication became a form of exile. The financial and psychological consequences of excommunication were deeply feared because the excommunicated were, in effect, socially dead.

Calvin's theology extended the insights of Luther and Zwingli to their logical conclusion. This pattern was most obvious in his understanding of justification by faith. Luther had argued that the Christian could not earn salvation through good works and that faith came only from God. Calvin reasoned that if an all-knowing, all-powerful God knew everything in advance and caused everything to happen, then the salvation of any individual was predetermined or, as Calvin put it, "predestined." Calvin's doctrine of predestination° was not new. In fact, it had long been

discussed among Christian theologians. But for Calvin two considerations made it crucial. First was Calvin's certainty that God was above any influence from humanity. The "majesty of God," as Calvin put it, was the principle from which everything else followed. Second, Calvin and other preachers had noticed that in a congregation attending a sermon, only a few listened and paid attention to what was preached, while the vast majority seemed unable or unwilling to understand. The reason for this disparity seemed to be that only the Elect could truly follow God's Word. The Elect were known only to God, but Calvin's theology encouraged the converted to feel the assurance of salvation and to accept a "calling" from God to perform his will on earth. God's calling° gave Calvinists a powerful sense of personal direction, which committed them to a life of moral activity, whether as preacher, wife, or shoemaker.

Calvin erected an elegant theological edifice, the *Institutes of the Christian Religion,* first published in six chapters in 1535 but constantly revised and expanded until it reached eighty chapters in the definitive 1559 edition. Calvin the lawyer wrote a tightly argued and reasoned work, like a trial attorney preparing a case. In Calvin's theology the parts fit neatly together like a vast, intricate puzzle. Calvin's

■ **Map 13.2 The Swiss Confederation**

Switzerland bound together thirteen fiercely proud regions, called cantons, three of which established their independence in 1291 from the Habsburg dynasty of the Holy Roman Empire.

work aspired to be a comprehensive reformed theology that would convince through reasoned deliberation.

Given its emphasis on building a holy community, Calvinism helped transform the nuclear family into a social unit for training and disciplining children, a family in which women had a vital educational function that in turn encouraged women's literacy. Calvinist communities also began to allow divorce for women who had been abused by their husbands. Calvinist women and men were both disciplined and liberated—disciplined to avoid physical and material pleasures, liberated from the necessity to do good works but guided by God's grace to do them anyway.

THE REFORMATION IN BRITAIN

Great Britain, as the island kingdom is known today, did not exist in the sixteenth century. The Tudor dynasty, which began in 1485 with Henry VII (see Chapter 11), ruled over England, Wales, and Ireland, but Scotland was still a separate kingdom with its own monarch and church institutions. These countries had distinctive political traditions, culture, and language, and as a result their Reformation experiences differed considerably. The Tudors imposed the Reformation as a matter of royal policy, and they were mostly successful in England and Wales. But they hardly made a dent in the religious culture of Ireland, which was a remarkable exception to the European pattern of conformity to the religion of the ruler. There the vast majority of the population were Catholics, a faith different from that of their Protestant monarch. Scotland, also an exception to the rule, wholeheartedly accepted the Protestant Reformation against the will of its Catholic queen and most of the clergy.

The Tudors and the English Reformation

In 1527 the rotund, self-absorbed, but crafty King Henry VIII (r. 1509–1547) announced that he had come to the pious conclusion that he had gravely sinned by marrying his brother's widow, Catherine of Aragon. By this time the couple had been married for many years, their only living child was the princess Mary, and at age 42 Catherine was unlikely to give birth to more children. Henry let it be known that he wanted a son, mostly to secure the English throne for the Tudor dynasty. He also had his eye on a beauty of the court, the ravishing Anne Boleyn, who was less than half Catherine's age. In the past popes had usually been cooperative when a powerful king needed an annulment, but Pope Clement VII (r. 1523–1534) was in no position to oblige Henry. At the time of the marriage, the papal curia had issued a dispensation for Henry to marry his brother's widow, a practice that is prohibited in the Bible. In effect, Henry was asking the papacy to admit it had made a mistake. In addition, at the moment when Henry's petition for divorce arrived, Clement was under the control of

Catherine's nephew, the Emperor Charles V, whose armies had recently captured and sacked the city of Rome. In 1531 Henry gave up trying to obtain papal approval and definitively separated from Catherine. Some eighteen months later he secretly married Anne Boleyn. England's compliant Archbishop Thomas Cranmer (1489–1556) pronounced the marriage to Catherine void and the one to Anne valid. But the marriage to Anne did not last. When she began to displease him, Henry had her arrested, charged with incest with her brother and adultery with other men. She was convicted and beheaded.

The English separation from the Roman Catholic Church, which took place in 1534 through Acts of Supremacy and Succession, has often been understood as a by-product of Henry's capricious lust and the plots of his brilliant minister, Thomas Cromwell (ca. 1485–1540). It is certainly true that Henry's desire to rid himself of Catherine led him to reject papal authority and to establish himself as the head of the Church of England. It is also certainly true that Henry was an inconstant husband: Of his six wives, two were divorced and two beheaded. However, the English Reformation cannot be explained simply as the consequence of royal whim or the machinations of a single minister.

The English Reformation began as a declaration of royal independence from papal supervision rather than an attempt to reform the practices of the Church. Under Henry VIII the English Reformation could be described as Catholicism without the pope. The concept of royal supremacy established control over the Church by granting to the king supervising authority over liturgical rituals and religious doctrines. Thomas Cromwell, who worked out the practical details for parliamentary legislation, was himself a Protestant, and no doubt his religious views emboldened him to reject papal authority. But the principal theorist of royal supremacy was a Catholic, Thomas Starkey (ca. 1499–1538). A sojourn in Italy had acquainted Starkey with Italian Renaissance political theory, which emphasized concepts of civic liberty—as we saw in Chapter 11. In fact, even many English Catholics found the change acceptable as long as it meant only abandoning submission to the pope in distant Rome. Those who opposed cutting the connection to Rome suffered for their opposition, however. Bishop John Fisher (ca. 1469–1535) and Sir Thomas More, the humanist author of *Utopia* and former chancellor of England, were both executed for their refusal to go along with the king's decision.

With this display of despotic power, Henry seized personal control of the English church, closed the monasteries, and confiscated their lands. He redistributed the monastic lands to the nobility in an effort to purchase their support. Henry's officials briefly flirted with some Protestant reforms, but theological innovations were largely avoided. The Reformation of Henry VIII was more significant for consolidating the dynastic power of the Tudors than for initiating wide-ranging religious reform.

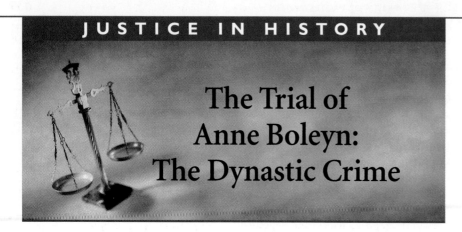

The Trial of Anne Boleyn: The Dynastic Crime

Anne Boleyn, the first of Henry VIII's wives to be executed, was beheaded in the Tower of London's courtyard in May 1536, just a few hundred feet from the hall in which she had celebrated her coronation three years earlier. She had been tried by a court of peers and unanimously convicted of high treason. The evidence against her was for adultery, but the alleged adultery of a queen was considered treason because it put in question the paternity of potential heirs to the throne. Queen Anne insisted on her innocence until the end, but her final address to the crowd did not protest her execution. Instead, she said, "According to the law and by the law I am judged to die, and therefore I will speak nothing against it."[9] To twenty-first century observers, Anne seems to accept her unjust fate passively. To sixteenth-century observers, however, she died "boldly," and her refusal to admit guilt and to accept the law was one of the best indicators of her innocence.

To understand Anne Boleyn's scaffold statement, it is necessary to look at the idea of a "fair trial" in sixteenth-century England. She was condemned for high treason because of her supposed adultery with five men, including her own brother. But her supposed lovers were in other places when the adulteries were alleged to take place—evidence that casts doubt on their truth. She was unable to present this evidence, which today would serve as an alibi for the defendant, because she heard the charges against her for the first time at the actual trial. The queen enjoyed no counsel for the defense, had no opportunity to call witnesses on her own behalf, and had no protection against self-incrimination. Because she was the queen of England, her trial was unusual, but these procedures were standard in the sixteenth century.

It was widely known that the king wished her death, but because her trial followed the accepted legal procedures, it was considered a fair trial by the standards of the sixteenth century. When Anne married Henry, who had recently divorced Catherine of Aragon, Anne's most important role was to provide the king with a male heir. Anne soon gave birth to a daughter, Elizabeth, but she then suffered two miscarriages. Some historians argue that Henry wanted to get rid of Anne in favor of her younger rival, Jane Seymour, but others have suggested that because the fetus of Anne's second miscarriage was deformed, she was suspected of witchcraft. Henry himself stated that he had been seduced by witchcraft, which was why God had not permitted him to have a son. He considered the marriage null and void because Anne's witchery had coerced him into the liaison. As far as Henry was concerned, Anne's failure to bear him a son was evidence of some sort of wrongdoing on her part. It remained only to construct a case against her.

The king and his prosecutors assembled a large number of statements about Anne's infidelity, which shocked observers of the trial. John Husee wrote, "I think verily, if all the books and chronicles . . . which against woman hath been penned, contrived, and written since Adam and Eve, those same were, I think, verily nothing in comparison of that which hath been

■ **Portrait of King Henry VIII**
This portrait by Hans Holbein the Younger depicts Henry as he looked shortly after Queen Anne's execution.

done and committed by Anne the Queen." James Spelman commented, "All the evidence was of bawdery and lechery, so that there was no such whore in all the realm."[10]

The quantity and offensive nature of the evidence was part of a propaganda campaign Henry orchestrated to convince the members of the nobility and the English people that Anne's execution was justified.

Despite the careful orchestration of the trial, the preponderance of the evidence, and the procedures that denied her systematic defense, Anne Boleyn managed to convince a number of observers that she was innocent. Charles Wriothesley recounted, "She made so wise and discreet answers to all things laid against her, excusing herself through her words so clearly as though she had never been faulty to the same."[11] Most telling was the opinion of Chapuys, the ambassador of Emperor Charles V to Henry's court. Chapuys had previously been hostile to Anne, but he considered the whole trial a sham. After the jury returned a guilty verdict, Anne herself shrewdly observed, "I believe you have reasons . . . upon which you have condemned me: but they must be other than those that have been produced in court."[12]

The trial of Anne Boleyn was a classic example of the triumph of judicial form over the substance of evidence. Since Henry and the prosecutors had followed the proper trial procedures, they believed they were above reproach on legal grounds. Anne had been justly condemned even if the evidence against her had been faked. ■

■ **Portrait Sketch of Anne Boleyn**
This portrait of Anne Boleyn may be by Hans Holbein the Younger. It was probably painted while Anne was queen of England.

Questions of Justice

1. Assuming that the evidence against Anne was false, why was her alleged treason defined as adultery rather than something else, such as witchcraft or heresy?

2. Explain Anne's reasoning behind the statement she made on the scaffold.

3. Characterize the relationship between Henry's continuing marital problems and the course of the English Reformation.

Taking It Further

Guy, John. *Tudor England.* 1990. Taking account of recent scholarship, this is the best general history of the period. It includes illuminating portraits of the principal figures.

Warnicke, Retha M. *The Rise and Fall of Anne Boleyn: Family Politics at the Court of Henry VIII.* 1991. Based on a careful examination of all the available evidence, Warnicke shows how the trial was a consequence of Henry VIII's desire to preserve his dynasty.

Under Henry's three children who succeeded him to the throne, the official religion of England gyrated wildly. Only ten years old when he followed his father to the throne, King Edward VI (r. 1547–1553) was the pawn of his Protestant protectors, some of whom pushed for a more thorough Protestant Reformation in England than Henry had espoused. After Edward's premature death, his half-sister, Queen Mary I (r. 1553–1558), daughter of Henry VIII and Catherine of Aragon, attempted to bring England back to obedience to the pope. Her unpopular marriage to the king of Spain and her failure to retain the support of the nobility, who were the foundation of Tudor government, damaged the Catholic cause in England.

Mary's successor and half-sister, Elizabeth Tudor, the daughter of Anne Boleyn, was an entirely different sort. Queen Elizabeth I (r. 1558–1603), raised as a Protestant, kept her enemies off balance and her quarrelsome subjects firmly in hand with her tremendous charisma and shrewd political judgments. Elizabeth became one of the most successful monarchs to ever reign anywhere, as Chapter 14 will demonstrate. Without the considerable talents of Elizabeth, England could easily have fallen into civil war over religion—as the Holy Roman Empire and France did and as England itself did some forty years after her death.

Between 1559 and 1563, Elizabeth repealed the Catholic legislation of Mary and promulgated her own moderately Protestant laws, collectively known as the Elizabethan Settlement, which established the Church of England (Episcopalian in the United States). Her principal adviser, William Cecil (1520–1598), implemented the details of the reform through reasonable debate and compromise rather than by insisting on doctrinal purity and rigid conformity. The touchstone of the Elizabethan Settlement was the Thirty-Nine Articles (finally approved by Parliament in 1571), which articulated a moderate version of Protestantism. It retained the ecclesiastical hierarchy of bishops as well as an essentially Catholic liturgy translated into English. This "middle way" between Roman Catholicism and militant Calvinism was ably defended by Richard Hooker (1553–1600), whose *Laws of Ecclesiastical Polity* emphasized how the law as promulgated by the royal government manifested the divine order.

The Church of England under Elizabeth permitted a wide latitude of beliefs, but it did not tolerate "recusants," those who as a matter of principle refused to attend Church of England services. These were mostly Catholics, who set up a secret network of priests to serve their sacramental needs and whom the government considered dangerous agents of foreign powers. Many others were militant Protestants who thought the Elizabethan Settlement did not go far enough in reforming religion. The most vocal and influential of the Protestant dissenters were the Puritans, who were influenced by Calvinism and demanded a church purified of what they thought were remnants of Roman Catholicism. As Chapter 15 will show, the hostility of the Puritans would eventually lead to civil war.

Scotland: The Citadel of Calvinism

While England groped its way toward moderate Protestantism, neighboring Scotland became one of the most thoroughly Calvinist countries in Europe. In 1560 the parliament of Scotland, with encouragement from Queen Elizabeth of England, overthrew Roman Catholicism against the will of Mary Stuart, Queen of Scots (1542–1587). The wife of the French king, Francis II, Mary was absent in France during the crucial early phases of the Reformation and returned to Scotland only after her husband's death in 1561. Despite her Catholicism, Mary proved remarkably conciliatory toward the Protestants by putting royal funds at the disposal of the new Reformed Kirk (Church) of Scotland. But the Scottish Calvinists never trusted her, and their mistrust would bring about her doom.

The Scots Confession of 1560, written by a panel of six reformers, established the new church. John Knox (ca. 1514–1572) breathed a strongly Calvinist air into the church through his many polemical writings and the official liturgy he composed in 1564, the *Book of Common Order*. Knox emphasized faith and individual Christian conscience over ecclesiastical authority, a priority that discouraged compromise among the Scots. Instead of the episcopal structure in England, which granted bishops the authority over doctrine and discipline, the Scots Kirk established a Presbyterian form of organization, which gave organizational authority to the pastors and elders of the congregations, all of whom had equal rank. As a result the Presbyterian congregations were more independent and subject to local variations than the episcopal structure allowed in the Anglican Church.

THE RADICAL REFORMATION

As we have seen, the magisterial reformers in Germany, Switzerland, England, and Scotland managed to obtain official sanction for their religious reforms, often at the cost of some compromise with governmental authorities. As a result, they were challenged by radicals from among their own followers who demanded faster, more thorough reform. In most places the radicals represented a small minority, perhaps never more than 2 percent of all Protestants. But their significance outstripped their small numbers, in part because they forced the magisterial reformers to respond to their arguments and because their enemies attempted to eradicate them through extreme violence.

The radicals can be divided into three categories: Anabaptists, who attempted to construct a holy community on the basis of literal readings of the Bible; Spiritualists, who abandoned all forms of organized religion to allow individuals to follow the inner voice of the Holy Spirit; and

Unitarians, who advocated a rational and tolerant religion that emphasized ethical behavior over ceremonies.

Anabaptists: The Holy Community

For Anabaptists, the Bible was a blueprint for reforming not just the church but all of society. Because the Bible reported that Jesus was an adult when he was baptized, the Anabaptists rejected infant baptism and adopted adult baptism (Anabaptism° means to rebaptize). An adult, they believed, could accept baptism as an act of faith, unlike an oblivious infant. Adult baptism allowed the creation of a pure church that included only the converted faithful, isolated from the sinfulness of the world. Anabaptists sought to obey only God and completely rejected all established religious and political authorities; they required adherents to refuse to serve in government offices, swear oaths, pay taxes, or fight in armies. Anabaptists sought to live in highly disciplined "holy communities," which excommunicated errant members and practiced simple services based on scriptural readings. Because the Anabaptist communities consisted largely of uneducated peasants, artisans, and miners, a dimension of economic radicalism colored the Anabaptist movement. For example, some Anabaptist radicals advocated the elimination of all private property and the sharing of wealth. On the position of women, however, Anabaptists were staunchly conservative, denying women any public role in religious affairs and insisting that they remain under the strict control of their fathers and husbands. Because the Anabaptists promoted such a radical reorganization of society along biblical lines, they provoked a violent reaction. In Zürich the city council decreed that the appropriate punishment was for all Anabaptists to be drowned in the local river where they had been rebaptizing themselves. By 1529 it became a capital offense in the Holy Roman Empire to be rebaptized, and during the sixteenth century perhaps as many as 5,000 Anabaptists were executed for the offense, a persecution that tended to fragment the Anabaptists into isolated, secretive rural communities.

During a brief period in 1534 and 1535, Anabaptists managed to seize control of the city of Münster in northern Germany. An immigrant Dutch tailor, John of Leiden, set up a despotic regime in Münster that punished with death any sin, even gossiping or complaining. John of Leiden introduced polygamy and collective ownership of property. John set an example by taking sixteen wives, one of whom he beheaded for talking back, stomping on her body in front of the other frightened wives. As the besieging armies closed in, John forced his followers to crown him king and worship him. After his capture, John was subjected to an excruciating torture, and as a warning to others his corpse was displayed for many years hanging in an iron cage.

"God opened the eyes of the governments by the revolt at Münster," as the Protestant reformer Heinrich Bullinger put it, "and thereafter no one would trust even those Anabaptists who claimed to be innocent."[13] The surviving Anabaptists abandoned the radicalism of the Münster community, embracing pacifism and nonviolent resistance. A Dutchman, Menno Simons (1496–1561), tirelessly traveled about the Netherlands and Germany, providing solace and guidance to the isolated survivors of the Münster disaster. His followers, the Mennonites, preserved the noblest features of the Anabaptist tradition of quiet resistance to persecution. Under Mennonite influence, Thomas Helwys founded the first Baptist church in England in 1612. As the leader of the English Baptists, Helwys wrote an unprecedented appeal for the absolute freedom of religion. In it he defended the religious rights of Jews, Muslims, and even atheists as well as all varieties of Christians. He was almost immediately put in prison, where he died.

The most significant measure of the influence of the Anabaptists is the fact that largest number of Protestants in the United States are Baptists. The modern Baptist movement has lost the social radicalism of its Anabaptist forbearers and now accepts the legitimacy of private property. Most Baptists have also forsaken pacifism, but during the civil rights movement of the 1950s and 1960s, it was a Baptist preacher, Dr. Martin Luther King, Jr., who reintroduced the principle of nonviolent resistance to persecution.

Spiritualists: The Holy Individual

Whereas the Anabaptists radicalized the Swiss Reformation's emphasis on building a godly community, the Spiritualists° radicalized Luther's commitment to personal introspection. Perhaps the greatest Spiritualist was the aristocratic Caspar Schwenckfeld (1490–1561), who was a friend of Luther's until he broke with the reformer over what he considered the weak spirituality of established Lutheranism. Schwenckfeld believed that depraved humanity was incapable of casting off the bonds of sin, which only a supernatural act of God could achieve. This separation from sinfulness was revealed through an intense conversion experience, after which the believer gained spiritual illumination. Schwenckfeld called this illumination the "inner Word," which he understood as a living form of the Scriptures written directly on the believer's soul by the hand of God. Schwenckfeld also prized the "outer Word," that is, the Scriptures, but he found the emotional experience of the inner Word more powerful than the intellectual experience that came from reading the Bible. Spiritualists reflected an inner peace evident in their calm physical appearance, lack of anxiety, and mastery of bodily appetites—a state Schwenckfeld called the "castle of peace."

The most prominent example of the Spiritualist tendency in the English-speaking world is the Quakers, who first appeared in England a century after the Lutheran Reformation. The Quakers, or Society of Friends, interpreted the priesthood of all believers to mean that God's spirit, which they called the Light of Christ, was given equally to all men and women. This belief led them to abandon entirely a separately ordained ministry and to replace organized worship with meetings in which any man, woman, or child could speak, read Scripture, pray, or sing, as the spirit moved them. The Quakers' belief in the sacredness of all human beings also inclined them toward pacifism and egalitarianism.

In no other religious tradition have women played such a prominent role for so long. From the very beginning of the movement, female Friends were prominent in preaching the Quaker gospel. In Quaker marriages, wives were completely equal to their husbands—at least in religious matters. Quakers long played a prominent role in various social reform movements as well. In the eighteenth century, they were the first to campaign for the abolition of slavery; in the nineteenth century, Quaker women were prominent in the movement to establish women's rights; and in the twentieth century they led antiwar movements and the campaign for nuclear disarmament.

Unitarians: A Rationalist Approach

Distinctive to Christian theology—in comparison to other monotheistic religions, such as Judaism and Islam—is the doctrine of the Trinity, which posits that the one God has three identities—God the Father, God the Son, and God the Holy Spirit. The doctrine of the Trinity made it possible for Christians to believe that God the Son "took on flesh" in what is called the "incarnation." At a particular moment in history, God became the human being Jesus Christ. The doctrine of the Trinity was officially established as Christian dogma at the Council of Nicea in 325, in response to the Arian heresy, which had denied Christ's divinity. The universal acceptance of the Trinity among Christians changed in the middle of the sixteenth century with the emergence of numerous radical sects that rejected the divinity of Christ. They were called Arians, Socinians, Anti-Trinitarians, or Unitarians°. The Italian Faustus Socinus (1539–1604) taught a rationalist interpretation of the Scriptures and argued that Jesus was a divinely inspired man, not God-become-man. Socinus's followers thus rejected the doctrine of the Trinity, which they found contrary to simple common sense and without support in Scripture. Socinus's ideas remain central to Unitarianism—the specific rejection of Trinitarian doctrine and the general emphasis on rationality.

Catholics and magisterial Protestants alike were extremely hostile to Unitarians, who tended to be well-educated humanists and men of letters. Unitarian views thrived in advanced intellectual circles in northern Italy and eastern Europe, but the most famous critic of the Trinity was the brilliant, if eccentric, Spaniard Michael Servetus (1511–1553). Trained as a physician and widely read in the literature of the occult, Servetus published influential Anti-Trinitarian works and daringly sent his provocative works to the major Protestant reformers. Based on a tip from the Protestants in Geneva, the Catholic inquisitor-general in Lyons, France, arrested Servetus, but he escaped from prison during his trial. While passing through Protestant Geneva on his way to refuge in Italy, he was recognized while attending a church service and again imprisoned. Although no law in Geneva allowed capital punishment, Servetus was convicted of heresy and burned alive.

The Anabaptists and Unitarians shared some early connections and similarities, but the two groups soon parted ways. Both Anabaptists and Unitarians followed the logic of their own beliefs and were unwilling to compromise with other Protestants. Anabaptists remained dogmatic and committed to a very narrow interpretation of Scripture. Unitarians were far stronger intellectually, and in eastern Europe they attracted support from the powerful. Much more open to debate, Unitarians became influential advocates for religious toleration, which they found in eastern Europe.

THE FREE WORLD OF EASTERN EUROPE

During the sixteenth century eastern Europe offered a measure of religious freedom and toleration unknown elsewhere in Europe. As a result, eastern Europe was open to considerable religious experimentation and attracted refugees from the oppressive princes of western Europe, none of whom tolerated more than one religion in their territories. Such religious toleration was made possible by the relative weakness of the monarchs in Bohemia, Hungary, Transylvania, and especially Poland-Lithuania, where the great land-owning aristocrats exercised nearly complete freedom on their estates. All of these kingdoms had Catholic monarchs, but the Reformation radicalized the aristocrats who dominated the parliaments, enabling Protestantism to take hold even against the wishes of the monarch.

As we have seen, in Bohemia (now in the Czech Republic), the Hussite movement in the fourteenth century had rejected papal authority and some of the sacramental authority of the priesthood long before the Protestant Reformation. After the Lutherans and Calvinists attracted adherents in Bohemia, the few surviving old Hussites and the new Protestants formed an alliance in 1575, which made common cause against the Catholics. In addition to this formal alliance, substantial numbers of Anabaptists found refuge from persecution in Bohemia and lived in complete freedom on the estates of tolerant landlords who were desperate for settlers to farm their lands.

The religious diversity of Hungary was also remarkable by the standards of the time. By the end of the sixteenth century, much of Hungary's diverse population had accepted some form of Protestantism. Among the German-speaking city dwellers and the Hungarian peasants in western Hungary, Lutheranism prevailed, whereas in eastern Hungary Calvinism was dominant.

No other country was as tolerant of religious diversity as Transylvania (now in Romania), largely because of the weak monarchy, which could not have enforced religious uniformity even if the king had wanted to do so. In Transylvania, Unitarianism took hold more firmly than anywhere else. In 1572 the tolerant ruler Prince István Báthory (r. 1571–1586) granted the Unitarians complete legal equality to establish their own churches along with Catholics, Lutherans, and Calvinists—the only place in Europe where equality of religions was achieved. Transylvania was also home to significant communities of Jews, Armenian Christians, and Orthodox Christians.

The sixteenth century was the golden age of the Polish-Lithuanian Commonwealth, which was by far the largest state in Europe. It escaped both the Ottoman invasions and the religious wars that plagued the Holy Roman Empire. From the Lutheran cities in the German-speaking north to the vast open plains of Great Poland, where Calvinism took hold among the independent-minded nobility, religious lines often had been drawn along ethnic or class divisions. When Sigismund August (r. 1548–1572) became king, he declared, "I am not king of men's conscience," and inaugurated extensive toleration of Protestant churches, even while the vast majority of peasants remained loyal to Orthodoxy or Catholicism. Fleeing persecution in other countries, various Anabaptist groups and Unitarians found refuge in Poland. This extensive religious diversity in Poland was later snuffed out during the Counter Reformation.

The Catholic and Counter Reformations

The terms Catholic Reformation and Counter Reformation refer to two distinct movements that profoundly revitalized the Catholic Church and established an institutional and doctrinal framework that persisted into the late twentieth century. The Catholic Reformation° was a series of efforts to purify the Church; they were not necessarily a reaction to the Protestant Reformation but evolved out of late medieval spirituality, driven by many of the same impulses that stimulated the Protestants. The most important of these efforts was the creation of new religious orders, especially the Society of Jesus, whose members are known as the Jesuits. The Counter Reformation° was a response to the Protestant Reformation and embraced defensive and offensive actions against Protestantism. The Counter Reformation propagandized Catholic doctrine, disciplined clergy and laity, and repressed heresy. The Counter Reformation established the Holy Office of the Inquisition, promulgated the *Index of Forbidden Books,* and implemented the decrees of the Council of Trent (1545–1563).

CHRONOLOGY	
The Diversity of Protestantism	
1520	Zwingli declared the People's Priest in Zürich
1529	Marburg Colloquy
1534	Parliament in England passes the Acts of Supremacy and Succession
1534–1535	Anabaptist control of Münster, Germany
1535	Execution of John Fisher and Thomas More; first edition of John Calvin's *Institutes of the Christian Religion*
1541	Calvin introduces the Reformation in Geneva
1559–1563	The Elizabethan Settlement of the Anglican Church
1560	Scots Confession

Whereas the Catholic Reformation came from the religious enthusiasm that welled up from the laity and lower clergy, the popes were primarily responsible for the Counter Reformation, which had a strongly international character. Counter Reformation Catholicism retained Latin, in contrast to Protestantism, which conducted services in vernacular languages such as German or English. The success of the Counter Reformation tended to obliterate differences in religious culture from one Catholic country to another, creating greater uniformity in Catholic practice and doctrine than had been the case in the medieval period. The international spread of the Counter Reformation was a source of tremendous strength in revitalizing the Church and in creating a distinctively Catholic culture. For 400 years after the Counter Reformation, Catholics who found themselves in a foreign land could experience something very familiar merely by attending a mass, spoken or chanted in the ancient Latin of the Church.

THE RELIGIOUS ORDERS IN THE CATHOLIC REFORMATION

The most dramatic and effective manifestation of the Catholic Reformation was the founding of new religious orders. These orders exhibited a religious vitality that had little to do with the Protestant threat. In fact, none of the new orders began near the centers of Protestantism, such as Germany. Italy, which remained strongly Catholic, produced the largest number of new orders, followed by Spain and France. All of the new orders remained committed to a very traditional Catholic theology, but they differed from the prayerful isolation of the traditional monastic orders by their commitment to an active ministry in the world.

Jesuits: The Soldiers of God

By far the most influential new order was the Society of Jesus. In 1534 a group of seven students at the University of Paris took a vow to go on a pilgrimage to Jerusalem after graduation. They were an international lot—a Portuguese, a Savoyard, an Aragonese, two Basques, and two Castilians. When the original seven plus some French companions gathered in Venice to take ship to Palestine, they found their way blocked by a war, a turn of events that led them to place themselves at the disposal of the pope. This loosely organized group of kindred spirits became the core of a new order. In 1540 they officially organized the Society of Jesus and elected Ignatius Loyola (1491–1556) the first General of the Society.

The dynamic personality and intense spirituality of Loyola gave the new order its distinctive commitment to moral action in the world. Loyola began his career as a courtier to King Ferdinand of Aragon and a soldier. In 1521 during a French attack on the Spanish garrison at Pamplona, Loyola's leg was shattered by a cannonball. Driven by vanity to keep his leg from looking deformed, he insisted on having his leg rebroken and reset several times despite the excruciating pain of the procedure. During the boredom of his convalescence, he turned to reading a life of Christ and the lives of the saints. From these he discovered tales of heroism superior to anything he had read of medieval knights. These revelations converted Loyola to Christ. Loyola's background as a courtier and soldier deeply influenced his religiosity. The Society of Jesus that he helped found preserved some of the better values Loyola had acquired as a courtier-soldier—social refinement, loyalty to authority, sense of duty, and high-minded chivalry.

Loyola's most impressive personal contribution to religious literature was the *Spiritual Exercises* (1548), which became the foundation of Jesuit practice. The *Spiritual Exercises* have been republished in more than 5,000 editions in hundreds of languages. The *Exercises* prescribe a month-long retreat devoted to a series of meditations in which the participant mentally re-experiences the spiritual life, physical death, and miraculous resurrection of Christ. Much of the power of the *Exercises* derives from the systematic employment of each of the five senses to produce a defined emotional, spiritual, and even physical response. Participants in the *Exercises* seem to hear the blasphemous cries of the soldiers at Christ's crucifixion, feel the terrible agony of His suffering on the cross, and experience the blinding illumination of His resurrection from the dead. Those who participated in the *Exercises* considered the experience life-transforming. These participants usually made a steadfast commitment to serve the Church.

The Jesuits distinguished themselves from other religious orders by extending their personal spirituality to minister to others. They did not wear clerical clothing, and on foreign missions or in dangerous situations they lived incognito for years. Jesuits became famous for their loyalty to the pope, and some took a special fourth vow (in addition to the three traditional vows of poverty, chastity, and obedience) to go on a mission if the pope requested it.

In Europe the Jesuit college system transformed the culture of the Catholic elite. These popular colleges provided free tuition to the poor, but they mostly attracted the sons of the aristocrats and the wealthy who absorbed from the Jesuit instructors the values of Renaissance humanism and the Catholic Reformation. Jesuit colleges were the equivalent of high schools, but some grew into universities or colleges within universities. By 1615 there were 372 Jesuit colleges in Europe; the system also spread to the major cities of the Americas. With the success of these colleges, education gradually replaced missionary work as the most important Jesuit activity.

The Jesuit order grew rapidly. At Loyola's death in 1556 there were about a thousand Jesuits, but by 1700 there were nearly 20,000, and many young men who wished to join had to be turned away because there were insufficient funds to train them. The influence of the Jesuits was even greater than their numbers would indicate, however. Besides their success in education, which shaped the values of the upper classes and guided intellectual life throughout Catholic Europe, Jesuits often served as the personal confessors to powerful figures, including several kings of France and Holy Roman emperors. By giving private advice on spiritual matters, confessors had many opportunities to influence royal policy, an influence the Jesuits were not shy to exercise.

Women's Orders: In But Not of the World

Creating a ministry that was active in the world was much more difficult for the female orders than for the Jesuits and the other male orders. Women who sought to reinvigorate old orders or found new ones faced hostility from ecclesiastical and civic authorities, who thought women had to be protected by either a husband or the cloister wall. Women in convents were supposed to be entirely separated from the world, "as if they were dead," but this principle was at odds with the desires of many devout women who wanted to help make the world a better place.

The cloistering of women was a highly controversial issue during the sixteenth century. Because it was cheaper to place a daughter in a convent than to provide her with a dowry for marriage, about one-third of the women of aristocratic families in Catholic countries found themselves in convents rather than on the marriage market. In some places, such as Venice during the late sixteenth century, more than three-quarters of the noblewomen were cloistered. In many convents, aristocratic women tried to live much as they would have in secular society, enjoying private apartments, servants, regular visits with relatives, musical entertainments, and even vacations. Many of these women felt like involuntary inmates living in a "Convent Hell," to quote the title of Arcangela Tarabotti's famous exposé of the nun's life (1654). The dreary experience of these reluctant nuns, however, contrasted with the genuine enthusiasm for convent life of many other women who were caught up in the religious enthusiasm of the Catholic Reformation.

The first task of those who were ardently religious was to reform convent life. The most famous model was provided by St. Teresa of Avila (1515-1582), who wrote a strict new rule for the long-established Carmelites, requiring mortifications of the flesh and complete withdrawal from the world. St. Teresa described her own mystical experiences in her *Autobiography* (1611) and in the *Interior Castle* (1588), a compelling masterpiece in the literature of mysticism. St. Teresa advocated a very cautious brand of mysticism, which was checked by regular confession and skepticism about extreme acts of self-deprivation. For example, she recognized that a nun who fell into an apparent rapture after extensive fasting was probably just having hallucinations from the hunger.

The Catholic convents of the sixteenth century presented many contradictions. On the one hand, they housed some women who had no special religious vocation, who did not want to be locked away from family and friends, and who suffered from the stifling boredom of living without apparent purpose. On the other hand, many women who willingly chose the religious life thrived in a community of women, were liberated from the rigors of childbearing, and were freed from direct male supervision. These women could devote themselves to cultivating musical or literary talents to a degree that would have been impossible in the outside world. Nuns created their own distinctly female culture, producing a number of learned women and social reformers, who had considerable influence in the arts, education, and charitable work such as nursing.

PAUL III, THE FIRST COUNTER REFORMATION POPE

Despite the Protestant threat, which was fully evident by 1519, the Church was slow to initiate its own reforms because of resistance among bishops and cardinals of the Church hierarchy who worried that reform would threaten their income. More than twenty years after Luther's defiant stand at the Diet of Worms in 1521, Pope Paul III (r. 1534–1549) finally launched a systematic counterattack. As a member of the powerful Farnese family who had long treated church offices as their private property, Paul seemed an unlikely reformer. But more than any other pope, Paul understood the necessity to respond to the political winds of change. It was Pope Paul, for example, who formally approved the Jesuits and began to employ them as missionary soldiers for the Church.

In 1541, in an attempt to resolve the dangerous religious disputes provoked by the Lutherans, Paul sent a representative to a discussion between Catholic and Protestant theologians held in conjunction with the Imperial Diet of Regensburg. Despite the best efforts of the pope's reform-minded representative, the meeting failed, making it stunningly clear how wide the gap had become between Protestant and Catholic theology. The failure of Regensburg shifted Pope Paul's efforts from a plan of hesitant accommodation to a defensive strategy devoted to building a Catholic bulwark against Protestant ideas.

In 1542 on the advice of an archconservative faction of cardinals, Paul III reorganized the Roman Inquisition, called the Holy Office. The function of the Inquisition was to inquire into the beliefs of all Catholics primarily to discover indications of heresies such as those of the Protestants. Jews, for example, were exempt from its authority, although Jews who had converted or been forced to convert to Christianity did fall under the jurisdiction of the Inquisition. There had been other inquisitions, but most had been local or national. The Spanish Inquisition was controlled by the Spanish monarchs, for example. In contrast, the Holy Office came under the direct control of the pope and cardinals and termed itself the Universal Roman Inquisition. Its effective authority did not reach beyond northern and central Italy, but it set the tone for the entire Counter Reformation Church and created a climate of caution, if not fear, especially among intellectuals.

The Inquisition immediately began to crack down on suspected heretics. One of the first victims was Bernardino Ochino (1487–1563), the most popular preacher in Rome and the Minister General of the Capuchin order. When summoned to answer questions before the Holy Office, he

CHRONOLOGY

The Catholic and Counter Reformations

1534–1549	Pontificate of Pope Paul III
1540	Founding of the Society of Jesus
1541	Imperial Diet of Regensburg
1542	Reorganization of the Roman Inquisition or Holy Office
1545–1563	Meetings of the Council of Trent
1548	*Spiritual Exercises* of Ignatius Loyola
1549	*Index of Forbidden Books*

The Ecstasy of St. Teresa of Avila: The Body and the Soul

St. Teresa of Avila (1515–1582) eloquently expressed the intimate connection between physical and spiritual experiences that was a common feature of Catholic mysticism. She was a Spanish Carmelite nun whose accounts of her own mystical experiences made her a model for other nuns throughout the world. Filled with religious ardor, she devoted herself to an ascetic regime of self-deprivations so intense that she fell ill and suffered paralysis.

Often afflicted by an intense pain in her side, Teresa reported that an angel had stuck a lance tipped with fire into her heart. This "seraphic vision," which became the subject of Gianlorenzo Bernini's famous sculpture in Santa Maria della Vittoria in Rome (1645–1652), epitomized the Catholic Reformation sensibility of understanding spiritual states through physical feelings. In St. Teresa's case, her extreme bodily deprivations, paralysis, and intense pain conditioned how she experienced the spiritual side of her nature. Many have seen an erotic character to the vision, which may be true, but the vision best demonstrates a profound psychological awareness that bodily and spiritual sensations cannot be precisely distinguished. As St. Teresa put it, "it is not bodily pain, but spiritual, though the body has a share in it—indeed, a great share." She described the paralysis of her soul and her body as interconnected: "The soul is unable to do either this or anything else. The entire body contracts and neither arm nor foot can be moved." She then described, in remarkably graphic terms, her repeated vision:

It pleased the Lord that I should sometimes see the following vision. I would see beside me, on my left hand, an angel in bodily form—a type of vision which I am not in the habit of seeing, except very rarely. . . . I pleased the Lord that I should see this angel in the following way. He was not tall, but short, and very beautiful, his face so aflame that he appeared to be one of the highest types of angel who seem to be all afire. . . . In his hands I saw a long golden spear and at the end of the iron tip I seemed to see a point of fire. With this he seemed to pierce my heart several times so that it penetrated to my entrails. When he drew it out, I thought he was drawing them out with it and he left me completely afire with a great love for God. The pain was so sharp that it made me utter several moans; and so excessive was the sweetness caused me by this intense pain that one can never wish to lose it, nor will one's soul be content with anything less than God. . . . So sweet are the colloquies of love which pass between the soul and God that if anyone thinks I am lying I beseech God, in His goodness, to give him the same experience.[14]

Visions such as this one were difficult to interpret. Exactly what was going on in those sweet colloquies between St. Teresa's soul and God? St. Teresa associated these visions with intense physical pain, as if she had to suffer in order to receive divine illumination, which she described as a sweet conversation between her soul and God. Her sensibility about the necessary relationship between physical pain and spiritual experiences was especially pronounced among sixteenth-century Catholics. Pain and suffering were understood as a form of penance, and thus the body could play a positive and redemptive role in enabling spirituality. The best way to transcend this world was in bodily pain, because through pain the Christian escaped the temptations of the flesh and renounced the attractions of the world. ■

■ **The Ecstasy of St. Teresa**
In this sculpture St. Teresa lies suspended in air in a swoon induced by a vision. An angel is about to pierce her side with an arrow.

For Discussion

How was pain understood to have religious value? What was happening around St. Teresa that might explain her preoccupation with pain?

fled to Geneva. His defection to Calvin's Geneva caused an enormous sensation and fueled the clamor for more intense repression. Any form of criticism of the Church within earshot of an informant of the Inquisition became very dangerous. The Inquisition could subject defendants to lengthy interrogations and stiff penalties, including prison sentences and even execution in exceptional cases.

A second effort to stop the spread of Protestant and other ideas deemed heretical led to the first *Index of Forbidden Books,* drawn up in 1549 in Venice, the capital of the publishing industry in Italy. The *Index* censored or banned many books that the Church considered detrimental to the faith and the authority of the Church. Most affected by the strictures were books about theology and philosophy, but books of moral guidance were also prohibited or butchered by the censors, such as the works of Erasmus, and classics of literature, such as Giovanni Boccaccio's *The Decameron.* The official papal *Index* of 1559 even prohibited translations of the Bible into vernacular languages such as Italian. It remained possible to buy certain heretical theological books "under the counter," much as people today find ways to obtain illegal drugs, but possessing such books could be dangerous if agents of the Inquisition conducted a raid.

THE COUNCIL OF TRENT

By far the most significant of Pope Paul III's contributions to the Counter Reformation was his call for a general council of the Church, which began to meet in 1545 in Trent on the border between Italy and Germany. The Council of Trent launched a new direction for the Catholic Church that guided it for the next 400 years.

Between 1545 and 1563 the council met under the auspices of three different popes in three separate sessions, with long intervals of as much as ten years between sessions. The objective of these sessions was to find a way to respond to the Protestant criticisms of the Church, to reassert the authority of the pope, and to launch reforms that would guarantee a well-educated and honest clergy. The decrees of the Council of Trent, which had the force of legislation for the entire Church, defied the Protestants by refusing to yield any ground on the traditional doctrines of the Church. The decrees confirmed the efficacy of all seven of the traditional sacraments, the reality of Purgatory, and the spiritual value of indulgences.

The prelates at Trent were more reluctant in announcing reforms that would apply to themselves; although they ordered bishops to reside in their dioceses or regions, they left a large loophole for the pope to grant exemptions. They decreed that every diocese should have a seminary to train priests, providing a practical solution to the problem of clerical ignorance.

The Council of Trent represented a dramatic reassertion of the authority of the papacy, the bishops, and the priesthood. The actual implementation of the decrees varied considerably from country to country and from diocese to diocese, however. The model for enforcing the decrees was Archbishop Carlo Borromeo (archbishop, 1565–1584) of Milan. His energetic visitations of his diocese and attention to administrative detail became an example for others. Despite the hopes of some of the participants in the council, it had no effect whatsoever in luring Protestants back into the Catholic fold.

The Reformation in the Arts

Most of the paintings, sculptures, and musical compositions created before and during the sixteenth century were destined for churches or had some kind of religious function. But with the tensions brought about during the Reformation, one of the major issues dividing Protestants and Catholics was defining the proper role of the arts in Christian worship. Except among the most radical Protestants, who entirely rejected any role for the arts in religious worship, the difference between the two was more one of degree than of kind. Catholics considered religious images and religious music, properly regulated, vital for devotion. Protestants, however, were uneasy about religious art because they worried about confining divine truths within any kind of visual representation.

PROTESTANT ICONOCLASM

Protestants sometimes initiated reform by vandalizing churches through acts of iconoclasm, the removing, breaking, or defacing of religious statues, paintings, and symbols such as crucifixes. The destruction of religious works of art more often than not took place even when the reformers themselves discouraged or denounced it. Nevertheless, in town after town in the thrall of reform enthusiasm, laypeople destroyed religious art, including some of the greatest masterpieces of the Middle Ages and Renaissance. Their violence against property was seldom matched by violence against people. Protestant mobs were much more likely to rip down an altar painting than to attack a priest.

Three factors likely explain iconoclasm. One was that people feared the power of such images. Guillaume Farel, the reformer of Geneva before Calvin, told how his parents had taken him as a child to the shrine of the Holy Cross at Tallard. A priest stationed at the shrine told the pilgrims that the Cross shook violently during storms. What Farel remembered most about the Cross was his fear, reinforced by the apprehension of his parents. The implication was that images possessed great powers that could be used both to protect and to destroy. The problem with religious images, therefore, was not that they were a form of idolatry but that they were perceived to be too powerful and potentially dangerous.

A second reason for iconoclasm was that religious images devoured financial resources that could be better spent on the poor. Ulrich Zwingli was especially articulate on this point. He hoped that the assets devoted to paying for paintings and statues could be transformed into "food of the poor." In this sense iconoclasm was part of a pious project to redirect the energy of Christians toward solving the social problems of the community. Great paintings were given to hospitals to serve as fuel, and crucifixes were sold as lumber with the proceeds going to the indigent.

Many reformers spoke of a third concern about images. They worried that a church filled with works of art distracted worshipers from paying attention to the Word of Scripture. They found the meaning of images too ambiguous, too subject to misinterpretation. Instead they wanted to ensure that their preaching provided the interpretation of Scripture. In effect, they wanted to substitute the Word of God for the image of God. In many reformed Dutch churches, for example, the walls were stripped bare of images and whitewashed. Passages of scripture were then painted on the walls in place of the images.

Although skeptical of the role of images in churches, propagandists for the Reformation had no such reservation about woodcuts and engravings, which could be reproduced in multiple copies and cheaply sold to thousands of people. These images, the visual by-product of the printing revolution, promoted the Reformation to the masses in a simple graphic way by lampooning the pope and ridiculing the wealth of the clergy. These images were the prototype for modern political cartoons. Also popular were portraits of the reformers. Many a pious Lutheran household replaced an image of the Madonna with an engraving of Martin Luther and his wife, Katherine von Bora.

COUNTER REFORMATION ART

The Catholic Church retained a strong commitment to the religious value of the arts. However, the Counter Reformation recognized that abuses had taken place in works of art that depicted events that did not appear in Scripture and placed artists under much closer surveillance than before. Artists were enjoined to avoid representing impieties of any sort and to use their art to teach correct doctrine and to move believers to true piety. Religious art had to convey a message simply, directly, and in terms that unlettered viewers could understand. The best Counter Reformation art employed dramatic theatrical effects in lighting and the arrangement of figures to represent deep emotional and spiritual experiences. Through contemplating these pictures, viewers were supposed to create similar experiences within themselves. In this sense an aesthetic and a spiritual appreciation of art were inseparable.

The Council of Trent forced a reevaluation of previous trends in the arts and a number of existing works of art.

The Italian Renaissance, in particular, had glorified the human body, often represented in the nude. In earlier generations churchmen and even popes had not objected to the display of naked figures in churches and chapels, but after the Council of Trent many influential ecclesiastics disapproved this practice in the strongest terms. Michelangelo's *The Last Judgment,* a fresco painted in the Sistine Chapel in the Vatican in Rome between 1534 and 1541, came under severe attack the year after the last session of Trent. The polemical *Dialogue on the Errors of Painters* criticized Michelangelo for subordinating the representation of Christian truths to his own stylistic interests in the human nude. Genitals and bare breasts in *The Last Judgment* were painted over, disfiguring one of the greatest masterpieces of the Renaissance. The crude overpainting was not removed until the fresco was cleaned during the 1990s.

Everywhere in Catholic Europe, offending body parts were painted over. In the Catholic parts of the Netherlands, paintings and statues deemed indecent were even destroyed, in an odd echo of Protestant iconoclasm. In Venice the Inquisition got involved. In a celebrated inquiry in 1573, the inquisitor dragged in the painter, Paolo Veronese, to answer why he put into a painting of the Last Supper various figures that did not appear in the Bible. The inquisitor noticed a figure dressed like a German and badgered Veronese with the allegation that this might indicate Lutheran sympathies. Ordered to change the painting, Veronese quietly changed its title instead.

Since artists' livelihoods depended on the patronage of aristocrats and high ecclesiastical officials, most quickly fell into line with the new requirements. Artistic rebels were unknown in the late sixteenth-century Catholic world. In 1577 the pope founded a new academy in Rome to create guidelines for artists in promoting Christianity, and the Jesuits proved very influential in defining a new path for artists. Many prominent artists across Europe enthusiastically embraced the Counter Reformation. Some became friends of Jesuits, undertook commissions for Jesuits, and practiced the *Spiritual Exercises,* thereby suffusing a Jesuit sensibility throughout Catholic culture.

SACRED MUSIC: PRAISING GOD

The Protestants' concern that the Word of God be intelligible to ordinary believers also influenced their attitude toward music. Luther, in particular, recognized the power of music to move the souls of the congregation. In the Lutheran mass he retained much of the traditional chant, but he translated the words into German and encouraged congregational singing so that believers sang the text themselves rather than passively listened to a choir. A number of new hymns were composed for the Lutheran service, some by Luther himself. One of the lasting masterpieces of the Reformation is Luther's great hymn, "A Mighty Fortress Is Our God." The Lutheran hymnbook laid the foundations for the magnificent tradition of Protestant church music that culminated in the compositions of Johann Sebastian Bach (1685–1750).

Zwingli, less certain about the value of music, banished organs from churches because he thought they obscured the clarity of the biblical text. Some radicals eliminated all music from churches, creating an austere form of worship practiced in houses or bare chapels, in which nothing was allowed to distract from the preaching of God's Word and the direct influence of the Holy Spirit. In these radical sects, the intimate connection between Western Christianity and the arts, which had been so pronounced for centuries, came to an abrupt end. Radical Protestants such as Anabaptists left a lasting legacy of hostility toward creative artists.

Ego sum Papa
(Ich bin der Papst).

Französischer Holzschnitt gegen den lasterhaften Papst Alexander VI.

■ **Anti-Catholic Propaganda**

This woodcut, titled *I am the Pope,* satirizes the papacy by depicting Pope Alexander VI as a monster. Alexander was infamous for allegedly conducting orgies in the Vatican. This kind of visual propaganda was an effective way to undermine support for the papacy.

■ **The Last Judgment**
In this fresco by Michelangelo, the figure with the raised hand in the upper center is Christ. On his right sits the Virgin Mary. Both figures were painted over with clothing to hide their nudity.

The Council of Trent spent more than a year debating the reform of sacred music. The Council decreed that the purpose of liturgical music was to encourage a sense of worship in the congregation. This meant that unlike Protestant music, which appealed to the laity by employing folk tunes, Catholic composers should not borrow from secular music, but like the Protestants, the style of composition must allow for the words to be clearly heard. The Catholics did not follow the Protestant emphasis on congregational singing and rejected virtuoso vocal or instrumental displays. Catholic liturgical performances consisted only of the organ either accompanying voices or playing solos.

The new music of the Catholic Reformation remained firmly rooted in the innovations of Renaissance music and consisted of compositions for various forms of the Latin mass. The most important Catholic composer of church music in the later sixteenth century was Giovanni Pierluigi da Palestrina (ca. 1525–1594). Palestrina spent most of his career in Rome, where he worked as an organist and choir master. His more than 100 masses demonstrated to the often skeptical prelates, who wanted to abolish all elaborate compositions, that music could reflect the meaning of the words while not obscuring their audibility. Palestrina amplified the sumptuous effects of the unaccompanied choir, employing a exotic mixture of harmonic and melodic purity, carefully controlled dissonance, and a sensuous sound. For many generations his music served as the model for Catholic composers.

■ **The Inquisition Criticizes a Work of Art**

This painting was originally intended to represent the Last Supper when Christ introduced the mass to his apostles. Because there are many figures in it who are not mentioned in the biblical account and the supper appears as if it were a Renaissance banquet, the artist, Paolo Veronese, was obliged to answer questions from the Inquisition. Ordered to remove the offending figures, Veronese instead changed the name of the painting to depict the less theologically controversial supper in the house of Levi.

THE INQUISITION INTERROGATES PAOLO VERONESE

In 1572 the prominent painter Paolo Veronese was called before the Inquisition in the city of Venice to answer questions about a painting of the Last Supper that he had created for the refectory of the friars of Santi Giovanni e Paolo. Paintings of the Last Supper were particularly sensitive during the controversies of the Reformation because Catholics believed Christ had instituted the mass at the Last Supper.

[The inquisitor] said to him, "Who do you think was really present at that supper?"

He answered, "I believe that Christ and his apostles were present. But if there is space left over in the picture I decorate it with figures of my own invention."

Said to him, "Did anyone commission you to paint Germans and clowns and the like in that picture?"

He answered, "No, my lords; my commission was to adorn that picture as I saw fit, for it is large and can include many figures, or so I thought."

It was said to him, "When you, the painter, add these decorations to your pictures, is it your habit to make them appropriate to the subject and to proportion them to the principal figures, or do you really do as the fancy takes you, without using any discretion or judgment?"

He answered, "I make the pictures after proper reflection, within the limits of my understanding."

He was asked, "Did he think it proper to depict at the Lord's last supper clowns, drunkards, Germans, dwarfs, and other lewd things?"

He answered, "No, my lords."

He was asked, "Why, then, did you paint them?"

He answered, "I did them on the understanding that they are not within the place where the supper is being held."

He was asked, "Do you not know that in Germany and other places infected with heresy they are accustomed, by means of outlandish paintings full of indecencies and similar devices, to abuse, mock and pour scorn on the things of the Holy Catholic Church, in order to teach false doctrine to foolish and ignorant people?"

He answered, "I agree, my lord, that it is bad; but I must say again that I am obliged to follow the example of my predecessors." [He was referring here to Michelangelo's Last Judgment in the Sistine Chapel of the Vatican.]

The inquisitors ordered Veronese to correct the painting, but he merely changed its name from The Last Supper *to* The Feast in the House of Levi. *It now hangs in the Accademia Gallery in Venice.*

Source: From *Venice: A Documentary History, 1450–1630*, edited by David Chambers and Brian Pullan, with Jennifer Fletcher. Published by Blackwell Publishers (Oxford, 1992). Reprinted by permission.

CONCLUSION
Competing Understandings

During the Reformation the West was permanently divided into two discordant religious cultures of Protestant and Catholic. The religious unity of the West achieved during the Middle Ages had been fruit of many centuries of diligent effort by missionaries, monks, popes, and crusading knights. That unity was lost through the conflicts between, on the one hand, reformers, city magistrates, princes, and kings who wanted to control their own affairs and, on the other, popes who continued to cling to the medieval concept of the papal monarchy. In the West, Christians no longer saw themselves as dedicated to serving the same God as all other Christians. Instead, Catholics and Protestants emphasized their differences.

The differences between these two cultures had lasting implications for how people understood and accepted the authority of the Church and the state, how they conducted their family life, and how they formed their own identities as individuals and as members of a larger community. The next chapter will explore all of these themes.

As the result of intransigence on the part of both cultures, the division had tragic consequences. From the late sixteenth century to the late seventeenth century, European states tended to create diplomatic alliances along this ideological and religious divide, they allowed technical disputes about doctrine to prevent peaceful reconciliation, and they conducted wars as if they were a fulfillment of God's plan. Even after the era of religious warfare ended, Protestant and Catholic cultures remained ingrained in all aspects of life, influencing not just government policy but painting, music, literature, and education. This division completely reshaped the West into a place of intense religious and ideological conflict, and by the eighteenth century undermined the very idea that the West was necessarily a Christian civilization.

Suggestions for Further Reading

For a comprehensive list of suggested readings, please go to www.ablongman.com/levack/chapter13

Bireley, Robert. *The Refashioning of Catholicism, 1450–1700: A Reassessment of the Counter Reformation.* 1999. A fair reappraisal of the major events by one of the most prominent historians of Catholicism in this period.

Bossy, John. *Christianity in the West, 1400–1700.* 1985. A short study not of the institutions of the Church but of Christianity itself, this book explores the Christian people, their beliefs, and their way of life. The book demonstrates considerable continuities before and after the Reformation and is especially useful in understanding the attitudes of common lay believers as opposed to the major reformers and Church officials.

Cameron, Euan. *The European Reformation.* 1995. The most comprehensive general survey, this bulky book covers all the major topics in considerable detail. It is excellent in explaining theological issues.

Hsia, R. Po-chia. *The World of Catholic Renewal 1540–1770.* 1998. An excellent survey of the most recent research.

Koenigsberger, H. G., George L. Mosse, and G. Q. Bowler. *Europe in the Sixteenth Century,* 2nd ed. 1989. A good beginner's survey. Strong on political events.

McGrath, Alister E. *Reformation Thought: An Introduction,* 3rd. rev. ed. 1999. Indispensable introduction for anyone seeking to understand the ideas of the European Reformation. Drawing on the most up-to-date scholarship, McGrath offers a clear explanation of these ideas, set firmly in their historical contexts.

Muir, Edward. *Ritual in Early Modern Europe.* 1997. A broad survey of the debates about ritual during the Reformation and the implementation of ritual reforms.

Oberman, Heiko A. *Luther: Man Between God and the Devil,* trans. Eileen Walliser-Schwarzbart. 1992. First published to great acclaim in Germany, this book argues that Luther was more the medieval monk than history has usually regarded him. Oberman claims that Luther was haunted by the Devil and saw the world as a cosmic battleground between God and Satan. A brilliant, intellectual biography that is sometimes challenging but always clear and precise.

O'Malley, John. *Trent and All That: Renaming Catholicism in the Early Modern Era.* 2000. O'Malley works out a remarkable guide to the intellectual and historical developments behind the concepts of Catholic reform, the Counter Reformation, and, in his useful term, Early Modern Catholicism. The result is the single best overview of scholarship on Catholicism in early modern Europe, delivered in a pithy, lucid, and entertaining style.

Ozment, Steven. *The Age of Reform, 1250–1550: An Intellectual and Religious History of Late Medieval and Reformation Europe.* 1986. Firmly places the Protestant Reformation in the context of late medieval spirituality and theology, particularly strong on pre-Reformation developments.

Reardon, Bernard M. G. *Religious Thought in the Reformation,* 2nd ed. 1995. A good beginner's survey of the intellectual dimensions of the Reformation.

Scribner, R. W. *The German Reformation.* 1996. A short and very clear analysis of the appeal of the Reformation by the leading social historian of the period. Pays attention to what people actually did rather than just what reformers said they should do.

Notes

1. *Correspondence of Erasmus,* trans. R. A. B. Mynors and D. F. S. Thomson, annotated by Wallace K. Ferguson (1974–1994), no. 858, pp. 167–177.
2. *Desiderius Erasmus, The Essential Erasmus,* ed. John P. Dolan (1964), p. 148.
3. Quotation from Gordon Rupp, *Luther's Progress to the Diet of Worms* (1964), p. 29.
4. Ibid., p. 33
5. Quote from an anonymous caricature reproduced in A. G. Dickens, *Reformation and Society in Sixteenth-Century Europe* (1966), fig. 46, p. 61.
6. Translated and quoted in Thomas Head, "Marie Dentière: A Propagandist for the Reform," in Katharina M. Wilson, ed., *Women Writers of the Renaissance and Reformation* (1987), p. 260.
7. Quoted in Peter Blickle, "The Popular Reformation," in *Handbook of European History 1400–1600: Late Middle Ages, Renaissance and Reformation,* vol. II: *Visions, Programs and Outcomes,* eds. Thomas A. Brady, Jr., Heiko A. Oberman, and James D. Tracy (1995), p. 171.
8. Quoted in Heiko A. Oberman, *Luther: Man between God and the Devil,* trans. Eileen Walliser-Schwarzbart (1989), p. 240.
9. E. W. Ives, *Anne Boleyn* (1986), p. 398.
10. Quoted in Margery Stone Schauer and Frederick Schauer, "Law as the Engine of State: The Trial of Anne Boleyn," *William and Mary Law Review* 22 (1980), p. 68.
11. Quoted in Ives, p. 387.
12. Quoted in Schauer and Schauer, p. 70.
13. Quoted in Dickens, p. 134.
14. Quoted in Irving Lavin, *Bernini and the Unity of the Visual Arts* (1980), p. 107.

The Age of Confessional Division, 1550–1618

O N JULY 10, 1584, A CATHOLIC EXTREMIST FRANÇOIS GUION, WITH A BRACE of pistols hidden under his cloak, surprised William the Silent, the Prince of Orange, as he was leaving the dining hall of his palace and shot him at point-blank range. William had been the leader of the Protestant nobility in the Netherlands, which was in revolt against the Catholic king of Spain. Guion masqueraded as a Protestant for seven years in order to ingratiate himself with William's party, and before the assassination he had consulted three Catholic priests who had confirmed the religious merit of his plan. Spain's representative in the Netherlands, the Duke of Parma, had offered a reward of 25,000 crowns to anyone who killed William, and at the moment of the assassination four other fanatics were in Delft trying to gain access to the duke.

The murder of William the Silent introduced an ominous new figure into Western civilization—the religiously motivated assassin. There had been many assassinations before the late sixteenth century, but the assassins had usually been motivated by the desire to gain political power or to avenge a personal or family injury, not by religious differences. The idea that killing a political leader of the opposing faith would serve God's plan injected into politics a measure of blind fanaticism that has persisted to our own times. The assassination of William introduced patterns of violence that have become all too familiar— deception by the assassin to gain access to his victim, the vulnerability of leaders who wish to mingle with the public, the lethal potential of easily concealed pistols (a new weapon at that time), the corruption of politics through vast sums of money, and the obsessive hostility of zealots against their perceived enemies. After the Protestant Reformation, the widespread acrimony among the varieties of Christian faith created a climate of religious extremism during the late sixteenth and early seventeenth centuries. These various forms or expressions of

St. Bartholomew's Day Massacre: This Protestant painter, François Dubois, depicted the merciless slaughter of Protestant men, women, and children in the streets of Paris in 1572. The massacre was the most bloody and infamous in the French Wars of Religion and created a lasting memory of atrocity.

Christianity were called confessions° because their adherents believed in a particular confession of faith, or statement of religious doctrine.

Religious extremism was just one manifestation of an anxiety that pervaded European society at the time—a fear of hidden forces controlling human events. In an attempt to curb that anxiety, the European states allied themselves with the churches. The combined effort of state and church sought to discipline common people, persecute deviants of all sorts, and combat enemies through a religiously driven foreign policy. During this age of confessional division, European countries polarized along confessional lines, and governments persecuted followers of minority religions, whom they saw as threats to public security. During this period there was no place for the modern ethical principles of religious toleration, separation of church and state, and human rights. Anxious believers everywhere were consumed with pleasing an angry God, but when they tried to find God within themselves many Christians seemed only to find the Devil in others.

By attempting to discipline the people of Europe and make them better Christians, educated and elite society directly confronted a thriving popular culture. In many respects, the culture they encountered was nearly as alien as the native cultures in the newly discovered America. Certainly, the peoples of early modern Europe considered themselves Christian, but what they meant by Christianity was quite at odds with that of the reformers who had pushed through the Protestant and Catholic Reformations. In a confused, haphazard, and sometimes violent fashion, members of the elite attempted to blot out many elements of popular culture that they suspected might be remnants of pre-Christian beliefs and practices. One of the most curious consequences of the Reformations during the sixteenth and seventeenth centuries was a dramatic conflict between two cultures, that of the educated elite and that of the ordinary people. However, the disciplining of the people was primarily confined to western Europe. In eastern Europe religious diversity and popular culture thrived largely due to the relative weakness of the eastern European monarchs in comparison with those in western Europe.

The religious controversies of the age of confessional division redefined the West. During the Middle Ages, the West came to be identified with the practice of Latin Catholic Christianity. The Reformation of the early sixteenth century broke up the unity of medieval Christian Europe by dividing westerners into Catholic and Protestant camps. During the period from 1550 to 1618, governments reinforced religious divisions and attempted to unify their peoples around a common set of beliefs. Between the sixteenth century and the end of the eighteenth, these confessional religious identities changed in some places into more secular political ideologies, such as the belief in the superiority of a republic over a monarchy, but the assumption that all citizens of a state should believe in some common

ideology remained. The period from about 1500 to 1800—the Early Modern period in European history—produced the lasting division of the West into national camps that were based on either religious confessions or ideological commitments.

The pervasive anxiety of the late sixteenth and early seventeenth centuries raises several questions that this chapter will explore: (1) How did the expanding population and price revolution exacerbate religious and political tensions? (2) How did religious and political authorities attempt to discipline the people? (3) How did religious differences provoke violence and start wars? (4) How did the countries of eastern Europe during the late sixteenth century become enmeshed in the religious controversies that began in western Europe during the early part of the century?

The Peoples of Early Modern Europe

During the tenth century if a Russian had wanted to see the sights of Paris—assuming he had even heard of Paris—he could have left Kiev and walked under the shade of trees all the way to France, so extensive were the forests and so sparse the human settlements of northern Europe. By the end of the thirteenth century, the nomadic Russian would have needed a hat to protect him on the shadeless journey. Instead of human settlements forming little islands in a sea of forests, the forests were by then islands in a sea of villages and farms, and from any church tower the sharp-eyed traveler could have seen other church towers, each marking a nearby village or town. At the end of the thirteenth century, the European continent had become completely settled by a dynamic, growing population, which had cleared the forests for farms.

As we saw in Chapter 10, during the fourteenth century all of that changed. A series of crises—periodic famines, the catastrophic Black Death, and a general economic collapse—left the villages and towns of Europe intact, but a third or more of the population was gone. In that period of desolation, many villages looked like abandoned movie sets, and the cities did not have enough people to fill in the empty spaces between the central market square and the city walls. Fields that had once been put to the plow to feed the hungry children of the thirteenth century were neglected and overrun with bristles and brambles. During the fifteenth century a general European depression and recurrent plagues kept the population stagnant.

In the sixteenth century the population began to rebound, but the sudden swell brought dramatic and destabilizing consequences that contributed to a pervasive anxiety. An important factor in the population growth was the transformation of European agriculture from subsistence to commercial farming, an uneven transformation that impoverished some villages while it enriched others. Moreover, the expanded population transformed the balance of power, as northern Europe recovered its population more successfully than southern Europe. As the population grew, young men and women flocked to the cities, creating enormous social strains and demands on local governments. Perhaps most disruptive was the price revolution, which brought inflation that ate away at the buying power of everyone from working families to kings and queens. The anxiety produced by these circumstances lasted into the early seventeenth century.

THE POPULATION RECOVERY

During a period that historical demographers call the "long sixteenth century" (ca. 1480–1640), the population of Europe began to grow consistently again for the first time since the late thirteenth century. In 1340, on the brink of the Black Death, Europe had about 74 million inhabitants, or 17 percent of the world's total. By 1400 the population of all of Europe had dropped to 52 million (less than one-fifth of the population of the United States today), or 14 percent of the world's total. Over the course of the long sixteenth century, Europe's population grew from 60.9 million to 77.9 million, just barely surpassing the pre-Black Death level.

The table to the right shows some representative population figures for the larger European countries during the sixteenth century. Two stunning facts emerge from these data. The first is the much greater rate of growth in northern Europe compared to southern Europe. England grew by 83 percent, Poland grew by 76 percent, and even the tiny, war-torn Netherlands gained 58 percent. During the same period Italy grew by only 25 percent and Spain by 19. These trends signal a massive, permanent shift of demographic and economic power from the Mediterranean countries of Italy and Spain to northern, especially northwestern, Europe. The second fact to note from these data is the overwhelming size of France, which was home to about a quarter of Europe's population. Once France recovered from its long wars of religion, its demographic superiority overwhelmed competing countries and made it the dominant power in Europe, permanently eclipsing its chief rival, Spain. Because Germany lacked political unity, it was unable to take advantage of its position as the second-largest land.

What explains the growth in the population and the economy? To a large extent, it was made possible by the transformation from subsistence to commercial agriculture in certain regions of Europe. Subsistence farmers, called peasants, had worked the land year in and year out, raising grains for the coarse black bread that fed their families, supplemented only by beer, grain porridge, and occasionally

European Population, 1500–1600 (in millions)

	1500	1550	1600
England	2.30	3.10	4.20
Germany	12.00	14.00	16.00
France	16.40	19.00	20.00
Netherlands	0.95	1.25	1.50
Belgium	1.25	1.65	1.30
Italy	10.50	11.40	13.10
Spain	6.80	7.50	8.10
Austria-Bohemia	3.50	3.60	4.30
Poland	2.50	3.00	3.40

Source: Jan de Vries, "Population," in *Handbook of European History 1400–1600: Late Middle Ages, Renaissance and Reformation,* Vol. 1: Structures and Assertions, edited by Thomas A. Brady, Jr., Heiko A. Oberman, and James D. Tracy, (1994), Table 1, p. 13.

vegetables. Meat was rare and expensive. Peasants consumed about 80 percent of everything they raised, and what little was left over went almost entirely to the landlord as feudal dues and to the church as tithing—the obligation to give to God one-tenth of everything earned or produced. Peasant families lived on the edge of existence. In a bad year some starved to death, usually the vulnerable children and old people. But during the sixteenth century, in areas with access to big cities, subsistence agriculture gave way to commercial crops, especially wheat, which was hauled to be sold in town markets. Profits from this market agriculture stimulated farmers to raise even greater surpluses in the agricultural regions around the great cities—in southern England around London; in the Netherlands around Antwerp and Amsterdam; in France the Ile-de-France near Paris; in northern Italy near Milan and Venice; in Catalonia near Barcelona; and in scattered places in Germany. Commercial crops and the cash income they produced meant fewer starving children and a higher standard of living for those who were able to take advantage of the new opportunities. As commercial agriculture spread, the population grew.

THE PROSPEROUS VILLAGES

Success in commercializing agriculture could make an enormous difference in the lives of peasants. The village of Buia tells the story of many similarly prosperous hamlets. Situated in Friuli, a region in the northeast corner of Italy, it served as part of the agricultural hinterland of the great metropolis of Venice. For centuries the peasants of hilly and pleasant Buia had lived in thatched hovels surviving at the subsistence level. But during the fourteenth and fifteenth centuries serfdom disappeared in the region and the peasants' legal status changed. Now free to sell their labor to the highest bidder, peasant families contracted with a landlord to lease a plot of land for a certain number of years in

■ The Rise of Commercial Agriculture
During the sixteenth century commercial agriculture began to produce significant surpluses for the expanding population of the cities.

exchange for annual rent payments in kind. A typical yearly rent might include two bushels of wheat, two of oats, one of beans, one of millet, three barrels of wine, two chickens, one ham, three guinea hens, thirty eggs, two cartloads of firewood, and two days' work mowing hay. In contrast to the servitude of serfdom, which tied peasants to the land, agricultural leases created a measure of economic freedom. They allowed landlords to find labor at a time when laborers were scarce, and they enabled peasants to negotiate for a better reward for their labor.

Unlike some neighboring villages that were still under the heel of their lords, Buia had incorporated as a town, a status that provided it with more autonomy from its lords, the Savorgnan family. Moreover, Buia had diversified its economy, branching out into cattle raising and marketing its fierce pear brandy and smooth white wine. But Buia's crucial economic advantage derived from its access to capital. The Savorgnan lords liberally lent money to their tenants in Buia, which enabled them to survive hard times and to invest in commercial profit-making enterprises. Unlike other families, the Savorgnans were willing to invest in their tenants, because they had established political and economic ties with the nearby commercial metropolis of Venice whose bankers were more than happy to bankroll

the Savorgnan family. From the commercial banks of Venice, money flowed through the hands of the Savorgnan to the peasants of the little village of Buia, who in turn produced crops that could be sold in the markets of Venice, a flow of money and goods that enriched everyone involved—the peasants, their Savorgnan landlords, and the Venetian bankers. With the increased income from commercial agriculture, Buia even began to look more affluent during the sixteenth century, boasting a substantial church, a tavern, and a simple one-room town hall where citizens could gather to debate their affairs.

The success of commercial agriculture during the sixteenth century depended on a free and mobile labor supply, access to capital for investment, and proximity to the markets of the big cities. What happened in Buia happened in many places throughout Europe, but overall the amount of land available could not provide enough work for the growing farm population. As a result, the growth of the rural population created a new class of landless, impoverished men and women, who were forced to take to the road to find their fortunes. These vagabonds, as they were called, foreshadowed the social problems that emerged from the uneven distribution of wealth generated by the new commerce.

THE REGULATED CITIES

By the 1480s cities began to grow, largely through migration from the more prosperous countryside, but the growth was uneven with the most dramatic growth occurring in the cities of the North, especially London, Antwerp, and Amsterdam (see Map 14.1). The surpluses of the countryside, both human and agricultural, flowed into the cities during the sixteenth century. Compared to even the prosperous rural villages, such as Buia, the cities must have seemed incomparably rich. Half-starved vagabonds from the countryside would have marveled at shops piled high with food (white bread, fancy pies, fruit, enormous casks of wine, roasting meats); they would have wistfully passed taverns full of drunken, laughing citizens; and they would have begged for alms in front of magnificent, marble-faced churches.

Every aspect of the cities exhibited dramatic contrasts between the rich and poor, who lived on the same streets and often in different parts of the same houses. Around 1580 Christian missionaries brought a Native American chief to the French city of Rouen. Through an interpreter he was asked what impressed him the most about European cities, so unlike the villages of North America. He replied that he was astonished that the rag-clad, emaciated men and women who crowded the streets did not grab the plump, well-dressed rich people by the throat.

The wretched human surplus from the farms continuously replenished and swelled the populations of the cities, which were frequently depleted by high urban death rates.

■ **Map 14.1 Population Distribution in the Sixteenth Century**
The population of Europe concentrated around the cities of northern Italy, the Danube and Rhine River valleys, Flanders and northern France, and southeastern England. During the late sixteenth century, northwestern Europe began to grow significantly more rapidly than southern Europe.

As wealthy as the cities were, they were unhealthy places: human waste overflowed from open latrines because there were no sewage systems; garbage, manure, dead animals, and roaming pigs and dogs made the streets putrid and dangerous; and water came from polluted rivers or sat stale in cisterns for months. Under such conditions, entire neighborhoods could be wiped out in epidemics. Both ends of the lifespan were vulnerable: one in three babies died in the first year of life; old people did not last long in cold, drafty houses. When the plague struck, which it continued to do about every twenty years until 1721, the rich escaped to their country retreats while the poor died in the streets or in houses locked up and under quarantine.

Despite the danger from disease in the cities, rural immigrants were less likely to starve than those who remained in small villages where they lacked land. Every city maintained storehouses of grain and regulated the price of bread and the size of a loaf so that the poor could be fed. The impulse to feed the poor was less the result of humanitarian motives than a recognition that nothing was more dangerous than a hungry mob. Given the contrasts in wealth among its inhabitants, cities guarded carefully against revolts and crime. Even for petty crime, punishment was swift, sure, and gruesome. The beggar who stole a loaf of bread from a baker's cart would have his hand amputated on a chopping block in the market square. A shabbily dressed girl who grabbed a lady's glittering trinket would have her nose cut off so that she could never attract a man. A burglar would be tortured, drawn, and quartered, and have his severed head impaled on an iron spike at the town gate as a warning to others.

To deal with the consequences of commerce and massive immigration, European cities attempted to regulate the lives of their inhabitants. Ringing bells measured each working day, and during the sixteenth century many cities erected a large mechanical clock in a prominent place so that busy citizens could keep to their schedules. The richer citizens elected from among themselves municipal officers who were responsible for protecting their financial interests. These officers inspected the weights and measures in the city market, regulated the distribution of produce to guarantee an abundant food supply, and repaired the streets and city walls. However talented or enterprising, new arrivals to the city had very limited opportunities. They could hardly start up their own business because all production was strictly controlled by the guilds. Recall from Chapter 10 that guilds were associations of merchants or artisans organized to protect their interests. Guilds rigidly regulated their membership; they required an apprenticeship of many years, prohibited technological innovations, guaranteed certain standards of workmanship, and did not allow branching out into new lines. A member of the goldsmiths' guild could not make mirrors; a baker could not sell fruit on the side; a house carpenter could not lay bricks. Given the limited opportunities for new arrivals, immigrant men and women begged on the streets or took charity from the public dole. The men picked up any heavy-labor jobs they could find. Both men and women became servants, a job that paid poorly but at least guaranteed regular meals.

Among the important social achievements of both Protestant and Catholic Reformations were efforts to address the problems of the destitute urban poor, who constituted at least a quarter of the population, even in the best of times. In Catholic countries such as Italy, Spain, southern Germany, and France, there was an enormous expansion of credit banks, which were financed by charitable contributions in order to provide small loans to the poor. Catholic cities established convents for poor young women who were at risk of falling into prostitution and for other women who had retired from the sex trade. Catholic and Protestant cities established orphanages, hospitals for the sick, hospices for the dying, and apartments lent out for a modest rent to poor widows. Both Catholic and Protestant cities attempted to distinguish between the "honest" poor—those who were disabled and truly deserving—and the "dishonest" poor who were thought to be malingerers. Protestant cities established poorhouses, which segregated the poor, subjected them to prisonlike discipline, and forced the able-bodied to work.

The more comfortable classes of the cities enjoyed large palaces and luxurious lifestyles. They hired extensive staffs of servants, feasted on meat and fine wines, and purchased exotic imports such as silk cloth, spices from the East, and, in the Mediterranean cities, slaves from eastern Europe, the Middle East, or Africa. The merchants whose fortunes came from cloth manufacturing, banking, and regional or international trade maintained their status by marrying among themselves, providing municipal offices to those whose fortunes had fallen, and educating their children in the newly fashionable humanist schools. The wealthy of the cities were the bastions of social stability. They possessed the financial resources and economic skills to protect themselves from the worst consequences of economic instability, especially the corrosive wave of price inflation that struck the West after about 1540.

THE PRICE REVOLUTION

Price inflation became so pervasive during the last half of the sixteenth century that it contributed to the widespread fear that events were being controlled by hidden forces. The effects of inflation are illustrated by the experience of the students at Winchester College in England. These young men were the privileged sons of English aristocrats and country gentlemen, who were destined for leisured wealth and public responsibility. The curriculum of Winchester emphasized the unchanging values of aristocratic privilege and Christian rectitude, but the dusty account books, kept in meticulous detail by generations of college stewards, reveal that change was very much a fact of college life during the sixteenth century. For example, in 1500 a piece of cloth large enough to make a student's uniform cost forty shillings. By 1580 the cost had doubled, and by 1630 it had tripled. During the sixteenth century the cost of a dozen sheets of parchment doubled, the cost of a dozen candles quadrupled, and the cost of a twelve-gallon barrel of wine (yes, the college served wine to its teenaged students) rose from eight to sixty-four shillings. English masons' experience of price inflation during this period was far more painful. Over the course of the century their wages doubled, but the price of bread increased four- or fivefold, and because the survival of their families depended on the cost of bread, price inflation seriously threatened their lives.

The finances of English college students and masons reveal the phenomenon that historians call the Price Revolution°. After a long period of falling or stable prices that stretched back to the fourteenth century, Europe experienced sustained price increases, beginning around 1540. The inflation lasted a century, forcing major economic and social changes that permanently altered the face of Western society. During this period overall prices across Europe multiplied five- or sixfold.

What caused the inflation? The basic principle is simple. The price paid for goods and services is fundamentally the result of the relationship between *supply* and *demand*. If the number of women who wish to wear silk gowns expands faster than the supply of silk, prices go up. This happens simply because those who most want silk will be willing to pay a higher price to get it. If the supply of available silk increases at a greater rate than the demand, then prices go down. The equation gets a little more complicated when taking into account two other factors that can influence price. One factor is the *amount of money in circulation.* If the amount of gold or silver available to make coins increases, there is more money in circulation. When more money is circulating, people have more money to buy more things, which creates the same effect as an increase in demand—prices go up. The other factor is called the *velocity of money in circulation,* which refers to the number of times money changes hands to buy things. When people buy commodities with greater frequency, it has the same effect as increasing the amount of money in circulation or of increasing demand—again, prices go up.

The precise combination of these factors in causing the great Price Revolution of the sixteenth century has long been a matter of considerable debate. Most historians would now agree that the primary cause of inflation was population growth, which increased demand. As Europe's population finally began to recover, it meant that more people needed and desired to buy more things. This explanation is most obvious for commodities that people need to survive, such as grain to make bread. These commodities have what economists call *inelastic demand,* that is, consumers do not have a great deal of discretion in purchasing them. Everybody has to eat. The commodities that people could survive without if the price is too high are said to have *elastic demand,* such as dancing shoes and lace collars. In England between 1540 and 1640 overall prices rose by 490 percent. More telling, however, is that the price of grain (inelastic demand) rose by a stunning 670 percent, whereas the price of luxury goods (elastic demand) rose much less, by 204 percent.

Monetary factors also contributed to inflation. The Portuguese brought in significant amounts of gold from Africa, and newly opened mines in central Europe increased the amount of silver by fivefold as early as the 1520s. The discovery in 1545 of the fabulous silver mine of Potosí (in present-day Bolivia) brought to Europe a flood of silver, which Spain used to finance its costly wars. As inflation began to eat away at royal incomes, financially strapped monarchs all across western Europe debased their money because they believed, mistakenly, that producing more coins containing less silver would buy more. In fact, the minting of more coins meant each coin was worth less and would buy less. Debasement was especially disastrous in England, where it was the major source of inflation during the 1540s and 1550s.

During the sixteenth century, no one understood these causes, however. People only experienced the effects of inflation, and then only gradually. The real wages of workers declined, causing widespread suffering and discontent. Incomes eroded for those dependent on fixed incomes—clergymen, pensioners, government clerks, and landlords who rented out land on long leases. Landlords who were willing to be ruthless and enterprising survived and even prospered. Those who were more paternalistic or conservative in managing their estates often lost their land to creditors.

The Price Revolution severely weakened governments. Most monarchs derived their incomes from their own private lands and from taxes on property. As inflation took hold, property taxes proved dangerously inadequate to cover royal expenses. Even frugal monarchs such as England's Elizabeth I were forced to take extraordinary measures, in her case to sell off royal lands. Spendthrift monarchs faced disaster. Spain was involved in the costly enterprise of nearly continuous war during the sixteenth century. To pay for the wars, Charles V resorted to a form of deficit financing in which he borrowed money by issuing *juros,* which provided lenders an annuity yielding between 3 and 7 percent on the amount of the principal. By the 1550s, however, the annuity payments of the *juros* consumed half of the royal revenues. Charles's son, Philip II, inherited such an alarming situation that in 1557, the year after he assumed the throne, he was forced to declare bankruptcy. Philip continued to fight expensive wars and borrow wildly, and thus failed to get his financial house in order. He declared bankruptcy again in 1575 and 1596. Philip squandered Spain's wealth, impoverishing his own subjects through burdensome taxes and contributing to inflation by borrowing at high rates of interest and debasing the coinage. As the greatest power of the sixteenth century, Spain sowed the seeds of its own decline by fighting on borrowed money.

Probably the most serious consequence of the Price Revolution was that the hidden force of inflation caused widespread human suffering. During the late sixteenth and early seventeenth centuries, people felt their lives threatened, but they did not know the source and so they imagined all kinds of secret powers at work, especially supernatural ones. Catholics suspected Protestants, Protestants suspected Catholics, both suspected Jews, and they all worried about witches. Authorities sought to relieve this widespread anxiety by looking in all the wrong places, by disciplining the populace, hunting for witches, and battling against enemies from the opposite side of the confessional divide.

Disciplining the People

The first generation of the Protestant and Catholic Reformations had been devoted to doctrinal disputes and to either rejecting or defending papal authority. Subsequent generations of reformers in the last half of the sixteenth and the early seventeenth centuries faced the formidable task of building the institutions that would firmly establish a Protestant or Catholic religious culture. Leaders of all religious confessions attempted to revitalize the Christian community by disciplining nonconformists and enforcing moral rigor. Members of the community came to identify responsible citizenship with conformity to a specific Christian confession.

Whether Lutheran, Calvinist, Catholic, or Anglican, godly reformers attacked popular culture. They reformed or abolished wild festivals, they imprisoned town drunks, they decreased the number of holidays, and they tried to regulate sexual behavior. Many activities that had once been accepted as normal came to be considered deviant or criminal. The process of disciplining the people required cooperation between church and secular authorities, but discipline was not entirely imposed from above. Some people wholeheartedly cooperated with moral correction and even encouraged reformers to go further. Others passively, actively, or resentfully resisted it.

ESTABLISHING CONFESSIONAL IDENTITIES

Between 1560 and 1650 religious confessions reshaped European culture, and loyalty to a single confession governed the relationships between states. A confession consisted of the adherents to a particular statement of religious doctrine—the Confession of Augsburg for Lutherans, the Helvetic Confessions for Calvinists, the Thirty-Nine Articles for Anglicans, and the decrees of the Council of Trent for Catholics. Based on these confessions of faith, the clergy disciplined the laity, exiled nonconformists, and promoted distinct religious institutions, beliefs, and culture.

The process of establishing confessional identities did not happen overnight; it lasted for centuries and had far-reaching consequences. During the second half of the sixteenth century, Lutherans turned from the struggle to survive within the hostile Holy Roman Empire to establishing a confessional identity in the parts of the empire where Lutheranism was the chosen religion of the local prince. They had to recruit Lutheran clergy and provide each clergyman with a university education, which was made possible by scholarship endowments from the Lutheran princes of Germany. Once established, the Lutheran clergy became a branch of the civil bureaucracy, received a government stipend, and enforced the will of the prince. Calvinist states followed a similar process.

Catholics responded with their own aggressive plan of training new clergymen, propagandizing the laity, and reinforcing the bond between church and state. Just as with the Lutheran princes, Catholic princes in Germany associated conformity to Catholicism with loyalty to themselves, making religion a pillar of the state. Everywhere in western Europe (except for Ireland and for a time France) the only openly practiced religion was the religion of the state.

The authorities primarily formed confessional identities among the laity by promoting distinctive ritual systems. These ritual systems embodied ways of acting and even of gesturing that literally transformed the way people moved their bodies so that a Catholic and a Protestant might be instantly recognized by certain telltale signs of posture, speech, and comportment.

The Catholic and Protestant ritual systems differed primarily in their attitude toward the sacred. Whereas Catholic ritual behavior depended on a repertoire of gestures that indicated reverence in the presence of the sacred, Protestant ritual depended on a demonstration of sociability that identified people as members of a certain congregation or church. For example, until the late sixteenth century Europeans greeted one another either by raising a hand, palm outward, which meant "welcome," or with a bow by which someone of lower status recognized the superiority of another. Some radical Protestants, however, insisted that all gestures of deference, such as bows and curtsies, were an affront to God and introduced a new form of greeting, the handshake. Shaking hands was completely egalitarian, and one could identify English Quakers or Scottish Calvinists, for example, simply by the fact that they shook hands with one another.

A particularly revealing ritual difference can be seen in the contrasting ways that Scottish Calvinists and Spanish Catholics reintegrated repentant sinners into the Church. In Calvinism disciplinary authority rested with the presbytery, a board of pastors and elders elected by the community. If a Scottish Calvinist blasphemed God, the presbytery could discipline him, shun him, or banish him from the community. If he wished to be reinstated and the presbytery agreed, he would be obliged to come before the entire congregation to confess sincerely his wrongs and beg forgiveness. The congregation would make a collective judgment about his acceptability for renewed membership. The pain inflicted on the Calvinist sinner was the social pain of having his transgression openly discussed and evaluated by his friends and neighbors.

If a Spanish Catholic blasphemed, he would be subjected to an extended ritual of penance, the auto-da-fé°, which meant a theater of faith. The auto-da-fé was designed to promote fear and to cause physical pain because, according to Catholic doctrine, bodily suffering in this world was necessary in order to free the soul from worse suffering in the next. An *auto* was a public performance in which dozens or sometimes hundreds of sinners and criminals were paraded through the streets in a theatrical demonstration of the authority of the Church and the power of penance. The *auto* culminated in a mass confirmation of faith in which the repentant sinners utterly subjected themselves to the authority of the clergy, while those who refused to repent or were relapsed heretics were strangled and their corpses burned.

Whereas the punishment of the Calvinist community was primarily a rite of social humiliation, the auto-da-fé involved physical torture as well as social degradation. The nub of the difference was that Calvinists had to demonstrate the sincerity of their social conformity; Catholics had to go through a performance that emphasized the authority of the clergy and that purified sin with physical pain.

POLICING THE FAMILY

One matter on which Calvinists, Lutherans, and Catholics agreed was that the foundation of society was the authority fathers had over their families. This principle, known as patriarchy, was discussed in Chapter 11. The confessions that emerged from the Reformation further strengthened patriarchy because it so usefully served the authoritarian needs of church and state. According to an anonymous treatise published in 1586 in Calvinist Nassau, the three pillars of Christian society were the church, the state, and the household. This proposition made the father's authority a reflection of the authority of clergy and king—a position that all the confessions would have accepted. The enforcement of patriarchy required the policing of gender roles. And during the otherwise discordant sixteenth century, the one issue on which virtually all men and many women agreed was that women should be subservient to men.

Marriage and Sexuality:
The Self-Restrained Couple

During the Early Modern period, the structure of the European family underwent a major transformation. The result was a new type of family that now seems normal to most people in the Western world. The new family type first appeared in northwestern Europe—in Britain, Scandinavia, the Netherlands, northern France, and western Germany.

In these regions, couples tended to wait to marry until their mid- or late twenties, well beyond the age of sexual maturity. And when these couples married, they established their own household separate from either of their parents. Husbands were usually only two or three years older than their wives. By contrast, in southern Europe, men in their late twenties or thirties married teenaged women, and in eastern Europe, both spouses married in their teens and resided in one of the parental households for many years. The pattern established in northwestern European required that the couple be economically independent before they married, which meant both had to accumulate savings or the husband needed to inherit from his deceased father before he could marry.

This new marriage pattern required prolonged sexual restraint by young men and women until they were economically self-sufficient. In addition to individual self-control, sexual restraint required social control by church and secular authorities. These efforts seem to have been generally successful. For example, in sixteenth-century Geneva, where the elders were especially wary about sexual sins, the rates of illegitimate births were extremely low. The elders were particularly vigilant about disciplining women and keeping them subservient, often making and enforcing highly minute regulations. In 1584 Calvinist elders in another Swiss town excommunicated Charlotte Arbaleste and her entire household because she wore her hair in curls, which the elders thought were too alluring.

The new family also tended to be a smaller family. Despite the Christian precept that encouraged as many children as possible, married couples in northwestern European began to space their children through birth control and family planning. These self-restrained couples practiced withdrawal, the rhythm method, or abstinence. When mothers no longer relied on wet nurses and nursed their own infants, often for long periods, they also reduced their chances of becoming pregnant. Thus, limiting family size became the social norm in northwestern Europe, especially among the educated and urban middle classes. Protestant families tended to have fewer children than Catholic families, but Catholics in this region also practiced some form of birth control, even though Church law prohibited all forms except abstinence.

For prospective couples, parental approval remained more important than romantic love. In fact, a romantic attachment between a husband and wife was frowned upon as unseemly and even dangerous. More highly prized in a marriage partner were trust, dependability, and the willingness to work. Many married couples certainly exhibited signs of affection—addressing one another lovingly in letters, nursing a sick mate, mourning a dead one—but overly sentimental attachments were discouraged as contrary to the patriarchal authority that ideally characterized family life. Most husbands and wives seem to have treated one another with a certain coolness and emotional detachment.

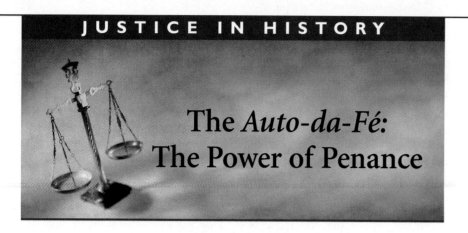

The *Auto-da-Fé:*
The Power of Penance

Performed in Spain and Portugal from the sixteenth to eighteenth centuries, the auto-da-fé merged the judicial processes of the state with the sacramental rituals of the Catholic Church. An *auto* took place at the end of a judicial investigation conducted by the inquisitors of the Church after the defendants had been found guilty of a sin or crime. The term auto-da-fé means "theater of faith," and the goal was to persuade or force a person who had been judged guilty to repent and confess. Organized through the cooperation of ecclesiastical and secular authorities, autos-da-fé brought together an assortment of sinners, criminals, and heretics for a vast public rite that dramatized the essential elements of the sacrament of penance: contrition, by which the sinner recognized and felt sorry for the sin; confession, which required the sinner to admit the sin to a priest; and satisfaction or punishment, by which the priest absolved the sinner and enacted some kind of penalty. The auto-da-fé transformed penance, especially confession and satisfaction, into a spectacular affirmation of the faith and a manifestation of divine justice.

The *auto* symbolically anticipated the Last Judgment, and it provoked deep anxiety among those who witnessed it about how God would judge them. By suffering bodily pain in this life the soul might be relieved from worse punishments in the next. The sinners, convicts, and heretics, now considered penitents, were forced to march in a procession that went through the streets of the city from the cathedral to the town hall or place of punishment. These processions would typically include some thirty or forty penitents, but in moments of crisis they could be far larger. In Toledo in 1486 there were three *autos*—one parading 750 penitents and two displaying some 900 each.

A 1655 *auto* in Córdoba illustrates the symbolic character of the rites. Soldiers bearing torches that would light the pyre for those to be burnt led the procession. Following them came three bigamists who wore on their heads conical miters or hats painted with representations of their sin, four witches whose miters depicted devils, and three criminals with harnesses around their necks to demonstrate their status as captives. The sinners carried unlit candles to represent their lack of faith. Criminals who had escaped arrest were represented in the procession by effigies made in their likeness, and those who had died before punishment were carried in their coffins. The marching sinners appeared before their neighbors and fellow citizens stripped of the normal indicators of status, dressed only in the emblems of their sins. Among them walked a few who wore the infamous *sanbenitos,* a kind of tunic or vest with a yellow strip down the back, and a conical hat painted with flames. These were the *relajados,* the unrepentant or relapsed sinners who were going to be "relaxed" (strangled and burned) at the culminating moment of the *auto.*

The procession ended in the town square at a platform from which penances were performed as on the stage of a theater. Forced to their knees, the penitents were asked to confess and to plead for readmission into the bosom of the church. For those who did confess, a sentence was announced that would rescue them from the pains of Purgatory and the flames of the *auto.* The sentence required them to join a penitential procession for a certain number of Fridays, perform self-flagellation in public, or wear a badge of shame for a prescribed period of time. Those who failed to confess faced a more immediate sentence.

The most horrendous scenes of suffering awaited those who refused to confess or who had relapsed into sin or heresy, which meant their confession was not considered sincere. If holdouts confessed prior to the reading of the sentence, then the *auto* was a success, a triumph of the Christian faith over its enemies, and everything that could possibly elicit confessions was attempted, including haranguing, humiliating, and torturing the accused until their stubborn will broke. If the accused finally confessed after the sentence was read, then they would be strangled before burning, but if they held out to the very end, they would be burned alive. From the ecclesiastics' point of view, the refusal to confess was a disaster for the entire Church because the flames of the pyre opened a window into Hell. They would certainly prefer to see the Church's authority acknowledged through confession than to see the power of Satan manifest in such a public fashion.

■ **Auto-da-fé in Lisbon**

A procession conducted the sinners, many with hats or aprons identifying their sins, to a stage and pyre where relapsed heretics were burned.

It is reported that crowds witnessed the violence of the autos-da-fé with silent attention in a mood of deep dread, not so much of the inquisitors, it seems, as for the inevitability of the final day of divine judgment that would arrive for them all. The core assumption of the auto-da-fé was that bodily pain could save a soul from damnation. As one contemporary witness put it, the inquisitors removed "through external ritual [the sinners'] internal crimes." It was assumed that the public ritual framework for the sacrament of penance would have a salutary effect on those who witnessed the *auto* by encouraging them to repent before they too faced divine judgment. ■

Questions of Justice

1. How did the auto-da-fé contribute to the formation of an individual and collective sense of being a Catholic?

2. How did the auto-da-fé reveal the difference between Spanish Catholic and Scottish Calvinist forms of discipline?

3. In the auto-da-fé, inflicting physical pain was more than punishment. How was pain understood to have been socially and religiously useful? Compare the role of pain here with that in St. Teresa of Avila's experience of pain, discussed in Chapter 13 (p. 448).

Taking It Further

Flynn, Maureen. "Mimesis of the Last Judgment: The Spanish *Auto de fe*," *Sixteenth Century Journal* 22 (1991): 281–297. The best analysis of the religious significance of the auto-da-fé.

Flynn, Maureen. "The Spectacle of Suffering in Spanish Streets," in Barbara A. Hanawalt and Kathryn L. Reyerson, eds., *City and Spectacle in Medieval Europe*. 1994. In this fascinating article Flynn analyzes the spiritual value of physical pain.

The moral status of marriage also changed during this period. Protestants no longer considered husbands and wives as morally inferior to celibate monks and nuns, and the wives of preachers in Protestant communities certainly had a respected social role never granted to the concubines of priests. But the favorable Protestant attitude toward marriage did not necessarily translate into a positive attitude toward women. In Germany the numerous books of advice, called the Father of the House literature, encouraged families to subordinate the individual interests of servants, children, and the mother to the dictates of the father, who was encouraged to be just but who must be obeyed. Even if a wife was brutally treated by her husband, she could neither find help from authorities nor expect a divorce.

Children: Naturally Evil?

Beginning in the fifteenth century, the middle classes began to adopt a new attitude toward children, placing greater emphasis on their welfare, education, and moral upbringing. The Reformation contributed to this process by emphasizing the family's responsibility for their children's moral guidance and religious education. One of the obligations of Protestant fathers was to read and teach the Bible in the home. This directive may have been more a theoretical ideal than a practical reality, but the rise in literacy among both boys and girls in Protestant countries attests to the increased importance of education.

Discipline also played a large role in the sixteenth-century family. Parents had always demonstrated love toward their children by indulging them with sweets and toys and protecting them from danger. But during the sixteenth century some authors of advice books and many preachers began to emphasize that parental love must be tempered by strict discipline. In effect, the clergy attempted to impose their own authoritarian impulses on the emotional lives of the family. The Protestant emphasis on the majesty of God and a belief in original sin translated into a negative view of human nature. Calvinist theologians who held such a view placed a special emphasis on family discipline. The *Disquisition on the Spiritual Condition of Infants* (1618) pointed out that from a theological point of view, babies were naturally evil. The godly responsibility of the father was to break the will of his evil offspring, taming them so that they could be turned away from sin toward virtue. The very title of a 1591 Calvinist treatise revealed the strength of the evil-child argument: *On Disciplining Children: How the Disobedient, Evil, and Corrupted Youth of These Anxious Last Days Can Be Bettered*. The treatise also advised that the mother's role should be limited to her biological function of giving birth. It directed fathers to be vigilant so that their wives did not corrupt the children, because women "love to accept strange, false beliefs, and go about with benedictions and witches' handiwork. When they are not firm in faith and the Devil comes to tempt them . . . they follow him and go about with supernatural fantasies."[1]

In order to break the will of their infants, mothers were encouraged to wean them early and turn them over for a strict upbringing by their fathers. The ideal father was to cultivate both love and fear in his children by remaining unemotional and firm. He was to be vigilant to prevent masturbation, to discourage frivolity, and to toughen little children by not allowing them to eat too much, sleep too long, or stay too comfortably warm. Although discouraged from being unnecessarily brutal, the godly father was never to spare the rod on either his children or his wife.

It is clear that disciplining children was an important theoretical guideline in sixteenth- and seventeenth-century Europe. It is less clear whether this was as true in practice as in theory. Historians disagree on the issue. It is likely that then, as now, there were many different ways of raising children, and each family exhibited its own emotional chemistry. And it is also likely that sixteenth-century parents did not consider firm discipline as unloving.

DISCIPLINING CHILDREN AND ENCOURAGING INFORMANTS

During the sixteenth and seventeenth centuries, schools began to rely on the monitor system for enforcing discipline among the pupils. The goal of the system was to control every moment of the students' lives, but it was impossible for school masters to achieve such regimentation by themselves, so they relied on student observers and informants. Youngsters were obliged to report any fellow student who spoke in the vernacular rather than Latin, lied, cursed, acted indecently, stayed in bed in the morning, talked in church, or missed prayers. The following account comes from a self-described "good pupil" at Cordier's College in Geneva.

We dined in the room, sitting quietly and making no murmur or noise; I gently reproved those whom I heard laughing foolishly or speaking in vain or frolicking; I told the observer about those who paid no attention to my warning so that he should take note of them . . . The master walked up and down the middle of the room, holding a book and frequently telling the observer to take note of those who played the fool . . . While we were finishing dinner, the last bell was rung, each of us picked up his books, and we went into the common room, the register of each class was read out according to custom, those who were present answered to their name, I answered too, and the absentees were recorded on the nomenclators' registers.

Source: From Philippe Ariès, *Centuries of Childhood: A Social History of Family Life*, translated by Robert Baldick, New York: Vintage Books, 1962.

■ **The Ideal Family**
During the late sixteenth century, idealized depictions of harmonious family life became very popular. This etching, which was sold in multiple copies at modest prices much as a wall poster would be today, depicts a prosperous peasant family.

SUPPRESSING POPULAR CULTURE

The family was not the only institution that sixteenth-century educated reformers sought to discipline. Their efforts also targeted many manifestations of traditional popular culture. The reformers or puritans, as they came to be called in England, wanted to purify society, to remake it into a "godly community" by imposing a rigid moral regimen, particularly on undisciplined youths and members of the lower classes. The suppression of popular culture had two aspects. One was a policing effort, aimed at ridding society of presumably un-Christian practices. The other was a missionary enterprise, an attempt to bring the Protestant and Catholic Reformations to the people through instruction and popular preaching.

Overall the godly reformers sought to encourage an ethic of asceticism, which valued thrift, modesty, chastity, and above all self-control. This ethic was neither Protestant nor Catholic but was promoted by clerics of all religious confessions. The traditional popular culture they so de-spised stressed other values such as spontaneity, emotional freedom, and generosity.

Once the reformers had cleaned up the churches by eliminating idolatry, unnecessary holidays, and superfluous rituals, they turned to the secular world, and they found much to criticize. The reformers saw impiety in comedians, dancing, loud music, rough sports, dice and card games, public drinking, dressing up in costumes, puppets, and above all actors. The Bishop of Verona condemned preachers who told stories that made the congregations laugh. To the reformers, these things were despicable because they seemed to be vestiges of pre-Christian practices and because they led people into sin.

The festival of Carnival° came under particularly virulent attack. The most popular annual festival, also known as Mardi Gras, Carnival took place for several days or even weeks before the beginning of Lent and included all kinds of fun and games—silly pantomimes, bear baiting, bullfights, masquerades, dances, lots of eating and drinking, and illicit sex. The *Discourse Against Carnival* (1607) complained about the temptations to sin and the money wasted in Carnival play. Catholics attempted to reform Carnival by eliminating the most offensive forms of behavior, especially those that led to violence or vice. Other popular festivals and entertainments suffered a similar fate of scornful criticism, regulation, or even abolition.

Pieter Brueghel the Elder's painting *The Battle Between Carnival and Lent* (1559) illustrates the role of festivals in the popular culture. In the painting, a fat man riding on a wine barrel engages in a mock joust with an emaciated, stooped figure of uncertain gender who rides a wheeled cart pulled by a monk and nun. The two figures represent two festival seasons. The fat man represents Carnival, a time of joyous, gluttonous, drunken feasting; the lean one represents Lent, a period of sexual abstinence and fasting that precedes Easter. The figures might also represent the passionate side of popular culture that was devoted to bodily pleasure (Carnival) and the clerical urge to suppress bodily desires and reform popular festivities (Lent).

What Catholics reformed, Protestants abolished. Martin Luther had been relatively tolerant of popular culture, but later reformers were not. The most famous German Carnival, the *Schembartlauf* of Nuremberg, was abolished; in England the great medieval pageants of York, Coventry, Chester, Norwich, and Worcester disappeared; in Calvinist Holland, the Christmas tradition of giving children gifts was strongly denounced.

The Carnival festival was highly resilient, however. Along with many other forms of popular culture, it persisted, even

■ **The Battle Between Carnival and Lent**
In this allegory, called *The Battle Between Carnival and Lent* (1559) by Pieter Brueghel the Elder, the festive season of Carnival is represented by a fat man riding a wine barrel. He is engaged in a mock joust with an emaciated figure representing Lent, the season for fasting. Behind Carnival, people engage in games, drinking, dancing, and flirtations. Behind Lent, a procession of the pious leads back into a church.

if less openly public. The moralist attack on popular culture meant that some activities retreated from outside to inside—into sports arenas, taverns, theaters, and opera houses. And some were professionalized by athletes, entertainers, actors, and singers. The attempts of dour clerics to abolish fun also provoked open resistance. In 1539 in Nuremberg the Lutheran pastor Andreas Osiander, who had preached against Carnival, found himself lampooned by a float in the shape of a ship of fools, in which he was depicted as the captain.

The attempts to suppress popular culture produced a confrontation between the educated elites of Europe and the workers, peasants, servants, and artisans who surrounded them and served them. Although not entirely successful, by the late sixteenth century the suppression had the effect of broadening the cultural gap between the educated few and the masses. Practices that previously had been broadly accepted forms of public entertainment, in which even members of the clergy participated, came to be seen as unworthy of educated people.

HUNTING WITCHES

The most catastrophic manifestation of the widespread anxiety of the late sixteenth and seventeenth centuries was the great witch-hunt°. The judicial prosecution of alleged witches in either church or secular courts dramatically increased about the middle of the sixteenth century and lasted until the late seventeenth, when the number of witchcraft trials rapidly diminished and stopped entirely in western Europe.

Throughout this period, people accepted the reality of two kinds of magic°. The first kind was natural magic, such as the practice of alchemy or astrology, which involved the manipulation of occult forces believed to exist in nature.

The fundamental assumption of natural magic was that everything in nature is alive. The trained magician could coerce the occult forces in nature to do his bidding. During the Renaissance many humanists and scientific thinkers were drawn to natural magic because of its promise of power over nature. Natural magic, in fact, had some practical uses. Alchemists, for example, devoted themselves to discovering what they called the "philosopher's stone," the secret of transmuting base metals into gold. In practice this meant that they learned how to imitate the appearance of gold, a very useful skill for counterfeiting coins or reducing the content of precious metals in legal coins. Natural magic was practiced by educated men and involved the human manipulation of the occult, but it did not imply any kind of contact with devils. Most practitioners of natural magic desired to achieve good, and many considered it the highest form of curative medicine.

People of the sixteenth and seventeenth centuries also believed in a second kind of magic—demonic magic. The practitioner of this kind of magic—usually but not always a female witch—called upon evil spirits to gain access to power. Demonic magic was generally understood as a way to work harm by ritual means. Belief in the reality of harmful magic and of witches had been widespread for centuries, and there had been occasional witch trials throughout the Middle Ages. Systematic witch-hunts, however, began only when ecclesiastical and secular authorities showed a willingness to employ the law to discover and punish accused witches. The Reformation controversies of the late sixteenth century and the authorities' willingness to discipline deviants of all sorts certainly intensified the hunt for witches. Thousands of people were accused of and tried for practicing witchcraft. About half of these alleged witches were executed, most often by burning. Cases of alleged witchcraft rarely occurred in a steady flow, as one would find for other crimes. Typically, witchcraft trials took place during localized hunts when a flareup of paranoia and torture multiplied allegations against vulnerable members of the community. Most allegations were against women, in particular young unmarried women and older widows, but men and even young children could be accused of witchcraft as well.

People in many different places—from shepherds in the mountains of Switzerland to Calvinist ministers in the lowlands of Scotland—thought they perceived the work of witches in human and natural events. The alleged demonic magic of witchcraft appeared in two forms: *maleficia* (doing harm) and *diabolism* (worshipping the devil). The rituals of *maleficia* consisted of a simple sign or a complex incantation, but what made them *maleficia* was the belief that the person who performed them intended to cause harm to someone or something. There were many kinds of *maleficia,* including coercing an unwilling lover by sprinkling dried menstrual blood in his food, sickening a pig by

HOW WOMEN CAME TO BE ACCUSED OF WITCHCRAFT: A WITCH'S CONFESSION

Walpurga Hausmännin, an elderly widow and midwife from a small town near Augsburg in the Holy Roman Empire, was accused in 1587 of killing more than forty children. Her confession, extracted out of her through fear and torture, is tragic but typical, complete with lurid details of sexual intercourse with the Devil, the Devil's mark, a pact with the Devil, and riding on a broomstick to a witches' sabbath. This excerpt from her confession, which lists some of her alleged victims, illustrates how the collective fears of the community were channeled into imagined crimes against children.

[T]he Devil] also compelled her to do away with and to kill young infants at birth, even before they had been taken to Holy Baptism. This she did, whenever possible. These as follows:

1 and 2. About ten years ago, she had rubbed Anna Hämännin, who dwelt far from Dursteigel, with her salve on the occasion of her first childbirth and also otherwise damaged her so that mother and child remained together and died.

3. Dorothea, the stepdaughter of Christian Wachter, bore her first child ten years before; at its birth she made press on its little brain so that it died. The Devil had specially bidden her destroy the first-born.

5. When, four years ago, the organist's wife was awaiting her confinement, she touched her naked body with her salve whereby the child promptly died and came stillborn.

8. Three years ago when she was called to a mill to the miller's wife there she had let the child fall into the water and drown.

11. When six years ago, she partook of food with Magdalena Seilerin, called *Kammerschreiberin* (wife of the chamber scribe), she had put a salve in her drink, so that she was delivered prematurely. This child she, Walpurga, secretly buried under the doorway of the said wife of the scribe on the pretext that then she would have no other miscarriage. The same she also did with many others. When she was questioned under torture for the reasons of this burial, she admitted that it was done in order to cause disunion between two spouses. This her Devil-Paramour had taught her.

15. She had also rubbed a salve on a beautiful son of the late Chancellor, Jacob by name: this child had lovely fair hair and she had given him a hobby-horse so that he might ride on it till he lost his senses. He died likewise.

Source: From George T. Matthews, ed., *News and Rumor in Renaissance Europe: The Fugger Newsletters,* pp. 137–143. Copyright © 1959 by G. P. Putnam's Sons.

cursing it, burning a barn by marking it with a hex sign, bringing wasting diarrhea to a child by reciting a spell, and killing an enemy by stabbing a wax statue of him. Midwives and women who specialized in healing were especially vulnerable to accusations of witchcraft. The intention behind a particular action they might have performed was often obscure, making it difficult to distinguish between magic designed to bring beneficial results, such as the cure of a child, and *maleficia* designed to bring harmful ones. With the high infant mortality rates of the sixteenth and seventeenth centuries, performing magical rituals for a sick baby could be very risky. The logic of witchcraft beliefs implied that a bad ending must have been caused by bad intentions.

While some people may have attempted to practice *maleficia*, the second and far more serious kind of ritual practice associated with demonic magic, *diabolism*, almost certainly never took place. Diabolism was a fantasy that helped explain events that could not otherwise be explained. The theory behind diabolism asserted that the witch had sold her soul to the Devil, whom she worshipped as her god. These witches had made a pact with the Devil, worshiped the Devil in the ritual of the witches' sabbath, flew around at night, and sometimes changed themselves into animals. The two core beliefs of the pact with the Devil and the witches' sabbath created the intellectual and legal conditions for the great witch-hunt of the sixteenth and seventeenth centuries.

A pact with the devil was believed to give the witch the ability to accomplish *maleficia*, in exchange for which she was obliged to serve and worship Satan. The most influential witchcraft treatise, *The Hammer of Witches* (1486), had an extensive discussion of the ceremony of the pact. After the prospective witch had declared her intention to enter his service, Satan appeared to her, often in the alluring form of a handsome young man who offered her rewards, including a demonic lover, called an *incubus*. To obtain these inducements, the witch was obligated to renounce her allegiance to Christ, usually signified by stomping on the cross. The Devil rebaptized her in a disgusting substance, guaranteeing that her soul belonged to him. To signify that she was one of his own, the Devil marked her body in a hidden place, creating a sign, which could easily be confused with a birthmark or blemish. To an inquisitor or judge almost any mark on the skin might confirm guilt.

One of the fullest accounts of beliefs in the witches' sabbath comes from the tragic trial of the Pappenheimer family in Bavaria in 1600. The Pappenheimers, consisting of a mother, a father, and their sons, were vagrants arrested for killing babies and cutting off their hands for the purposes of witchcraft. In her confession under torture, Anna Pappenheimer gave a full account of her participation in a fantastic witches' sabbath that supposedly took place at night on a hill outside of the village of Tettenwang. She claimed that witches arrived from near and far flying in

■ **The Witches' Sabbath**
The myth of the witches' sabbath depicted witches paying homage to an enthroned Satan. The typical sabbath motifs included the ability to fly and cannibalism of Christian babies, as shown on the lower right. The figures walking on their hands reveal a world literally turned upside down.

■ Burning of Witches at Dernberg in 1555
One of the witches is being taken away by a flying demon to whom she had sold her soul.

on broomsticks and pitchforks. The assembled company largely consisted of women, young and old and most of them naked, but there were a few male witches (known as warlocks) and even some children. With a clap of thunder and a profusion of smoke, Satan himself suddenly appeared with his eyes glowing, dressed in black and smelling horribly. The assembled witches and warlocks bowed low before him, praying in a travesty of the Lord's Prayer, "Our Satan which art in Hell. . . ." There followed an infernal banquet of disgusting foods, including horse meat, ravens, crows, toads, frogs, and boiled and roasted infants. After the feast, an orchestra of demons played tuneless, screeching dance music that aroused a mad lust in the witches and their demon lovers, who began a wild spinning dance that finally broke down into a indiscriminate orgy. The family and some other drifters were grotesquely tortured and burned alive.

Between about 1550 and 1650, some 100,000 people in Europe were tried for witchcraft. About 50,000 of these were executed. Approximately half of the trials were in the German-speaking lands of the Holy Roman Empire. Prosecutions were also extensive in Switzerland, France, Scotland, Poland, Hungary, Transylvania, and Russia. Some 10,000 people were tried in Spain and Italy, but these were mostly for minor offenses of *maleficia,* and very few people were executed, probably none in Italy. As the product of collective beliefs and collective paranoia, witchcraft beliefs could be applied to all kinds of people, but allegations were most commonly lodged against poor, older women in small rural villages. In most of Europe, about 80 percent of the witches were female, but in Essex County, England, and Basel, Switzerland, more than 90 percent were female. In Russia and Estonia, however, men made up the majority of witches. These differences in the gender of alleged witches illustrate how the witchcraft myth was adapted to local conditions and assumptions about who was dangerous in society.

The Confessional States

The Religious Peace of Augsburg of 1555 provided the model for a solution to the religious divisions produced by the Reformation. According to the principle of *cuius regio, eius religio* (he who rules determines the religion of the land), each prince in the Holy Roman Empire determined the religion to be followed by his subjects, and those who disagreed were obliged to emigrate elsewhere. Certainly, forced exile was economically and personally traumatic for those who emigrated, but it preserved what was almost universally believed to be the fundamental principle of successful rulership—one king, one faith, one law. In other words, each state should have only one church. Except in the notoriously weak states of eastern Europe and a few small troubled ones in Germany, hardly anyone thought it desirable to allow more than one confession in the same state.

The problem with this political theory of religious unity, of course, was the reality of religious divisions created by the Reformation. In some places there were as many as three active confessions—Catholic, Lutheran, and Calvinist—in addition to the minor sects, such as the Anabaptists and the Jewish communities. The alternative to religious unity would have been religious toleration, but hardly anyone in a position of authority was willing to advocate that. Calvin had expelled advocates of religious toleration, and Luther had been aggressively hostile to those who disagreed with him on seemingly minor theological points. After 1542 with the establishment of the Universal Inquisition, the Catholic Church was committed to exposing and punishing anyone who professed a different faith with the exception of Jews in Italy who were under papal protection. Geneva and Rome became competing propaganda centers, each spewing out a

Catholic and Protestant Churches

The distinction between Catholic and Protestant was clearly evident in the appearance of churches. Two fundamental assumptions governed what Catholics considered appropriate for a church. The first was the presence of relics on or beneath altars. A relic was the physical remains of a saint, or some object associated with the saint, and Catholics believed one of the purposes of a church was to house these sacred objects.

As a result, Catholic churches tended to have many altars, each housing relics, because the more relics a church possessed the greater the presence of the sacred in it. The second assumption was that the more magnificent and beautiful the physical appearance of the church, the

■ **A Catholic Church** A Catholic church is resplendent with marble, statues, and relics.

A Protestant Preacher Protestant preaching was always from the Bible. Both preacher and congregation followed the passage that was read from the scripture. Sermons were long—notice the hour-glass.

Separate Sides A blind man points to the separated sides of the Church, so bitterly divided between Protestant and Catholic. Attempts to unite the divided Church are known as "ecumenical movements."

■ **Two Kinds of Preaching** This German woodcut highlights the differences between Catholic and Protestant preaching. In Germany, the Bible, often crudely set in type, was available by the end of the fifteenth century. Printing was partially responsible for making the Reformation possible.

Plain and Simple Protestant ministers dress simply in a black gown and their pulpits are plain; no ornaments distract the congregation from the Word of God.

Teaching Children All Christians saw the importance of teaching children. In the Protestant tradition, schools were seen as an invitation to teach children the truth of Scripture.

greater the honor offered to God. Relics were usually kept in reliquaries, boxes made of silver or gold and sometimes decorated with jewels. Altars were built of rare marbles, surrounded by rich brocades, covered by embroidered white lace altar cloths, and bedecked with silver candelabra. Above the altars were paintings and sculptures, the more beautiful the better, because the mean, ugly, and cheap were considered an insult to God.

In contrast, Protestant churches reflected a sense of cautious reserve and unease about material display. The vast majority of Protestant churches had once been Catholic. During the course of the sixteenth century they were conformed to Protestant sensibilities by stripping

A Calvinist Church Bare walls and clear glass windows characterized a Calvinist church. At the head of the congregation is a simple communion table, a lectern holding the Bible, and a raised pulpit for preaching.

Gutenberg Bible Many of the Bibles were printed in the vernacular rather than Latin.

them of unnecessary vanities. Down came the statues and paintings, many of which were destroyed. The rich furnishings of silver and gold reliquaries were sold to provide alms for the poor. The walls of the churches were denuded of decorations. In Holland the walls were usually whitewashed, creating a visual impression of stark simplicity. In place of images, scriptural verses were sometimes painted on the bare walls. Altars were turned around so that ministers would face the congregation. The focus of attention shifted from the altar to the pulpit from which the minister would preach the Word of God. The aim of the architecture in Protestant churches changed dramatically—from creating visual impressions that stimulated piety and honored God to facilitating the ability of the congregation to hear the preacher.

To both Catholics and Protestants, the church was understood as the house of God. The difference, however, was in the kind of furnishings and the kind of behavior God found appropriate in His house.

Catholic Preaching Catholic preaching in the years before the Reformation took place only on certain days. It was moralistic and wide-ranging, and could therefore move far from the text of the Bible. The preacher here is shown without a Bible before him. Preaching was not the high point of the service.

Decoration in Devotion to God The decorated pulpit and the robes of the Catholic priest are aspects of the visual nature of Catholic devotion. The rest of the church would also have been decorated, and stained-glass windows may have shown stories from the Bible. Devotion was made tangible by the prayer beads used by the congregation, who are not necessarily listening to the sermon. "Telling the beads" is the practice of saying the sequence of prayers known as the rosary.

For Discussion

How would the different experiences of being in a church influence the understanding Catholic and Protestant children developed of their faith and confessional identity?

475

■ **Map 14.2   Religious Divisions in Europe About 1600**

After 1555 the religious borders of Europe became relatively fixed, with only minor changes in confessional affiliations to this day.

flood of polemical tracts and specially trained missionaries willing to risk their lives by going behind the enemy lines to console their co-religionists and evangelize for converts.

Wherever there were significant religious minorities within a state, the best that could be hoped for was a condition of anxious tension, omnipresent suspicion, and periodic hysteria (see Map 14.2). The worst possibility was civil war. Between 1560 and 1648 several religious civil wars broke out, including the French Wars of Religion, the Dutch revolt against Spain, the Thirty Years' War in Germany, and the English Civil War. (The latter two will be discussed in Chapter 15.)

During the late sixteenth century a new word appeared to describe a personality type that may not have been entirely new but was certainly much more common—the fanatic°. Originally referring to someone possessed by a demon, a fanatic came to mean a person who expressed immoderate enthusiasm in religious matters, a person who pursued a supposedly divine mission, often to violent ends. Fanatics from all sides of the religious divide initiated waves of political assassinations and engaged in grotesque mas-

sacres of their opponents. François Guion, the assassin of William the Silent, whose story began this chapter, was in many ways typical of fanatics in his steadfast pursuit of his victim and his willingness to masquerade for years under a false identity. During the sixteenth and seventeenth centuries, no religious community had a monopoly on fanatics. They presented themselves as serving the pope as well as the Protestant churches.

The sharp confessional divisions that produced fanatics and assassins also stimulated writers, poets, and dramatists to examine the human condition. Perhaps no period in the history of the West produced so many great works of literature as the late sixteenth and early seventeenth centuries.

THE FRENCH WARS OF RELIGION

When King Henry II (r. 1547–1559) of France died unexpectedly from a jousting accident, he left behind his widow, the formidable Catherine de Médicis (1519–1589), and a brood of young children—including his heir, Francis II

(r. 1559–1560), who was only 15. Henry II had been a peacemaker. He succeeded in keeping France from civil war by carefully pacifying the quarrelsome nobles of the realm, and at the Peace of Cateau-Cambrésis (1559) he finally brought an end to more than sixty years of war with Spain. In contrast, Catherine and her children, including three sons who successively ascended to the throne, utterly failed to keep the peace, and for some forty years France was torn apart by a series of desperate civil wars.

The Huguenots:
The French Calvinist Community

By 1560 Calvinism had made significant inroads into predominantly Catholic France. Pastors sent from Geneva had been especially successful in the larger provincial towns, where their evangelical message appealed to enterprising merchants, professionals, and skilled artisans. Some 10 percent of the population had become Calvinists, or Huguenots° as French Protestants were called. The political strength of the Huguenots was greater than their numbers might indicate, because between one-third and one-half of the lower nobility professed Calvinism. Calvinism was popular among the French nobility for two reasons. One was patronage. The financial well-being of any noble depended on his patron, an aristocrat of higher rank who had access to the king and who could distribute jobs and lands to his clients. When a high aristocrat converted to Protestantism, he tended to bring his noble clientele into the new faith as well. As a result of a few aristocratic conversions in southwest France, Calvinism spread through "a veritable religious spider's web,"[2] as one contemporary put it.

Even more important than networks of male clientele was the influence of aristocratic women. The sister of King Francis I (r. 1515–1547), Marguerite of Angoulême (1492–1549), married the King of Navarre and created a haven in Navarre for Huguenot preachers and theologians. Her example drew other aristocratic ladies to the Huguenot cause, and many of the Huguenot leaders during the French Wars of Religion were the sons and grandsons of these early female converts. Marguerite's daughter, Jeanne d'Albret, sponsored Calvinist preachers for several years before she publicly announced her own conversion in 1560, and her son, Henry Bourbon, became the principal leader of the Huguenot cause during the French Wars of Religion° and the person responsible for eventually bringing the wars to an end.

The Origins of the Religious Wars

Like all civil wars, the French Wars of Religion exhibited a bewildering pattern of intrigue, betrayal, and treachery. Three distinct groups constituted the principal players. The first group was the royal family, consisting of Queen Catherine de Médicis and her four sons by Henry II—King Francis II (r. 1559–1560), King Charles IX (r. 1560–1574),

King Henry III (r. 1574–1589), and Duke Francis of Alençon (1554–1584)—and her daughter, Marguerite Valois (1553–1615). The royal family remained Catholic but on occasion reconciled themselves with the Huguenot opposition, and Marguerite married into it. The second group was the Huguenot faction of nobles led by the Châtillon family and the Bourbon family who ruled Navarre. The third group was the hard-line Catholic faction led by the implacable Guise family. These three groups vied for supremacy during the successive reigns of Catherine de Médicis' three sons, none of whom proved to be effective monarchs.

During the reign of the sickly and immature Francis II, the Catholic Guise family dominated the government and raised the persecution of the Huguenots to a new level. In response to that persecution, a group of Protestant nobles plotted in 1560 against the Guises, and some Calvinist ministers provided scriptural justifications for vengeance against tyrants. The Guises got wind of a conspiracy to kill them and surprised the plotters as they arrived in small groups at the royal chateau of Amboise. Some were ambushed, some drowned in the Loire River, some hanged from the balconies of the chateau's courtyard. A tense two years later in 1562, the Duke of Guise was passing through the village of Vassy just as a large congregation of Protestants was holding services in a barn. The duke's men attacked the worshipers, killing some 740 of them and wounding hundreds of others.

Following the massacre at Vassy, civil war broke out in earnest. For nearly forty years a series of religious wars sapped the strength of France. Most of the battles were indecisive, which meant neither side sustained military superiority for long. Both sides relied for support on their regional bases: The Protestant strength was in the southwest, the Catholic in Paris and the north. Besides military engagements, the French Wars of Religion were characterized by political assassinations and massacres.

Massacre of St. Bartholomew's Day

After a decade of bloody yet inconclusive combat, the royal family tried to resolve the conflict by making peace with the Protestants, a shift of policy signified by the announcement of the engagement of Marguerite Valois, daughter of Henry II and Catherine de Médicis, to Henry Bourbon, the son of the Huguenot King of Navarre. At age 19, Marguerite—or Queen Margot, as she was known—was already renowned for her brilliant intelligence. But she was renowned also for her wanton morals, and to complicate the situation further, on the eve of the wedding she was having an affair with another Henry, the young new Duke of Guise who was the leader of the intransigent Catholic faction. The marriage between Marguerite and Henry of Navarre was to take place in Paris in August 1572, an event that brought all the Huguenot leaders to the heavily armed

Catholic capital for the first time in many years. The gathering of all their enemies in one place presented too great a temptation for the Guises who hatched a plot to assassinate the Huguenot leaders. Perhaps because she had become jealous of the Huguenots' growing influence on her son, King Charles IX, the mercurial Catherine suddenly switched sides and became implicated in the plot.

Catherine somehow convinced the weak-willed king to order the massacre of the Huguenot nobles gathered in Paris. On August 14, 1572, St. Bartholomew's Day, the people of Paris began a slaughter. Some 3,000 to 4,000 Huguenots were butchered in Paris and over 20,000 more were put to death throughout the rest of France. Henry of Navarre saved his life by pretending to convert to Catholicism, while most of his companions were murdered.

After the Massacre of St. Bartholomew's Day, both sides tried to interpret the events to their own advantage. Catholics celebrated. The pope marked the occasion by having a medal struck and frescoes painted in the Vatican. King Philip II of Spain wrote that the massacre "was indeed of such value and prudence and of such service, glory, and honor to God and universal benefit to all Christendom that to hear of it was for me the best and most cheerful news which at present could come to me."[3] For Catholics the massacre was a great service to God. Protestants had a very different reaction, and presented it as a great affront to God.

Catherine's attempted solution for the Huguenot problem failed to solve anything, however. Henry of Navarre escaped his virtual imprisonment in the royal household, set Marguerite up in an isolated castle, returned to Navarre and his faith, and reinvigorated Huguenot resistance. Two Huguenot political thinkers laid out a theory justifying political revolution, François Hotman in *Francogallia* (1573) and Théodore de Bèze in *Right of Magistrates* (1579). They argued that since the authority of all magistrates, including even low-ranking nobles, came directly from God, the Huguenot nobles had the right and obligation to resist a tyrannical Catholic king. During the same period, Catholic moderates known as the *politiques* rejected the excesses of the Guises and argued for an accommodation with the Huguenots.

The wars of religion continued until the assassination of King Henry III, brother of the late Charles IX. Both Charles and Henry had been childless, a situation that made Henry Bourbon of Navarre the rightful heir to the throne, even though he was a Huguenot. Henry Bourbon became King Henry IV (r. 1589–1610) and recognized that predominantly Catholic France would never accept a Huguenot king, and so in 1593 with his famous quip, "Paris is worth a mass," Henry reconverted to the ancient faith, and most opposition to him among Catholics collapsed. Once he returned to Catholicism he managed to have the pope annul his childless marriage to Marguerite so that he could marry Marie de' Medici and obtain her huge dowry. Affable, funny, generous, and exceedingly tolerant, "Henry the

---

THE ST. BARTHOLOMEW'S DAY MASSACRE: THE POLITICS OF MEMORY

The Duke of Sully (1560–1641) became an ambassador and finance minister for French King Henry IV and was the principal architect of the Edict of Nantes, which provided a measure of religious toleration for Protestants in France after 1589. During the St. Bartholomew's Day Massacre he was 12 years old, but he never forgot what he witnessed. Sully was one of the few members of Henry of Navarre's personal entourage to survive the massacre.

Intending on that day to wait upon the king my master [Henry of Navarre, later King Henry IV of France], I went to bed early on the preceding evening; about three in the morning I was awakened by the cries of people, and; the alarm-bells, which were everywhere ringing. . . . I was determined to escape to the College de Bourgogne, and to effect this I put on my scholar's gown, and taking a book under my arm, I set out. In the streets I met three parties of the Life-guards; the first of these, after handling me very roughly, seized my book, and, most fortunately for me, seeing it was a Roman Catholic prayer-book, suffered me to proceed, and this served me as a passport with the two other parties. As I went along I saw the houses broken open and plundered, and men, women, and children butchered, while a constant cry was kept up of, "Kill! Kill! O you Huguenots! O you Huguenots!" This made me very impatient to gain the college, where, through God's assistance, I at length arrived, without suffering any other injury than a most dreadful fright.

Source: From "The Saint Bartholomew's Day Massacre" in Bayle St. John, ed., *Memoirs of the Duke of Sully, Vol. 1* (London: George Bell and Sons, 1877).

Great" became the most popular king in French history, reuniting the war-torn country by ruling with a very firm hand. With the Edict of Nantes° of 1598, he allowed the Huguenots to build a quasi-state within the state, giving them the right to have their own troops, church organization, and political autonomy within their walled towns, but they were banned from the royal court and the city of Paris.

Henry encouraged economic development under his minister the Duke of Sully, who retired the crushing state debt and built up a fiscal surplus by reforming finances and eliminating corruption. Henry declared that his ambition was for even the poorest peasant to be able to afford a chicken in his pot every Sunday, and even though he did not achieve this laudatory goal, his public works included the beautification of Paris and an impressive canal system to facilitate transportation.

Despite his enormous popularity, Henry too fell victim to fanaticism. After surviving eighteen attempts on his life, the king was fatally stabbed by a Catholic fanatic, who took advantage of the opportunity presented when the royal coach unexpectedly stopped behind a cart loading hay. Unlike the aftermath of the St. Bartholomew's Day massacre, Catholics all over France mourned Henry's death and considered the assassin mad. Henry's brilliant conciliatory nature and the horrors of the religious wars had tempered public opinion.

PHILIP II, THE KING OF PAPER

France's greatest rivals were the Habsburgs, who had regularly helped finance the Catholic cause during the French Wars of Religion. During the late sixteenth century, Habsburg Spain took advantage of French weakness to establish itself as the dominant power in Europe. When Emperor Charles V abdicated his thrones in 1556, the Habsburg possessions in Germany and the throne of the Holy Roman Empire went to his brother, Ferdinand I, and the balance of his vast domain to his son, Philip II (r. 1556–1598). Philip's inheritance included Milan, Naples, Sicily, the Netherlands, scattered outposts on the north coast of Africa, colonies in the Caribbean, Central America, Mexico, Peru, the Philippines, and most important of all, Spain. In 1580 he also inherited Portugal and its far-flung

CHRONOLOGY	
The French Wars of Religion	
1559	Peace of Cateau-Cambrésis between France and Spain
1560	Protestant conspiracy of Amboise
1572	Massacre of St. Bartholomew's Day
1573	François Hotman publishes *Francogallia*
1579	Théodore de Bèze publishes *Right of Magistrates*
1593	King Henry IV of France converts to Catholicism
1598	Edict of Nantes granting Protestants religious toleration

overseas empire, which included a line of trading posts from West Africa to the Spice Islands and the vast colony of unexplored Brazil.

Ruling over these enormous territories was a gargantuan task that Philip undertook with obsessive seriousness. From the rambling palace of El Escorial, which was also a mausoleum for his father and a monastery, Philip lived in semimonastic seclusion and ruled as the "King of Paper," an office-bound bureaucrat rather than the rule-from-the-saddle warrior his father had been and many of his contemporary monarchs remained. Philip kept himself to a rigid daily work discipline that included endless committee meetings and long hours devoted to poring over as many as 400 documents a day, which he annotated extensively in his crabbed hand. Because of his inability to delegate authority and his immersion in minutiae, Philip tended to lose his grasp of the larger picture, especially the shaky finances of Spain.

This grave, distrustful, rigid man saw himself as the great protector of the Catholic cause and committed Spain to perpetual hostility toward Muslims and Protestants. On the Muslim front he first bullied the Moriscos, the descendants of the Spanish Muslims. The Moriscos had received Christian baptism, but they were suspected of secretly practicing Islam, and in 1568 Philip issued an edict that banned all manifestations of Muslim culture and ordered the Moriscos to turn over their children to Christian priests to educate. The outraged Moriscos of Granada rebelled but were defeated with vicious cruelty. At first dispersed throughout Spain, the surviving Moriscos were eventually expelled from the country in 1609. Philip hardened his policy toward the Moriscos because he feared, not unreasonably, that they would become secret agents on Spanish soil for his great Mediterranean rivals, the Ottoman Turks. To counter the Turkish threat, Philip maintained expensive fortresses on the North African coast. In 1571 he joined the Venetians and the pope to check Turkish advances after the Ottomans captured Cyprus, Venice's richest colony. The Christian victory at Lepanto in the Gulf of Corinth, which destroyed more than one-third of the enemy's fleet, was heralded as one of the greatest events of the sixteenth century, proving that the Turks could be beaten. Lepanto renewed the crusading spirit in the Catholic world. Although the victory at Lepanto was a valuable propaganda tool, it had slight military significance because the Turks quickly rebuilt their fleet and forced Venice to cede Cyprus to them. The island remains divided between Christian and Turkish populations to this day.

Philip once said he would rather lose all his possessions and die a hundred times than be the king of heretics. His attitude toward Protestants showed that he meant what he said. Through his marriage to Queen Mary I of England (r. 1553–1558), Philip encouraged her persecutions of Protestants, but they got their revenge. After Mary's death her half-sister, Queen Elizabeth I, refused his marriage proposal and in 1577 signed a treaty to assist the Protestant Netherlands, which was in rebellion against Spain. To add insult to injury, the English privateer Sir Francis Drake (ca. 1540–1596) conducted a personal war against Catholic Spain by raiding the Spanish convoys bringing silver from the New World. In 1587 Drake's embarrassing successes culminated with a daring raid on the great Spanish port city of Cadiz where, "singeing the king of Spain's beard" he destroyed the anchored Spanish fleet and many thousands of tons of vital supplies. Philip retaliated by building a huge fleet of 132 ships armed with 3,165 cannons, which sailed from Portugal to rendezvous with the Spanish army stationed in the Netherlands and launch an invasion of England in 1588. As the Invincible Armada, as it was called, passed through the English Channel, it was met by a much smaller English fleet, assembled out of merchant ships refit for battle. Unable to maneuver as effectively as the English in the fluky winds of the channel and mauled by the rapid-firing English guns, the Spanish Armada° suffered heavy losses and was forced to retreat to the north, where it sustained further losses in storms off the coast of Scotland and Ireland. Barely more than half of the fleet finally straggled home. The Spanish quickly replaced the lost ships, but Philip's sense of invincibility was severely shaken.

The reign of Philip II illustrated better than any other the contradictions and tensions of the era. No monarch had at his grasp as many resources and territories as Philip, and yet defending them proved extremely costly. The creaky governmental machinery of Spain put a tremendous burden on a conscientious king such as Philip, but even his unflagging energy and dedication to his duties could not prevent military defeat and financial disaster. Economic historians remember Philip's reign for its series of state bankruptcies and for the loss of the Netherlands, the most precious jewel in the crown of Spain.

THE DUTCH REVOLT

The Netherlands boasted some of Europe's richest cities, situated amid a vast network of lakes, rivers, channels, estuaries, and tidal basins that periodically replenished

CHRONOLOGY

Spain and the Netherlands

1548	Annexation of the northern provinces of the Netherlands to the Spanish crown
1568	Edict against Morisco culture
1571	Christian victory over Ottoman Turks at Lepanto
1580	King Philip II inherits Portugal and the Portuguese Empire
1581	Seven northern provinces of the Netherlands declare independence from Spain
1584	Assassination of William the Silent
1588	Defeat of the Spanish Armada
1609	Expulsion of the Moriscos from Spain
1648	Treaty of Westphalia recognizes independence of the Netherlands

The Netherlands During the Dutch Revolt, ca. 1580

- United Provinces
- Spanish Netherlands
- Bishopric of Liège

ENGLAND

North Sea

Amsterdam

HOLLAND

Utrecht

ZEELAND

Antwerp

Ghent

Flemish-speaking

Brussels

FLANDERS

French-speaking

HOLY ROMAN EMPIRE

Rhine R.

Meuse

LUXEMBOURG

FRANCE

Luxembourg

0   50 km
0   50 mi

■ **Map 14.3 The Netherlands During the Dutch Revolt, ca. 1580**

During the late sixteenth century the northern United Provinces separated from the Spanish Netherlands. The independence of the United Provinces was not recognized by the other European powers until 1648.

the exceptionally productive soil through flooding. The Netherlands consisted of seventeen provinces, each with its own distinctive identity, traditions, and even language. The southern provinces were primarily French-speaking; those in the north spoke a bewildering variety of Flemish dialects. In 1548 Emperor Charles V annexed the northern provinces that had been part of the Holy Roman Empire to the southern provinces he had inherited from his father. His decision meant that when his son, Philip II, became king of Spain, all of the Netherlands was included with the Spanish crown. With his characteristic bureaucratic mentality, Philip treated Dutch affairs as a management problem rather than a political sore spot, an attitude that subordinated the Netherlands to Spanish interests. Foreign rule irritated the Dutch, who had long enjoyed ancient privileges including the right to raise their own taxes and muster their own troops.

Consolidating the Netherlands under the Spanish crown deprived the Dutch princes of the right to chose the official religion of their lands, a right they would have enjoyed had the provinces remained in the Holy Roman Empire where the Religious Peace of Augsburg granted princes religious freedom. Philip's harsh attitude toward Protestants upset the delicate balance among Catholic, Lutheran, Calvinist, and Anabaptist communities. Huguenot refugees from the French Wars of Religion heightened the anti-Catholic fanaticism of the local Calvinists, who in 1566 occupied many Catholic churches and destroyed paintings and statues.

In response to the rapidly deteriorating situation in the Netherlands, Philip issued edicts against the heretics and strengthened the Spanish Inquisition. The Inquisition in Spain was an arm of the monarchy charged with ensuring religious conformity among the extremely diverse cultures of the Iberian peninsula. The Spanish Inquisition had been preoccupied with investigating the Christian sincerity of former Jews, who after the expulsions of 1492 had converted to Christianity in order to stay in Spain. When introduced in the Netherlands, the Inquisition became an investigating agency devoted to finding, interrogating, and, if necessary, punishing Protestants. Philip also dispatched 20,000 Spanish troops under the command of the Duke of Alba (1508–1582), a veteran of the Turkish campaigns in North Africa and victories over the Lutheran princes of Germany. Alba directly attacked the Protestants. He personally presided over the military court, the Council of Troubles, which became so notoriously tyrannical that the people called it the Council of Blood. As an example to others, he systematically razed several small villages where there had been incidents of desecrating Catholic images, slaughtering every inhabitant. Alba himself boasted that during the campaign against the rebels, he had some 18,000 people executed, in addition to those who died in battle or were massacred by soldiers. The Prince of Orange, William the Silent (1533–1584), accompanied into exile some 60,000 refugees, who constituted about 2 percent of the population. While abroad William began to organize resistance to Alba.

Alba's cruelty backfired by steeling Protestant opposition to the Spanish. Alba also lost support among otherwise loyal Catholics when he attempted to introduce a 10 percent tax on trade. His policies a failure, Alba was recalled to Spain in 1573. Meanwhile the sea-beggars, as the Dutch Calvinist privateers were called, had begun to achieve some success against the Spanish. Within a few short years, William the Silent seized permanent control of the provinces of Holland and Zeeland, which were then flooded by Calvinist refugees from the southern provinces. After Alba's departure, no one kept control of the unpaid Spanish soldiers, who in mutinous rage turned against cities loyal to Spain, including Brussels, Ghent, and most savagely Antwerp, the rich center of trade. Antwerp lost 7,000 citizens and one-third of its houses to the "Spanish fury," which permanently destroyed its prosperity. Alba's replacement, the shrewd statesman and general, the Duke of Parma (r. 1578–1592), ultimately subdued the southern provinces, which remained a Spanish colony. The seven northern provinces, however, united in 1579 and declared independence from Spain in 1581 (see Map 14.3). William the Silent became the *stadholder* (governor) of the new

United Provinces, and after his assassination his 17-year-old son, Maurice of Nassau, inherited the same title.

The Netherlands' struggle for independence transformed the population of the northern provinces from mixed religions to staunch Calvinism. The Dutch Revolt° became ensnared in the French Wars of Religion through Huguenot refugees, and the alliance with England, which provided much needed financial and moral support, reinforced the Protestant identity of the Dutch. The international Protestant alliance created by the Dutch Revolt and centered in the Netherlands withstood both Philip's fury and Parma's calm generalship. The failure of the Spanish Armada to land Parma's men in England guaranteed the survival of an independent Netherlands. The Dutch carried on a sporadic and inconclusive war against Spain until the end of the Thirty Years' War in 1648, when the international community recognized the independent Republic of the United Provinces.

LITERATURE IN THE AGE OF CONFESSIONAL DIVISION

Churches and monarchs everywhere demanded religious conformity in word and deed, a situation that would seem to stifle creativity, and yet the late sixteenth and early seventeenth centuries was one of the most remarkable periods in the history of creative literature. During this period the native or vernacular languages of western Europe became literary languages, replacing Latin as the dominant form of expression, even for the educated elite. Italian was the first vernacular to be prized for its literary qualities and considered a worthy alternative to Latin. The availability of cheap printed books and the Bible reading encouraged by the Protestant Reformation stimulated literature in other vernacular languages so that by the late sixteenth century great literary figures were writing in French, Portuguese, Spanish, and English.

French Literature During the Religious Turmoil

In France royal decrees in 1520 and 1539 substituted French for Latin in official legal and government documents. A century later with the founding of the Académie Française, it became government policy to promote, protect, and refine the French language. The greatest masters of French prose during this crucial period were François Rabelais (ca. 1483–1553) and Michel de Montaigne (1533–1592). Trained as a lawyer, Rabelais became a friar and priest but left the Church under a cloud of heresy to become a physician. Rabelais's satirical masterpiece, a series of novels recounting the fantastic and grotesque adventures of Gargantua and Pantagruel, combined an encyclopedic command of humanist thought with stunning verbal invention that has had a lasting influence on humorous writ-

ers to this day. One of Rabelais's most remarkable creations was the imaginary Abbey of Thélème, inhabited by a kind of antimonastic community of monks and nuns for whom "all their life was regulated not by laws, statutes, or rules, but according to their free will and pleasure." This was an abbey for hedonists who lived by the motto, "DO WHAT YOU WILL, because people who are free, well-born, well-bred, and easy in honest company have a natural spur and instinct which drives them to virtuous deeds and deflects them from vice."[4] Rabelais's optimistic vision of human nature represented a startling contrast to the growing anxiety provoked by the religious controversies of his time. Rabelais's controversial work was banned, and he was briefly forced into exile.

It is ironic that Montaigne became a master of French prose. His mother was a Catholic of Spanish-Jewish origins, and the young Michel spoke only Latin for the first six years of his life because his German tutor knew no French. After a modestly successful legal career, Montaigne retired to the family chateau to discover himself by writing essays, a literary form well suited to reflective introspection. In his essays, Montaigne struggled with his lasting grief over the premature death from dysentery of a close friend, reflected on his own experience of the intense physical pain of illness, and diagnosed the absurd causes of the French Wars of Religion. Montaigne's essays are a profound series of meditations on the meaning of life and death, presented in a calm voice of reason to an age of violent fanaticism. In one essay, for example, he exposed the presumption of human beings: "The most vulnerable and frail of all creatures is man, and at the same time the most arrogant." Montaigne thought it presumptuous that human beings picked themselves out as God's favorite creatures. How did they know they were superior to other animals? "When I play with my cat, who knows if I am not a pastime to her more than she is to me?"[5] His own skepticism about religion insulated him from the sometimes violent passions of his era.

Stirrings of the Golden Age in Iberia

The literary tradition in the Iberian peninsula differed from that of other regions in Europe in that Iberia is a polyglot region in which several languages are spoken—Basque, Galician, Portuguese, Castilian, and Catalan. The greatest lyric poet of the peninsula, Luís Vaz de Camões (1524–1580), lost an eye in battle and was sent to the Portuguese East Indies after he killed a royal official in a street brawl. When he returned years later, he completed his epic poem, *The Lusiads* (1572), which became the national poem of Portugal by celebrating Vasco da Gama's discovery of the sea route to India. This great work was modeled on the ancient epics, especially the *Aeneid*, the greatest Latin epic of ancient Rome, and even included the gods of Olympus as commentators on the human events of Camões's time. In the opening lines, Jupiter spoke of contemporary Portugal:

Eternal dwellers in the starry heavens, you will not have forgotten the great valor of that brave people the Portuguese. You cannot therefore be unaware that it is the fixed resolve of destiny that before their achievements those of Assyrians, Persians, Greeks and Romans shall fade into oblivion. Already with negligible forces—you were witnesses—they have expelled the Moslem, for all his strength and numbers . . .; while against the redoubtable Castilians they have invariably had heaven on their side. Always, in a word, they have known victory in battle and have reaped, with its trophies, fame and glory too.[6]

By connecting Portugal directly to the glories of the ancient empires, Camões managed to elevate the adventures of his fellow Portuguese in Asia to an important moment in the history of the world.

Because Spain was unified around the crown of Castile, the Castilian language became the language we now call Spanish. The period when Spain was the dominant power in Europe coincided with the Golden Age of Spanish literature. The greatest literary figure was Miguel de Cervantes Saavedra (1547–1616), an impoverished son of an unsuccessful doctor with little formal education. Like Camões, Cervantes survived many adventures, losing the use of his left hand at the naval battle of Lepanto and spending five years languishing in a Turkish prison after he was captured by Algerian pirates. In order to survive, the disabled veteran was forced to write plays for the Madrid theater and to work as a tax collector, but he was still imprisoned several times for debts. Desperate to make money, Cervantes published a serial novel in installments between 1605 and 1615. It became the greatest masterpiece in Spanish literature, *Don Quixote*.

The prototype of the modern novel form, *Don Quixote* was a satire of chivalric romances. Cervantes presented reality on two levels, the "poetic truth" of the master and dreamer Don Quixote and the "historic truth" of his squire and realist Sancho Panza. Don Quixote's imagination persistently ran away with him as he tilted at windmills, believing they were fierce dragons. It remained to Sancho Panza to point out the unheroic truth. Cervantes pursued the interaction between these two incongruous views of truth as a philosophical commentary on existence. For Cervantes there was no single, objective truth, only psychological truths revealed through the interaction of the characters, an idea that contrasted with the notion of dogmatic religious truth that dominated the time. Despite the extensive popularity of *Don Quixote*, Cervantes died a pauper, buried in an unmarked grave in Madrid.

The Elizabethan Renaissance

During the reign of Elizabeth I (r. 1558–1603), the Renaissance truly arrived in England. The daughter of Henry VIII and Anne Boleyn, Elizabeth faced terrible insecurity as a girl. Her father had her mother beheaded, she was declared illegitimate, and her sister Mary imprisoned her for treason in the Tower of London. After she ascended to the throne in 1558, however, she proved to be a brilliant leader. She prevented the kind of religious civil wars that broke out in France by establishing a moderate form of Protestantism as the official religion. She presided over the beginnings of England's rise as a major European power. Perhaps most remarkably, she became the patron and inspiration for England's greatest age of literature. Never

■ **Queen Elizabeth I of England**

Elizabeth presided over the greatest age of English literature.

married, Elizabeth used her eligibility for marriage as a lure in diplomacy, and even though she may have had real lovers, she addressed her subjects as if they were her only love. Her "golden speech" delivered before a divided House of Commons in 1601 exemplifies her ability to inspire exuberant loyalty:

> *Though God hath raised me high, yet this I account the glory of my crown, that I have reigned with your loves. . . . It is not my desire to live or reign longer than my life and reign shall be for your good. And though you have had, and may have, many mightier and wiser princes sitting in this seat, yet you never had, nor shall have any that will love you better.*[7]

Among Elizabeth's courtiers were major literary figures, including the adventurer-poet Sir Walter Raleigh (ca. 1552–1618), the soldier-poet Sir Philip Sidney (1554–1586), and Edmund Spenser (ca. 1552–1599), whose great poem *The Faerie Queen* was a personal tribute to Elizabeth.

The principal figure of the Elizabethan Renaissance, however, was not a courtier but a professional dramatist, William Shakespeare (1564–1616). In a series of theaters, including the famous Globe on the south side of the Thames in London, Shakespeare wrote, produced, and acted in comedies, tragedies, and history plays. Shakespeare's enormous output of plays, some of which made veiled allusions to the politics of Elizabeth's court, established him not only as the most popular dramatist of his time but the greatest literary figure in the English language. The power of his plays derives from the subtle understanding of human psychology found in his characters and the stunning force of his language. For Shakespeare, as for Montaigne, the source of true knowledge was self-knowledge. One character advises,

> *Neither a borrower nor a lender be,*
> *For loan oft loses both itself and friend*
> *And borrowing dulls the edge of husbandry.*
> *This above all: To thine own self be true,*
> *And it must follow, as the night the day,*
> *Thou canst not then be false to any man.*
> (Hamlet I, iii, 75–80)

Unlike most contemporary authors, Shakespeare wrote for a broad audience of paying theatergoers that included common workers as well as highly educated members of Elizabeth's court. This need to appeal to a large audience who gave instant feedback helped him hone his skills as a dramatist.

Some of these literary figures found their works banned, as did Rabelais. Some had political or personal troubles with their monarch, as did Montaigne, Camões, Raleigh, and Sidney. But the controversies of the day seemed to have stimulated rather than inhibited these writers. Political and religious turmoil led them to ask penetrating questions about the meaning of life and to rise above the petty squabbles that preoccupied so many of their contemporaries.

States and Confessions in Eastern Europe

In contrast to the confessional states of western Europe, eastern Europe during the early sixteenth century escaped the religious controversies that linked religious conformity to political loyalty. Bohemia and Poland, in particular, allowed levels of religious diversity unheard of in the West. During the last decades of the sixteenth and early seventeenth centuries, however, dynastic troubles compromised the relative openness of the eastern states, enmeshing them in conflicts among themselves that had an increasingly strong religious dimension. In Germany and central Europe, the weakness of the mad Emperor Rudolf permitted religious conflicts to fester, setting the stage for the disastrous Thirty Years' War (1618–1648) that pitted Catholic against Protestant.

Around the Baltic Sea, rivalries among Lutheran Sweden, Catholic Poland-Lithuania, and Orthodox Russia created a state of almost permanent war in a tense standoff among three very different political and religious states. The enormous confederation of Poland-Lithuania struggled to sustain the most decentralized, religiously diverse state anywhere in Europe. By the end of the century, it remained politically decentralized but had become an active theater of the Counter Reformation where dynastic policy firmly supported Catholicism. Russia began to strengthen itself from obscurity under the authoritarian rule of the tsars, who began to transform it into a major European power.

THE DREAM WORLD OF EMPEROR RUDOLF

In Goethe's *Faust*, set in sixteenth-century Germany, drinkers in a tavern sing:

> *The dear old Holy Roman Empire,*
> *How does it hang together?*[8]

Good question. How did this peculiarly decentralized state—neither Holy, nor Roman, nor an empire—hang together? In the late sixteenth century the empire consisted of the following components: 1 emperor; 7 electors, comprising 4 secular princes and 3 archbishops; 50 other bishops and archbishops; 21 dukes, margraves, and landgraves; 88 independent abbots and assorted prelates of the Church; 178 counts and other sovereign lords; about 80 free imperial cities; and hundreds of free imperial knights. The emperor presided over all, and the Imperial Diet served as a parliament, but the Holy Roman Empire was, in fact, a very loose confederation of semi-independent, mostly German states, many of which ignored imperial decrees that did not suit them. During the first half of the sixteenth century the empire faced a number of challenges—the turmoil within the empire presented by Martin

Luther, endless French enmity on the western borders, and the tenacious Ottoman threat on the eastern frontier. Only the universal vision and firm hand of Emperor Charles V kept the empire together. The universal vision and firm hand disappeared in the succeeding generations of emperors, to be replaced by petty dynastic squabbles and infirm minds.

The crippling weakness of the imperial system became most evident during the reign of Rudolf II (r. 1576–1612). The Habsburg line had a strain of insanity going back to Joanna "The Mad," the mother of Emperors Charles V (r. 1519–1558) and Ferdinand I (r. 1558–1564), who happened to be Rudolf's two grandfathers, giving him a double dose of Habsburg genes. Soon after his election to the imperial throne, Rudolf moved his court from bustling Vienna to the lovely quiet of Prague in Bohemia. Fearful of noisy crowds and impatient courtiers, standoffish toward foreign ambassadors who presented him with difficult decisions, paranoid about scheming relatives, and prone to wild emotional gyrations from deep depression to manic grandiosity, Rudolf was hardly suited for the imperial throne. In fact, many contemporaries, who had their own reasons to underrate him, described him as hopelessly insane. Rudolf certainly suffered from moments of profound melancholy and irrational fears that may have had genetic or organic causes, but he was probably unhinged by the conundrum of being the emperor, a position that trapped him between the glorious universal imperial ideal and the ignoble reality of unscrupulous relatives and petty rivalries.

Rudolf was not the only sixteenth-century prince in the Holy Roman Empire driven to distraction by the pressures of court life. At least twenty German princes and princesses were confined or deposed due to symptoms of serious mental disorder. Certainly inbreeding within a small pool of princely families contributed to the patterns of madness, but the most unhealthy emotional pressure was produced by the code of manners required of all courtiers, most particularly princes and princesses. This strictly-maintained code demanded the repression of all spontaneous feelings, a repression that resulted in a prevailing sense of shame. When religious rigidity and extreme political conflict were mixed into this volatile psychological concoction, it is not surprising that some personalities shattered. Since the entire political system depended on the prince's guidance, a mad prince could seriously disrupt an entire society.

Incapable of governing, Rudolf did not abandon the imperial ideal of universality, he just transmuted it into a strange dream world. In Prague he gathered around him a brilliant court of humanists, musicians, painters, physicians, astronomers, astrologers, alchemists, and magicians. These included an eclectic assortment of significant thinkers—the great astronomers Tycho Brahe and Johannes Kepler, the notorious occult philosopher Giordano Bruno, the theoretical mathematician and astrologer John Dee, and the remarkable inventor of surrealist painting Giuseppe Arcimboldo. As Chapter 16 will explain, many of these figures are considered the immediate forerunners of the Scientific Revolution. But Rudolf also fell prey to fast-talking charlatans, including the illusionist and opera-set designer Cornelius Drebber, who claimed to have invented a perpetual-motion machine. This weird court, however, was less the strange fruit of the emperor's hopeless dementia than the manifestation of a striving for universal empire. Rudolf sought to preserve the cultural and political unity of the empire, to eradicate religious divisions, and to achieve peace at home. Rudolf's court in Prague was perhaps the only place left during the late sixteenth century where Protestants, Catholics, Jews, and even radical heretics such as Bruno could gather together in a common intellectual enterprise, the goal of which was to discover the universal principles that governed nature, principles that would provide the foundations for a single unifying religion and a cure for all human maladies. It was a noble, if utterly improbable, dream.

While Rudolf and his favorite courtiers isolated themselves in their dream world, the religious conflicts within the empire reached a boiling point. Without a strong emperor, the Imperial Diets were paralyzed by confessional squabbles. In 1607 in the imperial free city of Donauworth in south Germany, a conflict between the Lutheran town council and the substantial Catholic minority gave the Catholic Duke of Bavaria the excuse to annex the city to his own territories. Despite the illegality of the duke's action, Rudolf passively acquiesced, causing fear among German Protestants that the principles of the Religious Peace of Augsburg of 1555 might be ignored. In the following decade, more than 200 religious revolts or riots took place. In 1609 the insane Duke John William of Jülich-Cleves died without a direct heir, and the most suitable claimants to the Catholic duchy were two Lutheran princes. Were one of them to succeed to the dukedom, the balance between Catholics and Protestants in Germany would have been seriously disrupted. Religious tensions boiled over. As Chapter 15 will describe, in less than a decade the empire began to dissolve in what became the Thirty Years' War.

THE RENAISSANCE OF POLAND-LITHUANIA

During the late sixteenth and early seventeenth centuries, Poland-Lithuania experienced a remarkable cultural and political renaissance. It was inspired by influences from Renaissance Italy linked to strong commercial and diplomatic ties to the Republic of Venice and intellectual connections with the University of Padua. As the major power in eastern Europe, Poland-Lithuania engaged in a tug-of-war with Sweden over control of the eastern Baltic and virtually constant warfare against the expansionist ambitions of Russia (see Map 14.4). The most remarkable achievement of Poland-Lithuania during this contentious time was its unparalleled and still controversial experiments in government. Poland-Lithuania had an elected king but called itself a republic. The king was a figurehead, and Poland-Lithuania was a republic in the sense that it was effectively governed by assemblies of nobles.

Very loosely joined since 1336, Poland and Lithuania legally merged in 1569, creating a confederation in which Poland supplied the king, but the Grand Duchy of Lithuania was considered an equal partner and allowed to retain its own laws, administration, and army. The novel feature of the confederation was how the nobles reserved power for themselves through their control of regional assemblies, which in turn dominated the central diet. These nobles elected the king and treated him, at best, as a hired manager. They resisted all attempts to exert royal power by asserting the legal right to form local armed confederations against the king and by exercising the principle of unanim-

ity in the diet, which prevented the king or a strong faction from dominating affairs. In the last half of the seventeenth century Poland-Lithuania fell into chaos under this system, but for nearly three-quarters of a century it worked well enough—at least for the nobles.

The rule of the nobles in Poland-Lithuania came at a great cost to the Polish peasants, however, who were ruthlessly forced into serfdom and deprived of their legal rights. Peasants were prohibited from leaving the land without permission from their landlords, and they were denied the ability to appeal the legal judgments of their local lords. In this regard, Poland-Lithuania moved in the opposite direction from western European states, which at this time were extending the right of judicial appeal and allowing serfdom to fade away. Moreover, the Polish kings could not stop the gradual erosion of their authority so that Poland-Lithuania, the greatest power in the East, enfeebled itself through the

■ Map 14.4 Poland-Lithuania and Russia

These countries were the largest in Europe in the size of their territories but were relatively under-populated compared to the western European states.

grasping hands of a notoriously self-interested and proud nobility.

Poland-Lithuania contained an incomparable religious mixture of Roman Catholics, Lutherans, Calvinists, Russian Orthodox, Anabaptists, Unitarians, and Jews, but these communities were strongly divided along geographic and class lines. Lutheranism was a phenomenon of the German-speaking towns, the peasants of Poland remained Catholic, those in Lithuania were Orthodox, and many of the nobles were attracted to Calvinism. During the late sixteenth century, however, Christians in Poland almost completely returned or converted to the Roman Catholic faith. The key to the transformation was the changing attitude of the Polish nobles, who had tolerated religious diversity because they believed that religious liberty was the cornerstone of political liberty. The return to Catholicism owed a great deal to Stanislas Hosius (1504–1579), who had studied in Italy before he returned to Poland to become successively a diplomat, bishop, and cardinal. Imbued with the zeal of the Italian Catholic Reformation, Hosius invited the Society of Jesus into Poland and worked closely with the papal *nuncios* (the diplomatic representatives of the pope), who organized a campaign to combat all forms of Protestantism. Between 1565 and 1586, forty-four young Polish nobles studied at the Jesuit college in Rome and when they returned took up the most influential church and government offices in Poland. Jesuit colleges sprouted up in many Polish towns, attracting the brightest sons of the nobility and urban bourgeoisie. A close alliance between the kings of Poland and the Jesuits enhanced the social prestige of Catholicism.

The cultural appeal of all things Italian helped lure the Polish nobility back to Catholicism. Through the spread of elite education, Catholicism returned to Poland largely through persuasion rather than coercion. But the transformation did not occur without violent repercussions. Lutheran, Calvinist, and Bohemian Brethren churches were burned. In Cracow armed confrontations between Protestant and Catholic militants led to casualties. However, Poland did not degenerate into civil war, as did France or the Netherlands over much the same issues. As the monarchy progressively weakened, the Catholic Church became the only solid institutional pillar of Polish national identity and Polish culture.

THE TROUBLED LEGACY OF IVAN THE TERRIBLE

While Poland experimented with a decentralized confederation dominated by nobles that severely restricted the king's initiative, Russia evolved in the opposite direction. During the late fifteenth and sixteenth centuries, the grand dukes of Moscow who became the tsars of Russia eclipsed the authority of the great landed nobles and snuffed out the independence of the towns. The authoritarian tendencies of the tsars harmed the Russian peasants, however, just as royal weakness harmed the Polish peasants. After 1454 Moscow's creation of military fiefs (*pomestye*) to supply soldiers against the Tartars (Mongol tribes) allowed the nobles to push the peasants back into serfdom. Refusing to accept enserfment, the peasants fled the fields in massive numbers, depopulating central Russia as they found refuge among the Cossack colonies along the borders to the southeast.

Russia was already well-integrated into the European diplomatic community and engaged in trade with its Western neighbors. But for more than 300 years Russia had been under the "Tartar Yoke," a term describing the Mongolian tribes that overran the country, pillaging and depopulating it. Ivan III, "The Great" (1462–1505), succeeded in gradually throwing off the Tartar Yoke by refusing to continue to pay tribute to the Mongols. Ivan married Zoë, the niece of the last Greek emperor of Constantinople. The marriage gave him the basis for claiming that the Russian rulers were the heirs of Byzantium and the exclusive protectors of Orthodox Christianity, the state religion of Russia. Following the Byzantine tradition of imperial autocracy, Ivan practiced Byzantine court ceremonies, and his advisers developed the theory of the Three Romes. According to this theory, the authority of the ancient Roman Empire had passed first to the Byzantine Empire, which God had punished with the Turkish conquest, and then to Moscow as the third and last "Rome." Ivan celebrated this theory by assuming the title of tsar (or "Caesar"). With his wife's assistance, he hired Italian architects to rebuild the grand ducal palace, the Kremlin. Ivan captured the vast northern territories of the city-state of Novgorod, expanding the Russian state north to the White Sea and east to the Urals. Ivan's invasion of parts of Lithuania embroiled Russia in a protracted conflict with Poland that lasted more than a century. Like his fellow monarchs in western Europe, Ivan began to bring the aristocrats under control by incorporating them into the bureaucracy of the state.

CHRONOLOGY

States and Confessions in Eastern Europe

1480	Grand Duke and later Tsar Ivan III, "The Great," of Russia refuses to pay tribute to Tartars
1569	Merging of Poland and Lithuania
1606	Emperor Rudolf declared incapable of ruling by his family
1604–1613	Time of Troubles in Russia
1613	Michael Romanov elected Tsar of Russia

Ivan III's grandson, Ivan IV, "The Terrible" (1533–1584), succeeded his father at age 3 and became the object of innumerable plots, attempted coups, and power struggles among his mother, uncles, and the boyars (the upper-level nobles who dominated Russian society). The trauma of his childhood years and a painful disease of the spine made him inordinately suspicious and prone to acts of impulsive violence. When at age 17 Ivan was crowned, he reduced the power of the dukes and the boyars by forcing them to exchange their hereditary estates for lands that obligated them to serve the tsar in war. In weakening the boyars, Ivan gained considerable support among the common people and was even remembered in popular songs as the people's tsar. Nevertheless, Ivan distrusted everyone. He often arrested people on charges of treason, just for taking a trip abroad. In a cruel revenge on his enemies among the boyars, he began a reign of terror in which he personally committed horrendous atrocities. His massacre in 1570 of the inhabitants of Novgorod, whom he suspected of harboring Polish sympathies, contributed to his reputation as a bloody tyrant. By setting aside half of the realm as his personal domain, he created a strong financial base for the army, which led to military successes in the prolonged wars against Poland, Lithuania, and Sweden. During his reign, however, the Polish threat and boyar opposition to his rule revealed signs of the fragility of Russian unity.

During the "Time of Troubles°" (1604–1613), Russia fell into chaos. Boyar families struggled among themselves for supremacy, the Cossacks from the south led a popular revolt, and Poles and Swedes openly interfered in Russian affairs. Finally, the Time of Troubles ended when in 1613 the national assembly elected Tsar Michael Romanov, whose descendants ruled Russia until they were deposed in 1917. During the seventeenth century the Romanovs gradually restored order to Russia, eroded the independence of local governments, and strengthened the institution of serfdom. By the end of the seventeenth century Russia was strong enough to reenter European affairs as a major power.

CONCLUSION
The Divisions of the West

During the late sixteenth and early seventeenth centuries, hidden demographic and economic pressures eroded the confidence and security of many Europeans, creating a widespread sense of unease. Most people retreated like confused soldiers behind the barricades of a rigid confessional faith, which provided reassurance that was unavailable elsewhere. To compensate for the absence of predictability in daily life, societies everywhere imposed strict discipline—discipline of women, children, the poor, criminals, and alleged witches. The frenzy for social discipline displaced the fear of those things that could not be controlled onto the most easily controllable people, especially the weak, the subordinate, and those perceived to be different.

The union between religion and political authority in the confessional states bolstered official religious faith with the threat of legal or military coercion. Where different religious confessions persisted within one state—most notably France and the Netherlands—the result was riots, assassinations, and civil war. The West had become divided along religious lines in two ways. The first kind of division was within countries with religiously mixed populations, where distinctive religious communities competed for political power and influence. In these countries religion became the cornerstone to justify patriotism or rebellion, loyalty or disloyalty to the monarch. The second kind of division was international. The confessional states formed alliances, crafted foreign policies, and went to war, with religion determining friend and foe. The West split into religiously driven national camps. Over the subsequent centuries, religious differences mutated into ideological differences, but the sense that alliances among states should be linked together by a common set of beliefs has persisted to this day as a legacy from the sixteenth century.

During the period of the middle seventeenth to eighteenth centuries, confessional identity and the fear of religious turmoil led monarchs throughout Europe to build absolutist regimes, which attempted to enforce stability through a strengthened, centralized state. The principles of religious toleration and the separation of church and state were still far in the future. They were made possible only as a consequence of the hard lessons learned from the historical turmoil of the late sixteenth and seventeenth centuries.

Suggestions for Further Reading

For a comprehensive list of suggested readings, please go to www.ablongman.com/levack/chapter14

Anderson, M. S. *The Origins of the Modern European State System, 1494–1618.* 1998. The best short study for students new to the subject of the evolution of the confessional states in Europe. This book is very good at establishing common patterns among the various states.

Burke, Peter. *Popular Culture in Early Modern Europe.* 1994. This wide-ranging book includes considerable material from eastern Europe and Scandinavia, as well as the more extensively studied western European countries. Extraordinarily influential, it practically invented the subject of popular culture by showing how much could be learned from studying festivals and games.

Davies, Norman. *God's Playground: A History of Poland,* rev. ed., 2 vols. 1982. By far the most comprehensive study of Polish history, this is particularly strong for the sixteenth and seventeenth centuries. Davies offers a Polish-centered view of European history that is marvelously stimulating even if he sometimes overstates his case for the importance of Poland.

Dukes, Paul. *A History of Russia: Medieval, Modern, Contemporary, ca. 882–1996,* 3rd ed. 1998. A comprehensive survey that synthesizes the most recent research.

Dunn, Richard S. *The Age of Religious Wars, 1559–1715,* 2nd ed. 1980. An excellent survey for students new to the subject.

Evans, R. J. W. *Rudolf II and His World: A Study in Intellectual History, 1576–1612.* 1973. A sympathetic examination of the intellectual world Rudolf created. Evans recognizes Rudolf's mental problems but lessens their significance for understanding the period.

Holt, Mack P. *The French Wars of Religion, 1562–1629.* 1996. A lucid short synthesis of the events and complex issues raised by these wars.

Hsia, R. Po-chia. *Social Discipline in the Reformation: Central Europe 1550–1750.* 1989. An excellent, lucid, and short overview of the attempts to discipline the people in Germany.

Huppert, George. *After the Black Death: A Social History of Early Modern Europe.* 1986. Engaging, entertaining, and elegantly written, this is the best single study of European social life during the Early Modern period.

Levack, Brian P. *The Witch-Hunt in Early Modern Europe,* 2nd ed. 1995. The best and most up-to-date short examination of the complex problem of the witch-hunt. This is the place to begin for students new to the subject.

Ozment, Steven E. *Ancestors: The Loving Family in Old Europe.* 2001. This comprehensive study of family life demonstrates that families were actually far more loving than the theory of patriarchy would suggest.

Parker, Geoffrey. *The Dutch Revolt,* rev. ed. 1990. The classic study of the revolt by one of the most masterful historians of the period. This study is especially adept at pointing to the larger European context of the revolt.

Parker, Geoffrey. *The Grand Strategy of Philip II.* 1998. Rehabilitates Philip as a significant strategic thinker.

Wiesner, Merry E. *Women and Gender in Early Modern Europe.* 1993. The best short study of the subject. This is the best book for students new to the subject.

Notes

1. Quoted in R. Po-Chia Hsia, *Social Discipline in the Reformation: Central Europe, 1550–1750* (1989), 147–148.
2. Quoted in R. J. Knecht, *The French Wars of Religion, 1559–1598,* 2nd ed. (1996), 13.
3. Quoted in John Neale, "The Massacre of St. Bartholomew," reprinted in Orest Ranum, ed., *Searching for Modern Times,* vol. 1, 1500–1650 (1969), 176.
4. François Rabelais, *The Histories of Gargantua and Pantagruel,* trans. J. M. Cohen (1955), 159.
5. Michel de Montaigne, *Essays and Selected Writings,* trans. and ed. Donald M. Frame (1963), 219–221.
6. Luís Vaz de Camões, *The Lusiads,* trans. William C. Atkinson (1952), 42.
7. Quoted in "Elizabeth I," *Encyclopedia Britannica* 8 (1959), 364b.
8. Quoted in Norman Davies, *Europe: A History* (1996), 529.

Absolutism and State Building in Europe, 1618–1715

I N 1651 THOMAS HOBBES, AN ENGLISH PHILOSOPHER LIVING IN EXILE IN FRANCE, was convinced that the West had descended into chaos. As he looked around him, Hobbes saw nothing but political instability, rebellion, and civil war. The turmoil had begun in the late sixteenth century, when the Reformation sparked the religious warfare described in the last chapter. In 1618 the situation deteriorated when another cycle of internal political strife and warfare erupted. The Thirty Years' War (1618–1648) began as a religious and political dispute in Germany but soon became an international conflict involving the armies of Spain, France, Sweden, and England as well as those of many German states. The war wreaked economic and social havoc in Germany, decimated its population, and forced governments throughout Europe to raise large armies and tax their subjects to pay for them. The entire European economy suffered as a result.

During the 1640s, partly as a result of that devastating conflict, the political order of Europe virtually collapsed. In England a series of bloody civil wars led to the destruction of the monarchy and the establishment of a republic. In France a civil war over constitutional issues drove the royal family from Paris. In Spain the king faced rebellions in no fewer than four of his territories, while in many European kingdoms peasants had risen in protest against the taxes their governments were collecting. Europe was in the midst of a profound and multi-faceted crisis.

Hobbes, a man plagued by anxiety even since he was a child, proposed a solution to this crisis. In 1651 he published a book, *Leviathan,* about the origin and exercise of political power. He began by observing that people had a natural tendency to quarrel among themselves and seek power over each other. If left to their own devices in a hypothetical state of nature, in which government did not exist, they would find themselves in constant conflict. In these circumstances, which Hobbes referred to as a state of war, people would be unable to engage in

Chapter Outline

- The Nature of Absolutism

- The Absolutist State in France and Spain

- Absolutism and State Building in Central and Eastern Europe

- Resistance to Absolutism in England and the Dutch Republic

Louis XIV: Portrait of Louis XIV in military armor, with his plumed helmet and his crown on the table to the right. The portrait was painted during the period of French warfare. In the background is a French ship.

■ **The Frontispiece of Thomas Hobbes's Treatise** *Leviathan,* **Published in London in 1651**
The ruler is depicted as incorporating the bodies of all his subjects, since they collectively authorized him to govern.

trade or agriculture or pursue cultural interests. Life would soon become, in Hobbes's famous words, "solitary, poor, nasty, brutish, and short." The only way for people to find peace in this dangerous and unproductive world would be to agree with their neighbors to form a political society, or a state, by surrendering their independent power to a ruler who would make laws, administer justice, and maintain order. In this state the ruler would wield great power, and he would not share it with others. His subjects, having agreed to endow him with such extensive power, and having agreed to submit to his rule, could not resist or depose him.

Hobbes wrote *Leviathan* not simply as an abstract study of political philosophy but as a solution to the problems that plagued the West in the middle of the seventeenth century. He was suggesting that the best way to achieve peace and security was for people to submit themselves to the authority of a single ruler. The term used to designate this type of government is absolutism°. In the most general

terms, absolutism means a political arrangement in which one ruler possesses complete and unrivaled power.

The political history of the West during the seventeenth and early eighteenth centuries can be written largely in terms of the efforts made by European monarchs to introduce absolutism. Those efforts were accompanied by policies intended to make the states they ruled wealthier and more powerful. Attempts to introduce absolutism and to strengthen the state took place in almost every country in Europe. In all these countries a succession of encounters took place between rulers who were trying to enlarge the power of the state and those who resisted their efforts. The outcome of these encounters varied from country to country, but for the most part the advocates of state building and absolutism prevailed. By the end of the seventeenth century the West comprised a number of large states, governed by rulers who had achieved unrivaled power and who commanded large, well-equipped armies. The West had entered the age of absolutism, which lasted until the outbreak of the French Revolution in 1789.

Not only did the West acquire a clear political identity during the seventeenth century, but its geographical boundaries also began to shift. Russia, which Europeans thought of as part of the East, began a program of imitating Western governments and became a major player in European diplomacy and warfare. At the same time Russia's southern neighbor, the Ottoman Empire, which had long straddled the boundary between East and West, was increasingly viewed by Europeans as part of a remote, Asian world.

This chapter will address the following questions: (1) What did absolutism mean, both as a political theory and as a practical program, and how was absolutism related to the growth of the power of the state? (2) How did the encounters that took place in France and Spain during the seventeenth century result in the establishment of absolutism, and how powerful did those two states become in the seventeenth century? (3) What was the nature of royal absolutism in central and eastern Europe, and how did the policies of the Ottoman Empire and Russia help to establish the boundaries of the West during this period? (4) Why did absolutism fail to take root in England and the Dutch Republic during the seventeenth century?

The Nature of Absolutism

Seventeenth-century absolutism had both a theoretical and a practical dimension. Theoretical absolutists included writers like Hobbes who described the nature of power in the state and explained the conditions for its acquisition and continuation. Practical absolutists were the rulers who took concrete political steps to subordinate all other political authorities within the state to themselves. Efforts to introduce royal absolutism in Europe began in the late sixteenth and early seventeenth centuries, but only in the late seventeenth century, after the Thirty Years' War and the political turmoil of the 1640s, did many European rulers consolidate their political positions and actually achieve absolute power.

The word *absolutism* usually conjures up images of despotic kings terrorizing every segment of the population, ruling by whim and caprice, and executing their subjects at will. Nothing could be further from the truth. Absolute monarchs succeeded in establishing themselves as the highest political authorities within their kingdoms, but they never attained unlimited power. Nor could they exercise power in a completely arbitrary manner. Theoretical absolutists never sanctioned this type of arbitrary rule, and the laws of European states never permitted it. Even if European monarchs had wished to act in this way, they usually could not because they did not have the political or judicial resources to impose their will on the people. The exercise of royal power in the seventeenth century, even when it was considered absolute, depended on the tacit consent of noblemen, office holders, and the members of local political assemblies. Kings usually could not afford to risk losing the support of these prominent men by acting illegally or arbitrarily, and when they did, they found themselves faced with rebellion.

THE THEORY OF ABSOLUTISM

When seventeenth-century political writers referred to the monarch as having absolute power, they usually meant that he possessed the highest legislative power in his kingdom. In particular, they meant that he did not share the power to make law with representative assemblies like the English Parliament. The French magistrate Jean Bodin (1530?–1596), who was one of the earliest proponents of absolutist theory, argued in *Six Books of a Commonweal* (1576) that absolute power consisted of several attributes, the most important of which was the power to make law. In similar fashion Hobbes referred to the absolute ruler as "sole legislator." Absolute monarchs, therefore, were rulers who could make law by themselves.

In order to bolster their authority, absolute monarchs frequently asserted that they received their power directly from God and therefore ruled by divine right. This idea was hardly new in the seventeenth century. The Bible proclaimed that all political authorities were "of God" and that people must therefore be obedient to them. In the fourteenth century European monarchs asserted that since God had given them the right to rule, the pope could not depose them. In the sixteenth century the idea of divine right was used to discourage rebellion, for to resist the king was to attack God's representative on Earth. In the seventeenth century many theorists of absolutism—although not

Hobbes—used the idea of divine right to insist that kings were accountable only to God, rather than to their subjects.

Absolute rulers often claimed that they were above the law. This meant that when monarchs acted for reason of state, that is, for the benefit of the entire kingdom, they were not strictly bound by the law of their kingdoms. Being above the law also meant that they could not be held legally accountable for their actions, since they were the highest judges in the land. Being above the law did not mean kings or queens could act arbitrarily, illegally, or despotically, even though some of them did so from time to time. Absolute rulers, no less than those who shared power with representative assemblies, were always expected to observe the individual rights and liberties of their subjects as well as the moral law established by God. They were expected, for example, to try people in a court of law rather than execute them at will. The French preacher Jacques Bossuet (1627–1704), who wrote an absolutist treatise on the authority of kings in 1670, insisted that even though kings were not subject to the penalties of the law, they still were not freed from the obligation to observe that law. No less than their subjects, kings were subject to the "equity of the laws." This meant that they should not rule despotically or arbitrarily.

Theorists of absolutism made distinctions between European monarchs and rulers in other parts of the world, such as Turkish sultans, Russian tsars, and the kings of Asian and African lands. In those so-called Eastern countries, according to Bodin, "the prince has become the lord of the goods and the persons of his subjects," by which Bodin meant that the rulers of those lands could seize the possessions of their subjects or execute them without due process of law. Only in the West, wrote Bodin, did royal subjects live under a regime that abided by the rule of law. Bodin exaggerated the powers of both Turkish sultans and Russian tsars, who had much in common with the absolute rulers of western and central Europe. But by emphasizing the rule of law and the king's obligation to abide by it, Bodin identified one of the distinctive features of Western politics during the age of absolutism.

THE PRACTICE OF ABSOLUTISM

What steps did the European monarchs who claimed absolute power take to establish and maintain themselves as the supreme authorities within the state? The first strategy they employed was the elimination or the weakening of national representative assemblies, such as Parliament in England, *Diets* in German states, and the *Cortes* in Spain and Portugal. In France, which is considered to have been the most absolutist state in seventeenth-century Europe, the monarchy stopped summoning its national assembly, the Estates General, in 1614. This assembly did not meet again until the late eighteenth century. In similar fashion, the Portuguese Cortes did not meet after 1640. In

Brandenburg-Prussia the representative assembly for the entire electorate, the Diet, met for the last time in 1652.

In the main Spanish kingdom of Castile, the process was more gradual. Spanish kings gradually reduced the importance of the Cortes in the sixteenth century, but they did not stop calling them until 1664. In the kingdoms of England and Sweden, where absolutism never triumphed, kings who aspired to absolute rule succeeded in dispensing with representative institutions only for brief periods of time. Charles I of England (r. 1625–1649) refused to summon Parliament between 1629 and 1640, while Charles XII of Sweden (r. 1697–1718) did not convene the Swedish *Riksdag* during his entire reign. His successor, however, re-established parliamentary rule in 1722. Charles XII also indicated his preference for absolutism by crowning himself at his coronation, thus symbolizing his belief that he derived his power from no other human authority.

The second strategy of absolutist rulers was to secure the support of smaller regional, provincial, and municipal assemblies that controlled local government. These institutions represented much less of a direct challenge to royal authority, especially since they usually could not act in concert with other political bodies. Most of them therefore managed to survive during the age of absolutism. In fact, these local assemblies proved extremely useful to absolute monarchs, in that they could often be persuaded to grant taxes and recruit soldiers in exchange for the maintenance of their own institutional privileges and liberties. Thus French monarchs regularly convened the provincial assemblies of Languedoc, Brittany, and other provinces long after they had stopped calling the Estates General. The rulers of Prussia continued to meet with provincial *Landtagen* after they stopped calling the general Diet, while in Austria the Habsburg emperors summoned provincial diets throughout the seventeenth and early eighteenth centuries. The only time the king needed to control or suppress these smaller assemblies was when they threatened to become independent of the state. This is what happened when the Spanish principality of Catalonia staged a revolt against the crown in 1640. After the suppression of the revolt the king did not summon the Cortes of Catalonia again until 1701. Absolute monarchs tolerated provincial or local assemblies only to the extent that they served the purposes of the king.

The third strategy of absolute monarchs was to subordinate the nobility to the king and make them dependent on his favor. This was a demanding task, often requiring considerable political skill. After all, the king himself belonged to this wealthy and powerful social group. Traditionally noblemen participated in the government of the kingdom, serving as royal councilors and as members of the representative assemblies that the king summoned in order to make laws and levy taxes. Noblemen also provided the king with soldiers in time of war and led them into battle. The king was therefore dependent upon his noblemen, and to a cer-

tain extent he shared power with them. Their privileges and powerful political and social position, however, often led them to participate in rebellions and conspiracies against the king, with the goal of either replacing him or gaining control of his government.

Monarchs who aspired to a position of unrivaled power within their kingdoms could not tolerate challenges of this sort from the ranks of the nobility. They therefore took steps to keep the nobility in line, not only by suppressing rebellion and quashing conspiracies but also by appointing men from different social groups as their chief ministers. Another tactic was to demand that noblemen spend at least part of the year at court, where it was less likely that they could organize collective action against the king and where the king could keep an eye on them. At the same time, however, the king could not afford to alienate the same men, upon whom he still relied for running his government and maintaining order in the localities. Absolute monarchs, therefore, offered nobles special privileges, such as exemption from taxation, positions in the king's household, and freedom to exploit their peasants in exchange for their recognition of the king's superiority and their assistance in maintaining order in the localities. In this way nobles became junior partners in the management of the absolutist state.

The final strategy of absolute monarchs was to gain effective control of the administrative machinery of the state and to use it to enforce royal policy throughout their kingdoms. Absolute monarchs were by nature state builders. They established centralized bureaucracies that extended the reach of their governments down into the smallest towns and villages and out into most remote regions of their kingdoms. The business conducted by these centrally controlled bureaucracies included collection of taxes, recruitment of soldiers, and operation of the judicial system. Some absolute monarchs used the central machinery of the state to impose and maintain religious conformity. As the seventeenth century advanced, they also used the same machinery to regulate the price of grain, stimulate the growth of industry, and relieve the plight of the poor. In these ways the policies pursued by absolute monarchs had an impact on the lives of all royal subjects, not just noblemen and royal councilors.

WARFARE AND THE ABSOLUTIST STATE

Much of the growth of European states in the seventeenth century can be related in one way or another to the conduct of war. During the period from 1600 to 1721, European powers were almost constantly at war. The entire continent was at peace for only four of those years. To meet the demands of war, rulers kept men under arms at all times. By the middle of the seventeenth century, after the Thirty Years' War had come to an end, most European rulers had acquired such standing armies. These armies not only served their rulers in foreign wars but also helped them maintain order and enforce royal policy at home. Standing armies thus became one of the main props of royal absolutism.

During the seventeenth and early eighteenth centuries European armies became larger, in many cases tripling in size. In the 1590s Philip II of Spain had acquired mastery of Europe with an army of 40,000 men. By contrast, in the late seventeenth century Louis XIV of France needed an army of 400,000 men to become the dominant power on the continent. The increase in the size of these forces can be traced to the invention of gunpowder and its more frequent use in the fifteenth and sixteenth centuries. Gunpowder led to the widespread use of the musket, a heavy shoulder firearm carried by a foot soldier. The use of the musket placed a premium on the recruitment and equipment of large armies of infantry, who marched in square columns with men holding long pikes (long wooden shafts with pointed metal heads) to protect the musketeers from enemy attacks. As the size of these armies of foot soldiers grew, the role of mounted soldiers, who had dominated medieval warfare, was greatly reduced.

Changes in military technology and tactics also necessitated more intensive military training. In the Middle Ages mounted knights had acquired great individual skill, but they did not need to work in precise unison with other men under arms. Seventeenth-century foot soldiers, however, had to learn to march in formation, to coordinate their maneuvers, and to fire without harming their comrades in arms. Therefore they needed to be drilled. The introduction of volley fire, by which one successive line of soldiers stepped forward to fire while the others were reloading, placed an even greater premium on precise drilling. Drilling took place in peacetime as well as during war. The wearing of uniforms, which began when the state assumed the function of clothing its thousands of soldiers, gave further unity and cohesion to the trained fighting force.

The cost of recruiting, training, and equipping these mammoth armies was staggering. In the Middle Ages individual lords often had sufficient financial resources to assemble their own private armies. By the beginning of the seventeenth century the only institution capable of putting the new armies in the field was the state itself. The same was true for navies, which now consisted of heavily armed sailing ships, each of which carried as many as 400 sailors. To build these large armies and navies, as well as to pay the increasing cost of waging war itself (which rose 500 percent between 1530 and 1630), the state had to identify new methods of raising and collecting taxes. In times of war as much as 80 percent of the revenue taken in by the state went for military purposes.

The equipment and training of military forces and the collection and allocation of the revenue necessary to subsidize these efforts stimulated the expansion and refinement of the state bureaucracy. Governments found it necessary to employ thousands of new officials to supervise the collection of new taxes, and in order to make the system of tax collection system more efficient, governments often introduced entirely new administrative systems. Some states completely reorganized their bureaucracies to meet the demands of war. New departments of state were created to supervise the recruitment of soldiers, the manufacture of equipment and uniforms, the building of fleets, and the provisioning of troops in time of war. Rulers of European states recognized that the exercise of absolute power greatly facilitated the utilization of state power for these purposes.

The Absolutist State in France and Spain

The two European countries in which royal absolutism first became a political reality were France and Spain. The histories of these two monarchies in the seventeenth century followed very different courses. The kingdom of France, especially during the reign of Louis XIV (r. 1643–1715), became a model of state building and gradually emerged as the most powerful country in Europe. The Spanish monarchy, on the other hand, struggled to introduce absolutism at a time when the overall economic condition of the country was deteriorating and its military forces were suffering a series of defeats. Spain established the forms of absolutist rule, but the monarchy was not able to match the political or military achievements of France in the late seventeenth century.

THE FOUNDATIONS OF FRENCH ABSOLUTISM

Efforts to make the French monarchy absolute began in response to the disorder that occurred during the wars of religion in the late sixteenth century. Bodin wrote his treatises during those wars, and the threat of renewed civil war between Protestants and Catholics affected French politics throughout the seventeenth century. The first steps toward the achievement of absolutism were taken during the reign of Henry IV (r. 1589–1610), the Huguenot who converted to Catholicism in 1594 and who ended the wars of religion by granting freedom of worship and full civil rights to French Protestants by the Edict of Nantes (1598). This decree brought internal religious peace to the kingdom, while the progressive financial and economic policies of Henry's brilliant minister, the Duke of Sully, helped restore the financial strength of the crown and involve the government in a process of commercial recovery and expansion. Despite this success, Henry could not prevent the great nobles from conspiring against him, and his policy of religious toleration encountered resistance from Catholics committed to the suppression of Protestantism. In 1610 a fanatical

Catholic, François Ravaillac, stabbed the king to death in his carriage on a Parisian street.

On Henry's death the crown passed to his young son, Louis XIII (r. 1610–1643), while the queen mother, Marie de Medici, assumed the leadership of a government acting in the king's name during his youth. This period of regency, in which aristocratic factions vied for supremacy at court, exposed the main weakness of the monarchy, which was the rival power of the great noble families of the realm. The statesman who addressed this problem most directly was Louis's main councilor, Cardinal Armand Jean du Plessis de Richelieu (1585–1642). A member of an old and wealthy family, Richelieu rose to power through the patronage of the queen mother and then, after losing her support, maintained his preeminent position with the support of the king himself. He became the king's chief minister in 1628. Richelieu was arguably the greatest statebuilder of the seventeenth century. He directed all his energies toward centralizing the power of the French state in the person of the king.

Richelieu's most immediate concern was bringing the independent nobility to heel and subordinating their local power to that of the state. This he accomplished by suppressing several conspiracies and rebellions led by noblemen and by restricting the independent power of the provincial assemblies and the eight regional parlements°, which were the highest courts in the country. His great administrative achievement was the strengthening of the system of the intendants°. These paid crown officials, who were recruited from the professional classes and the lower ranks of the nobility, became the main agents of French lo-

cal administration. Responsible only to the royal council, they collected taxes, supervised local administration, and recruited soldiers for the army. Since they could not come from the districts to which they were assigned, they had no vested interest in maintaining local customs or privileges.

Richelieu also modified the religious policy embodied in the Edict of Nantes. According to that document, Huguenots not only had freedom of worship but could also fortify the towns in which they lived. Richelieu resented the maintenance of these citadels of local power, which represented a challenge to the type of absolutist state he envisioned. He also suspected that rivals of the king from the nobility were using the Huguenot towns as a means of maintaining their independent power. A series of military confrontations between the government and the Protestants in the late 1610s and 1620s brought the country to the brink of civil war. Following the successful siege of the town of La Rochelle in 1627–1628, the government razed the fortifications of the Huguenot cities, melted down their cannons, and disarmed their Protestant citizens. A peace treaty signed in 1629 ratified the government's victory, but it did not deny the Huguenots their right to worship freely.

The most challenging task for Richelieu, as it was for all French ministers in the early modern period, was increasing the government's yield from taxation, a task that became more demanding during times of war. Levying taxes on the French population was always a delicate process, since the needs of the state conflicted with the privileges of various social groups, such as the nobles, who were exempt from taxation, and the estates of individual provinces such as Brittany that claimed the right to tax the people them-

■ **Cardinal Richelieu**

Triple portrait of Cardinal Richelieu, who laid the foundations of French absolutism.

selves. Using a variety of tactics, including negotiation and compromise, and relying heavily on the support of the provincial intendants, Richelieu managed to increase the yield from the *taille*, the direct tax on land, as much as threefold during the period 1635–1648. He supplemented the taille with taxes on office holding. Even then, the revenue was insufficient to meet the extraordinary demands of war.

Opposition to Richelieu's financial policies lay at the root of the main problem the government faced after the cardinal's death in 1642. The minister who succeeded him was his protégé Jules Mazarin (1602–1661), a diplomat of Italian birth who had entered French government service during Richelieu's administration. Mazarin dominated the government of Louis XIV (r. 1643–1715) during the period when the king, who inherited the throne at age 5, was still a boy and while his mother was serving as regent. Mazarin continued the policies of his predecessor, but he was unable to prevent civil war from breaking out in 1648. This challenge to the French state, known as the *Fronde* (a pejorative reference to a Parisian game in which children flung mud at passing carriages), had two phases. The first, the Fronde of the Parlement (1648–1649), began when the members of the Parlement of Paris, the most important of all the provincial parlements, refused to register an edict of the king that had required them to surrender four years' salary. This act of resistance led to demands that the king sign a document limiting royal authority. Barricades went up in the streets of Paris, and the royal family was forced to flee the city. A blockade of the city by royal troops led to an uneasy compromise in 1649. Revolts in three other parlements, each of which had its own dynamic and which were not coordinated with that of Paris, came to a similar resolution. The second and more violent phase was the Fronde of the Princes (1650–1653), during which the Prince de Condé and his noble allies waged war on the government and even formed an alliance with France's enemy, Spain. Only after Condé's military defeat did the entire rebellion collapse.

The Fronde stands as the great crisis of the seventeenth-century French state. It revealed the strength of the local, aristocratic, and legal forces with which the king and his ministers had to contend. These forces managed to disrupt the growth of the French state, drive the king from his capital, and challenge his authority throughout the kingdom. But in the long run they could not destroy the achievement of Richelieu and Mazarin. By the late 1650s the damage had been repaired and the state had resumed its growth.

CHRONOLOGY

France in the Age of Absolutism

1598	The Edict of Nantes grants toleration to French Calvinists, known as Huguenots
1610	Assassination of Henry IV of France, who was succeeded by Louis XIII (r. 1610–1643)
1628	Cardinal Richelieu becomes chief minister of Louis XIII of France
1643	Death of Louis XIII of France and accession of Louis XIV; Louis's mother, Anne of Austria, becomes queen regent with Cardinal Mazarin as his minister
1648–1653	The Fronde
1661	Death of Cardinal Mazarin; Louis XIV assumes personal rule
1685	Revocation of the Edict of Nantes
1715	Death of Louis XIV of France; succeeded by his grandson, Louis XV

ABSOLUTISM IN THE REIGN OF LOUIS XIV

The man who presided over the development of the French state for the next fifty years was the king himself, Louis XIV, who assumed direct control of his government after the death of Mazarin in 1661. In an age of absolute monarchs, Louis towered among his contemporaries. He is widely regarded as the most powerful king of the seventeenth century. This reputation comes as much from the image he conveyed as from the policies he pursued. Artists, architects, dramatists, and members of his immediate entourage helped the king project an image of incomparable majesty and authority. Paintings and sculptures of the king depicted him in sartorial splendor, holding the symbols of power and displaying expressions of regal superiority that bordered on arrogance. At Versailles, about ten miles from Paris, Louis constructed a lavishly furnished palace that became his main residence and the center of the glittering court that surrounded him. The palace was built in the baroque° style, which emphasized the size and grandeur of the structure while also conveying a sense of unity and balance among its diverse parts. The sweeping façades of baroque buildings gave them a dynamic quality that evoked an emotional response from the viewer. The baroque style, criticized by contemporaries for its exuberance and pomposity, appealed to absolute monarchs who wished to emphasize their unrivaled position within society and their determination to impose order and stability on their kingdoms.

Court life at Versailles revolved entirely around the king. Court dramas depicted Louis, who styled himself "the sun king," as Apollo, the god of light. The paintings in the grand Hall of Mirrors at Versailles, which recorded the king's military victories, served as reminders of his unrivaled accomplishments. Louis's formal routine in receiving visitors created appropriate distance between him and his courtiers while keeping his subjects in a state of subservient anticipation of royal favor. His frequent bursts of anger achieved the same effect. When an untitled lady took the seat of a noblewoman at a dinner in his presence, he described the act as one of "incredible insolence" that "had thrown him into such a rage that he had been unable to eat." After rebuking the offending lady for her "impertinence," he became so angry that he left the room.

The image of magnificence and power that Louis conveyed in art and ceremony mirrored and reinforced his more tangible political accomplishments. His greatest achievement was to solve the persistent problem of aristocratic independence and rebellion by securing the complete loyalty and dependence of the old nobility. This he achieved first by requiring the members of these ancient families to come to Versailles for a portion of every year, where they stayed in apartments within the royal palace itself. At Versailles Louis involved them in the elaborate cultural activities of court life and in ceremonial rituals that emphasized their subservience to the king. At the same time, he excluded the nobles from holding important offices in the government of the realm, a strategy designed to prevent them from building an independent power base within the bureaucracy. Instead he recruited men from the mercantile and professional classes to run his government. This policy of taming the nobility and depriving them of central ad-

ministrative power could work only if they received something in return. Like all the absolute monarchs of western Europe, Louis used the patronage at his disposal to grant members of the nobility wealth and privileges in exchange for their loyalty to the crown. In this way the monarchy and the nobility served each other's interests.

In running the actual machinery of government Louis built upon and perfected the centralizing policies of Richelieu and Mazarin. After the death of Mazarin in 1661 the king, now 23 years old, became his own chief minister, presiding over a council of state that supervised the work of government. An elaborate set of councils at the highest levels of government set policy that was implemented by the department ministers. The provincial intendants became even more important than they had been under Richelieu and Mazarin, especially in providing food, arms, and equipment for royal troops. It was the intendants' job to secure the cooperation of the local judges, city councils, and parish priests as well as the compliance of the local population. If necessary they could call upon royal troops in order to enforce their will, but for the most part they preferred to rely on the more effective tactics of negotiation and compromise with local officials. The system, when it worked properly, allowed the king to make decisions that directly affected the lives and beliefs of his 20 million subjects.

A further manifestation of the newfound power of the French state in the late seventeenth century was the government's active involvement in the economic and financial life of the country. The minister who was most responsible for this series of undertakings was Jean Baptiste Colbert

(1619–1683), a protégé of Mazarin who in 1661 became controller general of the realm. Born into a family of merchants, and despised by the old nobility, Colbert epitomized the type of government official Louis recruited into his service. Entrusted with the supervision of the entire system of royal taxation, Colbert managed to increase royal revenues dramatically simply by reducing the cut taken by the agents whom the government hired to collect taxes.

Even more beneficial to the French state was the determination of Colbert to use the country's economic resources for its benefit. The theory underlying this set of policies was mercantilism°, which held that the wealth of the state depended on its ability to import fewer commodities than it exported. Its goal was to secure the largest possible share of the world's monetary supply. In keeping with those objectives, Colbert increased the size of France's merchant fleet, founded overseas trading companies, and levied high tariffs on France's commercial rivals. To make France economically self-sufficient he encouraged the growth of the French textile industry, improved the condition of the roads, built canals throughout the kingdom, and reduced some of the burdensome tolls that impeded internal trade.

The most intrusive exercise of this power of the state during Louis XIV's reign was the decision to enforce religious uniformity. The king always considered the existence of a large Huguenot minority within his kingdom an affront to his sense of order. Toleration was divisive and dangerous, especially to someone who styled himself as "Most Christian King." Even after Richelieu had leveled the walls of the fortified Huguenot towns, the problem of religious pluralism remained. In 1685 Louis addressed this problem by revoking the entire Edict of Nantes, thereby denying freedom of religious worship to about one million of his subjects. The enforcement of this policy was violent and disruptive, with the army being called upon to enforce public conversions to Catholicism. Protestant churches were closed and often destroyed, while large numbers of Huguenots were forced to emigrate to the Netherlands, England, and Protestant German lands. Few exercises of absolute power in the seventeenth century caused more disruption in the lives of ordinary people than this attempt to realize the king's ideal of "one king, one law, one faith."

LOUIS XIV AND THE CULTURE OF ABSOLUTISM

A further manifestation of the power of the French absolutist state was Louis's success in influencing and transforming French culture. Kings had often served as patrons of the arts by providing income for artists, writers, and musicians while endowing cultural and educational institutions. Louis took this type of royal patronage to a new level, making it possible for him to control the dissemination of ideas and the very production of culture itself. During Louis's reign royal patronage, emanating from the court, extended the king's influence over the entire cultural landscape. The architects of the palace at Versailles, the painters of historical scenes that hung in its hallways and galleries, the composers of the plays and operas that were performed in its theaters, the sculptors who created busts of the king to decorate its chambers, and the historians and pamphlet writers who celebrated the king's achievements in print all benefited from Louis's direct financial support.

Much of Louis's patronage went to cultural institutions, thereby enabling the king to influence a wider circle of artists and have a greater effect on the cultural life of the nation. He took over the Academy of Fine Arts in 1661, founded the Academy of Music in 1669, and chartered a theater company, the *Comédie Française*, in 1680. Two great French dramatists of the late seventeenth century, Jean Baptiste Molière (1622–1673), the creator of French high comedy, and Jean Racine (1639–1699), who wrote tragedies in the classical style, benefited from the king's patronage. Louis even subsidized the publication of a new journal, the *Journal des savants*, in which men of letters advanced their ideas. In 1666 Louis extended his patronage to the sciences with the founding of the Royal Academy of Sciences, which had the twofold objective of advancing scientific knowledge and glorifying the king. It also benefited the state by devising improvements in ship design and navigation.

Of all the cultural institutions that benefited from Louis XIV's patronage, the *Académie Française* had the most enduring impact on French culture. This academy, a society of literary scholars, had been founded in 1635 with the support of Cardinal Richelieu. Its purpose was to standardize the French language and serve as the guardian of its integrity. In 1694, twenty-two years after Louis became the academy's patron, the first official French dictionary appeared in print. This achievement of linguistic uniformity, in which words received authorized spellings and definitions, reflected the pervasiveness of Louis's cultural influence as well as the search for order that became the defining characteristic of his reign.

Louis introduced order and uniformity into every aspect of his own life and that of his country. He followed a precise routine in ordering his daily life, created ceremonies that ordered the life of his court, and insisted on the court's adoption of table manners that followed strict rules of politeness. He created a bureaucracy that was organized along rational, orderly principles, and he sought to ensure that all his subjects would practice the same religion. The establishment of a clearly defined chain of command in the army, which Louis's minister the Marquis de Louvois introduced, gave organizational cohesion and hierarchical order to the large military force the king and his ministers assembled. Nearly all areas of French public life were transformed by the king's desire to establish order and uniformity and his use of the power of the state to enforce it.

One indication of the extent of Louis's achievement was the conspicuous attempt of other monarchs to imitate

REVOCATION OF THE EDICT OF NANTES, OCTOBER 25, 1685

....

In 1685 King Louis XIV of France revoked the Edict of Nantes, the decree of King Henry IV that had granted freedom of worship to French Protestants in 1598. Before the revocation was published, the government sent dragoons (cavalry who arrived on horseback but fought on foot) to terrorize Protestant households and make them convert to Catholicism. The terms of the revocation were particularly harsh, and despite the prohibition against leaving the country, hundreds of thousands of Huguenots emigrated to England, the Dutch Republic, and North America.

. . . Therefore we decided that there was nothing better we could do to erase from memory the troubles, the confusion and the evils that the growth of this false religion had caused in our kingdom and that gave rise to the said Edict and to so many other edicts and declarations that preceded it, than to revoke entirely the said Edict of Nantes and the detailed articles attached to it and everything that has been done since on behalf of the said Supposedly Reformed Religion [Calvinism].

1. We therefore for these reasons and in full knowledge, power and authority, by means of the present perpetual and irrevocable edict, do suppress and revoke the Edict of the King, our grandfather, issued at Nantes in April 1598. . . . As a result we desire and it is our pleasure that all the temples of the Supposedly Reformed Religion situated in our kingdom, county, lands and seigneuries within our obedience be immediately demolished.

2. Our subjects of the Supposedly Reformed Religion are not to assemble for worship in any place or house for any reason.

3. Noble lords are not to hold worship services in their houses or fiefs of any sort on pain of confiscation of goods and property.

4. Ministers of the Supposedly Reformed Religion who have not converted are to leave the kingdom within fifteen days and are not to preach or perform any functions in the meantime, or they will be sent to the galleys.

5. Ministers who convert, and their widows after their death, are to receive the same exemptions from taxes and troop lodgings that they had as ministers . . .

6. Converted ministers can become lawyers or doctors of law without the usual three years of study and for half the fees usually charged by the universities.

7. Special schools for the children of the Supposedly Reformed Religion are prohibited.

8. Children of [Huguenot] parents are to be baptized by the chief priests of their parishes and raised as Catholics, and local judges are to oversee this.

9. If Protestants who left the kingdom before this edict was issued return within four months, they can regain their property and resume their lives. If, however, they do not return within four months, their goods will be confiscated.

10. All subjects belonging to the Supposedly Reformed Religion and their wives and children are forbidden to leave the country or to send out their property and effects. The penalty for men is the galleys and women confiscation of their persons and property.

11. The declarations already issued concerning those who relapse are to be executed in full.

And in addition, those who adhere to the Supposedly Reformed religion, while waiting until it pleases God to enlighten them like the others, may continue to live in the cities and communities of our realm, continue their commerce, and enjoy their property without being bothered or hindered because of the Supposedly Reformed Religion, on condition, however, of not practicing their religion or assembling for prayers or worship or for any other pretext, with the penalties stated above.

Source: Copyright ©2000 by Bedford/St. Martin's. From *Louis XIV & Absolutism: A Brief Study with Documents* by William Beik. Reprinted with permission of Bedford/St. Martin's.

France, even in the eighteenth century. The absolute monarchs in Prussia, Austria, and Russia, as well as aspiring ones in England and Sweden, not only experimented selectively with French political methods but imported many of the features of French culture that Louis had supported. They built palaces in the same architectural style as that of Versailles, designed French gardens to surround them, imported the fashions and decorative styles of the French court, staged French ballets and operas in their capitals, and even spoke French, which had replaced Latin as the language of international diplomacy, when conducting official business. The power of the French monarchy had made French culture the dominant influence in the courts and capitals of Europe.

THE WARS OF LOUIS XIV, 1667–1714

The seventeenth-century French state was designed not only to maintain internal peace and order but also to wage war against other states. Colbert's financial and economic policies, coupled with the military reforms of the Marquis de Louvois, had laid the foundations for the creation of a formidable military machine. In 1667 Louis XIV began unleashing its full potential. Having assembled an army that was twenty times larger than the French force that had invaded Italy in 1494, Louis deployed this armed force against an array of European powers in no fewer than four separate wars between 1667 and 1714. His goal in all these wars, as it had been in all French international conflicts since 1635, was territorial acquisition (see Map 15.1). In this case Louis set his sights mainly on the German and Spanish territories in the Rhineland along the eastern borders of his kingdom. Contemporaries suggested, however, that he was thinking in grander terms than traditional French dynastic ambition. Propagandists for the king in the late 1660s claimed that Louis harbored visions of establishing a "universal monarchy" or an "absolute empire," reminiscent of the empires of ancient Rome, Charlemagne in the ninth century, and Charles V in the sixteenth century.

Louis never attained the empire of his dreams, but concerted action by almost all the other European powers was required to stop him. France's acquisition of new territories along its eastern boundaries between 1668 and 1684 confirmed the fears of other European states that the king had imperial ambitions. After Louis had launched an offensive against German towns along the Rhine River in 1688, signaling the beginning of yet another round of European warfare, Great Britain, the Dutch Republic, Spain, and Austria formed a coalition against him. Finally matched by the combined military forces of these allies, forced to wage war on many different fronts (including North America), and unable to provide adequate funding of the war on the basis of its system of taxation, France felt compelled to conclude peace in 1697. The Treaty of Ryswick marked the turning point in the expansion of the French state and laid the groundwork for the establishment of a balance of power° in the next century, an arrangement whereby various countries form alliances to prevent any one state from dominating the others.

The Treaty of Ryswick, however, did not mark the end of French territorial ambition. In 1701 Louis went to war once again, this time as part of an effort to place a French Bourbon candidate, his grandson Duke Philip of Anjou, on the Spanish throne. The impending death of the mentally weak, sexually impotent, and chronically ill King Charles II of Spain (r. 1665–1700) without heirs had created a succession crisis. In 1698 the major European powers had agreed to a treaty in which Spanish lands would be divided between Louis himself and the Holy Roman Emperor, both of whom happened to be Charles's brothers-in-law. By his will, however, Charles left the Spanish crown and all its overseas possessions to Philip. This bequest offered France more than it would have received on the basis of the treaty. If the will had been upheld, the Pyrenees mountains would have disappeared as a political barrier between France and Spain, and France, as the stronger of the two kingdoms,

would have controlled unprecedented expanses of European and American territory.

Dreaming once again of universal monarchy, Louis rejected the treaty in favor of King Charles's will. The British, Dutch, and Austrians responded by forming a Grand Alliance against France and Spain. After a long and costly conflict, known as the War of the Spanish Succession (1701–1713), the members of this coalition were able to dictate the terms of the Treaty of Utrecht (1713). Philip, who suffered from fits of manic depression and went days without dressing or leaving his room, remained on the Spanish throne as Philip V (r. 1700–1746), but only on the condition that the French and Spanish crowns would never be united. Spain ceded its territories in the Netherlands and in Italy to the Austrian Habsburg Monarchy and its strategic port of Gibraltar at the entrance to the Mediterranean to the British. The treaty not only confirmed the new balance of

Map 15.1 French Territorial Acquisitions, 1679–1714

The main acquisitions were lands in the Spanish Netherlands to the north and Franche Comté, Alsace, and Lorraine to the east. Louis thought of the Rhine River as France's natural eastern boundary, and territories acquired in 1659 and 1697 allowed it to reach that limit.

French Territorial Acquisitions, 1679–1714

- French gains to 1659
- French gains to 1679
- French gains to 1679 later lost
- French gains by Treaty of Ryswick 1697
- French frontier 1713/1714

DUTCH REPUBLIC
SOUTHERN (SPANISH) NETHERLANDS
Cologne
Aachen
HOLY ROMAN EMPIRE
Amiens
Luxembourg
Phillippsburg
Verdun
Landau
Paris
Strasbourg
FRANCE
LORRAINE
ALSACE
Freiburg
FRANCHE-COMTÉ
SWISS CANTONS
SAVOY-PIEDMONT

Rhine R.
Moselle R.
Marne R.
Seine
Saône R.
Rhône R.

0   100 km
0   100 mi

The French Bourbons and the Spanish Succession
1589–1700

Henry IV = Marie de Medici
(r. 1589–1610)

Louis XIII = Anna of Austria,
(r. 1610–1643)   d. of Philip III of Spain

Maria Theresa = **Louis XIV**   Philip = Elizabeth-Charlotte
of Spain   (r. 1643–1715)   duc d'Orleans

Louis = Maria Anna of Bavaria
(d. 1711)

Louis = Marie Adelaide   Philip, duke of Anjou   Charles,
(d. 1712)   of Savoy   and **Philip V**, king of Spain   duc de Berry
            (r. 1700–1746)

Louis XV
(r. 1715–1774)

power in Europe but also resulted in the transfer of large parts of French Canada, including Newfoundland and Nova Scotia, to Great Britain.

The loss of French territory in North America, the strains placed on the taxation system by the financial demands of war, and the weakening of France's commercial power as a result of this conflict made France a less potent state at the time of Louis's death in 1715 than it had been in the 1680s. Nevertheless the main effects of a century of French state building remained, including a large, well-integrated bureaucratic edifice that allowed the government to exercise unprecedented control over the population and a military establishment that remained the largest and best equipped in Europe.

ABSOLUTISM AND STATE BUILDING IN SPAIN

The history of Spain in the seventeenth century is almost always written in terms of failure, since the country endured a long period of economic decline that began in the late sixteenth century with a precipitate drop in the size of its population and stretched well into the eighteenth century. The monarchy became progressively weaker during the seventeenth century, as it was occupied by a succession of ineffective kings who exercised far less power than their French counterparts. To make matters worse, Spain in the seventeenth century suffered a long series of military defeats, most of them at the hands of the French, and it lost the position it had held in the sixteenth century as the major European power (see Map 15.2). By the early eighteenth

century Spain was a shadow of its former self, and its culture reflected uncertainty, pessimism, and nostalgia for former imperial greatness. None of this failure, however, should obscure the fact that Spain, like France, underwent a period of state building during the seventeenth century, and that its government, like that of France, gravitated toward absolutism.

The Spanish monarchy in 1600 ruled more territory than did France, and the various kingdoms and principalities that it comprised possessed far more independence than even the most remote and peripheral French provinces. The center of the monarchy was the kingdom of Castile, with its capital at Madrid. This kingdom, the largest and wealthiest territory within the Iberian peninsula, had been united with the kingdom of Aragon in 1479 when King Ferdinand II of Aragon (r. 1479–1516), the husband of Queen Isabella of Castile (r. 1474–1504), ascended the throne. These two kingdoms, however, continued to exist as separate states after the union, each having its own representative institutions and administrative systems. Each of them, moreover, contained smaller, semiautonomous kingdoms and provinces that retained their own distinctive political institutions. The kingdom of Valencia and the principality of Catalonia formed part of the Crown of Aragon, while in the sixteenth century the kingdoms of Navarre and Portugal had been annexed to the Crown of Castile. Outside the Iberian peninsula the Spanish monarchy ruled territories in the Netherlands, Italy, and the New World.

The only institution besides the monarchy itself that provided any kind of administrative unity to all these

■ Map 15.2 The Decline of Spanish Power in Europe, 1640–1714

Revolts in the United Provinces of the Netherlands and Portugal account for two of the most significant losses of Spanish territory. Military defeat at the hands of the French in 1659 and Austria in 1714 account for the loss of most of the other territories.

Spanish territories in the seventeenth century was the Spanish Inquisition, a centralized ecclesiastical court with a supreme council in Madrid and twenty-one regional tribunals in different parts of Spain, Italy, and America. Its function was to enforce religious uniformity and maintain the purity of the Catholic faith.

The great challenge for the Spanish monarchy in the seventeenth century was to integrate the various kingdoms and principalities of Spain into a more highly centralized state while at the same time making the machinery of that state more efficient and profitable. The statesman who made the most sustained efforts at realizing these goals was the energetic and authoritarian Count-Duke of Olivares (1587–1645), the contemporary and counterpart of Richelieu during the reign of the Spanish king Philip IV (1621–1665). The task Olivares faced was more daunting than anything the French cardinal had ever confronted. As a result of decades of warfare, the Spanish monarchy in the 1620s was penniless, the kingdom of Castile had gone

bankrupt, and the entire country had already entered a period of protracted economic decline.

To deal with these deep structural problems Olivares proposed a reform of the entire financial system, the establishment of national banks, and the replacement of the main tax, the *millones*, which was levied on the consumption of basic commodities such as meat and wine, with proportional contributions from all the towns and villages in the kingdom. At the same time he tried to address the problem of ruling a disparate and far-flung empire, making all the kingdoms and principalities within the monarchy contribute to national defense on a proportionate basis. His ultimate goal was to unify the entire peninsula in a cohesive Spanish national state, similar to that of France. This policy involved suppression of the individual liberties of the various kingdoms and principalities and direct subordination of each area to the king himself. It was, in other words, a solution based on the principles of absolutism.

Olivares was unable to match the state-building achievement of Richelieu in France. His failure, which was complete by the time he fell from office in 1643, can be attributed to three factors. The first was the opposition he confronted within Castile itself, especially from the cities represented in the Cortes, over the question of taxation. The second, a problem facing Spain throughout the seventeenth century, was military failure, in this case the losses to France during the final phase of the Thirty Years' War. That failure aggravated the financial crisis and prevented the monarchy from capitalizing on the prestige that usually attends military victory. The third and most serious impediment was opposition to the policy of subordinating the outlying Spanish regions to the kingdom of Castile. The kingdoms and provinces on the periphery of the country were determined to maintain their individual laws and liberties, especially the powers of their own Cortes, in the face of the pressures to centralize power in Madrid. The problem became more serious as Olivares, in the wake of military defeat by the French and Dutch, put more pressure on these outlying kingdoms and provinces to contribute to the war effort.

Provincial resistance to a policy of Castilian centralization lay at the root of the Spanish crisis of the seventeenth century. This crisis did not throw Castile itself into a state of civil war. Unlike Paris during the Fronde, Madrid itself remained peaceful. Throughout the 1640s the crown managed to maintain order within its main kingdom, probably because it had learned the art of negotiating directly with the thousands of towns and villages that ran local government. Instead, the Spanish crisis took the form of separatist revolts in Portugal, Catalonia, Sicily, and Naples. With the exception of Portugal, which recovered its sovereignty in 1640, the monarchy met this test and managed to maintain control of its provincial and Italian territories. In the aftermath of the revolts, however, the monarchy failed to bring the areas within the sphere of effective central government control.

The relative weakness of the Spanish monarchy, especially in comparison with that of France, became most apparent in the late seventeenth century, the age of Louis XIV. In two important respects the Spanish government failed to match the achievement of the French. First, it could never escape the grip that the old noble families had on the central administration. The unwillingness of the nobility to recruit ministers and officials from the mercantile and professional groups within society (which were small to begin with in Spain) worked against the achievement of bureaucratic efficiency and made innovation virtually impossible. Second, unlike the French government during Colbert's ministry, the Spanish government failed to take steps to encourage economic growth. The hostility of the aristocratic ruling class to mercantile affairs, coupled with a traditional Spanish unwillingness to follow the example of foreigners (especially when they were Protestants)

CHRONOLOGY

International Conflict in the Seventeenth Century

1609	Truce between the seven Dutch provinces and Spain
1618	Bohemian revolt against Habsburg rule; beginning of the Thirty Years' War
1619	Imperial forces defeat Bohemians at Battle of White Mountain
1648	Treaty of Westphalia, ending the Thirty Years' War; Treaty of Münster, ending the Dutch War of Independence
1667	Beginning of the wars of Louis XIV
1672	William III of Orange-Nassau becomes captain-general of Dutch; beginning of the war against France (1672–1678)
1688–1697	War of the League of Augsburg (Nine Years' War); England and Scotland join forces with Prussia, Austria, the Dutch Republic, and many German states against France
1697	Treaty of Ryswick
1700–1721	Great Northern War in which Russia eventually defeated Sweden; emergence of Russia as a major power
1701–1713	War of the Spanish Succession
1713	Treaty of Utrecht

prevented the country from stemming its own economic decline and the government from solving the formidable financial problems facing it. To make matters worse, the Spanish government failed to make its system of tax collection more efficient.

The mood that prevailed within the upper levels of Castilian society in the seventeenth century reflected the failure of the government and the entire nation. The contrast between the glorious achievements of the monarchy during the reign of Philip II (r. 1555–1598) and the somber realities of the late seventeenth century led most members of the ruling class to retreat into that past, a nostalgia that only encouraged further economic and political stagnation. The work of Miguel de Cervantes (1547–1616), the greatest Spanish writer of the seventeenth century, reflected this change in the Spanish national mood. In 1605 and 1615 Cervantes published (in two parts) *Don Quixote*, the story

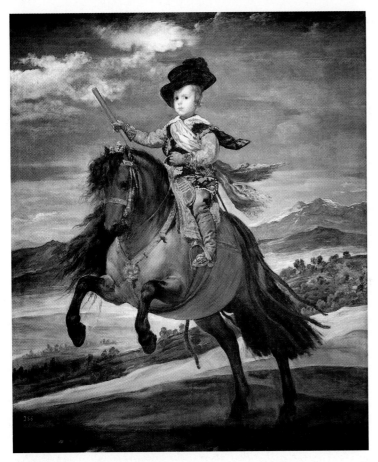

■ **Diego de Velázquez, Portrait of the Prince Baltasar Carlos, Heir to the Spanish Throne**

The depiction of the six-year-old prince on a rearing horse was intended to suggest military and political power at a time when the monarchy was losing both. The prince died in 1646, before he could succeed to the throne.

of an idealistic wandering nobleman who pursued dreams of an elusive military glory. This work, which as we have seen in Chapter 14 explored the relationship between illusion and reality, served as a commentary on a nobility that had lost confidence in itself.

Spanish painting, which paradoxically entered its Golden Age at the time the country began to lose its economic, political, and military vitality, was less willing to accept the decline of Spain. There was very little in the paintings of the great Spanish artist Diego de Velázquez (1599–1660) that would suggest the malaise that was affecting Spain and its nobility at the time. Velázquez painted in the baroque style that was in favor at court throughout Europe, depicting his subjects in heroic poses and imbuing them with a sense of royal or aristocratic dignity. One of his historical paintings, *The Surrender of Breda* (1634), commemorated a rare Spanish military victory over the Dutch in 1625 and the magnanimity of the Spanish victors toward their captives. All this was intended to reinforce the prestige of the monarchy, the royal family, and the nation itself at a time when the imperial grandeur of the past had faded. Velázquez's painting reflected the ideals of absolutism but ignored the realities of Spanish political and military life.

■ **Diego de Velázquez, *The Surrender of Breda,* 1634**

The Spanish victory over the Dutch in 1625 gave Velázquez a rare opportunity to depict Spanish soldiers in a role they had frequently played in the sixteenth century.

505

Absolutism and State Building in Central and Eastern Europe

T he forces that led to the establishment of absolutism and state building in France and Spain also made an impact on central and eastern Europe. In Germany the Thirty Years' War led to the establishment of two absolutist states, Prussia and the Austrian Habsburg Monarchy. Further to the East, the Ottoman and Russian Empires, both of them on the margins of the West, also developed absolutist political systems that shared many of the same characteristics as those in western and central Europe. Russia, previously thought of as belonging to an Eastern, Asian world, entered upon a program of Westernization and staked a claim to be considered a Western power. At the same time the Ottoman Empire, whose political development followed a Western pattern in many respects, was increasingly dismissed by Europeans as part of a distant, non-Western world.

GERMANY AND THE THIRTY YEARS' WAR, 1618–1648

Before 1648 the main political power within the geographical area known as Germany was the Holy Roman Empire. This large political formation was a loose confederation of kingdoms, principalities, duchies, ecclesiastical territories, and cities, each of which had its own laws and political institutions. The emperor, who was elected by a body of German princes, exercised immediate jurisdiction only in his own dynastic possessions and in the imperial cities. He also convened a legislative assembly known as the *Reichstag*, over which he exercised limited influence. But the emperor did not have a large administrative or judicial bureaucracy through which he could enforce imperial law in the localities. The empire was not in any sense a sovereign state, even though it had long been a major force in European diplomacy. It had acquired and maintained that international position by relying on the military and financial contributions of its imperial cities and the lands controlled directly by the Habsburg emperors.

A GERMAN WRITER DESCRIBES THE HORRORS OF THE THIRTY YEARS' WAR

In 1669 the German writer H. J. C. Grimmelshausen (1625–1676) published an imaginary account of the adventures of a German vagabond, to whom he gave the name Simplicissimus. The setting of the book was the Thirty Years' War in Germany, which Grimmelshausen had experienced firsthand. At age 10 Grimmelshausen, like the character Simplicissimus in the book, was captured by Hessian troops and later became a camp-follower. In this chapter Simplicissimus describes how the palace of his father was stormed, plundered, and ruined.

T he first thing that these troops did was, that they stabbed their horses; thereafter each fell to his appointed task, which task was either more or less than ruin and destruction. For though some began to slaughter and to boil and to roast, so that it looked as if there should be a merry banquet forward, yet others there were who did but storm through the house above and below the stairs. . . . All that they had no mind to take with them they cut in pieces. Some thrust their swords through the hay and straw as if they had not enough sheep and swine to slaughter; and some shook the feathers out of the beds and in their stead stuffed in bacon and other dried meat and provisions as if such were better and softer to sleep upon. Others broke the stove and the windows as if they had a never-ending summer to promise. Housewares of copper and tin they beat flat, and packed such vessels, all bent and spoiled, in with the rest. Bedsteads, tables, chairs and benches they burned, though there lay many cords of dry wood in the yard. . . .

Our maid was so handled in the stable that she could not come out; which is a shame to tell of. Our man they laid bound upon the ground, thrust a gag into his mouth, and poured a pailful of filthy water into his body; and by this, which they called a Swedish draught, they forced him to lead a party of them to another place where they captured men and beasts, and brought them back to our farm, in which company were my dad, my mother, and our Ursula.

And now they began first to take the flints out of their pistols and in place of them to jam the peasants' thumbs in and so to torture the poor rogues as if they had been about the burning of witches. For one of them they had taken they thrust into the baking oven and there lit a fire under him, although he had as yet confessed no crime; as for another, they put a cord round his head and so twisted it tight with a piece of wood that the blood gushed from his mouth and nose and ears. In a word each had his own device to torture the peasants, and each peasant had several torture.

Source: Reprinted from *The Adventurous Simplicissimus: Being the Description of the Life of a Strange Vagabond Named Melchior Sternfels Von Fuchshaim* by H. J. C. Grimmelshausen. Published by the University of Nebraska Press.

Map 15.3 Europe After the Treaty of Westphalia, 1648

The Holy Roman Empire no longer included the Dutch Republic, which was now independent of Spain. Some of the lands of the Austrian Habsburg Monarchy and Brandenburg-Prussia lay outside the boundaries of the Holy Roman Empire. Italy was divided into a number of small states in the north, while Naples, Sicily, and Sardinia were ruled by Spain.

The Thirty Years' War permanently altered the nature of this vast and intricate political structure. That war began as a conflict between Protestant German princes and the Catholic emperor over religious and constitutional issues. The incident that triggered it in 1618 was the so-called Defenestration of Prague, when members of the predominantly Protestant Bohemian legislature, known as the Diet, threw two royal officials out a castle window as a protest against the religious policies of their recently elected king, the future emperor Ferdinand II. The Diet proceeded to depose Ferdinand, a Catholic, and elect a Protestant prince, Frederick V of the Palatinate, to replace him. The war soon broadened into a European-wide struggle over the possession of German and Spanish territory, as the Danes, Swedes, and French successively entered the conflict against

the emperor and his Spanish Habsburg relatives. For a brief period in the late 1620s England also entered the conflict against Spain. The war, which was fought mainly on German soil, had a devastating effect on the country. More than one million soldiers marched across German lands, sacking towns and exploiting the resources of local communities. Germany lost up to one-third of its population, while the destruction of property retarded the economic development of the country for more than fifty years.

The political effects of the war were no less traumatic. By virtue of the Treaty of Westphalia, which ended the war in 1648, the empire was permanently weakened, although it continued to function until 1806 (see Map 15.3). The individual German territories within the empire developed more institutional autonomy than they had before the war.

They became sovereign states themselves, with their own armies, foreign policies, and central bureaucracies. Two of these German states soon surpassed all the others in size and military strength and became major European powers. The first was Brandenburg-Prussia, a collection of various territories in northern Germany that was transformed into the kingdom of Prussia at the beginning of the eighteenth century. In the nineteenth century Prussia would unify Germany under its leadership. The second state was the Austrian Habsburg Monarchy, which in the eighteenth century was usually identified simply as Austria. The Habsburgs had long dominated the Holy Roman Empire and continued to secure election as emperors after the Treaty of Westphalia. In the late seventeenth century, however, the Habsburg Monarchy acquired its own institutional identity, distinct from that of the empire. It consisted of the lands that the Habsburgs controlled directly in the southeastern

part of the empire and other territories, including the kingdom of Hungary, which lay outside the territorial boundary of the empire. Both Prussia and Austria developed their own forms of absolutism during the second half of the seventeenth century.

THE GROWTH OF THE PRUSSIAN STATE

In 1648, at the end of the Thirty Years' War, Prussia could barely have claimed the status of an independent state, much less that of an absolute monarchy. The core of the Prussian state was Brandenburg, which claimed the status of an electorate, since its ruler cast one of the ballots to elect the Holy Roman Emperor. The lands that belonged to the elector of Brandenburg lay scattered throughout northern Germany and stretched into eastern Europe. As

■   **Map 15.4   The Growth of Brandenburg-Prussia, 1618–1786**
By acquiring lands throughout northern Germany, Prussia became a major European power. The process began during the early seventeenth century, but it continued well into the eighteenth century. The Prussian army, which was the best trained fighting force in Europe in the eighteenth century, greatly facilitated Prussia's growth.

a result of the Thirty Years' War, the archbishoprics of Magdeburg and East Pomerania were annexed to Brandenburg. The Hohenzollern family, in whose line the electorate of Brandenburg passed, also owned or controlled various parcels of German territory in the Rhineland, near the borders of the Spanish Netherlands. In 1618 the Hohenzollerns had acquired the much larger but equally remote duchy of Prussia, a Baltic territory lying outside the boundaries of the Holy Roman Empire. As ruler of these disparate and noncontiguous lands, the elector of Brandenburg had virtually no state bureaucracy, collected few taxes, and commanded only a small army. Most of his territories, moreover, lay in ruins in 1648, having been devastated by Swedish and imperial troops at various times during the war.

The Great Elector Frederick William (r. 1640–1688) began the long process of turning this ramshackle structure into a powerful and cohesive German state (see Map 15.4). His son King Frederick I (r. 1688–1713) and grandson Frederick William I (r. 1713–1740) completed the transformation. The key to their success, as it was for all aspiring absolute monarchs in eastern Europe, was to secure the compliance of the traditional nobility, who in Prussia were known as Junkers°. The Great Elector Frederick William achieved this end by granting the Junkers a variety of privileges, including exemption from import duties and the excise tax. The most valuable concession was the legal confirmation of their rights over the serfs. During the previous 150 years Prussian peasants had lost their freedom, becoming permanently bound to the estates of their lords and completely subject to the Junkers' arbitrary brand of local justice. The Junkers had a deeply vested interest in perpetuating this oppressive system of serfdom, and the lawgiver Frederick was able to provide them with the legal guarantees they required.

With the loyalty of the Junkers secure, Frederick William went about the process of building a powerful Prussian state. A large administrative bureaucracy, centralized under a General Directory in Berlin, governed both financial and military affairs throughout the elector's lands. At first it was staffed by members of the nobility, but eventually educated commoners were recruited into the system. The taxes that the government collected, especially from the towns, went in large part to fund a standing army, which had come into being in the late 1650s.

The Prussian army grew rapidly, rising to 30,000 men in 1690 and 80,000 by 1740. It consisted of a combination of carefully recruited volunteers, foreign mercenaries, and, after 1713, conscripts from the general population. Its most famous regiment, known as the Blue Prussians or the Giants of Potsdam, consisted of 1,200 men, each of whom was at least six feet tall. Commanded by officers drawn from the nobility and reinforced by Europe's first system of military reserves, this army quickly became the best trained fighting force in Europe. Prussia became a model military

state, symbolized by the transformation of the royal gardens into an army training ground during the reign of Frederick William I.

As this military state grew in size and complexity, its rulers acquired many of the attributes of absolute rule. Most significantly they became the sole legislators within the state. The main representative assembly in the electorate, the Diet of Brandenburg, met for the last time in 1652. Frederick William and his successors, however, continued to consult with smaller local assemblies, especially in the matter of taxation. The elevation of Frederick I's status to that of king of Prussia in 1701 marked a further consolidation of power in the person of the ruler. His son's style of rule, which included physical punishment of judges whose decisions displeased him, suggested that the Prussian monarchy not only had attained absolute power but could occasionally abuse it.

THE AUSTRIAN HABSBURG MONARCHY

The Austrian Habsburgs were much less successful than the Hohenzollerns in building a centralized, consolidated state along absolutist lines. The various territories that made up the Austrian Habsburg Monarchy in the late seventeenth century were larger and more diverse than those that belonged to the king of Prussia. In addition to the collection of duchies that form present-day Austria and that then served as the core of the monarchy, it embraced two subordinate kingdoms, which were themselves composed of various semiautonomous principalities and duchies. The first of these, lying to the north, was the kingdom of Bohemia, which had struggled against Habsburg control for nearly a century and included Moravia and Silesia. The second, lying to the southeast, was the kingdom of Hungary, including the large semiautonomous principality of Transylvania. The Habsburgs regained Hungary from the Ottoman Empire in stages between 1664 and 1718. In 1713 the monarchy also acquired the former Spanish Netherlands and the Italian territories of Milan and Naples.

The Austrian Habsburg monarchs of the seventeenth and early eighteenth centuries never succeeded in integrating these ethnically, religiously, and politically diverse lands into a unified, cohesive state similar to that of France. The problem was a lack of a unified bureaucracy. The only centralized administrative institutions in this amalgam of kingdoms were the Court Chamber, which superintended the collection of taxes throughout the monarchy, and the Austrian army, which included troops from all Habsburg lands. Like many European military forces it had become a standing army in 1648, and by 1716 it had a troop strength of 165,000 men. Even these centralized institutions had difficulty operating smoothly. The council of the army had trouble integrating units drawn from separate kingdoms, while the Court Chamber never developed a uniform system of tax collection. For all practical purposes the Habsburgs had to rule their various kingdoms separately.

In governing its Austrian and Bohemian lands, this decentralized Habsburg monarchy did nonetheless acquire some of the characteristics of absolutist rule. This development toward absolutism began long before the Treaty of Westphalia in 1648. After defeating the Bohemians at the Battle of White Mountain in 1620 during the Thirty Years' War, Emperor Ferdinand II (r. 1618–1637) had decided to strengthen his authority in the areas under his direct control. Bohemia, which had led the revolt against him, was the main target of this policy, but the emperor used this opportunity to increase his power throughout his territories. After punishing the rebels and exiling many of the Protestant nobility, he undertook a deliberate expansion of his legislative and judicial powers, and he secured direct control over all his administrative officials.

A policy of severe religious repression accompanied this increase in the emperor's authority. Like Cardinal Richelieu of France, Ferdinand assumed that Protestantism served as a justification for rebellion, and he therefore decided that its practice could not be tolerated. Protestants in all the emperor's territories were forced to take a Catholic loyalty oath, and Protestant education was banned. Protestant towns were destroyed at exactly the same time that Richelieu was razing the fortifications of the Huguenot town of La Rochelle. These efforts at reconversion continued right through the seventeenth century. They amounted to a policy of religious or "confessional" absolutism.

While the Habsburgs succeeded in imposing some elements of absolutist rule on the Austrians and the Bohemians in the early seventeenth century, they encountered much more resistance when they attempted to follow the same course of action with respect to Hungary in the late seventeenth and eighteenth centuries. Hungarians had a long tradition of limited, constitutional rule in which the national Diet had exercised powers of legislation and taxation, just as Parliament did in England. Habsburg emperors made some limited inroads on these traditions but they were never able to break them. They also were unable to achieve the same degree of religious uniformity that they had imposed on their other territories. In Hungary the Habsburgs encountered the limits of royal absolutism.

THE OTTOMAN EMPIRE: BETWEEN EAST AND WEST

In the seventeenth and early eighteenth centuries the southeastern border of the Habsburg monarchy separated the kingdom of Hungary from the Ottoman Empire. This militarized frontier marked not only the political boundary between two empires but a deeper cultural boundary between East and West.

As we have seen in previous chapters, the West is not just a geographical but also a cultural realm, and the people who inhabit this realm, although distinct from one another, share many of the same religious, political, legal, and philosophical traditions. The Ottoman Turks, who posed a recurrent military threat to the Habsburg monarchy and who reached the gates of Vienna in 1683, were generally thought of as not belonging to this Western world. Because the Ottoman Turks were Muslims, Europeans considered them enemies of Christianity, infidels who were bent on the destruction of Christendom. In the sixteenth century Catholics and Protestants alike claimed that the military victories of the Turks over European forces were signs of divine punishment for the sins European Christians had committed. Ottoman emperors, known as sultans, were considered despots who ruled over their subjects as slaves. The sultans were also depicted in Western literature as cruel and brutal tyrants, the opposite of the ideal Christian prince of Europe. One French play of 1612 depicted the mother of the sultan Mehmed the Conquerer (r. 1451–1481) as drinking the blood of a victim.

These stereotypes of the Turks served the function of giving Europeans a sense of their own Western identity. Turks became a negative reference group with whom Europeans could favorably compare themselves. The realities of Ottoman politics and culture, however, were quite different from the ways in which they were represented in European literature. Turkish despotism, the name Europeans gave to the Ottoman system of government, existed only in theory. Ever since the fourteenth century Ottoman writers had claimed for the sultan extraordinary powers, including the right to seize the landed property of his subjects at will. In practice he never exercised unlimited power. His prerogatives were limited by the spirit of Muslim law, and he shared power with the grand vizier, who was his chief executive officer. In practice there was little difference between the rule of the sultans and that of European absolute monarchs.

Even the high degree of administrative centralization for which the Ottoman Empire was famous did not encompass all the regions under its control. Many of its provinces, especially those in the Balkans, enjoyed a considerable measure of autonomy, especially in the seventeenth century. The Balkans, which were geographically part of Europe, never experienced the full force of direct Turkish rule. In all the Ottoman provinces there was a complex pattern of negotiation between the central imperial administration and local officials. In this respect the Ottoman Empire was similar to the absolutist monarchies of western and central Europe. The Ottoman Empire bore the closest resemblance to the Spanish monarchy, which also ruled many far-flung territories in Europe. Like the Spanish monarchy, the Ottoman Empire declined in power during the seventeenth century and lost effective control of some of its outlying provinces.

Ottoman Turks and Europeans frequently went to war against each other, but there was a constant pattern of diplomatic, economic, and cultural interaction between them. The Turks had been involved in European warfare since the fifteenth century, and they had formed diplomatic alliances with the French against the Austrian Habsburgs on a number of occasions. Europeans and Ottomans often borrowed military technology from each other, and they also shared knowledge of administrative techniques. Trade between European countries and the Ottoman Empire remained brisk throughout this period. Europe supplied hardware and textiles to the Turks while they in turn shipped coffee, tobacco, and tulips to European ports. Communities of Turks and other Muslims lived in European cities, while numerous European merchants resided in territories under Ottoman control.

These encounters between Turks and Europeans suggest that the militarized boundary between the Habsburgs and the Ottoman Empire was much more porous than its fortifications would suggest. Military conflict and Western contempt for Muslim Turks disguised a much more complex process of political and cultural interaction between the two civilizations. Europeans tended to think of the Ottoman Empire as "oriental," but it is more accurate to view it as a region lying between the East and the West.

RUSSIA AND THE WEST

The other seventeenth-century power that marked the boundary between East and West was the vast Russian Empire, which stretched from its boundary with Poland in the west all the way to the Pacific Ocean in the east. Until the end of the seventeenth century, the kingdom of Muscovy and the lands attached to it seemed, at least to Europeans, part of the Asiatic world. Dominated by an Eastern Orthodox branch of Christianity, Russia drew very little upon the cultural traditions associated with western Europe. Unlike its neighboring Slavic kingdom of Poland, it had not absorbed large doses of German culture. It also appeared to Europeans to be another example of "Oriental despotism," a state in which the ruler, known as the tsar, could rule his subjects at will, "not bound up by any law or custom."

During the reign of Tsar Peter I, known as Peter the Great (r. 1682–1725), Russia underwent a process of Westernization, bringing it more into line with the culture of European countries and becoming a major European power. This policy began after Peter visited England, Holland, northern Germany, and Austria in 1697 and 1698. Upon his return he directed his officials and members of the upper levels of Russian society to adopt Western styles of dress and appearance, including the removal of men's beards. (Scissors were kept in the customs house for this purpose alone.) Beards symbolized the backward, Eastern, Orthodox culture from whose grip Peter hoped to extricate his country. Young Russian boys were sent abroad for their

education. Women began to participate openly in the social and cultural life of the cities, in violation of Orthodox custom. Smoking was permitted despite the Church's insistence that Scripture condemned it. The calendar was reformed and books were printed in modern Russian type. Peter's importation of Western art and the imitation of Western architecture complemented this policy of enforced cultural change. Westernization, however, involved more than a change of manners and appearance. It also involved military and political reforms that changed the character of the Russian state.

During the first twenty-five years of his reign Peter had found himself unable to achieve sustained military success against his two great enemies, the Ottoman Turks to the south and the Swedes to the west. During the Great Northern War with Sweden (1700–1721) Peter introduced a number of military reforms that eventually turned the tide against his enemy. These reforms were based on the knowledge he had acquired of military technology, organization,

■ **Peter the Great at the Battle of Poltava (1709), at Which Russia Defeated Swedish Forces**
Standing 6 feet 7 inches tall, at a time when the average male height was 5 feet 8 inches, Peter was great in military and political achievements as well as in stature.

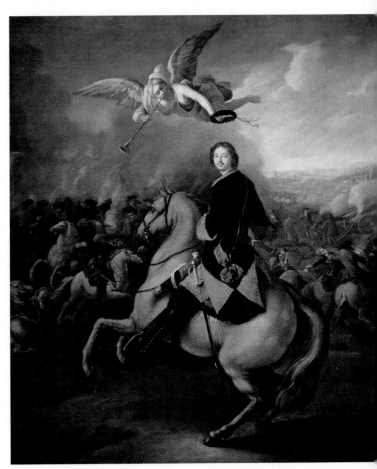

and tactics of Western European states, especially Prussia and, ironically, Sweden itself. Having introduced a program of conscription, Peter assembled a large standing army of more than 200,000 men, which he trained and disciplined in the Prussian manner. All of this was supported by the imposition of new taxes on a variety of commodities, including beards, and the encouragement of Russian industry in much the same way that Colbert had encouraged French industry. A central council, established in 1711, not only directed financial administration but also levied and supplied troops, not unlike the General Directory of the electorate of Brandenburg.

This new military state also acquired many of the centralizing and absolutist features of western European monarchies. Efforts to introduce absolutism in Russia had begun during the reigns of Alexis (r. 1645–1676) and Fedor (r. 1676–1682), who had achieved limited success in strengthening the central administration, controlling the nobility, and brutally suppressing peasant rebellions. Peter built upon his predecessors' achievement. He created an entirely new structure for managing the empire, appointing twelve governors to superintend Russia's forty-three separate provinces. He brought the Church under state control. By establishing a finely graded hierarchy of official ranks in the armed forces, the civil administration, and the court, Peter not only improved administrative efficiency but also made it possible for men of nonaristocratic birth to attain the same privileged status as the old landowning nobility. At the same time he won the support of all landowners by introducing primogeniture (inheritance of the entire estate by the eldest son), which prevented their estates from being subdivided, and supporting the enserfment of the peasants. In dealing with his subjects Peter claimed more power than any other absolute monarch in Europe. During the trial of his own son, Alexis, for treason in 1718, he told the clergy that "we have a sufficient and absolute power to judge our son for his crimes according to our own pleasure."

The most visible sign of Peter's policy of Westernization was the construction of the port city of St. Petersburg on the Gulf of Finland, which became the new capital of the Russian Empire. One of the main objectives of Russian foreign policy during Peter's reign had been to secure "a window to Europe" on the Baltic, which would open up trade with the West and allow Russia to become a Western naval power. By draining a swamp at the estuary of the Neva River, Peter laid the basis for the construction of an entirely new city, which was designed with the assistance of French and Italian architects in a style characteristic of European cities. In this enterprise Peter benefited from the nearly unlimited power he had over his subjects. He commanded every stonemason in Russia to relocate to the new construction site, and he used his powers over the serfs to assemble a labor force of more than 150,000 men. Construction began in 1703, and within twenty years St. Petersburg had a population of 100,000 people. With his new capital city now

CHRONOLOGY

The Age of Absolutism in Central and Eastern Europe

1618	Ferdinand II becomes Holy Roman Emperor (r. 1618–1637)
1640	Beginning of the reign of Frederick William, the Great Elector of Brandenburg Prussia (r. 1640–1688)
1657	Leopold I becomes Holy Roman Emperor (r. 1657–1705)
1682	Accession of Tsar Peter the Great of Russia (r. 1682–1725)
1688	Accession of Frederick as elector of Prussia; becomes king of Prussia in 1701
1703	Foundation of St. Petersburg, Russia's new capital and "window on the West"
1705	Joseph I (r. 1705–1711) becomes Holy Roman Emperor
1711	Charles VI (1711–1740), brother of Joseph I, becomes Holy Roman Emperor

looking westward, and an army and central administration reformed on the basis of Prussian and French example, Peter could enter the world of European diplomacy and warfare as both a Western and an absolute monarch.

Resistance to Absolutism in England and the Dutch Republic

The kingdom of England and the northern provinces of the Netherlands stand out as the two great exceptions to the dominant pattern of political development in seventeenth-century Europe. Both of these countries successfully resisted the establishment of royal absolutism, and neither underwent the rigorous centralization of power and the dynamic growth of the state that usually accompanied the establishment of absolutist rule. In England the encounter between the proponents and opponents of absolute monarchy was more pronounced than in any other European country. It resulted in the temporary destruction of the monarchy in 1649 and the establishment of parliamentary supremacy after the Glorious Revolution of 1688. In the northern provinces of the Netherlands, known as the Dutch Republic, an even more emphatic rejection of absolutism occurred. During their long struggle to win their independence from Spain, the Dutch established a republican, decentralized form of government, but that did not prevent them from acquiring considerable military strength and dominating the world's economy during the seventeenth century.

THE ENGLISH MONARCHY

At various times in the seventeenth century English monarchs tried to introduce royal absolutism, but the political institutions and the political culture of the country stood as major obstacles to their designs. As early as the fifteenth century, the English writer and diplomat Sir John Fortescue (ca. 1395–1477) had celebrated England's parliamentary system of government by contrasting it with that of France, where he claimed the king could make laws by himself and impose his will on his subjects. Fortescue's treatise contributed to the pride Englishmen had in what they considered their distinctive set of political and legal traditions. The most important of these traditions was the making of law and the levying of taxes by the two Houses of Parliament, the House of Lords and the House of Commons, with the king holding the power to sign or veto the bills they passed.

In the early seventeenth century the perception began to arise, especially among certain members of the House of Commons, that this tradition of parliamentary government was under attack. The first Stuart king, James I (r. 1603–1625), who succeeded the last Tudor monarch, Elizabeth I, aroused some of these fears as early as 1604, when he called his first parliament. James thought of himself as an absolute monarch, and in a number of speeches and published works he emphasized the height of his independent royal power, which was known in England as the prerogative°. James also spoke often about his divine right to rule, and he claimed that the main function of Parliament was simply to give the king advice, rather than to make law. These statements had the effect of antagonizing members of Parliament, leading them to defend their privileges, including the right they claimed to discuss foreign policy and other affairs of state.

James believed that he was an absolute monarch, but he did not actually try to put his ideas into practice. For example, he did not try to make laws or levy taxes without the consent of Parliament or deny men their legal rights, such as freedom from arbitrary imprisonment. The real political fireworks did not begin until James's son, Charles I (r. 1625–1649), succeeded him. Charles believed in absolutism every bit as much as his father, but unlike James, Charles actually put his theories into practice. His efforts to force his subjects to lend money to the government during a war with Spain (1625–1629) and his imprisonment of men who refused to make these loans led

Parliament to pass the Petition of Right in 1628. This document declared boldly that subjects possessed fundamental rights that kings could not violate under any circumstances, even when the country was at war.

Charles consented to the Petition of Right, but when Parliament met again in 1629, further conflict between the king and certain members of the House of Commons developed over taxation and the king's religious policies. Charles had been collecting duties on exports without parliamentary approval since 1625. He had also begun to favor conservative clergymen known as Arminians, leading the more zealous English Protestants, the Puritans, to fear that the English Church was leaning in the direction of Catholicism or "popery." Faced with this opposition over constitutional and religious issues, Charles decided to dismiss this parliament and to rule indefinitely without calling another one.

This period of nonparliamentary government, known as the personal rule°, lasted until 1640. During these years Charles, unable to collect taxes by the authority of Parliament, used his prerogative to bring in new revenues, especially by asking all subjects to pay "ship-money" to support the outfitting of ships to defend the country against attack. During the personal rule the king's religious policy fell under the control of William Laud, who was named archbishop of Canterbury in 1633 and who became one of the king's main privy councilors. Laud's determination to restore many of the rituals associated with Roman Catholicism alienated large numbers of Puritans and led to a growing perception that members of the king's government were engaged in a conspiracy to destroy both England's ancient constitution and the Protestant religion.

This period of absolutism might have continued indefinitely if Charles had not once again been faced with the financial demands of war. In 1636 the king tried to introduce a new religious liturgy in his northern kingdom of Scotland. The liturgy included a number of rituals that the firmly Calvinist Scottish population considered popish. The new liturgy so angered a group of women in Edinburgh that they threw their chairs at the bishop when he introduced it. In response to this affront to their religion, the Scots signed a National Covenant (1638) pledging themselves to defend the integrity of their Church, abolished episcopacy (government of the church by bishops) in favor of a Presbyterian system of church government, and mobilized a large army. To secure the funds to fight the Scots, Charles was forced to summon his English Parliament, thereby ending the period of personal rule.

THE ENGLISH CIVIL WARS AND REVOLUTION

Tensions between the reconvened English Parliament and Charles led to the first revolution of modern times. The Short Parliament, called in April 1640, lasted only two months, but a Scottish military victory against the English in that year forced the king to call a second parliament. The Long Parliament, which met in November 1640, impeached many of the king's ministers and judges, and it dismantled the judicial apparatus of the eleven years of personal rule, including the courts that had been active in the prosecution of Puritans. Parliament declared the king's nonparliamentary taxes illegal, and it enacted a law limiting the time between the meetings of Parliament to three years.

This legislation did not satisfy the king's critics in Parliament. Their suspicion that the king was conspiring against them and their demand to approve all royal appointments created a poisoned political atmosphere in which neither side trusted the other. After the king and his armed guards forced their way into the House of Commons to arrest five members for treason, there was little hope of reconciliation. In August 1642 civil war began between the Parliamentarians, known as Roundheads because many of the artisans who supported them had close-cropped hair styles, and the Royalists or Cavaliers, who often wore their hair in long flowing locks. Parliament, which was supported by the Scots and which benefited from the creation in 1645 of a well-trained, efficient fighting force, the New Model Army, ultimately won this war in 1646 and took Charles prisoner. The king's subsequent negotiations with the Scots and the English Presbyterians, both of whom had originally fought against him, led to a second civil war in 1648. In this war, which lasted only a few months, the New Model Army once again defeated Royalist forces.

This military victory led to a series of revolutionary changes in the English system of government. Believing with some justification that Charles could never be trusted, and eager to bring about an end to years of political uncertainty, members of the army purged Parliament of its Presbyterian members, leaving only a small group of Independents. These men, who favored a form of church government in which the congregations had a high degree of autonomy, had broken off negotiations with Charles I. The remaining members of Parliament were known as the Rump, because they were all that was left of the Long Parliament elected in 1640. This small group of Independents in Parliament, following the wishes of the army, set up a court to try Charles in January 1649. The trial resulted in Charles's conviction and execution, and shortly thereafter the Rump destroyed the House of Lords and the monarchy itself. As Parliament had already destroyed the episcopal structure of the English Church in 1646, these

CHRONOLOGY

A Century of Revolution in England and Scotland

1603	James VI of Scotland (r. 1567–1625) becomes James I of England (r. 1603–1625)
1625	Death of James I and accession of Charles I (r. 1625–1649)
1628	Parliament passes the Petition of Right
1629–1640	Personal rule of Charles I
1638	Scots sign the National Covenant
1640	Opening of the Long Parliament
1642–1646	Civil War in England, ending with the capture of King Charles I
1648	Second Civil War; New Model Army defeats English Presbyterians and Scots
1649	Execution of Charles I of England and the beginning of the Republic
1653	End of the Long Parliament; beginning and dissolution of Barebones Parliament; Oliver Cromwell becomes Protector of England, Scotland, and Ireland
1660	Restoration of the monarchy in the person of Charles II; House of Lords and the Church of England also restored
1685	Death of Charles II and accession of his brother, James II (r. 1685–1688)
1688–1689	Glorious Revolution in England and Scotland
1707	England and Scotland politically joined to form the United Kingdom of Great Britain

actions completed a genuine revolution, a political transformation that destroyed the very system of government and replaced it with new institutions.

The revolution resulted in the establishment of a republic, in which the House of Commons possessed supreme legislative power in the name of the people of England. This change in the system of government, however, did not lead to the introduction of a more democratic form of government. A government of this sort, in which a very large percentage of the adult male population would be allowed to vote, was the goal of a political party, the Levellers, which originated in the New Model Army and attracted considerable support in London and the towns. In 1647 at Putney Bridge, near London, the Levellers participated in a debate with more conservative army officers concerning the future constitution of the country. The spokesmen for the Levellers called for annual parliaments, the separation of powers between the executive and legislative branches of government, and the introduction of universal suffrage for men. The army officers argued against this proposed constitution, arguing that the vote should be entrusted only to men who owned property. The officers made sure that the Leveller program would not be accepted. The Levellers eventually mutinied in the army, their leaders were imprisoned, and the party collapsed.

The fate of the Levellers and their program underlines the fact that the English revolution was brought about by men of property, especially by the gentry or lesser aristocracy who sat in the House of Commons and who served as officers in the New Model Army. Although these men defeated and executed the king and secured the right to participate regularly in the governance of the kingdom, they were also determined to keep political power in the hands of their own class.

The republican government established in 1649 did not last. Tension between the army and the Rump, fueled by the belief that the Rump was not creating a godly society, resulted in the army's dissolution of the Long Parliament in 1653 and the selection of a small parliament of zealous Puritans, nominated by the army. Known as the Barebones Parliament for one of its members, Praise-God Barebones, this assembly soon became hopelessly divided between radicals who wished to eliminate state support of the Church, the Court of Chancery, and the universities, and the moderates who opposed these measures. Unable to overcome its divisions, it too was dissolved after sitting for only five months.

At that point Oliver Cromwell (1599–1658), the commander-in-chief of the army and the most prominent member of the Council of State after 1649, had himself proclaimed Protector of England, Scotland, and Ireland. Cromwell had been a leader of the revolution, a zealous Puritan who had provided crucial support for the execution of the king and the establishment of the republic. At the same time, however, Cromwell feared that the Levellers and now the radical Puritans of Barebones Parliament would destroy the social order. The establishment of the Protectorate, in which Cromwell shared legislative power with Parliament, represented an effort to return to a more traditional system of government. Cromwell would not, however, go so far as to accept a petition of 1657 to make him king. After Cromwell's death in 1658 and the brief rule of his son Richard, the Protectorate collapsed. A period of political instability, in which there was renewed hostility between the army and the members of Parliament, led the army to restore the monarchy in 1660.

LATER STUART ABSOLUTISM AND THE GLORIOUS REVOLUTION

Charles II (r. 1660–1685) and his brother James II (r. 1685–1688) were both absolutists who admired the political achievement of their cousin, Louis XIV of France. At

---

A LEVELLER ATTACKS THE LEADERS OF THE ENGLISH REVOLUTION

Within a month of King Charles I's execution in 1649, members of the Leveller party suspected that the officers of the army had abandoned their pledge to implement political reforms. They feared that the army was establishing an oligarchic regime that was just as repressive as that of Charles I. One of the Leveller leaders, John Lilburne, wrote this powerful and eloquent statement of the betrayal of the English revolution by its leaders.

Insomuch that we are even aghast and astonished to see that notwithstanding the production of the highest notions of freedom that ever this Nation or any people in the world have brought to light, notwithstanding the vast expense of blood and treasure that hath been made to purchase those freedoms, notwithstanding the many eminent victories God hath been pleased to honor our just cause withall, notwithstanding the extraordinary gripes and pangs this House hath suffered more than once at the hands of your own servants, and that at least for the obtaining these our native liberties. . . .

That yet after all these things have been done and suffered . . . behold, in the close of it all we hear and see what gives us fresh and pregnant cause to believe that the contrary is really intended, and that all those specious pretenses and high notions of Liberty with those extraordinary courses that have of late been taken . . . appear to us to have been done and directed by some secret powerful influences, the more securely and unsuspectingly to attain to an absolute dominion over the commonwealth.

Source: From *England's New Chains Discovered* by John Lilburne, 1649.

---

the same time, however, they realized that they could never return to the policies of their father, much less adopt those of Louis. Neither of them attempted to rule indefinitely without Parliament, as Charles I had. Their main objective was to destroy the independence of Parliament by packing it with their own supporters and use the prerogative to weaken the force of the parliamentary statutes to which they objected.

The main political crisis of Charles II's reign was the attempt by a group of members of Parliament, headed by the Earl of Shaftesbury (1621–1683) and known by their opponents as Whigs, to exclude the king's brother, James, from the throne on the grounds that he was a Catholic. Charles opposed this strategy because it violated the theory of hereditary divine right, according to which God sanctioned the right of the king's closest heir to succeed him. Those members of Parliament who supported Charles on

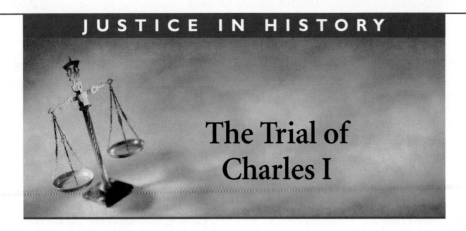

The Trial of Charles I

In January 1649, after the New Model Army had defeated the royalist forces in England's second civil war and purged Parliament of its Presbyterian members, the few remaining members of the House of Commons voted by a narrow margin to erect a High Court of Justice to try King Charles I. This trial, which resulted in Charles's execution, marked the only time in European history that a monarch was tried and executed while still holding the office of king.

The decision to try the king formed part of a deliberate political strategy. The men who arranged the proceeding knew that they were embarking upon a revolutionary course by declaring that the House of Commons, as the elected representative of the people, was the highest power in the realm. They also knew that the republican regime they were establishing did not command a large body of popular support. By trying the king publicly in a court of law and by ensuring that the trial was reported in daily newspapers (the first such trial in history), they hoped to prove the legitimacy of their cause and win support for the new regime.

The decision to bring the king to justice created two legal problems. The first was to identify a crime upon which the trial would be based. For many years members of Parliament had insisted that the king had violated the ancient laws of the kingdom. The charge read that he had "wickedly designed to erect an unlimited and tyrannical power" and he had waged war against his people in two civil wars. His prose-cutors claimed that those activities amounted to the crime of treason. The problem was that treason in England was a crime committed by a subject against the king, not by the king against his subjects. In order to try the king for this crime, his accusers had to construct a new theory of treason, according to which the king had attacked his own political body, which they identified with the kingdom or the state.

The second problem was to make the court itself a legitimate tribunal. According to English constitutional law, the king possessed the highest legal authority in the land. He appointed his judges, and the courts represented his authority. Parliament could vote to erect a special court, but the bill authorizing it would become law only if the king agreed to it. In this case the House of Commons had set up the court by its own authority, and it had named 135 men, most of whom were army officers, to serve as its judges. The revolutionary nature of this tribunal was difficult to disguise, and Charles made its illegality the basis of his defense. When asked how he would plead, he challenged the legitimacy of the court.

"By what power am I called hither?" he asked. "I would know by what authority—I mean lawful authority. There are many unlawful authorities in the world—thieves and robbers by the highways. And when I know what lawful authority, I shall answer. Remember I am your king, your lawful king. . . . I have a trust committed to me by God by old and lawful descent; I will not betray it to answer to a new unlawful authority."

By taking this position Charles put himself on the side of the law, and by refusing to enter a plea he also prevented his prosecutors from presenting the evidence against him.

The arguments that King Charles and John Bradshawe, the president of the court, presented regarding the legitimacy of the court reflected the main constitutional conflict in seventeenth-century England. On the one hand was the doctrine of divine-right absolutism, according to which the king received his authority from God. He was therefore responsible to God alone, not to the people. His subjects could neither try him in a court of law nor fight him on the battlefield. "A king," said Charles, "cannot be tried by any superior jurisdiction on earth." On the other hand was the doctrine of popular sovereignty, which held that political power came from the people. As Bradshawe said in response to Charles's objection, "Sir, as the law is your superior, so truly Sir, there is something that is superior to the law, and that is indeed the parent or author of law, and that is the people of England." This trial, therefore, involved not only a confrontation between Charles and his revolutionary judges but an encounter between two incompatible political ideologies.

In 1649 the advocates of popular sovereignty triumphed over those of divine right. Charles was convicted as a "tyrant, traitor, murderer, and public enemy of the good people of this nation." The verdict was never in doubt, although only 67 of the 135 men originally appointed as judges voted to convict the king, and a mere 59 signed the death warrant. The trial succeeded only to the extent that it facilitated the establishment of the new regime. With Charles gone, the Rump could move ahead with the abolition of the monarchy and the establishment of a republic. But in dramatic terms the trial was a complete failure. Charles, a small shy man with a nervous stammer, was expected to make a poor impression, but he spoke eloquently when he refused to plead, and he won support from spectators in the gallery. In the greatest show trial of the seventeenth century, the royal defendant stole the show.

When Charles's son, Charles II, was restored to the throne in 1660, royalists finally had their revenge against the judges of this court. Those who could be found alive were hanged, disemboweled, and quartered. For those who were already dead, there was to be another type of justice. In 1661 Royalists exhumed the badly decomposed corpses of Bradshawe, Henry Ireton, and Oliver Cromwell, the three men who bore the largest responsibility for the execution of the king. The three cadavers were hanged and their skulls were placed on pikes on top of Westminster Hall. This macabre ritual served as the Royalists' way of vilifying the memory of the judges of this illegal and revolutionary trial, and their unpardonable sin of executing an anointed king. ■

Questions of Justice

1. The men who brought King Charles to trial often spoke about bringing him to "justice." How is justice best understood in this context?

2. Why was it so important for the members of the High Court of Justice to make this trial conform to traditional common-law procedure? Did they succeed?

3. How does this trial reveal the limitations of divine-right absolutism in England?

Taking It Further

Peacey, Jason, ed. *The Regicides and the Execution of Charles I.* 2001. A collection of essays on various aspects of this episode and the men who signed the death warrant.

Wedgewood, C. V. *The Trial of Charles I.* 1964. Presents a full account and analysis of the trial by one of the great historical stylists of the twentieth century.

this issue, whom the Whigs called Tories, thwarted the designs of the Whigs in three successive parliaments between 1679 and 1681.

An even more serious political crisis occurred after James II succeeded to the throne in 1685. James began to exempt his fellow Catholics from the penal laws, which prevented them from worshipping freely, and from the Test Act of 1673, which had denied them the right to hold office under the crown. Catholics began to secure appointments in the army, the court, and local government. These efforts by the monarchy to grant toleration and political power to Catholics revived the traditional English fears of absolutism and popery. Not only the Whigs but also the predominantly Anglican Tories became alarmed at the king's policies. The birth of a Catholic son to James by his second wife, the Italian princess Mary of Modena, in June 1688 created the fear that the king's religious policy might be continued indefinitely. A group of seven Whigs and Tories, including the Bishop of London, drafted an invitation to William III of Orange, the captain general of the military forces of the Dutch Republic and James's nephew, to come to England to defend their Protestant religion and their constitution. William was married to James's eldest daughter, the Protestant Princess Mary, and as the king's nephew he also had a claim to the throne himself.

Invading with an international force of 12,000 men, William gathered substantial support from the English population, and when James's army defected, he was forced to flee to France without ever engaging William's forces in battle. The Convention, a special parliament convened by William in 1689, offered the crown to William and Mary while at the same time securing their assent to the Declaration of Rights, a document that later became the parliamentary statute known as the Bill of Rights. This bill, which is considered a cornerstone of the English constitution, corrected many of the abuses of royal power at the hands of James and Charles, especially the practice of exempting individuals from the penalties of the laws made by Parliament. By proclaiming William king and by excluding Catholics from the throne, the Bill of Rights also destroyed the theory of hereditary divine right.

It would be difficult to argue that this sequence of events, which is known as the Glorious Revolution, amounted to a revolution in the full sense of the word, since it did not change the basic institutions of English government. The revolution simply replaced one monarch with a king and queen who were more acceptable to the nation's political elite. But the events of 1688–1689 were decisive in defeating once and for all the absolutist designs of the Stuart kings and in guaranteeing that Parliament would

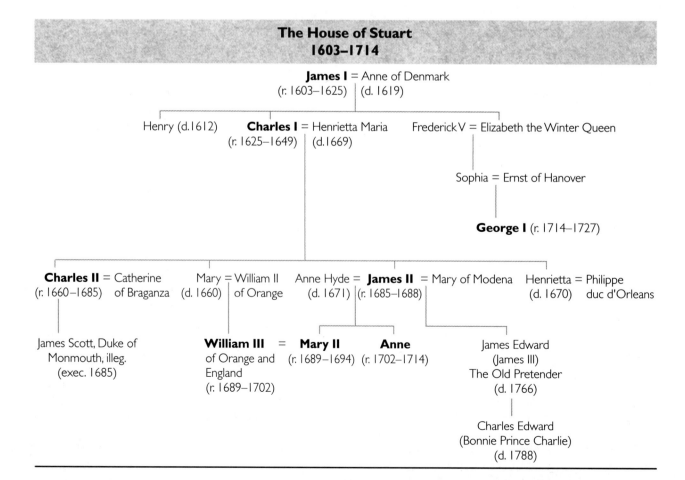

The House of Stuart
1603–1714

James I = Anne of Denmark
(r. 1603–1625) | (d. 1619)

Henry (d. 1612)   **Charles I** = Henrietta Maria   Frederick V = Elizabeth the Winter Queen
(r. 1625–1649) | (d. 1669)

Sophia = Ernst of Hanover

George I (r. 1714–1727)

Charles II = Catherine   Mary = William II   Anne Hyde = **James II** = Mary of Modena   Henrietta = Philippe
(r. 1660–1685)   of Braganza   (d. 1660) of Orange   (d. 1671) | (r. 1685–1688)   (d. 1670)   duc d'Orleans

James Scott, Duke of   **William III** = **Mary II**   **Anne**   James Edward
Monmouth, illeg.   of Orange and   (r. 1689–1694) (r. 1702–1714)   (James III)
(exec. 1685)   England   The Old Pretender
                         (r. 1689–1702)   (d. 1766)

Charles Edward
(Bonnie Prince Charlie)
(d. 1788)

■ **The Landing of William of Orange's Fleet in England, November 1688**
The declared objective of this expedition was "for the restoration of the Constitution and the True
Religion of England, Scotland and Ireland." After arriving in England, James II fled the country. William
and his wife Mary became king and queen of England and Scotland in February 1689.

form a permanent and regular place in English government. That Parliament has in fact met every year since
1689, and its legislative power grew considerably when the
crown vetoed a bill for the last time in 1707.

For the English aristocracy, the peers and gentry who
sat in Parliament, the revolution guaranteed that they
would occupy a paramount position within English politics and society for more than a hundred years. The revolution also had profound effects on British and European
diplomacy, since it quickly brought England and Scotland
into a war against Louis XIV of France, the great antagonist
of William III. The main reason William had come to
England and secured the crown in the first place was to secure British entry into the European alliance he was building against France.

Even if the Glorious Revolution has been misnamed, it
prompted the publication of a genuinely revolutionary political manifesto, John Locke's *Two Treatises of Government*
(1690). Locke was a radical Whig; he had written the
Treatises in the early 1680s as a protest against the absolutist
policies of Charles II, but only after the abdication and
flight of James II could he safely publish his manuscript.
Like Hobbes, Locke argued that men left the state of nature
and agreed to form a political society in order to protect
their property and prevent the chaos that characterized a
state of war. But unlike Hobbes, Locke asserted that the

government they formed was based on trust and that governments that acted against the interests of the people
could be dissolved. In these circumstances the people, in
whom sovereignty was always vested, could establish a new
regime. Locke's treatises constituted an uncompromising
attack on the system of royal absolutism, which he equated
with slavery. His work gave the people permission to take
up arms against an oppressive regime even before that
regime had consolidated its power. Since its publication, the
Two Treatises of Government has been pressed into the service of various revolutionary and radical causes, most notably in the Declaration of Independence by the United
States of America in 1776.

The Glorious Revolution had a direct bearing on the
growth of the English state. As long as Parliament had remained suspicious of the Stuart kings, it had been reluctant
to facilitate the growth of the state, which until 1688 was
under direct royal control. Once the king's power had been
permanently restricted, however, and Parliament had begun to emerge as the highest power within the country,
members of Parliament had less to fear from the executive
branch of government. The inauguration of a long period
of warfare against France in 1689 required the development
of a large army and navy, the expansion of the bureaucracy,
government borrowing on an unprecedented scale, and an
increase in taxes. Members of Parliament, especially those

in the Whig party, which had formed the main opposition to the monarchy before the revolution and had long opposed standing armies as a threat to English liberty, supported this expansion of the state as well as the war effort itself. By 1720 the kingdom of Great Britain, which had been created by the parliamentary union of England and Scotland in 1707, could rival the French state in military power, wealth, and diplomatic prestige. In fact, with its system of parliamentary government, Great Britain proved to be more successful than absolutist France in tapping the wealth of the people in the form of taxation to support its military establishment.

THE DUTCH REPUBLIC

In many respects the United Provinces of the Netherlands, known as the Dutch Republic, forms the most striking exception to the pattern of state building in seventeenth-century Europe. Formally established in 1588 during its revolt against Spanish rule, the Dutch Republic was the only major European power to maintain a republican form of government throughout the entire seventeenth century. As a state it also failed to conform to the pattern of centralization and consolidation that became evident in virtually all European monarchies. Having successfully resisted the centralizing policies of a large multinational Spanish monarchy, the Dutch Republic never acquired much of a centralized bureaucracy of its own. The provinces formed little more than a loose confederation of sovereign republican states. Each of the provinces sent deputies to the States General, where unanimity was required on all important issues, such as the levying of taxes, the declaration of war, and the ratification of treaties. Executive power was vested in a Council of State, which likewise consisted of deputies from the provinces. Even the individual provinces, the most important of which was Holland, were themselves decentralized, with the cities and rural areas sending delegates to a provincial assembly known as the States. Only the province of Holland invested one official, known as the grand pensionary, with extraordinary executive power.

This system of decentralized republican rule was much better suited for domestic affairs than the conduct of foreign policy. During most of the seventeenth century the Dutch were at war. After finally securing Spanish recognition of their independence by the Treaty of Münster in 1648, the Republic engaged in three commercial naval wars against England (1652–1654, 1665–1667, 1672–1674) and a much longer struggle against the territorial ambitions and economic policies of Louis XIV of France (1672–1678, 1689–1697, 1701–1713). The conduct of Dutch foreign policy and the coordination of the military forces of the seven provinces required some kind of central direction. During the 1650s John de Witt, the grand pensionary of Holland, assumed an informal presidency of the republic and directed the state's foreign policy in the first two wars against

England. After 1672 William III, a prince of the hereditary house of Orange-Nassau, gave further unity and coordination to Dutch state policy. William, who served as the stadholder or governor of each of the seven provinces, became the captain-general of the republic's military forces when war with France began in 1672.

The House of Orange, which had a permanent vote in the States General, represented the royal, centralizing force within the Dutch Republic, and it led a party within the republic that favored a modification of republican rule. These princes never acquired the same type of constitutional authority that monarchs exercised in other European states. William III of Orange, who became William III of England and Scotland in 1689, exercised far more power in his new British kingdoms than he did in the Dutch Republic. Nevertheless the House of Orange played a crucial role in the rise of this tiny republic to the status of a world power. During the period of its influence the size of the Dutch military forces increased dramatically, from 50,000 men in 1670 to 73,000 in 1690 and 130,000 in 1710. During the same period of time the size of the Dutch navy doubled. In this one respect the republican, decentralized United Provinces participated in the same process of state building as the other great powers of Europe. The main reason the government was able to support this large standing army was the enormous wealth it had accumulated by virtue of the country's thriving international trade.

Political power in the Dutch Republic lay mainly with the wealthy merchants and bankers who served as regents in the councils of the towns. These same men represented the towns in the States of each province. The rural areas, which predominated only in the eastern provinces, were represented by the aristocracy. The country was therefore ruled by an oligarchy, but the men who belonged to it represented a predominantly urban, mercantile elite rather than a rural nobility. The members of this bourgeois elite did not tend to seek admission to landed society in the way that successful English merchants often did. Nor were they lured into becoming part of an ostentatious court in the manner of the French nobility. As men completely immersed in the world of commerce, they remained part of mercantile society and used their political power to guarantee that the Dutch state would serve the interests of trade.

The political prominence of Dutch merchants reflected the highly commercial character of the Dutch economy. Shortly after its truce with Spain in 1609, the Dutch cities, especially the rapidly expanding port city of Amsterdam in Holland, began to dominate European and world trade. The Dutch served as middlemen and shippers for all the other powers of Europe, transporting grain from the Baltic, textiles from England, timber from Scandinavia, wine from Germany, sugar from Brazil and Ceylon, silk from Persia and China, and porcelain from Japan to markets throughout the world. The Dutch even served as middlemen for their arch-enemy Spain, providing food and manufactured goods to

■ **The Amsterdam Stock Exchange in 1668**
Known as the Bourse, this multi-purpose building served as a gathering point for merchants trading in different parts of the world. The main activity was the buying and selling of shares of stock in trading companies during trading sessions that lasted for two hours each day.

the Spanish colonies in the New World in exchange for silver from the mines of Peru and Mexico. As part of this process Dutch trading companies, such as the Dutch East India Company, began to establish permanent outposts in India, Indonesia, North America, the Caribbean, South America, and South Africa. Thus a relatively small country, with one-tenth the population of France and one-third that of Great Britain, became a colonial power.

To provide support for their dynamic mercantile economy, Dutch cities developed financial institutions favorable to trade. An Exchange Bank in Amsterdam, which had a monopoly on the exchange of foreign currencies, allowed merchants to make international transactions by adding sums to or deducting sums from their accounts whenever they imported or exported goods. The Dutch also developed rational and efficient methods of bookkeeping. A stock market, also situated in Amsterdam, facilitated the buying and selling of shares in commercial ventures. Even lawyers contributed to these commercial enterprises. In *The Freedom of the Sea* (1609), the great legal and political philosopher Hugo Grotius (1583–1645) defended the freedom of merchants to use the open seas for trade and fishing, thereby challenging the claims of European monarchs who wished to exclude foreigners from the waters surrounding their countries. Grotius, who also wrote *The Law of War and Peace* (1625), gained a reputation as the father of modern international law.

One of the most striking contrasts between the Dutch Republic and the kingdom of France in the seventeenth century lay in the area of religious policy. Whereas in France the revocation of the Edict of Nantes represented the culmination of a policy enforcing religious uniformity and the suppression of Protestant dissent, the predominantly Calvinist Dutch Republic gained a reputation for religious toleration. The Dutch Reformed Church did not always deserve this reputation, but secular authorities, especially in the cities, proved remarkably tolerant of different religious groups. Amsterdam, which attracted a diverse immigrant population during its period of rapid growth, contained a large community of Jews, including the philosopher Baruch Spinoza (1632–1677). The country became the center for religious exiles and political dissidents, accommodating French Huguenots who fled their country after the repeal of the Edict of Nantes in 1685 as well as English Whigs (including the Earl of Shaftesbury and John Locke) who were being pursued by the Tory government in the 1680s. In keeping with this Dutch tradition of toleration, Dutch courts became the first to stop the prosecution of witches, executing the last person for this crime in 1608.

This tolerant bourgeois republic also made a distinct contribution to European culture during the seventeenth century, known as its Golden Age. The Dutch cultural achievement was greatest in the area of the visual arts, where Rembrandt van Rijn (1606–1669), Franz Hals (ca. 1580–1666) and Jan Steen (1626–1679) formed only part of an astonishing concentration of artistic genius in the cities of Amsterdam, Haarlem, and Leiden. Dutch painting of this era reflected the religious, social, and

■ **Rembrandt, *Syndics of the Clothmakers of Amsterdam* (1662)**
Rembrandt's realistic portrait depicted wealthy Dutch bourgeoisie, who had great political as well as economic power in the Dutch Republic.

political climate in which painters worked. The Protestant Reformation had brought an end to the tradition of didactic and devotional religious painting that had flourished during the Middle Ages, leading many Dutch artists to adopt more secular themes for their work. At the same time the absence of a baroque court culture, such as that which still flourished in Spain and France as well as in the Spanish Netherlands, reduced the demand for royal and aristocratic portraiture as well as for paintings of heroic classical, mythological, and historical scenes. Instead the Dutch artists of the Golden Age produced intensely realistic portraits of merchants and financiers, such as Rembrandt's famous *Syndics of the Clothmakers of Amsterdam* (1662). Realism became one of the defining features of Dutch painting, evident in the numerous street scenes, still lifes, and landscapes that Dutch artists painted and sold to a largely bourgeois clientele. At the same time Dutch engravers perfected the art of political printmaking, much of

it highly satirical, an achievement that was encouraged by the political tolerance of the country.

In the early eighteenth century the Dutch Republic lost its position of economic superiority to Great Britain and France, which developed even larger mercantile empires of their own and began to dominate world commerce. The long period of war against France, which ended in 1713, took its toll on Dutch manpower and wealth, and the relatively small size of the country and its decentralized institutions made it more difficult for it to recover its position in European diplomacy and warfare. As a state it could no longer fight above its weight, and it became vulnerable to attacks by the French in the nineteenth century and the Germans in the twentieth. But in the seventeenth century this highly urbanized and commercial country showed that a small, decentralized republic could hold its own with the absolutist states of France and Spain as well as with the parliamentary monarchy of England.

CONCLUSION
The Western State in the Age of Absolutism

Between 1600 and 1715 three fundamental political changes, all related to each other, helped redefine the West. The first was the dramatic and unprecedented growth of the state. During these years all Western states grew in size and strength. They became more cohesive as the outlying provinces of kingdoms were brought more firmly under central governmental control. The administrative machinery of the state became more complex and efficient. The armies of the state could be called upon at any time to take action against internal rebels and foreign enemies. The income of the state increased as royal officials collected higher taxes, and governments became involved in the promotion of trade and industry and in the regulation of the economy. By the beginning of the eighteenth century one of the most distinctive features of Western civilization was the prevalence of these large, powerful, bureaucratic states. There was nothing like them in the non-Western world.

The second change was the introduction of royal absolutism into these Western states. From one end of the European continent to the other, efforts were made to establish the monarch as a ruler with complete and unrivaled power. These efforts achieved varying degrees of success, and in two states, England and the Dutch Republic, they ended in failure. Nevertheless, during the seventeenth and eighteenth centuries the absolutist state became the main form of government in the West. For this reason historians refer to the period of Western history beginning in the seventeenth century as the age of absolutism.

The third change was the conduct of a new style of warfare by Western absolutist states. The West became the arena where large armies, funded, equipped, and trained by the state, engaged in long, costly, and bloody military campaigns. The conduct of war on this scale threatened to drain the state of its financial resources, destroy its economy, and decimate its civilian and military population. Western powers were not unaware of the dangers of this type of warfare. The development of international law and the attempt to achieve a balance of power among European powers represented efforts to place restrictions on the conduct of seventeenth-century warfare. These efforts, however, were not completely successful, and in the eighteenth and nineteenth centuries warfare in the West entered a new and even more dangerous phase, aided by the technological innovations that the scientific and industrial revolutions made possible. To the first of those great transformations, the revolution in science, we now turn.

Suggestions for Further Reading

For a comprehensive list of suggested readings, please go to www.ablongman.com/levack/chapter15

Aylmer, G. E. *Rebellion or Revolution.* 1986. A study of the nature of the political disturbances of the 1640s and 1650s.

Beik, William. *Louis XIV and Absolutism: A Brief Study with Documents.* 2000. An excellent collection of documents.

Collins, James B. *The State in Early Modern France.* 1995. The best general study of the French state.

Elliott, J. H. *Richelieu and Olivares.* 1984. A comparison of the two contemporary absolutist ministers and state builders in France and Spain.

Harris, Tim. *Politics under the Later Stuarts.* 1993. The best study of Restoration politics, including the Glorious Revolution.

Hughes, Lindsey. *Russia in the Age of Peter the Great.* 1998. A comprehensive study of politics, diplomacy, society, and culture during the reign of the "Tsar Reformer."

Israel, Jonathan. *The Dutch Republic: Its Rise, Greatness and Fall, 1477–1806.* 1996. A massive and authoritative study of the Dutch Republic during the period of its greatest global influence.

Parker, David. *The Making of French Absolutism.* 1983. A particularly good treatment of the early seventeenth century.

Parker, Geoffrey. *The Military Revolution.* 1988. Deals with the impact of the military revolution on the world as well as European history.

Rabb, Theodore K. *The Struggle for Stability in Early Modern Europe.* 1975. Employs visual as well as political sources to illustrate the way in which Europeans responded to the general crisis of the seventeenth century.

Schama, Simon. *The Embarrassment of Riches: An Interpretation of Dutch Culture in the Golden Age.* 1987. Contains a wealth of commentary on Dutch art and culture during its most influential period.

Wilson, Peter H. *Absolutism in Central Europe.* 2000. Analyzes both the theory and the practice of absolutism in Prussia and Austria.

The Scientific Revolution

I N 1609 GALILEO GALILEI, AN ITALIAN MATHEMATICIAN AT THE UNIVERSITY OF Padua, introduced a new scientific instrument, the telescope, which revealed a wealth of knowledge about the stars and planets that filled the night skies. Having heard that a Dutch artisan had put together two lenses in such a way that magnified distant objects, Galileo built his own such device and directed it toward the heavens. Anyone who has looked through a telescope or seen photographs taken from a satellite can appreciate Galileo's excitement at what he saw. Objects that appeared one way to the naked eye looked entirely different when magnified by his new "spyglass," as he called it. The Milky Way, the pale glow that was previously thought to be a reflection of diffused light, turned out to be composed of a multitude of previously unknown stars. The surface of the moon, long believed to be smooth, uniform, and perfectly spherical, now appeared to be full of mountains, craters, and other irregularities. The sun, which was also supposed to be perfect in shape and composed of matter that could not be altered, was marred by spots that appeared to move across its surface. When turned toward Jupiter, the telescope revealed four moons never seen before. Venus, viewed over the course of many months, appeared to change its shape, much in the way that the moon did in its various phases. This latter discovery provided evidence for the relatively new theory that the planets, including Earth, revolved around the sun rather than the sun and the planets around the Earth.

Galileo shared the discoveries he made not only with fellow scientists but with other Europeans. In 1610 he published *The Starry Messenger*, a treatise in which he described his discovery of the new moons of Jupiter. Twenty-two years later he included the evidence he had gained from his telescope in another book, *Dialogue Concerning the Two Chief World Systems*, to support the claim that the Earth orbited around the sun. He also staged a number of public demonstrations of his new astronomical instrument, the first of which took place on top of one

The Telescope: The telescope was the most important of the new scientific instruments that facilitated discovery. This engraving depicts an astronomer using the telescope in 1647.

of the city gates of Rome in 1611. To convince those who doubted the reality of the images they saw, Galileo turned the telescope toward familiar landmarks in the city. Interest in the new scientific instrument ran so high that a number of amateur astronomers acquired telescopes of their own.

Galileo's observations and discoveries formed one facet of the development that historians call the Scientific Revolution. A series of remarkable achievements in astronomy, physics, chemistry, and biology formed the centerpieces of this revolution, but its effects reached far beyond the observatories and laboratories of seventeenth-century scientists. The Scientific Revolution brought about fundamental changes in Western thought, altering the way in which Europeans viewed the natural world, the supernatural realm, and themselves. It stimulated controversies in religion, philosophy, and politics and brought about changes in military technology, navigation, and economic enterprise. The revolution added a new dimension to Western culture and provided a basis for claims of Western superiority over people in other lands. For all these reasons the Scientific Revolution marked a decisive turning point in the history of Western civilization, and it set the West apart from contemporary civilizations in the Middle East, Africa, and Asia.

The scientific culture that emerged in the West by the end of the seventeenth century was the product of a series of cultural encounters. It resulted from a complex interaction among scholars proposing different accounts of how nature operated. In some cases the scientists who advanced the revolutionary ideas were themselves influenced by ideas drawn from different cultural traditions. Some of these ideas had originated in Greek philosophy, while others came from orthodox Christian sources. Still other ideas came from a tradition of late medieval science, which had in turn been heavily influenced by the scholarship of the Islamic Middle East. A skeptical refusal to rely on any inherited authority whatsoever had its own religious and philosophical sources.

In this chapter we will explore the scope and development of the Scientific Revolution and the changes it brought about in Western thought and culture. Five questions will structure our exploration of this subject: (1) What were the scientific achievements and discoveries of the late sixteenth and seventeenth centuries that historians refer to as the Scientific Revolution? (2) What methods did scientists use during this period to investigate nature, and how did they think nature operated? (3) Why did the Scientific Revolution take place in western Europe at this particular time? (4) How did the Scientific Revolution influence the development of philosophical and religious thought in the seventeenth and early eighteenth centuries? (5) How did the Scientific Revolution change the way in which seventeenth- and eighteenth-century Europeans thought of their relationship to the natural world?

The Discoveries and Achievements of the Scientific Revolution

Unlike political revolutions, such as the English Revolution of the 1640s discussed in the last chapter, the Scientific Revolution developed gradually and over a long period of time. It began in the middle and later decades of the sixteenth century and continued into the early years of the eighteenth century. Even though it took a relatively long time to unfold, it was revolutionary in the sense that it brought about a radical transformation of human thought, just as political revolutions have produced fundamental changes in systems of government. The most important changes in seventeenth-century science took place in the fields of astronomy, physics, chemistry, and biology.

ASTRONOMY: A NEW MODEL OF THE UNIVERSE

The most significant change in astronomy was the acceptance of the view that the sun, not the Earth, was the center of the universe. Until the middle of the sixteenth century, most natural philosophers—as scientists were known at the time—subscribed to the writings of the Greek astronomer Claudius Ptolemy (100–170 C.E.). Ptolemy's observations and calculations had given considerable support to the cosmology° (a theory regarding the structure and nature of the universe) proposed by the Greek philosopher Aristotle (384–322 B.C.E.). According to Ptolemy and Aristotle, the center of the universe was a stationary Earth, around which the moon, the sun, and the other planets revolved in circular orbits. Beyond the planets a large sphere carried the stars, which stood in a fixed relationship to each other, around the Earth from east to west once every twenty-four hours, thus accounting for the rising and setting of the stars. Each of the four known elements—earth, water, air, and fire—had a natural place within this universe, with the heavy elements, earth and water, being pulled down toward the center of the Earth and the light ones, air and fire, hovering above it. All heavenly bodies, including the sun and the planets, were composed of a fifth element, called ether, which unlike matter on Earth was thought to be eternal and could not be altered, corrupted, or destroyed.

This traditional view of the cosmos had much to recommend it, and some educated people continued to subscribe to it well into the eighteenth century. The authority of Aristotle, predominant in late medieval universities, was reinforced by the Bible, which in a few passages referred to the motion of the sun. The motion of the sun could be confirmed by simple human observation. We do, after all, see the sun "rise" and "set" every day, while the idea that the Earth rotates at a high speed and revolves around the sun contradicts the experience of our senses. Nevertheless, the Earth-centered model of the universe failed to provide an explanation for many patterns that astronomers observed in the sky, most notably the paths followed by planets. In the sixteenth century natural philosophers began to consider alternative models of the universe.

The first major challenge to the Ptolemaic system came from a Polish cleric, Nicolaus Copernicus (1473–1543), who in 1543 published *The Revolutions of the Heavenly Spheres*, in which he proposed that the center of the universe was not the Earth but the sun. The book was widely circulated, but it did not win much support for the sun-centered theory of the universe. The mathematical arguments Copernicus presented in the book were so abstruse that only the most erudite astronomers could understand them. Even those who could appreciate his detailed plotting of planetary motion were not prepared to adopt the central thesis of his book. In the late sixteenth century the great Danish astronomer Tycho Brahe (1546–1601) accepted the argument of Copernicus that the planets revolved around the sun but still insisted that the sun continued to revolve around the Earth.

■ **Two Views of the Ptolemaic or Pre-Copernican Universe**
(a) In this sixteenth-century engraving the Earth lies at the center of the universe and the elements of water, air, and fire are arranged in ascending order above the Earth. The orbit that is shaded in black is the firmament or stellar sphere. The presence of Christ and the saints at the top reflects the view that Heaven lay beyond the stellar sphere. (b) A medieval king representing Atlas holds a Ptolemaic cosmos. The Ptolemaic universe is often referred to as a two-sphere universe: The inner sphere of the Earth lies at the center and the outer sphere encompassing the entire universe rotates around the Earth.

(a)

(b)

Significant support for the Copernican model of the universe among scientists began to materialize only in the seventeenth century. In 1609 a German astronomer, Johannes Kepler (1571–1630), using data that Brahe had collected, confirmed the central position of the sun in the universe. In his treatise *New Astronomy,* Kepler also demonstrated that the planets, including the Earth, followed elliptical rather than circular orbits and that the planets moved in accordance with a series of physical laws. Kepler's book, however, did not reach a large audience, and his achievement was not fully appreciated until many decades later.

Galileo Galilei (1564–1642) was far more successful than Kepler in gaining support for the sun-centered model of the universe. In some respects Galileo was more conservative than Kepler. For example, Galileo never took issue with the traditional idea that the planets followed circular orbits. But Galileo had the literary skill, lacking in Kepler, of being able to write for a broad audience. Using the evidence gained from his observations with the telescope, and presenting his views in the form of a dialogue between the advocates of the two competing worldviews, he demonstrated the plausibility and superiority of Copernicus's theory.

The publication of Galileo's *Dialogue Concerning the Two Chief World Systems—Ptolemaic and Copernican* in 1632 won many converts to the sun-centered theory of the universe, but it lost him the support of Pope Urban VIII, who had been one of his patrons. Urban believed that by naming the character in *Dialogue* who defended the Ptolemaic system Simplicio (that is, a simple person), he was mocking the pope himself. In the following year Galileo was tried before the Roman Inquisition, an ecclesi-

(a)

■ **Two Early Modern Views of the Sun-Centered Universe**

(a) The depiction by Copernicus. Note that all the orbits are circular, rather than elliptical, as Kepler was to show they were. The outermost sphere is that of the fixed stars. (b) A late-seventeenth-century depiction of the cosmos by Andreas Cellarius in which the planets follow elliptical orbits. It illustrates four different positions of the Earth as it orbits the sun.

(b)

COPERNICUS PROPOSES HIS SUN-CENTERED THEORY OF THE UNIVERSE

....

In the dedication of his book On the Revolution of the Heavenly Spheres *(1543) to Pope Paul III, Copernicus explains that in his search for an orderly model of the universe he drew inspiration from a few ancient philosophers who had imagined that the Earth moved. He then explained how he had bolstered his theory through long and frequent observations. Anticipating condemnation from those who based their astronomical theories on the Bible, he appeals to the pope for protection while showing contempt for the theories of his opponents.*

. . . I began to chafe that philosophers could by no means agree on any one certain theory of the mechanism of the Universe, wrought for us by a supremely good and orderly Creator . . . I therefore took pains to read again the works of all the philosophers on whom I could lay my hand to seek out whether any of them had ever supposed that the motions of the spheres were other than those demanded by the mathematical schools. I found first in Cicero that Hicetas had realized that the Earth moved. Afterwards I found in Plutarch that certain others had held the like opinion. . . .

Taking advantage of this I too began to think of the mobility of the Earth; and though the opinion seemed absurd, yet knowing now that others before me had been granted freedom to imagine such circles as they chose to explain the phenomena of the stars, I considered that I also might easily be allowed to try whether, by assuming some motion of the Earth, sounder explanations than theirs for the revolution of the celestial spheres might so be discovered.

Thus assuming motions, which in my work I ascribe to the Earth, by long and frequent observations I have at last discovered that, if the motions of the rest of the planets be brought into relation with the circulation of the Earth and be reckoned in proportion to the circles of each planet . . . the orders and magnitudes of all stars and spheres, nay the heavens themselves, become so bound together that nothing in any part thereof could be moved from its place without producing confusion of all the other parts and of the Universe as a whole. . . .

It may fall out, too, that idle babblers, ignorant of mathematics, may claim a right to pronounce a judgment on my work, by reason of a certain passage of Scripture basely twisted to serve their purpose. Should any such venture to criticize and carp at my project, I make no account of them; I consider their judgment rash, and utterly despise it.

Source: From Nicolaus Copernicus, *De Revolutionibus Orbium Caelestium* (1543), translated by John F. Dobson and Selig Brodetsky in *Occasional Notes of the Royal Astronomical Society,* Vol. 2, No. 10, 1947. Reprinted by permission of Blackwell Publishing.

astical court whose purpose was to maintain theological orthodoxy. The charge against him was that he had challenged the authority of Scripture and was therefore guilty of heresy, the denial of the theological truths of the Roman Catholic Church. (See "Justice in History: The Trial of Galileo" later in this chapter.)

As a result of this trial Galileo was forced to abandon his support for the Copernican model of the universe, and *Dialogue* was placed on the Index of Prohibited Books, a list compiled by the papacy of all printed works containing heretical ideas. Despite this setback, support for Copernicanism grew during the seventeenth century, and by 1700 it commanded widespread support among scientists and the educated public. *Dialogue,* however, was not removed from the Index until 1822.

PHYSICS: THE LAWS OF MOTION AND GRAVITATION

Galileo made his most significant contributions to the Scientific Revolution in the field of physics, which deals with matter and energy and the relationship between them.

In the seventeenth century the main branches of physics were mechanics (the study of motion and its causes) and optics (the study of light). Galileo's most significant achievement in physics was to formulate a set of laws governing the motion of material objects. His work, which laid the foundation of modern physics, effectively challenged the theories of Aristotle regarding motion.

According to Aristotle, whose views dominated science in the late Middle Ages, the motion of every object except the natural motion of falling toward the center of the Earth required another object to move it. If the mover stopped, the object fell to the ground or simply stopped moving. One of the problems with this theory was that it could not account for the continued motion of a projectile, such as a discus or a javelin, after it left the hand of the person who threw it. Galileo's answer to that question was a theory of inertia, which became the basis of a radical new theory of motion. According to Galileo, an object continues to move or to lie at rest until something external to it intervenes to change its motion. Thus motion is neither a quality inherent in an object nor a force that it acquires from another object; it is simply a state in which the object finds itself.

Galileo also discovered that the motion of an object occurs only in relation to things that do not move. A ship moves through the water, for example, but the goods carried by that ship do not move in relationship to the moving ship. This insight served the immediate purpose of explaining to the critics of Copernicus how the Earth can move even though we do not experience its motion. Galileo's most significant contribution to the study of mechanics was his formulation of a mathematical law of motion that explained how the speed and acceleration of a falling object are determined by the distance it travels during equal intervals of time.

The greatest achievements of the Scientific Revolution in physics belong to English scientist Sir Isaac Newton (1642–1727). Newton was one of those rare geniuses whose research changed the way future generations viewed the world. As a boy Newton found himself out of place while working on his mother's farm in a small hamlet in Lincolnshire and while attending school in the same county. Fascinated by mechanical devices, he spent much of his time building wooden models of windmills and other machines. When playing with his friends he always found ways to exercise his mind, calculating, for example, how he could use the wind to win jumping contests with his classmates. While he was still an adolescent, it had become obvious to all his acquaintances that the only place where he would be comfortable would be at a university. In 1661 he entered Trinity College, Cambridge, a step that introduced him to the broader world of ideas. In 1667 he became a fellow of the college and two years later, at age 27, he became the Lucasian Professor of Mathematics.

At Cambridge Newton pursued a wide range of intellectual interests, including the study of biblical prophecy. His great discoveries, however, were in the disciplines of mathematics and natural philosophy. During the 1680s Newton formulated a set of mathematical laws that governed the operation of the entire physical world. In 1687 he published his theories in *Mathematical Principles of Natural Philosophy*. The centerpiece of this monumental work was the universal law of gravitation°, which demonstrated that the same force holding an object to the Earth also holds the planets in their orbits. Newton established that any two bodies attract each other with a force that is directly proportional to the product of their masses and inversely proportional to the square of the distance between them. This law represented a synthesis of the work by Kepler on planetary motion, Galileo on inertia, the English physicist Robert Hooke (1635–1703) on gravity, and the Dutch scientist Christian Huygens (1629–1695) on centrifugal force. Newton's *Mathematical Principles* superseded the works of

CHRONOLOGY

Discoveries of the Scientific Revolution

1543 Andreas Vesalius publishes *On the Fabric of the Human Body*, the first realistic depiction of human anatomy; Copernicus publishes *The Revolutions of the Heavenly Spheres*, challenging the traditional Earth-centered cosmos

1609 Johannes Kepler publishes *New Astronomy*, identifying elliptical orbits of the planets

1628 William Harvey publishes *On the Motion of the Heart and Blood in Animals*, demonstrating the circulation of the blood

1632 Galileo publishes *Dialogue Concerning the Two Chief World Systems*, leading to his trial

1638 Galileo publishes *Discourses on the Two New Sciences of Motion and Mechanics*, proposing new laws of motion

1655 Evangelista Torricelli conducts experiments on atmospheric pressure

1659 Robert Boyle invents the air pump and conducts experiments on the elasticity and compressibility of air

1673 Christian Huygens publishes *On the Motion of Pendulums*, developing his theories of gravitation and centrifugal force

1687 Newton publishes his *Mathematical Principles of Natural Philosophy*, presenting a theory of universal gravitation

all these scientists by establishing the existence of a single gravitational force and by giving it precise mathematical expression. At the same time it revealed the unity and order of the entire physical world. It provided, in Newton's words, "a system of the world."

Newton extended his study of motion to the science of optics by demonstrating that light consists of small particles that also follow the laws of motion. Newton's theory prevailed until the early nineteenth century, when a series of experiments provided support for a new theory of light, according to which light should be thought of as waves, similar to those that cross a pond after a stone is dropped. Later in the nineteenth century the wave theory itself gave way to the view that light is a form of electromagnetic radiation. The most revolutionary change in our understanding of light, however, came with Newton in the seventeenth century.

CHEMISTRY: DISCOVERING THE ELEMENTS OF NATURE

At the beginning of the seventeenth century, the branch of science today called chemistry had little intellectual respectability. It was not even an independent discipline, since it was considered a part of either medicine or alchemy°, the magical art of attempting to turn base metals into precious ones. The most famous chemist of the sixteenth century was the Swiss physician and natural magician Paracelsus (1493–1541), who rejected the theory advanced by the Greek physician Galen (129–200 C.E.) that diseases were caused by the imbalance of the four "humors" or fluids in the body—blood, phlegm, black bile, and yellow bile. The widespread medical practice of drawing blood from sick patients to cure them was based on Galen's theory. Paracelsus began instead to treat his patients with chemicals, such as mercury and sulfur, to cure certain diseases. Paracelsus and his followers also believed that chemistry would provide a new basis for the understanding of nature, and he interpreted the biblical account of the Creation as the chemical unfolding of nature. Paracelsus is often dismissed for his belief in alchemy, but his prescription of chemicals to treat specific diseases helped to give chemistry a respectable place within medical science.

During the seventeenth century chemistry became a legitimate field of scientific research, largely as the result of the work of the English natural philosopher Robert Boyle (1627–1691). Boyle destroyed the prevailing idea that all basic constituents of matter share the same structure. He contended that the arrangement of their components, which Boyle identified as corpuscles or atoms, determine their characteristics. Boyle also conducted experiments on the volume, pressure, and density of gas and the elasticity of air. His most famous experiments, undertaken with the help of an air pump, proved the existence of a vacuum. Largely as a result of Boyle's discoveries, chemists won acceptance as legitimate members of the company of scientists.

BIOLOGY: THE CIRCULATION OF THE BLOOD

The English physician William Harvey (1578–1657) made one of the great medical discoveries of the seventeenth century by demonstrating in 1628 that blood circulates throughout the human body. Harvey, who had studied medicine at the University of Padua and who became the royal physician to both James I and Charles I in England, challenged the traditional theory regarding the motion of the blood advanced by Galen and perpetuated by medieval philosophers. According to this traditional theory, blood originated in the liver, where it was converted from food and then flowed outward through the veins, providing nourishment to the organs and the other parts of the body. A certain amount of blood was also drawn from the liver into the heart, where it passed from one ventricle to the other and then traveled through the arteries to different parts of the body. During its journey this arterial blood was enriched by a special *pneuma* or "vital spirit" that originated in the atmosphere and was necessary to sustain life.

When this enriched blood reached the brain, it became the body's "psychic spirits," which eventually traveled to the nerves and influenced human behavior.

During the late sixteenth century a succession of Italian scientists called specific aspects of Galen's theory into question. It was Harvey, however, who proposed an entirely new framework for understanding the motion of the blood. Through a series of experiments on human cadavers and live animals in which he weighed the blood that the heart pumped every hour, Harvey demonstrated that the blood circulates throughout the body, traveling outward from the heart through the arteries and returning to the heart through the veins. The heart, rather than sucking in blood, performed the essential function of pumping it by means of its contraction and constriction. The only gap in Harvey's theory was the question of how blood goes from the ends of the arteries to the ends of the veins. The answer to this question came in 1661, when scientists, using another new magnifying instrument known as a microscope, could see the capillaries connecting the veins and arteries. Harvey, however, had provided the basis for understanding how blood circulates through the body, and he had set a standard for the conduct of future biological research.

■ **Biology**
William Harvey discovered the circulation of the blood.

Dissecting the Human Corpse

As medical science developed in the sixteenth and seventeenth centuries, the dissection of human corpses became a standard practice in European universities and medical schools. Knowledge of the structure and composition of the human body, which was central to the advancement of physiology, could best be acquired by cutting a corpse to reveal the organs, muscles, and bones of human beings. The practice reflected the emphasis scientists placed on observation and experimentation in conducting scientific research. In the sixteenth century the great Flemish physiologist Andreas Vesalius (1514–1564), who published the first realistic drawings of human anatomy in 1543, cut limbs and extracted organs in his lectures on anatomy at the University of Padua. A century later, the English physician William Harvey dissected human cadavers in his path-breaking study of the circulation of the blood.

The physicians who performed dissections had difficulty securing an adequate supply of corpses. A preference developed for the bodies of recently hanged criminals, mainly because rulers claimed jurisdiction over the bodies of the condemned and could dispose of them at will. Criminals, moreover, were generally young or middle-aged and in fairly good health, thus making them desirable specimens for dissection. Demand for corpses became so great in the late seventeenth and eighteenth centuries that surgeons were willing to pay a price for them, thus turning the dead human body into a commodity. In eighteenth-century England the demand for bodies of the hanged often resulted in brawls between the agents whom the surgeons paid to snatch the bodies from the scaffold and the relatives and friends of the deceased, who wanted to claim the corpses in order to guarantee a decent burial.

During the sixteenth and seventeenth centuries, dissection underwent two transformations. The first was the expansion of the audience from a small group of medical students to a large cross-section of scholars who attended in order to learn more about the relationship between human beings and the natural world. The audiences also began to include artists, who learned from these exercises how to depict the human body more accurately. The second change was the transformation of dissection into a public spectacle, controlled by municipal authorities. During the seventeenth century, the city of Bologna staged dissections every year before crowds of as many as 200 people.

To these public dissections, which took place in many other European cities, people from the lower classes were often admitted together with scholars, students, and artists. The uneducated men and women who attended were attracted by the entertaining aspects of the event and the eagerness to witness the violence done to the corpse, just as they were at public executions. They were particularly eager to see the dissection of the genital organs, so much so that some authorities restricted access to that part of the dissection in the interest of public decency.

The holding of public anatomy lessons had much less to do with the popularization of science than with the satisfaction of the popular taste for blood and sex. Only in the late eighteenth century, during the age of the Enlightenment, did a new sensitivity to blood and human torment and an unprecedented repugnance of death bring about an end to public dissections, together with the public executions with which they were closely associated. ▪

For Discussion

What interests were served by holding public dissections of human corpses in the seventeenth and eighteenth centuries?

■ **Dissection**
Rembrandt van Rijn, *The Anatomy Lesson of Dr. Nicholaes Tulp* (1632). This dissection, unlike many others in Europe during the seventeenth century, was performed in private. The observers were not medical students or curious public observers but members of the Amsterdam Company of Surgeons.

532

The Search for Scientific Knowledge

The natural philosophers who made these various scientific discoveries worked in different academic disciplines, and each followed his own procedures for discovering scientific truth. In the sixteenth and seventeenth centuries there was no such thing as a single "scientific method." Many natural philosophers, however, shared similar views regarding the way in which nature operated and the means by which humans could acquire knowledge of it. In searching for scientific knowledge, these scientists engaged in extensive observation and experimentation, used a process of deductive reason to solve scientific problems, expressed their theories in mathematical terms, and argued that nature operated like a machine. Taken together, these common features of scientific research ultimately defined a distinctly Western approach to solving scientific problems.

OBSERVATION AND EXPERIMENTATION

The most prominent feature of scientific research in sixteenth- and seventeenth-century Europe was the extensive observation of nature, combined with the testing of hypotheses by means of rigorous experimentation. This was primarily a process of induction°, in which theories emerged only after the systematic accumulation and analysis of large amounts of data. It assumed a willingness to abandon all preconceived notions, whether they were those of Aristotle, Galen, or medieval philosophers, and to base scientific conclusions on experience and observation.

The English philosopher Francis Bacon (1561–1626) promoted this empirical, experimental approach in his book *New Organon* (1620), in which he complained that all previous scientific endeavors, especially those of ancient Greek philosophers, relied too little on experimentation. By contrast, Bacon's approach involved the thorough and systematic investigation of nature, a process which Bacon, who was a lawyer and judge, compared to the interrogation of a person suspected of committing a crime. Bacon claimed that scientific experimentation was "putting nature to the question" in order to obtain the truth, a phrase that referred to questioning a prisoner under torture to determine the facts of a case.

All the great scientists of the sixteenth and seventeenth centuries abandoned preconceived notions and based their theories on the facts of nature, but the most enthusiastic practitioners of carefully planned and controlled experimentation came from England. Two of its most tireless advocates were Boyle, who performed a succession of experiments with an air pump to prove the existence of a vacuum, and Robert Hooke, whose experiments with a pendulum provided one of the foundations for Newton's

■ **Portrait of Robert Boyle with His Air-Pump in the Background (1664)**
Boyle's pump became the center of a series of experiments carried on at the Royal Society in London.

theory of universal gravitation. Harvey belongs to the same English experimental tradition, although his commitment to this methodology originated at the University of Padua. Galileo and some other Italian scientists matched the English in their insistence on experimentation, but Galileo's experiments were designed more to demonstrate the validity of his theories than to help him establish them in the first place.

DEDUCTIVE REASONING

The second feature of sixteenth- and seventeenth-century scientific research was the application of deductive reasoning to scientific problems. Unlike the inductive experimental approach, which found its most enthusiastic practitioners in England, the deductive approach had its most zealous advocates on the European continent. The men who took this approach were just as determined as Bacon and Boyle to replace the testimony of human authorities with what they discovered from nature itself. Their main method, however, was to establish basic scientific truths or propositions from which other ideas or laws could be deduced logically. The French philosopher and mathematician René Descartes (1596–1650) became the champion of this methodology. In his *Discourse on the Method* (1637) he recommended that in solving any intellectual problem a person should first establish fundamental principles or truths and then proceed deductively from those ideas to more specific conclusions.

The model for deductive reasoning was mathematics, in which one also moves logically from certain premises to conclusions by means of equations. Rational deduction° proved to be an essential feature of scientific methodology, although some scientists relied too heavily on it at the expense of a more experimental approach. The limitations of an exclusively deductive approach became apparent when Descartes and his followers deduced a theory of gravitation from the principle that objects could influence each other only if they actually touched. The theory, as well as the principle upon which it was based, lacked an empirical foundation°, which is one based on observation and experience, and eventually had to be abandoned.

MATHEMATICS AND NATURE

The third feature of scientific research in the sixteenth and seventeenth centuries was the application of mathematics to the study of the physical world. The mathematical treatment of nature was undertaken by scientists working in both the experimental and the deductive traditions. Descartes shared with Galileo, Kepler, and Huygens the conviction that nature had a geometrical structure and that it could therefore be understood in mathematical terms. The physical dimensions of matter, which Descartes claimed were its only properties, could of course be expressed mathematically. Galileo claimed that mathematics was the language in which philosophy was written in "the book of the universe."

This mathematical way of looking at the physical world had a long history. The Greek philosophers Pythagoras (582–507 B.C.E.) and Plato (ca. 428–348 B.C.E.) had both emphasized the geometric structure of the cosmos and therefore considered numbers to hold the key to its secrets. In the fifteenth century Renaissance philosophers revived this ancient Greek emphasis on mathematics. Copernicus, who was influenced by Platonic thought, criticized the Islamic and western European medieval philosophers who had accepted an Earth-centered universe for their mathematical miscalculations. Copernicus advocated a rigorous application of mathematics to astronomical writing. One of the reasons his book *The Revolutions of the Heavenly Spheres* was so demanding was that he described planetary motion in technical, mathematical terms.

In the seventeenth century Isaac Newton's work provides the best illustration of the application of mathematics to scientific problems. Newton used observation and experimentation to confirm his theory of universal gravitation, but the work in which he presented his theory, *Mathematical Principles of Natural Philosophy*, was written in the language of mathematics. Just as Newton had synthesized previous work in physics to arrive at the law of universal gravitation, he also combined the experimental and deductive approaches to acquire scientific truth. His approach to solving scientific problems, which became a model for future scientific research, involved generalization on the basis of particular examples derived from experiments and the use of deductive, mathematical reasoning to discover the laws of nature.

THE MECHANICAL PHILOSOPHY

Much of the scientific experimentation and deduction undertaken in the seventeenth century proceeded on the assumption that the natural world operated as if it were a machine made by a human being. This philosophy of nature, which is often referred to as the mechanical philosophy°, cannot be attributed to a single person; but its most comprehensive statement can be found in the work of Descartes. The scholastic philosophers of the fourteenth and fifteenth centuries insisted that nature was fundamentally different from a machine or any other object built by man. According to the scholastics, natural bodies had an innate tendency to change, whereas artificial objects, that is, those constructed by humans, did not. Descartes, Kepler, Galileo, and Bacon all denied that assumption, arguing that nature operated in a mechanical way, just like a clock or some other piece of machinery. The only difference was that we cannot readily observe the structures of natural mechanisms, in the way that we can see the structure of a pump or a wagon.

According to mechanists—scientists who subscribed to the mechanical philosophy—nature consisted of many machines, some of them extremely small. The human body was itself a machine, and the center of that human machine, the heart, was in Harvey's words "a piece of machinery in which, though one wheel gives motion to another, yet all the wheels seem to move simultaneously." Since the human body was made by God, it was superior to any human-made machine, but it was still nothing more than a machine.

According to Descartes, the only part of a human being that was not a machine was the mind, which was completely different from the body and the rest of the material world. Unlike the body, the mind was an immaterial substance that could neither be extended in space nor divided. Nor could it be measured mathematically, in the way one could record the dimensions of the human body. Because Descartes made this sharp distinction between the mind and the human body, we speak of his philosophy as being dualistic°.

The mechanical philosophy presented just as bold a challenge to those philosophers known as Neoplatonists° as

■ **René Descartes**

Although Descartes was a scientist who made contributions to the study of biology and optics, he is best known for the method he proposed to attain certain knowledge and his articulation of the mechanical philosophy.

it did to the scholastics. Neoplatonists were inspired by the work of Plotinus (205–270 C.E.), the last great philosopher of antiquity who had synthesized the work of Plato with that of other Greek philosophers. Plotinus also drew on many traditions of ancient Persian religion. Neoplatonic thought experienced a revival in the fifteenth and sixteenth centuries at the time of the Renaissance (see Chapter 11). Neoplatonists believed that the natural world was animistic—that is, it possessed a soul (known to them as a world soul) and was charged with various occult forces and spirits. The English natural philosopher William Gilbert (1544–1603), who wrote extensively on the phenomenon of magnetism, adopted a Neoplatonic worldview when he declared that the Earth and other planets were actually alive. Kepler clearly recognized the incompatibility of this outlook with that of the mechanical philosophy when he insisted that "the machine of the universe was not similar to a divine animated being."

Descartes and other mechanists argued that matter was completely inert or dead. It had neither a soul nor any innate purpose. Its only property was extension, or the physical dimensions of length, width, and depth. Without a spirit or any other internal force directing its action, matter sim-

ply responded to the power of the other bodies with which it came in contact. According to Descartes, all physical phenomena could be explained by reference to the dimensions and the movement of particles of matter. He once claimed, "Give me extension and motion and I will construct the universe." Even the human body contained no "vital spirits." It consisted only of flesh and the blood pumped by the mechanism of the heart. The only difference between the human body and other machines was that the mind (or soul) could move it, although how it did so was a matter of great controversy, as we shall see in a later section.

The view of nature as a machine implied that it operated in a regular, predictable way in accordance with unchanging laws of nature. Scientists could use reason to discover what those laws were and thus learn how nature performed under any circumstances. The scientific investigations of Galileo and Kepler were based on those assumptions, and Descartes made them explicit. The immutability of the laws of nature implied that the entire universe was uniform in structure, an assumption that underlay Newton's formulation of the laws of motion and of universal gravitation. Newton's theory of gravity denied Descartes's view of matter as inert, but he nonetheless accepted his view that the universe operated like a machine.

The Causes of the Scientific Revolution

.... ■ ....

Why did the Scientific Revolution take place at this particular time, and why did it originate in western European countries? What prompted natural philosophers in Italy, France, England, and the Dutch Republic to develop new ways of looking at the world? There are no simple answers to these questions. We can, however, identify a number of developments that inspired this remarkable set of scientific discoveries. Some of these developments were internal to science, in the sense that they arose out of earlier investigations conducted by natural philosophers in the late Middle Ages, the Renaissance, and the sixteenth century. Others were external to the development of science, arising out of the religious, political, social, and economic life of Europe during the early modern period.

DEVELOPMENTS WITHIN SCIENCE

The three internal causes of the Scientific Revolution were the research into the motion conducted by scholastic natural philosophers in the fourteenth century, the scientific investigations conducted by humanists at the time of the Renaissance, and the collapse of the dominant conceptual frameworks that had governed scientific inquiry and research for centuries.

Late Medieval Science

Modern science can trace some of its origins to the fourteenth century, when the first significant modifications of Aristotle's scientific theories began to emerge. These challenges came not only from theologians, who objected that Aristotle was a pagan philosopher, but from natural philosophers, who refined some of the basic ideas of Aristotle's physics.

The most significant of these refinements was the theory of impetus. Aristotle, as we have seen, had argued that an object would stop as soon as it lost contact with the object that moved it. The scholastic philosophers who modified this principle claimed that objects in motion acquire a force that stays with them after they lose contact with the mover. The theory of impetus did not bring about a full-scale demolition of Aristotle's mechanics, but it did begin to call Aristotle's authority into question. The theory of impetus was known in Galileo's day, and it influenced some of his early thought on motion.

Scholastic philosophers of the fourteenth century also began to recommend direct, empirical observation in place of the traditional scholastic tendency to accept preconceived theories regarding the operation of nature. This approach to answering scientific questions did not result in the type of rigorous experimentation that Bacon demanded three centuries later, but it did encourage scientists to base their theories on the facts that emerged from an empirical study of nature.

The contribution of late medieval science to the Scientific Revolution should not be exaggerated. Scholastic natural philosophers continued to accept the cosmology of Ptolemy. They still perpetuated the anatomical theories of Galen. The restraints that theology exercised over scientific thought in the Middle Ages also prevented the emergence of new scientific ideas.

Renaissance Science

Natural philosophers during the Renaissance made more tangible contributions to the rise of modern science than the scholastics of the late Middle Ages. Renaissance natural philosophers made those contributions despite the fact that the Renaissance, the revival of classical antiquity in the fifteenth and sixteenth centuries, was not conducive to the type of scientific research that Galileo, Descartes, Boyle, and Newton conducted. Renaissance humanism was mainly a literary and artistic movement, and humanists were not particularly interested in scientific knowledge. Humanism also cultivated a tradition of deferring to the superior wisdom of classical authors, whereas the new science defined itself largely in opposition to the theories of the ancients, especially Aristotle, Ptolemy, and Galen. The main philosophical movement of the Renaissance, moreover, was

Neoplatonism, which as we have seen, promoted an animistic view of nature that mechanists like Descartes and Kepler rejected.

The natural philosophers of the Renaissance did nonetheless make a number of important contributions to the birth of modern science. Many of the discoveries of the late sixteenth and seventeenth centuries drew their inspiration from Greek scientific works that had been recovered in their original form during the Renaissance. Copernicus found the original idea of his sun-centered universe in the writings of Aristarchus of Samos, a Greek astronomer of the third century B.C.E. whose work had been unknown during the Middle Ages. The theory that matter was divisible into small measurable particles known as atoms was inspired at least in part by the recovery of the texts of the ancient philosophers, most notably Democritus, who flourished around 480 B.C.E. Sixteenth-century editions of the works of Archimedes (287–212 B.C.E.), which had been virtually unknown in the Middle Ages, stimulated interest in the science of mechanics. The recovery and translation of previously unknown texts also made scientists aware that Greek scientists did not always agree with each other and thus provided a stimulus to independent observation and experimentation as a means of resolving their differences.

The Renaissance philosophy of Neoplatonism, despised by mechanists, also played an important role in the Scientific Revolution. In addition to the belief that the natural world had a soul, Neoplatonists adopted a geometric view of the universe and therefore encouraged the application of mathematics to the study of the natural world. Kepler developed his third law of planetary motion by applying to the cosmos the Neoplatonic idea of a harmony between numbers. The Neoplatonic tendency to think in terms of large, general categories also encouraged scientists like Kepler, Galileo, and Newton to discover universal laws of nature. Even alchemy, which many Neoplatonists practiced during the Renaissance, involved natural philosophers in experiments that gave them a limited sense of control over the operations of nature. The followers of Paracelsus, whose alchemy was tinged with Neoplatonic mysticism, were firm advocates of the observation of nature and experimentation.

Some of the most prominent natural philosophers of the seventeenth century were influenced to some extent by the cultural traditions that we associate with the Renaissance. Kepler became involved in the study of magic at the court of the Holy Roman Emperor Rudolf II. From his reading in Neoplatonic sources, Kepler acquired his belief that the universe was constructed according to geometric principles. Bacon gained some of his enthusiasm for experimentation from his interest in natural magic°, which was the use of magical words and drawings to manipulate forces in the physical world without calling on supernatural beings for assistance. Newton was fascinated by the subject of magic and studied alchemy intensively. The original inspiration of

Newton's theory of gravitation probably came from his professor at Cambridge, the Neoplatonist Henry More, who insisted on the presence of spiritual and immaterial forces in the physical world.

These contributions of the Renaissance to the new science were so important that some historians have identified the sixteenth century, when learned magic was in vogue and when the mechanical philosophy had not yet taken hold, as the first stage of the Scientific Revolution, to be followed by the mechanical phase when the discoveries of Galileo, Boyle, and Newton took center stage. Modern science resulted not so much from the victory of the mechanical philosophy over its Neoplatonic predecessor but from this encounter between these two worldviews.

The Collapse of Paradigms

The third internal cause of the Scientific Revolution was the collapse of the intellectual frameworks that had governed the conduct of scientific research since antiquity. The key to understanding this development is the recognition that scientists in all historical periods do not strive to introduce new theories but prefer to work within an established conceptual framework, or what the scholar Thomas Kuhn has referred to as a paradigm°. Scientists strive to solve puzzles that are presented by the paradigm. Every so often, however, the paradigm that has governed scientific research for an extended period of time collapses because it can no longer account for many different observable phenomena. A scientific revolution occurs when the old paradigm collapses and a new paradigm takes its place.

The revolutionary developments we have studied in astronomy and biology can be explained at least in part by the collapse of old paradigms. In astronomy the paradigm that had governed scientific inquiry in antiquity and the Middle Ages was the Ptolemaic system, in which the sun and the planets revolved around the Earth. Whenever ancient or medieval astronomers confronted a new problem as a result of their observations, they tried to accommodate the results to the Ptolemaic model. In the process they had to refine the basic concept that Ptolemy had presented. By the sixteenth century the paradigm had been modified or adjusted so many times that it no longer made sense. As scientists gradually added numerous "epicycles" of planetary motion outside the prescribed spheres, and as they identified numerous "eccentric" or noncircular orbits around the Earth, Ptolemy's paradigm of a harmoniously functioning universe gradually became a confused collection of planets and stars following different motions. Faced with this situation, Copernicus began to look for a simpler and more plausible model of the universe. The sun-centered theory that he proposed became the new paradigm within which Kepler, Galileo, and Newton all worked.

In the field of biology a parallel development occurred when the old paradigm constructed by Galen, in which the blood originated in the liver and was drawn into the heart and from there traveled through the arteries to the brain and nerves, also collapsed. By the seventeenth century the paradigm of Galen could no longer satisfactorily explain the findings of medical scholars, such as the recognition that blood could not easily pass from one ventricle of the heart to the other. It was left to Harvey to introduce an entirely new paradigm, in which the blood circulated through the body. As in astronomy, the collapse of the old paradigm led to the Scientific Revolution, and Harvey's new paradigm served as a framework for subsequent biological research.

DEVELOPMENTS OUTSIDE SCIENCE

A number of nonscientific developments also encouraged the development and acceptance of new scientific ideas. These developments outside science include the spread of Protestantism, the patronage of scientific research, the invention of the printing press, military and economic change, and voyages of exploration.

Protestantism

The growth of Protestantism in the sixteenth and seventeenth centuries encouraged the rise of modern science. Catholics as well as Protestants engaged in scientific research, and some of the most prominent European natural philosophers, including Galileo and Descartes, were devout Catholics. Protestantism, however, encouraged the emergence of modern science in three indirect ways.

First, Protestant countries proved to be more receptive than Catholic ones to new scientific ideas. Protestant churches, for example, did not prohibit the publication of books that promoted novel scientific ideas on the grounds that they were heretical, as the Papal Index did. The greater willingness of Protestant governments, especially those of England and the Dutch Republic, to tolerate the expression of unorthodox ideas helps to explain why the main geographical arena of scientific investigation shifted from the Catholic Mediterranean to the Protestant North Atlantic in the second half of the seventeenth century.

The second connection between Protestantism and the development of science was the emphasis Protestant writers placed on the idea that God revealed his intentions not only in the Bible but also in nature itself. Protestants claimed that individuals had a duty to discover what God had revealed to them in this way, just as it was their duty to read the Scripture to gain knowledge of God's will. Kepler's claim that the astronomer was "as a priest of God to the book of nature," a reference to the Protestant idea of the priesthood of all believers, serves as an explicit statement of this Protestant outlook.

The third contribution of Protestantism to the new science was the strong Protestant belief in the millennium, the second coming of Christ predicted in the Book of Revelation in the New Testament. Many Protestants believed that the event was about to occur and after Christ's arrival he would rule the world with the saints for a thousand years. In preparation for this climactic event, many English scientists, including Boyle and Newton, called for the use of scientific knowledge to achieve the general improvement of society. They also took seriously the biblical prediction that as the millennium approached, knowledge and understanding would increase.

Patronage

Although the intellectual problems that scientists grappled with may have inspired them to pursue their research and conduct experiments, they could not have succeeded without some kind of financial and institutional support. Only with the acquisition of an organizational structure could science acquire a permanent status, develop as a discipline, and give its members a professional identity. The universities, which today are known for their support of scientific research, did not serve as the main source of that support in the seventeenth century. One reason was that most universities, which were predominantly clerical institutions, had a vested interest in the defense of scholastic theology and Aristotelian science. They were therefore unlikely to provide the type of free academic atmosphere in which new scientific ideas might flourish. Moreover, within the university the only subject that allowed for the exploration of nature was that of philosophy. As long as science was considered a branch of philosophy, it could not establish its autonomy as a discipline and gain recognition as a legitimate pursuit in its own right.

Given limited support from the universities, scientists became dependent upon the patronage of wealthy and politically influential individuals. For the most part this patronage came from the kings, princes, and great noblemen who ruled European territorial states. During the seventeenth century, scientists found this type of patronage in two different types of institutions. The first were the courts of Italian and German princes. Galileo, for example, was the beneficiary of the patronage of Vincenzio Pinelli of Padua, the Venetian patrician Giovanfrancesco Sagredo, the Grand Duke of Tuscany Cosimo II de' Medici, the Roman aristocrat Prince Federico Cesi, and even Pope Urban VIII. These patrons, who were eager to display their interest in and support of learning, were actually responsible for securing Galileo's university appointments.

The terms of these appointments could be very generous. Galileo's appointment as Chief Mathematician at the University of Pisa, which Cosimo II secured for him in 1610, did not even require him to reside or teach there. Galileo's patrons gave him the opportunity to engage in his scientific work, and they circulated his publications at foreign courts. They did not, however, provide him with a permanent institutional base in which he could work.

Patronage from one politically powerful ruler rarely outlived the death of the patron, and the client could also lose the support of his patron, as Galileo did when he fell out of favor with Pope Urban VIII in 1632. Scientists who secured their livelihood at court also had to conduct themselves and their research in such a way as to maintain the favor of their patrons. Galileo referred to the new moons of Jupiter that he observed through his telescope as the Medicean stars in order to add luster to the image of the Medici family. His publications were inspired as much by his obligation to glorify Cosimo as by his belief in the validity of the sun-centered theory.

The second type of scientific institutions that provided patronage to scientists were academies in which groups of scientists could share ideas and work collectively. One of the earliest of these institutions was the Academy of the Lynxes in Rome, founded in 1603 by Prince Cesi. In keeping with the aristocratic values of its founder, it was modeled on an order of knights. Galileo became a member of this academy in 1611, and it published many of his works. In 1657 Cosimo II founded a similar institution, the Academy of Experiment, in Florence. These academies offered a more regular source of patronage than scientists could acquire from individual positions at court, but they still served the function of glorifying their founders, and they depended on patrons for their continued existence. The royal academies established in the 1660s, however, especially the Royal Academy of Sciences in France and the Royal Society in England, reduced that dependence on their patrons. These academies became in effect public institutions; even though they were established by the crown, they operated with a minimum of royal intervention. The royal academies also acquired a permanent location that made possible a continuous program of work.

The mission of the Royal Society in England was the promotion of scientific knowledge through a program of experimentation. It also served the political purpose of placing the results of scientific research at the service of the state, as we shall see shortly. This had been Francis Bacon's objective in his *New Organon*, and many of the members of the society, including Robert Boyle and Robert Hooke, were

---

CHRONOLOGY

The Formation of Scientific Societies

1603	Prince Cesi founds the Academy of the Lynxes in Rome
1657	Cosimo II de' Medici founds the Academy of Experiment in Florence
1662	Founding of the Royal Society of London under the auspices of Charles II
1666	Founding of the Academy of Sciences in Paris

■ **The Frontispiece of Thomas Sprat's *The History of the Royal Society of London* (1667)**
Fame places a laurel on a bust of Charles II, the patron of the society, while the president of the society, Lord Brouncker, sits to the left, pointing to the king's name. The late Sir Francis Bacon, whose emphasis on experimentation defined the purpose of the society, sits to the right and points to the navigational devices and firearms that he had predicted would lead to European control of the globe. They are sitting in a room filled with books and scientific instruments, including a telescope. In the background the Thames River, the gateway to the British Empire, suggests a further link between science and empire.

committed to the implementation of Bacon's plans. The research that members of the Royal Society did on both ship construction and military technology gave some indication of this commitment. These attempts to use scientific technology to strengthen the power of the state show that two of the most important developments of the seventeenth century, the growth of the modern state and the emergence of modern science, were related.

The Printing Press

The scientific academies and societies of the seventeenth century gave natural philosophers an opportunity to discuss their findings among themselves, but these scientists also needed to communicate the results of their research to scientists in more distant localities. The introduction and spread of printing throughout Europe made it much easier for scientists to share their discoveries with others who were working on similar problems. During the Middle Ages, when books were handwritten, the dissemination of scientific knowledge was limited by the number of copies that could be made of a manuscript. Moreover, errors could easily creep into the text as it was being copied. The advent and

spread of printing helped to correct this problem: Scientific achievements could be preserved in a much more accurate form and presented to a broader audience. The availability of printed copies also made it much easier for other scientists to correct or supplement the data that the authors supplied. In this way the entire body of scientific knowledge became cumulative, as it is today. Printing also made possible the reproduction of illustrations, diagrams, tables, and other schematic drawings that helped to convey the author's findings.

It remains uncertain how large a role printed materials played in the development of science. Scientists certainly read the work of others, but they also devoted large amounts of time to their own experiments, and those experiments in the long run were more important than books in the development of scientific knowledge. Printing may have accomplished more by making members of the non-scientific community aware of the latest advances in physics and astronomy than by leading scientists themselves to make new discoveries. In this way printing helped to make science an integral part of the culture of educated Europeans. The printing press also facilitated the growth of opposition to the new science, since it made possible the publication of treatises attacking the theories of Copernicus, Galileo, and Descartes.

Military and Economic Change

The Scientific Revolution occurred at roughly the same time that both the conduct of warfare and the European economy were undergoing dramatic changes. As territorial states increased the size of their armies and their military arsenals, they naturally demanded more accurate weapons with longer range. Some of the work undertaken by physicists during the seventeenth century, especially concerning the trajectory and velocity of missiles, gravitation, and air resistance, had the specific intention of improving military weaponry. Members of the Royal Society in England conducted extensive scientific research on these topics, and in so doing followed Francis Bacon's recommendation that scientists place their research at the service of the state.

The practical needs of capitalist enterprise also had a bearing on the direction of scientific research. The seventeenth century was a formative period in the emergence of a new capitalist economy, one in which private individuals engaged in trade, agriculture, and industry in order to realize ever-increasing profits. Some of the questions discussed at the meetings of the Royal Society suggest that its members undertook research with the specific objective of making such capitalist ventures more productive and profitable. The research did not always produce immediate results, but ultimately it increased economic profitability and contributed to the growth of the English economy in the eighteenth century. Knowledge of the displacement of water by ships led to improvements in methods of ship construction, which benefited merchants engaged in overseas trade. The determination of longitude by means of an accurate measurement of time at sea, a problem with which many seventeenth-century scientists grappled and which was finally solved in the eighteenth century with the invention of the chronometer, improved navigation. The study of mechanics led to new techniques to ventilate mines and raise coal or ore from them, thus making mining more profitable.

Voyages of Exploration

Closely related to the economic causes of the Scientific Revolution were the oceanic voyages of exploration that European mariners began to make in the late fifteenth century. As these voyages began long before the seventeenth century, they did not exercise an immediate or direct influence on the development of science. Most of the voyages, moreover, were undertaken by Portuguese and Spaniards, who did not play a major role in the Scientific Revolution. Nevertheless, these voyages revealed to mariners a number of natural phenomena that conflicted with the inherited traditions of Greek and late medieval science. They disproved, for example, much of what Ptolemy had written about the moistness of land in the Southern Hemisphere and what Aristotle had written about the difficulty of living in tropical areas. These inconsistencies led European natural philosophers to call into question the inherited authority of the Greeks on a variety of scientific

■ **The Frontispiece to Francis Bacon's**
The Great Instauration (1620)

The ship is shown sailing beyond the Straits of Gibraltar and the two pillars of Hercules, which had symbolized the limits of human knowledge. The biblical prophecy below the engraving reads: "Many shall pass to and fro and science will be increased." Bacon intended to show that the opening of the world to navigation and commerce complemented the further discovery of scientific knowledge. Both involved the discovery of new worlds.

matters and to base their views on the empirical observation of nature. In writing about the experimental method, Bacon frequently cited the body of evidence that had come from these voyages.

The Intellectual Effects of the Scientific Revolution

The Scientific Revolution had a profound impact on the intellectual life of educated Europeans. The discoveries of Copernicus, Kepler, Galileo, and Newton, as well as the assumptions upon which their work was based, influenced the subjects that people in the West studied, the way in which they approached intellectual problems, and their views regarding the supernatural realm.

EDUCATION

The philosophy of Aristotle, especially in its Christianized, scholastic form, had proved remarkably durable at European universities during the sixteenth century. It had successfully withstood the challenge of Neoplatonism, but the new science and the mechanical philosophy represented a more potent challenge to its supremacy. Over the course of the seventeenth and early eighteenth centuries, especially between the years 1680 and 1720, science and the new philosophy that was associated with it acquired academic respectability and became an important component of university education. Outside academia, knowledge of science increased as the result of its promotion by learned societies, attendance at public lectures, the discussion of science in coffeehouses, and the publication of scientific textbooks. As this knowledge was diffused among the educated classes, science secured a permanent foothold in Western culture.

The spread of science did not go unchallenged. It encountered academic rivals committed not only to traditional Aristotelianism but also to Renaissance humanism, which had gradually penetrated the curriculum of the universities during the sixteenth and seventeenth centuries. Beginning in the late seventeenth century a conflict arose between "the ancients," who revered the wisdom of classical authors, and "the moderns," who emphasized the superiority of the new scientific culture. The most concrete expression of this conflict was the Battle of the Books, an intellectual debate that raged in England and on the Continent in the late seventeenth and early eighteenth centuries over the question of which group of thinkers had contributed more to human knowledge. The battle accentuated the differences between two distinct components of western European culture. The Battle of the Books ended with no clear winner, and the conflict between the ancients

and the moderns has never been completely resolved. The humanities and the sciences, while included within the same curriculum at many universities, are still often regarded as representing two separate cultural traditions.

SKEPTICISM AND INDEPENDENT REASONING

One of the most significant intellectual effects of the Scientific Revolution was the encouragement it gave to the habit of skepticism, the tendency to doubt what we have been taught and are expected to believe. This skepticism formed part of the method that seventeenth-century scientists adopted in their efforts to solve philosophical problems. As we have seen, Descartes, Bacon, Galileo, and Kepler all refused to acknowledge the authority of classical or medieval texts, preferring instead to rely upon the knowledge they acquired from the observation of nature and the use of their own rational faculties.

In *Discourse on the Method*, Descartes showed the extremes to which this skepticism could be taken by doubting the reality of his own sense perceptions and even his own existence. He eventually found a way out of this dilemma when he realized that the very act of doubting proved his existence as a thinking being. As he wrote in words that have become famous, "I think, therefore I am." Upon this foundation Descartes went on to prove the existence of God and the material world, thereby conquering the skepticism with which he began his inquiry. In the process, however, Descartes had promoted an approach to solving intellectual problems that asked people to question the authority of others and to think clearly and systematically for themselves. The effects of this method began to become apparent in the late seventeenth century, when Descartes's methodology was invoked in challenging a variety of orthodox opinions regarding the supernatural world.

Some of the most radical of those opinions came from the mind of Baruch Spinoza (1632–1677), who grew up in Amsterdam in a community of Spanish and Portuguese Jews who had fled the Inquisition. Although educated in the Orthodox Jewish manner, Spinoza also studied Latin and read the works of Descartes and other Christian writers of the period. From Descartes, Spinoza had learned "that nothing ought to be admitted as true but what has been proved by good and solid reason." This skepticism and independence of thought led to his excommunication from the Jewish community at age 24, at which time he changed his first name from its Jewish form, Baruch, to Benedict. A skilled lens grinder by trade, Spinoza spent much of his life developing his philosophical ideas.

Spinoza challenged Descartes's separation of the mind and the body and the radical distinction between the spiritual and the material. For Spinoza there was only one substance in the universe, which he equated with nature or God. This pantheism, in which all matter became spirit and was comprehended within God, challenged not only the ideas of Descartes but also a fundamental tenet of Christianity—the distinction between God as pure spirit and the material world that he had created. In his most famous book, *A Treatise on Religion and Political Philosophy* (1670), Spinoza developed these ideas and also called for complete freedom from intellectual restraints.

The type of freethinking that Spinoza advocated aroused considerable suspicion. His followers, most of whom lived in the Dutch Republic, were constantly exposed to the danger of prosecution for atheism and blasphemy. Spinoza's skeptical approach to solving philosophical and scientific problems revealed the radical intellectual potential of the new science. The freedom of thought that Spinoza advocated, as well as the belief that nature followed immutable laws and could be understood in mathematical terms, served as important links between the Scientific Revolution and the Enlightenment of the eighteenth century. Those connections will be studied more fully in Chapter 17.

SCIENCE AND RELIGION

The most profound intellectual effects of the Scientific Revolution occurred in the area of religious thought. The claims of the new science presented two challenges to traditional Christian belief. The first involved the apparent contradiction between the sun-centered theory of the universe and biblical references to the sun's mobility. Since the Bible was considered the inspired word of God, the Church took everything it said, including any passages regarding the operation of the physical world, as literally true. The Bible's reference to the sun moving across the sky served as the basis of the official papal condemnation of sun-centered theories in 1616 and the prosecution of Galileo in 1633.

The second challenge to traditional Christian belief was the implication that if the universe functioned as a machine, on the basis of immutable natural laws, then God apparently played a very small role in its operation. This position, which was adopted by the late-seventeenth- and eighteenth-century thinkers known as Deists°, was considered a denial of the Christian belief that God superintended the operation of the world and was continually active in its governance. None of the great scientists of the seventeenth century actually adopted this position, but the acceptance of the mechanical philosophy made them vulnerable to the charge that they denied Christian doctrine. Because of his support for the mechanical philosophy, Descartes was suspected of atheism.

CHRONOLOGY

The Impact of the Scientific Revolution

1620	Sir Francis Bacon publishes *The New Organon,* arguing for the necessity of rigorous experimentation
1633	Galileo tried by the Roman Inquisition
1637	René Descartes publishes *Discourse on the Method,* recommending the solution of intellectual problems through a process of deduction
1670	Baruch Spinoza publishes *Treatise on Religion and Political Philosophy,* challenging the distinction between spirit and matter
1686	Bernard de Fontenelle publishes *Treatises on the Plurality of Worlds,* a fictional work exploring the possibility of extraterrestial life
1682	Edict of Louis XIV ending most witchcraft trials in France
1685	Last execution for witchcraft in England
1691–1693	Balthasar Bekker publishes *The Enchanted World* in four volumes, denying the intervention of the Devil in the operation of the natural world
1709	Thomas Newcomen invents the first steam engine

Although the new science and seventeenth-century Christianity appeared to be on a collision course, a number of scientists and theologians insisted that there was no conflict between them. One argument they made was that religion and science were separate disciplines that had very different concerns. Religion dealt with man's relationship with God, while science explained how nature operated. As Galileo wrote in a letter to the Grand Duchess Christina of Tuscany in 1615, "The Holy Ghost teaches us how to go to Heaven, not how the heavens go." Scripture was not intended to explain natural phenomena, but to convey religious truths that could not be grasped by human reason. In making these points Galileo was pleading for the separation of religion and science by freeing scientific inquiry from the control of the Church. To some extent, that separation has taken place over the course of the last three centuries. Theology and science have gradually become separate academic disciplines, each with its own objectives and methodology. Even the papacy eventually accepted the position of Galileo on this question in 1992. Nevertheless, conflicts between the claims of science and those who believe in the literal truth of the Bible have not disappeared, especially regarding the theory of evolution.

Another argument for the compatibility of science and religion was the claim that the mechanical philosophy, rather than relegating God to a role of a retired engineer, actually manifested his unlimited power. In a mechanistic universe God was still the creator of the entire physical world and the formulator of the laws of nature that guaranteed its regular operation. He was still all-powerful and present everywhere. According to Boyle and Newton, moreover, God played a supremely active role in governing the universe. Not only had he created the universe, but, in a theory developed by Boyle, he also continued to keep all matter constantly in motion. This theory served the purpose of redefining God's power without diminishing it in any way. Newton arrived at a similar position in his search for an immaterial agent who would cause gravity to operate. He proposed that God himself, who he believed "endures always and is present everywhere," made bodies move according to gravitational laws. Throughout the early eighteenth century this feature of Newtonian natural philosophy served as a powerful argument for the existence and immanence of God.

As the new science became more widely accepted, and as the regularity and immutability of the laws of nature became more apparent, religion itself began to undergo a transformation. Instead of denying the validity of the new science, many theologians, especially Protestants, accommodated scientific knowledge to their religious beliefs. Some Protestants welcomed the discoveries of science as an opportunity to purify the Christian religion by combating the superstition, magic, and ignorance that they claimed the Catholic Church had been promoting. Clerics who accepted the new science, including those who became members of the Royal Society, argued that since God worked through the processes of nature, human beings could acquire theological knowledge of him by engaging in scientific inquiry. For them religion and science were not so much separate but complementary forms of knowledge, each capable of illuminating the other.

The most widespread effect of the new science on religion was a new emphasis on the compatibility of reason and religion. In the Middle Ages scholastic theologians such as Thomas Aquinas had tried to reconcile the two, arguing that there was a body of knowledge about God, called natural theology, that could be obtained without the assistance of revelation. Now, however, with the benefit of the new science, theologians and philosophers began to expand the role that reason played in religion. In the religious writings of the English philosopher John Locke, the role of reason became dominant. In *The Reasonableness of Christianity* (1695), Locke argued that reason should be the final arbiter of the existence of the supernatural and it should also determine the true meaning of the Bible. This new emphasis on the role of reason in religion coincided with a rejection of the religious zeal that had characterized the era of the Reformation and the wars of religion. Political and ecclesiastical authorities looked down on religious enthusiasm not only as politically dangerous, since it had inspired revolution and rebellion throughout Europe, but as a form of behavior that had no rational basis.

The new emphasis on the reasonableness of religion and the decline of religious enthusiasm are often viewed as evidence of a broader trend toward the secularization of European life, a process in which religion gave way to more worldly concerns. In one sense this secular trend was undeniable. By the dawn of the eighteenth century, theology had lost its dominant position at the universities, the sciences had become autonomous academic disciplines, and religion had lost much of its intellectual authority. Religion also began to exercise less influence on the conduct of politics and diplomacy and on the regulation of economic activity.

Religion had not, however, lost its relevance. Throughout the eighteenth century it remained a vital force in the lives of most European people. Religious books continued to be published in great numbers. Many of those who accepted the new science continued to believe in a providential God and the divinity of Christ. Moreover, a small but influential group of educated people, following the lead of the French mathematician, physicist, and religious philosopher Blaise Pascal (1623–1662), insisted that although reason and science have their place, they represent only one sphere of truth. In his widely circulated book *Reflections*, which lay unfinished at his death but was published in 1670, Pascal argued that religious faith occupied a higher sphere of knowledge that reason and science could not penetrate. Pascal, the inventor of a calculating machine and the promoter of a system of public coach service in Paris, had been an advocate of the new science. He endorsed the Copernican model of the universe and opposed the condemnation of Galileo. But on the question of the relationship between science and religion, Pascal presented arguments that could be used against Spinoza, Locke, and all those who considered reason the ultimate arbiter of truth.

MAGIC, DEMONS, AND WITCHCRAFT

The new science not only changed many patterns of religious thought but also led to a denial of the reality and effectiveness of magic. Magic is the use of a supernatural, occult, or mysterious power to achieve extraordinary effects in the physical world or to influence the course of human events. The effects can be beneficial or harmful. Magicians claimed to be able to use their special powers to cure a person or inflict disease, acquire political power, stimulate love or hatred in another individual, predict the future, or produce any number of natural "marvels," including changes in the weather. In the sixteenth and seventeenth centuries men and women believed in and practiced two forms of magic. Natural magic, such as the practice of alchemy, involved the manipulation of occult forces that were believed to exist in nature. As we have seen, many

The Trial of Galileo

The events leading to the trial of Galileo for heresy in 1633 began in 1616, when a committee of eleven theologians reported to the Roman Inquisition that the sun-centered theory of Copernicus was heretical. Those who accepted this theory were declared to be heretics not only because they called the authority of the Bible into question but because they denied the exclusive authority of the Catholic Church to determine how the Bible should be interpreted. The day after this report was submitted, Pope Paul V instructed Cardinal Robert Bellarmine, a theologian who was on good terms with Galileo, to warn him to abandon his Copernican views. Galileo had written extensively in support of the sun-centered thesis, especially in his *Letters on Sunspots* (1613) and his *Letter to the Grand Duchess Christina* (1615), although he had never admitted that the theory was proved conclusively. Now he was being told that he should not hold, teach, or defend in any way the opinion of the sun's stability or the Earth's mobility. If he were to ignore that warning, he would be prosecuted as a heretic.

During the next sixteen years Galileo published two books. The first, *The Assayer* (1623), was an attack upon the views of an Italian philosopher regarding comets. The book actually won Galileo considerable support, especially from the new pope, Urban VIII, who was eager to be associated with the most fashionable intellectual trends. Urban took Galileo under his wing and made him the intellectual star of his court. Urban even went so far as to declare that support for Copernicanism was not heretical but only rash.

The patronage of the pope may have emboldened Galileo to exercise less caution in writing his second book of this period, *Dialogue Concerning the Two Chief World Systems* (1632). This treatise was ostensibly an impartial presentation of the rival Ptolemaic and Copernican cosmologies, but in its own quiet way it served the purpose of promoting Copernicanism. Galileo sought proper authorization from ecclesiastical authorities to put the book in print, but he eventually allowed it to be published in Florence before it received official approval from Rome.

The publication of *Dialogue* precipitated Galileo's fall from the pope's favor. Urban, who at this time was coming under criticism for leniency with heretics, ordered the book taken out of circulation in the summer of 1632 and appointed a commission to investigate Galileo's activities. After receiving the report from the committee a few months later, he turned the matter over to the Roman Inquisition, which charged Galileo with heresy.

The Roman Inquisition had been established in 1542 to preserve the Catholic faith. Its main concern was the prosecution of heresy. Like the Spanish Inquisition, this Roman ecclesiastical court has acquired a reputation for being harsh and arbitrary, for administering torture, for proceeding in secrecy, and for denying the accused the right to know what the charges were in advance of the trial. There is some validity to these criticisms, although the Roman Inquisition did not torture Galileo or deny him the opportunity to present a defense. The most unfair aspect of the proceeding, and of inquisitorial justice in general, was the determination of the outcome of the trial by the same judges who had brought the charges against the accused and conducted the interrogation. This meant that in a politically motivated trial such as Galileo's, the verdict was a foregone conclusion. To accept Galileo's defense would have been a sign of weakness and a repudiation of the pope.

Although the underlying substantive issue in the trial was whether Galileo was guilty of heresy for denying the sun's motion and the Earth's immobility, the more technical question was whether by publishing *Dialogue* he had violated the prohibition of 1616. In his defense Galileo claimed that the only reason he had written *Dialogue* was to present "the physical and astronomical reasons that can be advanced for one side or the other." He denied holding Copernicus's opinion to be true.

In the end the court determined that by publishing *Dialogue*, Galileo had violated the injunction of 1616. He had disseminated "the false opinion of the Earth's motion and the sun's stability" and he had "defended the said opinion already condemned." Even Galileo's efforts "to give the impression of leaving it undecided and labeled as probable" was still a very serious error,

■ The Trial of Galileo, 1633

Galileo is shown here presenting one of his four defenses to the Inquisition. He claimed that his book, *Dialogue Concerning the Two Chief World Systems,* did not endorse the Copernican model of the universe.

since there is no way that "an opinion declared and defined contrary to divine Scripture may be probable." The court also declared that Galileo had obtained permission to publish the book in Florence without divulging to the authorities there that he was under the injunction of 1616.

Throughout the trial every effort was made to distance the pope from his former protégé. There was real fear among the members of the papal court that since the pope had been Galileo's patron and had given him considerable latitude in developing his ideas, he himself would be implicated in Galileo's heresy. Every step was taken to guarantee that information re-garding the pope's support for Galileo did not surface. The court made sure, for example, that no one from the Medici court, which had provided support for Galileo, would testify on Galileo's behalf. The trial tells us as much about the efforts of Urban VIII to save face as about the Catholic Church's hostility to the new science.

Galileo was required to formally re-nounce of his views and to avoid any further defense of Copernicanism. After making this humiliating submission to the court, he was sent to Siena, and later that year was allowed to re-turn to his villa in Arcetri near Florence, where he remained under house arrest until his death in 1642. ■

Questions of Justice

1. Galileo was silenced because of what he had put into print. Why had he published these works, and why did the Church consider his publications a serious threat?

2. Why did Galileo accept the verdict of the court?

3. Is a court of law an appropriate place to resolve disputes between science and religion? Why or why not?

Taking It Further

Finocchiaro, Maurice, ed. *The Galileo Affair: A Documentary History.* 1989. A collection of original documents regarding the controversy between Galileo and the Roman Catholic Church.

Sharratt, Michael. *Galileo: Decisive Innovator.* 1994. A study of Galileo's place in the history of science that provides full coverage of his trial and papal reconsiderations of it in the late twentieth century.

SKEPTICISM REGARDING THE DEVIL

···················

Balthasar Bekker, a Dutch Calvinist minister, wrote a four-volume attack on the belief in witchcraft entitled The Enchanted World *in 1691–1693. The book denies the possibility that the Devil could exercise power over the natural world or that he could appear as a human being. Bekker reflects the skepticism and rationalism of Descartes as well as the belief of natural theologians that God works through the processes of nature.*

There is no argument so absurd as that of attributing an unusual effect to an occult or unknown cause, but above all, to these sorts of intellects [demons], as people want to do, in order to draw as a consequence that they have the power and the capacity to do such things. Why not rather investigate deeply into the knowledge of Nature in order to unite things corporeal to things corporeal? For if I encounter something which has not yet been proven, but which nevertheless is of the same nature as something else, what reason do I have to look for another cause than that which I already have found at work in the other? . . . I have not investigated the secrets of nature in such a way that I could know what she is yet capable of doing again, and I have not thumbed through books in such a way that there could not be in them certain things formerly known to be natural things, but that pass today for witchcraft. . . .

Man is forced, as soon as he meets something that arrests his judgment, to throw it back upon the Devil. He can do this in all safety, and without being fearful of passing for idiotic, stupid, wicked or impious. But if he should happen to put into doubt, and even more if he should deny that the Devil can be the author of the thing, he is called an atheist. . . . As if there had to be no God if it were not true that the Devil acted upon men in all sorts of encounters? If you answer yes, why could He not do by means of his angels the things which cannot be done naturally, or rather, by the force of nature, of which man still does not know the thousandth part?

Source: From Balthasar Bekker, *The Enchanted World* (1691) in Alan C. Kors and Edward Peters, *Witchcraft in Europe, 1100–1700: A Documentary History.* Copyright © 1972 by The University of Pennsylvania Press, Inc. Reprinted by permission of the University of Pennsylvania Press.

Neoplatonists believed in the possibility of this type of magic, and many of them actually practiced it. Demonic magic°, on the other hand, involved the invocation of evil spirits so that one might gain access to their supernatural power. The men who were most committed to the mechanical philosophy denied the effectiveness of both types of magic. By claiming that matter was inert, they challenged the central notion of natural magic, which is the belief that material objects are animated by occult forces, such as a sympathy for another object. If matter was not alive, it contained no forces for a magician to manipulate.

The denial of the reality of demonic magic was based on a rejection of the powers of demons. Seventeenth-century scientists did not necessarily deny the existence of angelic or demonic spirits, but the mechanical philosophy posed a serious challenge to the belief that those spirits could influence the operation of the physical world. The belief in demons experienced a slow death. Many scientists struggled to preserve a place for them in the physical world, arguing that demons, like God, could work through the processes of nature. Ultimately, however, the logic of the mechanical philosophy expelled them from the worldview of the educated classes. By the beginning of the eighteenth century, scientists and even some theologians had labeled the belief in demons as superstition, which originally had meant false or erroneous religion but which was now redefined to mean ignorance of mechanical causes. As Thomas Sprat, an English clergyman, declared in his history of the Royal Society, "Experiments have proven demons don't exist."

The denial of the power of magic, together with the rejection of the belief in the power of demonic spirits, also explains why many educated Europeans began to deny the reality of witchcraft in the later half of the seventeenth century. Witches were individuals, mostly women, who stood accused of using magic to bring harm upon their neighbors, their animals, or their crops. They were also accused of having made a pact with the Devil, the means by which they received their magical powers. In many cases it was claimed that witches worshipped the Devil collectively at nocturnal orgies known as sabbaths. At these assemblies, so it was claimed, witches danced naked, had sexual intercourse with demons and other witches, and sacrificed unbaptized children to the Devil. To someone who subscribed to the mechanical philosophy, this entire set of beliefs about witches was highly questionable. Demons could not intervene in the operation of the physical world, much less make pacts with human beings and copulate with them at the sabbath.

The most emphatic, comprehensive, and unequivocal attack on the entire body of witch beliefs during the seventeenth century came from the pen of a Dutch minister and follower of Descartes, Balthasar Bekker, whose four-volume study, *The Enchanted World* (1691–1693), denied that the Devil could exercise any jurisdiction over the natural world. The mechanical philosophy was not the only basis for Bekker's skepticism. A biblical scholar, Bekker produced many passages from Scripture indicating that God exercised complete sovereignty over the Devil and had in fact chained him to Hell. In this way the Devil had been rendered incapable of causing physical destruction in the world, either with or without the assistance of witches.

Skeptics such as Bekker played only a minor role in bringing about the decline and end of witchcraft prosecutions. As we discussed in Chapter 14, thousands of Europeans, most of them women, were tried and executed for witchcraft during the sixteenth and seventeenth centuries. These unfortunate people were accused not only of harming their neighbors but of belonging to a vast diabolical conspiracy to destroy Christian civilization. Beginning in the 1620s the number and frequency of these witchcraft trials began to decline. The reason for this decline was not so much the triumph of the mechanical philosophy, which spread within ruling elites only gradually, but the growing recognition by judges and magistrates that large numbers of innocent people had been forced under torture to confess to crimes they had not committed. In order to avoid any further miscarriages of justice, courts abandoned the use of torture and demanded that convictions for witchcraft satisfy very strict standards of legal proof. In such circumstances the number of convictions and executions was reduced to a mere trickle. The trials did not come to a complete end, however, until political authorities recognized that witchcraft was an impossible crime. Only then did they take steps to ensure that no one could ever be tried for it again. Between 1682 and 1776 the laws that had authorized the prosecution and execution of witches in France, Prussia, Great Britain, Sweden, Austria, Poland, and Russia were all repealed.

The skeptical views that many educated people acquired regarding witchcraft and magic were usually not shared by people who remained illiterate. For them magic and witchcraft remained very real, and they continued to suspect and accuse their neighbors of engaging in diabolical practices until the early nineteenth century. In a number of instances they took the law into their own hands, stoning accused witches, drowning them, or burning them alive. All of this served to highlight a widening gap between the views of the educated and those of the common people. There had always been differences between learned and popular culture, but there also had been many aspects of culture that educated and uneducated people shared. Both groups, for example, took part in the same religious services and rituals, and both groups also shared some of the same beliefs about magic and witchcraft. In the late seventeenth century, however, this common cultural ground began to disappear, and members of the educated classes began to develop unprecedented contempt for the ignorance and superstition of the common people. The education of the upper classes in the new science and in Descartes's philosophy only aggravated what was already a noticeable trend.

The development of two separate realms of culture became one of the main themes of eighteenth-century history, and it contributed directly to the formation of class divisions. On the one side were the educated upper classes who prided themselves on their rational and enlightened views; on the other were the illiterate peasants who continued to believe in magic, witchcraft, and what the educated referred to as "vulgar superstition."

Humans and the Natural World

The spread of scientific knowledge not only redefined the views of educated people regarding the supernatural realm, but it also led them to reconsider their relationship to nature. This process involved three separate but related inquiries. The first was to determine the place of human beings in a sun-centered universe; the second to investigate how science and technology had given human beings greater control over nature; and the third to reconsider the relationship between men and women in light of new scientific knowledge regarding the human mind and body.

THE PLACE OF HUMAN BEINGS IN THE UNIVERSE

The astronomical discoveries of Copernicus and Galileo offered a new outlook regarding the position of human beings in the universe. The Earth-centered Ptolemaic cosmos that dominated scientific thought during the Middle Ages was also human-centered. Not only was the planet that human beings inhabited situated at the center of the universe, but on Earth humans occupied a privileged position. This is not to say that the human condition was always viewed in positive terms. Trapped on a stationary Earth, which itself was corruptible, individuals were always vulnerable to the temptations of the demonic spirits that medieval clerics told them were constantly hovering in the atmosphere. But human beings nonetheless remained the absolute physical and moral center of this universe. They were, after all, created in the image of God, according to Christian belief. Renaissance Neoplatonism reinforced this medieval view. By describing human beings as having the characteristics of both angels and beasts, with the capacity to ascend toward God or descend to the level of animals, Neoplatonists accentuated the centrality and importance of humankind in the world.

The acceptance of a sun-centered model of the universe began to bring about a fundamental change in these views of humankind. Once it became apparent that the Earth was not the center of the universe, human beings began to lose their privileged position in nature. The Copernican universe was neither Earth-centered nor human-centered. Scientists such as Descartes continued to claim that human beings were the greatest of nature's creatures, but their habitation of a tiny planet circling the sun inevitably reduced the sense of their own importance. Moreover, as astronomers began to recognize the incomprehensible size of the cosmos, the possibility emerged that there were other habitable worlds in the universe, calling into further question the unique status of humankind.

In the late sixteenth century and seventeenth centuries a number of literary works explored the possibility of other inhabited worlds and forms of life. In *The Infinite Universe and World* (1584), the Neoplatonist monk Giordano Bruno (1548–1600), who was eventually burned as a heretic, postulated the existence of other rational beings and suggested that they might be more intelligent than humans. Kepler's *Somnium, or Lunar Astronomy* (1634), a book that combined science and fiction, described various species of moon dwellers, some of whom were rational and superior to humans. This was followed by a number of works of fiction on travel to the moon, including Francis Godwin's *The Man in the Moon* (1638) and Cyrano de Bergerac's *The Other World* (1657). The most ambitious and fascinating of all these books was a fictional work by the French dramatist and poet Bernard de Fontenelle, *Treatises on the Plurality of Worlds* (1686). This work, which became immensely popular throughout Europe, was more responsible than any purely scientific discovery of the seventeenth century for leading the general reading public to call into question the centrality of humankind in Creation.

THE CONTROL OF NATURE

The Scientific Revolution bolstered the confidence human beings had in their ability to control nature. By disclosing the laws governing the operation of the universe, the new science gave humans the tools they needed to make nature serve their own purposes more effectively than it had in the past. This confidence in human mastery over nature found its most articulate expression in the writings of Francis Bacon. Instead of accepting the traditional view that humans were either passively reconciled with nature or victimized by it, Bacon believed that knowledge of the laws of nature could restore the dominion over nature that humans had lost in the biblical Garden of Eden. Bacon believed that nature existed for human beings to control and exploit for their own benefit. His famous maxim, "knowledge is power," conveyed his confidence that science would give human beings this type of control over nature.

In the same spirit Descartes announced that as human beings we had the capacity "to turn ourselves into the masters and possessors of nature." For him nature included animals or beasts, which, unlike human beings, did not have souls and were therefore merely corporal machines. (For this reason, he was not at all reluctant to dissect live animals.) Later in the seventeenth century the members of the Royal Society proclaimed their intention to make scientific knowledge "an instrument whereby mankind may obtain a dominion over things." This optimism regarding human control of nature found support in the belief that God permitted such mastery, first by creating a regular and uniform universe and then by giving people the rational faculties by which they could understand nature's laws.

Many scientists of the seventeenth century emphasized the practical applications of their research, just as scientists often do today. Descartes, who used his knowledge of optics to improve the grinding of lenses, contemplated ways in which scientific knowledge might improve the drainage of marshes, increase the velocity of bullets, and use bells to make clouds burst. He even dreamed of making the blind see and enabling men to fly. As we mentioned earlier, members of the Royal Society discussed how their experiments would help miners, farmers, and merchants. They even discussed the possibility of making labor-saving machines. These efforts to apply scientific knowledge to practical problems encouraged the belief, which has persisted to the present day, that science could improve human life.

The hopes of seventeenth-century scientists for the improvement of human life by means of technology remained in large part unfulfilled until the eighteenth century. Only then did the technological promise of the Scientific Revolution begin to be realized, most notably with the innovations that preceded or accompanied the Industrial Revolution. The first steam engine, for example, which utilized the scientific study of atmospheric pressure conducted by a student of Galileo in the 1650s, was not invented until 1709. The great improvements in the construction of canals and the use of water power to drive machinery, which were based upon the study of Newtonian mechanics, likewise did not take place until the eighteenth century. In similar fashion, research on the internal structure of grains and the breeding of sheep did not significantly increase food production until the eighteenth century, at the time of the agricultural revolution.

By the middle of the eighteenth century, the belief that science would lead to an improvement of human life became an integral part of Western culture. Much less apparent at that time, however, was a recognition of the destructive potential of applied science. Governments supported scientific research on ballistics to gain military advantage, but it was not until the twentieth century, especially with the construction of engines of mass destruction, that people began to recognize technology's potential to cause permanent harm to the human race. In the seventeenth and eighteenth centuries, those who possessed scientific knowledge thought mainly in terms of the benefits that science and technology could confer. Their faith in human progress became one of the main themes of the Enlightenment, which will be discussed in Chapter 17.

WOMEN, MEN, AND NATURE

The new scientific and philosophical ideas of the seventeenth century challenged ancient and medieval notions regarding women's physical and mental inferiority to men. At the same time the new science left other traditional ideas about the roles of men and women unchallenged.

Until the seventeenth century, a woman's sexual organs were thought to be imperfect versions of a man's, an idea that made woman an inferior version of man and in some respects a freak of nature. During the sixteenth and seventeenth centuries, a body of scientific literature advanced the new idea that women had sexual organs that were perfect in their own right and served distinct functions in reproduction. Another traditional biological idea that came under attack during this period was Aristotle's view that men made a more important contribution to reproduction than did women. The man's semen was long believed to contain the form of the body as well as the soul, while the only contribution the woman was believed to have made to the process was the formless matter upon which the semen acted. By the beginning of the eighteenth century, a scholarly consensus had emerged that recognized equal contributions from both sexes to the process of reproduction.

Some seventeenth-century natural philosophers also called into question ancient and medieval ideas regarding women's mental inferiority to men. In this regard Descartes supplied a theory that presupposed intellectual equality between the sexes. In making a radical separation between the mind and the human body, Descartes found no difference between the minds of men and women. As one of his followers wrote in 1673, "The mind has no sex." A few upper-class women provided solid evidence to support this revolutionary claim of female intellectual equality. Princess Elisabeth of Bohemia, for example, carried on a long correspondence with Descartes during the 1640s and challenged many of his ideas on the relationship between the body and the soul. The privately educated English noblewoman

ELISABETH OF BOHEMIA CHALLENGES DESCARTES

······················

Elisabeth of Bohemia, the daughter of King Frederick of Bohemia and granddaughter of King James I of England, engaged in a long correspondence with Descartes regarding his philosophy. Privately educated in Greek, Latin and mathematics, Elisabeth was one of a small group of noblewomen who participated in the scientific and philosophical debates of the day. The letter concerns the relationship between the soul (or mind), which Descartes claimed was immaterial, and the body, which is entirely composed of matter. One of the problems for Descartes was to explain how the mind can move that body to perform certain functions. In the letter Elisabeth plays a deferential, self-effacing role but in the process exposes one of the weaknesses of Descartes's dualistic philosophy.

The Hague, 20 June 1643

Monsieur Descartes,

. . . The life I am forced to lead does not leave me the disposition of enough time to acquire a habit of meditation according to your rules. So many interests of my family that I must not neglect, so many interviews and civilities that I cannot avoid, batter my weak spirit with such anger and boredom that it is rendered for a long time afterward useless for anything else. All of which will excuse my stupidity, I hope, not to have been able to understand the idea by which we must judge how the soul (not extended and immaterial) can move the body by an idea we have in another regard of heaviness, nor why a power—which we have falsely attributed to things under the name of a quality—of carrying a body toward the center of the Earth when the demonstration of a contrary truth (which you promised in your Physics) confirms us in thinking it impossible. The idea of a separate independent quality of heaviness—given that we are not able to pretend to the perfection and objective reality of God—could be made up out of ignorance of that which truly propels bodies towards the center of the Earth. Because no material cause represents itself to the senses, one attributes heaviness to matter's contrary, the immaterial, which nevertheless I would never be able to conceive but as a negation of matter and which could have no communication with matter.

I confess that it is easier for me to concede the matter and the extension of the soul than to concede that a being that is immaterial has the capacity to move a body and to be moved by it. For if the former is done by giving information, it is necessary that the spirits which make the movement be intelligent, which you do not accord to anything corporal. And although, in your meditations, you show the possibility of the soul being moved by the body, it is nevertheless very difficult to comprehend how a soul, as you have described it, after having had the faculty and habit of good reasoning, would lose all that by some sort of vapors, or that being able to subsist without the body and having nothing in common with it, would allow itself to be so ruled by the body.

Source: From *The Princess and the Philosopher: Letters of Elisabeth of the Palatine to René Descartes* by Andrea Nye. Copyright © 1999 by Rowman & Littlefield Publishers, Inc. Reprinted by permission.

■ **Astronomers in Seventeenth-Century Germany**
Elisabetha and Johannes Hevelius working together with a sextant in a German astronomical observatory. More than 14 percent of all German astronomers were female. Most of them cooperated with their husbands in their work.

Margaret Cavendish (1623–1673) wrote scientific and philosophical treatises and conversed with the leading philosophers of the day. In early eighteenth-century France, small groups of women and men gathered in the salons or private sitting rooms of the nobility to discuss philosophical and scientific ideas. In Germany it was not uncommon for women to help their husbands run astronomical observatories.

Although seventeenth-century science laid the theoretical foundations for a theory of sexual equality, it did not challenge other traditional ideas that compared women unfavorably to men. Most educated people continued to ground female behavior in the humors, claiming that because women were cold and wet, as opposed to hot and dry, they were naturally more deceptive, unstable, and melancholic than men. They also continued to identify women with nature itself, which had always been depicted as female. Bacon's use of masculine metaphors to describe science and his references to "man's mastery over nature" therefore seemed to reinforce traditional ideas of male dominance over women. His language also reinforced traditional notions of men's superior rationality. In 1664 the secretary of the Royal Society, which excluded women from membership, proclaimed that the mission of that institution was to develop a "masculine philosophy." At the same time the tradition of depicting science as a female goddess, such as Minerva, began to disappear.

The new science provided the theoretical foundations for the male control of women at a time when many men expressed concern over the "disorderly" and "irrational" conduct of women. In a world populated with witches, rebels, and other women who refused to adhere to conventional standards of proper feminine behavior, the adoption of a masculine philosophy was associated with the reassertion of patriarchy.

CONCLUSION
Science and Western Culture

The Scientific Revolution was a uniquely Western phenomenon. It had no parallel in the Eastern world. During the Middle Ages the Islamic civilizations of the Middle East produced a rich body of scientific knowledge that had influenced the development of science in western Europe, but by the time of the Scientific Revolution Islamic science had entered a period of decline. Other civilizations, most notably in China and India, also possessed impressive scientific traditions, but they too failed to undergo a transformation similar to that which occurred in western Europe in the seventeenth century.

In all these non-Western civilizations, religious traditions had prevented philosophers from undertaking an objective study of the natural world. Either nature was viewed as an entirely secular (that is, not religious) entity and hence not worthy of study on its own terms, or it was viewed as something so heavily infused with spiritual value that it could not be subjected to rational analysis. Only in Europe did religious and cultural traditions allow the scientist to view nature as both a product of supernatural forces and something that was separate from the supernatural realm. Nature could therefore be studied objectively without losing its religious significance. Only when nature was viewed in this dual way, as both the creation of God and as something independent of the deity, could it be subjected to mathematical analysis and brought under human domination.

The Scientific Revolution gave the West a new source of identity. The West could be distinguished not only by its Christianity, its capitalist economic system, its large bureaucratic states, and its massive standing armies, but also by the scientific content of its education, its approach to the natural world, and its science-based technology. By the beginning of the eighteenth century, modern science became an essential component of Western culture. It also laid the foundations of the Enlightenment, another distinctively Western phenomenon, which will be discussed in the next chapter.

The rise of Western science and technology had profound implications for the encounters that took place between Western and non-Western peoples in Africa, Asia, and the Americas. By the eighteenth century, European science provided explicit support for European empires, which will be discussed in Chapters 19 and 23. Science gave Western states the military and navigational technology that allowed them to establish their control over non-Europeans. Knowledge of botany and agriculture allowed Western powers to develop the resources of the areas they colonized and to use these resources for the improvement of their own societies. Most important, the possession of scientific knowledge and technology encouraged people in the West to think of themselves as superior to the people they subjugated or controlled. Scientific theories regarding biological and physiological differences between the people who inhabited the West and natives of other countries also contributed to those attitudes. Western imperialism had its roots in the Scientific Revolution of the seventeenth century.

Suggestions for Further Reading

For a comprehensive list of suggested readings, please go to www.ablongman.com/levack/chapter16

Biagioli, Mario. *Galileo, Courtier: The Practice of Science in the Culture of Absolutism.* 1993. Argues that Galileo's desire for patronage determined the type of research he engaged in and the scientific questions he asked.

Cohen, H. Floris. *The Scientific Revolution: A Historiographical Inquiry.* 1995. A thorough account of all the different interpretations of the causes and significance of the Scientific Revolution.

Dear, Peter. *Discipline and Experience: The Mathematical Way in the Scientific Revolution.* 1995. Explains the importance of mathematics in the development of seventeenth-century science.

Debus, Allen G. *Man and Nature in the Renaissance.* 1978. Deals with the early history of the Scientific Revolution and develops many of its connections with the Renaissance.

Drake, Stillman, ed. *Discoveries and Opinions of Galileo.* 1957. Includes four of Galileo's most important writings, together with a detailed commentary.

Easlea, Brian. *Magic, Witch-Hunting and the New Philosophy.* 1980. Relates the end of witch hunting to the spread of mechanical philosophy.

Kuhn, Thomas S. *The Copernican Revolution.* 1957. The most comprehensive and authoritative study of the shift from an Earth-centered to a sun-centered model of the universe.

Popkin, Richard. *The History of Skepticism from Erasmus to Spinoza.* 1979. Discusses skepticism as a cause as well as an effect of the Scientific Revolution.

Schiebinger, Londa. *The Mind Has No Sex? Women in the Origins of Modern Science.* 1989. Explores the role of women in all aspects of scientific endeavor.

Shapin, Steven. *The Scientific Revolution.* 1996. A study of the origins of the modern scientific worldview that emphasizes the social influences on the production of knowledge and the social purposes for which scientific knowledge was intended.

Shapin, Steven, and Simon Schaffer. *Leviathan and the Air Pump.* 1989. Study of the difference between Robert Boyle and Thomas Hobbes regarding the value of experimentation.

Thomas, Keith. *Man and the Natural World. A History of the Modern Sensibility.* 1983. A study of the shifting attitudes of human beings toward nature during the period from 1500 to 1800.

Webster, Charles. *The Great Instauration: Science, Medicine and Reform, 1626–1660.* 1975. Explores the relationship between Puritanism and the Scientific Revolution in England.

Westfall, Richard S. *Never at Rest: A Biography of Isaac Newton.* 1980. A superb biography of the most influential scientist in the history of the West.

Eighteenth-Century Society and Culture

I N 1745 THOMAS BROWN AND ELEVEN OTHER MEN LIVING ON THE ESTATE OF THE Earl of Uxbridge, an English nobleman, were jailed for up to one year for shooting deer and rabbits on the earl's land. All twelve defendants were poor. Brown eked out a living as a coal miner in the earl's mines and rented a cottage and five acres of land from him. Like many of his fellow villagers, Brown supplemented his family's diet by shooting game from time to time, usually as he was walking to work through the earl's vast estate. This poaching violated a set of English parliamentary statutes known as the game laws, which restricted the shooting or trapping of wild animals to the members of the landed class.

The earl and other noblemen defended the game laws on the grounds that they were necessary to protect their property. The laws, however, served the even more important purpose of maintaining social distinctions between landowners and the common people. Members of the landed class believed that only they should have the right to hunt game and to serve deer, pheasants, and hares at lavish dinners attended by their social equals. For a poor person like Thomas Brown, who was described in a court document as "a rude disorderly man and a most notorious poacher," to enjoy such delicacies was a challenge to the social order.

This mid-eighteenth-century encounter between the Earl of Uxbridge and his tenants, which took the form of a criminal prosecution, reflected the tensions that simmered beneath the calm surface of eighteenth-century European society. These tensions arose between the members of the aristocracy, a small but wealthy governing elite, and the masses of tenants and laborers who formed the overwhelming majority of the European population. The aristocracy occupied a dominant position in eighteenth-century society. They controlled an enormous portion of the wealth in their countries, much of it in land. They staffed the state bureaucracies, legislative assemblies, the military officer corps, and the judiciaries of almost all European states. They dominated and set the

Chapter Outline

- The Aristocracy
- Challenges to Aristocratic Dominance
- The Enlightenment
- The Impact of the Enlightenment

First Lecture in the Salon of Madame Geoffrin, 1755: The speaker is lecturing on Voltaire's *The Orphan of China* before a predominantly aristocratic audience of men and women.

553

tone of high cultural life in Europe. Together with the monarchy and the church, with which they were socially and politically linked, the aristocracy formed what today is often referred to as "the Establishment."

By 1800 the social and political dominance of the aristocracy had begun to wane. Their legitimacy as a privileged elite was increasingly called into question. In a few countries political power began to pass from them to different social groups. The aristocracy did not surrender all their power, but they lost their stranglehold over society. This change began during a period of political stability between 1750 and the outbreak of the French Revolution in 1789.

The decline of the aristocracy was the result of a series of cultural encounters. The first were the tense and occasionally violent interactions between landowners and peasants who resented the repressive features of upper-class rule. The second were criticisms of the aristocracy and the demands for reform that came from the increasingly literate, politically active people from the middle ranks of society, such as merchants, financiers, industrialists, and skilled artisans. The third was the cultural and intellectual movement known as the Enlightenment. Even though many of the Enlightenment's most prominent thinkers came from the ranks of the aristocracy, they advanced a set of political, social, economic, and legal ideas that ultimately inspired the creation of a more egalitarian society.

The aristocracy did not relinquish power willingly or quickly. Although they faced severe criticism and challenges to their dominance, they managed to preserve much of their wealth and maintain at least some of their political influence. To insulate themselves from criticisms from less powerful social groups, they adopted many of the values of the people who occupied the middle ranks of society and subscribed to many of the ideas of the Enlightenment, including those that criticized their own class. Internal encounters between different social groups, just like external encounters between Western and non-Western peoples, rarely result in total domination of one group over the other. Instead both parties change their thinking and behavior as a result of their interaction.

These encounters, especially those that took place at the time of the Enlightenment, resulted in a redefinition of the West. In the last chapter we saw how the Scientific Revolution completely changed the face of Western culture. In the eighteenth century the Enlightenment, which was inspired to a great extent by the ideas of the Scientific Revolution, produced a set of political and social ideals that served as the basis for a new Western identity.

This chapter will address four main questions about eighteenth-century society and culture: (1) What social groups belonged to the aristocracy and how did they exercise their power and influence during the eighteenth century? (2) How did subordinate social groups, most notably the rural peasantry and those who lived in the towns, challenge the aristocracy during the late eighteenth century? (3) What were the main features of Enlightenment thought and how did it present a threat to the old order? (4) What impact did the Enlightenment have on Western culture and politics?

The Aristocracy

During the eighteenth century a relatively small, wealthy group of men dominated European society and politics. This social and ruling elite is often referred to as the aristocracy°, a term derived from a Greek word meaning the people who were the most fit to rule. In the eighteenth and nineteenth centuries the term *aristocracy* began to be applied not just to those few men who exercised political power but to the wealthiest members of society, especially those who owned land.

Within the aristocracy those who received official recognition of their hereditary status, including their titles of honor and special legal privileges, were known as the nobility°. In the Middle Ages the nobility consisted mainly of warriors who prided themselves on their courage and military skill. Over the course of many centuries these military functions became less important, although many noblemen, especially in central and eastern Europe, continued to serve as military officers in the armies of the state during the eighteenth century.

The aristocracy for the most part lived on their estates in the countryside, but they also spent time in the cities and towns, where many of them maintained townhouses or even large palaces. In cities that were centers of national government, such as Madrid and Berlin, aristocrats were prominent members of the royal court. As royal judges, some members of the aristocracy also took an active part in the administration of the law in the cities, just as they did in the provinces. The aristocracy, therefore, maintained a visible and powerful presence in urban society.

By the eighteenth century most European aristocracies included a relatively small group of titled noblemen (such as dukes and counts) who possessed great wealth and political influence and a much larger group of lesser aristocrats, occasionally referred to as gentry, who sometimes did not even bear hereditary titles. In Spain a vast gulf separated a few hundred titled noblemen, the *titulos*, and thousands of sometimes poverty-stricken *hidalgos*. In Britain a few hundred titled noblemen, known as peers, took precedence over some 50,000 families that belonged to the gentry. In Poland the nobility, known as the *szlachta*, was divided between a tiny, powerful group of magnates and some 700,000 noblemen of much more modest means who constituted more than 10 percent of the entire population.

MERCHANTS BECOME MEMBERS OF THE ARISTOCRACY IN ENGLAND

·················

Daniel Defoe is most famous for his novels, such as Robinson Crusoe *(1719) and* Moll Flanders *(1722), but he also wrote commentaries on contemporary English politics and society. In* The English Tradesman *(1726), which is excerpted here, Defoe argued that the wealth of England "lies mainly among the trading part of the people." To support his argument he presented evidence that many members of the English aristocracy came from trading backgrounds. England was unusual in the opportunities it offered for this type of upward social mobility, but Defoe nonetheless overstated his case. Even the English aristocracy of the eighteenth century was not open to such frequent entry from below.*

This being the case in England, and our trade being so vastly great, it is no wonder that the tradesmen in England fill the lists of our nobility and gentry; no wonder that the gentlemen of the best families marry tradesmen's daughters, and put their younger sons' apprentices to tradesmen; and how often do these younger sons come to buy the elder sons' estates, and restore the family, when the elder and head of the house, proving rakish and extravagant, has wasted his patrimony, and is obliged to make out the blessing of Israel's family, where the younger son brought the birthright, and the elder was doomed to serve him?

Trade is so far here from being inconsistent with a gentleman, that in short trade in England makes gentlemen, and has peopled this nation with gentlemen; for after a generation or two the tradesmen's children, or at least their grand-children, come to be as good gentlemen, statesmen, parliament-men, privy counselors, judges, bishops and noblemen, as those of the highest birth and the most ancient families; and nothing too high for them. Thus the earl of Haversham was originally a merchant; the late Secretary Craggs was the son of a barber; the present Lord Castlemaine's father was a tradesman, the great grandfather of the present Duke of Bedford the same, and so of several others . . .

We see the tradesmen of England, as they grow wealthy, coming every day to the herald's office, to search for the coats of arms of their ancestors, in order to paint them upon their coaches, and engrave them upon their furniture, or carve them upon the pediments of their new houses; and how often do we see them trace the registers of their families up to the prime nobility, or the most ancient gentry of the kingdom?

Source: From Daniel Defoe, The Complete English Tradesman, *Volume I, 1726.*

The aristocracy was not completely closed to outsiders. Commoners could gain entrance to it, especially its lower ranks, on the basis of acquired wealth or government service. It was not unusual for lawyers, wealthy merchants, or accomplished state servants to accumulate wealth during their careers, use that wealth to purchase land, and then receive a recognition of their new status in the form of a title of nobility. Many of the men to whom Peter the Great of Russia gave titles of nobility in the early eighteenth century were commoners. In France, where the old "nobility of the sword" could be distinguished from the "nobility of the robe" that ascended through state service, more than 20 percent of mid-eighteenth-century noblemen could not trace their noble status back further than two generations.

It was also possible for prosperous farmers to enter the aristocracy by purchasing land, hiring manual laborers to perform agricultural work, and then adopting the leisured lifestyle, dress, and manners of aristocrats. These men did not bear titles, but they expected to be regarded as having the same status as other members of the lesser aristocracy. Occasionally women of nonnoble birth gained entry into aristocratic society by marriage. This usually occurred when a nobleman who was greatly in debt arranged to marry his son to the daughter of a wealthy merchant in order to secure the dowry from the father of the bride. The dowry became the price of the daughter's admission to the nobility.

In the sixteenth and seventeenth centuries the size of the aristocracy had grown faster than the general population, both as a result of economic prosperity and the expansion of the state bureaucracy. In eastern Europe monarchs had increased the number of hereditary noblemen in order to gain their services for the state. In the eighteenth century the size of the aristocracy became stabilized and in many countries declined, as nobles took steps to restrict the number of newcomers from the lower orders. It was never a very large social group. The number of titled nobles was almost always less than 1 percent of the total population, and even when lesser nobles or gentry are taken into account, their total numbers usually amounted to no more than 4 percent. Only in Poland and Hungary did the percentages climb to more than 10 percent. Because of the small size of this social group, many nobles knew each other, especially those who were members of the same political assembly or who served together at court. The aristocracy was in fact the only real class° in European society before

■ **Marriage into the Nobility**

This painting by William Hogarth, in a series titled *Marriage à la Mode,* depicts the negotiation of a
marriage contract between an English earl and a wealthy London merchant. The earl, seated to the
left and pointing to his family tree, is negotiating with the merchant sitting across the table. The marriage will take place between the earl's vain son, sitting to the far right, and the distracted daughter of
the merchant, sitting next to him. The two individuals who are about to be married have no interest
in each other. The earl has incurred large debts from building the large mansion depicted in the rear,
and he intends to use the dowry to recover financially. By virtue of this transaction the daughter will
enter aristocratic society.

the early nineteenth century, in the sense that they formed a
cohesive social group with similar economic and political
interests, which they were determined to protect.

THE WEALTH OF THE ARISTOCRACY

The aristocracy was without question the wealthiest social
group in all European countries, and during the eighteenth
century many members of this group became even wealthier. The most prosperous aristocratic families lived in stu-
pendous luxury. They built magnificent homes on their
country estates and surrounded them with finely mani-
cured gardens. In the cities, where service at court demanded more of their time, they built spacious palaces, entertained guests on a lavish scale, and purchased everything
from expensive clothes to artistic treasures. They consumed
the best food and wines they could find at home or abroad.
This ostentatious display of wealth was intended to confirm
their social importance and status.

Most of the income that supported the lifestyle of the
aristocracy came directly or indirectly from land. In all
European countries the aristocracy owned at least one-
third of all the land, and in some countries, such as England
and Denmark, they owned more than four-fifths of it. Even
in the Italian states, where many of the nobility had come
from families of merchants, they controlled large estates.
Land provided the aristocracy with either feudal dues or
rents from the peasants who lived and worked on their
estates. Since noblemen did not engage in manual labor
themselves, it is not surprising that they later came to be
seen as unproductive parasites living off the labor of others.

During the first half of the eighteenth century the collective wealth of the European aristocracy reached new
heights. In eastern Europe that increase in wealth derived
mainly from the dramatic increase in the size of the population. With more serfs under their control, the landed nobility could increase the wealth they gained from their labor and dues. In western European countries, most

Size of the Aristocracy in European States in the Eighteenth Century

Country	Date	Number of Nobles and Lesser Aristocrats	Percent of the Population
Austria	1800	90,000	1.15%
France	1775	400,000	1.60
Great Britain & Ireland	1783	50,000	3.25
Hungary	1800	400,000	11.25
Poland	1800	700,000	11.66
Russia	1800	600,000	1.66
Spain	1797	402,000	3.80
Sweden	1757	10,000	0.50
Venice	1797	1,090	0.80

Sources: A. Corvisier, *Armies and Society in Europe, 1494–1789* (1976), pp. 113, 115; J. Meyer, *Noblesses et pouvoirs dans l'Europe d'Ancien Régime* (1973); M. Reinard and A. Armenguard, *Histoire Générale de la Population Modiale* (1961); J. Dewald, *The European Nobility* (1996), pp. 22–27.

notably Britain and France, the members of the aristocracy increasingly participated in other forms of economic activity. They operated rural industries such as mining and forestry. They entered the financial world by lending money to the government, thus serving the state in the process. They became involved in urban building projects and in the economic development of overseas colonies. Those who came from old families considered these pursuits to be beneath the status of a nobleman, but by investing at a distance nobles could give the impression that they were not actually engaged in the sordid transactions of the marketplace.

The members of the eighteenth-century aristocracy are often described as social and economic conservatives who were unable or unwilling to act in an entrepreneurial manner. The financial and commercial projects that many noblemen engaged in suggest that this reputation of the aristocracy is not fully deserved. Even on their landed estates, the aristocracy often behaved in a capitalistic manner during the seventeenth and eighteenth centuries. Many members of the aristocracy, both titled and untitled, adopted capitalist techniques of estate management to make their lands more productive. In England a nobleman, Charles Townshend, became widely known as "Turnip Townshend" when he introduced a crop rotation that included the lowly turnip. This type of agrarian entrepreneurship accounts for the accumulation of many great eighteenth-century aristocratic fortunes.

THE POLITICAL POWER OF THE ARISTOCRACY

The mid-eighteenth century also marked the apex of political power for the aristocracy in Europe. Having recovered from the economic and political turmoil of the mid-seventeenth century, when they suffered economic losses and experienced a temporary eclipse of their power, noblemen pursued various strategies to increase or preserve their share of local and national political power. In England, where royal power was greatly restricted as a result of the Glorious Revolution, the aristocracy gained political dominance. A small group of noblemen sat in the House of Lords, while the gentry formed the large majority of members of the House of Commons. After 1689 the English king could not rule without the cooperation of these two Houses of Parliament. The monarchy tried to control the proceedings of that assembly by creating parties of royal supporters within both houses. Since those parties were controlled by the king's ministers, who were themselves members of the nobility, the system allowed the aristocracy to dominate.

A similar situation prevailed in Poland and Hungary, where only the nobility were represented in the legislative assemblies of those countries. In Sweden and most German states the nobility formed a separate group that voted by themselves within the representative assemblies of those kingdoms. The country in Europe where members of the aristocracy exercised the least power and influence was the Dutch Republic. The traditional Dutch landed nobility remained a force to be reckoned with in eighteenth-century politics, but wealthy merchants and bankers held the balance of power in the seven Dutch provinces.

In absolute monarchies, where rulers had succeeded in restricting independent aristocratic power, members of the aristocracy exercised political power by controlling the institutions through which royal power was exercised. As we have seen in Chapter 15, absolute monarchs appeased the aristocracy by giving them control over provincial government and by recruiting them to occupy offices in the central bureaucracy of the state. The large bureaucracy of the eighteenth-century French state, for example, was run mainly by noblemen of the robe, a privileged group of approximately 2,000 officials who owed their noble status to their appointment to office rather than to heredity. In Russia during the early eighteenth century, tsars granted the nobility privileges and strengthened their powers over their serfs in order to secure the assistance the tsars needed to administer the Russian state at the local level.

The aristocracy exercised political power not only through bureaucratic institutions and provincial governments, but also through the judiciary. Members of the aristocracy often served as judges of the law courts of their kingdoms. In England noblemen and gentry served as the judges of almost all the common law courts, hearing cases both at the center of government at Westminster and in the provinces. In France noblemen staffed the nine regional *parlements* that registered royal edicts and acted as a court of appeal in criminal cases. The nobility controlled the central tribunals of the German kingdoms and principalities. At the local level the nobility exercised either a personal jurisdiction over the peasants who lived on their lands or an official jurisdiction as magistrates, such as the justices of the peace in each English county.

Britain provides a vivid example of the way in which the members of the landed class could use their judicial power to keep the lower classes in line: punishing petty crimes with harsh penalties. During the eighteenth century the incidence of crimes against property increased, especially when war created shortages of basic commodities. Those who occupied the middle ranks of society were the most frequent victims of these crimes, but as men of great wealth the aristocracy believed that all crimes against property threatened them as well. The aristocracy responded to this threat by passing legislation making even minor crimes against property, such as petty theft, capital offenses punishable by death. One victim of this harsh policy was John Burton, a lowly paid wagon driver who was hanged in 1744 for stealing two woolen caps.

Not all those convicted of such petty crimes suffered the same punishment as Burton. A few public executions every year were deemed sufficient to deter crime in a country that did not have a police force. Most convicted criminals were pardoned or had their sentences reduced. These displays of judicial mercy also served the purposes of the aristocracy by making people from the lower ranks of society dependent upon them for their lives. Exercising the power of pardon also strengthened their authority and made them appear sympathetic to the poor. In this way the British aristocracy helped to maintain the traditional deference paid to them from the lower ranks of society.

THE CULTURAL WORLD OF THE ARISTOCRACY

During the eighteenth century the aristocracies in western European countries followed a lifestyle that emphasized their learning, refinement, and appreciation of the fine arts. It had not always been that way. As late as the fifteenth century the aristocracy, which in the Middle Ages had been a warrior class, had a reputation for their indifference or even hostility to learning, and their conduct was often uncouth if not boorish. In eastern Europe a tradition of aristocratic illiteracy persisted into the eighteenth century. In western and central Europe, however, the pattern began to change in the sixteenth century, when members of the aristocracy started providing for the education of their children either at universities or in private academies. Even more important, aristocratic families began to acquire the manners and social graces that would be acceptable at court. By the eighteenth century the aristocracy, especially its upper ranks, became the backbone of what was then called "polite society."

The aristocracy also developed a sophisticated appreciation of high culture. Their homes housed large private collections of artwork that occasionally rivaled or even surpassed those of contemporary European monarchs. They were the main participants in the cultural life of European cities, especially Paris, London, Rome, Vienna, and Berlin. They formed the audiences of musical recitals, attended plays and operas in large numbers, and frequented the art galleries that were established in all the capitals of Europe. They also became the patrons of musicians, writers, and artists.

The homes of the eighteenth-century aristocracy reflected their preference for classicism°, a style in art, architecture, music, and literature that emphasizes proportion, adherence to traditional forms, and a rejection of emotion and enthusiasm. The classicism of the eighteenth century marked a step away from the more dynamic, imposing baroque style, which had flourished in the seventeenth century. Classicism celebrated the culture of ancient Greece and Rome. The revival of that culture in the eighteenth century in art and architecture is often referred to as neoclassicism°. The residences of the eighteenth-century aristocracy built in the classical style were perfectly proportioned and elegant without being overly decorated. Their Greek columns and formal gardens, lined with statues of classical figures, served as symbols of their cultural heritage. The classical architecture of the eighteenth century reflected the quiet confidence of the aristocracy that they, like their Greek and Roman forebears, occupied a dominant position in society.

Eighteenth-century music, which is likewise referred to as classical, reflected a concern for formal design, proportion, and concise melodic expression. The two greatest composers of the eighteenth century, Franz Joseph Haydn (1732–1809) and Wolfgang Amadeus Mozart (1756–1791), whose music was played before predominantly aristocratic audiences, became the greatest composers in this tradition. Classical music appealed less to the emotions than either the baroque music of the seventeenth century or the romantic music of the nineteenth century. The dominance of

■ **Chiswick House**

This house was built by Lord Burlington as library and reception hall on his estate near London about 1725. Symmetrical, balanced, and restrained, the building embodies many of the features of classicism. Chiswick House was modeled on the architecture of the Italian Andrea Palladio (1518–1580), who in turn drew his inspiration from the buildings of ancient Rome.

classicism in music as well as architecture during the eighteenth century reflected broader cultural currents in European intellectual life, when science and philosophy placed the highest value on the rationality and order of all material and human life.

Challenges to Aristocratic Dominance

Starting around the middle of the eighteenth century, the aristocracy endured increasingly acrimonious challenges to their power and criticisms of their values and lifestyles. They gradually lost the respect that they commanded from the lower ranks of society. By the end of the century European aristocracies had been significantly weakened. Their values had been called into question, while their political power and privileges had been eroded. A claim of nobility began to be viewed more as a sign of vanity than as a natural right to rule. The revolution that took place in France in the last decade of the eighteenth century, followed by the reform movements that developed in its wake throughout Europe in the early nineteenth century, brought the age of aristocracy to an end. Members of the aristocracy managed to regain some of what they had lost in the French Revolution, and they also showed their re-

sourcefulness by accommodating themselves to the new order, but they never recovered the dominant position they had held in the eighteenth century.

ENCOUNTERS WITH THE RURAL PEASANTRY

One set of challenges to the aristocracy came from the peasants and serfs who lived and worked on landed estates. This was the social group over whom the aristocracy exercised the most direct control. The control was most oppressive in central and eastern Europe, where the rural masses were serfs and therefore had no personal freedom. Landlords not only determined where serfs lived and when they married, but they also collected burdensome financial duties from them. Their plight was relieved only partially by the elimination of some of the burdens of serfdom. In Prussia and Austria these obligations were abolished by royal edict. The monarchs who instituted these reforms may have been responding to the demands of philosophes°, the intellectuals and writers of the age, who condemned the institution of serfdom for its cruelty and inefficiency. (See the section on the Enlightenment later in this chapter.) A more powerful motive, however, was the desire of monarchs to collect taxes from a peasantry that was spending the greater part of its income on financial duties owed to aristocratic landowners. Since the peasants still remained overburdened by financial obligations, emancipation did little to improve their lot.

In western Europe, where serfdom had for the most part given way to tenant ownership and leasehold tenure, the condition of the rural masses was only marginally better. After 1720, famines became less common than they had been in the late seventeenth century, making it possible for peasants to eke out an existence, but other economic pressures, including the elimination of common pasture rights and an increase in taxation, continued to weigh down on them. Over the course of the eighteenth century the number of peasants owning small plots of land declined. Many of those who leased land were forced to sell it as landowners consolidated their holdings. Consequently the number of landless laborers who worked for wages increased. By 1789 almost half the peasants in France had no land at all.

Under these circumstances the relationship between peasants and landowners continued to deteriorate. The realities of the marketplace gradually eroded the paternalistic concern that the nobility had traditionally shown for the welfare of their serfs or tenants. As the relationship between landlord and peasant became predominantly economic, the two parties became more distant. At the same time the gap between the culture of the elite and that of the common people, which as we have seen in Chapter 16 began in the seventeenth century, became more pronounced. The distance between landlord and peasant assumed real geographical form as landlords built their mansions away from the local village. By surrounding their homes with acres of parkland and gardens, they shielded themselves from the sight of the peasants working in the fields. Visual and personal contact between lord and peasant therefore became less frequent. The most direct contact a landlord made with the members of the lower classes was with the servants who worked in their homes.

As economic pressures on the peasants mounted, conflict between them and the aristocracy increased. Peasant resistance to their landlords could take a number of different forms. In some countries, most notably France, peasants could bring their grievances before village assemblies. These democratic institutions often succeeded in upholding peasants' demands, especially when royal officials in the provinces, who wished to collect their own taxes from the peasants, sided with them against the nobility.

Another option was to file a lawsuit against the lord, often with the assistance of the royal government. In Burgundy numerous peasant communities hired lawyers to take their seigneurs° or lords to court in order to prevent the imposition of new financial dues or the confiscation of communal village land. They were often aided in these efforts by the agents of the royal government, who wanted the peasants to be able to pay higher taxes imposed by the king. In these lawsuits, which became very common in the second half of the eighteenth century, peasants challenged not only the imposition of seigneurial dues but the very institution of aristocratic lordship. In 1765 one lawyer representing a peasant community in Champagne argued that the rights claimed by landowners "derive from the violence of

seigneurs" and had always been "odious." The language used in these cases inspired much of the rhetoric employed in the abolition of feudal privilege at the time of the French Revolution (see Chapter 18).

Peasants occasionally took more direct action against their landlords. In eastern France the number of incidents of rural violence against the property of seigneurs who tried to collect new duties increased toward the end of the eighteenth century. In Ireland a group known as the Whiteboys maimed cattle and tore down fences when landowners denied tenants their common grazing rights. Other forms of peasant action included poaching on the lands of landowners who claimed the exclusive right to hunt or trap game on their lands. The hunting activities of the tenants of the Earl of Uxbridge discussed at the beginning of this chapter are just one example of this type of lower-class resistance to aristocratic privilege.

In western Europe these acts of resistance did not develop into widespread peasant rebellion until the outbreak of the French Revolution in 1789. During the late eighteenth century incidents of rural violence were largely confined to individual villages. The reduction in the incidence of famine in the eighteenth century provides one possible explanation for this pattern of isolated, localized resistance. Without recurrent subsistence crises, the plight of the rural masses was not sufficiently desperate to provoke large-scale rebellion. The only expressions of collective unrest over the supply of food in western Europe during the eighteenth century were urban riots. These food riots usually took place in market towns or ports where grain was being exported. The violence was not directed against landlords but merchants or officials who were suspected of hoarding grain or fixing the price of bread.

The economic and social situation in eastern Europe differed from that of France, Britain, and other western European countries. In the east the deteriorating economic condition of the peasantry led to large-scale rebellion. Bohemia, Hungary, and Croatia, all of which lay within the boundaries of the Austrian Habsburg monarchy, witnessed large peasant revolts in the 1780s. The bloodiest of these revolts occurred in the province of Transylvania in 1784, when 30,000 peasant rebels butchered hundreds of noblemen and their families after those landowners had raised the dues owed to them as much as 1,000 percent.

The largest eastern European rural rebellion took place in Russia between 1773 and 1774. Pretending to be the murdered Tsar Peter III (d. 1762), the Cossack Emelian Pugachev (1726–1775) set out to destroy the Russian government of Catherine the Great and the nobility that served it. Pugachev assembled an army of 8,000 men, which staged lightning raids against government centers in the southern Urals. The most serious phase of this uprising took place when these troops marched into the agricultural regions of the country and inspired as many as three million serfs to revolt. Pugachev promised to abolish serfdom, end taxation, and eliminate the lesser aristocracy. The rebellion took a heavy toll, as the serfs and soldiers murdered some 3,000 nobles and officials. The Russian upper class feared that the rebellion would spread and destroy the entire social order, but government troops prevented that from happening by brutally suppressing the rising. Pugachev was transported to Moscow in an iron cage, where he was hanged, quartered, and burned.

Neither Pugachev nor the serfs who joined his rebellion envisioned the creation of a new social order. They still spoke in conservative terms of regaining ancient freedoms that had been lost. But this massive revolt, like others that resembled it, reflected the depth of the tension that prevailed between landlord and peasant, between noblemen and serf in the apparently stable world of the eighteenth century. That tension serves as one of the most striking and ominous themes of eighteenth-century social history.

THE SOCIAL POSITION OF THE BOURGEOISIE

In the cities and towns the most serious challenges to the aristocracy came not from the urban masses, who posed an occasional threat to all urban authorities, but from the bourgeoisie°. This social group was more heterogeneous than the aristocracy. It consisted of untitled people of property who lived in the cities and towns. The word *bourgeoisie* refers to those who were burghers—or those who had voting rights in the towns. Prosperous merchants and financiers formed the upper ranks of the bourgeoisie, while members of the legal and medical professions, second-tier government officials, and emerging industrialists occupied a social niche just below them. The bourgeoisie also included some skilled artisans and shopkeepers, sometimes referred to as the "petty bourgeoisie," who were far more prosperous than the large mass of urban laborers. The size of the bourgeoisie grew as the urban population of Europe expanded during the eighteenth century, even before the advent of industrialization. This social group was far more numerous in the North Atlantic countries of France, the Dutch Republic, and Britain than in the states of central and eastern Europe. In England the bourgeoisie accounted for about 15 percent of the total population in 1800, whereas in Russia they constituted no more than 3 percent.

Because it was possible for some members of the bourgeoisie to achieve upward social mobility and join the ranks of the aristocracy, the social and economic boundaries separating these wealthy townsmen from the lower ranks of the nobility could become blurred. In French towns it was often difficult to distinguish between wealthy financiers and noble bureaucrats. Although the two groups received their income from different sources, they both belonged to a wealthy, propertied elite. The middle and lower ranks of the bourgeoisie, however, gradually emerged as a social group that acquired its own social, political and cultural identity, distinct from that of the aristocracy.

Bourgeois identity was rooted in the towns, which had their own political institutions and their own social hierarchies. The bourgeoisie also possessed the means of effectively communicating with each other and thus were capable of forming common political goals. Their high rates of literacy made them the core of the new political force of public opinion that emerged in the cities and towns in the eighteenth century. The bourgeoisie made up the main audience of the thousands of newspapers, pamphlets, and books that rolled off the presses during the eighteenth century. A "public sphere" of activity, in which politically conscious townsmen participated, became a peculiar feature of bourgeois society. During the eighteenth and early nineteenth centuries the bourgeoisie became the leaders of movements seeking political change. They organized and became the main participants in the protest movements,

■ **Joshua Reynolds, *Mary, Duchess of Richmond* (ca. 1765)**

At a time when most European noblewomen were attracting criticism for their luxury and vanity, this prominent English duchess was depicted as being engaged in the simple domestic task of needlepoint. Some members of the aristocracy were able to deflect criticism of their lifestyle by adopting the habits of the bourgeoisie.

petitioning drives, and ultimately the revolutionary steps taken to challenge and replace established regimes.

THE BOURGEOIS CRITIQUE OF ARISTOCRACY

At the core of bourgeois identity lay a set of values that contrasted with those attributed to the aristocracy, especially the noblemen and noblewomen who gathered at court. Not all members of the bourgeoisie shared these values, nor did all members of the nobility embody those attributed to them. Nonetheless, the bourgeois critique of aristocratic society, which flourished mainly among the lower or petty bourgeoisie rather than the great merchants and financiers, contributed to the formation of bourgeois identity and helped to erode respect for the traditional aristocracy.

The bourgeois critique of the aristocracy consisted of three related themes. First was the allegation that the aristocracy lived a life of luxury, hedonism, and idleness that contrasted with the thrifty, sober, hardworking petty bourgeoisie. Unlike the aristocracy, the bourgeoisie did not display their wealth. Second, court nobles were accused of being sexually promiscuous and immoral, while their wives were depicted as vain flirts. There was some foundation to this charge, especially since the predominance of arranged marriages within the nobility had induced many noble husbands and wives to seek sexual partners outside marriage, a practice that was widely tolerated within aristocratic circles. By contrast, the bourgeoisie tended to enter into marriages in which both partners remained faithful to each other. Third, the members of the aristocracy were considered participants in a decadent international culture that often ignored or degraded the more wholesome, patriotic values of the bourgeoisie.

This critique of the aristocracy had profound political implications. It laid the foundation for the demands for equal political rights and the advancement of careers on the basis of talent rather than inherited wealth. These demands came not from the wealthy financiers, merchants, and capitalists who had the opportunity to ascend into the ranks of the nobility but from men of more modest wealth: holders of minor political offices, shopkeepers, and even skilled artisans. These people from the middle ranks of society, especially those who lived in the cities and towns, were most responsible for eventually reducing the influence of the aristocracy in European political and social life.

Criticism of aristocratic values and demands for liberty and equality received support from intellectuals who are usually identified with the movement known as the Enlightenment°. Not all of these thinkers and writers came from the middle ranks of society. Many of them were in fact members of the aristocracy or the beneficiaries of aristocratic patronage. Nevertheless their goal was to bring about the reform of society, and that inevitably led to a critique of aristocratic values and practices.

The Enlightenment

The Enlightenment was the defining intellectual and cultural movement of the eighteenth century. This complex movement had roots in the seventeenth century; the Scientific Revolution and the growth of philosophical skepticism were particularly important influences (see Chapter 16). Contemporaries used the word "Enlightenment" to describe their own intellectual outlook and achievements. For Immanuel Kant (1724–1804), the renowned German philosopher and author of *Critique of Pure Reason* (1781), enlightenment was the expression of intellectual maturity, the attainment of understanding solely by using one's reason without being influenced by dogma, superstition, or another person's opinion. For Kant enlightenment was both the process of thinking for oneself and the knowledge of human society and human nature that one achieved as a result. His famous exhortation, "Have the courage to know!" could serve as a slogan for the entire Enlightenment.

The Enlightenment is often referred to as a French movement, and it is true that the most famous of the European writers and thinkers of the Enlightenment, known as philosophes, were French. But French philosophes were inspired by seventeenth-century English sources, especially the writings of Isaac Newton (1647–1727) and John Locke (1632–1704), while German, Scottish, Dutch, Swiss, and Italian writers made their own distinctive contributions to Enlightenment thought. The ideas of the Enlightenment also spread to the Americas, where they inspired movements for political reform and national independence. The men and women of the Enlightenment thought of themselves not so much as French, British, or Dutch but as members of an international Republic of Letters, not unlike the international community of scholars that had arisen within the ancient Roman Empire and again at the time of the Renaissance. This cosmopolitan literary republic knew no geographical boundaries, and it was open to ideas from all lands. Its literary achievements, however, bore a distinctly Western stamp, and the idea they promoted became essential components of Western civilization.

THEMES OF ENLIGHTENMENT THOUGHT

Since the Enlightenment spanned the entire continent and lasted for more than a century, it is difficult to establish characteristics that all its participants shared. The Enlightenment was more a frame of mind, an approach to obtaining knowledge, as Kant claimed, than a set of clearly defined beliefs. Enlightenment writers, however, emphasized several intellectual themes that gave the entire movement a certain degree of unity and coherence.

Reason and the Laws of Nature

The first theme emphasized by Enlightenment thinkers was the elevation of human reason to a position of paramount philosophical importance. Enlightenment thinkers placed almost unlimited confidence in the ability of human beings to understand how the world operates. In previous ages philosophers had always found a place for human reason, but they also placed limits on it, especially when it came into conflict with religious faith. Medieval scholastic philosophers had tried to reconcile faith and reason, and that effort continued through the seventeenth century, particularly in scientific circles. In the eighteenth century, however, greater emphasis was placed on reason alone, which was believed to be superior to religious faith and the final arbiter of all disputes.

Confidence in human reason was closely associated with the belief that the operation of the entire universe was governed by natural laws that human reason could discover. This belief in natural law can be traced back to the ancient Greeks and to its revival and assimilation to Christian theology by the scholastics in the Middle Ages. Natural law acquired a distinctive character at the time of the Scientific Revolution. The search for and discovery of the laws governing such phenomena as gravitation, the circulation of the blood, and dynamics gradually led to the belief that all activity, including the behavior of human beings, was governed by similar laws.

The application of natural law to human society was the most novel and distinctive feature of Enlightenment thought. According to Enlightenment thinkers, scientific laws governed the functioning of society. There were even laws governing the passions and the operation of the human psyche. In his *Treatise of Human Nature* (1739–1740), the Scottish philosopher David Hume (1711–1776) offered a science of the human mind, which could be applied to politics and other human endeavors. Economics, too, received the same treatment. The Scottish economist Adam Smith (1723–1790), who described the operation of economic life in *The Wealth of Nations* (1776), believed that the economy was subject to inviolable laws, just like those that governed the movement of the heavens. The Enlightenment therefore gave birth to modern social science. Economics, political science, sociology, anthropology, and psychology all trace their origins as intellectual disciplines to this time. They were all based on the premise that reason could discover the laws or principles of human nature.

The search for natural laws governing all human life provides one explanation for the unprecedented interest of eighteenth-century writers in non-European cultures. During the Enlightenment a vast literature subjected the peoples of the world to detailed description, classification, and analysis. The first thorough, scholarly studies of Indian, Chinese, and Arab cultures were published during the middle and late eighteenth century. Egypt, a country that had been a part of the Ottoman Empire and isolated from the West since the sixteenth century, became the subject of a sizable literature, especially after the French occupied the country in 1798. There also was an increase in travel literature describing the societies that Europeans were encountering, some of them for the first time. Descriptions of the indigenous peoples of northwestern Canada, Australia, and Tahiti became readily available in the bookshops of Paris and London.

This cross-cultural scholarship, which was facilitated by the rapid growth of overseas empires after 1660, served the purpose of providing intellectuals with information enabling them to discover laws governing the behavior of all people. Some of the non-European countries that these scholars studied, such as China, had highly developed civilizations, whereas those of Native Americans and the indigenous people of the South Sea islands were far less developed. In both cases, however, educated people in the West began to consider these non-Western societies valid subjects of intellectual inquiry.

Religion and Morality

The spread of scientific knowledge in the eighteenth century gave the men of the Enlightenment a new understanding of God and his relationship to mankind. The Christian God of the Middle Ages and the Reformation period was an all-knowing, personal God who often intervened in the life of human beings. He could be stern and severe or gentle and merciful, but he was always involved in the affairs of humankind, which he governed through Providence. The gradual recognition that the universe was of unfathomable size and that it operated in accordance with natural laws made God appear to be more remote. Most philosophes believed that God was still the creator of the universe and the author of the natural laws that governed it, but they did not believe that he was still actively involved in its operation. God was the playwright of the universe, but not its director. This belief that God had created the universe, given it laws, and then allowed it to operate in a mechanistic fashion is known as deism°. In deism there was no place for the traditional Christian belief that God became human in order to redeem humankind from original sin.

Enlightenment thinkers, especially those who were deists, believed that human beings could use reason to discover the natural laws God had laid down at the time of creation. This inquiry included the discovery of the principles of morality, which no longer were to be grounded in Scripture. To observe the laws of God now meant not so much keeping his commandments but discovering what was natural and acting accordingly. In a certain sense God was being remade in a human image and was being identified with the natural instincts of human beings. In this way religion could become equated with the pursuit of human happiness.

If one believed that God established natural laws for all humanity, then doctrinal differences between religions became less important. All religions were valid to the extent that they led to an understanding of natural law. There was no one true religion, a point that the German dramatist and philosopher Gotthold Lessing (1729–1781) made in his play *Nathan the Wise* (1779) in response to the persistent questioning of a fictional Turkish sultan. This denial of the existence of one true religion led naturally to a demand for toleration of all religions, including those of non-Western peoples.

Enlightenment thinkers were highly critical of the superstitious and dogmatic character of contemporary Christianity, especially Roman Catholicism. French philosophes in particular had little use for priests, whom they castigated relentlessly in their letters and pamphlets. They minimized the importance of religious belief in the conduct of human life and substituted rational for religious values. They had little respect for the academic discipline of theology. The Swiss-born Parisian writer Baron d'Holbach (1723–1789), one of the few philosophes who could be considered an atheist—denying the existence of God at all—dismissed theology as a "pretended science." He claimed that its principles were "only hazardous suppositions, imagined by ignorance, propagated by enthusiasm or knavery, adopted by timid credulity, preserved by custom, which never reasons, and revered solely because not understood."

Epitomizing the new religious outlook of the Enlightenment was the Scottish moral philosopher David Hume, who is most famous for his treatise *An Enquiry Concerning Human Understanding* (1748). In that work he challenged the argument of the great rationalist philosopher René Descartes that God implants a number of clear and distinct ideas in our minds, from which we are able to deduce other truths. Hume's position was that our understanding derived from sense perceptions, not innate ideas. Even more important, he denied that there was any certain knowledge, thereby calling into question the authority of revealed truth and religious doctrine.

CREDULITY, SUPERSTITION, & FANATICISM.

Published by Longman, Hurst, Rees, & Orme, Jan.y 1.st 1809.

■ William Hogarth, *Credulity, Superstition, and Fanaticism* (1762)

Hogarth was a moralist who embodied the rationalism and humanitarianism of the Enlightenment. In this engraving he exposes the effects of fanatical religion, witchcraft, and superstition. The sermon has whipped the entire congregation into a highly emotional state. The woman in the foreground is Mary Tofts, who was believed to have given birth to rabbits. The boy next to her, allegedly possessed by the devil, vomits pins. The Protestant preacher's wig falls off, exposing the shaven head of a Roman Catholic monk. An unemotional Turk observes this scene from outside the window.

■ **David Hume, the Scottish Philosopher Who Represents the Mainstream of the Enlightenment in Great Britain**

Like John Locke, Hume explored the process by which the human mind reaches an understanding of the material world. Hume was committed to the application of science to the human psyche.

Hume's writing on religion reflected his skepticism. Raised a Presbyterian, he nevertheless rejected the revealed truths of Christianity on the ground that they had no rational foundation. The concept of Providence was completely alien to his philosophical position. An avowed deist, he expressed contempt for organized religion, especially Catholicism in France and Anglicanism in England. Organized religion, according to Hume, "rendered men tame and submissive, is acceptable to the magistrate, and seems inoffensive to the people, till at last the priest, having firmly established his authority, becomes the tyrant of human society."

Progress and Reform

Theories regarding the stages of human development, coupled with the commitment of philosophes to the improvement and ultimate transformation of society, contributed to a belief in the progress of civilization. Until the eighteenth century the very notion of progress was alien to even the most highly educated Europeans. Those who held political power had dedicated themselves to maintaining the social and political order, not its transforma-

tion. Programs of reform were almost always associated with the restoration of a superior golden age rather than the realization of something new and different. If movement took place, it was cyclical rather than progressive. Even the original meaning of the word *revolution* was the path of a planet that came full circle in its orbit, not the creation of a new order. Now, however, the possibility of improvement began to dominate philosophical and political discussion. The Enlightenment was largely responsible for making this belief in progress, especially toward the attainment of social justice, a prominent feature of modern Western culture.

Some Enlightenment thinkers, using evidence gained from encounters with non-Western people, argued that all civilizations progressed gradually from relatively simple to more complex economies and societies. David Hume, Adam Smith, and their fellow Scotsman Adam Ferguson (1723–1816) identified four stages of human development. The first was characterized by hunting and gathering, the second by pastoral farming, the third by agriculture, and the last by commerce. The French philosophe the Marquis de Condorcet (1743–1794) focused more on intellectual progress. In *A Sketch for a Historical Picture of the Progress of the Human Mind* (1795), Condorcet identified nine distinct epochs in human history. He predicted that in the tenth and final epoch humankind would achieve a state of perfection in which rational moral judgments would inform efficient government policy.

Another source of the Enlightenment's belief in progress was the conviction that corrupt institutions could be reformed, thereby allowing societies to advance to a higher level and realize their full potential. The system of taxation, bureaucratic institutions, established churches, and the institution of monarchy itself all became the targets of Enlightenment reformers. The judicial institutions of government were particularly susceptible to this type of reforming zeal. Campaigns arose to eliminate the administration of judicial torture as well as capital punishment. All of this was intended to establish a more humane, civilized society.

The intellectual inspiration to this movement for legal reform was the work of the Italian jurist Cesare Beccaria (1738–1794). In his *Essay on Crimes and Punishments* (1764), Beccaria argued that punishment should be used not to exact retribution for crimes but to rehabilitate the criminal and to serve the interests of society. "In order that every punishment may not be an act of violence committed by one man or by many against a single individual," wrote Beccaria, "it ought to be above all things public, speedy, necessary, and . . . proportioned to the crime." He called for the abolition of capital punishment and the imprisonment of convicted felons. The prison, which prior to the eighteenth century had been little more than a jail or holding facility, was now to become a symbol of the improvement of society.

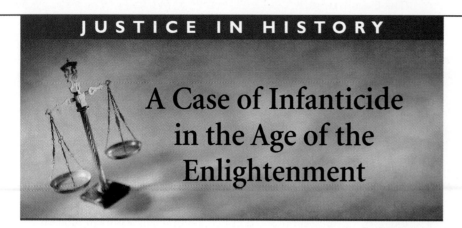
A Case of Infanticide in the Age of the Enlightenment

A mid-eighteenth century trial of a young French woman charged with killing her new-born child provides a window into the life of women who occupied the lower rungs of French society, in contrast to those who frequented the court and met in salons. The trial also raises the larger questions, debated in French and European judicial circles during the time of the Enlightenment, of how society should deal with the mothers of illegitimate children and whether the punishments prescribed for infanticide, or the killing of a young child, were proportionate to the crime.

In August 1742 Marie-Jeanne Bartonnet, a 21-year-old unmarried woman from a small French village in Brie, moved to Paris, where she took up residence with Claude le Queux, whom she had known in her youth, and Claude's sister. At that time Bartonnet was seven months pregnant. On October 22 Bartonnet caused a ruckus in the middle of the night when she went to the toilet and began groaning loudly and bleeding profusely. When her neighbors found her, and when she asked for towels for the blood, they suspected that she had had a miscarriage and called for a midwife. By the time the midwife arrived, it was clear that the delivery had already taken place and that the infant had fallen down the toilet to the cesspool five stories below. Suspecting that Bartonnet had killed the baby, the proprietress of the building reported her to the nearest judicial officer. The next day judicial authorities returned

to the building and found the body of the dead infant in the cesspool. An autopsy revealed that the child's skull had been dented either by a blunt instrument or a fall. After a medical examination of Bartonnet revealed the signs of having just delivered a baby, she was arrested and imprisoned for the crime of infanticide.

Bartonnet came very close to being executed, but the strict procedures of French justice saved her from paying the ultimate price for her apparent crime. In the seventeenth and eighteenth centuries French criminal justice had established clear criteria for determining the guilt or innocence of a person accused of a crime. These procedures involved a systematic interrogation of the accused (only rarely under torture), the deposition of witnesses, the evaluation of physical evidence, and the confrontation of the accused with the witnesses who testified against her. There also was a mandatory review of the case, which involved a further interrogation of the defendant, before the Parlement of Paris, the highest court in northern France.

The interrogations of Bartonnet did not give her judges much evidence on which they could convict her. When asked the name of the village where she had lived in Brie, she told her interrogators, "It's none of your business." She denied that she even knew she was pregnant, refused to name the man with whom she had had intercourse, and claimed that she had mistaken her labor pains for colic or diar-

rhea. She denied picking her baby off the floor of the toilet after the delivery and throwing it into the cesspool. When presented with the baby's corpse, she claimed she did not recognize it.

After this interrogation, Bartonnet was given the opportunity to challenge the testimony of the witnesses who had seen her the night of the delivery. The most damning testimony came from Madame Pâris, the wife of the proprietor, who had found Bartonnet on the toilet and thus could verify the circumstances of the clandestine delivery. Bartonnet's inability to challenge the testimony of Madame Pâris led directly to her initial conviction. After reviewing the entire dossier of evidence, the king's attorney recommended conviction for concealing her pregnancy, hiding her delivery, and destroying her child. French criminal procedure entrusted the decision of guilt or innocence to the judges themselves, and on November 27 they voted that Bartonnet should be executed by hanging.

Marie-Jeanne Bartonnet's fate, however, was not yet sealed. When her case went on appeal to the Parlement of Paris, Bartonnet repeated her statement that she went to the toilet but did not know whether she had given birth. Even though her execution was warranted by terms on an edict of 1557 that defined the crime of infanticide, the judges of this court voted to commute her sentence to a public whipping, banishment from the jurisdiction of the parlement of Paris, and confis-

■ **A Woman Accused of Murder in the Eighteenth Century**

With the exception of infanticide—the crime for which Marie-Jeanne Bartonnet was tried and convicted—few women were tried for capital crimes in the eighteenth century. One exception was Sarah Malcolm, a 22-year-old Englishwoman, shown here in a portrait by William Hogarth (1733). Malcolm was executed for slitting the throat of a wealthy lady in London.

cation of her property. The basis of this decision appears to have been the absence of any proof that she had deliberately killed her baby. Indeed, its injuries could have been caused by its fall down the drain pipe into the cesspool. There was also the persistent refusal of the defendant to make a confession. She may have been lying, but it is equally possible that once she had delivered the baby, which happened very quickly, she convinced herself that it had not happened.

Bartonnet's trial for infanticide stands at the end of a long period of intense prosecution of this crime. Trials of this sort declined as cities and towns built foundling hospitals for abandoned infants and as the moral outrage for illegitimacy was redirected from the pregnant mother to the illegitimate father. The new legal values promoted at the time of the Enlightenment, moreover, made it less likely that any woman or man would be executed for this or any other crime. ■

Questions of Justice

1. As in many trials, the facts of this case can be used to support different claims of justice. If you had been the prosecutor in this trial, what position would you have taken to prove the crime of infanticide? If you had been defending Marie-Jeanne Bartonnet, what arguments would you have used in her defense?

2. In his *Essay on Crimes and Punishments* (1764), Beccaria recommended that punishments be determined strictly in accordance with the social damage committed by the crime. What would Beccaria have said about the original sentence of death in this case? What would he have said about the modified sentence handed down by the Parlement of Paris?

Taking It Further

Michael Wolfe, ed. *Changing Identities in Early Modern France.* 1997. Gives a full account of Marie-Jeanne Bartonnet's trial for infanticide.

VOLTAIRE AND THE SPIRIT OF THE ENLIGHTENMENT

The philosophe who captured all the main themes as well as the spirit of the Enlightenment was the writer and philosopher François Marie Arouet (1694–1778), known universally by his pen name, Voltaire. Born into a French bourgeois family, Voltaire became one of the most prominent and prolific writers of the eighteenth century. Although he wrote for a fairly broad, predominantly bourgeois audience, and although he waged war against the injustices of aristocratic society, he was comfortable in the homes of the nobility and at the courts of European monarchs, especially that of Frederick the Great of Prussia. Voltaire's main career was as an author. He wrote plays and novels as well as poems, letters, essays, and history. These writings revealed his commitment to scientific rationality, his contempt for established religion, and his unflagging pursuit of liberty and justice.

Like many men of the Enlightenment, Voltaire developed a deep interest in science. He acquired much of his scientific knowledge from a learned noblewoman, Madame du Châtelet, a scientist and mathematician who translated the works of Newton into French. Madame du Châtelet became Voltaire's mistress, and the two lived together with her tolerant husband in their country estate in eastern France. The sexual freedom they experienced was characteristic of many Enlightenment figures, who rejected the Christian condemnation of sexual activity outside marriage and who justified their behavior on the basis of natural law and the pursuit of happiness. From Madame du Châtelet, Voltaire acquired not only an understanding of Newton's scientific laws but also a commitment to women's education and equality. Voltaire lived with her until she died in 1749 while giving birth to a child that was fathered neither by Voltaire nor her husband.

Voltaire's belief in a Newtonian universe—one governed by the universal law of gravitation—laid the foundation for his deism and his attacks on contemporary Christianity. In his *Philosophical Dictionary* (1764), he lashed out at established religion and the clergy, Protestant as well as Catholic. In a letter to another philosophe attacking religious superstition he pleaded, "Whatever you do, crush the infamous thing." In Voltaire's eyes Christianity was not only unreasonable; it was vulgar and barbaric. He condemned the Catholic Church for the slaughter of millions of indigenous people in the Americas on the grounds that they had not been baptized, as well as the executions of hundreds of thousands of Jews, witches, and heretics in Europe. All of these people were the victims of "barbarism and fanaticism."

Voltaire's indictment of the Church for these barbarities was matched by his scathing criticism of the French government for a series of injustices, including his own imprisonment for insulting the regent of France. While living in England for three years, Voltaire became an admirer of English legal institutions, which he considered more hu-

■ **The Calas Family in Prison**
When Jean Calas was accused of having murdered his son, Marc-Antoine, to prevent his conversion to Catholicism, he was imprisoned together with his wife, another son, two daughters, a servant, and a guest who had been in the house the night Marc-Antoine had hanged himself. Jean Calas was tortured and executed. Voltaire intervened in the case, leading King Louis XV to reverse the judgment and compensate the Calas family.

mane and just than those of his native country. Using England as a model, he appealed for the implementation of various political reforms in France. He deplored those "who reduce men to a state of slavery by force and downright violence." A tireless advocate of individual liberty, he became a regular defender of victims of injustice, including Jean Calas, a Protestant shopkeeper from Toulouse who had been tortured and executed for allegedly murdering his son because he had expressed a desire to convert to Catholicism. The boy had in fact committed suicide.

Voltaire showed a commitment to placing his knowledge in the service of humanitarian causes. In his most famous novel, *Candide* (1759), the character by that name challenges the smug confidence of Dr. Pangloss, the tutor who repeatedly claims that they lived in "the best of all possible worlds." At the end of the novel Candide responds to this refrain by declaring that "we must cultivate our garden." Voltaire, instead of being content with the current condition of humankind, was demanding that we put our theories into practice by working actively to improve society.

ENLIGHTENMENT POLITICAL THEORY

Enlightenment thinkers are known most widely for their political theories, especially those that supported the causes of liberty and reform. The men and women of the Enlightenment did not, however, share a common political ideology, nor did they agree on the most desirable type of political society. They did share a belief that politics was a science, which like the cosmos had its own natural laws. The title of one of David Hume's treatises, *That politics may be reduced to a science* (1741), reflects a belief that most Enlightenment political writers endorsed. They also thought of the state in secular rather than religious terms. There was little place in Enlightenment thought for the divine right of kings. Nor was there a place for the Church in the government of the state. On other issues, however, there was little consensus. Three thinkers in particular illustrate the range of Enlightenment political thought: Montesquieu, Rousseau, and Paine.

Baron de Montesquieu:
The Separation of Powers

The most influential political writer of the Enlightenment was the French philosophe Charles-Louis de Secondat, Baron de Montesquieu (1689–1785). The son of a nobleman of the robe from Bordeaux, Montesquieu had a legal education and also developed an early interest in science. His political thought owed as much to his study of history and anthropology as to the study of law and science. His first book, *The Persian Letters,* published anonymously in Holland in 1721, was a brilliant satire of Western government and society through the eyes of two Persian aristocrats traveling in Europe. It laid the groundwork for a much more scholarly and substantial contribution to political

CHRONOLOGY

Literary Works of the Enlightenment

1687	Isaac Newton, *Mathematical Principles of Natural Philosophy*
1690	John Locke, *An Essay Concerning Human Understanding*
1721	Baron de Montesquieu, *The Persian Letters*
1738	Voltaire, *Elements of the Philosophy of Newton*
1739	David Hume, *Treatise of Human Nature*
1748	Baron de Montesquieu, *Spirit of the Laws*
1748	David Hume, *An Enquiry Concerning Human Understanding*
1751	First volume of Diderot and d'Alembert's *Encyclopedia*
1755	Jean-Jacques Rousseau, *Discourse on the Origin of Inequality among Men*
1759	Voltaire, *Candide*
1762	Jean-Jacques Rousseau, *The Social Contract* and *Emile, or on Education*
1763	Voltaire, *Treatise on Toleration*
1764	Cesare Beccaria, *Essay on Crimes and Punishments*
1764	Voltaire, *Philosophical Dictionary*
1776	Adam Smith, *The Wealth of Nations*
1781	Immanuel Kant, *Critique of Pure Reason*
1791	Thomas Paine, *The Rights of Man*
1792	Mary Wollstonecraft, *A Vindication of the Rights of Woman*
1795	Marquis de Condorcet, *Progress of the Human Mind*

theory, *Spirit of the Laws* (1748). Often compared to Aristotle because of the range of his thought, Montesquieu interwove commentaries on natural-law, religion, morals, virtue, climate, and liberty. Unlike Hobbes, Locke, and the other natural law philosophers who preceded him, Montesquieu was not concerned with the origin of government or with the establishment of a universal model of politics. Rather, he treated the laws of a country in historical perspective and within the context of that country's religion, morality, climate, geography, and culture. His political writing was scientific mainly in its empirical approach to its subject, and in the comparisons it made between politics on the one hand and Newtonian physics on the other.

Montesquieu argued that there were three forms of government: republics, monarchies, and despotisms, each of which had an activating or inspirational force. In republics that force was civic virtue, in monarchies it was honor, and in despotisms it was fear. In each form of government there was a danger that the polity could degenerate: The virtue of republics could be lost, monarchies could become corrupt, and despotisms could lead to repression. The key to maintaining moderation and preventing this degeneration of civil society was the law of each country. Ideally the law of a country should provide for the separation and balance of political powers. Only in that way could degeneration be avoided and moderation assured.

Montesquieu used his knowledge of the British political system, which he had studied firsthand while living in England for two years, to propose that the key to good government was the separation of executive, legislative, and judicial power. He was particularly concerned about the independence of the judiciary. Montesquieu was unaware of how legislative and executive powers actually overlapped in eighteenth-century Britain, but his emphasis on the importance of a separation of powers became the most durable of his ideas. It had profound influence on the drafting of the Constitution of the United States of America in 1787.

Jean-Jacques Rousseau: The General Will

Also influential as a political theorist was the Swiss philosophe Jean-Jacques Rousseau (1712–1778), who as a young man moved from Geneva to Paris and became a member of a prominent intellectual circle. Rousseau does not conform to the model of the typical Enlightenment thinker. His distrust of human reason and his emotionalism separated him from Hume, Voltaire, and another great French philosophe, Denis Diderot (1713–1784). That distrust laid the foundations for the romantic reaction against the Enlightenment in the early nineteenth century (see Chapter 21.) Instead of celebrating the improvement of

---

MONTESQUIEU SATIRIZES EUROPEAN WOMEN

·················

Montesquieu's first publication, The Persian Letters *(1721), is a clever satire on French society. The book consists of a series of letters written to and from two fictional Persian travelers, Usbek and Rica. Because the characters come from a radically different culture, Montesquieu was able to avoid official censure for presenting his irreverent views. The Persians refer to the king as a great magician who has the power to persuade men to kill one another though they have no quarrel, and to the pope as "an old idol worshipped out of habit." Montesquieu's satire was all the more biting because Europeans harbored deep contempt for the world of the Middle East, which they thought of as a region ruled by oriental despots and inhabited by people with lax standards of sexual morality. In this passage from one of Usbek's early letters to one of his wives in the harem, Montesquieu presents a favorable image of the oriental harem to contrast with the aristocratic women of eighteenth-century France.*

Usbek to Roxana, at the seraglio in Ispahan

How fortunate you are, Roxana, to live in the gentle land of Persia and not in these poisoned regions where neither shame nor virtue are known! You live in my seraglio as in the bower of innocence, inaccessible to the assaults of mankind; you rejoice in the good fortune that makes it impossible for you to fall. No man has sullied you with lascivious glances; even your father-in-law, during the freedom of the festivals, has never seen your lovely mouth, because you have never failed to cover it with a sacred veil. . . .

If you had been raised in this country, you would not have been so troubled. Women here have lost all restraint. They present themselves barefaced to men, as if inviting conquest; they seek attention, and they accompany men to the mosques. On walks, even to their rooms; the service of eunuchs is unknown. In place of the noble simplicity and charming modesty which is the rule among you, one finds here a barbaric impudence, to which one cannot grow accustomed. . . .

When you enhance the brilliance of your complexion with lovely coloring, when you perfume all your body with the most precious essences, when you dress in your most beautiful garments, when you seek to distinguish yourself from your companions by the charm of your dancing or the delight of your song, when you graciously compete with them in beauty, sweetness and vivacity, then I cannot imagine that you have any other object than that of pleasing me. . . .

But what am I to think of European women? Their art in making up their complexions the ornaments they display, the care they give to their bodies, their preoccupation with pleasing are so many stains on their virtue and outrages to their husbands.

Source: From Baron de Montesquieu, *The Persian Letters*, translated by George R. Healy (Hackett, 1999), Letter 26. Reprinted by permission of Hackett Publishing Company, Inc. All rights reserved.

■ **Differences Among the Philosophes**

This satirical print shows Rousseau, to the left, and Voltaire engaged in heated debate. The two men were both major figures in the Enlightenment, but they differed widely in temperament and in their philosophical and political views. Rousseau was very much the rebel, who unlike Voltaire distrusted reason and articulated highly egalitarian political principles.

isting political and social order with an uncompromising attack on aristocracy and monarchy. He linked absolute monarchy, which he referred to as despotism, with the court and especially with the vain, pampered, conceited, and overdecorated aristocratic women who wielded political influence with the king and in the salons. As an alternative to this aristocratic, monarchical, and feminized society Rousseau proclaimed the sovereignty of the people. Laws were to be determined by the General Will, by which he meant the consensus of a community of citizens (but not necessarily the vote of the majority).

As a result of his writings Rousseau became associated with radical republican and democratic ideas that flourished at the time of the French Revolution. One indication of that radicalism was the fact that *The Social Contract* was banned not only in absolutist France but in the republics of the Netherlands and Switzerland as well. Rousseau was also criticized for justifying authoritarian rule. His argument that the General Will placed limits on individual civil liberty and encouraged autocratic leaders, such as the radical Maximilien Robespierre at the time of the French Revolution, to claim that their dictatorial rule embodied that General Will.

Thomas Paine: The Rights of Man

Of all the Enlightenment political theorists, the English publicist and propagandist Thomas Paine (1737–1809) was arguably the most radical. Paine was influenced by Rousseau, Diderot, and Voltaire, but his radicalism was cultivated mainly by his intense involvement in the political world of revolutionary America, where he became politically active in the 1770s. In *Common Sense* (1776) Paine presented the case for American independence from Britain. This included a passionate statement of human freedom, equality, and rationality. It also involved a vicious attack on hereditary monarchy and an eloquent statement for the sovereignty of the law. At the time of the French Revolution, Paine continued to call for the establishment of a republic in France and in his native country. In his most widely circulated work, *The Rights of Man* (1791), he linked the institution of monarchy with the aristocracy, which he referred to as "a seraglio of males, who neither collect the honey nor form the hive but exist only for lazy enjoyment."

The title of *The Rights of Man* identified a theme that appeared in much Enlightenment writing. Like Diderot and Rousseau, Paine spoke the language of natural rights. Until

society as it evolved into higher forms, Rousseau had a negative view of the achievements of civilization. In his novel *Emile, or on Education* (1762) he wrote, "All our wisdom consists of servile prejudices, all our customs are but enslavement, constraint, or bondage. Social man is born, lives and dies enslaved. At birth he is bound up with swaddling clothes; at his death he is nailed down in a coffin. For the whole of his existence as a human being he is chained up by our institutions." Rousseau idealized the uncorrupted condition of human beings in the state of nature, providing support for the theory of the "noble savage." Human beings could not ever return to that original natural state, but Rousseau did hold out the hope of recreating an idealized golden age when they were not yet alienated from themselves and their environment.

Rousseau's political theories were hardly conventional, but they appealed to some segments of the reading public. In his *Discourse on the Origin of Inequality among Men* (1755) and *The Social Contract* (1762) he challenged the ex-the Enlightenment, rights were considered legal privileges acquired by royal charter or by inheritance. One had a right, for example, to a particular piece of land or to elect representatives from one's county or town. Those rights could be surrendered under certain circumstances, such as when a person sold land. The new emphasis on natural law, however, led to the belief that simply by being a human being one acquired natural rights that could never be taken away. The American Declaration of Independence (1776), which was drafted by Thomas Jefferson, presented an eloquent statement of these God-given inalienable rights, which included "life, liberty and the pursuit of happiness." In defending that independence, Paine claimed that "a government of our own is our natural right." Since the eighteenth century those rights have been extended to include newly defined activities, such as the right to privacy, but the language in which such rights are asserted is a legacy of the Enlightenment.

WOMEN AND THE ENLIGHTENMENT

The claim advanced by Enlightenment thinkers that all human beings are equal in a state of nature did not lead to a widespread belief that on the basis of natural law men and women are equal. Quite to the contrary, many philosophes, including Diderot and Rousseau, argued that women were different in nature from men and that they should be confined to an exclusively domestic role as chaste wives and mothers. Rousseau also insisted on the separate education of girls.

This patriarchal argument supported the emerging theory of separate spheres°, which held that men and women should conduct their lives in different social and political environments. The identification of women with the private, domestic sphere laid the foundation for the ideology of female domesticity, which became popular in bourgeois society in the nineteenth century. But it denied them the freedom that aristocratic women in France had acquired during the eighteenth century, especially those who participated in polite society. It also continued to deny them civil rights. Like women in ancient Sparta, whose situation served as the model for a number of Enlightenment thinkers, eighteenth-century women could not vote and could not initiate lawsuits on their own authority. They were not full members of civil society.

Only in the 1790s did writers begin to use the language and ideas of the Enlightenment to advance the argument for the full equality of men and women. The first of these appeals came from Condorcet, who published *On the Admission of Women to the Rights of Citizenship* in 1789. In that pamphlet he proposed that all women who own property be given the right to vote. He later called for universal suffrage for all men and women on the grounds that they all shared a common human nature. A similar appeal came from the French dramatist and revolutionary activist Marie Olympe Aubrey de Gouges (1748–1793). At the very begin-

ning of the French Revolution, de Gouges, the daughter of a butcher, proposed that the revolutionary manifesto adopted by the French National Assembly, *Declaration of the Rights of Man and Citizen* (1789), be extended to include women as well as men.

De Gouges drafted her most famous publication, *The Rights of Woman* (1791), as a proposed appendix to that constitutional document. She took the authors of the *Declaration* to task for their failure to address the problem of women's civil rights and responsibilities with the same determination and enthusiasm they had manifested in proclaiming the rights of men. Revealing her debt to Rousseau, she proposed in Article VI of her document that "the law must be the expression of the general will. All citizens, men and women, must concur, personally or through their representatives, in its creation. It must be the same for everyone: every citizen, man and woman, being equal in its eyes, must be equally eligible for all high honors, public offices, and positions according to their merits . . ." Using more of Rousseau's language, she went on to propose a "social contract" between man and woman that recognized, among other things, common ownership of property. None of de Gouges's proposals were implemented by the French government, but she did succeed in drawing attention to the contradictions between the rhetoric and the reality of natural rights.

De Gouges's English contemporary, Mary Wollstonecraft (1759–1797), was the most famous of the Enlightenment's advocates of women's rights. Inspired by the events of the French Revolution, and angered by the conservative English response to the events taking place in France, Wollstonecraft wrote *A Vindication of the Rights of Woman* (1792). This treatise, which embodies a stinging critique of eighteenth-century polite society, has become a founding document of modern feminism. In it Wollstonecraft made an eloquent appeal for extending civil and political rights to women and even proposed that women elect their own representatives to legislatures. Her most original and innovative proposals, however, dealt with education. She claimed that in order for women to take control of their lives and to become the full equals of men within marriage and in the political realm, girls had to acquire greater knowledge and skill and learn how to support themselves. Wollstonecraft insisted that the education of women must be made equal and identical to that of men. In this way she challenged the arguments presented by Rousseau and many other male Enlightenment thinkers that cultural and social differences between men and women should be maintained because they were "natural."

THE ENLIGHTENMENT AND SEXUALITY

One facet of Enlightenment thought that had a profound effect on the position of women in society was the appeal for greater sexual permissiveness. Many philosophes, including Voltaire, Diderot, and Holbach, remained openly

DIDEROT CRITICIZES WESTERN RELIGION AND MORALITY

In 1771 Louis-Antoine de Bougainville published Voyage, *an account of life on the recently discovered island of Tahiti in which he attributed to the natives a high degree of sexual permissiveness. The following year Denis Diderot wrote a supplement to this piece of travel literature in which he imagined an encounter between a French priest and a Tahitian man. Diderot, who was a critic of Western colonialism, used this opportunity to criticize the repressive morality of European society and the religion that upheld that moral code. In this exchange Orou, a Tahitian man, offered the chaplain the opportunity to sleep with either his wife or one of his three daughters.*

The chaplain replied that his religion, his holy orders, his moral standards and his sense of decency all prevented him from accepting Orou's invitation. Orou answered: "I don't know what this thing is that you call 'religion,' but I can only have a low opinion of it because it forbids you to partake of an innocent pleasure to which Nature, the sovereign mistress of us all, invites everybody. It seems to prevent you from bringing one of your fellow creatures into the world, from doing a favor asked of you by a father, a mother and their children, from repaying the kindness of a host, and from enriching a nation by giving it an additional citizen. I don't know what it is that you call 'holy orders' but your chief duty is to be a man and to show gratitude. I am not asking you to take my moral standards back with you to your own country, but Orou, your host and your friend, begs you merely to lend yourself to the morality of Tahiti. Is our moral code a better or worse one than your own? This is an easy question to answer. Does the country you were born in have more people than it can support? If it does, then your morals are neither better nor worse than ours. Or can it feed more people than it now has? Then our morals are better than yours. . . ."

Source: From Denis Diderot, *Rameau's Nephew and Other Works,* translated by Jacques Barzun and Ralph H. Bowen. Copyright © 1956 by Jacques Barzun and Ralph H. Bowen. Reprinted 2001 by Hackett Publishing Company, Inc. Reprinted by permission of Hackett Publishing Company, Inc. All rights reserved.

---

critical of the strict standard of sexual morality enforced by Christian churches. The basic argument of the philosophes was that sexual activity should not be restricted because it was pleasurable and a source of happiness. The arbitrary prohibitions imposed by the Church contradicted human nature. European encounters with pagan natives of the South Pacific, who were reported to have enjoyed great sexual permissiveness, were used to reinforce this argument based on human nature. Diderot appealed to the sexual code of the Tahitians in his attack upon Christian sexual morality.

Many philosophes, including Voltaire, practiced what they preached and lived openly with women out of wedlock. Other members of wealthy society adopted an even more libertine lifestyle. The Venetian adventurer and author Giacomo Casanova (1725–1798), who was expelled from a seminary for his immorality, gained fame for his life of gambling, spying, and seducing thousands of women. To one young Spanish woman, who resisted his advances in order to protect her virginity, he said: "You must abandon yourself to my passion without any resistance, and you may rest assured I will respect your innocence." Casanova's name soon became identified with sexual seduction.

The violent excesses to which this type of eighteenth-century sexual permissiveness could lead can be seen in the career of Alphonse Donatien François, the Marquis de Sade (1740–1814). The author of licentious libertine narratives, including his own memoirs and an erotic novel, *Justine* (1793), de Sade described the use of violence in sexual en-counters and thus gave rise to the word *sadism* to describe the pleasurable administration of pain. He spent twenty-seven years in prison for his various sexual offenses.

It makes sense that noblemen like Casanova and de Sade would have adopted the libertine values of the Enlightenment thinkers. Somewhat more remarkable was the growth of public sexual permissiveness among all social groups, including the rather prim and proper bourgeoisie and the working poor. Erotic literature, such as John Cleland's *Memoirs of a Woman of Pleasure* (1749), and pornographic prints achieved considerable popularity in an increasingly commercialized society, while prostitution became more open and widespread. Voltaire and Diderot might not have approved of this literature or these practices, but their libertine, anti-Christian, materialist outlook helped to prepare the ground for their acceptance.

The Impact of the Enlightenment

The ideas of the Enlightenment spread to every country in Europe as well as to the Americas. They inspired programs of reform and radical political movements. Enlightenment thought, however, did not become the property of the entire population. It appealed mainly to the educated and the relatively prosperous and failed to penetrate the lower levels of society.

THE SPREAD OF ENLIGHTENED IDEAS

The ideas of the Enlightenment spread rapidly among the literate members of society, mainly by means of print. During the eighteenth century, print became the main medium of formal communication. The technology of printing allowed for the publication of materials on a scale unknown a century before. Pamphlets, newspapers, and books poured off presses, not only in the major cities but in provincial towns as well. Literacy rates increased dramatically throughout western Europe. The highly educated still constituted a minority of the population, but the better part of the aristocracy and many of those who occupied the middle ranks of society could read and write. By 1750 more than half the male population of France and England could read basic texts. The foundation of public libraries in all the major cities of western Europe made printed materials more widely available. In many bookshops, rooms were set aside for browsing in the hope that readers would eventually purchase the books they consulted.

One of the most widely circulated publications of the Enlightenment was the *Encyclopedia* compiled by the philosophe Denis Diderot and the mathematician Jean le Rond d'Alembert. This massive seventeen-volume work, which was published between 1751 and 1765, contained thousands of articles on science, religion, politics, and the economy. The entries in the *Encyclopedia* were intended not only to promote knowledge but also to advance the ideas of the Enlightenment. Included, for example, were two entries on natural law, which was described as being "perpetual and unchangeable." The entry on intolerance makes a passionate plea against religious persecution, asserting that "If we may tear out one hair of anyone whose opinions differ from ours, we could also claim the whole head, for there is no limit to injustice." Other articles praised the achievements of science and technology and gave special attention to industrial crafts and trades. Underlying the entire enterprise was the belief that knowledge was useful, that it could contribute to the improvement of human life. In these respects the *Encyclopedia* became the quintessential statement of the worldview of the Enlightenment, and its publication stands as a crowning achievement of the entire movement.

Encyclopedias, pamphlets, newspapers, and novels were not the only means by which the ideas of the Enlightenment spread. A number of informal institutions promoted the exchange of ideas. Literary societies and book clubs, which proliferated in the major cities of western Europe, encouraged the public reading and discussion of the latest publications. Scientific societies sponsored lectures on the latest developments in physics, chemistry, and natural history. One of the most famous of these lectures demonstrated the power of electricity by charging a young boy, suspended from the ground, with static electricity. This "electrified boy," who was not harmed in the process, attracted objects from a stool placed below him. Lectures like this one attracted large crowds.

Equally important in the spread of the scientific and cultural ideas of the Enlightenment were museums, where scientific and cultural artifacts, many of them gathered from around the world, could be viewed by an increasingly curious and educated public. The museums often sponsored exhibits and lectures. Paris became home to a number of these museums in the 1780s, and they could be found in all the major cities of Europe by the end of the eighteenth century. A more informal set of cultural institutions were the coffeehouses that sprang up in cities across Europe. These commercial establishments were open to everyone who could pay the fare, and therefore they proved to be immensely successful in facilitating the spread of ideas within the bourgeoisie. Newspapers were often read aloud at coffee houses, and they became the setting for many political debates.

Another set of institutions that promoted the ideas of the Enlightenment were the secret societies of men and women known as freemasons°. Freemasons strove to create a society based on reason and virtue, and they were committed to the principles of liberty and equality. Freemasonry first appeared in England and Scotland in the seventeenth century and then spread to France, the Dutch Republic, Germany, and as far east as Poland and Russia during the eighteenth century. Some of the most famous figures of the Enlightenment, including Voltaire, belonged to masonic lodges. In the 1770s there were more than 10,000 freemasons in Paris alone. The lodges were places where philosophes interacted with merchants, lawyers, and government leaders. The pope condemned the freemasons in 1738, and many civil authorities expressed deep suspicion of the political and religious ideas they fostered.

The most famous informal cultural institutions of the Enlightenment were the salons, the private sitting rooms of wealthy women where men and women were invited to discuss philosophy, science, literature, and politics. The salons were more socially exclusive than the literary and scientific societies and the masonic lodges, but they too encouraged the spread of the ideas of the Enlightenment among members of both aristocratic and bourgeois society.

THE LIMITS OF THE ENLIGHTENMENT

The ideas of the Enlightenment spread rapidly across Europe, but their influence was limited. The market for books by philosophes like Voltaire and Rousseau was quite small. Diderot and d'Alembert's *Encyclopedia* sold a remarkable 25,000 copies by 1789, but that was exceptional, and many sales were to libraries. Paine's *The Rights of Man* also reached a fairly broad audience, mainly because it was written in a simple direct style and its price was deliberately kept low. Most books on social and political theory, however, like scholarly works on science, did not sell very well. Rousseau's *The Social Contract* was a commercial failure.

Books on other topics had much better sales. Inspirational religious literature continued to be published in large quantities, indicating the limits of Enlightenment secularism. Novels, a relatively new genre of fiction that appealed to the bourgeoisie, were almost as successful. We can readily see why Rousseau and Voltaire both used novels to advance their radical social views. In France, books that were banned because of their pornographic content or their satirical attacks on the monarchy, the clergy, or ministers in the government also proved to be best-sellers in the huge underground French book market.

One segment of the popular press that revealed a limited influence of the Enlightenment was the literature on popular science. The reading public did not show much interest in technical scientific books, but they did purchase publications on such technological developments as hot-air balloons, which became a new fad in the 1780s. Descriptions of monsters found in distant lands and other extraordinary natural occurrences also sold thousands of copies. Some of this interest in the preternatural originated in the work of highly educated scholars, but the reports of new discoveries increasingly lent themselves to sensational treatment in the popular press.

Another subject of popular literary interest was mesmerism°. The Viennese physicist and physician Franz Anton Mesmer (1734–1815), who moved to Paris in 1778, claimed that he had discovered a fluid that permeated and surrounded all bodies and was the source of heat, light, electricity, and magnetism. Sickness was caused by the obstruction to the flow of this fluid in the human body. To restore this flow patients were massaged, hypnotized, or "mesmerized" with the intention of producing a convulsion or crisis that restored health. Mesmerism developed into a form of spiritualism in which its patients engaged in séances with spirits, and its practitioners dabbled in the occult. This pseudoscience, which was rejected by the French Academy of Science as a hoax, became the subject of numerous pamphlets and newspaper articles that fascinated the reading public.

Those who read books about mesmerism had only a tenuous connection with the learned world of the Enlightenment. Among those who were illiterate or barely literate, Enlightened ideas made even fewer inroads. The only exposure these people may have had to the ideas we associate with the Enlightenment would be through the actions and attitudes of their social superiors. From the elitist perspective of the philosophes, the intellectual world of the illiterate was characterized by the superstition and ignorance that the philosophes were determined to eliminate.

The growing gap between a learned culture shared by philosophes and members of salons on the one hand and the popular culture of the lower classes on the other can be seen in the perpetuation of beliefs regarding magic and witchcraft among the uneducated. During the late seventeenth and eighteenth centuries, educated people in Europe gradually abandoned their belief in magic and witchcraft. As we have seen in Chapter 16, belief in the operation of a mechanical universe, religious skepticism, and rationalism had gradually eroded many beliefs regarding the operation of a supernatural realm, especially the possibility of demonic intervention in the natural world. Among the lower classes, however, this skeptical outlook found very little fertile ground. Popular belief in a world charged with supernatural and magical forces continued to lead villagers to accuse their neighbors of having harmed them by means of witchcraft. After European courts stopped prosecuting witches in the late seventeenth and early eighteenth centuries, local communities often took justice into their own hands and lynched the suspects themselves. It was left to the government to prosecute those who engaged in this illegal form of local justice.

The gap between the high culture of the Enlightenment and that of the lower classes can also be seen in the condemnations of certain sports and amusements. Popular culture was known for its blood sports, especially cockfighting, and the baiting of bulls, bears, and badgers by tying the animals down and allowing dogs to attack them. These blood sports, which could attract thousands of spectators at a single event, resulted in the serious injury or the death of animals. Enlightenment thinkers, especially those from the bourgeoisie, condemned this activity for its cruelty and its barbarism. Just like the torture and execution of criminals, these "barbarous" pastimes had no place in polite society. Popular sports, however, could not be easily eradicated. It was not until the nineteenth century that they began to disappear, often as the result of campaigns conducted by clergymen rather than philosophes. The persistence of blood sports reveals the strength of popular culture and the inability of the Enlightenment to transform it.

ENLIGHTENED ABSOLUTISM

When we turn to Enlightened political ideas, we confront an even more difficult task of determining the extent of their impact. The main figures of the Enlightenment were intellectuals—men of letters who did not occupy positions of great political importance and who did not devote much thought to the challenging task of putting their theories into practice. The audience for their books did not always include people with the power to implement their proposals. Rulers often treated Enlightenment thinkers with suspicion, if only because they criticized established authority. Nevertheless, Enlightenment thought did make its mark on eighteenth-century politics in two strikingly different ways.

The first was through the reforms enacted by those rulers who are often referred to as enlightened despots°. These rulers exercised absolute power and used that power to implement changes that Enlightenment thinkers had proposed. The term *despot* is misleading, since these enlightened rulers were rarely despotic in the sense of exercising power cruelly and arbitrarily. The connection between Enlightenment and royal absolutism is not as unnatural as it might appear. It is true that philosophes tended to be critical of the Old Regime, the eighteenth-century

The Salon: Bringing Women and Men Together

Duxing the eighteenth century there were few higher academic institutions open to women. The universities excluded women as a matter of policy, and the same was true for all scientific societies, except in Italy. Only a handful of provincial academies and literary societies invited women to join their ranks. There was, however, one informal institution, the salon, in which women not only exchanged ideas with men but which women actually controlled.

The salon was a sitting room or parlor in the private home of an upper-class, learned lady where guests of both sexes gathered to discuss philosophy, religion, literature, art, and science. Salons became particularly prominent in Paris, where the salons of Madame Geoffrin and Madame du Deffand won international fame. The women who hosted these meetings invited the participants, entertained those who attended, and used their conversational skills to direct and facilitate the discussions that took place in the salons. They also used their influence to secure aristocratic patronage of the young male writers and scientists whom they cultivated. The success of a new book was often determined by its initial reception in the salon. Most of the prominent male figures of the French Enlightenment participated in these meetings, at least during the early years of their careers.

The overwhelming majority of the women of the salons came from the nobility. Their social status became a source of a criticism. Rousseau in particular had

Jean-Jacques Rousseau   He was the Enlightenment figure who was most highly critical of the culture of the salons.

■ **Madame de Staël**
Her salon in Paris was considered "the most brilliant in Paris."

■ **A Salon in Paris in the Late Eighteenth Century**

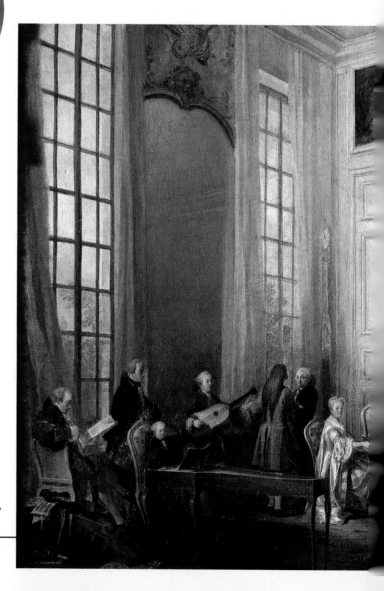

a very low opinion of the salons, objecting to the false charm and artifice of the women who presided over them and to the overly courteous and disingenuous conversations that took place there. He objected to the "female wits" who performed at these staged meetings. He expressed a preference for "a homely girl, simply brought up" over "a learned lady and a wit who would make a literary circle of my house and install herself as its president." Others objected to women participating in the public intellectual life of the city in this way. Montesquieu once remarked that "the society of women corrupts the morals and forms the taste." A further complaint was that the leadership exercised by women in the salons and their enforcement of the conventions of polite society were making French men effeminate.

■ **Literature** Abbé Delille reciting his poem *La Conversation* in the salon of Madame Geoffrin.

■ **Madame Geoffrin** Her salon was called "one of the wonders of the social world."

Rousseau claimed that "Every woman at Paris gathers in her apartment a harem of men more womanish than she." Women, so it was claimed, were diluting the valiant and warrior traditions of the old nobility. The salon thus became a focal point of strong antifeminine prejudice.

This kind of criticism betrays the truly revolutionary role that the salons performed in Old Regime France. First, they brought men and women into intellectual dialogue with each other at a time when other such public meetings were practically impossible to arrange. Second, while the membership of the salons was predominantly aristocratic, they did make possible the intermingling and the interaction of different social groups. Less than half of salon women came from the old nobility of the sword. Many of the others were women whose fathers had recently risen into the nobility or who had merely purchased their noble status. The men who attended the meetings had even fewer ties to the traditional aristocracy. Critics complained that the only requirement for membership in the salons was personal wealth, thus resulting in the debasement of the nobility.

The salons were places where old and new noble blood intermingled, where social refinement was even more important than inherited nobility. What mattered most in the salons was the quickness of one's wit, the quality of one's conversational skills, and the appeal of one's views. Thus the salon succeeded in opening elite society to the talented. In this way the salons helped to dissolve the bonds that held together the Old Regime and contributed to the creation of a society based on merit rather than birth alone.

For Discussion

To what extent did the salons represent a challenge to the traditional status of aristocratic women? What did Rousseau's critique of the salons reveal about the limits of the Enlightenment?

Figura III   Latus IV

Vorstellung des bereits in der Luft aufgezogenen
Inquisiten

■ Torture

The torture of a defendant as depicted in the published version
of the criminal code promulgated by Empress Maria Theresa in
1769. This form of torture, the *strappado*, used a pulley to hang
the accused from the ceiling. Weights could be attached to the
feet to make the pain more excruciating. The purpose of judicial
torture was to extract a confession. Torture was eliminated from
the law codes of most continental European countries during the
Enlightenment.

political order that had been dominated by an absolute
monarch and a privileged nobility and clergy. But many of
them, including Voltaire, had little sympathy with democracy and social equality, and preferred to entrust absolute
monarchs with the implementation of the reforms they
advocated. Among the philosophes the prospect of a
philosopher-king had widespread appeal.

Rulers of central and eastern European countries were
particularly open to Enlightenment thought. These monarchs had read widely in the literature of the Enlightenment
and introduced Western intellectuals to their courts. The
most famous of the enlightened absolutists was King
Frederick II of Prussia, known as Frederick the Great

(r. 1740–1786). Frederick, a deist who wrote poetry and
played the flute, was enamored of all things French. When
the French philosophe d'Alembert visited his court, the
king hosted a dinner at which he spoke only French, leaving many of the Prussian guests to sip their soup in stunned
silence. Frederick corresponded extensively with Voltaire
and invited him to take up residence at his French-style
royal palace, "Sans Souci," at Potsdam. The relationship between king and philosopher, however, was often stormy,
and when Frederick publicly burned a publication in which
Voltaire had lampooned a royal favorite, Voltaire left
Potsdam in 1752.

The departure of Voltaire did not weaken Frederick's
determination to implement a number of policies that
reflected the ideals of the Enlightenment. The most noteworthy of these was the introduction of religious toleration throughout his predominantly Lutheran kingdom.
Protestants of all denominations and Catholics (but not
Jews) received the protection of the law and even benefited
from royal patronage. Frederick also introduced a number
of legal reforms with the intention of realizing the
Enlightenment ideal of making the law both rational and
humane. He authorized the codification of Prussian law
(which was completed after his death in 1794), abolished
judicial torture, and eliminated capital punishment. In order to provide for the training of future servants of the
state, he began a system of compulsory education throughout the country. Like most enlightened rulers, Frederick
never abandoned his commitment to absolute rule, which
he strengthened by winning the support of the nobility. He
also remained committed to the militaristic and expansionist policies of his father, Frederick William I. For him there
was no contradiction between his style of rule and his commitment to Enlightenment ideals.

In neighboring Austria two Habsburg rulers, Maria
Theresa (r. 1740–1780) and her son Joseph II (r. 1780–
1790), pursued reformist policies that gave them the reputation of being enlightened monarchs. Most of Maria
Theresa's reforms were of an administrative nature.
Stunned by the Prussian invasion and occupation of the
Habsburg province of Silesia in 1740, Maria Theresa set
out to strengthen the Habsburg monarchy by gaining complete control over taxation and by reorganizing the military and civil bureaucracy. She also took steps to make the
serfs more productive, mainly by restricting the work they
performed on their lords' lands and by abolishing the feudal dues they paid.

These efforts won the applause of philosophes, but the
policies of Maria Theresa's that most clearly bore the stamp
of the Enlightenment were her legal reforms. Inspired by
Beccaria and Montesquieu, she established a commission to
reform the entire corpus of Austrian law. A new code of
criminal law was promulgated in 1769, and seven years later
Maria Theresa issued an edict abolishing judicial torture.
Joseph continued this program of legal reform by reorga-

■ Catherine the Great

Catherine II of Russia on the day she succeeded in taking the throne from her husband, Peter III, at Peterhof in 1762. Catherine, who despised her husband, joined a conspiracy against him right after his accession to the throne. Catherine, like Peter, had a number of lovers, and her two children, including the future emperor Paul, were reputedly conceived by members of the nobility.

She later corresponded with Voltaire and d'Alembert and employed the famous salon hostess Madame Geoffrin at her court. At Catherine's invitation Diderot visited St. Petersburg for six months.

Early in her reign, Catherine embarked on a program of reform similar to those of other enlightened absolutists. In 1767 she appointed a commission to codify Russian law on the basis of western European principles. Her recommendations to the commission included the abolition of torture and inhumane punishment and the establishment of religious toleration. She was eventually forced to disband the commission, which could not agree on a new code, but she later abolished torture and capital punishment on her own authority. Like Maria Theresa, she instituted a number of administrative and educational reforms, including the introduction of primary schooling in the provinces. Catherine, who became known as Catherine the Great, also tried unsuccessfully to provide for the education of girls as well as boys.

Catherine gained a reputation for being an enlightened European monarch, but her acceptance of traditional Russian culture and the need to maintain her rule prevented her from fully embracing the ideals of the Enlightenment. She even admitted that it was much easier to subscribe to the ideals of the Enlightenment than actually to implement them. The strength of vested interests within Russian society accounted for the failure of the law commission of 1767. After putting down the Pugachev rebellion in 1774, she began to question the desirability of social reform, and the experience of the French Revolution in the 1790s (see Chapter 18) led her to disavow the ideals of the Enlightenment.

On the issue of serfdom, which most Enlightenment thinkers wished to see abolished, she would not yield. She preserved that social system in order to secure the loyalty of the Russian nobility, and she extended it to Ukraine and parts of Poland after Russia incorporated those regions into the empire. Catherine also catered to the imperialistic ambitions of the Russians, gaining vast territories in eastern Europe, east Asia, and Alaska. Thus she expanded the Russian empire at the very time when the ideals of the Enlightenment were leading some philosophes to call for the dissolution of large imperial structures.

nizing the entire central court system and by eliminating capital punishment. He also revealed the influence of the Enlightenment by granting religious toleration, first to Protestants and eastern Orthodox Christians in 1781, and then to Jews in 1782. With respect to social issues, he completed his mother's work of abolishing serfdom altogether.

The efforts of Catherine II of Russia (r. 1762–1796) to implement the ideas of the Enlightenment followed a different course from those of Maria Theresa and Joseph. The daughter of a German prince, Catherine received an education grounded in a traditional curriculum of history, geography, and Lutheran theology. In 1745 she was married to a distant cousin, Peter, who was in line to inherit the Russian throne from his aunt, the childless Empress Elizabeth (r. 1741–1762). After arriving in St. Petersburg Catherine not only acquired a knowledge of Russian language, literature, and religion but also read widely in western European sources, including the works of Enlightenment thinkers.

THE ENLIGHTENMENT AND REVOLUTION

The second mark that Enlightenment thought made on eighteenth-century politics was the inspiration it gave to movements for reform and revolution in western Europe and the Americas. The emphasis placed by Enlightenment thinkers on individual liberty, natural rights, and political reform put pressure on both monarchs and the traditional nobility either to make concessions or to relinquish power altogether.

In Britain, for example, the movement for parliamentary reform and the expansion of the franchise°, as well as the first appeals for women's rights, were partially inspired by the Enlightenment. The radical democrat Thomas Paine, the feminist Mary Wollstonecraft, and the parliamentary reformer Joseph Priestley all based their demands for political reform on Enlightenment ideas of natural rights and civil liberty. It took considerable time, however, for these reforms to be realized. Only in 1832 did the British Parliament agree to a modest extension of the franchise, and women did not receive the vote until the early twentieth century. Nevertheless the movements to achieve these reforms were inspired by ideals born of the Enlightenment.

In France the influence of the Enlightenment on the momentous changes that took place during the French Revolution (1789–1799) has been a matter of debate among historians. The complexity of the revolution, which will be discussed in Chapter 18, and the diversity of Enlightenment thought make this a particularly difficult debate to resolve. Many of the revolutionaries of the 1790s were steeped in the ideas of the Enlightenment, but these did not necessarily inspire the revolution itself. The French philosophes of the eighteenth century denounced the evils of the Old Regime and proposed many ideas about how governments should function, but they did not make serious efforts to introduce actual reforms, much less topple the government. Many philosophes had personal connections with aristocratic society, and very few shared the democratic and egalitarian ideas that came to the fore at the time of the Revolution. Some lesser journalists and literary hacks were more successful than the most renowned philosophes in fostering contempt for the Old Regime before the Revolution. Their merciless satires of the court and the clergy were more responsible than the grand treatises of the philosophes for stimulating a crisis of confidence in the French government and eroding the traditional respect for authority that made possible the violent overthrow of the Old Regime.

We can nevertheless establish some connections between the ideas and programs of the philosophes and the events that transpired in France during the 1790s. Some of the figures of the Enlightenment contributed to the new critical spirit evident after 1750 or provided some inspiration for the creation of a new political culture once the revolution began. The towering reputation of Voltaire during the French Revolution—and the anger of conservatives who exhumed and burned his bones after it had ended—suggest that his passionate criticisms of the Old Regime and his pleas for human freedom at the very least helped to set the stage for the revolutionary events of the 1790s. The

same is true of the radical Rousseau, whose concept of the General Will served as the basis of a revolutionary ideology. Rousseau's democratic and republican ideas were used to justify some of the most important changes that took place during the revolution. Contemporaries glorified or attacked him, depending on their political philosophy, for having actually caused the revolution. One book published in 1791 was titled *On Jean-Jacques Rousseau Considered as One of the First Authors of the Revolution.*

Yet another application of enlightened ideas to politics took place in the Americas. The advocates of colonial independence from their mother countries, such as Thomas Jefferson in Virginia and Símon Bolívar in Venezuela and Colombia, were all deeply influenced by the Enlightenment concepts of natural law, natural rights, liberty, and popular sovereignty. The Declaration of Independence, which was written by Jefferson, betrayed its debt to the Enlightenment in its reference to the inalienable rights of all men and to the foundation of those rights in "the law of nature and Nature's God." Of course the American Revolution cannot be explained solely in terms of these Enlightenment ideas. The colonists found inspiration in many different sources, including English common law. But the American colonists did wish to create an entirely new world order, just as did many Enlightenment thinkers. They also adopted some of the most radical political ideas of the Enlightenment, which identified the people as the source of political power.

More generally, the Enlightenment fostered a critique of all efforts to establish overseas empires. The French renegade Jesuit priest Guillaume Thomas Raynal (1713–1796) wrote a condemnation of colonialism titled *The Philosophical and Political History of the Settlement and Commerce of Europeans in the Two Indies* (trans. 1776). Diderot and a number of lesser known philosophes contributed to the final version of this massive work, which was published at Geneva in 1780. The book, which was the first to treat European imperialism in both hemispheres in the same context, praised the civilizing effects of commerce but condemned colonialism for the effects it had on those who emigrated. Cut off from their homeland, colonists brought with them only the prejudices of the civilizations they left behind and became hopelessly corrupt and degenerate. The English political theorist Richard Price developed a similar critique of all overseas empires, claiming that simply by their size and their diversity they could not promote the happiness of a community and the "fellow-feeling that takes place between persons in private life." According to Price, sprawling overseas empires by their very nature violated the standards of humanity.

ENLIGHTENMENT AND WESTERN IDENTITY

The Enlightenment was a distinctly Western phenomenon. It arose in the countries of western Europe and then spread to central and eastern Europe (Germany, Austria, Poland

and Russia) and to the Americas. Most traditions that are identified today as "Western values" either had their origin or received their most cogent expression in the Enlightenment. In particular, the commitment to individual liberty, civil rights, toleration, and rational decision making all took shape during this period.

It would be misleading to make a simple equation between the ideas of the Enlightenment and the Western intellectual tradition. First, the ideals of the Enlightenment have never been never fully accepted within Western societies. Ever since their original formulation, the ideas of the philosophes and publicists of the Enlightenment have been challenged by conservatives who argued that those ideas would lead to the destruction of religion and the social order. Those conservative criticisms, which are voiced even today, became intense at the time of the French Revolution and during the early years of the nineteenth century, and we shall discuss them in Chapters 18 and 21. Second, claims that the ideas promoted by the Enlightenment are exclusively Western can also be disputed. A celebration of reason and an insistence on religious tolerance, for example, can be found in the cultures of ancient India and China. The claim that the West is more rational than the East is itself a product of long-standing Western prejudice, an assertion that studies of other cultures undertaken by Enlightenment writers only served to strengthen.

Nevertheless, the ideas and traditions of the Enlightenment, despite the challenges they have endured, have become deeply ingrained in Western law and politics. They are less often found embedded in the political and legal traditions of non-Western lands, and when they are, such as in the twentieth-century socialist legal system of China, their presence is more often the result of Western influence than the legacy of native Eastern thought.

The acquisition of the values of the Enlightenment, even though they were never universally adopted, gave Europeans a clear sense of their own identity with respect to the rest of the world. Educated people who prided themselves on being enlightened knew that their scientific, rational worldview was not shared by Asians, Africans, indigenous Americans, or South Pacific islanders. It did not matter whether Enlightenment thinkers had a positive view of those other cultures, like Voltaire or Rosseau, or a negative one, like Montesquieu. What mattered was that they shared a similar mental outlook and a commitment to individual liberty, justice, and the improvement of civilization. For all of them religious faith was less important, both as an arbiter of morality and as a source of authority, than it was in these other cultures. The men and women of the Enlightenment all looked to the law as a reflection of natural law and as the guardian of civil liberty. Their writings helped their European and colonial public audiences think of themselves as even more distinct from non-Western people than they had in the past.

As these Enlightened Western cultural values were spreading, the boundaries between East and West remained fluid and contested. The geographical region where this contest took place was what we now call eastern Europe. As we have seen in Chapter 15, the countries that occupied this buffer zone between East and West had long-standing cultural ties with Asia, especially the Middle East, but they also developed an attraction to Western culture beginning in the late seventeenth century. In Russia, this process of westernization began with Peter the Great, who integrated his country into European social, political and diplomatic life. But it was carried further by Catherine the Great, who invited *philosophes* to her court and introduced Western reforms. This adoption of Western ideas made her appear to be a model Enlightened ruler and her country part of the Western world, but Russia's inclusion became and has remained a matter of debate. The very term "eastern Europe," which was coined during the Enlightenment, reflected the ambiguous relationship between this part of the world and the West. It provides a further illustration of the fact that the West was a cultural realm whose geographical boundaries have frequently changed.

Change and Continuity in the Eighteenth Century

The eighteenth century is often viewed as a period of stability in the West. In political terms, that characterization makes some sense. During the years from 1700 to 1789 Europe stood between the turmoil of the mid-seventeenth century, which witnessed massive rebellions throughout Europe, and the upheaval of the French Revolution. In Great Britain, where Parliament had established its supremacy over the monarchy and where party factionalism ultimately resulted in the implementation of one-party rule by the Whigs, political peace was most apparent. A similar peace also dawned in countries where royal absolutism was in full force. In France, Spain, Prussia, Austria, and Russia, powerful central governments maintained tight control of the provinces and secured the suppression of the relatively few rebellions that broke out. In all these countries the political order remained intact. The aristocracy contributed to this stability. In their determination to preserve their own power, they placed financial burdens on their tenants, subjected the lower classes to harsh criminal prosecutions, and promoted a culture that celebrated the virtues of order and deference.

This picture of eighteenth-century stability is deceptive. Beneath the relatively placid surface of eighteenth-century European life, an array of historical forces was challenging the social and political order. These forces would ultimately bring about some of the most important transformations of the modern world. The growth of a wealthy and influential bourgeoisie, concentrated almost exclusively in the towns and cities, threatened to take power from the aristocracy and replace the values of that social elite with those of their own. The lower classes, beaten into submission by wealthy landlords and victimized by the brutalities of the criminal justice system, had developed their own strategies for denying the rulers the deference they expected and demanded. Finally, the thinkers of the Enlightenment, many of them drawn from the nobility itself, developed devastating critiques of both monarchy and aristocracy and set in motion movements for the reform of politics and the improvement of society. Instead of a stable and peaceful society, a picture emerges of a world in which all prevailing values and power structures were being challenged. These challenges all came to a head in the era of the French Revolution, to which we now turn.

Suggestions for Further Reading

For a comprehensive list of suggested readings, please go to www.ablongman.com/levack/chapter 17

Alexander, John T. *Catherine the Great: Life and Legend.* 1989. A lively biography of the remarkable "enlightened despot."

Beckett, J. V. *The Aristocracy in England 1660–1914.* 1986. A comprehensive study of this landholding and governing elite. Makes the important distinction between the aristocracy and the nobility.

Darnton, Robert. *The Forbidden Best-Sellers of Pre-Revolutionary France.* 1995. A study of the salacious, blasphemous, and subversive books that sold more copies than those of the philosophes in eighteenth-century France.

Dewald, Jonathan. *The European Nobility 1500–1800.* 1996. A comprehensive study of this social class that emphasizes its adaptability.

Doyle, William. *The Old European Order, 1660–1800.* 2nd ed. 1999. The best general study of the period.

Houston, R. A. *Literacy in Early Modern Europe: Culture and Education.* 1991. The best survey of the subject for the entire period.

Lugee, Carolyn. *Le Paradis des Femmes: Women, Salons and Social Stratification in 17th-Century France.* 1976. A social study of the women of the salons.

Outram, Dorinda. *The Enlightenment.* 1995. A balanced assessment of the major historiographical debates regarding the Enlightenment.

Root, Hilton. *Peasants and King in Burgundy: Agrarian Foundations of French Absolutism.* 1979. A study of peasant communal institutions and their relationship with the crown as well as the nobility.

Williams, David, ed. *The Enlightenment.* 1999. An excellent collection of political writings with a long introduction.

The Age of the French Revolution, 1789–1815

O N JULY 12, 1789, THE FRENCH JOURNALIST CAMILLE DESMOULINS addressed an anxious crowd of Parisian citizens gathered outside the royal palace. Playing upon fears that had been mounting during the past two months, Desmoulins claimed that the royal government of Louis XVI was preparing a massacre of Parisians. "To arms, to arms," Desmoulins cried out, as he roused the citizens to their own defense. That night Parisians responded to his call by invading arsenals in the city in anticipation of the violence they thought was about to descend upon them. The next day they continued to seize weapons and declared themselves members of the National Guard, a volunteer militia of propertied citizens.

On the morning of July 14, crowds of Parisians moved into one of the suburbs of the city, where royal troops were stationed in an ancient fortress known as the Bastille. The Parisians feared that the troops in the Bastille would take violent action against them, and they also wanted to capture the ammunition stored inside the fortress, which served as both an arsenal and a prison. Negotiations with the governor of the Bastille were interrupted when some of the militia, moving into the courtyard of the fortress, demanded the surrender of the troops. Shots were fired from both sides, and the exchange led to a full-scale assault upon the Bastille by the National Guard.

After three hours of fighting and the death of eighty-three people, the governor surrendered. He was then led by his captors, bearing the arms they had seized, to face charges before the officers of the city government. The crowd, however, crying for vengeance against their oppressors, attacked the soldiers and crushed them one by one underfoot. The governor was stabbed hundreds of times, hacked to pieces, and decapitated. The chief magistrate of the city suffered

Chapter Outline

- The First French Revolution, 1789–1791

- The French Republic, 1792–1799

- Cultural Change in France During the Revolution

- The Napoleonic Era, 1799–1815

- The Legacy of the French Revolution

The Storming of the Bastille, July 14, 1789: The Bastille was attacked not because it was a symbol of the Old Regime, but because it contained weapons that the Parisian citizens needed to protect themselves from royalist troops.

the same fate for his reluctance to issue arms to its citizens. The crowd then placed the heads of the two men on spears and paraded through the city.

The storming of the Bastille was the first of many violent episodes that occurred during the sequence of events called the French Revolution. That revolution brought about some of the most fundamental changes in European political life since the end of Roman rule. It heralded the destruction of the Old Regime, the eighteenth-century political order that had been dominated by an absolute monarch and a privileged nobility and clergy. It led to the submission of the Catholic Church to state control. A more radical phase of the revolution, beginning in 1792, resulted in the destruction of the French monarchy and the declaration of a republic. It also led to a period of state-sponsored terrorism in 1793 and 1794, during which one group of revolutionaries engaged in a brutal campaign to eliminate their real and imagined enemies.

The excesses of the revolution led to a conservative reaction. Between 1795 and 1799 a moderate republican government, known as the Directory, modified the egalitarianism of the revolution by limiting the right to vote to men of property. Between 1799 and 1814 the reaction continued under the direction of Napoleon Bonaparte, a military officer who dominated the Consulate, a new political structure established in 1799, and then proclaimed himself emperor in 1804. Although Napoleon declared his loyalty to many of the principles of the revolution, his authoritarian rule undermined or reversed many of its achievements. In 1815 Napoleon fell from power and the monarchy was restored, marking the end of the revolutionary period. The ideas of the revolution, however, especially its commitment to democratic republicanism and its concept of the nation, continued to dominate politics in the West for the next hundred years. The French Revolution permanently changed the political culture of the West.

In this chapter we shall address five questions regarding the era of the French Revolution: (1) Why did the Old Regime in France collapse in 1789, and what revolutionary changes took place in French government and society during the next two years? (2) How did a second, more radical revolution, which began with the establishment of the Republic in 1792, lead to the creation of a regime that used the power of the state to institute the Reign of Terror? (3) In what ways did the political events of the revolution change French cultural institutions and create a new political culture? (4) How did the authoritarian rule of Napoleon Bonaparte from 1799 to 1814 confirm or betray the achievements of the French Revolution, and what impact did his military conquests have on Europe and the world? (5) What did the French Revolution ultimately achieve and in what ways did it change the course of European and Western history?

The First French Revolution, 1789–1791

One of the main characteristics of political revolutions is that they involve a fundamental change in the political *system*, not simply in the personnel of government. On the basis of this criterion the French Revolution consisted of two distinct revolutions. The first revolution, which began in 1789, resulted in a destruction of royal absolutism and the drafting of a constitution. The second and more radical revolution began in 1792 with the abolition of the monarchy and the formation of the French Republic.

Like all revolutions, the first French revolution had deep-seated causes. As we discussed in Chapter 17, a constant barrage of satirical literature directed at the royal family and the court lowered the prestige of the government and thus weakened its authority. The publication of thousands of pamphlets advocating reform, including many written by philosophes of the Enlightenment, fostered a critical attitude toward the French government and led to demands for political and economic change. Conflicts between the nobility and the crown over constitutional issues, a source of tension throughout the age of absolutism, led to charges that the government was acting despotically. Encounters between the landowning nobility and the peasantry, which increased in the last half of the eighteenth century, also contributed to the disaffection with the Old Regime and played a major role in stimulating demands for a restriction of the privileges enjoyed by the nobility. Ongoing food shortages in the cities created a militant citizenry ready to take action against authorities they considered responsible for the high price of bread.

The immediate cause of the revolution was a major economic crisis that bankrupted the monarchy and deprived it of its authority. This crisis led to a revolt of the nobles against the crown and brought down the entire system of royal absolutism. Only after this collapse of royal government did various groups that had had long-standing grievances against the regime take the initiative and establish a new political system. These groups never actually planned the revolution; they simply filled a void created by the absence of effective governmental power.

THE BEGINNING OF THE REVOLUTION

The financial crisis that brought about the collapse of the French government peaked in the late 1780s. The government of Louis XVI (r. 1774–1792) had inherited considerable debts from that of his grandfather, Louis XV (r. 1715–1774) as a result of protracted periods of warfare with Great Britain. The opening of a new phase of this warfare in 1778, when France intervened in the American War of Independence on the side of the United States, pushed the government further into debt and put a strain on the entire French economy. Attempts to solve the crisis by implementing financial reforms made the situation only worse. In 1787 the government had a revenue of 475 million livres and expenses of just under 600 million livres. More than half of the revenue went to pay interest on the accumulated debt. As the crisis deepened, protests from the ranks of the nobility against royal policy became more vocal.

In 1787 the king made efforts to win the support of the nobility by convening an Assembly of Notables, a handpicked group of 144 nominees, the great majority of whom were noblemen. The purpose of the meeting was to gain approval for a new system of taxation that would include a direct tax on all landowners. These proposals encountered formidable opposition from the members of the assembly, and the meeting was adjourned. Some of the nobles in the assembly had been willing to pay the taxes, but only if the king would convoke the Estates General, a national legislative body that had not met since 1614. Convening the Estates General, they argued, would provide them with guarantees against royal despotism. Louis resisted these pressures, since he did not want to give up the right to make law by his own authority.

The king then tried to gain approval of new taxes from the regional parlements, the provincial law courts whose powers included the registration of royal edicts. There too the crown met resistance. The Parlement of Paris, which was the most important of all the parlements, refused to comply with the king's request. The other parlements followed suit, claiming that only the Estates General had the power to approve new taxes. Constitutional tension was heightened when the king demanded the registration of edicts for new loans without the approval of the parlements, a step that even he acknowledged was illegal. He then suspended the parlements, thereby deepening the constitutional crisis.

The deterioration of the government's financial condition finally forced the king to yield to the demands of the nobles and the increasingly hostile popular press. When tax returns dried up as the result of an agricultural crisis in the summer months of 1788, the government could no longer pay its creditors. In a desperate effort to save his regime, Louis announced that he would convene the Estates General. By this time there was little hope for Louis. His absolutist government had completely collapsed.

The meeting of the Estates General was set for May 1789, and during the months leading up to its opening, public debates arose over how the delegates should vote. The Estates General consisted of representatives of the three orders or social groups, known as estates, that made up French society: the clergy, the nobility, and the Third Estate.

CHRONOLOGY

The First French Revolution, 1789–1791

1787		
	February 22	Convening of the Assembly of Notables
1788		
	August 8	Announcement of the meeting of the Estates General
1789		
	May 5	The Estates General opens at Versailles
	June 17	The Third Estate adopts the title of the National Assembly
	June 20	Oath of the Tennis Court
	July 11	The king dismisses his finance minister, Jacques Necker
	July 14	The storming of the Bastille
	Late July	The Great Fear in rural areas
	August 4	Abolition of feudalism and privileges
	August 26	*Declaration of the Rights of Man and Citizen*
	October 5	March to Versailles; Louis XVI and National Assembly move to Paris
	November 2	Church property is nationalized
1790		
	July 12	Civil Constitution of the Clergy
	July 14	Feast of the Federation
	November 27	Decree requiring oath of loyalty from the clergy
1791		
	June 20	Royal family flees to Varennes, is apprehended by the National Guard
	October 1	Newly elected Legislative Assembly opens

The Third Estate technically contained all the commoners in the kingdom (about 96 percent of the population), ranging from the wealthiest merchant to the poorest peasant. The elected representatives of the Third Estate, whose numbers had doubled by a recent order of the king, were propertied nonnoble elements of lay society, including many lawyers and military officers.

Before the meeting a dispute arose among the representatives whether the three groups would vote by estate, in which case the first two estates would dominate the assembly, or by head, in which case the Third Estate would have numerical parity. Each side claimed that it was the best representative of the "nation," a term meaning the entire body of French people. The nobles maintained that the nation was represented by the nobility and clergy from all the provinces, especially the members of the provincial parlements, who had been critical of royal power during the past few decades. The members of the Third Estate advanced the claim that *they* represented the nation. The cleric Emmanuel-Joseph Sieyès (1748–1836), who joined the Third Estate during this dispute, claimed that it "has within itself all that is necessary to constitute a nation. . . . Nothing can go on without it, and everything would go on far better without the others . . . This privileged class (nobility and clergy) is assuredly foreign to the nation by its do-nothing uselessness."

The question of voting within the Estates General was not resolved when that body met at Versailles on May 5, 1789. After the king indicated that he would side with the clergy and nobility, the Third Estate took the dramatic step of declaring itself a National Assembly and asking members of the other estates to vote with them on the basis of "one man, one vote." Many members of the lower clergy and a few noblemen accepted this invitation. In a conciliatory response to this challenge, the king planned to summon all three estates to a special "royal session" to announce some concessions. In preparation for this meeting, however, he locked the Third Estate out of its meeting hall without explanation. The outraged members of the Third Estate went to a nearby indoor tennis court and took a solemn oath that they would not disband until the country had been given a constitution. One week later, after more clerics and noblemen had joined the ranks of the Third Estate, the king ordered the nobility and the clergy to join the National Assembly.

As this political crisis was reaching a climax, a major social crisis caused by the high price of bread was causing a breakdown of public order. For many years French agriculture had had difficulty meeting the demands of an expanding population. These problems, aggravated in the 1780s by a succession of poor harvests, climaxed in a widespread harvest failure in 1788. As the price of bread soared, demand for manufactured goods shrank, thus causing widespread unemployment among artisans. An increasing number of bread riots, peasant revolts, and urban strikes contributed to a sense of panic at the very time that the government's financial crisis deepened. In Paris the situation reached a critical point in June 1789.

At this point the king, a man with little political sense, made two ill-advised decisions. The first was to send 17,000 royal troops to Paris to restore order. The arrival of the troops gave the impression that the government was planning an attack on the people of the city. The second decision was the dismissal of the king's popular finance minister, Jacques Necker, who had favored the meeting of the Estates General and demonstrated real concern for the welfare of the populace. His dismissal sent a signal that the king was contemplating a move against the National Assembly. It was in this atmosphere of public paranoia that Parisians formed the National Guard and stormed the Bastille.

The fall of the Bastille unnerved the king. When he asked one of his aides, "Is it a revolt?" the aide replied, "No, sire, it is a revolution." The revolution had just begun. It moved into high gear two weeks later when the National Assembly responded to the outbreak of social unrest in the provinces. The scarcity of grain in the countryside gave rise to false rumors that the nobles were engaged in a plot to destroy crops and starve the people into submission. Peasants armed themselves and prepared to fight off the hired agents of the nobility. Some of these peasants burned the mansions of noblemen, together with the deeds that gave the nobles title to their lands and the right to collect dues from their tenants. A widespread panic, known as the "Great Fear," gripped the entire country. Townspeople and peasants amassed in large numbers to defend themselves and save the harvest. In response to this panic, which reached its peak in the last two weeks of July, the National Assembly began to pass legislation that destroyed the Old Regime and created a new political order.

THE CREATION OF A NEW POLITICAL SOCIETY

Between August 1789 and September 1790 the National Assembly took three revolutionary steps. The first was the elimination of noble and clerical privilege. In August the assembly abolished the feudal dues that peasants paid their lords, the private legal jurisdictions of noblemen, the collection of tithes by the clergy, and the exclusive rights of noblemen to hunt game on their lands. The privileges of provinces and local towns met the same fate, and ten months later the nobility lost their titles. Instead of a society divided into various corporate groups, each with its own privileges, France would now have only citizens, all of them equal at law. Social distinctions would be based on merit rather than birth. There were no longer any intermediary powers between the king and the individual subject.

The second step, taken on August 26, was the promulgation of the *Declaration of the Rights of Man and Citizen*.

DECLARATION OF THE RIGHTS OF MAN AND CITIZEN (1789)

·················

The passage of the Declaration of the Rights of Man and Citizen *by the National Assembly on August 26, 1789, is one of the earliest and most enduring acts of the French Revolution. A document of great simplicity and power, it was hammered out during many weeks of debate. Its concern with the natural rights of all people and equality before the law reflected the ideas of the Enlightenment.*

1. Men are born free and remain free and equal in rights. Social distinctions may be founded only on the common good.

2. The aim of all political association is the preservation of the natural and imprescriptible rights of man. These rights are liberty, property, security and resistance to oppression.

3. The principle of all authority rests essentially in the nation. No body nor individual may exercise any authority which does not emanate expressly from the nation.

4. Liberty consists in the freedom to do whatever does not harm another; hence the exercise of the natural rights of each man has no limits except those which assure to the other members of society the enjoyment of the same rights. These limits can only be determined by law. . . .

6. Law is the expression of the general will. Every citizen has the right to participate personally or through his representative in its formation. It must be the same for all, whether it protects or punishes. All citizens, being equal in the eyes of the law, are equally eligible to all dignities and to all public positions and occupations, according to their abilities, and without distinction except that of their virtues and talents.

7. No man may be indicted, arrested, or imprisoned except in cases determined by the law and according to the forms prescribed by law. . . .

10. No one should be disturbed for his opinions, even in religion, provided that their manifestation does not trouble public order as established by law.

11. The free communication of thoughts and opinions is one of the most precious of the rights of man. Every citizen may therefore speak, write, and print freely, but shall be responsible for any abuse of this freedom in the cases set by the law. . . .

17. Property being an inviolable and sacred right, no one may be deprived of it except when public necessity, determined by law, obviously requires it, and then on the condition that the owner shall have been previously and equitably compensated.

Source: From P.-J.-B. Buchez and P.-C. Roux, *Histoire parlementaire de la Révolution française.* (Paris: Paulin, 1834).

This document reveals the main influence of the Enlightenment on the revolution. It declared that all men, not just Frenchmen, had a natural right to liberty, property, equality before the law, freedom from oppression, and religious toleration. The statement that the "law is the expression of the general will" reflects the influence of Rousseau's *The Social Contract* (1762), while the statement that every citizen has the right to participate in the formation of that law either personally or through a representative embodies the basic principle of democracy. The *Declaration* differed from the English Bill of Rights of 1689 by grounding the rights it proclaimed in the natural law rather than in the law of one country. The provisions of the French document therefore serve as statements of broad principle rather than as confirmations of specific rights that the government had allegedly been violating.

The third step in this revolutionary program was a complete reorganization of the Church. In order to solve the problem of the national debt, the National Assembly placed land owned by the Church (about 10 percent of all French territory) at the service of the nation. The Civil Constitution of the Clergy of July 1790 in effect made the Church a department of the state, with the government paying the clergy directly. In order to retain their positions, the clergy were required to take an oath of loyalty to the nation. At the same time the Church was reorganized into eighty-three dioceses, one for each of the *départments* or administrative units into which the country was also now divided. The bishops of these dioceses were to be elected by laymen. The parishes, which were the basic units of ecclesiastical administration, would become uniform in size, each administering to some 6,000 parishioners.

In 1791 a newly elected Legislative Assembly—replacing the National Assembly—confirmed and extended many of these changes. A constitution, put into effect in October, formalized the end of royal absolutism. The king became a constitutional monarch, retaining only the power to suspend legislation, direct foreign policy, and command the armed forces. The constitution did not, however, give all men the right to vote. Only "active citizens," who paid the equivalent of three days' wages in direct taxes, had the right to vote for electors, who in turn chose representatives to the legislature.

The new constitution formally abolished hereditary legal privileges, thus providing equality of all citizens before the law. Subsequent legislation granted Jews and Protestants full civil rights and toleration. A law eliminating primogeniture (inheritance of the entire estate by the eldest son) gave all heirs equal rights to inherited property. The establishment of marriage as a civil contract and the right to end a marriage in divorce supported the idea of the husband and wife as freely contracting individuals. The largely symbolic abolition of slavery in France was consistent with the proclamation of equality of all men, but the failure to extend that emancipation to French colonies suggests that there were limits to the concept of liberty proclaimed by the assembly.

This body of legislation amounted to nothing less than a revolution. The Old Regime had been destroyed and a new one had taken its place. Although the form of government remained a monarchy, the powers of that monarchy were drastically curtailed. Unlike the English revolutions of the 1640s and 1688, this revolution did not disguise the extent of the changes that had transpired by using the language of conservatism, claiming that the revolution had recovered lost freedoms. It did not appeal to the French past at all. It promoted a new view of French society as a nation composed of equal citizens possessing natural rights, in place of the older concept of a society consisting of different corporate groups, each with its own privileges. Contemporaries recognized the significance of these changes. The Portuguese ambassador to France, who witnessed the events of 1789 firsthand, reported back to his government, "In all the world's annals there is no mention of a revolution like this."

RESPONSES TO THE FIRST FRENCH REVOLUTION

During the early years of the revolution, events in Paris and Versailles dominated the political scene. The revolution was not confined, however, to the metropolis. In the provinces groups of ordinary townspeople and peasants, frightened that the members of the nobility might be taking counteraction against them, took the law into their own hands and brought about a new revolutionary political and social order. In many places the local rulers who had exercised political power in towns and villages were overthrown and replaced by supporters of the new regime. At the same time there was considerable opposition to the revolutionary government. In many parts of the country the clergy's refusal to take the oath of loyalty to the nation led to violent clashes with the provincial authorities. In the south nobles began to organize resistance to the new regime, while militant Catholics attacked Protestants, who had been granted toleration and who generally supported the revolution.

The revolutionary events of 1789–1791 quickly gained the attention of countries outside France. In England the nonconformist Protestant minister Richard Price urged members of the British Parliament to follow the example of their French neighbors and abolish the laws that restricted hunting on aristocratic lands. Prussian reformers took

heart that the events of the revolution would portend the destruction of absolutism in their country and in other European lands. A Prussian official who had studied with the philosopher Immanuel Kant called the revolution "the first practical triumph of philosophy . . . the hope and consolation for so many of those ancient ills under which mankind has suffered."

Not all foreign assessments of the revolution were positive. In November 1790 the British politician Edmund Burke published *Reflections on the Revolution in France,* in which he expressed horror at the way in which abstract philosophy had destroyed the traditional social order in France. Pope Pius VI condemned the *Declaration of the Rights of Man and Citizen* and then, outraged at the attack upon the Roman Catholic Church, issued a sweeping condemnation of the Civil Constitution of the Clergy. The absolute monarchs of western Europe, sensing rightly that their regimes were in danger of a contagious revolutionary ideology, not only planned an invasion of France to restore the old order but took action against dissent in their own territories. When Polish legislators wrote a new constitution in 1791, modeled on that of France, Catherine the Great of Russia, who controlled a portion of Poland at the time, claimed that it was the product of French radicalism. She shut down the presses, revived censorship, turned against the philosophes whom she had admired, and banned the works of Voltaire.

The French Republic, 1792–1799

Beginning in 1792 France experienced a second revolution that was much more radical than the first. During this revolution France was transformed from a constitutional monarchy into a republic. The state claimed far greater power than it possessed under the constitutional monarchy established in 1791, and it used that power to bring about a radical reform of French society.

THE ESTABLISHMENT OF THE REPUBLIC, 1792

During the first two years of the revolution it appeared that the building of a new French nation would take place within the framework of a constitutional monarchy. Absolutism had suffered an irreversible defeat, but there was little sentiment among the members of the Legislative Assembly, much less among the general population, in favor of abolishing the institution of monarchy. The only committed republicans—those supporting the establishment of a republic—in the Legislative Assembly belonged to a party known as the Jacobins°, who found support in political clubs in Paris and in other parts of the country. By

■ Sans-Culottes

Male and female dress of the *sans-culottes*, the armed Parisian radicals who supported the Republic. The men did not wear the breeches (*culottes*) that were in style among the members of the French nobility.

the late summer of 1792 this group of radicals, drawing upon the support of militant Parisian citizens known as *sans-culottes* (literally, those without breeches, the pants worn by noblemen), succeeded in bringing about the second, more radical revolution.

King Louis himself was in part responsible for this destruction of the monarchy. The success of constitutional monarchy depended on the king's willingness to play the new role assigned to him as a constitutional figurehead. In October 1789 Louis had agreed, under considerable pressure, to move his residence from Versailles to Paris, where the National Assembly had also relocated. The pressure came mainly from women, who formed the large majority of 10,000 demonstrators who marched from Paris to Versailles demanding a reduction in the price of bread. The king yielded to their demands and came to Paris. As he entered the city, accompanied by soldiers, monks, and women carrying guns and pikes, he reluctantly agreed to wear the liberty cap with the tricolor cockade (a badge) to symbolize his acceptance of the revolution. Louis, however, could not disguise his opposition to the revolution, especially to the ecclesiastical settlement. This opposition led many people to suspect that he was encouraging the powers of Europe to invade France to restore the Old Regime.

Louis XVI had few personal resources upon which he might draw to win the confidence of his subjects. He was not as intelligent as his grandfather, Louis XV, nor did he have the skills necessary to dispel his subjects' growing distrust of him. Neither Louis nor his Austrian wife, Marie Antoinette, commanded much respect among the people. For many years the royal couple had been the object of relentless, sometimes pornographic satire. He had been lampooned for his rumored sexual inadequacies and she for a series of alleged infidelities with the king's brother and a succession of female partners. Whatever confidence Parisian citizens might have retained in the royal couple evaporated in June 1791, when the king and queen attempted to flee the country. The National Guard apprehended them at Varennes, close to the eastern French border, and forced them to return to Paris, where they were kept under guard at the palace of the Tuileries. Even that development, however, failed to destroy the monarchy, which had been preserved in the constitution implemented in October.

The development that actually precipitated the downfall of the monarchy and led to the establishment of a republic was the decision to go to war. Until the summer of 1791 European powers had been involved in various conflicts and had resisted pleas from French émigrés to support a counterrevolutionary offensive against the new French regime. After the flight to Varennes and the capture of the royal family, however, Frederick William II of Prussia (r. 1786–1797) and Emperor Leopold II of Austria (r. 1790–1792), the brother of Marie Antoinette, signed an alliance and called upon the other monarchs of Europe "to restore to the King of France complete liberty and to consolidate the bases of monarchical government." No action would be taken, however, unless all European sovereigns agreed to cooperate.

The actual declaration of war came not from the monarchs of Europe but from the French Legislative Assembly. A small group of republicans, headed by the eloquent orator Jacques-Pierre Brissot (1754–1793), convinced the assembly that an international conspiracy against the revolution would end in an invasion of their country. Brissot and his supporters also believed that if France could be lured into a foreign war, the king and queen would be revealed as traitors and the monarchy would be destroyed. Exploiting xenophobic as well as revolutionary sentiment, and claiming that the strength of a citizen army would win a quick and decisive victory, Brissot and his allies won the support of the entire assembly. They also appealed to the international goals of the revolution, claiming that the French army would inspire revolution against "the tyrants of Europe" everywhere they went.

The Legislative Assembly declared war on Austria in April 1792. Instead of a glorious victory, however, the war resulted in a series of disastrous defeats at the hands of Austrians and their Prussian allies in the Netherlands. This military failure contributed to a mood of paranoia in France, especially in Paris. Fears arose that invading armies, in alliance with nobles, would undermine the revolution. In May members of the assembly learned that the Austrian minister, in cooperation with a group of the king's advisers, was plotting the destruction of the assembly itself. In July the assembly officially proclaimed the nation to be in danger, calling for all citizens to rally against the enemies of liberty at home and abroad. Women petitioned for the right to bear arms. When the Austrians and Prussians threatened to torch the entire city of Paris and slaughter its population if anyone laid a hand on the royal family, citizens in Paris immediately demanded that the king be deposed.

On August 10 a radical republican committee overthrew the Paris commune, the city government that had

■ **Tricolor Cockade**
Louis XVI wearing the red liberty bonnet with the tricolor cockade in 1789. The king was forced to wear the liberty cap during his humiliating ride through Paris in October 1789.

been installed in 1789, and set up a new, revolutionary commune. A force of about 20,000 men, including volunteer troops from various parts of the kingdom, invaded the Tuileries, which was defended by about 900 Swiss guards. When the members of the royal bodyguard fled, they were pursued by members of the Paris crowds, who stripped them of their red uniforms and hacked 600 of them to death with knives, pikes, and hatchets. The attack on the Tuileries forced the king to take refuge in the nearby Legislative Assembly. The assembly promptly suspended the monarchy and turned the royal family over to the commune, which imprisoned them in the Temple, a medieval fortress in the suburbs of the city. The assembly then ordered its own dissolution and called for the election of a new legislative body that would draft a new constitution.

The fall of the monarchy did nothing to allay the siege mentality of the city, especially after further Prussian victories in early September escalated fears of a Prussian invasion. Individuals suspected of plotting against the regime were imprisoned, and when it was rumored that they would escape and support the Prussian enemy, angry crowds pulled 1,200 prisoners (most of whom were being held for nonpolitical crimes) from their cells and killed them. The feared foreign invasion that had inspired this "September Massacre" never did materialize. On September 20, 1792, a surprisingly well-disciplined and well-trained army of French citizens, inspired by dedication to France and the revolution, repulsed the armies of Austria and Prussia at Valmy. This victory saved the revolution. The German poet Johann Wolfgang von Goethe (1749–1832) claimed that the battle marked the beginning of "a new epoch in the history of the world." Delegates to a new National Convention, elected by universal male suffrage°, had already arrived in Paris to write a new constitution. On September 22 the convention declared that the monarchy was formally abolished and that France was a republic. France had now experienced a second revolution, more radical than the first, but dedicated to the same principles of liberty, equality, and fraternity.

■ **The Attack on the Palace of the Tuileries**

On the night of August 10, 1792, Parisian crowds and volunteer soldiers attacked the royal palace in Paris. The puffs of smoke in the building are coming from the Swiss guards, who were entrusted with the defense of the royal family and the palace. The royal family escaped and took refuge in the Legislative Assembly, but 600 of the Swiss guards were killed. Those that retreated were hunted down in the streets of Paris, stripped of their uniforms, and their heads placed on the end of spears.

THE JACOBINS AND THE REVOLUTION

Before the Republic was established, different political factions had begun to vie for power, both in the Legislative Assembly and in the country at large. The first major division to emerge was between the Feuillants, who supported a constitutional monarchy, and the Jacobins, many of whom favored the creation of a democratic republic. By the time the Republic had been declared, the Jacobins had become the major political party. Soon, however, factional divisions began to develop within Jacobin ranks. The main split occurred between the followers of Brissot, known as Girondins°, and the radicals known as Montagnards°, or "the Mountain." The latter acquired their name because they occupied the benches on the side of the convention hall, where the floor sloped upward. The Girondins occupied the lower side of the hall, while the uncommitted deputies, known as "the Plain," occupied the middle. Both

the Mountain and the Girondins claimed to be advancing the goals of the revolution, but they differed widely on which tactics to pursue. The Mountain took the position that as long as the state was endangered by internal and external enemies, the government needed to centralize authority in the capital. The Mountain thought of themselves as the representatives of the common people, especially the *sans-culottes* in Paris. Many of their leaders, including Georges-Jacques Danton (1759–1794), Jean-Paul Marat (1743–1793), and Maximilien Robespierre (1758–1794), were in fact Parisians. Their mission was to make the revolution even more egalitarian and to establish a republic characterized by civic pride and patriotism, which they referred to as the Republic of Virtue.

The Girondins, known as such because many of their leaders came from the southwestern *département* of Gironde, took a more conservative position than the Mountain on these issues. Favoring the economic freedom and local control desired by merchants and manufacturers, they were reluctant to support further centralization of state power. They believed that the revolution had advanced far enough and should not become more radical. They were also afraid that the egalitarianism of the revolution, if unchecked, would lead to a leveling of French society and result in social anarchy.

The conflict between the Girondins and the Mountain became apparent in the debate over what to do with the deposed king. Louis had been suspected of conspiring with the enemies of the revolution, and the discovery of his correspondence with the Austrian government led to his trial for treason against the nation. The Girondins had originally expressed reluctance to bring him to trial, preferring to keep him in prison. Once the trial began, they joined the entire National Convention in voting to convict him, but they opposed his execution. This stance led the Mountain to accuse the Girondins of being secret collaborators with the monarchy. By a narrow vote the convention decided to put the king to death, and on January 21, 1793, Louis was executed at the Place de Revolution.

The instrument of death was the guillotine, an efficient and merciful but nonetheless terrifying decapitation machine first pressed into service in April 1792. It took its name from Dr. Joseph-Ignace Guillotin, who had the original idea for such a device, although he did not invent it. The guillotine was inspired by the conviction that all criminals, not just those of noble blood, should be executed in a swift, painless manner. The new device was to be put to extensive use during the next eighteen months, and many Girondins fell victim to it.

The split between the Mountain and the Girondins became more pronounced as the republican regime encountered increasing opposition from foreign and domestic enemies. Early in 1793 Great Britain and the Dutch Republic allied with Prussia and Austria to form the First Coalition against France, and within a month Spain and the kingdoms of Sardinia and Naples joined them. The armies of these allied powers defeated French forces in the Austrian Netherlands in March of that year, and once again an invasion seemed imminent. At the same time internal rebellions against the revolutionary regime took place in various outlying provinces, especially in the district of the Vendée in western France. These uprisings were led by nobleman and clerics, but they also had popular support, especially from tenant farmers who resented the increased taxation imposed by the new revolutionary government.

In the minds of Robespierre and his colleagues, the Girondins were linked to these provincial rebels, whom

CHRONOLOGY

The French Republic and the Terror, 1792–1794

1792

April 20	Declaration of war against Austria
August 10	Attack on the Tuileries; monarchy is suspended
September 2–6	September Massacre of prisoners in Paris
September 20	French victory at the Battle of Valmy
September 21	National Convention meets
September 22	Abolition of the monarchy and establishment of the Republic

1793

January 21	Execution of Louis XVI
February 1	Declaration of war against Great Britain and the Dutch Republic
March 11	Beginning of rebellion in the Vendée
June 2	Purge of Girondins from the Convention
June 24	Ratification of a republican constitution
July 27	Robespierre elected to the Committee of Public Safety
August 23	The Convention decrees the *levée en masse*
October 5	Adoption of the revolutionary calendar
October 16	Execution of Marie Antoinette

1794

July 28	10th of *Thermidor*; execution of Robespierre
November 12	Jacobin clubs are closed

they labeled as federalists° because they opposed the centralization of the French state and thus threatened the unity of the nation. In June twenty-nine Girondins were expelled from the convention for supporting local officials accused of hoarding grain. This purge made it apparent that any political opponent of the Mountain, even those with solid republican credentials, could now be identified as an enemy of the revolution.

In order to repel the coalition of foreign powers, the convention ordered a *levée en masse*, a conscription of troops from the entire population. This step, taken in August 1793, created an unprecedented military force, a massive citizen army drawn from all segments of the population and committed to the prosecution of the war. In the past the rank and file of European armies, whether mercenaries or regular troops, had been filled with men on the margins of society: the poor, the unemployed, and even criminal outcasts. The conscription of males from all ranks of society might have promoted a sense of national unity among the troops, but it also caused resentment and resistance against this use of state power. It led to increased federalist resistance to the radical Jacobin government.

THE REIGN OF TERROR, 1793–1794

In order to deal with its domestic enemies, the republican government claimed powers that far exceeded those exercised by the monarchy in the age of absolutism. The convention passed laws that set up special courts to prosecute enemies of the regime and authorized special procedures that deprived those accused of their legal rights. These laws laid the legal foundation for the Reign of Terror°, a campaign to rid the state of its internal enemies. A Committee of Public Safety, consisting of twelve members entrusted with the executive power of the state, superintended this process. Although technically subordinate to the convention, the Committee of Public Safety became in effect a revolutionary dictatorship.

The man who emerged as the main figure on the Committee of Public Safety was Maximilien Robespierre. A brilliant student as a youth, Robespierre was affronted when the king's carriage splashed him with mud as he was waiting to read an address to the king. A man with little sense of humor, he was passionate in his quest for justice. As a lawyer who defended indigent clients, Robespierre was elected to the Third Estate in 1789 and became a favorite of the *sans-culottes,* who called him "The Incorruptible." That he may have been, but he was also susceptible to the temptation to abuse power for partisan political purposes. Like Rousseau, whose work he admired, he was also willing to sacrifice individual liberty in the name of the collective General Will. His logic was that since the General Will was indivisible, it could not accommodate dissent. Robespierre was primarily responsible for pushing the revolution to new extremes and for establishing the program of state repression that began in the autumn of 1793.

The most intense prosecutions of the Terror took place between October 1793 and June 1794, but they continued until August 1794. By that time the revolutionary courts had executed 17,000 persons, while 500,000 had suffered imprisonment. Another 20,000 either died in prison or were killed without any form of trial. Among the victims of the Terror were substantial numbers of clergy and nobility, as we might expect, but the overwhelming majority were artisans and peasants. One Parisian stableboy was guillotined for having said "f . . . the Republic," while a baker from Alsace lost his head for predicting that "the Republic will go to hell with all its partisans." Many of the victims came from the outlying regions of the country, especially the northeast, where foreign armies were threatening the Republic, and the west, where a brutal civil war between the French army and the advocates of federalism was raging. These provincial enemies of the regime were identified by special surveillance committees and then were tried by revolutionary tribunals. The guillotine was by no means the only method of execution. In November and December 1793, about 1,800 rebels captured during the uprising in the Vendée were tied to other prisoners, placed in sinking boats, and drowned in the chilly waters of the Loire River.

The most visible and alarming of the executions took place in the capital. The execution of Marie Antoinette and other royalists might have been justified on the basis of their active subversion of the regime, but trumped-up charges against Girondins exposed a process that would destroy republicans as well. As one victim of the Terror said in a speech before he went to the guillotine, the revolution, like the mythical Roman god Saturn, devoured its own children. Some of the most prominent figures of the Enlightenment fell victim to this paranoia. Among them was the Marquis de Condorcet, who believed passionately that all citizens, including women, had equal rights. Having campaigned against capital punishment, he committed suicide in a Parisian prison, just before he was to be executed. Another figure of the Enlightenment, the famous chemist Antoine Lavoisier (1743–1794), who had devoted himself to improving social and economic conditions in France, was executed at the same time. So too was the feminist Olympe de Gouges, who as we discussed in Chapter 17 had petitioned for the equal political rights of women. Many French revolutionaries, including Robespierre, used the political ideas of the Enlightenment to justify their actions, but the Terror struck down some of the most distinguished figures of that movement. In that sense the Terror marked the end of the Enlightenment in France.

The Committee of Public Safety then went after Danton and other so-called "Indulgents," who had decided that the Terror had gone too far. Danton's execution made everyone, especially moderate Jacobins, wonder who would be the next victim of a process that had spun completely out of control. In June 1794 the Terror reached a climax, as 1,300 people were sent to their deaths. In order to stop the process, a group of Jacobins in the convention, headed by Joseph Fouché (1759–1820) and Paul Barras (1755–1829), organized a plot against Robespierre. Calling him a tyrant, they arrested him and hundreds of his followers and guillotined them on July 28, 1794. An equally swift retaliation was exacted against the Jacobins in the provinces, when members of the White Terror, so named for the white Bourbon flag they displayed, executed leaders of the local revolutionary tribunals. With these reprisals, which used the very same methods that had been perfected by Robespierre and his followers, the most violent and radical phase of the French revolution came to an end.

The Reign of Terror had ended, but its memory would never be extinguished. Its horrors served as a constant

The Trial of Louis XVI

After the abolition of the monarchy and the proclamation of the French Republic in September 1792, the National Convention considered the fate of the deposed king. There was a broad consensus that Louis was guilty of treason against the nation and that he should answer for his crimes, but how he should do so was a matter of heated debate. The convention was divided between the Girondins and the Mountain. Of the two, the Girondins were more inclined to follow legal forms, whereas those of the Mountain considered themselves to be acting as a revolutionary tribunal that should adhere to standards of justice not specifically included in the law of the land. The convention thus became a forum where Louis's accusers expressed competing notions of revolutionary justice.

The most divisive and revealing issue was whether there should be a trial at all. The Mountain originally took the position that because the people had already judged the king on August 10, when the monarchy had fallen and the king taken prisoner, there was no need for a second judgment. They should proceed immediately to carrying out the death sentence. Robespierre argued that to have a trial would be counterrevolutionary, for it would allow the revolution itself to be brought before the court to be judged. A centrist majority, however, decided that the king had to be charged with specific offenses in a court of law and found guilty by due process before being sentenced.

A second issue, closely related to the first, was the technical legal question of whether the king could be subject to legal action. Even if the legislative branch of the government was considered the equal of the king in a constitutional monarchy, it did not possess authority over him. A further argument was that the king could not be tried for actions for which he had already suffered abdication. This claim was challenged on the most basic principle of the revolution—that the nation was higher than the king and his crimes were committed against that nation, which is the people. The king, moreover, was no longer king but was now a citizen and therefore subject to the law in the same way as anyone else.

The third issue was Louis's culpability for the specific charges in the indictment. These crimes included refusing to call the Estates General, sending an army to march against the citizens of Paris, and conducting secret negotiations with France's enemies. The journalist and deputy Jean-Paul Marat added that "he robbed the citizens of their gold as a subsidy for their foes" and "caused his hirelings to hoard, to create famine, to dry up the sources of abundance that the people might die from misery and hunger."

Nonetheless the king, who appeared personally to hear the indictment and then to respond to the charges on December 26, presented a plausible defense. He based it on the laws in force at the various times he was supposed to have committed his crimes. Thus he defended his sending of troops to Paris

on the grounds that in June and July 1789 he could order troops wherever he wanted. In the same vein he argued that he had used force solely in response to illegal intimidation. These legalisms, however, only made the members of the convention more contemptuous of the king. His defense failed to persuade a single convention deputy. He was convicted of treason by a vote of 693–0.

This unanimous conviction of the king did not bring an end to the factional debates over the king's fate. Knowing that there was extensive support for the king in various parts of the country, the Girondins asked that the verdict be appealed to the people. Their argument was that the convention, dominated by the Mountain and supported by militants in Paris, had usurped the sovereignty of the people. Pierre-Victurnien Vergniaud, a lawyer from Bordeaux, pleaded that "To take this right from the people would be to take sovereignty from them, to transfer it . . . to the hands of the representatives chosen by the people, to transform their representatives into kings or tyrants." Vergniaud's motion to submit the verdict to the people for ratification lost by a vote of 424–283.

The last vote, the closest of all, determined the king's sentence. Originally it appeared that a majority might vote for noncapital punishment. The Marquis de Condorcet, for example, argued that although the king deserved death on the basis of the law of treason, he could not bring himself to vote for capital punishment on

MORT DE LOUIS CAPET 16ᵉ DU NOM LE 21 JANVIER 1793.

■ **Execution of Louis XVI, January 21, 1793**
Although the king was convicted of treason by a unanimous vote, the vote to execute him carried by a slender majority of only twenty-seven votes.

principle. The radical response to this argument came from Robespierre, who appealed to the "principles of nature" in stating that the death penalty could be justified "only in those cases where it is vital to the safety of private citizens or of the public." Robespierre's impassioned oratory carried the day. By a vote of 361–334 the king was sentenced to "death within 24 hours" rather than the alternatives of imprisonment followed by banishment after the war or imprisonment in chains for life. The following day Louis was led to the guillotine.

All public trials, especially those for political crimes, are theatrical events, in that the various parties play specific roles and seek to convey certain mes-

sages to their audiences. The men who voted to put Louis XVI on trial wanted to create an educational spectacle in which the already deposed monarch would be stripped of any respect he might still have commanded among the people. Louis was to be tried like any other traitor, and he was to suffer the same fate, execution by the guillotine. The attempt to strip him of all privilege and status continued after his death. His corpse, with his head placed between his knees, was taken to a cemetery, placed in a wooden box, and buried in the common pit. The revolutionaries were determined to guarantee that even in death the king would have the same position as the humblest of his former subjects. ■

Questions of Justice

1. How would you describe the standard of justice that the members of the National Convention upheld in voting to execute the king? How did this standard of justice differ from the standard to which King Louis XVI appealed?
2. Evaluate the argument of Robespierre that the death penalty can be justified only in cases of public safety. Compare his argument to the Enlightenment critique of capital punishment presented by Cesare Beccaria. (See Chapter 17.)

Taking It Further

Jordan, David P. *The King's Trial: The French Revolution vs. Louis XVI.* 1979. The most thorough account of the trial.

Walzer, Michael (ed.). *Regicide and Revolution: Speeches at the Trial of Louis XVI.* 1974. A valuable collection of speeches with an extended commentary.

warning against the dangers inherent in revolutionary movements. The guillotine, the agent of a dysfunctional and indiscriminate state terrorism, became just as closely identified with the French Revolution as its famous slogan of "Liberty, Equality, Fraternity." The contrast between those two symbols, each of them emblematic of a different stage of the revolution, helps to explain how both conservatives and liberals in the nineteenth century would be able to appeal to the experience of the revolution to support their contradictory ideologies.

THE DIRECTORY, 1795–1799

A desire to end the violence of the Terror allowed moderates in the National Convention to regain control of the state apparatus that Robespierre and his allies had used to such devastating effect. The Paris Commune was dismantled and the Committee of Public Safety abolished. In November 1794 the Jacobin clubs throughout the country, which had provided support for the Terror, were closed. The moderates who now controlled the government still hoped to preserve the gains of the revolution, while returning the country to more familiar forms of authority. A new constitution of 1795 bestowed executive power on a five-man Directorate, while an assembly consisting of two houses, the Council of the Ancients and the Council of Five Hundred, proposed and voted on all legislation. The franchise was limited to property holders, allowing only 2,000,000 men out of an adult male population of 7,000,000 to vote. A system of indirect election, in which a person voted for electors who then selected representatives, guaranteed that only the wealthiest members of the country would sit in the legislative assembly.

The establishment of the Directory formed part of a more general reaction against the culture of the republic. The austere, egalitarian dress of the *sans-culottes* gave way once again to fancy and opulent clothes, at least among the bourgeoisie. Low necklines, officially out of favor during the Reign of Terror, once again came back into fashion among wealthier members of society. The high social life of the capital experienced a revival. Some dances took place on the sites of churches that Jacobins had desecrated. Jacobin theaters were shut down and Jacobin works of art destroyed. France was still a republic, but it was no longer Robespierre's Republic of Virtue.

Some of the more entrepreneurial citizens of Paris welcomed the new regime, but opposition soon arose, mainly from Jacobins and *sans-culottes*. When the government relaxed the strict price controls that had been in effect under the Jacobins, the soaring price of bread and other commodities caused widespread social discontent among the population. This situation was aggravated by the continuation of the interminable war against the foreign powers in the First Coalition. Wherever French troops went, their constant need of food and other goods resulted in serious shortages of these commodities.

By the end of 1798 conditions had grown even worse. Inflation was running out of control. The collection of taxes was intermittent at best. The paper money known as *assignats,* first issued by the government in 1791 and backed by the value of confiscated church lands, had become almost worthless. Late in 1797 the Directory had been forced to cancel more than half the national debt, a step that further alienated wealthy citizens who had lent money to the government. Military setbacks in 1798 and 1799 brought the situation to a critical point. An expedition to Egypt, which was intended to gain for France a

CHRONOLOGY

The Directory, 1795–1799

1795

August 22	The National Convention approves a new constitution
October 5	Napoleon suppresses a royalist insurrection in Paris
October 26	End of the Convention; beginning of the Directory

1796

| February 19 | The issuing of *assignats* is halted |
| April 12 | Beginning of a series of victories by Napoleon in Italy |

1798

May 13	Napoleon's expedition departs for Egypt
May	Second Coalition (Britain, Austria, Russia, Naples, and Turkey) is formed against Napoleon
July 21	Napoleon wins the Battle of the Pyramids
August 1	Nelson destroys the French fleet at the Battle of the Nile

1799

| November 9–10 | Napoleon's coup on the 18th of *Brumaire*; Consulate is established |

■ **Jean Charles Tardieu, *The French Army Halts at Syene, Upper Egypt, on February 2, 1799***

This painting depicts a cultural encounter between French soldiers and Egyptians in the city of Syene (now Aswan) during the Egyptian campaign of 1798–1799. The soldiers are scribbling on the ruins of ancient Egypt, indicating a lack of respect for Egyptian culture.

foothold in the Middle East, had resulted in a number of victories against the Turks, but the British destroyed the French fleet at the Battle of the Nile in 1798. The next year a series of revolts against French rule in Italy and in the Austrian Netherlands pushed the French armies back to France's earlier boundaries. The formation of a Second Coalition of European powers in 1799, which included Russia, Naples, and Turkey as well as Britain and Austria, represented a formidable challenge to French power and ensured that the war would not end soon. These military events produced a swing to the political left and raised the specter of another Jacobin coup.

In the face of this instability, Emmanuel-Joseph Sieyès, who had been elected as one of the directors two years earlier, decided to overthrow the government. Sieyès provided a link between the early years of the revolution, when he had defended the Third Estate, and the current government of the Directory. Unlike many other prominent political figures, he had managed to avoid prosecution as the revolution had become more radical. When asked what he had done during the Reign of Terror, Sieyès replied, "I survived." The goal of the planned coup was to provide the country with strong government, its greatest need in a period of political, economic, and social instability. The person Sieyès

selected as his partner in this enterprise, and the man who immediately assumed leadership of the coup, was Napoleon Bonaparte (1769–1821), a 30-year-old general who in 1795 had put down a royalist rebellion in Paris with a "whiff of grapeshot."

Napoleon had already established impressive credentials as a military leader. In 1796 and 1797 he had won major victories in Italy, leading to the Treaty of Campo Formio of 1797. Those victories and his short-lived success at the Battle of the Pyramids in Egypt had made him enormously popular in Paris, where he was received as a hero when he assumed command of the armed forces in 1799. His popularity, his demonstrated military leadership, and his control of a large armed force made this "man on horseback" appear to have the best chance to replace the enfeebled civilian regime of the Directory.

On November 9, 1799, Napoleon addressed the two legislative councils. He reported that another Jacobin conspiracy had been uncovered and that in order to deal with such insurrections a new constitution must be written to give the executive branch of the government more authority. Napoleon encountered resistance from some members of the Council of Five Hundred, who demanded that he be declared an outlaw. At this stage the president of the council,

599

Napoleon's brother Lucien, intervened and called in troops to evict the members who opposed him. The following day France had a new government, known as the Consulate.

Executive power in the new government was to be vested in three consuls—Napoleon, Sieyès, and Roger Ducos (1754–1816), a former member of the National Convention who had voted to execute Louis XVI. It soon became clear, however, that Napoleon would be the dominant member of this triumvirate, and in the new constitution of December 1799, which the electorate ratified by means of a plebiscite, Napoleon was named First Consul. This appointment made him the most powerful man in France and for all practical purposes a military dictator. Republican forms of government were preserved in the new constitution, but they were easily manipulated to produce what the consuls desired. A Senate appointed by the consuls chose men from a list of 6,000 "notables" to form a body known as the Tribunate, which would discuss legislation proposed by the consuls. Another assembly, the Legislative Body, would vote on those measures without debate.

With the establishment of the Consulate the French Republic was a thing of the past. It had been replaced by a military dictatorship in all but name. This transformation of the republic into a military dictatorship had been predicted by both the radical democrat Robespierre and the British conservative Edmund Burke many years before. The dictatorship became more apparent in 1802, when Napoleon was named Consul for Life, and in 1804, when he crowned himself emperor of the French.

Cultural Change in France During the Revolution

The French Revolution was primarily a political revolution. It brought about fundamental change in the system of government. It resulted in the destruction of the monarchy and the establishment of a republic. It inspired the drafting of new constitutions, led to the creation of new legislative assemblies, and endowed the state with unprecedented power. The French revolution also brought about profound changes in French culture. It transformed the cultural institutions of the Old Regime and created a new revolutionary culture.

THE TRANSFORMATION OF CULTURAL INSTITUTIONS

Between 1791 and 1794 most of the cultural institutions of the Old Regime were either destroyed or radically transformed, and new institutions under the control of the state took their place.

Schools

The confiscation of church property in 1790, followed by the abolition of the monastic religious orders, had a devastating effect on the traditional parish schools, colleges, and universities, most of which were run by the clergy. Without sufficient endowments, many of these schools were forced to close. During the Terror, schools suspected of having aristocratic associations and teaching counterrevolutionary doctrines came under further assault. Thousands of teachers lost their salaries and sought employment elsewhere. In September 1793 the universities were suppressed.

The government gradually realized that the entire educational process was collapsing. Recognizing the necessity of using education to encourage loyalty to the republican regime, the National Convention established a system of universal primary education. Instruction would be free, and the teachers would receive their salaries from the state. Unfortunately, the state did not have enough money to pay for the system, so the schools continued to languish.

The state was only slightly more successful in providing secondary education by converting abandoned colleges, monasteries, and libraries into "central schools," which were intended to provide a standardized form of state education. By 1799, the central schools had 10,000 students, 40,000 fewer than were in the colleges in 1789. The system was improved significantly during the Napoleonic period when the government established thirty-six secondary schools known as *lycées* while also allowing private and religious schools to continue to function.

Academies

The Parisian scientific and artistic academies established by Louis XIV (see Chapter 15) had a monopoly over the promotion and transmission of knowledge in the sciences and the visual arts. The academies were the epitome of privilege. They controlled their own membership, determined the recipients of their prizes, and had a monopoly of their particular branch of knowledge. They were also heavily aristocratic institutions; as many as three-quarters of their members were nobles or clergy.

During the revolution the academies were abolished as part of a general attack on corporate bodies. The work they did was taken over by various government committees. For example, the Commission on Weights and Measures, which had been part of the Academy of Science, became an independent commission. Its task had been to provide uniform weights and measures for the entire kingdom. In 1795 it established the meter, calculated as one ten-millionth of the distance from the North Pole to the equator, as the standard measure of distance. The metric system and the decimal system, which were introduced at the same time, have subsequently been adopted as universal standards in all European countries except Great Britain.

The Royal Academy of Arts, dissolved by a vote of the National Convention in 1793, was replaced by the Popular

■ **Destruction of the Statue of Louis XIV in the Place de Victoires, August 11, 1792**

The leaders of the Republic attempted to eliminate the memory of the institution of monarchy by destroying statues as well as the tombs of France's kings.

Le XI Aout 1792, les parisiens reprennent une mesure qu'ils avoient eu tort de ne pas mettre a execution le 20 Juin 1791. Ils abbatirent les Statues de Louis XIV, Place des Victoires et place vendôme.

and Republican Society of the Arts. The inspiration for this new republican society, which was open to artists of all social ranks, was Jacques-Louis David (1748–1825), the greatest painter of his generation. Employed at the court of Louis XVI, David became a vocal main critic of the academy at the time of the revolution. He painted some of the most memorable scenes of the revolution, including the oath taken at the tennis court by the members of the National Assembly in 1789. During the Republic David depicted heroes of the revolution such as Jean-Paul Marat, and after the empire was established he was appointed First Painter to Napoleon. David presided over a revival of classicism in French painting, employing Greek and Roman motifs and exhibiting a rationalism and lack of sentiment in his work.

Libraries

Shortly after the revolution had begun, thousands of books and manuscripts from the libraries of monasteries, royal castles, residences of the nobility, and academies came into the possession of the state. Many of these were funneled into the Royal Library, which grew five times in size between 1789 and 1794 and was appropriately renamed the National Library. The government also intended to inventory and catalog all the books held in libraries throughout the country. This effort to create the General Bibliography of France was never completed, and while the books were being cataloged, the government decided to get rid of those that dealt with "theology, mysticism, feudalism, and royal-

ism" by sending them to foreign countries. This decision did not lead to the export of books to other parts of Europe, but it initiated a frenzy of book sales, mainly to private individuals. Altogether about five million books were lost or sold during these years.

Museums and Monuments

The day after the abolition of the monarchy the National Assembly created a Commission of the Museum, whose function was "to collect paintings, statues and other precious objects from the crown possessions" as well as from the churches and houses of the émigrés. The museum was to be located in the Louvre, a royal palace that also served as an art gallery. When it opened in August 1793 the Louvre included a majority of paintings with religious themes, most of them confiscated from royal and émigré residences. The incompatibility of these religious works of art with the republican rejection of Christianity can be explained only by the assumption that this museum was intended to be entirely historical and to have no relevance to contemporary politics. The Louvre and the Museum of French Monuments represented an attempt to quarantine the religious French past from its secular present, lest it contaminate the revolution itself.

The revolutionaries did not have the same respect for the bodies of their former kings. On August 10, 1793, the first anniversary of the deposition of Louis XVI, the National Convention ordered the destruction of all the tombs of past French kings. One by one the tombs were opened and the corpses, embalmed in lead, were removed. Metals and valuables were melted down for use in the war effort. The corpses were either left to disintegrate in the atmosphere or dragged unceremoniously to the cemetery, where they were thrown into the common pit. The corpse of Louis XIV landed on top of that of Henry IV. This disrespectful treatment of the remains of France's former kings was intended to erase the memory of monarchy.

THE CREATION OF A NEW POLITICAL CULTURE

As the state was taking over and adapting the cultural institutions of the Old Regime, revolutionaries engaged in a much bolder and original undertaking: the production of a new, revolutionary political culture. Its sole purpose was to legitimate and glorify the new regime. It symbolized the political values of that regime: liberty, equality, and fraternity in 1789 and republicanism after 1792. This culture was almost entirely political; all forms of cultural expression were subordinated to the realization of a pressing political agenda.

One of the main characteristics of this culture was that it was popular—it was shared by the entire populace, not simply by a small upper-class or literate elite. The fundamental political doctrine of the revolution was popular sovereignty°: the claim that the people were the highest political power in the state. The revolutionaries claimed that this power could never be alienated. The move of the National Assembly from Versailles to Paris actually enabled the people to be present in the gallery during political debate, and deputies were always conscious of their presence. "Learn," claimed one of them in 1789, "that we are deliberating here in front of our masters and we are answerable to them for our opinions." The political culture that emerged—the textual and literary symbols spoken, written, and drawn to reflect this sovereignty of the people—would become the property of the entire population, especially in Paris, where the revolutionary cause found its most passionate popular support. The very words used to identify revolutionary institutions, such as the National Assembly and the National Guard, formed the texture of this new political culture.

The common people who embraced this new culture most enthusiastically were the *sans-culottes*—the radical shopkeepers, artisans, and laborers of Paris. The dress of these people influenced a change in fashion among the wealthier segments of society. A simple jacket replaced the ruffled coat worn by members of the upper classes, their powdered wigs gave way to natural hair, and they too now wore long trousers. They also donned the red liberty cap, to which a tricolor cockade was affixed. The tricolor, which combined the red and blue colors of Paris with the white symbol of the Bourbon monarchy, identified the adherents of the revolution.

Symbols of revolution could be found everywhere. The commercialization of the revolution guaranteed that the tricolor flag, portraits of revolutionary figures, and images of the Bastille would appear on household objects as constant reminders of the public's support for the revolution. By an order of the government in 1792 all men were required to wear the tricolor cockade. Liberty trees, first planted by peasants as protests against local landlords, became a symbol of the revolution. By May 1792 more than 60,000 had been planted throughout the country.

The press, no longer tightly controlled by the government and the printers' guild, became a crucial agent of revolutionary propaganda and a producer of the new culture. Pamphlets, newspapers, brochures, and posters all promoted a distinctive revolutionary language, which became one of the permanent legacies of the revolution. Political leaders used the same rhetoric in their political speeches. *Sans-culottes* sang satirical songs and ballads, many of them to the same tunes well known in the Old Regime. The most popular of the songs of the revolutionary period was the *Marseillaise,* first sung by soldiers preparing for battle against the Austrians but soon adopted by the civilian population and sung at political gatherings. The theaters, which had been privileged corporations in the Old Regime but also carefully regulated, were now free to engage in political satire that strengthened the ties of the people to the revolution.

Much of this new political culture stemmed from the conviction that the doctrine of popular sovereignty should be practiced in everyday life. *Sans-culottes* did this by joining the political clubs organized by different factions within the National Assembly, by addressing others as citizens, and by using the more familiar form of the pronoun *you* (*tu* rather than *vous*) in all conversations. They also participated in the revolution by taking public oaths. On the first anniversary of the fall of the Bastille, as many as 350,000 people, many of them members of the "federations" of National Guards throughout the country, gathered on the royal parade ground outside Paris to take an oath "to the Nation, to the Law, to the King." Direct democracy was not possible in a society of 27 million people, but these cultural practices allowed people to believe that they were participating actively in the political process.

The new revolutionary culture was emphatically secular. In its most extreme form, it was blatantly anti-Christian. In September 1793 the radical Jacobin and former priest Joseph Fouché inaugurated a program of de-Christianization°. Under his leadership, radical Jacobins closed churches and removed religious symbols such as crosses from cemeteries and public venues. In an effort to establish a purely civic religion, they forbade the public practice of religion and renamed churches "temples of reason." In their public pronouncements the architects of de-Christianization avoided reference to the Christian period of French history, which covered the entire national past.

This de-Christianization campaign became the official policy of the Paris Commune, and the National Convention issued a few edicts to enforce it. The program, however, did not win widespread support, and even some Jacobins claimed that in rejecting Christianity it had undermined a belief in God and the afterlife. In 1794 Robespierre attempted to modify the excesses of de-Christianization by launching the Cult of the Supreme Being. He promoted a series of festivals acknowledging the existence of a deity and the immortality of the soul. This new cult paid lip service to traditional religious beliefs, but it still served secular purposes. In fact, the cult was designed to direct the spiritual yearnings of the French people into patriotic undertakings and promote republican virtue.

The new secular revolutionary culture incorporated many elements of the Christian culture that had prevailed before the revolution began. The new pageants and festivals designed to promote a civic religion were modeled on traditional Catholic processions. Revolutionaries co-opted some of the religious holy days for their own purposes. Churches were converted to temples honoring revolutionary heroes. An effigy of Jean-Paul Marat, who was murdered in 1793, appeared on the altar of a Parisian church, next to a female statue of liberty. Jacques-Louis David's portrait of the murdered Marat depicted the slain victim in the manner of the dead Christ in Michelangelo's *Pietà*. Meetings of revolutionaries often took on the atmosphere of religious revivals, as men and women wept in response to orations. Secular catechisms taught young children the virtues of republicanism in the same way that they had instructed them in Christian doctrine during the Old Regime.

■ **Oath Taking**

On July 14, 1790, the first anniversary of the fall of the Bastille, as many as 350,000 people gathered on a field outside Paris to take an oath of loyalty to the new French nation. The event was referred to as the Feast of the Federation, since most of the oath takers were members of the regional federations of National Guards. The oath taking, which had many characteristics of a religious gathering, was led by the king himself, and it marked the most optimistic period of the revolution.

■ **Jacques-Louis David, *The Death of Marat* (1793)**
The Jacobin journalist Jean-Paul Marat was stabbed to death in his bathtub by a noblewoman, Charlotte Corday, in July 1793. The painting depicts Marat as having suffered a martyr's death. Marat holds the letter from his murderer that gave her entrance to his residence.

In order to destroy all vestiges of the Old Regime, the government also instituted a new calendar in October 1793. The dates on the calendar began with September 22, 1792, the day the Republic was established. That became the first day of the year I, while the weeks now had ten days instead of seven. The new months were given names to evoke the different seasons, such as *Brumaire* for the first month of wintry weather, *Germinal* for the season of planting, and *Thermidor* for the warmest month of the summer. Hostile British contemporaries gave their own humorous renditions of these names, translating them as Freezy, Flowery, Heaty, and so on. The new calendar was intended to make the revolution a part of people's everyday consciousness. It remained in effect until the last day of 1805.

The new revolutionary culture was disseminated widely, but it was always contested. Royalists trampled on the tricolor cockade, refused to adopt the new style of dress, and pulled up the liberty trees. This resistance from counter-revolutionary forces guaranteed that when the revolution

was reversed, much of the new political culture would disappear. Napoleon did little to perpetuate it, and the restored monarchy was openly hostile to it. Like the political revolution, however, some elements of revolutionary culture, such as the tricolor and the rhetoric of the revolutionary press, could never be suppressed. Not only did these cultural innovations inspire revolutionaries for the next hundred years, but they also became part of the mainstream of Western civilization.

CULTURAL UNIFORMITY

One of the most striking features of the new revolutionary culture was its concern for standardization and simplicity. The division of France into *départments,* all roughly equal in size, population, and wealth, and the further subdivision of each *départment* into uniform districts and communes, serves as one manifestation of this compulsion. The establishment of a national school system, at least on paper, serves as another. When the *lycées* were founded by Napoleon, each of the schools was given the exact same curriculum, and the same 3,000 books, chosen by a central committee, were deposited in all *lycée* libraries. The adoption of the metric system and the decimal system and the plan to establish one body of French law for the entire country, eventually brought to fruition by Napoleon, reflected the same impulse. So too did the efforts begun during the Terror to make French the official language in regions of the country that spoke Breton, Occitan, Basque, or other regional dialects.

The main source of this drive toward cultural uniformity was the desire to build a new French nation composed of equal citizens. Linguistic, legal, educational, or administrative diversity only made the realization of that program more difficult. The quest for cultural and political standardization did not, however, originate during the revolution. Many of the projects of the 1790s, especially the desire to establish standard weights and measures, began during the Old Regime. They were often the product of the rationalism of the Enlightenment, which, as we have seen in Chapter 17, sought to make society conform to the operation of universal laws.

The Napoleonic Era, 1799–1815

The coup d'état on November 9, 1799, or the eighteenth of *Brumaire* on the revolutionary calendar, marked a turning point in the political history of France. The Consulate ushered in a period of authoritarian rule. Liberty was restricted in the interest of order; republicanism gave way to dictatorship. The French Revolution had apparently run its course. But the period between 1799 and 1815 was also a time of considerable innovation, especially in the realm of politics and diplomacy. Those innovations were primarily the work of one man, Napoleon Bonaparte, who controlled the French government for the next fifteen years.

NAPOLEON'S RISE TO POWER

Napoleon Bonaparte was born on the Mediterranean island of Corsica. His father, Charles-Marie de Buonaparte, was an attorney who had supported the Corsican patriot Pascale de Paoli in winning the independence of the island from the Italian state of Genoa. His mother, Letizia, had come from an old noble family from Lombardy in Italy. In 1770 the new French government, which had gained control of the island the previous year, accepted the Buonaparte family as nobility. In 1779 the young Napoleon, whose native language was Corsican, received an appointment to a French military school. He survived both the rigors of the course of study and the taunting of his classmates, who mocked him for his accent and his poverty. Displaying a natural gift for military science, he won a position in the artillery section of the national military academy in Paris.

Until the beginning of the French Revolution, Napoleon seemed destined to pursue a successful but unspectacular career as an officer in the royal army. The events of the revolution made possible his rapid ascent to military prominence and political power. When the revolution broke out,

Napoleon returned to Corsica, where he organized the National Guard and petitioned the government to grant full rights of citizenship to his people. As the revolution became more radical he became a Jacobin, and he was commissioned to attack federalist and royalist positions in the south of France. Unlike many of his fellow Jacobins, he managed to survive the Terror and then found favor with the Directory. In 1796 Napoleon was given command of the Army of Italy, at which time he abandoned the Italian spelling of his name for Bonaparte. His decisive victories against the Austrians and his popularity in Paris attracted the attention of Sieyès and others who wished to give the country strong, charismatic leadership.

Napoleon's personality was ideally suited to the acquisition and maintenance of political power. A man of unparalleled ambition, he was driven by an extraordinarily high assessment of his abilities. After one of his military victories he wrote, "I realized I was a superior being and conceived the ambition of performing great things." To the pursuit of his destiny he harnessed a determined and a stubborn will. Temporary setbacks never seemed to thwart his single-minded pursuit of glory. He brought enormous energy to his military and political pursuits. He wrote more than 80,000 letters during his life, many of them transmitting orders to his officers and ministers. Authoritarian by nature, he used intimidation as well as paternal concern to cultivate the loyalty of his subordinates. Like many

■ **Charles Meynier,** *Napoleon on the Island of Lobau after the Battle of Essling, 1807*

This painting depicts the loyalty of Napoleon's troops to him and his concern for those who had been injured in battle.

THE FRENCH PEOPLE ACCEPT NAPOLEON AS EMPEROR, 1804

·················

The Countess de Rémusat was the wife of one of Napoleon's chamberlains. In this letter she explains why the French people accepted Napoleon as their emperor. Her comments reflect the fear of disorder that permeated French society at the end of the eighteenth century.

I can understand how it was that men worn out by the turmoil of the Revolution, and afraid of that liberty which had long been associated with death, looked for repose under the dominion of an able ruler on whom fortune was seemingly resolved to smile. I can conceive that they regarded his elevation as a decree of destiny and fondly believed that in the irrevocable they should find peace. I may confidently assert that those persons believed quite sincerely that Bonaparte, whether as Consul or Emperor, would exert his authority to oppose the intrigues of faction and would save us from the perils of anarchy.

None dared to utter the word Republic, so deeply had the Terror stained that name, and Directorial Government had perished in the contempt with which its chiefs were regarded. The return of the Bourbons could only be brought about by the aid of a revolution; and the slightest disturbance terrified the French people, in whom enthusiasm of every kind seemed dead. Besides, the men in whom they had trusted had one after the other deceived them; and as, this time, they were yielding to force, they were at least certain that they were not deceiving themselves.

The belief, or rather the error, that only despotism could at that epoch maintain order in France, was very widespread. It became the mainstay of Bonaparte; and it is due to him to say that he also believed it. The factions played into his hands by imprudent attempts which he turned to his own advantage; he had some grounds for his belief that he was necessary; France believed it too; and he even succeeded in persuading foreign sovereigns that he constituted a barrier against Republican influences which, but for him, might spread widely. At the moment when Bonaparte placed the imperial crown upon his head, there was not a king in Europe who did not believe that he wore his own crown more securely because of that event. Had the new emperor granted a liberal constitution, the peace of nations and of kings might, in sober seriousness, have been for ever secured.

Source: *Memoirs of Madame de Rémusat,* translated by C. Hoey and John Lillie (D. Appleton and Co., 1880).

---

authoritarian leaders, he had difficulty delegating authority, a trait that was to weaken his regime. Finally, in an age dominated by high-minded causes, he exhibited an instinctive distrust of ideology and the doctrinaire pronouncements of philosophes like Rousseau. Napoleon's military training led him to take a pragmatic, disciplined approach to politics, in which he always sought the most effective means to the desired end.

Napoleon's acquisition of power was systematic and shrewd. Playing on the need for a strong leader, and using the army he controlled as his main political tool, he maneuvered himself into the position of first consul in 1799. In 1802 he became consul for life, and two years later he crowned himself emperor of the French and his wife Josephine empress. The title of emperor traditionally denoted the height of monarchical power. It identified a ruler who not only ruled more than one kingdom or state but also did not share power with any other political authority. That was certainly the case with Napoleon. During his rule the Legislative Body, the Senate, and the Tribunate, all of which had been instituted during the Consulate, were reduced to performing only ceremonial functions.

It is certainly ironic that Napoleon, while continuing to hunt down and execute royalists, accepted a title of royalty himself and made his position, just like the French kingship, hereditary. In 1804 a group of royalists, including the members of the Bourbon family, were convicted of and executed for trying to assassinate Napoleon. One of them declared ironically, "We have done more than we hoped. We meant to give France a king, and we have given her an emperor." That emperor moreover, appeared to the royalists and to many others to be a tyrant who would trample on the rights of the French people. Napoleon's coronation also made a negative impression outside France. The great German composer Ludwig van Beethoven, having dedicated his *Third Symphony* (1803) to Napoleon for overthrowing tyranny in France, scratched Napoleon's name from the dedication after Napoleon assumed his new position as emperor.

NAPOLEON AND THE REVOLUTION

What was the relationship between Napoleon's rule and the French Revolution? Did Napoleon consolidate the gains of the revolution or destroy them? Did he simply redirect the revolutionary commitment to liberty, equality, and fraternity into new and more disciplined channels of expression after 1799? Or did he reverse the political trends that had prevailed from 1789 to 1799, crushing liberty in all its forms and establishing a ruthless, authoritarian dictatorship? Napoleon always thought of himself as the heir of the revolution rather than its undertaker. Certainly he was able to use the radical vocabulary of the revolution to characterize his domestic programs and his military campaigns. He presented himself as the ally of the common man against entrenched aristocratic privilege. He proclaimed a love for the French people and gave his support to the doctrine of popular sovereignty. He often referred to the rulers of other European countries as tyrants and presented himself as the liberator of their subjects.

This view of Napoleon as a true revolutionary, however, ignores the fact that his commitment to liberty was almost entirely rhetorical. Behind the appeals to the slogans of the revolution lurked an authoritarian will that was far stronger than that of any eighteenth-century absolute monarch. He used the language of liberty and democracy to disguise a thoroughgoing authoritarianism, just as he used the rhetoric of republicanism to legitimize his own dictatorial regime. The practice of holding carefully orchestrated and controlled elections to ratify the changes he made in French government guaranteed that his rule would appear to have emanated from the will of the people. At the establishment of the Consulate, Napoleon paid lip service to representative forms of government, which he maintained but then proceeded to render totally ineffective. When the empire was established he told his troops that they had the freedom to vote for or against the new form of government but then told them that if they voted against it, they would be shot.

We can make a stronger case for Napoleon's egalitarianism. He spoke of equality of opportunity. He synthesized the egalitarianism of the revolution with the authoritarianism of the Old Regime. He supported the equality of all Frenchmen (but not Frenchwomen) before the law. This egalitarianism laid the foundation for the support he received from the peasants, soldiers, and workers. It might be said that he brought both equality and political stability to France in exchange for political liberty.

There are two other ways in which we might legitimately consider Napoleon the heir of the revolution. The first is that he continued the centralization and growth of state power and the rational organization of the administration that had begun in 1789. Each of the successive regimes between 1789 and 1815, even the Directory, had contributed to this pattern of state building, and Napoleon's contribution was monumental. The second was his continuation and extension of France's military mission to export the revolution to its European neighbors. The two achievements are related to each other, since it was the war effort that necessitated the further growth and centralization of state power.

NAPOLEON AND THE FRENCH STATE

Once Napoleon had gained effective control of the French state, he set about the task of strengthening it, making it more efficient, highly organized, and powerful. In addition to turning the government into a de facto dictatorship, he settled the long struggle between Church and state, laid down an entirely new law code that imposed legal uniformity on the entire country, and made the civil bureaucracy more centralized, uniform, and efficient. All of this was done with the intention of making the state an effective instrument of social and political control.

Concordat with the Papacy

Napoleon's first contribution to the development of the French state, achieved during the Consulate, was to bring about a resolution of the bitter struggle between Church and state. A committed secularist, Napoleon was determined to bring the Church under the direct control of the state. This had been the main purpose of the Civil Constitution of the Clergy of 1790. Napoleon also realized, however, that this policy had divided the clergy between those who had taken an oath to the nation and those who had refused. Clerical independence had also become a major rallying cry of royalists against the new regime, thereby threatening the stability of the country.

Napoleon's solution to this problem was to reach an agreement with the Church that would satisfy clerics and royalists yet not deprive the state of its authority over the Church. With the Church safely under state control, Napoleon could also use religion to maintain respect for authority and to encourage loyalty and service to the state. "In religion," he wrote, "I do not see the mystery of the Incarnation but the mystery of the social order." In a new catechism published after Napoleon became emperor, children were taught: "Christians owe to the princes who govern them, and we owe in particular to Napoleon I, our Emperor, love, respect, obedience, fidelity, military service, and the tributes laid for the preservation and defense of the Empire."

The death of Pope Pius VI (r. 1775–1799), the implacable foe of the revolution, gave Napoleon the opportunity to address this problem. The new pope, Pius VII (r. 1800–1823), who was more sympathetic to liberal causes, was eager to come to terms with a French government that had become more moderate under the Consulate. The Concordat, which Napoleon and Pope Pius agreed to in 1801 and which was published the following year, gave something to both sides, although Napoleon gained more than he conceded. The pope agreed that all the clergy who refused to swear their loyalty to the nation would resign their posts, thus ending the bitter divisions of the past twelve years. The pope would appoint new bishops, but only with the prior approval of Napoleon. The state would pay all clerical salaries, and the Church would abandon any claims it still had to the ecclesiastical lands seized by the state at the beginning of the revolution.

These provisions represented formidable concessions to state power, and many French bishops found the terms of the Concordat too unfavorable to the Church. But the pope did manage to secure a statement that Roman Catholicism was the religion of the majority of citizens, and Napoleon agreed to scrap the secular calendar introduced in 1793, thereby restoring Sundays and holy days. Church attendance began to increase after having reached historic lows during the period of the Republic. The Church regained its respect as well as its legitimacy and its freedom to function in French society. More young recruits joined the clergy. Napoleon did not make many concessions to the Church, but they were significant enough to alienate a group of liberal philosophers and writers known as the Ideologues°, who objected to what they saw as the return of "monkish superstition."

With the pope at least somewhat appeased, Napoleon took unilateral steps to regulate the administration of the French Church. In a set of regulations known as the Organic Articles, which were added to the Concordat in 1802, the French church became a department of state, controlled by a minister of religion, just like the treasury or any other bureaucratic ministry. Pronouncements from the pope required prior government approval, and the clergy were obliged to read government decrees from the pulpit. Protestant congregations, which were also given freedom of worship and state protection by the terms of the Concordat, were likewise brought under state control, and their ministers were paid by the state. Jews received the protection of the state, but the government did not pay the salaries of rabbis.

The Civil Code

Napoleon's most enduring achievement in the realm of state building was the promulgation of a new legal code, the Civil Code of 1804, later known as the Napoleonic Code°. A legal code is an authoritative and comprehensive statement of the law of a particular country. The model for modern legal codes in Europe was the *Corpus Juris Civilis* of the Roman Empire, which Justinian decreed at Constantinople between 529 and 534 C.E. That code had replaced the thousands of constitutions, customs, and judicial decisions that had been in effect during the Roman republic and empire. In compiling the new French code Napoleon, who had just proclaimed himself emperor of the French, was imitating Justinian's legal achievement.

The Napoleonic Code also met a long-standing set of demands to reform the confusing and irregular body of French law. Ever since the Middle Ages, France had been governed by a multiplicity of laws. In the southern provinces of the country, those closest to Italy, the law had been influenced by Roman law. The *Corpus Juris Civilis* had

CHRONOLOGY	
The Consulate and the Early Years of the Empire, 1799–1806	
1799	
December 15	Proclamation of the Constitution of the Consulate
1801	
July 15	Signing of the Concordat with the Papacy
1802	
March 27	Peace of Amiens
April 8	Organic Articles added to the Concordat
1803	
May	Renewal of the war with Britain
1804	
March 21	The Civil Code is promulgated
December 2	Napoleon is crowned emperor of the French
1805	
August	Third Coalition (Britain, Austria, and Russia) is formed against France
October 21	Defeat of the French navy in the Battle of Trafalgar
October 29	The French defeat the Austrian army at Ulm
December 2	The French defeat Russian and Austrian armies at Austerlitz
December 31	End of the revolutionary calendar
1806	
October 14	French victories at the battles of Jena and Auerstädt
November 21	Proclamation of the Continental Blockade of British goods
August 6	Formal dissolution of the Holy Roman Empire

been revived in the Middle Ages and had been incorporated into the written law of these southern French provinces and municipalities. In the north the law was based on local or provincial customs that had not originally existed in written form. France needed a common law for all its people. Efforts to produce an authoritative written code began during the revolution, but Napoleon completed the project and published the code.

The Civil Code, which consisted of more than 2,000 articles, reflected the values that were ascendant in Napoleonic French society. The ideals of the revolution were enshrined in the articles guaranteeing the rights of private property, the equality of all people before the law, and freedom of religion. The values it promoted, however, did not include the equality of the sexes. It granted men control of all family property. Women could not buy or sell property without the consent of their husbands. Only adult men could witness legal documents. All male heirs were entitled to inherit equal shares of a family estate, but daughters were excluded from the settlement.

The Civil Code, which dealt only with the rights and relationships of private individuals, was the first and most important of six law codes promulgated by Napoleon. Others dealt with civil procedure (1806), commerce (1807), and criminal law (1811). Renamed the Napoleonic Code in 1806, the Civil Code had an impact on the law of several countries outside France. It became the basis for the codification of the laws of Switzerland, northern Italy, and the Netherlands, and it served as a model for the numerous codes that were compiled in the German territories controlled by France during the Napoleonic period. The Napoleonic Code also influenced the law of French-speaking North America, including the civil law of the state of Louisiana, which bears signs of its influence even today.

Administrative Centralization

Napoleon laid the foundation of modern French civil administration, which acquired the characteristics of rational organization, uniformity, and centralization. All power emanated from Paris, where Napoleon presided over a Council of State. This body consisted of his main ministers, who handled all matters of finance, domestic affairs, and war and oversaw a vast bureaucracy of salaried, trained officials. The central government also exercised direct control over the provinces, which lost the local privileges they had possessed under the Old Regime. In each of the departments an official known as a *prefect*, appointed by the central government, implemented orders emanating from Paris. Paid the handsome annual salary of 20,000 francs, the prefects were responsible for the maintenance of public order. The power of the prefects was far greater than that of the *intendants* of the Old Regime. The prefects enforced conscription, collected taxes, and supervised local public works, such as the construction and improvement of roads.

The men who served in the government of the French Empire belonged to one of two elaborate, hierarchical institutions: the civil bureaucracy and the army officer corps. The two were closely related, since the main purpose of the administrative bureaucracy was to prepare for and sustain the war effort. Both institutions were organized hierarchically, and those who held positions in them were trained and salaried. Appointment and promotion were based primarily on talent rather than birth.

The idea of "a career open to all talents," as Napoleon described it, ran counter to the tradition of noble privilege. This was one of the achievements of the revolution that Napoleon perpetuated during the empire. All of the twenty-six marshals who served under him in the army were of nonnoble blood. Three of them had been sergeants in the army before 1789 and another three had been privates. The new system did not amount to a pure meritocracy, in which advancement is determined solely by ability and performance, since many appointments were made or influenced by Napoleon himself on the basis of friendship or kinship. Napoleon's brother, Lucien, for example, became minister of the interior. The system did, however, allow people from the ranks of the bourgeoisie to achieve rapid upward social mobility. In order to recognize their new status, Napoleon created a new order of nonhereditary noblemen, known as *notables*. As men ascended through the ranks of the bureaucracy and army they were given the titles of duke, count, baron, and chevalier. Instead of basing their status on their ancestry, these men acquired their titles by virtue of their service to the state. Napoleon created more than 3,500 notables during his rule. In this way he encouraged service to the state while also strengthening loyalty to it.

NAPOLEON, THE EMPIRE, AND EUROPE

Closely related to Napoleon's efforts to build the French state was his creation of a massive European empire. The empire was the product of a series of military victories against the armies of Austria, Prussia, Russia, and Spain between 1797 and 1809. By the latter date France controlled, either directly or indirectly, the Dutch Republic, the Austrian Netherlands, Italy, Spain, and large parts of Germany and Poland. The instrument of these victories was the massive citizen army that Napoleon was able to assemble. Building on the *levée en masse* of 1793, which he supplemented with soldiers from the countries he conquered, Napoleon had more than one million men under arms by 1812. More than three times the size of Louis XIV's army in 1700, it was the largest military force raised under the control of one man up to this time in European history.

These troops engaged in a military offensive that was more massive, wide-ranging, and sustained than Alexander the Great's invasion of Egypt, Persia, and northern India between 334 and 326 B.C.E. Napoleon's invasion began with the great victories against Austria and Prussia in 1797. Two years later, shortly after Napoleon had become first consul, he directed his army to further military successes that paved the way to French dominance of Europe. The defeat of Austria in 1800 confirmed earlier territorial gains in Italy as well as French control over the southern Netherlands, now called Belgium. With Austria defeated and Russia involved with the Ottoman Turks, France and Britain concluded peace at Amiens in 1802. This peace gave Napoleon free rein to reorganize the countries that bordered on France's eastern and southeastern boundaries. In Italy he named himself the president of the newly established Cisalpine Republic, and he transformed the cantons of Switzerland

■ **Emperor Napoleon Crowning His Wife, Josephine, Empress of the French in the Cathedral of Notre Dame, 1804**

This painting by Jacques-Louis David depicts secular and religious figures gathered around Napoleon not as members of privileged orders but as representatives of the nation. Pope Pius VII remains seated as Napoleon places the crown on Josephine's head. Napoleon had already crowned himself emperor of the French.

into the Helvetic Republic. These acquisitions gave substance to the title of emperor that he assumed in 1804, since now he controlled many different kingdoms. France had not had an emperor since the ninth century, when Charlemagne and his heirs had ruled as Roman emperors, and Napoleon's territories were more extensive than those under Charlemagne's jurisdiction.

These stunning military successes as well as those that were to follow have secured Napoleon's reputation as one of the most brilliant and successful military leaders in modern history. The reasons for that reputation are a matter of some controversy. Napoleon made terrible strategic blunders in many of his campaigns and tactical mistakes in many of his battles. Somehow he seemed to make up for these mistakes by his careful planning, unbounded energy, and decisive moves. He spent hours studying his opponents' position beforehand but made quick decisions once the battle had begun. "Everything," he once said, "is in the execution." The combination of infantry, artillery, and cavalry in the same units or *corps* allowed him to move these forces easily on the battlefield. He struck quickly, usually at the center of en-

emy lines, using superior numbers to overwhelm his opponent. Attacks on enemy lines of communication often prevented his opponents from calling up reinforcements. Once they began their retreat, he would pursue them rather than stop to celebrate. In his campaigns he benefited from the loyalty of his troops and the ideological zeal that continued to inspire them, even as his wars lost their ideological purpose of exporting the ideals of the revolution.

Napoleon was far less successful at sea than on land. With no real experience in naval warfare, he could not match the dominance of the British navy, which retained its mastery of the seas throughout the entire revolutionary period. Only in the West Indies, where Britain was never able to send sufficient naval forces, did the French navy manage to hold its own. This naval weakness also explains Napoleon's failure to build or regain an overseas empire. His expedition to Egypt in 1798, which was dominated by dreams of colonial conquest in the Middle East and South Asia, was checked by the British destruction of the French fleet at the Battle of the Nile. In the Western Hemisphere financial problems and a false hope of limiting British power induced Napoleon to sell the vast North American territory of Louisiana, which he had acquired from Spain in 1796, to the United States in 1803. The following year the French Caribbean colony of St. Domingue became independent as the result of the violent revolution staged by free blacks and slaves, which we shall discuss in the next chapter. Informed of that loss, Napoleon shouted "Damn sugar, damn coffee, damn colonies!"

The most significant French naval defeat came in 1805, shortly after Britain, Austria, and Russia had formed the Third Coalition against France. As Napoleon was preparing for an invasion of Britain from northern French ports, the British navy, under the command of the diminutive, one-eyed Admiral Horatio Nelson, won one of the most decisive battles in the history of naval warfare. Nelson broke the line of a Franco-Spanish fleet that was preparing to strike off the Cape of Trafalgar near Gibraltar. The British destroyed or captured half the enemy ships, thus breaking the back of French sea power. The battle is commemorated at Trafalgar Square in London, which is overlooked by a towering statue of Nelson, who died of wounds inflicted during the battle.

Nelson might have survived if he had not insisted on wearing glimmering medals on his uniform, thereby attracting the notice of French marksmen.

The monumental naval defeat at Trafalgar did not prevent Napoleon from continuing his wars of conquest in central Europe. In October 1805 he defeated an Austrian army at Ulm, and in December of that year he overwhelmed the combined forces of Austria and Russia at Austerlitz. These victories brought him new German and Italian territory, which he ceded to some of the larger German states; the smaller German states became satellites of France and fought with him until the collapse of his empire. A defeat of Prussian forces at Jena and Auerstedt in 1806 and the subsequent occupation of Berlin gave him the opportunity to carve the new German kingdom of Westphalia out of Prussian territory in the Rhineland and to install his brother Jerome as its ruler. In the East he created the duchy of Warsaw out of Polish lands controlled by Prussia. In 1806 he formally dissolved the ancient Holy Roman Empire and replaced it with a loose association of sixteen German states known as the Confederation of the Rhine. By 1807, in the

THE FRENCH ENCOUNTER THE EGYPTIANS

·················

When the French army occupied Egypt in 1798, Napoleon brought with him 165 scholars who were organized into a Commission of Science and Arts. Their purpose was to give Napoleon information on the people and the resources of the country so that he could more easily control the country. A small group of these scholars set up an Institute of Egypt, whose mission was to propagate the Enlightenment and to undertake research on the history, people, and economy of the country. One of the members of the Institute, Vivant Denon, published Travels in Upper and Lower Egypt *in 1803. The following excerpt describes three of the ethnic groups in Egypt whom the French encountered: Arabs, Turks, and Greeks.*

After the Copts come the Arabs, the most numerous of the inhabitants of modern Egypt. Without possessing an influence proportioned to their numbers, they seem to be placed there to people the country, to cultivate the lands, to tend the flocks, or to be themselves in the degraded state of animals. They are, however, lively, and have a penetrating physiognomy. Their eyes, which are sunk in and overarched, are replete with vivacity and character; all their proportions are angular; their beard is short and hanging in filaments; their lips are thin and open, displaying fine teeth; their arms are fleshy and, in other respects, they are more active than handsome and more muscular than well shaped. . . .

The beauties of the Turks are more dignified and their shape more delicate. Their thick eyelids allow little expression in the eyes; the nose is thick; the mouth and lips handsome; the beard long and heavy; and this solemnity of gait, which, notwithstanding the nullity of their authority, inspires a certain degree of awe, they mistake for dignity. They possess a beauty which cannot be defined, or a reason given why it should be considered as such. This is not the case with the Greeks, who must be classed among the foreigners by whom societies distinct from those of the indigenous inhabitants are formed. The fine delineations of their form, their arch and penetrating eyes, and the delicacy and flexibility of their traits bring to the remembrance all that their monuments have transmitted to us to attest their elegance and taste. The degraded state to which they have been reduced, through a dread which the superiority of their intellectual faculties still inspires, has rendered many of them wily knaves. Were they, however, left to themselves, they would perhaps become, in a little time, who they formerly were, subtle and ambitious. Of all the nations on earth, this is the one which longs the most ardently for a revolution from whatever quarter it may come.

Source: From Vivant Denon, *Travels in Upper and Lower Egypt During the Campaigns of General Bonaparte in Their Country,* Volume I (Heard and Foreman, 1803).

Map 18.1 The Empire of Napoleon in 1812

By establishing dependent states in Spain, Italy, Germany, and Poland, France controlled far more territory than the areas technically within the French Empire.

words of one historian, Napoleon had "only allies and victims" on the Continent (see Map 18.1).

Napoleon inserted the last piece in this imperial puzzle by invading and occupying the kingdom of Spain in 1807. This campaign began as an effort to crush Portugal, the ally of Britain, which he was never able to defeat. In May 1808, as French armies marched through Spain en route to Lisbon, the Portuguese capital, a popular insurrection against Spanish rule occurred in Madrid. This spontaneous revolt, which led to the abdication of King Charles IV and the succession of his son Ferdinand VII, was the first of many developments that caused the collapse of the Spanish Empire in America. In Europe it led to the absorption of Spain into the French Empire. Sensing that he could easily add one more territory to his list of conquests, Napoleon forced Ferdinand to abdicate and summoned his own brother, Joseph Bonaparte, who was then ruling the dependent kingdom of Naples, to become king of Spain.

Joseph instituted some reforms in Spain, but the abolition of the Spanish Inquisition and the closing of two-thirds of the Spanish convents triggered a visceral reaction from the Spanish clergy and the general populace. Fighting for Church and king, small bands of local guerillas subjected French forces to intermittent and effective sabotage. An invasion by British forces under the command of Arthur Wellesley, later the Duke of Wellington (1769–1852), in what has become known as the Peninsula War (1808–1813), strengthened Spanish and Portuguese resistance.

The reception of the French in Spain revealed that the export of revolution, which had begun with the French armies of 1792, was a double-edged sword. The overthrow of authoritarian regimes in other European states won the support of progressive, capitalist, and anticlerical forces in those countries, but it also triggered deep resentment against French rule. The ideology of nationalism in Germany and Italy arose more because of a reaction against French rule than because the armies of France had tried to stimulate it. In Italy during the 1790s young educated *patrioti*, imbued with enthusiasm for liberty, equality, and progress, supported the newly proclaimed republics and envisioned the establishment of a single Italian state, at least in the north of Italy. By the middle of the Napoleonic years that vision had changed. Many of the *patrioti* had become disillusioned and joined secret societies to press for further political and social change and to plot insurrections against the new republics.

In Germany many of those who supported the French cause during the early years of the Republic turned away from it during Napoleon's wars of expansion. In 1809 a German student who attempted to assassinate Napoleon shouted "Long live Germany" at his execution. In 1813 the German writer Johann Gottlieb Fichte (1762–1814) appealed to the German nation to resist Napoleon in order to regain their liberty. For all his political astuteness, Napoleon could not comprehend that his own policies were responsible for the growth of this reactive sentiment, which formed one of the foundations of nineteenth-century nationalism. We shall discuss this topic more fully in Chapter 21.

THE DOWNFALL OF NAPOLEON

The turning point in Napoleon's personal fortunes and those of his empire came in 1810. After securing an annulment of his marriage to Josephine in late 1809, he married Marie-Louise, the daughter of the Habsburg emperor. This marriage, which the following year produced a son and heir to the throne, should have made the French Empire more secure, but it had the opposite effect. For the first time during his rule, dissent from both the right and the left became widespread. Despite the most stringent efforts at censorship, royalist and Jacobin literature poured off the presses. The number of military deserters and those evading conscription increased. Relations with the papacy reached a breaking point when Napoleon annexed the Papal States, at which point Pope Pius VII, who had negotiated the Concordat of 1801, excommunicated him.

Dissent at home had the effect of driving the megalomaniacal emperor to seek more glory and further conquests. In this frame of mind Napoleon made the ill-advised decision to invade Russia. The motives for engaging in this overly ambitious military campaign were not completely irrational. Victory over Russia promised to give France control of the Black Sea, and that in turn would ultimately lead to the control of Constantinople and the entire Middle East. More immediately, defeating Russia would be necessary to enforce the French blockade of British goods, which Russia had refused to support.

■ **Francisco Goya, *The Third of May 1808***
This painting of the suppression of the popular revolt in Madrid in 1808 captures the brutality of the French occupation of Spain. A French unit executes Spanish citizens, including a monk in the foreground. Goya was a figure of the Enlightenment and a Spanish patriot.

The problem with a Russian invasion was that it stretched Napoleon's lines of communication too far and his resources too thin, despite the support of the Austrians and Prussians whom he had defeated. Even before the invasion it was becoming increasingly difficult to feed, equip, and train the huge army he had assembled. The Grand Army that crossed from Poland into Russia in 1812 was not the efficient military force that Napoleon had commanded in the early years of the empire. Many of his best soldiers were fighting in the guerilla war in Spain. Casualties and desertions had forced Napoleon to call up new recruits who were not properly trained. Half the army, moreover, had been recruited from the population of conquered countries, making their loyalty to Napoleon uncertain.

The tactics of the Russians contributed to the failure of the invasion. Instead of engaging the Grand Army in combat, the Russian army kept retreating, pulling Napoleon further east toward Moscow. On September 7 the two armies clashed at Borodino, suffering a staggering 77,000 casualties in all. The Russian army then continued its retreat eastward. When Napoleon reached Moscow he found it deserted, and fires deliberately set by Muscovites had destroyed more than two-thirds of the city. Napoleon, facing the onset of a dreaded Russian winter and rapidly diminishing supplies, began the long retreat back to France. Skirmishes with the Russians along the way, which cost him 25,000 lives just crossing the Beresina River, conspired with the cold and hunger to destroy his army. During the entire Russian campaign his army lost a total of 380,000 men to death, imprisonment, or desertion. In the midst of this horror Napoleon, oblivious to the suffering of his troops, reported back to Paris, "The health of the emperor has never been better."

Not to be discouraged, Napoleon soon began preparing for further conquests. Once again his enemies formed a coalition against him, pledging to restore the independence of the countries that had become his satellites or dependents. Napoleon scored a few victories in the late summer of 1813, but in October allied forces inflicted a crushing defeat on him in the Battle of the Nations at Leipzig. Austrian troops administered another blow to the French in northern Italy, and the British finally drove them out of Spain. As a result of these defeats, Napoleon's army was pushed back into France. A massive allied force advanced into Paris and occupied the city. After extensive political maneuvering, including a vote by the Senate to depose Napoleon, the emperor abdicated on April 6, 1814. The allies promptly exiled him to the Mediterranean island of Elba. As he made the journey to the coast, crowds surrounding his coach shouted "Down with the tyrant!" while some villagers hanged him in effigy.

This course of events led to the restoration of the Bourbon monarchy. By the terms of the first Treaty of Paris of May 1814, the allies restored the brother of Louis XVI, the Count of Provence, to the French throne as Louis XVIII (r. 1814–1824). Louis was an implacable foe of the revolution, and much of what he did was intended to undermine its achievements. The white Bourbon flag replaced the revolutionary tricolor. Catholicism was once again recognized as the state religion. Exiled royalists returned to their high-ranking positions in the army. Nonetheless, Louis accepted a Constitutional Charter that incorporated many of the changes made between 1789 and 1791. Representative government, with a relatively limited franchise, replaced the absolutism of the Old Regime. Equality before the law, freedom of religion, and freedom of expression were all reaffirmed. Even more important, the powers of the state that the National Assembly and the Directory had extended and Napoleon had enhanced were maintained. The administrative division of France into departments continued, and the Napoleonic Code remained in force. France had experienced a counterrevolution in 1814, but it did not simply turn the political clock back to 1788. Some of the political achievements of the previous twenty-five years were indeed preserved.

Despite his disgrace and exile, Napoleon still commanded loyalty from his troops and from large segments of the population. While in power he had constructed a legend that drew on strong patriotic sentiment. Supporters throughout France continued to promote his cause in the same way that royalists had maintained that of the Bourbon monarchy since 1792. The Napoleonic legend held great appeal among the lower classes, who were persuaded that Napoleon, the patriot and the savior of the revolution, had made it possible for every Frenchman to achieve wealth and fame. The strength of the Napoleonic legend became apparent in March 1815, when Napoleon escaped from Elba and landed in southern France. Promising to rid the coun-

CHRONOLOGY

The Downfall of Napoleon, 1807–1815

1807	
November– December	French military intervention in Spain and Portugal begins
1808	
May	Beginning of the Spanish rebellion
July 20	Joseph Bonaparte appointed king of Spain
1809	
December 15	Annulment of marriage of Napoleon and Empress Josephine
1810	
April 2	Marriage of Napoleon to Marie-Louise
1812	
September 7	Battle of Borodino
September 14	Napoleon enters Moscow
October	Retreat from Moscow begins
1813	
October 16–19	Battle of the Nations at Leipzig
1814	
April 6	Abdication of Napoleon
May 30	First Treaty of Paris
September	Congress of Vienna assembles
1815	
March	Napoleon escapes from Elba
June 18	Battle of Waterloo
November 20	Second Treaty of Paris

try of the exiled royalists who had returned and to save the revolutionary cause that he claimed had been abandoned, he won over peasants, workers, and soldiers. Regiment after regiment joined him as he marched toward Paris. By the time he arrived, Louis XVIII had gone into exile once again, and Napoleon found himself back in power.

But not for long. The allied European powers quickly began to assemble yet another coalition. Fearing that the allies would launch a massive invasion of France, Napoleon decided to strike first. He marched an army of 200,000 men into the Austrian Netherlands, where the allies responded by amassing 700,000 troops. Near the small village of Waterloo, south of Brussels, he met the British forces of the

Duke of Wellington, who had turned the tide against him during the Peninsula War. Reinforced by Prussian troops, Wellington inflicted a devastating defeat on the French army, which lost 28,000 men and went into a full-scale retreat. Napoleon, captured in the battle, abdicated once again. He was exiled to the remote South Atlantic island of St. Helena, from which escape was impossible. He died there in 1821.

Even before the battle of Waterloo, the major powers of Europe had gathered in Vienna to redraw the boundaries of the European states that had been created, dismembered, or transformed during the preceding twenty-five years (see Map 18.2). Under the leadership of the Austrian foreign

■ **Map 18.2   Europe After the Congress of Vienna, 1815**
The four most important territorial changes that took place in 1815 were the scaling back of the boundaries of France to their status in 1790, the Austrian acquisition of territory in western and northeastern Italy, the establishment of the new kingdom of the Netherlands, and the formation of the new German Confederation.

minister, Prince Clemens von Metternich (1773–1859), this conference, known as the Congress of Vienna°, worked out a settlement that was intended to preserve the balance of power in Europe and at the same time uphold the principle of dynastic legitimacy. By the terms of a separate Treaty of Paris (the second in two years) the boundaries of France were scaled back to what they had been in 1790, before it had begun its wars of expansion. To create a buffer state on the northern boundary of France, the Congress annexed the Austrian Netherlands to the Dutch Republic, which now became the kingdom of the Netherlands with William I, a prince of the House of Orange, as its king. Territory along the Rhineland in the state of Westphalia was ceded to Prussia, while Austria gained territory in Italy, both along the French border in the west and in northern Italy to the east. In place of the defunct Holy Roman Empire, the Congress established a new German Confederation, a loose coalition of thirty-nine separate territories with a weak legislative assembly, whose members were appointed and instructed by their governments. The five major powers that had drawn this new map of Europe— Britain, Austria, Prussia, Russia, and France—agreed to meet annually to prevent any one country, especially France but also Russia, from achieving military dominance of the European Continent.

The Legacy of the French Revolution

With the conclusion of the Congress of Vienna a tumultuous period of European and Western history finally came to an end. Not only had France experienced a revolution, but every country in Europe and America had felt its effects. Governments were toppled in countries as far apart as Poland and Peru. Added to this turbulence was the experience of incessant warfare. France was at war for more than twenty years during the period of the Republic and the empire, and it had brought almost all European powers into the struggle. With armies constantly in need of provisions and supplies, high taxation, galloping inflation, and food shortages inflicted economic hardship on a large portion of the European population.

The cost of all this instability and warfare in terms of human life is staggering. Within the space of one generation almost two million European soldiers were killed in action, wasted by disease, or starved or frozen to death. In France alone just under 500,000 soldiers died during the revolutionary wars of 1792–1802 and another 916,000 during the wars of the empire. Internal political disturbances took the lives of hundreds of thousands of civilians from all ranks of society, not only in France but throughout Europe. The violence was fed at all levels by unprecedented fears of internal and external subversion. Government officials, collaborators, counterrevolutionaries, and imagined enemies of the state were all executed. This spate of violence and death—much of it in the name of liberty—was inflicted almost entirely by the state or its enemies.

What was achieved at this extraordinary price? How did the France of 1815 differ from the France of 1788? What on balance had changed? For many years historians, especially those who believed that economic forces determined the course of history, claimed that as a result of the revolution the bourgeoisie, composed of merchants, manufacturers, and other commoners of substantial wealth, had replaced the nobility as the dominant social and political class in the country. The bourgeoisie, so they argued, had started the revolution in order to acquire political power that was commensurate with their economic power, and they had ultimately prevailed.

This assessment can no longer be sustained. The nobility certainly lost many of their privileges in 1789, and many of them went into exile during the revolutionary period; however, the position they had in French society in 1815 did not differ greatly from what it had been under the Old Regime. In both periods there was considerable blurring of the distinctions between nobility and bourgeoisie. Nor did the revolutionary period witness the emergence of a new class of industrial entrepreneurs. The only group who definitely profited from the revolution in the long run were men of property, regardless which social category or "class" they may have belonged to. Men of property emerged triumphant in the Directory, they found favor during the Napoleonic period, and they became the most important members of political society after the monarchy was restored.

It would be difficult to argue that *women* of any social rank benefited from the revolution. During the early years of the revolution, women participated actively in public life. They were involved in many demonstrations in Paris, including the storming of the Bastille and the march to Versailles to pressure the king to move to Paris. Women as well as men filled the ranks of the *sans-culottes,* and women donned their own female version of nonaristocratic dress. During the early years of the revolution, many women joined patriotic clubs, such as the Club of Knitters or the unisex Fraternal Society of Patriots of Both Sexes. In 1790 the Marquis de Condorcet had published *On the Admission of Women to the Rights of Citizenship,* and the following year Olympe de Gouges published *The Rights of Women,* in which she called for the granting of women's equal rights. Both of these advocates of women's rights had been influenced by Enlightenment thought, as we have discussed in Chapter 17.

The goal advanced by Condorcet and de Gouges was not to be realized. The radical Jacobins dealt it a terrible setback when they banned all women's clubs and societies on the grounds that their participation in public life would be harmful to the institution of the family. This action, coupled with the imprisonment and death of both de Gouges and Condorcet during the Terror, signaled an end to the extensive participation of women in political life, which had begun during the eighteenth century, especially in the salons. During the nineteenth century women were generally considered to occupy a separate sphere of activity from that of men. They were expected to exercise influence in the private sphere of the home, but not in the public sphere of politics. As we shall discuss in Chapter 20, the changes wrought by the Industrial Revolution reinforced this segregation of men and women by excluding many married women from the workforce.

It is even more difficult to identify permanent economic changes as a result of the revolution. The elimination of the remnants of feudalism may have made France marginally more capitalist than it had been before the revolution, but agricultural and mercantile capitalism had long been entrenched in French society. Nor did the Continental System, the blockade of British goods from all European ports initiated in 1806, allow French industry to catch up with that of Great Britain. Whatever economic gains were made under the protective shield of the state were offset by the adverse economic effects of twenty-two years of nearly continuous warfare. In the long run the revolutionary period delayed the process of industrialization that had entered its preliminary stages in France during the 1780s and retarded the growth of the French economy for the remainder of the nineteenth century.

The permanent legacy of the French Revolution lies in the realm of politics. First, the period from 1789 to 1815 triggered an enormous growth in the competence and power of the state. This was a trend that had begun before the revolution, but the desire of the revolutionaries to transform every aspect of human life in the service of the revolution, coupled with the necessity of utilizing all the country's resources in the war effort, gave the state more control over the everyday life of its citizens than ever before. Fifteen years of Napoleonic rule only accentuated this trend, and after 1815 many of those powers remained with the government.

An even more significant and permanent achievement of the French Revolution was the promotion of the doctrine of popular sovereignty. The belief that the people constituted the highest political authority in the state became so entrenched during the revolution that it could never be completely suppressed, either in France or in the other countries of Europe. Napoleon recognized its power when he asked the people to approve political changes he had already made by his own authority. He also arranged for such plebiscites to secure approval of the new states he had set up in Europe. After the restoration of the monarchy the doctrine of popular sovereignty was promoted mainly by the press, which continued to employ the new revolutionary rhetoric to keep alive the high ideals and aspirations of the revolution. The doctrine also contributed to the formation of two nineteenth-century ideologies, liberalism and nationalism, which will be discussed in Chapter 21.

The third permanent political change was the active participation of the citizens in the political life of the nation. This participation had been cultivated during the early years of the revolution, and it had been accompanied by the creation of a new political culture. Much of that culture was suppressed during the Napoleonic period, but the actual habit of participating in politics was not. The franchise was gradually expanded in Europe during the nineteenth century. The press spread political ideas to a large segment of the population. People from all walks of life participated in marches, processions, and demonstrations. All of this followed from the acceptance of the French revolutionary doctrine that the people are sovereign and have a right therefore to participate in the political life of the state.

CONCLUSION

The French Revolution and Western Civilization

The French Revolution was a central event in the history of the West. It began as an internal French affair, reflecting the social and political tensions of the Old Regime, but it soon became a turning point in European and Western history. Proclamations of the natural rights of humanity gave the ideals of the revolution widespread appeal, and a period of protracted warfare succeeded in disseminating those ideals outside the boundaries of France.

Underlying the export of French revolutionary ideology was the belief that France had become the standard-bearer of Western civilization. French people believed they were *la grande nation,* the country that had reached the highest level of political and social organization. They did not believe they had acquired this exalted status by inheritance. Unlike the English revolutionaries of the seventeenth century, they did not claim that they were the heirs of a medieval constitution. French republicans of the 1790s attributed none of their national preeminence to the monarchy, whose memory they took drastic steps to erase. They considered the secular political culture that emerged during the French Revolution to be an entirely novel development.

The export of French revolutionary political culture during the Republic and the empire brought about widespread changes in the established order. Regimes were toppled, French puppets acquired political power, boundaries of states were completely redrawn, and traditional authorities were challenged. Liberal reforms were enacted, new constitutions were written, and new law codes were promulgated. The Europe of 1815 could not be mistaken for the Europe of 1789.

The ideas of the French Revolution, like those of the Enlightenment that had helped to inspire them, did not go unchallenged. From the very early years of the revolution they encountered determined opposition, both in France and abroad. As the revolution lost its appeal in France, the forces of conservatism and reaction gathered strength. At the end of the Napoleonic period, the Congress of Vienna took steps to restore the legitimate rulers of European states and to prevent revolution from recurring. It appeared that the revolution would be completely reversed, but that was not the case. The ideas born of the revolution would continue to inspire demands for political reform in Europe during the nineteenth century, and those demands, just like those in the 1790s, would meet with fierce resistance.

Suggestions for Further Reading

For a comprehensive list of suggested readings, please go to www.ablongman.com/levack/chapter18

Blanning, T. C. W. *The French Revolutionary Wars 1787–1802.* 1996. An authoritative political and military narrative that assesses the impact of the wars on French politics.

Chartier, Roger. *The Cultural Origins of the French Revolution.* 1991. Explores the connections between the culture of the Enlightenment and the cultural transformations of the revolutionary period.

Cobban, Alfred. *The Social Interpretation of the French Revolution.* 1971. Challenges the Marxist interpretation of the causes and effects of the revolution.

Doyle, William. *The Oxford History of the French Revolution.* 1989. An excellent synthesis.

Ellis, Geoffrey. *Napoleon.* 1997. A study of the nature and mechanics of Napoleon's power and an analysis of his imperial policy.

Furet, François. *The French Revolution, 1770–1814.* 1992. A provocative narrative that sees Napoleon as the architect of a second, authoritarian revolution that reversed the gains of the first.

Hardman, John. *Louis XVI: The Silent King.* 2000. A reassessment of the king that mixes sympathy with criticism.

Higgonnet, Patrice. *Goodness beyond Virtue: Jacobins during the French Revolution.* 1998. Explores the contradictions of Jacobin ideology and its descent into the Terror.

Hunt, Lynn. *Politics, Culture and Class in the French Revolution.* 1984. Analyzes the formation of a revolutionary political culture.

Kennedy, Emmet. *The Culture of the French Revolution.* 1989. A comprehensive study of all cultural developments before and during the revolution.

Landes, Joan B. *Women and the Public Sphere in the Age of the French Revolution.* 1988. Explores how the new political culture of the revolution changed the position of women in society.

Lefebvre, Georges. *The Great Fear of 1789: Rural Panic in Revolutionary France.* 1973. Shows the importance of the rural unrest of July 1793 that provided the backdrop of the legislation of August 1789.

Schama, Simon. *Citizens: A Chronicle of the French Revolution.* 1989. Depicts the tragic unraveling of a vision of liberty and happiness into a scenario of hunger, anger, violence, and death.

The West and the World: Empire, Trade, and War, 1650–1850

I N 1789 OLAUDAH EQUIANO, A FREED SLAVE LIVING IN GREAT BRITAIN, PUBLISHED an autobiographical account of his experiences in captivity. In this narrative Equiano recounted his seizure in the Gambia region of Africa and his transportation on a slave ship to the British Caribbean colony of Barbados. He described the unmerciful floggings to which the Africans on his ship were subjected, the unrelieved hunger they experienced, and the insufferable heat and smells they endured in the hold of the ship. He witnessed the suicide of those who threw themselves into the sea in order to avoid further misery. He was terrified that his white captors would eat him, and he wished for a merciful death.

Once the ship had reached its destination Equiano related how the Africans were herded into pens where white plantation owners examined, purchased, and branded them. The most moving part of Equiano's narrative is his account of the cries he heard as family members were sold to different masters. "O you nominal Christians," wrote Equiano, "might not an African ask you, learned you this from your God? Is it not enough that we are torn from our country and friends to toil for your luxury and lust of gain? Must every tender feeling be sacrificed to your avarice? Surely this is a new refinement in cruelty, which, while it has no advantage to atone for it, thus aggravates distress and adds fresh horrors to the wretchedness of slavery."

The journey that Equiano was forced to take across the Atlantic Ocean and the emotions he described were experienced by millions of African men and women during the period from 1650 to 1850. The forced emigration of Africans from their homelands, their sale to white landlords, and their subjection to inhumane treatment number among the abiding horrors of Western civilization. To understand how these horrors could have occurred, especially at the hands of men who proclaimed a commitment to human freedom, we must study the growth of European empires during these centuries.

Chapter Outline

- European Empires in the Americas and Asia

- Warfare in Europe, North America, and Asia

- The Atlantic World

- Encounters Between Europeans and Asians

- The Crisis of Empire and the Atlantic Revolutions

Samuel Scott, *A Thames Wharf* (1750s): British merchants conducted a brisk trade with Asia and the Americas in the eighteenth century.

As European states grew in size, wealth, and military power in the sixteenth and seventeenth centuries, the most powerful of them acquired large overseas empires. By the end of the seventeenth century the British, French, and Dutch had joined the Portuguese and the Spanish as overseas imperial powers. As we discussed in Chapter 12, the first stage of empire building, which lasted from 1500 until about 1650, had many different motives. The search for gold and silver, the mission to Christianize the indigenous populations, the desire of some colonists to escape religious persecution, the urge to plunder, the efforts of monarchs to expand the size of their dominions, and the desire to profit from international trade all figured in the process. In 1625 the English government recognized many of these motives when it declared the purpose of the colony of Virginia to be "the propagation of the Christian religion, the increase of trade, and the enlarging of the royal empire."

During the second stage of empire building, which lasted from roughly 1650 to 1850, the economic motive for acquiring overseas possessions became dominant. More than anything else, imperial policy was shaped by the desire for profit within a world economy. As far as the governments of western Europe were concerned, all colonies were economic enterprises. Whether these colonies were primarily involved in commerce or agriculture or mining was only a minor distinction. The main consideration was that they provided economic benefits to the European countries. They supplied the parent country, often referred to as the metropolis°, with agricultural products, raw materials, and minerals. Overseas colonies also provided the metropolis with markets for its manufactured goods.

The growth of these empires resulted in the expansion of the geographical boundaries of the West. It also resulted in the spread of Western ideas, political institutions, and economic systems to Asia and the Americas. At the same time, encounters between Europeans and non-Western peoples, especially those of Asia, brought about significant changes in the cultures of the West.

To understand the relationship between empire, trade, and war during this period, and their impact on the changing definition of the West, this chapter will address five main questions: (1) How did the composition and the organization of European empires change during the seventeenth and eighteenth centuries? (2) In what ways did the wars waged by European powers during this period involve competition for overseas possessions and trading routes? (3) How did European empires create an Atlantic economy in which the traffic in slaves was a major feature? (4) What cultural encounters took place between European and Asian peoples during this period of empire building, and how did these encounters change Western attitudes toward outsiders? (5) Why did European powers begin to lose control of some of their colonies, especially those in the Americas, between 1775 and 1825?

European Empires in the Americas and Asia

The main political units in Europe during this long period of history are usually referred to as states°. A state is a consolidated territorial area that has its own political institutions and recognizes no higher authority. Thus we refer to France, England (which became Great Britain after its union with Scotland in 1707), Prussia, the Dutch Republic, and Portugal as states. As we have discussed in Chapter 15, most of these states acquired larger armies and administrative bureaucracies during the sixteenth and seventeenth centuries, mainly to meet the demands of war. Consequently they became more highly integrated and cohesive political structures.

Many European states formed the center or core of much larger political formations known as empires°. The main characteristic of an empire in the seventeenth and eighteenth centuries was that it comprised many different kingdoms or territorial possessions outside the geographical boundaries of the state itself. These imperial territories were controlled by the metropolis, but they were not fully integrated into its administrative structure. Some of the territories that formed a part of these empires were located in Europe. The Austrian Habsburg monarchy, for example, had jurisdiction over a host of separate kingdoms and principalities in central and eastern Europe, including Hungary and Bohemia. This arrangement made Austria an empire, a designation it formally acquired in 1806. In like manner the Spanish monarchy, which also was an empire, controlled many different kingdoms and provinces in the Iberian peninsula as well as territories in southern Italy and the Netherlands. On the eastern and southeastern periphery of Europe lay two other empires: the Russian and the Ottoman, which controlled vast expanses of land not only in eastern Europe but also in the adjacent areas of Asia. As in previous centuries, the Russian and Ottoman empires marked the ever-shifting and often blurred boundaries between East and West.

Beginning in the fifteenth century, as the result of transoceanic voyages of exploration and the establishment of overseas colonies, western European states acquired, settled, or controlled territories in the Americas, Africa, and Asia. Mastery of these lands came much more quickly in the New World than in Asia. The peoples of North and South America whom the Europeans encountered when they arrived were able fighters, but they were not organized politically, and diseases introduced by the Europeans drastically reduced their numbers. European settlers, who had the added advantage of superior military technology, were able to gain the upper hand in battle, seize or purchase their lands, and force those who survived to retreat into less inhabited areas.

When Europeans started to develop extensive trading routes in Asia, however, that continent was already highly developed politically and militarily. Three Muslim empires—the Ottoman, the Safavid (Persia), and the Mughal (India)—as well as the neighboring Chinese Empire in East Asia occupied the mass of land from the Balkans to the Pacific Ocean. It was only when these Asian empires began to fall apart, giving greater autonomy to the smaller, subordinate states within their boundaries, that Europeans were able to exploit the situation and secure favorable trading arrangements and ultimately control of Asian territory itself.

Until the late eighteenth century European governments usually allowed their colonies a considerable degree of political autonomy. Although monarchs claimed sovereignty over all their imperial possessions, the distance of these lands from the metropolis made direct rule difficult. The solution to this problem was to delegate the functions of government either to officials who represented royal authority in the colony or to some corporate body. In the British, Dutch, and French empires, trading companies that engaged in commerce with the East Indies assumed many of these functions. These companies could negotiate treaties, raise military forces, and govern the population of the colonies. In many ways the companies became small states themselves, operating under the authority of the Crown. In North America and the Caribbean, imperial governments usually granted charters to their colonies, authorizing them to establish their own legislative assemblies.

Colonists were granted considerable autonomy as long as they conducted trade exclusively with the metropolis. Metropolitan governments were determined to use the colonies to realize the objectives of gaining the largest possible share of world trade, acquiring a supply of gold and other precious metals, and collecting import and export duties on the colonial trade. To accomplish these ends they passed legislation forcing the colonists to trade exclusively with the metropolis. When colonists tried to break this monopoly by trading with other nations or colonies, they came into direct conflict with their own governments in Europe.

The earliest of the European overseas empires were established by the Spanish and the Portuguese. During the period we are considering here, three rising European powers—Great Britain, France, and the Dutch Republic—began to rival the older empires. By the end of the period the British had emerged as the dominant imperial power. During the third period of imperial expansion in the late nineteenth and early twentieth centuries, the imperial rivalries that had developed in earlier years continued in different forms, and new European powers, most notably Germany and Italy, joined in the competition.

THE RISE OF THE BRITISH EMPIRE

The fastest-growing of these new European overseas empires during this period was that of Great Britain. England had begun its overseas empire in the late twelfth century, when it conquered the neighboring island of Ireland, but only in the seventeenth century did it begin to acquire lands in the New World and Asia. Attempts to establish colonies on the Atlantic coast of North America in the late sixteenth century had failed, most notably at Roanoke (in present-day North Carolina) in 1584. After Spain agreed not to contest English claims of territory north of Florida, the English succeed in settling a series of colonies along the Atlantic seaboard, the first of which was at Jamestown, Virginia, in 1607.

By 1700 this English empire in the New World included a number of colonies on the North American mainland, a vast territory in the northern part of Canada, and a cluster of islands in the Caribbean, most notably Barbados, Jamaica, and the Bahamas. These West Indian colonies developed an economy that used slave labor, and therefore blacks brought there from Africa soon outnumbered Europeans by a significant margin. In the colonies on the mainland of North America, however, most of the colonists were white. This was true even in the southern colonies, where slave labor was also introduced. Only in South Carolina, which was settled by Caribbean planters, did the black population exceed 50 percent.

A number of English colonists, especially in the northern colonies, had emigrated so that they might practice their religion without legal restraint. During the 1630s communities of English Protestants known as Puritans settled in New England. They objected to the control of the English Church by bishops, especially during the period from 1633 to 1641, when William Laud served as Archbishop of Canterbury. Their main complaint was the church services authorized by Laud too closely resembled those of Roman Catholicism. At the same time small groups of English Catholics, who often faced prosecution in English courts for practicing their religion, had taken refuge in Maryland. In the late seventeenth century a dissenting Protestant sect known as Quakers (so called because their founder, George Fox, told them to quake at the word of the Lord), smarting under legislation that denied them religious freedom and political power, emigrated to Pennsylvania.

Many other British colonists had come to America as indentured servants, usually serving for a period of seven years in order to gain their freedom. By this time the size of the indigenous American population in the colonies had become negligible. The Indians of North America either had been pushed westward beyond the frontiers of these colonies, had died of diseases to which they were highly vulnerable, or had been killed in skirmishes with the English.

During the seventeenth century the English also established a number of trading posts, known as factories°, along the coast of India. The first of these factories was Surat, which was settled in 1612, and it was soon followed by Madras (1640), Bombay (1661), and Calcutta (1690). There were significant differences between these mercantile outposts and the colonies in the Caribbean and the North American mainland. The number of British settlers in India, most of whom were members of the East India Company, remained extremely small, and they did not establish large plantations like those in the Caribbean colonies and the southern mainland colonies. Consequently they did not introduce slave labor into these countries.

In contrast to the situation in North America and the Caribbean, the British in India had to deal with a large native population. At first they had contact with that population only when they were engaged in trade. In the second half of the eighteenth century, however, the British began to gain direct political control of Indian provinces, and by 1850 they controlled a large portion of the South Asian subcontinent. Not only did the British eventually subject the Indians to their rule, but they also drove out their French and Dutch commercial rivals, who had established their own factories along the coast.

In addition to their settlements in America and India, the British acquired influence and ultimately political control of the area from Southeast Asia stretching down into the South Pacific. In the late seventeenth century the British began to challenge the Dutch and the Portuguese for control of the trade with Indonesia, and in the second half of the eighteenth century British merchants established a thriving trade with the countries on the Malay peninsula. In the late eighteenth century the British also began to explore the South Pacific, which remained the last part of the inhabited world that Europeans had not yet visited and settled. In 1770 the British naval officer and explorer Captain James Cook (1728–1779) claimed the entire eastern coast of Australia for Great Britain, and in 1788 the British established a penal colony in the southeastern corner of the continent at Botany Bay. Cook also visited New Zealand and many of the islands in the South Pacific, including Fiji, but colonies were not established at those locations until the middle of the nineteenth century.

The British Empire of the late seventeenth and eighteenth centuries possessed little administrative coherence; it was a hodge-podge of colonies, factories, and territories that had different relationships to the royal government in Britain (see Map 19.1). In India the provinces brought under British control were run by a trading corporation that exercised many functions of government. Some colonies in America, such as Maryland and Pennsylvania, operated under charters granted to members of the aristocracy. Most of the colonies on the North American mainland and in the Caribbean had their own legislatures. None of these colonies, however, sent representatives to the British Parliament. The only bond of unity among all the colonists is that they, like British subjects living in England or Scotland, owed their allegiance to the monarch and were under the monarch's protection. All of these colonists were therefore British subjects.

THE SCATTERED FRENCH EMPIRE

French colonization of North America and India paralleled that of Great Britain, but it never achieved the same degree of success. As the British were establishing footholds in the West Indies and the mainland of North America, the French acquired their own islands in the Caribbean and laid claim to large sections of Canada and the Ohio and Mississippi River valleys in the present-day United States. In the West Indies the French began the process of colonization by introducing indentured servants for periods of three years, but in the eighteenth century they began to follow the British and Spanish pattern of importing slaves to provide the labor for the sugar plantations. In North America French settlers did not require a large labor supply, since their main economic undertakings were the fur trade and fishing. Consequently slaves were not introduced to those areas. The European population of French possessions in North America also stayed well below that of the British colonies.

The parallel between French and British overseas expansion extended to India, where in the early eighteenth century the French East India Company established factories at Pondicherry, Chandenagar, and other locations. Rivalry with the British also led the French to make alliances with native governors of Indian provinces, and with this support the French fought the British both on land and sea at different critical times between 1744 and 1815. The British ultimately prevailed in this struggle, and by the turn of the nineteenth century the French presence in India had been reduced to a few isolated factories.

The waning of French influence in India coincided with a series of territorial losses in the New World. Defeats suffered at the hands of the British during the Seven Years' War (1756–1763) resulted in the transfer of French Canada and the territory east of the Mississippi River to Great Britain. During that conflict France also ceded the vast region of Louisiana between the Mississippi River and the Rocky Mountains to Spain. France regained Louisiana in 1801 but then promptly sold the entire territory to the United States in 1803. The following year the French Caribbean colony of Saint Domingue became independent, although France retained possession of its other West Indian colonies.

The only overseas area where France continued to expand after 1800 was much closer to home, on the Mediterranean shores of North Africa. French influence in this area had begun in the seventeenth century, and it persisted until the twentieth century. France occupied Egypt briefly from 1798 until 1801, and it acquired Algeria in

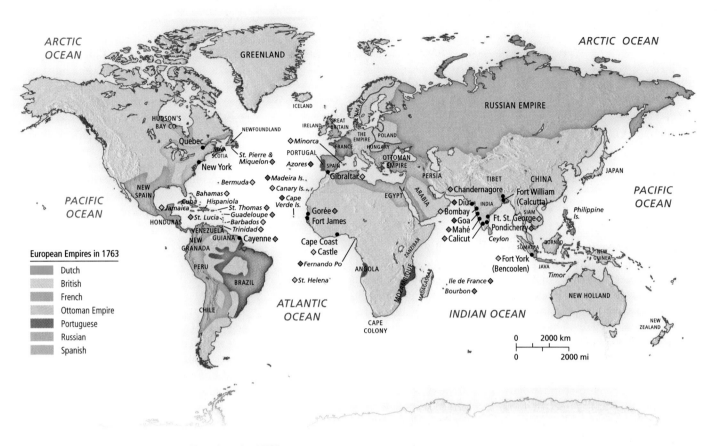

■ **Map 19.1 European Empires in 1763**

This map shows the overseas possessions of Britain, France, the Dutch Republic, Spain, and Portugal. Russian overseas expansion into North America had not yet begun.

1830. It was not until the third stage of imperialism in the late nineteenth century that France took possession of large territories in the interior of Africa and in Asia (see Chapter 23).

THE COMMERCIAL DUTCH EMPIRE

The tiny Dutch Republic acquired almost all of its overseas possessions in the first half of the seventeenth century, at about the same time that the British and French were establishing their first colonies in Asia and the New World. The formation of the Dutch empire went hand in hand with the explosive growth of the Dutch economy in the seventeenth century. At that time the Dutch Republic became the very center of a global economy, and its overseas colonies in the New World, Asia, and Africa helped the republic maintain its commercial supremacy. Dutch overseas settlements, just like the port cities of the metropolis, were dedicated almost exclusively to serving the interests of trade.

The Dutch were more eager than other European powers to use military and naval power to acquire and fortify trading depots. They also used military force to seize factories that had been established earlier by other countries, es-

pecially Portugal. With more than 1,400 vessels that could be used as warships and 250,000 sailors, they had a distinct military advantage over the Portuguese, who could not muster half those numbers. They seized two trading posts from the Portuguese on the West African coast in 1637, and in 1641 they also acquired from Portugal the African islands of São Tomé and Principe. In 1624 the Dutch, operating through their West Indian Company, seized the northern coast of Brazil, and after its return to Portugal in 1654 they acquired two small West Indian islands and a number of small plantation colonies on the Guiana coast of South America, mainly in present-day Surinam. From these small settlements in Africa and the Caribbean the Dutch carried on trade with the Spanish, Portuguese, French, and British colonies. Through these ports the Dutch brought more than 500,000 slaves to Brazil, the Spanish colonies, and the French and British West Indies.

In addition to their African and Caribbean possessions, the Dutch established a presence in three other parts of the world. In the early seventeenth century they settled a colony in the Hudson River valley on the North American mainland. They named the colony New Netherland and its main port, at the mouth of the river, New Amsterdam. In

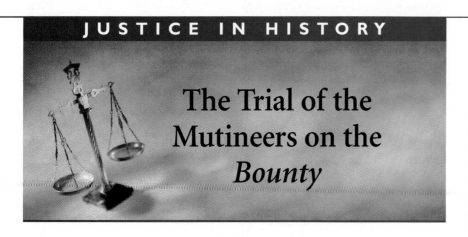

The Trial of the Mutineers on the *Bounty*

In December 1787 a British ship named the *Bounty,* under the captainship of William Bligh, left Portsmouth, England, on a momentous journey to Tahiti, an island in the South Pacific that Captain James Cook had first visited in 1769. The goal of the voyage of the *Bounty* was neither exploration nor colonial expansion but to bring home breadfruit trees that Cook had discovered on his second trip to the island in 1773. The trees, so it was hoped, would be introduced to the West Indies as a source of food for the slaves and hence the survival of the plantation economy. The voyage of the *Bounty* was therefore part of the operation of the new global economy that European expansion had made possible. The total size of the crew, all of whom had volunteered for service, was forty-six. The master's first mate, who became the main leader of a mutiny against Bligh, was Fletcher Christian.

The mutiny did not take place until after the ship had remained at Tahiti for a number of months, loaded its cargo of more than a thousand breadfruit plants, and begun its return voyage. The main reason for the mutiny was Captain Bligh's abusive and humiliating language. Unlike many other officers who faced the task of maintaining order on their ships and commanding the obedience of their crews, Bligh did not flog his men. In that regard Bligh's behavior was mild. Instead he went into tantrums and verbally abused them, belittling them and calling them scoundrels. Just before the mutiny Bligh called Fletcher Christian

a cowardly rascal and falsely accused him of stealing from him. On the morning of April 28, 1788 Christian arrested Bligh at bayonet point, tied his hands behind his back, and threatened him with instant death if he should speak a word. Claiming that "Captain Bligh had brought all this on himself," Christian and his associates put Bligh and eighteen other members of the crew into one of the ship's small launch boats and set them adrift, leaving them to reach a nearby island by their own power.

The mutineers sailed on to the island of Tubuai, where after a brief stay they split into two groups. Nine of them, headed by Christian and accompanied by six Tahitian men and twelve women, established a settlement on Pitcairn Island. The remaining sixteen mutineers returned to Tahiti. All but two of these men were apprehended in

1791 by Captain Edwards of the H.M.S. *Pandora,* which had been sent to Tahiti with the objective of arresting them and returning them to England for trial. At the beginning of its return voyage the *Pandora* was shipwrecked, and four of the prisoners drowned. The rest reached England aboard another ship in 1792. They were promptly charged before a navy court-martial with taking the *Bounty* away from its captain and with desertion, both of which were offenses under the Naval Discipline Act of 1766.

The trial took place aboard a British ship, H.M.S. *Duke,* in Portsmouth harbor in September 1792. The proceeding had all the markings of a state trial, one initiated by the government for offenses against the crown. Mutiny and desertion represented challenges to the state itself. During the second period of imperial expansion navies became major instruments of state power. Even when ships were used for purposes of exploration rather than naval combat, they served the interests of the state. The captain of the ship represented the power of the sovereign at sea. Because of the difficulty of maintaining order in such circumstances, he was given absolute authority. He could use whatever means necessary, including the infliction of corporal

■ **Sextant**

Eighteenth-century ships like the *Bounty* used this instrument to determine nautical position by means of the stars.

■ *The Mutineers Casting Bligh Adrift in the Launch,*
Engraving by Robert Dodd (1790)
This was the central act in the mutiny led by Fletcher Christian. Captain Bligh is standing in the launch in his nightclothes. Some of the breadfruit trees loaded on the ship at Tahiti can be seen on the top deck.

punishment, to preserve order. To disobey or challenge him was interpreted as an act of rebellion.

The trial was based on the assumption that the mutiny was illegal and seditious. The only question was the extent of individual involvement in the act itself. The degree of involvement was measured by evidence of one's cooperation with Christian or his loyalty to Bligh. The mere fact that some men had remained with Christian on the *Bounty* did not prove that they had supported the mutiny. Four of those men gave little evidence of having voluntarily cooperated with Christian, and those four men were eventually acquitted. The testimony of Captain Bligh, who testified that those four crew members had been reluctant to put him in the launch boat, was decisive in securing their nonguilty verdicts.

The remaining six men were convicted and sentenced to die by hanging. Three of those men were eventually spared their lives. Peter Heywood and James Morrison were well connected to influential people in the navy and the government and received royal pardons. William Muspratt, one of only three mutineers to hire a lawyer, entered a protest against the procedures of the court. In a court-martial, unlike a criminal trial at the common law, a prisoner could not call witnesses in his own defense. At the time of his conviction Muspratt protested that he had been "debarred calling witnesses whose evidence I have reason to believe would have tended to prove my innocence." The difference between the two systems of criminal justice, he claimed, "is dreadful to the subject and fatal to me." On this ground Muspratt was reprieved.

The three men who were executed died as model prisoners, proclaiming the illegality of their rebellion. Although the government had executed only a small minority of the mutineers, by securing their conviction and dramatizing it with a widely publicized hanging, it had upheld its authority and thus reinforced the power of the crown. ■

Questions of Justice

1. How would you characterize the different ideals of justice used by the mutineers and the British admiralty court as the bases of their actions?

2. How would you explain the differences in the sentences handed down to the mutineers?

3. What does the journey of the *Bounty* tell us about the role of the British navy in the process of imperial expansion? What problems were inherent in using British ships for these purposes?

Taking It Further

Rutter, Owen, ed. *The Court-Martial of the "Bounty" Mutineers.* 1931. Contains a full transcript of the trial.

1664 the Dutch lost the colony to the English, who renamed the colony and the port New York. The second area was in Asia, where the Dutch East India Company established a fort at Batavia (now Jakarta in Indonesia) and factories in India, China, and Japan. These possessions allowed the Dutch to engage in trade throughout Asia. In the eighteenth century, however, the British began to take control of Dutch trading routes.

The third area was the southern tip of Africa, where in 1652 the Dutch settled a colony at the Cape of Good Hope, mainly to provide support for ships engaged in commerce with the East Indies. In this colony some 1,700 Dutch settlers, most of them farmers known as boers°, developed an agricultural economy on plantations that employed slave labor. The loss of this colony to the British at the end of the eighteenth century reflected a more general decline of Dutch military and imperial strength.

THE VAST SPANISH EMPIRE

Of all the European overseas empires, the lands under the control of the Spanish monarchy were the most extensive. At the height of its power in 1650, the Spanish Empire covered the western part of North America from California to Mexico and from Mexico down through Central America. It also included Florida and the Caribbean islands of Cuba, San Domingo, and Puerto Rico. It embraced almost all of South America except Brazil, which was under Portuguese control. In Asia the main Spanish possessions were the Philippine Islands, named for the future King Philip II in 1542 and conquered with little bloodshed after 1564. The Philippines served as the main base from which the Spanish engaged in trade with other Asian countries.

Spanish overseas possessions were never ruled as closely as the royal government in Madrid ruled the smaller kingdoms and principalities on the Iberian peninsula. Spanish overseas possessions were, however, integrated into a much more authoritative imperial system than were those of the British. Until the eighteenth century a hierarchy of councils, staffed by men appointed by the crown, exercised political control of the various large territories or viceroyalties into which the empire was divided. Like all mercantilist enterprises, the Spanish colonial empire was designed to serve the purposes of trade. Until the eighteenth century a council known as the House of Trade, situated in Seville, exercised a monopoly over all colonial commerce. It funneled trade with the colonies from the southwestern Spanish port of Cadiz and to selected ports on the eastern coasts of Spanish America, from which it was then redirected to other ports. The ships returned to Spain carrying the gold and silver that had been extracted from the mines of Mexico and Peru. The entire journey was made under the protection of Spanish warships.

The Bourbon kings of Spain, who were installed on the throne in 1700, introduced a number of political reforms

■ **The Dutch Factory of Batavia in Indonesia, ca. 1665**
The Dutch Republic dominated the Asian trade in the seventeenth century. Batavia (now Jakarta) was the most important of their settlements in Southeast Asia. The efforts of the Dutch to transplant their culture is evident in this building's Dutch style of architecture.

that were intended to increase the volume of the colonial trade and prevent the smuggling that had always threatened to undermine it. On the one hand, they opened up the colonial trade to more Spanish and American ports and also permitted more trade within the colonies. On the other hand, the Bourbons, especially Charles III (r. 1759–1788), brought the viceroyalties under more direct control of Spanish royal officials and increased the efficiency of the tax collection system. These Bourbon reforms made the empire more manageable and profitable, but they also created tension between the Spanish-born bureaucrats and the creoles°, the people of Spanish descent who had been born in the colonies. These tensions eventually led in the early nineteenth century to a series of wars of independence from Spain that we shall discuss in a later section.

THE DECLINING PORTUGUESE EMPIRE

The Portuguese had been the first European nation to engage in overseas exploration and colonization. During the late fifteenth and sixteenth centuries they had established colonies in Asia, South America, and Africa (see Chapter 12). By the beginning of the eighteenth century, however, the Portuguese Empire had declined in size and wealth in relation to its rivals. The Portuguese continued to hold a few ports in India, most notably the small island of Goa. They also retained a factory at Macao off the southeastern coast of China. In the New World the major Portuguese plantation colony was Brazil, which occupied almost half the land mass of South America and which supplied Europe with sugar, cacao (from which chocolate is made), and other agricultural commodities. Closely linked to Brazil were the Portuguese colonies along and off the West African coast. These possessions were all deeply involved in the transatlantic trade, especially in slaves. The Portuguese also had a series of trading stations and small settlements on the southeastern coast of Africa, including Mozambique.

The contraction of the Portuguese Empire in the seventeenth and eighteenth centuries resulted in the transfer of land to other European countries. A relatively weak European power, Portugal did not fare well in the fierce military conflicts that ensued in South America and Asia over control of the colonial trade. Portugal's main military

and economic competition came from the Dutch, who seized many of its Asian, African, and South American colonies, and who acquired many Portuguese trading routes. Most of those losses took place in Asia between 1600 and 1670. The Portuguese Empire suffered further losses when the crown relinquished Bombay and the northern African port of Tangier to the English as part of the dowry for the Portuguese princess Catherine of Braganza when she married King Charles II in 1661.

Brazil remained by far the most important of the Portuguese possessions during the late seventeenth and eighteenth centuries. The colony suffered from an unfavorable balance of trade with Portugal, but it expanded in population and wealth during this period, especially after the discovery of gold and diamonds led to large-scale mining in the interior. The slave trade increased in volume in order to provide additional labor in the mines and on the sugar plantations. In the first quarter of the nineteenth century, as the British slave trade declined and came to an end, Portuguese ships carried 871,600 slaves to Brazil. Between 1826 and 1850 the number increased to an astonishing 1,247,700. As a result of this massive influx of Africans,

■ **Rio de Janeiro, the Major Slave Port in Brazil, Receiving Slaves**
More slaves went to Brazil than to any other country in the Americas. The trade continued until 1851, and only in 1888 was the institution of slavery abolished.

slaves accounted for approximately 40 percent of the entire Brazilian population by the beginning of the nineteenth century.

Like most other European countries, Portugal tightened the control of its imperial possessions during the second half of the eighteenth century. During the ministry of the dictatorial Marquis of Pombal from 1755 to 1777, efforts were made to increase the control exercised by the crown over all aspects of colonial life. Pombal also took steps to encourage the growth of the colonial trade, and he legalized intermarriage between whites and indigenous peoples. Like the Bourbon reforms in Spanish America, this legislation created considerable resentment among the creoles against the Portuguese bureaucrats who controlled the government. As in Spanish America, these tensions led to demands for Brazil's autonomy in the nineteenth century.

THE RUSSIAN EMPIRE IN THE PACIFIC

The only eastern European state that established an overseas empire during the eighteenth century was Russia. Between the fifteenth and the early eighteenth centuries Russia had gradually acquired a massive overland empire stretching from St. Petersburg in the west across the frigid expanse of Siberia to the Pacific Ocean. The main impulse of Russian expansion had been the search for exotic furs that were in high demand in the colder climes of Russia and northern Europe. During the reign of the Empress Catherine the Great (r. 1762–1796), Russia entered a period of further territorial expansion. On its western frontier it took part in the successive partitions of Poland between 1772 and 1795, while to the south it held the Crimean region within the Ottoman Empire between 1783 and 1792.

During the late eighteenth and early nineteenth centuries Russia also extended its empire overseas. Russian traders and explorers undertook numerous expeditions to Hawaii and other islands in the Pacific Ocean, sailing as far south as Mexico. They did not, however, establish colonies in these locations. Further expeditions brought Russia across the northern Pacific, where they encroached upon the hunting grounds of the native Aleuts in Alaska. The Russian-American Company, established in 1789, built a number of trading posts along the Pacific seaboard from Alaska down to Fort Ross in northern California. These claims led to a protracted territorial dispute with Spain, which had established a string of missions and settlements on the California coast as far north as San Francisco. In this way the two great European empires of Russia and Spain, advancing from opposite directions, confronted each other on the western coast of North America. Russian expansion into Alaska and California also led to territorial disputes with the United States, which was engaged in its own process of territorial expansion westward toward the Pacific during the nineteenth century.

Warfare in Europe, North America, and Asia

Until the middle of the seventeenth century, European states engaged each other in battle almost exclusively within their own continent. The farthest their armies ever traveled was to the Middle East to fight the Turks or to Ireland to conquer the native Celts. The acquisition of overseas empires and the conflicts that erupted between European powers over the control of global trade brought those European conflicts to new and distant military theaters. Wars that began over territory in Europe were readily extended to America in one direction and to Asia in the other. The military forces that fought in these imperial battles consisted not only of metropolitan government troops but also those of the colonists. These colonial forces were often supplemented by the troops drawn from the local population, such as when the French recruited Native Americans to fight with them against the British in North America. This pattern of recruiting soldiers from the indigenous population, which began in the eighteenth century, became the norm during the third and final phase of empire building in the nineteenth and early twentieth centuries.

Wars fought overseas placed a premium upon naval strength. Ground troops remained important, both in Europe and overseas, but naval power increasingly proved to be the crucial factor. All of the Western imperial powers either possessed or acquired large navies. Great Britain and the Dutch Republic rose to the status of world powers on the basis of sea power, while the French strengthened their navy considerably during the reign of Louis XIV. The Dutch used their naval power mainly against the Portuguese and the British, while the British directed theirs against the French and the Spanish as well as the Dutch. The overwhelming success that the British realized in these conflicts resulted in the establishment of British maritime supremacy.

MERCANTILE WARFARE

An increasingly important motive for engaging in warfare in the late seventeenth and eighteenth centuries was the protection and expansion of trade. The theory that underlay and inspired these imperial wars was mercantilism. As we discussed in Chapter 15, those who subscribed to this theory, such as Louis XIV's minister Jean-Baptiste Colbert, believed that the wealth of the state depended upon its ability to import fewer commodities than it exported and thus to acquire the largest possible share of the world's monetary supply. In order to achieve this goal, mercantilists encouraged domestic industry and placed heavy customs duties or tariffs on imported goods. Mercantilism was therefore a policy of protectionism°, the shielding of domestic industries from foreign competition. Mercantilists also sought to increase the size of the country's commercial fleet, establish colonies in order to promote trade, and import raw materials from the colonies to benefit domestic industry. The imperial wars of the seventeenth and eighteenth centuries, which were fought over the control of colonies and trading routes, thus formed part of a mercantilist policy.

Of course the older, more traditional motives for waging war, especially the desire of rulers for territorial expansion, did not disappear. The acquisitive impulses of France, Prussia, Austria, and Russia remained a recurrent source of international conflict throughout this period. But the mercantile motive, which began to emerge only in the 1650s, soon became a major feature of European warfare, and it explains why military conflict was extended from Europe to the colonies. As this motive for going to war became more important, wars fought primarily for religious or ideological reasons, which had been the norm during the period of the Reformation, virtually disappeared.

The first of the great mercantile wars that involved conflict overseas arose between England and the Dutch Republic in the middle and late seventeenth century (1652–1654, 1664–1667, 1672–1675). As these wars were fought between two Protestant powers, little about these conflicts could be attributed to religious zeal. Instead they were fought mainly for mercantile advantage between the two emerging commercial giants of Europe. The two countries were engaged in heated competition for control of the transatlantic trade, and the Dutch resented the passage of English laws, known as the Navigation Acts, that excluded them from trade with the English colonies. The Dutch claimed the right to trade with all ports in the world as well as to fish in the waters off British shores. Not surprisingly, many of the engagements in these wars took place at sea and in the colonies. The most significant outcome of these Anglo-Dutch wars was the loss of the port city of New Amsterdam to the English. That city, renamed New York, later became the leading port and financial center in the Western Hemisphere.

Shortly after the first Anglo-Dutch War, England also went to war against Spain (1655–1657). Although this conflict pitted a Protestant against a Catholic power, it too reflected the new emphasis on mercantile objectives. The main battles of this war were not fought in the English Channel, as they had been when the Spanish Armada had descended on England in 1588, but in the Caribbean. The war resulted in the British acquisition of one of its most important Caribbean colonies, Jamaica, in 1655. The Anglo-Spanish tensions that surfaced in this conflict continued into the eighteenth century, when Britain tried to smuggle more goods than it was allowed by the Treaty of Utrecht (1713) into the Spanish trading post of Portobelo on the isthmus of Panama. The Spanish retaliated by cutting off

the ear of Robert Jenkins, an English captain, and this incident led to the War of Jenkins' Ear in 1739. In 1762, during another war against Spain (as well as France), armed forces from Britain and the North American colonies seized the Cuban port of Havana as part of an effort to monopolize the Caribbean trade. The following year, however, Britain returned the city to Spain in exchange for Florida. This acquisition gave the British control of the entire North American eastern seaboard.

ANGLO-FRENCH MILITARY RIVALRY

Anglo-Spanish conflict paled in comparison with the bitter commercial rivalry between Great Britain and France during the eighteenth century. Anglo-French conflict was one of the few consistent patterns of eighteenth-century European warfare. It lasted so long and had so many different phases that it is known as the second Hundred Years' War, a recurrence of the bitter period of warfare between England and France from the middle of the fourteenth to the middle of the fifteenth century. The great difference between the two periods of warfare was that the first

CHRONOLOGY

A Century of Anglo-French Warfare

1701–1713	War of the Spanish Succession (Queen Anne's War in North America): Spain is allied with France
1740–1748	War of the Austrian Succession (Europe): France is allied with Spain, Prussia, and Russia; Britain is allied with Austria
1744–1748	King George's War (North America)
1754–1763	French and Indian War (North America): French and British are allied with different Indian tribes
1756–1763	Seven Years' War (Europe): France is allied with Austria; Britain is allied with Prussia
1775–1783	American War of Independence: France is allied with United States against Britain in 1778
1781–1783	Warfare in India
1792–1815	French Revolutionary and Napoleonic Wars: Britain is allied at various times with Austria, Prussia, Spain, and the Dutch Republic; warfare at various times in the West Indies as well as in India

Hundred Years' War involved military conflicts in France, while the second was marked by periodic naval and military engagements not only in Europe but in Asia and North America as well.

The Wars of the Spanish and Austrian Successions, 1701–1748

This eighteenth-century Anglo-French rivalry had its roots in the war of the Spanish Succession (1701–1713). The war began as an effort to prevent France from putting Louis XIV's grandson, Philip, on the Spanish throne (see Chapter 15). The implications of this dynastic conflict for the British and French colonial empires were monumental. By uniting French and Spanish territory the proposed succession would have created a massive French-Spanish empire not only in Europe but in the Western Hemisphere as well. This combination of French and Spanish territory and military power threatened to eclipse the British colonies along the North American coast and deprive British merchants of much of their valuable trade.

The ensuing struggle in North America, known by British colonists as Queen Anne's War, was settled in Britain's favor by the Treaty of Utrecht in 1713. Philip V, the first Spanish king from the Bourbon dynasty (r. 1700–1746), was allowed to remain on the throne, but French and Spanish territories in Europe and America were kept separate. Even more important, the French conceded their Canadian territories of Newfoundland and Nova Scotia to the British. The treaty, which also gave Britain the contract to ship slaves to the Spanish colonies for thirty years, marked the emergence of Britain as Europe's dominant colonial and maritime power.

The next phase of Anglo-French warfare, the War of the Austrian Succession (1740–1748), formed part of a European conflict that engaged the forces of Austria, Prussia, and Spain as well as those of Britain and France. In this conflict European dynastic struggles once again intersected with competition for colonial advantage overseas. The ostensible cause of this war was the impetuous decision by the new king of Prussia, the absolutist Frederick II (r. 1740–1786), to seize the large German-speaking province of Silesia from Austria upon the succession of Maria Theresa (r. 1740–1780) as the ruler of the hereditary Habsburg lands. Using the large army that his militaristic father Frederick William I had assembled, Frederick struck with devastating effectiveness, and by terms of the treaty that ended the war he acquired most of the province.

Frederick's aggression enticed other European powers to join the conflict. Eager to acquire some of the Habsburg territories in different parts of Europe, France and Russia both declared war on Austria. Britain then entered the war against France, mainly to keep France from acquiring Austria's possessions in the Netherlands. Britain's main concern in the European phase of this war, as it had been in the War of the Spanish Succession, was to maintain the balance of power among European states.

The colonial phase of this war, known in British North America as King George's War, opened in 1744, when the French supported the Spanish in a separate war that Spain had been waging against Britain since 1739 over the Caribbean trade. Clashes between French and British trading companies in India also began in the same year. The main military engagement of this war was the seizure of the French port and fortress of Louisbourg on Cape Breton Island in Canada by 4,000 New England colonial troops and a large British fleet. At the end of the war, however, the British returned Louisbourg to the French in exchange for the factory of Madras in India, which the French had taken during the war.

The Seven Years' War, 1756–1763

European and colonial rivalries became even more entangled in the next round of Anglo-French warfare, known as the Seven Years' War (1756–1763) in Europe and the French and Indian War (1754–1763) in North America. In Europe the conflict arose as a result of Maria Theresa's eventually unsuccessful attempt to regain Silesia. In this encounter, however, she joined forces with her former enemies, France and Russia, after Great Britain signed a defensive alliance with Prussia. This "diplomatic revolution" of 1756 shifted all the traditional alliances among European powers, but it did not affect Anglo-French rivalry in the colonies, which continued unabated.

The fighting in this North American theater of the war was particularly brutal and inflicted extensive casualties. In their struggle to gain control of eastern port cities and interior lands, the British and the French secured alliances with different Indian tribes. Among the many victims were some of France's Indian allies who contracted smallpox when British-American colonists sold them blankets deliberately contaminated with the disease—the first known use of germ warfare in the West. This colonial war also had an Asian theater, in which French and British forces, most of them drawn from the trading companies of their respective countries, vied for mercantile influence and the possession of factories along the coast of the Indian Ocean. This conflict led directly to the British acquisition of the Indian province of Bengal in 1765.

The Treaty of Paris, which ended this round of European and colonial warfare in 1763, had more profound implications in the colonies than in Europe. In Europe, Prussia managed to hold on to Silesia, although its army incurred heavy casualties and its economy suffered from the war. In North America, however, monumental changes occurred. As a result of British naval victories, all of French Canada east of the Mississippi, including the entire province of Quebec, with its predominantly French population and French system of civil law, passed into

British control (see Map 19.2). Even more important, the treaty secured British naval and mercantile superiority in the Atlantic, Caribbean, and Indian oceans. By virtue of its victories over France, Britain gained control of the lion's share of world commerce. This commercial superiority had profound implications for the economic development of Britain. Partially because of its ability to acquire raw materials from its colonies and to market its products throughout the world, Britain became the first country to experience the Industrial Revolution, as shall be discussed fully in Chapter 20.

The American and French Revolutionary Wars, 1775–1815

Despite the British victory over the French in 1763, the long conflict between the two countries continued into the early nineteenth century. During the American War of Independence (1775–1783), which we shall consider later, the North American colonists secured French military aid. During that war a British fleet attacked the French colony of Martinique, while the French dispatched an expedition against the British at Savannah that included hundreds of Africans and mulattos, or people of mixed race, drawn

■ **Map 19.2   British Possessions in North America and the Caribbean After the Treaty of Paris**

The British acquisition of French territory marked a decisive moment in the expansion of the British Empire.

from the population of the West Indies. In India further conflicts between the French and British occurred, mainly between 1781 and 1783. These simultaneous military engagements in various parts of the world turned this phase of Anglo-French conflict into the first truly global war.

Anglo-French rivalry entered yet another phase between 1792 and 1815, during the era of the French Revolution (see Chapter 18). The British were able to maintain their military and naval superiority, although once again it required an alliance with many European powers and the creation of a new balance of power against France. Even during this later phase of this French-British rivalry the British pursued imperial objectives. They expanded their empire in India and consolidated their territory there under the governorship of Richard Wellesley (1760–1842). In 1795, in the midst of the war against France, the British also acquired the Dutch colony at the Cape of Good Hope, giving them a base for their claims to much larger African territories in the nineteenth century.

The Atlantic World

By the beginning of the eighteenth century, the territorial acquisitions of the five European maritime powers had moved the geographical center of the West from the European continent to the Atlantic Ocean itself. The Atlantic, rather than separating large geographical land masses, became a central, unifying geographical entity. The boundaries of this new Western world were the four continents that bordered the Atlantic: Europe, Africa, North America, and South America. The main thoroughfares that linked them were maritime routes across the Atlantic and up and down its coasts. The main points of commercial and cultural contact between the four continents, until the end of the eighteenth century, were the coastal areas and ports that bordered on the ocean. Within this Atlantic world arose new patterns of trade and economic activity, new interactions between ethnic and racial groups, and new political institutions. The Atlantic world also became the arena in which political and religious ideas were transmitted across the ocean and developed within a new environment.

THE ATLANTIC ECONOMY

The exchange of commercial goods and slaves between the western coasts of Europe, the African coasts, and the ports of North and South America created an economic enterprise that became one of the most active in the entire world

(see Map 19.3). The ships that had brought the slaves from Africa to the Americas used the profits gained from their transactions to acquire precious metals and agricultural products for the European market. They then returned to western European Atlantic ports, where the goods were sold.

This Atlantic economy was fueled ultimately by the demand of a growing European population for agricultural products that could not be obtained in Europe and were more costly to transport from Asia. Sugar was the most important of these commodities, but tobacco, cotton, rice, cacao, and coffee also became staples of the transatlantic trade. At the same time the North and South American colonists created a steady demand for manufactured goods, especially cutlery and metal tools, that were produced in Europe.

Two of the commodities that were imported from the colonies, tobacco and coffee, were criticized for the harmful effects they had on the human body. Both products had originally come from the Middle East or India, but lower transportation costs made the American source more desirable. Tobacco was the target of a number of attacks written in the seventeenth century. Even at that early date critics recognized the adverse physical effects of this product, which had been used widely among Native Americans. "Tobacco, that outlandish weed," read one popular rhyme, "It spends the brain and spoils the seed." Critics also believed that it had a hallucinatory effect on those who inhaled its smoke.

Coffee was another stimulant that originally came exclusively from the Middle East but later began to be shipped from Haiti and after 1809 from Brazil. Like tobacco, coffee was controversial because of the effects it had on the human body. In the late seventeenth and eighteenth centuries it was believed to be a source of political radicalism, probably because the coffeehouses where it was consumed served as gathering places for political dissidents. Contemporaries also identified coffee's capacity to produce irritability and depression.

The Atlantic economy had its own rhythms, but it was also part of a global economy that had taken shape during the seventeenth century. As Europeans had expanded the volume of their imports from Asia, those markets were fully integrated into this world system. The system was capitalist in the sense that the production and distribution of commodities were undertaken by private individuals, in a systematic way, for the purposes of profit. European governments had an interest in this capitalist economy because as mercantilists they wanted their countries to acquire the largest possible share of world trade, but they did not control the actual operations of the marketplace. Their role was mainly to authorize individuals or trading companies to conduct trade in a particular geographical area.

Hudson Bay

GREAT BRITAIN

NETH.

NEW FRANCE

QUEBEC

LOUISIANA

NEWFOUNDLAND
(to Great Britain, 1713)

Furs

FRANCE

Manufactured goods

ACADIA
(NOVA SCOTIA)
(to Great Britain, 1713)

PORTUGAL

SPAIN

MEXICO

Tobacco, Rice, Timber

Silver

FLORIDA

Sugar, Cacao, Coffee

Canary Is.
(Spain)

ATLANTIC
OCEAN

AFRICA

CUBA

HISPANIOLA

PUERTO RICO

JAMAICA

LESSER
ANTILLES
(English and French
since about 1630)

Cape Verde Is.
(Port.)

Cape Verde

ASIENTO
(Spain to
Great Britain, 1713)

Portobelo

Sugar

European forts and trading stations

NEW
GRANADA

DUTCH
GUIANA

FRENCH
GUIANA

Amazon R.

Slaves

PERU

BRAZIL

ANGOLA

PACIFIC
OCEAN

The Atlantic Economy

- British
- Dutch
- French
- Portuguese
- Spanish

* Scale varies with perspective.

■ **Map 19.3   The Atlantic Economy in the Mid-Eighteenth Century**

Commodities and African slaves were exchanged between the four continents of North America, South America, Europe, and Africa.

■ **A Satire Against Coffee and Tobacco**
A seventeenth-century satirical depiction of two European women smoking tobacco and drinking coffee. Turkey, represented by the figure to the right, was the main source of these products in the seventeenth century. An African servant, to the left, pours the coffee.

THE ATLANTIC SLAVE TRADE

The slave trade became the very linchpin of the Atlantic economy, and all five Western European imperial powers—Britain, France, the Dutch Republic, Spain, and Portugal—engaged in it. The trade arose to meet the demand of plantation owners in the New World for agricultural labor. In the seventeenth century, after the indigenous Indian population had been ravaged by disease and the indentured whites who emigrated from Europe in search of a more secure future had gained their freedom, this demand became urgent. Slave labor possessed a number of advantages over that of free labor. Slaves could be disciplined more easily, they could be forced to work longer hours, and they could be used to build a plantation economy in which the growing, harvesting, and processing of sugar and other agricultural commodities could be directed by one authority. The use of slave labor also allowed the economies of European countries, especially Great Britain, to develop. Those who had invested in the colonial trade received attractive returns

on their investment, while agricultural profits acquired from crops produced by slaves encouraged the growth of domestic manufacturing.

The slave trade formed the crucial link in the triangular pattern of commercial routes that began when European vessels traveled to ports along the western coast of Africa. There they exchanged European goods, including guns, for slaves that African merchants had captured in the interior and had marched to the sea. At these ports the slaves were branded with initials indicating to which nation they belonged. They were then crowded into ships that transported them across the Atlantic to the coast of South America, to the Caribbean, or as far north as Maryland. This was the famous and often deadly Middle Passage, the second leg of the triangular journey, which was completed when the ships returned to their point of origin. Once they had arrived in the Americas, the slaves sold to the owners of plantations in the tropical areas of the Caribbean and the south Atlantic and in the more moderate climates of the North American mainland.

Slavery has been present throughout world history. It was a major feature of classical civilization and it was also present in medieval Europe before 1200. In Greece and Rome it had often been the result of captivity in war, whereas in the Middle Ages it was reserved for individuals who had been denied certain liberties. As Islam expanded in the ninth century, Arabs began the enslavement of foreign peoples, including black slaves from east Africa, and they continued that traffic into the early modern period. In the sixteenth and seventeenth centuries Barbary pirates in the Mediterranean captured approximately 850,000 white Europeans during sea raids and forced them into slavery in Muslim North Africa.

Within this long history of world slavery, the African slave trade conducted by Europeans is unique in two respects. The first distinction is its size. As a demographic phenomenon this involuntary transportation of Africans to the New World is without parallel in world history. It is the largest transoceanic migration recorded in written documents. Between 1519 and 1867 more than 11 million slaves were shipped from Africa to the New World. Deaths at sea reduced the number of slaves who actually arrived in the Americas to about 9.5 million. The peak years of the trade were from 1751 to 1800, when nearly four million slaves left African shores. As the volume of the slave trade increased during the eighteenth century, the percentage of African slaves among all immigrants arriving in the New World rose to more than 75 percent. Nine out of every ten slaves were sent to Brazil or the Caribbean region, including the northern coast of South America. The great majority of these slaves were sold to the owners of sugar and coffee plantations. Only about 4 percent of all slaves were destined for the British colonies on the North American mainland (after 1776 the United States), and almost all of those slaves were sent to the southern colonies.

The second distinctive feature of the European slave trade was its highly commercial nature. Acting in concert with African chieftains, European slave traders seized people who had performed no acts of aggression in their homelands, transported them overseas and sold them to the highest bidders. In this way African slaves were turned into commercial commodities and treated in a manner that deprived them of all human dignity. Slaves have never been treated well in any society, but slavery in the Americas has acquired a reputation for being particularly exploitative and barbaric, and this has much to do with its commercial character.

One harrowing incident on the British slave ship *Zong* reveals the way in which financial calculations determined the fate of slaves. The *Zong* set sail in 1781 from the African island of São Tomé with 442 African slaves on board. When the slaves began to fall ill and die because of a shortage of water, the captain of the ship, Luke Collingwood, feared

Volume of the Transatlantic Slave Trade from Africa, 1519–1867

1519–1600	266,100
1601–1650	503,500
1651–1675	239,800
1676–1700	510,000
1701–1725	958,600
1725–1750	1,311,300
1751–1775	1,905,200
1776–1800	1,921,100
1801–1825	1,645,100
1826–1850	1,621,000
1851–1867	180,800
Total	**11,062,000**

Source: David Eltis, "The Volume and Structure of the Transatlantic Slave Trade: A Reassessment," *William and Mary Quarterly*, 3rd series, 58 (2001), Table II. 6

■ Carlos Julião, *Extraction of Diamonds*

In addition to their labor on plantations, slaves in Latin America were put to work mining precious metals and jewels. This watercolor depicts African slaves mining diamonds in eighteenth-century Brazil.

that the owners of the ship would suffer a financial loss. If, however, the slaves were to be thrown overboard on the pretext that the safety of the crew was in jeopardy, the loss would be absorbed by those who had insured the voyage. Accordingly Collingwood decided to tie 132 slaves together, two by two, and fling them into the sea. When the ship owners went to court to collect the insurance, they argued that slaves were no different from horses and that they had a perfect right to throw the slaves overboard in order to preserve the safety of the ship.

Differences in the treatment and survival of slaves in the various parts of the New World had more to do with economic conditions, climate, and population trends than with the nationality or the religion of the slave masters. The crucial factor was the nature of the labor to which the slaves were subjected. Slaves who worked in the plantations, especially the sugar plantations, usually died within a few years. They were—simply said—worked to death. In the French colony of Saint Domingue, more than 500,000 of the 800,000 slaves brought to the colony between 1680 and 1780 perished. As long as the slave trade was still open, it was more profitable simply to replace those who died with new slaves than to try to extend the life of those the plantation owners already had. It was for this reason that the slave population did not start to grow internally in most areas until the slave trade ended in the nineteenth century.

Another factor influencing the treatment and survival of slaves was the ratio of the black to the white populations. When that ratio was high, as in all the Caribbean colonies, the codes regulating slave life were particularly harsh and created a reign of terror within the slave community. Yet another factor was climate. The absence of tropical diseases

A FORMER SLAVE PROTESTS AFRICAN SLAVERY

·················

In 1787 Quobna Ottobah Cugoano (1757–1791), a former slave, published an abolitionist treatise, Thoughts and Sentiments on the Evil and Wicked Traffic of the Slavery and Commerce of the Human Species. *Like the narrative written by Olaudah Equiano quoted at the beginning of this chapter, Cugoano's account describes the horrors of the African slave trade that he himself had experienced. In this passage Cugoano deplores the effect that the slave trade had on his native Africa.*

That base traffic of kid-napping and stealing men was begun by the Portuguese on the coast of Africa, and as they found the benefit of it for their own wicked purposes, they soon went on to commit further depredations. The Spaniards followed their infamous example, and the African slave trade was thought most advantageous for them, to enable themselves to live in ease and affluence by the cruel subjection and slavery of others. The French and English, and some other nations in Europe, as they founded settlements or colonies in the West Indies or in America, went on in the same manner, and joined hand in hand with the Portuguese and Spaniards to rob and pillage Africa as well as to waste and desolate the inhabitants of the western continent. But the European depredators and pirates have not only robbed and pillaged the people of Africa themselves; but, by their instigation, they have infested the inhabitants with some of the vilest combinations of fraudulent and treacherous villains, even among their own people, and have set up their forts and factories as a reservoir of public and abandoned thieves and as a den of desperadoes, where they may ensnare, entrap and catch men. So that Africa has been robbed of its inhabitants, its freeborn sons and daughters have been stole, and kid-napped and violently taken away and carried into captivity and cruel bondage. And it may be said in respect to that diabolical traffic which is still carried on by the European depredators, that Africa has suffered as much and more than any other quarters of the globe.

Source: Quobna Ottobah Cugoano, *Thoughts and Sentiments on the Evil and Wicked Traffic of the Slavery and Commerce of the Human Species* (London, 1787).

---

in the more temperate zone of the North American colonies provides the best explanation why in these colonies the numbers of births equaled and eventually exceeded the number of deaths long before they did in the Caribbean and South American colonies.

The slave trade itself became the object of intense competition, as each country tried to establish a monopoly over certain routes. During the seventeenth century the British managed to make inroads into the French slave trade, and eventually they surpassed the Portuguese and the Dutch as well. By 1700 British ships were transporting more than 50 percent of all slaves to the Americas. The dominance that Britain established in the slave trade was closely related to its growing maritime and commercial strength. With an enormous merchant marine and a navy that could support it, the British came to dominate the slave trade in the same way they came to dominate the entire world economy. Both revealed how far mercantile capitalism had triumphed in Britain and its overseas possessions.

For the British merchants who engaged in this trade there was no conflict between their traditional beliefs in individual liberty and their subjugation of African slaves. Theories of racial and national superiority removed Africans as well as other non-Europeans from the category of human beings who lived in a free society and who enjoyed individual rights. As long as those rights were tied to a particular national or racial group, such as freeborn Englishmen, slavery presented no challenge to British political ideas.

Not until the late eighteenth century did the enslavement of black Africans become a source of widespread moral concern. The movement to end the slave trade and slavery itself arose almost simultaneously in all European countries. It was inspired mainly by religious zeal, especially from evangelical Protestants in Great Britain and the Jesuits in Spain and Portugal. Societies were formed to campaign for the legislative prohibition of the transportation and sale of slaves. These appeals found support in the calculations by European capitalists, especially in Britain, that slavery was no longer economically advantageous. Goods produced by free labor, especially by machine, made slavery appear less cost-effective than in the past, and the entire system of slavery began to be viewed as a costly encumbrance.

By the first decade of the nineteenth century opposition to slavery began to achieve limited success, and by 1851 it had brought about an end to the entire slave trade. The United States refused to allow any of its ports to accept slave ships after 1808, the same year in which the British parliament legislated an end to the trade within its empire. The Dutch ended their slave trade in 1814, the French in 1815, and the Spanish in 1838. The Portuguese continued to import slaves to Brazil until 1851 and ended the practice only because the British were subjecting Portuguese slave traders to constant harassment. Liberation of the slaves generally came later, except in Haiti (formerly Saint Domingue), where slavery was abolished in 1794. The British dismantled the system within their empire between 1834 and 1838. Slavery persisted until 1848 in the French Caribbean, 1863 in the southern United States, 1886 in Cuba, and 1888 in Brazil.

CULTURAL ENCOUNTERS IN THE ATLANTIC WORLD

European countries had always possessed some ethnic diversity, but the emigration of people from many different parts of Europe and Africa to America, followed by their intermarriage, created societies of much greater complexity. Even the composition of the white European communities in the colonies was more varied than in the metropolis. In the British colonies, for example, English, Scots, and Irish were joined by large numbers of Germans, French, and Swiss. In 1776 Thomas Paine argued that all of Europe, rather than just England, was the true parent country of North American colonists. Ethnic divisions were further complicated by those of religion, especially in North America, where Protestants of many different denominations, as well as Roman Catholics, lived in close proximity to each other.

The ethnicity of colonial populations was more varied in Latin American colonies than in North America. The higher proportion of Africans in those colonies, more extensive patterns of intermarriage, and the free status achieved by large numbers of blacks and mulattos created highly stratified societies by the end of the eighteenth century. In these colonies divisions arose not only between the recently arrived Europeans and the creoles, but between the various groups considered by Europeans to be below them. The social structure of Brazil was more complex than that of any other country in the New World. At the top of the social hierarchy were Portuguese bureaucrats and below them was a large and wealthy group of planter creoles. These two elite groups dominated a lower-class social hierarchy of mestizos (people of mixed white and Indian ancestry), indigenous people, mulattos, freed blacks, and slaves.

Encounters between Europeans and Africans in the New World fostered the growth of ideas of white racial superiority that were grounded in the unbalanced power relationship between the dominant white and subordinate black populations. The circumstances under which physical contact between the races took place made the imbalance of this relationship readily apparent. Blacks appeared at the slave trading stations after having already been beaten into submission by their captives and forced to march hundreds of miles. The demeaning medical exams to which the slaves were subjected and their reduction to the status of a commodity for sale could readily deprive them of any sense of pride or self-respect. Their lack of formal education and literacy put them in a position of cultural inferiority, further reducing them to the status of beasts in the eyes of their white masters. In such circumstances references to the reputed blackness of the biblical Cain (Adam and Eve's first son, who murdered his brother Abel) only confirmed or reinforced the sense of superiority that white people took for granted.

THE TRANSMISSION OF IDEAS

The Atlantic Ocean became a corridor for the transmission of political and religious ideas. Political ideologies that developed in Europe were spread from the Old World to the New World mainly by the large volume of printed works that were exported during the eighteenth century. The ancient idea that a republic was the best form of government, which had found widespread support in Renaissance Italy and in seventeenth-century England, appealed to many political leaders in colonial North America. Eighteenth-century French and Scottish ideas regarding the rights of man and the responsibility of the government to bring about the improvement of society found fertile ground in many parts of North and South America. At the time of the French Revolution, ideals of liberty and equality were spread not only throughout Europe but in the Americas as well. Legal ideas embodied in English common law, French civil law, and Spanish customary law were also transported to the New World and became the legal foundation of the new societies that were formed there.

The traffic in political ideas did not flow in only one direction. Political ideologies that were formed out of British and European ideas of liberty at the time of the American Revolution were sent back to European countries in a new form, where they inspired reform and revolution in Britain, France, and Ireland. These same ideas of liberty exerted a powerful influence in the Caribbean colonies and in South America. In Haiti, where French and American ideas of liberty inspired a revolution in the 1790s, radical ideas of racial equality developed within the new republic and then spread outward to other colonies and the United States.

Religious ideas experienced a similar transmission and transportation. The Calvinist belief in predestination, which had been formulated in Switzerland and modified by Puritans in England during the sixteenth century, was adopted and further modified by colonists in New England during the seventeenth century. Catholic theological ideas that were introduced into Spanish and Portuguese America, including those regarding the role of the Devil in human society, interacted with those of indigenous peoples and African slaves and produced new religious syntheses. In religion as well as politics, these exchanges of ideas enriched the intellectual worlds of Europeans and colonists alike.

Encounters Between Europeans and Asians

The period from 1650 to 1850 was decisive in the development of European empires in Asia. These overseas possessions, like the American colonies, formed important components of the empires of European states and were also essential to the operation of the global economy. European dominance of world trade was exercised not only in the Atlantic world but also in the Middle East and Asia. The history of the European presence in these areas, however, is very different from that which occurred in the New World. A first difference was that of simple numbers. Prior to the eighteenth century the European presence in Asia had been limited to the activities of missionaries and merchants in places such as Jakarta, Macao, and Manila. During the eighteenth century the number of European colonists in Asia, even in India, remained relatively small in comparison with the numbers who settled in America, especially in British North America.

A second major difference between European empires in the East and in the West during the period from 1650 to 1850 is that in Asia European powers initially did not try to acquire and govern large land masses and subjugate their populations. Europeans first came to Asia to trade, not to conquer. They did not engage in fixed battles with Asians, take steps to reduce the size of their populations, or force them to migrate, as they did in the New World. Only in a handful of Southeast Asian islands did a pattern of conquest, similar to that which had occurred in the New World, take place. When Europeans used military force in Asia, it was almost always against rival European powers, not the indigenous population. When European countries did eventually use force against Asians, they discovered that victory was much more difficult than it had been in the New World. Indeed, Asian peoples already possessed or were acquiring sufficient military strength to respond to European military might. In China and Japan the possession of this military power prevented Europeans from even contemplating conquest or exploitation until the nineteenth century. Establishment of European hegemony in Asia, therefore, took longer and was achieved more gradually than in the Americas.

POLITICAL CONTROL OF INDIA

Despite their original intentions, Europeans eventually began to acquire political control over large land masses in Asia and subject Asians to European rule. The first decisive steps in this process took place in India during the second half of the eighteenth century. Until that time the British in

India, most of whom were members of the British East India Company, remained confined to the factories that were established along the Indian coast. The main purpose of these factories was to engage in trade not only with Europe but also with other parts of Asia. In conducting this trade the British had to deal with local Indian merchants and to compete with the French, the Portuguese and the Dutch, who had established factories of their own. They also found it advantageous to make alliances with the provincial governors, known as nawabs°, who controlled the interior of the country. It became customary for each European power to have its own candidate for nawab, with the expectation that he would provide favors for his European patrons once he took office.

■ **Warren Hastings**

Hastings (1732–1818), who was appointed the first governor-general of India in 1773, represented the ambiguities of early British rule in that country. An officer in the British East India Company, he was sympathetic to Indian culture. He was, however, accused of gross misconduct in the management of Indian affairs. His impeachment by the British Parliament in 1786 for corruption in his administration, and cruelty toward some of the native people in Bengal, lasted 145 days but resulted in an acquittal in 1787.

■ **Map 19.4 The Sequence of British Territorial Acquisitions in India, 1765–1856**
British political control of large territories on the South Asian subcontinent began more than a century after the establishment of the first factories along the coast.

The Sequence of British Territorial Acquisitions in India, 1765–1856

- Indian states and provinces
- British Territory in 1765
- British Territory in 1805
- British Territory in 1856
- Other European possessions
- Independent states
- ✕ Battle

Military Conflict and Territorial Acquisitions, 1756–1856

In 1756 this pattern of trading and negotiating resulted in armed military conflict in the city of Calcutta in the northeastern province of Bengal. The British had established a factory at Calcutta in 1690, and they continued to carry on an extensive trade there with Indian merchants, many of whom were Hindus. The nawab of Bengal, the Muslim Siraj-ud-Daulah, had contempt for all Europeans, especially the British, and he was determined that he would not be beholden to any of them. He was also deeply hostile to the Hindu merchants who were trading with the British. In June 1756 he sent an army of 50,000 Muslims against Calcutta, burning and plundering the city and beginning a siege of the East India Company's Fort William, which was manned by 515 troops in the service of the company. The entire British population of the city, together with more than 2,000 Hindus, had taken refuge in the fort. After a long struggle, which resulted in the death of hundreds of Indians, the fort fell to the nawab's forces, and some of the British officers and magistrates, including the governor of Calcutta, fled by sea.

During this siege the shooting death of a Bengali guard led to an incident that became permanently emblazoned on the emerging imperial consciousness of the British people. Officers in the nawab's army crammed the entire remaining British contingent, a total of 146 men and women, into the fort's lockup or prison, known as the Black Hole of Calcutta. Measuring 18′ × 14′ 10″, it was meant to hold only three or four prisoners overnight. The British prisoners were stifled by the insufferable heat and a lack of water and air. The stench was so bad that many prisoners vomited on the people squeezed next to them. Only twenty-two men and one woman survived until the next morning, when the nawab released them. The remainder had either been trampled to death or had asphyxiated.

The deaths of these British men and women in the Black Hole of Calcutta led the British to seek swift and brutal retribution against the nawab. In 1757, under the direction of the British military officer Robert Clive, a force of 800 British troops and 2,000 native Indian soldiers known as sepoys° retook Calcutta and routed Siraj-ud-Daulah's army

of 50,000 men at the battle of Plassey. Siraj-ud-Daulah was executed and replaced by a nawab more amenable to the British. A few years later the British East India Company secured the right to collect taxes and thus exercised political control over the entire province of Bengal. The enormous revenue from these taxes enabled the company to acquire a large army, composed mainly of sepoys. This force grew to 115,000 men by 1782. The British then used these military forces, which were equipped with Western military technology, to gain control of other provinces in India as well as to defeat their French rivals in subsequent engagements during the early nineteenth century.

These further acquisitions of Indian territory led to the eventual establishment of British rule throughout the south Asian subcontinent (see Map 19.4). New territories were brought under British control in the early years of the nineteenth century, and during the tenure of Lord Dalhousie as governor-general of India from 1848 to 1856 the British annexed eight Indian states, including the great Muslim state of Oudh in 1856. This policy of annexation went hand in hand with the introduction of Western technology and literature, the English language, and British criminal procedure.

The Sepoy Mutiny, 1857–1858

The British policy of annexation in India, coupled with the attitude of cultural superiority it encouraged, lay at the

641

root of the greatest act of rebellion by Indians against British rule in the nineteenth century. This rebellion, which began in 1857, is often known as the Sepoy Mutiny, since it originated in the ranks of the Indian troops serving in the armed forces of the British East India Company. The main source of resentment was the British annexation of Oudh, which many sepoys considered their homeland. The incident that actually provoked the rebellion was the issue of rifle cartridges coated with beef fat, which violated Hindu law, and pork fat, which violated Muslim law. Although this insensitivity to native Indian culture was not unprecedented, in this case it struck a particularly raw nerve and led to a mutiny by the Bengali army. The cities of Delhi and Lucknow came under siege, and dreadful atrocities, including the hacking to death of British women and children, occurred. British reprisals were equally savage and eventually succeeded in suppressing the rebellion.

In the wake of the mutiny the British government abolished the British East India Company and assumed direct rule of India. Queen Victoria (r. 1837–1901), the constitutional monarch of the United Kingdom, acquired much greater power over her Indian empire. Although the British government did take steps to confirm the lands and titles of Indian princes and to give them local power, their relationship with their British overlords remained one of strict subordination.

CHANGING EUROPEAN ATTITUDES TOWARD ASIAN CULTURES

This second phase of European imperialism in Asia, which lasted from 1650 to 1850, played a crucial role in the formation of Western identity. The steadily increasing numbers of Europeans who had contact with these lands—merchants, missionaries, writers and colonial administrators—and to a lesser extent the public who read about these foreign places, gained a clearer sense of who they were once they compared themselves to Indians, Chinese, and Polynesians. Until the seventeenth century Europeans thought of "the East" mainly as the Middle East, an area that was largely subsumed within the Ottoman Empire. Europeans expressed a generally negative view of the culture of this region (see Chapter 15), and over the years that perception had not changed. The political system of the Ottoman Empire was considered despotic and its religion, Islam, the antithesis of Christianity. The Far East, comprising South Asia (India), East Asia (China, Japan), and Southeast Asia (Burma, Siam, Indonesia), generally did not enter into these perceptions of "the Orient." There was little contact with this part of the world, and the little that was known about it was shrouded in mystery. During this period Europeans viewed the Far East mainly as an exotic land, rich in spices, silk, and other luxury commodities.

As Western missionaries and merchants made more frequent contacts with Asian society, Europeans developed more informed impressions of these distant lands and peoples. Some of those impressions were negative, especially when the power of Asian rulers was discussed, but many other characterizations of the East were positive. Interest in and admiration for both Indian and Chinese culture were most widespread during the middle years of the eighteenth century. The systematic study of Asian languages, especially Chinese and Sanskrit, began during this period. A preference for things Asian became characteristic of Enlightenment philosophes like Voltaire, who regarded

AN EIGHTEENTH-CENTURY CRITICISM OF NABOBS

The eighteenth-century English comedy The Nabob *reveals some popular prejudices against these merchants who had made fortunes in India and returned to England, where they flaunted their wealth. In this scene the mayor of the parliamentary borough of Bribe 'em has arrived at the house of the nabob, Sir Matthew Mite, to negotiate terms for the sale of the borough's seat. The mayor engages in this exchange with Mr. Touchit, who defends the nabob's wealth.*

Mayor: But how comes it about? And where do these here people get all their wealth?

Touchit: The way is plain enough; from our settlements and possessions abroad.

Mayor: Oh, maybe so. I've been often minded to ask you what sort of things them there settlements are; because why as you know, I have been never beyond sea.

Touchit: Oh, Mr. Mayor, I will explain that in a moment; Why, here are a body of merchants that beg to be admitted as friends, and take possession of a small spot in a country, and carry on a beneficial commerce with the inoffensive and innocent people, to which kindly they give their consent.

Mayor: Don't you think that is very civil of them?

Touchit: Doubtless. Upon which, Mr. Mayor, we cunningly encroach upon and fortify by little and little, till at length, we growing too strong for the natives, we turn them out of their lands, and take possession of their money and jewels.

Mayor: And don't you think, Mr. Touchit, that is a little uncivil in us?

Touchit: Oh nothing at all, these people are but a little better than Tartars or Turks.

Mayor: No, no, Mr. Touchit, just the reverse; it is *they* have caught the Tartars in us.

Source: From *The Nabob: A Comedy, in Three Acts* by Samuel Foote (London: T. Sherlock, 1778), Act II.

■ **Brighton Pavilion**

This building, designed by John Nash, reflected the incorporation of Eastern styles into English architecture, and was inspired by the description of Kubla Khan's palace in Samuel Taylor Coleridge's poem "Kubla Khan" (1816).

Asian cultures as superior to those of a corrupt Europe. Voltaire also found the East unaffected by the superstition and the fanaticism that characterized Western Christianity, which he loathed. To him, the main philosophical tradition of China, Confucianism, which embodied a strict moral code, was a more attractive alternative. Eastern religion, especially Hinduism, was also admired for its ethical content and its underlying belief in one God.

This mid-eighteenth-century admiration of Asian culture even extended to Chinese and Indian political institutions. The despotic Chinese empire was transformed through Voltaire's perceptions into an enlightened monarchy. There was less to admire in the Mughal empire in India, but Guillaume Thomas Raynal's condemnation of European imperialism, which we discussed in Chapter 17, idealized the "purity and equity" of the ancient Indian political system. Comparison of contemporary Indian politics with the corruption of the old regime in Europe made native Asian political systems look good by comparison. In Britain there was more disrespect for the members of the East India Company known as nabobs°, who returned to England to flaunt the wealth they had recently acquired in India, than there was for native Indian officials. There was

also more interest in reforming the British East India Company than in reforming Indian politics.

This intellectual respect for Asian philosophy and politics coincided with a period of widespread Asian influences on Western art, architecture, and design. Eastern themes began to influence British buildings, such as in the Brighton Pavilion, designed by John Nash. Small cottages, known as bungalows, owed their inspiration to Indian models. French architects built pagodas (towers with the roof of each story turning upward) for their clients. Chinese gardens, which unlike classical European gardens were not arranged geometrically, became popular in England and France.

A new form of decorative art which combined Chinese and European motifs, known in French as chinoiserie°, became highly fashionable. Wealthy French people furnished their homes with Chinese wallpaper and hand-painted folding screens. The demand for Chinese porcelain, known in English simply as china, was insatiable. Vast quantities of this porcelain, which was technically and aesthetically superior to the stoneware produced in Germany and England, left China for the ports of western Europe. Even the dress of Europeans was influenced by Asian styles. Indian and Chinese silks were in high demand, and

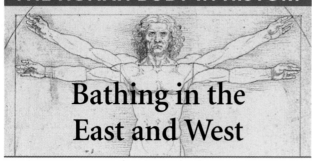

Bathing in the East and West

One of the most striking differences between Eastern and Western culture in the eighteenth century concerned the bathing of the human body. Among the Indians who practiced the Hindu religion, bathing had deep religious significance and was a daily ritual. The same was true for Muslims, for whom water possessed a sacred purifying role and prepared the bather for prayer or sacrifice. In the West bathing was not invested with similar religious significance. Christianity had emphasized purity of heart, not of the body. Without a religious inspiration, bathing the body rarely occurred in Western nations during the early modern period. Europeans might wash various parts of their body, especially the hands and face, but total immersion was almost unheard of. The few who did bathe usually did so no more than once a year, and tubs or basins were not widely available. Swimming in rivers and lakes was dangerous and often resulted in drowning. Even medical opinion conspired against bathing. According to one seventeenth-century French doctor, "bathing outside the practice of medicine was not only superfluous but very damaging to health."

By the beginning of the nineteenth century, many Europeans had begun to take regular baths. The sale of wash basins and commercially produced soap soared. This change occurred as a result of three distinct factors. The first was the insistence by many eighteenth-century Protestants that Christianity did indeed demand a clean body as well as a clean soul. The eighteenth-century founder of Methodism, the English preacher John Wesley, coined a new proverb when he declared that "cleanliness is indeed next to godliness."

A second reason was that cleanliness became associated with gentility and good manners. Bodily cleanliness became one of the ways in which members of society who considered themselves civilized made themselves attractive to the people with whom they associated. This explains why bathing the body all over first was adopted by the upper classes, who contrasted themselves with the dirty lower classes. It also became more common among women than men. The third reason was a change in medical opinion, which began to view bathing as a means to keep the pores of the skin open and thus promote perspiration. Bathing came to be viewed as a means of curing numerous diseases and as a key to long life.

The acceptance of bathing in the West owed something to Eastern influence. Eighteenth-century Western writers often commented on the daily bathing of Turks and Hindus, and Europeans who lived in the East had the opportunity to witness firsthand a custom that contrasted strikingly with their own. The period of most pronounced influence was the mid-eighteenth century, when many other features of Eastern culture penetrated the West. In the early nineteenth century a Hindu noted that bathing in the West was still very different from that practiced in his own country. Nevertheless, the reluctant European adoption of immersing the body in water had brought about a minor accommodation between Eastern and Western practice. ■

■ **Chaste Susanna at Her Bath (1865), by Jean-Jacques Henner**
By the nineteenth century, Europeans had adopted the practice of bathing the entire body.

For Discussion

What does the widespread practice of bathing in Asia and the reluctance of Europeans to adopt this practice tell us about the differences between Eastern and Western cultures in the eighteenth century?

Europeans expressed a preference for Indian cotton over that produced in the New World. A style of Indian nightwear, known as pajamas, became popular in England. Even a new sport, polo, which had originated to India, made its entry into upper-class European society at this time.

During the late eighteenth and early nineteenth centuries the European idealization of Asian culture came under direct attack. As the European presence in Asia became larger and more powerful, as the British began to exercise more control in India, and as merchants began to monopolize the Asian trade, Western images of the East became more unfavorable. Chinese philosophy, instead of being viewed as a repository of ancient ethical wisdom, was labeled as irrational when compared with that of the West. Confucianism fell out of favor, and Eastern religion in general was despised as being inferior to Christianity. Enlightenment thinkers such as Montesquieu and Diderot ranked Asian political systems below those of the more "advanced" countries of Europe. The English scholar George Anson claimed that the Chinese reputation for industry and ingenuity was undeserved and that their scientific thought was inferior to that of Europeans. The English writer Samuel Johnson (1709–1784) expressed this sense of Western intellectual superiority when he had an Arab poet in his novel *Rasselas* (1759) state that Europeans "are more powerful . . . than we, because they are wiser; knowledge will always predominate over ignorance."

Expressions of Western superiority over Asians were reinforced by emerging ideas of racial difference. Sixteenth- and seventeenth-century ideas of Europeans' superiority over black Africans and the indigenous peoples of the Americas on the basis of differences in skin color and facial features were now extended to the Chinese, dark-skinned South Asians, and Polynesians. Intellectual theories of race, which are a distinctly Western creation and were developed mainly during the late eighteenth century, provided an apparently empirical and scientific foundation for these assumptions. The color of one's skin in India, which had determined the position of a person in the Hindu caste system, was now used by Westerners to identify South Asians as "coloreds."

By the same token Chinese people, previously described as white by Westerners who admired China, were now referred to as being nonwhite or yellow. By the beginning of the nineteenth century, Westerners had acquired an ideology of superiority over Asians as well as Africans and indigenous American people that included racial difference as one of its main components. This ideology prepared Europeans intellectually and emotionally for the conquest of numerous countries in Asia and Africa in the second half of the nineteenth century. This third and final period of European imperial expansion, which began around 1870 and reached its peak around 1900, brought 84 percent of the Earth's surface under Western control.

The Crisis of Empire and the Atlantic Revolutions

During the period from 1780 to 1825, European empires experienced a crisis that marked the end of the second stage of European overseas expansion. As a result of this crisis British, French, and Spanish governments lost large segments of their empires, all in the Americas. New states and nations were carved out of the older sprawling empires. The crisis was to some extent administrative. Having acquired large expanses of territory overseas, European states were faced with the challenging problem of governing them from a distance. They not only had to rule large areas inhabited by non-European peoples (Indians and African slaves), but they also faced the difficulty of maintaining the loyalty of people of European descent who were born in the colonies.

These European colonials or creoles became the main protagonists in the struggles that led to the independence of the North American colonies from Britain in 1776 and the South American colonies from Spain a generation later. In the French colony of Saint Domingue, the location of the only successful revolution in the Caribbean region during this period, a very different set of pressures led to independence. In this colony, which became the republic of Haiti in 1804, the revolution was led not by white creoles but by people of color, including the slaves who worked on the plantations. In Britain's European colony of Ireland, where an unsuccessful revolution against British rule took place in 1798, the urge for independence came both from settlers of British descent and the native Irish population.

THE AMERICAN REVOLUTION, 1775–1783

The first Atlantic revolution was the revolt of the thirteen North American colonies and the establishment of their independence from British rule. During the second half of the eighteenth century, a number of tensions arose between the British government and its transatlantic colonies. All of these overseas colonies had developed traditions of self-government, and all of them had their own representative assemblies. At the same time the colonies were controlled by various governmental bodies responsible to the British Parliament, such as the Board of Trade. The colonies had their own militias, but they also received protection from British troops when conflicts developed with the French or other hostile powers.

The crisis that led to the American Revolution had its roots in the situation that emerged at the end of the French and Indian War. In order to maintain the peace agreed to in 1763, the government stationed British troops on the frontiers of the colonies. It argued that since the troops were protecting the colonists, they should contribute financially to their own defense. To this end the government began imposing a number of new taxes on the colonists. In 1765 the British Parliament passed the Stamp Act, which forced colonists to purchase stamps for almost anything that was printed. This piece of legislation raised the central constitutional issue of whether Parliament had the power to legislate for British subjects in lands that did not elect members of that Parliament. "Taxation without representation is tyranny" became the main rallying cry of the colonists. Opposition to the Stamp Act was so strong that Parliament repealed the act the following year, but at the same time it passed a statute declaring that it had the authority to tax the colonists as it pleased. When the government imposed new taxes on the tea imported from Britain in 1773, a number of colonists, dressed as Indians, threw the tea into the Boston Harbor.

■ *The Bostonian's Paying the Excise Man or Tarring and Feathering (1774)*
This satirical engraving reflects the hatred of colonial Americans at the collection of taxes levied on them without their consent. The Boston Tea Party is depicted in the background. The colonists are forcing the tax collector to drink the tea on which he is trying to collect taxes.

The government responded to this "Boston Tea Party" by passing a series of statutes, known in the colonies as the Intolerable Acts, in 1774. One of these acts specified that the port of Boston be closed until the colonists had repaid the cost of the tea. The Intolerable Acts led to organized resistance to British rule, and in the following year military conflict broke out at Lexington and Concord in Massachusetts. On July 4, 1776, thirteen of the colonies on the North American mainland, stretching from New Hampshire to Georgia, approved a Declaration of Independence from Great Britain. A long revolutionary war, in which the colonists received assistance from France in 1778, ended with the defeat of British troops at Yorktown in 1781 and the recognition of the republic of the United States of America in the Treaty of Paris in 1783.

The case that the American colonists made for independence from Britain drew upon a body of ideas that were embodied in hundreds of printed pamphlets and in speeches made before colonial legislatures. The most prominent of these ideas were first expressed by John Locke and other radical Whigs in the late seventeenth century. Locke, who justified resistance against the Stuart monarchy at the time of the Glorious Revolution and who placed limits on legislative as well as executive power, became the main inspiration of the Declaration of Independence, which was drafted by Thomas Jefferson. These ideas found support in the customs and traditions embodied in the English common law, especially the principle that men could not be deprived of their rights without their own consent. Republican ideas, drawn both from ancient Greece and Rome and revived at the time of the Renaissance, gave colonists a model of a community of virtuous men joined in a commitment to the body politic, which they defined in colonial terms. Finally there was the influence of the ideas of the Enlightenment, which emphasized the natural right of all men to life, liberty, and the pursuit of happiness.

Although the American Revolution was inspired by many of the ideas that had originated in the two English revolutions of the seventeenth century, it differed from those earlier revolutions in that it was directed more against the British Parliament than the king. The Declaration of Independence severed the bonds between the colonists and King George III, to whom they formally owed allegiance, but the constitutional powers against which they protested, especially that of taxation, were those of Parliament. It was taxation by the British Parliament, rather than nonparliamentary taxes like those levied in the 1640s, that led to the American Revolution.

THE HAITIAN REVOLUTION, 1789–1804

The second successful revolution in the Atlantic world took place in the French Caribbean colony of Saint Domingue, known later as Haiti, which occupied the western portion of the island of Hispaniola. This revolution resulted in the establishment of the colony's independence, but the revolt was directed not so much against French rule as against the island's white planters. Just like their counterparts in Spanish and British Caribbean colonies, these planters, known in Haiti as colons°, had little desire for national independence. They wished to remain within the protective custody of the French state. Since they formed a distinct minority of the total population, they did not think of themselves as constituting a separate national community. Any resistance to imperial rule, moreover, would have required that they arm their slaves in order to make the movement succeed, and that would have threatened their control of the black population.

The real threat of revolution in all the Caribbean colonies came not from the elite or ruling class but from the subordinate members of the population. In Saint Domingue the revolution began in 1789 with a rebellion of people defined legally as free coloreds, most of whom were mulattos. The development that triggered this revolt, organized under the leadership of Vincent Ogé, was the refusal of the white planters, who were creoles, to give the free coloreds representation in the revolutionary French National Assembly as well as in local assemblies in Saint Domingue.

The free colored rebellion of 1789 led directly to a massive slave revolt in 1791. At that time slaves constituted about 90 percent of the population. Their uprising took place after the French National Assembly voted to abolish slavery in France but not in the French colonies. In this revolt 12,000 African slaves, armed with machetes and reacting to their brutal treatment by their masters, destroyed a thousand plantations and killed hundreds of whites. Their tactics, which included cutting white planters in half, raping their wives and daughters, and decapitating their children, were matched by those of the planters, who retaliated by torturing blacks and hanging them in the streets.

Spanish and British armies, frightened that this slave rebellion would spread to their colonies, occupied Saint Domingue and massacred thousands of slaves, many of them after they surrendered. In 1795, however, the Spanish withdrew from Saint Domingue and ceded their portion of the island of Hispaniola to France. The British were likewise forced to leave the colony in 1798, having lost as many as 40,000 soldiers, most of them from disease. The man who had assumed the leadership of the slave revolt, the freed slave Toussaint L'Ouverture, then proceeded to conquer the entire island in 1801, abolish slavery, and proclaim himself the governor-general of an autonomous province.

In 1801, after Napoleon had assumed control of the French government and the idealism of the French Revolution had evaporated, a French army of 20,000 men occupied Saint Domingue. The purpose was to make the colony the centerpiece of a restored French Empire, including Florida, Louisiana, French Guiana, and the French

---

THOMAS PAINE SUPPORTS THE AMERICAN CAUSE

····················

Thomas Paine (1737–1809) was a radical Whig reformer who supported the cause for American independence. In Common Sense (1776), a pamphlet written to support the American cause in the year of the Declaration of Independence, Paine refutes the arguments of the British that they served the interests of the American colonists. Paine protests not only the commercial exploitation of the colonies but also the way in which Great Britain has involved them in warfare with continental rivals.

I have heard it asserted by some, that as America has flourished under her former connection with Great Britain, the same connection is necessary towards her future happiness, and will always have the same effect. Nothing can be more fallacious than this kind of argument. We may as well assert that because a child has thrived upon milk, that it is never to have meat, or that the first twenty years of our lives is to become a precedent for the next twenty. But even this is admitting more than is true; for I answer roundly that America would have flourished as much, probably much more, had no European power taken any notice of her. The commerce by which she hath enriched herself are the necessaries of life and will always have a market while eating is the custom of Europe.

But she has protected us, say some. That she hath engrossed us is true, and defended the Continent at our expense as well as her own, is admitted; and she would have defended Turkey from the same motive, *viz.* for the sake of trade and dominion.

Alas! We have been long led away by ancient prejudices and made large sacrifices to superstition. We have boasted the protection of Britain without considering that her motive was *interest,* not *attachment;* and that she did not protect us from *our enemies* on *our account* but from *her enemies* on *her own account,* from those who had no quarrel with us on any *other account,* and who will always be our enemies on the *same account.* Let Britain waive her pretensions to the Continent, or the Continent throw off the dependence, and we should be at peace with France and Spain, were they at war with Britain. The miseries of Hanover last war ought to warn us against connections.

Source: From Thomas Paine, *Common Sense* (Philadelphia: W.T. Bradford, 1776).

■ **The British Surrender at Yorktown in 1781**
This battle ended the American War of Independence, although the peace treaty was not signed for
another two years.

West Indies. This assertion of French imperial control secured the surrender of L'Ouverture. When it was learned
that the French were planning to reintroduce slavery, however, two black generals, Jean-Jacques Dessalines and Henri
Christophe, whom the French had enlisted to suppress the
revolt, united freed blacks and slaves against the French
forces. In 1803 these united forces drove the French out of
the colony, and in 1804 they established an independent
state of Haiti.

This new state of Haiti was far different from that of the
United States, in that it was governed entirely by people of
color and it banned slavery. It proclaimed racial equality by
defining all Haitians as black. The plantation system was
destroyed and the land was redistributed among free blacks;
foreigners were forbidden to hold property. Deciding upon
the form of government took time, however, as the new
rulers of the country were divided between those who
wished to establish a monarchy and those who favored a republic. Those divisions led to a prolonged civil war from
1807 until 1822, when the warring northern and southern
provinces were integrated into a single republic.

The Haitian revolution was the most radical and egalitarian of the Atlantic revolutions of the late eighteenth

and early nineteenth centuries. Whereas the American
Revolution was mainly a political movement that established a new republic, the Haitian revolution was a genuine
social and economic revolution as well. Its unqualified declaration of human equality and its abolition of slavery
served as an inspiration to abolitionist movements in other
countries, including the United States, throughout the
nineteenth century. The destruction of the plantation system, however, brought about a revolutionary transformation of the country's economy. As a French possession Saint
Domingue was quite possibly the richest colony in the
world, producing about two-fifths of the world's sugar and
half of its coffee. After the revolution, with its economy severed from that of France, the country could no longer compete successfully in the Atlantic economy.

THE IRISH REBELLION, 1798–1799

Within the British Empire the country that was most directly inspired by the success of the American Revolution
was the kingdom of Ireland. Unlike the residents of the
thirteen colonies in North America, the Gaelic people of
Ireland had long thought of themselves as a distinct nation.

The English, however, had begun a conquest of this Irish nation in the eleventh century, and during the next 500 years they had struggled to rule it effectively. One of their methods was to settle English landlords on Irish lands. They had done this in the Middle Ages by giving large estates to English feudal lords, but those old Anglo-Irish families had gradually begun to think of themselves as Irish, and after the Reformation they had remained Catholic, while most English people had become Protestant.

In the sixteenth century the English government had begun to settle colonies of English Protestants on plantations in various parts of Ireland. The purpose of this policy was to gain tighter control over the country and to promote the loyalty of Irish landowners to the English government. In the early seventeenth century James VI of Scotland (who had also become James I of England in 1603) had settled both Scottish Presbyterians, later known as the Scots Irish, as well as English Anglicans, in the northern Irish province of Ulster. These Protestants of Scottish and English descent had become the core of the ruling establishment throughout Ireland, especially after Catholic rebellions in 1641–1649 and again in 1689–1690 had failed.

In the eighteenth century Irish Protestants began to resent their subservient relationship to the British government. Just like the American colonists, they recognized the way in which the Irish economy was serving British rather than Irish interests, and they resented the control that Britain had over the Irish parliament. A reform association known as the Society of United Irishmen, led by the Protestant Ulsterman Wolfe Tone, succeeded in building common ground between Protestants and Catholics. The United Irishmen demanded the repeal of the laws that denied Catholics the right to hold office and sit in the Irish parliament.

The ideals of the United Irishmen drew on many different sources. A long tradition of Presbyterian republican radicalism found reinforcement in the ideals of the American Revolution. The Irish objected to paying tithes to the established Anglican church, and like the American colonists in the 1760s they resented the taxes they were asked to pay to aid in the British war against the French during the 1790s. French revolutionary ideas of liberty, equality, and fraternity had a pervasive influence in Ireland as well.

In 1798 the United Irishmen aligned themselves with lower-class Catholic peasants known as Defenders, and these Irish groups staged a rebellion against British rule with the intention of establishing an Irish republic. Like the American colonists, the Irish revolutionaries sought French aid, but it came too little and too late, and the rebellion failed. The revolt, which was marred by atrocities on both sides, resulted in the death of 30,000 people.

The British government recognized that its arrangement for ruling Ireland, in which the nationalist republican movement had originated, could no longer work. The British government decided therefore to bring about a complete union between Great Britain and Ireland. By the terms of this arrangement, which took effect in 1801, Ireland's parliament ceased to meet; instead the Irish were to elect a limited number of representatives to sit in the British parliament. Ireland thus became a part of the United Kingdom, just as Scotland had done in 1707. The proximity of Ireland to Britain, which made the prospect of Irish independence much more dangerous, was a major factor in making the British determined to hold on to this "internal colony." The forces of Irish nationalism could not be contained, however, and during the nineteenth century new movements for Irish independence arose.

NATIONAL REVOLUTIONS IN SPANISH AMERICA, 1810–1824

The final set of revolutions against European imperial powers occurred between 1810 and 1824 in a number of Spanish American colonies. These struggles, like the American Revolution, turned colonies into new states and led to the building of new nations. The first of these revolutions began in Mexico in 1810; others soon arose in Argentina, Colombia, Chile, and Peru. In these revolutions creoles played a leading role, just as they had in the American War of Independence. The main sources of creole discontent were the Bourbon reforms, which ironically had been intended to make the Spanish Empire more efficient and thus to preserve it. The reforms had achieved this goal, however, by favoring commercial interests at the expense of the traditional aristocracy, thereby reversing or threatening the position of many creole elites. The creoles also faced increasingly heavy taxation, as the Spanish government sought to make them support the expenses of colonial administration.

CHRONOLOGY

The Atlantic Revolutions, 1775–1824

1775–1783	United States of America
1789–1804	Haiti
1798–1799	Ireland
1810–1822	Mexico
1810–1819	Colombia
1810–1821	Venezuela
1810–1816	Argentina
1810–1818	Chile
1821–1824	Peru

■ **Símon Bolívar Presenting the Flag of Liberation to Soldiers After the Battle of Carabobo, 1821**
Bolívar was the man most directly responsible for liberating South American countries from Spanish rule. He liberated his native Venezuela in 1821 and defeated Spanish forces in Peru in 1824.

During the late eighteenth century Spanish creole discontent had crystallized into demands for greater political autonomy, similar to the objectives of British American colonists. South American creoles began to think of themselves as Spanish Americans and sometimes simply as Americans. Like British American colonists, they also read and were inspired by the works of Enlightenment political philosophers. They protested against the Bourbon reforms. Nevertheless, the Spanish creole struggle against imperial rule did not commence until some thirty years after the North American colonies had won their independence. One reason for this slow development of revolutionary action was that Spanish American creoles still looked to the Spanish government to provide them with military support against the threat of lower-class rebellion. When, for example, a rebellion of this sort against Spanish rule occurred in Peru in 1780, creole planters not only refused an invitation to join the revolt but also supported the Spanish forces that crushed it. Faced with this lower-class threat, which continued to plague them even after independence, creoles were cautious about abandoning the military and police support provided by the metropolis.

The event that eventually precipitated these wars for national independence was the collapse of the Spanish monarchy after Napoleon's French army invaded Spain in 1807 (see Chapter 18). This development left the Spanish Empire, which had always been more centralized than the British Empire, in a weakened position. In an effort to reconstitute the political order in their colonies, creoles sought to establish greater autonomy. Once the monarchy was restored, this demand for autonomy led quickly to armed resistance. This resistance began in Mexico, but it soon spread throughout Spanish America and quickly acquired popular support.

The man who took the lead in these early revolts against Spanish rule was the fiery Venezuelan aristocrat Símon Bolívar (1783–1830). Educated in the ideas of the Enlightenment, Bolívar led uprisings in his homeland in 1812 and 1814 and eventually defeated the Spanish there in 1819. Unlike most creoles, Bolívar was not afraid to recruit free coloreds and blacks into his armies. His hatred of European colonial governors knew few boundaries. At one point he reportedly commanded his soldiers to shoot and kill any European on sight. He vowed never to rest until all of Spanish America was free. Bolívar carried the struggle for liberation to Peru, which became independent in 1824, and created the state of Bolivia in 1825. Often compared to George Washington, he was more responsible than any one individual for the liberation of Spanish America from Spanish rule. Independent states were established in Argentina in 1816, Chile in 1818, Colombia in 1819, and Mexico in 1822. By then the Spanish, who in the sixteenth century had the largest empire in the world, retained control of only two colonies in the Western Hemisphere: Puerto Rico and Cuba.

CONCLUSION

The Rise and Reshaping of the West

During the second period of European empire building, from 1650 until 1850, the West not only expanded geographically but also acquired a large share of the world's resources. By dominating the world's carrying trade, and by exploiting the agricultural and mineral resources of the Americas, Western states gained control of the world economy. The slave trade, with all its horrors, formed an important part of this economy and served as one of the main sources of Western wealth.

Western economic power laid the foundations for Western political control. In Asia European states assumed political control over territories slowly and reluctantly, as Britain's gradual and piecemeal acquisition of territory in India revealed. In the Americas, European powers acquired territory with relative ease, and European possessions in the New World soon became part of the West. By 1700, as we have seen, the geographical center of the West had become the Atlantic Ocean.

The American territories that were brought under European political control also became, at least to some extent, culturally part of the West. The European colonists who settled in the Americas preserved the languages, the religions, and many of the cultural traditions of the European countries from which they came. When some of the British and Spanish colonies in the Americas rebelled against European regimes in the late eighteenth and early nineteenth centuries, the identity of the colonists who led the resistance remained essentially Western. Even the political ideas that inspired national resistance to European regimes had their origins in Europe.

The assertion of Western political and economic power in the world cultivated a sense of Western superiority. The belief that Europeans, regardless of their nationality, were superior to those from other parts of the world originated in the encounters that took place between Europeans and both African slaves and the indigenous peoples in the Americas. In the late eighteenth century a conviction also developed, although much more slowly, that the West was culturally superior to the civilizations of Asia. This belief in Western superiority became even more pronounced when the economies of Western nations began to experience more rapid growth than those of Asia. We now turn to the source of this new Western economic strength, the Industrial Revolution.

Suggestions for Further Reading

For a comprehensive list of suggested readings, please go to www.ablongman.com/levack/chapter19

Bailyn, Bernard. *Ideological Origins of the American Revolution.* 1967. A probing analysis of the different intellectual traditions upon which the American colonists based their arguments for independence.

Blackburn, Robin. *The Making of New World Slavery: From the Baroque to the Modern, 1492–1800.* 1997. Places European slavery in a broad world perspective.

Boxer, C. R. *The Dutch Seaborne Empire, 1600–1800.* 1965. A thorough account covering the entire period of Dutch expansion.

Davis, Ralph. *The Rise of the Atlantic Economies.* 1973. A readable study of economic development on both sides of the Atlantic.

Eltis, David, *The Rise of African Slavery in the Americas.* 2000. An analysis of the different dimensions of the slave trade based on a database of slave ships and passengers.

Goody, Jack. *The East in the West.* 1996. Challenges the idea that Western cultures are more rational than those of Asia.

Greene, Jack P. *Peripheries and Center: Constitutional Development in the Extended Polities of the British Empire and the United States 1607–1788.* 1986. A study of the composition of the British Empire and its disintegration in North America.

Kamen, Henry. *Empire: How Spain Became a World Power.* 2003. Explains how Spain established the most extensive empire the world had ever known.

Langley, Lester D. *The Americas in the Age of Revolution, 1750–1850.* 1996. A broad comparative study of revolutions in the United States, Haiti, and Latin America.

Liss, Peggy K. *The Atlantic Empires: The Network of Trade and Revolutions, 1713–1826.* 1983. Places the American Revolution in a broader comparative setting and includes material on early Latin American independence movements.

Mungello, D. E. *The Great Encounter of China and the West, 1500–1800.* 1999. Studies China's acceptance and rejection of Western culture as well as the parallel Western reception of China.

Pagden, Anthony. *Lords of All the World: Ideologies of Empire in Spain, Britain and France ca. 1500–ca. 1800.* 1996. Discusses the theoretical foundations of the Atlantic Empires.

Said, Edward. *Orientalism.* 1979. A study of the way in which Western views of the East have assumed its inferiority.

The Industrial Revolution, 1760–1850

I N 1842 A 17-YEAR-OLD GIRL, PATIENCE KERSHAW, TESTIFIED BEFORE A BRITISH PAR-liamentary committee regarding the practice of employing children and women in the nation's mines. When the girl made her appearance, the members of the committee observed that she was "an ignorant, filthy, ragged, and deplorable-looking object, such as one of uncivilized natives of the prairies would be shocked to look upon." Patience, who had never been to school and could not read or write, told the committee that she was one of ten children, all of whom had at one time worked in the coal mines, although three of her sisters now worked in a textile mill. She went to the pit at five in the morning and came out at five at night. Her job in the mines was to hurry coal, that is, to pull carts of coal through the narrow tunnels of the mine. Each cart weighed 300 pounds, and every day she hauled eleven of them one mile. The carts were attached to her head and shoulders by a chain and belt, and the pressure of the cart had worn a bald spot on her head. Patience hurried coal for twelve hours straight, not taking any time for her midday meal, which she ate as she worked. While she was working, the men and boys who dug the coal and put it in the carts would often beat her and take sexual liberties with her. Patience told the committee, "I am the only girl in the pit; there are about 20 boys and 15 men. All the men are naked. I would rather work in a mill than a coal pit."

Patience Kershaw was one of the human casualties of an extraordinary development that historians usually refer to as the Industrial Revolution. This process, which brought about a fundamental transformation of human life, involved the extensive use of machinery in the production of goods. Much of that machinery was driven by steam engines, which required coal to produce the steam. Coal mining itself became a major industry, and the men who owned and operated the mines tried to hire workers, many of them children, at the lowest possible wage. It was this desire to maximize profits that led to the employment, physical hardship, and abuse of girls like Patience Kershaw.

Chapter Outline

- The Nature of the Industrial Revolution

- Conditions Favoring Industrial Growth

- The Spread of Industrialization

- The Effects of Industrialization

- Industry, Trade, and Empire

Exhibit of Machinery at the Crystal Palace Exhibition in London in 1851: During the Industrial Revolution the manufacture of heavy machinery itself became an industry.

■ **Child Labor in the Mines**
A child hurrying coal through a tunnel in a mine.

The story of the Industrial Revolution cannot be told solely in terms of the exploitation of child or even adult workers. Many of its effects can be described in positive or at least morally neutral terms. The Industrial Revolution resulted in a staggering increase in the volume and range of products made available to consumers, from machine-produced clothing to household utensils. It made possible unprecedented and sustained economic growth. The Industrial Revolution facilitated the rapid transportation of passengers as well as goods across large expanses of territory, mainly on the railroads that were constructed in all industrialized countries. It brought about a new awareness of the position of workers in the economic system, and it unleashed powerful political forces intended to improve the lot of these workers.

The Industrial Revolution played a crucial role in redefining and reshaping the West. Until the late nineteenth century industrialization took place only in Western nations. During that century "the West" gradually became identified with those countries which had industrial economies. When some non-Western countries introduced mechanized industry in the twentieth century, largely in imitation of Western example, the geographical boundaries of the West underwent a significant alteration.

In this chapter we shall consider five basic questions: (1) To what economic and social developments does the term Industrial Revolution refer? (2) What social and economic changes made industrial development possible? (3) How did industrialization spread from Great Britain to the European continent and America? (4) What were the economic, social, and cultural effects of the Industrial Revolution? (5) What was the relationship between the growth of industry and Britain's dominance in trade and imperial strength during the middle years of the nineteenth century?

The Nature of the Industrial Revolution

The Industrial Revolution was a series of economic and social changes that took place in Great Britain during the late eighteenth and early nineteenth centuries and on the European continent and in the United States after 1815. Some economic historians claim that the use of the term *revolution*, which suggests radical and abrupt change, is misleading in this context, since the economic and social changes to which the term refers occurred gradually over a long period of time. Even so, the term is still appropriate because it conveys the radical nature and profound significance of the changes it identifies. Like the Scientific Revolution of the seventeenth century, which also took place gradually, the Industrial Revolution reshaped Western civilization.

The Industrial Revolution consisted of four closely related developments: the introduction of new industrial technology, the utilization of mineral sources of energy, the concentration of labor in factories, and the development of new methods of transportation.

NEW INDUSTRIAL TECHNOLOGY

The Industrial Revolution ushered in the machine age, and to this day machines are the most striking feature of modern industrial economies. In countries that have become industrialized, virtually every human-made commodity can be mass-produced by some kind of machine. In the late eighteenth century such machines were novelties, but their numbers increased dramatically in the early nineteenth century. For example, the power loom, a machine used for weaving cloth, was invented in Britain in 1787 but not put into widespread use until the 1820s. By 1836 there were more than 60,000 power looms in just one English county.

Machines became so common in Britain that machine making itself became a major industry, supplying its products to other manufacturers rather than to individual consumers. Machines were introduced in the textile, iron, printing, papermaking, and engineering industries and were used in every stage of manufacture. Machines extracted minerals that were used as either raw materials or sources of energy, transported those materials to the factories, saved time and labor in the actual manufacturing of commodities, and carried the finished products to market. Eventually machines were used in agriculture itself, facilitating both the plowing of fields and the harvesting of crops.

The most significant of the new machines, which changed the entire industrial process, were those used for spinning and weaving in the textile industry and the steam engine, first used in mining and the iron industry. These pieces of machinery became almost synonymous with the Industrial Revolution, and their invention in the 1760s appropriately marks its beginning.

Textile Machinery

Until the late eighteenth century, the production of textiles throughout Europe, which involved both the spinning of yarn and the weaving of cloth, was done entirely by hand, on spinning wheels and hand looms respectively. This was the practice for wool, which was the main textile produced in Europe during the early modern period, as well as for a new material, cotton, which became immensely popular in the early eighteenth century, mainly because of its greater comfort. The demand for cotton yarn was greater than the quantities spinners could supply. To meet this demand a British inventor, James Hargreaves, in 1767 constructed a new machine, the spinning jenny, which greatly increased the amount of cotton yarn that could be spun and thus made available for weaving. The original jenny, a hand machine used in the homes of spinners, consisted of only eight spindles, but it later accommodated as many as 120.

The spinning of yarn on the jenny required a stronger warp, the yarn that ran lengthwise on a loom. A power-driven machine, the water frame, introduced by the barber and wigmaker Richard Arkwright in 1769, made the pro-

CHRONOLOGY	
Technological Innovations of the Industrial Revolution	
1763	James Watts's rotative steam engine
1767	James Hargreaves's spinning jenny
1769	Richard Arkwright's water frame
1779	Samuel Crompton's mule
1787	Edmund Cartwright's power loom
1815	George Stephenson's steam locomotive
1846	Elias Howe's sewing machine

duction of this stronger warp possible. In 1779 Samuel Crompton, using tools he had purchased with his earnings as a fiddle player at a local theater, combined the jenny and the frame in one machine, called the mule. Crompton worked on his machine only at night, in order to keep it secret, and the strange noises that came out of his workshop made his neighbors think his house was haunted. The mule, which could spin as much as 300 times the amount of yarn produced by one spinning wheel, became the main spinning machine of the early Industrial Revolution. Both the water frame and the mule required power, and that requirement led to the centralization of the textile industry in large rural mills located near rivers so that their water wheels could drive the machinery.

The tremendous success of the mule eventually produced more yarn than the weavers could handle on their hand looms. Edmund Cartwright, an Oxford-educated clergyman, supported by monies from his heiress wife, addressed that need with the invention of the power loom in 1787. In that same year he put his new invention to use in a weaving mill he built near the town of Doncaster. The power loom, like the spinning jenny, the water frame, and the mule, met a specific need within the industry. It also gave the producer a competitive advantage by saving time, reducing the cost of labor, and increasing production. Two power looms run by a 15-year-old boy, for example, could produce more than three times what a skilled hand loom weaver could turn out in the same time using only the old hand device, the flying shuttle. The net effect of all these machines was the production of more than 200 times as much cotton cloth in 1850 as in 1780. By 1800 cotton became Britain's largest industry, producing more than 20 percent of the world's cloth, and by 1850 that percentage had risen to more than 50 percent. Indeed, by midcentury, cotton accounted for 70 percent of the value of all British exports.

The Steam Engine

The steam engine was even more important than the new textile machinery since it was used in almost every stage of the productive process, including the operation of textile machinery itself. The steam engine was invented by a Scottish engineer, James Watt, in 1763. It represented an improvement over the engine invented by Thomas Newcomen in 1709, which had been intended mainly to drain water from deep mines. The problem with Newcomen's engine was that the steam, which was produced in a cylinder heated by coal, had to be cooled in order to make the piston return, and the process of heating and cooling had to be repeated for each stroke of the piston. The engine was therefore inefficient and expensive to operate. Watt created a separate chamber where the steam could be condensed without affecting the heat of the cylinder. The result was a more efficient and cost-effective machine that could provide more power than any other source. Watt's pride in his invention was matched only by his pride in his Scottish nationality. Upon receiving a patent for the new device, he boasted, "This was made by a Scot."

After designing the steam engine, Watt teamed up with a Birmingham metal manufacturer, Matthew Boulton, to produce it on a large scale. Boulton provided the capital necessary to begin this process and to hire the skilled laborers to assemble the machines. He also had ambitious plans for marketing the new invention throughout the world. "It would not be worth my while to make for three countries only," Boulton said, "but I find it well worth my while to make for the whole world."

The steam engine soon became the workhorse of the Industrial Revolution. Not only did it pump water from mines, but it helped raise minerals like iron ore that were extracted from those mines. It provided the intense blast of heat that was necessary to re-smelt pig iron into cast iron, which in turn was used to make industrial machinery, buildings, bridges, locomotives, and ships. Once the engine was equipped with a rotating device, it was used to drive the factory machinery in the textile mills, and it eventually powered the railroad locomotives that carried industrial goods to market.

The widespread adoption of steam power came fairly late in the Industrial Revolution. Only in the 1840s and 1850s, after its efficiency had been greatly improved, did it become the main source of energy in the textile industry. Until then rural water power was the preferred method of running the cotton mills. Only after the introduction of coal-driven steam power did the factories locate in the cities, especially those of northern England, such as Manchester. The 1840s and 1850s were also the decades when the railroads, using the steam locomotive invented by the English engineer George Stephenson in 1815, began to crisscross the European continent. By midcentury the steam engine had become the predominant symbol of the Industrial Revolution.

MINERAL SOURCES OF ENERGY

Until the late eighteenth century, most economic activity, including the transportation of goods, was powered by either humans or beasts. Either people tilled the soil themselves, using a spade, or they yoked oxen to pull a plow. Either they carried materials and goods on their backs or they used horses to transport them. In either case the energy for these tasks came ultimately from organic sources, the food that was needed to feed farmers or their animals. If workers needed heat, they had to burn an organic material, wood or charcoal, to produce it. The amount of energy that could be generated in a particular region was therefore limited by its capacity to produce sufficient wood, charcoal, or food. By the middle of the eighteenth century, for example, the forests in Britain were no longer capable of producing sufficient quantities of charcoal for use in the iron industry.

Organic sources of energy were of course renewable, in that new crops could be grown and forests replanted, but the long periods of time that these processes took, coupled with the limited volume of organic material that could be extracted from an acre of land, made it difficult to sustain economic growth. The only viable alternatives to these organic sources of energy before the eighteenth century were those that tapped the forces of nature: windmills, which were used mainly in the Netherlands for purposes of field drainage, and water wheels, which were driven by water pressure from river currents, waterfalls, or human-made channels that regulated the flow of water. The potential of those natural sources of energy was both limited and difficult to harness, and it could be tapped only in certain locations or at certain times. Moreover, those sources could not produce heat.

The decisive change in the harnessing of energy for industrial purposes was the successful use of minerals, originally coal but in the twentieth century oil and uranium as well, as the main sources of energy used in the production and transportation of goods. These minerals were not inexhaustible, as the decline of coal deposits in Europe during the twentieth century has shown, but the supplies could last for centuries, and they were much more efficient than any form of energy produced from organic materials, including charcoal and peat. Coal produced the high combustion temperatures necessary to smelt iron, and unlike charcoal it was not limited by the size of a region's forests. Coal therefore became the key to the expansion of the British iron industry in the nineteenth century. That industry's dependence on coal was reflected by the relocation of iron works from the mines that supplied the ore itself to the coal fields that supplied the energy. Coal also became the sole source of heat for the new steam engine.

As the Industrial Revolution progressed, it relied increasingly on coal as its main fuel. The change, however, occurred gradually. In 1830 a majority of factories still used

■ **Philippe Jacques de Loutherbourg, *Coalbrookdale by Night* (1801)**
This painting depicts the intense heat produced by the coal bellows used to smelt iron in
Coalbrookdale, an English town in the Severn Valley that was one of the key centers of industrial ac-
tivity at the beginning of the nineteenth century.

water power, and steam power did not realize its most spectacular increases until after 1870. Nevertheless, largely because of the demands of the mining, textile, and metal industries, coal mining became a major industry itself with
an enormous labor force. By 1850 British mines employed
about 5 percent of the entire national workforce. These
miners were just as instrumental as textile workers in making Britain an industrial nation.

THE GROWTH OF FACTORIES

One of the most enduring images of the Industrial
Revolution is that of the large factory, filled with workers,
laboring amid massive machinery driven by either water or
steam power. Mechanized factory production evolved out
of forms of industry that had emerged only during the early
modern period (1500–1750). In the Middle Ages virtually
all industry in Europe was undertaken by skilled craftsmen
who belonged to urban guilds. These artisans, working
either by themselves or with the assistance of apprentices or
journeymen, produced everything from candlesticks and
hats to oxcarts and beds. During the early modern period
the urban craftsman's shop gave way to two different types
of industrial workplaces, the rural cottage and the large
handicraft workshop. Both of these served as halfway
houses to the large factory.

Beginning in the sixteenth century, entrepreneurs began
employing families in the countryside to spin and weave
cloth and make nails and cutlery. By locating industry in
the countryside the entrepreneurs were able to escape the
regulations imposed by the guilds regarding employment
and the price of finished products. They also paid lower
wages, since the rural workers, who also received an income
from farming, were willing to work for less than the residents of towns. Another attraction of rural industry was
that all the members of the family, including children, participated in the process. In this "domestic system" a capitalist entrepreneur provided the workers with the raw materials and sometimes the tools they needed. He later paid them
a fixed rate for each finished product. The entrepreneur was
also responsible for having the finished cloth dyed and for
marketing the commodities in regional towns.

Rural household industry was widespread not only in
certain regions of Britain but also in most European countries. In the late eighteenth century it gradually gave way to
the factory system. The great attraction of factory production was mechanization, which became cost-efficient only
when it was introduced in a central industrial workplace. In
factories, moreover, the entrepreneur could reduce the cost
of labor and transportation, exercise tighter control over
the quality of goods, and increase productivity by concentrating workers in one location. Temporary labor shortages

■ **Mule Spinning**
A large mechanized spinning mill in northern England, about 1835. The workers did not require any great skill to run the machinery.

sometimes made the transition from rural industry to factory production imperative.

The second type of industrial workplace that emerged during the early modern period was the large handicraft workshop. Usually located in the towns and cities, rather than in the countryside, these workshops employed relatively small numbers of people with different skills who worked collectively on the manufacture of a variety of items, such as pottery and munitions. The owner of the workshop supplied the raw materials, paid the workers' wages, and gained a profit from selling the finished products.

The large handicraft workshop made possible a division of labor°—the assignment of one stage of production to each worker or group of workers. The effect of the division of labor on productivity was evident even in the manufacture of simple items such as buttons and pins. In *The Wealth of Nations* (1776), the economist Adam Smith (1723–1790) used a pin factory in London to illustrate how the division of labor could increase per capita productivity from no more than twenty pins a day to the astonishing total of 4,800.

Like the cottages engaged in rural industry, the large handicraft workshop eventually gave way to the mechanized factory. The main difference between the workshop and the factory was that the factory did not require a body of skilled workers. When production became mechanized, the worker's job was simply to tend to the machinery. The only skill factory workers needed was manual dexterity to operate the machinery. Only those workers who made industrial machinery remained craftsmen or skilled workers in the traditional sense of the word.

With the advent of mechanization, factory owners gained much tighter control over the entire productive process. Indeed, they began to enforce an unprecedented discipline among their workers, who had to accommodate themselves to the boredom of repetitive work and a timetable set by the machines. Craftsmen who had been accustomed to working at their own pace now had to adjust to an entirely new and more demanding schedule. "While the engine runs," wrote one critical contemporary, "the people must work—men, women, and children yoked together with iron and steam. The animal machine—breakable in the best case, subject to a thousand sources of suffering—is chained fast to the iron machine which knows no suffering and no weariness."

Despite the growth and development of the factory system, the factory did not become the most common type of industrial workplace until the early twentieth century. In Britain, Germany, France, and the United States most manufacturing continued to take place in handicraft workshops in the cities or in rural households. Indeed, many of the industries that became mechanized spawned a variety of secondary crafts and trades, such as the dyeing and finishing of cloth and the sewing of clothes, which were conducted mainly in rural households.

NEW METHODS OF TRANSPORTATION

As industry became more extensive and increased its output, transport facilities, such as roads, bridges, canals, and eventually railroads, grew in number and quality. Increased industrial productivity has always depended on efficient movement of raw materials to places of production and transportation of finished products to the market. During the early phase of the Industrial Revolution in Britain, water transportation supplied most of these needs. A vast network of navigable rivers and human-made canals, eventually more than 4,000 miles in length, was used to transport goods in areas that did not have access to the coast. The canals that were built after 1760, with their systems of locks and their aqueducts spanning roads and rivers, were a product of the technology that the Scientific Revolution had made possible. For routes that could not be reached by water, the most common method of transportation was by horse-drawn carriages on newly built turnpikes or toll roads, many of them made of stone so that they were passable even in wet weather.

The most significant innovation in transport during the nineteenth century was the railroad. Introduced as the Industrial Revolution was gaining momentum, the railroad provided quick, cheap transportation of heavy materials like coal and iron over long distances. Its introduction in Britain during the 1820s and throughout Europe and America during the following decades serves as one of the best illustrations of the transition from an economy based on organic sources of energy to one based on mineral sources of energy. Driven by coal-burning, steam-powered locomotives, the railroads freed transport from a dependence on animal power, especially the horses that were used to pull coaches along turnpikes, barges along canals, and even carts along parallel tracks in mines. Railroads rapidly became the main economic thoroughfares of the industrial economy. They linked towns and regions that earlier had not been easily accessible to each other. They also changed the travel habits of Europeans by making it possible to cover distances in one-fifth the time it took by coach.

ADAM SMITH DESCRIBES THE DIVISION OF LABOR

Adam Smith, a Scottish economist who is considered the founder of the classical school of economics, was the great theorist of modern laissez-faire *capitalism. In* An Inquiry into the Nature and Causes of the Wealth of Nations *(1776), he challenged the mercantilist assumption that there was only a fixed supply of wealth for which nations had to compete. He also argued that in an unregulated economy, the pursuit of self-interest would work in the interest of the public welfare. In this selection Smith discusses the division of labor. Smith wrote* The Wealth of Nations *during the very early stages of industrialization. The place of production that he uses in this example is not a large mechanized factory but a small urban workshop, often referred to as a manufactory.*

To take an example, therefore, from a very trifling manufacture; but one in which the division of labour has been very often taken notice of, the trade of the pin-maker; a workman not educated to this business (which the division of labour has rendered a distinct trade), nor acquainted with the use of the machinery employed in it (to the invention of which the same division of labour has probably given occasion), could scarce, perhaps, with his utmost industry, make one pin in a day, and certainly could not make twenty. But in the way in which this business is now carried on, not only the whole work is a peculiar trade, but it is divided into a number of branches, of which the greater part are likewise peculiar trades. One man draws out the wire, another straits it, a third cuts it, a fourth points it, a fifth grinds it at the top for receiving the head; to make the head requires two or three distinct operations; to put it on is a peculiar business, to whiten the pins is another; it is even a trade by itself to put them into the paper; and the important business of making a pin is in this manner, divided into about eighteen distinct operations, which in some manufactories, are all performed by distinct hands, though in others the same man will sometimes perform two or three of them. I have seen a small manufactory of this kind where ten men only were employed, and where some of them consequently performed two or three distinct operations. But though they were very poor and indifferently accommodated with the necessary machinery, they could, when they exerted themselves, make about twelve pounds of pins a day. There are in a pound upwards of four thousand pins of a middling size. Those ten persons, therefore, could make among them upwards of forty-eight thousand pins in a day. Each person, therefore making a tenth part of forty-eight thousand pins, might be considered as making four thousand eight hundred pins in a day.

Source: From Adam Smith, *An Inquiry into the Nature and Cause of the Wealth of Nations*, 5th Edition, 1789, Book I, Chapter 1.

The construction and operation of railroads became a major new industry, employing thousands of skilled and unskilled workers and providing opportunities for investment and profit. The industry created an unprecedented demand for iron and other materials used to build and equip locomotives, tracks, freight cars, passenger cars, and signals, thus giving a tremendous boost to the iron industry and the metalworking and engineering trades. By the 1840s the railroads had become the main stimulus to economic growth throughout western Europe and the United States. Transport in industrialized economies continues to experience frequent innovation. During the twentieth century, for example, new methods of transportation, including automobiles, airplanes, and high-speed rails, have sustained economic growth in all industrialized countries, and like the railroads they have become major industries themselves.

Transport facilities, unlike factories, can seldom be built entirely by their individual owners. The cost of building locomotives and laying railroad tracks is almost always too great to come from the profits accumulated in the normal conduct of one's business. The funds for these facilities must come from either private investment, governments, or international financial institutions. In Britain the capital for the railroads came entirely from individual investors. In the United States, which built the world's largest railroad system in the nineteenth century, most of the capital also came from private investment, but many state and city governments helped finance early railroads. In other industrialized countries, governments played a more important role. In Belgium, which was the second European country to experience an Industrial Revolution, and in Russia, which was one of the last, the governments of those countries assumed the responsibility for building a national railroad system.

Conditions Favoring Industrial Growth

The immediate causes of the Industrial Revolution were the competitive pressures that encouraged technological innovation, the transition to coal power, the growth of factories, and the building of the railroads. These developments, however, do not provide a full explanation for this unprecedented economic transformation. Certain social and economic conditions were present in Britain that allowed industrialization to progress—a large population, improved agricultural productivity, the accumulation of capital, a group of people with scientific knowledge and entrepreneurial skill, and sufficient demand for manufactured goods. In this section we will look at the historical experience of Great Britain, which was the first country to industrialize, to see how these conditions made industrial economic development possible.

POPULATION GROWTH

Industrialization requires a sufficiently large pool of labor to staff the factories and workshops of the new industries. One of the main reasons why the Industrial Revolution occurred first in Britain is that its population during the eighteenth century increased more rapidly than that of any country in continental Europe. Between 1680 and 1820 the population of England more than doubled, while that of France grew at less than one-third that rate, and that of the Dutch Republic hardly grew at all. One of the reasons this growth took place was that famines, which had occurred periodically throughout the early modern period, became less frequent during the eighteenth century. The last great

Increase in European Population, 1680–1820

Population Totals (millions)

	1680	1820
France	21.9	30.5
Italy	12.0	18.4
Germany	12.0	18.1
Spain	8.5	14.0
England	4.9	11.5
Netherlands	1.9	2.0
Western Europe	71.9	116.5

Percentage Growth Rates, 1680–1820

England	133%
Spain	64
Italy	53
Germany	51
France	39
Netherlands	8
Western Europe	73

Source: E. A. Wrigley, "The Growth of Population in Eighteenth-Century England: A Conundrum Resolved," *Past and Present* 98 (1983), 122.

famine in Britain took place in 1740, only a generation before industrialization began. There was also a decrease in mortality from epidemic diseases, especially typhus, influenza, and smallpox. Bubonic plague, which had decimated the European population periodically since the fourteenth century, struck England for the last time in the Great Plague of London of 1665. It made its last European appearance at Marseilles in 1720 but did not spread beyond the southern parts of France.

Even more important than this reduction in mortality was an increase in fertility. More people were marrying, and at a younger age, which increased the birth rate. The spread of rural industry seems to have encouraged this early-marriage pattern. Wage-earning textile workers tended to marry a little earlier than agricultural workers, probably because wage earners did not have to postpone marriage to inherit land or to become self-employed, as was the case with farm workers.

This increase in population facilitated industrialization in two ways. First, it increased demand for the goods that were being manufactured in large quantities in the factories. The desire for these products, especially the new cottons, played an important role in enlarging the domestic market for manufactured goods, as we shall see shortly. Second, it increased the supply of labor, freeing a substantial portion of the population for industry, especially for factory labor. At the same time, however, this increase was not so large as to have had a negative effect on industrializa-

tion, as it did in a number of underdeveloped countries in the twentieth century. If population growth is too rapid, it can lead to declining incomes, put pressure on agriculture to feed more people than is possible, and prevent the accumulation of wealth. Most important, it can discourage factory owners from introducing costly machinery, because if labor is plentiful and cheap, it might very well cost less for workers to produce the same volume of goods by hand. Industrialization therefore requires a significant but not too rapid increase in population—the exact scenario that occurred in Britain during the eighteenth century.

AGRICULTURAL PRODUCTIVITY

Between 1700 and 1800 British agriculture experienced a revolution, resulting in a substantial increase in productivity. A major reason for this increase was the consolidation of all the land farmed by one tenant into compact fields. During the Middle Ages and most of the early modern period, each tenant on a manorial estate leased and farmed strips of land that were scattered throughout the estate. The decisions regarding the planting and harvesting of crops in these open fields were made collectively in the manorial court. Beginning in the sixteenth century, some of the wealthier tenants on these estates agreed to exchange their strips of land with their neighbors in order to consolidate their holdings into large compact fields, whose boundaries were defined by hedges, bushes, or walls. The main benefit of this process of enclosure° was that it allowed individual farmers to exercise complete control over the use of their land. In the eighteenth and nineteenth centuries the number of these enclosures increased dramatically, as the British Parliament passed legislation that divided entire estates into a number of enclosed fields. This legislation benefited all landowners, including the members of the aristocracy who passed the legislation.

With control of their lands, farmers could make them more productive. The most profitable change was to introduce new crop rotations, often involving the alternation of grains like rye or barley with root crops like turnips or grasses like clover. These new crops and grasses restored nutrients to the soil and therefore made it unnecessary to let fields lie fallow once every three years. Farmers also introduced a variety of new fertilizers and soil additives that made harvests more bountiful. Farmers who raised sheep took advantage of discoveries regarding scientific breeding that improved the quality of their flocks.

More productive farming meant that fewer agricultural workers were required to feed the population. This made it possible for more people to leave the farms to work in the factories and mines. The expanded labor pool of industrial workers, moreover, was large enough that factory owners did not have to pay workers high wages; otherwise the prospect of industrializing would have lost much of its appeal. The hiring of children and women to work in the factories and mines also kept the labor pool large and the costs of labor low.

CAPITAL FORMATION AND ACCUMULATION

The term capital° refers to all the assets used in production. These include the factories and machines that are used to produce other goods (fixed capital) as well as the raw materials and finished products that are sent to market (circulating capital). Other forms of capital are the railroads and barges used for transporting raw materials to the place of production and finished products to market. Mechanized industry involves the extensive and intensive use of capital to do the work formerly assigned to human beings. An industrial economy therefore requires large amounts of capital, especially fixed capital.

Capital more generally refers to the money that is necessary to purchase these physical assets. This capital can come from a number of different sources: It can come from individuals, such as wealthy landlords, merchants, or industrialists who invest the profits they have accumulated in industrial machinery or equipment. In many cases the profits derived from industrial production are reinvested in the firm itself. Alternatively, capital can come from financial institutions in the form of loans. Very often a number of individuals make their wealth available to an industrial firm by buying shares of stock in that company's operations. This of course is the main way in which most capital is accumulated today. In countries that have only recently begun to industrialize in Latin America and Southeast Asia, capital often comes from public sources, such as governments, or from international institutions, such as the International Monetary Fund.

In Great Britain the capital that was needed to achieve industrial transformation came almost entirely from private sources. Some of it was raised by selling shares of stock to people from the middle and upper levels of society, but an even larger amount came from merchants who engaged in domestic and international trade, landowners who profited from the production of agricultural goods (including those who owned plantations in America), and the industrial entrepreneurs who owned mines, ironworks, and factories. In Britain, where all three groups were more successful than in other parts of Europe, the volume of capital made available from these sources was substantial. These people could invest directly in industrial machinery and mines or, more commonly, make their wealth available to others indirectly in the form of loans from banks where they kept their financial assets.

Banks supplied a considerable amount of the funds necessary for industrialization. In Britain the possibilities for such capital were maximized in the late eighteenth century when financial institutions offered loans at low interest rates, and when the development of a national banking system made these funds readily available throughout the country, especially in the new industrial cities such as Leeds, Sheffield, and Manchester. The number of English banks went from a mere dozen in 1750 to more than 300 in 1800. Many bankers had close ties with industrialists, thereby facilitating the flow of capital from the financial to the industrial sector of the economy. Banks played an even more central role in the industrialization of Germany, which was economically not as advanced as Britain and less capable, therefore, of generating capital through the accumulation of profits.

TECHNOLOGICAL KNOWLEDGE AND ENTREPRENEURSHIP

The process of industrialization involves the application of technological knowledge to the manufacturing process. It also involves entrepreneurship, the ability to make business ventures profitable. The mechanization of industry demanded scientifically trained people not only to introduce new forms of machinery but also to mass produce that machinery for other manufacturers. The development of new modes of transportation required the skill of an entire class of civil engineers who could design and construct locomotives, ships, canals, railroads, and bridges. At the same time, industrialization required a group of business experts who knew how to run the factories and market their products. These requirements help explain why countries that are industrializing today often import technological and financial personnel from other countries to assist them in the process of industrialization and take steps to train and educate people from their own countries to carry on this work.

As we have discussed in Chapter 16, the geographical center of the Scientific Revolution shifted from the Mediterranean to the North Atlantic, especially to England, in the late seventeenth century. At the same time, England took the lead in making science an integral part of the nation's culture. In no other European country was so much attention given to the dissemination of scientific knowledge in public lectures, the meetings of local scientific societies, and the publication of scientific textbooks. Much of this popular scientific education focused on Newtonian mechanics and dynamics. These were precisely the areas of science that lent themselves most readily to technological application. The only area that was developed more fully in France than in Britain was thermodynamics, the branch of physics dealing with heat and its conversion into other forms of energy, such as steam power. To some extent the technological innovations and engineering achievements that took place in Britain during the Industrial Revolution can be considered the product of this unparalleled diffusion of scientific knowledge. Those who made these innovations also required extensive mathematical skill. The education given to British schoolchildren in the eighteenth century included more instruction in mathematics than was given in any other European country.

Industrial entrepreneurs, the people who actually ran the factories and superintended the industrial process, also needed a certain level of technological and mathematical skill, but their talents lay much more in their ability to run a variety of capitalist enterprises for a profit. Britain had no shortage of this type of talent in the eighteenth century. Even before the advent of mechanization there had developed an entire class of merchant capitalists who had organized the domestic system of rural industry or run the large handicraft workshops in London and other towns.

The invention and production of the steam engine readily illustrate the way in which technological and entrepreneurial skills reinforced and complemented each other. The partnership between the Scotsman James Watt, who invented the steam engine, and the Englishman Matthew Boulton represented a dynamic British alliance of science and capitalism. Of the two men, Watt had more scientific and mathematical knowledge, having taught himself geometry and trigonometry as well as having read textbooks on mechanics. He was familiar with the work of Joseph Black, the chemist at the University of Glasgow who studied steam, and he had acquired a knowledge of scientific instruments from his father's business as an outfitter of ships. Even though he was not an academic, he thought he was as smart as the famous French chemist Antoine Lavoisier. He was also a shrewd businessman who figured out various ways to use his knowledge of engineering to turn a profit and acquire a competitive advantage over others. Boulton was the classic eighteenth-century English entrepreneur who manufactured a variety of small metal objects from toys and buttons to teakettles and watch chains. His contribution to the partnership was assembling workers with the requisite skills to mass-produce the engine. Boulton was also scientifically knowledgeable, and both he and Watt were members of the Lunar Society of Birmingham, a voluntary scientific society where they shared similar interests. Both men thought of themselves as scientists, just as both of them acted as entrepreneurs.

Demand from Consumers and Producers

The conditions for industrialization that we have discussed so far all deal with supply°, that is, the amounts of capital, labor, food, and skill that are necessary to support the industrial process. The other side of the economic equation is demand°, that is, the desire of consumers to purchase industrial goods and of producers to acquire raw materials and machinery. Much of the extraordinary productivity of the Industrial Revolution arose from the demand for industrial products. Many of the technological innovations that occurred at the beginning of the revolution also originated as responses to the demand for more goods. For example, the demand for more cotton goods spurred the introduction of the spinning jenny, the water frame, and the mule.

Likewise the demand for coal for industrial and domestic use led to the development of an efficient steam engine in order to drain mines so that those supplies of coal could be extracted.

During the early years of industrialization, only about 35 percent of all British manufactured goods were exported. This statistic indicates that as the Industrial Revolution was taking hold, the domestic market was still the main source of demand for industrial products. The demand was especially strong among the bourgeoisie. Within that group a "consumer revolution" had taken place during the eighteenth century. This revolution was based on an unprecedented desire to acquire goods of all sorts, especially clothing and housewares, such as pottery, cutlery, furniture, and curtains. The consumer revolution was fueled in large part by a desire to imitate the spending habits of the aristocracy. It was assisted by commercial manipulation of all sorts, including newspaper advertising, warehouse displays, product demonstrations, and the distribution of samples. An entirely new consumer culture arose, one in which women played a leading role. Advertisements promoting the latest female fashions, housewares, and children's toys became more common than those directed at adult male consumers. One ad in a local British paper in 1777, capitalizing on reports that mice were getting into ladies' hair at night, promoted "night caps made of silver wire so strong that no mouse or even a rat can gnaw through them." Advertisements therefore created a demand for new products as well as increasing the demand for those already on the market.

If this consumer revolution had been restricted to the middle class, it would have had only a limited effect on the Industrial Revolution. The bourgeoisie in the eighteenth century constituted at most only 20 percent of the entire population of Britain, and most of the goods they craved, with the exception of the pottery produced in Josiah Wedgwood's factories (which is still made today), were luxury items rather than the types of products that could be easily mass-produced. A strong demand for manufactured goods could develop only if workers were to buy consumer goods such as knitted stockings and caps, cotton shirts, earthenware, coffeepots, nails, candlesticks, watches, lace, and ribbon. The demand for these products came from small cottagers and laborers as well as the middle class. The demand for stockings for both men and women was particularly strong. In 1831 the author of a study of the impact of machinery on British society declared, "Two centuries ago not one person in a thousand wore stockings; one century ago not one person in five hundred wore them; now not one person in a thousand is without them."

Demand for manufactured products from the lower classes was obviously limited by the amount of money that wage earners had available for non-essential goods, and real wages did not increase very much, if at all, during the eighteenth century. Nevertheless the income of families in which the wife and children as well as the father worked for wages did increase significantly both during the heyday of rural industry and during the early years of industrialization. With these funds available, a substantial number of workers could actually afford to buy the products that they desired. As the population increased, so too did this lower-class demand, which helped to sustain an economy built around industrial production.

The Spread of Industrialization

The Industrial Revolution, like the Scientific Revolution of the sixteenth and seventeenth centuries, did not occur in all European countries at the same time. As we have seen, it began in Britain in the 1760s and for more than four decades was confined exclusively to that country (see Map 20.1). It eventually spread to other European and North American countries, where many industrial innovations were modeled on those that had taken place in Britain. Belgium, France, Germany, Switzerland, Austria, Sweden, and the United States all experienced their own Industrial Revolutions by the middle of the nineteenth century. Only in the late nineteenth century did countries outside the traditional boundaries of the West, mainly Russia and Japan, begin to industrialize. By the middle of the twentieth century, industrialization had become a truly global process, transforming the economies of a number of Asian and Latin American countries.

GREAT BRITAIN AND THE CONTINENT

Industrialization occurred on the European continent much later than it did in Great Britain. Only after 1815 did Belgium and France begin to industrialize on a large scale, and it was not until 1840 that Germany, Switzerland, and Austria showed significant signs of industrial growth. Other European countries, such as Italy and Spain, did not begin serious efforts in this direction until the late nineteenth century. It took continental European nations even longer to rival the economic strength of Britain. Germany, which emerged as Britain's main competitor in the late nineteenth century, did not match British industrial output until the twentieth century.

Why did it take so long for other countries to industrialize? Virtually all of them had developed extensive rural industry in the late eighteenth century. The governments of European countries, in keeping with mercantilist philosophy, had a long tradition of encouraging the development of domestic industry. Population growth on the Continent during the late eighteenth century, while less dramatic than in Great Britain, should have been sufficient to stimulate consumer demand and increase the supply of labor. Overall

■ Map 20.1   The Concentrations of Industry in Great Britain, 1750–1820
The most heavily industrialized regions were in the north, where the population of cities such as Manchester, Liverpool, and Sheffield grew rapidly.

economic growth in France during that time almost matched that of Great Britain. Scientific education, while not as widespread as in Britain, was hardly lacking, especially in France. Nonetheless, industrialization on the Continent, especially in heavy industry, lagged far behind that of Great Britain, and the process was for the most part painfully slow.

One explanation for the slower development of industrialization on the Continent relates to the political situations in those countries. Well into the nineteenth century, most continental European countries had numerous internal political barriers that could impede the transportation of raw materials and goods from one part of the country to another. In Germany, for example, which was not politically united until 1871, scores of small sovereign territorial units charged tariffs whenever goods crossed their territorial boundaries. Only in 1834 was a customs union, the *Zollverein*, created to eliminate some of these barriers. In France, which had achieved a formal territorial unity during the reign of Louis XIV, local rights and privileges impeded internal trade until the early nineteenth century. This political situation was aggravated by the relatively poor state of continental roads and the inaccessibility of many seaports from production sites.

The contrast between the situation on the Continent and that which prevailed in Great Britain is striking. After 1707, when Scotland was united to England and freedom of internal trade was established between the two countries, the United Kingdom of Great Britain constituted the largest free trade zone in Europe. Thus raw materials and finished products could pass from one place within Great Britain to another, up to a distance of more than 800 miles, without payment of any internal customs or duties. The system of inland waterways was complete by 1780, and seaports were accessible from all parts of the country.

The industrial potential of many continental European countries was also weakened by the imposition of protective tariffs on goods imported from other countries. The purpose of this mercantilist policy was to develop national self-sufficiency and to maintain a favorable balance of trade, but it also had the negative effect of limiting economic growth. For example, in the Dutch Republic (the kingdom of the Netherlands after 1815) a long tradition of protecting established industries prevented that country from importing the raw materials and machines needed to develop new industries. Since protectionism invited retaliation from trading partners, it also tended to shrink the size of potential overseas markets. Britain adopted a policy of free trade during the 1840s, and it applied pressure on other European countries to adopt the same policy.

A further obstacle to European industrialization was aristocratic hostility, or at least indifference, to industrial development. In Britain the aristocracy, which consisted of noblemen and gentry, were themselves often involved in capitalist enterprise and did not have the same suspicion of industry and trade that their counterparts in France and Spain often harbored. Many members of the British aristocracy, such as the entrepreneur "Turnip Townshend" (see Chapter 17), were agricultural capitalists who improved the productivity of their estates. Others were involved in mining. The Duke of Devonshire encouraged the exploitation of the copper mines on his estate, while the Duke of Bridgewater employed the engineer James Brindley to build a canal from the duke's coal mines in Worsley to Manchester in 1759. He later had Brindley extend the canal from Manchester to the mouth of the Mersey River, connecting the textile region of Manchester with the large northern industrial city of Liverpool.

One reason for the British aristocracy's support for economic growth was that many of its members, especially the gentry, rose into its ranks from other social and economic groups. These individuals tended to be sympathetic to the values of a commercial and an industrial society. The same attitude toward commerce and industry simply did not exist among the nobility in France before the revolution, much less among German *Junkers*. These groups had little connection with industrial or commercial society, whose values they held in very low regard. Consequently they rarely invested in industry.

Even among the European middle classes, the same type of competitive entrepreneurial spirit that was exhibited by men like Matthew Boulton seems to have been in large part lacking. Capitalism was by no means absent in European countries, but the conduct of business was characterized by greater caution and less willingness to obtain new capital from loans or the sale of stock to investors. This went hand in hand with a reluctance to innovate as well as a distaste for competition and the maximizing of profits. Consequently continental European countries failed to produce many counterparts to the captains of industry who had contributed much of the capital, technology, and entrepreneurial spirit to the Industrial Revolution in Britain.

A final reason for the slow industrialization of continental European countries was that they lacked the abundant raw materials that were readily accessible in Britain. The natural resources that Britain had in greatest quantities were coal and iron ore, both of which were indispensable to industrialization. At the same time British farms provided ample supplies of raw materials for the wool and leather industries. The French and the Germans had some coal deposits, but they were more difficult to mine, and they were not located near ocean ports. Continental countries also lacked the access to other raw materials that Britain could import through its vast trading network, and in particular from its overseas colonies. With a large empire on four continents and the world's largest merchant marine, Britain had abundant supplies of raw materials such as cotton as well as the capacity to import them cheaply and in large quantities. The greater difficulty European countries had in obtaining these raw materials did not prevent them from industrializing; it simply made the process slower.

FEATURES OF CONTINENTAL INDUSTRIALIZATION

During the first half of the nineteenth century, especially after 1830, Belgium, France, Switzerland, Germany, and Austria began to introduce machinery into the industrial process, use steam power in production, concentrate labor in large factories, and build railroads. This continental European version of the Industrial Revolution is usually described as an imitative process, one in which entrepreneurs or government officials simply tried to duplicate the economic success that Britain had achieved by following British example. Continental European nations did indeed rely to some extent on British industrial machinery. Some of them also relied on British skilled labor when they began to build their first factories and ironworks. In a few instances, in violation of British law, foreign agents actually smuggled blueprints, models, or machine parts out of Britain. British engineers, entrepreneurs, and managers were also occasionally hired to run British-style factories in France and Germany. But each European nation, responding to its own unique combination of political, economic, and social conditions, followed its own course of industrialization.

One distinctive feature of continental European industrialization was that once countries like Belgium and Germany began to industrialize, their governments played a much more active role in encouraging and assisting in the process. In contrast to Britain, whose government allowed private industry to function with few economic controls, continental governments became active partners in the industrial process. They supplied capital for many economic ventures, especially the railroads and roads. In Prussia the government ran the mines. Many continental governments also imposed protective tariffs to prevent an influx of cheap British goods from underselling the products of their own fledgling industries. In a few cases continental European governments even provided financial support for investors in an effort to encourage capital formation. In some places, such as Austria, the state eliminated the regulations of urban guilds that had restricted industrial development in rural regions.

A second major feature of continental European industrialization is that banks, particularly in Germany and Belgium, played a central role in industrial development. This was necessitated by the low level of capital formation on the Continent and the reluctance of entrepreneurs to take risks by investing money themselves. Banks in Germany and Belgium played a particularly active role in stimulating industry. Drawing on the resources of both small and large investors, these corporate banks became in effect industrial banks, building railroads and factories themselves in addition to making capital available for a variety of industrial ventures.

A third distinct feature of continental European industrialization is that the railroads actually contributed to the beginning of industrial development. In Great Britain the railroads were introduced some sixty years after industrial-

■ **Medal Struck in 1835 to Commemorate the First German Railroad, from Nuremberg to Fürth**

Industry is depicted as a female figure with her arm resting on a winged wheel. The first railroad in Europe had opened in England in 1825. German engineers had modeled their first locomotive on that of George Stephenson.

ization had begun and thus helped sustain a process of economic development that had been long afoot. By contrast the railroads on the Continent provided the basic infrastructure of its new economy and became a major stimulus to the development of all other industries. Railroads also gave continental European governments the ability to transport military troops quickly in time of war, which helps to explain why governments supported railroad construction with such enthusiasm. In Belgium, which was the first continental European nation to industrialize, the new government built a national railroad system during the 1830s and 1840s, not only to stimulate industry but also to unify the newly independent nation.

Of all the European countries that industrialized, only Belgium appears to have followed the British model closely by developing coal, iron, and textiles as the three main sectors of the new economy. Other countries tended to concentrate their activity in one specific area. France emphasized textiles, especially those like worsted woolens that did not compete with British cottons. France's coal production and consumption never matched that of Great Britain or Belgium, and after 1850 it fell behind that of Germany as well. In 1860 France was importing 43 percent of its coal, and it was still relying on charcoal rather than coal to smelt pig iron. In Germany the main economic advances, which did not begin until 1850, occurred mainly in the area of heavy industry, that is, coal, iron, and engineering rather than textiles. Together with the United States, Germany began to offer the main economic competition to the British economy by the end of the nineteenth century.

INDUSTRIALIZATION IN THE UNITED STATES

Industrialization in the United States began during the 1820s, not long after Belgium and France had begun to experience their own industrial revolutions. It occurred first in the textile industry in New England, where factories using water power produced goods for largely rural markets. New England also began producing two domestic hardware products—clocks and guns—for the same market. Between 1850 and 1880 a second region between Pittsburgh and Cleveland became industrialized. This region specialized in heavy industry, especially steelmaking and the manufacture of large machinery, and it relied on coal for fuel.

American industrialization conformed to many of the patterns established in Britain and on the European continent. As in Britain and France, the development of cottage industry preceded industrialization. Most of the industrial machinery used in the United States during the nineteenth century was modeled on imports from Britain. The most significant American technological innovation before 1900 was the sewing machine, which was patented by Elias Howe in 1846 and then developed and improved upon by Isaac Singer in the 1850s. This new machine was then introduced in Europe, where it was used in the production of ready-to-wear garments.

After 1865, when American industrialization began to spread rapidly across the entire country, American entrepreneurs made a distinctive contribution to the industrial process in the area of business organization, especially the operation of international firms. Toward the beginning of the twentieth century, American manufacturers streamlined the production process by introducing the assembly line, a division of labor in which the product passes from one operation to the next until it is fully assembled. The assembly line required the production of interchangeable parts, another American innovation, first used in the manufacture of rifles for the U.S. government.

Like Great Britain, the United States possessed vast natural resources, including coal. It also resembled Britain in the absence of governmental involvement in the process of industrialization. The main difference between the industrialization of the two countries is that during the nineteenth century labor in America was in relatively short supply. This placed workers in a more advantageous situation in dealing with their employers and prevented some of the horrors of early British industrialization from recurring on the other side of the Atlantic. Only with the influx of European immigrants in the late nineteenth century did the condition of American workers deteriorate and begin to resemble the early nineteenth-century British pattern.

INDUSTRIAL REGIONALISM

Although we have discussed the industrialization of entire nations, the process usually took place within smaller geographical regions. There had always been regional specialization in agriculture, with some areas emphasizing crops and others livestock. During the Industrial Revolution, however, entire economies acquired a distinctly regional character. Regional economies began to take shape during the days of the domestic system, when merchants employed families in certain geographical areas, such as Lancashire in England, to produce textiles. In these regions there was a close relationship between agricultural and industrial production, in that members of the same household participated in both processes. Related industries, such as those for finishing or dyeing cloth, also sprang up close to where the cotton or wool yarn was spun and the cloth woven.

As industrialization spread outside Britain, this regional pattern became even more pronounced. In France the centers of the textile industry were situated near the northeastern border near Belgium and in the area surrounding Lyons in the east-central part of the country. Both of these areas had attracted rural household industry before the introduction of textile machinery. In Germany the iron industry was centered in the Ruhr region, where most of the country's coal was mined. In the city of Essen on the Ruhr River the industrialist Alfred Krupp (1812–1887) established an enormous steelmaking complex that produced industrial machinery, railroad equipment, and guns for the Prussian army. Within the Habsburg Empire most industry was located in parts of Bohemia (now the Czech Republic). The region in Ireland that experienced the most significant measure of industrialization was the northern province of Ulster, a linen-producing area that became Europe's leading producer of ready-to-wear women's undergarments and men's shirts in the 1850s.

The development of regional economies did not mean that markets were regional. The goods produced in one region almost always served the needs of people outside that particular area. Markets for most industrial goods were national and international, and even people in small agricultural villages created a demand for manufactured goods. The French iron industry, for example, was centered in the eastern part of the country, but it catered to the needs of the wealthier segments of its own and other European populations, as did the iron industry in the Ruhr region in Germany and the textile industry in the north of England.

The development of regional industrial economies helps to explain the striking contrast that persisted well into the twentieth century between the parts of countries that had become heavily industrialized and those that retained at least many of the appearances of a preindustrial life. In Britain and the rest of Europe industrial machinery and factories were not introduced into every village. Some areas remained exclusively agricultural, while others continued a tradition of rural industry. This pattern was particularly evident in France, where mechanized industry was concentrated in a limited number of centers in the northeastern half of the country. In 1870 more than two-thirds of the French population still lived in rural areas. As economic growth and industrial development continued, however, agricultural regions eventually began to lose their traditional character. Even if industry itself did not arrive, the

■ **A Colossal Steam-Driven Hammer, Nicknamed "Fritz," Installed by Alfred Krupp at His Steelworks in Essen in 1861**
Krupp's factory was located in the Ruhr region of Germany, the main center in that country for heavy industry.

larger industrial economy made its mark. Agriculture itself became mechanized, while railroads and other forms of mechanized transport integrated these areas in a national economy.

The Effects of Industrialization

The Industrial Revolution had a profound impact on virtually every aspect of human life. It encouraged the growth of the population and the economy, affected the conditions in which people lived, changed family life, created new divisions within society, and transformed the traditional rural landscape. The changes that it brought about were most evident in Britain, but in time they have occurred in every country that has industrialized, including the United States.

POPULATION AND ECONOMIC GROWTH

The most significant of these changes was the sustained expansion of both the population and the economy. As we have seen, the Industrial Revolution in Britain was facilitated by a significant population increase in the eighteenth century. That growth had created a plentiful supply of relatively cheap labor, which in turn had helped to bring about a marked increase in industrial output. As industry grew, population kept pace, and each provided a stimulus to the growth of the other.

Most contemporary observers in the late eighteenth century did not believe that this expansion of both the population and the economy could be sustained indefinitely. The most pessimistic of these commentators was Thomas Malthus (1766–1834), an English cleric who wrote *An Essay on the Principle of Population* in 1798. Malthus argued that population had a natural tendency to grow faster than the food supply. Thus, unless couples exercised restraint by marrying late and producing fewer children, the population would eventually outstrip the resources necessary to sustain it, resulting in poor nutrition, famine, and disease. These "positive checks" on population growth, which sometimes were initiated or aggravated by war, would drive population back to sustainable levels. These checks would also end periods of economic expansion, which generally accompany increases in population. For example, in the fourteenth century the Black Death, which killed about one-third of the European population, also ended a significant period of economic growth. A similar but less severe contraction of the European population and economy occurred in the second half of the seventeenth century, marking the end of the economic expansion that had begun in the sixteenth century. In both these instances the increase in population put pressure on the food supply, raised the price of food, reduced employment, and lowered wages. The scarcity of food and the reduced nutritional levels that followed had made the population vulnerable to disease. If these demographic and economic patterns were to recur, we might expect that the significant expansion of the population and the economy that took place in eighteenth-century England would likewise reach its limits, just around the time that Malthus was writing.

This predicted cyclical contraction of both the population and the economy did not take place. Europe for the first time in its history managed to escape the "Malthusian population trap." Instead of being sharply reduced after 1800, the population continued to expand at an ever faster rate, doubling in Great Britain between 1800 and 1850 and following a similar pattern of rapid growth in all other countries that had industrialized. At the same time the economy, instead of contracting or collapsing, continued to grow and diversify.

It is not absolutely clear how Europe avoided the Malthusian trap in the nineteenth century. Part of the answer lies in the greater productivity of agriculture, which resulted from either private initiative, as in Britain, or governmental agrarian reforms, as in Austria. The importation of grain from central and eastern Europe also helped to feed the larger, more urbanized population. Improvements in medicine and public health reduced mortality during the

THOMAS MALTHUS WRITES ABOUT THE LIMITATION OF POPULATION

....

Thomas Malthus was an English cleric who studied at Cambridge University and then took a position as a curate in a country parish in Surrey. In 1798 he published anonymously An Essay on the Principle of Population, *in which he advanced the argument that population tends to grow faster than the food supply, resulting in periodic subsistence crises that keep population in check. In the greatly expanded second edition of this book, published in 1803, Malthus distinguished between preventive and positive checks on the growth of population.*

The checks to population, which are constantly operating with more or less force in every society, and keep down the number to the level of the means of subsistence, may be classed under two general heads: the preventive and the positive.

The preventive check is peculiar to man and arises from that distinctive superiority in his reasoning faculties, which enables him to calculate distant consequences. . . . But man cannot look around him and see the distress which frequently presses upon those who have large families . . . These considerations are calculated to prevent a great number of persons in all civilized nations from pursuing the dictate of nature in an early attachment to one woman.

The positive checks to population are extremely various and include every cause, whether arising from vice or misery, which in any degree contributes to shorten the natural duration of human life. Under this head therefore may be enumerated all unwholesome occupations, severe labour and exposure to the seasons, extreme poverty, bad nursing of children, great towns, excesses of all kinds, the whole train of common diseases and epidemics, wars, pestilence, plague and famine.

On examining the obstacles to the increase of population which I have classed under the heads of preventive and positive checks, it will appear they are all resolvable into moral restraint, vice and misery. Of the preventive checks, the restraint from marriage, which if not followed by irregular gratifications may properly be termed moral restraint. Promiscuous intercourse, unnatural passions, violations of the marriage bed, and improper arts to conceal the consequences of irregular connexions clearly come under the head of vice. Of the positive checks, those which appear to arise unavoidably from the law of nature may be called exclusively misery; and those which we bring upon ourselves, such as wars, excesses and many others it would be in our power to avoid, are of a mixed nature. They are brought upon us by vice, and their consequences are misery.

Source: From Thomas Malthus, *An Essay on the Principle of Population, 2nd Edition,* 1803.

nineteenth century, helping to maintain the size of the industrial population. But it was mainly developments in industry itself, especially the increased accumulation of capital, that kept Europe from succumbing to yet another cycle of depopulation and economic contraction. The accumulation of capital over a long period of time was so great that industry was able to employ large numbers of workers even during the 1790s and 1800s, when Europe was at war. Since they had income from wages, workers were willing to marry earlier and have larger families, and with lower food prices because of higher agricultural productivity they could afford to maintain a healthier diet and purchase more manufactured goods as well. Thus the Industrial Revolution itself, coupled with the changes in agriculture that accompanied it, proved Malthus wrong.

While the rapid growth of population in industrialized societies up until the late twentieth century is incontestable, the record of economic growth is not so clear. In order to claim that the Industrial Revolution has resulted in sustained economic growth, we have to take a broad view, looking at an overall pattern of growth and ignoring certain cyclical recessions and depressions. Nations that have industrialized, beginning with European countries in the nineteenth century, have all experienced a significant increase in both gross national product and per capita income over the long run. Although the contrast between the size of these industrial economies and those of preindustrial, agrarian countries is staggering, economic growth in industrialized countries was not always rapid or continuous. During the first six decades of industrialization in Britain, for example, economic growth was actually fairly slow, mainly because so much capital went into subsidizing the long war against France (1792–1802; 1804–1815). During this period Britain spent an average of 60 million English pounds, or 25 percent of its national income, on war. Nevertheless, there still was steady growth, and more important, the type of Malthusian economic contraction or collapse that had followed all previous periods of expansion did not occur. To that extent we can say that the Industrial Revolution has resulted in sustained economic growth in the West.

STANDARDS OF LIVING

Ever since the early years of the Industrial Revolution, a debate has raged over the effect of industrialization on the standard of living and the quality of life of the laboring population. The supporters of the two main schools of thought on this issue have been called the optimists and the pessimists. The optimists have always emphasized the positive effects of both the process of mechanization and the system of industrial capitalism that arose during the revolution. They have focused on the success that industrialized nations have achieved in escaping the Malthusian trap and in achieving sustained economic growth. The Industrial Revolution, so they argue, has resulted in an unprecedented rise in individual income, which has made it possible for the mass of a country's population to avoid poverty for the first time in human history. In the second half of the twentieth century many optimists claimed that the industrialization of Western nations provided a blueprint for African, Asian, and Latin American countries that wished to escape from the poverty of a predominantly agrarian economy relying on organic sources of energy.

The main yardstick that the optimists have used to measure the improvement in living standards is per capita real income, that is, income measured in terms of its actual purchasing power. Real income in Great Britain rose about 50 percent between 1770 and 1850 and more than doubled during the entire nineteenth century. This increase in income allowed workers to improve their diets as well as to purchase more clothing and other basic commodities. These improvements, however, did not affect the lives of most workers for a long period of time—in Great Britain not until 1820, about sixty years after the beginning of industrialization. The increases that occurred after that date, moreover, were only averages, concealing disparities among workers with different levels of skill. Only in the late nineteenth and twentieth centuries did industrialization raise the real income of all workers to a level that made the benefits of industrialization apparent.

Even if the pessimists concede a long-term increase in real income, it has never been substantial enough to persuade them that industrialization was on balance a positive good, at least for the working class. The pessimists have always stressed the negative effects of industrial development on the life of the lower classes. In their way of thinking, industrialization was an unmitigated disaster. The cause of this disaster in their eyes was not the process of mechanization but the system of industrial capitalism°. This form of capitalism is characterized by the ownership of factories by private individuals and by the employment of wage labor. Like earlier forms of mercantile and agricultural capitalism, it involved a systematic effort to reduce costs and maximize profits. In the pursuit of this goal, employers tried to keep wages as low as possible and to increase production through labor-saving technology, thus preventing workers from improving their lot.

Pessimists regarding the Industrial Revolution over the past two centuries have usually claimed a moral basis for their position. In this respect they follow in a tradition begun by the poet William Blake (1757–1827), who referred to the new factories as "satanic mills," and the socialist Friedrich Engels, who in *The Condition of the Working Class in England in 1844* (1845) accused the factory owners in England of mass murder and robbery. Much pessimist writing has also been used to support a program of social or political reform. The German social philosopher Karl Marx (1818–1883), with whom Engels often collaborated and whose views we shall discuss more fully in Chapter 21, used his critique of industrial capitalism to call for a communist revolution in which the working class would seize political power and acquire ownership of the means of production.

Most of the evidence that social critics have used to support the pessimist position has come from the early period of industrialization in Britain, when incomes were either stagnant or declining and when conditions in factories and industrial and mining towns were most appalling. It is difficult to measure these living standards statistically, but the weight of qualitative evidence suggests that they deteriorated during the nineteenth century. Working-class housing was makeshift and crowded, and there were few sanitary facilities. A new word, *slum,* was coined to refer to these poverty-stricken working-class neighborhoods. Poor drainage and raw sewage gave rise to a host of new hygienic problems, especially outbreaks of typhus and cholera. Between 1831 and 1866 four epidemics of cholera killed at least 140,000 people in Britain, most of whom lived in poorer districts.

The impact of industrialization and urbanization on the environment was no less harrowing. The burning of coal and the use of industrial chemicals polluted the urban atmosphere. The famous London fogs, which were actually smogs caused by industrial pollutants, presented a serious public health problem throughout the nineteenth century and did not begin to disappear until the introduction of strict regulations on the burning of coal in the 1950s.

While life in the city was bleak and unhealthy, working conditions in the factory were monotonous and demeaning. Forced to submit to a regimen governed by the operation of the machine, workers lost their independence as well as any control whatsoever over the products of their labor. They were required to work long hours, often fourteen hours a day, six days a week, with few breaks. Factory masters locked the doors during working hours, and they assessed fines for infractions such as opening a window when the temperature was unbearable, whistling while working, and having dirty hands while spinning yarn. Work in the mines was a little less monotonous, but it was physically more demanding and far more dangerous.

WOMEN, CHILDREN, AND INDUSTRY

During the early Industrial Revolution in Great Britain, large numbers of children and women were recruited into the workforce, especially the textile and mining industries. In the woolen industry in the western part of England, for example, female and child labor together accounted for 75 percent of the workforce. Children under age 13 made up 13 percent of the cotton factory workforce, and those under age 18 made up 51 percent. This pattern of employment reflects the demands of industrialists, who valued the hand skills and dexterity that children possessed as well as the greater amenability of both children and women to the discipline of factory labor. Some of the machines that were in-

troduced into the textile industry in the late eighteenth century were specifically designed for women and children.

Female and child labor was both plentiful and cheap. Children received only one-sixth to one-third the wages of a grown man, while women generally took home only one-third to one-half of that adult male income. There was no lack of incentive for women and children to take one of these low-paying jobs. In a family dependent on wages, everyone needed to work, even when a large labor pool kept wages depressed.

The participation of both women and children in the workforce was not new. In an agricultural economy all members of the family contributed to the work, with parents and children, young and old, all being assigned specific roles. Rural industry also involved the labor of all members of the family. When people began working in the factories, however, they were physically separated from the home, making it impossible for workers to combine domestic and occupational labor.

As the workplace became distinct from the household, family life underwent a fundamental change, although this change did not occur immediately. During the early years of the Industrial Revolution, members of many families found employment together in the factories and mines. Factory owners also tried to perpetuate many aspects of family life in the new industrial setting, defining the entire factory community as an extended family, in which the factory owner played the paternalistic role. Gradually, however, mothers found it impossible to care for their youngest children on the job, and most of them dropped out of the full-time workforce. The restriction of child labor by the British Factory Act of 1833 reinforced this trend and led to the establishment of a fairly common situation in which the male wage earner worked outside the home while his wife stayed home with the children. As one young girl who worked in the mines testified before a parliamentary commission investigation of child labor in 1842, "Mother takes care of the children."

As more and more mothers left the factories, the female workforce became increasingly dominated by those who were unmarried. The few female workers who were married with children either came from the very poorest segments of society or took jobs only because their husbands were ill or unemployed. Neither the pay these women received nor the jobs they performed gave them financial autonomy or social prestige. Becoming an independent wage earner meant little when women's wages were on average one-third to one-half those of men. The jobs assigned to women within industry, such as operating textile machinery, generally required the least skill. When men and women were employed in the same workplace, the women were invariably subordinated to the authority of male workers or foremen, thereby perpetuating the patriarchal patterns that prevailed in preindustrial society. The Industrial Revolution did nothing to improve the status of women, and even their

The Sadler Committee on Child Labor

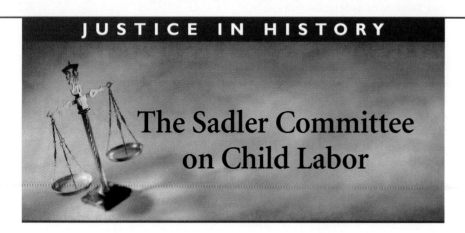

The widespread use of child labor in Britain during the early decades of the Industrial Revolution led to efforts by social reformers and members of Parliament to regulate the conditions under which children worked. Parliament passed legislation restricting the number of hours that all children could work in textile mills in 1819 and 1829, but neither of these laws were enforced effectively, and they did not apply to all industries. Complaints of inhumane treatment, moral degradation, and exploitation of child workers continued to surface. In 1831 Michael Sadler (1780–1835), a Tory member of the British Parliament, introduced a bill in Parliament to limit the number of hours that all children could work to ten hours per day. Like many social reformers, Sadler was inspired by what he considered his Christian duty to protect dependent members of the community.

Sadler chaired the committee to which his bill was referred. In order to muster support for the bill, Sadler held hearings in which child workers themselves came before the committee to report on the conditions under which they lived and worked. The success of his bill was by no means guaranteed. Many members of Parliament were deeply committed to the policy of *laissez-faire,* according to which the government should not intervene in the operation of the economy, treating it instead as a self-regulating machine. Sadler had to convince his colleagues

that they should modify that policy in the case of children, on the grounds that the state was obliged to provide for the welfare of children when their parents were unable to do so. He also needed to make the members of Parliament and the broader public aware of the brutality of the conditions under which the children worked.

The hearings that took place were not a trial in the strict sense of the word, but they possessed many of the features of a judicial investigation, not unlike those conducted by grand juries in criminal cases. The committee's proceedings were intended to expose, condemn, and ultimately remedy misconduct by the factory owners. Procedurally the committee members had more latitude than did courts of law. Since these parliamentary committees were designed to extract information rather than to bring offenders to trial, they did not need to adhere to any established judicial guidelines. There was no cross-examination of witnesses, nor could factory owners present a defense. The witnesses in this investigation were chosen because Sadler knew they would reveal the evils of the factory system.

The testimony presented to the Sadler Committee produced abundant

Child Workers
These children are on their way to work in the Yorkshire textile mills.

evidence of the exploitation and physical abuse of child workers. Some of the most harrowing testimony came from the examination of a 17-year-old boy, Joseph Hebergam, on July 1, 1832. Hebergam revealed that he had begun the work of worsted spinning at age 7, that he worked at the factory from five A.M. until eight P.M., and that he had only thirty minutes for lunch at noon, leaving him to eat his other meals while standing on the job. In the factory there were three overlookers, one of whom was responsible for greasing the machinery and another for whipping the workers. The latter overlooker walked continually up and down the factory with whip in hand.

When asked where his brother John was working, Joseph replied that he had died three years before at age 16. Sadler then inquired into the cause of his brother's death. The boy responded, "It was attributed to this, that he died from working such long hours and that it had been brought on by the factory. They have to stop the flies [part of the textile machinery] with their knees, because they go so swift they cannot stop them with their hands; he got a bruise on the shin by a spindle-board, and it went on to that degree that it burst; the surgeon cured that, then he was better; then he went to work again; but when he had worked about two months more his spine became affected, and he died." The witness went on to explain that his own severe labor had damaged his knees and ankles so much so that he found it painful to walk. His brother and sister would help carry him to the factory, but when they arrived late, even by as little as five minutes, the overlooker beat all three of them "till we were black and blue." At the request of the committee, Joseph then stood up to show the condition of his limbs. He reported the death of another boy who had sustained massive injuries when he was caught in the shaft of the machinery he was running. Joseph concluded his testimony by recounting how the factory owners had threatened him and his younger brothers with losing their jobs if they testified before the committee.

The hearings of the Sadler Committee were widely publicized, but they fell short of realizing their original objective. The bill, which eventually was approved by Parliament as the Factory Regulations Act of 1833, prohibited the employment of children under age 9 in all factories. Boys and girls were allowed to work up to nine hours a day from age 9 until their thirteenth birthdays, and up to twelve hours a day from age 13 until their eighteenth birthdays. The long-term effect of this legislation was to establish in Western industrialized countries the principle that childhood was a period of life set aside for education rather than work. ■

■ **Child Labor in the Textile Industry**
Factory girls operate machinery in a textile mill under the tight supervision of the factory owner.

Questions of Justice

1. Sadler's opponents could have objected that his "investigation" was a setup, since Sadler had chosen and coached the witnesses. In what ways was this proceeding fair? In what ways was it unfair?

2. This investigation was concerned with the achievement of social justice rather than the determination of criminal culpability. What were the advantages of using legislative committees in such an undertaking?

3. Child labor was not a new phenomenon in the early eighteenth century. Why did the Industrial Revolution draw attention to this age-old practice?

Taking It Further

Horn, Pamela. *Children's Work and Welfare, 1780–1890.* 1996. An examination of the scale and nature of child employment in Britain and changing attitudes toward the practice.

exclusion from certain occupations, such as mining by an act of Parliament in 1842, only reinforced a new sexual division of labor that was even more rigid than that which had prevailed in preindustrial society.

CLASS AND CLASS CONSCIOUSNESS

As Europe became more industrialized and urbanized, and as the system of industrial capitalism became more entrenched, writers began to use a new terminology to describe the structure of society. Instead of claiming that society consisted of a finely graded hierarchy of ranks to which individuals belonged by virtue of their occupations or their legal status, they divided society into three classes that could be distinguished by the type of property people owned and the manner in which they acquired it. At the top of this new social hierarchy was the aristocracy, consisting of those who owned land and received their income in the form of rent. The middle class or bourgeoisie, which included the new factory owners, possessed capital and derived their income from profits, whereas the working class

owned nothing but their own labor and received their income from wages.

This new model of society served a number of different purposes. Marx and Engels used it to construct a comprehensive theory of historical development. According to this theory, the middle class had struggled for centuries to seize power from the aristocracy, while the working class would eventually take power from the middle class. For Marx and Engels, conflicts over control of the means of production created a state of continuous class conflict. David Ricardo (1772–1823), an English social philosopher whose political and social allegiances were very different from those of Marx, used a similar model of society to illustrate the crucial role that the middle class played in the economy. Ricardo compared society to a coach in which the middle class was the driver guiding the vehicle, the working class was the horse that provided the labor, and the aristocracy was the nonpaying passenger.

Historians and social scientists disagree over the extent to which men and women in the nineteenth century were actually conscious of their membership in these classes. Marxist historians have claimed that the growth of wage

---

THE EMPLOYMENT OF WOMEN

....

The German social philosopher Friedrich Engels (1820–1895) was one of the founders of modern socialism. He and Karl Marx collaborated in writing The Communist Manifesto *(1848), and he edited the final two volumes of Marx's* Capital *after Marx died. Having served as a manager in a factory in Manchester, Engels described these conditions throughout Britain in one of his earliest works,* The Condition of the Working Class in England in 1844 *(1845). He emphasized the exploitation and brutalization of the lower classes as they were turned into a wage-earning proletariat. In this passage Engels describes the negative effects of factory labor on women and the family.*

The employment of women at once breaks up the family; for when the wife spends twelve or thirteen hours every day in the mill, and the husband works the same length of time there or elsewhere, what becomes of the children? They grow up like weeds; they are put out to nurse for a shilling or eighteen pence a week, and how they are treated may be imagined. Hence the accidents to which little children fall victims in the factory districts multiply to a terrible extent . . . Women often return to the mill three or four days after confinement, leaving the baby of course; in the dinner hour they must hurry home to feed the children and eat something, and what kind of suckling that can be is also evident. Lord Ashley repeats the testimony of several work women: "M.H., twenty

years old, has two children, the youngest a baby, that is tended by the other, a little older. The mother goes to the mill shortly after five o'clock in the morning, and comes home at eight at night; all day the milk pours from her breasts so that her clothing drips with it". . . . The use of narcotics to keep the children still is fostered by this infamous system and has reached a great extent in the factory districts. Dr. Johns, Registrar in Chief for Manchester, is of opinion that this custom is the chief source of the many deaths from convulsions. The employment of the wife dissolves the family utterly and of necessity, and this dissolution in our present society, which is based upon the family, brings the most demoralising consequences for parents and children. A mother who has no time to trouble herself about her child, to perform the most ordinary loving services for it during its first year, who scarcely indeed sees it, can be no real mother to the child, must inevitably grow indifferent to it, treat it unlovingly like a stranger. The children who grow up under such conditions are utterly ruined for later family life, can never feel at home in the family which they themselves found, because they have always been accustomed to isolation, and they contribute therefore to the already general undermining of the family in the working-class.

Source: From Friedrich Engels, *The Condition of the Working Class in England in 1844,* translated by F. K. Wischnewtzky (London: S. Sonnenshein, 1892).

■ **Capital and Labor**
This cartoon, drawn by the illustrator Gustave Doré, depicts wealthy industrialists gambling with workers tied together as chips.

labor, the exploitation of the working class, and conflicts between capital and labor encouraged workers to think of themselves not so much as individuals who claimed a certain social status but as members of a large class of workers who shared the same relationship to the means of production. These historians have pointed to the growth of trade unions, political campaigns for universal male suffrage, and other forms of working-class organization and communication as evidence of this awakening of class consciousness.

Other historians have claimed that people were less conscious of their class position. True, at certain times in the early nineteenth century some workers thought of themselves as members of a class whose interests were in conflict with those of factory owners and financiers. It was much more common, however, for them to think of themselves primarily as practitioners of a particular craft, as members of a local community, or as part of a distinct ethnic minority, such as the Irish. When they demanded the right to vote, workers based their claim on their historic constitutional rights, not on the interests of all wage earners. When they demonstrated in favor of the ten-hour working day, they did so to improve the conditions in which they worked, not to advance the struggle of all workers against the middle class. The work experiences of laborers were too varied to sustain an awareness among most of them that they belonged to one homogeneous group.

The various capitalists, shopkeepers, and factory owners who belonged to the bourgeoisie also lacked a clear sense of their membership in a single middle class. These people were capable of achieving solidarity on certain occasions, such as when they feared that workers threatened their interests. As we discussed in Chapter 17, the bourgeoisie often criticized the lifestyle and values of the landed aristocracy in print. But like the working class, the bourgeoisie was too diverse to allow for the development of a unifying class consciousness inspired by an identity of economic interest against those who occupied social positions either above or below them.

Working men and women showed a marked reluctance to engage in militant or violent action against their employers. Appeals for working-class solidarity to a large extent fell on deaf ears. It is true that on certain occasions workers took violent action against their employers. In 1812 groups of hand-loom weavers in the highly industrialized Midland region of England engaged in a determined campaign to destroy the new power looms that they blamed for rising unemployment and low wages. Often disguised and operating at night, these "Luddites," who took their name from their mythical leader Ned Ludd, smashed the new textile machinery that factory owners had introduced. (Even today people who object to the introduction of new technology are referred to as Luddites.) The government sent an army of 12,000 men to suppress the Luddites, a task made difficult by the protection given them by their communities.

The Luddites did not, however, represent the majority of the English working class. Factory workers in particular seemed reluctant to join working-class organizations. Most of the workers who participated in these associations and who campaigned for the rights of the workers were independent artisans who had little interest in the struggle that Marx and Engels had predicted would result in the victory of the working class.

The incident that contributed most directly to the formation of working-class consciousness in Britain in the early decades of the nineteenth century was the so-called Peterloo Massacre. In August 1819 some 60,000 people, most of them workers and their families, gathered at St. Peter's Field in the northern English city of Manchester. The purpose of the meeting was to demonstrate support for universal male suffrage, annual parliaments, and relief from low wages, high prices, and long hours. Shortly after the meeting began, a violent confrontation took place between the demonstrators and the volunteer cavalry (known as yeomen), who belonged to the city's bourgeoisie. Frightened by the size of the demonstration and determined to prevent concessions that would reduce their profits, the yeomen decided to disperse the meeting by force. In the confrontation that ensued, the yeomen trampled hundreds of demonstrators and slashed many others with their swords, killing 11 people and wounding more than 400. "Over the whole field," wrote one observer, "were strewed caps, bonnets, hats, shawls, and shoes, and other parts of male and female dress, trampled, torn and bloody."

The Peterloo Massacre has been referred to as class warfare. The events of that day may have occurred too spontaneously to justify the claim that they conformed to a pattern of deliberate middle-class violence against the working class. There is little doubt, however, that the demonstration and the brutal response to it contributed to the growth of class solidarity, especially among the workers. The massacre inspired a number of calls for working-class revolution. The young poet Percy Shelley (1792–1822), upon hearing of what had occurred in Manchester, called the working class to action:

> *Rise like lions after slumber*
> *In unvanquishable numbers*
> *Shake your chains to earth like dew*
> *Which in sleep had fallen on you.*
> *You are many—they are few.*

The British working class did not respond to Shelley's summons. The Peterloo Massacre did not lead to a working-class revolution in Britain. This violent encounter did, however, lead to the further organization of British labor, most notably in the Chartist movement, which staged a number of demonstrations in favor of parliamentary reform and the improvement of working conditions. (We shall discuss the activities of the Chartists more fully in Chapter 21.) The Peterloo Massacre also contributed to the growth of class consciousness in Britain. In the age of the Industrial Revolution, the division of society on the basis of class became increasingly apparent to workers

■ **The Industrial City of Sheffield in 1858**
Factories dominated the landscape of the city of Sheffield, which specialized in the production of steel, silver-plated items, and other metal goods.

■ **Pont Cysyllte Aqueduct in Wales**

This cast-iron bridge, 1,000 feet in length, carried the water of the Caledonian Canal across the River Dee, 127 feet below. It was built in 1805.

and members of the middle and working classes, as well as to social commentators such as David Ricardo and Karl Marx.

THE INDUSTRIAL LANDSCAPE

As industry spread throughout Europe and reached into areas that previously had been untouched by mechanization, urban and rural areas underwent dramatic changes. The most striking of these changes took place in the new industrial towns and cities, some of which had been little more than country towns before the factories were built. Manchester, for example, grew from a modest population of 23,000 people in 1773 to a burgeoning metropolis of 105,000 by 1820. Large factories with their smokestacks and warehouses, ringed by long rows of houses built to accommodate the armies of new industrial workers, gave these cities an entirely new and for the most part a grim appearance.

Cities experienced the most noticeable changes in physical appearance, but the countryside also began to take on a new look, mainly as a result of the transport revolution. The tunnels, bridges, and viaducts that were constructed to accommodate the railroad lines and the canals that were built to improve inland water transportation made an indelible imprint on the traditional terrain. In many ways this alteration of the landscape served as a statement of the mastery over nature that human beings had achieved at the time of the Scientific Revolution. The Industrial Revolution finally fulfilled the technological promise of that earlier revolution, and one of its effects was the actual transformation of the physical world.

The advent of modern industry also brought about a change in attitudes toward the landscape. The destruction of natural beauty in the interest of economic progress stimulated an appreciation of nature that had not been widespread during the medieval and early modern periods. Before the Industrial Revolution many features of the countryside, especially mountains, were viewed as obstacles to either travel or human habitation, not as sources of aesthetic appreciation. Urbanization and industrialization changed those perceptions, triggering a nostalgic reaction that became one of the sources of the romantic movement, which we shall consider in greater detail in the next chapter. Some of the idyllic landscapes of the English romantic painter John Constable (1776–1837), for example, represented an imaginative recreation of a countryside that had already been transformed by the advent of industry by the time he painted them.

Industry did not always form a blight on the landscape or offend artistic sensibilities. Some of the new industrial architecture, especially the viaducts and aqueducts that traversed valleys in the mountainous regions of the country, were masterpieces of modern engineering and architecture. Sir Walter Scott (1771–1832), the Scottish romantic novelist, claimed that the cast-iron Pont Cysyllte aqueduct in Wales, which carried the waters of the Caledonian Canal 127 feet above the River Dee, was the most beautiful work

■ **Joseph M. W. Turner, *Rain, Steam and Speed: The Great Western Railway* (1844)**

This was one of the first oil paintings that had the railroad locomotive as its theme.

of art he had ever seen. The railroads also had the ability to inspire the artistic imagination, as they did in Joseph Turner's (1775–1851) romantic painting *Rain, Steam and Speed,* which captured the railroad's speed and beauty.

Industry, Trade, and Empire

As the middle of the nineteenth century approached, Britain towered above all other nations in the volume of its industrial output, the extent of its international trade, and the size of its empire. In industrial production it easily outpaced all its competitors, producing two-thirds of the world's coal, about half of its cotton cloth, half of its iron, and 40 percent of its hardware. Little wonder that Britain became known as "the workshop of the world." Britain controlled about one-third of the world's trade, and London had emerged as the undisputed financial center of the global economy. Britain's overseas empire, which included colonies in Canada, the Caribbean, South America, India, Southeast Asia, and Australia, eclipsed that of all other European powers and would continue to grow during the second half of the century.

These three great British strengths—industry, trade, and empire—were closely linked. Britain's colonies in both Asia and in the Americas served as trading depots, while the promotion of trade led directly to the acquisition of new imperial possessions. Even when Britain did not formally acquire territory, it often established exclusive trading relationships with those countries, thereby creating an informal "empire of trade." Trade and empire in turn served the purposes of industry. Many of the raw materials used in industrial production, especially cotton, came from Britain's imperial possessions. At the same time, those possessions provided markets for Britain's mass-produced manufactured goods. Such imperial markets proved immensely valuable when France blockaded its ports during the Napoleonic wars and thereby cut into British trade with the entire European continent (see Chapter 18).

The great challenge for Britain during the nineteenth century was to find new markets for its industrial products. Domestic demand had been strong at the beginning of the Industrial Revolution, but by the 1840s British workers did not possess sufficient wealth to purchase the increasingly large volume of hardwares and textiles manufactured in the mills and factories. Britain had to look overseas to find markets to sell the bulk of its industrial products. One possibility was to market them in other European countries, such as France and Germany, where demand for manufactured goods was high. These countries, however, were in the midst of their own industrial revolutions, and their governments had often legislated high protective tariffs against British goods to encourage the growth of their own industries. Britain therefore chose instead to market its goods in the less economically developed parts of the world, including its own colonies. We can see this trading pattern in the relationships that Britain had with three different regions: East Asia, India, and Latin America. In all three areas, moreover, British military power and diplomatic influence were enlisted in the cause of industry, trade, and empire.

EAST ASIA: THE OPIUM WAR, 1839–1842

British conflict with China provides the best illustration of the way in which the British desire to promote trade led to the acquisition of new colonies. For three centuries the Chinese had tightly controlled their trade with European powers. By 1842, however, British merchants, supported by the British government, managed to break down these barriers and give Britain a foothold in China, allowing it to exploit the East Asian market.

The conflict arose over the importation of opium, a narcotic made from poppy seeds and produced in great quantities in India. This drug, which numbed pain but also had hallucinogenic effects and could cause profound lethargy, was in widespread use in Europe and had an even larger market in Asia. In China opium had became a national addiction by the middle of the eighteenth century, and the situation became much worse when British merchants increased the volume of illegal imports from India to China in the early nineteenth century. The Chinese government prohibited the use of opium, but since it had difficulty enforcing its own edicts, it decided to put an end to the opium trade.

Chinese efforts to stop British merchants from importing opium led to an increase in tensions between China and Britain. The situation reached a climax in 1839, when the Chinese seized 20,000 chests of opium in the holds of British ships and spilled them into the China Sea. It is unknown what effect the opium had on the fish, but the incident led to a British attack on Chinese ports. In this conflict, the first Opium War (1839–1842), the British had the advantage of superior naval technology, itself a product of the Industrial Revolution. The first iron-clad, steam-driven gunboat used in combat, the *Nemesis,* destroyed Chinese batteries along the coast, and an assault by seventy-five British ships on Chinkiang forced the Chinese to come to terms. In a treaty signed in 1842 China ceded the island of Hong Kong to the British, reimbursed British merchants for the opium it had destroyed, and opened five Chinese ports to international trade. As part of this settlement, each of these ports was to be governed by a British consul who was not subject to Chinese law. In this way Britain expanded its empire, increased its already large share of world trade, and found new markets for British manufactured goods in East Asia.

INDIA: ANNEXATION AND TRADE

The interrelationship of industry, trade, and empire became even clearer in India, which became known as the jewel in Britain's imperial crown. As we have seen in Chapter 19, Britain gained control of the Indian province of Bengal in the eighteenth century and subsequently acquired a number of other Indian states. After the Sepoy Mutiny of 1857 the British government brought all of India under its direct control.

Political control of India during the nineteenth century served the interests of British trade in two ways. First, it gave British merchants control of the trade between India and other Asian countries. Second, Britain developed a favorable balance of trade with India, exporting more goods to that country than it imported. Taxes paid to the British government by India for administering the country and interest payments on British loans to India increased the flow of capital from Calcutta to London. The influx of capital from India was in large part responsible for the favorable balance of payments that Britain enjoyed with the rest of the world until World War I. The capital that Britain received from these sources as well as from trade with China was funneled into the British economy or invested in British economic ventures throughout the world.

Control of India also served British interests by supplying British industries with raw materials while giving them access to the foreign markets they needed to make a profit. This promotion of British industry was done at the expense of the local Indian economy. The transportation of cotton grown in India to British textile mills, only to be returned to India in the form of finished cloth certainly retarded, if it did not destroy, the existing Indian textile industry. Resentment of this economic exploitation of India became one of the main sources of Indian nationalism in the late nineteenth century.

LATIN AMERICA: AN EMPIRE OF TRADE

British policy in Latin America developed differently from the way it had in China and India, but it had the same effect of opening up new markets for British goods. Great Britain was a consistent supporter of the movements for independence that erupted in South America between 1810 and 1824 (see Chapter 19). Britain supported these movements not simply because it wished to undermine Spanish and Portuguese imperialism, but because it needed to acquire new markets for its industrial products. Britain did not need to use military force to open these areas to British trade, as it did in China. Once the countries became independent, they attracted large volumes of British exports. In 1840 the British cotton industry shipped 35 percent of all its exports to Latin American countries, especially to Argentina, Brazil, Uruguay, Mexico, and Chile. Britain also exported large amounts of capital to these Latin American countries by investing vast sums of money in their economies. Britain thus established an informal "empire of trade" in Latin America. These countries were not controlled by Britain, but they had the same economic relationship with Britain as did Canada, Australia, and other parts of the British Empire.

British investment and trade brought the newly independent nations of Latin America into the industrial world economy. In so doing, however, Britain assigned these countries to a dependent position in that economy, not unlike the position that India occupied in Asia about the same time. One effect of this dependence was to transform the small, self-sufficient village economies that had developed alongside the large plantations in Central and South America. Instead of producing goods themselves and selling them within their own markets, these villages now became suppliers of raw materials for British industry. At the same time the Latin American population became more dependent upon British manufactured goods. This transformation not only retarded or destroyed native Latin American industry but also created huge trade deficits for Latin American countries by the middle of the nineteenth century.

CONCLUSION
Industrialization and the West

By 1850 the Industrial Revolution had begun to bring about some of the most dramatic changes in human life recorded in historical documents. Not since the Neolithic Age, when people began to live in settled villages, cultivate grains, and domesticate animals, did the organization of society, the patterns of work, and the landscape undergo such profound changes. In many ways the Industrial Revolution marked the watershed between the old way of life and the new. It gave human beings unprecedented technological control over nature, made employment in the home the exception rather than the rule, and submitted industrial workers to a regimentation unknown in the past. It changed family life, gave cities an entirely new appearance, and unleashed new and highly potent political forces, including the ideologies of liberalism and socialism, which shall be discussed in depth in the next chapter.

Industrialization changed the very definition of the West. In the Middle Ages the predominant cultural values of Western countries were those of Christianity, while in the eighteenth century those values were more often associated with the rational, scientific culture of the Enlightenment. Now, in the nineteenth century, the West was increasingly becoming identified with industrialization and the system of industrial capitalism it had spawned. In discussing the prospects of industrialization in the Ottoman Empire in 1856, a British diplomat wrote that "Europe is at hand, with its science, its labor, and its capital," but that the Qur'an and other elements of traditional Turkish culture "are so many obstacles to advancement in a Western sense." The Industrial Revolution was creating new divisions between the West and the non-Western world.

Until the late nineteenth century, industrialization took place only in nations that have traditionally formed a part of the West. Beginning in the 1890s, however, countries that lay outside the West or on its margins began to introduce industrial technology and methods. Between 1890 and 1910 Russia and Japan underwent a period of rapid industrialization, and in the second half of the twentieth century a number of countries in Asia and Latin America, as well as Turkey, followed suit. This process of industrialization and economic development is often described as one of Westernization, and it has usually led to conflicts within those countries between Western and non-Western values. The industrialization of these nations has not always been fully successful, and even when it has, doubt remains as to whether those nations should now be included within the West. Industrialization outside Europe and the United States reveals once again that the composition of the West changes from time to time and that its boundaries are often difficult to define.

Suggestions for Further Reading

For a comprehensive list of suggested readings, please go to www.ablongman.com/levack/chapter20

Ashton, T. A. *The Industrial Revolution,* reprint edition with preface by P. Hudson. 1992. The classic statement of the optimist position, identifying the benefits of the revolution.

Berg, Maxine. *The Age of Manufactures, 1700–1820: Industry, Innovation and Work in Britain.* 1994. A study of the process and character of specific industries, especially those employing women.

Brinley, Thomas. *The Industrial Revolution and the Atlantic Economy: Selected Essays.* 1993. Essays challenging the view that Britain's Industrial Revolution was a gradual process.

Deane, Phyllis. *The First Industrial Revolution.* 1967. The best study of technological innovation in Britain.

Gutmann, Myron. *Toward the Modern Economy: Early Industry in Europe, 1500–1800.* 1988. A study of cottage industry, especially in France.

Hobsbawm, E. J. *Industry and Empire.* 1968. A general economic history of Britain from 1750 to 1970 that analyzes the position of Britain in the world economy.

Jacob, Margaret. *Scientific Culture and the Making of the Industrial West.* 1997. An exploration of the spread of scientific knowledge and its connection with industrialization.

Morris. R. J. *Class and Class Consciousness in the Industrial Revolution, 1780–1850.* 1979. A balanced treatment of the link between industrialization and class formation.

Pollard, Sidney. *Peaceful Conquest: The Industrialization of Europe, 1760–1970.* 1981. A linking of coal supplies to economic development.

Rule, John. *The Vital Century, England's Developing Economy, 1714–1815.* 1992. A general economic history establishing the importance of early eighteenth-century developments.

Stearns, Peter. *The Industrial Revolution in World History,* 2nd ed. 1998. The best study of industrialization in a global context.

Teich, Mikulas, and Roy Porter, eds. *The Industrial Revolution in National Context: Europe and the USA.* 1981. Essays illustrating similarities as well as national differences in the process of industrialization.

Wrigley, E. A. *Continuity, Chance and Change: The Character of the Industrial Revolution in Britain.* 1988. Includes the best discussion of the transition from an advanced organic economy to one based on minerals.

Ideological Conflict and National Unification, 1815–1871

O N MARCH 18, 1871, THE PRESIDENT OF THE FRENCH GOVERNMENT, Adolphe Thiers, sent a small unit of troops to Paris to seize cannons that had been used against Prussian forces during their siege of the city a few months before. The artillery was in the possession of the National Guard, the citizen militia of Paris. The members of the National Guard felt that the government had abandoned them by recently concluding an armistice with the Prussians, who were still camped outside the city. They also believed that the government was determined to gain control of the city, which had refused to comply with the orders of the national government. When the troops reached the city, they encountered a hostile crowd of Parisians, many of whom were armed. The crowd surrounded the two generals who led the detachment, placed them up against a wall, and executed them.

This action by Parisian radicals led to a full-scale siege of Paris by government troops. In the city a committed group of radicals formed a new municipal government, the Paris Commune, which was a revival of the commune established during the French Revolution in 1792. The Commune took steps to defend the city against the government troops, and during its short life it implemented several social reforms. The Communards, as the members were known, set up a central employment bureau, established nurseries for working mothers, and recognized women's labor unions. For many decades the Commune served as a model of working-class government.

The Paris Commune lasted only a few weeks. On May 21 the troops of the provisional government poured through the gates of the city, and during the "bloody week" that followed they took the city street by street, demolishing the barricades and executing the Communards. The Communards retaliated by executing a number of hostages, including the archbishop of Paris. They also burned

Chapter Outline

- New Ideologies in the Early Nineteenth Century

- Ideological Encounters in Europe, 1815–1848

- National Unification in Europe and America, 1848–1871

- Ideology, Empire, and the Balance of Power

The Proclamation of the German Empire in the Hall of Mirrors at Versailles, January 21, 1871: King William I of Prussia, standing on the dais, is being crowned Emperor of Germany. At the center of the picture, dressed in a white uniform jacket, is Otto von Bismarck, the person most responsible for the unification of all German territory in one empire.

down the Tuileries Palace, the hall of justice, and the city hall. During this one week at least 25,000 Communards were killed, and since many bodies were burned in the fires that consumed the city, the numbers were probably much higher.

The short life of the Paris Commune marks the climax of a tumultuous period of European history. Between 1815 and 1871 Europe witnessed numerous movements for reform, periodic uprisings, and several revolutions. The people who participated in these momentous developments were inspired in large part by ideologies°, theories of society and government that lay at the basis of political programs. The ideologies that developed during this period—liberalism, conservatism, socialism, and nationalism—were the product of historical developments that had arisen in the West, and they endowed the West with a distinctive political culture. These four ideologies also provide a framework for understanding the complex and often confusing political and social history of the West from 1815 until 1871.

In this chapter we shall address four questions: (1)What were the main features of the ideologies that inspired people to political action during those years? (2) How did the encounters among the people who espoused these ideologies shape the political history of Europe between 1815 and 1848? (3) How did liberal and conservative leaders use the ideology of nationalism as a tool to unite the people of various territories into nation-states between 1848 and 1871? (4) What role did ideology play in international warfare and diplomacy, especially in efforts to maintain the balance of power during this period?

New Ideologies in the Early Nineteenth Century

In the wake of the French Revolution, four new ideologies—liberalism, conservatism, socialism, and nationalism—led thousands of Europeans to call for profound changes in the established political order. These ideologies had their roots in the works of eighteenth-century writers, but they developed into integrated systems of thought and inspired political programs in the first half of the nineteenth century. All four were influenced by the two great transformations of the West that we have discussed in Chapters 18 and 20: the French Revolution and the Industrial Revolution.

LIBERALISM: THE PROTECTION OF INDIVIDUAL FREEDOM

Liberalism° is anchored in the beliefs that political, social, and economic freedoms are of supreme importance and that the main function of government is to protect those freedoms. The political agendas of nineteenth-century liberals varied from one country to another, but they all pursued three main objectives. The first objective was to establish and protect individual rights, such as the freedom of the press, freedom of religion, and freedom from arbitrary arrest and imprisonment. Liberals sought to guarantee these rights by having them enumerated in written constitutions. Opposed to aristocratic privilege, liberals supported the principle of equality before the law. They also tended to be anticlerical, a position that led to frequent tension between them and the Roman Catholic Church. As defenders of individual freedom they often campaigned to end slavery and serfdom.

The second objective of liberals was the extension of the franchise (the right to vote) to all property owners, especially those in the middle class. For the most part liberals were opposed to giving the vote to the lower classes, on the grounds that poor people, with little property of their own, could not be trusted to elect representatives who would protect property rights. Liberals also were opposed to giving the vote or any other form of political power to women. They justified the exclusion on the grounds that the proper arena for female activity was the home, where women occupied their natural domain. In this way liberals subscribed to the theory of separate spheres, which assigned men and women different gender roles. As we know from Chapter 17, this theory was based on the belief that women were different in nature from men and that they should be confined to an exclusively domestic role as chaste wives and mothers. Liberals believed that only male property holders should be allowed to participate in public affairs.

The third objective of liberals was to promote free trade with other nations and to resist government regulation of the domestic economy. This economic dimension of liberal ideology, which is grounded in the writings of the Scottish economist Adam Smith and other advocates of free-market capitalism, is usually referred to as laissez-faire°, a phrase that means "let (people) do (as they choose)." Advocates of *laissez-faire* held that the government should intervene in the economy only if it is necessary to maintain public order and protect property rights. As merchants and manufacturers, liberals favored a policy of *laissez-faire* because it offered them the freedom to pursue their own self-interest without governmental interference and thereby realize greater profits.

Some of the earliest expressions of liberal ideology appear in the works of John Locke and his fellow Whigs in England during the late seventeenth century (see Chapter 15). In arguing against the absolutist policies of Charles II and James II, the Whigs emphasized the inviolability of private property rights, freedom from state economic control, and the rights of those who held property to participate in government. In the eighteenth century these ideas were developed by Enlightenment thinkers who defended natural rights, and they found eloquent expression at the time of the American Revolution and the early years of the French

Revolution. Liberal ideas were also embodied in the constitutions implemented in France, Germany, and Spain at the end of the Napoleonic period. When those constitutions and their principles came under attack after 1815, liberals sought to restore the freedoms they had lost without destroying public order. At that time liberalism became a distinct ideology.

Some liberals sought to realize their goals through the establishment of a republic, but the ideal form of government for most early nineteenth-century liberals was a limited monarchy—one in which the ruler did not act arbitrarily and suppress representative assemblies. As we shall see, liberal reformers in Britain during the 1830s wished to preserve the monarchy, and in France Louis-Philippe, the bourgeois citizen king installed during the Revolution of 1830, sought to implement liberal programs. In Germany, Belgium, and Greece, liberal revolts ended in the establishment of a constitutional monarchy.

Liberalism found its greatest strength among the urban middle class: merchants, manufacturers, and members of the professions. These people formed the group that felt most aggrieved by their exclusion from political life during the eighteenth and early nineteenth centuries and most eager to have government protect their property. Their substantial wealth provided the basis for their claim to acquire a share of political power, and as manufacturers and merchants they had the most to gain from an economy unfettered by government regulations.

Liberal economic theory found its most articulate proponents in England, where industrial capitalism achieved its earliest and most significant successes. Two of the most prominent liberals in early nineteenth-century Britain were the utilitarians Jeremy Bentham and David Ricardo. Utilitarians° advocated economic and social policies which in their view would provide the greatest good to the greatest number of people. In pursuit of that goal, Bentham (1748–1832), a legal scholar and political philosopher, proposed that a government should give its people as much freedom as possible and impose only those laws that were socially useful. The economist Ricardo (1772–1823), the son of a Dutch Jewish banker, argued that the absence of government intervention would spur economic growth and thus contribute to the benefit of all people. This *laissez-faire* argument was far more persuasive to manufacturers than to workers. In *Principles of Political Economy and Taxation* (1819), Ricardo argued that if wages were left to the law of supply and demand, they would fall to near subsistence levels. This "iron law of wages" made it clear that *laissez-faire* liberalism would not benefit the working class.

CONSERVATISM: PRESERVING THE ESTABLISHED ORDER

Throughout human history people have demonstrated a desire to maintain the established order and to resist change. In the early nineteenth century, however, the ideals of the Enlightenment and the radical changes ushered in by the French Revolution led to the formulation of a new ideology of conservatism°, a set of ideas intended to prevent a recurrence of the revolutionary changes of the 1790s. The main goal of conservatives after 1815 was to preserve the monarchies and aristocracies of Europe against liberal and national movements.

The new conservatism justified the existing political order as the product of gradual change. This defense was most clearly expressed in the writings of the fiery, Irish-born parliamentary orator Edmund Burke (1729–1797). Burke was no reactionary; he advocated a number of changes in British public life, including electoral reform and a reorganization of the British Empire. But Burke, who is regarded as the founder of modern conservatism, had enormous respect for the existing social order, which he considered the handiwork of God. Society according to Burke was a partnership between the living, the dead, and those who had yet to be born. Only within this historical partnership could change take place, and all changes would have to be gradual.

On the basis of this view of the social order, Burke attacked the liberal and radical ideas that had inspired the French Revolution. In *Reflections on the Revolution in France* (1790), he asserted that equality was a dangerous myth; its effect would be to allow those at the bottom to plunder those at the top and thus destroy the social order. Unlike the French revolutionaries, Burke had no faith in the people, whom he referred to as the "swinish multitude." In Burke's view rights did not derive from human nature, as they did for the philosophes of the Enlightenment; rights were privileges that had been passed down through the ages and could be preserved only by a hereditary monarchy. By claiming abstract rights for all men, the French had rejected their inheritance.

Conservative ideology justified the institution of monarchy on the basis of religion. The French writer Louis de Bonald (1754–1840) argued that Christian monarchies were the final creation in the development of both religious and political society. Only monarchies of this sort could preserve public order and prevent society from degenerating into the savagery witnessed during the French Revolution. De Bonald and his fellow French writer, Joseph de Maistre (1754–1821), rejected the entire concept of natural rights and reiterated the traditional doctrine of divine right, by which all political power came from God. De Maistre also reinforced the alliance between the throne and the altar by considering the monarchy and the Church as the foundations of the social order. In the nineteenth century, conservatives throughout Europe thought of religion as the basis of society. This view was especially strong in Catholic countries such as France and Austria, but Burke had put forth the same argument in Protestant England.

A fine line separates conservatism, which allows for gradual change, and reaction, which is the effort to reject any changes that have taken place and return to the old order. Early nineteenth-century conservatism provided an ideological foundation for the reactionary movements that arose throughout Europe after 1815. These movements had both national and international dimensions. In all western European countries, groups of influential and powerful individuals, usually nobles and churchmen, were determined to return to the days when they had more power. Internationally, the rulers of Europe, under the leadership of the Austrian foreign minister Clemens von Metternich, established a mechanism known as the Concert of Europe° to preserve the map of Europe as it was drawn at the Congress of Vienna (see Chapter 18). To do so meant taking concerted action against liberals and nationalists who attempted to unseat dynastic rulers.

In keeping with the identification of conservatism with religion, three of the four original powers in the Concert of Europe—Prussia, Russia, and Austria—gave their alliance a religious mission. At the Congress of Vienna Tsar Alexander I drafted a document in which the cooperation among European monarchs, whom he referred to as "the delegates of Providence," would be based "upon the sublime truths which the holy religion of Our Savior teaches." The British refused to subscribe to this document, claiming that it was "sublime mysticism and nonsense." So too did the future Louis XVIII of France (which was only a probationary member of the Concert of Europe until 1818) and even the pope. But Alexander's commitment to defend Christian values in what he called the Holy Alliance provided a religious foundation for the reactionary and repressive policies that Russia, Prussia, and Austria took steps to implement.

SOCIALISM: THE DEMAND FOR EQUALITY

Socialism, the third new ideology of the early nineteenth century, arose in response to the development of industrial capitalism and the liberal ideas that justified it. Socialism calls for the ownership of the means of production (such as factories, machines, and railroads) by the community, with the purpose of reducing inequalities of income, wealth, opportunity, and economic power. In small communities, such as some early nineteenth-century socialist settlements, ownership could be genuinely collective. In a large country, however, the only practical way to introduce socialism would be to give the ownership of property to the state, which represents the people.

The main appeal of socialism was the prospect of remedying the deplorable social and economic effects of the Industrial Revolution. As we have seen in Chapter 20, the short-term effects of industrialization included wretched working conditions, low wages, a regimentation of the labor force, and a declining standard of living. Socialists did not object to the mechanization of industry as such. Like liberals, they wanted society to be as productive as possible.

They did, however, object to the system of industrial capitalism that accompanied industrialization and the liberal economic theory that justified it.

The earliest socialists were known as Utopian socialists, a name given to them because they envisioned the creation of ideal communities in which perfect social harmony and cooperation would prevail. One of these Utopian socialists, the British industrialist and philanthropist Robert Owen (1771–1858), actually turned his mill in New Lanark, Scotland, into a model socialist community in which the principles of cooperation prevailed and where the workers were housed and their children were educated. In 1825 he established a similar community in New Harmony, Indiana. Utopian socialism was not particularly concerned with the granting of political rights to workers, nor did it encourage class consciousness or class tensions.

A second generation of socialists became more concerned with using the power of the state to improve their lot. The most influential of these socialists was the French democrat Louis Blanc (1811–1882), who proposed that the state guarantee workers' wages as well as employment in times of economic depression. He also wanted the state to support the creation of workshops in which workers would sell the product of their labor directly without a intermediary. The principle underlying Blanc's concept of the social order was, "From each according to his abilities; to each according to his needs." Blanc's brand of socialism began a long tradition in which workers tried to improve their lot by influencing government. This initiative was closely related to the radical democratic goal of universal male suffrage, which became one of the main objectives of many socialists after 1840.

The most radical form of nineteenth-century socialism was formulated by the German social philosopher Karl Marx (1818–1883). Marx was much more preoccupied than other socialists with the collective identity and political activities of the working class. Reading about working conditions in France during the early 1840s, he became convinced that workers in industrial society were the ultimate example of human alienation and degradation. In 1844 he began a lifetime association with another German-born philosopher, Friedrich Engels (1820–1895), who as we have seen in the preceding chapter exposed the wretchedness of working class life in Manchester. Marx and Engels began to think of workers as part of a capitalist system, in which they owned nothing but their labor, which they sold to capitalist producers for wages.

Marx and Engels worked these ideas into a broad account of historical change in which society moved inevitably and progressively from one stage to another. They referred to the process by which history advanced as the dialectic°. Marx acquired the idea of the dialectic from the German philosopher Georg Wilhelm Friedrich Hegel (1770–1831), who believed that history advanced in stages as the result of the conflict between one idea and

■ **Karl Marx**

Karl Marx, the German social philosopher who developed the revolutionary socialist doctrine of communism.

another. Marx disagreed with Hegel on the source of historical change, arguing that material or economic factors rather than ideas determined the course of history. Hence Marx's socialist philosophy became known as dialectical materialism°.

According to Marx and Engels, the first stage of the dialectic had taken place when the bourgeoisie, who received their income from capital, seized political power from the aristocracy, who received their income from land, during the English and French revolutions. Marx and Engels predicted that the next stage of the dialectic would be a conflict between the bourgeoisie and the working class or proletariat°, which received its income from wages. This conflict, according to Marx and Engels, would result in the triumph of the working class. Led by a committed band of revolutionaries, the proletariat would take control of the state, establish a dictatorship so that they could implement their program without opposition, and usher in a classless society.

Marx and Engels issued this call to action in *The Communist Manifesto* (1848), which ended with the famous words, "Working men of all countries unite!" Marx's brand of socialism, communism°, takes its name from this book. Communism is a revolutionary ideology that advocates the overthrow of "bourgeois" or capitalist institutions and the transfer of political power to the proletariat. Communism differs from other forms of socialism in its call for revolution, its emphasis on class conflict, and its insistence on complete economic equality. Communism belongs to a tradition that originated among members of the extreme wing of the democratic movement at the height of the French Revolution. One of those radicals, François-Noël Babeuf (1760–1797), demanded economic as well as political equality, called for the common ownership of land, and spoke in terms of class warfare. Marx's achievement was to place Babeuf's radical ideas in a new philosophical and historical framework. That framework, dialectical materialism, was explained in great detail in Marx's monumental three-volume work, *Das Kapital,* or *Capital* (1867–1894).

NATIONALISM: THE UNITY OF THE PEOPLE

Nationalism, the fourth new ideology of the early nineteenth century, also took shape during and after the French Revolution. A nation° in the nineteenth-century sense of the word refers to a large community of people who possess a sense of unity based on a belief that they have a common homeland and share a similar culture. The ideology of nationalism° is the belief that the people who form this nation should have their own political institutions and that the interests of the nation should be defended and promoted at all costs.

The geographical boundaries of nations do not often correspond to the geographical boundaries of states, which are administrative and legal units of political organization. For example, in the early nineteenth century Germans often referred to their nation as comprising all people who spoke German. At that time, however, there were several German states, such as Prussia, Bavaria, and Baden. A primary goal of nationalists is to create a nation-state°, a single political entity that governs all the members of a particular nation. The doctrine that justifies this goal is national self-determination°, the claim that any group that considers itself a nation has the right to be ruled only by members of its own nation and to have all the members of the nation included in this state.

The ideology of nationalism had roots in the French Revolution. Most of the revolutionary steps taken in France during the 1790s were undertaken in the name of a united French people. Article 3 of the *Declaration of the Rights of Man and Citizen* (1789) declared that "the principle of all authority rests essentially in the nation." The French Republic was constructed as the embodiment of the French nation. It gave an administrative unity to the French people and encouraged them to think of themselves as sharing a

KARL MARX AND FRIEDRICH ENGELS, *THE COMMUNIST MANIFESTO* (1848)

·····················

These excerpts from the final pages of The Communist Manifesto *provide a summary of the communist plan for establishing a socialist society by means of revolution. They reveal Marx's view of history as a succession of class conflicts and his prediction that the proletariat will become the ruling class. The appeal for working-class solidarity and revolution illustrates the power of socialist ideology to inspire people to action.*

The history of all past society has consisted in the development of class antagonisms, antagonisms that have assumed different forms at different epochs. But whatever form they may have taken, one fact is common to all past ages, viz., the exploitation of one part of society by the other . . .

We have seen above that the first step in the revolution by the working class is to raise the proletariat to the position of ruling class, to win the battle of democracy. The proletariat will use its political supremacy to wrest, by degrees, all capital from the bourgeoisie, to centralize all means of production in the hands of the state, i.e., of the proletariat organized as the ruling class, and to increase the total of productive forces as rapidly as possible.

If the proletariat during its contest with the bourgeoisie is compelled by the force of circumstances, to organize itself as a class, if by means of a revolution it makes itself the ruling class, and as such sweeps away by force the old conditions of production, then it will, along with these conditions, have swept away the conditions for the existence of class antagonisms and of classes generally, and will thereby have abolished its own supremacy as a class. . . .

Communists disdain to conceal their views and aims. They openly declare that their ends can be attained only by the violent overthrow of all existing social conditions. Let the ruling classes tremble at a Communist revolution. The proletarians have nothing to lose but their chains. They have a world to win. WORKING MEN OF ALL COUNTRIES UNITE!

Source: From Karl Marx and Friedrich Engels, *The Communist Manifesto,* 1848, translated in English by Friedrich Engels in 1888.

---

common cultural bond. Instead of a collection of regions, France had become *la patrie,* or the people's native land.

Nationalists emphasized the antiquity of nations, arguing that there had always been a distinct German, French, English, Swiss, or Italian people living in their respective homelands. This claim involved a certain amount of fiction, since in the past the people living in those lands possessed little cultural unity. There was little uniformity, for example, in the languages spoken by people who were identified as German, French, or Italian. Until the eighteenth century most educated Germans wrote in French, not German. Only a small percentage of Italians spoke Italian, and the main language of many Italian nationalists of the nineteenth century was French. Even after nation-states were formed, a large measure of linguistic, religious, and ethnic diversity has persisted within those states and has made true cultural unity impossible. The nation is therefore something of a myth—an imagined community to which nationalists believe they belong, but which in reality has never existed.

The ideal of the nation-state has proved almost impossible to realize. The boundaries of nations and states have never fully coincided. Patterns of human settlement are too fluid to prevent some members of a particular cultural group from living as a minority in a neighboring state. Germans, for example, have always lived in Poland, Spaniards in Portugal, and Italians in Switzerland. France at the time of the French Revolution probably came closest to realizing the ideal of a nation-state, claiming jurisdiction over most French people. Nevertheless, different regional identities and languages, such as that of the people of the southern province of Languedoc who spoke their own dialect, prevented the emergence of a powerful sense of national identity in all parts of France until the late nineteenth or early twentieth century.

In Britain the creation of a nation-state has been a complicated process. National consciousness, which is a people's belief that they belong to a nation, developed earlier in England than in any other country in Europe. In the sixteenth century almost all English people spoke the same language, and they were also subject to the same common law. In 1536, however, Wales was united to the kingdom of England, thereby including two nations, the English and the Welsh, in the same state. In 1707 England and Scotland were united in a new state, the United Kingdom of Great Britain, and in 1801 Ireland was brought into the United Kingdom as well. Thus the United Kingdom now included four nations: the English, the Welsh, the Scots, and the Irish. The task of building a British, as opposed to an English or a Scottish, nation in this multinational state has taken time, and to this day Britons are more accustomed to think of themselves as primarily English or Scottish than as British.

Other peoples have faced even more daunting obstacles than the British in constructing nation-states. Many nations have been subsumed within large empires, such as Hungarians and Croatians in the Habsburg Empire and Greeks and Serbs in the Ottoman Empire. In those empires, nationalist movements have often taken the form of separatist revolts or wars of independence, in which a nationalist group attempted to break off and form a nation-state of its own. A very different situation prevailed in Germany and Italy, where people who shared some linguistic and cultural traditions lived under the control of many different sovereign states of varying size. In these cases nationalist movements have sought to unite the smaller states into a larger nation-state.

One of the great paradoxes of nationalism is that the acquisition of colonies overseas often strengthened nationalist sentiment at home. The military conquest of these lands became a source of pride for the people in the metropolis, and also gave them a sense of cultural superiority. The main source of British national pride was the rapid spread of British control over one-quarter of the world's surface during the eighteenth and nineteenth centuries. Nationalism could also promote the supremacy of one's own nation over others. The French revolutionaries who conquered a large part of the European continent in the early nineteenth century justified their expansion on the grounds that they were superior to the rest of the human race. In 1848 a fervent German nationalist declared his support for "the preponderance of the German race over most Slav races." The Italian national leader Giuseppe Mazzini (1805–1872), whom we shall discuss in detail shortly, preferred to be called a patriot rather than a nationalist on the grounds that nationalists were imperialists who sought to encroach on the rights of other peoples.

Nationalism was often linked to liberalism during the early nineteenth century, when both movements supported revolutionary programs to realize the goal of national self-determination. Liberals believed that representative government and a limited expansion of the franchise would provide a firm foundation for the establishment of the nation-state, both in nations like Spain with a long tradition of self-rule as well as in countries like Greece that were seeking their independence from autocratic rulers. In Germany and Italy, where there was no central state, nationalists and liberals joined together to create one. There was, however, a difference of emphasis between the two ideologies, even in the early years of the nineteenth century. Liberalism stressed individual freedom, whereas nationalism was more concerned with political unity. At times those different ideals came into conflict with each other. The liberal doctrine of free trade, for example, ran into conflict with the doctrine of economic nationalism, which encouraged the protection of national industries. The nationalist German economist Friedrich List (1780–1846) claimed that free trade benefited only the wealthy and the powerful; he advocated instead protective tariffs to benefit German businesses.

Nationalism was just as capable of supporting conservatism as liberalism in the early nineteenth century. Since the nation was often viewed as having deep roots in the distant past, some nationalists glorified the monarchical and hierarchical political arrangements that prevailed in the Middle Ages. In 1848 conservative Prussian landlords rallied around the cause of "God, King, and Fatherland." Later in the nineteenth century, nationalism became identified almost exclusively with conservatism when the lower middle classes began to prefer the achievement of national glory, either in warfare or in imperialistic pursuits, to the establishment of individual freedom.

CULTURE AND IDEOLOGY

As the four great ideologies of the Western world were developing during the nineteenth century, they were influenced by two powerful cultural traditions: scientific rationalism and romanticism. These two traditions represented two sharply divergent sides of modern Western culture.

Scientific Rationalism

Scientific rationalism is a manner of thinking that traces its origins to the Scientific Revolution and reached its full flowering in the Enlightenment. This tradition has provided a major source of Western identity ever since the late eighteenth century. It has stressed the powers of human reason and considered science superior to all other forms of knowledge. Scientific rationalism is essentially a secular tradition, in that it does not rely on theology or Christian revelation for its legitimacy. The effort to construct a science of human nature, which was central to Enlightenment thought, belongs to this tradition, while the Industrial Revolution, which involved the application of scientific knowledge to production, was one of its products.

During the nineteenth century, scientific rationalism continued to have a powerful influence on Western thought and action. As scientific knowledge continued to grow, and as more people received a scientific education, the values of science and reason were proclaimed more boldly. Scientific knowledge and an emphasis on the importance of empirical data (that which can be tested) became essential components of much social thought. The clearest statement that science was the highest form of knowledge and would lead inevitably to human progress was the secular philosophy of positivism°.

The main elements of positivism were set forth by the French philosopher Auguste Comte (1798–1857). Like many thinkers in the Enlightenment tradition, Comte argued that human society passed through a succession of historical stages, each leading to a higher level. It had already passed through two stages, the theological and the metaphysical, and it was now in the third, the positive or scientific stage. The word *positive* in this context means that which has substance or concrete reality, as opposed to that which is abstract or speculative. Comte predicted that in the final positive stage of history the accumulation of factual or scientific knowledge would enable thinkers, whom we now call sociologists, to discover the laws of human behavior and thus make possible the improvement of society. This prediction of human progress, and Comte's celebration of the liberation of knowledge from its theological shackles, had particular appeal to liberals, especially those who harbored hostility to the Roman Catholic Church.

The values of science and the belief in its inevitable advance also influenced the social thought of Karl Marx. His ideology of communism has been referred to as scientific socialism, in that it too is based on a vision of history determined solely by positive, in this case material or economic, developments. Marxism rejects the metaphysical, idealistic world of Hegel and the theology of all Christian religion and thus fits into the same scientific tradition to which positivism and earlier Enlightenment thought belongs.

Romanticism

The cultural tradition that posed the greatest challenge to scientific rationalism was romanticism°. This tradition originated as an artistic and literary movement in the late eighteenth century, but it soon developed into a more general worldview. The artists and writers who identified themselves as romantics recognized the limits of human reason in comprehending reality. Unlike scientific rationalists, they used intuition and imagination to penetrate deeper levels of being and to comprehend the entire cosmos. Romantic art, music, and literature therefore appealed to the passions rather than the intellect.

Romantics did not think of reality as being simply material, as did the positivists. For them it was also spiritual and emotional, and their purpose as writers and artists was to communicate that non-empirical dimension of reality to their audiences. Romantics also had a different view of the relationship between human beings and nature. Instead of standing outside nature and viewing it objectively, in the manner of a scientist analyzing data derived from experiments, they considered themselves a part of nature and emphasized its beauty and power.

As an art form, romanticism was a protest against classicism and in particular the classicism that prevailed in the late eighteenth century. As we discussed in Chapter 17, classicism reflects a worldview in which the principles of orderliness and rationality prevail. Classicism is a disciplined style that demands adherence to formal rules that governed the structure as well as the content of literature, art, architecture, and music. By contrast romanticism allows the artist much greater freedom. In literature the romantic protest against classicism led to the introduction of a new

poetic style involving the use of imagery, symbols, and myth. One example of this new approach is "Rime of the Ancient Mariner" (1798) by the English romantic poet Samuel Taylor Coleridge (1772–1834), which uses the sun and moon as powerful symbols in describing a nightmarish sea voyage.

Many romantic works of literature, such as the novels of the Scottish author Sir Walter Scott (1771–1832), were set in the Middle Ages, a period often associated with superstition rather than science and enlightenment. Other romantic prose works explore the exotic, the weird, the mysterious, and even the satanic elements in human nature. Mary Shelley's introspective novel *Frankenstein* (1818), an early example of science fiction that embodies a critique of scientific rationalism, incorporates many of these themes.

Within the visual arts, romanticism also marked a rebellion against the classicism that had dominated eighteenth-century culture. Classicism emphasized formality and symmetry in art, and it celebrated the culture of an ideal Greek and Roman past. By contrast, romantic painters depicted landscapes that evoked a mood and an emotion rather than an objective pictorial account of the surroundings. Romantic paintings were intended to evoke feeling rather than to help the viewer achieve intellectual comprehension. John Martin's landscape *Sadak in Search of the Waters of Oblivion* (1812) conveys the power of nature and the eeriness of its animal life.

Romantic music, which also appealed to the emotions, marked a similar but more gradual departure from the formal classicism that was triumphant during the eighteenth century. The inspirational music of Ludwig van Beethoven (1770–1827), the son of a German court musician from Bonn, marked the transition from classical to romantic forms. Beethoven's early work conformed to the conventions of classical music, but his later compositions, which were completed as he became progressively deaf and which defied traditional classical harmonies, were intended to evoke an emotional response. His famous "Ode to Joy," in his ninth and final symphony, remains unequaled in its ability to rouse the passions. In the view of one critic, Beethoven's music "opens the floodgates of fear, of terror, of horror, of pain, and aroused that longing for the eternal which is the essence of romanticism."

Another early romantic composer, Franz Schubert (1797–1828), who was born in Vienna, blended classical forms with romantic themes by incorporating Hungarian and gypsy folk music into his compositions. The emotionally powerful operas of the German composer Richard Wagner (1813–1883), which were set in the mythical German past, marked the height of the romantic movement in music. That style attained its greatest popularity during the second half of the nineteenth century with the lyrical symphonies and concertos of Johannes Brahms (1833–1897) in Germany and the symphonies, ballets, and operas of Peter Tchaikovsky (1840–1893) in Russia.

■ **John Martin,** *Sadak in Search of the Waters of Oblivion* **(1812)**
This painting reflects the romantic concern with the fantastic or the bizarre as well as its intention to convey the power of nature.

Romanticism, like the rational and scientific culture it rejected, had powerful political implications, leaving its mark on the ideologies of the modern world. In the early nineteenth century, romanticism appealed to many liberals because it involved a protest against the established order and emphasized the freedom of the individual. Romantic writers were themselves often outsiders, and therefore their protests took many different forms. The French romantic author Victor Hugo (1802–1885), whose epic novels *The Hunchback of Notre Dame* (1831) and *Les Misérables* (1862) depicted human suffering with great compassion, identified romanticism as "liberalism in literature." For Hugo a relationship existed between liberty in art and liberty in society. In France wealthy liberal bourgeoisie generally patronized romantic music and literature, while nobles and clerics denounced them. Romanticism could, however, provide support for conservatism by idealizing the traditional social and political order of the Middle Ages and the central importance of religion in society. The hostility of romantics to the culture of the Enlightenment could also lead to political conservatism. Sir Walter Scott and Samuel Taylor Coleridge were both conservatives, while the German writer Johann Wolfgang von Goethe (1749–1832), whose poems reflected many of the themes of romantic literature, opposed all liberal and republican movements in Germany.

Romanticism has a closer association with nationalism than with any other ideology. In the most general sense romanticism invested the idea of "the nation" with mystical qualities, thus inspiring devotion to it. Romantics also had an obsessive interest in the cultural, literary, and historical roots of national identity. This connection between romanticism and nationalism can be seen in the work of the German philosopher and literary critic Johann Gottfried von Herder (1744–1803), who was one of the leaders of the *Sturm und Drang* (storm and stress) literary movement. This movement, which developed in the 1770s and 1780s and included works by Goethe and Friedrich von Schiller (1759–1805), encouraged subjectivity and the youthful revolt of genius against accepted classical standards. Herder promoted the study of German language, literature, and history with the explicit purpose of giving the German people a common sense of national unity. He claimed that "a people may lose its independence, but it will survive as long as its language survives." Like many romantics, Herder idealized the Middle Ages and cultivated many of the myths that surrounded that epoch in Germany's history.

In other parts of Europe, especially in Poland and the Balkans, romantic writers and artists gave nationalists the tools necessary to construct a common culture and history of their nations. The Polish romantic composer Frédéric

Mary Shelley's *Frankenstein:* The Body in Romantic Literature

In 1818, Mary Shelley, the twenty-year-old daughter of the feminist Mary Wollstonecraft and the wife of the poet Percy Shelley, published a novel, *Frankenstein: or, The Modern Prometheus,* that became a literary sensation in contemporary England and has inspired books and films down to the present day. The depiction of the human body in the novel reflects the attitude of romantic writers toward nineteenth-century science.

The novel tells the story of an idealistic Swiss scientist, Victor Frankenstein, who discovers the secret of giving life to inanimate matter. Using his knowledge of chemistry, anatomy, and physiology, Frankenstein pieces together bones and flesh from corpses to construct the frame of a human being, which he then infuses with life. The creature turns out to be a freak of nature: a gigantic, ugly, and deformed monster with watery eyes, yellow shriveled skin, and straight black lips. Frankenstein is horrified by what he has wrought, and his rejection leads the monster to turn on his creator, eventually killing his brother, his friend, and his wife on their wedding night. Frankenstein pursues the creature to the Arctic region, but the monster brings about Frankenstein's death. Filled with self-loathing for having murdered "the lovely and the helpless," the monster declares that Frankenstein will be his last victim and sets off to throw himself on his own funeral pyre.

The body of the monster created by Frankenstein is unnatural in the manner of creation, its size, its features, and its preternatural strength. The depiction of monstrous creatures in literature was common during the early modern period, as a way of indicating supernatural intervention in the world. Shelley's depiction of this monster, which reflects the preoccupation of romantic literature with the exotic and the mysterious, differs from that older tradition in that it identifies modern science, not supernatural forces, as the source of the monster's abnormality. In trying to unite the body and the soul, Frankenstein produced a creature he called a daemon, a body inhabited by an evil spirit who commits multiple murders. Science had produced a moral and a physical aberration.

One of the important theological questions in the history of Christianity has been whether an evil spirit or demon can inhabit or possess a human body. Shelley was preoccupied by this issue, as evidenced by Victor Frankenstein's deep interest in the figure of Satan in the novel. Frankenstein's monster was a demonic figure, but unlike the Satan of the Bible, he was the product of science and its attempt to control nature. The real monster becomes science itself, whose power nineteenth-century intellectuals desired but at the same time feared.

Mary Shelley, like many romantic writers, thought of nature as a life force with which human beings should be in harmony. The novel reinforces this theme by showing how a human being's attempt to control nature leads to nature's revenge. Frankenstein's loss of physical and mental health, the thwarting of his ability to have children with his wife, and his eventual death are all penalties for his violation of nature. ■

■ Depiction of the Monster Created by Victor Frankenstein

The creation of the monster in Mary Shelley's novel embodied a critique of scientific rationalism.

For Discussion

How does *Frankenstein* reflect the themes of romanticism and in particular its critique of scientific rationalism?

Chopin (1810–1849), who emigrated to Paris in 1831, inspired Polish nationalists by drawing on native Polish dances in his works for the piano. At the same time the romantic poet Adam Mickiewicz (1798–1855), another Polish exile in Paris, wrote *The Books of the Polish Nation* (1832), exalting his country as the embodiment of freedom and predicting that by its long suffering it would eventually liberate the human race.

Ideological Encounters in Europe, 1815–1848

The four new ideologies of the nineteenth century—liberalism, conservatism, socialism, and nationalism—interacted in a variety of ways, sometimes reinforcing each other and at other times leading to direct and violent political conflict. During the years between 1815 and 1831 the main ideological encounters occurred between liberalism, sometimes infused with nationalism, and conservatism. In 1815, at the time of the Congress of Vienna, it appeared that conservatism would carry the day. The determination of Metternich, the Austrian minister, to employ all the resources of the Holy Alliance to suppress any signs of revolutionary activity made the future of liberalism and nationalism appear bleak. The power of the new ideologies, however, could not be completely contained. Liberal and nationalist revolts took place in three distinct periods: the early 1820s, 1830, and 1848. During the latter two periods the demands of workers, sometimes expressed in socialist terms, added to the ideological mixture. In all these encounters conservatives had their say, and in most cases they emerged victorious.

LIBERAL AND NATIONALIST REVOLTS, 1820–1825

Between 1820 and 1825 a sequence of revolts in Europe revealed the explosive potential of liberalism and nationalism and the determination of conservatives to crush those ideologies. These revolts also reflected the strength of movements for national self-determination. The three most significant revolts took place in Spain, Greece, and Russia.

The Liberal Revolts of 1820 in Spain and Portugal

The earliest clash between liberalism and conservatism occurred in Spain, where liberals ran into determined opposition from their king, Ferdinand VII (r. 1808–1833). Ferdinand had been restored to power in 1814 after his forced abdication in 1808. In 1812, during the rule of

CHRONOLOGY

Liberal and Nationalist Revolts, 1820–1833

1820	Liberal Revolt in Spain; liberal army officers seize power in Portugal
1821	Beginning of Greek revolt against the Ottoman Empire
1825	Decembrist Revolt in Russia against Nicholas I
1829	Liberals gain majority in French Chamber of Deputies
1830	Revolution in Paris, Louis-Philippe I becomes king of France; Belgium becomes independent and adopts a liberal constitution; beginning of the Polish Rebellion against Nicholas I of Russia
1833	Greece becomes independent; Otto I becomes king

Joseph Bonaparte, the Spanish *cortes*—the representative assembly in that kingdom—had approved a liberal constitution. This constitution provided a foundation for a limited monarchy and the protection of Spanish civil liberties. In keeping with the ideas of the French Revolution, it also declared that the Spanish nation, not the king, possessed sovereignty. The tension began when King Ferdinand declared that he would not recognize this constitution. Even worse for the disheartened liberals was Ferdinand's decision to reestablish the Spanish Inquisition, invite exiled Jesuits to return, and refuse to summon the *cortes*. In 1820, when the Spanish Empire in the New World had already begun to collapse (see Chapter 19), liberals in Madrid, in alliance with some military officers, seized power.

This liberal revolt proved to be a test for the Concert of Europe. Metternich urged intervention, and although the British refused because they wanted to protect their trading interests with the Spanish colonies, the members of the Holy Alliance supported the invasion of Spain by a French army of 200,000 men. Ferdinand was restored once again to the throne, and once again he renounced the liberal constitution of 1812. The liberals not only lost this struggle, but they also suffered bitter reprisals from the government, which tortured and executed their leaders. The situation became only marginally better in 1833, when Ferdinand died and the liberal ministers of his young daughter, Queen Isabella II (r. 1833–1868), drew up another constitution. Her reign was marked by civil war, instability, and factional strife in which liberals made few substantial gains.

Shortly after the Spanish revolt of 1820, a similar rebellion based on liberal ideas took place in Portugal. The royal family had fled to Brazil during the Napoleonic wars, leaving Portugal to be governed by a regent. A group of army officers removed the regent and installed a liberal government, which proceeded to suppress the Portuguese Inquisition, confiscate church lands, and invite King John (r. 1816–1826) to return to his native land as a constitutional monarch. After the king returned in 1822, his enthusiasm for liberal government waned. His granddaughter, Maria II (r. 1826–1853), kept the liberal cause alive, relying on support from Portugal's traditional ally, Britain, but she struggled against the forces of conservatism and had only limited success.

The Nationalist Revolt of 1821 in Greece

A revolt in Greece in 1821, inspired more by nationalism than liberalism, achieved greater success than did the rebellions of 1820 in Spain and Portugal. It succeeded because other members of the Concert of Europe, not just Britain, lent their support to the revolt. Greece had long been a province in the sprawling Ottoman Empire, but a nationalist movement, organized by Prince Alexander Ypsilantis (1792–1828), created a distinct Greek national identity and inspired the demand for a separate Greek state. In 1821 a series of revolts against Ottoman rule took place on the mainland of Greece and on some of the surrounding islands. These rebellions received widespread support in Europe from scholars who considered Greece the cradle of Western civilization and from religiously inspired individuals who saw this as a struggle of Christianity against Islam. Hundreds of European volunteers joined the Greek rebel forces. Thus the insurrection became not only a liberal and national revolt but a broad cultural encounter between East and West. The English romantic poets George Lord Byron (1788–1824) and Percy Shelley (1792–1822) became active and passionate advocates for Greek independence, while the romantic painter Eugène Delacroix (1798–1863) depicted the horror of the Turkish massacre of the entire population at the island of Chios in 1822. The link between nationalism and romanticism could not have been made more explicit.

The Greek revolt placed the powers allied in the Concert of Europe in a quandary. On the one hand they were committed to intervene on behalf of the established order to crush any nationalist or liberal revolts, and they condemned the insurrection on those grounds when it first erupted. On the other hand they were Western rulers who identified the Ottoman Turks with everything that was alien to Christian civilization. Moreover, Russia wanted to

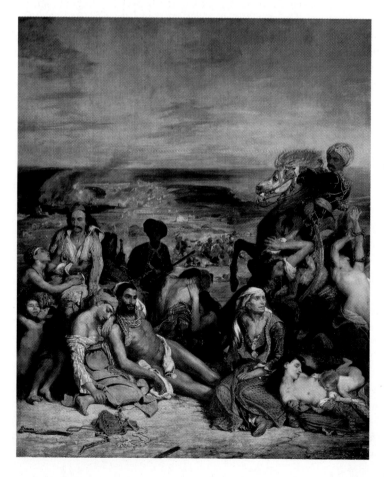

■ **Eugène Delacroix,**
***The Massacre at Chios* (1824)**

In 1821 the Greeks on the Aegean Islands rebelled against their Turkish rulers, and in April 1822 Turkish reprisals reached their peak in the massacre of the inhabitants of Chios. Romantic paintings were intended to evoke feelings, in this case horror, at the genocide perpetrated by the Turks against the Greek rebels. The painting reveals the close association of romantic art with the causes of liberalism and nationalism.

use this opportunity to dismember its ancient enemy, the Ottoman Empire. The European powers eventually took the side of the Greek rebels. In 1827 Britain, France, and Russia threatened the Turks with military intervention if they did not agree to an armistice and grant the Greeks their independence. When the Turks refused, the combined naval forces of those three countries destroyed the fleet of the Turks' main ally, Egypt, at Navarino off the Greek coast. This naval action turned the tide in favor of the Greeks, who in 1833 finally won their independence and placed a Bavarian prince, Otto I (r. 1833–1862), on the throne. Thus the Greek war of independence effectively ended the Concert of Europe. Originally intended to crush nationalist and liberal revolts, the Concert had in this case helped one succeed.

The Decembrist Revolt of 1825 in Russia

The least successful of the early liberal revolts took place in Russia, where a number of army officers, influenced by liberal ideas while serving in western Europe during the Napoleonic wars, staged a rebellion against the government of Tsar Nicholas I (r. 1825–1855) on the first day of his reign. The officers, together with other members of the nobility, had been meeting for almost a decade in political clubs, such as the Society of True and Faithful Sons of the Fatherland in St. Petersburg. In these societies they articulated their goals of establishing a constitutional monarchy and emancipating the serfs.

The rebels, known as Decembrists° for the month in which their rebellion took place, could not agree on the precise form of government they wished to institute. That disagreement, coupled with a reluctance to take action at the critical moment, led to their failure. When Tsar Alexander I died suddenly in 1825, the Decembrists hoped to persuade his brother Constantine to assume the throne and establish a representative form of government. Their hopes were dashed when Constantine refused to tamper with the succession and accepted the reign of his brother Nicholas. The reactionary Nicholas had no difficulty suppressing the revolt, executing its leaders, and leaving Russian liberals to struggle against police repression for the remainder of the nineteenth century.

LIBERAL AND NATIONALIST REVOLTS, 1830

A second cluster of early nineteenth century liberal and national revolts in 1830 achieved a greater measure of success than the revolts of the early 1820s. These revolutions took place in France, the kingdom of the Netherlands, and the kingdom of Poland.

The French Revolution:
The Success of Liberalism

The most striking triumph of liberalism in Europe during the early nineteenth century occurred in France, where a revolution took place fifteen years after the final defeat of Napoleon at Waterloo. This liberal success did not come easily. During the first few years of the restored monarchy conservatives had their way, as they did elsewhere in Europe. Louis XVIII had approved a Charter of Liberties in 1814, but he was hardly receptive to any further liberal reforms. Between 1815 and 1828 French politics was dominated by the ultraroyalists, who sponsored a "white terror" (so called because they displayed the white flag of the Bourbon monarchy) against liberals and Protestants. The terror was led by two men nicknamed Three Slices and Four Slices, indicating the number of pieces into which they butchered their Protestant enemies.

In 1824, when the conservative Charles X (r. 1824–1830) ascended the throne and took steps to strengthen the Church and the nobility, there appeared to be little hope for liberalism. Nevertheless liberal opposition to the monarchy gained support from merchants and manufacturers, as well as from soldiers who still kept the memory of Napoleon alive. When liberals became frightened that Charles would claim absolute power, and when a serious economic crisis afflicted the country in 1829, liberals at last gained a majority in the Chamber of Deputies, the French legislature.

Charles then embarked upon a perilous course. In what became known as the July Ordinances he effectively undermined the principles of the Charter of 1814. These ordinances dissolved the new Chamber of Deputies, ordered new elections under a highly restrictive franchise, and censored the press. The public reaction to this maneuver caught the king by surprise. Thousands of students and workers, liberals and republicans alike, poured onto the streets of Paris to demonstrate. Skirmishes with the king's troops only made the situation worse, and when the tricolor flag of the French Revolution appeared on top of Notre Dame Cathedral, protesters blocked the streets with barricades. Unable to restore order, the king abdicated in favor of his grandson, but the liberals offered the crown instead to the Duke of Orléans, who was crowned as Louis-Philippe I (r. 1830–1848).

Louis-Philippe accepted a revised version of the Charter of 1814 and doubled the franchise, giving the vote to middle-class merchants and industrialists. The king catered to this bourgeois constituency by encouraging economic growth and restricting noble privilege. His reign, which is often referred to as the "bourgeois monarchy," also achieved a measure of secularization when the Chamber of Deputies declared that Roman Catholicism was no longer the state religion. In keeping with mainstream liberal ideals, however, he did nothing to encourage republicanism or radical democracy, much less socialism. Efforts to depict him as the heir to the French Revolution did not persuade the bulk of the population. When the government brought the ashes of Napoleon from St. Helena to Paris, thousands of French men and women turned out to pay homage to the former emperor. Much to his disappointment, Louis-Philippe

■ **Scene from the French Revolution of 1830 in Paris**

Demonstrations by students and workers led to the abdication of King Charles X and the establishment of a liberal government. Tricolor flags of the French Revolution hang from the windows.

gained little political benefit from the move. France had acquired a liberal monarchy, but it stood on a precarious foundation.

The Belgian Revolution: The Success of Nationalism

The French Revolution of 1830 triggered the outbreak of a liberal and nationalist revolution in the neighboring country of Belgium. At the Congress of Vienna the Austrian Netherlands were united with the Dutch Republic in a new kingdom of the Netherlands. This union of the Low Countries did not work out, and soon after the formation of the new kingdom the Belgians began pressing for their independence as a nation. With a Dutchman, William I, as king and with the seat of government in Holland, the Dutch were the dominant partner in this union, a situation that cause considerable resentment in Belgium. Belgians spoke Flemish or French rather than Dutch, which had become the kingdom's official language. Moreover, most Belgians were Catholics, whereas the majority of Dutch people were Protestants. With their own language, religion, and culture, as well as their own history, Belgians thought of themselves as a separate nation. They also were more liberal than their Dutch neighbors, advocating free trade and the promotion of industry, while resenting the high tariffs imposed by the Dutch government.

The two main political parties in Belgium, the Liberals and the Clericals, joined forces to achieve autonomy. When the news of the Revolution in Paris reached Brussels, fighting broke out between workers and government troops. A national congress gathered to write a new constitution, and when the Dutch tried to thwart the rebellion by bombarding the Belgian city of Antwerp, Britain assembled a conference of European powers to devise a settlement. The powers agreed to recognize Belgium's independence, and they arranged for a German prince, Leopold of Saxe-Coburg, uncle of the future British Queen Victoria, to become king. The Dutch, however, refused to recognize the new government, and they renewed their military attacks on Belgium. Only in 1839 did all sides accept the new political arrangement.

The Polish Rebellion: The Failure of Nationalism

The French Revolution of 1830 triggered a second uprising, this one unsuccessful, in the kingdom of Poland (see

■ **Map 21.1 European Centers of Rebellion and Revolution, 1820–1848**

All these political disturbances were inspired by ideology.

European Centers of Rebellion and Revolution, 1820–1848

✳ Centers of revolution, 1820s and 1830s
✴ Centers of revolution, 1848

Map 21.1). Poland had suffered many partitions at the hands of European powers during the eighteenth century, and in 1815 the Congress of Vienna had redefined its borders once again. After incorporating much of the eastern portion of the country into the Russian Empire, the Congress established a separate Polish kingdom, with Warsaw as its capital and the Russian Tsar, Alexander I, as its king (r. 1815–1825).

With a Russian king the independence of Poland was a mere fiction, but Alexander had approved a liberal Polish constitution in 1815. He grew to regret this decision, and his rule as king of Poland gradually alienated Polish liberals within the national legislature, the *sejm*. The accession of Nicholas in 1825 only aggravated those tensions. An uncompromising conservative, Nicholas accused the Polish opposition of complicity with the Russian Decembrist rebels, and he brought them to the brink of rebellion when he made plans to send the Polish army, together with Russian troops, to suppress the French revolution of 1830 and to prevent the Belgians from receiving their independence.

The revolt began within the school of army cadets, who attacked the residence of the Grand Duke Constantine, but it quickly gained the support of the entire army and the urban populace. The revolt appealed to both liberals and nationalists, and it drew inspiration from a group of romantic poets who celebrated the achievements of the Polish past. A provisional government was established at Warsaw, but the liberal members of the elected national assembly were unwilling to enlist the peasantry in the conflict, fearful that they would rise against Polish landlords rather than the Russians. When the powers of western Europe refused to intervene on behalf of this liberal cause, Nicholas was able to crush the rebellion, abolish the *sejm*, and deprive the kingdom of Poland of its autonomous status. Nicholas visited a terrible revenge upon the leaders of the revolt, confiscated the lands of those who had emigrated, and shut down the University of Warsaw. His brutal repression set back the cause of liberalism and nationalism in Poland for another two generations.

LIBERAL REFORM IN BRITAIN, 1815–1848

The challenges that liberals faced in Britain were somewhat different from those they confronted in most other European countries. Having maintained the status quo during the era of the French Revolution, the forces of British conservatism, which bore the ideological stamp of Edmund Burke, remained formidable. At the same time, however, Britons already enjoyed many of the rights that liberals on the European continent demanded, such as freedom of the press and protection from arbitrary imprisonment. The power of the British monarchy was more limited than in almost any other European country. The ideology of liberalism, which originated in England and had deep roots in British political and social philosophy, defined the political creed of many Whigs, who formed the main opposition to the ruling Conservative or Tory party after 1815.

In this relatively favorable political climate, British liberals pursued three major goals, which amounted to a program for reform rather than revolution. The first was parliamentary reform and the expansion of the franchise. The British had a long tradition of representative government, which had been secured by the Glorious Revolution of 1688, but the titled nobility in the House of Lords effectively controlled elections to the House of Commons, while the members of the gentry or lesser aristocracy held most of the seats in the House of Commons. In some boroughs real representation was a sham; the electorate consisted entirely of the borough councils, who elected the nominees of the noblemen who controlled them. Very few people lived in some of these "rotten boroughs"—one was nothing but a pasture—whereas large segments of the population in the recently industrialized north had no representation at all in Parliament.

The Great Reform Bill of 1832, which was pushed through Parliament by the Whig prime minister, Lord Grey, marked a victory for British liberalism. The bill expanded the franchise to include most of the urban middle class. It eliminated the rotten boroughs and created a number of new ones in heavily populated areas. It also established a uniform standard for the right to vote in all parliamentary boroughs. In keeping with the principles of liberalism, however, the bill restricted the vote, and hence active citizenship, to property owners. It rejected the demands of radicals for universal male suffrage, and by using the phrase "male person" to identify eligible voters, the bill denied all women the vote.

The second liberal cause was the repeal of legislation that denied political power to Catholics and also to Protestants who did not attend the service of the Anglican Church. In the seventeenth century a body of legislation had denied both of these religious minorities the right to hold national or local political office. Catholics suffered the additional liability of being denied the right to sit in Parliament. Liberals provided the basis of support for the political "emancipation" of Catholics and Protestant nonconformists. Liberals were opposed on principle to religious discrimination, and many of them belonged to Protestant nonconformist congregations. Conservatives opposed the repeal of this legislation, but they feared a civil war in Ireland if Catholics were not allowed to sit in the British Parliament. The Tory prime minister, the Duke of Wellington, who had defeated Napoleon at Waterloo, eventually agreed to liberal demands. The Protestant nonconformists were emancipated in 1828, while the Catholics had to wait until one year later. One of the first Catholics elected to Parliament in 1830 was Daniel O'Connell (1775–1847), an Irishman who worked tirelessly to improve the lot of his countrymen within the limits of the Irish union with Britain.

The third liberal cause was free trade. The target of this campaign was a series of protective tariffs on the import or export of hundreds of commodities, including raw materials used in production. The most hated protective tariff was on grain (known in Britain as corn), which kept the price of basic food commodities high in order to protect the interests of landlords and farmers. In this respect the desire of liberals for free trade collided against the desire of Parliament to defend the economic interests of its largely aristocratic membership. In 1837 a group of indus-

AN IRISH OFFICIAL CRITICIZES BRITISH POLICY DURING THE POTATO FAMINE

....

The potato famine of 1845–1848, which was caused by a blight on Ireland's staple crop, the potato, killed thousands of Irish people and drove more than one million others to emigrate. As the extent of the famine became apparent in November 1845, the Lord Mayor of Dublin sent the following resolution to the Lord Lieutenant of Ireland, the highest-ranking official of the British government in that country.

. . . . That we have ascertained beyond the shadow of doubt that considerably more than one-third of the entire of the potato crop in Ireland has been already destroyed by the potato disease; and that such disease has not, by any means, ceased its ravages . . . That we arraign in the strongest terms, consistent with personal respect to ourselves, the culpable conduct of the present administration, as well in refusing to take any efficacious measure for alleviating the present calamity with all its approaching hideous and necessary consequences; as also for the un-

equivocal crime of keeping the ports closed against the importation of foreign provisions, thus either abdicating their duty to the people or their sovereign, whose servants they are, or involving themselves in the enormous guilt of aggravating starvation and famine, by unnaturally keeping up the price of provisions, and doing this for the benefit of a selfish class who derive at the present awful crisis pecuniary advantage to themselves by the maintenance of the oppressive Corn laws . . . Yet, whilst the Irish harbours are closed against the importation of foreign food, they are left open for the exportation of Irish grain, which has already amounted in the present season to a quantity nearly adequate to feed the entire people of Ireland, and to avert the now certain famine; thus inflicting upon the Irish people the abject misery of having their own provisions carried away to feed others, while they themselves are left contemptuously to starve.

Source: From John O'Rourke. *The History of the Great Irish Famine of 1847*. Dublin: 1902.

■ **The Last Great Chartist Rally in Britain, April 10, 1848**

Government precautions, including the appointment of special constables to handle the crowd, and rain kept the number of demonstrators in London lower than anticipated. The government ordered the leader of the movement, Feargus O'Connor, to stop the planned march to Parliament.

trialists and radical reformers formed the Anti–Corn Law League with the purpose of bringing about the repeal of the Corn Law of 1815, which greatly restricted the importation of foreign grain into Britain. This campaign against protectionism did not succeed until 1845, when the Conservative prime minister, Sir Robert Peel, brought about repeal by securing the votes of some of his own party and combining them with those of the Whigs, all of whom favored free trade.

Peel took this action only after the advent of the Great Famine in Ireland (1845–1848), which was caused by a blight on potatoes, the main crop on which the Irish population relied. The repeal of the corn laws allowed the importation of foreign grain into Ireland, but it did not solve the problem. More than one million Irish people died as a result of the famine, and another million were forced to emigrate, many of them to the United States and Canada.

Unlike the liberals, socialists and radical democrats achieved little success in Britain during the first half of the nineteenth century. In 1834 the Utopian socialist Robert Owen established the Grand National Consolidated Trades Union, the purpose of which was to unite all workers in a peaceful struggle to realize his idealist goals. Owen had hoped that his union would give "the productive classes a complete dominion over the fruits of their own industry."

The refusal of many unions to join this association, coupled with opposition from the government, led to its disintegration. In its wake workers and radicals decided that economic improvement could come only through political means. In 1837 the newly formed London Workingman's Association, in collaboration with a few radical Members of Parliament, drew up a People's Charter, calling for the implementation of a program of radical democracy. Their demands included universal male suffrage, annual parliaments, voting by secret ballot, equal electoral districts, the elimination of property qualifications for Members of Parliament, and the payment of salaries to those same members. The workers who supported this cause became known as Chartists.

The strength of the Chartist movement fluctuated between 1837 and 1848, gaining the greatest popular participation when economic conditions deteriorated. Most Chartists restricted their activities to meetings to support candidates for Parliament and petitioning Parliament. A few of the more militant, like the Irish immigrant Feargus O'Connor, called for "a holy and irresistible crusade" against the government. The British government and the upper classes became most frightened in 1848, when revolution broke out in France, Italy, and Germany, and when the Chartists decided to draft a new charter and threatened to form a revolutionary national assembly like that of France if Parliament were to reject the new document.

Within the next few years the Chartist movement died. British workers revealed, as they would throughout the remainder of the nineteenth century, that they had little inclination to take to the streets, especially after good economic times returned. The government's reduction of indirect taxes during the 1840s, coupled with the effective use of the police force and the strict enforcement of the criminal law, also helped prevent Britain from experiencing revolution in 1848. The price of this failure was that further liberal reforms, such as the extension of the franchise, did not take place in Britain for another two decades.

THE REVOLUTIONS OF 1848

Unlike Britain, almost every country in Europe experienced revolution in 1848. A wave of revolutionary activity spread rapidly throughout the Continent. The revolutions took place during a period of widespread economic discontent. European countries had suffered bad harvests in 1845 and 1846 and an economic recession in 1847, leading to a temporary decline in the standard of living among industrial as well as agricultural workers. Discontent took the form of mass protests and demonstrations, which increased the likelihood of violent confrontation. The revolutions of 1848 were more widespread than the revolts of the 1820s and 1830, and they involved greater popular participation. These revolutions also gave greater attention to both nationalist and socialist issues.

The French Revolutions of 1848

The first of the revolutions of 1848 took place in France, where the liberal government of Louis-Philippe faced mounting criticism. Declining economic conditions, which prevailed throughout Europe during the 1840s, provided an environment that brought the country to a crisis point. A series of demonstrations in Paris in favor of the right of workers to vote and to receive state assistance for their trades was the final precipitant. When troops from the Paris National Guard fired on the demonstrators and killed forty people, the barricades once again appeared in the streets and the rebels seized government buildings. France was experiencing its third revolution in sixty years. In an effort to

CHRONOLOGY	
The Revolutions of 1848	
1848	
February	Revolution in Paris
March	Insurrection in Berlin, peasant unrest in the countryside, formation of liberal governments in Prussia and other German states; revolutions in Milan and Venice, Ferdinand II issues a new constitution in Naples
April	Elections for a new National Assembly in France
May	Meeting of the Frankfurt Parliament; meeting of the Prussian Assembly
June	Suppression of working-class resistance in Paris; Pan-Slav Congress in Prague; suppression of the rebellion in Prague
October	Suppression of revolution in Vienna
December	Election of Louis-Napoleon as president of the Second French Republic; Frankfurt Parliament issues *Declaration of the Basic Rights of the German People*; Frederick William dissolves Prussian Assembly
1849	
March	King Frederick William rejects the German crown offered by the Frankfurt Parliament
April	Frankfurt Parliament promulgates a new constitution; Hungarian Diet proclaims Magyar independence
May–June	Fall of the liberal ministries in German states
August	Venetian Republic surrenders to Austrian forces; suppression of the Hungarian movement for independence

save his regime, Louis-Philippe abdicated in favor of his grandson, but the revolutionaries abolished the monarchy and declared the Second French Republic.

A provisional government selected by the Chamber of Deputies was headed by nine republicans, but it included liberals and radical democrats. Most significantly it also included two socialists, Louis Blanc and a worker who preferred to be called by the single name of Albert. The French Revolution of 1848 offered the socialists the first opportunity to realize their goal of a democratic and socialist republic. Many of the 200 clubs formed in Paris at this time, some of which were exclusively female, were either republican or socialist in their orientation. The socialist agenda included not only universal male suffrage, which was granted immediately by the government, but also active support for the masses of unemployed workers. Louis Blanc secured the establishment of national workshops to give the unemployed jobs on public projects. Ordinances reduced the length of the workday to ten hours in the city and twelve hours in rural areas, and the government authorized a commission to study working conditions.

These bold socialist initiatives did not last long. By the summer the euphoria of the revolution had dissipated and the aspirations of workers had been crushed. The elections held in April 1848 to constitute a new National Assembly and write a new constitution seated an overwhelming majority of conservative monarchists and only a small minority of republicans and socialists. Resentment of the provisional government's assistance to urban workers and anger at the levying of a surtax to pay for government programs revealed the lack of broad popular support for radical political programs. Tension between the new conservative assembly and the forces of the left mounted when the government closed the workshops and Parisian workers were either drafted into the army or sent to the provinces.

These newly adopted policies led to further working-class violence in Paris in June 1848. When General Louis Cavaignac, known as "the butcher," was called in to suppress this insurgency with regular army troops, there was a devastating loss of life. No fewer than 1,500 insurgents were killed in the streets or in summary executions, while another 4,000 were sent into exile in French colonies. These confrontations appeared to Karl Marx to constitute class warfare, a prelude to the proletarian revolution he predicted for the future. Louis Blanc, who was implicated in these uprisings, fled to England, where Marx himself would soon arrive and spend the rest of his life.

The revolution ended with the election of Napoleon's nephew, Louis-Napoleon Bonaparte (1808–1873), as the president of the Second French Republic in December 1848. Until the February Revolution it seemed highly unlikely that Louis-Napoleon, an impetuous adventurer and conspirator, would ever come to power. After staging two unsuccessful coups against the government of Louis-Philippe in 1836 and 1840, he was sentenced to life imprisonment. He managed to escape to England, however, and the events of February 1848 gave him the opportunity to return to France. He became a member of the new National Assembly, and then easily defeated Cavaignac in the presidential election.

As president, Louis-Napoleon drew support from conservatives, liberals, and moderate republicans. He also benefited from the legend that his uncle had created and the nationalist sentiment it inspired. Because the first Napoleon had become emperor, even those who preferred an empire to a republic could vote for his nephew. The younger Napoleon followed in his uncle's footsteps, seizing power in December 1851 and proclaiming himself emperor of the French one year later. He called himself Napoleon III, in deference to the dynastic rights of the uncrowned Napoleon II, the son of Napoleon I who had died in 1823.

The Revolutions of 1848 in Germany, Austria, Hungary, and Bohemia

Until French revolutionaries built barricades in the streets of Paris in 1848, liberalism and nationalism had achieved little success in Germany. German university students, inspired by the slogan "Honor, Freedom, Fatherland," had staged a number of large rallies during the early years of the nineteenth century, but the forces of conservatism had kept them in check. The Carlsbad Decrees of 1819, intended to suppress university radicalism, inaugurated a period of severe repression throughout Germany. The only success achieved by German liberals and nationalists prior to 1848 was the establishment of the *Zollverein,* a customs union of the various German states, in 1834. Even that project, which promoted free trade within German lands, did not attract support from all liberals.

A major opportunity for the liberal cause in Germany came in 1848 in the immediate wake of the February Revolution in France. As in France, however, this opportunity was complicated by the more radical demands of democrats and socialists for universal suffrage, including equal rights for women. German radicals also demanded government assistance to artisans and workers who had suffered economic hardship as a result of industrialization. In Berlin, the capital of Prussia, these discontents led radicals to barricade the streets. The situation became more serious after troops fired into the crowd, killing some 250 people. The violence spread to the countryside, where peasants demanded that landlords renounce their privileges and grant them free use of their lands. In response to these pressures, King Frederick William IV summoned an assembly, elected by universal male suffrage, to write a new Prussian constitution. Other German states also yielded to liberal pressure, establishing liberal governments known as the "March ministries."

As these events were unfolding, the contagion of revolution spread to Austria, the other major German kingdom, which formed the nucleus of the sprawling Habsburg Empire. News of the revolution in Paris led to demonstrations by students and workers in Vienna. An assortment of Austrian liberal aristocrats, middle-class professionals, and discontented workers demanded an end to the long rule of the conservative minister, Clemens von Metternich. In response to the demands of these groups, Emperor Ferdinand I (r. 1835–1848) summoned a constitutional assembly and installed a moderate government. A conservative Prussian observer feared that these concessions had broken "the most secure dam against the revolutionary tide."

The main difference between the revolutions of 1848 in Austria and the other German lands was that events in

THE CARLSBAD DECREES, 1819
·····················

The main source of liberal and national ideas in Germany after 1815 were university students, who often belonged to secret societies or fraternities. Conservatives considered these students dangerous revolutionaries and tried to expel them from the universities. When a student assassinated a conservative writer in 1819, the princes of the German Confederation issued a set of decrees that called for the monitoring of the lectures given at the universities, the removal of liberal professors, the expulsion of students, and the censorship of the press.

2. The confederated governments mutually pledge themselves to remove from the universities or other public educational institutions all teachers who, by obvious deviation from their duty, or by exceeding the limits of their functions, or by the abuse of their legitimate influence over youthful minds, or by propagating harmful doctrines hostile to public order or subversive to existing governmental institutions, shall have unmistakably proven their unfitness for the important office entrusted to them. No teacher who shall have been removed in this manner shall be again appointed to a position in any public institution of learning in another state of the Confederation.

3. Those laws which have for a long period been directed against secret and unauthorized societies in the universities shall be strictly enforced. The governments mutually agree that such persons as shall hereafter be shown to have remained in secret or unauthorized associations, or shall have entered such associations, shall not be admitted to any public office.

4. No student who shall be expelled from a university by a decision of the university senate which was ratified or prompted by the agent of the government, or shall have left the institution in order to escape expulsion, shall be received in any other university.

So long as this decree shall remain in force no publication which appears in the form of daily issues, or as a serial not exceeding twenty sheets of printed matter, shall go to press in any state of the union without the previous knowledge and approval of the state officials.

Source: From *Readings in European History: 1789 to the Present,* 2nd Edition by John L. Heineman. Copyright © 1994 by Kendall/Hunt Publishing Company. Used with permission.

Vienna awakened demands of Hungarians and Czechs for national autonomy within the Empire. In Hungary the nationalist leader Lajos Kossuth (1802–1894) pushed for a program of liberal reform and national autonomy. This initiative created further tensions between the Magyars and the various national minorities within the kingdom of Hungary. Similar problems arose in Bohemia, where a revolution in Prague led to demands from the Czechs for autonomy within the Habsburg Empire. In June 1848 the Czech rebels hosted a Pan-Slav Congress in Prague to advance a nationalist plan for achieving unity of all Slavic people within the empire. This idealistic proposal could not be realized, for there were many distinct Slavic nationalities, each of which had a desire to preserve its autonomy. In addition, there was a large German-speaking population within Bohemia that identified with other German territories in the Confederation.

The most idealistic and ambitious undertaking of the revolution in central Europe was the meeting of the Frankfurt Parliament in May 1848. Some 800 middle-class liberals, many of whom were lawyers, officials, and university professors, came from all the German states to draft a constitution for a united Germany. The Parliament produced powerful speeches in support of both liberal and nationalist ideals, and in December 1848 it promulgated a *Declaration of the Basic Rights of the German People.* This document recognized the equality of all German people before the law; freedom of speech, assembly, and religion; and the right to private property. Like so many liberal assemblies, however, the Frankfurt Parliament failed to address the needs of the workers and peasants. The delegates rejected universal male suffrage as a "dangerous experiment" and refused to provide protection for craftsmen who were being squeezed out of work by industrialization. For these reasons the Parliament failed to win broad popular support.

In April 1849 the Frankfurt Parliament drafted a new constitution for a united Germany, which would have a hereditary "emperor of the Germans" and two houses of parliament, one of which would be elected by universal male suffrage. Austria, however, voted against the new plan, and without Austrian support the new constitution had little hope of success. The final blow to German liberal hopes came when King Frederick William of Prussia refused the Frankfurt Parliament's offer of the crown, which he referred to as coming from the gutter and "reeking of the stench of revolution." At that point the Frankfurt Parliament disbanded and the efforts of German liberals to unite their country and give it a new constitution came to an inglorious end.

By the middle of 1849, conservative forces had triumphed in the various German territories and the

■ **The German National Assembly Gathered in St. Paul's Church in Frankfurt, 1848**
The Parliament ultimately failed in its goal to give a liberal constitution to a united Germany.

Habsburg Empire. In Prussia the efforts of the newly elected assembly to restrict noble privilege triggered a reaction from the conservative nobles known as *Junkers*. Frederick William dismissed his liberal appointees, sent troops to Berlin, and disbanded the assembly. A similar fate befell the other German states, such as Saxony, Baden, and Hanover, all of which had installed liberal governments in the early months of the revolution. In Austria Prince Alfred Windischgrätz, who had crushed the Czech rebels in June, dispersed the rebels in Vienna in October. When Hungary proclaimed its independence from the empire in April 1849, Austrian and Russian forces marched on the country and crushed the movement.

The Revolutions of 1848 in Italy

The revolutions of 1848 also spread to Austrian possessions in the northern Italian territories of Lombardy and Venetia. In Milan, the main city in Lombardy, revolutionary developments followed the same pattern as those in Paris, Berlin, and Vienna. When the barricades went up, some of the Milanese insurgents used medieval pikes stolen from the opera house to fight off Austrian troops. Their success triggered rebellions in other towns in Lombardy, in Venice, and in the southern kingdom of the

Two Sicilies. In that kingdom the Spanish Bourbon king, Ferdinand II (r. 1830–1859), after suppressing a republican revolt in January, was forced to grant a liberal constitution. The spread of these revolts inspired the hope of bringing about the unification of all Italian people in one state.

This Italian nationalist dream had originated among some liberals and republicans during the first half of the nineteenth century. Its most articulate proponent was Giuseppe Mazzini, a revolutionary from Genoa who envisioned the establishment of a united Italian republic through direct popular action. In his youth Mazzini had been a member of the *Carbonari*, a secret conspiratorial society pledged to drive foreigners out of the Italian states, to secure constitutional liberties, and to bring about some form of Italian unity. His arrest led to one of many periods of exile in London, where he continued to pursue the cause of republicanism and democracy. In 1831 Mazzini founded Italy's first organized political party, Young Italy, which was pledged to realize national unification, democracy, and greater social equality. Mazzini combined a passionate commitment to the ideals of liberalism, republicanism, and nationalism. For him the nation was the highest ideal to which one could pledge devotion, one possessing almost mystical qualities. "We have beheld in Italy," he wrote, "the purpose,

Prostitution, Corporal Punishment, and Liberalism in Germany

In March 1822 Gesche Rudolph, a poor, uneducated twenty-five-year old woman from the northern German city of Bremen, was arrested by municipal authorities for engaging in prostitution without registering with the police. Ever since the days when troops from five different European nations had occupied her neighborhood, Rudolph had been selling her sexual services as her only form of livelihood. After her arrest she was not given a formal trial but was summarily expelled from the city and banned from ever returning. Unable to earn a living through prostitution in a village outside the city, where she resided with a brother who physically abused her, Rudolph returned to the city, where she was arrested once again for prostitution. This time she was sentenced to fifty strokes of the cane and six weeks in jail, after which she was once again expelled from the city. Returning again to Bremen, she was arrested in a drunken stupor in a whorehouse and subjected to a harsher sentence of three months' imprisonment and 150 strokes before another expulsion. This pattern of arrest and punishment, expulsion and return occurred repeatedly during the next two decades, with the number of strokes rising to 275 and the period of imprisonment to six years. During a portion of her prison sentence she was given only bread and water for nourishment.

Rudolph's arrest in 1845 at the end of a six-year imprisonment and her subsequent expulsion and return to Bremen led to the appointment of a liberal lawyer, Georg Wilhelm Gröning, to represent her. After reviewing her case and calculating that she had been whipped a total of 893 times and imprisoned for a cumulative period of eighteen years, Gröning appealed her sentence to the senate of Bremen on the grounds that her treatment was not only futile but immoral. His appeal addressed an issue that went far beyond this particular case or even the prosecution of the crime of prostitution. Gröning's action raised the highly controversial issue of the legitimacy and value of corporal punishment, an issue that divided liberals and conservatives, who had different notions of justice.

Until the eighteenth century the penal systems of Europe had prescribed corporal punishments, administered publicly, for most crimes. These punishments ranged from whippings and placement in the stocks for minor offenses to mutilation, hanging, and decapitation for felonies. They were justified mainly on the grounds that they provided retribution for the crime and deterred the criminal and those who witnessed the punishment from committing further crimes. These two main functions of retribution and deterrence are the same functions that capital punishment allegedly serves today. Corporal punishments were also intended to humiliate the criminal both by violating the integrity of the body and by subjecting the prisoner to the mockery and sometimes the maltreatment of the crowd. The torture of suspects to obtain evidence also served some of these functions, although judicial torture took place during the trial, not as part of the sentence.

The entire system of corporal punishment, as well as that of torture, came under attack during the eighteenth century. In Prussia torture was abolished in 1754, and the General Law Code of 1794 eliminated many forms of corporal punishment. The General Law Code reflected the concern of Enlightenment thinkers that all such assaults on the body were inhumane and a denial of the moral dignity of the individual. Because corporal punishments in Prussia and elsewhere were administered mainly against people from the lower classes, they also were a violation of the liberal principle of equality before the law.

Despite these efforts at reform, the illegal administration of corporal punishment by public and private authorities continued in Prussia and the other German states. Conservatives, who had a different notion of justice from that of the liberals, defended these sentences on the grounds that all punishment, including imprisonment, was intended to deny the criminal freedom and hence his or her dignity. For them any reference to natural rights and human dignity were "axioms derived from abstract philanthropic speculation." The president of the Prussian police, Julius Baron von Minutoli, expressing the conservative position on the issue, claimed that corporal punishment was more effective than imprisonment in preventing crime, since it alone could instill terror in the criminal.

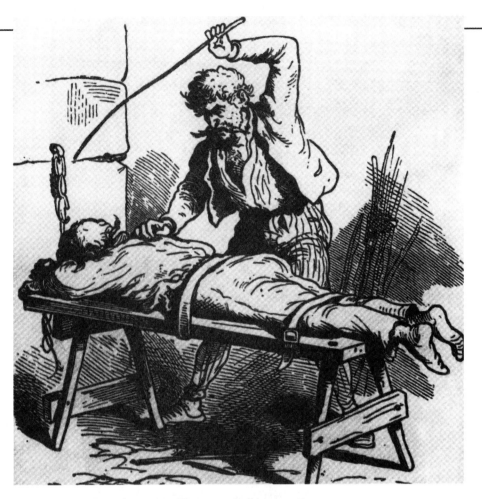

■ **Corporal Punishment in Nineteenth-Century Germany**
Whipping in prisons continued long after public corporal punishment was abolished in the middle of the nineteenth century.

It was apparent that in the case of Gesche Rudolph, 893 strokes had not instilled terror in her or brought about any transformation of her spirit. The Senate made the young woman Gröning's ward and suspended her sentence. Gröning arranged for Rudolph to live in the countryside under the strict supervision of a competent countryman. This compromise solution at least broke the cycle of expulsion, return, and punishment that had failed to reform her. We do not know whether she gave up her life of prostitution.

Soon after Gesche Rudolph became Gröning's ward, the liberal critics of corporal punishment in Germany celebrated a victory. King Frederick William IV of Prussia formally abolished the practice in his kingdom in May 1848. Shortly thereafter the Frankfurt Parliament included freedom from physical punishment by the state in its *Declaration of the Basic Rights of the German People.* Most German states and municipalities, including Bremen, wrote this right into law in 1849. The failure of the Frankfurt Parliament, however, and the more general failure of liberalism in Germany after 1849 led to a strong conservative campaign to reinstate corporal punishment in the 1850s. They succeeded only in maintaining corporal punishment within the family, on manorial estates, and in the prisons. Liberalism had not succeeded in completely establishing its standard of justice, but it did end exposure to public shame as a punishment for crime. ■

Questions of Justice

1. Many societies equate "justice" with the administration of punishments. In what ways were the authorities who whipped and imprisoned Gesche Rudolph upholding a standard of justice?
2. Why did liberals object to corporal punishment?
3. In addition to inflicting physical pain, corporal punishment produces social shame. What is the difference between social shame and legal guilt? In what ways does shame still play a role in punishments today?

Taking It Further

Evans, Richard. *Tales from the German Underworld: Crime and Punishment in the Nineteenth Century.* 1998. Provides a full account of the prosecution of Gesche Rudolph.

the soul, the consolidation of our thoughts, the country chosen of God and oppressed by men."

The ruler who assumed the nationalist mantle in 1848 was Charles Albert of Piedmont-Sardinia, the most economically advanced of the Italian states. This initiative began successfully, as Charles Albert's army, which included volunteers from various parts of Italy, marched into Lombardy and defeated Austrian forces. Instead of moving forward against Austria, however, Charles Albert decided to consolidate his gains, hoping to annex Lombardy to his own kingdom. This decision alienated republicans in Lombardy and in other parts of Italy as well as the rulers of the other Italian states, who feared that Charles Albert's main goal was to expand the limits of his own kingdom at their expense. By August 1848 the military tide had turned. Fresh Austrian troops defeated the Italian nationalists outside Milan. The people of that city turned against Charles Albert, forcing him to return to his own capital of Turin. The Italian revolutions of 1848 had suffered a complete defeat.

The Failure of the Revolutions of 1848

The revolutions of 1848 in France, Germany, the Habsburg Empire, and Italy resulted in victory for conservatives and defeat for liberals, nationalists, and socialists. All the liberal constitutions passed during the early phase of the revolutions were eventually repealed or withdrawn. The high hopes of national unity in Germany, Italy, and Hungary were dashed. Workers who built the barricades in the hope of achieving improvements in their working conditions gained little from their efforts.

Divisions among the different groups that began the revolutions were in large part responsible for their failure. The most serious division—in fact, one that was fatal—was the split between the liberals who formulated the original goals of the revolution and the lower-class participants who took to the streets. Liberals used the support of the masses to bring down the governments they opposed, but their ideological opposition to broad-based political movements and their fear of further disorder sapped their revolutionary fervor. Divisions also emerged between liberals and nationalists, whose goals of national self-determination required different strategies from those of the liberals who supported individual freedom.

The failure of nationalism in the revolutions of 1848 did not, however, portend the death of the ideologies of liberalism, nationalism, and socialism. They all continued to manifest strength during the following two decades, and they often influenced the policies of the conservative governments that returned to power after the revolutions. In Germany, for example, the goal of nationalists was realized under conservative auspices and even mustered a measure of liberal support, while in France liberalism made some inroads into the conservative and nationalist government of the Second French Empire after 1860.

National Unification in Europe and America, 1848–1871

Prior to 1848 the forces of nationalism, especially when combined with those of liberalism, had little to show for their efforts. Besides the Greek rebellion of 1821, which succeeded largely because of international opposition to the Turks, the only successful nationalist revolution in Europe took place in Belgium. Both of these nationalist movements were secessionist in that they involved the separation of smaller states from larger empires. Efforts in 1848 to form nations by combining smaller states and territories, as in Italy and Germany, or by uniting all Slavic people, as proposed at the Pan-Slav Congress, had failed. Between 1848 and 1871, however, movements for national unification succeeded in Italy, Germany, and the United States, each in a different way. In the vast Habsburg Empire a different type of unity was achieved, but it did little to promote the cause of nationalism.

ITALIAN UNIFICATION: BUILDING A FRAGILE NATION-STATE

The great project of Italian nationalists, the unification of Italy, faced formidable obstacles. Austrian military control over the northern territories, which in the end had thwarted the nationalist movement of 1848, meant that national unification would not be achieved peacefully. The dramatic economic disparities between the prosperous north and the much poorer south posed a challenge to any plan for economic integration. A long tradition of local autonomy within the kingdoms, states, and principalities made submission to a strong central government unappealing. The unique status of the papacy, which controlled its own territory and which influenced the decisions of many other states, served as another challenge. Despite these obstacles, the dream of a resurgence of Italian power, reviving the achievements of ancient Rome, had great emotive appeal. Hatred of foreigners who controlled Italian territory, which dates back to the fifteenth century, gave further impetus to the nationalist movement.

The main question for Italian nationalism after the failure of 1848 was who could provide effective leadership of the movement. It stood to reason that Piedmont-Sardinia, the strongest and most prosperous Italian kingdom, would be central to that undertaking. Unfortunately the king, Victor Emmanuel II (r. 1849–1861), was more known for his hunting, his carousing, and his affair with a teenage mistress than his statesmanship. Victor Emmanuel did, however, appoint as his prime minister a nobleman with liberal leanings, Count Camillio di Cavour (1810–1861). Cavour displayed many of the characteristics of nineteenth-

■ Map 21.2   The Unification of Italy, 1859–1870
The main steps to unification took place in 1860, when Piedmont-Sardinia acquired Tuscany, Parma, Modena, and the Romagna and when Garibaldi seized control of the Kingdom of the Two Sicilies in the name of King Victor Emmanuel of Piedmont-Sardinia.

century liberalism. He favored a constitutional monarchy, the restriction of clerical privilege and influence, and the development of a capitalist and industrial economy. He was deeply committed to the unification of the Italian peninsula, but only under Piedmontese leadership, and preferably as a federation of states. In many ways he was the antithesis of the republican Mazzini, the other central figure in Italian unification. Mazzini's idealism and romanticism led him to think of national unification as a moral force that would lead to the establishment of a democratic republic, which would then undertake an extensive program of social reform. Mazzini often wore black, claiming that he was in mourning for the unrealized cause of unification.

Mazzini's strategy for national unification involved a succession of uprisings and invasions. Cavour, however, adopted a diplomatic course of action intended to gain the military assistance of France against Austria. In 1859 French and Piedmontese forces defeated the Austrians at Magenta and Solferino and drove them out of Lombardy. One year later Napoleon III signed the Treaty of Turin with Cavour, allowing Piedmont-Sardinia to annex Tuscany, Parma, Modena, and the Romagna, while ceding to France the Italian territories of Savoy and Nice. This treaty resulted in the unification of all of northern and central Italy except Venetia in the northeast and the Papal States in the center of the peninsula (see Map 21.2).

The main focus of unification efforts now turned to the Kingdom of the Two Sicilies in the south. A rebellion against the Bourbon monarch Francis II, protesting new taxes and the high price of bread, had taken place there in 1860. At that point the militant republican adventurer Giuseppe Garibaldi (1807–1882) intervened with decisive force. Garibaldi, who was born in Nice and spoke French rather than Italian as his main language, was determined no less than Cavour and Mazzini to drive all foreigners out of Italy and achieve its unification. Originally a supporter of Mazzini's republican goals, Garibaldi gave his support in the 1860s for Italian unification within the framework of a monarchy. A charismatic military leader, Garibaldi put together an army of volunteers, known as the Red Shirts for their colorful makeshift uniforms. In 1860 he landed in Sicily with an army of 1,000 men, took the main Sicilian city of Palermo, and established a dictatorship on behalf of King Victor Emmanuel. He then landed on the mainland and took Naples. Shortly thereafter the people of Naples, Sicily, and most of the Papal States voted their support for union with Piedmont-Sardinia. In March 1861 the king of Sardinia assumed the title of King Victor Emmanuel of Italy (r. 1861–1878). Complete unification was achieved when Austria ceded Venetia to Italy in 1866 and when French troops, which had been protecting a portion of the Papal States, withdrew from Rome in 1870.

The unification of Italy owed more to the statecraft of Cavour than the passion of Mazzini and Garibaldi. Their achievement did not fully realize the lofty nationalist goals of creating a culturally unified people or a powerful central state. Economic differences between northern and southern Italy became even greater after unification than before. The overwhelming majority of the people continued to speak their local dialects or even French rather than Italian. Traditions of local political autonomy and resentment against the concentration of wealth in the north retarded the development of loyalty to the new Italian state and inspired a series of bloody rebellions in the former Kingdom of the Two Sicilies during the 1870s and 1880s.

This instability was aggravated by the widespread practice of banditry in the southern mainland. Bandits were peasants who, in the hope of maintaining a world that appeared to be vanishing, swept through towns, opened jails, stole from the wealthy, and sacked their houses. Closely related to banditry was the growth in Sicily of the Mafia°, organizations of armed men who took control of local politics and the economy. The Mafia originated during the struggle for unification in the 1860s and strengthened their position in Sicily once the country had been unified. Their power, the prevalence of banditry, and the enduring strength of Italian loyalty to the local community all made it difficult for the new Italian state to flourish. The movement for national unification had driven the French and the Austrians out of the peninsula, but it had failed to create a model nation-state.

GERMAN UNIFICATION: CONSERVATIVE NATION-BUILDING

Like Italy, Germany experienced a successful movement for national unification after the disappointments of 1848. The German movement, like the Italian, benefited from the actions of crafty statesmen and from the decisions made by other states. Unlike Italy, however, Germany achieved unification under the direction of highly conservative rather than liberal forces. One reason for this was that the severity of the reaction to the Revolution of 1848 had forced the emigration of many German liberals and nationalists to Great Britain and the Netherlands and as far west as the hill country of central Texas. Nevertheless a number of liberals, such as those who belonged to a Pan-German association known as the National Union, still kept alive the hopes of the Frankfurt Parliament for a German constitutional republic.

■ **Giuseppe Garibaldi**
The uniform he is wearing was derived from his days as a guerilla fighting in the civil war in Uruguay, 1842–1846. Garibaldi also spent two years in asylum in the United States.

The main dilemma regarding German unification was whether Prussia or Austria would form the nucleus of any new political structure. In the end, Prussia, with its almost entirely German-speaking population, its wealth, and its strong army, assumed leadership of the movement. The key figure in this process was Count Otto von Bismarck (1815–1898), a lawyer and bureaucrat from an old *Junker* family whom King William I of Prussia appointed as his prime minister in 1862. By birth, training, and instinct Bismarck was an inflexible conservative, determined to preserve and strengthen the Prussian nobility and monarchy and to make the Prussian state strong and powerful. In the words of the liberal British ambassador to Berlin, Robert Morier, "not one mustard seed of faith in liberal principles exists in Count Bismarck's nature." Bismarck did not hesitate, however, to make alliances with any political party, including the liberals, to achieve his goals. This subordination of political means to their ends, and Bismarck's willingness to use whatever tactics were necessary, regardless of any moral considerations, made him a proponent of *Realpolitik*, the adoption of political tactics solely on the basis of their realistic chances of success.

Bismarck pursued the goal of national unification through the exercise of raw military and political power. "The great questions of the time," he said in 1862, "are not determined by speeches and majority decisions—that was the error of 1848 and 1849—but by iron and blood." Bismarck did not share the romantic devotion of other German nationalists to the fatherland or their desire to have a state that embodied the spirit of the German people. His determination to achieve German national unification became synonymous with his goal of strengthening the Prussian state. This commitment to the supremacy of Prussia within a united Germany explains his steadfast exclusion of the other great German power, Austria, from his plans for national unification.

Bismarck's achievement of German unification was based mainly on Prussian success in two wars (see Map 21.3). The first, the Austro-Prussian War of 1866, resulted in the formation of a new union of twenty-two states, the North German Confederation. This new structure replaced the old German Confederation, the loose association of thirty-nine states, including Austria, that had been established in 1815 by the Congress of Vienna. The North German Confederation had a centralized political structure with its own legislature, the *Reichstag;* the king of Prussia became its president and Bismarck its chancellor. The foundation of the North German Confederation was, however, only one step toward the unification of all Germany. Bismarck laid the foundation for the realization of this larger goal by strengthening the *Zollverein,* which included the southern German states. By encouraging free trade among all the German states he also won support for unification from German liberals.

■ **Otto von Bismarck, Chancellor of Prussia**
Bismarck used state power to achieve the unification of Germany. He became known as the "iron chancellor," a reference to his exercise of raw political power.

The second war, which completed the unification of Germany, was the Franco-Prussian War of 1870–1871. This conflict began when Napoleon III, the French emperor, challenged Prussian efforts to place a member of the Prussian royal family on the vacant Spanish throne. Bismarck welcomed this opportunity to take on the French, who controlled German-speaking territories on their eastern frontier and who had cultivated alliances with the southern German states. Bismarck played his diplomatic cards brilliantly, guaranteeing that the Russians, Austrians, and British would not support France. He then used the army that he had modernized to invade France and seize the towns of Metz and Sedan. The capture of Napoleon III during this military offensive precipitated the end of France's Second Empire and the establishment of the Third French Republic in September 1870.

As a result of the war Prussia annexed the predominantly German-speaking territories of Alsace and Lorraine. Much more important, it led to the proclamation of the German Empire with William I of Prussia as emperor.

Officially the structure of the new empire, a term used to indicate that it embraced many separate states, was that of a federation, just like that of the North German Confederation that preceded it. In fact the government of the empire, like that of Prussia, was highly centralized as well as autocratic, and the liberal middle classes did not participate in it, as they did in the governments of Britain, France, and Italy. The German imperial government won the support of the middle class by adopting policies supporting free trade, but the ideologies that underpinned the new German Empire were those of conservatism and na-

tionalism, which encouraged devotion to "God, King, and Fatherland."

UNIFICATION IN THE UNITED STATES: CREATING A NATION OF NATIONS

At the same time that Italy and Germany were achieving national unification, the United States of America engaged in a bitter process that preserved and strengthened the federal union it had instituted in 1787. The thirteen colonies

■ **Map 21.3   The Unification of Germany, 1866–1871**
Prussia assumed leadership in uniting all German territories except Austria. Prussia was responsible for the formation of the North German Confederation in 1866 and the German Empire in 1871.

The Unification of Germany, 1866–1871

▨	Prussia before 1866
▨	Conquered by Prussia in Austro-Prussian War, 1866
▨	Austrian territories excluded from North German Confederation, 1867
▨	Joined with Prussia to form North German Confederation, 1867
▨	South German states joining with Prussia to form German Empire, 1871
▨	Won by Prussia in Franco-Prussian War, 1871
✕	Major battles
——	German Confederation boundary, 1815–1866
——	Bismarck's German Empire, 1871

that proclaimed their independence from Great Britain in 1776 shared common constitutional grievances against the mother country or metropolis, but each colony had its own identity. The U.S. Constitution, drawn up in 1787, sought to preserve this balance between the states and the federal government by dividing sovereignty between them, leaving to the states control over all matters it had not specifically given to the federal government. This arrangement generated friction and debate between the Federalists, who wished to strengthen the central government, and the Anti-Federalists, who feared that a strong central government would lead to corrupt, arbitrary rule. The Federalists won some early victories, including the establishment of a national bank, but they were unable to create a truly united people. The great victory of the Anti-Federalists was the Bill of Rights, the first ten amendments to the U.S. constitution, which was ratified by the states in 1791. By enumerating the rights of the citizens in a formal constitution, including freedom of speech and freedom of assembly, the Bill of Rights embodied one of the main elements of liberal ideology.

Throughout the early years of the republic Americans continued to think of themselves as citizens of particular states more than as members of a single national community. In the early nineteenth century, President Thomas Jefferson (1801–1809) imagined a new American nation, a people "with one heart and one mind," but nationalist sentiment, such as had developed in European countries on the basis of a common language and culture, had difficulty materializing in the United States. The American republic was originally the product of English-speaking colonists who shared the same language and culture as the British against whom they had rebelled. After the revolution, efforts were made to build a new nation on the basis of a distinctly American culture. *The American Dictionary of the English Language,* compiled by Noah Webster (1758–1843) in 1812, made one contribution to this endeavor by listing thousands of American words that had never been included in English dictionaries. Patriotic sentiment, especially after the defeat of British forces at the battle of New Orleans in 1815, also helped to give Americans a sense of common purpose and destiny.

These efforts at building an American nation became more challenging as the young republic began to incorporate Western territories into the federal union. Lands acquired by purchase or conquest were formed into territories and then gradually admitted into the union as states. This process of unification, which proceeded in a piecemeal fashion, took much longer than the unifications of Italy and Germany in the 1860s. It was marked by sustained military action against the Native American population and a war against Mexico between 1846 and 1848. Florida was annexed in 1819, while Texas, an independent republic for nine years, was admitted in 1845 and California in 1850. This process of gradual unification did not end until 1912,

when New Mexico and Arizona, the last territories in the contiguous forty-eight states, were admitted to the union.

As the United States expanded westward into the Spanish-speaking Southwest, and as immigrants from various European nations swelled the population of the eastern as well as the western states, the country became more rather than less culturally diverse. Assimilation to a dominant Protestant English-speaking culture, even one that was gradually becoming distinct from that of Great Britain, could not provide the same commitment to the homeland that inspired Italians and Germans to support national unification. Americans might be patriotic, in that they proclaimed their allegiance to the federal republic, but they had more difficulty thinking that they shared a common culture with the people from different parts of the country. Building a nation-state in America was a task fraught with obstacles.

The great test of American national unity came during the 1860s, when eleven southern states, committed to the preservation of the economic system of slavery, and determined that it should be extended into new territories acquired by the federal government, seceded from the union and formed a confederation of their own. The issue of slavery had helped to polarize North and South, creating deep cultural and ideological divisions that made the goal of national unity appear even more distant. America had its own ideological and cultural encounters that paralleled those that prevailed in European countries.

The constitutional issue underlying the civil war was the preservation of the union. In a famous speech President Abraham Lincoln (1861–1865) declared that "a house divided against itself cannot stand . . . this government cannot endure permanently half slave and half free." When the war ended, and slavery was abolished, that union was not only preserved but strengthened. Amendments to the U.S. Constitution provided for equal protection of all citizens under the law. The South, which had its own regional economy, was integrated into the increasingly commercial and industrial North. The whole process of national unification, both economic and social, was greatly facilitated by the building of railways. In the United States, even more than in Europe, railroads linked otherwise isolated communities and facilitated the spread of products and ideas across vast distances. Gradually the people of the United States began to think of themselves as a united people, drawn from many different nations of the world. The United States became "a nation of nations."

NATIONALISM IN EASTERN EUROPE: PRESERVING MULTINATIONAL EMPIRES

The national unifications that took place in Germany, Italy, and the United States formed part of a *western* European pattern in which the main units of political organization

■ **Map 21.4 Nationalities Within the Habsburg Empire**
The large number of different nationalities within the Habsburg Empire made it impossible to accommodate the demands of all nationalities for their own state.

would be nation-states. Ethnic minorities would of course always live within the boundaries of these states, but the state itself would encourage the growth of a national identity among all its citizens. We can observe this process at work in France, Britain, and Spain, all of which had undergone a process of national unification before the nineteenth century. Minority populations within these large western European states have occasionally threatened to establish a separate political identity as nations, but with the one notable exception of Ireland, the southern portion of which became independent of Britain in the twentieth century, the large states of western Europe have maintained their unity and promoted nationalist sentiment to sustain it.

In *eastern* Europe a very different pattern prevailed, especially in the Habsburg and Russian Empires. Instead of becoming unified nation-states, these two empires remained large, multinational political formations, embracing many different nationalities. This pattern was most obvious in the large, sprawling Habsburg Empire, which encompassed no fewer than twenty different ethnic groups, each of which thought of itself as a nation (see Map 21.4). The largest of these nationalities were the Germans in Austria and Bohemia and the Magyars in Hungary, but the Czechs, Slovaks, Poles, Slovenes, Croats, Rumanians, Bulgarians, and Italians (before 1866) all formed sizable minority populations. Map 21.4 only begins to reveal the full complexity of this diversity. The various nationalities

within the empire had little in common except loyalty to the Habsburg emperor, who defended the Catholic faith and the privileges of the nobility. National unification of the empire would have presented a much more formidable task than the ones that confronted Cavour and Bismarck.

During the era of national unification the ideology of nationalism threatened to tear apart this precariously unified empire. It awakened demands of Hungarians, Czechs, and others for national autonomy and also spawned a movement for the national unity of all Slavs. The emperor, Francis Joseph, recognized the danger of nationalist ideology. He also feared that liberalism, which was often linked to nationalism, would at the same time undermine his authority, which he had reasserted with a vengeance after the failure of the revolutions of 1848. He therefore repressed these nationalist aspirations at every turn. This policy had disastrous consequences for the future history of Europe, since Slavic nationalism and separatism have remained a source of political instability of southeastern Europe until the present day.

The one concession that Francis Joseph did make during this volatile period was to establish the Dual Monarchy of Austria-Hungary in 1867. This significant increase of Hungarian power within the empire came in the wake of the disastrous defeats of Austrian forces by the French and Piedmontese in 1859 and the Prussians in 1866. Austrian liberals took this opportunity to call for the introduction of constitutional government, while the second-largest ethnic group within the empire, the Magyars, demanded more autonomy for Hungary. The *Ausgleich* (Settlement) of 1867, which was proposed by the wealthy Hungarian nobleman and lawyer Ferenc Deák (1803–1876), created a dual monarchy in which Francis Joseph would be both king of Hungary and emperor of Austria. Each monarchy would have its own parliament and bureaucracy, although matters of foreign policy and finance would be handled in Vienna. This arrangement represented a concession to Magyar nationalism but gave very little to all the other nationalities within both kingdoms. The *Ausgleich* officially recognized the equality of all nationalities within the empire, and allowed schooling to be conducted in the local language, but it permitted only Germans in Austria and Magyars in Hungary to acquire their own political identity. Instead of a unified nation-state the emperor now presided over two multinational monarchies.

Ideology, Empire, and the Balance of Power

The new ideologies of the early nineteenth century, and the movements for national unification to which they gave rise, had a disruptive impact on the conduct of international affairs. The original framework for international action after 1815 was the Concert of Europe, which was intended to prevent the recurrence of revolution and preserve the balance of power. It achieved much greater success in pursuing the second goal than it did the first. The five European powers in the Concert—Britain, Austria, Russia, Prussia, and France—could never contain the liberal and national forces that the French Revolution had unleashed, but as a group the five powers prevented any one of them from establishing a dominant position in Europe.

Challenges to the balance of power during this period came mainly from governments engaged in a process of imperial expansion. The first of these challenges arose in the Western Hemisphere during the 1820s, the second occurred in the 1850s in the Balkans, and the third took place after the Franco-Prussian War of 1870–1871.

BRITAIN, THE UNITED STATES, AND THE MONROE DOCTRINE OF 1823

In North America a clash of empires threatened to engulf European powers in a new round of imperial expansion and warfare during the early 1820s. As Spanish power in the Western Hemisphere began to collapse, the young republic of the United States feared that Austria or France might intervene in the new Latin American nations. The United

States was also alarmed about Russian expansion down the western coast of North America, as we have discussed in Chapter 19. In order to prevent imperial expansion by any of these European powers, the United Sates found an ally in Britain, which even after the loss of the thirteen North American colonies still ruled a large empire of its own in Canada, the Caribbean, and South America. Britain did not wish to compromise the dominant influence it exercised in this area.

British and U.S. resistance to continental European imperialism in the Western hemisphere had a foundation in liberal ideology. The United States, with its constitutional protection of individual liberty and its success in achieving national self-determination in the American Revolution, had become the very embodiment of European liberalism. No wonder it supported the independence of Latin American nations on ideological as well as diplomatic grounds. In Britain, as we have already seen, the liberal tradition was stronger than in other parts of Europe. Britain's liberal heritage also helps to explain its refusal to join the Holy Alliance of 1815. The British government viewed the Concert of Europe as a mechanism for preserving the balance of power, not for supporting autocratic regimes.

In 1823, President James Monroe (1817–1825) declared that the United States would consider any future attempts by European powers to colonize the Americas as hostile acts. The enforcement of this policy, which became known as the Monroe Doctrine, depended mainly on the support of the British navy, since the United States was not yet capable of taking on the powers of Europe by itself. During the next ten years Britain provided that naval support.

The main effect of the Monroe Doctrine, and Britain's enforcement of it, was to preserve the balance of power in the Western Hemisphere. The doctrine also created the concept of two hemispheres, one old and one new, each refraining from interference in each other's affairs. The broader ideological significance of the Monroe Doctrine was that it provided support for liberalism and nationalism both in Europe and in the Americas. Monroe's speech made explicit reference to the opposition of the United States to the repressive political systems of the allied powers, support for the liberal revolutions that had taken place in Spain and Portugal in 1820, and approval of the revolutions against Spanish rule in Latin America.

RUSSIA, THE OTTOMAN EMPIRE, AND THE CRIMEAN WAR, 1853–1856

The second major challenge to the balance of power occurred as a result of Russian imperial ambitions in the Balkans, resulting in the first major war among European powers since the defeat of Napoleon at Waterloo in 1815. The Crimean War (1853–1856), which claimed almost a million casualties on all sides, was the direct result of Russian imperial expansion. It began when Russia occupied the principalities of Moldavia and Wallachia (present-day Romania) in the Ottoman Empire in order to gain access to the Straits of Constantinople and thus to the Aegean and Mediterranean seas. The weakness of the Ottoman Empire had invited Russian expansion into this area, which Russians justified by claiming they were protecting the Orthodox Christianity of people in the Balkans from their Turkish Muslim oppressors. They also claimed that they were promoting the national unity of all Slavic people under Russian auspices. This Russian version of Pan-Slavism differed from that developed by Czech Slavs at the Pan-Slav Congress of 1848. In effect it was an extreme form of Russian imperialism that rivaled the nationalism of individual Slavic nationalities.

Britain resisted the Russian occupation of Moldavia and Wallachia, ostensibly to protect its trade with the Turks but more urgently to prevent Russia from becoming too powerful. In this respect it was adhering to the principles of the Concert of Europe by trying to preserve the balance of power in Europe. The underlying British fear was that Russia might invade India, Britain's most important colony. When the Turks declared war on the Russians, therefore, the British followed suit and were joined by the French. Both powers sent large armies to begin a siege of the port of Sebastopol on the Black Sea.

The poorly trained British forces, commanded by officers who had purchased their commissions and who had no sound knowledge of military tactics, suffered staggering losses, more of them from disease than from battle. The most senseless episode of the war occurred when a British cavalry unit, the Light Brigade, rode into a deep valley, only to be cut down by Russian artillery perched on the surrounding hills. The slaughter was memorialized in a poem by the British poet Alfred Lord Tennyson (1850–1892), "The Charge of the Light Brigade."

Nevertheless, the British, French, and Turks prevailed, handing Russia its most humiliating defeat of the nineteenth century. The defeat led to a curtailment of Russian expansion for the next twenty years and preserved the balance of power in Europe. Within Russia the defeat contributed to a crisis that led to a series of liberal reforms during the rule of Tsar Alexander II (1855–1881). Alexander, an indecisive man who had inherited the throne in the middle of the Crimean War, was hardly a liberal (he once referred to the French system of government as "vile"), but he did yield to mounting liberal pressure to emancipate the serfs in 1861, a step that occurred two years before the emancipation of slaves in the United States.

THE GERMAN EMPIRE AND THE PARIS COMMUNE, 1870–1871

A third, and in the long run the most serious, challenge to the balance of power in Europe came from Prussia. As we have seen, Prussian victories over Austria in 1866 and France in 1871 allowed Bismarck to complete the unification of Germany. The newly created German Empire, which now possessed the strongest army in Europe, replaced Austria as the predominant power in central Europe. The growth of German military power, coupled with its expansionist territorial ambitions, soon made it a formidable rival to other European countries and threatened to upset the delicate balance of power. In the twentieth century Germany's territorial ambitions led ultimately to two world wars.

German military success in the Franco-Prussian War of 1870–1871 played a crucial role in French politics, exposing the complex ideological contradictions of the Second French Empire and laying the groundwork for the Third French Republic. After Napoleon III had established the Second Empire in 1852, he tried to mask his usurpation of power by preserving the tradition of universal male suffrage and by submitting his rule to popular ratification, just as his uncle had done. During the 1860s his government became known as "the Liberal Empire," a strange mixture of conservatism, liberalism, and nationalism. Although "the little Napoleon" ruled as an emperor, he gradually allowed a semblance of real parliamentary government to return, relaxed the censorship of the press, and encouraged industrial development. To this mixture he added a strong dose of nationalist sentiment by evoking the memory of Napoleon I.

These efforts failed to save Napoleon III's regime. His moderate liberal policies angered conservatives on the one hand and failed to satisfy the demands of republicans and socialists on the other. These complex ideological encounters came to a head in 1870 during the Franco-Prussian War, which Napoleon himself was in large part responsible for starting. Napoleon took the field at the Battle of Sedan and was captured. The Prussians allowed him to go into exile in England, where he lived until his death in 1873. On September 4, 1870, a large crowd invaded the Legislative Assembly in Paris and forced the deputies who still remained to join them in declaring the end of the Second Empire and the beginning of the Third Republic. Shortly thereafter Prussian troops surrounded Paris and began a long siege of the city, forcing hungry city dwellers to eat cats and dogs roaming the streets and an elephant seized from the Paris zoo.

In January 1871 Adolphe Thiers (1797–1877), a veteran statesman who had served as prime minister during the liberal government of the 1830s, negotiated an armistice with Bismarck. Thiers hoped to establish a conservative republican regime or possibly a restoration of the monarchy at the conclusion of the war. This prospect gained strength when elections to the new National Assembly, which Bismarck permitted so that the French legislature could conclude a formal peace treaty, returned a majority of monarchists. The National Assembly then elected Thiers as president of the provisional government.

■ **Execution of Paris Communards, May 1871**
Troops of the provisional French government killed at least 25,000 Parisians during the uprising.

The National Assembly, which sat at Bordeaux, and the provisional government, which took up residence at Versailles, were determined to assert their authority over the entire French nation. In particular, they wanted to curb the independence of the city of Paris, which was determined to carry on the struggle against Prussia and to keep alive the French radical tradition that had flourished in the city in 1792 and again in 1848. The radicalism of the Paris Commune drew its strength from the large working-class population in the industrialized districts on the northern, eastern, and southern edges of the city. The socialist and republican ideals of the Commune's leaders, coupled with their determination to preserve the independence of the city, culminated in the bloodshed described at the beginning of this chapter. The crushing of the Commune marked a bitter defeat for the forces of French socialism and radicalism. The Third French Republic that was established in September 1870 endured, but its ideological foundation was conservative nationalism, not liberalism or socialism.

CONCLUSION
The Ideological Transformation of the West

The ideological encounters that took place between 1815 and 1871 resulted in significant changes in the political culture of the West. As the early nineteenth-century ideologies of liberalism, conservatism, socialism, and nationalism played out in political movements and revolutions, the people who subscribed to these ideologies often redefined their political objectives. Many British and French socialists, for example, recognizing the necessity of assistance from liberals, abandoned their call for creating a classless society and sought instead to increase wages and improve working conditions of the lower classes. The demands of so-cialists for greater economic equality pressured liberals to accept the need for more state intervention in the economy. The realities of conservative politics led liberal nationalists in Germany and Italy to accept newly formed nation-states that were more authoritarian than they had originally hoped to establish. Recognizing the strength of the ideologies to which they were opposed, conservative rulers like Emperor Napoleon III and Tsar Alexander II agreed to adopt liberal reforms. Liberals, conservatives, socialists, and nationalists would continue to modify and adjust their political and ideological positions during the period of mass politics, which began in 1870 and which will be the subject of the next chapter.

The Western ideologies that underwent this process of adaptation and modification had a broad influence on world history. In the twentieth century, three of the four ideologies discussed in this chapter have inspired political change in parts of the world that lie outside the geographical and cultural boundaries of the West. Liberalism has provided the language for movements seeking to establish fundamental civil liberties in India, Japan, and several African countries. In its radical communist form, socialism inspired revolutions in Russia, a country which for many centuries had straddled the boundary between East and West, and in China. Nationalism has revealed its explosive potential in countries as diverse as Nepal, Thailand, and Zaire. Ever since the nineteenth century, Western ideologies have demonstrated a capacity both to shape and to adapt to a variety of political and social political circumstances.

Suggestions for Further Reading

For a comprehensive list of suggested readings, please go to www.ablongman.com/levack/chapter21

Anderson, Benedict. *Imagined Communities: Reflections on the Origin and Spread of Nationalism.* 1991. A discussion of the ways in which people conceptualize the nation.

Clark, Martin. *The Italian Risorgimento.* 1999. A comprehensive study of the social, economic, and religious context of Italian unification as well as its political and diplomatic dimensions.

Gellner, Ernest. *Nations and Nationalism.* 1983. An interpretive study that emphasizes the social roots of nationalism.

Hamerow, Theodore S. *Restoration, Revolution, Reaction: Economics and Politics in Germany, 1815–1871.* 1966. An investigation of the social basis of ideological encounters in Germany.

Honour, Hugh. *Romanticism.* 1979. A comprehensive study of romantic painting.

Hunczak, Tara, ed. *Russian Imperialism from Ivan the Great to the Revolution.* 1974. A collection of essays that illuminate Russian nationalism as well as imperialism over a long period of time.

Lichtheim, George. *A Short History of Socialism.* 1970. A good general treatment of the subject.

Nipperdey, Thomas. *Germany from Napoleon to Bismarck, 1800–1866.* 1996. An exploration of the creation of German nationalism as well as the failure of liberalism.

Onuf, Peter S. *Jefferson's Empire: The Language of American Nationhood.* 2000. A study of Jefferson's expansionary nationalism.

Pflanze, Otto. *Bismarck and the Development of Germany: The Period of Unification, 1815–1871.* 1963. The classic study of both Bismarck and the unification movement.

Pinckney, David. *The French Revolution of 1830.* 1972. The best treatment of this revolution.

Seton-Watson, Hugh. *Nations and States.* 1977. A clearly written study of the nation-state.

Sperber, Jonathan. *The European Revolutions, 1848–1851.* 1994. The best study of the revolutions of 1848.

Tombs, Robert. *The War Against Paris, 1871.* 1981. A narrative history of the Paris Commune.

The Coming of Mass Politics: Industrialization, Emancipation, and Instability, 1870–1914

I N THE SPRING OF 1881, A HARROWING SCENE TOOK PLACE IN ST. PETERSBURG, CAPI-
tal of the vast Russian Empire. A 28-year-old woman, Sofiia Perovskaia, was
scheduled to be executed for her part in the assassination of Tsar Alexander II.
Born into the ranks of wealth and privilege, Perovskaia had rejected her traditional role in order to join the revolutionary socialist movement. She became a
leader of the People's Will, a small revolutionary group that sought to undermine
the tsarist regime through a program of sabotage and assassination. These revolutionaries dared to set their sights on assassinating the tsar himself, and on
March 1, 1881, they achieved this goal. Led by Perovskaia, six People's Will members (all under age 30) stationed themselves at prearranged points along the
streets of St. Petersburg. At Perovskaia's signal, they released their bombs and assassinated one of the most powerful men in Europe.

Despite the death of the tsar and the audacity of the crime, however, the
tsarist regime did not crumble. The six assassins were quickly arrested and sentenced to death by hanging. (One of the six was pregnant and therefore allowed
to live.) On the day of Perovskaia's execution, she mounted the scaffold calmly,
but when the noose was placed around her neck, she grabbed hold of the platform below with her feet. It took the strength of two men to pry her feet loose so
that she could hang.

The image of Sofiia Perovskaia clinging to the platform with her bare feet
while her two executioners strained to push her to her death captures the ferocity
of political struggle not only in Russia but throughout Europe at the end of the
nineteenth century. As Chapter 21 explained, the ideological competition among
liberalism, conservatism, socialism, and nationalism shaped the political culture
of the West in the nineteenth century. Economic developments after 1870 both
intensified and widened this competition. Individuals and groups that had traditionally been excluded from power demanded a voice in political affairs. Even in

Chapter Outline

- Economic Transformation

- Defining the Political Nation

- Broadening the Political Nation

- Outside the Political Nation? The Experience of Women

Mass Society on the Move: European immigrants arriving in the United States, New York Harbor, 1906.

authoritarian Russia, the political nation could not long remain the preserve of the titled and wealthy. Neither economic modernization nor the coming of mass politics ensured the victory of democracy, however. Like Sofiia Perovskaia's executioners, the governing classes often struggled hard to pry newcomers off the platform of political power—and they often won.

Four questions will structure our exploration of this period: (1) How did the economic transformation of Europe after 1870 help shape the encounters between established political elites and newcomers to the political process? (2) How did the ruling classes of the Western powers respond to the new threats and opportunities provided by mass political participation? (3) What was the relationship between modern nationalism and the emergence of mass politics? (4) In what ways did the emergence of feminism in this period demonstrate the potential as well as the limits of political change?

Economic Transformation

Europe's political development between 1870 and 1914 is inextricably linked to its economic transformation. Four important economic developments helped shape European actions and attitudes during these years: the onset of economic depression in 1873, the expansion of the Industrial Revolution into new geographic regions and economic sectors, the emergence of new patterns in the production and consumption of industrial goods, and accelerated urbanization and immigration. Together, these developments not only altered the daily life of the ordinary European, they also exacerbated social tensions and accelerated political change. The resulting series of often violent encounters within societies helped transform the political structures and ideologies of the West.

ECONOMIC DEPRESSION

In 1873, Europe's economy tilted sharply downward—prices, interest rates, and profits all fell, and remained low in many regions until the mid-1890s. Contemporaries referred to this as the Great Depression in Trade and Agriculture°. In hindsight, "Great Depression" may seem an inaccurate label for a period that saw a continuing rise in world production and growing levels of foreign investment in new industrial economies, but to many Europeans living in these decades, this Great Depression seemed depressing indeed. Agriculture was hardest hit of all economic sectors. By the 1890s, the price of wheat had fallen to only one-third of what it had been in the 1860s. Farm owners and laborers across Europe found it difficult to remain on the land and make a living. Business, too, faced hard times after 1873.

Profit margins were squeezed as the prices of finished products fell, often by as much as 50 percent, while labor and production costs tended to remain much more static.

What caused this depression? Ironically, it was rooted in the very success of the Industrial Revolution. The development of the steamship and the expansion of railway lines across Europe and the United States sharply reduced the cost of transporting both agricultural and industrial goods. Cheaper transportation costs opened the breadbaskets of the American Midwest and Ukraine to European consumption. With wheat and other agricultural goods now flooding the market, farmers were forced to accept increasingly lower prices for their products. More generally, as regions and nations industrialized, they of course produced more goods. Yet many industrial workers, agricultural laborers, and landowning peasants still stood on the very edge of subsistence, with little money to spend on industrial products. In other words, by the 1870s, a mass consumer society had not yet emerged. Thus in many regions of Europe production exceeded consumption, and the result was a long-term agricultural and industrial depression.

INDUSTRIAL EXPANSION

The onset and impact of economic depression is, then, closely linked to the second important economic development of this period—the continued expansion of the Industrial Revolution. As Chapter 20 detailed, the period between 1760 and 1860 saw gradual, spotty, but still dramatic changes in economic production, first in Britain, then in portions of western Europe. But throughout much of the nineteenth century many of the inhabitants of central, eastern, and southern Europe continued to live and work in ways not far removed from those of their great-grandparents. They used simple horse- or oxen-drawn plows, they harvested with scythes fueled by their own arms and backs, they celebrated births and mourned deaths with rituals embedded in centuries-old peasant cultures. And they had little contact with unsettling ideas as high rates of illiteracy continued—almost 90 percent in some rural regions of the Austrian Empire, for example.

This cultural and economic isolation was breaking down by the time World War I erupted in 1914. Railways, which increasingly linked Europe's diverse regions into a single economic network, played a crucial role. Between 1870 and 1914 the world's rail network grew by 500 percent. In the 1880s, agriculture still employed the majority of Europe's population in all countries except Britain, Belgium, France, the Netherlands, and Switzerland, but even peasants still farming in traditional ways were caught up in the momentum of the industrial economy.

Imperial Russia serves as a good example of the breakdown of social and cultural isolation. By 1914 Russia had developed a significant industrial zone, one that tied it more closely than ever before to Western economic struc-

■ **Pre-Industrial Continuities**

This photograph of French peasant women taking time off for a meal highlights the patchy nature of industrialization even in western Europe. Not until the 1880s and 1890s did many rural regions come within the embrace of the modern industrial economy.

tures. In the 1890s, Russia underwent dramatic industrialization under the leadership of Sergei Witte (1849–1915), Alexander III's finance minister. Before serving the tsar in this capacity, Witte had a successful career in the railway industry. He used this experience to carry out a program of planned economic development. The state-owned railway network doubled in size. This impressive engineering achievement, which included the 5,000-mile Trans-Siberian railway (begun in 1891), accelerated the movement of both goods and laborers across the vast expanse of Russian territory. Witte also placed Russia on the gold standard, making the Russian ruble easily convertible into other currencies and so fostering international trade. High taxes and protective tariffs generated some of the capital to fuel industrial expansion, but foreign investment was also crucial. French, British, German, and Belgian capital poured into Russia, up from 98 million rubles in 1880 to 911 million by 1900. By the turn of the century, as a result of such policies, Russian steel production was ranked fourth worldwide, behind only Britain, Germany, and the United States And Russia supplied 50 percent of the oil used by the industrialized world. Coal mines and steel mills dotted Ukraine, and huge state-run factories dominated Moscow and St. Petersburg.

THE SECOND INDUSTRIAL REVOLUTION

The expansion of the Industrial Revolution coincided with a shift in the processes of industrialization itself. The decades after 1870 witnessed a new phase in the techniques and technologies of both production and consumption, a phase that some historians regard as so important that they call it the "Second Industrial Revolution°." Mechanical processes were altered with the development of more specialized lathes and the mechanization of tasks such as grinding that had previously been completed by hand. By the late 1870s, a series of technological innovations ensured that for the first time steel could be produced cheaply and in huge quantities. The availability of steel, more durable and more flexible than iron, expanded production in industries such as railroads, shipbuilding, and construction.

The construction industry itself was transformed. New technological advances in the production of not only steel but also iron, cement, and plate glass, combined with the inventions of the mechanical crane and stone cutter, allowed architects and builders to reach to the skies. Cityscapes changed dramatically as these spectacular new constructions thrust upward. In 1885, the engineering firm of Gustave Eiffel (1832–1923) proposed the construction of an iron and steel tower to celebrate the Paris World's Fair of 1889. Modeled on the structural supports of railway viaducts, the Eiffel Tower was ridiculed by critics as a "truly tragic street lamp" and a "half-built factory pipe," but it soon came to symbolize both Paris and the new age of modernity.

This same era saw the development of electric power. In 1866 the English scientist Michael Faraday (1791–1867) designed the first electromagnetic generator. Four years later the first commercially viable generator was produced. Once electricity could be cheaply generated and delivered to homes and shops, it then needed to be converted into usable forms. In 1879, the American Thomas Edison (1847–1931) invented the light bulb and illuminated the

14 Août 1888   14 Septembre 1888   26 Décembre 1888   20 Janvier 1889

■ **The Eiffel Tower Reaches to the Sky**
Engineer Gustave Eiffel designed the Eiffel Tower for an international exposition in Paris in 1889.

practical possibilities of electric power. These developments created a huge new energy-producing industry. They also accelerated the production and distribution of other industrial goods as factories and shops, as well as the train and tram lines that serviced them, were linked to the city power grid.

One important characteristic that distinguished this new phase of industrialization was the role of the state in encouraging economic modernization. Governments implemented policies of economic regulation and intervention, such as the construction of state-owned and -operated railway networks and the provision of financial assistance to private business ventures. The challenge posed by the Great Depression hastened the retreat from the free-trade principles of economic liberalism. Faced with declining profits and increased competition, businessmen demanded that their governments act to protect domestic industries from foreign competition. In this period, only Britain, Denmark, and the Netherlands retained the liberal commitment to free trade and refused to construct tariff walls designed to overprice the goods of outside competitors.

The emergence of much larger and more complicated organizational structures also characterized this new industrial phase. As a result of the economic pressures of the Great Depression, businesses grew much bigger. Faced with the necessity of trimming production costs in a time of declining profits, business owners developed new organizational forms, including both *vertical integration*—buying up the companies that supplied their raw materials and those that bought their finished products—and *horizontal inte-*

gration—linking up with companies in the same industry to fix prices, control competition, and ensure a steady profit. The Standard Oil Company exemplifies both trends. Formed in 1870 by the American industrialist John D. Rockefeller (1839–1937), Standard Oil monopolized 75 percent of the petroleum business in the United States by the 1890s, and in addition controlled iron mines, timberland, and various manufacturing and transportation businesses.

Within these new, huge, often multinational companies, organization grew more complex and impersonal. The small family firm run by the owner who knew the name of every employee grew increasingly rare as an ever-expanding layer of managers and clerical staff separated worker from owner. Moreover, identifying "the owner" grew increasingly difficult. The need for capital to fuel these huge enterprises drove businesses to incorporation—the sale of "shares" in the business to numerous stockholders, each of whom now shared ownership in the company.

The development of more complicated organizational patterns at the production end of the economic process interacted with changes in the way goods were marketed. During these decades, a revolution in retailing occurred, one that culminated in a new type of business aimed at middle-class customers—the department store. In a traditional shop, the retailer (who was often also the producer) offered a single product—gloves, for example—in limited quantity at a fairly high price. Often, this price was not set. The customer haggled with the tradesperson until they agreed on a price. "Browsing" was unheard of; an individual who entered a shop was expected to make a purchase. The department stores changed these practices. These new commercial establishments—Bon Marche in Paris, Macy's in New York, Marshall Field's in Chicago, Whiteley's in London—offered a vast array of products in huge quantities. They made their profits not from high prices, but from a quick turnover of a very large volume of low-priced goods. To stimulate sales, they sought to make shopping a pleasant experience. Thus, they provided huge, well-lighted expanses filled with appealing goods sold by courteous, well-trained clerks. In-store reading rooms and restaurants pampered the weary shopper. Another innovation, mail-order catalogs, offered the store's delights to potential customers stranded in distant rural regions and traditionally reliant for their goods on the itinerant peddler and the seasonal fair. Advertising became a crucial industry in its own right, as business sought to persuade potential customers of new needs and desires.

ON THE MOVE:
EMIGRATION AND URBANIZATION

These three economic developments—the onset of the Great Depression, the expansion of industrialization, and the Second Industrial Revolution—accelerated already existing patterns of urbanization and immigration, and so helped widen the borders of local, regional, and national communities across Europe. The Great Depression hit agricultural regions particularly hard, at just the same time that continuing population growth exerted greater pressure on land and jobs. In addition, industrial expansion undercut rural manufacturing and handicraft production, crucial sources of income for rural populations. As a result, men and women from traditional villages sought new economic opportunities in the industrializing cities of Europe, or further abroad, in the United States, Canada, South America, and Australia.

European cities grew dramatically after 1870. In 1800, only 23 European cities had more than 100,000 inhabitants. By 1900, 135 cities of such a size had sprung up. The European population as a whole continued to expand in this period, but the cities increased at a much faster pace. For example, in 1800 the city of Odessa in Ukraine held 6,000 inhabitants. By 1914, Odessa contained 480,000 people. In the same period, Hungary's Budapest expanded from 50,000 to 900,000 inhabitants. Even within these expanding cities, Europeans were on the move. Take the example of Berlin. In 1890, 12 percent of the city's population had arrived just that year; 8.5 percent of the population was on its way out. Another 56 percent moved to a new location within the city itself.

The migration flow was not all one-way. Farm laborers moved to the cities when times were tough and then moved home again after they had earned some money. Most urban immigrants came to the cities from the surrounding countryside, and often stayed for less than a year. Duisberg, a steel and tool-making center located in Germany's Ruhr Valley, grew in population from 8,900 to 106,700 between 1848 and 1904. Almost one-third of its newcomers in the 1890s came from villages less than fifteen miles away. No fewer than two-thirds of these immigrants eventually returned to their rural villages.

By 1910, however, one-sixth of Duisberg's immigrants came from other countries, particularly Italy and the Netherlands. The combined impact of agricultural crisis and urban industrial expansion broke down national boundaries to create an international industrial workforce by 1914. Inhabitants of industrially underdeveloped regions were drawn to more economically advanced areas. Italians

■ **The Bicycle Revolution**

The bicycle revolutionized daily life for ordinary Europeans. The introduction of equal-sized wheels in 1886 and of pneumatic tires in 1890 allowed for a far more comfortable ride than had been the case with the bone-breaking cycles built earlier. Mass industrial production made the bicycle affordable, and for the first time, ordinary individuals, far too poor to afford a horse or motorcar, could dare to purchase their own private means of transportation, which would get them where they wanted to go in one-quarter of the time that walking required. No longer confined to their village for work opportunities or social contacts, bicycle owners discovered that their daily world had widened fourfold.

A LETTER HOME

For immigrants to the United States, the "new world" offered the chance to break free from the cultural and religious restraints that had governed their lives in their villages at home. Many found the changes unsettling and distressing. Others were thrilled with their new freedom, as this letter reveals. The letter never made it to Goodstein's "auntie," but was instead confiscated by Russian tsarist authorities in an effort to discourage illegal emigration from its Polish territories.

San Bernadino [California], 28 November 1890

Dearest Auntie!

How happy I was a little while ago when finally I received a letter from You. Reading it and hearing about your good health gave me great pleasure and joy. . . .

This past 4 November, it was exactly one year since I left home. On 4 December I arrived in New York and on the 12th I reached San Bernadino. I can tell You for sure that I should have left home 15 years earlier. It would have been much better for me, a thousand times better because I am not able even to describe it to You, how I looked at first and how different I look now. I do not want to write about it because if I start I may never finish with it. I would like to ask the people at home just this one question: why is it forbidden for a young man to take a walk with a girl, to talk to her and to become acquainted with her. I do not consider it a sin. . . . Only You [the Jews in Poland] . . . are so backward. . . .

I do not mean to insult You, but it is especially true that in Your small towns within a half hour everything is known all over and becomes gossip. And so when a young man from there arrives here, what kind of an impression does he make? . . . when he gets together with people, he does not know how to behave and how to have a good time. . . . He also does not know how to hold a knife or a fork or a table napkin. And he does not know how to sing or raise a toast in company. At home we only used to say, "*Lehayim.*" At home we only sang *zmires.**

. . .

In our store, we also sell women's dresses and even underwear. And it may happen that a young man has to sell to some young girl some such things or whatever. We also sell, here, undershirts, shirts, collars, fine ties, pocket watches, top hats and overcoats. All this the young man was not acquainted with at home. . . .

Be well, Dear Auntie, and please write again to Your forever loving nephew.

Your nephew,
M. Goodstein

------

*"*Lehayim*" = "to life"; a toast. "*Zmires*" = sabbath songs.*

Source: From Witold Kula et al., *Writing Home: Immigrants in Brazil and the United States 1890–1891*, edited and translated by Josephine Wtulich (New York: Columbia University Press, 1986). Reprinted by permission of East European Monographs.

---

headed to France and Switzerland, while the Irish poured across the Irish Sea into Liverpool and Glasgow. Earlier in the century large numbers of Germans had sought new lives in the United States, but after 1880 emigration from Germany dwindled. As its industrial economy boomed, Germany became a net importer of labor from Poland and other eastern and central European regions.

Some immigrants headed not for the nearest city, but for an entirely different continent. Between 1860 and 1914, over 52 million Europeans crossed the ocean in quest of a better life. Seventy-two percent of these transoceanic immigrants traveled to North America, 21 percent to South America, and the rest to Australia and New Zealand.[1] Irish and English immigration to the United States remained high throughout this period, but after the 1880s eastern Europeans accounted for an ever-larger share of those bound for America. One hundred thousand Poles moved to the United States over the course of the 1880s; in the first decades of the twentieth century, between 130,000 and 175,000 Poles were immigrating to the United States each year.

By the 1890s, a truly global labor market had developed. Both technological developments (primarily the shift from sailing to steam ships) and competition among shipping firms considerably reduced the cost of transoceanic travel. As a result, men from villages in southern Italy and Spain could cross the Atlantic in time for the fall harvest of wheat in Argentina, travel to Brazil to pick coffee beans, and then head back home in May. Clearly, in such societies, the borders between local villages and the rest of the world had become permeable.

GROWING SOCIAL UNREST

Rapid economic change, combined with accelerated urbanization and immigration, heightened social tensions and destabilized political structures. The freefall in prices that characterized the Great Depression eroded capitalist profit margins, shattered business confidence, and increased middle-class resistance to workers' demands. Class hostilities rose as workers responded angrily to businessmen's efforts to protect their profit margins by reducing the number of their employees and increasing labor productivity. In rural regions such as Spain and Ireland, the devastating collapse in agricultural prices fostered serious social and economic crises. Increasingly desperate, agricultural laborers and peasants turned to violence to enforce their calls for a fairer distribution of land. The spread of industrialization into southern and eastern Europe also led to social unrest as handicraft producers and independent artisans fought to maintain their traditional livelihoods in the face of the industrial onslaught.

In regions such as Britain and parts of Germany, traditional producers had lost their battle against industrialization in the preceding generation, but the onset of the Second Industrial Revolution brought new social strains. The expansion of office and sales jobs widened the ranks of the lower middle class (or *petty bourgeoisie*). This increasingly important social group exhibited extreme class consciousness and an often fierce hostility toward the working class. With an income no higher than that of a skilled worker, the clerk had to fight hard to maintain middle-class status. The erosion of objective differences such as income levels accentuated the importance of subjective differences—wearing the correct clothing, speaking with the proper accent, living on the right street, keeping the children in school.

The flow of immigrants into Europe's cities also sent social and ethnic tensions soaring. Cities were often unable to cope with the sudden and dramatic increases in population, despite the spread of public health provisions such as water and sewer systems. Housing shortages and poor living conditions exacerbated social tensions as newcomers battled with established residents for jobs and apartments. The mixture of different nationalities and ethnic groups often proved particularly explosive.

Defining the Political Nation

These encounters between rival social groups within European societies changed European politics. Faced with rising social tensions, political leaders sought ways to quell social discontent and to ensure the political loyalty of their populations. At the same time, they faced a new world of mass politics—a new political culture characterized by the participation of men outside the upper and middle classes. Across Europe in the decades after 1870, those in power had to figure out how to stay there. They had to devise ways to incorporate the newly politicized masses into the nation while at the same time suppressing actual and potential unrest.

MAKING NATIONS

After 1870, all but the most authoritarian of European political leaders recognized the importance of "making nations," of creating a sense of national identity powerful enough to overcome the conflicting regional, social, and political loyalties that divided their citizens and subjects. In this nation-making effort, both education and nationalistic ritual proved essential. (See Map 22.1).

State elementary schools served as important tools in the effort to build internally united and externally competitive nation-states. During the last third of the nineteenth century, most of the nations of western and central Europe established free public elementary education systems. In Austria-Hungary, for example, free and compulsory education was decreed in 1869. Of course, passing legislation is one thing, ensuring compliance another. Because children's wages contributed to the family income, many poor families deeply resented the laws that made school attendance mandatory. In poorer districts of Austria-Hungary such as Bukovina, only 36 percent of children attended school, despite the law. In Italy communities were required to provide free education to needy children as early as 1859, but as late as 1912 only 31 percent of the children in the southern region of Calabria were in school.

Despite these difficulties, the schools constituted an essential link in the chain of national identity. Schools broke the cultural barriers imposed by illiteracy. Individuals who could read had access to newspapers, magazines, and books that drew them far beyond the borders of their local village or neighborhood. Both political leaders and intellectuals recognized the power of education in creating a national community. In the 1880s, for example, French student teachers were instructed that "their first duty is to make [their pupils] love and understand the fatherland."[2]

Schools thus helped forge a national identity in very specific ways. First, they ensured the triumph of the national language. Required to abandon their regional dialect (and sometimes brutally punished if they did not), children learned to read and write in the national language. Second, history and geography lessons taught children particular versions of the past that buttressed their sense of belonging to a superior people, and often served a specific political agenda. For example, French classrooms after 1870 displayed wall maps of France—maps that clearly included the provinces of Alsace and Lorraine, even though these regions belonged to Germany, which had seized them as the spoils of victory after the Franco-Prussian War. Finally, the schools, with their essentially captive populations, participated fully in newly designed nationalistic rituals, such as singing aggressive patriotic songs like "Deutschland Über Alles" ("Germany Over All") or "Rule Britannia," and observing special days to commemorate military victories or national heroes.

Nationalistic ritual was not confined to the schoolroom and playground. Making nations often meant *inventing* traditions to captivate the imagination and capture the loyalty of the mass electorate. German policymakers, for example, developed "Sedan Day." This national holiday, which celebrated the battle that helped create the new German state, featured parades, flag raisings, and special services to foster a sense of German nationalism among its citizens. At the same time, the person of the emperor, or *kaiser,* became the center of nationalistic ceremony and loyalty, particularly after the accession of William II (r. 1888–1918), the first emperor to identify himself as truly German rather than Prussian. William used personal appearances, militaristic pageantry, and civic ritual to link together monarchy and subjects in a sturdy chain of nationalism.

The monarchy was even more central to British nationalism. Whereas Queen Victoria's coronation in 1837 had been a small, disorganized affair, by the final decades of the century the anniversaries of her accession to the throne (the Silver Jubilee of 1887 and the Diamond Jubilee of 1897) were dramatically different. Elaborately staged, beautifully costumed, and carefully orchestrated, these events were designed to make ordinary individuals feel part of a wider,

powerful, meaningful national community. The new technologies of mass printing and mass production helped support this new mass politics of nationality. At the Jubilees, participants could purchase colorfully illustrated commemorative pamphlets, ceramic plates etched with the Queen's silhouette, teapots in the shape of Victoria's head, or even an automated musical bustle that played "God Save the Queen" whenever the wearer sat down.

RUSSIA: REVOLUTION AND REACTION

Across Europe, politicians and policymakers used both education and nationalistic ritual to blend disparate groups into a cohesive national community. As the example of Russia illustrates, failure to construct such a national com-

■ **Map 22.1 Europe at the End of the Nineteenth Century**

A comparison of this map with Map 18.2 ("Europe After the Congress of Vienna in 1815," p. 615) shows the impact of modern nationalism on European political geography. The most striking change is the formation of the new states of Italy and Germany (the German Empire). In addition, nationalist movements succeeded in carving away large chunks of the Ottoman Empire's European territories. By the 1880s, Bosnia and Herzegovina were under Austrian administration, and Greece, Serbia, Montenegro, Rumania, and Bulgaria had all achieved independence.

Russian situation. As we saw in Chapter 21, Marx stressed that revolution would come from the ranks of the urban working class, but in Russia, the number of urban workers remained relatively small (3 million in 1914, out of a population of 170 million) and the chances of a genuinely working-class revolution appeared slight. Many Russian revolutionaries, then, rejected Marx's brand of socialism as a Western ideology unsuited for export eastward. Arguing that Russia must follow its own, non-Western path, they looked not to the urban working class but to the peasantry as the source of a genuinely popular socialist revolution. Calling themselves *Populists* ("of the people") they fanned out across the countryside, living and working with peasants and endeavoring to build a new Russia from the bottom up. Some, such as Sofiia Perovskaia and the other members of the People's Will, turned to terrorism.

As we saw at the opening of this chapter, revolutionary populists succeeded in assassinating Tsar Alexander II, but not in toppling the tsarist regime. With the use of repressive legislation and an ever-expanding secret police force, both Alexander III (r. 1881–1894) and Nicholas II (r. 1894–1917) drove political dissenters—liberal, Marxist, and populist—underground or into exile. They could not, however, quell the social unrest produced by economic change. By the turn of the century, rapid, state-sponsored industrialization had built an industrial structure in Russia, but it stood on a very faulty foundation. Russia remained a largely agricultural nation, with peasants still accounting for over 75 percent of the population. Heavy taxation and rapid population growth, which increased competition for land, heightened social and economic anxiety among the peasant masses.

Within the industrial cities, social unrest also simmered. Factory workers labored more than twelve hours a day in wretched working conditions for very little pay. Any protest against these conditions was regarded as protest against the tsar and was quickly repressed. The workers

The Mass Marketing of National Identity

Advertising and mass production allowed ordinary Britons to participate in the glamour of royalty by purchasing inexpensive trinkets, like this 1902 coronation souvenir.

munity threatened political rulers with revolutionary consequences. Convinced that God had appointed them to rule, Russia's tsars clung to absolutism. To catch up with the West, the tsarist regime adopted Western industrialization but it had no intentions of accepting Western ideas of representative government. It could not, however, completely block the flow of these ideas into the Russian Empire. By the 1880s, many members of Russia's small but growing middle class espoused liberal political goals such as a written constitution and limited representational government. Other Russians went further and embraced socialism. Both liberalism and socialism constituted revolutionary ideological challenges to tsarist absolutism, and both met with fierce repression.

Socialists faced not only harsh political repression but also a major intellectual dilemma—the problem of adapting the political and economic ideas of Karl Marx to the

CHRONOLOGY

Instability Within the Russian Empire

1881	Assassination of Tsar Alexander II; accession of Alexander III
1882	May Laws reimpose restrictions on Russian Jews
1890s	Industrialization accelerates under Witte
1894	Accession of Nicholas II
1904	Outbreak of Russo-Japanese War
1905	Revolution
1906–1910	Nicholas II stifles political revolution

■ **The Revolution of 1905 in the Movies**

On Bloody Sunday, January 22, 1905, Russian troops opened fire on more than 100,000 citizens who had gathered in St. Petersburg to present a petition to the tsar. Rather than subduing the revolt, the massacre sparked a revolution. This photograph, supposedly of the moment when the tsar's troops began to shoot the demonstrators, is one of the most familiar images of the twentieth century—yet it is *not* in fact a documentary record. Instead, it is a still taken from *The Ninth of January*, a Soviet film made in 1925.

themselves remained peasants in their loyalties and mindset. Separated from their families who remained behind in the village, they lived in crowded state dormitories and traveled regularly back to their villages to plant and harvest. They had little sense of belonging to the Russian nation, or of participating in the political structures that governed their lives.

In 1905, popular discontent flared into revolution. That year Japan trounced Russia in a war sparked by competition for territory in Asia. The military debacle of the Russo-Japanese War revealed the incompetence of the tsarist regime and provided an opening for reformers to demand political change. On a day that became known as "Bloody Sunday" (January 22, 1905), a group of 100,000 workers and their families attempted to present to the tsar a petition calling for higher wages, better working conditions, and the right to participate in political decision making. Government troops opened fire on the unarmed crowd; at least 70 people were killed and more than 240 were wounded.

The massacre horrified and radicalized much of Russian society. Across the Russian Empire, cities came to a standstill as workers went on strike and demanded both economic and political rights. In June, portions of the navy mutinied. By the fall, the empire was in chaos, with transportation, communications, energy, and water supplies all facing disruption. Taking advantage of this upheaval, states on the fringes of the empire, such as the Baltic regions, rose up in revolt against imperial rule, and middle-class liberals

demanded limited representative government. In October, Tsar Nicholas II gave in and acceded to demands for the election of a legislative assembly. The Revolution of 1905 appeared to be a success.

By 1910, however, the tsar had regained much of his autocratic power. Revolutionary fervor dissipated as rival groups jostled for political influence. The tsar, with his army still loyal, refused to carry out many of the promised reforms. Tsarist autocracy remained intact, but so too did the causes of the discontent that had led to the revolution. Russia lacked an authentic national community, as Nicholas would discover during the First World War. We shall see in Chapter 24 that total war finally snapped the very fragile links that connected the tsarist regime to the peasant masses, and a new revolution destroyed the Russian imperial state.

GERMANY: IDENTIFYING THE ENEMY

In the new states of Germany and Italy, political rulers made a concerted effort to shape a national community, in contrast to the tsarist regime in Russia. Military victories constructed the borders of the new united Germany. Constructing a sense of nationhood within these borders, however, turned out to be more difficult. We saw in Chapter 21 that the new German state remained politically authoritarian, despite its democratic appearance. All adult males had the right to elect representatives to the German Reichstag (the lower house of parliament) but the Reichstag was fairly powerless. Real power lay in the hands of William I (r. 1861–1888), the first emperor (or *kaiser*) of the unified Germany, and his chancellor, the conservative aristocrat Otto von Bismarck. Appointed—and fired—at the emperor's whim, Bismarck did not answer to the legislature or the electorate. He could not entirely ignore the Reichstag, however, because it possessed the power of the purse. It had to approve the budget and appropriate the funds necessary to run the government. Bismarck thus faced the task of ensuring a sympathetic majority in the Reichstag while at the same time maintaining the emperor's authority, protecting the social and political privileges of the aristocracy, and pacifying the masses.

One way to unite these disparate interests was by identifying a common enemy. In the 1870s, that enemy was the Catholic Church. Convinced that loyalty to the Roman papacy compromised German Catholics' loyalty to the new state, Bismarck initiated what he rather grandly called the *Kulturkampf* (the "struggle of civilization"), a series of measures designed to limit the power of the Catholic Church in Germany. But Bismarck lost this battle. Catholics organized into an opposition political party and resisted Bismarck's efforts to marginalize them or to paint them as in any way "non-German." In 1874 the Catholic Center party won 25 percent of the seats in the Reichstag, and by 1878 Bismarck was forced to recognize that his anti-Catholic policies were threatening rather than strengthening his hold on German politics.

At this point Bismarck shifted his aim to a new target: German socialists. As we will see in the next section, powerful socialist political parties emerged in Europe during this era. To Bismarck, socialist loyalty to an international workers' movement was like the Roman Catholics' loyalty to the pope—an outside allegiance that weakened national unity.

Alarmed by socialist electoral victories, Bismarck outlawed the German Social Democratic Party (SPD) in 1878 and authorized the federal police to disband all socialist meetings and organizations.

This attack on the SPD appealed to antisocialist groups such as conservative landowners, Roman Catholics, and liberal businessmen, and thus gave Bismarck the Reichstag majority that he needed. The antisocialist strategy, however, risked alienating the growing urban working class. To attract the support of this vital social segment and weaken the

■ **German Emperor William II and His Entourage**

William preferred to wear military regalia when he appeared in public. In this way, William himself symbolized the link between the German state and Germany's military might.

appeal of the SPD at the same time, Bismarck introduced some of the most thoroughgoing social welfare measures yet seen in Europe. He initiated sickness benefits in 1883, coverage for industrial accidents in 1884, and old-age pensions and disability insurance in 1889. Even so, the outlawed SPD continued to attract growing numbers of working-class supporters.

In 1890, however, the new German emperor, William II (r. 1888–1918), fired Bismarck and let the antisocialist legislation lapse. William believed he could cement a sense of common German national identity among its various social groups—Catholics and socialists, aristocrats and workers, liberals and military officers, industrialists and landowners—through aggressive militarization and imperial expansion. These policies helped clear the way for World War I, a war that would at first unify but then destroy the German imperial state.

ITALY: THE ILLUSION OF TRANSFORMATION

The development of national unity in Italy ran up against two key obstacles: the papacy and poverty. As we saw in Chapter 21, Rome and the surrounding region remained outside the borders of the new Italian nation-state until 1870, when the French troops that had been protecting the pope withdrew to fight in the Franco-Prussian War. The Italian army marched in and claimed Rome as the capital of Italy. Pope Pius IX (r. 1846–1878) shut himself within the Vatican, refused to recognize the new state, and forbade Catholics (almost the entire Italian population) from voting or running for office. Many Catholics ignored the pope's prohibition, but the hostility between the papacy and the new government undermined the state's legitimacy.

An even more serious obstacle to national unity was raised by severe levels of poverty and economic underdevelopment, particularly in southern Italy. The south remained a region of huge, inefficiently run agricultural estates, unable to support its expanding population, particularly after cheap North American grain flooded the European markets and gutted agricultural prices. Small landowners were unable to make a profit, while the large aristocratic landholders responded to the economic crisis by "rationalizing" the management of their estates, a practice that usually included firing large numbers of agricultural laborers. As a result, much of the south seethed with social discontent. Immigration to France, Switzerland, South America, and the United States relieved some of the pressure, but both small landholders and the landless laborers who worked on the large estates found it increasingly difficult to make ends meet. Economically desperate and receptive to radical political ideas, the rural poor began to demand the breakup of large landholdings.

By the 1880s, the social unrest resulting from the agricultural crisis and the spread of revolutionary socialist ideologies so frightened the upper classes that they voted to widen the franchise in the hopes of depriving socialism of some of its appeal. In 1882 the assembly expanded the franchise from 8 percent of the adult male population (2 percent of the total population) to 25 percent of adult males. This action alone could not make a nation, however. Most peasants remained disenfranchised, without any sense of ownership in the new national political system. Poverty persisted as a key obstacle to national unity. The wealthy southern landholders who formed a solid bloc in the national assembly insisted on maintaining high tariffs on imported grain—a policy that protected their profits while increasing food prices. Taxes also rose rapidly as politicians favored balancing the budget over alleviating the plight of the poor.

The political system could not meet the challenge of creating a national community. No single party had a majority in the national assembly. Instead, Italian politicians developed a system of *trasformismo*, building and maintaining coalition governments by transforming opponents into allies through bribery and patronage. Because political leaders needed the votes of southern landowners to stay in power, the system stifled any chance to implement programs of economic development or land reform. Thus the politics of transformation actually ensured that no real social transformation occurred in Italy. By the 1890s, the government had to call out the army to put down labor strikes in the northern industrial cities, and imposed martial law over much of the south, which had erupted in revolt.

In a vain attempt to build national consensus through military glory, the Prime Minister Francesco Crispi (1819–1901), one of the heroes of Italian unification and a dominant figure in post-unification politics, authorized a disastrous invasion of Ethiopia. Italy's defeat in Ethiopia led to the fall of the Crispi government in 1896 and to a period of political confusion. Anarchist bombings, socialist-led

CHRONOLOGY

The Coming of Mass Politics in Italy

1870	Rome occupied by Italian army
1896	Italian invasion of Ethiopia defeated; fall of Crispi government
1900	Anarchists assassinate King Humbert
1903	First ministry of Giovanni Giolitti
1911	Universal manhood suffrage enacted
1912	Successful invasion of Libya
1914	Red Week

urban uprisings, violent labor strikes, and agricultural riots escalated.

In the first decade of the twentieth century, however, Italy appeared to take a new course under the premiership of Giovanni Giolitti (1842–1928), who sought ways for both rural and urban workers to feel a part of the nation. Alarmed by the growing appeal of Italy's revolutionary socialist parties, Giolitti embarked on a conscious policy of improving workers' lives and so convincing their political leaders that real change did not require revolution. Giolitti legalized trade unions, nationalized the railroads, established public health and life insurance programs, cracked down on child labor, established a six-day workweek, and in 1911 introduced universal manhood suffrage to Italy. Like Crispi, he turned to imperial expansion to foster a sense of "Italianness" among diverse groups. Unlike Crispi's humiliating failure in Ethiopia, however, Giolitti's colonial venture succeeded. In 1912 Italy annexed Libya.

Yet Giolitti's efforts to create a more inclusive political nation in Italy faltered. The Italian Socialist Party rejected his plan to incorporate it within the existing political system. During "Red Week" in June 1914, anarchist and socialist-inspired revolts spread across northern Italy. Perhaps most seriously, Giolitti, like his predecessors, relied on the support of southern landowners in the assembly and therefore ignored the crying need for economic development in the south. On the eve of the First World War, Italy remained seriously divided between north and south, between peasant and landowner, between industrialist and worker. No single vision of "Italianness" fused these groups into a single nation.

FRANCE: A CRISIS OF LEGITIMACY

Unlike Germany and Italy, France had long existed as a nation-state, but a century of almost continuous political revolution ensured that in the final decades of the nineteenth century no consensus existed on who or what France actually was. After Napoleon III's capture by Prussian troops in 1871, his empire collapsed and the French returned to a republican form of government, based on universal manhood suffrage. Born in the humiliation of military defeat, the Third Republic faced a crisis of legitimacy. Key sectors of the population argued that the Republic had been foisted on the French by their Prussian conquerors, and that it was therefore not a legitimate state and not worthy of their loyalty or support. This crisis of legitimacy was worsened by the failure of French politicians to generate much enthusiasm. A dozen different parties jostled for control of the legislature. Because no single party controlled a majority, the only way to form a government was through forging coalitions, and thus compromise, political wheeling and dealing, financial corruption, and constant reshuffling of officeholders became the common tools of parliamentary politics.

CHRONOLOGY

The Coming of Mass Politics in France

1870	Franco-Prussian War
1871	Formation of Third Republic
1885	Construction of the Eiffel Tower begins
1894	Anarchists assassinate President Sadi Carnot; Captain Alfred Dreyfus convicted of treason
1900	Women allowed to practice law
1906	Dreyfus exonerated; Marie Curie becomes first woman on university faculty

The lackluster nature of French politics accentuated the appeal of those who wished to destroy the French Republic—monarchists who wanted a king back on the throne, Bonapartists longing for the glory days of Napoleonic empire, Roman Catholics disturbed by republican efforts to curb the political power of the Church, aristocrats opposed to democracy. To perceive the depth of opposition to the Republic, it is essential to understand that "republicanism" in France meant more than "no king, no emperor." Rooted in the radical Jacobin Republic of 1792, republicanism rested on a vision of an ideal France consisting of male equals—small shopkeepers and independent artisans, governed by reason rather than religion. Such a vision directly conflicted with the interests and ideals of monarchists, Bonapartists, and Roman Catholics, as well as of the growing number of working-class socialists. The encounter of these rival ideologies generated chaos in French politics throughout this era.

This fundamental lack of consensus about the nature or shape of France was strikingly revealed by the eruption of the Dreyfus Affair°. In 1894, on the basis of hearsay evidence and forged documentation, a French military court convicted Captain Alfred Dreyfus (1859–1935) of espionage. Prominent French intellectuals took up Dreyfus's case, and it became a full-fledged "affair," as supporters and opponents of Dreyfus battled in the streets and in the legislature. Support for Dreyfus, who was Jewish, became linked to support for the secular and egalitarian ideals of the Republic; the anti-Dreyfusards, in contrast, saw Dreyfus's Jewishness as a threat to France's Catholic identity and argued that to question the army hierarchy was to undermine France's military might. The Dreyfus Affair so dominated French politics that in 1899, when René Waldeck-Rousseau, a prominent politician, formed a governing coalition comprising members of a number of political parties, its unifying principle was support for Dreyfus.

The Dreyfus Affair: Defining National Identity in France

On September 27, 1894, the five officers that made up the counterespionage section of France's War Ministry examined a disturbing document—an unsigned, undated, torn piece of paper that had clearly served as a cover letter for a packet of documents containing information on French military equipment and training. The officers found no envelope, but they concluded that the letter was intended for Lieutenant Colonel Maximilian von Schwartzkoppen, the German military attaché in Paris. Thus, this torn piece of paper constituted evidence of treason. Someone in the French officer corps was selling military secrets to the Germans.

After a brief investigation and a cursory comparison of handwriting samples, the French investigators concluded that the traitor was Captain Alfred Dreyfus, a candidate officer on the General Staff. An unlikely traitor, Dreyfus had compiled a strong record during his military career and, by all accounts, was a staunch French patriot. Moreover, because of his marriage to a wealthy woman, he had no need to sell his country for money. He was, however, an aloof and arrogant man, disliked by most of his fellow officers and without a strong backer among his superiors. He was also a Jew.

Despite the lack of solid evidence, Dreyfus was convicted of treason. After a ceremony of military degradation, he was exiled in 1895 to a specially constructed prison hut on Devil's Island, a former leper colony twelve miles off

the coast of French Guyana. Many French men and women believed he had gotten off too lightly. Both public and press clamored for his execution.

With Dreyfus safely imprisoned on his island, his case seemed closed. But in July 1895, Major Marie-Georges Picquart was named chief of the Intelligence Bureau. An ambitious man determined to make a name for himself, Picquart soon discovered that the sale of military secrets to the Germans had continued even after Dreyfus's imprisonment. Ignoring his superiors' instructions to leave the Dreyfus case alone, Picquart set out to trap the man he first believed to be Dreyfus's accomplice. The evidence he uncovered, however, led him to conclude that Dreyfus was in fact innocent.

Picquart's investigations raised serious doubts about Dreyfus's conviction. These doubts were transformed into sensational charges on January 13, 1898, when one of France's most famous authors, Émile Zola, alleged in a Paris daily newspaper that the French military was engaged in a colossal cover-up. In an article headlined "J'accuse!" ("I accuse!"), Zola charged that the General Staff had knowingly convicted an innocent man. Zola's accusations aroused enormous public attention, and over the next six weeks, riots broke out in French cities.

Retried before a second military court in 1899, Dreyfus was again found guilty—although this time "with extenuating circumstances," a ridiculous verdict (there are no extenuating circum-

stances for the crime of treason) concocted to salvage the military's position despite Dreyfus's obvious innocence. In the subsequent riots that broke out in Paris, 100 people were wounded and 200 jailed. Ten days later, the French president pardoned Dreyfus in an effort to heal the divisions opened by the trial. Finally, in 1906, a French high court set aside the court-martial verdict and exonerated Dreyfus. Not until 1995, however, did the French military acknowledge the captain's innocence.

The Dreyfus Affair drew international attention, polarized French politics, and tore apart Parisian society. It sparked not only violent protests but also numerous duels and a series of related trials for assault, defamation, and libel. To uphold Dreyfus's conviction, high-ranking military officials falsified evidence, even to the point of forging entire documents. The question "Are you for or against Dreyfus?" divided families and destroyed friendships. During the height of the controversy, for example, the painter Edgar Degas spoke contemptuously of paintings by Camille Pisarro. When reminded that he had once admired these very same works, Degas said, "Yes, but that was before the Dreyfus Affair." Degas was a passionate anti-Dreyfusard; Pisarro believed Dreyfus was innocent.[3]

What about the Dreyfus Affair so aroused personal passion as to alter one painter's perception of another's work? What made this trial not simply a case, but an *affair*, a matter of public debate and personal upheaval, a cause of violent rioting and political turmoil?

To comprehend the Dreyfus Affair, we must understand that it was less about Captain Alfred Dreyfus than about the very existence of the French Third Republic. The intellectuals and politicians who rallied in support of Dreyfus were defenders of the Republic, men and women who sought to limit the army's involvement in France's political life, who linked both monarchy and empire to national disaster rather than national glory, and who believed in a secular definition of the nation that would treat Roman

■ The Dreyfus Affair
Captain Alfred Dreyfus before his judges, 1899.

pointed to the successes of assimilated Jews such as Dreyfus—not only in the army but also in the universities, the professions, and business life—as evidence of what they perceived as the threat of Jewish "domination" of French culture.

Declared innocent in 1906, Dreyfus resumed his military career and served his country with distinction in the First World War. Like Dreyfus, the Third Republic survived the Dreyfus Affair. It was probably even strengthened by it. Outrage over the army's cover-up led republican politicians to limit the powers of the military and so lessened the chances of an anti-republican military coup. Anti-Semitism, however, remained a pervasive force in French politics and cultural life well into the twentieth century. ■

Catholics no differently from Protestants, Jews, or atheists. Dreyfus's opponents, in contrast, regarded the establishment of the Third Republic as a betrayal of the true France—a hierarchical, Roman Catholic, imperial state, steeped in military traditions. Defending the military conviction of Dreyfus became a way to express support not only for the army, but also for the authoritarian traditions that the Republic had jettisoned. The Dreyfus Affair was thus an encounter between competing versions of French national identity.

The question "What is France?" however, could not be answered without considering a second question: "Who belongs in France?"—or more specifically, "What about Jews?" France's small Jewish community (less than 1 percent of the total population) had enjoyed the rights of full citizenship since 1791—much longer than in most of Europe. Yet the Dreyfus Affair clearly demonstrated that even in France, the position of Jews in the national community was far from assured. Although anti-Semitism proba-

bly played little role in the initial charges against Dreyfus, it quickly became a dominating feature of the affair. More than seventy anti-Semitic riots ravaged France during this period. Anti-Semitic politicians and publications placed themselves in the vanguard of the anti-Dreyfus forces. For many anti-Dreyfusards, Dreyfus's Jewishness explained everything. The highly acclaimed novelist and political theorist Maurice Barres insisted, "I have no need to be told why Dreyfus committed treason . . . That Dreyfus is capable of treason I conclude from his race."[4]

Anti-Semites like Barres regarded Jewishness as a kind of genetic disease that made Jews unfit for French citizenship. To the anti-Semitic nationalist, the Jew was a person without a country, unconnected by racial or religious ties to the French nation—the very opposite of a patriot. As a symbol of rootlessness, "the Jew" came to represent for many anti-Dreyfusards the forces of unsettling economic and political change that appeared to be weakening the French nation. Anti-Semites

Questions of Justice

1. Dreyfus was tried both in military courts and in public opinion. What does the Dreyfus Affair reveal about the emergence of the mass media as an agent of judgment in popular culture? What sorts of evidence were used to convict him in the court of public opinion? How did this evidence differ from that used in the military trial?

2. What does the Dreyfus Affair reveal about definitions of national identity in late-nineteenth-century Europe?

Taking It Further

Cahm, Eric. *The Dreyfus Affair in French Society and Politics.* 1994. A wide-ranging history.

Kleeblatt, Norman, ed. *The Dreyfus Affair: Art, Truth, and Justice.* 1987. This richly illustrated collection of essays explores the cultural as well as political and legal impact of the case.

Lindemann, Albert S. *The Jew Accused: Three Anti-Semitic Affairs (Dreyfus, Beilis, Frank) 1894–1915.* 1991. An illuminating comparative study.

Snyder, Louis L. *The Dreyfus Case: A Documentary History.* 1973. An accessible collection of primary documents.

Dreyfus was finally declared not guilty in 1906, but the consequences of the affair were far-reaching. The Dreyfus Affair revealed the strength of anti-republicanism in France, and so drove the Republic's supporters to seize the offensive. The government pushed through measures placing the army under civilian control, prohibiting members of Catholic religious orders from teaching in public *or private* schools, and removing the Catholic Church from its privileged position in French political life. With these measures politicians aimed to separate citizenship from religious affiliation and social rank and to redefine France in republican terms.

In 1914, the success of this effort at redefinition remained unclear. National political life was dominated by the Radical Party, which represented the interests of small shopkeepers and independent artisans, not industrial workers, and drew its support from rural and small-town constituencies, not the growing cities. The Radicals' grip on power thwarted any significant efforts to address the grievances of the urban working class. Radicals opposed the high taxes necessary to establish social welfare programs and dragged their feet on social legislation such as the ten-hour workday (not passed until 1904) and old-age provisions (not established until 1910). As a result, workers increasingly turned to violent ideologies and actions, such as anarchism and sabotage. Although by 1914 the Third Republic was far stronger than it had been in the early 1870s, it clearly had not yet gained the approval of all segments of French society.

BRITAIN: NATION, CLASS, AND RELIGION

Unlike Germany and Italy, Britain was not a new nation; unlike France, it did not have to reconstruct its political structures after the humiliation of military defeat. Yet in Britain, too, the upper classes faced the task of responding to working-class demands for a political voice. They also confronted the problem of a regional divide even wider than the gap between north and south in Italy. Although the single political entity of the United Kingdom comprised England, Wales, Scotland, and Ireland, a chasm yawned between the first three overwhelmingly Protestant and industrialized nations, and the Roman Catholic, economically backward, peasant culture of Ireland. By the end of the century, the British political nation had broadened to include working-class men but proved incapable of embracing the Irish peasantry.

	CHRONOLOGY
	The Coming of Mass Politics in Britain
1867	Vote extended to urban male workers; formation of National Society for Women's Suffrage
1873	Onset of Great Depression in Trade and Agriculture
1874–1880	Conservative government of Benjamin Disraeli passes social reform legislation
1880	Elementary education made compulsory
1886	Regulation of prostitution ended
1893	Defeat of Second Irish Home Rule Bill in Britain; dockworkers' strike in Hull met with navy gunboats
1897	Queen Victoria's Diamond Jubilee
1898	Formation of Sinn Fein in Ireland
1903	Formation of suffragette movement
1906	Formation of Labour Party
1905–1912	Liberal government lays foundation of British social welfare state

While the English, Scottish, and Welsh economies flourished under the impact of industrialization, the Irish economy stagnated. Still devastated by the famine of the 1840s, the island remained a land of absentee English Protestant landowners and poor Irish Catholic tenants. Peasant desperation fueled revolutionary Irish nationalism, as the economic grievances of the Irish fused with their sense of political and religious repression, and convinced many Irish Catholics of the need for independence from Britain. In the 1860s, the Irish Republican Brotherhood, or Fenian movement, endeavored to overthrow British rule by force. The Fenian "Rising" of 1867 failed dismally, but it planted a seed that took deep root in Irish soil—the belief that the British constituted an occupying force that must be violently resisted.

Faced with growing Irish nationalism, the British resorted to military rule, accompanied by attempts to alleviate peasant grievances through land reform. Such measures were always too little, too late. In the 1880s, the British Liberal leader William Gladstone (1809–1898) embraced the cause of Irish "Home Rule"—limited political autonomy for Ireland—and for a short time it appeared as if parliamentary measures would solve the Irish problem. Home Rule, however, met fierce opposition not only from British Conservatives, but also from Irish Protestants. The descendants of English and Scottish settlers in Ireland, these

Protestants constituted a minority of the Irish population as a whole, but made up the majority of the population in the northernmost province of Ulster. Frightened by the idea of belonging to a Catholic state, the Ulster Protestants made it clear that they would fight to the death to remain a part of Britain.

The defeat of Home Rule bills introduced in 1886 and 1893 persuaded Irish Catholic nationalists of the futility of working with the British. In 1898 they organized themselves as Sinn Fein (pronounced "shin fane"—Gaelic for "Ourselves Alone"), a political movement devoted to complete independence for Ireland by any means necessary. Sinn Fein grew rapidly, and by 1914 could call to arms a paramilitary force of 180,000 fighters. As the success of Sinn Fein demonstrated, Irish Catholics had developed their own sense of nationhood, which refused to be subordinate to or absorbed by the British political nation.

Unable to contain Catholic Ireland, the borders of the British political nation proved flexible enough to incorporate most adult men in England, Scotland, and Wales. In the first half of the nineteenth century, the landed elite had accommodated middle-class demands for greater influence without relinquishing its own grasp on political power. Aristocrats and landed gentlemen played leading roles in both major political parties—the Liberals and the Conservatives (also called "Tories")—but both parties also pursued policies that encouraged industrial growth and benefited the middle classes. In the last third of the century, this system expanded to include working-class men. In 1867, many urban working men won the right to vote, and in 1884 this right was extended to rural male laborers.

Both the Conservative and the Liberal parties sought the support of these new working-class voters with programs designed to benefit ordinary people. In the 1870s, the Conservative government of Benjamin Disraeli (1804–1881) strengthened trade union rights, established the beginnings of a public housing program, expanded the state's program of inspecting factories, and assumed some responsibility for the population's safety by beginning to monitor the sale of food and drugs. The most substantial foundations of Britain's welfare state were, however, constructed in the early twentieth century by the Liberal government. Between 1906 and 1912, the Liberals enacted a series of welfare measures, including state-funded lunches for schoolchildren, pensions for the elderly, and sickness and unemployment benefits for some workers. As with Bismarck's pioneering social measures in Germany and Giolitti's reforms in Italy, this legislation was intended not only to attract workers' votes, but also to ensure working-class loyalty to the nation and its political leaders. In 1906, however, an independent working-class Labour Party emerged, thus signaling that not all working-class voters were willing to accept upper- and middle-class versions of national identity.

Broadening the Political Nation

The expansion of the suffrage in Britain was not unusual. Across Europe in the last third of the nineteenth and opening decades of the twentieth centuries, both aristocratic and middle-class politicians enacted measures extending the vote to lower-class men. Many middle- and upper-class Europeans regarded franchise reform as a preventive measure, a way to avoid socialist revolution by incorporating potential revolutionaries within the system. Even conservative politicians came to realize that mass suffrage did not always mean radical political change.

THE POLITICS OF THE WORKING CLASS

Yet not all new voters from the laboring classes remained loyal to their traditional superiors. The era of franchise expansion also witnessed the escalation of class hostilities, expressed in the rise of working-class socialist political parties and the emergence of new, more radical forms of trade unionism. Workers often rejected the political vision offered by their bosses and landlords, and instead fought hard to broaden the political nation on their own terms.

The Workers' City

In the decades after 1870, the combined impact of agricultural crisis and industrial expansion created large working-class communities in the rapidly growing industrial cities. These working-class communities tended to be increasingly isolated from the middle and upper class. Technological developments such as electrified tram lines, together with the expansion of the railway system, enabled Europe's middle classes to retreat from overcrowded, dirty, disease-ridden city centers to new and burgeoning suburbs. Workers knew members of the middle class only within the limited context of the "boss-employee" relationship—a relationship that was growing more hostile as economic depression drove middle-class employers to try to limit wages and raise productivity.

Within the sprawling industrial cities, industrial workers created a vibrant community life. They developed what sociologists call "urban villages," closely knit neighborhoods in which each family had a clear and publicly acknowledged place. Sharply defined gender roles played an important part in ordering this world. The home became the woman's domain (although many working-class women continued to work outside the home as well). In many regions, the wife controlled the family income and made most of the decisions about family life. Men built up their own cultural and leisure institutions, free from middle-class (and from female) participation and control—the corner pub, the music hall, the football club, the choral society, the brass

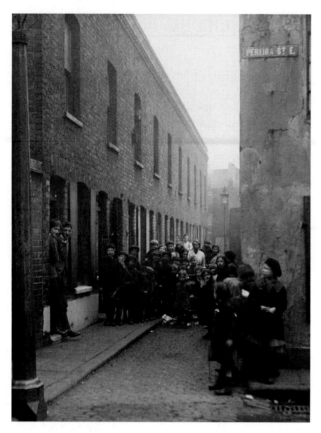

■ **Urban Villages**
Crowded into slums, European workers developed a separate working-class culture.

band. These institutions provided an escape from the physical and emotional confines of work and home; they also secured the bonds of male working-class identity, one that rested on a sharp distinction between "Us"—the ordinary men, the workers, the neighbors—and "Them"—the bosses, the owners, the landlords, the people with privilege and power.

Working-Class Socialism and the Revolutionary Problem

This heightened class identity and hostility were embodied in the emergence of working-class socialist political parties. In the decades after 1870, socialism established itself as a powerful force in European parliamentary politics, the means by which workers sought to claim a place in the political nation. By 1914, socialist parties had been formed in twenty European countries.

Why socialism? As we saw in Chapter 21, by 1870 Karl Marx had published a series of books outlining his economic and political theory of revolutionary socialism. Not many workers had the time, education, or energy necessary for the study of Marx's complex ideas. But Marx's basic points, presented to workers by socialist party activists and

organizers, resonated with many workers. Quite simply, most workers had already identified their boss as the enemy, and Marx assured them that they were right. His insistence that class conflict was inherent within the industrial system accorded with their own experience of social segregation and economic exploitation. In addition, the onset of economic depression in the 1870s appeared to confirm Marx's prediction that capitalism would produce ever more serious economic crises, until finally it collapsed under its own weight.

The most dramatic socialist success story was in Germany. Even after it was outlawed in 1878, the German Social Democratic Party (the SPD) continued to attract supporters. In 1890, the SPD emerged from the underground as the largest political party in Germany. By 1914, it held 40 percent of the seats in the German Reichstag, and served as the model for socialist parties founded in the Netherlands, Belgium, Austria, and Switzerland. Even more important, German socialists constructed a set of institutions that provided German workers with an alternative community. If they chose, they could send their children to socialist day care centers and bury their parents in socialist cemeteries. They could spend their leisure time in socialist bicycling clubs and gymnastic groups and choral societies and chess teams. They could read socialist newspapers, sing socialist songs, save their money in socialist savings banks, and shop at socialist co-operatives.

By the 1890s, the rapid growth of socialist parties such as the SPD persuaded many socialists that working-class revolution was just around the corner. In 1885 SPD leader August Bebel (1840–1913) told Marx's colleague Friedrich Engels, "Every night I go to sleep with the thought that the last hour of bourgeois society strikes soon."[5] Six years later in a speech before the SPD congress, Bebel told the gathered crowd, "I am convinced that the fulfillment of our aims is so close, that there are few in this hall who will not live to see the day."[6]

By the time Bebel made this promise, however, unexpected economic and political developments were creating serious problems for Marxist theory and practice. When Bismarck's antisocialist legislation was not renewed in 1890, the SPD faced a time of new opportunity, but also new challenges. To improve workers' wages and working conditions, the SPD worked in close connection with the rapidly growing German trade union movement—from 300,000 members in 1890 to 2.5 million in 1913. Such activity raised the fundamental question: What was the role of a socialist party within a nonsocialist state? To continue to attract voters, the SPD needed to push through legislation that would appeal to workers; yet the passage of such legislation, by improving workers' lives within a nonsocialist system, made the possibility of socialist revolution ever more remote. Why should workers resort to violent revolution when participation in parliamentary politics was clearly paying off?

The SPD's dilemma was shared by socialist parties across western Europe. According to Marx, capitalism would generate its own destruction—the growing misery of workers would fuel a social and political revolution. But in western European industrial nations in the last decades of the nineteenth century, working-class living standards were generally rising rather than deteriorating. In addition, the expansion of the franchise seemed to indicate that workers could gain political power without violent revolution. As socialist political parties grew in strength, then, they faced crucial and often divisive questions: Should they work for gradual reforms that would make life better for the worker—and risk making capitalism more acceptable? Could socialists participate in coalition governments with nonsocialists—and so lend legitimacy to parliamentary systems they condemned as oppressive and unequal?

The quest for answers to these questions led some socialists to socialist revisionism°, a set of political ideas most closely associated with the German socialist theorist Eduard Bernstein (1850–1932). Bernstein rejected the Marxist faith in inevitable violent revolution and argued instead for the gradual and peaceful evolution of socialism through parliamentary politics. Questioning Marx's insistence on the centrality of class struggle in modern politics, Bernstein called for German socialists to abandon their commitment to revolution, to form alliances with liberals, and to carry out immediate social and economic reforms.

In 1899, the German socialist party congress condemned Bernstein's revisionism and reaffirmed its faith in the inevitability of capitalism's collapse and working-class revolution. Bernstein had lost the battle—but he won the war. For regardless of what the congress affirmed as socialist theory, in practice the SPD acted like any other parliamentary party. It focused on improving the lot of its constituency through immediate and incremental legislative change. In the words of one socialist intellectual, the SPD was "a party which, while revolutionary, does not make a revolution."[7] Its effect, although not its aim, was thus to make the existing political system more responsive to the needs of working-class constituents. Despite the almost hysterical fears of many middle- and upper-class Europeans, the successes of socialist political parties probably worked less to foment revolution than to strengthen parliamentary political systems.

Radical Trade Unions and the Anarchist Threat

To many at the end of the nineteenth century, however, revolution appeared a genuine possibility. The Great Depression, which shattered middle-class confidence and shrank capitalists' profit margins, led businesses to look for ways to cut costs. As management sought to reduce the number of laborers, to increase the rate of production, and to decrease wages, workers began to organize themselves in new and threatening ways.

THE SOCIALIST CULTURE

Songs played a vital role in the socialist culture developed in Germany at the end of the nineteenth century. Workers organized singing societies, which competed in local, regional, and national competitions. Rejecting the nationalist and religious songs of the middle-class choral society repertoire, workers often expressed their political ideals in their music. These overly didactic lyrics reveal not only the rage against economic injustice that fueled the socialist movement, but also its fundamental faith in human rationality and in parliamentary politics as an avenue of change.

"YOU MEN, ALL OF YOU" BY ERNST KLAAR

Already on all sides and throughout the world
The proletariat rises up together—
The fate of the poor is to be changed,
And to be changed through the state.
O, if we stand together firmly,
Who will be able to refuse us our right?
Upward, upward, you new generation,
Defiant let your banner wave!
 Put in the eight-hour day!
 Reduce the misery of toil!
 To our victorious march
 The drum now beats.
 Eight hours are enough!

Source: From "You Men, All of You" by Ernst Klaar, translated by Vernon L. Lidtke in *The Alternative Culture*, 1985. Reprinted by permission.

The expansion and radicalization of trade unions highlighted growing working-class militancy. For example, in Britain between 1882 and 1913, union membership increased from 750,000 to 4,000,000. While size alone set apart the new unions from their midcentury predecessors, two additional differences marked them as much more subversive. First, the new unions were much more willing to resort to large-scale strikes and to violence. Second, the unions sought to better the lives of a wide range of workers, not just an elite of the highly skilled. In contrast to the unions of the 1850s and 1860s, which had tended to be small, craft-based groupings of skilled workers, the new unions aimed to organize all the male workers in an entire industry—for example, all male textile workers, rather than just the skilled weavers. (Unionists, fighting for higher pay, often resisted the unionization of female workers both because women earned much less than did men and because a central union aim was the "family wage"—a pay rate high enough for a man to support a family without his wife's second income.)

■ **The Unions' Challenge**
In 1911 the British government deployed troops in the city of Liverpool to put down working-class labor unrest. In one confrontation, two people were killed.

Political leaders reacted ferociously to the unionist challenge. In the coastal port of Hull in Britain, striking dockworkers in 1893 confronted Royal Navy gunboats. A little over a decade later, the British government responded to a transport workers' strike in Liverpool by quartering 14,000 soldiers in the city and stationing two warships off the coast. Increasingly, "class war" seemed an appropriate label for interactions between workers and their middle-class employers. Even the simple act of getting a shave could prove dangerous for a member of the bourgeoisie: Unionized workers in barbershops were encouraged to "inflict nonfatal cuts on the clients of their capitalist masters."[8]

In the first decade of the twentieth century, the European labor movement became further radicalized by its encounter with the new ideology of syndicalism°. Syndicalists worked to overturn the existing social and political order by marshaling the economic might of the laboring classes. They focused on the general strike as a means of change. In the syndicalist vision, if every worker in a nation went on strike, the resulting disruption of the capitalist economy would lead to working-class revolution. Thus they placed their revolutionary faith in economic rather than political action—in unions rather than parties, in the strike rather than the vote, and in compulsion rather than compromise. According to the French syndicalist theorist Georges Sorel (1847–1922), workers had to embrace violence to destroy the capitalist state. Sorel did not actually believe that a general strike was possible, but he believed that the idea of the general strike was crucial. In Sorel's view, the general strike served as an essential myth, an inspirational idea that would give workers the motivation and self-confidence they needed to overthrow the state.

In their rejection of parliamentary politics and in their willingness to utilize violent means to achieve their revolutionary ends, syndicalists were heavily influenced by anarchism°. In contrast to socialists who formed political parties to claim for workers a place in the political nation, anarchists shunned parliamentary politics. Opting for direct and violent action such as street fighting and assassination, anarchists aimed to destroy rather than control the state. The Russian anarchist Mikhail Bakunin (1814–1876) insisted that the great obstacle to achieving a just and egalitarian society was the state itself, not capitalism or the industrial middle class.

The combined impact of both syndicalism and anarchism created a climate of social unrest and political turmoil in much of Europe before 1914. In France, where a strong non-Marxist revolutionary tradition already existed, both syndicalism and anarchism possessed significant appeal. Impatient with parliamentary politics, anarchists resorted in the 1890s to a terrorist campaign in Paris, which began with a series of bombings and culminated in the fatal stabbing of President Sadi Carnot in 1894. Other prominent victims of assassination included Empress Elisabeth of Austria-Hungary in 1898, King Humbert of Italy in 1900, and U.S. president William McKinley in 1901.

NATIONALIST MASS POLITICS

The rise of socialist political parties and the spread of revolutionary ideologies such as anarchism and syndicalism fostered middle- and upper-class fears of a worker revolution. But the emergence of mass politics was not limited to left-wing ideologies. In the age of the masses, the right-wing ideas offered by nationalist, racist, and anti-Semitic parties also answered the demands of many ordinary people for a political voice. These parties possessed a special appeal in areas that industrialized late and so still contained a large peasant class profoundly threatened by the economic changes wrought by the continuing Industrial Revolution. Socialist politics also possessed little appeal for members of the petty bourgeoisie, who regarded the vision of working-class rule as a frightening nightmare. Instead, they turned to the new mass politics of nationalism.

Unlike the men who had dominated politics in the past, most newly enfranchised voters possessed only a basic education; they had little time for reading or sustained intellectual work; they worked long hours and therefore needed to be entertained. They needed a new style of politics—one based more on visual imagery and symbolism than on the written word, one that relied on emotional appeals rather than on intellectual debate. Nationalist politics fit the bill perfectly. Unlike socialists, who placed great faith in education and in rational persuasion, nationalist politicians did not recruit supporters with reasoned arguments. Instead, by waving flags, parading in historical costumes or military uniforms, and singing folk songs, they tapped into powerful personal and community memories to persuade voters of their common identity, one based not on shared political ideas or economic interests but rather on ethnic, religious, or linguistic ties. This was as much a politics of exclusion as of inclusion—it defined the nation by identifying who was "not in" as well as who belonged.

Austria-Hungary: The Politics of Division

Nationalist mass politics proved very powerful in the multi-ethnic, industrially underdeveloped Habsburg Empire. We saw in Chapter 21 that in 1867, Hungarian nationalism forced the administrative division of the empire into Austria in the west and the kingdom of Hungary in the east, thus creating what is called the Dual Monarchy, or simply Austria-Hungary. Straining under the social and economic pressures of late industrialization, Austria-Hungary contained numerous ethnic and linguistic groups competing for power and privileges. (See Map 21.4, p. 714.)This competition intensified as the franchise was gradually widened in the 1880s and 1890s. (The Austrian half of the empire achieved universal manhood suffrage in 1907.)

Language became a key battleground. In a multilingual empire, which language would be taught in the schools? Which language would be required in official communications? Which language would guarantee career advancement? Not surprisingly, individuals tended to agitate for the primacy of their own native language, and to jostle for the political power needed to ensure that primacy. In Hungary, the ruling Magyar-speaking Hungarian landlords redrew constituency boundaries to give maximum influence to Magyar speakers and to undercut the power of other ethnic and linguistic groups. This policy of "Magyarization" in governmental offices and in the schools bred widespread resentment among non-Hungarians and fostered their own nationalist ambitions.

At the same time in the Austrian half of the empire, Czechs succeeded in gaining greater political power and official support for the Czech language. Germans within Austria resented Czech gains and called for closer ties with Germany and even a complete break of the link with Hungary.

By 1900 the struggle over language laws in the Czech portion of the Austrian empire had become so intense that no party could establish a majority in the Reichsrat (the legislative assembly), and Emperor Francis Joseph (r. 1848–1916) resorted to ruling by decree.

The Appeal of Anti-Semitism

Anti-Semitism played a central role in the new nationalist mass politics. In the final third of the nineteenth century, Jews bore the brunt of the blame for Europe's economic, social, and cultural crises. They were charged with causing the Great Depression and masterminding terrorist conspiracies. Urban overcrowding, rising drug and alcohol addictions, the collapse of small corner shops unable to compete with large department stores, the rise of socialism—Jews received the blame for these diverse developments as well. As anti-Semitism grew, so too did anti-Jewish violence. In Russia, this violence often took the form of pogroms, mass attacks on Jewish homes and businesses, sometimes organized by local government officials. Although pogroms did not occur in western Europe, Jews in France, Britain, and other industrialized nations also experienced increasing hostility.

To explain the heightened anti-Semitism of this period, we need to understand three developments: the increased emphasis on racial identity, the upsurge in the numbers of Jewish immigrants into Western cities, and Jewish industrial and professional success. First, the triumph of nationalism meant a new concern with group boundaries and a greater focus on racial identity. Nationalism raised the question of "who does *not* belong?" For many Europeans and Americans, race provided the answer. The new nationalism meant new perceptions of common "racial roots." Ideas about "the English race" or of the shared racial heritage of the French had no scientific basis, but these perceptions of racial links nonetheless proved extremely powerful. In this new nationalistic climate, then, "Jewishness" was

CHRONOLOGY

The Coming of Mass Politics in Austria-Hungary

1867	Administrative division of Habsburg Empire: formation of Austria-Hungary; emancipation of Jews within Austria-Hungary
1869	Elementary education made compulsory and free
1881	Assassination of Russian Tsar Alexander II; upsurge in Jewish immigration into Vienna
1897	Karl Lueger elected mayor in Vienna on anti-Semitic platform
1898	Assassination of Empress Elisabeth
1907	Universal manhood suffrage enacted in Austria

increasingly defined not only as a matter of religious belief but also as a racial identity. As a racial marker, Jewishness was not a matter of choice but of blood—something that could not be changed. A Jew who no longer ascribed to the Jewish faith or even a Jew who converted to Christianity remained a Jew. This shift to a more racial definition of Jewishness is one of the factors behind the upsurge in anti-Semitic actions and attitudes at the end of the nineteenth century. If national identity grew from supposedly racial roots, then in the eyes of many Europeans, Jews were a foreign plant. They were non-English, or non-French, or non-German—essentially outsiders whose very presence could be seen as a threat to national unity.

This perception of Jews as outsiders was also exacerbated by the growth in immigrant Jewish urban populations after 1881. After the assassination of his father in 1881, Tsar Alexander III blamed Russia's Jewish community for his father's death. He responded by reimposing restrictions on Jewish economic and social life with the May Laws of 1882. Fleeing this repression, Jews from the Russian Empire settled in Paris, London, Vienna, and other European cities. The encounter between these immigrant Jewish communities and their hosts was often hostile. Extremely poor, the immigrants spoke Yiddish rather than the language of their new home, dressed in distinctive clothing, and sometimes practiced an ardently emotional style of Judaism that resisted assimilation. As the numbers of Jews escalated in Europe's cities, these new, impoverished, clearly identifiable immigrants were easily blamed for unemployment, the spread of disease, soaring crime rates, and any other difficulty for which desperate people sought easy explanations.

Many anti-Semites, however, associated Jews not with poverty but with wealth and power. One of the most striking developments of nineteenth-century history was what one historian has labeled the "rise of the Jews." [9] At the start of the nineteenth century, not only were Jews barred from political participation in most of Europe, but in the south and east they were also frequently confined to certain territories or city districts. Jews in Russia, for example, could not live outside the area defined as the "Pale of Settlement." Swiss Jews were confined to the canton of Aargau, and Jews in Rome had to reside in a certain district, or *ghetto*. The second half of the century, however, witnessed the emancipation of European Jewry as Jews gained civil and political rights. By 1900 many had benefited greatly from political and economic change.

Moving into new regions and new economic and political roles, Jewish communities quickly assumed a significant presence in European economic and political life. In Budapest in 1900, for example, Jews formed 25 percent of the population, yet they accounted for 45 percent of the city's lawyers, more than 40 percent of its journalists, over 60 percent of its doctors, and 50 percent of its qualified vot-

ers. A few Jewish families, such as the internationally connected Rothschild banking dynasty, possessed spectacular fortunes. Most important, in many cities Jewish businessmen clustered in certain areas of the emerging modern economy. In Germany, for example, almost all the large department stores were owned by Jewish businessmen, and in the cities of Frankfurt, Berlin, and Hamburg all the large daily newspapers were in the hands of Jewish proprietors. As a result, the small craftspeople and artisans with a great deal to lose from economic modernization often linked big-business capitalism to Jewishness. Like Tsar Nicholas II, who blamed the Russian Revolution of 1905 on Jewish conspirators, ordinary men and women reacted to their own personal reversals of fortune by seeking a scapegoat. Jews became the embodiment of threatening change to many newly enfranchised European voters.

Politicians quickly realized the power of anti-Semitism in the new age of mass politics. Across Europe, explicitly anti-Semitic parties emerged, while established conservative parties adopted anti-Semitic rhetoric to attract voters. In Germany, the widespread belief that Jews had conspired to cause the Great Depression fueled anti-Semitic politics; by the 1890s anti-Semitic parties had won seats in the Reichstag. In France, nationalists linked Jewish prosperity to French national decline and grew increasingly anti-Semitic in their ideology and rhetoric, until finally the Dreyfus Affair made explicit the connections between hatred of Jews and right-wing French nationalism. Many of Dreyfus's opponents saw "Jewishness" and "Frenchness" as incompatible, and regarded Dreyfus himself as part of a vast Jewish conspiracy to undermine France's religious, military, and national strength.

Anti-Semitic politics also proved extremely powerful in Vienna, capital of the Austrian half of the ancient Habsburg Empire. Vienna stood at the center of cultural, professional, and political life for German-speaking Austrians. As the city attracted both Austrian Jews from the surrounding countryside and Jewish emigrants fleeing Russian pogroms, Vienna's Jewish population grew from 118,000 in 1890 to 147,000 in 1900. Jews maintained a high profile in the city. At the University of Vienna, for example, one-quarter of the law students and almost one-half of the medical students were Jewish, although Jews made up only one-tenth of the Austrian population.

This growing Jewish presence provided the opportunity for Karl Lueger (1844–1910), a lawyer, self-made man, and power-hungry politician. Lueger's Christian Social party demonstrates how hate-based politics could overcome social and economic divisions among members of a single ethnic or religious community. Lueger used both anti-Semitism and promises of social reform to unite artisans and workers with conservative aristocrats in a German nationalist party. His proposals to exclude Jews from political and economic life proved so popular that he was elected mayor of Vienna in 1897, despite the opposition of Emperor Francis Joseph. Lueger was still the mayor in 1908, when 18-year-old Adolf Hitler, hoping to attend art school, moved to Vienna. Hitler's application to study art was denied, but he remained in Vienna for several years, soaking in the anti-Semitic political culture.

Zionism: Jewish Mass Politics

The heightened anti-Semitism of the last quarter of the nineteenth century convinced some Jews that the Jewish communities of Europe would be safe only when they gained a political state of their own. The ideology of Jewish nationalism was called Zionism°, as Jewish nationalists called for a return to Zion, the Biblical land of Palestine. Most Jews in western nations such as France and Britain viewed Zionism with skepticism, but it had a potent appeal in eastern Europe, home to more than 70 percent of the world's Jewish community—and to the most vicious forms of anti-Semitism.

Zionism became a mass movement under the guidance of Theodor Herzl (1860–1904). An Austrian Jew born in Budapest, Herzl was living in Vienna when Karl Lueger was elected mayor. Confronted with the appeal of anti-Semitism to the mass electorate, Herzl began to doubt whether Jews could ever be fully accepted as Austrian citizens. His experience as a journalist reporting on the Dreyfus Affair from Paris confirmed these doubts. The vicious display of anti-Jewish hatred in a prosperous, industrialized, western European state convinced Herzl that Jews would always be outsiders within the existing European nations. In 1896, he published *The Jewish State,* a call for Jews to build a nation-state in Palestine. Herzl gained the financial support of wealthy Jewish businessmen such as Baron Edmund James de Rothschild, but he recognized that for Zionism to succeed, it must capture the imagination and loyalties of ordinary Jews. Through newspapers, popular publications, large rallies, and his own enthusiasm, Herzl made Zionism into an international mass movement.

As a mass movement, Zionism faced strong opposition. Many Jewish leaders argued that Zionism played into the hands of anti-Semites by insisting that Jews did not belong in Europe. In addition, by marking out Palestine as the Jewish "homeland," Zionists ran into a huge political obstacle. Palestine still belonged to the Ottoman Empire, which opposed European Jewish immigration into the region as a destabilizing force. Nevertheless, 90,000 Jews had settled in Palestine, where they hoped to fulfill the Zionist dream, by 1914.

The Limits of Black Emancipation in the United States

The example of Jewish emancipation shows that the widening of the political nation to embrace adult working men in Europe did not always advance democratic values.

CHRONOLOGY

The Limits of Emancipation in the United States

1865	End of the Civil War
1877	End of Reconstruction in the American South
1880s–1890s	Passage of Black Codes and Jim Crow laws in Southern states
1896	*Plessy vs. Ferguson:* "separate but equal" institutionalized

The process of extending the suffrage often accentuated perceptions of racial difference and so heightened rather than subdued racist rhetoric and violence. In the United States, efforts to widen the political nation to include African-American men largely foundered on the rocks of racism.

We saw in Chapter 21 that the end of the Civil War in 1865 led to black emancipation. Amendments to the Constitution abolished slavery, granted citizenship to former black slaves, and gave black men the right to vote. The stationing of federal troops in the former slave states enforced the efforts of the Republican Party to reconstruct the American South. Failure to carry out any sort of land reform in the region, however, limited the impact of these reforms. Wealthy, white landowners had lost their slaves but retained their economic supremacy.

Reconstruction ended in 1877 when President Rutherford Hayes (1822–1893) withdrew federal troops from the South. Over the next two decades, the dominant landowning class succeeded in effectively depriving black citizens (and many poor whites) of the right to vote and in ensuring that blacks remained in an inferior economic and social position. "Black Codes" passed by Southern legislatures limited the type of property and occupation open to blacks, while literacy tests, poll taxes, and violent intimidation ensured that few blacks dared to vote. The threat of lynching was omnipresent. In the decade after 1889, an average of 187 blacks were lynched in the United States each year, 80 percent of these in the Southern states.

At the same time, the passage of Jim Crow° legislation (named after a black minstrel singer) mandated racial segregation in almost every aspect of Southern American society. Jim Crow laws meant that blacks could not travel in the same train cars with whites; that white nurses could refuse to work on wards with black patients; that blacks and whites could not be educated in the same schools, fed in the same restaurants, or buried in the same cemeteries.

Interracial marriage was illegal. In the important case of *Plessy vs. Ferguson* in 1896, the U.S. Supreme Court declared Jim Crow to be constitutional. The Court ruled that "separate but equal" facilities did not violate the rights of black citizens. Yet the separate facilities reserved for blacks were never equal. Jim Crow, like the literacy tests and poll taxes that deprived black men of the right to vote, made it clear that in the eyes of many powerful whites, blacks were not and should not be members of the political nation.

Outside the Political Nation? The Experience of Women

Extending the suffrage to men outside the middle and upper classes also called attention to gender differences, as middle-class women demanded that they, too, be made part of the political nation. The campaign for women's suffrage, however, was only part of a multifaceted international middle-class feminist movement° that, by the 1870s, demanded a reconsideration of women's roles. To the feminist movement, the vote was not an end in itself, but a means to an end, a way of achieving a radical alteration in cultural values and expectations. At the core of nineteenth-century feminism stood a rejection of the liberal ideology of separate spheres—the insistence that both God and biology destined middle-class men for the public sphere of paid economic employment and political participation, and women for the private sphere of the home. In seeking a place in the political nation, feminists sought not just to enter the public, masculine sphere, but in fact to obliterate many of the distinctions between the public and private spheres altogether and so to reconfigure political and social life.

During this period the feminist movement remained largely middle-class in its membership and its concerns. Working-class and peasant women were occupied by the struggle for survival; obtaining the vote seemed fairly irrelevant to a woman listening to her children cry from hunger. Politically active working-class women tended to agree with Karl Marx that class, not gender, constituted the real dividing line in society. For help in bettering their lives, they turned to labor unions and to working-class political parties rather than middle-class feminist organizations. The British working-class feminist Selina Cooper (1868–1946), for example, fought hard for women's rights, but within the context of the British Labour movement. Cooper, who was sent to work in a textile mill at age 10, viewed the widening of women's opportunities and the achievement of working-class political power as two sides of the same coin. Similarly, in Germany, the SDP activist Clara Zetkin (1857–1933) argued that the fight against class oppression was inextricably linked to the fight against women's oppression.

CHANGES IN THE POSITION OF MIDDLE-CLASS WOMEN

The middle-class women's movement operated within changing economic and social conditions that were pushing middle-class women into more public positions in European society. Married women moved into a new public role as consumers during this period. It was the woman who was the principal target of the new advertising industry, the woman whom the new department stores sought to entice with their lavish window displays and courteous shop clerks, the woman who rode the new tram lines and subways to take advantage of sale days.

The largest change for married middle-class women was much more basic, however. In the last third of the nineteenth century, middle-class men and women began to limit the size of their families. In Britain in the 1890s, the average middle-class family had 2.8 children, a sharp reduction in family size from the middle of the century, when the typical middle-class family had 6 children. This enormous change, characteristic of all the advanced industrial nations, reflected both economic and social developments. As the Great Depression cut into business profits and made economic ventures ever more precarious, middle-class families looked for ways to cut expenses and yet maintain a middle-class lifestyle. At the same time, the growing tendency to keep both boys and girls in school longer meant added financial obligations for the middle-class family. Limiting births, through the use of already well-known methods such as abstinence, withdrawal, and abortion, provided the answer. Smaller families meant middle-class married women no longer spent much of their married adult life pregnant or nursing. This change not only meant better health, it also freed women for other activities and interests, including feminist activism.

In contrast, working-class families continued to remain large because a worker's children were economic assets rather than liabilities. Working-class children left school by age 11 or 12 and so began to contribute to the family income much earlier. Middle-class women, then, were freed from the constant round of childbearing, while their working-class counterparts remained far more constrained by domestic duties.

The expectations of unmarried middle-class women were also transformed during this period. In 1850, the unmarried middle-class woman who had to support herself had little choice but to become a governess or a paid companion to an elderly widow. By 1900 her options had widened. As we shall see, the women's movement played a crucial role in this expansion of opportunity, but so also did two more general economic and political developments: the expansion of the state and the Second Industrial Revolution.

The expansion of state responsibilities in this period significantly widened opportunities for women. By the final

THE HUMAN BODY IN HISTORY

Men in Black

Within a span of about fifty years, upper- and middle-class European and American men transformed the way they presented their bodies to the world. Before the late eighteenth century, social rank outweighed gender in determining clothing styles. Thus an aristocratic man dressed more like an aristocratic woman than like a male laborer. Aristocrats, both men and women, decorated themselves with expensive jewels, shaped their bodies with corsets and pads, powdered their faces and hair, sported huge hats decorated with ribbons, carried lacy fans, wore high heels, and dressed in brightly colored and elaborately ruffled silks and taffetas. By the middle of the nineteenth century, however, the man had lost his plumage, and decoration had become a distinctly female attribute. The aristocratic man of the 1850s looked like his middle-class counterpart. He dressed in darkly colored, loose-fitting trousers and jackets; wore sensible shoes; and put on a top hat when he went outside. Cosmetics, perfume, ruffles and lace, elaborate jewelry, hats, and fans all retreated to the woman's sphere.

Whether he was engaged actively in business or lived a life of leisure, the new man in black now presented a sharp contrast to his female companions. His clothing associated him with the world of practicality and production; her costume, however, was designed to reinforce the prevailing notions about women's incapacity for public or economic roles.

Middle- and upper-class women's clothing not only remained brightly colored, decorative, and luxurious, it also became increasingly constrictive. The full crinolines and hoop skirts of the 1850s and 1860s, for example, made the simple task of sitting down a tricky endeavor, while tight corseting placed strenuous physical activity beyond reach of fashionable women.

Changes in clothing reflect new ideas about the relationships between a man's and a woman's identities and their physical bodies. After 1850 men's clothing styles deemphasized their bodies. Whereas eighteenth-century aristocrats wore attention-grabbing colors, silk stockings that outlined their legs, short jackets that emphasized their waist, and tight-fitting breeches that highlighted the sexual aspects of the male body, the long loose jackets and trousers of the later nineteenth-century man masked rather than highlighted their wearer's physical characteristics. In contrast, women's fashions increasingly accentuated female sexuality. By shrinking the waist, tightly laced corsets made the bust and hips appear fuller. In the 1880s, the addition of the bustle emphasized the woman's bottom. Such clothing styles fortified the view that a woman's body in many ways determined her destiny, that women were designed to be wives and mothers.

Economic developments led to important changes in women's fashions in the 1890s. As middle-class women began to enter the workforce in large numbers, fashions adapted to fit their new roles. Dresses became more streamlined: Skirts moved slightly above the ankles and shrank in width, and bustles disappeared. But it took the demands of the First World War, when women assumed previously all-male positions in industry, agriculture, and transportation, to effect radical alterations in the way women presented their bodies and themselves to the world. ■

For Discussion

Changes in women's employment patterns clearly had an impact on women's dress styles. What other economic developments during this period may help explain changes in fashion?

■ **Men in Black**
Painting by James Tissot, *Cercle de la Rue Royale,* detail (1868). Although most are barons, marquises, or counts, the men whose portraits Tissot captured in this high-society painting dress like bankers or stockbrokers.

decade of the nineteenth century, local governments took over many tasks traditionally assigned to church volunteers and especially women charity workers, such as training the poor in proper hygiene and nutrition. Middle-class women quickly claimed both paying and elected positions in the new local bureaucracies, on the argument that women possessed an expertise in managing households and raising children that could be directly translated into managing poorhouses and running schools. Women served on school and welfare boards, staffed government inspectorates, voted in local elections, and were elected to local office. For example, in Britain between 1870 and 1914, approximately 3,000 women were elected to county and municipal governing bodies. In Germany, 18,000 women worked as local welfare officials by 1910. But the largest employers of middle-class women before 1914 were the new state-funded elementary schools. The implementation of compulsory mass education created a voracious demand for teachers and thus a new career path for unmarried women from the middle class as well as from the upper ranks of the working class.

The emergence of new technologies and the retail revolution also created new jobs for women, positions that did not involve manual labor and so did not mean a descent into the working class. Middle-class women moved into the work world as typists, telephone and telegraph operators, sales clerks, and bank tellers. During the 1860s in England, the number of women working as commercial clerks and accountants increased tenfold.

Middle-class women thus found new ways to make a living; they did not, however, find the same opportunities as their male counterparts. A woman earned an average of between one-third and two-thirds less than a man working in the same job. The entry of large numbers of women into any job was certain to result in a recasting of that position as unskilled and low-paying. Unlike men, women lost their jobs when they married and found most supervisory positions closed to them.

By the 1880s, an international women's movement had emerged to challenge the legal, political, and economic disabilities facing European and American women. Consisting of a vast web of interconnected organizations, publications, and correspondence networks, the middle-class women's movement sought to challenge the ideology of separate spheres and to establish a new basis for both private and public relations. Its multifaceted campaigns focused on four fronts: the legal impediments facing married women, employment opportunities and higher education for girls and women, the double standard of sexual conduct enshrined in European laws, and national women's suffrage.

WOMEN AND THE LAW

European legal systems strongly reinforced the liberal ideology of separate spheres for men and women. Law codes often classified women with children, criminals, and the insane. Article 231 of the Napoleonic Code, the legal system of France and the basis of the legal codes of much of western and central Europe, declared that the wife was the dependent of the husband; hence, "the husband owes protection to his wife; the wife owes obedience to her husband." The Russian legal code agreed: "The woman must obey her husband, reside with him in love, respect, and unlimited obedience, and offer him every pleasantness and affection as the ruler of the household." In Russia a woman could not travel without her father's or husband's permission. The

■ **Women at Work**

The expansion of local and central government interference in daily life created many opportunities for women's paid employment. Here government health inspectors check a schoolgirl for head lice.

husband was also the legal guardian of all children; he alone had the authority to pick their schools, determine their punishments, and approve their marriage partners. Similarly, in Prussia the law declared that only the husband could decide when his baby should stop breastfeeding. English common law, based on tradition and precedent rather than on a single, systematized code, proclaimed much the same idea. As Sir William Blackstone explained in his famous *Commentaries on the Laws of England* (1765–1769), "the husband and wife are one person in law," and that person was the husband. A married woman simply disappeared in the eyes of the British common law. Most property brought into a marriage, or given to her or earned by her while married, became the property of her husband.

From the middle of the nineteenth century on, women's groups fought to improve the legal rights of married women. By the end of the 1880s, English married women had won rights to own their own property, control their own income, and keep their children. Two decades later, French women could claim similar rights. In contrast, the German women's movement suffered a sharp defeat with the promulgation of the Civil Code in 1900. The Civil Code, which formulated a single uniform legal system for Germany, proclaimed that "the husband takes the decisions in all matters affecting married life." It granted all parental authority to the husband—over his stepchildren as well as his own children. By German law, "if the parents disagree, the father's opinion takes precedence." While it allowed married women to keep money they earned while married, it declared that all property owned by the wife before marriage or given to her after marriage became the husband's.

FINDING A PLACE: EMPLOYMENT AND EDUCATION

In addition to their legal campaigns, feminists also worked to widen women's educational and employment opportunities as part of their effort to enter the public sphere. At the core of this aspect of the women's movement was a simple demographic reality—women outnumbered men in almost every region in Europe. In England by 1900, the higher rates of male emigration and infant mortality meant that there were 1,064 females for every 1,000 males. Clearly, not all women could marry. Thus, providing respectable jobs for middle-class single women was a high priority for early European and American feminists.

The problem of women's jobs quickly proved to be inseparable from the issue of women's education. Even girls from privileged families rarely received rigorous educations before 1850. The minority of girls who did go to school spent their time learning ladylike occupations such as fancy embroidery, flower arranging, and piano playing. Proper posture was more important than any literary or scientific attainments. Widening the world of women's education, then, became a crucial feminist aim and proved to be an

area in which they achieved considerable, but still limited, success.

Feminists' educational campaigns in the second half of the nineteenth century had two main emphases: first, improving the quality as well as expanding the number of girls' secondary schools, and second, opening universities to women. The fight to upgrade the quality of girls' secondary education was often difficult. Many parents opposed an academic curriculum for girls, a position reinforced by medical professionals who argued that girls' brains simply could not withstand the strain of an intellectual education. Dorothea Beale (1831–1906), a pioneer in girls' education in England, established one of the first academically oriented high schools for girls in London in the 1850s, but she faced an uphill battle in persuading reluctant parents to allow her to teach their daughters mathematics. In France, feminists achieved their goal of a state-funded and state-run system of secondary schools for girls in the 1880s. They lost the battle for a university-preparatory curriculum, however, which made it difficult for girls to pass the exams necessary to enter the French university system.

Not surprisingly, the number of women in French universities remained very small throughout this period. Opportunities for university education for women varied enormously. In the United States, women accounted for one-third of all students in higher education as early as 1880, while in Germany, women were not admitted to full-time university study until 1901. In Russia, the development of women's higher education was particularly sporadic. Full-time university study became available to women in Moscow in 1872, and by 1880, women in Russia had some of the best opportunities for higher education in all of Europe. But the involvement of Sofiia Perovskaia—an educated woman—in the assassination of Tsar Alexander II in 1881 convinced the authorities that revolutionary politics and advanced female education went hand in hand. Most educational avenues for Russian women were blocked for more than two decades after the assassination.

Despite such limitations and reverses, the range of jobs open to women did broaden during this period. In 1900, French women won the right to practice law, and in 1903 in the French city of Toulouse, a woman lawyer presented a case in a European court for the first time. In 1906, the physicist and Nobel Prize winner Marie Curie became the first woman to hold a university faculty position in France. By the opening decades of the twentieth century, women doctors, although still unusual, were not unheard of. In Russia, women accounted for 10 percent of all physicians by 1914.

NO MORE ANGELS

The campaigns for women's legal rights and an expansion of employment and educational opportunities helped women move out of the private and into the public sphere.

But the third goal of feminist activity—to eradicate the double standard of sexual conduct—posed a more radical challenge to nineteenth-century middle-class culture and its ideology of separate spheres. By arguing that the same moral standards should apply to both men and women, feminists questioned whether two separate spheres should exist at all.

The ideology of separate spheres glorified women's moral purity and held that the more aggressive, more animal-like natures of men naturally resulted in such male pastimes as heavy drinking and sexual adventurism. The laws as well as the wider culture reflected these assumptions. For example, in France, a woman with an illegitimate child could not institute a paternity suit against the father: Premarital sex was a crime for the woman, but not for the man. Similarly, the English divorce legislation of 1857 declared that a woman's adultery was all that was necessary for a husband to sue for divorce, but a man's adultery was not a sufficient reason to end a marriage. For a wife to divorce her husband, she had to prove that he had committed additional crimes such as bigamy, incest, or bestiality.

To feminists, applying different moral standards to men and women degraded men and blocked women's efforts to better their own lives and society as a whole. As the French feminist leader Maria Desraismes explained, "To say that woman is an angel is to impose on her, in a sentimental and admiring fashion, all duties, and to reserve for oneself all rights . . . I decline the honor of being an angel."[10]

In their effort to erase the moral distinctions between men and women, feminists fought on a variety of fronts. One key area of struggle was the regulation of prostitution. By the 1870s, many European countries, as well as the United States, had established procedures that made it safer for men to hire prostitutes, while still treating the women involved as criminals. In England, the Contagious Diseases Act, passed in 1870 to address the problem of venereal disease, declared that any woman suspected of being a prostitute could be stopped by the police and required to undergo a genital exam. Men, however, were subject to no such indignities. Feminists such as Josephine Butler (1857–1942) contended that such legislation made it easier for men to indulge their sexual appetites, while punishing the impoverished women who were forced to sell their bodies to feed themselves and their children. For almost twenty years Butler led a concerted campaign both to repeal the legislation that regulated prostitution and to focus public attention on the lack of employment opportunities for women.

Abuse of alcohol was another key battleground for the women's movement. Arguing that the socially accepted practice of heavy male drinking had devastating consequences for women, in the form of both family poverty and domestic violence, feminist activists backed the temperance or prohibitionist cause. The movement triumphed in the United States in 1919 when decades of agitation from groups such as the Women's Christian Temperance Union led to the passage of the Eighteenth Amendment prohibiting the manufacture and sale of alcoholic beverages. "Prohibition," however, did little to transform gender relations; instead, it simply created new ways for organized crime syndicates to make money. The American prohibition experiment ended in 1933 with the repeal of the Eighteenth Amendment.

In general, feminist moral reform campaigns achieved only limited success. The regulation of prostitution did end in England in 1886 and in the United States, France, and the Scandinavian countries by 1914, but remained in effect in Germany. By 1884 in France, a husband's adultery, like a wife's, could end a marriage, but in England, the grounds for divorce remained differentiated by gender until 1923. In all European countries and in the United States, the sexual double standard remained embedded in both middle- and working-class culture far into the twentieth century.

THE FIGHT FOR WOMEN'S SUFFRAGE

The slow pace and uneven progress on both the legal and moral fronts convinced many feminists that they would achieve their goals only if they possessed the political clout of the *national* suffrage. In 1867 the National Society for Women's Suffrage was founded in Britain; over the next three decades suffrage societies emerged on the Continent. The French suffragist Hubertine Auclert (1848–1914) described the vote as "the keystone that will give [women] all other rights." As the editor of *La Citoyenne* ("The Citizeness"), Auclert agitated for full citizenship rights for adult women. In an imaginative move, she refused to pay taxes, on the grounds of "no taxation without representation." Auclert was also the first woman to describe herself as a "feminist," a word that entered the English language from the French around 1890.

Auclert and other American and European suffragists had little success. Only in Finland (1906) and Norway (1913) did women gain the national franchise in this period. (By 1913, women also possessed the vote in twelve American states.) The social upheaval of World War I brought women the vote in Russia (1917), Britain (1918), Germany (1919), Austria (1919), the Netherlands (1919), and the United States (1920). Women in Italy had to wait until 1945; French women did not gain the vote until 1946, Greek women not until 1949. Women in Switzerland did not vote until 1971.

Feminists faced a number of significant obstacles in their battle for the national franchise. In Catholic countries such as France and Italy, the women's suffrage movement failed to become a political force not only because the Church remained fiercely opposed to the women's vote, but also because in Catholicism—in its veneration of the Virgin Mary and other female saints, in its exaltation of family life, in the opportunity for religious vocation as a nun—women found a great many avenues for emotional expression and

IN FAVOR OF THE VOTE FOR WOMEN

Many supporters of women's suffrage believed that education, reason, and persuasion would achieve the vote. If suffragists made their case in logical, reasonable terms, they would be able to convince a majority of male voters of the rightness of their cause. This excerpt from a French suffragist pamphlet, published in 1913, is very typical both in its effort to persuade its reader through a careful marshaling of factual evidence and in its belief that the women's vote would transform political life. French women did not win the vote for another thirty years.

We are going to try to prove that the vote for women is a just, possible and desirable reform.
. . .

A woman has responsibility in the family; she ought to be consulted about the laws establishing her rights and duties with respect to her husband, her children, her parents.

Women work—and in ever greater numbers; a statistic of 1896 established that . . . the number of women workers was 35 per cent of the total number of workers, both male and female.

If she is in business, she, like any businessman, has interests to protect. . . .

If a woman is a worker or a domestic, she ought to participate as a man does in voting on unionization laws, laws covering workers' retirement, social security, the limitation and regulation of work hours, weekly days off, labor contracts, etc.
. . .

Finally, her special characteristics of order, economy, patience and resourcefulness will be as useful to society as the characteristics of man and will favor the establishment of laws too often overlooked until now.

The woman's vote will assure the establishment of important social laws.

All women will want:

To fight against alcoholism, from which they suffer much more than men;
To establish laws of health and welfare;
To obtain the regulation of female and child labor;
To defend young women against prostitution;
Finally, to prevent wars and to submit conflicts among nations to courts of arbitration.

Source: From a report presented to Besancon Municipal Council by the Franc-Comtois Group of the Union Française pour le Suffrage des Femmes. Besancon, March 1913, pp. 6–9.

intellectual satisfaction. Feminism had a much harder time taking root in these countries.

In central and eastern Europe the obstacles were even greater. In much of this region, economic development was far behind that of the western areas of Europe, and thus middle-class culture—the social base of feminism—was also underdeveloped. In the Russian Empire, the middle class was small and any political organization independent of the tsar was seen as a form of treason. No women's suffrage movement existed there until the revolution of 1905 dramatically changed the political equation. After the Revolution won the vote for men but failed to extend it to women, an organized and vocal women's suffrage campaign emerged.

In contrast to Russia, in England the middle class was both large and politically powerful, and the political structure had shown itself capable of adaptation and evolution. Yet even in England, the site of the first and the strongest European female suffrage movement, women failed to win the vote in the nineteenth century. As a result, a small group of activists resorted to more radical tactics. Led by the imposing mother-and-daughters team of Emmeline (1858–1928), Christabel (1880–1958), and Sylvia Pankhurst (1882–1960), the suffragettes° formed a breakaway women's suffrage group in 1903. Convinced that the mainstream suf-

fragists' tactics such as signing petitions, publishing reasoned arguments, and lobbying politicians would never win the vote, the suffragettes threw respectability to the winds. They adopted as their motto the slogan "Deeds, Not Words," and declared that women would never earn the vote through rational persuasion. Instead, they had to grab it by force. The suffragettes broke up political meetings with the cry "Votes for Women!," they chained themselves to the steps of the Houses of Parliament, shattered shop windows, burned churches, destroyed mailboxes, and even, in a direct attack on a cherished citadel of male middle-class culture, vandalized golf courses.

In opting for violence, the suffragettes staged a full frontal assault on a central fortification of middle-class culture—the ideal of the passive, homebound woman. The fortress they were attacking proved well-defended, however. Their opponents reacted with fury. Police broke up suffragette rallies with sexually focused brutality: They dragged suffragettes by their hair, stomped on their crotches, punched their breasts, and tore off their blouses. Once in jail, hunger-striking suffragettes endured the horror of forced feedings. Several jailers pinned the woman to her bed while the doctor thrust a plastic tube down her throat, often lacerating her larynx in the process, and pumped in food until she gagged.

CONCLUSION

The West in an Age of Mass Politics

The clash between the suffragettes and their jailers was only one of a multitude of encounters, many of them violent, among those seeking access to political power and those seeking to limit that access, in the era from 1870 to the start of World War I in 1914. At the same time, changing patterns of industrialization and accelerated urbanization gave rise to other sorts of encounters–between the manager seeking to cut production costs and the employee aiming to protect his wages, for example, or among the newly arrived immigrants in the city, struggling to survive in an unfamiliar culture, and the long-established residents who spoke a different language.

Out of such encounters emerged key questions about the definition of "the West." Where, for example, did the West end? Did it include Russia? "Yes," replied the small revolutionary groups who embraced Karl Marx's socialist theories and argued that Russia would follow Western patterns of economic and political development. "No," replied the Russian populists who rejected Western models and sought a revolutionary path unique to Russia. The expansion of the franchise and the processes of making nations raised even more fundamental questions. Was the West defined by democracy? Should it be? Was it synonymous with white, western European men or could people with olive-colored or black skin—or women of any color—participate fully in Western culture and politics? Was "the West" defined by its rationality? In the eighteenth century, Enlightenment thinkers had praised the power of human rationality and looked to reason as the path to social improvement. The rise of a new style of politics, based on emotional appeal and often irrational racist hatred, challenged this faith in reason. But at the same time, developments in industrial organization and technologies, which helped expand European national incomes, seemed to point to the benefits of rational processes.

As we will see in the next chapter, the expansion of Western control over vast areas of Asia and Africa in this period led an increasing number of Europeans and Americans to highlight economic prosperity and technological superiority as the defining characteristics of the West. Confidence, however, was accompanied by anxiety as these years also witnessed a far-reaching cultural and intellectual crisis. Closely connected to the development of mass politics and changes in social and gender relations, this crisis slowly eroded many of the pillars of middle- and upper-class society and raised searching questions about Western assumptions and values.

Suggestions for Further Reading

For a comprehensive list of suggested readings, please go to www.ablongman.com/levack/chapter22

Evans, Richard. *The Feminists: Women's Emancipation Movements in Europe, America, and Australasia 1840–1920.* 1977. A helpful comparative overview.

Kern, Stephen. *The Culture of Time and Space 1880–1918.* 1983. An innovative work that explores the cultural impact of technological change.

Lidtke, Vernon. *The Alternative Culture: Socialist Labor in Imperial Germany.* 1985. Looks beyond the world of parliamentary politics to assess the meaning and impact of working-class socialism.

Lindemann, Albert. *Esau's Tears: Modern Anti-Semitism and the Rise of the Jews.* 1997. A comprehensive and detailed survey that challenges many assumptions about the roots and nature of modern anti-Semitism.

Mayer, Arno. *The Persistence of the Old Regime: Europe to the Great War.* 1981. Argues that landed elites maintained a considerable amount of economic and political power throughout the nineteenth century.

Milward, A. S., and S. B. Saul. *The Development of the Economies of Continental Europe, 1850–1914.* 1977. A helpful survey.

Moch, Leslie. *Moving Europeans: Migration in Western Europe Since 1650.* 1992. Filled with maps and packed with information, Moch's work explodes many easy assumptions about the movement of Europeans in the nineteenth century.

Nord, Philip. *The Republican Moment: Struggles for Democracy in Nineteenth-Century France.* 1996. Illuminates the struggle to define and redefine France.

Pilbeam, Pamela. *The Middle Classes in Europe, 1789–1914: France, Germany, Italy, and Russia.* 1990. A comparative approach that helps clarify the patterns of social change.

Richards, Thomas. *The Commodity Culture of Victorian England: Advertising and Spectacle 1851–1914.* 1990. Fascinating study of the manufacturing of desire.

Stearns, Peter N. *Lives of Labor: Work in a Maturing Industrial Society.* 1975. Explores changing economic and social patterns.

Steenson, Gary P. *After Marx, Before Lenin: Marxism and Socialist Working-Class Parties in Europe, 1884–1914.* 1991. Examines both ideology and political practice within Europe's socialist parties.

Weber, Eugen. *Peasants into Frenchmen: The Modernization of Rural France, 1870–1914.* 1976. A very important work that helped shape the way historians think about "nation making."

Notes

1. Leslie Moch, *Moving Europeans: Migration in Western Europe Since 1650* (1992), 147.
2. Quoted in Eugen Weber, *Peasants into Frenchmen: The Modernization of Rural France, 1870–1914* (1987), 332–333.
3. Norman Kleeblatt, *The Dreyfus Affair: Art, Truth, and Justice* (1987), 96.
4. Quoted in Eric Cahm, *The Dreyfus Affair in French Society and Politics* (1994), 167.
5. Quoted in Robert Gildea, *Barricades and Borders: Europe 1800–1914* (1987), 317.
6. Quoted in Leslie Derfler, *Socialism Since Marx: A Century of the European Left* (1973), 58.
7. Karl Kautsky, quoted in Eric Hobsbawm, *The Age of Empire 1875–1914* (1987), 133.
8. Eugen Weber, *France, Fin-de-Siecle* (1986), 126.
9. Albert Lindemann, *Esau's Tears: Modern Anti-Semitism and the Rise of the Jews* (1997).
10. Maria Desraismes, "La Femme et Le Droit," *Eve dans l'humanite* (1891), 16–17.

The West and the World: Cultural Crisis and the New Imperialism, 1870–1914

N THE AUTUMN OF 1898, BRITISH TROOPS MOVED INTO THE SUDAN IN NORTHEAST Africa to claim the region for the British Empire. On September 2, the British Camel Corps faced an army of 40,000 fighters. The Sudanese soldiers, Islamic believers known as dervishes who possessed a reputation for military fierceness, were fighting on their home ground against an invading force. Nevertheless, after only five hours of fighting, 11,000 dervishes lay dead. Their opponents lost just forty men. While the dervishes, armed with swords and spears, surged forward in a full-scale frontal assault, the British troops sat safely behind fortified defenses, and, using repeating rifles and Maxim guns (a type of early machine gun), simply mowed down their attackers. According to one participant on the British side, the future prime minister Winston Churchill, the biggest danger to the British soldiers during the battle of Omdurman was boredom: "the mere physical act [of loading, firing, and reloading] became tedious." The dervishes had little chance of boredom. Churchill recalled, "And all the time out on the plain on the other side bullets were shearing through flesh, smashing and splintering bone; blood spouted from terrible wounds; valiant men were struggling through a hell of whistling metal, exploding shells, and spurting dust—suffering, despairing, dying."[1]

The slaughter of 11,000 Sudanese in just over five hours formed but one episode in what many historians call the age of new imperialism, a period that witnessed both the culmination of, and a new phase in, Europe's conquest of the globe. This often-violent encounter between Europe and the regions that Europeans emphatically defined as non-Western was closely connected to the political and economic upheavals examined in Chapter 22. An understanding of the new imperialism, however, demands a close look not only at political

Chapter Outline

- Scientific Transformations

- Cultural Crisis and the Birth of Modernism

- The New Imperialism

Paul Gauguin, _Matamoe_ ("Peacocks in the Country"), 1892: The Fauvist painter Paul Gauguin fled Europe for Tahiti in an effort to restore to his art the strong colors and emotions that he believed characterized non-Western cultures. The sights, sensibilities, and symbolism of Tahitian society profoundly affected his painting—and helped shape modernist art.

rivalries and economic structures, but also at scientific, intellectual, and cultural developments in the last third of the nineteenth century. At the same time that European and American adventurers risked life and limb to chart Africa's rivers, exploit its resources, and subjugate its peoples, Western artists and scientists embarked on explorations into worlds of thought and perception far deeper than the surface reality accessible to the senses, and in so doing challenged the social order and even the meaning of reality itself.

The final decades of the nineteenth century and the opening years of the twentieth thus comprised an era of internal fragmentation and external expansion. The scientific, artistic, and physical explorations that are the subject of this chapter redefined the West and its relationship with the rest of the world. As Western dominance over Africa and Asia expanded, states such as Russia and Japan embarked on conscious efforts to westernize their societies and thereby compete successfully with the West's industrial and military might. Areas of white European settlement such as Australia, South Africa, and the United States moved more firmly inside Western boundaries. The tendency to color the West white, however, meant that members of the non-white populations of these regions were rarely accepted by whites as fully Western.

This chapter addresses three questions: (1) How did scientific developments during this period lead to not only greater intellectual and cultural optimism but also deepened anxiety? (2) What factors led many Europeans in this period to believe they were living in a time of cultural crisis? (3) What were the causes and consequences of the new imperialist ideology for both the West and non-Western societies?

Scientific Transformations

During the final third of the nineteenth century, Europeans encountered in new ways both the human body and the wider physical universe. Forced by urbanization to cram more bodies into limited space, men and women grew increasingly aware of the human body, and of the way it interacted with other bodies, both human and microscopic. At the same time, the work of geologists and biologists highlighted the way the body itself had evolved to meet the challenges of survival, while the experiments of chemists and physicists revealed the inadequacies of accepted models for understanding the physical world.

These developments affirmed a central assumption of the dominant middle-class worldview—that human reason and endeavor can guarantee social, intellectual, and moral progress. Scientific advances in the final third of the nineteenth century helped improve the health and hygiene of the Western world. Yet these changes in scientific understandings of both the body and the cosmos also threatened to destabilize Western society and therefore deepened the cultural anxiety of Europeans and Americans in this period.

MEDICINE AND MICROBES

In the second half of the nineteenth century, and particularly after 1870, a series of developments transformed the practice of Western medicine. Before this time, Western physicians assumed that illness was caused by bad blood and so relied on practices such as leeching (attaching leeches to the skin) and bloodletting (slicing open a vein). These procedures drained large amounts of blood, further weakening already ill patients. Admission into a hospital was sometimes a death sentence. Ignorant of the existence of bacteria and viruses, doctors commonly attended one patient after another without bothering to wash their hands or surgical instruments. The only anesthetic available was alcohol; pain was regarded as inevitable, something to be endured rather than eased.

Urbanization posed a fundamental challenge to such traditional medical practice, and helped transform Western medicine. Expanding urban populations served as fertile seedbeds for contagious diseases. Cholera outbreaks, such as the epidemics that ravaged British cities in 1831 and 1848, forced doctors and public officials to pay attention to the relationship between overcrowding, polluted water, and epidemic disease. Hamburg was one of the first cities to undertake the construction of a modern water and sewer system in 1842; in 1848 the London cholera epidemic persuaded public officials to build a vast sewer system (most of which is still in use today).

It was not until the 1860s, however, that germ theory was developed. By exploring the transmission of disease among plants and animals in the French agricultural industry, the chemist Louis Pasteur (1822–1895) discovered that the source of contagion is not air, water, or odor, but microscopic living organisms—bacteria. Astonishingly productive, Pasteur developed vaccines against anthrax, hog fever, sheep pox, various poultry and cattle diseases, and rabies. (His process of purifying milk and fermented products is still known as pasteurization.) Following Pasteur, Robert Koch (1843–1910), professor of public health in Berlin, isolated the tuberculosis bacillus in 1882 and the bacteria that cause cholera in 1883.

The work of Pasteur, Koch, and other scientists in tracing the transmission of disease was crucial in improving Western medical practice. Between 1872 and 1900, the number of European deaths from infectious diseases dropped by 60 percent. Once physicians and surgeons

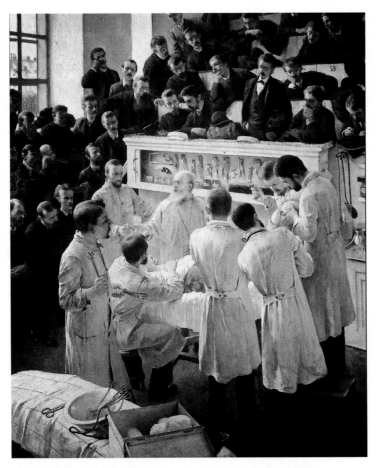

■ **Adelbert Seligmann, *German Surgeon Theodor Billroth at Work in Vienna* (1890)**
Modern surgery in the making: The patient has been anesthetized, but the modern operating room does not yet exist, nor are the doctors wearing gloves or masks. Billroth, the director of the Second Surgical Clinic in Vienna, pioneered surgical techniques for gastrointestinal illnesses and cancer.

genuine confidence that the conquest of nature through science would create a healthier environment. But the widespread awareness of germs also heightened anxiety. Isolation of the bacilli that caused an illness did not immediately translate into its cure, and viral infections remained often lethal. Measles, for example, continued to kill at least 7,000 people per year in Britain throughout the nineteenth century. After the 1870s, Europeans were aware that they lived in a world populated by potentially deadly but invisible organisms, carried on the bodies of their servants, their employees, their neighbors, and their family members. Those who could afford to isolate themselves from the danger often did so. As a result, this era witnessed striking growth in the number of seaside resorts, as middle- and upper-class Europeans fled from urban centers of contagion.

THE REVOLUTION IN PHYSICS

The transformation in medical practice was not the only dramatic scientific change that occurred in the late nineteenth century. Between 1880 and 1910 a revolution in physics occurred as well. Although the most dramatic consequences of this revolution—atomic weapons and nuclear energy—would not be realized for another half century, this transformation in scientific understanding contributed to both the exhilaration and the uncertainty that characterized the intellectual and cultural history of Europe in the decades before World War I.

At the core of this scientific revolution lay the question, "What is matter?" For most of the nineteenth century, the answer was simple: Matter was what close observation and measurement, as well as common sense, showed it to be. Material bodies, made up of the building blocks called atoms, rested and moved against a fixed backdrop of space and time. Matter was three-dimensional, defined by height, width, and depth. Accessible to reason, observation, and common sense, the material world could be understood and controlled.

As the new century opened, this picture of the universe began to crumble. A series of discoveries and experiments challenged this commonsense view of the universe and offered in its place a much more mysterious and unsettling vista. The discovery of the X-ray in 1895 had already disrupted prevailing assumptions about the solidity and predictability of matter. They were shaken even further in 1898 when the Polish-French chemist Marie Curie (1867–1934) discovered a new element, radium, which did not behave the way matter was supposed to behave. Because

accepted that microscopic organisms caused disease, they began to develop techniques to control their spread. The development of antiseptic surgery in the later 1860s improved the patient's odds of surviving the operating table.

The increasing use of anesthetics in the second half of the nineteenth century also improved those odds. In 1847 a Scottish physician performed the first delivery of a baby using chloroform to dull the mother's pain. Although condemned by many Christian theologians (who regarded pain as both ennobling and a necessary part of sinful human existence), the use of anesthetics spread fairly quickly. Britain's Queen Victoria, who gave birth to nine children, probably articulated the feelings of many patients when she greeted the use of anesthetics in the delivery room with unfettered delight: "Oh blessed chloroform!"

Medical advances such as anesthetic techniques and an understanding of how diseases are spread gave Europeans it continually emitted subatomic particles, radium did not possess a constant atomic weight. Two years later, the German scientist Max Planck (1858–1947) theorized that a heated body radiates energy not in the continuous, steady, predictable stream most scientists envisaged, but rather in irregular clumps, which he called *quanta*. Although at first dismissed by most scientists as contrary to common sense, Planck's quantum theory accorded with the emerging picture of a changeable universe.

These scientific discoveries provide the context for the work of Albert Einstein (1879–1955), certainly the most famous and readily recognizable scientist of the twentieth century. Bored by his job as a patent clerk, Einstein passed the time speculating on the nature of the cosmos. In 1905, he rang the death knell for the Newtonian universe by publishing an article that introduced to the world the theory of relativity. Einstein rejected the nineteenth-century assumption of the absolute nature of time and space. Instead, he argued, time and space shift relative to the position of the observer. Similarly, matter itself shifts. Mass depends on motion, and thus time, space, and matter intermingle in a universe of relative flux. The result of Einstein's vision was a revolution in perspective. The universe is not three- but four-dimensional: To height, width, and depth, Einstein added *time*.

This new understanding was much harder to grasp than that offered by Newtonian science. With the revolution in physics, much of science became incomprehensible to ordinary men and women, even educated ones. The new science also challenged the basic assumptions that governed nineteenth-century thought by offering a vision of the universe in which what you see is *not* what you get, in which objective reality might well be the product of subjective perception.

SOCIAL THOUGHT: THE REVOLT AGAINST POSITIVISM

Just as the revolution in physics presented a new and more disturbing picture of the physical universe, so social thinkers in the last third of the nineteenth century began to formulate troubling theories about the nature of human society. As Chapter 21 explained, the mainstream of nineteenth-century thought was positivist: It placed great faith in human reason and therefore in the validity of applying methods drawn from the natural sciences to the study of human affairs. Positivism viewed the world as eminently knowable and progress as ultimately guaranteed, given the capacity of rational human beings to understand and therefore control both physical and human nature. This faith in human reason, however, came under attack in the last decades of the century. In this era, social thinkers (writers and scientists whose work would lay the foundations for new academic disciplines such as sociology, psy-

chology, and anthropology) began to emphasize the role of nonrational forces in determining human conduct.

Social thinkers confronted the power of the nonrational first in the new mass politics of this era. The rise of racist and nationalist political parties demonstrated that individuals were often swayed more by emotion than by rational argument. In an effort to understand and therefore to manipulate political demonstrations, the French theorist Gustave LeBon (1841–1931) developed the discipline of crowd or collective psychology. He showed how appeals to emotion, particularly in the form of symbols and myths, can influence crowd behavior. In LeBon's view, democracy relinquished political control to the easily swayed masses and so would lead only to disaster.

Unlike LeBon, the German social theorist Max Weber (1864–1920) believed in democracy, but he, too, recognized the role of the nonrational in influencing the mass electorate. Weber was both fascinated and frightened by the development of modern industrial society. His studies focused on the "bureaucratization" of modern life—the tendency of both political and economic institutions to become increasingly standardized and to grow ever larger and more impersonal. Weber judged the triumph of bureaucracy as the victory of reason and science over individual prejudice and interest-group politics, and so as a generally progressive force. But at the same time he recognized that because growing bureaucracies could crush both ideals and individuals, they posed a real threat to personal and political freedom. Troubled by the vision of individuals trapped within "the iron cage of modern life," Weber in 1898 suffered a nervous breakdown. After four years Weber was able to free himself from the grip of debilitating depression, but he remained profoundly pessimistic about the future, which he described as "a polar night of icy darkness and hardness."[2]

According to his wife, when Weber fell into depression, "an evil something out of the subterranean unconscious . . . grasped him by its claws."[3] This view of the individual as a captive of the unconscious was central to the revolt against positivism, and reached its fullest development in the highly influential work of the Viennese scientist and physician Sigmund Freud (1856–1939). Freud argued that the conscious mind plays only a very limited role in shaping the actions of each individual. His effort to treat patients suffering from nervous disorders led him to hypnosis and dream analysis, and to the conviction that behind the conscious exterior existed a deeper, far more significant reality—the unconscious. In *The Interpretation of Dreams* (1900), Freud argued that beneath the rational surface of each human being surge all kinds of hidden desires, including such irrational drives as the longing for death and destruction.

Freud thought of himself as a scientist. He believed that he could understand human behavior (and treat mental illness) by diving below the rational surface and exploring the submerged terrain of unconscious desire. Yet the emergence of Freudian psychology convinced many educated Western

individuals not that the irrational could be uncovered and controlled, but rather that the irrational was *in* control.

THE TRIUMPH OF EVOLUTIONARY THEORY

During the same period that social thought was
outlining new ways to understand human behavior and raising serious doubts about the essential
rationality of that behavior, developments in geology and biology also led to both confidence and
anxiety. Evolutionary theory provided a scientific
framework in which educated Europeans could
understand and justify their own superior social
and economic positions. It also, however, challenged basic religious assumptions and depicted
the natural world in new and unsettling ways.

Traditionally, Europeans had relied on the
opening chapters of the Bible to understand the
origins of both nature and humanity. By the
1830s, however, the work of geologists challenged the biblical account. Although a literal
reading of the Bible dated the Earth at only 6,000
years old, geologists such as Charles Lyell
(1797–1875) argued on the basis of the fossil
record and existing geological formations that
the Earth had formed over millions of years.
Lyell's most famous work was the *Principles of
Geology*, first published in 1830 and a nineteenth-century best-seller that went through
eleven editions. In three volumes of very readable prose, packed with illustrative examples,
Lyell gently but rigorously refuted the orthodox
Christian position that geological change and the
extinction of species could be explained by the
biblical account of the flood or other such supernatural interventions. Instead, he and others argued that
the material world must be seen as the product of natural
forces still at work, still observable today.

But how could one explain the tremendous variety of
plant and animal species in the world today on the basis of
natural processes? In 1859, the British scientist Charles
Darwin (1809–1882) answered this question in a way that
proved quite satisfying to large numbers of educated
Europeans—and quite horrifying to others. Darwin had
spent two decades thinking about the data he collected during a five-year expedition to the South Pacific in the 1830s.
Serving as an unpaid naturalist on the H.M.S. *Beagle* between 1831 and 1836, Darwin observed that certain species
of animal and plant life, isolated on islands, had developed
differently from related species on the coast. After returning
to Britain, Darwin read the population theory of Thomas
Malthus (1766–1834). Malthus argued that population

THAT TROUBLES OUR MONKEY AGAIN.

Female descendant of Marine Ascidian:—"REALLY, MR. DARWIN, SAY WHAT YOU LIKE ABOUT MAN; BUT I WISH YOU WOULD LEAVE MY EMOTIONS ALONE!"

■ **Darwin as a Monkey**

Simplified and often ridiculous versions of Darwin's ideas almost immediately
entered popular culture. In this cartoon, he is being scolded by a woman for
his theory that women blush when men look at them because a man's gaze
directs a woman's attention to the visible parts of her body, which causes a
change in her "capillary circulation."

growth would outstrip food supply, and that in all species,
more offspring are produced than can actually survive.
Putting together Malthus's theory with his own observations, Darwin concluded that life is a struggle for survival,
and that even quite small biological variations might help
an individual member of a species win out in this struggle.
From this understanding came the Darwinian theory° of
the evolution of species.

Darwin's evolutionary theory rested on two basic ideas:
variation and *natural selection*. Variation refers to those
small but crucial biological advantages that assist in the
struggle for survival: A bird with a slightly longer beak, for
example, might gain easier access to scarce food supplies.
Over generations, the individuals more adapted for survival
displace those without the positive variation. Variation,
then, provides the means of natural selection, the process
by which new species evolve.

THE DESCENT OF MAN

First published in 1871, The Descent of Man *continued and completed Charles Darwin's theory of the evolution of species first introduced in his* Origin of Species *(1859). Darwin's work in many ways affirmed central prejudices and assumptions of his middle-class readers, as the following excerpts demonstrate.*

We have now seen that man is variable in body and mind; and that the variations are induced, either directly or indirectly, by the same general causes, and obey the same general laws, as with the lower animals. Man has spread widely over the face of the earth, and must have been exposed, during his incessant migration, to the most diversified conditions.... The early progenitors of man must also have tended, like all other animals, to have increased beyond their means of subsistence; they must, therefore, occasionally have been exposed to a struggle for existence, and consequently, to the rigid law of natural selection. Beneficial variations of all kinds will thus, either occasionally or habitually, have been preserved and injurious ones eliminated....

Man in the rudest state in which he now exists is the most dominant animal that has ever appeared on this earth. He has spread more widely than any other highly organised form, and all others have yielded before him. He manifestly owes this immense superiority to his intellectual faculties, to his social habits, which lead him to aid and defend his fellows, and to his corporeal structure....

The belief that there exists in man some close relation between the size of the brain and the development of the intellectual faculties is supported by the comparison of the skulls of savage and civilized races, of ancient and modern people, and by the analogy of the whole vertebrate series ... the mean internal capacity of the skull in Europeans is 92.3 cubic inches; in Americans 87.5; in Asiatics 87.1; and in Australians only 81.9 inches ... Nevertheless, it must be admitted that some skulls of very high antiquity, such as the famous one of the Neanderthal, are well developed and capacious.

Source: From *The Descent of Man,* 2nd edition, by Charles Darwin, 1874.

Darwin provided a persuasive explanation for evolutionary change, but the fact that the laws of genetic heredity were not yet understood resulted in two key weaknesses in his formulation—first, its extreme gradualness, in that the process of variation required many, many generations; and second, the lack of a precise explanation of how variations first emerge and how they are inherited. Answers to both problems lay embedded in the research of an Austrian monk, Gregor Mendel (1822–1884). Experimenting in his vegetable garden with what we now call selective breeding, Mendel developed the laws of genetic heredity. Mendel's work was ignored almost completely until the end of the century, when the Dutch botanist Hugo DeVries (1848–1935) used his data to hypothesize that evolution occurred through radical mutations in the reproductive cells of an organism. These mutations are passed on to offspring at the moment of reproduction and, if they offer an advantage in the struggle for existence, enable the offspring to survive and to produce more mutant offspring. Thus evolution can proceed by leaps, rather than gradually over a very long period of time.

Long before these genetic underpinnings of evolution were understood, however, Darwin's theories proved extraordinarily influential. Published in 1859, *The Origin of Species* aroused immediate interest and controversy. This controversy intensified when, in 1871, Darwin published *The Descent of Man,* in which he firmly placed humanity itself within the evolutionary process. Many Christians re-

acted with horror to a theory that they believed challenged the biblical narrative of Creation and denied a special place for humankind within the physical universe. But the most troubling aspect of Darwin's theory was its view of nature. According to orthodox Christian theology, nature, like the Bible, reveals God to the believer. In the Darwinian universe, however, nature was not a harmonious, well-ordered system that revealed the hand of God. Instead, it was the arena of brutal and bloody competition for survival—"nature red in tooth and claw," as the British poet Alfred Lord Tennyson put it. In such a universe, ideas of purpose and meaning seemed to disappear. Faced with this disturbing vision, many Christians opposed Darwinian evolutionary theory.

Many other Christians welcomed Darwin's theory, however. They argued that evolution did not banish divine purpose from the universe but instead showed God's hand at work in the gradual development of more perfect species. Enthusiastically applying the idea of evolution to the ethical universe, they contended that the history of humanity showed that the morally fittest proved victorious in the ethical sphere, just as the strongest triumphed in the natural world.

By 1870, three-quarters of British scientists surveyed accepted evolutionary theory. More important, many middle-class Europeans and Americans welcomed Darwin's ideas as providing a coherent explanation of change that accorded with their worldview. They saw Darwin's work as a scientific confirmation of their faith in the virtues of competition and in the inevitability of progress. As Darwin himself wrote in *The Origin of Species,* because "natural selection works solely by and for the good of each being, all corporeal [bodily] and mental development will tend to progress toward perfection."

SOCIAL DARWINISM AND RACIAL HIERARCHIES

Darwin's evolutionary theory contributed to a new understanding of biological relationships and of the connections between humanity and the natural world. In the last quarter of the nineteenth century, however, a growing number of writers and social theorists insisted that evolutionary theory could and should be applied more broadly. One of the most influential of this group was the British writer Herbert Spencer (1820–1902). Trained as a civil engineer, Spencer became convinced that evolution held the key to engineering a better human society. A self-confident, eminently practical thinker, Spencer coined the phrase "the survival of the fittest" to describe what he viewed as the most basic explanation of development in both nature and human society. He believed that human societies evolve like plant and animal species. Only the fittest, those able to adapt to changing conditions, survive. A great champion of *laissez-faire* economics (see Chapter 21), Spencer contended that government interference in economic and social affairs interfered with the natural evolutionary process and so hindered rather than assured progress.

Spencer's essentially biological vision of society proved influential in shaping the theories of Social Darwinism°. Arguing that racial hierarchy was the product of natural evolution, the Social Darwinists applied Spencer's ideas about the importance of individual competition and the survival of the fittest to entire races. In their view, the nonwhite races in Africa and Asia had lost the game. Their so-called backward way of life showed they had failed to compete successfully with white Europeans and thus displayed their biological inferiority. The very popular British novelist Rider Haggard, in his best-selling thriller *She* (1887), summed up the Social Darwinist worldview: "Those who are weak must perish; the earth is to the strong . . . We run to place and power over the dead bodies of those who fail and fall; ay, we win the food we eat from out the mouths of starving babes. It is the scheme of things."

In their effort to construct a scientifically based racial hierarchy, Social Darwinists made use not only of Darwin's idea of natural selection but also of the theory of "recapitulation," first proposed by the German zoologist Ernst Haeckel (1834–1919). According to Haeckel, as an individual matures, he or she moves through the same stages as did the human race during the course of its evolution. For example, the gill slits of a human embryo "recapitulate" the

fish stage through which the human race had evolved. The idea of recapitulation enabled scientists to fill in the gaps left by the fossil record. By observing the development of children into adults, they argued, we can witness the evolutionary maturation of the human race.

Social Darwinists used the theory of recapitulation to argue that only white European males had reached the pinnacle of evolutionary development. They contended that nonwhite men, as well as all women, embodied the more primitive stages of evolution through which the white European male had already passed. In other words, the nonwhite races and white women were suffering from arrested development. Their bodies and brains bore witness to their low-ranking position on the evolutionary ladder. Such ideas permeated much of Western culture in the late nineteenth century. Sigmund Freud, for example, argued that "the female genitalia are more primitive than those of the male," while Gustave LeBon compared the average female brain to that of a gorilla. G. A. Henty, a best-selling British novelist, insisted that the "intelligence of the average negro is about equal to that of a European [male] child of ten years old."[4]

Firmly convinced that the inferiority of women and nonwhites was a biological fact, nineteenth-century scientists and large sections of the European public welcomed evolutionary theory as scientific proof of deeply embedded cultural assumptions, such as the benefits of competition, the rightness of white rule and male dominance, and the superiority of Western civilization. Yet evolutionary science also worked to undermine European confidence because with the idea of evolution came the possibility of regression: Was the traffic on the evolutionary ladder all one-way, or could species descend to a lower evolutionary level? Could humanity regress back to its animal origins?

The concept of the "inheritance of acquired characteristics," associated with the work of the French scientist Jean-Baptiste Lamarck (1744–1829), played a crucial role in fostering these fears of regression. More than fifty years before Darwin published his *Origin of Species,* Lamarck theorized that acquired characteristics—traits that an individual develops in response to experience or the environment, such as the stooped back of a miner, the poor vision of a lace maker, or the deep tan of an agricultural laborer—could be passed on to the individual's offspring. Because the process of genetic reproduction was not understood until the twentieth century, Lamarck's theories remained very influential throughout the nineteenth century, and possessed deeply disturbing implications. Middle-class Europeans began to speculate that the conditions of urban industrial life were producing undesirable characteristics among urban workers. In their view, characteristics such as physical weakness, sexual promiscuity, and violent criminality were being passed from one generation to the next, and were threatening to reverse the evolutionary ascent of Western civilization.

■ **A page from *Criminal Man* (1876), by Cesare Lombroso**

An Italian physician, Lombroso established the new social science of criminology. In *Criminal Man,* he argued that individuals with certain physical characteristics, such as a narrow forehead or linked eyebrows, are likely to be criminals. According to Lombroso, the criminal body is the result of evolutionary regression. In the face, skull, and physique of the criminal we can see evidence of a reversion to a more primitive evolutionary state. The images shown here are grouped alphabetically as follows: A: shoplifters; B, C, D, F: swindlers; E: murderers; G: fraudulent bankrupts; H: purse-snatchers; I: burglars.

Cultural Crisis: The Fin-de-Siècle and the Birth of Modernism

The fear of evolutionary regression contributed to a growing cultural crisis. The sense that Western civilization was declining, that degeneration and decay characterized the contemporary experience, was summed up in a single French phrase: *fin-de-siècle*°. Literally translated as "end of the century," fin-de-siècle served as a shorthand term for the mood of cultural uneasiness, and even despair, that characterized much of European society in the final decades of the nineteenth century and the opening years of the twentieth. Uncertainty colored many aspects of European thought and culture. Fast-moving economic and social change, coupled with the new scientific ideas, convinced many Europeans that old answers were no longer sufficient. The quest for new answers fostered the birth of what would become known as modernism, a broad label for a series of unsettling developments in thought, literature, and art. Many Europeans celebrated modernism as a release from the restraints imposed by middle-class cultural codes. Others, however, responded fearfully. Both exhilaration and anxiety, then, characterize this time of cultural crisis.

THE FIN-DE-SIÈCLE

A series of social problems common to increasingly urbanized nations reinforced Europeans' fear of degeneration. As cities spread, so too did the perception of a rising crime rate. This perception of a more criminal society went hand-in-hand with the reality of increasing drug and alcohol use. Diners in high society finished their sumptuous meals with a dessert course consisting of strawberries soaked in ether; respectable bourgeois men offered each other cocaine as a quick "pick-me-up" at the end of the working day; middle-class mothers fed restless babies opium-laced syrups; workers bought enough opium-derived laudanum on Saturday afternoon to render them unconscious until work on Monday morning. Using Lamarck's theory of the inheritance of acquired characteristics, scientists contended that addictions could be passed on from generation to generation, thus contributing to national decline and a culture of decadence.

Popular novels of the fin-de-siècle also contributed to the fear of degeneration by depicting Western culture as diseased or barbaric. In a twenty-volume work, the French novelist Émile Zola (1840–1902) traced the decline of a once-proud family to symbolize the decay of all of France. As alcoholism and sexual promiscuity pollute succeeding generations, the family disintegrates. In *Nana* (1880), Zola used the title character, a prostitute, to embody his country. Watching as French soldiers march off to defeat in the Franco-Prussian War, Nana is dying of smallpox, her face "a charnel-house, a heap of pus and blood, a shovelful of putrid flesh."[5] Novels such as *Dr. Jekyll and Mr. Hyde* (1886) and *Dracula* (1897) showed that beneath the cultured exterior of a civilized man lurked a primitive, bloodthirsty beast and so revealed a deep sense of anxiety.

The most influential advocate of the idea that Western culture had degenerated was the German philosopher and poet Friedrich Nietzsche (1844–1900). In Nietzsche's view, most people were little more than sheep, penned in by outdated customs and conventions. Bourgeois morality, rooted in Christianity, helped sap Western culture of its vitality. "Christianity has taken the side of everything weak," Nietzsche claimed. He traced the weakness of Western culture beyond Christianity, however, and back to ancient Greece, to Socrates's exaltation of rationality. In Nietzsche's view, an overemphasis on rational thought had deprived Western culture of the power of more primal urges, such as the irrational, emotional, and instinctive aspects of human nature.

Even more fundamentally, Nietzsche argued that the belief that human reason has direct access to scientific fact is an illusion. Trained as a classical philologist, Nietzsche's study of language convinced him that everything we know must be filtered through a symbolic system—through language or some other means of artistic or mathematic representation. We can know only the representation, not the thing itself. Not even science can uncover "reality." Even the style of Nietzsche's publications worked to expose the limits of reason. Rather than write carefully constructed essays that proceeded in a logical, linear fashion from fact to fact, Nietzsche adopted an elusive, poetic style characterized by disconnected fragments, more accessible to intuitive understanding than to rational analysis.

Nietzsche's writings attracted little attention until the 1890s, when his ideas first exploded in Germany and Austria, and then spread throughout Europe. Nietzsche's call to "become what you are" attracted young enthusiasts, who embraced his conviction that the confining assumptions and aspirations of bourgeois society held back the individual from personal liberation. "God is dead," Nietzsche proclaimed, "and we have killed him." If God is dead, then "there is nobody who commands, nobody who obeys, nobody who trespasses."

TIGHTENING GENDER BOUNDARIES

The fear of degeneration evident throughout European culture and society in the last decades of the nineteenth century also expressed itself in a multifaceted effort to draw more tightly the boundaries around accepted definitions of "maleness" and "femaleness." Both the feminist and the homosexual joined the alcoholic, the drug addict, the prostitute, and the criminal in the list of dangerous and degenerate beings.

As discussed in Chapter 22, the years after 1850 and particularly after 1880 witnessed the birth of modern feminism. The emergence of legal, educational, and political reform campaigns challenged nineteenth-century middle-class domestic ideology. Antifeminists viewed these campaigns with alarm. They insisted that a woman's physiology demanded that she remain in the home. In the view of antifeminists, a woman who chose political activism or paid employment not only risked her own physical and mental breakdown, she also tended to produce physically and morally degenerate children.

Like feminists, homosexuals were also singled out as threats to the social order. Before 1869, *homosexual* was not a word: Coined by a Hungarian scientist seeking a new label for a new concept, it entered the English language in 1890. Traditionally, Europeans and Americans had viewed same-sex sexual practice as a form of immoral behavior, indulged in by morally lax—but otherwise normal—men. (Few considered the possibility of female homosexual behavior.) In the last third of the nineteenth century, however, the emphasis shifted from *actions* to *identity*, from condemning a specific type of sexual behavior to denouncing a certain group of people now considered abnormal and dangerous. Scientists argued that "the homosexual" was diseased—and that he could communicate this disease to others.

These ideas gained in force as homosexual subcultures increased in number in European and American cities. The anonymity and mobility of urban life offered homosexuals the possibility of creating a space for themselves in which a new, more confident and assertive homosexual identity could be expressed. But these subcultures soon encountered fierce repression as the moral and medical condemnation

The Trial of Oscar Wilde

In March 1895 the Marquis of Queensberry left a message with the porter of a gentleman's club in London. The message, written on Queensberry's calling card, read "To Oscar Wilde, posing as a *somdomite.*" What Queensberry meant to write was *sodomite,* a common term for a man who engaged in sexual relations with other men. By handing the card to the porter, Queensberry openly accused Wilde, a celebrated novelist and playwright, of homosexual—and therefore criminal—activity. Ten years earlier the British Parliament had declared illegal all homosexual activity, even consensual relations between adults in a private home. Queensberry's accusation, then, was extremely serious. Oscar Wilde responded by suing Queensberry for libel—and set in motion a legal process that led to Wilde's imprisonment, and indirectly, to his early death.

Wilde made a reckless mistake when he chose to sue for libel, for in fact Queensberry had not libeled him. Wilde was a homosexual, and he and Queensberry's son, Lord Alfred Douglas, were lovers. Why, then, did Wilde dare to challenge Queensberry? Perhaps the fact that he was married, with two children, seemed to provide a certain shield against the charge of homosexuality. Or perhaps Wilde's successes as a novelist and playwright gave him a misguided sense of invulnerability. With two of his plays currently appearing on the London stage to favorable reviews, Wilde stood at the pinnacle of his career in the spring of 1895.

Wilde had built that career on a deliberate flouting of middle-class codes of morality. He saw himself as an artist, and insisted that art should be freed from social convention and moral restraint. His "High Society" comedies about privileged elites living scandalous lives and exchanging witty epigrams were far from the morally uplifting drama expected by middle-class audiences. He also used his public persona to attack the conventional, the respectable, and the orthodox. Widely recognized for his outrageous clothing and conversation, Wilde had consciously adopted the mannerisms of what nineteenth-century Britons called a "dandy"—a well-dressed, irreverent, artistic, leisured, and most of all, effeminate man. Before the Oscar Wilde trial, such effeminacy did not serve as a sign of, or a code for, homosexual inclinations, but it did signal to many observers a lavish—and loose—lifestyle. Oscar Wilde, then, was a man many British men and women loved to hate.

Even so, when his trial opened Wilde appeared to be in a strong position, the prosecutor rather than the defendant. Because Wilde had Queensberry's card with the "sodomite" charge written right on it, Queensberry faced certain conviction unless he could show that Wilde had engaged in homosexual activity. Wilde knew, of course, that Queensberry would not risk bringing the legal spotlight to bear on his own son's homosexuality.

At first, Queensberry's attorney, Edward Carson, focused on Wilde's published works, trying to use Wilde's own words against him. It proved an ineffective strategy. On the witness stand, Wilde reveled in the attention, and ran circles around Carson.

On the second day of the libel trial, however, Wilde's witticisms proved insufficient as Carson began to question him about his frequent visits to a male brothel and his associations with a number of young, working-class men who worked as male prostitutes. Suddenly the issue was no longer the literary merit or moral worth of Wilde's published writings, but rather his sexual exploitation of working-class boys. At this point, Wilde withdrew his libel charge against Queensberry, and the court declared the Marquis not guilty.

If Queensberry was not guilty of libel in calling Wilde a sodomite, then by clear implication, Wilde was guilty of homosexual activity and therefore a criminal. Within days he was charged with "gross indecency" with another male. The jury in that case failed to reach a verdict, but the state was determined to obtain a conviction and brought the charges again. Wilde was refused bail, and on May 20 he was back in court.

On May 25, 1895—just three months after Queensberry had left his misspelled message with the club porter—Wilde's promising literary career ended. He was found guilty of seven counts of gross indecency with other men. The presiding judge, Sir Alfred Wills, characterized the trial as "the worst case I have ever tried," and declared, " I shall under the circumstances be expected to pass the severest sentence the law allows. In my judgment it is totally inadequate for such a case." He sentenced Wilde to two years at hard labor. The physical punishment took its toll. Wilde died in 1900 at age 46.

In sentencing Wilde, Wills described him as "the centre of a circle of extensive corruption of the most hideous kind." How do we account for the intensity of Wills's language, as well as the severity of Wilde's sentence? Homosexual activity had long been condemned on religious grounds, but this condemnation grew much more fierce in the closing decades of the nineteenth century. In a time of rapid and threatening change, the marking of gender boundaries became a way to create and enforce social order. Wilde crossed those boundaries, and so had to be punished. Moreover, by the end of the nineteenth century, the state had assumed new responsibilities. Desperate to enhance national strength in a period of heightened international competition, governments intervened in areas previously considered to be the domain of the private citizen. By the turn of the century, western European governments were compelling working-class parents to send their children to school, regulating the hours adults could work, supervising the sale of food and drugs, providing limited forms of old-age pensions and medical insurance—and policing sexual boundaries.

The policing of sexual boundaries became easier after the Wilde trial because it provided a homosexual personality profile, a "Wanted" poster to hang on the walls of Western culture. For many observers of his very well-publicized trial, Wilde became the embodiment of "the homosexual," a particular and peculiar type of person, and a menace to cultural stability. The Wilde trial linked "dandyism" to the new image of the homosexual. Outward stylistic choices such as effeminacy, artistic sensibilities, and flamboyant clothing and conversation became, for many observers, the telltale signs of substantial inner corruption. Thus the Wilde case marked an important turning point in the construction, as well as the condemnation, of a homosexual identity. ■

■ Oscar Wilde and Lord Alfred Douglas
Although the British government pursued its case against Wilde, it made no effort to put together a case against Douglas.

Questions of Justice

1. What does this trial reveal about changing definitions of "public" and "private" in the last decades of the nineteenth century?

2. How does this trial illustrate the role of medical, legal, and cultural assumptions in shaping sexual identity?

Taking It Further

An Ideal Husband. 1999. Film adaptation of Oscar Wilde's very funny play, which exemplifies his lighthearted but devastating critique of conventional manners and morals.

Ellman, Richard. *Oscar Wilde.* 1988. An important biography of Wilde.

Hyde, H. Montgomery. *The Trials of Oscar Wilde.* 1962. Includes extensive quotations from the trial transcripts as well as photographs of some of the documentary evidence.

McLaren, Angus. *The Trials of Masculinity: Policing Sexual Boundaries 1870–1930.* 1997. Places the Wilde trial within a wider cultural context.

of male homosexuality became enshrined in legislation. The Penal Code of the new Germany stipulated severe punishment for homosexuality, while the British government in 1885 made illegal all homosexual acts, even those between consenting adults in the privacy of their own home.

The new concern about homosexuality was nurtured by a wider anxiety about the man's role in society, an anxiety provoked not only by the challenge of feminism, but also by the economic changes associated with the rise of corporate capitalism (see Chapter 22). Required by liberal ideology to be aggressive, independent, self-reliant initiators, middle-class males increasingly found themselves bound to desks, demoted from being those who delivered orders to those who received them. No longer masters of their own fates, they were now bit players in the drama of corporate capitalism. Thus the fear of both feminism and homosexuality arose in part from the compelling need to shore up masculine identity.

The new science of sexuality also heightened this concern about the definition of the "normal" man and woman. During the final decades of the nineteenth century, scientists invaded the most intimate areas of human behavior and made important breakthroughs in the understanding of human reproduction and sexual physiology. In 1875, for example, a German physiologist discovered the basic process of fertilization—the union of male and female sex cells. Four years later, scientists for the first time witnessed,

with the aid of the microscope, a sperm cell penetrating an egg. In the following decade, scientific research uncovered the link between hormonal secretions and sexual potency, affirmed the existence of erogenous zones, and began to explore the role of chromosomes in reproduction.

This greater understanding of sexual *physiology* went hand in hand with the effort to apply the scientific method to sexual *practice*. With data drawn from biology, anthropology, and human physiology, scientists in Europe and the United States sought to define "normal" sexual behavior. In seven weighty volumes, the British scientist Havelock Ellis (1859–1939) explored the range of child and adult sexuality. Ellis used his data to argue for sex education, legalization of contraception and nudism, and tolerance of homosexuality. Other sex researchers, however, turned to science to buttress middle-class moral codes. The German scientist Richard von Krafft-Ebing labeled homosexuality a pathology in 1886, while many publications condemned masturbation and frequent sexual intercourse. Other works offered support for antifeminism by arguing that female physiology incapacitated women for public life.

Heightened concern about gender boundaries also pervaded the visual art of late-nineteenth-century Europe. Women often appeared as elemental forces, creatures of nature rather than civilization, who threatened to trap, emasculate, engulf, suffocate, or destroy the unwary man. In *Medicine,* by the Austrian painter Gustav Klimt

---

SEX AND CHARACTER

....

Otto Weininger's Sex and Character, *first published in 1903, was an immediate best-seller. It quickly appeared in numerous translations, became the center of conversation among educated Europeans, and remained in print in Germany until the 1950s. In the enthusiastic response to the work, we can see that anxiety over changing gender roles permeated middle-class European society.*

. . . The female must be described as absolutely without the quality of genius. The male has everything within him . . . It is possible for him to attain to the loftiest heights, or to sink to the lowest depths; he can become like animals, or plants, or even like women, and so there exist women-like female men. The woman, on the other hand, can never become a man.

Woman's thought is a sliding and gliding through subjects, a superficial tasting of things that a man, who studies the depths, would scarcely notice; it is an extravagant and dainty method of skimming which has no grasp of accuracy. A woman's thought is superficial.

. . . no woman ever believes herself to be anything but beautiful and desirable . . . What is the source of this form of vanity, peculiar to the female? It comes from the absence of an intelligible ego, the only begetter of a constant and positive sense of value; it is, in fact, that she is devoid of a sense of personal value. As she sets no store by herself or on herself, she endeavours to attain to a value in the eyes of others by exciting their desire and admiration.

It has been exhaustively proved that the female is soulless and possesses neither ego nor individuality, personality nor freedom, character nor will.

Woman does not wish to be treated as an active agent; she wants to remain always and throughout—this is just her womanhood—purely passive, to feel herself under another's will. She demands only to be desired physically, to be taken possession of, like a new property . . . a woman is brought to a sense of her existence only by her husband or children.

Source: From *Sex and Character* by Otto Weininger. London: William Heinemann, 1906.

■ **Gustav Klimt,** *Medicine* **(1901)**
Klimt was commissioned by the University of Vienna to create a work that would celebrate medicine's great achievements. Not surprisingly, the painting he produced provoked great controversy. The woman in the forefront is Hygeia, the Greek goddess of health, but behind her swim images of female sexuality and death. Klimt's paintings often featured women as alluring but engulfing elemental forces.

(1862–1918), the liquid portraits of women flow between and into images of sex and death in a disturbing and powerful painting. Such images recur even more graphically in the work of Klimt's student, Egon Schiele (1890–1918). In his very short life Schiele created more than 3,000 works on paper and 300 paintings, many of these depictions of the dangerous female. In works such as *Black-Haired Girl with Raised Skirt* (1911), harsh colors and brazen postures present an unsettling vision of female sexuality. A series of Schiele's paintings with titles such as *Dead Mother* place children in the arms of dead or expressionless women—a direct challenge to the middle-class glorification of motherhood.

THE BIRTH OF MODERNISM

Schiele's disturbing paintings exemplify the new modernist movement. Although the term modernism° was not commonly used until the 1920s, the main developments it embraced were well underway by 1914. It is a difficult term to define, in part because it refers to a variety of artistic, literary, and intellectual styles. Despite this variety, however, modernist art and literature expressed a set of common attitudes and assumptions that centered on a rejection of established authority. In the final decades of the nineteenth century, many artists tossed aside accepted standards and rules and embarked on a series of bold experiments. Oscar Wilde (1854–1900), the British playwright whose dramas mocked Victorian conventions and outraged middle-class sensibilities, wrote, "It is enough that our fathers believed. They have exhausted the faith-faculty of the species. Their legacy to us is the skepticism of which they were afraid."[6] At the core of modernism was a questioning of all accepted standards and truths, particularly those that shaped the middle-class liberal worldview.

In that liberal worldview, the arts served a useful purpose and were a vital part of civilized society. Going to art galleries, for example, was a popular activity, rather like going to the movies today. Respectable workers and middle-class men and women crowded into exhibitions where they viewed paintings that told an entertaining story and had a clear moral message. Modernism shattered this community between artist and audience. It rejected the idea of art as an instrument of moral or emotional uplift. Modernists argued that art is autonomous—it stands alone, of value in and of itself rather than for any impact it may have on society. Modernist painters, for example, did not seek to tell a story or to preach a sermon, but rather to experiment with line, color, and composition.

In addition to rejecting the idea that art must be useful, modernists also challenged middle-class liberalism by insisting that history is irrelevant. Nineteenth-century culture was "historicist." Fascinated with the process of change over time—with the evolution not only of species but also of ideas and societies—the prevailing mindset viewed history as the orderly forward march of progress. In contrast, modernists argued that fast-moving industrial and technological change had shattered the lines connecting history and modernity. Painters such as the Futurists in Italy and the Vorticists in Britain (two of the many artistic movements that clustered under the modernist umbrella) reveled in the new machine age, a world cut off from anything that had gone before. In their paintings they depicted human beings as machines in motion, moving too fast to be tied down to history.

New musical styles emerging in both popular and high culture in these decades also demonstrated the modernist sense of discontinuity. Ragtime, for example, combined

The Soccer Stadium

On a typical Saturday in 1910, all across Britain, approximately 300,000 mostly working-class men paid their six pennies for a ticket, pushed past turnstiles, and headed up concrete steps. Their destination? The terraces—simple concrete expanses, without seats, without restrooms, and without roofs or any protection from the often cold and rainy British weather—on which hundreds of men packed together in order to cheer on and swear at a relatively new type of being: the professional soccer (in European terms, football) player.

The emergence of professional soccer was closely linked with the solidification of an urban working-class culture in Britain. Modern soccer originated in clubs formed by middle-class reformers who hoped to lure working-class boys away from the corruption of the streets and onto the healthy playing fields (and, then, they hoped, into church pews). But workers quickly made soccer their own. They not only took over the soccer clubs, they also rejected the middle-class value system that defined the true sportsman as the amateur who played strictly for love of the game. Love of the game could not pay the rent. By the mid-1880s, a significant number of clubs were recruiting skilled players from other cities, and paying for their services. These clubs found it made economic sense to enclose their fields and to charge for admission: Professional soccer was born. By 1910, six million people were attending professional soccer games in Britain each year. Every major city had at least one professional team, and large cities had two or more. In Glasgow, no fewer than six professional teams

attracted thousands of supporters each Saturday of the season.

Soccer assumed a central role in urban working-class male culture. As cities grew, soccer became a way to create a sense of community, to overcome the anonymity of city life and forge bonds between men who were otherwise strangers. A shortened workweek (most factories released their employees at noon on Saturday by the 1880s), higher pay rates, and the construction of intracity rail networks all made possible regular outings to the soccer

England vs. Scotland, 1905 With the formation of national teams, professional soccer provided an important outlet for the expression of national identity.

Wembley Stadium in England, ca. 1924 By the 1920s, professional sports had developed into a major industry with its own infrastructure. Sports stadia, such as Wembley pictured here, became an integral part of the urban landscape.

THE STADIUM, BRITISH

stadium. At the stadium, working-class men constructed a world of their own, one that was separate from and opposed to both the woman-dominated space of the home and, even more important, the boss-controlled space of the factory. Both the players on the field and the supporters on the terraces expressed a set of values that sharply opposed the moral framework of the middle classes. To a team's supporters, winning was what mattered. Workers knew from their own brutal experience that the best man doesn't always win, and that life was not fair, so why value "fair play" on the field? Thus fans enthusiastically cheered illegal kicks and welcomed any referee error that benefited their side. At the Swindon vs. Barnsley Cup semifinal of 1912, the star player for Swindon was, unusually, a middle-class theological student. From the opening kickoff until he was carried off the field so badly injured that he could not play for a year, he was brutally kicked by the Barnsley players—to the delight of their cheering fans.

Even the game itself rejected middle-class values. The game first introduced by middle-class reformers to urban workers was intensely individualistic, with all the players scrambling to get the ball and then dribble it straight down the field for a goal. But workers changed the way soccer was played. By the 1890s, professional soccer had assumed its present form as a quintessential team sport with a clear division of labor: the defense holding off the opposing players, halfbacks linking up the defense and

■ **Bootham School Soccer Team, York, England, ca. 1885** Unlike the players on the professional teams, the boys on this school team would have been almost exclusively middle class.

offense, and forwards passing the ball into position. Victory on the field, like survival in the working-class world, depended not only on hard work and sheer ability, but also on possessing reliable mates and catching a good break now and then.

■ **Transportation for the Masses** By the turn of the century, the availability of cheap railway tickets not only made seaside excursions affordable for working people (as advertised here), but also enabled supporters to attend professional soccer matches.

For Discussion

What does the professionalization and division of labor in sport indicate about late-nineteenth century European society?

Wyndham Lewis was one of the founders of Vorticism, a pre–World War I English modernist movement. The name *Vorticist* comes from the word "vortex"—a whirlwind, a constant flow of energy. The Vorticists passionately embraced the new machine age and argued that the art of the era needed to reflect its energy and ceaseless movement.

■ **Egon Schiele, *Nude Self-Portrait with Open Mouth* (1910)**
Schiele's paintings exemplify the Expressionist movement with their bold use of color and their no-holds-barred exploration of human emotion and sexuality.

syncopation with unexpected rhythms and sudden stops, while jazz, which developed around the turn of the century in black urban neighborhoods in the United States, created a musical universe of constant change. At the same time, symphonic musicians such as Russian composer Igor Stravinsky (1882–1971) and his Austrian counterpart Arnold Schoenberg (1874–1951) shocked their audiences by tossing aside the convention that a piece should state a central theme, which is then repeated in a sequence of variations. In Stravinsky's ballet *The Rite of Spring* (1913), the meter changes no fewer than twenty-eight times in the final thirty-four bars of the central dance. Similarly, Schoenberg eliminated repetition from his works and used rapid tempo changes.

Modernism also rejected the dominant nineteenth-century faith in the power of human reason and observation, and instead emphasized the role of individual emotion and experience in shaping human understanding. In Paris, for example, a group of artists centered on the Spaniard Pablo Picasso (1881–1973) dared to juxtapose different perspectives and points of view on a single can-

vas. They called themselves Cubists°. Just as Albert Einstein revolutionized physics by arguing that time and space shift as the position of the observer changes, so Cubism transformed Western visual culture by revealing the incompleteness and even incoherence of individual perception. In one cultural historian's apt description, "Cubists cracked the mirror of art."[7] Their fragmented, jagged, energetic works no longer reflected the world "out there," but instead revealed the artist's fluid and contradictory vision (see page 774).

This emphasis on art as a form of personal expression is also seen in the Expressionist° movement, centered not in France as was Cubism, but in central and eastern Europe. Expressionists such as Egon Schiele argued that art should express the artist's interior vision, not the exterior world. In nude self-portraits, Schiele depicted himself as ugly and emaciated, a graphic expression of his tormented internal universe. His fellow Expressionist, the Russian painter Wassily Kandinsky (1866–1944), went even further in shattering artistic boundaries and splashing his emotions all over the canvas. Kandinsky sought to remove all form from his painting, to create a universe of pure color that would express a fundamental spiritual reality. In the process, he produced the first purely abstract paintings in Western art.

Because they so radically challenged middle-class and liberal standards and assumptions, modernist works were greeted with incomprehension and outrage. At the first performance of Schoenberg's *Five Orchestral Pieces* (1909) in London in 1912, one listener reported that "the audience laughed audibly all through . . . and hissed vigorously at the end." The next year in Vienna, the performance of a different Schoenberg piece had to be abandoned after the audience rioted. Modernist painting was routinely condemned as sick, pornographic, anarchic, and simply insane. One London reviewer dismissed the painter Paul Cézanne

(1869–1954) as "an artist with diseased retinas." Most middle-class men and women remained firmly within a cultural milieu in which paintings revealed pretty scenes, novels told a moral tale, and music offered harmonious charm. At the same time that Picasso was shattering perspective, one of the most popular pieces of art in the English-speaking world was *The Light of the World* by William Holman Hunt (1827–1910) (see following page). This moralistic piece with its easy-to-understand and uplifting story, completely at odds with every modernist principle, triumphantly toured the British Empire from 1905 to 1907. In cities throughout Australia, South Africa, Canada, and Britain, enthusiastic crowds jostled for tickets and hailed the painting as both a religious and an artistic masterpiece.

POPULAR RELIGION AND SECULARIZATION

As the response to Holman Hunt's depiction of Jesus shows, religious belief remained a powerful force in the decades after 1870. In Britain, regular Sunday worship continued to be a central aspect of middle-class culture, and the still-strong Sunday School movement as well as religious instruction in state schools ensured that working-class children were taught the fundamentals of the Christian faith. On the Continent, many Europeans connected revolutionary anarchy with unbelief after revolutionaries executed the Archbishop of Paris in 1871 (see Chapter 21). The excesses of the Paris Commune thus contributed to a religious

■ **Wassily Kandinsky, *Composition VII* (1913)**
Kandinsky's experiments in color and form led him to pure abstraction.

■ **William Holman Hunt,**
***The Light of the World* (1903)**
This devotional painting is rich in Christian symbolism. Jesus, the light of the world, stands knocking at the closed door of a lost soul. The overgrown weeds and fallen fruit symbolize sin; the lantern stands for Christ's illuminating power; while the stars and crescents on it represent Christ's appeal to Jews and Muslims.

revival. Much of this popular Catholic religiosity focused on the cult of the Virgin Mary: By the 1870s, the shrine at Lourdes, site of Mary's miraculous appearance in 1858, was attracting hundreds of thousands of Catholic pilgrims.

Three additional factors contributed to the religiosity of late-nineteenth-century Europe. First, the high rate of immigration, which meant that large groups of people often found themselves searching for something familiar in foreign cities, fostered attachments to the religious cultures of the homeland. In English cities, for example, Irish immigrants looked to the local Roman Catholic Church for spir-

itual solace, material support, and social contacts. Second, in many regions nationalism also shored up religious belief and practice. Hence, for Polish nationalists dreaming of independence from Russian rule, Roman Catholicism was a key part of a separate national identity. Finally, as we shall see in the next section, imperialism became interwoven with Western Christianity. Missionary publications and societies not only lobbied intensely for continued Western expansion abroad, but also served to inspire and unite Western Christians at home. Foreign mission work gave Western Christians a sense of both purpose and power as imperial expansion appeared to provide clear evidence of the ongoing triumph of Christianity.

Yet this triumphalism met growing anxiety, as Christians faced a series of challenges, most obviously those posed by science. As we saw in our discussion of Darwin, developments in geology and biology undermined the orthodox Christian view of a harmonious, divinely directed, natural world. Medical advances also worked to narrow the appeal of traditional religion. Tragedies once accepted as "acts of God," such as epidemic disease, now appeared to be curable and controllable. Increasingly, scientists seemed able to answer questions once thought the province of the theologians.

At the same time, the emergence of the social sciences posed a direct challenge to Christian belief by simply dismissing the question of religious truth and asking instead, what is the function of religious belief in a society? Emile Durkheim (1858–1917), one of the founders of French sociology, dared to lump Christianity with "even the most barbarous and the most fantastic rites and the strangest myths." Durkheim insisted that no religion is more true than any other; each fills a social need.[8]

The Christian response to these challenges varied. Some Christians embraced the scientific method as a gift from God, and argued that the Christian faith must adapt to the ongoing expansion of human knowledge. To many theologians as well as ordinary believers, the study of the Bible as an historical and literary document—as a collection of divinely inspired texts produced by all-too-human writers—promised to free Christians *from* antiquated beliefs impossible to sustain in the new scientific age, and *for* a more worldly, reform-oriented religious life. Other Christians, however, resisted any accommodation to the scientific age. Protestant fundamentalists insisted on retaining a belief in the literal, historical, and scientific accuracy of the Christian scriptures, a stance that led them to oppose science as the enemy of religion.

Similarly, the Roman Catholic papacy adopted a defiant pose in the face of the scientific challenge. In 1864, Pope Pius IX (r. 1846–1878) issued a *Syllabus of Errors*, which condemned not only materialism but also the idea that the pope should "harmonize himself with progress, with liberalism, and with modern civilization." Five years later, a church council—the first called since the sixteenth-century Catholic Reformation—proclaimed the doctrine of papal infallibility. According to this doctrine, any decrees issued by the pope with regard to faith and morals were free from error and good for all time and all places. The proclamation of the doctrine of papal infallibility was a sharp rebuff to Catholic theologians who argued that Christianity must adapt to the modern world.

The Roman Catholic Church also faced a crucial political challenge from both liberal and socialist movements. In Roman Catholic countries, the Church's alliance with conservatism pushed anticlericalism° to a dominant position on the liberal agenda. In France, for example, Roman Catholics were in the forefront of the conservative forces seeking to overturn the Republic established in 1871 and to return to monarchical or authoritarian rule. As a result, Frenchmen who wanted the Republic to survive fought to reduce the Church's influence over French politics and culture. At the same time, the spread of socialism provided European workers with an alternative belief system and source of communal life. The result was to widen the secular sphere and limit the influence of traditional Christianity.

The most significant challenge faced by Christianity after 1870, however, emerged not from scientific laboratories, parliamentary assemblies, or socialist rallies but rather from the department stores and playing fields. In the growing industrial cities, both working- and middle-class individuals enjoyed new, secular sources of entertainment, inspiration, and desire. Energies once focused on Christian devotion were now increasingly displaced onto the activities of consumption and recreation. Whereas shared religious worship had once cemented community life, the increasingly elaborate rituals of spectator sports now forged new bonds of loyalty and identity. At the same time, the delectable array of colorful products displayed in shop windows promised fulfillment and satisfaction in the here and now, an earthly paradise rather than a heavenly reward.

The New Imperialism

M any of those items on display behind the new plate-glass shop windows were the products of imperial conquest. After 1870, Europe entered not only a new age of mass consumption but also a new era of imperialist expansion. Imperialism intertwined with many of the economic, scientific, and cultural developments already examined in this chapter. Telegraphs ensured rapid communication from far-flung empires while mass printing technologies guaranteed that illustrated tales of imperial achievement made their way into homes and schools; Social Darwinism supplied a supposedly scientific justifica-

tion for the conquest of peoples deemed biologically inferior; swift and decisive victories over other lands and societies helped quell anxiety about European degeneration. For many Europeans, particularly the British who presided over the largest empire in the world, imperialist domination served as reassuring, even incontrovertible, evidence of the superiority of Western civilization.

UNDERSTANDING THE NEW IMPERIALISM

Imperialism was not, of course, new to Europe. In the fifteenth century, Europeans had embarked on the first phase of imperialism, with the extension of European control across coastal ports of Africa and India, and into the New World of the Americas. In the second phase, which began in the late seventeenth century, European colonial empires in both Asia and the Western Hemisphere expanded as governments sought to augment their profits from international trade. Trade motivated much of the imperial activity after 1870 as well, with the need to protect existing imperial possessions often impelling further imperialist conquests. The desire to protect India—the "Jewel in the Crown" of the British Empire—explains much of British imperial acquisition throughout the nineteenth century. Britain's annexation of Burma and Kashmir, its establishment of a sphere of influence in Persia, and its interests along the coast of Africa were all vitally linked to its concerns in India.

Neither defense of existing empires nor commercial considerations, however, fully explain the headlong rush into empire in the later nineteenth century. After 1870 and particularly after 1880, Europe's expansion into non-European territories became so much more aggressive that historians label this third phase the age of new imperialism°. A few figures illustrate the contrast: Between 1800 and 1880, European colonial empires grew by 6,500,000 square miles, but between 1880 and 1910, these empires increased by an astonishing 8,655,000. In just thirty years, European control of the globe's land surface swelled from 65 to 85 percent. In addition, new players joined the expansionist game. Recently formed nation-states such as Germany and Italy jostled for colonial territory in Africa, the United States began to extend its control over the western hemisphere, and Japan initiated its imperialist march into China and Korea. What factors lay behind this new imperialism?

Technology, Economics, and Politics

Part of the answer lies in the economic developments examined in Chapter 22. The new technologies characteristic of the Second Industrial Revolution meant that industrial Europe increasingly depended on raw materials available only in non-Western regions such as Asia, Africa, and South America. Rubber, for example, was essential not only for tires on the new automobiles, but also for insulating the electrical and telegraph wires now encircling the globe. Palm oil from Africa provided the lubricant needed for industrial machinery. Africa's once-plentiful elephant herds were slaughtered to provide the ivory for many of the new consumer goods now displayed prominently in department store windows and middle-class parlors—piano keys, billiard balls, knife handles. Increasingly dependent on these primary resources, European states were quick to respond to perceived threats to their economic interests. The Germans even coined a word to describe this fear of losing access to essential raw materials: *Torschlusspanik,* or "fear of the closing door."

Competition for markets also accelerated imperial acquisition. With the onset of economic depression in 1873 (discussed in Chapter 22), industrialists were faced with declining demand for their products in Europe. Imperial expansion seemed to provide a solution, with annexed territories seen as captive markets. As an editorial in the largest French mass circulation newspaper explained in 1891, "every gunshot opens another outlet for French industry."[9]

By the mid-1890s, however, the Great Depression had ended in most regions, and Europe embarked on the longest investment boom it had yet experienced. Western European capital spread across the globe, underwriting railway lines, digging mines, and erecting public utilities in the United States, Latin America, Russia, Asia, and Africa. This global investment boom also contributed to new imperialism. With each railroad or coal mine or dam, European interests in non-European regions expanded, and so did the pressure on European governments to assume formal political control should those interests be threatened, whether by the arrival of other European competitors or by local political instability.

Britain provides an important example of the link between empire and economics. By the end of the nineteenth century, the British Empire covered one-quarter of the globe and contained one-quarter of the world's population. This empire reflected Britain's position at the center of the world's economy, as the chief agent of global economic exchange. Despite the emergence of Germany and the United States as industrial powerhouses, Britain remained the world's largest trading nation. Even more important, British stockbrokers, currency traders, and banks managed the global exchange system that emerged in the last third of the nineteenth century. In this era British loans abroad were larger than the combined investments of its five largest competitors—France, Germany, the Netherlands, the United States, and Belgium.

Imperialism was motivated by more than economic concerns. Political pressures also contributed to imperialist acquisition. First, in the age of mass politics, political leaders needed to find issues that would both appeal to new voters and strengthen the status quo. Imperialism was one such issue. It assured ordinary men that they were part of a superior, conquering people. Tales of dangerous explorations and decisive military victories engaged the emotions and prodded the ordinary individual to identify more closely with the national group.

A second political factor motivating new imperialism was nationalist competition. As Chapter 21 outlined, the unification of Germany upset the balance of power in Europe. In this climate of tension, governments looked to enhance national strength. Newly formed nations such as Italy and Germany itself sought empires outside Europe as a way to gain both power and prestige within Europe. The nineteenth-century German historian Heinrich von Treitschke explained, "All great nations in the fullness of their strength have desired to set their mark on barbarian lands and those who fail to participate in this great rivalry will play a pitiable role in time to come." Similar concerns

The first step towards lightening

The White Man's Burden

is through teaching the virtues of cleanliness.

Pears' Soap

is a potent factor in brightening the dark corners of the earth as civilization advances, while amongst the cultured of all nations it holds the highest place—it is the ideal toilet soap.

■ **Pears' Soap Ad**

This advertisement brings together many of the assumptions of the imperial idea. Imperial rule is held to be a benevolent force, bringing both physical and moral hygiene to inferior peoples. At the same time, it brings profit to Western manufacturers.

about status and strategic advantages motivated nations such as Britain and France both to defend and expand their existing empires.

The Imperial Idea

New imperialism was not simply a policy embraced by elites for economic, political, and strategic advantage. One of its most distinctive features was the way it functioned as a belief system, as an idea that permeated middle-class and mass culture in the decades after 1870. Images of empire proliferated, appearing in boys' adventure stories, glossy ads for soap and chocolates, picture postcards, cookie tins, and cheap commemorative china plates and mugs. In the music halls and theaters, imperialist songs and dramas received popular applause. At exhibitions and world's fairs, both goods and peoples from conquered regions were put on display to educate the crowds of viewers in the "imperial idea."

At the center of this idea stood the assumption of the *rightness* of white European dominance over the world. Europeans would not have sought to remake the world in the European image had they not been convinced of the superiority of that image. What led white Europeans to believe they had both the right and the responsibility to take charge of other cultures and continents?

One key factor was the perceived link between Western Christianity and "civilization." Christian missionaries served as a vanguard of Western culture throughout the nineteenth century. The celebrated Scottish explorer David Livingstone (1813–1873), who mapped out much of central and southern Africa, was a Protestant missionary (although not a very successful one—his only convert eventually renounced the Christian faith). Moreover, missionary society publications introduced their readers to exotic territories, while the societies themselves served as powerful political interest groups that often lobbied for Western territorial expansion to promote the spread of Christian missionary activity.

Europeans also pointed to their advanced technologies as evidence of their material and moral superiority, and as a justification for their imperial rule. Before the nineteenth century, the technological gap between European and non-European societies had not loomed large; in some cases, such as China, non-European societies had held the technological advantage. Industrialization, however, gave Europe the technological edge. Thus Mary Kingsley (1862–1900), a British adventurer who was actually unusually admiring of African culture and customs, wrote, "when I come back from a spell in Africa, the thing that makes me proud of being one of the English is . . . a great railway engine . . . [I]t is the manifestation of the superiority of my race."[10]

■ **British Men at Ease in Burma in the 1890s**
Ordinary middle-class men could live like aristocrats in the colonies, where labor was extremely cheap.

Although many European Christians regarded the West's technological advantages as a sign that God intended Europe to Christianize (that is, Westernize) the globe, a growing number of prominent thinkers, writers, and policymakers viewed the force that conferred this civilizing duty upon Europeans as natural rather than supernatural—biology rather than God. As we have already seen in this chapter, the age of new imperialism was also the age of pseudoscientific racism. Social Darwinism lent a seemingly scientific authority to the imperial idea by supposedly proving the mental and moral superiority of white Europeans over all peoples of color. Thus the British Lord Milner (1854–1925) explained in a speech in South Africa in 1903: "The white man must rule, because he is elevated by many, many steps above the black man; steps which it will take the latter centuries to climb, and which it is quite possible that the vast bulk of the black population may never be able to climb at all."

Often white Europeans presented the idea of a biologically ordained imperial destiny in somber terms. They saw imperial rule as a heavy responsibility that must be shouldered by the civilized. Men and women in the West had a moral duty to bring the benefits of their civilization to the rest of the world. This idea of the burden of imperialism was dramatically expressed by Rudyard Kipling (1865–1936), the preeminent British poet of new imperialism. In 1899, Kipling urged American policymakers to complete their conquest of the Philippines with these words:

■ **Pablo Picasso, *Les Desmoiselles d'Avignon* (1907)**
Many art historians argue that Cubism was born with this painting. One of
Picasso's sources of inspiration was an exhibition of African masks held in Paris.
Like many modernists, Picasso saw in primitive art a passion and an elemental
clarity that he sought for in his own work.

Take up the White Man's burden—
  Send forth the best ye breed—
Go bind your sons to exile,
  To serve your captives' need;
To wait in heavy harness
  On fluttered folk and wild—
Your new-caught sullen peoples,
  Half devil and half child.

Not all Europeans embraced the idea of the "White
Man's burden," and many rejected the imperialist assumption of Western superiority. Some modernist artists, for example, looked to non-Western cultures for artistic inspiration and argued that these societies had much to teach the
West. The Fauves ("wild beasts"), a Paris-based circle of
artists that included Henri Matisse (1869–1954) and Paul
Gauguin (1848–1903), condemned most Western art as
overrefined and artificial, and sought in their own brilliantly colored works to rediscover the vitality that they
found in non-Western cultures (see page 752).

Critics of empire often focused on its domestic political
and economic implications. The British economist J. A.
Hobson (1858–1940) charged that overseas empires benefited only wealthy capitalists while distracting public atten-

tion from the need for domestic political and
economic reform. Hobson argued that unregulated capitalism led almost inevitably to imperialist expansion. While impoverishing the
masses, the capitalist system generates huge
surpluses in capital for a very small elite, who
must then find somewhere to invest these surpluses. Hobson's ideas proved very influential
among European socialists, who condemned
imperialism along with capitalism.

Many liberals also condemned imperialism.
The British prime minister William Gladstone
(1809–1898) clung fast to the liberal belief that
free trade between independent nations fostered international peace. Gladstone and other
liberals were uneasy about the expense of empire and acutely aware of the contradictions
between liberal ideals and imperialist practice.
It was difficult, for example, to reconcile the
liberal commitment to individual freedom
with the widespread use of forced labor in
colonial Africa.

Yet between 1880 and 1885—while
Gladstone was prime minister—the British
Empire expanded at the rate of 87,000 square
miles per year, with Gladstone himself ordering the bombardment of Alexandria and the
military occupation of Egypt. When Gladstone
did hold firm to his anti-imperialist ideals and
ordered British troops to withdraw from the
Sudan in 1885, he outraged the British public.
Critics of empire were in the minority, not
only in Britain but throughout Europe. The
imperial idea permeated European and much of American
culture in the final decades of the nineteenth century.

THE SCRAMBLE FOR AFRICA

New imperialism reached its zenith in Africa. In 1875
European powers controlled only 11 percent of the African
continent. By 1905, 90 percent of Africa was under
European control. In just thirty years, between 1875 and
1905, Europeans established thirty new colonies and pro-
tectorates encompassing ten million square miles of territory and controlling 110 million Africans (see Map 23.1).
The conquest of the African continent was so rapid and
dramatic that as early as 1884 mystified Europeans began to
talk about the Scramble for Africa°.

Overcoming the Obstacles

When the nineteenth century began, Europeans knew little
more about the continent of Africa than the ancient Greeks
had known. A vast and profitable trading network between
European merchants and Africa's coastal regions had developed, centering on the exchange of European goods for
African gold and slaves. European efforts to establish settle-

(a)

Africa Before the Scramble, 1876

- Indigenous power
- British
- French
- Portuguese
- Turkish (Ottoman) Suzerainty

Alien powers shown in italics

0   800 km
0   800 mi

■ **Map 23.1 (a) Africa Before the Scramble, 1876 and (b) Africa After the Scramble, 1914**

A comparison of these two maps reveals the dramatic impact of the new imperialism on African societies. Indigenous empires such as the Sokoto Caliphate in West Africa came under Western rule, as did tribal societies such as the Herero. Even indigenous states ruled by whites of European descent came under European rule, as the examples of the Transvaal and the Orange Free State in South Africa illustrate. Only Ethiopia preserved its independence.

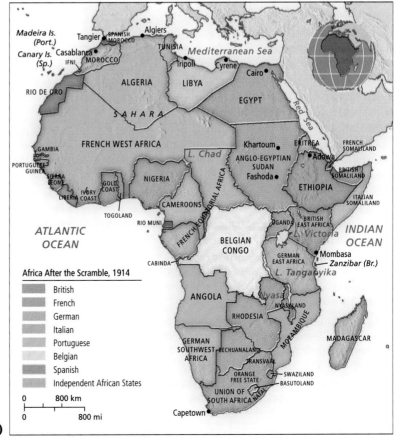

Africa After the Scramble, 1914

- British
- French
- German
- Italian
- Portuguese
- Belgian
- Spanish
- Independent African States

0   800 km
0   800 mi

(b)

ments in the interior, however, faced three key obstacles—the climate, disease, and African resistance.

Africa was known as "the white man's grave," deservedly so. Seventy-seven percent of the white soldiers sent to West Africa in the early nineteenth century died there, and another 21 percent became invalids. Temperatures of over 100 degrees Fahrenheit in some regions and constant rainfall in others made travel extremely difficult. The mosquito and the tsetse fly made it deadly. Mosquito bites brought malaria, while the tsetse fly carried trypanosomiasis, or sleeping sickness, an infectious illness that began with a fever and ended in a deadly paralysis. Sleeping sickness also posed a grave danger to livestock and so aggravated the problem of transportation within the African interior. In regions with endemic trypanosomiasis, such as equatorial, southern, and eastern Africa, the use of horses and oxen was impossible. Despite the dangers posed by the climate and disease, Europeans did endeavor to establish inland settlements in Africa but then faced the obstacle of African resistance. In the seventeenth century, for example, the Portuguese set up forts and trading centers in modern Zimbabwe but were driven out by local African populations.

Beginning around 1830, a series of developments altered the relationship between Europe and Africa, and prepared the groundwork for European conquest. First, the efforts of European explorers changed the Western vision of Africa. Between 1830 and 1870, adventurers mapped out the chief geographical features of Africa's interior and so illuminated the "Dark Continent" for Europeans. They discovered that central Africa was not the vast, empty desert that Europeans had assumed, but rather a territory with abundant agricultural and mineral resources—and lots of people, all of them potential consumers of European goods.

The shift in the European vision of Africa—from empty desert to potential treasure house—coincided with important changes within Africa itself. In the first half of the nineteenth century, various forces destabilized African political structures and so weakened the African ability to withstand conquest in later decades. Although the precise nature of the destabilizing forces varied by region, one common denominator prevailed—the unsettling impact of early encounters with the West. In the 1830s, for example, Britain and other European powers, pressured by humanitarian and missionary lobby groups, embarked on an effort to stamp out the West African slave trade. They succeeded but only in West Africa. The slave trade shifted to the central and eastern regions of the continent and wreaked havoc with political arrangements there. African slaving nations relied on frequent military raids to obtain their human merchandise. These raids—carried out by Africans against Africans—disrupted agricultural production, shattered trade networks, and undermined the authority of existing political rulers. With political systems in disarray, many African regions were vulnerable to European encroachment.

CHRONOLOGY

The Scramble for Africa

1876	Leopold II begins European settlement in the Congo
1882	British army lands in Egypt
1884	Berlin Conference; Hiram Maxim invents the machine gun
1896	Battle of Adowa: Italian army defeated by Ethiopia
1898	Battle of Omdurman in the Sudan
1908	Belgian government ends Leopold II's personal rule over the Congo

Finally, three specific developments shifted the balance of power in the West's favor—the steamship, the "quinine prophylaxis," and the repeating, breech-loading rifle. The steam revolution was inaugurated in 1807 when the *Clermont,* a ship powered by a steam engine invented by the American Robert Fulton, chugged its way along the Hudson River between Albany and New York City. By the 1820s, steamships were widely in use on European lakes and rivers. Steam proved crucial in enabling Western imperialists to overcome the obstacles to traveling through Africa by allowing them to use the continent's extensive but shallow river system.

But until the 1850s and the development of the "quinine prophylaxis," such journeys almost guaranteed death sentences because of the risk of malaria. Steam enabled Westerners to penetrate the African interior; quinine helped them survive once they got there. Produced commercially from 1827 on, quinine was prescribed by doctors for malaria. Death and disability rates from the disease remained high, however, until a series of chance discoveries revealed the importance of taking quinine prophylactically—of saturating the system with quinine before any risk of infection. By the 1860s, Westerners were routinely ingesting quinine in preparation for postings in Africa—and their death rates dropped dramatically.

African death rates, however, soared because of the third crucial technology of imperialism—the repeating, breech-loading rifles carried by Europeans from the 1870s on. Before the invention of these rifles, Europeans used muskets or muzzle-loading rifles that had to be loaded one ball or cartridge at a time while standing up, and were prone to foul easily, particularly in damp weather. Such weapons did not provide Europeans with much of a military advantage, even over spears. With the repeating rifle, however, "any European infantryman could now fire lying down, undetected, in any weather, fifteen rounds of ammunition in as many seconds at targets up to half a mile away." As we saw at the beginning of this chapter, in regions such as the Sudan, where armor-clad cavalrymen fought with spears, swords, and arrows like medieval knights, the repeating breech-loader and its descendant the machine gun made the European conquest "more like hunting than war."[11]

Slicing the Cake: The Conquest of Africa

In the decades after 1870, convinced that the conquest of African territories would guarantee commercial prosperity and strengthen national power, European states moved quickly to beat out their rivals and grab a piece of the continent. As King Leopold II of Belgium (1865–1909) explained in a letter to his ambassador in London in 1876, "I do not want to miss a good chance of getting us a slice of this magnificent African cake."[12]

Leopold's slice proved to be enormous. Presenting himself as a humanitarian whose chief concern was the abolition of the slave trade, he called on the other European leaders to back his claim to the Congo, a huge region of central Africa comprising territory more than twice as large as central Europe. After a decade of controversy and quarreling, representatives of the European powers met in Berlin in 1884 and agreed to Leopold's demands. At the same time, they used the Berlin Conference to regulate the Scramble for Africa. According to the terms established in Berlin, any state claiming a territory in Africa had to establish "effective occupation" and to plan for the economic development of that region.

But as the history of the Congo Free State demonstrated, colonialism in Africa was far from a humanitarian endeavor. Leopold's personal mercenary army turned the Congo into a hellhole of slavery and death. By claiming all so-called vacant land, Leopold deprived villagers of the grazing, foraging, and hunting grounds they needed to survive. He levied impossibly high rubber quotas for each village, forcing villagers to harvest wild rubber for up to twenty-five days each month while their families starved. Brutal punishments ensured compliance: Soldiers chopped off the hands of villagers who failed to meet their rubber quota. In other cases, babies were chained in sweltering huts until their mothers delivered their quota. At the same time, the Belgians forced black Africans to serve as human mules. This practice spread sleeping sickness from the western coast into the interior. Between 1895 and 1908, an epidemic of sleeping sickness decimated the already weakened population. As an estimated three million people died from the combined effects of forced labor, brutal punishments, starvation, and disease, the enormous profits from the Congo enabled Leopold II to indulge his hobby of building elaborate tourist resorts on the Riviera.

King Leopold's personal brand of imperialism proved so scandalous that in 1908 the Belgian government replaced Leopold's personal rule with state control over the Congo. Yet the king's exploitation of the Congo differed

Congo Atrocities

Harsh punishments were used by Leopold's forces to subdue the Congoese people and increase his personal profits.

only in degree, not in kind, from the nature of European conquest elsewhere in Africa. Forced labor was common throughout European-controlled areas, as were brutal punishments for any Africans who dared resist. Faced with tribal revolt in Southwest Africa, the German colonial army commander in 1904 ordered that the entire Herero tribe be exterminated. Twenty thousand Africans, including children, were forcibly driven from their villages into the desert to die of thirst.

African Resistance

As the Herero rebellion demonstrates, Africans frequently resisted the imposition of these often-brutal imperial regimes, but to no avail. The only successful episode of African resistance to European conquest occurred in northern Africa, in the kingdom of Ethiopia (also called Abyssinia). After four centuries of isolation, Ethiopia modernized in the 1850s. By the time of the European Scramble for Africa, Ethiopia had developed not only a modern standing army but also an advanced infrastructure and communications system. These factors enabled the Ethiopian nation, in 1896, to defeat the Italian army at the battle of Adowa.

Adowa, however, was the exception. Most African resistance was doomed by the technological gap that yawned between the indigenous peoples and their European conquerors. A booming arms trade developed between European rifle manufacturers and African states desperate to obtain guns. Frequently, however, the arms shipped to Africa were inferior models—muskets or single-firing muzzle-loaders rather than the up-to-date and deadly efficient repeating rifles and early machine guns possessed by the European invaders.

African military leaders who did obtain advanced weaponry often did not make the strategic leap necessary to adapt their military tactics to new technologies. (As we will see in Chapter 24, European military leaders made similar mistakes in World War I.) In the 1890s, for example, the West African state of Dahomey imported repeating rifles to enable it to resist French annexation. A prosperous, highly centralized state, Dahomey possessed a 4,000-soldier standing army with a deservedly fierce reputation. Dahomey's military command, however, failed to change the attack drill devised for a musket-based regiment. The troops advanced forward at a run, fired from the hip, and withdrew—a strategy that worked well with muskets because they did not have to be aimed, but that proved disastrous with more advanced weapons. In 1892, French forces, outnumbered six to one, annihilated the Dahomian army. By 1900, Dahomey had become part of the French empire.

Yet even African resistance leaders who did adapt military strategy as well as adopt modern military weapons could not stand for long against the industrial might of Western powers. The most famous African resistance leader, Samori Ture (1830–1900), built a vast West African empire of 115,000 square miles and held off the forces of French imperialism for fifteen years, but he, too, was conquered in the end. Utilizing information obtained by spies sent to infiltrate the French military, Samori trained his massive infantry in modern military maneuvers and armed his elite cavalry troops with 6,000 repeating rifles, used with deadly effect against the French in a series of battles in the 1880s. Even more important, Samori was one of the first military commanders to conceive of the tactics of modern guerilla warfare—hit-and-run attacks, night battles, the crucial advantage of knowing the land. These measures enabled him to elude French capture for more than seven years after the French in 1891 sent a massive force to destroy the Samorian state. Yet 6,000 repeating ri-

fles and guerilla tactics could not hold off the vast weight of French imperialism. Ambushed in 1898, Samori died in exile two years later, with his empire in European control.

The Scramble for Africa provides the most dramatic illustration of new imperialism but certainly not the only one. The same era witnessed the extension of European empires throughout Asia. Moreover, it was in Asia that non-European powers—the United States and Japan—entered the imperial game, and that Russia made its bid for empire.

ASIAN ENCOUNTERS

Unlike most of Africa, many of the diverse states of Asia had already been woven into the web of the Western economy well before 1870. Pacific states such as Java and Malaysia formed a part of the eighteenth-century mercantilist empires established by Dutch, British, Portuguese, and French trading companies. Throughout the nineteenth century, European governments formalized their control over many of these island states, primarily to protect trade routes or to ensure access to profitable commodities such as rubber, tin, tobacco, and sugar. The Dutch, for example, gradually expanded their East Indies empire, moving from control of the island of Java in 1815 to domination over almost the

---

CHRONOLOGY

Asia Encounters the West

1840–1842	The Opium War: "treaty port system" in China established
1853	Commodore Matthew Perry forces Japan to open its markets to the United States
1868	The Meiji Restoration In Japan. Japan begins rapid modernization
1885	Russia establishes control over Central Asia
1893	Union of French Indochina includes Laos, Cambodia, Tonkin, and Annam
1894–1895	The Sino-Japanese War
1898	Spanish-American War; United States annexes Puerto Rico, Philippines, Hawaii, and Guam; establishes protectorate over Cuba
1899	"Open door" policy in China proclaimed by United States
1900–1903	Boxer Rebellion in China
1901	Commonwealth of Australia formed
1904–1905	Russo-Japanese War
1911	Revolution in China: overthrow of Manchu Dynasty

entire archipelago several decades later. Similarly, Britain steadily expanded its control over India throughout the nineteenth century (see Map 23.2).

A number of factors accelerated the pace of imperialist acquisition in Asia beginning in the 1870s. In the age of steam, the Pacific islands took on strategic significance because European powers and the United States needed coaling stations for their commercial and naval fleets. At the same time, new industrial processes often heightened the economic value of many of these regions. The development of a process for producing dried coconut, for example, made Samoa so valuable that Germany, Britain, and the United States competed for control over the tiny islands. As in Africa, however, the most important factor in imperialist

expansion after 1870 was a phenomenon we can call the *scramble effect*: Imperialist gains by one power led to anxiety and a quicker pace of expansion by its rivals. The steady erosion of Chinese political stability—itself a result of encounters with the West—intensified this Asian scramble. Competition for access to Chinese markets was an important factor in determining the course of Western imperialism throughout much of Asia. The quest for a protected trade route to China, for example, impelled the French to extend their control over neighboring Indochina. By 1893, the Union of French Indochina included the formerly independent states of Laos, Cambodia, Annam, and Tonkin—the latter two better known by their contemporary name of Vietnam.

Map 23.2   Imperialism in Asia, 1914

The impact of the new imperialism on Asia was not as dramatic as in Africa, but the spread of Western rule is significant nonetheless. This map shows a key development: the entry of non-European powers—Japan and the United States—into the imperialist game. What it does not show is the extent of Western and Japanese influence in China. Profoundly destabilized by foreign intervention, China in 1914 was in the midst of revolution.

The United States and Empire

The U.S. embrace of empire may seem surprising, given its own history of rebellion from British colonial rule. American imperialism was, in fact, somewhat furtive. American policymakers tended to label their imperial territories "dependencies" rather than colonies, and few politicians in the United States spoke openly about the "American empire." Yet nineteenth-century American history was the story of imperial expansion and consolidation. War with Mexico in 1846 resulted in the acquisition of California (as well as New Mexico and part of Arizona) and so extended the reach of the United States from the Atlantic to the Pacific. The completion of the transcontinental Union Pacific railroad in 1869 both symbolized this coast-to-coast dominion and accelerated the pace of westward settlement. The conquest of the continent, however, depended on the defeat of its indigenous peoples. The decades from 1860 through 1890 were punctuated by a series of Indian Wars throughout the American West. As in Africa, however, even those Indians who acquired repeating rifles, such as Crazy Horse's troops who wiped out General George Armstrong Custer (1839–1876) at Little Big Horn in 1876, could not hold out for long against the industrial might of the United States.

With its borders touching the Pacific Ocean, the United States emerged as an imperialist power in Asia. In 1853, Commodore Matthew Perry used the potent threat of his squadron of four warships to force the opening of Japan to American commerce, and during the 1860s and 1870s the United States participated with the European powers in chipping away at China's national sovereignty to ensure favorable terms of trade there. By the end of the century, the United States had annexed Hawaii and part of Samoa, and as a result of the Spanish-American War had acquired Guam, the Philippines, Cuba, and Puerto Rico.

The Continued Expansion of the Russian Empire

Russia was also a key player in the game of Asian empire during this era. By 1914, the Russian Empire stretched from Warsaw in central Europe to Vladivostok on the Sea of Japan—8,660,000 square miles, or one-seventh of the global land surface. Ethnic Russians comprised only 45 percent of the population of this vast empire.

Beginning in the sixteenth century, Russian peasants had made their way into Siberia, seeking land and freedom from the obligations of serfdom. After the tsarist regime abolished the death penalty in 1744, these peasant colonialists were joined by less willing settlers: Deportation to Siberia became a common punishment for criminals, religious dissenters, and political dissidents. In the nineteenth century, immigration into Siberia accelerated, as peasants fled the debts imposed on them by the emancipation legislation of 1861 (see Chapter 21) and as the construction of the Trans-

Siberian railway was completed in the 1890s. Between 1800 and 1914, seven million Russians settled in or were deported to Siberia.

As in the United States, the indigenous population of this land was rapidly displaced. Until 1826 Siberian aborigines were traded as slaves. Two additional factors were even more devastating. First, the immigrants brought with them new epidemic diseases, which decimated the native population. And second, the booming fur trade depleted the animal herds that served as the aborigines' main food source.

During the nineteenth century Russia also expanded its control southward into central Asia, primarily as a preemptive response to the expansion of British power in India. Fearing that the British might push northward, the Russians pushed south. By 1885, the Black Sea region, the Caucasus, and Turkestan had all fallen to Russian imperial control. Over the next three decades the oil fields of the Caucasus would become a crucial part of the Russian industrial economy.

As the tsarist regime expanded its Asian empire, it increasingly encroached upon Chinese territory, a move that contributed to the destabilization of China and to growing hostilities between Russia and Japan. By 1860, Russia had gained from China a sizable chunk of land along the Pacific coast and began pressing into Manchuria. Manchuria, however, was a region also coveted by Japanese imperialists. The growing antagonism between Russia and Japan led to the outbreak of the Russo-Japanese War in 1904 and, as we noted in Chapter 22, to a dramatic Japanese victory. Military defeat by a people regarded as racially inferior shocked Russians and led to demands for radical political change. With Tsar Nicholas II's regime clearly weakened and his troops tied up in Manchuria, this domestic discontent exploded in the Russian Revolution of 1905. The return of his soldiers from the Manchurian front enabled Nicholas to withstand this challenge to his authoritarian rule. His regime, however, was fundamentally weakened: Imperialism could be a risky business.

Japanese Industrial and Imperial Expansion

Japan's victory over Russia in 1905 vividly illustrated its remarkable rise to global power and its emergence as an imperialist player. Until 1853, Japan had remained sealed off from the West, a result of a decision made by the Japanese emperor in the 1630s to close Japanese ports to all foreigners except a small contingent of Dutch and Chinese traders confined to the city of Nagasaki. But by the 1850s, Japan's isolation annoyed both the United States and the European powers with interests in Asia. American whalers, for example, fished off the coast of Japan and desired to use its ports to supply their ships, while American commercial interests in California, aiming to establish a steamer route across the Pacific, also looked longingly at Japanese ports. The Japanese government rebuffed all Western overtures until

1853, when Commodore Perry's warships forced Japan to open two of its ports to American ships. The next fifteen years were tumultuous, as Western powers pushed to expand their economic influence in Japan and as Japanese elites fought over the question of how to respond to the West. Anti-Western terrorism became endemic, civil war broke out, and a political revolution ensued.

In 1868, Japan emerged from this turbulent time with a new government. For more than 200 years effective political control had rested in the hands not of the Japanese emperor, but rather of the "Shogun," the military governor of Japan. When the Shogun adopted pro-Western policies, Japan's warrior nobility tossed him from power and restored the young Emperor Mutsuhito (1867–1912) to effective rule—the Meiji Restoration. Even more dramatically, these anti-Western elites determined that the only way to resist Western domination was by adopting Western industrial and military technologies and techniques. The next four decades witnessed a thoroughgoing revolution from the top as Japan's feudalist political system was dismantled, replaced by a modern centralized state modeled on France. Young Japanese men traveled to Europe and the United States to be educated in Western ways. Western technologies and techniques helped modernize the Japanese economy.

Modernization was not an end in itself, however. The purpose of opening Japan to the West was to build up its national wealth, and with this wealth, to remake Japan as a global military power. Thus funds poured into building a modern navy, modeled on Britain's, and a powerful conscript-based army, modeled on Germany's. Beginning in the 1890s, Japan used its now formidable military force to push its way into the imperialist game. War with China in 1894 and Russia in 1904 led to the Japanese seizure of Taiwan and Korea, and to expanded Japanese economic influence in Manchuria. One Japanese writer, Tokutomi Soho (1863–1957) proclaimed that Japan's imperial conquests showed that "civilization is not a monopoly of the white man."[13] Certainly imperialist violence was not a white man's monopoly: The Japanese brutally punished Koreans and Taiwanese who dared to protest against their new rulers.

■ **Japanese Sailors Waiting for Battle Against Russia, 1904**

The Japanese began the war with a surprise attack on Russian ships in Port Arthur. Many in Britain and the United States admired the Japanese for the audacity of their offensive—rather ironically, given the moral outrage that greeted a similar surprise attack carried out by the Japanese against American forces at Pearl Harbor in 1941.

"A DREAM OF THE FUTURE"

·················

In 1878, Tachibana Mitsuomi published his "Dream of the Future" in Hochi Shimbun, *the newspaper that he edited. Tachibana's dream is a nightmare. It reveals the anxiety prevalent in Japan during its time of rapid modernization and increasing contact with Western economies and ideas. In this excerpt, Tachibana projects the consequences of an imaginary decision to lift regulations on the importation of Western capital. In actual fact, no such decision was made. The Japanese government borrowed technology, techniques, and institutions from the West, but restrained the inflow of Western capital, thus retaining control over the Japanese economy.*

Tachibana's story opens with his bewilderment at suddenly finding himself on a busy street in Tokyo in 1967:

The houses in the surrounding streets were splendidly built and some of them three, and others five stories high; flags from every merchant's house were waving in the air; all kinds of precious articles were displayed in the shops and carriages and horses were incessantly passing to and fro. Indeed, a most flourishing trade was actually before my eyes. Greatly puzzled at this, I went into a shop and found that the master of the shop was a White man with blue eyes and red hair, wearing handsome clean clothes and sitting in an easy position by a desk; and that those wearing scanty and torn apparel and in the employment of the master of the house, were none but the yellow-coloured and high-cheek-boned brethren of ours. . . . I was informed that . . . all the large houses in the main streets [were] occupied by the Whites. . . .

". . . I then passed into the [side] streets and on looking at the state of the houses, I saw none but immense numbers of my countrymen flocking together like sheep or pigs, in a few poorly-built houses . . . their scanty dress leaving portions of their body uncovered . . . their wives were weeping from the cold, and the children crying from hunger, the husbands being employed by the Western people, and were earning scarcely sufficient wages to fill the mouths of their families. . . .

"I, seeing this, could hardly keep from weeping and was sorely puzzled why my countrymen should have fallen to such misery . . . I saw a respectable looking gray-haired old man standing on the bridge . . . I approached him and after bowing to him, I asked, 'Is this country Japan? Is this the capital, Tokei [Tokyo]? How is it that the Western people alone are enjoying such great wealth, whilst the Japanese are in such a miserable state? . . .'"

The old man explains to Tochibana that the Japanese "were outdone by the superior strength of capital and intellect" from the West. As a result of lifting regulations on Western investment and ownership within Japan, "those who have control over the wealth of Japan . . . are none but the Western people." Tochibana concludes, "At this, I was very sad and deeply affected, and I was on the point of bursting into tears, when I suddenly awoke and found that it was all a dream."

Source: From Tachibana Mitsuomi, "A Dream of the Future," *Hochi Shimbun,* October 17, 1878. For the full version and a commentary, refer to Ian Inkster, *Japanese Industrialisation: Historical and Cultural Perspectives* (Routledge: London and New York, 2001), pp. 1–6.

Scrambling in China

While Japan used its encounter with the West to modernize and militarize its society, China proved far less successful in withstanding Western encroachment. Throughout the nineteenth century, Chinese national sovereignty slowly eroded, as European powers, soon joined by Russia, the United States, and Japan, jostled for access to China's markets and resources.

For much of the nineteenth century, China's encounter with the West was structured by the treaty port system, a diplomatic and trading arrangement first forced on China by the British after their victory in the Opium War in 1842. The treaty port system granted to foreign representatives the right to live and trade in specific ports (and eventually in railheads within the Chinese interior). The system was inherently unequal. Low customs duties ensured that the profits flowed out from rather than into China. Even more significant, the principle of "extraterritoriality" declared foreign residents subject only to their own country's laws and so placed Westerners entirely outside the Chinese legal system, while granting Chinese residents in Western countries no such equivalent rights. Thus the provisions of the treaty port system worked to diminish Chinese national sovereignty.

The Western powers realized that the treaty port system was profitable but risky. If the Chinese government was forced to cede too much of its sovereignty to foreign interests, it might cease to control the country—and revolutions are rarely good for business. In 1858, Lord Elgin, who supervised British affairs in China, warned European traders to be careful not to "kill the goose that lays the golden eggs, throw the country into confusion and imperil the most lucrative trade you have in the world."[14] Taking to heart Elgin's warning, Western governments agreed to put the goose on life support—to assist the Chinese government in reforming its financial, administrative, and military systems. By 1890, China appeared to have stabilized as these reforms proceeded apace under the supervision of the Empress Dowager Cixi (Tzu Hsi) (1835–1908).

This stability proved to be short-lived, however. Western actions after 1895 fatally weakened China's central government. The Sino-Japanese War of 1894–1895 revealed China to be far weaker than the Western powers had realized. Over the next five years, these powers scrambled to create spheres of influence throughout China. The European powers and the United States did agree in 1899 to back the American "open door" policy, which opposed the formal partitioning of China (as had just occurred in Africa), but Western economic and political involvement continued to expand.

Chinese opposition to this intensified Western encroachment provoked greater outside interference—and the collapse of the Manchu dynasty that had governed China since the seventeenth century. In 1900, a secret society devoted to purging China of Western influence began attacking foreigners. The Boxer Rebellion (a rough translation of "Harmonious Fists," a name that refers to the society's commitment to the discipline of martial arts) received the covert support of the Chinese government. With more than 200 missionaries and several thousand Chinese Christians killed, and European diplomatic headquarters under attack in Beijing, the West responded in fury. A combined military force, drawing 16,000 soldiers from Russia, Germany, Austria-Hungary, France, Britain, Japan and the United States, crushed the rebellion and sacked Beijing. Required to pay a large indemnity to the West and to grant further trade and territorial concessions to its invaders, the Chinese central government was fatally weakened. In 1911, revolution engulfed China and propelled it into four decades of political and social tumult.

"White Australia"

The story of imperialist conquest in Asia also extends to the island continent of Australia. Discovered and claimed for the British Crown by Captain James Cook in 1770, Australia was used by Britain as a dumping ground for convicts for the next several decades. But with the establishment and expansion of the wool industry in the decades after 1830, the six British colonies established in Australia became a center of British immigration. In 1901, these colonies were joined together in the Commonwealth of Australia, part of the British Empire but a self-governing political entity—and a self-defined "Western" nation, despite its geographical location in the Eastern Hemisphere. Many Australians, including the new nation's first prime minister, Edmund Barton, identified the "West" as "white." Barton, who campaigned on a platform calling for a "White Australia," regarded his country as an outpost of Western civilization.

At the very start of Britain's occupation of Australia in 1787, King George III had forbidden anyone to "wantonly destroy [the Aboriginal peoples] or give them any unnecessary interruption in the exercise of their several occupations."[15] But the landing of whites intent on building cities, planting farms, and fencing in land for pastures clearly interrupted the nomadic way of life for the estimated 500,000 inhabitants of Australia, living in scattered tribal groupings. In 1795, the first major clash between Aborigines and British settlers occurred. Over the next hundred years, these clashes were frequent—and disastrous for the Aboriginal populations.

The British were divided over how to treat the Aborigines. To many British settlers, and as the decades passed, to many in the growing group of Australia-born whites, the Aborigines constituted a clear and violent threat that had to be eradicated. Massacres of Aborigines resulted. Christian and humanitarian groups, as well as the British government in London, opposed this sort of violence and insisted that the Aborigines should be westernized and Christianized. From the 1820s on, mission stations were established for housing and educating Aboriginal children. Forcibly removed from their homes, these children were educated in British ways and then at age 15 placed in employment as apprentices and domestic servants. Despite these missions, few Aborigines assimilated to the Western way of life. Thus the final decades of the nineteenth century saw a shift in official policy from assimilation to "protection." Aborigines and mixed-race individuals were declared legal wards of the state and required to live on reserves. Not until 1967 did Aborigines receive Australian citizenship.

White Australians also perceived Asian immigrants as a threat to their Western identity. By the 1850s, tens of thousands of Chinese had emigrated to Australia. Arriving as indentured servants, they worked under brutal conditions. Many, for example, labored in the gold mines, where they received one-twelfth of the wages paid to a European. As the numbers of Chinese immigrants grew, so, too, did anti-Chinese sentiment. Most British immigrants and white native Australians, often fiercely divided in their vision of what sort of nation Australia should be, agreed that it should be colored white. One newspaper editor noted, "The Chinese question never fails. At every meeting, somebody in the hall has a word to say in regard to it, and visions of millions of the barbarians swooping upon the colony in a solid body rise in the mental horizons of every man present."[16] In 1888, the Australian government turned back ships containing Chinese immigrants; restrictive immigration legislation soon followed.

A GLIMPSE OF THINGS TO COME: THE BOER WAR

Writing at the time of the Opium War (1840–1842), a British journalist in China urged the Chinese to accept what he regarded as the crucial lesson of history: "Ever since the dispersion of man, the richest stream of human

Map 23.3   South Africa

After the defeat of the Boer states—the Transvaal and the Orange Free State—in the Boer War, the Union of South Africa comprised the Cape Colony and the two Boer republics.

and children, and their black African servants, in poorly provisioned concentration camps. Diseases such as diphtheria and typhus soon took their toll. Almost 20,000 Boer women and children, and at least 14,000 blacks, died in these camps.

The British finally defeated the Boers in April 1902, but this victory was limited. The Boer states were brought under British control but the Boers (or Afrikaners, as they were increasingly called) outnumbered other whites in the newly created Union of South Africa (see Map 23.3). After South Africa received self-government in 1910, the Afrikaners dominated the political system and created a nation founded on segregation and racist oppression. More immediately, Britain emerged from the war with both its military and its humanitarian reputation severely tarnished. The war aroused strong opposition inside Britain and made clear that popular support for imperialism could be rapidly eroded if the costs of imperial conquest proved too high. The conflict between the war's opponents and supporters inside Britain was one that would be repeated within imperialist countries many times over the course of the next several decades as nationalist challenges against imperial rule multiplied and as the imperial idea grew less and less persuasive. More ominously, the sight of noncombatants confined—and dying—in concentration camps would soon become all too familiar. The Boer War thus served as a fitting opening to the twentieth century.

blessings has, in the will of Providence, followed a western course." To many Europeans, Australians, and Americans, the rapid expansion of Western imperial control over much of the world after 1870 confirmed this lesson. At the very end of the nineteenth century, however, the British found themselves embroiled in a bloody imperial conflict that challenged this complacent view. The Boer War of 1899–1902 shook British self-confidence and in many ways foreshadowed both the total warfare and the crumbling of empires that would mark the experience of the West in the twentieth century.

The Boer War was the culmination of a century of hostility among British imperialists, Dutch settlers (called Boers, the Dutch word for "farmer"), and indigenous Africans in the southern triangle of Africa. Germany's move into southwest Africa in 1884 worsened this conflict: The British in the Cape Colony feared that the Boers would work with Germany to limit British expansion in the region. But even more important was the discovery in 1886 of diamonds and gold in the Transvaal, an independent Boer republic. British investors in the profitable diamond and gold mines resented Boer taxation and labor policies, and pressed the British government to use military force to place the Boer republics under British rule.

In 1899, these imperialists got the war they had demanded, but it turned out to be rather different from what they expected. Skilled riflemen who were fighting for their very homes, the Boers proved to be fierce enemies who successfully adopted guerilla tactics against their numerically superior foe. By the spring of 1901, the war had reached a stalemate. The British military command in South Africa then decided to smoke out the Boer fighters through a scorched-earth policy: British troops burned more than 30,000 farms to the ground and confined the Boer women

CHRONOLOGY

The Struggle for Control in South Africa

1806	Britain takes control of the Cape Colony from the Dutch
1837	Boers establish independent republics of Transvaal and Orange Free State
1884	German annexation of Southwest Africa
1886	Gold discovered in the Transvaal
1899	Anglo-Boer War begins
1910	Self-government granted to South Africa

CONCLUSION

Reshaping the West: Expansion and Fragmentation

Africans and Asians who saw their political and social structures topple under the imperialist onslaught would probably have agreed with the Austrian poet Hugo von Hoffmansthal (1874–1929) when he wrote in 1905 that "what other generations believed to be firm is in fact sliding." Hoffmansthal, however, was commenting not on Africa or Asia or any other region of imperialist conquest, but rather on the Western cultural and intellectual landscape, which, like colonial political boundaries, underwent enormous and disturbing change in the period between 1870 and the outbreak of World War I in 1914. In this era, matter itself began to slide, as the Newtonian conception of the world gave way to a new, much more unsettling picture of the physical universe. At the same time, changes in medical practice, the revolt against positivism, and the triumph of Darwin's evolutionary theory helped undermine established assumptions and contributed to the sense that the foundations of Western culture were shifting; so, too, did the birth of modernism as well as broader cultural changes such as the move of middle-class women into the public sphere and the redefinition of sexual boundaries.

In the decades after 1870, then, a series of encounters reshaped the West. Its geographic boundaries expanded as non-European regions such as the United States emerged as significant economic and imperial powers. With Australians claiming Western identity, "the West" even spilled over into the Eastern Hemisphere. Yet fragmentation as well as expansion characterized the Western experience after 1870. At the same time that some social thinkers were proclaiming white cultural superiority, European artists such as Gauguin and Picasso were embracing the visual forms of non-European, nonwhite societies in an effort to push open the boundaries of Western culture. While scientific and technological achievements convinced many Europeans and Americans that the West was destined to conquer the globe, others regarded these scientific and technological changes with profound uneasiness.

The next chapter will show that the sense that old certainties were slipping led some Europeans to welcome the outbreak of war in 1914 as a way to restore heroic values and clear purpose to Western society. The trenches of World War I, however, provided little solidity. Many nineteenth-century political, economic, and cultural structures slid into ruin under the impact of total war.

Suggestions for Further Reading

For a comprehensive list of suggested readings, please go to www.ablongman.com/levack/chapter23

Adas, Michael. *Machines as the Measure of Men: Science, Technology, and Ideologies of Western Dominance.* 1989. A superb study of the way in which the ideology of empire was inextricably connected with cultural and intellectual developments within the West.

Betts, Raymond F. *The False Dawn: European Imperialism in the Nineteenth Century.* 1975. A general survey that looks at the ideas that underlay imperialism as well as the events that shaped it.

Bowler, Peter. *Evolution: The History of an Idea.* 1989. Looks at the development of evolutionary theory both before and after Darwin.

Butler, Christopher. *Early Modernism: Literature, Music, and Painting in Europe, 1900–1916.* 1994. Wide-ranging and nicely illustrated.

Dijkstra, Bram. *Idols of Perversity: Fantasies of Feminine Evil in Fin-de-Siècle Culture.* 1986. This richly illustrated work shows how anxiety over the changing role of women permeated artistic production at the end of the nineteenth century.

Dodge, Ernest. *Islands and Empires: The Western Impact on the Pacific and East Asia.* 1976. A useful study of Asian imperialism.

Ellis, John. *The Social History of the Machine Gun.* 1975. Lively, nicely illustrated, and informative.

Gould, Stephen Jay. *The Mismeasure of Man.* 1996. A compelling look at the manipulation of scientific data and statistics to provide "proof" for racist and elitist assumptions.

Headrick, Daniel R. *The Tools of Empire: Technology and European Imperialism in the Nineteenth Century.* 1981. Highlights the important role played by technology in determining both the timing and success of Western imperialism.

Hochschild, Adam. *King Leopold's Ghost.* 1998. Blistering account of Leopold's imperialist rule in the Congo.

Pick, Daniel. *Faces of Degeneration: A European Disorder c. 1848–1918.* 1993. Argues that concern over degeneration formed a central theme in European culture in the second half of the nineteenth century.

Showalter, Elaine. *Sexual Anarchy: Gender and Culture at the Fin de Siècle.* 1990. An illuminating look at the turbulence that characterized gender relations in the fin de siècle.

Sperber, Jonathan. *Popular Catholicism in Nineteenth-Century Germany.* 1984. A look at the religious dimensions of popular culture.

Thornton, A. P. *The Imperial Idea and Its Enemies: A Study in British Power.* 1959; reprinted 1985. An older but still-important look at imperialist ideology and opposition.

Vandervort, Bruce. *Wars of Imperial Conquest in Africa, 1830–1914.* 1998. An up-to-date study by a military historian.

Wesseling, H. L. *Divide and Rule: The Partition of Africa 1880–1914.* 1996. A solid survey of complex developments.

Notes

1. Winston Churchill, *The River War: An Account of the Reconquest of the Sudan* (New York, 1933); quoted in Daniel Headrick, *The Tools of Empire: Technology and European Imperialism in the Nineteenth Century* (1981), 118.

2. Quoted in H. Stuart Hughes, *Consciousness and Society: The Reorientation of European Social Thought 1890–1930* (1958), 332.

3. Quoted in Hughes, 296.

4. Quoted in Anne McClintock, *Imperial Leather: Race, Gender, and Sexuality in the Colonial Contest* (1995), 50.

5. Quoted in Shearer West, *Fin De Siècle*, (1993) 24.

6. Quoted in Christopher Butler, *Early Modernism: Literature, Music, and Painting in Europe, 1900–1916* (1994), 2.

7. Stephen Kern, *The Culture of Time and Space, 1880–1918* (1983), 195.

8. From *Elementary Forms.* Quoted in Hughes, 284–285.

9. Quoted in William Schneider, *An Empire for the Masses: The French Popular Image of Africa, 1870–1900* (1982), 72.

10. *West African Studies* (1901), 329–330.

11. Headrick, 101. Headrick is the historian who identified the crucial role of the steamship, the quinine prophylaxis, and the breech-loading, repeating rifle in the conquest of Africa.

12. Quoted in Thomas Pakenham, *The Scramble for Africa 1876–1912* (1991), 22.

13. Quoted in W. G. Beasley, *Japanese Imperialism, 1894–1945* (1987), 31–33.

14. Quoted in Beasley, 19.

15. Quoted in F. K. Crowley (ed.), *A New History of Australia* (1974), 6.

16. Quoted in Crowley, 207.

The First World War

O N THE MORNING OF JULY 1, 1916, IN THE FIELDS OF NORTHERN FRANCE near the Somme River, tens of thousands of young British soldiers crawled out of ditches and began to walk across a muddy expanse filled with shards of metal and decomposing human bodies. Encumbered with backpacks weighing more than sixty pounds, the men trudged forward. For the past week their heavy artillery had pummeled the Germans who lay on the other side of the mud. Thus they expected little opposition. In less than sixty seconds, expectations and reality horribly diverged. The German troops, who had waited out the bombardment in the safety of "dugouts"—fortified bunkers scooped from the earth beneath the trenches—raced to their gunnery positions and raked the evenly spaced lines of British soldiers with machine-gun fire. The slowly walking men made easy targets. Those who were lucky enough to make it to the enemy lines found their way blocked by barbed-wire fences—still intact, despite the bombardment. Standing in front of the wire, they were quickly mown down. Over 20,000 British soldiers died that day, thousands within the first minutes of the attack. Another 40,000 were wounded. Yet the attack went on. Between July 1 and November 18, 1916, when the Battle of the Somme finally ended, almost 420,000 British soldiers were killed or wounded. Their French allies lost 200,000 men to death or injury. German casualties are estimated at 450,000.

Such carnage became commonplace during the First World War. At the Battle of Verdun, which began before the Somme conflict and continued after, the French and Germans suffered total casualties of at least 750,000, while in the disastrous Gallipoli offensive of 1915, ANZAC (Australia and New Zealand) troops experienced a casualty rate of 65 percent. Between 1914 and 1918, European commanders sent more than eight million men to their deaths in a series of often futile attacks. The total number of casualties—killed, wounded, and missing—reached over 37 million.

Chapter Outline

- The Origins of the First World War
- The Experience of War
- War and Revolution

Death on the Western Front: This movie still comes from *The Battle of the Somme,* a documentary filmed during the battle and the first "war movie" shown in Britain.

These casualty figures were in part the products of the Industrial Revolution. Between 1914 and 1918 the nations of the West used their factories to churn out ever more efficient tools of killing. The need for machine guns, artillery shells, poison gas canisters, and other implements of modern warfare meant that World War I was the first total war°, a war that demanded that combatant nations mobilize their industrial economies as well as their armies, and thus a war that erased the distinction between civilian and soldier. In total war, victory depended on the woman in the munitions factory as well as the man on the front lines.

The First World War challenged many core assumptions of Western culture and reshaped economic and political structures. By shattering the authoritarian empires of eastern and central Europe and integrating the United States more fully in European affairs, the war ensured that commitment to democratic values became central to one dominant twentieth-century definition of "the West." But the war also strengthened antidemocratic forces: It catapulted into power a communist regime in Russia, intensified eastern Europe's ethnic and nationalist conflicts, and undermined many of the economic structures on which Western stability and prosperity rested. The years after the war, then, would see an acceleration of the fragmentation of Western cultural and social life already underway in the prewar period.

Three questions inform this chapter's examination of the origins and experience of the First World War: (1) What factors led Europe into war in 1914? (2) What were the characteristics of the war experience on both the front lines and on the home front? (3) What were the consequences of this war for the European and the global social, political, and international order?

The Origins of the First World War

On June 28, 1914, the heir to the throne of Austrian-Hungarian Empire, Archduke Franz Ferdinand (1863–1914), was assassinated by ethnic Serbian terrorists. Austrian officials accused the Serbian government of involvement with the assassination. One month after the archduke's death, Austria declared war on Serbia. One week later, Europe was at war. Germany entered the war on Austria's side. These two Central Powers°, as they were known, squared off against not only small Serbia but also the colossal weight of Russia, France, and Britain, called the Allies°. Soon the Ottoman Empire and Bulgaria joined the Central Powers, with Greece, Romania, Italy, and Portugal jumping in on the Allied side. By the time the war ended in late 1918, the conflict had embraced nations from around the globe.

The origins of the First World War have fascinated historians ever since. Why did the murder of one man on the streets of a Balkan city lead to the deaths of millions in theaters of war ranging from muddy ditches in northern

■ **Arrest of Gavrilo Princip**

Princip was only 18 years old when he assassinated the Archduke Franz Ferdinand and set into motion the sequence of events that led to the First World War. Because of his young age, he did not receive the death penalty but instead was sentenced to twenty years in prison. He did not serve out his term; he died at age 22 of tuberculosis.

France to beaches along the Mediterranean, from the mountains of Italy to the deserts of northern Africa and the depths of the Atlantic? To understand the war's origins, we need to examine four interlocking developments: first, the destabilizing effects of nationalist political movements in eastern Europe; second, the heightened international economic and military competition among the European powers, which resulted in the creation of rival alliance systems; third, the widening gap between the expectations of traditional diplomacy and the requirements of an industrialized military; and finally, a strengthening "will to war," the conviction among both policymakers and ordinary people that war would provide a resolution to social and cultural crisis.

NATIONALISM IN EASTERN EUROPE: AUSTRIA-HUNGARY AND THE PROBLEM OF SERBIA

The roots of the First World War extend deep into the soil of nationalist conflict in eastern Europe. Western European national identities coalesced in accordance with existing political boundaries; in eastern Europe, however, the "nation" was defined by ethnic, religious, or linguistic identities rather than political citizenship. More than 27 million subjects of the Habsburg monarchy, for example, did not identify themselves with the Austrian-Hungarian Empire's dominant German or Magyar (Hungarian) peoples.[1] For the Czechs or Slovenians or Serbs, translating national into political identity—creating a "nation-state"—demanded the breakup of empires and a radical redrawing of political boundaries. Unlike in much of western Europe, then, in the East nationalism served as an explosive rather than a unifying force.

The divisive impact of nationalism explains why officials within the vast Austrian-Hungarian Empire regarded the small state of Serbia as a major threat. As a multiethnic, multilinguistic empire, Austria-Hungary's very survival depended on damping down the fires of nationalism wherever they flamed up. Yet much of Serbian politics centered on fanning the nationalist flame. In 1903, a group of Serbian army officers had shot Serbia's despised king and queen, chopped their bodies into little bits, and threw the pieces out the window. The new king, a member of a rival Serbian royal dynasty, recognized that his position on the throne was precarious, to say the least. To remain in power he catered to the demands of radical nationalists, who sought the unification of all Serbs in eastern Europe into a Greater Serbian state. Given the fact that over seven million Serbs lived not in Serbia but in the confines of Austria-Hungary, it is not surprising that the Austrian monarchy regarded the call for Serbian unification as a direct threat to its existence.

The hostile relations between Serbia and Austria-Hungary led directly to the outbreak of World War I. In 1908 Austria annexed Bosnia, a region with a large Serbian population. The Serbian government responded by encouraging the formation of Bosnian Serb separatist groups. After one such group, the Black Hand, succeeded in assassinating Archduke Franz Ferdinand in the summer of 1914, Austrian officials decided to crush Serbia once and for all. On July 23 a representative of the Empire presented the Serbs with an ultimatum, a set of demands that would have given Austria-Hungary the right to an unprecedented degree of involvement in Serbian internal affairs. Austrian diplomats informed the Serbian government that anything short of unconditional acceptance of the impossible ultimatum within just forty-eight hours would be taken as a declaration of war. Serbian officials agreed to comply with every demand except one. On July 28 Austria-Hungary declared war on Serbia.

INTERNATIONAL COMPETITION AND THE ALLIANCE SYSTEM

But why did war between Austria-Hungary and Serbia mean war across Europe? To understand what transformed this Austro-Serbian conflict into a continental war, we need to look beyond the unsettling impact of nationalism in eastern Europe to the heightened international competition that divided Europe into rival alliance systems. Concerned with protecting and enhancing the economic and military might of their states in an increasingly unsettled international climate, diplomats wove a web of alliances across Europe. As we will see, these alliances helped escalate a regional conflict into a European and then a global war.

One crucial factor in the growing intensity of international competition in the prewar years was Germany's unification as a state in 1871. By creating a military and economic powerhouse in the middle of Europe, the unification of the German states upset the balance of power on the Continent. Until 1890, however, the diplomatic maneuvers of Otto von Bismarck (1815–1898), the chancellor of the new nation, ensured a certain degree of stability. Bismarck recognized that Germany's position in the center of Europe made it vulnerable to encirclement by hostile powers. To avoid such an encirclement, Bismarck patched up relations with Austria in the aftermath of the Austrian-Prussian War, an effort that resulted in the signing of the Dual Alliance between Germany and the Austrian Empire in 1879. In 1882, the Dual Alliance became the Triple Alliance° when Italy joined the two Central Powers in a defensive treaty. At the same time, Bismarck was careful to maintain an alliance with Russia. By the terms of the Reinsurance Treaty of 1887, Russia and Germany agreed to remain neutral if either was attacked. Bismarck thus ensured that if Germany were to go to war against its old enemy, France, it would not face battle on two fronts.

But in 1888, a new emperor, Kaiser William II (r. 1888–1918), succeeded to the German throne. William, an ambitious and impatient young man, dismissed Bismarck in 1890 and launched Germany down a more dangerous path. The new kaiser made a fatal break with Bismarck's policies in two areas. First, William let the Reinsurance Treaty with Russia lapse, thus allowing fiercely anti-German France to form a partnership with Russia, formalized as the Franco-Russian Alliance of 1894. Germany now faced exactly the sort of encirclement by hostile powers, and the resulting threat of a two-front war, that Bismarck had sought to avoid.

Second, William favored a new "world policy" for Germany that pushed Britain toward allying with Russia and France. Whereas Bismarck had insisted that Germany's interests were confined to Europe, William and many prominent Germans wanted to see Germany claim its "place in the sun" as a global imperial and naval power. In 1898 Germany passed a naval law mandating the construction of nineteen battle ships; a second law passed in 1900 doubled the number of ships. At the same time Germany adopted a more aggressive stance in Africa.

Such policies were guaranteed to aggravate and alienate Britain. As an island nation with a vast overseas empire, Britain based its military defense system on its naval supremacy. From the British point of view, a strong German navy was nothing less than a direct challenge to British national security, just as an expanding German empire was bound to come into conflict with British imperial interests.

Hostility toward German ambitions overcame Britain's long tradition of "splendid isolation" from continental entanglements. In the first decade of the twentieth century, a series of military, imperial, and economic arrangements formed ever-tighter links between Britain and both Russia and France. These arrangements cleared the way for the formation of the Triple Entente° among France, Russia, and Britain. An informal association rather than a formal alliance, the Triple Entente did not require Britain to join in a war against Germany. There is no doubt, however, that British officials increasingly viewed Germany as the major threat to British interests.

By the first decade of the twentieth century, then, Europe had split into two opposing camps: the Triple Alliance versus the Triple Entente. To German policymakers, it appeared that Germany stood surrounded by hostile powers. With Italy regarded as unreliable, Germany's alliance with Austria-Hungary took on greater and greater importance. Strengthening this crucial ally became paramount. These considerations guided German policymaking in July 1914. When Austrian officials debated their response to the assassination of Franz Ferdinand, Kaiser William and his chancellor Theobold von Bethmann-Hollweg (1856–1921) urged a quick and decisive blow against Serbia. According to the Austrian ambassador, the kaiser told him "he would

regret if we did not make use of the present moment, which is all in our favour."[2] In what some historians have described as an act akin to issuing a "blank check," the kaiser assured the ambassador that Germany would stand by Austria, even at the risk of a war with Russia.

Both German and Austrian policymakers recognized that an attack on Serbia translated into a threat against Russian interests. Eager to expand Russian influence in the Balkan region, the Russian Empire had for decades positioned itself as the champion of Slavic nationalism in the Balkans and as the protector of small independent Slavic states such as Serbia. Its loss in the Russo-Japanese War of 1905 (discussed in Chapter 23) had exposed Russia's military weaknesses, but by 1914 the tsarist empire was re-arming quickly. German officials gambled that Russia was not yet strong enough to risk war on Serbia's behalf. But what if they were wrong and Russia did mobilize? Then, as Bethmann-Hollweg explained, certainly Germany's chances of winning were "better now than in one or two years' time," when Russia would be a more formidable foe.[3]

The escalation of the Austro-Serbian conflict into a European war is partly explained, then, by the existence of rival alliances. Germany's support for Austria emboldened Austrian policymakers to embark on an aggressive attack on Serbia. The links between Serbia and Russia made it very likely that this attack against Serbia would pull in the Russian Empire, which of course did not stand alone but was allied with France. No open and formal alliance required Britain to join a continental war, but a series of treaties with France and Russia demonstrated that British policymakers viewed Germany as a major threat to their imperial, military, and economic interests.

MOBILIZATION PLANS AND THE INDUSTRIALIZED MILITARY

Alliances alone do not explain the transformation of the Austro-Serbian conflict into a European war, however. Consider the case of Italy. Although a member of the Triple Alliance, Italy did not join Germany and Austria in August 1914. In fact, when Italy did enter the war in 1915, it did so on the opposing side. Even more significantly, no alliance required either Russia or Britain to enter the fray. To understand why these powers entered the war when they did, we need to look not only at the alliance systems but also at a third factor in the origins of World War I—the widening gap between the expectations of traditional diplomacy and the requirements of an increasingly industrialized military. This growing gap ensured that when preparations for war were underway in the summer of 1914, control of the situation slipped out of the hands of the diplomats and their political superiors and into the grasp of the generals. The generals had planned for a European war. Once set in motion, their plans began to dictate events (see Map 24.1).

In the decades before 1914 military planning was dominated by a new reality, the railroad. The criss-crossing of the European continent with train tracks gave military planners a new and incredibly powerful weapon: the ability to move large numbers of men quickly to precise locations. The speed with which nations could now throw armies into battle almost obliterated the distinction between mobilization and actual war. *Mobilization* refers to the transformation of a standing army into a fighting force—calling up reserves, requisitioning supplies, enlisting of volunteers or draftees, moving troops to battle stations. Traditionally, mobilization meant preparation for a possible fight, a process that took months and could be halted if the diplomats succeeded in avoiding war. But the railroads accelerated the mobilization process and thereby changed the very nature of military plans. Aware that the enemy could also mobilize quickly, military planners stressed the importance of preventive attacks, of striking

■ **Map 24.1 Europe, August 1914**

In August 1914 each of the Central Powers faced the challenge of war on two fronts, but the entry of the Ottoman Empire into the war on the side of the Central Powers in November 1914 blocked Allied supply lines to Russia through the Mediterranean.

Europe, August 1914

The "Central Powers"

States formerly associated with the Central Powers, but remaining neutral on the outbreak of war, and later joining the Allies

The "Entente" or "Allies", following the German attack on Belgium and the Austrian attack on Serbia

Neutral, later joining the Central Powers

Neutral, later joining Allies

(a)   **(b)**

■ **Map 24.2** **The Schlieffen Plan, 1905 (a) and The Actual German Advance, 1914 (b)**

Count Alfred von Schlieffen's original plan of 1905 called for the sleeves of the German soldiers on the right flank to brush the English Channel—in a daring move, the German army would sweep in a huge arching movement west. In the fall of 1914 Helmut von Moltke modified Schlieffen's plan: The crucial right flank was only three times stronger than the left, rather than eight times stronger as Schlieffen stipulated, and Moltke moved his troops north and east of Paris instead of south and west. Military historians today still argue over whether Schlieffen's original plan could have succeeded.

before being struck. Once a nation mobilized, therefore, the momentum toward war became almost irresistible.

These factors help explain the origins and impact of the military blueprint that structured German actions—and Allied reactions—in the summer of 1914. This scheme was the Schlieffen Plan°. The Franco-Russian Alliance meant that beginning in 1894, German military planners had to prepare for the possibility of a two-front war. The Schlieffen Plan was devised for just that eventuality. It aimed for a quick knockout blow against France, which would then allow the German army to concentrate on defeating the much larger force of Russia. The rationale here was that

Russia's mobilization would take time. Its territory was so vast, and its industrial infrastructure so underdeveloped, that Russian troops would not pose an immediate threat to German borders. According to the Schlieffen Plan, the smaller Austrian army would hold off the slowly mobilizing Russians while the German army moved with lightning speed against France (see Map 24.2).

The need for speed dictated the next step in the plan—an attack against France via Belgium. German planners knew that the French expected any German attack to come through Alsace and Lorraine (the provinces taken from France by the victorious Germans after the Franco-

Prussian War in 1870). The Schlieffen Plan called for the bulk of the German army to avoid France's heavily fortified northeastern border and instead swing to the west. Moving rapidly in a wide arc, the German army would flood into France through Belgium, encircle Paris, and scoop up the French forces before their generals knew what had hit them. With France out of the fight, the German troops would then board trains and head back to the Eastern Front to join their Austrian allies in defeating the Russians.

The need for speed—the key factor in the Schlieffen Plan—placed enormous pressure on German politicians to treat a Russian declaration of mobilization as a declaration of war itself. And that is what happened. Only two days elapsed between Russia's order of mobilization and the German declaration of war. As soon as Russia began to mobilize, German military leaders pressured their political counterparts to break off diplomatic negotiations so that the troop-laden trains could set off.

Moreover, the plan for a speedy thrust into France meant that Germany went ahead with its invasion of Belgium—a decision that brought Britain into the war. Belgium was a neutral nation, with its neutrality protected by Britain under a long-standing treaty. German policymakers gambled that Britain would stay out of the conflict, but their gamble failed. Germany's unprovoked and brutal invasion of Belgium provided the British government with the public-pleasing moral justification it needed to enter the war with mass support. Thus, just six weeks after an Austrian archduke died in Sarajevo, British and German soldiers were killing each other in the mud of northern France.

CHRONOLOGY

The Outbreak of the First World War, 1914

June 28	Assassination of Archduke Franz Ferdinand
July 28	Austrian-Hungarian declaration of war against Serbia
July 30	Russian mobilization
July 31	French, Austrian, and German mobilization
August 1	German declaration of war on Russia
August 3	German declaration of war on France
August 4	German invasion of Belgium; British declaration of war against Germany

THE WILL TO WAR

The events that pushed those soldiers into that mud were dictated not by diplomatic maneuvers but by the needs of an industrialized military. Unable to rein in the new forces of industrial warfare, diplomats also faced new pressures from public opinion. This public pressure, or the "will to war," constitutes the fourth factor that helps explain the outbreak of World War I in 1914.

Still drawn largely from the aristocracy, diplomats moved from elaborate hall to exclusive dinner, secure in their belief that with their secret agreements and coded

■ **German Volunteers**

In western Europe, the public welcomed the news that war had begun. The middle-class young men in this photograph are marching up *Unter den Linden*, the main street of Berlin, on their way to volunteer to fight. Enthusiasm for the war was less marked in working-class and peasant communities.

dispatches they could manipulate international affairs. Mired in traditional protocol, they also remained enmeshed in traditional assumptions. Prominent among these assumptions was the notion of balancing power among the principal European states. But they sought to maintain a balance of power in a world increasingly unbalanced by the forces of nationalism, mass politics, and industrial change. To these men, the traditions of secret diplomacy made perfect sense. They believed only a small elite possessed the education, temperament, and background to understand and control international affairs. Increasingly, however, foreign affairs interested and excited the mass public, whose assumptions about the course of international events clashed strongly with those of the career diplomats.

A number of developments accounted for this mass interest in foreign affairs. First, new technologies such as the telegraph, telephone, and camera collapsed distances and made international news much more immediate and accessible. Second, the rise of the popular press—cheap newspapers marketed to a semiliterate public—changed the coverage of foreign affairs. The competition to attract readers increased the pressure on editors and reporters to simplify and color their coverage, to make the often dull, dense, gray complexities of foreign relations into a compelling drama of Good Guys versus Bad Guys. Finally, the emergence of mass nationalism played an important role in shaping public opinion. Well-schooled in national identity, the European masses by 1914 viewed international relations as a vast nationalistic competition. They wanted evidence that "we" were ahead of "them."

Public opinion, therefore, constituted a new ingredient in international affairs in the years before the outbreak of World War I. Public opinion also constituted a real, although impossible-to-measure factor in the war's outbreak. In the last weeks of July, pro-war crowds gathered in large cities. In Berlin, for example, a crowd of 30,000 young men and women paraded through the streets on the evening of July 25, singing patriotic songs and massing around statues of German heroes. Not all Europeans greeted the prospect of war with enthusiasm. Middle-class men and women, particularly students, predominated in the cheering crowds. In the countryside, farmers and villagers were more fearful, while in working-class neighborhoods anti-war demonstrations received solid support in July. The declaration of war, however, silenced these demonstrations. Opposition to the war was very much a minority movement after August 1914, even among working-class socialists. The German Social Democratic Party (SPD), for example, sponsored anti-war parades in July, but when war was declared in August, voted overwhelmingly to approve war appropriations. Socialist parties throughout Europe did likewise; national loyalties proved far stronger than class solidarity. In Britain, a total of 2.5 million men volunteered to fight in the war, with 300,000 enlisting in the first month.

What made the idea of war so appealing to so many men and women in 1914? For some Europeans, war constituted a purging force, a powerful cleanser that would scour the impurities and corruptions from European society. As Chapter 23 explained, the years before 1914 witnessed a widespread cultural crisis in Europe, marked by fears of racial degeneration and gender confusion. War seemed to provide an opportunity for men to reassert their virility and their superiority. It also offered them the chance to be part of something bigger than themselves—to move beyond the boundaries of their often-restricted lives and join in what was presented as a great national crusade. As Carl Zuckmayer, a German playwright and novelist and a volunteer in the conflict, explained later, men like him welcomed the war as bringing

WAR AS A UNIFYING FORCE

Many Europeans welcomed the outbreak of war because it offered a chance to step aside from peacetime quarrels and factions. This excerpt from The Diary of a French Army Chaplain, *first published in 1915, illustrates the way political party competition was forgotten as French society mobilized for war. The author, Felix Klein, contrasts the prewar political infighting of the French legislature with the spirit of unity expressed in the declaration of war on August 4, 1914.*

Where, but a few weeks ago, could be found a more grievous spectacle than the first sittings of the new Chamber? And where, even in turning over the annals of many Parliaments, could be found a more admirable scene than that it offered on the 4th August. . . . And in this hot-bed of dissensions, quarrels, selfish desires, boundless ambitions, what trace remained of groups, of rivalries, of hates? Unanimous the respect with which the Presidential message was received; unanimous the adhesion to the Chief of the Government and his noble declaration: "It is the liberties of Europe that are being attacked of which France and her allies and friends are proud to be the defenders. . . ." And without debate, with no dissentient voice, all the laws of national defense, with the heavy sacrifices they imply, are at once voted. . . .

The fact is that we know ourselves no longer; barriers are falling on every side which, both in public and private life, divided us into hostile clans. . . . The relations between citizens are transformed. In the squares, in the streets, in the trains, outside the stations, on the thresholds of houses, each accosts the other, talks, gives news, exchanges impressions; each feels the same anxiety, the same hopes, the same wish to be useful, the same acceptance of the hardest sacrifices.

Source: From *Diary of a French Army Chaplain* by Felix Klein. London: Melrose, 1915.

"liberation . . . from that which we—consciously or unconsciously—felt as the saturation, the stuffy air, the petrifaction of our world."[4]

For political leaders, war provided the opportunity to mask social conflicts, to displace domestic hostilities onto the battlefield. We saw in Chapter 22 that the decades before 1914 were characterized by the rise of aggressive and often violent trade union movements and the increasing strength of socialist political parties, as well as anarchist-inspired assassinations and ethnic terrorism. To many European elites, their society seemed on the verge of disintegration. But, as the future British prime minister Winston Churchill explained, war united societies with "a higher principle of hatred."

The war for which university students cheered and for which the politicians and generals had planned was not anything like the war that actually happened, however. Most anticipated a short war. Theorists argued that in the new industrial age, the cost of waging war was so high that no nation would be able to sustain a conflict for very long. Everything depended on throwing as many men and as much materiel as possible into the battlefield at the very beginning. The men who marched off in August 1914 expected that they would be home by Christmas. Instead, if they survived, which few of them did, they would spend not only that Christmas, but the next three, in the midst of unspeakable and unprecedented horror.

The Experience of War

Expecting a German attack through Alsace and Lorraine, French military commanders in August 1914 poured their troops into these provinces. Counting on *élan*, the French military spirit, to see them to victory, the French troops swung into battle sporting bright red pants and flashy blue tunics. At their head rode the cream of the French military education system, the graduates of the elite Saint-Cyr military academy, who charged forward wearing their parade dress of white gloves and plumed hats. All that color and dash made easy targets for the German machine guns. As one military historian has written, "Never have machine-gunners had such a heyday. The French stubble-fields became transformed into gay carpets of red and blue."[5] Those "gay carpets," colored with the blood and broken bodies of young French men, signaled that this would be a war that shattered expectations, a war of revolutionary possibilities and devastating slaughter. It was a war fought not only in northern France—what became known as the "Western Front"—and in the Balkans, but throughout eastern Europe, down into Africa, across Asia, and out into the Atlantic Ocean. It eventually drew in the United States, Japan, and many of the countries of Central and South America. As the economic demands of total war escalated, governments assumed unprecedented powers, women stepped into new roles, and social tensions rose. Thus at the same time the war spread beyond European borders, it also transformed relations within Europe.

THE WESTERN FRONT: STALEMATE IN THE TRENCHES

Implementing a modified version of the Schlieffen Plan (see Map 24.2), the German troops swept into Belgium in August 1914. By the first week of September the German troops had swung into France and seemed poised to take Paris. The Germans had overstretched their supply lines, however, and in a remarkable military feat, French and British forces turned back the German offensive at the Marne River. They had saved Paris, but they were unable to push the German army out of France. By the middle of October, the German, British, and French forces were huddling in trenches that eventually extended more than 300 miles from the Belgian coast to the borders of Switzerland. There they stayed for the next four years.

■ **French Soldiers**
These French soldiers are stationed in a listening post near the front lines. Note the typical trench features: barbed wire at the top, the sandbag walls, the omnipresent and always necessary shovel.

The Troglodyte War

Literary scholar Paul Fussell has used the phrase "the troglodyte war" to sum up what the soldiers experienced on the Western Front.[6] Like prehistoric cavemen, the men on both sides of the conflict found themselves confined to underground dwellings. As British poet and World War I veteran Siegfried Sassoon explained, "when all is said and done, this war was a matter of holes and ditches."

From the strategic point of view, these holes and ditches—the trenches—were defensive fortifications, and the long stalemate on the Western Front shows that they worked well. Despite numerous attempts between the fall of 1914 and the spring of 1918, neither side was able to break through the enemy line. The defensive advantages of the trench system are easy to comprehend. Attacking infantry units faced the dreadful task of walking forward against troops armed with machine guns and sheltered behind wide barbed-wire fences and a thick wall of dirt and sandbags (see Map 24.3).

A discussion of trench strategy, however, conveys nothing of the appalling misery summed up by the term "trench warfare." Imagine standing in a ditch that is about seven or eight feet deep and about three or four feet wide. The walls of the ditches are packed mud, propped up with sandbags. Wooden boards cover the floor, but the mud squelches between them. The top side of the ditch facing the enemy is reinforced with piled sandbags and barbed-wire barricades, thus deepening your sense of being underground. Moreover, the trenches do not run in tidy straight lines. If they did, an enemy machine gunner in the right position would be able to slaughter an entire platoon in a matter of seconds. Instead, the trenches zigzag at sharp angles, restricting the range of fire for enemy snipers but also ensuring that everywhere you look you see a wall of mud. Because you are in northern France, it is probably raining. Thus you are standing not on but *in* mud—if you are lucky. In some parts of the line, soldiers stand in muddy water up to a foot deep. On the other side of your sandbag defenses stretches no-man's-land°, the territory dividing the British and French trench systems from the German. Pocked with deep craters from heavy shelling, often a sea of mud churned up by the artillery, no-man's-land is littered with stinking corpses in various states of decomposition—all that is left of the soldiers who died during previous attacks. Your constant com-

EXPECTATIONS VS. REALITY

Written by two young upper-middle class British writers, the following poems illustrate the shift from the initial enthusiasm for the war to later disillusionment and despair. In the first poem, written just as the war began, Rupert Brooke welcomes the war as an ennobling and purifying force that will bring genuine peace. In contrast, Wilfred Owen's later piece flatly describes a soldier asphyxiated by poison gas. Brooke died of blood-poisoning on his way to Gallipoli in 1915; Owen was killed in battle in 1918, just days before the war ended.

1914. *Peace* by Rupert Brooke

Now, God be thanked Who has matched us with His hour,
And caught our youth, and wakened us from sleeping,
With hand made sure, clear eye, and sharpened power,
To turn, as swimmers into cleanness leaping,
Glad from a world grown old and cold and weary
Leave the sick hearts that honor could not move,
And half-men, and their dirty songs and dreary,
And all the little emptiness of love.

Dulce et Decorum Est by Wilfred Owen

Bent double, like old beggars under sacks,
Knock-kneed, coughing like hags, we cursed through sludge,
Till on the haunting flares we turned our backs
And towards our distant rest began to trudge.
Men marched asleep. Many had lost their boots

But limped on, blood-shod. All went lame; all blind;
Drunk with fatigue; deaf even to the hoots
Of tired, outstripped Five-Nines that dropped behind.
Gas! Gas! Quick, boys!—An ecstasy of fumbling,

Fitting the clumsy helmets just in time;
But someone still was yelling out and stumbling
And flound'ring like a man in fire or lime. . .
Dim, through the misty panes and thick green light,
As under a green sea, I saw him drowning.
In all my dreams, before my helpless sight,
He plunges at me, guttering, choking, drowning.

If in some smothering dreams you too could pace
Behind the wagon that we flung him in,
And watch the white eyes writhing in his face,
His hanging face, like a devil's sick of sin;
If you could hear, at every jolt, the blood
Come gargling from the froth-corrupted lungs,
Obscene as cancer, bitter as the cud
Of vile, incurable sores on innocent tongues,—
My friend, you would not tell with such high zest
To children ardent for some desperate glory,
The old Lie: "Dulce et decorum est
Pro patria mori."*

———————
* "It is good and right to die for one's country."

Sources: From "Peace" from *"1914" Five Sonnets* by Rupert Brooke. London: Sidgwick & Jackson, 1915; "Dulce et Decorum Est" from *Poems* by Wilfred Owen, with an Introduction by Siegfried Sassoon. London: Chatto and Windus, 1920.

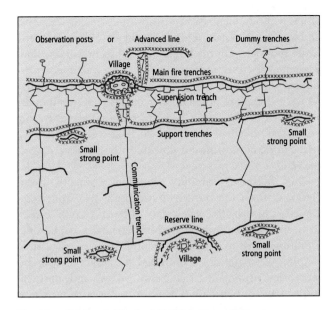

Map 24.3 A Typical British Trench System

The trench system consisted of three parallel lines: the front or fire trenches, the support trenches, and the reserve trenches, all connected by intersecting communications trenches. If the enemy succeeded in gaining the front trenches, the defending forces could withdraw to the support or even the reserve trenches, and still hold the line. (Source: From Tony Ashworth, *Trench Warfare, 1914–1918: The Live and Let Live System*, Pan Books, 2000. Copyright © 1980 by Tony Ashworth. Reprinted by permission of Macmillan, London, UK.

panions are lice (the term *lousy* was coined on the Western Front) and rats. For the rats, the war is an endless feast as they grow enormously fat, nibbling their way through the piles of dead.

From 1915 on, the horror of the Western Front escalated with the introduction of a new killing tool—poison gas, first deployed against enemy troops by the Germans in the spring of 1915. The Allies condemned the use of poison gas as inhumane, but within a matter of months the British and French, too, were firing poison gas canisters across the lines. The consequences were appalling: blinded eyes, blistered skin, seared lungs, death by asphyxiation. Gas proved to be an unreliable weapon, however. A sudden wind shift, and artillery units found they had asphyxiated their own troops. By 1916, with the gas mask a standard part of every soldier's uniform, military companies resembled hordes of insects. And, like insects, they were easily squashed. In the summer of 1915 an average of 300 British men became casualties on the Western Front every day, not because they were wounded in an attack but because they were picked off by snipers, felled by an exploding shell, or wasted by disease brought on by living in the mud amidst putrefying corpses.[7]

The Offensives

The offensives, the attacks launched by both sides on the Western Front, sent the numbers of dead and wounded

soaring. None of the elderly commanders—the Germans Helmut von Moltke and Erich von Falkenhayn, the French Joseph Joffre and Ferdinand Foch, and the British Douglas Haig and John French—knew what to make of trench warfare. Both Haig and French had been cavalry generals, and expected war to be fought at a gallop. Schooled to believe that war is about attacking, they sought vainly to move this conflict out of the ditches by throwing vast masses of both artillery and men against the enemy lines. But time and time again these mass attacks were foiled by the machine gun. One British captain described the compelling power of this weapon: "To the south of the wood Germans could be seen, silhouetted against the sky-line, moving forward. I fired at them and watched them fall, chuckling with joy at the technical efficiency of the machine."[8]

The Battle of the Somme, described in the opening of this chapter, provides a classic illustration of a failed offensive. The Somme, however, was only one of a number of fruitless attacks launched by both sides on the Western Front. By the end of 1917, the death tolls on the Western Front were astonishing, yet neither side had gained much ground. Soldiers, who enlisted not for a specific term or tour of duty but "for the duration"—until the war ended—became convinced that only the dead escaped from the trenches.

THE WAR IN EASTERN EUROPE

The Western Front was only one in a number of theaters of war. Floundering in the snows of the Italian Alps, the Italian and Austrian armies fought each other along a stationary front for two brutal years after Italy, enticed by the promise of territorial gain, joined the war on the Allies' side. Characterized by futile offensives and essential immobility, the war in Italy mirrored the conflict on the Western Front. In eastern Europe, however, a different plot unfolded. For three years, massive armies surged back and forth, as the plains and mountains of eastern Europe echoed with the tumult of spectacular advances, headlong retreats, and finally political revolution.

The Eastern Front: A War of Movement

Much of the movement in eastern Europe consisted of Russians running—running forward in surprising advances, running back in terrifying retreats. When the war began in August 1914, Russia shocked its enemies by fielding a much stronger army much more quickly than German and Austrian military planners had expected. In a two-pronged onslaught, Russian troops headed against the Germans in East Prussia and against the Austrians in Galicia, the northeastern region of the Austrian empire. Surprised by the speed of the Russian advance, German troops in East Prussia at first fell back, but brilliant maneuvering by the German commanders Paul von Hindenburg (1847–1934) and Erich von Ludendorff (1865–1937) turned the Russian tide at the

Battle of Tannenberg at the end of August. Within two weeks the Germans had shoved the Russian troops back across the border. In the subsequent months, the Germans advanced steadily into Russian imperial territory. At the same time, a combined German and Austrian assault forced the Russian army to retreat from Austrian Galicia—and over 300 miles into its own territory. Russian casualties in the offensive stood at 2.5 million. Over the next two years the pattern of Russian advances and retreats continued. Russian soldiers pushed into Austria-Hungary in June 1916, but could not sustain the attack. The summer of 1917 saw another initially successful Russian advance, but it too soon disintegrated into a retreat (see Map 24.4).

These defeats revealed that Russia's economic and political structures could not withstand the pressures of total war. Russian supply lines were so overextended that the poorly fed and inadequately clothed Russian troops found themselves without ammunition and unable to press ahead. Demoralized by defeat and by the daily grind

of life without adequate rations or uniforms or weapons or barracks, Russian soldiers began to desert in ever-larger numbers. On the home front Russian workers and peasants grew ever more impatient with wartime deprivations and demands. This disaffection led to revolution. As we will explore in detail later in this chapter, the tsar was forced to abdicate in March 1917. In November, the Bolsheviks, a small group of socialist revolutionaries, seized control and moved quickly to pull Russia out of the war.

The Bolshevik military withdrawal finally freed Germany from the burden of waging a two-front war. Signed in March 1918, the Treaty of Brest-Litovsk° ceded to Germany all of Russia's western territories, containing a full one-third of the population of the prewar Russian Empire. Germany now controlled the imperial Russian territories in Poland, the Baltic states, and part of Byelorussia. But because it had to commit large numbers of troops to controlling this new territory, Germany

■ **Map 24.4   The Eastern Front, 1915–1918**

Unlike the Western Front, the Eastern Front was far from stationary. By 1918, the Central Powers occupied Serbia, Romania, and much of European Russia.

reaped less advantage from this victory than might have been expected.

The Forgotten Front: The Balkans

The new Balkan states were no strangers to war by 1914. After shrugging off Ottoman control, Greece, Bulgaria, Romania, and Serbia fought each other in the First and Second Balkan Wars of 1912 and 1913. In southeastern Europe, World War I was thus in many ways the "Third Balkan War," yet another installment in an ongoing competition for territory and power. Bulgaria joined the Central Powers in 1915, hoping to gain back the territory it had lost in the Second Balkan War. To protect its hold on this territory, Romania entered the war on the Allies' side in August 1916 and quickly found itself crushed between invading Bulgarian, German, and Austrian-Hungarian troops.

The Serbian experience was even more bleak. In the first year of the war Austrian and Serbian troops jostled back and forth for control of the country, but in October 1915 Bulgarian, German, and Austrian forces advanced into Serbia from three different directions. By November, the Serbian army had been pushed to the Albanian border. Two hundred thousand Serbian soldiers fled over the snow-swept mountains of Albania to the Adriatic Sea, in a disastrous "Winter March." Serbia was occupied by Austrian troops and placed under military rule, as were the adjoining nations of Albania and Montenegro. Like most military occupations, this one was brutal. By the war's end, approximately 25 percent of Serbian citizens lay dead.

CHRONOLOGY

Major Developments in the First World War, 1914–1916

1914

September	First Battle of the Marne: Anglo-French forces halt German advance on the Western Front Battles of Tannenburg and the Masurian Lakes: Germans halt Russian advance on the Eastern Front
October–November	First Battle of Ypres: German offensive, no gains, trenches dug on the Western Front

1915

	Stalemate continues on Western Front
April	Allied landing on Gallipoli: British and ANZAC troops quickly pinned down
May	Russian retreat from Austria
June	First battle between Italy and Austria; stalemate continues for next two years
October–December	German-Bulgarian invasion of Serbia; Serbian "Winter March"

1916

January	Allied withdrawal from Gallipoli
February–December	Battle of Verdun: German offensive, no gains
July–November	Battle of the Somme: British offensive, no gains, stalemate continues on the Western Front

■ **The Winter March**

Of the 200,000 soldiers who attempted the "Winter March" in 1915, at least 40,000 died and another 60,000 were wounded.

THE WORLD AT WAR

The imperialist expansion of the later nineteenth century ensured that as soon as the war began, it jumped outside European borders. The British and French empires supplied the Allies with invaluable military and manpower resources. Australia, New Zealand, Canada, India, South Africa, and Ireland supplied no less than 40 percent of Britain's military manpower during the war. More than 650,000 men from Indochina, Algeria, and French West Africa assisted the French war effort. (One of these men was Ho Chi Minh, who would later lead the Vietnamese struggle against France and then the United States.)

Fighting fronts multiplied around the globe as the major combatants struggled for imperial as well as European supremacy (see Map 24.5). Portugal joined the Allies largely because it hoped to expand its colonial possessions in Africa. Japan, too, entered the war for colonial gain. When the war began in August 1914, Japan seized the opportunity to snatch German colonial possessions in China. In return, Japan contributed to the Allied war effort by using its navy to protect Allied troop and supply ships in both the Pacific and the Mediterranean. By the end of 1914, most of Germany's colonies in the Far East had been occupied by Japanese and ANZAC troops.

The Middle East also became a key theater. When the Ottoman Empire joined the war on the side of Germany and Austria-Hungary in 1914, it posed a serious threat to Britain's economic and military interests in the Mediter-

■ **Map 24.5 The World at War**

Imperialist relationships and global economics ensured that a European conflict became a world war. In Africa both Portuguese and South African troops fought a bush war against German and native soldiers. The entry of the Ottoman Empire on the side of the Central Powers in November 1914 extended the conflict into the Middle East. Japan, the first non-European power to enter the war, occupied German colonial territories in Asia and the Pacific region. When the United States joined the Allies in April 1917, a number of Latin American countries also declared war on Germany.

■ **Sikh Cavalry Officers**
Sikh cavalry officers from India patrol on the Western Front. India provided 1.3 million men to assist the British war effort. Indian troops fought—and more than 49,000 Indian soldiers died—in battles in the Middle East, in East Africa, and on the Western Front.

ranean and Middle East. Britain was desperate to protect Allied access both to the Suez Canal—a vital link to the soldiers and supplies of India, Australia, and New Zealand—and to Persian oil fields, an important source of fuel for the British navy. But by 1915 Ottoman armies had beaten back Allied attempts to advance through Arabia. They also occupied the Sinai peninsula, and threatened Britain's control of Egypt.

Struggling to establish a foothold on the shifting sands of the Middle East, the Allies joined with Arab groups seeking to free themselves from Ottoman rule. Led by a British soldier named T. E. Lawrence (1888–1935)—better known as "Lawrence of Arabia"—and inspired by promises of postwar national independence, Arab nationalists used guerilla warfare to undermine the Ottoman Empire's hold on the Arabian peninsula. This strategy proved successful. By 1917 British troops had pushed Ottoman forces out of Sinai, Arabian nationalists had lifted Ottoman control from almost the entire coastal region of the Arabian peninsula bordering the Red Sea, and Lawrence had captured Jerusalem.

THE END OF THE WAR

Despite the losses of its ally in the Middle East, at the beginning of 1918 Germany looked to be in winning position. Engulfed in revolution, Russia had dropped out of the war and relieved Germany of the burden of fighting on two fronts. With Serbia and Romania both occupied by their forces, the Central Powers could claim to have won the war in eastern Europe. Yet Germany was far weaker

than any map of its eastern conquests in 1917 could indicate. Germany was being strangled from the sea.

The War at Sea and the Entry of the United States

While infantrymen rotted in trenches and froze in mountain passes, the German and British navies fought a critical war at sea. German submarines sought to cut Britain's imperial lifeline and starve out its civilian population by sinking ships before they could reach British ports. Almost 14,000 British sailors and civilians died in these submarine attacks. In turn, British destroyers stretched a blockade across all ocean and sea passageways to Germany and its allies. The Allied blockade proved effective in preventing food and other essential raw materials from reaching Germany, Austria-Hungary and their associates. Food shortages sparked riots in more than thirty German cities in 1916. When the potato crop that year failed and eliminated one of the only sources of nutrition left, children's rations were limited to *one-tenth* of their actual needs.

Desperate to win the war quickly, German policymakers in 1917 took a huge gamble when they decided to up the tempo of their submarine war against Britain. Suspecting that supposedly neutral American passenger ships were delivering essential war materiel to Britain, they ordered their submarines to sink without warning any ship heading for British shores. The Germans were well aware that attacking American ships would very likely pull the United States into the war. In May 1915, a German submarine had torpedoed the British passenger liner *Lusitania* and killed almost 1,200 people, including 128 Americans. The furious response from the United States had forced Germany to restrict its submarine attacks. By 1917, however, Germany stood on the brink of economic collapse, and German policymakers decided they had no choice but to resume unrestricted submarine warfare. They gambled they could defeat Britain in a last-ditch effort before the addition of the United States to the Allies could make much of a difference. Over the next eight months German submarines sank 500 British merchant ships.

The United States declared war on Germany in April 1917. Outrage over American deaths at sea served as the most immediate cause of American entry into the war. Four other factors, however, also played a role. First, Franco-British news stories about German atrocities during the invasion of Belgium had persuaded many Americans that right rested on the Allied side. Second, the Russian Revolution of March 1917 removed an important obstacle to American cooperation with the Allies—the tsarist regime. Americans had balked at the idea of allying with the repressive government of Tsar Nicholas II, but the March Revolution, which overthrew Nicholas, reminded many in the United States of the American Revolution and offered American policymakers a more ideologically acceptable wartime partner. Third, by the time President Woodrow Wilson asked the U.S. Congress for a declaration of war, the American economy was thoroughly intertwined with that of the Allies. Trade between the United States and the Allied nations had grown from $825 million in 1914 to more than

$3 billion in 1916, and American bankers had loaned more than $2 billion to the Allied governments. Finally, the German government committed a serious blunder in the spring of 1917 when it offered to back Mexico in recovering New Mexico, Arizona, and Texas in exchange for Mexican support should war break out between Germany and the United States. American interception of a telegram sent by the German foreign minister Arthur Zimmermann exposed this offer and inflamed anti-German sentiment in the United States. The German resumption of unrestricted submarine warfare, then, simply put flame to kindling that was already in place.

The U.S. declaration of war (followed by those of Brazil, Costa Rica, Cuba, Guatemala, Haiti, Honduras, Nicaragua, and Panama) provided an immediate psychological boost for the Allies, but several months passed before American troops arrived on the battlefield in significant numbers. By July 1918, however, the United States was sending 300,000 fresh soldiers to Europe each month. The Allies now had access to an almost unlimited supply of materiel and men. Eventually nearly two million American soldiers were sent to Europe and almost 49,000 American soldiers died in battle.

Back in Motion: The Western Front in 1918
Faced with the prospect of having to fight fresh American forces, German policymakers decided to gamble one more time. On March 2, 1918—before the bulk of the U.S. army had been deployed—the German army launched a massive

■ **Harlem Hell Fighters**
The American expeditionary forces sent to France contained 200,000 black soldiers. This photograph shows the "Harlem Hellfighters," an all-black, all-volunteer regiment that served in front-line combat longer than any other American unit, saw half its men die, and received more than 170 medals of honor from the French government.

ground assault against British and French lines. The gamble almost succeeded. In just thirty minutes the German troops broke through the British front line; in seven days, German soldiers advanced forty miles; by April the German army stood just fifty miles from Paris.

What explains this sudden shift on the Western Front from a conflict characterized by stalemate and deadlock to a war of rapid and decisive movement? The answer is that after three and a half years of relentless, pointless slaughter, the German High Command in 1918 finally developed strategies that matched offensive techniques with industrialized killing technology. As we have seen, in the first years of the war commanders remained committed to offensive techniques suited to an age of preindustrial warfare—the mass charge, the cavalry attack. What they failed to realize was that industrial technologies such as the machine gun had transformed the power of defensive war. Certainly Western commanders were well-acquainted with the power of the machine gun. In the imperial conflicts discussed in Chapter 23, the machine gun enabled small European forces to mow down enormous indigenous armies. But on the Western Front, both sides possessed the machine gun. In other words, both sides were good on defense but poor on offense.

In 1918, however, the Germans came up with a new offensive strategy. They did not simply throw masses of men against machine guns. Instead of a frontal assault dictated by commanders sitting well behind the lines, Germany's offensive of 1918 consisted of a series of small group attacks aiming to cut behind British and French positions rather than straight on against them. In addition, the Germans in 1918 scrapped the massive preliminary artillery barrage that signaled when and where an attack was about to begin. In place of the barrage they employed sudden gas and artillery bursts throughout the offensive. The rapid German advance in the spring of 1918 showed that technique had caught up with technology.

In July, however, the Allies stopped the German advance; in August they broke through the German lines and began to push the German army backward. Throughout the summer the push continued. By September the Western Front, which had stood so stationary for so long, was being rolled eastward at a rapid clip. The final German gamble failed for three reasons: First, the German advance was so rapid that it overstrained German manpower and supply lines; second, the Allies learned from their enemies and adopted the same new offensive strategies; and third, the Allies figured out how to make effective use of a new offensive technology—the tank. Developed in Britain, the tank obliterated the defensive advantages of machine-gun-fortified trenches. A twentieth-century offense met a twentieth-century defense,

CHRONOLOGY

The End of the War, 1917–1918

1917	
	Stalemate continues on the Western Front
March	Collapse of the Russian imperial government
April	U.S. declaration of war on Germany
November	Bolshevik Revolution in Russia
December	Bolsheviks sign armistice with Germany; capture of Jerusalem by British troops
1918	
March	Treaty of Brest-Litovsk
March–July	German offensive on Western Front, rapid gains
July–November	Allied counteroffensive begins
September	Bulgaria and Allies sign armistice
November 3	Austria-Hungary sues for peace with Allies
November 9	Kaiser Wilhelm abdicates
November 11	Fighting ends on Western Front at 11:00 A.M.

and the war turned mobile. Reinforced with fresh American troops and the promise of more to come, the Allied forces surged forward against the hungry and demoralized Germans. When the Bulgarian, Ottoman, and Austrian armies collapsed in September and October, Germany stood alone. On November 11, 1918, German leaders signed an armistice and the war ended.

THE HOME FRONT

Four years of warfare had transformed the societies to which the soldiers returned. The term "home front" was coined during these years to highlight the fact that this war was fought not only by soldiers on the front lines, but also by civilians at home. Industrialization had created total war, a war that demanded that the productive capacity of a nation be utilized in the war effort, a war that recast and in some cases revolutionized not only the economic but also the political and social relations of the nations involved.

War in the Factories

World War I was the first industrial war. Everywhere we look on the Western Front we see the products of industrialization. Poison gas, the machine gun, barbed wire, canned foods, mass-produced uniforms and boots, and of course shovels all poured out of Europe's factories and helped shape this distinctive style of warfare. Even more important, industrialization made it possible for governments to deploy the vast masses of men mobilized in this conflict. Consider this comparison: The Battle of Waterloo, which ended the Napoleonic Wars in 1815, involved 170,000 men; the Battle of Sedan, which ended the Franco-Prussian War in 1870, involved 300,000 soldiers. The first Battle of the Marne, however, fought between the Germans and the French in September 1914, involved one million combatants. Only industrialized production could keep these huge armies supplied with weapons, ammunition, and other necessities.

It soon became clear that this war would be won in the factories as much as on the front lines. Those nations that collapsed did so at least in part because they lost the war at home. In Austria-Hungary, factories could not produce enough uniforms to clothe the empire's soldiers. Similarly, Russia's underdeveloped industrial sector and infrastructure meant that its soldiers failed to receive needed supplies. In the end, the Allies (minus Russia) won the war in large part because of their greater economic power. The contrast between the United States, with its vast industrial potential, and Germany, unable to feed its population, was pivotal, but even before U.S. entry, Germany was in trouble. Despite inflicting huge human and economic losses, the German submarine attacks were unable to stop the British empire from supplying Britain's factories with the raw materials they needed to crank out rifles, bullets, poison gas canisters, artillery shells, trucks, ambulances, and all the other makings of modern war.

At first, no government realized the crucial role that industrial labor would play in this war. Both military and political leaders believed that the war would end quickly, and that success depended on throwing as many men as possible into the front lines. In France, even munitions factories were shut down and their workers sent to the front. Governments practiced "business as usual"—letting the free market decide wages, prices, and supply—with disastrous results. Soaring rates of inflation, the rapid expansion of the black market, growing public resentment over war profiteering (the practice of private businessmen making huge profits off the war), and, most crucially, shortages of essential military supplies, including shells, proved that a total war economy needed total regulation.

Beginning in 1915, both the Allied and Central Powers governments gradually assumed the power to requisition supplies, dictate wages, limit profits, and forbid workers to change jobs. In Germany, the increasing regulation of the economy was called "war socialism," a misleading term because it was big business rather than ordinary workers who benefited. In Germany, the army worked in partnership with large industrial firms to ensure the supply of war materiel to the front lines, while the Auxiliary Service Law of 1916 drafted all men age 17 to 60 for war work. Measures such as these greatly expanded the size

and power of the central governments in the combatant states. For example, in 1914 the British office in charge of military purchases employed twenty clerks. By 1918, it had become the Department of Munitions, an enormous bureaucratic empire with 65,000 employees overseeing over three million men and women working in government-owned and -operated munitions plants.

The Individual and the State

One of the most striking aspects of the war experience on the home front was this expansion of governmental power. Even in Britain, bastion of liberalism, the demands of total war seriously restricted individual freedom. Flying in the face of tradition, in 1916 Britain's government imposed the draft—a clear example of the requirements of the state overriding the desires of the individual. By the war's end, governments had moved further, not only dictating all as-

■ **War Propaganda**
"Daddy, What Did You Do in the Great War?" This British poster achieved postwar notoriety for its rather crude attempt to embarrass men into volunteering to fight.

Daddy, what did YOU do in the Great War?

pects of economic life but also controlling many areas of social and intellectual choice. The British government restricted the hours that pubs could be open, as a way of encouraging workers to show up for work sober. It also tampered with time itself, introducing Daylight Saving Time as a means of maximizing war production.

To ensure that their citizens remained committed to the war effort, governments regulated the production and distribution of ideas. First, they eliminated ideas they viewed as dangerous. Pacifists and war objectors faced prison sentences and even execution. The French prime minister Georges Clemenceau (1841–1929) adopted a particularly harsh stance toward all dissenting opinion. Journalists and rival politicians—even the former prime minister—who dared suggest that France negotiate with Germany rather than fight on for total victory were thrown in prison. Second, governments worked to create ideas that would encourage a total war mentality. The First World War demonstrated the importance of propaganda as a political and social tool. Newspapers were carefully censored and photographs doctored to ensure that the public received a positive image of the war. In Britain, the government produced a series of now-legendary posters to shame men into enlisting. In Germany, giant wooden statues of the war hero Hindenburg were paraded around the nation to rally war enthusiasm.

The Politics of Total War

The war's reliance on industrial production greatly empowered industrial producers—the workers. In 1915 both France and Britain abandoned political party competition and formed coalition governments, which included socialist and working-class representatives. At the same time, political leaders welcomed labor unionists as partners in shaping the wartime economy. In return, French and British union leaders agreed to a ban on labor strikes and the "deskilling" of certain jobs—a measure that allowed unskilled laborers, particularly women, to take the place of skilled workers at much lower rates of pay.

Despite these "no strike" agreements, both Britain and France witnessed a sharp rise in the number of labor strikes in 1916 and in 1917. Faced with the potential of disintegration on the home front, political leaders in Britain and France reacted similarly. Both countries witnessed the emergence of war governments committed to total victory. In Britain, David Lloyd George (1863–1945) became prime minister at the end of 1916. A Welsh artisan's son who had fought hard to reach the top of Britain's class-bound, English-dominated political system, Lloyd George was not a man to settle for a compromise peace. One year later, Georges Clemenceau became prime minister of France. Nicknamed the "Tiger," Clemenceau demanded victory. When asked to detail his government's program, he replied simply, "*Je fais la guerre!*" ("I make war!").

Making war, however, was not possible without public support, as officials in both France and Britain realized. They cultivated this support in two ways. First, they sought to depict the war as a struggle between democracy and authoritarianism—a crusade not simply for national power or economic gain but for a better world. Second, they recognized that if civilian morale were to be sustained, the basic needs of ordinary citizens had to be met. Both governments intervened regularly in the economy to ensure that workers received higher wages, better working conditions, and a fair distribution of food stocks.

The situation in Germany differed significantly. The working class in Germany was never as successfully integrated into the political process as it was in Britain and in France. The parliamentary political voice of the working class, the Social Democratic Party (SPD), was not invited to participate in a coalition government. Instead, until the very last weeks of the war German political leadership remained in the hands of the conservative aristocracy. Increasingly, the aristocratic generals Hindenburg and Ludendorff—the heroes of the Battle of Tannenberg—called the political shots. The army and big industrial firms seized control of German economic life. Given the power to set prices and profit margins, industrialists—not surprisingly—made a killing. Their incomes soared, while ordinary workers were ground down by escalating inflation and chronic food shortages. By 1917, industrial unrest had slowed German war production, and civilian discontent had reached dangerous levels. Unlike the British and the French, the German government proved unable to control the unrest. The success of the Allied blockade meant Germans were starving. In contrast, living standards among employed workers in France and in Britain rose during the war.

War Against Civilians

Total war meant that the productive labor of the civilian was just as crucial as the killing work of the soldier. A logical, if horrifying, consequence of this fact was the deliberate targeting of civilian populations by military forces. The First World War eroded the distinction between civilian and combatant; as we will see in Chapter 26, in the Second World War this distinction almost disappeared. During World War I, both the German submarine attacks on passenger ships and the Allied blockade of Germany were aimed at civilians. Warfare on civilians also came from the skies. In the spring of 1915, the Germans began a series of zeppelin or airship raids against British cities. From airship decks, the zeppelin crews dropped bombs and grenades on civilian centers. Two years later, after the Germans shifted from zeppelins to airplanes, the British followed suit with air attacks against German cities. By the war's end, 7,300 British and German civilians had been killed and wounded in air attacks.

■ Turkish Massacre of Armenians
The Turkish massacre of more than one million Armenians illustrates the destructive consequences of combining nationalist hatred with total war. This criminal horror is often seen as foreshadowing the Jewish Holocaust during World War II.

The most horrifying civilian suffering, however, occurred on the Eastern Front, where hundreds of thousands of Serbs, Montenegrins, Romanians, and others died from starvation, disease, and brutal military occupation. The Armenian population living in the Turkish heartland of the Ottoman Empire also experienced intense suffering. Massacres of Armenians had punctuated the two decades before the outbreak of the war. Recognizing that Armenian loyalty to imperial rule was shaky, the Ottomans decided to eliminate the Armenian population from Turkey and the conquered territories of southern Russia through forced deportation and wholesale slaughter. Over one million Armenian men, women, and children died.

A MODERNIST WAR

On both the home front and the front lines, the war introduced men and women to new realities—often horrifying, sometimes liberating, always unsettling. But for

■ *We Are Making a New World* by Paul Nash (1918)
Nash's wartime paintings turned the landscape genre from an evocation of natural beauty into a cry of pain.

Returning to the Trenches by Christopher Nevinson (1914–1915) Nevinson's work demonstrates the close parallels between wartime reality and modernist representation.

some Europeans, the war confirmed rather than revolutionized their perceptions. In disturbing ways, the landscape of the war conformed to the canvases that modernist artists had painted in the decades before 1914. We saw in Chapter 23 that in these earlier decades, modernist styles and idioms were condemned as outrageous, degenerate, and removed from reality. By 1918, however, these forms seemed to offer an accurate, even realistic means of conveying the horror of the war experience. As the British cultural historian Samuel Hynes has argued, "modernism had not changed, but reality had."[9]

During the war many modernist artists abandoned "art for art's sake," the idea that art had no moral purpose or social responsibility, that it conveyed no message. Instead, they used their art to communicate their moral outrage against the war. Paul Nash (1889–1940), a British landscape painter and army volunteer, explained in 1918, "I am no longer an artist, interested and curious, I am a messenger who will bring back word from the men who are fighting to those who want the war to go on forever. . . . may it burn their lousy souls."[10] Before the war, Nash had painted pastoral scenes; his wartime experience, however, pushed him to employ modernist techniques. Nash's *We Are Making a New World* (1918)—a title dripping in irony—is one of the finest paintings produced during the war.

The war itself sometimes seemed like a modernist painting that had escaped its frame. The qualities that characterized a modernist painting—fragmentation, surprising juxtaposition, an emphasis on the isolation and the incommunicability of each individual's perception—also characterized a soldier's experience in the trenches. His vision is fragmented. Confined on all sides by mud walls, he can see only a bit of sky. When sent "over the top," he knows

only his own little part.* He cannot see the battlefield, or comprehend the battle plan, in its entirety. Every day he encounters surprising juxtapositions: a tired soldier resting against the wall of a trench out of which juts the arm of a corpse, for example. And in letters home he finds he simply cannot communicate to his parents or to his lover the reality in which he is living and expects to die.

Like modernist artists, soldiers quickly learned to question accepted truths, to mistrust the past, and to doubt the power of human reason. Recruited with promises of glory, they watched rats eat the bodies of their friends. While the generals clung to their history books, which taught that offensives won wars, soldiers died in great numbers. Not surprisingly, the modernist rejection of history resonated in the trenches. The past seemed to offer little of value in this new kind of war. Similarly, the war revealed the absurdity of the nineteenth-century faith in human reason. As the weeks, months, and years wore on, and the death tolls climbed higher and higher, many soldiers were struck by the senselessness, the sheer irrationality, of the conflict. The war, in fact, seemed to be governed not by rational men but rather by unthinking machines.

The mechanical nature of this war became a dominant theme in soldiers' accounts, just as machines dominated prewar modernist art. In this conflict, soldiers not only used machines, they became machines. Seeking the chance to be heroes, men volunteered to fight, and found themselves reduced to interchangeable parts in a colossal war machine. Like the gears on a machine, army companies moved in

---

* Now either a cliché applied to fund-raising drives or a colloquialism for "outrageous," the phrase over the top originated in World War I to describe the action of climbing out of a trench to mount an attack.

circles: from the firing trenches to the reserve trenches to the support trenches to behind the lines and back to the firing trenches. Thus in works such as *Returning to the Trenches*, British artist Christopher Nevinson (1889–1946) used modernist techniques to represent the reality of mechanized war. In Nevinson's work, the men cease to be individuals. Welded into a single machine, they are propelled into the trenches by a force beyond their control, components of a purely mechanized landscape. French war veteran and writer Georges Duhamel (1884–1966) even likened the front-line ambulances to factory repair shops. The function of the ambulances was to repair the broken-down parts (the soldiers) of the war machine and get them back into production.

War and Revolution

The machinery of total war tore at the social and political fabric of European societies. As seams began to fray and gaping holes appeared, many welcomed what they saw as the opportunity to tear apart the old cloth and create something entirely new. Some of these revolutionaries were Marxists aiming to build a socialist world order. Others were nationalists, determined to assert the rights of their ethnic or linguistic group. But it was not only in politics that total war opened the door to revolutionary change. Even relations between men and women faced a revolutionary challenge. Nor did all revolutionaries belong to underground terrorist groups. One individual who dared to demand a new world order was the president of the United States, Woodrow Wilson. The peace settlement, however, fell far short of creating a new Europe. Many of the conflicts that had caused the war remained unresolved, with disastrous consequences for the next generation.

THE WORLD TURNED UPSIDE DOWN

By the war's end, changes in the relations among classes and between men and women caused many Europeans to feel as if their world had turned upside down. Total war not only expanded the power of the state, it also enhanced the position of the working class. The result was a growing radicalism among European workers, as they realized the possibilities of their own collective power and the potential of the state as an instrument of social change. The fact that by 1917 many of these workers were women also had revolutionary implications. In the work world and in society at large, gender roles, like class relations, underwent a marked shift.

In the trenches and on the battlefields, the war had a leveling effect. For many young middle- and upper-class soldiers, the war provided their first sustained contact with both manual labor and manual laborers. In letters home, they testified to a newfound respect for both, as the horrors of the war experience broke down rigid class barriers.

On the home front, however, social relations grew more rather than less hostile. During the war years, inflation

---

THE BREAKDOWN OF CLASS BARRIERS

For many young middle- and upper-class officers, their time in the trenches offered their first sustained contact with men of the working class. Marc Bloch, who became one of the best-known historians of medieval Europe, was one of these young officers in the French army. In this excerpt from his war memoirs, Bloch records both his contempt for his commanders and his growing respect for his men.

I was by no means always satisfied with our officers. Often I found them insufficiently concerned with their men's well-being, too ignorant of their physical condition, and too uninterested to find out. The words "Let them cope". . . were still too often on their lips. . . .

When I remember the face of Corporal M., I cannot restrain a smile. He was a miner, stocky and rather heavy-footed, with a square face. . . . Though an indefatigable walker, he was unaccustomed to shoes, so he traveled the roads of Lorraine and Champagne barefoot. He was so careless and so stupid that it now seems to me I did little

during the first six weeks of the campaign but hunt for him from one end of the camp to the other, to transmit orders he never understood. But I should not forget that the last thing I did not succeed in making him understand, on the morning of September 10, was that his place was not at the head of the platoon. When we went into action that day, he fell, whether killed or wounded I do not know. . . .

Of all my comrades who fell in Champagne or the Argonne, there is none I mourned more than F., who was the sergeant of my second half platoon. F.'s line of work was not one usually considered important. He ran a shop for a wine merchant near the Bastille. He had scant education and could barely read. Yet no one has done more to make me understand the beauty of a truly noble and sensitive soul. . . . Unquestionably his main desire and his greatest effort was to ensure that his half platoon should "get along well together." When I lost him, I lost a moral support.

Source: From Marc Bloch, *Memoirs of War, 1914–15,* translated by Carole Fink (Cornell University Press, 1980), 161–166. Reprinted with the permission of Cambridge University Press.

eroded the savings of the middle class and left bourgeois men and women desperately seeking ways to maintain their social and economic status. In Germany and throughout eastern Europe, drastic food shortages and falling real wages produced a revolutionary situation. By contrast, in both Britain and France, a rising standard of living demonstrated to workers the benefits of an active and interventionist state. After the disastrous "business as usual" approach of the first year of the war, the French and British governments recognized that maintaining civilian morale was crucial if industrial and agricultural production levels were to increase. The results were high wage rates and improved working conditions. In state-owned munitions factories, workers for the first time received benefits such as communal kitchens and day care. Food rationing (although not implemented until quite late in the war) actually improved the diets of many poor families. Yet the result of these new policies was not social peace. Class hostilities rose as workers, having finally tasted the economic pie, fought for a bigger piece, while the middle class fought to defend its shrinking share. Many workers began to demand that the state act on their behalf during peacetime as well.

Many of these workers were women. By 1916, labor shortages in key military industries, combined with the need to free up as many men as possible for fighting, meant that governments on both sides actively recruited women for the paid workforce. Women were suddenly everywhere in very visible roles: as bus drivers, elevator operators, train conductors, and sales clerks. In eastern Europe, the agricultural labor force came to consist almost entirely of women. In western Europe, women joined labor unions in unprece-dented numbers. They took on extremely dangerous positions in munitions factories; they worked just behind the front lines as ambulance drivers and nurses; in 1917 and 1918, they often led the way in walking off the job to demand better conditions.

The impact of the war on women's roles should not be exaggerated, however. Throughout the war, more women continued to work in domestic service—as cooks, maids, nannies—than in any other sector of the economy. The great majority of those women who did move into skilled industrial employment were not new to the world of paid employment. Before 1914 they had worked in different, lower-paying jobs. And they certainly were not treated as men's equals. In government-run factories in Britain, women were paid as little as 50 percent of men's wages for the same job.

Nevertheless, for many women, the war constituted a profoundly liberating experience. With their husbands away, many wives made decisions on their own for the first time. The average wages of female munitions workers in Britain were three times higher than their prewar earnings. But just as crucially, the war validated women's claims to citizenship. Total war made the female civilian into a combatant. For example, the *Win the War Cookery Book* (1917) urged British housewives to view the preparation of meals in a time of food shortages as part of the war effort: "The British fighting line shifts and extends now *you* are in it. The struggle is not only on land and sea; it is in *your* larder, *your* kitchen and *your* dining room. Every meal you serve is now literally a battle."[11] With "women's work" as central to national survival as

Shell Shock: From Woman's Malady to Soldier's Affliction

Broken in mind as well as body, the casualties of World War I forced medical practitioners to think anew about the connections among emotional anguish, physical disabilities, and gender roles. Doctors discovered to their horror and surprise that in the trenches of total war, men's bodies began to act like women's. Pouring into hospital units came thousands of men with the symptoms of a malady that before the war was considered a woman's disease—hysteria.

The word *hysteria* comes from the Greek word *hystera*, for "womb" or "uterus," and for much of Western history doctors believed that women were doomed to suffer from hysteria because of their physical makeup—because they were afflicted with wombs. Physicians long considered the uterus to be an inherently weak and unstable organ, prone even to detach itself from its proper place and wander about the body causing havoc. By the end of the nineteenth century, however, the diagnosis had changed. Doctors continued

■ Shell Shock

French troops under artillery fire during the Battle of Verdun, 1916. Such battles produced psychological as well as physical casualties.

to regard hysteria as primarily a woman's disease but they were more inclined to view it as a neurosis, a mental and emotional disorder. The symptoms varied enormously but included bouts of shrieking, emotional problems such as depression or breakdown, and physical ailments without any clear physical cause—ranging from abnormal fatigue or insomnia to the inability to walk.

With war came thousands of soldiers with the symptoms of hysteria—men who could not stop shaking, men with healthy limbs who could not move, men certain that rats were nibbling at their bodies. At first, doctors dismissed such symptoms as signs of cowardice: These were men faking illness to avoid doing their duty. But by 1916, with such men accounting for 40 percent of the casualties in British combat zones alone, doctors realized they were dealing with an epidemic of male hysteria.

The war illustrated that hysteria was linked not to the uterus or the weak female nervous system but rather to an environment of immobility and passivity. Neither the length of time a soldier had served nor the intensity or horror of his combat experience were significant in producing breakdowns. Instead, the most important factor was his level of immobility. Men on the Western Front suddenly found themselves in positions of passivity and confinement. Deprived of the ability to make decisions, to determine their future, to act, many men broke down.

Yet the reincarnation of what had been considered a woman's malady as a soldier's affliction did not lead doctors to reexamine their understanding of the woman's body or the woman's role. Instead, they reconfigured the disease. Hysteria became "shell shock." The treatment differed as well. Convinced that female hysteria was a result of the overstimulation of the nervous system, doctors prescribed total rest cures for their female patients. Women found themselves confined to rooms with bare walls and shuttered windows, forbidden to read or to receive visitors. In contrast, doctors ordered male soldiers with shell shock to engage in intense physical and mental activity. Thus, despite the upheaval in gender roles caused by total war, doctors continued to view women's bodies as inherently passive and men's as naturally active. The findings of medical science remained linked to cultural conventions. ■

For Discussion

Why does the contrast between the medical treatment of hysteria and that of shell shock indicate that the war had a limited impact on gender roles? What evidence in this chapter points to the opposite conclusion?

men's work, women were regarded as an integral part of the national community.

Middle-class women, especially, testified to the freedom the war brought. Before 1914, the position of middle-class women in Europe had undergone important changes, as Chapter 22 detailed. From 1870 on, the numbers of women in higher education and paid employment expanded, women increasingly served in local government, and a European-wide women's suffrage campaign emerged. Despite the rise of these strong challenges to the ideology of separate spheres, however, the predominant idea remained that women were biologically suited for the private confines of home and family, and men for the public arena of work and politics. Many middle-class girls continued to live lives marked by immobility and passivity—sheltered within the family home, subject to paternal authority, waiting for a marriage proposal. The war, however, threw women into the public space. The middle-class girl who before 1914 was forbidden to travel without a chaperone might be driving an ambulance, splashing through the mud and blood, or washing the bodies of naked working-class soldiers.

At the same time that the war smashed many of the boundaries to which women had been confined, it sharply narrowed the world of the middle-class male soldier. While women were in charge and on the move—driving buses, flying transport planes, ferrying the wounded—men were stuck in the mud, confined to narrow ditches, waiting for orders. Expecting to be heroes, men of action, they found themselves instead living the sort of immobile, passive lives that had characterized the prewar middle-class women's experience. Ironically, then, at the same time the war gave women new power, it introduced many men, particularly middle-class men, to new levels of powerlessness. In total war, even gender roles turned upside down.

Yet when the war ended, some of these radical changes proved to be very temporary indeed. The much-heralded wartime movement of women into skilled factory jobs and public positions such as bus drivers and train conductors was rapidly reversed. For example, by the terms of the British Restoration of Pre-War Practices Act (1919), women who had taken up skilled factory jobs received two weeks' pay and a train ticket home.

Other changes appeared more permanent. In France in 1919, there were ten times as many female law students and three times as many female medical students as there had been in 1914. British women over age 30 received the vote on a limited basis while in the United States, Germany, and most of the new states in eastern Europe, the achievement of female suffrage was more complete. (Women in France, Italy, Switzerland, and Greece remained unenfranchised.) Cultural changes also seemed to signal a gender revolution. Women began to smoke in public; trousers became acceptable female attire;

hemlines rose dramatically; the corset and bustle disappeared for good.

THE RUSSIAN REVOLUTIONS

Tsarist Russia also disappeared. It began the war already sharply divided, its 125 million inhabitants splintered into more than one hundred different national groups—from Inuits in the north to Kazakhs in the southeast to Germans in the west. Ethnic hostilities sapped Russia's defenses from the very start. In Poland, for example, many of the four million Jews under Russian imperial rule welcomed the German army as liberators from tsarist violence and repression. In the regions of Latvia and Lithuania, anti-Russian sentiment flared high, and nationalists saw the war as opening the door to national independence.

The war brought political chaos to Russia. Nicholas II (r. 1894–1917), a man of limited intelligence and a remarkable capacity for self-delusion, insisted on going to the front and commanding his army. He left political affairs in the hands of his wife Alexandra (1872–1918) and her spiritual mentor Grigorii Rasputin (1869–1916). Rasputin is one of the more intriguing characters in twentieth-century history. An illiterate, unwashed faith healer from a peasant background, he possessed a well-documented and still-unexplained ability to stop the bleeding of Alexei, the young hemophiliac heir to the throne. To many high-ranking Russians, however, Rasputin was not a miracle worker but a traitor. Because Rasputin opposed the war against Germany, they perceived him as a voice of treason whispering in the German-born tsarina's ear. In 1916 Russian noblemen murdered Rasputin, in hopes of restoring authority and stability to the tsarist government.

The March Revolution

Rasputin's removal was not enough to stop the forces of revolution stirred up by total war. The political disarray he observed at the highest levels of government dumbfounded the French ambassador, who wrote in January 1917, "I am obliged to report that, at the present moment, the Russian Empire is run by lunatics."[12] The lack of effective political leadership, combined with Russian losses on the battlefield, brought to a boil the simmering disaffection with the tsarist government. Almost two million Russian soldiers had died and many more had been wounded or taken prisoner. Economic and communications networks had broken down, bread prices were rising, and people were hungry. Even members of the tsarist government began to ask not *if* revolution would occur, but *when*.

The answer came on March 8, 1917. A group of women workers in Petrograd staged a demonstration to protest against inadequate food supplies. Over the course of the next few days, similar demonstrations flickered across the city; on March 11, they coalesced into a major revolutionary fire when the troops who were ordered to put down the

REVOLUTION IN THE FRONT LINES

At age 25, Maria Botchkareva, a poor Russian woman who had been forced to work as a prostitute, volunteered for service as a soldier. Women served as nurses, ambulance drivers, and transport plane pilots on both sides of the war, but only in Russia did women serve in combat, and even there the presence of a woman on the front lines was quite exceptional. Botchkareva earned a well-deserved reputation as a fierce fighter, and was honored for her bravery. In 1917, she was serving at the front with her company when she heard startling news from the capital.

The first swallow to warn us of the approaching storm was a soldier from our Company who had returned from a leave of absence at Petrograd: "Oh my! If you but knew, boys, what is going on in the rear! Revolution! Everywhere they talk of overthrowing the Tsar. The capital is aflame with revolution.". . . Finally, the joyous news arrived. The Commander gathered the entire Regiment to read to us the glorious words. . . . The miracle had happened! Tsarism, which enslaved us and thrived on the blood and marrow of the toiler, had fallen. Freedom, Equality and Brotherhood! How sweet were these words to our ears! We were transported. There were tears of joy, embraces, dancing. It all seemed a dream, a wonderful dream. Who ever believed that the hated regime would be destroyed so easily and in our own time?

The Commander read to us the manifesto, which concluded with a fervent appeal to us to hold the line with greater vigilance than ever, now that we were free citizens, to defend our newly won liberty from the attacks of the Kaiser and his slaves. . . . Then came Order No. 1, signed by the Petrograd Soviet of Workmen and Soldiers. Soldiers and officers were now equal, it declared. All the citizens of Free Russia were equal henceforth. . . .

We were dazzled by this shower of brilliant phrases. The men went about as if intoxicated. For four days the festival continued unabated. . . . There were meetings, meetings, and meetings. . . . All duty was abandoned. . . . The front became a veritable insane asylum.

One day, in the first week of the revolution, I ordered a soldier to take up duty at the listening-post. He refused.

Source: From Maria Botchkareva, *Yashka: My Life as Peasant, Officer and Exile* (New York: Frederick A. Stokes Company, 1919), 139–145.

---

protest joined it instead. Governmental orders lost all authority, and on March 15 Tsar Nicholas was forced to abdicate. The Russian Revolution had begun.

Who now controlled Russia? Two competing centers of power soon emerged: the Provisional Government and the Petrograd Soviet. On March 12, the Duma, or Russian parliament, created a Provisional Government from among its members. Like the Duma, the new Provisional Government was dominated by members of the gentry and middle classes: professionals, businessmen, intellectuals, bureaucrats. These men tended to be liberals who believed that Russia was now moving along the path toward a parliamentary democracy. They quickly enacted important reforms such as universal suffrage, the eight-hour workday, and civic equality for all citizens.

But at the same time that the Provisional Government was struggling to bring order to the chaos of revolutionary Russia, across the empire industrial workers and soldiers formed soviets°, or councils, to articulate their grievances and hopes. As Russian revolutionary socialists in exile across Europe returned to their homeland in the weeks after the March Revolution began, they assumed leading roles in the Petrograd Soviet, which soon became a powerful political rival to the less radical Provisional Government.

The revolution, however, did not originate with nor was it controlled by either the liberals in the Provisional Government or the socialists in the Petrograd Soviet.

Nicholas II was overthrown by a popular revolution, and at the core of this popular revolution stood a simply stated demand: "Peace, Land, Bread." Soldiers—and most Russians—wanted an immediate end to a war that had long ceased to make any sense to them. Peasants, as always, wanted land, their guarantee of survival in a chaotic world. And city dwellers wanted bread—food in sufficient quantities and at affordable prices.

The Provisional Government could not satisfy these demands. It did promise the gradual redistribution of royal and monastic lands, but peasants, inspired by the revolution and unconstrained by the liberal regard for law and the rights of private property, wanted land immediately. More important, by the summer of 1917 no Russian government could have provided bread without providing peace. Russia no longer had the resources both to continue its war effort and to reconstruct its economy. The population of the cities began to dwindle as food disappeared from the shops, factories ceased operation because of shortages of raw materials, and currency had little value. Peace appeared impossible, however. Not only did Russia have commitments to its allies, but German armies stood deep within Russian territory. A separate peace with Germany would mean huge territorial losses. And so the war continued.

But so, too, did the revolution. Peasants effected their own land reform by simply seizing the land they wanted.

Soldiers declared their own peace by deserting in huge numbers. (Of every 1,000-man troop sent to the front, fewer than 250 men actually made it into combat. The rest deserted.) The Provisional Government grew increasingly unpopular. Not even the appointment of the popular socialist and Petrograd Soviet member Alexander Kerensky (1881–1970) as prime minister could stabilize the government's position.

The November Revolution

This tumultuous situation created the opportunity for the Bolsheviks°, one of the socialist factions in the Petrograd Soviet, to emerge as a powerful revolutionary force. In April 1917, the Bolshevik leader, Vladimir Lenin (1870–1924), returned from almost twenty years in exile. While still in his teens, Lenin had committed himself to revolution, after his older brother was executed for trying to assassinate Tsar Alexander III. Iron-willed and ruthlessly pragmatic, Lenin argued that a committed group of professional revolutionaries could force a working-class revolution on Russia immediately.

By the fall of 1917, Bolshevik membership had grown from 10,000 to 250,000, and the party had achieved a majority in the Petrograd Soviet. Lenin now demanded the immediate overthrow of the Provisional Government. "Insurrection is an art," he declared, something to be made, not something that happens spontaneously. By promising "Peace, Land, Bread," Lenin would take control. On November 9, Bolshevik fighters captured the Winter Palace in Petrograd, where the Provisional Government had been sitting.

The *second* Russian Revolution was underway. The Bolsheviks declared a policy of land and peace—land partition with no payment of compensation to estate owners

and an immediate peace with Germany, regardless of the cost. (And as we have seen, the cost was high: According to the terms of the Treaty of Brest-Litovsk, signed with Germany in 1918, Russia lost its western territories.) Not everyone in Russia was won over by promises of peace and land, however. Confronted with a diverse array of opponents, the Bolsheviks turned to the methods of terror. After an assassination attempt against Lenin in August 1918, the Bolshevik secret police received the power to execute without trial. More than 500 individuals were shot in a single day in Petrograd.

During the next two years, the Bolsheviks waged a brutal war against domestic and international opponents of their Communist Revolution. This civil war proved Lenin's

CHRONOLOGY

Revolution in Russia, 1917–1921

1917	
March 8	St. Petersburg/Petrograd women's protest; revolution begins
March 12	Establishment of Provisional Government
March 15	Abdication of Tsar Nicholas II
November 9	Bolshevik overthrow of the Provisional Government
1918–1921	Civil war

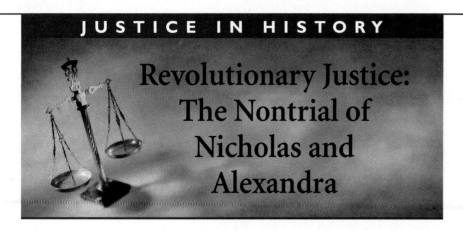

Revolutionary Justice: The Nontrial of Nicholas and Alexandra

. . . he saw all the members of the Tsar's family lying on the floor with numerous wounds to their bodies. The blood was gushing. The heir was still alive—and moaning. [The commander] walked over to him and shot him two or three times at point blank range. The heir fell still.[13]

On July 16, 1918, Bolshevik revolutionaries shot and killed Nicholas II, Tsar of Russia; his wife, the Tsarina Alexandra; his heir, 14-year-old Alexei; their four daughters—Olga (age 23), Tatiana (age 21), Maria (age 19), and Anastasia (age 17); their three servants; and their physician. When news of the deaths reached other countries, the killings were condemned as murders. The Bolsheviks, however, termed them executions, acts of revolutionary justice.

When Nicholas II abdicated on March 15, 1917, after twenty-three years on the throne, he expected to embark on a life of exile in Britain. Instead, the Provisional Government placed the tsar and his family under house arrest, and appointed a Commission of Inquiry to investigate the persistent rumors that the tsar's German-born wife had conspired with Germany to destroy Russia. The Commission found no evidence to convict the tsar or his wife of treason, but by the autumn of 1917, its findings were irrevelant. The war with Germany was effectively over, whereas the war against all that the tsar had stood for had just begun.

The civil war that followed the Bolshevik Revolution proved fatal for the royal family. Faced with counter-revolutionary challenges on all sides, the Bolsheviks feared that if Nicholas escaped, he would serve as a symbolic center for these antirevolutionary forces. They decided to move him to a region firmly under Bolshevik control. In April 1918, a special train transported the tsar and his family to Ekaterinburg (about 900 miles east of Moscow), where they were placed in the hands of the Bolshevik-dominated Ural Regional Soviet. Meanwhile, the revolutionary Bolshevik government prepared to try Nicholas publicly for his crimes against the Russian people. The charge was no longer secret contacts with Germany—the Bolsheviks themselves had negotiated with Germany and ended Russia's participation in the war—but rather the tsar's both real and symbolic leadership of a politically repressive regime. Leon Trotsky, the head of the Petrograd Soviet, planned to present the case against Nicholas.

But the case was never made. By July, an anti-Bolshevik army was approaching Ekaterinburg from the east. If these troops freed the imperial family, they would score a crucial victory. Told that Ekaterinburg might fall to the enemy within days, the Ural Soviet decided to execute the tsar and his family immediately, most likely with Lenin's approval.

Pavel Medvedev, one of the tsar's guards, later offered a detailed account of the events of the evening of July 16. His interviewer recorded what Medvedev had told him:

[He said,] The Tsar, the Tsaritsa [Tsarina], the Tsar's four daughters, the doctor, the cook and the lackey came out of their rooms. The Tsar was carrying the heir [Alexei] in his arms. . . . In my presence there were no tears, no sobs and no questions. . . .

Medvedev then testified that he was ordered out of the room. When he returned a few minutes later:

What Medvedev's understated account did not relate were the more gruesome details of the execution. In an effort to preserve part of the family fortune, the tsar's daughters were wearing corsets into which had been sewn diamonds. When they were shot, the bullets, in the words of one eyewitness, "ricocheted, jumping around the room like hail."[14] Even after several pistols were emptied, one of the girls remained alive. The guards resorted to bayonets.

The killing of not only the tsar but also his wife and children was a startling act, as the Bolsheviks themselves recognized. The Ural Regional Soviet announced the tsar's execution, but said nothing about his family, while the official statement from Moscow reported that "the wife and son of Nicholas Romanov were sent to a safe place."[15]

These omissions and lies reveal the Bolsheviks' own uneasiness with the killings. Why, then, was the entire family shot? The Bolsheviks' determination to win the civil war regardless of the cost provides part of the answer. According to Trotsky, Lenin "believed we shouldn't leave the Whites [the anti-Bolshevik forces] a live banner to rally around."[16] Any of the tsar's children could have served as such a banner. The rapid approach of the White army meant the royal family had to be disposed of quickly. But Trotsky also viewed the killings as an essential and absolute break with the past. In his words, "the execution of the Tsar's family was needed not only to frighten, horrify, and to dishearten the enemy, but also in order to shake up our own ranks, to show them that there was no turning back, that ahead lay either complete victory or complete ruin."[17] For the Bolsheviks, there was no middle ground.

The killing of Tsar Nicholas and his family thus forms part of the pattern of escalating violence that characterized the First World War's revolutionary aftermath. But in the blood of these killings we can also see reflected two ideas that had a powerful impact on postwar political life—first, the subordination of law to the revolutionary State; second, the concept of collective guilt.

The Bolsheviks offered a different idea of justice. As a Bolshevik publication explained in a discussion of the tsar's killing:

> Many formal aspects of bourgeois justice may have been violated. . . . However, worker-peasant power was manifested in the process, making no exception for the All-Russian murderer, shooting as if he were an ordinary brigand. . . . Nicholas the Bloody is no more.[18]

In the Bolshevik model, the law was not separate from but rather subordinate to the state. Legal rights and requirements—the "formal aspects of bourgeois justice"—could be suspended in the service of "worker peasant power," as embodied in the revolutionary state.

This concept of the law subordinate to the state helps us understand the tsar's execution without trial; the concept of collective guilt provides a context for the killing of his children. The Bolshevik model of socialism assumed that *class* constituted objective reality. Simply by belonging to a certain social class, an individual could be—and was—designated an enemy of the revolution. The Bolshevik constitution equated citizenship with social class. Workers and peasants received the vote, but seven categories of people, such as those who lived off investment interest, were disenfranchised. For the next two decades, aristocratic and middle-class origins served as an indelible ink, marking a person permanently as an enemy of the revolutionary state—regardless of that person's own actions or inclinations. Thus, from the Bolshevik perspective, the tsar's children bore the taint of their royal origins. When their continuing existence threatened the revolution, they were shot. Over the next four decades, the concept of collective guilt would result in the deaths of millions in the new Soviet Union.

When World War I ended and representatives of the Allied victors met in Paris in 1919 to build the new postwar world, they sought to establish nationalist-based democracies, in which the rule of law would guarantee the rights of individuals. These two interlinked concepts of law and human rights became for many the defining features of "the West," of democracy, and of civilization itself. The Bolsheviks challenged this definition. They offered instead a definition of democracy based on class and an understanding of the law resting on the demands of continuing revolution. ■

Questions of Justice

1. In what ways did the Bolshevik refusal to accept bourgeois principles of justice mean that the newly established Soviet Union placed itself outside the boundaries of the West?

2. Compare and contrast attitudes toward the law and "revolutionary justice" in the "nontrial" of Tsar Nicholas with those revealed in the trials of Charles I in seventeenth-century England and Louis XVI in eighteenth-century France. (See "Justice in History" in Chapters 15 and 19.) What factors explain the differences?

Taking It Further

Kozlov, Vladimir, and Vladimir Khrustalëv. *The Last Diary of Tsaritsa Alexandra.* 1997. Translation of the tsarina's diary from 1918.

Rosenberg, William, ed. *Bolshevik Visions: First Phase of the Cultural Revolution in Soviet Russia.* 1990. The section on "Proletarian Legality" explores the Bolsheviks' effort to develop a legal system that embodied their revolutionary ideals.

Steinberg, Mark, and Vladimir Khrustalëv. *The Fall of the Romanovs.* 1999. Detailed account of the last two years of the tsar and his family, based on recently opened archives.

■ **Tsar Nicholas II and Family**
Tsar Nicholas II, the Tsarina Alexandra, and their family.

■ **Spartacist Revolution**

The effort to establish a soviet government in Berlin took the form of street fighting. This photograph shows one street skirmish that occurred in the city's newspaper district.

promises of "Peace, Land, Bread" to be hollow. Peasant farms were transformed into battlefields as five years of civil war killed off more combatants than had World War I. In the resulting famine, death tolls reached as high as five million. Yet, as the next chapter shows, the Bolsheviks emerged victorious. The Russian Empire was remade as the Soviet Union, a communist state.

THE SPREADING REVOLUTION

The victory of the Bolsheviks in Russia inspired socialists across Europe and around the world. In January 1919, communists in Buenos Aires, Argentina, led by Russian immigrants, controlled the city for three days until they were crushed by the Argentine army. British dockworkers struck in support of the Bolshevik Revolution, and in French cities general strikes caused chaos. In Austria, revolutionaries attempted to take control of government buildings in Vienna but were quickly defeated by the Austrian army. In Hungary, Bela Kun, a journalist who had come to admire the Bolsheviks while a prisoner of war in Russia, established a short-lived soviet regime in the spring of 1919.

Revolution also swept through defeated Germany. Disillusion with the kaiser's regime had set in long before Germany had lost the war. Defeat simply accentuated the desire for radical political change. But the first revolutionary step in Germany was a response not to popular desire but to American demands. In October 1918, Germany's military commanders recommended that the German government enter into peace negotiations. U.S. President Woodrow Wilson, however, saw the war as a democratic crusade and so refused to allow the Allies to negotiate with representatives of the kaiser's authoritarian regime. To placate Wilson, the kaiser was forced to overhaul Germany's political system. For the first time, representatives of left-wing and centrist parties—including the SPD, the largest socialist party in Europe—were invited to join the government.

This "revolution from above" coincided with and was challenged by a "revolution from below." Inspired by the success of the Bolshevik Revolution, many German workers rejected the SPD's vision of socialism as too moderate. The members of the SPD believed in working for gradual social reform through parliamentary action and debate. A much more radical alternative was offered by a breakaway socialist faction called the Spartacists (after Spartacus, the gladiator who led a slave revolt against Rome in the first century B.C.E.). Directed by Karl Liebknecht (1871–1919) and Rosa Luxemburg (1870–1919), the Spartacists wanted Germany to follow Russia down the path to communist revolution. In Berlin, thousands rallied behind Liebknecht and Luxemburg. By November 8, communists had declared the establishment of a Soviet republic in the province of Bavaria; the Red Flag—symbol of communism—was flying over eleven German cities; and revolutionaries had seized control of all the main railroad junctions.

On November 9, the head of the SPD, Friedrich Ebert (1871–1925), became chancellor of Germany and the kaiser abdicated. One of Ebert's colleagues in the SPD triumphantly proclaimed from the window of the Reichstag building in Berlin that Germany was now a parliamentary democracy. Almost at that very moment, Karl Liebknecht stood at another window (in the occupied royal palace) and announced that Germany was now a revolutionary communist state. With two opposing versions of revolution on offer, civil war raged until the spring of 1919, when the SPD defeated the communists for control of the new Germany.

THE NATIONALIST REVOLUTIONS

In both Germany and Russia, the war created the opportunity for *social* revolution. In other areas, both within and outside Europe, the war kindled the fires of *nationalist* revolution. As the war progressed, both sides used nationalism against the enemy. The British, for example, fostered Arab nationalism to undermine Ottoman strength while the

Germans sought to encourage uprisings in both India and Ireland as a way to weaken Britain. For peoples seeking political statehood, the war held great promise.

The Disintegration of Austria-Hungary

Nationalist divisions plagued Austria-Hungary from the very start of the war. On the average, of every 100 soldiers mobilized, twenty-five spoke German, twenty-three Magyar, thirteen Czech, nine Serbo-Croatian, eight Polish, eight Ukrainian, seven Romanian, five Slovak, three Slovene, and one Italian.[19] Such linguistic confusion created overwhelming administrative and logistical difficulties. But much more important, this linguistic diversity symbolized a lack of the fundamental national cohesion needed to unite the empire's peoples behind the war effort. Large sections of the population of the Austrian-Hungarian Empire opposed the war; both Czech and Serb soldiers defected to the Russian side. Throughout the war years, minority groups within the empire faced brutal repression. Over 500 Bosnian Serbs and hundreds of Ukrainians were shot without trial because they sympathized with the enemy.

When the war turned decisively against the Central Powers in 1918, Austria-Hungary broke into pieces. In May, mutinies erupted among Slovenian, Ruthenian, Serbian, and Czech troops. Throughout the summer of 1918, the Allied army advanced up from Greece through the Balkan peninsula, and restored independent status to Serbia, Albania, and Montenegro. Inspired by the resurrection of these nationalist states and sure that Austria-Hungary was defeated, nationalist politicians made their move. By the end of October, they had declared independent governments in Poland, Hungary, Czechoslovakia, and what would become Yugoslavia.

Promises in the Middle East

World War I also resulted in the collapse of the Ottoman Empire. When war broke out in 1914, Ottoman control still stretched far into the Middle East, embracing Palestine and the western coast of the Red Sea. As we have seen, this region became a key battleground, with both oil and the Suez Canal as strong lures for the armies of both sides. Allied victory and the collapse of the Ottoman Empire opened the door to revolutionary change. As in eastern Europe, a new map would have to be drawn and new political structures erected.

The defeat of the Ottoman forces in this region owed an enormous debt to the revolutionary impact of Arab nationalism. By the late nineteenth century, Arab intellectuals had begun to dream of overthrowing Ottoman rule. When war came, Arab nationalists joined with the Allies to defeat the Ottoman forces. The British welcomed Arab support with promises of Arab national independence after the war.

But the British also promised to support a Jewish state in the same region. Eager to win the backing of the American Jewish community for U.S. participation in the war, the British government in 1917 issued the Balfour Declaration°, a pledge of British support for a Jewish national homeland in Palestine. With Jews often the first victims of escalating hatred and ethnic violence, the Zionist argument that Jews needed their own nation-state seemed more and more compelling to many Europeans. To the 700,000 Arabs living in Palestine, however, the Balfour Declaration was a betrayal. Contradictory promises of an independent Palestinian homeland made to both Arabs and Jews set the stage for disaster in future decades.

War and the European Empires

The Middle East was not the only region in which the war heightened nationalist aspirations. In Ireland, revolutionary nationalists saw the war as an opportunity for revolt. Counting on the war to distract the British, they mounted an armed rebellion on Easter Monday in 1916. Quickly and brutally suppressed, the "Easter Rising" was fairly unusual: Few colonial territories saw armed uprisings during the war years. But throughout the regions of European empires, the desire for political independence gained in strength as the war changed economic relationships and strengthened nationalist identities.

The war eroded many of the economic connections between European nations and their empires. Germany's submarine warfare and the Allies' blockade sharply limited both the imports of colonial raw materials and foods into Europe and the exports of European industrial products to the imperial territories. The war thus stimulated the development of more diversified and industrialized—and therefore more independent—economies in regions such as Australia, India, South Africa, and much of South America.

Less directly, but just as important, the war undermined the sense of superiority that had bolstered European imperialism. In the latter decades of the nineteenth century, imperialist ideologues defended empire making as the spread of a superior civilization to primitive regions and peoples. They described inhabitants of Asia, Africa, and South America as barbarians who needed the guidance and discipline of the more advanced European white races. But by 1918, in the wake of the war, at least some Europeans were asking, "Who is the barbarian now?"

In what the British called the "white Dominions"—Australia, New Zealand, Canada, and South Africa—the war accelerated the formation of national as opposed to imperial identities. By 1914, these regions had already received a great deal of autonomy within the structure of the British Empire, with the nonwhite populations firmly subjugated to the white colonial classes. When the British government declared war against Germany, the Dominions found themselves at war as well. Serving as part of the British forces, the Dominion regiments nonetheless remained distinct—Canadians fought alongside Canadians, Australians with Australians. The performance of these Dominion troops during the war became a matter of intense national pride.

For example, in 1915, British political and military leaders devised a plan to win the war by heading up the Gallipoli peninsula to the Ottoman capital of Constantinople. (See Map 24.4). On April 25, British and ANZAC troops moved onto the peninsula. At one of the landing sites, the troops were put ashore on the wrong beach, a narrow stretch of sand butting against tall cliffs on the top of which sat Turkish soldiers armed with machine guns. It was an impossible situation, yet for the next six months they clung there, heroically if futilely, until at last British commanders admitted defeat and evacuated the peninsula. For many Australians, the word *Gallipoli* became synonymous with national suffering and national courage. The heroism of their soldiers (and what they perceived as the stupidity of the British planners) accentuated their sense of themselves as Australian rather than British.

The war proved even more influential—and more destabilizing—in imperial territories without large white populations. Small nationalist movements existed in many of these regions before 1914, but the war strengthened and energized them. In Egypt, British requisitions of food, livestock, and forced labor aroused great resentment and fostered the birth of the Wafd, a nationalist group fighting for Egyptian independence. Throughout the British empire, Muslims faced divided loyalties. If they fought for Britain, they fought against their religious leader, the caliph, sultan of the Ottoman Empire. Discontent spread among non-Muslims as well. In countries such as India, which lost almost 50,000 of its soldiers in the war, more and more people—Hindu and Muslim—began to question the right of a small group of men in a government far, far away to involve their people in a war.

The nationalist cause in India took on added impetus in 1916 when a British-educated lawyer returned from South Africa, where he had spent twenty years fighting to improve the lot of indentured Indian laborers. As the war was drawing to a close, Mohandas Gandhi (1869–1948) introduced India and the world to a new form of revolution. He called on his followers to fight the British not with armed weapons but with moral force—with nonviolent protest and civil disobedience. Unlike many revolutionaries (such as Lenin), Gandhi did not believe that a small elite could or should dictate the course of events. He transformed Indian nationalism from the pastime of Western-educated intellectuals to a mass movement. By the end of the war, he and his followers stood ready to challenge British rule over India.

WILSON'S REVOLUTION

At the beginning of 1919, the representatives of the victorious Allied nations gathered in Paris to draw up the treaties that would wrap up the war. Yet their aims were far higher

■ Wilson and the Peace
Setting sail for the Paris Peace Conference on December 4, 1918, Wilson believed he was also embarking on a journey in which he would lead Europe into political democracy and international peace.

than simply ending the war; they wished to construct a new Europe and to reconfigure the conduct of international affairs. At the center of this high endeavor was the American college-professor-turned-president Woodrow Wilson. Like the Bolsheviks, Wilson offered a vision of a radical new future. He based *his* version of revolutionary change on the ideal of national self-determination—a world in which "every people should be left free to determine its own polity, its own way of development, unhindered, unthreatened, unafraid, the little along with the great and powerful." The map of Europe would be redrawn, the old empires replaced with independent, ethnically homogenous, democratic nation-states (see Map 24.6).

These new nation-states would interact differently from the empires of the past. In what he called his Fourteen Points, Wilson demanded a revolution in international affairs. He argued that "Points" such as freedom of the seas, freedom of trade, and open diplomacy (an end to secret treaties) would break down barriers and guarantee peace and prosperity for all peoples. The cornerstone of this new world order would be an international organization, the League of Nations°, which would oversee the implementation of these new measures and would have the power to resolve disputes between nations. Wilson and other planners of the postwar era envisioned the league as a truly revolutionary organization, one that would guarantee that World War I was "the war to end all wars." To replace the system of secret diplomacy and Great Power alliances that had led to the horrors of total war, the league offered an international forum in which all states, big and small, European and non-European, would have a voice and in which negotiations would be conducted openly and democratically. War would become outmoded.

THE FAILURE OF THE PEACE SETTLEMENT

At the end of the war, then, Europe seemed to stand on the brink of revolutionary change. But as we shall see in Chapter 25, soaring social and political expectations went unrealized, as Europeans sought not to build a new world but to reconstruct the one the war had obliterated. The peace treaties that ended the war played a crucial role in shattering the

■ **Map 24.6 Europe and the Middle East after World War I**
A comparison of this map with Map 24.1 on page 793 illustrates the vital role played by the war in shaping eastern Europe and the Middle East.

dreams of a new Europe and in undermining the international political and economic stability of the postwar era. In Paris in 1919 and 1920, the Allies and their defeated enemies signed a series of treaties named after the French palaces in which they were signed—the Treaty of Versailles, with Germany; the Treaty of St. Germain, with Austria; the Treaty of Neuilly, with Bulgaria; the Treaty of Trianon, with Hungary; and the Treaty of Sèvres, with Turkey. In drawing up the treaties, the Allies' writers sought to create a new international order based on three features: a democratic Germany, national self-determination in eastern Europe, and the League of Nations. They failed in all three areas.

The Treaty of Versailles and German Democracy

At the center of the new Europe envisioned by Woodrow Wilson was to be a new democratic Germany. French leader Georges Clemenceau did not share this vision. He had lived through two German invasions of his homeland and wished to ensure that Germany could never again threaten France. Clemenceau proposed the creation of a Rhineland state out of Germany's industrialized western region, both as a neutral buffer zone between France and Germany and as a way to reduce Germany's economic power. The British leader, David Lloyd George, who had just won an election on the campaign slogan "Hang the Kaiser" and who had promised his people that he would squeeze Germany "until the pips squeak," publicly supported Clemenceau's hardline approach to the peace settlement with Germany. In private, however, he expressed fear that such an approach would backfire by feeding the flames of German resentment and undermining the structures of German democracy.

Lloyd George's fears proved well-grounded. The German people bitterly resented the Versailles Treaty°, which they perceived as unjustly punitive. By the terms of the treaty, Germany lost all of its overseas colonies, 13 percent of its European territory, 10 percent of its population, and its ability to wage war. The German army was limited to a defensive force of 100,000 men and was allowed no aircraft or tanks. Clemenceau failed in his effort to create a separate Rhineland state, but the Rhineland was demilitarized, emptied of German soldiers and fortifications. In addition, the coalfields of the Saar region were ceded to France for fifteen years. Even more significantly, the Versailles Treaty declared that German aggression had caused the war, and therefore that Germany must recompense the Allies for its cost. In 1921, the Allies presented Germany with a bill for reparations° of 132 billion marks ($31.5 billion). As we will see in the next chapter, this reparations clause set up an economic cycle that was to prove devastating for both global prosperity and German democratic politics.

The Failure of National Self-Determination

The map of Europe drawn by the peace treaties appeared to signal the establishment of a new international order.

The old authoritarian empires of eastern and central Europe disappeared, replaced with independent nation-states. In keeping with the principle of national self-determination, Poland once again became an independent nation, with pieces carved out of the German, Austrian, and Russian empires. One entirely new state was formed out of the rubble of the Austrian-Hungarian Empire—Czechoslovakia. Romania, Greece, and Italy all expanded as a result of serving on the winners' side, while Serbia became the heart of the new Yugoslavia. The defeated nations shrunk, some dramatically. Austria, for example, became a mere rump of what had been the mighty Habsburg Empire, while Hungary was reduced to one-third of its prewar size. All that remained of the Ottoman Empire was Turkey.

These changes were heralded as the victory of "national self-determination." But as Woodrow Wilson's own secretary of state, Robert Lansing, complained, "This phrase is simply loaded with dynamite. It will raise hopes which can never be realized." Wilson had called for "every people" to be left free to determine its political destiny—but who constituted "a people"? Did, for example, the Macedonians? Should there be an independent Macedonia? Macedonians said yes, but the Paris peace negotiators answered no. Macedonia was enveloped by Yugoslavia and Greece, and in consequence, throughout the 1920s and 1930s Macedonians waged a terrorist campaign in the Balkans. Wilson's peaceful new world seemed far, far away when in 1923, a Macedonian nationalist group kidnapped the Bulgarian prime minister, chopped off his head, and sliced off his limbs.

The Macedonians were far from the only dissatisfied ethnic group in eastern Europe. Even after the peace settlements redrew the map, no fewer than 30 million eastern Europeans remained members of minority groups. Less than 70 percent of Hungarians, for example, lived in Hungary—more than three million were scattered in other states. Over nine million Germans resided outside the borders of Germany. In the newly created Czechoslovakia, one-third of the population was neither Czech nor Slovak. The new state of Yugoslavia contained an uneasy mixture of several ethnic groups, most resentful of the dominant Serbs. Rather than satisfying nationalist ambitions, then, the peace settlements served to inflame them, thus creating a volatile situation for the post–World War I world.

The Limits of the League

True to Wilson's vision of a new international order, the treaty makers included the Covenant of the League of Nations in each of the treaties. The league, however, never realized Wilson's high hopes of making war obsolete. Three factors help explain the league's failure. First, it did not represent every state. When the league met for the first time in 1920, three significant world powers had no representative present: Germany and the Soviet Union were excluded, and, in a stunning defeat for President

Wilson, the U.S. Senate rejected membership. The failure of these three states to participate in the League at its beginning stripped the organization of much of its potential influence. Second, the League had no military power. Although it could levy economic sanctions against states that flouted its decisions, it could do nothing more. Finally, the will to make the League work was lacking.

With Wilson removed from the picture, European leaders were free to pursue their own rather more traditional visions of what the League should be. French politicians, for example, believed that the League's primary reason for existence was to enforce the provisions of the Versailles Treaty—in other words, to punish Germany rather than to restructure international relations.

CONCLUSION

The War and the West

Sparked by nationalist fervor, international competition, and a widespread will to believe that in war lay the solution to political divisions and cultural fears, World War I quickly slipped out of the control of both the diplomats and the generals. Industrialization changed the face of combat. Total war smashed the boundaries of the battlefield, eroded the distinction between soldier and civilian, and demanded an overhaul of each combatant nation's political, economic, and social structures.

The idea of "the West" also changed as a result of the impact of this war. The entry of American forces in the final year of the war signaled that in the twentieth century, the United States would have to be factored into any definition of "Western culture" or "Western civilization." At the same time, the spread of the war to the Middle East and Africa and the significant role played by soldiers from imperial territories such as Tunisia, India, and Australia demonstrated the global framework that complicated and constrained Western affairs. The war's revolutionary aftermath also had profound consequences for formulations of "Western identity." With the triumph of the Bolshevik Revolution, two versions of modernity now presented themselves—one associated with the United States and capitalism, and the other represented by the new Soviet Union and its communist ideology. Soviet communism's intellectual roots lay in Marxism, a quintessentially Western ideology, one shaped by Western ideals of evolutionary progress and the triumph of human reason. But after the Russian Revolution, communism was increasingly viewed in the West as something foreign, essentially Eastern, the Other against which the West identified itself.

The carnage of World War I also challenged the faith of many Europeans that through industrial development the West was progressing morally as well as materially. In the final decades of the nineteenth century, European and American soldiers had used repeating rifles and machine guns to conquer huge sections of the globe in the name of Western civilization. In 1914, European and American soldiers turned their machine guns on each other. The world the war had created was one of unprecedented destruction. Millions lay dead, with millions more maimed for life. Vast sections of northern France and eastern Europe had been turned into giant cemeteries filled with rotting men and rusting metal. Across central and eastern Europe, starvation continued to claim thousands of victims, while a worldwide influenza epidemic, spread in part by the marching armies, ratcheted up the death tolls even higher. In the new world shaped by relentless conflicts such as the Battle of the Somme, the pessimism and sense of despair that had already invaded much of the arts in the decade before the war became more characteristic of the wider culture. For many Europeans, the optimism and confidence of nineteenth-century liberalism died in the trenches.

Yet, paradoxically, the war also fostered high hopes. Wilson declared that this had been the war to end all wars. The fires of revolution burned high and many in the West believed that on top of the ashes of empire they would now build a better world. The task of reconstruction, however, proved immense; as we shall see in Chapter 25, in many areas, retrenchment replaced revolution. Seeking stability in an increasingly unsettled world, many

Europeans and Americans did their best to return to prewar patterns. The failure of the peace settlement ensured that the "war to end all wars" set the stage for the next, far more destructive total war.

Suggestions for Further Reading

For a comprehensive list of suggested readings, please go to www.ablongman.com/levack/chapter24

Cork, Richard. *A Bitter Truth: Avant-Garde Art and the Great War.* 1994. A beautifully illustrated work that looks at the cultural impact of the war.

Eksteins, Modris. *Rites of Spring: The Great War and the Birth of the Modern Age.* 1989. Explores the links among modernism, the war experience, and modernity.

Ferguson, Niall. *The Pity of War.* 1999. A bold reconsideration of many accepted interpretations of the origins and experience of the war.

Fitzpatrick, Sheila. *The Russian Revolution, 1917–1932.* 1994. As the title indicates, Fitzpatrick sees the revolutions of 1917 as the opening battle in a more than ten-year struggle to shape the new Russia.

Gilbert, Martin. *The First World War: A Complete History.* 1994. A comprehensive account, packed with illuminating detail.

Gilbert, Martin. *The Routledge Atlas of the First World War.* 1994. Much more than a set of maps, Gilbert's atlas provides a very clear and useful survey of both the causes and results of the war.

Higonnet, Margaret. *Lines of Fire: Women's Visions of World War I.* 1998. An important study of women's experiences.

Joll, James. *The Origins of the First World War.* 1984. One of the best and most carefully balanced studies of this complicated question.

Read, Christopher. *From Tsar to Soviets: The Russian People and Their Revolution, 1917–1921.* 1996. An up-to-date study of the popular revolution and its fate.

Winter, J. M. *The Experience of World War I.* 1989. Despite the title, this richly illustrated work not only covers the war itself but also explores the factors that led to its outbreak and outlines its chief consequences.

Winter, J. M., and R. M. Wall, eds. *The Upheaval of War: Family, Work and Welfare in Europe, 1914–1918.* Cambridge, 1988. A series of essays examining the home front experiences.

Notes

1. Figures from Alan Sharp, "The Genie That Would Not Go Back into the Bottle: National Self-Determination and the Legacy of the First World War and the Peace Settlement," in Seamus Dunn and T. G. Fraser, eds., *Europe and Ethnicity*, (1996), p. 10.
2. Quotation from Karl Kautsky et. al. eds., *The Outbreak of the World War: German Documents* (1924), 76.
3. Quoted in Niall Ferguson, *The Pity of War* (1999), 152.
4. Quoted in Eric Leeds, *No Man's Land: Combat and Identity in World War I* (1979), 17.
5. Allister Horne, *The Price of Glory: Verdun, 1916* (1967), 27.
6. Paul Fussell, *The Great War and Modern Memory* (1975).
7. Figure from Tony Ashworth, *Trench Warfare 1914–1918* (1980), 15–16.
8. Quoted in Martin Gilbert, *A History of the Twentieth Century, Vol. 1* (1997), 417.
9. Samuel Hynes, *A War Imagined: The First World War and English Culture* (1991), 195.
10. Quoted in Richard Cork, *A Bitter Truth* (1994), 198.
11. Quoted in Sheila Rowbotham, *A Century of Women* (1997), 72.
12. Quoted in W. Bruce Lincoln, *Red Victory: A History of the Russian Civil War* (1989), 32.
13. Quoted in Edvard Radzinsky, *The Last Tsar*, trans. Marian Schwartz (1993), 336.
14. From the written account of Yakov Yurovsky, quoted in Radzinsky, *The Last Tsar*, 355.
15. Quoted in William Henry Chamberlin, *The Russian Revolution, 1917–1921. Volume 2. From The Civil War to the Consolidation of Power* (1987), 91.
16. Quoted in Lincoln, *Red Victory*, 151.
17. *Ibid.*, Quoted in Lincoln, 155.
18. Quoted in Radzinsky, *The Last Tsar*, 326.
19. Figures from Robert O. Paxton, *Europe in the Twentieth Century*, 3rd ed. (1997), 109.

Reconstruction, Reaction, and Continuing Revolution: The 1920s and 1930s

O N SEPTEMBER 14, 1927, AN OPEN CAR ACCELERATED DOWN A STREET IN Nice in southern France. In its passenger seat sat a woman, who let her long silk shawl whip in the wind. This woman in free-flowing clothing, speeding down the streets in a convertible, provides a fitting image for Western culture in the decade after World War I. Entranced by the automobile, Americans and Europeans embraced its promise of mobility and freedom. They perceived themselves as moving ahead, breaking through traditional barriers and heading off into new directions. Even more fitting was the identity of that female passenger: Isadora Duncan, by 1927 one of the most famous artists in Europe. In the years before World War I, the American-born Duncan had rejected classical ballet as an artificial form that restricted and deformed the female body. She cast aside ballet's confining toe shoes and tutus, and opted for bare feet and simple tunics. For Duncan, dance was not a force imposed on the body from outside; instead, dance flowed from the body itself. In her break with the highly regulated system of classical ballet, her quest for more natural forms, and her desire to liberate women, both physically and artistically, Duncan serves as an apt symbol for modernity. Moreover, as an American, Duncan appeared to personify the new culture that for many Europeans represented the world of the future. Even her clothing—loose tunics, free-flowing scarves, fluid shawls—symbolized a love of freedom and movement.

Yet freedom is sometimes dangerous and movement can be violent. On that autumn day in 1927 Duncan's long scarf became entangled in the wheel of her car and strangled the dancer. Gruesome as it is, the image of Duncan's sudden death serves as an appropriate introduction to the history of the West in the 1920s and 1930s, the turbulent interlude between two tragic world wars. The

Chapter Outline

- Cultural Despair and Desire

- Out of the Trenches: Reconstructing National and Gender Politics in the 1920s

- The Rise of the Radical Right

- The Polarization of Politics in the 1930s

- European Empires in the Interwar Era

"This Hand Guides the Reich: German Youth Follow It in the Ranks of the Hitler Youth": In this German propaganda poster from the 1930s, the Nazi government promises order and strong leadership, and at the same time allies itself with youth and vigor. During the 1930s, governments from across the political spectrum borrowed techniques from mass advertising to spread their ideas and win support.

American president Woodrow Wilson had hailed World War I as the "final war for human liberty." Many Europeans agreed; they thought that the war would propel their society down a new road, yet in much of Europe the drive toward freedom ended quickly. The interwar period saw the strangulation of democracy in eastern and southern Europe and the rise of political and cultural ideologies that viewed human liberty as an illusion and mass murder as a tool of the state.

These developments had profound implications for the idea of the West. In the Wilsonian vision, "the West" stood as a culture that promoted individual freedom through democratic politics and capitalist economics. But the success of antidemocratic and anticapitalist ideologies in capturing the hopes and allegiances of large numbers of Europeans illustrated that Wilson's definition of the West was only one among many, and that the link between "Western" and "democratic" remained fragile.

Understanding the developments that shaped the interwar era demands close consideration of the way Europeans responded to the revolutionary aftermath of World War I. Hopes for radical social and political change often clashed with the desire to restore the prewar order. Five questions will guide our examination of this confusing period: (1) What was the impact of the war on European cultural life? (2) In what ways did reconstruction rather than revolution characterize the postwar period? (3) What circumstances explain the emergence of the Radical Right? (4) What factors led to the polarization of European politics in the 1930s? (5) How did the interaction between Europe and the world outside the West change after the war?

Cultural Despair and Desire

To many Europeans in the 1920s and 1930s, World War I seemed to have torn a huge and irreparable gash in the fabric of culture and society. It appeared as the sudden and horrifying end to an age of science and progress, an era of technological improvement and social optimism. Yet this perception of a radical cultural break masked fundamental continuities. As we observed in Chapter 23, beginning in the 1870s, anxiety intermingled with optimism in European culture, and widespread fear of degeneration and decay marked Western society. Well before World War I, modernist painters, musicians, and poets were pushing beyond the limits of nineteenth-century art and articulating disturbing visions of a world in purposeless flux. The real change in the years after the war was that modernism's fragmented canvases and dissonant choruses no longer seemed alien; they echoed the

sensibilities of societies shattered by total war. But the war had also injected art with an often passionate political intensity. Excitement as well as anxiety thus marked the art and the age. The interwar era was a time of contradictions, one in which many Europeans despaired at the future of their society but many others dreamed of building a new and better world.

THE WASTE LAND

Within just a few years of the war's end, war memorials were erected in cities, towns, and villages throughout France and Britain. Significantly, these memorials rarely celebrated the Allies' victory; instead, they focused on dead soldiers. Slaughter, not success, was the dominant theme. At Verdun, for example, the memorial was an ossuary, a gigantic receptacle for the skulls and bones of 130,000 men. In some ways, European culture after the war took on the form of an ossuary, as intellectuals and artists looked at the death tolls from the war, and concluded that the end product of human reason and scientific endeavor was mass destruction.

In the English-speaking world, the American expatriate poet T. S. Eliot (1888–1965) supplied the most evocative portrait of postwar disillusion. In 1922, Eliot published a lengthy poem called "The Waste Land," which became a metaphor used by many Europeans to express their own sense of the waste wrought by the war. Arising out of Eliot's own personal anguish, "The Waste Land" contains no straightforward narrative. Instead, like a Cubist collage painting, it comprises fragments of conversation, literary allusions, disjointed quotations, mythological references, all clashing and combining in a modernist cry of despair.

The heightened anxiety and loss of certainty that characterized much of Western literature after the war is also clear in the realms of theology and philosophy. In the nineteenth century, theologians emphasized the harmony of religion and science. Their argument that God is present in the world, guiding its rational and progressive evolution, was difficult to sustain in a society that had experienced the absurd slaughter of World War I. In his postwar writings, the Swiss theologian Karl Barth (1886–1968) emphasized human sinfulness and argued that an immense gulf separated humanity from God. Neither scientific analysis nor historical inquiry could bridge the gap. Reaching God demanded a radical leap of faith.

Barth's German colleague Rudolf Bultmann (1884–1976) made the leap of faith even more radical. Bultmann argued that the Jesus Christ depicted in the New Testament—the foundation of Christianity—was largely fictional. In Bultmann's view, the Gospels were something like Eliot's "Waste Land" poem, a collection of fragments originating from myth and folk tale, layered on one another and capable of multiple interpretations. Rational inquiry and scien-

THE WASTE LAND

T. S. Eliot's "The Waste Land" comprises 434 lines; the excerpt given here is thus just one small piece of a much larger and complex poetic work that provides an evocative portrait of a despairing age. One of its central images, drawn from the English legends of King Arthur, is of an impotent and sickly king, reigning over a dried-up land.

April is the cruellest month, breeding
Lilacs out of the dead land, mixing
Memory and desire, stirring
Dull roots with spring rain.
Winter kept us warm, covering
Earth in forgetful snow, feeding
A little life with dried tubers.
. . . .

But at my back in a cold blast I hear
The rattle of the bones, and chuckle spread
    from ear to ear.

A rat crept softly through the vegetation
Dragging its slimy belly on the bank
While I was fishing in the dull canal
On a winter evening round behind the gashouse
Musing upon the king my brother's wreck
And on the king my father's death before him.
White bodies naked on the low damp ground
And bones cast in a little low dry garret,
Rattled by the rat's foot only, year to year.

Source: From "The Waste Land" by T. S. Eliot. First published in 1922. Reprinted by permission of Faber and Faber Ltd.

---

tific methods cannot deliver a certain image of the historical Jesus, who remains essentially unknowable, obscured by the myths built up over centuries. Yet Bultmann, a Lutheran pastor, did not discard his Christian beliefs. Instead, he argued that within and through the Christian mythology rests ultimate spiritual—although not scientific or historical—truth.

Bultmann's form of Christianity is often called Christian existentialism° because Bultmann put a Christian twist on the existentialist philosophy taught by his friend, the philosopher Martin Heidegger (1889–1976). At the core of existentialism was a profound despair. The human condition is one of anxiety and alienation, even *Nausea*, as Heidegger's student Jean-Paul Sartre (1905–1980) entitled one of his most famous works. For Barth and Bultmann, the way out from this anxiety was through submission to God. As an atheist, Heidegger found this route blocked. Instead, he taught that the individual must struggle to rise above mere existence to a consciousness of the genuine and authentic. Sartre's version of existentialism was more pessimistic. At a time when, as we will see, dictatorships were rising across Europe, Sartre insisted that the fundamental fact of human existence is that "man is condemned to be free" in a universe devoid of meaning or reason. Yet Sartre, too, offered a way out from this prison of freedom: Individuals must recognize that they are free to make choices, and then must do so. During World War II, Sartre's own heroic acts in the French Resistance against the Nazis exemplified his insistence on the necessity of making moral choices in an absurd world.

A sense of absurdity and waste dominates much of the visual art of the period. War veteran Otto Dix (1891–1969) filled his canvases with crippled ex-soldiers. The vivid colors and distorted figures of the Expressionist style enabled Dix to articulate his outrage at the world he saw about him. In *Flanders,* painted in 1934, Dix depicted a nightmare of trench soldiers, rotting like blasted trees. Here there is no heroism, only horror (see page 830).

BUILDING SOMETHING BETTER

Stuck in the mud, the soldiers in Dix's *Flanders* provide a haunting image of European culture in the interwar years. A very different image takes shape when we examine the work of Dix's contemporaries in the *Bauhaus.* Established in Berlin in 1919 as a school for architects, craftsmen, and designers, the Bauhaus epitomized not the despair but rather the near-utopianism of much of European culture after the war. Bauhaus sought to eliminate the barriers between "art" (what we put on our walls or see in museums) and "craft" (what we actually use in daily life: furniture, textiles, dishes, and the like), and so to enhance daily living by making it more effective, efficient, and beautiful. Its founder, Walter Gropius (1883–1969), hoped his students would become nothing less than "the architects of a new civilization."[1]

Gropius's belief that the arts could serve a social purpose was commonly shared in the interwar years. As the British poet W. H. Auden (1907–1973) explained, although good poetry is "not concerned with telling people what to do," it should "[lead] us to the point where it is possible for us to make a rational and moral choice."[2] Many artists abandoned the prewar modernist ideal of "art for art's sake," and produced work steeped in political passion and a desire for a better world. The murals of the Mexican artist Diego Rivera (1906–1957) exemplify this postwar turn toward political engagement.

Much of the near-utopianism of European culture focused on the transforming power of technology. The "machine aesthetic" triumphed most completely in the Soviet Union, where the Bolsheviks encouraged artistic experiment and innovation as part of their revolution. The engineer became the image of a communist hero, and industrial motifs permeated Soviet culture in the 1920s. In the revolutionary theater of Vsevelod Meyerhold, mechanical gestures replaced naturalistic expressions and sets consisted of scaffolding. Similarly, a factory whistle opens the chorus of Dmitri Shostakovich's *Second Symphony* (1927), written to praise industrial labor.

Postwar architecture in the West also provides a vivid illustration of this mechanical faith. A house, explained the Swiss architect Le Corbusier (1887–1965), was "a machine for living in." Le Corbusier and his fellow modernist architects stripped their buildings of all ornament and frequently exposed the essential machinery—the supporting beams, the heating ducts, the elevator shafts. Concrete, steel, and glass became the building materials of choice as modernist skyscrapers—glittering rectangles—transformed urban skylines and testified to the triumph of the human-made.

Closely related to the worship of the machine in the interwar period was a celebration of movement and speed.

The automobile evolved from a rich man's toy to a middle-class necessity, made possible by the assembly-line techniques developed in Henry Ford's Detroit factories. The assembly line, which reduced the entire industrial workforce of a factory to a single efficient machine, was imported from the United States into Europe in the later 1920s. The airline industry also took off in this era. In 1919 the first air passenger service between London and Paris began; the next decade saw Europe's major cities linked by air networks. The car and the plane became potent symbols of a new age of possibility and opportunity. In 1927, when the American Charles Lindbergh (1902–1974) became the first person to fly across the Atlantic alone, he was hailed not only as a national but as an international hero, an icon of human resourcefulness and technological mastery.

The idea that Western society was moving rapidly and that anything was possible in a world of change shaped much of the culture of the interwar era. Take the popular dance craze of the 1920s—the Charleston. Arms outstretched and legs firing like pistons, the entire body becomes a fast-moving machine. Another American import, Hollywood's "moving pictures," even more clearly represented and stimulated the ideal of a society in motion. The Italians and the French had dominated the movie industry before 1914, but during the war film production in Europe halted. American filmmakers quickly filled the void. After the war, moviegoing became a truly popular pastime—and most of the movies on the screen were made in America.

■ **Otto Dix, *Flanders* (1934–1935)**

In this painting, the Flanders landscape is literally shaped by the bodies of soldiers. Like these soldiers—and much of postwar European culture—Dix could not escape the war. His paintings reveal a man permanently wounded.

■ **Diego Rivera, *The Distribution of Arms* (1928)** Like many other artists in the 1920s and 1930s, Diego Rivera combined political activism with his artistic pursuits. A member of the Mexican Communist Party, Rivera's pro-Soviet sympathies are evident in this mural depicting a workers' revolution.

Hollywood presented European audiences with an appealing, if unrealistic, picture of the United States as a land of fabulous wealth, technological modernity, and unlimited mobility.

Out of the Trenches: Reconstructing National and Gender Politics in the 1920s

As we saw at the end of Chapter 24, in the years immediately following World War I Europe stood on the brink of revolutionary change. The war toppled empires and redrew the map of eastern and central Europe. Gender roles turned upside down, imperial patterns shattered, and social expectations were raised. The American president Woodrow Wilson promised a radically new world of peace and democracy. In Russia, the Bolshevik Revolution offered an even more radical vision of communist freedom. Despite these expectations and fears, however, retrenchment rather than revolution characterized much of the immediate postwar period. In many areas, World War I was the turning point that failed to turn, as Europeans sought to reconstruct the structures toppled by total war.

THE RECONSTRUCTION OF RUSSIA: FROM TSAR TO COMMISSAR

Even in the newly formed Soviet Union, the nation that epitomized revolution, important aspects of prewar society re-emerged in the postwar period. By 1922 and against all odds, the Bolsheviks had won the civil war and established their authority over most of the regions of the old tsarist empire. The Bolsheviks also re-established many features of the tsarist regime: authoritarian rule built on violent coercion, a highly centralized state, a large bureaucratic elite living in conditions of privilege that cut it off from ordinary people, and a peasant economy.

How do we explain the continuity of authoritarian rule in Russia? The first crucial factor was the impact of civil and international war. Across Russia in 1919 the Bolsheviks faced fierce opposition from rival bands of socialists, middle-class liberals, and aristocratic supporters of the tsar. These opponents of the Bolshevik revolution—called the "Whites" to distinguish them from the "Red" Bolsheviks—were supported by foreign troops. Fearing the spread of communist revolution, fourteen different countries (including the United States, Britain, France, and Japan) sent more than 100,000 soldiers to fight in Russia. In addition to these forces, the new Bolshevik state confronted numerous attempts by non-Russian nationalists to throw off the yoke of Russian rule. This was warfare at its most savage. When Ukrainian peasants resisted Russian

■ **"Whites" and "Reds"**
These U.S. sailors, on board the cruiser *Des Moines* in 1919, are on their way to fight against the Bolsheviks in Russia. They disembarked at Archangel, a northern Russian port held by the Allied armies. Even with the assistance of American and west European troops, the "Whites" were unable to defeat the Bolsheviks, and the "Reds" won the Russian Civil War.

control, the Bolsheviks resorted to methods of mass reprisal. Entire villages were burned, the men executed, the women and children sent to slower deaths in prison camps. The Bolsheviks did not have a monopoly on murder, however. White forces in the Ukraine massacred over 100,000 Jews.

As the scale of savagery escalated, so too did Russia's economic disintegration. In the cities, residents faced anarchic conditions. Transportation systems shut down, the water supply ceased to run, and furniture became the only source of fuel. When the furniture ran out, entire families froze to death inside apartment blocks. The urban areas emptied as their inhabitants fled to the countryside. By 1921, Moscow had lost half its residents and Petrograd (formerly St. Petersburg) had lost two-thirds. Yet conditions in the countryside were also brutal. To feed the cities, the Bolsheviks adopted the policy of "War Communism": requisitioning (stealing) food and seed stores from the peasants. The peasants resisted, both actively, in violent revolt, and passively, by reducing the amount they planted. Food shortages and other war-related hardships increased the population's vulnerability to epidemic disease. Between 1918 and 1921, the number of deaths from the combined impact of the civil war, starvation, and typhus surpassed the number of those who died in World War I.

The need to impose order on this chaotic situation led the Bolsheviks to adopt increasingly authoritarian measures. Like the Jacobins in 1792 during the French Revolutionary Wars, the Bolsheviks turned to terror to defeat their enemies, both domestic and foreign. In the first six years of Bolshevik rule, the Cheka (Lenin's secret police force) executed at least 200,000 people. In contrast, in the fifty years before the Bolsheviks came to power, 14,000 Russians had died at the hands of the tsarist secret police.

But the antidemocratic nature of the Bolshevik regime was not solely a response to the pressures of war. Ideology is the second crucial factor that helps explain the continuity of authoritarian rule in post-tsarist Russia. Faced with the task of building a communist state in an isolated, economically backward, peasant society, the Bolshevik leader Vladimir Lenin modified Marxist theory. In a peasant society, Lenin argued, the agent of revolutionary change could not be the working class: There simply were not enough industrial workers in Russia. Instead, the Bolshevik or Communist Party, an elite of highly disciplined, politically aware and committed individuals, would be the "vanguard" of revolution. Debate and disagreement could not be permitted—at the Tenth Communist Party Congress in 1921, party leaders agreed to Lenin's proposal to ban all political factions. Because the masses could not be trusted to make their own decisions, government officials, strictly controlled by the party, would make these decisions for them. The number of bureaucrats multiplied, and by 1925, had become a privileged elite, with access to the best jobs, food, clothing, and apartments. The rule of the tsar had been replaced not with democracy but with the rule of the commissar, the Communist Party functionary.

In the economic sphere, as in the political system, important continuities shaped the Russian experience. By 1921 the Bolshevik policy of "War Communism" had produced famine in the countryside and widespread peasant unrest. Material necessity forced Lenin to backpedal from communist ideology and announce a New Economic Policy (NEP)°. Under NEP, peasants were allowed to sell their produce for profit. Although the state continued to control heavy industry, transport, and banking, NEP encouraged the proliferation of small private businesses and farms—just as the tsar's economic policymakers had done before the war.

THE RECONSTRUCTION OF NATIONAL POLITICS IN EASTERN AND CENTRAL EUROPE

U.S. President Woodrow Wilson's vision of a new international order based on democratic politics offered the war-torn states of Europe a sharp alternative to Bolshevik one-party rule. But in the new states of eastern Europe, democracy proved to be fragile, and in most cases short-lived. Much of old Europe survived the war intact.

The Defeat of Democracy in Eastern Europe

After the peace negotiations concluded in 1922, postwar eastern Europe certainly looked markedly different from its prewar counterpart (see Map 25.1). The Russian, Austrian-Hungarian, and Ottoman Empires had all disappeared, replaced by a jigsaw puzzle of small independent nations. But lines on the map did not change key political and economic realities. Three important threads tied these new states to their prewar past: ethnic disputes, economic underdevelopment, and antidemocratic politics.

As we saw at the end of Chapter 24, the Allies paid lip service to the ideal of national self-determination but found it impossible to create ethnically homogenous nation-states in eastern Europe. As a result, nationalist-ethnic divisions continued to haunt postwar political structures. In the new Yugoslavia, for example, ethnic struggles dominated interwar politics. Croats and Slovenes had expected a federalist system that would grant them local autonomy. Instead, they found themselves in a centralized state under Serbian control. As a result, Croat representatives refused even to sit in the new parliament.

Economic difficulties also threatened eastern European stability. In many regions, eastern Europe remained a world

■ **Map 25.1   Europe in the 1920s and 1930s**

The map shows the consequences of not only World War I but also such successor conflicts as the Irish-English struggles, which resulted in the formation of the Irish Free State; the war between Bolshevick Russia and its enemies, which widened the western frontiers of the Soviet state; and the Turkish uprising, which kept Turkey intact and independent.

of peasants and aristocratic landlords. In Romania, Poland, and Hungary, at least 60 percent of the population worked the land; in Bulgaria and Yugoslavia the figure was 80 percent—versus 20 percent in industrialized Britain. With little industrial growth in these regions and few cities to absorb labor, unemployment rates and land hunger were both high.

Thus ethnic divisions and economic underdevelopment helped destabilize eastern Europe's new democratic political systems. The result was the collapse of democracy across eastern Europe. As the chronology (right) shows, with the exception of Czechoslovakia, every eastern European nation returned to authoritarian politics during the 1920s or early 1930s. In Poland, for example, democracy crumbled in 1926 when the World War I hero Marshal Josef Pilsudski (1867–1935) seized power in a military coup, after parliamentary representatives proved unable to overcome class and ethnic divisions. Pilsudski told the squabbling legislators, "The time has come to treat you like children, because you behave like children."[3] In Yugoslavia, the death of democracy was even more dramatic. Years of escalating ethnic violence peaked in 1928 when a popular Croatian political leader was shot to death on the floor of the legislature. The ensuing ethnic unrest gave King Alexander (a Serb) the excuse he needed to abolish the constitution and replace parliamentary democracy with a royal dictatorship. A brutal repression of Alexander's opponents followed. In Bulgaria, Albania, Hungary, and Romania, too, continuing ethnic conflicts and economic underdevelopment ensured the destruction of democracy.

The Weakness of the Weimar Republic

In Germany, as in the new states of eastern Europe, the appearance of radical change masked crucial continuities between the pre- and postwar eras. The kaiser's empire gave way to the Weimar Republic°, led by a democratically elected parliamentary government. This democratic political structure, however, sat uneasily atop fundamentally antidemocratic social and political foundations.

The survival of authoritarian attitudes and institutions resulted in part from the civil war that raged throughout Germany in the fall of 1918 and the first months of 1919. In this struggle, communists, inspired by the Bolshevik Revolution, fought their one-time colleagues in the more moderate socialist party (the SPD) for control of the new Germany. Anxious to impose order on a potentially anarchic situation, the SPD leaders who now controlled the German government chose not to replace the existing state bureaucracy—the elite corps of aristocratic civil servants that had served the kaiser—but to work with it. To put down the communist threat, they also abandoned their longstanding loathing of the German military and deployed both regular army units and the "Free Corps" (volunteer paramilitary units, often comprising demobilized soldiers addicted to violence). By the spring of 1919, this strange alliance of moderate socialists, traditional aristo-

---

CHRONOLOGY

The Return of Authoritarian Rule to Eastern Europe

1923	Boris III establishes a royalist dictatorship in Bulgaria
1926	Marshal Josef Pilsudski establishes a military dictatorship in Poland
1928	A new constitution gives King Zog in Albania almost unlimited powers
1929	Alexander I establishes a royal dictatorship in Yugoslavia
1932	Fascist leader Gyula Gombos appointed prime minister in Hungary
1938	King Carol establishes a royal dictatorship in Romania

---

crats, and military men had triumphed. In January 1919, Free Corps officers murdered the communist leaders Karl Liebknecht and Rosa Luxemburg in Berlin. Three months later, an equally savage repression crushed the communist soviet in Munich, with the Free Corps killing more than 600 people.

The SPD had won. Yet it lost. By allying with the aristocratic civil service, the army, and the Free Corps, the SPD crushed more than the communist revolution; it also crushed its own chances of achieving significant social change. The officers in the army and the bureaucrats in the civil service were representatives of the old Germany, vehemently opposed to not only communism but also parliamentary democracy. Continuing in positions of authority and influence, they constituted a formidable anti-democratic force at the very heart of the new Germany. The approximately 400,000 men who made up the Free Corps also regarded democratic ideals and the new German republic with contempt—"an attempt of the slime to govern."[4] The attitude of the Free Corps men is summed up in their slogan: "Everything would still have been all right if we had shot more people."[5]

The antidemocratic nature of the Free Corps became clear in 1920, after the Allies imposed restrictions on the size of Germany's military force and most Free Corps units were officially dissolved. Disaffected corpsmen joined the rightwing politician Wolfgang Kapp (1858–1922) and the World War I hero Erich von Ludendorff in an effort to overthrow the Weimar regime. This "Kapp Putsch" quickly fizzled out, defeated by both divisions in the ranks of the rebels and a general strike, but the threat posed by the Free

Corps did not disappear. Disguising themselves as athletic societies, haulage companies, and even circuses, many corps units continued their violent anti-Weimar activities. In 1923, some of these corpsmen tried once again to overthrow the Weimar government by force, with another "putsch," this time originating in a beer hall in Munich and led by a former army corporal named Adolf Hitler. Like the Kapp Putsch, Hitler's "Beer Hall Putsch°" did not succeed. The laughably light sentences imposed on its participants, however, made clear the strength of anti-Republican sentiments not only among disgruntled Free Corps men but also far up the ranks of the Weimar judicial system.

Antidemocratic forces in the Weimar Republic fed on the widespread resentment among Germans aroused by severity of the Versailles Treaty. Many Germans could not separate the birth of the Republic from the national humiliation imposed by Versailles. They blamed the moderate socialist government that signed the treaty for this humiliation. Army officers encouraged the idea that Germany could have kept on fighting had it not been "stabbed in the back" by the socialists. This "stab-in-the-back" legend helped undermine support not only for the SPD's moderate socialism but even for democracy itself.

The Death of Money: The Causes and Consequences of Hyperinflation

The shaky foundations of democracy in Weimar Germany were eroded further by the dramatic events of 1923. In that year, the German mark collapsed completely and paper money ceased to have any value. Germans used wheelbarrows full of cash to purchase a single loaf of bread. In later years, Germans spoke of 1923 as "the time when money died." With the death of money came the collapse of many other assumptions. Inflation not only gutted the currency but it also exposed as hollow many of the conventions and standards by which many Germans had ordered their lives. The result was a long-lasting cultural crisis that paved the way for the collapse of German democracy in the 1930s.

What the Germans experienced in 1923 was a phenomenon economists labeled hyperinflation°, the unintended by-product of the Weimar government's effort to force the Allies to reconsider reparations. In 1922, the Weimar government halted the payment of reparations and demanded a new economic settlement. The French responded by sending troops to occupy the Ruhr Valley, Germany's principal coal-mining and industrial region, and to seize coal as a form of reparations payment. To the surprise and dismay of French politicians, however, German coal miners simply refused to head down into the mines. This policy of passive resistance received the full support of the German government. It vowed to pay the coal miners for not working, and it raised the funds to do so by printing money. By January 1923, the mark, which in 1914 could be traded for the American dollar at a rate of 4:1, had plummeted to an exchange rate of 22,400:1. Within a few weeks, Germans were being paid three times a day, so they could run out and spend their wages before prices rose once again. And prices did keep rising. By October, the exchange rate from mark to dollar was at 440,000,000:1.

Despite—or in some ways because of—the economic disaster of hyperinflation, the Weimar government's strategy worked. The French army pulled out of the Ruhr Valley and in 1924 Allied and German representatives renegotiated reparations. The resulting Dawes Plan stretched the payments over a longer period. But the social costs of this victory were enormous. Middle-class men and women, who had lived frugally and saved carefully all their lives, found their retirement accounts completely wiped out in the course of a single afternoon. Peasant families who had scrimped for years to acquire dowries for their daughters found that they had only enough money to buy half a loaf of bread. The world turned topsy-turvy; old rules no longer applied. Respectable families were forced to send their daughters out as prostitutes to service the American tourists who lived in luxury for just pennies a day. Small businessmen went bankrupt while large industrialists, with their much greater resources, borrowed freely and expanded ruthlessly.

By the end of 1924, the German economy had stabilized; the later 1920s were years of relative prosperity. Yet for many Germans, the Weimar Republic was now indelibly stained by the memory of hyperinflation. For these Germans, democracy meant disorder and degradation. They looked with longing back to the prewar period, an era of supposed social stability and national power.

CHRONOLOGY	
The Instability of the Early Weimar Republic	
1918	Civil war: moderate socialists fight communists
1919	
January	Free Corps murder Karl Liebknecht and Rosa Luxemburg
March	Communist soviet in Munich crushed
1920	Kapp Putsch
1922	French occupation of the Ruhr
1923	Hyperinflation destroys German economy; Beer Hall Putsch
1924	Dawes Plan

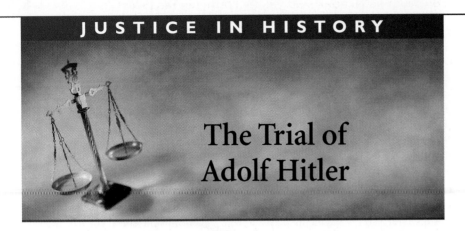

The Trial of Adolf Hitler

On February 24, 1924, Adolf Hitler appeared in court in Munich to confront a charge of high treason following his pathetic attempt three months earlier to overthrow the Weimar government by armed rebellion. The trial marked a crucial point in Hitler's career. It gave him a national platform and, even more important, convinced him of the futility of an armed offensive against the state. From 1925 on, Hitler would work through the parliamentary system in order to destroy it. But the trial of Adolf Hitler is also significant in what it reveals about the power of antidemocratic forces in the new Germany. The trial made clear that many in positions of authority and responsibility in the Weimar Republic shared Hitler's contempt for the democratic state. By treating Hitler not as a traitorous thug but rather as an honorable patriot, his prosecutors helped weaken the already fragile structures of German democracy.

Hitler's attempt to overthrow the Weimar Republic by force occurred at the height of hyperinflation and the ensuing political chaos. By November 8, 1923, when Hitler took up arms, the German mark was worth only one trillionth of its prewar value. As its currency eroded, the Weimar Republic saw its political legitimacy seeping away as well. Separatist movements in several states threatened the sovereignty of the central government in Berlin. Separatist politics attracted the

support of many men from aristocratic backgrounds, members of the traditional conservative elite who viewed Weimar democracy as a foreign and unwelcome import.

Hitler had little interest in the separatist movement, but he believed he could channel its antidemocratic sentiments into a national revolution. He attracted a number of supporters, including one of the most important men in Germany, the World War I hero General Erich von Ludendorff. Seeking to avoid the blame for Germany's defeat in 1918, Ludendorff insisted that his army could have won the war had it not been stabbed in the back by the Social Democratic politicians who now ran the government. Like many German conservatives—and like Hitler—he viewed the Weimar Republic as illegitimate.

On November 8 Hitler made his move. His men surrounded a Munich beer hall where 2,000 supporters of Bavarian separatism had gathered. Hitler declared that both the Bavarian and the national governments had been overthrown and that he was now the head of a new German state, with Ludendorff as his commander-in-chief. Around noon the next day, Hitler, Ludendorff, and several thousand of their followers marched toward the regional government buildings located on one of Munich's main squares. Armed police blocked their passage. In the ensuing firefight, seventeen men were killed. Despite the bullets

whizzing through the air, Ludendorff marched through the police cordon and stood in the square awaiting arrest. Hitler ran away. Police found him two days later, cowering in a supporter's country house about thirty-five miles outside of Munich.

The Beer Hall Putsch had clearly, utterly, completely failed. In jail awaiting trial, Hitler contemplated suicide. Yet later he described his defeat as "perhaps the greatest stroke of luck in my life." The defeat meant a trial; the trial meant a national audience—and an opportunity for Hitler to present his case against the Weimar Republic. He admitted that he had conspired to overthrow the democratically elected Republican government, but he insisted he was not therefore guilty of treason. The real treason had occurred in November 1918, when the Social Democratic government had surrendered to the Allies: "I confess to the deed, but I do not confess to the crime of high treason. There can be no question of treason in an action which aims to undo the betrayal of this country in 1918. . . . I consider myself not a traitor but a German." He argued that he was not aiming for personal power: "In what small terms small minds think! . . . What I had in mind from the very first day was a thousand times more important than becoming a minister. I wanted to become the destroyer of Marxism." Thus Hitler depicted himself as a patriot, a nationalist motivated by love of Germany and hatred

Hitler in Landsberg Prison, 1924
This photo of Hitler during his short imprisonment was made into a postcard, to be purchased by his supporters.

of communists and socialists. "The eternal court of history," according to Hitler, would judge him and his fellow defendants "as Germans who wanted the best for their people and their Fatherland, who were willing to fight and to die."[6]

Despite Hitler's own admission of conspiring against the government, the presiding judge could convince the three lay judges (who took the place of a jury) to render a guilty verdict only by arguing that Hitler would most likely be pardoned soon. The reluctance of the judges to convict Hitler highlights the extraordinary sympathy shown to him and his political ideas throughout the trial and during his imprisonment. The chief prosecutor offered a rather surprising description of an accused traitor: "Hitler is a highly gifted man, who has risen from humble beginnings to achieve a respected position in public life, the result of much hard work and dedication. . . . As a soldier he did his duty to the utmost. He cannot be accused of having used the position he created for himself in any self-serving way." In delivering the verdict, the judge emphasized Hitler's "pure patriotic motives and honorable intentions." Rather than being deported as a foreign national convicted of a serious crime (Hitler was still an Austrian citizen), Hitler was given a slight sentence of five years, which made him eligible for parole in just six months. In prison he was treated like a visiting dignitary—

exempted from work and exercise requirements, provided with prisoners to clean his rooms, even given a special table, decorated with a swastika banner, in the dining hall. When he was released in September, his parole report described him favorably as "a man of order."[7]

Hitler's gentle treatment reveals the precarious state of democratic institutions in Germany after World War I. Many high-ranking Germans in positions of power and influence (such as judges and prosecutors) viewed parliamentary democracy with loathing. The trial also reveals the willingness of conservative aristocrats to ally with Radical Right groups such as the Nazis. Still not very strong, the Nazis in 1923 were easily reined in. A decade later, however, the conservatives who thought they could ride Hitler to power suddenly found that they were no longer in control. ◼

Questions of Justice

1. Imagine you are a German war veteran reading about this case in the newspaper in 1924. Why might you be attracted to the party of Adolf Hitler?

2. Compare Hitler's trial with that of Alfred Dreyfus in France in 1895 (see "Justice in History" in Chapter 22). How did both trials reveal key points of instability within the political systems in which they occurred?

Taking It Further

Gordon, Harold Jr. *Hitler and the Beer Hall Putsch.* 1972. This lengthy study (over 600 pages) provides a detailed account of the putsch and its aftermath.

The Hitler Trial before the People's Court in Munich, trans. H. Francis Freniece, Lucie Karcic, and Philip Fandek (3 vols.). 1976. English translation of the court transcripts.

THE RECONSTRUCTION OF GENDER

Many of the patterns that shaped interwar national politics also characterized the politics of gender in these years. World War I wrought a profound upheaval in gender roles in European society. The demands of total war had meant that women moved into economic areas previously designated as "men only." Middle-class conventions collapsed as women shrugged off both their corsets and their chaperones, and jumped into the drivers' seats of ambulances and buses. The war, therefore, seemed an important turning point in the history of women in the West. But here again the turning point failed to turn. Important changes in women's expectations did occur, but nineteenth-century gender roles were quickly reconstructed after the war.

The New Woman

At first sight, the postwar period seems an era of profound change in the roles of women. In the films, magazines, novels, and popular music of the 1920s, the "New Woman" took center stage. Living, working, and traveling on her own, sexually active, she stepped out of the confines of

■ **The "New Woman"**

Almost every aspect of the "New Woman" captured in this 1928 French photograph caused offense to traditionalists: short skirts and bobbed hair, smoking in public, the association with a car and therefore with mobility and illicit sex—all crossing the border into masculine terrain.

home and family. Women's dress reinforced this idea of a new woman. Whereas nineteenth-century women's clothing had accentuated the womanly body while restricting the woman's movement, the clothing of the 1920s ignored a woman's curves and became much less confining. Complementing this revolution in clothing came a revolution in hairstyle. Women chopped off the long locks regarded for generations as a sign of femaleness and sported fashionable new bobs.

This perception of the New Woman rested on important changes in women's political and economic expectations. By 1920 women in the United States and many European countries had received the right to vote in national elections and to hold national office. In all the industrialized countries, the expansion of both the health care and service sectors meant new jobs for women as nurses, social workers, secretaries, telephone exchange operators, and clerks. Women's higher education opportunities also widened in this period.

The biggest change affecting the lives of ordinary women was the spreading practice of limiting family size. We saw in Chapter 22 that by the 1870s middle-class women in Western nations were practicing forms of birth control. In the 1920s and 1930s, an increasing number of working-class women began to do so as well. In Britain, for example, between 1911 and 1931 the average number of children per family fell from 3.4 to 2.2, with most of this decrease resulting from changes in working-class family size. Fewer pregnancies and fewer mouths to feed meant a significant improvement in women's health and living standards.

The Reconstruction of Traditional Roles

Despite these important changes, however, women's roles actually altered little in the two decades after World War I. These years witnessed a strong reaction against the wartime gender upheaval and a concerted effort to reconstruct nineteenth-century masculine and feminine ideals.

Both the war's lengthy casualty lists and the drop in the average family size provoked widespread fear about declining populations—and thus declining national strength. Governments, religious leaders, and commercial entrepreneurs joined together to convince women that their destiny lay in motherhood. Sale and purchase of birth control devices became illegal during the 1920s in France, Belgium, Italy, and Spain. France outlawed abortions in 1920. In Britain after 1929, a woman who had an abortion could be sentenced to life imprisonment.

To encourage population growth, governments also turned to more positive incentives ranging from the symbolic to the economic. Mother's Day, an American invention, crossed into Europe during the 1920s. In France from 1920 on, women who gave birth to at least five children received a bronze medal; those who bore seven or more children earned the silver; and mothers who produced ten offspring brought home the gold. German women had an easier time: They needed only seven children to get the gold. Of more lasting importance was the expansion of welfare services—family allowances, subsidized or state-provided housing, school lunches, health insurance, prenatal and well-baby clinics—with the express aim of strengthening the family, encouraging women to stay at home, and raising the birth rate. Eugenics played an important role in this legislation. National leaders wanted to increase not only the quantity but the quality of the population. On the positive side, this meant improving the health of babies and mothers. More ominously, much of the rhetoric focused on separating the "fit" from the "unfit," with both class and race among the factors that determined who was "fit" to produce children for the nation.

Despite the calls for women to remain at home, many women had to work in paid employment. In the work world, just as in the family, traditional roles were strengthened after World War I. Most working women returned to jobs in domestic service or to factory positions labeled unskilled and therefore low-paying. Women tended to be barred from management positions, assigned to the most repetitive tasks, and paid by piecework, with the result that the wage gap between male and female laborers remained wide. In both Germany and Britain, unemployment benefits were frequently denied to married women workers, even though they had regularly paid into the insurance system while they were working. The numbers of women employed in the clerical and service sectors did rise in this era, but the movement of women into these positions meant such jobs were reclassified as "women's work," a guarantee of low pay and little power.

Women and the Bolshevik Revolution

In sharp contrast to these efforts to buttress the traditional family structures, in Russia the Bolsheviks promised to revolutionize gender roles. Lenin believed that the family was a middle-class institution doomed to "wither away." In the ideal communist society, marriage would be a mutually beneficial—and in many cases temporary—arrangement between two equally educated and equally waged partners, and both housework and child care would move from the private domestic household into the public sphere of paid employment. To create such a society, the Bolsheviks turned to legislation. One month after seizing power, they legalized divorce and civil marriages. In October 1918, a new family legal code declared women and men equal under the law, made divorce readily available, and abolished the distinction between legitimate and illegitimate children. To free women from housework—described by Lenin as "barbarously unproductive, petty, nervewracking, and stultifying drudgery"[8]—the Bolsheviks established communal child care centers, laundries, and dining rooms. In 1920, just as other nations were outlawing abortion, the practice became legal in Bolshevik Russia.

By 1922, however, the newly created Soviet Union seemed about to self-destruct, and as we have already seen, Lenin retreated from rigorous communist economic ideology to institute the New Economic Policy. NEP also meant significant reversals in the gender revolution. By 1923, the dining halls had been closed and more than half of the day care centers had shut down. The decade of the 1920s was a time of high unemployment for Soviet women. Those who did find jobs received wages that averaged only 65 percent that of men's. An increasing number turned to prostitution. In addition, the traditional patriarchal peasant household—with women in a clearly subordinate role—remained firmly intact. Even in revolutionary Russia, therefore, certain continuities linked the pre- and postwar experience of women.

The Rise of the Radical Right

·· ▬ ··

As the revolution in gender roles was reversed, as Lenin's communist revolution shifted into a lower gear, and as Wilson's democratic revolution ran out of gas, a very different sort of revolution was occurring in Italy, a region long on the periphery of European power. The fascist revolution introduced Europe to a new sort of politics, the politics of the Radical Right. Like conservatism, the new Radical Right ideologies—fascism° and its younger cousin, Nazism—dismissed equality as a socialist myth and emphasized the importance of authority. But neither fascism nor Nazism was conservative. These radical political systems sought to use the new technologies of the mass media to mobilize their societies for a program of violent nationalism.

THE FASCIST ALTERNATIVE

Conceived in the coupling of wartime exhilaration and postwar despair, fascism offered an alternative to the existing political ideologies. Fascism was more than a set of political ideas, however. As presented by its creator, Benito Mussolini (1883–1945), fascism was an ongoing performance, a spectacular sound-and-lights show with a cast of millions.

Mussolini's Rise to Power

Fascism originated in Italy. In 1915 after a fierce internal debate that widened the already huge gaps in Italian society, Italy entered the war on the side of the Allies. Many pro-war Italians believed that parliamentary politics, with its emphasis on compromise, committees, and endless discussion, was sapping the vitality from Italian society. Calling for violent action, they viewed the war as a cleansing force, a powerful disinfectant that would leave Italian society stronger

THE CULT OF THE LEADER

The personality cult *characterized not only the Radical Right ideologies of Italian fascism and German Nazism, but also the ideological system that stood at the opposite end of the political spectrum: Stalinist communism. Searching for a way to mobilize the masses without granting to them actual political power, Mussolini, Hitler, and Stalin erected around themselves leadership cults. Their own images came to embody the nation. As the following set of excerpts shows, the cults of Mussolini, Hitler, and Stalin took on religious dimensions, with all three men adored as secular saviors.*

I. DESCRIPTION OF MUSSOLINI'S VISIT TO TRIESTE IN 1938

Finally we have seen and heard Him! . . . These first reactions, expressed with indescribable joy, eyes moved to tears and an ineffable, agonizing joy . . . It is not easy to describe the expression on most faces, on those of the little people as on those of the educated, of the mass as a whole. Expressions of wonderful contentment and pride among those who saw Him pass close by—especially among the dockworkers He visited yesterday—and those whose eyes He met, those who caught His eye. "Never such eyes! The way he looks at you is irresistible! He smiled at me . . . I was close, I could almost touch him . . . When I saw him my legs trembled" . . . and a thousand other similar statements show and confirm the enormous fascination exercised by his person.

II. DESCRIPTION OF AN EARLY NAZI RALLY BY LOUISE SOLMITZ, SCHOOLTEACHER

The April sun shone hot like summer and turned everything into a picture of gay expectation. There was immaculate order and discipline . . . the hours passed. . . . Expectations rose. There stood Hitler in a simple black coat and looked over the crowd. Waiting. A forest of swastika pennants swished up, the jubilation of this moment was given vent in a roaring salute. . . . How many look up to him with a touching faith! As their helper, their savior, their deliverer from unbearable distress—to him who rescues the Prussian prince, the scholar, the clergyman, the farmer, the worker, the unemployed, who leads them from the parties back into the nation.

III. SPEECH BY A WOMAN DELEGATE AT A WORKERS' CONFERENCE IN THE SOVIET UNION

Thank you comrade Stalin, our leader, our father, for a happy, merry kolkhoz life!

He, our Stalin, put the steering-wheel of the tractor in our hand. . . . He, the great Stalin, carefully listens to all of us in this meeting, loves us with a great Stalinist love (*tumultuous applause*), day and night thinks of our prosperity, of our culture, of our work . . .

Long live our friend, our teacher, the beloved leader of the world proletariat, comrade Stalin! (*Tumultuous applause, rising to an ovation. Shouts of 'Hurrah!'*)

Sources: "I. Description of Mussolini's Visit to Trieste in 1938," reprinted by permission of the publisher from *The Sacralization of Politics in Fascist Italy* by Emilio Gentile, translated by Keith Botsford, p. 147, Cambridge, Mass.; Harvard University Press. Copyright © 1996 by the President and Fellows of Harvard College. "II. Description of an Early Nazi Rally by Louise Solmitz, Schoolteacher," copyright © 1988 by Claudia Koonz. From *Mothers in the Fatherland: Women, the Family, and Nazi Politics* by Claudia Koonz. Reprinted by permission of St. Martin's Press, LLC. "III. Speech by a Woman Delegate at a Worker's Conference in the Soviet Union," from *Stalin's Peasants: Resistance and Survival in the Russian Village after Collectivization* by Sheila Fitzpatrick. Copyright © 1996 by Oxford University Press, Inc. Published by Oxford University Press, Inc.

and more powerful. Mussolini, a socialist journalist, shared these views. Because the Socialist Party opposed Italy's entry into the war, Mussolini broke with the socialists, joined the army in 1915, and fought courageously until he was wounded in 1917. When the war ended, he sought to create a new form of politics that would translate the military camaraderie and the exhilaration of violent action from the trenches to peacetime society. The result was fascism. Mussolini condemned conservatism, liberalism, and socialism as all outdated. Socialism exalted the working class; liberalism viewed the individual as the core of society; conservatism clung to social hierarchy. Fascism, however, identified the *nation* as the dominant social reality. With a strong leader at the wheel, with violent action as its fuel, the fascist nation would crash through social and economic barriers and transport its people into a new and more powerful age.

In March 1919, Mussolini and a little more than 100 men and some women gathered in Milan and declared themselves the fascist movement. Like Mussolini, many of these "fascists of the first hour" were war veterans; a number had served in the *arditi*, elite commando units that fought behind enemy lines. The arditi uniform, a severe black shirt, became the fascist badge of identity. The arditi slogan, "*me ne frego*" ("I don't give a damn") became the blackshirts' creed, a fitting summary of their willingness to throw aside conventional standards and politics.

Just three and a half years after the first fascist meeting in Milan, Mussolini became prime minister of Italy. His astonishing rise to power occurred against a backdrop of social turmoil. In 1919 and 1920, more than one million workers were on strike, factory occupations became commonplace, and a wave of land seizures spread across the countryside. Increasingly frightened that revolution would engulf Italy just as it had destroyed tsarist Russia, large landowners and industrialists, as well as the professional and commercial middle classes, looked to Mussolini's fascists for help. Fascist squads disrupted Socialist Party meetings, vandalized the offices of socialist newspapers, broke up strikes, beat up trade unionists, and protected aristocratic estates from attack. By 1922, the fascists were a formidable political force and Mussolini was engaged in negotiations aimed at bringing the fascists into a coalition government. Fascist violence proved persuasive. In October 1922, King Victor Emmanuel III (1900–1946) asked Mussolini to become not only a member of the government but its prime minister. Mussolini agreed. In a carefully orchestrated display of muscle, fascists from all over Italy converged in the "March on Rome," a piece of street theater designed to demonstrate Mussolini's mass support, as well as the disciplined might of his followers.

The Fascist Revolution in Italy

Over the next four years Mussolini used both legal and illegal methods, including murder, to eliminate his political rivals and remake Italy as a one-party state. By 1926,

he had succeeded. Party politics, an independent press, and the trade union movement ceased to exist. Victor Emmanuel remained on the throne, the official head of state, but power lay in Mussolini's hands. The restored death penalty and a strong police apparatus stood ready to enforce Mussolini's will.

In a sharp break with previous governments, Mussolini won the support of the Catholic Church. For more than fifty years, successive popes had regarded themselves as prisoners in the Vatican, surrounded by a hostile, secular state. In the mid-1920s, Mussolini, a self-proclaimed atheist, suddenly recognized the Church as a possible ally. After consecrating his marriage in a religious ceremony and arranging the baptism of his children, he ordered crucifixes placed in all schools and courtrooms and increased the amount of state funds flowing into the Church coffers. In the Lateran Pact of 1929, Mussolini declared Catholicism the state religion and guaranteed the Church freedom to control spiritual matters. In exchange, Pope Pius XI (r. 1922–1939) became the first Catholic prelate to recognize the Italian state. The pope declared Mussolini "a man sent by Providence" to defeat socialism, feminism, and other threats to the social order.

As Mussolini's alliance with the Church indicated, Mussolini's supposedly radical revolution reinforced traditional elite interests. Fascist economic theory, such as it

■ The March on Rome, October 28, 1922

The fascist march on Rome was a carefully orchestrated show of power, not an armed rebellion. Mussolini had already been offered the premiership of Italy, as is clear from his clothing: He has changed his black shirt for a proper suit.

was, promised to replace capitalist competition and the profit motive with corporatism: committees (or "corporations") made up of representatives of workers, employers, and the state were to direct the economy for the good of the nation. In actuality, workers' rights disappeared from fascist Italy while private property and industrial profits remained untouched. At the same time, landed aristocrats prospered. Early fascist promises of land redistribution were quickly forgotten, and the end of democracy meant that the control of local government rested not with elected officials but rather with Mussolini's appointees—usually drawn from the ranks of the traditional agrarian elite.

Mussolini's revolution, then, was not about leveling society. Mussolini had no intention of giving *actual* political power to ordinary people; he did, however, recognize the importance of giving them the *illusion* of power. Participation was the key. The fascist revolution offered individuals a sense of power by giving them the chance to participate in the life of the nation. A series of "after-work" occupational and recreational groups served as a channel for fascist propaganda and connected ordinary people more closely to the fascist state, while at the same time occupying their leisure hours. By 1939, four million Italians were participating in fascist sporting clubs, holiday camps, and cultural outings.

The "Cult of the Duce" also provided an important means of fostering a sense of participation in the life of the nation. Mussolini insisted, "I am Fascism." Carefully choreographed public appearances gave ordinary Italians the chance to see, hear, and adore their Duce ("Leader"), and through contact with his person, to feel a part of the new Italy. To stimulate public adoration of himself, Mussolini paid careful attention to his public image. He ordered that the press ignore his birthdays and the births of his grandchildren: The Duce could not be seen to age. Instead, in photograph after photograph, Mussolini appeared as a man of action. Depicted in planes, in trains, and in racing cars, he was always on the move, always pressing forward. At the same time, Mussolini combined up-to-date advertising and the latest mass media technologies with age-old rituals inspired largely by the Catholic Church. Huge public rallies set in massive arenas, carefully staged with lighting and music, inspired his followers. A popular fascist slogan summed up the leadership cult: "Believe, Obey, Fight." Italians were not to think or question; they were to *believe*. What were they to believe? Another slogan provides the answer: "Mussolini is always right."

THE GREAT DEPRESSION AND THE SPREAD OF FASCISM AFTER 1929

The simple certainty offered by a slogan such as Mussolini's proved highly appealing throughout much of Europe after 1929. During the 1930s, fascist movements emerged in almost every European state. The key factor in the spread of

---

CHRONOLOGY

Mussolini's Rise to Power

1915–1917	Serves in the Italian army
1919	Participates in the creation of the fascist movement
1921	Fascist Party wins thirty-five seats in parliament
1922	Becomes prime minister
1925–1926	Abolishes party politics and establishes himself as dictator
1929	Signs Lateran Accords with the Roman Catholic Church

---

fascism was the Great Depression°. On October 24, 1929, the American stock market collapsed. Over the next two years, the American economic crisis evolved into a global depression. Banks closed, businesses collapsed, and unemployment rates rose to devastating levels. Even by the end of the 1930s, the production rates of many nations remained low. Desperate people looked for desperate answers. Fascism provided some of these.

Why did the Depression spread so quickly and last so long? The explanation lies with the changing role of the United States in Europe. World War I accelerated the shift of the world's economic center away from Europe and toward America. New York's stock market emerged to rival London's, and U.S. businesses increasingly displaced European competitors as the chief suppliers of industrial goods to regions such as Latin America. While European nations sold off their domestic and foreign assets and borrowed heavily to pay for the war, the United States moved from the position of debtor to creditor nation. By the end of 1918 Allied nations owed the United States more than $9 billion—and American officials made it clear that they expected this money to be repaid in full, with interest.

The problem of wartime indebtedness quickly became entangled with the issue of German reparations. Britain, France, and Italy could pay off their debts to the United States only if Germany paid reparations to them. Hyperinflation and the near-collapse of the German economy in 1923 made clear, however, that the reparations schedule established by the Versailles Treaty would have to be revised. In 1924 and again in 1928 American and European financial representatives met to reconfigure (and in 1928 to reduce) the payments. American credit became the fuel that kept the European economy burning. From 1925 on, American investors loaned money to Germany, which used the money to pay reparations to the Allies, which in turn used the money to pay back the United States. The system worked for a short time. Fueled by loans, the German economy kicked into gear. Currencies stabilized, production rose, and American money flowed not only into Germany but into all of Europe. If these loans dried up, however, Europe faced disaster.

In 1929 that disaster struck. With the collapse of the U.S. stock market, savings portfolios lost between 60 and 75 percent of their value almost overnight. Scrambling to scrape up any assets, American creditors liquidated their European investments, and European economies tumbled. Germany, the country whose economy was most directly linked to the United States, saw its industrial output fall by 46 percent, while its number of jobless grew to over six million.

The political and social disarray that accompanied the Great Depression enhanced the appeal of fascist promises of stability, order, and national strength. In the 1930s, fascist movements emerged across Europe. Although few succeeded in seizing the reins of government, the emergence of popular fascist movements placed enormous pressure on existing authoritarian regimes and forced them to adopt many fascist trappings. For example, Romania's King Carol II (r. 1930–1940) faced a strong challenge to his rule from the Iron Guard, the first mass fascist movement in the Balkans. To compete with the Guard, Carol embraced its language of national renewal, as well as typically fascist features such as uniformed paramilitaries, a youth group, and mass rallies. In 1938 he abolished all political parties, placed the judicial system under military control, and declared himself a royal dictator. He then dissolved the Iron Guard and had its leader garroted.

THE NAZI REVOLUTION

In Germany, the Nazi Party offered a different version of Radical Right ideology. Just as the emergence of fascism was inextricably linked to the career of one man, Benito Mussolini, so Nazism° cannot be separated from Adolf Hitler (1889–1945). To understand the Nazi Revolution in Germany, we need first to explore Hitler's rise to power and then to examine the impact of Nazi rule on ordinary people.

Hitler's Rise to Power

Hitler, an ardent German nationalist, was not a citizen of Germany for most of his life. Born in Austria, Hitler came of age in Vienna, where he made a meager living as a painter while absorbing the anti-Semitic German nationalism that permeated the capital city of the Habsburg Empire. When World War I broke out, Hitler grabbed at the chance to fight the war in a German rather than an Austrian uniform. He regarded army life as "the greatest of all experiences." Hitler served as a German soldier for almost the entire length of the war until he was temporarily blinded by poison gas in 1918. After the war he settled in Munich, home to large bands of unemployed war veterans. Munich

became a fertile breeding ground of far right-wing political factions that espoused various versions of German nationalism laced with antidemocratic, antisocialist, and often anti-Semitic imagery and ideas.

The Nazi Party began as one of these small fringe groups, with Hitler quickly emerging as its leader. *Nazi* is shorthand for *National Socialist German Workers' Party,* but this title is misleading—the Nazis were *not* a socialist party. Like fascism, Nazism was fiercely opposed to socialism, communism, trade unionism, and any political analysis that emphasized class conflict or workers' rights. Hitler, however, inserted these common fascist ideas into an astonishing apocalyptic story. In the tale told by Hitler, Germany was destined to become a powerful empire controlling central and eastern Europe. This new age would dawn only after a mighty battle between the racially superior Germans and their numerically superior enemy: the forces of "Judeo-Bolshevism." In Hitler's distorted vision, communism and Jewishness were two parts of the same evil whole. He saw the Bolshevik victory in Russia and the call for communist world revolution as part of a much larger struggle for Jewish world domination. Like Mussolini, Hitler exalted the nation, but Hitler's Nazism, much more so than Mussolini's fascism, focused on *race* as the key social reality. To Hitler, all history was the history of racial struggle, and in that racial struggle, the Jews were always the principal enemy. Hitler regarded Jewishness as a biological rather than a religious identity, as a sort of toxic infection that could be passed on to future generations and that posed a threat to the racially pure "Aryans"—white northern Europeans. (*Aryan* is actually a linguistic term referring to the Indo-Aryan or Indo-European language groups. Hitler misapplied the term to racial groups to lend a supposedly scientific authority to his racism.)

In its early days Nazism appealed to men like Hitler, individuals without much power or, apparently, much chance of getting it—demobilized and now unemployed soldiers, small shopkeepers wiped out by postwar inflation, lower middle-class office clerks anxious to preserve their shaky social status, and workers who had lost their jobs. Nazism offered a simple explanation of history, a promise of future glory, and a clear and identifiable scapegoat for both personal and national woes. By the time of the Beer Hall Putsch in November 1923, party membership stood at about 55,000.

As we saw earlier in the discussion of postwar Germany, the Beer Hall Putsch failed in its aim to overthrow the Weimar Republic, but it did bring Hitler before a national audience. Both his speeches during the ensuing trial for treason and *Mein Kampf* (My Struggle), the book he wrote while in prison, publicized his racialized view of German political history. After Hitler emerged from prison, he concentrated on transforming the Nazis into a persuasive political force. To infiltrate German society at all levels, Nazis formed university and professional groups, labor unions, and agrarian organizations, while the Nazi paramilitary organization, the SA (the *Sturmabteilung*), terrorized opponents. The party held meetings and rallies incessantly, not just during election periods, and so ensured that Germany was saturated with its message. Even so, in the elections of 1928, Nazi candidates won only 2.6 percent of the vote.

It was the Great Depression that gave the Nazis their chance at power. After 1929, unemployment rates skyrocketed and the Weimar political system began to collapse. No German political leader was able to put together a viable governing coalition. Parliamentary power dwindled; in all of 1932 the federal parliament was in session for only thirteen days. As the mechanisms of parliamentary democracy faltered, the German chancellor Heinrich Bruning was increasingly forced to rely on a stopgap measure in the German constitution—the presidential emergency decree. The constitution declared that in emergency situations, decrees signed by the German president could become law without parliamentary consent. But this practice meant that power shifted from the parliament to the president, the World War I hero General Paul von Hindenburg. Already in his eighties, Hindenburg was a weak man easily manipulated by a small circle of aristocratic advisors and cronies.

In this unstable political climate, political polarization accelerated. In elections in 1930 both the Communist and Nazi parties attracted an increasing number of votes as Germans looked for extreme solutions to extreme problems. By July 1932, the Nazis had become the largest party in the parliament, winning the support of 37 percent of the German voters. Support for their communist rivals also continued to grow.

Terrified of the threat posed by communism and convinced that Hitler could be easily controlled, a small group of conservative politicians persuaded Hindenburg to offer Hitler the position of chancellor in January 1933. One of the group, Baron Franz von Papen, reassured a friend that Hitler posed "no danger at all. We have hired him for our act. In two months' time we'll have pushed Hitler so far into the corner, he'll be squeaking."[9] But von Papen was wrong.

Within six months Hitler had destroyed what remained of democracy in Germany and established a Nazi dictatorship. Almost as soon as he took office he persuaded Hindenburg to pass an emergency decree mandating the seizure of all Communist Party presses and buildings. Then in February a mentally unstable Dutch transient set fire to the German parliament building. Declaring that the fire was part of a communist plot against the state, Hitler demanded the power to imprison without warrant or trial. Mass arrests of more than 25,000 of his political opponents

CHRONOLOGY

Hitler's Rise to Power

1914–1918	Serves in the German army
1919–1923	Establishes himself as a right-wing activist in Munich
1923	Fails to overthrow the government with the Beer Hall Putsch
1929	Collapse of the U.S. stock market; onset of Great Depression
1930	Nazis win 107 seats in German parliament
1932	Nazis win 230 seats; become largest party in German parliament
1933	
January	Becomes chancellor
February	Uses Reichstag fire as pretext to gain emergency powers
March	Uses the Enabling Act to destroy democracy in Germany

followed—not only communists but also social democrats and anyone who dared oppose him openly. At the end of March, German politicians, cowed by Nazi threats of imprisonment, passed the Enabling Act. This key act gave Hitler the power to suspend the constitution and pass legislation without a parliamentary majority. By the summer of 1933, parliamentary political life had ceased to exist in Germany.

The Nazi dictatorship was designed to give maximum power to Hitler. Often presented as a model of authoritarian efficiency, it was actually a confusing mass of overlapping bureaucracies, in which ambitious officials competed with each other for power and influence. This planned chaos ensured that none of Hitler's deputies acquired too much authority. It also enhanced the mystery of the state. The individual citizen attempting to make a complaint or resolve a problem would soon feel like he was engaged in a battle with a multilimbed monster.

This multilimbed monster, however, had only one head: Adolf Hitler. The entire system was designed to make clear that there was only one man in charge, one leader—the *Führer*. Like Mussolini, Hitler realized the importance of personalizing his rule. During election campaigns before 1933 and in the early years of power after, Hitler was constantly on the move, using cars and planes to hit city after city, to deliver speech after speech, to touch person after person. In 1932 and 1933, he conducted election campaigns from the sky, often visiting four or five cities in a single night. He always arrived late, so that his plane could fly above the packed stadium, the focus of every upturned face. Leaders of the Hitler Youth were required to take this oath: "Adolf Hitler is Germany and Germany is Adolf Hitler. He who pledges himself to Hitler pledges himself to Germany."[10]

National Recovery

Jews, communists, socialists, and other groups defined as enemies of the state faced the constant threat of persecution and imprisonment under the Nazi regime during the 1930s. But for many Germans not in these groups, life got better. Nazi rule brought economic prosperity, restoration of national pride, and a cultural revolution that linked the power of nostalgia to the dynamism of modernity.

Economic depression gave the Nazis the chance at power; economic prosperity enabled them to hold on to this power. Because Hitler perceived himself as a revolutionary, bound by no existing rules, he was able to adopt the

■ Hitler Opening the Construction of the German Autobahn, 1933

Hitler's program of public works was designed both to provide employment and to rebuild Germany as a world power. One of his most cherished projects was the Autobahn, the highway system of modern Germany. The Autobahn was not only of economic importance, in terms of providing an efficient means of moving goods and people across Germany, but also of great symbolic significance: It associated Nazi Germany with mobility and modernity.

aggressive and ultimately successful economic policy suggested by Hjalmar Schacht (1877–1970), his finance minister. The rules of economic orthodoxy dictated that in times of depression, a government should cut spending and maintain a balanced budget. Schacht broke the rules and instead embarked on a program of massive state expenditure. The result was the most impressive economic recovery in Europe. Industrial output rose by almost 30 percent while unemployment dropped from 44 percent in 1932 to 14.1 percent in 1934 to under 1 percent in 1938. In contrast, double-digit unemployment rates persisted in Britain while in France industrial production remained below 1929 levels through the 1930s. Under the Nazis, social welfare programs expanded and the "Strength through Joy" program (directly inspired by Mussolini's "after-work" organizations) provided workers with cheap vacations, theater and concert tickets, and weekend outings. Although real wages fell under Nazi rule and independent trade unions were outlawed, the fact that jobs were now available in abundance made Hitler an economic savior to many Germans.

Many also viewed him as a national savior, a leader who restored Germany's pride and power. Payment of war reparations, demanded by the humiliating Versailles Treaty, halted in 1930 because of the global economic crisis. Hitler never resumed payment. He also ignored the treaty's military restrictions and rebuilt Germany's armed forces. By 1938, parades featuring row after row of smartly uniformed troops, impressive displays of tanks, and flybys of military aircraft all signaled the revitalization of German military might. For many ordinary Germans, traumatized and shamed by the sequence of national disasters—military defeat, loss of territory, hyperinflation, political and fiscal crises, unemployment—the sight of troops goose-stepping under the German flag meant a personal as well as a national renaissance. As one Nazi song proclaimed, "And now the me is part of the great We."[11]

To create the "great We," Hitler utilized modern techniques and technology. In his election campaigns in the early 1930s he demonstrated that, like Mussolini, he understood the power of the new mass media. For just one election, his staff distributed 50,000 records of his speeches. The Nazis published a glossy illustrated magazine, produced their own films, and littered cities with campaign posters. Impressed by Mussolini's use of the radio to popularize fascism, Hitler subsidized the production of radios in Germany so that by the end of the 1930s most Germans had access to a radio—and to Hitler's radio talks. He also recognized the power of the cinema, and hired the brilliant filmmaker Leni Riefenstahl (1902–2003) to film Nazi rallies. These still-astonishing films show an overwhelming mass spectacle, in which an entire nation appears to be marching in step behind Hitler.

But Hitler also recognized the power of nostalgia for many Germans. He used modern techniques and technologies to establish the Nazis as bulwarks of tradition. In speeches, posters, and films, the Nazis painted a picture of a mythic Germany, an idyllic community peopled by sturdy blond peasants, small shopkeepers, and independent craftsmen. The Nazis promised that under their leadership, individual Germans would regain meaning and purpose as part of a single national community. International corporations, large department stores, and supermarket chains were all demonized as elements of a vast Jewish-controlled conspiracy to deprive ordinary people of their livelihoods.

Campaigns of Repression and Terror

Part of the appeal of the "great We" that Hitler was creating relied on the demonization and violent repression of the "not Us," those defined as outside or opposed to the nation. Hitler used the existing German police force as well as his own paramilitary troops—the brownshirted SA and the blackshirted SS (the *Schutzstaffeln*)—to terrorize those he defined as enemies of the nation. The Nazis first targeted political opponents. By 1934 half of the 300,000 German Communist Party members were in prison or dead; most of the rest had fled the country. The Nazis also persecuted specific religious groups on the basis of their actual or presumed opposition to the Nazi state. Roman Catholics were banned from government service and subject to constant harassment, and about half of Germany's 20,000 Jehovah's Witnesses were sent to concentration camps.

The groups that the Nazis deemed biologically inferior suffered most severely. Beginning in 1933, the Nazi regime forced the sterilization of the Roma (Gypsies), the mentally and physically handicapped, and mixed-race children (in most cases, the offspring of German women and black African soldiers serving in the French occupation force in the Rhineland). By 1939, 370,000 men and women had been sterilized.

The Jewish community—less than 1 percent of the German population—bore the brunt of Nazi racial attacks. To Nazi anti-Semites, Hitler's accession to the German chancellorship was like the opening of hunting season. They beat up Jews in the streets, vandalized Jewish shops and homes, threatened German Christians who associated with Jews, and violently enforced boycotts of Jewish businesses. Anti-Jewish legislation piled up in an effort to convince Germans of the separateness, the "non-Germanness," of Jewish cultural and racial identity. In 1933, "non-Aryans" (Jews) were dismissed from the civil service and the legal profession, and the number of Jewish students in high schools and universities was restricted. Every organization in Germany—youth clubs, sports teams, labor unions, charitable societies—was subject to "Nazification," which meant Jewish members had to be dismissed and Nazis appointed to leadership roles. In 1935, the "Nuremberg Laws" labeled as Jewish anyone with three or more Jewish grandparents. Marriage or sexual relations between German Jews and non-Jews now became a serious crime.

WOMEN AND THE RADICAL RIGHT

Much of the appeal of both fascism and Nazism lay in the promise to restore order to societies on the verge of disintegration. Restoration of order meant the return of women to their proper place. According to Nazi propaganda, "the soil provides the food, the woman supplies the population, and the men make the action."[12] Hitler proclaimed, "the Nazi Revolution will be an entirely male event." Mussolini agreed: "Woman must obey. . . . In our State, she must not count."[13]

In Nazi Germany, the restoration of order translated into a series of financial and cultural incentives to encourage women to stay at home and produce babies. Incentives ranged from marriage loans (available only if the wife quit her job) to income tax deductions to the opportunity to participate in housewives' discussion, welfare, and leisure groups. Disincentives were also utilized. One of the first actions of the new Nazi government was to dismiss women from the civil service. Women physicians could work only in their husbands' practices. By 1937, both women physicians and women Ph.D.s had lost the right to be addressed as "Doctor" or "Professor." The Nazis abolished coeducation and replaced female principals with males. Birth control became illegal and penalties for abortion increased while prosecutions doubled.

In Italy, Mussolini's government focused its legislation on both men and women. Unmarried men over age 30 had to pay double income tax (priests were exempt), homosexual relations between men were outlawed, and fatherhood became a prerequisite for men in high-ranking public office. As in the democracies, the fascist government established a wide-ranging social welfare program: Family allowances, maternity leaves, birth and marriage loans, and family health clinics were all established to strengthen the Italian "race." Quotas limited the number of women employed in both the civil service and in private business, while women found themselves excluded entirely from jobs defined as "virile," a varied list that included boat captains, diplomats, high school principals, and history teachers.

The Polarization of Politics in the 1930s

To Europeans and Americans disenchanted with the response of the democracies to the challenge of the Great Depression, fascist Italy and Nazi Germany offered powerful alternatives. The Soviet Union provided yet another option. While the capitalist nations struggled with high unemployment rates and falling industrial output, the

Soviet Union appeared to be performing economic miracles. Politics in the West thus became polarized between communism on the left and fascism and Nazism on the right. In both the United States and Europe, however, politicians and policymakers sought to maintain the middle ground, to retain democratic values in a time of extremist ideologies.

THE SOVIET UNION UNDER STALIN: REVOLUTION RECONSTRUCTED, TERROR EXTENDED

Many Europeans looked with envy at the Soviet Union in the 1930s. Unemployment had disappeared; huge industrial cities transformed the landscape; the development of new industries such as chemicals and automobiles, together with a full-scale exploitation of the Soviet Union's massive natural resources (gold, timber, coal), sent production indices soaring. But this economic transformation rested on dead bodies, millions of dead bodies. During the 1930s, mass murder became an integral part of the Soviet regime under Joseph Stalin (1879–1953).

Stalin's Rise to Power

By 1928, Stalin was the uncontested head of the party. At the time of Lenin's death in 1924, however, few observers would have predicted Stalin's success. A stalwart Bolshevik, he was overshadowed by more charismatic, intellectually able colleagues. How, then, did Stalin seize control of the Communist party and the Soviet state?

One key factor in Stalin's rise to power was the changing nature of the Communist Party. The party that made the revolution in 1917 comprised only 24,000 members. Following a massive recruitment campaign to honor Lenin's memory, party membership in 1929 stood at over one and a half million—and only 8,000 of these had been members in 1917. In other words, the vast majority of communists in 1929 had not fought in the revolution. For them, communism was not a revolutionary ideology challenging the tsarist political order; it was itself the political order. Party membership was not a revolutionary act; it was a guarantee of privileged status and career opportunities. Moreover, unlike the original Bolshevik revolutionaries, most of the new members were not well-educated or well-versed in communist ideology. In fact, 25 percent of the party membership was functionally illiterate.

As party secretary from 1922 on, Stalin had led the recruitment drive that enlisted many of these new party members. Other party leaders dismissed Stalin as the "card-index Bolshevik"—the paper-pusher, the gray guy with the boring job. But Stalin, an astute politician, recognized that

CHRONOLOGY

Stalin's Rise to Power

1917	
March	Popular Russian Revolution
November	Bolshevik Revolution
1918–1921	Russian Civil War
1921	New Economic Policy (NEP) begins
1922	Stalin appointed General Secretary of the Central Committee of the Communist Party
1924	Death of Lenin
1925–1928	Leadership disputes; Stalin emerges as the head of the Communist Party
1929	NEP ended; collectivization begins
1934	The Congress of Victors
1934–1938	The Great Purge

his card index held enormous power. Not only did he determine the fate of party membership applications, he also decided who got promoted to what and where. Thus, throughout the 1920s Stalin slowly built up a broad base of support within the party. Vast numbers of ordinary communists owed their party membership, and in many cases their livelihoods, to Stalin.

While Stalin expanded his support at the grassroots, a fierce ideological struggle at the highest levels of the Communist Party distracted his rivals for the party leadership. By the time of Lenin's death, the New Economic Policy (NEP) had restored economic stability to the Soviet Union. The nation, however, remained far behind its capitalist competitors in both agricultural and industrial productivity. All communists agreed on the need to launch the Soviet economy into industrialization. The problem was, how could this backward nation obtain the capital it needed for industrial development? One faction of the party, led by Leon Trotsky (1879–1940), argued that the answer was to squeeze the necessary capital out of the peasantry through high taxation and even, if necessary, the confiscation of crops. Trotsky wanted to abandon NEP and its encouragement of small private farming initiatives. The opposing faction, led by Nikolai Bukharin (1888–1938), pointed to the lessons taught by western European industrialization. In the West, industrial capital came from agricultural profits. Bukharin insisted on the need for gradualism: Agricultural development must precede industrialization. "Enrich the peasant," Bukharin argued.

Stalin at first backed Bukharin and those who wished to continue on the NEP course, because he perceived that the more immediate threat to his ambitions came from the charismatic Trotsky. Once Trotsky had been expelled from the party, however, Stalin reversed course and turned on Bukharin. Painting this veteran Bolshevik as an antisocialist, Stalin pushed Bukharin to the margins of Soviet politics. In 1928, Stalin emerged as the sole leader of the party and as a fierce advocate of the abandonment of NEP, the total socialization of the Soviet economy, and a fast march forward into full-scale industrialization.

The "Revolution from Above": Collectivization and Industrialization, 1928–1934

As party leader, Stalin placed the Soviet Union firmly back on a revolutionary course, with the aim of catapulting the Soviet Union into the ranks of the industrialized nations. The first step in what was called "the revolution from above" was collectivization°, the replacement of private and village farms with large cooperative agricultural enterprises run by communist managers according to directives received from the central government. Collectivization had both economic and political aims. Regarded as more modern and efficient, collective farms were expected to produce an agricultural surplus and thereby raise the capital needed for industrialization. But in addition, collectivization would realize communist ideals by eradicating the profit motive, abolishing private property, and transforming the peasants into modern state employees.

The peasants resisted this transformation, however. They burned their crops and slaughtered their livestock. Famine followed. The numbers of deaths resulting from collectivization and the famine of 1931–1932 remain the subject of intense controversy; the available quantitative evidence points to death figures between five million and seven million. Ukraine and Kazakhstan were hardest hit. Almost 40 percent of the Kazakh population died from starvation or typhus; the number of dead in Ukraine alone may have reached four million.[14] Perhaps as many as ten million peasants were deported in these years; many of these died either on the way to or in forced labor camps.

While class war raged in the countryside, city dwellers embarked on the second stage of the "revolution from above"—industrialization. In 1931 Stalin articulated the task facing the Soviet Union: "We are fifty or a hundred years behind the advanced countries. We must catch up this distance in ten years. Either we do it or we go under."[15]

■ "Pictures Can't Lie . . ."

Stalin was not Lenin's closest associate, nor did Lenin select him as his successor. To claim and consolidate his position as sole leader of the Communist Party and of the Soviet Union, Stalin had to falsify history and present himself as Lenin's chosen heir. Murder and mass executions could remove competitors from the present, but to erase them from the past, Stalin turned to the airbrush and the scissors rather than the gun. Pictures showing other Bolsheviks standing next to Lenin were cropped, leaving him with Stalin, or if such a pairing could not be achieved, standing alone. This illustration shows the process at work. Compare the photo shown on page 815 of Chapter 24 with the photo on the right. In the first photo, taken just seconds before the one shown here, Lev Kamenev and Leon Trotsky—leading Bolsheviks and rivals with Stalin for the party leadership after Lenin's death—stand on the steps to Lenin's left. But in this picture, Kamenev and Trotsky have been cut out and some steps have been drawn in. Stalin sought to airbrush Trotsky and Kamenev out of Soviet history, just as he eliminated them from Soviet politics. Trotsky was forced into exile in 1929 and murdered in 1940, Kamenev was executed in 1936.

Doing it demanded, first, unprecedented levels of labor output. Despite the massive investment in heavy industry, the Soviet Union throughout the 1930s remained undermechanized. What it lacked in technology, however, it possessed in population. Thus Soviet industry was highly labor-intensive. To ensure that workers produced at the levels needed, the Soviet state under Stalin imposed fierce labor discipline. Only productive workers received ration cards. Internal passports restricted workers' freedom of movement. If fired, a worker was automatically evicted from his or her apartment and deprived of a ration card.

Catching up with the West also demanded reducing already-low levels of personal consumption. Eighty percent of all investment went into heavy industry, while domestic construction and light industry—clothing, for example, or furniture—were ignored. Scarcity became the norm, long lines and constant shortages part of every urban resident's existence. Economists estimate that Soviet citizens endured a 40 percent fall in their already low standard of living between 1929 and 1932.

Yet in the midst of this suffering was great enthusiasm. For young communists in the 1930s, these years of hardship were also years of heroism, an era in which they believed they were building a new society. They volunteered to organize collective farms, to work in conditions of extreme brutality at construction sites, to labor long hours in factories and mines. Babies born in this decade received names like "Little-Five Years" (for girls) and "Plan" (for boys), reflecting their parents' enthusiasm for the series of Five-Year-Plans issued by the central government as outlines for the new world order. Much of this enthusiasm was stirred up by propaganda campaigns aimed at persuading laborers to work ever harder and sacrifice ever more. Ordinary workers who achieved record-breaking feats of production were featured in newspaper articles and rewarded with medals, special ceremonies, and material gifts. Immense publicity focused on the gargantuan engineering achievements of the era—the cities built atop swampland, the hydroelectric projects with their enormous dams and power plants, the Moscow subway system. Such publicity made party members feel part of a huge and powerful endeavor. A popular song announced, "We were born to make fairy tales come true."[16]

Just as important as the propaganda campaigns was the reality of unprecedented opportunity. The Soviet Union in the 1930s has been called "the quicksand society," one in which traditional structures and relations (and people too) were swallowed up at a breathtaking pace. Yet as these traditional structures disappeared, new ones emerged, bringing tremendous geographic and social mobility to Soviet society. For example, Nikita Khrushchev (1894–1971), who would succeed Stalin as the head of the party and state in the 1950s, was the son of a poor peasant.

No propaganda campaign and no amount of effort from enthusiastic young communists, however, could provide the Soviet Union with the labor it needed to catch up with the West in ten years. Forced labor was crucial. Throughout the 1930s, as many as five million men, women, and children—peasants, political opponents of Stalin, religious dissenters, ethnic minorities—labored in prison camps.[17] By some estimates, forced labor accounted for no less than 25 percent of all construction work in the Soviet Union in the 1930s. Many of the huge engineering triumphs of the decade rested on the backs of prisoners and deportees.

By the end of the 1930s, Stalin's "revolution from above" had achieved its aim. The pouring of resources into heavy industry and the wringing of every ounce of labor out of an exhausted, cold, and hungry populace succeeded in building the foundations of an industrial society. This society would stand the test of total war in the 1940s.

But Stalin's revolution failed to convert Soviet agriculture into a modern, prosperous sector of the economy. Rural regions remained backward. Peasant villages, for example, were not electrified until the later 1950s. Most peasants regarded the collective farm as belonging not to them or to the community but to the state, just another in a long line of harsh landlords. Under Stalin, peasants were second-class citizens, ineligible for internal passports, with little access to the benefits of Soviet industrialization. Like

■ **Forced Labor in the Soviet Union**

Deported peasants and political prisoners construct the Stalin-Belomor canal in northern Russia in 1933. Death rates were high as slave laborers toiled in brutal conditions to achieve Stalin's industrial goals. At least 30,000 prisoners died on this project.

their ancestors under serfdom, peasants at the end of the 1930s found themselves tied to a particular village, saddled with forced labor obligations, and compelled to spend the bulk of their time farming for someone else's profit. Most peasants viewed the state, and Stalin, as the enemy, to be ignored when possible, tricked if necessary, and endured no matter what.

Stalin's Consolidation of Power: The Great Purge and Soviet Society, 1934–1939

By the mid-1930s, the worst seemed to be over. Most villages were collectivized and the mass violence had ended. The 17th Party Congress in 1934 was known as the "Congress of Victors," as the party celebrated its industrial successes and the achievement of collectivization. But for many of the men and women at this Congress the worst was yet to come. Within five years, half of the 2,000 delegates had been arrested; of the 149 elected members of the Congress's Central Committee, 98 were shot dead. These Congress delegates, and hundreds of thousands of other Soviet citizens, were victims of the "Great Purge°." In the purge, Stalin's effort to eliminate any possible rival to his power converged with widespread paranoia and economic crisis to produce a nationwide witch hunt and mass executions.

The beginning of the purge is often dated from December 1, 1934, when Leningrad Communist Party Chief Sergei Kirov was assassinated. Some historians argue that Stalin himself engineered Kirov's assassination because he feared the Leningrad chief's popularity. Stalin's exact role in the assassination remains opaque, but it is clear that once Kirov was dead Stalin used the murder for his own political ends. The hunt for Kirov's killers became the pretext for a purge of the Communist Party. The investigation into the assassination sparked a wave of arrests and executions, first in Leningrad, and soon throughout the entire Soviet Union.

The early victims of the purge tended to be top-ranking Communist Party officials, many of whom had opposed Stalin on various issues during the 1920s. By charging these powerful men with conspiring against the communist state, Stalin reduced the chances that any competitor might oust him. In a series of three spectacular show trials attended by journalists from all over the world, leading Bolsheviks—some of the Soviet Union's most respected men such as Nikolai Bukharin—pleaded guilty to charges of conspiracy and sabotage, and were immediately executed. Numerous smaller trials replicated the process throughout the Soviet Union. Non-Russians suffered heavily. By the end of the 1930s, for example, 260 of the 300 party secretaries in Georgia had been killed. The purge also swept the armed forces. Those executed included three of the five Soviet marshals, thirteen of fifteen army commanders, and fifty-seven of eighty corps commanders.

Two factors spread the purge beyond the top ranks of the party and military. First, the purge coincided with the military resurgence of Germany as well as heightened hostilities between the Soviet Union and Japan. By the later 1930s the Soviet press carried frequent articles about the possibility of a two-front war, and lent credence to popular fears of spies. With the show trials indicating that even the highest-level Bolsheviks were not to be trusted, people began to suspect that traitors lurked within every factory and local party gathering. Second, the purge came at a time of agricultural crisis and the beginnings of an industrial slowdown. In 1936, exceptionally bad weather resulted in a dangerously poor harvest. By 1937, food was once again in short supply. At the same time the shortcomings of an overly centralized and poorly run economy were multiplying. Subject to an endless stream of ever-changing and often irrational program and policy directives, managers falsified key economic statistics, while poorly trained workers misused machines and cut all available corners. People were anxious and hungry, and eager to find someone to blame for breakdowns and failures. The purge made it easy to point the finger, to charge this manager with deliberately failing to order tractors or that engineer with implementing the wrong system of crop rotation to sabotage production.

Thus the Great Purge quickly spun out of control to embrace low-level party members, managers in state agencies, factory directors, and engineers. Family members, neighbors, clients, and friends all became victims. So, too, did the "usual suspects"—anyone with a black mark on his or her record, one-time well-to-do farmers, former priests and nuns, anyone who had opposed the Bolsheviks or Stalin at any time or place. Many were killed without trial, others executed after a legal show. Many of those purged were deported to slave labor camps to be worked to death on Stalin's vast construction projects. Death estimates vary widely; at least 750,000 people died, with the numbers of those arrested, imprisoned, or deported running into the millions.[18]

The Great Purge consolidated Stalin's hold on the Soviet Union. It not only eliminated all potential competitors, it also tied huge numbers of people more tightly to Stalin and his version of revolution. The shocking thing about the Great Purge was its popularity. The purge hit primarily urban managers. For the most part, ordinary workers and peasants were safe from its onslaught. These ordinary citizens, who had been ordered about, reprimanded, fined, insulted, and assaulted by these self-same managers, tended to believe that the purge's victims got what they deserved. Moreover, the purge can also be seen as a huge job creation program. Individuals who moved into the positions left vacant by the purge's victims had an enormous material as well as psychological stake in viewing the purge as an act of justice.

Stalin and the Nation

The popularity of the purge was also closely linked with the emergence of a Stalin-centered personality cult. By the time the purge began, the cult was an omnipresent part of Soviet urban life. Huge posters and statues ensured that Stalin's figure remained constantly in front of Soviet citizens. Every scientific, technological, or economic advance in the Soviet Union was linked to the person and power of Stalin. Textbooks rewrote the history of the Bolshevik Revolution to highlight Stalin's contribution. The scores of letters personally addressed to Stalin that poured into central government offices testify to the success of this cult. To many Soviet citizens, Stalin personified the nation.

Increasingly it was the *nation*—not the worker, not socialism, not the revolution—that was emphasized. Lenin had condemned Russian nationalism as a middle-class ideology to be eradicated along with capitalism. The working class, not the nation, was what mattered. But Stalin reversed this aspect of Lenin's revolution. In the 1930s, "Russia" and "the motherland/fatherland" both reappeared in political discourse. The tsarist past, which Lenin had condemned or ignored, was resurrected to emphasize Russian greatness. The imperial anthem resounded once again, while films and books praised strong Russian leaders such as Peter the Great. While this resurgence of Russian nationalism was popular in Russia itself, it spelled real difficulties for the 50 percent of the Soviet population who lived outside of Russia and who found it necessary to repress their own sense of national identity—or face deportation.

Exalting the motherland went hand in hand with exalting the mother. Just as Stalin resurrected Russian nationalism in the 1930s, so he sought to resurrect the Russian family. He promoted the family as a vital prop of the national order, an institution to be strengthened rather than encouraged to wither away (as Lenin had insisted). In 1936, Stalin's regime outlawed abortion and made divorce more difficult. Like Western leaders, Stalin also sought to increase the national birth rate by granting pregnant women maternity stipends and increasing the number of prenatal health clinics. There was no effort to pull women out of the workforce, however. Of the more than four million new workers entering the labor force between 1932 and 1937, 82 percent were women. The Soviet Union continued to provide women with access to higher education and professional jobs—women worked as doctors, engineers, scientists, and high-ranking public officials. (And women were deported and executed in huge numbers—one could argue that Stalin was an equal-opportunity killer.)

THE SEARCH FOR MIDDLE GROUND

The apparent economic successes of fascism and Nazism on the right, and Stalinism on the left, polarized European politics. For many Europeans in the 1930s, it seemed that the middle ground was collapsing beneath their feet, that democracy had failed and that they had no choice but to scramble to one extreme or the other. Yet in both western Europe and in the United States, important steps were taken to assure that democracy not only survived but that it eventually delivered a decent standard of living to the great mass of ordinary people.

A Third Way?
The Social Democratic Alternative

The effort to meet the challenge of the depression without embracing either the Radical Right or Stalinism accelerated the development of the political model that would dominate western Europe after World War II: social democracy°. In a social democracy, a democratically elected parliamentary government assumes the role of ensuring a decent standard of living for its citizens. To achieve this goal, the government assumes two important functions—first, regulating an economy containing both private enterprise and nationalized or state-controlled corporations; and second, overseeing a welfare state, which guarantees the citizen access to unemployment and sickness benefits, pensions, family allowances, and health services. Although social democracy did not triumph in western Europe until after the massive bloodletting of another total war, the interwar years witnessed important steps toward this third path, an alternative to the extremes of both the Radical Right and Stalinism.

One of the most striking experiments in changing the relationship between democratic governments and the economy occurred in the United States. Franklin Delano Roosevelt (1882–1945) became president in 1932 at the height of the Great Depression, when unemployment stood at 24 percent (15 million workers were without jobs) and Washington, D.C., witnessed federal troops called out to quell rioting among unemployed veterans. Promising a "New Deal" of "Relief, Recovery, Reform," Roosevelt tackled the depression with an activist governmental policy that included agricultural subsidies, public works programs, and the Social Security Act of 1935, which laid the foundations of the U.S. welfare program.

Yet even with this sharp upswing in governmental activity, unemployment remained high—ten million workers were without jobs in 1939—and the gross national product (GNP) did not recover to 1929 levels until 1941. In the view of some economists, Roosevelt failed to solve the problem of unemployment because he remained committed to the ideal of a balanced budget. In contrast, the British economist John Maynard Keynes (1883–1946) insisted that in times of depression, the state should not reduce spending and endeavor to live within its budget, but instead should adopt a program of deficit spending to stimulate economic growth. Only when prosperity returned, Keynes advised, should governments increase taxes and cut expenditures to recover the deficits.

The experience of Sweden appeared to confirm Keynes's theory. The Swedish Social Democratic Party took office in 1932 with the intention of using the powers of central government to revive the depressed economy. The government allowed its budget deficit to climb while it financed a massive public works campaign, as well as an increase in welfare benefits ranging from unemployment insurance to maternity allowances to subsidized housing. By 1937 unemployment was shrinking rapidly as the manufacturing sector boomed.

Throughout most of western Europe, however, governments proved far more reluctant to advocate radically new policies, despite an expansion of the state's role in economic affairs. In Britain, for example, social spending did rise during the interwar decades. Government spending on social benefits—ranging from old-age pensions to health and unemployment insurance to school meals—grew from 4.2 percent of the gross national product in 1910 to 11.3 percent of the GNP by 1938. In addition, a housing program made two million new houses available to families on low incomes. In general, however, the British government remained reluctant to intervene in the economy. Britain's limited economic recovery in the later 1930s was based largely on private initiatives such as an expansion in housing construction and the emergence of new industries aimed at domestic consumption (radios and other small electronics, household goods, automobiles). In the areas hardest hit by depression—the heavy export industries such as coal, shipbuilding, textiles, and steel, located primarily in northern Britain—the lack of government intervention meant continuing high unemployment rates and widespread poverty and deprivation throughout the 1930s.

The Popular Front in France

The limited success of democratic governments in addressing the problems of the Great Depression meant that many experienced the 1930s as a hard, hungry decade when democracy failed to deliver a decent standard of living. The example of France illustrates both the political polarization occurring in Europe in the 1930s and the sharp limits on governments seeking both to maintain democratic politics and to improve the living conditions of their citizens. The Great Depression hit France later than most other European nations, but by 1931 the nation was experiencing a sharp economic downturn. France lacked such basic welfare benefits as old-age pensions and unemployment insurance. As the economy plummeted, therefore, social unrest rose, and so, too, did the appeal of the fascist movement. In 1934, right-wing antigovernment riots left seventeen dead and more than 2,000 injured.

The increasing strength of fascism, combined with the deepening national emergency, led to the formation of the Popular Front, a coalition comprising the centrist Radical Party, the moderate leftist Socialist Party, and the Stalinist Communist Party. In 1936, the Popular Front won the national elections. The Socialist Party leader Leon Blum (1872–1950) took office as prime minister in the midst of a general strike involving two million workers. He settled the strike to the workers' benefit by granting them a 15 percent pay raise and the right to collective bargaining. Over the next year, Blum nationalized the key war industries and gave workers further pay increases, paid holidays, and a forty-hour work week.

For many French voters, Blum's policies of social reform represented not a new democratic alternative but rather the first step on the road to Stalinism. Thus they cried, "Better Hitler than Blum!"—in other words, better the Radical Right than the Stalinist Left. The response of the global business community was a massive pullout of capital from France, resulting in a major financial crisis and the devaluation of the French franc. Dependent on foreign loans, Blum's government faced sharp pressure to pull back from its program of social and economic reforms. When it tried to do so, its working-class constituency rose in revolt. In May 1937 the suppression of a left-wing demonstration left seven dead and 200 injured. Blum resigned the next month. The Popular Front in France quickly disintegrated.

THE SPANISH CIVIL WAR

Spain became the arena in which the struggle of Europe's polarized political forces turned into outright war. In 1931, a democratically elected republican government replaced the Spanish monarchy and in 1936, a Popular Front government, comprising both socialists and communists, took office. In July, army officers led a right-wing rebellion against this government.

The struggle between the left-wing Republican government and the right-wing rebels quickly became an international issue. Both fascist Italy and Nazi Germany supported the rebellion, enabling General Francisco Franco (1892–1975) and his crack Moroccan troops to cross into Spain from their station in North Africa and launch an all-out offensive against the Republic. The Republican government appealed to the democracies for aid, but the only government that came to its assistance was that of the Soviet Union. Soviet tanks and aircraft enabled the besieged city of Madrid to hold out against Franco's forces but at the same time the Soviet intervention split the Republican movement, with anarchists and socialists resisting Stalinist control. Unnerved by the Soviet involvement, the governments of France, Britain, and the United States remained neutral. Appalled by this official inaction, many citizens of these countries served in the International Brigade, which fought for the cause of democracy in Spain.

The Spanish Civil War raged until March 1939, when the last remnants of the Republican forces finally surrendered to Franco. Four hundred thousand men and women died in the war; in the following four years, another 200,000 were executed. The war resulted in the death of democracy in Spain and the establishment of an authoritarian government led by Franco. Even more crucially, Spain became a

THE EXPANSION OF EMPIRE

During the final years of World War I, the Allies claimed to be fighting for national self-determination, but they had no intention of allowing the nations under their imperial rule to determine themselves. Belgium and Portugal retained their African colonies, and Britain and France divided up Germany's African possessions between themselves. In Asia, some of the spoils went to Japan, Australia, and New Zealand (see Map 25.2).

Similarly, in the Middle East the victorious Allies carved up the Ottoman Empire but replaced it with French and British control. Arab leaders had fought for the Allies against their Ottoman rulers with the expectation that when the war ended they would govern independent Arab kingdoms. These expectations seemed on the brink of fulfillment in October 1918, when the Arab leader Husein's son Faisal entered Damascus at the head of an Arab nationalist army. But less than two years later, in what the Arabs called *am an-nakba*—"the year of catastrophe"—Faisal was deposed by the French. The League of Nations devised a new system of "Mandates," by which territories that the league recognized as states but deemed "not yet able to stand by themselves under the strenuous conditions of the modern world" were placed under Western supervision. France took over Syria and Lebanon; Britain established control of Iraq, Palestine, and Transjordan. The British also retained a dominant influence in both Egypt and the new state of Saudi Arabia.

The British thus emerged from the war with a firmer hold on the Middle East. At the same time, the war altered the imperial structures within Britain's so-called white settlement colonies. As Chapter 24 explained, Canada, Australia, New Zealand, and South Africa emerged from the war with a strong sense of their own unique national identities. In 1931 the Statute of Westminster confirmed this sense by placing the parliaments of these states on an equal footing with the British Parliament—no longer would London reign supreme within what was increasingly called the British Commonwealth°. Because both the British and their former colonial subjects viewed the Commonwealth states as *extensions of* the West, this loosening of imperial control was hailed as a triumph of Western culture and civilization rather than as a challenge to ideas of Western superiority and to the structures of Western empire.

During the interwar period, European imperial nations placed new emphasis on the necessity and desirability of their imperial connections. The Belgian government promoted the Congo as a "model colony," while Portugal embarked on an intensive economic development campaign in its imperial territories. Throughout the 1920s and 1930s, the French government promoted colonial investments so that by 1940, over 45 percent of French overseas investment went to its empire. In Britain, a series of colonial

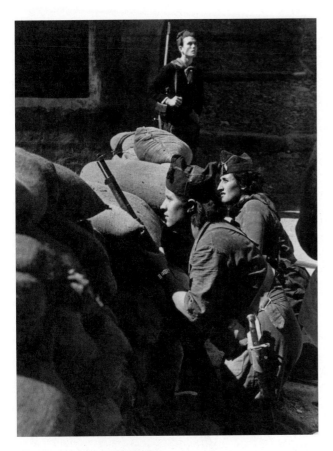

■ **The Spanish Civil War**
The Spanish Civil War mobilized women as well as men. These soldiers, fighting in the uniform of the anarchist militia, are defending the barricades of Barcelona against rebel attack.

potent symbol for all of Europe. To both fascists and their democratic opponents, Franco's victory served as one more step in the forward march of the Radical Right.

European Empires in the Interwar Era

The polarization of European politics was one important consequence of the First World War. The war also had significant—but contradictory—consequences for the structures of European empires. On the one hand, the war seemed to strengthen European imperialism: Both France and Britain emerged from the war with their empires expanded and their commitment to imperialism intact. On the other hand, the economic, social, and political changes wrought by the war accelerated the formation of mass nationalist movements that challenged imperial control.

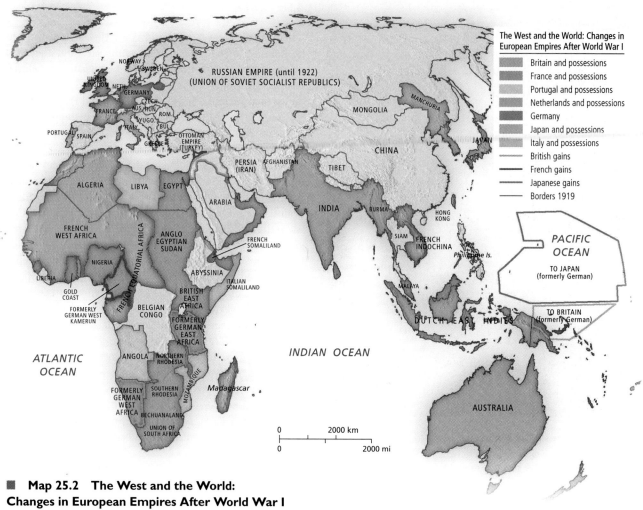

■ **Map 25.2 The West and the World: Changes in European Empires After World War I**
Britain, France, and Japan were the principal beneficiaries of Germany's loss of empire after World War I.

exhibitions impressed on the British public the importance of the empire to Britain's economic prosperity, while popular British filmmakers and novelists found that imperial settings formed the perfect backdrop for tales of heroic Englishmen triumphing against all odds. In both Britain and France, imperial history became a required part of school curricula, thus indoctrinating the post–World War I generations in the values of empire.

THE EROSION OF EMPIRE

This period also witnessed the emergence of important challenges to the imperial idea. For Britain, one of the most dramatic of these challenges occurred in its oldest and closest imperial territory. In 1921, ground down by over two years of guerilla warfare waged with consummate skill by the Irish Republican Army (IRA), the British government offered independence to most of Ireland. (Ireland's six

northern counties, dominated by Protestants who opposed Irish independence, remained part of Britain.) The Irish victory was unique; throughout the regions of empire, however, shifting global economic relationships and communist ideology accelerated the spread of mass nationalist movements and so worked to erode imperial control.

Economics and Mass Nationalism

The economic demands of total war had forced Europe's imperial powers to utilize fully their colonial resources, a strategy that brought with it unintended but far-reaching social changes, including the increasing migration of workers, the expansion of cities, and the enveloping of once isolated villages in the global economic web. These unsettling changes provoked resistance, often in the form of anti-Western agitation, because colonial subjects equated Western social, political, and cultural styles with imperialist oppression. In Africa, anti-Western religious movements increased in number and popularity in this era. Conversions to Islam multiplied. In the growing cities, immigrants who were cut off from their village and its religious practices found that Islam provided an alternative cultural identity to that on offer from their European rulers.

The Great Depression further accelerated the spread of mass nationalism throughout Asia and Africa. Because of the Depression, the prices of primary products fell sharply. The result was disastrous for the undeveloped regions of the world that relied on income from the sales of agricultural products and raw materials. At the same time, the benefits of imperial governance diminished. Looking for ways to reduce expenditures, European governments cut funds to colonial schools, public services, and health care. Direct taxation rates rose while unemployment rates soared. In response, nationalist movements exploded. For example, challenges to French imperialist rule escalated during the 1930s in Tunisia, Algeria, Indochina, and Trinidad.

The Impact of Communism: The Case of China

Economics accounted for only part of the spread of nationalism in imperial territories in the interwar era. Communist ideology also played a role. Lenin had argued that imperialism was the logical outcome of capitalism and its quest for markets, and thus that anticapitalism and anti-imperialism went hand in hand. Under Lenin, the Soviet Union declared itself the defender of oppressed nationalities everywhere, and provided assistance to nationalist independence movements in Indonesia, Indochina, Burma, and most significantly, China.

Soviet advisors helped form the Chinese communist Party in 1921. The communists quickly formed an alliance with the Guomindang, a Western-oriented reform movement seeking to bring order to revolution-torn China through industrial and political modernization. By 1925, when Chiang Kai-Shek (1887–1975) became the Guomindang leader, Soviet political and military advisors had helped reorganize the Guomindang, reform its army, and solidify its power base. Chiang was able to establish Guomindang rule over most of China. Despite Chiang's Soviet links, Americans and Europeans with economic interests in the region welcomed China's stabilization under the Guomindang. Emboldened by Western support, Chiang broke with the communists in 1927. Communism, however, remained a potent force in China even after this break. Led by Mao Zedong (1893–1976), China's communists would revolutionize Chinese society after World War II and offer a potent challenge to Western models of modernity.

THE QUESTION OF WESTERNIZATION: THE CASES OF TURKEY AND INDIA

The question of the relationship between modernity and the West was a crucial one for nationalists in non-Western regions. These nationalists sought not only political independence but also economic modernization. They wanted to establish prosperous nations on a level equal with Europe and the United States. But could modernization be achieved without Westernization? Developments in Turkey and India offer two different answers to this question.

To Mustafa Kemal Pasha (1881–1938), the leader of Turkey, "modernity" and "the West" seemed inseparable. A war hero, Kemal led a postwar nationalist revolt that defeated the Anglo-French plan to partition the Ottoman Empire's Turkish heartland among themselves. Kemal forced a new peace settlement in which Turkey remained intact and independent. Kemal had no intentions of letting Western powers govern in Turkey, but he was not anti-Western. He viewed the West as modern, and he intended to modernize Turkey. As a state-led industrialization program began to transform the economy, Kemal declared Turkey a secular republic and abolished both the sultanate and the Islamic caliphate. He also attempted to westernize Turkish culture. He outlawed polygamy, granted women civil and legal rights, and required all Turks to take surnames—he became known as Kemal "Ataturk" ("the Turk"). The Latin alphabet replaced Arabic script and a mass literacy program was established. Schoolmasters who dared use Arabic lettering were arrested. Ataturk even insisted that citizens of the new state change their clothes. Western suits replaced Eastern robes, and the bowler hat replaced the fez, which Ataturk claimed was "an emblem of ignorance, negligence, fanaticism, hatred of progress and civilization."[19]

Westernization and modernization, however, did not mean democratization. Despite setting up a parliament elected by universal suffrage, Ataturk made full use of emergency executive powers to govern with an iron grip over a one-party state. He also continued the Ottoman policies of repression toward Turkey's Armenian minority.

In India, the nationalism of Mohandas Gandhi (1869–1948) offered a striking contrast to Ataturk's pro-Western approach. Gandhi transformed the Indian National Congress into a mass nationalist movement by appealing to Indian customs and religious identity. He was not opposed to modernization, but he argued that modernization did not necessarily mean Westernization, that India could follow its own path. Thus Gandhi (a lawyer educated in England) rejected Western dress and presented himself in the role of the religious ascetic, a familiar and deeply honored figure in Indian culture. In his insistence that the nationalist struggle be one of "moral force" rather than a physical fight, Gandhi drew on the Hindu tradition of nonviolence. He was careful, however, not to equate "Indian" with "Hindu." He worked hard to incorporate the minority Muslim community into the nationalist movement, and he broke with the traditional Hindu caste system by campaigning for the rights of those deemed "untouchable." Ordinary Indians surged into the movement,

GANDHI ON TRIAL

When World War I ended, Mohandas Gandhi transformed the Indian National Congress into a mass movement. He and his supporters embarked on a campaign of noncooperation with British rule. The campaign was designed to undermine British political and economic structures in India, while at the same time building the nationalist cause on the moral foundations of nonviolence. In 1922, however, a number of violent episodes occurred, including the murder and subsequent burning of twenty-one Indian policemen by nationalists in the town of Chauri-Chaura. Gandhi declared that he would fast until the violence stopped. Following further mass civil disobedience (and more violence in Bombay and Madras), Gandhi was arrested. The following excerpt is from Gandhi's confession at his trial, and shows clearly why Gandhi won the admiration of so many in the Western world.

I wish to endorse all the blame that the Advocate General has thrown on my shoulders in connection with the Bombay occurrences, the Madras occurrences, and the Chauri-Chaura occurrences . . . He is quite right when he says that as a man of responsibility, a man having received a fair share of education, having had a fair share of experience in this world, I should know the consequences of every one of my acts. I knew them. I knew that I was playing with fire. I ran the risk, and if I were set free I would still do the same. I would be failing in my duty if I did not do so . . . I wanted to avoid violence; I want to avoid violence. Non-violence is the first article of my faith. It is the last article of my faith. But I had to make my choice; I had either to submit to a system which I consider has done irreparable harm to my country, or to incur the risk of the mad fury of my people bursting forth when they understood the truth from my lips. I know that my people have sometimes gone mad; I am deeply sorry for it; and I am therefore here to submit, not to a light penalty but to the highest penalty. I do not ask for mercy.

Source: From a speech by Mohandas K. Ghandi at his defense trial, March 18, 1922.

calling Gandhi "Mahatma," or "great-souled," a term of great respect.

Unable to decide whether to arrest Gandhi as a dangerous revolutionary or to negotiate with him as a representative of the Indian people, the British did both. In 1931, Gandhi and the viceroy of India (literally the "vice-king," the highest British official in India) met on equal terms for a series of eight meetings. A few months later Gandhi was in prison, along with 66,000 of his nationalist colleagues. Successive British governments did pass a series of measures granting Indians increasing degrees of self-government, but Gandhi and the Indian National Congress demanded full and immediate national independence. The resulting impasse led to escalating unrest and terrorist activity, despite Gandhi's personal commitment to nonviolence. India remained the jewel in Britain's imperial crown, but the glue holding it in place was deteriorating rapidly by the end of the 1930s.

THE POWER OF THE PRIMITIVE

Gandhi's rejection of any notion of Western superiority was not unique. Just as nationalists outside of the West began to challenge the idea of Western supremacy in this era, so too did Westerners themselves. For nineteenth-century European culture, "civilization" was what gave the West the right to rule the rest of the world. But after Verdun and the Somme, many Europeans found it hard to believe in the superiority of Western civilization. One of the bestsellers in Europe during the 1920s was Oswald Spengler's *The Decline of the West* (1919), in which Spengler argued that western European civilization was marching along a path of inevitable decline. The poet Ezra Pound was more succinct; he described European civilization as "an old bitch, gone in the teeth."

Developments in psychology further undermined the idea of Western superiority by eroding the boundaries between so-called primitive and modern cultures. In his postwar writings, Sigmund Freud (1856–1939) emphasized that human nature was fundamentally aggressive, even bestial. Freud's three-part theory of personality, developed in the 1920s, argued that within each individual the *id*, the unconscious force of primitive instinct, battles against the controls of the *ego*, or conscious rationality, and the *superego*, the moral values imposed by society. Although Freud taught that the continuity of civilization depended on the repression of the id, many Freudian popularizers insisted that the individual should allow his or her primitive self to run free. The work of Freud's one-time disciple Carl Jung (1875–1961) also stressed the links between the primitive and the modern. Jung contended that careful study of an individual's dreams will show that they share common images and forms—"archetypes"—with ancient mythologies and world religions. These archetypes point to the existence of the "collective unconscious," shared by all human beings, regardless of when or where they lived. Thus, in Jung's analysis the boundary between "civilized" and "primitive," "West" and "not West," disappeared.

■ The Power of the Primitive

When the American dancer Josephine Baker first hit the stage in Paris in 1925, her audience embraced her as the image of African savagery, even though Baker was a city kid from Philadelphia. A Parisian sensation from the moment she arrived, Baker's frenetic and passionate style of dancing, as well as her willingness to appear on stage wearing nothing but a belt of bananas, seemed to epitomize for many Europeans the essential freedom they believed their urbanized culture had lost, and that both the United States and Africa retained. As Baker's belt of bananas, designed by her white French employer, makes clear, much of this idealization of the primitive was deeply embedded in racist stereotypes. But it is also clear that both Baker's blackness and her Americanness represented a positive image of liberation to many Parisians.

In the work of other thinkers and artists, that boundary remained intact, but Western notions of cultural superiority were turned upside down. The belief that white Western culture was anemic, washed out, and washed up led to a new openness to alternative intellectual and artistic traditions. This era saw a lasting transformation of popular music as the energetic rhythms of African-American jazz worked their way into white musical traditions. Many writers argued that the West needed to look to outside its borders for vibrancy and vitality. The German novelist Herman Hesse (1877–1962) condemned modern industrial society as spiritually barren and celebrated Eastern mysticism as a source of power and wisdom. Similarly, the *Négritude* movement stressed the history and intrinsic value of black African culture. Founded in Paris in 1935 by French colonial students from Africa and the West Indies, Négritude condemned European culture as weak and corrupted, and called for blacks to recreate a separate cultural and political identity. The movement's leading figures, such as Leopold Senghor (1906–2001), who later became the first president of independent Senegal, vehemently opposed the continuation of European empires and demanded African self-rule. Drawing together Africans, Afro-Caribbeans, and black Americans, Négritude assumed the existence of a common black culture that transcended national and colonial boundaries. The movement stole the white racists' stereotype of the "happy dancing savage" and refigured it as positive: Black culture fostered the emotion, creativity, and human connections that white Western industrial society destroyed.

CONCLUSION

The Kingdom of Corpses

I n 1921, the Goncourt Prize, the most prestigious award in French literature, was awarded not to a native French writer but to a colonial: René Maran, born in the French colony of Martinique. Even more striking than Maran's receiving the prize was the content of the novel for which he was honored. In *Batouala*, Maran mounted a fierce onslaught against Western culture: "Civilization, civilization, pride of the Europeans and charnel house of innocents . . . You build your kingdom on corpses."[20]

For many in the West, Maran's description of Europe as a kingdom of corpses seemed apt in the aftermath of total war. The 1920s and 1930s witnessed a dramatic re-evaluation of Western cultural and political assumptions. Both Soviet communism on the left and Nazism and fascism on the right rejected such key Western ideals as individual rights and the rule of law. Such extremist ideologies seemed persuasive in the climate of despair produced not only by the war, but by the postwar failure of democracy in eastern Europe and the collapse of the global economy after 1929. As a result, the kingdom of corpses grew: in Nazi Germany, in Spain, and most dramatically in the Soviet Union. The kingdom of corpses was, however, a particularly expansionist domain. As the 1930s ended, the West and the world stood on the brink of another total war, one in which the numbers of dead would spiral to nearly incomprehensible levels.

Suggestions for Further Reading

For a comprehensive list of suggested readings, please go to www.ablongman.com/levack/chapter25

Bookbinder, Paul. *Weimar Germany: The Republic of the Reasonable.* 1996. An innovative interpretation.

Brendon, Piers. *The Dark Valley: A Panorama of the 1930s.* 2000. Fast-paced but carefully researched and comprehensive overview of the histories of the United States, Germany, Italy, France, Britain, Japan, Russia, and Spain.

Carrère D'Encausse, Hélène. *Stalin: Order through Terror.* Vol. 2, *A History of the Soviet Union, 1917–1953.* 1981. A brief but convincing account of the way Stalin seized and held power in the Soviet Union.

Fischer, Conan. *The Rise of the Nazis.* 1995. Summarizes recent research and includes a section of primary documents.

Fitzpatrick, Sheila. *Everyday Stalinism. Ordinary Life in Extraordinary Times: Soviet Russia in the 1930s.* 1999. Explores the daily life of the ordinary urban worker in Stalinist Russia.

Fitzpatrick, Sheila. *Stalin's Peasants: Resistance and Survival in the Russian Village after Collectivization.* 1995. Superb history from the bottom up.

Getty, J. Arch, and Oleg V. Naumov. *The Road to Terror: Stalin and the Self-Destruction of the Bolsheviks, 1932–1939.* 1999. Interweaves recently discovered documents with an up-to-date interpretation of the Great Purge.

Gilbert, Bentley Brinkerhoff. *Britain 1914–1945: The Aftermath of Power.* 1996. Short, readable overview, designed for beginning students.

Jackson, Julian. *The Popular Front in France: Defending Democracy, 1934–1938.* 1988. A political and cultural history.

Kershaw, Ian. *Hitler.* 1991. A highly acclaimed recent biography.

Mack Smith, Denis. *Mussolini: A Biography.* 1983. An engaging read.

Pedersen, Susan. *Family, Dependence, and the Origins of the Welfare State: Britain and France, 1914–1945.* 1993. Shows how welfare policy was inextricably linked to demographic and eugenic concerns.

Rothschild, Joseph. *East Central Europe between the Wars.* 1974. An older source, but still one of the best accounts of this tumultuous region in this tumultuous time.

Thomas, Hugh. *The Spanish Civil War.* 1977. An authoritative account.

Whittam, John. *Fascist Italy.* 1995. A short synthesis of recent research. Includes a section of primary documents and an excellent bibliographic essay.

Notes

1. Quoted in Peter Gay, *Weimar Culture* (1970), 99.
2. Quoted in T. W. Heyck, *The Peoples of the British Isles from 1870 to the Present* (1992), 200.
3. Quoted in Martin Gilbert, *A History of the Twentieth Century, Vol. I* (1997), 700.
4. Quoted in Michael Burleigh, *The Third Reich: A New History* (2000), 36.
5. Quoted in Burleigh, 52.
6. Quoted in Joachim Fest, *Hitler* (1973), 190–193.
7. Quoted in Fest, 192, 218.
8. Quoted in Wendy Goldman, *Women, the State, and Revolution: Soviet Family Policy and Social Life, 1917–1936* (1993), 5.
9. Quoted in Claudia Koonz, *Mothers in the Fatherland* (1987), 130.
10. Quoted in Fest, 445.
11. Quoted in Koonz, 194.

12. Quoted in Koonz, 178.

13. Quoted in Koonz, 56; Victoria DeGrazia, *How Fascism Ruled Women: Italy, 1922–1945* (1992), 234.

14. See J. Arch Getty and Roberta Manning, *Stalinist Terror: New Perspectives* (1993), 11, 265, 268, 280, 290.

15. Quoted in Mark Mazower, *Dark Continent: Europe's Twentieth Century* (1998), 123.

16. Quoted in Sheila Fitzpatrick, *Everyday Stalinism*, 68.

17. See Stephen G. Wheatcroft, "More Light on the Scale of Repression and Excess Mortality in the Soviet Union in the 1930s," in Getty and Manning, *Stalinist Terror*, 275–290.

18. "Appendix 1: Numbers of Victims of the Terror," in J. Arch Getty and Oleg V. Naumov, *The Road to Terror: Stalin and the Self-Destruction of the Bolsheviks, 1932–1939* (1999), 587–594.

19. Quoted in Felix Gilbert, *The End of the European Era* (1991), 162.

20. Quoted in Tyler Stovall, *Paris Noir: African Americans in the City of Light* (1996), 32.

World War II and Its Aftermath, 1931–1949

O N JUNE 22, 1940, FRENCH DELEGATES SIGNED AN ARMISTICE ACKNOWL-edging their army's defeat by the forces of Nazi Germany. After sweeping through Norway, Denmark, the Netherlands, and Belgium in a startling spring offensive, the German army had conquered France in just six weeks. Nazi Germany now dominated the European continent. To mark this achievement, Chancellor Adolf Hitler announced plans for the rebuilding of the German Empire. These plans included the physical transformation of Berlin and forty other cities. The past would be wiped out, replaced by the new Nazi order. Hitler's urban redesigns called for the construction of triumphal arches and monumental public buildings to proclaim to the world the power of the German state, and for broad, straight streets to serve as visual reminders of Nazi values—discipline over freedom, regimentation over spontaneity, uniformity over individualism.

Five years later, Berlin and much of Germany had been leveled—not by Nazi urban planners, however, but by Soviet artillery and by British and American bombs. The rebuilding of German cities after World War II took place in a context far removed from Hitler's grandiose and gruesome visions of race-based imperial rule. On top of the rubble of the past, a new European order emerged. This new order was based not on a German continental empire, as Hitler had hoped, but rather on German partition and the division of Europe into two opposing camps—western Europe allied with the United States, eastern Europe dominated by the Soviet Union.

This chapter examines the way that World War II transformed European society, politics, and culture. The war was not confined to Europe, however. In Hitler's quest to conquer the European continent, he joined hands with an un-likely ally: Japan. Japan's desire for a Pacific empire clashed with American and

Chapter Outline

- The Coming of War
- Europe at War, 1939–1941
- The World at War, 1941–1945
- The Home Fronts
- A Dubious Peace, 1945–1949

Wilhelm Becker, *Bombing Raid in Berlin* (1943): The intentional and intensive bombing of civilian centers was one of the defining characteristics of the Second World War.

British interests in the region and transformed World War II into a global conflict. Japanese imperial ambitions arose from the efforts of governing elites to insulate their nation's economic and political structures from Western influence. The Pacific war constituted the most brutal in a long series of violent clashes resulting from the encounter between the West and the world. Understanding World War II, then, demands that we look not only at Germany and the results of the twisted perversions of Nazi ideology but also at global power relations, patterns of economic dependency, and the changing relationship between the West and the rest of the world.

To examine this second round of total war, this chapter focuses on five questions: (1) What were the expectations concerning war in the 1920s and 1930s, and how did these hopes and fears lead to armed conflict in both Europe and Asia? (2) How did Nazi Germany conquer the continent of Europe by 1941? (3) Why did the Allies win in 1945? (4) What did total war mean on the home fronts? (5) How and why did Europe step directly from World War II into the Cold War?

The Coming of War

The 1914–1918 war had been proclaimed the "war to end all wars." Instead, a little more than twenty years later, total war once again engulfed Europe and then the world. Adolf Hitler's ambitions for a German Empire in eastern Europe account for the immediate outbreak of war in September 1939. But other, longer-term factors also contributed, and help explain the origins of World War II. During the 1930s, the uneasy peace was broken by a series of military conflicts. These confrontations underlined the fragility of the post–World War I international settlement and foreshadowed the horrors to come in World War II.

AN UNEASY PEACE

The origins of the Second World War are closely tied to the settlement of the First. Rather than ending war for all time, the treaties negotiated after 1918 created an uneasy peace, one that could not be sustained. As we have already seen, much of Hitler's appeal to his German followers lay in his openly displayed contempt for the economic and military terms of the Versailles Treaty. But the peace settlement of World War I led to World War II in other, less direct ways as well. First, the redrawing of the map of eastern and central Europe fostered political instability in these regions. The mapmakers failed to fulfill the nationalist ambitions of many groups—the Macedonians, the Croats, the Ukrainians, and a host of others—and created as many territorial resentments as they resolved. For ex-

ample, Germans could not forget that parts of Silesia now belonged to Poland, and Hungarians mourned the loss of traditionally Hungarian lands to Czechoslovakia, Romania, and Yugoslavia. Demands for boundary revisions, as well as ethnic hostilities and economic weaknesses, debilitated the new central and eastern European states carved out of the prewar Austrian-Hungarian, Russian, and German Empires.

Second, the League of Nations, created to replace the competitive alliance systems that many blamed for starting World War I, could not realize the high hopes of its planners. Poorly organized, lacking military power, boycotted by the United States and at various times excluding the key nations of Germany and the Soviet Union, the league proved too weak to serve as the basis of a new international order. Instead, alliances, such as that between the French and Polish governments or the "Little Entente" of Czechoslovakia, Yugoslavia, and Romania, formed the framework of a more traditional and very precarious international system.

Finally, the peace settlements created resentments among the war's winners as well as its losers. Italian nationalists argued that their nation's contribution to the Allies' victory should have been more fully compensated, and looked longingly at territories granted to Yugoslavia, Austria, and Albania. Japanese nationalists, too, felt betrayed by the peace. Japan had cooperated fully with Britain and the United States during the First World War, and expected this cooperation to be rewarded in the postwar era. Instead, many Japanese contended that the peace settlement disregarded Japan's economic needs and international ambitions. The results of the postwar Washington Conference, for example, enraged Japanese nationalists. The conference, convened in Washington, D.C., in 1921, assembled representatives of the war's nine victorious powers—Britain, France, Italy, the United States, Belgium, the Netherlands, Portugal, China, and Japan—who pledged themselves to uphold China's territorial integrity and political independence. European and especially American capital poured into China during the 1920s while Western advisers assisted in the reform of the Chinese tax and currency systems. Japanese nationalists viewed a united, Western-oriented China not as a guarantor of regional stability but rather as a threat to Japanese political power and economic development.

THE 1930s: PRELUDE TO WORLD WAR II

The onset of the Great Depression in 1929 heightened international instability. Throughout Europe economic nationalism intensified as nations responded to economic collapse by throwing up tariff walls in an effort to protect their own industries. In addition, leaders sought escape from economic difficulties through territorial expansion. In Japan, for example, the collapse of export markets for

Japanese raw silk and cotton cloth made it difficult for the Japanese to pay for their vital imports of oil and other industrial resources. Anti-Western Japanese nationalists contended that Western capitalism was terminally ill and that the time had come for Japan to embark on a course of aggressive imperialist expansion to ensure its access to vital resources. In 1931, Japanese forces seized Manchuria.

Similarly, Mussolini proclaimed empire as the answer to Italy's economic woes, as well as a way to recreate the glories of ancient Rome. Seeking to expand Italy's North African empire and to avenge Italy's humiliating defeat at the Battle of Adowa in 1896, when Ethiopian troops had beaten back an Italian invasion, Mussolini ordered his army into Ethiopia in 1935. The Italian forces inflicted on the Ethiopian people many of the horrors soon to come to the European continent, including the saturation bombing of civilians, the use of poison gas, and the establishment of concentration camps. At the end of June 1936, Ethiopia's now-exiled Emperor Haile Selassie (1892–1975) addressed the Assembly of the League of Nations and warned, "It is us today. It will be you tomorrow."[1]

One year after Italian troops invaded Ethiopia, civil war broke out in Spain. As Chapter 25 explained, the war between the elected republican government and General Franco's rebels quickly became an international conflict. Hitler and Mussolini sent troops and equipment to assist Franco, and Stalin responded by sending aid to communists fighting on the republican side. Reluctant to ally with Stalin, the governments of France, Britain, and the United States remained neutral, and seemed, therefore, to signal that aggressors could act with impunity.

While the Spanish Civil War raged, the Japanese resumed their advance in China. The Japanese conquest was brutal. In what became known as the Rape of Nanking (Nanjing), soldiers used babies for bayonet practice, gang-raped as many as 20,000 young girls and women, and left the bodies of the dead to rot in the street. The League of Nations had condemned Japan's seizure of Manchuria in 1931 but could do little else.

Against this backdrop of military aggression and the democracies' inaction, Hitler made his first moves to establish a German Empire in Europe (see Map 26.1). In 1933, he withdrew Germany from the League of Nations and two years later announced the creation of a German air force and the return of mass conscription—in deliberate violation of the terms of the Versailles Treaty. In 1936, Hitler al-

CHRONOLOGY

On the Road to World War II

1919	Versailles Treaty
1921–1922	Washington Conference
1929	Onset of the Great Depression
1931	Japan invades Manchuria
1933	Hitler becomes chancellor of Germany
1935	Hitler announces a German air force and military conscription; Italy invades Ethiopia
1936	German troops occupy the Rhineland; civil war breaks out in Spain; Hitler and Mussolini form the Rome-Berlin Axis
1937	Japan advances against China; Rape of Nanking
1938	
March	Germany annexes Austria (the *Anschluss*)
September	Munich Conference: Germany occupies the Sudetenland
1939	
March 15	Germany invades Czechoslovakia
August 23	German-Soviet Non-Aggression Pact
September 1	Germany invades Poland
September 3	Great Britain and France declare war on Germany

lied with Mussolini in the Rome-Berlin Axis° and again violated his treaty obligations when he sent German troops into the Rhineland, the industrially rich region on Germany's western border. Yet France and Britain did not respond. Two years later, in March 1938, Germany broke the Versailles Treaty once more by annexing Austria after an intense Austrian Nazi propaganda campaign punctuated by violence.

After the successful *Anschluss* ("joining") of Germany and Austria, Hitler demanded that the Sudetenland, the western portion of Czechoslovakia inhabited by a German-speaking majority, be joined to Germany as well. He seemed finally to have gone too far. France and the Soviet Union had pledged to protect the territorial integrity of Czechoslovakia. In September 1938, Europe stood on the brink of war. The urgency of the situation impelled Britain's prime minister Neville Chamberlain (1869–1940) to board an airplane for the first time in his life and fly to Munich to negotiate with Hitler. After intense negotiations that excluded the Czech government, Chamberlain and French prime minister Edouard Daladier agreed to grant Hitler the right to occupy the Sudetenland immediately. Assured by Hitler that this "Munich Agreement" satisfied all his territorial demands, Chamberlain flew home to a rapturous welcome. Crowds cheered and church bells rang when he claimed to have achieved "peace in our time."

"Peace in our time" lasted for six months. In March 1939, German troops occupied the rest of Czechoslovakia and Hitler's promises proved to be worthless. On August 23, Hitler took out an insurance policy against fighting a two-front war by persuading Stalin to sign the German-Soviet Non-Aggression Pact°. The pact publicly pledged the two powers not to attack each other; it also secretly divided Poland between them and promised Stalin substantial territorial gains—much of eastern Poland and the Baltic regions of Latvia, Estonia, and parts of Lithuania. On September 1, 1939, German troops invaded Poland. The British and French declared war against Germany on September 3. Two weeks after German troops crossed

Poland's borders in the west, the Soviets pushed in from the east and imposed a regime of murderous brutality. The Second World War had begun.

EVALUATING APPEASEMENT

Could Hitler have been stopped before he catapulted Europe into World War II? The debate over this question has centered on British policy during the 1930s. France advocated an aggressive policy toward Germany in the 1920s, even to the point of sending troops into the Rhineland in 1923 to seize reparations. But during the 1930s, debilitating economic and political crises left France too weak to respond strongly to Hitler. With the United States remaining aloof from European affairs and the now-communist Soviet Union regarded as a pariah state, Britain assumed the initiative in responding to Hitler's rise to power and his increasingly aggressive actions.

■ **Map 26.1   The Expansion of Germany in the 1930s**

Beginning with the remilitarization of the Rhineland in 1936, Hitler embarked on a program of German territorial expansion. This map also indicates the expansion of the Soviet Union into Poland as a result of the secret terms of the German-Soviet Non-Aggression Pact.

■ Pablo Picasso's *Guernica* (1937)

The bombing of the undefended city of Guernica during the Spanish Civil War has come to symbolize the horror of modern aerial warfare, and Picasso's depiction of this horrific event has become one
of the most well-known works of the twentieth century.

After World War II broke out, one term came to be equated with passivity and cowardice in the face of aggression. That term was appeasement°—the policy of conciliation and negotiation that British policymakers, particularly Neville Chamberlain, pursued in their dealings with Hitler in the 1930s. Chamberlain, however, was not a coward and was far from passive. Convinced he had a mission to save Europe from war, he actively sought to accommodate Hitler. Chamberlain thought like the businessmen who voted for him. He believed that through negotiation a suitable agreement—the "best price"—can always be found. His fundamental failure was not passivity or cowardice but rather his insistence that Hitler was a man like himself. Chamberlain could not believe that Hitler would find a war worth the price Germany would need to pay.

For Chamberlain, and many other Europeans, the alternative to appeasement was a total war that would surely destroy Western civilization. They remembered the last war with horror, and agreed that the next war would be even worse, for it would be an air war. The years after 1918 saw the aviation industry come into its own in Europe and the United States, and both military experts and ordinary people recognized the disastrous potential of airborne bombs. Stanley Baldwin (1867–1947), Chamberlain's predecessor as prime minister, told the British public that there was no defense against a bomber force: "The bomber will always get through." The horrendous civilian casualties inflicted by the Italian air force in Ethiopia and by the bombing of Spanish cities in the Spanish Civil War convinced many

Europeans that Baldwin was right, and that war was completely unacceptable. Just two years after the British Peace Pledge Union was founded in 1934, it had 100,000 supporters pledged not to fight in a war.

Motivated by the desire to avoid another horrible war, appeasement also rested on two additional pillars—first, the assumption that many of Germany's grievances were legitimate; second, the belief that only a strong Germany could neutralize the threat posed by Soviet communism. During the 1920s, many historians, political scientists, and policymakers studied the diplomatic records concerning the outbreak of World War I and concluded that the treaty makers at Versailles were wrong in blaming Germany for starting the war. During the 1920s, then, British leaders sought to renegotiate reparations, to press the French into softening their anti-German policies, and to draw Germany back into the network of international diplomatic relations. Hitler's rise to power gave added impetus to a policy already in place. British leaders argued that they could rob Hitler of much of his appeal by rectifying legitimate German grievances.

British policymakers' fear of communism reinforced their desire to stabilize Germany. Many politicians applauded Hitler's moves against German communists and welcomed the military resurgence of Germany as a strong bulwark against the threat posed by Soviet Russia. The startling announcement of the German-Soviet Non-Aggression Pact in the summer of 1939 revealed the hollowness of this bulwark, just as the German invasion of

Czechoslovakia in March had exposed Hitler's promises of peace as worthless.

Europe at War, 1939–1941

German soldiers crossed the Polish border on September 1, 1939; just two years later, Hitler appeared to have achieved his goal of establishing a Nazi Empire in Europe. By the autumn of 1941, almost all of continental Europe was either allied to or occupied by Nazi Germany.

A NEW KIND OF WARFARE

During these two years, the German army moved from triumph to triumph as a result of its mastery of the new technology of offensive warfare. Executing a strategy of attack that fully utilized the products of modern industry, the German military demonstrated the power of a mobile, mechanized offensive force. Germany's only defeat during these years came in the Battle of Britain, when Germany confronted a mobile, mechanized defense. Like Germany's victories, this defeat highlighted the central role of industrial production in modern warfare.

The Conquest of Poland

In its attack on Poland, the German army made use of a new kind of warfare. As Chapter 24 explained, in World War I a full frontal infantry assault proved no match for a deeply entrenched defensive force armed with machine guns. In the 1920s and 1930s, military strategists theorized that the way to avoid the stalemate of trench warfare was to use both the airplane and the tank to construct an "armored fist" strong and swift enough to break through even the most well-fortified enemy defenses. The bomber plane provided a mobile bombardment, one that shattered enemy defenses, broke vital communication links, and clogged key transport routes. Simultaneously, motorized infantry and tank formations punched through enemy lines.

Germany's swift conquest of Poland provided the world with a stunning demonstration of this new offensive strategy. Most of the German army, like all of the Polish, moved on foot or by horseback, as soldiers had done for centuries.

IN THE TANKS

If World War I was the war of the trenches, then World War II was the war of the tanks. In the Battle of Kursk on the eastern front, for example, the Russians and Germans sent a thousand tanks into combat on a single day (July 12, 1943). In the first two years of the war, just the sight of these armored monsters crashing through barriers could demoralize an entire infantry regiment. By 1942, however, both sides had developed effective antitank defensive systems. For the men in the tanks, the experience of combat was harrowing.

ALAN GILMOUR, 48TH ROYAL TANK REGIMENT (BRITAIN), TUNISIA, 1943

In the low padded compartment . . . we crouch, the two of us shapeless figures engulfed in a miasma of smoke and dust through which the facia lights barely penetrate. Behind us in the turret the crew are choking with the fumes of cordite which the fans are powerless to dissipate. Cut off from visible contact with the outside world, the wireless operator, wedged in his seat, cannot possibly know in which direction the vehicle is moving. To all five of us, the intercom, our lifeline, relays a bedlam of orders, distortions, and cries from another world.

NAT FRANKEL, AMERICAN PRIVATE, FRANCE, 1944

It takes twenty minutes for a medium tank to incinerate; and the flames burn slowly, so figure it takes ten minutes for a hearty man within to perish. You wouldn't even be able to struggle for chances are both exits would be sheeted with flame and smoke. You would sit, read *Good Housekeeping*, and die like a dog. Steel coffins indeed!

ANONYMOUS BRITISH TANK COMPANY COMMANDER, ITALIAN FRONT, 1944

We were ordered to make the attack in the face of an anti-tank screen firing down the line of advance. We knew that we should not get far. . . . armour-piercing shot seemed to come from all directions. . . . the tanks were knocked out one by one. Most of them burst into flames immediately. A few were disabled, the turrets jammed or the tank made immobile. As the survivors jumped out, some of them made a dash across the open. . . . but they were almost all mown down by German machine gun fire.

Sources: From Bryan Perrett, *Through Mud and Blood: Infantry.* Published by Robert Hale, 1975. Reprinted by permission of Watson, Little, Ltd., licensing agents.; from Nat Frankel and Larry Smith, *Patton's Best: An Informal History of the 4th Armored Division.* Hawthorne Books, New York, 1978.; and from Douglas Orgill, *The Gothic Line,* Heinemann, 1967. Reprinted by permission of John Johnson Limited.

Fast-moving motorized divisions, however, bludgeoned through the Polish defenses, penetrated deep into enemy territory, and secured key positions. While these units wreaked havoc on the ground, the Luftwaffe—the German air force—rained ruin from the air. Thirteen hundred planes shrieked across the Polish skies and in just one day destroyed the far smaller, less modern Polish air force, most of whose planes never left the ground. Warsaw surrendered after just ten days.

Blitzkrieg in Western Europe

Western newspaper reporters christened this new style of warfare blitzkrieg°—lightning war. Western Europeans experienced blitzkrieg firsthand in the spring of 1940. The German army invaded Denmark and Norway in early April, routed the French and British troops sent to aid the Norwegians, and moved into western Europe in May. The Netherlands fell in just four days; Belgium, supported by French and British units as in World War I, held out for two weeks.

On May 27, 1940, the British army and several divisions of the French force found themselves trapped in a small pocket on the northern French coast called Dunkirk. Their destruction seemed certain. But over the next week, the only Allied success in the campaign unfolded. The British Royal Air Force (RAF) succeeded in holding off the Luftwaffe and enabling the British navy and a flotilla of fishing and recreational boats manned by British civilians to evacuate these troops. By June 4, 110,000 French and almost 240,000 British soldiers had been brought safely back to Britain. But, as the newly appointed British prime minister Winston Churchill (1874–1965) reminded his cheering people, "wars are not won by evacuation."

Over the next two weeks the Germans steadily advanced through northern France, and on June 14, German soldiers marched into Paris. The French Assembly voted to disband and to hand over power to the World War I war hero Marshal Philippe Pétain (1856–1951), who established an authoritarian government. On June 22 this new Vichy regime° (named after the city Pétain chose for his capital) signed an armistice with Germany that pledged French collaboration with the Nazi regime. Theoretically, Pétain's authority extended over all of France, but in actuality the Vichy regime was confined to the south, with Germany occupying France's western and northern regions, including Paris, as well as the Atlantic seaboard. One million French soldiers became prisoners of war. Germany, with its allies and satellites, held most of the continent.

The Battle of Britain

After the fall of France, Hitler hoped that Britain would accept Germany's domination of the continent and agree to a negotiated peace. But his hopes went unrealized. Military disaster in Norway had thoroughly discredited Prime Minister Chamberlain and his halfhearted approach to war making. A member of Chamberlain's own party, Leo Amery, spoke for the nation when he shouted at Chamberlain, "In the name of God, go!" Chamberlain went. Party politics were suspended for the duration of the war, and the British government passed to an all-party coalition headed by Winston Churchill, a vocal critic of Britain's appeasement policy since 1933. Never a humble man, Churchill wrote that when he accepted the position of prime minister, "I felt as if I were walking with Destiny, and that all my past life had been but a preparation for this hour and this trial . . . I was sure I should not fail." In his first speech as prime minister, Churchill promised, "Victory—victory at all costs."

Faced with the British refusal to negotiate, Hitler ordered his General Staff to prepare for a land invasion of Britain. But placing German troops in the English Channel while Britain's Royal Air Force (RAF) still flew the skies would be a certain military disaster. Thus, a precondition of invasion was the destruction of the RAF. On July 10, German bomber raids on English southern coastal cities opened the Battle of Britain, a battle waged in the air—and in the factories. Fortunately for Britain, from 1935 on the government's defense policy had accorded priority to the RAF. In the summer of 1940, British factories each month produced twice the number of fighter aircraft coming out of German plants in the same period. Preparing for air attack, the British had constructed a shield comprising fighter

■ **Victory Celebration, July 1940**
Young German girls in Berlin prepare a carpet of flowers for Hitler.

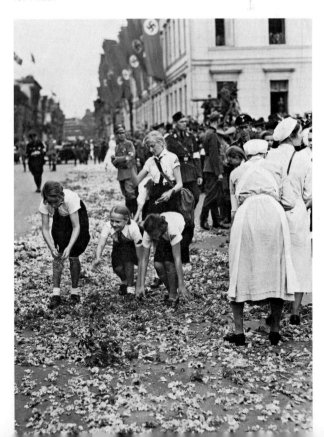

planes, anti-aircraft gun installations, and a chain of radar stations. These preparations, its higher production rates of aircraft, and the fact that RAF pilots were fighting in the skies above their homes gave the British the advantage. On September 17, 1940, Hitler announced that the invasion of Britain was postponed indefinitely.

THE INVASION OF THE SOVIET UNION

War against Britain had never been one of Hitler's central goals, however. His dreams of the "Third Reich," a renewed Germanic European empire that was to last a thousand years, centered on conquest of the Soviet Union. Hitler believed that the rich agricultural and industrial resources of the vast Russian empire rightly belonged to the superior German race. He also believed that Soviet communism was an evil force and a potential threat to German stability and prosperity. Moreover, as the next chapter will show, one of Hitler's aims in invading the Soviet Union was to realize his dream of a new racial order in Europe. This dream demanded a war against the Jews, the majority of whom lived in Poland and the Soviet Union.

A Crucial Postponement

In July 1940, at the very start of the Battle of Britain, Hitler ordered his military advisers to begin planning a Soviet invasion. By December the plan was set: German troops were to invade the Soviet Union in April 1941. But they did not. Hitler postponed the invasion for two crucial months because the ambitions of an incompetent ally—Mussolini—threatened to undermine the economic base of the Nazi war machine.

Italy was ill-equipped to fight a broad-based war. Its military budget was only one-tenth the size of Germany's, its tanks and aircraft were outdated, it had no aircraft carriers or anti-aircraft defenses, and most crucially, it lacked an adequate industrial base. Yet in 1940 Mussolini's hopes of rebuilding the Roman Empire drove him to launch just such a war. In July 1940, Italian troops invaded British imperial territories in North Africa, and in October Mussolini's soldiers marched into Greece. But by the spring of 1941, the Italian advance was in trouble. The British army in North Africa pushed the Italians back into Libya while the Greeks mounted a fierce resistance against the invaders.

Hitler feared the consolidation of British power in Africa and was even more terrified that Mussolini's adventurism would pull the British into eastern Europe. If Britain were able to build air bases in Greece, the Balkans would lie open to British bombing runs. The British could then cripple the German war effort. Germany received 50 percent of its cereal and livestock from the Balkan region, 45 percent of its aluminum ore from Greece, and 90 percent of its tin from Yugoslavia. Most crucially, the oil fields of Romania

CHRONOLOGY	
Europe at War	
1939	
September	German-Soviet conquest of Poland
1940	
April 9	German blitzkrieg against Denmark and Norway begins
May 10	Germans attack western Europe
June 22	Fall of France
July 10	Battle of Britain begins
September 7	London Blitz begins
September 17	Hitler cancels plans for invasion of Britain
1941	
March	U.S. Congress passes Lend-Lease Act
April	German invasion of the Soviet Union postponed; German offensives in Yugoslavia, Greece, and North Africa
June 22	German invasion of the Soviet Union begins
September	German siege of Leningrad begins
December	German advance halted outside Moscow

constituted Germany's chief source of this vital war-making resource. Without oil, there would be no blitz in blitzkrieg.

These economic considerations led Hitler to delay the invasion of the Soviet Union while the German army mopped up Mussolini's mess in the Balkans and North Africa. In April 1941, German armored units punched through Yugoslavian defenses and encircled the hapless Yugoslav army. Greece came next. The British sent troops, as well as state-of-the-art tanks and airplanes to aid the Greeks, but by the end of April Greece was in German hands. Meanwhile, in North Africa German field marshal Erwin Rommel's (1891–1944) Afrika Korps recaptured all the territory taken by the British the previous year.

In the summer of 1941, then, Germany stood triumphant, with dramatic victories in North Africa and the Balkans (see Map 26.2). But these victories came at a high price. They had postponed the German invasion of the Soviet Union. By the winter of 1941, the delay in beginning the Soviet invasion would imperil the German army.

Early Success

On June 22, 1941, the largest invading force the world had yet seen began to cross the Soviet borders. Three million German soldiers, equipped with 2,770 modern aircraft and

3,350 tanks, went into battle. In a matter of days, most of the Soviet air force was destroyed. By October 1941, only four months after the invasion began, German tanks were within eighty miles of Moscow, Kiev had fallen, and Leningrad was besieged. An astonishing 45 percent of the Soviet population was under German occupation, and the Germans controlled access to much of the Soviet Union's natural and industrial resources, including over 45 percent of its grain and 65 percent of its coal, iron and steel.

The early German victories in the Soviet campaign illustrated the power of blitzkrieg. Although the bulk of the German army traveled on foot or horseback (the Germans went into the Soviet Union with 700,000 horses), its spear-

head force consisted of tank and motorized infantry divisions. This force shattered the Soviet defensive line and then moved quickly to seize key targets. Two additional factors contributed to the initial German success. First, Stalin's stubborn refusal to believe that Hitler would violate the Non-Aggression Pact and attack the Soviet Union weakened Russian resistance. Soviet intelligence sources sent in more than eighty warnings of an imminent German attack; all, however, were classified as "doubtful" and a number of the messengers were punished, some even executed. Even as German troops poured over the border and German bombs fell on Soviet cities, Stalin distrusted the news of a German invasion and ignored his generals' pleas for a counterassault.

■ **Map 26.2 The Nazi Empire in 1942**

By 1942, Nazi Germany occupied or was allied to not only most European countries but also much of North Africa and the Middle East. Spain, Portugal, Ireland, Iceland, Sweden, and Switzerland remained neutral. Great Britain and the Soviet Union east of Moscow remained unconquered.

■ **Stuck in the Mud**
Climate and geography proved unbeatable foes for the German Army in the Soviet Union. The thaw following an October snowfall turned the roads to mud, and greatly slowed the German advance. The onset of real winter the following month brought far worse conditions.

A second factor that contributed to the early German victories was the popularity of the invasion among many of the peoples being invaded. The initial German advance occurred in territories where Stalin's rule had brought enormous suffering. In areas that had come under Soviet rule in the previous two years—eastern Poland and the Baltic states—anti-Soviet sentiment was especially high. Ceded to the Soviets by the German-Soviet Non-Aggression Pact, these regions were still bleeding from the imposition of Stalinist terror after 1939. Over two million ethnic Poles had been thrown into cattle cars and sent to Siberian labor camps. Thousands had been shot, including 10,000 Polish army officers who were marched to the Katyn forest and gunned down in front of mass graves. To many in these regions, then, the Germans at first seemed like liberators.

The Fatal Winter

On October 10, Hitler's spokesman announced to the foreign press corps that the destruction of the Soviet Union was assured. German newspapers proclaimed, "CAMPAIGN IN THE EAST DECIDED!"[2] But within just a few months, the German advance had stalled. Leningrad resisted its besiegers and Moscow remained beyond the Germans' reach.

Three obstacles halted the German invasion: stiffening Soviet resistance, the difficulty of supplying the Germans' overstretched lines, and the Russian weather. German troops rapidly squandered the huge reserves of anti-Stalinist sentiment in occupied Soviet territory by treating the local populations with fierce cruelty. Both SS and German army units moved through Soviet territories like a plague of locusts, stripping the regions of livestock, grain, and fuel. The Nazi governor of Ukraine insisted, "I will pump every last thing out of this country."[3] By 1941, both Ukraine and Galicia were devastated by human-made famine. German atrocities in the occupied territories

strengthened the will to resist among the Soviets still in the Germans' path. Anti-German partisan units worked behind the German lines, sabotaging their transportation routes, hijacking their supplies, and murdering their patrols. They found the Germans especially vulnerable to this sort of attack because of their overstretched supply lines. Ironically, the Germans had succeeded too well: Since June they had advanced so far so fast that they overstrained their supply and communication lines.

The weather worsened these logistical problems. An early October snowfall, which then melted, turned Russia's dirt roads to impassable mud. By the time the ground froze several weeks later, the German forces, like Napoleon's army 130 years earlier, found themselves fighting the Russian winter. Subzero temperatures wreaked havoc with transportation lines. Horses froze to death, and machinery refused to start. Men fared just as badly. Dressed in lightweight spring uniforms and forced to camp out in the cold, German soldiers fell victim to frostbite. By the end of the winter, the casualty list numbered more than 30 percent of the German East Army.

At the close of the winter of 1941–1942, the German army still occupied huge sections of the Soviet Union and controlled the vast majority of its agricultural and industrial resources. Over three million Soviet soldiers had been killed and another three million captured. But the failure to deal the Soviets a quick death blow in 1941 gave Stalin and his military high command a crucial advantage—*time*. In the zones soon to be occupied by the German army, Soviet laborers dismantled entire factories and shipped them eastward to areas out of German bombing range. Between August and October 1941, 80 percent of the Soviet war industry was in pieces, scattered among railway cars, heading to safety in Siberia. With time, these factories could be rebuilt and the colossal productive power of the Soviet Union geared for the war effort. And that is what happened.

By 1943, Russia was outproducing Germany: 24,000 tanks versus 17,000; 130,000 artillery pieces versus 27,000; 35,000 combat aircraft versus 25,000. In a total war, in which victory occurs on the assembly line as well as on the front line, these were ominous statistics for Hitler and his dreams of a German Empire.

The World at War, 1941–1945

I n December 1941, as the German advance slowed in the Soviet Union, Japanese expansionism in the Pacific fused with the war in Europe and drew the United States into the conflict. Neither Japan nor Germany could compete with the United States on the factory floor. Over the next four years, as millions of soldiers, sailors, and civilians lost their lives in a gargantuan and complicated conflict, industrial production continued to supply a crucial advantage to the Allies.

THE GLOBALIZATION OF THE WAR

Even before 1941, Europe's imperialist legacy ensured that World War II was not confined to Europe. As we have seen, Mussolini's desire to expand his North African empire pushed the fighting almost immediately outside European borders. In addition, Britain would never have been able to stand alone against the German-occupied continent without access to the manpower and materials of its colonies and Commonwealth. German efforts to block British access to these resources spread the war into the Atlantic, where British merchant marines battled desperately against German submarines to keep open the sea lanes into Britain.

Britain also drew heavily on the resources of the United States. Throughout 1941 the United States maintained a precarious balance between neutrality and support for the British war effort, as American naval escorts accompanied supply ships loaded with goods for Britain across the Atlantic. In March, the U.S. Congress passed the Lend-Lease Act°, which guaranteed to supply Britain all needed military supplies, with payment postponed until after the war ended. The passage of Lend-Lease was one of the most important decisions in all of World War II. It gave first Britain and then the Soviets access to the incredible might of American industry.

At the same time that the United States was drawing closer to Britain, its relations with Japan were growing increasingly hostile. In 1941 the Japanese occupied Indochina, and the United States responded by placing an embargo on trade in oil with Japan. Threatened with the loss of a key resource, Japanese policymakers viewed this boycott as tantamount to an act of war. Japan's imperial ambitions demanded that it move decisively before its oil ran out. The South Pacific, a treasure house of mineral and other resources, beckoned.

Between December 7 and 10, 1941, Japanese forces attacked American, British, and Dutch territories in the Pacific—Hong Kong, Wake and Guam islands, the Philippines, Malaya, Molucca in the Dutch East Indies, and most dramatically, the U.S. Pacific fleet base at Pearl

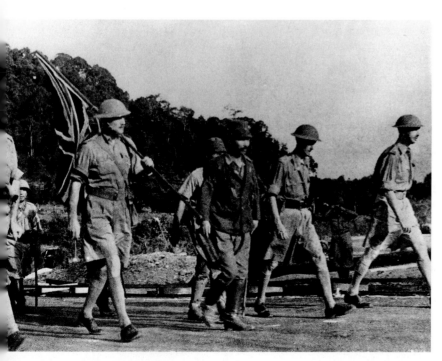

■ **The Surrender of Singapore**

In one of the most humiliating moments in British military history, General Arthur Percival surrenders the Union Jack, and Singapore, to the Japanese in February 1942. Over 130,000 troops were taken prisoner by a Japanese force containing half that number. The Japanese had captured the island's water reservoirs and so had placed Percival in a helpless situation.

Map shows the following labels:

Irkutsk, Ulan Bator, MONGOLIA, CHINA, MANCHUKUO (MANCHURIA), REHE, Beijing, Vladivostok, KOREA, Sea of Japan, Sakhalin, Kamchatka, Kurile Islands, Aleutian Islands, Chongqing, Nanjing, Shanghai, RICE, Tokyo, PACIFIC OCEAN, Midway Is., Calcutta, OIL, COAL, LEAD, OPIUM, RICE, Guangzhou, Okinawa, TAIWAN (Formosa), Hong Kong, Iwo Jima, Hawaiian Islands, Pearl Harbor, INDIA, Mandalay, OIL, RUBBER, Hanoi, Hainan, LUZON, HEMP, Mariana Islands, BURMA, Rangoon, THAILAND, RICE, FRENCH INDO-CHINA, Manila, Philippine Islands, TIN, GOLD, Bangkok, RICE, COAL, Saigon, MINDANAO, RICE, Marshall Islands, South China Sea, Caroline Islands, COAL, TIN, MALAYA, COAL, GOLD, SARAWAK, OIL, Gilbert Islands, RUBBER, TIN, GOLD, RUBBER, Singapore, OIL, GOLD, BORNEO, CELEBES, Phoenix Islands, SUMATRA, COAL, RUBBER, DUTCH EAST INDIES, NEW GUINEA, PAPUA, RUBBER, Bismarck Arch., New Ireland, Solomon Islands, Ellice Islands, Tokelau Islands, Samoa Islands, Society Islands, OIL, JAVA, Timor, Port Moresby, Fiji Islands, Darwin, INDIAN OCEAN, Townsville, New Hebrides, New Caledonia, AUSTRALIA, NEW ZEALAND

Japan's Territorial Ambitions
■ Japanese Empire
■ Occupied by Japan by 1941

0 — 1000 km
0 — 1000 mi

■ Map 26.3 Japan's Territorial Ambitions

Lacking its own supply of natural resources, Japan embarked on imperial conquest.

Harbor. After an attack that lasted only a few hours, the American Pacific fleet in Hawaii lay gutted. Guam fell immediately; Wake held out until December 23; Hong Kong surrendered on Christmas Day; by February, Malaya had been defeated. On February 15, 1942, the garrison of 130,000 British, Indian, Australian, and local troops surrendered Singapore to a Japanese force less than half its size. By May, this astounding success had been cemented with the conquest of Indonesia, Burma, and the Philippines. In just a few months, the Japanese had established themselves as imperial overlords of the South Pacific, with its wealth of raw materials (see Map 26.3).

The audacity of the Japanese attack impressed Hitler. Although he had long feared American industrial power, he declared war on the United States on December 11, 1941. In Europe Germany now faced the alliance of Britain, the Soviet Union, and the United States. Even against such an alliance, Germany appeared to occupy a

strong position. By January a spectacular offensive in North Africa had brought Rommel's forces within two hundred miles of the strategically vital Suez Canal. And in June the German army resumed its advance in the Soviet Union. Within a few months German troops stood at the borders of Russia's oil fields in the southern Caucasus. With Germany on the offensive in the east and Japan controlling the Pacific, the Allies looked poised to lose the war.

FROM ALLIED DEFEAT TO ALLIED VICTORY

Twelve months later the situation had changed, and the Allies were on the road to eventual victory. This road, however, proved long and arduous. The period from 1943 through 1945 was marked by horrendous human suffering, unprecedented attacks on civilians, and cataclysmic military battles. Yet in the end American and Soviet industrial supremacy, allied with a superior military strategy, pushed the balance in the Allies' favor.

The Turning Point: Midway and Stalingrad

The second half of 1942 proved the turning point as two very different battles helped transform the course of the war. In the Pacific, victory at the Battle of Midway gave the U.S. forces a decisive advantage. In Europe, the Battle of Stalingrad dealt Germany a blow from which it never recovered.

The Battle of Midway was the result of the Japanese effort to ensure its air supremacy by drawing the U.S. Pacific fleet's aircraft carriers into battle. To do so, the Japanese attacked Midway Island, a U.S. outpost in the Pacific, on June 4, 1942. By midmorning the Japanese had shot down two-thirds of the American planes. But then an American dive-bomber group, which earlier in the morning had overflown its target and gotten lost, suddenly found itself above the main Japanese carriers. Caught in the act of refueling and rearming the strike force, their decks cluttered with gas lines and bombs, the carriers made remarkably combustible targets. In five minutes, three of Japan's four carriers were destroyed; the fourth was sunk later in the day. Japan's First Air Fleet was decimated. The destruction of the Japanese fleet dealt Japan a blow from which it could not recover. The United States possessed the industrial resources to rebuild its lost ships and airplanes. Japan did not. In five explosive minutes the course of the Pacific war changed.

The Battle of Stalingrad could not have been more different from the Battle of Midway. Extending over months, it tested human endurance to its very limits. In July 1942 the German army was sweeping southward toward the oil-rich Caucasus. Hitler ordered the southern offensive split into two, with one arm reaching up to conquer Stalingrad on the Volga River. The conquest of Stalingrad would give the Germans control over the main waterway for the transport of oil and food from the Caucasus to the rest of the Soviet Union. These resources were vital to the Soviet war effort now that Ukraine was held by Germany. But by dividing his offensive, Hitler widened his front from 500 to 2,500 miles. By the time the German Sixth Army reached Stalingrad on August 23, German resources were fatally overstretched.

Recognizing Germany's vulnerability, Stalin's generals assured him they could attack the exposed German lines and then encircle the German Sixth Army—but only if Stalingrad's defenders could hold on for almost two months while they assembled the necessary men and machinery. An epic urban battle ensued, with the Russian and German soldiers fighting street by street, house by house, room by room. By November, the Russians had surrounded the Germans. When the German commander, General Friedrich von Paulus (d. 1953), requested permission to surrender, Hitler replied, "The army will hold its position to the last soldier and the last cartridge."[4] Paulus finally

disobeyed orders and surrendered on January 30, 1943, but by then his army had almost ceased to exist. The Germans were never able to make up the losses in manpower, material, or morale they suffered at Stalingrad. The colossal struggle turned the course of the European war, as the Battle of Midway turned the course of the Pacific war.

The Allies on the Offensive

The Allies were now on the offensive. In 1942 British bomber command ordered the intensive bombing of German civilian centers. Soon joined by the American air force, the RAF bombers brought the war home to the German people. In October 1942 Rommel's North Afrika Korps suffered a decisive defeat to the British at the Battle of El Alamein. In November, a joint landing of British and American troops in French North Africa forced the Germans to send reinforcements to Rommel. After fierce fighting, the Anglo-American forces finally claimed victory in North Africa in the spring of 1943.

The Allies followed their victory in North Africa with an invasion of Italy. This campaign was a response, first, to Stalin's pleas that his Allies open a "Second Front" in Europe and so relieve the pressure on Russian troops and, second, to Churchill's desire to protect British economic and imperial interests in the Mediterranean. The Italian offensive began on July 10, 1943, when Anglo-American forces landed in Sicily, prepared to push up into what Churchill called the "soft underbelly" of German-controlled Europe. Within just fifteen days, Mussolini had been overthrown in a high-level coup and his successor opened peace negotiations with the Allies. But then German muscle hardened the "soft underbelly": The German army occupied Italy. British and American soldiers faced a long, brutal, slow-moving push up the peninsula. Ridged with mountains and laced with rivers, Italy formed a natural defensive fortress. In an eight-month period, the Allied forces advanced only seventy miles.

The European war was decided, then, not in the mountains of Italy but on the eastern front. Beginning in the summer of 1943, the Russians steadily pushed back the Germans. By the spring of 1944 the Red Army had reached the borders of Poland. In August Soviet troops turned south into Romania and Hungary. By February 1945 they were within 100 miles of Berlin (see Map 26.4).

Two interconnected factors proved vital in the Soviet victory over the Germans in the east. The first was the evolution of Soviet military strategy. By 1943, the Red Army had learned important lessons from being on the receiving end of blitzkrieg. It had not only increased its tank units, but it had concentrated these into armies in which motorized infantry regiments accompanied massive numbers of tanks, antitank battalions, and mobile antiaircraft artillery. In addition, a vast expansion in the number of radios and field telephones overcame the organizational chaos that had greeted the German invasion in 1941.

These changes in technique and technology were closely connected to achievements in industrial production, the

■ Map 26.4 Allied Victory in Europe, 1942–1945
Beginning in late 1942, Allied forces moved onto the offensive.

second key factor in the Soviet victory. Mobile armored forces depended on factories churning out steel, rubber, oil, and all the various machine parts needed by a modern army. Access to the industrial wealth of the United States provided the Soviet Union with assistance in this task. By 1943, Lend-Lease deliveries of aircraft and tanks were pouring into Soviet ports. Lend-Lease supplied the Soviet Union with the basics needed to keep its army moving: rails and locomotives, jeeps, trucks and gasoline, plus 15 million pairs of boots. Yet the Soviets did not rely only on imports. The Soviet industrial effort was enormous. In 1943, Russia manufactured four times as many tanks as it imported, and Soviet production of tanks and antitank guns was double that of Germany.

The Fall of Germany

As the Red Army closed in on Germany from the east, the British and Americans pushed in from the west. On June 6, 1944, the Allies carried out the largest amphibious operation the world had ever seen. Five seaborne divisions (two American, two British, and one Canadian) and three airborne divisions (two American and one British) crossed the English Channel and landed on a sixty-mile stretch of coastline in northern France. The "D-Day" landings illustrated the Allied advantage in manpower and material. Against the Allies' eight divisions, the Germans had four; against the Allies' 5,000 fighter planes, the Germans could send up 169.

CHRONOLOGY

The Long March Toward Allied Victory

1943

February	German surrender at Stalingrad; Red Army goes on the offensive; Allied round-the-clock bombing of Germany begins; Japanese surrender at Guadalcanal
May	German surrender in North Africa
July 10	Allied invasion of Italy begins

1944

January	Lifting of the siege of Leningrad
June 4	Allies liberate Rome
June 6	D-Day landings; Allied offensive in France begins
August 24–26	Allied liberation of Paris
September	Allies liberate the Netherlands, Belgium, Luxembourg
October	U.S. invasion of Philippines

Yet the strength of the German resistance—particularly on Omaha Beach, where the U.S. landing encountered more than 4,000 casualties—signaled that the road to Berlin would not be easy. The Allies faced the formidable task of uprooting the Germans from territory where they had planted themselves five years earlier. For ten long months, the British, American, Canadian, and imperial

■ **The Battle for Berlin**
On April 20, 1945, Hitler celebrated his fifty-sixth birthday, and made a rare visit out of his Berlin bunker to visit with the troops defending his city. As this photograph shows, these "soldiers" were just children. Ten days later, Hitler committed suicide.

The GI

On January 26, 1942, the first soldiers from the United States arrived in Britain to prepare for the invasion of Nazi-controlled Europe. By the spring of 1944, Britain was host to a million and a half American soldiers, sailors, and airmen, awaiting the opening of the Second Front in Europe. The coming of the "Yanks" to war-weary, bomb-blasted Britain was an event of more than military significance. For the majority of individuals on both sides, it was their first prolonged encounter with another culture, another way of life. Cultural clashes were commonplace. Forgetting that most essential items were strictly rationed, the GIs (slang that comes from the military label "government issue") at times infuriated their hosts with insensitive complaints about cold rooms, inadequate food, and the shabby style of British dress. The British found the Americans naive, supremely self-confident, alarmingly friendly, and most of all, BIG.

The *bigness* of the GI is a constant theme in British descriptions and recollections. One British man, urging greater toleration for the GIs, explained to his countrymen, "An American is like a large dog trying to be friendly with everyone in the room, whilst wrecking everything with its tail wagging." A Lancashire nurse recalled her first sight of GIs: "They all seemed to be handsome six-footers with friendly grins and toothpaste advert teeth." But we know that not every GI stationed in Britain was tall and husky; the average height of American servicemen in this era was 5' 10". How do we explain this focus on the bigness of the GI body?

A number of factors helped shape British perceptions. First, the bigness of America in general was a constant obsession of both the GIs and their British hosts. *Meet the U.S. Army,* a publication distributed in British schools, told the children, "In the USA, you can get in a car—a high-powered car at that—and drive for a week or more in a comparatively straight line without running into the sea." Second, the Americans *looked better.* The GI's uniform was of a higher-quality fabric and a closer fit than that of the average British soldier's: American privates often found that their flashy uniforms led not only British civilians but

even British soldiers to mistake them for officers. Third, compared to the British, the Americans were big eaters and big spenders. An American private earned five times as much as his British counterpart—and spent it with abandon. British pubgoers were sometimes dismayed to find that American soldiers had already consumed the pub's entire stock of beer. Undisciplined by rationing, American appetites seemed huge to the British. One soldier enjoyed his dinner in a British home: "Only afterwards did I discover that I had eaten the family's special rations for a *month.*" GIs also had access to items such as chocolate and canned fruit that had long been unobtainable in Britain. And finally, different cultural norms magnified the impact of the GI's presence. Americans spoke more loudly. They used exaggerated expressions that struck the more understated British as boastful. They tended to lounge, to slouch, to lean against walls, to throw their bodies around in ways that startled many British, schooled in more restrained patterns of public behavior. All of these factors combined to ensure that the GI made an indelible impression on British culture.

Embraced with enthusiasm by many British citizens (particularly women), derided by others (particularly men) as "overfed, overpaid, oversexed, and over here," the GI's body became a symbol, a shorthand reference to American power, influence, and plenty. As World War II ended and the Cold War began, and as the United States took on a new role as the undisputed leader of the "West," the American soldier became a familiar figure throughout western Europe, the visible reminder of the reconfiguration of military and economic dominance.[5] ■

For Discussion

What other bodies became symbols or shorthand references during World War II? What did these bodies symbolize?

■ **Wartime Encounters**
British women entertain GIs heading for the front line in France.

troops fought a series of hard-won battles. By March 1945, as the Russian army approached Berlin from the east, the British and American armies reached Germany's Rhine border and by mid-April stood within fifty miles of Berlin.

The Allies agreed, however, to leave the conquest of Berlin to the Soviet Army. In this climactic battle of the European war, 320,000 Germans, many of them young boys, fought three million Soviet troops. Even so, it took eleven days before the city's commander surrendered on May 2. Two days earlier, Hitler had taken a cyanide capsule and then shot himself with his service pistol. On May 7, 1945, General Alfred Jodl (1890–1946) signed the unconditional surrender of German forces.

The Fall of Japan

When Germany surrendered, the war in the Pacific was still raging. After the Midway battle of 1942, the United States steadily, but slowly, agonizingly, pushed the Japanese back island by island. Japanese industry could not make up for the weapons and ammunition expended in these brutal battles. In contrast, American factories were just gearing up. Whereas in 1940 American assembly lines produced only a little more than 2,000 aircraft, by 1944 they had manufactured over 96,000 bombers and fighters. American productivity per worker hour was five times that of Japan.

While U.S. troops moved, island by island, closer to the Japanese mainland, British and Indian troops rebuffed a Japanese attempt to invade India and pushed the Japanese out of Burma. Australian forces, with American assistance, held the line at New Guinea and forestalled a Japanese invasion of Australia. By February 1945, when U.S. Marines landed on the small island of Iwo Jima, just 380 miles from Japan's home islands, the Japanese war effort was in tatters and an Allied victory was ensured.

Obtaining this victory was not easy. In the month of fighting for Iwo Jima, one-third of the American landing force was killed or wounded. The April conquest of Okinawa was even more hard-won. Outnumbered two to one, the Japanese endured a week-long preliminary bombardment designed to pulverize their defenses and suffered unbelievable casualties—110,000 of the 120,000 soldiers on the island died. They were still able to inflict serious losses on the attacking force: 50,000 Americans were killed or wounded. (Nobody bothered to count how many Okinawans died in a battle they had done nothing to provoke: Estimates range as high as 160,000.)

The conquest of Iwo Jima and Okinawa gave the United States the bases it needed to launch a relentless bombardment of Japanese cities. By July 1945, much of Japan lay in waste. At the same time, a U.S. naval blockade cut Japan off from its supply lines. Already in its death throes, the Japanese war effort was abruptly terminated in August

when the United States dropped atomic bombs on the cities of Hiroshima and Nagasaki (see Chapter 27), and the Soviet army finally entered the Pacific war with an attack on Japanese forces in China. On August 15, the Japanese emperor Hirohito (1901–1989) announced his country's surrender.

The Home Fronts

......................■........................

While soldiers fought and died in numerous theaters of war, European civilian life was transformed to meet the demands of total war. As governments mobilized their economies for the war effort, gender roles shifted and the demand for radical social change grew. Far more than in World War I, the distinction between the home front and the front lines collapsed, with bombing raids and enemy occupation bringing war onto the civilian's doorstep.

THE OTHER WARS

During World War II in Europe the home front was not a place of safety or normalcy but a place where other wars were fought. Civilians joined the Resistance against Nazi occupation; rival political and ethnic groups engaged in savage struggles for dominance; and both Allied and Axis bombers targeted noncombatants. At the same time, Europeans living in the areas occupied by the Germans endured an increasingly repressive regime.

The Limits of Resistance

Throughout the war individuals and groups in occupied Europe performed heroically, hiding Jews and others on the run, sabotaging equipment, disrupting transportation systems, and relaying secret information to the Allies. In the Soviet Union and in mountainous regions of Yugoslavia, Italy, and southern France, where the terrain offered shelter for guerillas, anti-Nazi fighters formed partisan groups that attacked German army units.

Both men and women participated in the Resistance, the struggle against Nazi rule. In Yugoslavia, 100,000 women fought as soldiers in the partisan ranks: 25,000 were killed and 40,000 injured. Most women in the Resistance were not in combat units. Instead, they played gender stereotypes to great advantage: They hid bombs in baby carriages, tucked vital messages under their shopping, disarmed Germans with feminine charm. One Italian partisan used to catch rides on German trucks to deliver her illegal communications: "What was there to fear? You only had to give them a few smiles."[6] With men at risk of being rounded up for forced labor in Germany, women often shouldered the burden of distributing clandestine publications, delivering supplies and arms, and finding safe houses.

But only a minority of Europeans, men or women, fought in the Resistance. As the Dutch historian Louis de Jong has noted of European actions and attitudes under Nazi occupation, "Unwilling adjustment was the rule, intentional resistance the exception."[7] Why did so few Europeans join the Resistance? Important factors include the Germans' military might, their success at infiltrating Resistance organizations, and their willingness to use brutal force to crush any threat. The German network of concentration camps throughout occupied Europe possessed enormous deterrent value. Concerned for their own and their families' safety, most Europeans hoped simply to keep their heads down and survive the war.

The German practice of exacting collective retribution for Resistance actions particularly undercut mass support for anti-German efforts. In 1942, for example, British intelligence forces parachuted Czech agents into German-held Czechoslovakia. The agents assassinated the chief SS official in the region, Reinhard Heydrich (1904–1942), but they were immediately betrayed by one of their own. In retaliation, the Germans massacred the entire population of the village of Lidice. Similarly, an assassination attempt against Hitler in 1944 led to mass arrests and the executions of an estimated 5,000 Germans.

In Germany itself and in countries allied to rather than conquered by the Germans, potential resisters had to convince themselves that patriotism demanded working against their own government. In France until 1943, resistance meant opposing the lawfully instituted but collaborationist Vichy government of Marshal Pétain. As a World War I hero, Pétain had an almost godlike reputation in France and was popular even with those who did not share his au-

thoritarian conservatism. As a result, in the early years of the war many French men and women viewed the members of the Resistance as traitors against France, rather than as heroes fighting against the Nazis. By 1943, however, an alternative focus of national loyalty had emerged: the Free French headed by General Charles De Gaulle (1890–1970), a career military man who had gone into exile rather than accept the armistice with Nazi Germany. After the Anglo-American landing in North Africa in November 1942, De Gaulle claimed Algeria as a power base and declared himself the head of a Free French provisional government. French patriots could declare themselves loyal to this alternative government, and fight in the Resistance against both Nazi rule and Vichy collaboration.

In many areas—for example, much of Italy after the German army occupied the country in 1943—a genuine spirit of unity characterized the Resistance struggle, with socialists, communists, and Catholics working together not only to defeat the Nazis but also to create the foundations of a better society. In other areas, divisions within the Resistance limited its impact. Conservative army officers fighting to preserve the prewar status quo clashed with

■ The Resistance

A Yugoslav partisan signals his defiance before he is hanged by his German captors.

LIVING UNDER THE BOMBS

·················

During the 1930s, European statesmen and politicians condemned the aerial bombing of civilian populations as an act of barbarity and criminality. Once World War II began, the targeting of civilians in order to break home front morale and impede industrial production became commonplace. Analysts disagree about the military effectiveness of urban bombing, but no one can dispute the human horror.

In this first excerpt, an elderly air warden from Hull, one of Britain's northern port cities, is speaking. One night, when he returned from his post, he found that his street:

Was as flat as this 'ere wharfside—there was just my 'ouse like—well, part of my 'ouse. My missus were just making me a cup of tea for when I come 'ome. She were in the passage between the kitchen and the wash'ouse, where it blowed 'er. She were burnt right up to 'er waist. 'Er legs were just two cinders. And 'er face—The only thing I could recognize 'er by was one of 'er boots—I'd 'ave lost fifteen 'omes if I could 'ave kept my missus. We used to read together. I can't read mesen [myself]. She used to read to me like. We'd 'ave our armchairs on either side o' the fire, and she read me bits out o' the paper. We 'ad a paper every evening. Every evening.

In the following excerpt, a German woman, 19 years old on July 28, 1943, recalls the bombing of Hamburg and the firestorm it induced:

We came to a door which was burning just like a ring in a circus through which a lion has to jump. . . . I struggled to run against the wind in the middle of the street but could only reach a house on the corner. . . . We got to the Loschplatz [park] all right but I couldn't go across the Eiffestrasse [street] because the asphalt had melted. There were people on the roadway, some already dead, some still lying alive but stuck in the asphalt. They must have rushed on to the roadway without thinking. Their feet had got stuck and then they put out their hands to try to get out again. They were on their hands and knees screaming.

Sources: Excerpt from a Mass-Observation typescript report, filed at Mass-Observations offices, no. 844, August 23, 1941. Copyright © by the Trustees of the Mass-Observation Archive. Reprinted by permission.; and from Martin Middlebrook, *The Battle of Hamburg*, Allen Lane, 1980. Reprinted by permission of the author.

guerilla groups that espoused radical political goals. Fighting among Resistance factions shaded into civil war. In Ukraine, nationalists fought against communist partisans as well as the Germans. In Greece, the communist-dominated National Liberation Front battled not only the Nazis but also a rival Resistance group, the royalist National Greek Democratic Union.

Civil War in Yugoslavia

The fiercest struggle occurred in Yugoslavia, where political and ethnic divisions split both the country and the Resistance. Wartime Yugoslavia experienced a bloodletting unmatched anywhere in Europe except in the German-occupied regions of Poland and the Soviet Union. Parts of the country such as Slovenia and Macedonia were occupied by German or German-allied armies and endured brutal repression. The scale of violence peaked in the fascist state of Croatia, created after the German invasion of 1941. This Nazi-sponsored regime immediately embarked on a savage program of ethnic homogenization, with a ferocious campaign of terror against Jews, Bosnian Muslims, and Serbs.

In Yugoslavia, therefore, the Resistance was not simply or even primarily aimed at the Germans. Guerilla bands of Serbian soldiers called *Chetniks* supported the now-exiled Yugoslav monarchy and regarded the Croatian regime as their main enemy, although, like the Croatian fascists, the Chetniks also slaughtered both Muslims and Jews. In the midst of this bloody free-for-all, a second Resistance group emerged, one based not on ethnicity but on political ideology. Led by communist Josip Broz (1892–1980), alias "Tito," these partisans saw the war as a chance for social revolution and promised equality for all in a reunited Yugoslavia. Tito's partisans focused on fighting Germans (diverting ten German divisions from the eastern front), but they also fought their fellow Yugoslavs, with the royalist Chetniks fiercely opposing Tito's aim of a communist state.

Tito's partisans won the civil war. In 1944 they fought alongside the Soviet army and liberated Yugoslavia from German control. With 90 percent of the vote in the first postwar election, Tito assumed control of the new communist state of Yugoslavia, a position he held for the next thirty-five years. Beneath the uniform surface created by communist ideology, however, the jagged edges of ethnic division remained sharp.

The Bombing War

For many Europeans, World War II was the war of the bomber. The new technologies and techniques of military aviation ensured that the men, women, and children living in areas targeted by enemy bombers suffered severely. In Britain, until late 1941, civilian deaths outnumbered military, and most of these deaths came from bombing raids. During the autumn of 1940, Londoners endured the "Blitz"—seventy-six consecutive nights of mass bombing.

By May 1941, almost every main industrial city in Britain had been bombed, and 43,000 noncombatants lay dead.

While German bombers were killing British civilians, British bombers, joined in 1943 by the American air force, retaliated in kind, and as the war wore on, developed new techniques of airborne destruction. In May 1942, British planes destroyed Cologne with the world's first 1,000-bomber raid. At the end of July 1943, the British introduced the world to the horror of the firestorm with the bombing of Hamburg. In this human-made catastrophe, fires caused by incendiary bombs combine with winds to suck the oxygen out of the air and raise temperatures to combustible levels. As one survivor recalled, "The smallest children lay like fried eels on the pavement."[8] In a single night, 45,000 of Hamburg's residents were killed. In total, over 500,000 German civilians died in bombing attacks. Twenty percent of the dead were children.

Under Occupation

In occupied Europe, Nazi racial ideology shaped the experience of both soldiers and civilians. The Nazis drew a sharp line between the peoples of western Europe—the Dutch, Norwegian, Danes, and Flemish, all considered of racially superior "Germanic stock"—and the Slavs of eastern Europe. The ferocity of Nazi brutality increased exponentially in the eastern occupied regions. The Nazis drew the sharpest line of all at the Jews, and as Chapter 27 details, sought to murder every Jew in Europe.

The German treatment of prisoners of war (POWs) illustrates the contrast between the western and eastern European experience during World War II. By the end of 1941, 2.5 million Soviet soldiers had been captured. By February 1942, two million of these had died, both from starvation and from epidemic diseases nurtured by the poor conditions in the camps. In contrast, of the over one million French soldiers captured by the Germans in 1940, nineteen out of twenty returned home at the end of the war. When dealing with western European POWs, the Germans abided by international rules; in eastern Europe, World War II was a game without rules and without limits.

In the "General Government" (the portion of Poland not directly annexed to Germany but rather treated as an enemy state under occupation), civilians struggled to survive in barbaric conditions. Political, economic, and intellectual elites faced imprisonment or execution; ordinary Poles endured extreme hunger, hard labor, constant shortages, and the omnipresent threat of death. By the time the war ended in 1945, more than 20 percent of Poland's population had died. Poland's substantial Jewish population endured a hell beyond imagining.

In the occupied regions of the Soviet Union, conditions also reached barbaric levels. Almost 63,000 Soviet civilians were killed in the first five weeks after the German invasion. In planning for the invasion, German policymakers assumed that after a quick and easy victory, the industrial and particularly the agricultural resources of the Soviet Union would be theirs for the taking. They intended to strip the conquered nation of its food, with no provision made for feeding the defeated Soviets. According to Alfred Rosenberg (1893–1946), the Nazi minister of the eastern occupied territories, the deaths of "many tens of millions" from starvation was to be regarded as "a stern necessity, beyond the realm of all sentiment."[9] Although German plans for a quick conquest in the Soviet Union were soon shattered, German willingness to regard the Soviet population as expendable remained unchanged.

The German occupation of western Europe was less heavy-handed, particularly during the first half of the war. The Nazis believed that "Germanic" peoples such as the Dutch could be taught to become good Nazis and therefore spared them the extreme violence and mindless brutality that characterized the German occupation in the east. Moreover, in western Europe the Germans sought to work with rather than to annihilate political and economic elites. For example, in both Belgium and the Netherlands civil servants continued to do their prewar jobs. Nonetheless, the German occupation in the west, even in the first two years of the war, was far from lenient. The Nazis forced occupied countries to pay exorbitant sums to cover the costs of their own occupation. In addition, they were required to sell both manufactured products and raw materials to Germany at artificially low prices. Anyone who spoke out against the Nazis faced imprisonment or death. The occupation grew even more harsh after 1943 as German military losses piled up, stocks of food and essential supplies dwindled, and German demands for civilian labor increased.

Foreign Laborers in Germany

For millions of European men and women, the war meant forced labor in Germany. With the need to free up German men for the front lines, the Nazis faced crucial labor shortages in almost every sector of the economy. Placing the economy on an all-out war footing would have meant imposing unpopular measures such as the conscription of women for industrial labor, lengthening working hours, and prohibiting holidays. The Nazis chose instead to recruit labor from conquered territories. Within days of the invasion of Poland, Polish POWs were working in German fields. By August 1944, German farmers and factory owners employed over 5.7 million foreign civilian laborers (one-third of whom were women) and almost two million POWs. These foreign workers accounted for more than half the labor in German agriculture and in German munitions plants, and one-third of the labor force in key war industries such as mining, chemicals, and metals.

Hostile, hungry, often untrained for the jobs in which they were placed, foreign workers proved to be less productive than German laborers. Nevertheless, foreign labor played a crucial role in wartime Germany, not only in fueling the German war machine, but also in maintaining

German civilian morale. Foreign labor cushioned German civilians from the impact of total war and reassured them that they belonged to a superior race. Many German factory owners were relieved to find they now had a labor force with few political rights. The director of one aircraft manufacturing firm explained, "The great advantage of employing foreigners . . . is that we only have to give orders. There is no refusal, no need to negotiate."[10] The labor of foreigners also benefited the German working class. Nazi regulations stipulated that German workers were to regard themselves as the masters of the foreign laborers working alongside them. Thus ordinary Germans held positions of privilege and power. Some families even found themselves able to afford new luxuries. Beginning in 1942, the Nazi regime brought Russian women into Germany to serve as maids in German households. As a result, according to a report in January 1943, "even those households with many children, whose financial situation previously did not permit them to hire domestic help, can now afford to maintain a worker."[11]

WOMEN'S WORK

The obliteration of the distinction between soldier and civilian, between the home front and the front lines, meant that this was a women's war. As we have seen, women joined the ranks of the Resistance (and in the Soviet Union, the regular army as well). Women also tended to bear the brunt of home front deprivation, as they were the ones who had to get a meal on the table and clothe their children in the face of severe rationing. Basic household goods such as frying pans, toothbrushes, bicycle tires, baby bottles, and batteries almost disappeared; food was in short supply; clothing had to be recycled. It was Europe's women who became experts at "make do and mend," as British government pamphlets advised.

British women were fully mobilized. They did not serve in combat, but they were drafted for service in civilian defense, war-related industry, or the armed forces. Women accounted for 25 percent of the civilians who worked in Britain's Air Raid Protection services as wardens, rescuers, and telephone operators. All citizens—male or female—working less than 55 hours per week had to perform compulsory fire-watching duties from 1941 on. The numbers of women employed in male-dominated industries such as metals and chemicals rose dramatically.

Only the Soviet Union mobilized women more fully than Britain. Soviet women constituted 80 percent of the agricultural and 50 percent of the industrial labor force. All Soviet adult

men and women under age 45 who were not engaged in essential war work were required to work eleven hours a day constructing defenses. Unlike in Britain, Russian women also served in combat. By 1944, 246,000 women were in front-line units. For all Soviet citizens, male and female, life on the home front meant endless labor, inadequate food supplies, and constant surveillance under martial law. Stalin demanded an all-out war against not only the German invaders but also anyone at home who undermined the war effort in any way. The Soviet government established a compulsory sixty-hour workweek and issued ration cards only to those who worked.

Until 1943, the German home front contrasted sharply with that of Britain and the Soviet Union. The Nazi policy toward female employment rested on Hitler's conviction that Germany had lost World War I in part because of the collapse of morale on the home front. As a result, Hitler placed a high priority on maintaining civilian morale. Generous allowances for soldiers meant that their wives,

■ **The Women's War**
Russian women dig trench defenses at the outskirts of Moscow in 1941. No other state mobilized its women as fully as did the Soviet Union.

unlike in Britain, did not have to work to feed their families. In the first years of the war, the Nazi government rationed clothing and food supplies but did not dramatically cut consumption levels. Most significantly, Hitler hesitated to conscript middle-class German women for industrial labor. For Hitler, ideology came before economics. He believed that the future of the "German race" depended on middle-class women being protected from the strains of paid labor so that they could bear healthy Aryan babies.

In Germany the use of foreign labor took the place of the full-scale mobilization of women. Top-ranking Nazis explicitly linked the use of foreign workers to gender considerations. At the end of 1941, for example, Hermann Göring (1893–1946) announced that Soviet workers would be brought into Germany to guarantee "that in future, the German women should not be so much in evidence in the work process."[12] The number of women in the German workforce actually fell by 500,000 between 1939 and 1941. German women who did work were prohibited from working long hours or at night, and from performing heavy physical labor. Instead, eastern European workers (many of them women) were given the tough jobs and the poor hours. At the Krupp metalworks factory, for example, German women worked for six hours at light jobs during the day; Russian women did the heavy labor during the twelve-hour night shift.

Military necessity eventually undercut Nazi gender ideology. The fall of Stalingrad marked a turning point in Nazi policy toward German women at work. With losses on the Eastern front averaging 150,000 men per month, the German army desperately needed more men. At the same time, the German war economy demanded more workers. In response, Hitler's deputy Joseph Goebbels (1897–1945) declared that Germany must fight a total war, which meant total mobilization of the home front. The final, desperate year of the war saw a concentrated use of female labor in Nazi Germany.

Of all the combatant states, the United States stands out as unique with regard to the home front. The United States never fully mobilized its economy, and over 70 percent of its adult women remained outside the paid workforce. Rationing was comparatively minimal and consumption levels in the United States high. In fact, for many families, the war years brought prosperity after years of economic depression. But most important, American cities were never bombed, and thus the United States was able to maintain a clear distinction between soldier and civilian, man and woman—a distinction that was blurred in other combatant nations.

WHAT ARE WE FIGHTING FOR?

To mobilize their populations for total war, governments had to convince their citizens of the importance of the war effort. Maintaining morale and motivating both civilians and soldiers to endure deprivation and danger demanded that leaders supply a persuasive answer to the question: What are we fighting for?

Myth Making and Morale Building

All nations—democratic or authoritarian—rely on myths, on stories of national origins and identity, to unify disparate individuals, classes, and groups. In times of total war, such myths become crucial. During World War II, the process of myth making was institutionalized by government agencies responsible for propaganda. In Britain, the newly formed Ministry of Information (democracies tend to shy away from using the word *propaganda*) took on the task of propping up civilian morale. Staffed by upper-class men, the MOI's efforts often betrayed its class composition: Many of its posters and leaflets adopted a hectoring tone, subjecting ordinary citizens to a barrage of do's and don'ts. Far more effective were the speeches of Prime Minister Winston Churchill, whose romantic vision of Britain as a still-great power destined to triumph was exactly the myth that the beleaguered British needed. In Germany, strict censorship had already subordinated the arts and entertainment industries to the demands of the state. The war heightened this control as censorship tightened even further, paper shortages limited the production of books and periodicals, and the threat of being drafted for the eastern front kept artists in line.

In all the combatant nations, governments enlisted artists, entertainers, and the technologies of the mass media for myth making and morale building. The British artist Henry Moore's (1898–1986) drawings of ordinary people in air raid shelters (completed under an official commission) evoke the survival of civilized values in the midst of unspeakable degradation. Perhaps the most famous musical work from the war is Dmitri Shostakovich's (1906–1975) *Seventh Symphony*—now universally known as the *Leningrad Symphony* and a symbol of human resilience. Shostakovich composed the early drafts of this work in Leningrad while German shells were falling, and it was actually performed in Leningrad in August 1942, while the city was still under siege.

During the war, film came into its own as an artistic form capable of creating important myths of national unity. Laurence Olivier's version of Shakespeare's *Henry V* (1944) comforted British moviegoers with its classic story of a stirring English military victory against huge odds. In Italy, a group of filmmakers known as the Neo-Realists created a set of films that dramatized the Resistance spirit of national unity. Shot on location, with amateur actors and realistic sets, films such as Roberto Rossellini's *Open City* (1945) depicted lower-class life with honesty and respect, and called for the creation of a better society from the rubble of the old.

■ **Henry Moore, *Tube Shelter Perspective* (1941)**
Inadequate public provision of air raid shelters forced working-class Londoners to take matters into their own hands. They began to use London subway stations for shelter during nighttime bombing raids. Impressed by the resilience and good humor of these ordinary people, Moore paid homage to their courage in a series of striking drawings.

Planning for Reconstruction

Rossellini's call for the creation of a new society was echoed throughout Europe during the war. Across Europe a consensus emerged on the need for social democracy, a society in which the state intervenes in economic life to ensure both public welfare and social justice. As early as December 1942, a government committee set out a radical plan for a new Britain. In rather unusual language for an official document, the committee's report identified "five giants on the road to reconstruction": Want, Disease, Ignorance, Squalor, and Idleness. To slay these giants, the committee recommended that the state assume responsibility for ensuring full employment and a minimum standard of living for all through the provision of family allowances, social welfare programs, and a national health service. The Beveridge Report (named after the committee's chairman) became a bestseller in Britain and the basis for a number of postwar European social welfare plans. Churchill, however, reacted lukewarmly to its proposals—a major reason for his defeat in the election of June 1945. The Labour Party, which enthusiastically endorsed the Beveridge Report and campaigned with slogans such as "Fair Shares for All," won by a landslide. Similarly, Charles De Gaulle, a political conservative, found that in order for his Free French Committee to be recognized as the provisional government of France, he had to display a commitment to democracy and radical social reform. Thus he espoused women's suffrage, and his government promised not only free medical services and expanded family allowances, but also the nationalization of key industries and economic planning.

Four factors explain this radical reorientation of European politics. First, and most important, as the war dragged on and the death tolls mounted, European men and women demanded that their suffering be worthwhile. They wanted to know that they were fighting not to rebuild the depressed and divided societies of the 1930s, but to construct a new Europe. Second, the war (and the ongoing revelations of Nazi atrocities) completely discredited the politics of the far right. This sort of politics, whether fascist, Nazi, or conservative-authoritarian, disappeared from legitimate political discussion. But in Europe (although not in the United States) the liberal ideal of the free and self-interested individual competing in an unregulated economy also lay in ruins, the victim of the prewar Great Depression. The new Europe, then, had to be built along different lines. The third factor that explains the radical reorientation of European politics was the combatant nations' success in mobilizing their economies for total war. If governments could regulate economies to fight wars, why could they not regulate economies for peacetime prosperity? Finally, the important role of socialists and communists in the Resistance enhanced the respectability of radical political ideas. Out of the Resistance came a determination to break the mold of prewar politics and create a new Europe. In France, for example, the Resistance Charter of 1944 demanded the construction of a "more just social order" through the nationalization of key industries, the establishment of a comprehensive social security system, and the recognition of the rights of workers to participate in management.

More generally, the Resistance raised key questions about the role of the individual in modern society. In the 1930s, many Europeans had been persuaded by Hitler, Mussolini, and other far-right theorists that the individual was not important, that only the state mattered. But what the Resistance revealed is the power of human choice and the need for individual action in a world run amuck. Despite—even because of—the horrors of the war, Europeans such as the French writer Albert Camus (1913–1960) emerged convinced of the power of human action: "A pessimist with respect to the human condition, I am an optimist with respect to man." Thus democracy reclaimed the activist state from fascism and Nazism on the one hand, and Stalinism on the other. Europeans saw that the power of the state could be used to improve the well-being of its citizens without at the same time trampling on the rights of the individual.

A Dubious Peace, 1945–1949

Reconstruction seemed far off in 1945, however. World War II ended, but the killing did not. In 1947, Winston Churchill asked, "What is Europe now?" and he answered in the bleakest terms: "A rubble-heap, a charnel house, a breeding ground of pestilence and hate."[13] Postwar purges and deportations ensured that the death totals continued to mount after 1945, and in many regions, particularly in eastern Europe and Southeast Asia, World War II gave way to civil and imperial wars. Most significantly, as the "hot" war waned, the Cold War between the Soviet Union and the United States began.

DEVASTATION, DEATH, AND CONTINUING WAR

If there was peace in Europe and Asia in 1945, it was the "peace of a graveyard," with an estimated 55 million people dead. These deaths were not distributed equally among combatant nations. The greatest losses occurred in the regions Hitler marked as the ground for his new racial empire. Estimates for Soviet deaths—both civilian and military—run up to 25 million.

In the immediate postwar period, the death statistics continued to rise as the victors turned with vengeful fury against the vanquished. In Czechoslovakia, purges killed 30,000 collaborators between 1945 and 1948. In Yugoslavia, Tito ordered the massacre of anticommunists. No one knows how many died: Some estimates range as high as 60,000.

For those left alive, the task of rebuilding was overwhelming. In the Soviet Union, 70 percent of the factories and 60 percent of the transportation facilities had been destroyed. In some German cities, almost every house was uninhabitable. Throughout Europe and Japan, the bombers had rendered most highways, rail tracks, and waterways unusable. With laborers, seed, fertilizer, and basic farming equipment all in short supply, agricultural production in 1945 stood below 50 percent of prewar levels. Less visible, but just as devastating, was the destruction of the financial system. Britain had become the world's largest debtor

nation. Few European currencies were worth much. In occupied Germany, cigarettes replaced marks as the unit of exchange.

One of the most serious problems facing Europe was that of the refugees or displaced persons (DPs). The war, and Hitler's attempt at racial reordering, had uprooted millions from their homes. The DP problem grew even larger as a result of the peace settlement. The Soviet Union kept the Polish territories it had claimed in 1939 and in recompense, Poland received a large chunk of what had been prewar Germany. The new Polish government then expelled the German inhabitants from this region. In Czechoslovakia, Romania, Yugoslavia, and Hungary, too, ethnic Germans were forced out of their homes and onto the road toward Germany. Over 11 million Germans suffered from this forced deportation. As many as two million, suffering from inadequate food, clothing, and shelter, died en route to Germany.

■ **Victors' Vengeance**
The bodies of Mussolini and his mistress hang in the Piazza Loreto in Milan. One year earlier, this piazza was the site of the shooting of Italian hostages by the German military.

Ethnic Germans were not the only ones to endure forced deportation as part of the postwar settlement. Between 1945 and 1948, seven million refugees from other ethnic groups were forcibly transferred, as eastern European governments found a brutal solution to the ethnic divisions that had destabilized prewar political structures. The deportations, together with the Nazis' slaughter of the Jewish population in these regions (see Chapter 27), transformed the ethnic map of Europe. Thus, Poland, whose prewar ethnic minorities composed 32 percent of its population, emerged with a postwar minority population of 3 percent.

Mass deportations also occurred in the Soviet Union. As the Red Army slowly pushed the Germans out of Soviet territory, many of the inhabitants of these regions found that liberation from German occupation did not mean freedom. Following the "liberation" of the Caucasus in the fall of 1943 and the spring of 1944, Stalin accused hundreds of thousands of men, women, and children of collaborating with the Germans. The accused were loaded onto freezing freight cars without adequate supplies of food, water, or warm clothing, and shipped eastward. Entire ethnic groups, such as the Chechens, were accused of collaboration and deported. An estimated 25 percent of these people died on the journey or in the first few years of barren existence in their new homes. Deportations continued after 1945. In the late 1940s and early 1950s, tens of thousands were shipped out of Ukraine, Byelorussia, Moldavia, Latvia, Lithuania, and Estonia.

These deportations can be understood as a continuation of war—a war carried out by governments against groups marked as dangerous because of their ethnic makeup. Other forms of war also continued after 1945. In the Baltic states, the "Forest Brothers" opposed the reimposition of Soviet rule over their homelands by waging guerilla warfare against the government. In Lithuania, partisan fighters posed such a military threat that more than 70,000 Soviet troops were deployed against them in 1948. Similarly, Ukrainian nationalists kept up a guerrilla war against the Soviets until the early 1950s. In many regions, World War II led directly to civil war as compatriots with clashing visions of the postwar future battled each other. In Greece civil war between communist and anticommunist forces raged until 1949, while in Trieste (along the Italian-Yugoslav border) civil war continued until 1954. In Poland, sporadic fighting between the new communist regime and anticommunist guerilla units based in the marshes and forests continued until 1956.

IMPERIAL ENCOUNTERS

World War II also sparked a series of bloody colonial encounters. In the Pacific region, many colonial nationalists had sided with the Japanese against the British, Dutch, and French, whom they regarded not as defenders of democracy but as imperial overlords. The Japanese internment of the Dutch population in Indonesia in 1942 allowed nationalists to assume positions in the country's government. In Burma, the student-based nationalist movement, led by Aung San (1915–1947), supported the Japanese invasion. Similarly, the Indian nationalist Subhas Chandra Bose (1897–1945) formed a National Army that fought alongside the Japanese and against the British. Of the 45,000 Indian troops captured by the Japanese in the conquests of Malaya and Singapore, 40,000 chose to join Bose's army.

When World War II ended, nationalist elites in colonial regions resisted Western efforts to reimpose imperial rule. They pointed to the inherent contradiction between the Allies' claim to be fighting for democracy and the fact that many Allied nations were imperialist states that denied democratic rule to the colonial regions they controlled. The result was a series of bloody colonial conflicts. In Indonesia, war raged from 1945 to 1949, when the Dutch finally abandoned their attempt to regain control of the region. In Indochina, the nationalist leader Ho Chi Minh (1890–1969) adopted the U.S. Declaration of Independence for his model when he proclaimed Indochinese independence from French colonial rule in September, 1945. A thirty-year war in Vietnam followed, first against the French and then against the Americans.

This era also witnessed a dramatic contraction of the British Empire. Throughout the war Churchill had placed a high priority on preserving the British Empire intact, but World War II had significantly weakened the British state, with its forces stretched to the breaking point. Clement Attlee (1883–1967), who succeeded Churchill as prime minister in July 1945, sought to retain Britain's hold on its essential imperial interests by jettisoning those that Britain no longer needed—or could no longer afford. In just two years—1947 and 1948—Britain relinquished control of India, Burma, and Palestine.

As in much of eastern and central Europe, ethnic and religious hatred devastated these regions in the late 1940s. The proclamation of the new state of Israel in 1948 coincided with the first in a series of Arab-Israeli wars, which left in its wake 500,000 Arab refugees. In India, the Muslim nationalists led by Muhammad Ali Jinnah (1876–1948) refused to accept citizenship in an independent state dominated by Hindus, and won from the British the creation of a separate Muslim state—Pakistan. The partition of the subcontinent led to mass slaughter. Sikhs, frustrated in their desires for an independent Sikh state, saw their Punjabi homeland divided between the two new nations and responded with violence, while Hindus and Muslims also clashed fiercely. More than ten million people fled their homes and became refugees—Muslims fearing Hindu rule, Hindus fearing Muslim rule, Sikhs fearing both. Mahatma Gandhi traveled from village to village in some of the most devastated areas and begged for an end to the killing, but the death tolls reached 250,000—and included Gandhi himself, who was shot by an assassin just six months after Indian independence was proclaimed.

FROM HOT TO COLD WAR

The conflict that aroused the most alarm and posed the greatest threat to the dubious peace after 1945 was the Cold War°, the struggle for global supremacy between the United States and the Soviet Union. Within just a few years of the defeat of Germany and Japan, the allies became enemies, and what Winston Churchill called an "Iron Curtain" dropped between eastern and western Europe. The divisions of the Cold War were rooted in World War II, nurtured by the fears and hopes it aroused.

Interests, Aims, and Armies

Stalin's principal concern in planning for the postwar period was to secure the Soviet Union's western border, to construct for his nation a cushion or buffer zone that could absorb the impact of any future invasion from the west, such as had occurred twice in Stalin's lifetime. The buffer zone Stalin demanded comprised the states of eastern Europe.

Stalin's demand that eastern Europe be regarded as a Soviet sphere of influence conflicted with his allies' public commitment to establish representative democratic political structures throughout Europe. Like Woodrow Wilson in World War I, U.S. president Franklin D. Roosevelt believed that the establishment of European democracies, committed to the liberal economic principles and practices, was crucial for American international security and economic prosperity. British prime minister Winston Churchill's major concerns were the postwar balance of power in Europe and the maintenance of the British Empire. He recognized that once Germany was defeated, a power vacuum would exist in central and eastern Europe and he feared that the Soviets might prove too eager to fill that vacuum. The possibility of Soviet expansion in the Balkans alarmed Churchill, who viewed a Soviet presence in the region as a threat to British military and economic interests in Greece and throughout the Mediterranean.

Fraying Seams, 1943–1945

The "Big Three°," then, came to the negotiating table with clashing interests and aims; even before the war ended, the fabric of the alliance was under strain. In face-to-face meetings—at Tehran in November 1943 and at Yalta in February 1945—disagreements on key questions were already fraying the seams of the alliance. These questions included German reparations and the political and territorial shape of postwar Poland.

Reluctant to place too much pressure on these fraying seams, Roosevelt opted for postponing the hard decisions.

He was not seeking simply to sidestep controversy. Rather, he hoped that the controversial questions would be settled after the war by a new international body, the United Nations (UN). In Roosevelt's vision, such a body could succeed where the now-discredited League of Nations had failed: It could guarantee that conciliation and negotiation would replace armed conflict in settling disputes between countries. Roosevelt recognized that if the Soviet Union refused to participate in the United Nations, the UN, like the league, would be a failure. Therefore he sought to avoid confrontations that might give Stalin a reason to block Soviet membership in the UN.

Roosevelt also hoped that new international economic structures would provide a framework for settling the disputes that divided the Allies. In 1944 leading American and European economists gathered in New Hampshire to construct a system for postwar economic revival. Well aware of the economic chaos that had followed World War I, and desperate to avoid a repeat of the Great Depression of the 1930s, they drew up the Bretton Woods Agreement°, which became the basic framework for the Western postwar economic order. To keep the global economy running smoothly, Bretton Woods established the American dollar as the world's reserve currency and fixed the currency exchange rates of its forty-four participating nations. It also established two new international economic institutions— the International Monetary Fund (IMF), to maintain the stability of member currencies, and the World Bank, to encourage global economic development.

Through the establishment of such international organizations as the IMF and the UN, Roosevelt sought "the end of the system of unilateral action, the exclusive alliances, the spheres of influence, the balances of power, and all the expedients that have been tried for centuries and have always failed." Yet neither Stalin nor Churchill shared Roosevelt's vision. Standing on opposite ends of the political spectrum, the Russian communist and the English aristocrat both continued to believe in precisely those "spheres of influence, the balances of power" that Roosevelt proclaimed outmoded. In the worldview of both Stalin and Churchill, armed force, not a new international organization, would determine the shape of the postwar world. As Stalin pointed out to Tito, the Yugoslav communist leader, "Everyone imposes his own system as far as his armies can reach. It cannot be otherwise."

By 1945, Stalin's army had a long reach. To prevent Soviet domination of eastern Europe, Churchill had earlier in the war pressed for an Anglo-American invasion of the Balkans. When the Big Three met in Tehran in 1943, however, they agreed that the Anglo-American invasion would be a single, concentrated attack across the English Channel into France (the D-Day invasion of June 1944). Although the decision led to a successful offensive and the defeat of Germany, it left the Balkans open to the Red Army. By the time the Big Three met in Yalta in the spring of 1945, the communist partisans under Tito controlled Yugoslavia, and the Soviet Army had occupied Romania, Bulgaria, Hungary, and much of Czechoslovakia. A conquering army possesses strongly persuasive powers. The Red Army's presence in eastern Europe ensured that American and British objections to Soviet actions remained confined to words only. No American or British policymaker—political or military—was prepared to advocate an armed confrontation with the Soviet Union in 1945.

At Yalta, then, the presence of the Red Army in eastern Europe weakened the negotiating positions of Churchill and Roosevelt. Roosevelt's desire to obtain Stalin's commitment to enter the war against Japan also reduced his bargaining power. The result was a series of problematic compromises. Stalin signed a declaration promising free elections in eastern Europe; at the same time, Roosevelt and Churchill agreed that such freely elected governments should be pro-Soviet.

The Yalta agreements also left undecided the future of Germany. With his country devastated by the ruinous German invasion and occupation, Stalin insisted that Germany be forced to pay reparations to the Soviet Union. Both Roosevelt and Churchill feared that a weak or partitioned German state would invite Soviet expansion into central Europe. The Big Three left open the question of German reparations but stipulated the division of Germany, and the symbolically and strategically vital city of Berlin, into occupation zones controlled by the United States, the Soviet Union, France, and Britain.

Ripping Apart, 1945–1946

In July 1945, when the Allied leaders met again in the German city of Potsdam, Stalin faced two unfamiliar negotiating partners. The new U.S. president Harry Truman (1884–1972) replaced Roosevelt, who had died in April, and midway through the summit, the new prime minister, Labour Party leader Clement Attlee, arrived to take Churchill's place. These leadership changes complicated the Big Three negotiations. Attlee lacked Churchill's prestige, and Stalin had far less rapport with Truman than he had enjoyed with Roosevelt. More important, during the conference Truman received a telegram informing him of the world's first successful atomic bomb test, a development

CHRONOLOGY

The Outbreak of the Cold War

1943	
November	Tehran Conference
1944	
August	Soviet Army advances into Balkans
October	Soviets link up with Tito's partisans in Yugoslavia
1945	
January	Soviet Army advances into Poland
February	Yalta Conference
July	Potsdam Conference
August	United States drops atomic bombs on Hiroshima and Nagasaki
1946	
March	Churchill gives his "Iron Curtain" speech in Missouri
1947	
February	Truman Doctrine announced
June	Marshall Plan announced
1948	Stalinist terror in eastern Europe underway
1949	
April	Formation of North Atlantic Treaty Organization (NATO)
May	Official formation of West Germany (Federal Republic of Germany)
August	Soviet atomic bomb test

that reduced Western incentives for placating Stalin. (See Chapter 27.)

But in July 1945 Cold War divisions were not yet solid. Throughout the rest of 1945 and 1946 Truman continued to hope to resolve the differences dividing the one-time allies and resisted the idea of a permanent American military presence in Europe. Stalin, too, was unwilling to push too far. He feared American military might, he hoped to retain access to western economic assistance and expertise, and he wanted to scale back military expenditures. Thus he proceeded with rapid demilitarization: Soviet army strength went from 12 million men in 1945 to 3 million by 1948. At the same time, Stalin adopted a policy of passivity for communist parties operating in regions that he viewed as part of the Western sphere of influence. He refused to assist

■ **The Big Three I (Yalta, February 1945)**
From 1941 until April 1945, the Big Three meant Stalin, Roosevelt, and Churchill. At the very end of
the war, however, the composition of the Big Three suddenly changed, as Harry Truman replaced
Roosevelt and Clement Attlee replaced Churchill.

Greek communists seeking to overthrow the British-backed monarchical regime, and he ordered communist parties in western Europe to participate with noncommunists in coalition governments.

During this period, however, the British pushed Truman to adopt a hard line toward Stalin and his demands. British foreign policy was in the hands of the foreign secretary, Ernest Bevin (1881–1951). A labor leader with a history of fighting against communist efforts to control British unions, Bevin was a fierce anti-Stalinist. He was also an ardent British nationalist who regarded the maintenance of the British Empire, particularly in the Mediterranean and the Middle East, as crucial to preserving Britain's Great Power status in the postwar world. Bevin thus urged the United States to stand tough when the Soviets demanded a stake in what had been Italy's North African empire and he urged a strong response when Stalin delayed pulling Russian troops out of Iran. (Soviet and British troops had occupied Iran during the war to keep its oil supplies out of German hands.)

The alliance finally fell apart not over the Mediterranean or the Middle East but over Germany. At Potsdam, Truman and Attlee had agreed to Stalin's demand for German reparations. By 1946, however, British and American authorities became convinced that Germany faced mass starvation. To feed the Germans in the British zone, Attlee's government had to impose bread rationing on the British public—a drastic step never taken during the war itself. The British and Americans decided that the immediate priority must be German economic recovery. They combined their zones into a single economic unit and stopped reparations deliveries to the Soviets. All pretense of a united Allied policy in Germany was dropped, making almost inevitable the eventual division of Germany into two hostile states. The French soon merged their occupation zone with that of the British and Americans, and in 1949 this territory became the Federal Republic of Germany (West Germany), while the Soviet-occupied zone became the German Democratic Republic (East Germany).

Torn in Two, 1947–1949

Within just a few years of the war's end, therefore, clashing aims and interests had shredded the wartime alliance. Because the Cold War was not a shooting war, it is difficult to pinpoint its precise start, but two key developments of 1947—the Truman Doctrine° and the Marshall Plan°—played crucial roles in transforming allies into enemies.

Like the division of Germany, the Truman Doctrine was linked to Britain's postwar economic crisis. In February 1947 Attlee's government informed Truman's administration that it could not afford to continue its fight against communist rebels in Greece. The United States immediately assumed Britain's role in the Mediterranean. Truman used this development to issue the Truman Doctrine, a broad policy statement committing the American government "to support free people who are resisting attempted subjugation by armed minorities or by outside pressures."[14] The Truman Doctrine inaugurated the policy of containment°—resisting communist expansion wherever in the world it occurred. After the declaration of the Truman Doctrine, the ideological division of Europe proceeded swiftly. Under strong pressure from American political and financial interests, the French and Italian governing coalitions expelled their communist members in May 1947.

The Marshall Plan furthered the division of Europe into two hostile camps. In June 1947, U.S. secretary of state General George Marshall (1880–1959) proposed that the United States underwrite Europe's economic recovery. Initially, Marshall's proposal received little attention in the United States, but in Britain, Foreign Secretary Ernest Bevin heard a report of it on the radio. Believing that British interests demanded a firm American commitment to Europe, Bevin perceived the Marshall Plan as the first step toward establishing this ongoing U.S. presence. He called the plan "a lifeline to sinking men." Bevin's French counterpart, Foreign Minister Georges Bidault (1899–1983), shared his enthusiasm, and together they helped make the Marshall Plan a reality. With representatives from twelve other European states, Bevin and Bidault drew up a list of European resources and requirements, and devised a four-year plan for European economic reconstruction. In 1948, the first food shipments from the United States reached European ports. Eventually $17 billion in aid poured into Europe. A new international body, the Organization for European Economic Cooperation (OEEC), worked to coordinate aid, eliminate trade barriers, and stabilize currencies. The formation of the OEEC was the first step in integrating western European economies, a process that eventually led to the establishment of the European Union (EU), as we will see in Chapters 28 and 29.

The Marshall Plan helped unify western Europe, but at the same time it accelerated the division of East and West. Stalin saw the Marshall Plan as an effort to undercut Soviet influence in Europe, and he was right. Marshall's intentions were explicitly anticommunist. A tour of Europe's still-devastated regions in the spring of 1947 had convinced Marshall that if the United States did not jump-start Europe's economies, its peoples would turn readily to communism. Marshall Plan aid was available to any country that chose to accept it, including the Soviet Union and the nations of eastern Europe. Participating states, however, were required to join in the OEEC—a requirement the Soviets would not accept. Stalin had already refused to participate in the Bretton Woods system, which he saw as an instrument of American economic domination.

In April 1949 nine western European nations[18] joined together with the United States and Canada in the North Atlantic Treaty Organization (NATO)°, a military alliance specifically aimed at repelling a Soviet invasion of western Europe. Months later, on August 29, 1949, the Soviet Union conducted a successful test explosion of an atomic bomb. Over the next few years, Stalin forced his eastern European satellites into an anti-Western military alliance, finalized as the Warsaw Pact° in 1955. Europe was divided into hostile military blocs, each possessing an atomic arsenal.

Terror in Eastern Europe

The onset of the Cold War accelerated a Stalinist campaign of terror already underway in eastern Europe. Stalin launched the terror in the Soviet satellite states in direct response to developments in Yugoslavia. Led by Tito, Yugoslav communists resisted Stalin's efforts to dictate their foreign and domestic policies. This quarrel became a permanent break in 1948, when Stalin lost all control over Yugoslavia. Alarmed, Stalin sought to eliminate any potential Tito imitators from the rest of eastern Europe. The Cold War provided Stalin with additional weaponry in this battle against any possible threat to his personal power. Stalin insisted that a Western conspiracy to divide and conquer the Soviet bloc could be defeated only by a thoroughgoing purge of the communist ranks.

Over the next five years, Stalin prodded eastern European governments to institute a campaign of terror in their countries. Arrested, charged with sabotage and espionage for the West, and savagely tortured, prominent communists were convicted in public show trials at which they recited the confessions that had been prepared for them. The terror quickly spread beyond the ranks of prominent communists. Factory supervisors were assigned quotas; they knew if they did not come up with a required number of names of "criminals," they would be imprisoned. In Budapest, frightened citizens watched the police vans that slid through the street every Monday, Wednesday, and Friday night at 2 A.M., picking up the next allotment of victims. The security forces targeted anyone remotely connected to "the West," including veterans of the Spanish Civil War and members of international organizations such as the Boy Scouts. Jews, considered "cosmopolitan" and therefore potentially pro-Western, were particularly suspect. For eastern Europeans, World War II had ended, but the peace never really began.

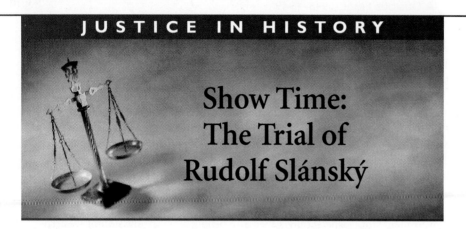

Show Time: The Trial of Rudolf Slánský

On the night of July 31, 1951, Rudolf Slánský–general secretary of the Communist Party of Czechoslovakia (CPC) and the second most powerful man in Prague—left his 50th birthday party, and headed home, a frightened man. Outwardly, nothing was wrong. The CPC had celebrated the day in style. The communist president, Klement Gottwald, presented to Slánský the medal of the Order of Socialism, the highest honor awarded in Czechoslovakia. Telegrams of congratulations poured in from all over the country. But the huge stack of congratulatory telegrams contained no greeting from Stalin. Slánský knew he was in trouble.

At another place and in another time, Slánský's fear could be dismissed as mere paranoia. But in the upper ranks of the Communist Party in Czechoslovakia in 1951, signs of Stalin's approval or disapproval were literally a matter of life or death. The Stalinist purge of eastern Europe was well underway, with thousands arrested, tortured, imprisoned, or killed.

Slánský knew he was vulnerable on three counts. First, he held a rank high enough to ensure a spectacular show trial. As the Soviet Great Purge of the 1930s had demonstrated, trials and executions of leading communists worked both to terrorize Stalin's potential rivals and, by rousing ordinary citizens to perpetual vigilance, to cement mass loyalty to the regime. But for a trial to be a genuine show, the defendant had to be worth showing.

Slánský, as the CPC general secretary, was the perfect defendant.

Slánský was a target for Stalin's purge, second, because he was a Czech, and Stalin viewed his Czech colleagues with particular suspicion. Czechoslovakia was the only state in eastern Europe with a history of successful democracy and without Soviet troops in occupation after 1945. Moreover, the CPC had participated with noncommunists in a coalition government longer than any other eastern European communist party.

Such differences linked the CPC to the ideology of "national communism," which taught that the Soviet path to communism was not the only one, that each nation must find its own route. "National communism" became a heresy in Stalin's eyes after his break with the Yugoslav communist leader Tito in 1948. Tito had dared to lead Yugoslavia down a different path, and had dared to defy Stalin's leadership. Determined to prevent any additional defections from his eastern European empire, Stalin embarked on a quest for real or potential "titoists". To save his own skin, CPC leader Klement Gottwald needed to demonstrate his willingness to uproot titoism from his party and his government. Slánský became that demonstration.

Finally, Slánský was vulnerable because he was a Jew. When the purges in eastern Europe began in 1948, anti-Semitism played no prominent role, but by 1950 the intersection of Middle Eastern power plays, Cold War hostilities, Stalin's paranoia, and the still-

powerful tradition of Jew-hating in eastern European culture made Jewish communists particularly suspect. Aiming to establish a Soviet presence in the Middle East after the war, Stalin had tried to persuade the new state of Israel to align with the Soviet Union by offering the new Israeli government diplomatic recognition and arms deals. But Stalin's efforts failed. By 1950, Israel had become an ally of the United States. Stalin responded with fury. All Jews came under suspicion of "Zionist" (that is, pro-Israel and therefore pro-Western) tendencies.

Stalin's failure to send Slánský a birthday telegram signaled that Slánský was now on the list of suspects. Over the following months Soviet advisors and homegrown Czech torturers pressured prisoners already caught in the net of the purge to confess that they were part of a Slánský-led conspiracy to overthrow the communist government and to turn Czechoslovakia against the Soviet Union. These torture-induced confessions were then used to prepare a flimsy case against Slánský and thirteen other men (eleven of them Jews).

Shortly before midnight on November 24, 1951, security agents arrested Slánský at his home. A lifelong atheist, Slánský could say nothing except "Jesus Maria." He knew what was coming. Instrumental in initiating the Stalinist purge in Czechoslovakia, Slánský had approved the arrests and torture of many of his colleagues. Ironically, he had drafted the telegram asking Stalin to send Soviet advisors to ahead of abstractions such as "truth." Slánský may have believed that his confession, false though it was, served the party. As one experienced interrogator noted about a different defendant, "He'll confess; he's got a good attitude toward the party."[16] In addition, Slánský may have been promised, as were other show trial defendants, that his life would be spared and his family protected if he confessed.

In his closing statement, Slánský said, "I deserve no other end to my criminal life than that proposed by the state prosecutor."[17] The prosecutor demanded the death penalty. Slánský was executed on December 3, 1952. Ten of his co-accused also hanged. Their families were stripped of their party memberships and privileges, deported with only the barest essentials to designated districts, and assigned to manual labor. ■

assist in the Czech purge—the very same advisors who decided to target Slánský.

For the next year, Slánský endured mental and physical torture, directed by these advisors. Common torture tactics included beatings and kickings; prolonged periods without sleep, food or water; all-night interrogation sessions; and being forced to stand in one place or march in circles for days on end. One interrogator recalled, "Instead of getting evidence, we were told that they were villains and that we had to break them."[15] Breaking Slánský took six months; the remaining months were spent defining and refining the details of his imaginary crimes against the communist regime, and rehearsing for the all-important show trial.

Slánský's trial, which began on November 20, 1952, was in every sense a show. Before the trial began, party officials had already determined the verdict and the sentences. Prosecutors, defense attorneys, judges, and the accused spoke the lines of a script written by security agents. Thus, one year after his arrest, Slánský stood up in court and pled guilty to the crimes of high treason, espionage, and sabotage. A founding member of the CPC, he said he had conspired to overthrow the communist government. A resistance fighter during World War II, he confessed to working with the Nazis against the communists. A zealous Stalinist, he announced that he was a titoist-Zionist, who had plotted to hand Czechoslovakia to the Americans.

Why did Slánský make such a ludicrous confession? Fear of further torture is clearly one motive, but other factors also came into play. Communists such as Slánský believed that the interests of the party always came first, ahead of individual rights,

Questions of Justice

What sort of justice was served in the trial of Rudolf Slánský?

Taking It Further

Lukes, Igor. "The Rudolf Slánský Affair: New Evidence." *Slavic Review* 58, 1 (Spring 1999): 160–187. Illuminating study of the role of Cold War intrigue in determining Slánský's fate.

Kaplan, Karel. *Report on the Murder of the General Secretary.* 1990. Kaplan emigrated from Czechoslovakia to West Germany in the late 1970s, with a stack of hidden documents, and wrote this report.

CURTAINS AND CAMPS

The Cold War gave rise to a new set of metaphors, as politicians, diplomats, and journalists struggled to find ways to explain the new world order. Two of the most compelling metaphors arose very early: the "Iron Curtain," coined by Winston Churchill in 1946, and "the two camps," used in a speech by Stalin's spokesman Andrei Zhdanov in 1947.

In 1946, Churchill was still the leader of Britain's Conservative Party, but was no longer prime minister. On a visit to the United States, he gave a pivotal speech that warned of a divided Europe.

From Stettin in the Baltic to Trieste in the Adriatic, an iron curtain has descended across the Continent. Behind that line lie all the capitals of the ancient states of Central and Eastern Europe. Warsaw, Berlin, Prague, Vienna, Budapest, Belgrade, Bucharest and Sofia, all these famous cities and the populations around them lie in what I must call the Soviet sphere, and all are subject in one form or another, not only to Soviet influence but to a very high and, in many cases, increasing measure of control from Moscow. . . .

At the founding meeting of the Cominform in September 1947, Zhdanov delivered a speech that clearly articulated the postwar division of the world into two hostile blocs.

In the post-war period sharp changes have taken place in the international situation . . . Two opposite political lines took shape: at one pole, the policy of the USSR and the democratic countries, aimed at undermining imperialism and strengthening democracy; at the other pole the policy of the USA and Britain, aimed at strengthening imperialism and strangling democracy. . . .

Thus two camps have come into being . . .

The Truman-Marshall Plan is only one component part . . . of a general plan of worldwide expansionist policy that is being carried out by the USA in all parts of the world . . . Yesterday's aggressors, the capitalist magnates of Germany and Japan, are being groomed by America for a new role, that of serving as an instrument of the USA's imperialist policy in Europe and Asia. . . . Under these conditions it is essential for the anti-imperialist and democratic camp to close ranks, work out a common programme of actions and develop its own tactics against the main forces of the imperialist camp. . . .

Sources: From a speech by Winston Churchill, delivered to Westminster College, Fulton, Missouri, March 5, 1946.; and from G. Procacci (ed.), *The Cominform: Minutes of the Three Conferences 1947, 1948, 1949*, Milan, 1994.

CONCLUSION

The New Europe, The New West

Adolf Hitler had promised his allies and his enemies that he would create a new Europe. And so he did. As Europeans emerged from their bomb shelters, returned home from their army units, or searched desperately for family members among the DP camps, they faced an uncertain future in a radically changed world. World War II and the Cold War that succeeded it created a new European—and a new global—order, but one dramatically different from that envisioned by Hitler.

World War II also reshaped the dominant idea of the "West." Hitler offered a set of ideas that promised a dramatic reconfiguration of Western values along racist, authoritarian lines. In the Nazi vision, the West comprised white, northern Europeans, marching in step to the dictates of the antidemocratic state. The wartime encounter with this vision was crucial; from it emerged a sharpened commitment within the West to the processes and values of democracy.

But to present the Second World War as a conflict between democracy and Nazism is to oversimplify. To defeat Nazi Germany, the democracies of Britain and the United States allied with Stalin's Soviet Union, a dictatorial regime that matched Hitler's Germany in its contempt for democratic values and human rights and surpassed it in state-sanctioned mass murder. The Soviet Union emerged from the war as the dominant power in eastern Europe; the presence of the Red Army obliterated any chance to establish democratic governments in this region.

The tensions inherent in the Anglo-American alliance with the Soviets led directly to the Cold War, the ideological and political conflict that dominated the post–World War II world and that once again forced a redefinition of the West. From 1949 until 1989, it was easy to draw the West on any map: One simply shaded in the United States and those countries allied to it. But at the same time a new division emerged. World War II marked the beginning of the end of European imperial control over the non-European world. As a result, the postwar era would see growing tensions between "North" and "South"—between the industrially developed nations and the underdeveloped regions seeking to shrug off their colonial past.

Much of the impetus for imperial control over non-European regions came from the conviction of European supremacy. During the war, however, Japanese victories had exposed the illusion of European military invincibility. And after the war, the gradual realization of the full horror of what became known as the Holocaust—Hitler's war against the Jews—demolished any lingering claim to European cultural superiority. Few could doubt the technological preeminence of the nation that emerged as "Leader of the Western World" (the United States), but in the aftermath of the atomic bombings of Japanese cities, disturbing questions surfaced about the implications and consequences of such technologies in a democratic society. These two key developments of the war, the Holocaust and Hiroshima, are the subject of the next chapter.

Suggestions for Further Reading

For a comprehensive list of suggested readings, please go to www.ablongman.com/levack/chapter26

Calder, Angus. *The People's War: Britain, 1939–1945.* 1969. Lengthy but worth the effort for students wishing to explore the war's impact on British society. (Those who want a shorter account can turn to Robert Mackay, *The Test of War: Inside Britain 1939–45* [1999].)

Gross, Jan T., ed. *The Politics of Retribution in Europe: World War II and Its Aftermath.* 2000. This series of essays makes clear that war did not end in Europe in May 1945.

Iriye, Akira. *The Origins of the Second World War in Asia and the Pacific.* 1987. Part of Longman's Origins of Modern Wars series aimed at university students, this short and readable study highlights the major issues and events.

Keegan, John. *The Second World War.* 1989. Provides clear explanations of military technologies and techniques; packed with useful maps and vivid illustrations.

Kitchen, Martin. *Nazi Germany at War.* 1995. A short and nicely organized survey of the German home front.

Milward, A. S. *War, Economy, and Society, 1939–1945.* 1977. A solid survey by a leading economic historian.

Moore, Bob, ed. *Resistance in Western Europe.* 2000. A collection of essays that explores recent research on this controversial topic.

Overy, Richard. *Russia's War: A History of the Soviet War Effort, 1941–1945.* 1997. A compelling account, written to accompany the television documentary *Russia's War.*

Paxton, Robert. *Vichy France: Old Guard and New Order, 1940–1944.* 1972. A now-classic study of the aims and evolution of France's collaborationist government.

Rock, William R. *British Appeasement in the 1930s.* 1977. A balanced and concise appraisal.

de Senarclens, P. *From Yalta to the Iron Curtain: The Great Powers and the Origins of the Cold War.* 1995. A look at the diplomatic, political and military concerns that created the Cold War.

Weinberg, Gerhard. *A World at Arms: A Global History of World War II.* 1994. Places the war within a global rather than simply a European context.

Wyman, Mark. *DPs: Europe's Displaced Persons, 1945–1951.* 1989. An important study of an often-neglected topic.

Notes

1. Quoted in Piers Brendon, *The Dark Valley: A Panorama of the 1930s* (2000), p. 282.
2. Quoted in Richard Overy, *Russia's War* (1998), p. 95.
3. Quoted in Mark Mazower, *Dark Continent: Europe's Twentieth Century* (1999), p. 157.
4. Quoted in Joachim Fest, *Hitler* (1973), p. 665.
5. Quotations from Juliet Gardiner, *"Over Here"—The GIs in Wartime Britain* (1992), p. 62, 53, 132.
6. Quoted in Jane Slaughter, *Women in the Italian Resistance 1943–1945* (1997), p. 63.
7. Quoted in Bob Moore, ed., *Resistance in Western Europe* (2000), p. 210.
8. Quoted in Richard Rhodes, *The Making of the Atomic Bomb* (1988), p. 474.
9. Quoted in Ulrich Herbert, *Hitler's Foreign Workers* (1997), p. 139.
10. Quoted in Herbert, p. 306.
11. Quotations from Herbert, pp. 149, 189.
12. Quoted in Herbert, p. 149.
13. Quoted in Derek Urwin, *A Political History of Western Europe Since 1945* (1997), p. 320.
14. Quoted in Robert Paxton, *Europe in the Twentieth Century* (1997), p. 512.
15. Quoted in Karel Kaplan, *Report on the Murder of the General Secretary* (1990), p. 159.
16. Quoted in Kaplan, p. 242.
17. Quoted in Kaplan, p. 231.
18. The original signatories of the NATO treaty were Iceland, Norway, Great Britain, Belgium, the Netherlands, Luxembourg, France, Italy, and Portugal. Greece and Turkey joined the alliance in 1951, West Germany in 1954, Spain in 1982. Sweden, Finland, Switzerland, Austria, Yugoslavia, and Albania remained nonaligned with either the United States or the Soviet Union.

The Holocaust, the Bomb, and the Legacy of Mass Killing

I N THE WEEKS IMMEDIATELY PRECEDING AND FOLLOWING THE END OF THE SECOND World War in Europe, many Allied soldiers faced their most difficult assignment yet. Hardened combat veterans, accustomed to scenes of slaughter and destruction, broke down and wept as they encountered a landscape of horror beyond their wildest nightmares: the world of the Nazi concentration and death camps. As one American war correspondent put it, "we had penetrated at last to the center of the black heart, to the very crawling inside of the vicious heart."[1] The American soldiers who opened the gates of the camp in Mauthausen, Austria, never forgot their first sight of the prisoners there: "By the thousands they came streaming . . . Hollow, pallid ghosts from graves and tombs, terrifying, rot-colored figures of misery marked by disease, deeply ingrained filth, inner decay. . . . squat skeletons in rags and crazy grins."[2]

Similarly, the British troops who liberated Bergen-Belsen in Germany were marked indelibly by what they encountered within the camp's walls. By the end of 1944, Bergen-Belsen had become the dumping ground for tens of thousands of prisoners evacuated from camps in eastern Europe, as the Nazi SS desperately retreated in front of the advancing Soviet army. Already sick and starving, these prisoners were jammed, 1,200 at a time, into barracks built to accommodate a few hundred. By March 1945, both drinking water and food had disappeared, human excrement dripped from bunk beds until it coated the floors of the barracks, and dead bodies piled up everywhere. In these conditions, the only living beings to flourish were the microorganisms that cause typhus. When the British entered Bergen-Belsen, they found 60,000 emaciated and diseased prisoners, half of them Jews. Floundering in this sea of human want, British soldiers, doctors, and nurses did what they could; even so, 28,000 of Bergen-Belsen's inmates died in the weeks following liberation. The photographs of the mass graves taken by the Allies when they opened the camps produced an enduring image of mass

Chapter Outline

- Toward the Final Solution: From Emigration to Extermination

- Responding to the Holocaust

- The Race for the Atom Bomb

- The Dawn of the Nuclear Age

The Crematoria at Buchenwald: The Nazis used industrial technologies, such as industrial-scale bake ovens, to commit mass murder. At Buchenwald, one of the many camps within the Nazi system of concentration and death camps, victims' bodies were cremated..

■ **Mass Grave at Bergen-Belsen**
This concentration camp was liberated by British soldiers on April 15, 1945.

killing, one that has become emblematic of what is now called the Holocaust°, the murder of approximately six million European Jews, and three to five million other victims, including Polish and Russian Christians, Jehovah's Witnesses, Roma (Gypsies), homosexuals, and political opponents of the Nazi regime.

A few months later, another compelling photographic image stunned the world: the mushroom cloud. In August 1945, U.S. planes dropped two atomic bombs on the Japanese cities of Hiroshima and Nagasaki. Tens of thousands died within seconds, and the mushroom cloud immediately became seared on Western consciousness. Yet the image of the billowing cloud, monstrous and beautiful, focused not on mass death but rather on the power and mystery of the new atomic age. Soon, however, other images entered Western consciousness: staggering figures, barely recognizable as human, with their melted eyeballs dripping from their sockets and their flesh peeling off in sheets, the stumbling and blinded survivors of the atomic bombs. As Europeans and Americans encountered the awesome destructive power of first-rate physics allied to military might, they were forced to confront the possibility of mass killing on an unprecedented, even incomprehensible, scale. With the development of the hydrogen bomb in the early 1950s, governments possessed the ability to destroy not just single cities, but entire civilizations and perhaps the world itself.

How can we understand the events that led to both the Holocaust and Hiroshima? Hitler's war against the Jews and the atomic bombings in Japan were not equivalent acts.

Both, however, ensured the centrality of *mass killing* in any discussion of the experience or meaning of the twentieth century. The assembly-line techniques of mass murder developed by the Nazis and, in very different ways, the sheer efficiency of the atom bomb in obliterating urban populations forced both individuals and their political leaders to confront the destructive potential of modern technologies and techniques. Both also challenged key assumptions about the identity of the "West" and so demanded the creation of new frameworks—cultural, political, and international—in the postwar world. In their use of Western science and technology to achieve fundamentally irrational and evil ends, the Nazi death camps upset settled assumptions about both the benevolent role of science in society and the supposed moral superiority of Western civilization. In very different ways, the Bomb, too, caused widespread questioning about basic Western ideals and values. Originating in the desire to save the West from Nazi domination, its use against Japan continues to provoke heated controversy about Western motivations and to raise important questions about the implications of advanced technology for democratic decision making.

To explain how these two events helped shape Western identity and consciousness since World War II, this chapter will address four questions: (1) How and why did the Nazis devise a plan aimed at killing every Jew in Europe? (2) How did Europeans and Americans respond to the Nazi effort to annihilate the Jews—both at the time, and in the decades since the death camps were revealed to the world? (3) What were the factors that led to the Allies' decision to drop atomic bombs on Japanese cities? (4) What were the consequences of this decision?

Toward the Final Solution: From Emigration to Extermination

························ ■ ························

Central to an examination of the Holocaust is the question of *origins:* When and why was the plan for the annihilation of Europe's Jewish population first conceived? The question is not as simple as it may first appear. Anti-Semitism was a central component of both Adolf Hitler's worldview and Nazi ideology, yet anti-Semitism alone cannot explain the Holocaust, nor was the Holocaust the product of a detailed plan carefully plotted out by Hitler long before he came to power. The decision to murder the Jews evolved over time. More specifically, the Holocaust originated as a response to, and by-product of, total war.

ANTI-SEMITISM: THE NECESSARY PRECONDITION

Anti-Semitism alone cannot explain the Holocaust, but it was its necessary precondition. As Chapter 22 explained, modern anti-Semitism emerged in the nineteenth century. The lifting of discriminatory laws in this period benefited Jews, many of whom moved into the mainstream of European economic, political, and intellectual life, particularly in areas such as Austria and Germany. At the same time, however, the spread of industrialization created an unstable economic and social climate. Those people who viewed themselves as victims in the new modern world—the small shopkeeper put out of business by the large department store, the skilled artisan replaced by new technology, the farmer who watched agricultural prices plummet in the new global marketplace—looked for someone to blame for their woes.

They did not have far to look. European Christians had long blamed Jews for evils of all kinds. Christian doctrine identified the Jews as responsible for the crucifixion of Jesus, while during the Middle Ages Jews were widely believed to have caused the bubonic plague. In the less industrialized regions of Europe, such as outlying portions of the Russian and Austrian-Hungarian Empires, religious anti-Semitism remained powerful until well into the twentieth century. In the more urban and industrial regions, however, this traditional, religion-based hatred of Jews loosened its grip on European culture. Instead, the rise of quasi-scientific theories of racial difference ensured that in a more secular society, Jews were regarded with suspicion not only because of their religion but more so because of their race, a supposed biological fact that could not be altered or escaped.

The rise of racist pseudoscience interacted with the spread of both socialist and mass nationalistic politics to produce a virulently anti-Semitic atmosphere throughout much of Europe by the beginning of the twentieth century. The fact that many Jewish intellectuals had embraced Karl Marx's critique of capitalist society and that a number of leading socialist politicians were Jewish led some desperate Europeans to lump together Jewishness and socialism as partners in a plot to destroy European stability. At the same time, nationalism became a potent force in European politics. Increasingly, ethnic and national identity were seen as inseparable: Germans should have a Germany, Serbs a Serbia, Bulgarians a Bulgaria, and so on. But in this world of competing ethnic nationalisms, where did Jews belong? If national identity depended on ethnicity, then, ominously, the answer was: Not here.

Already firmly established by 1914, modern anti-Semitism flourished in the chaos of post–World War I Europe. The Bolshevik victory in the newly established Soviet Union sparked widespread fear that socialist or communist revolutions would spread across Europe. To desperate, hate-filled men like Adolf Hitler, "the Jew" and "the communist" were indistinguishable. More generally, the existence of large ethnic minorities in the new nation-states established after the war ensured that ethnic tensions continued to rage in central and eastern Europe, with Jews frequently spotlighted as outsiders and potential threats. In addition, the onset of worldwide economic depression in 1929 intensified the quest for scapegoats. Jews, who played a prominent role in European banking industries, were easy targets.

Modern or racial anti-Semitism had thus infected much of European society in the years before Hitler took power in Germany. It was particularly virulent in central and eastern Europe, where traditional peasant societies continued to exist and where ethnic nationalism proved especially potent. Once the Holocaust was underway, Hitler would find ready allies for his war against the Jews among these populations. But the existence of anti-Semitism does not explain the origins or the course of the Holocaust. In order to understand what actually happened, we need to place the Holocaust within the context of both Hitler's racial state and World War II.

INTENSIFIED PERSECUTION OF THE JEWS IN GERMANY, 1938–1939

Hitler talked of exterminating European Jews in his writings and speeches, but he had no specific plan for killing all European Jews when he came to power in 1933. He did clearly identify Jews as a threat to German revival, and he instituted practices designed to drive Jews out of Germany. We saw in Chapter 25 that as soon as the Nazis assumed power, they began to implement a series of laws and policies aimed at constructing what they viewed as a "racially pure" German state. Not only Jews but also the Roma (Gypsies) and the handicapped were singled out for persecution on the grounds that they posed a threat to the health of the supposed German race. By 1938, these policies had driven about 25 percent of Germany's Jews elsewhere; more than 350,000 Jewish German citizens, however, remained.

That year marked an intensification of Nazi persecution of German Jews. With the economic recovery of Germany well underway, the Nazis were less dependent on foreign trade and less vulnerable to the threat of foreign sanctions. And, as we saw in Chapter 26, Nazi Germany achieved two remarkable foreign policy victories in 1938—the Anschluss with Austria in March and the seizure of the Sudetenland from Czechoslovakia in September. The willingness of Western nations to yield on these issues helped persuade Hitler that he could pursue his anti-Semitic programs more aggressively. In 1938 Jews were excluded from all commercial activity and forced to register all property holdings. Jewish firms either were forced to shut down or were taken over by the state or by "Aryan"-owned firms.

On the night of November 9, 1938, anti-Jewish violence in Germany reached new heights. The assassination of a German official in the Paris embassy by a 17-year-old Jewish student provided the pretext for Nazi-encouraged anti-Jewish rioting across Germany. Over 300 synagogues were burned. Although Jews were the victims of the rioting, looting, and vandalism, over 35,000 Jews were sent to concentration camps, and the Nazi government levied a fine of one billion marks against the Jewish community. Because so many windows and store fronts were destroyed in the frenzy of violence—the value of broken glass alone was put at 24 million marks—the episode became known as Kristallnacht°: the Night of the Broken Glass. But more than glass shattered that night. One hundred German Jews were murdered. In the subsequent weeks, one thousand of the Jews sent to the prison camps died.

Faced with the increasing tempo of Nazi persecution, another 150,000 German Jews fled the Reich after Kristallnacht. Yet by September 1939, not only had emigration failed to remove all Jews from Germany, but the numbers of Jews under German control had actually risen. The unification of Germany and Austria in 1938, followed by the seizure first of the Sudetenland and then all Czechoslovakia, meant 300,000 more Jews in the expanded Germany.

These numbers skyrocketed with the outbreak of war. The invasion of Poland brought almost two million more Jews under German control. Pushing Jews to emigrate no longer seemed a workable solution to what the Nazis defined as the "Jewish Problem." As a result, a new sense of urgency characterized the Nazis' effort to find a way to clear Jews out of German-occupied territories. But even more

important, the fact of war itself made a radicalization of policy and a turn toward murderous violence much more acceptable.

THE GERMAN DRIVE EASTWARD AND THE RADICALIZATION OF THE "FINAL SOLUTION"

The rapid German conquest of Poland in September 1939 not only initiated World War II, as Chapter 26 detailed, but also inaugurated the Nazis' war against the Jews. The German occupation of Poland marked the first step toward the Nazi construction of a new racial order in Europe. In the Nazi vision, Germany was destined to expand its holdings eastward—space for the superior race. The Slavic populations of eastern Europe, defined in Hitler's racist hierarchy as biologically inferior, were to serve as a vast labor

CHRONOLOGY

The Holocaust

1939

September	World War II begins; racial reordering of Poland underway

1941

June 22	German invasion of Soviet Union, Einsatzgruppen actions underway
October	Himmler orders halt to all Jewish emigration
December	Chelmno death camp begins operation

1942

January 20	Wannsee Conference

1943

February	German surrender at Stalingrad; Soviet army on the offensive
April	Warsaw Ghetto uprising

1944

June 6	D-Day; British, French, and American armies on the offensive
November	Forced marches from death camps to Germany underway

1945

January	Auschwitz liberated by Soviet army
April	Hitler's suicide; Soviet army enters Berlin; British army liberates Bergen-Belsen

pool. Jews were to be "eliminated" from the region. At this point, however, "elimination" did not yet mean total extermination but instead referred to vaguely articulated plans for mass deportations.

As a first step to begin building this new racial world order, the Nazi government divided defeated Poland in two. Germany directly annexed the northern and western regions of Poland and moved in German settlers to join ethnic Germans already living in these areas, displacing huge numbers of Poles from their homes and lands. The rest of German-occupied Poland formed the "General Government," a region envisaged as a huge work camp, home to an army of Polish slave labor that would help create the economic foundations of a vast German empire.

In the General Government, the Nazis embarked on a wholesale destruction of Polish society and culture. Universities and high schools were closed; businesses, farms, and bank accounts were seized; Polish place names were replaced with German. SS squads toured the countryside, searching for so-called "Aryan"-looking babies and children. Tens of thousands of blonde, blue-eyed Polish youngsters were kidnapped and sent to Germany, where they underwent a series of pseudoscientific tests to judge their "racial type." If they passed, they were given German names, forced to speak German, and given for adoption to SS-approved German couples. Mass murder accompanied mass kidnapping. To reduce the Polish people to slaves, the Nazis murdered Polish intellectuals and professionals, whose very existence contradicted Hitler's insistence that Poles were biologically suited only for manual labor.

Within the context of this larger plan of racial reordering, Nazi policy toward the Jews initially focused on "ghettoization." Polish Jews were forcibly expelled from their homes and confined in ghettos that were sealed off from the non-Jewish population. They were soon joined by Jews deported from Germany and Austria. Packed into overcrowded apartments, with inadequate food rations and appalling sanitary conditions, Jews lived in a nightmare of disease, starvation, and death. In Warsaw, for example, the Jewish ghetto comprised only 100 square blocks surrounded by a nine-foot wall. In this small area were crammed 400,000 people, living in rooms that contained on average six to nine individuals. The daily ration was 336 calories—far below starvation levels.

In the period between the invasion of Poland on September 1, 1939, and the invasion of the Soviet Union on June 22, 1941, an estimated 30,000 Jews were either directly murdered or died of starvation and disease as a result of Nazi policies. Yet the suffering had only begun.

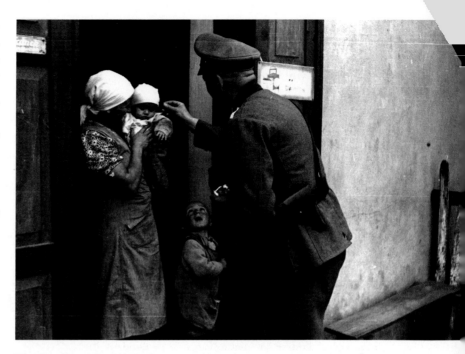

■ **The New Racial Order**

A Nazi soldier assesses the racial characteristics of two young Polish children; their proud mother seems unaware that if her children are judged "Aryan" enough, they will be taken from her and given to a German family.

Some time in the spring or summer of 1941, the Nazis' definition of what they termed the Final Solution° to the "Jewish problem" shifted from emigration and expulsion to extermination. Historians disagree on the exact timing, but it is clear that the Nazi invasion of the Soviet Union provided the catalyst for the shift. Hitler may have already decided on genocide in the months of planning leading up to the June invasion. Alternatively, the decision to murder all the Jews in Europe may not have been taken until after the invasion was underway. It is clear that by the summer of 1941 SS squads were shooting thousands of Jews at a time. In October SS leader Heinrich Himmler (1900–1945) ordered that no Jew be allowed to emigrate from German-controlled territory. The doors of German-occupied Europe slammed shut; genocide was now the official German policy.

In planning for war with the Soviets, Hitler had determined that this would be no conventional military conflict between nation-states. Instead, it would be a battle of races and ideologies. From the early 1920s, Hitler had insisted that two key obstacles blocked the road to a revived German empire—communism and the Jewish people. Hence, war against the Soviet Union, the world's first communist state and home to millions of Jews, was no ordinary war. In Hitler's feverish and hate-filled imagination, Jews were the chief "carriers" of the communist or Bolshevik "virus." He thus perceived the war against the Soviet Union as a struggle to the death against "Judeo-Bolshevism," a powerful enemy that threatened to undermine not only Germany's military and economic strength but even its cultural identity. In such a war, the only rule would be that of absolute destruction. Only the most ferocious would survive.

THE WAR AGAINST THE JEWS

On June 22, 1941, the Nazi army invaded the Soviet Union. Marching with the forces of the regular army were special mobile units of the SS called Einsatzgruppen° ("strike forces"). With the army providing logistical support, these small motorized units (about 3,000 men in all) took on the task of liquidating the enemies of the Nazi Reich—which meant killing not only communist leaders and activists but also, and especially, Jews. Such a task was immense: Over five million Jews lived in the Soviet Union in 1941, and about four million of these lived in the territories invaded by the Germans.

In their war against the Jews, the Einsatzgruppen found ready allies among large sectors of the occupied population. The earliest stages of the German invasion of the Soviet Union took place in the territories that had been seized by the Soviets in 1939 as a result of the German-Soviet Non-Aggression Pact. The local populations often welcomed the German troops as liberators, and aided the SS in hunting down and killing Jews. In Lvov in eastern Galicia, for example, anti-Soviet Ukrainian fighters turned on the large Jewish community and in two days of violence killed at least 7,000 Jews—*before* the Einsatzgruppen had even arrived.

The ferocity of the war against the Jews intensified in the fall and early winter of 1941–1942. Two interconnected factors help explain this intensification. First, as Chapter 26 detailed, in these months the German military offensive ground to a halt. Second, the brutality with which the German occupiers treated the defeated populations in the occupied territories stirred up armed resistance in the form of guerrilla warfare. Seeking a scapegoat for their military losses, Germans blamed the Jews (many of whom did join guerilla combat units).

The horror of what has come to be known as Babi Yar helps illustrate the way in which German military frustration interacted with the slaughter of Jews. In the fall of 1941, German troops surrounded the city of Kiev. Despite sure defeat, Soviet forces held out for almost a month and then planted delayed-action bombs in the city, so that when the German troops entered on September 24, hundreds of Germans died in explosions and the resulting fires. Furious, the German officials blamed the Jews for the explosions. They rounded up all the Jews they could find—mostly old men, women, and young children—and drove them to Babi Yar, a ravine outside the city. The unarmed Jews were stripped, brutally beaten, and herded in small groups down a path into the ravine. Once at the bottom, they were shoved onto the ground and shot, one by one. Their bodies stacked up in layers. The corpses eventually numbered nearly 34,000.

Babi Yar was not unique. In Riga, Latvia, for example, 20,000 Jews perished in two separate actions in November and December 1941. In Lithuania, 10,000 Jews died in massacres in Kovno and 25,000 in Vilna. Estimates of the final death count of the Einsatzgruppen actions range from 1.5 to 2 million. Most of these murders followed the same general pattern: Jews were forcibly rounded up and marched in batches to a field or woods. The first batch was ordered to dig a large ditch. They were then stripped of their clothing, lined up on the edge of the ditch, and shot. Subsequent batches were lined up and shot as well, so that by the end of a day's worth of killing, the ditch would be filled with dead and dying bodies. It was then covered with a thin layer of soil, transformed from a ditch into a mass grave.

■ *Einsatzgruppen* **Action**
A soldier shoots the last remaining Jew in a Ukrainian village.

THE "JAGER REPORT"

....

Karl Jager was a German businessman who joined the SS in 1932. In 1941 he was appointed commander of Einsatzkommando 3 of Einsatzgruppe A, the unit ordered to rid Lithuania of Jews. The following is an excerpt from his nine-page report on his squad's activities in the summer and fall of 1941. The first six pages contain a day-by-day tally of the number of "executions" (murders) carried out. The final total: 137,346 Jews killed. Jager became a farm laborer after the war, but in 1959 he was arrested; he hanged himself before he could be tried for war crimes.

KAUEN [KAUNAS], 1 DECEMBER 1941.
SECRET REICH BUSINESS!

. . . . Today I can confirm that our objective, to solve the Jewish problem for Lithuania, has been achieved by EK 3. In Lithuania there are no more Jews . . . It was only possible to achieve our objective . . . by forming a raiding squad consisting of specially selected men led by SS-Obersturmführer Hamann, who grasped my aims completely and understood the importance of ensuring cooperation with the Lithuanian partisans and the relevant civilian authorities.

The execution of such actions is first and foremost a matter of organization. The decision to clear each district of Jews systematically required a thorough preparation of each individual action and a reconnaissance of the prevailing conditions in the district concerned. The Jews had to be assembled at one or several places. Depending on the number of Jews a place for the graves had to be found and then the graves dug. . . .

In Rokiskis 3,208 people had to be transported $4\frac{1}{2}$ km before they could be liquidated. In order to get this work done within 24 hours, over sixty of the eighty available Lithuanian partisans had to be detailed for cordon duty. The rest, who had to be relieved constantly, carried out the work together with my men . . . It was only through the efficient use of time that it was possible to carry out up to five actions of week, while still coping with any work that arose in Kauen, so that no backlog was allowed to build up.

The actions in Kauen itself, where there was an adequate number of reasonably well-trained partisans available, were like parade-ground shootings in comparison with the often enormous difficulties which had to be faced elsewhere.

All the officers and men in my Kommando took an active part in the major actions in Kauen . . . I consider the Jewish action more or less terminated as far as Einsatzkommando 3 is concerned.

Source: Reprinted with the permission of The Free Press, a Division of Simon & Schuster Adult Publishing Group, from *"The Good Old Days": The Holocaust as Seen by Its Perpetrators and Bystanders* by Ernst Klee, Willi Dressen, and Volker Reiss, translated by Deborah Burnstone. Copyright © 1988 by S. Fischer Verlag, GmbH. Translation, copyright © 1991 by Deborah Burnstone.

THE EVOLUTION OF THE DEATH CAMPS

On January 20, 1942, senior German officials met in a villa in Wannsee, outside Berlin, to devise a plan for destroying European Jewry. SS Lieutenant Colonel Adolf Eichmann (1906–1962) listed the number of Jews in every country; even the Jewish populations in neutral countries such as Sweden and Ireland were added to the target list. The Wannsee Conference marked the beginning of a more systematic approach to killing European Jews, one that built on the experience gained by the Einsatzgruppen in the Soviet war.

To accomplish their task of mass murder, the Einsatzgruppen had become killing machines. By trial and error, they discovered the most efficient ways of identifying and rounding up Jews, shooting them quickly, and burying the bodies. But the Einsatzgruppen actions also revealed the limits of conventional methods of killing. Shooting unarmed civilians, particularly women and children, proved to be emotionally wearing on even the best-trained and carefully indoctrinated men. Most of the Einsatzgruppen killings occurred at very close range; the shooters were often covered with blood and pieces of flesh by the day's end. A systematic approach needed to be wedded to more advanced technology that would comfortably distance the killers from those they killed. This perceived need resulted in a key Nazi innovation, the death camp. The death camps emerged from the synthesis of three already existing realities in German-governed Europe—the "euthanasia" program, forced emigration and population resettlement, and the concentration camp system.[3]

"Life Unworthy of Life":
The "Euthanasia" Program

The technologies and techniques of mass murder used in the Polish death camps were first developed in the so-called "euthanasia" campaign within Germany. (*Euthanasia* means mercy killing; no element of mercy motivated the Nazis.) This campaign grew out of the Nazi perception of biology as destiny. To shape the new Germany, the Nazis sought not only to eliminate the "racially impure"—the Jews—from German society but also to weed out non-Jewish Germans who were deemed unfit to be members of

Baltic Sea

Poland and the Death Camps

- ☒ Concentration camp
- ☒ Extermination camp
- ☒ Concentration and extermination camp
- Annexed by Germany, 1939
- General Government occupied by Germany, 1939
- Territory occupied by USSR in 1939 and Germany in 1941

Note: In addition to the concentration and extermination camps shown here, there were hundreds of forced labor camps for Jews, Poles, Gypsies, Russians, and other victims of the Nazis.

■ **Map 27.1 Poland and the Death Camps**
The Nazis set up a vast network of concentration and labor camps across Europe, but built death camps only in Poland.

the "Master Race." Beginning in the winter of 1939, government officials and medical personnel began the secret and systematic killing of the mentally and physically impaired, many of them young children. All across Germany doctors were required to identify the handicapped in their care. Individuals judged unfit to be Germans—what the Nazis labeled "life unworthy of life"—were sent to killing centers within Germany, where they were gassed and their bodies burned in crematoria. At least 80,000 Germans were killed.

After two years of secret mass murder, Hitler ordered the killing centers shut down because an increasing number of German citizens grew suspicious and began to protest against the program. (Throughout the war, however, Nazi officials continued to encourage German doctors to withhold medical care and food from patients they judged "unworthy of life.") In 1941, the killing centers' personnel were transferred to Poland to assist in setting up and running the death camps there. They took with them the technologies and techniques of mass murder that they had developed,

including the use of both gas for asphyxiating their victims and crematoria for disposing of the bodies.

Moving People into Place

In addition to these technologies, the functioning of the death camps depended on a workable policy of forced emigration and population resettlement. Once the decision was made to exterminate all the Jews in Europe, the Nazis made use of the policies of deportation and ghettoization that they had developed in Poland over the previous two-and-a-half years. From 1939 on, the Nazis forcibly resettled Poles to make room for Germans and experimented with confining Jews in ghettos. Beginning in 1942, these policies of deportation and ghettoization were extended across Europe to catch the continent's Jewish peoples in an ever-widening net. Faced with moving much larger populations across a much broader area, the Nazis made systematic use of the European railroad system to transport their victims efficiently.

In early 1942 the trains conveying Jewish victims to the death camps began to rumble across Europe. The Polish ghettos were systematically emptied as their inhabitants were sent in batches to their deaths. Individuals selected for extermination were ordered to gather at the railway station for deportation to "work camps" further east. They were then crammed onto cattle cars, more than 100 people per car, all standing up for the entire journey. Deprived of food and water, with hardly any air, and no sanitary facilities, often for several days, many Jews died en route. Those who survived emerged into the nightmare world of the death camps (see Map 27.1).

The Camps

The death camps grew most directly out of the already existing system of concentration camps, the third element needed to implement the "Final Solution." Beginning in 1933, the Nazi government set up concentration camps, in which the inmates were often forced to endure brutal manual labor. Communists, Jehovah's Witnesses, the Roma, and anyone else defined as an enemy of the regime soon filled their barracks. By the end of 1938 the concentration camp system held about 30,000 prisoners. After the war began in 1939, the concentration camps expanded dramatically in both size and number, and increasingly served as vital reserves of forced labor for German industry. Scattered throughout Nazi-controlled Europe, concentration camps became an essential part of the Nazi war economy. Firms that used camp labor included well-known businesses such as Bayer, Krupp, BMW, and Volkswagen. Some firms, such as the huge chemical conglomerate I. G. Farben, established factories inside or right next to camps.

Concentration camp inmates died in huge numbers from the brutal physical labor, torture, and diseases brought on by malnutrition and inadequate housing and sanitary facilities. At some camps, the SS guards indulged regularly in mass murder. The notorious Mauthausen camp in Austria centered on a stone quarry. Prisoners worked eleven hours a day, carrying—often at a run—impossibly heavy loads of rock up a steep staircase of 186 steps. When bored, the guards played a game they called "parachutes": They pushed the prisoners off the quarry edge to be smashed on the rocks below. At Mauthausen prisoners were also regularly shot en masse, drowned in groups of thirty in the shower rooms, and gassed. Gassings took place first in specially equipped vans and, from August 1941 on, in a gas chamber.

Mauthausen illustrated the way in which a labor camp also became a camp for mass killing. But it was in Poland, in a short period between late 1941 and early 1942, that the Germans developed the death camp, a specialized concentration camp with only one purpose—murder, primarily the murder of Jews.

Auschwitz and the Death Camp System

In the Polish camps of Chelmno, Treblinka, Belzec, and Sobibor, the only living inhabitants, besides the SS staff and their Ukrainian POW assistants, were small groups of slave laborers employed in sorting through the victims' belongings and disposing of the bodies. Jews went straight from the transport trains into a reception room, where they were told to undress, and then herded into a "shower room"— actually a gas chamber. Carbon monoxide gas, piped in from gas or diesel engines running outside the chamber, killed the victims. After the gas had done its work, the bodies were either buried or burned. Shut down in late 1943,

these camps, together with that of a fifth camp, Maidanek, killed more than two million Jews.

Maidanek combined a prison and labor camp with a death camp. So, too, did Auschwitz°, which stood at the center of the death camp system. The history of Auschwitz helps explain the way a concentration camp evolved into a death camp, with the use of the technologies of mass murder developed in the "euthanasia" program within Germany and the techniques of mass concentration and deportation perfected in the occupation of Poland. Auschwitz originated in 1940 as a concentration camp for Polish, then Soviet, prisoners of war. It became a huge industrial complex involving both state-owned and private industry and covering several square miles, with barracks for 70,000 prisoners who slaved in its coal mines, synthetic rubber and oil factories, and several smaller military industries. Its inmate population soon comprised not only Poles and Russians but also a cross-section of peoples from across Europe. A special section of the camp was reserved for the Roma after December 1942, when Himmler ordered all European Gypsies to be deported to Auschwitz. Given hardly enough food for survival (the official diet permitted a prisoner to remain alive for an average of three months), Auschwitz's inmates endured daily hard labor in the mines and factories and the constant, indiscriminate brutality of their captors.

In the middle of 1942, Auschwitz's cruel empire expanded to encompass a death camp as well. The previous fall, Nazi experiments had shown how effective the pesticide Zyklon-B was in killing Soviet prisoners of war.

■ **Walking to the Gas Chambers at Auschwitz**

For most Jews, their first glimpse of Auschwitz was their last. Only a small percentage survived the initial selection process.

Jewish Victims of the Nazis

Region	Jews in 1939	Jews murdered
Poland	3.35 million	3 million
Soviet Union	2.2 million	1.3 million*
Romania	750,000	350,000
Germany	500,000	200,000
Hungary	450,000†	300,000
France	350,000	75,000
Czechoslovakia	255,000	185–190,000
Austria	185,000	65,000
Netherlands	140,000‡	105,000
Belgium	90,000	40,000
Greece	77,000	60,000
Yugoslavia	75,000	60,000
Italy	57,000	7,500
Bulgaria	50,000§	—
Denmark	8,000	
Luxembourg	3,000	800
Finland	2,000	—
Norway	1,800	760

*Figure includes 200,000 Baltic Jews.

†In 1938.

‡Figure includes 30,000 German and Austrian refugees.

§In prewar borders.

Beginning in the summer of 1942, trainloads of Jews arrived in Birkenau, the death camp built within the Auschwitz complex. Those deemed strong enough (never more than 20 percent of a typical transport) were selected for hard labor in the main camp; the rest perished in Birkenau's gas chambers, poisoned with Zyklon-B. The writer Elie Wiesel, deported to Birkenau-Auschwitz with his family when he was fifteen, recalled the selection process:

> "Men to the left! Women to the right!" Eight words spoken quietly, indifferently, without emotion. Eight short, simple words. Yet that was the moment when I parted from my mother.[4]

Wiesel's mother and younger sister, and hundreds of thousands of others, went immediately to the gas chamber. Their bodies were burned in one of Auschwitz's five crematoria. At least one million people were gassed at Auschwitz, most of them Jews.

The gas chambers stopped operating at Auschwitz in November 1944. Faced with imminent defeat in the war, the Nazis scrambled to cover up the evidence of their crimes. Himmler ordered Auschwitz destroyed. The SS sent the remaining prisoners from Auschwitz and other camps on brutal forced marches westward. Exact figures are impossible to calculate, but it is estimated that of the more than

700,000 inmates in the Nazi camp system in January 1945, at least one-third died in the following few months, either on the march or in the overcrowded disease-ridden German camps in which they were crammed. Half of these dead were Jews.

These final victims joined the millions who starved or died of disease in the ghettoes, suffocated in the cattle cars, or were shot in mass graves, worked to death in the labor camps, or asphyxiated in the gas chambers. Children were especially vulnerable. Of the Jewish children living in 1939 in the regions already or soon to be under German control, only 11 percent survived. In total, the Holocaust claimed the lives of approximately six million Jews. The numbers of Roma victims remains unclear. Somewhere between 200,000 and 600,000 died in what the Roma call the *Porajmos*—the Devouring. Jews and Gypsies were the only groups singled out for total extermination based on their supposed biological identity. But Hitler's drive to create his new Germany claimed three to five million other victims as well. Five to fifteen thousand homosexuals perished. So, too, did as many as three million Polish Christians.

Responding to the Holocaust

In their effort to destroy European Jewry, the Nazis were not completely unaided or completely unhindered. Victims, bystanders, accomplices, and perpetrators all faced crucial choices when confronted with the Holocaust.

JEWISH RESISTANCE

One of the most frequently asked questions about the Holocaust is, why did the Jews not respond more aggressively to the Nazi threat? Jewish leaders, in particular the members of the Jewish Councils (groups of Jewish leaders appointed by the Nazis to implement their directives in the ghettos), have been harshly condemned for cooperating with the Nazis. Their options were few, however. Resistance almost always meant certain death. Instead, they followed orders, hoping that by doing so they would save not only themselves and their families, but also their communities. In most cases, they were hoping to buy time, to ensure the survival of at least part of European Jewry. As we saw in Chapter 26, few Europeans—Jew or non-Jew—violently resisted the Nazis; armed rebellion against Nazi oppression was the choice of only a small minority in all subjugated countries.

Some Jews did opt for violent resistance. Thousands of Jews fought in the underground resistance throughout Europe; in a number of ghettos violent uprisings marked the Jewish response to deportations; in occupied Poland, Jews formed more than thirty guerilla groups; rebellions

■ The Resistance

Increasingly aware that the Nazi fiction of "resettlement" was in fact a death sentence, Jews such as these refugees from the Vilna ghetto fled to the forests. Formed into partisan units, they waged guerilla warfare against the German army.

even occurred in the death camps of Treblinka, Sobibor, and Auschwitz. In the best-known case of violent resistance, the Jews in the Warsaw ghetto rose up in the spring of 1943 after a series of deportations that decimated the ghetto's population. Armed with only one or two submachine guns and a scattering of pistols, rifles, hand grenades, and gasoline bombs, Jewish fighters held off the far superior German military force for over a month. In the end, however, the ghetto was leveled, and all its survivors deported to the death camps.

The majority of Jews relied on other means of resisting the Nazis. Because the Nazis viewed Jews as sub-humans that had to be exterminated, any action that affirmed their human identity was, for Europe's Jews, a form of resistance. When Jews in the Polish ghettos formed schools, lending libraries, drama companies, and chamber music groups, they proclaimed their own humanity and so directly confronted Nazi lies. Every bar mitzvah (the Jewish coming-of-age ceremony), every poetry reading, every song, every dance, every family meal, every birth celebration and funeral service conducted by Jews in this time of horror marked an act of profound and fundamental resistance to Nazi degradation.

THE WIDENING CIRCLE OF RESPONSIBILITY

Who participated in the effort to exterminate the Jews? It is clear that the most direct responsibility for the Holocaust lies with Hitler, high-ranking Nazi officials, the Einsatzgruppen, and the Death's Head SS, which ran the death camps. But the circle of responsibility extended far beyond the ranks of these elites.

The complicity of ordinary Germans in the Holocaust has been a subject of great controversy. Many people simply tried not to watch while the horror unfolded. The villagers living around the Mauthausen camp, for example, saw the shuffling columns of starving and beaten prisoners regularly walking the almost three miles from the train station to the camp. Those living near the camp heard the screams, woke to find ashes coating their farms, gagged at the stench of burning human bodies—and learned not to look. One farmer nearby did write a letter of complaint, noting that prisoners were often shot and left to die in the ditch bordering her farm: "I request that it be arranged that such inhuman deeds be discontinued, or else be done where one does not see it."[5]

Many other Germans were more directly involved. Recent research has established that members not only of the SS but also of regular German army units and even reserve police battalions regularly rounded up and murdered Jews. Moreover, German civilians (many, if not most, of whom were *not* members of the Nazi Party) participated in the vast administrative machine needed to perpetrate the Holocaust. The deportations, for example, constituted a colossal operation involving local civil servants; bank, post office, and insurance clerks; and countless others. Consider, for example, the participation of the officials, engineers, and travel agents of the German rail network in the transportation of Jews to the death camps. These ordinary Germans handled preparations for mass deportations as a business arrangement. With money confiscated from Jews, the SS paid four pennies per kilometer for each Jewish "passenger," with children under age 10 traveling at half-fare, and children under age 4 for free. The SS purchased only

A GHETTO DIARY

·····················

Zelig Kalmanovich (1881–1943), a Jewish scholar, recorded his observations, his deepening sense of Jewish identity, and his abiding faith in God in a diary that he kept while living in the Vilna ghetto. His diary bears witness to the horrendous choices that confronted Jews during the Holocaust. As the following excerpt records, Jews found themselves carrying out the selection of Nazi victims. It also makes clear that men like Kalmanovich were under no illusions about the destiny of those Jews selected for "transport": He knew that selection meant death.

SUNDAY, OCTOBER 11 [1942]

[The eve of Simhat or Simchath Torah, a Jewish holiday] . . . There was singing and dancing . . . I said a few words: "Our song and dance are a form of worship. Our rejoicing is due to Him who decrees life and death. Here in the midst of this small congregation, in the poor and ruined synagogue, we are united with the whole house of Israel . . ."

[SUNDAY], OCTOBER 25 [1942]

. . . All our Jewish brethren in the Vilna district were gathered into one ghetto . . . Our policemen were sent with passes to be distributed among the . . . workers, and to turn over the rest of the people, "the superfluous," [those without work permits] to the hands of the authorities to do with them what is customary these days. The young men took upon themselves this difficult task. They donned their official caps, with the "Star of David" upon them, went there and did what they were supposed to do. The result was that more than 400 people perished: the aged, the infirm, the sick, and retarded children. Thus 1,500 women and children were saved. Had outsiders, God forbid, carried out this action, 2,000 people would have perished.

The [Jewish] commandant said: "To be sure, our hands are stained with the blood of our brethren, but we had to take upon ourselves this dreadful task. We are clean before the bar of history. We shall watch over the remaining. Who knows if any more victims will be demanded from us here, as they were demanded there. We shall give them only the old and the sick. Children we will not give them. They are our hope."

Source: From the Diary of Zelig Kalmanovich, YIVO Archives, New York, Sutzkever-Kaczerginski Collection. Reprinted by permission of the YIVO Institute for Jewish Research.

---

one-way tickets; Jewish "travelers" did not make return journeys from the gas chambers.

By mechanizing and dividing up the labor of killing, the Nazis made it easier for any single individual involved to escape a sense of personal responsibility or criminal culpability. Few Germans were able to see the entire process at work; few wanted to know. Each could claim, "I was only doing my job."

The circle of responsibility embraces more than Germany. As described earlier, the Einsatzgruppen relied on local people for assistance in slaughtering the Jews in the Russian, Ukrainian, and Baltic regions. In western Europe, a different situation prevailed. The occupied west contained a network of concentration and labor camps that by the spring of 1945 housed a starving and disease-ridden inmate population. But those territories had no death camps nor were Jews shot en masse there. Nevertheless, the Nazis relied heavily on local populations to implement the process that delivered western Jews to the death camps. In countries such as France, the Netherlands, and Belgium, local bureaucrats and police officers took charge of registering, rounding up, and finally deporting Jews.

Some governments in both western and eastern Europe *did*, however, endeavor to slow or sidetrack the German war against the Jews. In the most dramatic case of resistance, the Danes rallied as a people to sneak most of the 8,000 Jews in Denmark across the narrow sea to safety in neutral Sweden. Fascist Italy, too, proved a haven for many Jews. Anti-Semitism was not part of the fascist platform in Italy until 1938, and even then it remained essentially foreign and secondary. Despite the alliance with Germany, Italians undercut anti-Jewish measures by noncompliance, obstruction, and evasion.

Even in nations with anti-Semitic governments at the helm, the "Final Solution" ran into obstacles. In Vichy France, as in German satellite countries in eastern Europe such as Romania, Hungary, and Bulgaria, officials who had proved willing to pass anti-Jewish legislation, and even to turn over Jews of other nationalities to the Germans, hesitated to comply with orders for mass roundups and deportations of their own Jewish citizens. Nationalism apparently outweighed racism in these instances. In Bulgaria, efforts to delay the deportations proved successful: Most Bulgarian Jews survived. In Hungary, the Jewish community remained intact throughout most of the war, only to be targeted for extermination at Auschwitz in the spring and summer of 1944. Of Hungary's 750,000 Jews, at least 300,000 died. The rest survived only because the Russian invasion forced the Germans to abandon Auschwitz.

Just as most of the nations of Europe bear some measure of responsibility for the Holocaust, so too does the Christian Church, both Protestant and Catholic. Certainly individual Christians displayed great heroism in resisting the Nazis. For example, the German Lutheran theologian Dietrich Bonhoeffer (1906–1945) assumed a leading role in resisting the Nazi co-option of the Lutheran church. He directed an underground seminary that worked to train pastors independently of Nazi control, and in 1945, he participated in a failed plot to assassinate Hitler. Bonhoeffer was executed by the Nazis shortly before the end of World War II.

Yet the courage and conviction displayed by Bonhoeffer was unusual. Other German Protestant leaders did little to stop the Nazi effort to murder European Jewry. From 1933 on, the established church of Germany, the Lutheran Church (to which 60 percent of the population belonged), was led by a Hitler appointee, Ludwig Muller, a former army chaplain and an ardent Nazi. No Protestant bishop found the courage to take a public stand against Hitler's anti-Jewish policies. Protestant military chaplains did protest the army's involvement in killing Jews, but they did so on behalf of the *soldiers,* who found the task of murder an emotional strain. Moreover, both Protestant and Roman Catholic clergymen assisted the Nazi regime in identifying German Jews by providing the baptismal and marriage records used to prove "Aryan" status.

The record of the Roman Catholic Church is ambiguous. On the one hand, in localities such as Slovakia and Croatia, Catholic churchmen participated enthusiastically in explicitly anti-Semitic fascist governments. On the other hand, as we noted in Chapter 25, German Catholics faced persecution under the Nazi regime. The Catholic Center Party was outlawed and the Civil Service Law of 1933 purged from government posts not only Jews but also Catholic Center Party activists. Throughout the 1930s, Catholic schools faced a constant onslaught from enthusiastic local Nazi officials who sought to replace religious education with Nazi propaganda. Church doctrine also placed Roman Catholics in direct opposition to Nazi eugenics programs, particularly the forcible sterilization of the handicapped and of mixed-race children. Yet, while many Roman Catholic clergy and laypeople took courageous stands in defense of their religious beliefs, few acted on behalf of the Jews. The largely Catholic outcry against the regime's "euthanasia" policies forced the Nazis to halt the program; no such outcry emerged in response to the deportation of German Jews.

Many Catholics looked to the pope for guidance through the darkness of the war years. The question of the papacy's passivity in the face of the Holocaust is highly controversial. From 1933 on, the Catholic leadership had struggled with the question of how to respond to the Nazi regime's anti-Semitic policies. In 1937, the aging Pope Pius XI (r. 1922–1939) issued the encyclical *Mit brennender Sorge* ("With Deep Anxiety"), a clear condemnation of Hitler's government. Significantly, however, the encyclical focused on the Nazis' mistreatment of Catholics, not Jews.

Pius XI died in February 1939. His successor, Pius XII (r. 1939–1958), was an austere, authoritarian figure who knew Germany well. He had served there as *papal nuncio* (the Vatican's diplomatic representative) from 1917 to 1929, and in 1933 he had negotiated the Vatican's *concordat* or treaty with Hitler's regime. In exchange for Hitler's promise (soon broken) to allow Catholics religious freedom and his guarantee to safeguard Catholic schools, the Vatican agreed to follow a policy of noninterference in the Nazi regime's political and social policies. As a result, the Catholic Center Party, an important anti-Nazi voice in German politics, was silenced.

Once the war began, Pius XII adopted a policy of careful neutrality, one that prohibited him from clearly condemning the Nazi murder of Jews, even though the Vatican's sophisticated diplomatic and intelligence network ensured that it was well-informed of the mass killings from very early on. In his Christmas Eve radio address of 1942, Pius XII came close to condemning Nazi Germany when he called on all peoples to vow to serve God, a vow owed, he insisted, "to those hundreds of thousands who, without any fault of their own, sometimes only by reason of their nationality or race, are marked down for death or gradual extinction." The pope did not, however, explicitly name Hitler, or Nazi Germany, or the Jews.

THE ALLIES' RESPONSE

How did the Allied governments respond to the Nazis' war against the Jews? To answer this question, we must ask when and what the Allies learned about the Holocaust. A crime of such unprecedented proportions could not and did not take place in total secrecy. In fact, British code breakers translated German military radio transmissions throughout the summer of 1941. As the German army—and the Einsatzgruppen—moved into the Soviet Union, British officials confronted intercepted messages such as this one from August 27: "Regiment South shot 914 Jews; the special action staff with police battalion 320 shot 4,200 Jews."

From nearly the beginning of the Nazi effort to exterminate European Jewry, then, Allied leaders had access to surprisingly accurate and horrific information about the Holocaust. By June 1942, this information included details about the death camps. That month, Polish authorities in exile in London released a report, based on information smuggled out by the Polish underground, describing the Nazis' effort to exterminate Polish Jews. This report not only discussed large-scale gassings but also emphasized that such gassings were part of a coordinated plan. The report erred, however, in estimating that 700,000 Jews had been murdered. By June 1942, the Nazi regime was responsible for the deaths of at least two million Jews.

Such information quickly became accessible to ordinary people. From 1941 on, British and American newspaper readers and radio listeners received numerous reports about Jewish massacres and, after 1942, they heard or read about the existence of the death camps. For example, the Babi Yar massacre was reported in the Western press two months after it occurred. These reports had to compete with other war news, however. In addition, many of these articles were written in a skeptical tone, as both reporters and editors had a difficult time believing that such atrocities could be taking place. Newspaper readers, faced with horror on a scale they simply could not conceive, retreated to comfortable positions. They assured themselves that the reports must be exaggerated, that atrocities always take place during wars, that things simply could not be so bad. Many recalled that during World War I, atrocity stories had circulated that later were revealed to be simply propaganda. But even when they believed what they were reading, people often could not grasp its full meaning. As theologian and Dutch Protestant leader W. A. Visser't Hooft explained, "people could find no place in their consciousness for such an unimaginable horror . . . It is possible to live in a twilight between knowing and not knowing."[6]

But not everyone remained in the twilight. British and American Jewish groups mobilized to force the Allied governments to do something to help European Jews before it was too late. Pressure from Jewish and non-Jewish public-interest groups did succeed in pushing the British and American governments to issue an inter-Allied declaration in December 1942 that in no uncertain terms announced and condemned Hitler's effort to exterminate European Jewry. This declaration was broadcast all over the world.

Yet despite official and public acknowledgment of the mass murder of Jews, the Allies did not act directly to stop the killings. Should the Allies be considered bystanders in the crime of the Holocaust? As we saw in Chapter 26, the Soviets put an enormous amount of effort into evacuating factories from their western territories to safety in the east—but Stalin's government made no effort to evacuate Jews. Even more controversial is the failure of the United States and Britain to act more decisively on behalf of Europe's Jews. Some scholars, for example, have highlighted the role of anti-immigration sentiment in limiting the western Allies' response. Scarred by the experience of the Great Depression, both Americans and British often proved reluctant to welcome refugees. If Jewish refugees were rescued, where would they go? Who would pay for their maintenance? Who would find them jobs? By the fall of 1941, however, such questions meant little: Himmler's order that no Jew leave German-occupied territory alive halted Jewish immigration.

The key question is: How did the western Allies respond to the Holocaust from 1942 on? Many historians have contended that anti-Semitism in both British and American society structured the Allies' strategic priorities and prevented political leaders from exploring alternative strategies, such as sending in commando units, bombing the rail lines into the death camps, or even bombing the camps themselves.

Other historians argue these alternatives were not militarily feasible, and that the Allies did the only thing they could do on the Jews' behalf—win the war as quickly as possible.

AFTER AUSCHWITZ: REMEMBERING THE HOLOCAUST

In the months after the war ended, Allied leaders struggled to bring Nazi leaders to trial to account for their crimes. What one participant called "the greatest trial in history" opened on November 14, 1945. For eleven months, a tribunal of four judges and four alternates—American, British, French, and Soviet—sat in a courtroom in the German city of Nuremberg to judge nineteen prominent German military, political, and industrial leaders. In 403 open sessions they heard 94 witnesses and pored over the written testimonies of 143 more. (The published proceedings of the trial take up forty-two volumes.) The cascade of information, broadcast by the crowds of journalists packed into the courtroom, offered the world its first encounter with the Holocaust. The Nuremberg trials° of 1945–1946 highlighted the Nazi onslaught against European Jewry as one of the most horrendous of the Nazis' many "crimes against humanity," a category first introduced into international law by the Nuremberg tribunal. The Nuremberg indictment noted that "Jews were systematically persecuted since 1933" and that "Since 1 September 1939 . . . millions of Jews from Germany and from the occupied Western Countries were sent to the Eastern Countries for extermination." The main charge against the defendants, however, was not attempted genocide but rather conspiring to destroy the peace of Europe via an aggressive war that carried the murder of millions in its wake. The centrality of Hitler's anti-Semitism to both his worldview and his war-making did not become clear in the trials.

In the moral and physical exhaustion that followed the end of World War II, as in the Nuremberg trials, the Holocaust tended to recede from view. Nevertheless, reaction to the Holocaust did play a central role in one of the most dramatic consequences of the war—the establishment of the state of Israel. Many Holocaust survivors embraced Zionism, the ideology of Jewish nationalism (see Chapter 22). From 1945 on, European Jewish refugees poured into British-controlled Palestine. Many soon found themselves waging guerilla warfare against the British, who sought to limit Jewish immigration in order to pacify the local Muslim and Christian populations and to maintain political stability in the region. Faced with mounting violence as well as growing international pressure to grant Jewish demands for statehood, the British turned the problem over to the United Nations in spring of 1947. At the end of that year, the UN adopted a plan calling for the partition of Palestine into Jewish and Arab sectors forming a Jewish and Arab state. Faced with opposition to the plan from the surrounding Arab nations, the British pulled out their troops in May 1948 without transferring authority to either Jews or Arabs. Jewish leaders immediately proclaimed the new state of Israel and the region erupted into an all-out war between Israel and the surrounding Arab nations. After nine months of fighting, an uneasy peace descended, based on a partition of Palestine among Israel, Jordan (which held the region around Jerusalem known as the West Bank), and Egypt (which occupied the Gaza Strip). Approximately 750,000 Palestinian Arabs became stateless refugees, an embittered population confined to camps in Syria, Lebanon, and Jordan, as well as the West Bank and Gaza (see Map 27.2). Not all Holocaust survivors emigrated to Israel, but most of the tens of thousands who turned instead to the United States supported Israel with financial contributions and emotional commitment.

Just as the fact and memory of the Holocaust helped shape the new nation of Israel, so too did it influence the new West Germany. In communist-controlled East Germany, state censorship of political and historical studies guaranteed that the Holocaust was shunted aside as a fascist crime that had little to do with the new communist nation. In contrast, the government of West Germany in 1952 acknowledged German responsibility for the Holocaust when it agreed to pay reparations to individual Jews, to the state of Israel, and to Jewish communities throughout the world.

Despite these developments, the Western world did not begin to grapple with the meaning and memory of the Holocaust until the early 1960s. The reception of *The Diary of Anne Frank,* a simple day-by-day account written by a young Dutch Jewish girl during World War II, illustrates the way in which the central facts of the Holocaust were easily evaded. Published in 1947 and translated into over fifty languages, the book became an international bestseller as well as the basis of a much-acclaimed stage play and movie in the late 1950s. Hiding with her family in a secret annex located behind her father's factory in Amsterdam, Anne used her diary to try to find order and meaning in a world gone mad. The diary abruptly ends on August 1, 1944; three days later Anne and her family were arrested. Anne Frank died of typhus in Bergen-Belsen, shortly before British troops liberated the camp. By telling the story of a horrifying tragedy through the eyes of one ordinary yet extraordinarily appealing young girl, the book forced its readers to confront evil—but not, in fact, to confront the Holocaust. Both the play and film version depicted Anne as a universal symbol of innocence destroyed by the evil of war, not as a Jewish girl killed because she was Jewish.

But in 1960, the world was forced to confront the Holocaust in a very dramatic way. That year the prime minister of Israel captured the world's attention by announcing that the Israeli secret service had found and kidnapped Adolf Eichmann, a leading Nazi administra-

tor charged with overseeing "Jewish Affairs" during World War II. Worldwide coverage of Eichmann's subsequent trial presented for the first time to a large audience the basic narrative of the Holocaust. In the years that followed, the Holocaust became the subject of numerous historical, literary, and artistic works.

For writers and artists in West Germany, the Holocaust became closely connected to questions of collective guilt and national identity. What did it mean to be German in the post-Holocaust world? Nobel Prize–winning novelists Heinrich Böll (1917–1985) and Günter Grass (b. 1927) struggled to find answers. Called "the conscience of a nation," Böll conveyed the dehumanization wrought by the war in a series of carefully crafted novels. Grass's work has been more varied, ranging from sculpture to plays to novels and short stories. From his first and most well-known novel, *The Tin Drum* (1959), in which a small boy caught in

■ Map 27.2   Israel and Its Neighbors, 1949

The map inset outlines the United Nations' plan to partition Palestine into Jewish and Arab sectors, with Jerusalem as an international zone. This plan was not implemented.

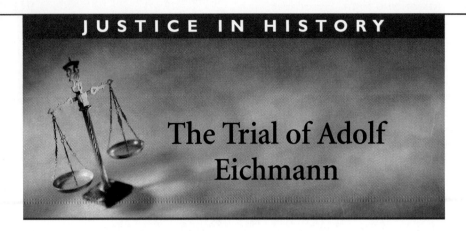

The Trial of Adolf Eichmann

On May 23, 1960, David Ben-Gurion (1886–1973), the prime minister of Israel, made a spectacular announcement: Israeli secret service agents had kidnapped Adolf Eichmann, a wanted Nazi war criminal, and smuggled him into Israel to await trial. Eichmann, the head of the Gestapo's Jewish Affairs unit, had implemented Nazi policies on Jewish emigration and deportation. His office sorted through the complicated bureaucratic procedures to ensure that the trains laden with Jews kept to their schedules and delivered their human cargo to the gas chambers on time. It was to Eichmann that Jewish leaders came to plead for emigration visas and for work permits. It was with Eichmann that Jewish leaders negotiated about the timing, size, and composition of deportations. For many Jews, then, Eichmann represented German power and came to personify Nazi evil. He had disappeared in the chaotic final days of World War II and eventually made his way to Argentina, where, as "Ricardo Klement," he lived a quiet, respectable life with his wife and children—until 1960.

From the moment of Ben Gurion's sensational announcement, the Eichmann case occupied the attention of the world. Six hundred foreign correspondents attended the trial, which was one of the first to be filmed by television cameras. Over 1,500 documents were submitted and 120 witnesses testified in the 114 sessions held between April 11 and August 14, 1961. Three judges, each of whom had been

born in Germany and had emigrated to Palestine in 1933, heard the evidence. On December 15, they sentenced Eichmann to death. He died by hanging on May 31, 1962, the first execution in Israel, which had abolished capital punishment for all crimes except genocide.

The Eichmann trial told the story of Jewish suffering during World War II to the widest possible audience. Both Ben-Gurion and the chief prosecutor Gideon Hausner stated publicly that the trial aimed to construct "a living record of a gigantic human and national disaster," and so educate both young Israelis and the entire world in the causes and consequences of the Holocaust.[7] As Hausner explained in his emotional opening statement, he saw himself as the spokesman for "six million accusers . . . [whose] ashes were piled up in the hills of Auschwitz and in the fields of Treblinka, or washed away by the rivers of Poland."[8] Hausner (who, like many Israelis, had lost most of his relatives in the Nazi death camps) called more than 100 witnesses, many of them death camp survivors. Their testimony, published or broadcast throughout the world, painted an unforgettable and detailed picture of the horror of genocide.

By the time the prosecution rested its case, no one could doubt that Eichmann was a guilty man, one who had played an essential role in the murder of millions. Yet the Eichmann trial attracted an enormous amount of criticism, and continues to arouse great controversy. Critics charged that

to achieve moral justice for Holocaust victims and survivors, the Israeli court committed a legal injustice against Eichmann. The trial was not only made possible by a violation of international law (Eichmann's kidnapping), it also was filled with irregularities, including the introduction of testimony that did not pertain to the specific crimes charged. Critics also disputed Israel's legal right to try Eichmann: The crimes had not occurred in Israeli territory, nor were Eichmann's victims Israeli citizens. (Israel did not exist until 1948.)

In reply to these critics, Hausner and other supporters of the prosecution insisted that justice demanded that Eichmann be brought to trial, and that the Israeli government had pursued the only course of action open to it. In the Eichmann trial, then, we confront a case in which what was legal on the one hand and what was just on the other appeared very much at odds. There is no doubt that Eichmann was guilty of horrendous crimes; there is also no doubt that the Israeli government stepped beyond the boundaries of international law in kidnapping Eichmann.

The Eichmann trial also raised important questions about the nature of the Holocaust. Was it a crime perpetrated by a few very evil men, or did the evil penetrate deep into German, and European, society? The prosecution's case sought to depict Eichmann as a monster, a brilliant and demonic mastermind responsible for the deaths of millions of Jews. As Hausner con-

■ Eichmann on Trial
Eichmann sits on the left in a cage of bulletproof glass.

tended, "it was [Eichmann's] word that put gas chambers into action; he lifted the telephone, and railway trains left for the extermination centers; his signature it was that sealed the doom of tens of thousands."[9] Such a depiction provided a comforting explanation for the Holocaust—it was perpetrated not by ordinary human beings but by monstrous devils.

Yet many trial observers and subsequent historians argued that such a depiction was simply wrong. This argument appeared in forceful terms in the most well-known critique of the prosecution—Hannah Arendt's *Eichmann in Jerusalem: A Report on the Banality of Evil*, published in 1963. Arendt (1906–1975), a Jewish philosopher who had fled Nazi Europe in 1941, argued that the evidence provided in the trial showed Eichmann to be a fairly commonplace man, motivated by ambition as much as by ideology, a rather plodding bureaucrat obsessed with trivial details—in other words, an ordinary man, capable of extraordinary evil.

Must ordinary men be held responsible for following evil orders? This is the final question raised by the Eichmann trial. Defense attorney Robert Servatius insisted that the Holocaust was an "act of state," a crime carried out by a political regime, for which no civil servant could bear the blame. Eichmann only followed orders. Servatius concluded his arguments by asking Eichmann how he viewed "this question of guilt." Eichmann replied,

Where there is no responsibility, there can be no guilt. . . . The questions of responsibility and conscience are for the leadership of the state. . . . I condemn and regret the act of extermination of the Jews which the leadership of the German state ordered. But I myself could not jump over my own shadow. I was a tool in the hands of superior powers and authorities.[10]

Eichmann's judges disagreed. In declaring Eichmann guilty of genocide, they argued,

We reject absolutely the accused's version that he was nothing more than a 'small cog' in the extermination ma-
chine. . . . He was not a puppet in the hands of others. His place was among those who pulled the strings.[11] ■

Questions of Justice

1. Even if Eichmann's assertion that he was simply "a tool in the hands of superior powers and authorities" could be proven correct, to what degree was he culpable for his actions?

2. In the Eichmann case, the letter of the law and justice appeared to be at odds. In what situations—if any—must the law be broken to ensure that justice prevails?

Taking It Further

Laqueur, Walter. "Hannah Arendt in Jerusalem: The Controversy Revisited," in Lyman H. Legters, ed., *Western Society After the Holocaust.* 1983. Examines the impact of Arendt's critique of the trial.

The Trial of Adolf Eichmann: Record of Proceedings in the District Court of Jerusalem. Vols. 1–9, 1993–1995. The basic primary source.

■ **Anselm Kiefer, *Germany's Spiritual Heroes* (1973)**
In much of his work, Kiefer struggled with the legacy of German history.

the trauma of the Nazi era refuses to grow up, to *My Century* (1999), one hundred short tales that convey his personal history of Germany in the twentieth century, Grass explored the moral issues posed by Germany's past.

In contrast to Böll and Grass (both of whom were POWs), the artist Anselm Kiefer, born in 1945, had no direct experience of World War II. Yet, as Kiefer's works show, Germans born after the war continued to grapple with its legacy for personal and national identity. Adding straw, sand, shells, and clay to large canvases or woodcuts, Kiefer built up multitextured works that commented both ironically and allusively on the troubled German past. Painted on six strips of burlap sewn together, *Germany's Spiritual Heroes* (1973) evokes both a crematorium and a memorial hall, and so challenges the viewer to question the national myths that made Germany vulnerable to Nazi ideology. A decade after he painted this work, Kiefer completed a set of paintings that offered haunting images of the death camps.

By the 1980s, many West Germans argued that the Holocaust had come to assume far too large a place in German cultural identity. In journal and newspaper articles, historians fought a well-publicized battle (the *Historikerstreit*) over the proper place of the Holocaust in history. Conservative historians argued that the Holocaust, while an act of enormous criminality, was far from unique; other countries had experienced other outbreaks of mass slaughter. They insisted that Germany, like other nations, needed a usable past rather than "a negative myth of absolute evil."[12]

The Historikerstreit revealed that historians disagree about the meaning of the Holocaust. Was it a unique incident in Western civilization, or was it one more episode in

the lengthy history of mass slaughter? Perhaps the best answer is: It was both. The Holocaust does not stand alone as an example of the way in which ideology can fuel mass murder. Chapter 25 showed how Joseph Stalin's political ideas and personal paranoia led to mass death in the Soviet Union. At least two million people died "unnatural deaths" in the Soviet Union during the 1930s, with 750,000 of these executed in the Great Purge alone. An additional four to five million people starved in the famine of 1932, the direct consequence of Stalin's collectivization drive. In the decades after the Holocaust, the world encountered other tragic examples of ideological frenzy resulting in mass death. In the late 1950s, an estimated 30 million Chinese died as a result of the Chinese Communist leader Mao Zedong's (1893–1976) decision to catapult his nation into industrialization through what he called the "Great Leap Forward." Twenty years later in Cambodia, the Khmer Rouge, a communist group inspired by Mao, declared that all city dwellers were enemies of the communist peasant utopia they sought to establish. In less than four years, 1.7 million people—20 percent of the Cambodian population—died as a result of this idea.

The Holocaust occurred at the intersection of modern nationalism and modern war, as did many other episodes of twentieth-century mass murder. During the First World War, the Armenian minority population in Turkey was accused of collaborating with the invading Russian enemy. Six hundred thousand Armenian men, women, and children were massacred, and another 400,000 died in the course of forced deportations. In World War II, 487,000 Serbs in the Nazi-allied state of Croatia fell victim to state-sanctioned ethnic slaughter. Viewed in this context, Hitler's effort to destroy the Jews of Europe was a particularly horrendous act in an ongoing tragedy.

Yet the Turks did not aim to kill every Armenian in Europe, nor did the Croatian fascists hope to eradicate Serbians from the continent. Hitler wanted to kill every Jewish man, woman, and child in Europe. Moreover, the Holocaust was not just a product of ideological or nationalist passion; it was also the result of careful calculation. In the death camps we encounter some of the most highly developed products of human reason used for evil and irrational ends. The gas chamber, for example, is a triumph of industrial *technology*—a sophisticated construction designed to deliver complex chemical products efficiently. But far more important is the centrality of industrial *techniques* to the Holocaust—the adaptation of the assembly line to facilitate mass murder. The Nazis approached the slaughter of a people as an engineering problem, one to be solved with the rational application of both machinery and method. They constructed a vast machine of death, with slave laborers as the key components, each with identification numbers tattooed onto their forearms, a type of human "bar coding." Like manufacturers everywhere, the Nazis sought to eliminate bottlenecks in the "production" process: Mass graves had to be dug when the crematoria could not keep up with the output from the gas chambers. And, like businessmen, the Nazis strove to make profitable use of every aspect of their raw material. The victims' hair, gold tooth fillings, and clothes were all recycled into the Nazi economy. Within these death factories constructed according to the highest standards of efficiency, the human raw material moved along a murderous assembly line—from arrival through selection to the undressing rooms to the gas chamber to the crematoria.

The Nazi death machine thus uniquely challenged, and continues to challenge, the widely held belief that rationality and progress are automatically linked, and that the dominant position of rationality in Western culture assures the West's claim to the label "civilized." For who would agree that the Nazis were civilized? By using the tools of civilization for barbaric ends, the Nazis called into question the very meaning of Western civilization. As one historian has argued, "the realisation that some men will construct a factory in which to kill other men raises the gravest questions about man himself. We have entered an age which we cannot avoid labeling 'After Auschwitz.'"[13]

The Race for the Atom Bomb

Western civilization has also entered an era that we cannot avoid labeling "After the Atom Bomb." During the summer of 1945, Western civilization came face-to-face with the destructive potential of scientific rationality not only in the remains of the Nazi death camps but also in the radioactive rubble of two Japanese cities, Hiroshima and Nagasaki. After the atom bomb the world would never be the same. Scientific theory and military technology had together produced weapons of awesome destructive capability that created an entirely new global balance of power—and the horror of mass death. But before we examine both the immediate and long-term consequences of the atomic bombings, we need to explore two central questions: What factors led scientists to pressure the Allied governments into creating weapons of such destructive power? Once these bombs had been made, why were they dropped on Japanese cities?

SPLITTING THE ATOM

The atom bomb resulted from the profound intellectual revolution occurring in science in the first decades of the twentieth century. At its most basic level, this revolution overthrew the mechanistic explanation of the universe that had held sway since the first scientific revolution in the seventeenth century (see Chapter 16). The triumph of the theories of Isaac Newton had ensured that for 200 years, educated Westerners regarded the natural world as a precise and predictable machine. But Newton's theories could not account for new realities such as X rays, radioactivity, and the discovery that atoms were not solid but actually made up of mobile electrons, nuclei, and empty space. In the first half of the twentieth century, scientists began to replace Newton's now-discredited universe with a new, more complicated model based on Albert Einstein's theory of relativity. As Chapter 23 explained, Einstein's model replaced Newton's static universe with a world in which space, time, matter, and energy are all interchangeable.

The effort to construct an entirely new understanding of the cosmos electrified the discipline of physics and attracted some of the most brilliant young thinkers of the twentieth century. Students traveled across Europe and the United States in pursuit of the best teachers and in hopes of joining research teams in both university and state-funded laboratories.

Much of the funding for all of this scientific activity came from governments. World War I, with its poison gas and bomber planes, had shown that in the new technological age, military victory depended as much on science as it did on soldiers. As one observer said in 1919, "The decisive assaults upon mankind now proceed from the drawing boards and the laboratory." Realizing the practical potential of scientific research, governments began to pour funds into university science departments and to establish research laboratories.

In the 1920s few of these political leaders realized that Einstein's concept of matter as "frozen energy" had profound implications for military technology. But in theory, if the energy could be "thawed out," then this energy could be released—a process that would produce a terrific explosion.

■ **Hiroshima After the Atom Bomb**
The buildings left standing had been reinforced against earthquakes.

But could this theory become reality? In 1936, the distinguished British scientist Ernest Rutherford (1871–1937) answered that question with a resounding "no" when he dismissed as "moonshine" the idea of unlocking the atom to release energy. Yet, just four years earlier, a scientist working in Rutherford's own laboratory had in fact found the key to unlocking the atom's energy. In 1932, James Chadwick (1891–1974) discovered that atoms contain not only positively charged protons and negatively charged electrons, but also neutrons. Because neutrons possess no electrical charge, they are not repelled by either an atom's protons or its electrons. Bombarded with heavy neutrons, an atom's nucleus could, in theory, be split open—a process called nuclear fission. Moreover, the split nucleus would itself emit neutrons, which would then burst open other atoms, which in turn would emit further neutrons . . . and on and on in a nuclear chain reaction. The result: a colossal burst of energy, an explosion, an atom bomb.

The atom bomb, however, remained purely theoretical—or pure "moonshine," in Rutherford's words—until 1938, when two scientists working in Berlin proved Rutherford wrong. Otto Hahn (1879–1968) and Fritz Strassmann (1902–1980) bombarded uranium with a stream of neutrons, and broke open the uranium atom. Matter had been

unlocked. As one historian has noted, "Physicists viewed the discovery of nuclear fission like the finding of a lost treasure map."[14] Within a year, over 100 articles on the implications of this discovery were published in scientific journals around the world.

One of the many scientists who recognized the path-breaking nature of the Hahn-Strassmann experiment was the brilliant Hungarian physicist Leo Szilard (1898–1964). Szilard had emigrated to Germany to take advantage of the first-rate scientific opportunities available in interwar Berlin. In 1933, however, Szilard, who was Jewish, recognized that he had no place in the new Nazi Reich. Like many German and eastern European Jewish scientists (including Albert Einstein and Sigmund Freud), Szilard fled to the West. He emigrated first to England, and then, in 1937, to the United States.

An avid reader of British science fiction writer H. G. Wells, Szilard had always been intrigued by the atomic bombs that Wells imagined in his stories. Once Hahn and Strassman published the results of their experiment with nuclear fission, Szilard recognized that the atom bomb had moved from the world of fiction into the realm of actual possibility. The discovery of nuclear fission in Germany occurred within just three weeks of the events of Kristallnacht, the night on which Nazis murdered more than 100 Jews, terrorized countless others, and burned Jewish businesses, homes, and synagogues. Appalled by the thought of Nazi Germany gaining access to the atomic bomb, Szilard began a vigorous campaign for a Western nuclear weapons program.

THE THREAT OF THE GERMAN BOMB

Szilard was just one of a large number of central and eastern European scientists who emigrated to Britain or the United States during the 1930s. Ironically, during the 1920s, many eastern European Jewish scientists had made their way to Germany, because it was perceived as far more enlightened and far less anti-Semitic than countries such as Poland and Hungary. But this situation changed abruptly in 1933. One of the Nazis' first measures on taking power was to limit the number of Jews employed in universities and the civil service. The University of Göttingen dismissed its top seven scientists, all of them Jewish. At the same time, Jewish scientists found themselves subject to professional persecution and verbal abuse. The Nazis derided Einstein's work, for example, as "Jewish world-bluff."

Acutely aware of the threat that Nazism posed to civilization, many of these émigré scientists were convinced after 1938 that Germany, with its stellar tradition of scientific research and magnificent laboratories, possessed the potential for developing an atom bomb. They and other scientists in the West began to pressure the British and American governments to devote the necessary resources to an atomic weapons program. In 1939, Leo Szilard met with Einstein (who by then was living in the United States) and asked him to use his considerable prestige to influence President Roosevelt. Einstein agreed, and six weeks after the start of the war in Europe, Roosevelt received a letter, signed by Einstein but actually written by Szilard, that warned both of the possibility of "extremely powerful bombs of a new type," and of rumors that Germany was building up its uranium supplies.

Roosevelt declared that "this requires action," but the United States was not yet at war in 1939 and little was done to respond to Szilard and Einstein's warnings. It was left to Britain to take the initial lead in the quest for the atom bomb. There, two refugee scientists, Otto Frisch (1904–1979) and Rudolph Peierls (1907–1995), had been barred (because of their German citizenship) from participating in the top-secret development of radar. They turned instead to exploring the means of developing and detonating an atom bomb. By April 1940, their work had impressed the British government enough to spark the creation of a committee to oversee atomic energy research.

American officials in the spring of 1941 dismissed the British atomic research project as "a wild goose chase." But by the summer of that year, the British had convinced the Americans that an atom bomb could be constructed. In October, Roosevelt suggested to British prime minister Winston Churchill that Britain and the United States pool their efforts and create an atomic partnership. The result was the Manhattan Project°.

THE BEST AND THE BRIGHTEST: THE MANHATTAN PROJECT

The Manhattan Project, the code name for the joint British-American effort to construct an atom bomb, was an extraordinary endeavor, the biggest and most expensive weapons

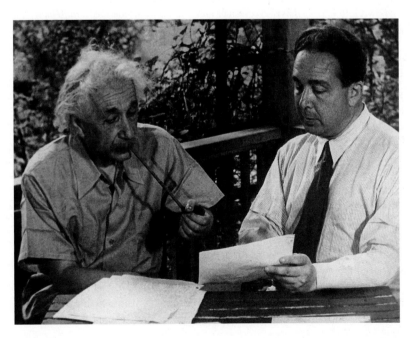

■ **Albert Einstein and Leo Szilard**
In 1946, Einstein and Szilard reenacted the signing of their letter to Roosevelt for the cameras.

research and development project up to that point in history. Comprising thirty-seven installations in nineteen American states and in Canada, it employed 120,000 individuals. Yet this colossal effort was top-secret. Until U.S. president Harry Truman announced the drop of an atom bomb on Hiroshima in August 1945, few American, British, or Canadian citizens had any inkling that nuclear weapons had jumped from the pages of science fiction and into the world of brutal fact.

The Manhattan Project recruited the best and the brightest, the very top scientists in their fields. In 1943, twenty of the thirty-three nuclear physicists regarded as "leaders in the field" worked on the Manhattan Project. Many of these scientists were astonishingly young; the average age of the scientists working at the core of the project in Los Alamos, New Mexico, was 25.

The Manhattan Project was run by the American military, although its scientific research was directed by the brilliant Berkeley professor of physics, Robert Oppenheimer (1904–1967). In late 1942, Brigadier General Leslie Groves (1896–1970), an engineer who had overseen construction of the Pentagon building in Washington, D.C., became the project's officer-in-charge. The scientists successfully resisted Groves's efforts to place them in military uniform and assign them military rank, but they quickly discovered that they were now servants of the state. Oppenheimer himself found that his telephone conversations were bugged, his movements monitored, his mail screened. His wife's Communist Party membership, and his own left-wing political leanings, made him the subject of intense military scrutiny.

For most of the project scientists, the discomforts of life in Los Alamos (and in other installations in Oak Ridge, Tennessee, and Hanford, Washington) and the unfamiliar military regulations were small prices to pay to participate in what they perceived as the race against Nazi Germany. Throughout 1942, Oppenheimer, Szilard, and other scientists worried that Allied progress was too slow, and that Germany might construct an atom bomb first.

Then, on December 2, 1942, the Italian physicist Enrico Fermi (1901–1954) and other scientists working at the University of Chicago produced a nuclear chain reaction. Once this breakthrough occurred, progress on the atom bomb moved ahead quickly. At 5:29 A.M., on July 16, 1945, the world's first atomic explosion was detonated over the desert of New Mexico. Oppenheimer gave this test explosion its code name—Trinity. American scientist Isidor Rabi (1898–1988) described the sight:

CHRONOLOGY

The Road to the Atom Bomb

1932	Discovery of the neutron
1933	Hitler appointed chancellor of Germany; emigration of many leading eastern European and German scientists to Britain and the United States
1938	First successful splitting of the atom
1939	Szilard and Einstein's letter to President Roosevelt
1940	Creation of British atomic bomb project
1941	Establishment of joint Anglo-American atomic bomb project
1942	Manhattan Project underway; first nuclear chain reaction
1945	
February	Bombing of Dresden
March	Bombing of Tokyo
May	German surrender; end of war in Europe
July	Potsdam Conference; Trinity test explosion
August 6	Atom bomb dropped on Hiroshima
August 8	Soviet declaration of war on Japan
August 9	Atom bomb dropped on Nagasaki
August 15	Japanese surrender

Suddenly, there was an enormous flash of light, the brightest light I have ever seen or that I think anyone has ever seen. It blasted; it pounced; it bored its way right through you . . . Finally, it was over, diminishing, and we looked toward the place where the bomb had been; there was an enormous ball of fire which grew and grew and it rolled as it grew . . . It looked menacing. It seemed to come toward one. A new thing had just been born.

Robert Oppenheimer recalled a line from the Hindu scripture, the *Bhagavad Gita:* "Now I am become Death, the destroyer of worlds." Kenneth Bainbridge (1904–1996), an experimental physicist from Harvard and director of the test, put it more simply: "Now we are all sons-of-bitches," he told Oppenheimer.[15]

THE DECISION TO DROP THE BOMB

By the time of the Trinity test, Nazi Germany had fallen to the Allies. Months before V-E Day (Victory-in-Europe Day—May 8, 1945), Allied military leaders had realized that the Allies would defeat Germany without an atom bomb. In the spring of 1945, as the Allied armies pushed across

■ The Mushroom Cloud
The detonation of the atomic bomb over Hiroshima on August 6, 1945, produced what would become one of the most familiar images of the post–World War II age.

Europe, a special intelligence unit discovered that the Germans had never come close to developing atomic weapons. Hence, the original aim of the Manhattan Project, to beat the Germans to a superweapon, was no longer valid by 1945. But almost a year earlier, American military planners had already shifted the atomic target to Japan (see Map 27.3).

By August 1945, Japan was staggering under the combined effects of an American naval blockade and nightly bombing raids. In addition, the Soviet Union stood poised to enter the Pacific War on the Allies' side. Japan had clearly lost the war, and important members of the Japanese cabinet began to press for peace, although Japan's military leaders were determined to fight on to the bitter end. The end, however, was clear. The question was not if but when Japan would surrender.

Given this situation, the decision to use atom bombs against Japan generated controversy from the very start. In the weeks before Hiroshima, scientists at the University of Chicago section of the project (including Leo Szilard) protested against plans to drop the bomb on Japan without warning. Important American military officials such as General Dwight Eisenhower (1890–1969), supreme commander of the Allied forces in Europe, and General Douglas MacArthur (1880–1964), supreme commander of the Allied forces in the Pacific, opposed the use of the atom bombs as (in MacArthur's words) "completely unnecessary."[16]

The decision to drop the bombs involved several considerations. Historians have highlighted four factors that influenced the decision: the desire to save American lives, domestic pressure for Japan's unconditional surrender, international political concerns, and the widespread use of mass air bombing in both Europe and the Pacific during the war.

First, both Truman and his advisers aimed to end the war quickly and thereby save the lives of American servicemen. By the summer of 1945 U.S. forces had reversed Japan's expansion into the Pacific, destroyed most of Japan's navy, and blockaded Japan itself. But these victories exacted a high price. In the spring campaigns on the islands of Iwo Jima and Okinawa, almost 20,000 Americans and 131,000 Japanese lost their lives.

The fierce Japanese resistance encountered at Iwo Jima and Okinawa convinced military planners, ordinary servicemen, and the American public that an invasion of Japan's home islands would result in horrifying casualties. In mid-June 1945, the Joint War Plans Committee estimated that a November invasion of Japan's southern island of Kyushu, followed by a March invasion of the main island of Honshu, would result in 40,000 Americans killed, 150,000 wounded, and 3,500 missing. Admiral William Leahy (1875–1959) noted to President Truman that if casualty rates at Kyushu were as high as those on Okinawa, then the numbers of Americans killed in the first phase of the invasion could reach as high as 50,000.

The desire to end the war quickly and so avoid the deaths of American servicemen thus played an important role in the decision to drop the atom bomb. An invasion of the Japanese home islands was, however, not a foregone conclusion in the spring and summer of 1945. Admiral Leahy, who opposed using the Bomb, argued that the blockade of Japan would end the war *without* an invasion. In 1946, the U.S. Strategic Bombing Survey concluded that Leahy was correct: "Certainly prior to 31 December 1945, and in all probability prior to 1 November 1945 [the scheduled date of the Kyushu invasion], Japan would have surrendered . . . even if no invasion had been planned or contemplated."

Of course, the Strategic Bombing Survey officials had the benefit of hindsight, an advantage denied to Truman and his advisers. But it is clear that there were alternatives to

■ **Map 27.3 Japan in 1945**

By the summer of 1945, American bombing raids had decimated many Japanese cities, including Tokyo. Hiroshima escaped unscathed until August 6, 1945. Nagasaki received the second atom bomb on August 9 only because clouds obscured the primary target of Kokura.

both an invasion and the atom bomb. Continuing the blockade and conventional bombing of Japan constituted one such alternative; another was exploring diplomatic avenues for ending the war. American and British policymakers knew that in April, members of the Japanese government had approached the Soviet Union with tentative offers of a Japanese surrender, on the condition that the Japanese emperor be allowed to remain on his throne.

Why were these peace initiatives not pursued? Domestic politics proved to be a crucial constraining factor. The demand for Japan's "unconditional surrender" was extremely popular with both the British and American publics, and most historians agree that Truman—in office only a few months and with far less prestige than Roosevelt—would have found it politically impossible to abandon such a popular policy. The memory of Japan's surprise attack on the American air force base in Pearl Harbor, Hawaii, in 1941, combined with the savagery with which the Pacific war had been waged, ensured that Americans wanted nothing less than Japan's unconditional surrender. Moreover, by the spring of 1945, the Manhattan Project had cost almost two billion dollars. To have spent such a sum of money, and then not to use the resulting weapon while American lives were being lost every day in a dreadful conflict, was, finally, unacceptable.

International politics also played a role in the dropping of the Bomb—specifically, the desire to impress the Soviet Union with American power. By 1945, as Chapter 26 detailed, the fundamental conflicts that divided the Allies could no longer be papered over. It is significant that although Britain and the United States cooperated in the Manhattan Project, they excluded the other principal member of the alliance, the Soviet Union. Concerns over Soviet expansion into both eastern Europe and Asia dominated the thoughts of Truman and his advisers in the final year of the war. American and British officials hoped that the use of the atom bomb, by ending the war quickly, would not only save Allied lives but also stall the Soviet advance in the Pacific. (The Soviets declared war on Japan on August 8, 1945.) Both American and British leaders gambled that a dramatic demonstration of the awesome destructive power of the atom bomb would force the Soviets to recognize that the United States held the winning card and that they must therefore play the postwar game according to American rules.

Finally, the decision to drop the atom bombs must be seen within the context of total war, and, in particular, the strategic mass bombing of civilian centers. In 1939, both Roosevelt and British prime minister Neville Chamberlain publicly condemned aerial bombing of noncombatants as an unacceptable atrocity. But after the German Luftwaffe began bombarding British cities in the fall of 1940, the British Royal Air Force retaliated with air attacks on German civilian centers. Flying in massive formations, bomber planes dropped incendiary bombs and set Germany ablaze. Tens of thousands of noncombatants died in these attacks. The most notorious occurred in 1945, when the Allies destroyed Dresden. A German city with great historical but no military or industrial value, Dresden housed thousands of refugees and over 26,000 American POWs. The bombing, together with the subsequent firestorm, resulted in 130,000 casualties.

In the first years of the war, American military officials had hesitated to follow the British lead in targeting civilian centers. But by 1945 the U.S. air command had adopted massive bombing raids as a key strategy in the war against Japan. In a single March evening, American planes bombed residential areas in Tokyo. Eighty-five thousand Japanese civilians died in the firestorm that night. In the next five months, American bombers hit sixty-six Japanese cities, burned 180 square miles, and killed approximately 330,000 Japanese.

By 1945, then, killing huge numbers of noncombatants had become commonplace. Years of immersion in the savage barbarity of World War II made the use of atom bombs acceptable. The atom bomb's appeal was not in its potential to kill tens of thousands in a single night; conventional bombs were already doing that, and doing it rather effectively. But the idea of massive casualties, caused by a single bomb, dropped by a single plane, promised to have an enormous psychological impact on the Japanese, and so to end the war more quickly.

The Dawn of the Nuclear Age

At 8:15 A.M. on August 6, 1945, a light "brighter than a thousand suns" flashed above the city of Hiroshima. For the first time ever, an atom bomb had been dropped on human beings. Ten days later, Japan surrendered to the Allies, and World War II ended. But the detonation of the atom bomb signaled more than the end of the war; it was a flashpoint of both a new political phase—the emerging Cold War—and a new cultural era. What, then, were the results, both immediate and long-term, of the atomic bombings of Hiroshima and Nagasaki? How did the cultural and political landscape shift after the atom bomb?

"THE GREATEST THING IN HISTORY"

On the day the first bomb was dropped, Truman received a telegram announcing the atomic bombing of Hiroshima: "Results clear-cut successful in all respects." Truman exulted, "This is the greatest thing in history."[17] The atom bomb dropped on Hiroshima caused greater damage than its creators had predicted. Temperatures at the site of the atomic explosion reached 5,400 degrees Fahrenheit. All those exposed within two miles of the center suffered primary thermal burns—their blood literally boiled and their skin peeled off in strips. The combined impact of the blast wave and the thermal flash started fires, which quickly coalesced into a firestorm. Of the 76,000 buildings in Hiroshima, 70,000 were damaged or destroyed. Human losses matched the material damage. Of a wartime population of 400,000, 140,000 died by the end of 1945, with another 60,000 dying in the next five years, primarily due to radiation poisoning. Scientists calculated that the atom bomb produced casualties 6,500 times more efficiently than an ordinary bomb.

Selected in May for atomic bombing, Hiroshima had been deliberately preserved from aerial attack to heighten the Bomb's psychological impact as well as to ensure that the atom bomb's force could be reliably measured. Government press releases about the bombing inaccurately described the city as "an important Japanese army base." Hiroshima did house 43,000 soldiers (a little over 3,000 of whom were killed by the atom bomb), but it was in fact an industrial city, populated by ordinary civilians.

The Japanese reacted to the Hiroshima bombing with incomprehension and confusion. They literally did not know what had hit them. One Japanese woman recalled, "I just could not understand why our surroundings had changed so greatly in one instant . . . I thought it might have been something which had nothing to do with the war, the collapse of the earth which it was said would take place at the end of the world."[18] Within the high levels of the Japanese government, gradual realization of the atomic bomb's power, coupled with U.S. threats of sending a "rain of ruin" on Japan if it did not surrender, strengthened the position of those officials who recognized that Japan must now give up. A hardline faction of the military, however, wished to fight on.

On August 8, the Soviet Union declared war on Japan. The next day, a second atom bomb fell on Japan. Not even named on the original target list, Nagasaki received the second atom bomb by chance. Because the original objective, Kokura, was shielded by heavy cloud cover, the pilot turned toward his secondary target. The atom bomb in Nagasaki killed 70,000 outright, with another 70,000 dying over the next five years. On August 10, Emperor Hirohito met with his military leaders. Viewed in the West as an implacable war lord, Hirohito was actually a man with fairly limited political power who had been pressing for peace since June. Now he insisted the time had come to surrender.

Negotiations between the Allies and the Japanese cabinet over the position of the emperor in a postwar Japan continued until August 15, when peace was announced. In Hiroshima and Nagasaki, however, another battle was raging, this time against an unseen and at first unrecognized enemy—radiation. On September 5, 1945, a journalist for the London *Daily Express* reported,

In Hiroshima . . . people are still dying, mysteriously and horribly—people who were uninjured in the cataclysm from an unknown something which I can only describe as the atomic plague.[19]

The lingering horror of radiation sickness, accounts of which were at first dismissed by many Americans as Japanese propaganda, signaled that the atom bomb was not just a bigger weapon, not simply more bang for the buck. A revolutionary new force, it introduced the world to new horrors and new possibilities.

COLD WAR CONCERNS AND THE NUCLEAR ARMS RACE

The scientists who created the atom bomb recognized that it had the potential to revolutionize international power relations. The eminent Danish scientist Niels Bohr (1886–1962) urged both Roosevelt and Churchill in 1944 to inform Stalin of the Manhattan Project and prepare a postwar plan for international control of atomic weapons. Bohr feared that failure to include the Soviets in the development

"A GOOD DOSE OF PROPAGANDA"

························

The following is an excerpt from a declassified transcript (originally marked "Top Secret") of a telephone conversation between General Leslie Groves, the head of the Manhattan Project, and Lt. Col. Rea, a military physician at Oak Ridge Hospital. Groves, concerned about media reports of radiation sickness among Hiroshima survivors, called on Rea for reassurance and advice. The excerpt begins with Groves quoting from a disturbing report.

Groves: Then it goes on: "Radioactivity caused by the fission of the uranium used in atomic bombs is taking a toll of mounting deaths and causing reconstruction workers in Hiroshima to suffer various sicknesses and ill health."

Rea: I would say this: You yourself, as far as radioactivity is concerned, it isn't anything immediate, it's a prolonged thing. I think what these people have, they just got a good thermal burn, that's what it is. . . .

Groves: Now then, he says—this is the thing I wanted to ask you about particularly—"an examination of soldiers working on reconstruction projects one week after the bombing showed that their white corpuscles had diminished by half and a severe deficiency of red corpuscles."

Rea: I read that, too—I think there's something hookum about that.

Groves: Would they both go down?

Rea: They may, yes, they may, but that's awfully quick, pretty terrifically quick. Of course it depends—but I wonder if you aren't getting a good dose of propaganda . . . Of course those Jap scientists over there aren't so dumb either and they are making a play on this, too. They evidently know what the possibility is. Personally, I discounted a lot of it, as it's too early, and in the second place, I think that a lot of these deaths they are getting are just delayed thermal burns.

. . .

Groves: This is the kind of thing that hurts us—"The Japanese, who were reported today by Tokyo radio, to have died mysteriously a few days after the atomic bomb blast, probably were the victims of a phenomenon which is well known in the great radiation laboratories of America." That, of course, is what does us the damage.

Rea: I would say this: You will have to get some big-wig to put a counter-statement in the paper.

Source: Excerpts from Groves, 201 File. Manhattan Engineer District Records. National Archives.

---

of the atomic bomb would fuel Soviet suspicion of the West and result in a frightening race to amass nuclear arms.

After the Japanese bombings, many Manhattan Project scientists and other leading intellectuals—including Albert Einstein and Leo Szilard—joined with Bohr in demanding that a radical new world order be created. The resulting "scientists' movement" attempted to use the great prestige of nuclear scientists after Hiroshima to influence the reconstruction of postwar political structures. The movement called for the development of transnational institutions that would not only control the world's supply of nuclear weapons but also work to redistribute the world's wealth more rationally and reduce nationalistic competition. The alternative, scientists warned, was World War III—a nuclear conflict that could destroy civilization.

The efforts of the scientists to head off a nuclear arms race proved futile. To political leaders in the United States and Britain, demands that the U.S. government turn over its nuclear weapons technology to an international body seemed misguided, at best. The Manhattan Project, although rooted in fear of a German atom bomb, was also shaped by American and British convictions that the Soviet Union would be the West's principal postwar adversary. General Groves, the military head of the Manhattan Project, recalled that "there was never . . . any illusion on

my part but that Russia was our enemy, and the Project was conducted on that basis."[20] Churchill, Roosevelt, and Truman all viewed the atom bomb not only as a war-winning weapon, but also as a postwar diplomatic tool, a device to control the Soviets once peace was declared.

Possession of the atomic "secret" thus shaped Anglo-American attitudes and actions toward the Soviet Union in the final months of the war. Truman scheduled the Potsdam Conference, the "Big Three" summit called to negotiate postwar power relations, to coincide with the Trinity test explosion. He knew that if the test was successful, he would have a weighty bargaining chip in his negotiations with Stalin. The Trinity test report transformed Truman's very demeanor at Potsdam. According to Churchill, Truman "was a changed man. He told the Russians just where they got on and off, and generally bossed the whole meeting." As Truman's adviser James Byrnes (1882–1972) explained, Truman gambled that the Bomb would "put us in a position to dictate our own terms at the end of the war."[21]

The gamble did not pay off. The Soviets responded not by acquiescing to Anglo-American demands but by accelerating their own nuclear weapons research. American policymakers wagered that the Soviets would be unable to develop atomic weapons for at least ten years. They did not realize, however, how advanced the Soviet atomic project already was. Soviet scientists were some of the best in the world and Stalin authorized the spending of huge sums of money on the project. In addition, Soviet spies on the Manhattan Project had passed crucial scientific information on to Russian scientists who, like their Western counterparts, were motivated by a mixture of patriotism and scientific curiosity to press forward rapidly toward an atomic weapon. Fear also played a role: Soviet atomic scientists knew that if they failed, their lives were forfeit. When Stalin's deputy Beria warned against giving scientists too much freedom, Stalin replied, "Leave them in peace. We can always shoot them later."[22]

In August, 1949, the Soviets detonated "Joe I," the first Soviet atom bomb. The nuclear arms race° was on. Within three years the atom bomb was outmoded. The United States won the race for the hydrogen bomb, a weapon more than one thousand times more destructive than the atomic bombs used against Japan. The United States detonated the world's first hydrogen bomb in November 1952, but the Soviets followed in August 1953 with a technologically more sophisticated device. In the second half of the 1950s the nuclear arms race veered onto a new track, with the focus less on the bombs themselves than on their delivery systems. In August 1957, the Soviets tested the world's first intercontinental ballistic missile (ICBM); the U.S. version followed one year later. By the mid-1960s, both the United States and the Soviet Union had replaced the manned bomber plane with nuclear submarines and missiles.

The nuclear arms race had important consequences for the postwar world. In international relations, the nuclear arms race raised the stakes of the Cold War conflict, as both superpowers sought to ensure that their nuclear arsenal equaled or surpassed that of their rival. It also enhanced the position of the superpowers vis-à-vis other allied and rival powers. Other nations did acquire access to nuclear weapons, but none could afford the vast nuclear stockpiles built up by the Soviet Union and the United States. The nations belonging to the two rival Cold War alliances, NATO and the Warsaw Pact, relied on the superpowers for their nuclear defense. Curiously, however, possession of nuclear weapons also limited Soviet and American power. The nuclear threat proved to be a restraining force; behind every potential military action rested the question, "Is this worth the risk of a nuclear war?"

Another consequence of the nuclear arms race was a far-reaching militarization of ordinary life. In a nuclear conflict, to be attacked is to be destroyed; hence, the only possibility of victory rests in launching a surprise attack, in hitting the enemy before it has a chance to hit you. In the 1950s, then, citizens on both sides of the Cold War divide learned that destruction might rain from the skies at any moment. In the United States, the Soviet Union, and Britain, civil-defense campaigns sought to buttress civilian morale by preparing them for nuclear war. American

CHRONOLOGY

The Nuclear Arms Race

1942	Manhattan Project underway; Soviet spies keep Stalin informed
1945	Hiroshima and Nagasaki bombings; acceleration of Soviet atomic bomb project
1949	First test of Soviet atomic bomb
1952	First test of British atomic bomb
	First test of American hydrogen bomb
1953	First test of Soviet hydrogen bomb
1957	First test of British hydrogen bomb
	First test of Soviet ICBM
1958	Formation of Campaign for Nuclear Disarmament (CND) in Britain; first test of American ICBM
1960	First test of French atomic bomb
1964	First test of Chinese atomic bomb

schoolchildren practiced diving under their desks and covering their heads with their hands—"duck-and-cover drills"—to ready them for nuclear attack. Soviet citizens were taught how to dig shelters in which to shield themselves from post-attack radiation.

The superpowers clearly dominated the nuclear race, yet other nations also sought to enter the contest. For many nations, the possession of nuclear weapons technology seemed an important guarantor of national prestige and power. By the end of the twentieth century, the nuclear club included as its members not only the Soviet Union and the United States but also Britain, France, China, Israel, India, Pakistan, and, it is believed, South Africa and Brazil.

LEARNING TO LIVE WITH THE BOMB

Nuclear weapons presented a cultural as well as political and military challenge. While the science behind the bomb eluded the grasp of all but those with advanced scientific educations, the implications of this new weapon were much more readily accessible. From the moment that the Hiroshima bombing was announced, people recognized that the world stood on the brink of an unknown era. Amidst the rejoicing and relief over the war's ending arose fear and apprehension about the dawn of the atomic age. As the

American magazine *Time* noted in its end-of-the-year issue, "What the world would best remember of 1945 was the deadly mushroom clouds over Hiroshima and Nagasaki . . . In their giant shadows . . . all men were pygmies."

With astonishing swiftness, speculations emerged about new and bigger bombs, and the annihilation of entire civilizations. In 1945 Manhattan Project scientists had only begun to explore the possibility of a hydrogen bomb; yet popular culture immediately grasped that Hiroshima was only the beginning. Within just a few months after the atomic bombings, for example, American newspapers featured stories predicting atomic wars that would devastate not just single cities but the entire Earth, leaving behind "a barren waste, in which the survivors of the race will hide in caves or live among ruins."[23]

Threads of sparkling hope interwove with these somber expressions of fear. The fact of the atom bomb made the realization of other seemingly farfetched dreams seem possible. Abundant energy "too cheap to meter," a cure for cancer and inherited diseases, plentiful harvests and giant fruits, deserts turned to lush tropical paradises—all were promised in the immediate aftermath of the destruction of Hiroshima and Nagasaki.

By the 1960s, World War III had not devastated civilization, nor had the world been transformed into paradise, yet Europeans and Americans found themselves struggling to come to terms with the new nuclear age. A growing understanding of radiation and its dangers introduced new fears into ordinary life. The Australian Nevil Shute's (1899–1960) *On the Beach,* published first as a novel in 1959 and then produced as a film in 1962, articulated the widespread cultural anxiety. In Shute's unrealistic but unforgettable fiction, the inhabitants of a southern Australian community await inevitable death from invisible clouds of radiation already responsible for obliterating human life on the rest of the planet.

Scientists scoffed at Shute's fictional radiation clouds, but his novel seemed convincing to many readers who had learned during the previous decade that poisonous clouds were far more than fantasy in the nuclear age. Aboveground nuclear testing in the American West, various South Pacific island clusters, and the Soviet Union had introduced a new word into the world's vocabulary: *fallout.* Scientists had assumed that the radioactive effects of a nuclear explosion would be confined to the blast area, but they were wrong. These explosions ejected into the air radioactive particles, which formed pinkish clouds that drifted across the skies and later settled to the ground in the form of fallout, often appearing as a light dust or ash—or, to children, a sort of snow in which they delighted to play. In 1954, fallout rained down on four Japanese fishermen caught unaware near a U.S. hydrogen bomb test. The resulting death of one of the fishermen became a worldwide scandal that sparked awareness of and protests against nuclear testing.

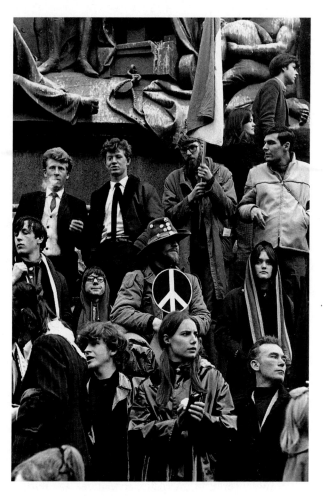

■ **Nuclear Protest**

CND supporters gather in Trafalgar Square, London, for the annual Easter march to the British nuclear weapons research establishment at Aldermaston. The circular CND symbol quickly transcended the movement itself and became a global peace symbol.

The most significant of these protests emerged in Britain at the start of 1958 when a group of middle-class men and women formed the Campaign for Nuclear Disarmament (CND). Its founders—journalists and intellectuals with a long history of participation in respectable protest and humanitarian campaigns—envisioned CND as an elite pressure group that would lobby Parliament to abandon Britain's separate nuclear weapons program. Much to their surprise and discomfort, CND mushroomed into the first significant postwar mass movement, drawing up to 100,000 supporters onto its annual Easter march and expressing an unfocused but deeply felt sense of uneasiness with the nuclear age. It quickly sparked the formation of similar campaigns in western Europe and the United States, while its symbol, a circle containing a broken cross (actually a combination of the semaphore signals for

N [nuclear] and D [disarmament]), became an instantly recognizable global icon of postwar protest. In many ways, CND foreshadowed the larger and more well-known protests of the 1960s (see Chapter 28). Its young, blue-jeans-clad marchers, stepping to the beat of jazz bands, voiced their anger at having been sidelined while the superpowers played a dangerous nuclear game.

In this period, the Bomb also permeated American and European cultural consciousness. Because figurative painting seemed utterly incapable of capturing the power and terror of the atomic age, the bomb reinforced the hold of abstract art over the avant-garde. But abstract art itself changed. Rejecting the very formal, carefully composed, geometric abstractions that had characterized much of modernist art in the period before the war, Abstract Expressionists sought to develop more spontaneous, emotional styles. Jackson Pollack (1912–1956), for example, invented an entirely new way of painting. Placing the canvas on the ground, he moved around and in it, dripping or pouring paint. Such a technique rested on intuition rather than intellect, and demanded that the artist almost throw himself into the painting itself. As Pollack explained, "New needs need new techniques . . . The modern painter cannot express his age, the airplane, the atom bomb . . . in the old forms."[24] In Pollack's works, the canvas has no clear center, no focal point. Instead, it disintegrates, like matter itself.

Musicians, too, responded to the challenge of the nuclear age. For Polish composer Krzysztof Penderecki (b. 1933), the revolution in warfare wrought at Hiroshima demanded radical changes in musical composition. He created new notational devices and constructed a work for no fewer than fifty-two stringed instruments. Penderecki's *Threnody* [a song of lamentation] *for the Victims of Hiroshima* was praised as one of the best musical works of the year when it was performed in Warsaw in 1961. Probably the best-known musical response to Hiroshima, Penderecki's piece, with its polytonal dissonances, absorbs its listener into a world of pain and anger.

Most people confronted their nuclear fears not in concert halls or art galleries, but rather in movie theaters. Here various nuclear-spawned terrors, including giant spiders, ants, and turtles, wreaked weekly havoc on the Western world. Fittingly enough, many of these films were produced in Japan.

Throughout the 1950s, nuclear war and the postnuclear struggle for survival also filled the pages of popular fiction.

■ **Jackson Pollack,** *Shimmering Substance* **(1946)**

Many of Pollack's postwar works—huge paintings that pulse with power—show an obsession with heat and light, surely no coincidence in the dawn of the nuclear age.

■ **Peter Sellers as Dr. Strangelove**
This blackly comic character's strange love for the technologies of mass destruction linked together Nazism and the nuclear age.

Probably the most important "nuclear" novel, however, confined mention of atomic bombs to a single sentence. In *The Lord of the Flies* (1954), British author William Golding (1911–1993) told the simple and brutal story of the conflict between savagery and civilization. Fleeing an England under atomic attack, a group of upper-class boarding-school boys are stranded on an island. Their moral deterioration poses basic questions about the meaning of civilization, a question brought to the forefront of Western culture by the use of advanced science to obliterate civilian populations.

The Lord of the Flies showed how quickly the veneer of civilization disintegrates in a world without advanced technology; other cultural productions of the postwar period spotlight technology itself as a threat to civilization. The fear of technology out of control served as the dramatic impulse behind two notable films released in 1964. The first, *Fail-Safe,* used a compelling but conventional narrative to dramatize the failure of supposedly "fail-safe" weapons-control devices and the resulting nuclear devastation of Moscow and New York. But it took filmmaker Stanley Kubrick's (1928–1999) masterpiece, *Dr. Strangelove; or, How I Learned to Stop Worrying and Love the Bomb* (1964), to capture the widespread fear of a nuclear war sparked by accident, by a combination of human error and technological determinism. Unlike *Fail-Safe* (and most films about nuclear war), *Dr. Strangelove* was a comedy; it subverted conventional Cold War orthodoxies by daring to laugh at nuclear war. In its pervasive sense of uneasiness with the power delivered by science into human hands, we can discern the cultural fallout of the nuclear age.

CONCLUSION
The West, Progress, and Power

The title character of Kubrick's film, Dr. Strangelove, is a German scientist who cannot resist thrusting his arm forward in a Nazi salute and yelling, "Heil Hitler!" at inappropriate moments. In these scenes of black comedy, Kubrick linked the Nazi obsession with power to the postwar quest for nuclear dominance. It is a linkage that resonates in Western culture after Auschwitz and the atom bomb. As one scholar has argued, two images "have haunted mankind since the Second World War—the barbed wire and emaciated figures of Hitler's death camps, and the blinding white flash over the city of Hiroshima."[25]

Just as the Holocaust raised crucial questions about the meaning of Western civilization, so too did the bombings of Hiroshima and Nagasaki and their nuclear aftermath. With the best of intentions, some of the greatest minds in the Western world had produced weapons designed to kill and maim tens of thousands of civilians. For centuries, the use of the methods of scientific inquiry to uncover truth and achieve both material and moral progress had supported Westerners' self-identification and their sense of cultural superiority. The carnage of

World War I had eroded these assumptions; World War II and particularly the Holocaust and the atom bomb threatened to level them entirely. The war years demonstrated that the best of science could produce the worst of weapons, that technology and technique could combine in factories designed for mass murder. The task of accepting this knowledge, and facing up to its implications, helped shape Western culture after 1945.

Suggestions for Further Reading

For a comprehensive list of suggested readings, please go to www.ablongman.com/levack/chapter27

Alperovitz, Gar. *Atomic Diplomacy: Hiroshima and Potsdam. The Use of the Atomic Bomb and the American Confrontation with Soviet Power*. 1994. The first edition of this book, published in 1965, sparked an ongoing scholarly debate about the role of Cold War concerns in shaping U.S. decision making at the end of World War II.

Arad, Yitzhak, ed. *The Pictorial History of the Holocaust*. 1990. An excellent introduction.

Browning, Christopher. *Ordinary Men: Reserve Police Battalion 101 and the Final Solution in Poland*. 1992. A powerful account of the participation of a group of "ordinary men" in mass murder.

Frayn, Michael. *Copenhagen*. 1998. A remarkable play in which Frayn dramatizes a meeting (which actually did occur) between the German atomic physicist Werner Hiesenberg and his Danish anti-Nazi colleague Niels Bohr. Contains both extremely clear explanations of the workings of atomic physics and a provocative exploration of the moral issues involved in the making of the atom bomb.

Friedlander, Saul. *Nazi Germany and the Jews, 1933–1939*. 1998. An important study of the evolution of Nazi anti-Semitic policy before the war.

Hersey, John. *Hiroshima*. 1985. This edition of Hersey's classic account (first published in 1946) contains an added chapter that tells the stories of the survivors forty years after the bombing.

Hilberg, Raul. *Perpetrators, Victims, Bystanders: The Jewish Catastrophe, 1933–1945*. 1992. As his title indicates, Hilberg looks at the three principal sets of participants in the Holocaust.

Marrus, Michael R. *The Holocaust in History*. 1987. A clearly written, concise account of historians' efforts to understand the Holocaust. Highly recommended.

Niewyk, Donald L., ed. *The Holocaust: Problems and Perspectives of Interpretation*. 1992. Looks at areas of dispute such as the origins of the Holocaust, the extent of Jewish resistance, and the possibilities of rescue.

Nobile, Philip, ed. *Judgment at the Smithsonian: The Bombing of Hiroshima and Nagasaki*. 1995. Includes an extremely sensible essay by historian Barton Bernstein on both the historiography and popular mythology of the bombings.

Rhodes, Richard. *Masters of Death: The SS-Einsatzgruppen and the Invention of the Holocaust*. 2002. Compelling account of the Einsatzgruppen actions during the German invasion of the Soviet Union.

Rhodes, Richard. *The Making of the Atomic Bomb*. 1986. A lengthy but very readable account; very good at explaining the complicated science involved.

Sherwin, Martin J. *A World Destroyed: Hiroshima and the Origins of the Arms Race*. 1987. Focuses on the diplomatic and political context.

Notes

1. Quoted in Robert H. Abzug, *Inside the Vicious Heart: Americans and the Liberation of Nazi Concentration Camps* (1985), p. 19.
2. Quoted in Gordon Horwitz, *In the Shadow of Death, Living Outside the Gates of Mauthausen* (1991), p. 167.
3. This argument is made by Christopher Browning in *The Path to Genocide: Essays on the Launching of the Final Solution* (1992).
4. Elie Wiesel, *Night*, (1958), p. 39.
5. Quoted in Horwitz, p. 35.
6. Quoted in Walter Laqueur, *The Terrible Secret: An Investigation into the Suppression of Information about Hitler's "Final Solution"* (1982), p. 100.
7. Gideon Hausner, *Justice in Jerusalem* (1966), p. 291.
8. Hausner, pp. 323–324.
9. From Hausner's opening statement; quoted in Moshe Pearlman, *The Capture and Trial of Adolf Eichmann* (1963), p. 149.
10. Quoted in Pearlman, pp. 463–465.
11. Quoted in Pearlman, p. 603; Hausner, p. 422.
12. The quotation is from Ernst Nolte, translated and quoted by Charles Maier, in *The Unmasterable Past: History, Holocaust, and German National Identity* (1997), p. 32.
13. Karl A. Schleunes, *The Twisted Road to Auschwitz: Nazi Policy Toward German Jews, 1933–39* (1970), p. 1.
14. Martin J. Sherwin, *A World Destroyed: Hiroshima and the Origins of the Arms Race* (1987), p. 17.
15. Quoted in Richard Rhodes, *The Making of the Atomic Bomb* (1986), pp. 672, 675, 676.

16. Quoted in Ronald Takaki, *Hiroshima: Why America Dropped the Bomb* (1995), p. 3.
17. Quoted in Takaki, p. 46.
18. Quoted in Robert Jay Lifton, *Death in Life: The Survivors of Hiroshima* (1967), pp. 22-23.
19. Quoted in Paul Boyer, *By the Bomb's Early Light: American Thought and Culture at the Dawn of the Atomic Age* (1985), p. 187.
20. Quoted in Sherwin, p. 62.
21. Churchill to Henry L. Stimson, Stimson Diary; quoted in Sherwin, p. 199.
22. Quoted in John Lewis Gaddis, *We Now Know: Rethinking Cold War History* (1997), p. 96.
23. Quotation from the *Chicago Tribune;* quoted in Boyer, p. 15.
24. Quoted in Jonathan Fineberg, *Art Since 1940: Strategies of Being* (1995), p. 89.
25. Michael Bess, *Realism, Utopia, and the Mushroom Cloud* (1993), p. xv.

INFORMATION
LIBRE

Redefining the West After World War II

ON ONE APPARENTLY ORDINARY DAY IN AUGUST 1961, WESTERN EUROPEAN television viewers witnessed an extraordinary sight. While the news cameras rolled, policemen from East Berlin played tug-of-war with firemen from West Berlin. Between them was not a length of rope, but rather a middle-aged German woman. This horrifying contest had been set in motion by the construction of the Berlin Wall. Appalled by the growing numbers of East German citizens who were fleeing communist rule through the gateway of West Berlin, the East German and Soviet authorities decided to shut the gate. In the early morning hours of August 13, East German workers erected a barbed-wire fence along Berlin's east-west dividing line. In some cases, this line ran right through apartment buildings. For the next few weeks, these apartments provided literal "windows to the west." West Berlin firemen waited with blankets ready to catch anyone willing to jump out of a window—and out of communist eastern Europe. These windows closed quickly. The communist authorities bricked them up; later they leveled entire apartment buildings to create a moat in front of what was now the armed fortress of East Berlin. The barbed-wire fence became a concrete wall buttressed by gun towers, lit by searchlights and patrolled by armed guards with "shoot to kill" orders.

The unidentified woman in this scene, literally caught between West and East, serves as an appropriate symbol for Europe during the 1950s and 1960s. In these decades, the Cold War between the United States and the Soviet Union influenced European politics, culture, and society. European governments and their populations found their freedom of maneuver checked by Cold War constraints. The woman's desperation to reach the West reminds us that American influence in western Europe should not be equated with Soviet control of eastern Europe: Cultural and economic dominance are not the same as political tyranny.

Chapter Outline

- The Cold War, the West, and the World
- Imperial Encounters: Decolonization in a Cold War Context
- After Stalin: The Soviet Union and Eastern Europe in the 1950s and 1960s
- The West: Integration and Affluence
- Culture and Society in the Age of Consumption

Protest Poster, Paris 1968: Many of the protest movements of the 1960s questioned the democratic nature of Western governments. Protesters in Paris in 1968 used posters such as this one to articulate their sense that, despite constitutional guarantees and universal suffrage, Western political systems actually suppressed free speech.

Tug-of-War at the Berlin Wall
Caught by the television cameras, this woman sought to escape through her window into West Berlin. She succeeded.

Nevertheless, many Europeans in the West as well as the East felt that they no longer controlled their own societies.

The Cold War was an encounter of two clashing ideologies, as much a battle of ideas and values as weapons and warriors. Both sides laid claim to universal cultures—to have achieved a way of life that would benefit *all* human societies. This ideological encounter forced a redefinition of "the West." Previous chapters have described the way in which this cultural construct shifted over time. By the late nineteenth century, Christianity, although still important, played a less central role in defining "the West" than did a mix of other factors, including the possession of industrial technology, the illusion of white superiority based on pseudoscientific racist theorizing, and faith in both capitalist economics and liberal political values. The Cold War added an anti-Soviet stance and a fear of communist ideology to the mix. These additions at times eroded the Western commitment to democracy, particularly within the developing world.

Significantly, the Cold War turned "hot" not in Europe but in places such as Korea, Cuba, and Vietnam. The developing world served as the site of crucial Cold War conflicts

in this era. The postwar years witnessed the widening of the economic gap between "North" and "South"—between the industrialized nations, largely located in the Northern Hemisphere, and the economically underdeveloped regions (many but certainly not all of which were situated south of the equator), now shrugging off colonial rule and seeking both political independence and economic prosperity. Thus, as Europeans encountered each other across the Cold War divide, they also encountered non-Europeans across a huge economic gulf. Two very different contests—North versus South and West versus East—quickly became entangled with each other as the Cold War moved beyond Europe's borders to the developing regions.

These encounters created postwar Western culture. To understand their impact, this chapter addresses five questions: (1) What shape did the global Cold War assume after 1949? (2) What was the impact of decolonization on both the former imperial powers in western Europe and on the global balance of power? (3) What patterns characterized the history of the Soviet Union and eastern Europe after the death of Stalin? (4) What developments produced the unprecedented political stability and economic prosperity in western Europe in this era? (5) How do we explain social and cultural trends in this time of fast-paced change?

The Cold War, the West, and the World

The specter of a Third World War loomed over Europe in the 1950s. An American anthropologist living in a small French village, for example, found his neighbors reluctant to make any long-range plans. As one farmer explained, "Plant an apricot orchard so the Russians and Americans can use it as a battlefield? Thanks, [I'm] not so dumb."[1] The postwar era saw the leaders of the superpowers struggling with the new horrible possibilities created by nuclear weapons. At the same time, anticolonial nationalist movements and Cold War rivalries flowed together in an unstable and at times combustible mixture.

THE COLD WAR GOES GLOBAL: THE CHINESE REVOLUTION AND THE KOREAN WAR, 1949–1953

China provided the first example of this inflammable mixture. In 1949, the Communists under Mao Zedong won their decades-long battle to assume control of China. Mao followed in Stalin's footsteps, establishing a one-party state and identifying entire social classes as "enemies of the people." To many Western observers, particularly in the United States, Mao's victory heralded a disturbing expansion of communist power. As Mao triumphantly proclaimed, "The East is Red!" The United States refused to recognize China's communist government as legitimate, and international tensions deepened.

In 1950, this vision of a Red East turned the Cold War hot in Korea. A part of the Japanese empire since 1910, Korea regained political independence after Japan's defeat in 1945, but was immediately divided. A Soviet-allied communist regime took over North Korea, and an anti-communist state propped up by the United States was established in the south. In 1950, Stalin gave in to pressure from North Korea's leader, Kim Il-Sung (1912–1994), and agreed to supply arms for an invasion of South Korea. This civil war was quickly swallowed up by the Cold War. A UN-sponsored, largely American army fought alongside South Korean troops, while soldiers from Communist China supported North Korea.

The Korean War accelerated the globalization of the Cold War. U.S. policymakers became convinced that communism was on the march throughout Asia and had to be stopped. As a result of the Korean conflict, the French government was able to persuade Truman's administration to support its struggle against communist nationalists in Indochina, thus drawing the United States into supporting a colonial regime and onto the path that would lead to its war in Vietnam. The conflict in Korea also welded Japan firmly into the Western alliance. As the U.S. army turned to the Japanese for vital military supplies, over $3.5 billion poured into and rejuvenated the Japanese economy. (American military orders for trucks guaranteed the success of a struggling new Japanese firm called Toyota.) Transformed from an occupied enemy to a staunch ally and an economic powerhouse, Japan became the dam holding back "the red tide that threatens to engulf the world."[2] Thus, in a curious way, Japan—geographically as far "East" as one can get—became a part of the "West."

The Korean War demonstrated not only the globalization of the Cold War but also its limits. After three years of fighting and more than three million deaths, Korea remained divided. Stalin refused to send the Red Army into the conflict, and Truman resisted pressure to invade Communist China. This restraint was imposed, at least in part, by new military realities. By 1950, both sides possessed the atomic bomb. Both realized that expanding the war would almost guarantee the use of nuclear weapons. The question, "Is this worth a nuclear war?" proved inescapable.

Often seen as an American affair, the Korean War did involve small numbers of European troops. Far more important, it fostered intense political controversy within western Europe and raised important questions about the role of the United States in European affairs. Fearing that the war's outbreak signaled a more aggressive Soviet policy in Europe as well as Asia, western European leaders pushed for the transformation of NATO from a loose defensive alliance to a coordinated and formidable fighting

CHRONOLOGY

The Cold War, 1950–1962

1950	Outbreak of the Korean War
1953	First American and Soviet hydrogen bomb tests; death of Joseph Stalin; end of the Korean War
1955	First Geneva summit
1956	Hungarian uprising and its repression by Soviet troops
1957	Launch of *Sputnik*
1959	Khrushchev's visit to the United States
1961	Berlin Wall built
1962	Cuban Missile Crisis

force. This transformation, however, came at a price. As the U.S. military budget exploded from $13.5 billion to $50 billion per year, Truman's administration demanded that its European allies strengthen their own military forces and permit the rearmament of West Germany. Konrad Adenauer (1876–1967), West Germany's first chancellor, argued that only a rearmed West Germany could prevent the forcible reunification of Germany on Soviet terms, but with the trauma of German conquest and occupation so recently behind them, many Europeans were horrified by German rearmament. Britain's prime minister Clement Attlee warned, "The policy of using Satan to defeat Sin is very dangerous." Even within West Germany the proposal aroused strong opposition. After four years of controversy and a failed effort to create a western European army (the European Defense Community, or EDC), West Germany rearmed, as the United States had initially demanded, under the NATO umbrella.

BRIDGES AND BRINKMANSHIP: THE COLD WAR, 1953–1963

In 1953, both sides in the Cold War changed leaders. Stalin died in March 1953, just a few months after a new Republican administration headed by President Dwight Eisenhower (1890–1969) took office in the United States. This change of leadership heralded a new phase in the Cold War in which both sides sought to build bridges—to improve communications, find common ground, and thereby ease tensions. But at the same time, both players utilized the contradictory strategy of brinkmanship°, which relied on the threat of nuclear war. Eisenhower's Secretary of State John Foster Dulles (1888–1959) articulated the classic brinkmanship argument: "If you try to run away from [nuclear war], if you are scared to go to the brink, you are lost."[3] With the Cold War veering sharply back and forth between bridge building and brinkmanship, the period from 1953 until 1963 was characterized by heightened hopes and deepening fears, by thawing superpower relations followed by the icy blasts of renewed hostilities.

Summit Talks and Spy Planes

Eisenhower was elected in 1952 with a promise of an aggressive new approach to foreign affairs. He and Dulles rejected Truman's policy of *containing* communism as defeatist, a "negative, futile and immoral policy . . . which abandons countless human beings to a despotism and Godless terrorism."[4] Instead, they committed the United States to *roll back* communism and insisted that communist aggression would be met with massive nuclear retaliation.

The new American brinkmanship was matched on the other side of the Cold War divide. After a period of uncertain leadership following Stalin's death in 1953, Nikita Khrushchev (1955–1964) emerged in 1955 as the new Soviet leader. Loud and boisterous, given to off-the-cuff remarks and spontaneous displays of emotion, Khrushchev contrasted sharply with the disciplined, reserved Stalin. (It is hard to imagine Stalin taking off his shoe and beating it on a table, as Khrushchev did in front of the television cameras at an assembly of the United Nations.) Khrushchev played a dangerous game of nuclear bluff, in which he persistently and often quite successfully convinced allies and foes alike that the Soviet Union possessed a far stronger nuclear force than it actually did.

Both Khrushchev and Eisenhower, however, recognized that the hydrogen bomb made total war unwinnable and both sought ways to break out of the positions into which they were frozen by Cold War hostilities. In July 1955, representatives of Britain, France, the United States, and the Soviet Union met in Geneva for the first summit of the Cold War. Although this summit produced no substantial policies, it marked a crucial psychological step, a bridge across the Cold War divide. In April 1956, Khrushchev traveled on a state visit to Britain—the first Cold War visit of a Soviet leader to a Western nation.

The Cold War froze once again in October 1956, when Khrushchev sent tanks into Hungary to crush a nationalist rebellion there. Less than one year later, the Soviets launched into space the first human-made satellite, *Sputnik*. The crushing of the Hungarian Revolution showed that the Soviets would permit no challenge to their authority in eastern Europe, while the success of *Sputnik* seemed to shift the military balance of power. Khrushchev claimed—falsely—that the Soviets possessed an advanced intercontinental ballistic missile (ICBM) force and that Soviet factories were producing rockets "like sausages from a machine."[5] Many in the West feared that the Soviets were winning the Cold War. To western

Europeans, *Sputnik* had ominous implications. The development of ICBMs meant that American cities were vulnerable to a Soviet nuclear strike. Europeans began to ask themselves whether the United States would actually risk Chicago to save Paris: If the Soviets invaded western Europe with conventional forces, would the Americans respond with nuclear weapons and so open their own cities to nuclear retaliation?

Yet in the late 1950s, the Cold War ice seemed to be breaking once again. In 1958 the Soviet Union announced a voluntary suspension on nuclear testing. The United States and Britain followed suit and nuclear test ban talks opened in Geneva. The next year Khrushchev spent twelve days touring the United States—much to his regret, security concerns kept him from visiting Disneyland. The communist leader impressed Americans as a down-to-earth, ordinary sort of guy, a man rather than a monster. Khrushchev

■ **"We Will Bury You!"**
In sharp contrast to the reserved, taciturn Stalin, Khrushchev often exploded in anger. This *Time* magazine cover from September 1961 shows Khrushchev in a familiar bombastic pose, as the Soviet Union announced that it was resuming above-ground testing of its hydrogen bombs. One of Khrushchev's most memorable lines was his warning to the West about the coming economic supremacy of the Soviet system: "We will bury you!"

ended his U.S. visit with the promise of another four-power summit in 1960.

The summit never happened. A few weeks before the summit was to convene in France, the Soviet Union announced it had shot down an American spy plane and captured its pilot. The summit was aborted, and Cold War relations froze solid once again.

On the Brink: The Berlin Wall and the Cuban Missile Crisis

These incidents initiated one of the most dangerous periods in the Cold War. Soviet defense spending rose by one-third from 1959 to 1963. In the United States, Herman Kahn's *On Thermonuclear War* became a bestseller. Kahn argued that although thermonuclear war would mean the deaths of millions, it remained a winnable scenario. General Tommy Powers, the commander of the U.S. Strategic Air Command (the nuclear strike force), insisted, "At the end of the war, if there are two Americans and one Russian, we win." Europeans found this idea less than reassuring.

Many Europeans and Americans expected nuclear war to begin in the divided city of Berlin. Khrushchev once noted, "Berlin is the testicles of the West . . . Every time I want to make the West scream, I squeeze on Berlin."[6] Yet throughout the 1950s, it was the East, not the West, that found Berlin a rather tender spot on the collective communist body politic. Germans from the East regularly crossed into West Berlin to work, shop—and disappear. All totaled, 2.8 million East Germans (one-sixth of the population) fled west through Berlin between 1949 and 1961. This torrent of emigration seriously weakened the East German economy by siphoning off its most productive citizens. Almost 75 percent of those who emigrated were below age 45, and most were skilled workers or professionals. The continuing destabilization of East Germany and pressure from the East German communist leader Walter Ulbricht (1893–1973) pushed Khrushchev to adopt a dramatic solution in 1961— the construction of the Berlin Wall°, literally a concrete symbol of the Cold War divide.

The new American president, John F. Kennedy (1917–1963), asserted that "a wall is a hell of a lot better than a war,"[7] but relations between the superpowers remained very tense. Kennedy had campaigned for the presidency in 1960 on a strong anticommunist platform, warning Americans (incorrectly) of the Soviet Union's nuclear superiority: "We will mold our strength and become first again. Not first if. Not first but. Not first when. But first period."[8] Two weeks after the Wall went up, the Soviet Union ended a three-year moratorium on nuclear testing. Kennedy increased military spending and called for an expanded civil defense program to prepare the American public for nuclear war. In Britain, the Conservative government stepped up its own civil defense program, while across Europe men and women feared that if nuclear war occurred, their countries would become a wasteland.

Such a war was narrowly avoided in the fall of 1962. This time the battleground was not Berlin but Cuba, as once again the Cold War intersected with a nationalist struggle. In 1959, a nationalist revolutionary movement led by Fidel Castro (b. 1926) succeeded in toppling Fulgencio Batista y Zaldivar (1901–1973), Cuba's corrupt but pro-U.S. dictator. At the time of the revolution, Castro was not a communist. Faced with American hostility to his plans for radical land reform, however, Castro drew closer to the Soviet Union, which offered both economic and military assistance—and revolutionary enthusiasm. The Communist deputy premier Anastas Mikoyan (1895–1978) explained to an American official, "You Americans must realize what Cuba means to us old Bolsheviks. . . . it makes us feel like boys again!"[9] By 1962, Castro and Cuba were firmly within the Soviet communist camp.

Against such a background, the Cuban Missile Crisis unfolded. Aware of American efforts to assassinate Castro and emotionally committed to preserving the Cuban Revolution, Khrushchev decided "to throw a hedgehog at Uncle Sam's pants."[10] NATO nuclear missiles, stationed in Turkey, were aimed at Soviet cities; Khrushchev chose to retaliate in kind. In October 1962, Kennedy received photos, taken by a spy plane, of nuclear missile bases under construction in Cuba. When operational, the missiles would be able to reach every major mainland American city except Seattle. What the photographs did not show, and what Kennedy did not know, was that the Soviet forces in Cuba were armed with nuclear weapons—and with the discretionary power to use these weapons if U.S. forces attacked. Some of Kennedy's advisers urged just such an attack, but instead the president used secret diplomatic channels to lead Khrushchev to a compromise. Khrushchev removed the missiles and in exchange, Kennedy guaranteed that the United States would not invade Cuba and agreed to withdraw the NATO missiles from Turkey (while claiming that the removal of the Turkish missiles was unrelated to events in Cuba).

The Cuban Missile Crisis marked a watershed in the history of the Cold War. In the aftermath of the crisis, both the United States and the Soviet Union backed off from brinkmanship. In 1963, the superpowers agreed to stop aboveground nuclear testing with the Nuclear Test Ban Treaty, and set up between them the "hotline," a direct communications link (at first not a telephone but a system of telegraph lines and teleprinters) to encourage immediate personal consultation in the event of a future crisis.

BREAKING THE BLOCS: THE COLD WAR AFTER THE CRISIS

In the decade after the Cuban Missile Crisis, a series of diplomatic shifts reconfigured global alignments. The rigid bipolarization characteristic of the Cold War during the

1950s broke down; by the early 1970s, multiple poles of power had emerged.

Ostpolitik: Stabilizing Central Europe

The first of these diplomatic shifts occurred in central Europe. During the Cuban Missile Crisis, European political leaders on both sides of the Iron Curtain found themselves powerless, faced with what the British historian Arnold Toynbee described as "annihilation without representation." As a result, the crisis accelerated European efforts to forge paths less controlled by Cold War concerns. It was no coincidence that just one year later, in 1963, West Germany's Social Democratic Party (SPD) demanded a new *Ostpolitik* or "Eastern policy"—the opening of diplomatic and economic relations between West Germany and the Soviet Union and its satellite states.

In 1969, the West Berlin mayor and SPD leader Willy Brandt (1913–1992) became the chancellor of the West German government and proceeded to make *Ostpolitik* a reality. In treaties with both Poland and the Soviet Union, Brandt's government accepted Germany's wartime territorial losses and opened up economic links. In 1972 East and West Germany recognized the legitimacy of each other's existence and finally resolved the long-standing Berlin crisis: Brandt's government accepted that East Berlin was part of East Germany, while the Soviet Union guaranteed West German civilians access to West Berlin. In 1973, both Germanies entered the United Nations, a triumphant climax to *Ostpolitik*.

Detente: Controlling the Arms Race

With *Ostpolitik*, nations such as West Germany, Poland, and East Germany took the initiative in bridging the Cold War divide. But during this era, the leaders of the superpowers also acted to break down the bipolarities of the Cold War. By the end of the 1960s, both the Soviet Union and the United States faced stagnating economies, and both were spending $50 million per day on nuclear weapons. These economic pressures led Soviet and American leaders to embrace detente°, the effort to stabilize superpower relations through negotiations and arms control. In November 1969 Soviet and American negotiators began the Strategic Arms Limitation Talks (SALT). Signed in 1972, the agreement froze the existing weapons balance. With both superpowers possessing sufficient nuclear weaponry to destroy the globe several times over, SALT may seem to have been inconsequential, but it helped arrest the armaments spiral and, more important, revealed a shift in Cold War power relations.

The Sino-Soviet Split and Ping-Pong Diplomacy

This same era witnessed important changes in relations within the communist world. Throughout the 1930s and 1940s, the Chinese Communist leader Mao Zedong was an obedient disciple of Stalin, whom he regarded as an authoritative "elder brother" in the family of communism. But

CHRONOLOGY

The Cold War, 1963–1973

1963	Nuclear Test Ban treaty signed; contacts between China and Soviet Union suspended; West German SPD demands a new *Ostpolitik*
1964	Khrushchev ousted; beginning of the Brezhnev era; first successful Chinese atomic bomb test
1966	SPD joins West German coalition government
1969	Willy Brandt elected chancellor of West Germany; *Ostpolitik* accelerated; SALT negotiations begin
1970	West Germany signs treaties with Poland and the Soviet Union
1972	West Germany signs treaty with East Germany; SALT I signed; Nixon visits China
1973	West Germany and East Germany join United Nations

from the mid-1950s on, the communist family grew more and more dysfunctional, as Mao opposed Khrushchev's efforts to reform the Soviet system (discussed shortly) and rejected Khruschev's aim of "peaceful co-existence" with the West. Khrushchev, in turn, opposed Mao's "Great Leap Forward," an effort to accomplish in a single year what had taken the Soviet Union twenty years to achieve—the transformation of a peasant agricultural society into an industrial powerhouse. An estimated 30 million Chinese starved to death as a result of Mao's fantasies. Mao took these deaths in stride but his Soviet partners were horrified and in 1960, Khrushchev suspended economic aid to China. In 1963 China refused to sign the Nuclear Test Ban Treaty, and all contacts between the two states were broken. By the time the first Chinese atomic bomb exploded in 1964, the split between China and the Soviet Union was open and irrevocable. The Sino-Soviet border became a militarized zone, the site of frequent clashes as a million Soviet and a million Chinese soldiers stood head to head. In 1969 the Soviets deployed nuclear missiles on the border, and Mao ordered underground nuclear shelters built in every Chinese city. The East was still Red, but red came in two clashing shades.

President Richard Nixon (1913–1994) and his national security adviser Henry Kissinger (b. 1923) decided to take advantage of the growing hostilities between China and the Soviets, and act according to the ancient proverb, "The enemy of my enemy is my friend." In the spring of 1971, Nixon announced the lifting of travel and trade restrictions with China. Mao responded to the American initiative by inviting the U.S. Ping-Pong team to make a highly publicized visit to Beijing. In July 1971, Nixon—a politician who had built his career on fervent anticommunism—sent shock waves through the world by announcing that he would visit China. In the 1950s, "East versus West" had formed a basic building block of international relations. With part of the East now reconciled to the West, the shape of international politics looked much less clear.

Imperial Encounters: Decolonization in a Cold War Context

The Chinese Communist victory in 1949, the outbreak of the Korean War in 1950, and the Cuban Missile Crisis of 1962 all illustrated that the Cold War was not confined to European borders. Across Africa and Asia in the 1950s and 1960s the Soviet Union and the United States used economic and military aid, as well as covert action, to cajole and coerce newly independent nations into choosing sides in the global Cold War conflict. The superpowers served as magnetic poles, drawing toward themselves competing nationalist forces and so entangling Cold War concerns with nationalist independence struggles throughout the world (see Map 28.1).

THE END TO EMPIRE

These struggles grew fierce during the postwar era. As Chapter 26 explained, World War II had strengthened colonial nationalist movements, while at the same time eroding the economic and military resources needed by European governments to hang on to their imperial possessions. The immediate postwar era witnessed the birth of several new nations—India and Pakistan in 1947, Israel in 1948, and Indonesia in 1949. But it is a mistake to think that European governments emerged from the Second World War committed to decolonization. Imperial ties seemed more crucial than ever in the economic hard times following the war. Moreover, faced with the reality of superpower domination in Europe, nations such as Britain and France looked to their imperial possessions to give them international power and prestige. As the British foreign minister Ernest Bevin explained, empire provided the means "to develop our own power and influence to equal that of the U.S. of A. and the U.S.S.R."[11]

During the 1950s, then, the British adopted a "yes, but later" approach to African independence. They sought to diminish the force of colonial nationalism by diverting it down channels of constitutional reform and complicated systems of power sharing—and then fiercely and futilely stomping down on nationalists who broke out of these channels. Many African leaders, such as Kwame Nkrumah (1957–1966) in Ghana and Jomo Kenyatta (1963–1978) in Kenya, moved from British prison cells to prime ministerial or presidential offices.

France also resisted decolonization. In 1954, the French army suffered a decisive defeat at Dien Bien Phu in North Vietnam. Dien Bien Phu marked the end of France's eight-year war against the communist nationalist forces of Ho Chi Minh and the end of France's empire in Indochina. Humiliated by this defeat, French army officers responded ferociously to the outbreak of a nationalist revolt in Algeria that same year. Many prominent politicians and ordinary men and women shared the army's view that France had

■ **Imperial Retreat**
On May 7, 1954, French forces surrendered to Vietnamese rebels at Dien Bien Phu. The battle quickly became a symbol of the retreat of Europe from its imperialist strongholds.

■ Map 28.1 After Empire: Africa and the Middle East

In just three decades, between 1880 and 1919, European nations divided up between them almost the entire African continent in the notorious "scramble for Africa" (see Chapter 23). In just one decade African nationalists effected an even more dramatic scramble *out* of sub-Saharan Africa. In the ten years after Ghana (formerly the British Gold Coast) became independent in 1957, thirty-two independent states were formed.

GREAT BRITAIN
NETH.
BEL
FRANCE
ITALY
PORTUGAL SPAIN
TURKEY
CYPRUS 1960 SYRIA 1946
LEBANON 1946 IRAQ IRAN
ISRAEL 1948 KUWAIT 1961
MALTA 1964 (from Great Britain)
TUNISIA 1957
MOROCCO 1956
ALGERIA 1962
LIBYA 1951
EGYPT
JORDAN 1946
UNITED ARAB EMIRATES 1971
BAHRAIN 1971 (from Great Britain)
QATAR 1971 OMAN
WESTERN SAHARA (MOROCCO) 1975
MAURITANIA 1960
MALI 1960
NIGER 1960
CHAD 1960
SUDAN 1956
YEMEN 1967 P.D.R. OF YEMEN 1967 (unified with Yemen 1990)
SENEGAL 1960
BURKINA FASO 1960
GAMBIA 1965
GUINEA 1958
GUINEA-BISSAU 1974
SIERRA LEONE 1961
CÔTE D'IVOIRE 1960
GHANA 1957
BENIN 1960
NIGERIA 1960
CENTRAL AFRICAN REPUBLIC 1960
ETHIOPIA
DJIBOUTI 1977
LIBERIA 1820s
TOGO 1960
CAMEROON 1960
SOMALIA 1960
EQUATORIAL GUINEA 1968
GABON 1960 CONGO 1960
UGANDA 1962 KENYA 1963
DEMOCRATIC REPUBLIC OF CONGO (ZAIRE) 1960
RWANDA 1962
BURUNDI 1962
TANZANIA 1964
ATLANTIC OCEAN
INDIAN OCEAN
ANGOLA 1975
MALAWI 1964
ZAMBIA 1964
MOZAMBIQUE 1974
MADAGASCAR 1960
MAURITIUS 1968 (from Great Britain)
NAMIBIA 1990
ZIMBABWE 1980
BOTSWANA 1966
SWAZILAND 1968
LESOTHO 1966
SOUTH AFRICA (Republic 1961)

After Empire: Africa and the Middle East

- Great Britain
- France
- Netherlands
- Italy
- Belgium
- Portugal
- Spain

Date is year independence was achieved.
Shading indicates former ruler.

0   1000 km
0   1000 mi

been pushed too far, and must now stand fast. The result was the Franco-Algerian War, a brutal fight that raged until the early 1960s. Like the Dreyfus Affair of the 1890s (see Chapter 22), the Algerian conflict divided friendships and families. Supporters of the French army in Algeria saw it as a force fighting on behalf of Western civilization against barbarism (both Arab and communist). Critics, pointing to the evidence that the French army used torture against its enemies, argued that the war threatened to corrupt French society.

By the time Algeria claimed independence in 1962, approximately 200,000 Algerian nationalist fighters had been killed or imprisoned, 15,000 French soldiers and auxiliary forces were dead, and almost 23,000 civilians in both France and Algeria had fallen victim to terrorist attack. Another casualty of this conflict was the Fourth Republic, the political structure erected in France after World War II. With France on the brink of civil war in 1958—French army officers were preparing an assault on Paris—Charles De Gaulle forced through a new constitution, which sharply tilted the balance of power in French domestic politics toward the president (conveniently De Gaulle himself).

As the Algerian crisis showed, decolonization was not something that just happened "out there" in the world beyond western Europe; rather it had an often profound impact on European political life. The loss of empire also led to a series of cultural encounters within European societies. Decolonization resulted in an upsurge in immigration. White settlers retreated back to their country of origin, and colonial "losers"—indigenous groups that had allied with the now-defeated colonial powers—fled because they feared discrimination, retribution, or perhaps simply a loss of status. In France, for example, Algerian independence led to the influx not only of Algeria's white French population but also of 80,000 Algerian Harkis whose loyalty to the colonial administration jeopardized their place in the new Algeria. The white settler groups often brought with them hardened racist attitudes, while the presence of nonwhite minority groups, clustered in certain cities, sparked resentment in societies unused to cultural diversity. Thus racism became more overt in European political and social life.

In the United States, too, decolonization had a significant cultural impact. The burgeoning African-American civil rights movement compared the systemic racism of American society to the repression endured by colonial populations. Organizations such as the National Association for the Advancement of Colored People (NAACP), founded in 1910, had long fought against racial discrimination in the United States, but in the 1950s the civil-rights struggle became a mass movement with an innovative program of "freedom rides," lunch counter sit-ins, boycotts, and voter registration campaigns. Martin Luther King Jr. (1929–1968) and other civil-rights leaders directly linked the civil-rights struggle to the colonial independence movements happening at the same time. In King's words, "the determination of Negro Americans to win freedom from all forms of oppression springs from the same deep longing that motivates oppressed peoples all over the world."[12]

THE IMPERIALIST LEGACY

The legacy of imperialist rule lingered long, particularly in areas with large white European settlement such as Rhodesia and South Africa. Despite UN sanctions and a violent black nationalist movement, white settlers in Rhodesia (present-day Zimbabwe) retained a lock on political and economic power until 1980. In South Africa, the white supremacist Afrikaner Nationalist Party assumed control in 1948 and implemented the policies of apartheid°, the rigid segregation of communities based on race. To break down any chance of resistance, the apartheid regime deliberately accentuated tribal divisions among black South Africans and denied them basic human rights. The "No Trial Act" of 1963, for example, gave the government the right to detain anyone, without charge or trial, for as long as it chose.

Imperialism also left a long-lasting economic legacy. European states lost their monopoly on the raw materials and markets of their one-time colonies, yet in the postcolo-

CHRONOLOGY

The End to European Empire

1946	French colonial war in Indochina begins
1947	India, Pakistan, and Burma achieve independence from British rule
1948	State of Israel established; apartheid regime in South Africa comes into power
1949	Indonesia achieves independence from Dutch rule
1954	Defeat of French forces in Indochina; partition of North and South Vietnam; beginning of Franco-Algerian War
1955	Bandung Conference: the "Third World" is born
1956	Suez Crisis
1957	Kwame Nkrumah becomes first prime minister of independent Ghana
1960	Congo achieves independence from Belgian rule; Nigeria achieves independence from British rule; most French colonies in tropical Africa become independent
1962	Algeria achieves independence from French rule
1963	Jomo Kenyatta becomes first prime minister of independent Kenya
1965	U.S. bombing of North Vietnam begins
1967	Suharto ousts Sukarno as leader of Indonesia

nial era, African states grew more economically dependent than ever on the West, a development that anti-Western African nationalists labeled "neo-colonialism." Desperate for cash, newly independent African governments increased production of cash crops for export—cotton, coffee, nuts, sugar—and also expanded their mining industries, producing uranium, lithium, copper, tin, gold, diamonds, and zinc for Western markets. Such exports were extremely vulnerable to fluctuations in demand and prices. At the same time, African nations became ever more dependent on importing manufactured goods from the industrialized West, with aid from Western nations often contingent on trading deals requiring such imports.

For many of the newly independent nations of Africa and Asia, political stability proved as elusive as economic prosperity. To be solid, democratic political structures must rest on a foundation of popular participation, yet almost a century of imperialist rule made such participation very problematic. For example, when the Congo became independent in 1960, it possessed only sixteen university graduates out of a population of 13 million—the result of the Belgian policy of restricting Congolese children to a basic education. In Africa as a whole, 80 percent of the African people could not read or write. Not surprisingly, then, by 1966 military regimes had replaced elected governments in the former colonial territories of Nigeria, Congo Brazzaville, Burkina Faso, Algeria, the Benin Republic, and the Central African Republic. In many newly independent states, competition between rival groups for power led to civil war. Nigeria, which gained independence from Britain in 1960, was overcome by political corruption and regional secession. In its civil war, which began in 1966, at least one million people died, either in battle or from starvation. The Congo stepped directly from Belgian rule in 1960 into a protracted civil war.

COLD WAR EMPIRES

Both superpowers played a role in the Congolese civil war, a good example of the way decolonization became entangled with Cold War rivalries. While Stalin had directed Soviet aid to regimes sharing borders with the Soviet Union (such as North Korea), Khrushchev opted for a far more aggressive approach, using military and economic aid to foster communist movements in Asia, Africa, and South America. Seeking to limit communist expansion, as well as to ensure access to crucial energy and mineral resources, the United States responded by using its economic and military power to cultivate pro-Western (but not always democratic) regimes.

In many regions, superpower influence replaced imperial control. The abrupt withdrawal of Belgium from the Congo in 1960, for example, catapulted that nation into a cauldron of political upheaval and diplomatic maneuvering. Both overt and covert superpower involvement brought the situation to a boil. U.S. intervention included an aborted CIA plot to assassinate the Congo's first elected leader, Patrice Lumumba. (Lumumba was murdered in 1961, but by political rivals rather than American intelligence operatives).

Increasingly in the Middle East, the United States replaced Britain and France as the regional powerbroker. This important reworking of the global power equation became dramatically evident in 1956, when the British and French governments attempted a military invasion of Egypt in an effort to return the Suez Canal to European control. The resulting "Suez Crisis" proved a disaster for France and Britain, when the United States used its economic clout to push Britain to the brink of financial collapse and so force British troops to withdraw.

REJECTING THE WEST

················

Born in Martinique, Frantz Fanon became a champion of Algerian independence. He died of leukemia in 1961, shortly before an independent Algeria came into being. His writings, published posthumously, articulated clearly the discontent of the colonized. Riveting dissections of the relations of power in Western capitalism, they also helped inspire the protests of 1968.

"The last shall be first and the first last."* Decolonization is the putting into practice of this sentence.... The naked truth of decolonization evokes for us the searing bullets and bloodstained knives which emanate from it. For if the last shall be first, this will only come to pass after a murderous and decisive struggle between the two protagonists.

.... As soon as the native begins to pull on his moorings, and to cause anxiety to the settler, he is handed over to well-meaning souls who in cultural congresses point out to him the specificity and wealth of Western values. But ... it so happens that when the native hears a speech about Western culture he pulls out his knife—or at least he makes sure it is within reach. The violence with which the supremacy of white values is affirmed and the aggressiveness which has permeated the victory of these values over the ways of life and thought of the native mean that, in revenge, the native laughs in mockery when Western values are mentioned in front of him.

.... For centuries the capitalists have behaved in the under-developed world like nothing more than war criminals. Deportations, massacres, forced labour and slavery have been the main methods used by capitalism to increase its wealth, its gold or diamond reserves, and to establish its power.... So when we hear the head of a European state declare with his hand on his heart that he must come to the help of the poor under-developed peoples, we do not tremble with gratitude. Quite the contrary; we say to ourselves: "It's a just reparation which will be paid to us."

---

* Fanon is quoting Jesus' words in Matthew 19:30. But as the rest of the excerpt makes clear, Fanon's interpretation of this verse contrasts with the usual Christian emphasis on submission.

Source: From Frantz Fanon, *The Wretched of the Earth*, translated by Constance Farrington. Copyright © 1963 by Présence Africaine. Used by permission.

Map 28.2 After Empire: Independent Asia

After Empire: Independent Asia

- Great Britain
- France
- Netherlands
- United States

Date is year independence was achieved.
Shading indicates former ruler.

0 ——— 1000 km

0 ——— 1000 mi

Dates of national formation often give no indication of the continuing political upheaval and violence that afflicted the countries of Asia in the postwar period. The formation of the nations of Vietnam, Laos, and Cambodia in 1953–1954, for example, did not mean an end to warfare in Indochina.

But it was in Vietnam where superpower rivalries were most dramatically superimposed onto a colonial conflict. The withdrawal of French imperial forces from Indochina in 1954 after the French army's humiliating defeat at Dien Bien Phu opened the door to superpower intervention in the region. The Indochinese peninsula was divided, with communist North Vietnam propped up by the Soviet Union, and anticommunist South Vietnam buttressed by American economic and military aid (see Map 28.2). Under the Kennedy presidency (1961–1963), the number of military advisors in Vietnam expanded rapidly, as did American involvement in South Vietnamese politics. When Kennedy's successor, Lyndon Johnson (1908–1973), took office, he issued a clear order, "Win the war!" In 1964, the American Congress granted Johnson the authority to take "all necessary measures" to do so. By 1966, 429,000 American soldiers were fighting in Vietnam. From the U.S. perspective, the Vietnam War was an episode in the Cold War, an effort to block the expansion of communism in Southeast Asia. But to the North Vietnamese leader Ho Chi Minh, the fight against American troops was another chapter in a decades-long struggle against Western colonial rule.

Many newly independent nations sought to resist being pulled into the orbit of either superpower. In 1955, Ahmed Sukarno (1949–1966), the nationalist leader who had led Indonesia out from under Dutch rule six years before, hosted the Bandung Conference of "nonaligned" nations. Bandung signaled the desire of many national leaders to find a place for their nations between or apart from the United States or the Soviet Union. French journalists at the conference gave these nations a collective label—neither the first (Western, capitalist) nor the second (Eastern, communist) but rather the Third World°. Few of these nonaligned nations had much power on their own, but the General Assembly of the United Nations provided them with an important forum for making their voice heard. As the pace of decolonization accelerated, the number of independent nations voting in the UN grew. But genuine independence proved difficult to retain, as the example of Indonesia demonstrates. Despite Sukarno's call for nonalignment, the need for material and military assistance pushed him to lead Indonesia into the Soviet sphere of influence. Then, in 1967, General Mohamed Suharto (b. 1921) succeeded Sukarno after a bloody coup. With his country's rivers clogged with the headless corpses of 100,000 victims, Suharto aligned Indonesia with the West.

After Stalin: The Soviet Union and Eastern Europe in the 1950s and 1960s

Divided by the Cold War, eastern and western Europe followed separate paths in the postwar era (see Map 28.3). Yet despite the ideological divide, certain commonalities linked both sides. Eastern and western Europeans alike lived under the threat of nuclear war, even as both sets of peoples benefited from the Cold War's deflection of military conflict away from the European continent to other parts of the globe. Intra-European rivalries decreased. Populations on both sides of the divide also experienced greater prosperity and a rise in living standards. Thus, in contrast to the sharp bends and turns of international affairs in this era, European domestic politics achieved remarkable stability.

In the East, however, this stability was imposed by force and transposed into stagnation. After a time of tumult

The Soviet Bloc in the Postwar Era

1953	Death of Stalin; relaxation of terror in eastern Europe and Soviet Union; "New Course" in Hungary underway under Nagy
1955	Khrushchev emerges as new Soviet leader
1956	Khrushchev's "Secret Speech," de-Stalinization accelerates; unrest in Poland results in new regime under Gomulka; Hungarian Revolution crushed by Soviet forces
1964	Khrushchev ousted; Brezhnev era begins
1968	Prague Spring crushed

associated with de-Stalinization°, or Khrushchev's efforts to reform the communist system, maintaining the status quo became the *raison d'être* of its ruling elites. To sustain the system and their positions in it, they sought to improve the living conditions of their populations without surrendering effective political and economic control.

THE SOVIET UNION: FROM DE-STALINIZATION TO STAGNATION

Emerging as the new Soviet leader in 1955, Khrushchev was determined to prove the superiority of communism over capitalism—to his own people and to the world. A true communist success story, Khrushchev was born to illiterate peasants, began work as a coal miner at age 14, and rose to the top of the Soviet system. Recognized as a man with talent by the Communist Party, he was trained as an engineer and helped build the Moscow subway system. Khrushchev owed everything to the Communist Party, and he never forgot it. Confident in the moral and material superiority of communism, Khrushchev believed that the Soviet Union would win the Cold War on the economic battlefield. But this ultimate victory would take place only if Soviet living standards substantially improved, and only if the Stalinist systems of terror and rigid centralized control were dismantled.

Khrushchev's determination to set communism on a new course became clear in February 1956 when, in a lengthy speech before the Twentieth Congress of the Communist Party, he shocked his listeners by detailing and condemning Stalin's crimes. Although delivered to a closed session, the speech soon appeared in the Western press and gained worldwide attention. This "Secret Speech" marked the beginning of de-Stalinization, a time of greater openness in the Communist bloc as governments dismantled many of the controls on speech and publication, and for the first time in years dissent and debate reappeared in public life.

The most dramatic sign of de-Stalinization was the release of at least four and a half million prisoners from slave labor camps. As one Soviet citizen recalled, their return was disturbing: "in railway trains and stations, there appeared survivors of the camps, with leaden grey hair, sunken eyes, and a faded look; they choked and dragged their feet like old men."[13] These survivors often returned to

find their spouses remarried, their children embarrassed by their presence, their world destroyed. Some, such as Alexander Solzhenitsyn, wrote horrifying accounts of their experiences. Solzhenitsyn's books narrated the daily degradation of prison life and provided a detailed map of the network of slave labor camps that he christened "The Gulag Archipelago."

De-Stalinization did not mean an end to all political and cultural repression in the Soviet Union. In 1959 the Gulag still held at least a million prisoners. Religious believers found that conditions worsened under Khrushchev. As part

■ Map 28.3 Europe in the Cold War

As this map shows, during the Cold War the "West" was defined culturally and politically, rather than in geographic terms. Greece and Turkey stand far to the east in Europe, yet their membership in NATO placed both within the "West."

of his effort to revitalize communist culture, Khrushchev embarked on a massive offensive against religious practice, which included the razing of churches, the arrest of clergy, the closure of seminaries and monasteries, and even in some cases the forcible removal of children from Christian homes. The number of both Orthodox and Protestant churches dropped by 50 percent. At the same time, anti-Semitism continued to mark communist policy and practice, with Soviet Jews targeted for harassment and repression.

De-Stalinization also failed to remedy the long-term economic weaknesses of the Soviet Union. In 1962, per capita consumption of consumer goods stood at only 40 to 60 percent that of France, West Germany, and Britain. In agriculture, the economic sector where the Soviet Union lagged the furthest behind the West, Khrushchev embarked on an ambitious reform program, which included rapid mechanization, a massive chemical fertilizer program, and the plowing of virgin lands. He refused to retreat from collectivization, however. As a result, the fundamental productivity problem remained unsolved—and in fact worsened in the long term as immense ecological damage was inflicted on the Soviet countryside. Soil erosion increased exponentially, nitrogen runoff from fertilized fields contaminated water supplies, and overirrigation led to salinization and a decline in soil fertility. The full force of these problems would not be felt until the 1980s, but as early as 1963 the Soviet Union had to import Western grain, a humiliating admission of failure for Khrushchev's regime.

Khrushchev's reforms unsettled many high-ranking communists; as a result, he was forced out of office in 1964. After a short period of collective leadership, Leonid Brezhnev (1906–1982) emerged as the new Soviet leader, a position he held until his death in 1982. A polite man with no interest in literature, art, or original ideas, Brezhnev was far more reassuring to Soviet bureaucrats than the flamboyant Khrushchev, whose boisterous embrace of new ideas and ambitious schemes had proven so destabilizing. Fifty-eight years old and already physically ailing when he assumed the party leadership, the increasingly decrepit Brezhnev matched his era.

Under Brezhnev the Soviet economy stagnated. Growth rates in both industrial production and labor productivity slowed during the second half of the 1960s. In the 1970s, growth virtually ceased. This economic stagnation was, however, masked by improving living standards. Brezhnev continued policies implemented by his predecessor such as free higher education and rising wages, while accelerating the expansion of consumer goods. In addition, state subsidies ensured that the cost of utilities, public transport, and rents remained far lower than in the West (although apartments were in short supply), and an extensive welfare system eased pressures on ordinary people.

By the middle of the 1960s, the Soviet Union appeared to have achieved a sort of stability. It was, however, a stability built on repression as well as stagnation. Judging de-Stalinization to be a risky business, Brezhnev and his colleagues embarked on a rehabilitation of Stalin's reputation. As statues of the dictator began to reappear, the limited cultural and intellectual freedoms introduced under Khrushchev vanished. Rigid censorship and repression once again characterized Soviet society. Those who expressed dissident views soon found themselves denied employment and educational opportunities, imprisoned, sent to the Gulag, or confined indefinitely in a psychiatric ward.

Yet dissent did not disappear. Soviet society may have resembled a stagnant pond by the 1970s, but beneath the surface churned dangerous currents that, in the late 1980s, would engulf the entire communist system. Reviving a practice employed by reformers under the tsarist regime, dissidents evaded the censors by *samizdat* or "self-publishing." Novels, plays, poetry, political treatises, and historical studies were circulated privately, copied by hand or duplicated on treasured (and often confiscated) typewriters and photocopiers and distributed more widely.

Nationalism among the non-Russian populations served as the source of much discontent within the Soviet Union during this era. As the Soviet economy grew, Russian managers and technicians were sent to places such as oil-rich Kazakhstan. Russian immigration to the Baltic states was particularly dramatic: In 1970, native Latvians made up only 59 percent of the Latvian population. Resentment of these Russian immigrants, perceived as the privileged representatives of a colonialist power, escalated. Non-Russians increasingly equated centralized economic and political control with Russian dominance rather than with communist ideology. By the mid-1960s, clandestine nationalist political organizations had emerged in almost every non-Russian republic of the Soviet Union.

DIVERSITY AND DISSENT IN EASTERN EUROPE

Despite the uniformity imposed by Soviet-style communist systems during these decades, the nations of eastern Europe developed in different ways. De-Stalinization contributed to this diversification. In his "Secret Speech" of 1955, Khrushchev declared, "it is ridiculous to think that revolutions are made to order"[14] and so signaled that communist nations could follow paths diverging from the road traveled by the Soviet Union.

But just how far from the Soviet road could those paths go? The contrasting fates of Poland and Hungary in 1956 provide the answer. In Poland, popular protests against rigid Stalinist controls proved strong enough in 1956 to bring back into power Władysław Gomułka (1905–1982), an influential Polish communist who had been purged in the Stalinist terror of 1951. Under Gomułka, Poland abandoned the economically disastrous policy of collectivization. Gomułka made clear, however, that Poland could not leave the Warsaw Pact.

Events took a different course in Hungary. Between 1953 and 1956, Hungary pursued a de-Stalinizing "New Course" under the leadership of the reformist communist Imre Nagy (1896–1958). Like Gomułka, Nagy broke with Stalinist economics, permitting a slower pace of industrialization, the production of more consumer goods, and the relaxation of agricultural collectivization. But unlike Gomułka, Nagy proved unable to resist demands for a break with the Soviet Union. By October 1956, hundreds of thousands of Hungarians were on the streets of Budapest, chanting, "We will never again be slaves." On October 31, Hungary withdrew from the Warsaw Pact—or tried to. Four days later, Khrushchev sent in the tanks. As many as 20,000 Hungarians may have died in early November as the Red Army crushed all resistance.[15] Nagy was executed in 1958.

The repression of the Hungarian revolt defined the limits of de-Stalinization in eastern Europe: The Soviet Union's satellite states could not follow paths that led out of the Warsaw Pact. Within the confines of this structure and of the one-party state, however, the governments of eastern Europe continued to pursue different courses. East Germany, for example, became the most industrially advanced and urbanized country in eastern Europe, while Poland's countryside was dotted with family farms. In Hungary, Nagy was succeeded not by a hardline Stalinist but by János Kádár (1912–1989), a reformist communist who had survived torture and imprisonment during the Stalinist purge of the early 1950s. Kádár's Hungary became the most liberal country in the Eastern bloc, with debate encouraged within the Communist Party, censorship loosened on film studios and publishers, and private business ventures encouraged. In sharp contrast, Romanians endured the reign of the "mini-Stalins." Gheorghe Gheorghiu-Dej (1901–1965) and Nicolae Ceauşescu (1918–1989) imposed not only one-party but one-man control over the country through Stalinist methods of terror. Their monomaniacal construction schemes, which dwarfed even Stalin's efforts, destroyed the Romanian economy. Yet at the same time, they pursued a remarkably independent foreign policy that included negotiating economic aid from the United States and France.

Within the diverse experiences of eastern Europeans, certain commonalities characterized the history of this era. Except in Romania and even more oppressive Albania, living standards improved. Educational opportunities expanded, the supply of consumer goods increased, and political repression became less overt. Even so, overcentralization, bureaucratic mismanagement, and political corruption ensured that living standards remained below those of the West. Moreover, the very consumer goods that

■ **De-Stalinization**

On October 31, 1956, Hungarian demonstrators pulled down a huge statue of Joseph Stalin and then dragged it two miles through the city center. Stalin's head still sits at an intersection in Budapest.

were supposed to persuade Soviet and eastern European citizens of the superiority of the communist system instead demonstrated its deficiencies. With a radio, a Hungarian teenager could tune into Radio Free Europe, and through its rock-and-roll programs, hear of a livelier, more abundant society in the West. In East Germany, television watchers could view West German networks and catch a glimpse of Western prosperity.

PRAGUE 1968: THE DESTRUCTION OF SOCIALISM WITH A HUMAN FACE

Discontent and dissent simmered throughout the eastern bloc during the 1960s. Samizdat publishing, so important a feature of the dissident movement in the Soviet Union, also tied together reform movements throughout eastern Europe. In 1968, however, these reform efforts received a fatal blow. When eastern bloc armies crushed a multifaceted popular protest in Czechoslovakia, they also crushed all hopes that the communist system could be reformed.

During the 1960s, a reform movement emerged in the ranks of the Czechoslovakian Communist Party. It included both Slovaks, who believed that the regime's highly centralized policies favored Czechs, and the new elite of highly educated technocrats who resented the power of poorly educated party superiors. At the beginning of 1968, this resentment fueled an intraparty revolution. Longtime communist leader Antonín Novotný (1952–1968) was removed

■ **Crushing the Prague Spring, 1968**
Confronted with the overwhelming might of the Warsaw Pact armies, many Czechs tried to reason with the invading soldiers, who could do little but shrug and say they were only obeying orders.

from office and replaced by the reformist Communist (and Slovak) Alexander Dubček (1921–1992). Dubček embarked on a program of radical reform, aimed at achieving "socialism with a human face." This more humane socialism included freedom of speech, press, assembly, and travel; the removal of Communist Party controls from social and cultural life; and decentralization of the economy. Dubček's effort to reform the system from the top quickly merged with a wider popular protest movement that had arisen among intellectuals, artists, students, and workers. The result was the "Prague Spring"°—the blossoming of political and social freedoms throughout Czechoslovakia, but especially in the capital city of Prague.

Well aware of the fate of Hungary in 1956, Dubček reassured Brezhnev and the other Soviet leaders that these reforms would not lead Czechoslovakia out of the Warsaw Pact. But by the summer of 1968, many of the ideas of the Prague activists were filtering through to other eastern European countries and to the Soviet Union itself. In Ukraine, nationalist protesters looked to Prague for inspiration, while in Poland, student riots, which broke out in all the major cities, featured placards reading "Poland is awaiting its own Dubček." Frightened communist leaders throughout the eastern bloc demanded that Brezhnev act to stifle the Prague Spring.

On the night of August 20–21, 80,000 troops—drawn not only from the Soviet Union but also Poland, Hungary, and East Germany—crossed the Czech border. They were immediately confused: Czechs had removed road signs and painted over street numbers in order to confound the invaders. Thirty Czechs died on the first day of the invasion,

and hundreds more were injured. The resistance spread. Workers went on strike, 20,000 Czechs marched in Prague to protest the invasion, and children ran in front of the tanks, shaking their fists. But over the next several weeks, the Prague Spring was crushed. The scientists, artists, and intellectuals who had supported the movement found themselves either in prison or unemployed. As one Communist Party journal explained, the new regime "will not permit all flowers to blossom. We will cultivate, water, and protect only one flower, the red rose of Marxism."

But that rose needed an army to hold it up. In the fall of 1968, Brezhnev acknowledged that Soviet domination in eastern Europe rested on force alone when he articulated what came to be known as the "Brezhnev Doctrine." Formally a commitment to support global socialism, the Brezhnev Doctrine was essentially a promise to use the Red Army to stomp on any eastern European effort to achieve fundamental change.

Even more important, after 1968 eastern Europeans recognized the futility of attempting to reform a system that had now been revealed as beyond reform. Many, perhaps most, eastern Europeans retreated to private worlds of friendship and family life (or to the easy escape provided by alcohol). Others, however, refused to give up or to give in to a system they now viewed as utterly corrupt. They sought, in the words of the Czech playwright and dissident Václav Havel (b. 1936), to "live in truth" in the midst of a society based on lies. As the Polish author Konstanty Gebert explained, living in truth raised "a small, portable barricade between me and silence, submission, humiliation, shame. Impregnable for tanks, uncircumventable. As long as I man it, there is, around me, a small area of freedom."

The West: Integration and Affluence

As in eastern Europe, Cold War concerns helped shape postwar societies in western Europe. Fear of communism furthered the integration of Europe's economies and helped define the political centrism characteristic of western Europe in the 1950s and 1960s. The dominant fact of the postwar years was, however, material prosperity as western European economies embarked on two decades of dramatic economic growth and consumer spending.

THE TRIUMPH OF POLITICAL CONSENSUS

In both the United States and Europe during this era, the Cold War constricted the parameters of political debate. Joseph McCarthy (1908–1957), a senator from Wisconsin, catapulted himself to international prominence by charging that communists occupied key positions in the U.S. State Department, the Hollywood establishment, and American universities. Writers, actors, film producers, social activists, scientists, and intellectuals found themselves on trial, stigmatized, unemployable. In western Europe, anticommunism never dominated political culture to this extent; it did, however, accelerate a broad retreat from the radicalism of the immediate postwar years. With the exception of the Scandinavian countries, conservative parties held power throughout western Europe during the 1950s. In West Germany, the Communist Party was banned in 1956. In France and Italy, communist parties remained popular, drawing 20 to 30 percent of the vote, but their exclusion from office after 1947–1948 effectively marginalized them.

With the communists outlawed or isolated, and with the ideologies of the extremist Right such as fascism and Nazism thoroughly discredited by the horrors of the war, western European politics took on a new and marked stability during the 1950s and early 1960s. Even France, severely divided by colonial crises and subject to nineteen different governments between 1948 and 1958, witnessed the emergence of a basic consensus on the outlines and aims of domestic political life. The Cold War placed strong pressure on Social Democratic parties to moderate or even abandon their Marxist ideology, in order to carve out a place for themselves in the anticommunist political culture. In sharp contrast to the interwar years, the parties in power in western Europe in the 1950s and 1960s, and the voters who put them there, agreed on the viability and virtues of parliamentary democracy. The new constitutions of France, West Germany, and Italy guaranteed the protection of individual rights, and French and Italian women achieved suffrage. The democratic ideal of the universal franchise had finally been realized in most of western Europe.

After 1945, citizenship took on a wider meaning in the West. It embraced not only the right to vote but also the right to a decent standard of living. Through the nationalization of key industries, the establishment of public agencies to oversee and encourage investment and trade, and the manipulation of interest rates and currency supplies, governments assumed the task of ensuring full employment and industrial prosperity for their citizens. A slogan of the German Social Democratic Party—"as much competition as possible, as much planning as necessary"—sums up an approach common to much of western Europe at this time. This commitment, however, embraced a variety of national styles. The British stressed the nationalization of heavy industry, while the French emphasized the role of centralized planning. Led by the pragmatic visionary Jean Monnet (1888–1979), France's postwar Planning Commission set economic targets and directed investment. In contrast, in West Germany, where centralized direction of the economy was linked to Nazism, politicians chose a more free-market path to industrial success.

Yet even in West Germany, citizens had access to an extensive welfare system. With the construction of comprehensive welfare states, postwar governments undertook to guarantee their citizens adequate incomes and medical care. By the end of the 1950s, the average western European working class family received 63 percent of its income from wages. The substantial remaining income came from welfare benefits such as family allowances, national health services, sickness and disability insurance, and old-age pensions. In addition, state-run vaccination and inoculation programs, stricter sanitation regulation, and the development of policies to control communicable diseases all meant an improvement in the health of Europe's populations.

The postwar political consensus was reflected in the triumph of centrist politics. Christian Democratic° parties—which have no American or British counterpart—flourished on the Continent during the postwar era. Drawing on a Roman Catholic base for their support and espousing a largely conservative social ideology combined with a progressive commitment to the welfare state, Christian Democratic parties dominated much of European politics in the 1950s and 1960s. Christian Democratic parties played significant roles in the political life of France and Belgium, governed West Germany between 1949 and 1969, and provided every prime minister except two in Italy between 1945 and 1993.

Three factors account for Christian Democracy's success. First, as anticommunists and advocates of the free market, Christian Democrats benefited from Cold War anxieties and more directly from American aid and support. Second, because they were based on religion (Roman Catholicism) rather than class, Christian Democratic parties were able to appeal to both middle-class and working-class voters, and particularly to women, who tended to vote more conservatively than men. But finally and most important, the triumph of Christian Democracy rested on its dramatic transformation from a right-wing to a centrist

CHRONOLOGY

Conservatives in Power in Western Europe

1945	Christian Democrat De Gaspari becomes prime minister of Italy
1949	Christian Democrat Adenauer becomes first chancellor of West Germany
1951	Conservatives replace Labour in power in Britain
1958	French Fourth Republic replaced by more authoritarian regime of De Gaulle

political movement. In the interwar period, Christian Democracy, rooted in a religious and political tradition based on hierarchy and authoritarianism, had veered close to fascism. But during World War II, many Catholics served in the resistance movement, where they absorbed progressive political ideas. This war-inspired desire to use the power of the state to improve the lives of ordinary people blended with more traditional Catholic paternalism. After the war the Christian Democrats not only jettisoned their authoritarianism and embraced democracy, they also supported the construction of comprehensive welfare states.

ECONOMIC INTEGRATION: THE COMMON MARKET

Just as western European societies became more politically integrated within their borders, so they became more economically integrated across their borders. The formation of the European Economic Community° (EEC) or Common Market° in 1957 marks a significant moment in not only the economic history of western Europe but also in its wider political and social development. As we will see in Chapter 29, from the 1980s on the states within this economic union moved steadily toward greater political integration as well.

The idea of European union took shape during World War II as Europeans, fighting in conditions of unprecedented horror, looked for ways to guarantee a lasting peace. In 1943, Jean Monnet, who would oversee French economic planning in the postwar era, declared, "there will be no peace in Europe, if the states are reconstituted on the basis of national sovereignty." Resistance fighters, already drawn to radical ideas, embraced Monnet's vision of a Europe no longer divided by national boundaries. In July 1944, resistance leaders from France, Italy, the Netherlands, and a number of other countries met in Geneva and declared their support for a federal, democratic Europe.

No such radical restructuring of Europe occurred, but the push toward greater European union moved forward in the years after the war. Cold War concerns played a significant role. Opposition to Stalin helped western Europeans see themselves as part of a single region with common interests. At the same time, American postwar planners—anxious to restore economic prosperity to Europe in order to lessen the appeal of communism—urged their European colleagues to dismantle trade barriers and coordinate national economic plans. As Chapter 26 explained, recipients of Marshall Plan aid were required to develop transnational institutions to oversee the distribution and use of American funds. Looking back on this early stage of European integration, the Belgian prime minister (and ardent proponent of European union) Paul-Henri Spaak (1899–1972) wrote in the later 1960s, "Europeans, let us be modest. It is the fear

of Stalin and the daring views of Marshall which led us into the right path."[16]

Spaak was a socialist, but many Christian Democrats also promoted European economic union, including Konrad Adenauer, the first chancellor of West Germany; Alcide de Gaspari, the postwar prime minister of Italy; and the French foreign minister Robert Schuman (1886–1963). Schuman's upbringing opened him to an internationalist perspective. Reared in Alsace under both German and French rule, Schuman had served as a German army officer before he entered French politics.

Desperate to break down the nationalist and economic rivalries that had led to World War II, Schuman in 1950 proposed the merger of the German and French coal and steel industries. The resulting European Coal and Steel Community (ECSC), established in 1952, comprised not only Germany and France, but also Italy and the Benelux countries (Belgium, the Netherlands, and Luxembourg). It proved to be an economic success, promoting the efficient exploitation of western European steel and coal resources and stimulating economic growth throughout the member economies. But advocates of European union, such as Schuman and Jean Monnet, saw the ECSC as far more than an economic arrangement. In Monnet's words, the ECSC was "the first expression of the Europe that is being born."[17]

Heartened by the success of the ECSC, the six member nations in 1957 formed the European Economic Community. The EEC sought to establish not only an enormous free trade zone across member boundaries, but also to coordinate policies on wages, prices, immigration, and social security. It worked. Between 1958 and 1970, trade among its six member states rose five times. The rapid movement of goods, services, and even workers ensured that the economies of member states flourished. In contrast, Britain, which had chosen to remain outside the EEC in order to preserve its preferential trading relationships with its former and current colonies, struggled to compete, with growth rates below those of its continental competitors.

THE AGE OF AFFLUENCE

If a European living in 1930 had been transported by a time machine to the Europe of 1965, he or she would probably have been most astonished not by political consensus or European economic unity but by the cornucopia of consumer goods spilling over the lives of ordinary Europeans. On the average, western European economies were growing by 4 percent a year during the 1950s, with some states growing even faster. Growth in Italian industrial production averaged over 8 percent per year, as firms such as Vespa and Olivetti cornered the international market with their motor scooters and typewriters.

It is not surprising that after years of wartime rationing, Europeans went on a spending spree. What is surprising is

THE AGE OF AFFLUENCE

·················

Full employment and rising real wages meant that the European working class joined the mass consumer society in the postwar era. In Alan Sillitoe's novel Saturday Night and Sunday Morning, *20-year-old Arthur Seaton seethes with unarticulated anger over continuing class divisions and his own powerlessness; yet, he is well aware of the stark material contrast between the 1930s and the 1950s. Seaton credits the war, not the welfare state, with the material improvements he observes around him. He confronts his father on Monday morning before heading to work:*

"You'll go blind one day, dad," he said, for nothing, taking the words out of the air for sport, ready to play with the consequences of whatever he might cause.

Seaton turned to him uncomprehendingly, his older head still fuddled. It took ten cups of tea and as many Woodbines [cigarettes] to set his temper right after the weekend. "What do you mean?" he demanded, intractable at any time before ten in the morning.

"Sittin' in front of the TV. You stick to it like glue from six to eleven every night. It can't be good for yer. You'll go blind one day. You're bound to. I read it in the *Post* last week that a lad from the Medders went blind . . ."

"Ye're barmy," Seaton said. "Go an tell yer stories somewhere else . . ."

The subject was dropped. His father cut several slices of bread and made sandwiches with cold meat left from Sunday dinner. Arthur teased him a lot, but in a way he was glad to see the TV standing in a corner of the living-room, a glossy panelled box looking, he thought, like something plundered from a spaceship. The old man was happy at last, anyway, and he deserved to be happy, after all the years before the war on the dole [on unemployment benefit], five kids and the miserying that went with no money and no way of getting any. And now he had a sit-down job at the factory, all the Woodbines he could smoke, money for a pint [of beer] if he wanted one, though he didn't as a rule drink, a holiday somewhere, a jaunt on the firm's trip to Blackpool [a seaside resort], and a television-set to look into at home. The difference between before the war and after the war didn't bear thinking about. War was a marvellous thing in many ways, when you thought about how happy it had made so many people in England.

. . . . Once out of doors they were aware of the factory rumbling a hundred yards away . . . The thousands that worked there took home good wages . . . With the wages you got you could save up for a motor-bike or even an old car, or you could go on a ten-day binge and get rid of all you'd saved. Because it was no use saving your money year after year. A mug's game, since the value of it got less and less and in any case you never knew when the Yanks were going to do something daft like dropping the H-bomb on Moscow.

Source: From *Saturday Night and Sunday Morning* by Alan Sillitoe, copyright © 1958 by Alan Sillitoe. Used by permission of Alfred A. Knopf, a division of Random House, Inc.

---

that this spree simply did not stop. A swift and unprecedented climb in real wages—by 80 percent in England, for example, between 1950 and 1970—helps explain why. So too does the construction of the welfare state. With full employment and comprehensive welfare services offering unprecedented financial security, Europeans shrugged off habits of thrift.

The postwar period witnessed a boom in housing construction. The annual volume of construction rose by 80 percent between 1950 and 1957. With new houses came new household goods. Items such as refrigerators and washing machines, once unaffordable luxuries, now became increasingly common in ordinary homes. In France, for example, the stock of home appliances rose by 400 percent between 1949 and 1957. By the 1970s, half of British families owned their own homes, two-thirds possessed washing machines, three-quarters owned refrigerators, and a whopping 90 percent had television sets.

While such purchases transformed the interiors of European homes and apartments, outside the automobile revolutionized much of both the rural and urban landscape. Highways, few and far between in 1950, cut across the countryside, and parking meters, unknown in Europe before 1959, dotted city streets. In 1964, the archbishop of Florence presided over a thanksgiving service in a gas station to celebrate the completion of a highway linking Milan and Naples. Out-of-town shopping centers, geared to the convenience of car owners, proliferated; city centers decayed.

Spending begot more spending. Credit buying (what the British called "buying on the never-never") became commonplace and made possible even more consumption. Television commercials (first seen in the mid-1950s), the Yellow Pages (first distributed in Europe in the early 1960s), and color advertising supplements in the Sunday newspapers (an innovation, again, of the early 1960s) all encouraged a culture of consumption.

Culture and Society in the Age of Consumption

The new affluence brought with it a sense of new possibilities, together with a fear that the abundance of material goods could actually work to restrict rather than open up opportunities. A variety of cultural and social developments and responses shaped, and were shaped by, western Europeans' efforts to make sense of the new material world.

CULTURAL ENCOUNTERS: AMERICANIZATION AND IMMIGRATION

Affluence meant greater economic interchange, which in turn meant increased interactions across diverse cultures. During the postwar era, two sets of cultural encounters particularly shaped European societies. First, Europeans found themselves inundated with American products, people, and ideas. Second, rising numbers of immigrants from non-Western societies brought to Europe greater cultural diversity.

The American Challenge

In western Europe in the 1950s and 1960s, consumption often meant the consumption of American goods. U.S.-based corporations scattered branch offices throughout western Europe, and U.S.-produced goods filled the shelves of European shops. In France, the best-selling book of the 1960s was entitled *The American Challenge,* and argued that Europe was fast becoming nothing more than a subcontractor for American business.

Western Europeans also struggled with American domination in science and technology. The United States invested more in scientific research and development, produced more graduates in the sciences and engineering than all other Western countries combined, and came out on top in terms of numbers of papers published and patents registered. Between 1945 and 1967, fifty-four scientists from the United States (fourteen foreign-born) won the Nobel Prize; the rest of the world produced sixty-eight scientific winners. Europeans spoke with alarm about the "brain drain" as scientists and academics headed across the Atlantic to the richer universities of the United States.

The United States particularly dominated the realm of popular culture. Immediately after World War II, the U.S. government forced European states to dismantle quotas on American film imports by threatening to withhold much-needed loans. By 1951, American productions accounted for 61 percent of film showings in western Europe. American television, too, quickly established a central position in European mass culture. In the mid-1950s, few

European households had a television, while the average American family was watching more than five hours of programming every day. In the second half of the decade, then, as the number of television owners in Europe began to expand rapidly (more than doubling between 1955 and 1956), American television networks were well-situated to take advantage of this new market. By 1960, CBS, ABC, and NBC were selling their programs to the world. The popular *Lone Ranger* series appeared in twenty-four countries. Language itself seemed subject to American takeover. More than 80 percent of the songs played on Austrian radio in the early 1960s were written by Americans and sung in English. Words such as *babysitter* and *comics* entered directly into German, while French children coveted *les jeans* and *le chewing-gum.*

While the pursuit of profit provided the primary motivating force for the export of these cultural goods, the Cold War also played a role. Seeking to fortify western Europe against communist ideas as well as communist armies, the United States embarked on a full-scale cultural assault during the 1950s. The U.S. Central Intelligence Agency (CIA) covertly funded not only western European anticommunist political parties but also cultural and scientific organizations and publications that it believed would promote values and ideas antithetical to Marxist ideology. Films, art exhibits, books and magazines, radio shows, and scholarly exchange programs all became weapons in the cultural Cold War. Ironically, the effort to fight communism with American culture went hand in hand with censorship, with the works of left-wing authors and composers banned from American-funded libraries and public information centers throughout western Europe. More positively, exhibitions of American modernist paintings were sent on tour to persuade western Europeans that capitalism nurtured artistic innovation. Even rock music was enlisted in the Cold War. In 1958, a writer in a NATO journal argued, "Whenever a rock and roll or calypso tune imbeds itself in a communist mind, it tends to erode other things." By the early 1960s, Radio Free Europe regularly included Western rock music in its programming.

Many Europeans enthusiastically embraced American culture but some Europeans argued that even as Europe was losing its colonial possessions, it was itself undergoing colonization, or at least "coca-colonization," as Coca-Cola and other American products seemed poised to conquer European markets and transform European tastes.[18] Opponents to "coca-colonization" came from both the right and the left of the political spectrum, with conservative nationalists joining pro-Soviet communists in denouncing American influence over European culture.

One of the most powerful voices protesting American hegemony was France's conservative leader Charles De Gaulle. De Gaulle sought to reduce American influence in Europe by pursuing independent foreign and military policies. He extended diplomatic recognition to China in

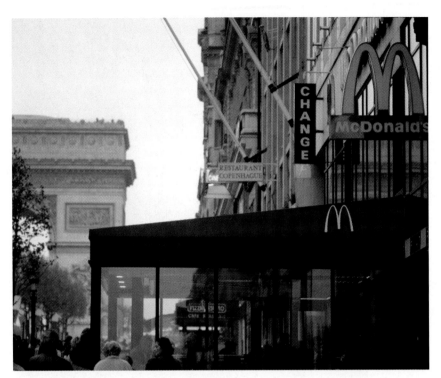

■ **McDonald's on the Champs-Elysées in Paris**
In the postwar era, the United States functioned as a symbol of modernity. The McDonald's hamburger franchise represented the United States to many Europeans because it typified modernity's standardization and mass consumerism. Assembly-line production lowered costs and made the standardized experience of eating fast food affordable to the masses.

1964 and two years later made a state visit to Moscow. In 1960 France exploded its own atomic bomb and in 1966 French forces withdrew from NATO command, although France remained formally part of the Atlantic alliance. De Gaulle was deeply anticommunist and fiercely opposed to the Soviet Union, but he believed that the more immediate threat to the French way of life came from American culture. Taken in 1960 to view a new highway in California, De Gaulle gazed somberly at the sight of cars weaving in and out on a traffic cloverleaf and commented, "I have the impression that all this will end very badly."[19] De Gaulle's anti-Americanism was largely rooted in his pro-Frenchness: He wanted to reduce American influence in Europe in order to restore France to a position of grandeur and glory. In De Gaulle's imagination, France was "like the princess in the fairy stories or the Madonna in the frescoes, as dedicated to an exalted and exceptional destiny . . . France cannot be France without greatness."[20]

American cultural and economic influence in postwar Europe was very real, yet the fear of Europe becoming a secondhand version of the United States was misplaced. Throughout this era, Europeans consumed American products with great gusto, but in the process they adapted these products to suit their own needs. In the late 1950s, for example, four young working-class men from the northern British seaport of Liverpool latched on to the new American rock and roll, mixed in their own regional musical styles, and transformed popular music not only in Europe but also in the United States. The impact of the Beatles testified to the power of European culture to remake American cultural products. Even McDonald's, when it arrived in European cities in the 1960s, made subtle changes to the composition of its fast food to appeal to the differing tastes of the new markets. Thus the cultural history of this era is one of reciprocal encounters rather than one-way Americanization.

Immigration and the Challenge of Diversity

At the same time, the immigration of new communities into western European countries brought new and in many cases non-Western cultural traditions into contact with those of the host nation. Immigration was the result of economic prosperity. As their economic growth rates soared in the 1950s, northern and western European nations were experiencing a slowing rate of population increase. Scrambling for workers to fill their fields and factories, staff their new hospitals, and build their new houses and transportation systems, governments undertook to recruit foreign labor. Beginning in 1955, the West German government negotiated a series of immigration contracts with Italy, Greece, Turkey, Yugoslavia, and the North African states. In Britain, both public and private agencies turned for workers to the West Indies, India, and Pakistan. France recruited workers from Spain and Italy, as well as its colonial territories such as Algeria, Morocco, Tunisia, Senegal, Mali, and Guadeloupe. By the beginning of the 1970s, the nations of northern and western Europe were home to approximately nine million immigrants, half of these from the less prosperous Mediterranean states of Portugal, Spain, Italy, and Greece. The other half came from Turkey, Yugoslavia, and countries in Asia, Africa, and the Caribbean.

■ **Immigrants Arriving in Britain, 1956**
Many immigrants from regions within the British Empire had been taught that Britain was the "mother country" or "home." They were shocked to discover that once in Britain, they were regarded as foreign and as inferior.

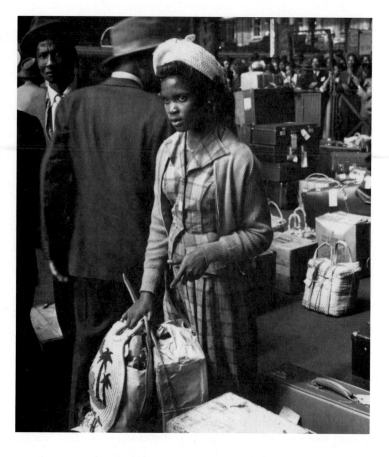

These workers did the dirtiest, most dangerous, least desirable jobs. They worked the night shifts, emptied the bedpans, dug the ditches, and cleaned the toilets. They lived in substandard housing, often confined to isolated dormitories or inner-city slums, and accepted low, often illegally low, pay rates. The reason they did so is starkly presented in the table below: Despite racial discrimination and economic exploitation, western Europe offered greater economic opportunities than were available in the immigrants' homelands.

Until the 1970s, the majority of these immigrants were single men, who saw themselves, and were seen by their host countries, as "guestworkers," temporary laborers who would earn money and then return home to their native lands. By the mid-1960s, however, families were beginning to join these men, and a second generation of "immigrants" was being born, a generation who did not know their supposedly "native" land. This generation changed the face of Europe. Chapter 29 will show that by the 1980s European societies had become multiethnic. The emergence of urban subcultures immeasurably enlivened European cultures and economies (and diets); it also complicated domestic politics and raised challenging questions about the relationship between national and ethnic identity. In the 1950s and 1960s, however, few Europeans could yet discern the multicolored patterns that were emerging.

THE SECOND SEX?

In 1949, the French writer Simone de Beauvoir (1908–1986) published *The Second Sex*. In this enormously influential critique of gender divisions in Western industrial society, de Beauvoir argued that women remained the "second sex." Despite changes in their political and legal status, women were still defined by their relationship to men rather than by their own actions or achievements. Over the next two decades, the new prosperity pushed women into higher education and the labor force and so, in the long run, worked to undermine the traditional gender

The Appeal of Immigration—Annual Per Capita Gross National Product in the Mid-1960s

Pakistan	$125
Turkey	$353
Jamaica	$520
Spain	$822
Italy	$1,272
Britain	$1,977
France	$2,324

Source: Leslie Page Moch, *Moving Europeans: Migration in Western Europe Since 1650* (1992), p. 177.

roles that de Beauvoir described; in the short run, however, affluence accentuated women's domestic identity.

A number of changes both reflected and reinforced postwar domesticity. The most important were demographic. Marriage rates rose and the marriage age dropped in the postwar years. In the United States, between 1940 and 1957, the fertility rate rose by 50 percent. Europe experienced a baby "boomlet" rather than a baby boom. European birth rates rose in the late 1940s but dropped again in the 1950s (whereas U.S. fertility rates remained high into the 1960s). Nevertheless, although family sizes were small, a higher percentage of western European women than ever before had children.

By exalting women's maternal identity, both religion and popular culture provided a potent ideology for these demographic changes. The Roman Catholic Church of the 1950s placed renewed emphasis on Mary, the paragon of motherhood. Pope Pius XII (r. 1939–1958) particularly encouraged the growth of devotion to Mary during the last years of his papacy. The pope, who believed he had experienced his own personal Marian visitation, proclaimed in 1950 that Mary had ascended bodily into heaven (the Doctrine of the Assumption) and designated 1954 as the Year of Mary. This Marian devotion encouraged women to regard motherhood as a holy calling, and as the very core of female identity.

Popular culture reinforced this religious message. Programming aimed at families dominated the new television schedules and established new images of what families should look like and how they should interact. So, too, did the articles and advertisements of women's magazines. In both, the woman stayed at home, presiding over an expanding array of household machines that, in theory, reduced her housework burden and so freed her to focus on the satisfactions of motherhood.

At the same time, a number of cultural, economic, and technological changes transformed the Western home into a much more private place. Because of the boom in house building, by the mid-1950s couples forced by wartime deprivation to live with their parents could now move into their own apartment or house. Accelerated suburbanization, made possible by the expansion of private car ownership and the spread of highway networks, meant that relatives now lived farther apart. "Family" increasingly meant the nuclear family. Prosperity accentuated the family's isolation. Economic growth translated into a rapid drop in the number of domestic servants as workers turned to better-paying jobs and household appliances took their place. Because the new houses and apartment buildings possessed modern conveniences such as indoor plumbing, communal baths, toilets, and washhouses gradually disappeared. Television moved the social center away from cinemas, cafés, and pubs to the family living room.

Cold War concerns also accentuated the Western woman's domestic role in two very different ways. First, anticommunist propaganda hailed domesticity as a sign of Western superiority, by contrasting the favorable lot of Western women to their Soviet counterparts, who led lives of almost endless labor. The vast majority of Soviet women combined their domestic duties with full-time outside employment, often in jobs involving heavy manual labor, and they spent a substantial portion of each day lining up to purchase scarce goods. Second, the nuclear age made the nuclear family seem all the more important. Feeling increasingly helpless in a superpower-dominated world on

■ **The Kitchen Debate**

The kitchen—stocked with an abundance of attractively packaged foods and a glittering array of time-saving appliances—symbolized not only material plenty but also moral stability. In the Western domestic ideal, the kitchen represented the center of family life, and the woman's proper domain. When Vice President Richard Nixon traveled to Moscow in 1959 to open an American exhibition, he pointed to the display model of a suburban kitchen as evidence of Western superiority. Khrushchev refused to be impressed. Nixon and Khrushchev's argument became known as the "Kitchen Debate."

the brink of nuclear annihilation, Europeans tended to withdraw for shelter to family life.

For some women, this shelter was more like a prison. In *The Captive Wife,* published in 1966, the British sociologist Hannah Gavron (b. 1944) asked, "Have all the great changes in the position of women in the last one hundred and fifty years come to nothing?" In *The Feminine Mystique* (1963), the American journalist Betty Friedan (b. 1921) identified what she called "the problem that had no name," a crisis of identity and purpose among middle-class, educated women confined in the role of housewife and mother.

Whether a nightmare or a dream, the domestic ideal remained removed from the reality of many women's lives in the postwar era. In the poorer social classes, women by necessity continued to work outside the home, as they always had. At the same time, the new culture of consumption demanded that many women, clinging precariously to the middle rungs of the social ladder, take on paid employment to pay for the ever-expanding list of household necessities. In many countries, such as Britain, the number of female workers, including married women with children, rose. In 1951, 21 percent of British married women were in the paid workforce; by 1971 the figure was 47 percent.

In general, a new pattern of employment emerged that reconciled the new domesticity with the needs of expanding economies. It was increasingly expected that single women, including those in the middle class, would work until they married. Many continued to do so until the first child arrived, and resumed paid employment after the last child had left home or at least started school. This work was regarded, however, as secondary to their main job—the making of a home and the rearing of children. Part-time employment, with lower wages and few or no benefits, expanded accordingly. Everywhere pay rates remained unequal. In Britain in 1950, single women earned about half of what their male colleagues were paid; in France two decades later, married women workers earned one-third less than married men. Inequalities in legal status continued as well. Until 1964 and the passage of the Matrimonial Act, a married French woman could not open her own bank account, run a shop, or apply for a passport without her husband's permission. Traditional gender roles remained firmly intact, despite the material and political changes of the postwar era.

HIGH CULTURE IN THE AGE OF CONSUMPTION

Continuity also marked the high culture of the 1950s. Neorealism, which had first appeared in Italian cinema during World War II (see Chapter 26), continued to exert a powerful influence not only in the European film world but also in British and French fiction. For example, the novels of the British "Angry Young Men" of the 1950s, like

Italian movies of the 1940s, presented realistic depictions of working-class lives and concerns. At the same time, both existentialism and modernism retained their dominant position in high culture in the decade after World War II. By the beginning of the 1960s, however, existentialist concerns and modernist assumptions were losing their hold. In very general terms, artists retreated from engagement with the horrors of World War II and the overwhelming challenges of the Cold War. Instead, they produced works that reflected, commented on, and reveled in the cascade of consumer abundance that was transforming western European and American social life.

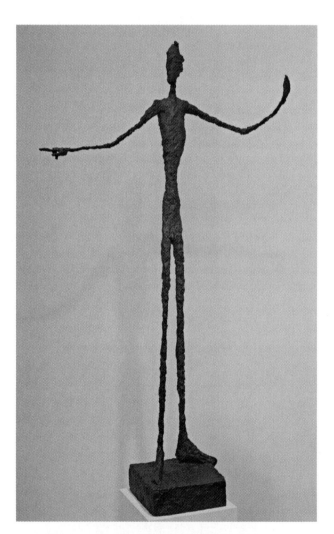

■ **Alberto Giacometti, *Man Pointing* (1947)**
Giacometti's sculptures embodied existentialist anguish. His account of this piece's creation seems to be lifted from a Samuel Beckett play or one of Jean-Paul Sartre's novels: "Wanting to create from memory [the figures] I had seen, to my terror the sculptures became smaller and smaller; they had a likeness only when they were small, yet their dimensions revolted me, and tirelessly I began again, only to end several months later at the same point."

Meaning and Absurdity

Forged in the despair of the 1930s and hammered into shape by the horrors of the Second World War, existentialism remained a powerful cultural force in the early postwar era. Jean-Paul Sartre's conviction that existence has no intrinsic meaning, and yet that the individual retains the freedom to act and therefore make meaning, resounded loudly in a world that had experienced both the Holocaust and the Resistance. The existentialist emphasis on individual action as the source of meaning could lead to a life of political activism—Sartre, for example, worked with the French Resistance and became a prominent participant in left-wing political causes in the 1950s and 1960s. On the other hand, existentialism also justified political disengagement. In the Irish-French playwright Samuel Beckett's (1906–1989) existentialist masterpiece *Waiting for Godot* (1952), two tramps sit in an empty universe, waiting for someone who never comes. In this absurd void, politics has no relevance or resonance.

Existentialist themes echo throughout the visual arts in the 1950s. The sculptures of the Swiss artist Alberto Giacometti (1901–1966) are the embodiments of existentialist anguish—fragile, insubstantial, they appear ready to crack under the strain of being. While Giacometti's sculptures embody existentialist terror, the works of the preeminent British painter of the 1950s, Francis Bacon (1909–1992), evoke outright nausea. Bacon's disturbing canvases are case studies in the power of the subconscious. He painted the people he saw around him, but his perceptions were of a society disfigured by slaughter. Slabs of meat, dripping in blood, figure prominently. Bacon explained, "When you go into a butcher's shop . . . you can think of the whole horror of life, of one thing living off another."[21] By the end of the decade, solitary figures, secluded in claustrophobic settings and embodying Sartre's description of human existence as essentially isolated, recurred frequently in Bacon's work.

Moving into Post-Modernism

The works of Bacon and Giacometti remained well under the umbrella of modernism (see Chapter 23). As the consumer revolution poured through Western culture, however, it forced a dramatic transformation in the content and purpose of the visual arts. Fascinated by the plethora of material objects pouring off assembly lines and onto department store shelves, artists began to turn away from ex-

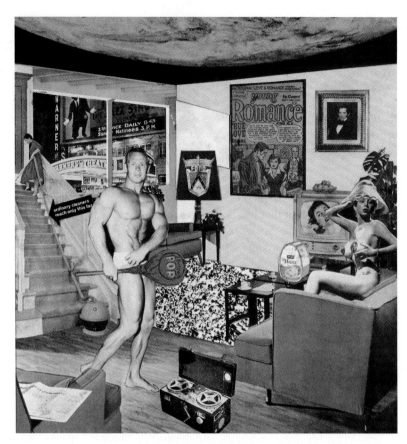

■ **Richard Hamilton, "Just What Is It That Makes Today's Homes So Different, So Appealing?" (1956)**
British artist Richard Hamilton was one of the leading figures in the Pop Art of the 1950s.

istentialist concerns and to focus on the material stuff of everyday existence. Technology, too became a source of artistic inspiration. Works such as "Just What Is It That Makes Today's Homes So Different, So Appealing?" (1956), by British artist Richard Hamilton (b. 1922) signaled this artistic shift. This playful collage satirizes and yet celebrates the postwar emphasis on material consumption and on private family life. Hamilton was a leading force in the Independent Group, a loose association of British artists, designers, and architects that sought in their work to embody the "aesthetics of plenty"—the idea that consumer affluence had smashed the barriers between fine art and popular culture. The Independent Group, along with other movements such as "New Realism" in France and "Capitalist Realism" in West Germany, helped shape what became known as pop art°. Pop artists dismissed the anguish of Bacon and Giacometti as the concerns of an older generation still mired in World War II. Pop art looked outward rather than inward, and focused on the material rather than the spiritual. Pop artists spoke in the vocabulary of mass material culture, and even relied on mass production and mass marketing.

The result was a revolution in Western art. These young artists broke with modernism, and catapulted the art world into what would become postmodernism (as we shall see in Chapter 29). Pop artists challenged accepted ideas about the role of both art and the artist in Western society. Works such as *Flag* (1954–1955) by the American Jasper Johns (b. 1930) raised fundamental questions about the difference between a thing and the artist's interpretation of that thing. *Flag* consists of small pieces of newspapers dipped into wax and then sealed onto fabric in the pattern of the American flag—in other words, the work is not just an image of a flag; it *is* a flag. Where, then, is the line between reality and representation? And if that line disappears, where does the artist stand? When the American pop artist Andy Warhol (1930–1987) called his studio "The Factory" and employed assistants to mass-produce his works, he overturned the modernist idea of the artist as a uniquely inspired individual. His German counterpart Gerhard Richter (b. 1932) went even further when he placed himself in the furniture display of a West German department store and called the resulting "piece" *Living with Pop* (1963). Richter turned the artist, as well as art, into a commodity, something to be bought and sold just like anything else. In the age of consumption, the individual artist's intentions and attitudes became unimportant, and concepts such as artistic genius or lasting meaning became irrelevant.

The demotion of the individual and the abandonment of meaning characteristic of pop art also characterized developments in social thought. Existentialism had elevated the individual as the only source of meaning in an absurd universe. In the late 1950s, however, a new social theory—structuralism°—emerged to challenge existentialism's hold on Western intellectual formations. Rooted in linguistics and anthropology, structuralism transformed a number of academic disciplines, including literary criticism, political theory, sociology, and even history. Structuralism was first introduced to a wide audience by the French anthropologist Claude Lévi-Strauss (b. 1908). Levi-Strauss argued that the myths told in all cultures, whether that of Brazilian Indian tribes still using stone-age tools or medieval French peasants or contemporary Londoners, shared certain "deep structures," repeated patterns such as pairings and oppositions that help give order to the cultural world. The actual stories are unimportant. To use a newspaper metaphor offered by the intellectual historian Roland Stromberg, the structuralist is interested not in the content of the articles but in the layout of the page—the arrangement of articles, the juxtaposition of images, the shape of headlines. By analyzing the "layout" of cultures, the structuralist can uncover the basic structures of human thought. In structuralism, then, as in pop art, the individual matters little. Human beings exist within a ready-built structure that shapes and dictates the way they perceive the world.

SCIENCE AND RELIGION IN AN AGE OF MASS CONSUMPTION

At the same time that structuralists depicted the individual as stuck within a cultural and linguistic web, his or her choices firmly constrained by the sticky fibers of that web, radical breakthroughs in the biological sciences posited that perhaps the web lay inside the individual, its fibers comprising chemicals and chromosomes that set sharp limits on individual capabilities. While Levi-Strauss sought to decipher human culture, biologists embarked on the task of decoding humanity's genetic structure. In 1962, the British biologist Francis Crick (b. 1916) and his American colleague James Watson (b. 1928) received the Nobel Prize in Medicine and Physiology for mapping the structure of DNA, the basic building block of genetic material, which they had discovered in 1953. Crick and Watson's model of the "double helix," the intertwined spirals of chemical units that, in a sense, issue the instructions for an individual's development, caught the attention of the world. As biologists and geneticists furthered their investigations into human genetic inheritance, they raised exciting yet potentially disturbing possibilities, such as the cloning of living organisms and genetic manipulation, and added a new dimension to the perennial debate about individual freedom.

Other scientific developments assured human beings more freedom from their physical environment than ever before. Motivated by the Cold War, the space race launched humanity beyond the confines of Earth, culminating in 1969 with the American astronaut Neil Armstrong's moon walk. Medical breakthroughs in this era seemed to promise that infectious diseases could be eradicated. Large-scale production of penicillin transformed ordinary medical care, as did rapid development of vaccines against many childhood killers such as measles. In 1953, the American Jonas Salk announced the first successful clinical trial of a polio vaccine. In this era, blood transfusions become more commonplace, along with the development of organ transplants, following the first successful kidney transplant in Chicago in 1950. Like washing machines and television sets, a long and healthy life suddenly appeared accessible to most people.

While scientists were claiming more control of the physical environment than ever before, the organized churches continued to offer spiritual authority and sustenance. Church attendance, which had declined in most Western countries in the interwar period, rose during the 1950s. In the United States between 1942 and 1960, church membership per capita grew faster than at any time since the 1890s. No European nation shared this dramatic religious upsurge; nevertheless, except in Scandinavia, western Europe experienced what we can call a gentle religious revival. In Britain during the 1950s, church membership, Sunday school enrollment, and the numbers of baptisms and religious marriages all increased. In West Germany, the rate of churchgoing rose among Protestants from 1952 until 1967. Throughout Catholic Europe, the vibrancy of Christian Democratic politics reflected the vital position of the Catholic Church in society.

In the 1960s, however, the situation changed dramatically. Europeans (followed a generation later by their American counterparts) abandoned the churches in favor of the shops, sports fields, and television sets. Declining rates of church attendance, a growing number of civil rather than religious marriage ceremonies, and an increased reluctance to obey Church teaching on issues such as premarital sexual relations all pointed to the secularization of European society. As we will see in Chapter 29, by the 1970s, churchgoing rates in both Protestant and Catholic countries were in freefall. In what had once been called "Christendom," the fastest-growing religious community was Islam.

The churches did not remain stagnant during this time of change. A number of Protestant theologians argued that Christianity could maintain its relevance in this more secular society only by adapting the biblical message to a modern context. The British theologian (and Anglican bishop) John Robinson achieved great notoriety in 1963 with his *Honest to God,* a short but provocative book that challenged belief in a supernatural God and argued that the language in which Christians articulate their faith must be updated to make sense in the modern world.

The biggest change occurred in Roman Catholicism. In 1963 the Second Vatican Council—widely known as Vatican II°—convened in Rome, the first catholic council to meet since 1870. In calling the council, Pope John XXIII (r. 1958–1963) sought to modernize and rejuvenate the Church, a process that, he recognized, would demand "a change in mentalities, ways of thinking and prejudices, all of which have a long history."[22] John did not live to see this change in mentalities take place, but his successor Paul VI (r. 1963–1978) presided over a quiet revolution.

The Church that emerged from Vatican II was a great deal less hierarchical and a great deal more open than its pre–Vatican II predecessor. The council embraced ecumenism, the effort to overcome the divisions between the separate Christian branches. For the first time, Roman Catholics were allowed to receive communion in non-Roman churches (under certain conditions). Reversing Pius XII's emphasis on the absolute power of the papacy, Vatican II granted more authority to local and regional councils. For ordinary Catholics, the most striking changes occurred in the worship service. To make the service more accessible to the laity, Latin was scrapped in favor of the vernacular (in France, services were in French; in Britain, in English; and so on). A number of reforms narrowed the gap between priest and people. During the mass, for example, the priest stood behind the altar, facing the congrega-

CHRONOLOGY

Medical Breakthroughs

1950	First kidney transplant
1952	First sex-change operation
1953	Discovery of DNA
1954	Polio vaccine developed
1957	CAT scan developed
1967	First heart transplant

tion, rather than in front, with his back to the people, and all worshipers, not only the priest, received the wine at communion.

Vatican II was less revolutionary in its approach to sexual issues and gender roles. The council said nothing about homosexuality (still a largely taboo subject throughout the Western world), reaffirmed the traditional doctrine of clerical celibacy, and insisted that only men could be ordained as priests. It did, however, abandon over one thousand years of Church teaching when it insisted that the purpose of marriage was not simply to produce children but also to establish "an intimate partnership of life and love" between a man and a woman.[23] Following up on this crucial break, the council declared that parents had the right and responsibility to determine how many children they should have and when they should have them—but, in obedience to Paul VI's order that contraception was not a subject suitable for conciliar debate, it left open the question of birth control. Three years later, the pope closed the question. In the papal document *Humanae Vitae* he declared contraceptive use to be contrary to Church teaching.

The issues of clerical celibacy, women's ordination, and contraceptive use would bedevil the Church for the rest of the century. Nevertheless, Vatican II did reinvigorate global Catholicism. It also made clear that, as one popular contemporary folk song put it, "the times they are a'changin'." A quiet and cautious administrator, Paul seemed an unlikely revolutionary, yet he became the first pope to travel outside Italy since 1809 and the first to fly on an airplane. If the pope could fly, who knew what else might happen?

1968 AND THE END OF THE POSTWAR ERA

Events in 1968 seemed to indicate that the answer might be: Just about anything. As we have already seen, that year eastern Europe witnessed the most serious challenge to Soviet hegemony in eastern Europe since 1956. In the West, too,

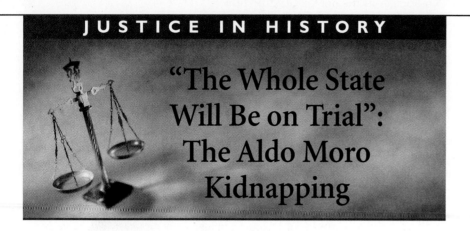

"The Whole State Will Be on Trial": The Aldo Moro Kidnapping

On March 16, 1978, while on his way to pray before going to Parliament, the former prime minister of Italy and leader of the Christian Democratic Party, Aldo Moro, was kidnapped in broad daylight in a Roman suburb. In a carefully planned and brilliantly executed operation, a woman driving a white car backed in front of Moro's official dark blue Fiat and caused an accident. She and her male companion sprang from their car and blasted automatic weapons into the front seat of the Fiat, killing Moro's chauffeur and bodyguard. Moro, who had been quietly reading the morning paper when the attack began, was pulled unhurt from the backseat and hurried away in an escape vehicle. Thus began Aldo Moro's horrible ordeal, and one of the most daring instances of organized terrorist violence in the postwar era.

Moro was kidnapped by the Red Brigade, a terrorist group that emerged out of the student protest movement. During the 1960s, many young Italians became convinced that Italy needed fundamental change. These students believed that Italy's traditional left-wing political parties (the Socialists and the Communists) could never transform Italy's political or social structures in any meaningful way. The Communists were sunk in inertia; the Socialists had shown themselves to be just another group of politicians interested in personal power when they joined the Christian Democrats in a governing coalition in 1962. The stu-

dents turned instead to the street protest of the "New Left." In 1967, students occupied the University of Trento. Over the next several months, student protest spread throughout the country.

The New Left ideology of the student movement was broadly Marxist, but opposed to Soviet-style communism. Spontaneity, a mistrust of authority in any form, a rejection of political doctrine (in some cases, a rejection of any books at all), and an insistence on direct democracy all characterized the movement in its first days. By 1970, however, the movement had altered. Heartened by the spread of the most serious labor unrest in Italian industry since World War II, students shifted their focus from the universities to the factories. As students joined striking workers spontaneity disappeared; doctrine and discipline returned with a vengeance. The movement adopted Soviet-style authoritarianism and factionalized into small revolutionary groups, each of which demanded conformity to its brand of ideological purity.

One of these factions was the Red Brigades, led by former student activist Renato Curcio. The Red Brigades declared an "attack on the heart of the state." By targeting politicians, judges, journalists, and professors, the Brigades hoped to terrorize the ruling elite, destabilize the Italian state, and push Italian society into revolution. In 1976 and 1977, fifteen people died and over fifty were wounded in Brigade attacks.

Then, in the spring of 1978, the Red Brigades kidnapped Aldo Moro.

Just a few weeks before, the Italian state had brought to trial fifteen captured Red Brigadiers, including Curcio. Kept in a cage in the courtroom in Turin, the defendants screamed insults and made obscene gestures at the judges and jury. It was from this cage that Curcio shouted to the world, "Moro is in our hands!" Curcio then explained, "The real trial is taking place elsewhere . . . Moro is in the hands of the proletariat, and the whole state will be on trial."

To the Red Brigadiers, Moro represented the kind of compromise-based politics that prevented any fundamental transformation of Italian society. Moro had spent much of his political career working to ensure that Italy's traditional left-wing parties posed no radical threat. During the 1960s, under Moro's leadership, the Christian Democrats had formed coalition governments with the Italian Socialists. Moro believed that by including the Socialists in government, he could tame them—and he was right. Once in office, the Socialists abandoned much of their radical rhetoric and most of their radical goals. In the 1970s, Moro sought to cooperate with the Communists, in hopes of domesticating them just as he had tamed the Socialists a decade earlier. To the Brigades, then, Aldo Moro was "the most authoritative leader, the undisputed theorist and strategist of the

Christian Democratic regime, which for thirty years has oppressed the Italian people."

The so-called trial conducted by the Red Brigades had nothing to do with proving a case against Moro but consisted of repeatedly badgering him with allegations. The goal was to keep Moro in complete terror and to break down his will. After a month the Red Brigades announced the completion of the Aldo Moro trial. The verdict: "ALDO MORO IS GUILTY AND IS THEREFORE CONDEMNED TO DEATH."

On May 9 the Red Brigades brought the affair to a dramatic finale. They telephoned Moro's assistant and told him where to find his boss. The former prime minister's bullet-riddled body lay in the back of a red Renault station wagon across the street from the American Cultural Center, which stood almost exactly halfway between the headquarters of the Christian Democratic and Italian Communist parties. By leaving Moro's body in this spot, the Brigades expressed their contempt for the entire Italian political establishment. Moreover, by managing to park a car containing Moro's bloody body in plain view in a city swarming with policemen, the Brigadiers taunted the government with their apparent invincibility. From his cage in the Turin courtroom, Renato Curcio declared, "This is only the beginning. You have not understood what will happen in Italy during the coming days and months."

But Curcio was wrong. Moro's death utterly failed to ignite the revolution. Appalled by Moro's murder, Italians from across the political spectrum supported a new antiterrorist offensive mounted by the government. By 1982 many of the Brigadiers had been arrested. Much to the surprise of many Italians, Italian society emerged from its bloody encounter with "revolutionary justice" not only intact, but even, it can be argued, more united than before—exactly the opposite of what the Brigades had intended. ■

Questions of Justice

1. How does the killing of Aldo Moro compare to an earlier episode of "proletarian justice"—the "Nontrial of Nicholas and Alexandra"? (See "Justice in History" in Chapter 24, p. 816.)

2. How might the Aldo Moro affair be considered an episode in the history of the Cold War?

Taking It Further

Drake, Richard. *The Aldo Moro Murder Case.* 1995. Based on the extensive records of two parliamentary inquiries and four sets of criminal trials, this book is the most thorough examination of all the available evidence about the Moro murder.

Wagner-Pacifici, Robin Erica. *The Moro Morality Play: Terrorism as Social Drama.* 1986. This book is less concerned with the evidence of who did what than how the Moro kidnapping constituted one of the most striking social dramas of the twentieth century.

■ **The Death of Aldo Moro**
By killing Moro, the Red Brigades hoped to spark a revolution. Instead, they horrified their potential supporters.

■ **The Protests of 1968**
French student demonstrators and
their supporters gather at the Place
Denfert-Rochereau, Paris.

the end of the 1960s saw the rise of widespread protests against the postwar order. In 1968, demonstrations disrupted university campuses in almost every Western country and in the East and the Third World as well. Students from Addis Ababa to Warsaw, from Berkeley to Berlin, rose up in protest. In Italy half a million students were on strike. In Mexico City, a series of confrontations between students and police resulted in a police massacre that killed 300 students. In France, a student demonstration blossomed into a full-scale social revolt, which for a time looked set to topple De Gaulle's government. The events in Paris began in May, when police used brutal methods to clear a Parisian courtyard occupied by protesting students. The unwarranted violence of the police action, broadcast throughout France in newspaper photographs and television news reports, aroused support for the students from the wider population. Within a few days, eight million French men and women were on strike.

The common theme among these protests was the demand for a voice, for the right of ordinary people to participate in the processes and structures that determined their lives. More specifically, protesters drew on the ideas of the New Left° to articulate a profound uneasiness with the power of the state in the West. Before World War II, activists and thinkers on the left of the political spectrum had sought to expand the power of the state to counterbalance the inegalitarian consequences of capitalism and so make

possible genuine democracy. But by the late 1950s and early 1960s, New Left thinkers, appalled by the excesses of Stalinism and concerned about the growth of state power in the West, warned that the expansive state, with its staff of experts, threatened the individuality and independence of the ordinary citizen. The German philosopher Herbert Marcuse (1898–1979) condemned the "repressive tolerance" of Western democracies. According to Marcuse, debate seemed open, but the range of actual political choices was limited. Throughout the West, the concept of "citizenship" was being degraded, defined by voting alone rather than by active participation in decision making. Building on this idea, the student movement called for "participatory democracy," the revitalization of active citizenship.

Armed with these New Left ideas, student protesters quickly moved beyond the university context to mount a broadly based challenge to the Cold War status quo. In their view, the superpower conflict threatened the world with nuclear annihilation at the same time that it restricted domestic political freedoms and denied individuals an effective political voice. Rejecting both Soviet-style communism and free-market capitalism, they turned for inspiration to the newly emerging nations of the Third World. Idealizing such Third World revolutionaries as Ernesto Che Guevara, one of the leaders of the Cuban revolution, and the Algerian nationalist leader Frantz Fanon, the students identified their struggle for a more open politics with the colo-

ROCK AND REVOLUTION

....

In 1967, the Beatles, already global superstars, released Sgt. Pepper's Lonely Hearts Club Band. *Called the "most influential rock album ever produced," Sgt. Pepper's revolutionized rock music. The complexity of its compositions impressed serious music critics, who for the first time acknowledged that rock music was worth listening to. The album's lyrics, too, received unprecedented praise, with one reviewer comparing the last song on the album ("A Day in the Life") to T. S. Eliot's modernist masterpiece, "The Waste Land" (see Chapter 24). Although not overtly political, Sgt. Pepper's illustrates many of the themes of the protests that marked the era in which it was produced. Infused with a sense of playfulness and celebration, the album called its listeners to burst out of the confines of order, authority, and rationality, and embrace instead the values of human community and emotional liberation.*

SHE'S LEAVING HOME

Wednesday morning at five o'clock as the day begins
Silently closing her bedroom door
Leaving the note that she hoped would say more
She goes downstairs to the kitchen clutching her
    handkerchief
Quietly turning the backdoor key
Stepping outside she is free.
She (We gave her most of our lives)
is leaving (Sacrificed most of our lives)
home (We gave her everything money could buy)

She's leaving home after living alone
For so many years. Bye, bye
Father snores as his wife gets into her dressing gown
Picks up the letter that's lying there
Standing alone at the top of the stairs
She breaks down and cries to her husband
Daddy our baby's gone.
Why would she treat us so thoughtlessly
How could she do this to me.
She (We never thought of ourselves)
is leaving (Never a thought for ourselves)
home (We struggled hard all our lives to get by)
She's leaving home after living alone
For so many years. Bye, bye
Friday morning at nine o'clock she is far away
Waiting to keep the appointment she made
Meeting a man from the motor trade.
She (What did we do that was wrong)
is having (We didn't know it was wrong) fun
Fun is the one thing that money can't buy
Something inside that was always denied
For so many years. Bye, bye
She's leaving home bye bye

nial independence movements (see Rejecting the West, on p. 940). Vietnam served as a central issue, with the protesters regarding the U.S. not as "the leader of the free world" but rather as an imperialist oppressor.

Discarding orthodox political solutions went hand in hand with overturning traditional social rules. In their demand for "liberation," the students focused as much on cultural as on economic and political issues. Commentators began to talk about a sexual revolution as practices became commonplace that in the 1950s were labeled immoral or bohemian—couples living together before marriage or individuals engaging in sexual relationships with a variety of partners.

The global protest subsided in the early 1970s, but the movement had a significant impact. As we shall see in the next chapter, two of its offshoots, environmentalism and feminism, mounted a radical challenge to political relations and economic practices throughout the West from the 1970s onward and helped define the contemporary era. The protest movement also survived in the distorted form of terrorism. Frustrated with their failure to effect real change through protest and persuasion, a small minority of student activists turned to organized violence. The Weathermen in the United States, the Red Brigades in Italy, and Baader-Meinhof and the Red Army Faction in West Germany all dived underground and resorted to bombings, assassinations, abductions, and hijackings in an effort to weaken the structures of Western capitalism. In Italy a terrorist culture emerged, with approximately 2,000 acts of terrorism committed each year during the 1970s, including a yearly average of 40 murders and 300 *reported* kidnappings. With its dramatic rejection of the processes of democratic decision making, terrorism challenged some of the most basic assumptions of the postwar order in the West.

CONCLUSION
New Definitions, New Divisions

The Cold War was an ideological encounter, with both sides laying claim to the title "democratic." When Soviet tanks rolled through the streets of Budapest in 1956, they flattened not only the Hungarian Revolution but also any illusions about the democratic nature of Soviet-style communism. Yet the hope that the communist system could be reformed, that Marx's original concern for social justice and political equality could be reclaimed, remained—until twelve years later when the tanks rolled again in an eastern European city. The crushing of the Prague Spring destroyed any hope of a democratic eastern Europe within the confines of the Cold War.

In contrast, democracy took firm root in western Europe during the postwar era, even in nations with antidemocratic cultural traditions such as West Germany and Italy. Yet in 1968, protesters in Paris and in cities throughout the world challenged the easy linkage of "the West" with democracy. They pointed out that the increasing scale and complexity of industrial society deprived ordinary people of opportunities for genuine participation in political decision making. And they pointed to the way that Cold War divisions superseded democratic commitments. Despite its abandonment of democratic practices to reinforce racial apartheid, for example, South Africa considered itself, and was considered by other powers, as part of "the West." Within the Cold War context, "the West" sometimes seemed to mean simply "anti-Soviet."

By the early 1970s, the sharp bipolarities of West versus East had begun to break down. Over the next three decades, economic crisis, combined with revolutionary changes in eastern European and Soviet affairs, would reshape the contemporary world. By the early 1990s, the Cold War was over and nationalist conflicts, often fueled by vicious ethnic and religious hatreds, once again played front and center, after twenty years of being upstaged by superpower hostilities.

Suggestions for Further Reading

For a comprehensive list of suggested readings, please go to www.ablongman.com/levack/chapter28

Ansprenger, Franz. *The Dissolution of Colonial Empires.* 1989. A clear and comprehensive account (that unfortunately includes no maps).

Castles, Stephen, et al. *Here for Good: Western Europe's New Ethnic Minorities.* 1984. A useful exploration of the impact of postwar immigration, despite the rather rigid Marxist analysis.

Crampton, R. J. *Eastern Europe in the Twentieth Century—And After.* 1997. Detailed chapters on the 1950s and 1960s, including a substantial discussion of the Prague Spring.

Cronin, James. *The World the Cold War Made: Order, Chaos, and the Return of History.* 1996. An intelligent and thought-provoking overview of the impact of the Cold War.

Fineberg, Jonathan. *Art Since 1940: Strategies of Being.* 1995. A big, bold, lavishly illustrated volume that makes the unfashionable argument that individuals matter.

Fink, Carole, et al. *1968: The World Transformed.* 1998. A collection of essays that explores both the international and the domestic political context for the turmoil of 1968.

Isaacs, Jeremy, and Taylor Downing. *Cold War: An Illustrated History.* 1998. The companion book to the CNN television series. Filled with memorable photographs.

Judge, Edward, and John Langdon. *A Hard and Bitter Peace: A Global History of the Cold War.* 1999. An extremely useful survey for students. Excellent maps.

Keep, John. *Last of the Empires: A History of the Soviet Union, 1945–1991.* 1995. Looks beyond the Kremlin to explore social, cultural, and economic developments.

Mazrui, Ali, and Michael Tidy. *Nationalism and New States in Africa.* 1984. Offers a thematic rather than chronological account of African state-building.

Poiger, Uta. *Jazz, Rock, and Rebels: Cold War Politics and American Culture in a Divided Germany.* 2000. Explores the interplay among youth culture, Americanization, and political protest.

Stromberg, Roland. *After Everything: Western Intellectual History Since 1945.* 1975. A swiftly moving tour through the major intellectual developments.

Urwin, Derek. *A Political History of Western Europe Since 1945.* 1997. Readable, reasonably up-to-date, and comprehensive.

Zubok, Vladislav, and Constantine Pleshakov. *Inside the Kremlin's Cold War: From Stalin to Khrushchev.* 1996. A close examination of the Cold War on the Soviet side.

Notes

························· ▬▬ ·························

1. Lawrence Wylie, *Village in the Vaucluse* (1964), p. 33.
2. Quotation from *Time* magazine, 1950; quoted in Martin Walker, *The Cold War and the Making of the Modern World* (1993), pp. 66–67.
3. Quoted in Stephen Ambrose, *Rise to Globalism* (1971), p. 225.
4. Quoted in Walker, p. 83.
5. Quoted in Donald W. White, *The American Century* (1996), p. 286.
6. Quoted in Jeremy Isaacs and Taylor Downing, *Cold War: An Illustrated History* (1998), p. 170.
7. Quoted in Isaacs and Downing, p. 182.
8. Quoted in Walker, p. 132.
9. Quoted in John Lewis Gaddis, *We Now Know: Rethinking Cold War Evidence* (1997), p. 181.
10. Quotation from Isaacs and Downing, p. 190.
11. Quoted in John D. Hargreaves, *Decolonization in Africa* (1996), p. 113.
12. Quoted in White, *The American Century* (1996), p. 328.
13. Quoted in John L. H. Keep, *Last of the Empires: A History of the Soviet Union, 1945–1991* (1995), p. 79.
14. Quoted in Walker, p. 105.
15. Official Hungarian statistics reported 3,000 dead. John Lewis Gaddis places the number at 20,000 in *We Now Know: Rethinking Cold War Evidence* (1997).
16. Quoted in Robert Paxton, *Europe in the Twentieth Century* (1997), p. 578.
17. Quoted in Derek Urwin, *A Political History of Western Europe Since 1945* (1997), p. 84.
18. Reinhold Wagnleitner, *Coca-Colonization and the Cold War: The Cultural Mission of the United States in Austria After the Second World War* (1994).
19. Quoted in Richard Kuisel, *Seducing the French: The Dilemma of Americanization* (1993), p. 147.
20. Quoted in Felix Gilbert, *The End of the European Era, 1890 to the Present* (1991), p. 429.
21. Quoted in Jonathan Fineberg, *Art Since 1940: Strategies of Being* (1995), p. 144.
22. Quoted in Adrian Hastings, *Modern Catholicism: Vatican II and After* (1991), p. 29.
23. Quoted in Hastings, p. 267.

The Contemporary Era, 1973 to the Present

O N THE EVENING OF NOVEMBER 9, 1989, EAST GERMAN BORDER GUARDS stationed at the wall that divided East and West Berlin gazed out nervously at an unprecedented sight. Thousands of their fellow citizens had gathered in front of the gates, and were demanding to be let through into the western half of the city. This demand was extraordinary; in the twenty-eight years that the Berlin Wall had stood, over 200 people had been shot trying to cross it. But the autumn of 1989 was no ordinary time. A radically reformist regime had emerged in the Soviet Union and publicly proclaimed that its eastern European allies could no longer rely on the Soviet army to assist them in putting down domestic dissent. Poland and Hungary were in the process of replacing communist governments with pluralist parliamentary systems. And in East Germany, 200,000 disaffected citizens had taken advantage of relaxed border controls in Hungary and Czechoslovakia to flee to the West in just a few weeks, while over one million had joined illegal protest demonstrations.

On November 9, in response to overwhelming public pressure, the East German government announced that it would drastically relax the requirements for obtaining an exit visa to visit or emigrate to the West. In a press conference to announce the upcoming changes, the East Berlin Communist Party boss Gunter Schabowski gave a carelessly worded reply to a reporter's question about the new travel policy—and sparked a revolution. Schabowski indicated, wrongly, that as of the next morning, anyone who wanted to head to the West could obtain an automatic exit visa at the border. The news spread quickly, and huge crowds gathered at the checkpoints that dotted the Berlin Wall. The nervous border guards had no idea what to do. Neither did their superiors, who refused to issue the guards any clear instructions. As the crowds pressed forward, the guards gave in and opened the gates. While television cameras broadcast the scene to an astonished world, tens of thousands of East Germans walked, ran, and danced

Chapter Outline

- A New and Uncertain Era: The 1970s and 1980s
- Revolution in the East
- Rethinking the West

And the Wall Came Tumbling Down: Berliners celebrate the fall of the Berlin Wall in November 1989.

across the border that had for so long literally and symbolically divided West from East. Elated with their new freedom and energized with a sense of power and possibility, they then turned on the wall itself. Jumping on top of it, they transformed it from an instrument of coercion and division into a platform for partying. Caught, the East German government saw no way to close the gates. Within a few days, and again without any official approval, ordinary Germans, equipped with hammers and chisels, began to dismantle the wall that the politicians had erected almost three decades earlier.

As extraordinary as the fall of the wall was, the events that followed over the next two years proved even more dramatic—the collapse of communist regimes throughout eastern Europe, the end of the Cold War, the disintegration of the Soviet Union, and the onset of civil war in Yugoslavia and in many formerly Soviet regions. Over the next decade, both governments and ordinary people—not only throughout Europe but across the globe—struggled to build new structures to suit the vastly changed geopolitical landscape. With the collapse of communism and the sundering of the Iron Curtain that had once divided Europe, the meaning of "the West" itself changed, as new enemies emerged to take the place of the Soviet Union. Clearly, then, the dramatic developments of 1989–1991 deserve close study, but they must be set within a context of causes and consequences. To explain that context, this chapter will address three questions: (1) How did economic and political developments in the 1970s and 1980s interact to bring about an end to the international structures of the postwar era and to create a volatile situation within the Soviet bloc? (2) What factors explain not only the outbreak but also the success of the revolutions of 1989–1991, and what were the consequences of these revolutions for the societies of eastern Europe? (3) What were the implications of these developments for the meaning of "the West" itself?

A New and Uncertain Era: The 1970s and 1980s

In the early 1970s, the United States and Europe—both East and West—entered a new era, one defined by economic crisis, widening social divisions, heightened political polarization, and a renewed Cold War.

ECONOMIC CRISIS AND ITS CONSEQUENCES IN THE WEST

Economic crisis was the defining fact of the history of the West after 1973. Before the 1970s, inflation and unemployment seemed to be mutually exclusive—robust economies featured little or no unemployment but tended toward inflation; slower-moving economies were devoid of inflation, but suffered from high unemployment rates. The 1970s, however, brought an unprecedented combination of high inflation rates (in the double digits in many countries by the end of the 1970s) and high unemployment rates (also reaching the double digits in a number of regions). Commentators labeled this new reality stagflation°—the escalating prices of a boom economy combined with the joblessness of an economy going bust. Between 1974 and 1976 the average annual growth rate within western European nations dropped to zero, a sharp contrast to the 1960s' average of 4.8 percent. The prosperous postwar era appeared to be over. By 1984, one-quarter of western European workers under age 25 were unemployed.

Causes of the Economic Crisis

What caused this economic crisis? There is no easy answer, but clearly war and oil played important roles. In October 1973, Egyptian and Syrian armies attacked Israel. When Soviet forces began airlifting supplies to the invading troops, Israel appealed to the U.S. for military aid. In retaliation for American assistance to Israel, the oil-producing states, or OPEC (Organization of Petroleum Exporting Countries), imposed an embargo on American sales, cut back production, and drove up prices from $3 to $16 per barrel of oil. In 1979 political revolution in Iran sparked an even more dramatic price rise—up to $35 per barrel by 1981. These price increases vastly accelerated the inflationary spiral and dealt the death blow to the easy affluence of the postwar era.

Yet rising oil prices were not the sole cause of the economic crisis of the 1970s and 1980s. Two other factors also contributed. First, in 1973 U.S. President Richard Nixon decided to let the dollar "float," to let market forces rather than fixed currency exchange rates determine the dollar's value against other currencies. This decision gutted the Bretton Woods agreements, which had governed international economic affairs since World War II (see Chapter 26), and introduced a more volatile economic era. Whereas the Bretton Woods system had worked to direct the flow of capital to countries in need of investment, the new unregulated system allowed capital to surge into markets where investors could reap immediate gains. National economies lay vulnerable to speculative attacks. No fewer than sixty-nine countries experienced serious banking crises, and the annual economic growth rates of the developed nations fell by one-third in the decades that followed the collapse of Bretton Woods.

A second factor in the economic crisis of the 1970s was international competition. Both the western European and American economies struggled to compete with the emerging Asian and South and Latin American economies. Western societies possessed aging industries and a politicized workforce that demanded relatively high wages and

Inflation and Economic Performance in the West

	France	Great Britain	Italy	United States	West Germany
Inflation over Previous Year (percent)					
1970	5.2%	6.4%	5.0%	5.9%	3.4%
1975	11.8	24.2	17.0	9.1	6.0
1979	9.1	13.4	14.8	11.3	4.1
Gross Domestic Product (Percentage Growth/Decline over Previous Year)					
1970	+5.7%	+2.3%	+5.3%	−0.3%	+5.1%
1975	+0.2	−0.6	−3.6	−0.1	−1.6
1979	+3.3	+2.4	+2.7	+2.4	+4.2

Source: Martin Walker, *Cold War: A History*, 1993, p. 234.

extensive social services. Increasingly, manufacturing concerns moved south and east, to take advantage of the lack of labor regulation and protection in the developing world.

Heightened Social Tensions

The economic crisis had stark social consequences. As the economic pie grew smaller, competition for slices grew more fierce. The 1970s saw a resurgence of industrial unrest in western Europe. In Britain, conflict with the unions brought down three successive governments in a decade. In both Italy and West Germany, workers became increasingly militant and succeeded in winning large wage increases. These industrial settlements only worsened the problem of inflation. Workers demanded large pay increases to meet the rising cost of living, but employers, faced with having to pay higher wages, raised the prices of their goods and services. And so the cost of living continued to climb.

The new economic climate of austerity also led to heightened racial conflict throughout much of western Europe. As we saw in Chapter 28, postwar governments struggling to cope with labor shortages had encouraged immigration, both from the poorer countries of southern and eastern Europe and from colonial or former colonial regions such as Algeria, India, and Jamaica. By 1971, nine million immigrants were living in northern and western Europe.

With the onset of economic crisis, these immigrant communities soon found themselves under attack. European governments reacted to rising unemployment rates by halting labor immigration. By 1975 West Germany, France, the Netherlands, Britain, Belgium, Sweden, and Switzerland had all banned further immigration. Because it explicitly (although incorrectly) linked the presence of immigrants to unemployment, anti-immigration legislation helped solidify racist attitudes among many sectors of the European population. Violence against immigrants began to escalate. In 1973, thirty-two Algerians were murdered in France. White working-class youths in London indulged in what

they termed "paki-bashing": beating up individuals of Southeast Asian descent.

Ironically, anti-immigration legislation actually increased the size of immigrant communities. West Germany saw its number of foreign residents rise by 13 percent between 1974 and 1982; in the same period, France witnessed a 33 percent increase. Foreign workers scrambled to get into western Europe before the doors shut, and once they were in, were reluctant to leave because of the well-grounded fear that they would not be able to return. Family members came too—only Switzerland banned the entry of dependents.

In the 1980s, then, what sociologists call "migration streams" were solidifying into ethnic minority communities—not "guestworkers," but rather a permanent part of western European societies. By 1991, 25 percent of the inhabitants of France were either immigrants or the children or grandchildren of immigrants. For both economic and social reasons, minority groups clustered in certain areas in certain cities. In West Germany in the early 1980s, ethnic minorities constituted 6 percent of the population as a whole, but 24 percent of the population of Frankfurt—and in the city's central district, 80 percent.

The resulting encounters among peoples of different religious and ethnic traditions reshaped European culture. In Britain, for example, Afro-Caribbean styles of dress and music had a profound influence on white working-class youth culture. These encounters also posed a potent challenge to ideas of national identity. By the 1980s, British journalists were writing about "third-generation immigrants," as if someone born in Britain to British citizenship was somehow less British than other British citizens. Such terminology indicated a deep reluctance to classify individuals with brown or black skin as British, an inability to conceive of national identity as anything but white. In France, the highly centralized education system became the site of hostile encounters, as Islamic parents fought for the rights of their daughters to attend school in traditional Muslim headdress, a practice resisted by some French authorities

"YOUNG, BRITISH, AND WHITE"

During the 1980s, racist violence increased in Britain, as throughout much of Europe. Overtly racist political parties, such as the National Front, capitalized on anti-immigrant sentiment to recruit new members for their movements. In this document, the American journalist Bill Buford describes a birthday party held in a pub for one young member of the National Front. The excerpt begins with a dangerous moment: football (soccer) rivalries are threatening to divide the partygoers.

On the far side, some of the new members had started in on their football chants, just as Neil had feared. These appeared to be West Ham supporters. They were then answered, from the other side of the room, by Chelsea supporters.* A contrapuntal chorus of West Ham and Chelsea songs followed, one that sent Neil scurrying through his record collection. It was time to change the music . . . It was time to play the White Power music.

None of the songs was played on any of the established radio stations or sold in any of the conventional shops. It was a mail-order or cash-in-hand music trade, and from the titles you could see why: "Young, British, and White"; "England Belongs to Me"; "Shove the Dove"; "England" and "British Justice." These were the lyrics of "The Voice of Britain":

> Our old people cannot walk the streets alone.
> They fought for this nation and this is what they get back.

> They risked their lives for Britain, and now Britain belongs to aliens.
> It's about time Britain went and took it back.

> This is the voice of Britain.
> You'd better believe it.
> This is the voice of Britain
> C'mon and fly the flag now.
> . . .

The music was delivered with the same numbing, crushing percussion that had characterized everything else that had been played that evening . . . There was one refrain I could follow, and that was because it was played repeatedly, and because, each time, everyone joined in. It seemed to be the theme song.

> Two pints of lager[†] and a packet of crisps.[‡]
> Wogs[§] out! White power!
> Wogs out! White power!
> Wogs out! White power!

It was interesting to contemplate that the high-point of the evening was organized around this simple declaration of needs: a lad needed his lager; a lad needed his packet of crisps; a lad needed his wog.

---

[*] *West Ham and Chelsea = rival English soccer teams.*
[†] *"Lager" = beer.*
[‡] *"Packet of crisps" = bag of potato chips.*
[§] *"Wog" = racially derogatory term for Southeast Asians.*

Source: From *Among the Thugs: The Experience, and the Seduction, of Crowd Violence* by Bill Buford. Copyright © 1991, 1990 by William Buford. Used by permission of W. W. Norton & Company, Inc. and The Random House Group Limited.

---

who feared that "Frenchness" would be diluted if immigrants failed to accept the traditions of the host society.

In both France and Britain, immigrants could become or already were legal citizens. In West Germany, Switzerland, and the Scandinavian countries, however, foreign workers remained foreign, with no chance of obtaining citizenship. Thus by the 1980s, a dangerous situation had emerged in these countries, with the children of foreign workers growing up in a society in which they had no political rights. These "foreigners" experienced widespread discrimination in education, housing, and employment. In West Germany in the late 1970s, over 40 percent of foreign workers lived in housing without a bath or shower. (Only 6 percent of German citizens did so.) Forced to live in such substandard accommodation by poverty, immigrants were often then stereotyped as dirty and uncivilized.

Explicitly racist political parties capitalized on the new anti-immigration sentiment. In France, for example, Jean-Marie Le Pen (b. 1928), a veteran of the Algerian war,

created the *Front National* in 1974 as an anti-immigration party. In Le Pen's view, "Everything comes from immigration. Everything goes back to immigration." Unemployment, rising crime rates, an increase in illegitimate births, crowded schools, AIDS—Le Pen blamed it all on nonwhite immigrants. Appealing particularly to young, male working-class voters, Le Pen's party attracted between 9 and 11 percent of the votes in elections in the mid-1980s, and remained a threatening political presence for the next two decades. In the presidential race of 2002, Le Pen beat out sixteen competitors and came in second only to the incumbent, the Gaullist Party leader Jacques Chirac.

A Changing Political Culture

The economic crisis called into question the main assumptions that had governed political life since World War II. Western Europeans had emerged from the horror of total war in 1945 determined to build better societies. Rejecting the extremes of communism on the left and fascism on the right, they took the centrist social democratic path. Two features characterized social democracies—first, mixed economies that combined nationalization of key industries with private enterprise, and second, an interventionist state that took responsibility for maintaining full employment and providing extensive welfare services. The stagflation of the 1970s, however, seemed to indicate that these social democratic solutions no longer worked.

Alternative answers appeared, clustered under the label of New Conservatism°, epitomized by the Republican Ronald Reagan in the United States (1911–), the Christian Democrat Helmut Kohl in West Germany (1930–), and the Conservative Margaret Thatcher in Britain (1925–). On the most fundamental level, the New Conservatives rejected the postwar emphasis on social improvement in favor of policies intended to create more opportunities for individual achievement. Thatcher even insisted, "There is no such thing as society." In the New Conservative worldview, there was instead the individual, freely competing in a world governed by market forces rather than governmental regulations or state planning. As Kohl demanded during his

■ The New Conservatism

Britain's first female prime minister, Margaret Thatcher, called herself a "conviction" rather than a "consensus" politician. She held office from 1979 to 1990—the longest term of any British prime minister in the twentieth century.

Spending on Social Services as a Percentage of the Gross Domestic Product

	France	West Germany	Sweden	United Kingdom
1960	13.2	15.5	11.0	10.8
1965	15.6	16.5	13.8	11.8
1970	15.1	17.1	18.6	13.1
1975	23.9	23.7	25.0	17.1
1980	26.3	24.0	31.9	18.1
1985	28.7	23.8	30.7	20.3

Source: Susan Pedersen, *Family, Dependence, and the Origins of the Welfare State: Britain and France, 1914–1945*, 1993, p. 416. Reprinted with the permission of Cambridge University Press.

1983 campaign, "Less state, more market; fewer collective burdens, more personal performance; fewer encrusted structures, more mobility, self-initiative, and competition." Privatization of nationalized or state-owned industries constituted a key part of the New Conservative agenda—removing the state from the economy and allowing private enterprises to compete. In Britain under Thatcher, the coal industry, transport, and utilities were all shifted to private ownership.

New Conservatives also mounted an attack on the welfare state, insisting that rising social expenditures, funded by rising taxes, lay at the heart of the economic crisis that had afflicted the West since the early 1970s. They pointed to the fact that the years between 1960 and 1981 had seen a dramatic rise in social spending (for programs such as health, disability, and unemployment insurance; pensions; and family allowances). Minimizing the successes of these social programs in reducing poverty, New Conservatives instead linked rising social expenditures to surging inflation and declining economic growth rates.

New Conservative fiscal policies did not actually break sharply from their social democratic predecessors. Reagan, for example, used deficit spending to finance skyrocketing military budgets (up by 40 percent during his administration). The real break lay in the New Conservatives' willingness to tolerate high unemployment rates in order to lower inflation. By imposing high interest rates on their economies, Thatcher and Reagan engineered a recession in the early 1980s that brought inflation under control. Inflation rates in Britain fell from 18 percent in 1980 to 4.5 percent in 1983. High interest rates, however, overvalued the British pound and the American dollar. As a result, manufacturers found it hard to sell their products abroad and many went under. In Britain, 13 percent of the workforce was unemployed by 1984. In West Germany, too, Kohl's policies of holding down taxes and government expenditures were accompanied by unemployment rates of over 9 percent in the mid-1980s. Inflation-busting came at a high social cost, as riots erupted in English cities in 1981 and beggars reappeared on British streets.

By the end of the 1980s, as a result of falling global oil prices and the Reagan military spending spree that primed the pump of the global economy, Western economies returned to growth (and by 1990, inflation rates had begun to rise again). But the average late-1980s growth rates of 2 to 3 percent per year were lower than those of 5 to 6 percent that had characterized Western economies in the 1950s and 1960s. At the same time, unemployment rates tended to hover between 5 and 7 percent—levels that would have been regarded as unacceptably high in the earlier period. A new political culture, based on lowered expectations, had come into being.

Even Europe's social democratic parties had to adapt to this new political culture. In Sweden, the Social Democrats returned to office in 1982 after eight years out of power, but under the leadership of Olaf Palme (1926–1986), the chastened party followed a centrist path, marked by moderate wage agreements and reductions in tax rates. Socialist governments in Italy, Greece, and Spain during the 1980s also followed the path of reduced health and social security expenditures, rising utility and public transport fees, and wage cuts.

The most dramatic example of social democratic adaptation occurred in France. In 1981, French voters elected Socialist Party leader François Mitterrand (1916–1996) to the presidency. In his first year in office, Mitterrand implemented a series of radical social democratic measures, including a rise in the minimum wage, a reduction in the workweek and an increase in holiday time, and expanded social welfare. He nationalized the country's banking system and imposed higher taxes on the wealthier sections of society. But in 1982, Mitterrand was forced by a series of economic catastrophes—falling exports, rising trade and budget deficits, and soaring inflation rates—to cut social spending, to reverse his nationalization program, and to implement "austerity" measures, which led to higher unemployment rates.

FROM DETENTE TO RENEWED COLD WAR, 1975–1985

At the same time that economic crisis undermined political consensus, rising superpower tensions put an end to the era of detente—and caused greater rifts within western European societies. In the early 1970s, detente had appeared to be flourishing, with the United States and the Soviet Union signing the first major arms control agreement in 1971. The culmination of detente came in 1975 at the Helsinki Conference in Finland. Thirty-two European states, Canada, the United States, and the Soviet Union declared their acceptance of all existing European borders, agreed to a policy of joint notification of all major military exercises (thus reducing the chances of accidental nuclear war), and promised to safeguard the human rights of their citizens.

Ironically, the Helsinki Accords marked the beginning of the end of the detente era. Using the Helsinki human rights clauses to demand political reform, eastern European and Soviet dissidents such as the Soviet scientist and Nobel Peace Prize–winner Andrei Sakharov (1921–1989) began to publicize the human rights abuses committed by their governments. The human rights issue weakened U.S.-Soviet relations, particularly after the election of Jimmy Carter (1976–1980) to the U.S. presidency. Carter insisted on placing human rights at the center of his foreign policy. Soviet leaders reacted in fury to what they perceived as Carter's meddling in their internal affairs—and heightened their persecution of dissidents. Sakharov, for example, was imprisoned in 1979.

As detente crumbled, the arms race accelerated. Alarmed by the Soviet deployment of a new intermediate-range nuclear missile in 1977, western European leaders pressured Carter to approve the development of NATO's own intermediate-range weapon, the cruise missile. In 1979, the governments of West Germany, Britain, Italy, Belgium, and the Netherlands agreed to the deployment of the cruise missiles on their soil. Carter pledged a 5 percent increase in the U.S. defense budget, with even more dramatic increases promised for years to come.

The final blow to detente came in 1979 with the Soviet invasion of Afghanistan. In 1978 Afghan communists had seized control of their government and soon found themselves under attack from Islamic rebels. The prospect of a fundamentalist Islamic regime in Afghanistan alarmed the Soviet government, which feared the spread of Islamic nationalism into its own Central Asian republics. In December 1979, on the same day that NATO announced the deployment of its cruise missiles, the Politburo voted to send troops into Afghanistan (at a meeting in which Soviet leader Leonid Brezhnev was so drunk he could not participate). Calling the invasion "the most serious threat to peace since the Second World War," Carter cut economic and cultural links with the Soviet Union, approved CIA aid for anti-Soviet Islamic guerrilla groups, and warned that if the Soviets moved toward the Middle East, he would not hesitate to use nuclear weapons. The era of detente was over.

With the election of New Conservatives such as Reagan and Thatcher, the renewal of the Cold War took on a greater intensity. Both Reagan and Thatcher viewed detente as a policy of weakness. Pointing to the triumph of communist regimes in Ethiopia, Vietnam, Mozambique, and Angola, they argued that the Soviet Union had gained the advantage over the West in the struggle for global supremacy. Reagan labeled the Soviet Union the "Evil Empire"—a reference to the popular *Star Wars* film series that was first released in the 1970s—and revived the anticommunist attitudes and

■ The Greenham Common Protests

In the spring of 1983, protesters formed a fourteen-mile-human chain across Greenham Common in England to protest against NATO's deployment of cruise missiles. The protest was part of a much wider movement in western Europe and the United States, which articulated widespread public discontent with the renewal of the Cold War. It also played a pivotal role in British feminism, as female activists established a women-only camp at the Greenham Common military base.

rhetoric of the 1950s. Thatcher strongly supported Reagan's decision to accelerate the arms buildup begun by Carter. Her hard-line anticommunism won her the nickname the "Iron Lady" from Soviet policymakers.

The renewal of the Cold War, like the end of economic prosperity, opened up large rifts within European societies. The NATO decision to deploy cruise missiles proved enormously unpopular with many ordinary Europeans. Hundreds of thousands of protesters turned out in the streets of London, Bonn, Amsterdam, and other cities. Many of these protesters demanded not only the cancellation of the cruise missiles but also a withdrawal from NATO's nuclear umbrella and a reorientation of European political life and international affairs away from nuclear weapons—and away from the United States.

NEW CHALLENGES AND NEW IDENTITIES IN THE WEST

In the wake of economic crisis and the renewed Cold War, new cultural and political forces emerged in western Europe and the United States. In the 1970s and 1980s, feminism and radical environmentalism demanded a shift in the political status quo.

Changing Women's Roles

New feminism° emerged directly out of the student protest movement of the 1960s. Female activists grew frustrated at being denied a voice in the movement—"we cook while the men talk of revolution."[1] At the same time, they were increasingly eager to connect analyses of political subordination to experiences of sexual repression. Their efforts to liberate women from political and cultural limits and expectations gave birth to what was, by the 1980s, an international feminist movement.

Economic changes buttressed the new feminism. The numbers of women working outside the home rose in these decades—up by 50 percent in Italy between 1970 and 1985, for example. By the late 1970s, women in France accounted for over 34 percent of the labor force; in Britain, 31 percent; in West Germany, 37 percent. As unemployment took a particularly high toll on male, unionized, full-time, skilled manual laborers, many homes saw the wife emerge as the chief breadwinner.

Demographic changes also supported the new feminism. In 1970, the age at which men and women first married began to climb (reversing the trend of two decades), and birth rates continued to fall. Women were also far more likely to have children outside marriage—25 percent of all

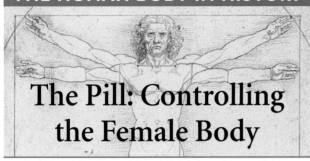

The Pill: Controlling the Female Body

In the postwar period, all sorts of pills appeared on the shelves of American and European pharmacies. Offered in a myriad of colors and sizes, they promised all sorts of remedies for all sorts of ailments. But only one earned the designation "*the* Pill"—the oral contraceptive, first marketed in the United States in 1960. In 1993, the *Economist* (a respected British weekly news magazine) listed the Pill as one of the seven wonders of the modern world. A revolutionary contraceptive, the Pill helped alter the place of the female body in Western culture.

The Pill's entry into the mass market coincided with two other developments. First, sexual practices and attitudes changed significantly among some sectors of the population—particularly middle-class men and women with university educations. Second, the birth rate slowed throughout the United States and western Europe. Thus it is often assumed that the Pill caused both a sexual and demographic revolution.

This assumption is incorrect. Although by 1965 the Pill was the most popular form of birth control in the United States (used by 80 percent of white, non-Catholic, college graduates between ages 20 and 24), in Europe it became a part of women's lives much more slowly. Introduced to Britain in 1961, the Pill was not mass-marketed there until the late 1960s. In France and Czechoslovakia, withdrawal remained the most popular form of birth control until well into the 1970s, when the Pill began to be distributed widely. In Italy, contraceptives of all types, including the Pill, were illegal until 1971. In Ireland, they remain illegal for unmarried men and women. In the Soviet Union, the Pill was never widely accessible. Most Soviet women relied on withdrawal, rhythm, and abortion—on the average, four to six abortions during the childbearing years. Moreover, throughout Europe and the United States, the Pill always remained more popular with the wealthier sectors of society. Because women who wanted to use it were required to visit their doctor every six months, many poor women viewed the Pill as prohibitively expensive (and many single women simply could not obtain a prescription).

The Pill, then, did not cause the sexual revolution. It did, however, have a radical impact. The Pill offered a new, yet ambivalent way of viewing the female body. Other methods of birth control dealt with the consequences of sexual intercourse (the barrier methods, withdrawal, and abortion) or sought to limit its practice (rhythm). The Pill, however, was not an external object to be inserted or applied or fitted. By manipulating the female reproductive cycle, it actually altered the body itself, permitting women to experience what had been defined as an exclusively male prerogative—the detachment of sexual intercourse from pregnancy. At the same time, the Pill allowed women to distance themselves from their bodies. One of the problems with other forms of female contraceptives was that they required women to touch their genitals, a requirement that many European and American women found distasteful.

The Pill also raised important questions about controlling the female body. During the course of the twentieth century, childbirth had altered radically in the Western world. No longer occurring at home and presided over by women, childbirth now occurred in the hospital, where doctors—usually male—were in charge. It had become "medicalized": The birthing woman had become a patient, a medical problem, in need of drugs and other scientific devices. The Pill fit with this process. Although many women hailed it as a liberator that allowed them to control their own bodies, the Pill was initially marketed to doctors very differently. In its advertising, the Searle pharmaceutical company assured doctors that the Pill would allow them to supervise and regulate their patients' birth control practices. The Pill, then, offered the promise of controlling the female body: The question was, who was in charge? ∎

∎ **One Little Pill**

In 1967, *Time* magazine's cover story on the Pill was entitled "Freedom from Fear."

For Discussion

Why has the Pill become a powerful symbol of changes in women's roles in the contemporary era?

births in Britain in 1988; in Sweden and Denmark, almost 50 percent. Marriage itself became optional. By the late 1970s, almost half of the couples who married were already cohabiting.

Institutional politics responded slowly to the changes in women's roles. In many countries, women had lost ground since World War II. Whereas thirty women had sat in France's National Assembly in 1945, in 1973 only nine remained. Slowly, these numbers climbed back up. In the British general elections of 1992, twice as many women stood as parliamentary candidates compared to 1979. The most dramatic changes occurred in Scandinavia. By the mid-1980s, women averaged about one-third of the members of parliament in Sweden, and women members accounted for approximately half of Norway's cabinets.

The new feminist movement refused to confine its focus to the world of party politics, recognizing instead that "the personal is political." Much of the new feminist critique focused on the female body—its image, its oppression, its control. Feminists challenged feminine stereotypes through attacks on beauty pageants and critiques of the fashion industry, and sought the reform of legal codes to outlaw spousal rape and to legalize abortion. Legalization of abortion occurred first in northern Europe: in Britain in 1967, in Denmark in 1970. Catholic Europe followed: In Italy abortions became legally available in 1978, in France in 1979.

In the economic and educational spheres, feminists demanded equal pay for equal work and greater access to educational and professional opportunities. They pressed for more generous parental leave policies, family allowances, and child care provisions. In addition, with women accounting for approximately half of the university students in many Western countries, feminists began to alter the content of the curriculum. Challenging the male biases that had regarded women's contributions as irrelevant and women's lives as insignificant, for example, feminist historians brought to light the "hidden history" of women.

Environmental Awareness and Activism

Environmentalists added their voice to the political cacophony of the 1970s and 1980s. Conservationist groups seeking to protect this species or preserve that plant had long existed in the industrial world, but the radical environmentalism that emerged in the later 1960s was something new. Radical environmentalists saw problems such as species elimination or pollution as part of a larger ecological breakdown. They challenged the fundamental structures of industrial economies (whether capitalist or communist), particularly their inherent emphasis on "more, bigger, faster, now." The movement embraced the ideas of unorthodox economists such as Britain's E. F. Schumacher (1911–1977), who insisted that quantitative measures of economic growth (such as the GNP) failed to factor in environmental destruction and social dislocation, and that in many con-

■ **Spaceship Earth**
The photographs of the globe taken by the Apollo space teams in the 1960s provided humanity with a powerful new visual image, one that proved influential in shaping radical environmentalism. Suspended in space, the Earth seemed suddenly vulnerable, its limits very clear, a single spaceship hurtling through a vast infinity.

texts, "small is beautiful." At the heart of radical environmentalism was the concept of natural limits, of "Spaceship Earth"—the vision of the planet as a "single spaceship, without unlimited reservoirs of anything."[2]

New media-savvy organizations like Greenpeace publicized the environmentalist cause with colorful protests, such as sailing in small rubber dinghies to challenge whaling fleets. The most popular of radical environmentalist targets was nuclear power. From the mid-1970s on, protests against the construction of nuclear power plants in western Europe drew tens of thousands of supporters. The movement's slogan, "Nuclear Power? No Thanks," was translated into more than forty languages.

Environmental concern helped create a new sort of political party. By the late 1980s Green Parties had sprouted in fifteen western European countries. The Greens were the most successful in West Germany, where they sat in the legislature from 1983 and formed an important voting bloc. In the late 1990s, the members of the German Green Party joined the government.

Green politics° drew its ideas not only from environmentalism but also from both feminism and the mass protests against NATO's cruise missile deployment in the early 1980s. Strongly opposed to NATO and its reliance on nuclear weapons, the Greens appropriated the antinuclear movement's effort to break away from Cold War categories. To do so, they turned to feminist theory, contending that both the continuing Cold War and the degradation of the natural environment stemmed from the same root as discrimination against women—an obsession with physical power, a glorification of violence, and an unwillingness to tear down hierarchical structures. The Greens articulated a basic challenge to the political status quo: "We are neither left nor right; we are in front."

THE CRISIS OF LEGITIMACY IN THE EAST

Like the West, eastern Europe was rocked by the transformation in the global economy after 1973, but the impact was delayed, its consequences not fully felt until the 1980s. Even during the apparent prosperity of the 1970s, however, both structural economic weaknesses and spreading political disillusion undermined the stability of the Soviet bloc.

The Illusion of Prosperity

While Western countries in the 1970s struggled with stagflation and disappearing economic growth rates, the Soviet Union posted record-breaking production figures. By 1984, for example, the Soviet Union was producing 80 percent more steel and six times more iron ore than the United States. But Soviet prosperity was an illusion. Published growth and productivity statistics had little to do with actual economic performance. The Soviet economy continued to be hampered by overcentralization. The state planning commission, GOSPLAN, had the impossible task of coordinating the production of over four million different products in at least 50,000 factories. "Success" in Soviet industry continued to mean fulfilling arbitrary quotas, regardless of the quality of goods produced, the actual demand for the product, or the cost of producing it. The Soviet command economy also proved far too rigid to keep pace with global economic change. While triumphantly proclaiming its fulfillment of the heavy industrial expansion planned by Khrushchev in the early 1960s, Soviet leaders in the 1970s failed to recognize that increasingly, microchips counted for far more than iron ore—that fiber optics, not steel, would buttress the new modernity. When the first Soviet home computer reached the market in the 1980s, it cost ten times the comparable Western model. The few consumers who could afford the machine soon found that no floppy disks were available to run it.

By the 1980s, the only growth sectors in the Soviet economy were oil and vodka—and then the bottom dropped out of the oil market. After peaking at $35 per barrel in 1981, oil prices began a steady decade-long fall. In 1985, a barrel of oil averaged at $26; a year later, prices had dropped to between $12 and $20 per barrel. For the Soviet economy, the results were catastrophic.

The Soviet leadership was incapable of responding to the economic crisis. Throughout the 1970s, the General Secretary of the Communist Party (and thus the de facto ruler of the Soviet Union) was Leonid Brezhnev, whose increasing physical frailty mirrored that of the country at large. Like many of his colleagues, Brezhnev had been a child at the time of the Russian Revolution; he knew only Soviet rule and had risen into major office very young because of the employment opportunities created by Stalin's Great Purge. In 1982, the average age of members of the Politburo was 68. These men had a vested interest in maintaining the status quo, not in carrying out fundamental reform.

The Soviet Union's satellite states in eastern Europe also lurched from apparent prosperity into economic crisis during this period. During the 1970s, the Soviets provided oil to their eastern European satellites at prices far below the market value and so shielded these economies from some of the tensions afflicting their western European rivals. At the same time, eastern European governments borrowed heavily from Western banks. They used the loans to increase the flow of consumer goods to their populations (and thus to quell dissent) and also to import the latest industrial technologies, in hopes that modernization would invigorate their stagnant economies.

These hopes went unrealized. Western loans did not solve fundamental problems such as overcentralization and the divorce of prices from production costs. Despite an increased standard of living, eastern European consumption levels remained well behind those in the West. And unlike Soviet citizens, eastern Europeans were acutely aware of this fact. Travel restrictions were less severe than in the Soviet Union, and many eastern Europeans had access to Western television and radio stations. In East Germany, the prosperity of West Germany just across the border was a particular source of discontent. While West Germans drove some of the best-made cars in the world, East Germans endured long waiting periods before purchasing the Trabant, a plastic car with a two-cylinder, two-stroke motor that pumped out clouds of polluting exhaust.

In the 1980s, the debt-laden economic structures of eastern Europe began to collapse. Two factors were crucial. First, governments found they had to borrow simply to service their existing debt. Second, as oil prices fell, the Soviet Union responded by charging market value for their oil sales to their satellites, thus depriving these economies of a crucial support. Ordinary people soon felt the impact of this economic crisis, as governments restricted the flow of consumer goods and imposed higher prices.

The Moment of Solidarity, the Moment of Punk

Events in Poland at the end of the decade illustrated how economic discontent and political dissent could create a revolutionary situation. Faced with negative economic growth rates, the Polish government announced price increases for meat and other essentials in July 1980. Poles hit

■ **The Moment of Solidarity**
Lech Wałęsa addresses workers in the Gdansk shipyard in 1980. Note the pictures of the pope and the Virgin Mary—Roman Catholicism served as a vital source of national unity and identity, one opposed to communism.

the streets in angry protest. Workers at the Lenin Shipyard in Gdansk went on strike, a legal impossibility in a communist state. Led by a charismatic and politically savvy electrician named Lech Wałęsa (b. 1943), the striking shipyard workers demanded the right to form a trade union independent of communist control. One month later, they did so—and Solidarity° was born. Solidarity was far more than a trade union, however. When Wałęsa and his co-workers announced their demands, they not only included the right to unionize and strike, but also called for the liberation of political prisoners and an end to censorship. They demanded a rollback of the state's power and sharp restrictions on its repressive apparatus. Within just a few months, ten million Poles had joined the ranks of Solidarity.

Fearing Soviet military intervention, the Polish communist government cracked down. In December 1981 Prime Minister Wojciech Jaruzelski declared martial law, arrested more than 10,000 Solidarity members (including Wałęsa), banned all independent trade unions, and imposed price increases of 75 percent. For the next eighteen months, Poles lived in fear; they could not leave their home city without police permission and phone lines were openly wiretapped.

Like the Hungarian revolution in 1956 and the Prague Spring of 1968, Solidarity seemed to be one more futile and defeated protest in eastern Europe. But two factors made the Solidarity story end very differently. First, Poland's economic crisis continued to deepen. Its debt to the West climbed inexorably upward, food shortages became endemic, unemployment rates rose, and real wages fell. The average Polish worker's monthly wage was half the

cost of living, and the waiting time for an apartment was fifteen years. Second, Solidarity simply refused to be defeated. Both in prison and out, its members resolved to act as if they were free. They met in small groups, published six illegal newspapers and ran a radio station, and organized election boycotts. To a far greater degree than many observers in the West realized at the time, Solidarity remained a political presence and a moral force in Polish society throughout the 1980s, and in 1989 it emerged to lead Poland into democracy.

Before 1989 no other eastern European country experienced a protest movement as dramatic as Solidarity, yet throughout the region economic hardship fed widespread political alienation and a deepening longing for radical change. One sign of the widening gap between the communist authorities and the people they governed was the emergence of punk music as a cultural force among eastern European youth. Punk had first appeared in Britain in the mid-1970s, the product of economic decline and social division. Dressed in clothes that deliberately mocked the consumerism and respectability of mainstream middle-class society—ripped trousers held together with safety pins, dog collars, spiked and outrageously colored hair—punks promoted a do-it-yourself style of rock music that also spat on middle-class standards. Punk rockers rarely had any musical training or expertise; even talent was not actually necessary. All that was needed was rage, which was readily available.

The nihilistic message of bands such as Britain's Sex Pistols—"no future for you, no future for me"—resonated in eastern Europe. With names like Doom, Crisis, Shortage, Paralysis, Sewage, and Dead Organism, Eastern punk bands, like their Western models, often expressed utter despair: "No goal, no future, no hope, no joy!" But this nihilism butted against explicit political protest. At punk concerts in Poland, bands and their audiences stood in silent homage to Solidarity. In Hungary, the members of one punk group received prison sentences for a performance in which they mocked their government as a "rotten, stinking communist gang" while tearing up a live chicken.[3]

Nature and the Nation

The dissatisfaction expressed by punk bands permeated eastern European society, and increasingly took political form. Just as the emergence of radical environmentalism demonstrated a strong current of dissatisfaction with the political order in the West, so similar movements in the East pushed for radical change.

For decades, the conquest of nature had been a key part of Soviet ideology: "We cannot wait for favors from nature; our task is to take from her."[4] Beginning in the 1930s, Soviet engineers sought to fill what they regarded as nature's "empty spaces" with exotic plant and animal life, thus wreaking havoc with the ecological balance of much of the Soviet environment. In the early 1960s, Khrushchev's "Virgin Lands" scheme introduced intensive chemical fertilization and irrigation across huge swathes of Soviet territory, resulting in the fall of lake water levels, the destruction of wetlands, and the salinization of extensive stretches of land. The situation worsened in the 1970s. The rapid expansion of heavy industry focused on churning out products, not on human safety or environmental sustainability. The most basic environmental precautions were ignored within Soviet and eastern European cities; untreated sewage was often dumped directly into lakes and rivers. By 1977, Soviet scientists concluded that Lake Baikal—the most voluminous and deepest freshwater lake in the world, home to more than 800 plant and 1,500 animal species—had experienced irreversible environmental degradation.

As a result of this environmental destruction, environmentalist protest groups emerged in the Soviet Union and throughout eastern Europe. Because Soviet officials regarded the environment as insignificant, they tended to view environmentalist protest as unimportant, as a "safe" outlet for popular frustration. Thus environmentalism became one of the few areas in Soviet society that permitted ordinary people free expression and in which public opinion was allowed a voice. Environmental activism worked like a termite infestation, nibbling away from within at the structures of Soviet communism.

Environmentalism also proved crucial in underlining nationalist identity and fueling nationalist protest. The various national and ethnic groups within the vast Soviet empire watched their forests disappear, their lakes dry up, and their ancient cities bulldozed, as a result of decisions made in faraway Moscow by men they regarded as foreigners—as *Russians* rather than *comrades*. By the 1980s, schools in Latvia issued gas masks as a routine safety precaution because of the dangers of chemical spills. Many Latvians concluded that they would be better off independent of Soviet control.

Revolution in the East

Between 1989 and 1991, revolution engulfed eastern Europe and the Soviet Union. The appointment of Mikhail Gorbachev (1985–1991) as Soviet Communist Party Secretary in 1985 proved pivotal. Gorbachev's efforts to reform the Soviet system led to a series of breathtaking changes: Soviet control over eastern Europe ended, the Cold War came to an abrupt halt, the Soviet Union itself ceased to exist. Ironically, Gorbachev set in motion the first two of these developments precisely to avoid the third. But Gorbachev did not control the story. Ordinary people developed their own plot lines. What Czech dissident Václav Havel called "the power of the powerless" proved to be powerful indeed. In the decade following the revolutions, however, a sense of powerlessness returned to eastern Europe, as economic and social crisis followed in the wake of communism's fall.

GORBACHEV AND RADICAL REFORM

In 1982, the decrepit Leonid Brezhnev died—and so, in rapid succession, did his two successors, Yuri Andropov (1982–1984) and Konstantin Chernenko (1984–1985). The time had come for a generational change. When Mikhail Gorbachev succeeded Chernenko, he was 54 years old. Compared to his elderly colleagues on the Politburo, he looked like a teenager.

Gorbachev's biography encompassed the drama of Soviet history. He was born, in 1931, into the turmoil of collectivization. One-third of the inhabitants of his native village in Stavropol were executed or imprisoned or died from famine or disease in the upheavals of the early 1930s. Both of his grandfathers were arrested on trumped-up charges. Yet Gorbachev's family continued to believe in the Communist dream. During World War II his father served in the Red Army (and was twice wounded), and in 1948 Gorbachev and his father together won the Order of Red Banner of Labor for harvesting almost six times the average crop. Because of this award and his academic abilities, Gorbachev won entry to Moscow University. After earning degrees in economics and law, he rose through the ranks of the provincial Communist Party. In 1978, at age

47, he became the youngest member of the Communist Party Central Committee, the key leadership body in the Soviet Union.

Gorbachev came to power in 1985, convinced that the Soviet system was ailing, and that the only way to restore it to health was through radical surgery. What he did not anticipate was that such surgery would in fact kill the patient. His surgical tools were glasnost and perestroika, two Russian terms without direct English equivalents.

Glasnost°, sometimes translated as "openness," "publicity," or "transparency," meant abandoning the deception and censorship that had always characterized the Soviet system, for a policy based on open admission of failures and problems. To Gorbachev, "Broad, timely, and frank information is testimony of faith in people . . . and for their capacity to work things out themselves."[5]

Not surprisingly, Soviet citizens remained wary of Gorbachev's talk of glasnost—until April 1986 and the Chernobyl nuclear power plant disaster. Operator error at the Ukrainian power plant led to the most serious nuclear accident in history. In the days following the accident, thirty-five plant workers died; over the next five years the clean-up effort would claim at least 7,000 lives. The accident placed more than four million inhabitants of Ukraine and Belarus at risk from excess radiation, and spread a radioactive cloud that extended all the way to Scotland. When news of the accident first reached Moscow, party officials acted as they had always done: They denied anything had happened. But monitors in Western countries quickly picked up on the excess radiation spewing into the atmosphere. Gorbachev initiated an about-face and insisted that the accurate information about the disaster be released to the public. Chernobyl became the first Soviet media event. In 1986, 93 percent of the Soviet population had access to a television set and what they saw on their screens convinced them that glasnost was real. A powerful change had occurred in Soviet political culture.

Through glasnost Gorbachev aimed to overcome the alienation and apathy that he perceived as endemic in Soviet culture, to convince citizens of the importance of participating in the structures of political and economic life. At the same time, he sought to change those structures through perestroika°, often translated as "restructuring" or "reconstruction." Gorbachev believed he could reverse his nation's economic decline only through a series of reforms focusing on modernization, decentralization, and the introduction of a limited market.

Gorbachev knew, however, that even limited reforms threatened the vested interests of communist bureaucrats. Thus the success of economic perestroika depended on political perestroika. The culmination of political restructuring came in May 1989, when Soviet voters entered the voting booths to elect the Congress of People's Deputies, and for the first time in Soviet history they had a choice of candidates. All of these candidates were members of the Communist Party, but in 1990, the Communist Party monopoly was ended, and the Soviet Union entered the brave new world of multiparty politics.

A NEW INTERNATIONAL ORDER

Restructuring Soviet economics and politics led almost inevitably to restructuring international relations. By the 1980s, at least 18 percent of the Soviet GNP was absorbed by the arms race; Gorbachev concluded that the Soviet Union simply could not afford the Cold War. In just a five-year period, between 1987 and 1991, the international order was transformed. The Cold War ended, the Soviet Union released its hold on eastern Europe, and the communist regimes put in place in the late 1940s collapsed.

These dramatic changes began with Gorbachev's efforts to reduce Soviet military spending. As soon as Gorbachev took office, he signaled to the West his desire to resume arms control negotiations. In December 1987, Gorbachev and U.S. president Ronald Reagan signed the INF (Intermediate Nuclear Forces) Treaty, agreeing to the total elimination of land-based intermediate-range nuclear missiles. In 1990, the Soviet Union, the United States, and twenty-two European countries agreed to cut conventional forces. A year later, the Soviets and Americans signed the Strategic Arms Reduction Treaty (START I), pledging themselves to a mutual reduction of intercontinental ballistic missiles (ICBMs). At the same time, Gorbachev moved to reduce Soviet military commitments abroad. In 1989, he ended the Soviet war in Afghanistan, pulled the Red Army from Mongolia, and removed Soviet-sponsored Cuban forces from Angola.

Even more remarkable changes occurred within Europe. By the end of 1990, the Red Army had withdrawn from every nation in eastern Europe except East Germany and Poland (and would soon clear out of these countries as well). In 1991, the Warsaw Pact was dissolved.

The Soviet retreat from eastern Europe was linked to Gorbachev's aim of economic perestroika. The Soviet Union could not afford its empire. In his first informal meetings with eastern European leaders in 1985, Gorbachev told them they should no longer expect Soviet tanks to enforce their will on rebellious populations. By the time Gorbachev addressed the UN General Assembly at the end of 1988 and declared that the nations of eastern Europe were free to choose their own paths, dramatic changes were already underway.

Hungary and Poland were the first to jettison communist rule. Even before Gorbachev took power, economic crisis had driven both of these states to embrace fundamental reforms. In the early 1980s Hungary moved toward a Western-oriented, market-driven economy by joining the World Bank and the International Monetary Fund (IMF) and establishing a stock market. Political reforms accompanied these economic changes. In 1983, Hungarian voters for the first time had a choice of candidates (all still Communist Party members); eighteen months later, independent candidates were allowed to run—and many were elected. In Poland, Jaruzelski's government also began experimenting with restoring some measures of a market economy and with political liberalization. Once martial law ended in 1983, censorship loosened considerably.

CHRONOLOGY

Revolution in Eastern Europe

1989

January	Noncommunist parties and unions legalized in Hungary
February	Roundtable talks between Polish government and Solidarity
June	Free elections in Poland
September	Solidarity forms government in Poland; Hungary opens its borders to the West; thousands of East Germans emigrate
November	Fall of Berlin Wall; reformist communists overthrow Zhivkov in Bulgaria
December	Collapse of communist government in Czechoslovakia and East Germany; execution of Ceauşescu in Romania

1990

March	Free elections in East Germany and Hungary
October	Reunification of Germany
December	Wałęsa elected president of Poland

Newspapers published criticisms of governmental policy that would never have been permitted before 1980.

With Gorbachev in power, the pace of reform in both Poland and Hungary accelerated rapidly. In January 1989, Hungary took the leap into political pluralism by legalizing noncommunist political parties and trade unions. In February, Solidarity and Polish communist officials began "round table talks" aimed at restructuring Poland's political system. In June, Poland held the first free elections in the Soviet bloc. Solidarity swept the contest and formed the first noncommunist government in eastern Europe since 1948.

A bewildered world waited to see if Gorbachev would send in the tanks. Only one day before the Polish elections, the Chinese communist government, oblivious to the television cameras that broadcast the horrible scenes around the globe, had used brutal force to crush a student pro-democracy uprising centered in Beijing's Tiananmen Square. Hundreds died. Horrified by the carnage, Gorbachev insisted that "the very possibility of the use or threat of force [in Poland] . . . is totally unacceptable."[6]

With the prop of the Red Army removed, the communist states of eastern Europe were easily toppled. In November 1989, the Berlin Wall fell. The collapse of the wall echoed to the sound of communist governments crashing throughout eastern Europe. In December, after a year of ever-widening protest demonstrations, the communist government in Czechoslovakia resigned. Alexander Dubček, the hero of the Prague Spring of 1968, returned in triumph to assume the leadership of parliament, and the playwright and leading dissident Václav Havel (1936–) became the Czech president. In March 1990, the Christian Democrats took over the government from the communists in East Germany; seven months later the states of East and West Germany ceased to exist, and a single Germany was reborn. At the end of the year, reform-minded Communist Party members in Bulgaria overthrew the government of Todor Zhivkov, who had been in power for thirty-five years.

All of these revolutions occurred with very little bloodshed. The pace of change in Czechoslovakia was so smooth, in fact, that the events earned the nickname "the Velvet Revolution." But in Romania, the revolutionary cloth came soaked in blood. In December 1989, Romania's dictator Nicolae Ceaușescu ordered the army to fire on a peaceful protest; hundreds died. In a matter of days, however, the soldiers turned against Ceaușescu. Fighting spread across the nation as the dictator's security forces battled with both the demonstrators and the army. Ceaușescu and his wife

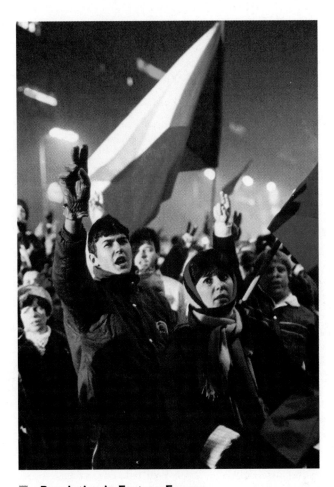

■ **Revolution in Eastern Europe**
Students in Prague give the V for Victory signal in November 1989.

went into hiding, but on Christmas Day they were caught and executed by a firing squad. The televised pictures of their dead bodies were broadcast around the world. A new government was formed under Ion Iliescu (b. 1930), a reformist communist who had attended Moscow University with Gorbachev.

FROM SUCCESS TO FAILURE: THE DISINTEGRATION OF THE SOVIET UNION

By 1990, Gorbachev was one of the best-known leaders in the Western world. His leadership was seen as pivotal in accomplishing radical change in eastern Europe with a minimum of bloodshed and in ending the Cold War. But for Gorbachev, these changes in the international structure were means to an end—freeing the Soviet economy for prosperity and thereby saving the communist system. But prosperity eluded his grasp, and the system he sought to save disintegrated. Between 1985 and 1991, Gorbachev's administration started and stopped twelve different national economic plans, in ever-more-desperate attempts to prop up the Soviet economy. Yet these reforms seemed only to worsen the economic crisis. By 1990, food and other essential goods were scarce, prices had risen by 20 percent since the year before, and productivity was falling. In 1991, the average net income in Russia fell by 17 percent. Dramatic increases in the number of prostitutes (accompanied by a tripling of the rate of venereal disease in Moscow), abandoned babies, and the homeless population all signaled a society in the midst of economic breakdown.

By the early 1990s Gorbachev faced fierce opposition not only from hard-line communists who opposed his reforms, but also from more liberal reformers who viewed the communist system as utterly broken, and who wanted to accelerate the shift to a capitalist economy. These reformers found a spokesman in Boris Yeltsin (1931–), a charismatic, hard-drinking, boisterous politician who became the president of Russia (as distinct from the Soviet Union) in 1991. As Gorbachev increasingly began to tack toward the right, Yeltsin emerged as the leader who would keep the revolution on course. When communist hard-liners attempted to overthrow Gorbachev in August of 1991, it was Yeltsin who led the popular resistance movement that defeated the coup attempt.

Gorbachev was finally defeated not by a political coup but by the power of nationalism. Glasnost had allowed separatist nationalist movements within the Soviet Union to surface from the underground, but Gorbachev, despite his commitment to freedom of choice for eastern Europe, firmly opposed the breakup of the Soviet Union. In 1990, he deployed troops to quell nationalist rioting in both Azerbaijan and Georgia, and to counter independence movements in the Baltic states of Latvia, Estonia, and Lithuania. Short of an all-out civil war, however, there was little Gorbachev could do to hold the union together. By

December 1991, the Soviet Union had broken apart (see Map 29.1). On December 25, Gorbachev resigned his office as president of a state that no longer existed.

THE RETURN OF HISTORY: RUSSIA AND EASTERN EUROPE AT THE END OF THE TWENTIETH CENTURY

With the Cold War over and the long struggle between communism and capitalism clearly won by the latter, one best-selling author talked of the "end of history," by which he meant the end of the ideological struggles that had so defined the last two centuries of historical development.[7] But such talk was premature. "History" returned with a vengeance in the 1990s. As nationalism replaced the capitalist-communist struggle, many of the divisive issues that had led to world war in 1914 and 1939 moved back on the center stage. Patterns of prewar politics reasserted themselves.

The Former Soviet Union in Crisis

For many ordinary Russians, the ending of the Soviet regime meant freedom of the worst kind—freedom to be hungry, freedom to be homeless, freedom to be afraid. In January 1992, Yeltsin applied "shock therapy" to the ailing Russian economy. He lifted price controls, abolished subsidies, and privatized state industries. By mid-1994, the state sector of the Russian economy had shrunk to under 40 percent. But the economy did not prosper. Prices climbed dramatically, and the closure of unproductive businesses sent unemployment rates upward, while at the same time cuts in government spending severed welfare lifelines. By 1995, 80 percent of Russians were no longer earning a living wage. Food consumption fell to the same level as the early 1950s, with meat almost disappearing from the diets of many.

The economic situation worsened in 1998, when Russia effectively went bankrupt. The value of the ruble collapsed

■ **Map 29.1   The Former Soviet Union**

In December 1991, the Soviet empire disintegrated. In its place stood fifteen independent and very diverse republics, ranging from tiny and impoverished Moldova to relatively affluent and Europeanized Latvia to Russia itself, still the dominant power in the region, but economically stagnant.

and the state defaulted on its loans. Even Russians with jobs found it difficult to make ends meet. Workers at the Moscow McDonald's, for example, had regarded themselves as privileged: They were paid regularly and well. But overnight in 1998, the value of their paycheck dropped by 70 percent. Workers in state jobs simply weren't paid at all.

For many Russians, capitalism meant lawlessness. Managers of state industries were often able to manipulate privatization for their own private enrichment, so they grew fabulously wealthy, while ordinary employees experienced sharp pay cuts or the loss of their jobs. The prime minister Viktor Chernomyrdin (1938–), for example, moved from his position as the head of the state natural gas monopoly to become the largest shareholder of the privatized natural gas company. By the mid-1990s, a new force had appeared in Russian life—the "Russian Mafia," crime syndicates with international links that used extortion and intimidation to seize control of large sectors of the economy.

In the non-Russian republics, often the situation was even worse. The end of the Soviet Union meant the end of Soviet subsidies for these impoverished regions. Tajikistan, for example, depended on Soviet financial aid to prop up the extensive irrigation system that allowed its farmers to grow cotton for export. The collapse of the Soviet Union meant the collapse of the Tajikistan economy. By the end of the 1990s, almost half of Tajikistan's 6.2 million inhabitants were struggling to survive in the face of severe food shortages. In Moldova, the economy shrank by 60 percent between 1991 and 2001, while life expectancy rates fell by five years. One Moldovan elementary school principal admitted she was "hungry for Soviet days," which she recalled as a time when salaries were steady and health care universally available.[8] In the post-Soviet era, Moldovans resorted to marketing their body organs to Western entrepreneurs for $3,000 each.

The economic and social collapse that followed the end of the Soviet Union fostered a climate of desperation in which extremist nationalism flourished. Independence did not mean stability in the republics of Georgia, Armenia, and Azerbaijan, all of which experienced civil war in the 1990s. In Russia itself, Yeltsin faced strong opposition from nationalist groups who viewed the breakup of the Soviet Union as a humiliation for Mother Russia. In elections at the end of 1993, the party of ultranationalist Vladimir Zhirinovsky (b. 1946) won 23 percent of the vote, more than any other single party.

The sharpest nationalist challenge to Yeltsin came from Chechnya, one of twenty-one autonomous republics within the larger Russian Federation. When the Soviet Union broke up, Chechnya became part of independent Russia. But the Chechens demanded their own state, and in 1991 declared Chechnya independent. The Chechen-Russian dispute simmered until 1994 when Yeltsin committed 30,000 troops to forcing Chechnya back within Russia's embrace.

In the ensuing twenty-month conflict, 80,000 died and 240,000 were wounded—80 percent of these Chechen civilians. Yeltsin negotiated a truce in the summer of 1996, but four years later his successor, Vladimir Putin (1952–), renewed the war against Chechnya.

Eastern Europe After Communism

Like the former Soviet Union, the countries of eastern Europe found the path from communist rule to democracy far from easy. All the states of eastern Europe experienced high inflation rates, high unemployment, and economic instability in the wake of the revolution. The dissolution of the Soviet bloc meant that economic networks established over the last four decades suddenly disintegrated. In addition, Western advisors and the IMF, which controlled access to much-needed loans, insisted that the new governments follow programs of "austerity" aimed at cutting government spending and curbing inflation. The result was economic hardship far beyond what any Western electorate would have endured. In Poland, for example, the new Solidarity-led government instituted the "Big Bang" on New Year's Day, 1990. Controls disappeared and overnight prices jumped between 30 and 600 percent. The inflation rate for 1990 in Poland was a remarkable 550 percent. Even in 1995, when the economy had stabilized, inflation remained at 20 percent, while joblessness stood at 15 percent. In 1996 the Gdansk shipyard, where Solidarity had been born in 1980, closed and half its workers lost their jobs.

But by the second half of the 1990s, it was clear that despite these costs, Poland was succeeding in moving from communism to capitalism. With some measures of market reform already in place before 1988, both Poland and Hungary were the best prepared for the transition from a command to a capitalist economy. The Czech Republic and the Baltic nations also moved fairly rapidly through the most difficult stages of this transition. In countries such as Romania, Bulgaria, Albania, and of course Russia itself, severe economic instability continued, with the majority of their populations experiencing hardship.

Political stability was also hard-won during this decade. The revolutionary coalitions that had led the charge against communist rule in 1989–1990 quickly fragmented as their members moved from the heady idealism of challenging authoritarianism to the nitty-gritty of parliamentary politics. Political parties proliferated: forty-five in Hungary in 1990, sixty-seven in Poland in 1991, seventy-four in Romania in 1992. One unexpected result of the end of the communist monopoly on power was a worsened political position for women. Under communism, a quota system had ensured that women occupied 30 percent of the parliamentary seats in eastern European governments. In the postcommunist era of the mid-1990s, the percentages were far lower, ranging from 7 percent in Romania to 13 percent in Bulgaria and Poland.

Yet signs of emerging political stability were evident in the 1990s. Former communists entered the political mainstream. Given the seriousness of the economic crisis in eastern Europe in the 1990s, it is not surprising that ex-communists soon were back in power as disenchanted voters turned to the people who represented a more stable past. Between 1993 and 1995, the "Velvet Restoration" occurred, as ex-communists returned to power in Lithuania, Hungary, Bulgaria, and Poland. In Romania, they had never left. Yet Western fears that the revolutions of 1989 would be reversed proved groundless. Ex-communists continued with the economic liberalization programs of their opponents, although in many cases opting for a more gradual and thus, they hoped, less socially divisive transition. No former communist regime returned to authoritarian rule or a centralized state-run economy.

A far greater threat to eastern European democracy was posed by the revival not of communism but of pre–World War II political ideas and styles. For example, the claim of Josef Antall, Hungary's prime minister in the early 1990s, to be the leader of "all Hungarians" (two million of whom lived in Romania and another 600,000 in Slovakia) recalled the vehement Hungarian nationalism of the 1920s and 1930s. In Romania escalating discrimination against the Hungarian and Roma minority populations stirred up memories of interwar racist violence. Throughout eastern Europe, anti-Semitic rhetoric returned to political discourse. In 1990, Lech Wałęsa's election campaign was tainted by anti-Jewish references; graffiti appeared on the walls of Warsaw buildings: "Jews to the ovens."

The resurgence of pre–World War II ethnic identities did not always mean violence, however. In Czechoslovakia, Václav Havel's Civic Forum could not bridge the regional-ethnic divide that opened up between the Czech half of the country and Slovakia. In 1993, Czechoslovakia ceased to exist, replaced by the separate nations of the Czech Republic and Slovakia. Significantly, the breakup of Czechoslovakia was accomplished without violence, negotiated in conference rooms rather than fought out in the streets.

The German Problem

The problems that engulfed Germany after its eastern and western halves reunited in October 1990 illustrated the difficulties faced by eastern Europeans as they struggled to adjust to a post–Cold War, post-Soviet world. Almost half the population of East Germany crossed the border into West Germany in the first week after the fall of the Berlin Wall. They returned home dazzled by the consumer delights they saw in store windows and eager for a chance to grab a piece of the capitalist pie. West German chancellor Helmut Kohl recognized the power of these desires, and skillfully forced the pace of reunification. When the two Germanies united at the end of 1990, Kohl became the first chancellor of the new German state.

Kohl trusted that West Germany's economy was strong enough to pull its bankrupt new partner into prosperity, but he proved overly optimistic. The residents of the former East Germany soon found their factories closing and their livelihoods gone. These economic troubles quickly leached over into the western regions of Germany. By 1997, unemployment in Germany stood at 12.8 percent—the highest since World War II. In the eastern regions, over 20 percent of the population was out of work.

For the women of the former East Germany, life in the new Germany meant an intense culture clash. The concept of the male breadwinner/head of household was enshrined in the West German legal code until the end of the 1970s and prominent in West German culture for a long time after. This concept was alien to many East German women. In East Germany, all women were expected to be in full-time employment, the state provided day care and school holiday care, abortion was readily available, and contraceptives were free. In the new united Germany, which adhered to West German legal and cultural traditions, more conventional gender roles and conceptions of sexual morality dominated. For at least some East German women, then, the end of communist rule was not unambiguously liberating.

Economic despair throughout much of the former East Germany resulted in racial violence. Looking for scapegoats, eastern German youths targeted the foreign workers in their cities. Violent attacks against Turkish workers escalated in the 1990s, as did support for neo-Nazi organizations. In 1998, these economic and social problems led German voters to reject Kohl and the Christian Democrats. The Social Democrats, out of office since 1982, took charge under the leadership of Gerhard Schroeder (b. 1944). Schroeder, however, was unable to reverse the economic slide. By 2001, the German economy was standing still, with a GDP growth rate of little over zero.

THE BREAKUP OF YUGOSLAVIA

In Yugoslavia the "return of history" proved most marked and, given the nature of that history, most horrific. When the communist guerilla leader Tito seized control of the Yugoslav state after World War II, he sought to free Yugoslavia from the divisive and bloody battles of its recent past. But in the 1980s and 1990s, the revival of nationalist hostilities within Yugoslavia led to civil war and state-sanctioned mass murder, to scenes of carnage and to mass atrocities not seen in Europe since the 1940s.

Although Yugoslavia had appeared on European maps since the end of World War I, one could argue it did not really exist until after World War II. During the 1920s and 1930s, the subjects of the Serbian monarchy did not regard themselves as "Yugoslavs"; they were Serbs or Croats,

■ Map 29.2 The Former Yugoslavia

The breakup of Yugoslavia began in June 1991, with the Slovenian and Croatian declarations of independence. Bosnia and Macedonia soon followed.

Muslims or Montenegrins, Albanians or Slovenians. And during World War II, as we saw in Chapter 26, Serbs and Croats fought each other with a savage intensity–a bitter reminder of the lack of a single national Yugoslav identity.

To construct a united nation out of Yugoslavia's diverse and often hostile cultures, Tito utilized two tools—federalism and communism. A federal political structure consisting of six equal republics prevented Serbia, or any other of the republics, from dominating Yugoslavia. Communism served as a unifying ideology, a cluster of ideas that transcended the divisions of race, religion, and language. Recognizing the divisive and bloody potential of ethnic nationalism, Tito refused to allow it to break through the surface of Yugoslav political life. Aspiring politicians knew that an appeal to ethnic hatred would bar them from career advancement in the communist hierarchy. Ethnic identities and rivalries were declared unacceptable, part of the bourgeois past that had supposedly been left behind.

Yugoslavs often said, however, that their nation consisted of "six nationalities, five languages, four religions, . . . and one Tito." According to this folk wisdom, Tito—not communism, not federalism—was the glue that held together this diverse state. In 1980, Tito died. Ominously, the year after his death saw the outbreak of riots between ethnic Albanians and Serbs in the province of Kosovo. Even more ominously, Tito's death coincided with the onset of serious economic crisis. The drastic rise in oil prices in 1979 under-

cut the Yugoslav economy, as did its rising debt load. Between 1979 and 1985 real wages fell in Yugoslavia by almost 25 percent. By 1987, inflation was raging at 200 percent per year and two years later it had burst through into hyperinflation—200 percent *per month.*

Under pressure from this economic crisis, the federal structure built by Tito began to collapse, as the wealthier Yugoslav republics such as Croatia sought to loosen the ties that bound them to the poorer republics such as Serbia. Then, in 1989, the revolutions that swept through the Soviet satellite states shattered the hold of communism on Yugoslavia as well. Ethnic nationalism, long simmering under the surface of Yugoslavian political life, poured into the resulting ideological void. New leaders emerged with new agendas. In Serbia, the former communist functionary Slobodan Milosevic (b. 1941) transformed himself into a popular spokesman for aggressive Serbian nationalism. Milosevic used rallies and the mass media, which he controlled, to convince Serbs that their culture was under attack and to paint himself as the defender of that culture. To enhance Serbia's power—and his own—Milosevic fiercely opposed any talk of destroying the Yugoslav federation. Moreover, Milosevic possessed a powerful weapon to enforce his will. The Yugoslav army, the fourth largest fighting force in Europe, was dominated by Serbs.

Thus, when Croatia declared independence in June 1991, the result was civil war (see Map 29.2). Milosevic

A GLOBAL YOUTH CULTURE?

The following excerpt, from an interview with rock singer and Serbian nationalist Sonja Karadzic, first appeared in a Serbian magazine in September 1992, at the height of the war in Bosnia. Daughter of Radovan Karadzic, the political leader of the Bosnian Serbs, Sonja Karadzic condemned her fellow Serbs who had fled the war in Bosnia for the safety of Serbia. She also offered a disturbing definition of "Western civilization": one characterized not by democratic freedom and the protection of human rights, but rather by a culture of violence fostered by American television and films.

If the Americans come to Bosnia, they'll see that our soldiers look at the world like theirs do. We aren't Vietnamese or Iraqis, we are fighters who think in terms of the same images and music as their soldiers do. The Serbian chetnik fighters have grown up with a Coke in their hand and watching the same TV spots as someone their own age in Alabama, and we're into the latest styles just the way guys or girls from Florida are. Together we got our battle ethics from the movies about Mad Max and Terminator, Rambo and Young Guns. And what happened when the war began—we started identifying with the me-

dia images and heroes. Our fighters got into battle dress, short Rambo boots and modern weapons of destruction. They call themselves chetniks—but Mad Max Chetniks, Serbian Terminators. And most important, it doesn't matter what sex you are. Nobody is dirty or sloppy or smelly or unshaven—we're still into good cigarettes and Coca-Cola, nice perfume and makeup, and we're up on the latest movies and music. And we still like a good laugh—not the Moslem nonsense down in town. We're building a new lifestyle in a new country.

Fortunately for us only the best fighters, the real ones have stayed. The others have helped us perform a natural selection by running away from the homeland they weren't prepared to defend and build up . . .

For us the Serbian chetniks . . . will always be our heroes, our Serbian Terminators. With fighters like them we are already the victors in this war and leaders in the creation of a new civilization.

Source: From an interview with Sonja Karadzic, by Nenad Stefanovic, *Duga* (Belgrade), September 12–26, 1992. Excerpted and translated by Ann Clymer Bigelow. Reprinted by permission.

(a)

(b)

■ Bosnian War Atrocities

(a) Serbian heads, found after Serb fighters raided a Muslim base in northern Bosnia in 1993. (b) The mass grave of Muslim civilians, Pilica, northwest of Srebrenica, in the spring of 1996. Twelve thousand of the men and boys of Srebrenica tried to flee to safety—about half made it; many of those that didn't were forced by Serb fighters to dig their own graves and then shot in front of them. The citizens of Srebenica who did not flee were told by Bosnian Serbian General Ratko Mladic, "No one will harm you." Mladic then ordered his soldiers to shoot all Muslim men between ages 17 and 60. Reviewing the evidence against Mladic, the UN tribunal noted, "These are truly scenes from hell, written on the darkest pages of human history."

mobilized the Yugoslav army against the Croatian separatists. In 1992 the war spread to Bosnia-Herzegovina after its government, too, declared independence. The war quickly degenerated into an ethnic bloodbath, with memories of World War II shaping the conflict. Serbs viewed Croats as the direct heirs of the murderous Nazi-backed Croatian Ustace regime, responsible for the mass slaughter of Serbs in World War II. In turn, Croats called all Serbs "Chetniks," linking them to the anti-Croat Serbian guerrilla bands of the war years. The presence of paramilitary forces also heightened the brutality of the war. With no military discipline and often possessing criminal records, the volunteers in these units plunged into a fury of plunder, murder, and rape.

This war introduced the world to the horrors of ethnic cleansing° and rape camps. By 1994, all sides within the Bosnian war were practicing ethnic cleansing, although it is clear that Serbs initiated the practice and used it most extensively. To create all-Serb zones within Croatia and Bosnia, Serb paramilitary units embarked on a campaign of terror designed to force Muslims and Croats to abandon their homes and villages. They burned mosques, closed schools, and vandalized houses. Most villagers fled; the paramilitaries tortured and often killed those who stayed. Women were sometimes rounded up and placed in special camps where they were subjected to regular, systematic rape. An estimated 20,000 women, most of them Muslim, endured this peculiarly vicious effort to subjugate and humiliate a people.

Outrage against these atrocities forced Western governments to intervene. In 1994, NATO planes began bombing Serb positions, the first time in its history that NATO had gone into combat. The Dayton Accords, signed in Dayton, Ohio, in December 1995, brought an uneasy peace to Bosnia. The accords declared Bosnia to be one state with two parts—the Muslim-Croat Federation (consisting of 51 percent of Bosnian territory) and the Serbian Republic (holding the remaining 49 percent), each with its own military, taxation, and judicial powers. Keeping the peace in this strange creation was the job of 60,000 UN soldiers.

Peace eluded Serbia during this period, however. The sort of vicious nationalism embodied by Milosevic demanded a constant supply of enemies and a continuous cycle of violence. In 1998, large-scale fighting between Serbs and Albanians erupted in the province of Kosovo. Ethnic cleansing, mass rape, and a huge exodus of refugees began

once again. After a NATO bombing campaign in Serbia, NATO and Russian troops moved into Kosovo, and in 2001, a police helicopter transported Milosevic to the Netherlands to be tried for genocide before the International War Crimes Tribunal.

CHRONOLOGY

The Shattering of Yugoslavia

1989	Slobodan Milosevic becomes president of Yugoslavian Republic of Serbia
1991	
July	Civil war in Croatia begins
1992	
April	Civil war in Bosnia begins
1994	
April	NATO air strikes against Bosnian Serb positions begin
1995	
December	Dayton Accords
1998	Large-scale fighting in Kosovo between Albanians and Serbs
1999	
March	NATO air strikes against Serbia
June	Ceasefire in Kosovo
2000	
October	Milosevic defeated in Serbian elections
2001	
June	Milosevic extradited to the Hague to be tried for genocide

Rethinking the West

——————

A t the start of the 1990s, a sense of triumphalism characterized much of Western culture—at its simplest, expressed as "we won the Cold War." But who was "we"? For forty years, the Cold War had provided a clear enemy and thus a clear identity: The West was anti-communist, anti-Soviet, anti–Warsaw Pact. Communism's loss of credibility, the disintegration of the Soviet Union, and the dismantling of the Warsaw Pact all demanded that the West revise itself. New enemies moved into prominent positions, the relationship between the United States and Europe had to be renegotiated, and even the definition of

"Europe" became problematic. At the same time, a series of intellectual and cultural forces challenged many facets of Western identity, while Western nations, like those in the rest of the world, found their scope of autonomous action increasingly limited as they were caught up in the web of global economic, technological, and environmental change.

OLD AND NEW ENEMIES

This textbook has traced the way in which "the West" changed meaning, largely in response to places and peoples defined as "not West." With the ending of the Cold War, the West lost its main enemy—but replacements stood readily at hand. In 1996, the American president Bill Clinton (1946–) identified terrorism as "the enemy of our generation." Terrorism in many ways replaced communism as the new foe against which the West defined itself. Because terrorists seek to achieve political ends through the means of violence and intimidation, terrorism short-circuits the democratic process: Decision-making power shifts from the ballot box to the bomb. Thus terrorism directly opposed what many regarded as the bedrock of Western culture—a commitment to democracy and the rule of the law.

Yet the equation of the West with law and democracy conveniently ignored other, less palatable, products of Western political culture such as fascism, Nazism, and terrorism itself. Terrorism grew out of late nineteenth-century anarchism, which advocated violence as a means of political change (see Chapter 22). Like the Russian populists who assassinated Tsar Alexander II or the Serbian nationalists who shot the Archduke Franz Ferdinand and sparked World War I, contemporary terrorists belonged to groups lacking access to political power. Unable to achieve their goals through political persuasion (lobbying, campaigning, winning votes), they endeavored to destabilize the societies they opposed through acts of terror. Thus small groups of western European and American student activists, disillusioned by the failures of 1968, went underground in the 1970s, embarking on bombing and assassination campaigns. Thwarted nationalism provided even more fertile soil for the growth of terrorism. In Spain, the Basque separatist group Eta engaged in a three-decades-long campaign of terror to achieve its aim of an independent Basque state. In Northern Ireland, assassinations, bombings, and kneecappings became commonplace after the Irish Republican Army (IRA) turned to terror to pressure the British government to relinquish its control over the province.

Terrorism is thus one of the negative aspects of "Western civilization." Yet, by the 1980s, terrorism was often perceived as the antithesis of the West, as an outside threat, usually bearing an Arabic face. Popular perceptions often linked "terrorism" and "Islam," with Islam defined as emphatically "not West"—fanatical, violent, antidemocratic.

What factors forged this perceived link between Islam and terrorism? One of the most important was the continuing Israeli-Palestinian crisis. Frustrated by the failure of the United Nations to implement its 1947 resolution promising a Palestinian state, Palestinian nationalists in 1964 formed the Palestine Liberation Organization (PLO). Like the IRA or Eta, the PLO saw violence as its only means to its nationalist ends. The PLO's commitment to terrorism deepened after the Arab-Israeli War of 1967, which led to Israel occupying East Jerusalem, all land west of the Jordan River (the West Bank), and the Golan Heights. In response, the PLO took its campaign of terror around the world, bombing airports, targeting tourists, and persuading many in the West that "Arab," "Muslim," and "terrorist" were interchangeable terms.

At the same time, U.S. support for Israel convinced many Muslims that "the West" (often equated simply with the United States) was an enemy. Between 1949 and 1998, Israel received more American aid than any other country. As relations between Palestinians and Israelis deteriorated in the late 1980s and 1990s, Palestinians and their supporters argued that the United States was bankrolling a repressive regime and that Israel was a Western colonialist outpost (see Map 29.3).

The conflict in Israel served as a backdrop to the emergence of a militant, anti-Western form of Islam, fueled by fear of Western culture as well as the West's willingness, during the Cold War, to prop up unpopular and corrupt governments. Events in Iran illustrate this process. In 1979, a popular revolution overthrew the autocratic, U.S.-backed Shah of Iran, and vaulted into power the Ayatollah Khomeini (1901–1989). Khomeini rapidly reversed the westernizing and modernizing policies of the Shah. The Sharia (the religious law of Islam) became the law of the state, and strict Islamic codes of behavior were required for all Iranians. Women, for example, could not appear in public without being veiled. Then in November 1979, Iranian students, obeying instructions from religious leaders, took over the U.S. Embassy in Tehran and captured sixty-six Americans, the bulk of whom spent over a year in captivity—an episode of state-sanctioned terrorism that constituted an appalling tragedy for the hostages, and an international humiliation for the United States. Khomeini decried the United States as the "Great Satan," while the excesses of his regime strengthened the popular perception in the West that Islam fundamentally opposed Western values.

Two additional factors raised anti-Muslim sentiments throughout much of the Western world—oil and immigration. In 1979, OPEC responded to Khomeini's revolution in Iran by raising the base price of petroleum by almost 25 percent, thus (as we have seen earlier) catapulting the West into economic crisis. Although OPEC included non-Arab nations such as Venezuela, for most in the West it was seen as an "Arab cartel," and linked to an image of a resurgent

Islam. Even more important was the emergence in western Europe of permanent minority communities, many of them Muslim. As the minarets of mosques began to poke through the skylines of European cities, some non-Muslim Europeans argued that their own cultures were under threat. The decision of the Ayatollah Khomeini to issue a death sentence against the Anglo-Indian writer Salman Rushdie in 1989 forced many of these tensions and hostilities into the open but provided no easy answers.

During the 1990s, these hostilities grew more fierce as a result of the First Gulf War. In 1991 American and British forces led a twenty-eight country coalition in a military intervention to drive invading Iraqi forces out of tiny but oil-rich Kuwait. The war itself could not be construed as "the West versus Islam" or "the West versus the East": One Arab and Islamic country had invaded another. But in the aftermath of the war, U.S. forces remained in American-controlled bases in Saudi Arabia, home of some of the most holy sites in Islam. For Muslim radicals, the presence of the United States in this region was both an offense against Islam and an insult to Arabian political independence. Anti-Western Islamic movements grew stronger in many

Map 29.3 The Middle East in the Contemporary Era

Although placed under Palestinian self-rule in 1994, the West Bank and Gaza Strip remain contested areas, sites of frequent confrontations between Palestinians and Israelis.

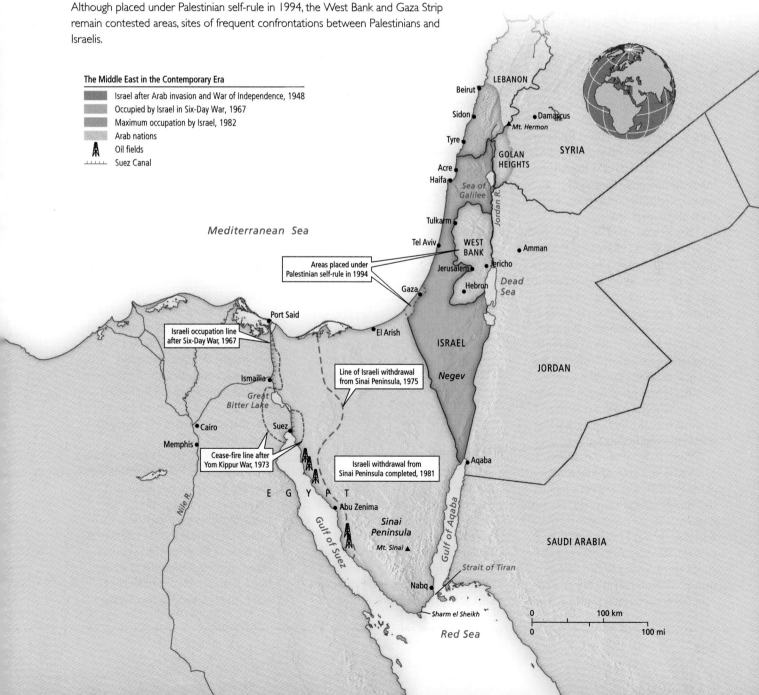

The Middle East in the Contemporary Era

- Israel after Arab invasion and War of Independence, 1948
- Occupied by Israel in Six-Day War, 1967
- Maximum occupation by Israel, 1982
- Arab nations
- Oil fields
- Suez Canal

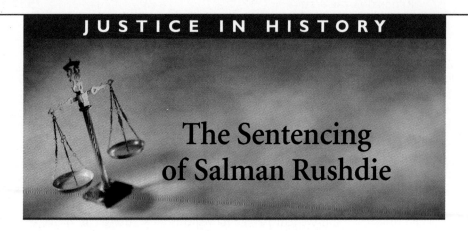

The Sentencing of Salman Rushdie

In February 1989, the Ayatollah Khomeini, political leader of Iran and spiritual head of the Shi'a Muslim community, issued a death sentence against the novelist Salman Rushdie and offered an award of $2.5 million to any faithful Muslim who succeeded in killing him. Rushdie, a British citizen who had never been tried in any Iranian or Islamic court, immediately went into hiding, where he remained for several years. His death sentence ignited the "Satanic Verses Affair," a tumultuous international crisis caused by a resounding clash of cultural assumptions and expectations.

The crisis centered on a book. In the early autumn of 1988 Viking Penguin published Rushdie's *The Satanic Verses,* a difficult novel about the complexities and contradictions of the modern immigrant experience. Born in India and raised in an Islamic home, Rushdie wrote *The Satanic Verses* to describe "migration, metamorphosis, divided selves, love, death, London, and Bombay."[9] The novel received immediate critical acclaim, with reviewers praising it as an astonishing work of postmodernist fiction.

Other readers judged it differently. Many Muslims around the world regarded the book as a direct attack on the foundations of their religious faith. One scene in the novel particularly horrified devout Muslims. In this episode, the central character has a psychotic breakdown and falls into a dream: Muhammad appears as a corrupt businessman and prostitutes in a brothel take on the names of the Prophet's wives.

The novel aroused intense controversy from the moment of its publication. The government of India banned it almost immediately; within a matter of weeks, several other states followed suit. Anti-Rushdie demonstrations in both India and Pakistan turned violent, resulting in fifteen deaths. Bookstores selling the novel received bombing and death threats. In western Europe, hostilities between Muslims and non-Muslims intensified. Then, on February 14, 1989, an announcer on Radio Tehran read aloud the text of a *fatwa,* or decree, issued by the Ayatollah Khomeini:

> I would like to inform all the intrepid Muslims of the world that the author of the book entitled The Satanic Verses, *which has been compiled, printed and published in opposition to Islam, the Prophet and the Koran, as well as those publishers who were aware of its contents, have been sentenced to death. I call on all zealous Muslims to execute them quickly, wherever they find them . . . Whoever is killed on this path will be regarded as a martyr, God willing.*

Western governments reacted quickly against Khomeini's call for Rushdie's death. The twelve nations of the European Community, the United States, Sweden, Norway, Canada, Australia, and Brazil all condemned Khomeini's judgment, recalled their ambassadors from Tehran, and cancelled high-level diplomatic contacts with Iran. British Prime Minister Margaret Thatcher provided police protection for Rushdie and dismissed British Muslim demands to ban the book: "It is an essential part of our democratic system that people who act within the law should be able to express their opinions freely."[10]

Large numbers of Muslims, including many who spoke out against Rushdie's book, also condemned Khomeini's fatwa. Some Muslim scholars contended that the Ayatollah's fatwa was a scholarly opinion, not a legally binding judgment; others argued that Rushdie could not be condemned without a trial, or that because Rushdie lived in a society without an Islamic government, he was not bound by Islamic law.

But many ordinary Muslims ignored these high-level theological and legal disputes and greeted the Ayatollah's fatwa with delight. The news of the Ayatollah's fatwa brought crowds of cheering Muslims into the city streets. In Manchester and Bradford, young British Muslim men insisted they would kill Rushdie if given the chance. In Paris, demonstrators marched to cries of "we are all Khomeinists!"

Why did Khomeini's fatwa arouse such popular enthusiasm within Western Muslim communities? A partial answer to this question is that many Muslims were frustrated with what they regarded as the unequal application of the laws of censorship. Faced with what they saw as a hate-filled, pornographic caricature of Islam, they demanded that Western

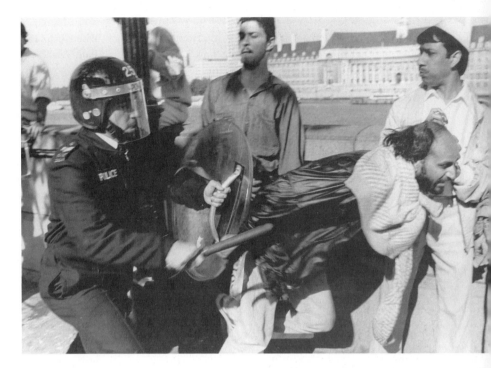

governments use the laws censoring pornography and banning hate crimes to block the publication of Rushdie's book. In Britain, Muslims were particularly outraged that the existing law against blasphemy protected only Christianity, the official state religion.

But the controversy was not simply a dispute about censorship. For some Muslims, Rushdie's *Satanic Verses* epitomized Western secular society, with its scant regard for tradition or religious values. As Dr. Kalim Siddiqui of the pro-Iranian Muslim Institute in Britain proclaimed, "western civilization is fundamentally an immoral civilization. Its 'values' are free of moral constraints."[11] From this perspective, Khomeini's fatwa condemned not just one book or one author, but an entire culture that seemed inherently opposed to Islam. Khomeini had already proven himself a forceful leader in the Iranian hostage crisis of 1979–1980, when he successfully thumbed his nose at American power. Now once again he seemed willing to take on the West to defend Islam.

The anti-Western stance of some radical Muslims was mirrored by the anti-Islam position soon occupied by some Rushdie supporters. In one of the most ironic twists in the entire Satanic Verses Affair, Rushdie's books, which condemned the endemic racism in British society and exposed the falsehood of Western claims to cultural superiority, were championed by individuals who articulated precisely the sort of Western cultural chauvinism against which Rushdie had written so

passionately. For example, Robert Maxwell, a multimillionaire communications tycoon, offered $10 million to any individual "who will, not kill, but civilise the barbarian Ayatollah" by forcing him to recite publicly the Ten Commandments.[12] Many western Europeans agreed with the conclusion drawn in this letter to a British daily newspaper: "The lesson of the Rushdie affair is that it was unwise to let Muslim communities establish themselves in our midst."[13] The lines were drawn, with Islam standing for irrationalism, barbarity, intolerance, and ignorance, while the "West" was linked to democracy, reason, freedom, and civilization. At precisely the moment when the crumbling of communism and the ending of the Cold War deprived the West of one of its defining attributes, the Satanic Verses Affair offered up a new Other against which the West could define itself. ■

Questions of Justice

1. On what grounds are publications censored in secular, Western societies? Given the existence of this censorship, should Rushdie's book have been banned?

2. In what ways does the Satanic Verses Affair illuminate the tensions within many European societies from the 1970s on, as communities struggled to adapt to the challenges of ethnic and religious diversity?

Taking It Further

Bowen, David G., ed. *The Satanic Verses: Bradford Responds*. 1996. This collection of essays and documents helps explains why many British Muslims viewed the British government's failure to censor Rushdie's book as an act of injustice.

regions of the world, including not only the Middle East but also the Philippines, Algeria, Bosnia, and Afghanistan.

The dangerous perception of some sort of fundamental opposition between "Islam" and "the West" led, on September 11, 2001, to one of the most dramatic episodes of terrorism ever. At 8:46 A.M., a jumbo jet hijacked by Muslim Arab terrorists smashed into one of the towers of the World Trade Center in New York City. Twenty minutes later, another hijacked plane hit the second tower. A third plane dove into the Pentagon, the U.S. military headquarters in Washington, D.C., and a fourth crashed in Pennsylvania. Almost 3,000 people died.

In the wake of the horrifying attack, U.S. president George W. Bush (1946–) declared a "war on terrorism." U.S. and European intelligence officers quickly linked the suicide pilots to a terrorist organization run by Osama bin Laden, a wealthy Saudi exile who espoused a fiercely anti-Western form of Islam. Bin Laden was backed by the

■ The Terrorist Age

A fireball erupts from one of the World Trade Center towers as it is struck by the second of two airplanes in New York on September 11, 2001. The terrorist attacks demonstrated the power of global communications in the contemporary world. By the time the first tower collapsed, just a little more than an hour after the first plane crash, television stations around the world were broadcasting live images of the scene. Thus viewers witnessed on their television screens the Hollywood-like scene of the towers' collapse.

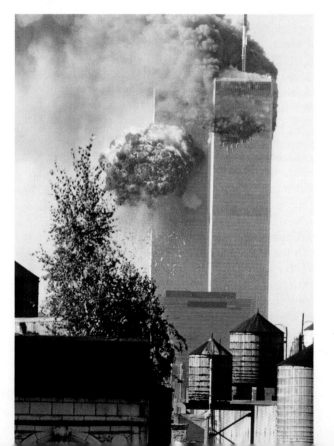

Taliban, a revolutionary Muslim group that had won control of Afghanistan in the early 1990s after the Soviet army withdrew from the region. The United States began air attacks against Afghanistan in October 2001. The Taliban regime fell within weeks, but the war against terrorism continued.

In March 2003, this widely ranging war took a new turn when U.S. and British forces, attacked Iraq in the Second Gulf War. No direct connection linked Osama bin Laden to Iraq's government, which was firmly controlled by Saddam Hussein, a secular dictator with a long history of torturing and killing radical Muslims who threatened his personal power. But in the world after "9/11", Saddam Hussein's refusal to allow United Nations' inspections of his weapons factories convinced both the American and British governments that Iraq possessed the ability to launch a terrorist strike, in the form of biological or chemical weapons, against Western targets. The result was the first preemptive war ever waged by U.S. forces and, after a three-week conflict involving both air strikes and land battles, the toppling of Saddam Hussein's dictatorial regime. Many Iraqis cheered the dictator's overthrow, but many Arabs in the surrounding nations condemned the Anglo-American intervention as yet another episode in a long history of Western imperial intrusions on Arab territory.

9/11 thus had important consequences for the West and the world. It not only resulted in military engagements in both Afghanistan and Iraq, but also accelerated the development of the United States as a military colossus. Even before the Second Gulf War, the U.S. defense budget outweighed that of the next nine largest defense budgets of other countries combined. In addition, 9/11 made it clear that terrorism had replaced communism as the West's new enemy, the "Them" against which the "Us" took shape. A series of mysterious anthrax outbreaks in the weeks following the September 2001 attacks provided an alarming demonstration of the risks terrorism posed in urban industrial society. Defense budgets could skyrocket, but there seemed little safety in a world in which every passenger plane could become a weapon of mass murder, and every envelope could contain deadly spores. Finally, in the aftermath of the attacks the question of Western identity was more troublesome than ever. European and American Muslims found their loyalties questioned, their religious beliefs regarded as grounds for suspicion. The long, complex history of Islam in the West was often ignored, replaced by a simplistic "Them" versus "Us" mentality.

THE EUROPEAN UNION

In the wake of 9/11, the status of the United States as the world's only superpower seemed dramatically confirmed; developments in Europe in this era, however, limited American hegemony. With the ending of the Cold War, the nations of western Europe, united under the umbrella of the European Union° (EU), moved to take on a much more important role in global affairs. We saw in Chapter 28 that the EU began in the 1950s as the Common Market or EEC (European Economic Community), an economic free-trade organization of six western European nations. By the end of the millennium, this organization had become a powerful entity possessing not only economic but also political clout, a potential counterweight to the United States.

From the EEC to the EU

During the 1970s and 1980s, the EEC widened both its membership and its areas of cooperation, and thus helped move the nations of western Europe toward greater economic and political unity. Britain, Denmark, and Ireland joined the European Community in 1973, Greece in 1981, Spain and Portugal in 1986. (Austria, Finland, and Sweden joined in the 1990s.) In 1979, a European parliament chosen directly by European voters met for the first time. Throughout these decades, the European Court of Justice gradually began to assert the primacy of the European Community over national law, thus breaching the walls of national sovereignty and pushing western Europe down the road toward political integration. A name change signaled this broadening of aims. The EEC—the European Economic Community—became the EC—the European Community, a political and cultural as well as economic organization.

The development of the EC made it clear that the "West" was no longer American-made. Even before expanding in the 1980s, the EC constituted the largest trading unit and consumer market in the world. By 1980, the U.S. share of global economic output had fallen from 38 percent in 1970 to 25 percent, while the EC saw its share rise in these same years from 26 to 30 percent. The "Western" economy gradually grew less American, and more and more European. The emergence of Europe as the strongest economic competitor to the United States broke the symbolic link between "America" and "modernity." One French businessman noted in 1983, "I remember when I first went to America thirty years ago. Everything looked bigger, newer, faster. Now, everything looks shabbier and older than here."[14]

The pace of change accelerated in the 1980s and 1990s as the Single European Act of 1985 and the Maastricht Agreements of 1991 replaced the European *Community* (EC) with the European *Union* (EU), defined by France's President Mitterrand as "one currency, one culture, one social area, one environment." The establishment of the EU meant visible changes for ordinary Europeans. They saw their national passports replaced by a common EU document, and border controls eliminated. The creation of a single EU currency—the euro, which replaced national currencies in 2002—tore down one of the most significant economic barriers between European countries. In what was labeled the largest peacetime logistical operation in European history, 6 billion notes and 37.5 billion coins re-

placed national currency in twelve EU states. At the same time, the powers of the European Parliament expanded. Member states moved toward establishing common social policies (such as labor rights) and a common defense system, with an EU rapid reaction force of 60,000 men created in 2003.

Old and New Obstacles

At the launch of the euro, the president of the European Central Bank announced that the single currency would "forever banish the horrors of past conflicts," thus underscoring the internationalist idealism that has driven forward European unification since the 1940s.[15] This process of European unification was controversial, however. French voters ratified the Maastricht treaty with a "yes" vote of only 51 percent, while Britain, Denmark, and Sweden refused to join the conversion to the euro, fearing a loss of national sovereignty and economic independence. "Euro-skeptics" questioned the economic value of unification. They pointed out that throughout the 1990s, the U.S. economy continued to outperform that of the EU, and European unemployment rates were often high. France's, for example, hovered between 10 and 12 percent in the mid-1990s. Small traders and independent producers opposed the seemingly endless stream of orders and regulations issued by EU bureaucrats and the way in which economic integration privileged large, international firms over small, local shops. In addition, the process of unification meant the loss of many of the symbols that people treasured as links to their national traditions. In Britain in 2001, a shopkeeper who refused to abandon traditional English ounces and pounds for the metric system (required by EU regulations) became a folk hero, seen by many as an English patriot who refused to give in to faraway faceless bureaucrats in Brussels.

The end of the Cold War posed an even sharper challenge to the EU. Should the European Union (often called simply "Europe") include East as well as West? Attracted by the undoubted prosperity of the EU, the nations of the former Soviet bloc answered that question with a resounding "yes." The leaders of western Europe, however, looked with trepidation at the prospect of joining their countries to eastern Europe's shattered economies and divided societies, and drew up a set of rigorous qualifications for applicant nations. To be recognized as belonging to "Europe," nations applying for EU membership had to meet a set of complex financial requirements that demonstrated both the essential stability of their economies and their commitment to market capitalism. Thus "Europe" was defined, first of all, as capitalist. But a set of political requirements made clear that "Europe" also meant a commitment to democratic politics. Applicants' voting processes, treatment of minority groups, policing methods, and judicial systems were all scrutinized, as the EU used its considerable economic clout to nurture fledgling democratic structures in eastern Europe. In 2003, the EU parliament voted overwhelmingly in favor of expanding the Union to include Estonia, Latvia,

Lithuania, Poland, the Czech Republic, Slovakia, Slovenia, and Hungary, as well as Cyprus and Malta (see Map 29.4).

That same year, however, the Second Gulf War opened a serious fissure in the European Union. While governments in eastern Europe supported the Anglo-American attack on Iraq, those of France, Germany, and Russia strongly opposed military intervention and stymied attempts to gain United Nations approval of military action. The split within Europe over the war revealed that the development of a common European foreign and defense policy would be difficult indeed.

CULTURE AND SOCIETY IN THE POSTMODERN ERA

While the formation of the EU, the end of the Cold War, and the revolutions of 1989 helped redefine the balance of power within the West, intellectual and artistic develop-

ments labeled as "postmodern" challenged the dominance of Western values, styles, and assumptions in global culture. At the same time, technological and economic developments worked in contradictory ways, producing a global culture that was at once more uniform than ever before and yet more fragmented, a collection of distinct subcultures.

The Making of the Postmodern

A grab-bag term covering a huge array of styles and stances, postmodernism° at its core constitutes the rejection of Western cultural supremacy. A diverse group of writers, thinkers, and artists began to challenge the idea that Western science and rationality had constructed a single, universally applicable form of "modernity." Postmodernism in this general sense resulted from the joining of three specific intellectual and cultural streams: postmodernist architecture, postmodernist art, and the literary theories of poststructuralism.

■ **Map 29.4 Contemporary Europe**
The revolutions of 1989 and their aftermath mark a clear turning point in European history, as a comparison of this map and that of "Europe in the Cold War" (p. 943) will show. Significant changes include the breakup of the Soviet Union and Yugoslavia, the replacement of Czechoslovakia by the Czech Republic and Slovakia, and the unification of Germany.

■ **Judy Chicago, *The Dinner Party*, (1973–1979)**

This installation sits on 2,300 white porcelain tiles, across which run the names of 999 women from Western history. Each of the thirty-nine place settings includes a ceramic or painted china plate and a needlework runner that use symbols to portray historical or mythological female figures. Like Chicago's work, much of the feminist art of the 1970s focused on celebrating femaleness, the ways in which women's bodies and experiences set them apart from men. Later in the era, many younger feminists criticized this work for reducing women to some sort of mythic female essence, and instead focused their art on exposing the dynamics of power and oppression in modern societies.

As Chapter 28 explained, with the pop art of the 1960s visual artists moved away from many of the central assumptions of modernism. It was in architecture, however, that postmodernism first clearly took form, perhaps because the failures of modernist architecture were so obvious by the early 1970s. Motivated by an intense faith in both human rationality and modern technology, modernist architects had sought to build new forms of housing that, they believed, would enable people to live better, more beautiful lives. But the concrete high-rises they constructed failed to connect with the needs and emotions of their inhabitants, and many became derelict, crime-ridden, graffiti-scarred tenements.

Faced with this sense of failure, a new generation—the postmodernists—insisted that architects needed to start communicating with ordinary people. The American architect Charles Jencks (b. 1939) argued that because people tend to rely on the familiar to make sense of their world, modernism was wrong to reject traditional forms. For example, most Europeans and Americans connect domestic housing with gabled roofs (ask a child to draw a picture of a house and see if he or she draws a flat roof). Was it surprising, Jencks asked, that the concrete rectangles used by modernists for housing proved profoundly alienating to many people? Postmodernist *anti-elitism* thus led to *eclecticism,* to re-creating and combining forms and styles from past eras (such as gabled roofs), and to efforts to revive local and regional styles. Why should the streets of Tokyo look like the center of London or downtown Chicago? Instead, postmodernists embraced an architecture rooted in the specifics of time and place. In addition to being anti-elitist and eclectic, then, postmodernist architecture was also *anti-*

universalist: It condemned modernism for its assumption that the same modern (and Western) ideals and forms fit all individuals and all societies.

The same sorts of criticism of modernism surfaced in the art world, as the wider political context of the late 1960s and early 1970s transformed the visual arts in three ways. First, in the wake of the protests of 1968, artists—many coming out of left-wing activist environments—rejected ideologies based on hierarchy and authority. This rejection led to an attack on the modernist idea of the "avant-garde," a small elite of artistic geniuses fighting to advance the frontiers of aesthetic excellence. Even more than their modernist predecessors, postmodernist artists celebrated the possibilities of the mass media and condemned distinctions between "high" and popular culture. Second, the experience of political protest led many artists to reject the modernist ideal of "art for art's sake," insisting instead that art had to say something to the world around it. To communicate with a wider public, they plundered both the past and popular culture for familiar forms and material. As the art critic Edit DeAk explained, postmodernist art relied on "the shock of recognition instead of the shock of the new."[16] Finally, feminism proved crucial in shaping the new art. Women began to challenge the dominance of men in the art world not only by highlighting the systematic exclusion of women from gallery and museum exhibitions, but also by questioning the aesthetic hierarchy that relegated to the lower status of "craft" traditionally female art forms such as weaving.

By the end of the 1970s, postmodernist practices in art and architecture were both reinforced by and in turn served to strengthen a growing body of literary and cultural theory often called *poststructuralism*. The theory of poststructuralism was associated with the work of an assorted group of French thinkers, whose ideas were taken up in American universities and then filtered back into European intellectual circles. These thinkers included Jacques Derrida (b. 1930) and Roland Barthes (1915–1980) in literary studies, Michel Foucault (1926–1984) in history, and Jacques Lacan (1901–1981) in psychoanalytic theory.

Like postmodernist theories in architecture and art, poststructuralism began as an exploration into the problems of communication. Jacques Derrida argued that the world we see and experience is a world structured by language—we cannot even understand or express our very selves apart from language. But because there is no inherent match between a word (what Derrida called a "signifier") and the thing or idea to which that word refers (the "signified"), communication is never straightforward. An endless variety of meanings and interpretations results, and thus, Derrida argued, we must abandon the idea of a fixed or single truth, of ultimate or universal meaning. In a related argument, Roland Barthes declared the "Death of the Author," by which he meant that the purpose of literary study is not to ask "What does the author mean?" but instead to explore the way in which the reader creates his or her own meanings.

This effort to challenge any center of authority (sometimes called "decentering") linked the poststructuralist concern with communication to its analysis of power. In their work, Michel Foucault and Jacques Lacan looked at hierarchies of authority (not only in the political sphere but also in academic disciplines, for example, or in the medical world), and the way these authorities created and manipulated seemingly objective bodies of knowledge to retain their hold on power.

Postmodernism in its most general form emerged by the later 1980s out of the blending of these poststructuralist theories of communication and power with the critique of modernism already flourishing in architecture and the arts. Thinkers, writers, and artists argued that Western elites had shaped global culture and had ignored or distorted the cultures of non-Western and minority groups. This view of culture as bound up in a global contest for power disturbed many more traditional thinkers (with "modernist" now increasingly perceived as traditional) who continued to insist that criteria of aesthetic excellence ("Beauty") and objective standards of knowledge ("Truth") did exist. These critics warned that cultural "decentering" would destroy the social cohesion and political stability of the West.

Postmodern Cultures and Postindustrial Technologies

In many ways popular culture confirmed postmodern theories. In Britain, for example, the "Big Beat" songs that dominated the club scene in the late 1990s were produced not by vocalists or instrumentalists but by disc jockeys who lifted snatches from old records, played them at different speeds, and combined them with contrasting styles. Like postmodernist paintings, Big Beat contained chunks of the past, recycled in startling new ways. More generally, a series of technological developments meant that popular culture was clearly "decentered," that at the very least a multitude of popular cultures coexisted and that the individual consumer of culture, like Barthes's reader, was free to make meaning as he or she chose. The video cassette recorder (VCR), first marketed in 1975, not only transported film viewing from the public to the private sphere, it also provided the film viewer with the possibility to tailor the film to his or her own preferences—to adjust the volume or choose another soundtrack entirely, to omit or fast-forward through certain scenes, to replay others endlessly. Similarly, the proliferation of cable and satellite television stations during the 1980s and 1990s fragmented the viewing audience and made it impossible to speak of popular culture in the singular.

Postmodernist concerns with communication and codes, with the way in which interpretations can be endlessly modified, and with the abolition of a single center of authority, certainly seemed appropriate for an era that many called "the Information Age" and others called the postindustrial society°. The industrial phase of economic development was characterized by an emphasis on production. But in the postindustrial phase, the *making* of things becomes less important than the *marketing* of them. A postindustrial society, in fact, is characterized less by *things* in general than by *images, ideas, and information*. If the factory symbolized industrial society, then the epitome of the postindustrial era is the home computer, with its capacity to disperse information, market products, and endlessly duplicate yet constantly alter visual and verbal images. By the end of the 1990s, relatively inexpensively priced home computers gave their users access to libraries, art galleries, and retail outlets from across the world, and provided, for entrepreneurs, the opportunity to make (and lose) enormous fortunes by exploiting this new image-oriented means of marketing products and information—all without any central regulating authority. Governments scrambled desperately to impose control on the proliferating technologies of the postindustrial age, but in true postmodern fashion the centers of authority broke down. Existing laws that regulated pornography, for example, proved difficult to apply to the Internet, the vast global communications web.

Similarly, developments in medical technologies raised important questions about authority and ownership. In 1978, Louise Brown was born in Britain, the world's first "test-tube baby." Over the next twenty years, assisted fertility treatment resulted in the births of more than a million babies. As the technology grew more sophisticated, so too did the ethical and political questions. Societies struggled to determine the legality of practices such as commercial surrogate motherhood, in which a woman rents her womb to a couple, and postmenopausal motherhood, in which a woman past childbearing age is implanted with a fertilized egg. Genetic research provoked even more debate about which authorities or what principles should guide scientific research. In 1996, British scientists introduced the world to Dolly the sheep, the first mammal cloned from an adult. Many scientists declared that the cloning of human beings, long part of science fiction and horror stories, was inevitable, even if declared immoral by religious leaders and illegal by political authorities. The announcement in February 2001 that the human genome had been decoded—that scientists had mapped the sequencing of the human genome, or set of instructions in every cell in the human body—immediately raised such questions as: Who owns this information? Who has the authority to decide how it is to be used?

Postmodern Patterns in Religious Life

Postmodern patterns—the fragmentation of cultures, the collapse of centers of authority, the supremacy of image—also characterized Western religious faith and practice after the 1970s. Christianity no longer served as a common cultural bond. In a time of increasing immigration and cultural diversity, Islam was the fastest-growing religious community in western Europe. In Britain, Muslims outnumbered Methodists by two to one. By the end of the twentieth century, established Protestant churches in western Europe faced a serious crisis, with regular churchgoers now a small minority of the population—less than 5 percent, in most countries. The decline of the mainline churches in the United States was also dramatic, although a greater percentage of Americans—25 to 30 percent—attended church regularly. Religious faith became a private matter, the mark of subcultures (often defined by an "Us versus Them" mentality), rather than a bond tying together individuals and groups into a cohesive national culture.

At the same time, however, the long-reigning Pope John Paul II (b. 1920, r. 1978–) experienced unprecedented popularity. The most well-traveled and populist-oriented of twentieth-century popes, John Paul II became a media star, met with the same sort of cheering crowds and T-shirt vendors that accompanied famous rock bands. Much of his popularity rested on his intimate connection with Poland's Solidarity, and therefore with an image of liberation. Born Karol Wojtyła, John Paul was the first non-Italian pope since 1523 and the first-ever Polish pope. Twelve million people—one-third of the Polish population—greeted the pope in Warsaw in 1979 when he made the first visit by any pope to a communist country. Many Solidarity members testified to the importance of this visit in empowering them to challenge the political order fourteen months later. But

CHRONOLOGY	
Medical Challenges	
1977	First diagnosed case of AIDS
1978	First test-tube baby
1980	Worldwide eradication of smallpox
1982	First use of genetic engineering (insulin manufactured from bacteria)
1983	First artificially created chromosome
1984	HIV identified
1985	First use of laser surgery to clear blocked arteries
1997	Successful cloning of sheep
2001	Human genome decoded

the pope's support for Solidarity did not mean he supported other forms of rebellion against authority. Opposing the promise of continuing change inherent in Vatican II (see Chapter 28), John Paul II adopted a thoroughly authoritarian approach to church government and took an uncompromising stand against birth control, married clergy, and the ordination of women. Confronted with the postmodernist message that authority had fragmented and that no universal truth existed, many Christians found the pope's uncompromising stand a source of great comfort.

Yet, the papacy of John Paul II confirmed as well as contradicted postmodernist ideas; much of the pope's popularity was based on image rather than authority. Despite censoring liberal Catholic theologians, the pope was unable to bring into line an increasingly rebellious flock throughout Europe and the United States. In the United States, millions turned out to cheer the pope waving from an open car (the "popemobile"), yet the percentage of American Catholics using birth control—in direct violation of papal teachings—mirrored that of the population at large. By the 1980s, Catholic Italy boasted the second-lowest birth rate in the world (after China), with the one-child family becoming the norm. It was hard to avoid the conclusion that in much of Western Roman Catholicism, as in much of postmodern society, image ruled while authority dissipated.

THE GLOBAL CHALLENGE

At the same time that postmodern artists and theorists were questioning the validity of Western cultural forms, economic and environmental developments called into doubt other key assumptions of Western societies. Both the globalization of market capitalism and a worldwide environmental crisis crashed down national borders, limited the scope of action open to individual governments, and raised significant questions about the ecological sustainability of Western habits of consumption.

The Global Economy

In the 1990s, a number of technological and economic developments helped make national borders even more permeable and accelerated the globalization of economic production. Personal computers, fax machines, and wireless telephones all ensured that "the office" could be anywhere. Fiber optic cables that transmitted signals 4,000 times faster than their copper predecessors made instant communication across national boundaries a reality.

Technological innovations demanded organizational change. In the postindustrial economy, firms had to be more flexible, able to respond immediately to rapidly changing markets and technologies. They did not want too much capital investment in one way of doing things, in one kind of machinery, in one labor force, in one stock of supplies. Rather than economies of scale, they looked for other economies, such as subcontracting, outsourcing, and downsizing. The worker became more vulnerable. Concepts such as "a job for life" or "loyalty to the firm" had little relevance as companies merged and fragmented, shedding large number of workers in the endless pursuit of efficiency and the competitive edge. In this global economy, multinational corporations, with quick access to cheap Third World labor and raw materials, possessed significant economic power. In 2000, corporations such as

THE WEST AND THE REST

....

In 1998, economic historian David Landes published The Wealth and Poverty of Nations: Why Some Are So Rich and Some So Poor. *Landes, a professor at Harvard University, had been writing on the history of industrial and technological change since the 1950s. Now he turned his attention to the present, and endeavored to answer one of the most pressing problems of the contemporary era. His introduction laid out the key issues.*

The old division of the world into two power blocs, East and West, has subsided. Now the big challenge and threat is the gap in wealth and health that separates the rich and poor. These are often styled North and South, because the division is geographic; but a more accurate signifier would be the West and the Rest, because the division is also historic. Here is the greatest single problem and danger facing the world of the Third Millennium. The only other worry that comes close is environmental deterioration, and the two are intimately connected, indeed are one. They are one because wealth entails not only consumption but also waste, not only production but also destruction. It is this waste and destruction, which has increased enormously with output and income, that threatens the space we live and move in.

How big is the gap between rich and poor and what is happening to it? Very roughly and briefly: the difference in income per head between the richest industrial nation, say Switzerland, and the poorest nonindustrial country, Mozambique, is about 400 to 1. Two hundred and fifty years ago, this gap between richest and poorest was perhaps 5 to 1, and the difference between Europe and, say, East or South Asia (China or India) was around 1.5 or 2 to 1.

. . . . Our task (the rich countries), in our own interest as well as theirs, is to help the poor become healthier and wealthier. If we do not, they will seek to take what they cannot make; and if they cannot earn by exporting commodities, they will export people. In short, wealth is an irresistible magnet; and poverty is a potentially raging contaminant: it cannot be segregated, and our peace and prosperity depend in the long run on the well-being of others.

. . . the best way to understand a problem is to ask: How and why did we get where we are? How did the rich countries get so rich? Why are the poor countries so poor? Why did Europe ("the West") take the lead in changing the world?

A historical approach does not ensure an answer. Others have thought about these matters and come up with diverse explanations. Most of these fall into two schools. Some see Western wealth and dominion as the triumph of good over bad. The Europeans, they say, were smarter, better organized, harder working; the others were ignorant, arrogant, lazy, backward, superstitious. Others invert the categories. The Europeans, they say, were aggressive, ruthless, greedy, unscrupulous, hypocritical; their victims were happy, innocent, weak—waiting victims and hence thoroughly victimized. We shall see that both of these manichean visions have elements of truth, as well as of ideological fantasy. Things are always more complicated than we would have them.

Source: From *The Wealth and Poverty of Nations: Why Some Are So Rich and Some So Poor* by David S. Landes. Copyright © 1998 by David S. Landes. Used by permission of W. W. Norton & Company, Inc.

■ North versus South

An Ethiopian farmer wages a losing war against drought and famine.

ExxonMobil and DaimlerChrysler had annual revenues that exceeded the GDP of Norway or Singapore.

Increasingly, however, it was the far more nebulous "markets" that dictated the course of economic and political affairs across the world. In the 1990s, the volatility that had characterized the global economy since the collapse of the Bretton Woods agreements in 1973 became even more intense as currency speculators moved their money in and out of currency markets with astonishing rapidity, and with often devastating consequences for the countries involved. In 1997, for example, Thailand was forced to devalue its currency, and the economic catastrophe of collapsing currencies and stock markets quickly spread to Indonesia, Malaysia, the Philippines, and South Korea. By 1998, the Japanese economy had slid into serious recession.

As the Asian economic crisis revealed, "the markets," rather than elected leaders, played an increasingly important role in determining a country's path. So, too, did the dictates of the World Bank and the IMF, the institutions that directed the flow of aid and loans throughout much of the world. The IMF, for example, insisted that governments receiving loans follow the orthodoxy of "austerity"—cutting government spending on social and welfare programs and restricting the flow of money supply to reduce inflation. Thus economists in offices far away, not elected leaders, called the shots. Moreover, both the World Bank and the IMF embodied the characteristic Western confidence of the postwar era. Local traditions and leaders were ignored, replaced instead by outside economists and agronomists who believed that an infusion of Western economic and technological expertise would set the rest of the world on the path to economic growth.

By the 1990s, the widening gap between "North" and "South," the rich and poor nations of the world, called into question these easy assumptions. Meetings of the World Bank, the IMF, and the "G8" (Japan, the United States, Britain, Canada, France, Germany, Italy, and Russia) were disrupted by "antiglobalization" campaigners who sought to call attention to the social costs of global capitalism, particularly the devastation wrought by what was called the "debt crisis." Over fifty of the world's poorest countries (thirty-six in Africa) were paying off their debts to Western banks and governments by withdrawing money from sanitation, health, and education programs. Relief organizations estimated that as many as seven million children died each year during the 1990s because of the debt crisis.

The Environmental Crisis

The urgency of the environmental crisis also revealed the limitations of Western expertise. By 1985, 257 multilateral treaties mandated some form of environmental protection—restrictions on trade in endangered species, wetlands preservation, forest conservation, regulation of industrial emissions. Almost half of these had been signed since 1970. Yet the degradation of the planet proceeded apace. At the end of the millennium, half of the world's rivers were polluted or running dry, and the number of people displaced by water crises stood at 25 million (versus 21 million war-related refugees). In the 1980s, almost half of the world's tropical forests were cleared, posing a serious threat to the planet's biodiversity.

The destruction of the rain forests contributed to what is perhaps the largest threat facing not only Western but global civilization at the beginning of the third millennium—global warming. Global warming is linked to industrial development. The burning of fossil fuels such as oil and coal (which releases carbon dioxide into the atmosphere) and deforestation (which reduces the "natural sinks" that absorb the gas) together produce the "greenhouse effect"—the trapping of solar radiation in the Earth's atmosphere, with rising temperatures as a result. Faced with predictions of widespread climate change (and resulting economic devastation on a colossal scale), representatives from 160 countries met in Kyoto in 1997 and agreed to cut "greenhouse gas emissions" by 10 percent. In 2001, however, U.S. President George W. Bush rejected the Kyoto Agreements. Without the cooperation of the world's largest producer of greenhouse gases, the Kyoto Agreements' impact would be minimal.

Europeans, both political leaders and ordinary citizens, reacted with fury to Bush's withdrawal from the Kyoto Agreements. They condemned the unilateral American action as that of a superpower out of control, no longer constrained by the Cold War to march in step with its allies.

This perception of the United States as a bullying "hyperpower" was strengthened in 2003 by the Second Gulf War. Across Europe, anti-war rallies drew huge crowds as Europeans protested against what they perceived to be an unwarranted use of American military force. As new divisions and alliances emerged both within and outside of Europe, the meaning of "the West" remained the subject of intense debate.

CONCLUSION

Where Is the West Now?

In England, the most popular fast food is not fish and chips, long the quintessential English national supper, nor is it the Big Mac, as opponents of economic globalization might predict. Instead it is curry, the gift of the minority South Asian immigrant community. In the new millennium, "the West" may no longer serve as an important conceptual border marker. By many of the criteria explored in this textbook—economic, technological, political, and cultural—Tokyo would be defined as a Western city. So, too, would Melbourne—or Budapest or Warsaw. Nevertheless, the economic and social trauma that afflicted Russia and the poorer nations of the former Soviet bloc such as Romania and Bulgaria in the 1990s and after demonstrates that the "West" retains its distinct identity, for clearly the gap between it and the "East" remains wide. The admittedly hesitant, still incomplete spread of the Western ideal of democracy has thrown a fragile bridge across that gap. But perhaps the real divide for the twenty-first century stretches between "North" and "South"—the huge and growing difference between the global Haves and the Have-Nots. Whether any bridge can stretch across that span remains to be seen.

Suggestions for Further Reading

For a comprehensive list of suggested readings, please go to www.ablongman.com/levack/chapter29

Ardagh, John. *Germany and the Germans: The United Germany in the Mid-1990s.* 1996. A snapshot of a society in the midst of social and economic change.

Hughes, H. Stuart. *Sophisticated Rebels. The Political Culture of European Dissent 1968–1987.* 1988. A perceptive and imaginative exploration of "dissenters," ranging from Solidarity and Soviet dissidents to German Greens, Welsh nationalists, and an assortment of novelists and philosophers.

Kavanagh, Dennis. *Thatcherism and British Politics: The End of Consensus?* 1987. Kavanagh answers the question posed in his title with a convincing "yes."

Lewis, Jane, ed. *Women and Social Policies in Europe: Work, Family and the State.* 1993. A series of essays exploring the position of women in western Europe. Packed with statistics and useful tables.

McNeill, John. *Something New Under the Sun: An Environmental History of the Twentieth Century.* 2000. Argues that twentieth-century human economic activity has transformed the ecology of the globe—an ongoing experiment with a potentially devastating outcome.

Ost, David. *Solidarity and the Politics of Anti-Politics: Opposition and Reform in Poland Since 1968.* 1990. Although the bulk of this account was written before the Revolution of 1989, it provides a compelling study of Solidarity's emergence, impact, and ideology.

Rogel, Carole. *The Breakup of Yugoslavia and the War in Bosnia.* 1998. Designed for undergraduates, this work includes a short but detailed historical narrative, biographies of the main personalities, and a set of primary documents.

Rosenberg, Tina. *The Haunted Land: Facing Europe's Ghosts After Communism.* 1995. Winner of the Pulitzer Prize, this disturbing account focuses on the fundamental moral issues facing postcommunist political cultures.

Sandler, Irving. *Art of the Postmodern Era: From the Late 1960s to the Early 1980s.* 1996. Much more broad-ranging than the title suggests, this well-written, blessedly jargon-free work sets both contemporary art and the theories of the postmodern within the wider historical context.

Stokes, Gale. *The Walls Came Tumbling Down: The Collapse of Communism in Eastern Europe.* 1993. A superb account, firmly embedded in history.

Young, John W. *Cold War Europe 1945–1991: A Political History.* 1996. A solid survey.

See also the works by Crampton, Cronin, Isaacs and Downing, Judge and Langdon, Keep, and Urwin listed at the end of Chapter 28.

Notes

1. Quoted in Robert Paxton, *Europe in the Twentieth Century* (1997), p. 613.
2. Kenneth Boulding, "The Economics of the Coming Spaceship Earth," first published in 1966, reprinted in *Toward a Steady-State Economy,* ed. Herman Daly (1973).
3. Quotations from Timothy W. Ryback, *Rock Around the Bloc: A History of Rock Music in Eastern Europe and the Soviet Union* (1990); pp. 184–185, 176.
4. Quoted in D. J. Peterson, *Troubled Lands: The Legacy of Soviet Environmental Destruction* (1993), p. 12.
5. Quoted in Archie Brown, *The Gorbachev Factor* (1996), p. 125.
6. Quoted in R. J. Crampton, *Eastern Europe in the Twentieth Century—And After* (1997), p. 408.
7. Francis Fukuyama, *The End of History and the Last Man* (1992).
8. Quoted in *The Observer* (London), April 8, 2001, p. 20.
9. Salman Rushdie, "Please, Read *Satanic Verses* Before Condemning It," *Illustrated Weekly of India,* October 1988, reprinted in M. M. Ahsan and A. R. Kidwai. *Sacrilege versus Civility: Muslim Perspectives on The Satanic Verses Affair* (1991), p. 63.
10. Quoted in Malise Ruthven, *A Satanic Affair: Salman Rushdie and the Wrath of Islam* (1991). p. 562.
11. Quoted in Ruthven, p. 100.
12. *Bookseller,* London, February 24, 1989; quoted in Lisa Appignanesi and Sara Maitland, *The Rushdie File* (1990), pp. 103–104.
13. *The Sunday Telegraph,* June 24, 1990; quoted in Ahsan and Kidwai, p. 80.
14. Quoted in J. Robert Wegs and Robert Landrech, *Europe Since 1945* (1996) p. 354.
15. Wim Duisenberg, quoted in *The Independent* (London), August 31, 2001, p. 1.
16. Quoted in Irving Sandler, *Art of the Postmodern Era* (1996), p. 4.

Glossary

absolutism (pp. 492–494) A form of government in the seventeenth and eighteenth centuries in which the ruler possessed complete and unrivalled power.

acropolis (p. 89) The defensible hilltop around which a polis grew. In classical Athens, the Acropolis was the site of the Parthenon (Temple of Athena).

Aeneid (p. 175) Written by Virgil (70–19 B.C.E.), this magnificent epic poem celebrates the emperor Augustus by linking him to his mythical ancestor, Aeneas, the Trojan refugee who founded the Roman people. Considered by many to be the greatest work of Latin literature, the poem has had enormous influence in the West.

agrarian capitalism (p. 420) A form of economic organization characteristic of European colonialism in which Europeans organized the production of certain kinds of commercial crops (such as sugar, tobacco, and indigo) on land expropriated from native peoples and with slave labor.

agricultural revolution (p. 273) Refers to technological innovations that began to appear during the eleventh century, making possible a dramatic growth in population. The agricultural revolution came about through harnessing new sources of power with water and wind mills, improving the pulling power of animals with better collars, using heavy plows to better exploit the soils of northern Europe, and employing a three-field crop rotation system that increased the amount and quality of food available.

agricultural societies (p. 15) Settled communities in which people depend on farming and raising livestock as their sources of food.

alchemy (p. 531) A form of learned magic that was intended to turn base metals into precious ones.

aldeias (p. 412) Settlements for natives who had converted to Christianity in Brazil. In these settlements the Jesuit fathers protected the natives from enslavement.

Allies (p. 790) During World War I, the states allied against the Central Powers of Germany and Austria-Hungary. During World War II, the states allied against the regimes of Nazi Germany, fascist Italy and imperial Japan.

Anabaptism (p. 443) Meaning "to rebaptize"; refers to those Protestant radicals of the sixteenth century who rejected infant baptism and adopted adult baptism. Anabaptists treated the Bible as a blueprint for reforming not just the church but all of society, a tendency that led them to reject the authority of the state, to live in self-governing "holy communities," and in some cases to practice a primitive form of communism.

anarchism (p. 740) Ideology that views the state as unnecessary and repressive, and rejects participation in parliamentary politics in favor of direct, usually violent, action.

anticlericalism (p. 771) Opposition to the political influence of the Roman Catholic Church.

Antonine Decree (p. 168) In 212 C.E. the emperor Aurelius Antoninus, called Caracalla, issued a decree that granted citizenship to all the free inhabitants of the Roman Empire. The decree enabled Roman law to embrace the entire population of the empire.

apartheid (p. 939) System of racial segregation and discrimination put into place in South Africa in 1948.

Apologists (p. 182) Christian writers in the second and third centuries C.E. who explained their religion to learned non-Christians. In the process they helped Christianity absorb much of Hellenistic culture.

appeasement (p. 865) British diplomatic and financial efforts to stabilize Germany in the 1920s and 1930s and so avoid a second world war.

Arians (p. 199) Christians who believe that God the Father is superior to Jesus Christ his Son. Most of the Germanic settlers in western Europe in the fifth century were Arians.

aristocracy (p. 554) A term that originally applied to those who were considered the most fit to rule and later identified the wealthiest members of society, especially those who owned land.

Asceticism (p. 201) The Christian practice of severely suppressing physical needs and daily desires in an effort to achieve a spiritual union with God. Asceticism is the practice that underlies the monastic movement.

Auschwitz (p. 905) Technically Auschwitz-Birkenau; death camp in Poland that has become the symbol of the Holocaust.

auto-da-fé (p. 465) Meaning literally a "theater of faith," an *auto* was practiced by the Catholic Church in early modern Spain and Portugal as an extended public ritual of penance designed to cause physical pain among the sinful and promote fear of God's judgment among those who witnessed it.

Babylonian Captivity of the Church (p. 338) Between 1305 and 1378 seven consecutive popes voluntarily chose to reside in Avignon, France, in order to escape anarchy in the streets of Rome. During this period the popes became subservient to the kings of France.

Babylonian Exile (p. 81) The period of Jewish history between the destruction of Solomon's temple in Jerusalem by Babylonian armies in 587 B.C.E., and 538 B.C.E., when Cyrus of Persia permitted Jews to return to Palestine and rebuild the temple.

balance of power (p. 501) An arrangement in which various countries form alliances to prevent any one state from dominating the others.

Balfour Declaration (p. 819) Declaration of 1917 that affirmed British support of a Jewish state in Palestine.

baroque (p. 497) A dynamic style in art, architecture, and music intended to elicit an emotional response. It was closely associated with royal absolutism in the seventeenth century.

Battle of Kadesh (p. 52) The battle between Egyptian and Hittite armies in Syria in 1274 B.C.E. that set the territorial limits of both empires in Canaan and the Middle East for a century during the International Bronze Age.

Beer Hall Putsch (p. 835) Failed Nazi effort to overthrow the German government by force in 1923.

Berlin Wall (p. 935) Constructed by the East German government, the wall physically cut the city of Berlin in two and prevented East German citizens from access to West Germany; stood from 1961 to 1989.

Big Three (p. 886) Term applied to the British, Soviet, and U.S. leaders during World War II: until 1945, Churchill, Stalin, and Roosevelt; by the summer of 1945, Attlee, Stalin, and Truman.

blitzkrieg (p. 867) "Lightning war;" offensive military tactic making use of airplanes, tanks, and motorized infantry to punch through enemy defenses and secure key territory. First demonstrated by the German army in World War II.

boers (p. 628) Dutch farmers in the colony established by the Dutch Republic in South Africa.

Bolsheviks (p. 815) Minority group of Russian socialists, headed by Lenin, who espoused an immediate transition to a socialist state. It became the Communist Party in the Soviet Union.

bourgeoisie (p. 561) A social group, technically consisting of those who were burghers in the towns, that included prosperous merchants and financiers, members of the professions, and some skilled craftsmen known as "petty bourgeoisie."

Bretton Woods Agreement (p. 886) Agreement signed in 1944 that established the post-World War II economic framework in which the U.S. dollar served as the world's reserve currency.

brinkmanship (p. 933) Style of Cold War confrontation in which each superpower endeavored to convince the other that it was willing to wage nuclear war.

British Commonwealth (p. 853) Loose organization of former British colonies and imperial territories.

bronze (p. 41) An alloy of tin and copper that produces a hard metal suitable for weapons, tools, ornaments, and household objects. Bronze production began about 3200 B.C.E.

bubonic plague (p. 327) An epidemic disease spread from rats to humans via flea bites. The infection enters the bloodstream, causing inflamed swellings called buboes (hence, "bubonic" plague) in the glands of the groin or armpit, internal bleeding, and discoloration. Although disputed by some, most experts consider bubonic plague the cause of the Black Death, which killed at least one-third of the population of Europe between 1348 and the early 1350s. Bubonic plague reappeared recurrently in the West between 1348 and 1721.

caliph (p. 283) After Muhammad's death in 632, the ruler of the Islamic state was called the caliph. The sectarian division within Islam between the Shi'ites and Sunni derived from a disagreement over how to determine the hereditary succession from Muhammad to the caliphate, which combined governmental and some religious responsibilities.

caliphate (p. 235) The Islamic imperial government that evolved under the leadership of Abu Bakr (r. 632–634), the successor of the prophet Muhammad.

calling (p. 438) The Calvinist doctrine that God calls the Elect to perform his will on earth. God's calling gave Calvinists a powerful sense of personal direction.

canon law (p. 297) The collected laws of the Roman Catholic Church. Canon law applied to cases involving the clergy, disputes about church property, and donations to the Church. It also applied to the laity for annulling marriages, legitimating bastards, prosecuting bigamy, protecting widows and orphans, and resolving inheritance disputes.

capital (p. 664) All the physical assets used in production, including fixed capital, such as machinery, and circulating capital, such as raw materials; more generally the cost of these physical assets.

caravels (p. 397) Hybrid three-masted ships developed about 1450 in the Iberian peninsula by combining the rigging of square with triangular lateen sails. These ships could be sailed in a variety of winds, carry large cargoes, be managed by a small crew, and be defended by guns mounted in the castle superstructure.

Carnival (p. 469) The most popular annual festival in much of Europe before modern times. Also known as Mardi Gras, the festival took place for several days or even weeks before the beginning of Lent and included all kinds of fun and games.

Carolingian Renaissance (p. 263) The "rebirth" of interest in ancient Greek and Latin literature and language during the reign of the Frankish emperor Charlemagne (r. 768–814). Charlemagne promoted the intensive study of Latin to promote governmental efficiency and to propagate the Christian faith.

Catholic Reformation (p. 445) A series of efforts during the sixteenth century to purify the Church that evolved out of late medieval spirituality and that included the creation of new religious orders, especially the Society of Jesus.

Central Powers (p. 790) Germany and Austria-Hungary in World War I.

Chalcedonians (p. 199) Christians who follow the doctrinal decisions and definitions of the Council of Chalcedon in 451 C.E. stating that Christ's human and divine natures were equal, but entirely distinct and united in one person "without confusion, division, separation, or change." Chalcedonian Christianity came to be associated with the Byzantine Empire and is called Greek Orthodoxy. In western Europe it is known as Roman Catholicism.

chinoiserie (p. 643) A French word for an eighteenth-century decorative art that combined Chinese and European motifs.

Christendom (p. 199) Collectively refers to the many Christian kingdoms of western Europe that used Latin as the language of worship, diplomacy, and law during the Middle Ages.

Christian Democracy, Christian Democratic parties (pp. 947–948) Conservative and confessionally based (Roman Catholic) political parties that dominated much of western European politics after World War II.

Christian humanists (p. 428) During the fifteenth and sixteenth centuries these experts in Greek, Latin, and Hebrew subjected the Bible to philological study in an attempt to understand the precise meaning of the founding text of Christianity.

circuit court (p. 311) Established by King Henry II (r. 1154–1189) to make royal justice available to virtually anyone in England. Circuit court judges visited every shire in England four times a year.

civic humanism (p. 375) A branch of humanism introduced by the Florentine chancellor Leonardo Bruni who defended the republican institutions and values of the city. Civic humanism promoted the ethic of responsible citizenship.

civilization (p. 13) The term used by archaeologists to describe a society differentiated by levels of wealth and power, and in which religious, economic, and political control are based in cities.

civitas (p. 162) The Roman term for a city. A city included the town itself, all the surrounding territory that it controlled, and all the people who lived in the town and the countryside.

clans or kin groups (p. 249) The basic social and political unit of Germanic society consisting of blood relatives obliged to defend one another and take vengeance for crimes against the group and its members.

class (p. 555) A large and often cohesive social group that was conscious of its shared economic and political interests.

classicism (p. 558) A style in art, architecture, music, and literature that emphasizes proportion, adherence to traditional forms, and a rejection of emotion and enthusiasm.

Cluny (p. 278) A monastery founded in Burgundy in 910 that became the center of a far-reaching movement to reform the Church that was sustained in more than 1,500 Cluniac monasteries, modeled after the original in Cluny.

Cold War (p. 886) Struggle for global supremacy between the United States and the Soviet Union, waged from the end of World War II until 1990.

collectivization (p. 848) The replacement of private and village farms with large cooperative agricultural enterprises run by state-employed managers.

colons (p. 647) White planters in the French Caribbean colony of Saint Domingue (Haiti).

Columbian exchange (p. 416) The trade of peoples, plants, animals, microbes, and ideas between the Old and New Worlds that began with Columbus.

Columbian question (p. 418) The debate among historians and epidemiologists about whether syphilis or its ancestor disease originated in the Americas and was brought to the Old World after Columbus's voyages.

Common Market (p. 948) Originally comprising West Germany, France, Italy, Belgium, Luxembourg, and the Netherlands, the Common Market was formed in 1957 to integrate its members' economic structures and so foster both economic prosperity and international peace. Also called the European Economic Community (EEC).

communes (p. 275) Sworn defensive associations of merchants and workers that appeared in north-central Italy after 1070 and that became the effective government of more than a hundred cities. The communes evolved into city-states by seizing control of the surrounding countryside.

communism (p. 689) The revolutionary form of socialism developed by Karl Marx and Friedrich Engels that promoted the overthrow of bourgeois or capitalist institutions and the establishment of a dictatorship of the proletariat.

Concert of Europe (p. 688) The joint efforts made by Austria, Prussia, Russia, Britain, and France during the years following the Congress of Vienna to suppress liberal and nationalist movements throughout Europe.

Conciliar Movement (p. 340) A fifteenth-century movement that advocated ending the Great Schism and reforming church government by calling a general meeting or council of the bishops, who would exercise authority over the rival popes.

Confessions (p. 464) The formal sixteenth-century statements of religious doctrine: the Confession of Augsburg for Lutherans, the Helvetic Confessions for Calvinists, the Thirty-Nine Articles for Anglicans, and the decrees of the Council of Trent for Catholics.

Congress of Vienna (p. 616) A conference of the major powers of Europe in 1814–1815 to establish a new balance of power at the end of the Napoleonic Wars.

conquistadores (p. 404) Spanish adventurers in the Americas who explored and conquered the lands of indigenous peoples, sometimes without legal authority but usually with a legal privilege granted by the king of Spain who required that one-fifth of all things of value be turned over to the crown. The conquistadores extended Spanish sovereignty over new lands.

conservatism (pp. 687–688) A nineteenth-century ideology intended to prevent a recurrence of the revolutionary changes of the 1790s and the implementation of liberal policies.

containment (p. 889) Cold War policy of blocking communist expansion; inaugurated by the Truman Doctrine in 1947.

Corpus of Civil Law (p. 215) The body of Roman law compiled by the emperor Justinian in Constantinople in 534. The Corpus became a pillar of Latin-speaking European civilization.

cosmology (p. 526) A theory concerning the structure and nature of the universe such as those proposed by Aristotle in the fourth century B.C.E. and Copernicus in the sixteenth century.

Counter Reformation (p. 445) The Catholic response to the Protestant Reformation by propagandizing Catholic doctrine, disciplining the clergy and laity, and repressing heresy. The Counter Reformation established the Holy Office of the Inquisition, promulgated the *Index of Forbidden Books*, and implemented the decrees of the Council of Trent (1545–1563).

counties (p. 263) Territorial units devised by the Carolingian dynasty during the eighth and ninth centuries for the administration of the empire. Each county was administered by a count who was rewarded with lands and sent to areas where he had no family ties to serve as a combined provincial governor, judge, military commander, and representative of the king.

courtly love (p. 319) An ethic first found in the poems of the late twelfth- and thirteenth-century troubadours that portrayed the ennobling possibilities of the love between a man and a woman. Courtly love formed the basis for the modern idea of romantic love.

creoles (p. 628) People of Spanish descent who had been born in Spanish America.

crusades (p. 292) Between 1095 and 1291, Latin Christians heeding the call of the pope launched eight major expeditions and many smaller ones against Muslim armies in an attempt to gain control of and hold Jerusalem.

Cubism (p. 768) Modernist artistic movement of the early twentieth century that emphasized the fragmentation of human perception through visual experiments with geometric forms.

cultural relativism (p. 420) A mode of thought first explored during the sixteenth century to explain why the peoples of the New World did not appear in the Bible. Cultural relativism recognized that many (but not necessarily all) standards of judgment are specific to particular cultures rather than the fixed truths established by natural or divine law.

culture (p. 12) The knowledge and adaptive behavior created by communities that helps them to mediate between themselves and the natural world through time.

cuneiform (p. 20) A kind of writing in which wedge-shaped symbols are pressed into clay tablets to indicate words and ideas. Cuneiform writing originated in ancient Sumer.

Curia (p. 297) The administrative bureaucracy of the Roman Catholic Church.

Cynic (p. 123) Cynics followed the teachings of Antisthenes (ca. 445–360 B.C.E.) by rejecting pleasures, possessions, and social conventions in order to find peace of mind.

Darwinian theory of evolution (p. 757) Scientific theory associated with nineteenth-century scientist Charles Darwin that highlights the role of variation and natural selection in the evolution of species.

Decembrists (p. 697) Russian liberals who staged a revolt against Tsar Nicholas I on the first day of his reign in December 1825.

de-Christianization (pp. 602–603) A program inaugurated in France in 1793 by the radical Jacobin and former priest Joseph Fouché that closed churches, eliminated religious symbols, and attempted to establish a purely civic religion.

deduction (p. 534) The logical process by which ideas and laws are derived from basic truths or principles.

deists (p. 542) Seventeenth- and eighteenth-century thinkers who believed that God created the universe and established immutable laws of nature but did not subsequently intervene in the operation of nature or in human affairs.

Delian League (p. 95) The alliance among many Greek cities organized by Athens in 478 B.C.E. in order to fight Persian forces in the eastern Aegean Sea. The Athenians gradually turned the Delian League into the Athenian Empire.

demand (p. 665) The desire of consumers to acquire goods and the need of producers to acquire raw materials and machinery.

democracy (p. 78) A form of government in which citizens devise their own governing institutions and choose their leaders; began in Athens, Greece, in the fifth century B.C.E.

demonic magic (p. 546) The invocation of evil spirits with the goal of utilizing their supernatural powers to change the course of nature or to alter human behavior.

de-Stalinization (p. 942) Khrushchev's effort to decentralize political and economic control in the Soviet Union after 1956.

detente (p. 936) During the 1970s, a period of lessened Cold War hostilities and greater reliance on negotiation and compromise.

dialectic (p. 688) The theory that history advanced in stages as the result of the conflict between different ideas or social groups.

dialectical materialism (p. 689) The socialist philosophy of Karl Marx according to which history advanced as the result of material or economic forces and would lead to the creation of a classless society.

division of labor (p. 660) The assignment of one stage of production to a single worker or group of workers to increase efficiency and productive output.

domestication (p. 14) Manipulating the breeding of animals over many generations in order to make them more useful to humans as sources of food, wool, and other byproducts. Domestication of animals began about 10,000 years ago.

Dreyfus Affair (pp. 733–735) The trials of Captain Alfred Dreyfus on treason charges dominated French political life in the decade after 1894 and revealed fundamental divisions in French society.

dualistic (p. 534) A term used to describe a philosophy, such as that of René Descartes, in which a rigid distinction is made between body and mind or between the material and the immaterial world.

Dutch Revolt (p. 482) The rebellion against Spanish rule of the seven northern provinces of the Netherlands between 1579 and 1648, which resulted in the independence of the Republic of the United Provinces.

Edict of Nantes (p. 478) Promulgated by King Henry IV in 1598, the edict allowed the Huguenots to build a quasi-independent state within the kingdom of France, giving them the right to have their own troops, church organization, and political autonomy within their walled towns, but banning them from the royal court and the city of Paris. King Louis XIV revoked the edict in 1685.

Einsatzgruppen (p. 902) Loosely translated as strike force or task force; SS units given the task of murdering Jews and Communist Party members in the areas of the Soviet Union occupied by Germany during World War II.

empires (pp. 43, 622) Large political formations consisting of different kingdoms or territories outside the boundaries of the states that control them.

enclosure (p. 663) The consolidation of scattered agricultural holdings into large, compact fields which were then closed off by hedges, bushes, or walls, giving farmers complete control over the uses of their land.

encomienda (p. 408) The basic form of economic and social organization in early Spanish America, based on a royal grant awarded to a Spaniard for military or other services that gave the grantee and his successors the right to gather tribute from the Indians in a defined area.

enlightened despots (p. 575) The term assigned to absolute monarchs who initiated a series of legal and political reforms in an effort to realize the goals of the Enlightenment.

Enlightenment (p. 562) An international intellectual movement of the eighteenth century that emphasized the use of reason and the application of the laws of nature to human society.

Epicureans (p. 121) Followers of the teachings of the philosopher Epicurus (341–271 B.C.E.). Epicureans tried to gain peace of mind by choosing pleasures rationally.

ethnic cleansing (p. 985) A term introduced during the wars in Yugoslavia in the 1990s; the systematic use of murder, rape, and violence by one ethnic group against members of other ethnic groups in order to establish control over a territory.

Etruscans (p. 130) A people native to Italy, the Etruscans established a league of militaristic cities in central Italy that grew rich from war and trade. Etruscans had a great influence on the formation of the Roman state.

Eucharist (p. 301) Also known as Holy Communion or the Lord's Supper, the Eucharistic rite of the Mass celebrates Jesus' last meal with his apostles when the priest-celebrant consecrates wafers of bread and a chalice of wine as the body and blood of Christ. In the Middle Ages the wafers of bread were distributed for the congregation to eat, but drinking from the chalice was a special privilege of the priesthood. Protestants in the sixteenth century and Catholics in the late twentieth century began to allow the laity to drink from the chalice.

European Economic Community (EEC) (p. 948) Originally comprising West Germany, France, Italy, Belgium, Luxembourg, and the Netherlands, the EEC was formed in 1957 to integrate its members' economic structures and so foster both economic prosperity and international peace. Also called the Common Market.

European Union (EU) (p. 991) A successor organization to the EEC; the effort to integrate European political, economic, cultural, and military structures and policies.

excommunication (p. 296) A decree by the pope or a bishop prohibiting a sinner from participating in the sacraments of the Church and forbidding any social contact whatsoever with the surrounding community.

existentialism (pp. 829, 955) Twentieth-century philosophy that emerged in the interwar era and influenced many thinkers and artists after World War II. Existentialism emphasizes individual freedom in a world devoid of meaning or coherence.

Expressionism (p. 769) Modernist artistic movement of the early twentieth century that used bold colors and experimental forms to express emotional realities.

factories (p. 624) Trading posts established by European powers in foreign lands.

fanatic (p. 476) Originally referring to someone possessed by a demon, a fanatic came during the sixteenth century to mean a person who expressed immoderate enthusiasm in religious matters or who pursued a supposedly divine mission, often to violent ends.

fascism (p. 839) Twentieth-century political ideology that rejected the existing alternatives of conservatism, communism, socialism, and liberalism. Fascists stressed the authoritarian power of the state, the efficacy of violent action, the need to build a national community, and the use of new technologies of influence and control.

federalists (p. 594) The name assigned by radical Jacobins to provincial rebels who opposed the centralization of the state during the French Revolution.

feminism, feminist movement (p. 744) International movement that emerged in the second half of the nineteenth century and demanded broader political, legal, and economic rights for women.

Fertile Crescent (p. 16) Also known as the Levantine Corridor, this twenty-five mile wide arc of land stretching from the Jordan River to the Euphrates River was the place where food production and settled communities first appeared in Southwest Asia (the Middle East).

feudalism (p. 267) A term historians use to describe a social system common during the Middle Ages in which lords granted fiefs (tracts of land or some other form of income) to dependents, known as vassals, who owed their lords personal services in exchange. Feudalism refers to a society governed through personal ties of dependency rather than public political institutions.

fief (p. 267) During the Middle Ages a fief was a grant of land or some other form of income that a lord gave to a vassal in exchange for loyalty and certain services (usually military assistance).

Final Solution (p. 901) Nazi term for the effort to murder every Jew in Europe during World War II.

fin-de-siecle (p. 760) French term for the "turn of the century"; used to refer to the cultural crisis of the late nineteenth century.

First Triumvirate (p. 144) The informal political alliance made by Julius Caesar, Pompey, and Crassus in 60 B.C.E. to share power in the Roman Republic. It led directly to the collapse of the Republic.

food production (p. 14) The practice of growing crops and raising livestock as opposed to hunting and gathering. Food production made civilization possible.

Forms (p. 105) In the philosophical teachings of Plato, these are eternal, unchanging absolutes such as Truth, Justice, and Beauty that represent true reality, as opposed to the approximations of reality that humans encounter in everyday life.

Forum (p. 129) The political and religious center of the city of Rome throughout antiquity. All cities in the empire had a forum in imitation of the capital city.

franchise (p. 580) The right to vote; also called the suffrage.

freemasons (p. 574) Members of secret societies of men and women that flourished during the Enlightenment, dedicated to the creation of a society based on reason and virtue and committed to the principles of liberty and equality.

French Wars of Religion (p. 477) A series of political assassinations, massacres, and military engagements between French Catholics and Calvinists from 1560 to 1598.

German-Soviet Non-Aggression Pact (p. 864) Signed by Stalin and Hitler in 1939, the agreement publicly pledged Germany and the Soviet Union not to attack each other, and secretly divided up Poland and the Baltic states between the two powers.

Girondins (pp. 593–594) The more conservative members of the Jacobin party who favored greater economic freedom and opposed further centralization of state power during the French Revolution.

glasnost (p. 977) Loosely translated as openness or honesty; Gorbachev's effort after 1985 to break with the secrecy that had characterized Soviet political life.

Gothic (p. 320) A style in architecture in western Europe from the late twelfth and thirteenth centuries, characterized by ribbed vaults and pointed arches, which drew the eyes of worshipers upward toward God. Flying buttresses, which redistributed the weight of the roof, made possible thin walls pierced by large expanses of stained glass.

grand jury (p. 311) In medieval England after the judicial reforms of King Henry II (r. 1154–1189), grand juries were called when the circuit court judge arrived in a shire. The sheriff assembled a group of men familiar with local affairs who constituted the grand jury and who reported to the judge the major crimes that had been committed since the judge's last visit.

Great Depression in Trade and Agriculture (p. 722) Downturn in prices and profits, particularly in the agricultural sector, in Europe from 1873 through the 1880s.

Great Depression (p. 842) Calamitous drop in prices, reduction in trade, and rise in unemployment that devastated the global economy in 1929.

Great Persecution (p. 191) An attack on Christians in the Roman empire begun by the emperor Galerius in 303 C.E. on the grounds that their worship was endangering the empire. Several thousand Christians were executed.

Great Purge (p. 850) Period of mass arrests and executions particularly aimed at Communist Party members. Lasting from 1934 to 1939, the Great Purge enabled Stalin to consolidate his one-man rule over the Soviet Union.

Great Schism (p. 339) The division of the Catholic Church (1378–1417) between rival Italian and French claimants to the papal throne.

Green movement, Green politics (p. 973) A new style of politics and set of political ideas resulting from the confluence of environmentalism, feminism, and anti-nuclear protests of the 1970s.

guilds (p. 335) Professional associations devoted to protecting the special interests of a particular trade or craft and to monopolizing production and trade in the goods the guild produced.

haciendas (p. 408) Large landed estates that began to be established in the seventeenth century replaced encomiendas throughout much of Spanish America.

Hallstatt (p. 127) The first Celtic civilization in central Europe is called Halstatt. From about 750 to about 450 B.C.E., Hallstatt Celts spread throughout Europe.

helots (p. 91) The brutally oppressed subject peoples of the Spartans. Tied to the land they farmed for Spartan masters, they were treated little better than beasts of burden.

heresies (p. 198) Forms of Christian belief that are not considered Orthodox.

hetairai (p. 98) Elite courtesans in ancient Greece who provided intellectual as well as sexual companionship.

Holocaust (p. 898) Adolf Hitler's effort to murder all the Jews in Europe during World War II.

Homo sapiens sapiens (p. 13) Scientific term meaning "most intelligent people" applied to physically and intellectually modern human beings that first appeared between 200,000 and 100,000 years ago in Africa.

hoplites (p. 90) Greek soldiers in the Archaic Age who could afford their own weapons. Hoplite tactics made soldiers fighting as a group dependent on one another. This contributed to the internal cohesion of the polis and eventually to the rise of democracy.

Huguenots (p. 477) The term for French Calvinists, who constituted some 10 percent of the population by 1560.

humanists (p. 373) During the Renaissance humanists were writers and orators who studied Latin and sometimes Greek texts on grammar, rhetoric, poetry, history, and ethics.

Hundred Years' War (p. 341) Refers to a series of engagements (1337–1453) between England and France over England's attempts to assert its claims to territories in France.

hyperinflation (p. 835) Catastrophic price increases and currency devaluation, such as that which occurred in Germany in 1923.

Iconoclasm (p. 231) The destruction of religious images in the Byzantine empire in the eighth century.

icons (p. 231) The Christian images of God and saints found in Byzantine art.

ideologies (p. 686) Theories of society and government that form the basis of political programs.

Ideologues (p. 608) A group of liberal writers and philosophers in France who objected to Napoleon's religious policy on the grounds that it would inaugurate a return of religious superstition.

induction (p. 533) The mental process by which theories are established only after the systematic accumulation of large amounts of data.

indulgences (p. 339) Certificates that allowed penitents to atone for their sins and reduce their time in purgatory. Usually these were issued for going on a pilgrimage or performing a pious act, but during the Babylonian Captivity of the Church (1305–1378) popes began to sell them, a practice Martin Luther protested in 1517 in an act that brought on the Protestant Reformation.

industrial capitalism (p. 672) A form of capitalism characterized by the ownership of factories by private individuals and the employment of wage labor.

intendants (p. 496) French royal officials who became the main agents of French provincial administration in the seventeenth century.

interdict (p. 297) A papal decree prohibiting the celebration of the sacraments in an entire city or kingdom.

Investiture Controversy (p. 296) A dispute that began in 1076 between the popes and the German emperors over the right to invest bishops with their offices. The most famous episode was the conflict between Pope Gregory VII and Emperor Henry IV. The controversy was resolved by the Concordat of Worms in 1122.

Jacobins (p. 590) A French political party supporting a democratic republic that found support in political clubs throughout the country and dominated the National Convention from 1792 until 1794.

Jim Crow (p. 743) Series of laws mandating racial segregation throughout the American South.

Junkers (p. 509) The traditional nobility of Prussia.

justification by faith alone (p. 431) Refers to Martin Luther's insight that humanity is incapable of performing enough religious good works to earn eternal salvation. Salvation is an unmerited gift from God called grace. Those who receive grace are called the Elect.

knight (p. 267) During the Middle Ages a knight was a soldier who fought on horseback. A knight was a vassal or dependent of a lord, who usually financed the knight's expenses of armor and weapons and of raising and feeding horses with a grant of land known as a fief.

Koine (p. 119) The standard version of the Greek language spoken throughout the Hellenistic world.

Kristallnacht (p. 900) The "Night of the Broken Glass"—on November 9, 1938, Nazi-directed mobs burned the synagogues and vandalized the homes and businesses of the German Jewish community.

La Tène (p. 127) A phase of Celtic civilization that lasted from about 450 to 200 B.C.E. La Tène culture became strong especially in the regions of the Rhine and Danube Rivers.

laissez-faire (p. 686) The principle that governments should not regulate or otherwise intervene in the economy unless it is necessary to protect property rights and public order.

lapis lazuli (p. 59) A precious, deep-blue gemstone found in the Middle East that was traded widely for jewelry during the International Bronze Age.

latifundia (p. 173) These huge agricultural estates owned by wealthy Romans, including the emperor, often used large slave-gangs as labor.

lay investiture (p. 278) The practice of nobles, kings, or emperors installing churchmen and giving them the symbols of office.

League of Nations (p. 821) Association of states set up after World War I to resolve international conflicts through open and peaceful negotiation.

Lend-Lease Act (p. 871) Passed in March 1941, the act gave Britain access to American industrial products during World War II, with payment postponed for the duration of the war.

Levantine Corridor (p. 16) Also known as the Fertile Crescent, this twenty-five mile wide arc of land stretching from the Jordan River to the Euphrates River was the place where food production and settled communities first appeared in Southwest Asia (the Middle East).

liberalism (pp. 686–687) An ideology based on the conviction that individual freedom is of supreme importance and the main responsibility of government is to protect that freedom.

linear perspective (p. 379) In the arts the use of geometrical principles to depict a three-dimensional space on a flat, two-dimensional surface.

liturgy (p. 276) The forms of Christian worship, including the prayers, chants, and rituals to be said, sung, or performed throughout the year.

lord (p. 267) During the Middle Ages a lord was someone who offered protection to dependents, known as vassals, who took an oath of loyalty to him. Most lords demanded military services from their vassals and sometimes granted them tracts of land known as fiefs.

Macedonian Renaissance (p. 280) During the Macedonian dynasty's rule of Byzantium (867–1056), aristocratic families, the Church, and monasteries devoted their immense riches to embellishing Constantinople with new buildings, mosaics, and icons. The emperors sponsored historical, philosophical, and religious writing.

Mafia (p. 710) Organizations of armed men who took control of local politics and the economy in late nineteenth-century Sicily.

magic (p. 470) Learned opinion described two kinds of magic: natural magic, which involved the manipulation of occult forces believed to exist in nature, and demonic magic, which called upon evil spirits to gain access to power. Widely accepted as a reality until the middle of the seventeenth century.

Magisterial Reformation (p. 436) Refers to Protestant churches that received official government sanction.

Magna Carta (p. 312) In 1215 some English barons forced King John to sign the "great charter," in which the king pledged to respect the traditional feudal privileges of the nobility, towns, and clergy. Subsequent kings swore to uphold it, thereby accepting the fundamental principle that even the king was obliged to respect the law.

Manhattan Project (p. 917) Code name given to the secret Anglo-American project that resulted in the construction of the atom bomb during World War II.

marches (p. 263) Territorial units of the Carolingian empire for the administration of frontier regions. Each march was ruled by a margrave who had special powers necessary to defend vulnerable borders.

Marshall Plan (p. 889) The use of U.S. economic aid to restore stability to Europe after World War II and so undercut the appeal of communist ideology.

mechanical philosophy (p. 534) The seventeenth-century philosophy of nature, championed by René Descartes, holding that nature operated in a mechanical way, just like a machine made by a human being.

mendicant friars (p. 299) Members of a religious order, such as the Dominicans or Franciscans, who wandered from city to city and throughout the countryside begging for alms rather than residing in a monastery. Mendicant friars tended to help ordinary laypeople by preaching and administering to the sick and poor.

mercantilism (p. 499) The theory that the wealth of a state depended on its ability to import fewer commodities than it exported and thus acquire the largest possible share of the world's monetary supply. The theory encouraged state intervention in the economy and the regulation of trade.

mesmerism (p. 575) A pseudoscience developed by Franz Anton Mesmer in the eighteenth century that treated sickness by massaging or hypnotizing the patient to produce a crisis that restored health.

metropolis (p. 622) The parent country of a colony or imperial possession.

Mishnah (p. 203) The final organization and transcription of Jewish oral law, completed by the end of the third century C.E.

Modern Devotion (p. 341) A fifteenth-century religious movement that stressed individual piety, ethical behavior, and intense religious education. The Modern Devotion was promoted by the Brothers of the Common Life, a religious order whose influence was broadly felt through its extensive network of schools.

modernism (p. 765) Term applied to artistic and literary movements from the late nineteenth century through the 1950s. Modernists sought to create new aesthetic forms and values.

monastic movement (p. 201) In Late Antiquity, Christian ascetics organized communities where men and women could pursue a life of spirituality through work, prayer, and asceticism. Called the monastic movement, this spiritual quest spread quickly throughout Christian lands.

Monophysites (p. 199) Christians who do not accept the Council of Chalcedon (see Chalcedonians). Monophysites believe that Jesus Christ has only one nature, equally divine and human.

monotheism (p. 78) The belief in only one god, first attributed to the ancient Hebrews. Monotheism is the foundation of Judaism, Christianity, Islam, and Zoroastrianism.

Montagnards (pp. 593–594) Members of the radical faction within the Jacobin party who advocated the centralization of state power during the French Revolution and instituted the Reign of Terror.

mosque (p. 234) A place of Muslim worship.

nabobs (p. 643) Members of the British East India Company who made fortunes in India and returned to Britain, flaunting their wealth.

Napoleonic Code (p. 608) The name given to the Civil Code of 1804, promulgated by Napoleon, which gave France a uniform and authoritative code of law.

nation (p. 689) A large community of people who possess a sense of unity based on a belief that they have a common homeland and share a similar culture.

nationalism (p. 689) The belief that the people who form a nation should have their own political institutions and that the interests of the nation should be defended and promoted at all costs.

national self-determination (p. 689) The doctrine advanced by nationalists that any group that considers itself a nation has the right to be ruled only by the members of their own nation and to have all members of the nation included in that state.

nation-state (p. 689) A political structure sought by nationalists in which the boundaries of the state and the nation are identical, so that all the members of a nation are governed by the same political authorities.

NATO (North Atlantic Treaty Organization) (p. 889) Defensive anti-Soviet alliance of the United States, Canada, and the nations of western Europe established in 1949.

natural magic (p. 536) The use of magical words and drawings to manipulate the occult forces that exist in nature without calling on supernatural beings for assistance.

nawabs (p. 640) Native provincial governors in eighteenth-century India.

Nazism (p. 843) Twentieth-century political ideology associated with Adolf Hitler that adopted many fascist ideas but with a central focus on racism and particularly anti-Semitism.

neoclassicism (p. 558) The revival of the classical art and architecture of ancient Greece and Rome in the eighteenth century.

Neoplatonism (pp. 205, 534–535) A philosophy based on the teachings of Plato and his successors that flourished in Late Antiquity, especially those of Plotinus. Neoplatonism influenced Christianity in Late Antiquity. During the Renaissance Neoplatonism was linked to the belief that the natural world was charged with occult forces that could be used in the practice of magic.

NEP (New Economic Plan) (p. 832) Lenin's economic turnaround in 1921 that allowed and even encouraged small private businesses and farms in the Soviet Union.

New Conservatism (p. 969) Political ideology that emerged at the end of the 1970s combining the free market approach of nineteenth-century liberalism with social conservatism.

new feminism (p. 971) Re-emergence of the feminist movement in the 1970s.

new imperialism (p. 771) The third phase of modern European imperialism, that occurred in the late nineteenth and early twentieth centuries and extended Western control over almost all of Africa and much of Asia.

New Left (p. 960) Leftwing political and cultural movement that emerged in the late 1950s and early 1960s; sought to develop a form of socialism that rejected the over-centralization, authoritarianism, and inhumanity of Stalinism.

nobility (p. 554) Members of the aristocracy who received official recognition of their hereditary status, including their titles of honor and legal privileges.

no-man's-land (p. 798) The area between the combatants' trenches on the Western Front during World War I.

nuclear arms race (p. 923) Product of the Cold War between the United States and the Soviet Union; each superpower endeavored to achieve military superiority through the acquisition of ever-more sophisticated nuclear bombs and nuclear weapons delivery systems.

Nuremberg trials (p. 910) Post-World War II trials of members of the Nazi Party and German military; conducted by an international tribunal.

Old Regime (p. 575) The political order of eighteenth-century France, dominated by an absolute monarch and a privileged nobility and clergy.

oligarchy (p. 97) A government consisting of only a few people rather than the entire community.

opera (p. 383) A musical form invented in the final decades of the sixteenth century by a group of humanist-musicians who thought the power of ancient Greek music could be recovered by writing continuous music to accompany a full drama.

orthodox (p. 198) In Christianity, the term indicates doctrinally correct belief. Definitions of Orthodoxy changed numerous times.

ostracism (p. 96) Developed in democratic Athens, this practice enabled citizens in the assembly to vote to expel any Athenian citizen from the city for ten years for any reason.

Ottonian Renaissance (p. 271) Under the patronage of the Saxon Emperor Otto I (936–973) and his brother Bruno, learned monks, Greek philosophers from Byzantium, and Italian scholars gathered at the imperial court, stimulating a cultural revival in literature and the arts.

paganism (p. 197) The Christian term for polytheist worship (worshiping more than one god). In the course of Late Antiquity, the Christian church suppressed paganism, the traditional religions of the Roman empire.

palimpsests (p. 254) Because parchment sheets used for copying were expensive, monks often scrubbed off an old text and copied another in its place. These reused sheets of parchment often contain layers of valuable texts that can be retrieved by scientists.

panhellenic (p. 90) This word means open to all Greek communities. It applies to the athletic games, such as the Olympic Games, in which competitors came from all over the Greek world.

papacy (p. 195) The bishop of the city of Rome is called the Pope, or Father. The papacy refers to the administrative and political institutions controlled by the Pope. The papacy began to gain strength in the sixth century in the absence of Roman imperial government in Italy.

paradigm (p. 537) A conceptual model or intellectual framework within which scientists conduct their research and experimentation.

parlements (p. 496) The highest provincial courts in France, the most important of which was the Parlement of Paris.

pastoralist societies (p. 15) Nomadic communities that move from place to place to find pastures for their herds of domesticated animals.

patricians (p. 131) In ancient Rome, patricians were aristocratic clans with the highest status and the most political influence.

patrons and clients (p. 138) In ancient Roman society, a powerful man (the patron) would exercise influence on behalf of a social subordinate (the client) in anticipation of future support or assistance.

Paul of Tarsus (p. 182) The most effective early Christian missionary, Paul preached the teachings of Jesus to non-Jewish audiences before his death in Rome about 65 C.E.

Pax Romana (p. 150) Latin for "Roman Peace", this term refers to the Roman Empire established by Augustus that lasted until the early third century C.E.

perestroika (p. 977) Loosely translated as "restructuring;" Gorbachev's effort to decentralize, reform, and thereby strengthen Soviet economic and political structures.

personal rule (p. 513) The period from 1629 to 1640 in England when King Charles I ruled without Parliament.

phalanx (p. 91) The military formation favored by hoplite soldiers. Standing shoulder to shoulder in ranks often eight men deep, hoplites moved in unison and depended on one another for protection.

philology (p. 373) A method reintroduced by the humanists during the Italian Renaissance devoted to the comparative study of language, especially to understanding the meaning of a word in a particular historical context.

philosophes (p. 559) The writers and thinkers of the Enlightenment, especially in France.

pilgrimage (p. 203) Religious journeys made to holy sites in order to encounter relics.

Pillars of Islam (p. 234) The five basic principles of Islam as taught by Muhammad.

plainchant (p. 322) A medieval form of singing based on a straightforward melody sung with simple harmony by a choir to accompany the recitation of the text of the liturgy.

plantation colony (p. 398) First appearing in the Cape Verde Islands and later in the tropical parts of the Americas, these colonies were established by Europeans who used African slave labor to cultivate cash crops such as sugar, indigo, cotton, coffee, and tobacco.

plebeians (p. 131) The poorest Roman citizens.

polis (p. 89) Or city-state, developed by Greeks in the Archaic Age. A polis was a self-governing community consisting of a defensible hilltop, the town itself, and all the surrounding fields farmed by the citizens of the polis. Poleis (plural) shared similar institutions: an assembly place for men to gather and discuss community affairs, a council of elders, and an open agora, which served as a market and a place for informal discussions.

polyphony (p. 322) A form for singing the Christian liturgy developed around 1170 in which two or more independent melodies were sung at the same time.

polytheistic (p. 30) Refers to polytheism, the belief in many gods.

pop art (p. 955) Effort by artists in the 1950s and 1960s both to utilize and to critique the material plenty of post-World War II popular culture.

popular sovereignty (p. 602) The claim that political power came from the people and that the people constituted the highest political power in the state.

portolanos (p. 397) Books of sailing directions that included charts and descriptions of ports. Portolanos appeared in the Mediterranean in the Late Middle Ages.

positivism (pp. 691–692) The philosophy developed by August Comte in the nineteenth century according to which human society passed through a series of stages, leading to the final positive stage in which the accumulation of scientific data would enable thinkers to discover the laws of human behavior and bring about the improvement of society.

postindustrialism, postindustrial society (p. 994) A service-rather than manufacturing-based economy characterized by an emphasis on marketing and information and by a proliferation of communications technologies.

postmodernism (pp. 992, 995) Umbrella term covering a variety of artistic styles and intellectual theories and practices; in general, a rejection of a single, universal, Western style of modernity.

Pragmatic Sanction of Bourges (p. 385) An agreement between the pope and king of France made in 1438 that guaranteed the virtual autonomy of the French Church from papal control.

Prague Spring (p. 946) Short-lived popular effort in 1968 to reform Czechoslovakia's political structures; associated with the phrase "socialism with a human face."

predestination (p. 438) The doctrine promoted by John Calvin that since God, the all-knowing and all-powerful being, knew everything in advance and caused everything to happen, then the salvation of any individual was predetermined.

prerogative (p. 513) The set of powers exercised by the English monarch alone, rather than in conjunction with Parliament.

Price Revolution (p. 463) After a long period of falling or stable prices that stretched back to the fourteenth century, Europe experienced sustained price increases between about 1540 and 1640, causing widespread social and economic turmoil.

priesthood of all believers (p. 432) Martin Luther's doctrine that all those of pure faith were themselves priests, a doctrine that undermined the authority of the Catholic clergy over the laity.

proletariat (p. 689) The word used by Karl Marx and Friedrich Engels to identify the class of workers who received their income from wages.

protectionism (p. 631) The policy of shielding domestic industries from foreign competition through a policy of levying tariffs on imported goods.

Radical Reformation (p. 436) Refers to Protestant movements that failed to gain official government recognition and were at best tolerated, at worst persecuted, during the sixteenth century.

Raiders of the Land and Sea (p. 66) The name given by Egyptians to the diverse groups of peoples whose combined naval and land forces destroyed many cities and kingdoms in the eastern Mediterranean and Anatolia, thereby bringing the International Bronze Age to an end.

Reign of Terror (p. 595) A purging of alleged enemies of the French state between 1793 and 1794, superintended by the Committee of Public Safety, that resulted in the execution of 17,000 people.

relics (pp. 203, 277) In Christian belief, relics are sacred objects that have miraculous powers. They are associated with saints, biblical figures, or some object associated with them. They served as contacts between Earth and Heaven and were verified by miracles.

Religious Peace of Augsburg (p. 435) In 1555 this peace between Lutherans and Catholics within the Holy Roman Empire established the principle of *cuius regio, eius religio*, which means "he who rules determines the religion of the land." Protestant princes in the Empire were permitted to retain all church lands seized before 1552 and to enforce Protestant worship, but Catholic princes were also allowed to enforce Catholic worship in their territories.

Renaissance (p. 362) A term meaning "rebirth" used by historians to describe a movement that sought to imitate and understand the culture of antiquity. The Renaissance generally refers to a movement that began in Italy and then spread throughout Europe from about 1350 to 1550.

reparations (p. 822) Payments imposed upon Germany after World War I by the Versailles Treaty to cover the costs of the war.

republicanism (p. 362) A political theory first developed by the ancient Greeks, especially the philosopher Plato, but elaborated by the ancient Romans and rediscovered during the Italian Renaissance. The fundamental principle of republicanism as developed during the Italian Renaissance was that government officials should be elected by the people or a portion of the people.

requeriemiento (p. 404) A document read by conquistadores to the natives of the Americas before making war on them. The document briefly explained the principles of Christianity and commanded the natives to accept them immediately along with the authority of the pope and the sovereignty of the king of Spain. If the natives refused, they were warned they would be forced to accept Christian conversion and subjected to Spain anyway.

revisionism, socialist revisionism (p. 739) The belief that an equal society can be built through participation in parliamentary politics rather than through violent revolution.

rhetoric (p. 373) The art of persuasive or emotive speaking and writing, which was especially valued by the Renaissance humanists.

Roman Republic (p. 128) The name given to the Roman state from about 500 B.C.E., when the last king of Rome was expelled, to 31 B.C.E., when Augustus established the Roman Empire. The Roman Republic was a militaristic oligarchy.

Romanesque (p. 320) A style in architecture that spread throughout western Europe during the eleventh and the first half of the twelfth centuries and characterized by arched stone roofs supported by rounded arches, massive stone pillars, and thick walls.

romanization (p. 167) The process by which conquered peoples absorbed aspects of Roman culture, especially the Latin language, city-life, and religion.

romanticism (pp. 692–695) An artistic and literary movement of the late eighteenth and nineteenth centuries that involved a protest against classicism, appealed to the passions rather than the intellect, and emphasized the beauty and power of nature.

Rome-Berlin Axis (p. 863) Alliance between Mussolini's Italy and Hitler's Germany formed in 1936.

Schlieffen Plan (p. 794) German military plan devised in 1905 that called for a sweeping attack on France through Belgium and the Netherlands.

scholasticism (p. 316) A term referring to a broad philosophical and theological movement that dominated medieval thought and university training. Scholasticism used logic learned from Aristotle to interpret the meaning of the Bible and the writings of the Church Fathers, who created Christian theology in its first centuries.

Scramble for Africa (p. 774) The frenzied imposition of European control over most of Africa that occurred between 1870 and 1914.

scriptorium (p. 253) The room in a monastery where monks copied books and manuscripts.

Second Industrial Revolution (p. 723) A new phase in the industrialization of the processes of production and consumption, underway in Europe in the 1870s.

Second Triumvirate (p. 145) In 43 B.C.E. Octavian (later called Augustus), Mark Antony, and Lepidus made an informal alliance to share power in Rome while they jockeyed for control. Octavian emerged as the sole ruler of Rome in 31 B.C.E.

seigneur (p. 560) The lord of a French estate who received payments from the peasants who lived on his land.

separate spheres (p. 572) The theory that men and women should conduct their lives in different social and political environments, confining women to the domestic sphere and excluding them from the public sphere of political involvement.

sepoys (p. 642) Indian troops serving in the armed forces of the British East India Company.

Septuagint (p. 120) The Greek translation of the Hebrew Bible (Old Testament).

serfs (p. 274) During the Middle Ages serfs were agricultural laborers who worked and lived on a plot of land granted them by a lord to whom they owed a certain portion of their crops. They could not leave the land, but they had certain legal rights that were denied to slaves.

settler colony (p. 398) A colony authorized when a private person obtained a license from a king to seize an island or parcel of land and occupied it with settlers from Europe who exported their own culture to the new lands. Settler colonies first appeared among the islands of the eastern Atlantic and portions of the Americas.

simony (p. 278) The practice of buying and selling church offices.

Social Darwinism (p. 759) The later-nineteenth-century application of the theory of evolution to entire human societies.

social democracy (pp. 851, 883, 969) Political system in which a democratically elected parliamentary government endeavors to ensure a decent standard of living for its citizens through both economic regulation and the maintenance of a welfare state.

Solidarity (p. 975) Trade union and political party in Poland that led an unsuccessful effort to reform the Polish communist state in 1981; survived to lead Poland's first non-communist government since World War II in 1989.

Sophists (p. 105) Professional educators who traveled throughout the ancient Greek world, teaching many subjects. Their goal was to teach people the best ways to lead better lives.

soviets (p. 814) Workers' and soldiers' councils formed in Russia during the Revolution of 1917.

Spanish Armada (p. 480) A fleet of 132 ships, which sailed from Portugal to rendezvous with the Spanish army stationed in the Netherlands and launch an invasion of England in 1588. The English defeated the Armada as it passed through the English Channel.

Spanish Reconquest (p. 286) Refers to the numerous military campaigns by the Christian kingdoms of northern Spain to capture the Muslim-controlled cities and kingdoms of southern Spain. This long, intermittent struggle began with the capture of Toledo in 1085 and lasted until Granada fell to Christian armies in 1492.

spiritualists (p. 443) A tendency within Protestantism, especially Lutheranism, to emphasize the power of personal spiritual illumination, called the "inner Word," a living form of the Scriptures written directly on the believer's soul by the hand of God.

stagflation (p. 966) Term coined in the 1970s to describe an economy troubled by both high inflation and high unemployment rates.

states (p. 622) Consolidated territorial areas that have their own political institutions and recognize no higher political authority.

Stoicism (p. 123) The philosophy developed by Zeno of Citium (ca. 335–ca. 263 B.C.E.) that urged acceptance of fate while participating fully in everyday life.

structuralism (p. 956) Influential post–World War II social theory that explored the common structures of language and thought.

Struggle of the Orders (p. 131) The political strife between patrician and plebeian Romans beginning in the fifth century B.C.E. The plebeians gradually won political rights and influence as a result of the struggle.

suffragettes (p. 749) Feminist movement that emerged in Britain in the early twentieth century. Unlike the suffragists, who sought to achieve the vote for women through rational persuasion, the suffragettes adopted the tactics of violent protest.

supply (p. 665) The amounts of capital, labor, and food that are needed to produce goods for the market as well as the quantities of those goods themselves.

Syncretism (p. 176) The practice of equating two gods and fusing their cults was common throughout the Roman Empire and helped to unify the diverse peoples and religions under Roman rule.

syndicalism (p. 740) Ideology of the late nineteenth and early twentieth century that sought to achieve a working-class revolution through economic action, particularly through mass labor strikes.

Talmuds (p. 203) Commentaries on Jewish law. Rabbis completed the Babylonian Talmud and the Jerusalem Talmud by the end of the fifth century C.E.

Tetrarchy (p. 190) The government by four rulers established by the Roman emperor Diocletian in 293 C.E. that lasted until 312.

During the Tetrarchy many administrative and military reforms altered the fabric of Roman society.

Third World (p. 942) Term coined in 1955 to describe nations that did not align with either the Soviet Union or the United States; commonly used to describe the industrially underdeveloped nations.

thomism (p. 318) A branch of medieval philosophy associated with the work of the Dominican thinker, Thomas Aquinas (1225–1274), who wrote encyclopedic summaries of human knowledge that confirmed Christian faith.

Time of Troubles (p. 488) The period from 1604 to 1613 when Russia fell into chaos, which ended when the national assembly elected Tsar Michael Romanov, whose descendants ruled Russia until they were deposed in 1917.

total war (pp. 790, 805) A war that demands extensive state regulation of economic production, distribution, and consumption.

trading posts (p. 404) Built by European traders along the coasts of Africa and Asia as a base for trade with the interior. Trading posts or factories were islands of European law and sovereignty, but European authority seldom extended very far beyond the fortified post.

transubstantiation (p. 301) A doctrine promulgated at the Fourth Lateran Council in 1215 that explained by distinguishing between the outward appearances and the inner substance how the Eucharistic bread and wine changed into the body and blood of Christ.

Treaty of Brest-Litovsk (p. 800) Treaty between Germany and Bolshevik-controlled Russia, signed in March, 1918, that ceded to Germany all of Russia's western territories.

trial by jury (p. 311) When disputes about the possession of land arose after the late twelfth century in England, sheriffs assembled a group of twelve local men who testified under oath about the claims of the plaintiffs, and the circuit court judge made his decision on the basis of their testimony. The system was later extended to criminal cases.

Triple Alliance (p. 791) Defensive alliance of Germany, Austria-Hungary, and Italy, signed in 1882.

Triple Entente (p. 792) Informal defensive agreement linking France, Great Britain, and Russia before World War I.

triremes (p. 93) Greek warships with three banks of oars. Triremes manned by the poorest people of Athenian society became the backbone of the Athenian empire.

troubadours (p. 319) Poets from the late twelfth and thirteenth centuries who wrote love poems, meant to be sung to music, which reflected a new sensibility, called courtly love, about the ennobling possibilities of the love between a man and a woman.

Truman Doctrine (p. 889) Named after U.S. president Harry Truman, the doctrine that in 1947 inaugurated the Cold War policy of resisting the expansion of communist control.

Twelfth-Century Renaissance (p. 317) An intellectual revival of interest in ancient Greek philosophy and science and in Roman law in western Europe during the twelfth and early thirteenth centuries. The term also refers to a flowering of vernacular literature and the Romanesque and Gothic styles in architecture.

tyrants (p. 91) Political leaders from the upper classes who championed the cause of hoplites in Greek city-states during the Archaic Age. The word "tyrant" gained its negative connotation when democracies developed in Greece that gave more political voice to male citizens than permitted by tyrants.

Unitarians (p. 444) A religious reform movement that began in the sixteenth century and rejected the Christian doctrine of the Trinity. Unitarians (also called Arians, Socinians, and Anti-Trinitarians) taught a rationalist interpretation of the Scriptures and argued that Jesus was a divinely inspired man, not God-become-man as did other Christians.

universal law of gravitation (p. 530) A law of nature established by Isaac Newton in 1687 holding that any two bodies attract each other with a force that is directly proportional to the product of their masses and indirectly proportional to the square of the distance between them. The law was presented in mathematical terms.

universal male suffrage (p. 592) The granting of the right to vote to all adult males.

Utilitarians (p. 687) Nineteenth-century British liberals who promoted social and economic policies that in their view would provide the greatest good for the greatest number of people.

vassals (p. 267) During the Middle Ages men voluntarily submitted themselves to a lord by taking an oath of loyalty. Vassals owed the lord certain services—usually military assistance—and sometimes received in exchange a grant of land known as a fief.

Vatican II (p. 957) Popular term for the Second Vatican Council that convened in 1963 and introduced a series of changes within the Roman Catholic Church.

Versailles Treaty (p. 822) Treaty between Germany and the victorious Allies after World War I.

Vichy, Vichy regime, Vichy government (p. 867) Authoritarian state established in France after defeat by the German army in 1940.

Warsaw Pact (p. 889) Military alliance of the Soviet Union and its eastern European satellite states in the Cold War era.

Weimar Republic (p. 834) The democratic German state constructed after defeat in World War I and destroyed by the Nazis in 1933.

wergild (p. 250) In Germanic societies the term referred to what an individual was worth in case he or she suffered an injury. It was the amount of compensation in gold that the wrongdoer's family had to pay to the victim's family.

witch-hunt (p. 470) Refers to the dramatic increase in the judicial prosecution of alleged witches in either church or secular courts from the middle of the sixteenth to the middle of the seventeenth centuries.

Zionism (p. 743) Nationalist movement that emerged in the late nineteenth century and sought to establish a Jewish political state in Palestine (the Biblical Zion).

Zoroastrianism (p. 86) The monotheistic religion of Persia founded by Zoroaster that became the official religion of the Persian Empire.

Credits

Unless otherwise acknowledged, all photographs are the property of Pearson Education, Inc. Page abbreviations are as follows: (T) Top, (B) Bottom, (L) Left, (R) Right, (C) Center.

The Human Body in History title panel image: Cameraphoto/ Art Resource, NY
Justice in History title panel image: Don Mason/Corbis

What Is the West?
2 Canali Photobank; 4 European Space Agency/Photo Researchers, Inc.; 6 Courtesy of Adler Planetarium & Astronomy Museum, Chicago, Illinois (W-264); 7 American Museum of Natural History Library (AMNH#314372)

Chapter 1
10 Victor R. Boswell, Jr./National Geographic Image Collection; 12 Augustin Ochsenreiter/South Tyrol Museum of Archaeology; 20 (L) Courtesy of the Trustees of the British Museum, London (BM116730); (R) Courtesy of the Trustees of the British Museum, London (WA15285); 23 (T) Robert Harding Picture Library; (B) George Gerster/Photo Researchers, Inc.; 25 Nimatallah/Art Resource; 27 Erich Lessing/Art Resource, NY; 28 Scala/Art Resource, NY; 30 Staatlisches Museum Ägyptischer Kunst; 31 Dagli Orti/The Art Archive; 32 (T) Borromeo/Art Resource, NY; (B) Robert Harding Picture Library; 36 From Grahame Clark, *World Prehistory,* third edition, p. 140, © 1977 Cambridge University Press; 37 Roger Ressmeyer/Corbis

Chapter 2
40 National Archaeological Museum, Athens/Dagli Orti/The Art Archive; 44 Réunion des Musées Nationaux/Art Resource, NY; 45 Egyptian Museum Cairo/Dagli Orti/The Art Archive; 47 British Museum, London/Bridgeman Art Library; 49 Osiride Head of Hatshepsut, originally from a statue. Provenance: Thebes, Deir el Bahri. Limestone, painted. H. 64 cm. H. with crown 124.5 cm. The Metropolitan Museum of Art, Rogers Fund, 1931, (31.3.157) Photograph © 1983 The Metropolitan Museum of Art; 51 AKG London; 54 (L) Degeorge/Corbis; (R) AKG London; 58 Private Collection, Paris/Dagli Orti/The Art Archive; 60 Nimatallah/Art Resource, NY; 62 Scala/Art Resource, NY; 64 Hirmer Fotoarchive; 69 (L) AKG London; 72 (T) Erich Lessing/Art Resource, NY; (B) Oriental Institute, University of Chicago

Chapter 3
76 Erich Lessing/Art Resource, NY; 82 Collection, Israel Museum, Jerusalem. Photo © Israel Museum/David Harris; 84 State Hermitage Museum, Moscow, Russia; 90 American Numismatic Society; 94 Paul Lipke/Trireme Trust USA; 98 (L) Foto Marburg/Art Resource, NY; (TR) Bridgeman Art Library; (B) Pedicini/Index s.a.s.; 99 Staatliche Äntikensammlungen und Glyphtothek, Munich; 100 Robert Harding Picture Library; 3.10 *Column krater* (missing bowl) (detail), Greek, Archaic Period (Late Corinthian), about 550 B.C.E., Place of manufacture: Greece, Corinthia, Corinth, Veramic, Black Figure, Height 33 cm (13 in); diameter: 41 cm (16 ⅛ in.), Museum of Fine Arts, Boston, Helen and Alice Coburn Fund (63.420) Photograph © 2003 Museum of Fine Arts, Boston;

104 Scala/Art Resource, NY; 106 Boltin Picture Library; 107 Scala/Art Resource, NY

Chapter 4
110 Scala/Art Resource, NY; 114 Dagli Orti/The Art Archive; 117 Réunion des Musées Nationaux/Art Resource, NY; 119 Nimatallah/Art Resource, NY; 122 Réunion des Musées Nationaux/Art Resource, NY; 123 Erich Lessing/Art Resource, NY; 128 (T) Erich Lessing/Art Resource, NY; (B) Staatliche Museen, Berlin/BPK, Berlin; 130 Robert Harding Picture Library; 137 *Statue of Cybele,* Roman, II Century A.D., Bronze, Length 139.1 cm. The Metropolitan Museum of Art, Gift of Henry G. Marquand, 1897. (97.22.24) Photograph by Schecter Lee, Photograph © 1985 The Metropolitan Museum of Art; 143 Alinari/Art Resource, NY

Chapter 5
148 Erich Lessing/Art Resource, NY; 154 SEF/Art Resource, NY; 155 Erich Lessing/Art Resource, NY; 156 Mimmo Jodice/Corbis; 158 Vasari/Index s.a.s.; 159 Leo C. Curran; 160 © Dorling Kindersley; 161 (T) (B) © Dorling Kindersley; (C) Scala/Art Resource, NY; 162 Robert Harding Picture Library; 171 AKG London; 177 Scala/Art Resource, NY; 178 Art Resource, NY; 181 Courtesy of the Trustees of the British Museum, London (BMC Vespasian 16)

Chapter 6
186 Österreichische Nationalbibliotek, Vienna; 188 Scala/Art Resource, NY; 189 SEF/Art Resource, NY; 190 Erich Lessing/ Art Resource, NY; 193 Alinari/Art Resource, NY; 196 Victoria & Albert Museum, London/Art Resource, NY; 200 Réunion des Musées Nationaux/Art Resource, NY; 202 Hanan Isachar/ Corbis; 209 Alinari/Art Resource, NY; 214 Erich Lessing/Art Resource, NY; 217 Réunion des Musées Nationaux/Art Resource, NY; 218 Courtesy of the Trustees of the British Museum, London 222 Art Resource, NY

Chapter 7
226 Balatoni Museum, Keszthely, Hungary; 227 *David and Goliath,* Byzantine, Made in Constantinople, 629–630; Early Byzantine, Silver, D. 1 ½ in. (3.8 cm); Diam. 19 ½ in (49.4 cm); The Metropolitan Museum of Art, Gift of J. Pierpont Morgan, 1917 (17.190.396) Photograph © 2000 The Metropolitan Museum of Art; 229 British Museum/The Art Archive; 230 Monastery of St. Catherine, Mt. Sinai, Egypt/Bridgeman Art Library; 230 Scala/Art Resource, NY; 232 Courtesy of His Eminence Archbishop Damianos and the Holy Council of the Fathers, Saint Catherine's Monastery. Photograph © Idryma Orous Sina, Mt. Sinai Foundation; 235 AP/Wide World Photos; 237 Courtesy of the Greer Gallery of Art, Smithsonian Institution, Washington, D.C. (F1930.60a); 238 Robert Harding Picture Library; 242 (TL) (TR) The Nasser D. Khalili Collection of Islamic Art; (BL) Bibliothèque Nationale de France (2001 A 83707); (BR) Bibliothèque Nationale de France (2001 A 83708); 245 British Museum/Eileen Tweedy/The Art Archive; 253 (T) Courtesy of the Trustees of the British Museum, London (EPS200642); (B) Courtesy of the Trustees of the British Museum, London (EPS200646); 254 By permission of the British Library (Cotton.Nerod.iv. fol. 211)

Chapter 8

258 Art Resource, NY; **263** Bibliothèque Nationale de France, Paris (Latin 9428 f. 71v/RC A 39420); **266** Erich Lessing/Art Resource, NY; **269** AKG London; **270** AKG London; **272** Bodleian Library, Oxford University (Ms Bodl. 624 fol. 81r); **273** Réunion des Musées Nationaux/Art Resource, NY; **274** Cambridge University Collection of Aerial Photography (ATV76); **276** Chitter Åhlin/The Museum of National Antiquities, Sweden; **277** Scala/Art Resource, NY; **279** State Historical Museum, Moscow; **286** Scala/Art Resource, NY

Chapter 9

290 Giraudon/Art Resource, NY; **294** Dagli Orti/The Art Archive; **295** Werner Forman Archive/Art Resource, NY; **299** Arthur Thévenart/Corbis; **301** Scala/Art Resource, NY; **302** Musée Condé, Chantilly/Bridgeman Art Library; **303** Cameraphoto/Art Resource, NY; **305** Bridgeman Art Library; **307** Bibliothèque Nationale de France, Paris; **311** Art Resource, NY; **317** BPK, Berlin; **320** Courtesy Achim Bednorz; **321 (L)** Courtesy Achim Bednorz; **(R)** Marc Garanger/Corbis

Chapter 10

324 Snark/Art Resource, NY; **328** Réunion des Musées Nationaux/Art Resource, NY; **329** Scala/Art Resource, NY; **337** Bibliothèque Nationale de France, Paris (M. 2643, folio 226 v.); **339** Santa Maria Novella, Florence/Index a.s.a.; **341** Honourable Society of Inner Temple London/Eileen Tweedy/The Art Archive; **342** Bibliothèque Nationale de France, Paris (MS. Fr. 2644 fol. 135); **344** Bibliothèque Nationale de France/Harper Collins Publishers/The Art Archive; **345** By permission of the British Library (Addt. mss.42130 fol 147v); **347** Bibliothèque Nationale de Rouen (MS U 49 fol. 1); **348** Stadtarchiv Soest (Bestand A Nr. 2771); **349** *Tomb Effigy of Jean d'Alluy,* mid-13th century, Limestone, 83 $\frac{1}{2}$ × 34 $\frac{1}{4}$ in. (212.1 × 87 cm) The Metropolitan Museum of Art, The Cloisters Collection, 1925. (25.120.201) Photography © 1979 The Metropolitan Museum of Art; **350 (T)** Réunion des Musées Nationaux/Art Resource, NY; **(B)** Bibliothèque Nationale de France, Paris (MS. Lat. 1156B, fol 163); **351** Réunion des Musées Nationaux/Art Resource, NY; **352** Réunion des Musées Nationaux/Art Resource, NY

Chapter 11

360 Scala/Art Resource, NY; **366** Scala/Art Resource, NY; **367** Ravenna/Index s.as.; **371** Kunsthistorisches Museum, Vienna/Art Resource, NY; **372** Erich Lessing/Art Resource, NY; **378** Orsi Battaglini/Index s.as.; **379** Art Resource, NY; **380 (T)** Alinari/Art Resource, NY; **(B)** Bridgeman Art Library; **381** Scala/Art Resource, NY; **382** Scala/Art Resource, NY; **383** Petrus Christus (Flemish [Bruges], active by 1444, died 1475–76), *A Goldsmith in His Shop,* Possibly Saint Elegius, 1449, Oil on wood; Overall: 39 $\frac{3}{8}$ × 34 $\frac{3}{4}$ in. (100.1 × 85.8 cm); Painted surface: 38 $\frac{5}{8}$ × 33 $\frac{1}{2}$ in. (98 × 85.2 cm). The Metropolitan Museum of Art, Robert Lehman Collection, 1975 (1975.1.110) Photograph © 1993 The Metropolitan Museum of Art

Chapter 12

392 Courtesy of the Trustees of the British Museum; **395** Bibliothèque Nationale de France, Paris (RCC1619); **397** Science Academy Lisbon/Dagli Orti/The Art Archive; **398** Bridgeman Art Library; **401** Scala/Art Resource, NY; **402** Scala/Art Resource, NY; **405** Snark/Art Resource, NY; **406 (T)** American Museum of Natural History Library (AMNH#314372); **(B)** American Museum of Natural History (AMNH# 315459); **408** New York Public Library, Rare Books Division. Astor, Lenox and Tilden Foundations; **411** Georgius Hoefnagle plate from Georg Braun (1542–1622), 5 vols. *Civitatis orbis terrarum* (Colonia Agrippinae, 1572–1618), Maps Division, Sterling Memorial Library, Yale University; **417** The Library of Congress; **418** Biblioteca Medicea Laurenziana (Med. Palat. 220, c. 460v)

Chapter 13

424 Scala/Art Resource, NY; **427** *Das Standebuch,* 1568; **428** Erich Lessing/Art Resource, NY; **429** Foto Marburg/Art Resource, NY; **434** M. Schneiders/Artephot; **440** Thyssen Bronemisza Collection, Madrid; **441** By courtesy of the National Portrait Gallery, London (NPG668); **448** Scala/Art Resource, NY; **450** The Granger Collection, New York; **452** Scala/Art Resource, NY; **453** Alinari/Art Resource, NY

Chapter 14

456 Musée de Beaux Arts Lausanne/Dagli Orti/The Art Archive; **460** Art Resource, NY; **467** AKG London; **469** Adriaen van Oastade (Dutch, 1610–1685). *The Family,* 1647. Etching on paper, 7 $\frac{1}{2}$ × 6 $\frac{5}{8}$ in. Georgia Museum of Art, University of Georgia; gift of Alfred H. Holbrook, GMOA 1967.1820.; **470** Erich Lessing/Art Resource, NY; **472** New York Public Library, Astor, Lenox and Tilden Foundations; **473** Mansell Collection/Time Life Pictures/Getty Images; **474 (B)** Museum of Rome/Dagli Orti/The Art Archive; **475 (T)** Germanisches National Museum, Nürnberg; **(C)** The Library of Congress; **(B)** © Dorling Kindersley; **479** Réunion des Musées Nationaux/Art Resource, NY; **483** Bedford Estate/Marquess of Tavistock

Chapter 15

490 Réunion des Musées Nationaux/Art Resource, NY; **496** Philippe de Champaigne, 1602–1674. *Triple Portrait of Cardinal Richelieu,* oil on canvas, 58.4 × 72.4 cm. © The National Gallery, London (NG798); **498** Réunion des Musées Nationaux/Art Resource, NY; **505 (T)** Museo del Prado/Art Resource, NY; **(B)** Scala/Art Resource, NY; **511** Scala/Art Resource, NY; **517** This item is reproduced by permission of the Huntington Library, San Marina, California; **519** AKG London; **521** Museum Boijmans van Beuningen, Rotterdam; **522** Rijksmuseum Foundation, Amsterdam

Chapter 16

524 © Archivo Iconografico, S.A./Corbis; **527 (L)** © 1982 Instructional Resources Corporation; **(R)** From *The Cosmographical Glass,* 1559; **528 (T)** The Library of Congress (LC USZ62-95165); **(B)** By permission of the British Library (Neg No. 2204); **531** By courtesy of the National Portrait Gallery, London (NPG5115); **532** Photograph © Mauritshuis, The Hague; **533** Ashmolean Museum, Oxford University (BI313); **535** Erich Lessing/Art Resource, NY; **539** Harry Ransom Humanities Research Center, University of Texas-Austin; **540** Harry Ransom Humanities Research Center, University of Texas-Austin; **545** Erich Lessing/Art Resource, NY; **550** Corbis

Chapter 17

552 Erich Lessing/Art Resource, NY; **556** © National Gallery, London; **559** AKG London; **561** By courtesy of the Trustees of the Goodwood Collection; **564** *Engravings by Hogarth,* plate 95;

565 Scottish National Portrait Gallery (PG1057); **568** Witt Library, Courtauld Institute of Art, London; **571** Bibliothèque Nationale de France, Paris; **576** (**L**) Réunion des Musées Nationaux/Art Resource, NY; (**R**) Erich Lessing/Art Resource, NY; **577** (**TR**) Corbis; (**TL**) BPK, Berlin; (**CL**) By permission of the Houghton Library, Harvard University; (**CR**) Mary Evans Picture Library; **578** From *Constituto Criminalis Theresiana*, 1769; **579** Art Resource, NY

Chapter 18
584 Erich Lessing/Art Resource, NY; **591** AKG London; **592** (**B**) Bibliothèque Nationale de France, Paris (80C 103369); **593** Bibliothèque Nationale de France, Paris (45B M89); **597** Giraudon/Art Resource, NY; **599** Réunion des Musées Nationaux/Art Resource, NY; **601** Annenberg Rare Book & Manuscript Library, University of Pennsylvania (Révolutions de Paris No. 161: Aug 4–11, 1792); **603** Photothèque des Musées de las Ville de Paris/Cliché: Andreani; **604** Giraudon/Art Resource, NY; **605** Réunion des Musées Nationaux/Art Resource, NY; **610** Réunion des Musées Nationaux/Art Resource, NY; **613** Erich Lessing/Art Resource, NY

Chapter 19
620 Victoria & Albert Museum, London/Art Resource, NY; **626** Private Collection Pairs/Dagli Orti/The Art Archive; **627** British Museum/Art Resource, NY; **629** Benson Latin American Collection, University of Texas-Austin; **637** Benson Latin American Collection, University of Texas-Austin; **640** Bridgeman Art Library; **643** Bridgeman Art Library; **644** Erich Lessing/Art Resource, NY; **646** The Library of Congress; **648** Art Resource, NY; **650** Museo Bolivar Caracas/Dagli Orti/The Art Archive

Chapter 20
654 Guildhall Library, Corporation of London/Bridgeman Art Library; **656** From *The White Slaves of England*, 1853; **659** Science Museum, London/Science and Society Picture Library; **660** From *History of the Cotton Manufacture in Great Britain*, 1836; **662** *Lewis Carroll's Album*. The Gernsheim Collection, Harry Ransom Research Center, University of Texas-Austin; **668** Deutsche Bahn Museum, Nurnberg; **670** AKG London; **674** Rickett Collection of Slides/The Slide Center; **677** *Punch*, 1847; **678** Sheffield Archives and Local Studies Library; **679** Rickitt Collection of Slides/The Slide Center; **680** © National Gallery, London

Chapter 21
684 Gemålde von Anton von Werner, 1995. Friedrichsruh, Bismarck-Museum, Bildarchiv Preussischer Kulturbesitz, Berlin; **689** The Granger Collection, New York; **693** Southampton Art Gallery/Bridgeman Art Library; **694** Bridgeman Art Library; **696** Réunion des Musées Nationaux/Art Resource, NY; **698** Giraudon/Art Resource, NY; **701** The Royal Archives © 2003 Her Majesty Queen Elizabeth II; **705** AKG London; **710** Hulton Archive/Getty Images; **711** AKG London; **717** AKG London

Chapter 22
720 The Library of Congress (811714 262-7307); **723** Roger-Viollet/Getty Images; **724** Hulton Archive/Getty Images; **725** The Mansell Collection/Time Life Pictures/Getty Images; **729** Courtesy Special Auction Services, England; **730** Eastphoto/Sovfoto; **731** Hulton Archive/Getty Images; **735** Hulton Archive/Getty Images; **738** Hulton Archive/Getty Images; **740** By permission of the People's History Museum; **745** Bridgeman Art Library; **746** By permission of the People's History Museum

Chapter 23
752 Erich Lessing/Art Resource, NY; **755** Erich Lessing/Art Resource, NY; **757** Cambridge University Library, Darwin Archive; **760** New York Public Library, Astor, Lenox and Tilden Foundations; **763** The Granger Collection, New York; **765** Schloss Immendorf, Austria/Bridgeman Art Library; **766** (**L**) Mary Evans Picture Library; (**B**) Corey Suppes/Ballparks.com; **767** (**TR**) AKG London; (**BR**) Science Museum, London/Science & Society Picture Library; **768** (**L**) Victoria & Albert Museum/Art Resource, NY; (**R**) Graphische Sammlung Albertina, Vienna, Austria/Bridgeman Art Library; **769** Eastphoto/Sovfoto; **770** Manchester City Art Galleries, UK/Bridgeman Art Library; **772** Wisconsin Historical Society (WHi-3104); **773** Hulton Archive/Getty Images; **774** © The Museum of Modern Art, New York/Art Resource, NY/© Estate of Pablo Picasso/Artists Rights Society (ARS), New York; **777** Anti-Slavery International; **781** Robert Hunt Picture Library

Chapter 24
788 Imperial War Museum, London; **790** Hulton Archive/Getty Images; **795** Ullstein Bilderdienst; **797** Imperial War Museum, London; **801** Robert Hunt Picture Library; **803** Imperial War Museum, London; **804** Hulton Archive/Getty Images; **806** Imperial War Museum, London; **808** (**T**) Hulton Archive/Getty Images; (**B**) Imperial War Museum, London; **809** National Gallery of Canada, Ottawa (No. 4800); **811** Imperial War Museum, London; **812** Hulton-Deutsch Collection/Corbis; **815** Hulton Archive/Getty Images; **817** Corbis; **818** AKG London; **820** AP/Wide World Photos

Chapter 25
826 Institute of Contemporary History and Wiener Library; **830** Bildarchiv Preussischer Kulturbesitz; **831** Schalwijk/Art Resource, NY/Reproduction authorized by Nacional Bellas Artes y Literatura/ © 2003 Banco de México, Diego Rivera & Frida Kahlo Museums Trust. Av. Cinco de Mayo No. 2, Col. Centro, Del. Cuauhtémoc 06059, México, D.F.; **832** Hulton Archive/Getty Images; **837** AKG London; **838** Photographie J. H. Lartigue/© Ministère de la Culture-France/A.A.J.H.L.; **841** AKG London; **845** AKG London; **848** David King/Sovfoto; **849** TASS/Sovfoto; **853** Robert Capa/Magnum Photos, Inc.; **857** AKG London

Chapter 26
860 Courtesy of the National Museum of the U.S. Army; **865** Art Resource, NY/© 2003 The Estate of Pablo Picasso/Artists Rights Society (ARS) New York; **867** Suddeutscher Verlag Bildarchiv; **870** AKG London; **871** TRH Pictures; **875** Popperfoto; **876** Hulton Archive/Getty Images; **878** Foto-Tanjug; **881** Sovfoto; **883** © Henry Moore Foundation. © Tate Gallery, London/Art Resource, NY; **884** AKG London; **888** Courtesy Franklin D. Roosevelt Library; **891** CTK Photo

Chapter 27
896 United States Holocaust Memorial Museum, Washington, D.C.; **898** Hulton Archive/Getty Images; **901** Bundesarchiv Bild (101I/12/11/19); **902** AKG London; **905** AKG London; **907** United States Holocaust Memorial Museum, Washington, D.C. Courtesy of Moshe Kaganovich; **913** Bettmann/Corbis;

Index

I-5

I-18

region, 906 (illus.); code of, 909; Protestants and Holocaust in, 909. *See also* German-Soviet Non-Aggression Pact (1939); Germany; Hitler, Adolf; Second World War

Nazi Party, 843, 907

Neanderthal people, 13

Neapolis (Naples), 89

Nebmertuf (Egyptian scribe), 44 (illus.)

Nebuchadnezzar II (Neo-Babylonian empire), 71, 81

Necker, Jacques (France), 588

Nefertiti (Egypt), 50

Négritude movement, 857

Negus, the (Ethiopia), 396

Neighborhoods: as "urban villages," 737–738

Nelson, Horatio, 611

Nemesis (ship), 681

Neo-Assyrian empire, 70, 71 (map)

Neo-Babylonian empire, 70–72, 73 (map)

Neo-colonialism, 939

Neolithic Age: trade in, 16; in Europe, 35–36, 35 (map), 36 (illus.)

Neo-Nazis: in Germany, 982

Neoplatonism, 534; Christianity and, 205–206; in Renaissance, 364; mechanical philosophy and, 534–535; human beings and, 547

Neorealism, 954; filmmakers and, 882

NEP. *See* New Economic Policy (NEP, Soviet Union)

Nero (Rome), 151, 152; Colossus of Nero (statue) and, 161 (illus.); Britain and, 166; Seneca and, 175; Christians and, 183

Nerva (Rome), 152, 153

Nestorian church, 240

Netherlands: trade in, 315; woolen cloth and, 335; Renaissance painting in, 382; Spain and, 387, 501, 509; Calvinism in, 437; iconoclasm in, 450; William the Silent in, 457; population growth of, 459; revolts in, 480–482, 481 (map), 599; Inquisition in, 481; Dutch Republic and, 512–513, 520–522, 698; kingdom of, 615 (map), 616, 667, 698; women's suffrage in, 748; Second World War and, 861, 867; Holocaust and, 908; in Benelux countries, 948. *See also* United Provinces of the Netherlands

Neuilly, Treaty of, 822

Neustria, kingdom of, 246–247

Neutrality: Russian-German treaty of, 791; of Catholic Church in Holocaust, 909

Neutrons, 916

Nevinson, Christopher, 809 (illus.), 810

New Amsterdam, 628, 631

New Astronomy (Kepler), 528

New Comedy: Hellenistic, 121, 137

Newcomen, Thomas, 658

New Conservatism, 969–970

New Economic Policy (NEP, Soviet Union), 832; Trotsky, Stalin, and, 832–833; gender policy and, 839

New England, 623; Calvinism in, 437; industrialization in, 668–669

Newfoundland, 412, 632

New Guinea: in Second World War, 877

New Harmony, Indiana, 688

New imperialism, 753–754, 771–784; Western Christianity vs. indigenous culture and, 773; idea of, 773–774; in Africa, 774–778; by Leopold of Belgium, 777; in Asia, 778–783, 779 (map); of United States, 780

New Kingdom (Egypt), 25, 48 (map); administration and government under, 44–45; empire in Canaan and Nubia, 45–49; justice in, 46–47; women in, 52–53

New Lanark, Scotland, 688

New Left: student movement and, 958; protests by, 960–961, 960 (illus.)

New Mexico: United States and, 713, 780

New Model Army (England), 514, 515

New Netherland, 625–628

New Organon (Bacon), 533, 538

"New Realism": in arts, 955

New Rome: Constantinople as, 194

New Spain, 407

Newspapers, 574

New Testament. *See* Bible (Christian)

Newton, Isaac, 530, 538, 915; mathematics and, 534; magic and, 536–537; on God, 543; Enlightenment and, 562; Voltaire and, 568; revolution in physics and, 756

"New Woman": after First World War, 838–839, 838 (illus.)

New World, 398; use of term, 403; peoples of, 419–420; French territorial losses in, 624; legal ideologies in, 639; imperialism by, 771. *See also* Americas; specific countries and regions

"New world order": of Nazis, 900–902, 901 (illus.)

New Year's Day, 196

New York (city), 631

New York (colony), 628

New Zealand: Britain and, 624; immigration to, 726; First World War and, 802; after First World War, 819; colonies of, 853

Nicaea, Council of, 198, 444

Nice, 709

Nicene Creed, 198

Nicholas I (Russia), 697, 699

Nicholas II (Russia), 739, 804; Revolution of 1905 and, 730; Jews and, 742; First World War and, 813; March Revolution and, 814–815; abdication and execution of, 816–817; family of, 817 (illus.). *See also* Russian Revolutions

Nietzsche, Friedrich, 761

Nigeria, 940

Night of the Broken Glass (Germany). *See* Kristallnacht (Germany)

Nika Revolt (Byzantium), 215

Nile, Battle of the, 599, 610

Nile River region: ancient Egypt and, 25; trade in, 28; Neo-Assyrian empire and, 70; Rome and, 169

Nimes, 154 (illus.)

Niña (ship), 402

Nineteenth dynasty (Egypt), 52

Ninety-Five Theses (Luther), 432

Nineveh, 70

Nixon, Richard: China and, 936–937; "kitchen debate" with Khrushchev and, 953 (illus.); floating dollar and, 966

Nkrumah, Kwame, 937

Noah (Bible): flood and, 83

Nobel Prize: Marie Curie and, 747; to U.S. scientists, 950

Nobility: in Rome, 138; in England, 311, 389, 699–700; lifestyle of, 350–352; hunting by, 350 (illus.); ducal castle of, 352 (illus.); in France, 385, 496, 588; in absolutist state, 494; in Prussia, 509; in Russia, 512; medieval, 554; entrance to, 555; marriage into, 555, 556 (illus.); French Revolution (1789) and, 587, 588; Napoleon and, 609. *See also* Aristocracy

Nogarola, Isotta, 375

Noguerol de Ulloa, Francisco, 410–411, 411 (illus.)

Nomads: lifestyle of, 15; Scythian, 84, 84 (illus.); Huns as, 207–208; Avars as, 211; empires of, 212 (map); Bulgars as, 226; Arab, 232; Mongols and Turks as, 330. *See also* Hapiru people

Nonaggression Pact (German-Soviet), 864

Nonaligned nations, 942

Non-European cultures: studies of, 563

Nonrational thought, 756–757

Nonviolent resistance: Baptists and, 443; Gandhi and, 820

Normandy: Vikings in, 266–267; French control of, 312

Normans: ships of, 266 (illus.); Byzantium and, 282

Norsemen (Northmen). *See* Vikings

North (industrial world), 893, 997 (illus.); gap with South, 997, 998

North Africa: Carthage in, 111, 226; Rome and, 169, 172; Germanic kingdoms in, 188; Vandals in, 207, 210, 215; Byzantium and, 226–227; Muslims in, 235, 238, 239; Frankish attacks on, 245; Shi'ite caliphate in, 284; Maghrib region in, 396; Spain and, 480; French in, 624–625; Italy and, 868; Nazis in, 868, 872; Germany and, 869 (map); Allied victory in, 874; after Second World War, 888

North Afrika Korps: at El Alamein, 873

North America: in Western world, 5; Scandinavian voyages to, 394; British Empire in, 412–413; European exploration and settlement of, 412–413; French wars in, 501; Napoleonic Code in, 609; France and, 611, 624, 632; empire in, 622; British empire and, 623, 632–633, 633 (map); Spanish in, 628; Russian trade in, 630; colonial wars in, 632; Seven Years' War in, 632–633; Atlantic economy and, 635 (map); slavery in, 636; ethnicity in, 639; republican government in, 639

North Atlantic Treaty Organization (NATO), 889, 933; cruise missiles in Europe and, 970, 971 (illus.); environmentalists and, 973–974; in Bosnia, 985

Northern Europe: expansion of, 281 (map); city population growth in, 461; marriage patterns in, 465

Northern Ireland violence in, 986

Northern Lights, 125

Northern Renaissance, 382, 383 (illus.), 428–430

North German Confederation, 711

North Korea, 933

Northumbria: kingdom of, 245; monasticism in, 253

North Vietnam, 941. *See also* Vietnam War

Northwest Passage: North America and, 412

Norway: Christian bishoprics in, 276; women's suffrage in, 748; Second World War and, 861, 867. *See also* Baltic region; Scandinavia

Notables: in Napoleonic France, 609

"No Trial Act" (South Africa, 1963), 939

Nova Scotia, 412, 632

Novels: *Don Quixote* as, 483; in Enlightenment, 574, 575. *See also* Literature; specific works

GREENLAND
(KALAALLIT NUNAAT)
(Den.)

ICELAND

ALASKA
(U.S.)

UNITED
KINGDOM

IRELAND

FRANCE

CANADA

SPAIN

PORTUGAL

UNITED STATES

AZORES (Port.)

ATLANTIC
OCEAN

MOROCCO

CANARY IS. (Sp.)

WESTERN SAHARA
(Mor.)

HAWAII (U.S.)

MEXICO

BAHAMAS
DOMINICAN
REPUBLIC
HAITI

PUERTO RICO (U.S.)
ST. KITTS AND NEVIS
ANTIGUA AND BARBUDA
DOMINICA
ST. VINCENT AND THE GRENADINES
BARBADOS

MAURITANIA

CUBA
JAMAICA
BELIZE
GUATEMALA
HONDURAS
EL SALVADOR
NICARAGUA

GUADELOUPE (Fr.)
MARTINIQUE (Fr.)
ST. LUCIA

CAPE
VERDE

SENEGAL

MALI

THE GAMBIA
GUINEA-BISSAU

GRENADA
TRINIDAD AND TOBAGO
GUYANA

GUINEA
SIERRA LEONE

COSTA RICA

PANAMA

VENEZUELA

SURINAME
FRENCH GUIANA (Fr.)

LIBERIA
CÔTE D'IVOIRE

COLOMBIA

BURKINA FASO
GHANA

PACIFIC OCEAN

GALÁPAGOS IS.
(Ec.)

ECUADOR

PERU

BRAZIL

WESTERN
SAMOA

AMERICAN
SAMOA (U.S.)

BOLIVIA

TONGA

FRENCH
POLYNESIA (Fr.)

PARAGUAY

CHILE

ATLANTIC
OCEAN

URUGUAY

ARGENTINA

0   1,500   3,000 Miles

0   1,500   3,000 Kilometers

**Contemporary
Political Map
of the World**

FALKLAND IS. (U.K.)

80°N
60°N
40°N
Tropic of Cancer
20°N
0° Equator
20°S
Tropic of Capricorn
40°S
60°S
Antarctic Circle
80°S

Arctic Circle

160°W   140°W   120°W   100°W   80°W   60°W   40°W   20°W